Merriam-Webster's Crossword Puzzle Dictionary

Merriam-Webster's
Crossword Puzzle
Dictionary

Third Edition

ISBN-10 0-87779-636-3
ISBN-13 978-0-87779-636-8

Printed in the United States of America
1234QW/B0605

Merriam-Webster, Incorporated
Springfield, Massachusetts, U.S.A.

Preface to the Third Edition

This new edition of MERRIAM-WEBSTER'S CROSSWORD PUZ-ZLE DICTIONARY represents a significant revision of those that have preceded it. Every entry has been reconsidered, the content has been thoroughly updated, and the page design has been enhanced for legibility.

In updating the work, we have added many terms that have recently entered the general English vocabulary: the names of computer languages (*Java, Perl*), new national currencies (*vatu, nakfa*), contemporary slang (*slacker, schlep, hoser, chill out, go-to guy, brewski, nebbish*), and much more. And numerous individuals and institutions that have emerged in recent years—soccer stars (*Hamm, Ronaldo*), auto companies (*Kia, Daewoo*), Nobel Prize winners (*Annan, Naipaul*), actors and actresses (*Depp, Swank*), and so on—have naturally also been added.

Drawing extensively on actual crossword puzzles, we have made a special effort to add examples of "crosswordese," words that show up unusually often in puzzle grids. Thus, you will find such distinctive words and names as those for Prince Valiant's wife (*Aleta*) and son (*Arn*), a former newspaper columnist (*Eda*), a sharp mountain ridge (*arête*), a hare's tail (*scut*), an eminent golfer (*Els*), Peer Gynt's mother (*Ase, Aase*), a puzzle-cube inventor (*Erno*), and a Scottish uncle (*eme*)—many of which might have been omitted if frequency of use in everyday English had been our only criterion.

While crossword clues have gotten cleverer in recent years, crossword answer words have gotten simpler, and archaic and obscure terms have gradually been disappearing from puzzle grids. For this new edition, it seemed unnecessary to retain words that were unlikely to show up in even the most challenging modern puzzles, and consequently a number of words that have fallen out of use have been deleted. Their absence has been more than made up for by additional entries and answer words, which now total substantially over 300,000.

We hope our revised edition, with its new orientation, will prove to be the most useful dictionary of its kind for a new century of puzzle solving.

———————————

The principal editors of this dictionary's first two editions were James G. Lowe and Michael G. Belanger. Editorial work on the new edition was carried out by Mark A. Stevens and C. Roger Davis with freelance help from Jocelyn White Franklin, Mike Nichols, Francesca M. Forrest, and Doris Maxfield. Eileen M. Haraty and Dr. Thomas W. Adams made valuable vocabulary contributions, and Robert D. Copeland and Ted Atanowski provided essential electronic assistance. The pages were typeset by Dianna Logan at Dedicated Business Services of Clarinda, Iowa.

Mark A. Stevens
Editor

Explanatory Notes

This dictionary is organized to make it easy to find answer words with a specific number of letters. Every answer word follows a numeral indicating the number of letters it contains. These words generally run from three to 13 letters. Two-letter words are omitted because such words almost never appear in crossword puzzles, and words longer than 13 letters are omitted because, when a puzzle calls for a longer answer, the answer is usually a phrase or part of a phrase rather than a single word or term. An exception to the 13-letter limit is made for multi-word titles of works, which occasionally run as long as 25 letters. The exception allows for those frequent crossword clues that omit one or two words from a title, perhaps enough for a five- or ten-letter answer.

As in any crossword dictionary, a single list of answer words will often include words representing various parts of speech. The entry for **quiet**, for example, includes synonyms for the noun *(silence),* the adjective *(placid),* and the verb *(soothe),* all in a continuous list. Since clues are often intentionally ambiguous as to what part of speech or meaning is intended, listing all the possible synonyms together is probably ideal for the puzzle solver.

Words that share a root with their entry word have usually been omitted from the answer lists, since puzzle creators rarely choose a clue that is related in this way to its answer. Therefore, *singular* does not appear at **single**, *basal* does not appear at **basic**, and *papa* does not appear at **pop**. On the other hand, since clues do occasionally share a standard prefix or suffix (such as *re-* or

-*ness*) with an answer word, we have retained many clue/answer-word pairs of this kind.

When one entry word simply adds a suffix to another entry word, as when **truthfulness** follows **truthful**, the answer list for the suffixed entry word will generally omit all the words that merely add the same suffix to a word in the stem word's list. For example, since **truthful** includes such answer words as *frank* and *candid,* the list at **truthfulness** omits *frankness* and *candidness.* When encountering a clue with a common suffix, therefore, the user will occasionally want to look at a neighboring entry to find all the possible synonyms.

When a personal name is entered as an answer term, the first name generally appears in parentheses and is ignored in the letter count. In cases where the first name is the one normally encountered—e.g., for historical figures such as Michelangelo and Raphael or fictional characters such as Tess Durbeyfield and Angel Clare—the last name is generally parenthesized instead. When a title begins with an article *(A, An,* or *The),* the article is parenthesized and omitted from the letter count. In a list of geographic entities such as mountains (lakes, gulfs, etc.), the generic word *Mount (Lake, Gulf,* etc.*)* is similarly omitted from the letter count. If you find that none of the answers as listed fits the blanks for a given puzzle clue, you should naturally check to see if any of the parenthesized or omitted elements might help provide the desired answer.

Many entries are broken into subentries by means of subheadings. Subheadings often consist of a single word, which is usually to be read as either preceding or following the main entry word. Thus, in the entry for **hair**, the subheadings include **animal** (which should be read as "animal hair") and **ornament** (which should be read as "hair ornament"). The subentry **combining form** lists the kinds of word fragments, usually Greek or Latin in origin, that are commonly called *roots.*

The dictionary is best used somewhat imaginatively.

If you fail to find a word at its own entry, look up a synonym; only rarely will you fail to find one. If a clue takes a form such as **Australian tree**, **garden tool**, or **Southeast Asian lake** and the dictionary provides no such entry, check at the entry for the generic term—**tree**, **tool**, **lake**, etc.—for a list, perhaps broken down by subheadings.

A

A1
4 best, tops 5 prime 7 optimal, perfect
8 superior 9 excellent, first-rate, front-rank,
matchless, top-drawer 10 blue-ribbon, first-
class

Aaron
brother: 5 Moses
father: 5 Amram
sister: 6 Miriam

aback
7 unaware 8 suddenly, unawares 10 by
surprise 12 unexpectedly

abaft
4 back 5 after 6 astern, behind
8 rearward 9 sternward

abalone
7 mollusc, mollusk 9 gastropod

abandon
4 cede, drop, dump, ease, jilt, junk, play,
quit 5 cease, chuck, ditch, leave, let go,
scrap, yield 6 desert, disown, give up,
laxity, maroon, reject, resign, strand, vacate
7 back out, bail out, cast off, discard, drop
out, forsake, freedom, liberty, license, pull
out, retreat 8 abdicate, give over, hand
over, renounce, wildness, withdraw
9 looseness, repudiate, surrender, throw
over 10 enthusiasm, exuberance,
relinquish, wantonness 11 discontinue,
leave behind, naturalness, spontaneity,
unrestraint 12 carelessness,
heedlessness, intemperance, recklessness,
unconstraint 13 impulsiveness

abandoned
4 free, lewd, lorn, wild 5 loose 6 gave up,
jilted, vacant, wanton 7 cast off, corrupt,
given up, outcast, uncouth 8 cast away,
depraved, derelict, deserted, desolate,
forsaken, stranded 9 cast aside,
debauched, destitute, discarded, dissolute,
eliminated, lecherous, neglected,
reprobate, shameless 10 degenerate,
dissipated, friendless, lascivious, left
behind, licentious, profligate, uninhibited,
unoccupied 12 incorrigible, relinquished,
uncontrolled, unrestrained

abase
5 lower, shame 6 debase, defame,
demean, demote, grovel, humble, lessen,
reduce 7 cheapen, degrade, devalue, put
down 8 belittle 9 denigrate, discredit,
disparage, downgrade, humiliate
10 depreciate, undervalue

abash
4 faze 5 mix up, shame, upset 6 dismay,
puzzle, rattle 7 confuse, mortify, mystify
8 confound 9 discomfit, embarrass
10 discompose, disconcert

abashment
6 unease 7 chagrin 8 disquiet
9 confusion 12 discomfiture, discomposure
13 embarrassment

abate
3 ebb, end 4 ease, fade, fall, omit, slow,
void, wane 5 allay, annul, close, let up,
quash, taper 6 deduct, lessen, negate,
recede, reduce, relent, weaken 7 abolish,
decline, deprive, die down, dwindle, ease
off, nullify, slacken, subside 8 decrease,
diminish, mitigate, moderate 9 alleviate,
eradicate 10 invalidate

abatement
6 ebbing, rebate, waning 8 decrease,
discount 9 declining, deduction, dwindling,
exemption, lessening, reduction, shrinkage
10 diminution, subsidence 11 subtraction

abattoir
8 shambles

abbey
6 friary 7 convent 8 cloister 9 monastery

abbot
female: 6 abbess

abbreviate
3 cut 4 clip, trim 5 prune 6 cut out, reduce
7 abridge, curtail, cut back, shorten
8 compress, condense, contract, cut short,
truncate

abbreviation
5 brief 6 digest, précis, sketch 7 acronym,
cutting, outline 8 abstract, clipping,
synopsis, trimming 10 abridgment,
shortening 11 curtailment
12 condensation

abdicate
4 cede, drop, quit 5 forgo, leave, waive,
yield 6 abjure, evade, give up, reject,
resign 7 abandon, cast off, discard,
disclaim 8 abnegate, hand over, renounce,
withdraw 9 repudiate, surrender
10 relinquish

abdomen
3 gut, pot 5 belly, tummy 6 middle, paunch
7 midriff, stomach 8 potbelly 9 bay
window 10 midsection 11 breadbasket
depression: 5 navel

abduct
4 grab, take 5 seize 6 kidnap, remove,
snatch 8 carry off, draw away, take away
9 carry away, steal away 10 spirit away
11 make off with

Abduction from the Seraglio composer
6 Mozart (Wolfgang Amadeus)

abecedarian
4 tyro 6 novice 7 amateur, dabbler, learner
8 beginner, initiate, neophyte 9 beginning,
smatterer 10 apprentice, dilettante,
elementary 11 rudimentary
12 alphabetical

Abel
brother: 4 Cain, Seth
father: 4 Adam
mother: 4 Eve
slayer: 4 Cain

Abelard
son: 9 Astrolabe
wife: 7 Heloise

abele
6 poplar

aberrant
3 odd 7 deviant, strange, unusual
8 abnormal, atypical, peculiar, straying
9 anomalous, deviating, different, eccentric,
irregular, unnatural, untypical
11 exceptional, nonstandard

aberration
4 slip 5 quirk 6 change, oddity 7 anomaly,
mistake 8 mutation 9 curiosity, deviation,
exception, straying, wandering
10 deflection, difference, distortion,
divergence 11 abnormality, peculiarity
12 eccentricity, irregularity

abet
3 aid, egg 4 ally, back, help, prod, spur,
urge 5 boost, egg on 6 assist, exhort,
foment, incite, second, stir up 7 condone,
endorse, forward, promote, support
8 advocate 9 encourage, instigate
11 countenance

abettor
4 aide, ally 6 backup, cohort, helper
7 inciter, partner 8 fomenter 9 accessory,
supporter 10 accomplice, instigator
11 confederate, conspirator
12 collaborator

abeyance
4 lull, rest 5 break, lapse, pause 6 recess
7 respite, time-out, waiting 8 breather,
interval 10 inactivity, quiescence,
suspension 12 intermission, interruption

abeyant
7 dormant 8 deferred, inactive, recessed
9 postponed, quiescent, suspended
11 interrupted

abhor
4 hate 5 scorn 6 detest, loathe, reject,
revile, vilify 7 contemn, despise, disdain,
dislike 8 execrate 9 abominate, excoriate,
repudiate

abhorrence
4 evil, hate 6 hatred, horror 7 disgust
8 aversion, distaste, loathing 9 repulsion,
revulsion 10 repugnance 11 abomination,
detestation

abhorrent
4 base, foul, vile 5 awful 6 horrid, odious
7 beastly, hateful, heinous 8 damnable,
horrific 9 atrocious, execrable, horrible,
invidious, loathsome, monstrous,
obnoxious, repellent, repugnant, repulsive,
revolting 10 abominable, deplorable,
despicable, detestable, disgusting 12 contemptible, reprehensible

abide
4 bear, last, live, stay, wait 5 await, brook,
dwell, exist, stand, tarry 6 accede, accept,
comply, endure, linger, remain, reside, stay
on, suffer 7 consent, hang out, inhabit,
keep on, persist, sojourn, stomach, subsist,

swallow, wait for **8** continue, live with, stand for, tolerate **9** put up with, withstand

abiding
4 fast, firm, sure **6** steady **7** durable, eternal, lasting, staying **8** constant, enduring, timeless **9** complying, perpetual, steadfast **10** continuing, persistent, persisting, unchanging **11** everlasting, unfaltering

abigail
4 maid

Abigail
brother: 5 David
husband: 5 David, Nabal
mother: 5 Amasa
son: 7 Chileah

ability
4 bent, gift **5** craft, flair, knack, might, savvy, skill **6** talent **7** aptness, command, faculty, know-how, mastery, prowess **8** aptitude, capacity, facility, faculty **9** adeptness, dexterity, expertise, handiness, ingenuity, potential **10** adroitness, capability, cleverness, competence, efficiency **11** proficiency, skillfulness **13** qualification

abject
3 low **4** base, mean, poor, vile **5** lowly, sorry **6** dismal, humble, ignoble, shabby, sordid **7** debased, fawning, forlorn, pitiful, servile **8** cast down, degraded, dejected, downcast, hopeless, pathetic, pitiable, rejected, resigned, wretched **9** afflicted, deplorable, destitute, groveling, miserable, worthless **10** obsequious, spiritless, submissive **11** deferential, downtrodden, subservient **12** contemptible, dishonorable, ingratiating

abjure
4 cede, deny **5** avoid, spurn **6** desert, disown, recall, recant, reject, refuse, revoke **7** abandon, disavow, decline, forsake, retract **8** disclaim, forswear, renounce, take back, withdraw **9** repudiate, surrender **10** relinquish **11** abstain from

ablaze
5 afire, aglow, fiery **6** aflame, alight, blazing, on fire **7** burning, flaming, excited, flaring, ignited, radiant

able
3 apt, fit **4** keen **5** adept, alert, sharp, smart **6** adroit, clever, expert, facile, suited **7** capable, skilled **8** skillful, talented **9** competent, effective, effectual, efficient,

qualified **10** proficient **11** intelligent, resourceful **12** accomplished, enterprising

able-bodied
3 fit **4** hale **5** hardy, lusty, sound, stout **6** brawny, hearty, robust, strong, sturdy **7** capable **8** stalwart, vigorous **9** strapping

ablution
6 laving **7** bathing, washing **8** lavation **9** cleansing, immersion **12** purification

abnegate
4 cede, deny, drop **5** forgo, waive, yield **6** abjure, give up, recant, revoke, vacate **7** disavow, gainsay **8** disallow, disclaim, forswear, renounce, withdraw **9** repudiate, surrender **10** contradict, contravene, relinquish

abnegation
6 denial **9** surrender **10** abstinence, self-denial **12** renouncement, renunciation

Abner
cousin: 4 Saul
father: 3 Ner
slayer: 4 Joab

abnormal
3 odd **5** freak, undue, weird **6** off-key **7** bizarre, deviant, unusual **8** aberrant, atypical, freakish, peculiar **9** anomalous, divergent, eccentric, irregular, unnatural **11** heteroclite **13** heteromorphic, preternatural

abnormality
4 flaw **6** oddity **7** anomaly **8** deviance **9** deviation, exception **10** aberration, difference **12** irregularity

abode
4 home, nest **5** house **7** address, lodging, sojourn **8** domicile, dwelling **9** residence **10** habitation

abolish
3 end **4** undo, kill, void **5** abate, annul, erase, quash **6** cancel, negate, recall, repeal, revoke, vacate **7** destroy, nullify, rescind, retract, reverse, wipe out **8** abrogate, disallow, dissolve, overturn, prohibit **9** eliminate, eradicate, terminate **10** do away with, extinguish, invalidate

abolitionist
4 Mott (Lucretia), Weld (Theodore) **5** Brown (John), Child (Lydia), Lundy (Benjamin), Smith (Gerrit), Stowe (Harriet Beecher) **6** Birney (James), Lowell (James Russell), Parker (Theodore), Tappan (Arthur), Tubman (Harriet) **7** Lincoln (Abraham) **8** Douglass (Frederick),

Garrison (William Lloyd), Phillips (Wendell), Whittier (John Greenleaf)

abominable

5 awful, nasty 6 cursed, horrid, odious 7 hateful 8 horrible, shocking, terrible, wretched 9 abhorrent, loathsome, offensive, repellent, repugnant, repulsive, revolting 10 deplorable, despicable, detestable, disgusting 12 contemptible

abominable snowman

4 yeti

abominate

4 damn, hate 5 abhor, curse, scorn 6 detest, loathe, revile 7 despise 8 execrate 9 repudiate

abomination

4 evil, hate 5 scorn 6 hatred, horror, plague 7 disdain, disgust, dislike 8 anathema, aversion, contempt, distaste, loathing 9 repulsion, revulsion 10 abhorrence, repugnance, repugnancy 11 detestation

aboriginal

5 first 6 native 7 ancient, endemic, primary 8 earliest, original, primeval 9 primitive 10 indigenous, primordial 13 autochthonous

aborigine

6 native 7 ancient 8 indigene 10 autochthon

abort

4 drop, halt, stop 5 check, expel, scrap, scrub 6 arrest, cancel 7 abandon, call off 8 cut short 9 interrupt, terminate

abortive

4 vain 5 empty 6 futile, unripe 7 failing, useless 8 immature, unformed 9 fruitless, worthless 10 unavailing, unfruitful 11 ineffective, ineffectual, unavailable, undeveloped 12 unproductive, unsuccessful

abound

4 flow, teem 5 burst, crawl, crowd, flood, swarm, swell 6 be full, throng 7 bristle, jam with 8 overflow, pack with 9 crawl with 11 be plentiful

abounding

4 full, rife 5 laden 6 filled, full of, jammed, packed 7 copious, profuse, replete, stuffed, teeming 8 abundant, swarming, thronged 9 alive with, bristling, plenteous, plentiful 11 overflowing

about

4 as to, back, in re, near, nigh, over 5 again, anent, circa, round 6 almost, around, moving, nearby, nearly 7 apropos, close to, roughly, through 8 backward, in general 9 as regards, engaged in, haphazard, in reverse, regarding 10 as concerns, concerning, encircling, in regard to, more or less, on all sides, oppositely, relating to, respecting 11 any which way, dealing with, on every side, practically, referring to, relative to, surrounding 12 here and there, with regard to 13 approximately, concerned with, in reference to, with respect to

about-face

4 turn 7 reverse 8 reversal 9 turnabout, volte-face

above

3 o'er 4 over, past 5 aloft, supra 6 beyond 8 overhead 9 exceeding
prefix: 4 over 5 hyper, super, supra

above all

7 chiefly 9 primarily 10 especially 11 principally 12 particularly

aboveboard

4 free, open 5 frank 6 candid, honest, openly 7 frankly, up front 8 candidly, honestly, straight 10 truthfully, forthright, scrupulous

abracadabra

5 charm, magic 6 babble, jargon 9 gibberish 10 double talk, mumbo jumbo 11 incantation 12 gobbledygook 13 mystification

abrade

3 bug, irk, rub 4 burn, fret, gall, rasp, wear 5 annoy, chafe, erode, grate, graze, upset, weary 6 bother, ruffle, scrape 7 corrode, eat away, perturb, provoke, roughen 8 irritate, wear away, wear down 9 aggravate, grind down

Abraham

brother: 5 Haran, Nahor
concubine: 5 Hagar
father: 5 Terah
grandfather: 5 Nahor
grandson: 4 Esau
nephew: 3 Lot
son: 5 Isaac, Medan, Shuah 6 Midian, Zimran 7 Ishmael
well: 9 Beer-Sheba
wife: 5 Sarah 7 Keturah

abrasion
5 chafe, scuff **6** scrape **7** chafing, erosion, grating, rubbing, scratch **8** friction, grinding, scraping, scuffing **10** irritation, scratching

abrasive
5 emery, rough, sharp **6** biting, pumice **7** wearing **8** annoying **9** smoothing, polishing **10** irritating, unpleasant

abreast
6 beside, next to, versed, with-it **7** versant **8** familiar, informed, up-to-date **9** au courant **10** acquainted, conversant **13** knowledgeable

abridge
3 cut **4** pare, trim **5** limit, prune **6** lessen, narrow, reduce **7** curtail, cut back, shorten **8** boil down, compress, condense, cut short, diminish, restrict, truncate **9** summarize **10** abbreviate

abridgment
5 brief **6** digest **7** capsule, cutting, short form, summary **8** abstract, synopsis **9** reduction **10** diminution, lessening, shortening **11** compression, contraction, curtailment, restriction **12** abbreviation, condensation

abroad
4 afar, away **6** afield, about, astray, widely **7** touring **8** overseas **9** elsewhere, traveling

abrogate
3 end **4** undo, void **5** abate, annul, quash **6** cancel, negate, repeal, revoke, vacate **7** abolish, blot out, nullify, rescind, reverse **8** dissolve **9** discharge **10** extinguish, invalidate, obliterate

abrupt
4 curt **5** bluff, blunt, brief, brisk, crisp, gruff, hasty, sharp, sheer, short, steep **6** cut off, snippy, sudden **7** arduous, brusque, hurried, rushing **8** headlong **9** broken off, impetuous **10** unexpected **11** precipitant, precipitate, precipitous **13** unceremonious

abruptly
5 short **6** curtly **7** quickly, steeply **8** suddenly **12** unexpectedly **13** precipitately, precipitously

abruptness
8 curtness **9** steepness **10** brusquerie **12** precipitance

Absalom
commander: **5** Amasa
father: **5** David
mother: **7** Maachah
sister: **5** Tamar
slayer: **4** Joab

abscess
4 boil, sore **5** botch, ulcer **6** lesion, pimple, trauma **7** blister, pustule **8** furuncle **9** carbuncle

abscond
4 bolt, flee, quit **5** break, leave **6** decamp, escape, run off **7** run away, take off **8** slip away, sneak off **9** disappear, sneak away, steal away

absence
4 AWOL, lack, need, void, want **6** dearth, defect, vacuum **7** default, drought, failure, vacancy **9** privation **10** deficiency, inadequacy **11** absenteeism, inattention **13** insufficiency

absent
4 away, AWOL, gone, lost **6** no-show **7** bemused, faraway, lacking, missing, omitted, wanting, without **8** distrait, heedless **9** elsewhere, forgetful, wandering **10** abstracted, distracted, not present **11** inattentive, preoccupied **12** not attentive

absentminded
4 lost **7** bemused, faraway **8** distrait, dreaming, heedless, unseeing **9** forgetful, oblivious, unheeding, unmindful **10** abstracted, distracted, unnoticing **11** inattentive, inconscient, preoccupied, unconscious, unobserving **12** unperceiving

absent without leave
4 AWOL

absolute
4 full, pure, real, true **5** ideal, sheer, total, utter **6** actual, entire, simple **7** eternal, factual, genuine, perfect, supreme, unmixed **8** autarkic, complete, despotic, flawless, infinite, outright, positive, ultimate, simplest, thorough, unflawed **9** arbitrary, autarchic, boundless, downright, embodying, imperious, masterful, sovereign, unalloyed, undiluted, unlimited **10** autocratic, autonomous, consummate, impeccable, monocratic, tyrannical **11** categorical, dictatorial, domineering, fundamental, independent, unequivocal, unmitigated, unqualified **12** indefectible, indisputable, totalitarian, unrestrained, unrestricted **13** authoritarian, incontestable, unconditional

absolutely
5 fully 6 wholly 7 utterly 8 entirely
9 doubtless, perfectly 10 completely,
definitely, positively, thoroughly
11 doubtlessly 13 unequivocally

absolution
6 pardon 7 amnesty, freeing, release
9 releasing, remission 10 letting off
11 exculpation, exoneration, forgiveness
12 dispensation

absolutism
9 Caesarism, despotism 12 dictatorship

absolve
4 free 5 clear, let go, remit, spare 6 acquit,
excuse, exempt, let off, pardon 7 forgive,
release, relieve, set free 8 dispense
9 discharge, exculpate, exonerate,
vindicate

absorb
4 bear, blot 5 imbue, learn, sop up, use up
6 assume, embody, endure, engage,
imbibe, infuse, ingest, soak up, sponge,
suck up, take in, take up 7 acquire,
consume, drink in, engross, immerse,
involve, receive, sustain 8 permeate
9 preoccupy, transform 10 assimilate
11 incorporate

absorbed
4 deep, into, lost, rapt 6 intent 7 engaged,
wrapped 8 caught up, immersed, involved
9 engrossed, wrapped up 10 captivated,
fascinated 11 preoccupied

absorbing
9 arresting, consuming 10 engrossing,
intriguing 11 captivating, fascinating,
interesting 12 monopolizing, preoccupying

abstain
4 curb, deny, diet, fast, keep, pass, stop
5 avoid, forgo, spurn 6 abjure, eschew,
give up, pass up, refuse, reject 7 decline,
forbear, refrain 8 abnegate, forswear, hold
back, keep from, renounce, swear off,
teetotal, withhold 9 constrain, do without
11 deny oneself

abstemious
5 sober, strict 7 ascetic, austere, chaste,
sparing 9 abstinent, continent, temperate
10 restrained 11 self-denying

abstinence
6 denial 7 fasting 8 chastity, sobriety
9 soberness 10 continence, self-denial,
temperance 12 renunciation 13 self-
restraint

abstract
5 brief, ideal 6 detach, digest, précis
7 epitome, neutral, outline, shorten,
summary, utopian 8 academic, breviary,
condense, detached, notional, separate,
synopsis 9 disengage, summarize
10 abridgment, conceptual, conspectus,
disconnect, dissociate, impersonal
11 appropriate, impractical, speculative,
theoretical 12 condensation, hypothetical,
transcendent 13 disinterested

abstracted
4 lost, rapt 6 absent, intent 7 bemused,
faraway 8 absorbed, distrait, heedless
9 engrossed, oblivious, unheeding,
unmindful, unminding, withdrawn
11 inattentive, inconscient, preoccupied
unconscious 12 absentminded

abstruse
4 deep 5 heavy 6 knotty, occult
7 complex 8 esoteric, hermetic, involved,
profound 9 difficult, intricate, recondite
11 complicated

absurd
5 balmy, comic, crazy, droll, funny, inane,
loony, potty, silly, wacky 6 insane
7 asinine, fatuous, foolish, idiotic 8 farcical,
illogical 9 laughable, ludicrous
10 irrational, ridiculous 11 harebrained
12 preposterous, unreasonable

absurdity
5 farce, folly 7 inanity 8 insanity, nonsense
9 craziness, dottiness, silliness
11 foolishness, incongruity, witlessness
13 irrationality, ludicrousness,
senselessness

abundance
6 bounty, excess, plenty, riches, wealth
9 affluence, profusion 10 lavishness,
prosperity 11 prodigality
Scottish: 5 routh

abundant
4 full, lush, rich, rife 5 ample, thick 6 filled,
lavish, plenty 7 copious, crammed,
crowded, fruitful, liberal, profuse, replete
8 adequate, generous, prolific
9 abounding, bounteous, bountiful,
extensive, luxuriant, plenteous, plentiful
10 sufficient

abuse
3 mar 4 harm, hurt, rail 5 anger, decry,
shame, spoil, wrong 6 damage, debase,
deride, impair, injure, misuse, revile, vilify
7 calumny, corrupt, cursing, exploit,
obloquy, oppress, outrage, pervert,

profane, pollute **8** belittle, berating, blaspheme, derision, derogate, discount, disgrace, harshness, ill-treat, maltreat, mistreat, reviling, swearing **9** contumely, desecrate, disparage, dispraise, invective, manhandle, mishandle, persecute, profanity, vehemence **10** defamation, depreciate, impose upon, malignment, revilement, scurrility **11** disapproval **12** billingsgate, condemnation, denunciation, vilification, vituperation

abusive
5 dirty, harsh **6** odious **7** corrupt **8** scurrile **9** injurious, insulting, invective, offending, offensive, truculent **10** calumnious, defamatory, scurrilous **11** blasphemous, castigating, opprobrious **12** calumniating, contumelious, sharp-tongued, vituperative, vituperatory

abut
4 join, link **5** flank, touch, verge **6** adjoin, border, butt on **8** border on, neighbor **9** lie beside **11** butt against, communicate

abutting
4 next **6** beside, joined, next to **7** joining, verging **8** adjacent, next door, touching **9** adjoining, bordering, impinging **10** connecting, contiguous, juxtaposed **11** bordering on, coextensive, coterminous, neighboring **12** conterminous

abysm
see **abyss**

abysmal
4 deep, vast **7** endless, unplumbed **8** infinite, profound, unending, wretched **9** boundless, cavernous, plumbless, soundless **10** bottomless, fathomless, unmeasured **11** illimitable, measureless **12** immeasurable, unfathomable

abyss
3 pit **4** gulf, hell, hole, void **5** abysm, chasm, depth, gorge, hades, Sheol **6** Tophet **7** fissure, Gehenna, inferno **8** crevasse, deepness **9** perdition **10** underworld

academia
10 university **12** professoriat

academic
3 don **5** pupil, tutor **6** closet, fellow, master **7** bookish, learned, scholar, student **8** abstract, gownsman, lecturer, pedantic, scholarly **9** professor **10** scholastic **11** book-learned, conjectural, impractical,

speculative, theoretical **12** conventional, hypothetical

academic period
4 term **7** quarter **8** semester **9** trimester

academy
6 lyceum **7** college, society **9** institute **10** prep school **12** conservatory

Academy Award winner
picture:
1927–28: **5** Wings
1928–29: **14** Broadway Melody
1929–30: **25** All Quiet on the Western Front
1930–31: **8** Cimarron
1931–32: **10** Grand Hotel
1932–33: **9** Cavalcade
1934: **18** It Happened One Night
1935: **17** Mutiny on the Bounty
1936: **16** The Great Ziegfeld
1937: **15** Life of Emile Zola
1938: **20** You Can't Take It with You
1939: **15** Gone with the Wind
1940: **7** Rebecca
1941: **19** How Green Was My Valley
1942: **10** Mrs. Miniver
1943: **10** Casablanca
1944: **10** Going My Way
1945: **11** Lost Weekend (The)
1946: **19** Best Years of Our Lives (The)
1947: **19** Gentleman's Agreement
1948: **6** Hamlet
1949: **14** All the King's Men
1950: **11** All About Eve
1951: **15** American in Paris (An)
1952: **19** Greatest Show on Earth (The)
1953: **18** From Here to Eternity
1954: **15** On the Waterfront
1955: **5** Marty
1956: **26** Around the World in Eighty Days
1957: **20** Bridge on the River Kwai (The)
1958: **4** Gigi
1959: **6** Ben-Hur
1960: **9** Apartment (The)
1961: **13** West Side Story
1962: **16** Lawrence of Arabia
1963: **8** Tom Jones
1964: **10** My Fair Lady
1965: **12** Sound of Music (The)
1966: **16** Man for All Seasons (A)
1967: **16** In the Heat of the Night
1968: **6** Oliver
1969: **14** Midnight Cowboy
1970: **6** Patton
1971: **16** French Connection (The)
1972: **9** Godfather (The)
1973: **5** Sting (The)

1974: 9 Godfather (Part Two)(The)
1975: 25 One Flew over the Cuckoo's Nest
1976: 5 Rocky
1977: 9 Annie Hall
1978: 10 Deer Hunter (The)
1979: 14 Kramer vs. Kramer
1980: 14 Ordinary People
1981: 14 Chariots of Fire
1982: 6 Gandhi
1983: 17 Terms of Endearment
1984: 7 Amadeus
1985: 11 Out of Africa
1986: 7 Platoon
1987: 11 Last Emperor (The)
1988: 7 Rain Man
1989: 16 Driving Miss Daisy
1990: 16 Dances with Wolves
1991: 17 Silence of the Lambs (The)
1992: 10 Unforgiven
1993: 14 Schindler's List
1994: 11 Forrest Gump
1995: 10 Braveheart
1996: 14 English Patient (The)
1997: 7 Titanic
1998: 17 Shakespeare in Love
1999: 14 American Beauty
2000: 9 Gladiator
2001: 13 Beautiful Mind (A)
2002: 7 Chicago
2003: 14 Lord of the Rings

actor:
1927–28: 8 Jannings (Emil)
1928–29: 6 Baxter (Warner)
1929–30: 6 Arliss (George)
1930–31: 9 Barrymore (Lionel)
1931–32: 5 Beery (Wallace), March (Fredric)
1932–33: 8 Laughton (Charles)
1934: 5 Gable (Clark)
1935: 8 McLaglen (Victor)
1936: 4 Muni (Paul)
1937: 5 Tracy (Spencer)
1938: 5 Tracy (Spencer)
1939: 5 Donat (Robert)
1940: 7 Stewart (James)
1941: 6 Cooper (Gary)
1942: 6 Cagney (James)
1943: 5 Lukas (Paul)
1944: 6 Crosby (Bing)
1945: 7 Milland (Ray)
1946: 5 March (Fredric)
1947: 6 Colman (Ronald)
1948: 7 Olivier (Laurence)
1949: 8 Crawford (Broderick)
1950: 6 Ferrer (José)
1951: 6 Bogart (Humphrey)
1952: 6 Cooper (Gary)
1953: 6 Holden (William)

1954: 6 Brando (Marlon)
1955: 8 Borgnine (Ernest)
1956: 7 Brynner (Yul)
1957: 8 Guinness (Alec)
1958: 5 Niven (David)
1959: 6 Heston (Charlton)
1960: 9 Lancaster (Burt)
1961: 6 Schell (Maximilian)
1962: 4 Peck (Gregory)
1963: 7 Poitier (Sidney)
1964: 8 Harrison (Rex)
1965: 6 Marvin (Lee)
1966: 8 Scofield (Paul)
1967: 7 Steiger (Rod)
1968: 9 Robertson (Cliff)
1969: 5 Wayne (John)
1970: 5 Scott (George C.)
1971: 7 Hackman (Gene)
1972: 6 Brando (Marlon)
1973: 6 Lemmon (Jack)
1974: 6 Carney (Art)
1975: 9 Nicholson (Jack)
1976: 5 Finch (Peter)
1977: 8 Dreyfuss (Richard)
1978: 6 Voight (Jon)
1979: 7 Hoffman (Dustin)
1980: 6 De Niro (Robert)
1981: 5 Fonda (Henry)
1982: 6 Kingsley (Ben)
1983: 6 Duvall (Robert)
1984: 7 Abraham (F. Murray)
1985: 4 Hurt (William)
1986: 6 Newman (Paul)
1987: 7 Douglas (Michael)
1988: 7 Hoffman (Dustin)
1989: 8 Day-Lewis (Daniel)
1990: 5 Irons (Jeremy)
1991: 7 Hopkins (Anthony)
1992: 6 Pacino (Al)
1993: 5 Hanks (Tom)
1994: 5 Hanks (Tom)
1995: 4 Cage (Nicholas)
1996: 4 Rush (Geoffrey)
1997: 5 Nicholson (Jack)
1998: 7 Benigni (Roberto)
1999: 6 Spacey (Kevin)
2000: 5 Crowe (Russell)
2001: 10 Washington (Denzel)
2002: 5 Brody (Adrien)
2003: 4 Penn (Sean)

actress:
1927–28: 6 Gaynor (Janet)
1928–29: 8 Pickford (Mary)
1929–30: 8 Shearer (Norma)
1930–31: 8 Dressler (Marie)
1931–32: 5 Hayes (Helen)
1932–33: 7 Hepburn (Katharine)
1934: 7 Colbert (Claudette)
1935: 5 Davis (Bette)

1936: 6 Rainer (Luise)
1937: 6 Rainer (Luise)
1938: 5 Davis (Bette)
1939: 5 Leigh (Vivien)
1940: 6 Rogers (Ginger)
1941: 8 Fontaine (Joan)
1942: 6 Garson (Greer)
1943: 5 Jones (Jennifer)
1944: 7 Bergman (Ingrid)
1945: 8 Crawford (Joan)
1946: 11 de Havilland (Olivia)
1947: 5 Young (Loretta)
1948: 5 Wyman (Jane)
1949: 11 de Havilland (Olivia)
1950: 8 Holliday (Judy)
1951: 5 Leigh (Vivien)
1952: 5 Booth (Shirley)
1953: 7 Hepburn (Audrey)
1954: 5 Kelly (Grace)
1955: 7 Magnani (Anna)
1956: 7 Bergman (Ingrid)
1957: 8 Woodward (Joanne)
1958: 7 Hayward (Susan)
1959: 8 Signoret (Simone)
1960: 6 Taylor (Elizabeth)
1961: 5 Loren (Sophia)
1962: 8 Bancroft (Anne)
1963: 4 Neal (Patricia)
1964: 7 Andrews (Julie)
1965: 8 Christie (Julie)
1966: 6 Taylor (Elizabeth)
1967: 7 Hepburn (Katharine)
1968: 7 Hepburn (Katharine) 9 Streisand (Barbra)
1969: 5 Smith (Maggie)
1970: 7 Jackson (Glenda)
1971: 5 Fonda (Jane)
1972: 8 Minnelli (Liza)
1973: 7 Jackson (Glenda)
1974: 7 Burstyn (Ellen)
1975: 8 Fletcher (Louise)
1976: 7 Dunaway (Faye)
1977: 6 Keaton (Diane)
1978: 6 Fonda (Jane)
1979: 5 Field (Sally)
1980: 6 Spacek (Sissy)
1981: 7 Hepburn (Katharine)
1982: 5 Streep (Meryl)
1983: 8 MacLaine (Shirley)
1984: 5 Field (Sally)
1985: 4 Page (Geraldine)
1986: 6 Matlin (Marlee)
1987: 4 Cher
1988: 6 Foster (Jodie)
1989: 5 Tandy (Jessica)
1990: 5 Bates (Kathy)
1991: 6 Foster (Jodie)
1992: 8 Thompson (Emma)
1993: 6 Hunter (Holly)

1994: 5 Lange (Jessica)
1995: 8 Sarandon (Susan)
1996: 9 McDormand (Frances)
1997: 4 Hunt (Helen)
1998: 7 Paltrow (Gwyneth)
1999: 5 Swank (Hilary)
2000: 7 Roberts (Julia)
2001: 5 Berry (Halle)
2002: 6 Kidman (Nicole)
2003: 6 Theron (Charlize)

accede

3 let 5 admit, agree, allow, grant, yield
6 accept, assent, comply, concur, give in,
permit 7 agree to, approve, concede,
consent 9 acquiesce, cooperate, subscribe

accelerando

6 faster 7 speed up 10 speeding up

accelerate

3 gun, rev 4 grow, roll 5 hurry, impel, rev
up, speed 6 hasten, open up, step up
7 quicken, speed up 8 expedite, go faster,
increase 9 fast track, gain speed 10 move
faster, peel rubber

acceleration

7 speedup 8 hurrying, spurring
9 hastening, increasing, revving up
10 quickening, speeding up, stepping up
12 moving faster

accent

4 beat, lilt, tone 5 acute, grave, meter,
pulse, throb 6 rhythm, stress, weight
7 cadence 8 emphasis 9 diacritic,
pulsation 10 inflection, intonation
Irish: 6 brogue
Scottish: 4 burr
Southern: 5 drawl

accept

3 bow, buy, see 4 bear, gain, okay, take
5 admit, adopt, agree, catch, favor, go for,
grasp, yield 6 accede, admire, affirm,
assent, endure, follow, take in, take on
7 agree to, approve, believe, receive,
respect, swallow, welcome 8 assent to,
bear with, hold with, live with, stand for,
tolerate, tough out 9 acquiesce, agree
with, undertake 10 capitulate,
comprehend, concur with, understand
11 acknowledge, countenance, subscribe
to

acceptable

4 good, okay 6 decent, worthy 7 average,
welcome 8 adequate, all right, bearable,
ordinary, passable, pleasing, standard,
suitable 9 endurable, tolerable
10 sufficient 11 commonplace,

respectable, supportable **12** satisfactory
13 unexceptional, unimpeachable

acceptably
4 well **5** amply, right **7** capably **8** properly,
suitably **9** fittingly, tolerably **10** adequately,
becomingly, fairly well **11** competently
12 sufficiently **13** appropriately

acceptant
4 open **8** amenable, friendly, swayable
9 favorable, receptive, recipient, welcoming
10 open-minded, responsive
11 persuadable, persuasible, susceptible
13 influenceable

acceptation
4 gist **5** point, sense **6** import **7** meaning,
message, purport **9** intention
10 intendment **12** significance, significancy
13 signification, understanding

accepted
5 usual **6** common, normal, proper
7 correct, ordinary, regular, routine
8 approved, everyday, expected, habitual,
orthodox, received **9** customary
10 accustomed, recognized, sanctioned
11 established, traditional **12** conventional

access
3 fit, way **4** adit, door, gust, pang, path,
road, turn **5** burst, entry, get at, onset,
route, sally, spell, throe **6** attack, avenue,
entrée **7** contact, flare-up, ingress,
passage, seizure **8** approach, entrance,
eruption, increase, outburst **9** admission,
explosion **10** admittance

accessible
4 near, open **5** handy **6** public, usable
8 possible **9** available, operative,
reachable **10** attainable, employable,
obtainable **11** practicable
12 approachable, unrestricted

accession
4 rise **5** raise **8** addition, approach,
increase, outburst, taking on **9** accretion,
adherence, increment, induction
10 admittance, assumption, attainment,
succession **11** acquisition
12 augmentation, inauguration

accessory
3 aid **4** aide, trim **5** extra, frill **6** helper
7 abettor, adjunct, fitting, insider, partner
8 addition, adjuvant, appendix **9** accretion,
adornment, ancillary, appendage, assistant,
associate, auxiliary, increment, secondary,
tributary **10** accomplice, coincident,
collateral, concurrent, decoration,

incidental, subsidiary **11** appurtenant,
concomitant, confederate, conspirator,
subordinate, subservient **12** appurtenance,
contributory **13** accompaniment, coco-
spirator, supplementary

accident
3 hap, lot **4** fate, luck, odds **5** fluke
6 chance, gamble, hazard, kismet, mishap
7 bad luck, destiny, fortune, lottery
8 calamity, casualty, fortuity, incident
9 adventure, mischance **10** misfortune
12 misadventure

accidental
3 odd **5** fluky **6** casual, chance, random
7 unmeant **8** by chance, careless
9 chromatic, dependent, extempore,
impromptu, unplanned, unwitting
10 coincident, contingent, fortuitous,
incidental, undesigned, unexpected,
unforeseen, unintended, unpurposed
11 conditional, inadvertent **12** coincidental,
nonessential, uncalculated
13 unintentional

acclaim
4 hail, clap, laud **5** cheer, éclat, exalt,
extol, glory, honor, kudos, roose
6 homage, praise, salute **7** applaud,
approve, commend, glorify, magnify,
ovation, root for **8** applause, plaudits
10 compliment

acclimate
5 adapt **6** adjust, change, harden, season
7 toughen **9** condition, habituate

accolade
4 bays, fame **5** award, badge, honor,
kudos **6** praise **7** laurels, tribute
8 approval **10** decoration **11** distinction

accommodate
3 fit **4** hold, put up, rent, suit **5** adapt, alter,
board, defer, favor, house, humor, lodge,
put up, yield **6** adjust, attune, bestow,
billet, change, encase, harbor, modify,
oblige, please, submit, tailor, take in
7 cater to, conform, contain, enclose,
furnish, indulge, quarter, receive, shelter,
8 accustom, allow for, domicile **9** entertain,
harmonize, integrate, reconcile **11** domiciliate, make room for

accommodating
7 amiable, helpful, willing **8** gracious,
obliging **9** adaptable **10** hospitable,
solicitous, thoughtful **11** considerate,
cooperative

accommodations
4 digs, keep, room 5 hotel, motel
7 housing, lodging, shelter 8 lodgment,
quarters 9 residence 12 room and board

accompaniment
4 back, mate 6 fellow, backup 7 adjunct,
comrade, consort, partner 8 addition
9 accessory, associate, attendant,
colleague, companion, corollary
10 assistance, complement, enrichment,
equivalent, supplement 11 concomitant,
enhancement 12 augmentation

accompany
4 join 5 bring, guide, pilot 6 attend,
convoy, escort, go with 7 combine,
conduct, consort 8 chaperon, come with
9 associate 10 appear with, go together
11 perform with

accompanying
8 incident 9 accessory, ancillary, attendant,
attending, secondary 10 associated,
coincident, collateral 11 concomitant

accomplice
4 aide, ally 5 aider 6 flunky, helper, stooge
7 abettor, partner 9 accessory, assistant,
associate 11 confederate, conspirator,
subordinate 13 coconspirator

accomplish
3 win 4 gain 5 reach, score 6 attain,
effect, fulfil, rack up 7 achieve, execute,
fulfill, perfect, pull off, realize, succeed
8 bring off, carry out, complete 9 discharge
10 bring about

accomplished
4 able 5 adept 6 expert 8 finished,
masterly, skilled 8 skillful, talented
9 perfected, practiced 10 proficient
11 beyond doubt

accomplishment
3 act, art 4 deed, feat 5 craft, doing, skill
6 action, effort, finish, talent 7 ability,
exploit 9 adeptness, expertise
10 attainment, capability, completion,
expertness 11 achievement, acquirement,
acquisition, proficiency

accord
4 deal, fuse, give, jibe, pact 5 agree,
award, blend, chime, fit in, grant, match,
merge, tally, union 6 affirm, assent, concur,
confer, treaty 7 compact, concert, concord,
conform, empathy, harmony, rapport
8 affinity, coalesce, coincide, dovetail,
sympathy 9 agreement, harmonize,
reconcile, vouchsafe 10 attraction,

conformity, consonance, correspond,
solidarity 11 concordance
13 understanding

accordant
8 agreeing 9 congruous, consonant
10 conforming, harmonious 13 correspondent

accordingly
4 duly, ergo, then, thus 5 hence
9 therefore, thereupon 12 consequently

accost
3 dog 4 call, dare, face, hail 5 annoy,
cross, front, hound, worry 6 bother, call to
7 affront, apply to, bespeak, outface,
outrage 8 approach, confront 9 challenge
10 buttonhole 11 memorialize

accouchement
7 lying-in 8 childbed, delivery 10 childbirth
11 confinement, giving birth, parturition

account
3 tab, use 4 bill, deem, note, rate, view
5 avail, basis, favor, score, story, track,
value, worth 6 assess, client, esteem,
reason, reckon, record, regard, report,
repute 7 analyze, explain, expound,
history, invoice, justify, recital, respect,
service, utility, version 8 appraise,
consider, customer, estimate, 9 advantage,
chronicle, narrative, probe into, rationale,
reckoning, relevance, statement, valuation
10 admiration, estimation, exposition,
importance, reputation, usefulness 11 consequence, distinction, explain away,
explanation, performance, rationalize
13 consideration, justification
book: 6 ledger

accountable
6 liable 8 amenable 10 answerable
11 explainable, responsible

accounting
11 bookkeeping

accoutre
3 arm, rig 4 deck, gear 5 adorn, dress,
equip, fix up, ready 6 attire, fit out, outfit,
supply 7 appoint, furnish, prepare, provide,
turn out 9 provision

accoutrement
3 kit 4 gear 6 outfit, tackle 7 regalia
8 tackling 9 accessory, apparatus,
equipment, machinery, trappings
10 provisions 11 furnishings, habiliments
12 appointments 13 paraphernalia

accredit
3 lay 4 okay 5 refer 6 assign, attest,

charge, credit, enable **7** approve, ascribe, certify, commend, empower, endorse, license, warrant **8** sanction, validate, vouch for **9** attribute, authorize, recognize, recommend **10** commission, credential

accretion
4 rise **5** raise **7** buildup, growth **8** addition, increase **9** accession, appendage, increment **10** attachment **11** enlargement **12** accumulation, augmentation

accrue
4 grow **5** amass **6** gather, pile up **7** build up, collect, compile **8** increase **10** accumulate, amalgamate **11** agglomerate

accumulate
4 heap, grow, mass, pile **5** add to, amass, hoard, lay by, lay in, lay up, stock, store **6** accrue, garner, gather, pile up, rack up, roll up **7** acquire, backlog, collect, compile, lay down, stack up, store up **8** assemble, increase **9** stockpile

accumulation
4 bank, heap, mass, pile **5** hoard, stock, store, trove **7** buildup, growth, reserve **8** increase **9** accretion, amassment **10** collection **11** aggregation, enlargement **13** agglomeration

accumulative
6 heaped **7** growing **8** additive, additory **9** summative **10** collective, increasing **11** aggregative **12** augmentative

accuracy
8 veracity **9** certainty, exactness, precision **10** definition, exactitude **11** correctness, preciseness **12** definiteness

accurate
4 just, nice, true **5** exact, right **6** actual, proper **7** certain, correct, factual, precise **8** definite, reliable, rigorous **9** authentic, error-free, errorless **10** dependable

accursed
4 vile **6** odious **7** hateful **8** damnable **9** abhorrent, execrable, loathsome, offensive, repugnant, revolting **10** abominable, despicable, detestable

accusation
3 rap **6** charge **9** complaint **10** allegation, indictment **12** denunciation **false: 7** calumny

accuse
3 tax **5** blame, brand **6** allege, charge,

delate, finger, impute, indict **7** arraign, ascribe, censure, impeach **8** admonish, denounce, reproach **9** criminate, criticize, inculpate, reprobate **10** denunciate **11** incriminate

accustom
3 use **4** wont **5** adapt, inure **6** adjust, harden, season **7** conform **9** habituate **11** acclimatize, familiarize

accustomed
3 set **5** usual **6** normal **7** chronic, regular, routine **8** accepted, everyday, familiar, habitual, ordinary, standard **9** customary **10** habituated **11** commonplace, established, traditional **12** conventional

ace
3 bit, jot, pip, top **4** atom, hair, iota, mite, star **5** crumb, defeat, minim, point, score, speck **6** master, winner **7** whisker **8** molecule, particle **9** first rate, hole in one **11** hairbreadth, tennis score

ace and face card
7 natural **9** blackjack

acedia
6 apathy **7** boredom

acerbate
3 vex **5** anger, annoy, peeve **6** madden **7** incense, inflame **8** embitter, irritate **9** aggravate **10** exasperate

acerbic
4 acid, sour, tart **5** acrid, harsh, rough, sharp **7** caustic, cutting, satiric **8** stinging **9** acidulous, corrosive, sarcastic **10** astringent

acerbity
7 acidity, sarcasm **8** acrimony, asperity, sourness, tartness **9** harshness, roughness, surliness **10** bitterness, causticity

Achates' companion
6 Aeneas

ache
3 yen **4** hurt, long, pain, pang, pine, pity, sigh **5** crave, smart, throb, yearn **6** hanker, hunger, stitch, suffer, thirst, twinge **8** yearning **11** commiserate **Scottish: 6** stound

Acheron
5 Hades, river

achieve
3 get, win **4** gain **5** reach, score **6** attain, effect, finish, obtain, rack up, secure **7** acquire, execute, fulfill, get done,

perform, realize, succeed **8** carry out, complete, conclude **9** actualize **10** accomplish

achievement
4 deed, feat **6** finish **7** exploit, success **10** attainment, completion **11** acquisition, tour de force

Achilles
adviser: 6 Nestor
companion: 9 Patroclus
father: 6 Peleus
horse: 7 Xanthus
lover: 7 Briseis
mother: 6 Thetis
slayer: 5 Paris
victim: 6 Hector
vulnerable part: 4 heel

aching
4 hurt, sore **6** in pain **7** hurtful, hurting, painful **8** yearning **9** disturbed **10** afflictive, distressed **13** compassionate

acicular
5 acute, peaky, piked, sharp **6** peaked, pointy, spiked **7** pointed

acid
4 sour, tart **5** acerb **7** acerbic, acetose, caustic **8** stinging **9** corrosive, sarcastic, vitriolic
bleaching: 6 oxalic
fatty: 6 capric **7** caproic, stearic **8** caprylic
found in apples: 5 malic
found in cranberries: 7 benzoic
found in grapes: 8 tartaric
found in lemons: 6 citric
found in rhubarb: 6 oxalic
found in sour milk: 6 lactic
indicator: 6 litmus
kind: 5 amino, boric, iodic, malic, oleic **6** acetic, bromic, formic, nitric, oxalic, tannic **7** nitrous, silicic **8** carbolic, carbonic, muriatic, sulfuric **9** aqua regia **12** hydrochloric
neutralizer: 4 base **6** alkali
tanning: 6 tannic **8** catechin
vinegar: 6 acetic

acidulous
3 dry **4** sour, tart **5** acerb, harsh, sharp **6** biting **7** acerbic, acetose, cutting, piquant, pungent **9** sarcastic

Acis
lover: 7 Galatea
slayer: 10 Polyphemus

acknowledge
3 own **4** avow, deem, tell, view **5** admit,

agree, allow, grant, let on, own up **6** accede, accept, fess up, reveal **7** concede, confess, declare, divulge, profess **8** announce, consider, disclose, proclaim **9** recognize

acknowledgment
6 assent, avowal, credit, notice **9** admission **10** confession **11** affirmation, declaration, recognition

acme
3 cap, top **4** apex, peak **6** apogee, climax, summit, tiptop, vertex, zenith **8** capstone, pinnacle, ultimate **9** high point **10** perfection **11** culmination

acorn sprouter
3 oak

acoustic
5 aural **6** audile **8** auditory **9** unplugged

acquaint
4 clue, tell, warn **6** advise, fill in, inform, notify, orient, reveal, wise up **7** apprise, disclose, divulge, present **8** accustom **9** enlighten, habituate, introduce **11** familiarize

acquaintance
4 mate **5** amigo, crony, grasp **6** friend **7** comrade, contact **9** associate, colleague, companion **10** cognizance, experience **11** familiarity

acquainted
6 versed **7** abreast, in touch **8** familiar, informed, up-to-date **9** au courant **10** conversant

acquiesce
3 bow, yes **5** agree, allow, bow to, yield **6** accede, accept, assent, comply, concur, give in, submit **7** consent, go along **9** reconcile, subscribe

acquiescence
6 assent **7** consent **8** giving in, yielding **9** deference **10** acceptance, compliance, conformity, submission **11** resignation

acquiescent
6 docile **7** passive **8** resigned, yielding **10** submissive **11** unresistant, unresisting **12** nonresistant, nonresisting

acquire
3 add, buy, get, win **4** earn, form, gain, land **5** amass, annex **6** garner, obtain, pick up, secure **7** bring in, collect, develop, procure **10** accumulate

acquirement
8 addition 9 accretion 11 acquisition

acquisition
4 gain 5 prize 7 winning 8 addition, learning, property, purchase 9 accretion

acquisitive
5 eager, itchy 6 grabby, greedy 8 covetous, desirous, grasping 10 avaricious

acquit
3 act 4 bear, free 5 carry, clear, let go 6 behave, deport, let off 7 absolve, comport, conduct, perform, release, set free 8 liberate 9 discharge, exculpate, exonerate, vindicate

acres
4 area, land 5 lands 6 estate, expanse 7 demesne, holding 8 property

acrid
4 acid, sour 5 harsh, nasty, sharp 6 biting, bitter 7 austere, burning, caustic, cutting, pungent 8 stinging 9 trenchant 10 astringent, irritating 11 acrimonious

acrimonious
3 mad 5 angry, cross, irate, sharp, testy 6 bitter, cranky, ireful 7 acerbic, biting, caustic, cutting 9 indignant, irascible, rancorous 11 belligerent, contentious, quarrelsome

acrimony
5 anger, spite 6 animus, malice, rancor 7 ill will 8 acerbity, asperity, mordancy 9 animosity, antipathy, harshness, virulence 10 bitterness 11 malevolence

Acrisius
daughter: 5 Danaë
slayer: 7 Perseus

acrobat
7 gymnast 9 aerialist, trapezist 11 funambulist

across
4 over 6 beyond 7 athwart 12 transversely
prefix: 5 trans

act
3 law, run 4 bear, bill, deed, fake, feat, mime, play, pose, sham, work 5 bluff, feign, front, put-on, serve, stunt 6 affect, appear, behave, shtick 7 exploit, operate, perform, portray, pretend, routine, statute 8 function, pretense, simulate 9 officiate 10 masquerade 11 counterfeit, impersonate

acting
6 pro tem 7 interim, playing 9 ad interim, dramatics, imitating, portrayal, temporary 10 pro tempore 12 entertaining

action
4 case, deed, move, step, stir, suit, work 5 cause, doing 6 battle, bustle, combat 7 lawsuit, process, service 8 activity, behavior, conflict, fighting, function 9 execution, operation, procedure 10 engagement, proceeding 11 performance

action painting
7 tachism

activate
4 stir, wake 5 rally, rouse, set up, waken 6 arouse, awaken, call up, turn on 8 energize, mobilize, motivate, vitalize 9 stimulate

active
4 busy, live, spry 5 agile, alert, alive, brisk, going 6 at work, in play, lively, moving 7 driving, dynamic, flowing, running, working 8 animated, bustling, emitting, erupting, spirited, vigorous 9 effective, energetic, operating, operative, sprightly 11 functioning, industrious 12 enterprising

activity
6 action, bustle, motion 7 process, pursuit, venture 8 exercise, exertion 10 exercising, liveliness 11 undertaking

actor
4 mime, star 5 mimic 6 mummer, player 7 trouper 8 thespian 9 performer 11 participant 12 impersonator
name: 3 Cox (Wally), Fox (James, Michael J.), Lee (Bruce), Lom (Herbert), Mix (Tom), Ray (Aldo) 4 Alda (Alan, Robert), Bean (Orson), Blue (Ben), Bond (Ward), Caan (James), Cage (Nicholas), Cobb (Lee J.), Coco (James), Culp (Robert), Dean (James), Depp (Johnny), Dern (Bruce), Duff (Howard), Egan (Richard), Falk (Peter), Ford (Glenn, Harrison), Foxx (Redd), Geer (Will), Gere (Richard), Grey (Joel), Hill (Arthur), Hope (Bob), Hurt (John, William), Ives (Burl), Kaye (Danny), Kean (Edmund), Keel (Howard), Ladd (Alan), Lahr (Bert), Lord (Jack), Lowe (Rob), Lunt (Alfred), Marx (Chico, Groucho, Harpo, Zeppo), Muni (Paul), Ngor (Haing S.), Peck (Gregory), Penn (Seán), Pitt (Brad), Raft (George), Roth (Tim), Ryan (Robert), Shaw (Robert), Tati (Jacques), Tone (Franchot), Torn (Rip), Tune (Tommy), Wahl (Ken), Webb (Clifton, Jack), Wynn (Ed, Keenan),

York (Michael) **5** Adler (Luther), Allen (Fred, Tim, Woody), Arkin (Adam, Alan), Asner (Ed), Autry (Gene), Ayres (Lew), Bacon (Kevin), Barry (Gene), Bates (Alan), Beery (Wallace), Benny (Jack), Berle (Milton), Boone (Richard), Booth (Edwin), Boyer (Charles), Brand (Neville), Burns (George), Caine (Michael), Candy (John), Chase (Chevy), Clift (Montgomery), Cosby (Bill), Dafoe (Willem), Davis (Clifton, Ossie, Sammy Jr.), Delon (Alain), Donat (Robert), Evans (Maurice), Ewell (Tom), Finch (Peter), Firth (Colin, Peter), Flynn (Errol), Fonda (Henry, Peter), Franz (Dennis), Gabin (Jean), Gable (Clark), Gould (Elliot), Grant (Cary, Hugh), Gwenn (Edmund), Hanks (Tom), Hardy (Oliver), Hauer (Rutger), Hawke (Ethan), Hayes (Gabby), Irons (Jeremy), Jaffe (Sam), Jones (Dean, James Earl, Tommy Lee), Kazan (Elia), Keach (Stacy), Keith (Brian, David), Kelly (Gene), Kiley (Richard), Kline (Kevin), Kotto (Yaphet), Lamas (Fernando, Lorenzo), Lanza (Mario), Lewis (Jerry, Richard), Lloyd (Harold), Lorre (Peter), Lukas (Paul), Lynde (Paul), March (Fredric), Mason (James), McCoy (Tim), Mills (John), Mineo (Sal), Moore (Dudley, Roger, Victor), Neill (Sam), Nimoy (Leonard), Niven (David), Nolte (Nick), Olmos (Edward James), O'Neal (Patrick, Ryan), Payne (John), Perry (Luke, Matthew), Pesci (Joe), Power (Tyrone), Price (Vincent), Pryce (Jonathan), Quaid (Dennis, Randy), Quayle (Anthony), Quinn (Aidan, Anthony), Rains (Claude), Reeve (Christopher), Scott (Campbell, George C., Randolph), Segal (George), Sheen (Charlie, Martin), Smits (Jimmy), Stack (Robert), Stamp (Terence), Sydow (Max von), Tracy (Spencer), Wayne (John), Wilde (Cornel), Wills (Chill), Woods (James), Young (Gig, Robert) **6** Abbott (Bud), Albert (Eddie), Ameche (Don), Arness (James), Backus (Jim), Balsam (Martin), Barker (Lex), Baxter (Warner), Beatty (Ned, Warren), Begley (Ed), Blades (Ruben), Bogart (Humphrey), Bolger (Ray), Brando (Marlon), Brooks (Albert, Mel), Burton (Richard), Caesar (Sid), Cagney (James), Cantor (Eddie), Cariou (Len), Carney (Art), Carrey (Jim), Carvey (Dana), Chaney (Lon), Cleese (John), Coburn (Charles, James), Colman (Ronald), Conrad (Robert, William), Conway (Tim, Tom), Coogan (Jackie), Cooper (Gary), Cotten (Joseph), Coward (Noël), Crabbe (Buster), Crenna (Richard), Cronyn (Hume), Crosby (Bing), Cruise (Tom), Culkin (Macaulay), Curtis (Tony), Dailey (Dan), Dalton (Timothy), Danson (Ted), Danton (Ray), Darren (James), De Niro (Robert), de Sica (Vittorio), De Vito (Danny), Dillon (Matt), Downey (Robert), Dullea (Keir), Duryea (Dan), Duvall (Robert), Ferrer (José, Mel), Fields (W.C.), Finney (Albert), Garcia (Andy), Garner (James), Gibson (Hoot, Mel), Glover (Danny), Graves (Peter), Greene (Lorne), Grodin (Charles), Harris (Ed, Richard), Harvey (Laurence), Hayden (Sterling), Heflin (Van), Heston (Charlton), Hingle (Pat), Holden (Bill), Hopper (Dennis, William), Howard (Leslie, Ron, Trevor), Hudson (Rock), Hunter (Jeffrey, Tab), Huston (John, Walter), Hutton (Jim, Timothy), Irving (Henry), Jacobi (Derek, Lou), Jagger (Dean), Keaton (Buster, Michael), Keitel (Harvey), Kilmer (Val), Knotts (Don), Landau (Martin), Landon (Michael), Laurel (Stan), Lemmon (Jack), Liotta (Ray), Lugosi (Bela), MacRae (Gordon), Malden (Karl), Martin (Dean, Steve), Marvin (Lee), Massey (Raymond), Mature (Victor), McCrea (Joel), Meeker (Ralph), Menjou (Adolphe), Mifune (Toshiro), Modine (Matthew), Morley (Robert), Mostel (Zero), Murphy (Audie, Eddie), Murray (Bill, Don), Neeson (Liam), Nelson (Ozzie), Newley (Anthony), Newman (Paul), O'Brian (Hugh), O'Brien (Edmund, Pat), Oldman (Gary), O'Toole (Peter), Pacino (Al), Parker (Fess), Poston (Tom), Powell (Dick), Reeves (Keanu, Steve), Reiner (Carl, Rob), Reiser (Paul), Rennie (Michael), Ritter (John, Tex), Rogers (Roy, Wayne, Will), Romero (Cesar), Rooney (Mickey), Rourke (Mickey), Schell (Maximilian), Seagal (Steven), Sharif (Omar), Slezak (Walter), Snipes (Wesley), Spacey (Kevin), Spader (James), Swayze (Patrick), Taylor (Robert, Rod), Thomas (Danny, Richard), Turpin (Ben), Vallee (Rudy), Vaughn (Robert), Voight (Jon), Wagner (Robert), Walker (Robert), Warden (Jack), Wayans (Damon, Keenen Ivory), Weaver (Dennis, Fritz), Welles (Orson), Werner (Oskar), Wildor (Gene), Willis (Bruce) **7** Abraham (F. Murray), Andrews (Dana), Astaire (Fred), Aykroyd (Dan), Baldwin (Alec, Daniel, Stephen, William), Bellamy (Ralph), Bogarde (Dirk), Branagh (Kenneth), Bridges (Beau, Jeff, Lloyd), Bronson (Charles), Brosnan (Pierce), Brynner (Yul), Burbage (Richard), Bushman (Francis X.), Buttons (Red), Calhern (Louis), Calhoun (Rory), Cameron (Rod), Carroll (Leo G.), Chaplin (Charlie), Clooney (George), Connery (Sean), Connors (Chuck), Conried

(Hans), Costner (Kevin), Crystal (Billy), Daniels (Jeff), da Silva (Howard), DeLuise (Dom), Dennehy (Brian), Donahue (Troy), Donlevy (Brian), Douglas (Kirk, Melvyn, Michael, Paul), Dreyfuss (Richard), Durante (Jimmy), Edwards (Vince), Feldman (Marty), Fiennes (Ralph), Freeman (Morgan), Garrick (David), Gazzara (Ben), Gielgud (John), Gleason (Jackie), Goodman (John), Gossett (Lou), Grammer (Kelsey), Granger (Farley, Stewart), Guinness (Alec), Hackman (Gene), Henreid (Paul), Hoffman (Dustin), Homolka (Oscar), Hopkins (Anthony), Hoskins (Bob), Janssen (David), Johnson (Ben, Don, Van), Jourdan (Louis), Jurgens (Curt), Karloff (Boris), Kennedy (Arthur, George), Klugman (Jack), Lawford (Peter), Leonard (Robert Sean, Sheldon), Lithgow (John), MacLane (Barton), Maharis (George), Mathers (Jerry), Matthau (Walter), McCarey (Leo), McGavin (Darren), McQueen (Steve), Milland (Ray), Mitchum (Robert), Montand (Yves), Navarro (Ramon), Newhart (Bob), O'Connor (Carroll, Donald), Olivier (Laurence), Palance (Jack), Paulsen (Pat), Peppard (George), Perkins (Anthony), Pickens (Slim), Pidgeon (Walter), Poitier (Sidney), Preston (Robert), Randall (Tony), Redford (Robert), Rickman (Alan), Robards (Jason), Robbins (Tim), Robeson (Paul), Roberts (Pernell, Tony), Sanders (George), Savalas (Telly), Scourby (Alexander), Selleck (Tom), Sellers (Peter), Shatner (William), Shepard (Sam), Silvers (Phil), Sinatra (Frank), Skelton (Red), Skinner (Otis), Steiger (Rod), Stewart (James, Patrick), Stooges (Three), Tamblyn (Russ), Ustinov (Peter), Van Dyke (Dick, Jerry), Wallach (Eli), Widmark (Richard), Wilding (Michael), Winters (Jonathan), Woolley (Monty) **8** Banderas (Antonio), Barrault (Jean-Louis), Basehart (Richard), Belmondo (Jean-Paul), Berenger (Tom), Blackmer (Sidney), Borgnine (Ernest), Buchanan (Edgar), Buchholz (Horst), Chandler (Jeff), Costello (Lou), Crawford (Broderick, Michael), Cummings (Robert), Day-Lewis (Daniel), DiCaprio (Leonardo), Eastwood (Clint), Forsythe (John), Garfield (John), Goldblum (Jeff), Griffith (Andy), Harrison (Noel, Rex), Hemmings (David), Holbrook (Hal), Holloway (Stanley), Houseman (John), Jannings (Emil), Kingsley (Ben), Langella (Frank), Laughton (Charles), Marshall (E.G., Herbert), McDowall (Roddy), McDowell (Malcolm), McLaglen (Victor), Meredith (Burgess),

Rathbone (Basil), Redgrave (Michael), Reynolds (Burt), Ritchard (Cyril), Robinson (Edward G.), Sarrazin (Michael), Scofield (Paul), Seinfeld (Jerry), Stallone (Sylvester), Stroheim (Erich von), Sullivan (Barry), Travolta (John), Turturro (John), Van Damme (Jean-Claude), Von Sydow (Max), Whitmore (James), Williams (Robin) **9** Amsterdam (Morey), Barrymore (John, Lionel), Brandauer (Klaus Maria), Broderick (Matthew), Carnovsky (Morris), Carradine (David, John, Keith, Robert), Courtenay (Tom), Depardieu (Gérard), Fairbanks (Douglas), Fishburne (Larry), Franciosa (Anthony), Hardwicke (Cedric), Harrelson (Woody), Hyde-White (Wilfrid), Lancaster (Burt), MacMurray (Fred), Malkovich (John), Montalban (Ricardo), Nicholson (Jack), Pleasance (Donald), Robertson (Cliff, Dale), Strasberg (Lee), Tarantino (Quentin), Valentino (Rudolph), Zimbalist (Efrem) **10** Fitzgerald (Barry), Hasselhoff (David), Montgomery (Robert), Richardson (Ralph), Sutherland (Donald, Kiefer), Washington (Denzel) **11** Chamberlain (Richard), Greenstreet (Sydney), Mastroianni (Marcello), Trintignant (Jean-Louis) **13** Kristofferson (Kris)

actor's
quest: 4 part, role
signal: 3 cue

actress
3 Bow (Clara), Cox (Courtney), Day (Doris), Dee (Ruby, Sandra), Dru (Joanne), Gam (Rita), Loy (Myrna), May (Elaine), Rae (Charlotte) **4** Ball (Lucille), Bara (Theda), Barr (Roseanne), Cass (Peggy), Cher, Coca (Imogene), Cruz (Penelope), Dahl (Arlene), Daly (Tyne), Dern (Laura), Diaz (Cameron), Dors (Diana), Down (Lesley-Ann), Duke (Patty), Duse (Eleonora), Eden (Barbara), Foch (Nina), Garr (Teri), Gish (Dorothy, Lillian), Grey (Jennifer), Gwyn (Nell), Hawn (Goldie), Holm (Celeste), Hunt (Helen, Linda, Marsha), Hurt (Mary Beth), Hyer (Martha), Ivey (Judith), Kahn (Madeline), Kerr (Deborah), Lake (Veronica), Lisi (Virna), Main (Marjorie), Mayo (Virginia), Neal (Patricia), Olin (Lena), Page (Geraldine), Raye (Martha), Rigg (Diana), Ross (Diana, Katharine), Rush (Barbara), Ryan (Meg, Peggy), Shue (Elisabeth), Weld (Tuesday), West (Mae), Wood (Natalie, Peggy), Wray (Fay), York (Susannah) **5** Adams (Maude), Aimee (Anouk), Allen (Joan, Gracie, Karen, Nancy), Alley (Kirstie), Arden (Eve), Astor

(Mary), Bates (Kathy), Berry (Halle), Black (Karen), Bloom (Claire), Blyth (Ann), Booth (Shirley), Brice (Fanny), Britt (May), Bruce (Virginia), Buzzi (Ruth), Caron (Leslie), Close (Glenn), Crain (Jeanne), Danes (Claire), Davis (Bette, Geena, Judy), Dench (Judi), Derek (Bo), Dunne (Irene), Eggar (Samantha), Evans (Edith), Falco (Edie), Field (Sally), Fonda (Bridget, Jane), Gabor (Eva, Zsa Zsa), Garbo (Greta), Gless (Sharon), Grant (Lee), Greer (Jane), Grier (Pam), Hagen (Uta), Hasso (Signe), Hayek (Salma), Hayes (Helen), Heche (Anne), Henie (Sonja), Howes (Sally Ann), Jones (Cherry, Jennifer, Shirley), Kazan (Lainie), Kelly (Grace, Patsy), Kurtz (Swoosie), Lahti (Christine), Lange (Hope, Jessica), Leigh (Janet, Jennifer Jason, Vivien), Lenya (Lotte), Lewis (Juliette), Loren (Sophia), Mason (Marsha, Pamela), Meara (Anne), Miles (Sarah, Vera), Moore (Demi, Julianne, Mary Tyler, Terry), North (Sheree), Novak (Kim), O'Hara (Maureen), Olson (Nancy), O'Neal (Tatum), Perez (Rosie), Picon (Molly), Pitts (Zasu), Reese (Della), Ricci (Christina), Roman (Ruth), Ruehl (Mercedes), Ryder (Winona), Saint (Eva Marie), Scott (Lizbeth, Martha), Shire (Talia), Smith (Alexis, Maggie), Stone (Sharon), Storm (Gale), Swank (Hilary), Tandy (Jessica), Terry (Ellen), Tomei (Marisa), Tyler (Liv), Tyson (Cicely), Watts (Naomi), Welch (Raquel), Wiest (Dianne), Wyatt (Jane), Wyman (Jane), Young (Sean, Loretta) **6** Adjani (Isabelle), Angeli (Pier), Arthur (Beatrice, Jean), Ashley (Elizabeth), Bacall (Lauren), Bardot (Brigitte), Barkin (Ellen), Barrie (Wendy), Baxter (Anne), Bening (Annette), Bergen (Candice, Polly), Bisset (Jacqueline), Blaine (Vivian), Brooks (Louise), Bujold (Genevieve), Butler (Brett), Cannon (Dyan), Carter (Dixie, Lynda, Nell), Cooper (Gladys), Crouse (Lindsay), Curtin (Jane), Curtis (Jamie Lee), Danner (Blythe), Davies (Marion), Delaney (Dana), Del Rio (Dolores), Dennis (Sandy), Diller (Phyllis), Draper (Ruth), Dumont (Margaret), Duncan (Sandy), Durbin (Deanna), Duvall (Shelley), Ekberg (Anita), Ekland (Britt), Fabray (Nanette), Farmer (Frances), Farrow (Mia), Feldon (Barbara), Fisher (Carrie), Foster (Jodie), Garner (Peggy Ann), Garson (Greer), Gaynor (Mitzi), Gordon (Ruth), Grable (Betty), Grimes (Tammy), Hannah (Daryl), Harlow (Jean), Harper (Jessica, Tess, Valerie), Harris (Barbara, Julie, Rosemary), Hedren (Tippi), Hiller (Wendy), Hunter (Holly, Kim),

Hussey (Ruth), Huston (Anjelica), Hutton (Betty), Irving (Amy), Keaton (Diane), Keeler (Ruby), Kidman (Nicole), Kinski (Nastassja), Knight (Shirley), Lamarr (Hedy), Lamour (Dorothy), Lasser (Louise), Laurie (Piper), Lillie (Beatrice), Louise (Tina), Lupino (Ida), MacRae (Sheila), Malone (Dorothy), Martin (Mary), Matlin (Marlee), McGraw (Ali), Merkel (Una), Merman (Ethel), Midler (Bette), Miller (Ann), Mirren (Helen), Monroe (Marilyn), Moreau (Jeanne), Moreno (Rita), Oberon (Merle), O'Brien (Margaret), Oliver (Edna May), Palmer (Lili), Paquin (Anna), Parker (Eleanor, Mary-Louise), Sarah Jessica, Suzy), Peters (Bernadette), Powers (Stephanie), Prowse (Juliet), Rainer (Luise), Rashad (Phylicia), Remick (Lee), Ritter (Thelma), Rivera (Chita), Rogers (Ginger), Scales (Prunella), Seberg (Jean), Sidney (Sylvia), Somers (Suzanne), Sommer (Elke), Spacek (Sissy), Streep (Meryl), Taylor (Elizabeth), Temple (Shirley), Theron (Charlize), Thomas (Marlo), Tiffin (Pamela), Tomlin (Lily), Turner (Kathleen, Lana), Walker (Nancy), Warren (Lesley Ann), Watson (Emily), Weaver (Sigourney), Wilson (Marie), Winger (Debra), Wright (Teresa), Wynter (Dana) **7** Allyson (June), Andress (Ursula), Andrews (Julie), Aniston (Jennifer), Bassett (Angela), Bennett (Constance, Joan), Bergman (Ingrid), Binoche (Juliette), Blethyn (Brenda), Buckley (Betty), Bullock (Sandra), Burnett (Carol), Burstyn (Ellen), Campbell (Mrs. Patrick), Colbert (Claudette), Collins (Joan, Pauline), Cornell (Katherine), Cushman (Charlotte), Darnell (Linda), DeCarlo (Yvonne), Deneuve (Catherine), Dukakis (Olympia), Dunaway (Faye), Dunnock (Mildred), Fawcett (Farrah), Fleming (Rhonda), Fricker (Brenda), Gardner (Ava), Garland (Judy), Gingold (Hermione), Goddard (Paulette), Grahame (Gloria), Grayson (Kathryn), Hayward (Susan), Heckart (Eileen), Hepburn (Audrey, Katharine), Hershey (Barbara), Jackson (Anne, Glenda, Kate), Langtry (Lillie), Learned (Michael), Lombard (Carole), MacGraw (Ali), Madonna, Magnani (Anna), Mangano (Silvana), McGuire (Dorothy), McKenna (Siobhan), McQueen (Butterfly), Meadows (Audrey, Jayne), Mimieux (Yvette), Miranda (Carmen), Mulgrew (Kate), Natwick (Mildred), Parsons (Estelle), Perlman (Rhea), Perrine (Valerie), Plummer (Amanda), Podesta (Rosanna), Portman (Natalie), Roberts (Julia), Russell (Jane, Rosalind, Theresa), Scacchi

(Greta), Sevigny (Chloë), Shearer (Norma), Shields (Brooke), Siddons (Sarah), Simmons (Jean), Sorvino (Mira), Sothern (Ann), Stevens (Connie, Stella), Stritch (Elaine), Swanson (Gloria), Swinton (Tilda), Thaxter (Phyllis), Thurman (Uma), Tierney (Gene), Ullmann (Liv), Winfrey (Oprah), Winslet (Kate), Winters (Shelley), Withers (Jane), Woodard (Alfre) **8** Anderson (Judith, Loni, Melissa Sue), Arquette (Patricia, Rosanna), Ashcroft (Peggy), Bancroft (Anne), Bankhead (Tallulah), Basinger (Kim), Blondell (Joan), Byington (Spring), Caldwell (Zoe), Channing (Carol, Stockard), Charisse (Cyd), Christie (Julie), Crawford (Joan), DeMornay (Rebecca), Dewhurst (Colleen), Dietrich (Marlene), Dressler (Marie), Fletcher (Louise), Fontaine (Joan), Fontanne (Lynn), Goldberg (Whoopi), Griffith (Melanie), Hayworth (Rita), Holliday (Judy), Lansbury (Angela), Lawrence (Gertrude), Leachman (Cloris), Leighton (Margaret), Lindfors (Viveca), Lockhart (June), Lovelace (Linda), MacLaine (Shirley), McDaniel (Hattie), Mercouri (Melina), Minnelli (Liza), Nelligan (Kate), Neuwirth (Bebe), O'Donnell (Rosie), Pfeiffer (Michelle), Pickford (Mary), Prentiss (Paula), Redgrave (Lynn, Vanessa), Reynolds (Debbie), Roseanne, Rowlands (Gena), Sarandon (Susan), Shepherd (Cybill), Signoret (Simone), Stanwyck (Barbara), Straight (Beatrice), Sullavan (Margaret), Talmadge (Norma), Thompson (Emma, Sada), Van Doren (Mamie), Williams (Esther), Woodward (Joanne) **9** Alexander (Jane), Barrymore (Drew, Ethel), Bernhardt (Sarah), Blanchett (Cate), Cardinale (Claudia), Christian (Linda), Clayburgh (Jill), Dandridge (Dorothy), DeGeneres (Ellen), Dickinson (Angie), Fairchild (Morgan), Henderson (Florence), Kellerman (Sally), Mansfield (Jayne), McDonnell (Mary), Moorehead (Agnes), O'Sullivan (Maureen), Pleshette (Suzanne), Plowright (Joan), Schneider (Romy), Singleton (Penny), Stapleton (Jean, Maureen), Strasberg (Susan), Streisand (Barbra), Struthers (Sally), Thorndike (Sybil), Vera-Ellen, Zellweger (Renée) **10** Ann-Margret, Lanchester (Elsa), Montgomery (Elizabeth), Richardson (Miranda, Natasha), Rossellini (Isabella), Rutherford (Margaret), Tushingham (Rita) **11** de Havilland (Olivia), McCambridge (Mercedes), Riefenstahl (Leni), Silverstone (Alicia), Steenburgen (Mary) **12** Bonham-Carter (Helena), Lollabrigida (Gina), Mastrantonio (Mary Elizabeth)

actual
4 hard, live, real, true **5** exact **6** extant, living **7** certain, current, factual, genuine **8** absolute, bona fide, concrete, definite, existent, existing, material, physical, positive, tangible **9** authentic, objective **10** legitimate, phenomenal, undeniable **12** indisputable

actuality
4 fact **5** being, truth **7** reality **9** existence, substance **10** embodiment **11** incarnation, materiality

actually
4 very **5** truly **6** indeed, in fact, really **7** de facto, no doubt **9** genuinely, in reality, veritably **10** absolutely

actuate
4 move, spur, stir **5** drive, impel, rouse **6** arouse, excite, propel, set off, turn on **7** provoke, trigger **8** activate, energize, mobilize, motivate, vitalize

act up
5 cut up **7** show off **9** misbehave **11** misfunction

acumen
3 wit **6** acuity, vision, wisdom **7** insight **8** keenness **9** acuteness, sharpness **10** astuteness, perception, shrewdness **11** discernment, penetration, percipience **12** perspicacity

acute
4 dire, keen **5** sharp **6** urgent **7** crucial, exigent, intense, pointed **8** critical, incisive, piercing, shooting, stabbing **9** knifelike, observant, trenchant **10** perceptive **11** penetrating, quick-witted, sharp-witted

ad _____
3 hoc, lib, rem **7** hominem, interim, nauseam **9** infinitum

adage
3 saw **4** rule **5** axiom, maxim, motto **6** byword, saying, truism **7** proverb **8** aphorism, apothegm

adagio
4 slow **5** tempo

Adah
husband: **4** Esau **6** Lamech
son: **5** Jabal, Jubal **7** Eliphaz

Adam
grandson: **4** Enos **5** Enoch
rib: **3** Eve

son: 4 Abel, Cain, Seth
wife: 3 Eve 6 Lilith

Adam
4 Bede 5 Smith

adamant
3 set 4 firm, hard 5 rigid, stiff, stone, tough
6 flinty 8 immobile, obdurate, resolute
9 immovable, unbending, unswaying
10 determined, inflexible, unbendable,
unyielding 11 unbreakable

adapt
3 fit 4 suit 5 alter, shape, yield 6 adjust,
change, modify, revise, square, tailor
7 arrange, conform, remodel 9 acclimate,
habituate, reconcile 11 acclimatize,
accommodate

adaptable
6 mobile, pliant, supple 7 ductile, plastic,
pliable 8 flexible, moldable 9 alterable,
malleable, versatile 10 adjustable,
modifiable 11 conformable

adaptation
6 change 8 revision 9 reworking
10 adjustment, alteration 12 modification

ad astra per
6 aspera

add
3 sum, tot 4 cast, foot, join, tote 5 affix,
annex, count, tally, total 6 append,
attach, figure, reckon, tack on, take on
7 augment, compute, count up, enlarge,
improve, include 8 compound, increase,
totalize 9 build onto, calculate 10 supplement

added
3 new 4 else, more 5 extra, fresh, other
7 another, farther, further 8 appended
9 accessory, increased 10 additional
13 supplementary

addendum
5 extra, rider 8 addition 10 supplement

adder
5 snake, viper 10 calculator 12 hognose
snake

addict
3 fan, nut 4 bias, buff 5 hound, lover
6 abuser, devote, junkie, zealot 7 booster,
devotee, fanatic, groupie, habitué
9 habituate, surrender 10 aficionado,
enthusiast

addition
4 plus, rise 5 annex, extra, raise, rider

7 accrual, adjunct 8 addendum, appendix,
increase 9 accession, accessory,
accretion, extension, increment
10 supplement 11 enlargement
12 appurtenance, augmentation

additional
see **added**

additionally
3 too 4 also, more, then 5 again 6 as well
7 addedly, besides, further 8 likewise,
moreover 9 along with 11 furthermore

additive
5 extra 8 extender 9 summative,
substance

addle
5 mix up, spoil 6 muddle, puzzle
7 confuse, fluster, nonplus, perplex
8 befuddle, bewilder, confound, distract,
throw off 9 dumbfound

add-on
7 adjunct 9 accessory 11 enhancement

address
3 aim, air, set, URL 4 hail, send, tact, talk
5 apply, court, grace, greet, level, place,
point, poise, remit, route, skill, speak, treat
6 call to, devote, direct, pursue, relate,
salute, speech 7 bearing, consign, deliver,
forward, know-how, lecture, location, speak
to, write to 8 appeal to, approach,
converse, deal with, deftness, delivery,
demeanor, dispatch, identify, petition,
position, presence, talk with, transmit
9 attention, dexterity, diplomacy, expertise
10 adroitness, competence, directions,
efficiency 11 communicate, comportment,
designation, proficiency, savoir faire,
tactfulness

adduce
3 lay 4 cite 5 claim, offer 6 allege, submit,
tender 7 advance, present, proffer,
propose, refer to, suggest 8 document
9 exemplify 10 illustrate

add up
3 sum 5 count, tally, total 6 amount,
reckon 7 compute 9 make sense

add up to
4 mean 5 spell 6 amount, denote, import,
intend 7 compute, connote, express,
signify

A Death in the Family author
4 Agee (James)

adept
3 pro 4 deft, whiz 5 crack, savvy 6 adroit,

expert, master, wizard **7** skilled
8 masterly, skillful, virtuoso **9** dexterous,
masterful **10** proficient **11** crackerjack
12 professional

adequacy
5 might **6** enough **7** ability **8** capacity
10 capability, competence, sufficient
11 sufficiency **13** qualification

adequate
6 common, decent, enough **8** all right,
passable, pleasing, standard, suitable
9 competent, sufficing **10** acceptable,
sufficient **11** comfortable **12** satisfactory
13 unexceptional, unimpeachable

adequately
4 well **5** amply, right **6** enough **8** all right,
passably, properly, suitably, tolerably
9 fittingly **12** sufficiently **13** appropriately

adhere
4 glue **5** cling, paste, stick **6** attach, bind
to, cement, cleave, cohere, fasten **7** stick
to **8** hold fast

adherence
4 bond **5** cling **7** loyalty **8** adhesion,
clinging, cohesion, fidelity, sticking
9 constancy **10** attachment **12** faithfulness

adherent
6 cohort, votary **7** devotee, sectary
8 disciple, follower, henchman, partisan,
stalwart **9** satellite, supporter
10 aficionado

adhering
6 clingy, gluing, sticky **7** binding,
8 clinging, sticking **9** attaching, cementing

adhesive
4 glue **5** gluey, gooey, gummy, stamp,
tacky **6** cement, clingy, gummed, sticky
7 holding, stickum **8** adhering, fastener,
mucilage, sticking **9** attaching

adieu
5 congé **6** bye-bye, so long **7** cheerio, good-
bye, parting **8** farewell **11** leave-taking

ad interim
6 acting, pro tem **9** temporary **10** pro
tempore **11** temporarily

adios
4 by-by, ciao, ta-ta **5** adieu, later **6** bye-
bye, so long **7** cheerio, goodbye, toodles
8 farewell, toodle-oo **10** hasta luego

adipose
3 fat **4** oily **5** fatty **6** greasy **7** fatlike

adit
3 way **4** door **5** entry **6** access, entrée,

tunnel **7** ingress, passage **8** entrance
9 mine entry **10** passageway **12** mine
entrance

adjacent
4 near **5** close **6** beside, nearby, next to
8 abutting, next door, touching **9** adjoining,
alongside, bordering **10** contiguous,
juxtaposed, near-at-hand **11** close-at-
hand, neighboring **12** conterminous

adjoin
3 add **4** abut, link, line, meet **5** annex,
touch, verge **6** append, attach, border, butt
on, couple **7** connect, impinge **8** neighbor
11 communicate

adjourn
4 move, rise, stay **5** defer, delay **6** hold
up, put off, recess, shelve **7** hold off,
suspend **8** dissolve, hold over, postpone,
prorogue **9** prorogate

adjudge
4 deem, rule **5** award, grant **6** decide,
settle, umpire **7** mediate, referee
9 arbitrate **10** adjudicate

adjunct
5 added, affix **6** joined **8** addendum,
addition, appanage, appendix, attached
9 accessory, accretion, appendage,
assistant, associate, auxiliary
10 attachment **12** appurtenance

adjure
3 beg, bid **4** urge **6** exhort **7** beseech,
entreat, command, implore, require
9 importune **10** supplicate

adjust
3 fit, fix, rig **4** suit, tune **5** adapt, order,
right **6** accord, attune, modify, orient,
settle, square, tailor, tune up **7** arrange,
conform, correct, rectify, resolve
8 modulate, regulate **9** habituate,
harmonize, reconcile **11** accommodate

adjuvant
4 aide **6** aiding, helper **8** enhancer,
modifier **9** accessory, ancillary, assisting,
auxiliary **10** collateral, subsidiary
11 appurtenant **12** contributory

ad-lib
9 extempore, improvise, impromptu
10 improvised, off-the-cuff, unprepared
11 extemporize, spontaneous, unrehearsed

Admetus
father: **6** Pheres
wife: **8** Alcestis

administer

3 run **4** boss, deal, give, head **5** issue
6 direct, govern, head up, manage
7 conduct, control, deal out, deliver, dole
out, execute, give out, mete out, oversee,
perform, provide **8** carry out, dispense,
share out **9** apportion, supervise
10 distribute, portion out

administration

7 control, regime **9** direction
10 governance, presidency
system of: **11** bureaucracy

administrator

4 boss, exec, head **5** chief **7** manager,
officer **8** director, official, overseer
9 executive **10** supervisor

admirable

6 august, worthy **8** laudable **9** deserving,
estimable, excellent, meritable
11 commendable, meritorious, outstanding
12 praiseworthy

admiral

American: **4** Byrd (Richard), Sims
(William) **5** Dewey (George), Stark
(Harold) **6** Halsey (Bull), Nimitz (Chester)
7 Zumwalt (Elmo) **8** Farragut (David),
Rickover (Hyman), Spruance (Raymond)
Confederate: **6** Semmes (Raphael)
Dutch: **5** Tromp (Maarten)
English: **5** Drake (Francis) **6** Nelson
(Horatio), Rodney (George), Vernon
(Edward) **7** Hawkins (John) **8** Beaufort
(Francis), Jellicoe (John), Villiers (George)
11 Mountbatten (Louis)
French: **10** Villeneuve (Pierre-Charles)
German: **4** Spee (Graf Maximilian von)
6 Dönitz (Karl), Raeder (Erich) **7** Doenitz
(Karl), Tirpitz (Alfred von)
Japanese: **4** Togo (Hideki) **5** Yonai
(Mitsumasa) **7** Yamamoto (Isoroku)
Spanish: **8** Menéndez (Pedro)

admiration

5 favor **6** esteem, praise, regard
7 account, delight, respect **8** applause,
approval, pleasure **9** affection
10 estimation **11** approbation
12 appreciation

admire

5 adore, honor, prize, value **6** esteem,
praise, regard, relish, revere **7** adulate,
applaud, approve, cherish, commend,
respect **8** consider, treasure **9** delight in
10 appreciate

admirer

3 fan **4** beau, buff **7** booster, devotee,

fancier **8** believer, follower, partisan
9 supporter **10** enthusiast

admission

3 way **4** door **5** entry **6** access, assent,
entrée **7** ingress **8** entrance
10 admittance, concession, confession
11 affirmation

admit

3 own **4** avow, take **5** agree, allow, enter,
grant, let in, let on, lodge, own up
6 accept, fess up, harbor, permit, suffer,
take in **7** concede, confess, receive,
shelter, welcome **8** entertain, introduce,
recognize **11** acknowledge

admix

5 blend, merge **6** mingle **7** combine
8 comingle, compound, immingle
9 commingle **11** intermingle

admixture

5 alloy, blend, combo **7** amalgam, fusion
8 compound **9** aggregate, composite
12 amalgamation

admonish

4 warn **5** alert, chide **6** lesson, monish,
rebuke, talk to **7** caution, counsel, reprove,
speak to **8** call down, forewarn, reproach
9 criticize, reprimand

admonition

3 tip **6** caveat, rebuke **7** caution, chiding,
reproof, warning **8** reproach **9** criticism,
reprimand **11** disapproval, forewarning

ado

4 fuss, stir **5** tizzy, whirl, worry **6** bother,
bustle, flurry **7** concern, problem, trouble,
turmoil **9** confusion **10** difficulty

adolescence

5 youth **7** puberty **8** minority **9** greenness
10 juvenility, pubescence **12** youthfulness

adolescent

4 teen **5** minor **6** teener **7** teenage
8 immature, preadult, teenager, youthful
9 pubescent

Adonai

3 God **4** YHWH **6** Elohim, Yahweh

Adonijah

brother: **5** Amnon **7** Absalom, Chileab
father: **5** David
mother: **7** Haggith
slayer: **7** Benaiah

Adonis

lover: **5** Venus **9** Aphrodite
mother: **5** Myrrh **6** Myrrha
slayer: **4** boar

adopt

4 pick, take 5 raise 6 accept, affect, assume, choose, select, take on, take up 7 care for, embrace, endorse, espouse

adoption

6 choice 7 raising, support 8 espousal, taking in 9 embracing, selection 11 embracement

adorable

4 cute, dear 7 darling, lovable, winsome 8 charming, pleasing, precious 9 appealing 10 attractive, delightful

adoration

4 love 5 ardor, honor 6 esteem, praise 7 passion, worship 8 devotion, idolatry 9 adulation, affection, reverence 10 admiration 11 idolization

adore

4 love 5 honor, prize 6 admire, dote on, esteem, revere 7 cherish, idolize, respect, worship 8 dote upon, treasure, venerate 9 affection, delight in, reverence

adorn

4 deck, grace, trim 5 fix up 6 bedeck, enrich, pretty 7 dress up, enhance, enliven, furbish, garnish, smarten 8 beautify, decorate, ornament, prettif 9 embellish

adornment

5 decor, frill 6 finery 7 garnish 8 ornament, trimming 9 accessory, caparison 10 decoration 13 embellishment

ad rem

3 apt 7 apropos, fitting, germane 8 apposite, material, relevant 9 pertinent 10 applicable, relevantly, to the point 11 applicative, applicatory

adrift

4 asea, lost 5 at sea, loose 6 afloat 7 aimless, mixed up 8 confused, floating, unmoored 10 anchorless, bewildered 11 disoriented, purposeless

adroit

3 apt 4 able, deft 5 adept, canny, handy, savvy, smart 6 astute, clever, expert, nimble, shrewd 7 cunning, skilled 8 skillful, talented 9 dexterous, ingenious 11 intelligent, quick-witted, resourceful 13 perspicacious

adroitness

3 art 5 craft, flair, gift, knack, savvy, skill 7 address, cunning, know-how, prowess 8 deftness 9 adeptness, dexterity, expertise, ingenuity, readiness 10 cleverness, expertness 12 intelligence

adulation

7 acclaim, baloney, blarney, fawning, tribute, worship 8 applause, flattery, soft soap 9 servility, sweet talk 10 overpraise 11 false praise 12 blandishment

adulatory

7 buttery, fawning 8 unctuous 9 kowtowing 10 flattering, obsequious, oleaginous 11 bootlicking, sycophantic

adult

4 aged, ripe 5 grown 6 mature 7 grown-up, matured, ripened 9 full-blown 10 fully grown 11 full-fledged

adulterate

3 cut 4 thin 5 alloy, dirty, taint, water 6 debase, defile, dilute, doctor, dope up, falsify, impair, weaken 7 cheapen, corrupt, defiled, degrade, devalue, diluted, pollute, tainted, thinned 8 degraded, denature, impurify, polluted, spurious 9 water down 10 tamper with 11 contaminate

adumbrate

3 dim, fog 4 bode, call, hint, mist, veil 5 augur, cloud 6 darken, shadow, sketch 7 becloud, bespeak, betoken, obscure, outline, portend, predict, presage, suggest 8 block out, disclose, forebode, forecast, foretell, indicate, intimate, prophesy 9 obfuscate, prefigure 10 foreshadow, overshadow 11 prefigurate 12 characterize

adumbration

4 hint, sign 5 shade, umbra 6 shadow 7 outline 8 penumbra 10 indication, intimation, suggestion

advance

3 aid 4 cite, help, lend, loan, move, rise 5 get on, march, money, raise, serve 6 assist, course, foster, mature, prefer, supply, uplift 7 deposit, develop, elevate, forward, furnish, further, headway, ongoing, present, proceed, promote, propose, upgrade 8 approach, get along, heighten, increase, progress 9 encourage, evolution, provision 10 accelerate, bring about 11 development, furtherance, improvement, progression 12 breakthrough

advanced

3 old 5 first 6 far out 7 forward, in front, leading, liberal, radical 8 far ahead, foremost 9 developed 10 precocious 11 broad-minded, progressive

advancement
4 gain, rise **5** boost, growth **7** headway
8 progress **9** elevation, promotion
10 betterment, preference
11 improvement, progression

advantage
4 boon, edge, gain, good, help, lead, odds
5 asset, avail, serve **6** better, profit
7 account, benefit, mastery **8** blessing,
interest, leverage **9** allowance, head start,
upper hand **10** ascendancy, domination,
leadership, prosperity **11** superiority
12 running start

advantageous
4 good **6** timely, toward, useful **7** benefic,
gainful, helpful **8** favoring, salutary
9 conducive, desirable, expedient,
favorable, fortunate, promising
10 beneficial, profitable, propitious,
worthwhile

advent
5 onset **6** coming **7** arrival **8** approach
9 beginning

adventitious
5 fluky **6** casual, chance **8** by chance
9 unplanned **10** accidental, contingent,
fortuitous, incidental, unexpected

adventure
3 try **4** feat, risk, trip **5** quest, wager
6 chance, gamble, hazard **7** exploit
8 escapade **9** undertake **10** enterprise,
experience

adventurous
4 bold, rash **5** brash, risky **6** daring
8 intrepid, reckless **9** audacious,
dangerous, daredevil, foolhardy,
hazardous, impetuous, imprudent **10** innovative **12** enterprising

adversary
3 con, foe **4** anti **5** enemy, rival **7** opposer
8 opponent, opposing **10** antagonist,
competitor

adverse
3 bad **4** anti **7** counter, harmful, hostile,
hurtful, opposed **8** contrary, damaging,
negative, opposing, opposite **9** injurious
11 deleterious, detrimental, obstructive,
unfavorable **12** antagonistic, antipathetic

adversity
4 dole **5** trial **6** misery, mishap **7** bad luck,
bad news, trouble **8** bad break, distress,
hard time, hardship **9** mischance, suffering
10 difficulty, ill fortune, misfortune

advert
4 cite, note **5** refer **6** allude, notice, remark
7 bring up, mention, observe **8** indicate,
point out

advertent
5 aware **7** heedful, mindful **9** attentive,
intentive, observant, regardful

advertise
4 drum, hype, plug, puff, push **5** boost,
pitch **6** blazon, herald, inform, notify, report
7 advance, apprise, build up, declare,
promote, publish, sponsor **8** announce,
ballyhoo, proclaim **9** broadcast, publicize
10 annunciate, promulgate

advertisement
4 bill, plug, sign **5** blurb, flyer, promo
6 notice, poster, want ad **7** affiche
9 billboard, broadcast, circular, promotion,
publicity **10** commercial **11** declaration,
publication **12** announcement,
proclamation

advice
3 aid, tip **4** help, news, view, word **6** notice
7 caution, counsel, input, opinion, tidings,
warning **8** guidance, teaching
10 admonition, suggestion **11** information,
instruction **12** intelligence

advisable
4 wise **5** sound **6** seemly **7** politic,
prudent **8** sensible, suitable, tactical
9 desirable, expedient, practical
10 worthwhile **11** recommended
12 advantageous

advise
3 tip **4** tell, tout, urge, warn **6** clue in,
confer, enjoin, fill in, guide, inform, notify,
wise up **7** apprise, caution, consult,
counsel, suggest, tip off **8** acquaint,
forewarn, instruct, point out **9** encourage,
prescribe, recommend

Advise and Consent author
5 Drury (Allen)

advised
7 studied, weighed **8** designed, intended
10 calculated, considered, deliberate,
thought out **11** intentional **12** premeditated

adviser
5 coach, guide **6** mentor **7** counsel, tipster
9 counselor **10** consultant, instructor

advisory
7 guiding, helping **9** educative **10** coun-
seling **12** consultative **13** informational

advocacy
3 aid **6** urging **7** backing, defense, support **9** promotion

advocate
4 back, push, tout, urge **5** favor **6** backer, defend, preach, uphold **7** promote, propose, support **8** argue for, backstop, champion, exponent, plump for, side with **9** encourage, expounder, proponent, recommend, spokesman, supporter **11** countenance

Aeacus
father: **4** Zeus
mother: **6** Aegina
son: **6** Peleus **7** Telamon

Aedon
brother: **7** Amphion
sister-in-law: **5** Niobe
son (victim): **6** Itylus

Aeëtes
daughter: **5** Medea
father: **6** Helios

aegis
4 care, ward **5** armor, guard **6** charge, shield **7** backing, control, defense, support **8** auspices, guidance, security **9** influence, patronage, safeguard **10** protection **11** sponsorship

Aegisthus
father: **8** Thyestes
lover: **12** Clytemnestra
mother: **7** Pelopia
slayer: **7** Orestes
victim: **6** Atreus **9** Agamemnon

Aeneas
companion: **7** Achates
father: **8** Anchises
mother: **5** Venus **9** Aphrodite
son: **5** Iulus **8** Ascanius
wife: **6** Creusa **7** Lavinia

Aeneid
author: **6** Vergil, Virgil
first words: **16** arma virumque cano
hero: **6** Aeneas

Aeolus
daughter: **7** Alcyone **8** Halcyone
father: **8** Poseidon

aeon
3 age **4** time **6** period **8** blue moon, duration

aerate
7 lighten, freshen, refresh **9** oxygenate, ventilate

aerial
4 high **5** lofty **6** flying, vapory **7** antenna, soaring **8** birdlike, elevated, ethereal, fanciful, towering, vaporous **9** pneumatic **10** impalpable **11** atmospheric, forward pass

aerie
4 nest **7** citadel, lookout **9** penthouse

aeronaut
4 Fogg (Phileas) **5** pilot **7** aviator **8** Zeppelin (Ferdinand, Graf von) **10** balloonist

Aerope
husband: **6** Atreus
lover: **8** Thyestes
son: **8** Menelaus **9** Agamemnon

aery
see **aerial**

Aesculapius
daughter: **6** Hygeia **7** Panacea
father: **6** Apollo
slayer: **4** Zeus **7** Jupiter
teacher: **6** Chiron
wife: **6** Epione

Aeson
brother: **6** Pelias
son: **5** Jason

aesthete
4 buff **6** expert **7** devotee **9** authority **10** dilettante **11** appreciator, cognoscente, connoisseur

aesthetic
6 artful, creative **8** artistic, pleasing **9** beautiful, sensitive **10** attractive, harmonious

afar
5 apart **6** remote **7** distant

affable
4 kind, open, warm **6** at ease, genial, gentle, kindly, polite **7** amiable, cordial **8** friendly, gracious, obliging, pleasant, sociable **9** congenial, courteous

affair
4 case, love **5** amour, worry **6** action, matter **7** concern, liaison, palaver, romance **8** business, function, interest, intrigue, occasion **9** happening, procedure **10** proceeding **12** relationship

affect
3 act **4** fake, move, sham, stir, sway **5** adopt, alter, bluff, change, fancy, feign, haunt, put on, touch **6** assume, strike **7** act upon, disturb, impress, inspire,

pretend **8** frequent, simulate **9** cultivate, influence **11** counterfeit

affectation
3 air **4** airs, pose, sham, show **6** facade **8** pretense **9** mannerism **10** pretension **13** artificiality

affected
5 false, moved, put-on **6** phoney **7** altered, assumed, changed, feigned, stilted **8** disposed, inclined, involved, mannered, precious, spurious **9** concerned, conscious, contrived, insincere, pretended, unnatural **10** artificial **11** overrefined, pretentious **13** self-conscious

affecting
3 sad **6** lively, moving **7** pitiful **8** exciting, poignant, touching **9** thrilling **10** disturbing, impressive **11** distressing, influential

affection
4 bias, love **5** trait **6** doting, liking, malady, virtue, warmth **7** ailment, concern, disease, emotion, feature, feeling, illness, leaning, passion, quality **8** devotion, disorder, fondness, interest, penchant, property, sickness, sympathy **9** attention, attribute, character, complaint, condition, sentiment **10** attachment, propensity, tenderness **12** predilection

affectionate
4 dear, fond, warm **6** caring, doting, loving, tender **7** devoted **8** friendly **11** sympathetic

affective
6 moving **7** emotive **8** stirring, touching **9** emotional

affectivity
7 emotion, feeling, passion **9** sentiment

affianced
7 engaged, pledged **8** intended, plighted, promised **9** betrothed, committed **10** contracted

affiche
4 bill, list **6** notice, poster **7** placard **8** handbill

affidavit
4 oath **9** testimony **11** affirmation, declaration

affiliate
4 ally, join **5** annex, unite **6** branch **7** combine, connect, partner **9** associate

affiliated
4 akin **5** bound **6** allied, joined, linked **7** kindred, related **9** connected, dependent **10** associated

affiliation
4 club **5** tie-in, union **6** hookup, league **7** cahoots, company, joining **8** alliance **10** connection, fellowship **11** association, combination, conjunction, partnership

affinity
6 simile **7** analogy, kinship, rapport **8** likeness, relation, sympathy **9** alikeness **10** attraction, similarity, similitude **11** resemblance **13** compatibility

affirm
3 say, yes **4** aver, avow, okay **5** state, swear, vouch **6** assent, assert, attest, depose, ratify, uphold **7** certify, confirm, declare, profess, protest, testify, witness **8** dedicate, validate **9** guarantee

affirmative
3 aye, yea, yes **4** yeah **6** assent **8** approval, positive **9** affirming, approving, asserting, assertion, confirming, endorsing, favorable, ratifying **10** supporting **11** affirmation

affix
3 add, tag **4** bind, glue, join, nail, stick, tack **5** annex, paste, put on, rivet, tag on **6** append, attach, fasten, tack on **7** impress, stick on, subjoin **8** addition **9** appendage **10** attachment

afflict
3 try, vex **4** pain, rack **5** annoy, beset, harry, press, smite, worry, wound, wring **6** bother, burden, harass, harrow, injure, martyr, pester, plague, strike, suffer **7** agonize, anguish, torment, torture, trouble **8** distress

afflicted
6 pained, rueful, woeful **7** doleful, injured, unhappy, worried **8** dolorous, stricken, troubled, wretched **9** disturbed, miserable, sorrowful, tormented **10** distressed

affliction
3 woe **4** care **5** cross, grief, trial **6** ordeal, plague, sorrow **7** anguish, illness, scourge, torment, trouble **8** distress, hardship, sickness **9** adversity, heartache, infirmity **10** misfortune **11** tribulation

afflictive
3 sad **4** dire, sore **6** aching, bitter, woeful **7** galling, hurtful, hurting, painful **8** grievous, mournful **9** sorrowful **10** calamitous, deplorable, lamentable **11** distasteful, distressing, regrettable, troublesome, unfortunate, unpalatable **13** heartbreaking

affluence
5 means, worth **6** bounty, influx, plenty, riches, wealth **8** opulence, property, richness **9** abundance, plenitude, profusion, resources **10** prosperity

affluent
4 full, rich **5** flush **6** loaded **7** copious, flowing, moneyed, opulent, wealthy, well-off **8** abundant, plentiful, well-to-do **9** bountiful, tributary, well-fixed **10** prosperous

afford
4 able, bear, give **5** allow, grant, incur, offer, spare, stand **6** bestow, confer, donate, impart, manage, supply **7** furnish, present, support, sustain

affordable
5 cheap **6** modest **7** low-cost **8** bearable **10** manageable, reasonable **11** inexpensive

affray
3 row **5** clash, fight, melee, scrap **6** fracas, rumpus **7** dispute, quarrel, ruction, scuffle **8** disorder, skirmish

affront
3 vex **4** face, meet, slap, slur **5** abuse, anger, annoy, wrong **6** injury, insult, offend, slight **7** offense, outrage, put down **8** contempt, rudeness **9** aspersion, criticize, encounter, indignity

Afghanistan
capital: **5** Kabul
city: **5** Herat **8** Kandahar **12** Mazar-i-Sharif
ethnic group: **7** Pashtun
language: **4** Dari **6** Pashto
monetary unit: **7** Afghani
neighbor: **4** Iran **5** China **8** Pakistan **10** Tajikistan, Uzbekistan **12** Turkmenistan

aficionado
3 fan **4** buff **5** hound, lover **6** expert **7** admirer, devotee, habitué **10** enthusiast **11** appreciator

afield
4 afar, away, awry **5** amiss, badly, wrong **6** abroad, astray **8** straying **9** elsewhere, off course

afire
3 hot **5** aglow, fiery **6** ablaze, aflame, alight, red-hot **7** blazing, burning, excited, flaming, flaring, ignited **8** inflamed, in flames **9** energized, excitable **10** passionate **11** conflagrant

afloat
4 asea **5** at sea **6** adrift, buoyed **9** supported, sustained

afraid
4 wary **5** chary, jumpy, loath, scary, sorry, timid **6** averse, scared, trepid **7** anxious, fearful, uneager, worried **8** cautious, hesitant, skittish, timorous **9** concerned, regretful, reluctant, unwilling **10** frightened **11** disinclined **12** apprehensive

afresh
3 new **4** anew, over **5** again, newly **6** de novo, encore **8** once more, repeated **9** once again

Africa
country: **4** Chad, Mali, Togo **5** Benin, Congo, Egypt, Gabon, Ghana, Kenya, Libya, Niger, Sudan, Zaire **6** Angola, Gambia, Guinea, Malawi, Rwanda, Uganda, Zambia **7** Algeria, Burundi, Comoros, Eritrea, Lesotho, Liberia, Morocco, Namibia, Nigeria, Senegal, Somalia, Tunisia **8** Botswana, Cameroon, Djibouti, Ethiopia, Tanzania, Zimbabwe **9** Cape Verde, Mauritius, Swaziland **10** Ivory Coast, Madagascar, Mauritania, Mozambique, Seychelles **11** Burkina Faso, Côte d'Ivoire, Sierra Leone, South Africa **12** Guinea-Bissau
ethnic group: **3** Ibo **4** Akan, Arab, Boer, Copt, Fula, Issa, Moor, Zulu **5** Bantu, Fulah, Galla, Hausa, Kongo, Mande, Pygmy, Swazi, Wolof **6** Berber, Fulani, Hamite, Herero, Kikuyu, Nubian, Somali, Tuareg, Ubangi, Yoruba **7** Ashanti, Bedouin, Bushman, Malinke, Swahili **8** Egyptian, Mandingo **9** Hottentot
language: **3** Ibo **5** Bantu, Galla, Hausa **6** Arabic, Berber, Somali, Yoruba **7** Amharic, Bambara, Swahili **8** Malagasy **9** Afrikaans

aft
5 after **6** astern **8** rearmost, rearward **9** sternward

after
3 aft, for **4** back, hind, next, past, rear **5** below, later, since **6** astern, back of, behind, beyond, hinder **7** by and by, ensuing **8** hindmost, in view of **9** following, posterior, sternward **10** subsequent **12** subsequently

after all
3 yet **5** still **6** at last, though **7** finally, however **8** in the end **11** nonetheless **12** nevertheless

aftereffect
5 issue, result, upshot 7 fallout, outcome
11 consequence, eventuality

afterlife
6 beyond 8 eternity 9 hereafter

aftermath
4 wake 6 effect, result, upshot
12 consequences, repercussion

afterward
4 next, soon, then 5 later 6 behind 7 by
and by, thereon 8 latterly 9 hereafter
10 thereafter 12 subsequently

afterword
8 epilogue

Agag
kingdom: 6 Amalek
slayer: 6 Samuel

again
4 also, anew, back, over 6 afresh, de novo,
encore 8 once more

again and again
3 oft 4 much 5 often 8 ofttimes
10 frequently, oftentimes, repeatedly

against
6 contra, facing, versus 7 vis-à-vis
8 fronting, opposite, touching
prefix: 4 anti 6 contra 7 counter

Agamemnon
avenger: 7 Orestes
brother: 8 Menelaus
daughter: 7 Electra 9 Iphigenia
father: 6 Atreus
slayer: 9 Aegisthus
son: 7 Orestes
wife: 12 Clytemnestra

agape
4 love, open 6 amazed, gaping 7 yawning
8 wide open 9 astounded, love feast
10 astonished, confounded
11 dumbfounded, overwhelmed
13 thunderstruck

agate
3 taw 4 type 6 marble, quartz 7 shooter
8 type size

Agave
father: 6 Cadmus
husband: 6 Echion
mother: 8 Harmonia
sister: 3 Ino 6 Semele 7 Autonoë
son: 8 Pentheus

age
3 eon, era 4 aeon, grow, span, time

5 epoch, ripen, stage 6 grow up, mature,
mellow, period 7 develop, grow old 8 blue
moon, division, interval, lifetime, long time,
majority, maturate 9 become old 10 generation

aged
3 old 4 ripe, worn 5 cured, hoary, olden
6 mellow, senior 7 ancient, antique,
elderly, matured, ripened 8 grown old,
timeworn 9 developed, senescent,
venerable 11 patriarchal 12 antediluvian

ageless
7 endless, eternal, lasting 8 dateless,
enduring, immortal, timeless 9 immutable
11 everlasting

agency
4 firm 5 cause, force, means, organ, power
6 action, bureau, medium, office
7 company, channel, function, vehicle
8 activity, auspices, business, division,
ministry 9 mechanism, operation
10 department, instrument 12 organization
13 establishment

agenda
6 docket, lineup 7 program 8 calendar,
schedule 9 timetable
entry: 4 item

Agenor
brother: 5 Belus
daughter: 6 Europa
father: 7 Antenor, Neptune 8 Poseidon
mother: 5 Libya
son: 6 Cadmus

agent
3 fed, spy 4 tool 5 actor, means, organ,
proxy, spook 6 deputy, factor, medium
7 channel, proctor, steward, vehicle
8 assignee, attorney, executor, minister,
ministry 9 activator, go-between,
middleman, operative 10 instrument,
procurator

age-old
5 olden 7 ancient, antique, elderly, forever
8 timeworn 9 venerable 10 immemorial
11 time-honored, traditional

agglomerate
4 heap, mass, pile, rock 6 gather 7 cluster
9 aggregate 10 collection 11 aggregation

agglomeration
4 heap 5 hoard, trove 7 cluster
9 aggregate, amassment, gathering
10 collection, cumulation 11 aggregation

aggrandize
4 hype 5 boost 6 beef up, expand, extend,
praise 7 augment, build up, enhance,

enlarge, ennoble, glorify, inflate, magnify **8** heighten, increase, multiply **11** distinguish

aggravate
3 vex **4** gall **5** anger, annoy, grate, mount, peeve, pique, rouse, upset **6** burn up, deepen, nettle, worsen **7** bedevil, disturb, enhance, inflame, magnify, perturb, provoke **8** heighten, increase, irritate **9** intensify **10** exacerbate

aggravation
4 pain **5** worry **6** bother **8** increase **9** annoyance, worsening **10** irritation **11** provocation

aggregate
3 all, sum **4** body, bulk, floc **5** add up, gross, total, whole **6** amount **8** entirety, quantity, totality **9** composite **10** cumulative **11** agglomerate **12** conglomerate **13** agglomeration

aggregation
4 body, mass **5** crowd, group, hoard, total, trove **7** cluster, company **8** assembly **9** amassment, gathering **10** assemblage, collection, cumulation **11** agglomerate **12** accumulation

aggression
4 push, raid **5** fight, onset **6** attack **7** assault, offense **8** invasion **9** hostility, incursion, offensive, onslaught, pugnacity **10** assailment **12** belligerence **13** combativeness

aggressive
5 pushy **6** fierce, severe **7** hostile, scrappy, vicious, warlike **8** emphatic, forceful, militant **9** assertive, attacking, combative, energetic, intrusive, offensive **11** belligerent, contentious, domineering, hard-hitting **12** enterprising

aggrieve
4 hurt, pain **5** annoy, harry, upset, worry, wrong **6** harass, injure, plague **7** afflict, oppress, torment, trouble **8** distress **9** constrain, persecute

aghast
4 agog, awed **6** afraid, amazed, scared **7** anxious, fearful, shocked, stunned **8** appalled, dismayed, startled **9** awestruck, horrified, terrified **10** astonished, confounded, frightened **11** dumbfounded, overwhelmed **13** thunderstruck

agile
4 deft, spry **5** alert, brisk, catty, lithe, quick, zippy **6** active, adroit, limber, lively, nimble,

supple **7** lissome **9** adaptable, dexterous, sprightly

agitate
4 move, rile, rock, stir, toss **5** argue, churn, peeve, shake, upset **6** arouse, bother, excite, flurry, joggle, ruffle, stir up **7** discuss, dispute, disturb, fluster, perturb, provoke, tempest, trouble, unhinge **8** disquiet, irritate **9** thrash out **10** discompose

agitation
4 flap, fuss, stir, to-do **5** clash, flurry **6** bustle, clamor, debate, lather, tumult **7** dispute, tempest, turmoil **9** commotion, confusion **10** turbulence **11** disturbance

agitator
5 rebel **6** shaker **7** inciter, stirrer **8** fomenter, inflamer **9** disrupter **10** instigator **11** provocateur

Aglaia
see **Graces**

Aglauros
father: 7 Cecrops
sister: 5 Herse **9** Pandrosos

aglow
4 warm **5** afire **6** bright, aflame, alight **7** excited, radiant, shining **8** gleaming, luminous

agnate
4 akin, like **5** alike **6** allied, joined, linked **7** cognate, connate, kindred, kinsman, related, similar **8** relation, relative **9** analogous **10** affiliated **11** consanguine **13** corresponding

agnostic
7 doubter, skeptic **8** doubting **10** questioner, undogmatic **11** uncommitted **12** noncommittal

Agnus ＿＿＿＿＿
3 Dei

ago
4 back, gone, past, yore **5** since **6** before

agog
4 avid, keen **5** eager **6** roused **7** excited, fervent **8** desirous **9** expectant, impatient **12** enthusiastic

agon
5 clash **6** battle **7** contest **8** conflict, struggle

agonize
4 fret, gall, hurt, pain, rack **5** chafe **6** harrow, squirm, suffer, writhe **7** afflict,

torment, torture, trouble **8** distress, stew over, struggle **10** excruciate

agonizing
6 fierce **7** extreme, intense, painful, racking, tearing **9** harrowing, suffering, torturing, torturous **10** tormenting **12** excruciating

agony
4 pain, pangs **5** dolor **6** misery **7** anguish, passion, torment, torture **8** distress, outburst, struggle **9** suffering **10** affliction

agora
11 marketplace **12** meeting place

agrarian
5 rural **6** rustic **8** pastoral **10** campestral **12** agricultural

agree
3 buy, set, yes **4** jibe, okay, suit **5** admit, check, equal, fit in, match, tally **6** accede, accept, accord, assent, concur, settle, square **7** buy into, comport, concede, concert, concord, conform, consent **8** check out, coincide, dovetail, side with **9** acquiesce, harmonize, recognize, subscribe **10** correspond **11** acknowledge

agreeable
4 nice, open **5** ready **7** affable, welcome, willing **8** amenable, in accord, pleasant, pleasing **9** approving, congenial, congruous, consonant, favorable, receptive **10** acceptable, compatible, concurring, consenting, consistent **11** pleasurable, sympathetic

agreed
3 aye, yea, yep, yes **4** okay **6** surely **8** all right, of course **9** certainly, positively **10** definitely

agreement
4 bond, deal, pact **6** accord, assent, treaty **7** bargain, compact, concord, consent, entente, harmony **8** contract, covenant **9** concordat **10** acceptance, consonance **11** arrangement, concordance, concurrence

agree with
3 fit **4** suit **5** befit **6** assist, become **7** support **10** go together

agricultural
7 bucolic **8** agrarian, pastoral

agriculture
7 farming, tillage **8** agronomy, ranching **9** husbandry **11** cultivation, soil culture

Agrippina
brother: 8 Caligula
husband: 8 Claudius
son: 4 Nero

aground
5 stuck **6** ashore, on land **7** beached, on shore **8** disabled, stranded

ague
3 flu **5** fever **7** malaria, shivers **9** influenza, shivering **10** blackwater

Ahab
daughter: 8 Athaliah
father: 4 Omri
wife: 7 Jezebel

Ahasuerus
kingdom: 6 Persia
wife: 6 Esther, Vashti

Ahaz
kingdom: 5 Judah
son: 8 Hezekiah
wife: 3 Abi

Ahaziah
father: 4 Ahab 5 Joram 7 Jehoram
kingdom: 5 Judah 6 Israel
mother: 7 Jezebel 8 Athaliah
sister: 9 Jehosheba 11 Jehosboeath

ahead
4 ante, fore **6** before, onward **7** earlier, forward, in front, leading, onwards **8** foremost, forwards, previous **9** in advance **10** beforehand **11** precedently

Ahinoam
father: 7 Ahimaaz
husband: 4 Saul 5 David
son: 5 Amnon

aid
4 abet, care, hand, help, lift **6** assist, helper, relief, rescue, succor **7** backing, comfort, help out, support, sustain **9** assistant, attendant, subsidize **10** assistance, benefactor, mitigation **11** alleviation

Aida
composer: 5 Verdi (Giuseppe)
father: 8 Amonasro
lover: 7 Radames
rival: 7 Amneris

aide
6 deputy, helper, second **7** orderly **8** adjutant. **9** assistant, attendant, coadjutor **10** coadjutant, lieutenant

aikido
10 martial art

ail
4 hurt, pain 5 upset, worry 6 bother
7 afflict, disturb, trouble 8 distress

ailing
3 ill, low 4 down, sick, weak 6 in pain,
poorly, sickly, unwell 8 below par, diseased
9 enfeebled 10 indisposed 11 debilitated

ailment
6 malady, unrest 7 disease, ferment,
illness, turmoil 8 disorder, disquiet,
sickness, syndrome 9 affection, complaint,
condition, infirmity 10 inquietude,
uneasiness 11 disquietude, restiveness
12 restlessness

aim
3 end, try 4 cast, goal, head, mark, mean,
plan, want, wish 5 angle, essay, focus,
level, point, slant, train 6 aspire, design,
desire, direct, intend, object, strive, target,
zero in 7 address, attempt, propose,
purpose 8 ambition, endeavor 9 objective
11 contemplate

aimless
6 random 7 wayward 8 goalless
9 desultory, haphazard, hit-or-miss,
irregular, pointless, unplanned 10 de-
signless 11 purposeless

air
3 sky 4 aura, mien, mood, song, tune, vent
5 style 6 manner, melody, reveal, strain
7 bearing, divulge, express, feeling, quality
8 demeanor 9 broadcast, character,
ventilate 10 atmosphere, deportment

aircraft
5 blimp, drone, plane 6 glider 7 airship,
balloon, chopper 8 aerodyne, aerostat,
airplane, jetliner, zeppelin 9 dirigible
10 helicopter
carrier: 7 flattop
designer: 6 Fokker (Anthony), Martin
(Glenn) 7 Junkers (Hugo), Tupolev
(Andrei) 8 Northrop (Jack), Sikorsky (Igor),
Yakovlev (Alexander) 13 Messerschmitt
(Willy)

airless
5 close 6 stuffy, sultry 8 stagnant, stifling
11 suffocating

airline
3 JAL, KLM, LOT, TWA 4 BOAC, El Al
5 Delta, Pan Am, USAir, Varig 6 Iberia,
Qantas, United, Virgin 7 Eastern, JetBlue,
Olympic 8 Aeroflot, Alitalia, American,
Swissair 9 Air France, Lufthansa,
Northwest, Southwest, U.S. Airways
11 Continental, Pan American

airman
5 flier, flyer, pilot 6 flyboy 7 aviator
8 aeronaut

air movement
4 gust, wind 5 draft 6 breath, breeze
7 updraft 9 downdraft

air navigation system
5 loran, navar, radar

airplane
3 jet 5 avion 6 bomber 7 fighter
8 autogiro, autogyro 9 transport
A-bomb-dropper: 8 Enola Gay
battle: 8 dogfight
body: 8 fuselage
engine: 3 jet 6 fanjet 7 propjet
8 turbofan, turbojet 9 turboprop
engine casing: 7 nacelle
engineless: 6 glider
instrument: 5 radar, radio 7 compass
9 altimeter, gyroscope 10 tachometer
11 transponder
maneuver: 4 buzz, dive, loop, roll
8 nosedive 9 chandelle 10 barrel roll
movement: 3 yaw 4 bank, spin 5 pitch
8 tailspin
part: 3 fin 4 flap, nose, prop, tail, wing
5 cabin, wheel 6 engine, rudder 7 aileron
8 airscrew, elevator 9 empennage,
propeller 10 stabilizer
pilotless: 5 drone
shelter: 6 hangar
target: 6 drogue
vapor: 8 contrail

air plant
6 orchid 7 epiphyte 9 bromeliad,
kalanchoe 11 Spanish moss 12 strangler
fig

airport
5 field 7 helipad 8 heliport 9 aerodrome
building: 8 terminal
flag: 8 windsock
name:
   Atlanta: 10 Hartsfield
   Boston: 5 Logan
   Chicago: 5 O'Hare 6 Midway
   Dublin: 7 Shannon
   London: 7 Gatwick 8 Heathrow
   New York: 3 JFK 7 Kennedy 9 La
      Guardia
   Paris: 4 Orly 8 DeGaulle 9 Le Bourget
   Rome: 7 Da Vinci

Washington: **6** Dulles, Reagan **8** National
part: **5** apron, tower **6** runway **7** taxiway

airs
4 pose, show **5** front **6** vanity **7** hauteur
8 pretense **9** loftiness, mannerism, vainglory **10** pretension **11** affectation, insincerity, ostentation **13** artificiality

airship
3 jet **5** blimp, plane **8** zeppelin **9** dirigible

airtight
4 shut **6** closed, sealed **7** certain
8 hermetic, ironclad **10** impervious
11 impermeable, irrefutable **12** indisputable, invulnerable **13** incontestable

airy
4 open, rare, thin **5** blowy, fresh, gusty, light, lofty, proud, windy **6** aerial, bouncy, breezy, dainty, unreal **7** buoyant, gaseous, soaring, tenuous **8** affected, animated, delicate, ethereal, graceful, illusory, rarefied, spirited, towering, vaporous, volatile **9** expansive, frivolous, pneumatic, resilient, sprightly, vivacious
10 diaphanous, ventilated **11** atmospheric, skyscraping **12** effervescent, high-spirited

A Is for Alibi author
7 Grafton (Sue)

Ajax
4 hero **5** Greek **7** warrior
father: **6** Oileus **7** Telamon
opponent: **6** Hector
participant: **9** Trojan War

akin
4 like, same **5** alike **6** allied **7** kindred, related, similar, uniform **8** parallel
9 analogous, consonant **10** affiliated, comparable, compatible **11** consanguine
13 corresponding

Alabama
capital: **10** Montgomery
city: **5** Selma **6** Mobile **10** Birmingham, Huntsville, Tuscaloosa **12** Muscle Shoals
college, university: **6** Auburn
8 Tuskegee
mountain: **6** Cheaha
nickname: **6** Cotton (State) **12** Heart of Dixie
river: **6** Mobile **7** Alabama **9** Tombigbee
state bird: **12** yellowhammer
state flower: **8** camellia
state tree: **12** longleaf pine

alacrity
8 dispatch **9** briskness, eagerness, quickness, readiness **10** enthusiasm, expedition, liveliness, promptness
11 promptitude, willingness
12 cheerfulness

alamo
6 poplar **10** cottonwood

a la mode
4 chic, tony **6** trendy **7** dashing, stylish
8 up-to-date **9** exclusive **11** fashionable
12 with ice cream

alarm
3 SOS **4** bell, fear, horn **5** alert, dread, panic, scare, siren, spook, upset **6** dismay, excite, fright, signal, terror, tocsin
7 anxiety, distress, disturb, startle, terrify, unnerve, warning **8** frighten **9** terrorize
11 forewarning, trepidation **12** apprehension **13** consternation

alas
3 heu, woe **5** alack, darn, drat, oy vey
7 woe is me

Alaska
capital: **6** Juneau
city: **4** Nome **5** Sitka **6** Barrow **9** Anchorage, Fairbanks **10** Prudhoe Bay
island group: **6** Kodiak **8** Aleutian, Pribilof
mountain, range: **6** Brooks **8** McKinley, Wrangell
nickname: **12** Last Frontier
park: **6** Denali, Katmai
river: **5** Yukon
state bird: **9** ptarmigan
state flower: **11** forget-me-not
state tree: **11** sitka spruce

alb
4 gown **8** vestment

Albania
capital: **6** Tirana, Tiranë
city: **5** Korçë, Vlorë **6** Durrës **7** Shkodër
ethnic group: **4** Gheg, Tosk
monetary unit: **3** lek
neighbor: **6** Greece, Serbia **9** Macedonia
part of: **7** Balkans
peninsula: **6** Balkan
sea: **8** Adriatic

albatross
5 check, goony, worry **6** burden, gooney
7 anxiety, seabird **9** hindrance, millstone, restraint **11** encumbrance

Albee play
7 Sandbox (The) 8 Seascape, Zoo Story
(The) 9 Tiny Alice 13 American Dream
(The) 14 Three Tall Women 16 A Delicate
Balance 25 Who's Afraid of Virginia Woolf?

albeit
5 still, while 6 even if, much as, though
7 despite, whereas 8 although 10 even
though

Alberta
capital: 8 Edmonton
city: 5 Banff 7 Calgary
lake: 6 Claire, Louise 9 Athabasca
mountain, range: 7 Rockies 8 Columbia
provincial flower: 8 wild rose
river: 4 Milk 5 Peace 9 Athabasca

Albion
7 England

album
4 book 6 jacket, record 7 garland,
omnibus 8 notebook, pictures, register
9 anthology, portfolio, scrapbook
10 collection, miscellany, recordings

Alcestis
father: 6 Pelias
husband: 7 Admetus
rescuer: 8 Heracles, Hercules

alchemist
10 Paracelsus

alchemy
5 charm, magic 7 panacea, sorcery
8 wizardry 9 conjuring 10 necromancy

Alcina
sister: 7 Morgana 10 Logistilla
victim: 6 Rogero 8 Astolpho, Ruggiero

Alcinous
daughter: 8 Nausicaa
wife: 5 Arete

Alcmaeon
father: 10 Amphiaraus
mother: 8 Eriphyle
wife: 10 Callirrhoe

Alcmene
husband: 10 Amphitryon
son: 8 Heracles, Hercules

alcohol
4 grog 5 booze, hooch, juice, sauce
6 hootch, liquor, red-eye, rotgut, tipple
7 spirits 8 home brew 9 aqua vitae,
firewater, moonshine
name: 4 amyl 5 butyl, cetyl, ethyl
6 glycol, methyl, sterol 7 butanol, ethanol,
mannite, menthol 8 glycerin, glycerol,
inositol, mannitol, methanol 9 isopropyl
11 cholesterol
used in perfumes: 5 nerol 7 borneol
8 geraniol, linalool

alcoholic
4 hard 5 drunk 6 brewed 8 drunkard
9 distilled, fermented, inebriant, inebriate,
spiritous 10 spirituous 11 dipsomaniac,
inebriating 12 intoxicating

alcoholic drink
see under **beverage**

alcove
4 nook 5 niche 6 gazebo, recess
9 belvedere 11 summerhouse
Japanese: 8 tokonoma

Alcyone
father: 5 Atlas 6 Aeolus
husband: 4 Ceyx
mother: 7 Pleione
sisters: 8 Pleiades

ale
3 nog 4 beer, nogg

aleatory
4 iffy 5 dicey, risky, shaky 6 chancy
9 hazardous, uncertain 10 contingent,
precarious, vulnerable 11 problematic,
speculative 13 unpredictable

alehouse
3 bar, pub 6 bistro, saloon, tavern
7 taproom 8 beer hall 10 beer garden
11 rathskeller

alembic
5 still 6 filter 9 distiller

alert
3 SOS 4 keen, warn 5 alarm, quick, ready,
sharp, smart 6 brainy, bright, clever, lively,
notify, tip off, tocsin 7 heedful, mindful, on
guard, red flag, wakeful 8 animated,
forewarn, open-eyed, vigilant, watchful
9 attentive, mercurial, sprightly, wide-awake
10 perceptive 11 intelligent, quick-witted
Scottish: 4 gleg 8 wakerife

Aleutian island
3 Fox 4 Adak, Atka, Attu, Near 5 Amlia,
Kiska 6 Unimak 8 Unalaska 9 Andreanof
town: 11 Dutch Harbor

alewife
4 fish 7 herring 8 menhaden

Alexander
birthplace: 5 Pella
conquest: 4 Tyre 5 Egypt, Issus
6 Greece, Persia 7 Parthia 8 Granicus

father: 6 Philip
general: 9 Antipater
horse: 10 Bucephalus
kingdom: 9 Macedonia
mother: 8 Olympias
teacher: 9 Aristotle
wife: 6 Roxana

alfalfa
3 hay 5 plant 6 forage, legume 7 lucerne
9 perennial

alfresco
7 open-air, outdoor, outside 8 outdoors
9 out-of-door 10 out-of-doors

alga
6 desmid, diatom 7 seaweed
blue-green: 6 nostoc
brown: 4 kelp 5 fucus 8 rockweed
green: 6 chlorella
red: 4 nori

algebra term
4 root 6 factor 8 binomial, equation,
monomial, variable 9 quadratic 10 poly-
nomial

Algeria
capital: 7 Algiers
city: 4 Bône, Oran 6 Annaba 11 Constantine
coast: 7 Barbary
desert: 6 Sahara
ethnic group: 4 Arab 6 Berber
language: 6 Arabic, Berber
monetary unit: 5 dinar
mountain range: 5 Atlas 12 Saharan
Atlas
neighbor: 4 Mali 5 Libya, Niger
7 Morocco, Tunisia 10 Mauritania

Algren novel
17 Walk on the Wild Side (A) 19 Man with
the Golden Arm (The)

Ali
son: 5 Hasan 6 Husayn
wife: 6 Fatima

alias
3 AKA 6 anonym, handle 7 moniker, pen
name 8 nickname 9 false name,
pseudonym, stage name 10 also called,
nom de plume 11 nom de guerre

alibi
4 plea 5 clear, cover, proof 6 answer,
excuse 7 account, cover up, defense,
pretext 9 assertion, exonerate
11 explanation

alien
6 exotic 7 foreign, opposed, strange

8 estrange, outsider, stranger, transfer
9 estranged, extrinsic, foreigner, outlander
10 extraneous, outlandish 12 incompatible

alienate
4 part 5 repel 6 assign, convey, divide,
offend, oppose 7 break up, turn off
8 disunify, disunite, estrange, separate,
sign over, transfer 9 disaffect 10 drive
apart, relinquish

alienation
5 break 6 breach 7 discord, divorce,
rupture 8 division 10 conveyance,
separation 11 breaking off 12 disaffection,
estrangement

alight
4 land 5 fiery 6 arrive, bright, settle
7 blazing, burning, deplane, descend,
detrain, flaming, flaring, get down, glowing,
ignited, on fire, shining 8 dismount 9 touch
down 11 conflagrant

align
4 ally, join, line, true 5 agree, array, order,
range 6 adjust, follow, line up 8 regulate
9 affiliate, associate 10 straighten

alike
4 akin, same 7 similar 8 parallel
9 analogous, consonant 10 comparable
13 corresponding

alikeness
6 simile 7 analogy 8 affinity, alliance
9 closeness, relation, semblance
10 comparison, connection, similarity,
similitude 11 resemblance

aliment
4 eats, fare, feed, food, grub 7 nourish,
nurture, sustain 9 nutriment
10 sustenance 11 nourishment

alimentary
9 nutritive 10 nourishing, sustaining
11 nutritional

alimentary canal
7 enteron

alimony
4 keep 5 bread 6 living, upkeep 7 support
9 allowance, provision 10 livelihood,
sustenance 11 maintenance, subsistence

alive
4 rife, spry 5 alert, awake, aware, brisk,
fresh, quick, ready, vital 6 active, extant,
living, viable 7 animate, dynamic, knowing,
moving, replete, running, teeming, working,
zestful 8 animated, existent, existing,
sensible, sentient, swarming, thronged

9 abounding, breathing, cognizant, conscious, energetic, operative, sensitive, wide-awake 11 functioning, overflowing

alkali
4 base, salt 9 substance 11 soluble salt
metal: 6 cesium, sodium 7 lithium 8 francium, rubidium 9 potassium 10 monovalent
opposite: 4 acid

alkaline
5 acrid, basic, salty 6 bitter, soluble 7 antacid, caustic 8 chemical

alkaline substance
3 lye 4 lime, soda 5 borax 6 potash 7 ammonia, antacid 8 pearl ash, saltwort 11 caustic soda

alkaloid
4 base
medicinal: 5 ergot 7 codeine, emetine, eserine, quinine 8 atropine, caffeine, lobeline, morphine 9 ephedrine, quinidine, reserpine 11 scopolamine
narcotic: 6 heroin 7 cocaine, codeine 8 morphine
poisonous: 8 atropine, nicotine, solanine 11 scopolamine

all
3 sum 4 each 5 every, gross, total, whole 6 entire, in toto, purely, wholly 7 exactly, totally, utterly 8 complete, entirety, everyone, outright, totality 9 aggregate, everybody 10 altogether, everything

all-around
7 general, overall, skilled 8 complete, sweeping, synoptic 9 adaptable, competent, many-sided, panoramic, universal, versatile 10 consummate, proficient 11 wide-ranging 12 encompassing 13 comprehensive

allay
4 balm, calm, ease, lull 5 abate, quiet, still 6 lessen, reduce, settle, soothe, subdue 7 assuage, compose, lighten, mollify, quieten, relieve 8 decrease, diminish, mitigate, moderate 9 alleviate 11 tranquilize

all but
4 most, much, nigh 5 about 6 almost, nearly 8 as much as, in effect 9 just about, virtually 11 essentially, practically 13 approximately

All Creatures Great and Small
author
7 Herriot (James)

allegation
5 claim 6 charge, report 9 assertion, statement 10 contention, profession 11 declaration

allege
3 say 4 avow, cite 5 claim, offer, state 6 adduce, assert, attest, charge, submit 7 advance, contend, declare, present, profess 8 maintain 10 put forward

alleged
6 stated 7 accused, dubious, reputed, suspect 8 asserted, declared, doubtful, so-called, supposed 9 described, pretended, professed, purported, soi-disant 10 ostensible, self-styled 12 questionable

allegiance
4 duty 5 ardor, piety 6 fealty, homage 7 loyalty 8 devotion, fidelity 9 adherence, constancy, obedience 10 dedication, obligation 11 devotedness 12 faithfulness

allegiant
4 firm, true 5 liege, loyal 6 ardent, steady 7 devoted, dutiful, staunch 8 constant, faithful, resolute 9 steadfast 10 dependable

allegorical
5 moral 6 fabled 8 mythical, symbolic 9 legendary, spiritual 10 emblematic, exegetical, fictitious, figurative 12 iconographic, illustrative, metaphorical

allegory
4 myth, tale 5 fable, story 6 emblem, symbol 7 parable 8 apologue 9 symbolism 10 figuration 12 typification

allegro
5 brisk 6 bouncy, lively 8 animated, spirited 9 sprightly

allergy
5 dread 6 hatred 7 disgust, dislike 8 aversion, distaste 9 antipathy, disliking, rejection, repulsion

alleviate
4 cure, ease 5 allay 6 lessen, reduce, remedy 7 assuage, lighten, mollify, relieve 8 decrease, diminish, mitigate

alleviation
4 ease 6 relief 7 decline 8 decrease, easement 9 lessening, reduction 10 diminution, mitigation

alley
4 lane, walk 6 marble, street 7 passage 10 backstreet

all-fired
7 totally, utterly 9 extremely 10 absolutely, completely 11 excessively

alliance
3 tie 4 bond, pact 5 union 6 accord, league, treaty 7 compact, concord 8 affinity, relation 9 coalition 10 connection, federation 11 affiliation, association, combination, confederacy, conjunction, partnership, unification 12 relationship 13 confederation

allied
4 akin 5 bound 6 agnate, joined, linked, united 7 cognate, connate, kindred, related, unified 8 in league 9 connected 10 affiliated, associated, connatural 11 consanguine

alligator
11 crocodilian
relative: 4 croc 6 caiman, cayman 9 crocodile

alligator pear
7 avocado

all in
4 dead, used, worn 5 spent, tired 6 bushed, done in, used up 7 drained, far-gone, worn-out 8 depleted 9 dead tired, exhausted, washed-out

all in all
5 in all 6 mainly 7 en masse, largely 9 generally 10 altogether, by and large, on the whole

allocate
4 give 5 allot, slice 6 assign, divide, divvy up 7 dish out, dole out, earmark, mete out 8 set apart 9 admeasure, apportion, designate 10 distribute

allocution
4 talk 5 spiel 6 sermon, speech 7 address, lecture, oration, oratory, pep talk 11 exhortation

allot
4 give 5 grant, share 6 accord, assign 7 deal out, divvy up, dole out, mete out 8 allocate, dispense, set aside 9 admeasure, apportion 10 distribute

allotment
3 cut, lot 4 bite, part 5 chunk, piece, quota, share, slice 6 ration 7 measure, portion 9 allowance, provision 13 apportionment

all-out
4 full 5 total 6 entire, utmost 7 maximum 8 absolute, complete, thorough 9 full-blown, full-scale, unlimited 12 totalitarian 13 thoroughgoing

all over
8 wherever 9 all around 10 everyplace, everywhere, far and near, far and wide, high and low, thoroughly, throughout

allow
3 let, lot, own 4 avow, give 5 admit, allot, brook, grant, leave, let on, stand 6 assign, endure, permit, suffer 7 concede, confess, consent, forbear, mete out 8 allocate, tolerate 9 apportion 11 acknowledge

allowance
3 aid, cut, lot, pay, sum 4 bite, edge, help, part 5 grant, leave, piece, quota, share, slice 6 amount, permit, ration 7 consent, handicap, measure, partage, portion, quantum, subsidy, vantage 8 handicap, pittance, quantity, sanction 9 advantage, allotment, head start, reduction 10 adjustment, allocation, assistance, concession, permission, sufferance, toleration 13 accommodation, apportionment, authorization

alloy
5 blend 6 fusion 7 amalgam, mixture 8 compound 9 admixture, composite 10 adulterant 11 interfusion 12 amalgamation, intermixture
brass-like: 6 latten
copper-sulfur: 6 niello
copper-tin: 6 bronze
copper-zinc: 5 brass 6 tombac
gold-like: 6 ormolu
gold-silver: 8 electrum
iron-carbon: 5 steel
iron-nickel: 5 invar
mercury: 7 amalgam
tin-lead: 5 terne 6 pewter, solder
used in jewelry: 6 tombac

all-powerful
6 mighty 7 supreme 8 absolute, almighty 10 invincible, omnipotent 11 controlling

all right
3 aye, yea, yep, yes 4 good, okay, safe, well 6 agreed, decent, proper, surely 7 average, 8 adequate, of course, passable, passably, pleasing, standard, very well 9 agreeable, certainly, tolerable, tolerably 10 , acceptably, adequately, definitely, positively, sufficient, well enough 12 satisfactory

all round
see **all-around**

All the King's Men author
6 Warren (Robert Penn)

All the Way Home author
4 Agee (James)

allude
4 hint 5 imply, point, refer 7 bring up, suggest 8 indicate, intimate

allure
4 draw, pull 5 charm, tempt 6 appeal, entice, lead on, seduce 7 attract, beguile, enchant, glamour, win over 8 charisma, inveigle, persuade 9 captivate, fascinate, magnetism, magnetize 10 attraction 11 enchantment, fascination

alluring
6 lovely 7 winning, winsome 8 charming, inviting, pleasing 9 appealing, beguiling, glamorous, seductive 10 appetizing, attractive, bewitching, enchanting 11 captivating, fascinating

ally
4 join 5 unite 6 friend, helper 7 comrade, partner 8 federate 9 accessory, affiliate, associate, auxiliary, bedfellow, colleague, supporter 10 accomplice 11 confederate 12 collaborator

almighty
4 very 6 hugely, mighty 7 awfully, godlike, supreme 8 absolute 9 extremely 10 invincible, omnipotent 11 all-powerful, exceedingly

almost
4 nigh 5 about 6 all but, nearly 8 as good as, as much as, just about, not quite, wellnigh 9 virtually 11 essentially, practically 13 approximately
Scottish: 6 feckly

alms
4 gift 6 relief 7 present 8 donation, offering 10 assistance 11 benefaction, beneficence 12 contribution

aloe
9 emollient, succulent

Aloeus
father: 7 Neptune 8 Poseidon
mother: 6 Canace
son: 4 Otus 9 Ephialtes
wife: 9 Iphimedia

aloft
4 high, over 5 above 6 on high, upward 7 skyward 8 in flight, overhead

aloha
4 by-by, ciao, hail 5 hello, howdy 6 bye-bye, good-by, so long 7 good-bye, welcome 8 farewell, greeting 9 greetings
State: 6 Hawaii

alone
4 only, sole, solo, stag 5 apart 6 singly, solely, unique, wholly 7 isolate, removed 8 detached, entirely, isolated, peerless, singular, solitary 9 matchless, unequaled, unmatched, unrivaled 10 nothing but, unequalled, unexampled, unexcelled 11 exclusively, unsurpassed 12 incomparable, unparalleled, unrepeatable 13 unaccompanied

aloneness
8 solitude 9 isolation, seclusion 10 uniqueness

along
3 too, yet 4 also, near, with 5 forth, there 6 as well, at hand, on hand, onward 7 besides, forward 8 likewise, moreover 11 furthermore 12 accompanying, additionally

alongside
6 beside, next to 8 touching 9 adjoining, bordering

aloof
3 shy 4 cold, cool 5 apart, proud 6 casual, chilly, frigid, offish, remote 7 distant, haughty, removed, stuck up 8 arrogant, detached, reserved, reticent, solitary 9 incurious, unbending, uncurious, withdrawn 10 disdainful, restrained, unfriendly, unsociable 11 constrained, indifferent, standoffish, unconcerned 12 uninterested 13 disinterested

alopecia
8 baldness

alp
4 peak 5 mount 8 mountain

alpaca
4 wool 5 cloth 6 mammal
habitat: 4 Peru 5 Andes 7 Bolivia

alpha
4 dawn 5 first, start 6 outset 7 dawning, genesis, opening 9 beginning 12 commencement

alphabet
4 ABC's 7 letters
Arabic: 3 ayn, dad, dal, gaf, jim, kaf, kha, lam, mim, nun, qaf, sad, sin, tha, waw, zay 4 alif, dhal, shin 5 ghayn
Greek: 3 chi, eta, phi, psi, rho, tau 4 beta, iota, zeta 5 alpha, delta, gamma, kappa,

omega, sigma, theta 6 lambda 7 epsilon,
omicron, upsilon
Hebrew: 3 mem, nun, sin, taw, tet, vav,
waw, yod 4 alef, ayin, beth, heth, kaph,
koph, qoph, resh, shin, teth 5 aleph, gimel,
lamed, sadhe, tsade, zayin 6 daleth,
samekh
Old Irish: 4 ogam 5 ogham
runic: 7 futhark

Alpheus
  beloved: 8 Arethusa
  father: 7 Oceanus
  form: 5 river
  mother: 6 Tethys

Alpine
  animal: 4 ibex 7 chamois
  dress: 6 dirndl
  house: 6 chalet
  lake: 4 Como, Iseo 5 Garda 6 Geneva
  7 Lucerne 8 Bodensee, Maggiore
  9 Constance, Neuchâtel
  pass: 3 col 5 Cenis 7 Brenner, Simplon
  9 St. Bernard
  peak: 5 Blanc, Eiger 7 Bernina
  8 Jungfrau 10 Matterhorn
  plant: 9 edelweiss
  primrose: 8 auricula
  resort: 5 Davos 7 Bolzano, Zermatt
  8 Chamonix, Grenoble 9 Innsbruck
  10 Interlaken 11 Saint Moritz
  river: 5 Rhine, Rhône
  snowfield: 4 firn, névé
  staff: 10 alpenstock
  state: 5 Tirol, Tyrol 7 Bavaria
  tunnel: 5 Blanc, Cenis 7 Arlberg, Simplon
  10 St. Gotthard
  wind: 4 bora, föhn 5 foehn

already
  4 even, once, prior 5 by now 6 before, by
  then 7 earlier, just now 8 formerly
  9 before now 10 by this time, heretofore,
  previously

also
  3 and, too 4 more, plus 5 again, along
  6 as well 7 besides, further 8 likewise,
  moreover 9 along with, including, similarly
  10 in addition 11 furthermore
  12 additionally

also-ran
  3 dud 5 loser 7 failure, washout
  8 defeated

altar
  6 shrine
  boy: 6 server 7 acolyte
  cloth: 4 pall 7 frontal
  constellation: 3 Ara

hanging: 6 dorsal, dossal
platform: 8 predella
screen: 7 reredos
shelf: 7 retable
site: 4 apse, bema
vessel: 5 cruet, paten 7 chalice
8 ciborium 10 monstrance

alter
  3 fix 4 geld, spay, turn, vary 5 adapt,
  neuter 6 adjust, change, doctor, modify,
  mutate, neuter, revamp 7 remodel
  8 castrate, moderate, modulate 9 refashion

alteration
  4 turn 5 shift 6 change 8 mutation,
  revision 9 variation 10 adaptation,
  adjustment, changeover, conversion,
  remodeling, transition 12 modification

altercate
  4 spat, tiff 5 argue, scrap 6 bicker, hassle
  7 dispute, quarrel, wrangle 8 squabble
  9 caterwaul

altercation
  3 row 4 beef, flap, spat, tiff 6 blowup,
  brawl, combat, fracas, hassle 7 contest,
  dispute, quarrel, rhubarb, wrangle
  8 argument, squabble 9 bickering
  10 falling-out 11 controversy, embroilment

alternate
  3 sub 5 proxy 6 backup, by turn, change,
  fill-in, rotate, second 7 another, relieve,
  stand-in 8 periodic, rotating 9 change off,
  fluctuate, recurrent, recurring, replacing,
  surrogate 10 equivalent, every other,
  periodical, substitute 11 every second,
  pinch hitter, replacement 12 intermittent

alternately
  6 in lieu, rather 7 instead 10 preferably

alternative
  5 other, proxy 6 backup, choice, option,
  second 7 another 8 atypical, druthers,
  election 9 different, selection, surrogate
  10 preference, substitute 11 contingency,
  nonstandard, possibility

Althaea
  father: 8 Thestius
  husband: 6 Oeneus
  son (victim): 8 Meleager

although
  4 when 5 still, while 6 albeit, even if, much
  as 7 despite, howbeit, whereas

altitude
  6 height 8 eminence 9 elevation, high
  level

altitudinous
4 high, tall 7 eminent 8 elevated

altogether
4 nude, well 5 fully, in all, quite 6 in toto, wholly 7 all told, en masse, exactly, totally, utterly 8 all in all, entirely 9 generally, perfectly 10 absolutely, by and large, completely, on the whole, thoroughly

altruism
7 charity 8 sympathy 10 compassion, generosity 11 benevolence 12 philanthropy, selflessness 13 unselfishness

altruistic
3 big 6 humane 8 generous 9 unselfish 10 benevolent, bighearted, charitable, open-handed 11 considerate, magnanimous, noble-minded 12 humanitarian 13 philanthropic

alum
4 grad 6 emetic 7 styptic 8 graduate 10 astringent

always
4 ever 7 forever 8 evermore, for keeps 9 at any rate, eternally 10 at all times, constantly, endlessly, in any event, invariably 11 continually, forevermore, in perpetuum, perpetually, unceasingly 12 consistently, continuously

Amahl and the Night Visitors composer
7 Menotti (Gian Carlo)

amalgamate
3 mix 4 ally, fuse, meld, pool 5 admix, alloy, merge, unify, unite 6 mingle 7 combine 8 coalesce, compound, intermix 9 commingle, integrate 11 consolidate, intermingle

amalgamation
5 alloy, blend, union 6 fusion, merger 7 joining, melding, merging, mixture, uniting 8 alliance, compound 9 admixture, coalition, composite 10 commixture 11 , intermixture 13 consolidation

Amalthea
form: 4 goat
horn: 10 cornucopia
nursling: 4 Zeus

amanita
8 death cap, mushroom 9 fly agaric

amanuensis
6 scribe 7 copyist 9 scrivener, secretary 11 transcriber 12 stenographer

amass
4 bulk, heap, make, pile 5 hoard, lay up, store, uplay 6 accrue, garner, gather, pile up, roll up 7 acquire, collect, compile, round up, store up 8 assemble, cumulate 9 aggregate, stockpile 10 accumulate 12 come together

amassment
4 pile 5 clump, group, hoard, stack, stock, store, trove 7 cluster 8 assembly, quantity 9 gathering, stockpile 10 assemblage, collection, cumulation 11 aggregation 12 accumulation 13 agglomeration

amateur
4 tyro 6 layman, novice, tinker, votary 7 admirer, dabbler, devotee, learner 8 aspirant, beginner, neophyte, putterer 9 greenhorn, smatterer 10 apprentice, dilettante, enthusiast, uninitiate 11 abecedarian

amateurish
3 raw 5 green 6 simple 7 artless 8 dabbling, inexpert 9 deficient, unskilled, untutored 10 dilettante, unfinished, unpolished, unskillful 12 dilettantist, unproficient 13 inexperienced

amative
see amorous

amatory
6 ardent, erotic, loving, tender 7 sensual 8 romantic 9 erogenous, seductive 10 passionate 11 aphrodisiac

amaze
4 daze 5 floor 6 wonder 7 astound, perplex, startle 8 astonish, bewilder, blow away, bowl over, confound, surprise 9 dumbfound 10 admiration 11 flabbergast

amazement
3 awe 6 marvel, wonder 8 surprise 9 marveling 10 admiration, perplexity, wonderment 12 astonishment, bewilderment, confoundment

amazing
7 awesome 8 striking, stunning, wondrous 9 marvelous, startling, wonderful 10 astounding, impressive, miraculous, stupendous, surprising 11 astonishing, bewildering, spectacular 12 breathtaking

Amazon
6 parrot 7 warrior 8 giantess 12 woman warrior

ambassador
5 agent, envoy 6 legate 8 diplomat, emissary 9 messenger
papal: 6 nuncio

amber
5 ocher, ochre, resin, rosin 6 orange, yellow 7 saffron

ambience
4 mood, tone 6 flavor, medium, milieu 7 climate 10 atmosphere 11 environment 12 surroundings

ambient
5 music 6 milieu 7 general, setting 8 everyday 9 prevalent 10 atmosphere, prevailing 11 atmospheric, environment, mise-en-scène 12 encompassing, surroundings 13 environmental

ambiguity
5 doubt 6 enigma, puzzle 7 evasion 9 equivoque, obscurity, vagueness 11 incertitude, uncertainty 12 doubt-fulness, equivocality, equivocation 13 double meaning

ambiguous
5 vague 6 opaque, unsure 7 cryptic, dubious, inexact, obscure, unclear 8 doubtful, puzzling 9 enigmatic, equivocal, tenebrous, uncertain, unsettled 10 indefinite, inexplicit 11 problematic 12 inconclusive, questionable

ambit
4 area, room 5 field, limit, orbit, range, reach, scope, space, sweep 6 border, bounds, extent, limits, radius, sphere 7 breadth, circuit, compass, expanse, purview 8 boundary, confines 9 extension, perimeter, periphery 13 circumference

ambition
3 aim 4 goal, hope, itch, push, wish, zeal 5 ardor, dream, drive, vigor 6 desire, energy, hunger, spirit, target, thirst 7 avidity, craving, purpose 8 appetite, striving, yearning 9 eagerness, intention, objective 10 aspiration, enterprise, enthusiasm, get-up-and-go, initiative, pretension

ambitious
4 avid, bold, keen 5 eager, pushy 6 driven, hungry, intent 7 driving, zealous 8 aspiring, desirous, striving 9 energetic 10 aggressive 11 hard-working 12 enterprising, enthusiastic

ambivalent
5 mixed 6 unsure 7 warring 8 clashing, wavering 9 equivocal, fluctuating, uncertain, undecided, vacillating 10 unresolved 13 contradictory

amble
4 gait, walk 5 dally, drift, mosey 6 dawdle, linger, stroll, wander 7 meander, saunter

ambrosia
6 dainty, regale 7 dessert, perfume 8 delicacy, ointment

ambrosial
5 balmy, spicy, sweet 6 savory 7 scented 8 aromatic, fragrant, heavenly, luscious, perfumed, pleasing, redolent 9 delicious 10 delectable, delightful 11 scrumptious

ambulate
4 hoof, move, pace, step, walk 5 tread, troop 6 foot it, hoof it 7 traipse

ambulatory
6 moving, on foot, roving 7 nomadic, roaming, walking 8 vagabond 9 itinerant 11 peripatetic

ambush
4 jump, lurk, trap 5 snare 6 assail, attack, entrap, lay for, waylay 7 assault, ensnare 8 surprise 9 ambuscade 11 concealment

ameliorate
3 fix 4 help, lift, mend 5 amend, raise 6 better, perk up, remedy, reform 7 elevate, enhance, improve, lighten, relieve, upgrade 8 mitigate 9 alleviate 10 convalesce, recuperate

amenable
4 open, tame 6 docile, liable, pliant, suited 7 plastic, pliable, subdued, subject, willing 8 biddable, in accord, obedient, yielding 9 adaptable, agreeable, complying, malleable, receptive, tractable 10 answerable, consenting, responsive, submissive 11 accountable, acquiescent, cooperative, responsible

amend
3 fix 4 help 5 alter, right 6 better, change, modify, reform, remedy, repair, revise, square 7 correct, improve, rectify 8 put right 9 meliorate 10 ameliorate

amendment
5 rider 6 change, remedy, reform 7 codicil, rectification, reformation, repair 8 addendum, revision 10 alteration, attachment, correction 11 enhancement, improvement 12 modification

amends
7 redress 8 reprisal 9 indemnity, quittance 10 recompense, reparation 11 restitution 12 compensation

amenities
5 mores 6 polish 7 decorum, manners 8 civility, courtesy 9 etiquette, propriety 12 social graces

amenity
5 charm, frill 6 luxury 7 comfort, quality 8 civility, courtesy, facility 9 advantage, etiquette, geniality, pleasance 10 affability, amiability, betterment, cordiality, enrichment, pleasantry, politeness 11 convenience, enhancement, improvement, sociability 12 agreeability, graciousness, pleasantness

ament
6 catkin

amerce
3 tax 4 dock, fine, levy 5 exact, mulct 6 punish 7 hit with, make pay 8 penalize

amercement
4 fine 5 mulct 7 damages, forfeit, penalty 10 assessment, punishment, reparation

American League
Baltimore: 7 Orioles
Boston: 6 Red Sox
Anaheim: 6 Angels
Chicago: 8 White Sox
Cleveland: 7 Indians
Detroit: 6 Tigers
Kansas City: 6 Royals
Milwaukee: 7 Brewers
Minnesota: 5 Twins
New York: 7 Yankees
Oakland: 9 Athletics
Seattle: 8 Mariners
Tampa Bay: 9 Devil Rays
Texas: 7 Rangers
Toronto: 8 Blue Jays

American Samoa
capital: 8 Pago Pago
island, island group: 4 Rose 5 Aunuu, Manua, Swains 7 Tutuila
language: 6 Samoan

America, the Beautiful
music: 4 Ward (Samuel Augustus)

words: 5 Bates (Katherine Lee)

Amfortas
father: 7 Titurel
opera: 8 Parsifal

amiability
7 amenity 9 geniality, pleasance 10 cordiality 11 sociability 12 complaisance, congeniality, friendliness, pleasantness, sociableness 13 agreeableness, enjoyableness

amiable
4 kind, warm 6 genial, gentle, kindly 7 affable, cordial, likable 8 cheerful, friendly, gracious, likeable, obliging, sociable 9 agreeable, congenial, courteous 10 responsive 11 complaisant, good-humored, good-natured, warmhearted

amicable
7 cordial, pacific 8 empathic, friendly, peaceful, sociable 9 congenial, peaceable 10 harmonious, like-minded, neighborly 11 sympathetic 13 understanding

amid
4 over 5 among, midst 6 during 7 amongst, between 10 throughout

amigo
3 pal 4 chum, mate, pard 6 friend 7 comrade, partner 8 sidekick 9 companion, confidant 12 acquaintance

amino acid
4 dopa 6 leucin, lysine, serine, toluid, valine 7 cystein, cystine, glycine, leucine, proline, toluide 8 cysteine, dopamine, histidin, thyroxin, toluidin, tyrosine

Amis, Kingsley
novel: 8 Lucky Jim
son: 6 Martin

amiss
3 bad 4 awry, poor 5 badly, wrong 6 afield, astray, faulty, flawed 7 wrongly 8 erringly, faultily 9 defective, imperfect 10 improperly, mistakenly, out of place 11 erroneously, imperfectly, incorrectly, unfavorably 12 inaccurately 13 inappropriate

amity
5 union 6 accord, comity, unison 7 concert, concord, harmony 8 alliance, goodwill 9 agreement 10 friendship, kindliness 11 concurrence, cordiality 12 friendliness

Ammonite
6 Semite
god: 6 Molech, Moloch

ammunition
4 shot 5 bombs 6 rounds, shells
7 charges 8 armament, grenades,
missiles, ordnance 10 cartridges
11 projectiles

Amneris's rival
4 Aïda

amnesty
6 pardon 7 freeing, release 8 immunity,
reprieve 9 discharge 10 absolution
11 forgiveness 12 dispensation

Amnon
father: 5 David
half sister: 5 Tamar
mother: 7 Ahinoam

amoeba
4 blob 8 rhizopod 9 protozoan

Amon
father: 8 Manasseh
son: 6 Josiah

Amonasro's daughter
4 Aïda

among
3 mid 4 amid 5 midst 6 amidst, within
7 between
prefix: 5 inter

amorist
4 rake, wolf 5 lover, Romeo 7 Don Juan,
gallant, playboy 8 Casanova, lothario,
paramour 9 womanizer 12 heartbreaker

amorous
6 ardent, erotic, in love 7 amative,
amatory, lustful 8 enamored, romantic
10 infatuated, passionate 11 aphrodisiac,
impassioned

amorousness
4 love, lust 5 amour, ardor 6 desire
7 passion 9 eroticism

amorphous
7 unclear 8 formless, inchoate, nebulous,
unformed, unshaped 9 shapeless,
undefined 10 indistinct 11 nondescript
12 disorganized 13 characterless

amortize
5 repay 6 pay off, reduce 7 pay down
8 write off

amount
4 bulk, dose 5 add up, equal, price, total
6 dosage, matter, number, upshot
7 purport, quantum 8 quantity
9 aggregate, substance
owed: 4 debt
small: 3 bit, jot 4 atom, drop, iota, mite,
whit 5 minim, spark, speck, trace
7 modicum, smidgen 8 molecule, particle
9 scintilla

amour
4 love 5 fling, lover 6 affair 7 liaison,
passion, romance 8 intimacy, intrigue
9 dalliance 10 love affair
12 entanglement, relationship

amour propre
5 pride 6 egoism, vanity 7 conceit,
egotism 8 self-love, vainness 9 vainglory
10 narcissism, self-
esteem, self-regard 11 self-conceit, self-
respect 12 pridefulness 13 conceitedness

amphetamines
5 speed 6 dexies, hearts, uppers
7 bennies, Dexoxyn 8 greenies, pep pills,
Preludin 9 Dexedrine 10 Benzedrine,
Methedrine

amphibian
burrowing: 9 caecilian
legless: 9 caecilian
tailed: 3 eft 4 newt 10 salamander
tailless: 4 frog, toad 8 bullfrog, tree toad
10 batrachian
wormlike: 9 caecilian
young: 7 tadpole 8 polliwog

Amphion
brother: 6 Zethus
conquest: 6 Thebes
father: 4 Zeus
mother: 7 Antiope
sister: 5 Aedon
wife: 5 Niobe

amphitheater
4 bowl 5 arena 7 stadium 8 coliseum
10 auditorium, hippodrome

Amphitrite
father: 6 Nereus
husband: 7 Neptune 8 Poseidon
mother: 5 Doris
son: 6 Triton

Amphitryon's wife
7 Alcmene

amphora
3 jar, jug, urn 4 ewer, vase 5 crock, flask
6 carafe, flagon, vessel

ample
4 wide 5 buxom, great, large, roomy
6 lavish, plenty, portly 7 copious, liberal,
profuse 8 abundant, generous, handsome,
spacious 9 bounteous, bountiful,
capacious, expansive, extensive,
plenteous, plentiful 10 commodious,
sufficient 11 substantial

amplify
5 boost, raise, swell 6 dilate, expand,
extend, jack up 7 augment, develop,
distend, enhance, enlarge, inflate, magnify
8 increase 9 elaborate, intensify
10 supplement

amplitude
4 size 5 range, scale, scope, space
6 amount, extent, spread 7 bigness,
breadth, expanse, stretch 8 distance,
fullness, wideness 9 abundance,
expansion, greatness, largeness,
magnitude, roominess 12 spaciousness
13 capaciousness

amulet
4 juju, luck 5 charm 6 fetish, grigri, mascot
7 periapt 8 gris-gris, talisman 10 lucky
piece, phylactery 11 rabbit's-foot

amuse
4 wile 5 charm, cheer 6 appeal, divert,
engage, occupy, please, regale, tickle
7 animate, beguile, delight, enchant,
enliven, gladden 8 distract, interest,
recreate 9 entertain, fascinate

amusement
3 fun 4 play 7 delight, pastime, pleasure
9 diversion, enjoyment 10 recreation
11 distraction 13 entertainment

amusing
3 fun 5 droll, funny 7 comical, risible
8 engaging, humorous, pleasing
9 diverting, enjoyable 9 laughable
12 entertaining

Amycus
father: 7 Neptune 8 Poseidon
friend: 8 Heracles, Hercules
mother: 5 Melia

ana
5 varia 7 sayings 9 anecdotes
10 collection, miscellany 11 memorabilia,
miscellanea

anabasis
5 march 7 advance, headway, retreat
8 progress 11 advancement, progression

anagogic
6 arcane, hidden, mystic, occult, secret
7 obscure 8 esoteric, mystical, telestic
9 spiritual 10 symbolical 11 allegorical

analects
5 album 6 digest 7 garland, omnibus
8 treasury 9 anthology, selection
10 compendium, miscellany
11 compilation, florilegium

analgesic
6 opiate 7 anodyne 10 anesthetic,
painkiller

analogous
4 akin, like 5 alike 7 kindred, similar,
related, uniform 8 parallel 9 consonant
10 comparable, equivalent, resembling

analogue
5 match 7 cognate 8 parallel 9 correlate,
similarity 11 correlation, counterpart,
equivalence 13 correspondent

analogy
6 simile 8 affinity, likeness, metaphor,
parallel, relation 9 agreement, alikeness,
semblance 10 comparison, similarity,
similitude 11 correlation, equivalence,
resemblance

analysis
5 assay, audit, proof, study 6 method,
review, report, survey 7 finding, inquiry
8 division 9 breakdown, partition, statement
10 dissection, inspection, resolution,
separation 11 examination 13 clarification

analytic
6 cogent, subtle 7 logical, testing
8 studious 9 organized 10 diagnostic,
scientific, systematic 11 proposition,
questioning 13 investigative, ratiocinative

analyze
4 part, test 5 assay, study 6 divide
7 dissect, examine, inspect, resolve
8 classify, consider, separate 9 anatomize,
break down, decompose, interpret
10 decompound, scrutinize
11 deconstruct, distinguish, investigate

analyze grammatically
5 parse

Ananias
4 liar 9 falsifier 12 prevaricator
father: 9 Nedebaeus
wife (coconspirator): 8 Sapphira

anarchism
4 riot 6 theory 7 misrule 8 disorder
9 distemper, rebellion 11 lawlessness

anarchist
5 rebel 6 rioter 8 agitator, mutineer,
provoker, revolter 9 dissident, insurgent

10 malcontent **11** provocateur
13 revolutionary

anarchy
4 riot **5** chaos **7** misrule, mob rule, turmoil
8 disarray, disorder **9** confusion,
distemper, mobocracy, rebellion
10 ochlocracy, revolution **11** lawlessness
13 nongovernment

anathema
3 ban **4** bane **5** curse, enemy, odium,
taboo **6** pariah **7** bugbear, censure,
malison, outcast, reproof **8** loathing
9 damnation, bête noire **10** black beast,
execration **11** abomination, commination,
detestation, imprecation, malediction
12 condemnation, denunciation

anathematize
3 ban **4** damn, oust **5** curse, expel
6 banish **7** condemn **8** denounce,
execrate **9** objurgate, proscribe **13** excommunicate

anatomical depression
5 fossa, fovea

anatomical tube
3 vas **4** duct **5** canal

anatomist
5 Wolff (Kaspar) **6** Harvey (William)
8 Vesalius (Andreas)

anatomize
5 cut up **7** analyze, dissect **8** separate
9 break down, decompose

anatomy
5 frame, mummy **6** makeup **8** analysis,
division, skeleton **9** framework, histology,
structure **10** dissection, morphology,
physiology **11** examination

Anaxo
brother: 10 Amphitryon
daughter: 7 Alcmene
father: 7 Alcaeus
husband: 9 Electryon

ancestor
8 forebear, foregoer **9** ascendant,
precursor, prototype **10** antecedent,
antecessor, forefather, forerunner,
progenitor **11** predecessor **12** primogenitor

ancestral
6 family, inborn, inbred, lineal **7** genetic
8 familial **10** bequeathed, hereditary,
inherited **11** consanguine, patrimonial
sequence: 8 pedigree **9** bloodline,
genealogy

ancestry
4 line, race **5** blood, breed, stock **6** family,
origin, source **7** descent, history, kindred,
lineage **8** heritage, pedigree **9** parentage
10 derivation, extraction

Anchises' son
6 Aeneas

anchor
4 moor **6** secure **7** grapnel, mooring
8 mainstay
part: 5 crown, fluke, shank

anchorage
4 port **5** haven, roads **6** harbor, refuge,
riding **7** mooring, shelter **9** harborage,
roadstead

anchorite
5 loner **6** hermit **7** recluse **8** solitary

anchors
6 aweigh

ancient
3 old **4** aged **5** hoary, olden **6** age-old,
primal **7** antique, archaic, elderly
8 Noachian, old-timer, primeval, timeworn
9 venerable **10** primordial **12** antediluvian

ancient capital
4 Susa **5** Aksum, Balkh, Calah, Isker,
Kalhu, Ninus, Pella, Petra, Sibir **6** Angkor,
Bactra, Nimrud, Sardis **7** Babylon,
Knossos, Memphis, Nineveh, Samaria,
Shushan **10** Persepolis

ancient city
Asia Minor: 4 Nice, Teos **5** Tyana
6 Edessa, Nicaea **7** Antioch
13 Halicarnassus
Babylonia: 4 Sura **5** Agade, Akkad, Eridu,
Larsa **7** Ellasar
Bengal: 4 Gaur **9** Lakhnauti
Canaan: 5 Gezer
Cyprus: 7 Salamis
Egypt: 5 Tanis **6** Thebes **7** Memphis
10 Heliopolis
Etruria: 4 Veii
Euphrates River: 7 Babylon
Greece: 5 Crisa **6** Athens, Sparta
7 Calydon **9** Lacedaemon
Ionia: 4 Myus, Teos **5** Chios, Samos
6 Priene **7** Ephesus, Lebedos, Miletus,
Phocaea **8** Colophon, Erythrae
10 Clazomenae
Italy: 5 Locri **7** Pompeii **8** Siracusa,
Syracuse **11** Herculaneum
Latium: 5 Gabii **9** Alba Longa
Mayan: 4 Cobá **5** Tikal, Tulum, Uxmal
8 Palenque **11** Chichén Itzá

Nile River: 5 Meroë
North Africa: 5 Utica 8 Carthage
Palestine: 4 Gaza 5 Ekron, Endor, Sodom 6 Beroea, Bethel, Gilead, Hebron 7 Jericho, Samaria 8 Ashkelon 9 Capernaum, Jerusalem
Peloponnesus: 5 Tegea 6 Sparta 7 Corinth
Sumeria: 4 Kish, Uruk 5 Erech, Larsa 6 Lagash
Turkey: 5 Assos, Assus 9 Byzantium

ancient country
Adriatic coast: 7 Illyria
Africa: 10 Mauretania
Arabian Peninsula: 5 Sheba
Asia: 4 Aram 5 Media, Minni, Syria 7 Armenia, Ash Sham, Bactria
Asia Minor: 5 Lydia, Mysia 6 Aeolis, Pontus 7 Cilicia, Phrygia 8 Bithynia
Balkan: 7 Macedon 9 Macedonia
Black Sea: 7 Colchis
Dead Sea: 4 Edom
Euphrates River: 9 Babylonia
Europe: 4 Gaul 5 Dacia 6 Gallia
gold-rich: 5 Ophir
Italy: 6 Latium 7 Etruria
Nile valley: 4 Cush
Peloponnesus: 4 Elis 7 Arcadia
Syria: 9 Phoenicia

ancient empire
6 Median 7 Hittite, Persian 8 Assyrian, Athenian, Chaldean, Seleucid 9 Ptolemaic 10 Babylonian

ancient kingdom
Anglo-Saxon: 6 Wessex
Asia: 4 Ghor, Ghur
Celtic: 7 Cumbria
China: 3 Shu
Euphrates valley: 4 Hira 7 Al-Hirah
Greece: 8 Pergamon, Pergamum
North Of Assyria: 3 Van 6 Ararat, Urartu
Palestine: 5 Judah 6 Israel
Persian Gulf: 4 Elam
Portugal: 7 Algarve
Spain: 4 Leon 6 Aragon 7 Castile, Galicia, Granada, Navarre
Syria: 4 Moab
Welsh: 5 Powys
West Sahara: 4 Gana 5 Ghana

ancient monument
6 sphinx 7 obelisk, pyramid

ancient royal forest
4 Dean 8 Sherwood

ancient town
Africa: 4 Zama

Armenia: 4 Dwin, Tvin
Asia Minor: 4 Soli 5 Derbe, Issus, Soloi
Attica: 6 Icaria
Black Sea: 5 Olbia 9 Apollonia
Greece: 4 Abae, Opus 8 Marathon
Italy: 4 Elea, Luna 5 Cumae, Velia
Latium: 5 Ardea, Cures
Macedonia: 5 Pydna, Stobi 9 Apollonia
Peloponnesus: 5 Asine
Persia: 6 Hormuz 8 Harmozia
Sicily: 5 Hybla
Spain: 5 Munda
Tatar: 5 Isker, Sibir
Wendish: 5 Julin

ancilla
3 aid 4 aide, ally, hand, help 6 helper 9 assistant, attendant, supporter

ancillary
5 extra 8 adjuvant, incident 9 accessory, attendant, attending, auxiliary, satellite, secondary 10 additional, coincident, collateral, subsidiary, supporting 11 appurtenant, concomitant, subordinate, subservient 12 accompanying, contributory 13 supplementary

andante
4 slow 5 tempo 7 relaxed, walking 8 moderate

Anderson, Maxwell
play: 7 High Tor 8 Key Largo 9 Winterset 11 Valley Forge 14 What Price Glory

Anderson, Sherwood
book: 9 Poor White 12 Dark Laughter 13 Winesburg Ohio

Andes native
4 Inca

andiron
7 firedog

Andorra
capital: 7 Andorra
language: 7 Catalan
liberator: 11 Charlemagne
monetary unit: 4 euro
mountain range: 8 Pyrenees
neighbor: 5 Spain 6 France
river: 6 Valira

Andrea
5 Doria 8 del Sarto

androgynous
7 epicene 8 bisexual 9 unisexual

android
5 robot 9 automaton

Andromache
husband: 6 Hector
son: 8 Astyanax, Molossus

Andromeda
father: 7 Cepheus
husband: 7 Perseus
mother: 10 Cassiopeia
rescuer: 7 Perseus

_____ and warp
4 weft, woof

anecdote
4 tale, yarn 5 story 7 account, episode,
recital 8 relation 9 narration, narrative
12 recollection, reminiscence

anemic
3 wan 4 pale, thin, weak 5 pasty 6 feeble,
pallid, sickly, watery 7 insipid 8 ischemic
9 bloodless, colorless 10 spiritless

anemone
9 buttercup 10 windflower

anent
4 as to, in re 5 about, as for 7 apropos
8 touching 9 as regards 10 concerning
13 with respect to

anesthetic
6 opiate 7 anodyne 9 analgesic
10 painkiller, palliative
medical: 5 ether 8 spinal 8 morphine,
procaine 9 halothane, novocaine
10 benzocaine, chloroform, tetracaine
11 scopolamine
suffix: 5 caine

anesthetize
4 numb, stun 6 benumb, deaden
8 etherize, knock out 9 narcotize
11 desensitize

anesthetized
4 dead, numb 5 inert 6 asleep, torpid
10 insensible 11 insensitive, unconscious

anew
4 over 5 again 6 afresh, de novo, lately, of
late 8 once more, recently

angel
6 backer, cherub, patron, seraph, surety
7 sponsor 8 backer-up, guardian
9 celestial, guarantor, supporter
10 benefactor 11 underwriter
biblical: 5 Uriel 7 Gabriel, Michael,
Raphael
fallen: 7 Lucifer
hierarchy: 6 powers 7 thrones, virtues
8 cherubim, seraphim 9 dominions
Mormon: 6 Moroni

of death: 6 Azrael

Angel Clare's bride
4 Tess

angelic
4 holy, pure 5 godly 6 divine 7 saintly
8 cherubic, ethereal, heavenly 9 celestial
11 beneficent

Angelica
father: 9 Galaphron
husband: 6 Medoro
lover: 7 Orlando

Angelou work
13 Heart of a Woman (The) 25 I Know
Why the Caged Bird Sings

anger
3 ire, irk, vex 4 bile, boil, burn, fume, fury,
gall, huff, rage, rant, rave, rile 5 annoy,
pique, storm, upset, wrath 6 blow up,
choler, dander, enrage, madden, nettle,
offend, seethe, stir up 7 affront, bristle,
dudgeon, flare up, incense, outrage,
provoke, steam up, umbrage 8 acrimony,
boil over, irritate 9 aggravate, annoyance,
animosity, displease, infuriate 10 antagonism, antagonize, exasperate
11 displeasure, indignation, infuriation
12 exasperation

angle
3 aim, bow 4 axil, bend, bias, fish, hand,
skew, turn 5 facet, slant 6 aspect, corner,
crotch, dogleg 7 flexure, outlook, turning
9 direction, viewpoint 10 standpoint

angler
6 fisher 8 monkfish 9 fisherman, goosefish

Anglo-Saxon
assembly: 4 moot 5 gemot 6 gemote
council: 9 heptarchy
county: 5 shire
court: 4 moot 5 gemot 6 gemote
crown tax: 4 geld
epic: 7 Beowulf
free servant: 5 thane, thegn
god: 3 Ing
goddess of fate: 4 Wyrd
historian: 4 Bede
king: 3 Ine, Ini 4 Edwy 5 Edgar, Edred
6 Alfred, Edmund, Edward, Egbert
8 Ethelred
kingdom: 4 Kent 5 Essex 6 Mercia,
Sussex, Wessex 10 East Anglia
11 Northumbria
king's council: 5 witan
letter: 3 edh, eth, wen, wyn 4 wynn
5 thorn
nobleman: 4 earl

poet: 4 scop
prince: 8 atheling
sheriff: 5 reeve
slave: 4 esne
warrior: 5 thane, thegn

Angola

capital: 6 Luanda
city: 6 Huambo 7 Lubango 8 Benguela
exclave: 7 Cabinda
language: 10 Portuguese
monetary unit: 6 kwanza
neighbor: 5 Congo 6 Zambia 7 Namibia
11 South Africa
river: 5 Congo

angora

3 cat 4 goat, hair, wool, yarn 6 mohair,
rabbit

angry

3 hot, mad 4 sore 5 irate, riled, riley,
upset, vexed, wroth 6 fuming, heated,
ireful, wrathy 7 enraged, furious, riled up
8 choleric, incensed, inflamed, maddened,
wrathful 9 indignant, irritated
10 aggravated, infuriated 11 acrimonious,
exasperated

angst

4 fear 5 worry 6 unease 7 anxiety,
concern 8 distress 10 insecurity
11 disquietude, fretfulness 12 apprehension

Anguilla

island, island group: 3 Dog 4 Seal
5 Scrub 7 Leeward
language: 7 English
location: 10 West Indies
territory of: 7 Britain

anguish

3 rue, woe 4 ache, care, dole, hurt, pain,
pang 5 agony, dread, grief, throe, worry
6 misery, regret, sorrow, throes 7 anxiety,
distress, torment, torture 8 hardship
9 heartache, suffering 10 affliction,
heartbreak 12 wretchedness

angular

4 bony, edgy, lank, lean, thin 5 gaunt,
lanky, spare, stiff 6 forked, skinny, zigzag
7 pointed, scraggy, scrawny 8 cornered,
rawboned, ungainly 9 roughhewn
10 unfinished, ungraceful, unpolished
13 sharp-cornered

ani

6 cuckoo

anima

4 soul 6 psyche, spirit 9 inner self

animadversion

4 slam, slur 7 censure, obloquy
9 aspersion, criticism 10 accusation,
imputation, reflection 11 insinuation
12 reprehension

animadvert

6 notice 7 observe 9 criticize

animal

5 beast, brute, feral 6 brutal, carnal, ferine
7 beastly, bestial, brutish, critter, fleshly,
sensual, swinish, wilding 8 creature,
wildling
antlered: 3 elk 4 axis, deer 5 moose
7 caribou 8 reindeer
aquatic: 3 eel 4 fish, frog, seal 5 otter,
whale 6 dugong, sea cow, walrus
7 dolphin, manatee, octopus 8 bryozoan,
porpoise 9 alligator, crocodile
arboreal: 4 bird 5 chimp, coati, koala,
lemur, sloth 6 gibbon, monkey 7 opossum,
tarsier 8 kinkajou, marmoset, squirrel
9 orangutan
burrowing: 4 mole 5 brock, ratel
6 badger, gopher, marmot, rabbit
7 echidna 9 armadillo, groundhog,
woodchuck
castrated: 5 capon, steer 6 barrow,
wether 7 gelding
draft: 3 yak 4 mule, oxen (plural) 5 horse
6 donkey 8 elephant
exhibit: 3 zoo
extinct: 3 moa 4 dodo, urus 6 quagga
7 mammoth 8 dinosaur, eohippus,
mastodon 9 trilobite
female: 3 cow, dam, doe, ewe, hen, pen,
roe, sow 4 mare, puss 5 bitch, goose,
jenny, nanny, vixen 6 jennet 7 lioness
four-footed: 9 quadruped
four-limbed: 8 tetrapod
free-swimming: 6 nekton
hibernating: 4 bear, frog, toad 5 skunk,
snake 7 polecat 8 chipmunk
9 groundhog, woodchuck
horned: 3 ram, yak 4 bull, goat, ibex,
kudu 5 addax, bison, eland, rhino 6 cattle,
koodoo 7 buffalo, gazelle, giraffe, unicorn
8 antelope
humped: 3 elk, yak 4 zebu 5 bison,
camel, moose
imaginary: 5 snark
insect-eating: 4 mole, newt 5 gecko,
shrew 7 echidna 8 aardvark, anteater,
hedgehog, pangolin, tamandua
10 salamander
male: 3 cob, ram, tom 4 boar, buck, bull,

cock, stag, stud **5** billy, steer **6** gander
7 gobbler, rooster **8** bachelor, stallion
many-celled: 8 metazoan
many-footed: 9 centipede, millipede
marsupial: 5 koala **6** wombat
7 opossum, wallaby **8** kangaroo
9 bandicoot, phalanger
meat-eating: 9 carnivore
mythical: 5 Hydra **6** dragon, kraken,
sphinx **7** centaur, griffin, mermaid,
Pegasus, unicorn **8** basilisk, Cerberus,
Minotaur
one-celled: 9 protozoan
Peruvian: 5 llama **6** alpaca, vicuña
plant-eating: 9 herbivore
skin disease: 5 mange
snouted: 5 coati, tapir **8** mongoose
(see also *animal insect-eating*)
spotted: 4 axis, paca **6** calico, jaguar,
ocelot **7** cheetah, leopard, piebald
8 skewbald **9** dalmatian
striped: 4 kudo **5** tiger, zebra **6** koodoo,
quagga
trail: 3 pug **4** foil, slot **5** spoor
tusked: 6 walrus **7** warthog **8** elephant
two-footed: 5 biped
web-footed: 4 duck, frog, toad **5** goose,
otter **6** beaver **8** duckbill, platypus
young: 3 cub, kid, kit, pup **4** calf, colt,
fawn, foal, joey, lamb **5** bunny, chick, kitty,
poult, shoat, stirk, whelp **6** cygnet, farrow,
heifer, kitten, piglet **7** bullock, gosling,
lambkin **8** suckling, yeanling, yearling
9 fledgling

animal behavior
study of: 8 ethology

animal fat
4 suet **6** tallow

animalism
4 lust **7** abandon **8** vitality **9** carnality
10 sensualism, sensuality **11** lustfulness,
physicality, unrestraint

animalize
4 warp **6** debase **7** corrupt, deprave,
pervert, vitiate **9** brutalize **10** bestialize,
demoralize

animal life
5 fauna

animal sound
3 arf, baa, bay, caw, coo, low, mew, moo
4 bark, bray, buzz, crow, hiss, hoot, howl,
meow, purr, roar, yelp **5** bleat, chirp, croak,
drone, growl, grunt, miaow, neigh, quack
6 bellow, gibber, gobble, warble **7** screech,
twitter

animate
4 fire, live, move, spur, stir, urge **5** alert,
alive, cheer, drive, exalt, impel, liven,
nerve, spark, steel **6** active, arouse, excite,
inform, kindle, lively, living, moving, viable,
vital, vivify **7** actuate, chirk up, dynamic,
enliven, hearten, inspire, quicken, refresh
8 activate, embolden, energize, inspirit,
motivate, spirited, vitalize **9** breathing,
encourage, energized, enhearten, make
alive, stimulate **10** invigorate

animated
3 gay **4** keen **5** alert, alive, peppy, quick,
vivid, vital **6** lively, living **7** dynamic,
excited, vibrant, zestful **8** spirited, vigorous
9 activated, energetic, energized,
exuberant, sprightly, vitalized, vivacious
12 high-spirited

animation
3 pep, vim **4** brio, dash, élan, life, zing
5 oomph, verve **6** energy, esprit, gaiety,
spirit **8** dynamism, vitality, vivacity
10 liveliness

animato
5 brisk, tempo **6** lively **8** spirited **9** energetic, sprightly

animosity
4 hate **5** venom **6** animus, enmity, hatred,
rancor **7** dislike, ill will **8** acrimony
9 antipathy, hostility **10** antagonism,
resentment

animus
4 plan, soul **6** design, enmity, intent,
pneuma, psyche, rancor, spirit **7** dislike, ill
will, meaning, purpose **9** antipathy, élan
vital, hostility, intention **10** antagonism,
intendment, opposition, vital force
11 disposition, malevolence

Anjou
4 pear
capital: 6 Angers
native: 7 Angevin

ankle
6 tarsus

annals
6 record **7** account, history **8** archives,
register **9** chronicle

annelid
4 worm **5** leech **9** earthworm

annex
3 add, arm, cop, ell, win **4** gain, hook, join,
land, take, wing **5** add on, affix, seize, tag
on **6** adjoin, append, attach, fasten, obtain,

pick up, secure, tack on, take on
7 acquire, connect, preempt, procure,
subjoin **8** accroach, addition, appendix,
arrogate, superadd, take over **9** extension
10 attachment, commandeer, subsidiary,
supplement **11** appropriate, expropriate,
incorporate

Annie Oakley
4 pass **10** free ticket, markswoman

annihilate
4 do in, kill, raze, rout, ruin, undo **5** abate,
annul, crush, erase, quash, quell, wrack,
wreck **6** murder, negate, quench, rub out,
squash, uproot, vanish **7** abolish, blot out,
destroy, expunge, nullify, put down, root
out, vitiate, wipe out **8** abrogate, demolish,
massacre, suppress, vanquish **9** eradicate,
extirpate, liquidate, slaughter
10 extinguish, invalidate, obliterate
11 exterminate

annihilation
7 killing **8** massacre **9** abolition **11** destruction, elimination, liquidation,
termination **12** obliteration **13** extermination

anniversary
hundredth: **9** centenary **10** centennial
tenth: **9** decennial
thousandth: **10** millennial

annotate
5 gloss **6** remark **7** comment, explain
8 footnote **9** elucidate, interpret
10 commentate

announce
4 call **5** augur, sound **6** attest, blazon,
herald, impart, issue, report, reveal, signal
7 bespeak, declare, divulge, forerun, give
out, portend, predict, presage, present,
publish, release, signify **8** disclose,
forecast, foreshow, foretell, indicate,
proclaim **9** advertise, broadcast, harbinger,
make known, publicize, state, tell, trumpet
10 give notice, make public, promulgate
11 preindicate

announcement
4 news **6** notice, report **7** message,
release **8** briefing, bulletin **9** broadcast,
statement **10** communiqué, disclosure
11 declaration, publication
12 proclamation, promulgation
13 advertisement, communication

announcer
5 emcee **6** deejay, herald, veejay
9 anchorman, voice-over **10** disc jockey,
disk jockey, newscaster **11** anchorwoman,
broadcaster, commentator
12 anchorperson, sportscaster

annoy
3 bug, irk, vex **4** bait, fret, gall, miff
5 chafe, chivy, harry, peeve, tease, upset,
worry **6** badger, bother, harass, heckle,
hector, needle, nettle, pester, plague, ruffle
7 agitate, bedevil, disturb, hagride, perturb,
provoke, tick off **8** distress, irritate
9 beleaguer
Scottish: **4** fash

annoyance
4 drag, to-do **5** trial, upset, worry **6** bother,
nettle, plague, strain **7** problem, trouble
8 distress, headache, irritant, nuisance,
vexation **10** affliction, disturbance,
harassment, irritation **11** aggravation,
botheration, indignation, provocation
12 exasperation

annoying
5 pesky **8** tiresome, vexatious **9** troubling
10 disturbing, irritating **11** aggravating,
distressing, troublesome **12** exasperating

annual
5 plant **6** flower, yearly **7** almanac **8** each
year, yearbook, yearlong **9** every year

annul
4 undo, void **5** abate, erase, quash
6 cancel, delete, efface, negate, revoke,
vacate **7** abolish, blot out, expunge, nullify,
redress, rescind, retract, reverse, vitiate,
wipe out **8** abrogate, dissolve **9** cancel
out, discharge, frustrate **10** annihilate,
counteract, extinguish, invalidate,
neutralize, obliterate **11** countermand

annunciate
see **announce**

anodyne
4 balm **5** bland **6** opiate, relief, remedy
7 soother **8** narcotic, nepenthe, painless,
sedative **9** analgesic, calmative,
innocuous, soporific **10** anesthetic,
depressant, pain-killer, palliative
11 inoffensive, unoffending **12** tranquilizer

anoint
3 rub **4** daub, laud, name **5** anele, apply,
bless, honor, smear **6** choose, hallow,
ordain **7** confirm, massage **8** dedicate,

sanctify, set apart, venerate **9** designate
10 consecrate

anomalous
3 odd **6** off-key **7** deviant, strange,
unusual **8** aberrant, abnormal, atypical,
peculiar **9** deviating, deviatory, divergent,
irregular, unexpected, unnatural, untypical
11 heteroclite, incongruous, paradoxical
12 inconsistent **13** nonconforming,
preternatural

anomaly
5 freak, quirk **6** oddity **9** departure,
deviation, exception **10** aberration,
divergence **11** abnormality, peculiarity
12 idiosyncrasy, incongruity, irregularity
13 inconsistency

anomie
4 flux **6** unrest **7** anxiety, inertia **10** alienation, insecurity **11** disquietude, instability,
uncertainty **12** disaffection, estrangement,
indifference, restlessness

anon
4 soon **5** later **7** by and by, shortly
8 directly **9** presently **10** before long
11 after a while

anonym
5 alias **6** handle **7** pen name **8** nickname
9 pseudonym **10** nom de plume
11 assumed name, nom de guerre

anonymous
7 unknown, unnamed **8** nameless, not
named, unsigned **9** incognito
10 innominate **11** unspecified **12** undesignated, unidentified, unrecognized

anorak
5 parka

another
3 new **4** else, more **5** added, fresh
7 farther, further, one more **9** different
10 additional **11** alternative, someone else
13 something else

anschluss
5 union **6** league **8** alliance **9** coalition
10 federation **11** confederacy
13 confederation

answer
4 fill, meet, plea **5** atone, plead, rebut,
reply, serve, solve **6** come in, explain,
refute, rejoin, result, retort, return
7 conform, defense, explain, fulfill, respond,
satisfy **8** antiphon, rebuttal, response,

solution **9** rejoinder **10** refutation
11 recriminate **13** countercharge

answerable
5 bound **6** liable **7** obliged, subject
8 amenable **9** compelled, duty-bound,
obligated **11** accountable, constrained,
responsible

ant
5 emmet **9** carpenter
relating to: 6 formic

Antaean
4 huge **5** giant **6** heroic **7** mammoth,
titanic **8** colossal, enormous, gigantic
9 cyclopean, Herculean **10** gargantuan

Antaeus
father: 7 Neptune **8** Poseidon
mother: 4 Gaea
slayer: 8 Heracles, Hercules

antagonism
3 con **5** animus, enmity, hatred, rancor
7 discord **8** conflict, friction **9** animosity,
antipathy, hostility **10** antithesis,
contention, dissension, opposition,
resistance **11** contrariety **12** disagreement

antagonist
3 con, foe **4** anti **5** enemy, match
6 muscle **7** opposer **8** chemical, opponent
9 adversary, contender

antagonistic
4 anti **6** averse **7** adverse, hostile,
opposed **8** clashing, contrary, inimical,
opposing **9** bellicose, combative,
rancorous, truculent, vitriolic **10** discordant
11 belligerent, conflicting, contentious
12 antipathetic

Antarctica sea
4 Ross **7** Weddell **8** Amundsen

ante
3 bet, pay, pot **4** cost, risk **5** level, pay up,
price, put up, stake, wager **6** stakes
7 produce

anteater
see **animal** *insect-eating*

antecede
7 forerun, precede, predate **8** foredate, go
before

antecedence
8 priority **10** precedence, precession,
preference

antecedent

4 fore, line 5 cause, prior 6 former, reason
7 earlier 8 ancestor, anterior, forebear,
foregoer, occasion, previous 9 condition,
foregoing, precedent, preceding, precursor,
prototype 10 forerunner, progenitor
11 determinant, predecessor

antedate

7 forerun, precede 11 anachronize
12 occur earlier

antediluvian

3 old 4 aged, fogy 5 hoary, passé 6 age-
old, fogram, fossil, square 7 ancient,
antique, archaic 8 mossback, Noachian,
obsolete, outdated, outmoded, primeval,
primitive, timeworn 9 out-of-date
10 antiquated, fuddy-duddy 12 old-
fashioned 13 stick-in-the-mud

antelope

3 gnu 4 kudu, oryx 5 addax, bongo, eland,
nyala, serow 6 dik-dik, duiker, impala,
koodoo, lechwe 7 blesbok, chamois,
gazelle, gemsbok, gerenuk, sassaby
8 bushbuck, reedbuck, steinbok
9 springbok, waterbuck 10 hartebeest
female: 3 doe
male: 4 buck
young: 3 kid
(see also **gazelle**)

antenna

4 wire 6 aerial, device, dipole, sensor
8 monopole, receiver

antennae

4 ears 11 sensitivity 13 receptiveness

anterior

4 past 5 prior 6 former 8 previous
9 foregoing, precedent, preceding
10 antecedent

anteroom

5 entry, foyer, lobby 6 alcove 9 vestibule

Anteros

brother: 4 Eros
father: 4 Ares, Mars
mother: 5 Venus 9 Aphrodite
opposite: 4 Eros

anthem

4 hymn, song 5 chant, paean, psalm
8 canticle

anthology

3 ana 5 album 6 digest, reader 7 garland,
omnibus 8 analects, treasury 9 selection
10 assortment, collection, compendium,
miscellany 11 compilation, florilegium

anthropoid

3 ape 5 biped 6 monkey 7 bipedal,
gorilla, manlike, primate 8 hominoid,
humanoid 10 chimpanzee

anthropologist

4 Boas (Franz), Dart (Raymond, Mead
(Margaret) 5 Sapir (Edward), Tylor
(Edward Burnett) 6 Frazer (James
George), Geertz (Clifford), Leakey (Louis),
Morgan (Lewis Henry) 7 Bateson
(Gregory), Kroeber (Alfred Louis)
8 Benedict (Ruth) 10 Malinowski
(Bronisaw) 11 Lévi-Strauss (Claude)

anti

3 con 6 averse 7 adverse, against,
counter, opposed, opposer 8 contrary,
opponent, opposing 9 adversary, opposed
to 10 antagonist 12 antagonistic,
antipathetic, in opposition

antiaircraft fire

4 flak

antibiotic

7 colicin 8 neomycin, viomycin 9 poly-
myxin 10 bacitracin, novobiocin, penicillin
11 bacteriocin, tyrothricin 12 streptomycin,
tetracycline

antic

3 gag 4 dido, joke, lark, romp 5 caper,
comic, prank, trick 6 frisky, frolic, lively
7 comical, foolish, playful 8 escapade,
farcical, prankish, spirited 9 high jinks,
laughable, ludicrous, sprightly
10 frolicsome, rollicking, shenanigan,
tomfoolery 11 mischievous, monkeyshine
12 monkeyshines 13 practical joke

anticipate

3 see 4 wait 5 await, check 6 divine,
expect 7 counter, count on, foresee,
prepare, presage, prevent, wait for
8 forecast, foreknow, foretell 9 apprehend,
forestall, prevision, visualize 10 prepare for

anticipation

7 inkling, outlook, promise 8 awaiting,
forecast, prospect 9 awareness, foresight,
foretaste 10 expectancy 11 expectation,
realization 12 apprehension
13 visualization

Anticlea

father: 9 Autolycus
husband: 7 Laertes
son: 7 Ulysses 8 Odysseus

antidote

4 cure, drug 6 remedy 7 negator
8 medicine 9 nullifier 10 corrective,

counteract, preventive **11** counterstep,
neutralizer **12** counteragent
13 counteractant, counteractive

Antigone
brother: **9** Polynices **10** Polyneices
father: **7** Oedipus
mother: **7** Jocasta
sister: **6** Ismene
uncle: **5** Creon

Antigua and Barbuda
capital: **7** St. Johns
island: **7** Antigua, Barbuda, Redonda
language: **7** English
monetary unit: **6** dollar

Antilochus
father: **6** Nestor
friend: **8** Achilles
slayer: **6** Memnon

Antiope
father: **6** Asopus
husband: **5** Lycus **7** Theseus
queen of: **7** Amazons
son: **6** Zethus **7** Amphion **10** Hippolytus

antipasto
9 appetizer **11** hors d'oeuvre **12** hors
d'oeuvres

antipathetic
5 loath **6** averse, loathe **7** adverse,
hostile, opposed **8** aversive, clashing,
contrary, inimical, opposing, opposite
9 abhorrent, disliking, loathsome, repellent,
repugnant, repulsive **10** discordant,
unfriendly **11** conflicting, distasteful, ill-
disposed, uncongenial **12** antagonistic
13 contradictory

antipathy
4 hate **6** animus, enmity, hatred, rancor
7 allergy, dislike, ill will **8** aversion,
distaste, loathing **9** animosity, hostility
10 abhorrence, antagonism, opposition,
repellency

antiphon
5 psalm, reply, verse **6** answer, anthem,
return **7** respond **8** response

antipodal
5 polar **7** adverse, counter, opposed,
reverse **8** contrary, converse, opposite
9 diametric **11** conflicting, contrasting,
diametrical **12** antithetical **13** contradictory

antipode
6 contra **7** counter, reverse **8** contrary,
converse, flip side, opposite **9** other side
10 antithesis **11** counterpole

antiquate
7 make old, outdate, outmode **8** obsolete
9 obsolesce **12** superannuate

antiquated
3 old **4** aged **5** dated, fusty, hoary, moldy,
passé **6** old hat **7** ancient, antique, archaic
8 obsolete, out-of-date, old-timey,
outmoded **10** oldfangled, out-of-style
11 discredited, obsolescent
12 antediluvian, old-fashioned,
superannuated **13** inappropriate

antique
3 old **4** aged **5** dated, hoary, olden, passé,
relic **6** age-old, bygone, rarity **7** ancient,
archaic, vintage **8** artifact, heirloom, old-
timey, outdated, outmoded, timeworn
9 ancestral, objet d'art, out-of-date,
venerable **10** antiquated, oldfangled
12 antediluvian, old-fashioned

antiseptic
6 iodine **7** alcohol, sterile **8** hygienic,
peroxide, sanitary **9** boric acid, carvacrol,
germicide, merbromin **10** gramicidin,
sterilized **12** carbolic acid, disinfectant
pioneer: **6** Lister (Joseph)

antisocial
7 ascetic, austere, hostile **8** eremitic,
solitary **9** alienated, reclusive, withdrawn
10 unfriendly **11** standoffish
12 antagonistic, misanthropic

antithesis
3 con **6** contra **7** counter, reverse
8 antipode, antipole, contrary, contrast,
converse, opposite **10** antagonism,
opposition **11** counterpole

antithetical
5 polar **7** counter, reverse **8** contrary,
converse, opposite **9** antipodal, diametric
10 antipodean **11** diametrical
13 contradictory

antitoxin
4 sera (plural) **5** serum **11** neutralizer

antiwar
6 irenic **8** pacifist **10** nonviolent, pacifistic

Antony, Mark
defeat: **6** Actium
friend: **6** Caesar
lover: **9** Cleopatra
wife: **7** Octavia

anxiety
4 care, fear **5** doubt, dread, panic, worry
6 unease **7** concern **8** , distress, mistrust,
suspense **9** self-doubt, suffering

anxious
10 uneasiness 11 disquietude, uncertainty
12 apprehension

anxious
4 avid, keen 5 eager 6 afraid, ardent,
scared, uneasy 7 alarmed, fearful, worried
8 agitated, desirous, troubled, worrying
9 impatient, perturbed, terrified
10 breathless, disquieted, frightened
12 apprehensive

any
3 all 4 a bit, some 5 at all, every 7 a little,
several 8 whatever

anyhow
6 random 7 however 8 at random,
randomly 9 hit-or-miss 10 carelessly
11 any which way, haphazardly, regardless
13 helter-skelter

anymore
3 now 5 today 8 nowadays 9 presently,
these days

anyone
3 all 9 everybody

anything
5 at all

anytime
4 ever 5 at all 8 whenever

anyway
4 ever, once 5 at all 7 however
12 nevertheless

anywhere
5 at all 7 all over 10 at any point

anywise
5 at all

apace
4 fast 6 versed 7 abreast, flat-out, hastily,
quickly, rapidly, swiftly 8 informed, up-to-
date, speedily 9 posthaste 12 lickety-split
13 expeditiously

Apache
chief: 7 Cochise 8 Geronimo
subgroups: 7 Cibecue 9 Jicarilla,
Mescalero 10 Chiricahua

apart
5 alone, aside 6 singly 7 asunder,
removed 8 detached, isolated, one by one
9 severally 10 separately 12 individually
13 independently, unaccompanied
prefix: 3 dis

apart from
3 bar, but 4 save 6 except, saving
7 barring, besides 9 except for, excepting,
excluding, other than, outside of
11 exclusive of

apartheid
8 division 9 partition 10 separation,
separatism 11 segregation 12 separateness

apartment
4 flat, room 5 rooms, suite 6 rental
7 chamber, housing, lodging 8 building,
dwelling 9 residence 13 accommodation

apathetic
4 dull, flat, limp 5 inert 6 stolid, torpid
7 languid, passive, unmoved 8 sluggish
9 impassive, untouched 10 anesthetic,
insensible, phlegmatic, spiritless
11 emotionless, indifferent, insensitive
12 unresponsive 13 disinterested

apathy
6 torpor 8 coldness, dullness, lethargy,
obduracy, stoicism 9 aloofness, disregard,
inertness, lassitude, passivity, stolidity,
torpidity, unconcern 10 detachment,
dispassion 11 callousness, disinterest,
impassivity 12 heedlessness, indifference,
listlessness 13 insensibility, insensitivity

ape
4 copy, mime, mock 5 mimic 6 baboon,
bonobo, gibbon, monkey, parody, pongid,
simian 7 copycat, emulate, gorilla, imitate,
siamang, take off 8 simulate, travesty
9 burlesque, orangutan 10 anthropoid,
caricature, chimpanzee 11 impersonate

aperçu
5 brief 6 digest, précis, sketch, survey
7 insight, outline 8 syllabus
10 compendium, impression

aperitif
4 whet 5 drink 8 cocktail 9 appetizer

aperture
3 gap 4 hole, vent 6 outlet 7 opening,
orifice, pinhole

apery
7 mimicry 9 imitation

apex
3 cap, tip, top 4 acme, cusp, peak, roof
5 crest, crown, limit, point 6 apogee,
climax, summit, vertex, zenith 8 capstone,
pinnacle, ultimate 9 crescendo, sublimity
11 culmination, ne plus ultra
12 quintessence

aphorism
3 saw 4 rule 5 adage, axiom, maxim, moral

6 dictum, saying, truism 7 precept, proverb
8 apothegm

aphrodisiac
6 erotic 7 amative, amatory, amorous,
lustful 8 excitant 10 passionate

Aphrodite
Roman counterpart: 5 Venus
consort: 4 Ares 6 Vulcan 10 Hephaestus
father: 4 Zeus 7 Jupiter
goddess of: 4 love
mother: 5 Dione
son: 4 Eros 6 Aeneas 7 Priapus

apiarist
9 beekeeper

apical
3 top 7 highest, topmost 8 loftiest
9 uppermost

apiculture
10 beekeeping

apiece
3 per 4 a pop, each 6 singly, to each 7 for
each 8 one by one 9 per capita, severally
10 separately 12 individually, respectively

apish
5 phony, silly 7 slavish 8 affected
9 emulative, imitative 10 artificial

aplenty
4 full 5 ample 6 galore, indeed 7 copious,
greatly 8 abundant, very much
9 extremely

aplomb
4 ease 5 poise 6 polish 8 coolness,
easiness 9 assurance, certainty, certitude,
composure 10 confidence, equanimity
11 nonchalance, savoir faire 12 self-
reliance 13 self-assurance

apocalypse
6 augury, oracle, vision 8 disaster,
prophecy 10 Armageddon, prediction,
revelation

apocalyptic
4 dire 5 awful 7 baleful, baneful, fateful,
fearful, ominous 8 Delphian, dreadful,
oracular, terrible 9 appalling, climactic,
grandiose, prophetic 10 foreboding,
predicting 11 foretelling, prophetical,
threatening 12 inauspicious
book: 10 Revelation 11 Revelations

apocryphal
5 false, wrong 6 untrue 7 dubious
8 doubtful, spurious 9 incorrect,

ungenuine, unverified 10 ficticious,
inaccurate 11 unauthentic 12 questionable

apogee
4 acme, apex, peak 6 climax, summit,
zenith 8 capstone, meridian, pinnacle
9 high point 11 culmination

Apollo
6 Helios 7 Phoebus
beloved: 6 Cyrene, Daphne 8 Calliope
birthplace: 5 Delos
father: 4 Zeus 7 Jupiter
mother: 4 Leto 6 Latona
oracle: 6 Delphi
sister: 5 Diana 7 Artemis
son: 3 Ion 7 Orpheus
temple: 6 Delphi

apologetic
5 sorry 6 rueful 8 contrite, penitent
9 regretful, repentant 10 remorseful
11 penitential 12 compunctious

apologia
4 plea 6 excuse, reason 7 defense
8 argument 11 elucidation, explanation
13 clarification, justification

apologize
5 atone 6 lament, regret, repent 7 confess
9 beg pardon 10 make amends

apologue
4 myth, tale 5 fable, story 7 parable
8 allegory

apology
4 plea 6 amends, excuse 7 redress,
regrets 8 mea culpa 9 admission,
makeshift 10 concession, confession

apostasy
7 perfidy 9 defection, desertion, disavowal,
falseness, rejection 11 abandonment,
repudiation 12 disaffection, renunciation

apostate
7 heretic, traitor 8 defector, deserter,
recreant, renegade, turncoat 9 turnabout

apostatize
4 turn 6 defect, desert 7 abandon,
forsake, sell out 8 renounce 9 repudiate

a posteriori
9 inductive

apostle
4 John, Jude, Paul 5 James, Judas, Peter,
Silas, Simon 6 Andrew, Philip, Thomas
7 Matthew 8 Barnabas, disciple, follower,

apothecary

Matthias, preacher **9** missioner
10 colporteur, evangelist, missionary
11 Bartholomew **12** propagandist
of Germany: 8 Boniface
of Ireland: 7 Patrick
of the English: 9 Augustine
of the French: 5 Denis
of the Gauls: 8 Irenaeus
of the Gentiles: 4 Paul
of the Goths: 7 Ulfilas
to the Indians: 9 John Eliot

apothecary

7 chemist **8** druggist, pharmacy
9 drugstore **10** pharmacist

apothegm

see **aphorism**

apotheosis

6 height **7** epitome **8** exemplar, last word,
ultimate **9** archetype, elevation
10 exaltation **11** deification, embodiment,
ennoblement, idolization, lionization
12 enshrinement, quintessence
13 glorification

appall

3 awe **4** faze **5** alarm, shake, shock
6 dismay **7** horrify, outrage, overawe,
perturb **8** confound, distress **10** disconcert
11 consternate

appalled

6 aghast **11** dumbfounded

appalling

5 awful **6** horrid **7** fearful **8** daunting,
dreadful, horrible, horrific, shocking, terrible
9 atrocious, dismaying, frightful, loathsome
10 disgusting, formidable, horrifying

appanage

5 grant, right **7** adjunct **8** property
9 endowment, privilege **10** birthright,
perquisite **11** prerogative

apparatus

4 gear, tool **5** gizmo **6** device, outfit, tackle
7 utensil **8** matériel, tackling **9** equipment,
implement, machinery **10** instrument
11 contraption, habiliments
13 accouterments, accoutrements,
paraphernalia

apparel

4 clad, duds, garb, gear, robe, suit, togs
5 adorn, array, dress, getup, habit **6** attire,
clothe, outfit **7** clothes, costume, garment,
glad rags, raiment, threads **8** clothing,
enclothe, vestment **9** embellish
11 habiliments

apparent

5 clear, plain **6** patent **7** evident, obvious,
seeming, visible **8** distinct, manifest,
palpable **9** succedent **10** noticeable,
observable **11** discernible, perceivable,
unambiguous, unequivocal
12 successional

apparition

5 ghost, shade, umbra **6** shadow, spirit,
vision, wraith **7** phantom, specter
8 illusion, phantasm **10** appearance,
phenomenon **13** hallucination

appeal

3 ask, beg, bid **4** call, lure, plea, pray, pull,
suit, urge **5** apply, brace, charm, crave,
plead **6** accuse, allure, charge, excite,
invoke, sue for **7** attract, beseech, entreat,
glamour, implore, request **8** call upon, charisma, entreaty, interest, intrigue, petition
9 fascinate, importune, magnetism,
seduction **10** allurement, attraction,
supplicate **11** application, fascination,
imploration **12** drawing power, solicitation,
supplication

appealing

8 alluring, charming, pleading, pleasant,
pleasing **9** agreeable, imploring
10 attracting, attractive, bewitching,
enchanting, entreating **11** captivating,
fascinating

appear

4 come, look, loom, rise, seem, show
5 arise, issue, occur, sound **6** arrive,
emerge, show up **7** be clear, emanate
8 look like, resemble **9** be evident, come
forth **10** be manifest **11** materialize

appearance

3 air **4** face, form, look, mien, pose, show
5 debut, dress, front, guise, image
6 advent, aspect, facade, manner **7** arrival,
bearing, display, seeming **8** attitude,
demeanor, illusion **9** semblance
10 impression, occurrence, simulacrum
11 countenance **13** manifestation

appease

4 calm, ease **5** allay, quiet **6** buy off,
pacify, soothe **7** assuage, concede,
content, gratify, mollify, placate, relieve,
satisfy, sweeten **10** conciliate, propitiate

appellation

4 name **5** brand, label, nomen, style, title
7 moniker **8** cognomen **10** identifier
11 designation **12** denomination

append
3 add **5** add on, affix, annex, tag on
6 adjoin, attach, tack on **7** subjoin
10 supplement

appendage
3 arm, fin, leg, tab, tag **4** barb, flap, horn,
limb, seta, tail, wing **5** extra **6** cercus,
member **7** adjunct, antenna, elytron,
stipule **8** pedipalp, pendicle, tentacle
9 accessory, auxiliary, extremity
10 attachment, collateral, incidental,
projection, supplement **12** appurtenance,
nonessential, protuberance

appendix
5 notes, rider **7** adjunct, codicil
8 addendum, addition **9** accessory,
appendage **10** attachment, supplement
12 appurtenance

apperception
5 grasp **9** awareness **10** cognizance
11 realization, recognition
12 apprehension, assimilation
13 comprehension, introspection,
understanding

appertain
4 bear **5** apply, refer **6** bear on, belong,
relate **8** bear upon **10** be relevant **11** be
connected, be pertinent

appetence
3 yen **5** taste, thirst **6** desire, hunger,
relish **7** craving, longing, stomach
8 fondness

appetent
4 agog, avid, keen **5** eager **6** ardent
7 anxious, craving, lusting, thirsty
8 desirous, yearning **9** impatient
10 breathless

appetite
3 yen **4** bent, itch, lust, urge **5** taste
6 desire, hunger, liking, relish **7** craving,
leaning, longing, passion, stomach
8 cupidity, fondness, gluttony, penchant,
soft spot, voracity, weakness, yearning
9 hankering **10** preference, proclivity,
propensity **11** inclination

appetizer
4 whet **5** snack **6** canapé, savory, tidbit
8 aperitif, cocktail, stimulus **9** antipasto
11 hors d'oeuvre

appetizing
5 tasty **6** savory **8** saporous, tempting
9 agreeable, appealing, aperitive, flavorful,
palatable, relishing, toothsome

10 delectable, flavorsome **11** tantalizing
13 mouth-watering

applaud
4 clap, hail, laud, root **5** bravo, cheer, extol
6 praise, rise to **7** acclaim, approve,
commend **9** recommend **10** compliment

applause
4 hand **5** round **6** bravos, cheers, praise
7 acclaim, hurrahs, ovation, rooting
8 accolade, approval, cheering, clapping,
plaudits **11** acclamation, commendation

apple
4 crab, Fuji, Gala, pome **6** Empire, pippin,
russet **7** Baldwin, costard, Duchess,
Winesap **8** Braeburn, Cortland, greening,
Jonagold, Jonathan, McIntosh **9** Delicious
10 Rome Beauty **11** Granny Smith,
Gravenstein, Northern Spy, Transparent
dessert: 5 crisp
juice: 5 cider

applejack
5 cider **6** brandy, liquor **8** calvados **9** hard
cider

apple knocker
see **rustic**

apple-polish
4 fawn **5** toady **6** kowtow **7** cater to,
flatter, honey up, truckle **8** butter up,
10 curry favor, ingratiate

apple-polisher
5 toady **6** yes-man **8** bootlick, groveler,
lickspit **9** flatterer, sycophant **11** lickspittle

applesauce
5 hooey **6** bunkum **7** baloney, rubbish,
twaddle **8** malarkey, nonsense
9 poppycock

appliance
6 device **7** utensil **9** implement **10** instrument **11** application
kitchen: 4 oven **5** mixer, range, stove
6 fridge **7** blender, toaster **9** can opener,
microwave **10** dishwasher **12** refrigerator

applicability
3 use **7** account, fitness, utility
9 advantage, relevance **10** usefulness

applicable
3 apt, fit **4** just, meet **5** ad rem **6** seemly,
suited, useful **7** apropos, fitting, germane
8 apposite, material, relevant, suitable
9 befitting, pertinent **10** felicitous
11 appropriate

applicant
6 seeker 7 hopeful 8 aspirant, inquirer
9 candidate, job-hunter, job-seeker

application
3 use 4 form, heed, plea, suit, solicitation,
suit 5 study 6 appeal, debate, effort, letter
7 request 8 entreaty, exercise, exertion,
industry, petition 9 assiduity, attention,
diligence, operation, treatment 10 dedication, employment 11 requisition,
utilization 13 concentration, consideration

appliqué
5 decal

apply
3 dab, use 4 bend, give, turn, urge
5 press, refer 6 accost, affect, appeal,
assign, bear on, bestow, devote, direct,
employ, engage, handle, relate, resort, take
on 7 address, beseech, concern, entreat,
execute, implore, involve, pertain, utilize
8 approach, bear upon, exercise, petition,
set about 9 appertain, implement,
importune, undertake 10 administer,
buckle down

appoint
3 arm, fix, rig, set, tap 4 gear, name
5 equip 6 assign, decide, fit out, outfit,
supply 7 dress up, furbish, furnish,
provide, turn out 8 accouter, accoutre,
accredit, delegate, nominate 9 authorize,
designate, determine, embellish, provision
10 commission

appointment
3 job 4 date, meet, post, spot 5 berth,
place, tryst 6 billet, choice, office
7 meeting 8 election, position
9 equipment, selection, situation
10 assignment, connection, engagement,
rendezvous 11 arrangement, assignation,
designation

appointments
7 fitting 8 equipage, equipment 9 trappings 12 furnishings 13 accoutrements

apportion
3 cut, lot 4 give, mete, part 5 allot, allow,
cut up, divvy, quota, serve, share, slice,
split 6 assign, bestow, divide, parcel, ration
7 deal out, dish out, divvy up, dole out,
measure, mete out, prorate, split up
8 allocate, dispense, separate, share out
9 admeasure, partition 10 administer,
distribute

apportionment
3 cut, lot 4 part 5 piece, quota, share,
slice, split 6 ration 7 measure, quantum

9 allotment, allowance 10 allocation,
assignment

apposite
3 apt 4 just 5 ad rem 6 proper, suited,
timely 7 apropos, fitting, germane, right on
8 material, on target, relevant, suitable
9 pertinent 10 applicable, appropriate

appositeness
7 aptness, fitness 9 relevance
10 pertinence, timeliness 11 suitability

appraisal
5 stock 6 rating, survey 7 pricing
8 estimate, judgment 9 valuation
10 assessment, estimation, evaluation

appraise
3 eye, fix, set 4 rate, size 5 assay, audit,
gauge, judge, price, set at, value 6 assess,
figure, size up, survey 7 adjudge, examine,
inspect, measure, valuate 8 estimate,
evaluate, look over 9 calculate, figure out

appreciable
5 clear, plain 6 marked 7 evident, obvious
8 apparent, clear-cut, concrete, manifest,
material, palpable, sensible, tangible
10 detectable, measurable, noticeable,
observable 11 discernible, perceptible,
substantial 12 considerable

appreciate
4 gain, go up, grow, know, like, love, rise
5 enjoy, grasp, judge, prize, savor, value
6 admire, esteem, fathom, regard, relish
7 apprize, cherish, cognize, enhance,
improve, inflate, realize, respect
8 evaluate, increase, treasure
9 apprehend, delight in, recognize 10 comprehend, understand

appreciation
4 gain, rise 6 growth, regard, thanks
7 tribute 8 increase, judgment 9 awareness, gratitude, inflation 10 evaluation,
perception 11 recognition, sensitivity,
testimonial 12 gratefulness

apprehend
3 dig, get, nab, see 4 bust, fear, grab,
know, nail, read, take, twig 5 catch, grasp,
pinch, run in, seize, sense 6 absorb,
accept, arrest, collar, detain, digest, divine,
fathom, pick up, take in, wise up 7 capture,
catch on, cognize, compass, foresee, make
out, preknow, previse, realize 8 conceive
9 penetrate, recognize, visualize
10 anticipate, appreciate, understand

apprehensible
5 clear, lucid, plain 7 evident, obvious

8 distinct, explicit, knowable, luminous
9 graspable 10 fathomable

apprehension
3 ken 4 care, fear, idea 5 alarm, angst,
dread, grasp, pinch, worry 6 arrest, notion,
pickup, unease 7 anxiety, capture,
concern, seizure, thought 8 disquiet,
judgment 9 agitation, awareness,
detention, knowledge, misgiving, suspicion
10 conception, foreboding, perception,
solicitude, uneasiness 11 disquietude,
premonition 13 comprehension,
understanding

apprehensive
5 alive, awake, aware, sharp 6 afraid,
astute, scared, uneasy 7 anxious, fearful,
knowing, worried 8 sensible, sentient,
troubled 9 cognizant, conscious, observant,
perceptive, sensitive 10 discerning,
disquieted, insightful

apprentice
4 bind, tyro 5 pupil, serve 6 novice, rookie
7 learner, starter, student, trainee, work for
8 beginner, freshman, neophyte, newcomer
9 novitiate 10 tenderfoot

apprenticed
5 bound 7 obliged, pledged 8 articled
9 obligated 10 indentured

apprise
4 clue, post, tell, warn 6 advise, clue in, fill
in, impart, inform, notify, reveal, wise up
7 let know 8 acquaint, announce, describe,
disclose 9 make known 11 communicate

apprize
5 value 6 admire, esteem, regard, relish
7 cherish 8 hold dear, treasure
10 appreciate, rate highly

approach
4 near, nigh 5 reach, rival, touch, verge
6 access, advise, amount, avenue, border,
gain on 7 address, advance, apply to,
attempt, consult, descent, request 8 come
up to, draw near, endeavor, overture
9 come close 11 approximate

approachable
7 affable 8 friendly, sociable 9 agreeable,
congenial, reachable, receptive
10 accessible, attainable

approaching
6 coming 7 nearing 8 expected, imminent,
oncoming, upcoming 11 forthcoming

approbate
4 back, like 5 favor 6 accept, assent,

praise 7 applaud, approve, commend,
consent, endorse, support 8 sanction
9 recommend 11 countenance

approbation
3 nod 4 okay 5 favor 6 esteem, praise
7 acclaim, consent, support 8 applause,
approval, sanction 10 admiration,
permission 11 endorsement,
commendation, recognition

appropriate
3 apt, cop, due, fit 4 grab, just, lift, meet,
take, true 5 allot, annex, claim, exact, filch,
grasp, pinch, right, seize, steal, swipe,
usurp 6 assign, assume, budget, devote,
pilfer, proper, snatch, snitch, timely, useful,
worthy 7 apropos, desired, earmark, fitting,
germane, merited, preempt, purloin
8 accroach, apposite, arrogate, deserved,
eligible, entitled, relevant, rightful, set apart,
set aside, suitable 9 befitting, opportune,
pertinent, requisite 10 acceptable,
admissible, applicable, commandeer,
compatible, confiscate, convenient,
felicitous, seasonable

appropriately
4 well 5 amply, aptly, right 8 properly,
suitably 9 fittingly 10 acceptably,
adequately, becomingly

appropriateness
3 use 5 order 7 account, aptness, fitness,
service, utility 8 meetness 9 advantage,
propriety, relevance, rightness
10 expediency, usefulness 13 applicability

appropriation
5 grant 7 funding, stipend, subsidy
9 allotment, allowance 10 allocation,
assignment, earmarking, subvention

approval
4 okay 5 favor, leave 6 assent 7 consent,
go-ahead, license, support 8 applause,
blessing, sanction, suffrage
10 acceptance, compliment, concurrence,
green light, permission, ratification 11 approbation, benediction, endorsement
12 commendation 13 authorization,
confirmation

approve
4 okay 5 clear, favor, go for 6 accept, back
up, praise, ratify, uphold 7 applaud, certify,
commend, condone, confirm, endorse,
initial, mandate, stand by, support, sustain
8 accredit, hold with, sanction 9 approbate,
authorize, encourage 10 compliment
11 countenance

approximate
4 near 5 close, rough, touch 6 almost
7 similar, verge on 8 approach, come near
10 resembling 11 comparative

approximately
4 most, nigh 5 about, circa 6 all but,
almost, nearly 7 close to 8 well-nigh
9 just about, very close 11 practically

approximation
8 likeness, nearness 9 closeness
10 similarity 11 resemblance

appurtenance
7 adjunct 8 addition, appendix, ornament
9 accessory, apparatus, appendage
10 attachment 11 furnishings
13 accompaniment

appurtenant
5 extra 8 adjuvant 9 accessory, ancillary,
auxiliary 10 additional, collateral,
subsidiary 11 subordinate, subservient
12 accompanying, contributory

a priori
8 provable, reasoned 9 deducible,
deductive, derivable, inferable, inferential
11 presumptive

apron
5 stage 6 shield 7 garment 8 pinafore
9 extension

apropos
3 apt 4 as to, in re, meet 5 about, ad rem,
anent, aptly, as for 6 proper, timely
7 fitting, germane, related 8 apposite,
material, pointful, relevant, suitable,
suitably, touching 9 as regards, opportune,
pertinent, regarding 10 applicable, as
respects, concerning, relevantly,
respecting, seasonably 11 applicative,
applicatory, bearing upon, in respect to,
opportunely, pertinently 13 with respect to

apt
3 fit 4 just 5 alert, given, prone, quick,
ready, savvy, smart 6 bright, clever, liable,
likely, prompt, proper 7 apropos, fitting,
germane, tending 8 apposite, disposed,
inclined, relevant, suitable 9 befitting,
pertinent, qualified 10 felicitous,
responsive 11 appropriate, intelligent

aptitude
4 bent, gift 5 flair, knack, savvy 6 genius,
liking, talent 7 ability, faculty, fitness
8 capacity, tendency 10 capability,
cleverness, proclivity, propensity

11 disposition, inclination, suitability
12 predilection

aptness
4 bent, gift 5 flair, knack, skill 6 genius,
talent 7 ability, faculty, fitness 8 tendency
9 propriety, readiness 10 capability,
cleverness, expediency, likelihood
11 inclination, suitability 12 intelligence

aquanaut
5 diver 10 scuba diver

aqua vitae
4 grog 5 booze, drink, hooch 6 liquor,
tipple 7 alcohol, spirits

aqueduct
5 canal 6 course 7 channel, conduit,
passage 8 waterway 11 watercourse

aqueous
5 fluid 6 liquid, watery 9 liquefied

Aquila
13 constellation
representation: 5 eagle
star: 6 Altair

Aquitaine
7 Guienne
queen: 7 Eleanor

aquiver
5 shaky 7 quaking, shaking, trembly
9 shivering, trembling, tremulant, tremulous

Arab
chief: 4 emir 5 sheik 6 sheikh, sultan
country: 4 Iraq, Oman 5 Egypt, Libya,
Qatar, Sudan, Syria, Yemen 6 Jordan,
Kuwait 7 Algeria, Bahrain, Lebanon,
Morocco, Tunisia 11 Saudi Arabia

arable
7 fertile 8 fruitful, tillable 10 cultivable,
productive

Arachne
father: 5 Idmon
form: 6 spider
mother: 6 Cyrene
rival: 6 Athena 7 Minerva

arachnid
4 mite, tick 6 acarus, spider 8 scorpion
9 arthropod, phalangid, tarantula
10 harvestman 13 daddy longlegs

arbiter
5 judge 6 expert, umpire 7 referee
8 mediator 9 authority, moderator
11 adjudicator

arbitrary
4 rash **6** chance, random **7** erratic, offhand, wayward, willful **8** fanciful, heedless **9** frivolous, impetuous, whimsical **10** capricious, subjective **10** irrational **12** unreasonable **13** discretionary

arbitrate
5 judge **6** settle, umpire **7** adjudge, mediate, referee **9** intervene **10** adjudicate **12** intermediate

arbitrator
5 judge **6** umpire **7** referee, settler **8** mediator **9** moderator **11** adjudicator

arbor
4 axle, beam **5** bower, frame, shaft **7** pergola, shelter, spindle

arc
3 bow, lob **4** arch, bend, path **5** curve, round **7** rainbow **9** curvation, curvature **11** measurement, progression

arcade
6 arches **7** gallery **10** passageway

arcadia
4 Eden, Zion **6** heaven, utopia **7** Elysium, nirvana **8** paradise **9** fairyland, Shangri-la **10** wonderland **12** promised land

arcane
6 hidden, mystic, occult, opaque, secret **7** obscure, unknown **8** esoteric **9** recondite **10** cabalistic, mysterious, unknowable **11** inscrutable **12** impenetrable **13** unaccountable

Arcas
father: **4** Zeus **7** Jupiter
mother: **8** Callisto

arch
3 bow, coy, sly **4** bend, hump, pert **5** curve, fresh, saucy, vault **6** camber, cheeky, impish **7** playful, roguish, waggish **8** flippant, malapert **9** curvature **10** coquettish **11** mischievous
inner curve: **8** intrados
kind: **4** ogee **5** ogive, round, Tudor **6** lancet **7** rampart, trefoil **9** horseshoe, primitive, segmental **10** shouldered **11** equilateral
outer curve: **8** extrados
part: **6** impost **8** keystone, springer, voussoir

archaeological site
Africa: **8** Zimbabwe **13** Great Zimbabwe
Britain: **7** Avebury **9** Skara Brae, Sutton Hoo **10** Stonehenge
Cambodia: **6** Angkor **9** Angkor Wat

Crete: **7** Knossos
Egypt: **4** Giza **5** Luxor **6** Abydos, Karnak, Naqada, Thebes **7** Memphis **9** El-Bahnasa **11** Oxyrhynchus
Greece: **7** Delphi **7** Mycenae, Olympia
Guatemala: **5** Tikal
Honduras: **5** Copán
Indonesia: **9** Borobudur
Iran: **10** Persepolis
Iraq: **4** Isin, Nuzi **6** Nimrud **7** Babylon, Nineveh, Samarra
Israel: **7** Jericho
Italy: **7** Pompeii **11** Herculaneum
Lebanon: **6** Byblos **7** Baalbek
Mexico: **5** Mitla, Tulum, Uxmal **8** Palenque **10** Monte Albán **11** Chichén Itzá
Peru: **11** Machu Picchu
Syria: **7** Palmyra
Tunisia: **8** Carthage, Kairouan
Turkey: **4** Troy **6** Knidos **8** Hisarlik, Pergamon **9** Hissarlik
Uzbekistan: **9** Samarkand

archaeologist
4 Dart (Raymond) **5** Evans (Arthur) **6** Carter (Howard), Childe (V. Gordon), Kidder (Alfred), Petrie (Flinders) **7** Thomsen (Christian), Woolley (Leonard), Worsaae (Jens) **8** Breasted (James Henry), Goodyear (William) **10** Schliemann (Heinrich) **11** Champollion (Jean-François), Winckelmann (Johann)

archaic
3 old **5** dated, olden, passé **6** bygone **7** ancient, antique **8** obsolete, outdated **9** out-of-date, primitive, unevolved **10** antiquated **11** undeveloped **12** old-fashioned

archangel
5 Uriel **7** Gabriel, Michael, Raphael

arched
4 bent **5** bowed, round **6** curved **7** curving, rounded

archer
4 Tell (William) **5** Cupid **6** bowman **9** Robin Hood **11** Sagittarius

archery
9 toxophily

archetypal
5 ideal, model **7** classic, perfect, typical **9** classical, exemplary **10** consummate **12** paradigmatic, prototypical

archetype
4 idea **5** ideal, model **6** mirror **7** epitome,

essence, example, pattern **8** exemplar, original, paradigm, standard **9** beau ideal, prototype **10** apotheosis, embodiment, protoplast **12** quintessence

archfiend
5 demon, devil, Satan **6** diablo **7** Lucifer

Archimedes
5 Greek **8** inventor
cry: 6 eureka
discovery: 5 screw **8** buoyancy
9 principle **11** water raiser

archipelago
Asian: 5 Malay
Canada: 6 Arctic
Japan: 4 Goto **9** Gotoretto
Norway: 11 Spitsbergen
Papua New Guinea: 8 Bismarck
9 Louisiade
Philippines: 4 Sulu
off Scotland: 7 Orcades, Orkneys
United States: 9 Alexander

architect
5 maker **7** creator **8** designer, inventor
9 generator **10** originator
American: 3 Pei (I. M.) **4** Hood
(Raymond), Kahn (Louis) **5** Gehry (Frank),
McKim (Charles), Meier (Richard), Roche
(Kevin), Stone (Edward Durell), Weese
(Harry), White (Stanford) **6** Breuer
(Marcel), Fuller (Buckminster), Gilbert
(Cass), Graves (Michael), Morgan (Julia),
Neutra (Richard), Rogers (Isaiah), Soleri
(Paolo), Upjohn (Richard), Walter
(Thomas), Warren (William), Wright (Frank
Lloyd) **7** Burnham (Daniel), Johnson
(Philip), Latrobe (Benjamin), Olmsted
(Frederick Law), Renwick (James), Sturgis
(John Hubbard), Venturi (Robert)
8 Bulfinch (Charles), Saarinen (Eero, Eliel),
Sullivan (Louis), Thornton (William),
Yamasaki (Minoru) **10** Richardson (Henry
Hobson)
Austrian: 4 Loos (Adolf) **6** Wagner (Otto)
Brazilian: 8 Niemeyer (Oscar)
Canadian: 6 Safdie (Moshe)
Dutch: 8 Rietveld (Gerrit)
English: 4 Nash (John), Shaw (Richard),
Wood (John), Wren (Christopher) **5** Jones
(Inigo), Scott (George Gilbert), Wyatt
(James) **6** Foster (Norman), Rogers
(Richard), Street (George Edmund),
Voysey (Charles) **7** Lutyens (Edwin)
8 Vanbrugh (John)
Finnish: 5 Aalto (Alvar) **8** Saarinen (Eero,
Eliel)
French: 6 Perret (Auguste) **7** Garnier

(Tony), L'Enfant (Pierre-Charles) **11** Le
Corbusier **12** Viollet-le-Duc (Eugène)
German: 8 Schinkel (Karl) **10** Men-
delsohn (Erich)
German-American: 7 Gropius (Walter)
Israeli: 6 Safdie (Moshe)
Italian: 5 Nervi (Pier Luigi) **6** Romano
(Giulio), Soleri (Paolo) **7** Alberti (Leon
Battista), Bernini (Gian Lorenzo), da Vinci
(Leonardo), Orcagna, Peruzzi
(Baldassare), Raphael, Vignola (Giacomo
da) **8** Bramante (Donato), Leonardo (da
Vinci), Palladio (Andrea), Sangallo
(Giuliano da), Terragni (Giuseppe)
9 Borromini (Francesco), Sansovino
(Jacopo) **12** Michelangelo
Japanese: 5 Tange (Kenzo)
Roman: 9 Vitruvius
Scottish: 10 Mackintosh (Charles Rennie)
Spanish: 7 Gaudí (Antonio)
Swedish: 7 Asplund (Erik Gunnar)

architecture
6 design, makeup **9** formation **11** composition **12** constitution, construction
ornament: 4 boss, fret **5** gutta **6** finial,
volute **7** cabling, console, crocket, diglyph
8 triglyph, vignette **9** arabesque, modillion
style: 5 Doric, Ionic, Tudor **6** Gothic,
Norman, Rococo **7** Baroque **8** Colonial,
Georgian **9** Byzantine, Victorian
10 Corinthian, Romanesque

archive
4 file **6** record **7** collect, history, library,
records **8** document, register **9** chronicle
10 collection, repository

archon
10 magistrate

arctic
3 icy **4** cold **5** chill, gelid **6** chilly, frigid,
frosty, wintry **7** glacial, numbing
8 freezing, hibernal **11** hyperborean
animal: 3 auk, fox **4** bear, hare, seal, vole
5 sable, whale **6** ermine, marten
7 caribou, lemming **8** reindeer **9** polar
bear, ptarmigan
base: 4 Etah **5** Thule **6** Barrow **11** Point
Barrow
bird: 3 auk
cetacean: 7 narwhal
current: 8 Labrador
dog: 5 husky **7** Samoyed **8** malamute
explorer: 4 Byrd (Richard), Cook
(Frederick) **5** Bylot (Robert), Davis (John),
Peary (Robert) **6** Baffin (William), Bering
(Vitus), Henson (Matthew), Hudson (Henry),
Nansen (Fridtjof), Nobile (Umberto)
7 Barents (Willem), Bennett (Floyd), Wilkins

(George), Wrangel (Ferdinand)
8 Amundsen (Roald) **9** Ellsworth (Lincoln),
Mackenzie (Alexander), MacMillan (Donald)
10 Stefansson (Vilhjalmus)
forest: **5** taiga
jacket: **5** parka **6** anorak
people: **4** Lapp **5** Aleut, Inuit, Yakut
6 Eskimo, Tungus **7** Chukchi, Samoyed
sea: **4** Kara **6** Laptev **7** Barents, Chukchi
8 Beaufort
transport: **7** dogsled
treeless plains: **6** tundra

ardent
3 hot **4** agog, avid, keen, true **5** eager,
fierce, fiery, loyal **6** fervid, heated, intent,
red-hot, strong, torrid **7** blazing, burning,
devoted, earnest, fervent, flaming, glowing,
intense, shining, staunch, zealous **8** constant, desirous, faithful, powerful, resolute,
sizzling, vehement, white-hot **9** allegiant,
impatient, impetuous, impulsive, perfervid,
scorching, steadfast **10** breathless, hot-
blooded, passionate **11** impassioned
12 enthusiastic

ardor
4 fire, heat, zeal, zest, zing **5** gusto, verve,
vigor **6** energy, fealty, fervor, spirit, warmth
7 avidity, loyalty, passion **8** devotion,
fidelity **9** eagerness, intensity, vehemence
10 allegiance, enthusiasm, excitement
12 faithfulness

arduous
4 hard **5** harsh, rough, sheer, steep, tight,
tough **6** severe, taxing, tiring, trying, uphill
7 labored **8** grueling, rigorous, toilsome
9 difficult, effortful, gruelling, laborious,
punishing, strenuous **10** formidable
11 precipitate, precipitous

area
4 belt, turf, zone **5** field, place, range,
realm, scene, space, tract **6** domain,
locale, region, sector, sphere **7** expanse,
stretch **8** district, locality, province, vicinity
9 bailiwick, territory **12** neighborhood
unit: **4** acre **7** hectare

arena
5 field, scene, stage **6** sphere **7** stadium,
theater **8** activity, building, coliseum,
province **10** hippodrome **12** amphitheater

Ares
Roman counterpart: **4** Mars
consort: **9** Aphrodite
father: **4** Zeus
mother: **4** Enyo, Hera
sister: **4** Eris

son: **5** Remus **7** Romulus

arête
5 crest, ridge

Arethusa
5 nymph **6** spring **9** wood nymph
pursuer: **7** Alpheus

argent
6 silver **7** silvern, silvery **9** whiteness

Argentina
capital: **11** Buenos Aires
city: **6** Paraná **7** Córdoba, La Plata,
Rosario, Santa Fe **11** Mar del Plata
desert: **9** Patagonia
language: **7** Spanish
leader: **5** Perón (Juan)
monetary unit: **4** peso
mountain, range: **5** Andes **9** Aconcagua
neighbor: **5** Chile **6** Brazil **7** Bolivia,
Uruguay **8** Paraguay
plain: **6** Pampas
river: **5** Plata (Río de la) **6** Paraná
8 Colorado **12** Río de la Plata
volcano: **5** Maipo **9** Tupungato

Arges
7 Cyclops
brother: **7** Brontes **8** Steropes
father: **6** Uranus
mother: **4** Gaea

Argonaut
4 hero **10** adventurer **13** paper nautilus
leader: **5** Jason

argosy
4 ship **5** fleet **6** armada, supply **8** flotilla

argot
4 cant **5** idiom, lingo, slang **6** jargon,
patois, patter **7** dialect **10** vernacular

arguable
4 moot **7** dubious **8** doubtful **9** debatable,
in dispute, uncertain **10** disputable
11 contestable, problematic
12 questionable

argue
5 claim, clash, prove **6** assert, attest,
bicker, debate, differ, induce, object, reason
7 agitate, canvass, contend, discuss,
dispute, dissent, justify, protest, quarrel,
quibble, stickle, testify, witness, wrangle
8 announce, conflict, consider, disagree,
indicate, maintain, persuade, polemize,
squabble **9** thrash out **10** polemicize
11 expostulate, remonstrate

argument
3 row 4 case, feud, flap, fuss 5 claim,
proof, set-to, theme, topic 6 debate,
dustup, hassle, motive, reason, rumpus,
thesis 7 defense, dispute, polemic, sorites,
subject, summary, wrangle 8 abstract,
evidence, rebuttal 9 amplitude, assertion,
discourse 10 contention, discussion,
dissension, squabbling 11 controversy,
disputation, embroilment 12 disagreement

argumentation
6 debate 7 dispute, oratory 8 forensic,
rhetoric 9 dialectic, reasoning
10 discussion 11 controversy, disputation

argumentative
4 moot 9 in dispute, litigious, polemical
11 contentious, quarrelsome
12 disputatious, questionable
13 controversial

Argus
father: 4 Zeus
mother: 5 Niobe
slayer: 6 Hermes

Argus-eyed
5 alert 9 all-seeing

argyle
4 sock 6 design 7 diamond, pattern
8 Campbell

aria
3 air, lay 4 hymn, lied, solo, song, tune
5 ditty 6 melody 7 descant

Ariadne
father: 5 Minos
husband: 7 Theseus
island home: 5 Naxos
mother: 8 Pasiphaë

arid
3 dry 4 drab, dull, sere 5 dusty, vapid
6 barren, boring, desert, dreary, jejune
7 bone-dry, insipid, parched, sterile,
tedious, thirsty 8 droughty, lifeless, weariful
9 dryasdust, infertile, unwatered, waterless,
wearisome 10 lackluster, spiritless,
unfruitful 12 moistureless 13 uninteresting

Ariel
6 spirit
master: 8 Prospero

Aries
3 ram 13 constellation

aright
4 well 5 fitly 6 justly, nicely 8 decently,
properly 9 correctly, fittingly, precisely
10 accurately, decorously

Ariosto epic
14 Orlando Furioso

arise
4 go up, lift, soar, wake 5 awake, begin,
get up, issue, mount, occur, start 6 appear,
ascend, aspire, come up, crop up, emerge,
spring, uprear, wake up 7 emanate,
proceed 8 commence 9 originate

Aristaeus
father: 6 Apollo
mother: 6 Cyrene
son: 7 Actaeon
wife: 7 Autonoe

aristocracy
5 elite, state 6 gentry, jet set 7 who's who
8 nobility, noblesse 9 beau monde, blue
blood, gentility, haut monde
10 government, patricians, patriciate, upper
class, upper crust

aristocrat
9 blue blood, gentleman, patrician
ancient Greek: 8 eupatrid
Russian: 5 boyar 6 boyard

aristocratic
5 aloof, elite, noble 6 lordly 7 courtly,
elegant, genteel, haughty, refined, stately
8 highborn, well-born, well-bred 9 dignified,
exclusive, patrician 10 privileged, upper-
class, upper-crust 11 blue-blooded

Aristophanes play
5 Birds (The), Frogs (The), Wasps (The)
6 Clouds (The), Plutus

arithmetic
4 math 8 addition, counting, figuring
9 ciphering, reckoning 10 estimation
11 calculation, computation, mathematics

Arizona
capital: 7 Phoenix
city: 4 Mesa, Yuma 5 Tempe 6 Bisbee,
Sedona, Tucson 8 Glendale, Prescott
9 Flagstaff 10 Scottsdale
mountain: 9 Humphreys (Peak)
nickname: 11 Grand Canyon (State)
park: 15 Petrified Forest
river: 4 Gila, Salt 8 Colorado
state bird: 10 cactus wren
state flower: 7 saguaro (cactus)
state tree: 9 palo verde

ark
3 den 4 ship 5 chest, haven 6 adytum,
asylum, refuge 7 convent, retreat, shelter
8 hideaway 9 safe house, sanctuary
10 repository, Torah chest
landfall: 6 Ararat

wood: 6 gopher 7 cypress

Arkansas
capital: 10 Little Rock
city: 4 Hope 9 Fort Smith, Pine Bluff
10 Hot Springs 11 Bentonville
12 Fayetteville
mountain, range: 5 Ozark 8 Magazine
nickname: 17 Land of Opportunity
river: 3 Red 8 Arkansas
state bird: 11 mockingbird
state flower: 12 apple blossom
state tree: 12 loblolly pine

arm
3 bay, ell, gun, rig 4 cove, gear, gulf, wing
5 annex, bayou, equip, firth, force, inlet,
power 6 fit out, harbor, muscle, outfit,
slough, weapon 7 appoint, furnish, turn out
8 accouter, strength 9 extension
bone: 4 ulna 6 radius 7 humerus
combining form: 6 brachi 7 brachio
muscle: 6 biceps 7 triceps

armada
4 navy 5 boats, fleet, force, group, ships
7 vessels 8 flotilla, warships

armadillo
relative: 5 sloth 8 anteater

armament
4 arms 5 armor 6 weapon 7 defense
8 ordnance, security, weaponry
9 munitions, safeguard 10 ammunition,
protection

armamentarium
4 fund 5 stock, store 6 supply 9 inventory

armchair
6 remote 8 fauteuil 9 vicarious
11 theoretical

armed forces
4 army, navy 6 troops 8 air force, military
10 servicemen

Armenia
capital: 7 Yerevan
city: 6 Gyumri 8 Vanadzor
lake: 5 Sevan
monetary unit: 4 dram
mountain, range: 7 Aragats 8 Caucasus
neighbor: 4 Iran 6 Turkey 7 Georgia
10 Azerbaijan
river: 5 Araks

armistice
5 truce 9 agreement, cease-fire
10 suspension

armor
4 mail 5 aegis, cover, guard 6 shield

7 buckler 8 security 9 safeguard
10 protection
arm: 8 brassard
body: 7 cuirass
armpit: 8 pallette
buttocks: 5 culet
coat: 7 hauberk 10 brigandine
face: 5 visor 6 beaver
flexible: 4 mail
foot: 8 solleret
hand: 7 gantlet 8 gauntlet
head: 6 helmet
horse: 4 bard 5 barde 8 chamfron
leg: 6 greave 7 jambeau
mail: 4 coif 7 hauberk
suit: 7 panoply
thigh: 5 tasse 6 tuille
throat: 6 gorget

armory
4 dump 5 depot, plant, range, store
7 arsenal, factory 8 magazine
10 collection, storehouse

armpit
6 axilla 8 underarm
Scottish: 5 oxter

arms
7 ensigns, warfare 8 weaponry

army
4 host 5 flock, horde 6 legion 7 militia
9 multitude
combat arm: 5 armor 8 infantry
9 artillery
commission: 6 brevet 7 reserve
Fort: 3 Dix, Lee, Ord 4 Drum, Hood,
Knox, Myer, Polk, Sill 5 Bliss, Bragg, Irwin,
Lewis, McCoy, Meade, Riley, Story
6 Carson, Eustis, Gillem, Gordon, Greely,
McNair, Monroe, Rucker 7 Belvoir,
Benning, Detrick, Jackson, Ritchie, Shafter,
Stewart 8 Buchanan, Campbell, Hamilton,
Holabird, Huachuca, Monmouth
9 McClellan, McPherson 10 Richardson,
Sam Houston, Wainwright 11 Leavenworth
mascot: 4 mule
meal: 4 chow, mess
mine layer: 6 sapper
NCO: 8 corporal, sergeant
officer: 5 major 7 captain, colonel,
general, warrant 10 lieutenant
post: 4 base, camp, fort
postal abbreviation: 3 APO
relating to: 7 martial 8 military
school: 3 OCS, OTS 7 academy 9 West
Point
store: 10 commissary 12 post exchange
unit: 5 corps, squad, troop 7 brigade,

cavalry, company, platoon **8** division,
regiment **9** battalion
vehicle: 4 jeep, tank **6** Abrams, Humvee
7 Bradley **9** half-track

aroma
4 balm, odor **5** scent, smell, spice **6** flavor
7 bouquet, incense, perfume **9** fragrance,
redolence

aromatic
5 balmy, spicy, sweet **6** savory **7** odorous,
perfumy, pungent, scented **8** fragrant,
perfumed, redolent **9** ambrosial

around
4 near, nigh **5** about, circa **6** nearby
7 through
prefix: 4 ambi, peri **5** amphi **6** circum

around-the-clock
8 constant, unending **9** ceaseless,
continual, incessant, perpetual, unceasing
10 continuous **11** unremitting
13 uninterrupted

arouse
4 fire, stir, wake, whet **5** alert, awake,
pique, rally, waken **6** awaken, bestir, excite,
fire up, foment, incite, kindle, work up
7 agitate, inflame **9** challenge, stimulate

arraign
3 tax, try **5** blame **6** accuse, charge, indict,
summon **9** criminate, inculpate
11 incriminate

arrange
4 plan, sort **5** adapt, array, chart, order,
score, unify **6** assort, codify, design,
devise, lay out, line up, map out, scheme,
set out, settle **7** dispose, marshal, prepare,
work out **8** organize, sequence
9 blueprint, harmonize, integrate,
methodize **10** bring about, categorize,
instrument, symphonize, synthesize
11 choreograph, orchestrate, systematize

arrangement
5 array, order, setup **6** format, layout,
lineup, series **8** grouping, ordering,
sequence **9** structure **10** adaptation
11 disposition **12** distribution
floral: 4 posy **7** bouquet, garland

arrant
4 rank **5** gross, total, utter **6** brassy,
brazen **7** blatant, extreme, flat-out
8 absolute, complete, impudent, infernal,
overbold **9** barefaced, downright,
egregious, out-and-out, shameless,
unabashed **10** immoderate, unblushing

arras
6 screen **7** drapery **8** curtains, tapestry

array
3 lot **4** clad, garb, pomp, show **5** adorn,
batch, bunch, clump, dress, group, order
6 attire, bundle, clothe, draw up, finery,
lineup, marshal, panoply, raiment, variety
7 apparel, arrange, cluster, display, dispose, garment,
marshal, panoply, raiment, variety
8 clothing, decorate, enclothe, organize,
spectrum **9** formation **10** assortment
11 systematize

arrears
3 due **4** debt **5** claim, debit **7** deficit
9 liability **10** balance due, obligation
12 indebtedness

arrest
3 nab, tab, tag **4** bust, grab, halt, hold, jail,
slow, snag, stay, stem, stop **5** block, catch,
check, pinch, run in, seize, stall **6** collar,
detain, haul in, lock up, pick up, pull in,
retard, take in **7** capture, contain, seizure
8 imprison, obstruct, restrain **9** apprehend,
detention, interrupt **11** incarcerate
12 apprehension

arresting
6 marked, signal **7** salient **8** striking
9 affective, appealing, prominent
10 attractive, compelling, enchanting,
impressive, noticeable, remarkable
11 conspicuous, eye-catching, outstanding

arrival
6 advent, coming **7** landing, success
8 entrance, incoming **9** emergence
10 appearance

arrive
4 come, land, show **5** get in, get to, reach
6 appear, show up, thrive, turn up
7 prosper, succeed **8** flourish

arriviste
7 parvenu, upstart **8** roturier **12** nouveau
riche

arrogance
3 ego **4** airs, gall **5** brass, cheek, pride
6 hubris **7** conceit, disdain, hauteur **8** self-
love **9** loftiness **11** haughtiness

arrogant
5 cocky, proud **6** lordly, snooty **7** haughty,
pompous **8** cavalier, fastuous, insolent,
superior **9** egotistic **10** disdainful, high-
handed, peremptory **11** domineering,
magisterial, overbearing **12** supercilious
13 high-and-mighty, self-important

arrogate
4 grab, take **5** annex, claim, seize, usurp
6 assume, demand **7** ascribe, preempt
8 accroach, take over **9** sequester

10 commandeer, confiscate
11 appropriate, expropriate

arrow
4 dart 5 shaft
poison: 4 upas 6 curare

arrowroot
5 plant, tuber 6 starch 7 coontie

Arrowsmith's wife
5 Leora

arroyo
3 gap 4 draw 5 brook, chasm, cleft, clove,
creek, gorge, gulch, gully 6 coulee, ravine
7 channel 11 watercourse

arsenal
4 dump 5 depot, stock, store 6 armory,
supply 7 factory, weapons 8 magazine,
ordnance 9 stockpile 10 depository,
repertoire, repository, storehouse

arson
6 firing 8 torching 9 pyromania
12 incendiarism

arsonist
5 firer, torch 7 firebug 10 incendiary

art
5 craft, skill 6 métier 7 finesse, know-how
8 artifice, painting, vocation 9 dexterity,
expertise, sculpture 10 handicraft
faddish: 6 kitsch
style: 3 pop 4 dada 6 cubist, rococo
7 fauvist, realist, surreal 8 abstract, futurist
9 classical 10 naturalist, surrealist 12 nat-
uralistic, surrealistic 13 expressionist,
impressionist

art deco
5 style 6 design
designer: 4 Erté

Artemis
Roman counterpart: 5 Diana
birthplace: 5 Delos
brother: 6 Apollo
father: 4 Zeus
mother: 4 Leto
priestess: 9 Iphigenia

artery
3 way 4 duct, line, path, road, tube
5 aorta, track 6 avenue, course, street,
vessel 7 carotid, channel, conduit,
highway, passage, pathway 8 coronary
9 boulevard 12 thoroughfare

artful
3 sly 4 foxy, wily 5 adept, sharp, slick,
smart, suave 6 adroit, astute, clever, crafty,
smooth, tricky 7 cunning, shrewd

8 guileful, skillful 9 dexterous, ingenious
10 artificial, diplomatic

arthropod
3 bee, fly 4 crab, mite, moth, tick 6 beetle,
insect, shrimp, spider 7 lobster
8 arachnid, barnacle, diplopod, myriapod,
scorpion 9 butterfly, centipede, cockroach,
millipede, trilobite 10 crustacean
body segment: 6 somite, telson
8 metamere

Arthur
see **King Arthur**

article
3 the 4 bind, item, part 5 essay, paper,
piece, point, theme, thing 6 matter, object
7 element, feature, passage, section
10 particular 11 composition, stipulation

articled
5 bound 10 indentured

articulate
3 say 4 join, link, oral 5 clear, hinge, joint,
lucid, shape, speak, state, talk, utter, vocal,
voice 6 couple, fluent, prolix, relate,
spoken, voiced 7 connect, express, jointed
8 coherent, definite, distinct, eloquent,
integrate, vocalize 9 effective, enunciate,
harmonize, integrate, pronounce, verbalize
10 coordinate, expressive 11 concatenate
12 intelligible, smooth-spoken

artifact
5 curio, relic 6 legacy, rarity, trophy
7 remnant, spin-off, vestige 8 creation,
heirloom 9 by-product, handcraft,
handiwork 10 handicraft 11 contrivance,
fabrication

artifice
4 play, ploy, ruse, wile 5 craft, feint, guile,
skill, trick 6 deceit, device, gambit
7 cunning, slyness 8 facility, foxiness,
trickery, wiliness 9 adeptness, canniness,
chicanery, duplicity, ingenuity, stratagem
10 adroitness, artfulness, cleverness,
craftiness

artificial
4 fake, faux, mock, sham 5 bogus, dummy,
faked, false, phony, put-on 6 ersatz,
forced, hollow, unreal 7 assumed, feigned,
in vitro, labored, man-made, plastic,
pretend 8 affected, mannered, spurious
9 contrived, imitation, insincere, simulated,
synthetic, unnatural 10 fabricated,
factitious, fictitious, substitute

artillery
4 arms 5 canon, force 6 rocket 7 battery,

bazooka, gunnery, weapons **8** cannonry, howitzer, ordnance, weaponry **9** munitions

artisan
6 worker **7** builder, workman **8** producer **9** carpenter, craftsman **12** craftsperson

artist
7 painter **8** sculptor, virtuoso
garb: 5 smock
knife: 7 spatula
medium: 3 oil **5** paint **6** pastel **7** tempera **8** charcoal **10** watercolor
pigment board: 7 palette
stand: 5 easel
workshop: 6 studio **7** atelier
(see also **painter**)

artless
4 free, open, pure, true **5** crude, naive, plain **6** direct, honest, simple **7** genuine, natural, sincere, unaware **8** trusting **9** childlike, guileless, ingenuous, unstudied **10** above-board, forthright, unaffected, uncultured, unschooled **12** unartificial, unsuspicious

arty
5 showy **6** pseudo **8** affected, imposing **9** overblown **11** pretentious **12** high-sounding

Aruba
capital: 10 Oranjestad
language: 5 Dutch **10** Papiamento
monetary unit: 6 florin
part of: 11 Netherlands

as
3 for, who **4** coin, like, that, when **5** being, since, which, while **6** though **7** because **11** considering, for instance

as a pin
4 neat

as a rule
6 mainly, mostly **7** usually **8** commonly **9** generally **10** frequently, ordinarily

Ascanius
5 Iulus
father: 6 Aeneas

ascend
4 go up, lift, rise, soar **5** arise, climb, crest, mount, scale **6** aspire, move up, occupy **7** lift off, take off **8** escalade, escalate, surmount

ascendancy
4 rule **5** power, reign **7** command, control, mastery **8** dominion **9** authority, dominance, influence, supremacy **10** domination, prepotency

11 preeminence, sovereignty **13** preponderance

ascendant
6 master, rising **7** regnant **8** ancestor, dominant, forebear, relative, superior **9** paramount, precursor, prevalent, sovereign **10** commanding, forefather, forerunner, prevailing, progenitor **11** controlling, overbearing, predecessor, predominant, predominate **12** preponderant, primogenitor

ascension
4 rise **6** rising **7** going up, scaling **8** climbing, mounting

ascent
4 ramp, rise **5** climb, grade, slope **6** rising **7** advance, incline **8** gradient, progress **9** acclivity, elevation, uplifting

ascertain
5 learn **7** catch on, find out, unearth **8** discover, make sure **9** determine, establish, figure out

ascetic
5 stoic **6** hermit, severe **7** austere, eremite, recluse **9** abstinent, anchoress, anchorite, mortified **10** abstemious, astringent, forbearing, restrained **11** disciplined, self-denying
ancient Hebrew: 6 Essene
Buddhist: 5 bonze
early Christian: 7 stylite
Hindu: 4 yogi **5** fakir, Yogin

Asclepius
see **Aesculapius**

ascribe
3 lay **4** cite **5** infer, refer **6** assign, charge, credit, impute **8** accredit **9** attribute, reference **10** conjecture

Asenath
husband: 6 Joseph
son: 7 Ephraim **8** Manasseh

aseptic
4 cool, flat **5** clean **7** sterile **8** germ-free, hygienic, sanitary **9** unfeeling **10** restrained, sterilized **11** emotionless, unemotional

asexual
6 agamic

as for
4 in re **5** about, anent **7** apropos **9** regarding **10** concerning, respecting **12** with regard to

as good as
4 nigh **6** all but, almost, nearly **8** in effect, well-nigh **9** basically, in essence, just about, virtually **11** essentially, practically

ash
4 soot, tree, wood **7** cinders, residue **8** clinkers

ashamed
6 abased, abject, guilty **7** abashed, humbled **8** contrite, penitent **9** chagrined, mortified, repentant **10** humiliated **11** discomfited, embarrassed

ashen
3 wan **4** gray, pale **5** faded, pasty, waxen **6** doughy, pallid, sallow, sickly **7** ghostly **8** blanched, bleached **9** bloodless, colorless **10** corpselike

Asher
daughter: **5** Serah
father: **5** Jacob
mother: **6** Zilpah
son: **4** Isui **6** Beriah, Ishuah, Jimnah

ashes
5 ruins **6** pallor **7** remains

ashy
3 wan **4** drab, pale **5** livid, waxen **6** doughy, leaden, pallid **7** ghastly, greyish **8** blanched **9** bloodless, colorless, washed-out **10** cadaverous

Asia
country: **4** Laos **5** Burma, China, India, Japan, Korea, Nepal **6** Bhutan, Russia, Taiwan **7** Armenia, Georgia, Myanmar, Vietnam **8** Cambodia, Malaysia, Mongolia, Pakistan, Sri Lanka, Thailand **9** Indonesia, Kampuchea, Kazakstan, Singapore **10** Azerbaijan, Bangladesh, Kazakhstan, Kyrgyzstan, North Korea, South Korea, Tajikistan, Uzbekistan **11** Afghanistan, Philippines **12** Turkmenistan
ethnic group: **3** Han, Lao, Tai **4** Arab, Kurd, Moor, Shan **5** Karen, Khmer, Malay, Tajik, Tamil, Uzbek **6** Burman, Lepcha, Manchu, Mongol, Sindhi **7** Baluchi, Bengali, Persian, Punjabi, Tibetan **8** Armenian, Assyrian, Javanese **9** Dravidian, Indo-Aryan, Sinhalese **10** Circassian, Montagnard, Singhalese
language: **3** Lao **4** Urdu **5** Hindi, Malay, Tamil, Uzbek **6** Arabic, Bahasa, Korean, Nepali **7** Bengali, Burmese, Khalkha, Kurdish, Persian, Tibetan, Turkish **8** Armenian, Japanese, Javanese, Mandarin **9** Cambodian **10** Vietnamese

Asia Minor
8 Anatolia
country: **6** Turkey

Asian inland sea
4 Aral

aside
4 away **5** apart **7** tangent **8** away from **9** in reserve, privately **10** digression, discursion **11** parenthesis

aside from
3 bar, but **4** save **6** bating, except **7** barring, besides **9** excepting, excluding, other than, outside of **11** exclusive of

Asimov, Isaac
forte: **5** sci-fi
work: **6** I Robot **9** Nightfall **10** Foundation (Trilogy) **14** Gods Themselves (The)

asinine
5 crazy, daffy, silly **6** absurd, simple **7** fatuous, foolish, idiotic, puerile, witless **8** mindless **9** brainless **10** irrational, ridiculous **11** nonsensical

ask
3 beg, bid **4** pray, quiz, seek **5** crave, exact, grill, plead, query **6** appeal, demand, desire, invite **7** beseech, call for, canvass, consult, enquire, entreat, examine, implore, inquire, request, require, solicit **8** petition, question **9** catechize, importune **10** supplicate **11** interrogate
Scottish: **5** speer, speir

askance
8 sidelong, sideways **9** cynically, obliquely **10** critically, doubtfully, doubtingly, scornfully **11** skeptically **12** suspiciously **13** distrustfully, mistrustfully

asker
6 beggar, prayer, suitor **7** speaker **9** suppliant **10** petitioner, questioner, supplicant **11** supplicator

askew
4 awry **6** turned **8** cockeyed **9** crookedly

aslant
4 awry **5** askew **7** crooked **8** cockeyed, sideways, sidewise **9** obliquely

asleep
4 dead, idle, numb **5** inert **6** dozing, numbed **7** defunct, dormant, napping **8** benumbed, deadened, inactive, in repose, not alert, sluggish **9** senseless, unfeeling **10** insensible, slumbering, unanimated **11** indifferent, unconscious **12** anesthetized

as long as
3 for **5** since **6** seeing **7** because, whereas **10** inasmuch as **11** considering **12** provided that

as much as
6 all but, almost **8** well-nigh **11** essentially, practically

aspect
3 air **4** look, mien, side **5** angle, facet, phase, scene, slant **6** regard, status **7** bearing, seeming **8** exposure, position **9** direction **10** appearance **11** perspective

aspen
4 tree **6** poplar

asperity
5 rigor **8** acerbity, acrimony, grimness, hardness, hardship, mordancy, severity, tartness **9** harshness, roughness, sharpness **10** bitterness, difficulty, unevenness **12** irregularity, irritability

asperse
4 slur **5** libel, smear, sully **6** attack, defame, insult, malign, vilify **7** baptize, slander, tarnish, traduce **8** bad mouth, dishonor, sprinkle **9** denigrate, insinuate **10** calumniate

aspersion
4 muck, slam, slur **5** abuse **7** calumny, obloquy, slander **9** invective, stricture **10** defamation, detraction **11** denigration **12** vilification, vituperation **13** animadversion

asphalt
4 pave **7** bitumen, surface **8** blacktop, pavement

asphyxiate
4 kill **5** choke, drown **6** stifle **7** smother **8** strangle, throttle **9** suffocate

aspirant
6 seeker **7** hopeful, seeking **9** applicant, candidate, contender

aspiration
3 aim **4** goal, urge, wish **5** dream **6** desire, intent, object **7** craving, longing, passion, pursuit **8** ambition, striving, yearning **9** breathing, objective **10** pretension **13** ambitiousness

aspire
3 aim, try **4** long, pant, rise, seek, soar, want, wish **5** arise, mount, strive, yearn **6** ascend, desire, hunger, thirst

aspiring
7 longing, seeking, wanting, wishful **8** striving, vaulting, yearning **9** ambitious

as regards
4 in re **7** apropos **8** touching **10** concerning, respecting

ass
4 dolt, fool, jerk, moke, mule **5** burro, dunce, idiot **6** donkey, nitwit **8** bonehead, imbecile **10** nincompoop
female: **5** jenny
male: **4** jack
wild Asian: **5** kiang **6** onager

assai
4 very

assail
4 bash, beat **5** abuse, beset, blast, pound, storm **6** attack, berate, buffet, charge, fall on, malign, oppugn, pummel, revile, strike, vilify **7** assault, bombard, break down **8** fall upon, lambaste

assassin
3 gun **5** bravo **6** gunman, hit man, killer **7** torpedo **8** murderer **9** cutthroat **10** hatchet man, triggerman
of Caesar: **6** Brutus **7** Cassius
of Garfield: **7** Guiteau (Charles Julius)
of J. F. Kennedy: **6** Oswald (Lee Harvey)
of M. L. King: **3** Ray (James Earl)
of Lincoln: **5** Booth (John Wilkes)
of Marat: **6** Corday (Charlotte)
of McKinley: **8** Czolgosz (Leon)
of R. F. Kennedy: **6** Sirhan (Sirhan)

assassinate
4 do in, kill, slay **6** finish, murder, rub out **7** bump off, execute, gun down, put away, take out **8** dispatch, knock off **9** eliminate, liquidate

assault
3 mug, war **4** raid **5** beset, fight, onset, set-to, storm **6** assail, attack, charge, fall on, strike, threat **7** aggress, besiege, mugging, offense **8** fall upon, invasion, storming **9** incursion, offensive, onslaught, violation **10** aggression

assay
3 try **4** rate, seek, test **5** judge, offer, prove, trial, value, weigh **6** assess, result, rating, strive, survey **7** analyze, attempt, inspect, measure, valuate, venture **8** analysis, appraise, endeavor, estimate, evaluate, examine, struggle **9** appraisal, undertake, valuation **10** assessment, evaluation, inspection, measurement **11** examination

assemblage

5 crowd, group **6** muster **7** company, turnout **8** audience **9** gathering **10** collection **11** aggregation, composition, convergence **12** congregation

assemble

4 call, form, make, mass, meet, mold **5** amass, build, clump, group, shape, unite **6** gather, muster, summon **7** cluster, collect, convene, convoke, fashion, marshal, produce, round up **8** congress, contrive **9** aggregate, forgather **10** accumulate, congregate **11** fit together, manufacture, put together **12** call together, come together **13** bring together

assembly

4 bevy **5** bunch, covey, crowd, flock, group, party, rally, set-up **6** muster, troupe **7** cluster, meeting **8** conclave **9** congeries, gathering **10** collection **11** association, fabrication, get-together, manufacture **12** congregation, construction
American Indian: 6 powwow
ancient Greek: 8 ecclesia
ancient Roman: 7 comitia
Anglo-Saxon: 4 moot **5** gemot **6** gemote **8** folkmoot, folkmote
ecclesiastical: 5 synod **10** consistory
legislative: 4 diet **6** senate **8** congress **10** parliament
place: 4 hall, room **5** agora **10** auditorium
Russian: 4 duma
witches': 6 sabbat **7** sabbath

assent

3 nod, yes **4** okay **5** agree **6** accede, accord, concur, say yes **7** approve, consent, embrace **8** approval, sanction, thumbs-up **9** accession, acquiesce, agreement, subscribe **10** acceptance, admission, permission **11** affirmation, concurrence **12** acquiescence

assert

3 say **4** aver, avow **5** argue, claim, posit, state, utter, voice **6** adduce, affirm, allege, attest, avouch, defend, depose, insist, submit **7** advance, contend, declare, express, justify, profess, protest, publish, warrant **8** announce, maintain, proclaim **9** broadcast, postulate, predicate **10** promulgate

assertion

6 avowal **8** averment **9** affidavit, statement **10** allegation, avouchment, contention, deposition, disclosure, insistence, profession **11** affirmation, attestation, declaration **12** asseveration **13** pronouncement

assertive

4 firm, sure **5** pushy, strong **7** assured, certain, decided, pushing **8** cocksure, emphatic, forceful, positive **9** confident, energetic, insistent **10** aggressive, resounding **11** affirmative, distinctive, self-assured **13** self-confident

assess

3 fix, tax **4** deem, levy, rate **5** assay, exact, judge, put on, set at, value, weigh **6** charge, figure, impose, reckon, survey **7** account, compute, subject, valuate **8** appraise, consider, estimate, evaluate **9** determine

assessment

3 fee, tax **4** duty, levy, toll **6** charge, impost, rating, tariff **8** estimate, judgment **9** appraisal, valuation **10** estimation, evaluation **12** appraisement

asset

4 boon, good **5** merit **6** credit **7** benefit **8** blessing, resource **9** advantage **11** distinction
opposite: 9 liability

assets

5 items, means, money **6** wealth **7** capital **8** bankroll, property **9** resources, valuables **11** possessions

asseverate

4 aver, avow **5** state **6** affirm, assert, attest, avouch, depose, insist **7** certify, contend, declare, profess **8** maintain, proclaim **9** pronounce

assiduous

4 busy **5** eager **6** active **7** moiling, zealous **8** diligent, sedulous, tireless **9** attentive, laborious **10** persistent, unflagging **11** hard-working, industrious **13** indefatigable

assiduously

4 hard **6** busily **9** earnestly, intensely **10** diligently, thoroughly **11** intensively **12** exhaustively, meticulously, persistently **13** painstakingly, unremittingly

assign

3 fix, lay, set **4** cede, deed, give, name **5** allot, allow, refer **6** charge, convey, credit, define, impute, remise, settle **7** appoint, ascribe, earmark, lay down, mete out, specify, station **8** accredit, allocate, delegate, make over, relegate, sign over, transfer **9** admeasure, apportion, attribute, designate, establish, prescribe **10** pigeonhole

assignation

4 date **5** tryst **7** meeting **9** allotment **10** engagement, rendezvous **11** appointment, get-together

assignee

5 agent, proxy **6** deputy, factor **7** officer **8** attorney, delegate

assignment

3 job **4** beat, duty, post, task, work **5** chore, stint **6** office **8** homework, position, transfer **9** allotment **10** allocation, delegation, obligation **11** designation

assimilate

5 adapt, adopt, grasp, learn, liken, match **6** absorb, adjust, digest, equate, imbibe, soak up, take in, take up **7** blend in, compare, conform **8** parallel **10** comprehend, understand **11** incorporate

assimilation

8 taking in **9** awareness **10** absorption, conversion **11** mindfulness, recognition **12** apperception **13** consciousness, incorporation

assist

3 aid **4** abet, back, help, lift **5** boost, do for, serve, stead **6** relief, succor **7** backing, benefit, comfort, help out, secours, service, support, work for **8** benefact, work with **9** cooperate, open doors

assistance

3 aid **4** hand, help, lift **5** boost, **6** relief, succor **7** backing, benefit, comfort, secours, service, subsidy, support **8** abetment **9** upholding **10** subvention, supporting **11** cooperation

assistant

3 aid **4** aide, ally, help **5** aider **6** backer, backup, deputy, flunky, helper, second **7** acolyte, ancilla, orderly **8** adjutant, henchman **9** attendant, auxiliary, coadjutor **10** accomplice, aide-de-camp, coadjutant, lieutenant **12** right-hand man

assistive

6 aiding, useful **7** helpful **10** beneficial **11** serviceable

assize

3 law **4** rule, writ **5** canon, edict **6** decree **7** finding, inquest, precept, statute, verdict **8** standard **9** ordinance, prescript **10** regulation

associate

3 pal **4** ally, chum, join, link, mate, pair, yoke **5** blend, buddy, crony, group, match, merge, unite **6** cohort, comate, couple, fellow, friend, hobnob, relate, worker **7** bracket, combine, compeer, comrade, conjoin, connect, consort, partner **8** confrere, coworker, employee, familiar, federate, identify, intimate **9** affiliate, bedfellow, colleague, companion, copartner, secondary **10** accomplice, amalgamate, compatriot, complement **11** concomitant, confederate, correlative, counterpart, running mate, subordinate **12** acquaintance **13** accompaniment

association

3 tie **4** band, bloc, bond, clan, club, crew, hint **5** group, guild, order, tie-up, union **6** hookup, league **7** circuit, concert, linkage, linking, society **8** alliance, congress, overtone, relation, sodality, teamwork **9** coalition, undertone **10** conference, connection, federation, fellowship, fraternity, mental link, suggestion **11** affiliation, brotherhood, combination, conjunction, connotation, cooperation, implication, partnership **12** conjointment, organization, relationship, togetherness **13** collaboration

assort

5 class, group, order **6** codify, divide **7** arrange **8** classify, stratify **9** associate, designate, harmonize, methodize **10** categorize, distribute, pigeonhole **11** systematize

assorted

4 like **5** mixed **6** fitted, motley, suited, sundry, varied **7** adapted, diverse, matched, similar, various **9** different **11** diversified, conformable **12** conglomerate, multifarious **13** heterogeneous, miscellaneous

assortment

4 olio **5** array, group **6** choice, jumble, medley **7** mélange, mixture, variety **8** mishmash, mixed bag, pastiche **9** diversity, potpourri, selection **10** collection, hodgepodge, miscellany **11** gallimaufry

assuage

4 calm, cool, ease **5** allay, quiet **6** lessen, pacify, quench, reduce, soften, soothe, temper **7** appease, lighten, mollify, placate, relieve, sweeten **8** decrease, mitigate, moderate **9** alleviate **10** conciliate, propitiate

as such
5 per se　8 by itself　9 in essence, virtually
11 essentially　12 by definition
13 fundamentally, intrinsically

assumably
6 likely, surely　7 no doubt　8 probably
9 doubtless　10 most likely, presumably

assume
3 act, don　4 fake, sham, take　5 adopt,
bluff, feign, put on, seize, usurp　6 affect,
draw on, expect, reckon, slip on, take in,
take on, take up　7 believe, imagine,
preempt, premise, presume, pretend,
receive, suppose, suspect　8 accroach,
arrogate, shoulder, simulate, take over
9 undertake　10 commandeer, presuppose,
understand　11 appropriate, counterfeit

assumed
4 fake, sham　5 bogus, false, put on, tacit
6 made-up, phoney　7 feigned　8 affected,
delusory, putative, spurious, supposed
9 deceptive, pretended, simulated
10 artificial, fictitious

assumption
5 posit　6 belief, thesis　7 conceit, premise,
seizure, surmise　8 takeover　9 arrogance,
postulate　10 acceptance, arrogation,
conjecture, pretension, usurpation　11 expectation, supposition, undertaking　13 appropriation

assurance
4 oath, word　5 nerve, troth　6 aplomb,
parole, pledge, safety, surety　7 promise,
support, warrant　8 audacity, boldness,
safeness, security, sureness, temerity,
warranty　9 assertion, brashness, certainty,
certitude, cockiness, composure,
guarantee, hardiness, self-trust
10 brazenness, confidence, conviction,
equanimity, profession　11 affirmation,
presumption

assure
4 aver　5 bet on, cinch, pledge, swear
6 affirm, attest, ensure, insure, secure,
soothe　7 certify, comfort, confirm, promise,
satisfy　8 convince, persuade　9 guarantee
11 make certain

assured
3 set　4 cool　5 fixed　6 secure　7 certain,
decided, settled　8 clear-cut, composed,
definite, positive, sanguine, undoubted
9 assertive, collected, confident, unruffled
10 guaranteed, pronounced　11 beyond
doubt, made certain, unflappable
13 imperturbable, self-confident, self-
satisfied

assuredly
9 certainly, doubtless　10 positively
11 confidently, undoubtedly, without fail

assuredness
6 surety　9 certainty, certitude　10 confidence, conviction

Assyria
capital:　5 Calah　7 Nineveh
city:　5 Ashur, Assur
god:　3 Sin　4 Nabu　5 Ashur, Nusku
6 Tammuz　7 Ninurta
goddess:　6 Ishtar
king:　3 Pul　6 Sargon　11 Sennacherib,
Shalmaneser　12 Ashurbanipal
language:　7 Aramaic
queen:　9 Semiramis
river:　6 Tigris
writing:　9 cuneiform

asterisk
4 star　6 symbol　9 character

astern
3 aft　4 rear, tail　5 abaft　6 back of, behind
8 backward, rearmost, rearward

asteroid
5 Ceres

Asterope
father:　5 Atlas
mother:　7 Pleione
sisters:　8 Pleiades

asthma
7 allergy　8 disorder

as to
4 in re　5 about, anent　7 apropos
9 regarding　10 concerning, respecting
11 according to

astonish
4 daze, stun　5 amaze, floor, shock
7 astound, stagger, startle, stupefy　8 blow
away, bowl over, confound, dumfound,
surprise　9 dumbfound, take aback
11 flabbergast

astonishing
7 amazing　8 stunning, wondrous
9 marvelous, startling, wonderful
10 astounding, miraculous, prodigious,
staggering, stupendous, surprising
11 spectacular　12 breathtaking

astonishment
3 awe　5 shock　6 wonder　8 surprise
9 amazement, confusion　10 perplexity,
wonderment　12 bewilderment,
stupefaction　13 consternation

astound

4 daze, stun 5 amaze, shock 7 confuse
8 astonish, bewilder, confound, dumfound,
surprise 9 dumbfound, overwhelm, take
aback 11 flabbergast

Astraea

father: 4 Zeus 7 Jupiter
mother: 6 Themis

astral

6 dreamy, starry 7 exalted, highest, stellar
8 elevated, sidereal 9 celestial, top-drawer,
unworldly, visionary 10 top-ranking
11 high-ranking 12 otherworldly

astray

4 awry 5 amiss, badly, wrong 6 adrift,
afield 7 in error 9 off course

astride

8 bridging, spanning 10 on each side,
straddling

astringent

4 acid, keen 5 acerb, acrid, harsh, sharp,
stern 6 biting, bitter, severe, strict
7 acerbic, ascetic, austere, caustic, cutting,
puckery, pungent, styptic 8 incisive
10 irritating, stinging 11 contracting
12 constrictive

astrolabe successor

7 sextant

astrologer

5 Dixon (Jeane), Faust 9 stargazer,
Zoroaster 11 horoscopist, Nostradamus

astrological aspect

5 trine 7 sextile 8 quartile 10 opposition
11 conjunction

astronaut

4 Ride (Sally) 5 Glenn (John), White
(Edward), Young (John) 6 Aldrin (Edwin),
Cooper (Gordon), Lovell (James), Worden
(Alfred) 7 Bluford (Guion), Collins
(Michael), Gagarin (Yuri), Grissom (Gus),
Jemison (Mae), Schirra (Walter), Shepard
(Alan), Yegorov (Boris) 8 Stafford
(Thomas) 9 Armstrong (Neil), Carpenter
(Scott), McAuliffe (Christa) 10 Tereshkova
(Valentina)

astronomer

American: 3 See (Thomas Jefferson)
5 Sagan (Carl) 6 Hubble (Edwin), Lowell
(Percival) 7 Langley (Samuel), Newcomb
(Simon), Shapley (Harlow) 8 Bowditch
(Nathaniel), Mitchell (Maria), Tombaugh
(Clyde) 9 Pickering (Edward)
11 Schlesinger (Frank)

Austrian: 13 Schwarzschild (Karl)
Danish: 5 Brahe (Tycho)
Dutch: 4 Oort (Jan Hendrik) 6 Sitter
(Willem de) 7 Huygens (Christiaan)
English: 4 Ryle (Martin), Wren
(Christopher) 6 Halley (Edmond), Lovell
(Bernard) 7 Lockyer (Joseph), Parsons
(William) 8 Herschel (Caroline, John,
William)
French: 6 Picard (Jean) 7 Laplace
(Pierre-Simon de)
German: 4 Wolf (Maximilian) 5 Vogel
(Hermann) 6 Kepler (Johannes), Müller
(Johann), Struve (Otto)
Greek: 12 Eratosthenes
Italian: 7 Galileo (Galilei) 12 Schiaparelli
(Giovanni)
Persian: 11 Omar Khayyám
Polish: 10 Copernicus (Nicolaus)
Swedish: 7 Celsius (Anders)
Swiss: 6 Zwicky (Fritz)

astute

3 sly 4 deep, foxy, keen, wily 5 cagey,
canny, heady, quick, savvy, sharp 6 artful,
clever, crafty, shrewd, tricky 7 cunning,
knowing 8 guileful 9 insidious, sagacious
11 calculating 13 perspicacious

astuteness

3 wit 6 acumen 8 keenness, wiliness
9 canniness 10 craftiness, shrewdness
11 discernment, percipience
12 perspicacity

Astyanax

father: 6 Hector
mother: 10 Andromache

asunder

4 torn 5 apart, split 7 divided 9 into parts,
separated

as usual

8 normally, wontedly 9 routinely
10 habitually, ordinarily 11 customarily
12 consistently

as well

3 and, too, yet 4 also, even, just, more,
plus 7 besides, further 8 likewise,
moreover 9 along with, including, similarly
10 in addition 11 furthermore
12 additionally

as well as

3 and 4 plus 7 besides 9 along with
11 not counting 12 in addition to, together
with

as yet

5 so far, to now 7 earlier, thus far
8 hitherto, until now 10 to this time 12 to
the present

asylum
4 home, port 5 cover, haven 6 covert, harbor, refuge 7 retreat, shelter 8 hospital, security 9 harborage, safe house, sanctuary 10 protection, sanatorium 11 institution

asymmetric
6 uneven 7 not even, unequal 8 lopsided 9 irregular 10 unbalanced 12 over-balanced

Atalanta
husband: 8 Melanion
suitor: 10 Hippomenes

at all
4 ever, once 6 anyway 7 anytime

atavism
9 reversion, throwback 10 recurrence

ataxia
5 chaos, snarl 6 huddle, muddle 7 clutter 8 disarray, disorder 9 confusion

atelier
6 studio 8 workroom, workshop

Athamas
daughter: 5 Helle
father: 6 Aeolus
son: 7 Phrixos, Phrixus 8 Learchus
wife: 3 Ino 7 Nephele

Athena
Roman counterpart: 7 Minerva
attribute: 3 owl 5 Aegis 7 serpent
city: 6 Athens
father: 4 Zeus
names: 4 Nike 6 Pallas 9 Parthenos
shield: 5 Aegis
statue: 9 Palladium
temple: 9 Parthenon

athenaeum
6 museum 7 library 8 archives 10 repository

Athens
citadel: 9 Acropolis
founder: 7 Cecrops
last king: 6 Codrus
marketplace: 5 agora
rival: 6 Sparta
senate: 5 boule
temple: 9 Parthenon

athirst
4 avid, keen 5 eager 6 ardent 7 anxious 8 desiring, desirous, yearning 9 impatient

athlete
4 jock 5 sport 6 player 7 acrobat, gymnast, tumbler 9 sportsman 10 competitor 11 sportswoman

athlete's foot
8 ringworm 10 tinea pedis

athletic
6 brawny, robust, sinewy 8 muscular, sporting, vigorous 9 energetic, strapping, strenuous
contest: 4 agon, game 5 match
field: 4 oval, ring, rink 5 arena, court 7 diamond, stadium 8 gridiron
prize: 3 cup 5 medal 6 trophy

athletics
5 games, races 6 events, sports 7 contest 8 exercise 9 exercises 10 gymnastics, recreation 12 calisthenics

athwart
4 over 5 cross 6 across, beyond 9 crossways, crosswise, opposed to 12 transversely

Atlanta's civic center
4 Omni

Atlas
brother: 10 Prometheus
daughter: 5 Hyads 6 Hyades 8 Pleiades 10 Atlantides
father: 7 Iapetus
mother: 7 Clymene
race: 5 Titan
wife: 7 Pleione

at last
7 finally

Atli
wife (slayer): 6 Gudrun

atmosphere
3 air 4 aura, mood, tone 6 medium, milieu 7 ambient, climate, feeling, quality 8 ambiance, ambience 11 environment, mise-en-scène 12 surroundings
stratum: 9 exosphere 10 ionosphere, mesosphere 11 chemosphere, ozonosphere, troposphere 12 stratosphere, thermosphere
sun's: 12 chromosphere

atmospheric
4 airy 6 aerial 8 ethereal

atoll
6 island
equatorial area: 5 Baker
Indian Ocean: 4 Male
Kiribati: 4 Beru
Marshall Islands: 6 Bikini 8 Eniwetok
Tuamotu: 4 Anaa 5 Chain
Tuvalu: 8 Funafuti

atom

3 bit, jot 4 iota, mite, whit 5 minim, speck, touch, trace 6 tittle 7 modicum, smidgen 8 particle 9 scintilla
charged: 3 ion 5 anion
group: 7 radical

atomic particle

3 ion 4 beta, muon, pion 5 alpha, boson, meson 6 baryon, hadron, lepton, proton 7 fermion, hyperon, neutron, nucleon 8 electron, mesotron, neutrino, positron, thermion
hypothetical: 5 quark 6 parton

atomize

4 nuke, ruin 5 smash, wreck 6 divide, rub out 7 break up, destroy, shatter 8 demolish, destruct, disperse, dynamite, fragment, nebulize 9 break down, devastate, pulverize 10 disconnect

at once

3 now 4 away, both 6 pronto 8 directly, first off, right now, together 9 forthwith, instantly, right away 11 immediately, straightway 12 concurrently, straightaway, without delay

atone

3 pay 6 redeem, repair, repent 7 correct, expiate, rectify, redress, satisfy 10 compensate, make amends, recompense

atoner

8 penitent

atop

4 upon

Atossa

father: 5 Cyrus
husband: 6 Darius 7 Smerdes 8 Cambyses
son: 6 Xerxes

at random

5 about 6 anyhow 7 anywise 8 by chance 9 aimlessly, haphazard 10 carelessly 11 any which way, haphazardly 12 accidentally 13 helter-skelter

at rest

4 dead 5 still 8 inactive, lifeless, reposing, sleeping, tranquil, unmoving 9 quiescent 10 motionless, stationary, untroubled 11 trouble-free

Atreus

brother: 8 Thyestes
father: 6 Pelops
mother: 10 Hippodamia
slayer: 9 Aegisthus
son: 8 Menelaus 9 Agamemnon 11 Pleisthenes
victim: 11 Pleisthenes
wife: 6 Aerope

atrocious

4 foul, vile 5 awful, cruel 6 brutal, horrid, odious, savage, wicked 7 heinous, noisome, obscene 8 barbaric, horrible, shocking, terrible 9 appalling, desperate, execrable, loathsome, monstrous, offensive, repulsive, revolting, sickening 10 abominable, despicable, detestable, disgusting, horrifying, outrageous, scandalous 12 contemptible

atrocity

4 evil 5 crime 6 horror, infamy 7 cruelty, outrage 8 enormity, savagery 9 barbarity, brutality 11 abomination, heinousness 13 monstrousness

atrophy

7 decline, wasting 9 decadence, waste away 10 devolution 11 declination 12 degeneration 13 deterioration

attach

3 add, fix, tie 4 bind, hook, link, take 5 affix, annex, latch, rivet, stick, unite 6 adhere, append, assign, fasten, secure 7 ascribe, connect 8 make fast 9 associate, attribute

attached

5 fixed 7 sessile

attachment

3 tie 4 bond, link, love 6 fealty 7 loyalty, seizure 8 addition, adhesion, devotion, fastener, fidelity, fondness 9 accessory, adherence, affection, connector, constancy 10 allegiance, connection 12 faithfulness

attack

4 bout, jump, raid, rush 5 beset, blitz, drive, fight, foray, onset, sally, siege, spasm, spell, storm, throe 6 access, ambush, assail, banzai, battle, charge, fall on, harass, have at, invade, irrupt, onrush, sortie, strike, tackle 7 aggress, assault, barrage, besiege, bombard, offense, seizure 8 fall upon, invasion, outbreak, paroxysm 9 beleaguer, incursion, offensive, onslaught, pugnacity 10 aggression, blitzkrieg

attain

3 get, win 4 gain 5 reach, score 6 arrive, come to, effect, make it, obtain, rack up 7 achieve, fulfill, pull off, realize, succeed 8 bring off, complete 10 accomplish

attainment

4 feat 6 finish 7 arrival 10 completion
11 achievement, acquirement, acquisition,
fulfillment, realization

attempt

3 bid, try 4 seek, shot, stab 5 assay,
crack, essay, offer, trial 6 attack, effort,
strive, tackle 7 assault, venture
8 endeavor, striving, struggle 9 undertake
11 undertaking 12 make an effort

attend

3 aid, see 4 be at, go to, hear, heed, help,
mark, mind, note 5 apply, catch, nurse,
see to, serve, visit, watch 6 assist, convoy,
doctor, drop in, escort, go with, listen,
notice, show up, turn up, wait on 7 be
there, care for, conduct, hearken, oversee,
pay heed, work for 8 chaperon, stay with,
wait upon 9 accompany, chaperone,
companion, look after, supervise
11 concentrate

attendant

4 aide 5 valet 6 escort, helper, lackey
7 orderly, servant 9 ancillary, assistant
10 bridesmaid, coincident 11 chamberlain,
concomitant 12 accompanying
ancient Roman: 6 lictor
in court: 7 bailiff 8 tipstaff

attendants

5 suite, train 7 cortege, retinue
9 entourage

attendee

4 goer

attention

4 care, heed, mark, note 5 study 6 notice,
regard, remark 7 amenity, command,
concern, respect, service, thought 8 civility,
courtesy, industry, scrutiny 9 assiduity,
awareness, deference, diligence, gallantry,
spotlight, treatment 10 absorption,
cognizance, observance, politeness
11 application, mindfulness, observation,
sensibility 12 deliberation
13 concentration, consciousness,
consideration

attention getter

4 ahem 5 gavel

attentive

4 kind 5 alert, awake, aware, civil 6 intent,
polite 7 devoted, gallant, heedful, mindful
8 gracious, obliging, open-eyed
9 advertent, courteous, observant,
regardful 10 interested, respectful,
solicitous, thoughtful 11 considerate
13 concentrating

attenuate

3 sap 4 rare, slim, thin 5 abate, blunt,
reedy 6 lessen, rarefy, shrink, slight, stalky,
subtle, twiggy, weaken 7 cripple, deflate,
disable, reduced, slender, squinny, subtile,
tenuous, unbrace 8 contract, enfeeble,
mitigate, rarefied, tapering, wiredraw
9 constrict, dissipate, undermine
10 become thin, become fine, become less,
debilitate

attest

4 aver, show 5 argue, prove, swear, vouch
6 adjure, affirm, assert, verify 7 certify,
confirm, declare, display, exhibit, point to,
support, sustain, swear to, testify, warrant,
witness 8 announce, indicate, manifest
9 establish 10 asseverate 11 bear
witness, demonstrate 12 authenticate

attestation

5 proof 7 witness 8 evidence 9 testament,
testimony 10 validation 11 declaration,
testimonial 12 confirmation

attic

4 loft, room 6 garret 7 storage 8 cockloft

Attica

6 Greece
division: 4 deme

at times

9 sometimes 10 now and then, on
occasion 11 now and again 12 here and
there, occasionally

attire

4 clad, duds, garb, gear, togs, wear
5 array, drape, dress, getup, habit, tog up
6 clothe, fit out, outfit 7 apparel, clothes,
costume, garment, raiment, threads
8 clothing, garments, glad rags
11 habiliments

attitude

4 pose, view 5 angle, stand 6 manner,
stance 7 bearing, mind-set, outlook,
posture 8 carriage, demeanor, position,
pretense 10 standpoint 11 inclination,
perspective, point of view

attitudinize

4 mask, pose, sham 6 affect 7 pass for,
pass off, posture, pretend, show off
10 masquerade

attorney

5 agent, proxy 6 deputy, factor, lawyer
7 counsel 8 advocate, assignee
9 barrister, counselor, solicitor
10 counsellor, legal eagle, mouthpiece

attract
4 draw, lure, wile 5 charm, court, tempt
6 allure, appeal, beckon, draw in, entice,
invite, seduce 7 beguile, bewitch, enchant,
solicit 8 appeal to, interest, intrigue,
inveigle 9 captivate, fascinate, influence,
magnetize

attraction
4 bait, call, draw, lure, pull 5 charm
6 allure, appeal, liking 8 affinity, cynosure,
sympathy 9 affection, chemistry,
magnetism, seduction 10 allurement
12 drawing power

attractive
4 cute, fair, sexy 5 bonny, dishy 6 comely,
lovely, luring, pretty 7 Circean, likable,
winsome 8 alluring, charming, engaging,
enticing, fetching, handsome, inviting,
magnetic, mesmeric, tempting 9 appealing, beauteous, beautiful, beckoning,
glamorous, seductive 10 bewitching,
enchanting 11 captivating, fascinating,
good-looking, tantalizing 13 prepossessing

attractiveness
5 charm 6 appeal, beauty, glamor
7 glamour

attrbute
3 lay 4 mark, sign 5 apply, facet, pin on
point, refer, trait 6 aspect, assign, charge,
credit, emblem, impute, symbol, virtue
7 ascribe, connect, earmark, explain,
feature, quality 8 accredit, classify,
property 9 adjective, character, designate

attrition
3 rue 4 ruth, wear 6 sorrow 7 erosion,
penance, remorse, rubbing, wearing
8 abrasion, friction, grinding 9 penitence,
penitency, reduction, weakening
10 repentance 12 contriteness

attritional
5 sorry 6 rueful 8 contrite, penitent
9 regretful, repentant 10 apologetic,
remorseful 11 penitential

attune
6 accord, adjust 7 balance, conform
9 harmonize, integrate, reconcile
10 coordinate, proportion 11 accommodate

atypical
3 odd 5 queer 7 deviant, strange, unusual
8 aberrant, abnormal, peculiar
9 anomalous, deviative, different, divergent,
irregular, unnatural 11 exceptional,
heteroclite, nonstandard 13 preternatural

auberge
3 inn 5 hotel, lodge 6 hostel, tavern
7 hospice 8 hostelry 9 roadhouse
11 caravansary, public house

Auber opera
10 Fra Diavolo

auburn
4 rust 5 henna 6 russet 8 chestnut
11 burnt sienna 12 reddish-brown

au courant
3 mod 4 up on 5 awake, aware, hep to, hip
to, savvy 6 modern, modish, versed
7 abreast, current, in touch, knowing,
stylish, versant, witting 8 familiar, informed,
sentient, up-to-date 9 cognizant,
conscious, plugged in 10 acquainted,
conversant 11 fashionable
12 contemporary 13 up-to-the-minute

auction
4 sale, sell

audacious
4 bold, rash 5 brash, brave, cocky, risky,
saucy 6 brazen, cheeky, daring 7 valiant
8 arrogant, fearless, impudent, insolent,
intrepid, reckless, unafraid, uncurbed
9 daredevil, dauntless, foolhardy,
shameless, undaunted, venturous
10 courageous, ungoverned, unhampered
11 adventurous, impertinent, temerarious,
uninhibited, untrammeled, venturesome
12 unrestrained 13 adventuresome

audacity
4 gall 5 brass, cheek, moxie, nerve, spunk
6 mettle, spirit 7 courage 8 boldness,
chutzpah, rashness, temerity 9 assurance,
arrogance, brashness, cockiness,
disregard, hardihood, hardiness,
impudence, insolence 10 brazenness,
effrontery 12 recklessness

audible
5 aural, clear, heard 8 distinct 9 auricular

audibly
5 aloud 7 aurally, clearly, out loud

audience
5 crowd, group, house 6 public 7 hearing,
gallery, hearers, meeting 8 admirers,
assembly, audition, devotees 9 clientele,
following, gathering, interview
10 assemblage, listeners, spectators

audile
see **auditory**

audio
5 sound

audit
4 scan 5 check, probe 6 go over, report, review, survey, verify 7 analyze, balance, checkup, inspect 8 analysis, examine, scrutiny 10 inspection, scrutinize 11 examination 13 investigation

audition
4 test 5 trial 6 tryout 7 hearing, reading

auditor
8 examiner, listener 9 inspector 10 accountant, controller 11 comptroller

auditory
5 aural 8 acoustic

au fait
4 able 5 right 6 decent, proper, versed 7 abreast, capable, correct, versant 8 becoming, decorous, familiar, informed 9 befitting, competent, informed, qualified 10 acquainted, conforming, conversant, to the point

au fond
8 at bottom 9 basically, in essence 11 essentially 13 fundamentally

Augean
9 difficult 10 formidable 11 distasteful
stable: 3 sty 4 sink 5 filth, Sodom 7 cesspit 8 cesspool

auger
3 bit 5 borer, drill, screw 6 gimlet, trepan, wimble 9 corkscrew

Auge's son
8 Telephus

aught
3 all, nil, nix, zip 4 nada, zero 5 zilch 6 cipher 7 nothing 8 anything, goose egg 10 everything

augment
3 wax 4 grow, hike, rise 5 add to, boost, build, exalt, mount, raise 6 beef up, expand, extend 7 build up, develop, enhance, enlarge, magnify 9 intensify, reinforce 8 compound, heighten, increase, multiply 10 aggrandize, supplement 11 make greater

augmentation
4 rise 5 annex, extra, raise 7 adjunct, buildup 8 addition, increase 9 accession, accretion, increment 10 complement, enrichment 11 enhancement, enlargement

augur
4 bode, seer 6 herald, oracle 7 betoken, diviner, portend, predict, presage, promise, prophet, suggest 8 forebode, forecast, foreshow, foretell, indicate, prophesy, soothsay 9 adumbrate, foretoken, harbinger, predictor, prefigure 10 forecaster, foreshadow, foreteller, prophesier, soothsayer, vaticinate 11 Nostradamus 13 prognosticate

augury
4 omen, sign 5 token 6 herald 7 auspice, portent, presage, warning 8 bodement, forecast, prophecy 9 foretoken, harbinger 10 divination, forerunner, prediction, prognostic 11 forewarning

august
5 grand, noble, regal 6 lordly 7 eminent, stately 8 baronial, imposing, majestic, princely, splendid 9 dignified, grandiose 11 magnificent

auk
5 alcid 7 seabird
genus: 4 Alca

au lait
4 café

au naturel
3 raw 4 nude 5 naked, plain 6 unclad 8 stripped 9 unclothed, undressed 10 stark naked

aura
3 air 4 feel, glow, halo, mood, tone, vibe 5 aroma, vibes 6 nimbus 7 aureole, feeling, quality 8 ambience, mystique, radiance, sensation, stimulus 9 emanation, semblance 10 atmosphere

aural
6 audile 7 audible 8 acoustic, auditory 9 auricular

aureate
6 florid, golden 7 flowery, orotund 8 sonorous 9 bombastic, grandiose, overblown 10 euphuistic, rhetorical 11 declamatory 13 grandiloquent

aureole
4 aura, halo, ring 5 crown, light 6 circle, corona, nimbus 8 radiance

au revoir
4 by-by, ciao, ta-ta 5 adieu, adios 6 bye-bye, so long 7 farewell, good-bye 11 arrivederci

auricular
see **aural**

Auriga star
7 Capella

aurora
4 dawn, morn 7 dawning, morning, sunrise
8 cockcrow, daybreak

Aurora
Roman counterpart: 3 Eos
goddess of: 4 dawn
husband: 8 Tithonus
son: 6 Memnon

auslander
5 alien 7 inconnu 8 outsider, stranger
9 foreigner

auspice
4 omen, sign 10 divination

auspices
5 aegis 6 charge 7 backing, support
8 guidance 9 influence, patronage
11 sponsorship, supervision

auspicious
6 bright, lucky, timely 7 hopeful
9 favorable, fortunate, opportune,
promising, well-timed 10 prosperous
11 encouraging, propitious

Austen, Jane
novel: 4 Emma 10 Persuasion
13 Mansfield Park 15 Northanger Abbey
17 Pride and Prejudice 19 Sense and
Sensibility

Auster
see **Notus**

austere
4 bare, cold, dour, firm, grim, hard 5 acrid,
bleak, grave, harsh, plain, rigid, sharp,
spare, stern 6 bitter, severe, simple,
somber, strict 7 ascetic, serious, spartan
8 exacting 9 stringent, unadorned,
unfeeling 10 astringent, restrained 11 self-
denying

austerity
5 rigor 6 thrift 7 economy 8 acerbity,
asperity, coldness, grimness, hardness,
rigidity, severity 9 harshness, parsimony,
privation, solemnity, spareness, sternness,
stiffness 10 self-denial, simplicity,
strictness, stringency 11 unadornment
13 self-restraint

Australia
capital: 8 Canberra
city: 5 Perth 6 Darwin, Sydney
8 Adelaide, Brisbane 9 Melbourne,
Newcastle
desert: 10 Great Sandy 13 Great Victoria
ethnic group: 9 Aborigine
island: 6 Fraser 8 Kangaroo, Melville,
Tasmania
lake: 4 Eyre
monetary unit: 6 dollar
mountain, range: 9 Ayers Rock
9 Kosciusko 13 Great Dividing
reef: 12 Great Barrier
river: 4 Swan 6 Murray 7 Darling
8 Flinders 11 Cooper Creek 12 Coopers
Creek
strait: 4 Bass 6 Torres

Austria
capital: 6 Vienna
city: 4 Graz, Linz 8 Salzburg 9 Innsbruck
10 Klagenfurt
lake: 10 Neusiedler
monetary unit: 4 euro
mountain: 13 Grossglockner
mountain range: 4 Alps
neighbor: 5 Italy 7 Croatia, Germany,
Hungary 8 Slovakia, Slovenia
11 Switzerland 13 Czech Republic,
Liechtenstein
river: 3 Ems 6 Danube

autarchy
see **autocracy**

autarkic
4 free 8 separate 9 sovereign
10 autonomous, self-ruling 11 independent, self-reliant 13 self-governing

autarky
7 freedom 8 autonomy 12 independence,
self-reliance

authentic
4 real, true 5 legit, pukka, right, solid,
sound, valid 6 actual, trusty 7 certain,
credible, factual, for real, genuine
8 accurate, bona fide, credible, faithful,
reliable 9 undoubted, veritable
10 convincing, dependable, legitimate,
sure-enough 11 indubitable, trustworthy
12 questionless

authenticate
5 prove, vouch 6 adduce, attest, verify
7 bear out, certify, confirm, justify, voucher,
warrant 9 accredit, validate 11 corroborate
12 substantiate

author
5 maker 6 penman, scribe, writer
7 creator 8 inventor, novelist, prosaist
9 generator 10 originator
American: 3 Bly (Robert), Fox (Paula),

Nin (Anaïs), Poe (Edgar Allan), Tan (Amy) **4** Agee (James), Buck (Pearl S.), Cook (Robin), Dana (Richard Henry), Fast (Howard), Ford (Richard), Grey (Zane), King (Stephen), Jong (Erica), King (Stephen), Mann (Thomas), Puzo (Mario), Rand (Ayn), Rice (Anne), Roth (Philip), Shaw (Irwin), Uris (Leon), West (Nathanael), Wouk (Herman) **5** Aiken (Conrad), Alger (Horatio), Banks (Russell), Barth (John), Benét (Stephen Vincent), Blume (Judy), Boyle (T. Coraghessan), Brown (Rita Mae), Clark (Mary Higgins), Crane (Hart, Stephen), Dunne (Dominick, John Gregory), Elkin (Stanley), Ellis (Bret Easton), Foote (Horton), Harte (Bret), Henry (O.), Jakes (John), James (Henry), Levin (Ira), Lewis (Sinclair), Lurie (Alison), Mason (Bobbie Ann), Oates (Joyce Carol), O'Hara (John), Ozick (Cynthia), Paine (Thomas), Paley (Grace), Potok (Chaim), Price (Reynolds, Richard), Steel (Danielle), Stein (Gertrude), Stone (Irving), Stout (Rex), Stowe (Harriet Beecher), Turow (Scott), Twain (Mark), Tyler (Anne), Vidal (Gore), Welty (Eudora), White (Edmund, E. B., T. H.), Wolfe (Thomas, Tom), Wylie (Elinor) **6** Alcott (Louisa May), Asimov (Isaac), Auster (Paul), Bellow (Saul), Berger (Thomas), Bierce (Ambrose), Bowles (Paul), Cabell (James Branch), Capote (Truman), Cather (Willa), Chopin (Kate), Clancy (Tom), Conroy (Pat), Cooper (James Fenimore), Dickey (James), Didion (Joan), Ellroy (James), Ferber (Edna), French (Marilyn), Gaddis (William), Gaines (Ernest J.), Gilroy (Frank), Godwin (Gail), Hailey (Arthur), Harris (Frank, Joel Chandler), Hawkes (John), Heller (Joseph), Hersey (John), Hinton (S. E.), Holmes (Oliver Wendell), Hughes (Langston), Irving (John, Washington), Jewett (Sarah Orne), Kidder (Tracy), Koontz (Dean), Krantz (Judith), L'Amour (Louis), L'Engle (Madeleine), Le Guin (Ursula K.), London (Jack), Mailer (Norman), McBain (Ed), Miller (Arthur, Henry, Joaquin, May), Morley (Christopher), Morris (Wright), Mosley (Walter), Norris (Frank), Parker (Dorothy), Piercy (Marge), Porter (Katherine Anne, William Sydney), Proulx (E. Annie), Runyon (Damon), Sarton (May), Singer (Isaac Bashevis), Smiley (Jane), Styron (William), Taylor (Peter), Updike (John), Walker (Alice), Waller (Robert James), Warren (Robert Penn), Wilder (Laura Ingalls, Thornton), Wilson (August, Edmund, Harriet, Lanford), Wister (Owen), Wright (James, Richard) **7** Baldwin (Faith, James), Beattie (Ann), Cheever (John),

Clemens (Samuel Langhorne), Collins (Jackie), Connell (Evan), Cozzens (James Gould), DeLillo (Don), Dreiser (Theodore), Ellison (Ralph), Erdrich (Louise), Farrell (James T.), Francis (Dick), Franzen (Jonathan), Gardner (Erle Stanley), Garland (Hamlin), Glasgow (Ellen), Goldman (William), Grafton (Sue), Grisham (John), Hammett (Dashiell), Heyward (DuBose), Howells (William Dean), Hurston (Zora Neale), Jackson (Shirley), Jarrell (Randall), Johnson (Diane, James), Keillor (Garrison), Kennedy (William), Kerouac (Jack), Kincaid (Jamaica), Lardner (Ring), Leonard (Elmore), Malamud (Bernard), Masters (Edgar Lee), McCourt (Frank), Miller (Henry), Mumford (Lewis), Nabokov (Vladimir), O'Connor (Flannery), Pynchon (Thomas), Rexroth (Kenneth), Richter (Conrad), Roberts (Elizabeth Madox, Kenneth, Nora), Saroyan (William), Sheehan (Neil), Sheldon (Sidney), Theroux (Paul), Thoreau (Henry David), Thurber (James), Wallace (Lew), Wharton (Edith) **8** Anderson (Maxwell, Poul, Regina, Sherwood), Benchley (Peter), Bradbury (Ray), Bradford (Barbara Taylor), Caldwell (Erskine), Chandler (Raymond), Cornwell (Patricia), Crichton (Michael), Doctorow (E. L.), Faulkner (William), Kingston (Maxine Hong), Marquand (John P.), McCarthy (Cormac, Mary), McMillan (Terry), McMurtry (Larry), Melville (Herman), Michener (James), Mitchell (Donald Grant, Margaret, S. Weir), Morrison (Toni), Remarque (Erich Maria), Rinehart (Mary Roberts), Salinger (J. D.), Sandburg (Carl), Sinclair (Upton), Spillane (Mickey), Stockton (Frank R.), Vonnegut (Kurt), Wambaugh (Joseph) **9** Burroughs (Edgar Rice, John, William S.), Dos Passos (John), Hawthorne (Nathaniel), Hemingway (Ernest), Hillerman (Tony), Isherwood (Christopher), McCullers (Carson), Steinbeck (John), Wodehouse (P. G.), Woollcott (Alexander) **10** Cunningham (Michael), Fitzgerald (F. Scott), Kingsolver (Barbara), Tarkington (Booth) **11** Auchincloss (Louis), Matthiessen (Peter)

Argentinian: **6** Borges (Jorge Luis)
Australian: **4** West (Morris L.) **5** Stead (Christina), White (Patrick) **6** Davies (Robertson) **7** Clavell (James) **8** Keneally (Thomas) **10** McCullough (Colleen), Richardson (Henry Handel)
Austrian: **5** Kafka (Franz) **7** Jelinek (Elfriede), Suttner (Bertha) **8** Bernhard (Thomas) **10** Schnitzler (Arthur)
Canadian: **3** Roy (Camille, Gabrielle) **5** Kirby (William), Moore (Brian), Munro

(Alice) **6** Atwood (Margaret), Davies (Robertson) **7** Leacock (Stephen), Raddall (Thomas), Richler (Mordecai), Service (Robert), Shields (Carol) **8** Woodcock (George) **9** de la Roche (Mazo), MacLennan (Hugh)
Chilean: 6 Donoso (José) **7** Allende (Isabel)
Chinese: 5 Han Yu
Colombian: 7 Márquez (Gabriel García)
Czech: 5 Capek (Karel), Hasek (Jaroslav) **7** Kundera (Milan)
Danish: 4 Rode (Helge), Wied (Gustav) **6** Jensen (Johannes Vilhelm) **7** Dinesen (Isak), Holberg (Ludwig)
Dutch: 6 Vondel (Joost van den)
Egyptian: 7 Mahfouz (Naguib)
English: 4 Amis (Kingsley, Martin), Dahl (Roald), Ford (Ford Madox, John), Lyly (John), Saki, Snow (C. P.), Ward (Mrs. Humphry), West (Rebecca) **5** Byatt (A. S.), Defoe (Daniel), Doyle (Authur Conan), Eliot (George, Thomas Stearns), Evans (Mary Ann), Frayn (Michael), Hardy (Thomas), James (Henry, P. D.), Lewis (C. S., Monk, Wyndham), Lowry (Malcolm), Milne (A. A.), Munro (H. H.), Powys (John Cowper, Llewelyn, Theodore Francis), Reade (Charles), Spark (Muriel), Waugh (Alec, Evelyn), Wells (Charles Jeremiah, H. G.), White (T. H.), Wilde (Oscar), Woolf (Leonard, Virginia), Young (Arthur, Edward, Francis Brett) **6** Ambler (Eric), Archer (Jeffrey), Austen (Jane), Belloc (Hilaire), Brontë (Anne, Charlotte, Emily), Bunyan (John), Butler (Samuel), Clarke (Arthur C.), Conrad (Joseph), Fowles (John), Graves (Robert), Greene (Graham, Robert), Hilton (James), Hudson (W. H.), Huxley (Aldous), Malory (Thomas), McEwan (Ian), O'Brian (Patrick), Orwell (George), Potter (Beatrix), Powell (Anthony), Sayers (Dorothy L.), Sterne (Laurence), Storey (David), Walton (Izaak) **7** Ballard (J. G.), Burgess (Anthony), Burnett (Frances Hodgson), Carroll (Lewis), Collins (Wilkie), Dickens (Charles), Dodgson (Charles), Durrell (Lawrence), Fleming (Ian), Follett (Ken), Forster (E. M.), Forsyth (Frederick), Golding (Louis, William), Kipling (Rudyard), Le Carré (John), Lessing (Doris), Lofting (Hugh), Maugham (Robin, W. Somerset), Murdoch (Iris), Naipaul (V. S.), Rendell (Ruth), Rowling (J. K.), Sassoon (Siegfried), Shelley (Mary Wollstonecraft, Percy Bysshe), Sitwell (Edith, Osbert, Sacheverell), Southey (Robert), Stewart (Mary), Stoker (Bram), Surtees (Robert Smith), Tolkien (J. R. R.), Walpole (Horace, Hugh), Wyndham (John) **8** Christie

(Agatha), Fielding (Henry), Forester (C. S.), Koestler (Arthur), Lawrence (D. H., T. E.), Macaulay (Rose, Thomas Babington), Meredith (George), Sillitoe (Alan), Smollett (Tobias), Strachey (Lytton), Trollope (Anthony), Zangwill (Israel) **9** De Quincey (Thomas), Du Maurier (Daphne, George), Goldsmith (Oliver), Mansfield (Katherine), Masefield (John), Priestley (J. B.), Radcliffe (Ann), Stevenson (Robert Louis), Thackeray (William Makepeace), Wodehouse (P. D.) **10** Chesterton (Gilbert Keith), Galsworthy (John), Isherwood (Christopher), Richardson (Dorothy, Samuel) **12** Quiller-Couch (Arthur Thomas)
Finnish: 7 Waltari (Mika) **9** Sillanpää (Frans Eemil)
French: 4 Gide (André), Hugo (Victor), Kock (Charles-Paul de), Sade (Marquis de), Sand (George), Zola (Emile) **5** Beyle (Marie Henri), Camus (Albert), Dumas (Alexandre), Genet (Jean), Sagan (Françoise), Staël (Germaine de), Verne (Jules), Vigny (Alfred-Victor) **6** Balzac (Honoré de), Daudet (Alphonse), France (Anatole), Proust (Marcel), Sartre (Jean-Paul) **7** Cocteau (Jean), Colette, Gautier (Léon, Théophile), Malraux (André), Mauriac (Claude, François), Maurois (André), Merimée (Prosper), Rolland (Romain), Romains (Jules), Simenon (Georges) **8** Beauvoir (Simone de), Flaubert (Gustave), Marivaux (Pierre), Rabelais (François), Stendhal, Voltaire **9** Giraudoux (Jean) **10** Maupassant (Guy de), Saint-Simon (Duke de) **12** Robbe-Grillet (Alain), Saint-Exupéry (Antoine de)
German: 4 Böll (Heinrich), Mann (Thomas) **5** Grass (Gunter), Hesse (Hermann), Kafka (Franz), Storm (Theodor), Tieck (Ludwig), Zweig (Stefan) **6** Goethe (Johann Wolfgang von), Toller (Ernst) **7** Fontane (Theodor), Richter (Jean Paul), Wieland (Christoph Martin) **8** Hoffmann (E. T. A., Heinrich), Remarque (Erich Maria), Schlegel (August Wilhelm von, Friedrich von, Johann Elias) **9** Hauptmann (Gerhart), Sudermann (Hermann) **10** Wassermann (Jakob)
Greek: 6 Lucian **11** Kazantzakis (Nikos)
Hungarian: 5 Jókai (Mór)
Icelandic: 7 Laxness (Halldór)
Indian: 7 Rushdie (Salman)
Irish: 5 Behan (Brendan), Doyle (Roddy), Joyce (James), Moore (Brian), Wilde (Oscar) **6** O'Brien (Edna), Stoker (Bram) **7** Beckett (Samuel), O'Connor (Frank), Russell (George William) **8** O'Faolain

(Julia, Sean), Stephens (James) **9** O'Flaherty (Liam)
Italian: 3 Eco (Umberto) **5** Verga (Giovanni) **6** Silone (Ignazio) **7** Calvino (Italo), Manzoni (Alessandro), Moravia (Alberto) **9** Boccaccio (Giovanni), Vittorini (Elio) **10** Pirandello (Luigi), Straparola (Gianfrancesco)
Japanese: 7 Mishima (Yukio) **8** Kawabata (Yasunari), Murakami (Haruki), Murasaki (Shikibu) **9** Yokomitsu (Riichi), Yoshikawa (Eiji)
Lebanese: 6 Gibran (Khalil) **7** Fuentes (Carlos)
Nigerian: 6 Achebe (Chinua) **7** Soyinka (Wole), Tutuola (Amos)
Norwegian: 3 Lie (Jonas) **6** Hamsun (Knut), Undset (Sigrid) **7** Rolvaag (Ole) **8** Bjornson (Bjornstjerne), Kielland (Alexander)
Peruvian: 11 Vargas Llosa (Mario)
Polish: 7 Reymont (Wladyslaw) **8** Zeromski (Stefan) **11** Sienkiewicz (Henryk)
Portuguese: 6 Pessoa (Fernando) **8** Saramago (José)
Roman: 5 Pliny, Varro (Marcus Terentius)
Russian: 5 Gogol (Nikolai), Gorki (Maxim), Gorky (Maxim) **7** Chekhov (Anton), Pushkin (Alexander), Tolstoy (Leo) **8** Andreyev (Leonid), Turgenev (Ivan), Zamyatin (Yevgeny) **9** Ehrenburg (Ilya), Lermontov (Mikhail), Pasternak (Boris), Sholokhov (Mikhail) **10** Dostoevsky (Fyodor) **11** Dostoyevsky (Fyodor), Yevtushenko (Yevgeny) **12** Solzhenitsyn (Alexander)
Scottish: 4 Lang (Andrew) **5** Scott (Alexander, Walter) **6** Barrie (James M.), Buchan (John) **8** Urquhart (Thomas) **9** Stevenson (Robert Louis)
South African: 6 Fugard (Athol) **8** Gordimer (Nadine)
Spanish: 6 Baroja (Pio) **7** Alarcón (Pedro Antonio de) **9** Cervantes (Miguel de)
Swedish: 7 Johnson (Eyvind), Rydberg (Viktor) **8** Lagerlöf (Selma) **10** Lagerkvist (Pär), Strindberg (August)
Swiss: 4 Wyss (Johann Rudolf) **5** Spyri (Johanna) **6** Frisch (Max) **9** Spitteler (Carl)
Trinidadian: 7 Naipaul (V. S.)
Welsh: 4 Owen (Alun, Daniel, Goronwy, John) **5** Evans (David, Evan), Wynne (Ellis)
Yiddish: 4 Asch (Sholem) **6** Singer (Isaac Bashevis) **8** Aleichem (Sholem)

authoritarian

5 harsh, rigid **6** despot, severe, strict, tyrant **8** absolute, autocrat, despotic, dictator, dogmatic **9** imperious, stringent

10 absolutist, autocratic, oppressive, totalistic, tyrannical **11** dictatorial, doctrinaire, domineering, magisterial **12** totalitarian

authoritative

4 sure, true **5** legal, legit, sound **6** lawful, proven **7** factual **8** accepted, accurate, approved, attested, dogmatic, official, orthodox, reliable, verified **9** canonical, cathedral, confirmed, imperious, trustable validated **10** autocratic, commanding, definitive, dependable, documented, dominating, ex cathedra, legitimate, sanctioned **11** dictatorial, doctrinaire, domineering, irrefutable, magisterial, overbearing, trustworthy **12** indisputable

authority

4 rule, sway **5** clout, force, power, right, say-so **6** agency, charge, credit, expert, master, weight **7** command, control, grounds, license, mastery, warrant **8** citation, decision, dominion, prestige **9** influence, testimony **10** domination, governance, government, management **12** jurisdiction

authorization

4 okay, word **5** leave **6** permit **7** consent, go-ahead, mandate **8** approval, sanction **9** agreement, allowance, clearance **10** green light, permission, sufferance **11** approbation

authorize

3 let **4** okay, vest **5** allow **6** affirm, enable, invest, permit **7** approve, confirm, empower, endorse, entitle, license, qualify, warrant **8** accredit, sanction, vouch for **9** give leave, recognize **10** commission **11** countenance

auto

see **automobile**

autobahn

7 highway **8** turnpike **10** expressway **12** superhighway

autobiography

4 life, vita **5** diary **6** memoir **7** account, journal **9** life story **11** confessions **13** reminiscences

autochthonous

6 native **7** endemic **8** original **10** ab-original, indigenous

autocracy

7 czarism, tyranny **8** monarchy **9** despotism, monocracy **12** absolute rule, dictatorship

autocrat
4 czar, duce, emir, lord, raja, shah, tsar, tzar 5 mogul, rajah, ruler 6 caliph, despot, sultan, tyrant 7 magnate, monarch 8 dictator, oligarch, overlord 9 potentate, sovereign 10 absolutist

autocratic
7 haughty 8 absolute, arrogant, despotic 9 arbitrary, imperious, tyrannous 10 monocratic, tyrannical 11 dictatorial, domineering, overbearing

autodidactic
10 self-taught 12 self-educated

autograph
3 ink, pen 4 sign 5 write 7 endorse 8 original 9 signature, subscribe 11 endorsement, John Hancock

Autolycus
daughter: 8 Anticlea
father: 6 Hermes 7 Mercury

automated
7 robotic 9 by machine, motorized 10 electrical, electronic, mechanical, mechanized, programmed 12 computerized

automatic
6 reflex 8 habitual 9 impulsive, reflexive 10 mechanical, self-acting, unprompted 11 instinctive, involuntary, perfunctory, spontaneous, unmeditated
prefix: 4 self

automaton
5 droid, golem, robot 7 android, machine 9 mechanism

automobile
3 bus, car 5 buggy, coupe, racer, sedan 6 jalopy, tourer, wheels 7 flivver, hardtop, machine 8 dragster, motorcar, roadster, runabout 9 hatchback, limousine 11 convertible
American: 3 Reo 4 Cord, Ford, Jeep, Nash 5 Buick, Dodge, Eagle, Essex, Lexus 6 DeSoto, Hudson, Model A, Model T, Saturn, Willys 7 LaSalle, LeBaron, Maxwell, Mercury, Mustang, Packard, Pontiac, Rambler, Seville 8 Cadillac, Chrysler, Corvette, Eldorado, Franklin, Lincoln, Plymouth 9 Chevrolet, Hupmobile 10 Duesenberg, Oldsmobile, Studebaker 11 Continental, Pierce-Arrow, Thunderbird 12 Kaiser-Frazer
British: 4 Mini 6 Anglia, Austin, Cooper, DeSoto, Jaguar, Morris 7 Bentley, Daimler, Hillman, Sunbeam, Triumph 8 Vauxhall

10 Range Rover, Rolls-Royce 11 Aston Martin, Land Rover 12 Austin-Healey
French: 5 Simca 7 Citroën, Peugeot, Renault
German: 3 BMW 4 Audi, Benz, Opel 7 Daimler, Porsche 8 Mercedes 10 Volkswagen 12 Mercedes-Benz
Italian: 4 Fiat 6 Lancia 7 Bugatti, Ferrari 8 Maserati 9 Alfa-Romeo 11 Lamborghini
Japanese: 5 Honda, Isuzu, Mazda 6 Datsun, Nissan, Subaru, Toyota 10 Mitsubishi
Korean: 3 Kia 6 Daewoo 7 Hyundai
Swedish: 4 Saab 5 Volvo

automotive pioneer
4 Benz (Carl Friedrich), Ford (Henry), Olds (Ransom), Otto (Nikolaus), Pope (Albert) 5 Evans (Oliver), Rolls (Charles), Roper (Sylvester) 6 Cugnot (Nicholas Joseph), Duryea (Charles E., J. Frank), Lenoir (Etienne), Winton (Alexander) 7 Bugatti (Ettore), Citroën (André-Gustave), Daimler (Gottlieb), Peugeot (Armand), Stanley (Francis, Freelan) 8 Morrison (William) 10 Lanchester (Frederick William)

Autonoë
father: 6 Cadmus
husband: 9 Aristaeus
mother: 8 Harmonia
sister: 5 Agave
son: 7 Actaeon

autonomous
4 free 8 autarkic, separate 9 sovereign 10 self-ruling 11 independent 12 self-governed, self-reliant, uncontrolled 13 self-contained, self-governing

autonomy
7 autarky, freedom 8 home rule, self-rule 11 sovereignty 12 independence

autopsy
6 assess 7 examine 8 evaluate, necropsy 10 assessment, dissection, evaluation, postmortem 11 examination

auto racer
4 Foyt (A. J.), Hill (Graham) 5 Clark (Jim), Mears (Rick), Petty (Richard), Unser (Al, Bobby) 6 Carter (Pancho), Fangio (Juan), Vogler (Rich) 7 Brabham (Jack), Stewart (Jackie) 8 Andretti (Mario, Michael), Johncock (Gordon) 9 Earnhardt (Dale) 10 Rutherford (Johnny)

autumn
4 fall 6 season 8 maturity

auxiliary
4 aide 5 spare 6 backup, helper

7 reserve **8** adjutant, adjuvant
9 accessory, ancillary, assistant, coadjutor, secondary **10** accomplice, additional, collateral, subsidiary **11** appurtenant, subservient **12** contributory
13 complementary, supplementary
verb: 3 are, can, did, had, has, may, was
4 been, does, have, must, were, will
5 could, might, ought, shall, would
6 should

avail
3 aid, use **4** gain, good, help **5** asset, serve **6** profit **7** account, benefit, fitness, satisfy, service **9** advantage, relevance
10 usefulness **13** applicability

available
5 handy, on tap, ready, valid **6** at hand, on hand, usable **7** present, willing **8** prepared
9 qualified **10** accessible, attainable, convenient, obtainable, procurable
11 purchasable

avalanche
4 mass, rush **5** drown, flood, slide
6 deluge **7** overrun, smother **8** inundate, mudslide, overflow, rockfall **9** landslide, overwhelm, rockslide, snowslide
10 inundation **12** accumulation

Avalon
8 paradise

avant-garde
7 radical **8** advanced, contempo **10** innovative, pioneering **11** cutting-edge, leading-edge, progressive **12** experimental
13 up-to-the-minute

avarice
5 greed **7** avidity **8** cupidity, rapacity, voracity **10** greediness **12** covetousness

avaricious
6 grabby, greedy, stingy **7** miserly
8 covetous, esurient, grasping, ravenous
9 mercenary, rapacious **11** acquisitive

avatar
4 type **5** image **7** epitome **8** exemplar
9 archetype **10** apotheosis, embodiment, expression **11** incarnation, reification
13 manifestation

avaunt
4 away **5** hence, leave, scram **6** beat it, depart, get out

ave
4 hail **8** farewell, greeting

avenge
5 repay, right **6** punish **7** get even, pay

back, redress, requite **9** fight back, retaliate, vindicate

avenue
3 way **4** path, road **5** drive, means, route, track **6** access, artery, street **7** channel, course, parkway, pathway **8** approach
9 boulevard **10** passageway
12 thoroughfare

aver
4 avow **5** prove, state, swear **6** affirm, allege, assert, attest, avouch, depose, insist, verify **7** declare, profess, protest, testify, warrant **8** maintain **9** guarantee, predicate

average
3 par **4** fair, mean, norm **5** usual
6 common, divide, equate, figure, median, medium, middle, normal **7** balance, even out, typical **8** everyday, midpoint, moderate, ordinary **12** intermediate

averagely
4 so-so **6** enough, fairly, rather **8** passably
9 tolerably **10** moderately

averse
5 balky, loath **6** afraid **7** hostile, opposed, uneager **8** allergic, hesitant **9** reluctant, resistant, unwilling **10** indisposed
11 disinclined **12** antipathetic

aversion
4 fear, hate **5** dread **6** hatred, horror
7 allergy, disgust, dislike **8** disfavor, distaste, loathing **9** antipathy, disliking, repulsion, revulsion **10** abhorrence, antagonism, repugnance **11** abomination, detestation, displeasure **13** indisposition

aversive
8 ungenial **9** repellent, repugnant
11 uncongenial **12** antipathetic **13** unsympathetic

avert
4 foil, halt, turn, veer, ward **5** avoid, check, deter **6** thwart **7** deflect, fend off, forfend, obviate, prevent, rule out, ward off **8** go around, stave off, turn away **9** forestall, frustrate, turn aside

avian
6 flying, winged **8** birdlike, ornithic

aviary
4 cage **8** birdcage, dovecote **9** birdhouse, enclosure

aviator
3 ace **4** Post (Wiley) **5** flier, pilot
6 airman, flyboy, Wright (Orville, Wilbur),

Yeager (Chuck) **7** birdman, Earhart (Amelia) **8** aeronaut **9** bush pilot, Lindbergh (Charles) **10** Richthofen (Manfred von) **12** (Eddie)

avid
4 agog, keen **5** eager **6** ardent, greedy, hungry **7** anxious, athirst, craving, fervent, thirsty, zealous **8** appetent, covetous, desirous, grasping **9** impatient **10** breathless, insatiable **12** enthusiastic

avidity
4 zeal **5** greed **6** fervor, thirst **7** avarice, craving **8** cupidity, keenness, rapacity **9** eagerness **10** greediness

Avis
competitor: 5 Hertz

avis
4 rara

avocation
5 hobby **7** pastime, pursuit **8** sideline **9** amusement, diversion **10** recreation

avoid
4 bilk, duck, miss, shun, snub **5** annul, avert, dodge, elude, evade, shirk, skirt **6** bypass, divert, escape, eschew, pass up **7** abstain, prevent, refrain **8** preclude, sidestep, stay away, withdraw **9** keep clear **11** refrain from **12** keep away from

avoidance
5 dodge **6** escape **7** dodging, elusion, evasion **8** escaping, escapism, eschewal, shirking, shunning **9** runaround **10** abstinence

avouch
3 own **4** aver, avow **5** admit, claim, state, swear **6** affirm, assert, depose, insist **7** certify, confess, confirm, declare, profess, testify **9** predicate, pronounce **11** acknowledge, corroborate

avow
3 own **4** aver **5** admit, allow, grant, let on, own up, state, swear **6** affirm, assert, avouch, depose **7** concede, confess, declare, profess, protest **8** disclose, maintain, proclaim **9** predicate **11** acknowledge

avowal
6 assent **9** admission, assertion, statement **10** profession **11** affirmation, attestation, declaration

avowedly
6 openly **7** frankly **8** candidly **9** allegedly **10** apparently, ostensibly, supposedly

await
4 bide, hope, stay **5** abide **6** expect **7** count on, look for **8** watch for **10** anticipate, hang around

awake
4 stir **5** alert, alive, aware, rouse **6** active, arouse, bestir, excite, revive, roused, stir up **7** animate, aroused, excited, on guard **8** activate, sensible, sentient, vigilant, watchful **9** attentive, cognizant, conscious, observant, stimulate, stirred up

award
4 gift, give, kudo **5** allot, badge, endow, grant, honor, kudos, medal, prize **6** accord, bestow, confer, donate, trophy **7** concede, laurels, tribute **8** accolade, citation, donation **9** vouchsafe **10** blue ribbon, decoration, distribute **11** distinction
motion picture: 5 Oscar **7** Academy **11** Golden Globe
mystery novel: 5 Edgar
record: 6 Grammy
science-fiction: 4 Hugo
television: 4 Emmy
theater: 4 Tony

aware
4 onto **5** alert, alive, awake **7** heedful, knowing, mindful, tuned in, witting **8** informed, sensible, sentient, vigilant **9** attentive, au courant, cognizant, conscious, observant **10** conversant, perceptive **12** apprehensive **13** knowledgeable

awash
4 full **6** afloat, filled, jammed, loaded, packed **7** brimful, covered, crammed, crowded, flooded, run-over, stuffed **8** brimming, chockful **9** chock-full **11** overflowing

away
3 far, fro, now, off, out **4** afar, gone **5** along, apart, aside, forth, hence **6** abroad, absent, afield, far off **7** distant, lacking, missing, not here **9** elsewhere **11** incessantly **12** continuously

away from
6 beyond

awe
5 alarm, amaze, scare **6** wonder **7** inspire, startle **8** astonish **9** amazement, reverence **10** veneration, wonderment **11** flabbergast **12** astonishment

aweless
4 bold **5** brave **7** valiant **8** fearless,

intrepid, unafraid **9** dauntless, undaunted **10** courageous

awesome
6 august **7** amazing, sublime **8** imposing, terrific, wondrous **10** formidable, impressive **11** astonishing **12** breathtaking **13** extraordinary

awful
3 bad **4** very **5** nasty **6** odious **7** hateful **8** dreadful, horrible, horrific, shocking, terrible, terrific **9** appalling, atrocious, extremely, frightful, loathsome, offensive **10** deplorable, disgusting, formidable

awfully
4 much, very **6** hugely, vastly **7** greatly **8** terribly, whopping **9** extremely, immensely **10** dreadfully, enormously **11** exceedingly

awhile
7 briefly **8** for a time **11** temporarily

awkward
5 gawky, inept, messy, nerdy, splay **6** clumsy, gauche, klutzy, wooden **7** artless, gawkish, halting, lumpish, unhandy, unhappy **8** bumbling, bungling, tactless, ungainly **9** graceless, ham-handed, ill-chosen, inelegant, lumbering, maladroit **10** blundering, ungraceful, unskillful **11** heavyhanded, unfortunate **12** embarrassing, incommodious, inconvenient, infelicitous

awl
4 tool **7** piercer

awning
6 canopy **7** marquee **8** sunshade
ancient Roman: 8 velarium

awry
5 amiss, askew, wrong **6** astray **7** askance, crooked **8** cockeyed **9** cock-a-hoop, crookedly
Scottish: 5 agley

ax, axe
3 can, hew **4** adze, boot, chop, fire, sack **6** bounce **7** boot out, chopper, cleaver, dismiss, hatchet, kick out **8** tomahawk **9** discharge, terminate
blade: 3 bit
handle: 5 helve

axiom
3 law **4** rule **5** adage, maxim, moral, truth **6** dictum, truism **7** precept, theorem **8** aphorism, apothegm **9** postulate, principle **10** principium **11** fundamental

axiomatic
5 given **7** assumed, certain, obvious **8** accepted, absolute, manifest, provable **10** aphoristic, understood **11** fundamental, indubitable, self-evident **12** unquestioned

axis
4 line, pole, stem **5** point, pivot **8** alliance **9** continuum, plant stem **11** partnership **12** straight line, turning point

axle
3 bar, pin, rod **4** beam **5** bogie, shaft **7** spindle, support

aye
3 yea, yep, yes **4** amen, okay, ever, vote **6** agreed, always **8** all right **11** affirmative, continually

Azerbaijan
capital: 4 Baku
city: 5 Gäncä **8** Sumqayit
exclave: 8 Naxçivan **11** Nakhichevan
monetary unit: 5 manat
neighbor: 4 Iran **6** Russia **7** Armenia, Georgia
river: 4 Kura **5** Araks
sea: 7 Caspian

Azores
capital: 12 Ponta Delgada
city: 5 Horta
island: 4 Pico **5** Corvo, Faial, Lajes **6** Flores **8** São Jorge, Terceura **9** São Miguel **10** Santa Maria
part of: 8 Portugal

Aztec
capital: 12 Tenochtitlán
conqueror: 6 Cortés, Cortéz
emperor: 9 Moctezuma, Montezuma
god: 4 Xipe **6** Tlaloc **9** Xipetotec **12** Quetzalcoatl
hero: 4 Nata
language: 7 Nahuatl
temple: 8 teocalli

azure
3 sky **4** blue **5** color **7** sky blue

B

baa
5 bleat

Babbitt
10 conformist, middlebrow, philistine
author: 5 Lewis (Sinclair)

babble
3 gab, jaw, yak, yap 4 blab, chat, go on,
gush, rant, rave 5 clack, prate, run on
6 burble, drivel, gibber, gossip, jabber,
murmur, patter, piffle, rattle, yammer
7 blabber, blather, chatter, maunder,
palaver, prattle, twaddle 8 nonsense, idle
talk 9 gibberish 11 jabberwocky

babe
3 cub, tot 4 doll, girl 5 bairn, child, chick,
cutie, woman 6 infant, hottie 7 bambino,
papoose, neonate, newborn 8 bantling,
nursling

babel
3 ado, din, row 4 to-do 5 hoo-ha
6 bedlam, clamor, hubbub, jangle, outcry,
racket, ruckus, tumult, uproar 7 clangor,
discord, ferment, turmoil 8 brouhaha,
clangour, foofaraw 9 cacophony,
commotion, confusion 10 dissonance,
hullabaloo, hurly-burly, turbulence
11 pandemonium 12 vociferation

baboon
3 oaf 4 clod, dolt, goon, lout 6 chacma,
galoot, simian 7 palooka 8 lunkhead,
mandrill, meathead 9 hamadryas

babushka
6 granny 7 bandana 8 bandanna, kerchief

baby
3 pet, tot 4 tiny 5 bairn, sissy, spoil
6 cocker, coddle, cosset, dote on, infant,
pamper, bambino, cater to, indulge,
neonate, newborn, papoose, toddler
8 bantling, dote upon, nursling, suckling,
weanling 11 mollycoddle
ailment: 5 colic, croup

bed: 4 crib 6 cradle 8 bassinet
bedroom: 7 nursery
breechcloth: 6 diaper
cap: 6 biggin, bonnet
carriage: 4 pram 5 buggy 8 stroller
12 perambulator
doctor: 12 pediatrician
food: 3 pap 4 milk 6 pablum 7 pabulum
garment: 7 rompers
Italian: 7 bambino
napkin: 3 bib
outfit: 7 layette
powder: 4 talc
shoe: 6 bootee
Spanish: 4 bebé, nene

baby grand
5 piano

babyhood
7 infancy 10 diaper days, immaturity

babyish
5 petty 7 foolish, puerile, spoiled
8 childish, immature, juvenile 9 infantile,
infantine

Babylonian
6 lavish 9 luxurious
abode of the dead: 5 Aralu
capital: 7 Babylon
chaos: 4 Apsu
city: 5 Akkad 6 Cunaxa
crown prince: 10 Belshazzar
division: 5 Akkad, Sumer
earth mother: 6 Ishtar
first ruler: 6 Nimrod
god: 3 Bel 6 Marduk, Tammuz
goddess: 5 Belit 6 Ishtar
hero: 9 Gilgamesh
king: 6 Sargon 9 Hammurabi
12 Ashurbanipal
river: 6 Tigris 9 Euphrates
sun god: 3 Bel 7 Shamash
tower: 5 Babel 8 ziggurat
waters: 4 Apsu 6 Tiamat
winged dragon: 6 Tiamat

baccalaureate
6 degree 9 bachelor's 10 graduation

bacchanal
6 maenad
see also **bacchanalia**

bacchanalia
4 bash, orgy 5 binge, revel, spree
6 bender, excess 7 blowout, carouse,
debauch, revelry, wassail 8 carnival,
festival, wingding 11 celebration,
dissipation, merrymaking

bacchanalian
4 wild 7 drunken, riotous 8 frenzied
9 debauched, orgiastic 12 intoxicating
cry 4 evoe 5 evohe

Bacchus
8 Dionysus
attendant: 6 maenad 9 bacchante
father: 4 Zeus 7 Jupiter
lover: 5 Venus 9 Aphrodite
mother: 6 Semele
son: 7 Priapus
staff: 7 thyrsus

Bach, Johann Sebastian
birthplace: 8 Eisenach
genre: 5 fugue, motet, suite 6 sonata
7 cantata, chorale, partita, prelude, toccata
8 concerto, fantasia, oratorio, sinfonia
home: 7 Leipzig
instrument: 5 organ 11 harpsichord
musical style: 7 baroque
religion: 8 Lutheran

back
3 aft, aid 4 abet, fund, help, hind, rear
5 abaft, about, dorsa (plural), spine, stake
6 assist, astern, dorsum, hinder, recede,
uphold 7 endorse, finance, promote,
retract, retreat, reverse, sponsor, support
8 advocate, bankroll, champion, rearward,
side with 9 in reverse, posterior, retrocede,
subsidize 10 retrograde
ailment: 7 lumbago 10 rheumatism
of an arthropod: 6 tergum
of an insect: 5 notum
of the neck: 4 nape 6 scruff
prefix: 4 post 5 retro
relating to: 6 dorsal

back answer
3 lip 6 retort 7 riposte 8 comeback,
repartee, wisecrack 9 rejoinder 10 return
shot 11 parting shot

backbite
4 slam, slur 5 abuse, decry, knock, libel,
smear, sully, taint 6 defame, defile, malign,

vilify 7 asperse, put down, run down,
slander, traduce 8 bad-mouth, belittle,
besmirch, derogate, diminish 9 denigrate,
discredit

backbiter
6 gossip 7 defamer, traitor 9 detractor,
slanderer 10 talebearer

backbiting
5 abuse, smear, spite 6 gossip 7 abusing,
calumny, obloquy, scandal, slander
8 libelous, smearing 9 aspersion,
cattiness, gossiping, invective, maligning,
traducing, vilifying 10 calumnious,
defamation, defamatory, scandalous,
slandering, slanderous 11 denigration
12 belittlement, depreciation, spitefulness,
vituperation 13 disparagement

backbone
4 base, grit, guts, will 5 basis, moxie,
nerve, spine, spunk 6 mettle, pillar, rachis
7 resolve, support 8 mainstay, tenacity
9 character, fortitude, framework,
toughness, vertebrae 10 foundation, moral
fiber, resolution 12 spinal column
13 determination, steadfastness

backbreaking
6 taxing, tiring 7 arduous, onerous
8 grueling, toilsome 9 fatiguing, gruelling,
laborious, punishing, strenuous, torturous,
wearisome 10 burdensome, exhausting

backchat
6 banter, gossip 10 persiflage

backcomb
5 tease

backcountry
4 bush 6 sticks 7 boonies, outback
8 frontier, interior 9 boondocks 10 hinterland

backcourtman
5 guard

back down
4 balk 5 admit, demur, welsh, yield 6 beg
off, bow out, cry off, give in, give up, recall,
recant, renege 7 concede, disavow, retract,
retreat 8 withdraw 9 surrender, take back,
weasel out 10 chicken out

backdrop
6 milieu 7 climate, context, scenery, setting
8 stage set 10 atmosphere, background
11 environment, mise-en-scène
12 surroundings

backer
4 ally 5 angel 6 patron, surety 7 sponsor
8 advocate, defender, exponent, follower,
promoter 9 auxiliary, guarantor, investor,
proponent, supporter 10 bankroller,
benefactor, meal ticket

backfire
4 fail 5 blast 6 fizzle, go awry 7 go amiss,
go wrong 8 miscarry, ricochet
9 boomerang, discharge, explosion
10 disappoint, spring back 11 fall through
13 counteraction

backgammon
board section: 5 table
piece: 5 stone
wedge: 5 point

background
4 base, tone 6 milieu 7 history, scenery,
setting 8 heritage 9 education, training
10 experience, supporting
13 circumstances, qualification

backhanded
7 devious, oblique 8 indirect, derisive,
sneering 9 insulting, sarcastic
10 roundabout 12 disingenuous
13 condescending
compliment: 6 insult, slight 7 put-down
9 aspersion

backing
3 aid 4 help 5 aegis, funds 7 harmony,
support 8 auspices 9 patronage,
promotion 10 assistance 11 endorsement,
sponsorship 13 accompaniment,
encouragement

backland
see **backcountry**

backlash
5 slack 6 recoil 8 kickback, reaction,
response, ricochet 11 retaliation
12 repercussion

backlog
4 pile 5 hoard, stock, store 6 pile up,
supply 7 nest egg, reserve 9 inventory,
reservoir, stockpile 12 accumulation

back of
5 abaft 6 behind 9 following

back off
see **back down**

back out
4 quit 5 leave, welsh, yield 6 beg off,
desert, give up, renege 7 forsake
8 withdraw 9 surrender

backpack
4 gear, hike 5 tramp 6 duffel, ramble
8 knapsack, rucksack 9 haversack

backpedal
see **back down**

backset
see **setback**

backside
3 bum 4 butt, rear, rump, seat, tail, tush
5 fanny, hiney, stern 6 behind, bottom,
breech, far end, heinie 8 buttocks,
derriere, haunches 9 fundament, posterior
12 hindquarters

backslide
4 fall, sink, slip 5 lapse 6 return, revert
7 go wrong, regress, relapse 9 retrovert
10 degenerate, go downhill, recidivate
11 deteriorate

backstabbing
4 slur 5 smear 6 malice 7 calumny,
scandal, slander 8 betrayal 9 treachery
10 defamation, detraction, traitorous
11 treacherous 12 belittlement,
depreciation, vilification 13 disparagement

backstairs
6 covert, secret, sneaky, sordid 7 furtive
8 hush-hush 9 secretive 10 scandalous
11 clandestine, underhanded
13 surreptitious

backstop
5 fence 6 screen, uphold 7 bolster,
support 8 advocate, champion, side with

back talk
3 lip 4 guff, sass 5 cheek, mouth, sauce
9 freshness, impudence, insolence
12 impertinence

backtrack
7 regress, retrace, retreat, reverse 8 turn
tail

backward
4 dull, slow, rear 5 abaft, dense 6 averse,
astern, behind stupid 7 awkward, delayed,
moronic 8 ignorant, inverted, rearward,
retarded, reversed, stagnant 9 benighted,
dim-witted, in reverse 10 half-witted,
retrograde, slow-witted, uncultured
11 thickheaded, turned around,
undeveloped 12 feebleminded,
simpleminded, uncultivated
13 unprogressive

backwoods
see **backcountry**

backwoodsman
4 hick, rube 5 swain, yokel 6 rustic
7 bumpkin, hayseed 9 hillbilly 10 clodhopper, country boy, provincial
11 mountaineer

bacon
side: 6 flitch, gammon
slice: 6 rasher

Bacon, Francis
work: 12 Novum Organum

bacteria
5 cocci 7 bacilli, vibrios 8 spirilla
culture medium: 4 agar
destroyer: 10 antibiotic

bacterial disease
6 plague, typhus 7 anthrax, leprosy,
tetanus, typhoid 8 botulism, syphilis
9 gonorrhea, pneumonia 10 diphtheria,
infection, meningitis 11 shigellosis

bacteriologist
American: 6 Enders (John Franklin)
7 Noguchi (Hideyo), Theiler (Max)
British: 7 Fleming (Alexander)
French: 5 Widal (Fernand) 7 Nicolle
(Charles-Jean-Henri), Pasteur (Louis)
German: 4 Cohn (Ferdinand Julius), Koch
(Robert) 5 Klebs (Edwin) 7 Behring (Emil
von), Löffler (Friedrich) 10 Wassermann
(August von)
Japanese: 8 Kitasato (Shibasaburo)
Russian: 11 Metchnikoff (Elie)
Swiss: 6 Yersin (Alexandre-Emile-John)

bad
3 ill, low 4 evil, foul, sour 5 amiss, awful,
lousy, wrong 6 crummy, putrid, rancid,
rotten, sinful, wicked 7 harmful, hateful,
hurtful, immoral, naughty, noisome,
noxious, spoiled, tainted, vicious
8 damaging, dreadful, inferior, perverse,
terrible, wretched 9 abhorrent, defective,
execrable, injurious, loathsome, obnoxious,
offensive, putrefied, reprobate, repulsive,
sickening 10 disgusting, iniquitous 11 deleterious, detrimental, distasteful, intolerable
12 unacceptable 13 objectionable
comparative: 5 worse
prefix: 3 dys, mis
superlative: 5 worst

Badebec
husband: 9 Gargantua
son: 10 Pantagruel

Baden
3 spa 6 resort 9 hot spring

badge
3 pin 4 arms, logo, mark, seal, sign
5 award, honor, kudos, medal, token
6 button, emblem, ensign 7 laurels
8 accolade, hallmark, insignia 10 coat of
arms, decoration 11 distinction, purple
heart

badger
3 bug, nag 4 bait, goad, ride 5 annoy,
brock, chivy, harry, hound 6 chivvy, harass,
hassle, heckle, hector, needle, pester,
plague 7 torment 8 bullyrag 9 importune

Badger State
9 Wisconsin

badinage
4 play 6 banter, joking 7 jesting, joshing,
kidding, ribbing, teasing 8 backchat,
chitchat, repartee 9 cross talk
10 persiflage

badland
4 wild 5 waste, wilds 6 barren, desert
7 outback 8 wildness 10 wilderness
11 hill country

bad mark
3 gig 7 demerit 9 poor grade

bad-tempered
4 dour, sour 5 cross, sulky, surly, testy
6 crabby, cranky, crusty, grumpy, ornery,
sullen, touchy 7 grouchy, peevish
8 choleric, petulant 9 crotchety, dyspeptic,
irascible, irritable, splenetic 10 ill-humored,
ill-natured, unpleasant 11 quarrelsome
12 cantankerous, curmudgeonly,
disagreeable, misanthropic

Baedeker
5 guide 6 manual 8 handbook
9 guidebook, vade mecum 10 compendium 11 enchiridion, travel guide

baffle
4 balk, foil 5 addle, block, floor, mix up,
stump 6 bemuse, hinder, impede, muddle,
puzzle 7 thwart 7 barrier, confuse, flummox,
mystify, nonplus, perplex 8 befuddle,
bewilder, confound 9 deflector,
dumbfound, frustrate 10 circumvent,
disappoint, disconcert

bafflement
9 confusion 10 bemusement, perplexity
12 bewilderment

bag
3 cop, nab, kit, net, sag, win 4 flop, grip,

hook, kill, land, nail, poke, sack, tote, trap
5 biddy, bulge, catch, crone, forgo, pouch,
purse, seize, shoot, snare, steal, udder
6 beldam, collar, duffel, duffle, give up,
secure, valise **7** abandon, acquire,
capture, satchel **8** backpack, knapsack,
reticule, suitcase **9** apprehend, haversack
12 protuberance

bagatelle
6 trifle, whimsy **9** plaything

baggage
4 gear **5** hussy, stuff, tramp, trull, wench
6 burden, things, wanton **7** carry-on,
effects, jezebel, luggage, parcels, trollop
8 obstacle, matériel, slattern, strumpet
9 equipment, hindrance, prostitute
10 impediment **11** impedimenta
13 paraphernalia

baggy
5 loose

Baghdad
founder: 6 Mansur
river: 6 Tigris

bagnio
4 crib, stew **7** brothel, lupanar **8** bordello,
cathouse **10** bawdy house, whorehouse

bagpipe
part: 5 drone **7** bourdon, chanter
sound: 5 skirl

Bahamas
capital: 6 Nassau
island: 3 Cat **5** Abaco **6** Andros, Inagua
7 Watling **9** Eleuthera, Mayaguana
11 Grand Bahama, San Salvador **13** New
Providence
language: 7 English
monetary unit: 6 dollar
neighbor: 4 Cuba

Bahrain
capital: 6 Manama
island: 6 Sitrah **7** Bahrain **10** Al
Muharraq
language: 6 Arabic
monetary unit: 5 dinar

bail
3 bar, dip **4** bond, flee, lade **5** ladle, scoop
6 handle, pledge, surety **7** release
8 guaranty, security, warranty **9** guarantee
10 collateral **12** recognizance

bailiwick
4 area, turf, zone **5** field, realm **6** domain,
sphere **7** demesne, purview, terrain
8 district, dominion, province **9** champaign,
specialty, territory **10** discipline
12 jurisdiction

bailout
3 aid **6** relief, rescue **7** subsidy
11 benefaction, deliverance

bairn
3 kid, tot **4** babe, baby, tyke **5** child
6 infant

bait
3 nag, try, vex **4** lure, ride, trap **5** abuse,
chase, chivy, decoy, harry, hound, leger,
snare, taunt, tease, tempt, worry **6** allure,
badger, come-on, entice, entrap, harass,
heckle, hector, lead on, molest, pester,
seduce **7** beguile, torment, torture **8** bullyrag, inveigle, ridicule **9** persecute,
seduction, sweetener **10** attraction,
allurement, enticement, temptation
and switch: 4 lure **5** trick **8** inveigle
10 substitute

bake
4 burn, char, cook, fire, kiln **5** broil, roast,
toast **6** scorch **7** scallop, scollop, swelter

baked clay
7 ceramic

baker's dozen
8 thirteen

bakers' yeast
6 leaven **9** leavening

baking
3 hot **5** fiery **6** red-hot, torrid **7** burning
8 broiling, scalding, sizzling, white-hot
9 scorching
chamber: 4 kiln, oven

baksheesh
3 tip **4** alms **5** bribe, favor **6** grease,
reward **7** payment **8** gratuity
9 emolument **12** compensation

Balaam
beast: 3 ass **6** donkey
father: 4 Beor

balance
4 rest **5** level, scale, weigh **6** adjust,
excess, make up, offset, set off, square,
stasis **7** harmony, remains, remnant,
residue **8** atone for, equalize, outweigh,
residual, residuum, symmetry
9 composure, congruity, equipoise,
harmonize, remainder, stability
10 compensate, counteract, difference,
equanimity, neutralize, proportion,
steadiness **11** consistency, countervail,
equilibrium, self-control **12** counterpoise

balanced
4 fair **5** equal **6** offset, stable, steady

7 equable, weighed 9 equitable, impartial
10 evenhanded, harmonized, stabilized

balcony
6 piazza 7 catwalk, gallery 8 platform
9 mezzanine
section: 4 loge

bald
4 bare, nude 5 blunt, naked, plain, stark
6 barren, severe, shaven, smooth
8 glabrous, hairless, palpable, treeless
9 depilated, unadorned, uncovered
10 deforested, forthright 11 undisguised,
unvarnished

baldachin
4 silk 6 canopy, fabric

Balder, Baldur
father: 4 Odin
mother: 5 Frigg 6 Frigga
slayer: 3 Höd 4 Hoth, Loke, Loki
5 Hoder, Hothr
wife: 5 Nanna

balderdash
3 rot 4 bosh, bull, bunk 5 bilge, crock,
hooey 6 blague, bunkum, drivel
7 baloney, eyewash, garbage, hogwash,
palaver, rubbish, twaddle 8 buncombe,
claptrap, malarkey, nonsense, tommyrot
9 poppycock 10 tomfoolery 11 foolishness
13 horsefeathers

bald-faced
4 bold 6 arrant, brazen 7 blatant, defiant
8 impudent, insolent 9 audacious,
shameless, unabashed 11 impertinent

baldness
8 alopecia 12 hairlessness

baldpate
7 widgeon 8 skinhead

Baldwin, James
essay: 17 Nobody Knows My Name,
Notes of a Native Son
novel: 12 Fire Next Time (The)
13 Giovanni's Room 14 Another Country
21 Go Tell It on the Mountain
play: 21 Blues for Mister Charlie

balefire
6 beacon 9 watchfire

baleful
4 dire, evil 6 deadly, malign 7 direful,
fateful, harmful, hostile, malefic, ominous
8 menacing, sinister
9 ill-boding, ill-omened, malignant
10 maleficent, malevolent, pernicious
11 apocalyptic, threatening 12 unpropitious

balk
3 bar, gag, jib, shy 4 beam, dash, foil, ruin
5 block, check, demur, stall 6 baffle,
boggle, desist, flinch, hinder, plank, rafter,
refuse, thwart 7 prevent, scruple, stumble
8 hang back, hesitate, obstruct 9 frustrate,
hindrance 10 circumvent, disappoint

balky
5 loath 6 averse, ornery, mulish, unruly
7 froward, restive, wayward, willful
8 contrary, hesitant, perverse
9 immovable, obstinate, reluctant, stubborn
10 unreliable 11 intractable, wrongheaded
12 cross-grained, recalcitrant
13 uncooperative, unpredictable

ball
3 orb, wad 4 prom 5 dance, globe, round
6 sphere 8 spheroid
batted high: 3 fly
batted straight: 5 liner
of thread or yarn: 4 clew
ornamental: 6 pom-pom, pompon
tiny: 7 globule

ballad
3 lay 4 poem, song
singer: 8 minstrel 10 troubadour

ballast
4 load 5 poise 6 steady 7 balance, freight
8 balancer 9 stabilize 10 dead weight,
stabilizer, weigh down 12 counterpoise
13 counterweight

ballerina
6 dancer 8 coryphée, danseuse 9 toe
dancer 11 dancing girl
see **dancer**

ballet
4 Agon 6 Apollo, Giselle, Jewels, Sylvia
7 Orpheus 8 Bayadère (La), Coppélia,
Firebird (The), Raimonda, Raymonda,
Swan Lake, Sylphide (La) 9 Fancy Free,
Petrushka, Sylphides (Les) 10 Don
Quixote, Nutcracker (The), Petrouchka
12 Rite of Spring (The)
costume: 4 tutu 6 tights 7 leotard
dancer: 7 danseur 8 coryphée, danseuse
9 ballerina
for two: 9 pas de deux
handrail: 5 barre
jump: 4 jeté 9 entrechat
knee bend: 4 plié
position: 6 pointe 8 attitude 9 arabesque
step: 3 pas 8 glissade
turn: 6 chaîné 9 pirouette

ball game
see at **game**

Ballo in Maschera composer
5 Verdi (Giuseppe)

balloon sail
9 spinnaker

ball-shaped
7 globoid, globose 8 globular, spheroid
9 globulous, spherical

ball up
4 clew, daze 5 addle 6 fuddle, jumble,
muddle, puzzle, tangle 7 confuse, fluster
8 befuddle, bewilder, bollix up, confound,
distract, throw off 9 disorient

ballyhoo
4 hype, tout 6 blazon, herald, hoopla,
hubbub, tumult 7 promote, trumpet
8 brouhaha 9 commotion, publicity
12 extravaganza

balm
4 lull 5 aroma, cream, quiet, salve, scent,
spice 6 chrism, relief, remedy, solace
7 anodyne, bouquet, comfort, incense,
perfume, soother, unction, unguent
8 easement, ointment 9 emollient,
fragrance, redolence 10 palliative
11 consolation, restorative

balmacaan
8 overcoat

balm of Gilead
6 poplar 8 restorer 9 balsam fir, soother
11 restorative 12 balsam poplar

balmy
4 calm, daft, mild, nuts, soft 5 crazy, loony,
nutty, potty, silly, sweet, wacky 6 gentle,
insane, smooth 7 cracked, foolish, lenient,
summery 8 aromatic, deranged, fragrant,
perfumed, peaceful, pleasant, pleasing,
redolent, soothing, tropical 9 agreeable,
ambrosial, temperate

baloney
3 rot 4 bosh, bull, bunk 5 bilge, hokum,
hooey 6 bunkum, humbug 7 hogwash,
rubbish 8 buncombe, claptrap, nonsense
9 poppycock 10 balderdash
11 foolishness

balsam poplar
9 tacamahac 12 balm of Gilead

Balthazar's gift
5 myrrh

Baltic
native: 4 Lett 7 Latvian 8 Estonian
10 Lithuanian
state: 6 Latvia 7 Estonia 9 Lithuania

Baltic native
4 Lett, Sorb, Wend 7 Latvian 8 Estonian,
Prussian 10 Lithuanian

balustrade
4 rail 5 fence 7 railing 8 banister, handrail

Balzac character
4 Pons (Cousin) 5 Bette (Cousin) 6 Goriot
(Père), Vidocq 7 Chabert (Colonel),
Eugénie (Grandet), Grandet, Vautrin
8 Rubempré (Lucien de) 9 Birotteau,
Rastignac (Eugène de) 13 Henri de
Marsay

Bambi author
6 Salten (Felix)

bambino
3 kid, tot 4 babe, baby, tyke 5 bairn, child
6 cherub, Christ, infant, moppet, nipper
7 toddler

bamboozle
3 con 4 bilk, dupe, fool, gull, hoax, scam
5 stump, trick 6 baffle, befool, diddle,
puzzle 7 chicane, confuse, deceive,
defraud, mislead, perplex, swindle
8 befuddle, confound, flimflam, hoodwink,
throw off 9 frustrate 11 hornswoggle

ban
3 bar 5 curse, taboo 6 enjoin, forbid,
outlaw 7 censure, exclude 8 anathema,
prohibit, suppress 9 damnation, interdict,
proscribe 10 injunction 11 forbiddance,
malediction, prohibition, suppression
12 denunciation, interdiction, proscription

Ban
ally: 6 Arthur
son: 8 Lancelot

banal
4 blah, dull, flat 5 bland, corny, ho-hum,
tired, trite, usual, vapid 6 common, jejune,
stupid 7 clichéd, humdrum, insipid,
prosaic, sapless, trivial 8 ordinary,
9 hackneyed, quotidian, wearisome
10 namby-pamby, pedestrian, uninspired,
wishy-washy 11 commonplace

banality
5 ennui 6 cliché, old saw, truism
7 bromide, inanity, old song 8 chestnut,
monotony, prosaism 9 platitude
10 dreariness, shibboleth, triviality
11 commonplace, old chestnut,
tediousness

banausic
4 blah, drab, dull, poky 6 dreary, earthy,
stodgy 7 humdrum, mundane, routine,

secular, sensual, tedious, worldly
8 everyday, material, plodding, temporal, workaday **9** practical, pragmatic **10** monotonous, pedestrian **11** acquisitive, utilitarian **13** materialistic, uninteresting

band
4 belt, bevy, club, crew, gang, gird, sash, tape **5** bunch, corps, covey, group, horde, party, strap, strip, troop, unite **6** concur, fillet, girdle, league, outfit, ribbon, team up, troupe **7** cluster, combine, company, coterie **8** cincture, engirdle, ensemble, symphony **9** cooperate, orchestra **10** federation
Mexican: 8 mariachi
neck: 8 torque
small: 5 combo

bandage
4 bind **5** cover, dress, gauze, truss **6** swathe **7** plaster, swaddle **8** compress, dressing

bandanna
8 babushka, kerchief **9** headscarf **11** neckerchief

bandeau
3 bra **5** strip **6** fillet, ribbon, stripe **7** tube top **8** swimwear **9** brassiere

banderilla
4 dart

banderole
4 flag, jack **6** banner, burgee, colors, ensign, pennon, scroll **7** pennant **8** bannerol, standard, streamer

bandicoot
3 rat

bandit
6 outlaw, raider, robber, sacker **7** brigand, cateran, forager, ravager **8** marauder, pillager **9** cutthroat, desperado, holdup man, plunderer **10** freebooter, highwayman **11** bushwhacker

bandleader
7 maestro **9** conductor

bandolier
4 belt, sash

bandwagon
3 fad **4** chic, mode, rage **5** craze, style, trend, vogue **7** fashion

bandy
3 bat **4** flip, swap, toss **5** argue, bowed **6** banter **7** discuss, shuffle **8** exchange **9** bowlegged, pass about **11** interchange

bane
3 woe **4** pest, ruin **5** curse, death, venom, virus **6** blight, burden, plague, poison **7** bugaboo, bugbear, scourge, torment, undoing **8** anathema, calamity, downfall, nuisance **9** bête noire, contagion, destroyer, ruination **10** affliction, pestilence **11** destruction

baneful
4 dire, evil **5** fatal **6** deadly **7** fateful, harmful, hurtful, malefic, noxious, ominous **9** ill-boding, ill-omened, injurious, malignant, pestilent, unhealthy **10** disastrous, pernicious **11** apocalyptic, deleterious, pestiferous, threatening **12** pestilential, unpropitious

bang
3 bat, box, hit, pop, rap **4** bash, beat, belt, blow, boom, bump, clap, peal, push, rape, shot, slam, sock, wham, whop **5** blast, burst, crack, crash, noise, pound, punch, smack, smash, sound, vigor, whack **6** fringe, report, strike, thrill, wallop **7** collide, exactly, resound **8** smack-dab, squarely **9** explosion **10** detonation

banger
7 athlete, sausage

Bangkok native
4 Thai

Bangladesh
capital: 5 Dacca, Dhaka
city: 6 Khulna **10** Chittagong
former name: 6 Bengal
language: 7 Bengali
monetary unit: 4 taka
neighbor: 5 Burma, India **7** Myanmar
river: 5 Padma **6** Ganges, Jamuna **11** Brahmaputra

bangle
4 disk **5** charm **6** anklet, bauble **7** pendant, trinket **8** bracelet, wristlet

bang-up
3 ace **4** fine **5** dandy, primo, super **6** far-out, superb **7** capital **8** champion, fabulous, five-star, splendid, top-notch **9** excellent, first-rate **10** first-class **11** spectacular

banish
3 ban **4** oust **5** debar, eject, evict, exile, expel **6** deport, dispel, put out, run out **7** cast out, dismiss, exclude, shut out, turn out **8** drive out, relegate, send away, transport **9** discharge, ostracize, rusticate **10** expatriate **13** excommunicate

banishment
5 exile 7 banning 8 eviction 9 discharge,
expulsion, ostracism 10 dispelling,
relegation 11 deportation, dissolution
12 displacement

banister
3 bar 4 rail 7 railing 10 balustrade

bank
3 row 4 edge, heap, hill, mass, pile, rank,
save, tier, tilt 5 amass, array, beach, coast,
group, hoard, levee, mound, pitch, shore,
slope, stack, stash 6 coffer, dealer, invest,
margin, rivage, strand 7 deposit, incline,
lay away, pyramid 8 lakeside, lay aside,
salt away, seafront, set aside, sock away,
squirrel, treasury 9 riverside 10 repository,
storehouse 11 credit union 12 squirrel
away

bank on
5 trust 7 believe

bankroll
4 back, fund 5 endow, funds, stake 6 pay
for 7 capital, finance, sponsor, support
9 grubstake, subsidize 10 capitalize,
underwrite

bankrupt
4 bare, bust, do in, ruin 5 break, drain,
empty, strip, spent, use up, wreck
6 broken, divest, failed, fold up 7 deplete,
deprive, exhaust, lacking, sterile
8 depleted, indebted 9 destitute,
exhausted, pauperize, penniless
10 impoverish 12 impoverished

bankruptcy
4 lack, ruin 6 penury 7 failure 9 depletion,
ruination, sterility, total loss 10 barrenness,
exhaustion, insolvency 11 destitution,
liquidation

banned
5 taboo 6 barred 7 illegal, illicit, tabooed
8 enjoined, verboten 9 forbidden
10 contraband, disallowed, prohibited,
proscribed 11 interdicted

banner
4 flag, jack 6 burgee, ensign, pennon
7 pendant, pennant 8 banderol, gonfalon,
standard, streamer 9 banderole
Roman: 7 labarum 8 vexillum

bannerol
see banderole

banquet
4 feed 5 feast 6 dinner, regale, repast,
spread

banquette
4 seat, sofa 5 bench, shelf 8 platform,
sidewalk

Banquo
5 ghost
murderer: 7 Macbeth

banshee
6 keener, wailer

bantam
3 wee 4 arch, fowl, mini, pert, runt, tiny
5 dwarf, saucy, small 6 cheeky, little, petite
8 insolent, malapert 9 combative,
undersize 10 diminutive, undersized

banter
3 fun, kid, rag, rib, wit 4 fool, jest, jive,
joke, josh, razz 5 chaff, dally, jolly, tease
7 jesting, joshing, kidding, mockery,
ragging, razzing, ribbing, teasing
8 backchat, back talk, badinage, challenge,
chitchat, drollery, exchange, repartee
9 small talk 10 persiflage, pleasantry
11 give-and-take

bantling
4 babe, baby 5 bairn 6 infant 7 bambino,
newborn, papoose

baptize
3 dip, dub 4 call, name, soak 5 title
6 anoint, douse, drench, purify 7 asperse,
cleanse, entitle, immerse 8 christen,
dedicate, initiate, sprinkle 9 designate
10 consecrate, denominate, regenerate

bar
3 ban, dam, pub, rod, tap 4 curb, dive,
halt, save, stop 5 block, court, estop, ingot,
limit, stick, strip 6 bistro, except, impede,
lounge, saloon, tavern 7 barrier, cantina,
delimit, exclude, gin mill, rule out, taproom
8 alehouse, blockade, count out, obstacle,
obstruct, restrict, tribunal 9 barricade,
eliminate, honky-tonk, nightclub, roadhouse
11 obstruction, rathskeller 12 circumscribe,
watering hole
type: 3 raw 4 cash, fern, open, roll, tiki
6 sports

barb
3 dig 4 dart, hook 5 quill, shaft, thorn

Barbados
capital: 10 Bridgetown
language: 7 English
location: 10 West Indies
monetary unit: 6 dollar

barbarian
3 Hun 4 Goth, lout, rude, wild 5 beast,

crude, brute **6** savage, Vandal **7** lowbrow, uncouth **8** Visigoth **9** foreigner, Ostrogoth, primitive **10** uncultured **11** uncivilized **12** uncultivated

barbaric
4 wild **5** crude **6** brutal, coarse, rough, savage, beastly, boorish, brutish, loutish, uncouth **8** churlish **9** atrocious, monstrous, primitive, unrefined **11** uncivilized

barbarism
8 malaprop, rudeness, solecism **9** vulgarism, vulgarity **10** coarseness, corruption **11** impropriety, malapropism **12** backwardness, unseemliness

barbarity
7 cruelty **8** atrocity, savagery **9** brutality, depravity **10** inhumanity, savageness **11** viciousness **12** ruthlessness **13** monstrousness

barbarous
4 base, fell, grim, rude, vile, wild **5** cruel, harsh **6** brutal, fierce, Gothic, savage, unholy, vulgar, wicked **7** brutish, Hunnish, inhuman, lowbrow, uncivil, ungodly, vicious, wolfish **8** backward, fiendish, inhumane, ruthless, sadistic **9** benighted, ferocious, graceless, heartless, merciless, monstrous, primitive, tasteless, truculent **10** abominable, outlandish, outrageous, philistine, unmerciful **11** unchristian, uncivilized **12** uncultivated

Barbary state
5 Tunis **7** Algiers, Morocco, Tripoli

barbecue
5 grill, roast **7** cookout, roaster

barber
3 bob, cut **4** clip, crop, trim **5** shave, shear **6** shaver **7** clipper, cropper **8** coiffeur **9** coiffeuse **10** beautician, haircutter **11** hairdresser, hair stylist

Barber of Seville
author: **12** Beaumarchais (Pierre-Augustin)
character: **6** Figaro, Rosina, Rosine **7** Bartolo, Basilio **8** Almaviva, Bartholo
composer: **7** Rossini (Gioacchino) **9** Paisiello (Giovanni)

bard
4 muse, poet, scop **5** skald **8** jongleur, minstrel **9** balladist **10** Parnassian, troubadour

Bard of Avon
11 Shakespeare (William)

bare
4 bald, mere, nude, void **5** empty, naked, shorn, stark, strip **6** barren, denude, devoid, expose, peeled, reveal, unclad, unveil, vacant **7** denuded, disrobe, emptied, exposed, uncover **8** bankrupt, disclose, stripped **9** unclothed, uncovered, undressed

barefaced
4 bald, bold, open **5** blunt, naked **6** arrant, brassy, brazen **7** blatant, glaring, obvious **8** flagrant, impudent, overbold **9** audacious, beardless, shameless, unabashed **10** unblushing **11** temerarious, unconcealed

barefoot
6 unshod **8** shoeless **9** discalced

bareheaded
7 hatless

barely
4 just **6** hardly, scarce **7** faintly **8** meagerly, scarcely

bargain
3 buy **4** bond, deal, pact, swap **5** agree, steal, trade, truck, value **6** barter, confer, dicker, haggle, higgle, palter, pledge **7** chaffer, compact, savings, traffic **8** closeout, contract, covenant, exchange, giveaway, good deal, huckster, markdown, transact **9** agreement, good value, negotiate, reduction **10** compromise, convention, loss leader, pennyworth **11** arrangement, transaction **13** understanding

barge
4 scow **5** clump, stump **6** lumber **7** galumph, stumble

baritone
4 Prey (Hermann) **5** Gobbi (Tito) **6** Bailey (Norman), London (George), Milnes (Sherrill), Terfel (Bryn), Warren (Leonard) **7** Hampson (Thomas), MacNeil (Cornell), Merrill (Robert), Tibbett (Lawrence) **8** Raimondi (Ruggero), Warfield (William)

bark
3 arf, bay, yap, yip **4** snap, woof, yelp **5** snarl **6** bellow

barkeeper
see **bartender**

barker
6 hawker 8 pitchman

Barlow epic
9 Columbiad

barman
see **bartender**

Barmecidal
5 empty, false 6 unreal 7 fictive
8 apparent, illusive, illusory 9 imaginary
10 chimerical, ostensible 13 insubstantial

barn
6 stable
area of: 4 loft 7 hayloft

barnacle
5 leech 7 sponger 8 hanger-on, nuisance,
parasite 9 dependent, free rider
10 crustacean, freeloader

barnstorm
8 campaign

Barnum
elephant: 5 Jumbo
midget: 8 Tom Thumb
partner: 6 Bailey

barnyard
4 foul, rude 5 crass, crude, dirty, nasty
6 coarse, earthy, filthy, ribald, smutty,
vulgar 7 obscene, raunchy, uncouth
8 indecent 9 tasteless 10 indelicate
12 scatological

baron
4 lord, peer 5 mogul, noble 6 tycoon
7 kingpin, magnate 8 overlord
13 industrialist

baronial
5 ample, grand, noble 6 august, lordly
7 stately 8 imposing, majestic, princely
9 grandiose 10 commanding, impressive
11 magnificent, resplendent

baroque
6 florid, ornate, rococo 7 complex
8 dramatic 9 excessive, grotesque,
irregular 10 flamboyant, ornamented
11 embellished, extravagant 12 ostentatious 13 overdecorated

Baroque
architect: 4 Wren (Christopher) 7 Bernini
(Gian Lorenzo), Guarini (Guarino),
Maderno (Carlo) 9 Borromini (Francesco)
composer: 4 Bach (Johann Sebastian)
5 Lully (Jean-Baptiste) 6 Handel (George
Frideric), Rameau (Jean-Philippe), Schütz

(Heinrich) 7 Corelli (Arcangelo), Purcell
(Henry), Vivaldi (Antonio) 8 Albinoni
(Tommaso), Couperin (François), Telemann
(Georg Philipp) 9 Pachelbel (Johann),
Scarlatti (Alessandro, Domenico)
10 Monteverdi (Claudio)
painter: 4 Hals (Frans) 5 Steen (Jan)
6 Claude (Lorrain), Rubens (Peter Paul)
7 El Greco, Holbein (Hans), Poussin
(Nicolas), Van Dyck (Anthony), Vermeer
(Jan) 8 Carracci (Agostino, Annibale,
Lodovico), Ter Borch (Gerard)
9 Rembrandt (van Rijn), Velázquez (Diego)
10 Caravaggio
sculptor: 5 Puget (Pierre) 7 Bernini (Gian
Lorenzo), Coustou (Guillaume, Nicholas),
Pigalle (Jean-Baptiste) 8 Coysevox
(Antoine), Girardon (François)

barrack
4 jeer, root 5 cheer, scoff, taunt 6 billet,
casern, deride, hector 7 caserne
8 quarters

barrage
3 dam 4 fire, hail, mass 5 blitz, burst,
salvo, storm, surge 6 deluge, shower,
stream, volley 7 gunfire, torrent
8 drumfire, shelling 9 broadside,
cannonade, crossfire, fusillade, onslaught
11 bombardment

barranca
4 bank 5 bluff, gully 6 arroyo

barrel
3 keg, tun, vat 4 butt, cask, drum, peck,
race, rush, tear 5 hurry 6 firkin, hasten
8 hogshead
maker: 6 cooper
part: 4 hoop 5 stave
stopper: 4 bung
support: 6 gantry

barrelhouse
4 dive 5 hurry, joint 7 hangout 9 honky-
tonk

barren
3 dry 4 arid, bare, poor 5 bleak, empty,
stark, stony, waste 6 desert, devoid, effete,
futile, fallow, wanting 7 badland, lacking,
parched, sterile 8 desolate, heirless,
impotent 9 childless, fruitless, infertile,
unbearing, unfertile, wasteland
10 unfruitful, untillable 11 unrewarding
12 hardscrabble, unproductive, unprofitable

barricade
5 block, fence 7 barrier 8 blockade
9 roadblock
of trees: 6 abatis

Barrie character
4 John, Nana 5 Peter, Tommy, Wendy
7 Michael 8 Crichton 9 Tiger Lily 10 Tinker
Bell 11 Captain Hook

barrier
see **barricade**

barring
3 but 4 save 6 bating, except, saving
7 besides, without 9 aside from, excluding,
excepting, outside of 11 exclusive of

barrio
4 slum, turf, ward 6 ghetto 7 quarter,
section 8 district, precinct 12 neighborhood

barrister
6 lawyer 7 counsel 8 advocate,
attorney 9 counselor

barroom
3 pub 6 lounge, saloon, tavern 7 gin mill,
rum room, taproom 8 alehouse, beer hall,
dramshop, drinkery, groggery, grogshop
9 beer joint, roadhouse 12 watering hole

bartender
7 tapster 8 boniface 10 mixologist
12 saloonkeeper

barter
4 swap 5 trade, truck 7 bargain, traffic
8 exchange

Bartered Bride composer
7 Smetana (Bedrich)

Barth novel
7 Chimera 12 Giles Goat-Boy 13 Sot-
Weed Factor (The)

Baruch
father: 6 Neriah, Zabbai
occupation: 6 scribe

basal
5 basic, vital 6 bottom, lowest 7 minimal,
primary, radical 8 simplest 9 beginning,
essential, undermost 10 bottommost,
elementary, primordial, underlying
11 fundamental, preliminary, rudimentary
12 foundational

base
3 bad, bed, fix, key, low 4 camp, evil, foot,
foul, home, mean, poor, post, prop, rest,
root, seat, site, ugly, vile 5 build, cheap,
dirty, found, hinge, lousy, lowly, nadir, plant,
set up, sorry, stand 6 bottom, coarse,
common, depend, derive, filthy, ground,
humble, menial, origin, paltry, scurvy,
shoddy, sleazy, sordid, source, trashy,
wicked 7 bedrock, caitiff, essence, footing,

ignoble, lowborn, low-down, pitiful, servile,
squalid, support 8 beggarly, buttress,
cowardly, garrison, inferior, pedestal,
plebeian, recreant, unwashed, unworthy,
wretched 9 construct, dastardly,
degrading, establish, framework,
loathsome, low-minded, predicate, principle
10 abominable, despicable, foundation,
groundwork, substratum, unennobled
11 disgraceful, humiliating, ignominious
12 contemptible, meanspirited,
substructure, underpinning

baseball
abbreviation: 3 ERA, HSP, LOB, MVP,
PCT, RBI
reputed founder: 9 Doubleday (Abner)
glove: 4 mitt
official: 3 ump 6 umpire
pitch: 4 drop, heat 5 curve, smoke
6 change, heater, sinker, slider, slurve
7 spitter 8 change-up, fadeaway, fastball,
fork ball, knuckler, palm ball, spitball
9 brushback, screwball 11 knuckleball
12 change of pace, knuckle curve
player: 6 batter 7 baseman, catcher,
fielder, pitcher 9 infielder, shortstop
10 outfielder 11 left fielder 12 right fielder
13 center fielder
term: 3 bag, bat, box, fan, fly, out, run, tag,
tap, tip 4 balk, ball, base, bean, bunt,
cage, deck, foul, hook, line, mitt, pill, pole,
save, walk 5 alley, apple, bench, bloop,
clout, count, drive, error, flare, fungo, glove,
homer, liner, mound, pop-up, slide, swing
6 assist, clutch, double, dugout, groove,
ground, inning, inside, pop fly, pop-out,
powder, putout, rubber, runner, single,
strike, triple, windup 7 battery, blooper,
bullpen, cleanup, diamond, floater, fly ball,
home run, infield, manager, outside, pickoff,
rhubarb, sidearm, squeeze, stretch
8 baseline, beanball, delivery, foul ball,
grounder, keystone, outfield, pinch-hit,
rosin bag, southpaw 9 full count, home
plate, hot corner, line drive, sacrifice,
strikeout, two-bagger 10 double play,
frozen rope, ground ball, scratch hit, strike
zone 11 knuckleball, pinch hitter, squeeze
play, three-bagger

baseballer
3 Ott (Mel) 4 Bell (George), Cobb (Ty),
Cone (David), Dean (Dizzy), Fisk (Carlton),
Ford (Whitey), Foxx (Jimmy), Kaat (Jim),
Mays (Willie), Rice (Jim), Rose (Pete), Ruth
(Babe), Ryan (Nolan), Sosa (Sammy)
5 Aaron (Henry), Anson (Cap), Banks
(Ernie), Belle (Albert), Bench (Johnny),
Berra (Yogi), Boggs (Wade), Bonds (Barry),

Brett (George), Brock (Lou), Brown (Kevin), Carew (Rod), Clark (Will), Damon (Johnny), Davis (Mark), Green (Shawn), Grove (Lefty), Gwynn (Tony), Henke (Tom), Jeter (Derek), Kiner (Ralph), Maris (Roger), Mauer (Joe), Paige (Satchel), Perez (Tony), Perry (Gaylord), Smith (Lee), Spahn (Warren), Staub (Rusty), Tiant (Luis), Viola (Frank), Weeks (Rickie), Young (Cy), Yount (Robin) **6** Dawson (Andre), Feller (Bob), Foster (George), Franco (John), Garvey (Steve), Gehrig (Lou), Gibson (Bob, Josh, Kirk), Gooden (Dwight), Herzog (Whitey), Hunter (Catfish), Koufax (Sandy), Lajoie (Nap), Maddux (Greg), Mantle (Mickey), Morgan (Joe), Murphy (Dale), Murray (Eddie), Musial (Stan), Palmer (Jim), Piazza (Mike), Raines (Tim), Ripken (Cal), Seaver (Tom), Sisler (George), Sutter (Bruce), Sutton (Don), Thomas (Frank), Vaughn (Mo), Wagner (Honus), Walker (Larry) **7** Bagwell (Jeff), Canseco (José), Carlton (Steve), Clemens (Roger), Coleman (Vince), Collins (Eddie), Delgado (Carlos), Fingers (Rollie), Griffey (Ken), Hornsby (Roger), Hubbell (Carl), Jackson (Joe, Reggie), Johnson (Randy, Walter), Justice (David), Leonard (Buck), McGwire (Mark), Mondesi (Raul), Puckett (Kirby), Reardon (Jeff), Schmidt (Mike), Simmons (Al), Speaker (Tris) **8** Anderson (Sparky), Blyleven (Bert), Clemente (Roberto), DiMaggio (Joe), Guerrero (Vladimir), Martinez (Pedro), Mitchell (Kevin), Righetti (Dave), Robinson (Brooks, Frank, Jackie), Williams (Bernie, Ted), Winfield (Dave) **9** Alexander (Grover), Eckersley (Dennis), Gehringer (Charlie), Greenberg (Hank), Henderson (Rickey), Hernandez (Willie), Hershiser (Orel), Killebrew (Harmon), Mathewson (Christy), Mattingly (Don), Rodriguez (Alex), Sheffield (Gary) **10** Campanella (Roy), Conigliaro (Tony), Strawberry (Darryl), Valenzuela (Fernando) **11** Garciaparra (Nomar), Yastrzemski (Carl)

baseball team
  see **American League; National League**

baseboard
  7 molding **8** skirting

baseless
  4 idle, thin, vain **5** empty, false, wrong
  6 feeble, flimsy **9** frivolous, pointless,
  senseless, unfounded, untenable
  10 fallacious, gratuitous, groundless,
  inadequate, incredible, ungrounded
  11 uncalled-for, unconfirmed, unnecessary,
  unsupported, unsustained, unwarranted

12 indefensible, contemptible,
unpersuasive **13** unjustifiable

basement
  6 bottom, cellar, ground **7** bedrock
  10 foundation, groundwork, substratum
  12 substructure

base on balls
  4 walk

bash
  3 bat, hit **4** belt, blow, fete, gala, slam,
  whop **5** blast, crack, crash, party, pound,
  smack, smash, thump, whack **6** attack,
  pummel, soiree, strike, wallop **7** blowout,
  shindig **8** wingding

Bashemath
  father: **7** Ishmael
  husband: **4** Esau
  sister: **8** Nebaioth

bashful
  3 coy, shy **5** chary, mousy, timid
  6 demure, modest, nervous **7** abashed
  8 blushing, reserved, retiring, timorous
  9 diffident, reluctant, shrinking, unassured
  11 unassertive

basic
  3 key **4** main **5** chief **6** bottom **7** capital,
  central, element, minimum, primary, radical
  8 cardinal, inherent, rudiment **9** beginning,
  elemental, essential, intrinsic, primitive,
  principal, unadorned **10** elementary,
  underlying **11** fundamental **12** foundational

basically
  6 au fond, mainly, mostly **7** at heart,
  chiefly, firstly, overall **8** in effect
  9 generally, in essence, primarily

basic point
  4 crux, gist, pith **5** heart **6** kernel
  7 essence

basilica
  6 church **7** minster **9** cathedral

basin
  3 dip, pan, sag **4** bowl, sink **6** cirque,
  hollow **7** sinkage **8** sinkhole, washbowl
  9 concavity **10** depression
  liturgical: **5** stoup **7** piscina

basis
  3 bed **4** crux, root, seat, seed **5** heart,
  nexus **6** bottom, ground, reason
  7 bedrock, essence, footing, grounds,
  nucleus, premise, support, warrant
  9 authority, postulate, principle
  10 assumption, foundation, groundwork,

substratum **11** fundamental, presumption **12** substructure, underpinning **13** justification

bask
3 sun **4** loll **5** glory, revel, relax **6** lounge, wallow, welter **7** indulge **8** sunbathe **9** luxuriate

basket
6 bushel, gabion **7** pannier
angler's: **5** creel

basketball
inventor: **8** Naismith (James)
official: **6** umpire **7** referee
player: **5** cager, guard **6** center **7** forward **8** hoopster, swingman **10** point guard
team: **4** five **5** quintet
term: **3** gun, jam, key **4** cage, dunk, pass **5** board, lay-up, press, shoot, tip-in **6** freeze, tap-off, tip-off, travel **7** dribble, keyhole, rebound, throw-in, time-out **8** alley-oop, jump ball, slam dunk **9** backboard, backcourt, field goal, free throw **11** ball control

basketballer
3 Bol (Manute) **4** Bird (Larry), Ming (Yao), Nash (Steve), Redd (Michael), Reed (Willis), West (Jerry, Mark) **5** Allen (Ray), Barry (Rick), Brand (Elton), Cousy (Bob), Davis (Baron), Ewing (Patrick), Mikan (George), O'Neal (Shaquille), Price (Mark) **6** Baylor (Elgin), Blount (Mark), Boozer (Carlos), Bryant (Kobe), Carter (Vince), Cowens (Dave), Duncan (Tim), Erving (Julius), Gervin (George), Jordan (Michael), Malone (Jeff, Karl, Moses), McAdoo (Bob), McHale (Kevin), Miller (Brad, Reggie), Parish (Robert), Pierce (Paul, Ricky), Pippin (Scottie), Skiles (Scott), Thomas (Kenny), Thorpe (Otis), Walton (Bill), Worthy (James) **7** Barkley (Charles), Billups (Chauncey), Dawkins (Darryl), Dampier (Erick), Duncan (Tim), Edwards (James), Frazier (Walt), Garnett (Kevin), Hilario (Nene), Houston (Allan), Iverson (Allen), Jackson (Lauren), Jamison (Antawn), Johnson (Magic), McGrady (Tracy), Russell (Bill), Rollins (Tree), Taurasi (Diana), Wallace (Ben), Wilkins (Dominique) **8** Auerbach (Red), Cardinal (Brian), Havlicek (John), Olajuwon (Akeem), Magloire (Jamaal), Nowitzki (Dirk), Randolph (Zach), Robinson (David), Stockton (John), Thompson (Tina), Williams (Buck) **9** Donaldson (James), Ferdinand (Marie), Holdsclaw (Chamique), Robertson (Oscar) **10** Stojakovic

(Predrag), Williamson (Corliss) **11** Abdul-Jabbar (Kareem), Chamberlain (Wilt)

Basmath's father
7 Solomon

Basque
6 bodice
cap: **5** beret
game: **6** pelota **7** jai alai
mountains: **8** Pyrenees
province: **5** Alava **7** Vizcaya **9** Guipúzcoa

bass
3 low **4** deep **6** singer **8** cabrilla
famous: **5** Hines (Jerome), Pinza (Ezio), Ramey (Samuel), Siepi (Cesare), Tozzi (Giorgio) **6** Hotter (Hans), London (George), Morris (James) **7** Plishka (Paul), Robeson (Paul), Talvela (Martti) **8** Flagello (Ezio), Ghiaurov (Nicolai), Raimondi (Ruggero) **9** Chaliapin (Fyodor), Christoff (Boris)

Bassanio's beloved
6 Portia

bassinet
6 cradle, basket

bastard
5 cross **6** by-blow, hybrid **7** mongrel **9** love child **12** natural child
combining form: **4** noth **5** notho

bastardize
4 warp **5** taint **6** debase, defile **7** corrupt, debauch, degrade, deprave, pervert, pollute, vitiate **9** brutalize **10** adulterate, bestialize, demoralize, depreciate **11** contaminate

baste
3 sew **4** beat, drub, lash, mill, pelt, rail, tack, whip **5** paste, scold **6** batter, berate, larrup, pummel, revile, stitch, thrash, wallop **7** bawl out, belabor, chew out, clobber, moisten, tell off, trounce, upbraid **8** bless out, chastise **9** dress down **10** tongue-lash

bastille
4 jail **6** prison **9** bridewell

bastinado
3 bat, rod **4** bash, beat, blow, cane, club **5** birch, crack, pound, smack, smash, stick, whack **6** cudgel, paddle, strike, switch, thwack, wallop **8** bludgeon **9** truncheon

bastion
5 tower **7** bulwark, citadel, parapet, rampart, redoubt **8** fastness, fortress **10** breastwork, stronghold **13** fortification

bat
3 bag, bop, hag 4 belt, biff, blow, bust, club, slam, sock, swat, whop, wink 5 biddy, blink, crone, smack 6 cudgel, thwack 7 meander 8 bludgeon 9 flying fox, truncheon 10 knobkerrie, shillelagh 11 pipistrelle

batch
3 lot, set 5 array, bunch, clump, crowd, group 6 bundle, clutch, parcel 7 cluster 8 quantity, shipment 10 assemblage, assortment, collection 11 aggregation 12 accumulation

bate
3 bar 4 omit 5 check 6 deduct, except, reduce 7 cut back, exclude, suspend 8 diminish, moderate, restrain, subtract

bateau
4 boat, dory 5 craft, skiff 6 dinghy, launch 7 shallop

bath
3 spa, tub 4 soak, wash 5 hydro, wells 6 shower 7 springs 8 ablution 13 watering place

bathe
3 dip, lap, lip, sop, tub, wet 4 bask, lave, soak, soap, swim, wash 5 clean, douse, flood, rinse, flush, souse, steep 6 shower 7 cleanse, immerse, pervade, suffuse 8 irrigate

bathetic
5 mushy, soppy, stale, tired, trite 6 drippy 7 clichéd, cloying, gushing, maudlin, mawkish 9 emotional, hackneyed, schmaltzy 10 lachrymose 11 commonplace, sentimental, stereotyped, tearjerking 13 anticlimactic, overemotional, stereotypical

bathhouse
5 sauna 6 cabana

bathing suit
6 bikini, trunks 7 bandeau, maillot

bathos
7 letdown 8 banality, comedown 9 triteness 10 anticlimax

bathroom
3 loo 4 john 5 privy 6 toilet 8 lavatory, outhouse

Bathsheba
father: 5 Eliam
husband: 5 David, Uriah
son: 7 Solomon

bathtub gin
5 hooch 6 rotgut 7 bootleg 8 homebrew 9 moonshine 11 mountain dew

Batman creator
4 Kane (Bob)

baton
3 rod 4 club, mace, wand 5 billy, staff, stick 6 cudgel 7 war club 8 bludgeon 9 billy club, truncheon 10 nightstick

_____ Bator
4 Ulan

batrachian
4 frog, toad 9 amphibian

battalion
4 army, host, unit 5 force, horde 6 legion, throng, troops 8 squadron 10 contingent, detachment

batter
4 bash, beat, drub, hurt, maul, mush 5 baste, break, dough, paste, pound, wreck 6 bruise, buffet, bung up, hitter, mangle, pommel, pummel, thrash, wallop 7 assault, belabor, bombard, clobber, coating, contuse, cripple, lambast 8 demolish, lambaste

battery
3 lot, set 4 body, guns 5 abuse, array, batch, bunch, clump, group, suite 6 bundle, cannon, series 7 assault, beating, cluster 8 thumping 9 artillery, onslaught 10 energy cell 11 gunnery unit

battery terminal
5 anode 7 cathode

battle
4 fray 5 brush, clash, fight 6 action, assail, attack, combat, sortie 7 assault, contend, contest 8 conflict, skirmish, struggle 9 encounter, onslaught, scrimmage 10 engagement 11 hostilities

battle-ax
5 harpy, scold, shrew 6 virago 8 harridan 9 termagant, Xanthippe

Battle Born State
6 Nevada

battle cry
6 banzai

battlement
4 wall 7 barrier, bastion, bulwark, parapet, rampart 10 protection

batty
3 mad 4 daft, nuts, zany 5 barmy, crazy, kooky, loony, nutty, potty, wacky 6 crazed,

cuckoo, insane, maniac, screwy, whacko
7 bananas, bonkers, cracked, idiotic,
lunatic **8** deranged **9** bedlamite

bauble
3 toy **5** curio **6** gewgaw, trifle **7** bibelot,
novelty, trinket, whatnot **8** gimcrack,
ornament **9** objet d'art, plaything
10 knickknack

Baucis's husband
8 Philemon

Bavaria
6 Bayern
capital: 6 Munich
city: 8 Augsburg, Bayreuth, Würzburg
9 Nuremberg
king: 6 Ludwig
patron saint: 6 Rupert

bawd
4 drab, moll, tart **5** madam, tramp, whore
6 floozy, harlot, hooker **7** trollop
8 strumpet **10** prostitute **11** nightwalker
12 streetwalker

bawdy
4 blue, lewd **5** crude, dirty **6** coarse,
erotic, ribald, risqué, smutty, vulgar
7 obscene **8** indecent, prurient
9 lecherous, offensive, salacious
10 lascivious, libidinous, licentious,
suggestive

bawdy house
4 crib, stew **6** bagnio **7** brothel, lupanar
8 bordello

bawl
3 cry, sob **4** howl, roar, rout, wail, weep,
yell, yowl **5** shout **6** bellow, berate,
boohoo, clamor, holler, outcry, scream,
shriek, squall **7** blubber, bluster

bawl out
3 wig **4** lash **5** baste, scold **6** berate,
rebuke **7** censure, chew out, condemn, tell
off, upbraid **8** bless out, castigate,
denounce, tear into **9** dress down,
reprimand **10** tongue-lash

bay
3 arm **4** cove, gulf, howl, nook, wail
5 award, bight, crown, firth, honor, inlet,
niche **6** harbor, laurel, recess **7** garland,
laurels **8** accolade **10** decoration
Aegean Sea: 5 Anzac
Africa: 6 Walvis
Alaska: 7 Glacier
Antarctica: 3 Ice **8** Amundsen
Argentina: 6 Blanca

Australia: 5 Anson, Shark **6** Botany,
Sharks **9** Discovery
Baltic: 4 Hano, Kiel **6** Danzig, Kieler
9 Pomerania **10** Pomeranian,
Pommersche
Beaufort Sea: 7 Prudhoe **9** Mackenzie
Brazil: 9 Guanabara
Bristol Channel: 10 Carmarthen
California: 5 Morro **8** Monterey, San
Diego
Canada: 5 Fundy
Capetown: 5 Table
Caribbean Sea: 5 Limon **8** Chetumal
Central America: 7 Fonseca
Cuba: 10 Guantánamo
East River: 8 Flushing
Egypt: 6 Abu Qir
Eire: 4 Clew **7** Brandon
English Channel: 3 Tor **4** Lyme
Europe: 6 Biscay
Florida: 8 Biscayne
Greenland: 6 Baffin **8** Melville
Gulf of Alaska: 12 Resurrection
Gulf of California: 5 Adair
Gulf of Guinea: 5 Benin **6** Biafra
Gulf of Mexico: 5 Tampa **6** Mobile
7 Aransas **8** Campeche, Sarasota
9 Matagorda, Pensacola **10** San Antonio,
Terrebonne **11** Atchafalaya, Ponce de
Leon **12** Apalachicola, Corpus Christi
Gulf of St. Lawrence: 5 Bonne, Gaspé
Hawaii: 5 Koloa, Lawai
Hong Kong: 4 Deep
Honshu: 3 Ise **5** Mutsu, Osaka, Owari,
Tokyo **6** Atsuta, Sagami
Indian Ocean: 6 Bengal
Indonesia: 8 Humboldt
Irish Sea: 4 Luce **7** Dundalk
Jamaica: 4 Long
Japan: 4 Tosa
Java Sea: 7 Batavia **8** Djakarta
Lake Erie: 8 Sandusky
Lake Huron: 7 Saginaw, Thunder
Lake Michigan: 5 Green **13** Grand
Traverse
Lake Ontario: 11 Irondequoit
Lake Superior: 5 Huron **8** Keweenaw
9 Whitefish
Long Island Sound: 6 Oyster
Maine: 5 Casco **7** Machias **9** Penobscot
Maryland-Virginia: 10 Chesapeake
12 Chincoteague
Massachusetts: 6 Boston **7** Cape Cod
8 Buzzards, Plymouth
New Brunswick: 13 Passamaquoddy
Newfoundland: 4 Hare **5** White
7 Fortune

New Jersey: 5 Great **6** Newark **7** Raritan **8** Barnegat
New York: 7 Jamaica
North Carolina: 6 Onslow
Northwest Territories: 5 Wager **7** Repulse **8** Franklin **9** Frobisher
Oregon: 4 Coos
Puerto Rico: 5 Sucia
Quebec: 6 Ungava
Rhode Island: 12 Narragansett
Sea of Japan: 13 Peter the Great
South Carolina: 4 Bull, Long
South China Sea: 5 Subic **7** Camranh
Spain: 5 Cadiz
Strait of Gibraltar: 7 Tangier
Sydney: 6 Botany
Tasmania: 5 Storm
Texas: 7 Trinity
Tyrrhenian Sea: 6 Naples **7** Paestum
Wales: 10 Caernarfon, Caernarvon
Washington: 5 Dabob **6** Skagit
West Indies: 5 Coral

bayou
5 creek, marsh **6** slough **9** everglade, tributary
Louisiana: 5 Macon **9** Barataria, Lafourche **10** Terrebonne
Mississippi: 9 Chickasaw

Bay State
13 Massachusetts

bay window
3 gut, pot **5** oriel, tummy **6** paunch **8** potbelly **9** beer belly, spare tire **11** corporation, breadbasket

bazaar
4 fair, mall, mart, souk **6** market **7** benefit **8** emporium, exchange **11** marketplace

bazooka's target
4 tank

be
4 live **5** exist

beach
4 bank **5** Cocoa, coast, shore **6** Malibu, Pebble, strand, Venice **7** seaside, shingle, Waikiki **8** cast away, lakeside, littoral **9** lakeshore, seashore **10** Clearwater, Copacabana, oceanfront, run aground

_____ Beach
3 Amy **4** Long, Palm, Vero **5** Dover, Miami, Omaha **6** Delray, Myrtle, Ormond **7** Daytona, Riviera, Waikiki **8** Imperial, Virginia

beached
6 ashore **7** aground **8** grounded, marooned, stranded **9** abandoned

beachhead
8 foothold

beachwear
see **bathing suit**

beacon
4 buoy, sign **5** flare, guide **6** pharos, signal **7** bonfire, lantern **8** balefire **9** watchfire **10** lighthouse, signal fire **11** inspiration, transmitter **12** guiding light

bead
3 dab, dot, pea **4** blob, drop **6** bubble **7** driblet, globule **8** spherule

beak
3 neb, nib **4** bill, nose **5** snoot, snout, spout **6** pecker, schnoz **7** schnozz **8** mandible **9** proboscis, schnozzle

beaker
3 cup **6** carafe, goblet, vessel **8** decanter

beaklike part
7 rostrum

be-all and end-all
3 sum **4** pith, root, soul **5** total, whole **6** bottom **7** essence **8** entirety, sum total, totality **9** aggregate, substance **10** prime cause **12** quintessence

beam
3 bar, ray **4** balk, boom, burn, glow, grin, spar **5** flare, flash, gleam, joist, plank, shaft, shine, shoot, smile, strut **6** girder, lintel, rafter, signal, streak, stream, timber **7** radiate **8** transmit **9** broadcast

beaming
6 bright, joyful, lucent **7** fulgent, lambent, radiant **8** animated, cheerful, luminous **9** brilliant, effulgent, refulgent **12** incandescent

bean
3 soy, wax **4** bush, conk, dome, head, lima, mung, navy, pate, pole, poll, snap, soya **5** baked, brain, broad, horse, jelly, pinto **6** belfry, coffee, frijol, kidney, legume, noddle, noggin, noodle, string **7** jumping **9** headpiece **10** stringless
of India: 3 urd

beanery
4 café **5** diner, grill **9** hash house **10** coffee shop, restaurant **11** greasy spoon **12** luncheonette

beano
5 bingo

Bean Town
6 Boston

bear
3 lug 4 tote 5 abide, allow, beget, bring, brook, bruin, carry, stand, touch 6 accept, behave, convey, deport, endure, permit, suffer 7 comport, condone, conduct, deliver, stomach, support, sustain, swallow, undergo 8 engender, generate, shoulder, tolerate 9 procreate, propagate, reproduce, transport 10 bring forth 11 countenance
Alaskan: 5 polar 6 Kodiak
Australian: 5 koala
genus: 5 Ursus
kind: 3 sun 5 black, brown, honey, koala, polar, sloth 6 Kodiak 7 grizzly 10 spectacled
relating to: 6 ursine
young: 3 cub

bearable
7 livable, tenable 8 adequate, passable 9 allowable, endurable, tolerable 10 acceptable, admissible, good enough, manageable, sufferable 11 supportable, sustainable

bearcat
5 panda

beard
4 dare, defy, face, fuzz 5 brave, front 6 goatee 7 outface, stubble, Vandyke 8 confront, imperial, whiskers 9 challenge
on grain: 3 awn

bearded
5 bushy, fuzzy, hairy 6 shaggy, tufted 7 bristly, goateed, hirsute, stubbly 8 unshaven 9 whiskered 11 bewhiskered

bear down
4 rout 5 crush, quell 6 burden, defeat, reduce, subdue 7 conquer, overrun, trample 8 overcome, vanquish 9 emphasize, overpower, overwhelm, subjugate

bearer
4 mule 5 envoy 6 coolie, porter, runner 7 carrier, courier 8 conveyor, emissary 9 go-between, messenger 11 internuncio

bear hug
6 clinch

bearing
3 air, set 4 look, mien, pose 5 poise
6 aspect, manner, stance 7 address, conduct, display, posture 8 attitude, behavior, carriage, delivery, demeanor, presence, relation 9 demeanour, direction 10 connection, deportment 11 comportment

bearish
4 curt 5 gruff, rough, terse, surly 6 cranky, ornery 7 anxious, dubious, prickly, uncouth 8 cautious, vinegary 9 crotchety, irascible 10 ill-humored 11 pessimistic 12 cantankerous

bearlike
6 ursine

bear out
4 show 5 prove 6 attest, uphold, verify 7 certify, confirm, justify 8 validate, vouch for 9 vindicate 11 corroborate, demonstrate 12 authenticate, substantiate

bear up
4 cope, fare, prop 5 brace, get by 6 endure, uphold 7 bolster, support, sustain 8 buttress, get along, maintain, underpin

beast
5 brute 6 animal 7 critter, monster, varmint 8 behemoth, creature

beastly
4 foul, mean, vile 5 awful, brute, feral, nasty 6 animal, brutal, odious 7 bestial, brutish, inhuman, ogreish, swinish 8 horrible, terrible 9 barbarous, revolting 10 abominable, detestable

beat
3 box, get, gyp, hit, lam, rap, tan, top 4 balk, belt, best, cane, dash, drub, drum, dump, flap, flog, foil, lash, lick, maul, pelt, rout, ruin, stir, tick, trim, whip, whop 5 baste, cheat, cozen, excel, forge, lay on, meter, outdo, paste, pound, pulse, punch, rhyme, route, scoop, scour, smear, stick, stump, swing, throb, tread, tromp, whack, whisk 6 baffle, batter, better, buffet, cudgel, defeat, diddle, exceed, forage, hammer, larrup, muss up, patrol, pummel, rhythm, rounds, strike, thrash, thresh, thwart, wallop 7 belabor, clobber, circuit, conquer, exhaust, fashion, fatigue, lambast, lay down, prevail, pulsate, ransack, rough up, shellac, surpass, swindle, triumph, trounce 8 bewilder, bludgeon, Bohemian, lambaste, outshine, outsmart, outstrip, overcome, precinct 9 exhausted, frustrate, palpitate, pulsation, transcend, vibration 10 circumvent, pistol-whip 11 oscillation

beating
4 rout **5** lumps **6** defeat, hiding, mayhem
7 assault, setback **9** hammering, pulsation,
throbbing **11** palpitation, shellacking

beatitude
3 joy **5** bliss **7** delight, ecstasy, rapture
8 euphoria, gladness, rhapsody
9 happiness, transport **10** exaltation,
joyfulness **11** blessedness **12** blissfulness

Beatles
4 John (Lennon), Paul (McCartney)
5 Ringo (Starr) **6** George (Harrison)

beatnik
5 rebel **6** hippie **7** radical **8** Bohemian
9 dissident **11** flower child
13 nonconformist

beat-up
6 rickety, shabby **7** worn-out **8** decrepit,
tattered **9** crumbling **10** broken-down,
ramshackle, tumble-down **11** dilapidated

beau
5 dandy, flame, lover, swain, wooer
6 steady, suitor **7** admirer, beloved
8 paramour, truelove, young man
9 boyfriend **10** sweetheart

Beau Brummell
3 fop **5** dandy, swell **7** coxcomb, gallant
8 macaroni **11** petit-maître **12** lounge
lizard

beau ideal
5 guide, model **6** mirror **7** epitome,
example, paragon, pattern **8** exemplar,
paradigm, standard **9** archetype
12 quintessence

Beaumarchais hero
6 Figaro

beau monde
5 elite **6** gentry, jet set **7** society **8** smart
set **10** glitterati, upper crust

beauteous
see **beautiful**

beautiful
4 fair **5** bonny **6** comely, lovely, pretty,
radiant **8** glorious, gorgeous, handsome,
splendid, stunning **9** exquisite
10 attractive **11** good-looking, resplendent,
well-favored

beautiful people
6 jet set **8** smart set **9** haut monde
10 glitterati **11** high society

beautify
4 deck, gild, trim **5** adorn, array, fix up,
grace, prank, primp **6** bedeck, doll up

7 dress up, festoon, garland, garnish,
gussy up, enhance, improve **8** decorate,
ornament, prettify, spruce up **9** embellish,
glamorize

beauty
5 asset, belle, dream, merit, peach
6 appeal, eyeful, looker, lovely **7** charmer,
dazzler, stunner **8** knockout **9** eye-opener,
good looks **10** good-looker, loveliness

beaver
6 rodent
project: 3 dam
home: 5 lodge
young: 3 kit, pup

Beaver State
6 Oregon

becalm
4 hush, lull, stop **5** allay, quiet, stall, still
6 arrest, pacify, sedate, settle, soothe,
steady, subdue **7** assuage, compose,
quieten **11** tranquilize

because
3 for, now **4** that **5** since **7** being as,
whereas **8** being how, as long as, seeing
as **10** inasmuch as

because of
4 over **5** due to **7** owing to, thanks to,
through **10** by reason of **11** on account of

Beckett work
4 Not I, Play, Watt **6** Molloy, Murphy
7 Endgame **9** Happy Days, Unnamable
(The) **10** Eleutheria, Malone Dies
14 Krapp's Last Tape **15** Waiting for Godot

beckon
3 bid, nod **4** lure, wave **6** allure, entice,
invite, motion, signal, summon **7** attract

becloud
3 dim, fog **4** blur, hide, veil **5** addle, bedim,
befog, cloak, muddy **6** impair, darken,
muddle, puzzle, shroud **7** confuse, eclipse,
obscure, perplex **8** befuddle **9** obfuscate
10 overshadow

become
3 fit, get, wax **4** grow, suit **5** befit **6** go
with **7** enhance, flatter **8** turn into

becoming
3 apt **5** right **6** decent, proper, seemly
7 correct, fitting **8** decorous, suitable,
tasteful **9** befitting **10** attractive, flattering,
well-chosen **11** appropriate, comme il faut

bed
3 cot **4** base, bunk, crib, sack, twin
5 basis, berth, layer **6** bottom, cradle,
double, ground, Murphy, pallet **7** bedrock,

stratum, trundle **8** rollaway **10** foundation, substratum
of India: 7 charpoy

bedaub
4 coat **5** cover, smear **6** smudge
7 overlay, plaster

bedazzle
4 daze **5** blind

bedcover
5 duvet, quilt **6** afghan, spread **7** blanket
8 coverlet **9** comforter **11** counterpane

bedeck
4 trim **5** adorn, array, prank **6** attire,
bedaub, jazz up **7** appoint, bedizen, dress
up, festoon, furbish, garland, garnish,
gussy up **8** accouter, beautify, decorate,
ornament, prettify **9** embellish

bedevil
5 annoy, harry, spoil, tease, worry
6 harass, needle, nettle, pester, plague
7 hagride, provoke, torment, trouble
8 bewilder **10** exasperate

bedevilment
6 bother **7** torment, trouble **8** disorder,
vexation **9** annoyance, confusion
10 irritation **11** aggravation
12 bewilderment

bedfellow
4 ally **5** crony **7** comrade **9** associate,
colleague **10** compatriot **11** confederate
12 collaborator

bedim
3 fog **4** blur, mask, veil **5** befog, blear,
cloud, gloom, shade, shroud **6** darken,
muddle, shadow **7** becloud, confuse,
eclipse, obscure **9** obfuscate

bedizen
4 deck, garb, gild **5** adorn, array, endue
6 doll up, dude up, invest, outfit, rig out
7 costume, dandify, dress up, garnish,
gussy up, turn out **8** beautify, ornament
9 caparison, embellish

bedlam
3 ado **5** chaos, furor **6** asylum, clamor,
furore, hubbub, tumult, uproar, welter
7 turmoil **8** foofaraw, madhouse, upheaval
9 commotion, maelstrom **10** hurly-burly
11 pandemonium

bedlamite
3 mad, nut **4** loon, nuts **5** batty, crazy,
loony **6** insane, madman, maniac
7 cracked, lunatic **8** demented, deranged

bedouin
4 Arab **5** nomad

bedraggled
5 faded, seedy **6** shabby, ragtag, untidy
7 muddied, rundown, unkempt **8** decrepit,
dripping, slovenly, tattered **10** disheveled,
disarrayed, disordered, down-at-heel,
ramshackle, threadbare **11** dilapidated

bedridden
6 laid up, shut-in **8** confined
12 hospitalized

bedrock
4 base, core, foot, root **5** axiom, basic,
basis, floor, nadir **6** bottom, depths, ground
7 footing, support **10** foundation,
groundwork, substratum **11** fundamental
12 substructure, underpinning

bedroom
7 boudoir, chamber

bedspread
8 coverlet **11** counterpane

bed-wetting
8 enuresis

bee
food: 6 nectar
glue: 8 propolis
group: 5 swarm **6** colony
house: 6 apiary, hive
kind: 5 drone, mason, queen **6** mining,
sewing, worker **8** quilting, spelling
9 carpenter
nest: 4 hive, skep
product: 3 wax **5** honey
relating to: 8 apiarian
wax cells: 9 honeycomb

beechnuts
4 mast

beef
4 crab, fuss, meat **5** bitch, brawn, gripe
6 grouse, muscle **7** grumble **8** strength
9 bellyache, complaint, grievance
10 falling-out
cut: 3 rib **4** loin, rump, side **5** chuck,
flank, plate, round, shank **7** brisket, sirloin
10 tenderloin
grade: 5 prime **6** choice **7** utility
8 standard **10** commercial
order: 4 rare **6** medium **8** well-done

beefeater
5 guard **6** sentry, warder, yeoman

beefy
5 bulky, burly, hefty, husky, meaty
6 brawny, fleshy, robust, stocky, sturdy
7 massive **8** muscular, thickset
9 strapping **11** substantial

Beehive State
4 Utah

beekeeper
8 apiarist 12 apiculturist

beekeeping
10 apiculture

beeline
3 fly, nip, zip 4 race, whiz 5 hurry, speed
6 bullet, hasten, hustle, rocket 7 hotfoot
8 expedite, highball 10 make tracks
12 shortest path

Beelzebub
5 devil, fiend, Satan 6 diablo 7 Evil One,
Lucifer, Old Nick, serpent 8 Apollyon
9 adversary, archfiend

beer
3 ale 4 bock, brew, suds 5 draft, lager,
stout, weiss 6 porter 7 brewski, cerveza,
pilsner 8 pilsener
vessel: 3 mug 4 toby 5 stein 6 flagon,
seidel 7 tankard 8 schooner 9 blackjack
drinking place: 3 bar, inn, pub 6 saloon,
tavern
ingredient: 4 hops, malt 5 yeast 6 barley
maker: 6 brewer
mythical inventor: 9 Gambrinus
plant: 7 brewery
Russian: 5 kvass
Scottish: 10 barley-bree

beer hall
3 pub 6 saloon, tavern 7 taproom
8 alehouse 11 public house, rathskeller

Beeri
daughter: 6 Judith
son: 5 Hosea

beet
5 chard 6 mangel, wurzel 10 Swiss chard
family: 9 goosefoot

Beethoven, Ludwig van
birthplace: 4 Bonn
opera: 7 Fidelio
overture: 6 Egmont 7 Leonore
10 Coriolanus, Prometheus
sonata: 7 Tempest 8 Kreutzer
9 Moonlight, Waldstein 10 Pathétique
12 Appassionata
symphony: 6 Choral, Eroica 8 Pastoral

beetle
3 bug, jut 5 bulge 6 insect, scarab, scurry
7 project 8 overhang, protrude, stand out,
stick out
click: 6 elater 7 firefly
dung: 6 scarab 9 tumblebug
front wing: 6 elytra (plural) 7 elytron

fruit-eating: 8 curculio
insect-eating: 7 ladybug 8 ladybird
kind: 4 bean, dung, fire, June, stag
5 click, flour, grain, tiger, water 6 carpet,
chafer, ground, May bug, museum
7 blister, cadelle, carabid, firefly, goldbug,
goliath, June bug, vedalia 8 ambrosia,
Japanese 9 longicorn, potato bug
10 cockchafer, rhinoceros
order: 10 Coleoptera
snouted: 6 weevil 7 billbug 8 curculio
9 wood borer
young: 4 grub 5 larva 6 larvae (plural)
8 wireworm

beet soup
6 borsch 7 borscht

befall
3 hap 5 ensue, occur 6 betide, chance,
follow, happen 7 come off, develop, fall out
8 happen to, transpire 9 come about,
eventuate

befit
4 meet, suit 6 become, go with 9 agree
with, chime with 10 accord with, be right
for 11 be proper for

befitting
3 apt 4 just, meet 5 happy, right 6 decent,
proper, seemly 7 correct 8 becoming,
decorous, suitable 10 conforming,
felicitous 11 appropriate, comme il faut

befog
3 dim 4 blur, hide, veil 5 bedim, blear,
cloak, cloud, muddy 6 darken, puzzle
7 becloud, confuse, eclipse, envelop,
obscure, perplex 8 bewilder, confound
9 obfuscate, overcloud 10 overshadow

befool
4 dupe, gull, hoax, play 5 cozen, trick
6 delude 7 chicane, deceive, mislead
8 hoodwink 9 bamboozle, victimize
11 hornswoggle

before
3 ere 4 ante, once, till, up to 5 ahead, until
6 facing, sooner, up till 7 ahead of, already,
earlier, prior to 8 formerly 9 in advance, in
front of, preceding 10 previously 11 in
advance of
prefix: 3 pre, pro 4 ante, fore

befoul
3 mar, tar 4 slur, soil 5 dirty, smear, spoil,
sully, taint 6 defame, defile, malign,
smudge 7 blacken, pollute, profane,
spatter, tarnish, traduce 8 besmirch

9 bespatter, denigrate 10 adulterate
11 contaminate

befuddle
4 daze 5 addle, mix up 6 ball up, baffle,
bemuse, muddle 7 confuse, fluster,
perplex, stupefy 8 bewilder, confound,
disorient, distract, throw off

befuddlement
3 fog 4 daze, haze, maze 5 mix-up
6 muddle, stupor 9 confusion
10 perplexity, puzzlement 11 distraction

beg
3 ask, bum, dun, nag, sue 4 pray, urge
5 brace, cadge, crave, evade, hit on, plead,
press, worry 6 adjure, appeal, apply call
on, demand, entreat, invoke, pester
7 beseech, besiege, conjure, entreat,
implore, request, solicit 8 petition, sidestep
9 importune, panhandle 10 supplicate

beget
4 bear, sire 5 breed, bring, cause, hatch,
spawn, yield 6 create, effect, father, forge
7 produce 8 engender, generate, multiply,
result in 9 procreate, propagate, reproduce
10 bring about

beggar
4 hobo, defy, ruin 5 tramp 6 bummer,
cadger, fellow, pauper, prayer, sponge,
suitor 7 moocher, sponger 8 bankrupt,
deadbeat, vagabond 9 overwhelm,
pauperize, schnorrer, suppliant 10 down-
and-out, freeloader, impoverish,
panhandler, petitioner, supplicant 11 bindle
stiff, supplicator 12 street person

beggared
4 flat, poor 5 broke, needy 6 ruined
7 drained 8 bankrupt, dirt poor, indigent,
strapped, wiped out 9 destitute, penniless,
penurious, tapped out 10 pauperized
11 impecunious, insolvent, overwhelmed
12 dispossessed, impoverished

beggarly
3 low 4 base, mean, poor 5 cheap, lowly,
nasty, petty, sorry 6 cheesy, meager,
measly, paltry, scanty, scurvy, shabby,
shoddy, sorry, trashy 7 ignoble, miserly,
pitiful, squalid 8 pitiable, inferior, wretched
9 miserable, niggardly 10 despicable,
despisable 11 ignominious 12 contemptible, parsimonious

Beggar's Opera
music: 7 Pepusch (John)
painting: 7 Hogarth (William)

text: 3 Gay (John)

beggarweed
6 dodder 9 knotgrass 11 tick trefoil

beggary
4 need, want 6 penury 7 bumming,
cadging, poverty 8 mooching, pleading
9 indigence, neediness, pauperism,
privation 10 meagerness, mendicancy
11 destitution, panhandling

begin
4 dawn, open, rise 5 arise, cause, create,
dig in, enter, found, mount, set to, start
6 appear, attack, be born, broach, effect,
emerge, get off, induce, invent, launch,
spring, sprout, tackle, take up, tee off
7 break in, embark on, emanate, jump off,
kick off, lead off, prepare, usher in 8 activate, commence, embark on, engender,
initiate 9 establish, instigate, institute,
introduce, originate 10 embark upon,
inaugurate, issue forth 11 break ground

beginner
4 colt, tiro, tyro 6 newbie, new kid, novice,
rookie 7 recruit, starter, student, trainee
8 freshman, neophyte, newcomer
9 fledgling, greenhorn, novitiate
10 apprentice, catechumen, tenderfoot
11 abecedarian

beginning
4 dawn, font, rise, root 5 alpha, basal,
birth, fount, onset, start 6 day one, origin,
outset, primal, source, spring 7 dawning,
genesis, infancy, initial, kickoff, nascent,
opening 8 creation, exordium, outstart,
prologue, rudiment, simplest 9 elemental,
emergence, inception, incipient
10 appearance, elementary, incipiency,
initiative, initiatory, opening gun, rudimental
11 origination, rudimentary 12 commencement, inauguration, introductory

begird
3 hem 4 belt, bind, ring 5 beset, fence,
hem in, round 6 circle, corral, girdle,
immure 7 confine, enclose, wreathe
8 encircle, engirdle, surround
9 encompass 12 circumscribe

beg off
5 demur, welsh 6 bow out, cop out, opt
out, pass up, refuse, renege 7 back out,
bail out, decline, drop out, pull out 8 back
down, withdraw

begone
5 leave, scram. split 6 beat it, decamp,
depart, get out 7 buzz off, get lost,
skiddoo, take off, vamoose 8 clear out,

begrime

hightail, shove off **9** skedaddle **10** make
tracks

begrime
3 tar **4** foul, soil, spot **5** dirty, muddy,
smear, spoil, sully, taint **6** defile, mess up,
muck up, smirch, smooch, smudge, smutch
7 blacken, corrupt, pollute, tarnish
8 besmirch **11** contaminate

begrudge
4 envy **6** resent

beguile
3 con **4** draw, dupe, fool, hoax, lure, play,
snow, wile **5** bluff, charm, fleet, trick
6 beckon, betray, delude, divert, entice,
humbug, seduce, take in **7** attract, bewitch,
deceive, enchant, engross, exploit, finesse,
mislead **8** distract, hoodwink, intrigue,
maneuver **9** captivate, fascinate, while
away **10** manipulate **11** double-cross

beguiling
4 wily **5** false **6** artful, subtle **8** alluring,
deluding, delusive, delusory **9** deceitful,
deceiving, deceptive, insidious, seductive
10 bewitching, chimerical, enchanting,
fallacious, misleading **11** enthralling

Behan's autobiography
10 Borstal Boy

behave
3 act, run **5** carry, react **6** acquit, be good,
deport, direct, manage **7** comport,
conduct, disport, perform **8** function

behavior
3 act, air, way **4** mien, tone, ways
6 action, aspect, custom, habits, manner
7 bearing, conduct **8** demeanor, presence,
response **10** deportment **11** comportment

behead
4 head, kill **7** execute **9** decollate
10 decapitate, guillotine

beheaded noblewoman
8 Jane Grey (Lady) **9** Catherine (Howard)
10 Anne Boleyn

behemoth
5 giant, jumbo, whale **7** goliath, mammoth,
monster **8** colossus **9** leviathan
11 monstrosity

behemothic
4 huge **5** jumbo **7** mammoth, massive,
titanic **8** colossal, gigantic, towering
9 Herculean, monstrous **10** gargantuan
11 elephantine

behest
3 say **4** will, wish, word, writ **5** edict, order
6 charge, demand, urging **7** bidding,
command, dictate, mandate, precept,
request **9** direction, enjoinder, ordinance,
prescript, prompting **10** injunction **11** commandment, exhortation, instruction
12 solicitation

behind
3 can **4** late, next, rump **5** after, fanny
6 back of, bottom, heinie **7** backing
8 backside, buttocks, derriere, trailing
9 following, posterior **10** supporting
12 subsequent to
prefix: 4 post **5** retro

behindhand
3 lax **4** late, slow **5** slack, tardy **6** in debt,
lesser, remiss **7** belated, delayed, laggard,
overdue **8** backward, careless, derelict,
sluggish **9** in arrears, negligent, unmindful
10 delinquent, neglectful, regardless,
subordinate, unpunctual **11** undeveloped
13 unprogressive

behold
3 see **4** espy, note, view **6** descry, notice
7 discern, observe, witness
French: 5 voilà
Latin: 4 ecce

beholden
5 bound **7** obliged **8** grateful, indebted
9 duty-bound, obligated

beholder
4 seer **6** gawker, viewer **7** watcher,
witness **8** observer, onlooker, passer-by
9 bystander, spectator **10** eyewitness
12 rubbernecker

beige
3 tan **4** buff, ecru **7** vanilla

being
3 man **4** body, life, self, soul **5** human,
stuff, thing **6** entity, matter, mortal, nature,
object, person, spirit **7** essence
8 creature, existent, material **9** actuality,
character, existence, personage,
something, substance **10** individual
11 personality **12** essentiality
13 individuality

bejeweled
7 studded **8** sequined **9** encrusted,
spangled **10** bespangled, gem-studded,
ornamented

Bel
Sumerian counterpart: 5 Enlil
wife: 5 Belit **6** Beltis

Bel _____
  3 Air 5 Paese

bel _____
  5 canto 6 esprit

Bela
  father: 4 Beor 8 Benjamin
  son: 3 Ard

belabor
  4 beat, drub, flog 5 baste, pound, scold
  6 batter, berate, buffet, pummel, thrash,
  wallop 7 lambast, scourge, tell off, upbraid
  8 chastise, lambaste, tear into 9 criticize,
  fulminate, overstate 10 flagellate
  11 overexplain

Belarus
  capital: 5 Minsk
  city: 6 Homyel 7 Vitebsk 8 Mahilyow
  9 Vitsyebsk
  language: 7 Russian 10 Belarusian
  11 Belarussian
  monetary unit: 5 rubel, ruble
  neighbor: 6 Latvia, Poland, Russia
  7 Ukraine 9 Lithuania
  river: 3 Bug 5 Neman 7 Dnieper, Pripyat

belated
  4 late, slow 5 tardy 6 remiss 7 delayed,
  laggard, overdue 10 behindhand, behind
  time, unpunctual

Belau
  see **Palau**

belch
  4 burp, emit, gush, spew, vent, void
  5 eject, eruct, erupt, expel, issue, spout,
  spurt, vomit 6 hiccup, irrupt 7 explode,
  extrude 8 disgorge 10 eructation
  11 expectorate

beldam
  3 hag 5 crone 8 old woman

beleaguer
  3 bug, dog, hem, nag, vex 4 gnaw
  5 annoy, beset, erupt, hound, siege, storm,
  tease, worry 6 assail, attack, badger,
  bother, fall on, harass, invest, pester,
  plague 7 bedevil, besiege, hagride, put
  upon, set upon, trouble 8 blockade, fall
  upon

belfry
  7 steeple 8 carillon 9 bell tower,
  campanile
  dweller: 3 bat

Belgium
  capital: 8 Brussels

  city: 4 Gent 5 Ghent, Liège 7 Antwerp
  9 Charleroi
  ethnic group: 7 Fleming, Flemish,
  Walloon
  language: 5 Dutch 7 Flemish
  monetary unit: 4 euro
  neighbor: 6 France 7 Germany
  10 Luxembourg 11 Netherlands
  plain: 8 Flanders
  port: 7 Antwerp 8 Oostende
  river: 4 Yser 5 Meuse 7 Schlede
  sea: 5 North

belie
  4 deny, hide, warp 5 color, twist 6 expose,
  doctor, garble 7 conceal, confute, distort,
  falsify, gainsay, pervert, trump up
  8 confront, denounce, disagree, disguise,
  disprove, miscolor, misstate, negative
  9 disaffirm, gloss over, repudiate 10 contradict, contravene, controvert
  11 dissimulate 12 misrepresent

belief
  3 ism 4 idea, mind, view 5 axiom, credo,
  creed, dogma, faith, hunch, tenet, trust
  6 assent, avowal, credit, surety, theory,
  thesis 7 concept, feeling, opinion, precept,
  surmise, theorem 8 credence, doctrine,
  firmness, religion, sureness 9 assurance,
  certainty, certitude, intuition, postulate,
  principle, sentiment 10 acceptance,
  assumption, confidence, contention,
  conviction, hypothesis, impression,
  persuasion 11 supposition

believable
  5 solid, sound, valid 6 cogent, likely,
  smooth, steady, trusty 7 logical, swaying,
  tenable, up front 8 credible, possible,
  probable, rational, reliable 9 authentic,
  colorable, plausible 10 convincing,
  creditable, impressive, meaningful,
  persuasive, presumable, reasonable,
  satisfying, supposable 11 conceivable,
  substantial, trustworthy 12 satisfactory

believe
  3 buy 4 deem, hold, know 5 lap up, think,
  trust 6 accept, affirm, assume, credit,
  expect, reckon 7 fall for, imagine, profess,
  suppose, suspect, swallow 8 conceive,
  consider 10 conjecture, presuppose,
  understand

belittle
  3 cut, pan 5 abuse, decry, knock, scorn
  6 deride, insult, jeer at, revile 7 cut down,
  put down, run down, sneer at 8 bad-
  mouth, derogate, diminish, discount,
  minimize, write off 9 criticize, discredit,

disparage, dispraise, downgrade, underrate **10** depreciate, undervalue **13** underestimate

belittlement
5 abuse, scorn **7** calumny, jeering, scandal, slander **8** derision, ridicule **9** aspersion **10** backbiting, defamation, detraction **11** denigration **12** backstabbing, depreciation **13** disparagement

Belize
capital: **8** Belmopan
city: **10** Belize City
ethnic group: **4** Maya **5** Mayan
language: **7** English, Spanish
monetary unit: **6** dollar
mountain: **8** Victoria
neighbor: **6** Mexico **9** Guatemala
river: **5** Hondo
sea: **9** Caribbean

bell
4 peal **5** chime, knell **6** tocsin

belle
5 siren **6** beauty, eyeful **7** charmer **8** knockout, ornament **11** enchantress, femme fatale

Bellerophon
father: **7** Glaucus **8** Poseidon
grandfather: **8** Sisyphus
horse: **7** Pegasus
victim: **7** Chimera

belles lettres
10 literature

belletrist
8 novelist **4** poet **6** author, writer **9** dramatist **10** playwright

bellflower
9 campanula

_____ belli
5 casus

bellicose
6 ornery **7** hawkish, hostile, martial, scrappy, warlike **8** factious, fighting, militant **9** assertive, combative, truculent **10** aggressive, pugnacious, rebellious **11** belligerent, contentious, disputatious, hot-tempered, quarrelsome **12** gladiatorial

belligerence
5 fight **6** attack, enmity, rancor, spleen **7** ill will **9** hostility, militancy, petulance, pugnacity **10** aggression, antagonism, truculence **11** bellicosity **12** churlishness **13** combativeness

belligerent
6 ardent, fierce **7** fighter, hostile, opponent, scrappy, soldier, warlike, warring, warrior **8** battling, churlish, fighting, invading, militant, petulant **9** aggressor, attacking, bellicose, combatant, combative, disputant, splenetic, truculent **10** aggressive, antagonist, pugnacious **11** contentious, hot-tempered, quarrelsome **12** antagonistic, disputatious

Bellini
opera: **5** Norma **6** Pirata (II) **8** Puritani (I) **10** Sonnambula (La)
sleepwalker: **5** Amina

bell metal
6 bronze

bellow
3 bay, cry, moo **4** bark, bawl, bray, howl, roar, rout, yowl **5** shout **6** clamor, holler **7** bluster

Bellow character
4 Rose (Billy) **5** Chick **6** Herzog (Moses E.) **7** Citrine (Charlie), Sammler (Arthur) **8** Humboldt, Fonstein (Harry) **9** Henderson **10** Ravelstein (Abe), Augie March

bell ringer
6 toller **9** Quasimodo **12** carillonneur **13** campanologist

bell ringing
11 campanology

bell-shaped
11 campanulate

bell sound
4 bong, boom, ding, dong, peal, ring, ting, toll **5** chime, clang, knell **6** tinkle

bell tower
6 belfry **7** clocher **8** carillon **9** campanile

_____ bellum
4 ante, post

bellwether
4 dean, lead **5** doyen, guide, pilot **6** leader **7** pioneer **9** lodestar **9** harbinger **10** forerunner **11** trend setter

belly
3 gut, pot **5** tummy **6** paunch, venter **7** abdomen, midriff, stomach **9** bay window **10** midsection **11** breadbasket, front porch
Scottish: **4** wame

bellyache
4 beef, carp, crab, fret, fuss, moan, yawp **5** bitch, bleat, colic, gripe, whine **6** grouse, snivel, squawk, yammer **7** grumble

8 complain **11** let off steam
12 collywobbles

bellyacher
4 crab **5** crank **6** griper, grouch, whiner
7 grouser **8** grumbler, sourpuss
10 complainer, crosspatch, malcontent
11 faultfinder

belly button
5 navel

belong
3 fit, set **4** suit, vest **5** agree, apply, befit,
chime, fit in, match, tally **6** accord, attach,
become, reside **7** pertain **9** correlate,
harmonize **10** correspond

belongings
3 kit **4** gear **5** goods, stuff **6** assets,
estate, legacy, things **7** baggage, effects
8 chattels, movables, property **9** patrimony
11 attachments, impedimenta, inheritance,
possessions **13** appurtenances

beloved
3 pet **4** baby, beau, dear, idol, love
5 flame, honey, lover, swain, sweet
6 adored, steady **7** darling, dearest, dear
one, doted on, sweetie **8** favorite, idolized,
ladylove, old flame, precious, truelove
9 boyfriend, cherished, inamorata,
treasured **10** girlfriend, heartthrob,
sweetheart, sweetie pie

below
5 infra, under **7** beneath **10** underneath
prefix: 3 sub **5** infra

belt
3 bat, bop **4** area, band, bash, biff, blow,
gird, loop, ring, sash, slam, slug, sock,
whap, whop, zone **5** smack, smash, strap,
strip **6** begird, cestus, circle, engird, girdle,
region, wallop **7** baldric, clobber, stretch
8 begirdle, ceinture, cincture, encircle,
engirdle **9** bandoleer, bandolier, territory,
waistband **10** cummerbund
celestial: 6 zodiac

beltway
8 ring road

Belus
brother: 6 Agenor
daughter: 4 Dido
father: 7 Neptune **8** Poseidon
mother: 5 Libya
son: 6 Danaus **7** Cepheus, Phineus
8 Aegyptus

belvedere
6 alcove, cupola, gazebo, pagoda
7 balcony, terrace **10** widow's walk

11 garden house, summerhouse,
observatory

bemedaled
9 decorated **10** beribboned

bemired
4 miry, oozy **5** boggy, dirty, grimy, gummy,
gunky, muddy, stuck, swampy **6** filthy,
soiled, swamped

bemoan
3 rue **4** wail, weep **6** bewail, grieve,
lament, oppose, regret **7** deplore
8 complain, object to **10** sorrow over
12 disapprove of

bemuse
4 daze **5** addle **6** absorb, muddle, puzzle
7 confuse, mystify, nonplus, perplex
8 bewilder, distract **10** disconcert

bemused
3 wry **4** lost **6** absent, remote **7** faraway
8 distrait **9** distraite **10** abstracted,
distracted **11** preoccupied
12 absentminded **13** lost in thought

bench
5 court **6** settee, settle, thwart **7** counter
8 platform **9** worktable
church: 3 pew
outdoor: 6 exedra
upholstered: 9 banquette

benchmark
4 norm **5** basis, gauge, guide, model, scale
7 measure **8** exemplar, paradigm,
standard **9** criterion, guideline, milestone,
yardstick **10** touchstone

bend
3 arc, bow, sag **4** arch, bank, cave, curl,
flex, hang, hook, lean, mold, sway, tend, tilt,
turn, veer, warp **5** angle, crook, curve,
round, shape, shift, stoop, twist, yield
6 compel, corner, buckle, direct, double,
fasten, kowtow, subdue, submit, zigzag
7 deflect, dispose, distort, flexure, turning
8 lean over **9** curvature, deviation,
genuflect **10** compromise, predispose

bendable
5 lithe **6** limber, pliant, supple **7** elastic,
plastic, pliable **8** flexible, moldable
9 malleable, tractable **11** manipulable

bender
see **binge**

_____ **bene**
4 nota

beneath
5 below, under

prefix: 3 hyp, sub **4** hypo **5** infra

_____ Benedict
4 eggs

benediction
4 boon, okay **5** favor, grace **6** orison, thanks **7** benefit, benison, godsend **8** approval, blessing **9** advantage **11** approbation, consecration **12** thanksgiving

benefaction
4 alms, care, fund, gift, help **5** favor, grant **6** relief **7** charity, comfort, largess, service, subsidy **8** donation, handout, largesse, oblation, offering, windfall **9** endowment, patronage **10** assistance **12** contribution, ministration

benefactor
5 angel, donor **6** backer, patron **7** grantor, sponsor **9** supporter, sustainer **11** contributor, underwriter

beneficence
see **benefaction**

beneficent
4 kind **6** benign, caring, giving **8** generous **10** altruistic, bighearted, charitable, ungrudging **11** kindhearted, magnanimous **13** compassionate, philanthropic

beneficial
4 good **5** brave, tonic **6** benign, toward, useful **7** helpful **8** favoring, salutary, valuable **9** favorable, healthful, nurturing, wholesome **10** profitable, propitious, salubrious **12** advantageous, constructive

beneficiary
4 heir **5** donee, payee **7** grantee, heiress, legatee **8** assignee **9** inheritor, recipient

beneficiate
5 treat **6** reduce **7** prepare, process

benefit
3 aid **4** boon, gain, good, help, perk, sake **5** avail, extra, favor, serve **6** assist, behalf, better, profit, relief, succor **7** account, advance, charity, further, godsend, improve, promote, relieve, welfare **8** blessing, interest **9** advantage, well-being **10** ameliorate, fund-raiser, prosperity **11** good fortune **12** contribute to

benevolence
4 boon, gift, help **5** amity, favor, grant **6** comity, relief **7** caritas, charity **8** altruism, clemency, goodness, goodwill, humanity, kindness **10** compassion, compliment, kindliness **11** magnanimity

benevolent
4 good, kind, warm **6** caring, do-good, humane, kindly **7** helpful, liberal **8** generous, tolerant **10** altruistic, beneficent, bighearted, charitable, openhanded **11** considerate, magnanimous, warmhearted **12** elee-mosynary, humanitarian **13** compassionate, philanthropic, tenderhearted

Ben Hur author
7 Wallace (Lew)

benighted
6 obtuse, unread **8** backward, ignorant, untaught **9** untutored, unwitting **10** illiterate, uneducated, uninformed, unlettered, unschooled **11** know-nothing **12** uncultivated **13** unenlightened, unprogressive

benign
4 kind, mild **6** genial, gentle, humane, kindly, mellow **7** amiable, clement **8** gracious, harmless, merciful, pleasant **9** favorable, fortunate, healthful, temperate, remediable, wholesome **10** auspicious, benevolent, charitable, forbearing, propitious **11** good-hearted **12** noncancerous

Benin
capital: 9 Porto-Novo
city: 7 Cotonou
coast: 5 Slave
ethnic group: 3 Fon **6** Fulani, Yoruba
former name: 7 Dahomey
language: 3 Fon **6** French
monetary unit: 5 franc
neighbor: 4 Togo **5** Niger **7** Nigeria **11** Burkina Faso
river: 5 Ouémé

benison
5 grace **8** blessing **11** benediction **12** consecration

Benjamin
brother: 6 Joseph
father: 5 Jacob
mother: 6 Rachel

bent
3 set **4** bias, gift **5** arced, bowed, flair, knack **6** arched, curved, intent, talent **7** decided, faculty, leaning **8** aptitude, capacity, penchant, resolute, resolved, tendency **10** determined, proclivity, propensity **11** disposition, inclination **12** predilection

benumb
4 daze, dull, stun 5 blunt, chill 6 deaden, freeze 7 petrify, stupefy 8 etherize, paralyze 10 immobilize 11 desensitize

benumbed
4 cold 6 frozen 9 unfeeling 10 insensible 11 insensitive 12 anesthetized

Beowulf
drink: 4 mead
monster: 7 Grendel

bequeath
4 gift, will 5 endow, grant, leave 6 bestow, commit, confer devise, hand on, impart, legate, pass on 7 furnish, present 8 hand down, make over, transmit

bequest
3 lot 4 gift 5 share, trust 6 devise, estate, legacy 7 portion 8 heritage 10 settlement 11 inheritance

berate
3 jaw 4 rail, rate 5 chide, scold 6 rebuke, reprove, revile 7 bawl out, chew out, condemn, reproach, tell off, upbraid 8 admonish, chastise 9 castigate, criticize, reprimand 10 tongue-lash, vituperate

berceuse
7 lullaby 10 cradlesong

bereave
3 rob 4 lose 5 seize, strip 6 divest, remove 7 deprive 8 take away 10 confiscate, disinherit, dispossess 11 appropriate, requisition

bereaved
8 mourning 9 sorrowful, sorrowing 10 distressed 11 heartbroken 13 grief-stricken

bereavement
3 rue, woe 4 loss 5 dolor, grief 6 misery, pining, regret, sorrow 7 anguish, despair, remorse, sadness 8 grieving, mourning 9 dejection, heartache 10 affliction, depression, desolation 11 deprivation, despondency, lamentation, tribulation

bereft
5 shorn 6 devoid, robbed 7 fleeced, forlorn, wanting 8 beggared, deprived, desolate, divested, stripped 9 destitute 10 despondent 12 disconsolate, dispossessed, impoverished

Bergen's dummy
7 Charlie (McCarthy) 8 Mortimer (Snerd)

Berger novel
12 Little Big Man

Bergman role
4 Ilsa

berm
4 path 5 ledge, mound, shelf 8 shoulder

Bermuda
capital: 8 Hamilton
territory of: 7 Britain

Bernice
brother: 7 Agrippa
father: 5 Herod
husband: 6 Polemo
lover: 5 Titus 9 Vespasian

berry
5 cubeb, fruit, grape 7 currant, madrona, madrone 8 allspice 9 saskatoon

berserk
3 ape 4 amok 5 amuck, crazy 6 crazed, insane 7 bonkers, lunatic 8 demented, deranged, frenzied

berth
3 bed, cot 4 dock, moor, pier, port, post, quay, slip 5 cabin, jetty, levee, place, wharf 6 billet, office 8 position 9 anchorage, situation 10 connection 11 appointment, compartment 13 accommodation

beseech
see **beg**

beset
3 dog, hem, try, vex 4 gird, ring 5 harry, hem in, storm, worry 6 assail, attack, badger, circle, fall on, harass, infest, pester, plague, strike 7 assault, besiege, overrun, trouble, torture 8 blockade, encircle, fall upon, surround 9 beleaguer, encompass, overswarm

besetment
3 nag 4 bane, pain, pest 5 curse, trial 6 blight, bother, gadfly, pester, plague 7 torment 8 irritant, nuisance, vexation 9 annoyance 10 affliction, botherment, holy terror 11 aggravation, botheration

besetting
6 urgent 7 driving 8 dominant 9 obsessive 10 compelling, persistent 11 omnipresent 12 overwhelming

beside
4 near, nigh 6 next to

besides
3 too 4 also, else, plus, save 5 added, extra 6 and all, as well, beyond, except, to boot 7 barring, farther, further, without 8 as well as, likewise, moreover, more than

9 aside from, along with, exceeding, excluding, other than, otherwise, outside of 10 in addition 11 exclusive of, furthermore, not counting 12 additionally, together with

besiege
3 nag 4 ring, trap 5 beset, hem in, hound 6 assail, attack, circle, girdle, harass, pester, plague 7 assault, confine, environ, trouble 8 blockade, encircle, surround 9 beleaguer, encompass

besmear
see smear

besmirch
4 blot, foul, slur, soil 5 dirty, libel, stain, sully, taint 6 defile, damage, impugn, malign 7 asperse, slander, tarnish 8 disgrace, dishonor

besom material
5 twigs

besotted
5 dotty, drunk 7 charmed, muddled, smitten 8 enamored 9 enchanted 10 captivated, fascinated, infatuated, spellbound 11 intoxicated

bespatter
see spatter

bespeak
3 ask 4 book, hire, show 5 imply 6 accost, attest, desire, evince, reveal 7 address, apply to, betoken, connote, lecture, portend, request, reserve, signify, solicit, suggest, testify, witness 8 announce, approach, foretell, indicate, intimate, petition 9 preengage 10 prearrange

bespoke
8 tailored 10 custom-made

best
3 gem, top 4 beat, pick, tops 5 cream, elite, excel, model, outdo, pride, prime, prize 6 choice, defeat, exceed, finest 7 conquer, greatest, leading, optimal, optimum, paragon, premium, supreme, surpass 8 exemplar, foremost, nonesuch, outshine, outstrip, overcome 9 matchless, nonpareil, number-one, paramount, transcend, unequaled 11 outstanding 12 incomparable
combining form: 6 aristo

bestial
4 vile, wild 5 brute, cruel, feral 6 animal, brutal, carnal, fierce, malign, savage 7 beastly, brutish, inhuman, swinish, vicious

8 depraved, inhumane 9 ferocious 10 degenerate

bestialize
4 ruin, warp 5 abase 6 debase, defile 7 corrupt, debauch, degrade, deprave, pervert, pollute, subvert, vitiate, violate 9 brutalize 10 bastardize, demoralize

bestir
3 fly, rip 4 dash, flit, goad, race, rush, spur, stir, tear, urge, wake, whet 5 rally, rouse, scoot, waken, whirl 6 arouse, awaken, hasten, hustle, kindle 8 get going, scramble 9 challenge

bestow
4 give 5 apply, award, grant 6 confer, devote, donate, lavish 7 hand out, present 8 bequeath, give away
Scottish: 7 propine

bestower
5 donor, giver 6 patron 7 donator 8 altruist 9 conferrer, patroness, presenter 10 benefactor 12 benefactress 13 good Samaritan

bestrew
3 dot, sow 6 pepper, shower 7 diffuse, disject, scatter, speckle, stipple 8 disperse, sprinkle 9 broadcast, interlard 10 distribute 11 disseminate

bestride
5 mount, tower 8 dominate, loom over, straddle 9 stand over

bet
3 pot 4 ante, game, play, risk, shot 5 put on, stake, wager 6 gamble, hazard, parlay, pledge 7 lay odds, venture
racing: 6 exacta 8 perfecta, quinella, quiniela
taker: 6 bookie

Betelgeuse
4 star
constellation: 5 Orion

betel palm
5 areca

bête noire
4 hate, ruin 5 trial 6 animus, horror 7 bugbear, scourge, torment, undoing 8 anathema, aversion, downfall 9 ruination 10 black beast

bethink
4 cite, mind 6 call up, recall, remind, retain, review, revive 7 flash on 8 hark back, look back, remember, summon up 9 conjure up,

recollect, reminisce **10** call to mind, retrospect

Bethuel
daughter: 7 Rebekah
father: 5 Nahor
mother: 6 Milcah
son: 5 Laban
uncle: 7 Abraham

betide
4 fall **5** break, ensue, occur **6** befall, chance, happen **7** come off, develop, fall out **8** commence **9** come about, transpire

betimes
4 anon, soon **5** early **6** pronto, seldom, timely **7** too soon **8** directly, far ahead, fitfully, promptly **9** presently **10** before long, now and then, on occasion, seasonably **11** prematurely **12** occasionally, sporadically

betoken
4 bode, omen, show, warn **5** argue, augur **6** attest, denote, hint at **7** bespeak, point to, portend, presage, promise, signify, suggest, testify, witness **8** announce, forebode, evidence, foreshow, foretell, indicate, intimate, prophesy **9** prefigure **10** foreshadow **13** prognosticate

betray
4 dupe, jilt, name, sell, show, tell, trap **5** bluff, cheat, knife, rat on, snare, spill, split **6** delude, desert, entrap, evince, finger, inform, reveal, seduce, take in, tattle, tell on, turn in, unmask, unveil **7** abandon, beguile, betoken, deceive, divulge, ensnare, forsake, let down, let slip, mislead, sell out, traduce, uncover **8** blurt out, denounce, disclose, discover, evidence, give away, indicate, manifest **9** deliver up **10** apostatize, break faith, lead astray **11** demonstrate, double-cross **13** inform against

betrayal
4 leak **7** perfidy, treason **8** exposure **9** duplicity, falseness, Judas kiss, treachery **10** disclosure, infidelity, revelation **13** faithlessness

betrayer
3 rat **4** fink, nark **5** Judas **6** snitch **7** stoolie, tattler, traitor **8** apostate, defector, informer, quisling, renegade, squealer, turncoat **10** talebearer, tattletale **11** backstabber, stool pigeon

betroth
3 wed **5** marry **6** pledge **7** espouse **8** affiance

betrothal
6 pledge **8** espousal **10** engagement

betrothed
6 fiancé **7** engaged, fiancée, pledged **8** intended, plighted, promised, wife-to-be **9** affianced, bride-to-be, spoken for **10** contracted **11** husband-to-be

better
3 fix, top, win **4** beat, help, mend, more, well **5** amend, cured, elder, excel, finer, outdo **6** exceed, fitter, repair **7** advance, correct, enhance, further, greater, improve, largest, mending, rectify success, surpass, triumph, victory **8** greatest, improved, outshine, outstrip, stronger, superior, whip hand, worthier **9** advantage, desirable, excellent, healthier, improving, meliorate, preferred, transcend, upper hand **10** ameliorate, preferable, preferably, recovering, surpassing

bettor
7 gambler, wagerer

between
4 amid **5** among, twixt **6** within **7** betwixt
prefix: 5 inter, intra

betweentimes
11 at intervals

bevel
4 bias, cant **5** angle, grade, slant, slope **7** chamfer, incline, oblique **8** diagonal

beverage
3 ade, nog, pop, tea **4** cola, maté, milk, soda **5** cider, cocoa, drink, juice, mocha, shake **6** coffee, eggnog, frappe, malted, nectar **7** potable, soda pop **8** lemonade, libation, potation **9** drinkable, milk shake
alcoholic: 3 ale, gin, rum **4** beer, grog, mead, wine **5** cider, julep, negus, punch, stout, toddy, vodka **6** bishop, brandy, caudle, cooler, liquor, rickey, shandy, sherry, whisky **7** liqueur, martini, sangria, tequila, whiskey **8** cocktail, highball, sillabub, syllabub, vermouth
Arab: 4 arak **6** arrack
Australasian: 4 kava
Balkan: 9 slivovitz
British: 5 perry, stout
carbonated: 4 cola, soda **6** rickey **7** soda pop **8** root beer **9** ginger ale
central Asian: 6 kumiss **7** koumiss
Dutch: 7 schnaps **8** schnapps
from milk: 5 kefir **6** kumiss **7** koumiss

bevy

Greek: 4 ouzo 7 retsina
Irish: 6 poteen 10 usquebaugh
medicinal: 6 elixir
Mexican: 6 pulque 7 tequila
of the gods: 6 nectar
Oriental: 4 arak, sake, saki 6 arrack
Russian: 5 kefir, kvass, vodka
Scottish: 6 scotch
South American: 4 maté 5 yerba
9 yerba maté
Swedish: 5 glogg
Turkish: 4 raki
West Indies: 3 rum

bevy

3 mob 4 band, club, crew, gang, herd, knot, pack 5 bunch, covey, crowd, drove, flock, group, horde, party, swarm 6 clutch, gaggle, troupe 7 cluster, company, coterie 8 assembly 9 menagerie, multitude 10 assemblage, collection

bewail

3 rue 4 keen, moan, weep 5 mourn 6 bemoan, grieve, lament, regret 7 deplore

beware

4 heed, mark, mind, note, shun 5 avoid, watch 6 attend, notice 7 look out 8 take heed, watch out

bewhiskered

5 bushy 7 bearded, goateed, hirsute, stubbly 8 unshaven

bewilder

3 fog 4 daze, stun 5 addle, amaze, befog, mix up, stump 6 baffle, ball up, bemuse, fuddle, muddle, puzzle, rattle 7 confuse, fluster, mystify, nonplus, perplex, stumble 8 befuddle, confound, distract 9 disorient, dumbfound 10 disconcert

bewilderment

3 awe 4 daze 6 wonder 8 surprise 9 amazement, confusion 10 perplexity, puzzlement 11 distraction 12 astonishment, discomfiture, stupefaction 13 consternation

bewitch

3 hex 4 draw, pull, snow, take, wile 5 charm, spell, trick 6 allure, dazzle, delight, seduce, voodoo 7 attract, bedevil, beguile, control, enchant, possess 8 demonize, ensorcel, enthrall, entrance, intrigue, overlook 9 captivate, enrapture, ensorcell, fascinate, hypnotize, magnetize, mesmerize, spellbind

bewitching

4 foxy 5 siren 8 alluring, charming, engaging, enticing, magnetic, mesmeric 9 seductive 10 attractive 12 irresistible

bewitchment

3 hex 4 jinx 5 charm, magic, spell 6 trance 7 evil eye, sorcery 8 black art, wizardry 9 conjuring 10 necromancy 11 conjuration, enchantment, incantation, thaumaturgy

beyond

4 over, past 5 above, after 6 across, beside, yonder 7 besides, further, outside 8 as well as 9 afterlife, hereafter, otherwise 10 afterworld 12 over and above
prefix: 4 meta, over, para 5 extra, hyper, super, trans, ultra 6 preter

Bhutan

capital: 7 Thimphu
ethnic group: 6 Bhutia 8 Assamese, Nepalese 9 Mongolian, Sharcrops
language: 8 Dzongkha
monetary unit: 8 ngultrum
mountain range: 8 Himalaya 13 Great Himalaya
neighbor: 5 China, India, Tibet
plain: 5 Duars

bias

4 bend, bent, skew, sway, tilt, turn 5 angle, bevel, slant 7 beveled, bigotry, dispose, distort, incline, leaning, oblique, slanted 8 diagonal, penchant, slanting, tendency 9 crosswise, inclining, influence, prejudice, proneness, viewpoint 10 diagonally, favoritism, partiality, propensity, predispose, prepossess, proclivity, standpoint, transverse 11 disposition, inclination 12 one-sidedness, predilection 13 preconception

biased

6 racist, swayed, unfair, warped 7 bigoted, colored, partial, slanted 8 disposed, inclined, one-sided, partisan, slanting 9 jaundiced, sectarian, unneutral 10 influenced, interested, prejudiced 11 opinionated, predisposed, tendentious

bibelot

5 curio 6 bauble, gewgaw, trifle 7 memento, novelty, trinket, whatnot 8 gimcrack, ornament 9 objet d'art 10 knickknack

Bible

abbreviation: 3 Col, Cor, Dan, Eph, Gal, Gen, Hab, Heb, Hos, Jas, Jer, Jon, Lam, Lev, Mal, Mic, Neh, Num, Pet, Rev, Rom, Sam, Tim, Tit 4 Deut, Ezek, Josh, Judg,

Obad, Phil, Prov, Zech, Zeph **5** Chron, Thess **6** Eccles, Philem
Apocrypha book: 5 Tobit **6** Baruch, Esdras, Esther, Judith **7** Susanna **8** Manasseh, Manasses **9** Maccabees
New Testament book: 4 Acts, John, Jude, Luke, Mark **5** James, Peter, Titus **6** Romans **7** Hebrews, Matthew, Timothy **8** Philemon **9** Ephesians, Galatians **10** Colossians, Revelation **11** Corinthians, Philippians **13** Thessalonians
Old Testament book: 3 Job **4** Amos, Ezra, Joel, Ruth **5** Hosea, Jonah, Kings, Micah, Nahum **6** Daniel, Esther, Exodus, Haggai, Isaiah, Joshua, Judges, Psalms, Samuel **7** Ezekiel, Genesis, Malachi, Numbers, Obadiah **8** Habakkuk, Jeremiah, Nehemiah, Proverbs **9** Leviticus, Zechariah, Zephaniah **10** Chronicles **11** Deuteronomy **12** Ecclesiastes, Lamentations **13** Song of Solomon
part: 4 book **5** verse **7** chapter **9** testament
translator: 4 Knox (Ronald Arbuthnott) **5** Eliot (John) **6** Jerome, Luther (Martin) **7** Erasmus (Desiderius), Tyndale (William), Zwingli (Huldrych) **8** Andrewes (Lancelot), Wycliffe (John) **9** Coverdale (Miles)
version: 5 Douay **6** Coptic, Gothic, Syriac **7** Vulgate **9** Jerusalem, King James, Masoretic **10** New English, Septuagint

Biblical

animal: 8 behemoth
ascetic order: 6 Essene
battle: 7 Jericho
battle site: 10 Armageddon
charioteer: 4 Jehu
city, town: 4 Cana, Gaza, Tyre, Zoar **5** Endor, Golan, Haifa, Joppa, Sidon, Sodom **6** Asshur, Bethel, Emmaus, Gilgal, Hebron, Mizpah, Shiloh, Smyrna, Tarsus **7** Antioch, Baalbec, Bethany, Corinth, Ephesus, Ephraim, Jericho, Magdala, Nineveh, Samaria **8** Caesarea, Damascus, Gomorrah, Nazareth, Philippi, Tiberias **9** Beersheba, Bethlehem, Capernaum, Jerusalem
coin:
(see at **Hebrew**)
desert: 5 Sinai
garden: 4 Eden **8** Paradise
giant: 7 Goliath
giant slayer: 5 David
hill: 4 Zion **7** Calvary
hunter: 6 Nimrod
judge: 3 Eli **4** Ehud **6** Gideon, Samson, Samuel **7** Deborah, Jephtha **8** Jephthah

king: 3 Asa **4** Ahab, Amon, Elah, Jehu, Saul **5** David, Herod, Hiram **6** Josiah **7** Azariah, Menahem, Solomon **8** Hezekiah, Jeroboam, Manasseh, Rehoboam, Zedekiah **9** Zechariah **11** Jehoshaphat
land: 3 Nod **4** Aram, Elam, Moab, Seba **5** Judah, Judea **6** Canaan, Goshen, Israel **7** Chaldea, Galilee, Samaria **9** Palestine
land of plenty: 6 Goshen
measure:
(see at **Hebrew**)
mountain: 5 Horeb, Sinai **6** Ararat, Carmel, Gilboa, Gilead, Hermon, Moriah, Olivet, Pisgah **7** Lebanon
name: 3 Asa, Bel, Dan, Eli, Eve, Gad, Ham, Ira, Job, Lot, Uri **4** Abel, Adam, Ahab, Amon, Boaz, Cain, Elam, Enos, Esau, Jael, Jehu, Joel, John, Lael, Leah, Levi, Mark, Mary, Mica, Moab, Noah, Omar, Onan, Paul, Reba, Ruth, Sara, Saul, Seth, Shem **5** Aaron, Abner, Amram, Asher, Caleb, David, Dinah, Elias, Enoch, Ethan, Hagar, Heman, Herod, Hosea, Isaac, Jacob, James, Jared, Jesse, Jonah, Jubal, Judah, Judas, Laban, Micah, Moses, Naomi, Peter, Rufus, Sarah, Sheba, Simon, Tamar, Tubal, Uriah, Uriel, Zadok **6** Ashhur, Balaam, Baruch, Canaan, Daniel, Elijah, Elisha, Esther, Gideon, Gilead, Hannah, Hebron, Isaiah, Israel, Jeshua, Jethro, Joanna, Joseph, Joshua, Josiah, Judith, Martha, Miriam, Nathan, Nimrod, Pasach, Philip, Pilate, Rachel, Reuben, Salome, Samson, Samuel, Simeon, Thomas, Tobias
patriarch:
(see at **Hebrew**)
people: 6 Kenite, Levite **7** Amorite, Edomite, Elamite, Moabite **9** Israelite
plains: 6 Sharon **7** Jericho
plotter: 5 Haman
poem: 5 psalm
pool: 8 Bethesda
priest: 3 Eli **4** Levi **5** Aaron, Annas **8** Caiaphas
Promised Land: 6 Canaan
pronoun: 3 thy **4** thee, thou **5** thine
prophet:
(see **prophet**)
Psalmist: 5 David
punishment: 7 stoning
queen: 5 Sheba **6** Esther **7** Jezebel
river: 4 Nile **6** Jordan
sacred object: 4 urim **7** thummin
scribe: 6 Baruch
sea: 3 Red **4** Dead **7** Galilee
sea monster: 9 Leviathan
spice: 5 aloes, myrrh **6** cassia **7** calamus **8** cinnamon **12** frankincense

spy: 5 Caleb
temptress: 3 Eve 7 Delilah
thief: 8 Barabbas
tree: 5 cedar
valley: 4 Baca, Elah 6 Hinnon, Kidron, Shaveh, Siddim
witch's home: 5 Endor

bibliography
4 list 7 catalog, history 8 book list
13 reference list

bibliopole
7 bookman 10 book dealer, bookseller

bibulous
6 spongy 7 thirsty 8 drinking 9 absorbent
10 absorptive

bicker
3 row 4 spar, spat, tiff 5 argue, clack, fight, scrap 6 gurgle, hassle 7 brabble, clatter, contend, dispute, fall out, flicker, quarrel, quibble, wrangle 8 squabble

bickering
3 row 4 spat 5 brawl, run-in 6 blowup, fracas, hassle, ruckus, rumpus, strife
7 discord, dispute, quarrel, rhubarb, wrangle 8 squabble 11 altercation, embroilment

bicycle
4 bike
brake: 7 caliper, coaster
for two: 6 tandem
gear shift: 10 derailleur
rider: 6 cycler 7 cyclist

bid
3 ask, say, try 4 call, tell, warn, wish
5 essay, greet, offer, order 6 amount, charge, direct, effort, enjoin, invite, render, summon, tender 7 attempt, command, proffer, request, require, venture
8 endeavor, instruct, proposal 10 invitation, submission 11 proposition

biddable
4 mild 6 docile, pliant 7 amiable, pliable, willing 8 amenable, obedient, obliging
9 tractable 10 governable, manageable
11 acquiescent, cooperative, good-natured
13 accommodating

bidding
4 call, word 5 offer, order 6 behest, charge, demand, notice 7 auction, command, dictate, mandate, request, summons, tender 9 ordinance, summoning
10 injunction, invitation 11 commandment, instruction 12 proclamation

biddy
3 bag, bat, hag, hen 4 drab, trot 5 crone, witch 6 beldam 7 chicken

bide
4 live, stay, wait 5 await, dwell, tarry
6 hang in, linger, remain, reside 7 hang out, sojourn 8 continue, sit tight, tolerate
10 hang around 11 stick around

bier
10 catafalque

biff
3 bop, box, hit, jab, zap 4 bash, belt, blow, clip, ding, nail, slam, slug, sock, swat, whop
5 blast, catch, clout, pound, slosh, smack, thump, whack 6 strike, thwack, wallop

bifurcate
3 cut 4 fork 5 split 6 bisect, branch, cleave, divide, halve 8 separate 9 branch out 11 dichotomize, dichotomous

bifurcation
4 fork 6 branch 8 division 9 dichotomy, partition, radiation 10 separation

big
3 fat 4 full, hard, huge, main, tall, vast
5 adult, ample, chief, great, grown, heavy, hefty, husky, large, lofty, major, proud, roomy 6 bumper, hugely 7 capital, copious, crammed, crowded, eminent, grown-up, hulking, leading, liberal, mammoth, massive, monster, notable, popular, replete, sizable, stuffed, swollen, weighty 8 colossal, enormous, generous, gracious, imposing, inflated, material, oversize, princely, spacious, swelling
9 capacious, chock-full, distended, extensive, heavy duty, humongous, important, momentous, overblown, paramount, ponderous, principal, prominent, unselfish 10 commodious, large-scale, major-league, preeminent, prodigious, voluminous 11 heavyweight, magnanimous, overflowing, significant, substantial 12 considerable
13 comprehensive, consequential

big bang theorist
5 Gamow (George)

Big Bertha's birthplace
5 Essen

Big _____, Cal.
3 Sur

Big Dipper
constellation: 9 Ursa Major
star: 5 Alcor, Dubhe, Merak, Mizar

bigfoot
9 Sasquatch

biggety
4 bold, vain, wise 5 fresh, nervy, sassy
6 cheeky, snippy, snooty, uppity 7 forward,
stuck-up 8 impudent, insolent, puffed up,
snobbish 9 conceited 11 smart-alecky
13 self-important

bighearted
6 giving 7 liberal 8 generous 9 forgiving
10 altruistic, benevolent, charitable,
munificent, openhanded 11 magnanimous
13 compassionate

big house
3 can, jug, pen 4 coop, jail 5 clink, joint
6 cooler, lockup, prison 7 slammer
8 bastille, bridewell, hoosegow, stockade
11 reformatory 12 penitentiary

bight
3 arm, bay 4 cove, gulf 6 harbor

bigmouthed
4 loud, rude 8 boastful 10 boisterous

bigness
4 size 5 scale, scope 6 extent, volume
9 amplitude, immensity, magnitude
10 dimensions, importance

bigot
6 racist 8 jingoist, racialist 9 extremist
10 chauvinist 11 supremacist

bigoted
6 biased, narrow, unfair 9 hidebound,
illiberal, sectarian 10 brassbound,
intolerant, prejudiced 11 small-minded
12 narrow-minded

bigotry
4 bias 6 racism 9 apartheid, prejudice
10 xenophobia 11 intolerance

big shot
3 VIP 4 czar 5 celeb, mogul, nabob,
tycoon 6 bigwig, fat cat 7 kingpin, notable,
pooh-bah 8 higher-up, luminary, top brass
9 celebrity, dignitary, personage 13 high-
muck-a-muck

big-time
5 major 7 eminent, greatly, leading
8 renowned 9 high-level, important,
paramount, prominent 10 large-scale
11 influential, major-league

big top
4 tent 6 circus

bigwig
3 VIP 5 heavy, mogul, nabob 6 honcho,

kahuna 7 kingpin, magnate, notable
8 luminary, somebody 9 dignitary,
personage 11 heavy hitter, muckety-muck
13 high-muck-a-muck

bijou
3 gem 5 jewel 8 gemstone

bijouterie
6 jewels 7 jewelry 8 trinkets
10 decoration

bike
5 cycle 7 scooter 10 motorcycle
12 motorscooter

bilge
3 rot 4 bull, bunk, guff 5 hooey, trash
6 bunkum 7 baloney, garbage, hogwash,
malarky, rubbish, twaddle 8 claptrap,
nonsense 9 poppycock, silliness
10 balderdash 11 foolishness

bilk
3 con, gyp 4 balk, beat, dash, duck, dupe,
foil, fool, hoax, hose, kite, milk, ruin, scam
5 avoid, cheat, cozen, dodge, elude,
evade, shake, shaft, skirt, stiff, trick
6 baffle, chisel, chouse, diddle, double,
escape, eschew, fleece, rip off, sucker,
thwart 7 deceive, defraud, prevent, swindle
8 flimflam, hoodwink, sidestep, stave off
9 frustrate 10 circumvent

bill
3 dun, fin, neb, nib, tab 4 beak, bone,
buck, chit, list, note, skin 5 check, score,
visor 6 charge, damage, dollar, notice,
poster, roster 7 account, charges, invoice,
placard, program, sawbuck, smacker
8 mandible 9 greenback, reckoning,
smackeroo, statement

billet
3 bar, bed, gig, hut, job, rod 4 post, slab,
spar, spot 5 berth, board, house, ingot,
lodge, place, put up, stick, strip 6 bestow,
canton, harbor, office 7 quarter 8 domicile,
position, quarters, vocation 9 entertain,
situation 10 assignment, connection,
employment, encampment, livelihood,
profession, occupation 11 appointment

billet-doux
8 mash note 10 love letter

billfold
6 wallet

billiards term
3 cue 4 foot, head, jaws, kiss, long, peas,
pool, race, rack, spot 5 break, carom,
chalk, count, masse 6 bridge, cannon,

corner, crotch, inning, miscue, nurses, pocket, stance, string **7** bricole, cue ball, cushion, ferrule, kitchen, pyramid, scratch, shooter, snooker **8** apex ball, balkline, bank shot, cue stick, dead ball, jump shot, rotation, triangle **9** clean bank, eight ball **10** chuck nurse, head string, object ball **12** balance point

billingsgate
5 abuse **6** tirade **7** obloquy **9** contumely, invective **10** revilement, scurrility **12** vilification, vituperation

billion
British: 8 milliard
combining form: 4 giga

billionth
combining form: 4 nano

bill of fare
4 menu **7** program **11** carte du jour

billow
4 mass, wave **5** bulge, cloud, surge, swell **6** puff up, roller **7** balloon, upsurge

Billy Budd's captain
4 Vere

billy club
4 cane **5** baton **6** cudgel, paddle **8** bludgeon **9** bastinado, truncheon **10** knobkerrie, nightstick

bin
4 crib **5** frame, stall **6** bunker, hamper, trough **9** container **10** receptacle

binary
4 twin, dual **5** duple **6** double, duplex **7** coupled, paired, matched, twofold **9** dualistic

bind
3 tie **4** frap, gird, tape, wrap **5** chain, cinch, strap, tie up, truss **6** cement, commit, fasten, fetter, ligate, pinion **7** bandage, confine, enchain, shackle, trammel **8** enfetter, restrain **9** constrain, constrict, indenture

binder
4 file **5** cover **6** folder, jacket **7** wrapper

binding
8 required **9** mandatory, requisite **10** obligatory

bindlestiff
4 hobo

binge
3 jag **4** orgy, riot, soak, tear, time, toot **5** blast, booze, fling, party, revel, souse,

spree, stint **6** bender **7** blowoff, blowout, carouse, debauch, rampage, revelry, shindig, splurge, surfeit, wassail **8** carousal, gluttony **9** bacchanal, brannigan **10** debauchery, indulgence **11** bacchanalia, celebration **12** intemperance

bingo
3 yes **5** beano **7** correct

biographer
American: 5 Weems (Parson) **6** Parton (James) **7** Freeman (Douglas) **8** Bradford (Gamaliel), Sandburg (Carl) **10** McCullough (David)
English: 6 Aubrey (John), Morley (John), Walton (Izaak) **8** Strachey (Lytton)
French: 7 Maurois (André)
German: 6 Ludwig (Emil)
Greek: 8 Plutarch
Italian: 6 Vasari (Giorgio)
Roman: 9 Suetonius
Scottish 7 Boswell (James)

biography
3 bio **4** life, obit, vita **5** diary, story **6** memoir **7** history, profile **8** obituary **11** confessions

biological category
5 class, genus, order **6** family, phylum **7** kingdom, species, variety **10** subspecies

bionomics
7 ecology

Bip's creator
7 Marceau (Marcel)

bird
African: 6 barbet, bulbul, jabiru, turaco **7** courser, marabou, ostrich, touraco **8** hornbill, oxpecker, parakeet **9** broadbill, francolin
Antarctic: 4 skua **7** penguin **10** sheathbill
aquatic: 3 auk, mew **4** coot, duck, erne, gull, loon, skua, swan, teal, tern **5** booby, cahow, goose, grebe, murre **6** fulmar, gannet, petrel, puffin, scoter, wigeon **7** anhinga, dovekie, mallard, moorhen, pelican, penguin, skimmer, widgeon **8** baldpate, dabchick, murrelet **9** albatross, cormorant, gallinule, guillemot, kittiwake **10** sheathwater, sheathbill
arctic: 3 auk **4** knot, skua **5** murre **6** fulmar, jaeger **7** dovekie **9** guillemot, gyrfalcon
Asian: 4 myna, ruff, smew **5** mynah, pewit **6** chukar, drongo, dunlin, hoopoe, peewit **7** courser, lapwing, peacock **8** dotterel,

hornbill, parakeet, tragopan, wheatear
9 francolin
Australian: 3 emu 4 lory 5 galah
6 drongo 7 bustard 8 bellbird, cockatoo,
lorikeet, lyrebird, parakeet 9 cassowary
blackbird: 3 ani, daw 4 crow, rook
5 merle, ousel, ouzel, raven 6 chough,
magpie, thrush 7 grackle, jackdaw,
redwing
carrion-eating: 6 condor 7 buzzard,
vulture
Central American: 4 guan, ibis 5 booby,
macaw 6 barbet, jabiru, toucan 7 bittern,
jacamar, quetzal, tinamou 8 curassow,
troupial
chimney-nesting: 5 swift
class: 4 Aves
colony: 5 roost 7 rookery
combining form: 5 ornis 6 ornith
7 ornitho 8 ornithes (plural)
crow family: 3 daw, jay 4 rook 5 raven
6 chough, corbie, magpie 7 jackdaw
diving: 3 auk 4 smew 5 grebe, murre
6 petrel 8 murrelet 9 guillemot, merganser
European: 3 mew 4 rook, smew, wren
5 crake, egret, finch, merle, ousel, ouzel,
pewit, pipit 6 cuckoo, hoopoe, linnet,
martin, merlin, redleg, thrush 7 bustard,
jackdaw, kestrel, lapwing, martlet, ortolan,
redwing, sparrow, wagtail 8 blackcap, dabchick, nightjar, nuthatch, redstart, starling,
throstle, whimbrel, woodcock 9 chaffinch,
crossbill, stonechat 10 chiffchaff,
goatsucker, kingfisher 11 lammergeier
extinct: 3 moa 4 dodo 9 aepyornis,
solitaire
fabulous: 3 roc 7 phoenix
fish-eating: 4 erne 6 osprey
flightless: 3 emu, moa 4 dodo, kiwi, rhea
6 kakapo, ratite, takahe 7 apteryx, ostrich,
penguin 9 cassowary
game: 4 duck, rail, teal 5 brant, goose,
quail, snipe 6 chukar, grouse, turkey
7 bustard, mallard, pintail, widgeon
8 baldpate, bobwhite, moorfowl, pheasant,
shoveler, tragopan, wildfowl, woodcock
9 merganser, partridge, ptarmigan
ground-dwelling: 5 quail 6 grouse,
peahen, turkey 7 chicken, peacock,
peafowl 8 bobwhite, moorfowl, pheasant
9 partridge, ptarmigan
Indian: 6 bulbul 7 peacock 8 adjutant,
tragopan
Jamaican: 7 vervain
large: 3 emu, moa 5 eagle 6 curlew
7 bustard, ostrich, pelican 8 curassow,
shoebill
largest: 7 ostrich
Madagascar: 6 drongo 7 anhinga

marsh: 4 coot, rail 5 crane, snipe, stilt
9 gallinule
Mexican: 6 jacana
mythical: 3 roc 7 phoenix
New Zealand: 3 kea 4 kiwi 6 kakapo
7 apteryx
nocturnal: 3 owl 5 owlet 7 oilbird
8 guacharo, nightjar 9 nighthawk
10 goatsucker
North American: 3 ani, tit 4 coot, wren
5 booby, crane, egret, junco, murre, robin,
swift, veery, vireo 6 dunlin, fulmar, grouse,
phoebe, towhee, turkey, verdin, willet 7 anhinga, blue jay, catbird, flicker, grackle,
tanager 8 bobolink, bobwhite, cardinal,
killdeer, nuthatch, thrasher, titmouse
9 chickadee, crossbill, nighthawk,
partridge, snakebird 10 bufflehead
12 whippoorwill
of Arabian Nights: 3 roc
of brilliant plumage: 4 lory 5 macaw
6 oriole, parrot, toucan, trogon 7 jacamar
8 lorikeet, parakeet, pheasant, tragopan
of peace: 3 dove
of prey: 3 owl 4 hawk, kite 5 buteo,
eagle, harpy 6 condor, falcon, osprey,
raptor 7 buzzard, goshawk, harrier, kestrel,
vulture 8 caracara 9 accipiter 11 lammergeier
passerine:
(see **songbird** below)
razorbilled: 3 auk
relating to: 5 avian 8 ornithic
shore: 3 auk 4 gull, tern 5 snipe, stilt
6 avocet, curlew, dunlin, plover, puffin,
willet 7 lapwing, skimmer 8 killdeer,
whimbrel, woodcock 9 phalarope,
sandpiper, turnstone
small: 3 tit 4 wren 5 finch, pewee, pipit,
vireo 6 canary, tomtit, verdin 7 sparrow
8 titmouse 9 chickadee
songbird: 3 jay, tit 4 chat, crow, lark,
wren 5 finch, pipit, robin, veery, vireo
6 bulbul, canary, linnet, oriole, shrike,
thrush 7 catbird, creeper, kinglet, redwing,
skylark, sparrow, swallow, tanager, titlark,
wagtail, warbler, waxwing 8 bobolink,
brantail, cardinal, nuthatch, Philomel,
redstart, starling, thrasher, woodlark
9 chickadee, stonechat 10 chiffchaff,
flycatcher 11 nightingale
South American: 4 guan, loro, rhea
5 egret, macaw 6 jabiru, toucan
7 jacamar, limpkin, oilbird 8 caracara,
curassow, guacharo, screamer, troupial
9 trumpeter
talking: 4 myna 5 mynah 6 parrot
tropical: 3 ani 6 barbet, drongo, toucan,

trogon **7** jacamar, quetzal, sawbill, waxbill **8** troupial

turkey-like: 8 curassow

unfledged: 4 eyas **5** chick **8** nestling

wading: 4 ibis, rail **5** crane, egret, heron, stork **6** godwit, jabiru, jacana **7** bittern, limpkin, tattler **8** flamingo, shoebill **9** spoonbill

web-footed: 3 auk **4** duck, loon, swan **5** goose, murre **6** avocet, fulmar, gannet, petrel, puffin **7** anhinga, pelican, penguin **8** shoveler **9** albatross, cormorant, guillemot, merganser, razorbill, snakebird **10** shearwater

West Indian: 3 ani

birdbrain
4 dodo, goof **5** dummy, dunce, idiot, moron, ninny **6** nitwit **7** airhead, dullard, halfwit **8** dumbbell, imbecile, meathead, numskull **9** dumb bunny, ignoramus, numbskull, simpleton **10** nincompoop **11** featherhead

birdcage
6 aviary

birdlife
8 avifauna

bird pepper
9 chiltepin

birds' eggs
study of: 6 oology

birth
4 dawn, stem **5** arise, issue, onset, start **6** create, outset, spring **7** emanate, genesis, lineage, opening **8** delivery, generate, geniture, nascence, nascency, nativity, pedigree **9** beginning, originate **10** extraction **11** parturition **12** commencement

birth-control leader
6 Sanger (Margaret)

birth flower
April: 5 daisy
August: 9 gladiolus
December: 10 poinsettia
February: 8 primrose
January: 9 carnation
July: 8 sweet pea
June: 4 rose
March: 6 violet
May: 15 lily of the valley
November: 13 chrysanthemum
October: 6 dahlia
September: 5 aster

birthmark
4 mole **5** nevus, point, trait **7** feature **13** discoloration

Birth of a Nation director
8 Griffith (D. W.)

birthright
3 due, lot **6** legacy **7** bequest, portion **8** appanage, heirloom, heritage **9** patrimony **11** entitlement, inheritance

birthroot
8 trillium

birthstone
April: 7 diamond **8** sapphire
August: 7 peridot **8** sardonyx
December: 6 zircon **9** turquoise
February: 8 amethyst
January: 6 garnet
July: 4 ruby
June: 5 agate, pearl **11** alexandrite
March: 6 jasper **10** aquamarine, bloodstone
May: 7 emerald
November: 5 topaz
October: 4 opal **10** tourmaline
September: 8 sapphire **10** chrysolite

biscuit
4 rusk, snap **6** cookie **7** cracker **8** cracknel, hardtack

bishop
district: 7 diocese
headdress: 5 miter, mitre
seat of office: 3 see
skullcap: 9 zucchetto
staff: 7 crosier, crozier
throne: 8 cathedra

bishopric
3 see **7** diocese

bison
European: 6 wisent **7** aurochs
family: 7 Bovidae
North American: 7 buffalo

bistered
4 dark **5** brown, dusky, swart, tawny **6** brunet **7** swarthy, tanned **8** brunette **11** dark-skinned

bistro
3 bar, pub **4** café **5** joint **6** nitery, tavern **7** barroom, cabaret, hot spot, niterie, taproom **8** snack bar **9** nightclub, night spot **10** coffee shop **11** rathskeller **13** watering place

bit
3 dab, dot, end, jot, tad **4** atom, dash,

drop, iota, lump, mite, part, rein, tick, time, whet **5** borer, flake, grain, minim, pinch, scrap, shard, shred, slice, space, speck, spell, trace, while **6** minute, moment, morsel, rather, second **7** portion, segment, smidgen, stretch, trickle **8** fraction, fragment, molecule, mouthful, particle, somewhat

bit by bit
6 evenly **9** by degrees, gradually, piecemeal **12** continuously **13** slow and steady

bitch goddess
7 success

bite
3 cut, eat, lot, nip **4** chaw, chew, edge, etch, food, gnaw, kick, meal, pain, part, rust, snap, tapa, zest **5** champ, chomp, erode, munch, piece, quota, share, slice, snack, stink, taste, tooth **6** crunch, morsel, nibble **7** corrode, eat away, eat into, engrave, portion **8** dissolve, mouthful, piquancy **9** allotment, allowance, masticate, occlusion **10** laceration **11** refreshment

biting
3 raw **4** cold **5** bleak, crisp, harsh, nippy, sharp **6** bitter, severe **7** acerbic, caustic, cutting, mordant, satiric **8** freezing, incisive, piercing **9** sarcastic, scathing, trenchant **11** penetrating

bitter
4 acid, tart **5** acerb, acrid, harsh, sharp **6** severe **7** acerbic, caustic, galling, hostile, painful **8** grievous, ruthless, virulent **9** rancorous, vexatious, vitriolic **11** acrimonious, unpalatable **12** antagonistic

bitterness
4 gall **6** rancor **7** ill will **8** acidity, acrimony, asperity, coldness **9** animosity, antipathy **10** resentment

bittersweet
4 vine **8** poignant **10** nightshade

bitumen
3 tar **5** pitch **7** asphalt **8** blacktop

bivalve
4 clam, spat **6** cockle, mussel, oyster **7** geoduck, mollusk, piddock, scallop **9** lampshell **10** brachiopod

bivouac
4 camp, tent **6** billet, encamp, laager, maroon **7** shelter, sojourn **10** encampment

bizarre
3 odd **5** antic, queer, weird **7** curious, oddball, strange, uncanny, unusual **8** abnormal, atypical, freakish, peculiar, quixotic, singular **9** anomalous, eccentric, fantastic, grotesque, unearthly, unnatural **10** outlandish, outrageous **11** extravagant

bizarrerie
5 freak **6** oddity **7** anomaly, caprice, oddness **9** curiosity, weirdness **10** aberration

Bizet opera
6 Carmen

blab
3 gab, gas, jaw, yak **4** chat, leak, talk, tell **5** run on, spill **6** babble, betray, burble, gabble, gossip, inform, jabber, reveal, snitch, squeal, tattle, tell on, yammer **7** blather, chatter, divulge, let slip, palaver, prattle **8** blurt out, disclose, give away, go public

blabber
3 gab, rat **4** chat, fink **5** clack, drool, prate **6** babble, canary, drivel, gabber, gabble, gossip, jabber, magpie, prater, ramble **7** blather, chatter, palaver, prattle, twaddle **8** idle talk, jabberer, prattler **9** chatterer **10** chatterbox, tatttletale

blabbermouth
3 rat **4** fink **6** canary, gabber, gossip, magpie, prater, snitch **7** windbag **8** busybody, jabberer, prattler **10** chatterbox, talebearer, tattletale **11** stool pigeon

black
3 jet **4** ebon, inky, noir, onyx **5** ebony, raven, sable **6** pitchy **8** charcoal, funereal **9** pitch-dark
combining form: 3 mel **4** atro, mela, melo **5** melam, melan **6** melano

blackball
3 bar **4** veto, shun, snub **5** block, spurn **6** ice out, refuse, reject, strike **7** boycott, exclude, keep out, rule out **9** interdict, ostracize **11** vote against

black bass
7 sunfish

black beast
see bête noire

Black Beauty author
6 Sewell (Anna)

blackbird
see bird

black cohosh
7 bugbane

black crappie
7 sunfish 10 calico bass

black death
6 plague 13 bubonic plague

black diamond
4 coal 8 hematite 9 carbonado

blacken
3 dim, fog, ink 4 blot, burn, char, sear, slur, soil, soot 5 cloud, libel, shade, singe, smear, sully, taint 6 bruise, darken, defame, defile, malign, scorch, vilify 7 asperse, cloud up, eclipse, slander, traduce 8 besmirch, dishonor 10 calumniate

black eye
4 blot, onus, slur 5 stain 6 bruise, defeat, shiner, stigma 7 setback

blackfish
5 whale 6 tautog 10 pilot whale

Black Forest
11 Schwarzwald
city: 10 Baden-Baden
peak: 8 Feldberg
river: 5 Rhein, Rhine 6 Danube, Neckar

black gold
3 oil 9 petroleum

blackguard
4 heel, punk 5 abuse, cheat, knave, rogue 6 rascal 7 hoodlum, lowlife, ruffian, villain 8 hooligan, scalawag 9 charlatan, miscreant, reprobate, scoundrel 10 delinquent, mountebank 11 rapscallion

blackhead
3 zit 4 spot 5 sebum 6 pimple 10 larval clam

blackjack
3 oak, sap 4 bash, club, cosh 6 coerce 7 pontoon, tankard 8 bludgeon 9 twenty-one, vingt-et-un 10 sphalerite

black lead
8 graphite

black letter
6 Gothic 10 Old English

blacklist
3 bar 4 oust 5 expel, purge, smear 6 banish, impugn 7 boycott, condemn, exclude, shut out 8 denounce 9 ostracize, proscribe 10 stigmatize

blackmail
5 bleed 6 extort, payoff 7 milking, squeeze 8 chantage, coercion 9 extortion, hush money, shake down

black out
4 edit, wipe 5 annul, erase, faint, swoon 6 cancel, censor, cut off, darken, delete, efface, excise 7 conceal, eclipse, expunge 8 collapse, make dark, sanitize, suppress 9 eradicate, expurgate 10 blue-pencil, obliterate

blackpoll
7 warbler

Black Prince
6 Edward

Black Sea
city: 5 Yalta 6 Odessa 9 Constanta
peninsula: 6 Crimea 7 Crimean

Blackshirt
7 fascist

blacksmith
6 forger 7 farrier, striker 10 horseshoer

blacktail
8 mule deer

blackthorn
4 plum, sloe

black widow
6 spider

bladder
3 sac 4 cyst 5 pouch 7 blister, vacuole 7 vesicle

blade
4 beau, buck, dude, edge, leaf 5 knife, sword 6 runner 9 swordsman

blah
4 bosh, dull, flat, tame 5 ho-hum, hooey, tired, vapid 6 boring, bunkum, dreary, humbug, stodgy 7 humdrum 8 banausic, lifeless, mediocre, nonsense, plodding 10 balderdash, lackluster, monotonous, pedestrian 11 indifferent, uninspiring 13 uninteresting

blamable
see blameworthy

blame
3 rap 4 onus 5 fault, guilt, knock 6 accuse, charge, finger, indict 7 censure, condemn 8 denounce, reproach 9 criticize, liability, reprehend, reprobate 10 accusation, imputation 11 culpability

12 condemnation, denunciation, reprehension
Scottish: 4 wite, wyte **6** dirdum

blameless
4 good, pure **5** clean, moral **7** perfect, upright **8** innocent, unguilty, virtuous **9** crimeless, exemplary, faultless, guiltless, honorable, lily-white, righteous, unsullied **10** immaculate, impeccable, inculpable **13** unimpeachable

blameworthy
3 lax **5** amiss **6** guilty, liable, sinful **7** at fault **8** criminal, culpable, derelict **9** negligent **10** answerable, censurable, delinquent, indictable, punishable **11** disgraceful, inexcusable, responsible **12** dishonorable **13** reprehensible, objectionable

blanch
4 fade, pale **5** quail, scald, start **6** bleach, shrink, whiten **7** decolor, lighten, parboil **8** etiolate

blanched
3 wan **4** ashy, pale **5** ashen, faded, livid, peaky, waxen, white **6** anemic, doughy, pallid, peaked **7** ghostly **8** bloodless, colorless, washed out **10** cadaverous

Blancheflor's beloved
6 Flores, Floris

bland
4 dull, flat, blah, mild, soft **5** balmy, banal, vapid **6** boring, gentle, pablum **7** insipid, restful, sapless **8** soothing **9** calmative **10** complacent, flavorless, monotonous, namby-pamby, wishy-washy **12** ingratiating **13** nonirritating

blandish
3 con, woo **4** coax, fawn, urge **5** cozen **6** cajole, stroke **7** blarney, flatter, wheedle **8** butter up, inveigle, soft-soap **9** importune, sweet-talk **10** curry favor

blandishment
3 oil **5** honey **7** blarney, eyewash, incense, promise **8** flattery, soft soap **9** adulation, seduction, sweet talk **10** allurement, compliment, inducement, sycophancy, temptation

blank
3 gap **4** bare, dull, seal, skip, void **5** chasm, dazed, empty, space, virgin **6** stupid, vacant, vacuous **7** deadpan, obscure, unfilled **8** complete, omission, outright, spotless **9** impassive **10** empty, space, interstice, obliterate **11** featureless **12** inexpressive, unexpressive

blanket
4 bury, hide **5** cover, quilt, throw **6** afghan, stroud **7** overlay **8** coverlet, mackinaw, sweeping **10** overspread

blankness
6 vacuum **7** nullity, vacancy, vacuity **9** emptiness **10** desolation

blare
4 roar **5** blast, shout **6** clamor, jangle **7** trumpet

blaring
4 loud **5** sharp **6** brassy, shrill **7** clarion, jarring, roaring **8** blinding, piercing, strident **9** deafening, dissonant **10** stentorian **11** ear-piercing, penetrating, stentorious **12** earsplitting

blarney
3 con, oil **4** coax, bunk **5** charm, honey, hooey **6** bunkum, cajole, humbug **7** baloney, incense, wheedle **8** blandish, buncombe, cajolery, flattery, inveigle, nonsense, soft soap **9** adulation, sweet-talk **11** compliments **12** blandishment, inveiglement

blasé
4 cool **5** bored, jaded, sated **6** breezy **7** knowing, offhand, unmoved, worldly **9** apathetic, incurious, surfeited, unexcited **10** world-weary **11** indifferent, unconcerned, worldly-wise **12** disenchanted, uninterested **13** disillusioned, sophisticated

blaspheme
4 cuss **5** abuse, curse, swear **6** revile **7** pollute, profane **8** denounce, execrate **9** castigate, excoriate

blasphemous
6 coarse, sinful **7** godless, impious, obscene, profane, ungodly **10** irreverent **12** sacrilegious **13** disrespectful

blasphemy
3 sin **5** abuse, error **6** heresy **7** cursing, cussing, impiety, mockery **8** swearing **9** profanity, sacrilege, violation **10** execration, heterodoxy **11** desecration, iconoclasm, imprecation, irreverence, malediction, profanation

blast
3 din **4** bang, beat, blow, boom, clap, dash, gale, gust, kill, peal, ruin, slam, toot **5** blare, burst, crack, crash, salvo, shoot,

smash, wreck **6** attack, blight, blow up, damage, squall, wallop **7** destroy, lambast, shatter, shrivel, trumpet **8** dynamite, lambaste, outburst **9** explosion, castigate, discharge, overwhelm, shock wave **10** annihilate, detonation

blat

4 bray **5** blurt **6** cry out **7** exclaim **8** blurt out

blatant

4 bald, loud **5** clear, gaudy, naked, noisy, overt, saucy **6** arrant, brassy, brazen, crying, flashy, garish, patent, tawdry, vulgar **7** glaring, jarring, obvious **8** flagrant, immodest, impudent, insolent, manifest, overbold, strident **9** barefaced, clamorous, obtrusive, shameless, unabashed **10** boisterous, outrageous, scurrilous, unblushing, vociferous **11** conspicuous, loudmouthed, transparent **12** ear-splitting, obstreperous

blather

3 gab, gas, jaw, rot, yak **4** bosh, gush, rave, stir **5** bleat, drool, hokum, prate **6** babble, bunkum, drivel, effuse, gabble, jabber, natter, yammer **7** blabber, chatter, enthuse, palaver, prattle, rubbish, twaddle **8** chitchat, claptrap, idle talk, nonsense **9** commotion **10** balderdash, double-talk, flapdoodle **12** gobbledygook

blaze

4 burn, fire **5** burst, flame, flare, glare, shine **7** flare up **8** eruption, outburst **10** incandesce **13** conflagration
Scottish: 3 low **4** lowe

blazer

6 marker, reefer **9** sport coat **10** sports coat **12** sports jacket

blazes

4 hell **5** abyss, Hades, Sheol **6** Tophet **7** Gehenna, inferno **9** perdition **11** netherworld

blazing

4 keen **5** afire, fiery **6** aflame, alight, ardent, fervid, on fire, red-hot **7** burning, fervent, flaming, flaring, furious, glowing, ignited, intense, lighted **8** dazzling, feverish, powerful, speeding, white-hot **9** brilliant, perfervid **11** conflagrant, impassioned **12** incandescent **13** scintillating

blazon

4 deck **5** adorn, sound **7** declare, display, publish, trumpet **8** announce, proclaim

9 advertise, broadcast **10** coat of arms, promulgate **11** ostentation

bleach

3 dim **4** fade, pale **5** white **6** blanch, blench, purify, whiten **7** decolor, launder, wash out **8** etiolate, peroxide, sanitize **9** whitewash

bleak

3 raw, sad **4** bare, cold, dour, drab, grim, wild **5** chill, drear, empty, harsh, stark **6** barren, chilly, dismal, dreary, gloomy, lonely, severe, somber, wintry **7** austere, blighted, exposed, joyless **8** desolate, funereal, hopeless **9** cheerless, windswept, woebegone **10** depressing, despondent, oppressive, melancholy

blear

3 dim, fog **4** blur, dull, mist, murk, veil **5** bedim, faint, vague **6** shroud **7** becloud, hidden, obscure, shadowy, unclear **10** indistinct

bleary

3 dim **5** all in, faint, filmy, fuzzy, milky, spent, tired, vague **6** pooped, sapped, used-up, wasted **7** blurred, drained, obscure, shadowy, unclear, worn-out **8** depleted **9** enervated, exhausted, washed-out **10** indistinct

bleat

3 baa **4** blat, carp, crab, fuss, yawp **5** gripe, whine **6** bellow, grouse, grumble, squawk, yammer **7** blather, whimper **8** complain **9** bellyache

bleed

3 sap, run **4** milk, ooze, pity, seep **5** drain, exude, leech, mulct **6** extort, fleece **7** diffuse, extract **9** blackmail **10** hemorrhage

blemish

3 mar **4** blot, flaw, harm, mark, maim, mole, scar, spot, vice, wart **5** fault, nevus, spoil, stain **6** blotch, damage, deface, defect, distort, impair, injure, pimple, stigma **7** blacken, freckle, pervert, tarnish, vitiate **8** impurity, mutilate, pockmark **9** birthmark **12** imperfection **13** disfigurement

blench

3 shy **4** balk, duck, fade **5** blink, cower, quail, quake, start, wince **6** flinch, purify, recoil, shrink, whiten **7** launder, shy away, squinch, tremble **8** draw back, etiolate **9** whitewash

blend

3 fit, mix **4** brew, fuse, meld, weld **5** admix, alloy, merge, unify, union, unite

6 commix, fusion, go with, hybrid, mingle **7** amalgam, combine, mélange, mixture **8** beverage, coalesce, compound, conflate, immingle, intermix, mishmash **9** admixture, commingle, composite, harmonize, infusion, integrate **10** amalgamate, commixture, concoction, synthesize **12** adulteration, amalgamation, intermixture

blender setting
3 mix **4** whip **5** puree **7** liquefy

blesbok
8 antelope

bless
4 laud **5** exalt, extol, endow, favor, grace **6** anoint, bestow, hallow, praise, uphold **7** approve, beatify, glorify, magnify **8** enshrine, eulogize, make holy, sanctify **10** consecrate

blessed
4 holy **5** happy, lucky **6** joyous, sacred **7** saintly **8** beatific, hallowed **9** beatified, fortunate, venerated **10** inviolable, sacrosanct, sanctified **11** consecrated

blessedness
5 bliss **8** felicity, sanctity **9** beatitude, godliness, happiness **12** blissfulness

blessing
4 boon, good, okay **5** asset, favor, grace **6** assent, bounty, thanks **7** benefit, benison, consent, fortune, godsend, support **8** approval, good luck, windfall **9** advantage **10** invocation, permission **11** approbation, benediction, endorsement, good fortune, valediction **12** commendation, consecration, thanksgiving **13** encouragement

"_____ bleu!"
5 Sacré

blight
3 mar, nip **4** dash, ruin **5** blast, decay, spoil, wreck **6** canker, wither **7** disease, scourge, shrivel **9** withering **10** pestilence **13** deterioration

blimp
7 airship **8** zeppelin **9** dirigible

blind
4 daze, dull **5** decoy, front, shade, shill **6** dazzle **7** eyeless, muddled, shutter **8** bedazzle, unseeing **9** sightless **10** visionless

blind alley
6 pocket **7** dead end, impasse **8** cul-de-

sac, deadlock **9** stone wall **10** standstill **11** obstruction

blind god
4 Eros, Hodr, Hoth **5** Cupid, Hoder, Hodur, Hothr

blindworm
8 slowworm

blink
3 bat **4** wink **5** flash, yield **6** give in, squint **7** flicker, flutter, nictate, twinkle **9** nictitate **11** scintillate

blink at
4 omit **5** clear, let go **6** bypass, excuse, forget, ignore, slight **7** condone, connive, let pass, neglect **8** discount, overlook, pass over **9** disregard, exonerate, whitewash

blip
6 censor, screen **9** deviation, expurgate, radar spot **10** bowdlerize

bliss
3 joy **4** Zion **6** Canaan, heaven **7** ecstasy, elysium, nirvana, rapture **8** empyrean, euphoria, paradise **9** beatitude, happiness **10** exaltation **11** blessedness

blissful
5 happy **6** divine, elated, joyful, joyous **8** beatific, ecstatic, euphoric **9** ambrosial, delighted, entranced, rapturous **10** delightful, entrancing

blissfulness
3 joy **7** ecstasy **8** euphoria **9** beatitude, happiness **10** exaltation **11** contentment

blister
4 bleb, flay, lash **5** blain, bulla, slash **6** assail, canker, scathe, scorch **7** lambast, scarify, scourge, vesicle **8** lambaste **9** castigate, excoriate

blithe
3 gay **4** boon **5** happy, jolly, merry, sunny **6** bouncy, casual, cheery, chirpy, jaunty, jocund, jovial **7** gleeful **8** carefree, careless, cheerful, chirrupy, gladsome, heedless, mirthful **9** lightsome, sprightly, unworried, vivacious **10** untroubled **11** thoughtless **12** lighthearted

blithesome
see **blithe**

blitz
4 raid, rush **7** air raid, bombard, bombing **8** shelling **9** onslaught **10** mass attack **11** bombardment

blitzkrieg
6 attack 7 assault, bombing 9 offensive, onslaught 11 bombardment

blizzard
4 gale 6 squall 8 whiteout 9 snowstorm

bloat
5 bulge, swell 6 billow, expand, fatten, puff up 7 balloon, distend, enlarge, inflate 10 distension

bloated
5 puffy 6 puffed 7 pompous, swollen 8 arrogant, enlarged, inflated 9 distended, overblown, overlarge 11 pretentious 13 self-important

bloc
4 band, ring 5 cabal, party, union 6 clique, league 7 combine, faction 8 alliance 9 coalition 10 consortium, contingent, federation 11 association, combination 13 confederation

block
3 bar 4 clog, fill, hunk, plug, slab, stop, wall, wing 5 brick, choke, chunk, close, ingot 6 cut off, hinder, impede 7 barrier, congest, occlude, stopper 8 obstacle, obstruct 9 barricade, hindrance, intercept

blockade
3 bar 4 stop, wall 5 beset, hem in, siege 6 shut in 7 barrier, besiege 8 close off, encircle, obstruct, stoppage 9 barricade, beleaguer, blank wall, hindrance, roadblock 10 impediment 11 obstruction

blockage
3 bar 4 clog, halt 7 barrier 8 obstacle, stoppage 10 impediment 11 obstruction

blockbuster
4 bomb 11 spectacular

blockhead
3 oaf 4 clod, dolt, dope, fool 5 dummy, dunce, idiot, moron, ninny, nitwit 7 halfwit, imbecile 8 clodpole, clodpoll, dumbbell, numskull 9 ignoramus, lamebrain, numbskull, simpleton 10 nincompoop 12 featherbrain

blockheaded
4 dull, dumb 5 dense, thick 6 stupid 7 doltish, obtuse 9 brainless, dim-witted 10 slow-witted

block out
5 chart, close, draft, frame, mark 6 hinder, screen, sketch 7 obscure, outline, prepare, repress, shut off 8 indicate, obstruct 9 adumbrate, formulate

block up
3 dam 4 clog, fill, plug, stop 5 choke 7 congest

bloke
3 guy, man 4 chap, gent 6 fellow 9 gentleman

blond
4 fair, gold, pale 5 light, sandy, straw, tawny 6 flaxen, golden 7 towhead 8 platinum 9 champagne, towheaded 10 fair-haired 11 sandy-haired 12 honey-colored

blood
4 gore 7 descent, kindred, kinship, lineage 8 ancestry 10 extraction
cancer of: 8 leukemia
cell: 3 red 5 white 8 hemocyte, monocyte, platelet 9 corpuscle, leukocyte 10 lymphocyte 11 erythrocyte, granulocyte
clot: 8 thrombus
coloring matter: 10 hemoglobin
disease: 6 anemia 8 leukemia 10 hemophilia
fluid part: 5 serum 6 plasma
of the gods: 5 ichor
particle in: 7 embolus
poisoning: 6 pyemia 7 toxemia 10 septicemia
pressure: 8 systolic 9 diastolic
relating to: 5 hemic
serum: 6 plasma
study of: 10 hematology
sugar: 7 glucose

bloodbath
7 carnage 8 butchery, massacre, slaying 9 slaughter 10 decimation 12 annihilation 13 extermination

bloodless
3 wan 4 ashy, dull, pale, weak 5 ashen, waxen 6 anemic, feeble, pallid, sallow, torpid 8 listless 9 insensate, unfeeling 10 insensible, nonviolent 11 coldhearted, passionless, unemotional

bloodletting
4 gore 7 carnage, killing 8 butchery, shambles, violence 9 slaughter 10 phlebotomy 11 venesection

bloodline
6 family, strain 7 descent, lineage 8 ancestry, pedigree 10 family tree

bloodroot
7 puccoon

bloodshed
4 gore 7 carnage 9 slaughter

bloodstained
4 gory 6 grisly 7 imbrued, wounded
8 sanguine 10 sanguinary 11 ensanguined, sanguineous

bloodstone
10 chalcedony

bloodsucker
4 tick 5 lamia, leech 6 lizard, sponge
7 sponger, vampire 8 hanger-on, parasite
10 freeloader 12 lounge lizard

bloodthirsty
5 rabid 8 ravening, sanguine 9 cutthroat,
homicidal, murdering, murderous,
predatory, voracious 10 sanguinary
11 sanguineous

blood vessel
4 vein 5 aorta 6 artery 7 jugular
9 capillary
combining form: 3 vas 4 angi, vasi, vaso
5 angio

bloody
4 gory, grim, very 5 cruel 6 damage,
damned, deadly, grisly 7 blasted, hateful,
imbrued, wounded 8 accursed, infernal,
sanguine 9 cutthroat, homicidal,
murdering, murderous 10 detestable,
sanguinary 11 ensanguined, sanguineous
12 death-dealing, slaughtering

bloom
4 blow, glow, open, posy 5 blush 6 floret,
flower, thrive, unfold 7 blossom, burgeon,
coating, develop, dusting, prosper
8 flourish, rosiness 10 cloudiness,
effloresce 13 discoloration

blooper
4 goof, slip, trip 5 boner, break, error, fluff,
gaffe, lapse 6 boo-boo, bungle, howler,
slipup 7 blunder, faux pas, fly ball, misstep,
mistake, offense 8 solecism 9 indecorum,
false step 11 impropriety 12 indiscretion

blossom
3 bud, wax 4 blow, glow, grow, open, posy
5 bloom, blush, flush 6 expand, flower,
mature, thrive, unfold 7 burgeon, develop
8 flourish, floweret, progress, prosper
10 effloresce, peak period 13 effflores-
cence

blot
4 blur, mark, onus, slur, smut, soil, spot
5 brand, odium, smear, speck, stain, sully
6 absorb, smudge, stigma 7 bestain,
blemish, spatter, tarnish 8 black eye,
discolor, disgrace 9 bespatter, moral flaw

blotch
4 mark, spot 5 stain 6 macula, macule,
mottle, smudge 7 blemish, splotch
12 imperfection

blot out
4 raze, void 5 annul, crush, erase, quash,
quell, scrub 6 cancel, delete, efface,
squash 7 abolish, destroy, expunge
9 eliminate, eradicate, extirpat
10 annihilate, extinguish, obliterate
11 exterminate

blotto
see **drunk**

blouse
5 middy, shell, shirt, smock, tunic 6 guimpe

bloviate
4 rail, rant, rave 5 mouth, orate, spout
7 bluster, carry on, declaim, inveigh,
soapbox, talk big 8 harangue, perorate,
sound off, splutter 9 hold forth
10 vociferate

blow
3 bop, fan, hit, jar 4 bang, bash, belt, blff,
bump, cuff, damn, fail, gasp, gust, huff,
pipe, puff, slam, slug, swat, toot, whop,
wind 5 boast, botch, crack, drive, erupt,
leave, pound, punch, shock, slosh, smack,
smash, sound, spend, waste, whack
6 buffet, depart, impact, mishap, thwack,
wallop 7 assault, breathe, chagrin,
consume, debacle, explode, flounder,
flutter, fritter, trumpet 8 calamity, disaster,
knockout, squander 9 bombshell, collision,
dissipate, throw away 10 concussion,
misfortune, trifle away 11 catastrophe

blow-by-blow
4 full 5 fussy 6 minute 7 careful, precise
8 detailed, itemized, thorough
10 exhaustive, meticulous, scrupulous
13 thoroughgoing

blowhard
see **boaster**

blow in
4 land 5 pop by 6 appear, arrive, drop by,
show up, turn up 7 hit town 11 materialize

blowout
4 bash, fete, gala, riot, tear 5 binge, blast,
break, party, split, spree 6 frolic, shindy
7 shindig, victory 8 carousal, flat tire
9 festivity

blowsy
5 dingy, ruddy 6 florid, frowsy, sloppy,
untidy 7 flushed, healthy, unkempt
8 blooming, blushing 10 bedraggled

blow up

4 bomb, burn, fume, rage 5 bloat, burst, erupt, flare, go off, storm, swell 6 expand, seethe 7 bristle, distend, enlarge, explode, inflate, magnify, rupture, shatter 8 boil over, demolish, detonate, dynamite, heighten, mushroom 9 discredit, fulminate, overstate 10 aggrandize

blowy

4 airy, wild 5 fresh, gusty, windy 6 breezy, stormy 7 squally 8 blustery 9 windswept 11 tempestuous

blubber

3 cry, fat, sob 4 bawl, flab, keen, lard, pipe, wail, weep 5 flesh 6 snivel 7 carry on 8 whale fat

bludgeon

3 bat 4 club 5 baton, billy, bully 6 attack, cudgel, hector 7 bluster, war club 8 browbeat, bulldoze, bullyrag 9 bastinado, billy club, blackjack, strong-arm, truncheon 10 intimidate, nightstick
British: 4 cosh

blue

3 low, sad, sea 4 down, glum, lewd, navy, racy 5 bawdy, ocean, royal, salty, spicy 6 cobalt, gloomy, risqué 7 naughty, profane, unhappy 8 dejected, downcast, indecent, off-color 9 depressed, woebegone 10 despondent, dispirited, melancholy, suggestive 11 downhearted 12 disconsolate
dark: 5 perse 6 indigo
grayish: 5 merle, slate
greenish: 4 aqua, cyan, teal 5 beryl 6 cobalt 7 azurite 9 turquoise
reddish: 5 smalt 6 marine, purple, violet 7 cyanine, gentian, lobelia
sky: 5 azure 6 cerulean

___ Blue

3 Ben 9 Little Boy

blue blood

4 lady, lord, peer 5 elite, noble 6 aristo 7 royalty 8 nobleman 9 gentility, gentleman, patrician 10 aristocrat, noblewoman 11 gentle birth, gentlewoman

bluebonnet

4 Scot 11 Texas lupine

Blue Boy painter

12 Gainsborough (Thomas)

bluecoat

3 cop, law 4 fuzz 5 bobby 6 copper 9 constable, patrolman, policeman

Bluegrass State

8 Kentucky

Blue Grotto site

5 Capri

bluejacket

4 mate, salt, swab 5 limey 6 sailor, seaman 7 swabbie 9 sailorman

blue jeans

5 Levis 6 denims

blue moon

3 age, eon, era 4 aeon 5 epoch 7 dog's age 8 eternity, lifetime 10 generation

bluenose

4 prig 5 prude 7 puritan 9 Mrs. Grundy, nice Nelly 10 goody-goody

bluenosed

4 prim 5 rigid 6 prissy, proper, square, stuffy 7 prudish 8 overnice, priggish 9 Victorian 10 scrupulous, tight-laced 11 puritanical, straitlaced

blue-pencil

3 cut 4 edit, trim 5 emend 6 cut out, delete, excise, remove, revise 7 clean up 8 boil down, cross out 9 strike out, tighten up

bluepoint

6 oyster

blueprint

3 map 4 cast, plan, plot 5 chart, draft, frame, model, trace 6 design, devise, rubric, scheme, set out, sketch 7 arrange, diagram, outline, picture, project 8 game plan, strategy 9 delineate 10 conception, rough draft 11 description

blue-ribbon

3 top 5 prime 6 Grade A, tip-top 7 capital, premier 8 five-star, top-notch, superior 9 excellent, first-rate, top-drawer 10 first-class, top-quality, world-class 11 outstanding 12 prize-winning

blues

4 funk 5 dumps, gloom, grief 6 lament 7 sadness, trouble 8 doldrums, glumness 9 dejection, pessimism 10 depression, desolation, low spirits, melancholy, woefulness 11 despondency, melancholia, unhappiness 12 hopelessness, mournfulness

bluff

3 act, con 4 curt, fake, fool, jive, ruse, sham, show 5 blunt, cliff, feign, frank, gruff, rough, trick 6 abrupt, betray, candid, crusty, delude, direct, hearty, humbug

7 beguile, brusque, deceive, fake out, mislead, playact, pretend **8** headland, pretense **9** deception, outspoken, precipice, steep bank **10** escarpment, forthright, no-nonsense, promontory, subterfuge **11** counterfeit, double-cross, plainspoken, short-spoken **13** unceremonious

blunder
4 bull, gaff, goof, mess, muff, slip, trip **5** boner, botch, error, fluff, gaffe, gum up, lapse, lurch **6** bobble, bollix, bumble, bungle, foul up, fumble, goof up, howler, mess up, wander **7** blooper, failure, faux pas, louse up, misstep, mistake, screw up, stumble **8** disaster, flounder **12** indiscretion, misadventure

blunderbuss
3 gun **4** dolt **5** klutz **6** galoot, lummox **7** bungler, firearm **8** bonehead, numskull **9** blockhead, numbskull **10** stumblebum **13** butterfingers

blunt
4 bald, calm, curt **5** allay, bluff, brief, frank, gruff, plain, rough, terse **6** abrupt, benumb, candid, crusty, deaden, direct, lessen, obtuse **7** brusque, rounded, uncivil **8** enfeeble, not sharp, snippety **10** forthright **11** desensitize, insensitive, plainspoken, unvarnished **12** discourteous **13** unceremonious

blur
3 dim, fog **4** blot, dull, mist **5** befog, blear, cloud, muddy, smear, stain, taint **6** smudge, stigma **7** becloud, besmear, confuse, tarnish **8** besmirch, discolor **in printing: 6** mackle

blurb
4 hype, plug, puff **5** press **6** notice **7** write-up **8** good word **9** promotion **12** commendation

blurry
4 hazy **5** vague **6** cloudy **7** clouded, unclear **9** undefined, unfocused **10** indistinct

blurt
4 blab, blat, bolt **5** spill **6** cry out, let out **7** divulge, exclaim, let slip, spit out **8** disclose, give away **9** ejaculate

blush
4 burn, glow, rose, view **5** bloom, color, flame, flush, rouge **6** mantle, pinken, redden **7** blossom, crimson, redness, turn red **8** mantling, rosiness

bluster
4 bawl, crow, gust, huff, rage, roar, rout **5** blast, bully, prate, storm, strut, vaunt **6** bellow, clamor, hector, lean on **7** bombast, bravado, dragoon, roister, swagger, talk big **8** boasting, browbeat, bulldoze, bullyrag, domineer **9** gasconade **10** grandstand, intimidate **11** braggadocio

blustery
4 wild **5** blowy, gusty, rough **6** drafty, raging, raving, squally, stormy **7** furious, violent **9** truculent, tumultuous, turbulent **10** boisterous **11** tempestuous

boa
5 scarf, snake

boar
3 pig **4** male **5** swine

board
4 fare, feed, food, lath, slab, slat **5** catch, get on, hop on, house, lodge, meals, panel, plank, put up, table **6** billet, embark **7** emplane, entrain, quarter **9** directors **11** directorate
artist's: 7 palette

boarder
5 guest **6** lodger, renter, roomer, tenant

board game
see at **game**

boarding house
6 hostel **7** hospice, lodging, pension **8** pensione

boardwalk
7 gangway **9** esplanade, promenade

boast
3 own **4** blow, brag, crow, have, puff **5** exalt, exult, glory, mouth, prate, preen, strut, vaunt **6** parade **7** bluster, bombast, bravado, contain, enlarge, exhibit, inflate, possess, show off, swagger, talk big **9** gasconade **10** exaggerate, grandstand **11** rodomontade **12** exaggeration

boaster
6 gascon **7** egotist, peacock, show-off **8** big mouth, blowhard, braggart **11** braggadocio, rodomontade

boastful
4 vain **5** cocky **6** braggy **8** arrogant, braggart, puffed-up, vaunting **9** bigheaded, conceited, egotistic **11** egotistical, pretentious, swellheaded **12** vainglorious **13** swelled-headed
Scottish: 6 vaunty

boat

3 ark, hoy, tug 4 dhow, dory, junk, pram,
prau, proa, punt, scow, ship, yawl 5 barge,
canoe, coble, ferry, kayak, ketch, scull,
shell, skiff, sloop, smack, umiak, yacht
6 bateau, bugeye, caïque, cutter, dinghy,
hooker, lateen, lugger, packet, sampan,
vessel, wherry 7 caravel, coracle, currach,
curragh, gondola, lighter, pinnace, pirogue,
pontoon, shallop, steamer, trawler, vedette,
vidette 8 schooner, trimaran 9 catamaran,
hydrofoil

bottom projection: 4 keel
captain: 5 pilot 6 master 7 skipper
dock, basin: 6 marina
front end of: 3 bow 4 fore, prow
motor: 7 cruiser, inboard 8 outboard,
runabout
on a ship: 3 gig 6 launch 7 pinnace
race: 7 regatta
rear end of: 3 aft 5 stern
song: 6 chanty, shanty 7 chantey
9 barcarole 10 barcarolle

boatman

4 mate 5 limey 6 Charon, sailor
7 mariner, oarsman, paddler 8 deckhand,
water dog 9 gondolier, navigator

boat-shaped

8 scaphoid 9 navicular

Boaz's wife

4 Ruth

bob

3 jig, nod, rap, tap 4 buff, clip, crop, dock,
trim 5 bunch, float 6 bounce, curtsy, jiggle,
jounce, polish, trifle, wobble 7 cluster,
curtsey, nosegay 8 shilling 9 genuflect

bobbery

3 ado, din, row 4 fray, riot 5 babel, noise
6 bedlam, hubbub, racket, ruckus, rumpus
7 ferment, ruction 9 commotion, confusion
10 hullabaloo, hurly-burly 11 disturbance,
pandemonium

bobbin

4 pirn 5 quill, spool, wheel 7 spindle
8 cylinder

bobble

3 bob, dud 4 flub, fluff, goof, mess, muff
5 botch, error, gum up 6 ball up, bollix,
bumble, bungle, flub up, fumble, goof up,
muff up 7 blooper, failure, louse up,
mistake

bobby

3 law 6 copper, peeler 7 officer
9 constable, patrolman, policeman

bobwhite

5 quail 9 partridge

Boccaccio

beloved: 9 Fiammetta
tales: 9 Decameron

bode

4 hint 5 augur 6 signal, warn of
7 betoken, portend, presage, promise,
signify, suggest 8 foreshow, indicate
9 foretoken, prefigure 10 foreshadow

bodega

3 bar, pub 5 saloon 7 barroom, grocery
8 wineshop 12 general store

bodement

4 omen, sign 5 hunch 6 augury 7 portent,
presage 8 prophecy 9 foretoken,
harbinger 10 foreboding, intimation,
prediction, prognostic 11 premonition
12 presentiment

bodiless

7 ghostly 8 ethereal, spectral 9 unfleshly
10 discarnate, immaterial, unphysical
11 disembodied, incorporeal, nonmaterial
12 apparitional 13 insubstantial

bodily

6 carnal 7 en masse, earthly, fleshly,
sensual, somatic 8 corporal, entirely,
physical, totally, visceral 9 corporeal
10 altogether, completely 11 unspiritual

bodkin

4 shiv 5 blade, knife, shank 6 dagger,
lancet, needle 7 poniard 8 stiletto

_____ bodkins

4 odds

body

4 bulk, core, form, hull, mass, soma
7 frame, stiff, stock, torso 6 corpse, corpus
7 anatomy, cadaver, carcass, chassis,
corpora (plural), remains 8 physique
9 aggregate, substance
combining form: 4 dema, soma, some,
somi (plural) 5 somat, somia, somus
6 somata (plural), somato

body cavity

5 cecum, sinus 6 coelom 7 abdomen
8 hemocoel

body check

5 block

bodyguard

7 retinue 9 attendant, protector

body of water

3 bay, sea 4 cove, gulf, lake, pond, pool

5 bight, brook, creek, fiord, firth, fjord, inlet, ocean, river **6** harbor, lagoon, puddle, stream **7** channel, estuary **9** reservoir

body passage
4 duct, vein **5** canal **6** artery, meatus, ureter, vagina, venule, vessel **7** trachea, urethra **8** bronchus **9** arteriole, capillary, esophagus, intestine **10** bronchiole **13** bronchial tube, fallopian tube

body politic
5 state **6** nation **11** nation-state

boffo
3 gag, gas, hit **4** wild **5** laugh, scream **7** sold-out **8** smash-hit, smashing **10** successful **11** sensational

bog
3 fen **4** mire, quag **5** delay, marsh, swamp **6** impede, morass, muskeg, slough, slow up **8** quagmire **9** swampland

Bogart, Humphrey
film: 6 Sahara **7** Dead End, Sabrina **8** Big Sleep (The), Key Largo **10** Casablanca, High Sierra **11** Caine Mutiny (The) **12** African Queen (The) **13** Maltese Falcon (The) **15** Petrified Forest (The) **16** To Have and Have Not **24** Treasure of the Sierra Madre (The) **wife: 6** Bacall (Lauren)

bog down
4 flag, mire **5** choke, delay, stall **6** detain, falter, hang up, hinder, impede, retard, slow up **7** embroil, set back, slacken **8** encumber, keep back, obstruct, slow down **9** lose steam **10** decelerate

bogey
5 ghost, haunt, shade, spook **6** scarer, shadow, spirit, wraith **7** phantom, specter **8** phantasm, revenant **10** apparition

bogeyman
5 spook **7** bugbear, chimera, monster, phantom, specter, spectre **10** apparition

boggle
4 balk, mess, muff, stun **5** amaze, botch, fudge, gum up, shock, wreck **6** bollix, bungle, cobble, goof up, mess up, strain **7** astound, louse up, nonplus, stagger, stumble, stupefy **8** astonish, bewilder, bowl over, confound **9** dumbfound, mishandle, mismanage, overwhelm, take aback **11** flabbergast

bogus
4 fake, mock, sham **5** false, phony, snide **6** ersatz, forged, pseudo **7** fictive, pretend

8 invented, specious, spurious, trumped up **9** brummagem, concocted, imitation, pinchbeck, simulated **10** artificial, fabricated, fraudulent, mendacious **11** counterfeit

Bohème, La
character: 4 Mimi **7** Rodolfo
composer: 7 Puccini (Giacomo)
setting: 5 Paris

bohemian
5 artsy, gypsy, hippy **6** hippie **7** beatnik, dropout, oddball, offbeat **8** maverick, vagabond, wanderer **9** eccentric **10** avant-garde, iconoclast, unorthodox **13** nonconformist

boil
3 jet **4** bolt, brew, burn, cook, dash, foam, fume, gush, moil, race, rage, rush, spew, spot, stew, vent **5** anger, churn, erupt, fling, froth, poach, shoot, storm, swirl **6** blow up, bubble, charge, canker, coddle, pimple, seethe, simmer **7** abscess, agitate, bristle, ferment, flare up, pustule, smolder **8** furuncle **9** carbuncle, discharge **10** effervesce **11** excrescence

boil down
4 pare, trim **6** amount, reduce **7** distill **8** compress, condense, simplify, truncate **9** summarize, synopsize **10** streamline **11** concentrate, encapsulate

boiler suit
8 coverall

boiling
3 hot **5** fiery **6** baking, red-hot, sultry, torrid **7** burning, febrile **8** agitated, roasting, scalding, sizzling, tropical **9** scorching **10** blistering

boil over
4 burn, fume, rage **5** erupt **6** blow up, bridle, see red, seethe **7** bristle, flare up

boisterous
4 loud, wild **5** noisy, rowdy **6** lively, stormy, unruly **7** blatant, raucous, riotous **8** strident **9** clamorous, convivial, turbulent **10** disorderly, disruptive, rollicking, tumultuous, uproarious, vociferous **11** loudmouthed, tempestuous, ungovernable **12** high-spirited, obstreperous, rambunctious, unrestrained

Boito opera
11 Mefistofele

bold
4 free, pert, rude **5** bluff, brave, fresh,

gutsy, nervy, sassy, saucy, sheer, showy,
steep **6** arrant, bright, brazen, cheeky,
daring, heroic **7** doughty, forward, glaring,
obvious, valiant **8** cocksure, fearless,
impudent, insolent, intrepid, resolute,
unafraid, valorous **9** audacious, dauntless,
intrusive, prominent, shameless,
undaunted **10** courageous, pronounced
11 adventurous, impertinent, smart-alecky,
venturesome **12** enterprising,
presumptuous

boldness

4 gall, grit **5** drive, nerve, valor **6** aplomb,
mettle, spirit **8** audacity, backbone,
chutzpah, temerity **9** arrogance, challenge,
hardihood, impudence, insolence
10 brazenness, disrespect, effrontery
11 discourtesy **12** impertinence

Bolero composer

5 Ravel (Maurice)

Bolivia

ancient culture: 4 Inca **10** Tiahuanaco
capital: 5 La Paz, Sucre
city: 6 El Alto **9** Santa Cruz
10 Cochabamba
conqueror: 7 Pizarro (Hernando)
Indian people: 6 Aymara **7** Quechua
lake: 5 Poopó **8** Titicaca
language: 6 Aymara **7** Quechua, Spanish
monetary unit: 9 boliviano
mountain, range: 5 Andes **6** Sajama
neighbor: 4 Peru **5** Chile **6** Brazil
8 Paraguay **9** Argentina
river: 4 Beni **5** Abuna **6** Mamoré
7 Guaporé **9** Pilcomayo

bollix

4 flub, mess, muff, ruin **5** botch, gum up,
spoil, upset **6** bobble, bumble, bungle, foul
up, fumble, goof up, jumble, mess up,
muck up, muddle, muff up **7** confuse,
louse up, screw up **8** dishevel, disorder,
scramble, unsettle **9** mishandle,
mismanage

bolo

5 knife **7** machete

Bolshevik

3 Red **6** commie **7** comrade **8** Leninist,
tovarich, tovarish **9** communist

bolshevism

7 Marxism **8** Leninism **9** communism

bolster

3 aid **4** buoy, gird, help, prop **5** boost,
brace, carry, cheer **6** assist, bear up, buoy
up, pillow, upbear, uphold **7** bulwark,
cushion, fortify, hearten, shore up, support,

sustain **8** backstop, buttress, maintain
9 encourage, reinforce **10** strengthen
12 underpinning **13** reinforcement

bolt

3 bar, fly, rod, run **4** cram, dash, dart, flee,
gulp, jump, lock, race, rush, tear, wolf
5 arrow, blurt, bound, chase, dowel, flush,
hotfoot, rivet, scarf, scoot, shoot, skirr,
slosh, start **6** charge, decamp, devour,
gobble, guzzle, secure, spring **7** abscond,
exclaim, make off, missile, rigidly, scamper,
startle, take off **8** blurt out, hightail
9 skedaddle **10** make tracks, take flight
11 ingurgitate **13** thunderstroke

bomb

3 dud, hit **4** bust, dull, fail, flop, sink, zero
5 blast, blitz, lemon, loser, pound, shell
6 blow up **7** debacle, destroy, failure, home
run, success, washout, wipe out
8 detonate, disaster, fall flat, long pass,
long shot, spray can

bombard

4 pelt **5** blast, blitz, shell, storm **6** attack,
assail, cannon, catapult, hammer, pepper,
shower, strafe, strike **7** assault, barrage
9 cannonade

bombardment

4 hail **5** burst, salvo **6** attack, shower,
volley **7** barrage, battery **8** drumfire
9 broadside, cannonade, fusillade,
onslaught

bombardon

4 bass **8** bass tuba

bombast

4 rant **6** hot air **7** bluster, fustian, oration
8 rhapsody, tumidity **9** fancy talk,
pomposity, turgidity **10** pretension
11 rodomontade

bombastic

5 wordy **6** prolix **7** aureate, flowery,
orotund, pompous, swollen **8** inflated,
puffed-up **9** overblown **10** euphuistic,
rhetorical **11** declamatory, overwrought
12 magniloquent **13** grandiloquent

bombed

4 high **5** drunk, fried, stiff, tight **6** blotto,
stoned, wasted **8** comatose, tanked up
9 plastered **10** inebriated **11** intoxicated

bombinate

3 hum **4** buzz, purr, whir **5** drone, strum,
thrum **6** bumble, rumble **7** grumble

bombshell

4 blow, jolt **5** shock **6** marvel **8** surprise

9 curveball, sensation 10 revelation
11 thunderbolt

bona fide
4 real, sure, true 5 valid 6 actual
7 earnest, genuine, sincere 8 sterling
9 authentic, undoubted, veritable
10 legitimate, sure-enough 11 indubitable,
in good faith 13 authenticated

bona fides
6 candor 7 probity 8 goodwill 9 good
faith, sincerity 10 reputation 11 reliability,
sincereness

bonanza
4 mine 5 catch, hoard 7 pay dirt
8 Golconda, gold mine, treasure, treasury,
windfall 12 extravaganza 13 treasure
trove

bonbon
5 candy, sweet 7 fondant 9 sweetmeat,
sugarplum 10 confection

bond
3 tie 4 bail, fuse, knot, link, pact, yoke
5 nexus 6 cement, fetter, pledge, surety
7 bargain, compact, linkage, promise,
shackle, warrant 8 adhesive, affinity,
cohesion, contract, covenant, guaranty,
ligament, ligature, security, vinculum,
warranty 9 adherence, agreement,
coherence, guarantee 10 attachment,
connection, connective, obligation

bondage
4 yoke 6 chains, thrall 7 durance, fetters,
helotry, peonage, serfage, serfdom, slavery
9 captivity, detention, servitude, thralldom,
vassalage, villenage 10 subjection 11 enslavement, subjugation 12 imprisonment

bondsman
4 peon, serf 5 helot, slave 6 surety
7 chattel

bone
ankle: 5 talus 6 tarsus
arm: 4 ulna 6 radius 7 humerus
back: 5 spine 8 vertebra 9 vertebrae
(plural)
breast: 7 sternum
calf: 6 fibula
cavity: 5 fossa
change into: 6 ossify
cheek: 5 malar 6 zygoma
chest: 3 rib
collar: 8 clavicle
face: 5 malar, nasal 7 frontal 8 temporal
finger: 7 phalanx 8 phalange
foot: 6 tarsus 9 calcaneum, calcaneus
10 astragalus, metatarsus
hand: 10 metacarpus

head: 5 skull, vomer 7 cranium
8 parietal, sphenoid 9 occipital
heel: 6 calcaneum, calcaneus
hip: 5 ilium, pubis 6 pelvis 7 ischium
jaw: 7 maxilla 8 mandible
kneecap: 7 patella
leg: 5 femur, tibia 6 fibula 7 patella
lower back: 6 coccyx, sacrum
middle ear: 5 anvil, incus 6 hammer,
stapes 7 malleus, stirrup
relating to: 6 osteal
shin: 5 tibia
shoulder blade: 7 scapula
small: 7 ossicle
substance: 6 ossein
thigh: 5 femur
toe: 7 phalanx 8 phalange
U-shaped: 5 hyoid
wrist: 6 carpus

bonehead
4 clod 5 dunce, moron 6 cretin, dimwit,
nitwit 7 halfwit 8 clodpole, clodpoll,
lunkhead, numskull 9 ignoramus,
lamebrain, numbskull 12 featherbrain

bonelike
7 osseous, osteoid

boner
see **blooper**

bone up
4 cram 5 study 6 review, revise 8 pore
over

bong
4 bell, dong, peal, ring, toll 5 chime, knell,
sound 6 hookah, strike 7 resound 9 water
pipe 11 reverberate

boniface
7 barkeep 8 publican, taverner
9 barkeeper, innkeeper 12 saloonkeeper

bonkers
3 ape, mad 4 daft, loco, nuts, wild 5 batty,
crazy, giddy, loony, potty 6 cuckoo, insane
7 bananas, haywire 8 demented,
deranged, unhinged

bon mot
4 jest, quip 5 crack, sally 7 epigram,
riposte 8 one-liner, repartee 9 witticism

bonny
4 fair, fine 6 comely, lovely, pretty
7 winsome 8 pleasing 9 beauteous,
beautiful, excellent 10 attractive, delightful
11 good-looking

bon ton
4 élan 5 flair, style 6 gentry, jet set

7 fashion, society 8 elegance, smart set
9 haut monde, propriety 11 high society

bonus

4 gift, plus 6 reward 7 benefit, payment,
premium 8 dividend 12 compensation
13 fringe benefit

bon vivant

7 epicure, flaneur, gourmet, trifler
8 aesthete, gourmand 10 aficionado,
dilettante, gastronome 11 cognoscente,
connoisseur 12 boulevardier,
gastronomist, man-about-town

bony

4 lank, lean, thin 5 gaunt, lanky, spare
6 barren, skinny, twiggy 7 angular, osseous,
scraggy, scrawny, starved 8 rawboned,
skeletal, underfed 9 emaciated
10 cadaverous

boo

4 hiss, hoot, jeer, razz 6 bellow, deride,
heckle, revile 7 catcall 9 raspberry, shout
down

boob

3 oaf 4 dolt, dope, goof, goon, boor
5 chump, dunce, goose, ninny 6 breast,
dumb ox 7 blunder, fathead, mistake,
tomfool 8 lunkhead 9 simpleton
10 dunderhead, philistine

boo-boo
see **blooper**

booby hatch

6 asylum, bedlam 8 bughouse, loony bin,
madhouse, nuthouse 9 funny farm
11 institution

booby trap

4 mine 5 snare 6 hazard 7 pitfall, springe
8 deadfall, land mine

boodle

3 wad 4 bilk, haul, heap, loot, mint, perk,
take 5 booty, prize, spoil 6 bundle, packet,
payola, spoils 7 fortune, plunder, present
8 kickback 9 incentive 10 bribe money,
inducement

book

4 list, text, tome 5 album, bible, codex,
enter, folio, novel, tract 6 charge, engage,
enroll, folder, line up, manual, octavo,
quarto, record, script, volume 7 catalog,
edition, reserve 8 hardback, inscribe,
register, schedule, softback, treatise
9 hardcover, monograph, paperback,
preengage 10 compendium 11 publication
combining form: 6 biblio
of hours: 5 Horae

of psalms: 7 psalter

bookie
see **bookmaker**

bookish

5 nerdy 6 formal 7 erudite, learned
8 academic, cerebral, literary, pedantic,
studious, well-read 9 scholarly
10 longhaired 12 intellectual, professorial

bookkeeping term

4 loss 5 asset, audit, check, debit, entry,
yield 6 budget, credit, equity, income,
ledger, margin, profit, return 7 account,
accrual, balance, expense, invoice,
revenue, voucher 8 discount, dividend,
interest, write off 9 inventory, liability
10 appreciate, depreciate, fiscal year
11 double entry 12 amortization,
appreciation, balance sheet, depreciation,
variable cost

booklet

8 brochure, opuscule, pamphlet

bookmaker

6 binder, bookie, editor 7 printer 9 bet
holder, oddsmaker, publisher

book of account

6 ledger, record 7 journal 8 register

bookplate

5 label 8 ex libris

bookstall

5 kiosk 9 newsstand

boom

3 wax 4 bang, clap, grow, rise slam, spar,
wham 5 blast, boost, burst, crack, crash,
sound, smash, swell 6 do well, expand,
growth, rumble, thrive 7 explode, prosper,
resound, thunder 8 flourish, kick hard, long
beam 9 expansion 10 bull market,
detonation, prosperity 11 reverberate

boomerang

6 recoil 7 rebound 8 backfire, backlash,
come back, kick back, ricochet 10 bounce
back

booming

4 bass, deep 6 robust 7 roaring
8 affluent, resonant, sonorous, thriving
9 deafening 10 prospering, prosperous,
successful 11 flourishing

boon

3 aid, gay 4 gift, good, help 5 asset, grant,
favor, jolly, merry, token 6 blithe, bounty,
jocund, jovial 7 benefit, festive, gleeful,
godsend, largess, present 8 blessing, lar-

gesse, mirthful, windfall **9** advantage, convivial, privilege **10** indulgence **11** benediction, benefaction

boondocks
5 wilds **6** sticks **7** outback **8** backland, frontier **9** backwater, backwoods, rural area **10** hinterland **11** backcountry, countryside, provinces **12** back of beyond

boondoggle
4 cord, hoax, scam **5** fraud, hokum **6** hustle **7** fast one, hatband, lanyard, swindle **8** flimflam **10** fool around, mess around **11** horse around

boor
3 cad, oaf **4** lout, hick, rube **5** brute, chuff, churl, clown, yahoo, yokel **6** lummox, rustic **7** buffoon, bumpkin, hayseed, peasant **9** ignoramus, vulgarian **10** clodhopper, philistine, provincial

boorish
4 rude **5** crass, crude, rough **6** coarse, common, rugged, vulgar **7** ill-bred, loutish, lowbred, lumpish, uncivil, uncouth **8** churlish, cloddish, clownish, impolite, insolent, lubberly, swainish **9** graceless, offensive, tasteless, unrefined **10** philistine, provincial, robustious, uncultured, ungracious, unmannerly, unpolished, unsociable **11** bad-mannered, clodhopping, ill-mannered, uncivilized **12** discourteous, uncultivated **13** disrespectful

boost
3 aid **4** hike, lift, jump, plug, push, rise **5** raise, steal **6** assist, beef up, expand, extend, foster, jack up **7** advance, amplify, augment, elevate, magnify, promote, support **8** heighten, increase, shoplift **9** advertise, encourage, expansion, promotion **10** assistance **11** helping hand **13** encouragement

booster
3 fan **4** hypo, shot **6** backer, patron, rocket, rooter **7** vaccine **8** champion, defender, promoter, upholder **9** amplifier, expositor, injection, proponent, supporter **10** shoplifter **11** inoculation

boot
3 can **4** bang, fire, kick, sack **5** chuck, eject, evict, expel, start **6** bounce, thrill **7** dismiss, kick out, start up **8** throw out **9** discharge, dismissal, terminate
kind: 5 wader **6** arctic, chukka, gaiter, galosh, mukluk **7** jodhpur, shoepac **8** balmoral, cothurni (plural), overshoe, shoepack **9** cothurnus **10** Wellington

Boötes star
8 Arcturus

booth
4 nook **5** berth, bower, kiosk, stall, stand **6** carrel **9** enclosure **11** compartment

bootleg
3 hot, run **5** hooch **6** pirate **7** illicit, smuggle **9** irregular, moonshine **10** bathtub gin, contraband **11** black market, mountain dew **12** unauthorized

bootless
4 vain **5** empty **6** futile, hollow **7** useless **8** abortive, impotent, nugatory **9** fruitless, valueless, worthless **10** profitless, unavailing **11** ineffective, ineffectual **12** unproductive, unprofitable, unsuccessful

bootlick
4 fawn **5** cower, crawl, creep, stroke, toady **6** cringe, grovel, kowtow **7** cater to, flatter, truckle **8** blandish **9** brownnose, importune, seek favor **10** curry favor **11** apple-polish **12** bow and scrape

bootlicker
4 toad **5** toady **6** lackey, lapdog, minion, yes-man **7** doormat, spaniel **8** hanger-on **9** sycophant **11** lickspittle

booty
4 haul, lift, loot, pelf, swag, take **5** prize, spoil, yield **6** spoils **7** pillage, plunder, rear end, seizure, takings **8** buttocks

booze
4 brew, grog, swig **5** binge, drink, hooch, juice, quaff, sauce, souse, swill **6** guzzle, imbibe, liquor, rotgut, tank up, tipple **7** alcohol, carouse, put away, spirits, swizzle **8** cocktail, liquor up **9** aqua vitae, firewater, knock back, moonshine

boozehound
3 sot **4** lush, wino **5** drunk, souse **7** guzzler **8** drunkard **9** alcoholic, inebriate **11** dipsomaniac

boozer
see **boozehound**

bop
3 bat, box, hit, jab, pop, rap **4** bash, bean, belt, biff, boff, blow, clip, cuff, jive, slug, sock, swat, whop **5** clock, pound, smack, thump, whack **8** plant one

borax
4 junk

Bordeaux wine
district: 5 Médoc **6** Graves

grape: 6 Malbec, Merlot 8 Cabernet
name: 5 Arsac, Ludon, Macau 6 Moulis
7 Labarde, Margaux, Pomerol 8 Cantenac,
St. Julien, Pauillac 9 St. Emilion, St.
Estèphe, St. Laurent
red: 6 claret

bordello
see **brothel**

border
3 hem, lip, rim 4 abut, brim, edge, join,
line, pale, trim 5 bound, brink, flank, frame,
limit, march, skirt, touch, verge 6 adjoin,
bounds, butt on, define, fringe, limbus,
margin, trench 7 contour, outline, selvage
8 approach, boundary, frontier, neighbor,
sideline, surround 9 marchland, perimeter,
periphery 11 butt against, communicate
inlaid: 8 purfling
raised: 7 coaming

bordereau
4 note 6 record 7 account
10 memorandum

bordering
4 nigh 5 close 6 almost, next to
7 meeting, verging 8 abutting, adjacent,
touching 9 adjoining, alongside, close
upon, impinging 10 approximal,
contiguous, juxtaposed 11 coterminous,
neighboring, practically

borderland
5 march 6 fringe, margin 8 frontier
9 marchland

borderline
4 pale 6 almost, nearly 7 unclear
8 boundary, doubtful, dubious, marginal,
unstable 9 ambiguous, debatable,
dubitable, equivocal, perimeter, uncertain,
undecided, unsettled 11 demarcation,
problematic 12 intermediate
13 indeterminate

border state
8 Delaware, Kentucky, Maryland, Missouri,
Virginia

bore
3 irk 4 drag, drip, mine, peer, pill, ream,
sink, tire, yawn 5 auger, drill, drone,
gouge, prick, punch 6 burrow, pierce,
tunnel 7 bromide, caliber, fatigue
8 diameter, puncture 9 penetrate,
perforate 10 dullsville

boreal
3 icy 4 cold, cool 5 chill, gelid, polar
6 arctic, bitter, chilly, frosty, frigid, tundra
7 glacial, wintery 8 freezing, northern
9 northerly

Boreas
beloved: 8 Orithyia
brother: 5 Notus 8 Hesperus, Zephyrus
father: 8 Astraeus
mother: 3 Eos
son: 5 Zetes 6 Calais

boredom
5 blahs, ennui 6 apathy, stupor, tedium,
torpor 7 fatigue 8 doldrums, dullness,
flatness, monotony 9 lassitude, weariness
11 incuriosity, tediousness 12 indifference

Borgia
4 Juan 6 Alonso, Cesare 7 Alfonso,
Rodrigo 8 Lucrezia

boring
3 dry 4 arid, drab, dull, flat, zero 5 ho-
hum, dreary, stodgy, tiring, vapid
7 humdrum, tedious 8 bromidic, drudging,
lifeless, tiresome 9 wearisome
10 lackluster, monotonous, pedestrian,
unexciting 13 uninteresting

boring tool
5 drill, auger 6 trepan

Boris Godunov composer
10 Mussorgsky (Modest) 11 Moussorgsky
(Modest)

born
3 née 6 innate, native 8 destined, inherent
9 intrinsic 10 congenital, deep-seated
combining form: 3 gen 4 gene 6 genous
7 genetic

borne by the wind
6 aeolic, eolian 7 aeolian

Borneo
ethnic group: 4 Dyak 5 Dayak
mountain: 8 Kinabalu
nation: 6 Brunei
river: 6 Rabang

Borodin opera
10 Prince Igor

borough
4 town 5 burgh 7 village 8 township

bosh
see **bunkum**

Bosnia-Herzegovina
capital: 8 Sarajevo
language: 7 Serbian 8 Croatian
13 Serbo-Croatian
monetary unit: 4 mark 5 dinar
neighbor: 6 Serbia 7 Croatia
part of: 7 Balkans
sea: 8 Adriatic

bosom
4 bust, core, soul, teat 5 chest, close,
heart 6 breast 7 embrace 8 feelings,
intimate 10 affections, conscience

bosomy
5 built, busty, buxom, curvy 6 chesty
7 shapely, stacked 9 Junoesque 11 full-
figured

boss
4 head, stud 5 chief 6 direct, honcho,
leader, manage, master, survey
7 command, foreman, headman, oversee
8 director, employer, overlook, overseer,
superior 9 chieftain, supervise
10 supervisor, taskmaster 11 superintend
African: 5 bwana

bossy
3 cow 4 calf 7 studded 8 despotic,
imperial 9 arbitrary, assertive, imperious,
masterful 10 autocratic, high-handed,
imperative, peremptory, tyrannical
11 controlling, dictatorial, domineering,
magisterial, oppressive, overbearing

botanist
American: 4 Gray (Asa) 5 Sears (Paul
B.) 6 Bailey (Liberty), Bessey (Charles),
Carver (George Washington) 7 Bartram
(John, William), Burbank (Luther)
9 Fairchild (David)
Austrian: 6 Mendel (Gregor)
British: 6 Sloane (Sir Hans)
Danish: 7 Warming (Johannes)
Dutch: 7 De Vries (Hugo)
French: 7 Lamarck (Chevalier de)
German: 4 Cohn (Ferdinand), Mohl (Hugo
von) 5 Sachs (Julius von)
Irish: 6 Harvey (William)
Scottish: 5 Brown (Robert)
Swedish: 8 Linnaeus (Carolus)
Swiss: 6 Nägeli (Karl) 8 Candolle
(Augustin)

botany branch
7 ecology 8 algology, bryology, mycology
9 phycology 10 morphology, palynology,
physiology 11 hydroponics, paleobotany,
pteridology, systematics 12 bacteriology

botch
4 blow, flop, flub, foul, goof, mess, muck,
muff, ruin 5 fluff, gum up, mix-up, snarl,
spoil 6 bobble, boggle, bollix, bumble,
bungle, fiasco, fumble, goof up, mess up,
muddle 7 blunder, confuse, louse up,
washout 8 bugger up, disaster, disorder,
dishevel, mishandle, shambles
9 mishandle, mismanage, patchwork

10 discompose, hodgepodge, misconduct,
mishmash

botchy
5 messy 6 blowzy, frowsy, frowzy, sloppy,
untidy 7 chaotic 8 careless, confused,
slapdash, slipshod, slovenly

both
combining form: 3 bis
prefix: 4 ambi, amph 5 amphi

bother
3 ado, bug, irk, nag, vex 4 drag, fret, fuss,
gall, pest, pain 5 annoy, eat at, harry, trial,
upset 6 badger, flurry, harass, needle,
pester, plague, ruffle 7 afflict, agitate,
anxiety, bedevil, concern, disturb, fluster,
perturb, provoke, torment, trouble
8 disquiet, headache, irritant, nuisance,
vexation 9 aggravate, annoyance, intrude
upon 10 discompose, exasperate, irritation
11 aggravation 12 exasperation
13 inconvenience

botheration
4 damn, pain, pest 5 trial 6 plague
7 torment 8 headache, irritant, nuisance,
vexation 9 annoyance 10 difficulty,
irritation 11 aggravation, provocation
12 exasperation 13 inconvenience

Botswana
capital: 8 Gaborone
city: 11 Francistown
desert: 8 Kalahari
former name: 12 Bechuanaland
language: 6 Tswana 7 English
monetary unit: 4 pula
neighbor: 7 Namibia 8 Zimbabwe
11 South Africa
river: 5 Chobe 6 Molopo 7 Limpopo
8 Okavango

bottle
4 vial 5 cruet, cruse, flask, phial 6 ampule,
carafe, fiasco, flacon, magnum, vessel
7 ampoule 8 decanter, jeroboam
9 container

bottle gourd
8 calabash

bottleneck
5 choke 6 hinder, impede, narrow
7 impasse 8 obstacle, obstruct, paralyze,
slowdown, throttle 9 hindrance 10 choke
point, congestion, traffic jam 11 obstruction

bottom
3 bum 4 base, boat, core, foot, root, pith,
rump, seat, ship, sole, soul, tail, tush
5 basal, basic, basis, fanny, found, nadir

6 behind, breech, heinie, lowest, source
7 bedrock, essence, footing, primary, rear
end **8** backside, buttocks, derriere,
pedestal, pediment **9** establish,
fundament, lowermost, posterior, predicate,
principle, underbody, undermost, underside
10 foundation, nethermost, underbelly,
underlying, underneath **11** fundamental,
lowest point **12** undersurface

bottomless
4 deep, vast **7** abysmal, endless
8 baseless, enduring, profound, unending
9 boundless, unlimited **10** gratuitous,
groundless, unfillable, ungrounded
11 everlasting, immeasurable, inestimable,
never-ending, unfathomable **13** inexhaustible

bottommost
4 last **5** least **6** lowest **7** deepest

bough
3 arm **4** limb **5** shoot **6** branch **8** offshoot

boulevard
4 road **6** artery, avenue, street **7** terrace
8 main drag **9** esplanade, promenade
10 high street **12** thoroughfare

boulevardier
7 flaneur, trifler **9** bon vivant **10** aficionado, dilettante **11** cognoscente,
connoisseur **12** man-about-town

bounce
3 can, hop, pep, vim, zip **4** fire, jump, leap,
oust, sack, zest **5** expel, vault, verve, vigor
6 energy, hurdle, spirit, spring **7** bluster,
boot out, dismiss, kick out, rebound, saltate
8 buoyancy, ricochet, sparkle, vitality
9 animation, discharge, eliminate,
terminate **10** ebullience, elasticity,
liveliness

bounce back
5 rally **6** perk up, pick up, recoil, return,
revive **7** cheer up, improve, rebound,
recover **8** backfire **9** boomerang
10 recuperate, turn around

bounce off
5 carom **7** rebound **8** ricochet

bouncer
4 goon **5** guard **8** houseman, sentinel,
watchman **9** muscleman

bouncy
3 gay **4** airy **5** peppy, perky **6** blithe,
cheery, jaunty, jocund, lively **7** buoyant,
elastic **8** animated, volatile **9** ebullient,

energetic, expansive, exuberant, resilient,
sprightly **10** unsinkable **12** effervescent,
high-spirited **13** irrepressible

bound
3 end, hem, hop, rim **4** bolt, edge, jump,
leap, term, skip **5** caper, frisk, hem in, limit,
skirt, vault, verge **6** border, bounce, define,
demark, driven, finite, fringe, gambol,
hurdle, margin, spring, sprint **7** confine,
delimit, enclose, hotfoot, limited, mark out,
obliged, rebound, saltate **8** articled,
beholden, confined, confines, enslaved,
pledged, resolved, restrain, surround
9 compelled, demarcate, obligated
10 determined, indentured, limitation
11 apprenticed, responsible
12 circumscribe

boundary
3 hem **4** mete, pale **5** ambit, limit **6** limits,
margin **7** compass, outline **8** confines,
environs, perimeter, purlieus **9** precincts
10 borderline **13** circumference

bounder
3 cad, cur, dog **4** boor, worm **5** knave,
louse, rogue **6** rascal, rotter

boundless
4 vast **5** great **7** endless **8** infinite
9 excessive, limitless, unbounded,
unlimited **10** indefinite, unconfined,
unmeasured **11** illimitable, measureless
12 immeasurable, unrestricted
13 inexhaustible, unsurpassable

bounteous
5 ample **6** benign, lavish **7** copious,
liberal, profuse **8** abundant, generous,
handsome, prodigal **9** bountiful, capacious,
expansive, extensive, plenteous, plentiful,
unsparing **10** beneficent, big-hearted,
freehanded, munificent, openhanded,
voluminous **11** magnanimous, overflowing

bountiful
see **bounteous**

bounty
5 grant, prize, yield **6** deluge, plenty,
reward, wealth **7** payment, premium
8 plethora, richness **9** abundance,
affluence, plenitude, profusion, prosperity
10 cornucopia, generosity, inducement,
liberality, luxuriance **11** benevolence,
copiousness **12** compensation

Bounty captain
5 Bligh (William)

bouquet
4 balm, kudo, odor, posy, spray **5** aroma,

kudos, scent, spice 6 eulogy, medley
7 acclaim, corsage, essence, garland,
incense, nosegay, perfume 8 accolade,
encomium 9 fragrance, redolence
10 compliment 11 arrangement,
boutonniere 12 commendation

bourgeois
7 burgher 8 ordinary 10 conformist,
philistine 11 middle-class 12 conventional

bourgeoisie
11 middle class, third estate

Bourne Identity author
6 Ludlum (Robert)

bout
3 jag, run 4 game, meet, term, tour, turn
5 match, round, shift, siege, spell, spasm,
spree, stint, throe, trick 6 attack 7 contest,
session 8 outbreak 10 engagement

boutique
4 shop 8 emporium

bovine
3 cow, yak 4 anoa, bull, calf, gaur, neat,
zebu 5 bison, steer, stirk 6 heifer, placid,
torpid, wisent 7 aurochs, banteng, buffalo,
bullock, cowlike 8 longhorn
genus: 3 Bos
sound: 3 low, moo

bow
3 arc, bob, dip, nod 4 arch, bend, knot,
lout, prow, turn 5 angle, crook, curve,
debut, defer, hunch, round, stoop, yield
6 archer, congee, curtsy, give in, kowtow,
relent, salaam, salute, submit 7 concede,
curtsey, flexure, incline, rainbow, succumb,
turning 9 curvation, curvature, genuflect,
obeisance, surrender 10 capitulate
11 buckle under 12 knuckle under

Bow, Clara
6 It girl

bowdlerize
4 blip, edit 6 censor, cleanse, distort,
excise, purify, screen 7 abridge, launder
8 sanitize 9 expurgate 10 adulterate, blue-
pencil

bowed
4 bent 5 arced, bandy 6 arched, curved
11 bandy-legged, curvilinear

bowel
3 gut 6 paunch 9 intestine

bower
5 arbor 6 anchor 7 enclose, pergola,
retreat 9 apartment

bowery
7 skid row

bowfin
4 amia 7 mudfish

bowl
5 arena, basin, jorum, mazer, stade, tazza
6 tureen, vessel 7 stadium 8 coliseum
12 amphitheater

bowlegged
5 bandy

bowler
3 hat 5 derby 6 kegler

Bowl game
5 Super
Abilene: 5 Pecan
Anaheim: 7 Freedom
Atlanta: 5 Peach
Dallas: 6 Cotton
El Paso: 3 Sun
Fresno: 10 California
Honolulu: 5 Aloha
Houston: 10 Bluebonnet
Jacksonville: 5 Gator
Memphis: 7 Liberty
Miami: 6 Orange 8 Carquest
Mobile: 6 Senior
New Orleans: 5 Sugar
Orlando: 13 Florida Citrus
Pasadena: 4 Rose
San Diego: 7 Holiday
Shreveport: 12 Independence
Tampa: 10 Hall of Fame
Tempe: 6 Fiesta
Tucson: 6 Copper

bowling
7 kegling
British: 8 skittles
Italian: 5 bocce, bocci 6 boccie
term: 3 pin 4 hook, lane, spot 5 curve,
frame, spare, split 6 gutter, strike, string,
turkey 7 duckpin 9 candlepin

bowl over
3 awe, fell, wow 4 daze, stun 5 floor,
shock, throw 6 boggle, dismay 7 astound,
flatten, impress, stupefy 8 blow away,
surprise 9 bring down, dumbfound, knock
down, overwhelm 10 disconcert

bow out
4 exit, fold, quit 5 leave, welsh 6 beg off,
give up, retire 8 withdraw 9 surrender

box
3 bin 4 case, cell, chop, cuff, duke, loge,
slap, sock, spar 5 booth, chest, clout,
crate, fight, punch, smack, stall, trunk
6 buffet, carton, casket, coffer, coffin,

encase, hopper, packet **7** confine, enclose, package **9** container, enclosure, rectangle **10** pigeonhole, receptacle **11** compartment

boxer

7 fighter, palooka **8** pugilist **9** flyweight **11** heavyweight, lightweight **12** bantamweight, middleweight, welterweight **13** featherweight
champ: **3** Ali (Muhammad) **4** Bowe (Riddick) **5** Bruno (Frank), Jones (Roy), Lewis (Lennox), Louis (Joe), Moore (Archie), Tyson (Mike) **6** Hagler (Marvin), Hearns (Thomas), Holmes (Larry), McCall (Oliver), Moorer (Michael), Seldon (Bruce), Spinks (Leon, Michael), Tunney (Gene), Walker (Mickey) **7** Charles (Ezzard), Corbett (James), Dempsey (Jack), Douglas (Buster), Foreman (George), Frazier (Joe), Johnson (Jack), LaMotta (Jake), Leonard (Sugar Ray), Sharkey (Jack), Walcott (Joe) **8** Marciano (Rocky), Robinson (Sugar Ray), Sullivan (John L.) **9** Armstrong (Henry), Holyfield (Evander), Patterson (Floyd), Schmeling (Max)

boxing

8 pugilism **10** fisticuffs **13** prizefighting
term: **3** jab, TKO **4** blow, bout, duck, foul, hook, ring, rope, spar **5** break, count, feint, glove, match, parry, punch, round, swing **6** bucket, canvas, corner **7** low blow, referee **8** heavy bag, knockout, uppercut **9** knockdown **11** punching bag

boy

3 lad, son, tad **5** gamin, puppy, sonny **6** laddie, nipper, shaver **9** shaveling, stripling, youngster
combining form: **3** ped **4** paed, paid, pedo **5** paedo, paido
errand: **5** gofer **8** lobbygow
French: **6** garçon
Latin: **4** puer
mischievous: **6** urchin
Spanish: **4** niño

boyfriend

4 beau **5** swain **6** fiancé, old man, suitor **7** main man **9** inamorato

Boy Scout

founder: **11** Baden-Powell (Robert)
gathering: **8** jamboree
motto: **10** be prepared
rank: **4** Life (Scout), Star (Scout) **5** Eagle (Scout) **10** Tenderfoot
unit: **5** troop **6** patrol

Boys Town

founder: **8** Flanagan (Edward)
state: **8** Nebraska

bozo

3 oaf **4** boob, clod, dodo, dolt, dope, fool, goof, jerk, mutt, simp, yo-yo **5** chump, dummy, dunce, idiot, moron, ninny, noddy, stupe **6** dimwit, donkey, dum-dum, nitwit, noodle **7** airhead, dullard, pinhead **8** bonehead, clodpoll, dumbbell, dumbhead, imbecile, lunkhead, meathead, numskull **9** birdbrain, blockhead, ignoramus, lamebrain, numbskull, simpleton, thickhead **10** dunderhead, hammerhead, nincompoop **11** chowderhead, chucklehead, knucklehead

B.P.O.E. member

3 Elk

Brabantio's daughter

9 Desdemona

brabble

3 row **4** beef, feud, flap, riot, spat, tiff **5** argue, scrap, set to **6** bicker, blowup, fracas, grouse **7** dispute, fall out, palaver, quarrel, rhubarb, scuffle, wrangle **8** argument, squabble **9** altercate, bickering, brannigan, caterwaul, wrangling **10** falling-out **11** altercation, disputation, embroilment

brace

3 arm, bar, duo, tie **4** dyad, gird, pair, prop, stay **5** clamp, ready, shore, steel, strut, truss **6** accost, bear up, column, couple, demand, splint, steady, uphold **7** bolster, bracket, enliven, fortify, freshen, prepare, refresh, shore up, support, sustain, tighten, twosome **8** buttress, reinforce **10** cantilever, exhilarate, invigorate, strengthen **12** underpinning **13** underpropping

bracelet

6 bangle **7** manacle **8** wristlet

bracing

4 keen **5** brisk, crisp, fresh, nippy, sharp, tonic **6** biting, chilly **7** rousing **8** stirring **9** animating **10** energizing, quickening **11** restorative, stimulating, stimulative **12** exhilarating, invigorating

bracken

4 fern **5** brake, brush, scrub **11** undergrowth

bracket

3 arm **4** join, link, omit **5** brace **6** couple, relate, remove **7** combine, compare, conjoin, connect, embrace, encircle, enclose, include, support **8** buttress, leave out, put aside, set aside **9** associate, encompass **11** parenthesis **12** strengthener

brackish
4 sour **5** acrid, briny, salty **6** saline, salted **9** repulsive, sickening **10** nauseating

bract
4 leaf **5** glume, paleat **6** spathe **8** phyllary

brad
4 nail

Bradamant
brother: **7** Rinaldo
husband: **6** Rogero **8** Ruggiero

Bradbury's forte
5 sci-fi **7** fantasy

brae
4 bank, hill **5** slope **8** hillside

brag
3 gas **4** blow, crow, puff **5** boast, mouth, prate, vaunt **7** show off, swagger, talk big **9** cockiness, gasconade **10** grandstand **11** rodomontade

braggadocio
6 hot air **7** boaster, bombast, bravado, conceit, puffery, swagger, windbag **8** blowhard, boasting, braggart, bragging **9** arrogance, cockiness, pomposity **10** cockalorum, pretension, swaggering **11** fanfaronade

braggart
6 blower **7** boaster, egotist, vaunter, windbag **8** big mouth, blowhard **9** big talker, know-it-all, swaggerer, vulgarian **11** braggadocio

Brahmin
8 highbrow **9** blueblood, patrician **10** aristocrat

braid
4 plat **5** plait, queue **7** galloon, pigtail **8** soutache **9** interlace **10** intertwine, interweave

brain
3 wit **4** bean, conk, mind **7** concuss **9** intellect **10** gray matter **12** intelligence
bone: **5** skull **7** cranium
clot: **10** thrombosis
gland: **6** pineal **9** pituitary
layer: **6** cortex
lobe: **6** limbic, vermis **7** frontal **8** parietal, temporal **9** occipital
membrane: **3** pia **4** dura **6** meninx **8** pia mater **9** arachnoid, dura mater
part: **4** lobe **7** medulla **8** cerebrum,

thalamus **9** sensorium, ventricle **10** cerebellum, hemisphere **12** diencephalon
relating to: **8** cerebral **10** encephalic
ridge: **4** gyri (plural) **5** gyrus
vertebrate: **10** encephalon
wave record: **3** EEG

brainchild
4 idea, opus, work **6** animus, scheme, theory **7** coinage **9** handiwork, invention **10** hypothesis **11** achievement, chef-d'oeuvre, contrivance, innovation

brainiac
4 whiz **6** genius **7** prodigy

brainless
3 dim **5** dense, silly, thick **6** simple, stupid **7** asinine, foolish, idiotic, moronic, vacuous, witless **9** dim-witted, nitwitted **10** acephalous, feebleminded

brainpower
3 wit **5** sense **6** smarts **8** aptitude, capacity, sagacity **9** intellect, mentality, mother wit **10** perception **11** discernment, penetration **12** intelligence **13** comprehension

brainsick
3 mad **4** daft **5** batty, crazy, manic, potty **6** crazed, insane, mental **7** cracked, haywire, lunatic **8** aberrant, demented, deranged, maniacal, unhinged **9** bedlamite, delirious, disturbed **10** disordered, incoherent, irrational, unbalanced

brainstorm
3 rap, jaw **4** idea **6** confer **7** dream up, huddle, think up **8** cogitate, discuss, mull over **9** mental fit **10** groupthink, kick around, toss around **11** inspiration, put together

brainteaser
5 poser, rebus **6** puzzle, riddle **7** stumper **9** conundrum **10** cryptogram

brainwashing
10 propaganda **11** mind control, reeducation

brainy
4 keen **5** quick, savvy, sharp, smart **6** adroit, astute, bright, clever **9** egg-headed, brilliant, sagacious **10** discerning, precocious **11** intelligent, quick-witted, ready-witted **13** knowledgeable, perspicacious

brake
4 curb, slow, stop **5** block **6** damper, hinder, impede, retard, slough **7** barrier,

bracken, slacken **8** blockade, obstacle, obstruct, slow down **9** deterrent, hindrance **10** constraint, decelerate **11** bracken fern

bramble
4 burr **5** brier, furze, gorse, hedge, shrub, thorn **6** nettle **7** thistle

branch
3 arm **4** fork, limb, rami (plural), wing **5** bough, ramus **6** ramify **7** diverge, outpost **8** division **9** tributary **10** subsidiary

branched
6 ramate, ramose

brand
4 blot, blur, logo, make, mark, onus, sear, slur, sort, spot, type **5** badge, class, odium, stain, stamp, sword, taint, torch **6** accuse, charge, impute, stigma, stripe **7** species, variety **8** black eye, disgrace, insignia, logotype **9** trademark **10** stigmatize

brandish
4 wave **5** flash, shake, sport, swing, wield **6** flaunt, parade **7** display, exhibit, show off **8** flourish

brand-new
4 mint **5** fresh **6** latest, unused, virgin **8** up-to-date **9** untouched **11** cutting-edge **13** inexperienced

brandy
4 marc, ouzo, raki **5** Pisco **6** cognac, grappa, kirsch, Metaxa **7** liqueur **8** Armagnac, calvados, digestif, eau-de-vie **9** applejack, framboise, slivovitz

brannigan
3 row **4** bust, flap, spat, tiff **5** binge, fight, set-to, spree **6** bender, blowup, hassle, ruckus **7** brabble, discord, dispute, quarrel, wassail, wrangle **8** squabble **10** falling-out **11** altercation

brash
4 bold, flip, pert **5** cocky, gutsy, hasty, nervy, saucy **6** brassy, brazen, cheeky, madcap, uppish, uppity **7** brittle, forward **8** arrogant, cocksure, flippant, impudent, insolent, reckless, tactless **9** audacious, bumptious, ebullient, energetic, exuberant, hot-headed, impetuous, impolitic, maladroit, unabashed, untactful **10** ill-advised, incautious **11** overweening, thoughtless, unrestrained **12** high-spirited, presumptuous, undiplomatic **13** disrespectful, inconsiderate, irrepressible, self-assertive

brashness
4 gall, grit, guts **5** brass, cheek, crust,

nerve, pluck **6** aplomb, daring, mettle, spirit **8** audacity, temerity **9** assurance **10** confidence, effrontery **11** presumption

brass
4 gall **5** cheek, nerve **8** audacity, chutzpah **9** brashness, impudence, insolence **10** confidence, effrontery **11** presumption **12** impertinence

brassbound
3 set **5** brash, rigid **6** brazen, narrow **7** adamant, bigoted, forward **8** obdurate **9** illiberal, presuming, obstinate, unbending **10** implacable, inflexible, intolerant, relentless, unswayable, unyielding **11** opinionated, small-minded, unrelenting **12** narrow-minded, presumptuous, single-minded **13** dyed-in-the-wool, self-asserting, self-assertive

brasserie
10 restaurant

brass hat
3 VIP **4** boss **5** elder **6** better, senior **7** big shot **8** big wheel, higher-up, superior

brassica
4 kale, rape **5** colza **6** turnip **7** cabbage, mustard **8** broccoli, collards, kohlrabi, rutabaga **11** cauliflower

brass tacks
5 facts **7** details **11** nitty-gritty, particulars

brass worker
7 brazier

brassy
see **brazen**

brat
3 imp **4** punk **6** urchin **10** holy terror

bravado
5 bluff **6** hot air **7** bluster, bombast **8** audacity, boasting, boldness, bragging, defiance, vaunting **9** gasconade **10** blustering, grandiosity, pretension, swaggering **11** braggadocio **12** boastfulness

brave
4 bold, dare, defy, face, game, meet, risk **5** beard, gutsy, hardy, manly, nervy, noble, stout **6** daring, heroic, manful, plucky, spunky **7** defiant, doughty, gallant, take on, valiant, venture **8** confront, face down, fearless, intrepid, reckless, resolute, spirited, splendid, stalwart, unafraid, valorous **9** audacious, challenge, dauntless, excellent, steadfast, undaunted, withstand **10** courageous **11** boldhearted,

indomitable, lionhearted, undauntable, unflinching, venturesome **12** stouthearted **13** adventuresome

Brave New World author
6 Huxley (Aldous)

bravery
4 grit, guts **5** nerve, pluck, valor **6** daring, mettle, spirit **7** courage, heroism **8** audacity, boldness, temerity **9** derring-do, fortitude, gallantry **11** intrepidity **12** fearlessness, intrepidness
false: 7 bravado

bravo
3 olé **4** rave **5** cheer **6** gunman, hit man, killer **7** ovation, plaudit, villain **8** applause, assassin **9** desperado

bravura
4 bold **5** showy **6** daring, florid, ornate **8** dazzling, skillful, virtuoso **9** brilliant

brawl
3 row **4** feud, flap, fray, fuss, maul, riot, spar, spat, tiff **5** clash, broil, fight, melee, scrap, set-to **6** affray, battle, bicker, dustup, fracas, rumble, tussle **7** bobbery, brabble, contend, quarrel, rhubarb, ruction, scuffle, wrangle **8** dogfight, eruption, skirmish, slugfest, squabble, upheaval **9** fistfight, imbroglio, scrimmage **10** donnybrook, fisticuffs, free-for-all **11** altercation, disturbance **13** confrontation

brawn
4 beef, meat, thew **5** clout, flesh, might, power, sinew **6** muscle **8** strength **9** puissance **10** headcheese

brawny
5 beefy, burly, husky, lusty, tough **6** robust, sinewy, stocky, strong, sturdy **8** athletic, muscular, powerful, thickset, vigorous **9** strapping, well-built **10** able-bodied

bray
4 mill **5** crush, grind, pound **6** bellow, pestle, powder **7** atomize, trumpet **9** pulverize

brazen
4 bold, loud **5** brash, gaudy, noisy, showy **6** arrant, brassy cheeky **7** blatant, defiant, forward, glaring, jarring **8** flagrant, impudent, insolent **9** audacious, barefaced, obtrusive, shameless, unabashed **10** outrageous, procacious, unblushing **11** conspicuous, impertinent **12** contumelious, presumptuous **13** disrespectful

Brazil
capital: 8 Brasília
city: 5 Belém **6** Recife **8** Salvador, São Paulo **12** Rio de Janeiro **13** Belo Horizonte
discoverer: 6 Cabral (Pedro)
island: 6 Marajó **7** Caviana
language: 10 Portuguese
monetary unit: 4 real
neighbor: 4 Peru **6** Guyana **7** Bolivia, Uruguay **8** Colombia, Paraguay, Suriname **9** Argentina, Venezuela **12** French Guiana
river: 6 Amazon **8** Parnaíba **10** Alto Paraná **12** São Francisco

breach
3 gap **4** gash, hole, open, rent, rift, slit **5** break, chasm, cleft, crack, split **6** hiatus, lacuna, schism **7** break in, discord, disrupt, fissure, infract, interim, opening, rupture, violate **8** aperture, disregard, disunity, division, fracture, infringe, interval, trespass **9** severance, violation **10** alienation, contravene, infraction, separation, transgress **11** delinquency, dereliction **12** disaffection, disobedience, estrangement, infringement, interruption **13** contravention, discontinuity, noncompliance, nonobservance, transgression

bread
3 bun **4** food, pita, rusk **5** bagel, money, toast **6** living, muffin, sippet **7** biscuit, crouton, edibles, stollen **8** victuals, zwieback **9** provender **10** livelihood, provisions, sustenance **11** comestibles, maintenance, subsistence
communion: 4 host **5** wafer **9** Eucharist
from heaven: 5 manna
ingredient: 4 meal **5** flour, yeast **6** leaven
Jewish: 5 matzo **6** hallah, matzoh **7** challah
maker: 5 baker
Scottish: 7 bannock
spread: 3 jam **4** oleo **5** jelly **6** butter **9** margarine
unleavened: 5 matzo **6** matzoh

bread and butter
4 keep, work **6** basics, living **7** support **8** mainstay, victuals **10** employment, livelihood, occupation, sustenance **9** nutriment **11** maintenance, necessities, subsistence **12** alimentation

breadbasket
3 gut **5** belly, tummy **6** paunch

breadth

7 abdomen, stomach 8 potbelly 9 bay window, beer belly

breadth

4 area, size, span 5 range, reach, scope, space, sweep, width 6 extent, spread 7 compass, expanse, stretch 8 distance, fullness, latitude, vastness, wideness 9 amplitude, expansion, magnitude 10 liberality

break

3 gap 4 bust, dash, halt, leak, luck, rest, rift, ruin, tame 5 burst, clear, crack, inure, relief, sever, solve, spell 6 breach, chance, decode, divide, escape, exceed, hiatus, impair, lacuna, refute, reveal 7 destroy, divulge, fall out, interim, lighten, opening, respite, rupture, shatter, surpass, suspend, time-out, violate 8 accustom, bankrupt, breather, decipher, disclose, division, downtime, fracture, good luck, interval, moderate 9 interlude, interrupt 10 annihilate, controvert, impoverish, suspensions 11 discontinue, disjunction, dislocation, opportunity 12 intermission, interruption 13 discontinuity

breakable

4 weak 5 frail 6 flimsy 7 brittle, fragile, friable 8 delicate 9 frangible

breakaway

4 prop 7 escapee 8 offshoot, renegade, seceding

break down

4 fail, fold, sort, wilt 5 class, decay, index, 6 cave in, digest, give in 7 analyze, clarify, crumble, crumple, elucidate, give out, give way, go crazy, succumb 8 classify, collapse, dissolve 9 anatomize, decompose, fall apart 12 disintegrate

breakdown

5 crash, decay, smash, study, wreck 6 mishap 7 crack-up, debacle, failure, smashup 8 analysis, collapse, taxonomy 9 cataclysm, partition 10 disruption, dissection, resolution 11 dysfunction, examination, prostration

breaker

4 wave 6 billow, comber, roller

Breakfast at Tiffany's author

6 Capote (Truman)

breakfront

7 cabinet 8 bookcase

break in

4 tame 5 train 6 breach, burgle, gentle,

invade 7 intrude 8 initiate 9 condition, habituate, interfere, interpose, interrupt

breakneck

4 fast 5 fleet, hasty, quick, rapid, swift 6 racing, speedy, unsafe 8 meteoric 10 harefooted 11 precipitous

break off

3 end 4 drop, halt, kill, stop 5 abort, cease, scrub, sever 6 cancel, detach 7 curtail, scratch, suspend 8 cut short 9 terminate 11 discontinue

break out

4 bolt, flee 5 arise, erupt, flare 6 emerge, escape 7 explode 8 mushroom, separate

break through

5 burst 6 breach, emerge, pierce 7 rupture, surface 8 overcome 9 penetrate

breakthrough

4 find, gain, hike, leap, rise 5 boost 7 advance, radical, upgrade 8 advanced, increase, landmark 9 invention, milestone 10 avant-garde, innovation 11 cutting-edge, development, exceptional, progressive, quantum leap

break up

3 end 4 halt, part 6 divide, sunder 7 destroy, disband, disjoin, disrupt, rupture, scatter, shatter 8 disperse, dissever, dissolve, disunite, separate 9 decompose, dismantle, pulverize, terminate 12 disintegrate

breakup

4 rift 5 split 7 divorce 8 analysis, parting 9 dispersal 10 dissection, separation 11 dissolution

breakwater

5 jetty

breast

5 bosom, chest, heart
animal: 7 brisket
combining form: 3 maz 4 mast, mazo 5 masto, stern, steth 6 mastia (plural), sterno, stetho

breastbone

7 sternum

breast-feed

5 nurse 6 suckle 7 nourish

breastwork

7 barrier, bastion, bulwark, defense, parapet, rampart 9 barricade, earthwork 10 embankment 13 fortification, reinforcement

breath
4 gasp, gust, hint, puff 5 let-up, pause, trace, whiff 6 breeze 7 respite
10 exhalation, inhalation, suggestion

breathe
4 emit, sigh 5 exude, utter, voice
6 endure, exhale, expire, inhale, murmur
7 confide, express, give off, inspire, persist, radiate, respire, subsist, survive, whisper

breather
4 lull, rest, stay, vent 5 break, let-up, pause, spell 6 hiatus, recess 7 caesura, respite 8 downtime 9 remission
12 interruption

breathing
labored: 7 dyspnea
normal: 6 eupnea
rapid: 8 polypnea

breathing apparatus
10 respirator
underwater: 5 scuba

breathing orifice
4 nose 5 mouth 8 blowhole, spiracle

breathless
4 agog, avid, keen 5 eager 6 ardent
7 anxious, gasping, intense 8 gripping
9 expectant, impatient 11 short-winded
13 on tenterhooks

breathtaking
6 moving 7 awesome 8 dramatic, exciting, imposing, stunning, wondrous
9 panoramic, thrilling 10 impressive, staggering 11 astonishing, magnificent, spectacular 12 awe-inspiring, overwhelming 13 heart-stirring

Brecht play
4 Baal 13 Life of Galileo (The), Mother Courage 15 Seven Deadly Sins (The), Threepenny Opera (The) 20 Caucasian Chalk Circle (The)

breech
3 bum 4 duff, rear, rump, seat, tail 5 fanny
6 behind, bottom, heinie 7 keester, keister, rear end 8 backside, buttocks, derriere, haunches 9 fundament, posterior 12 hindquarters

breechclout
9 loincloth

breed
3 ilk 4 bear, grow, kind, make, mate, race, rear, sire, sort, type 5 beget, brand, cause, class, cross, genus, hatch, likes, raise, stock, yield 6 couple, create, father,

induce, nature, strain, stripe 7 bring up, develop, educate, lineage, nurture, produce, species, variety 8 copulate, engender, generate, mate with, multiply
9 cultivate, procreate, propagate, reproduce 10 discipline, extraction, give rise to, impregnate, inseminate

breeding
4 line 5 grace, taste 6 polish 7 culture, decorum, lineage, manners 8 ancestry, civility, courtesy, pedigree 9 genealogy, gentility, propriety 10 refinement, upbringing 11 cultivation

breeding ground
6 hotbed, origin 8 hothouse 10 forcing bed, mating spot 12 forcing house

breeze
3 zip 4 flit, sail, snap, waft 5 cinch, draft, waltz 6 zephyr 8 duck soup, kid stuff
10 child's play

breezy
4 airy, cool 5 fresh, gusty, windy 6 blithe, casual, drafty 7 offhand, relaxed
8 carefree, careless, detached, informal
9 easygoing 10 insouciant, nonchalant
11 unconcerned 12 devil-may-care, lighthearted

Breton
4 Celt

_____ breve
4 alla

breviary
5 brief 6 digest, précis 7 epitome, essence, outline, rundown, summary
8 abstract, boildown, synopsis 9 reduction
10 abridgment, conspectus, prayer book
11 abridgement 12 condensation, divine office

brevity
7 economy 8 laconism 9 briefness, concision, crispness, pithiness, shortness, terseness 10 transience

brew
3 ale, tea 4 beer, loom, mull, plan, plot
5 drink 6 cook up, foment, gather, impend, infuse, scheme, stir up 7 concoct, ferment
8 contrive

briar
4 burr, pipe 5 furze, gorse, shrub, thorn
6 nettle 7 bramble, thistle

Briareus
7 Aegaeon
father: 6 Uranus

bribe

mother: 4 Gaea

bribe
3 buy, fix, sop 6 buy off, payoff, payola,
square, suborn 7 corrupt 9 incentive
10 enticement, inducement, tamper with

bric-a-brac
6 curios 8 trinkets 9 ornaments 10 objets
d'art 11 gingerbread, knicknacks
13 embellishment

brick
5 block
layer: 5 mason
laying: 7 masonry
material: 4 clay, marl
oven: 4 kiln
row: 6 course
sun-dried: 5 adobe
trough for carrying: 3 hod

bridal
7 nuptial, spousal 8 conjugal 9 connubial
11 matrimonial

bridal wreath
6 spirea

bridewell
3 can, jug, pen 4 coop, jail 5 clink, joint
6 lockup, prison 7 slammer 8 bastille
12 penitentiary

bridge
4 join, link, span 5 unite 7 connect
8 overpass, traverse
great: 8 Brooklyn 10 Golden Gate
kind: 4 arch, draw, rope 5 swing, truss
7 bascule, covered, natural, pontoon,
trestle, viaduct 10 cantilever, suspension
term: 3 bid 4 book, east, pass, ruff, slam,
suit, void, west 5 bonus, dummy, north,
raise, south, trick, trump 6 double, renege,
rubber 7 auction, finesse, no-trump,
overbid 8 contract, jump call, redouble
9 grand slam, overtrick, singleton 10 little
slam, undertrick, vulnerable

bridgelike game
5 whist 6 hearts

bridle
3 bit 4 curb, fume, rein, rule 5 check, flare,
quell 6 govern, halter, hold in, manage,
master, rein in, ruffle, seethe, subdue
7 bristle, control, flare up, inhibit, repress
8 hold back, moderate, restrain, suppress,
withhold 9 constrain, deterrent,
hackamore, restraint

brief
4 curt 5 pithy, short, terse 6 abrupt, digest,
inform 7 brusque, concise, epitome,

laconic, outline, passing 8 abstract,
breviary, fleeting, succinct, summary,
synopsis 9 momentary, transient
10 abridgment, conspectus
11 abridgement, compendious
12 condensation 13 short and sweet

brig
3 can, jug, pen 4 coop, jail 5 clink
6 cooler, lockup, prison 7 slammer
8 stockade 9 guardroom 10 guardhouse

brigade
4 army, unit 5 force, group 6 troops
10 contingent, detachment

brigand
6 bandit, bummer, looter, pirate, raider,
rustler 7 cateran, corsair, forager
8 marauder, pillager 9 buccaneer,
plunderer 10 freebooter, highwayman

brigandage
7 pillage, sacking 10 despoiling,
ransacking 11 depredation

bright
4 fair, keen 5 aglow, alert, clear, light, lucid,
quick, shiny, smart, sunny, vivid 6 brainy,
cheery, clever, lively, lucent 7 beaming,
blazing, flaming, fulgent, glowing, lambent,
lighted, radiant 8 cheerful, dazzling,
gleaming, luminous, lustrous, sunshiny
9 brilliant, effulgent, favorable, refulgent,
sparkling 10 auspicious, glittering,
precocious, propitious, shimmering
11 illuminated, intelligent, quick-witted
12 incandescent 13 scintillating

brighten
4 buoy 5 cheer, clear, shine 6 look up,
perk up, polish, revive, solace 7 burnish,
cheer up, clear up, enhance, enliven,
furbish, gladden, hearten, improve
8 illumine 10 illuminate

brightness
5 éclat, shine 6 luster, lustre 8 radiance,
splendor 10 brilliance, effulgence,
luminosity
measure of: 3 lux 5 lumen 6 candle
7 candela 10 foot-candle

brilliance
see **brightness**

brilliant
6 ablaze, brainy, genius, lucent, superb
7 beaming, fulgent, lambent, radiant,
shining, stellar 8 dazzling, luminous,
masterly, striking 9 effulgent, ingenious,
refulgent, sparkling 10 glittering
11 exceptional 12 incandescent

brilliantine
6 pomade 9 hair cream

brim
3 hem, lip, rim 4 edge, fill, well 5 brink, skirt, verge, visor 6 border, fill up, fringe, margin 7 run over 8 overflow, well over 9 perimeter, periphery 13 circumference

brimful
see **brimming**

brimming
4 full 5 awash, flush 6 filled, jammed, loaded, packed 7 crammed, crowded, replete, stuffed, teeming, welling 8 bursting, overfull, suffused, swarming, swelling 9 chock-full, jam-packed 11 chockablock, running over

brimstone
6 sulfur

brine
3 sea 4 deep, main 5 ocean 8 seawater 9 salt water

bring
3 lug 4 lead, pack, tote 5 carry, fetch, gross, yield 6 convey 7 attract, produce 9 transport

bring about
3 win 5 beget, cause 6 create, draw on, effect, secure 7 procure, produce, trigger 8 engender, generate, result in 10 accomplish, effectuate, give rise to

bring around
4 hook, sway, turn 7 convert, win over 8 convince, persuade, talk into 9 argue into, prevail on, sweet-talk 11 prevail upon

bring back
5 renew 6 recall, recoup, return, revive 7 recover, reprise, restore, salvage 8 retrieve, revivify 9 reinstate 10 repatriate 11 reestablish

bring down
3 bag, hew 4 drop, fell, raze 5 floor, level, shoot 6 defeat, depose, ground, humble, lay low, reduce 7 depress, flatten 8 demolish, overturn 9 humiliate, overthrow, prostrate, undermine

bring forth
4 bear 5 beget, yield 6 create, elicit, invent 7 deliver, produce 8 generate 9 propagate, reproduce 10 give rise to

bring forward
6 adduce, submit, tender, unveil

7 advance, present, produce, proffer 9 introduce

bring in
3 pay, net, win 4 draw, earn, gain, sell 5 fetch, gross, yield 6 garner, return, secure 7 acquire, be worth, realize 9 introduce

bring off
6 effect, finish, rescue 7 achieve, execute, realize, succeed 8 carry out 9 discharge, implement 10 accomplish, consummate, effectuate 12 carry through

bring out
4 cull 5 educe, utter, voice 6 elicit, reveal 7 declare, enhance, explain, extract 8 disclose, introduce, showcase 9 elucidate, highlight

bring together
3 mix, wed 4 herd, join, link, yoke 5 amass, batch, blend, group, marry, merge, rally, unify, unite 6 corral, muster 7 collect, compact, compile, convene, round up 8 assemble 9 aggregate, integrate, reconcile, stockpile 10 synthesize 11 consolidate

bring up
4 moot, rear 5 breed, raise, refer, teach, train, vomit 6 advert, allude, broach, foster, school 7 advance, educate, mention, nurture, propose, suggest, touch on 8 point out, instruct 9 cultivate, introduce 10 put forward 11 regurgitate

brink
3 hem 4 bank, brim, edge 5 point, skirt, verge 6 border, fringe, margin 9 extremity, perimeter, periphery, threshold

briny
5 salty 6 saline

brio
3 pep, vim, zip 4 dash, élan, fire, gusto, life, zest, zing 5 ardor, flair, oomph, style, verve, vigor 6 bounce, esprit, fervor, spirit 7 panache, passion, sparkle 8 dynamism, vivacity 9 animation

brioche
4 roll

Briseis' lover
8 Achilles

brisk
4 busy, fast, keen, spry, yare 5 agile, fresh, nippy, quick, sharp, zippy 6 lively, nimble, snappy, speedy 7 bracing 8 animated,

bustling, vigorous **9** energetic, sprightly **10** refreshing **11** stimulating **12** invigorating

bristle
4 boil, burn, fume, seta **5** anger, quill, setae (plural), spine **6** chaeta, seethe **7** chaetae (plural), flare up
Scottish: 5 birse

British
air force: 3 RAF
cathedral city: 3 Ely **4** York **5** Ripon, Truro, Wells **6** Durham, Exeter **7** Chester, Lincoln **8** Coventry, Hereford, St. David's **9** Lichfield, Salisbury, Wakefield, Worcester **10** Canterbury, Gloucester
Channel Island: 4 Sark **6** Jersey **8** Alderney, Guernsey
coin, current: 5 pence (plural), penny, pound
coin, old: 3 bob **5** crown, groat, noble **6** bawbee, florin, George, guinea, tanner, teston **8** farthing, shilling **9** halfcrown, halfpenny, sovereign **10** threepence
colony, former: 4 Aden, Cape **5** Adana, Kenya, Malta, Natal **6** Ceylon, Cyprus, Gambia **7** Jamaica, Sarawak **9** Gold Coast, Singapore, Transvaal **10** Basutoland, New Zealand **11** Orange River, Sierra Leone **12** Bechuanaland
county: 4 Avon, Kent, York **5** Derby, Devon, Essex, Gwent **6** Dorset, Durham, Oxford, Surrey, Sussex **7** Bedford, Cumbria, Norfolk, Rutland, Suffolk, Warwick **8** Cheshire, Cornwall, Hereford, Hertford, Somerset, Stafford **9** Berkshire, Cleveland, Hampshire, Lancaster, Leicester, Wiltshire, Worcester **10** Cumberland, Gloucester, Humberside, Lancashire, Merseyside, Shropshire **11** Westmorland **12** Lincolnshire
court, local: 8 hustings
court, medieval: 4 eyre
forest: 5 Arden, weald **8** Sherwood
king, legendary: 3 Lud **4** Beli, Bran **6** Arthur, Artegal, Belinus, Elidure **8** Brannius
language, ancient: 6 Celtic, Cymric **9** Brythonic
legislature: 10 Parliament
news agency: 7 Reuters
nobleman: 4 duke, earl, peer **5** baron **6** prince **8** marquess, viscount
order: 6 Garter
people, early: 5 Celts, Jutes, Picts **6** Angles, Iceni, Saxons
political party: 4 Tory, Whig **6** Labour **12** Conservative

pope: 8 Adrian IV
prince: 5 Harry **6** Andrew, Edward **7** Charles, William
princess: 4 Anne **5** Diana **8** Margaret
prison: 5 Tower (of London) **7** Newgate **8** Dartmoor
queen, ancient: 8 Boadicea, Boudicca
resort: 4 Bath **7** Margate **8** Brighton **9** Blackpool
royal house: 4 York **5** Tudor **6** Stuart **7** Hanover, Windsor **9** Lancaster **11** Plantagenet
royal residence: 7 Windsor **8** Balmoral **10** Buckingham
school: 4 Eton **5** Rugby **6** Harrow **10** Winchester
school, military: 9 Sandhurst
spa: 4 Bath **5** Epsom **6** Buxton **7** Malvern, Matlock **8** Brighton **9** Harrogate **10** Cheltenham

British Columbia
capital: 8 Victoria
city: 6 Surrey **7** Burnaby **8** Richmond **9** Vancouver
mountain: 11 Fairweather
provincial flower: 7 dogwood (Pacific)

British Honduras
6 Belize

brittle
4 curt **5** crisp, frail, stiff **6** infirm **7** crumbly, fragile, friable **9** breakable, frangible, inelastic, irritable, sensitive **10** perishable, transitory

broach
3 tap **4** moot **6** open up **7** bring up, mention, propose, suggest **8** initiate **9** introduce **10** put forward

broad
4 wide **7** general, liberal **8** extended, generous, spacious, sweeping, tolerant **9** expansive, extensive
combining form: 4 eury, lati, plat **5** platy

broadcast
3 air, sow **4** beam, show **5** radio, strew **6** blazon, report, spread **7** bestrew, declare, publish, scatter **8** announce, proclaim, televise, transmit **9** advertise, publicize **10** bruit about, promulgate **11** communicate, declaration, disseminate, publication **12** announcement, proclamation, promulgation, transmission

broaden
4 open **5** swell, widen **6** dilate, expand, extend, fatten, spread **7** amplify, augment, distend, enlarge, thicken **8** increase **10** supplement

broadloom
6 carpet

broad-minded
4 open 7 liberal 8 catholic, eclectic, flexible, tolerant, unbiased 9 accepting, indulgent, unbigoted 10 forbearing, undogmatic 11 progressive 12 unjudgmental, unprejudiced

broadsheet
7 tabloid 9 newspaper

broadside
4 hail 5 burst, salvo, sheet, storm 6 shower, volley 7 barrage, torrent 8 at random 9 cannonade, fusillade, laterally, obliquely 11 bombardment

broadtail
4 hawk 5 sheep 7 karakul 8 lambskin

Brobdingnagian
4 huge 5 giant, jumbo 7 hulking, immense, mammoth, massive, titanic 8 colossal, gigantic, towering 9 cyclopean, humongous, monstrous 10 gargantuan, prodigious 11 elephantine

brochette
4 spit 6 skewer

brochure
5 flier, flyer 7 booklet 8 pamphlet

brogue
4 lilt, shoe 6 accent, oxford 7 dialect

broil
3 row 4 bake, burn, char, clash, cook, fray, riot, sear 5 brawl, fight, grill, melee, roast, run-in, toast 6 affray, fracas, ruction, tumult 7 bobbery, rhubarb, ruction, swelter, wrangle 8 disorder, squabble 10 donnybrook, free-for-all 11 disturbance

broiling
3 hot 5 fiery 6 baking, red-hot, torrid 7 blazing, burning 8 ovenlike, scalding, sizzling, white-hot 9 scorching 10 blistering, oppressive, sweltering

broke
4 poor 5 needy, spent 6 busted, ruined 7 drained 8 bankrupt, beggared, dirt poor, indigent, penniless, strapped, wiped out 9 destitute, insolvent, out of cash, penurious, played out 10 cleaned out 11 impecunious

broke-in
4 tame 5 tamed 6 docile

broken
4 shot 5 tamed 6 beaten, busted, cut off, faulty 7 crushed, haywire, humbled, subdued 8 bankrupt, defeated, violated, weakened 9 depressed, disrupted, fractured, heartsick, shattered, sorrowful 11 discouraged, demoralized, interrupted 12 disconnected, disheartened 13 discontinuous

broken-down
7 rickety 8 battered, decaying, decrepit 9 crumbling, neglected 10 threadbare, ramshackle 11 debilitated, dilapidated 12 deteriorated

brokenhearted
7 crushed, unhappy 8 dejected, dolorous, hopeless, wretched 9 depressed, heartsick, sorrowful 10 despairing, despondent 12 inconsolable 13 grief-stricken

broker
5 agent 6 factor 8 diplomat, mediator 9 financier, go-between, matchmaker, middleman 10 interagent, interceder, negotiator 11 intercessor 12 intermediary 13 intermediator

brolly
8 umbrella

bromide
4 bore, drip, lump, pill, yawn 5 drone, grind 6 cliché, old saw, truism 7 proverb 8 banality, chestnut, prosaism, sedative 9 platitude, soporific 10 shibboleth, triviality 11 commonplace, rubber stamp

bromidic
3 dry 4 arid, dull 5 banal, bland, dusty, stale, trite 6 boring 7 humdrum, insipid, tedious 8 shopworn, tiresome 9 dryasdust, moth-eaten, wearisome 10 monotonous, pedestrian, unoriginal 11 commonplace 13 unimaginative, uninteresting

bronco
5 horse 6 cayuse 7 mustang
Australian: 6 brumby

Brontë
character: 9 Catherine, Rochester 10 Heathcliff
novel: 7 Shirley 8 Jane Eyre, Villette 16 Wuthering Heights
sisters: 4 Anne 5 Emily 9 Charlotte

Bronx cheer
3 boo 4 hoot, jeer, razz 5 taunt 7 catcall 9 raspberry

brooch
3 pin 4 clip 5 clasp 8 fastener

brood

brood
3 set, sit 4 fret, mope, muse, stew, sulk
5 cover, flock, gloom, hatch, worry 6 litter,
ponder, repine 7 despond, progeny
8 children, meditate, ruminate 9 offspring

brook
4 bear, burn, gill, race, rill 5 abide, creek,
stand 6 arroyo, endure, rillet, runnel,
stream, suffer 7 rivulet, stomach, swallow
8 stand for, tolerate
Scottish: 6 burnie

Brookner novel
10 Hotel du Lac

broom
5 besom, brush, shrub, sweep, whisk
7 heather

broth
5 stock 8 bouillon, consommé

brothel
4 crib, stew 6 bagnio 7 lupanar
8 bordello, cathouse 9 call house
10 bawdy house, whorehouse

brother
3 kin 4 monk 5 friar 7 comrade, sibling
French: 5 frère
Italian: 3 fra 5 frate 8 fratello
Latin: 6 frater
relating to: 9 fraternal
Spanish: 7 hermano

brotherhood
4 club, gang 5 amity, guild, order, union
6 league 7 kinship, society 8 alliance,
sodality 10 fellowship, fraternity, friendship
11 association, camaraderie, comradeship,
confederacy 12 togetherness 13 consanguinity, secret society

brotherly
9 fraternal

Brothers Karamazov
4 Ivan 5 Mitya 6 Alexei, Alexey, Dmitri,
Dmitry 7 Alyosha 10 Smerdyakov

brouhaha
3 din 4 coil, to-do, fuss, riot 5 babel, broil,
hoo-ha, whirl 6 bedlam, clamor, fracas,
furore, hubbub, hurrah, jangle, pother,
racket, ruckus, rumpus, shindy, tumult,
uproar 7 ferment 8 foofaraw 9 agitation,
commotion 10 excitement, hullabaloo,
hurly-burly 11 pandemonium

brow
3 top 4 mien 5 front, crest, crown
8 forehead 9 gangplank 10 expression
11 countenance

browbeat
3 cow 5 beset, bully, harry, press
6 badger, carp at, coerce, harass, hector,
lean on 7 bluster, dragoon 8 bludgeon,
bulldoze, bullyrag, domineer, overbear,
pressure 9 tyrannize 10 intimidate

brown
4 sear 5 dusky, toast 6 scorch, tanned
7 swarthy
dark: 5 sepia, umber 9 chocolate
grayish: 3 dun 6 bister, bistre
light: 3 tan 4 ecru, fawn 5 beige, hazel,
khaki, tawny
moderate: 4 teak 6 sienna
reddish: 3 bay 4 roan 5 henna
6 auburn, russet, sorrel, titian 8 chestnut
yellowish: 6 bronze 12 butterscotch

Brown Bomber
5 Louis (Joe)

brown coal
7 lignite

brownie
3 elf, fay 5 fairy, pixie 6 sprite

Browning poem
8 Prospice, Sordello 11 Aurora Leigh,
Pippa Passes 12 Rabbi Ben Ezra 13 Fra
Lippo Lippi, My Last Duchess 14 How Do I
Love Thee?

brown recluse
6 spider

brownshirt
4 Nazi 12 storm trooper

browse
4 crop, feed, scan, shop, skim 5 graze,
munch 6 forage, nibble, peruse 7 dip into,
pasture 8 glance at, look over 10 glance
over 11 flip through, leaf through, look
through, skim through 12 thumb through

bruin
4 bear

bruise
5 pound, wound 6 batter, damage, injure,
injury 7 contuse 8 abrasion, discolor
9 contusion 13 discoloration

bruit about
6 blazon, gossip, report, spread 7 declare,
publish 8 announce, circulate, proclaim
9 advertise, broadcast 10 annunciate,
pass around, promulgate 11 blaze abroad

brume
3 fog 4 film, haze, mist, murk 5 vapor
6 miasma 8 haziness 11 obscuration

brummagem
4 fake, sham 5 bogus, false, gaudy, phony,
showy 6 ersatz, pseudo,
tinsel, tawdry 7 chintzy 8 spurious
9 imitation, pinchbeck, tasteless
10 fabricated, fictitious 11 counterfeit,
make-believe

Brunei
capital: 17 Bandar Seri Begawan
island: 6 Borneo
language: 5 Malay
monetary unit: 6 dollar
neighbor: 8 Malaysia
sea: 10 South China

brunet
3 jet 4 dark, onyx 5 dusky, ebony, raven,
sable, sooty, swart 6 swarth 7 swarthy
8 bistered, obsidian 10 dark-haired
11 brown-haired

Brunhild
5 queen 7 heroine 8 Valkyrie
husband: 6 Gunnar 7 Gunther
lover: 9 Siegfried

brunt
4 jolt 5 shock 6 burden, impact

brush
4 clip, kiss, skim 5 broom, clash, graze,
run-in, scrap, scrub, shave, sweep, whisk
6 glance, scrape, tussle 7 contact, thicket
8 skirmish 9 encounter, shrubbery,
sideswipe 11 undergrowth

brusque
4 curt, tart 5 bluff, blunt, brief, gruff, rough,
short, surly, terse 6 abrupt, crusty, snippy
7 uncivil 8 impolite, snippety, succinct
10 peremptory, ungracious 11 ill-mannered
12 discourteous

brutal
4 hard 5 cruel, feral, harsh 6 rugged,
savage, severe 7 beastly, bestial,
inhuman, swinish, vicious 8 barbaric,
callous, pitiless, ruthless, sadistic
9 barbarous, ferocious, merciless
10 relentless 11 cold-blooded,
remorseless 12 bloodthirsty

brutalize
5 abuse 6 debase, harden 7 corrupt,
debauch, deprave, pervert, roughen,
subvert, vitiate 8 maltreat, mistreat
9 manhandle 10 bestialize

brute
4 ogre 5 beast, cruel, feral 6 animal,
savage 7 beastly, bestial, inhuman,
piggish, swinish, varmint 8 creature
10 troglodyte 11 instinctive

brutish
3 low 4 base, vile 5 crude, feral, gross,
rough, stony 6 animal, carnal, coarse,
scurvy, strong 7 beastly, bestial, boorish,
inhuman, obscene, piggish, swinish,
uncivil, uncouth 8 barbaric, degraded,
depraved, inhumane, physical, sadistic
9 primitive, truculent, unrefined 11 animal-
istic, uncivilized

bryophyte
4 moss 8 hornwort 9 liverwort

Brythonic
see **Cymric**

bubble
3 sac 4 blob, boil, dome, fizz, foam, moil
5 churn, froth, slosh, spume, swash
6 burble, gurgle, seethe,
simmer 7 ferment, globule, vesicle
10 effervesce

bubbly
5 alive, fizzy, foamy, jolly, perky 6 cheery,
frothy, lively 7 buoyant, excited
8 animated, effusive 9 champagne,
ebullient, exuberant, sparkling
10 carbonated

buccaneer
5 rover 6 cowboy, pirate, sea dog
7 corsair, sea wolf 8 picaroon, sea rover
9 sea robber 10 freebooter

buck
3 fop, guy, lad, lug 4 balk, bear, bill, chap,
dude, jerk, load, move, note, oner, pack,
stag, tote, trip 5 cadet, carry, dandy, ferry,
fight, money, pitch, repel, stark, throw
6 combat, dollar, fellow, oppose, resist,
unseat 7 coxcomb, trestle 8 antelope,
bank note, sawhorse, traverse 9 greenback, withstand, workhorse 10 completely
11 Beau Brummel

bucket
3 fly, run 4 pail, rush, whiz 5 hurry, speed
6 barrel, basket, hasten, hustle, vessel
9 clamshell 10 receptacle

Buckeye State
4 Ohio

buckle
4 bend, clip, fold, hasp, kink, warp 5 catch,
clamp, clasp, heave, yield 6 cave in, fasten
7 contort, crumple harness 8 collapse
9 fastening 10 coffee cake

buckle under
3 bow 4 cave, fold, give 5 defer, yield
6 cave in, submit 7 concede, succumb

8 collapse **9** surrender **10** capitulate
11 admit defeat

Buck novel
9 Good Earth (The)

buckram
5 stiff, taut **6** wooden **8** starched
9 cardboard, unbending **10** inflexible
11 interlining

bucks
4 kale **5** bread, dough, money, moola
6 dinero, do-re-mi, moolah **7** lettuce
10 greenbacks

buck up
4 buoy, lift, rally **5** cheer **6** solace
7 comfort, console, gladden, improve,
refresh, smarten **8** brighten **9** encourage
10 strengthen

_____ buco
4 osso

bucolic
5 rural **6** rustic **7** georgic, halcyon, idyllic
8 agrarian, arcadian, pastoral
10 campestral, provincial **11** countrified,
picturesque

bud
4 germ, seed **5** gemma, spark **6** sprout
7 burgeon **9** pullulate **10** primordium
combining form: 5 blast **6** blasto

Buddha
7 Gautama **10** Siddhartha
dialogues: 5 sutra
disciple: 6 Ananda
enemy: 4 Mara
Japanese: 5 Amida, Amita
mother: 4 Maya
son: 6 Rahula
teachings: 6 dharma
wife: 9 Yasodhara

Buddhism
3 Son, Zen **4** Chan **5** Kegon **6** Huayan,
Tendai **7** Tiantai **8** Hinayana, Mahayana,
Nichiren, Pure Land **9** Theravada,
Vajrayana

Buddhist
chant: 6 mantra
dialogues: 5 sutra
enlightenment: 6 satori
evil spirit: 4 Mara
fate: 5 karma
language: 4 Pali
monk: 4 lama **5** arhat, bonze
sacred city: 5 Lhasa
saint: 5 arhat

scripture: 5 sutra **6** sutras **9** Pali canon
sect: 3 Zen
shrine: 4 tope **5** stupa **7** chorten
spell: 6 mantra
spiritual leader: 4 guru **9** Dalai Lama
state of happiness: 7 nirvana
temple: 6 pagoda
title: 7 mahatma
tree of enlightenment: 5 bodhi,
pipal

buddy
3 mac, pal **4** chum, mate **5** crony
6 comate, fellow, friend **7** compeer,
comrade, partner **8** coworker, playmate,
sidekick **9** associate, companion
10 accomplice **11** confederate

buddy-buddy
5 close, pally, thick, tight **6** chummy
8 intimate, palsy-walsy **11** inseparable

budge
4 move **5** shift, yield **7** give way

budgerigar
6 parrot **8** parakeet

budget
5 funds, means **6** amount, ration, supply
8 allocate, estimate **9** allowance,
apportion, resources

Buenos _____
5 Aires

buff
3 fan, nut, rub, tan **4** fawn, sand, wipe
5 beige, brush, fiend, freak, glaze, gloss,
lover, shine **6** addict, expert, polish, votary
7 admirer, burnish, devotee, fanatic,
fancier, furbish, groupie, habitué **8** follower
9 yellowish **10** aficionado, altogether,
enthusiast **11** connoisseur, yellow-brown

buffalo
4 bilk, faze **5** bison, bovid, stump **6** baffle,
muddle, rattle **7** carabao, confuse,
defraud, flummox, fluster, nonplus, perplex,
swindle **8** befuddle, bewilder, confound,
hoodwink **9** bamboozle, dumbfound

buffalo grass
5 grama

buffer
6 screen, shield **7** buckler, bulwark,
cushion **8** absorber, mediator, polisher
9 safeguard **10** protection **12** intermediary

buffet
3 box, hit, rap **4** beat, blip, blow, bump,
chop, cuff, drub, jolt, move, poke, slap,
sock **5** clout, drive, force, pound, punch,

smack, spank **6** batter, hammer, pummel, thrash, wallop **7** belabor, clobber, counter, lambast **8** lambaste, salad bar **9** sideboard

buffoon
3 wag **4** dolt, fool, goof, lout, zany **5** antic, clown, comic, droll, dunce, joker, yokel **6** jester **7** bumpkin, dullard **8** bonehead **9** blockhead, harlequin **10** clodhopper **11** merry-andrew

bug
3 fad, fan, irk, nag, nut, spy, tap, vex **4** buff, flaw, fret, gall, germ, mania, peeve **6** bother, defect, insect, malady, needle, nettle, pester, plague, zealot **7** disease, fanatic, microbe, provoke, wiretap **8** irritate, listen in, protrude, sickness **9** eavesdrop, infection, obsession **10** enthusiast **12** imperfection **13** micro-organism

bugaboo
see **bugbear**

bugbear
4 bane, bogy, fear, ogre **5** bogey, bogie, poser **6** goblin, teaser **7** bugaboo, problem, specter, spectre **8** anathema, bogeyman, phantasm **9** bête noire, boogerman, boogeyman, hobgoblin **10** black beast **11** abomination

buggy
4 cart, tram **6** go-cart, jalopy **8** carriage

bugle
call: 4 mess, taps **5** drill **6** sennet, tattoo **7** fanfare, retreat, tantara **8** assembly, reveille
relative: 6 cornet **7** trumpet **10** flugelhorn

build
3 wax **4** body, form, make, mode, mold, rise **5** boost, erect, forge, frame, habit, mount, put up, raise, set up, shape, swell **6** expand, figure **7** amplify, augment, compose, enlarge, fashion, magnify, produce, upsurge **8** assemble, compound, engineer, escalate, heighten, increase, multiply, physique **9** construct, establish, fabricate, institute, intensify, originate **10** accelerate, inaugurate, strengthen **11** fit together, manufacture **12** conformation, constitution

builder
5 mason **9** carpenter **10** bricklayer, contractor

builder's knot
10 clove hitch

building
3 hut **5** house **7** edifice **8** dwelling **9** structure
addition: 3 ell **4** wing **5** annex
compartment: 3 bay **4** room **6** office
connector: 9 breezeway
farm: 4 barn, crib, shed, silo
for apartments: 8 tenement
for arms: 7 arsenal
for gambling: 6 casino
for grain: 4 silo **7** granary **8** elevator
for horses: 6 stable
for manufacture: 4 shop **5** plant **7** factory
for music: 10 auditorium
for sports: 3 gym **4** bowl **5** arena **7** stadium **8** coliseum **9** gymnasium **10** hippodrome
material: 4 iron, wood **5** adobe, brick, glass, steel, stone **6** cement **8** concrete
projection: 3 bay, ell **4** wing **5** annex **6** dormer **7** cornice
round: 7 rotunda

building kit
5 Legos **10** Erector set **11** Lincoln Logs

build up
4 hype, plug, puff **5** boost, brace, erect **6** accrue, expand, extend, fortify, praise **7** collect, develop, enhance, improve, promote **8** buttress, heighten, increase **9** advertise, construct, establish, intensify, publicize **10** accumulate, aggrandize, strengthen

buildup
4 hype, puff, to-do **6** growth, hoopla **8** increase, ballyhoo **9** accretion, expansion, promotion, publicity **10** escalation **11** development, enhancement, enlargement **12** accumulation, augmentation **13** strengthening

built-in
6 inborn, inbred, innate **8** included, inherent **9** essential, ingrained, intrinsic **10** congenital, deep-seated, indwelling **11** established, fundamental **12** constitutive, incorporated

bulb
4 leek, lily, sego **5** onion, tulip **6** allium, garlic, squill **8** daffodil, hyacinth **9** amaryllis, narcissus
segment: 5 clove

bulb-like bud
4 corm **5** tuber **7** rhizome

Bulgaria

capital: 5 Sofia
city: 4 Ruse 5 Stara, Varna 6 Burgas, Pleven, Zagora 7 Plovdiv
monetary unit: 3 lev
mountain, range: 6 Balkan, Musala 7 Rhodope
neighbor: 6 Greece, Serbia, Turkey 7 Romania 9 Macedonia
part of: 7 Balkans
river: 6 Danube 7 Maritsa
sea: 5 Black

bulge

3 bag, jut, sac, sag 4 blob, bump, edge, lump, poke 5 bloat, bug out, pouch, swell 6 beetle, billow, bubble, dilate, excess, expand 7 balloon, distend, inflate, project, puff out 8 overhang, protrude, stand out, stick out, swelling 9 allowance, head start 10 distension, projection, promontory, protrusion 11 excrescence, protuberate 12 protuberance

bulk

4 body, core, loom, mass 5 fiber, swell, total 6 amount, corpus, expand, volume 7 bigness, quantum 8 majority, quantity, stand out 9 aggregate, magnitude, substance

bulky

3 fat 5 beefy, hefty, husky, large, obese, stout 7 massive 8 cumbrous 9 corpulent, ponderous 10 cumbersome, overweight, unwieldy 11 substantial

bull

4 bunk, male, slip, toro, trip 5 boner, edict, error, fluff, force, hooey, lapse 6 bovine, bungle, decree 7 baloney, blooper, blunder, hogwash, mistake 8 nonsense 11 detective
combining form: 4 taur 5 tauri, tauro

bulldoze

3 cow 4 move, push, raze 5 abash, bully, clear, cream, elbow, force, level, press, scare, shove 6 coerce, hector, hustle, jostle, lean on, menace, propel, thrust 7 bluster, clobber, dragoon, flatten, oppress, trounce 8 bludgeon, browbeat, bullyrag, demolish, domineer, restrain, shoulder 9 terrorize, tyrannize 10 intimidate, obliterate

bullet

6 dumdum, tracer 9 cartridge 10 projectile
size: 7 caliber, calibre

bulletin

4 news 5 flash, scoop 6 notice, report 7 account, catalog, gazette, message, missive, release 8 briefing, calendar, dispatch, magazine, register 9 catalogue, statement 10 communiqué, periodical 12 announcement

bull fiddle

10 contrabass, double bass

bullfighter

6 torero 7 matador, picador 8 toreador 11 cuadrillero 12 banderillero
famous: 6 Arruza 7 Ordóñez 8 Belmonte, Joselito, Manolete 9 Dominguin 10 El Cordobés

bullfighting

arena: 5 plaza
cheer: 3 olé
hero: 6 torero 7 matador 8 toreador
lancer: 7 picador
red cloth: 6 muleta
Spanish: 7 corrida
team: 9 cuadrilla

bullheaded

6 mulish 7 adamant, willful 8 contrary, obdurate, perverse, stubborn 9 insistent, obstinate, pigheaded 10 headstrong, refractory, self-willed, unyielding 11 intractable, stiff-necked 12 intransigent, pertinacious, strong-willed

bullish

4 rosy 6 brawny, rising, upbeat 7 booming 9 advancing, expanding, favorable 10 optimistic

bully

3 cow 4 goon, pimp, punk, thug 5 abuse, heavy, meany, tease, tough 6 harass, hector, meanie, menace, pander, pick on, rascal 7 bluster, buffalo, dragoon, harrier, oppress, ruffian, torment, torture 8 bludgeon, browbeat, bulldoze, bullyrag, harasser, threaten 9 bulldozer, persecute, victimize, tormenter, tyrannize 10 browbeater, corned beef, intimidate, persecutor 11 intimidator

bullyrag

see **bulldoze**

bulrush

4 reed 5 sedge 7 cattail, papyrus

bulwark

4 wall 6 screen, shield 7 barrier, bastion, parapet, rampart, seawall 8 buttress, fortress, palisade 9 earthwork, safeguard 10 breakwater, breastwork, embankment, stronghold 13 fortification

bum
3 beg, vag 4 bust, hobo, idle, laze, lazy, loaf, loll, slug 5 binge, cadge, drunk, hit up, idler, mooch, tramp 6 bottom, dawdle, loafer, loiter, lounge, slouch, unfair 7 depress, drifter, feel low, goof off, rear end, vagrant, wheedle 8 buttocks, derelict, fainéant, importune, slugabed, sluggard, vagabond 9 do-nothing, goldbrick, lazybones, panhandle, transient

bumbershoot
8 umbrella

bumble
3 mar 4 blow, flub, muff 5 botch, fluff, gum up, lurch, slip up 6 bobble, bollix, bungle, falter, fumble, mess up, muck up, rumble, teeter, totter 7 blunder, screw up, stagger, stumble 8 flounder

bumbling
5 inept 6 clumsy, gauche, gawky, klutzy 7 awkward, halting, unhandy 8 ungainly 9 all thumbs, graceless, ham-handed, maladroit, unskilled 11 heavy-handed, incapable, incompetent 13 butterfingers, uncoordinated

bummer
3 dud 4 drag, flop, hobo 5 tramp 6 beggar, cadger, downer, sponge, too bad 7 failure, forager, moocher, sponger 8 deadbeat, vagabond 9 tough luck 10 freebooter, panhandler, rotten luck, wet blanket

bump
3 bop, hit, jar, ram, rap, wen 4 bang, bash, bust, jolt, knot, lump, oust, slam 5 break, carom, clash, crack, crash, gnarl, knock, prang, shift, shock, shove, wound 6 demote, growth, impact, injury, jostle, jounce, nodule, remove, strike, wallop 7 collide, degrade, demerit, pothole, run into 8 demotion, dislodge, displace, swelling 9 carbuncle, collision, contusion, convexity 10 concussion, projection, protrusion 12 protuberance

bumpkin
3 oaf 4 boor, hick, lout, rube 5 clown, swain, yokel 6 rustic 7 hayseed, peasant 9 chawbacon, hillbilly, simpleton 10 clodhopper, country boy, countryman, provincial

bump off
3 ice 4 do in, kill, slay 5 erase, snuff 6 murder, rub out 7 butcher, execute, take out 8 knock off 9 eliminate, liquidate 11 assassinate

Bumppo, Natty
alias: 7 Hawkeye 10 Deerslayer, Pathfinder
creator: 6 Cooper (James Fenimore)

bumptious
5 cocky, pushy 8 arrogant, impudent 9 audacious, obnoxious, obtrusive, officious 13 self-assertive

bumpy
5 jerky, nubby, ridgy, rough 6 bouncy, jouncy, knobby, knotty, patchy, pimply, uneven 7 jolting, nodular 9 difficult, irregular

bun
4 load, roll 6 pastry

bunch
3 lot, set, wen 4 band, bevy, bump, clot, crew, knot, lump, mass, push 5 batch, clump, covey, crowd, flock, group, party, spray, stack, swell 6 bundle, circle, clutch, gather, huddle, parcel, throng 7 bouquet, collect, cluster 8 assembly, protrude, swelling 9 gathering 10 assemblage, assortment, collection, congregate 11 aggregation 12 accumulation

bunco steerer
3 gyp 6 con man, grifter 7 cheater, diddler, sharper 8 swindler 9 defrauder, trickster 12 double-dealer 13 confidence man

bundle
3 lot, pot, set, wad 4 bale, body, heap, mint, pack, pile, wrap 5 array, batch, bunch, clump, group, sheaf, truss 6 fardel, packet, parcel 7 cluster, fortune 10 assortment

bungalow
5 cabin, lodge 6 chalet 7 cottage

bungle
4 flub, goof, mess, mix up, muff, slip, trip 5 boner, botch, error, fluff, gum up, lapse, spoil 6 bollix, bumble, fiasco, foozle, foul up, fumble, goof up, mess up, muck up, muddle 7 blooper, blunder, failure, louse up, misstep, mistake, stumble 9 mishandle, mismanage

bungler
3 oaf 4 clod, dolt, goof 5 klutz 7 screw-up, tomfool 8 bonehead, goofball, shlemiel 9 blunderer, schlemiel 10 stumblebum 11 blunderbuss, incompetent 13 butter-fingers

bunglesome
6 clumsy, klutzy 7 awkward 8 bumbling 9 all thumbs 13 uncoordinated

bung up
4 beat, hurt 5 abuse, pound 6 batter, bruise, injure 7 contuse, disable 9 disfigure, manhandle

bunion
4 lump 8 swelling 10 protrusion, tumescence 11 enlargement

bunk
3 bed, cot, kip, rot 4 bosh, bull, guff, jazz 5 bilge, board, crash, hokum, hooey, house, lodge, pallet, put up 6 humbug, piffle 7 eyewash, baloney, hogwash, rubbish, twaddle 8 claptrap, domicile, flimflam, malarkey, nonsense, tommyrot 9 poppycock 10 balderdash

bunker
3 bin 6 dugout 7 bastion, chamber 10 embankment, stronghold 11 compartment

bunkum
3 rot 4 bosh, bull, guff, jazz 5 bilge, hokum, hooey 6 humbug, piffle 7 baloney, hogwash, rubbish, twaddle 8 claptrap, flimflam, malarkey, nonsense, tommyrot 9 poppycock 10 balderdash

bunting
5 flags 9 streamers

Bunyanesque
4 huge 5 giant, jumbo 7 mammoth, massive, titanic 8 behemoth, colossal, gigantic, towering 9 Herculean 10 gargantuan, prodigious

Bunyan's ox
4 Babe

buoy
4 lift, prop 5 boost, cheer, float, raise 6 assist, beacon, bear up, buck up, solace, uphold, uplift 7 bolster, comfort, gladden, hearten, signal, support, sustain 9 encourage

buoyancy
6 bounce, levity 7 jollity 8 airiness 10 ebullience, exuberance, exuberancy, liveliness, resilience 12 floatability 13 effervescence

buoyant
3 gay 4 airy 5 sunny 6 afloat, bouncy 7 elastic 8 cheerful, floating, volatile 9 expansive, floatable, resilient 10 unsinkable, weightless 12 effervescent, lighthearted

burble
3 gas, yak 4 blab, chat, gush, talk, wash 5 clack, plash, run on, slosh, swash 6 babble, bubble, gabble, gurgle, murmur, rattle, splash, yammer 7 chatter, prattle, sparkle

burden
3 tax, try 4 care, clog, core, duty, gist, haul, lade, load, onus, pile, pith, task, text 5 brunt, cargo, press, theme, weigh 6 amount, charge, chorus, cumber, hamper, lading, lumber, saddle, strain, stress, thrust, upshot, weight 7 afflict, anxiety, freight, oppress, payload, refrain, purport 9 encumber, handicap, obligate, overload 9 millstone, substance, weigh down 10 deadweight 11 encumbrance

burdensome
5 tough 6 taxing, trying 7 arduous, exigent, irksome, onerous, weighty 8 crushing, exacting, grievous 9 demanding, difficult, fatiguing, ponderous 10 exhausting, oppressive 11 troublesome 12 backbreaking, unmanageable

bureau
4 unit 5 chest 6 agency 7 dresser, section 8 ministry 10 department, chiffonier 11 writing desk

bureaucrat
8 mandarin, minister, official 11 functionary 12 civil servant, officeholder

burg
4 city, town 7 borough 8 fortress 10 metropolis, walled town 12 municipality

burgee
4 flag 6 banner, ensign, pennon 7 pendant, pennant 8 standard, streamer

burgeon
4 blow, boom, open 5 bloom, build, mount, run up 6 emerge, expand, flower, sprout, thrive, unfold 7 augment, blossom, develop, enlarge, fill out, prosper, run riot 8 flourish, heighten, increase, multiply, mushroom, snowball 9 germinate 10 burst forth, effloresce

burghal
5 civic, urban 8 citified 9 municipal 12 metropolitan

burgher
7 citizen, denizen 8 townsman

burglar
4 yegg 5 thief
loot: 4 swag

burglarize
see **burgle**

burglary
5 heist, theft 7 larceny

burgle
3 rob 4 lift, loot 5 heist, steal, strip 6 rip off, thieve 7 despoil, plunder, ransack 9 break into, knock over 10 housebreak

burgomaster
5 mayor 10 magistrate

Burgundy wine
grape: 5 Gamay 9 Pinot Noir 10 Chardonnay
red: 8 Mercurey 10 Beaujolais
white: 5 Rully 6 Chagny 7 Chablis 10 Montrachet 13 Pouilly-Fuissé

burial
4 tomb 5 grave 7 funeral 9 interment, obsequies, sepulcher, sepulchre, sepulture 10 entombment, inhumation
box: 6 casket, coffin
ceremony: 7 funeral, obsequy 9 obsequies
mound: 6 barrow 7 tumulus
tomb: 9 mausoleum, sepulcher, sepulchre

burial ground
8 boot hill, cemetery 8 boneyard, God's acre 9 graveyard 10 churchyard, necropolis 12 memorial park, potter's field
early Christian: 8 catacomb

Burkina Faso
capital: 11 Ouagadougou
ethnic group: 3 Gur 5 Mossi 7 Voltaic
former name: 10 Upper Volta
language: 4 Moré 5 Dyula 6 French
monetary unit: 5 franc
neighbor: 4 Mali, Togo 5 Benin, Ghana, Niger 10 Ivory Coast
river: 5 Volta (Black, Red) 6 Nazion 7 Mouhoun, Nakanbe 8 Red Volta 10 Black Volta

burlap
5 gunny 6 fabric 7 bagging, sacking
fiber: 4 hemp, jute

burlesque
3 ape 4 mock, sham 5 farce, spoof 6 parody, satire, send-up 7 lampoon, mockery, mocking, takeoff 8 pastiche, skin show, travesty 10 caricature, distortion, girlie show, lampoonery

burly
4 hale 5 beefy, hefty, husky, tough 6 brawny, robust, strong, stocky 8 athletic, heavyset, muscular, powerful, stalwart, thickset, vigorous 9 strapping

Burma
see **Myanmar**

burn
4 bake, char, cook, fire, fume, rage, sear 5 anger, blaze, broil, creek, flame, flare, gleam, roast, scald, singe, smart, smoke, sting, toast 6 ignite, kindle, scorch, seethe 7 bristle, combust, consume, cremate, flare up, inflame, radiate, smolder, swelter 8 smoulder 9 carbonize, cauterize 10 incinerate

burnable
8 volatile 9 flammable, ignitable 10 incendiary 11 combustible, inflammable

burned-out
4 beat, shot 5 spent, weary 6 sapped 7 drained, worn-out 8 consumed, fatigued 9 destroyed, exhausted, played-out 10 broken-down 11 debilitated 12 extinguished

burner
3 hob

burning
3 hot 5 afire, aglow, fiery 6 ablaze, aflame, alight, ardent, fervid, heated, hectic, red-hot, torrid, urgent 7 blazing, fervent, fevered, glowing, ignited, kindled, searing 8 broiling, feverish, pressing, sizzling, white-hot 9 scorching 10 imperative, passionate 11 conflagrant, impassioned 12 incandescent
combining form: 4 igni
malicious: 5 arson

burnish
3 rub, wax 4 buff 5 glaze, gloss, scour, sheen, shine 6 luster, patina, polish, smooth 7 furbish, varnish 8 brighten

burnished
5 shiny 6 glossy, satiny, sheeny 7 lambent, radiant, shining 8 gleaming, lustrous, polished 9 brilliant 10 glistening 11 resplendent

burnsides
8 whiskers 9 sideburns 10 sideboards 11 dundrearies, muttonchops 12 side-whiskers

burp
5 belch, eruct, expel

burro
3 ass 6 donkey 7 jackass

Burroughs hero
6 Tarzan

burrow

burrow
3 den, dig 4 hole, lair, mine, nook, snug
5 delve, gouge 6 cavity, cuddle,
nestle, nuzzle, tunnel 7 snuggle
10 excavation

burst
3 pop, run 4 bang, boom, clap, gush, gust,
rive, rush, slam, wham 5 blast, crack,
crash, erupt, flare, go off, lunge, sally,
salvo, smash, spasm, split, storm, surge
6 access, blow up, emerge, launch, plunge,
shiver, spring, shower, volley 7 assault,
barrage, explode, flare-up, fly open,
rupture, shatter, torrent 8 detonate,
drumfire, eruption, fragment, outbreak,
splinter, splitter 9 broadside, cannonade,
explosion, fusillade, onslaught
11 bombardment

Burundi
capital: 9 Bujumbura
ethnic group: 4 Hutu 5 Tutsi
former name: 6 Urundi
lake: 10 Tanganyika
language: 5 Rundi 6 French 7 Kirundi
monetary unit: 5 franc
neighbor: 5 Congo 6 Rwanda
8 Tanzania

bury
4 hide, sink, stow 5 cache, cover, embed,
inter, plant, stash 6 absorb, entomb,
inhume, mantle, shroud 7 blanket,
conceal, cover up, implant, lay away,
overlay, put away, secrete 8 ensconce,
submerge

bus
5 clear 7 missile, trolley, vehicle 9 hand
truck 10 spacecraft

bush
4 rose 5 lilac, shrub, wahoo 6 azalea,
cassis, privet 7 currant, thicket, weigela
8 backland, barberry, hazelnut
9 backwater, backwoods, forsythia,
manzanita 10 gooseberry, hinterland,
wilderness 11 pussy willow
12 rhododendron

bushel
3 ton 4 heap, load, pile 6 basket, hamper
7 pannier

bush-league
5 minor 6 junior, two-bit 8 inferior,
mediocre, small-fry 9 small-time
10 inadequate, second-rate 11 lightweight
13 insignificant

bushranger
6 outlaw 8 woodsman 12 frontiersman

bushwhack
4 trap 6 ambush, assail, attack, entrap,
waylay 7 assault 8 surprise 9 blindside

bushwhacker
6 bandit, outlaw, raider, sniper 8 guerilla,
woodsman 9 guerrilla 10 highwayman

bushy
5 bosky 6 fluffy, fuzzy, hairy, leafy, woolly
7 hirsute, unkempt 9 bristling, luxuriant,
overgrown 10 disordered 11 flourishing

business
3 job 4 firm, line, work 5 trade 6 affair,
custom, matter, métier, office, outfit, racket
7 calling, company, concern, pursuit, traffic
8 commerce, function, industry
9 patronage 10 employment, enterprise,
livelihood, occupation 11 corporation
13 establishment
expense: 8 overhead
syndicate: 6 cartel

businesslike
6 formal 7 orderly, serious 8 diligent,
thorough 9 competent, efficient, practical,
pragmatic 10 impersonal, methodical, no-
nonsense, purposeful, systematic
11 disciplined, hardworking
12 professional

businessman
6 broker, dealer, trader, tycoon 7 magnate
8 investor, merchant 9 bourgeois,
financier, tradesman, executive
10 capitalist, trafficker 12 entrepreneur,
merchandiser 13 industrialist

busker
8 minstrel, musician 11 entertainer

buss
4 kiss, peck 5 smack 6 smooch
8 osculate

bust
3 bag, cop, dud, hit, jag, nab, net 4 bomb,
bump, fail, flop, fold, raid, ruin, slug, sock,
tear, tour 5 binge, bosom, break, broke,
burst, catch, chest, crash, lemon, loser,
punch, smash, spell, spree, stint, torso,
trash, 6 arrest, bender, breast, collar,
demote, pick up 7 break up, carouse,
degrade, demerit, destroy, exhaust, failure,
rupture, wear out 8 bankrupt, demolish,
fracture 9 apprehend, break down,
destitute, downgrade, penniless 10 impoverish, police raid

bustle
3 ado, fly, run 4 flit, fuss, rush, stir, tear,
teem, to-do 5 hurry, whirl, whisk 6 action,
be busy, bestir, clamor, flurry, furore,

hassle, hasten, hubbub, hustle, motion, pother, scurry, tumult, uproar **7** ferment, turmoil **8** activity, to-and-fro **9** commotion, whirlpool, whirlwind **10** hurly-burly, excitement, liveliness

bustling
4 busy, rife **5** brisk, fussy, peppy **6** active, hectic, lively **7** dynamic, festive, hopping, humming, jumping **8** animated, swarming, vigorous **9** energetic, tumultuous **11** hard-working, industrious

busty
5 ample, buxom, curvy **6** bosomy, chesty, zaftig **7** shapely, stacked **10** curvaceous, voluptuous **11** full-bosomed, well-rounded

busy
5 brisk, fussy **6** active, at work, lively, on duty, tied up **7** engaged, hopping, humming, swamped, working **8** bustling, crowded, diligent, employed, energetic, hustling, meddling, occupied, overdone, sedulous, teeming **9** assiduous, congested, elaborate, intrusive, obtrusive, officious **10** meddlesome, overworked **11** impertinent, industrious, interfering, unavailable

busybody
5 prier, pryer, snoop, yenta **6** butt-in, gossip, old hen **7** meddler **8** informer, kibitzer, quidnunc **9** pragmatic **10** chatterbox, newsmonger, pragmatist, talebearer, tattletale **11** nosey parker, rumormonger **12** gossipmonger, rubbernecker, troublemaker

but
3 bar, yet **4** just, only, save **5** alone **6** except, merely, saving, unless **7** barring, besides, however **8** entirely **9** aside from, excepting, excluding, outside of **13** on the contrary

butcher
4 ruin, slay **5** botch, carve, clean, spoil, wreck **6** bollix, killer, mess up, slayer **7** cut meat, destroy, meat man **8** mutilate **9** slaughter **11** slaughterer

butcher-bird
6 shrike

butcherly
5 cruel **6** bloody, clumsy, savage **7** awkward **8** sadistic **9** ferocious, merciless **10** unskillful

butchery
7 carnage **8** abattoir, genocide, massacre **9** bloodbath, bloodshed, holocaust, slaughter **10** mass murder **12** annihilation **13** extermination

buteo
4 hawk **7** buzzard

butler
5 valet **7** steward **10** manservant

Butler, Samuel
novel: **7** Erewhon **13** Way of All Flesh (The)
poem: **8** Hudibras

butt
3 end, keg, tip, ram, tun, vat **4** base, cask, drum, dupe, join, push, rump, stub, stump, tail **5** chump, fanny, patsy, touch, verge **6** adjoin, barrel, border, bottom, firkin, pigeon, sucker, target, thrust, victim **7** collide, fall guy, rear end, run itno **8** derriere, hogshead, neighbor **9** cigarette, fundament, lie beside, pilgarlic, posterior, remainder **11** communicate, sitting duck **12** hindquarters **13** laughingstock

butter
artificial: **4** oleo **9** margarine **13** oleomargarine
Indian: **4** ghee
piece: **3** pat
semifluid: **4** ghee
tree: **4** shea

butterball
5 blimp, whale **8** dumpling, elephant **10** bufflehead

butterfish
6 gunnel

butterfly
4 blue **5** diana, satyr, zebra **6** copper, morpho **7** admiral, buckeye, monarch, satyrid, skipper, sulphur, vanessa, viceroy **8** crescent, grayling, milkweed, victoria **9** aphrodite, metalmark, nymphalid, wood nymph **10** fritillary, hairstreak **11** swallowtail
bush: **8** buddleia
fish: **6** blenny, chiton **7** gurnard
larva: **11** caterpillar
lily: **8** mariposa
order: **11** Lepidoptera
plant: **8** oncidium
pupa: **8** chrysalis
scientist: **13** lepidopterist

butter up
4 coax **5** charm **6** cajole, kowtow, praise, stroke **7** adulate, beguile, blarney, flatter, massage, wheedle **8** blandish, bootlick, soft-soap **9** brownnose, sweet-talk **10** overpraise

butt in

6 kibitz, meddle 7 intrude, obtrude
8 busybody, interpose, overstep
9 interfere, interlope, interrupt

buttinsky

7 meddler 8 busybody, kibitzer, quidnunc
9 loudmouth 10 trespasser
12 troublemaker

buttocks

4 rear, rump, seat, tail 5 fanny, nates
6 behind, bottom, breech, heinie 7 hind
end, hunkers, keister, rear end, tail end
8 backside, derriere, haunches
9 fundament, posterior

buttonball

8 sycamore 9 plane tree

button-down

6 square, stuffy 8 decorous, orthodox,
straight 10 restrained 11 straitlaced,
traditional 12 conservative, conventional

buttonwood

8 sycamore 9 plane tree

buttress

4 pier, prop, stay 5 brace, carry, shore,
strut, truss 6 back up, bear up, hold up,
column, uphold 7 bolster, bulwark, fortify,
shore up, support, sustain 9 reinforce,
stanchion 10 strengthen 12 underpinning
13 fortification, reinforcement

buxom

5 ample, busty, curvy 6 bosomy, chesty,
zaftig 7 shapely, stacked 10 curvaceous,
voluptuous 11 full-bosomed, full-figured,
well-rounded

buy

5 bribe 6 obtain, ransom, redeem
7 acquire, bargain, believe 8 purchase

buy back

6 ransom, recoup, redeem, regain
8 retrieve 10 repurchase

buyer

6 client, patron, vendee 7 shopper
8 consumer, customer 9 purchaser

buy off

3 fix, sop 5 bribe 6 settle 7 corrupt,
silence 9 influence 10 manipulate, tamper
with

buzz

3 fad, hum 4 call, fizz, high, hiss, news,
purr, ring, talk, whir, whiz 5 craze, drone,
hurry, rumor, strum, thrum, whirr, whish
6 bumble, fizzle, gossip, murmur, natter,
report, rumble, sizzle, summon, wheeze,
whoosh 7 chatter, scandal, whisper
8 sibilate 9 bombinate 11 reverberate,
scuttlebutt

buzzard

5 buteo 7 vulture 13 turkey vulture

by

3 per, via 4 away, near, nigh, past 5 along,
aside 6 at hand, beside, next to 7 through
9 alongside 10 incidental 11 according to
12 not later than

by and by

4 anon, soon 5 after, later 7 shortly
8 directly, latterly 9 afterward, presently
10 before long 12 subsequently

by and large

7 all told, broadly, en masse, overall,
usually 8 all in all, normally 9 generally,
typically 10 altogether, on the whole,
ordinarily 11 principally

by dint of

see **by means of**

bye-bye

4 ciao, ta-ta 5 adieu, adios 6 so long
7 cheerio 8 au revoir, farewell, sayonara,
toodle-oo

bygone

3 old 4 dead, late, lost, once, past
5 dated, fossil, of old, olden 6 former, of
yore, remote, whilom 7 antique, archaic,
belated, defunct, extinct, old-time, onetime,
quondam, vintage 8 departed, sometime,
obsolete, outdated, outmoded, vanished
9 erstwhile, out-of-date 10 antiquated,
oldfangled 12 antediluvian, old-fashioned

by means of

3 per, via 4 with 5 using 7 through
9 employing, utilizing

byname

6 handle 7 epithet, moniker 8 cognomen
9 sobriquet 10 diminutive, hypocorism
11 appellation

bypass

4 omit 5 avoid, burke, shunt, skirt
6 detour, ignore 7 highway 8 outflank, ring
road, sidestep 10 circumvent, pass around
11 deviate from

by-product

5 yield 6 effect, result 7 outcome, residue,
spin-off 8 offshoot 9 outgrowth
10 derivative, descendant 11 aftereffect,
consequence 12 repercussion

Byron work
4 Cain, Lara 5 Beppo 6 Giaour (The),
Werner 7 Corsair (The), Don Juan,
Manfred 12 Childe Harold

bystander
6 gawker, viewer 7 watcher, witness
8 beholder, observer, onlooker, passerby
9 spectator 10 eyewitness
12 rubbernecker

by stealth
5 slyly 7 sub rosa 8 covertly, in secret,
secretly 9 furtively, privately 10 under
cover 11 insidiously 13 clandestinely

by virtue of
see **by means of**

by way of
see **by means of**

byword
3 saw 5 adage, axiom, maxim, motto,
nomen 6 dictum, phrase, saying, slogan,
truism 7 epigram, epithet, precept,
proverb, refrain 8 aphorism, cognomen,
nickname 9 platitude, prescript, sobriquet
10 hypocorism, shibboleth 11 catchphrase,
commonplace, rallying cry

Byzantine
6 daedal, knotty 7 complex, devious
8 involved 9 elaborate, intricate
10 convoluted 11 complicated
12 labyrinthine 13 sophisticated,
surreptitious
emperor: 3 Leo 4 Zeno 5 Basil
6 Bardas, Justin, Phocas 7 Michael,
Romanus 9 Heraclius, Justinian
10 Nicephorus, Theodosius
empress: 3 Zoe 5 Irene 8 Theodora

C

cab
4 hack, taxi 6 jitney 7 hackney 8 carriage

cabal
3 mob 4 clan, club, plot, ring 5 coven, group, junta, mafia 6 cartel, circle, clique 7 coterie, faction, in-group 8 intrigue 9 camarilla 10 conspiracy 11 machination

cabaletta
4 aria, song

cabalistic
6 arcane, mystic, occult 8 esoteric 9 recondite 10 mysterious 11 inscrutable 12 impenetrable

caballero
6 knight 7 paladin 8 cavalier, horseman 9 chevalier

cabana
3 hut 5 shack 7 shelter

cabaret
4 café 6 bistro, nitery 7 hot spot 9 nightclub, nightspot 10 supper club 12 watering hole

cabbage
3 nab, nip 4 cash, hook, lift, palm 5 bread, dough, filch, kraut, money, moola, pinch, steal, swipe 6 dinero, do-re-mi, moolah, pilfer 7 purloin, scratch 10 greenbacks, sauerkraut
disease of: 6 mildew, mosaic 7 root rot, yellows 8 blackleg, club root
family: 4 cole, kale, rape 5 colza, savoy 6 turnip 7 collard, mustard 8 broccoli, colewort, kohlrabi, rutabaga 11 cauliflower

cabbagehead
see **dunce**

cabdriver
4 hack 5 cabby 6 cabbie

cabin
3 hut 4 camp, shed 5 berth, hovel, lodge, shack 6 cabana, chalet, lean-to, shanty 7 bivouac, cottage 9 stateroom

cabin cruiser
5 yacht 9 motorboat, powerboat

cabinet
4 case 6 bureau 7 armoire, chamber, commode, console, council, dresser 8 advisers, advisors, cupboard, ministry 9 presidium 10 chiffonier, collection, counselors

cabinetmaker
American: 5 Eames (Charles), Phyfe (Duncan) 6 Belter (John Henry) 7 Goddard (John, Stephen, Thomas) 8 McIntire (Samuel), Townsend (Christopher, Edmund, James, Job, John)
English: 4 Adam (James, Robert), Hope (Thomas), Kent (William) 8 Sheraton (Thomas) 11 Chippendale (Thomas), Hepplewhite (George)
French: 6 Boulle (André-Charles) 8 Caffieri (Jacques, Jean-Jacques, Philippe), Cressent (Charles)
German: 10 Weisweiler (Adam)

cable
4 rope, wire 5 braid, chain 6 stitch 8 transmit 9 telegraph

cabriolet
5 coupe 8 carriage

cache
4 bury, hide 5 cover, plant, stash, store 6 memory, wealth 7 conceal, lay away, nest egg, put away, reserve, secrete 8 ensconce, treasure 9 stockpile 10 accumulate 11 hiding place

cachet
4 rank, seal 5 motto, state 6 slogan, status 7 dignity, stature 8 approval, position, prestige, standing 11 consequence

cachinnate
4 crow, howl, roar 5 laugh, whoop
6 guffaw, shriek

cackle
3 gab, jaw 4 blab, chat, crow 5 clack,
cluck 6 babble, burble, gabble, gaggle,
gobble 7 blabber, blatter, chatter, prattle

cacoëthes
4 zeal 5 mania 6 desire 9 obsession

cacomistle
5 civet 7 raccoon 8 civet cat, ringtail

cacophonic
5 harsh 8 tuneless 9 dissonant, unmusical
10 discordant, unmelodious
12 unharmonious

cacophony
9 harshness 10 dissonance

cactus
5 nopal 6 cereus, cholla, mescal, peyote
7 opuntia, saguaro 11 prickly pear

cad
3 cur, dog 4 boor, heel, lout, rake 5 creep,
knave, louse, rogue 6 rascal, rotter
7 bounder 9 conductor, scoundrel

cadaver
4 body, mort 5 stiff 6 corpse 7 carcass,
remains 8 deceased

cadaverous
5 ashen, gaunt, livid 6 pallid, wasted
7 deathly, ghastly, ghostly, shadowy
8 skeletal, spectral 9 deathlike, emaciated,
ghostlike 10 corpselike

caddy
3 bin, box 4 aide 5 toter 6 casket
8 canister, tea chest

cadence
4 beat, flow, lilt 5 meter, pulse 6 rhythm
9 pulsation 10 conclusion, inflection,
intonation

cadet
4 pimp 5 plebe 7 student, trainee

cadge
3 beg, bum 5 mooch 6 hustle, sponge
8 freeload, scrounge 9 panhandle

Cadmus
daughter: 3 Ino 5 Agave 6 Semele
7 Autonoë
father: 6 Agenor
sister: 6 Europa
victim: 6 dragon
wife: 8 Harmonia

cadre
4 cell, core 5 frame, staff 6 cohort 7 in-
group 9 framework

caducity
3 age 6 dotage, old age 8 senility
10 senescence 11 senectitude

Caesar
assassin: 6 Brutus (Marcus Junius)
7 Cassius (Gaius)
battle: 4 Zela 9 Pharsalus
conquest: 4 Gaul 7 Britain
eulogist: 6 Antony (Marc) 7 Anthony
(Mark) 8 Antonius (Marcus)
message: 12 Veni vidi vici
river: 7 Rubicon
utterance: 9 Et tu Brute
wife: 7 Pompeia 8 Cornelia 9 Calpurnia

Caesarism
7 tyranny 9 authority, autocracy, despotism
10 absolutism 12 dictatorship

caesura
5 break, pause 12 interruption

café
5 diner 6 bistro, nitery 7 barroom,
beanery, cabaret, hot spot 8 cookshop
9 lunchroom, nightclub, nightspot
10 coffee shop, restaurant, supper club
12 luncheonette, watering hole
13 watering place

café _____
4 noir 6 au lait, filtre 7 society

caftan
4 gown, robe 6 muumuu 12 dressing gown

cage
3 hem, pen 4 cell, coop, jail 5 score
6 corral, immure, lock up, shut in 7 close
in, enclose, impound 8 imprison
9 enclosure 11 incarcerate

cagey
3 sly 4 foxy, wary, wily 5 canny, sharp
6 astute, clever, crafty, shrewd

cahier
6 record, report, review

cahoots
6 hookup, league 8 alliance 9 collusion
10 complicity 11 partnership

caiman
9 crocodile 11 crocodilian

Cain
brother: 4 Abel, Seth
father: 4 Adam
land: 3 Nod

mother: 3 Eve
nephew: 4 Enos
son: 5 Enoch
victim: 4 Abel

Caine Mutiny author
4 Wouk (Herman)

Cain novel
8 Serenade 13 Mildred Pierce 23 Postman Always Rings Twice (The)

cajole
3 con 4 coax, dupe 6 entice, seduce
7 beguile, blarney, deceive, wheedle
8 blandish, inveigle, maneuver, persuade, soft-soap 9 sweet-talk

cake
3 dry, set 4 coat, loaf, rime 5 cover, crust
6 harden, pastry 7 congeal, encrust, incrust 8 solidify
almond: 8 macaroon
flat: 5 cooky 6 cookie
oatmeal: 4 farl 5 scone 7 bannock
ring-shaped: 5 donut 6 jumble
8 doughnut
rum-soaked: 4 baba
Scottish: 4 farl 5 scone
shell-shaped: 9 madeleine
topping: 5 icing 8 frosting, streusel
without flour: 5 torte
without shortening: 6 sponge

Cakes and Ale author
7 Maugham (W. Somerset)

cakewalk
4 romp, rout, snap 5 cinch, dance, strut
6 breeze, prance 8 pushover, walkover

calaboose
3 can 4 brig, coop, jail, tank 5 clink, pokey
6 cooler, lockup, prison 7 slammer
8 hoosegow 9 jailhouse

calamitous
4 dire 5 fatal 6 woeful 7 ruinous
8 grievous 10 disastrous, lamentable
11 cataclysmic, devastating, unfortunate
12 catastrophic 13 heartbreaking

calamity
4 ruin 5 wreck 7 tragedy 8 disaster,
downfall 9 cataclysm 11 catastrophe,
tribulation

Calamity ____
4 Jane

calculate
4 rely 5 assay, count, gauge, judge, solve,
tally, tot up, value 6 assess, cipher, figure,
intend, reckon 7 compute, measure, work

out 8 appraise, estimate, evaluate,
forecast 9 ascertain, determine, figure out

calculated
6 likely 7 planned 8 intended 9 worked
out 10 deliberate 12 aforethought,
premeditated

calculating
3 sly 4 wary, wily 5 canny, chary, sharp
6 artful, crafty, shrewd 7 careful, cunning,
devious, politic 8 cautious, discreet,
guileful, scheming 9 designing
11 circumspect

calculating device
6 abacus
Peruvian: 5 quipu

calculation
8 analysis, counting, estimate, figuring,
prudence 9 ciphering, reckoning
10 arithmetic, estimation, prediction
11 computation

Caledonia
8 Scotland

calendar
3 log 4 card, sked 6 agenda, docket
7 almanac, program 8 schedule
9 timetable
abbreviation: 3 Apr, Aug, Dec, Feb, Fri,
Jan, Mar, Mon, Nov, Oct, Sat, Sep, Sun,
Tue, Wed 4 Sept 5 Thurs
ecclesiastical: 4 ordo

calenture
4 fire, zeal 5 ardor, fever 6 fervor
7 passion 10 enthusiasm

calf
hide: 3 kip
leather: 3 elk
meat: 4 veal
stray: 5 dogie
unbranded: 8 maverick

Caliban
5 slave
master: 8 Prospero
witch-mother: 7 Sycorax

caliber
4 bore 5 class, gauge, grade, merit, value,
worth 6 virtue 7 ability, quality, stature
8 diameter

calibrate
3 set 6 adjust, polish 7 measure 8 fine-
tune, regulate 9 ascertain 11 standardize

California
capital: 10 Sacramento

city: 4 Napa 6 Fresno, Sonoma
7 Anaheim, Oakland, San Jose 8 San
Diego, Santa Ana 9 Long Beach, Santa
Cruz 10 Los Angeles 12 San Francisco
college, university: 3 USC 4 UCLA
5 Mills 6 Pomona 8 Berkeley, Stanford,
Whittier 9 Loma Linda 10 Golden Gate,
Occidental, Pepperdine, Santa Clara
desert: 6 Mohave
fault zone: 10 San Andreas
lake: 5 Owens, Tahoe 9 Salton Sea
lowest spot: 11 Death Valley
motto: 6 Eureka
mountain, range: 5 Coast 6 Lassen
(Peak), Shasta 7 Whitney 12 Sierra
Nevada
nickname: 6 Golden (State)
park: 7 Sequoia 8 Yosemite 11 Kings
Canyon 14 Channel Islands
river: 10 Sacramento, San Joaquin
state bird: 5 quail
state flower: 11 golden poppy
state tree: 7 redwood, sequoia
wine region: 4 Napa 6 Sonoma

caliginous
3 dim 4 dark, dusk 5 dusky, foggy, misty,
murky 6 gloomy 7 obscure, sunless
8 nebulous 9 lightless, tenebrous

Caligula's mother
9 Agrippina

caliph's name
3 Ali 7 Abu Bakr

Calista's seducer
8 Lothario

calisthenics
7 workout 9 exercises

call
3 bid, cry 4 buzz, hail, lure, name, page,
ring, yell 5 phone, pop in, shout, visit
6 bellow, come by, drop by, drop in, holler,
salute, stop by, stop in, summon
7 convene, convoke, summons 8 estimate
9 designate, telephone

calla
4 lily

call down
5 chide, scold 6 rebuke 7 censure,
reprove 8 admonish, reproach
9 reprimand

called
5 named 6 chosen, picked, yclept
7 ycleped 8 selected

caller
5 guest, suitor 7 visitor

call for
3 ask, beg 4 seek 5 crave, plead
6 demand, entail, pick up 7 beseech,
entreat, implore, involve, require
11 necessitate

call forth
5 awake, educe, evoke, rouse 6 arouse,
elicit 7 conjure, provoke 9 conjure up

calligrapher
6 penman, scribe 7 copyist 9 engrosser,
scrivener

calligraphy
4 hand 6 script 7 writing 8 longhand
10 penmanship 11 handwriting

call in
5 phone 6 summon 7 convene, reclaim
8 retrieve, withdraw 9 repossess,
telephone

calling
3 job 4 duty, work 5 craft, trade 6 career,
métier 7 mission, pursuit, yelling
8 business, lifework, shouting, vocation
10 employment, obligation, occupation,
profession

call in sick
7 book off

Calliope
4 Muse
father: 4 Zeus 7 Jupiter
mother: 9 Mnemosyne
son: 7 Orpheus

Callisto
lover: 4 Zeus 7 Jupiter
son: 5 Arcas

Call It Sleep author
4 Roth (Henry)

call off
4 halt 5 abort, scrub 6 cancel, divert
8 distract

Call of the Wild
author: 6 London (Jack)
dog: 4 Buck

call on
5 visit 6 oblige 7 require

callosity
8 hardness 9 thickness

callous
5 stony 8 hardened, obdurate, uncaring
9 heartless, indurated, unfeeling 10 hard-
bitten, hard-boiled 11 coldhearted,
hardhearted, insensitive, unemotional

12 case-hardened, stonyhearted
13 unsympathetic

callow
3 raw 5 fresh, green, naive, young
7 puerile 8 immature, juvenile, youthful
9 unfledged 10 unseasoned
13 inexperienced, unexperienced

call's partner
4 beck

call up
5 draft, evoke 6 summon 8 mobilize,
retrieve 9 conscript

calm
4 cool, ease, hush, lull 5 allay, peace,
quiet, relax, salve, still 6 hushed, pacify,
placid, poised, repose, sedate, serene,
settle, smooth, soothe, stable, steady, stilly
7 appease, assuage, compose, halcyon,
mollify, pacific, placate, restful, resting
8 composed, inactive, peaceful, reposing,
serenity, tranquil 9 collected, composure,
easygoing, impassive, possessed,
quiescent, unruffled 10 phlegmatic,
untroubled 11 tranquility, tranquilize,
unflappable 12 even-tempered, self-
composed, tranquillity 13 imperturbable,
self-possessed

calmative
8 quietive, relaxing, sedative 9 soporific
12 tranquilizer

calmness
4 lull 5 quiet 6 phlegm 8 coolness,
serenity 9 composure, placidity, sangfroid
10 equanimity 11 tranquility 12 tranquillity

calumet
4 pipe 9 peace pipe

calumniate
5 libel, smear 6 defame, malign, vilify
7 asperse, slander, tarnish, traduce
8 besmirch 9 denigrate 10 scandalize

calumnious
8 libelous 9 maligning, traducing, vilifying
10 backbiting, defamatory, detracting,
scandalous, slanderous

calumny
7 scandal, slander 9 aspersion
10 backbiting, defamation, detraction
11 denigration 12 backstabbing,
belittlement, depreciation 13 disparagement

calvados
6 brandy 9 applejack

calvary
5 agony, cross, trial 6 misery, ordeal
7 anguish 8 distress 9 suffering
10 affliction, visitation 11 tribulation

Calypso
beloved: 7 Ulysses 8 Odysseus
island: 6 Ogygia

calyx part
3 cup 5 sepal

camaraderie
5 cheer 7 jollity 10 affability, fellowship
12 conviviality

camarilla
3 mob 4 camp, clan, ring 5 cabal, mafia
6 circle, clique 7 coterie, ingroup

Cambodia
9 Kampuchea
capital: 9 Phnom Penh
city: 10 Battambang 11 Kompong Cham
ethnic group: 8 Mon-Khmer
lake: 8 Tonle Sap
language: 5 Khmer
leader: 6 Pol Pot
monetary unit: 4 riel
neighbor: 4 Laos 7 Vietnam 8 Thailand
river: 6 Mekong
ruin: 9 Angkor Wat

camel
one-humped: 9 dromedary
two-humped: 8 Bactrian

camel-hair fabric
3 aba

camelopard
7 giraffe

Camelot
6 palace
lord: 6 Arthur

Camembert
6 cheese

cameo
6 brooch, relief, walk-on 8 portrait

cameraman
6 photog 7 lensman 12 photographer

Cameroon
capital: 7 Yaoundé
ethnic group: 4 Fang 5 Duala, Pygmy
6 Fulani 8 Bamileke
largest city: 6 Douala
monetary unit: 5 franc
neighbor: 4 Chad 5 Congo, Gabon
7 Nigeria
river: 5 Nyong 6 Sanaga

Camille's creator
5 Dumas (Alexandre)

Camino _____
4 Real

camouflage
4 mask 5 cloak 7 conceal, deceive
8 disguise 9 dissemble 11 dissimulate

camp
3 hut 4 bloc, shed 5 cabin, lodge, shack
6 clique, shanty 7 bivouac, coterie,
cottage, faction 10 settlement

campaign
4 push 5 blitz, drive, fight, lobby, stump
6 attack 7 agitate, canvass, crusade
8 movement, politick 9 barnstorm,
offensive 10 engagement, expedition
11 electioneer, whistle-stop

campaigner
8 activist 9 candidate

campanile
6 belfry 8 carillon 9 bell tower

campesino
6 farmer 7 peasant

campestral
5 rural 6 rustic, sylvan 7 bucolic, country,
idyllic 8 agrarian, pastoral 10 provincial
11 countrified

campus
see **college**

Camus work
4 Fall (The) 5 Rebel (The) 6 Plague (The)
8 Caligula, Stranger (The)

can
3 may, tin 4 boot, fire, sack 5 let go, put
up 7 dismiss 9 container, discharge
10 receptacle

Canaan
4 Zion 12 Promised Land
father: 3 Ham
grandfather: 4 Noah

Canaanite god
3 Mot 4 Baal 6 Molech, Moloch

Canada
bay: 5 Fundy, James 6 Baffin, Hudson,
Ungava 8 Georgian 9 Frobisher
capital: 6 Ottawa
city: 6 London, Oshawa, Quebec, Surrey
7 Burnaby, Calgary, Halifax, Moncton,
Regina, Toronto, Windsor 8 Edmonton,
Hamilton, Montreal, Moose Jaw, Victoria,
Winnipeg 9 Longueuil, North York,
Saskatoon, Vancouver 10 Lethbridge,
Thunder Bay 11 Fredericton, Scarborough
13 Charlottetown, Mississisauga
district: 6 riding
explorer: 6 Hudson (Henry) 7 Cartier
(Jacques) 9 Champlain (Samuel de)
Indian people: 4 Cree, Inuk 5 Blood,
Haida, Huron, Inuit, Métis, Niska, Slave
6 Abnaki, Beaver, Eskimo, Micmac,
Mohawk, Nootka, Ojibwa, Ojibwe, Ottawa,
Piegan, Seneca, Stoney 7 Kutenai,
Naskapi, Ojibway, Siksika, Wyandot
8 Algonkin, Chippewa, Iroquois, Kootenai,
Kootenay, Kwakiutl, Salishan, Tsattine
9 Algonkian, Algonquin, Blackfeet,
Blackfoot, Chipewyan, Tsimshian
10 Algonquian, Athapascan, Gros Ventre,
Montagnais 11 Assiniboine
island, island group: 5 Banks, Devon
6 Baffin 7 Belcher 8 Melville, Victoria
9 Anticosti, Elles-mere, Vancouver
10 Cape Breton 11 Southampton
12 Newfoundland, Prince Edward
lake: 6 Louise 7 Nipigon 8 Reindeer,
Winnipeg 9 Athabasca, Champlain, Great
Bear 10 Great Slave
language: 6 French 7 English
monetary unit: 6 dollar
mountain, range: 5 Coast, Logan, Rocky
10 Laurentian
national park: 5 Banff, Fundy 6 Jasper
7 Glacier, Nahanni 8 Kootenay 9 Gros
Morne 10 Grasslands, Point Pelee
11 Georgian Bay, Wood Buffalo
peninsula: 5 Bruce, Gaspé 6 Ungava
8 Labrador
prime minister: 4 King (W. L. Mackenzie)
5 Clark (Joe) 6 Abbott (John), Borden
(Robert Laird), Bowell (Mackenzie), Martin
(Paul), Tupper (Charles), Turner (John)
7 Bennett (Richard Bedford), Laurier
(Wilfrid), Meighen (Arthur), Pearson
(Lester), Trudeau (Pierre Elliott)
8 Campbell (Kim), Chrétien (Jean),
Mulroney (Brian), Thompson (John)
9 MacDonald (John), Mackenzie
(Alexander), St. Laurent (Louis)
11 Diefenbaker (John)
province: 6 Quebec 7 Alberta, Nunavut,
Ontario 8 Manitoba 10 Nova Scotia
12 New Brunswick, Newfoundland (and
Labrador), Saskatchewan 15 British
Columbia 18 Prince Edward Island
provincial park: 3 Gas 7 Rondeau
9 Garibaldi
river: 3 Red 5 Liard, Slave, Yukon
6 Albany, Fraser, Nelson, Ottawa, Severn
8 Columbia, Saguenay 9 Athabasca,
Churchill, Mackenzie 10 St. Lawrence
sea: 8 Beaufort, Labrador

symbol: 9 maple leaf
territory: 5 Yukon **9** Northwest

Canadian insurgent
4 Riel (Louis)

canaille
3 mob **6** masses, rabble **8** riffraff, unwashed **9** hoi polloi **11** proletariat, proletariat

canal
4 duct **6** course **7** channel, conduit **8** aqueduct **11** watercourse
Africa: 4 Suez **8** Ismailia
Belgium: 6 Albert
Canada: 7 Welland
Central America: 6 Panama
China: 7 Da Yunhe
Florida: 10 Saint Lucie
Germany: 4 Kiel
Greece: 7 Corinth
Michigan: 3 Soo
New York: 4 Erie **6** Oswego **9** Champlain
Ontario: 6 Rideau
Venice: 5 Grand

canapé
6 morsel **9** appetizer **11** hors d'oeuvre
spread: 4 paté

canard
3 fib, lie **4** tale, yarn **5** fraud, rumor, spoof **6** deceit **7** falsity, untruth chestnut **9** falsehood

canary
3 rat **4** fink, wine **5** finch **6** snitch **7** rat fink, stoolie **8** informer, squealer **11** stool pigeon

Canary Islands
5 Ferro, Lobos, Palma **6** Gomera, Hierro **7** Inferno **8** Graciosa, Tenerife **9** Alegranza, Lanzarote

cancel
3 end **4** drop, undo, x out **5** abort, annul, erase, scrub **6** delete, efface, negate, offset, repeal, revoke **7** blot out, call off, destroy, expunge, nullify, rescind, wipe out **8** black out, deletion **9** terminate **10** invalidate, neutralize, obliterate

cancer
5 tumor **9** carcinoma **10** malignancy
treatment: 5 chemo, X rays **9** radiation **12** chemotherapy

cancer-causing
12 carcinogenic
substance: 10 carcinogen

candescent
7 glowing **8** dazzling **9** refulgent

Candia
5 Crete

candid
4 fair, just, open **5** blunt, frank, plain **6** honest **7** sincere **8** unbiased **9** equitable, guileless, impartial, objective **10** aboveboard, forthright, scrupulous, unreserved **11** openhearted, unconcealed, undisguised **12** unprejudiced **13** dispassionate

candidate
6 seeker **7** hopeful, nominee, stumper **8** aspirant **9** applicant, contender **10** campaigner, contestant

Candide
author: 8 Voltaire
lover: 9 Cunegonde
tutor: 8 Pangloss
valet: 7 Cacambo

candle
5 taper **6** bougie
holder: 6 sconce **7** menorah, pricket **9** girandole **10** candelabra **11** candelabrum
material: 3 wax **4** wick **6** tallow **8** beeswax, stearin **8** paraffin
religious: 6 votive **7** paschal

candlefish
8 eulachon
relative: 5 smelt

candlelit service
5 vigil

candlepins
7 bowling

candor
7 honesty **8** fairness, openness **9** frankness, sincerity, whiteness **11** artlessness **13** guilelessness

candy
7 sweeten **9** sugarcoat **10** confection
kind: 4 rock **5** fudge, lolly, sweet, taffy **6** bonbon, comfit, dragée, jujube, nougat, toffee **7** brittle, caramel, fondant, gumdrop, penuche, praline **8** licorice, lollipop, lollypop, marzipan, sourball **9** chocolate, jelly bean, nonpareil, sweetmeat **10** confection **12** butterscotch
medicated: 7 lozenge **9** cough drop

cane
3 rod **4** beat, drub, flog, lash, reed, stem, swat **5** flail, grass, spank, staff, stave, stick, weave, whale **6** batter, buffet, cudgel, larrup, paddle, rattan, thrash, wallop

7 lambast, sorghum 8 lambaste
12 walking stick

Canea's land
5 Crete

canine
3 dog 4 tyke 5 hound, pooch

caning material
5 istle

Canis Major star
6 Sirius

Canis Minor star
7 Procyon

canker
4 rust, sore 5 stain 6 debase, infect
7 corrupt, debauch, deprave, pervert,
vitiate 8 necrosis 10 demoralize

cankered
8 infested, infected

canker sore
5 ulcer 6 lesion 10 ulceration

cannabis
3 pot 4 hemp 5 bhang, ganja, grass
7 hashish 9 marijuana

canned
5 drunk, fired 6 potted 11 prerecorded

Cannery Row author
9 Steinbeck (John)

canniness
7 caution, cunning, slyness 8 prudence,
wiliness 9 cageyness, foresight
10 artfulness, cleverness, craftiness,
discretion, precaution, providence,
shrewdness 11 forethought

cannon
6 pom-pom 8 howitzer, ordnance
9 artillery
part: 5 chase 6 breech 8 cascabel,
trunnion

cannonade
4 bomb 5 blitz, burst, salvo, shell
6 shower, volley 7 barrage, bombard
8 drumfire, shelling 9 broadside, fusillade
11 bombardment

cannonball
4 dive 5 speed 7 missile

cannoneer
6 gunner

cannon fodder
6 troops 8 infantry, soldiers

canny
3 sly 4 wary, wise 5 acute, cagey, chary,
quick, sharp, smart 6 adroit, clever, frugal,
saving, shrewd 7 cunning, knowing,
prudent, thrifty 9 ingenious, provident
10 economical 11 quick-witted, sharp-
witted 12 nimble-witted

canoe
6 dugout 7 pirogue
ancient: 7 coracle
Eskimo: 5 kayak, umiak

canon
3 law 4 list, rule 5 dogma, edict, round,
tenet 6 decree 7 precept, statute
8 doctrine, standard 9 clergyman, criterion,
ordinance 10 regulation

canonical
5 sound 6 lawful 7 classic 8 accepted,
approved, official, orthodox, received
10 authorized, recognized, sanctioned
13 authoritative

canonical hour
4 none, sext 5 lauds, prime, terce
6 matins, tierce 7 vespers 8 compline

canonicals
9 vestments

canoodle
3 hug, pet 5 spoon 6 caress, cuddle,
fondle

can opener
9 church key

canopy
5 cover, shade 6 awning 7 marquee,
shelter 8 covering, sunshade 9 baldachin
10 baldachino
canvas: 4 tilt

cant
3 tip 4 heel, lean, list, tilt 5 angle, argot,
bevel, idiom, lingo, piety, slang, slant, slope
6 humbug, jargon, patois, patter, speech
7 dialect, diction, incline, lexicon, palaver,
recline 8 language, singsong 9 hypocrisy
10 dictionary, pharisaism, sanctimony,
vernacular 11 inclination, insincerity
12 pecksniffery

cantaloupe
5 melon 9 muskmelon

cantankerous
4 dour, sour 5 cross, huffy, testy, waspy
6 crabby, cranky, crusty, grumpy, morose,
ornery 7 bearish, crabbed, grouchy,
peevish, prickly, waspish 8 cankered,
liverish, petulant, snappish, stubborn,

canter
vinegary **9** crotchety, difficult, dyspeptic, irascible, irritable, obstinate **10** ill-natured, irritating, vinegarish **12** cross-grained

canter
3 bum **4** gait, hobo, lope **5** tramp
6 beggar **7** drifter, vagrant **8** derelict, vagabond **11** bindle stiff

Canterbury
Archbishop: 3 Oda **6** Anselm, Becket (Thomas à), Parker (Matthew) **7** Cranmer (Thomas), Dunstan **9** Augustine

Canterbury Tales
author: 7 Chaucer (Geoffrey)
character: 8 Griselda, pardoner, summoner **10** wife of Bath
inn: 6 Tabard

canticle
3 ode **4** hymn, song **6** Te Deum
10 Benedicite, Benedictus, Magnificat
12 Nunc Dimittis

canticles
11 Song of Songs **13** Song of Solomon

cantilever
4 beam **6** bridge **7** bracket, support

cantillate
4 sing **5** chant **6** intone, recite

cantina
3 bar, pub **6** saloon, tavern **7** barroom

canton
5 state **6** billet **7** quarter, section **8** district, division

cantor
5 hazan **6** singer **9** precentor

canvas
4 duck, sail, tarp, tent **7** tenting **8** painting
9 sailcloth, tarpaulin

canvasback
4 duck

canvass
3 con, vet **5** argue, study **6** debate, survey
7 discuss, dispute, examine, inspect, solicit
8 campaign **9** check over **10** scrutinize
11 electioneer **12** authenticate

canyon
4 Glen, Zion **5** Bryce, chasm, gorge, Grand, gulch, Hells **6** Copper, coulee, ravine, valley

cap
3 tam, top **4** best **5** beret, cover, crest, crown, limit, trump **6** beanie, exceed, top off **7** calotte **9** culminate

clergyman's: 7 biretta **9** zucchetto
hoodlike: 4 coif
hunter's: 7 montero
jester's: 7 coxcomb **9** cockscomb
Jewish: 8 yarmulke
knitted: 5 toque, tuque **9** balaclava
military: 4 kepi
mushroom: 6 pileus
part: 4 bill, brim, flap, peak **5** visor
7 earflap
Roman: 6 pileus
Scottish: 3 tam **8** balmoral **9** glengarry
11 tam-o'-shanter
Turkish: 6 calpac **7** calpack

capability
5 craft, means, skill **7** ability, potency
8 adequacy, aptitude, capacity, efficacy, facility **9** potential **10** competence, efficiency **12** potentiality **13** effectiveness, qualification

capable
3 apt **4** able **5** adept **6** adroit, au fait
9 competent, efficient, qualified
10 proficient **11** susceptible

capacious
4 wide **5** ample, roomy **7** sizable
8 abundant, spacious **9** extensive
10 commodious **11** substantial

capacitance
unit of: 5 farad

capacity
4 bent, gift, rank, role, room **5** knack, range, reach, scope, skill, space **6** output, status, talent **7** ability, caliber, faculty
8 adequacy, aptitude, facility, position, standing **10** capability, competence
11 proficiency **13** qualification
unit of: 4 gill, peck, pint **5** liter, litre, minim, quart **6** bushel, gallon **10** fluid ounce, milliliter

Capaneus
slayer: 4 Zeus
wife: 6 Evadne

caparison
5 adorn **6** finery **7** apparel, panoply, raiment **9** adornment, trappings

cape
4 cope, ness **5** cloak, point **6** capote, mantle, tabard, tippet **7** manteau, pelisse
8 foreland, headland, mantelet, mantilla, pelerine **9** peninsula **10** promontory
clergyman's: 8 mozzetta

Cape
Africa: 4 Juby, Yubi **5** Blanc **6** Blanco
7 Agulhas

Alaska: 3 Icy 4 Nome 11 Krusenstern
Algeria: 3 Fer
Antarctica: 3 Ann 4 Dart 5 Adare
Arctic: 8 Nordkaap
Asia: 5 Aniva
Australia: 5 Byron, Otway, Sandy, Smoky 6 Arnhem 9 Van Diemen
Baffin Island: 4 Dyer
Black Sea: 5 Yasun
Borneo: 4 Datu 6 Datoek
Brazil: 4 Frio, Raso
California: 9 Mendocino
Colombia: 5 Aguja
Costa Rica: 5 Velas
Crete: 5 Plaka
Croatia: 5 Ploca 6 Planka
Cuba: 4 Cruz 5 Maisi
Denmark: 4 Skaw 6 Skagen
Desolación Island: 5 Pilar 6 Pillar
Djibouti: 3 Bir
Egypt: 5 Banas
England: 8 Bolerium, Lands End
Florida: 5 Sable 7 Kennedy 9 Canaveral
Greece: 4 Busa 5 Gallo, Malea, Papas, Vouxa 6 Araxos, Maleas 7 Akritas
Guinea: 5 Verga
Gulf of California: 5 Lobos
Gulf of Guinea: 5 Lopez
Gulf of Mexico: 4 Rojo
Hawaii: 5 Ka Lae 10 South Point 11 Diamond Head
Hispaniola: 5 Beata
Honshu: 3 Iro, Oma 5 Inubo, Kyoga, Nyudo
Indonesia: 4 Vals 5 False
Japan: 4 Esan, Nomo, Sata, Soya 5 Erimo, Kamui
Libya: 3 Tin 4 Milh
Long Island Sound: 10 Throgs Neck
Malay Peninsula: 5 Bulat
Malaysia: 4 Piai 5 Sirik
Massachusetts: 3 Ann, Cod
Mediterranean: 5 Ajdir
Mexico: 4 Buey
Morocco: 3 Sim 4 Guir, Rhir
Namibia: 4 Fria
Newfoundland: 5 Bauld
New Jersey: 3 May
New Zealand: 5 Brett
North Carolina: 4 Fear 7 Lookout 8 Hatteras
Northwest Territories: 8 Bathurst
Nova Scotia: 5 Canso 6 Breton
Oman: 3 Nus 4 Hadd

Ontario: 4 Hurd, Rich
Pakistan: 5 Monze, Muari
Portugal: 5 Roca
Puerto Rico: 4 Rojo
Quebec: 5 Gaspé
Red Sea: 5 Kasar
Sicily: 4 Boeo, Faro 7 Lilibeo, Passero, Pelorus
Solomon Islands: 5 Zelee
Somalia: 4 Asir 5 Assir, Hafun
South Africa: 8 Good Hope
South America: 4 Horn
Spain: 3 Nao 4 Gata 5 Creus, Penas
Syria: 5 Basit
Taiwan: 5 O-luan 7 Garam Bi
Tierra del Fuego: 5 Penas
Tunisia: 5 Blanc
Turkey: 3 Boz 4 Baba, Ince, Kara, Krio 6 Lectum 8 Bozburun 9 Inceburun, Karaburun
Vancouver Island: 5 Scott
Virginia: 5 Henry
Washington: 5 Alava

Čapek, Karel
coinage: 5 robot
play: 3 R.U.R.

caper
4 dido, lark, leap, romp 5 antic, frisk, prank, revel, shine, theft, trick 6 cavort, frolic, gambol, prance 7 roguery, rollick 8 escapade, mischief 10 shenanigan, tomfoolery 11 monkeyshine

Cape Town's famous son
5 Smuts (Jan)

Cape Verde
capital: 5 Praia
city: 7 Mindelo
island: 3 Sal 4 Fogo, Maio 5 Brava 8 Boa Vista, São Tiago 10 São Vicente, São Nicolau, Santa Luzia, Santo Antão
language: 7 Crioulo 10 Portuguese
monetary unit: 6 escudo

capillary
4 tube 6 tubule 8 hairlike 11 blood vessel

capital
4 main 5 basic, chief, funds, major, prime 6 assets, lethal, wealth 8 cardinal 9 essential, excellent, financing, first-rate, principal, resources 10 first-class, investment, preeminent, underlying 11 fundamental, outstanding, predominant, wherewithal
Afghanistan: 5 Kabul
Albania: 6 Tirana, Tiranë
Alberta: 8 Edmonton
Algeria: 7 Algiers

Angola: 6 Luanda
Antigua and Barbuda: 7 St. John's
10 Saint John's
Argentina: 11 Buenos Aires
Armenia: 7 Yerevan
Assam: 6 Dispur
Australia: 8 Canberra
Austria: 4 Wien 6 Vienna
Azerbaijan: 4 Baku
Bahamas: 6 Nassau
Bahrain: 6 Manama
Bangladesh: 5 Dhaka
Barbados: 10 Bridgetown
Belarus: 5 Minsk
Belgium: 8 Brussels
Belize: 8 Belmopan
Benin: 9 Porto-Novo
Bhutan: 7 Thimphu
Bolivia: 5 La Paz
Bosnia and Herzegovina: 8 Sarajevo
Botswana: 8 Gaborone
Brazil: 8 Brasília
Bulgaria: 5 Sofia
Burkina Faso: 11 Ouagadougou
Burma: 6 Yangon 7 Rangoon
Burundi: 9 Bujumbura
Cambodia: 9 Phnom Penh
Cameroon: 7 Yaoundé
Canada: 6 Ottawa
Cape Verde: 5 Praia
Central African Republic: 6 Bangui
Chad: 8 N'Djamena
Chile: 8 Santiago
China: 6 Peking 7 Beijing
Colombia: 6 Bogotá
Comoros: 6 Moroni
Congo (Zaire): 8 Kinshasa
Costa Rica: 7 San José
Côte d'Ivoire: 7 Abidjan 12 Yamoussou-
kro
Croatia: 6 Zagreb
Cuba: 6 Havana
Cyprus: 7 Nicosia
Czech Republic: 6 Prague
Denmark: 10 Copenhagen
Dominica: 6 Roseau
Dominican Republic: 12 Santo Domingo
East Timor: 4 Dili
Ecuador: 5 Quito
Egypt: 5 Cairo
El Salvador: 11 San Salvador
Equatorial Guinea: 6 Malabo
Eritrea: 6 Asmara
Estonia: 7 Tallinn
Ethiopia: 10 Addis Ababa
Faeroe Islands: 8 Tórshavn
Falkland Islands: 7 Stanley
Fiji: 4 Suva
Finland: 8 Helsinki

France: 5 Paris
French Guiana: 7 Cayenne
Gabon: 10 Libreville
Galápagos Islands: 12 San Cristóbal
Gambia: 6 Banjul
Georgia, Republic of: 6 Tiflis 7 Tbilisi
Germany: 6 Berlin
Ghana: 5 Accra
Greece: 6 Athens
Greenland: 8 Godthaab
Grenada: 9 St. George's 12 Saint
George's
Guam: 5 Agana
Guinea: 7 Conakry
Guyana: 10 Georgetown
Haiti: 12 Port-au-Prince
Honduras: 11 Tegucigalpa
Hungary: 8 Budapest
Iceland: 9 Reykjavík
India: 8 New Delhi
Indonesia: 7 Jakarta 8 Djakarta
Iran: 6 Tehran 7 Teheran
Iraq: 7 Baghdad
Ireland: 6 Dublin
Israel: 7 Tel-Aviv 9 Jerusalem
Italy: 4 Rome
Jamaica: 8 Kingston
Japan: 5 Tokyo
Jordan: 5 Amman
Kazakhstan: 6 Astana 7 Alma-Ata
Kenya: 7 Nairobi
Kiribati: 6 Tarawa 11 South Tarawa
Korea, North: 9 Pyongyang
Korea, South: 5 Seoul
Kuwait: 10 Kuwait City
Kyrgyzstan: 7 Bishkek
Laos: 9 Vientiane
Latvia: 4 Riga
Lebanon: 6 Beirut
Lesotho: 6 Maseru
Libya: 7 Tripoli
Liechtenstein: 5 Vaduz
Lithuania: 7 Vilnius
Macedonia: 6 Skopje
Madagascar: 12 Antananarivo
Malawi: 8 Lilongwe
Malaysia: 11 Kuala Lumpur
Maldives: 4 Male
Mali: 6 Bamako
Malta: 8 Valletta
Manitoba: 8 Winnipeg
Marshall Islands: 6 Majuro
Mauritania: 10 Nouakchott
Mauritius: 9 Port Louis
Micronesia: 7 Palikir
Moldova: 8 Chişinău, Kishinev
Mongolia: 9 Ulan Bator
Montserrat: 8 Plymouth
Morocco: 5 Rabat

Mozambique: 6 Maputo
Myanmar: 6 Yangon 7 Rangoon
Namibia: 8 Windhoek
Nauru: 5 Yaren
Nepal: 8 Katmandu 9 Kathmandu
Netherlands: 9 Amsterdam
Newfoundland: 10 Saint Johns
New Zealand: 10 Wellington
Nicaragua: 7 Managua
Niger: 6 Niamey
Nigeria: 5 Abuja
Northern Ireland: 7 Belfast
Northern Territory: 6 Darwin
North-West Frontier Province: 8 Peshawar
Northwest Territories: 11 Yellowknife
Norway: 4 Oslo
Nova Scotia: 7 Halifax
Oman: 6 Muscat
Pakistan: 9 Islamabad
Palau: 5 Koror 10 Babelthuap
Papua New Guinea: 11 Port Moresby
Paraguay: 8 Asunción
Peru: 4 Lima
Philippines: 6 Manila
Poland: 6 Warsaw
Portugal: 6 Lisbon
Prince Edward Island: 13 Charlottetown
Puerto Rico: 7 San Juan
Qatar: 4 Doha
Queensland: 8 Brisbane
Réunion: 7 St. Denis 10 Saint Denis
Romania: 9 Bucharest
Russia: 6 Moscow
Rwanda: 6 Kigali
Saint Helena: 9 Jamestown
Saint Kitts and Nevis: 10 Basseterre
Saint Lucia: 8 Castries
Samoa: 4 Apia
Saskatchewan: 6 Regina
Saudi Arabia: 6 Riyadh
Scotland: 9 Edinburgh
Senegal: 5 Dakar
Serbia and Montenegro: 8 Belgrade
Seychelles: 8 Victoria
Shetland: 7 Lerwick
Sicily: 7 Palermo
Sierra Leone: 8 Freetown
Sikkim: 7 Gangtok
Sind: 7 Karachi
Slovakia: 10 Bratislava
Slovenia: 9 Ljubljana
Solomon Islands: 7 Honiara
Somalia: 9 Mogadishu
South Africa: 8 Cape Town, Pretoria 12 Bloemfontein
South Australia: 8 Adelaide
South-West Africa: 8 Windhoek

Spain: 6 Madrid
Sri Lanka: 7 Colombo
Sudan: 8 Khartoum
Suriname: 10 Paramaribo
Swaziland: 7 Mbabane
Sweden: 9 Stockholm
Switzerland: 4 Bern 5 Berne
Syria: 8 Damascus
Tahiti: 7 Papeete
Taiwan: 6 Taipei
Tajikistan: 8 Dushanbe
Tanzania: 6 Dodoma 11 Dar es Salaam
Tasmania: 6 Hobart
Thailand: 7 Bangkok
Tibet: 5 Lhasa
Tirol: 9 Innsbruck
Togo: 4 Lomé
Tonga: 9 Nuku'alofa
Trinidad and Tobago: 11 Port-of-Spain
Tunisia: 5 Tunis
Turkey: 6 Ankara
Turkmenistan: 8 Ashgabat 9 Ashkhabad
Tuvalu: 8 Funafuti
Uganda: 7 Kampala
Ukraine: 4 Kiev
United Arab Emirates: 8 Abu Dhabi
United Kingdom: 6 London
Uruguay: 10 Montevideo
Uttar Pradesh: 7 Lucknow
Uzbekistan: 8 Tashkent
Vanuatu: 4 Vila
Venezuela: 7 Caracas
Victoria: 9 Melbourne
Vietnam: 6 Hanoi
Wales: 7 Cardiff
Western Australia: 5 Perth
Yemen: 4 Sana 5 Sanaa
Yugoslavia: 8 Belgrade
Yukon: 10 Whitehorse
Zambia: 6 Lusaka
Zimbabwe: 6 Harare

capitalist
6 backer, tycoon 7 magnate 8 investor
9 bourgeois, financier, plutocrat
12 entrepreneur

capitalistic
9 bourgeois

capitalize
4 back, fund 5 stake 6 profit 7 convert,
finance, promote, sponsor, support
8 bankroll 9 grubstake, subsidize

capital sin
see **deadly sin**

capitation
3 tax 7 payment, poll tax

Capitol Hill sound
3 aye, nay

capitulate
3 bow 4 cave 5 defer, yield 6 cave in,
give in, give up, relent, submit 7 concede,
succumb 9 acquiesce, surrender
12 knuckle under

capitulation
9 surrender 10 submission

capo
3 bar 4 boss, head 5 chief 9 godfather

capote
4 cope 5 cloak 6 mantle, tabard
7 manteau, pelisse 8 overcoat

capper
4 lure 5 blind, decoy, shill 6 climax, finale
8 clincher

capriccio
4 whim 5 caper, fancy, prank 6 notion,
vagary, whimsy 7 impulse

caprice
3 bee 4 mood, vein, whim 5 fancy, freak,
humor 6 foible, maggot, megrim, notion,
vagary, whimsy 7 conceit 8 crotchet

capricious
4 iffy 5 flaky, moody 6 chancy, fickle
7 erratic, flighty, wayward 8 fanciful,
unstable, variable, volatile 9 arbitrary,
impulsive, mercurial, uncertain, whimsical
10 changeable, inconstant
12 effervescent, incalculable
13 temperamental, unpredictable

caprid
4 goat

capriole
4 leap 5 caper

capsize
4 keel, roll, sink 5 upset 7 founder, tip over
8 collapse, overturn, turn over

capstone
4 acme, apex, peak 6 apogee, climax,
coping, summit, zenith 8 pinnacle 9 high
point 11 culmination

capsule
6 canned, pocket, potted 7 compact,
outline 9 condensed

capsulize
6 reduce 7 enclose 8 compress,
condense 9 summarize, synopsize

captain
6 master 7 skipper
fictional: 4 Ahab, Nemo 5 Queeg

historical: 5 Bligh (William)
pirate: 4 Kidd (William)

Captains Courageous author
7 Kipling (Rudyard)

caption
5 title 6 legend, rubric 7 cutline, heading
8 subtitle 9 underline

captious
5 testy 7 carping, peevish 8 caviling,
contrary, critical, exacting, petulant,
snappish 9 demanding, irritable
10 censorious, nit-picking 12 faultfinding,
overcritical 13 hypercritical

captivate
4 draw, grip, hold, take 5 charm 6 allure,
dazzle, please, ravish, seduce 7 attract,
beguile, bewitch, delight, enchant, gratify
8 enthrall 9 enrapture, fascinate,
hypnotize, infatuate, magnetize,
mesmerize, spellbind

captivating
8 charming, enticing, fetching, magnetic,
riveting 9 appealing, glamorous, seductive
10 bewitching, engrossing, intriguing
11 enthralling, fascinating

captive
5 bound, caged, taken 6 jailed 7 hostage
8 confined, detainee, internee, prisoner
10 enthralled, hypnotized, imprisoned

captivity
7 bondage, custody, slavery 9 detention
10 internment 11 confinement
12 imprisonment

capture
3 bag, get, nab, net, win 4 nail, take, trap
5 catch, lasso, prize, seize, snare 6 arrest,
collar, entrap, occupy, secure 7 conquer,
ensnare 8 preserve

Capuan
4 lush 5 plush 6 deluxe 7 opulent
8 luscious, palatial 9 luxuriant, luxurious,
sumptuous 11 upholstered

car
4 auto, heap 5 buggy, coach, crate, sedan,
wreck 6 jalopy, junker, wheels 7 clunker,
flivver 9 roadster 10 automobile
(see also **automobile**)

carafe
5 cruet, ewer 6 bottle, flacon, flagon
8 decanter

caravan
6 convoy, safari

caravansary
3 inn 4 khan 5 hotel, lodge, serai
6 hostel, tavern 10 campground

carbohydrate
5 sugar 6 starch 7 amylose, glucose,
lactose, maltose, sucrose 8 fructose,
glycogen 9 cellulose, galactose

carbolic acid
6 phenol

carbon
4 coal, coke, soot 8 charcoal, graphite,
plumbago 9 lampblack

carbonate
6 aerate

carbon copy
4 dupe, twin 5 clone, ditto, mimeo, repro,
Xerox 7 replica 8 knockoff 9 duplicate,
facsimile 10 dead ringer 11 replication
12 reproduction

carbonize
4 burn, char, sear 5 singe, toast 6 scorch

carbuncle
4 boil, sore 5 ulcer 6 garnet, pimple
7 abscess, pustule 8 cabochon

carcass
4 body, hulk, mort 5 frame, shell, stiff
6 corpse 7 cadaver, remains 8 skeleton

carcinoid
5 tumor 8 neoplasm

carcinoma
5 tumor 6 cancer 8 neoplasm

card
3 wag, wit 4 menu, sked 5 joker
6 agenda, docket 7 program 8 calendar,
comedian, humorist, schedule 9 timetable
fortune-telling: 5 tarot
performer's: 3 cue
spot: 3 pip

cardboard
5 stiff 6 unreal, wooden 7 bristol,
buckram, stilted 8 lifeless 10 unlifelike
11 stereotyped, unrealistic

card-carrying
4 true 7 genuine 8 bona fide 9 authentic,
certified 11 full-fledged

card game
see at **game**

cardiac stimulant
7 ouabain 9 digitalis

cardinal
3 key 4 main 5 basic, chief, prime, vital
6 ruling 7 central, leading, pivotal, primary
9 essential, important, principal
10 overriding, overruling 11 fundamental
12 constitutive
point: 4 east, west 5 north, south
suffix: 4 teen
virtue: 7 justice 8 prudence 9 fortitude
10 temperance

care
3 rue, woe 4 fear, heed, mind, tend, ward
5 alarm, grief, nurse, pains, serve, trust,
watch, worry 6 attend, charge, dismay,
effort, mother, regard, regret, sorrow, strain,
stress, unease, wait on 7 anguish, anxiety,
concern, conduct, custody, keeping, trouble
8 disquiet, exertion, handling, interest,
suspense 9 attention, curiosity, misgiving,
oversight, vigilance 10 affliction,
foreboding, management, solicitude,
uneasiness 11 disquietude, heedfulness,
maintenance, safekeeping, supervision
12 apprehension, guardianship,
watchfulness 13 consciousness,
consideration, consternation

careen
4 race, sway, tilt 5 lurch, pitch, speed,
swing, weave 6 repair, wobble 7 stagger

career
3 job 4 race, rush, tear, work 5 chase,
speed 6 charge, course 7 calling, passage
8 lifework, vocation 9 encounter
10 livelihood, profession

care for
4 like, love, mind, tend 5 nurse, treat
6 attend, foster 7 cherish, nurture
8 preserve 9 cultivate, look after

carefree
4 wild 6 blithe, breezy, jaunty 8 reckless
10 insouciant, untroubled 12 happy-go-
lucky, lighthearted 13 irresponsible

careful
4 safe, wary 5 chary, exact, fussy
7 dutiful, guarded, precise, prudent, studied
8 accurate, cautious, critical, discreet,
gingerly, thorough 9 attentive, provident
10 deliberate, meticulous, particular,
scrupulous 11 calculating, circumspect,
considerate, foresighted, painstaking,
punctilious 13 conscientious

carefully
6 warily 8 gingerly 10 cautiously,
discreetly 12 meticulously, scrupulously
13 painstakingly, punctiliously

careless
3 lax 5 hasty, messy, slack 6 casual, remiss, sloppy, untidy 7 cursory, offhand, unkempt 8 feckless, heedless, reckless, slapdash, slipshod, slovenly 9 forgetful, negligent, oblivious, unheeding, unmindful, unstudied 10 disheveled, inaccurate, incautious, neglectful, unthinking, untroubled 11 inadvertent, inattentive, indifferent, perfunctory, spontaneous, thoughtless, unconcerned 12 uninterested, unreflective 13 irresponsible

caress
3 pat, pet, toy 4 kiss, love 5 dally, touch 6 coddle, cosset, cuddle, dandle, fondle, nuzzle, pamper, stroke 7 cherish, indulge 8 canoodle 10 endearment

caressive
7 calming 8 soothing

caretaker
6 warden 7 curator, janitor 9 custodian

careworn
3 wan 4 drawn, faded, jaded 7 haggard, pinched, wearied 8 fatigued, troubled 9 exhausted 10 distressed

cargo
4 haul, load 6 burden, lading 7 freight, payload 8 shipload, shipment 11 consignment

caribe
7 piranha

caribou
8 reindeer

caricature
4 mock, sham 5 farce, phony 6 parody 7 cartoon, lampoon, mockery, takeoff 8 travesty 9 burlesque 10 distortion, pasquinade 12 exaggeration

Carlsbad feature
4 cave 6 cavern

Carmen
author: 7 Mérimée (Prosper)
composer: 5 Bizet (Georges)
lover: 7 Don José 9 Escamillo

carnage
4 gore 8 butchery, hecatomb, massacre 9 bloodbath, bloodshed, slaughter

carnal
4 lewd 6 animal, bodily, coarse, earthy, sexual, vulgar, wanton 7 earthly, fleshly, lustful, mundane, obscene, sensual, worldly 8 corporal, material, physical, sensuous, temporal 9 corporeal 10 lascivious

carnation
4 pink 5 color 6 flower

carnival
4 fair, fete 6 fiesta
attraction: 4 ride 6 midway 8 sideshow 10 concession
character: 5 shill 6 barker, hawker 7 grifter, spieler
New Orleans: 9 Mardi Gras
performer: 4 geek

carnivore
9 meat-eater 10 flesh-eater

carol
4 song 6 ballad
Christmas: 4 noel

carom
6 bounce, glance 7 rebound 8 ricochet

Caron role
4 Gigi, Lili 5 Fanny

carotid's relative
5 aorta

carousal
3 bat, jag 4 bash, tear 5 binge, booze, drunk, fling, revel, spree 6 bender, frolic 7 blowout, debauch, shindig 8 wingding 9 brannigan
Scottish: 6 splore

carouse
5 revel 6 cavort, frolic 7 roister
Scottish: 4 birl

carp
3 nag 4 carp, fuss 5 bream, cavil, scold 6 peck at, pester 7 henpeck 8 complain, cyprinid, sea bream 9 complaint, criticize, find fault

carpe _____
4 diem

carpenter
3 ant, bee 6 joiner, wright 7 builder, workman 10 woodworker

carpentry
7 joinery 10 timberwork

carper
6 critic, nagger 7 caviler, knocker nitpicker 10 complainer, criticizer 11 faultfinder

carpet
3 mat, rug 4 Agra 5 Herat, Heriz, Koula, Ladik, Sarok, tapis 6 Herati, Kerman, Keshan, Kirman, Sarouk, Tabriz, Wilton 8 moquette 9 Axminster, broadloom

carpet beetle
10 buffalo bug

carping
7 blaming, fussing, nagging, railing 8 captious, caviling, critical, scolding pestering 10 censorious, upbraiding 11 criticizing, reproachful 12 faultfinding, overcritical

carrageen
7 seaweed 9 Irish moss

carrefour
5 plaza 6 square 10 crossroads

carriage
3 rig 4 pose 5 coach 6 stance 7 posture, transit 8 attitude 9 transport 10 conveyance, deportment
American: 5 buggy 8 rockaway 9 buckboard
attendant: 6 flunky 7 footman
baby: 4 pram 5 buggy 8 stroller 12 perambulator
driver: 4 hack 5 cabby 7 hackney 8 coachman
folding top: 6 calash
four-wheeled: 4 trap 5 buggy, coupe 6 calash, fiacre, landau, surrey 7 hackney, phaeton 8 barouche, brougham, carryall, rockaway, stanhope, victoria 9 buckboard
Indian: 6 gharry
man-drawn: 8 rickshaw 10 jinricksha, jinrikisha
Russian: 6 troika 7 droshky
stately: 7 caroche
three-horse: 6 troika
two-wheeled: 3 gig 4 shay, trap 5 buggy, sulky 6 chaise, hansom 7 calèche, dogcart, tilbury 9 cabriolet
with attendants: 8 equipage

carriage trade
5 elite 6 gentry 7 quality 9 blue blood, gentility 10 upper class, upper crust 11 aristocracy

carrick bend
4 knot

carrier
4 mule 5 envoy 6 bearer, porter, runner, vector 7 airline, courier, shipper, vehicle 8 conveyor, emissary 9 go-between, messenger, transporter 11 internuncio

Carroll character
5 Alice, Bruno, snark 6 boojum, Sylvie 8 Dormouse, Red Queen 9 Mad Hatter, March Hare 10 Mock Turtle 11 White Rabbit 12 Humpty Dumpty

carrot
5 prize 6 reward 9 incentive 10 inducement

carry
3 get, lug 4 bear, haul, have, hump, keep, move, pack, send, take, tote, wear 5 bring, ferry, fetch, range, stock 6 affect, bear up, convey, uphold 7 comport, conduct, portage, possess, support, sustain 8 buttress, transfer, transmit 9 influence, transport

carrying case
7 holdall, satchel 8 carryall

carry off
4 kill 6 abduct, execute, kidnap, perform, realize, remove, spirit away 7 achieve, destroy 8 complete, conclude, dispatch, shanghai 10 accomplish

carry on
3 run 4 go on, keep, rant, rave, wage 6 direct, endure, manage, ordain 7 conduct, operate, persist, prattle, proceed 8 continue, sound off 9 persevere

carry out
6 effect, govern, render 7 achieve, execute, fulfill, oversee, perform, realize 8 bring off, complete, finalize, transact 9 discharge, prosecute 10 accomplish, administer, effectuate 12 administrate

carry over
6 deduct 7 persist 8 postpone, transfer

carry through
4 last 5 abide 6 effect, endure 7 execute, perdure, perform, persist, survive 8 bring off, complete, continue 10 accomplish, effectuate

Carson work
11 Sea Around Us (The) 12 Silent Spring

cart
3 gig 4 dray, haul 5 buggy, carry 6 barrow, convey, schlep 7 schlepp, trundle, tumbrel, tumbril 8 carriage 9 transport 11 wheelbarrow
Indian: 5 tonga
racing: 5 sulky

_____ **carte**
3 à la

_____ Carte
5 D'Oyly

carte blanche
3 say 5 power, right, say-so 7 freedom,
license 8 free hand, free rein 9 authority
10 blank check 11 prerogative

carte du jour
4 menu

cartel
4 bloc, pool 5 trust 7 combine 9 syndicate
10 consortium 12 conglomerate

Carthaginian
goddess of the moon: 5 Tanit 6 Tanith
queen: 4 Dido 6 Elissa

cartilage
7 gristle

cartographer
English: 5 Smith (William)
Flemish: 6 Kremer (Gerhard) 8 Mercator
(Gerardus), Ortelius
German: 13 Waldseemüller (Martin)
Greek: 7 Ptolemy

cartography
9 mapmaking

carton
3 box 4 pack

cartoonist
3 Lee (Stan) 4 Capp (Al), Kane (Bob), Lee
(Stan), Nast (Thomas), Szep (Paul)
5 Adams (Scott), Booth (George), Chast
(Roz), Crumb (R.), Davis (Jim), Gould
(Chester), Hanna (Bill), Jones (Chuck),
Kelly (Walt), Steig (William), Young (Chic)
6 Addams (Charles), Caniff (Milton), Disney
(Walt), Larson (Gary), Martin (Don), Schulz
(Charles), Walker (Mort) 7 Barbera (Joe),
Feiffer (Jules), Ketcham (Hank), Mauldin
(Bill), Thurber (James), Trudeau (Garry)
8 Goldberg (Rube), Groening (Matt),
Herblock, Hokinson (Helen), MacNelly
(Jeff), Oliphant (Pat) 9 Fleischer (Max)
10 Hirschfeld (Al)

cartouche
5 frame 6 shield 9 cartridge

cartridge
4 case, tube 5 shell 8 cassette, cylinder
9 cartouche, container

cartwheel
4 coin 6 dollar, tumble 10 handspring

carve
3 cut, hew 4 chip, etch, form, hack

5 shape, slice 6 chisel, cleave, incise,
sculpt 7 dissect, engrave, whittle
9 sculpture

Casablanca
actor: 5 Lorre (Peter), Rains (Claude)
6 Bogart (Humphrey) 7 Bergman (Ingrid)
11 Greenstreet (Sydney)
character: 4 Ilsa (Lund), Rick (Blaine)
6 Laszlo (Victor)
director: 6 Curtiz (Michael)

Casanova
4 rake, roué, wolf 5 Romeo 6 lecher,
masher, tomcat 7 amorist, Don Juan,
gallant, playboy, seducer 8 lothario,
paramour 9 adulterer, ladies' man,
libertine, womanizer 10 lady-killer,
voluptuary 11 philanderer

cascade
4 fall, gush, lace, pour, spew 5 chute, falls,
flood, spill 6 deluge, plunge, rapids,
shower, torrent, tumble 7 Niagara
8 cataract 9 avalanche, waterfall
10 outpouring

Cascade Mountains peak
6 Lassen, Shasta 7 Rainier

case
3 box, con, vet 4 etui, hull, husk, skin, suit
5 cause, event, shell 6 action, sample,
sheath 7 episode, examine, example,
inspect, lawsuit 8 argument, covering,
incident, instance, sampling, specimen
9 check over, condition, situation
10 occurrence, proceeding, scrutinize
11 eventuality 12 circumstance
grammatical: 6 dative 8 ablative,
genitive, vocative 9 objective 10 accusative, nominative, possessive

casebearer
5 larva 11 caterpillar

case-hardened
5 tough 7 callous 8 obdurate 9 indurated,
insensate, toughened, unfeeling
11 insensitive 12 thick-skinned

casement
4 sash 6 window

Casey at the Bat poet
6 Thayer (Ernest Lawrence)

cash
4 coin, jack 5 bread, dough, money, scrip
6 dinero, redeem, wampum 7 cabbage,
lettuce, scratch 8 currency
10 greenbacks, ready money 11 legal
tender

cashier

3 can 4 boot, fire, oust, sack 5 clerk, eject, expel, scrap 6 banker, bounce, bursar, reject, teller 7 boot out, discard, dismiss, kick out 8 jettison, throw out 9 discharge, eliminate, terminate, throw away 10 bookkeeper 11 bean counter, comptroller

cash in

3 die 4 conk, drop 5 croak 6 expire, pop off, redeem, retire 7 kick off, succumb 8 check out, drop dead, pass away, settle up 9 liquidate

casing

4 hull, husk, pipe, rind, skin, tire 5 frame, shell, space 7 wrapper 8 membrane

casino

attendant: 6 dealer 8 croupier
game: 4 faro 5 craps, monte, poker 6 tierce 8 baccarat, roulette 9 blackjack

cask

3 keg, tun 4 butt, drum, pipe 6 barrel, firkin 8 hogshead

casket

3 box 5 chest 6 coffer, coffin 8 jewel box

Caspian Sea

city: 4 Baku
feeder: 4 Ural

Cassandra

4 seer 7 prophet, seeress 8 doomster 9 doomsayer, pessimist, worrywart 10 prophetess
brother: 7 Helenus
father: 5 Priam
lover: 9 Agamemnon
mother: 6 Hecuba
slayer: 12 Clytemnestra

casserole

4 dish 5 crock 6 tureen

Cassiopeia

daughter: 9 Andromeda
husband: 7 Cepheus
kingdom: 8 Ethiopia

Cassio's mistress

6 Bianca

cassock

4 robe 7 soutane 8 vestment

cast

3 add, hue, sum, tot 4 drop, face, fire, form, hurl, kind, look, mold, shed, sort, tint, tone, toss, turn, type 5 color, fling, heave, leave, pitch, range, shade, shape, strew, throw, tinge, total, touch 6 actors, design, devise, direct, figure, nature, reject, slough, troupe, visage 7 arrange, company, quality, replica, scatter 8 abdicate, disperse, jettison, sprinkle 9 character, prognosis, throw away 10 appearance, conjecture, distribute, expression, prediction, strabismus, suggestion 11 countenance

cast about

4 hunt, seek 5 grope 6 search 7 seek out 8 contrive 9 search for, search out
a spell on: 3 hex 5 charm 7 beguile, bewitch 8 enthrall 9 captivate, enrapture, fascinate, hypnotize, infatuate, mesmerize, spellbind
overboard: 7 deep-six 8 jettison

castaway

5 leper, tramp 6 beggar, maroon, pariah 7 Ishmael, outcast, vagrant 8 deadbeat, derelict 10 Ishmaelite

cast down

see downcast

caste

5 class 6 degree, estate, status 7 station 8 division, prestige

cast head

4 bust

castigate

4 beat, flay, rail, whip 5 baste, chide, scold, slash 6 berate, pummel, punish, rebuke, scorch, thrash 7 belabor, blister, chasten, chew out, lambast, reprove, scarify, scourge, upbraid 8 chastise, lambaste, penalize 9 criticize, dress down, excoriate, reprimand 10 discipline, tongue-lash

castigation

3 rod 6 rebuke 7 reproof 8 punition, scolding 10 correction, discipline, punishment 12 chastisement

castle

5 manor, villa 7 alcazar, château, citadel, mansion 8 fortress 10 stronghold
adjunct: 4 moat
gate: 10 portcullis
ledge: 7 rampart
structure: 6 turret
tower: 4 keep 6 donjon
wall: 6 bailey 10 battlement

cast off

5 fling, flung, let go, loose, untie 6 jilted, untied 7 unhitch 8 cut loose, forsaken, rejected, unfasten, unmoored 9 discarded, unhitched 10 left behind, unfastened

Castor
brother: 6 Pollux 10 Polydeuces
constellation: 6 Gemini
father: 4 Zeus 9 Tyndareus
mother: 4 Leda
sister: 5 Helen
slayer: 4 Idas

castor oil
8 laxative 9 cathartic, lubricant, purgative

cast out
4 oust 5 eject, evict, exile, expel 6 banish,
deport 7 discard 9 eliminate, ostracize

castrate
3 fix 4 geld, spay 5 alter, unman, unsex
6 neuter 7 unnerve 8 enervate, mutilate
9 sterilize 10 emasculate 11 desexualize

castrato singer
9 Farinelli

casual
5 light, minor 6 breezy, chance, random,
remote 7 natural, offhand, relaxed, trivial,
unfussy 8 detached, informal, laid-back
9 easygoing, impromptu, irregular,
uncurious, unplanned, unserious
10 accidental, contingent, fortuitous,
improvised, incidental, insouciant,
nonchalant, occasional 11 indifferent, low-
pressure, spontaneous, unconcerned,
unimportant 12 uninterested
13 disinterested, insignificant

casualty
4 prey 5 death 6 mishap, victim
8 accident, calamity, disaster, fatality
9 mischance 10 misfortune 11 catastrophe 12 misadventure

casuistry
7 sophism 9 deception, sophistry
12 equivocation, speciousness
13 deceptiveness

casus _____
5 belli

cat
4 lion, lynx, puma, puss 5 felid, kitty, liger,
ounce, pussy, tiger, tigon 6 cougar, feline,
jaguar, mouser, ocelot 7 caracal, cheetah,
leopard, panther 12 mountain lion
Alice's: 5 Dinah
catlike animal: 6 civet, genet 7 linsang
combining form: 5 ailur 6 ailuro
disease: 9 distemper
domestic: 3 Mau, Rex 4 Manx 5 tabby
6 Angora, Birman, calico, exotic, Ocicat,

Somali 7 bobtail, Burmese, Persian,
Ragdoll, Siamese 8 longhair, Wirehair
9 Himalayan, Maine coon, shorthair,
Tonkinese 10 Abyssinian
extinct: 10 saber-tooth
fastest: 7 cheetah
female: 5 queen 7 lioness, tigress
9 grimalkin
genus: 5 Felis
grinning: 8 Cheshire
male: 3 gib, tom
relating to: 6 feline
ring-tailed: 6 serval
sound: 3 mew 4 hiss, meow, purr, roar
9 caterwaul
spotted: 4 pard 6 jaguar, margay, ocelot,
serval 7 cheetah, leopard, panther
striped: 5 tiger
tailless: 4 Manx
young: 6 kitten

cataclysm
5 flood 6 deluge 7 Niagara, torrent,
tragedy 8 calamity, cataract, disaster,
flooding 10 inundation 11 catastrophe,
devastation

cataclysmic
5 fatal 7 ruinous 10 calamitous, disastrous
11 devastating 12 catastrophic

catacomb
5 crypt, vault 8 cemetery 10 necropolis,
undercroft

catafalque
4 bier

catalog
4 list, roll 5 enter, index, tally 6 enroll,
roster 7 itemize, program 8 classify,
inscribe, register, roll call, schedule,
syllabus 9 enumerate, inventory
10 prospectus
of books: 11 bibliotheca
of saints: 9 hagiology

catalyst
4 goad, spur 7 impetus, impulse
8 stimulus 9 incentive, stimulant
10 incitation, incitement, motivation

catamaran
4 boat, raft

catamount
4 lynx, puma 6 bobcat, cougar 7 panther,
wildcat

cataract
5 falls, flood, rapid 6 deluge, rapids

7 cascade, Niagara, torrent 8 downpour
9 waterfall 10 inundation

catastrophe
3 woe 6 deluge, fiasco 7 debacle, tragedy
8 calamity, disaster, meltdown
9 cataclysm, emergency 11 devastation

catastrophic
5 fatal 6 deadly, tragic 7 ruinous
10 calamitous, disastrous 11 cataclysmic

Catawba
4 wine 5 river 6 Indian

catcall
4 hiss, hoot, jeer, razz 9 criticism,
raspberry 10 Bronx cheer

catch
3 bag, get, nab, net, see, wed 4 dupe, find,
fool, grab, grip, gull, haul, hoax, hook, nail,
snag, sock, spot, take, trap 5 block, clasp,
clout, grasp, hit on, marry, reach, round,
seize, smite, snare, stick, stump, trick,
watch, whack 6 accept, anchor, arrest,
clutch, collar, cut off, descry, detect,
engage, entrap, fasten, flurry, follow, put
out, rattle, secure, snatch, strike, take in,
tangle, turn up 7 capture, confuse,
deceive, disturb, ensnare, grapple, hit
upon, perplex, receive 8 confound,
contract, entangle, flimflam, fragment,
hoodwink, kick over, meet with, overhaul,
overtake 9 apprehend, bamboozle,
embarrass, encounter, intercept
10 comprehend, understand 12 come
down with

Catch-22 author
6 Heller (Joseph)

catchall term
3 etc.

Catcher in the Rye
author: 8 Salinger (J. D.)
character: 9 Caulfield (Holden)

catcher's glove
4 mitt

catching
6 taking 10 contagious, infectious
12 communicable

catch on
3 see 4 hear 5 learn 7 find out 8 discover
9 ascertain, determine, figure out

catchphrase
see **catchword**

catch up
4 hold 6 gain on 7 close in, ensnare
8 entangle, enthrall 9 fascinate,
mesmerize, spellbind

catchword
5 maxim, motto 6 slogan 10 shibboleth

catchy
6 fitful, spotty, tricky 7 erratic 8 sporadic
9 appealing, desultory, irregular,
memorable, spasmodic

catechist
7 teacher

catechize
3 ask 4 quiz 5 grill, query, train
7 examine, inquire 8 instruct, question
9 inculcate 11 interrogate

catechumen
6 novice 7 convert, student, trainee
8 initiate, neophyte

categorical
7 certain, decided, express 8 absolute,
clear-cut, definite, emphatic, explicit,
positive 9 downright 10 definitive,
forthright 11 unambiguous, unequivocal,
unqualified

categorize
3 peg 4 sort 5 class, group 7 put down
8 classify, identify 10 pigeonhole

category
4 rank, tier 5 class, genre, grade, group
6 league 7 section 8 division, grouping
10 pigeonhole

catenation
4 link 5 chain 6 series, string 7 linkage
10 connection, succession

catercorner
9 obliquely, slantways, slantwise
10 cornerwise, diagonally

caterpillar
5 larva 7 cutworm, webworm 8 army-
worm, silkworm 10 casebearer

cater to
5 humor 6 pamper, supply 7 furnish,
gratify, indulge

caterwaul
4 howl, meow, yowl 5 miaow 6 squall

catfish
see **fish**

catharsis
5 purge, tonic 7 purging 8 curative
9 cleansing, purgation, purgative
10 lustration 11 expurgation, restorative
12 purification

cathartic
5 purge, tonic 8 curative 9 castor oil,
purgative 11 restorative, therapeutic

Cathay
5 China

cathedral
5 duomo 6 church 8 basilica
feature: 4 apse, nave 5 altar 6 chapel
7 chancel 10 clerestory 8 buttress,
transept

Cather novel
8 Lost Lady (A) 9 My Antonia, One of
Ours, O Pioneers 13 Song of the Lark
15 Professor's House (The) 16 Shadows
on the Rock 23 Youth and the Bright
Medusa

catholic
5 broad 6 global 7 general, liberal
8 eclectic, tolerant 9 expansive, inclusive,
undivided, universal, worldwide
10 ecumenical 12 cosmopolitan
13 comprehensive

catholicity
7 breadth 9 tolerance 10 liberality
11 magnanimity 12 universality

catholicon
6 elixir 7 cure-all, nostrum, panacea

catkin
5 ament

catlike
6 feline 7 furtive 8 stealthy

catnap
3 nap 4 doze 6 siesta, snooze 10 forty
winks

Cato
title: 6 aedile, censor, consul 7 praetor,
tribune 8 quaestor

Cat on a _____ Tin Roof
3 Hot

cat's-paw
4 dupe, knot, pawn, tool 5 patsy 6 puppet,
stooge

cattail
4 reed, rush

cattle
4 cows, kine, neat, oxen 7 bovines
9 livestock
breed: 5 Angus, Devon, Kerry 6 Durham,
Jersey, Sussex 7 Brahman, Hariana, Red
Poll 8 Ayrshire, Galloway, Guernsey,
Hereford, Highland, Holstein, Limousin,
Longhorn 9 Charolais, Red Polled,
Shorthorn, Simmental 10 Brown Swiss
11 Dutch Belted
catching rope: 5 lasso 6 lariat
cry: 3 low, moo
dehorn: 4 poll
disease: 4 loco 5 bloat 6 nagana
7 anthrax, locoism, measles, murrain
8 blackleg, lumpy jaw, mastitis, staggers
10 rinderpest, Texas fever 11 brucellosis
extinct breed: 9 Teeswater
family: 7 Bovidae
feed: 6 fodder
genus: 3 Bos
goddess: 6 Bubona
grazing land: 5 range 7 pasture
group: 4 herd 5 drove
herdsman: 6 cowboy, drover, gaucho
7 vaquero 8 wrangler 10 cowpuncher
identification: 5 brand
pen: 6 corral
round up: 7 wrangle
stable: 4 barn, byre
steal: 6 rustle
wild flight: 8 stampede

catty
4 mean 5 nasty 6 barbed, bitchy, feline
7 furtive, vicious 8 spiteful, stealthy
9 malicious 10 backbiting, malevolent

Caucasian
capital: 4 Baku 6 Tiflis 7 Tbilisi, Yerevan
republic: 7 Armenia, Georgia
10 Azerbaijan

Caucasus
peak: 6 Elbrus
people: 5 Osset

caucus
4 bloc, sect 5 cabal, lobby 6 parley,
powwow 7 faction

caudal appendage
4 tail

caudillo
6 despot, tyrant 8 dictator 9 strongman

cauldron
3 pot 6 boiler, kettle 8 crucible

cause
4 case, make, root 5 evoke, hatch

6 compel, effect, elicit, induce, motive, origin, reason, source, spring 7 produce, provoke 8 engender, generate, occasion 9 incentive, necessity 10 antecedent, bring about, inducement, originator 11 determinant, precipitate 13 consideration

cause _____
7 célèbre

causerie
4 chat 5 essay 6 column 7 article, feature 8 colloquy, dialogue 12 conversation

caustic
4 acid, keen, tart 5 acerb, acrid, sharp 6 biting, bitter, ironic 7 acerbic, cutting, mordant, pungent 8 scathing, stinging 9 corrosive, sarcastic, trenchant 10 astringent
solution: 3 lye

cauterize
4 burn, numb, sear 6 deaden 11 anesthetize

caution
4 warn 6 caveat 7 warning 8 forewarn, monition, prudence 9 canniness, chariness, foresight, vigilance 10 admonition, discretion, providence 11 carefulness, forethought, forewarning 12 admonishment, discreetness

cautionary
7 warning 8 monitory 10 admonitory

cautious
4 wary 5 alert, cagey, canny, chary, leery 6 shrewd 7 careful, guarded, politic, prudent 8 gingerly, vigilant, watchful 9 judicious, provident 11 circumspect, considerate, foresighted

cavalcade
6 parade, series 7 cortege 8 sequence 10 procession, succession

cavalier
5 lofty, proud 6 casual, knight, lordly 7 gallant, haughty, offhand 8 arrogant, debonair, horseman, scornful, superior 9 caballero, gentleman 10 disdainful, dismissive, insouciant, nonchalant 12 aristocratic, supercilious

cavalryman
6 lancer 7 dragoon, trooper
Algerian: 5 spahi
horse: 5 waler
Prussian: 5 uhlan
Russian: 7 cossack
Turkish: 5 spahi
weapon: 5 lance, saber 7 carbine

cave
3 bow, den 4 bend, drop, give, grot, lair 5 antre, break, defer, yield 6 fold up, grotto, hollow, submit 7 crumple, knuckle, succumb 8 collapse 9 break down 10 capitulate, subterrane 11 buckle under 12 knuckle under, subterranean
dweller: 3 bat 4 bear, lion 6 hermit 9 Cro-Magnon 10 troglodite 11 Neanderthal
explorer: 9 spelunker
formation: 10 stalactite, stalagmite
France: 7 Lascaux 10 Rouffignac
Iceland: 7 Singing
Indiana: 9 Wyandotte
Iraq: 8 Shanidar
Kentucky: 7 Mammoth
New Zealand: 7 Waitomo
rock: 8 dolomite 9 limestone
Scotland: 7 Fingal's
South Africa: 5 Cango
Spain: 8 Altamira
study of: 10 speleology

caveat
6 notice 7 caution, warning 8 monition 10 admonition 11 explanation, forewarning

caveat _____
6 emptor

caveman
5 brute 6 savage 9 barbarian, Cro-Magnon 10 troglodyte

cavern
6 grotto 12 subterranean
Capri: 10 Blue Grotto
Montana: 13 Lewis and Clark
New Mexico: 8 Carlsbad
Tennessee: 10 Cumberland
Virginia: 5 Luray

cavernous
4 vast 6 gaping, hollow 7 yawning

caviar
3 roe 4 eggs 6 relish
source: 6 beluga 8 sturgeon

cavil
4 carp 7 nitpick, quibble 9 criticize, find fault

caviler
6 carper, critic 7 knocker 8 quibbler 10 criticizer 11 faultfinder

caviling
5 fussy 7 carping, finicky, nagging 8 captious, contrary, critical, exacting, niggling 10 censorious, nitpicking 12 faultfinding 13 hairsplitting

cavity
3 pit **4** bore, hole, void **5** decay **6** caries, hollow **7** vacuity **10** interstice
body: 5 antra (plural), sinus **6** antrum **8** follicle, hemocoel

cavort
4 leap, romp **5** caper, cut up, frisk, sport **6** frolic, gambol, prance **7** carry on, rollick **10** roughhouse **11** horse around

cavy
4 paca **6** rodent **9** guinea pig

caw
4 crow, yawp **6** squall, squawk

cay
3 key **4** isle, reef **5** islet **6** island

cayenne
6 pepper
genus: 8 Capsicum

cayman
see **caiman**

Cayman Islands
capital: 10 George Town
discoverer: 8 Columbus (Christopher)
territory of: 7 Britain

Cayuga chief
5 Logan (James)

cease
3 die, end **4** halt, quit, stop **5** close **6** desist, ending, finish **8** conclude, give over, knock off, leave off **9** terminate **10** conclusion **11** discontinue, termination

cease-fire
5 truce **9** armistice **10** suspension

ceaseless
7 endless, eternal, nonstop **8** constant, immortal, unending **9** continual, incessant, perennial, perpetual, sustained, unabating **10** continuing, continuous **11** everlasting, never-ending, unremitting **12** interminable **13** uninterrupted

Cecrops' daughter
5 Herse **8** Aglauros, Aglaurus **9** Pandrosos, Pandrosus

cede
4 deed **5** grant, leave, yield **6** assign, convey, give up **7** abandon, concede **8** alienate, hand over, make over, part with, renounce, sign over, transfer **9** surrender, vouchsafe **10** relinquish

ceinture
4 belt, sash **6** girdle **9** waistband

Celaeno
father: 5 Atlas
mother: 7 Pleione
sisters: 8 Pleiades

celebrate
4 fete, hold, hymn, keep, laud **5** bless, cry up, exalt, extol, honor, party, revel **6** praise **7** carouse, glorify, maffick, observe, perform, rejoice **8** eulogize **9** solemnize **11** commemorate

celebrated
5 famed, great, noted **6** famous **7** eminent, notable, partied **8** caroused, rejoiced, renowned **9** prominent, well-known **11** illustrious **13** distinguished

celebration
4 bash, fete, gala **5** party **6** fiesta **7** blowout, jubilee, revelry **8** ceremony, festival, jamboree, wingding **10** observance

_____ célèbre
5 cause

celebrity
3 VIP **4** fame, hero, lion, name, star **5** éclat, glory **6** renown, repute **7** notable **8** eminence, luminary, prestige, somebody **9** notoriety, personage, superstar **10** notability, prominence, reputation

celerity
4 pace **5** speed **8** alacrity, dispatch, rapidity, velocity **9** briskness, fleetness, quickness, swiftness **10** speediness

celestial
6 divine **7** blessed, elysian, sublime **8** beatific, empyreal, empyrean, ethereal, heavenly, Olympian, supernal **9** unearthly **12** otherworldly

celestial body
3 sun **4** moon, star **5** comet **6** meteor, nebula, planet **8** asteroid **9** satellite

Celestial Empire
5 China

celibate
5 chaste, single, unwed, virgin **8** virginal, virtuous **9** abstinent, continent

cell
4 room **5** cubby, zooid **6** alcove **7** chamber, cubicle **9** corpuscle, cubbyhole **11** compartment
blood: 8 hemocyte
disease: 6 cancer
division: 7 meiosis, mitosis
fertilized egg: 6 zygote

material: **3** DNA, RNA **7** protein
9 chromatin, cytoplasm **10** protoplasm
nerve: **6** neuron
part: **4** gene **7** nucleus, vacuole
8 ribosome **9** centriole **10** chromosome
reproductive: **3** egg **4** germ, ovum
5 sperm **6** gamete **8** gonidium

cellar
5 store **7** shelter **8** basement

cellist
American: **4** Rose (Leonard) **6** Lesser
(Laurence), Parnas (Leslie) **7** Nelsova
(Zara), Parisot (Aldo), Starker (Janos)
8 Fournier (Pierre), Schuster (Joseph)
10 Greenhouse (Bernard)
English: **5** du Pré (Jacqueline)
Russian: **11** Piatigorsky (Gregor)
12 Rostropovich (Mstislav)
Spanish: **6** Casals (Pablo)

cellophane
4 wrap **7** wrapper **8** wrapping
9 packaging

celluloid
4 film **7** plastic

Celt
4 Gael, Scot **6** Breton **8** Irishman,
Welshman **10** Cornishman, Highlander

Celtic
deity: **4** Bran **5** Epona, Lugus, Macha
6 Brigit **8** Rhiannon **9** Cernunnos
festival: **7** Beltane, Samhain

cement
4 bind, glue, join **5** grout, unify, unite
6 mortar **8** concrete
ingredient: **4** lime **6** silica **7** alumina
8 magnesia, pozzolan **9** iron oxide,
pozzolana

cemetery
8 boneyard, boot hill **8** God's acre
9 graveyard **10** churchyard, necropolis
12 burial ground, memorial park, potter's
field
underground: **8** catacomb

cenotaph
4 tomb **6** marker **8** memorial, monument

censer
8 thurible
carrier: **8** thurifer

censor
3 ban, cut **4** blip, edit **5** bleep, purge **6** cut
out, delete, excise, purify, screen **7** clean
up **8** black out, restrict, suppress, withhold

9 expurgate, red-pencil **10** blue-pencil,
bowdlerize

censorious
6 severe **7** carping **8** captious, critical
10 accusatory, condemning **11** reproachful
12 condemnatory, denunciatory,
disapproving, faultfinding, overcritical,
reprehending **13** hypercritical

censurable
5 wrong **6** guilty, sinful **7** heinous
8 blamable, blameful, culpable, improper,
wrongful **9** incorrect **10** deplorable,
despicable, detestable **11** blameworthy,
disgraceful, impeachable **12** unacceptable
13 discreditable, objectionable,
reprehensible

censure
5 blame, scold **6** rebuke, strafe **7** condemn, reprove, upbraid **8** chastise,
denounce, disallow, reproach **9** castigate,
criticize, reprehend, reprimand, reprobate
10 disapprove

centaur
6 Chiron, Nessus

Centaurus star
4 Beta **5** Alpha

Centennial State
8 Colorado

center
3 hub, mid **4** axis, core, crux, mean, pith,
root, seat **5** focus, heart, midst, pivot
6 inside, medial, median, middle, source
7 central, essence **8** interior, midpoint,
omphalos **10** focal point **11** equidistant
12 intermediary, intermediate

centerboard
4 keel

centerfold
7 foldout **8** gatefold

central
3 hub, key, mid **4** main, mean **5** basic,
chief, focal **6** medial, median, middle
7 leading, pivotal, primary, salient
8 cardinal, dominant, exchange, foremost,
moderate **9** essential, paramount, principal
10 overriding **11** fundamental, outstanding,
predominant **12** intermediate

Central African Republic
capital: **6** Bangui
former name: **11** Ubangi-Shari
language: **5** Sango, Zande **6** French
monetary unit: **5** franc

neighbor: 4 Chad 5 Congo, Sudan
8 Cameroon

Central America
country: 6 Panama 8 Honduras 9 Costa
Rica, Guatemala, Nicaragua 10 El
Salvador
language: 7 Nahuatl, Spanish

centralize
5 focus, unify 11 concentrate, consolidate

centripetal
8 afferent, focusing, unifying
10 converging 11 integrative
12 centralizing 13 concentrating,
consolidating

centurion
7 officer 9 commander

century plant
5 agave

cephalopod
5 squid 7 mollusc, mollusk, octopus
10 cuttlefish

Cepheus
daughter: 9 Andromeda
kingdom: 8 Ethiopia
wife: 10 Cassiopeia

cerate
4 balm 5 cream, salve 6 chrism
7 unction, unguent 8 dressing, liniment,
ointment 9 demulcent, emollient

Cerberus
5 guard 6 guardian, sentinel, watchdog
father: 6 Typhon
form: 3 dog
mother: 7 Echidna

cereal
4 meal, mush, samp 5 gruel 6 farina
7 oatmeal 8 cornmeal, porridge
grass: 3 rye 4 corn, oats, ragi, rice
5 emmer, maize, spelt, wheat 6 barley,
millet 7 sorghum 9 buckwheat
North African: 8 couscous
Russian: 5 kasha

cerebral
6 mental 7 bookish 8 highbrow
9 scholarly 10 highbrowed 12 intellectual

cerebrate
5 think 6 reason 7 reflect 8 cogitate
9 speculate 10 deliberate

cerebration
7 thought 9 brainwork 10 cogitation,
reflection 11 speculation 12 deliberation

ceremonial
6 august, formal, ritual, solemn 7 courtly,
stately, studied 8 mannered, stylized
10 liturgical 11 ritualistic 12 conventional

ceremonious
6 formal, proper, seemly, solemn 7 courtly,
stately 8 decorous, imposing, majestic
9 dignified, grandiose 10 impressive
11 punctilious 12 conventional

ceremony
4 form, pomp, rite 6 ritual 7 decorum,
liturgy, service 8 protocol 9 formality
10 observance
Jewish: 8 habdalah, havdalah 10 bar
mitzvah, bat mitzvah
university: 8 encaenia

Ceres
Greek counterpart: 7 Demeter
daughter: 10 Persephone, Proserpina,
Proserpine
father: 6 Cronus, Saturn
mother: 3 Ops 4 Rhea

certain
3 set 4 firm, some, sure, true 5 fated, fixed
6 divers, stated, sundry 7 assured, settled,
several, various 8 cocksure, credible,
definite, destined, positive, provable,
reliable, sanguine, specific, surefire,
unerring 9 authentic, certified, conclusive,
confident, convinced, necessary, plausible,
warranted 10 dependable, guaranteed,
inarguable, inevitable, infallible, stipulated,
undeniable, verifiable 11 confirmable,
indubitable, ineluctable, inescapable,
trustworthy, unavoidable 12 demonstrable,
indisputable, well-grounded
13 incontestable, predetermined,
uncontestable

certainty
5 faith 6 surety 8 firmness, sureness
9 assurance, certitude, sure thing
10 confidence, conviction 11 assuredness,
staunchness 12 absoluteness,
definiteness, positiveness

certificate
7 diploma, license, voucher 8 contract,
document 9 affidavit 10 credential

certifier
6 notary 7 auditor 9 registrar

certify
4 aver, avow, okay 5 state, swear, vouch
6 assert, assure, attest, verify 7 approve,
confirm, endorse, license, testify, warrant,

witness **8** accredit, guaranty, notarize
9 authorize, guarantee, recognize
10 commission **12** authenticate

Cervantes' hero
10 Don Quixote

cessation
3 end **4** halt, rest, stop **5** break, cease,
close, letup, pause **6** ending, finish, freeze,
hiatus, period, recess **7** respite
10 conclusion, suspension **11** termination
12 interruption

cesspool
3 den, pit, sty **4** sink **5** sewer, Sodom
6 cloaca, gutter, pigsty **8** Gomorrah
12 Augean stable

cetacean
5 whale **7** dolphin **8** porpoise

Cetus star
4 Mira

Ceylon
8 Sri Lanka

cgs unit
3 erg **4** dyne, gram, phot **5** gauss, poise,
stilb **6** second, stokes **7** lambert, maxwell,
oersted **10** centimeter

Chablis
4 wine **8** Burgundy **9** white wine

Chad
capital: 8 N'Djamena
city: 4 Sarh **6** Abéché **7** Moundou
lake: 4 Chad
language: 6 Arabic, French
monetary unit: 5 franc
neighbor: 5 Libya, Niger, Sudan **7** Nigeria
8 Cameroon
river: 5 Chari **6** Logone

chafe
3 irk, rub, vex **4** fret, gall, peel, rage, skin,
wear **5** annoy, erode **6** abrade, bother,
scrape **7** provoke **8** irritate, vexation

chaff
3 kid, rag, rib **4** jest, joke, josh, razz dregs,
husks, tease **6** banter, debris, refuse
7 remains **8** detritus **9** sweepings

chaffer
6 barter, dicker, haggle, higgle, palter
7 bargain, chatter **8** exchange, huckster

chagrin
3 ire, irk, vex **5** abash, annoy, peeve,
pique, upset **6** dismay **7** perturb

8 disquiet, distress, unsettle, vexation
9 annoyance, discomfit, displease,
embarrass, humiliate, petulance
10 disappoint, discompose, disconcert,
irritation **11** frustration, humiliation
12 discomfiture

chagrined
4 hurt **5** upset, vexed **6** shamed
7 ashamed **8** dismayed, distressed
9 disturbed, mortified, perturbed, unsettled
10 humiliated **11** discomposed,
embarrassed **12** disappointed,
disconcerted

chain
3 row **4** bind, bond, gyve **5** group, train,
trust **6** cartel, catena, fetter, hobble, series,
string, tether **7** combine, manacle, shackle
8 handcuff, sequence **9** syndicate **10** succession **11** concatenate, progression
12 conglomerate **13** concatenation
adjunct: 8 sprocket
collar: 6 torque
gang: 6 coffle
ornamental: 10 chatelaine
sound: 5 clank

chain ____
3 saw **4** gang, mail **5** store **6** letter
8 reaction

Chained Lady
9 Andromeda

chair
4 seat **5** stool **6** rocker, settee, settle
7 preside
back: 5 splat
bishop's: 8 cathedra
designer: 5 Eames
portable: 5 sedan
reclining: 12 chaise longue, chaise
lounge
royal: 6 throne
type: 4 club, easy **6** morris **7** rocking
8 captain's, electric **9** director's, reclining
10 Adirondack, ladder-back

chaise
4 sofa **5** chair, coach, divan **8** carriage

chalcedony
4 onyx, sard **5** agate, chert **6** jasper,
quartz **9** carnelian, cornelian **10** bloodstone **11** chrysoprase

chalet
3 hut **4** camp **5** lodge **7** cottage

chalice
3 cup **5** grail **6** goblet

chalk out
5 draft **6** sketch **7** outline **8** block out, rough out **11** skeletonize **12** characterize

chalk up
3 get, win **4** gain **6** attain, credit, impute, obtain, secure **7** achieve, acquire, ascribe, procure, realize **9** attribute

challenge
3 try **4** dare, defy, face, stir, wake **5** brave, claim, demur, doubt, exact, rouse, waken **6** arouse, awaken, demand, impugn, invite, kindle **7** calling, dispute, protest, require, solicit, venture **8** confront, defiance, demurral, demurrer, question, struggle **9** objection, postulate, stimulate **10** difficulty, insistence **12** remonstrance

challenger
5 rival **8** aspirant, opponent **9** adversary, contender **10** antagonist, competitor, contestant

chamber
4 cell, hall, room **5** haven, house **7** cubicle **9** apartment, enclosure **11** compartment
underground: 8 hypogeum

chambered seashell
8 nautilus

chamberlain
6 priest **7** officer, servant **9** attendant, treasurer

chameleon
6 lizard

chameleonic
6 fickle **7** protean **9** mercurial **10** changeable, inconstant

chamfer
5 bevel **6** groove

chamois
6 shammy **7** leather **8** antelope, ruminant
habitat: 4 Alps
Old Testament: 6 aoudad

chamois-like animal
4 goat, ibex

champ
3 gum **4** bite, chew, mash **5** gnash, munch **7** trample **8** macerate, ruminate **9** masticate

champagne
4 wine **6** bubbly
center: 5 Reims **6** Rheims

Champagne
capital: 6 Troyes

champaign
5 field, plain **7** expanse, terrain **11** battlefield

champignon
6 fungus **8** mushroom

champion
4 back, hero **5** first, prime **6** uphold, victor, winner **7** capital, contend, leading, paladin, premier, support, titlist **8** advocate, defender, exponent, fight for, foremost, medalist, unbeaten **9** excellent, nonpareil, number one, principal, proponent, protector, supporter **11** illustrious, outstanding, titleholder, white knight

championship
5 crown, title **6** laurel, trophy **7** contest, defense, laurels, pennant **8** advocacy **10** blue ribbon

chance
3 hap, hit, lot, odd **4** fate, luck, meet, odds, risk, shot **5** break, fluke, light, wager **6** befall, casual, gamble, happen, hazard **7** fortune, offhand, stumble, venture **8** accident, fortuity, occasion, prospect **9** advantage, transpire **10** accidental, fortuitous, incidental, likelihood **11** contingency, opportunity, possibility, probability
even: 6 toss-up

chancellor
5 judge **8** minister **9** secretary
German: 4 Kohl (Helmut) **6** Brandt (Willy), Erhard (Ludwig), Hitler (Adolf) **7** Schmidt (Helmut) **8** Adenauer (Konrad), Bismarck (Otto von) **9** Schroeder (Gerhard)

chancy
4 iffy **5** dicey, fluky, hairy, risky **6** touchy, tricky **8** perilous, ticklish **9** dangerous, haphazard, hazardous, uncertain **10** capricious, precarious **11** speculative, treacherous **12** incalculable **13** unpredictable

Chandler, Raymond
character: 7 Marlowe (Philip)
novel: 8 Big Sleep (The) **11** Long Good-Bye (The) **13** Murder My Sweet **16** Farewell My Lovely
screenplay: 10 Blue Dahlia (The) **15** Double Indemnity

change
3 fix **4** swap, turn, vary **5** alter, coins, money, morph, shift, trade **6** adjust, evolve, modify, mutate, reform, remake, revamp, revert, revise, switch **7** commute,

convert, novelty, replace, reverse **8** exchange, mutation, revision, transfer **9** alternate, deviation, diversify, fluctuate, refashion, transform, transmute, transpose, variation **10** alteration, conversion, divergence, innovation, substitute **11** interchange, permutation, transfigure, vicissitude **12** metamorphose, modification, transmogrify **13** metamorphosis, transmutation

sudden: 8 peripety **10** peripeteia

changeable
5 fluid **6** fickle, labile, pliant, shifty **7** flighty, mutable, plastic, protean, unfixed, varying **8** restless, shifting, slippery, ticklish, unstable, unsteady, variable, volatile **9** adaptable, alterable, impulsive, mercurial, uncertain, unsettled, whimsical **10** capricious, inconstant **11** chameleonic, fluctuating, vacillating **13** kaleidoscopic, temperamental, unpredictable

change decor
4 redo **10** redecorate

changeless
5 fixed **6** steady **7** abiding, regular, uniform **8** constant, enduring, resolute **9** immutable, perpetual, steadfast, unvarying **10** invariable

change off
6 rotate **9** alternate

change of heart
8 reversal

change of life
9 menopause **11** climacteric

change of pace
5 pitch, shift **9** slow pitch

changeover
5 shift **10** alteration, conversion, transition

channel
3 way **4** band, duct, pass, path, pipe **5** agent, canal, carry **6** agency, convey, course, funnel, groove, gutter, medium, siphon, strait, trough, tunnel **7** conduct, conduit, passage, vehicle **8** aqueduct, pipeline, transmit **10** instrument **11** watercourse
Africa-Madagascar: 10 Mozambique
Atlantic-Nantucket Sound: 8 Musketget
Atlantic-North Sea: 7 English
Ellesmere-Greenland: 7 Robeson
Ganges: 5 Hugli **7** Hooghly
Hawaii: 5 Kaiwi, Kauai
Japan: 5 Bungo
Northwest Territories: 9 M'Clintock

Pakistan: 4 Nara
Scotland: 5 Minch
Tierra del Fuego: 6 Beagle
Tigris-Euphrates: 11 Shatt al Arab
Virginia: 12 Hampton Roads
West Indies: 9 Old Bahama

channel bass
4 drum **7** red drum, redfish

Channel Islands
capital: 8 St. Helier **11** St. Peter Port
dependency of: 7 Britain
island: 4 Sark **6** Jersey **8** Alderney, Guernsey

chanson
4 song

"Chanson _____"
6 Triste

chanson de _____
5 geste

chant
4 sing, tune **5** drone **6** intone **8** vocalize **10** cantillate
Gregorian: 9 plainsong **12** cantus firmus
Jewish: 6 Hallel

chanteuse
6 singer **7** artiste **10** cantatrice

chanticleer
4 cock **7** rooster

chaos
6 bedlam, muddle **7** anarchy, clutter, entropy, turmoil **8** disarray, disorder **9** confusion **11** lawlessness

Chaos
daughter: 3 Nox, Nyx **4** Gaea
son: 6 Erebus

chaotic
7 jumbled, lawless **8** anarchic, confused, formless **9** amorphous, haphazard, scrambled **10** disordered, disorderly, topsy-turvy, tumultuous **11** harum-scarum, unorganized **12** disorganized **13** helter-skelter, unpredictable

chap
3 guy **4** gent **5** bloke **6** fellow

chaparral
5 scrub **7** thicket

chaparral cock
10 roadrunner

chapeau
3 hat **6** topper

chapel
6 bethel, church, shrine **7** chantry
9 sanctuary

chaperone
5 guide **6** attend, duenna, escort, matron
7 oversee **9** accompany, companion,
supervise **11** superintend

chapfallen
see **crestfallen**

chaplain
5 padre, pastor **8** minister, sky pilot

chaplet
5 crown **6** anadem, laurel, rosary, wreath
7 coronal, coronet, garland

chapter
4 unit **5** phase, stage **6** branch, period
7 episode, section **8** division **9** affiliate

char
4 burn **9** carbonize

character
3 ilk **4** bent, case, cast, kind, mark, mind,
name, rank, role, sign, sort, type **5** state,
trait **6** cipher, device, letter, makeup,
nature, oddity, repute, spirit, status, stripe,
symbol, temper, virtue **7** feature, oddball,
persona, quality, station, variety **8** capacity,
eminence, identity, position, standing
9 attribute, eccentric, rectitude, situation
10 reputation, uniqueness **11** description,
disposition, personality, temperament
13 individuality
chief: 4 hero **11** protagonist
defect: 8 hamartia

character assassination
5 libel **7** calumny, scandal, slander
10 backbiting, defamation **12** backstabbing

characteristic
4 mark, sign **5** badge, point, token, trait
6 aspect, innate, normal, proper **7** feature,
natural, quality, special, typical **8** especial,
peculiar, property, specific, tendency **9** attribute, birthmark, component, mannerism,
trademark **10** diagnostic, emblematic,
individual, particular **11** distinction,
distinctive, peculiarity, singularity
12 idiosyncrasy **13** idiosyncratic

characterize
4 mark **5** draft **6** define, sketch, typify
7 outline, portray **8** describe, identify
10 constitute, pigeonhole **11** distinguish,
individuate, personalize **12** discriminate
13 differentiate, individualize

characterless
4 flat **5** mousy **7** humdrum, insipid,
vacuous **8** mediocre **9** colorless
10 namby-pamby, wishy-washy
11 nondescript

charade
4 sham **5** farce, put-on **6** parody
8 disguise, pretense, travesty **9** deception
11 make-believe

chare
see **chore**

charge
3 ask, bid, fee, lay, tab, tax **4** bill, care,
cost, duty, fill, heap, kick, load, onus, race,
rate, rush, task, tell, toll, warn **5** choke,
debit, order, place, price, refer, trust
6 accuse, assign, attack, burden, credit,
direct, enjoin, exhort, impugn, impute,
indict, saddle, thrill **7** arraign, ascribe,
bidding, command, conduct, entrust,
expense, impeach, mandate, request,
solicit **8** accredit, handling, instruct, price
tag, reproach, stampede **9** attribute,
committal, electrify, inculpate
10 accusation, allegation, commitment,
injunction, management, obligation
11 incriminate, instruction, requirement,
supervision

chargeable
6 liable **7** subject **11** accountable,
responsible

chargeless
4 free **6** gratis **8** costless **10** gratuitous
13 complimentary

charger
5 horse, mount, steed **6** salver **7** courser,
platter **8** trencher, warhorse

chariness
7 caution **8** prudence **9** integrity
10 discretion

chariot
8 carriage
four-horse: 8 quadriga

charioteer
6 Auriga, driver

charisma
5 charm **6** allure, appeal, duende
7 glamour **9** magnetism **10** attraction
11 fascination

charitable
6 benign, giving, humane, kindly
7 clement, lenient, liberal **8** generous,
merciful, obliging, tolerant **9** forgiving,
indulgent **10** altruistic, beneficent,
benevolent, forbearing, thoughtful

11 considerate, kindhearted, sympathetic
12 eleemosynary, humanitarian 13 philanthropic

charity
4 alms, love 5 grace, mercy 6 lenity, relief
7 caritas 8 altruism, clemency, donation, goodwill, leniency, offering 10 generosity, humaneness, kindliness 11 benefaction, beneficence, benevolence 12 contribution

charivari
5 babel, melee 6 jangle, jumble, medley, racket, ruckus, uproar 7 farrago
8 serenade, shivaree 9 cacophony, confusion 10 hodgepodge 11 celebration

charlatan
4 sham 5 bluff, faker, fraud, quack 6 con man 8 imposter, impostor, swindler
10 mountebank 11 quacksalver
13 confidence man

Charlemagne
brother: 8 Carloman
father: 5 Pepin
knight: 6 Oliver, Roland 7 Olivier, paladin 8 douzeper
nephew: 6 Roland 7 Orlando
sword: 7 Joyeuse
traitor: 4 Gano 7 Ganelon

Charles's Wain
9 Big Dipper, Ursa Major

charleston
5 dance

Charley's Aunt author
6 Thomas (Brandon)

Charlie and the Chocolate Factory author
4 Dahl (Roald)

Charlie Brown creator
6 Schulz (Charles)

Charlie McCarthy
5 dummy 6 stooge
friend: 5 Snerd (Mortimer)
voice: 6 Bergen (Edgar)

charm
3 hex 4 juju, lure, rune, take, wile 5 grace, quark, spell 6 allure, amulet, appeal, enamor, fetish, mascot, seduce, voodoo
7 attract, beguile, bewitch, enchant, glamour 8 enthrall, entrance, talisman, witchery 9 captivate, enrapture, ensorcell, fascinate, hypnotize, magnetism, mesmerize 10 allurement, attraction, phylactery, witchcraft 11 fascination, incantation 13 agreeableness

charmed
5 lucky 7 blessed 8 enamored
9 bewitched, enchanted, entranced, fortunate 10 captivated, fascinated, infatuated

charmer
4 roué 5 magus 6 wizard 7 seducer, warlock 8 conjurer, lothario, magician, sorcerer 9 enchanter 11 spellbinder

charming
7 winsome 8 adorable, alluring, inviting, magnetic 9 appealing, glamorous, seductive 10 attractive, delightful, enchanting, entrancing 11 captivating

Charon
7 boatman 8 ferryman
father: 6 Erebus
mother: 3 Nox
river: 4 Styx

Charpentier opera
6 Louise

charpoy
3 bed, cot

chart
3 map 4 plan, plat, plot 5 graph, table
6 design, lay out, map out, sketch
7 arrange, diagram, outline, project
9 blueprint 10 tabulation

charter
3 let 4 deed, hire, rent 5 grant, lease
10 conveyance 12 constitution

Chartreuse
7 liqueur

chary
4 wary 5 cagey, canny 6 frugal, stingy
7 careful, guarded, miserly, prudent, sparing, thrifty 8 cautious, discreet, gingerly, hesitant 9 provident, reluctant
10 economical, restrained, suspicious, unwasteful 11 calculating, circumspect, constrained, disinclined

Charybdis
9 whirlpool
rock associated with: 6 Scylla

chase
3 run 4 bolt, dash, game, hunt, prey, race, rush, tear 5 chivy, drive, eject, evict, hound, shoot, speed, trail 6 career, charge, course, follow, hasten, pursue, quarry
7 boot out, hunting, kick out, pursuit 8 run after, throw out

chase away

chase away
4 rout, shoo

chaser
4 wolf 6 masher 7 Don Juan 8 Casanova
9 ladies' man, womanizer 10 lady-killer
11 philanderer

chasm
3 gap 4 gulf, rift 5 abyss, cleft, clove,
flume, gorge, gulch, split 6 ravine
8 crevasse

chasmal
6 gaping 7 echoing, yawning 9 cavernous

chassepot
5 rifle

chaste
4 pure 5 clean, moral 6 decent, modest,
proper, seemly, vestal, virgin 7 austere,
prudish 8 celibate, decorous, innocent,
maidenly, platonic, spotless, virginal,
virtuous 9 abstinent, continent, stainless,
undefiled, unsullied 10 immaculate
11 unblemished

chasten
5 abase, scold 6 humble, punish, rebuke,
refine, subdue 7 correct, upbraid
8 chastise 9 castigate, humiliate,
reprimand 10 discipline

chastise
4 beat, flog, whip 5 scold 6 punish,
rebuke, thrash 7 belabor, censure,
chasten, correct, reprove, scourge, upbraid
9 castigate 10 discipline

chastisement
3 rod 7 reproof 8 punition 10 correction,
discipline, punishment 11 castigation

chastity
6 purity, virtue 7 modesty 8 celibacy
9 innocence, integrity, virginity
10 abstention, continence, maidenhood

chasuble
8 vestment

chat
3 gab, jaw, rap, yak, yap 4 blab, gush, talk
5 prate, visit 6 babble, confab, gossip,
jabber, natter, parley, patter, yak-yak
7 chatter, palaver, prattle, twaddle
8 causerie, colloquy, converse, dialogue,
schmooze 9 tête-à-tête, yakety-yak
11 confabulate 12 conversation, tittle-tattle
13 confabulation

château
5 manor, villa 6 castle, estate 7 mansion
8 fortress 12 country house

chateaubriand
5 steak 10 tenderloin

Chateaubriand novel
4 René 5 Atala

chatelain
6 warden 8 governor 9 castellan

chatelaine
4 hook, wife 5 clasp 8 mistress

chattel
4 serf 5 slave 7 bondman 8 bondsman,
property

chatter
3 gab, jaw, yak 4 blab, bull 5 prate
6 babble, gabble, gibber, gossip, jabber,
natter, patter, yak-yak, yammer 7 blabber,
blather, palaver, prattle, vibrate 9 small
talk, yakety-yak 12 tittle-tattle

chatterbox
6 gabber, gossip, magpie, prater 7 blabber
8 jabberer, prattler 12 blabbermouth

chatty
5 gabby 7 voluble 9 garrulous, talkative
10 loquacious

Chaucer pilgrim
4 Cook, Monk 5 Clerk, Friar, Reeve
6 Miller, Parson, Squire 8 Franklin,
Manciple, Merchant, Summoner 10 Nun's
Priest, Wife of Bath

chauffeur
5 drive 6 driver 9 transport

chauvinism
6 sexism 8 jingoism 10 partiality,
patriotism 11 nationalism

cheap
4 mean, poor junky, tight 6 cheesy,
common, cruddy, flashy, measly, paltry,
shabby, shoddy, sleazy, stingy, tawdry,
trashy 7 chintzy, cut-rate, low-cost,
reduced, thrifty 8 inferior, trifling, uncostly
9 brummagem, low-priced economical
11 inexpensive 12 contemptible,
meretricious

cheapen
5 decry, lower 6 debase, reduce
7 devalue 8 mark down 9 devaluate,
downgrade 10 depreciate, undervalue

cheapjack
5 junky 6 hawker, cheesy, cruddy, shoddy,
sleazy, tawdry, trashy 7 haggler, higgler,
packman, peddler 8 huckster, inferior,
rubbishy 9 worthless 13 opportunistic

cheapskate
5 miser **7** niggard, scrooge **8** tightwad
9 skinflint **11** cheeseparer

cheat
3 con, gyp **4** bilk, burn, dupe, fool, gull, hoax, milk, ream, scam **5** bunco, cozen, crook, fraud, fudge, gouge, hocus, put-on, screw, shaft, short, slick **6** chisel, chouse, con man, deceit, delude, diddle, extort, fleece, humbug, rip-off, sucker, take in **7** beguile, chicane, deceive, defraud, diddler, mislead, sharper, shyster, swindle, two-time **8** flimflam, hoodwink, swindler, trickery **9** bamboozle, chicanery, deception, defrauder, imposture, overreach, trickster **11** double-cross **12** double-dealer **13** confidence man
on a check: 4 kite

check
3 tab, try **4** bill, curb, halt, jibe, stay, stop, test, tick **5** block, brake, draft, prove, score, stall **6** accord, arrest, baffle, bridle, damage, desist, hold in, square, thwart, verify **7** compare, conform, control, examine, inhibit, repress, setback **8** dovetail, hold back, hold down, preclude, restrain, reversal, suppress **9** constrain, criterion, interrupt, restraint **10** correspond, inspection **11** examination
13 investigation

checkered
5 plaid **6** motley **7** mutable, spotted **9** patchwork, patterned **10** variegated **11** diversified

checklist
7 catalog **9** catalogue, inventory **11** enumeration

checkmate
4 beat **6** corner, defeat **7** outplay **8** vanquish **9** finish off

check out
3 die, eye **5** leave **6** assess **7** examine, inspect **8** appraise, evaluate, look over

check over
3 con, vet **4** scan **5** audit, study **6** review, survey **7** analyze, canvass, examine, inspect **10** scrutinize

checkup
4 exam **8** physical **10** inspection **11** examination

cheek
4 gall **5** brass, nerve **8** audacity, chutzpah, temerity **9** brashness, impudence, insolence **10** confidence, effrontery **11** presumption **12** impertinence

cheekbone
5 malar

cheeky
4 bold, flip, pert, wise **5** brash, cocky, fresh, nervy, sassy, saucy, smart **6** brazen **7** forward **8** flippant, impudent, insolent **11** impertinent, smart-alecky **12** presumptuous

cheep
4 peep **5** chirp, tweet **7** chirrup, chitter, twitter

cheer
3 rah **4** buoy, hail, root **5** bravo, huzza, nerve **6** buck up, gaiety, hoorah, hooray, hurrah, hurray, huzzah, solace, spirit **7** animate, applaud, comfort, console, enliven, gladden, hearten **8** embolden, inspirit **9** animation, encourage **10** strengthen
corrida: 3 olé

cheerful
3 gay **4** glad, rosy **5** jolly, merry, perky, sunny **6** blithe, bouncy, bright, chirpy, hearty, jaunty, jocund, lively **7** beamish, buoyant, radiant **8** animated, carefree, chirrupy **9** vivacious **12** lighthearted

cheerio
3 bye **4** ta-ta **5** adieu **6** bye-bye, good-by, so long **7** good-bye, toodles **8** farewell, toodle-oo

cheerless
4 dour, drab, grim **5** bleak **6** dismal, dreary, gloomy, somber, sombre **7** forlorn, joyless **8** desolate, dolorous, funereal, mournful **9** dejecting **10** depressing, melancholy, oppressive, tenebrific **11** dispiriting

cheers
5 salud, skoal **6** cincin, l'chaim, prosit **7** l'chayim, sláinte **8** applause, approval, chinchin **9** bottoms up **10** jubilation **11** acclamation, approbation

cheery
5 happy, jolly, merry, sunny, upbeat **6** blithe, bouncy, chirpy, lively **7** buoyant, chipper, festive, gleeful **8** animated, carefree, gladsome **9** convivial, sparkling **12** lighthearted

cheese
3 pot **4** blue, jack **5** brick, cream **6** farmer **7** cottage, process, ricotta **9** smearcase

American: 8 Longhorn 11 Liederkranz
12 Monterey Jack
Belgian: 9 Limburger
curdling agent: 6 rennet, rennin
Danish: 7 Havarti
dish: 6 fondue 7 rarebit, soufflé
Dutch: 4 Edam 5 Gouda 6 Leyden
English: 7 cheddar, Stilton 8 Cheshire
10 Lancashire
French: 4 Brie 7 fromage, Livarot
9 Camembert, Reblochon, Roquefort
10 Neufchâtel 11 Pont l'Évêque, Port du
Salut
German: 6 Tilsit 7 Munster 8 Muenster,
Tilsiter
Greek: 4 feta
green: 7 sapsago
Italian: 6 Asiago, Romano 7 fontina,
ricotta 8 Bel Paese, Parmesan, pecorino
9 provolone 10 Gorgonzola, mozzarella
lover: 9 turophile
main ingredient: 6 casein
Norwegian: 9 Jarlsberg
protein: 6 casein
Scottish: 6 Dunlop, Orkney 7 kebbock,
kebbuck
Swiss: 6 Saanen 7 Gruyère, sapsago
8 Vacherin 10 Emmentaler
11 Emmentaler
uncured: 7 cottage
Welsh: 10 Caerphilly

cheesecloth
5 gauze

cheeselike
6 caseic 7 caseous

cheeseparer
5 miser 7 niggard, scrooge 8 tightwad
9 skinflint 10 cheapskate, pinchpenny

cheeseparing
4 mean 5 chary, cheap, mingy, tight
6 frugal, shabby, stingy 7 chintzy, miserly,
thrifty 8 grudging, skimping 9 niggardly,
penurious 11 closefisted, tightfisted
12 parsimonious 13 penny-pinching

cheesy
4 poor 5 cheap 6 common, shabby,
shoddy, sleazy, tawdry, trashy 7 caseous
8 rubbishy

Cheever, John
novel: 8 Falconer 14 Wapshot Scandal
(The) 16 Wapshot Chronicle (The)
story: 7 Swimmer (The)

chef
4 cook

chef d'oeuvre
7 classic 9 showpiece 10 magnum opus,
masterwork 11 masterpiece, tour de force

Chekhov, Anton
play: 6 Ivanov 7 Seagull (The) 10 Uncle
Vanya 12 Three Sisters 13 Cherry
Orchard (The)
story: 9 Black Monk (The)

chelonian
6 turtle 8 tortoise

chemical
agent: 8 catalyst
combining power: 7 valence
compound: 4 acid, base, diol, enol, imid,
oxim, salt, tepa, urea 5 amide, amine,
diene, ester, imide, imine, indol, orcin,
oxime, purin, pyran, salol, tolan, triol
6 alkali, benzin, benzol, diamin, emodin,
guanin, halide, hydrid, indole, inulin,
ionone, isatin, isolog, isomer, ketone,
lactam, maltol, metepa, natron, nitril, pterin,
purine, pyrone, pyrrol, quinol, retene,
silane, skatol, tannin, tetryl, thiram, thymol,
tolane, triene, trimer, uracil, ureide, yttria,
zeatin 7 barilla, benzene, benzole,
cumarin, diamide, diamine, diazine,
diazole, diester, flavone, guanine, heptose,
hydride, indamin, indican, indoxyl, isatine,
levulin, metamer, monomer, naphtol, nitrile,
orcinol, oxazine, phytane, picolin, polyene,
polymer, pyrrole, quinoid, quinone, salicin,
skatole, steroid, taurine, terpene, thiazin,
thiazol, thymine, tolidin, triazin, urethan,
uridine, vitamer, xylidin 8 cephalin,
cyanamid, disulfid, elaterin, fluorene,
furfural, guaiacol, hematein, hexamine,
indamine, isologue, kephalin, lichenin, limo-
nene, melamine, naloxone, naphthol,
palmitin, phenazin, phosphid, phthalin,
picoline, piperine, pristane, quinolin,
resorcin, salicine, santonin, siloxane,
sodamide, sorbitol, spermine, squalene,
stilbene, strontia, tautomer, thiazine,
thiazole, thiophen, thiotepa, thiourea,
tolidine, triazine, triazole, triptane, tyramine,
urethane, vanillin, warfarin, xanthene,
xanthine, xanthone, xylidine, ytterbia,
zaratite, zirconia
(see at **element**)
quantity: 4 mole
radical: 4 acyl, amyl, cyan 5 allyl, butyl,
ethyl, tolyl 6 acetyl, formyl, methyl, oxalic,
phenyl, propyl, toluyl 7 benzoyl
reaction: 5 redox
salt: 5 niter, nitre, urate, ziram 6 haloid,
humate, malate, oleate, phytin 7 ferrate,
formate, gallate, maleate, pectate, persalt,
picrate, tannate, toluate, zincate
8 fumarate, pyruvate, racemate, selenate,
silicate, stearate, tartrate, thionate, titanate,
valerate, vanadate, xanthate
suffix: 3 ane, ase, ate, ein, ene, ide, ile,

ine, ite, ium, oic, oin, one, ose, ous, yne
4 eine, idin, itol, oate, olic, onic **5** idine,
onium, oside, ylene
warfare agent: 7 tear gas **8** vesicant
10 mustard gas

chemin de fer
5 train **7** railway **8** railroad

chemise
4 slip

chemist
7 analyst **8** druggist **10** apothecary,
pharmacist
American: 4 Urey (Harold) **6** Remsen
(Ira), Sumner (James) **7** Onsager (Lars),
Pauling (Linus), Seaborg (Glenn)
8 Hoffmann (Roald), Langmuir (Irving),
Mulliken (Robert), Richards (Theodore),
Woodward (Robert)
Austrian: 4 Kuhn (Richard) **5** Pregl (Fritz)
British: 4 Abel (Frederick), Davy
(Humphry), Todd (Alexander) **5** Boyle
(Robert), Soddy (Frederick) **6** Dalton
(John), Ramsay (William) **7** Faraday
(Michael) **8** Smithson (James) **9** Priestley
(Joseph), Wollaston (William)
10 Williamson (Alexander)
Dutch: 8 van't Hoff (Jacobus)
French: 5 Curie (Irene, Marie, Pierre)
7 Moissan (Henri), Pasteur (Louis)
8 Sabatier (Paul) **9** Gay-Lussac (Joseph),
Lavoisier (Antoine), Berthelot (Marcellin)
German: 5 Haber (Fritz) **6** Bunsen
(Robert), Liebig (Justus von), Nernst
(Walther), Wittig (Georg), Wohler
(Friedrich) **7** Fischer (Emil, Ernst, Hans),
Hofmann (August), Ostwald (Friedrich),
Wallach (Otto), Wieland (Heinrich),
Windaus (Adolf), Ziegler (Karl)
9 Zsigmondy (Richard) **10** Erlenmeyer
(Richard), Staudinger (Hermann)
11 Willstatter (Richard)
Italian: 5 Natta (Giulio) **8** Avogadro
(Amedeo)
Russian: 8 Semyonov (Nikolay), Zelinsky
(Nikolay) **10** Mendeleyev (Dmitry)
Swedish: 8 Svedberg (The, Theodor)
9 Berzelius (J. J.)
Swiss: 6 Karrer (Paul), Werner (Alfred)
(see also under **Nobel Prize winner**)

chemist's vessel
4 vial **5** flask, phial **6** ampule, beaker,
mortar, retort **7** ampoule **8** crucible, test
tube

chemoreceptor
8 taste bud

cheongsam
5 dress

Cheops
5 Khufu

cherish
4 keep, save **5** adore, guard, honor, nurse,
prize, value **6** admire, cosset, defend, dote
on, esteem, foster, harbor, relish, revere,
shield **7** apprize, care for, nourish, nurture,
shelter, worship **8** conserve, hold dear,
preserve, treasure, venerate **9** cultivate,
delight in, entertain, reverence, safeguard
10 appreciate

Cherokee
chief: 4 Ross (John)
historian: 7 Sequoia, Sequoya
8 Sequoyah

cherry
dark: 4 bing
family: 4 rose **8** Rosaceae
genus: 6 Prunus
hybrid: 4 Duke
sour: 7 morello
sweet: 4 bing **7** mazzard, oxheart
wild: 7 mazzard **10** maraschino

cherry bomb
11 firecracker

Cherry Orchard author
7 Chekhov (Anton)

cherrystone
4 clam **6** quahog

Chersonese
9 peninsula

cherub
4 babe, baby **5** angel, child, cupid, putto
6 infant **7** bambino **8** amoretto, innocent

cherubic
4 cute, rosy **6** chubby **7** angelic
8 adorable, innocent

chess
champion: 3 Tal (Mikhail) **4** Euwe (Max)
6 Karpov (Anatoly), Lasker (Emanuel)
7 Fischer (Bobby), Kramnik (Vladimir),
Smyslov (Vassily), Spassky (Boris)
8 Alekhine (Alexander), Kasparov (Garry),
Steinitz (Wilhelm) **9** Botvinnik (Mikhail),
Petrosian (Tigran) **10** Capablanca (José)
draw game: 9 stalemate
goal: 4 mate **9** checkmate
move: 6 castle, gambit
opening: 6 gambit
piece: 4 king, pawn, rook **5** queen
6 bishop, knight
risk: 6 gambit
term: 5 check **7** capture, endgame

chest
3 box **4** kist **5** bosom, torso, trunk
6 breast, bureau, coffer, thorax **7** cabinet,
8 cupboard, treasury **9** exchequer

chesterfield
4 sofa **5** divan **8** overcoat **9** davenport

chestnut
4 tree **5** color, horse **6** cliché, marron
10 chinquapin
extract: 6 tannin
water: 4 ling

cheval glass
6 mirror

chevalier
5 noble **6** knight **8** horseman **9** caballero,
gentleman

chevet
4 apse

chevron
6 stripe

chew
3 eat, gum **4** bite, gnaw **5** champ, chomp,
munch **6** crunch, devour, nibble
7 consume **8** ruminate **9** masticate

chewing gum
6 chicle

chew out
3 jaw **5** scold **6** rebuke, revile **7** bawl out,
reprove, tell off, upbraid **8** lambaste,
reproach **9** castigate, criticize, reprimand
10 tongue-lash, vituperate

Chiang _____
7 Kai-shek

chic
4 mode, rage, tony **5** smart, style, swank,
swish, vogue **6** modish, trendy, with-it
7 dashing, elegant, fashion, stylish
10 dernier cri **11** fashionable

chicane
4 dupe, fool, gull, hoax, ploy, ruse, wile
5 cavil, cheat, feint, fraud, trick **6** gambit
8 artifice, flimflam, hoodwink, trickery
9 bamboozle, deception, duplicity,
stratagem, victimize **10** dishonesty, hanky-
panky **13** double-dealing

chicanery
4 plot, ruse **5** fraud, trick **6** gambit
8 intrigue, trickery **9** deception, duplicity
10 subterfuge **11** machination,
skulduggery

chichi
4 arty **5** gaudy, showy, swank **6** dressy,
frilly, la-di-da **7** splashy **8** affected,
précieux, precious **10** flamboyant,
preciosity **11** affectation, fashionable,
overrefined, pretentious **12** ostentatious
13 ornamentation

chick
3 kid, tot **4** girl **5** child **6** moppet, nipper,
pullet **7** toddler **8** juvenile, young one
9 youngster

chickadee
8 titmouse
family: 7 Paridae

chicken
4 fowl, funk **5** sissy, timid **6** coward,
craven **7** dastard, gutless **8** cowardly,
poltroon **11** lily-livered, yellowbelly
13 pusillanimous
breed: 4 Java **6** Cochin **7** Cornish,
Leghorn **9** Dominique, Orpington,
Wyandotte **11** Jersey Giant, Rock Cornish
castrated: 5 capon
cooking: 5 fryer **7** broiler, roaster
disease: 8 pullorum **11** coccidiosis
female: 3 hen **6** pullet
genus: 6 Gallus
male: 4 cock **7** rooster **8** cockerel
pen: 4 coop
small: 6 bantam
sound: 6 cackle

chicken feed
7 peanuts **8** pittance **11** chump change

chicken pox
9 varicella

chickpea
4 gram **8** garbanzo

chickweed
4 pink **7** potherb

chicle
3 gum **10** chewing gum

chicory
6 endive **7** witloof **9** radicchio

chide
3 kid **5** scold **6** berate, rebuke **7** chew
out, lecture, reprove, upbraid **8** admonish,
call down, reproach **9** castigate, reprimand

chiding
6 rebuke **7** reproof **8** reproach
9 reprimand **10** admonition **12** admonishment

chief
3 key **4** arch, boss, duce, head, lion, main,
star **5** first, major, prime **6** führer, honcho,
leader, master, primal, ruling, sachem

7 fuehrer, headman, highest, leading, premier, primary **8** cardinal, champion, dictator, dominant, eminence, foremost **9** number-one, principal, prominent **10** preeminent **11** outstanding, predominant
commander: 4 CINC
prefix: 4 arch
Spanish: 4 jefe

Chief Justice
3 Jay (John) **4** Taft (William Howard) **5** Chase (Salmon), Stone (Harlan Fiske), Taney (Roger), Waite (Morrison), White (Edward) **6** Burger (Warren), Fuller (Melville) Hughes (Charles Evans), Vinson (Fred), Warren (Earl) **8** Marshall (John), Rutledge (John) **9** Ellsworth (Oliver), Rehnquist (William)

chiefly
6 mainly, mostly, notably **7** largely, overall **9** generally, primarily **10** especially **11** principally **12** preeminently **13** predominantly

chiffchaff
4 bird **7** warbler

chiffonier
5 chest **6** bureau **7** armoire, dresser

chigger
4 mite **6** chigoe, red bug

chignon
3 bun **4** knot

chilblain
4 sore **8** swelling **12** inflammation

child
3 kid **5** minor, youth **6** cherub, infant, moppet, nipper, shaver, urchin **7** bambino, toddler **8** juvenile, small fry, young one **9** youngling, youngster
gifted: 7 prodigy
homeless: 4 waif
parentless: 6 orphan
Scottish: 5 bairn
spoiled: 4 brat
young: 3 tot **4** baby, tike, tyke **6** infant, kiddie **8** bantling, weanling

childish
5 naive **7** puerile **8** arrested, immature **9** infantile

childless
6 barren **7** sterile

childlike
5 naive **6** docile, filial **7** natural, puerile **8** innocent, trustful, trusting **9** ingenuous

children
4 kids, seed **5** brood, heirs, issue **6** scions **7** progeny **9** offspring, posterity **11** descendants

child's play
4 snap **5** cinch, setup **6** breeze, picnic **8** cakewalk, duck soup, kid stuff, pushover **11** piece of cake

Chile
capital: 8 Santiago
city: 6 Temuco **10** Concepción, Talcahuano, Viña del Mar **11** Antofagasta, Valparaíso
conqueror: 7 Almagro (Diego de) **8** Valdivia (Pedro de)
desert: 7 Atacama
island: 6 Easter **13** Juan Fernández
lake: 10 Llanquihue
language: 7 Spanish
leader: 7 Allende (Salvador) **8** Pinochet (Augusto)
monetary unit: 4 peso
mountain range: 5 Andes
neighbor: 4 Peru **7** Bolivia **9** Argentina
passage: 5 Drake
river: 6 Bío-Bío
strait: 8 Magellan

Chileab
father: 5 David
mother: 7 Abigail

chili con _____
5 carne

Chilion
father: 9 Elimelech
mother: 5 Naomi

chill
3 icy, raw **4** ague, cold, cool, hang **5** gelid, nippy **6** arctic, formal, freeze, frigid, frosty, wintry **7** distant, glacial, hostile **8** dispirit, freezing **10** demoralize, discourage, dishearten **11** emotionless, refrigerate

chiller
7 shocker **8** thriller

chilly
3 raw **4** cold **5** algid, brisk, crisp, nippy **6** frigid **7** bracing, coldish, hostile **10** unfriendly

chilopod
9 centipede

chime
3 din **4** bell, bong, dong, peal, ring, toll, tune **5** agree, clang, knell, sound **6** accord, strike **7** concord, harmony

8 carillon 9 agreement, harmonize
10 consonance, correspond

chime in
3 say 4 tell 5 state, utter inject 7 break in,
declare 9 interrupt

chimera
5 dream, fancy 7 fantasy, figment,
monster, specter, spectre 8 illusion,
phantasy 9 nightmare, pipe dream

Chimera
father: 6 Typhon
mother: 6 Echidna
slayer: 11 Bellerophon

chimerical
6 absurd, unreal 7 fictive, utopian
8 delusive, delusory, fabulous, fanciful,
illusory, mythical, spurious 9 ambitious,
beguiling, deceptive, fantastic, fictional,
imaginary, visionary 10 far-fetched,
fictitious, improbable, outlandish
11 extravagant, unrealistic
12 preposterous, supposititious

chiming
8 harmonic 9 consonant 10 harmonious

chimney
3 lum 4 flue, tube, vent 5 stack
10 smokestack
corner: 8 fireside 9 inglenook
output: 4 soot 5 fumes, smoke

chimpanzee
3 ape 7 primate 10 anthropoid
kin: 6 bonobo, gibbon 7 gorilla
9 orangutan

chin
3 gab, jaw, rap, yak 4 blab, chat, talk
8 converse

china
6 dishes 7 ceramic 8 crockery 9 porcelain,
tableware 11 earthenware
maker: 3 Bow 5 Hizen, Imari, Spode
6 Doccia, Sèvres 7 Bristol, Chelsea,
Dresden, Limoges, Meissen 8 Caughley,
Haviland, Wedgwood

China
bay: 8 Hangzhou
capital: 7 Beijing
city: 4 Sian, Xi'an 5 Wuhan 6 Canton,
Harbin, Mukden 7 Nanjing, Nanking,
Tianjin 8 Shanghai, Shenyang, Tientsin
9 Chongqing, Guangzhou
desert: 4 Gobi 10 Taklimakan
dynasty: 3 Han, Sui 4 Ch'in, Chou, Ming,

Sung, Tang, Yüan 5 Ch'ing, Shang
6 Manchu
ethnic group: 3 Han
gulf: 5 Bo Hai
heritage site: 9 Great Wall
island: 6 Hainan 8 Hong Kong
lake: 5 Tai Hu 8 Hongze Hu, Poyang Hu
10 Dongting Hu
language: 3 Han 8 Mandarin
leader: 9 Mao Zedong, Sun Yat-sen
10 Kublai Khan, Mao Tse-tung 12 Deng
Xiaoping 13 Chiang Kai-shek, Teng Hsiao-
p'ing
monetary unit: 4 yuan
monetary unit, former: 4 tael
mountain, range: 6 Kunlun 8 Himalaya
9 Altai Shan, Altay Shan, Himalayan
10 Gongga Shan
old name: 6 Cathay
peninsula: 7 Leizhou 8 Liaodong,
Shandong
province: 5 Anhui, Gansu, Hevei, Henan,
Hubei, Hunan, Jilin 6 Fujian, Shanxi,
Yunnan 7 Guizhou, Jiangsu, Jiangxi,
Qinghai, Shaanxi, Sichuan 8 Liaoning,
Shandong, Szechuan, Szechwan, Zhejiang
9 Guangdong 12 Heilongjiang
region: 5 Tibet 6 Xizang 10 Nei Monggol
12 Ningxia Huizu 13 Inner Mongolia,
Xinjiang Uygur
river: 4 Amur 5 Chang, Huang, Tarim
6 Mekong, Yellow, Zangbo 7 Salween,
Yangtze

china clay
6 kaolin

chinchilla
3 fur 6 rodent

chine
5 crest, ridge, spine 7 hogback
8 backbone

Chinese
aromatic root: 7 ginseng
bamboo: 7 whangee
boat: 4 junk 6 sampan
bow: 6 kowtow
cabbage: 7 bok choy, pak choi
card game: 6 fan-tan
cauterizing agent: 4 moxa
prefix: 4 Sino
conveyance: 7 pedicab 8 rickshaw
10 jinricksha, jinrikisha
date: 6 jujube
dialect: 4 Amoy 8 Mandarin
9 Cantonese, Pekingese
dictator: 9 Mao Zedong 10 Mao Tse-tung
12 Deng Xiaoping 13 Teng Hsiao-p'ing

dog: 4 chow, Peke 8 chow chow 9 Pekingese

dynasty: 3 Ch'i, Han, Qin, Sui, Wei, Yin 4 Ch'en, Ch'in, Chou, Hsia, Ming, Qing, Song, Sung, T'ang, Tsin, Yuan 5 Ch'ing, Liang, Shang 6 Manchu, Mongol, Shu Han

fabric: 6 pongee, tussah 8 shantung

feminine principle: 3 yin

feudal state: 3 Wei

food: 6 dim sum, lo mein, mantou, subgum, wonton 8 chop suey, chow mein 9 fried rice 10 egg foo yong, egg foo yung, Peking duck 11 egg foo young

fruit: 6 lichee, litchi, lychee, loquat 7 kumquat 8 mandarin

gambling game: 6 fan-tan

gong: 6 tam-tam

gruel: 6 congee

herb: 5 ramie 7 ginseng

idol: 4 joss

laborer: 6 coolie

legendary emperor: 7 Huangdi, Huang-ti

mandarin's residence: 5 yamen

masculine principle: 4 yang

money, silver: 5 sycee

musical instrument: 4 pipa

nurse: 4 amah

official: 8 mandarin

official seal: 4 chop

oil: 4 tung

ox: 4 zebu

porcelain: 4 Ming 7 celadon, Nankeen 8 mandarin

pottery: 4 Kuan, Ming 5 Chien

puzzle: 7 tangram

race: 9 Mongoloid

religion: 6 Taoism 8 Buddhism 12 Confucianism

sauce: 3 soy

secret society: 4 tong

sheep: 5 urial

silkworm: 6 tussah

tea: 5 bohea, hyson 6 congou, oolong 8 souchong

temple: 6 pagoda

tree: 4 tung 6 ginkgo, loquat 7 kumquat

vine: 5 kudzu

chink
4 rift, slit 5 caulk, cleft, crack, split 6 cranny 7 crevice, fissure, opening 8 aperture

chinquapin
3 nut 8 chestnut

chintzy
4 loud 5 cheap, gaudy, showy, tacky 6 flashy, garish, stingy, tawdry, vulgar 9 tasteless 12 meretricious

chip
4 flaw, nick 5 flake, notch, shard, slice, split, wafer, wedge 6 chisel, defect, paring, sliver 7 counter

chip in
6 ante up, kick in 7 pitch in 10 contribute 11 come through

chipper
4 spry 5 alert, brisk, perky, zesty 6 bright, lively, nimble 8 animated, spirited 9 sprightly, vivacious

chirk
4 buoy 5 cheer 7 animate, enliven, hearten 8 energize, inspirit 9 encourage 10 strengthen

chirography
6 script 8 longhand 10 penmanship 11 calligraphy, handwriting

chiromancy
9 palmistry

Chiron
7 centaur
father: 6 Cronus
mother: 7 Philyra
pupil: 5 Jason 8 Achilles, Heracles, Hercules 9 Asclepius 11 Aesculapius

chiropody
8 podiatry

chiropractic founder
6 Palmer (Daniel)

chirp
4 chip, peep, sing 5 cheep, trill, tweet 6 warble 7 chirrup, twitter

chirpy
3 gay 5 sunny 6 blithe, cheery, sparky 7 buoyant, sparkly 8 cheerful, sunbeamy 9 lightsome

chirrup
4 chip, peep, sing 5 cheep, tweet 6 warble 7 chipper, twitter

chisel
3 gyp, hew 4 beat, bilk, scam 5 carve, cheat, cozen, cut in, gouge, trick 6 butt in, diddle, fleece, horn in, sculpt 7 defraud, engrave, intrude, swindle

chit
3 IOU, kid 4 memo, note, slip 5 child 6 moppet 7 invoice, voucher 8 notation 9 youngster 10 memorandum

chitchat
3 gab 5 chaff 6 babble, banter, gossip

7 chatter, palaver, prattle badinage 9 small talk 12 tittle-tattle

chitter
4 chip, peep, sing 5 cheep, chirp, tweet 6 warble 7 chatter, chirrup, twitter

chivalric
see **chivalrous**

chivalrous
5 lofty, manly, noble 7 courtly, gallant, valiant 8 generous, gracious, knightly 9 honorable 10 benevolent, courageous 11 considerate, gentlemanly, magnanimous

chivy, chivvy
4 bait, ride 5 annoy, tease 6 badger, heckle, hector 7 torment 8 bullyrag

Chloe
11 shepherdess
beloved: 7 Daphnis

chlordane
11 insecticide

Chloris
father: 7 Amphion
husband: 6 Neleus 8 Zephyrus
mother: 5 Niobe
son: 6 Nestor

chloroform
7 anodyne, solvent 10 anesthetic 11 anaesthetic

chockablock
4 full 6 jammed, loaded, packed 7 brimful, crammed, crowded, stuffed 9 jam-packed

chocolate
5 brown, cacao, cocoa

Chocolate Soldier composer
6 Straus (Oscar)

chocolate tree
5 cacao

choice
3 top 4 best, pick, rare, vote 5 cream, elite, prime, prize 6 chosen, dainty, option, rating, select 7 elegant, verdict 8 decision, delicate, druthers, election, judgment, selected, superior, volition 9 exquisite, selection 9 selection 10 preference 11 alternative 13 determination
even: 6 toss-up

choir
6 chorus 7 chorale
area: 4 loft 7 chancel, gallery
leader: 6 cantor 8 choragus 9 precentor
member: 9 chorister
section: 4 alto, bass 5 tenor 7 soprano

vestment: 4 gown, robe 5 cotta 8 surplice

choke
3 gag 4 clog, plug, stop 5 block, close 6 stifle 7 congest, occlude, silence, smother 8 obstruct, strangle, throttle 9 constrict, suffocate 10 asphyxiate

choking
8 quashing, stifling 10 repression, smothering, squelching, strangling 11 suppression

choleric
5 angry, fiery, irate 6 fierce, heated 7 enraged, incensed, wrathful 9 irascible, splenetic 10 infuriated 11 hot-tempered 13 quick-tempered

cholla
6 cactus 7 opuntia

Chomolungma
7 Everest (Mt.)

chomp
4 bite, chew 5 munch 6 crunch 9 masticate

choose
3 opt 4 cull, mark, pick, take, want 5 adopt, elect, favor 6 decide, desire, opt for, prefer, select 7 embrace, pick out 8 decide on, handpick 9 single out

choosy
5 fussy, picky 7 finical, finicky 9 finicking, selective 10 fastidious, particular, pernickety 11 persnickety

chop
3 cut 4 dice, fell, hack, hash, seal, veer 5 cut up, grade, mince 7 quality

chop-chop
4 fast 6 presto, pronto, quick 7 quickly, rapidly 8 promptly, speedily 9 posthaste 12 lickety-split

chophouse
10 restaurant

Chopin, Frédéric
birthplace: 6 Poland
instrument: 5 piano
lover: 4 Sand (George)
work: 7 mazurka 8 nocturne 9 polonaise

choppy
4 wavy 5 jerky, rough 6 ripply, stormy, uneven 7 erratic 8 variable 9 turbulent, unsettled

choral section
5 altos 6 basses, tenors 8 sopranos

chord
5 triad 6 tetrad 7 harmony
sequence: 7 cadence 11 progression

chore
3 job 4 duty, task 5 stint, trial 6 devoir,
effort 7 routine 10 assignment, obligation
11 tribulation

choreograph
6 devise, direct, map out 7 arrange,
compose 11 orchestrate

choreographer
American: 4 Feld (Elliot), Holm (Hanya),
Lang (Pearl) 5 Ailey (Alvin), Fosse (Bob),
Limón (José), Shawn (Ted), Tharp (Twyla)
6 Duncan (Isadora), Dunham (Katherine),
Fokine (Michel), Graham (Martha), Morris
(Mark), Taylor (Paul), Tetley (Glen) 7 de
Mille (Agnes), Jamison (Judith), Joffrey
(Robert), Martins (Peter), Massine
(Leonide), Robbins (Jerome), St. Denis
(Ruth), Tamiris (Helen), Weidman (Charles)
8 Champion (Gower, Marge), Humphrey
(Doris), Nikolais (Alwin), Villella (Edward)
10 Balanchine (George), Cunningham
(Merce)
Australian: 8 Helpmann (Robert)
Cuban: 6 Alonso (Alicia)
Danish: 5 Bruhn (Erik) 7 Martins (Peter)
12 Bournonville (August)
English: 5 Dolin (Anton), Tudor (Antony)
6 Ashton (Frederick), Weaver (John)
7 Markova (Alicia), Rambert (Marie) 8 de
Valois (Ninette), Helpmann (Robert)
9 MacMillan (Kenneth)
French: 5 Lifar (Serge) 6 Béjart
(Maurice), Perrot (Jules), Petipa (Marius)
7 Camargo (Marie), Massine (Léonide),
Noverre (Jean-Georges)
German: 5 Jooss (Kurt)
Hungarian: 5 Laban (Rudolf)
Mexican: 5 Limón (José)
Russian: 5 Lifar (Serge) 6 Fokine
(Michel), Petipa (Marius) 8 Nijinska
(Bronislava), Nijinsky (Vaslav)

chorography
3 map 7 mapping 8 features 9 mapmaking

chortle
5 laugh 6 giggle, guffaw, hee-haw, titter
7 chuckle, snicker

chorus
5 choir 7 refrain

chorus girl
7 chorine

chosen
4 pick 5 elect, elite, named 6 called,
marked, pegged, picked, select 7 blessed
8 selected 9 appointed, delegated,
exclusive

Chou _____
5 En-lai

chouse
3 gyp 4 bilk, clip, dupe, herd 5 cheat,
cozen, drive, trick 6 diddle, fleece
7 defraud, swindle 8 flimflam

chow
4 eats, feed, food, grub, meal

chowchow
6 medley, relish 7 mélange

chowderhead
4 boob, clod, dodo, dolt, dope, fool
5 chump, dunce, idiot, noddy 6 dimwit,
nitwit, noodle 7 halfwit, schnook
8 dumbbell, numskull 9 lamebrain,
numbskull

chowhound
7 glutton 8 gourmand

chrism
3 oil 4 balm 5 cream, salve 6 cerate
7 unction, unguent 8 ointment

christen
3 dub 4 call, name, term 5 title 7 asperse,
baptize, immerse 8 dedicate, sprinkle
9 designate

christening
7 baptism

Christian
denomination: 6 Mormon, Quaker
7 Baptist, Friends 8 Anglican, Catholic,
Lutheran, Moravian, Nazarene, Reformed
9 Calvinist, Episcopal, Mennonite,
Methodist 10 Anabaptist 11 Pentecostal,
Unitarian 12 Episcopalian, Presbyterian,
Universalist
Eastern rite: 5 Uniat 6 Uniate
Egyptian: 4 Copt
love feast: 5 agape
martyr, first: 7 Stephen
symbol: 3 IHS 4 fish, rood 5 cross
6 Chi-Rhos 7 ichthus

Christiania
4 Oslo

Christian Science founder
4 Eddy (Mary Baker)

Christie, Agatha
  character: 6 Marple (Jane), Poirot (Hercule)
  novel: 14 Death on the Nile 24 Murder on the Orient Express
  play: 9 Mousetrap (The) 24 Witness for the Prosecution

Christina's World painter
  5 Wyeth (Andrew)

Christmas
  4 Noel, yule 8 Nativity, yuletide
  symbol: 7 Yule log

Christmas Carol, A
  author: 7 Dickens (Charles)
  character: 7 Scrooge (Ebenezer), Tiny Tim 8 Cratchit (Bob)

Christogram
  6 Chi-Rho

Christopher Robin creator
  5 Milne (A. A.)

chromatic
  8 colorful 10 accidental

chromatin thread
  7 spireme

chromosome component
  3 DNA 4 gene 8 telomere 10 centromere, chromomere

chronic
  5 usual 6 wonted 7 routine 8 constant, enduring, habitual 9 ceaseless, confirmed, continual, customary, incessant, perennial, perpetual, recurrent, recurring 10 accustomed, continuing, habituated, inveterate, persisting 11 unrelenting

chronicle
  4 list 6 annals, record, relate, report 7 account, history, narrate, recital, recount 8 describe 9 narration, narrative

chronicler
  8 narrator, recorder, reporter 9 historian

chronograph
  5 clock, watch 9 timepiece

chronology
  5 annal 6 annals, record 7 history 8 calendar, register, schedule 9 timetable

chronometer
  5 clock, watch 9 timepiece

chrysalis
  4 pupa 8 covering

Chryseis
  captor: 9 Agamemnon
  father: 7 Chryses

Chrysippus
  father: 6 Pelops
  slayer: 6 Atreus 8 Thyestes

chthonic
  6 Hadean, nether 7 hellish, satanic 8 accursed, infernal, plutonic 9 plutonian, Tartarean 10 sulphurous

chubby
  5 hefty, husky, plump, podgy, pudgy, round, tubby 6 chunky, fleshy, portly, rotund, stocky, zaftig 8 plumpish, roly-poly

chuck
  3 pat, tap 4 cast, hurl, junk, oust, shed, toss 5 ditch, fling, heave, nudge, pitch, scrap, throw 6 give up, reject 7 abandon, boot out, discard, dismiss, kick out 8 jettison, throw out 9 throw away

chucker
  7 bouncer

chuckle
  5 laugh 6 giggle, guffaw, hee-haw, titter 7 chortle, snicker

chucklehead
  see **chowderhead**

chuff
  3 oaf 4 boor, lout, rube 5 churl, clown, yahoo, yokel 7 bumpkin, hayseed 10 clodhopper

chum
  3 pal 4 mate 5 buddy, crony 6 friend, salmon 7 comrade 8 sidekick 9 companion

chummy
  4 cozy 5 close, pally, palsy, thick 8 familiar, intimate 10 buddy-buddy, palsy-walsy

chump
  3 oaf, sap 4 boob, dolt, dope, dupe, fool, goof, goon, gull, mark 5 booby, dummy, dunce, patsy 6 pigeon, sucker, turkey 7 fall guy, fathead 8 dolthead, lunkhead

chunk
  3 sum, wad 4 clod, hunk, lump, slab 5 clump 6 nugget

chunky
  5 beefy, dumpy, hefty, husky, plump, pudgy, squat, stout 6 chubby, fleshy, portly,

rotund, stocky, stubby, stumpy **8** heavyset, thickset

church
4 cult, fane, kirk, sect **5** creed, faith
6 temple **7** minster **8** basilica, religion
9 cathedral, communion **10** tabernacle
12 denomination
adjunct: 6 belfry **7** steeple **9** bell tower
basin: 4 font **5** stoup
bench: 3 pew
bishop's: 9 cathedral
calendar: 4 ordo
caretaker: 6 sexton
chapel: 7 oratory
council: 5 synod
court: 4 rota **10** consistory
creed: 6 Nicene **8** Apostles'
district: 6 parish **7** diocese
father: 5 Basil **6** Jerome, Justin, Origen
7 Ambrose, Clement **8** Ignatius
9 Augustine **10** Chrysostom, Tertullian, theologian
fund-raiser: 6 bazaar
governing body: 5 curia **7** classis
10 consistory, presbytery
head: 4 pope **7** pontiff
law: 5 canon
member: 11 communicant
of a monastery: 7 minster
officer: 5 elder, vicar **6** beadle, deacon, sexton, verger, warden **9** presbyter, sacristan
part: 4 apse, bema, loft, nave **5** aisle, altar, choir **6** vestry **7** chancel, gallery, narthex, steeple **8** sacristy, transept
9 baptistry, sanctuary **10** baptistery, clerestory
porch: 6 parvis **7** galilee
reader: 6 lector
recess: 4 apse
revenue: 5 tithe
room: 6 vestry **8** sacristy
Scottish: 4 kirk
seats for clergy: 7 sedilia
service: 4 mass **6** matins **7** vespers
8 evensong **9** communion
small: 6 chapel
tribunal: 4 rota
vault: 5 crypt

Churchill, Winston
daughter: 4 Mary **5** Diana, Sarah
father: 8 Randolph
mother: 6 Jennie
Order: 6 Garter
phrase: 11 Iron Curtain
son: 8 Randolph
trademark: 5 cigar
wife: 10 Clementine

church key
9 can opener

churchman
6 bishop, cleric, divine, parson, pastor, priest **8** minister, preacher, reverend
9 clergyman **12** ecclesiastic

churl
3 oaf **4** boor, clod, lout, rube **5** chuff, clown, yahoo, yokel **6** mucker **7** bumpkin, hayseed **10** clodhopper

churlish
4 base, curt, dour, rude **5** blunt, crude, gruff, surly **6** coarse, crusty, oafish, vulgar
7 boorish, brusque, loutish, lowbred, uncivil
8 cloddish, clownish **10** unmannerly
11 clodhopping, uncivilized
12 discourteous

churn
4 boil, foam, roil, stir **5** froth, swirl
6 bubble, seethe, simmer, stir up **7** agitate, ferment, smolder

chute
4 fall, ramp **5** falls, rapid, slide, spout
6 rapids **7** cascade, channel, descent
8 cataract **9** spinnaker, waterfall

chutzpah
4 gall **5** brass, cheek, moxie, nerve, spunk
8 audacity, temerity **10** effrontery

CIA
predecessor: 3 OSS

ciao
4 by-by, ta-ta **5** adieu, adios, aloha, hello, howdy **6** bye-bye, good-by, so long
7 good-bye, welcome **8** farewell
9 greetings

cicatrix
4 scar **13** scarification

Cicero
forte: 7 oratory
target: 8 Catiline **10** Mark Antony

cicerone
4 guru **5** coach, guide, tutor **6** docent, escort, mentor **7** adviser **9** counselor, tour guide

Cid, El (Le)
4 epic, hero, play, poem **5** opera
composer: 8 Massenet (Jules)
meaning: 4 lord
name: 4 Díaz (Rodrigo, Ruy) **5** Bivar
playwright: 9 Corneille (Pierre)
sword: 6 Colada, Tizona
wife: 6 Jimena, Ximena

cigar
5 stogy **6** corona, Havana, stogie
7 cheroot **8** panatela, perfecto
case: **7** humidor
color: **5** claro **6** maduro **8** colorado

cigarette
3 fag **4** butt **5** smoke **6** gasper **10** coffin
nail

cilium
4 hair, lash **7** eyelash

Cimmerian
4 dark **5** dusky **6** gloomy, murky **7** hellish,
shadowy, stygian **8** infernal, plutonic
9 plutonian

cinch
4 snap **5** girth, setup **6** assure, breeze,
ensure, fasten, insure, picnic, secure,
shoo-in **8** duck soup, kid stuff, pushover
9 certainty **10** child's play

cinchona bark extract
7 quinine

cincture
4 band, belt, sash **6** girdle **9** waistband

cinders
3 ash **4** coal, lava, slag **5** ashes, dross
embers **8** clinkers

cinema
4 film, show **5** flick, movie **6** movies
7 picture, theater, theatre **12** silver screen
13 motion picture

cinereous
4 ashy, gray, grey **5** ashen **7** ashlike

cinnabar
3 ore **7** mineral, pigment **9** vermilion
color: **3** red

cinnamon bark
6 cassia

cinnamon stone
6 garnet **8** essonite

cipher
4 code, zero **5** aught, count, digit **6** figure,
naught, nobody, number, reckon, symbol
7 compute, integer, numeral **8** estimate,
monogram **9** calculate, nonentity **11** whole
number

ciphering
8 figuring **9** computing, reckoning
10 arithmetic **11** calculation, computation

circa
4 near, nigh **5** about **6** around, roughly
13 approximately

circadian
5 daily **6** cyclic **7** diurnal, regular
9 quotidian

Circe
5 siren **9** sorceress
brother: **6** Aeëtes
father: **3** Sol **6** Helios
home: **5** Aeaea
lover: **7** Ulysses **8** Odysseus
niece: **5** Medea
son: **5** Comus **9** Telegonus

Circean
6 luring **8** alluring, enticing, fetching,
tempting **10** bewitching

circinate
6 coiled **7** rounded

circle
4 belt, gyre, hoop, loop, ring **5** crowd,
cycle, group, orbit, wheel, whorl **6** clique,
corona, girdle, gyrate, rotary, rotate
7 compass, coterie, cronies, friends,
revolve, rondure **8** surround **9** encompass
10 associates, companions, revolution
bisector: **8** diameter
colored: **6** areola
combining form: **3** gyr **4** cycl, gyro
5 cyclo
graph: **8** pie chart
luminous: **4** aura, halo **6** corona, nimbus
7 aureole
part: **3** arc **6** sector **8** quadrant
small: **4** disk **7** annulet

circlet
4 band, ring **6** bangle, diadem **8** bracelet,
headband
for head or helmet: **7** coronal

circuit
3 lap, way **4** loop, tour, trip, turn **5** ambit,
cycle, orbit, round, route, track **6** course,
hookup, league **7** compass, journey,
pathway, travels **8** district, rotation
9 perimeter, periphery, round trip
10 revolution, roundabout **11** association,
circulation **13** circumference

circuitous
7 devious, oblique, winding **8** circular,
indirect, tortuous **10** collateral, convoluted,
meandering, roundabout

circuit rider
5 judge **8** minister, preacher **9** clergyman

circular
4 bill 5 flier, flyer, round 7 annular, cycloid, discoid, handout, leaflet 8 handbill 9 throwaway
file: 11 wastebasket
motion: 4 eddy, gyre, spin 5 whirl 8 gyration, rotation 10 revolution
plate: 4 disc, dish, disk

circularize
4 poll 6 survey 7 canvass 9 advertise, publicize

circulate
4 flow 6 rotate, spread 7 diffuse, radiate, revolve 8 disperse 9 propagate 10 distribute 11 disseminate

circulation
4 flow 6 spread 8 currency 9 diffusion 11 propagation 12 transmission 13 dissemination

circumciser
5 mohel

circumcision, Jewish
4 bris 9 Brit Milah

circumference
3 rim 5 ambit 6 border, bounds, limits, margin 7 circuit, compass 8 boundary, confines 9 perimeter, periphery

circumflex
9 diacritic

circumjacent
11 surrounding

circumlocution
8 pleonasm, verbiage 9 euphemism, loquacity, prolixity, verbosity, wordiness 10 redundancy 11 periphrasis, verboseness

circumnavigate
5 skirt 6 bypass, detour 8 sidestep

circumnavigator
4 Cook (James) 5 Drake (Francis) 8 Magellan (Ferdinand), van Noort (Olivier) 9 Cavendish (Thomas)

circumscribe
5 cramp, limit 6 fetter, hamper 7 confine, delimit, enclose, mark off, outline, trammel 8 restrict, surround 9 constrict

circumscribed
5 bound, fixed 6 finite, narrow, strait 7 bounded, cramped, limited, precise 8 confined, definite, hampered 10 restrained, restricted 11 determinate

circumscription
5 cramp, limit, stint 6 border, margin 8 boundary 9 perimeter, restraint, stricture 10 constraint, definition, limitation 11 confinement, restriction 12 ball and chain, delimitation 13 constrainment

circumspect
4 safe, wary 5 chary 7 careful, guarded, prudent 8 cautious, discreet, gingerly 11 calculating

circumstance
4 fact, item 5 event, thing 6 detail, factor 7 adjunct, element, episode, feature 8 accident, incident, occasion 9 component, condition, happening 10 occurrence, particular 11 concomitant, constituent, eventuality

circumstantial
4 full 5 close, exact 6 strict 7 precise, replete 8 accurate, complete, detailed, thorough 9 elaborate, pertinent 10 blow-by-blow, ceremonial, exhaustive, incidental, particular

circumvent
5 avoid, elude, evade, hem in, skirt 6 bypass, detour 8 outflank, sidestep

circumvolution
4 gyre, turn 5 wheel, whirl 8 gyration, rotation 10 revolution

circus
4 ring 5 arena 6 big top 9 spectacle 12 amphitheater
animal: 4 bear, flea, lion, seal 5 horse, tiger 8 elephant
attraction: 5 freak 8 sideshow
owner: 6 Bailey (James), Barnum (P. T.) 8 Ringling (Bros.)
performer: 5 clown, tamer 7 acrobat, athlete, juggler, tumbler 9 aerialist, fire eater
worker: 10 roustabout

citadel
4 fort 7 redoubt 8 fastness, fortress 10 stronghold
of Carthage: 5 Bursa, Byrsa
Russian: 7 kremlin

citation
5 quote 6 eulogy 7 excerpt, mention, summons, tribute 8 accolade, encomium 9 panegyric, quotation, reference 12 commendation

cite
4 name, tell 5 offer, quote 6 adduce,

recall, summon **7** arraign, mention, present, refer to, specify **8** point out, remember **9** recollect

citizen
7 burgess, burgher, subject **8** civilian, national, resident, townsman **10** inhabitant

Citizen Kane director
6 Welles (Orson)

citron
4 tree **5** melon

citrus
family: 3 rue **8** Rutaceae
fruit: 4 lime, ugli **5** lemon **6** citron, orange, pomelo **7** kumquat, tangelo **8** bergamot, mandarin, shaddock **9** tangerine **10** grapefruit

city
4 burg **5** urban **7** burghal **9** municipal **10** metropolis
combining form: 5 polis
Eternal: 4 Rome
French: 5 ville
heavenly: 4 Sion, Zion
Latin: 4 urbs
Motor: 7 Detroit
of Bells: 10 Strasbourg
of Bridges: 6 Bruges
of Brotherly Love: 12 Philadelphia
of David: 9 Jerusalem
official: 6 mayor **7** manager **8** alderman **10** councilman
of God: 6 heaven **8** paradise
of Gold: 8 Eldorado
of Kings: 4 Lima
of Lights: 5 Paris
of Lilies: 8 Florence
of Masts: 6 London
of Rams: 6 Canton
of Refuge: 6 Medina
of Saints: 8 Montreal
of Seven Hills: 4 Rome
of the dead: 10 necropolis
of Victory: 5 Cairo
planner: 8 urbanist
section: 4 slum, ward **5** block, plaza **6** barrio, ghetto, square, uptown **8** business, downtown, red-light **11** residential
slicker: 4 dude
windy: 7 Chicago

city-state, Greek
5 Argos, polis **6** Athens, Delphi, poleis (plural), Sparta, Thebes **7** Corinth

city, town, village
(see also **capital**)

Afghanistan: 5 Balkh, Farah, Herat, Kushk **6** Konduz **8** Kandahar, Qandahar **9** Jalalabad
Alabama: 3 Opp **4** Arab, Boaz, Elba **5** Selma **6** Athens, Dothan, Mobile **7** Decatur, Florala **8** Prichard **10** Birmingham, Huntsville, Scottsboro, Tuscaloosa **12** Muscle Shoals
Alaska: 4 Nome **5** Kenai, Sitka **6** Barrow, Bethel, Kodiak, Valdez **9** Anchorage, Fairbanks, Ketchikan **11** Point Barrow
Albania: 4 Fier **5** Berat, Korçë, Kukës, Vlorë
Alberta: 4 Olds **5** Hanna, Leduc, Taber **7** Calgary **8** Edmonton **10** Lethbridge **11** Medicine Hat
Algeria: 4 Bône, Oran **5** Batna, Blida, Médéa, Saïda, Sétif **6** Annaba, Bechar **11** Constantine
Angola: 6 Huambo **7** Lubango **8** Benguela
Argentina: 4 Azul, Goya **5** Junin, Lanus, Lujan, Merlo, Salta, Tigre **6** Parana **7** Córdoba, La Plata, La Rioja, Mendoza, Rosario, San Juan, Santa Fe **9** Catamarca **11** Bahía Blanca, Mar del Plata
Arizona: 3 Ajo **4** Eloy, Mesa, Yuma **5** Globe, Tempe **6** Tucson **7** Sun City, Winslow **8** Glendale, Prescott **9** Flagstaff, Tombstone **10** Casa Grande, Scottsdale
Arkansas: 4 Mena **5** Beebe, Cabot, Earle, Ozark, Wynne **9** Fort Smith, Pine Bluff, Texarkana **10** Hot Springs
Armenia: 6 Gyumri **8** Vanadzor
Australia: 3 Ayr **5** Dalby, Dubbo, Perth, Unley **6** Darwin, Sydney **8** Adelaide, Brisbane, Randwick **9** Bankstown, Blacktown, Gold Coast, Melbourne, Newcastle **10** Kalgoorlie, Parramatta, Sutherland, Wollongong **12** Alice Springs
Austria: 4 Enns, Graz, Linz, Wels **5** Steyr, Traun **8** Salzburg **9** Innsbruck **10** Klagenfurt
Azerbaijan: 5 Gäncä **8** Sumqayit **9** Kirovabad
Bahamas: 8 Freeport
Bangladesh: 5 Bogra, Pabna **6** Khulna, Sylhet **7** Barisal, Comilla, Jessore, Rangpur, Saidpur **10** Chittagong
Belarus: 5 Brest, Gomel, Mozyr, Pinsk **6** Grodno, Homyel', Hrodna **7** Mogilev, Vitebsk **8** Babruysk, Mahilyow **9** Vitsyebsk
Belgium: 3 Ath, Hal, Huy, Mol **4** Amay, Dour, Geel, Genk, Gent, Hoei, Luik, Mons, Vise **5** Aalst, Arlon, Diest, Evere, Ghent, Halle, Ieper, Jumet, Leuze, Liège, Namur, Ronse, Theux, Wavre, Ypres **6** Bruges **7** Antwerp, Brugge, Hasselt, Louvain **8** Oostende **9** Charleroi

Benin: 5 Kandi **6** Abomey **7** Parakou
Bolivia: 5 Oruro, Uyuni **6** Potosí **9** Santa
Cruz **10** Cochabamba
Bosnia and Herzegovina: 5 Bihac, Brcko,
Jajce, Tuzla **6** Mostar, Zenica **9** Banja
Luka
Botswana: 4 Maun **5** Kanye
11 Francistown
Brazil: 4 Codo, Pará **5** Bahia, Bauru,
Belém, Ceara, Natal **6** Campos, Canoas,
Caxias, Ilheus, Maceio, Manaus, Olinda,
Recife, Santos **7** Aracaju, Caruaru,
Goiania, Jundiai, Marilia, Niteroi, Pelotas,
São Luis, Uberaba, Vitória **8** Campinas,
Caratinga, Fortaleza, Guarulhos, Rio
Grande **10** Guarapuava, Joao Pessoa,
Juiz de Fora, Nova Iguaçu, Pernambuco,
Petropolis, Piracicaba, Pôrto Velho, Santa
Maria, Santo André, São Gonçalo,
Uberlândia **11** Campo Grande, Caxias do
Sul, Ponta Grossa, Pôrto Alegre
12 Montes Claros, Rio de Janeiro, Teófilo
Otoni, Volta Redonda **13** Belo Horizonte,
Campina Grande, Duque de Caxias,
Florianopolis, Mogi das Cruzes, Riberião
Prêto
British Columbia: 5 Comox **6** Surrey
7 Burnaby **8** Richmond **9** Vancouver
Bulgaria: 3 Lom **4** Ruse **5** Varna, Vidin
6 Burgas **7** Plovdiv **11** Stara Zagora
California: 4 Brea, Galt, Lodi, Ojai
5 Arvin, Azusa, Ceres, Chico, Chino, Dixon,
Hemet, Indio, Norco, Ripon, Ukiah, Wasco,
Yreka **6** Downey, Encino, Fresno, Oxnard,
Pomona, Sonoma **7** Anaheim, Burbank,
Compton, Fremont, Hayward, Modesto,
Oakland, San Jose, Seaside, Soledad, Van
Nuys **8** Berkeley, Glendale, Palo Alto,
Pasadena, San Diego, Santa Ana,
Stockton, Torrance, Yuba City **9** El
Segundo, Hollywood, Long Beach, Menlo
Park, Riverside, Sausalito **10** Chula Vista,
Culver City, Los Angeles, San Leandro,
Santa Clara **11** Bakersfield, Laguna
Beach, Pebble Beach, Redwood City, San
Clemente, Santa Monica **12** Beverly Hills,
Mission Viejo, Redondo Beach, San
Francisco, Santa Barbara **13** San Bernar-
dino, San Luis Obispo
Cambodia: 8 Siem Reap **10** Battambang
11 Kompong Cham
Cameroon: 4 Buea, Edea **5** Kribi, Lomie
6 Douala **7** Bamenda, Foumban
9 Bafoussam
Canada: 4 York **5** Banff **6** London,
Oshawa, Ottawa, Regina, St. John
7 Brandon, Burnaby, Calgary, Halifax,

Iqaluit, Red Deer, St. John's, Sudbury,
Toronto, Windsor **8** Hamilton, Montreal,
Moose Jaw, North Bay, Saint John,
Victoria, Winnipeg **9** Dartmouth, Kitchener,
Longueuil, North York, Saint John,
Saskatoon, Vancouver **10** Lethbridge,
Saint John's, Sherbrooke, Thunder Bay,
Whitehorse **11** Fredericton, Medicine Hat,
Mississauga, Scarborough, Yellowknife
12 Peterborough, Prince Albert, Prince
George **13** Charlottetown, Trois-Rivières
Central African Republic: 5 Bouar
7 Bambari
Chad: 4 Sarh **6** Abéché
Chile: 4 Lebu, Lota, Tomé **5** Ancud,
Angol, Arica, Maipu, Penco, Rengo, Talca
6 Temuco **7** Copiapó, Iquique **8** Rancagua
10 Concepción, Talcahuano, Valparaíso
11 Antofagasta
China: 4 Amoy, Jian, Luan, Xi'an, Yaan
5 Hefei, Jilin, Jinan, Lhasa, Qinan, Ssuan,
Wuhan, Yibin, Yumen **6** Andong, Anqing,
Anshan, Anxian, Anyang, Beihai, Canton,
Dalian, Datong, Foshan, Fushun, Fuzhou,
Guilin, Haikou, Handan, Harbin, Hohhot,
Hoihao, Jilong, Luzhou, Mukden, Ningbo,
Pengbu, Suzhou, Urümqi, Xiamen, Xining,
Xuzhou, Yanggu, Yichun, Yining, Zhangi,
Zhaoan **7** Baoding, Changan, Chengdu,
Dandong, Guiyang, Huainan, Jiamusi,
Jiaxing, Kaifeng, Kunming, Lanzhou,
Luoshan, Luoyang, Nanking, Nanjing,
Nanning, Shantou, Tianjin, Taiyuan,
Wanxian, Weifang, Yizhang, Zhuzhou
8 Changchi, Changsha, Dangshan,
Hangzhou, Hanzhong, Hengyang,
Huangshi, Jiangmen, Jiujiang, Kueiyang,
Liaoyang, Nanchang, Shanghai, Shangrao,
Shaoyang, Shenyang, Tianshui, Ürümqi,
Yinchuan, Zhenjing **9** Changchun,
Chenjiang, Chongqing, Chungking,
Guangzhou, Huangshih, Zhengzhou,
Zhenjiang **10** Jingdezhen, Laojunmiao
11 Qinhuangdao, Zhangjiakou
Colombia: 4 Buga, Cali **5** Bello, Mocoa,
Neiva, Ocaña, Pasto, Tuluá, Tunja
6 Cúcuta, Ibagué **7** Ciénaga, Palmira,
Pereira, Popayán **8** Medellín, Montería
9 Cartagena, Manizales **10** Santa Marta
11 Bucaramanga **12** Barranquilla
Colorado: 6 Arvada, Aurora, Golden,
Salida **7** Alamosa, Boulder, Durango,
Greeley, La Junta **8** Brighton, Gunnison,
Lakewood, Longmont, Loveland, Montrose,
Thornton **9** Englewood, Estes Park,
Leadville, Littleton, Rocky Ford, Telluride
10 Broomfield, Castle Rock, Fort Lupton,
Fort Morgan, Monte Vista, Northglenn,

Wheat Ridge **11** Fort Collins **13** Grand
Junction
Congo (Zaire): 4 Boma **6** Bukavu
7 Kolwezi **8** Bandundu **9** Kisangani
10 Lubumbashi **12** Stanleyville
Congo-Brazzaville: 11 Pointe-Noire
Connecticut: 5 Byram **6** Darien, Easton,
Granby, Groton, Haddam **7** Ansonia,
Bethany, Danbury, Enfield, Meriden,
Milford, Newtown, Niantic, Norwalk,
Norwich, Old Lyme, Pomfret, Windham
8 Branford, Cromwell, East Lyme, Guilford,
New Haven, Simsbury, Stamford, Suffield,
Westport **9** Greenwich, New Canaan,
Newington, New London, Rocky Hill,
Southbury, Waterbury, Waterford
10 Bridgeport, Brookfield, East Haddam,
Farmington, Kensington, Litchfield, New
Britain, New Milford, North Haven,
Plainville, Ridgefield, Stonington, Torrington
11 Beacon Falls, Glastonbury, Middlefield,
Old Saybrook, Southington, Wallingford,
Willimantic **12** Wethersfield
Costa Rica: 8 Alajuela **10** Puntarenas
11 Puerto Limón
Croatia: 4 Pula **5** Sisak, Split, Zadar
6 Osijek, Rijeka, Zagreb **9** Dubrovnik
Cuba: 5 Banes, Bauta **6** Bayamo
7 Holguín **8** Camagüey, Marianao,
Matanzas, Santiago **10** Cienfuegos,
Guantánamo **11** Pinar del Río
Cyprus: 7 Kyrenia, Larnaca, Nicosia
8 Limassol **9** Famagusta
Czech Republic: 4 Brno, Zlín **5** Plzen
7 Liberec, Olomouc, Ostrava **10** Bratislava
Delaware: 6 Lewes **7** Seaford
10 Harrington, Wilmington, Winterthur
Denmark: 5 Arhus, Skive, Vejle **6** Alborg,
Odense, Viborg **13** Frederiksberg
Dominican Republic: 4 Azua, Bani, Moca
5 Bonao, Nagua **8** Barahona, Santiago
Ecuador: 4 Loja **5** Canar, Daule, Manta,
Pinas **7** Machala **8** Riobamba
9 Guayaquil
Egypt: 4 Giza, Idfu, Isna, Qena **5** Aswan,
Asyut, Benha, Disuq, Girga, Luxor, Minuf,
Tahta, Tanta **6** Helwan **7** El Arish, Zagazig
8 Damanhur, Damietta, El Faiyum, Ismailia,
Port Said **10** Alexandria
Eire: 4 Athy, Birr, Cobh, Cork, Naas, Tuam
5 Ennis, Sligo **6** Carlow, Galway, Tralee
7 Dundalk, Kildare, Wexford, Wicklow
8 Drogheda, Kilkenny, Limerick, Monaghan
9 Castlebar, Killarney, Tipperary, Waterford
10 Balbriggan
El Salvador: 7 La Unión **8** Santa Ana
9 Sonsonate
England: 4 Bath, Eton, Hove, Ryde, York
5 Brent, Brigg, Colne, Corby, Cowes,

Derby, Dover, Egham, Eling, Esher, Eston,
Goole, Leeds, Leigh, Lewes, Luton, Poole,
Ryton, Wigan **6** Bexley, Bolton, Dudley,
Durham, Exeter, Merton, Oldham, Oxford,
Torbay, Warley, Welwyn **7** Bristol, Bromley,
Croydon, Hackney, Ipswich, Malvern,
Norwich, Salford, Seaford, Walsall
8 Abingdon, Basildon, Bradford, Brighton,
Coventry, Hastings, Hatfield, Havering,
Hertford, Kingston, Lewisham, Plymouth,
Wallsend **9** Aylesbury, Blackpool,
Cambridge, Islington, Leicester, Liverpool,
Newcastle, Sheffield, Stratford,
10 Birkenhead, Birmingham, Canterbury,
Colchester, Manchester, Nottingham,
Portsmouth, Sunderland **11** Bournemouth,
Northampton, Southampton **12** Peter-
borough, Stoke-on-Trent, West Bromwich
13 Southend-on-Sea, Wolverhampton
Estonia: 5 Narva, Pärnu, Tartu
Ethiopia: 5 Aksum, Harer **6** Nazret
8 Dire Dawa
Finland: 4 Kemi, Oulu, Pori **5** Espoo,
Hango, Kotka, Lahti, Rauma, Turku, Vaasa
6 Vantaa **7** Tampere
Florida: 5 Largo, Miami, Ocala, Ocoee,
Oneco, Tampa **6** DeLand, Naples
7 Hialeah, Key West, Orlando, Sebring
8 Gulfport, Key Largo, Lakeland, Opa-
Locka, Sarasota **9** Boca Raton, Bradenton,
Fort Myers, Hollywood, Kissimmee, Palm
Beach, Pensacola, Vero Beach
10 Clearwater, Cocoa Beach, Fort Pierce,
Miami Beach, Punta Gorda, Titusville
11 Coral Gables, Gainesville, Key
Biscayne, St. Augustine, Winter Haven
12 Apalachicola, Daytona Beach, Ft.
Lauderdale, Jacksonville, Pompano Beach,
St. Petersburg **13** Chattahoochee
France: 3 Dax, Pau **4** Agde, Agen, Albi,
Ales, Auch, Caen, Gien, Laon, Lyon, Metz,
Nice, Orly, Rezé, Sens, Sète, Vire **5** Arles,
Arras, Auray, Auton, Avion, Berck, Blois,
Bondy, Brest, Creil, Digne, Dijon, Douai,
Dreux, Flers, Gagny, Laval, Le Puy, Lille,
Lunel, Lyons, Mâcon, Meaux, Melun,
Muret, Nîmes, Niort, Noyon, Reims, Revin,
Rodez, Rouen, Royan, Tours, Tulle, Vichy,
Vitre **6** Amiens, Angers, Calais, Cannes,
Dieppe, Evreux, Le Mans, Nantes, Nevers,
Rennes, Rheims, Thiers, Toulon, Troyes
7 Ajaccio, Antibes, Avignon, Béthune,
Bourges, Le Havre, Limoges, Lorient,
Lourdes, Orléans, Roubaix **8** Beauvais,
Besançon, Biarritz, Bordeaux, Chartres,
Gentilly, Grenoble, Nanterre, Poitiers,
Toulouse **9** Cherbourg, Dunkerque, Le
Creusot, Marseille, Montreuil, Perpignan
10 Draguignan, Marseilles, Strasbourg,

Versailles **11** Carcassonne, Montpellier **12** Saint-Etienne **13** Aix-en-Provence

Gabon: 4 Oyem **8** Bitam **10** Port-Gentil **11** Franceville

Gambia: 9 Serekunda

Georgia: 4 Adel, Alma, Arco **5** Jesup, Macon, McRae **6** Albany, Athens **7** Augusta, Calhoun **8** Americus, Columbus, Marietta, Savannah, Valdosta **9** Brunswick

Georgia, Republic of: 6 Batumi **7** Kutaisi, Rustavi, Sukhumi

Germany: 3 Aue, Hof, Ulm **4** Bonn, Gera, Goch, Hamm, Jena, Kehl, Kiel, Köln, Marl, Suhl **5** Aalen, Ahlen, Borna, Bruhl, Calbe, Celle, Düren, Emden, Essen, Forst, Fulda, Furth, Gotha, Greiz, Hagen, Halle, Hanau, Herne, Hurth, Kleve, Lemgo, Lobau, Mainz, Neuss, Peine, Pirna, Riesa, Stade, Thale, Trier, Wesel, Zeitz **6** Aachen, Bremen, Coburg, Dachau, Dessau, Erfurt, Kassel, Lübeck, Munich, Rheydt **7** Cologne, Cottbus, Dresden, Hamburg, Hanover, Koblenz, Krefeld, Leipzig, München, Munster, Potsdam, Rostock, Zwickau **8** Augsburg, Bayreuth, Chemnitz, Cuxhaven, Dortmund, Duisburg, Freiburg, Hannover, Mannheim, Nürnberg, Würzburg **9** Bielefeld, Brunswick, Darmstadt, Frankfurt, Göttingen, Karlsruhe, Magdeburg, Nuremberg, Offenbach, Oldenburg, Osnabrück, Remscheid, Stuttgart, Wiesbaden, Wuppertal **10** Baden-Baden, Düsseldorf, Heidelberg, Oberhausen, Regensburg, Salzgitter **11** Brandenburg, Bremerhaven, Saarbrücken **12** Braunschweig **13** Gelsenkirchen

Ghana: 4 Axim, Keta, Tema **5** Lawra, Yendi **6** Kumasi

Greece: 3 Kos **4** Arta **5** Argos, Lamia, Nemea, Volos **6** Sparta, Thebes **7** Corinth, Khalkis, Larissa, Piraeus, Tríkala **8** Salonika **12** Thessaloniki

Guatemala: 5 Cobán **13** Quezaltenango

Guinea: 4 Labé **5** Kankan, Kindia

Haiti: 8 Gonaïves **10** Cap Haitien

Hawaii: 4 Aiea, Hilo, Laie **5** Kapaa, Lihue, Maili **6** Kailua **7** Kaneohe, Waikiki, Wailuku

Honduras: 5 Danlí **7** La Ceiba **12** San Pedro Sula

Hong Kong: 7 Kowloon

Hungary: 3 Ozd **4** Eger, Györ, Pécs **5** Abony, Bekes **6** Szeged **7** Miskolc **8** Debrecen

Idaho: 4 Buhl **5** Nampa **6** Dubois, Moscow **7** Gooding, Payette, Rexburg **8** Caldwell **9** Blackfoot, Pocatello, Sandpoint, Sun Valley, Twin Falls **11** Coeur d' Alene, Grangeville **12** Mountain Home, Saint Anthony

Illinois: 6 DeKalb, Galena, Hardin, Joliet, Macomb, Moline, Paxton, Peoria, Skokie, Urbana **7** Chicago, Decatur, Glencoe, Oak Lawn, Oak Park, Tuscola, Watseka, Wheaton **8** Carthage, Evanston, Kankakee, La Grange, Monmouth, Rockford, Vandalia, Waukegan **9** Belvidere, Effingham, Galesburg, Park Ridge, Yorkville **10** Belleville, Carbondale, Carrollton, Des Plaines, Metropolis, Northbrook, Rock Island **11** Carlinville, Jerseyville, Lindenhurst, Murphysboro, Taylorville **12** Highland Park, Mount Carroll

India: 3 Mau **4** Agra, Ahwa, Bhuj, Durg, Gaya, Kota, Mhow, Pune, Puri, Rewa, Tonk, Ziro **5** Adoni, Aimer, Akola, Alwar, Arcot, Arrah, Banda, Barsi, Bidar, Bihar, Churu, Damoh, Delhi, Dewas, Eluru, Gonda, Jalna, Jammu, Karur, Miraj, Morvi, Nasik, Patan, Patna, Poona, Sagar, Satna, Sikar, Simla, Surat, Thana **6** Baroda, Bhopal, Bombay, Cochin, Guntur, Howrah, Indore, Jaipur, Jhansi, Kanpur, Madras, Meerut, Mysore, Nagpur, Raipur, Rajkot, Ranchi, Ujjain **7** Aligarh, Asansol, Belgaum, Bikaner, Burdwan, Cuttack, Gauhati, Gwalior, Jodhpur, Kurnool, Lucknow, Madurai, Mathura, Nellore, Patiala, Vellore **8** Amritsar, Bhatpara, Calcutta, Dehra Dun, Kolhapur, Ludhiana, Sholapur, Srinagar, Varanasi **9** Ahmadabad, Allahabad, Bangalore, Hyderabad **10** Ahmadnagar, Chandigarh, Trivandrum **11** Pondicherry

Indiana: 4 Gary **5** Berne, Paoli, Vevay **6** Delphi, Kokomo, Marlon, Muncie, Tipton **7** Bedford, Corydon, Elkhart, La Porte, Winamac **8** Bluffton, Kentland **9** Boonville, Fort Wayne, New Albany, Rushville, South Bend, Vincennes **10** Crown Point, Evansville, Logansport, Scottsburg, Terre Haute, Valparaiso **11** Bloomington, Greencastle, Noblesville, Shelbyville **12** Connersville, Lawrenceburg, Martinsville

Indonesia: 4 Pati **5** Ambon, Bogor, Garut, Kudus, Medan, Tegal, Turen **6** Batang, Kediri, Madiun, Malang, Manado, Padang **7** Bandung, Kendari **8** Semarang, Surabaja, Surabaya, Tjirebon **9** Palembang, Pontianak, Surakarta **10** Pekalongan **11** Tasikmalaja **12** Bandjarmasin

Iowa: 5 Onawa, Pella **6** Eldora, Harlan, Keokuk, Le Mars, Red Oak **7** Allison, Anamosa, Carroll, Clinton, Corydon,

Denison, Dubuque, Marengo, Osceola, Waverly **8** Clarinda, Ida Grove, Waterloo **9** Davenport, Fort Dodge, Indianola, Mason City, Muscatine, Oskaloosa, Sioux City, Storm Lake, West Union, Winterset **10** Emmetsburg, Rock Rapids, Spirit Lake **11** Cedar Rapids, Fort Madison **13** Council Bluffs

Iran: 3 Qom, Qum **4** Amul, Arak, Khoi, Sari, Yazd, Yezd **5** Ahvaz, Ahwaz, Babol, Rasht **6** Abadan, Meshed, Shiraz, Tabriz **7** Esfahan, Hamadan, Isfahan, Mashhad **9** Bakhtaran

Iraq: 3 Ana, Kut **4** Kufa **5** Al Kut, Amara, Basra, Erbil, Hilla, Mosul, Najaf, Rutba **6** Amarah, Hillah, Kirkuk, Ramadi, Rutbah **7** Falluja, Samarra **8** Fallujah, Nasiriya **9** Nasiriyah

Ireland: (see *Eire*, above)

Israel: 5 Afula, Haifa, Holon, Jaffa **7** Rehovot **8** Ashqelon, Nazareth, Ramat Gan **9** Beersheba

Italy: 4 Acri, Alba, Asti, Bari, Enna, Este, Fano, Gela, Iesi, Lodi, Lugo, Pisa **5** Adria, Agira, Anzio, Aosta, Arola, Cantù, Capua, Carpi, Crema, Cuneo, Eboli, Fermo, Fondi, Forlì, Gaeta, Genoa, Imola, Ivrea, Lecce, Lecco, Lucca, Massa, Melfi, Menfi, Milan, Monza, Padua, Parma, Prato, Siena, Turin **6** Ancona, Assisi, Foggia, Mantua, Milano, Modena, Naples, Napoli, Rimini, Torino, Venice, Verona **7** Bergamo, Bologna, Bolzano, Brescia, Catania, Firenze, Leghorn, Messina, Palermo, Perugia, Pescara, Potenza, Ravenna, Salerno, San Remo, Taranto, Trieste, Venezia **8** Brindisi, Cagliari, Florence, La Spezia, Piacenza, Siracusa, Syracuse

Ivory Coast: 6 Bouaké

Jamaica: 6 May Pen **10** Montego Bay

Japan: 3 Ina, Ise, Ito, Ota, Tsu, Ube, Uji, Yao **4** Ageo, Anan, Gifu, Hagi, Himi, Hofu, Iida, Joyo, Kaga, Kobe, Kofu, Kure, Miki, Mito, Naha, Nara, Noda, Oita, Otsu, Saga, Saku, Soka, Tosu, Ueda, Yono **5** Akita, Atami, Beppu, Chiba, Imari, Itami, Iwaki, Iwata, Izumi, Izumo, Kiryu, Kochi, Kyoto, Minoo, Odate, Ogaki, Okawa, Okaya, Omiya, Omuta, Osaka, Otaru, Oyama, Sabae, Saiki, Sakai, Sanjo, Suita, Tenri, Urawa **6** Akashi, Aomori, Himeji, Kadoma, Kurume, Matsue, Mitaka, Nagano, Nagoya, Numazu, Sasebo, Sendai, Suzuka, Toyama, Yonago **7** Fukuoka, Hitachi, Ibaraki, Imabari, Muroran, Niigata, Niihama, Nobeoka, Obihiro, Odawara, Okayama, Okazaki, Sapporo **8** Ashikaga, Fujisawa, Fukuyama, Hirakata, Hirosaki, Ichihara, Ichikawa, Kakogawa, Kamakura,

Kanazawa, Kawasaki, Miyazaki, Nagasaki, Onomichi, Shizuoka, Takasaki, Toyonaka, Wakayama, Yamagata, Yokohama, Yokosuka **9** Fukushima, Funabashi, Hiroshima, Kawaguchi, Yamaguchi, Yokkaichi

Jordan: 5 Aqaba, Irbid

Kansas: 4 Gove, Iola **5** Colby, Hoxie, Lakin, Leoti, Paola, Pratt **6** Atwood, Beloit, Girard, Holton, Salina **7** Abilene, Emporia, Garnett, Kinsley, Wichita **8** Cimarron, Goodland, La Crosse, Sublette **9** Coldwater, Fort Scott, Great Bend, Oskaloosa **10** Hutchinson **11** Leavenworth **12** Council Grove, Overland Park **13** Medicine Lodge

Kazakhstan: 6 Almaty, Aqtöbe, Guryev, Semey, Uralsk **7** Alma-Ata, Zhambyl **8** Balkhash, Chimkent, Dzhambul, Kyzl Orda, Pavlodar, Shymkent **9** Karaganda **10** Aktyubinsk

Kentucky: 4 Inez **5** Cadiz, Hyden, McKee **6** Elkton, Harlan **7** Ashland, Campton, Greenup, Hindman, Paducah, Stanton **8** Fort Knox, Mayfield **9** Bardstown, Covington, Cynthiana, Lexington, Maysville, Owensboro, Pikeville, Pineville, Southgate, Vanceburg **10** Booneville, Hawesville, Louisville, Whitesburg **11** Hardinsburg, Harrodsburg, Hodgenville, Leitchfield, Morganfield **12** Bowling Green

Kenya: 4 Embu **5** Nyeri **6** Kisumu, Nakuru **7** Mombasa

Kyrgyzstan: 3 Osh **5** Naryn

Laos: 5 Pakse **11** Savannakhet

Latvia: 7 Jelgava, Liepaja **9** Ventspils **10** Daugavpils

Lebanon: 4 Tyre **5** Sidon, Zahlé **7** Juniyah, Tripoli

Libya: 5 Homs **5** Derna, Zawia **6** Tobruk **8** Benghazi, Misratah

Lithuania: 6 Kaunas **8** Klaipeda

Louisiana: 4 Jena **5** Amite, Arabi, Houma, Mamou, Norco, Rayne **6** Colfax, Edgard, Gretna, Minden, Ruston **7** Arcadia, Bastrop, Marrero, Oberlin **8** Bogalusa, De Ridder, Metairie, New Roads, Oak Grove, Westwego **9** Abbeville, Chalmette, Hahnville, Leesville, New Iberia, Opelousas, Port Allen, Thibodaux, Winnfield, Winnsboro **10** New Orleans, Plaquemine, Shreveport **11** Lake Charles **12** Natchitoches

Macedonia: 6 Bitola, Prilep, Tetovo

Maine: 4 Saco **5** Orono **6** Auburn, Bangor, Gorham **7** Berwick, Kittery, Machias, Rumford **8** Lewiston, Portland, Rockland **9** Bar Harbor, Biddeford, Brunswick, Ellsworth, Kennebunk,

Skowhegan, Wiscasset **11** Millinocket, Presque Isle **13** Kennebunkport
Malawi: 5 Mzuzu, Zomba **8** Blantyre
Malaysia: 4 Ipoh **5** Gemas, Klang **6** Kelang, Penang, Pinang **11** Johore Bahru
Mali: 5 Kayes, Mopti, Ségou **7** Sikasso
Malta: 10 Birkirkara
Maryland: 5 Bowie **6** Denton, Elkton, Towson **8** Bethesda, Landover, Snow Hill **9** Baltimore, Rockville **10** Beltsville, Hagerstown **11** Chestertown, College Park, Leonardtown **12** Havre de Grace, Silver Spring
Massachusetts: 4 Ayer **5** Acton, Lenox, Salem **6** Agawam, Boston, Dedham, Lowell, Malden, Monson, Natick, Saugus, Woburn **7** Amherst, Danvers, Duxbury, Holyoke, Hyannis, Medford, Methuen, Needham, Swansea, Taunton, Walpole, Waltham, Wareham **8** Brockton, Chicopee, Falmouth, Plymouth, Rockport, Scituate, Yarmouth **9** Attleboro, Braintree, Brookline, Cambridge, Edgartown, Fall River, Fitchburg, Haverhill, Lexington, Nantucket, Southwick, Wilbraham, Worcester **10** Barnstable, Framingham, Gloucester, Greenfield, Leominster, New Bedford, North Adams, Pittsfield, Somerville, Swampscott **11** Northampton, Springfield **12** Mattapoisett, Provincetown, Williamstown
Mauritania: 4 Atar **5** Kaedi **6** Dakhla
Mexico: 4 León **5** Ameca, Choix, Tepic **6** Cancún, Celaya, Colima, Jalapa, Juárez, Mérida, Oaxaca, Puebla, Toluca, Tuxtla **7** Durango, Guasave, Morelia, Obregón, Reynosa, Tampico, Tijuana, Tlalpán, Torreón, Uruapan, Zapopan **8** Chetumal, Coyoacán, Culiacán, Ensenada, Mazatlan, Mexicali, Saltillo, Tuxtepec **9** Chihuahua, Fresnillo, Ixtacalco, Monterrey, Querétaro, Salamanca, Tapachula, Zacatecas **10** Cuernavaca, Hermosillo, Ixtapalapa, Xochimilco **11** Guadalajara, Nuevo Laredo **13** San Luis Potosí
Michigan: 4 Alma, Holt **5** Flint, Ionia, L'Anse, Niles **6** Otsego, Paw Paw, Warren **7** Allegan, Corunna, Detroit, Gladwin, Livonia, Midland, Saginaw **8** Ann Arbor, Bessemer, Dearborn, Escanaba, Grayling, Hastings, Houghton, Muskegon, Newberry, Petoskey, Sandusky **9** Cheboygan, Coldwater, Hillsdale, Kalamazoo, Menominee, Port Huron, Roscommon, Ypsilanti **10** Charlevoix, Grand Haven, West Branch, White Cloud **11** Battle Creek, Grand Rapids, Harrisville, Saint Ignace **12** Highland Park, Iron Mountain

Minnesota: 3 Ely **4** Mora **5** Anoka, Edina, Osseo **6** Aitkin, Benson, Duluth, Waseca, Windom, Winona **7** Glencoe, Hibbing, Mankato, Red Wing, St. Cloud, Wabasha **8** Brainerd, Elk River, Moorhead, Shakopee **9** Caledonia, Crookston, Faribault, Pipestone, Rochester, Saint Paul, Silver Bay **10** Park Rapids, Saint Cloud, Saint James, Saint Peter, Stillwater, Two Harbors **11** Bloomington, Fergus Falls, Long Prairie, Minneapolis, Worthington **12** Breckenridge, Granite Falls, Redwood Falls
Mississippi: 5 Iuka **6** Amory **6** Biloxi, Leland, McComb, Purvis, Sardis, Sumner, Tupelo, Winona **7** Belzoni, Brandon, Okolona, Quitman, Wiggins **8** Gulfport, Hernando, Meridian, Paulding, Rosedale, Walthall **9** Greenwood, Indianola, New Albany, Pittsboro, Vicksburg **10** Batesville, Booneville, Brookhaven, Clarksdale, Ellisville, Greenville, Hazlehurst, Pascagoula, Port Gibson, Starkville, Waynesboro **11** Coffeeville, Hattiesburg, Poplarville **12** Holly Springs
Missouri: 3 Ava **4** Linn **5** Eldon, Hayti, Ladue, Rolla **6** Galena, Neosho, Potosi **7** Hermann, Ironton, Kennett, Linneus, Osceola, Palmyra, Sedalia, St. Louis **8** Gallatin, Hannibal **9** Boonville, Hartville, Hillsboro, Maryville, Pineville, Tuscumbia, Warrenton **10** Kansas City, Kirksville, Marble Hill, Marshfield, Perryville, Saint Louis, Springfield, Steelville, Unionville, West Plains **11** Poplar Bluff, Saint Joseph, Warrensburg **12** Independence, Saint Charles
Moldova: 5 Balti **7** Tighina **8** Tiraspol
Mongolia: 5 Kobdo **6** Darhan **10** Choybalsan
Montana: 5 Butte, Havre, Libby **6** Hardin, Polson **8** Bozeman **8** Billings, Missoula, Red Lodge **10** Great Falls
Montenegro: 8 Titograd **9** Podgorica
Morocco: 3 Fès **4** Safi, Salé, Taza **5** Nador, Oujda **6** Agadir, Meknès **7** Kenitra, Tangier **9** Marrakech, Marrakesh **10** Casablanca
Mozambique: 5 Beira **7** Chimoio, Nampula **9** Quelimane, Quilimane
Myanmar: 3 Pyu **4** Paan **5** Akyab, Bhamo, Chauk, Katha, Magwe, Minbu, Mogok, Tavoy **7** Bassein **8** Mandalay, Moulmein
Namibia: 5 Outjo **6** Tsumeb **8** Oshakati **12** Keetmanshoop
Nebraska: 3 Ord **5** Cozad, Omaha, Ponca, Tryon, Wahoo **6** Elwood, Gering, McCook, Minden, Wilber **7** Burwell,

Fremont, Kearney, Kimball, Osceola, Tekamah **8** Beatrice, Fairbury, Hastings, Ogallala, Red Cloud, Schuyler, Tecumseh, Thedford **9** Fullerton, Papillion **10** Springview, Stockville **11** Grand Island, Hayes Center, North Platte, Plattsmouth
Netherlands: 3 Ede, Epe, Oss **4** Echt, Tiel, Uden **5** Aalst, Assen, Breda, Delft, Emmen, Hague, Soest, Vaals, Venlo, Vught, Weert, Weesp, Zeist **6** Arnhem **7** Haarlem, Tilburg, Utrecht **8** Enschede, Nijmegen, The Hague **9** Apeldoorn, Eindhoven, Groningen, Rotterdam, Zandvoort **10** Maastricht
Nevada: 3 Ely **4** Elko, Reno **6** Fallon, Minden, Pioche **7** Tonopah **8** Las Vegas, Lovelock **9** Goldfield, Yerington **10** Winnemucca
New Brunswick: 5 Minto **6** St. John **7** Moncton **9** Dalhousie, Saint John **10** Edmundston, Richibucto **12** Hopewell Cape, Perth Andover, Saint Andrews
Newfoundland: 5 Burin **6** Wabana **10** Mount Pearl **11** Corner Brook
New Hampshire: 5 Derry, Dover, Keene **6** Berlin, Exeter, Gorham, Nashua **7** Hanover, Laconia, Lebanon, Ossipee **8** Hinsdale, Seabrook **9** Littleton, Merrimack **10** Manchester, Portsmouth, Woodstock
New Jersey: 4 Atco, Lodi **6** Camden, Newark, Nutley, Rahway, Rumson **7** Bayonne, Cape May, Clifton, Hoboken, Paramus, Passaic, Raritan, Teaneck **8** Freehold, Metuchen, Paterson, Vauxhall, Woodbury **9** Belvidere, Bridgeton, Elizabeth, Glassboro, Lakehurst, Maplewood, Menlo Park, Montclair, Princeton, Riverside, Toms River **10** Asbury Park, Bloomfield, Cherry Hill, East Orange, Flemington, Hackensack, Jersey City, Morristown, Mount Holly, Perth Amboy, Piscataway, Plainfield, Somerville, West Orange **11** Mays Landing, South Orange **12** Atlantic City, New Brunswick **13** Palisades Park
New Mexico: 4 Taos **5** Belen, Hobbs, Raton **6** Clovis, Deming, Grants **7** Roswell, Socorro **8** Estancia, Los Lunas, Portales **9** Carrizozo, Las Cruces, Los Alamos, Lovington, Tucumcari **10** Alamogordo, Bernalillo, Fort Sumner **11** Albuquerque
New York: 4 Elma, Ovid, Troy **5** Depew, Ilion, Islip, Le Roy, Nyack, Olean, Owego, Utica **6** Attica, Cohoes, Delmar, Elmira, Hudson, Ithaca, Oneida **7** Batavia, Buffalo, Corning, Geneseo, Katonah, Mineola, Penn Yan, Suffern, Yonkers **8** Bay Shore,

Cortland, Herkimer, Hyde Park, Kingston, Lockport, Mayville, Ossining, Syracuse, Valhalla **9** Greenport, Hempstead, Patchogue, Riverhead, Rochester, Scarsdale, Schoharie **10** Binghamton, Glens Falls, Haverstraw, Huntington, Lackawanna, Lake George, Lake Placid, Mamaroneck, Massapequa, Mount Kisco, Plattsburg, Rensselaer, Watervliet **11** Canajoharie, Canandaigua, Cooperstown, Farmingdale, Hudson Falls, Plattsburgh, Port Chester, Saint George, Schenectady, Southampton, Watkins Glen, White Plains **12** Lake Pleasant, Poughkeepsie **13** Mechanicville, Port Jefferson
New Zealand: 4 Hutt, Tawa **5** Levin, Taupo, Waihi **7** Dunedin, Manukau **8** Auckland **12** Christchurch
Nicaragua: 4 León **5** Boaco, Rivas **6** Masaya **7** Granada
Nigeria: 3 Aba, Ado, Ede, Ife, Ila, Iwo, Jos, Owo, Oyo **4** Kano, Ondo **5** Akure, Enugu, Gusau, Lagos, Okene, Zaria **6** Ibadan, Ilesha, Ilorin, Kaduna, Mushin, Sokoto **7** Onitsha, Oshogbo **8** Abeokuta **9** Maiduguri, Ogbomosho **12** Port Harcourt
North Carolina: 4 Dunn **5** Ayden, Elkin, Erwin, Oteen, Sylva **6** Dobson, Durham, Lenoir, Manteo, Marlon, Shelby, Winton **7** Bayboro, Brevard, Edenton, Kinston, New Bern, Newland, Roxboro, Sanford, Tarboro **8** Asheboro, Beaufort, Gastonia, Hatteras, Snow Hill **9** Albemarle, Asheville, Charlotte, Currituck, High Point, Kitty Hawk, Louisburg, Lumberton, Morganton **10** Chapel Hill, Greensboro, Mocksville, Smithfield, Wilkesboro **11** Statesville, Yanceyville **12** Murfreesboro, Winston-Salem
North Dakota: 4 Mott **5** Cando, Fargo, Minot, Rolla **6** Amidon, Ashley, Bowman, Formon, Lakota, Linton, Medora, Mohall **8** Wahpeton, Washburn **9** Dickinson, Williston **10** Devils Lake, Grand Forks
Northern Ireland: 5 Derry, Larne, Newry, Omagh **6** Antrim, Armagh **9** Bally-mena, Coleraine, Craigavon, Dungannon **10** Ballymoney **11** Ballycastle, Downpatrick, Enniskillen, Londonderry **13** Carrickfergus
North Korea: 5 Haeju, Nampo **6** Wonsan **7** Hamhung, Kaesong, Sinuiju **8** Ch'ongjin, Kimchaek **9** P'yongyang
Northwest Territories: 6 Dawson **10** Whitehorse **11** Yellowknife
Norway: 4 Bodo **5** Hamar, Skien, Vardo **6** Bergen, Tromso **8** Kirkenes

9 Stavanger, Trondheim 10 Hammerfest
12 Kristiansand
Nova Scotia: 5 Digby 6 Pictou 7 Arichat,
Baddeck 8 Port Hood 9 Dartmouth,
Kentville, Lunenburg, Shelburne, Westville
10 Antigonish 11 Guysborough
Ohio: 4 Kent 5 Akron, Berea, Bryan,
Carey, Eaton, Heath, Logan, Niles, Parma,
Piqua, Solon, Xenia 6 Canton, Celina,
Dayton, Elyria, Euclid, Kenton, Lorain,
Marion, Medina, Sidney, Tiffin, Toledo
7 Ashland, Batavia, Bucyrus, Chardon,
Findlay, Ironton, Oakwood, Pomeroy,
Ravenna, Wauseon, Wooster 8 Conneaut,
Marietta, Sandusky 9 Ashtabula,
Cleveland, Coshocton, Mansfield
10 Cincinnati, Gallipolis, Wapakoneta,
Zanesville 11 Chillicothe, Circleville,
Millersburg, Mount Gilead, Painesville, Port
Clinton 12 Steubenville 13 Bellefontaine,
Cuyahoga Falls
Oklahoma: 3 Ada 4 Alva, Enid 5 Altus,
Atoka, Sayre, Tulsa 6 Durant, El Reno,
Guymon, Idabel, Lawton, Okemah, Poteau,
Wewoka 7 Antlers, Ardmore, Cordell,
Eufaula, Newkirk, Purcell, Sapulpa,
Watonga 8 Anadarko, Okmulgee,
Pawhuska, Sallisaw, Stilwell 9 Chickasha,
Claremore, Frederick, McAlester, Wilburton
10 Stillwater, Tishomingo 11 Pauls Valley
12 Bartlesville
Oman: 3 Sur 6 Matrah 7 Salalah
Ontario: 4 Ajax, Wawa, York 6 Barrie,
Guelph, Kenora, London, Oshawa, Sarnia,
Simcoe 7 Cobourg, Markham, Napanee,
Sudbury, Windsor 8 Brampton, Cochrane,
Goderich, Hamilton, North Bay, Pembroke,
Prescott 9 Brantford, Etobicoke, Kitchener,
L'Original, Newmarket, North York, Owen
Sound, Walkerton 10 Belleville, Brockville,
Burlington, Haileybury, Parry Sound,
Thunder Bay 11 Bracebridge, Fort
Frances, Mississauga, Scarborough
12 Peterborough, St. Catharines
Oregon: 5 Canby, Nyssa 6 Eugene
8 Coquille, La Grande, Portland, Roseburg
9 Clackamas, Corvallis, Gold Beach,
Pendleton, The Dalles, Tillamook
10 Grants Pass 12 Klamath Falls
Pakistan: 5 Bannu, Bhera, Kasur, Kohat
6 Gujrat, Lahore, Mardan, Multan, Quetta,
Sukkur 7 Karachi, Sialkot 8 Lyallpur,
Peshawar, Sargodha 9 Hyderabad
10 Bahawalpur, Faisalabad, Gujranwala,
Rawalpindi
Paraguay: 3 Itá 4 Yuty 5 Luque, Pilar
7 Caacupé, Caazapa 9 Paraguarí 10 San
Lorenzo

Papua New Guinea: 3 Lae 10 Mount
Hagen, Popondetta
Pennsylvania: 4 Erie, York 5 Avoca,
Darby, Muncy, Paoli 6 Easton 7 Altoona,
Bedford, Clarion, Hanover, Hershey,
Latrobe, Reading, Ridgway, Sunbury
8 Carlisle, Edinboro, Hazleton, Montrose,
Scranton, Somerset 9 Allentown,
Ebensburg, Honesdale, Jim Thorpe,
Lancaster, Lewisburg, Lock Haven,
Meadville, New Castle, Wellsboro
10 Bloomsburg, Brookville, Carbondale,
Clearfield, Gettysburg, Greensburg,
Huntingdon, Kittanning, McKeesport,
Middleburg, Pittsburgh, Pottsville,
Waynesburg 11 Stroudsburg, Valley
Forge, West Chester, Wilkes-Barre
12 Philadelphia, State College,
Williamsport
Peru: 3 Ica, Ilo 5 Ancon, Cuzco, Jauja,
Junin, Lamas, Pisco, Piura, Tacna 6 Callao
8 Arequipa, Chiclayo, Chimbote, Trujillo
Philippines: 3 Iba 4 Bago, Bais, Boac,
Bogo, Cebu, Daet, Jolo, Lipa, Mati
5 Basco, Bulan, Cadiz, Danao, Davao,
Digos, Gapan, Gubat, Iriga, Laoag, Ormoc,
Pasay, Silay, Tagum, Vigan 6 Butuan,
Iloilo, Quezon 7 Angeles, Bacolod, Basilan
8 Batangas, Calbayog, Caloocan 9 Zam-
boanga 10 Quezon City
Poland: 4 Lodz, Nysa, Pila, Zary
5 Bytom, Bytow, Chelm, Kutno, Lomza,
Luban, Lubin, Plock, Radom, Torun, Tychy
6 Elblag, Gdansk, Gdynia, Kalisz, Kielce,
Krakow, Lublin, Poznan, Rybnik, Zabrze
7 Chorzow, Dabrowa, Gliwice, Rzeszow,
Wroclaw 8 Gornicza, Katowice, Szczecin
9 Bialystok, Bydgoszcz, Sosnowiec,
Walbrzych 11 Czestochowa
Portugal: 4 Faro 5 Braga, Evora, Porto
6 Almada, Oporto, Queluz 7 Amadora
8 Barreiro, Santarém
Prince Edward Island: 10 Summerside
Puerto Rico: 5 Ponce 6 Caguas
7 Arecibo, Bayamón 8 Carolina,
Guaynabo, Mayagüez
Quebec: 4 Alma 5 Amqui, Anjou, Gaspé,
Laval, Lévis, Magog, Percé, Rouyn
6 Granby, Ham Sud, Matane, Ste.-Foy, Val
d'Or 7 Bedford, Lachute 8 Beauport, Cap
Santé, Joliette, Lac Brome, Maniwaki,
Montreal, Rimouski, Roberval, Sept-Iles,
Waterloo 9 Bécancour, Cookshire,
Iberville, Inverness, La Malbaie, La Prairie,
Longueuil, Montmagny, Sainte-Foy, Saint
Jean, Tadoussac, Vaudreuil 10 Baie-
Comeau, Chicoutimi 11 Beauharnois,
Louiseville, Mont-Laurier 12 Charlesbourg
13 Trois-Rivières

Rhode Island: 7 Newport, Rumford, Warwick 8 Apponaug, Coventry, Cranston, Tiverton, Westerly 9 Hopkinton, Pawtucket 10 Woonsocket 12 Narragansett, West Kingston

Romania: 3 Dej 4 Aiud, Arad, Cluj, Deva, Husi, Iasi 5 Anina, Bacau, Buzau, Carei, Lugoj, Sibiu, Turda 6 Braila, Brasov, Galati, Oradea 7 Craiova 8 Ploiesti 9 Constanta, Timisoara 10 Cluj-Napoca

Russia: 3 Kem, Ufa 4 Inta, Luga, Okha, Omsk, Orel, Orsk, Perm, Tula, Tura, Zima 5 Aldan, Artem, Chita, Ishim, Kansk, Kazan, Lysva, Onega, Penza, Pskov, Rzhev, Salsk, Serov, Sochi, Sokol, Tomsk, Tulun, Volsk, Yurga 6 Bratsk, Grozny, Kaluga, Kovrov, Kurgan, Rostov, Ryazan, Samara, Syzran, Tambov, Tyumen, Vyborg, Yelets 7 Irkutsk, Ivanovo, Izhevsk, Kalinin, Kolomna, Lipetsk, Magadan, Norilsk, Rybinsk, Saransk, Saratov, Shakhty, Vologda, Yakutsk, Zhdanov 8 Belgorod, Kemerovo, Kostroma, Murmansk, Nakhodka, Voronezh 8 Novgorod, Orenburg, Smolensk, Taganrog, Vladimir, Voronezh 9 Archangel, Astrakhan, Berezniki, Krasnodar, Serpukhov, Stavropol, Ulyanovsk, Volgograd, Yaroslavl 10 Cheboksary, Dzerzhinsk 11 Arkhangel'sk, Chelyabinsk, Cheremkhovo, Cherepovets, Kaliningrad, Krasnoyarsk, Novosibirsk, St. Petersburg, Vladivostok 13 Yekaterinburg

Saskatchewan: 8 Moose Jaw 9 Saskatoon 10 Assiniboia 12 Prince Albert

Saudi Arabia: 4 Jauf, Taif 5 Jedda, Jidda, Mecca, Tabuk 6 Jeddah, Jiddah, Medina 8 Buraydah

Scotland: 3 Ayr 4 Alva, Caol, Dyce, Oban 5 Alloa, Annan, Beith, Cowie, Cupar, Dalry, Ellon, Kelso, Kelty, Largs, Leven, Nairn, Patna, Troon 6 Dundee 7 Glasgow, Paisley 8 Aberdeen, Greenock, Hamilton 9 Inverness, Lockerbie 10 Kilmarnock 11 Dunfermline, John o'Groats

Senegal: 5 Thiès 6 Kaolak 7 Kaolack 10 Saint-Louis

Serbia: 3 Bor, Nis, Pec 4 Ruma 5 Becej, Cacak, Pirot, Sabac, Senta, Vrbas, Vrsac 7 Novi Sad 8 Subotica 10 Kragujevac

Slovakia: 5 Nitra 6 Kosice, Presov, Zilina

Slovenia: 4 Bled 5 Celje, Koper, Kranj 7 Maribor

Somalia: 3 Eil 5 Afgoi, Alula, Brava, Burao, Marka, Obbia 7 Berbera, Kismayu 8 Hargeysa, Kismaayo

South Africa: 5 Brits, Ceres, De Aar, Nigel, Paarl 6 Benoni, Durban, Soweto 7 Springs 8 Boksburg, Mafeking 9 Germiston, Kimberley, Ladysmith, Uitenhage 10 East London 11 Krugersdorp, Vereeniging 12 Johannesburg 13 Port Elizabeth

South Carolina: 5 Aiken, Cayce, Saxon 6 Sumter 7 Gaffney, Laurens, Manning, Pickens 8 Beaufort, Newberry, Rock Hill, Walhalla 9 Abbeville, Allendale, Greenwood, Kingstree, McCormick, Winnsboro 10 Charleston, Darlington, Greenville, Hilton Head, Orangeburg, Walterboro 11 Bishopville, Myrtle Beach, Spartanburg 12 Moncks Corner

South Dakota: 7 Sturgis, Yankton 8 Deadwood, Elk Point 9 Brookings, Rapid City 10 Sioux Falls

South Korea: 3 Iri 4 Yosu 5 Cheju, Masan, Mokpo, Pusan, Suwon, Taegu, Ulson, Wonju 6 Chinju, Chonju, Inchon, Kunsan, Taejon 7 Kwangju

Spain: 4 Adra, Baza, Elda, Jaca, Jaén, León, Loja, Lugo, Olot, Reus, Vich, Vigo 5 Albox, Alcoy, Alora, Baena, Cádiz, Ceuta, Cieza, Ecija, Eibar, Elche, Gijón, Ibiza, Jodar, Lorca, Mahon, Oliva, Osuna, Palma, Ronda, Soria, Ubeda 6 Bilbao, Burgos, Cuenca, Huelva, Lérida, Málaga, Mérida, Murcia, Oviedo, Toledo 7 Almadén, Almería, Cáceres, Córdoba, Durango, Granada, Segovia, Sevilla, Seville, Tarrasa, Vitoria 8 Albacete, Alicante, La Coruña, Pamplona, Sabadell, Valencia, Zaragoza 9 Algeciras, Barcelona, Salamanca, Santander, Saragossa, Tarragona 10 Hospitalet, Valladolid 12 San Sebastián

Sri Lanka: 5 Galle, Kandy 6 Jaffna 8 Dehiwala, Moratuwa 10 Batticaloa

Sudan: 4 Juba 5 Kodok, Kosti 7 El Obeid, Kassala 8 Omdurman

Sweden: 4 Lund, Täby, Umea 5 Falun, Gävle, Lulea, Malmö, Växjö, Visby 6 Orebro 7 Uppsala 8 Göteborg, Halmstad 9 Jönköping, Linköping 12 Kristianstad

Switzerland: 3 Zug 4 Biel, Chur, Sion, Thun 5 Aarau, Arbon, Baden, Basel, Koniz 6 Geneva, Lugano, St. Gall, Zürich 7 Lucerne, Zermatt 8 Lausanne, Montreux, St. Moritz 9 Neuchâtel, Saint Gall 11 Saint Moritz

Syria: 4 Hama, Homs 5 Idlib 6 Aleppo, Tartus 7 Latakia

Taiwan: 5 Chia-i 6 T'ai-nan 7 Chi-lung, Hsin-chu 8 Feng-shan, Pan-ch'iao, San-ch'ung, T'ai-chung 9 Kao-hsiung

Tanzania: 5 Lindi, Mbeya, Tanga 6 Arusha, Dodoma, Kigoma, Mwanza 8 Morogoro, Zanzibar 11 Dar es Salaam

Tennessee: 5 Alcoa, Erwin, Rives
6 Loudon, Ripley, Selmer 7 Memphis,
Waverly 8 Gallatin, Oak Ridge, Rutledge,
Tazewell, Wartburg 9 Dandridge,
Dyersburg, Jacksboro, Jonesboro,
Knoxville, Lewisburg, Maryville
10 Cookeville, Crossville, Somerville,
Waynesboro 11 Blountville, Chattanooga,
Clarksville, Greeneville, McMinnville,
Rogersville, Sevierville, Shelbyville 12 Eli-
zabethton, Lawrenceburg, Madisonville,
Murfreesboro

Texas: 4 Azle, Waco 5 Alvin, Anson,
Baird, Bowie, Bryan, Clute, Cuero, Emory,
Ennis, Freer, Hondo, Marfa, Mexia, Olney,
Pampa, Pecos, Pharr, Plano, Sealy, Vidor,
Wylie 6 Belton, Boerne, Bonham, Burnet,
Conroe, Dallas, Del Rio, Denton, El Paso,
Gilmer, Goliad, Jayton, Lamesa, Laredo,
Linden, Lufkin, Odessa, Seguin, Sinton,
Uvalde 7 Abilene, Anahuac, Bandera,
Bastrop, Brenham, Denison, Dimmitt,
Houston, Kaufman, Kountze, Lubbock,
Midland, Wharton 8 Amarillo, Angleton,
Beaumont, Beeville, Cleburne, Eastland,
Giddings, Gonzales, Granbury, Groveton,
Hemphill, La Grange, Lampasas,
Longview, McKinney, Monahans,
Montague, Pearsall, Rockwall, Stinnett
9 Arlington, Ballinger, Bellville, Big Spring,
Brownwood, Corsicana, Crosbyton, Eagle
Pass, Fort Worth, Galveston, Groesbeck,
Henrietta, Hillsboro, Kerrville, Levelland,
Palo Pinto, Plainview, San Angelo, San
Marcos, Woodville 10 Brownfield,
Coldspring, Gatesville, Jourdanton,
Kingsville, Port Arthur, Port Lavaca, San
Antonio, Sweetwater, Waxahachie
11 Brownsville, Floresville, Littlefield,
Nacogdoches, Weatherford 12 Brecken-
ridge, Daingerfield, Fort Stockton, New
Braunfels, Raymondville, Stephenville,
Wichita Falls 13 Corpus Christi,
Hallettsville

Thailand: 3 Nan, Tak 5 Phrae, Roi Et,
Surin 8 Songkhla 9 Chiang Mai
10 Nonthaburi

Tunisia: 4 Béja, Sfax 5 Gabès, Gafsa,
Susah 6 Ariana 7 Bizerte, Safaqis

Turkey: 5 Adana, Bursa, Izmir, Konya,
Sivas 6 Edirne, Erzurum, Samsun
7 Antakya, Antalya, Antioch, Kayseri,
Malatya 8 Istanbul 9 Eskisehir, Gallipoli,
Gaziantep 10 Diyarbakir

Turkmenistan: 8 Nebit Dag 9 Chardzhou,
Dashhowuz

Uganda: 3 Jinja, Mbale 7 Entebbe

Ukraine: 4 Lviv, Lvov, Sumy 5 Lutsk,
Rovno, Yalta 6 Odessa 7 Donetsk,
Kharkiv, Kharkov, Kherson, Luhansk,
Poltava 8 Mariupol, Vinnitsa, Zhitomir
9 Chernigov, Chernobyl, Krivoy Rog, Krivyy
Rih, Nikolayev 10 Kirovograd, Sebastopol,
Sevastopol, Simferopol, Zaporozhye

United Arab Emirates: 5 Ajman, Dubai
6 Dubayy 8 Fujairah, Fujayrah

Uruguay: 4 Melo 5 Minas, Pando, Rocha,
Salto 6 Rivera 8 Paysandú 10 Las
Piedras

Utah: 3 Loa 4 Lehi, Orem 5 Manti,
Ogden, Provo, Sandy 6 Dugway, Tooele
7 Parowan 8 Duchesne 9 Coalville
11 Saint George

Uzbekistan: 5 Nukus 6 Kokand
7 Bukhara, Fergana 8 Andizhan, Chirchik,
Namangan 9 Samarkand, Samarqand

Venezuela: 4 Coro 5 Anaco, Cagua
6 Cumaná, Mérida, Petare 7 Cabimas,
Guayana, Maracay 8 Valencia
9 Maracaibo 12 Barquisimeto, San
Cristóbal

Vermont: 5 Barre 7 Rutland 8 St. Albans
10 Bennington, Burlington, Middlebury
11 Brattleboro, Saint Albans, St. Johnsbury

Vietnam: 3 Hue 4 Vinh 5 Da Lat, Hoi An,
My Tho 6 Can Tho, Da Nang, Saigon
7 Bien Hoa, Nam Dinh, Qui Nhon
8 Haiphong, Nha Trang, Thanh Hoa
9 Long Xuyen

Virginia: 4 Tabb 5 Luray 6 Grundy
7 Accomac, Boydton, Fairfax, Hampton,
New Kent, Norfolk 8 Abingdon, Culpeper,
Leesburg, Manassas, Montross, Nottoway,
Poquoson, Powhatan, Rustburg, Tazewell
9 Arlington, Clintwood, Courtland,
Dinwiddie, Eastville, Farmville, Fincastle,
Goochland, Lunenburg, Lynchburg
10 Alexandria, Appomattox, Berryville,
Front Royal, Hillsville, Jonesville, King
George, Lovingston, Pearisburg,
Portsmouth, Rocky Mount, Wytheville
11 Heathsville, King William, Newport
News 12 Chesterfield, Prince George,
Spotsylvania, Williamsburg

Wales: 4 Rhyl 5 Neath, Risca, Tenby,
Tywyn 7 Cardiff, Cwmbran, Denbigh,
Harlech, Newport, Swansea 8 Aberdare,
Bridgend 10 Caernarfon, Caernarvon,
Llangollen 11 Aberystwith

Washington: 4 Omak 5 Brier, Camas,
Kelso, Lacey, Pasco, Selah 6 Asotin,
Colfax, Tacoma, Yakima 7 Ephrata,
Everett, Prosser, Redmond, Seattle,
Spokane 8 Bellevue, Chehalis, Colville,
Okanogan 9 Montesano, Ritzville,
Snohomish, Wenatchee 10 Bellingham,
Coupeville, Ellensburg, Goldendale, Walla

Walla, Waterville **11** Port Angeles, Port Orchard **12** Friday Harbor, Port Townsend
West Virginia: 5 Nitro, Welch **6** Elkins, Hamlin, Hinton, Keyser, Ripley **7** Beckley, Weirton **8** Kingwood, Philippi, Wheeling **9** Pineville, Wellsburg **10** Buckhannon, Clarksburg, Huntington, Moorefield, Morgantown, Petersburg, Williamson **11** Harrisville, Martinsburg, Moundsville, Parkersburg **12** Harpers Ferry, Summersville **13** New Cumberland, Point Pleasant
Wisconsin: 4 Kiel **5** Ripon, Tomah **6** Antigo, Barron, Oconto, Racine, Wausau **7** Baraboo, Chilton, Elkhorn, Hayward, Kenosha, Mauston, Merrill, Oshkosh, Shawano, Viraqua, Waupaca, Wautoma **8** Appleton, Green Bay, Kewaunee, La Crosse, Montello, Phillips, Washburn, Waukesha, West Bend **9** Eau Claire, Ellsworth, Fond du Lac, Green Lake, Ladysmith, Manitowoc, Marinette, Menomonie, Milwaukee, Sheboygan, Shell Lake, Wauwatosa, West Allis, Whitehall **10** Balsam Lake, Darlington, Dodgeville, Eagle River, Grantsburg, Janesville **11** Neillsville, Sturgeon Bay **12** Stevens Point, Whitefish Bay
Wyoming: 6 Casper, Lander **7** Laramie, Rawlins **8** Gillette, Kemmerer, Sheridan **10** Green River **11** Rock Springs
Yemen: 4 Aden **5** Taizz **7** Hodeida, Mukalla **8** Hudaydah
Zambia: 5 Kabwe, Kitwe, Mansa, Mbala, Mongu, Ndola **6** Kasama **7** Chipata
Zimbabwe: 5 Gweru **6** Hwange, Kadoma, Kwekwe, Mutare, Umtali **7** Mashava **8** Bulawayo, Masvingo

civet
3 cat
Madagascar: 5 fossa
relative: 5 genet

civic
5 urban **6** public, social **8** communal, national, societal **9** municipal

civil
6 polite, public, seemly, urbane **7** affable, cordial, courtly, genteel, refined **8** decorous, gracious, mannerly, national, obliging, well-bred **9** courteous, political **10** diplomatic **12** well-mannered **13** accommodating

civility
6 comity **7** amenity, decency, decorum, manners **8** courtesy **9** etiquette, gentility, propriety **10** politeness **11** correctness

civilization
7 culture

civilized
6 decent, proper, urbane **7** genteel, refined **8** decorous, mannerly, tasteful **9** courteous **10** cultivated **13** sophisticated

civil rights
leader: 4 King (Martin Luther)
organization: 4 ACLU, CORE **5** NAACP

Civil War
admiral: 8 Buchanan (Franklin), Farragut (David)
battle: 6 Shiloh **7** Bull Run **8** Antietam, Manassas **9** Mobile Bay, Nashville, Vicksburg **10** Cold Harbor, Gettysburg **11** Chattanooga, Chickamauga
general: 3 Lee (Robert E.) **4** Hood (John Bell), Pope (John) **5** Bragg (Braxton), Buell (Don Carlos), Ewell (Richard Stoddart), Grant (Ulysses S.), Meade (George), Sykes (George) **6** Hooker (Joseph) **7** Forrest (Nathan Bedford), Jackson (Thomas "Stonewall"), Sherman (Thomas West, William Tecumseh) **8** Burnside (Ambrose), Johnston (Albert Sidney, Joseph Eggleston), Sheridan (Philip) **9** McClellan (George Brinton), Rosecrans (William), Schofield (John) **10** Beauregard (Pierre)
ship: 7 Monitor **9** Merrimack

civil wrong
4 tort

clabber
5 curds

clack
3 gab, jaw, yak **4** blab, chat **5** prate **6** babble, cackle, gabble, gossip, jabber, rattle **7** blabber, chatter, clatter, palaver, prattle **9** yakety-yak

clad
4 face, side, skin **5** dress, faced **6** clothe, decked, garbed, outfit **7** attired, clothed, covered, dressed, overlay, sheathe **8** costumed, overlaid, sheathed **9** outfitted

claim
4 call, dibs, hold, plea, take **5** argue, exact, right, share, stake, title **6** adduce, allege, assert, defend, demand, insist **7** advance, call for, contend, declare, justify, profess, purport, require, solicit, warrant **8** interest, maintain **9** assertion, challenge, postulate, privilege **10** allegation, birthright **11** affirmation, declaration, prerogative, requisition **12** protestation

clairvoyance
3 ESP 7 insight 9 intuition, telepathy 10 sixth sense 11 penetration, second sight 12 precognition

clairvoyant
4 seer 5 sibyl 7 diviner 8 telepath 10 soothsayer

clam
4 buck 5 razor 6 dollar, quahog 7 bivalve, coquina, geoduck, mollusc, mollusk, smacker, steamer 11 cherrystone
genus: 3 Mya

clamant
4 dire 6 crying, urgent 7 blatant, burning, exigent 8 pressing 9 insistent 10 compelling, imperative

clamber
5 climb, crawl, scale, swarm 8 scrabble, scramble, struggle

clammy
4 cool, dank, damp 5 close, moist, slimy 6 sticky

clamor
3 cry, din 4 bawl, roar, to-do 5 babel, hoo-ha, noise 6 bellow, demand, hubbub, jangle, outcry, racket, ruckus, tumult, uproar 7 agitate, dispute, ferment, protest, turmoil 8 brouhaha, shouting 9 agitation, commotion 10 hullabaloo, hurly-burly 11 pandemonium

clamorous
5 noisy, vocal 6 crying, shrill, urgent 7 blatant, exigent, raucous, voluble 8 strident, vehement insistent 10 boisterous, imperative, tumultuous, vociferous 11 importunate 12 obstreperous

clamp
4 grip, hold, vise 5 clasp, grasp 6 clench, clinch, clutch, fasten, secure 7 grapple

clamshell
6 bucket 7 grapple

clan
3 mob 4 camp, folk, ring, sept 5 cabal, house, stock, tribe 6 circle, clique, family 7 coterie, kindred, lineage 9 camarilla
emblem: 5 totem

Clancy novel
12 Patriot Games 13 Sum of All Fears (The) 17 Hunt for Red October (The) 21 Clear and Present Danger

clandestine
6 covert, secret, sneaky 7 furtive, illicit 8 hush-hush, stealthy 10 undercover, under wraps 11 underhanded 12 hugger-mugger, illegitimate 13 surreptitious, under-the-table

clang
3 cry, din 4 ding, peal, slam 6 jangle 8 ding-dong

clangor
3 din 5 noise 6 clamor, jangle, racket, rattle, tumult, uproar 7 clatter, ringing 9 stridency 13 reverberation

clangorous
5 noisy 7 booming, rackety, ringing 8 clattery, sonorous 9 deafening 12 earsplitting

clap
3 pat 4 bang, blow, boom, clap, slam, slap 5 blast, burst, crack, crash, whack 6 strike 7 applaud 8 applause

claptrap
4 bull, bunk 5 cheap, hokum, showy, trash 6 bunkum, drivel, humbug, vulgar 7 baloney, eyewash, hogwash, twaddle 8 malarkey, nonsense 9 poppycock 10 balderdash, flapdoodle

Clara Bow
6 It girl

Clare Boothe _____
4 Luce

claret
3 red 4 wine 8 Bordeaux

clarify
5 clean, clear 6 define, filter, purify 7 analyze, cleanse, clear up, explain, resolve 8 simplify 9 elucidate 10 illuminate 13 straighten out

clarion
5 clear 7 ringing, rousing, trumpet 8 gleaming, stirring 9 brilliant

clarity
6 purity 8 accuracy, lucidity 9 clearness, limpidity, precision 10 exactitude, simplicity 12 transparency

Clarke novel
10 Earthlight 19 Fountains of Paradise (The)

clash
4 bump, jolt 5 brawl, crash, melee, set-to, smash 6 battle, fracas, impact, jangle 7 collide 8 conflict, mismatch, skirmish

9 collision, encounter **10** engagement
11 embroilment

clasp
3 hug, pin **4** clip, grip, hold **5** clamp, grasp, press **6** brooch, buckle, clench, clinch, clutch, enfold **7** embrace, grapple, squeeze **10** chatelaine

class
3 ilk **4** hold, kind, mark, part, rank, rate, sort, tier, type **5** allot, brand, caste, gauge, genre, genus, grade, grain, group, judge, order, score, stamp, style **6** assess, assign, assort, branch, course, league, nature, reckon, regard, stripe **7** bracket, caliber, quality, section, species, variety **8** appraise, category, consider, division, evaluate, grouping, separate **10** categorize, pigeonhole **11** description **12** denomination
middle: **11** bourgeoisie
school: **6** junior, senior **8** freshman **9** sophomore
working: **11** proletariat

classic
5 ideal, model, prime **7** capital, typical, vintage **8** champion, enduring, standard, superior, top-notch **9** authentic, canonical, classical, excellent, exemplary, tradition **10** magnum opus, masterwork **11** chef d'oeuvre, masterpiece, memorable, tour de force, traditional **12** paradigmatic, prototypical **13** authoritative

classical
4 pure **5** Attic, Greek, ideal, Latin, Roman **7** ancient, fitting, Grecian, perfect, typical, vintage **8** Hellenic, standard, sterling **9** canonical, exemplary **10** consummate **11** traditional **13** authoritative

classical musician
4 Böhm (Karl), Hess (Myra), Lind (Jenny), Muti (Riccardo), Pons (Lily), Shaw (Robert) **5** Arrau (Claudio), Biggs (E. Power), Borge (Victor), Boult (Adrian), Davis (Colin), du Pré (Jacqueline), Gould (Glenn), Masur (Kurt), Mehta (Zubin), Melba (Nellie), Ozawa (Seiji), Patti (Adelina), Pinza (Ezio), Price (Leontyne), Ramey (Samuel), Sills (Beverly), Stern (Isaac), Szell (George) **6** Abbado (Claudio), Battle (Kathleen), Boulez (Pierre), Callas (Maria), Caruso (Enrico), Casals (Pablo), Galway (James), Levine (James), Maazel (Lorin), Midori, Norman (Jessye), Peters (Roberta), Previn (André), Rampal (Jean-Pierre), Rattle (Simon), Reiner (Fritz), Serkin (Peter, Rudolf), Terfel (Bryn), Tucker (Richard), Upshaw (Dawn), Walter (Bruno) **7** Bartoli (Cecilia), Beecham (Thomas), Bocelli (Andrea), Brendel (Alfred), Cliburn (Van), Corelli (Franco), Domingo (Plácido), Farrell (Eileen), Fiedler (Arthur), Fleming (Renée), Glennie (Evelyn), Haitink (Bernard), Heifetz (Jascha), Karajan (Herbert von), Menuhin (Yehudi), Nilsson (Birgit), Ormandy (Eugene), Perlman (Itzhak), Pollini (Maurizio), Sargent (Malcolm), Segovia (Andrés), Tebaldi (Renata) **8** Anderson (Marian), Argerich (Martha), Bergonzi (Carlo), Carreras (José), Flagstad (Kirsten), Horowitz (Vladimir), Kreisler (Fritz), Marriner (Neville), Oistrakh (David), Schnabel (Artur), Te Kanawa (Kiri), Zukerman (Pinchas) **9** Barenboim (Daniel), Bernstein (Leonard), Chaliapin (Feodor), Klemperer (Otto), Landowska (Wanda), Pavarotti (Luciano), Stokowski (Leopold), Toscanini (Arturo) **10** Rubinstein (Arthur), Sutherland (Joan), Tetrazzini (Luisa) **11** Furtwängler (Wilhelm), Kostelanetz (André), Schwarzkopf (Elisabeth) **12** Rostropovich (Mstislav)

classification
4 sort, type **5** genre, genus, grade, order **6** family, phylum, rating **7** sorting, species **8** category, division, grouping, ordering, taxonomy, typology **11** arrangement, cataloguing

classified
6 secret, sorted **7** divided, ordered **9** top secret **11** categorized **12** confidential

classify
4 rank, rate, sort **5** grade, group **6** assort **7** arrange **9** break down **10** categorize, pigeonhole

classy
4 chic, tony **5** swank **6** modish **7** dashing, elegant, refined, stylish **8** gracious, tasteful, well-bred **9** courteous **11** fashionable

clatter
4 to-do **6** clamor, hubbub, pother, rattle, tumult, uproar **7** turmoil **9** commotion **10** hurly-burly
Scottish: **7** brattle

clattery
5 noisy **7** rackety **10** clangorous

Claudia's husband
6 Pilate

Claudio's beloved
4 Hero

Claudius
nephew: 6 Hamlet
predecessor: 8 Caligula
slayer: 6 Hamlet 9 Agrippina
successor: 4 Nero
wife: 8 Gertrude 9 Agrippina

Clavell novel
6 Gai-Jin, Shogun, Tai-Pan 7 King Rat

claw
3 dig 4 nail, rake, tear 5 chela, talon,
uncus 6 scrape 7 scratch

clay
3 cob 4 loam, lute, marl 5 argil, brick,
earth, gault, loess, ocher, ochre 6 kaolin
10 terra-cotta
baked: 4 tile 5 adobe, brick
box: 6 saggar, sagger
building: 5 adobe
ceramic: 10 terra-cotta
constituent: 6 silica 8 feldspar, silicate
9 kaolinite
in glass: 4 tear
made of: 7 fictile
porcelain: 6 kaolin
red: 8 laterite
rock: 5 shale
tobacco pipe: 6 dudeen
watery mixture: 4 slip
white: 6 kaolin

clay pigeon
6 target

clean
4 dust, fair, pure, swab, tidy, wash, wipe
5 bathe, fresh, groom, purge, scour, scrub,
sweep 6 bright, chaste, decent, neaten,
purify, spruce, vacuum, washed 7 clarify,
launder, sinless 8 hygienic, innocent,
sanitary, sanitize, spotless, unsoiled
9 blameless, faultless, sparkling, stainless,
undefiled, unsullied, untainted, wholesome
10 antiseptic, immaculate 11 unblemished
12 spick-and-span

clean-cut
4 trim 7 defined, precise 8 definite,
explicit, specific 9 wholesome 10 definitive
11 categorical, unambiguous, well-
groomed

cleaner
see **cleanser**

cleanhanded
8 innocent 9 blameless

clean-limbed
4 trim 7 shapely 8 handsome
10 statuesque

cleanse
4 wash 5 purge, rinse 6 purify, refine
7 clarify, launder 8 lustrate, sanitize
9 disinfect, expurgate, sterilize

cleanser
3 lye 4 soap 9 detergent 10 antiseptic
12 disinfectant

cleansing
7 purging 8 ablution 9 catharsis, purgation
10 lustration 11 expurgation
12 purification

clear
3 get, net, pay, rid, win 4 earn, fade, fair,
fine, free, gain, leap, lose, make, pure, well
5 close, empty, exact, fully, glean, lucid,
overt, pay up, plain, quite, repay, solve,
stark, sunny 6 acquit, gather, hurdle,
limpid, obtain, pay off, pick up, secure,
settle, simple, square, vacant, vacate,
vanish 7 absolve, acquire, approve,
audible, clarify, clarion, cleanse, clean up,
defined, evident, explain, improve, legible,
obvious, precise, rule out, satisfy, utterly
8 apparent, definite, distinct, entirely,
explicit, knowable, luminous, manifest,
palpable, pleasant, scot-free, shake off,
surmount 9 authorize, cloudless,
discharge, eliminate, elucidate, evaporate,
exculpate, exonerate, extricate, liquidate,
meliorate, negotiate, perfectly, unblurred,
unclouded, vindicate 10 ameliorate,
completely, illuminate, illustrate,
openhanded, see-through 11 conspicuous,
disentangle, open-and-shut, perceptible,
translucent, transparent, unambiguous,
unequivocal 12 recognizable,
unmistakable 13 uncomplicated

clearance
3 gap 4 sale 7 go-ahead, removal
8 approval 10 green light, permission
13 authorization

clear away
6 remove 7 take out

clear-cut
5 crisp, exact, plain 7 decided, precise
8 definite, distinct, explicit, manifest
10 definitive, pronounced, undisputed
11 categorical, indubitable, unambiguous,
unequivocal 12 unquestioned

clear-eyed
6 astute 9 judicious, observant
10 discerning, perceptive

clearheaded
4 calm, cool 10 perceptive

clearing
3 gap 5 field, glade 7 opening
10 settlement

clear out
5 scoot, scram, split 6 beat it, begone, bug
off, decamp, depart 7 buzz off, skiddoo,
take off, vamoose 8 shove off 9 drive
away, skedaddle 10 hightail it

clear-sightedness
6 acuity, acumen 8 keenness, sagacity
10 astuteness, shrewdness
11 discernment, penetration, percipience
12 perspicacity

clear up
5 solve 6 cipher, unfold 7 clarify, dope out,
explain, resolve, unravel 8 decipher
9 elucidate, figure out 10 illuminate

clearwing
4 moth

cleat
4 bitt 5 chock 6 batten 7 bollard, dolphin

cleavage
4 rift 5 chasm, cleft, split 6 schism
7 fissure 8 crevasse 9 splitting

cleave
3 cut, hew 4 chop, join, link, rend, rive
5 carve, cling, sever, slice, split, stick, unite
6 adhere, divide, sunder 7 combine
8 dissever, separate

cleft
3 gap 4 rift 5 chasm, chink, clove, crack,
gorge, gulch, split 6 clough, ravine, schism
7 crevice, fissure 8 cleavage

clemency
5 grace, mercy 6 lenity 7 caritas, charity
8 kindness, lenience, leniency, mildness
9 tolerance 10 compassion, gentleness,
indulgence, sufferance, toleration 11 forbearance

clement
4 fair, kind, mild 5 balmy 6 benign,
humane, kindly 7 lenient 8 merciful,
tolerant 9 indulgent 10 benevolent,
charitable, forbearing 13 compassionate

clench
4 grip, grit, hold 5 clamp, clasp, grasp
6 clutch 7 grapple

Cleopatra
attendant: 4 Iras 8 Charmian
brother: 7 Ptolemy
husband: 7 Ptolemy
killer: 3 asp
lover: 6 Antony (Marc), Caesar (Julius)
7 Anthony (Mark)
river: 4 Nile

Cleopatra's Needle
7 obelisk

clepsydra
9 timepiece 10 water clock

clerestory
7 gallery

clergy
7 canonry 8 ministry 9 churchmen,
diaconate, pastorate, rabbinate
10 priesthood 11 cardinalate 13 eccle-
siastics

clergyman
5 clerk, padre, vicar 6 bishop, cleric,
curate, divine, father, parson, pastor, priest,
rector 7 dominie, prelate 8 chaplain,
clerical, minister, preacher, reverend,
shepherd, sky pilot 9 churchman, pulpiteer
10 evangelist, missionary, sermonizer
12 ecclesiastic
American: 4 Hale (Edward Everett), King
(Martin Luther, Thomas Starr) 5 Eliot
(John), Moody (Dwight), Stone (Barton
Warren), Weems (Parson) 6 Dwight
(Timothy), Finney (Charles), Graham
(Billy), Holmes (John Haynes), Hooker
(Thomas), Mather (Cotton, Increase,
Richard), Merton (Thomas), Parker
(Samuel, Theodore), Sunday (Billy), Taylor
(Edward, Graham, Nathaniel William)
7 Beecher (Henry Ward, Lyman), Edwards
(Jonathan), Harvard (John), Russell
(Charles Taze) 10 Muhlenberg (Frederick
Augustus, Henry Melchior, John Peter
Gabriel)
English: 4 Ward (Nathaniel, Seth, William
George) 5 Donne (John), Paley (William),
Smith (Henry "Silver-Tongued," John "The
Sebaptist," Sidney) 6 Cotton (John), Fuller
(Andrew, Thomas), Taylor (Jeremy,
Rowland), Wesley (Charles, John)
7 Cranmer (Thomas), Parsons (Robert)
8 Kingsley (Charles) 10 Whitefield
(George)
home: 5 manse 6 priory 7 rectory
8 vicarage 9 monastery, parsonage

traveling: **12** circuit rider

cleric
see **clergyman**

clerisy
8 literati **10** illuminati **13** intellectuals

clerk
7 cashier **8** salesman **9** secretary **10** accountant, bookkeeper **11** salesperson **12** stenographer

clever
3 apt, sly **4** able, deft, good, keen **5** adept, alert, canny, funny, handy, quick, savvy, sharp, smart, witty **6** adroit, astute, brainy, bright, crafty, expert, shrewd, tricky **7** amusing, capable, cunning, knowing, skilled **8** fanciful, humorous, pleasing, skillful, talented **9** competent, dexterous, ingenious **10** proficient **11** intelligent, quick-witted, resourceful **12** entertaining

cliché
3 saw **6** truism **7** bromide **8** banality, buzzword, chestnut **9** platitude **10** shibboleth, stereotype **11** commonplace

clichéd
5 banal, bland, musty, stale, tired, trite, vapid **6** old-hat **7** humdrum, insipid, wornout **8** bromidic, shopworn, timeworn **9** hackneyed **10** pedestrian, unoriginal **11** stereotyped **13** platitudinous, unimaginative

click
3 fit **4** snap, tick, work **5** agree, match **6** go over, pan out **7** come off, succeed

client
6 patron **7** patient, protégé **8** customer **9** dependent

clientele
4 fans **5** trade, train **6** custom, market, public **7** patrons, traffic **8** audience, patients, regulars, shoppers **9** customers **10** purchasers, supporters **12** constituency

cliff
4 crag **5** bluff, scarp **8** headland, palisade **9** precipice **10** escarpment

climacteric
4 apex, crux, cusp **5** acute **6** crisis **7** crucial **8** critical **9** menopause **11** culmination **12** change of life, turning point

climactic
4 peak **7** crucial, pivotal **8** critical,

decisive, dramatic **9** momentous **10** definitive **11** culminating, determining

climate
6 medium, milieu **7** ambient **8** ambience **10** atmosphere **11** environment **12** surroundings

climax
3 cap **4** acme, apex, peak **5** crown **6** apogee, summit, top off **8** capstone, meridian, pinnacle **9** culminate **11** culmination

climb
4 go up, rise, soar **5** mount, scale, slope **6** ascend **7** clamber **8** escalate, increase

climbing
8 scandent

climbing iron
7 crampon

clinch
3 hug **4** grip, hold, seal **5** clamp, clasp, grasp, sew up **6** clutch, decide, ensure, lock up **7** confirm, embrace, grapple, squeeze **8** nail down

clincher
4 tire **5** proof **6** kicker **7** quietus **9** deathblow **10** smoking gun **11** affirmation, attestation, coup de grâce **12** confirmation **13** corroboration

cling
4 bond **5** stick **6** adhere, cleave, clutch, hold on, linger **8** adhesion **9** adherence

clingstone
5 peach

clink
3 can, jug, pen **4** brig, cell, coop, jail, stir **5** pokey, pound **6** cooler, jingle, lockup, prison, tingle, tinkle **7** slammer **8** hoosegow **9** calaboose

clinker
3 dud **4** bomb, bust, flop, goof, slag **5** botch, brick, error, lemon, loser **6** bummer, bungle, fiasco, howler, turkey **7** bloomer, blunder, failure, faux pas, mistake

clinkers
3 ash **4** slag **5** ashes **7** cinders

clinquant
5 gaudy **6** flashy, garish, tawdry, tinsel **8** specious **10** glittering **11** superficial

Clio
see **Muse**

clip

3 bob, cut, mow, pin **4** crop, hasp, pare, snip, sock, trim **5** block, clasp, prune, punch, shave, shear, slash **6** broach, brooch, fleece, reduce **7** curtail, cut back, cut down, shorten **8** magazine, truncate **10** abbreviate, overcharge

clique

3 set **4** camp, clan, club, gang, ring **5** cabal, crowd, mafia **6** circle **7** coterie, faction, in-group **9** camarilla

cloak

4 cape, mask, robe, veil, wrap **5** cover, guise **6** facade, joseph, mantle, screen, shroud, veneer **7** blanket, conceal, curtain, dress up, manteau, obscure **8** disguise **9** dissemble, semblance **10** camouflage **11** dissimulate
ancient Greek: 7 chlamys
ancient Roman: 7 pallium
Arab: 3 aba
fur: 7 pelisse
hooded: 6 capote **7** burnous **8** burnoose
liturgical: 4 cope
Moroccan: 8 djellaba
over armor: 6 tabard **7** surcoat
Spanish: 5 manta

clobber

4 belt, drub, flay, lick, slam, slug, whip, whup **5** blast, brain, clout, pound, smash **6** hammer, thrash, wallop **7** shellac, trounce **8** demolish, lambaste

clochard

3 bum, vag **4** hobo **5** tramp **6** beggar, canter **7** drifter, floater, moocher, vagrant **8** deadbeat, derelict, vagabond **9** transient **10** freeloader, panhandler **11** bindle stiff

cloche

3 hat **5** cover, toque, tuque

clock

4 time **9** timepiece **11** chronometer
water: 9 clepsydra

clocklike

5 exact **6** minute, prompt, strict, timely **7** precise, regular **8** accurate, punctual, reliable, thorough **9** assiduous **10** dependable, meticulous, scrupulous **11** painstaking **13** conscientious

clockmaker

10 horologist

clockwise

6 deasil **7** dextral **11** right-handed

Clockwork Orange author

7 Burgess (Anthony)

clod

3 gob, wad **4** boob, dolt, dope, hunk, lump, soil **5** chump, chunk, clump, dummy, dunce, earth **6** dimwit **8** dumbbell **9** blockhead, lamebrain

cloddish

7 boorish, ill-bred, loutish, uncouth **8** churlish, clownish **9** unrefined **10** uncultured, unpolished **11** uncivilized

clodhopper

4 boor, boot, hick, lout **5** chuff, churl, clown, yokel **6** rustic **7** bumpkin, hayseed, redneck **9** chawbacon

clog

3 gum, jam, tax **4** fill, glut, load, plug, stop **5** block, choke, close, stuff **6** hamper, hinder **7** congest **8** encumber, obstruct, overload **10** impediment **11** encumbrance

cloister

5 abbey, court **6** arcade, garden **7** convent, retreat, seclude, shelter **9** courtyard, monastery, sequester

Cloister and the Hearth author

5 Reade (Charles)

cloistered

7 recluse **8** confined, hermetic, secluded **9** seclusive, withdrawn **11** sequestered

cloistered one

3 nun **4** monk

clone

4 copy **5** ditto **6** double, carbon **7** replica **9** duplicate, facsimile, replicate, reproduce **10** carbon copy, simulacrum **12** reproduction

Clorinda

beloved: 7 Tancred
father: 6 Senapo
guardian: 6 Arsete
slayer: 7 Tancred

close

3 end **4** near, nigh, shut, slam **5** block, cease, choke, humid, muggy, tight **6** ending, finale, finish, narrow, nearby, sticky, stuffy, sultry, windup, wrap up **7** airless, compact, crowded, stopper **8** abutting, adjacent, complete, conclude, finalize, intimate, obstruct, stifling **9** adjoining, cessation, condensed, terminate **10** conclusion, consummate, convenient, near-at-hand **11** constricted, neighboring, termination **12** confidential

225

closed-minded
4 deaf 6 narrow 8 obdurate 9 hidebound, obstinate, pigheaded, unbending
10 bullheaded, hardheaded 11 intractable

closefisted
5 cheap, mingy 6 frugal, stingy 7 miserly, thrifty 9 niggardly, penurious 13 penny-pinching

close in
3 hem 4 cage 5 fence, hedge 6 corral, immure 7 advance, confine, enclose, envelop, impound 8 approach, converge, encircle, enshroud, imprison, surround

close-knit
8 intimate

closely
4 hard 7 sharply 8 intently, minutely
9 carefully 11 searchingly 12 meticulously, scrupulously, thoughtfully 13 punctiliously

close match
6 toss-up

closemouthed
3 mum 4 mute 6 silent 7 laconic
8 reserved, reticent, taciturn 12 tight-mouthed

closeness
8 intimacy

close off
4 clog, plug 5 block 6 stop up 7 isolate, occlude 8 insulate 9 segregate, sequester

closet
6 covert, inside, office 7 cabinet, chamber, furtive, private 8 wardrobe 11 speculative, theoretical

closing
3 end 4 last, stop 5 final 6 ending, finish, latest, period, windup, wrap-up 7 curtain
8 eventual, terminal, ultimate 9 cessation
10 concluding 11 termination

closure
3 cap, end, lid 6 ending, finish 8 fastener
9 cessation

clot
3 gel, set 4 curd, glob, jell, lump 5 clump
6 curdle, gelate 7 congeal 8 coagulum, thrombus 9 coagulate 10 gelatinize
combining form: 6 thromb 7 thrombo

cloth
see **fabric**

clothe
3 tog 4 deck, do up, garb, robe 5 array,
cloak, couch, drape, dress, endow, equip
6 attire, bedeck, outfit, swathe 7 apparel, costume, dress up 8 accouter

clothes
3 rig 4 duds, garb, rags, togs 5 array, dress, getup, habit 6 attire, outfit, things
7 apparel, costume, raiment, rigging, threads, toggery, vesture 8 garments, glad rags 9 vestments 11 habiliments
basket: 6 hamper
civilian: 5 mufti

clothes-moth genus
5 Tinea

clothespress
7 armoire 8 wardrobe

cloud
3 dim, fog, tar 4 blur, haze, mist, murk
5 addle, befog, brume, gloom, muddy, plume, smear, sully, taint 6 muddle, nebula, puzzle, shadow, smudge
7 besmear, confuse, obscure, perplex, tarnish 8 befuddle, besmirch, discolor, distract, overcast 9 obfuscate
type: 6 cirrus, nimbus 7 cumulus, stratus
11 altocumulus, altostratus
12 cirrocumulus, cirrostratus, cumulonimbus, nimbostratus 13 stratocumulus

cloudburst
6 deluge, shower 7 monsoon, torrent
8 downpour, drencher, rainfall
10 outpouring

clouded
5 dusky, murky, shady 6 dreary, gloomy, somber, sombre 7 dubious, ominous, sunless, unclear 8 doubtful, overcast
9 ambiguous, equivocal, uncertain, unsettled 11 problematic

cloudless
4 fair, fine 5 clear, sunny 7 clarion
8 pleasant, rainless, sunshiny

cloud-like mass
6 nebula

cloudy
4 dull, hazy 5 dusky, foggy, heavy, misty, murky, vague 6 gloomy, opaque, somber, sombre 7 louring, obscure, tainted, unclear
8 confused, darkened, lowering, nebulous, overcast, vaporous 10 indistinct

clout
3 box, hit, rag 4 blow, cuff, poke, pull, slam, slap, slug, sock, swat, sway 5 paste,

power, punch, smack, smite, whack
6 strike **9** influence

clove
4 bulb **5** spice **7** chopped, severed

clove hitch
4 knot

clover
5 lotus **6** alsike, ladino, lucern **7** alfalfa, berseem, lucerne, melilot, trefoil **8** four-leaf, shamrock **9** lespedeza
family: 3 pea
genus: 9 Trifolium

clown
3 wag **4** mime, zany **5** cutup, joker, Punch **6** jester, mummer **7** buffoon **8** comedian, jokester **9** harlequin, prankster **11** merry-andrew
French: 7 Pierrot
operatic: 5 buffo
Spanish: 8 gracioso

clownish
4 rude **6** clumsy, gauche, oafish **7** awkward, boorish, ill-bred, loutish, lumpish, uncouth **8** churlish, cloddish **9** unrefined

cloy
4 fill, glut, jade, pall, sate **5** gorge **6** sicken **7** satiate, surfeit **8** overfill

cloying
4 icky **5** gushy, mushy, sappy, soppy **6** sticky, sugary **7** fulsome, gushing, maudlin, mawkish **9** excessive, schmaltzy, sickening **10** disgusting, distasteful, lovey-dovey, nauseating, saccharine **11** sentimental

club
3 bat, sap **4** beat, cosh, iron, mace **5** baton, billy, guild, lodge, order, union **6** cudgel, league **7** society **8** bludgeon, sodality, sorority **9** blackjack, truncheon **10** fellowship, fraternity, knobkerrie, nightstick **11** association, brotherhood
Australian: 5 waddy
Irish: 10 shillelagh

clubfoot
7 talipes

cluck
4 dodo, dolt, dope, fool **5** dunce **6** dimwit, nitwit **7** pinhead

clue
3 cue **4** hint, idea, lead, sign, tell, warn **6** advise, inform, notify, notion, tip-off

7 inkling **8** evidence, telltale **10** indication, intimation, suggestion

clump
3 gob, wad **4** clod, hunk, lump, mass, mess, plod **5** batch, bunch, chunk, group, stomp, tramp **6** bumble, bundle, lumber, parcel **7** cluster, galumph, stumble

clump of grass
4 tuft **6** tuffet **7** tussock

clumsy
5 bulky, gawky, inept, splay **6** clunky, gauche, klutzy **7** awkward, hulking, lumpish, unhandy **8** bumbling, bungling, tactless, ungainly, unsubtle, unwieldy **9** all thumbs, graceless, ham-handed, inelegant, lumbering, maladroit **11** heavy-handed, inefficient

clumsy one
3 oaf **4** clod, goon, lout, slob **5** klutz **6** baboon, galoot, lummox **7** bumpkin, bungler, palooka **13** butterfingers

clunk
4 thud **5** clout, thump, whack **6** thwack, wallop

clunker
4 bomb, heap **5** crate, wreck **6** jalopy, junker **7** stinker **10** rattletrap

cluster
3 lot, set **4** band, bevy, crew, knot, pack **5** array, batch, bunch, clump, covey, group **6** bundle, clutch, gather **7** collect, package **8** assemble, assembly **9** aggregate, associate, gathering **10** accumulate

cluster bean
4 guar

clutch
4 grab, grip, hold, keep **5** catch, clamp, clasp, grasp, pinch, seize **6** bundle, clench, clinch, snatch **7** cluster, grapple

clutter
4 hash, mash, mess, muss, ruck **5** chaos, snarl, strew **6** jumble, litter, muddle **7** mélange, rummage **8** disarray, disorder, mishmash, shambles **9** confusion **10** hodgepodge

Clydesdale
5 horse **10** draft horse

Clymene
father: 7 Oceanus
husband: 7 Iapetus
mother: 7 Tethys
son: 5 Atlas **10** Epimetheus, Prometheus

Clytemnestra
brother: 6 Castor, Pollux 10 Polydeuces
daughter: 7 Electra 9 Iphigenia
father: 9 Tyndareus
husband: 9 Agamemnon
lover: 9 Aegisthus
mother: 4 Leda
slayer: 7 Orestes
son: 7 Orestes
victim: 9 Agamemnon, Cassandra

Clytie
beloved: 6 Apollo
form: 9 sunflower 10 heliotrope

coach
3 bus, car 5 drill, stage, train, tutor
6 chaise, mentor 7 prepare, trainer
8 carriage, instruct 10 instructor

coadjutor
3 aid 5 aide 6 bishop, deputy 9 assistant
10 aide-de-camp, lieutenant

coagulate
3 gel, set 4 clot, jell 6 curdle 7 congeal,
jellify, thicken 8 coalesce, condense,
solidify 10 gelatinize, inspissate
11 concentrate, consolidate

coal
distillate: 3 tar
dust: 4 smut, soot 5 slack
element: 6 carbon
fused leavings: 4 slag 7 clinker
glowing: 5 ember, gleed
hard: 10 anthracite
lump: 3 cob
miner: 7 collier
region: 4 Saar
residue: 4 coke
soft: 6 cannel 10 bituminous

coalesce
3 mix 4 fuse, join, link 5 blend, merge,
unite 6 mingle 7 combine, conjoin
10 amalgamate

coalition
4 bloc, ring 5 party, union 6 fusion,
league, merger 7 combine, melding,
merging 8 alliance 9 anschluss
10 federation 11 affiliation, association,
combination, confederacy, integration,
unification 13 confederation, consolidation

coarse
3 raw 4 rude 5 bawdy, crass, crude, dirty,
gross, rough, tacky 6 common, filthy,
grainy, ribald, smutty, vulgar 7 boorish,
obscene, raffish, raunchy, uncouth
8 granular, indecent 9 inelegant,
roughneck, unrefined 10 uncultured
11 particulate 12 uncultivated

coast
4 bank 5 beach, drift, shore, slide 6 strand
7 seaside 8 littoral, seashore
of Antarctica: 4 Knox

coastal
7 seaside 8 littoral, riverine

coaster
4 sled, tray 6 trader

coat
5 crust, glaze, gloss, layer, parka, plate,
tunic 6 blazer, duster, finish, jacket, patina,
raglan, reefer, ulster, veneer 7 cutaway
8 covering, mackinaw, tegument
9 newmarket, redingote 10 integument,
mackintosh 11 windbreaker
animal: 4 fur 5 hide, pelt, wool 6 pelage
fur-lined: 7 pelisse
kind: 3 pea, top 5 frock 6 trench
Levantine: 6 caftan
of arms: 5 crest 6 blazon, emblem,
shield, tabard 8 blazonry 10 escutcheon
of egg white: 5 glair 6 glaire
of mail: 7 hauberk
soldier's: 5 frock, tunic 6 capote
waterproof: 7 slicker 10 mackintosh

coating
4 film, leaf, scum, skin 5 glaze, gloss, layer
6 finish, patina, veneer 7 dusting, lacquer,
overlay, surface, varnish 8 covering

coax
4 lure, urge 5 cable, press, tempt 6 cajole,
entice, induce 7 blarney, wheedle
8 blandish, butter up, inveigle, persuade,
soft-soap 9 importune, sweet-talk

cob
3 ear 4 swan 5 adobe, horse

cobble
4 make, mend 5 patch, stone 6 repair
11 paving stone

cobbler
3 pie 5 drink 8 cocktail 9 shoemaker

cobbler's form
4 last

cobelligerent
4 ally

cobweb
3 net 4 mesh, trap 8 gossamer
9 confusion, spiderweb 12 entanglement

coccyx
8 tailbone

cochineal
3 dye 6 insect

cock
3 tap 4 boss, head, heap, hill, lord, mass, pile, rick, tilt 5 chief, mound, stack, strut, valve 6 faucet, honcho, leader, master, spigot 7 headman, hydrant, rooster, swagger 11 chanticleer

cock-a-hoop
4 awry 5 askew 7 askance, crooked 8 boastful, exultant, exulting, jubilant 9 triumphal 10 triumphant

Cockaigne
6 utopia 7 arcadia 9 Shangri-la 10 wonderland

cockalorum
7 bluster, bombast, bravado 8 blowhard, boasting, braggart, leapfrog 11 braggadocio

cockamamy
5 batty, crazy, daffy, flaky, kooky, loony, nutty, wacky 6 absurd 9 ludicrous 10 incredible, ridiculous 11 harebrained

cock-and-bull story
5 crock 6 canard 7 whopper 9 fairy tale

cockcrow
4 dawn, morn 5 sunup 7 morning, sunrise 8 daybreak, daylight

cocker
4 baby 5 humor, spoil 6 coddle, cosset, pamper 7 indulge, spaniel 11 mollycoddle

cockeyed
4 awry 5 askew 8 lopsided 11 harebrained

cockle
5 shell 6 dimple, furrow, groove, pucker, ripple 7 bivalve, mollusc, mollusk, wrinkle

cockleshell
4 boat

cockscomb
see **coxcomb**

cocksure
5 brash 6 cheeky 9 bumptious 13 overconfident

cocktail
5 Bronx, drink 6 gibson, gimlet, mai tai, mimosa, mojito, Rob Roy, zombie 7 gin fizz, martini, sidecar, stinger 8 aperitif, daiquiri, pink lady, salty dog, sombrero 9 Cuba libre, manhattan, margarita, mint julep, rusty nail 10 Bloody Mary, Tom Collins, wallbanger 11 grasshopper, screwdriver, whiskey sour 12 black russian, cosmopolitan, old-fashioned
fruit: 9 macedoine
gasoline: 7 Molotov

Cocktail Party author
5 Eliot (T. S.)

cocky
4 bold, sure 5 brash, pushy, sassy, saucy 6 brassy, cheeky, jaunty 8 arrogant, impudent, insolent 9 conceited 10 swaggering 11 self-assured 12 enterprising 13 overconfident, self-confident

coconspirator
7 abettor 9 accessory 10 accomplice 11 confederate

coconut
husk fiber: 4 coir
meat: 5 copra

coda
5 envoi, envoy 6 ending, finale 7 summary 8 epilogue, follow-up 9 afterword 10 conclusion

coddle
4 baby 5 humor, spoil 6 cosset, pamper 7 cater to, indulge

code
6 cipher, symbol 7 encrypt 8 encipher
kind: 3 zip 4 area 5 Morse, legal, penal
message in: 10 cryptogram 11 cryptograph

code word
see **communications code word**

codger
6 duffer, fellow

codicil
5 rider 8 addendum, addition, appendix 10 postscript, supplement

codswallop
see **nonsense**

coefficient
6 factor 7 measure 8 constant

coelenterate
5 coral 7 anemone, hydroid 9 cnidarian, jellyfish 10 sea anemone

coerce
3 cow 5 bully, force, impel, press 6 compel, menace, oblige 8 browbeat, bulldoze, dominate, threaten 9 blackjack,

constrain, strong-arm, terrorize
10 intimidate

coercion
5 force **6** duress, menace, threat
8 pressure **10** compulsion, constraint

Coeur d'_____
5 Alene

coeval
see **contemporary**

coexistent
see **contemporary**

coffee
alkaloid: 8 caffeine
bean: 3 nib
cake: 6 kuchen
cup: 9 demitasse
French: 4 café
grinder: 4 mill
kind: 4 drip, java **5** decaf, latte, mocha
7 arabica, instant **8** espresso **9** Americano, macchiato **10** café au lait,
cappuccino
maker: 10 percolator
pot: 3 urn

coffee shop
4 café **5** diner **8** snack bar **9** cafeteria,
hash house, lunchroom **11** greasy spoon
12 luncheonette

coffer
5 chest **6** casket **8** treasury **9** exchequer,
strongbox

coffin
3 box **4** kist **6** casket
carrier: 6 hearse **10** pallbearer
nail: 9 cigarette
stand: 4 bier **10** catafalque

cogency
5 force, point, power, punch **7** potency
8 strength, validity **9** relevance
10 conviction, pertinence **13** effectiveness

cogent
5 solid, sound, valid **6** potent **7** telling,
weighty **8** forceful, powerful, relevant
9 pertinent **10** compelling, convincing,
meaningful, persuasive **11** influential, well-
founded **12** well-grounded
13 consequential

cogitate
4 muse **5** think **6** ponder, reason **7** reflect
8 conceive, consider, meditate, mull over,
ruminate **9** cerebrate, speculate
10 deliberate

cogitation
7 thought **10** meditation, reflection,
rumination **11** cerebration, speculation
12 deliberation **13** consideration

cogitative
7 pensive **10** meditative, reflective,
ruminative, thoughtful **11** speculative
13 contemplative

Cogito _____ sum
4 ergo

cognac
6 brandy

cognate
4 akin, like **5** alike **6** allied, common
7 kindred, related, similar **8** parallel
10 affiliated, associated

cognition
9 awareness, knowledge, sentience
10 perception

cognizance
4 heed, note **6** notice **9** attention,
awareness, knowledge **12** jurisdiction

cognizant
5 aware **7** knowing, mindful **8** informed,
sensible **9** conscious **13** knowledgeable

cognize
4 know **5** grasp **6** fathom **7** realize
8 perceive **9** apprehend **10** appreciate,
comprehend, understand

cognomen
4 name **5** alias, title **7** epithet, moniker,
surname **8** nickname **11** appellation,
appellative, designation **12** denomination

cognoscente
5 judge **6** critic, expert **7** epicure
8 aesthete **9** authority **10** specialist
11 connoisseur

cognoscible
8 knowable **10** fathomable **13** apprehensible

cohere
4 fuse, join **5** agree, blend, cling, merge,
stick, unite **6** accord **7** combine, comport,
conform, connect **8** coalesce, dovetail
10 correspond **11** consolidate

coherence
4 bond **5** union, unity **8** adhesion,
cohesion **9** agreement, congruity, integrity
10 conformity, connection, consonance,
solidarity **11** consistency, integration

coherent
5 sound 7 logical, ordered, unified
8 rational 10 consistent, integrated,
meaningful 11 coordinated

cohesion
see **coherence**

coho
6 salmon 12 silver salmon

cohort
3 pal 4 ally, band, chum, crew, mate
5 buddy, crony, group 6 fellow, friend
7 comrade, partner 8 adherent, confrere,
disciple, follower, henchman, sidekick
9 assistant, associate, colleague,
companion, supporter 10 accomplice
11 demographic 12 collaborator

coif
3 cap, cut 4 hood, perm 6 hairdo
7 haircut 8 skullcap

coiffeur
6 barber 10 haircutter 11 hairdresser,
hairstylist

coiffure
6 hairdo
aid: 3 net, rat 5 snood

coil
4 curl, loop, ring, turn, wind 5 helix, twine,
twist 6 rotate, spiral 7 entwine, revolve,
wreathe 8 curlicue 9 corkscrew

coiled
6 spiral, volute 7 helical, voluted, whorled
9 circinate

coin
4 mint 6 invent, make up, strike
Afghanistan: 3 pul 7 afghani
Albania: 3 lek 9 quindarka
Algeria: 5 dinar 7 centime
ancient Greek: 4 obol
ancient Muslim: 5 dinar
ancient Roman: 8 denarius
Argentina: 4 peso 7 centavo
Austria: 4 euro 8 groschen 9 schilling
Bahrain: 4 fils 5 dinar
Belgium: 4 euro 5 franc 7 centime
Benin: 5 franc 7 centime
Bhutan: 7 chetrum 8 ngultrum
Bolivia: 7 centavo 9 boliviano
Botswana: 4 pula 5 thebe
Brazil: 4 real 7 centavo 8 cruzeiro
Bulgaria: 3 lev 8 stotinka
Burundi: 5 franc 7 centime
Cameroon: 5 franc 7 centime
Canada: 6 loonie, toonie, twonie
Cape Verde Islands: 6 escudo 7 centavo

Chile: 4 peso 7 centavo
China: 3 fen 4 jiao, yuan
Columbia: 4 peso 7 centavo
Costa Rica: 5 colón 7 centimo
Cuba: 4 peso 7 centavo
Czech Republic: 5 haler 6 koruna
defective: 4 fido
Denmark: 3 ore 5 krone
Dominican Republic: 4 peso 7 centavo
Ecuador: 5 sucre 7 centavo
edge: 7 milling
Egypt: 7 piastre
European gold: 5 ducat
Finland: 4 euro 5 penni 6 markka
former: 3 ecu, mil, pie, sol, sou 4 anna,
besa, doit, duit, kran, para, pice, reis
(plural) 5 fanam, litas, mohur, paisa, rupia,
shahi, soldo, toman 6 centas, denier,
heller, macuta, pagoda, tangka 7 santims,
sapeque 8 maravedi, skilling 9 rigsdaler
10 Indian head, reichsmark
13 reichspfennig
France: 4 euro 5 franc 7 centime
Gambia: 5 butut 6 dalasi
Germany: 4 euro, mark 7 pfennig
Ghana: 4 cedi 6 pesewa
Great Britain: 3 bob 5 crown, penny
6 guinea 7 ha'penny 8 farthing, shilling,
sixpence 9 halfpenny, sovereign
10 threepence
Greece: 4 euro 6 lepton 7 drachma
Guatemala: 7 centavo, quetzal
Guinea-Bissau: 4 peso
Haiti: 6 gourde 7 centime
Honduras: 7 centavo, lempira
Hungary: 5 pengo 6 filler, forint
Iceland: 5 aurar (plural), eyrir, krona
India: 5 paisa, rupee
Indonesia: 3 sen 6 rupiah
Iran: 4 rial 5 dinar
Iraq: 4 fils 5 dinar
Ireland: 4 euro 5 penny 8 farthing
Israel: 5 agora 6 shekel
Italy: 4 euro, lira 5 scudo
Japan: 3 rin, sen, yen
Jordan: 4 fils 5 dinar
Kenya: 8 shilling
Korea, North and South: 3 won 4 chon
Kuwait: 4 fils 5 dinar
large: 9 cartwheel
Lebanon: 5 livre 7 piastre
Lesotho: 4 loti 7 licente, lisente
Libya: 5 dinar 6 dirham
Luxembourg: 4 euro 5 franc
Madagascar: 5 franc
Malawi: 6 kwacha 7 tambala
Mauritania: 5 khoum 7 ouguiya
Mauritius: 5 rupee
Mexico: 4 peso 7 centavo

Monaco: 4 euro 5 franc
Morocco: 6 dirham
Mozambique: 7 metical
Nepal: 5 paisa, rupee
Netherlands: 4 euro 6 florin, gulden 7 guilder
Nicaragua: 7 centavo, córdoba
Nigeria: 4 kobo 5 naira
Norway: 3 ore 5 krone
Oman: 4 rial 5 baiza
Pakistan: 5 paisa, rupee
Panama: 6 balboa 9 centesimo
Papua New Guinea: 4 kina, toea
Paraguay: 7 centimo, guarani
Peru: 3 sol 7 centimo
Philippines: 4 piso 7 sentimo
Poland: 5 grosz, zloty
Portugal: 4 euro 6 escudo 7 centavo
Qatar: 5 riyal 6 dirham
Roman: 6 aureus, bezant 7 solidus
Romania: 3 ban, leu
Russia: 5 kopek, ruble 6 kopeck
San Marino: 4 lira
Saudi Arabia: 4 rial 6 halala
Seychelles: 5 rupee
side of a: 7 obverse
Slovakia: 5 haler 6 koruna
South Africa: 4 rand 10 Krugerrand
Spain: 4 euro 5 peseta 7 centimo
Sri Lanka: 5 rupee
stamping metal: 8 planchet
Suriname: 6 florin, gulden 7 guilder
Swaziland: 9 lilangeni
Sweden: 3 ore 5 krona 8 skilling
Switzerland: 5 franc 6 rappen
Syria: 7 piastre
Tanzania: 8 shilling
Thailand: 4 baht 5 tical 6 satang
Tonga: 6 pa'anga, seniti
Tunisia: 5 dinar
Turkey: 4 lira 5 kurus
Uganda: 8 shilling
United Arab Emirates: 6 dirham
United States: 4 dime 5 penny 6 dollar, nickel 7 quarter 10 half-dollar
Uruguay: 4 peso 9 centesimo
Vatican City: 4 lira
Venezuela: 7 bolivar
Samoa: 4 sene, tala
Zambia: 5 ngwee 6 kwacha

coinage
7 new word 8 creation, currency
9 invention, neologism 10 brainchild
11 contrivance

coincide
4 jibe 5 agree, equal, match, tally
6 accord, concur, square 7 comport,

conform 8 dovetail 9 harmonize
10 correspond

coincident
7 similar 9 consonant 10 concurrent
11 concomitant, synchronous 12 accompanying, contemporary, simultaneous

coincidentally
8 by chance, together 12 accidentally,
concurrently, fortuitously

coin-shaped
8 nummular

col
4 pass 5 ridge 6 saddle

_____ colada
4 piña

colander's cousin
5 sieve 6 sifter 8 strainer

cold _____
3 war 4 call, cash, cuts, feet, fish, sore,
wave 5 cream, frame, front, patch, steel,
sweat, water 6 turkey 7 comfort, storage
8 shoulder

cold
3 icy, raw 4 cool, dead, iced 5 aloof, chill,
crisp, frore, gelid, nippy, polar 6 arctic,
biting, chilly, frigid, frosty, frozen, glacial,
wintry 7 bracing, glacial, shivery 8 chilling,
comatose, freezing, lifeless
11 emotionless, passionless, unconscious,
unemotional 12 unresponsive
combining form: 4 cryo, kryo
common: 6 coryza
symptom: 5 cough, fever 6 sneeze
7 catarrh

cold-blooded
5 cruel 6 brutal 7 callous 8 hardened,
obdurate, pitiless, ruthless 9 heartless,
impassive, unfeeling 10 hard-boiled,
impersonal 11 emotionless, hard-hearted
12 matter-of-fact, stonyhearted
13 dispassionate, unimpassioned

cold feet
4 fear 5 alarm, doubt, dread, panic, worry
6 dismay, fright, terror 7 anxiety, jitters
8 timidity 9 cowardice 11 trepidation
12 apprehension

coldhearted
see **cold-blooded**

cold-shoulder
3 cut 4 snub 6 ignore, slight 9 ostracize

cold storage
8 abeyance, dormancy 10 quiescence, suspension 12 intermission, interruption

cole
4 kale, rape 7 cabbage 8 brassica, broccoli, kohlrabi 11 cauliflower

Coleridge poem
9 Dejection, Kubla Khan 10 Christabel

Colette character
4 Gigi 5 Cheri 8 Claudine

colewort
4 kale 7 cabbage

colic
5 gripe 9 bellyache 11 stomachache 12 collywobbles

coliseum
4 bowl 5 arena, stade 6 circus 7 stadium

collaborate
6 team up 7 collude 8 conspire 9 cooperate

collaborator
4 ally 6 helper 7 abettor, partner, traitor 8 coworker, henchman, quisling 9 accessory, assistant, associate, auxiliary, colleague 10 accomplice 11 confederate, conspirator

collapse
4 cave, drop, failruin 5 break, crash, smash, wreck 6 buckle, cave in, fold up 7 breakup, crack-up, crumple, debacle, deflate, downfall, failure, founder, give out, give way, pass out, shatter, smashup, succumb 8 condense 9 breakdown, cataclysm, fall apart, ruination 10 disruption 11 catastrophe, destruction, prostration 12 disintegrate

collar
3 bag, nab 4 grab, hook, nail, take 5 catch, seize 6 arrest, secure 7 capture 9 apprehend
armor: 6 gorget
boy's: 4 Eton
chain: 4 torc 6 torque
jeweled: 8 carcanet
lace-edged: 6 rebato
metal: 4 torc 6 torque
pleated: 4 ruff

collarbone
8 clavicle

collate
5 group, order 7 arrange, collect, compare, compile 8 assemble, contrast, organize 9 integrate

collateral
4 bond 6 allied, lineal, pledge, surety 7 cognate, kindred, oblique, related, subject 8 indirect, parallel, security 9 accessory, ancillary, attendant, auxiliary, dependent, secondary, tributary 10 coincident, coordinate, reciprocal, subsidiary 11 concomitant, subordinate, subservient 12 accompanying, confirmatory, contributory 13 complementary, corresponding, corroborative

colleague
4 aide 6 cohort, fellow, helper 7 partner 8 confrere, coworker, teammate 9 assistant, associate, companion 10 compatriot 11 confederate 12 collaborator

collect
4 draw 5 group, infer, raise 6 deduce, derive, gather, muster, prayer 7 build up, compile, compose, convene, dispose, marshal, round up 8 assemble, conclude, converge 10 accumulate, congregate, rendezvous

collected
4 calm, cool 5 quiet, still 6 poised, serene 7 assured 8 complete, composed, sanguine, tranquil 9 assembled, confident, unruffled 11 unflappable 13 imperturbable, self-possessed

collection
3 ana, kit, lot 4 band, bevy, crew, olio, ruck 5 bunch, crowd, hoard, trove 6 medley, muster 7 cluster, variety 8 assembly, caboodle 9 aggregate, anthology, congeries, gathering, stockpile 10 assemblage, assortment, cumulation, miscellany 11 aggregation 12 accumulation, congregation 13 agglomeration
miscellaneous: 4 hash, olio 6 jumble, medley 7 mélange, mixture 8 mishmash, pastiche 9 hodgepodge, salmagundi 11 olla podrida
of anecdotes: 3 ana
of animals: 3 zoo 8 menagerie
of artistic works: 6 museum 7 gallery
of clothes: 8 wardrobe
of dried plants: 9 herbarium
of literary pieces: 8 analects 9 anthology
of reports: 4 file 7 dossier
of trinkets: 10 bijouterie

collective
5 joint 7 commune, kibbutz, kolkhoz 11 cooperative

collector
of bird's eggs: 8 oologist
of books: 11 bibliophile
of coins: 11 numismatist
of fares: 9 conductor
of phonograph records: 10 discophile
of stamps: 11 philatelist

colleen
4 girl, lass 6 maiden
country: 4 Eire, Erin 7 Ireland

college
building: 3 gym, lab 4 dorm, hall
campus area: 4 quad 10 quadrangle
class meeting: 3 lab 7 lecture, seminar
8 tutorial, workshop
degree: 3 BLS, DST, LLB, LLD, MBA,
MEd, MFA, MLS, PhD 5 LittD
graduate: 6 alumna, alumni (plural)
7 alumnae (plural), alumnus
official: 4 dean 5 prexy 6 bursar, regent
7 proctor, provost 9 registrar
oldest in U.S.: 7 Harvard
oldest women's in U.S.: 12 Mount
Holyoke
relating to: 8 academic 10 collegiate
social group: 4 frat 8 sorority
10 fraternity
song: 9 alma mater
student class: 4 soph 5 frosh 6 junior,
senior 8 freshman 9 sophomore
teacher: 3 don 4 prof 8 academic
9 professor
term: 7 quarter, session 8 semester
9 trimester
VIP: 4 BMOC
woman: 4 coed

college team
Air Force: 7 Falcons
Alabama: 11 Crimson Tide
Arizona: 8 Wildcats
Arizona State: 9 Sun Devils
Arkansas: 10 Razorbacks
Arkansas State: 7 Indians
Army: 6 Cadets
Auburn: 6 Tigers
Baylor: 5 Bears
Boston College: 6 Eagles
Boston University: 8 Terriers
Brigham Young: 7 Cougars
Brown: 5 Bears
California: 11 Golden Bears
Central Michigan: 9 Chippewas
Cincinnati: 8 Bearcats
Citadel: 8 Bulldogs
Clemson: 6 Tigers
Colgate: 10 Red Raiders
Colorado: 9 Buffaloes

Colorado State: 4 Rams
Columbia: 5 Lions
Connecticut: 7 Huskies
Cornell: 6 Big Red
Dartmouth: 8 Big Green
Davidson: 8 Wildcats
Delaware State: 7 Hornets
Drake: 8 Bulldogs
Duke: 10 Blue Devils
Eastern Kentucky: 8 Colonels
Eastern Michigan: 6 Eagles
Florida: 8 Gators
Florida State: 9 Seminoles
Fresno State: 8 Bulldogs
Furman: 8 Paladins
Georgia: 8 Bulldogs
Georgia Tech: 13 Yellow Jackets
Harvard: 7 Crimson
Hawaii: 15 Rainbow Warriors
Holy Cross: 9 Crusaders
Houston: 7 Cougars
Howard: 6 Bisons
Idaho: 7 Vandals
Idaho State: 7 Bengals
Illinois: 6 Illini
Illinois State: 8 Redbirds
Indiana: 8 Hoosiers
Indiana State: 9 Sycamores
Iowa: 8 Hawkeyes
Iowa State: 8 Cyclones
Kansas: 8 Jayhawks
Kansas State: 8 Wildcats
Kent State: 13 Golden Flashes
Kentucky: 8 Wildcats
Lehigh: 9 Engineers
Louisiana State: 6 Tigers
Louisiana Tech: 8 Bulldogs
Maine: 10 Black Bears
Maryland: 5 Terps 9 Terrapins
Massachusetts: 9 Minutemen
Miami (Florida): 10 Hurricanes
Miami (Ohio): 8 Redskins
Michigan: 10 Wolverines
Michigan State: 8 Spartans
Minnesota: 7 Gophers
Mississippi: 6 Rebels
Mississippi State: 8 Bulldogs
Missouri: 6 Tigers
Montana: 9 Grizzlies
Montana State: 7 Bobcats
Navy: 10 Midshipmen
Nebraska: 11 Cornhuskers
Nevada: 6 Rebels 8 Wolfpack
New Hampshire: 8 Wildcats
New Mexico: 5 Lobos
New Mexico State: 6 Aggies
North Carolina: 8 Tar Heels
North Carolina State: 8 Wolfpack
Northeastern: 7 Huskies

Northwestern: 8 Wildcats
Notre Dame: 13 Fighting Irish
Ohio State: 8 Buckeyes
Ohio University: 7 Bobcats
Oklahoma: 7 Sooners
Oklahoma State: 7 Cowboys
Oregon: 5 Ducks
Oregon State: 7 Beavers
Pennsylvania: 7 Quakers
Pennsylvania State: 12 Nittany Lions
Pittsburgh: 8 Panthers
Princeton: 6 Tigers
Purdue: 12 Boilermakers
Rhode Island: 4 Rams
Rice: 4 Owls
Rutgers: 14 Scarlet Knights
San Diego State: 6 Aztecs
San Jose State: 8 Spartans
South Carolina: 9 Gamecocks
South Carolina State: 8 Bulldogs
Southern California: 7 Trojans
Southern Illinois: 7 Salukis
Southern Methodist: 8 Mustangs
Stanford: 9 Cardinals
Syracuse: 9 Orangemen
Temple: 4 Owls
Tennessee: 10 Volunteers
Tennessee State: 6 Tigers
Tennessee Tech: 12 Golden Eagles
Texas: 9 Longhorns
Texas A&M: 6 Aggies
Texas Christian: 11 Horned Frogs
Texas Southern: 7 Tigers
Texas Tech: 10 Red Raiders
Toledo: 7 Rockets
Tulane: 9 Green Wave
UCLA: 6 Bruins
UNLV: 12 Runnin' Rebels
Utah: 4 Utes
Utah State: 6 Aggies
Vanderbilt: 10 Commodores
Villanova: 8 Wildcats
Virginia: 9 Cavaliers
VMI: 7 Keydets
VPI: 8 Gobblers
Wake Forest: 12 Demon Deacons
Washington: 7 Huskies
Washington State: 7 Cougars
West Virginia: 12 Mountaineers
William & Mary: 5 Tribe
Wisconsin: 7 Badgers
Wyoming: 7 Cowboys
Yale: 4 Elis 8 Bulldogs

collide
3 hit, ram 4 bump 5 clash, crash, smash
6 impact, strike 7 impinge 8 conflict

collision
4 bump, jolt 5 clash, crash, shock, smash,
wreck 6 impact 7 crack-up, smashup
10 concussion

collocate
7 arrange 8 position 9 juxtapose

collogue
6 confer, huddle, parley, powwow 7 consult

colloid
3 gel, sol 4 agar 7 mixture 8 hydrogel,
hydrosol

colloquial
6 casual, vulgar 7 demotic 8 familiar,
informal 9 idiomatic 10 vernacular

colloquium
5 forum 7 palaver, seminar 9 symposium
10 conference, roundtable

colloquy
4 chat, talk 5 forum 6 debate, parley
7 palaver, seminar 8 dialogue
9 symposium 10 conference, discussion,
roundtable 12 conversation
13 confabulation

collude
4 plot 6 devise, scheme 7 connive
8 conspire, contrive, intrigue 9 machinate

collusion
4 plot 8 intrigue, skin game 10 conspiracy

collywobbles
5 colic, gripe 9 bellyache 11 stomachache

Colombia
capital: 6 Bogotá
city: 4 Cali 6 Ibagué 9 Cartagena,
Medellín 12 Barranquilla
language: 7 Spanish
liberator: 7 Bolivar (Simón)
monetary unit: 4 peso
mountain, range: 5 Andes, Chita
6 Puracé, Tolima 9 Cristóbal
neighbor: 4 Peru 6 Brazil, Panama
7 Ecuador 9 Venezuela
river: 6 Chauca 7 Orinoco 9 Magdalena
sea: 9 Caribbean

Colonel Blimp
4 fogy, Tory 6 fossil 7 old fogy
8 mossback 10 fuddy-duddy 11 reactionary

colonnade
4 stoa 9 peristyle

colony
7 outpost 9 satellite 10 settlement

color
3 dun, dye, hue, red, tan 4 aqua, blue,
cast, glow, gold, gray, grey, jade, lime,

navy, pink, puce, rose, teal, tint, tone
5 amber, azure, beige, belie, black, blush,
brown, coral, ebony, flush, green, hazel,
henna, ivory, khaki, lilac, mauve, ocher,
ochre, olive, paint, peach, rouge, shade,
stain, taupe, tinge, umber **6** auburn,
bronze, canary, copper, indigo, maroon,
orange, purple, redden, salmon, sienna,
silver, violet, yellow **7** crimson, emerald,
magenta, pigment, saffron, scarlet
8 chestnut, dyestuff, lavender, tincture
9 embellish, embroider, turquoise, vermilion
10 aquamarine, exaggerate
12 pigmentation
band: **5** facia, vitta **6** fascia
combining form: **5** chrom **6** chromo
7 chromat **8** chromato
primary: **3** red **4** blue **6** yellow
relating to: **9** chromatic
secondary: **5** green **6** orange, purple
soft: **6** pastel

Colorado
capital: **6** Denver
city: **4** Vail **5** Aspen **6** Aurora, Pueblo
7 Boulder **8** Lakewood **11** Fort Collins
college, university: **5** Regis **9** Fort Lewis
mountain, range: **5** Longs (Peak), Pikes
(Peak), Rocky **6** Elbert **7** Rockies
nickname: **10** Centennial (State)
park: **9** Mesa Verde
river: **8** Arkansas, Colorado **9** Rio Grande
state bird: **11** lark bunting
state flower: **9** columbine
state tree: **10** blue spruce

colorant
3 dye **5** stain **7** pigment **8** dyestuff,
tincture

colored
6 biased, warped **8** one-sided, partisan
9 jaundiced **10** prejudiced **11** tendentious

colorful
3 gay **5** gaudy, showy, vivid **6** bright,
flashy, florid, garish, motley **7** splashy

coloring
4 cast, tint **5** front, tinge **6** facade, nuance
7 pigment **8** overtone **10** camouflage,
complexion **12** embroidering
13 embellishment

colorless
3 wan **4** ashy, drab, dull, flat, pale
5 ashen, pasty, prosy, waxen, white
6 albino, doughy, pallid **7** insipid, neutral,
prosaic **8** abstract, blanched, bleached
10 achromatic, lackluster

Color Purple author
6 Walker (Alice)

colossal
4 huge, vast **7** mammoth, massive, titanic
8 enormous, gigantic, immense
9 cyclopean, monstrous **10** gargantuan,
stupendous **11** astonishing, elephantine

colossus
5 giant, titan **6** statue **7** goliath, mammoth,
monster **8** behemoth **9** leviathan

Colossus of _____
6 Rhodes

colporteur
10 evangelist, missionary **12** propagandist

colt
4 foal, tyro **6** novice, rookie **8** beginner,
freshman, neophyte, newcomer **9** fledgling
10 tenderfoot

coltish
6 frisky, impish **7** playful **10** frolicsome

Columbine
beloved: **9** Harlequin
father: **9** Pantaloon

Columbus, Christopher
birthplace: **5** Genoa
patron: **8** Isabella **9** Ferdinand
ship: **4** Niña **5** Pinta **10** Santa Maria
son: **5** Diego
starting point: **5** Palos

column
3 row **4** pier **5** shaft, stela **6** pillar
7 obelisk **8** pilaster
angle: **5** arris
base: **4** ordo **5** socle **6** plinth **9** stylobate
bulge: **7** entasis
female figure: **8** caryatid
male figure: **5** atlas **7** telamon **8** atlantes
(plural)
style: **5** Doric, Ionic **10** Corinthian
top: **7** capital **8** chapiter

coma
6 stupor, torpor **8** blackout, hebetude,
lethargy **9** lassitude

comate
3 pal **4** chum **5** buddy, crony **7** comrade,
partner **9** associate, colleague, companion

comatose
5 dopey **6** stupid, torpid **7** out cold
8 sluggish **9** lethargic **10** insensible
11 unconscious

comb
4 rake, sift, sort **5** crest, curry, probe,
scour, sweep, tease **6** search, winnow
7 ransack **8** untangle **10** straighten
11 investigate

combat
3 war 4 buck, duel, fray 5 fight, repel
6 action, battle, oppose, resist, strife
7 contend, contest, dispute 8 skirmish,
struggle 9 withstand 11 controversy

combatant
7 battler, fighter, soldier, warrior 8 militant,
opponent 9 adversary, aggressor,
assailant, contender, disputant, mercenary
10 antagonist, challenger, competitor,
contestant 11 belligerent

combative
6 feisty 7 scrappy, warlike 8 militant
9 agonistic, bellicose, truculent 10 aggressive, pugnacious 11 belligerent,
contentious, quarrelsome 12 disputatious,
militaristic

combativeness
9 pugnacity 10 aggression, truculence
11 bellicosity 12 belligerence

combe
4 dale, dell, glen, vale 6 dingle, valley

combination
3 mix 4 bloc, pool, ring 5 blend, union
6 fusion, hookup, merger 7 melding,
merging 8 alliance 9 aggregate, coalition,
composite, synthesis 10 connection
11 affiliation, association, conjunction,
partnership, unification 13 consolidation

combine
3 add, mix, wed 4 band, bloc, fuse, join,
link, pool, ring 5 blend, chain, group,
marry, merge, trust, unify, union, unite
6 cartel, league, mingle 7 bracket, conjoin,
connect, faction 8 coadjute, coalesce
9 associate, coalition, commingle,
cooperate, integrate, syndicate
10 amalgamate 11 consolidate,
incorporate 12 conglomerate
Japanese: 8 keiretsu, zaibatsu
Korean: 7 chaebol, jaebeol

combined action
7 synergy 9 synergism

combo
3 trio 4 band 5 group 6 septet, sextet
7 quartet, quintet 8 ensemble

combust
4 burn 6 ignite, kindle 10 incinerate

combustible
4 edgy, fuel 8 burnable, volatile
9 excitable, flammable, ignitable
11 inflammable

material: 3 gas, oil 4 coal, peat, wood
6 tinder

combustion
4 riot 7 burning 8 eruption, ignition,
kindling 9 explosion, oxidation
13 thermogenesis

come
4 flow, hail, stem 5 arise, issue, occur
6 arrive, derive, show up, spring, turn up
7 advance, emanate, proceed 8 approach
9 originate
a cropper: 4 fail, fall
across: 4 find, meet 8 discover
9 encounter
apart: 12 disintegrate
at: 6 attack
away: 5 leave 6 depart
before: 7 precede
clean: 7 confess
forth: 5 issue 6 appear, emerge
forward: 7 advance 9 volunteer
into: 5 enter 7 acquire
near: 5 verge 8 approach
round: 5 rally 7 get well, recover
to pass: 5 occur 6 happen
up: 5 arise
upon: 4 find, meet 8 discover
9 encounter

comeback
5 rally 6 answer, retort, return 7 rebound,
revival, riposte 8 rebuttal, recovery,
repartee, response 11 improvement
12 counterclaim, recuperation

come by
4 call 5 pop in, visit 6 drop in, look in
7 acquire, collect, inherit

comedian
3 wag, wit 4 card 5 clown, comic, droll,
joker 6 jester 7 farceur 8 funnyman,
humorist, jokester, quipster 11 entertainer

comedo
9 blackhead

comedown
4 dive, fall, ruin 5 crash 7 decline,
descent, failure, setback 8 collapse
9 ruination

come down with
3 get 5 catch 7 develop 8 contract

comedy
5 farce, humor 6 levity 8 drollery, hilarity
9 drollness, wittiness

come in
5 enter, reply 6 answer 7 respond

command

comely
4 fair **5** bonny, sonsy **6** lovely, pretty,
proper, sonsie **7** winsome **8** becoming,
decorous, handsome, pleasing
9 beauteous, beautiful, befitting
10 attractive **11** good-looking

come off
4 fare, seem **5** click, occur **6** appear, go
over, happen, pan out **7** develop, succeed
8 prove out **9** transpire

come-on
4 bait, lure, trap **5** decoy, snare
9 seduction **10** allurement, enticement,
inducement, invitation, temptation
12 blandishment, inveiglement, solicitation

come out
4 leak **5** break, debut, end up **6** emerge
9 transpire

come out with
3 say **4** tell **5** state, utter **6** report
7 declare, deliver, publish, release
8 announce, proclaim

comestible
6 edible **7** eatable **8** esculent

comestibles
4 feed, food **6** viands **7** edibles **8** victuals
9 provender **10** provisions

come through
6 chip in, endure **7** pitch in, prevail, survive
8 transmit **10** contribute

come together
4 mass, meet **5** merge, swarm **6** gather,
huddle **7** cluster, collect, combine,
convene **8** assemble, converge
10 congregate

come upon
4 find **7** run into, suncover, unearth
8 bump into, discover, trip over
9 encounter, run across

comeuppance
3 due **5** lumps **7** deserts

comfort
3 aid **4** help **5** cheer **6** assist, buck up,
luxury, relief, solace, soothe, succor
7 amenity, cheer up, console, relieve,
support **8** reassure, sympathy
10 assistance, sympathize
11 commiserate, consolation, contentment

comfortable
4 cozy, easy, homy, snug, soft **5** ample,
cushy, homey, roomy **7** content, easeful,
restful, well-off **8** adequate, homelike,

pleasant, pleasing, spacious, well-to-do
9 agreeable, satisfied, well-fixed
10 commodious, prosperous, sufficient,
well-heeled **11** substantial **12** satisfactory

comforter
4 down, pouf, puff **5** duvet, quilt
9 eiderdown

comfy
4 cozy, homy **5** cushy, homey

comic
3 wag, wit **5** antic, droll, funny, joker
6 jester **7** risible **8** comedian, farcical,
funnyman, humorist, jokester, quipster
9 laughable, ludicrous **10** ridiculous

comical
4 zany **5** droll, funny, goofy, silly **6** absurd
7 amusing, foolish, risible, waggish
8 farcical **9** laughable, ludicrous
10 ridiculous

comic strip
4 Pogo, Shoe **5** Hazel, Henry, Nancy
6 Archie, Popeye **7** Blondie, Dilbert, Far
Side (The), Peanuts **8** Alley Oop, Andy
Capp, Garfield, Krazy Kat, Li'l Abner,
Superman, Yellow Kid (The) **9** Betty Boop,
Dick Tracy, Flash Gordon, Marmaduke,
Mary Worth, Spider-Man **10** Doonesbury,
Joe Palooka, Little Nemo **11** Bloom
County, Brenda Starr, Mutt and Jeff, Rex
Morgan M.D., Steve Canyon **12** Beetle
Bailey **13** Captain Marvel, Gasoline Alley,
Prince Valiant

coming
3 due **4** next **5** fated, onset **6** advent,
future **7** arrival, ensuing, nearing
8 approach, expected, foreseen, imminent
9 following, impending **11** approaching
forth: 7 issuant

comity
5 amity **7** concord, harmony **8** goodwill
10 friendship **11** benevolence,
camaraderie **12** friendliness

comma
4 lull **5** pause **8** interval

command
3 bid **4** rule, sway **5** order **6** adjure,
behest, charge, compel, direct, enjoin
7 bidding, conduct, control, dictate,
mandate, mastery, precept **9** authority,
direction, directive, expertise, ordinance
10 domination, injunction **11** instruction
12 jurisdiction
to go: 4 mush **6** avaunt, begone
7 giddyap

to stop: 4 whoa 5 avast

commandeer
4 take 4 annex, seize, usurp 6 assume, hijack 7 preempt 8 accroach, arrogate 9 conscript, sequester 10 confiscate 11 appropriate, expropriate, requisition

commander
4 boss, head 6 honcho, leader, master 7 captain, general, headman, officer

commandment
3 law 4 fiat, rule 5 edict, order 6 decree 7 mitzvah, precept, statute

commedia dell' _____
4 arte

comme il faut
6 decent, polite, proper, seemly 7 correct 8 becoming, decorous, suitable

commemorate
4 keep 7 observe 8 eulogize, monument 9 celebrate, solemnize 11 memorialize 13 monumentalize

commemorative
8 memorial 10 dedicatory 11 celebratory

commence
4 begin, start 6 launch, set out 7 kick off 8 embark on, initiate 10 embark upon, inaugurate

commencement
4 dawn 5 birth, onset, start 6 outset 7 dawning, genesis, opening 9 beginning, inception 10 graduation 12 inauguration

commend
4 hail, laud 5 extol 6 commit, kudize, praise, salute, tender 7 acclaim, applaud, approve, consign, entrust 8 hand over, relegate, turn over 10 compliment

commendable
6 worthy 8 laudable 9 admirable, deserving, estimable, meritable, venerable 10 creditable 11 meritorious 12 praiseworthy

commensurable
see **commensurate**

commensurate
4 even 5 equal 10 comparable 11 coextensive 12 proportional 13 corresponding, proportionate

comment
4 note 5 opine 6 remark 7 mention, observe 8 critique, point out 9 criticism, interject 10 animadvert 11 observation 12 obiter dictum

commentary
5 gloss 6 review 8 analysis, critique, exegesis 9 editorial, narration, voice-over 10 annotation, exposition 11 explanation, observation 12 appreciation, obiter dictum

commerce
5 trade 7 contact, traffic 8 business, congress, dealings, exchange, industry 9 communion 11 interchange 13 communication

commercial
6 advert 8 economic 10 mercantile 13 advertisement

commie
3 Red 5 pinko 6 bolshy 7 bolshie 9 Bolshevik

commination
5 curse 8 anathema 10 accusation, execration 11 imprecation, malediction 12 denunciation

commingle
3 mix 4 meld 5 blend, merge, unify 8 compound, intermix 9 integrate 10 amalgamate

comminute
4 bray 5 crush, grind 9 granulate, pulverize

commiserate
4 pity 7 condole, feel for 9 empathize 10 sympathize 13 compassionate

commiseration
4 pity, ruth 7 empathy 8 sympathy 10 compassion, condolence

commission
3 bid, fee 4 name 5 board, order 6 agency, assign, charge, enable, engage, enjoin, enlist 7 appoint, command, council, empower, license, warrant 8 accredit, delegate, deputize 9 authorize, designate 10 delegation, deputation, percentage 11 certificate

commit
4 bind 5 allot, grant, refer 6 assign, convey, execute, invest, ordain, pledge, record, reveal 7 achieve, consign, deposit, entrust, execute, perform, promise, pull off, trustee 8 allocate, carry out, hand over, obligate, relegate, turn over 10 accomplish, perpetrate

commitment
3 vow 4 bond, deal, duty 6 charge, devoir, pledge 7 promise 8 contract

9 agreement, assurance, guarantee
10 obligation 11 undertaking

committal
see **commitment**

commixture
5 blend 6 fusion 7 amalgam, melange
8 compound, mingling 9 composite

commodious
4 wide 5 ample, roomy 8 spacious
9 capacious, expansive, luxurious
11 comfortable

commodities
5 goods, items, wares 8 articles, products
9 vendibles 11 merchandise

common
4 park 5 banal, daily, joint, plaza, trite,
usual 6 mutual, normal, shared 7 general,
generic, prosaic, regular, routine, typical
8 adequate, communal, conjoint, conjunct,
déclassé, everyday, familiar, frequent,
habitual, ordinary, standard, workaday
9 customary, prevalent, tolerable, universal
10 collective, pedestrian, prevailing,
unexciting, widespread 12 conventional,
run-of-the-mill, satisfactory
13 unexceptional, uninteresting

commonalty
3 mob 5 plebs 6 masses, people, plebes,
public, rabble 7 commune 8 populace
9 hoi polloi, multitude, plebeians
11 proletariat, rank and file, third estate

commoners
see **commonalty**

commonplace
5 stale, tired, trite, usual 6 cliché, normal,
truism 7 bromide, clichéd, humdrum,
mundane, obvious, prosaic, regular,
routine, typical 8 banality, bromidic,
chestnut, everyday, habitual, mediocre,
ordinary, well-worn, workaday
9 hackneyed, platitude, prevalent
10 pedestrian, shibboleth, stereotype,
uneventful 11 stereotyped
12 conventional, run-of-the-mill,
unremarkable 13 stereotypical,
unexceptional, uninteresting

common sense
6 wisdom 8 judgment, prudence
10 shrewdness

Common Sense author
5 Paine (Thomas)

commotion
3 ado, din, row 4 flap, fuss, moil, riot, stew,
stir, to-do 5 storm, whirl 6 bustle, clamor,
dither, flurry, fracas, furore, hoopla, hubbub,
hurrah, lather, outcry, pother, racket,
ruckus, rumpus, shindy, tumult, uproar,
upturn 7 ferment, tempest, turmoil
8 brouhaha, foofaraw 9 agitation,
confusion 10 convulsion, hullabaloo, hurly-
burly, turbulence 11 pandemonium

commove
5 rouse 6 excite 7 agitate, inspire,
provoke 9 electrify, galvanize, stimulate

communal
5 civil, joint 6 common, mutual, public,
shared 10 collective 11 socialistic

commune
10 collective
Israeli: 7 kibbutz
Russian: 3 mir 7 kolkhoz

communicable
8 catching 10 contagious, infectious
13 transmissible, transmittable

communicate
4 tell 6 convey, impart, inform, pass on,
relate, reveal, signal 7 connect, contact,
divulge 8 disclose, transmit 9 make known

communication
4 talk 7 contact, message, missive, talking
8 converse, exchange 9 directive
10 discussing, discussion 11 interchange,
intercourse 12 conversation
means: 3 Web 4 drum, mail, note 5 e-
mail, media, phone, radio 6 letter, medium,
pigeon, speech 8 Internet 9 telegraph,
telephone 10 television
system: 8 language

communications code word
4 Alfa, Echo, Golf, Kilo, Lima, Mike, Papa,
Xray, Zulu 5 Alpha, Bravo, Delta, Hotel,
India, Oscar, Romeo, Tango 6 Quebec,
Sierra, Victor, Yankee 7 Charlie, Foxtrot,
Juliett, Uniform, Whiskey 8 November

communicative
5 vocal 6 fluent, prolix 7 verbose, voluble
8 eloquent 9 expansive, garrulous,
talkative 10 articulate, expressive,
loquacious

communion
7 rapport, sharing 9 sacrament
10 connection, Eucharist, fellowship
cloth: 8 corporal
cup: 7 chalice
plate: 5 paten

communism
7 Marxism 8 Leninism 10 bolshevism
12 collectivism

Communist
3 red **5** lefty, pinko **6** bolshy, Maoist
7 bolshie, comrade, Marxist **8** Leninist
9 Bolshevik, Stalinist **10** Bolshevist,
Trotskyist

Communist leader
Chinese: 3 Mao **4** Deng **5** Jiang **8** Hu
Jintao **9** Mao Zedong **10** Jiang Zemin,
Mao Tse-tung **12** Deng Xiaoping **13** Teng
Hsiao-p'ing
Russian: 5 Lenin (Vladimir Ilyich) **6** Stalin
(Joseph) **7** Kosygin (Aleksey), Trotsky
(Leon) **8** Andropov (Yuri), Brezhnev
(Leonid) **9** Chernenko (Konstantin),
Gorbachev (Mikhail) **10** Khrushchev
(Nikita)

community
4 town **7** enclave, society **12** neighborhood
ecological: 10 biocenosis **11** biocoenosis

commute
5 alter, change, make up, modify, soften,
travel **7** convert, curtail, shorten, shuttle
8 decrease, exchange, mitigate, transfer
9 transform, translate, transmute,
transpose **10** compensate, substitute
11 interchange

Como está _____?
5 usted

Comoros
capital: 6 Moroni
island: 6 Mohéli **7** Anjouan **12** Grande
Comore
language: 6 Arabic, French **8** Comorian
monetary unit: 5 franc
volcano: 8 Karthala

compact
4 bond **5** close, dense, unify **7** bargain,
bunched, crowded, pressed **8** compress,
condense, contract, covenant
9 agreement, concordat **10** convention
11 concentrate, consolidate, transaction

compadre
3 pal **4** chum, mate **5** amigo, buddy, crony
6 friend **7** comrade, partner **8** confrere,
sidekick, intimate **9** associate, colleague,
companion

companion
3 pal **4** chum, mate **5** buddy, crony
6 cohort, escort **7** comrade, consort,
partner **8** sidekick **9** associate, attendant,
colleague

companionable
6 genial, social **7** affable, amiable
8 outgoing, sociable **9** agreeable,
congenial, convivial **10** gregarious
11 good-natured

companionship
7 company, society **8** intimacy
10 fellowship **11** camaraderie

company
4 band, club, crew, firm, gang, team
5 corps, group, party, troop **6** circle, clique,
guests, outfit, troupe **7** concern, coterie,
retinue, society, visitor **8** assembly,
business, ensemble, visitors **9** gathering
10 assemblage, enterprise, fellowship
11 association, camaraderie, corporation
12 congregation **13** companionship,
establishment

comparable
4 akin, like **5** alike **6** agnate **7** similar,
uniform **8** parallel **9** analogous
10 equivalent, homologous **12** commensurate **13** corresponding

comparative
4 near **8** relative **11** approximate

compare
5 liken, match **6** equate, relate **7** collate
8 contrast, parallel **9** correlate
10 assimilate

comparison
6 simile **7** analogy **8** affinity, contrast,
likeness **9** collation, semblance
10 similarity, similitude **11** correlation,
resemblance

compartment
3 bay **4** cell, nook, part, slot **5** berth,
booth, niche, stall **6** alcove, carrel, locker
7 chamber, cubicle, section **8** division
9 cubbyhole **10** pigeonhole **11** subdivision

compass
3 hem **4** ring **5** ambit, field, grasp, orbit,
range, reach, scope, sweep **6** bounds,
circle, domain, extent, girdle, limits, radius,
sphere **7** circuit, environ, purview
8 boundary, confines, environs
9 enclosure, extension, perimeter,
periphery **13** circumference
kind: 4 gyro **5** solar **8** magnetic
stand: 8 binnacle

compassion
4 pity, ruth **5** mercy **7** charity, empathy
8 clemency, humanity, kindness, sympathy
10 condolence, humaneness
11 benevolence **13** commiseration, fellow
feeling

compassionate
4 pity, warm **6** humane, tender **7** clement
8 merciful **10** benevolent, charitable,

solicitous **11** commiserate, kindhearted, softhearted, sympathetic, warmhearted

compassionless
5 stony **7** callous **8** obdurate **9** heartless, unfeeling **11** coldblooded, hard-hearted, ironhearted **12** stonyhearted

compass point
3 ENE, ESE, NNE, NNW, SSE, SSW, WNW, WSW **4** east, west **5** north, rhumb, south **7** bearing
Scottish: 4 airt

compatible
6 proper **8** suitable **9** agreeable, congenial, congruous, consonant **10** consistent, harmonious, like-minded **11** appropriate, sympathetic

compatriot
8 confrere **9** associate, colleague, companion

compeer
see **companion**

compel
4 hale, urge **5** drive, force **6** coerce, impose, oblige **7** enforce **9** constrain

compelling
4 dire **5** acute **6** cogent, crying, urgent **7** clamant, exigent, telling, weighty **8** forceful, pressing **10** convincing, persuasive **11** importunate, significant **12** well-grounded **13** authoritative

compendious
5 brief, pithy, short **7** compact, concise, summary **8** succinct **9** condensed **11** abbreviated

compendium
4 list **5** brief, guide **6** aperçu, digest, manual, précis, sketch, survey **7** epitome, summary **8** abstract, Baedeker, handbook, overview, syllabus, synopsis **9** anthology, guidebook, vade mecum **10** abridgment, collection, conspectus **11** abridgement, compilation, enchiridion

compensate
3 pay **5** atone, repay **6** make up, offset, pay off, redeem, set off **7** balance, guerdon, requite, satisfy **8** outweigh **9** indemnify, reimburse **10** counteract, neutralize, recompense, remunerate **11** countervail

compensation
6 amends, reward, salary **7** damages, payment, redress **8** earnings, reprisal, requital, solatium **9** atonement, indemnity,

quittance, repayment **10** recompense, reparation **11** restitution **12** remuneration

compete
3 vie **4** spar **5** fight **6** battle, strive **7** contend, contest **8** struggle

competence
5 skill **7** ability, know-how **8** adequacy, aptitude, capacity, facility **9** expertise **10** capability **11** proficiency, sufficiency **13** qualification

competent
3 fit **4** able **5** adept **6** au fait, decent, proper **7** capable, skilled **8** adequate **9** efficient, qualified **10** proficient, sufficient **12** satisfactory

competition
4 bout, game, meet, race **5** clash, fight, match, rival **6** strife **7** contest, matchup, rivalry **8** concours, conflict, striving, struggle, tug-of-war **10** antagonism, contention, tournament

competitor
5 enemy, rival **8** opponent **9** adversary **10** antagonist, contestant, opposition

compile
4 edit **5** amass **6** gather, select **7** build up, collate, collect **8** assemble **9** construct **10** accumulate **11** anthologize

complacency
5 pride **7** conceit **8** smugness **10** narcissism

complacent
4 smug **6** serene **7** assured **9** conceited, confident **11** self-assured, unconcerned **13** self-confident, self-contented, self-possessed, self-satisfied

complain
3 nag **4** beef, crab, fret, fuss, wail **5** gripe, grump, whine **6** grouch, grouse, lament, yammer **7** grizzle, grumble, protest **9** bellyache

complainer
4 crab **5** crank **6** griper, grouch **7** grouser **8** grumbler, sourpuss **10** malcontent **11** faultfinder

complaint
5 gripe **6** grouse, lament, malady **7** ailment, disease, protest **8** disorder, sickness, syndrome **9** condition, criticism, grievance, infirmity, objection **10** affliction, allegation **12** protestation

complaisant
4 easy, mild **7** amiable, lenient **8** generous, obliging **9** agreeable, compliant,

easygoing, indulgent **11** deferential, good-humored, good-natured **12** good-tempered **13** accommodating

complement

4 crew, rest **9** correlate, remainder **10** supplement **11** counterpart

complete

3 end **4** done, full, halt **5** close, ended, total, utter, whole **6** entire, finish, intact, wind up, wrap up **7** achieve, fulfill, perfect, perform, plenary **8** absolute, conclude, finalize, finished, integral, round out, thorough **9** concluded, out-and-out, terminate **10** accomplish, consummate, exhaustive, unabridged **11** categorical, unmitigated **13** thoroughgoing

completed

4 done, over **5** ended **7** through **8** done with, executed, finished **9** concluded, fulfilled **10** terminated **11** consummated **12** accomplished

completion

3 end **6** finish, windup, wrap-up **8** fruition **10** conclusion

complex

6 daedal, knotty, system, varied **7** chelate, gordian, network **8** abstruse, compound, involved, syndrome, tortuous **9** aggregate, Byzantine, composite, elaborate, intricate **10** convoluted **11** complicated **12** conglomerate, labyrinthine **13** heterogeneous, sophisticated

complexion

3 hue **4** cast, tint, tone **5** color, humor, tinge **6** aspect, makeup, nature, temper **8** tincture **9** character **10** appearance, coloration **11** disposition, temperament **13** individuality, pigmentation

compliance

7 consent **8** docility **9** agreement, deference, obedience **10** acceptance, conformity, submission **11** amenability, flexibility, resignation **12** acquiescence, tractability

complicate

5 mix up, ravel, snarl **6** jumble, muddle, tangle **7** confuse, involve **8** confound, disorder, entangle **9** aggravate, convolute **10** disarrange, exacerbate

complicated

6 daedal, knotty **7** complex, gordian, tangled **8** abstruse, involved, tortuous **9** Byzantine, elaborate, intricate, recondite **10** convoluted **12** labyrinthine **13** heterogeneous, sophisticated

complicity

8 abetment **9** collusion **10** connivance **11** involvement

compliment

4 hail, kudo, laud **5** extol, honor, kudos **6** praise, salute **7** acclaim, applaud, bouquet, commend, regards, tribute **8** accolade, encomium **9** laudation, recommend **11** recognition **12** appreciation, commendation, congratulate

complimentary

4 free **6** gratis **8** costless **9** favorable, laudatory **10** chargeless, gratuitous **12** appreciative

comply

4 obey **5** yield **6** accede, submit **7** conform **9** acquiesce

component

4 part **5** piece **6** factor **7** element, segment **10** ingredient **11** constituent

comport

4 bear, jibe **5** agree, carry, fit in, match, tally **6** accord, acquit, behave, demean, square **7** conduct **8** coincide, dovetail **9** harmonize **10** correspond

comportment

3 air **4** mien **7** address, bearing, conduct **8** attitude, behavior, carriage, demeanor, presence

compose

4 calm, cool, form, lull, make **5** forge, quiet, relax, still, write **6** becalm, create, devise, draw up, indite, invent, make up, settle, solace, soothe **7** collect, console, contain, control **8** comprise **9** construct, fabricate, formulate, originate **10** constitute
type: 3 set

composed

4 calm, cool **5** staid **6** poised, sedate, serene **9** collected, unruffled **11** unflappable **13** imperturbable, self-possessed

composer

6 scorer **8** melodist **9** balladist, songsmith, tunesmith **10** songwriter
American: 3 Kay (Hershy, Ulysses)
4 Bock (Jerry), Cage (John), Hill (Edward Burlingame), Ives (Charles), Kern (Jerome), King (Carole), Lane (Burton), Monk (Thelonious), Work (Henry Clay)
5 Adams (John), Arlen (Harold), Beach (Amy), Blake (Eubie), Bland (James A.),

Bloch (Ernest), Cohan (George M.), Friml (Rudolf), Glass (Philip), Gould (Morton), Grofé (Ferde), Handy (W. C.), Loewe (Frederick), Mason (Daniel Gregory, Lowell), Moore (Douglas), Reich (Steve), Sousa (John Philip), Still (William Grant), Styne (Jule), Zappa (Frank) **6** Barber (Samuel), Berlin (Irving), Carter (Elliott), Cowell (Henry), Emmett (Daniel), Foster (Stephen), Hanson (Howard), Harris (Roy), Herman (Jerry), Joplin (Scott), Kander (John), McHugh (Jimmy), McKuen (Rod), Menken (Alan), Morton ("Jelly Roll"), Oliver ("King"), Parker (Charlie "Bird," Horatio), Piston (Walter), Porter (Cole), Previn (André), Seeger (Pete), Taylor (Deems), Varèse (Edgard), Warren (Harry) **7** Babbitt (Milton), Brubeck (Dave), Copland (Aaron), Gilbert (Henry F.), Gilmore (Patrick), Goldman (Edwin Franko), Herbert (Victor), Loesser (Frank), Mancini (Henry), Menotti (Gian Carlo), Rodgers (Richard), Romberg (Sigmund), Schuman (William), Thomson (Virgil), Tiomkin (Dimitri), Willson (Meredith), Youmans (Vincent) **8** Anderson (Leroy), Billings (William), Burleigh (Henry Thacker), Damrosch (Leopold, Walter), Gershwin (George), Hamlisch (Marvin), Herrmann (Bernard), Korngold (Erich Wolfgang), Kreisler (Fritz), Marsalis (Wynton), Schuller (Gunther), Sessions (Roger), Sondheim (Stephen), Williams (John) **9** Bacharach (Burt), Bernstein (Elmer, Leonard), Donaldson (Walter), Ellington (Duke), Hovhaness (Alan), MacDowell (Edward) **10** Blitzstein (Marc), Carmichael (Hoagy), Gottschalk (Louis Moreau)
Argentinian: 9 Ginastera (Alberto)
Australian: 8 Grainger (Percy)
Austrian: 4 Berg (Alban), Wolf (Hugo) **5** Haydn (Franz Joseph) **6** Czerny (Karl), Mahler (Gustav), Mozart (Leopold, Wolfgang Amadeus), Straus (Oscar), Webern (Anton) **7** Strauss (Eduard, Johann, Josef) **8** Bruckner (Anton), Schubert (Franz) **10** Schoenberg (Arnold)
Belgian: 5 Ysaÿe (Eugène) **6** Franck (César)
Brazilian: 5 Jobim (Antonio Carlos) **10** Villa-Lobos (Heitor)
Czech: 3 Suk (Josef) **6** Dvořák (Antonín)

7 Janáček (Leoš), Martinu (Bohuslav), Smetana (Bedřich)
Danish: 7 Nielsen (Carl)
Dutch: 9 Sweelinck (Jan Pieterszoon)
English: 4 Arne (Thomas Augustine), Byrd (William) **5** Elgar (Edward), Holst (Gustav) **6** Delius (Frederick), Morley (Thomas), Tallis (Thomas), Walton (William), Wesley (Charles, Samuel) **7** Britten (Benjamin), Dowland (John), Gibbons (Orlando), Purcell (Henry), Weelkes (Thomas) **8** Sullivan (Arthur) **9** Dunstable (John) **11** Lloyd Webber (Andrew)
Finnish: 8 Palmgren (Selim), Sibelius (Jean)
Flemish: 5 Dufay (Guillaume), Lasso (Orlando di) **6** Lassus (Orlande de) **8** Willaert (Adriaan)
French: 4 Indy (Vincent d'), Lalo (Edouard) **5** Auber (Esprit), Bizet (Georges), Dukas (Paul), Fauré (Gabriel), Ibert (Jacques), Jarre (Maurice), Lully (Jean-Baptiste), Ravel (Maurice), Satie (Erik), Widor (Charles-Marie) **6** Boulez (Pierre), Campra (André), Franck (César), Gounod (Charles), Rameau (Jean-Philippe), Thomas (Ambroise) **7** Berlioz (Hector), Debussy (Claude), Delibes (Léo), Machaut (Guillaume de), Milhaud (Darius), Poulenc (Francis) **8** Chabrier (Emmanuel), Couperin (François, Louis), Honegger (Arthur), Massenet (Jules), Messiaen (Olivier) **9** Meyerbeer (Giacomo), Offenbach (Jacques) **10** Saint-Saëns (Camille)
German: 4 Bach (C. P. E., Johann Christian, Johann Sebastian, Wilhelm Friedemann), Orff (Carl) **5** Bruch (Max), Gluck (Christoph Willibald von), Reger (Max), Spohr (Louis, Ludwig), Weber (Carl Maria von), Weill (Kurt) **6** Brahms (Johannes), Handel (George Frideric), Schütz (Heinrich), Vogler (Abt), Wagner (Richard) **7** Hassler (Hans Leo), Strauss (Richard) **8** Korngold (Erich Wolfgang), Schumann (Robert), Telemann (Georg Philipp) **9** Beethoven (Ludwig van), Buxtehude (Dietrich), Hindemith (Paul), Meyerbeer (Giacomo), Pachelbel (Johann) **10** Praetorius (Michael) **11** Humperdinck (Engelbert), Mendelssohn (Felix), Stockhausen (Karlheinz)
Hungarian: 5 Léhar (Franz), Liszt (Franz) **6** Bartók (Béla), Kodály (Zoltán), Ligeti (György) **8** Dohnányi (Erno)
Italian: 4 Peri (Jacopo), Rota (Nino) **5** Berio (Luciano), Boito (Arrigo), Verdi (Giuseppe) **6** Busoni (Ferruccio) **7** Bellini (Vincenzo), Caccini (Giulio), Corelli

composite

(Arcangelo), Martini (Padre), Puccini
(Giacomo), Rossini (Gioacchino), Salieri
(Antonio), Tartini (Giuseppe), Vivaldi
(Antonio) **8** Albinoni (Tomaso), Clementi
(Muzio), Gabrieli (Andrea, Giovanni), Mascagni (Pietro), Paganini (Niccolò), Respighi
(Ottorino) **9** Cherubini (Luigi), Donizetti
(Gaetano), Pergolesi (Giovanni Battista),
Scarlatti (Alessandro, Domenico),
Tommasini (Vincenzo) **10** Boccherini
(Luigi), Monteverdi (Claudio), Palestrina (G.
P. da), Ponchielli (Amilcare), Zingarelli
(Niccolò) **11** Frescobaldi (Girolamo),
Leoncavallo (Ruggero) **12** Dallapiccola
(Luigi)
Mexican: 6 Chávez (Carlos)
Norwegian: 5 Grieg (Edvard)
Polish: 6 Chopin (Frédéric) **7** Gorecki
(Henryk) **10** Paderewski (Ignacy Jan),
Penderecki (Krzysztof), Wieniawski
(Henryk) **11** Lutoslawski (Witold),
Szymanowski (Karol)
Romanian: 7 Xenakis (Iannis)
Russian: 6 Glinka (Mikhail) **7** Borodin
(Aleksandr) **8** Glazunov (Aleksandr),
Scriabin (Aleksandr) **9** Balakirev (Mily),
Prokofiev (Sergey), Schnittke (Alfred)
10 Kabalevsky (Dmitri), Mussorgsky
(Modest), Rubinstein (Anton), Stravinsky
(Igor), Tcherepnin (Nikolay)
11 Tchaikovsky (Pyotr Ilich)
12 Khachaturian (Aram), Rachmaninoff
(Sergey), Shostakovich (Dmitry)
Spanish: 5 Falla (Manuel de) **7** Albéniz
(Isaac), Rodrigo (Joaquin) **8** Granados
(Enrique), Victoria (Tomas Luis de)

composite

3 mix **5** blend **6** fusion, hybrid **7** amalgam, complex, mixture **8** compound
11 combination **12** amalgamation

composition

4 opus **5** essay, paper, theme **6** design,
layout, makeup **7** article **9** formation
11 arrangement **12** architecture,
constitution, construction
choral: 4 mass **5** motet **8** oratorio
for eight: 6 octet
for five: 7 quintet
for four: 7 quartet
for nine: 6 nonet
for one: 4 aria, solo
for seven: 6 septet
for six: 6 sextet
for three: 4 trio
for two: 4 duet
instrumental: 3 jig **4** reel **5** étude, fugue,
gigue, march, rondo, suite **6** sonata
7 caprice, partita, prelude, scherzo

8 concerto, fantasia, overture, rhapsody,
saraband, sinfonia, symphony, tone poem
9 allemande, capriccio, sarabande
10 intermezzo
vocal: 4 aria, lied, mass, song **5** carol,
chant, motet, opera, round **6** arioso,
ballad, chanty **7** cantata, chanson,
chantey, chorale, lullaby, requiem
8 berceuse, madrigal, oratorio **9** plainsong,
spiritual

compos mentis

4 sane **5** lucid, sound **6** normal

composure

4 calm **5** poise **7** balance, dignity
8 calmness, coolness, evenness, serenity,
sobriety **9** sangfroid **10** equanimity
11 equilibrium

compound

3 mix **4** join, link **5** admix, alloy, blend,
union, unite **6** expand, extend, fusion,
make up, mingle **7** amalgam, augment,
complex, compost, enlarge, magnify,
mixture **8** coalesce, comingle, heighten,
increase, intermix, multiply **9** admixture,
aggravate, associate, commingle,
composite, intensify, synthesis
10 commixture, exacerbate **11** intermingle
12 amalgamation
chemical:
(see at **chemical**)
medicinal: 8 magnesia
protein: 7 peptone
sulfur: 5 thiol **7** sulfide, sulfone
8 sulfonyl, sulfuryl, sulphide

comprehend

4 know **5** catch, grasp **6** absorb, accept,
embody, fathom, take in **7** cognize,
compass, contain, discern, embrace,
include, involve, subsume **8** comprise,
perceive **9** encompass **10** appreciate,
understand

comprehensible

8 knowable **9** graspable **10** fathomable
12 intelligible

comprehension

3 ken **5** grasp **9** awareness, knowledge
10 cognizance, conception, perception
11 discernment **12** apperception
13 understanding

comprehensive

4 full, wide **5** broad **6** global **7** general,
overall **8** catholic, complete, sweeping
9 all-around, extensive, inclusive, universal
10 exhaustive **12** all-inclusive,
encyclopedic

comprehensiveness
5 range, reach, scope **7** breadth **8** fullness
9 amplitude

compress
3 jam **4** cram, push **5** crush, press
6 reduce, shrink, squash, squish, shrink
7 bandage, compact, squeeze
8 condense, contract **11** concentrate

comprise
4 form **6** make up **7** compose, contain,
embrace, include, subsume
10 comprehend, constitute

compromise
4 mean, pact, risk settle **7** bargain,
compact **8** contract, endanger, trade off
9 agreement, middle way **10** concession,
golden mean, jeopardize, settlement
12 middle ground

compulsion
4 itch, need, urge **5** drive, force **8** coercion
9 necessity **10** constraint

compulsive
7 driving **9** besetting, obsessive
12 irresistible, overwhelming

compulsory
7 binding **8** coercive, enforced, required
9 mandatory, requisite **10** imperative,
obligatory

compunction
4 pang **5** demur, qualm regret, unease
7 remorse, scruple **8** distress **9** hesitancy,
misgiving **10** conscience, hesitation

compunctious
5 sorry **8** contrite, penitent **9** regretful,
repentant **10** apologetic, remorseful
11 penitential

computation
8 figuring **9** ciphering, reckoning
10 arithmetic, estimation **11** calculation

compute
5 tally, total **6** cipher, figure, reckon
8 estimate **9** calculate, determine

computer
6 abacus, laptop **7** desktop **9** mainframe
10 calculator
component: 3 CPU **4** chip **5** mouse,
tower **7** monitor **8** keyboard **9** hard drive
information: 4 data
instruction: 5 macro
inventor: 7 Babbage (Charles)
language: 3 Ada, APL **4** Java, Lisp, Perl

5 ALGOL, BASIC, COBOL **6** Pascal
7 FORTRAN
type: 6 analog **7** digital

comrade
3 pal **4** ally, chum, mate **5** buddy, crony
6 cohort, comate, fellow **7** consort
8 sidekick, tovarich, tovarish **9** associate,
colleague, companion

con
3 gyp, vet **4** anti, bilk, coax, dupe, fool,
hoax, rook, scam **5** cheat, fraud, learn,
study, trick **6** cajole, fleece, gammon,
inmate, survey **7** against, blarney,
canvass, chicane, convict, deceive,
defraud, examine, inspect, swindle,
wheedle **8** blandish, flimflam, hoodwink,
inveigle, jailbird, memorize, negative,
opponent, persuade, prisoner, soft-soap
9 bamboozle, check over, sweet-talk
10 antithesis, manipulate, scrutinize
11 hornswoggle **12** tuberculosis

concatenate
4 join, link **5** unite **7** connect

concavity
3 dip, sag **4** bowl, dent, sink **5** basin
6 crater, hollow, trough **7** sinkage
8 sinkhole **10** depression

conceal
4 bury, hide, mask, veil **5** cache, cloak,
cover, stash **6** screen **7** obscure, secrete
8 ensconce, enshroud, palliate
10 camouflage

concealed
5 privy **6** buried, covert, hidden, secret
8 obscured, shrouded, ulterior
11 clandestine

concede
3 own **4** avow, fold **5** admit, allow, award,
grant, yield **6** accept, accord **7** confess
9 surrender, vouchsafe **10** capitulate,
relinquish **11** acknowledge

conceit
4 idea, whim **5** fancy, pride **6** egoism,
megrim, notion, vagary, vanity **7** caprice,
egotism, thought **8** crotchet, metaphor,
self-love, smugness, snobbery **9** self-pride,
vainglory **10** narcissism, self-esteem
11 complacence, complacency, self-
opinion, swelled head

conceited
4 vain **6** snobby, snooty **7** pompous,
stuck-up **8** immodest, puffed up, snobbish
12 narcissistic, vainglorious

conceitedness
6 vanity 8 self-love 9 vainglory
10 narcissism

conceivable
8 possible 9 plausible, thinkable
10 imaginable, supposable

conceive
4 form 5 beget, fancy, grasp, think
6 accept, assume, devise, expect, follow,
gather, ideate, ponder 7 believe, dream
up, feature, imagine, realize, suppose,
suspect, think up 8 cogitate, envisage,
envision, meditate, ruminate 9 apprehend,
formulate, originate, speculate, visualize
10 comprehend, excogitate, understand

concentrate
4 mass 5 focus 6 gather, shrink 7 collect,
compact 8 assemble, compress,
condense, contract, converge
10 accumulate 11 consolidate

concentrated
5 thick 6 intent, strong 7 focused, intense
8 vehement 9 intensive, undiluted,
undivided 12 undistracted

concentration
5 field, major, study 9 attention
10 absorption 11 application

concept
4 idea 5 image 6 notion, theory 7 conceit,
thought 10 impression, perception

conception
4 idea 5 birth, image, start 6 notion, origin,
outset, theory 7 conceit, genesis, thought
9 beginning 10 impression, perception

conceptual
5 ideal 8 abstract, notional 9 imaginary,
visionary 10 ideational 11 theoretical
12 hypothetical, intellectual

concern
4 care, firm, heed 5 doubt, worry 6 affair,
bear on, bother, engage, gadget, matter,
occupy, outfit, regard, unease 7 anxiety,
company, disturb, involve, perturb, trouble
8 business, deal with, disquiet, interest,
mistrust 9 attention, curiosity, misgiving,
suspicion 10 enterprise, skepticism,
solicitude, uneasiness 11 carefulness,
contrivance, uncertainty 12 apprehension
13 consciousness, consideration,
establishment

concerned
7 anxious, worried 8 affected, involved
10 implicated, interested

concerning
4 as to, in re 5 about, anent, as for
7 apropos 9 as regards, regarding
10 relating to, relative to, respecting

concert
5 agree, union 6 accord, concur, settle,
soiree 7 arrange, concord, harmony, recital
8 coincide, musicale 9 agreement,
cooperate, harmonize, negotiate 11 performance

concerted
5 joint 6 mutual, united 7 unified
8 combined 11 coordinated 13 collaborative

concert hall
5 arena, odeum 7 theater, theatre
10 auditorium

concession
5 favor, grant 8 giveback 9 admission,
allowance, privilege 10 compromise
12 acquiescence

conch
5 shell 7 mollusc, mollusk

concierge
6 porter, warden 7 doorman, janitor
9 custodian 10 doorkeeper

conciliate
4 calm, ease 6 disarm, pacify, soothe
7 appease, assuage, mollify, placate,
sweeten, win over 9 reconcile
10 propitiate

concise
5 brief, pithy, short, terse 7 compact,
laconic, summary 8 abridged, succinct
9 condensed 10 compressed, contracted
11 compendious 13 short and sweet

conclave
5 synod 6 caucus, powwow 7 meeting,
session 8 assembly 9 gathering
10 conference, consistory, convention
11 convocation

conclude
3 end 4 halt, stop 5 close, infer, judge
6 decide, deduce, derive, effect, figure,
finish, gather, reason, settle, wind up, wrap
up 7 collect, resolve 8 complete
9 determine, terminate

concluding
4 last 5 final 6 latest, latter 7 closing
8 eventual, terminal, ultimate

conclusion
3 end 4 stop 5 cease, close 6 ending,
epilog, finale, finish, period, result, windup
7 closing, closure, outcome, verdict
8 decision, epilogue, judgment, sequitur
9 cessation, deduction, inference,
summation 10 completion, denouement,
resolution, settlement 11 culmination,
termination 13 determination

conclusive
4 last 5 final 6 cogent 8 deciding,
decisive, ultimate 9 clinching
10 compelling, convincing, definitive,
undeniable 11 determinant, determinate,
irrefutable 12 irrefragable, unanswerable
13 determinative

concoct
3 mix 4 brew, cook 5 frame, hatch 6 cook
up, create, devise, invent 7 dream up
8 conceive, contrive 9 fabricate, formulate,
originate

concoction
4 brew, plan 5 blend 7 mixture, project
8 compound, creation 9 invention
11 combination, contrivance, fabrication,
preparation

concomitant
7 adjunct 8 adjuvant 9 accessory,
ancillary, associate, attendant, attending,
companion, satellite 10 coincident,
collateral 12 accompanying
13 accompaniment, supplementary

concord
4 pact 5 amity, peace, unity 6 accord,
comity, treaty 7 concert, entente, harmony,
rapport 8 goodwill 9 agreement
10 consonance

concordant
8 agreeing 9 congruous, consonant
10 compatible, consistent, harmonious
11 appropriate

concourse
5 foyer 6 throng 7 joining, meeting
8 junction 9 gathering 10 confluence,
crossroads

concrete
5 solid 6 actual 8 specific, tangible
10 particular 11 substantial
component: 4 sand 5 water 6 gravel

concubine
7 hetaera, hetaira 8 mistress 9 courtesan,
odalisque

concupiscence
4 lust 5 ardor 6 desire 7 lechery, passion
9 prurience, pruriency 11 lustfulness
13 lickerishness

concupiscent
3 hot 7 aroused, goatish, lustful 8 prurient
9 lecherous, lickerish, salacious
10 lascivious, libidinous, lubricious,
passionate

concur
4 jibe 5 agree, unite 6 accord, assent
7 approve, combine, concord, consent, go
along 8 coincide 9 cooperate, harmonize

concurrent
6 coeval 8 parallel 10 coexistent,
coexisting, convergent, synchronic
11 synchronous 12 contemporary,
simultaneous

concurrently
6 at once 8 together 12 coincidently

concuss
3 jar 4 rock, stun 5 shake, shock
7 agitate

concussion
3 jar 4 bump, jolt 5 clout, crash, shock
6 impact 7 jarring, jolting, shaking
8 pounding 9 agitation, collision

condemn
3 rap 4 damn, doom 5 blame, decry,
knock, seize 7 censure, convict, deplore
8 denounce, sentence 9 criticize,
deprecate, proscribe, reprehend, reprobate
10 denunciate

condensation
3 dew 5 brief 6 digest, précis 7 epitome,
outline, summary 8 abstract, synopsis
9 reduction 10 abridgment, conspectus
11 abridgement

condense
5 sum up 6 digest, reduce, shrink
7 abridge, compact, shorten 8 boil down,
compress, contract 9 constrict, epitomize,
summarize, synopsize 10 abbreviate
11 concentrate, consolidate, precipitate

condensed
7 concise, summary 10 boiled down
11 compendious

condescend
5 deign, stoop 6 unbend

condescending

5 lofty **6** lordly, snobby, snooty, uppish, uppity **7** haughty, pompous **8** affected, arrogant, cavalier, snobbish, superior **10** disdainful **11** patronizing, pretentious **12** supercilious

condign

3 apt, due, fit **4** fair, just **5** right **6** proper **7** fitting, merited **8** deserved, rightful, suitable **9** equitable, justified **11** appropriate

condiment

5 curry, sauce, spice **6** catsup, relish, tamari **7** chutney, ketchup, mustard **8** dressing, soy sauce **9** seasoning **10** mayonnaise

_____ con Dios!

4 Vaya

condition

5 shape, state, terms **6** fettle, malady, status **7** ailment, disease, fitness, proviso **8** syndrome **9** complaint, essential, exception, necessity, provision, requisite, situation **10** limitation, sine qua non **11** requirement, reservation, stipulation **12** prerequisite **13** qualification

conditional

7 reliant **8** relative **9** dependent, provisory, qualified, tentative, uncertain **10** contingent, restricted **11** provisional

condolence

3 rue **4** pity, ruth **6** solace **7** comfort **8** sympathy **10** compassion **13** commiseration

condonable

7 tenable **9** excusable, tolerable **10** acceptable, defensible, pardonable **11** justifiable

condone

5 remit **6** excuse, pardon **7** forgive **8** overlook

conduce

4 lead, tend **7** redound **10** contribute

conducive

7 helpful, leading, tending **9** favorable **10** beneficial, salubrious **11** efficacious, serviceable, stimulating **12** advantageous, contributory, instrumental **13** accommodating

conduct

3 act, run **4** bear, head, lead, show **5** guide, pilot, steer, usher **6** attend, behave, charge, convey, demean, deport, direct, escort, handle, manage **7** arrange, bearing, comport, control, manners, operate, oversee **8** behavior, demeanor, handling, shepherd, transmit **9** accompany, oversight, supervise **10** administer, deportment, management **11** comportment, supervision

conductor

5 guide **6** escort, leader **7** maestro **8** motorman **10** bandleader
American: **4** Shaw (Robert) **5** Stock (Frederick), Szell (George) **6** Levine (James), Maazel (Lorin), Previn (André), Reiner (Fritz), Thomas (Theodore, Michael Tilson), Walter (Bruno) **7** Fennell (Frederick), Fiedler (Arthur), Monteux (Pierre), Ormandy (Eugene), Schwarz (Gerard), Slatkin (Leonard) **8** Damrosch (Leopold, Walter), Williams (John) **9** Bernstein (Leonard), Leinsdorf (Erich), Rodzinski (Artur), Steinberg (William), Stokowski (Leopold) **11** Kostelanetz (André), Mitropoulos (Dimitri)
Argentinian: **7** Kleiber (Carlos) **9** Barenboim (Daniel)
Australian: **7** Bonynge (Richard)
Austrian: **4** Böhm (Karl) **6** Mahler (Gustav) **7** Karajan (Herbert von) **11** Weingartner (Felix)
Belgian: **5** Ysaÿe (Eugene)
British: **5** Solti (Georg)
Canadian: **6** Dutoit (Charles) **9** MacMillan (Ernest)
Czech: **7** Kubelik (Jan, Rafael)
Dutch: **7** Haitink (Bernard) **10** Mengelberg (Willem)
English: **4** Wood (Henry) **5** Boult (Adrian), Davis (Colin) **6** Rattle (Simon) **7** Beecham (Thomas), Leppard (Raymond), Malcolm (George), Pinnock (Trevor), Sargent (Malcolm) **8** Goossens (Eugene), Marriner (Neville) **9** Mackerras (Charles) **10** Barbirolli (John)
Finnish: **7** Salonen (Esa-Pekka)
French: **5** Munch (Charles) **6** Boulez (Pierre), Prêtre (Georges) **7** Monteux (Pierre)
German: **4** Muck (Carl, Karl) **5** Masur (Kurt) **6** Jochum (Eugen) **7** Kleiber (Erich) **9** Klemperer (Otto), Scherchen (Hermann) **10** Sawallisch (Wolfgang) **11** Furtwängler (Wilhelm), Mendelssohn (Felix)
Greek: **11** Mitropoulos (Dimitri)
Hungarian: **5** Seidl (Anton) **6** Doráti (Antal), Reiner (Fritz) **7** Nikisch (Arthur), Ormandy (Eugene), Richter (Hans)
Indian: **5** Mehta (Zubin)
Italian: **4** Muti (Riccardo) **6** Abbado (Claudio) **7** Chailly (Riccardo), Giulini

(Carlo Maria) **8** Cantelli (Guido), Sinopoli (Giuseppe) Toscanini (Arturo)
Japanese: 5 Ozawa (Seiji)
Polish: 9 Rodzinski (Artur)
Russian: 7 Gergiev (Valery) **10** Temirkanov (Yuri) **12** Koussevitzky (Serge)
Spanish: 6 Iturbi (José)
Swiss: 8 Ansermet (Ernest)
stick: 5 baton

conduit
4 duct, main, pipe **5** canal **6** course **7** channel **8** aqueduct, penstock, pipeline **11** watercourse

coney
4 pika **5** hyrax, lapin **6** rabbit **10** butterfish

confab
4 chat, talk **6** confer, huddle, parley, powwow **7** consult **8** collogue, colloquy, dialogue **10** conference, discussion **12** conversation, deliberation

confabulate
see **confab**

confabulation
see **confab**

confection
see **candy**

confederacy
5 cabal, union **6** league **7** compact **8** alliance **9** coalition, syndicate **10** conspiracy, federation

confederate
3 reb **4** ally **5** rebel, unite **6** fellow **7** abettor, partner **9** accessory, associate, colleague, Johnny Reb **10** accomplice **11** conspirator **12** collaborator **13** coconspirator
admiral: 6 Semmes
capital: 8 Richmond
color: 4 gray
general: 3 Lee (Robert E.) **4** Hill (Ambrose), Hood (John Bell) **5** Bragg (Braxton), Ewell (Richard Stoddart), Price (Sterling), Smith (Edmund Kirby) **6** Morgan (John Hunt), Stuart (J. E. B.) **7** Forrest (Nathan Bedford), Hampton (Wade), Jackson (Thomas Jonathan "Stonewall"), Pickett (George) **8** Johnston (Albert Sidney, Joseph Eggleston) **9** Pemberton (John Clifford) **10** Beauregard (Pierre G. T.), Longstreet (James)
president: 5 Davis (Jefferson)
soldier: 9 butternut
spy: 4 Boyd (Belle)
vice-president: 8 Stephens (Alexander)

confederation
see **confederacy**

confer
4 give, meet, talk **5** allot, award, grant, speak **6** accord, advise, bestow, confab, donate, huddle, parley, powwow **7** consult, discuss, present **8** collogue, converse **10** deliberate **11** confabulate

conference
4 talk **5** forum, synod **6** caucus, league, parley, powwow **7** meeting, palaver, seminar **8** assembly, colloquy, congress **9** symposium **10** colloquium, discussion, round-robin, roundtable **11** association, convocation **12** consultation, deliberation **13** confabulation

confess
3 own **4** avow, sing **5** admit, allow, grant, let on, own up **6** reveal **7** concede, divulge, profess **8** disclose **9** come clean **11** acknowledge

confession
5 creed **6** avowal **7** peccavi **9** admission, statement **10** disclosure

confidant
8 familiar, intimate

confide
4 tell **5** trust **6** bestow, commit, reveal **7** commend, consign, entrust, whisper **8** hand over, relegate, turn over

confidence
5 faith, poise, stock, trust **6** aplomb, surety **8** credence, reliance, sureness **9** assurance, certainty, certitude **10** conviction, equanimity
game: 4 scam **5** bunco, bunko, grift, sting **7** swindle **8** flimflam

confidence man
3 gyp **5** shark **7** diddler, grifter, scammer, sharper, sharpie **8** swindler **9** charlatan, defrauder, trickster **11** bunco artist

confident
4 bold, sure **5** brash, brave, cocky **6** secure **7** assured, certain **8** cocksure, fearless, intrepid, positive, sanguine, unafraid **9** dauntless, undaunted **10** courageous, undoubtful **11** self-assured, self-reliant **13** self-assertive, self-possessed

confidential
5 close, privy **6** hushed, inside, secret **7** private **8** familiar, hush-hush, intimate **9** auricular, classified

configuration
4 cast, form 5 shape 6 figure, layout, makeup 7 contour, gestalt, outline, pattern 9 structure 12 conformation

confine
3 box, mew, pen 4 cage, coop, crib, jail, term 5 bound, cramp, hem in, limit 6 immure, intern, lock up, shut in, shut up 7 delimit, enclose, impound, put away 8 encircle, imprison, localize, restrict 9 constrain 11 incarcerate 12 circumscribe

confinement
7 custody, lying-in 8 childbed 9 captivity, detention, restraint 10 constraint 12 accouchement, imprisonment 13 incarceration

confines
6 bounds, limits 7 borders, compass 8 boundary, environs, purlieus 9 precincts 10 boundaries

confirm
3 fix, set 5 check, prove, vouch 6 attest, ratify, uphold, verify 7 approve, bear out, certify, concede, endorse, justify, support 8 buttress, check out, validate 9 ascertain, reinforce 10 strengthen 11 corroborate 12 authenticate, substantiate

confirmation
5 proof 7 support, witness 8 approval, evidence 9 testimony 10 validation 11 attestation, endorsement, testimonial 12 ratification, verification 13 certification, corroboration

confirmed
3 set 5 fixed, sworn 6 proven 7 chronic, settled 8 deep-dyed, definite, habitual, hardened, ratified 10 accustomed, deep-rooted, deep-seated, entrenched, habituated, inveterate, persistent 13 bred-in-the-bone, dyed-in-the-wool

confiscate
4 grab, take 5 annex, seize, usurp 7 escheat, impound, preempt 8 arrogate 9 sequester 10 commandeer 11 appropriate, expropriate

confiture
3 jam 8 conserve, preserve 9 marmalade, preserves

conflagrant
5 afire, fiery 6 ablaze, aflame, alight 7 blazing, burning, flaming

conflagration
3 war 4 fire 5 blaze 7 inferno 8 conflict 9 holocaust

conflate
3 mix 4 fuse, join, meld, weld 5 blend, merge, mix up 6 mingle, muddle 7 combine, confuse, mistake 8 coalesce, confound 9 commingle

conflict
3 row, war 4 bout, duel, rift, vary 5 brawl, clash, fight, set-to 6 battle, combat, differ, fracas, strife 7 contend, contest, discord, dispute, rivalry, warfare 8 argument, disagree, mismatch, struggle, tug-of-war, variance 9 encounter, rencontre 10 contention, engagement 11 competition

conflicting
6 at odds 7 opposed, warring 8 clashing, contrary, opposing 9 dissonant 10 contending, discordant, discrepant 11 incongruent, incongruous, inconsonant 12 antagonistic, antipathetic, incompatible, inconsistent, inharmonious 13 contradictory

confluence
6 merger 7 joining, meeting, merging 8 junction 9 concourse, gathering 11 convergence

conform
3 fit 4 jibe, obey, suit 5 adapt, agree, fit in, match, yield 6 accord, adjust, attune, comply, follow, square, submit, tailor 8 dovetail 9 acquiesce, harmonize, reconcile 10 coordinate, correspond, proportion 11 accommodate

conformable
6 fitted, suited 7 adapted, matched 8 amenable, obedient, suitable 9 agreeable, compliant, congenial, consonant 10 submissive

conformation
4 cast, form 5 shape 6 figure 7 anatomy 9 structure 10 adaptation 11 arrangement 13 configuration

conforming
3 apt 6 decent, proper, seemly 7 correct, uniform 8 becoming, decorous, suitable 9 befitting, civilized 10 compatible, consistent 11 comme il faut

conformity
6 accord 7 decorum, harmony 9 agreement, coherence, congruity, obedience, orthodoxy 10 accordance,

allegiance, compliance, consonance, observance, submission **11** consistency **12** acquiescence

confound
4 damn, faze **5** befog, mix up, stump **6** baffle, puzzle, rattle, refute **7** confuse, mistake, mystify, nonplus, perplex, stupefy **8** befuddle, bewilder, disprove **9** discomfit, dumbfound, embarrass, frustrate **10** controvert, disconcert **11** misidentify

confounded
5 utter **6** blamed, cursed, cussed, damned **7** blasted, blessed, doggone, shocked **8** absolute, accursed, dismayed, infernal, outright **9** consarned, dad-blamed, execrable, out-and-out **11** dumbfounded, overwhelmed, unmitigated **13** thunderstruck

confrere
see **colleague**

confront
4 defy, face, meet **5** beard, brave, cross **6** accost, breast, oppose, take on **9** challenge, encounter

Confucian way of life
3 tao

confuse
3 fog **4** blur, daze, faze **5** abash, addle, befog, cloud, dizzy, mix up, muddy, stump, upset **6** baffle, ball up, bemuse, flurry, foul up, fuddle, garble, jumble, mess up, muddle, puzzle, rattle **7** agitate, becloud, derange, disrupt, distort, flummox, fluster, mislead, mistake, mystify, nonplus, perplex, perturb, snarl up **8** bedazzle, befuddle, bewilder, confound, disorder, disquiet, distract, throw off, unsettle **9** discomfit, disorient, embarrass **10** complicate, disarrange, discompose, disconcert **11** disorganize, misidentify **12** misrepresent

confused
4 lost **5** dazed, messy, muddy, muzzy, vague **6** addled **7** at a loss, chaotic, mixed up, muddled, puzzled **9** flustered, perplexed, unsettled **10** bewildered, nonplussed, topsy-turvy **11** disoriented **12** disconcerted

confusion
3 ado, din **4** flap, mess, stew **5** babel, chaos, havoc, mix-up, snafu, snarl **6** bedlam, dither, foul-up, hubbub, huddle, jumble, lather, muddle, tumult, unease **7** anarchy, clutter, turmoil **8** disarray,

disorder, shambles **9** abashment, agitation, commotion, imbroglio **10** hullabaloo, perplexity, puzzlement, turbulence, uneasiness **11** derangement, disturbance, pandemonium **12** bewilderment **13** embarrassment

confute
4 deny **5** evert, rebut **6** defeat, negate **8** confound, disprove, puncture **10** controvert, disconfirm

congé
3 bow **5** adieu **6** good-by **7** good-bye, molding, parting, sendoff **8** farewell **9** dismissal **11** leave-taking

congeal
3 dry, gel, set **4** clot, jell **5** jelly **6** curdle, harden **7** stiffen, thicken **8** solidify **9** coagulate **10** gelatinize

congener
6 agnate **7** cognate, sibling **8** relation, relative

congenial
4 nice **6** social **7** affable, amiable, cordial, kindred, welcome **8** amicable, friendly, gracious, pleasant, pleasing, sociable, suitable **9** agreeable, congruous, consonant, favorable **10** compatible, consistent, gratifying, harmonious **11** cooperative, pleasurable, sympathetic **13** companionable

congenital
6 inborn, inbred, innate, native **7** natural **8** inherent **9** essential, ingrained, intrinsic **10** deep-seated, indigenous, indwelling

conger
3 eel

congeries
5 group **7** company **8** assembly **9** gathering **10** assemblage, collection **11** aggregation **12** congregation

congest
3 jam **4** clog, fill, plug, stop **5** block, choke, close, crowd **6** plug up **7** occlude **8** obstruct

conglobate
4 ball **6** sphere **8** ensphere **9** spherical

conglomerate
4 mass, pool **5** chain, group, mixed, trust **6** cartel, motley **7** chaebol, combine **8** keiretsu, zaibatsu **9** aggregate, syndicate

11 aggregation 12 multifarious 13 heterogeneous

conglomeration
5 hoard, trove 8 mishmash 9 aggregate
10 collection, cumulation, hodgepodge,
miscellany 11 agglomerate, aggregation
12 accumulation

Congo, Democratic Republic of the
capital: 8 Kinshasa
city: 7 Kolwezi 9 Mbuji-Mayi
10 Lubumbashi
explorer: 7 Stanley (Henry Morton)
former name: 5 Zaire 12 Belgian Congo
lake: 4 Kivu 5 Mweru 6 Albert, Edward
10 Tanganyika
language: 6 French 7 English
monetary unit: 5 franc
neighbor: 5 Congo, Sudan 6 Angola,
Rwanda, Uganda, Zambia 7 Burundi
8 Tanzania
river: 5 Congo

Congo, Republic of
capital: 11 Brazzaville
city: 11 Pointe-Noire
former name: 11 Middle Congo
language: 6 French
monetary unit: 5 franc
neighbor: 5 Congo, Gabon 6 Angola
7 Cabinda 8 Cameroon
river: 5 Congo

congratulate
4 laud 6 salute 10 compliment, felicitate

congregate
4 meet 5 swarm 6 gather, muster
7 collect, convene 8 assemble, converge
9 forgather 10 foregather, rendezvous

congregation
4 mass 5 crowd, flock, group 7 meeting
8 assembly, audience 9 gathering
10 assemblage, collection 11 churchgoers
12 parishioners

congress
4 diet 5 synod 6 league 7 meeting,
society 8 assembly, conclave 10 convention, parliament 11 association, Capitol
Hill, legislature

congressman
5 solon 7 senator 8 delegate, lawmaker
10 legislator 14 representative

congruity
9 agreement, coherence 10 conformity
11 consistency

congruous
3 apt, fit 7 fitting 9 agreeable, befitting,

congenial, consonant 10 compatible,
concordant, consistent, harmonious
11 appropriate, sympathetic

conifer
3 fir, yew 4 pine 5 cedar, larch 6 spruce
7 cypress, hemlock, juniper 8 softwood
9 evergreen 10 arborvitae

conjectural
7 reputed 8 putative, supposed 11 speculative, theoretical 12 hypothetical,
suppositious 13 suppositional

conjecture
5 guess, infer 6 assume, theory
7 presume, suppose, surmise, suspect
8 theorize 9 inference, speculate
11 hypothesize, proposition, speculation,
supposition

conjoin
3 wed 4 band, link, yoke 5 unite 6 couple
7 combine, connect 8 federate 9 affiliate,
associate, cooperate 11 consolidate

conjoint
6 common, mutual, public, shared, united
7 unified 8 combined, communal
9 concerted 10 collective 11 coefficient,
cooperative, intermutual

conjointly
8 mutually, together

conjugal
6 wedded 7 marital, married, nuptial,
spousal 8 hymeneal 9 connubial
11 matrimonial

conjugality
7 wedlock 8 marriage 9 matrimony

conjugate
4 fuse, join, link, pair, yoke 5 yoked
6 couple, joined, linked 7 bracket,
combine, conjoin, connect, coupled
9 associate, connected

conjunct
5 joint 6 common, joined, mutual, shared,
united

conjunction
3 and, but, for, nor, yet 4 lest, once, than,
then, when 5 after, since, union, until,
where, which, while 6 before, either,
though, unless 7 because, however,
neither, whereas, whether 8 alliance,
although, moreover, whenever 9 therefore
10 connection 11 affiliation, association,
combination, concurrence

conjuration
4 oath 5 charm, spell, trick 7 sorcery
10 adjuration, hocus-pocus, invocation
11 abracadabra, incantation

conjure
3 beg 4 urge 6 appeal, invoke, summon
7 beseech, entreat, imagine, implore
8 contrive 8 importune 10 supplicate

conjurer
4 mage, seer 5 magus 6 Magian, wizard
7 warlock 8 magician, sorcerer
9 enchanter, trickster 11 illusionist,
necromancer

conjuring
5 magic 7 sorcery 8 wizardry 10 hocus-
pocus, necromancy 11 abracadabra,
legerdemain, thaumaturgy

conk
3 die, hit, rap 4 belt, swat 5 croak, faint,
knock, thump, whack 8 knock out

con man
see **confidence man**

connate
4 akin 6 allied, inborn, native 7 kindred,
related 8 inherent 9 congenial, elemental,
essential, ingrained, inherited, intrinsic
10 affiliated, congenital, indigenous,
indwelling 11 consanguine

connect
3 tie, wed 4 ally, bind, join, link, yoke
5 marry, unite 6 attach, bridge, couple,
fasten, relate 7 combine, conjoin
8 transfer 9 affiliate, associate, interlock

Connecticut
capital: 8 Hartford
city: 4 Avon 6 Darien 8 New Haven,
Stamford 9 Greenwich, New London,
Waterbury 10 Bridgeport
college, university: 4 Yale 7 Trinity
8 Wesleyan 9 Fairfield 10 Quinnipiac
nickname: 6 Nutmeg (State)
12 Constitution (State)
river: 6 Thames 10 Housatonic
11 Connecticut
state bird: 5 robin (American)
state flower: 14 mountain laurel
state tree: 8 white oak

connection
3 tie 4 bond, link 5 joint, nexus, tie-in,
union 6 hookup 7 joining, kinship, network
8 affinity, alliance, coupling, junction,
juncture 9 coherence, communion,
fastening 10 attachment, catenation,
continuity 11 affiliation, association,

combination, conjunction, partnership
12 relationship

connective
3 and, nor, not 4 then 6 either 7 neither
8 syndetic 11 conjunction, conjunctive

conniption
3 fit 4 bout 5 furor, spasm, spate, spell,
throe 6 attack, frenzy 7 seizure, tantrum
8 outburst, paroxysm 10 convulsion

connivance
8 intrigue 9 collusion 10 complicity,
conspiracy

connive
4 plot, wink 5 blink 6 devise, scheme, wink
at 7 blink at, collude 8 conspire, contrive,
intrigue 9 machinate

connoisseur
4 buff 6 expert 7 epicure, gourmet
8 aesthete, gourmand, highbrow
9 authority, bon vivant 10 dilettante,
gastronome 11 cognoscente

connotation
4 hint 7 meaning 8 overtone 9 undertone
10 intimation, suggestion 11 association,
implication, signification

connote
4 hint, mean 5 imply, spell 6 hint at, intend
7 betoken, express, signify, suggest
8 indicate, intimate 9 insinuate

connubial
6 wedded 7 marital, married, nuptial,
spousal 8 conjugal, hymeneal
11 matrimonial

connubiality
7 wedlock 8 marriage 9 matrimony
11 conjugality

conquer
4 beat, best, lick, tame, whip 5 crush
6 defeat, master, subdue 8 overcome,
surmount, vanquish 9 checkmate,
overpower, overthrow, overwhelm,
subjugate

conquest
3 win 4 rout 7 triumph, victory
9 overthrow, seduction 11 subjugation

Conrad, Joseph
character: 3 Jim 4 Axel, Lena 5 Flora,
Kurtz 6 Marlow, Verloc 7 Almayer
8 MacWhirr, Nostromo
work: 5 Youth 6 Chance 7 Lord Jim,
Typhoon, Victory 8 Nostromo 11 Secret

Conroy novel
Agent (The) **13** Almayer's Folly **15** Heart of Darkness

Conroy novel
10 Beach Music **11** Water Is Wide (The) **12** Great Santini (The) **13** Prince of Tides (The) **17** Lords of Discipline (The)

consanguineous
4 akin **6** agnate **7** cognate, connate, kindred, related

conscience
5 demur, honor, qualm **6** ethics, virtue **7** decency, remorse, scruple **8** morality, scruples **9** integrity **10** contrition **11** compunction

conscienceless
6 amoral **7** immoral **9** unethical **12** unprincipled, unscrupulous

conscientious
4 fair, just, true **5** exact **6** honest **7** careful, dutiful, upright **8** diligent, reliable, studious **9** honorable **10** high-minded, meticulous, principled, scrupulous **11** hard-working, painstaking, punctilious

conscious
5 alive, awake, aware **7** knowing, mindful, witting **8** sensible, sentient **9** attentive, cognizant **10** deliberate, perceptive

consciousness
4 heed, mind **6** regard **7** concern **9** alertness, awareness, knowledge **10** cognizance, perception **11** realization, recognition

conscribe
5 draft, limit **6** call up, enlist, enroll, muster **7** recruit

conscript
5 draft, elect **6** called, choose, chosen, enlist, enroll, induct, select **7** drafted, dragoon, impress, recruit, soldier **8** selected

consecrate
5 bless **6** anoint, devote, hallow, ordain, pledge **8** dedicate, sanctify

consecrated
4 holy **6** sacred **7** blessed **8** hallowed **10** sanctified
oil: 6 chrism

consecution
see **sequence**

consecutive
4 next **5** later **6** serial **7** ensuing, ordered, sequent **9** following, succedent **10** sequential, subsequent, succeeding, successive **11** progressive **12** successional

consent
3 yes **4** okay **5** agree, allow, leave, yield **6** accede, accord, assent, comply, concur, permit **7** approve, go-ahead **8** sanction **9** acquiesce, agreement, allowance, approval, subscribe **10** compliance, permission **12** acquiescence **13** authorization, understanding

consequence
4 fame, note, rank **5** issue, state **6** cachet, effect, import, moment, renown, repute, result, sequel, status, upshot, weight **7** account, conceit, dignity, fallout, outcome, stature **8** eminence, interest, position, prestige, reaction, standing **9** aftermath, inference, magnitude **10** importance, reputation **11** aftereffect, weightiness **12** repercussion, significance **13** momentousness

consequent
5 later, sound **7** ensuing, logical **8** rational **9** deduction, following, resulting

consequential
3 big **5** major **7** serious, weighty **8** egoistic, indirect, material **9** conceited, egotistic, important, momentous **10** collateral, incidental, meaningful, subsidiary **11** significant, substantial **12** considerable **13** self-important

consequently
4 ergo, thus **5** hence **9** as a result, therefore, thereupon **10** inevitably **11** accordingly

conservation
4 care **7** control **9** attention, husbandry **10** management, protection **11** safekeeping **12** guardianship, preservation

conservative
4 tory **6** proper **7** diehard **8** cautious, discreet, old-guard, old-line, orthodox, rightist, standpat **9** right-wing, temperate **10** restrained **11** circumspect, reactionary, right-winger, standpatter, traditional

conservatory
6 school **7** academy, nursery **8** hothouse **10** greenhouse **11** music school

conserve
3 can, jam **4** keep, save **5** hoard, lay up, put up, skimp, store **6** keep up **7** husband, protect, support, sustain **8** maintain, set aside, withhold **9** confiture, economize, safeguard, sweetmeat

consider

3 see **4** deem, feel, mind, muse, note, rate, view **5** fancy, judge, sense, study, think, weigh **6** credit, look at, notice, ponder, reason, reckon, regard **7** account, believe, examine, imagine, inspect, reflect, respect, suppose **8** appraise, cogitate, conceive, conclude, envisage, meditate, mull over, ruminate **9** speculate, think over **10** deliberate, excogitate, scrutinize, think about **11** contemplate

considerable

3 big **5** ample, hefty, large, major **7** notable, sizable, weighty **8** material, sensible, sizeable **9** extensive, important, momentous, plentiful **10** large-scale, meaningful **11** respectable, significant, substantial **13** consequential

considerably

3 far **4** well **5** quite **6** rather **7** notably **8** somewhat **10** noticeably **11** appreciably **13** significantly, substantially

considerate

4 kind **6** kindly, polite, tender **7** amiable, careful, patient, tactful **8** discreet, generous, obliging **9** attentive **10** chivalrous, forbearing, solicitous, thoughtful **11** circumspect, complaisant, sympathetic, warmhearted **13** compassionate

consideration

3 fee **4** heed, tact **5** cause, favor, issue, study **6** esteem, factor, motive, reason, regard **7** account, concern, payment, respect, thought **8** kindness **9** attention, awareness **10** admiration, cogitation, discussion, estimation, inducement, recompense, reflection, solicitude **11** application, forbearance, mindfulness **12** deliberation **13** attentiveness, concentration

considered

7 advised, studied, weighed **8** studious **10** deliberate, thought-out **11** intentional **12** aforethought, premeditated

consign

4 give, send, ship **5** agree, allot, award, remit, yield **6** commit, convey, devote, submit **7** address, commend, confide, deliver, entrust, forward **8** dispatch, hand over, relegate, transmit, turn over **9** surrender

consist

3 lie **4** rest **5** abide, agree, dwell, exist, fit in **6** accord, inhere, reside **7** comport, conform, consort, subsist **8** dovetail **10** correspond

consistency

7 aptness, concord, density, fitness, harmony, texture **8** evenness, firmness, likeness **9** agreement, coherence, congruity, thickness, viscosity **10** conformity, consonance, similarity **11** suitability

consistent

4 even, true **6** steady **7** regular, uniform **8** constant **9** accordant, agreeable, congenial, congruous, consonant, unfailing, unvarying **10** compatible, conforming, dependable, invariable, unchanging **11** homogeneous, sympathetic, undeviating

consistently

8 wontedly **9** regularly, routinely **10** habitually, invariably **11** customarily

console

4 calm, case **5** cheer **6** buck up, solace **7** cabinet, comfort, hearten

consolidate

3 mix, set **4** fuse, join, meld, pool **5** blend, merge, unify, unite **6** firm up, secure **7** compact, fortify **8** compress, condense, federate, solidify **9** integrate **10** amalgamate, strengthen **11** concentrate

consolidation

5 union **6** merger **7** melding, merging **9** coalition **11** combination, integration, unification **12** amalgamation

consonance

6 accord **7** concord, harmony **9** agreement, congruity, resonance **10** congruence

consonant

4 akin, like **6** agnate **7** musical, similar **8** blending, harmonic, resonant **9** congruous **10** compatible, harmonious **11** conformable **13** corresponding **kind:** **4** stop, surd **5** nasal, velar **6** atonic, voiced **7** lateral, palatal, spirant **8** alveolar, bilabial, unvoiced **9** fricative, voiceless

consort

3 set **4** mate, wife **5** agree, group, tally, unite **6** accord, attend, fellow, spouse, square, troupe **7** company, comport, conform, husband, partner **8** assembly, chaperon, dovetail **9** accompany, associate, companion, harmonize **10** correspond

consortium

4 bloc, club, ring 5 guild, trust, union
6 cartel, league 7 combine, society
8 alliance, congress 9 coalition, syndicate
10 federation 11 association
12 conglomerate

conspectus

5 brief 6 digest, précis, sketch, survey
7 epitome, outline, summary 8 abstract,
overview, synopsis 9 reduction
10 abridgment 11 abridgement
12 condensation

conspicuous

5 clear, overt, showy 6 marked, patent,
signal 7 blatant, evident, glaring, notable,
obvious, pointed, salient 8 apparent,
distinct, flagrant, manifest, striking
9 arresting, egregious, notorious, obtrusive,
prominent 10 celebrated, noticeable,
pronounced, remarkable 11 eye-catching,
illustrious, outstanding 12 ostentatious

conspiracy

4 plan, plot 5 cabal 6 scheme 8 intrigue
11 machination

conspirator

7 abettor, plotter, schemer 9 accessory,
intriguer 10 accomplice 11 confederate

conspire

4 plot 5 cabal 6 scheme 7 collude,
connive 8 intrigue 9 machinate

constable

6 deputy, lawman, warden 7 marshal,
sheriff

constancy

5 faith 6 fealty 7 loyalty, resolve
8 adhesion, devotion, fidelity, firmness
9 adherence, diligence, endurance,
fortitude 10 allegiance, attachment,
dedication, resolution, steadiness
11 staunchness 12 faithfulness,
perseverance 13 dependability,
steadfastness

constant

4 even, fast, firm, true 5 fixed, loyal
6 dogged, stable, steady, trusty 7 abiding,
chronic, endless, equable, lasting, nonstop,
staunch, uniform 8 enduring, faithful,
habitual, resolute, unending 9 ceaseless,
confirmed, continual, immovable,
immutable, incessant, obstinate, perpetual,
steadfast, sustained, unceasing, unfailing,
unmovable, unvarying 10 changeless,
consistent, continuous, dependable,

inflexible, invariable, inveterate, persistent,
persisting, unchanging, unwavering
11 everlasting, inalterable, unalterable,
unrelenting, unremitting 12 interminable,
unchangeable

Constantine

birthplace: 4 Nish
mother: 6 Helena
son: 7 Crispus
victim: 6 Fausta 7 Crispus
wife: 6 Fausta

constantly

4 ever 5 often 6 always 7 forever
9 eternally 10 frequently, invariably,
repeatedly 11 incessantly, perpetually
12 continuously

constellation

5 group 7 pattern 10 assemblage,
collection 11 arrangement
Altar: 3 Ara
Archer: 11 Sagittarius
Arrow: 7 Sagitta
Balance: 5 Libra 9 Ursa Major
Bear, Little: 9 Ursa Minor
Big Dipper: 9 Ursa Major
Bird of Paradise: 4 Apus
Bull: 6 Taurus
Centaur: 6 Centaurus
Chained Lady: 9 Andromeda
Chameleon: 10 Chamaeleon
Champion: 7 Perseus
Charioteer: 6 Auriga
Clock: 10 Horologium
Colt: 8 Equuleus
Crab: 6 Cancer
Crane: 4 Grus
Cross: 4 Crux
Crow: 6 Corvus
Crown: 6 Corona
Cup: 6 Crater
Dolphin: 9 Delphinus
Dove: 7 Columba
Dragon: 5 Draco
Eagle: 6 Aquila
Fishes: 6 Pisces
Fly: 5 Musca
Flying Fish: 6 Volans
Furnace: 6 Fornax
Graving Tool: 6 Caelum
Great Bear: 9 Ursa Major
Greater Dog: 10 Canis Major
Hare: 5 Lepus
Herdsman: 6 Boötes
Horned Goat: 11 Capricornus
Hunter: 5 Orion
Indian: 5 Indus
Keel: 6 Carina

Lady in the Chair: 10 Cassiopeia
Larger Bear: 9 Ursa Major
Larger Dog: 10 Canis Major
Lesser Dog: 10 Canis Minor
Lion: 3 Leo
Little Bear: 9 Ursa Minor
Little Dipper: 9 Ursa Minor
Little Fox: 9 Vulpecula
Lizard: 7 Lacerta
Lyre: 4 Lyra
Mariner's Compass: 5 Pyxis
Monarch: 7 Cepheus
Net: 9 Reticulum
Painter's Easel: 6 Pictor
Pair of Compasses: 8 Circinus
Peacock: 4 Pavo
Pump: 6 Antlia
Ram: 5 Aries
Rescuer: 7 Perseus
River Po: 8 Eridanus
Sails: 4 Vela
Scorpion: 8 Scorpius
Serpent: 7 Serpens
Serpent Holder: 9 Ophiuchus
Sextant: 7 Sextans
Shield: 6 Scutum
Smaller Bear: 9 Ursa Minor
Square: 5 Norma
Stern: 6 Puppis
Swan: 6 Cygnus
Table: 5 Mensa
Toucan: 6 Tucana
Triangle: 10 Triangulum
Twins: 6 Gemini
Unicorn: 9 Monoceros
Virgin: 5 Virgo
Water Carrier: 8 Aquarius
Water Monster: 5 Hydra
Water Snake: 6 Hydrus
Whale: 5 Cetus
Winged Horse: 7 Pegasus
Wolf: 5 Lupus

consternate
5 alarm, daunt, shake, shock **6** appall,
dismay **7** horrify, unnerve **8** distress

consternation
4 fear **5** alarm, dread, panic, shock
6 dismay, fright, horror, terror **11** trepidation
12 bewilderment

constituent
4 part **5** piece, voter **6** factor, member
7 element, portion **8** division, fraction
9 component, elemental, principal
10 ingredient

constitute
4 form, make **5** enact, found, set up, start
6 create, embody, make up **7** appoint,

compose **8** complete, comprise, organize
9 establish, institute, represent

constitution
3 law **4** code **5** build, canon **6** design,
makeup, nature **7** charter **8** physique
9 formation, structure **11** composition
12 architecture, construction

constitutional
4 walk **6** inborn, inbred, innate, lawful
7 built-in, essential, organic **8** inherent
9 essential, ingrained, intrinsic
10 congenital, deep-seated

Constitution State
11 Connecticut

Constitution, U.S.S.
12 Old Ironsides

constitutive
5 vital **8** cardinal **9** essential **11** fundamental **12** constructive

constrain
3 bar **4** curb, deny, jail **5** chain, check,
crush, force, impel, limit, press **6** bridle,
coerce, compel, enjoin, oblige, secure,
squash, squish **7** contine, deprive, inhibit,
refrain, squeeze **8** compress, hold back,
hold down, imprison, restrain, restrict
11 incarcerate

constraint
4 bond **5** check, force **6** duress
8 coercion, pressure **9** captivity, detention,
restraint **10** compulsion, diffidence,
inhibition, limitation, repression
11 confinement, restriction, suppression
13 embarrassment

constrict
4 curb **5** cramp, limit, pinch, strap
6 hamper, narrow, shrink **7** confine, inhibit,
squeeze, tighten **8** compress, condense,
contract, restrain, strangle, stultify
9 constrain **12** circumscribe

constrictor
3 boa **5** snake **6** muscle **8** anaconda
9 sphincter, strangler

construct
4 form, make **5** build, erect, forge, frame,
put up, raise, set up, shape **6** create,
devise **7** build up, compile, fashion,
produce **8** assemble, engineer
9 establish, fabricate **11** manufacture, put
together

construction
6 design, makeup **7** edifice, shaping
8 assembly, building **9** formation

constructive

10 fashioning 11 arrangement, engineering, fabrication, manufacture 12 architecture, constitution

constructive

6 useful 7 helpful, implied, virtual 8 implicit, positive, valuable 9 practical 10 beneficial

construe

5 educe, gloss, parse 6 induct 7 analyze, explain, expound 9 explicate, interpret 10 paraphrase, understand

consuetude

5 habit, usage 6 custom, manner 8 practice 10 convention

consult

3 ask 6 advise, confer, huddle, parley 7 examine, refer to 8 collogue, consider 11 confabulate

consume

3 eat, use 4 down, gulp, ruin 5 drain, drink, eat up, gorge, spend, use up, waste 6 absorb, devour, expend, finish, ingest, obsess, take up 7 deplete, destroy, engross, exhaust, put away, put down, swallow 8 squander 9 dissipate, finish off, polish off 10 annihilate, extinguish, monopolize, run through

consumer

4 user 5 buyer 6 client 7 shopper, end user 8 customer 9 purchaser

consumer advocate

5 Nader (Ralph)

consuming

6 ardent 7 fervent, intense 8 gripping, riveting 9 absorbing 10 engrossing 11 enthralling 12 monopolizing

consummate

3 end 4 ripe 5 close, crown, ideal, utter 6 finish, superb, wind up, wrap up 7 achieve, perfect, supreme 8 absolute, complete, conclude, finished, flawless, peerless, ultimate 9 faultless, matchless, perfected, virtuosic 10 accomplish, impeccable, inimitable 11 superlative 12 accomplished 13 thoroughgoing

consumption

3 use 5 decay, waste 6 intake 7 wasting 8 phthisis 9 depletion, ingestion 10 absorption 11 dissipation 12 tuberculosis

contact

4 meet 5 reach, touch 8 tangency, touching 9 closeness, communion, proximity 10 connection, contiguity

contagion

11 association, contingence 13 communication

contagion

3 pox 4 bane, meme 5 taint, venom, virus 6 miasma, plague, poison, scourge 7 disease, infection 8 epidemic 9 pollution 10 corruption, pestilence 13 contamination

contagious

6 catchy 8 catching, epidemic 9 spreading 10 infectious 12 communicable, pestilential 13 transmissible, transmittable

contain

4 hold, keep 5 check, house 6 embody, take in 7 collect, control, embrace, enclose, include, receive, repress, subsume 8 comprise, restrain 9 encompass 10 comprehend 11 accommodate

container

3 bag, bin, box, can, cup, jar, keg, mug, pod, pot, tin, tub, urn, vat 4 cage, case, cask, drum, etui, ewer, pail, sack, silo, tank, vase, vial, well 5 chest, crate, cruet, flask, glass, gourd, phial, pouch 6 basket, bottle, carafe, carton, casket, coffin, cooler, goblet, hamper, hatbox, holder, inkpot, shaker 7 bandbox, capsule, chalice, inkwell, package, pitcher, thermos 8 canister, catchall, decanter, envelope, hogshead, jerrican, puncheon 10 receptacle **liturgical:** 3 pyx 7 chalice 8 ciborium

contaminate

4 foul, soil 5 dirty, spoil, stain, sully, taint 6 befoul, debase, defile, infect, injure, poison 7 corrupt, deprave, pervert, pollute, profane, tarnish, vitiate 9 desecrate 10 adulterate

conte

4 tale 5 story 9 narrative

contemn

4 snub 5 abhor, scorn, spurn 6 deride 7 deplore, despise, disdain 8 ridicule 10 look down on

contemplate

4 mull, muse, view 5 study, think, weigh 6 behold, debate, gaze at, intend, look at, ponder, regard 7 examine, inspect, propose, reflect 8 meditate, gaze upon, look upon, mull over, ruminate, think out 9 think over 10 deliberate, excogitate, scrutinize

contemplation

5 study 6 musing 7 thought 8 thinking 9 intention, pondering 10 cogitation, meditation, reflection, rumination

11 cerebration, expectation, speculation
12 deliberation 13 consideration

contemplative

6 musing 7 pensive 10 cogitative, meditative, reflecting, reflective, ruminative, thoughtful 11 speculative 13 introspective

contemporary

3 new 6 coeval, extant, modern 7 current, present, recent, topical 8 existent, existing, up-to-date 9 au courant 10 coexistent, coexisting, coincident, concurrent, present-day, synchronic 11 synchronous 12 simultaneous

contempt

5 scorn, shame 7 despite, disdain, mockery 8 aversion, defiance, disfavor, disgrace, dishonor, distaste, ignominy 9 antipathy, discredit, disesteem, disrepute 10 disrespect, opprobrium, repugnance 12 disobedience, stubbornness

contemptible

3 low 4 base, mean, poor, vile 5 cheap, sorry 6 abject, odious, paltry, scummy, scurvy, shabby, sordid, squalid 7 hateful, ignoble, pitiful 8 inferior, pitiable, shameful, unworthy, wretched 9 abhorrent, loathsome 10 despicable, detestable, disgusting 11 ignominious
12 dishonorable

contemptuous

7 haughty 8 arrogant, derisive, scornful
10 disdainful 12 supercilious
13 condescending, disrespectful

contend

3 vie, war 4 aver, avow, cope, face, urge 5 argue, brawl, claim, fight 6 affirm, allege, assert, battle, charge, combat, debate, defend, insist, oppose, report, strive 7 compete, contest 8 confront, maintain, struggle 9 encounter, withstand

contender

5 match, rival 6 player 8 opponent 9 adversary, candidate, combatant 10 antagonist, challenger, competitor, contestant

_____ contendere

4 nolo

content

4 cozy, gist 5 happy 6 at ease, serene 7 appease, gratify, meaning, placate, satisfy 9 gratified, satisfied, substance 11 comfortable 12 significance

contention

3 war 4 beef, feud 6 combat, rumpus,

strife, thesis 7 discord, dispute, dissent, quarrel, rivalry, wrangle 8 argument, conflict, disunity, squabble 10 difference, dissension, dissidence 11 altercation, competition, controversy
Scottish: 5 sturt

contentious

5 fiery 7 carping, froward, peppery, scrappy, warlike 8 captious, caviling, contrary, militant, perverse 9 bellicose, combative, hotheaded, litigious, polemical, truculent 10 pugnacious 11 belligerent, quarrelsome 12 disputatious, faultfinding 13 argumentative, controversial

conterminous

10 coincident 11 coextensive

contest

3 vie 4 bout, duel, feud, fray, game, meet, race, tilt 5 clash, fight, match, repel, rival, trial 6 battle, combat, debate, oppose, resist, strife, strive 7 compete, dispute, rivalry, warfare 8 argument, conflict, endeavor, skirmish, struggle, tug-of-war 9 challenge, encounter, rencontre 10 engagement, tournament 11 competition

contiguity

9 adjacency, immediacy, proximity
11 propinquity

contiguous

4 next 8 abutting, adjacent, touching
9 adjoining, bordering 10 juxtaposed

continence

6 purity, virtue 8 chastity, sobriety 9 austerity 10 abnegation, abstinence, asceticism, chasteness, moderation, temperance 11 forbearance 12 renunciation 13 self-restraint

continent

4 Asia, mass 5 sober 6 Africa, chaste, Europe 8 celibate, mainland 9 abstinent, Australia, temperate 10 abstemious, Antarctica, restrained 11 abstentious 12 North America, South America
lost: 8 Atlantis

contingence

5 touch 7 contact 8 tangency, touching

contingency

4 pass 5 event 6 chance, crisis 8 exigency, juncture, occasion 9 emergency 10 likelihood 11 opportunity, possibility, probability, uncertainty

contingent

3 odd 4 band 5 group, party, troop 6 casual, chance, likely 7 reliant 8 possible, probable, relative 9 dependent,

empirical, entourage 10 accidental, delegation, deputation, detachment, fortuitous, incidental, uncertain, unforeseen 11 conditional 13 unanticipated, unforeseeable, unpredictable

continual
6 steady 7 abiding, endless, nonstop, regular, running 8 constant, enduring, timeless, unbroken, unending 9 ceaseless, incessant, perpetual, perennial, recurrent, recurring, unceasing, unfailing, unvarying 10 persistent, persisting, relentless, unchanging, unflagging 11 everlasting, unremitting 12 interminable 13 uninterrupted

continually
4 ever 6 always 7 forever 8 steadily, together 9 endlessly 10 constantly 11 incessantly, night and day 12 interminably, persistently, relentlessly, successively 13 consecutively

continuance
3 run 4 stay 5 delay 6 sequel 8 duration, survival 9 longevity 10 permanence 11 adjournment, persistence 12 postponement, prolongation

continuation
3 run 4 coda 6 sequel 8 appendix, duration, epilogue 9 endurance, extension 10 resumption 11 persistence, protraction 12 prolongation

continue
4 go on, last, stay 5 abide, renew, run on 6 endure, hang in, keep at, keep on, keep up, pick up, push on, remain, reopen, resume, retain, take up 7 carry on, persist, proceed, prolong, restart, survive 8 maintain, postpone, press on 9 carry over, persevere 10 recommence

continuing
5 fixed 6 steady 7 abiding, chronic, durable, eternal, lasting, ongoing 8 constant, enduring, lifelong, stubborn 9 long-lived, obstinate, perennial, prolonged, steadfast, tenacious, unabating 10 inveterate, persistent, persisting 11 long-lasting

continuity
4 flow 6 script 8 duration, scenario, sequence 9 endurance 11 persistence, progression

continuous
see **continual**

continuously
see **continually**

contort
4 knot, warp 5 twist, wring 6 deform, wrench, writhe 7 distort, grimace, torture 9 convolute, corkscrew, disfigure

contortionist
7 acrobat

contour
4 form, line 5 curve, lines, shape 6 figure 7 outline, pattern, profile 9 lineament, lineation 10 silhouette 11 delineation

contra
6 facing, toward 7 against, counter, reverse, vis-à-vis 8 converse, fronting, opposite 10 conversely

contraband
3 hot 5 taboo 6 banned 7 bootleg, illegal, illicit, smuggle 8 unlawful 9 forbidden 10 prohibited, proscribed 11 black market, bootlegging, trafficking

contract
4 bond, hire, pact, sink 5 catch, incur, lease 6 engage, induce, lessen, reduce, shrink, treaty, weaken 7 abridge, acquire, afflict, bargain, decline, dwindle, shorten, shrivel 8 compress, condense, covenant, decrease, diminish 9 agreement, constrict, succumb to 11 concentrate, transaction 12 come down with
part: 6 clause 7 article, proviso

contraction
3 he'd, he's, I'll, it's, I've, tic 4 ain't, can't, don't, flex, he'll, isn't, let's, she'd, she's, won't, you'd 5 aren't, cramp, didn't, hadn't, hasn't, she'll, spasm, they'd, wasn't, you'll, you're, you've 6 haven't, mustn't, needn't, they'll, they've, weren't 7 couldn't, elision, mightn't, wouldn't 8 shouldn't 9 reduction, shrinkage 10 abridgment 12 abbreviation
heart's: 7 systole
poetic: 3 e'en, e'er, o'er, 'tis 4 ne'er, 'twas 5 'twere, 'twill

contradict
4 deny 5 belie, cross, rebut 6 impugn, negate, refute, take on 7 confute, dispute, gainsay, traverse 9 challenge, disaffirm

contradiction
6 denial 7 paradox 8 antinomy, negation, rebuttal, variance 9 disparity 10 gainsaying, opposition, refutation 11 discrepancy, incongruity, inconsistency 12 disagreement, protestation

contradictory
7 counter, reverse 8 contrary, converse,

negating, opposite **9** antipodal
10 antipodean, antithesis, nullifying
12 antithetical

contraption

3 rig **5** gizmo **6** device, doodad, gadget
7 machine **9** apparatus, doohickey
11 contrivance

contrariety

10 antagonism, antithesis, opposition,
perversity, unlikeness

contrariwise

9 vice versa **10** conversely, oppositely

contrary

5 balky **6** averse, ornery, unruly
7 adverse, counter, froward, reverse,
wayward **8** converse, opposite, perverse,
stubborn **9** antipodal, diametric, dissident,
obstinate, vice versa **10** conversely,
discordant, headstrong, oppositely,
rebellious, refractory **11** conflicting,
intractable, wrongheaded **12** antagonistic,
antipathetic, antithetical, contumacious,
cross-grained, recalcitrant
prefix: 7 counter

contrast

6 differ **7** collate, compare, conflict, diverge
8 disagree **9** disparity, diversity
10 comparison, difference, divergence
11 distinction, distinguish **13** dissimilarity

contravene

4 defy, deny **5** break, cross, fight **6** abjure,
breach, disown, impugn, negate, offend,
oppose, reject **7** disobey, gainsay, violate
8 disclaim, infringe, renege on **9** disaffirm,
go against, repudiate **10** contradict,
transgress

contravention

6 breach **7** offense **8** trespass **9** violation
10 infraction **12** infringement
13 nonobservance, transgression

contretemps

3 row **4** slip, tiff **5** clash, run-in **6** dustup,
mishap, slip-up **7** dispute, quarrel
8 argument **9** mischance **10** falling-out,
misfortune

contribute

3 add **4** give, help, tend **5** grant **6** add in,
donate, kick in, submit, supply **7** conduce,
pitch in, redound **9** subscribe **11** come
through

contribution

4 alms, gift **5** input, share **7** charity,

payment, present **8** donation, offering
11 benefaction, beneficence

contributory

8 adjuvant **9** accessory, ancillary, auxiliary
10 collateral, subsidiary, supporting
11 appurtenant, subservient

contrite

5 sorry **8** penitent **9** regretful, repentant
10 apologetic, remorseful **11** penitential

contriteness

see **contrition**

contrition

3 rue **4** ruth **6** regret **7** penance, remorse
9 penitence **10** repentance
11 compunction **12** self-reproach

contrivance

4 ruse **6** device, gadget **7** gimmick
8 artifice **9** apparatus, expedient,
invention, stratagem **10** brainchild
11 contraption

contrive

3 rig **4** fake, make, move, plan, plot
5 frame, hatch **6** cook up, devise, invent,
make up, manage, scheme, vamp up,
wangle **7** arrange, concoct, connive,
develop, dream up, fashion, project, work
out **8** cogitate, conspire, engineer, intrigue
9 construct, elaborate, fabricate, formulate,
machinate

contrived

5 hokey **6** forced **7** labored **8** strained
9 concocted, insincere **10** artificial,
fabricated, factitious

control

3 run **4** curb, rein, rule, sway **5** guide,
power, steer **6** bridle, direct, govern,
handle, manage, master, rein in, subdue
7 command, conduct, mastery, oversee,
repress, reserve **8** dominate, dominion,
regulate, restrain **9** authority, direction,
restraint, supervise, supremacy
10 discipline, domination, management
11 supervision **12** jurisdiction

controlled

8 discreet, reserved **9** temperate
10 restrained

controversial

5 risky **6** touchy **7** awkward, charged,
eristic **8** delicate, disputed, ticklish
9 explosive, litigious, polemical
11 contentious, problematic **12** disputatious **13** argumentative

controversy
3 row 5 clash 6 debate, rumpus, strife
7 dispute, quarrel, wrangle 8 argument,
squabble 10 contention, falling-out
11 altercation, disputation, embroilment

controvert
4 deny 5 rebut 6 debate, oppose, oppugn,
refute 7 confute, counter, dispute, gainsay
8 disprove, question 9 challenge,
repudiate

contumacious
7 froward 8 contrary, insolent, mutinous,
obdurate, perverse 9 obstinate
10 rebellious, refractory 11 disobedient,
intractable 12 recalcitrant
13 insubordinate

contumacy
8 contempt, defiance 9 insolence
10 perversity 12 stubbornness
13 recalcitrance

contumelious
7 abusive 8 derisive, insolent, scornful
9 insulting, truculent 10 disdainful,
scurrilous 11 opprobrious 12 vituperative

contumely
5 abuse 6 insult 7 affront, mockery,
obloquy 8 contempt, ridicule, sneering
9 aspersion, invective 10 scurrility
12 vituperation

contuse
6 batter, bruise, injure 7 blacken

conundrum
5 poser 6 enigma, puzzle, riddle 7 baffler,
mystery, problem, puzzler, stumper
10 puzzlement 13 Chinese puzzle

convalesce
4 heal, mend 7 improve, recover
10 recuperate

convene
4 call, meet, 6 call in, gather, muster,
summon 7 convoke, summons
8 assemble 9 forgather 10 congregate
12 come together

convenience
4 ease 7 amenity, benefit, comfort, leisure
8 facility 9 handiness 10 assistance
13 accessibility

convenient
3 fit 4 near 5 close, handy, ready 6 at
hand, nearby, proper, useful 7 close by,
helpful 8 suitable 9 available, immediate,
opportune 10 accessible 11 appropriate,
comfortable 12 advantageous

convent
5 abbey 6 priory 7 nunnery 8 cloister
9 monastery, sanctuary

convention
3 law 4 bond, code, pact, rule 5 canon,
usage 6 accord, custom, treaty
7 compact, meeting, precept 8 assembly,
congress, contract, covenant, practice,
protocol 9 agreement, concordat, formality,
gathering, propriety, tradition
11 convocation 13 understanding

conventional
5 trite, usual 6 formal, normal, proper,
seemly, solemn, square 7 correct, regular,
routine, typical 8 everyday, habitual,
moderate, ordinary, orthodox, standard,
straight 9 bourgeois, customary 10 button-
down, conforming, prevailing, restrained,
unoriginal 11 commonplace, traditional
12 conservative

conventionalize
5 adapt 7 conform, stylize

converge
4 join, meet 5 focus, merge, unite
11 concentrate 12 come together

conversant
8 familiar 9 au courant 10 acquainted
11 experienced

conversation
4 chat, talk 6 confab, debate, parley
7 palaver, talking 8 causerie, colloquy,
dialogue, duologue, exchange, repartee
9 discourse, tête-à-tête 10 discussion
13 confabulation

conversation piece
5 curio 6 oddity 9 curiosity

converse
3 gab 4 chat, chin, talk 5 speak, visit
6 confer, contra, parley 7 chatter, counter,
reverse 8 antipode, contrary, opposite
9 antipodal, diametric 10 antithesis
12 antithetical 13 contradictory

conversely
9 vice versa 10 oppositely 12 contrariwise

conversion
5 shift 6 change, switch 7 novelty, rebirth,
turning 8 mutation, reversal 9 about-face
10 alteration, changeover 11 permutation
12 modification, regeneration
13 metamorphosis, transmutation

convert
4 sway 5 alter 6 change, modify, redeem,
reform, switch 7 commute, remodel
8 persuade, renovate 9 proselyte,
transform, translate, transmute, transpose

11 transfigure 12 metamorphose, transmogrify
Christian: 10 catechumen

convex
5 bowed, toric 6 arched, curved 7 bulging, curving, gibbous, rounded

convey
3 lug 4 bear, cart, cede, deed, pack, send, tell, tote 5 bring, carry, ferry 6 assign, impart, pass on 7 channel, conduct, consign, deliver, express, project 8 make over, sign over, transfer, transmit
9 transport 11 communicate

conveyance
3 car 4 auto, cart, deed, sled 5 coach, sedan, stage, title, wagon 7 charter, trailer, transit, vehicle 8 carriage, carrying
9 transport 10 automobile 12 transporting
public: 3 bus, cab 4 taxi, tram 5 plane, train 7 trolley 8 airplane, monorail, railroad, rickshaw 9 streetcar
10 jinricksha, jinrikisha

convict
5 felon, lifer 6 inmate, send up
7 condemn, put away 8 criminal, jailbird, prisoner, sentence, yardbird 10 find guilty

conviction
4 view 5 creed, faith 6 belief, surety
7 opinion 8 doctrine, sentence, sureness
9 assurance, certainty, certitude, sentiment
10 confidence, persuasion
12 condemnation

convince
6 assure, induce, prompt 7 satisfy, win over 8 persuade, talk into 9 influence, prevail on 11 bring around, prevail upon

convincing
5 solid, sound, valid 6 cogent 8 credible, faithful 9 plausible 10 believable, conclusive, persuasive, satisfying
11 trustworthy

convivial
3 gay 5 jolly, merry 6 hearty, jocund, jovial, lively, social 7 festive 8 mirthful, sociable 9 fun-loving, vivacious
10 gregarious 13 companionable

convocation
5 synod 7 council, meeting 8 assembly, conclave 9 gathering 10 assemblage
12 congregation

convoke
4 call 6 gather, invite, muster, summon
7 collect, convene 8 assemble 12 call together

convoluted
6 coiled 7 complex, tangled, winding
8 involved, tortuous 9 intricate
10 circuitous 11 anfractuous, complicated, labyrinthine

convoy
6 attend, escort 7 conduct 9 accompany

convulse
4 rock 5 shake 7 agitate, concuss
8 tetanize

convulsion
3 fit 5 spasm 6 attack, tumult, uproar
7 quaking, rocking, seizure, shaking
8 disaster, paroxysm, upheaval
9 commotion, trembling

cook
3 fix, fry 4 bake, boil, chef, heat, melt, stew
5 broil, grill, poach, roast, sauté, steam
6 braise, doctor, simmer 7 falsify, parboil, prepare, swelter

cooked
4 done, sham 5 bogus, faked, phony
6 made-up 7 altered 8 doctored, spurious
10 fictitious

cookery
7 cuisine
expert: 3 Yan (Martin) 4 Chen (Joyce), Kerr (Graham), Puck (Wolfgang), Root (Waverley) 5 Beard (James), Child (Julia), David (Elizabeth), Hines (Duncan), Smith (Jeff) 6 Bocuse (Paul), Carême (Marie-Antoine), Farmer (Fannie), Fisher (M. F. K.), Franey (Pierre), Waters (Alice)
7 Crocker (Betty), Stewart (Martha)
8 Bourdain (Anthony), Rombauer (Irma)
9 Claiborne (Craig), Escoffier (Auguste), Prudhomme (Paul)

cookie
4 snap 7 biscuit, brownie 10 gingersnap

cooking
appliance: 4 oven 5 mixer, range, stove
7 blender, toaster 9 microwave
10 rotisserie
implement: 3 cup, pan, pot, wok 4 olla
5 ladle, sieve, spoon, whisk 6 grater, masher, sifter, tureen 7 griddle, skillet, spatula, steamer 8 colander, teaspoon
9 eggbeater, frying pan 10 rolling pin, tablespoon 12 measuring cup
room: 6 galley 7 kitchen

Cook Islands
capital: 6 Avarua
dependency of: 10 New Zealand
island: 9 Rarotonga

cool

3 hep, hip, icy **4** calm, cold **5** abate, aloof, chill, gelid, nippy **6** arctic, chilly, frigid, frosty **7** assured, compose, control, decline, distant, dwindle, repress, subside **8** composed, decrease, detached, diminish, reserved, suppress **9** collected, confident, impassive, unruffled **10** nonchalant, phlegmatic, unsociable **11** indifferent, standoffish, unflappable **13** dispassionate, imperturbable, self-possessed

cooler

3 fan, jug, pen **4** brig, coop, jail **5** clink, pokey **6** fridge, icebox, lockup, prison **7** freezer, slammer **9** calaboose **11** refrigerant **12** refrigerator

cooling device

3 fan **6** fridge, icebox **7** freezer **12** refrigerator

coolness

5 chill, poise **6** aplomb, phlegm **7** reserve **9** composure, frigidity, sangfroid **10** dispassion, equanimity **11** nonchalance, self-control

coop

3 hem, jug, mew, pen **4** brig, cage, jail **5** cramp, fence, pokey, prison **6** cooler, corral, lockup, shut in **7** close in, confine, enclose, slammer **9** calaboose, enclosure

cooperate

5 agree, unite **6** concur, league **7** combine, conjoin, pitch in **8** coincide, conspire **11** collaborate, participate **12** work together

cooperation

8 alliance, teamwork **13** confederation

cooperative

5 joint **6** common, mutual, shared **8** coactive, conjoint, obliging **9** collegial, concerted **10** collective, synergetic **11** coordinated **13** accommodating, collaborative, uncompetitive

Cooper hero

7 Hawkeye **10** Deerslayer, Pathfinder **11** Natty Bumppo

coordinate

4 mate, mesh **5** align, equal, match, order **6** adjust, relate **7** coequal, conform **8** organize, parallel **9** companion, correlate, harmonize, integrate, reconcile **10** proportion, reciprocal **11** accommodate, correlative, counterpart

coot

4 bird, fogy **6** dotard, duffer, fellow, oddity, scoter, weirdo **7** oddball **9** character, eccentric

cootie

5 louse **9** body louse

cop

3 nab **4** lift, take **5** adopt, catch, filch, pinch, steal, swipe **6** pilfer **7** capture, officer **8** bluecoat **9** patrolman, policeman

copacetic

3 A-OK **4** fine, jake, okay **5** dandy, great, nifty **8** all right **9** excellent **12** satisfactory

cope

4 cape, hack **5** cloak, cover, get by, match, vault **6** canopy, endure, make do, manage, mantle **7** carry on, survive **8** vestment

copestone

5 crown

copious

4 lush, rich **5** ample **6** lavish, plenty **7** liberal, profuse, replete **8** abundant, generous **9** abounding, bounteous, bountiful, exuberant, luxuriant, plenteous, plentiful

Copland work

5 Rodeo **11** Billy the Kid **17** Appalachian Spring

cop-out

5 dodge **6** excuse **7** evasion, pretext, retreat

copper

4 cent, coin **5** metal, penny, token **9** butterfly, policeman
item: 4 cent **5** penny **6** kettle
sulfate: 7 vitriol **9** bluestone **11** blue vitriol

copperhead

5 snake, viper **8** pit viper

coppice

4 bosk, wood **5** copse, grove, woods **6** bosque, forest, growth **7** thicket **9** brushwood, underwood

copse

see **coppice**

Copt

8 Egyptian

copula

4 bond, link **5** joint, union **7** coupler

copy

3 ape **4** echo, fake, mock, sham **5** clone, ditto, forge, mimic, model **6** carbon, parrot,

repeat **7** emulate, forgery, imitate, replica, takeoff **8** knockoff, likeness, simulate **9** duplicate, facsimile, imitation, replicate, reproduce **10** impression, simulacrum, simulation, transcribe, transcript **11** counterfeit, counterpart, reduplicate, replication **12** reproduction

copyist
5 clerk **6** scribe **8** imitator **9** engrosser, transcriber **10** plagiarist

copyread
4 edit

coquet
3 toy **4** fool, vamp **5** dally, flirt, tease **6** trifle

coquette
4 vamp **5** flirt, tease

coquettish
3 coy **4** fickle **9** frivolous, kittenish **11** flirtatious

coral
3 red **4** pink, rosy **5** polyp **9** limestone

coral reef
3 cay, key **5** atoll
off Australia: 5 Wreck
world's largest: 12 Great Barrier

cord
3 tie **4** band, lace, pile, rope, whip, yarn **5** cable, nerve, stack **6** strand, string, tendon
twisted: 7 torsade

cordage
4 rope **5** ropes **7** rigging
fiber: 4 bast, hemp, jute, pita **5** sisal

Corday's victim
5 Marat (Jean-Paul)

Cordelia
father: 4 Lear
sister: 5 Regan **7** Goneril

cordial
4 warm **6** genial, hearty, jovial, tender **7** affable, liqueur, sincere **8** cheerful, friendly, gracious, sociable **9** congenial, convivial, heartfelt **10** hospitable **11** sympathetic, warmhearted **12** wholehearted

cordiality
6 warmth **7** amenity **9** geniality **10** amiability **12** agreeability, friendliness

cordon
4 lace, line, ring **5** braid **6** circle, ribbon **7** barrier **8** espalier
bleu: 4 chef, cook **6** ribbon **10** blue ribbon, decoration, master chef

core
3 hub, nub **4** base, crux, gist, meat, pith, root **5** basis, focus, heart, midst **6** center, depths, kernel, middle, upshot **7** essence, nucleus **8** interior, midpoint **9** substance **10** foundation

corium
5 cutis **6** dermis

cork
4 bark, plug, seal, stop **5** float **6** bobber **7** stopper, stopple

corker
4 lulu **5** beaut, dandy, dilly, doozy **6** doozie, killer **8** jim-dandy, knockout **9** humdinger **11** crackerjack **12** lollapalooza

corkscrew
4 coil, wind **5** helix, twist **6** spiral

cormorant
4 bird, shag **7** glutton

corn
5 grain, maize **6** hominy **9** granulate
bread: 4 pone **7** bannock
Indian: 5 maize **6** mealie
kind: 3 pop **5** flint, flour, sweet **6** Indian
pest: 5 borer
piece: 3 cob, ear **5** spike **6** kernel, nubbin

Corncracker State
8 Kentucky

corner
3 box, fix, jam, nab **4** hole, nook, trap, tree **5** angle, catch, coign, niche, seize **6** collar, cranny, dogleg, pickle, plight, recess, scrape **7** capture, dilemma, impasse, trouble **8** bottle up, monopoly **10** bring to bay **11** predicament **12** intersection
of eye: 7 canthus

cornerstone
4 base **5** basis **7** support **8** rudiment **10** foundation, groundwork

cornet
4 cone, horn **7** officer, trumpet **10** instrument

Cornhusker State
8 Nebraska

cornice
3 cap 4 band, eave 5 crown 7 molding

cornmeal
4 masa, samp 5 grits 6 hominy
7 hoecake
mush: 7 polenta

cornucopia
4 cone, horn 6 bounty, plenty, wealth
9 abundance, profusion 12 horn of plenty

Cornwallis, Charles
adversary: 6 Greene (Nathanael)
surrender site: 8 Yorktown

corny
5 banal, sappy, stale, trite 6 old hat
7 clichéd, mawkish 8 shopworn
9 hackneyed, schmaltzy 11 sentimental,
stereotyped

corollary
6 effect, result, sequel, upshot 8 parallel,
sequence 9 resulting 10 associated, end
product, equivalent 11 aftereffect,
consequence

corona
4 aura, glow, halo 5 cigar, crown, glory
6 circle, nimbus 7 aureola, aureole

coroner
8 examiner

coronet
5 crown, tiara 6 anadem, circle, diadem,
wreath 7 chaplet, circlet, garland
8 headband

Coronis
form: 4 crow
son: 9 Asclepius 11 Aesculapius

corporal
3 NCO 6 bodily, carnal 7 fleshly, somatic
8 physical

corporate
7 unified 8 combined 9 aggregate

corporeal
6 bodily, carnal, mortal 7 fleshly, somatic
8 material, physical, tangible 9 objective
10 phenomenal 11 substantial

corps
4 band, body 5 group, party, troop 6 outfit,
troupe 7 company

corpse
4 body 5 bones, stiff 7 cadaver, carcass,
carrion, remains
combining form: 4 necr 5 necro

corpselike
4 dead 5 gaunt 7 deathly, ghastly,
macabre lifeless, skeletal 10 cadaverous

corpulence
7 fatness, obesity 9 adiposity, rotundity
10 fleshiness

corpulent
3 fat 5 bulky, gross, heavy, obese, plump,
stout 6 fleshy, portly, rotund 7 porcine,
weighty 9 overblown 10 overweight

corpus
4 body, bulk, core, mass 6 oeuvre
9 principal, substance 10 collection
11 compilation

corpuscle
4 cell 8 hemocyte, monocyte 9 blood cell,
leukocyte 10 lymphocyte 11 erythrocyte,
granulocyte

corral
3 mew, pen 5 fence 6 gather, shut in
7 close in, collect, confine, enclose, round
up 8 surround 9 enclosure

correct
3 fit, fix 4 edit, just, mend, true 5 amend,
emend, exact, right 6 adjust, decent,
proper, punish, reform, remedy, repair,
revise, seemly 7 chasten, fitting, improve,
perfect, precise, rectify, redress
8 accurate, becoming, chastise, decorous,
flawless, set right 9 castigate, faultless
10 conforming, discipline, impeccable,
legitimate, meticulous, scrupulous 11 appropriate, comme il faut, punctilious
12 conventional
combining form: 4 orth 5 ortho

correction
3 rod 6 rebuke 7 reproof 8 revision
9 amendment 10 adjustment, discipline,
emendation, punishment 11 castigation

corrective
4 cure 6 remedy 8 antidote, punitive,
remedial 10 beneficial 11 counterstep,
restorative 12 counteragent
13 counteractive

correctness
7 decorum 8 accuracy, fidelity 9 precision,
propriety 10 exactitude

correlate
5 match 6 analog 7 pendant 8 analogue,
coincide, dovetail, parallel 9 harmonize
10 complement, correspond
11 counterpart

correlative
3 and, nor 4 both, then 6 either 7 neither, related 10 complement, reciprocal 11 counterpart 13 complementary, corresponding

correspond
4 jibe 5 agree, equal, match, write 6 accord, concur 7 comport, conform 8 dovetail 9 harmonize 11 communicate

correspondence
4 mail 7 analogy, letters 8 symmetry 9 agreement, congruity 10 conformity, similarity 11 consistency, correlation
mathematical: 7 mapping 8 function

correspondent
5 match 6 analog, pen pal, writer 7 fitting 8 analogue, parallel, reporter, suitable 9 correlate 10 conforming, journalist 11 commentator, contributor, counterpart

corresponding
4 akin, like 5 alike 6 agnate 7 related, similar 8 matching, parallel 9 analogous, consonant 10 comparable 11 correlative

correspondingly
4 also 7 equally 8 likewise 9 similarly 11 analogously

corrida
9 bullfight
shout: 3 olé

corridor
4 hall, lane, path 5 aisle, route, strip 6 artery, avenue 7 hallway, passage 10 passageway

corroborate
5 prove 6 uphold, verify 7 approve, bear out, certify, confirm, endorse, justify, support 8 document, validate 9 vindicate 12 authenticate, substantiate

corroborative
9 ancillary, auxiliary 10 collateral, supporting, supportive 12 confirmatory

corrode
4 rust 7 eat away, eat into, oxidize 8 wear away 9 undermine

corrosive
5 acerb 6 biting 7 acerbic, caustic, cutting 9 sarcastic

corrosiveness
7 sarcasm 8 acerbity

corrugation
4 fold, ruck 5 plica, ridge 6 crease, furrow, groove 7 crinkle, wrinkle

corrupt
3 rot 5 bribe, decay, spoil, stain, taint, venal 6 befoul, debase, defile, molder, rotten, smirch 7 crooked, debauch, degrade, deprave, pervert, putrefy, tarnish, vitiate 8 bribable, degraded, depraved, infected, perverse 9 decompose, dishonest, miscreant, reprobate, unethical 10 bastardize, degenerate 12 unprincipled, unscrupulous 13 untrustworthy

corruptible
5 venal 7 buyable 8 bribable

corruption
4 vice 5 decay, fraud, graft 7 bribery, jobbery 9 barbarism, depravity, turpitude 10 immorality, wickedness 11 impropriety

corsair
5 rover 6 pirate 8 picaroon, sea rover 9 buccaneer, pickaroon, privateer 10 freebooter

corset
5 stays 6 bodice, girdle 7 support

cortege
5 train 6 parade 7 retinue 9 entourage 10 attendants, procession

cortex
4 bark, husk, peel, rind 6 casing 8 peridium

Cortland
5 apple

corundum
4 ruby 5 emery, topaz 7 emerald 8 abrasive, amethyst, sapphire

coruscate
5 flash, gleam, glint, shine 7 glisten, glitter, sparkle, twinkle 11 scintillate

corvid
3 jay 4 crow 5 raven 6 magpie 9 passerine

Corvino's wife
5 Celia

corybantic
3 mad 4 wild 5 rabid 6 crazed 7 frantic, furious 8 ecstatic, frenetic, frenzied 9 delirious

coryphée
6 dancer 8 danseuse 9 ballerina

Cosí Fan Tutte composer
6 Mozart (Wolfgang Amadeus)

cosmetic
4 kohl **5** blush, rouge **6** ceruse, makeup, powder **7** blusher, bronzer, mascara **8** lip gloss, lipstick **9** eye shadow **10** decorative, nail polish, ornamental **11** beautifying, superficial

cosmetologist
10 beautician

cosmic
4 huge, vast **7** immense **8** infinite **9** planetary, spiritual, unbounded, universal **12** astronomical, metaphysical

cosmopolitan
6 global, urbane **7** worldly **8** catholic, cultured, polished **9** civilized, universal, worldwide **10** cultivated, ecumenical **11** worldly-wise **13** sophisticated

cosmos
6 flower **8** creation, universe

Cossack
army: 3 Don **4** Ural **5** Kuban
land: 7 Ukraine
leader: 5 Razin (Stenka) **6** ataman, hetman, Mazepa (Ivan) **7** Bulavin (Kondraty) **8** Pugachov (Yemelyan)
novel: 10 Taras Bulba

cosset
3 pet **4** baby, lamb, love **5** humor, spoil **6** caress, cocker, coddle, cuddle, dandle, dote on, fondle, pamper **7** cater to, indulge **11** mollycoddle

cost
3 tab **4** rate, toll **5** price **6** charge, damage, outlay, tariff **7** expense, payment **8** price tag **9** sacrifice **11** expenditure **12** disbursement
business: 8 overhead

Costa Rica
bay: 8 Coronado
capital: 7 San José
city: 8 Alajuela **10** Puntarenas **11** Puerto Limón
discoverer: 8 Columbus (Christopher)
language: 7 Spanish
leader: 5 Arias (Oscar)
monetary unit: 5 colón
neighbor: 6 Panama **9** Nicaragua
peninsula: 3 Osa **6** Nicoya
river: 7 San Juan
volcano: 5 Barba, Irazú **9** Turrialba

costermonger
6 hawker **7** peddler **9** barrow boy

costive
4 mean, slow **5** bound, close, tight **6** frugal, stingy **7** miserly **9** penurious **10** hardfisted, pinchpenny **11** closefisted **12** cheeseparing, parsimonious

costless
4 free **6** gratis **10** gratuitous **13** complimentary

costly
4 dear, rich **5** fancy **6** lavish, pricey **7** opulent, premium **8** precious, splendid, valuable **9** expensive, luxurious, priceless **10** exorbitant, high-priced, invaluable **11** extravagant

costume
3 rig **4** duds, garb, mode **5** dress, getup, guise, habit, style **6** attire, outfit **7** apparel, clothes, fashion, threads, turnout, uniform **8** disguise, ensemble, garments **9** trappings

cot
3 bed, hut **4** camp **5** cabin, lodge, shack **6** shanty
wheeled: 6 gurney

coterie
4 band, camp, clan, club, ring **5** cabal **6** circle, clique **7** in-group **9** camarilla

cotillion
4 ball, prom **5** dance

cottage
3 hut **4** camp **5** cabin, lodge, shack **6** shanty **8** bungalow
Russian: 5 dacha
Swiss: 6 chalet

cotton
cleaner: 3 gin **6** linter
cloth: 4 duck, jean, mull **5** baize, chino, denim, drill, khaki, scrim, terry, wigan **6** calico, canvas, chintz, dimity, muslin, oxford, sateen, velour **7** batiste, etamine, fustian, gingham, jaconet, nankeen, organdy, percale **8** corduroy, dungaree, moleskin, nainsook, tarlatan **9** grenadine, percaline, stockinet, swansdown **10** balbriggan **11** stockinette
cloth, Indian: 5 surah **6** madras **7** dhurrie, khaddar
comb: 4 card
fuzz remover: 6 linter
measure: 4 hank, pick, yard **5** count, skein
pad: 7 pledget
pod: 4 boll

refuse: **5** flock
seed separator: **3** gin
sheet: **4** batt
thread: **5** lisle

Cotton State
 7 Alabama

cottonwood
 5 alamo **6** poplar

cottony
 4 soft **6** fluffy

_____ Coty
 4 René

couch
 3 den, put **4** lair, sofa, word **5** divan, lodge
 6 burrow, chaise, daybed, lounge, phrase
 7 express, lie down, recline **9** davenport,
 formulate **12** chesterfield

couch potato
 7 slacker

cougar
 3 cat **4** puma **7** panther **9** catamount
 12 mountain lion

cough
 4 hack, hawk

cough drop
 6 troche **7** lozenge

cough up
 3 pay **5** spend **6** lay out, pay out
 7 deliver, dole out, fork out **8** fork over,
 hand over, shell out

couloir
 5 chasm, gorge, gulch, gully **6** ravine

council
 4 diet **5** board, junta **6** powwow, senate
 7 cabinet, meeting **8** assembly, conclave,
 congress, ministry **10** conference,
 federation **12** consultation
 ancient Greek: 5 boule
 church: 5 synod **10** consistory
 medieval English: 4 moot **5** gemot
 6 gemote **8** hustings
 Muslim: 5 divan
 Russian: 4 duma **6** soviet
 secret: 5 cabal, junto **9** camarilla
 Spanish: 7 cabildo

counsel
 4 urge, warn **6** advice, advise, charge,
 direct, enjoin, lawyer **7** consult, suggest
 8 advocate, attorney **9** prescribe,
 recommend **10** advisement
 12 deliberation

British: 9 barrister, solicitor

count
 3 add, sum, tot **4** bank, earl, mean, rely,
 tote **5** issue, score, tally, total, tot up,
 weigh **6** census, charge, depend, expect,
 figure, matter, number, reckon, result, tote
 up **7** compute, signify **8** estimate, militate,
 numerate, quantify **9** calculate, enumerate
 10 allegation

countenance
 3 mug **4** back, cast, face, look, mien, phiz
 5 favor, go for **6** accept, visage **7** approve,
 commend, condone, endorse, support
 8 advocate, features, hold with, sanction,
 tolerate **9** approbate, composure,
 encourage **10** expression
 11 physiognomy

counter
 3 pit, vie **4** anti **5** asset, check, match,
 polar, shelf **6** offset, oppose **7** adverse,
 against, hostile, obverse, opposed, reverse
 8 antipode, contrary, converse, opposing,
 opposite **9** antipodal, diametric **10** antipodean, antithesis, contravene
 12 antagonistic, antipathetic, antithetical
 13 contradictory

counteract
 3 fix **4** foil **5** annul **6** cancel, negate,
 oppose, resist, thwart **7** balance, correct,
 nullify, prevent, rectify, redress **8** negative
 9 cancel out, frustrate **10** balance out,
 neutralize

counteragent
 4 cure **6** remedy **8** antidote **9** antitoxin,
 antivenin **10** corrective

counterbalance
 6 cancel, make up, offset, redeem, set off
 7 ballast, correct, even out, rectify, redress
 8 equalize, outweigh **10** compensate

counterblow
 7 revenge **8** reprisal, requital, revanche
 9 vengeance **11** retaliation, retribution

counterclockwise
 4 levo **12** levorotatory

counterfeit
 4 copy, fake, hoax, sham **5** bluff, bogus,
 dummy, false, feign, forge, fraud, mimic,
 phony **6** affect, assume, deceit, ersatz,
 forged, pseudo **7** feigned, imitate, pretend
 8 delusive, delusory, knock off, simulate,
 spurious **9** brummagem, deception,
 deceptive, fabricate, imitation, imposture,
 insincere, pinchbeck, pretended, simulated
 10 fraudulent, misleading, simulacrum
 prefix: 5 pseud **6** pseudo

counterpane
4 pouf, puff 5 duvet 6 spread 8 bedcover, coverlet 9 bedspread, comforter, eiderdown

counterpart
4 like, twin 5 equal, match 6 analog, double 7 vis-à-vis 8 analogue, parallel 9 correlate, duplicate 10 complement, coordinate, equivalent 11 correlative 13 correspondent

counterpoise
6 make up, offset, redeem, set off 7 balance, ballast 8 outweigh 9 stabilize 10 compensate

countersign
8 password 9 watchword

countervail
4 foil 6 cancel, offset, oppose, redeem, set off, thwart 7 balance, correct, nullify, rectify 8 outweigh 9 frustrate 10 compensate, neutralize

countless
6 legion, myriad, untold 7 umpteen 11 innumerable

Count of Monte Cristo
6 Dantès (Edmond) **author:** 5 Dumas (Alexandre)

count out
5 expel 6 except 7 exclude 9 disregard, eliminate

countrified
5 rural 6 rustic 7 bucolic 8 homespun, pastoral 10 campestral

country
4 home, land, soil 5 rural 6 nation, region, rustic, sticks 7 boonies, bucolic, outland 8 homeland, pastoral 9 backwoods, boondocks 10 campestral, fatherland, motherland, provincial
dance: 3 jig 4 reel 10 strathspey
home: 5 manor, ranch, villa 8 hacienda
music: 9 bluegrass
road: 4 lane, path 5 byway

coup
4 blow, feat 5 upset 6 putsch, stroke 8 takeover

couple
3 duo 4 bond, dyad, fuse, join, link, mate, pair, span, team, yoke 5 brace, hitch, marry, merge, unite 6 hook up, link up 7 bracket, combine, conjoin, connect, doublet, harness, twosome

coupler
4 link, ring 5 hitch, joint 6 hookup 7 shackle 8 ligature
railroad: 7 drawbar

couplet
3 duo 4 dyad, pair 5 twins 7 distich, doublet, twosome

coupling
4 link, seam 5 joint, union 7 joining, pairing 8 junction, juncture 9 connector 10 connection

courage
4 dash, grit, guts 5 heart, moxie, nerve, pluck, spunk, valor 6 daring, mettle, spirit 7 bravery, heroism 8 audacity, backbone, boldness, firmness, temerity, tenacity, valiance, valiancy 9 assurance, fortitude, gallantry 10 resolution 11 doughtiness, intrepidity 12 fearlessness 13 dauntlessness

courageous
4 bold 5 brave, gutsy, nervy, stout 6 daring, heroic, manful, plucky, spunky, strong 7 doughty, gallant, valiant 8 fearless, intrepid, resolute, stalwart, unafraid, valorous 9 audacious, dauntless, tenacious, undaunted 11 venturesome 12 stouthearted

courier
5 envoy 6 legate, runner 8 emissary 9 go-between, messenger 11 internuncio

course
3 row, run, way 4 dart, dash, duct, flow, line, path, plan, race, road, rush, tack, tear 5 canal, chain, chase, class, hurry, orbit, order, range, route, scoot, scope, speed, surge, track, trend 6 career, design, hasten, hustle, manner, policy, policy, scheme, sequel, series, string, system 7 advance, channel, circuit, conduit, passage, pattern, program, regimen, routine, seminar 8 aqueduct, duration, progress, sequence, syllabus 9 procedure, racetrack 10 curriculum, succession 11 progression
dinner: 5 salad 6 entrée 7 dessert 9 blue plate

courser
4 bird 5 horse 7 charger 8 huntsman, warhorse

court
3 bar, woo 4 date, quad, yard 5 charm, motel, spark, suite, tempt 6 allure, homage, invite, palace, pursue 7 address, flatter, justice, retinue, romance, solicit

8 assembly, cloister, tribunal 9 captivate, curtilage, enclosure, entourage 10 magistrate, parliament, quadrangle 11 legislature
action: 4 suit 5 trial 6 appeal, assize 7 hearing, inquest, lawsuit 10 proceeding
calendar: 6 docket
call to: 7 summons 8 subpoena 11 arraignment
circuit: 4 eyre
crier's call: 4 oyez
decision: 6 assize 7 finding, verdict 8 judgment
ecclesiastical: 4 rota 5 Curia 10 consistory
Indian: 6 durbar
kind: 4 moot 5 civil 6 county, family 7 circuit, customs, federal, supreme 8 chancery, criminal, district, juvenile, kangaroo, superior 9 appellate, municipal 11 territorial
medieval English: 4 eyre, moot 5 gemot 6 gemote 8 hustings
of equity: 8 chancery
officer: 5 clerk, crier, judge 7 bailiff, justice, marshal, sheriff 10 prosecutor
order: 4 writ 5 edict 6 decree 7 summons 8 mandamus, subpoena
panel: 4 jury
relating to: 8 judicial 9 juridical
session: 6 assize 7 sitting 8 sederunt

courteous
5 civil 6 polite 7 courtly, gallant, genteel 8 mannerly, well-bred 9 attentive 10 chivalrous, thoughtful 11 considerate 12 well-mannered

courtesy
7 amenity, decorum, manners, service 8 chivalry, civility 9 attention, etiquette, gallantry 10 cordiality, indulgence 11 courtliness 12 graciousness 13 attentiveness, consideration

court game
see under **game**

courtly
5 noble 6 august, formal, urbane 7 elegant, gallant, refined, stately 8 gracious 9 dignified 10 chivalrous 11 ceremonious, flattering

courtship
4 suit 6 dating, wooing 7 romance 10 flirtation
former custom of: 8 bundling

courtyard
4 quad 5 garth, patio 9 curtilage 10 quadrangle

cousin
3 kin 7 kinsman 8 relative

Cousteau, Jacques
ship: 7 Calypso
vehicle: 11 bathysphere

couturier
8 clothier, costumer, designer 10 dressmaker

cove
3 arm, bay 4 nook 5 bight, firth, inlet, niche 6 harbor, recess 9 concavity

covenant
3 vow 4 bond, pact 5 agree, swear 6 pledge, treaty 7 compact, promise 8 contract 9 agreement 10 convention

Covent Garden offering
5 opera

cover
3 cap, lid 4 bury, hide, hood, mask, wrap 5 alibi, cloak, front, guise, stash, track 6 enfold, enwrap, facade, hiding, insure, refuge, screen, secure, shield, shroud, travel 7 blanket, conceal, embrace, enclose, envelop, obscure, overlay, protect, secrete, shelter, write up 8 disguise, ensconce, enshroud, traverse 9 encompass, safeguard, sanctuary, superpose 10 overspread 11 concealment, superimpose
rooflike: 6 awning, canopy
the eyes: 9 blindfold
the face: 4 mask, veil
the mouth: 6 muzzle
with asphalt: 4 pave
with cloth: 5 drape
with dirt: 7 begrime, blacken 8 besmirch
with straw: 6 thatch

coverall
8 jumpsuit 10 boilersuit

covered wagon
9 Conestoga

covering
anatomical: 5 theca, velum 6 tegmen 7 velamen 8 tegument 10 integument
close-fitting: 6 sheath 9 sheathing
cloth: 5 sheet
flap: 9 operculum
for a book: 4 case 6 jacket
for a cigar: 7 wrapper
for a coffin: 4 pall
for a corpse: 6 shroud 8 cerement
for a package: 7 wrapper
for concealment: 10 camouflage

for food: 4 cosy, cozy
for soil: 5 mulch
metal: 4 mail 5 armor
of a diatom: 6 lorica
of a plant ovary: 8 pericarp
of a seed: 4 aril, case 5 testa
of fruits: 4 peel, rind
of gloom: 4 pall
of grain: 4 hull, husk 5 chaff
shell-like: 8 carapace
thin: 4 film 6 patina, veneer
waterproof: 4 tarp 9 tarpaulin

coverlet
4 pouf, puff 5 duvet 6 spread 8 bedcover
9 bedspread, comforter 11 counterpane

covert
4 lair 5 haven, privy 6 hidden, masked,
refuge, secret, veiled 7 feather, furtive,
retreat, shelter, sub-rosa, thicket 8 hush-
hush, shrouded, stealthy 9 concealed,
disguised, sanctuary, sheltered
10 undercover 11 camouflaged,
clandestine, hiding place, underhanded
12 hugger-mugger 13 surreptitious, under-
the-table

covertly
7 sub-rosa 9 by stealth 12 hugger-mugger

covet
4 want 5 crave 6 desire

covetous
4 avid, keen 5 itchy 6 grabby, greedy
7 envious 8 desirous, esurient, grasping,
ravenous 9 rapacious, voracious
10 avaricious, gluttonous 11 acquisitive

covey
4 band, bevy, crew, nest 5 brood, bunch,
flock, group, party, troop 6 gaggle, troupe
7 cluster, company

cow
(see also **cattle**)
4 faze, kine (plural), neat 5 abash, bossy,
bully, daunt 6 appall, bovine, dismay,
hector, rattle 7 bluster, dragoon
8 bludgeon, browbeat, bulldoze, bullyrag
9 discomfit, embarrass, strong-arm
10 disconcert, intimidate
cud: 5 rumen
French: 5 vache
hornless: 5 muley 7 pollard
mammary gland: 5 udder
pen: 6 corral
shed: 4 barn, byre
Spanish: 4 vaca
young: 4 calf 5 stirk 6 heifer

coward
6 craven 7 caitiff, chicken, dastard,
milksop, nebbish 8 poltroon, recreant
9 jellyfish 10 scaredy-cat 11 yellowbelly

_____ Coward
4 Noël

cowardly
5 timid, wimpy 6 afraid, craven, yellow
7 caitiff, chicken, fearful, gutless
8 poltroon, recreant, timorous 9 dastardly
11 lily-livered, milk-livered, poltroonish
12 apprehensive, fainthearted, poor-
spirited, white-livered 13 pusillanimous

cowboy
5 rogue, waddy 6 drover, herder, waddie
7 puncher, rancher 8 buckaroo, herdsman,
maverick, wrangler 9 cattleman, ranch
hand 10 cowpuncher 12 broncobuster
contest: 5 rodeo
gear: 5 cuffs, quirt, spurs 6 duster
7 bedroll, slicker, Stetson
legendary: 9 Pecos Bill
leggings: 5 chaps
movie: 3 Mix (Tom) 4 Hart (William S.)
5 Autry (Gene), Wayne (John) 6 Gibson
(Hoot), McCrea (Joel), Murphy (Audie),
Ritter (Tex), Rogers (Roy, Will) 8 Cisco
Kid, Eastwood (Clint)
rope: 5 lasso, reata, riata 6 lariat
Spanish-American: 6 charro, gaucho
7 vaquero

cower
5 quail, wince 6 blench, cringe, flinch,
recoil, shrink

cowfish
6 dugong, sea cow 7 grampus, manatee
8 sirenian

cowl
4 cape, hood 5 cloak 6 mantle 7 capuche

cowpox
8 vaccinia

cowpuncher
see **cowboy**

coxcomb
3 fop 4 beau, buck, dude, fool 5 blood,
dandy, swell 7 peacock 8 macaroni
9 exquisite 11 Beau Brummel
12 clotheshorse, fashion plate, lounge
lizard

coy
3 shy 4 arch, cute, pert 5 saucy, timid
6 demure, modest 7 bashful, evasive,
playful 8 blushing, decorous, skittish
9 diffident, kittenish 10 capricious,

coquettish **11** flirtatious, mischievous
12 noncommittal

Coyote State
11 South Dakota

coypu
6 rodent
fur: 6 nutria

cozen
3 gyp **4** bilk, scam **5** cheat, trick **6** diddle,
fleece, take in **7** beguile, deceive, defraud,
swindle, wheedle **8** flimflam **9** bamboozle
11 double-cross

cozy
4 safe, snug, soft **5** comfy, cushy, pally,
tight **6** chummy, secure **8** familiar,
intimate **11** comfortable

crab
3 nag **4** beef, fuss, yawp **5** gripe, sidle
6 grinch, griper, grouch, kvetch, squawk,
yammer **7** decapod, grouser, growler
8 arthropod, complain, grumbler, sourpuss
9 bellyache, shellfish **10** bellyacher,
complainer, crosspatch, crustacean,
curmudgeon **11** faultfinder
claw: 5 chela **6** nipper
constellation: 6 Cancer
genus: 3 Uca **6** Birgus **7** Limulus,
Pagurus
kind: 3 pea **4** blue, king, pine, rock
5 ghost, purse **6** hermit, spider **7** fiddler
9 Dungeness, horseshoe
king, horseshoe: 7 limulus

crabbed
4 dour, glum, grim, sour **5** gruff, surly
6 crusty, gloomy, morose, sullen **9** illegible,
irascible, saturnine, splenetic

crablike
8 cancroid

crabwise
8 sidelong, sideward, sideways **9** laterally

crack
3 gag, gap, rap, try **4** bang, bash, belt,
blow, boom, clap, flaw, jest, joke, open,
peal, quip, rift, roll, shot, slam, slap, snap,
stab, wham, whop **5** adept, break, burst,
chink, cleft, crash, craze, knock, smack,
smash, solve, split, whack, whirl, wreck
6 breach, cranny, decode, expert, master,
moment, thwack **7** break up, crevice,
decrypt, destroy, fissure, instant, shatter,
skilled **8** crevasse, decipher, disorder,
interval, masterly, skillful, superior **9** break
into, excellent, interrupt, masterful, witticism
10 percussion, proficient

crackbrain
3 nut **4** kook **5** crank, wacko **6** cuckoo
7 dingbat, lunatic **9** ding-a-ling, fruitcake,
screwball

crackdown
5 purge **8** quashing **10** repression
11 suppression

cracked
3 mad **4** daft, nuts **5** balmy, batty, crazy,
daffy, loony, nutty **6** broken, crazed,
cuckoo, insane, screwy **7** bonkers, lunatic,
smashed **8** demented, deranged

cracker
5 wafer **6** hacker, rustic **7** biscuit, saltine,
snapper **8** Georgian **9** Floridian

crackerjack
3 ace **4** lulu **5** dandy, nifty, sharp **6** corker,
killer **8** jim-dandy, knockout **9** humdinger
12 lollapalooza

crackle
4 snap **7** glitter, sparkle, twinkle
9 crepitate **10** effervesce **13** effervescence

crackpot
3 nut **4** case, kook, loon **5** crank, loony,
wacko **6** cuckoo, madman **7** dingbat,
lunatic, oddball **9** ding-a-ling, eccentric,
fruitcake, harebrain, screwball

crack-up, crack up
5 crash, smash, wreck **6** fiasco **7** debacle
8 accident, collapse, disaster **9** breakdown
11 catastrophe

cradlesong
7 lullaby **8** berceuse

craft
3 art, job **5** guile, knack, skill, trade, wiles
6 career, deceit, métier **7** ability, calling,
cunning, know-how, slyness **8** artifice,
caginess, foxiness, vocation, wiliness
9 adeptness, canniness, dexterity, duplicity,
expertise, ingenuity, technique
10 adroitness, artfulness, competence,
occupation, profession, shrewdness
11 proficiency

craftiness
5 guile **7** cunning **8** artifice, subtlety

craftsman
5 smith **6** carter, carver, potter, weaver,
wright **7** artisan, builder, cobbler, jeweler
9 carpenter **10** blacksmith

crafty
3 sly **4** foxy, keen, wily **5** acute, cagey,
canny, sharp, slick **6** adroit, artful, astute,

clever, shrewd, tricky **7** cunning, devious, fawning, vulpine **8** guileful, scheming, skillful, slippery **9** deceitful, designing, ingenious, insidious **11** calculating, duplicitous
Scottish: 7 sleekit

crag
3 tor **4** hill **5** cliff

craggy
5 harsh, rocky, rough **6** jagged, rugged, uneven

cram
3 jam, ram **4** bolt, fill, gulp, heap, load, pack, wolf **5** crowd, crush, drive, force, press, shove, study, stuff, wedge **6** gobble, review, squash, thrust **7** jam-pack, overeat, squeeze

crammed
4 full **5** awash, flush **7** brimful **8** brimming **9** chock-full

cramp
4 kink, pain, pang **5** crick, hamper, limit, spasm **6** stitch **7** confine, inhibit, shackle **8** confined, restrain, restrict **9** restraint, stricture **10** constraint, limitation **11** confinement, restriction

cramped
5 close, tight **6** narrow **9** confining, two-by-four

crane
4 bird, boom, rail **5** heron **7** derrick, stretch
arm: 3 jib
genus: 4 Grus
ship's: 5 davit

Crane hero
12 Henry Fleming

cranium
5 skull **9** braincase

crank
3 nut **4** crab, kook **5** fancy **6** griper, grouch, notion, rotate, turn up, vagary **7** caprice, conceit, fanatic, grouser, oddball **8** crackpot, crotchet, grumbler, sourpuss **9** eccentric, screwball **10** bellyacher, crosspatch

cranky
5 cross, testy **6** crabby, crusty, cussed, grumpy, ornery, tetchy, touchy **7** bearish, crabbed, peevish, prickly **8** contrary, petulant, tortuous, vinegary **9** crotchety, irascible, irritable, obstinate **10** bad-

humored, ill-humored **12** cantankerous, disagreeable **13** unpredictable

cranny
3 gap **4** nook, slit **5** chink, crack, niche **6** corner **7** crevice

crash
3 din, jar, ram **4** bang, boom, bump, bust, clap, fail, fold, jolt, peal, slam, wham **5** blast, break, burst, crack, shock, smash, wreck **6** impact, pileup **7** collide, crack-up, debacle, decline, failure, smashup **8** accident, collapse **9** breakdown, collision **10** concussion

crass
4 rude **5** crude, gross **6** coarse, vulgar **7** boorish, loutish, uncouth **8** churlish **9** unrefined **13** materialistic

crate
3 box **4** heap **5** wreck **6** jalopy, junker **7** clunker

crater
3 pit **4** dent, hole, pock **5** crash **6** cavity, dimple, hollow, trough **7** caldera **8** collapse **10** depression
Hawaiian: 7 Kilauea

cravat
3 tie **4** band **5** ascot, scarf **7** necktie

crave
3 ask, beg **4** need, want, wish **5** covet **6** demand, desire **7** call for, entreat, implore, long for, require **8** yearn for

craven
4 funk **6** abject, coward **7** caitiff, chicken, dastard, fearful, gutless, ignoble **8** cowardly, cringing, poltroon, recreant **9** dastardly **11** lily-livered, poltroonish, yellowbelly **13** pusillanimous, yellowbellied

craving
4 itch, lust, urge **6** desire, hunger, thirst **7** longing, passion **8** appetite, yearning **9** hankering

crawl
4 flow, inch, teem **5** creep, swarm **6** abound, grovel **7** slither, wriggle **9** pullulate

crawling
6 repent

craze
3 fad **4** chic, rage **5** crack, fever, furor, mania, trend, vogue **6** dement, enrage, frenzy, furore, madden **7** derange, fashion,

unhinge **9** unbalance **10** dernier cri, enthusiasm

craziness
5 folly, mania **6** lunacy **8** hysteria, insanity **9** absurdity

crazy
3 fey, mad **4** daft, gaga, loco, nuts, wild **5** balmy, barmy, batty, daffy, dotty, goofy, kooky, loony, mental, nutty, rabid, silly, wacko, wacky **6** absurd, cuckoo, fruity, insane, psycho, screwy, teched, whacky **7** berserk, bonkers, cracked, foolish, frantic, lunatic, smitten, tetched, touched, unsound **8** cockeyed, crackpot, demented, deranged, frenetic, frenzied, maniacal, unhinged **9** bedlamite, delirious, eccentric, fanatical, foolhardy, ludicrous, possessed, screwball, senseless **10** crackbrain, moonstruck, ridiculous, unbalanced **11** harebrained, nonsensical **12** preposterous
British: 5 potty **6** scatty
Scottish: 3 wud

creak
4 rasp **5** grate, grind **6** scrape, squeak, squeal **7** grating, screech **9** squeaking

creaky
4 aged **5** rusty **7** rickety, run-down, squeaky, unsound, worn-out **8** decrepit **9** tottering **10** broken-down, ramshackle

cream
3 top **4** balm, beat, best, drub, pick, whip, whup **5** blast, elite, prime, salve **6** cerate, choice, defeat, finest, thrash **7** clobber, destroy, trounce, unguent **8** lambaste, liniment, ointment

crease
4 fold, ruck **5** graze, plica, ridge **6** furrow, groove, rumple **7** crinkle, wrinkle

create
3 dub **4** form, make, sire **5** beget, build, cause, forge, found, hatch, set up, spawn, start **6** author, design, devise, father, invent **7** compose, concoct, develop, fashion, produce **8** conceive, engender, generate, occasion **9** construct, establish, fabricate, formulate, institute, originate **10** constitute

creation
5 birth, world **6** cosmos, nature **7** genesis **8** universe **9** inception, macrocosm **10** conception **11** macrocosmos

creative
7 fertile **8** artistic, inspired, original **9** deceptive, demiurgic, ingenious,

inventive **10** innovative, innovatory **11** imaginative **12** innovational

creator
3 god **6** author **8** inventor **9** architect, generator, patriarch **10** originator, progenitor

creature
3 man **5** beast, being, brute, human **6** animal, mortal, person **7** critter, varmint
fabled: 3 elf, imp, orc, roc **4** ogre, puck, yeti **5** dwarf, fairy, ghost, giant, gnome, harpy, nymph, pixie, troll **6** dragon, goblin, gorgon, kraken, merman, sphinx, sprite **7** bigfoot, brownie, bugbear, centaur, chimera, gremlin, griffin, mermaid, monster, unicorn, vampire, wendigo **8** minotaur, werewolf **9** hobgoblin, manticore, sasquatch **10** cockatrice, hippogriff, leprechaun
(see also **monster**)

credence
5 faith, trust **6** belief, credit **8** reliance **9** sideboard **10** acceptance, confidence

credentials
6 papers **9** documents **10** references **12** certificates, testimonials **13** documentation, qualifications

credenza
6 buffet **8** bookcase **9** sideboard

credible
5 solid, sound, valid **6** trusty **8** reliable **9** authentic, colorable, plausible **10** believable, convincing, persuasive, reasonable **11** trustworthy **12** satisfactory

credit
4 deem, feel **5** asset, faith, honor, refer, sense, think, trust **6** accept, assign, belief, charge, impute, notice, weight **7** ascribe, believe **8** consider, credence, prestige, reliance **9** attribute, authority, influence **10** confidence, reputation **11** recognition

creditable
6 worthy **8** laudable, reliable **9** colorable, deserving, estimable, plausible, reputable **10** believable **11** commendable, meritorious, respectable **12** praiseworthy

credo
5 canon, creed, dogma, tenet **6** belief, tenets **7** beliefs, precept **8** doctrine, ideology **9** catechism, principle

credulous
5 naive **6** unwary **8** gullible, trustful,

trusting **9** believing **12** unsuspecting,
unsuspicious **13** unquestioning

creed
4 sect **5** canon, dogma, faith, tenet
6 belief, church, tenets **7** beliefs, precept
8 doctrine, ideology, religion **9** catechism,
communion, principle **12** denomination

creek
4 burn, rill **5** brook **6** arroyo, rillet, runlet,
runnel, stream **7** freshet, rivulet **8** brooklet
9 streamlet

creep
4 drag, edge, inch, lurk, slip **5** crawl, glide,
shirk, skulk, slide, slink, snake, sneak, steal
6 spread, tiptoe **7** gumshoe, slither, wriggle
9 pussyfoot

creeping
6 repent **7** gradual **9** prostrate

creepy
5 eerie, weird **6** spooky **7** anxious,
macabre, ominous, strange, uncanny
8 ghoulish, menacing, sinister **9** unnerving
10 disturbing, unpleasant, unsettling
11 hair-raising

crème de la crème
4 best **5** elect, elite **6** finest **8** very best

Cremona family
5 Amati **8** Guarneri

Creon
daughter: **6** Creusa, Glauce, Glauke
sister: **7** Jocasta
son: **6** Haemon
victim: **8** Antigone

crescendo
4 acme, apex, peak, rise **5** crest, surge,
swell **6** apogee, climax, growth, height,
zenith **8** increase, pinnacle **9** high point
11 culmination

crescent-shaped
5 bowed **6** lunate, sickle **7** falcate
body or surface: **8** meniscus

crest
3 cap, top **4** acme, apex, comb, noon,
peak, roof, tuft **5** arête, chine, crown,
plume, ridge **6** apogee, climax, summit,
vertex **7** hogback **8** pinnacle, surmount
9 high point **10** coat of arms, prominence
11 culmination
of a wave: **8** whitecap

crestfallen
3 low **4** blue, down **6** droopy **8** dejected,

downcast, drooping **9** depressed
10 dispirited **11** discouraged, downhearted
12 disappointed, disconsolate,
disheartened

Crete
ancient city: **7** Cnossus, Knossos
8 Phaistos
ancient name: **6** Candia
capital: **5** Canea
goddess: **8** Dictynna **11** Britomartis
guard: **5** Talos
king: **5** Minos **9** Idomeneus
maze: **9** labyrinth
monster: **8** Minotaur
mountain: **3** Ida
princess: **7** Ariadne

cretin
3 oaf **4** boob, clod, dolt, dope, fool, lout
5 dumbo, dummy, dunce, idiot, moron
6 dimwit, nitwit **7** half-wit **8** imbecile,
lunkhead, numskull **9** lamebrain,
numbskull, simpleton

Creusa
father: **5** Priam
husband: **6** Aeneas
mother: **6** Hecuba
son: **3** Ion **8** Ascanius

crevice
3 gap **4** seam, slit **5** chink, cleft, crack
6 cranny **7** fissure **8** cleavage
10 interstice

crew
4 band, bevy, gang, team **5** bunch, covey,
group, party **6** rowers, rowing **7** company,
sailors

crib
3 bed, bin, box, hut, key **4** pony, trot
5 cheat, crate, hovel, shack, stall, steal,
theft **6** cradle, crèche, manger, pilfer
7 barrier, brothel **8** bassinet, bedstead,
bordello **9** enclosure **10** plagiarism,
plagiarize

Crichton novel
11 Terminal Man (The) **12** Jurassic Park
15 Andromeda Strain (The)

cricket
period of play: **7** innings
team: **6** eleven
term: **3** leg, off, rot **4** bowl **5** pitch
6 bowler, wicket, yorker **7** batsman, striker
9 fieldsman
turn at bat: **4** over

crime
3 sin **4** evil, tort, vice **5** caper **6** breach,

delict, felony **7** misdeed, offense **8** atrocity, iniquity **9** diablerie, violation **10** corruption, illegality, infraction, wrongdoing **11** misdemeanor **13** transgression
instructor: 5 Fagin

Crimea
city: 5 Kerch, Yalta **10** Sebastopol, Sevastopol, Simferopol
river: 4 Alma
sea: 4 Azov
strait: 5 Kerch

criminal
4 hood, thug **5** crook, felon, shady **6** outlaw **7** convict, corrupt, crooked, hoodlum, illegal, illicit, lawless, mobster **8** culpable, fugitive, gangster, jailbird, offender, scofflaw, unlawful, wrongful **9** desperado, felonious, miscreant, nefarious, racketeer, wrongdoer **10** delinquent, lawbreaker, malefactor, trespasser **12** illegitimate, transgressor
habitual: 8 repeater **10** recidivist

criminate
see **incriminate**

crimp
4 bend, curb, wave **5** frizz **6** crease, hamper, hold in **7** crinkle, inhibit, wrinkle **8** hold back, obstacle, restrain **9** constrain, restraint **10** impediment **11** obstruction

crimson
3 red **4** rose **5** blush, color, flush **6** redden

cringe
4 duck **5** cower, hunch, quail, wince **6** blench, flinch, recoil, shrink

crinkle
4 ruck **5** crimp, plica, ridge **6** crease, furrow, pucker, ruck up, rumple, rustle **7** crackle, crumple, scrunch, wrinkle **11** corrugation

crinkly
5 crepy **6** crepey, frizzy **7** frizzed **8** wrinkled

cripple
4 lame, maim **6** mangle **7** disable **8** mutilate, paralyze **9** hamstring, undermine **12** debilitate, incapacitate

crippled
4 halt, lame **6** maimed **7** gnarled, mangled **8** battered, deformed, disabled, weakened **9** enfeebled, misshapen, mutilated, paralyzed **11** debilitated, handicapped

crisis
4 crux, pass **5** pinch **6** climax, crunch,

height, strait **7** impasse, straits **8** disaster, exigency, juncture, zero hour **9** emergency, extremity **10** crossroads **11** catastrophe, contingency **12** turning point

crisp
4 cold, cool, curl, deft, keen, neat, wavy **5** brisk, clean, crimp, curly, fresh, nippy, pithy, sharp, short **6** biting, chilly, lively, ripple, spruce **7** bracing, brittle, crunchy, cutting, wrinkle **8** clean-cut, clear-cut, incisive **9** trenchant **11** stimulating **12** invigorating

crisscross
3 net **4** grid, mesh **5** weave **7** network, overlap **8** reticule **9** confusion, decussate, intersect, reticular **10** reticulate

criterion
4 norm **5** canon, gauge, ideal, model, tenet **7** measure, precept **8** exemplar, paradigm, standard **9** benchmark, yardstick **10** touchstone

critic
5 judge **6** carper, pundit **7** arbiter, caviler **8** caviller, censurer, quibbler, reviewer **9** belittler, nitpicker **10** disparager, mudslinger **11** commentator, connoisseur, faultfinder

critical
4 dire **5** acute, fussy **7** carping, crucial, finicky, pivotal, weighty **8** captious, caviling, censorious, decisive **9** desperate, important, momentous **10** belittling, censorious, conclusive, precarious **11** disparaging, significant **12** faultfinding **13** consequential, determinative, hairsplitting
study: 6 examen **8** exegesis

criticism
4 flak, slap **5** blame, cavil, swipe **6** rebuke, review **7** censure, comment, opinion, reproof **8** analysis, judgment, reproach **9** appraisal, objection **10** assessment, commentary, evaluation, nitpicking **11** examination, observation **12** faultfinding

criticize
3 pan, rap **4** bash, carp **5** blame, blast, cavil, chide, fault, judge, knock, roast, scold **6** assess, rebuke, review, scathe **7** censure, condemn, nitpick, reprove **8** appraise, badmouth, chastise, denounce, evaluate, lambaste **9** castigate, disparage, dress down, excoriate, find fault, reprehend, reprimand, reprobate

critique
see **criticism**

critter
5 beast 6 animal 7 varmint

Crius
father: 6 Uranus
mother: 4 Gaea
son: 8 Astraeus

croak
3 die 6 cackle, expire, squawk 7 grumble

croaky
5 gruff, husky, raspy 6 hoarse 8 gravelly

Croatia
capital: 6 Zagreb
city: 5 Split 6 Osijek, Rijeka 9 Dubrovnik
monetary unit: 4 kuna
neighbor: 7 Hungary 8 Slovenia
part of: 7 Balkans
region: 8 Dalmatia, Slavonia

crock
3 jar, lie, pot 4 tale 6 tureen 7 cripple,
disable, fiction 9 break down
11 fabrication

crocked
3 lit 4 high 5 drunk, lit up, oiled, tipsy
6 bashed, blotto, bombed, juiced, potted,
soaked, soused, stewed, stoned, tanked,
wasted, zonked 7 drunken, pickled, pie-
eyed, sloshed 9 plastered
10 inebriated, liquored up 11 intoxicated

crocodile
7 reptile
bird: 6 plover
Indian: 6 gavial 7 gharial
relative: 9 alligator
South American: 6 caiman, cayman
Southeast Asian: 6 mugger

Croesus' kingdom
5 Lydia

croft
4 farm 5 field

crofter
4 hind 6 farmer

Cromwell, Oliver
13 lord protector
battle: 6 Naseby 11 Marston Moor
regiment: 9 Ironsides
son: 7 Richard

crone
3 hag 4 trot 5 biddy, witch 6 beldam
7 beldame

Cronus
5 Titan 6 Saturn
daughter: 4 Hera 6 Hestia 7 Demeter
father: 6 Uranus
mother: 4 Gaea
sister: 4 Rhea 6 Cybele, Tethys
son: 4 Zeus 5 Hades 7 Jupiter, Neptune
8 Poseidon
wife: 4 Rhea 6 Cybele

crony
3 pal 4 chum 5 buddy 6 cohort
7 comrade 8 sidekick 9 associate,
companion 10 accomplice 11 confederate

crook
3 bow 4 bend, flex, hook, wind 5 angle,
curve, staff, thief 6 bandit, robber
7 burglar, crosier, hoodlum, pothook
8 criminal

crooked
4 awry 5 askew, lying, shady, venal
6 curved, errant, jagged, shifty, skewed,
zigzag 7 bending, corrupt, devious, illegal,
illicit, slanted 8 cockeyed, criminal,
ruthless, tortuous, twisting 9 deceitful,
dishonest, nefarious, underhand, unethical
10 fraudulent, mendacious, untruthful
11 duplicitous, underhanded 12 unscrupulous 13 double-dealing

croon
4 sing 6 murmur, warble

crooner
4 Cole (Nat "King"), Como (Perry) 5 Laine
(Frankie), Tormé (Mel) 6 Crosby (Bing),
Martin (Dean), singer, Vallee (Rudy)
7 Astaire (Fred), Bennett (Tony), Sinatra
(Frank) 8 Eckstine (Billy), vocalist,
Williams (Andy)

crop
3 bob, cut, hew, lop, mow 4 chop, clip,
pare, snip, trim 5 prune, shave, shear,
stock, yield 6 gullet, handle, output
7 harvest, produce 8 fruitage, truncate
10 collection

croquet
5 roque

crosier
5 crook, staff

cross
3 mad 4 mule, rood, span 5 angry, surly,
testy, trial 6 betray, bridge, crabby, cranky,
grumpy, hybrid, negate, oppose, ordeal,
tetchy, touchy 7 athwart, calvary, carping,
gainsay, grouchy, mongrel, peevish 8 captious, choleric, confront, traverse
9 decussate, half blood, half-breed,
hybridize, intersect, irascible, irritable,
querulous, splenetic 10 affliction,

contradict, contravene, interbreed, transverse **11** tribulation **12** cantankerous **13** quick-tempered
a river: **4** ford
bearer: **8** crucifer
decoration: **4** Iron **8** Victoria
Egyptian: **4** ankh
kind: **3** tau **5** Greek, Latin, papal **6** Celtic, fleury, formée, moline, pommée, potent **7** avellan, botonée, Calvary, Maltese **8** crucifix, fourchée, Lorraine, quadrate **11** patriarchal **12** Saint Andrew's **13** Saint Anthony's
section: **5** slice
stroke of a letter: **5** serif

crossbow
8 arbalest, arbalist

crossbreed
4 mule **5** hybrid **7** bastard, mongrel **9** half blood, half-breed, hybridize **10** interbreed

cross-eye
6 squint **10** strabismus

crossing
8 junction, overpass, traverse **9** traversal, underpass **10** transverse **11** decussation, interchange, transversal **12** intersection

cross out
5 erase **6** cancel, delete, efface, excise **7** expunge

crosspatch
4 crab **5** crank, grump **6** griper, grouch **7** grouser **8** grumbler, sorehead, sourpuss **10** complainer, curmudgeon

crossroads
4 crux, pass **5** pinch **6** crisis, strait **8** exigency, juncture, zero hour **9** carrefour, emergency **11** contingency **12** intersection, turning point
goddess: **6** Hecate, Hekate, Trivia

cross-shaped
8 cruciate **9** cruciform

crossways
6 aslant **7** athwart, oblique **8** diagonal **9** obliquely **10** diagonally, transverse **11** kitty-corner **12** transversely

crotchet
3 bee **4** whim **5** fancy, freak, quirk, trick **6** foible, megrim, notion, vagary **7** caprice, conceit **11** quarter note **12** eccentricity

crotchety
5 testy **6** crabby, cranky, crusty, ornery, tetchy, touchy **7** bearish, peevish, prickly **8** contrary, snappish, vinegary **9** difficult,

eccentric, irascible **10** vinegarish **11** ill-tempered **12** cantankerous, cross-grained

crouch
4 bend, duck **5** cower, hunch, squat, stoop **6** cringe, huddle, shrink **10** hunker down

croup
3 bum **4** butt, hack, rear, rump, seat, tail **5** cough, edema, whoop **6** behind **7** keister, rear end, tail end **8** backside, buttocks, derriere, haunches **9** posterior

crow
4 blow, brag, puff **5** boast, exult, gloat, prate, vaunt **6** cackle **7** bluster **9** gasconade, humble pie
colony: **7** rookery
cry: **3** caw
family: **6** corvid **8** Corvidae
genus: **6** Corvus
relating to: **7** corvine
relative: **3** daw, jay **4** rook **5** raven **6** chough, magpie **7** jackdaw

crowbar
3 pry **5** jimmy, lever

crowd
3 jam, mob **4** army, bear, cram, fill, herd, host, mass, pack, pile, push, rout, ruck **5** bunch, crush, drove, flock, flood, group, horde, hurry, press, serry, shove, surge, swarm, troop **6** circle, clique, gaggle, huddle, jostle, legion, rabble, squash, squish, stream, throng **7** cluster, collect, company, coterie, squeeze **8** assembly **9** gathering, multitude **10** assemblage, collection **11** aggregation **12** congregation

crowded
4 full **5** awash, close, dense, thick, tight **6** loaded **7** brimful, compact, teeming **8** brimming, populous, swarming **9** chock-full, congested, jam-packed

crow-like
7 corvoid

crown
3 cap, top **4** acme, apex, peak, roof **5** cover, crest, tiara **6** climax, diadem, laurel, summit, top off, vertex, wreath, zenith **7** chaplet, coronal, coronet, garland, overlay, perfect **8** pinnacle, round off, surmount **9** culminate, finish off **10** consummate **9** culmination **11** culmination

crucial
4 dire **5** acute, vital **6** urgent **7** central, pivotal **8** critical, deciding, decisive **9** desperate, essential, important,

momentous, necessary **10** imperative
11 climacteric, significant

crucible
4 test **5** trial **6** ordeal **8** acid test
10 melting pot

crucifix
4 rood **5** cross

crucifixion site
7 Calvary **8** Golgotha

crucify
4 rack **6** impale, martyr **7** mortify, pillory,
torment, torture **10** excruciate

crud
3 goo **4** glop, gook, gunk, junk, muck
5 dreck, filth, slime, trash **6** debris, sludge
7 deposit, garbage, rubbish **12** incrustation

crude
3 raw **4** poor **5** crass, dirty, gross, rough
6 coarse, earthy, gauche, impure, ribald,
risqué, vulgar **7** boorish, ill-bred, loutish,
lowbred, obscene, obvious, raunchy,
uncivil, uncouth **8** backward, cloddish,
homespun, ignorant, indecent, inferior
9 elemental, graceless, inelegant,
makeshift, primitive, rough-hewn, unrefined
10 amateurish, unfinished, unpolished

cruel
4 fell, grim, mean **5** harsh **6** brutal, fierce,
savage **7** bestial, brutish, callous, heinous,
vicious **8** inhumane, ruthless, sadistic
9 atrocious, barbarous, ferocious,
heartless, merciless, monstrous, truculent
12 bloodthirsty

cruise
4 roam, rove, sail, surf, tour **5** drift, jaunt
6 junket, voyage **9** excursion

cruiser
4 boat **5** yacht **7** warship **8** squad car
9 patrol car, powerboat

crumb
3 bit **4** iota **5** ounce, scrap, shred
6 morsel, sliver **7** smidgen **8** fragment,
particle

crumble
5 decay **8** collapse **9** break down,
decompose **11** deteriorate **12** disintegrate

crumbly
7 friable

crummy
4 poor **5** dingy, lousy, seedy, tacky
6 cruddy, flimsy, shoddy, sleazy **8** inferior

crumple
3 wad **4** cave **5** crimp **6** buckle, cave in,
ruck up **7** crinkle, scrunch, wrinkle
8 collapse

crunch
4 chew **5** champ, chomp, grind, munch,
sit-up **6** crisis **7** compute, process,
squeeze **8** shortage, showdown

crusade
5 cause, drive **6** appeal **7** holy war
8 campaign, movement **9** offensive
10 expedition **11** undertaking

Crusader
English: 7 Richard (Lionheart)
French: 5 Louis (IX) **6** Philip, Robert
7 Baldwin, Charles, Godfrey, Raymond,
Raymund **8** Boniface, Montfort, Philippe,
Theobald
German: 6 Conrad **9** Frederick, Friedrich
10 Barbarossa
Norman: 7 Tancred **8** Bohemund
Preacher: 5 Peter (the Hermit), Urban (II)
7 Adhémar, Bernard **8** Innocent (III),
Pelagius

crusading
11 evangelical **12** evangelistic

crush
3 jam, mob **4** cram, mash, pulp, push, ruin
5 crowd, drove, grind, horde, pound, press,
quash, quell, smash, wreck **6** bruise,
burden, defeat, reduce, squash, squish,
subdue, throng **7** conquer, destroy, mortify,
oppress, passion, put down, repress,
scrunch, squeeze, squelch, trample **8** bear
down, beat down, demolish, overcome,
suppress, vanquish **9** humiliate, multitude,
overpower, overwhelm, pulverize, puppy
love, subjugate **10** annihilate, extinguish,
obliterate **11** infatuation

crust
4 cake, coat, rime, scab **7** coating, deposit
8 covering

crustacean
4 crab, flea **5** louse, prawn **6** isopod,
shrimp, slater, sow bug **7** copepod,
daphnia, decapod, lobster, pill bug
8 amphipod, barnacle, crawfish, crayfish,
ostracod, sand flea **9** arthropod, beach
flea, shellfish, water flea, wood louse
10 stomatopod, whale louse
11 branchiopod
aggregate of: 5 krill
appendage: 7 pleopod
body segment: 6 somite, telson
8 metamere

claw: 5 chela 6 pincer
covering substance: 6 chitin
larva: 8 nauplius

crusty
4 curt 5 bluff, blunt, gross, gruff, short, surly 6 cranky 7 brusque, crabbed, prickly 8 choleric 9 irascible, irritable, saturnine, splenetic

crux
3 nub 4 core, gist, meat, pith 5 focus, heart 6 kernel, thrust 7 essence, purport 9 substance

cry
(see also **exclamation**)
3 sob 4 bawl, blub, call, howl, keen, mewl, moan, pule, wail, weep, yawp, yell, yowl 5 bleat, motto, mourn, shout, whine, whoop 6 boohoo, furore, holler, lament, scream, snivel, squall, squawk, squeak, squeal 7 blubber, screech, ululate, whimper 10 vociferate
bacchanals': 4 evoe
calf: 5 bleat
cat: 3 mew 4 meow 5 miaow
cattle: 3 low, moo
chick: 4 peep 5 cheep
court: 4 oyez
crane: 5 clang
crow: 3 caw
dog: 3 arf 4 bark, woof
donkey: 4 bray 6 hee-haw
duck: 5 quack
frog: 5 croak
goat: 5 bleat
goose: 4 honk 5 clang
hen: 6 cackle
horse: 5 neigh 6 nicker, whinny 7 whicker
lion: 4 roar
owl: 4 hoot
pig: 4 oink 5 grunt
raven: 5 croak
sheep: 5 bleat
songbird: 5 chirp, tweet
turkey: 6 gobble

cry down
5 decry 6 defame, deride, malign, revile, vilify 7 condemn 8 belittle, denounce, derogate, diminish 9 denigrate, deprecate, discredit, disparage 10 calumniate, depreciate 11 detract from, opprobriate

crying
4 dire 5 acute, vital 6 urgent 7 blatant, burning, clamant, exigent, heinous 8 flagrant, pressing, shocking 9 atrocious, clamorous, desperate, monstrous,

notorious 10 compelling, imperative, outrageous, scandalous 11 importunate

crypt
5 vault 7 chamber 8 catacomb 9 mausoleum 10 undercroft

cryptic
5 vague 6 arcane, occult, opaque, secret 7 Delphic, obscure, unclear 8 abstruse, Delphian, esoteric, puzzling 9 ambiguous, enigmatic, recondite, tenebrous 10 mysterious, mystifying 12 unfathomable

crystal
4 lens 5 clear, lucid 6 limpid, lucent, quartz 8 clear-cut, luminous, pellucid 9 glassware, unblurred 11 translucent, transparent, transpicuous
gazer: 4 seer 7 psychic 11 clairvoyant

Cry, the Beloved Country author
5 Paton (Alan)

cry up
4 laud, puff 5 boost, extol 6 praise 7 acclaim

cub
3 pup 4 tyro 6 baby, novice, rookie 8 neophyte 9 offspring, youngster 10 apprentice

Cuba
capital: 6 Havana
city: 7 Holguín 8 Camagüey, Santiago 10 Guantánamo, Santa Clara
discoverer: 8 Columbus (Christopher)
language: 7 Spanish
leader: 6 Castro (Fidel) 7 Batista (Fulgencio)
monetary unit: 4 peso 6 dollar
sea: 9 Caribbean

cubbyhole
5 niche 6 alcove, recess 7 cubicle

cube
4 dice 5 mince

Cub Scout
rank: 4 Bear, Lion, Wolf 6 Bobcat 7 Webelos
unit: 3 den 4 pack

Cuchulain
father: 3 Lug 4 Lugh 5 Lugus
foe: 4 Medb 5 Maeve
kingdom: 6 Ulster
lord: 9 Conchobar
mother: 8 Dechtire
son: 8 Conlaoch
victim: 8 Conlaoch
wife: 4 Emer

cuckoo
3 mad, nut **4** daft, kook, nuts **5** batty, crank, crazy, daffy, loony, loopy, nutty, potty, silly, wacko, wacky **6** crazed, fruity, insane, screwy, whacky **7** bonkers, cracked, idiotic, lunatic, nutcase **8** crackpot, demented **9** ding-a-ling, harebrain, screwball **12** crackbrained
bird: 3 ani

cucumber
4 pepo **7** gherkin

cuddle
3 hug, pet **4** neck, snug **5** spoon **6** burrow, caress, clinch, cosset, dandle, fondle, nestle, nuzzle **7** embrace, snuggle, squeeze **8** canoodle

cuddlesome
7 lovable, snuggly **8** huggable **11** embraceable

cudgel
3 bat, sap **4** club, cosh, mace **5** baton, billy **7** war club **8** bludgeon **9** bastinado, billy club, blackjack, truncheon **10** knobkerrie, nightstick, shillelagh

cue
3 key, nod, rod, tip **4** clue, hint, lead, prod, sign **6** insert, notion, prompt, signal, tip-off **7** inkling, warning **8** high sign, reminder, telltale **10** indication, intimation, suggestion

cuff
3 box, hit **4** belt, blip, clip, poke, slap, sock **5** clout, fight, punch, smack, whack **6** bangle, buffet, wallop **7** clobber, scuffle **8** bracelet, wristlet

cul-de-sac
5 pouch **6** pocket **7** dead end, impasse **10** blind alley **12** diverticulum

cull
4 pick, sift, thin **5** elect, glean **6** choose, garner, gather, select, winnow **7** extract, thin out

culminate
4 peak **5** crest **6** climax

culmination
3 top **4** acme, apex, peak **6** apogee, capper, climax, height, payoff, summit, zenith **8** capstone, pinnacle **11** ne plus ultra **12** consummation

culpability
4 onus **5** blame, fault, guilt

culpable
6 guilty, liable, sinful **7** at fault **8** blamable, blameful **10** censurable, delinquent **11** blameworthy, impeachable, responsible **13** reprehensible

cult
3 fad **4** sect **5** creed, faith **6** church **8** religion **10** persuasion **12** denomination

cultivable
6 arable **8** tillable

cultivate
4 farm, grow, tend, till **5** breed, nurse, raise **6** enrich, foster, refine **7** cherish, develop, further, improve, nourish, nurture, produce, promote **9** encourage, propagate

cultivated
6 urbane **7** genteel, refined **8** cultured, polished, well-bred

cultivation
6 polish **7** culture **8** breeding **10** refinement **11** development

culture
4 grow **5** taste **6** foster **7** nurture **9** cultivate, erudition, gentility **10** refinement **11** cultivation **12** civilization **13** enlightenment

cultured
6 urbane **7** erudite, genteel, learned, refined **8** educated, highbrow, literate, polished, well-bred **9** civilized **10** cultivated **11** enlightened

culture medium
4 agar

cum _____ salis
5 grano

cumber
4 clog, lade, load **6** burden, hinder, hobble, impede, saddle **7** clutter **8** handicap **9** hindrance

cumbersome
5 bulky, heavy, hefty **6** clumsy **7** awkward **8** unwieldy **9** lumbering, ponderous, slow-moving

cumbrous
see **cumbersome**

cumshaw
3 fee, tip **5** bribe **6** payoff **7** present **8** gratuity, largesse **9** lagniappe, pourboire **10** perquisite

cumulate
4 heap **5** amass, hoard, lay up, store **6** garner, gather, pile up **7** collect, combine, store up **9** stockpile

cumulation
4 heap, mass, pile **5** cache, hoard, trove
9 stockpile **10** collection **11** aggregation
13 agglomeration

cumulative
8 additive, compound **9** summative
10 compounded, increasing

cunning
3 sly **4** cute, foxy, keen, wary, wily
5 acute, cagey, canny, craft, guile, savvy,
sharp, shifty, skill, slick, smart **6** adroit,
artful, astute, clever, crafty, deceit, tricky
7 finesse, know-how, slyness **8** artifice,
deftness, facility, foxiness, guileful, slippery,
subtlety, wiliness **9** adeptness, cageyness,
canniness, dexterity, dexterous, duplicity,
ingenious, ingenuity, insidious, sharpness,
slickness **10** adroitness, artfulness,
cleverness, craftiness, shiftiness,
shrewdness, trickiness

cup
3 mug **4** toby **5** grail, jorum, stein
6 beaker, goblet, seidel **7** chalice, tankard
8 schooner
handle: 3 ear, lug
liturgical: 5 calix **7** chalice
small: 6 noggin **8** cannikin, pannikin
9 demitasse
sports: 5 Davis, Ryder, World **6** Curtis,
Nextel **7** Stanley **8** America's, Wightman

cupbearer of the gods
4 Hebe **8** Ganymede

cupboard
5 ambry, cuddy **6** buffet, closet, larder,
pantry **7** armoire, cabinet **8** credence,
credenza **9** sideboard

Cupid
4 Amor, Eros **5** putto **6** cherub **8** amoretto
beloved: 6 Psyche
brother: 7 Anteros
father: 6 Hermes **7** Mercury
mother: 5 Venus **9** Aphrodite
title: 3 Dan

cupidity
4 lust **5** greed **6** desire **7** avarice, avidity,
craving, lechery, passion **8** rapacity,
voracity **9** eagerness, esurience
10 greediness **11** infatuation
12 covetousness **13** rapaciousness

cupola
4 dome **5** vault **6** turret **7** furnace, lookout

cur
3 dog **4** mutt **7** mongrel

curate
6 cleric, priest **9** churchman, clergyman

curative
4 pill **5** tonic **6** elixir, relief, remedy
7 healing, nostrum, panacea, therapy
8 antidote, healthful, remedial, salutary,
sanative, solution **9** medicinal, remedying,
treatment, wholesome **10** beneficial,
corrective **11** restorative, therapeutic
12 health-giving

curator
6 keeper, warden **9** caretaker, custodian
11 conservator

curb
3 bit **4** deny **5** check, frame, leash, tie up
6 border, bridle, edging, fetter, hamper,
hobble, hold in, subdue **7** abstain, contain,
control, inhibit, refrain, repress **8** hold
back, hold down, restrain, suppress,
withhold **9** constrain, entrammel, restraint
British: 4 kerb

curdle
4 clot, sour, turn **5** spoil **7** clabber,
congeal, thicken **9** coagulate

cure
3 age, spa **4** heal, mend **5** treat **6** elixir,
kipper, physic, pickle, relief, remedy
7 rectify, relieve, restore, therapy
8 antidote, medicant, medicine, preserve,
recovery, solution **10** ameliorate, corrective
12 counteragent **13** counteractive

cure-all
6 elixir **7** nostrum, panacea **10** catholicon

curio
6 oddity, whimsy **7** novelty

curiosity
5 freak **6** marvel, oddity, rarity, whimsy,
wonder **7** anomaly, concern, novelty
8 interest, nonesuch

curious
3 odd **4** nosy **5** nosey, novel, queer, weird
6 exotic, prying, quaint, snoopy **7** bizarre,
oddball, strange, unusual **8** meddling,
peculiar, puzzling, singular **9** inquiring,
intrusive **11** inquisitive, questioning

curl
4 coil, kink, wind **5** frizz, twine, twist
6 spiral **7** contort, crinkle, entwine, frizzle,
ringlet, wreathe **9** corkscrew

curling
match: 8 bonspiel
period of play: 3 end
team: 4 four
term: 3 tee **4** hack, rink **5** house, stone

curly
4 wavy **5** kinky **6** frizzy

currency

4 cash, coin **5** dough, lucre, money, scrip
7 coinage **8** banknote **10** acceptance,
prevalence **11** legal tender
unit:
(see **individual country**)

current

4 eddy, flow, flux, rush, tide **5** drift, flood,
spate, tenor, trend **6** extant, modern,
strain, stream **7** instant, ongoing, popular,
present, regnant, topical **8** accepted,
existent, existing, tendency, up-to-date
9 prevalent **10** present-day, prevailing,
widespread **11** fashionable **12** contemporary
air: 4 gale, gust, wind **5** blast, draft
6 breeze, squall, zephyr **7** cyclone, indraft,
updraft **9** downdraft **10** slipstream
ocean: 7 riptide **8** undertow **9** maelstrom,
whirlpool
unit: 3 amp **6** ampere

Currier's partner

4 Ives (James)

curry

4 beat, comb, seek, whip **5** groom
6 thrash

curse

4 bane, cuss, damn, evil, jinx, oath
5 swear **6** blight, plague, whammy
7 afflict, damning, malison, scourge,
torment **8** anathema, execration, execrate
9 bête noire, blaspheme, blasphemy,
expletive, imprecate, profanity, swearword
10 affliction, execration, misfortune,
pestilence **11** commination, imprecation,
malediction, profanation **12** anathematize,
denunciation

cursed

6 damned **7** blasted, dratted **8** damnable,
infernal **9** execrable **10** confounded
13 blankety-blank

cursive

6 fluent, smooth **7** flowing, running

cursory

5 hasty, quick, rapid **6** casual **7** hurried,
shallow, sketchy **8** careless **10** uncritical
11 perfunctory, superficial

curt

4 rude **5** bluff, blunt, brief, gruff, short, terse
6 abrupt, crusty **7** brusque, concise
8 succinct **10** peremptory

curtail

3 cut **4** clip, dock, trim **5** prune, slash
6 lessen, reduce **7** abridge, cut back,

shorten **8** diminish, pare down, retrench,
truncate **10** abbreviate

curtain

4 drop, veil **5** drape **6** screen **7** barrier
doorway: 8 portiere
holder: 3 rod
Indian: 6 purdah
rod concealer: 7 valance
sash: 7 tieback
stage: 4 drop **5** scrim **8** backdrop

curtains

3 end **4** ruin **5** death **6** demise, finish
7 decease **8** disaster

curtilage

4 quad, yard **5** court **8** cloister
9 courtyard, enclosure **10** quadrangle

curvaceous

5 buxom **7** rounded, shapely **9** Junoesque
10 statuesque, voluptuous **13** well-
developed

curvature

(see **curvation**)
of the spine: 8 kyphosis, lordosis
9 scoliosis

curve

3 arc, bow **4** arch, bend, turn, veer, wind
5 crook, round, twist **6** convex, spiral,
swerve **7** concave, flexure, rondure
of an arch: 8 extrados, intrados
pitcher's: 4 hook
plane: 7 cycloid, limaçon **8** parabola,
sinusoid, trochoid **9** hyperbola
S-shaped: 3 ess **4** ogee **7** sigmoid

curved

4 bent **5** arced, bowed, round **6** arched
7 arcuate, bending, embowed, falcate,
rounded, sigmoid, sinuous, twisted
implement: 6 sickle
molding: 4 ogee
sword: 7 cutlass **8** scimitar

curvilinear

see **curved**

curvy

see **curvaceous; curved**

Cush

father: 3 Ham
son: 6 Nimrod

cushion

3 mat, pad **5** squab **6** absorb, buffer,
pillow, soften **7** bolster, hassock, pillion
8 palliate, woolsack

cushy
4 cozy, easy, soft 11 comfortable, undemanding

cusp
3 tip 4 apex, edge, peak 5 point, verge 12 turning point

cuspid
6 canine 8 eyetooth

cuspidate
5 sharp 6 peaked, pointy 7 pointed

cuss
3 guy, man 4 chap, damn, dude, oath 5 curse, swear 6 fellow 9 expletive

cussed
4 dour 5 crude, gruff 6 crusty, cursed, grumpy, ornery 7 boorish, brusque, grouchy 8 churlish 9 obstinate 10 unyielding 11 contentious 12 antagonistic, cantankerous

cussword
4 oath 5 curse 9 expletive, swearword

custard
4 flan 7 pudding

custodian
5 super 6 keeper, porter, warden 7 curator, steward 8 guardian, overseer, watchdog, watchman 9 caretaker, concierge, protector 10 supervisor 11 conservator

custody
4 care, ward 5 guard, trust 6 charge 7 keeping 9 captivity, detention 10 caretaking, management, protection 11 confinement, safekeeping, supervision 12 guardianship

custom
3 use 4 norm 5 habit, mores (plural), trade, usage 6 groove, manner, praxis, ritual 7 folkway, precept, routine, traffic 8 business, habitude, practice 9 patronage 10 consuetude, convention

customary
5 usual 6 common, normal, wonted 7 general, regular, routine 8 accepted, everyday, familiar, frequent, habitual, ordinary, orthodox, standard 10 accustomed 11 established, traditional 12 conventional

custom-built
7 bespoke 10 tailor-made 11 made-to-order

customer
5 buyer 6 client, patron 7 shopper 8 consumer 9 purchaser
frequent: 7 habitué

customized
see **custom-built**

custom-made
see **custom-built**

cut
3 bob, hew, lop, mow, saw 4 bite, chop, clip, crop, dice, dock, fell, gash, hack, nick, pare, reap, sawn, slit, snip, snub, trim 5 carve, filet, lathe, lower, mince, notch, piece, prune, quota, sawed, sever, share, shave, shear, slash, slice, split, wound 6 cleave, delete, dilute, divide, excise, fillet, incise, reduce, scythe, sickle, sunder 7 abridge, curtail, dissect, operate, portion, scissor, section, segment, shorten 8 amputate, decrease, dissever, division, mark down, separate, truncate 9 allotment, allowance, reduction 10 abbreviate 12 cold-shoulder
of beef: 3 rib 4 loin, rump 5 baron, chine, chuck, flank, plate, roast, round, shank, steak 6 saddle 7 brisket, sirloin 8 shoulder 9 aitchbone

cut across
6 bisect 8 transect 9 transcend

cut-and-dried
5 stock 7 routine 9 formulaic 10 unoriginal 11 predictable 13 unimaginative

cutaneous
6 dermal

cutaway
4 coat, dive 5 tails

cut back
3 zag 4 clip, curb, dock, pare, trim 5 lower, prune, shave, slash 6 lessen, reduce 7 abridge, curtail, shorten 8 decrease, retrench, truncate 10 abbreviate

cut down
3 axe 4 chop, clip, fell, pare 5 lower, shave, slash 6 digest, reduce 7 abridge, shorten 10 abbreviate

cute
6 dainty, pretty 7 cunning 8 affected 10 attractive 11 impertinent, smart-alecky

cut in
7 include, intrude, obtrude 9 introduce

cutlass
5 saber, sabre, sword 7 machete
8 scimitar

cut off
3 axe, bar, end, lop 4 halt, kill, stop
5 abort, block, sever 6 disown 7 curtail,
destroy, isolate, suspend, 8 amputate,
obstruct, renounce, separate, truncate
9 intercept, interrupt, terminate
10 disinherit 11 discontinue

cut out
3 end 4 halt 5 leave, scram, usurp 6 beat
it, delete, depart, escape, excise, remove,
resect 7 defraud, deprive, take off
8 displace, supplant 9 eliminate, extirpate
10 disconnect

cutpurse
5 thief 10 pickpocket

cut short
3 bob 4 clip, crop, dock, halt, poll 5 abort,
check, scrub, shear 7 abridge, curtail
8 break off 9 interrupt, terminate
10 abbreviate

cuttable
7 sectile 8 scissile

cutthroat
5 bravo 6 gunman, hit man, killer
7 torpedo 8 assassin, murderer
10 hatchet man, triggerman

cutting
8 incisive, piercing 9 sarcastic, trenchant
11 penetrating
edge: 5 blade
remark: 3 dig 4 barb 5 taunt
tool: 3 axe, hob, saw 4 adze 5 knife,
lathe, mower, plane, razor 6 reaper,
scythe, shears, sickle 7 hatchet
8 scissors, tomahawk

cuttlefish
7 mollusc, mollusk 10 cephalopod
ink: 5 sepia
relative: 5 squid 7 octopus

cut up
4 dice, hash, romp 5 caper, clown, mince,
slash 6 cavort 7 carry on, show off
9 misbehave 10 roughhouse

cutup
3 wag 4 zany 5 clown, joker 6 madcap
7 buffoon, farceur 8 jokester

cyan
4 blue

Cybele
4 Rhea
beloved: 5 Attis

brother: 6 Cronus
father: 6 Uranus
husband: 6 Cronus
mother: 4 Gaea
son: 4 Zeus 7 Jupiter, Neptune
8 Poseidon

cyber
5 wired 10 electronic

cybernetics founder
6 Wiener (Norbert)

cycle
3 age, lap, set 4 bike, loop, ring 5 chain,
orbit, recur, round, wheel 6 circle, course,
period, series 7 circuit 8 rotation,
sequence 9 vibration 10 revolution,
succession, two-wheeler, velocipede
11 oscillation

cyclic
7 regular 8 periodic, repeated, rhythmic
9 iterative, recurring, repeating
10 isochronal 12 intermittent

cyclone
7 tornado, twister

cyclopean
4 huge 7 immense, mammoth, massive,
titanic 8 colossal, enormous, gigantic
9 monstrous 10 gargantuan, tremendous
11 elephantine

Cyclops
5 Arges 7 Brontes 8 Steropes
10 Polyphemus

Cycnus
father: 4 Ares, Mars
slayer: 8 Heracles, Hercules

cygnet
4 swan
dam (mother): 3 pen
sire (father): 3 cob

Cygnus
form: 4 swan
friend: 7 Phaeton
star: 5 Deneb

cylinder
4 drum, pipe, tube 5 spool 6 barrel,
bobbin, platen, roller

cylindrical
6 terete 7 tubular 8 tubelike

Cymbeline
daughter: 6 Imogen
son: 9 Arviragus, Guiderius
son-in-law: 9 Posthumus

Cymric
5 Welsh 6 Celtic 9 Brythonic

bard: 8 Taliesin
Elysium: 6 Annwfn
god: 5 Lludd
   of Elysium: 5 Arawn
   of the dead: 5 Pwyll
   of the seas: 3 Ler **4** Llyr **5** Dylan
   of the sky: 7 Gwydion
   of the sun: 4 Lleu, Llew
   of the underworld: 4 Gwyn
goddess: 3 Don **9** Arianrhod
magician: 6 Merlin

Cymru
   5 Wales

cynical
   8 derisive, sardonic, scornful **12** misanthropic

Cynthia
   4 Luna, moon **5** Diana **7** Artemis

cyprian
   4 bawd, jade, slut, tart **5** hussy, tramp
   6 floozy, harlot, hooker, wanton **7** jezebel,
   trollop **8** slattern, strumpet **10** prostitute

Cyprus
   capital: 7 Nicosia **8** Lefkosia
   city: 7 Larnaca **8** Limassol
   language: 5 Greek **7** Turkish
   monetary unit: 4 lira **5** pound
   mountain: 7 Olympus
   port: 9 Famagusta
   sea: 13 Mediterranean

Cyrano de Bergerac
   4 poet **7** duelist **8** duellist
   author: 7 Rostand (Edmond)
   beloved: 6 Roxane
   feature: 4 nose
   rival: 9 Christian

Cyrus
   conquest: 5 Lydia, Media **7** Babylon
   daughter: 6 Atossa
   empire: 7 Persian
   father: 8 Cambyses
   son: 8 Cambyses

cyst
   3 sac, wen **4** sore **5** pouch, spore
   6 growth **7** abscess, blister, capsule,
   vesicle **8** swelling

Cytherea
   4 isle **5** Venus **6** island **9** Aphrodite

czar
   5 chief, mogul **6** despot, honcho, tycoon,
   tyrant **7** emperor, kingpin, magnate
   8 autocrat
   Russian: 4 Ivan **5** Basil, Boris, Peter
   6 Alexis, Dmitry, Feodor, Fyodor, Vasily
   7 Dimitri, Michael, Romanov **8** Nicholas,

Romanoff, Theodore **9** Alexander **12** Boris
Godunov

czar's wife
   7 czarina

Czech Republic
   capital: 6 Prague
   city: 4 Brno **7** Ostrava
   monetary unit: 6 koruna
   neighbor: 6 Poland **7** Austria, Germany
   8 Slovakia
   region: 7 Bohemia, Moravia
   river: 4 Labe, Oder **5** March **6** Morava

D

dab
3 bit, pat **4** blob, blow, daub, peck, poke, spot **5** smear, touch **6** bedaub **7** besmear, plaster, splotch **8** flatfish

dabble
3 dip, dot, toy **4** fool, stud **5** fleck **6** dampen, fiddle, monkey, pepper, putter, splash, tinker **7** freckle, spatter, stipple **8** sprinkle **9** bespeckle, muck about **10** muck around

dabbler
4 duck, tyro **7** amateur **8** putterer, tinkerer **9** smatterer **10** dilettante

dabchick
5 grebe

dacha
5 villa **7** cottage **12** country house

dad
3 pop **4** papa **5** padre, pater **6** father, old man, parent

Dadaist
3 Arp (Jean), Ray (Man) **4** Ball (Hugo) **5** Ernst (Max), Grosz (George), Tzara (Tristan) **7** Duchamp (Marcel), Picabia (Francis) **10** Schwitters (Kurt)

daedal
6 knotty **7** complex **8** artistic, involved, skillful **9** elaborate, intricate **11** complicated **12** labyrinthine **13** sophisticated

Daedalus
7 builder **9** architect, artificer
construction: **9** Labyrinth
father: **6** Metion
son: **6** Icarus
victim: **5** Talos **6** Perdix

daffy
see **daft**

daft
3 mad **4** loco, nuts **5** balmy, crazy, dopey, flaky, loony, nutty, potty, silly, wacko, wacky **6** absurd, crazed, cuckoo, insane, screwy **7** cracked, foolish, idiotic, lunatic, witless **8** demented **10** unbalanced **11** hare-brained

Dag
father: **7** Delling
horse: **9** Skinfaksi
mother: **4** Nott

Dagda
chief god of the: **5** Gaels, Irish
daughter: **6** Brigit
instrument: **4** harp
son: **6** Aengus
wife: **5** Boann

dagger
4 dirk **5** skean, skene **6** bodkin, stylet **7** dudgeon, poniard **8** stiletto
handle: **4** hilt
Malay: **4** kris

_____ Dahl
5 Roald **6** Arlene

daikon
6 radish

daily
7 diurnal **8** everyday **9** circadian, quotidian

dainty
5 goody, tasty, treat **6** choice, morsel, select, tidbit **7** elegant, fragile **8** delicacy, delicate, ethereal, graceful, kickshaw **9** exquisite, recherché **10** delightful

dairy
8 creamery

dais
5 stage **6** podium **7** rostrum **8** platform

daisy
5 oxeye **6** Shasta
British: **10** moonflower
Scottish: **5** gowan

Daisy Miller author
5 James (Henry)

Dakota dialect
5 Teton

Daksha's father
6 Brahma

dale
4 dell, glen, vale 6 dingle, valley

dally
3 lag, pet, toy 4 drag, idle, play 5 delay, flirt, tarry 6 coquet, dawdle, diddle, linger, loiter, trifle 8 lollygag 9 hang about, waste time 10 fool around

dam
4 weir 5 block, check 7 barrier 8 hold back, restrain
major: 4 Oahe 6 Hoover 7 San Luis 8 Fort Peck, Garrison, Oroville 10 Bonneville, Glen Canyon 11 Grand Coulee

damage
3 mar 4 blot, harm, hurt, loss, maim, ruin 5 abuse, burst, cloud, spoil, stain, wound 6 blight, deface, impair, injure, injury, mangle, ravage, scathe 7 blemish, destroy, marring, tarnish, vitiate 8 maltreat, mischief, mistreat, mutilate, sabotage 9 devastate, vandalism 10 impairment 11 devastation

damaged
4 hurt, rent 6 broken, busted, dinged, flawed, marred 7 injured, spoiled, totaled 8 battered, blemished, impaired, ruptured 9 fractured, fragmented, imperfect, shattered

damaging
6 nocent 7 harmful, hurtful, nocuous 9 injurious 11 deleterious, detrimental, prejudicial

dame
4 lady 5 woman 6 gammer, matron 7 dowager 9 matriarch

Damien's island
7 Molokai

Damkina's son
6 Marduk

damn
4 cuss, darn, doom, drat 5 curse, swear 7 condemn, doggone 8 execrate, sentence 9 imprecate 10 vituperate 12 anathematize

damnable
6 blamed, cursed, cussed 7 blasted, dratted 8 accursed, infernal 9 abhorrent, execrable 10 abominable, detestable

damned
5 utter 6 blamed, cursed, cussed, darned, dashed, doomed 7 awfully, blasted, doggone, dratted, goldarn 8 accursed, infernal 9 condemned 10 confounded 13 anathematized

Damocles' _____
5 sword

Damon's friend
7 Pythias

damp
3 wet 4 dank, dewy 5 check, choke, humid, moist, musty 6 clammy 7 bedewed 8 humidify, humidity

dampen
4 cool, curb 5 chill 6 deaden 7 depress, moisten 8 diminish

damsel
3 gal 4 girl, lass, maid, miss 5 filly, wench 6 lassie, maiden

Dan
father: 5 Jacob
mother: 6 Bilhah
son: 6 Hushim

Danaë
father: 8 Acrisius
lover: 4 Zeus
son: 7 Perseus

Danaus
brother: 8 Aegyptus
daughters: 7 Danaïds 8 Danaïdes
father: 5 Belus
founder of: 5 Argos
grandfather: 7 Neptune 8 Poseidon

dance
3 hop, jig, tap 4 ball, flit, foot, heel, hoof, juba, leap, lope, reel, step, trip 5 bamba, brawl, galop, gigue, hover, lindy, mambo, mixer, polka, rumba, stomp, swing, tread, 6 ballet, bolero, boogie, Boston, cancan, chassé, foot it, formal, frolic, German, hoof it, rhumba, shimmy 7 beguine, coranto, courant, flicker, flitter, flutter, hoedown, one-step, shuffle 8 cakewalk, flamenco, galliard, glissade, rigadoon, rigaudon 9 allemande, cotillion, jitterbug, pas de deux
art of: 12 choreography
Austrian: 7 ländler

ballroom: 5 rumba, tango 6 cha-cha, rhumba 7 fox-trot, mazurka, two-step 8 merengue 9 cotillion 10 Charleston
Bohemian: 5 polka
Brazilian: 5 samba 6 maxixe 7 lambada 8 capoeira 9 bossa nova
combining form: 5 chore 6 choreo, chorio
country: 4 reel 8 hornpipe
couple: 5 polka 9 cotillion, malaguena 11 square dance
court: 6 canary, pavane 8 saraband 9 allemande, sarabande
Cuban: 5 conga, mambo, rumba 6 rhumba 8 habanera
designer: 13 choreographer
English: 6 morris
formal: 4 ball, prom 8 cotillion
French: 6 cancan 7 bourrée, gavotte 9 allemande 8 carmagnole
garment: 4 tutu 7 leotard
Haitian: 4 juba 8 merengue
Hungarian: 7 czardas
Indian: 6 nautch 7 bhangra
instrument: 8 castanet
Israeli: 4 hora
Italian: 10 saltarello, tarantella, villanella 11 passacaglia
lively: 3 jig 4 reel, trot 5 galop, gigue, polka, rumba 6 rhumba 7 bourrée 8 fandango, hornpipe, rigadoon, rigaudon 9 farandole, shakedown 10 Charleston, saltarello, tarantella
movement: 4 plié, step 8 capriole, glissade 9 pirouette
Muse of: 11 Terpsichore
1920's: 10 Charleston
Polish: 5 polka 7 mazurka 9 polonaise
Polynesian: 4 hula
Scottish: 3 bob 4 reel 5 fling 10 strathspey 11 schottische 13 Highland fling
shoes: 5 pumps 8 slippers
slipper: 7 toeshoe
slow: 6 adagio, minuet, pavane 8 habanera
South American: 7 carioca
Spanish: 4 jota 6 bolero 7 zapateo 8 cachucha, chaconne, fandango, flamenco, saraband 9 malaguena, sarabande 10 seguidilla
springy: 3 jig
square: 7 hoedown, lancers 9 cotillion, quadrille

stately: 5 pavan 6 pavane 8 saraband 9 polonaise, sarabande
step: 3 pas
woman's: 6 cancan

dancer
6 hoofer 7 chorine, clogger, danseur, stepper 8 coryphée, danseuse 9 ballerina, chorus boy 10 cakewalker, chorus girl
American: 4 Feld (Elliot), Holm (Hanya), Lang (Pearl), Tune (Tommy) 5 Ailey (Alvin), Fosse (Bob), Kelly (Gene), Shawn (Ted), Tharp (Twyla) 6 Castle (Irene, Vernon), Duncan (Isadora), Dunham (Katherine), Graham (Martha), Morris (Mark), Taylor (Paul), Verdon (Gwen) 7 Astaire (Fred), Bujones (Fernando), de Mille (Agnes), Farrell (Suzanne), Gregory (Cynthia), Jamison (Judith), Joffrey (Robert), Martins (Peter), Massine (Leonide), McBride (Patricia), Robbins (Jerome), St. Denis (Ruth), Tamiris (Helen) 8 Champion (Gower, Marge), d'Amboise (Jacques), Humphrey (Doris), Kirkland (Gelsey), Mitchell (Arthur), Nikolais (Alwin), Villella (Edward) 9 Tallchief (Maria) 10 Cunningham (Merce)
Cuban: 6 Alonso (Alicia)
Danish: 5 Bruhn (Erik) 7 Martins (Peter) 8 Tomasson (Helgi)
English: 5 Dolin (Anton), Somes (Michael), Tudor (Antony) 7 Fonteyn (Margot), Markova (Alicia), Rambert (Marie) 8 de Valois (Ninette), Helpmann (Robert)
French: 5 Lifar (Serge) 6 Béjart (Maurice), Perrot (Jules), Petipa (Marius) 7 Camargo (Marie), Massine (Leonide)
German: 5 Jooss (Kurt)
Italian: 5 Grisi (Carlotta)
Mexican: 5 Limón (José)
Russian: 5 Lifar (Serge) 6 Fokine (Michel), Petipa (Marius) 7 Massine (Leonide), Nureyev (Rudolf), Pavlova (Anna), Ulanova (Galina) 8 Danilova (Aleksandra), Makarova (Natalia), Nijinska (Bronislava), Nijinsky (Vaslav), Vaganova (Agrippina) 9 Karsavina (Tamara), Semyonova (Marina) 11 Baryshnikov (Mikhail), Plisetskaya (Maya)
Scottish: 7 Shearer (Moira)

dancing
6 ballet 12 choreography
mania: 9 tarantism

dandle
3 pet 4 play 6 caress, cosset, cradle, cuddle, pamper

dandruff
5 scall, scurf

dandy
3 fop 4 beau, buck, dude, fine, toff 5 nifty, swell 6 peachy 7 coxcomb, foppish 8 terrific 9 excellent, first-rate, hunky-dory 11 Beau Brummel, crackerjack 12 lounge lizard

dang
4 damn, darn 6 cursed, cussed, damned, darned 7 blasted, dratted, goldarn 8 infernal 10 confounded

danger
4 risk 5 peril 6 crisis, hazard, menace, plight, threat 7 pitfall, trouble 8 distress, jeopardy 9 emergency
signal: 4 bell 5 alarm, siren 6 tocsin

dangerous
5 risky 6 unsafe 7 parlous 8 insecure, menacing, perilous, unstable 9 hazardous 10 precarious 11 threatening

dangle
4 hang 5 droop, swing 6 depend 7 suspend

Daniel _____
pioneer: 5 Boone
statesman: 7 Webster

Danish
hero: 5 Ogier
king: 9 Christian, Frederick
queen: 9 Margrethe

dank
3 wet 4 damp 5 humid, moist 6 clammy 8 dripping

Dante
beloved: 8 Beatrice
birthplace: 8 Florence
daughter: 7 Antonia
deathplace: 7 Ravenna
party: 6 Guelph 7 Bianchi
patron: 5 Scala
teacher: 6 Latini
wife: 5 Gemma
work: 7 Inferno 8 Commedia, Paradiso 9 Vita Nuova 10 Purgatorio 12 Divine Comedy (The)

Dantean division
5 canto

Danton's colleague
5 Marat (Jean-Paul) 11 Robespierre (Maximilien)

Danzig
6 Gdańsk

Daphne
father: 5 Ladon 6 Peneus
form: 6 laurel 10 laurel tree
pursuer: 6 Apollo 9 Leucippus

Daphnis' lover
5 Chloe

dapper
4 neat, trim 5 doggy, natty, sassy, smart, swank 6 classy, jaunty, rakish, snazzy, spiffy, spruce, sprucy 7 bandbox, dashing, doggish, foppish, stylish 11 well-groomed

dapple
4 spot 5 fleck, patch 6 mottle 7 speckle, stipple

dappled
4 pied 6 motley 7 flecked, mottled, patched, piebald, spotted 8 brindled 10 variegated 11 varicolored

Dardanelles
10 Hellespont

Dardanus
descendants: 7 Trojans
father: 4 Zeus 7 Jupiter
mother: 7 Electra

dare
3 try 4 defy, risk 5 beard, brave 6 hazard 7 attempt, venture 8 confront, defiance 9 challenge

daredevil
see **daring**

darer
4 hero 6 risker

daring
4 bold, guts, rash 5 brash, brave, gutsy, moxie, nerve, nervy, pluck, valor 6 heroic, plucky 7 courage, heroism 8 audacity, boldness, bravery, fearless, reckless 9 audacious, derring-do, fortitude, venturous 10 courageous 11 adventurous, venturesome 13 adventuresome

Darius
battle: 8 Marathon
father: 9 Hystaspes
country: 6 Persia 7 Parthia
son: 6 Xerxes
wife: 6 Atossa

Darjeeling
3 tea

dark
3 dim 4 dusk, inky, murk 5 black, blind, cloud, dingy, dusky, ebony, murky, night, sable, shady, sooty, swart, umber, unlit, vague 6 brunet, cloudy, dismal, gloomy,

opaque, somber, sombre, wicked
7 obscure, ominous, rayless, satanic, shadowy, stygian, subfusc, sunless, swarthy, unclear **8** bistered, brunette, infernal, sinister **9** enigmatic, lightless, secretive, tenebrous, unlighted **10** caliginous, indistinct, mysterious, mystifying, pitch-black **11** crepuscular **13** unilluminated
poetic: 4 ebon

darken
3 dim **5** bedim, cloud, gloom, lower, shade, sully, umber **6** shadow **7** becloud, blacken, eclipse, obscure, tarnish **8** melanize, overcast **9** obfuscate, overcloud **10** overshadow
Scottish: 5 gloam

dark-haired
female: 8 brunette
male: 6 brunet

darkness
4 dusk, evil, murk **5** black, gloom, night, shade **6** shadow **8** blackout **9** nightfall, obscurity

darling
3 hon, pet **4** dear, duck, love **5** angel, deary, ducky, flame, honey, loved, sugar, sweet **7** beloved, dearest, sweetie **8** adorable, charming, favorite, precious **10** sweetheart, sweetie pie

darn
4 knit, mend **5** patch **6** blamed, cursed, cussed, damned, shucks **7** blasted, doggone, dratted **8** infernal **9** embroider **10** confounded

darn it
French: 3 zut

Darrow client
4 Debs (Eugene), Loeb (Richard) **6** Scopes (John) **7** Haywood (William), Leopold (Nathan)

dart
3 fly, run, zip **4** barb, bolt, buzz, dash, flit, leap, rush, sail, scud, skim, tear **5** arrow, bound, hurry, lance, pitch, scamp, scoot, shaft, shoot, skirr, spear, speed, spurt **6** glance, hasten, scurry, spring, sprint **7** javelin, missile, scamper
barbed: 10 banderilla

D'Artagnan's friends
5 Athos **6** Aramis **7** Porthos **10** musketeers

Dartmouth location
5 Devon **7** Hanover **12** New Hampshire

darts term
3 leg **4** bust **5** split **6** double, flight, hockey, treble **8** bull's-eye

Darwin, Charles
colleague: 7 Wallace (Alfred Russel)
ship: 6 Beagle
theory: 9 evolution, selection

dash
3 fly, nip, run **4** bolt, brio, cast, damn, dart, élan, foil, hurl, race, ruin, rush, slam, tear, zing **5** break, chase, flair, fling, pinch, smash, style, trace **6** esprit, hyphen, scurry, splash, sprint, thrust, thwart **7** bravura, depress, destroy, shatter, smidgen, spatter **8** confound **9** animation, frustrate

dashboard reading
4 fuel **5** speed **7** mileage **8** pressure **11** temperature

dashing
4 bold **5** smart **6** dapper, jaunty, lively, modish **7** gallant, stylish **8** animated, spirited **11** adventurous, fashionable

Das Kapital author
4 Marx (Karl)

dassie
4 pika **5** coney, hyrax

dastard
6 coward, craven **7** chicken, quitter **8** poltroon, recreant **9** scoundrel

dastardly
3 low **4** base, mean **6** craven, yellow **8** cowardly, shameful, skulking **11** treacherous, underhanded **13** pusillanimous

data
4 info **5** facts, input **7** figures **9** documents **11** information

date
3 age, era, woo **5** court, epoch, tryst **6** cutoff, escort **7** take out **8** deadline **9** accompany **10** engagement, rendezvous **11** anniversary, appointment, assignation

dated
3 old **5** passé **6** démodé, old hat **7** archaic, outworn **8** obsolete, outmoded **10** antiquated **12** old-fashioned **13** unfashionable

datum
4 fact

daub
4 blob, blot, spot 5 fleck, paint, smear
6 dapple, smudge, splash 7 besmear,
dribble, plaster, speckle, splotch

daughter
Blythe Danner's: 7 Paltrow (Gwyneth)
Bruce Dern's: 5 Laura
Bush's: 5 Jenna 7 Barbara
Carter's: 3 Amy
Cash's: 7 Rosanne
Cher's: 8 Chastity
Clinton's: 7 Chelsea
Cole's: 7 Natalie
Coppola's: 5 Sofia
Danny Thomas's: 5 Marlo
Debbie Reynolds's: 6 Carrie (Fisher)
Eddie Fisher's: 6 Carrie
Elizabeth II's: 4 Anne
Elvis's: 9 Lisa Marie
Fonda's: 4 Jane
Ford's (Gerald): 5 Susan
Freud's: 4 Anna
Garland's: 12 Liza Minnelli
Goldie Hawn's: 10 Kate Hudson
Ingrid Bergman's: 8 Isabella (Rossellini)
Janet Leigh's: 8 Jamie Lee (Curtis)
Joel Grey's: 8 Jennifer
Johnson's (Lyndon): 4 Lucy 5 Linda
Jon Voight's: 8 Angelina (Jolie)
Kennedy's (John F.): 8 Caroline
Klaus Kinski's: 9 Nastassja
Maureen O'Sullivan's: 3 Mia (Farrow)
Naomi Judd's: 7 Wynonna
Nat King Cole's: 7 Natalie
Nixon's: 5 Julie 6 Tricia
Pat Boone's: 5 Debby
Ravi Shankar's: 10 Norah Jones
Reagan's: 5 Patti 7 Maureen
Richard Burton's: 4 Kate
Ryan O'Neal's: 5 Tatum
Sinatra's: 5 Nancy
Tony Curtis's: 8 Jamie Lee (Curtis)

Daughter of the Moon
7 Nokomis

daunt
3 cow 4 alarm, deter 6 dismay, subdue
7 terrify 8 frighten 10 disconcert,
discourage, dishearten, intimidate

daunting
7 awesome 8 imposing 9 dismaying,
unnerving 10 forbidding, formidable
11 dispiriting 12 discouraging, intimidating,
overwhelming

dauntless
4 bold, game 5 brave 6 daring 7 gallant,
valiant 8 fearless, unafraid 9 unfearful,

unfearing 10 courageous 11 lionhearted
12 stouthearted

dauntlessness
4 guts 5 heart, nerve, pluck, spunk, valor
6 daring, mettle, spirit 7 bravery, cojones,
courage 8 boldness 10 resolution
12 fearlessness

davenport
4 desk, sofa 5 couch, divan 6 daybed
12 chesterfield

David
commander: 4 Joab 5 Amasa
companion: 8 Jonathan
daughter: 5 Tamar
father: 5 Jesse
rebuker: 6 Nathan
son: 5 Amnon 7 Absalom, Solomon
wife: 7 Abigail, Ahinoam 9 Bathsheba

_____ **David**
4 Camp 5 Magen, Mogen 6 Star of

David Copperfield
author: 7 Dickens (Charles)
character: 4 Dora, Heep 5 Uriah
6 Barkis 8 Micawber, Peggotty
9 Murdstone 10 Steerforth

Da Vinci Code author
5 Brown (Dan)

davit
5 crane

dawdle
3 lag 4 idle, laze, loaf, loll 5 dally, delay,
tarry 6 diddle, linger, loiter, lounge
8 lollygag 10 dillydally

dawn
4 morn 5 sunup 6 aurora 7 morning,
sunrise 8 cockcrow, daybreak, daylight
9 beginning 10 first light
goddess: 3 Eos 6 Aurora

day
abbreviation: 3 Fri, Mon, Sat, Sun, Thu,
Tue, Wed 4 Thur, Tues 5 Thurs
before: 3 eve
church calendar: 5 feria
French: 4 jour
German: 3 Tag
holy: 5 feast
hot: 8 scorcher
hour: 4 noon
Latin: 4 dies
Spanish: 3 día

daybreak
4 dawn, morn 5 sunup 6 aurora
7 dawning, morning, sunrise 8 cockcrow,
daylight

daydream
4 muse 5 fancy 6 vision 7 fantasy, reverie 8 phantasy 9 fantasize 10 woolgather 13 woolgathering

daystar
3 Sol, sun 5 Venus 7 phoebus

daze
3 fog 4 haze, stun 5 amaze, blind 6 dazzle, stupor, trance 7 astound, confuse, stupefy 8 astonish, bedazzle, befuddle, confound 9 dumbfound

dazed
5 woozy 6 groggy, punchy 7 dazzled, stunned 8 confused 9 stupefied 10 punch-drunk

_____ d'Azur
4 Côte

dazzle
5 amaze, blind, éclat, glitz, shine 7 impress 8 astonish, bewilder, confound, outshine 9 overpower

dazzling
6 flashy, garish 7 radiant 8 splendid, stunning 9 brilliant 11 confounding, resplendent 12 overpowering

deacon
6 clergy, cleric, layman 8 reverend 9 churchman

dead
4 cold, gone, late 5 passé, slain, stiff 6 buried, fallen 7 defunct, done for, expired, extinct 8 deceased, departed, lifeless 9 senseless 10 corpselike 11 unconscious 12 extinguished

deadbeat
3 bum 5 idler 6 debtor, loafer, slouch 7 lounger, shirker, slacker 10 delinquent, malingerer

dead duck
5 goner 8 casualty, fatality

deaden
4 dull, kill, mute, numb, stun 5 blunt, quiet 6 benumb, dampen, lessen, muffle, reduce, stifle, smother, stupefy 8 suppress, tone down 11 anesthetize, desensitize

dead end
4 halt, stop 6 pocket, unruly 7 impasse 8 cul-de-sac, standoff 9 stalemate, terminate 10 blind alley, bottleneck, standstill

deadened
4 numb 6 asleep, dulled, killed, numbed 7 blunted 8 benumbed, impaired 12 anesthetized

deadeye
5 block 8 marksman 12 sharpshooter

deadfall
4 trap 7 springe 9 booby trap, mousetrap

deadliness
8 fatality 9 lethality, mortality

deadlock
3 tie 4 draw 7 impasse 8 standoff, stoppage 9 checkmate, stalemate 10 standstill

deadly
5 fatal, toxic 6 lethal, mortal 7 capital, killing 8 lethally, unerring 10 implacable 11 destructive 12 pestilential

deadpan
5 blank, empty 6 vacant 9 impassive 10 poker-faced 11 inscrutable 12 inexpressive, unexpressive

Dead Souls author
5 Gogol (Nikolay)

dead to rights
9 red-handed

deadweight
4 load 6 weight

deal
4 dole, sale, sell 5 allot, serve, shake, share, trade, treat 6 barter, dicker, parcel 7 bargain, deliver, dish out, dole out, mete out, package, portion, traffic, wrestle 8 contract, disburse, dispense, share out 9 agreement, apportion, negotiate 10 administer, compromise, distribute, measure out 11 arrangement, transaction 13 understanding
great: 4 gobs, heap, lots, tons 5 heaps, horde, loads, scads 6 oodles, plenty, stacks
out: 8 disburse, dispense 9 apportion 10 administer, distribute
with: 5 serve, treat 6 handle, regard 7 concern, involve

dealer
5 agent 6 broker, seller, trader, vendor 8 chandler, merchant, operator 9 tradesman 10 negotiator, trafficker 11 businessman, distributer, distributor 12 merchandiser
British: 5 coper 6 draper, jobber, mercer 7 chapman

dealings
5 trade, truck 7 affairs, matters, traffic
8 business, commerce, concerns
11 intercourse 12 interactions,
transactions, undertakings

dean
4 head 5 chief, doyen, elder 6 leader

dear
3 pet 4 fond, lamb, love 5 honey, loved,
sweet 6 costly, doting, loving, prized,
scarce 7 beloved, darling, devoted,
lovable, machree, querida, tootsie
8 favorite, precious, valuable 9 cherished,
expensive, heartfelt, treasured 10 fair-
haired, honeybunch, sweetheart
12 affectionate
French: 4 cher **5** chère **6** cherie

dearth
4 lack, want 6 famine 7 absence, default,
paucity 8 scarcity, shortage, sparsity
9 privation, scantness 10 deficiency,
meagerness, scantiness

death
3 end 4 exit 6 demise, ending, expiry
7 decease, passing, quietus 8 casualty,
curtains, fatality, necrosis, thanatos
9 bloodshed, departure 10 expiration,
extinction, grim reaper 11 dissolution,
termination 12 annihilation
after: 10 posthumous
combining form: 6 thanat **7** thanato
music: 5 dirge, elegy **8** threnody
notice: 4 obit **8** obituary **9** necrology
of tissue: 8 gangrene
personification: 10 grim reaper
put to: 3 gas, hit, ice, zap **4** do in, hang,
kill, slay **5** drown, lynch, snuff, waste
6 murder, poison, rub out **7** bump off,
butcher, execute, smother, wipe out **8** blow
away, dispatch, immolate, knock off,
strangle, throttle **9** slaughter, suffocate
10 asphyxiate **11** assassinate, electrocute
rate: 9 mortality
rites: 7 funeral **8** exequies **9** interment,
obsequies

deathless
7 abiding, eternal, lasting, undying
8 enduring, immortal 11 everlasting
12 imperishable

deathlike
see **deathly**

deathly
5 fatal 6 lethal, mortal 7 macabre, stygian
12 pestilential

debacle
4 rout 6 defeat, fiasco 7 breakup, failure,
8 collapse, disaster 9 breakdown,
cataclysm 10 disruption

debar
3 ban 4 stop 6 forbid, outlaw 7 exclude,
prevent, rule out 8 preclude, prohibit
9 interdict

debark
4 land 6 alight, get off 11 decorticate

debase
3 mar 4 harm 5 lower, stain 6 damage,
defile, demean, dilute, impair, reduce,
weaken 7 cheapen, corrupt, degrade,
devalue, pervert, pollute, vitiate 8 dishonor
9 undermine 10 adulterate, depreciate
11 contaminate

debatable
4 iffy, moot 7 dubious 8 arguable, doubtful
9 contested, uncertain, undecided
10 disputable, unresolved 11 problematic
12 questionable

debate
4 moot 5 argue, bandy, plead 7 contend,
contest, discuss, dispute, quarrel, wrangle
8 argument, consider, forensic, question
9 dialectic, thrash out 10 controvert, toss
around 11 application, controversy,
disputation 12 deliberation 13 argumentation
art of: 9 forensics
expert: 7 eristic
place for: 5 forum

debauch
4 orgy, warp 6 seduce 7 corrupt, deprave,
pervert, vitiate 9 bacchanal, brutalize
10 lead astray, saturnalia 11 bacchanalia

debauched
6 wanton 8 degraded, depraved, vitiated
9 corrupted, dissolute, libertine, perverted
10 degenerate, licentious

debilitate
3 sap 6 impair, weaken 7 cripple, disable
8 enfeeble 9 attenuate, undermine
10 devitalize

debilitated
4 weak 6 feeble, infirm, sapped 7 run-
down, worn-out 8 weakened 9 enfeebled

debility
7 disease, malaise 8 weakness 9 infirmity
10 feebleness, infirmness, sickliness
11 decrepitude

Debir
kingdom: 5 Eglon

slayer: 6 Joshua

debit
4 bill, levy 6 charge 7 deficit 8 drawback
9 liability 11 encumbrance, shortcoming

debonair
5 suave 6 smooth, urbane 7 dashing,
elegant 10 nonchalant 12 lighthearted

Deborah's husband
9 Lappidoth

debris
4 junk, slag 5 trash, waste 6 litter, refuse,
rubble, spilth 7 garbage, rubbish
8 detritus, riffraff, wreckage
rock: 5 scree, talus 8 colluvia 9 colluvium

debt
3 due, sin 6 arrear, red ink 7 arrears,
default, deficit 8 mortgage, trespass
9 arrearage, liability 10 obligation
11 delinquency
acknowledgment: 3 IOU 4 bill 5 check

debtless
7 solvent

debunk
6 expose, reveal, show up, unmask 7 lay
bare, lay open, uncloak, uncover, undress
8 unshroud 9 demystify, discredit

Debussy's La _____
3 Mer

debut
3 bow 5 entry 6 entree 7 come out,
opening, present 8 entrance, premiere
9 beginning, coming out, introduce
12 introduction, presentation

decadence
5 decay 7 decline 10 degeneracy,
regression 11 degradation 12 degeneration 13 deterioration

decadent
6 effete 7 debased 8 decaying, degraded,
depraved 9 debauched, declining
10 degenerate, dissolute 13 self-indulgent

Decalogue verb
5 shalt

Decameron, The
author: 9 Boccaccio (Giovanni)
heroine: 8 Griselda

decamp
4 blow, bolt, exit, flee 5 leave, scram, split
6 beat it, begone, cut out, escape, get out,
retire 7 abscond, make off, pull out, run
away, skiddoo, take off, vamoose 8 clear
out, withdraw 9 skedaddle

decant
4 pour 7 draw off, pour out 8 transfer

decanter
5 cruet, flask 6 bottle, carafe, flagon,
vessel

decapitate
4 head 6 behead 9 decollate 10 guillotine

decapod
7 mollusc, mollusk 10 crustacean

decathlon champ
6 Jenner (Bruce), Morris (Glenn), O'Brien
(Dan), Schenk (Christian), Sebrle (Roman,
Toomey (Bill), Zmelik (Robert) 7 Doherty
(Ken), Johnson (Rafer), Mathias (Bob)
8 Campbell (Milton), Thompson (Daley)

decay
3 rot 4 ruin, wane 5 spoil, waste
6 molder, wither 7 atrophy, crumble,
decline, putrefy, rotting 8 putresce,
spoilage 9 decompose 11 deteriorate
12 dilapidation, putrefaction
13 deterioration

decayed
6 putrid, rotted, rotten, ruined 7 carious,
spoiled 8 decadent, moldered, overripe
9 putrefied 10 decomposed, degenerate

decease
3 die, end 4 fail, pass 5 death, sleep
6 demise, depart, dying, expire, finish, pass
on, perish 7 passing, quietus, release,
succumb 8 pass away 9 departure
10 expiration

deceased
4 body, dead, late 6 corpse 7 cadaver,
carcass, expired, remains 8 departed,
lifeless 9 inanimate

deceit
3 gyp 4 hoax, ruse, sham 5 fraud, guile,
trick 6 humbug 7 swindle 8 artifice,
flimflam, trickery 9 chicanery, deception,
duplicity, imposture 10 dishonesty
13 double-dealing

deceitful
3 sly 4 wily 5 false, lying 6 crafty, sneaky,
tricky 7 cunning, knavish, roguish
8 guileful, two-faced 9 deceptive,
dishonest, underhand 10 mendacious
11 underhanded 13 double-dealing

deceive
3 con 4 bilk, dupe, fool, gull, hoax 5 bluff,
cozen, lie to, trick 6 delude, humbug,
palter, take in 7 beguile, mislead, sandbag,
two-time 8 flimflam, hoodwink
9 bamboozle, four-flush 11 double-cross

deceiving
5 false 6 tricky 8 deluding, delusive, delusory, guileful, two-faced 9 beguiling, deceptive 10 fallacious, misleading 11 duplicitous, underhanded

decelerate
4 slow 5 delay 6 retard, slow up 7 slacken 8 slow down

decency
7 decorum, dignity, fitness, modesty 8 civility 9 etiquette, propriety 10 conformity, seemliness

decennium
6 decade

decent
4 fair, good 5 right 6 honest, modest, proper, seemly 7 correct, fitting, upright 8 adequate, all right 9 competent, honorable, tolerable 10 acceptable, conforming, sufficient 11 comme il faut, presentable, respectable 12 satisfactory

deception
3 gyp 4 gaff, hoax, hype, ruse, sham, wile 5 cheat, fraud, guile, put-on, trick 6 deceit, dupery, humbug, mirage 7 chicane, cunning, fallacy, fantasm, knavery, sophism 8 flimflam, illusion, intrigue, phantasm, trickery, trumpery, wiliness 9 casuistry, chicanery, duplicity, imposture, sophistry, treachery 10 artfulness, dishonesty, hanky-panky, subterfuge 11 indirection 12 speciousness, spuriousness 13 double-dealing

deceptive
5 false, phony 6 tricky 8 deluding, delusory, illusory, specious 9 beguiling, deceitful, deceiving 10 fallacious, misleading

decide
3 opt 4 rule, will 5 judge 6 settle 7 adjudge, resolve 8 conclude 9 determine 10 adjudicate

decided
3 set 4 firm 5 fixed 6 intent 7 assured, certain, obvious, settled 8 definite, resolute, resolved 10 determined, pronounced 11 established, unequivocal

decimate
4 raze, ruin 5 wreck 7 abolish, destroy, wipe out 8 demolish, massacre 9 slaughter 10 annihilate, obliterate 11 exterminate

decipher
4 read 5 break, crack, solve 6 decode, reveal 7 decrypt, resolve, unravel 8 unriddle 9 figure out, interpret, puzzle out, translate 12 cryptanalyze

decision
4 fiat 6 choice, ruling 7 finding, resolve, verdict 8 firmness, judgment, sentence 9 selection 10 conclusion, resolution, settlement 13 determination
rabbinical: 9 responsum

decisive
3 set 7 crucial, settled 8 critical, resolute 10 conclusive, convincing, determined, imperative, peremptory 11 determining 12 unmistakable

deck
4 trim 5 adorn, array, dress, equip, floor, level, porch, prank 6 attire, blazon, clothe 7 apparel, appoint, furnish, garland, garnish, terrace 8 accouter, accoutre, beautify, decorate, emblazon, ornament, platform 9 embellish
chief: 4 bos'n 9 boatswain
high: 4 poop
lowest: 5 orlop
out: 5 array, fix up, slick, spiff, tog up 6 clothe, doll up 7 dress up, gussy up 8 spruce up
part: 7 scupper

deckhand
3 gob 4 jack, swab 6 sailor, seaman 7 jack-tar, rouster, swabbie 10 bluejacket

declaim
4 rant 5 mouth, orate, speak 6 recite 7 deliver, lecture 8 bloviate, harangue, perorate 9 hold forth

declamatory
5 tumid, windy, wordy 6 florid, turgid 7 aureate, flowery, fustian, orotund, pompous, ranting, verbose 8 sonorous 9 bombastic, high-flown, overblown 10 euphuistic, oratorical, rhetorical 12 magniloquent 13 grandiloquent

declaration
5 edict 6 avowal, notice, report 7 promise 8 document, pleading 9 affidavit, manifesto, statement, testimony 10 confession, deposition, disclosure, expression, profession 11 affirmation, attestation 12 announcement, notification, proclamation 13 advertisement, pronouncement

declare
3 say, vow 4 aver, avow, tell, vent 5 claim, sound, state, swear, utter, voice 6 affirm,

allege, assert, avouch, blazon, depone, depose, herald, insist, ordain, report, reveal **7** certify, confirm, deliver, divulge, express, profess, signify, testify **8** announce, disclose, indicate, maintain, manifest, proclaim, propound **9** advertise, broadcast, enunciate, predicate, pronounce **10** annunciate, asseverate, promulgate **11** come out with, disseminate
a saint: 8 canonize
in cards: 3 bid **4** meld
invalid: 5 annul

declass
4 bump, bust **5** abase, lower **6** demote, reduce **7** degrade, set back **9** downgrade

déclassé
4 mean, poor **6** common, vulgar **7** ignoble, lowered **8** inferior, lowgrade, mediocre, middling **10** second-rate **11** second-class

declension
5 class, slope **7** decline, descent **8** downfall **9** downgrade **10** inflection **12** dégringolade **13** deterioration

declination
3 ebb **5** slant, slide **6** ebbing **7** refusal, incline **8** downturn **9** downgrade **10** deflection **12** dégringolade, turning aside **13** deterioration

decline
3 dip, ebb, jib, rot, sag, set **4** balk, dive, drop, fade, fail, fall, flag, loss, sink, slip, wane **5** abate, avoid, demur, droop, lapse, lower, say no, slide, slope, slump, spurn **6** ebbing, go down, recede, refuse, reject, renege, waning, weaken, worsen **7** abstain, atrophy, descend, descent, devolve, dismiss, drop-off, dwindle, failure, falloff, forbear, refrain, relapse, sell-off, sinkage, subside **8** comedown, decrease, downfall, downturn, languish, lowering, turn down **9** backslide, decadence, downgrade, downslide, downswing, downtrend, reprobate, repudiate, weakening **10** degeneracy, degenerate, depression, devolution, disapprove, falling off **11** backsliding, deteriorate **12** degeneration, dégringolade **13** deterioration

declivitous
5 steep **6** sloped **7** pitched, sloping **8** inclined **9** inclining **10** descending

declivity
3 dip **4** drop, fall **5** slope **7** decline, descent **8** downturn, gradient **9** downgrade **11** inclination

decode
see **decipher**

decollate
4 head, kill **6** behead **10** decapitate, guillotine

decolor
6 blanch, bleach, blench, whiten **7** wash out **11** achromatize

decompose
3 rot **5** decay, spoil, taint **6** fester, molder **7** analyze, break up, crumble, putrefy, resolve **8** dissolve, separate **9** anatomize, break down **12** disintegrate

decor
7 setting **8** backdrop, stage set **11** furnishings **13** ornamentation

decorate
4 do up, pink, trim **5** adorn, dress, frill **6** bedeck **7** bedizen, dress up, enhance, festoon, furnish, garnish, appliqué **8** beautify, emblazon, ornament **9** embellish
a border: 6 purfle

decorated
6 ornate **7** adorned, honored, wrought **9** bemedaled, decked out, garnished **10** beribboned, ornamented **11** embellished

decoration
4 bays **5** award, badge, honor, kudos, medal **6** doodad, plaque **7** garnish, laurels **8** accolade, filigree, fretting, fretwork, frippery, furbelow, ornament, trimming, vignette **11** distinction
cutout: 8 appliqué
furniture: 4 buhl **6** boulle

decorous
3 fit **4** meet, prim **5** right **6** au fait, comely, decent, proper, seemly **7** correct, elegant, fitting **8** becoming, mannerly, suitable, tasteful **9** befitting, civilized, de rigueur, dignified **10** conforming **11** appropriate, respectable, well-behaved

decorously
5 fitly **7** rightly **8** decently, properly, suitably **9** correctly, fittingly **11** befittingly, respectably

decorousness
7 decency **8** civility **9** propriety, rightness **10** seemliness **11** correctness, orderliness **12** correctitude

decorticate
4 bare, bark, flay, hull, husk, pare, peel,

skin **5** scale, scalp, shell, shuck, strip
6 denude **7** lay bare, pull off

decorum
5 order **7** decency, dignity, fitness,
modesty **9** etiquette, propriety, protocol
10 properness, seemliness
11 correctness, orderliness **12** correctitude

decoy
4 bait, fake, lure **5** plant, shill, tempt
6 allure, capper, delude, entice, lead on,
pigeon, seduce **7** deceive, mislead
8 inveigle **10** red herring

decrease
3 cut, ebb **4** bate, drop, ease, fall, loss,
wane **5** allay, lower **6** lessen, reduce,
shrink **7** abridge, curtail, cut back, cutback,
cut down, decline, die down, drop off,
dwindle, fall off, lighten, shorten, slacken,
subside **8** diminish, downturn, moderate,
rollback, taper off **9** abatement, alleviate,
reduction **10** abbreviate, depreciate,
diminution, falling off

decree
4 fiat, rule **5** canon, edict, enact, judge,
order, ukase **6** behest, charge, dictum,
impose, ordain, ruling **7** adjudge, appoint,
bidding, command, declare, dictate, lay
down, mandate, precept, statute
8 judgment, proclaim, sentence **9** directive,
judgement, ordinance, prescribe, prescript,
pronounce **10** adjudicate, injunction,
regulation **11** declaration **12** adjudication,
announcement, proclamation, promulgation
13 pronouncement
Muslim: 5 fatwa

decrepit
4 aged, weak, worn **5** frail, seedy, tacky
6 creaky, feeble, infirm, senile, shabby,
wasted, weakly **7** fragile, run-down, worn-
out **8** battered, impaired, weakened
10 bedraggled, broken-down, down-at-
heel, ramshackle **11** dilapidated

decrepitude
4 ruin **5** decay **7** frailty, wasting
8 collapse, debility, weakness **9** disrepair,
infirmity **10** exhaustion, feebleness,
infirmness **12** dilapidation, enfeeblement
13 deterioration

decretal
4 fiat, writ **5** edict, order, ukase **6** assize,
dictum, letter, ruling **7** dictate **8** decision,
judgment **11** declaration
13 pronouncement

decry
3 boo **4** bash, slam, slur **5** abuse
6 berate, malign, vilify **7** asperse, censure,

condemn, degrade, devalue, put down
8 bad-mouth, belittle, denounce, derogate,
reproach **9** criticize, deprecate, discredit,
disparage, dispraise, reprehend, reprobate
10 depreciate, disapprove **11** rail against

decrypt
see **decipher**

decumbent
4 flat **5** prone **6** supine **9** lying down,
prostrate, reclining **10** horizontal

decussate
5 cross **8** crosscut **9** intersect
10 crisscross, intercross

dedicate
3 vow **5** bless **6** commit, devote, hallow,
pledge **7** address **8** inscribe, restrict, set
apart **10** consecrate

deduce
5 infer, judge, trace **6** derive, evolve,
gather, reason, reckon **7** discern, make
out, surmise **8** conclude **9** figure out

deduct
4 bate **5** abate, infer, judge **6** gather,
remove **7** make out, take off, take out
8 conclude, knock off, perceive, subtract,
take away

deduction
3 cut **8** discount, illation, judgment,
sequitur, write-off **9** abatement, inference,
reasoning **10** conclusion **11** subtraction

deductive
7 a priori **8** dogmatic, illative, provable,
reasoned **9** derivable, inferable
10 consequent **11** inferential **13** ratiocinative

deed
3 act **4** cede, fact, feat, pact **5** doing, title
6 action, assign, convey, escrow, remise
7 charter, exploit **8** alienate, contract,
covenant, make over, sign over, transfer
9 adventure **10** conveyance, enterprise
11 achievement, performance, tour de
force
brutal: 8 atrocity
evil: 3 sin **11** malefaction
good: 7 mitzvah

deem
4 feel, hold **5** judge, think **7** account,
adjudge, believe **8** consider

de-emphasize
8 downplay, minimize, play down **9** gloss
over, soft-pedal, underplay
13 underestimate

deep
3 low **4** bass, rapt, sunk **5** abyss, grave, ocean **6** occult, orphic, secret **7** abyssal, obscure **8** abstruse, esoteric, hermetic, profound **9** engrossed, recondite **10** bottomless, fathomless, mysterious
pink: 5 coral

deepen
6 darken, worsen **7** enhance, enlarge, magnify, thicken **8** heighten **9** aggravate, intensify **10** strengthen

deepness
5 abyss **9** intensity **10** profundity

deep-seated
6 inborn, inbred, innate **7** settled **8** inherent, lifelong, profound, stubborn **9** confirmed, ingrained, intrinsic **10** congenital, entrenched, indwelling, inveterate **11** established **12** longstanding **13** bred-in-the-bone, dyed-in-the-wool, thoroughgoing

deep-six
4 dump, toss **5** chuck, scrap **7** discard, unload **8** jettison **9** eliminate

deep water
7 trouble **8** distress **10** difficulty

deer
3 elk, roe **4** buck, musk, stag **5** moose **6** wapiti **7** caribou, venison
Asian: 4 axis **6** sambar **7** muntjac
British: 4 hart
female: 3 doe **4** hind
Japanese: 4 sika
male: 4 buck, hart, stag **7** roebuck
meat: 5 jerky **7** venison
path: 3 run **5** trail
red: 7 brocket
relating to: 7 cervine
track: 4 slot **5** spoor
young: 3 kid **4** fawn

Deerslayer (The)
author: 6 Cooper (James Fenimore)
character: 5 Harry (Hurry) **6** Hutter (Thomas), Judith (Hutter) **11** Natty Bumppo **12** Chingachgook

deface
3 mar **4** harm, ruin **6** damage, deform, impair, injure **9** disfigure, vandalize

de facto
6 actual, really **8** actually, existing

defalcation
7 default, failing, failure **10** embezzling, inadequacy, negligence **12** embezzlement

defamation
5 libel, smear **7** calumny, obloquy, slander **10** backbiting **11** traducement **12** backstabbing **13** disparagement

defamatory
8 libelous **9** maligning, traducing, vilifying **10** backbiting, calumnious, slanderous **11** denigrating

defame
5 abase, libel, smear **6** malign, vilify **7** asperse, blacken, blemish, slander, traduce **8** dishonor **9** denigrate, discredit **10** calumniate

default
4 fail **5** welsh **7** absence, exclude, failure, forfeit, neglect **9** selection

defeasance
4 deed **6** defeat **9** overthrow **11** termination

defeat
3 tan **4** beat, best, down, drub, edge, foil, lick, loss, rout, sink, undo, whip, whup **5** crush, outdo, skunk, swamp, upset, waste, whomp **6** outgun, reduce, subdue, wallop **7** beating, conquer, destroy, failure, licking, mow down, nose out, nullify, outplay, overrun, setback, shellac, trounce, wipe out **8** knock out, outfight, outflank, overcome, vanquish, waterloo **9** frustrate, overpower, overthrow, overtrump, subjugate, thrashing, trouncing **10** obliterate **11** shellacking

defeatist
8 doomster **9** doomsayer, Gloomy Gus, pessimist, worrywart

defect
3 bug **4** flaw, lack, vice, want **5** botch, error, fault **6** damage, dearth, desert, foible, injury **7** blemish, default, failing **8** drawback, weakness **9** birthmark, deformity **10** apostatize, deficiency **11** shortcoming **12** imperfection, tergiversate
timber: 4 knot
visual: 6 myopia, squint **9** amblyopia, hyperopia **10** presbyopia, strabismus

defection
8 apostasy **9** desertion, forsaking, recreancy **10** disloyalty **11** abandonment

defective
5 amiss **6** broken, faulty, flawed **7** damaged, lacking, unsound, wanting **8** impaired **9** corrupted, deficient, imperfect

10 inaccurate, inadequate, incomplete
12 insufficient

defector
5 Judas 7 traitor 8 apostate, quisling, recreant, renegade, turncoat 9 turnabout
13 double-crosser

defend
4 back, hold, save 5 argue, cover, guard
6 screen, secure, shield, uphold
7 contend, justify, protect, support
8 advocate, champion, maintain, plead for, preserve 9 safeguard

defendable
see **defensible**

defendant
7 accused, libelee 8 libellee

defender
7 paladin, tribune 8 advocate, champion, guardian 9 protector 11 white knight

defense
4 fort, ward 5 aegis, alibi, armor, guard
6 excuse, sconce, shield 7 bulwark, rampart, shelter 8 apologia, armament, fastness, fortress, muniment, security
9 safeguard 10 protection, stronghold
11 exculpation, explanation 13 justification
organization: 4 NATO 5 NORAD, SEATO
10 Warsaw Pact

defenseless
4 open 7 exposed, unarmed 8 helpless, wide open 9 unguarded 10 vulnerable
11 unprotected

defensible
5 valid 7 tenable 8 passable 9 excusable, plausible 10 condonable, reasonable
11 justifiable

defer
3 bow 4 stay, wait 5 delay, remit, stall, table, yield 6 accede, hold up, put off, shelve, submit 7 hold off, lay over, put over, suspend 8 hold over, postpone, prorogue 9 acquiesce 13 procrastinate

deference
5 honor 6 esteem, homage, regard
7 respect 8 courtesy 9 obeisance
11 recognition

deferential
8 obliging 9 disarming, regardful
10 respectful 11 complaisant

defiance
4 dare 5 moxie 7 bravado 8 audacity, contempt 9 challenge, contumacy,

impudence, insolence 10 brazenness, effrontery 12 contrariness, stubbornness

defiant
4 bold 5 brash, gutsy, sassy, saucy
6 brazen, cheeky, daring 8 arrogant, impudent, insolent 9 audacious, obstinate, resistant 10 refractory 12 recalcitrant

deficiency
4 flaw, lack, want 5 fault, minus 6 dearth
7 absence, blemish, demerit, failing, failure, paucity 8 scarcity, shortage, weakness
9 privation 10 inadequacy, scantiness
11 defalcation, shortcoming
12 imperfection
mental: 6 idiocy 7 amentia

deficient
3 shy 5 minus, scant, short 6 faulty, flawed, meager, meagre, measly, scanty, scarce 7 failing, lacking, unsound, wanting
8 exiguous, impaired 9 defective, imperfect
10 inadequate, incomplete

deficit
4 lack, loss 6 red ink 8 shortage
10 impairment, inadequacy 12 disadvantage 13 insufficiency

defile
3 tar 4 foul, pass, rape, soil 5 dirty, gorge, march, shame, smear, spoil, stain, sully, taint 6 befoul, debase, ravish 7 besmear, corrupt, pollute, profane, tarnish, violate
8 deflower, dishonor 9 desecrate 11 contaminate

defiled
5 raped 6 impure 7 stained, unclean
8 profaned, polluted, ravished, violated
9 corrupted 10 deflowered, desecrated
12 contaminated

define
3 fix, hem, rim, set 4 edge 5 limit
6 assign, border, detail 7 clarify, delimit, lay down, mark off, mark out, outline, specify
9 delineate, demarcate, determine, establish 11 distinguish 12 characterize

definite
3 set 4 sure 5 clear, final, fixed, sharp, solid 7 certain, decided, express, precise, settled 8 clear-cut, distinct, explicit, specific 10 conclusive, pronounced
11 unambiguous, unequivocal
12 unmistakable

definiteness
8 accuracy, sureness 9 certainty, certitude, exactness, precision 10 exactitude

definitive
5 final **7** express **8** clear-cut, complete,
explicit, settling, specific, ultimate
10 concluding, conclusive, exhaustive
11 categorical, determining, unambiguous
13 authoritative

deflate
4 dash **6** humble, reduce, shrink
7 devalue, put down **8** contract, ridicule
9 humiliate, shoot down

deflect
5 avert, parry **6** divert **7** deviate, diverge,
hold off **9** turn aside

deflection
3 yaw **4** bend, tack, turn, veer **5** carom,
curve, shift **6** double, swerve **7** bending,
rebound, turning, veering **8** swerving
9 departure, deviation, diversion
10 divergence

deflower
4 rape **5** spoil **6** defile, ravish **7** despoil,
violate **9** desecrate

Defoe, Daniel
character: 6 Crusoe (Robinson), Friday,
Roxana **12** Moll Flanders

deform
4 warp **5** spoil **6** deface **7** contort, distort
8 misshape **9** disfigure

deformed
4 awry, bent **5** askew, bowed **6** warped
7 buckled, crooked **8** crippled **9** contorted,
misshapen, unshapely

deformity
4 flaw **6** defect **7** blemish **11** abnormality
12 imperfection, irregularity, malformation
13 disfigurement

_____ de France
3 Île

defraud
3 con, gyp **4** bilk, dupe, rook, scam
5 cheat, cozen, mulct, trick **6** fleece, rip off
7 swindle **8** flimflam **9** bamboozle

deft
3 apt **4** able **5** adept, agile, handy
6 adroit, clever **7** skilled **8** dextrous, skillful
9 dexterous

deftness
5 knack, skill **7** address, prowess **8** facility
9 adeptness, dexterity **10** capability

defunct
4 cold, dead, late **5** kaput **7** extinct
8 deceased, departed, lifeless, vanished

defy
4 dare, face, gibe, jeer, mock **5** beard,
brave, flout, stump **6** resist **7** affront,
outdare, outface **8** confront **9** challenge,
disregard, withstand

dégagé
6 breezy, casual **7** relaxed, unfussy
8 informal **9** easygoing **10** nonchalant,
unreserved **13** unconstrained

degeneracy
see **degeneration**

degenerate
4 sink **6** rotten, sunken, worsen **7** corrupt,
debased, decayed, decline, descend,
immoral, pervert, vicious, vitiate
8 decadent, degraded, depraved
9 backslide, dissolute **11** deteriorate

degeneration
7 atrophy, decline **8** downfall, lowering
9 decadence, depravity, downgrade
10 debasement, perversion, regression
11 degradation **12** dégringolade
13 deterioration

degradation
4 fall **7** decline, descent **8** demotion
9 abasement, decadence, depravity,
downgrade, reduction **10** corruption,
debasement, degeneracy, perversion
11 downgrading **12** degeneration

degrade
4 bump, bust **5** abase, break, decry, lower
6 debase, demean, demote, impair, lessen,
reduce **7** corrupt, declass, pervert, put
down **8** belittle, cast down, derogate,
diminish **9** decompose, discredit,
disparage, downgrade, humiliate

degree
3 peg **4** heat, rank, rate, rung, step, term,
tier **5** grade, honor, notch, order, pitch,
point, ratio, scale, shade, stage, stair
6 amount, extent, status **7** measure,
station **8** standing **9** dimension, intensity,
magnitude **10** proportion
academic: 3 BFA, BSc, DDS, LLB, LLD,
LLM, MBA, MFA, MSc, PhD **5** MPhil
7 master's **9** bachelor's, doctorate
highest: 8 cum laude **13** magna cum
laude, summa cum laude
of combining power: 7 valence
of height: 5 grade
of importance: 7 caliber, calibre
of outward slope: 5 splay
seeker: 9 candidate
slight: 4 hair
utmost: 4 acme

dégringolade
see **degeneration**

_____ de guerre
3 nom

dehydrate
3 dry 4 sear 5 parch 9 desiccate,
exsiccate

Deianira
brother: 8 Meleager
father: 6 Oeneus
husband: 8 Heracles, Hercules
mother: 7 Althaea
victim: 8 Heracles, Hercules

deific
5 godly 6 divine 7 godlike

deification
8 idolatry 10 apotheosis, glorifying
13 glorification

deify
5 exalt 7 glorify, idolize, worship
8 sanctify, venerate 11 apotheosize

deign
5 stoop 7 descend 9 vouchsafe
10 condescend

Deiphobus
brother: 5 Paris 6 Hector
father: 5 Priam
mother: 6 Hecuba
wife: 5 Helen

Deirdre
beloved: 5 Noisi
father: 5 Felim

deity
3 god 4 Lord 7 goddess, godhead,
godhood 8 Almighty, divinity 12 supreme
being
(see also at **Greek; Hindu; Norse;
Roman**)

deject
5 chill, cloud, daunt 6 dampen, dismay
7 depress 8 dispirit 9 disparage
10 demoralize, discourage, dishearten

dejected
3 low, sad 4 blue, down, glum, sunk
6 gloomy, morose, somber, sombre
7 doleful, hangdog, humbled, unhappy
8 downcast, wretched 9 cheerless,
depressed, woebegone 10 despondent,
spiritless 11 crestfallen, downhearted
12 disconsolate, disheartened

dejection
5 dumps, gloom 7 despair, sadness
10 melancholy 11 despondency,
unhappiness 12 mournfulness

Delaware
capital: 5 Dover
city: 10 Wilmington
nickname: 5 First (State) 7 Diamond
(State)
state bird: 14 blue hen chicken
state flower: 12 peach blossom
state tree: 13 American holly

delay
3 lag 4 drag, hold, slow, stay, wait 5 dally,
defer, stall, tarry, trail 6 dawdle, detain,
hang up, hinder, holdup, impede, linger,
loiter, put off, retard, slow up 7 bog down,
hold off, respite, set back, slacken,
suspend 8 hesitate, hold over, postpone,
prorogue, reprieve, slow down 10 dillydally, moratorium, suspension
13 procrastinate

delaying
8 dawdling, dilatory 10 postponing, putting
off

delectable
5 tasty, yummy 6 choice, savory
8 charming, heavenly, luscious, pleasing
9 ambrosial, delicious, enjoyable, exquisite,
toothsome 10 delightful, enchanting
11 scrumptious 13 mouthwatering

delectation
3 fun, joy 4 zest 5 gusto 6 relish 7 delight
8 gladness, pleasure 9 enjoyment

delegate
4 name, send 5 agent, envoy, proxy
6 assign, depute, deputy, legate 7 appoint,
consign, entrust 8 deputize, emissary,
transfer 9 authorize, catchpole, designate,
spokesman 10 commission, mouthpiece,
procurator

delete
4 drop, omit, x out 5 erase, purge
6 cancel, censor, cut out, efface, excise,
remove 7 blot out, destroy, expunge, take
out, wipe out 8 black out, cross out
9 eliminate, eradicate, strike out 10 blue-
pencil, obliterate

deleterious
3 bad 6 nocent 7 baneful, harmful, hurtful,
noxious, noxious, ruinous 8 damaging,
injurious 10 pernicious 11 destructive,
detrimental, mischievous, prejudicial

deletion
7 erasure, voiding 9 canceling

deliberate
10 deficiency 11 elimination 12 cancellation

deliberate
4 chaw, cool, muse, pore, slow 5 chary, meant, study, think, weigh 6 chew on, ponder, reason 7 careful, heedful, planned, reflect, studied, willful, willing, witting 8 cautious, cogitate, consider, intended, measured, meditate, mull over, ruminate, talk over 9 cerebrate, conscious, unhurried 10 calculated, considered, purposeful, thought-out 11 circumspect, intentional 12 premeditated

deliberately
9 knowingly, on purpose, purposely, willfully, wittingly 11 consciously 12 purposefully 13 intentionally

deliberation
5 study 6 debate 7 thought 10 conference, discussion, reflection 13 consideration

Delibes, Léo
ballet: 6 Sylvia 8 Coppélia, La Source
opera: 5 Lakmé

delicacy
5 goody, treat 6 dainty, luxury, morsel, nicety, tidbit 7 frailty 8 kickshaw, fineness 9 fragility, precision 10 daintiness, difficulty, indulgence, stickiness 11 awkwardness 12 ticklishness

delicate
4 fine, lacy, weak 5 frail 6 choice, dainty, flimsy, petite, queasy, sickly, slight, subtle, tender, touchy, tricky 7 elegant, fragile, refined, tactful, tenuous 8 ethereal, feathery, finespun, gossamer, graceful, pleasing, ticklish 9 exquisite, sensitive, squeamish 10 precarious

delicatessen
11 charcuterie

delicious
5 tasty, yummy 6 choice, divine, savory 8 heavenly, luscious 9 ambrosial, exquisite, toothsome 10 delectable, delightful 11 scrumptious 13 mouthwatering

delight
3 joy 4 glee 5 amuse, bliss, charm, enjoy, exult, glory, mirth, revel 6 divert, please, regale, relish 7 ecstasy, enchant, gladden, gratify, jollity, rapture, rejoice 8 enravish, entrance, fruition, hilarity, pleasure 9 delectate, enjoyment, enrapture, entertain 11 delectation

in: 4 love 5 adore, enjoy, savor 6 admire, relish 7 cherish 10 appreciate

delighted
4 glad 5 happy 6 joyful 8 ecstatic, euphoric

delightful
5 yummy 6 dreamy, lovely 8 charming, heavenly, luscious, pleasant, pleasing 9 congenial, enjoyable 10 delectable, enchanting, satisfying 11 captivating, fascinating, pleasurable, scrumptious 12 entertaining

Delilah's victim
6 Samson

DeLillo novel
5 Libra, Mao II 10 Underworld, White Noise

delimit
3 bar 5 bound, hem in 6 demark, define 7 confine, enclose 8 restrict 9 demarcate, determine 12 circumscribe

delineate
3 map 4 etch, limn 5 chart, image, trace 6 define, depict, detail, render 7 outline, picture, portray 8 describe, spell out 9 elucidate, interpret, represent 10 illustrate

delineation
5 draft, story 6 report 7 account, contour, drawing, outline, picture, profile 9 depiction, rendering 11 presentment

delinquency
4 debt 5 crime, fault, lapse 7 default, failure, misdeed, neglect, offense 8 omission 9 oversight 10 misconduct, nonpayment, wrongdoing 11 dereliction, misbehavior

delinquent
3 lax 5 slack 6 debtor 7 overdue 8 careless, offender 9 defaulter, in arrears, negligent 10 behindhand, neglectful

deliquesce
3 rot, run 4 flux, fuse, melt, thaw 5 decay 6 render, soften 7 liquefy, putrefy 8 dissolve, fluidize 9 decompose, disappear, waste away 12 disintegrate

delirious
3 mad 4 wild 5 crazy 6 crazed, insane, raving 7 frantic, lunatic 8 confused, demented, deranged, ecstatic, frenetic, frenzied, rambling 9 rapturous 10 bewildered, corybantic, distracted, irrational 11 lightheaded, overexcited, overwrought

delirium
5 furor, mania **6** fervor, frenzy **7** ecstasy, jimjams, rapture, seizure **8** dementia, hysteria **13** hallucination

delirium _____
7 tremens

deliver
4 bear, deal, feed, find, give, hand, save, send, ship, sing, take **5** bring, serve, speak, state, throw, utter **6** convey, redeem, rescue, strike, supply **7** consign, present, produce, provide, set free, release **8** hand over, liberate, turn over **9** pronounce, surrender **10** bring forth, emancipate **11** come out with, come through

deliverance
6 rescue **7** freeing, opinion, release, verdict **8** decision **9** acquittal, discharge, salvation **10** absolution, liberation

Deliverance author
6 Dickey (James)

delivery
4 drop **5** birth, labor **6** rescue **7** address, bearing **8** birthing, shipment **9** elocution, rendition, salvation **10** childbirth, conveyance, liberation **11** consignment, parturition, transferral **12** childbearing, transmission

dell
4 dale, glen, vale **6** dingle, hollow, valley

Delphic
4 dark **5** vatic **6** arcane, hidden, mantic, mystic, occult, veiled **7** cryptic, obscure **8** auguring, divining, esoteric, mystical, oracular **9** ambiguous, enigmatic, equivocal, prophetic, recondite, sibylline, vaticinal **10** mystifying, portentous **11** prophesying, prophetical

delta
5 plain **6** letter, symbol **7** deposit **8** triangle **9** increment

delude
3 con **4** dupe, fool, gull, hoax **5** bluff, cozen, trick **6** betray, humbug, juggle, take in **7** beguile, deceive, mislead **8** flimflam, hoodwink **11** double-cross

deluge
5 drown, flood, swamp **6** drench, engulf **7** Niagara, torrent **8** cataract, downpour, drencher, flooding, inundate, overflow **9** cataclysm, overwhelm **10** cloudburst, outpouring, inundation

delusion
4 hoax, sham **5** dream, fancy, snare **6** mirage **7** chimera, fallacy, fantasy, figment, phantom, specter **8** daydream, phantasm **9** deception **10** apparition **11** ignis fatuus **13** hallucination

delusive
5 false **8** fanciful, illusory, specious **9** beguiling, deceiving, deceptive, imaginary **10** chimerical, fallacious, misleading

delusory
see **delusive**

deluxe
4 lush, posh **5** grand, plush, ritzy, swank **6** choice, costly, swanky **7** elegant, opulent **8** luscious, splendid **9** expensive, exquisite, luxuriant, luxurious, sumptuous **10** first class

delve
3 dig, dip **4** mine **5** probe **6** dredge, fathom, hollow, quarry, search, shovel **7** inquire **8** excavate
into: 4 sift **5** probe **7** explore **8** prospect **11** investigate

delving
6 asking **7** inquest, inquiry, probing **8** research **9** inquiring, searching

demagnetize
7 degauss

demagogue
6 leader **7** inciter **8** agitator, fomenter **9** firebrand **10** instigator **11** provocateur **12** rabble-rouser

demand
3 ask, use **4** call, need, urge, want **5** claim, crave, exact, force, order **6** compel, direct, expect, insist **7** call for, request, require **11** requirement, requisition

demanding
4 hard **5** pushy, tough **6** taxing, trying **7** exigent, onerous, weighty **8** exacting, forceful, rigorous **9** assertive, difficult, insistent, strenuous, stringent **10** aggressive, burdensome, oppressive **11** challenging

demarcate
5 bound, limit **6** define, set off **7** delimit, mark off, outline **8** separate, set apart **9** delineate, determine **11** distinguish **12** circumscribe **13** differentiate

demarcation
9 outlining 10 border line, separation
11 distinction 12 delimitation

démarche
4 plan, ploy, ruse 5 feint 6 action, device,
gambit, scheme, tactic 7 protest 8 artifice,
maneuver, petition 9 stratagem
10 initiative 11 contrivance, machination

demean
4 bear 5 abase, carry, decry, lower
6 acquit, behave, debase, deport, humble
7 comport, conduct, degrade, detract
8 bad-mouth, belittle 9 disparage,
humiliate

demeanor
3 air 4 look, mien 6 aspect, manner
7 address, bearing, conduct 8 behavior,
carriage, presence 10 deportment
11 comportment

demented
3 mad 5 crazy, loony, nutty, wacko
6 crazed, insane, psycho 7 lunatic,
unsound 8 deranged, frenzied, maniacal
9 delirious 10 hysterical, unbalanced
12 psychopathic

_____ de mer
3 mal

demerit
4 mark 5 fault, stain 6 defect 7 blemish,
penalty 9 downgrade 10 deficiency,
punishment 11 shortcoming
12 imperfection

demesne
5 field, realm 6 domain, estate, region,
sphere 7 terrain 8 dominion, province
9 bailiwick, champaign, territory
house: 5 manor

Demeter
see Ceres

demigod
4 diva, idol 8 superman 9 superstar

demise
3 die, end 4 drop, pass 5 death, dying,
sleep 6 cash in, depart, ending, expire
7 decease, passing, quietus, release,
silence, succumb 8 pass away
9 cessation, departure 10 expiration,
extinction

demit
4 quit 6 bow out, give up, resign
8 abdicate, renounce, step down, withdraw

demiurgic
8 creative, original 9 formative, ingenious,
inventive 10 innovative 11 originative
12 innovational

demobilize
7 break up, disband, dismiss, scatter
8 disperse, separate 9 discharge,
disengage, muster out

democratic
7 popular 8 populist 10 self-ruling
11 egalitarian 13 self-governing

Democrats' symbol
6 donkey

démodé
5 dated, passé 7 antique, archaic 8 old-
timey, outdated 9 out-of-date 12 old-
fashioned

demoiselle
6 damsel, lassie, maiden 10 damselfish

demolish
4 raze, ruin 5 crush, level, smash, total,
wrack, wreck 7 destroy, flatten, wipe out
8 decimate, tear down 9 finish off
10 annihilate, obliterate

demolition
6 razing 8 leveling, wrecking 10 bulldozing
11 destruction 12 annihilation

demolition bomb
11 blockbuster

demon
3 imp 5 devil, fiend, genie, ghoul, jinni,
Satan 7 hellion, incubus 9 archfiend
Arabic: 5 afrit 6 afreet
female: 5 lamia 7 succuba, succubi
(plural) 8 succubae (plural), succubus

demonic
6 wicked 7 satanic 8 devilish, diabolic,
fiendish, infernal 9 possessed
10 diabolical

demonize
6 malign, revile, vilify 7 bedevil, censure,
slander 8 denounce 9 diabolize

demonstrate
3 try 4 mark, show, test 5 prove, rally
7 confirm, display, exhibit, explain, make
out, protest 8 evidence, manifest,
proclaim, validate 9 determine, establish
10 illustrate 12 authenticate

demonstration
4 expo, show, test 5 march, proof, rally,
trial 6 picket 7 display, protest 9 spectacle

10 exhibition, exposition, validation
12 presentation 13 corroboration, manifestation

demonstrative
4 open 8 effusive, outgoing, specific
9 emotional, expansive, exuberant, outspoken 10 outpouring, unreserved, validating 12 affectionate, unrestrained
13 unconstrained

demoralize
5 chill, daunt, shake, unman, upset
6 dampen, debase, deject, rattle, weaken
7 corrupt, debauch, deprave, unnerve, vitiate 8 dispirit, psych out 9 undermine
10 discourage, dishearten

Demosthenes
6 orator
oration: 9 Philippic

demote
4 bump, bust 5 lower 6 reduce 7 declass, degrade 9 downgrade

demulcent
4 balm 5 jelly, salve 7 unguent 8 liniment, ointment, soothing 9 softening

demur
5 qualm 6 object, oppose, resist 7 dispute, protest 8 question 9 challenge, hesitancy, objection 10 hesitation, indecision, reluctance 11 compunction, remonstrate

demure
3 coy, shy 5 timid 6 modest 7 bashful
8 reserved, reticent, retiring 9 diffident
11 unassertive 12 self-effacing

demurral
7 protest 9 challenge, objection
12 remonstrance 13 remonstration

demurrer
see **demurral**

den
4 base, cave, home, lair, room 5 study
6 burrow, cavern, hollow 7 dayroom, hideout, sanctum 8 hideaway, playroom
rabbit: 6 warren

denial
3 nay 6 heresy 7 refusal 8 disproof, negation, rebuttal 9 disavowal, rejection
10 abnegation, gainsaying, refutation
11 repudiation 12 renunciation

denigrate
5 decry, libel, smear, stain, sully 6 darken, defame, defile, impugn, malign, vilify
7 asperse, devalue, put down, slander,

tarnish, traduce 8 belittle, dishonor, tear down 9 discredit, disparage
10 calumniate, scandalize

denims
5 jeans 8 overalls 9 blue jeans, dungarees

denizen
5 liver 6 native 7 dweller, habitué, haunter, resider 8 habitant, occupant, resident
9 indweller, inhabiter 10 frequenter, inhabitant

Denmark
capital: 10 Copenhagen
city: 5 Århus 6 Ålborg, Odense
11 Helsingborg 13 Frederiksberg
island: 3 Fyn 7 Falster, Zealand
8 Bornholm 9 Sjaelland
monetary unit: 5 krone
neighbor: 6 Sweden 7 Germany
part of: 11 Scandinavia
peninsula: 7 Jutland
possession: 9 Greenland 12 Faroe Islands 13 Faeroe Islands
sea: 5 North 6 Baltic
strait: 5 Lille, Store 9 Langeland

denominate
3 dub 4 call, name, term 5 label, style, title
7 baptize, entitle 8 christen 9 designate

denomination
4 cult, name, sect 5 creed, faith, style, title
6 church 8 category, cognomen, religion
9 communion 10 persuasion
religious: 5 Amish 6 Mormon 7 Baptist
8 Lutheran, Moravian, Reformed
9 Adventist, Episcopal, Mennonite, Methodist, Unitarian 11 Pentecostal
12 Presbyterian, Universalist 13 Roman Catholic

denotation
4 name, sign 5 sense 6 import 7 meaning
10 indication, signifying 11 designation
13 signification, specification

denote
4 mark, mean, name, show 5 spell
6 import 7 add up to, betoken, express
8 announce, indicate 9 designate, represent

denouement
6 effect, result, upshot 7 outcome
10 conclusion 11 consequence, culmination

denounce
3 rap 4 skin 5 blame, blast, decry, knock
6 rebuke, scathe 7 censure, condemn,

de novo

upbraid **8** derogate, reproach **9** castigate, criticize, dress down, excoriate, reprehend, reprobate **10** denunciate, vituperate **11** incriminate **12** anathematize

de novo
4 anew, over **5** again, newly **6** afresh **8** once more **9** over again **11** from scratch

dense
4 dull, dumb **5** close, heavy, solid, thick, tight **6** obtuse, opaque, stupid **7** compact, crammed, crowded, doltish, serried **9** fat-headed, jam-packed **10** numskulled **11** blockheaded, numbskulled, thickheaded **12** impenetrable

dent
4 bash, ding, flaw, nick **5** tooth **6** dimple, hollow **10** depression, impression

denticulate
6 ridged **7** dentate, notched, serrate, serried, toothed **8** saw-edged, sawtooth, serrated **10** saw-toothed

dentin
6 enamel

denude
4 bare **5** strip **6** divest **7** disrobe, uncover, undress **8** unclothe

denunciate
see **denounce**

deny
5 cross, rebut **6** disown, forbid, negate, refuse, refute, reject, renege **7** disavow, gainsay **8** abnegate, disallow, disclaim, forswear, renounce, traverse, withhold **9** disaffirm **10** contradict, contravene

depart
3 die **4** exit, flee, pass, quit **5** leave, scram, split **6** begone, decamp, demise, desert, escape, expire, go away, go forth, move on, move out, perish, skidoo **7** decease, deviate, pass on, pull out, skiddoo, take off, vamoose **8** pass away, shove off, slip away, withdraw **9** skedaddle, take leave

departing
6 egress, exodus **7** good-bye **8** farewell **9** desertion **11** leave-taking, valedictory

department
5 arena **6** branch, domain, sphere **7** section **8** category, division, province **9** bailiwick, territory **11** subdivision

departure
4 exit **5** adieu, break, congé, going **6** egress, exodus, flight **7** leaving **8** farewell **9** deviation, diversion **10** aberration, decampment, deflection, divergence, embarkment, setting-out, withdrawal **11** embarkation, leave-taking
of a ship: 6 sortie
point: 7 outpost

dependable
4 sure, true **5** loyal, solid, tried **6** secure, steady, trusty **7** certain, staunch **8** accurate, constant, faithful, reliable, surefire **9** authentic, steadfast, unfailing **11** responsible, trustworthy **12** tried and true **13** authoritative
Scottish: 6 sicker

dependence
4 need **5** faith, habit, stock, trust **8** reliance **9** addiction **11** contingency, habituation

dependent
5 child **6** minion, vassal **7** reliant, relying **9** secondary **10** contingent, equivalent **11** conditional, subordinate

depend on
5 bet on, trust **6** bank on, hang on, look to, rely on, turn on **7** build on, count on, hinge on, stand on, swear by

depict
4 draw, limn, show **5** image, paint **6** relate, render, sketch **7** express, picture, portray **8** describe **9** delineate, represent **10** illustrate

depiction
5 image, sketch **7** drawing, picture **9** portrayal, rendering **11** delineation, portraiture, presentment **12** illustration, presentation

deplete
3 sap **4** milk **5** bleed, drain, eat up, empty, leech, use up **6** expend, lessen, reduce **7** consume, draw off, exhaust **8** decrease, diminish, draw down **9** undermine **10** run through

depleted
6 sapped, used up **7** drained, reduced **8** consumed, expended **9** exhausted, washed-out

deplorable
5 awful **6** rotten, woeful **8** dreadful, god-awful, grievous, terrible, wretched **9** execrable, miserable, sickening **10** calamitous, disastrous, lamentable **11** distressing, intolerable **12** contemptible,

disreputable, heartrending
13 heartbreaking, reprehensible

deplore
3 rue **5** abhor, mourn **6** bemoan, bewail, grieve, lament, regret **7** condemn **8** denounce, object to **9** deprecate **10** disapprove

deploy
3 use **5** array **6** muster, unfold **7** arrange, display, dispose, marshal, utilize **8** position

_____ de plume
3 nom

depone
5 state, swear **6** affirm, assert, attest **7** certify, confirm, declare, testify, warrant **11** corroborate **12** authenticate

deport
3 act **4** bear **5** carry, exile, expel **6** acquit, banish, behave, demean **7** conduct **8** displace, relegate **10** expatriate

deportee
5 exile **8** expellee

deportment
3 air, set **4** mien, port **6** aspect, manner **7** address, bearing, conduct, manners **8** behavior, carriage, demeanor, presence

depose
4 aver, avow, oust **5** state, swear **6** affirm, assert, avouch, remove, topple, unmake **7** declare, profess, testify, uncrown **8** dethrone, displace, throw out, unthrone **9** overthrow

deposit
3 lay **4** bank, drop, dump, fund, lees, pawn, save, stow **5** cache, chest, dregs, place, put by, stash, store **6** settle **7** consign, grounds, lay away **8** put aside, security, sediment, sock away **9** settlings **11** precipitate **13** precipitation
alluvial: 5 delta
black: 4 soot
calcium carbonate: 10 stalactite, stalagmite
containing gold: 6 placer
eggs: 5 spawn
geologic: 7 horizon
glacial: 4 till **5** drift, esker **7** moraine
loam: 5 loess
mineral: 4 lode **10** concretion
muddy: 6 sludge
sand: 4 bank **5** beach
sedimentary: 4 silt
skeletal: 5 coral

stolen goods: 5 fence
stream: 8 alluvium, sediment
tooth: 6 tartar

deposition
6 avowal **7** ousting, placing **9** affidavit, dismissal, testimony **10** testifying **11** attestation, declaration

depository
4 bank, dump, safe **5** attic, cache, depot, store, vault **7** archive, arsenal **8** magazine **9** warehouse **10** storehouse
for bones: 7 ossuary

depot
4 dump **5** cache, store **6** armory, garage **7** arsenal, station **8** magazine, terminal, terminus **9** warehouse **10** depository, repository, storehouse **12** station house

deprave
4 warp **6** debase **7** corrupt, debauch, pervert, vitiate **9** brutalize **10** bastardize, bestialize, demoralize

depraved
3 bad, low **4** base, evil, ugly, vile **6** putrid, rotten, wanton, warped, wicked **7** bestial, corrupt, debased, immoral, twisted, vicious **8** degraded, perverse, vitiated **9** corrupted, debauched, miscreant, nefarious, perverted, reprobate **10** degenerate

depravity
4 vice **8** baseness **9** abasement, decadence **10** corruption, debasement, debauchery, degeneracy, immorality, perversion **12** degeneration

deprecate
7 frown on, put down **8** belittle, derogate, disfavor, object to, play down, pooh-pooh **9** disparage **10** disapprove **12** disapprove of

depreciate
4 drop, fall **5** abate, decry, erode, lower **6** lessen, reduce, slight **7** cheapen, devalue, put down **8** belittle, decrease, derogate, diminish, discount, mark down, write off **9** devaluate, disparage, downgrade, underrate **10** devalorize, undervalue **11** detract from

depreciation
8 discount **10** denigration **12** belittlement **13** disparagement

depreciative
9 slighting **10** derogatory, detracting, pejorative **11** disparaging, underrating **12** undervaluing

depredate
4 sack 5 waste 6 ravage 7 despoil, pillage, plunder 8 desolate, lay waste, prey upon, spoliate 9 desecrate, devastate, vandalize

depredation
4 sack 5 havoc 7 pillage, plunder, sacking 8 ravaging 9 marauding, ruination 10 spoliation 11 desecration, destruction, devastation 12 despoliation

depredator
6 looter, raider 7 forager, spoiler, vandal 8 marauder 9 plunderer 10 freebooter

depress
4 damp, dash, dent 5 chill, daunt, lower 6 dampen, deject, dismay, sadden 7 afflict, trouble 8 dispirit, enfeeble 9 disparage, weigh down 10 discourage, dishearten

depressed
3 low, sad 4 blue, down, glum, sunk 6 broody, gloomy, glumpy, lonely, somber 8 cast down, dejected, downcast 9 bummed out, flattened, woebegone 10 dispirited, lugubrious, melancholy, spiritless 11 crestfallen, downhearted, melancholic 12 disconsolate 13 disadvantaged

depressing
3 sad 5 bleak 6 dismal, dreary, gloomy, somber, sombre 7 joyless 8 funereal, mournful 9 saddening 10 melancholy, oppressive 11 melancholic 13 disheartening

depression
3 dip, low, pit, sag 4 bust, drop, funk, hole, sink, vale 5 basin, blues, dolor, dumps, ennui, gloom, scoop, slump 6 cavity, crater, hollow, pocket, valley 7 cyclone, decline, sadness, sinkage 8 downturn, sinkhole, concavity, dejection 10 desolation, melancholy 11 melancholia, unhappiness
anatomical: 5 fossa, fovea 6 foveae (plural)
geographic: 7 Qattara
in ridge: 3 col
in snow: 8 sitzmark
small: 4 dent 6 dimple

depressive
4 blue, dour, glum 6 woeful 7 doleful 8 downbeat, downcast, mournful 9 miserable, woebegone 10 despondent, melancholy 11 low-spirited

deprivation
4 lack, loss 6 denial 7 forfeit, removal 10 forfeiture 11 bereavement, divestiture 13 dispossession

deprive
3 rob 5 strip 6 divest 8 disseise, disseize 10 disinherit, dispossess
of brilliancy: 4 dull 6 deaden
of courage: 7 unnerve
of sensation: 6 benumb

depth
4 base, drop, gulf 5 abyss, chasm, gorge 7 lowness 10 profundity
measure: 6 fathom
of water: 5 draft 7 draught

depthless
7 cursory, shallow, sketchy 10 uncritical 11 superficial

Dept. of _____
5 Labor, State 6 Energy 7 Defense, Justice 8 Commerce, Interior, Treasury 9 Education 11 Agriculture

deputize
4 name 6 assign 7 appoint, empower, warrant 8 delegate 9 authorize, designate 10 commission

deputy
4 aide 5 agent, proxy 6 backup, factor 8 delegate 9 assistant, catchpole, surrogate

derange
4 muss 5 craze, upset 6 madden, mess up 7 confuse, perturb, unhinge 8 confound, disarray, disorder, distract, unsettle 9 interrupt, unbalance 10 discompose 11 disorganize

deranged
3 mad 4 loco 5 crazy, wacko 6 crazed, insane, maniac 7 berserk, cracked, haywire, lunatic, unsound 8 demented, maniacal 9 disturbed 10 disordered, flipped out, unbalanced

derangement
4 mess 5 chaos, mania 6 lunacy, muddle 7 madness 8 dementia, disorder, insanity 9 confusion, unbalance 10 hodgepodge 11 distraction, disturbance, psychopathy

derby
3 hat 4 race 7 contest 9 horse race

derelict
3 bum 4 hobo, lorn 5 tramp 6 remiss, shabby 7 drifter, outcast, run-down, uncouth, vagrant 8 careless, deserted, vagabond 9 abandoned, negligent 10 neglectful 11 dilapidated

12 disregardful, undependable
13 irresponsible

dereliction
5 fault 7 default, failure, neglect
9 deviation, disregard, oversight
11 abandonment, delinquency, shortcoming

deride
3 rag, rap 4 gibe, jeer, jibe, lout, mock,
quiz, razz, twit 5 fleer, rally, scoff, scout,
sneer, taunt 6 dump on, insult 7 catcall
8 ridicule

de rigueur
5 right 6 au fait, decent, proper 7 correct
8 becoming, decorous, required
9 essential, mandatory, requisite
10 compulsory, obligatory, prescribed
11 comme il faut

derision
5 abuse, scorn 7 disdain, mockery, ribbing
8 contempt, raillery, ridicule, scoffing
9 contumely, invective

derisive
7 abusive, jeering, mocking 8 sardonic,
scoffing, scornful, taunting 9 insulting,
sarcastic 10 disdainful 12 contemptuous

derivable
7 a priori 9 deducible, deductive, traceable
10 obtainable 11 extractable
12 attributable, determinable

derivation
4 root 6 origin, source 7 descent
9 etymology 10 provenance, wellspring
11 origination, provenience

derivative
5 banal 7 spin-off 8 acquired, offshoot
9 by-product, imitative, outgrowth,
secondary 10 descendant, unoriginal

derive
3 get 4 draw, flow, rise, stem, take
5 adapt, arise, educe, infer, issue, trace
6 deduce, deduct, evolve, gather, obtain
7 descend, emanate, extract, proceed,
work out 8 arrive at, conclude 9 formulate,
originate

dernier cri
3 fad 4 chic, rage 5 craze, vogue 8 last
word

derogate
5 decry 6 berate, dump on, insult 7 put
down 8 bad-mouth, belittle, diminish,
minimize, write off 9 disparage, dispraise
10 depreciate 11 detract from

derogatory
5 snide 8 decrying, scornful, spiteful
9 degrading, demeaning, maligning,
slighting 10 belittling, detracting, disdainful,
pejorative 11 disparaging
12 contumelious, depreciative

derrick
5 hoist

derriere
3 bum 4 beam, butt, rear, rump, seat, tail
5 fanny 6 behind, bottom 7 rear end
8 backside, buttocks 9 posterior

derring-do
4 guts 5 nerve, pluck, spunk, valor
6 daring, mettle 7 bravado, bravery,
bravura, courage 8 boldness 9 gallantry
12 fearlessness 13 dauntlessness

dervish
4 monk, Sufi 9 mendicant
in Arabian Nights: 4 Agib
practice: 7 dancing 8 whirling
wandering: 5 fakir 8 calender

descant
4 sing 6 melody, remark, treble
7 comment, discuss, melisma, melodia,
oration, soprano 9 discourse, expatiate
12 counterpoint

Descartes's axiom
13 cogito ergo sum

descend
4 dive, drop, fall, pass, sink 5 slide, stoop,
swoop 6 alight, derive, go down, plunge,
worsen 7 decline 8 come down, dismount
9 originate 10 degenerate, retrograde
by rope: 6 rappel

descendant
4 heir 5 scion 7 progeny, spin-off
8 offshoot, relative 9 by-product, offspring,
outgrowth 10 derivative

descendants
4 seed 5 brood, heirs, issue, spawn 6 litter
7 progeny 8 children 9 offspring, posterity
11 progeniture

descent
3 dip 4 drop, fall 5 birth, blood, slide, slope
6 origin, plunge, tumble 7 decline, drop-off,
incline, lineage, sinkage 8 ancestry,
comedown, gradient, pedigree 9 declivity,
downgrade 10 derivation, devolution,
extraction
airplane: 8 approach
parachute: 4 jump 7 bailout

describe
4 limn 6 denote, depict, recite, relate,
render, report 7 explain, express, mark

out, narrate, outline, picture, portray,
recount **9** delineate, represent **10** illustrate
12 characterize

description
3 ilk **4** kind, sort, type **6** nature, report
7 account, picture, species **9** character,
depiction, narrative, portrayal
10 recounting

descry
3 see **4** espy, spot **6** behold, detect, spy
out, turn up **7** discern, find out, hit upon
8 discover, meet with, perceive
9 encounter, recognize

Desdemona
father: 9 Brabantio
husband: 7 Othello
slanderer: 4 Iago
slayer: 7 Othello

desecrate
4 sack **5** stain, sully, waste **6** befoul,
debase, defile, degrade, ravage **7** corrupt,
despoil, pillage, pollute, profane, violate
8 spoliate **9** depredate, devastate

desecration
5 abuse **7** impiety **9** blasphemy, sacrilege
10 debasement, defilement, spoliation
11 profanation **12** despoliation

desensitize
4 dull, numb **5** blunt **6** benumb, dampen,
deaden, freeze, sedate **11** anesthetize

desert
4 flee, quit **5** leave, waste **6** barren,
betray, decamp, defect, escape, maroon,
strand **7** abandon, abscond, badland,
forsake **8** renounce **9** repudiate,
wasteland **10** apostatize, wilderness
12 tergiversate
African: 5 Namib **6** Libyan, Sahara
7 Arabian **8** Kalahari
Arizona: 7 Painted
Asian: 4 Gobi, Thar **6** Syrian **7** Kara-Kum
8 Kyzyl Kum, Qizilkum **10** Great Sandy
basin bottom: 5 playa
beast: 5 camel **9** dromedary
California: 6 Mohave, Mojave
Chilean: 7 Atacama
clay: 5 adobe
dweller: 4 Arab **5** nomad **6** Berber,
Libyan, Malian, Nubian **7** bedouin
8 Algerian, Egyptian, Maghrebi, Maghribi,
Sudanese **11** Mauritanian
Egyptian: 7 Arabian
fertile area: 5 oases (plural), oasis
garb: 3 aba
hallucination: 6 mirage
Israeli: 5 Negev

region: 3 erg
Saudi Arabia: 7 Al-Nafud, An Nafud
Sudan: 6 Nubian
travel group: 7 caravan
wind: 7 sirocco

deserted
4 bare, lorn **6** barren, vacant **8** derelict,
desolate, forsaken, solitary **9** abandoned,
neglected **11** uninhabited

deserter
3 rat **4** AWOL **6** bolter **7** runaway
8 apostate, defector, fugitive, renegade,
runagate, turncoat

desertion
7 perfidy **8** apostasy **9** defection, forsaking
11 abandonment, dereliction

deserts
3 due **6** reward **8** requital **9** reckoning
10 recompense **11** comeuppance

deserve
3 win **4** earn, gain, rate **5** merit **6** demand
7 justify, warrant

deserved
3 apt, due **4** just **5** right **7** fitting, merited
8 rightful, suitable **9** befitting
11 appropriate **13** rhadamanthine

deserving
3 due **6** worthy **8** laudable **9** admirable,
estimable **10** creditable **11** commendable,
meritorious, thankworthy **12** praiseworthy

desiccate
3 dry **5** dry up, parch, wizen **6** wither
7 shrivel **9** dehydrate **10** devitalize

desiderate
4 want, wish **5** covet, crave **6** desire
7 long for, wish for **8** yearn for

design
3 aim **4** cast, draw, form, mean, mind,
plan, plot, will **5** chart, draft, frame, model,
motif **6** create, device, devise, figure,
intend, intent, invent, lay out, makeup, map
out, motive, scheme, set out, sketch, tailor
7 arrange, diagram, drawing, execute,
fashion, meaning, outline, pattern, prepare,
project, propose, tracing **8** contrive,
creation, game plan, intrigue, strategy,
thinking **9** blueprint, construct, delineate,
direction, formation, intention, invention
10 decoration, figuration **11** arrangement,
composition **12** architecture, construction
book: 8 vignette
carpet: 3 gul **9** medallion
incised: 8 intaglio

Indonesian: 5 batik
inlaid: 6 mosaic
intricate: 9 arabesque
of squares: 5 check
openwork: 8 filigree
perforated: 7 stencil
raised: 8 repoussé
skin: 6 tattoo
textile: 8 polka dot
velvety: 8 flocking

designate
3 dub, tap 4 call, name, pick, term 5 allot, elect, label, style, title 6 assign, choose, denote, depute, select 7 appoint, declare, earmark, reserve, signify, specify 8 allocate, christen, delegate, identify, set aside, stand for 9 apportion, stipulate 10 decide upon 11 appropriate 12 characterize

designation
4 name, sign 5 class, nomen, style, title 6 naming 8 cognomen, monicker 11 appellation

designed
7 devised, planned 8 intended, resolved 9 contrived, patterned 10 considered, deliberate, determined, thought-out 12 premeditated

designedly
9 expressly, knowingly, on purpose, purposely, willfully, wittingly 11 consciously, purposively 12 deliberately 13 intentionally

desirable
8 enviable, fetching 9 advisable, agreeable, preferred 10 attractive, beneficial 12 advantageous

desire
3 aim, yen 4 envy, eros, itch, lust, want, wish 5 covet, crave, fancy, go for, greed 6 pining, thirst 7 avarice, craving, long for, longing, passion 8 appetite, cupidity, petition, yearn for, yearning 9 eroticism, hankering, prurience, pruriency 10 aphrodisia, attraction, preference 11 inclination, lustfulness 13 concupiscence, lickerishness

desired
6 wanted 8 hoped-for 9 preferred, requested

desirous
6 greedy 7 athirst, craving, envious, longing, wishful, wishing 8 covetous, grasping 10 solicitous

desist
4 halt, quit, stop 5 cease, yield 7 forbear, hold off, refrain 8 knock off, leave off, surcease 11 discontinue

desistance
3 end 4 halt, stop 5 cease, close 6 ending, finish, period 8 stoppage, stopping 9 cessation 10 conclusion 11 termination

desk
5 booth, stand, table 7 counter, lectern, rolltop 8 lapboard 9 secretary 10 escritoire
adjunct: 8 inkstand, standish
item: 3 pad 7 blotter, inkwell
library: 6 carrel

desolate
4 bare, lorn, sack 5 alone, bleak, drear stark, waste 6 barren, devoid, dismal, dreary, gloomy, ravage 7 despoil, forlorn, joyless, finish, period, plunder 8 dejected, derelict, deserted, desolate, downcast, forsaken, lay waste, lifeless, lonesome, solitary, spoliate 9 abandoned, cheerless, depredate, desecrate, destitute, devastate, sorrowful 10 despondent 11 dilapidated 12 inconsolable 13 disheartening

desolation
3 woe 4 ruin 5 gloom, grief, waste 6 misery, sorrow 7 anguish, despair, sadness 8 bareness 9 bleakness, dejection, wasteland 10 loneliness 11 abandonment, devastation 12 wretchedness

despair
6 give up 8 lose hope

despairing
7 anxious, doleful, forlorn 8 dejected, desolate, hopeless, wretched 9 depressed 10 despondent 11 downhearted 12 disconsolate 13 brokenhearted

desperado
6 bandit, gunman, outlaw 7 bandito, brigand, convict, ruffian 8 criminal 9 cutthroat 10 gunslinger, highwayman, lawbreaker

desperate
4 bold, dire, rash 5 acute, risky 6 daring, futile 7 crucial, forlorn, frantic, useless, violent 8 critical, headlong, hopeless, reckless, shocking 9 foolhardy, impetuous 10 despondent, frustrated, outrageous, scandalous 11 climacteric, precipitate 12 overpowering 13 irretrievable

desperation
5 agony 7 anguish, despair 8 distress
11 distraction 12 hopelessness,
wretchedness

despicable
3 low 4 base, foul, grim, mean, ugly, vile
5 awful, cheap, gross, sorry 6 abject,
scurvy, shabby, sordid 7 beastly, hateful,
ignoble, pitiful 8 pitiable, shameful,
wretched 9 degrading, loathsome
10 deplorable, detestable 11 disgraceful,
ignominious 12 contemptible, disreputable
13 reprehensible

despise
4 hate, shun, snub 5 abhor, avoid, scorn,
spurn 6 detest, loathe, reject 7 contemn
8 execrate 9 abominate

despised one
6 pariah 7 outcast

despisement
4 hate 5 scorn 6 hatred, malice 7 disdain,
ill will 8 aversion, contempt, loathing
9 antipathy, contumely 10 abhorrence
11 detestation

despite
8 although 11 in the face of 12 regardless
of

despiteful
4 evil, mean 5 catty 6 bitchy, horrid,
malign, odious, wicked 7 baleful, baneful,
hostile, vicious 8 vengeful 9 malicious,
rancorous, repellent 10 despicable,
malevolent

despoil
4 sack 5 blast, strip, waste, wreck
6 denude, devour, maraud, ravage
7 pillage, plunder 8 desolate, spoliate
9 depredate, desecrate, devastate, strip
away, vandalize 10 wreak havoc

despoiler
6 looter, sacker, vandal 7 ravager, wrecker
8 marauder, pillager 9 plunderer, spoliator
10 depredator, freebooter

despond
4 fret, mope, wilt 5 brood, droop, worry
6 give up, sorrow 8 languish 9 dejection
12 hopelessness

despondency
5 blues, dumps, gloom 6 misery, sorrow
7 anguish, despair, sadness 8 glumness
9 dejection 10 depression, melancholy
11 desperation, unhappiness
12 hopelessness

despondent
3 low, sad 4 blue, down, glum 7 doleful,
forlorn 8 cast down, dejected, downcast,
grieving, hopeless, mourning 9 depressed,
desperate, heartsick, heartsore, sorrowful,
woebegone 10 dispairing, dispirited,
melancholy 11 discouraged, downhearted
12 disconsolate, disheartened

despot
4 czar, duce, tsar, tzar 5 ruler 6 tyrant
7 autarch, emperor 8 autocrat, dictator
9 oppressor, strong man

despotic
8 absolute 9 arbitrary, autarchic,
imperious, tyrannous 10 autocratic,
monocratic, tyrannical 11 dictatorial
12 totalitarian

despotism
7 czarism, tsarism, tyranny, tzarism
8 autarchy 9 autocracy 10 absolutism,
domination 12 dictatorship

desquamate
4 pare, peel 5 scale 7 peel off 8 flake off,
scale off 9 exfoliate

dessert
3 ice, pie 4 cake, flan, fool, tart 5 Betty,
bombe, crepe, crisp, fruit, grunt, halva, Jell-
O, melba, s'more, sweet, torte 6 afters,
blintz, Danish, éclair, fondue, frappe,
gâteau, halvah, hermit, junket, kuchen,
mousse, pastry, sorbet, sundae, trifle
7 brownie, cobbler, compote, custard,
gelatin, parfait, pudding, sabayon, sherbet,
soufflé, spumoni, strudel 8 ambrosia,
Bismarck, crostata, flummery, ice cream,
macaroon, meringue, napoleon, pandowdy,
streusel, tiramisu, turnover 9 charlotte,
cream puff, fruitcake, petit four, shortcake
10 blancmange, brown Betty, cheesecake,
frangipane, icebox cake, zabaglione
11 baked Alaska, banana split, crème
brûlée, gingerbread 12 hasty pudding,
zuppa inglese
French: 5 bombe 6 éclair, frappe, gâteau,
mousse 7 parfait, sabayon 9 petit four
10 blancmange, frangipane
frozen: 5 bombe 7 parfait, sherbet
German: 6 kuchen 7 strudel
Italian: 7 cannoli, spumoni 10 zabaglione
12 zuppa inglese
soft: 3 pud 7 pudding
Turkish: 5 halva 6 halvah

destination
3 aim, end, use 6 object, target 7 purpose
8 terminus 9 objective 10 appointing

destine
4 fate 6 assign, direct, intend 8 dedicate,
set aside 9 designate, determine,
preordain 10 foreordain 12 predetermine

destiny
3 lot 4 doom, fate 5 karma 6 design,
future, kismet, Moirai 7 fortune, portion
8 prospect 9 hereafter 12 circumstance

destitute
4 bare, poor, void 5 broke, empty, needy
6 bereft, devoid, ruined 7 drained, lacking
8 bankrupt, depleted, dirt poor, divested,
indigent, strapped, stripped 9 deficient,
exhausted, penurious 10 bankrupted,
stone-broke 11 impecunious
12 impoverished

destitution
6 penury 7 poverty 9 indigence, privation

destroy
3 axe, zap 4 doom, down, kill, nuke, raze,
ruin, sack, slay, undo 5 crush, erase,
quash, quell, smash, total, trash, waste,
wrack, wreck 6 finish, lay low, mangle,
ravage, rubble, rub out 7 abolish, atomize,
despoil, expunge, nullify, pillage, shatter,
wipe out 8 decimate, demolish, dispatch,
dynamite, lay waste, pull down, snuff out,
stamp out, tear down 9 devastate,
dismantle, eradicate, extirpate, liquidate,
pulverize 10 annihilate, extinguish
11 exterminate

destroyer
4 bane, ruin 6 tin can, vandal 7 undoing,
warship 8 downfall

destruction
4 loss, ruin 5 havoc 7 killing, sacking,
undoing 8 downfall 9 ruination
10 extinction 11 devastation, liquidation,
12 annihilation

destructive
7 baneful, harmful, ruinous 8 damaging
9 corrosive, injurious 10 shattering
11 deleterious, detrimental

desuetude
6 disuse 7 closure, neglect 9 cessation
11 abandonment

desultory
6 casual, chance, fitful, random, spotty
7 aimless, erratic, offhand, vagrant
8 shifting, slipshod, sporadic, wavering
9 haphazard, hit-or-miss, unplanned
10 capricious, digressive, disjointed
11 purposeless 12 unmethodical,
unsystematic

detach
4 free, part, undo, wean 5 sever 6 cut off,
remove, sunder 7 disjoin, divorce, release
8 separate, uncouple, withdraw
9 disengage 10 disconnect 12 disaffiliate

detached
5 alone, aloof, apart 6 remote 7 distant,
neutral, removed, severed 8 abstract,
isolated, separate, unbiased 9 incurious,
withdrawn 10 impersonal 11 indifferent,
unconcerned, unconnected 12 uninterested 13 disinterested, dispassionate,
unaccompanied

detachment
5 squad 7 divorce, rupture 8 disunion,
division 9 partition 10 neutrality,
separation 11 dissolution

detail
4 item, list, part 5 point 6 assign, nicety,
relate, report 7 appoint, article, element,
itemize, listing, minutia, specify 8 allocate,
spell out 9 enumerate, stipulate
10 assignment, particular 12 circumstance
13 particularize

detailed
4 full 6 minute 8 itemized, complete,
thorough 10 blow-by-blow, exhaustive,
meticulous, particular 13 thoroughgoing

detain
3 nab 4 bust, curb, hold, keep, mire, snag
5 check, delay, run in 6 arrest, collar, hang
up, hinder, hold up, impede, pick up, retard,
slow up 7 bog down, reserve, set back
8 hold back, keep back, restrain, slow
down, withhold 9 apprehend
10 buttonhole
in conversation: 10 buttonhole

detect
4 espy, find, spot 5 catch, dig up, hit on,
scent 6 descry, notice, turn up 7 discern,
hit upon, uncover, unearth 8 discover,
meet with 9 ascertain, encounter, ferret
out, track down

detectable
6 patent 7 evident, visible 8 sensible,
tangible 10 noticeable, observable
11 discernible, perceptible

detection

detection
9 discovery 10 unearthing
system: 5 radar, sofar

detective
4 dick, G-man 6 shamus, sleuth
7 gumshoe 8 hawkshaw, informer,
sherlock 9 inspector 10 private eye
12 investigator
fictional: 4 Chan (Charlie), Gray
(Cordelia), Moto (Mr.) 5 Banks (Alan),
Bosch (Harry), Brown (Father), Dupin
(Auguste), Lecoq, Lupin (Arsène), McGee
(Travis), Morse (Inspector), Queen (Ellery),
Rebus (John), Saint, Spade (Sam), Trent
(Philip), Vance (Philo), Wolfe (Nero)
6 Alleyn (Roderick), Archer (Lew), Carter
(Nick), Hammer (Mike), Holmes (Sherlock),
Marple (Miss Jane), McCone (Sharon),
Poirot (Hercule), Wimsey (Peter)
7 Campion (Albert), Charles (Nick, Nora),
Maigret (Jules), Marlowe (Philip)
8 Drummond (Bulldog), Millhone (Kinsey)
9 Dalgleish (Adam) 10 Robicheaux (Dave),
Warshawski (V. I.) 11 Father Brown

detective-story writer
3 Poe (Edgar Allan), Tey (Josephine)
4 Carr (John Dickson), Knox (Ronald)
5 Blake (Nicholas), Block (Lawrence),
Cross (Amanda), Doyle (Arthur Conan),
Green (Anna Katherine), Innes (Michael),
James (P. D.), Marsh (Ngaio), Queen
(Ellery), Stout (Rex) 6 Bramah (Ernest),
Buchan (John), Hansen (Joseph), McBain
(Ed), Mosley (Walter), Parker (Robert),
Peters (Ellis), Sayers (Dorothy L.)
7 Bentley (E. C.), Biggers (Earl Derr),
Collins (Wilkie), Francis (Dick), Freeman
(Austin), Gardner (Erle Stanley), Grafton
(Sue), Hammett (Dashiell), Hornung (E.
W.), Rendell (Ruth), Simenon (Georges),
Van Dine (S. S.), Wallace (Edgar)
8 Chandler (Raymond), Christie (Agatha),
Gaboriau (Emile), Marquand (John),
Paretsky (Sara), Rinehart (Mary Roberts),
Spillane (Mickey) 9 Allingham (Margery),
Hillerman (Tony), Lockridge (Frances,
Richard), Macdonald (Ross) 10 Chesterton
(Gilbert Keith)

detention
6 arrest 7 holding 10 internment
11 confinement 12 imprisonment

deter
5 avert, block 6 divert, hinder, impede,
thwart 7 forfend, inhibit, obviate, prevent,
rule out, shut out, ward off 8 dissuade,
preclude, restrain, stave off 9 forestall, turn
aside 10 discourage

deterge
4 wash 7 cleanse, wash off

detergent
4 soap 8 cleanser

deteriorate
3 rot 4 fade, fail, flag, sink, wear 5 decay,
lapse, slide, spoil 6 weaken, worsen
7 decline, regress 8 languish
9 decompose, fall apart 10 debilitate,
degenerate, depreciate, go downhill,
retrograde, retrogress 12 disintegrate

deterioration
4 ruin 5 decay 6 ebbing, waning
7 atrophy, decline, erosion, failing, rotting
8 decaying, spoiling 9 crumbling,
decadence, downgrade 10 debasement,
degeneracy 12 degeneration,
dégringolade

determinant
4 gene 5 agent, basis, cause, trait
6 factor, ground, reason 7 epitope, radical
9 attribute, influence

determinate
5 fixed 6 cymose 7 limited, precise,
settled 8 constant, definite 10 definitive,
restricted 11 established 13 circumscribed

determination
5 drive, spunk 6 fixing, mettle 7 finding,
opinion, purpose, resolve, verdict
8 decision, firmness, judgment, tenacity
9 assurance, hardihood, impulsion,
intention, resolving, willpower
10 conclusion, dedication, definition,
doggedness, resolution, settlement
11 decidedness, intrepidity
12 perseverance, resoluteness,
stubbornness 13 purposiveness

determine
3 fix, set 4 rule 5 bound, limit, prove
6 decide, figure, ordain, settle 7 control,
delimit, find out, mark out, measure,
preform, unearth 8 conclude, discover,
regulate 9 ascertain, demarcate, establish,
preordain, resolve on 10 delimitate,
foreordain, predestine, predispose

determined
3 set 4 bent 5 fixed 6 driven, intent
7 decided, earnest, serious, settled
8 decisive, hellbent, resolute, resolved,
stubborn 9 tenacious 10 persistent,
purposeful, unwavering 11 established,
persevering, unfaltering 12 foreordained,
unhesitating

detest
  4 hate 5 abhor, spurn 6 loathe 7 despise, dislike 8 execrate 9 abominate, repudiate

detestable
  4 foul, vile 6 damned, horrid, odious 7 hateful, heinous 9 abhorrent, execrable, loathsome 10 abominable, despicable 12 contemptible

detestation
  4 hate 6 hatred 8 anathema, aversion, loathing 9 repulsion, revulsion 10 abhorrence, execration, repugnance

dethrone
  4 oust 6 depose 7 uncrown 8 displace

detonate
  5 blast, burst, go off, spark 6 blow up, set off 7 explode 8 touch off

detonator
  3 cap 4 fuse 9 explosive 11 blasting cap

detour
  5 avoid, skirt 6 bypass 9 diversion

detract
  6 divert, lessen, reduce 8 decrease, diminish, minimize 10 depreciate

detraction
  9 aspersion, maligning, traducing 10 backbiting, belittling, derogation, slandering 11 denigration, deprecation, traducement 12 backstabbing, belittlement 13 disparagement

detractive
  9 maligning, slighting, traducing, vilifying 10 defamatory, derogatory, pejorative 11 denigrating, disparaging 12 depreciative, depreciatory

detriment
  4 harm, loss 6 damage, injury 7 marring 8 drawback 10 impairment 12 disadvantage

detrimental
  3 bad, ill 7 adverse, harmful, hurtful, nocuous 8 damaging, negative 9 injurious 11 deleterious, unfavorable

detritus
  4 tufa, tuff 5 scree, talus 6 debris, rubble 7 remains 11 odds and ends

Detroit
  county: 5 Wayne
  founder: 8 Cadillac (Sieur de)
  lake: 4 Erie 10 Saint Clair
  sobriquet: 6 Motown 9 Motor City

de trop
  5 extra, spare 7 too much, surplus 9 excessive, redundant 10 gratuitous 11 superfluous 13 supernumerary

Deucalion
  father: 10 Prometheus
  kingdom: 6 Phthia
  mother: 7 Clymene
  son: 6 Hellen
  wife: 6 Pyrrha

Deutschland über _____
  5 alles

Devaki's son
  7 Krishna

_____ De Valera
  5 Eamon

devaluate
  5 abase, decry, lower 6 reduce, weaken 7 cheapen, degrade 8 mark down, write off 9 undermine, underrate, write down 10 depreciate

devaluation
  7 decline 10 debasement, declension 11 declination

devalue
  see **depreciate**

devastate
  4 raze, ruin, sack 5 waste 6 ravage 7 despoil, pillage, plunder 8 demolish, desolate, lay waste, overcome, spoliate 9 depredate, desecrate, overpower, overwhelm

devastation
  4 loss, ruin 5 chaos, havoc, waste 6 ravage 7 pillage, plunder 8 disorder 9 confusion, ruination 10 demolition, desolation, spoliation 11 depredation

develop
  3 age 4 form, grow 5 occur, reach, ripen 6 attain, dilate, evolve, expand, grow up, happen, mature, mellow, open up, thrive, unfold, unfurl 7 achieve, acquire, advance, burgeon, enlarge, expound, promote 8 flourish 9 actualize, elaborate, establish, transpire 11 come to light, materialize

development
  5 phase 6 growth, result, spread 7 advance, buildup, outcome 8 ontogeny, progress, ripening 9 evolution, expansion, flowering, phylogeny, unfolding 10 maturation 11 elaboration, progression
  of life: 10 biogenesis

Devi
7 goddess
consort: 5 Shiva
father: 7 Himavat
name: 3 Uma 4 Kali 5 Durga, Gauri
6 Chandi 7 Parvati

deviant
4 bent 5 kinky, queer 6 off-key 7 twisted,
wayward 8 aberrant, abnormal, atypical,
perverse 9 anomalous, different, divergent,
irregular, unnatural 11 heteroclite

deviate
3 err, yaw 4 turn, vary, veer 5 sheer, stray
6 depart, swerve, wander 7 digress,
diverge 8 aberrant 9 eccentric, turn aside

deviation
3 yaw 4 bend, tack, turn 5 error, shift
6 change 7 anomaly, turning, veering
8 variance 9 departure, diversion
10 aberration, alteration, deflection,
divergence

device
4 ploy, tool 5 feint, gizmo, means, motif,
motto, shift, thing, trick 6 dingus, doodad,
emblem, figure, gadget, gambit, hickey,
jigger, medium, motive, symbol, widget
7 gimmick, machine, utensil, whatnot,
whatsit 8 artifice, creation, insignia
9 apparatus, appliance, doohickey,
expedient, implement, invention, makeshift,
mechanism, thingummy 10 instrument
11 contraption, contrivance, inclination,
thingamabob, thingamajig, thingumajig
automatic: 5 servo
binding: 5 clamp
fastening: 6 zipper
grasping: 4 tong
heating: 8 radiator
hoisting: 5 crane, lewis 8 windlass
holding: 4 vise 5 clamp

devil
5 beast, cloot, demon, fiend, rogue, Satan,
scamp 6 Belial, diablo, dybbuk, rascal,
spirit 7 Clootie, dickens, Lucifer, Old Nick,
serpent, tempter, villain 8 Apollyon,
Mephisto, scalawag, succubus
9 archfiend, Beelzebub, cacodemon,
scoundrel, skeezicks 10 blackguard, Old
Scratch 11 rapscallion

devilfish
3 ray 5 manta 7 octopus 8 manta ray
10 cephalopod

devilish
3 bad 4 evil 6 cursed, wicked 7 demonic,
hellish, roguish, satanic 8 accursed,
damnable, diabolic, fiendish, infernal,
sinister 9 nefarious 10 diabolical,
iniquitous, villainous 11 mischievous

devil-may-care
3 gay 4 rash, wild 6 rakish, sporty
7 raffish 8 carefree, rakehell, reckless
9 easygoing

devilry
7 knavery, roguery, sorcery, waggery
8 mischief 9 diablerie 10 wickedness,
witchcraft 11 roguishness, waggishness
12 sportiveness

devious
3 sly 4 foxy, wily 6 artful, crafty, errant,
erring, roving, shifty, sneaky, tricky
7 bending, crooked, cunning, curving,
erratic, winding 8 aberrant, guileful,
indirect, scheming, sneaking, twisting
9 deceptive, underhand, wandering
10 roundabout 11 out-of-the-way,
underhanded

devise
4 form, plan, plot, will 5 chart, forge, frame,
shape 6 cook up, create, design, invent,
legacy, legate, scheme 7 arrange,
bequest, concoct, connive, dope out,
dream up, hatch up, project 8 bequeath,
property 9 determine, formulate
11 inheritance

devitalize
3 sap 5 drain 6 deaden, weaken
7 exhaust 8 enfeeble 9 desiccate
10 eviscerate

devoid of
7 lacking, wanting 8 free from

devoir
3 job 4 duty, task, work 5 chore, stint
6 charge 9 committal 10 assignment,
commitment, obligation

devolution
5 decay 7 decline, passing 8 receding,
transfer 9 conferral, decadence, recession,
surrender 10 conveyance, declension,
degeneracy, regression, relegation,
transferal 11 degradation
12 degeneration, dégringolade,
retrograding, transference 13 retrogression

devolve
4 give, pass 6 pass on 8 hand down, hand
over, relegate, transfer 10 degenerate

devote
5 apply 6 commit, direct, donate, hallow
7 reserve 8 dedicate, give over, sanctify
9 confirm in, habituate 10 consecrate

devoted
4 dear, fond, true 5 loyal 6 ardent, caring, doting, fervid, loving 7 dutiful, fervent, zealous 8 constant, faithful 9 dedicated 10 thoughtful 12 affectionate
religiously: 6 oblate

devotee
3 fan, nut 4 buff 5 hound, lover 6 addict, votary, zealot 7 admirer, amateur, fanatic, fancier, habitué 8 follower 9 supporter 10 aficionado, enthusiast

devotion
4 love, zeal 5 ardor, piety 6 fealty, fervor, prayer 7 loyalty, passion 8 fidelity, fondness 9 adherence, adoration, reverence 10 allegiance, attachment, dedication, enthusiasm 12 faithfulness

devour
3 eat 5 eat up, enjoy 6 absorb, feed on 7 consume, destroy, feast on, pillage 8 prey upon, wolf down 9 delight in, feast upon, polish off, swallow up 10 annihilate

devouring
4 avid 6 greedy 8 esurient, ravenous 9 voracious 10 gluttonous

devout
4 holy 5 godly, loyal, pious 6 ardent 7 earnest, fervent, serious, sincere, zealous 8 faithful, reverent 9 pietistic, prayerful, religious

devoutness
4 zeal 5 ardor, piety 9 reverence 10 commitment

dew
5 sweat, tears 8 moisture 11 precipitate 12 perspiration 13 precipitation

dewy
3 wet 4 damp, pure 5 fresh, moist, naive 7 artless, natural 8 innocent, wide-eyed 9 credulous, guileless, ingenuous, unworldly

dexter
5 right

dexterity
4 ease 5 craft, grace, skill 7 ability, aptness, know-how, prowess, sleight 8 deftness, facility 9 adeptness, expertise, readiness 10 adroitness, nimbleness, smoothness 12 skillfulness

dexterous
3 apt 4 able, deft 5 adept, agile handy 6 adroit, artful, facile, nimble, smooth 7 skilled 8 masterly, skillful 10 proficient

_____ Dhabi
3 Abu

diablerie
7 devilry, roguery, sorcery, waggery 8 deviltry, iniquity, mischief, satanism 9 devilment 10 black magic, hellborn, witchcraft, wrongdoing 11 roguishness, waggishness 12 sportiveness

diabolical
4 evil 5 awful 6 impish, wicked 7 beastly, demonic, heinous, hellish, puckish, roguish, satanic 8 demoniac, devilish, dreadful, fiendish, god-awful, hellborn, infernal, rascally, sinister 9 execrable, malicious, monstrous, nefarious 10 degenerate, demoniacal, horrendous, iniquitous, scandalous, villainous 11 mischievous

diabolism
see **diablerie**

diacritic
5 acute, breve, grave, haček, tilde 6 macron, umlaut 7 cedilla 8 dieresis 9 diaeresis 10 circumflex
Arabic: 5 hamza 6 hamzah

diadem
5 crown 6 wreath 7 chaplet, coronal, coronet 8 headband

diagnose
4 spot 5 place 8 identify, pinpoint 9 determine, interpret, recognize 11 distinguish

diagnostic
8 analytic 10 analytical, expository, indicating, indicative 11 explanatory, exploratory 12 interpretive

diagonal
4 bias 5 bevel 6 biased 7 beveled, oblique, slanted 8 inclined, slanting 9 inclining, slantways, slantwise

diagonally
9 slantways, slantwise 10 cornerwise 11 catercorner, kitty-corner

diagram
3 map 5 chart, design, graph 6 layout, sketch 7 drawing, isotype 9 represent

dial
4 call, face, knob, tune, turn 5 phone 6 rotate 7 control 10 manipulate

dialect
4 cant, jive 5 argot, idiom, koine, lingo, slang 6 creole, jargon, patois, patter, pidgin, speech, tongue 8 language, localism 10 vernacular 11 regionalism, terminology 13 provincialism

Georgia: 6 Gullah
London: 7 cockney

dialectic

5 logic **6** debate **8** dialogue, forensic
9 reasoning **10** discussion **11** disputation
13 argumentation, investigation

dialogue

4 chat, talk **6** confer, parley, script
8 colloquy, converse **12** conversation
13 confabulation

diameter

4 bore **5** chord, width **7** breadth, caliber
8 bisector, wideness **9** broadness

diametric

7 counter, opposed **8** contrary, converse,
opposite **12** antithetical **13** contradictory

diamond

3 gem **5** field, stone
element: 6 carbon
famous: 4 Hope, Pitt **5** Sancy **6** Orloff,
Regent **8** Braganza, Cullinan, Kohinoor
9 Excelsior **10** Great Mogul
inferior: 4 bort
oval: 9 briolette
pattern: 6 argyle
playing card: 7 lozenge
state: 8 Delaware
surface: 5 facet

Diana

see **Artemis**

diapason

4 peal, stop **5** range, scale, scope
7 compass, measure **8** spectrum
10 tuning fork

diaper

5 nappy **7** pattern **8** ornament

diaphanous

5 filmy, gauzy, sheer, vague **6** flimsy
8 ethereal, gossamer **11** transparent
13 insubstantial

diaphragm

4 stop **6** septum **8** membrane **9** partition

diarist

4 Gide (André) **5** Frank (Anne), Pepys
(Samuel), Scott (Walter), Swift (Jonathan),
Woolf (Virginia) **6** Burney (Fanny), Evelyn
(John) **7** Boswell (James) **8** Robinson
(Henry Crabb) **10** chronicler, journalist

diary

3 log **6** record **7** daybook, diurnal, journal,
logbook **8** notebook, register **9** chronicle

diastase

6 enzyme **8** catalyst, reactant

diatribe

6 tirade **7** polemic **8** harangue, jeremiad
9 criticism, philippic **11** castigation
12 denunciation

dibs

4 gelt **5** claim, dough, money, title **6** rights
11 reservation

dice

4 cast, cube **5** bones, cubes, ivory, mince
11 devil's-bones
game: 5 craps
losing throw: 7 missout
singular: 3 die
throw: 7 boxcars **9** snake eyes

dicer

5 loser, risker **7** gambler

dicey

4 iffy **5** risky **6** chancy, tricky **8** ticklish
9 uncertain, whimsical **10** precarious,
problematic, speculative **13** unpredictable

dichotomize

5 halve **7** dissect **8** hemisect **9** bifurcate

dichotomous

5 split **6** forked **7** pronged **9** bifurcate
10 bifurcated

dichotomy

7 forking **8** division **9** bisection, branching,
splitting **11** bifurcation **13** contradiction

Dickens, Charles

birthplace: 10 Portsmouth
captain: 6 Cuttle
character: 3 Ada (Clare), Pip, Tim **4** Dick
(Mr.), Dora, Gamp (Sairey), Heep (Uriah),
Nell **5** Drood (Edwin), Emily, Fagin, Lucie
(Manette), Sikes (Bill) **6** Barkis, Bumble
(Mr.), Carton (Sydney), Cuttle (Capt.),
Darnay (Charles), Dombey (Fanny,
Florence, Paul), Dorrit (Amy), Oliver (Twist)
7 Barnaby (Rudge), Dedlock (Lady),
Defarge, Gargery (Joe), Manette (Dr.),
Scrooge (Ebenezer), Tiny Tim **8** Cratchit
(Bob), Havisham (Miss), Jarndyce (John),
Magwitch (Abel), Micawber (Mr.), Nickleby
(Nicholas), Peggotty (Clara, Daniel, Ham),
Pickwick (Mr.) **9** Bill Sikes, Gradgrind (Mr.),
Murdstone (Mr.), Pecksniff (Mr.), Uriah
Heep **10** Chuzzlewit (Anthony, Jonas,
Martin), Steerforth **11** Copperfield (David)
hero: 6 Carton (Sydney)
nationality: 7 English
pen name: 3 Boz

villain: 5 Fagin
work: 9 Hard Times **10** Bleak House
11 Oliver Twist **12** Barnaby Rudge,
Dombey and Son, Little Dorrit
14 Christmas Carol (A), Pickwick Papers
(The) **15** Our Mutual Friend, Tale of Two
Cities (A) **16** David Copperfield, Martin
Chuzzlewit, Nicholas Nickleby **17** Great
Expectations

dicker
4 deal, swap **5** argue, trade **6** barter,
haggle, higgle, palter **7** bargain, chaffer
8 contract, huckster **9** negotiate

dickey
10 shirtfront

Dickey novel
11 Deliverance

dictate
3 set **4** lead, rule, word **5** edict, order,
tenet **6** behest, decree, direct, enjoin,
govern, impose, ordain, recite **7** bidding,
command, control, lay down, mandate,
read off, summons **9** determine, direction,
directive, prescribe, principle, pronounce,
verbalize **10** injunction **12** prescription

dictative
5 bossy **8** despotic, dogmatic **9** imperious
10 peremptory **11** doctrinaire, magisterial
13 authoritarian

dictator
4 czar, duce **6** caesar, despot, tyrant
8 autocrat, martinet **9** oppressor,
strongman
German: 6 Hitler (Adolf)
Italian: 9 Mussolini (Benito)
military: 8 caudillo
Spanish: 6 Franco (Francisco)

dictatorial
5 bossy **8** despotic, dogmatic **9** arbitrary,
imperious, masterful **10** autocratic, ironhanded, peremptory, tyrannical
11 doctrinaire, domineering, overbearing
12 totalitarian **13** authoritarian

dictatorship
7 tyranny **9** autocracy, Caesarism,
despotism, supremacy **10** absolutism

diction
6 phrase, speech **7** wordage, wording
8 delivery, language, parlance, phrasing,
rhetoric, verbiage **9** elocution, verbalism
11 enunciation, phraseology

dictionary
7 lexicon **8** glossary, wordbook
10 repository **13** reference book

compiler: 7 Johnson (Samuel), Webster
(Noah) **13** lexicographer
geographical: 9 gazetteer
of synonyms: 8 thesauri (plural)
9 thesaurus

dictum
4 fiat **5** adage, axiom, edict, maxim, moral
6 ruling **7** mandate, opinion, precept,
proverb **11** declaration **13** pronouncement

didactic
5 moral **6** teachy **7** donnish, preachy
8 advisory, edifying, pedantic, sermonic,
teaching **9** hortative, pedagogic, teacherly
10 moralizing **11** informative, instructive

diddle
3 con, gyp, toy **4** beat, bilk, dupe, hoax,
fool, idle, laze, loaf, loll, rook, scam
5 cheat, cozen, delay, drone, trick **6** chisel,
chouse, dabble, dawdle, delude, fiddle,
fleece, loiter, lounge, rope in, take in
7 deceive, defraud, goof off, mislead,
swindle **8** flimflam, fool with, hoodwink,
lollygag **9** bamboozle, overreach,
victimize, waste time **10** dilly-dally, fool
around, hang around

diddler
3 gyp **4** sham **5** cheat, faker, fraud, rogue
6 con man **7** grifter, shammer, sharper
8 swindler **9** con artist, defrauder, trickster
11 flimflammer **12** double-dealer
13 confidence man

dido
4 jest, lark **5** antic, caper, curio, frill, prank
6 bauble, frolic, gewgaw, trifle, whimsy
7 bibelot, novelty, trinket **8** furbelow,
gimcrack, kickshaw, mischief **9** bagatelle,
plaything **10** knickknack, tomfoolery

Dido
6 Elissa
brother: 9 Pygmalion
city founded by: 8 Carthage
father: 5 Belus **8** Mutton
husband: 7 Acerbas **8** Sichaeus
lover: 6 Aeneas

Dido and Aeneas composer
7 Purcell (Henry)

die
4 drop, fall, mold, pass, stop, wane
5 cease, croak **6** cash in, demise, expire,
go west, matrix, pass on, peg out, perish,
pop off **7** decease, go south, kick off, snuff
it, succumb **8** cash it in, check out, drop
dead, pass away **9** disappear **10** buy the
farm **12** join the choir **13** kick the bucket

from hunger: 6 starve
loaded: 6 fulham

_____ die
4 sine

diehard
7 devoted, fanatic **8** true-blue **9** dogmatist
10 determined **11** bitter-ender, doctrinaire,
reactionary, standpatter **12** conservative,
intransigent **13** stick-in-the-mud

_____ diem
3 per **5** carpe

Dies _____
4 Irae

diet
4 eats, fare, fast, feed, menu **6** ration,
reduce, regime **7** regimen **8** assembly,
victuals **10** parliament **11** legislature,
nourishment

Diet of _____
5 Worms **6** Speyer, Spires **8** Augsburg

Dieu _____ (British motto)
10 et mon droit

_____-dieu
4 prie

differ
4 vary **5** demur **7** deviate **8** disagree

difference
7 discord, dispute, dissent **8** conflict,
contrast, variance **9** departure, deviation,
disparity, otherness, variation
10 dissension, divergence, unlikeness
11 controversy, discrepancy, distinction
12 disagreement **13** dissimilarity

different
5 other **6** divers, single, sundry, unlike
7 another, deviant, distant, diverse, several,
special, unalike, unequal, unusual, various
8 discrete, distinct, peculiar, separate
9 disparate, divergent **10** dissimilar, individual, particular **11** contrasting, distinctive

differentiate
4 vary **5** adapt **6** change, modify
8 contrast, separate, transform **9** diversify
11 distinguish, individuate **12** characterize,
discriminate

difficult
4 hard **5** tough **6** thorny, uphill **7** arduous,
awkward, labored, obscure, operose
8 exacting, perverse, puzzling, stubborn
9 demanding, effortful, herculean,
laborious, strenuous **10** refractory
11 problematic

difficulty
3 ado, fix, jam **4** beef **4** pass, snag
5 hitch, nodus, pinch, rigor, worry **6** bother,
hang-up, hassle, pickle, plight, scrape,
strait **7** dilemma, pitfall, problem, trouble
8 distress, hardness, hardship, hot water,
obstacle, quandary, quagmire, question,
squabble **9** adversity, bickering, challenge,
deep water, objection **10** falling-out,
impediment **11** aggravation, altercation,
arduousness, controversy, obstruction, predicament, vicissitude **12** complication,
disagreement **13** embarrassment,
inconvenience

diffidence
7 modesty, reserve, shyness **8** distrust,
meekness, timidity **9** quietness, restraint,
timidness **10** hesitation **11** bashfulness

diffident
3 shy **4** meek **5** timid **7** bashful
8 hesitant, reserved, retiring, timorous
9 reluctant, unassured **11** unassertive
12 self-effacing

diffuse
5 strew, wordy **6** prolix, spread **7** scatter,
verbose **8** disperse, rambling **9** broadcast,
dispersed, propagate, scattered, spreading,
spread out **10** distribute, long-winded,
widespread **11** disseminate, distributed

diffusion
6 spread **7** osmosis **9** broadcast,
dispersal, prolixity, spreading **10** dispersion, scattering **11** circulation,
propagation **12** broadcasting, promulgation

dig
3 jab **4** barb, grub, hole, like, mine, poke,
prod, root, site, stab **5** delve, ditch, enjoy,
gouge, nudge, probe, scoop, spade, taunt
6 burrow, plunge, quarry, relish, rootle,
shovel, thrust, trench, tunnel **7** explore,
root out, unearth **8** excavate, prospect
10 excavation **11** investigate
up: 6 exhume **7** unearth

digest
5 sum up **6** absorb, codify, précis
7 consume, stomach, summate, swallow
8 abstract, boil down, classify, compress,
condense, syllabus, synopsis
9 summarize, summation, synopsize
10 abridgment **12** condensation

digger
4 plow **5** miner **6** shovel **7** soldier

digit
3 toe **5** thumb **6** cipher, figure, finger,

number, pinkie **7** integer, numeral
9 character **11** whole number

dignified
4 prim **6** august, formal, proper, seemly
7 courtly, elegant, stately **8** cultured,
decorous, ennobled, polished **9** distingué,
patrician

dignify
5 adorn, exalt, grace, honor **7** ennoble,
elevate, glorify, sublime **11** distinguish

dignitary
3 VIP **4** lion **5** chief, nabob **6** leader,
worthy **7** notable **8** eminence, luminary
9 personage **10** notability **11** muckety-
muck **13** high-muck-a-muck

dignity
4 rank **5** honor, merit, poise, pride, worth
6 cachet, status, virtue **7** address,
decorum, gravity, hauteur, majesty, stature
8 grandeur, nobility, position, prestige,
standing **9** propriety **10** augustness,
seemliness **11** consequence, self-respect

digress
5 stray **6** depart, ramble, swerve, wander
7 deviate, diverge **8** divagate

digression
5 aside **7** episode, tangent **8** drifting,
excursus, rambling, straying **9** deviation,
wandering **10** deflection, divagation,
divergence **11** parenthesis

dig up
4 find **6** expose, reveal **7** nose out, root
out, uncover, unearth **8** discover **9** ferret
out, run across, search out, track down

dik-dik
8 antelope

dike
3 dam **4** bank **5** ditch, drain, levee
7 barrier **8** causeway **10** embankment
11 watercourse

dilapidate
4 ruin **5** decay, wreck **7** break up,
crumble, decline, neglect **9** break down,
decompose, disregard **10** deliquesce
12 disintegrate

dilapidated
5 dingy, seedy **6** beat-up, ragtag, ruined,
shabby **7** decayed, run-down **8** battered,
crumbled, decrepit **9** crumbling **10** broken-
down, down-at-heel, ramshackle
12 deteriorated

dilapidation
4 ruin **5** decay **7** atrophy **8** collapse,

decaying **9** crumbling, decadence,
disrepair **11** decrepitude **13** decomposition, deterioration

dilate
5 swell, widen **6** expand, extend
7 distend, enlarge, expound **9** discourse,
expatiate

dilatory
4 slow **5** slack, tardy **7** laggard **8** dallying,
delaying, sluggish **9** leisurely, lingering,
unhurried **11** time-wasting

dilemma
3 box, fix, jam **4** bind, hole, spot **6** choice,
corner, pickle, plight, scrape **7** catch-22,
problem **8** argument, quandary
10 difficulty **11** predicament

dilettante
4 tyro **7** amateur, dabbler **8** aesthete,
putterer **9** smatterer

dilettantish
see **amateurish**

diligence
4 zeal **8** industry **9** assiduity **10** commitment **11** application, persistence
12 perseverance, sedulousness
13 assiduousness

diligent
8 sedulous **9** assiduous **10** persistent,
persisting, unflagging **11** hardworking,
industrious, painstaking, persevering

dilly
4 lulu **5** dandy, doozy, peach **6** corker,
doozie, pippin, ripper, rouser **8** jim-dandy,
knockout **9** humdinger **10** ripsnorter
11 crackerjack

dillydally
see **delay**

dilute
3 cut **4** thin, weak **5** water **6** watery,
weaken **8** diminish, weakened
9 attenuate, water down **11** watered-down

dim
4 dull, dumb, hazy, pale, slow **5** befog,
blear, blind, cloud, dense, dusky, faint,
muddy, murky, muted, thick, vague
6 bleary, gloomy, stupid **7** becloud, low
beam, obscure, shadowy, subdued, unclear
9 tenebrous **10** ill-defined, indistinct,
lackluster, lusterless **11** unpromising

dime novel
4 pulp **7** chiller, shocker **8** dreadful, thriller
12 bloodcurdler **13** penny dreadful

dimension
4 size 5 reach, scale, scope, width
6 aspect, extent, spread 7 compass,
expanse, measure, quality 9 amplitude,
magnitude

diminish
3 ebb 4 bate, wane 5 abate, peter, quell,
taper 6 lessen, reduce, subdue, temper,
weaken 7 curtail, dwindle, subside
8 belittle, decrease, minimize, moderate,
restrain, taper off 9 attenuate, disparage,
dispraise 10 depreciate 11 detract from

diminishing
6 waning 8 receding 9 declining,
dwindling, lessening, subsiding, weakening
10 curtailing, decreasing 11 attenuating
12 depreciating

diminutive
3 wee 4 tiny 5 bitsy, dwarf, pygmy, small,
teeny, weeny 6 bantam, little, midget,
minute, peewee, petite, teensy
9 miniature, pint-sized, undersize
10 teeny-weeny 11 lilliputian 12 teensy-
weensy

_____ dimittis
4 Nunc

dimple
3 pit 4 dent, dint, fret, nick 5 notch
6 ripple 8 pockmark 10 depression
11 indentation

dimwit
3 oaf 4 clod, dodo, dolt, dope, fool, simp,
yo-yo 5 booby, chump, cluck, dummy,
dunce, idiot, moron, stupe 6 dum-dum
7 airhead, dullard, fathead, pinhead
8 bonehead, dumbbell, imbecile, lunkhead,
meathead, numskull 9 birdbrain,
blockhead, dumb bunny, dumb cluck,
ignoramus, lamebrain, numbskull,
simpleton 10 dunderhead, nincompoop
11 featherhead, knucklehead
12 featherbrain

dim-witted
4 dull, dumb, slow 6 stupid 7 doltish,
foolish, idiotic, moronic 8 backward,
imbecile, retarded 9 brainless, half-baked,
imbecilic 11 birdbrained, lamebrained
12 feebleminded, simpleminded

din
3 row 4 roar 5 babel, clash, noise
6 bedlam, clamor, deafen, hubbub, racket,
rattle, tumult, uproar 7 clangor, clatter,
resound 8 brouhaha 9 commotion,
stridency 10 hullabaloo, hurly-burly
11 pandemonium 13 clamorousness

Dinah
brother: 4 Levi 6 Simeon
father: 5 Jacob
mother: 4 Leah

dine
3 eat, sup 4 feed 5 feast 6 eat out
7 banquet, nourish

diner
4 café 5 eater 6 eatery 7 canteen
8 snack bar 9 hash house 10 coffee shop,
restaurant 11 greasy spoon 12 lunch
counter, luncheonette, sandwich shop

ding
3 mar 4 dent, nick 5 clang 7 blemish

ding-a-ling
3 nut 4 kook, yo-yo 5 flake, loony, wacko
6 cuckoo, nitwit, weirdo 7 lunatic
8 crackpot 9 fruitcake, harebrain,
lamebrain, screwball 10 crackbrain
12 scatterbrain

dinghy
5 skiff 7 rowboat, shallop 8 lifeboat, life
raft, sailboat

dingle
4 dale, dell, glen, vale 6 ravine, valley

dingus
5 gizmo 6 doodad, gadget, jigger, widget
7 whatsit 9 doohickey, thingummy
11 thingamabob, thingamajig, thingumajig

dingy
4 foul, mean 5 dirty, seedy, tacky 6 filthy,
grubby, grungy, scuzzy, shabby, soiled,
sordid 7 run-down, squalid, sullied,
unclean 8 begrimed

dinky
3 toy 4 tiny 5 small, teeny 9 undersize
10 locomotive

"Dinner _____"
7 at Eight

dinner
4 meal 5 feast 6 regale, repast, spread,
supper 7 banquet 8 luncheon 9 collation
10 table d'hôte
course: 4 meat, soup 5 salad 6 entrée
7 dessert 9 appetizer
jacket: 3 tux 6 tuxedo

dinosaur
6 fossil 7 has-been 8 theropod
11 anachronism

dinosauric

4 huge 5 passé 6 bygone 7 extinct,
mammoth 8 colossal, enormous, obsolete,
outmoded 9 cyclopean, leviathan, out-of-
date 10 antiquated, behemothic, fossilized,
gargantuan, mastodonic, oldfangled
11 elephantine 12 antediluvian, old-
fashioned, out-of-fashion 13 anachronistic

dint

4 nick 5 force, might, power 6 dimple, virtue
7 drive in, impress 10 impression
11 indentation

diocese

3 see 9 bishopric
Eastern Orthodox: 7 eparchy
subdivision: 6 parish

diode

9 rectifier 10 vacuum tube 12 electron
tube
component: 5 anode 7 cathode
9 electrode

Diomedes

city founded by: 4 Arpi
father: 4 Ares, Mars 6 Tydeus
foe: 6 Aeneas, Hector
slayer: 8 Hercules
victim: 6 Rhesus

Dione

5 Titan
cult partner: 4 Zeus
daughter: 5 Venus 9 Aphrodite
father: 7 Oceanus
lover: 4 Zeus
mother: 6 Tethys

Dionysus

see **Bacchus**

Dionyza's husband

5 Cleon

Dioscuri

5 twins 6 Castor, Gemini, Pollux
father: 4 Zeus 9 Tyndareus
mother: 4 Leda
sister: 5 Helen

dip

3 sag 4 bail, draw, drop, duck, dunk, fall,
lade, sink, skid, slip, slue, swim 5 basin,
ladle, lower, pitch, sauce, scoop, slope,
slump, spoon, stoop 6 go down, hollow,
plunge 7 decline, descend, descent, falloff,
immerse, sinkage 8 decrease, downturn,
sinkhole, submerge, submerse
9 concavity, declivity, downswing,
downtrend, immersion 10 depression

diphthong

7 digraph 8 ligature

diploma

6 degree 7 charter 8 document
9 sheepskin 10 credential

diplomacy

4 tact 7 address, finesse 8 delicacy
10 artfulness, discretion, statecraft
11 negotiation, savoir faire, tactfulness

diplomatic

4 deft 5 bland, suave 6 artful, astute,
polite, smooth, urbane 7 courtly, politic,
tactful 8 delicate, discreet 9 courteous
12 conciliating, conciliatory, paleographic
13 accommodating

diplomat's office

7 embassy, mission

diplopod

9 millipede

dipper

3 cup 4 bird 5 ladle, ouzel, scoop, stars
6 bucket 10 pickpocket, water ouzel

dippy

4 daft, zany 5 crazy, daffy, flaky, goofy,
kooky, loony, nutty, silly, wacky 6 stupid
7 doltish, foolish, witless 9 half-baked
11 harebrained 12 preposterous

dipsomania

10 alcoholism

dire

4 grim 5 acute, awful 6 dismal, horrid,
tragic, urgent, woeful 7 baleful, baneful,
crucial, extreme, fateful, ominous, ruinous
8 alarming, critical, dreadful, grievous,
horrible, horrific, menacing, shocking,
sinister, terrible 9 appalling, desperate,
frightful, ill-boding 10 calamitous,
deplorable, depressing, foreboding,
malevolent, oppressing, oppressive,
pernicious 11 apocalyptic, distressing,
threatening

direct

4 head, lead, show 5 apply, frank, guide,
label, level, order, pilot, plain, point, route,
steer, train 6 assign, charge, define,
devote, divert, enjoin, escort, extend,
govern, lineal, linear, manage, ordain,
settle 7 address, carry on, command,
conduct, control, genuine, nonstop,
operate, oversee, preside, project, request
8 dispatch, instruct, regulate, shepherd,
straight, unbroken, verbatim 9 determine,

firsthand, immediate, prescribe
10 administer, contiguous, continuous,
inevitable **11** categorical, undeviating,
unequivocal, word for word
a helmsman: 4 conn
proceedings: 7 preside

direction

3 way **4** east, line, path, side, west
5 angle, north, point, south, trend
6 course, design **7** bearing, channel,
command, purpose **8** guidance, tendency
9 clockwise, oversight, viewpoint
10 management, standpoint, trajectory
11 instruction, supervision
blowing: 7 leeward **9** windward
horizontal: 7 azimuth
(see also **compass point**)

directive

4 fiat, memo, word, writ **5** edict, order,
ukase **6** charge, decree, dictum, notice,
ruling **7** bidding, command, dictate,
mandate **8** deciding, managing
9 presiding **10** assignment, injunction,
memorandum **11** instruction, supervising,
supervisory **12** policy-making **13** communication, pronouncement

directly

3 due **4** anon, soon **5** right, spang **6** at
once, pronto **7** bluntly, by and by, shortly
8 first off, in person, promptly, squarely,
straight, verbatim **9** forthwith, instanter,
instantly, presently, right away **10** face-to-
face **11** immediately, straight off,
straightway, word for word **12** contiguously,
straightaway

director

4 boss, head **5** chief **6** leader, top dog
7 manager **8** overseer **9** conductor,
organizer **10** head honcho, supervisor

directory

4 list **5** guide, index **6** folder **7** catalog
8 register **9** catalogue **11** compilation

dirge

6 lament **7** requiem **8** threnody
11 lamentation
Gaelic: 8 coronach

dirigible

5 blimp **7** airship **8** zeppelin **9** steerable

dirk

4 stab **5** sword **6** dagger **7** poniard

dirt

3 mud **4** clay, dust, land, loam, mire, muck,
porn, smut, soil, spot **5** earth, filth, fraud,
grime, stain **6** gossip, ground **7** chicane,

squalor **9** chicanery, excrement, indecency
10 corruption, hanky-panky **11** pornography

dirt-poor

4 bust **5** broke **8** beggared, indigent
9 destitute, flat broke, penniless, penurious
10 stone-broke **12** impoverished

dirty

3 low, tar **4** base, foul, lewd, smut, soil
5 bawdy, foggy, grimy, messy, mucky,
muddy, murky, nasty, smear, sooty, stain,
sully, taint **6** basely, befoul, coarse,
debase, defile, filthy, grubby, impure,
smudge, smutty, soiled, sordid, vulgar
7 corrupt, defiled, hateful, immoral,
obscene, raunchy, smutchy, spotted,
squalid, squally, sullied, tainted, tarnish,
unclean, unkempt **8** begrimed, besmirch,
blustery, indecent, off-color, polluted,
unchaste, unwashed **9** ill-gotten, uncleanly
10 abominable, blustering, scandalous,
scurrilous **11** disgraceful, distasteful,
distressing, tempestuous, unlaundered
12 contaminated, contemptible,
disagreeable, dishonorable, scatological

Dis

see **Pluto**

disability

7 ailment **8** drawback, handicap
9 detriment, hindrance, infirmity, unfitness
10 affliction, impairment, impediment,
incapacity **11** restriction, shortcoming
12 disadvantage

disable

3 sap **4** maim **5** spoil **6** hobble, weaken
7 cripple **8** enfeeble, handicap, paralyze,
sabotage **9** hamstring, undermine
10 debilitate, immobilize **11** incapacitate
a racehorse: 6 nobble

disabled

7 hobbled **8** crippled **9** arthritic, paralyzed,
rheumatic **11** handicapped **13** incapacitated

disabuse

4 free **5** emend, purge **7** correct, deliver,
rectify, redress, release, relieve **8** liberate,
unburden **9** enlighten, undeceive
10 illuminate **11** disencumber, disillusion

disaccharide

7 lactose, maltose, sucrose

disaccord

3 jar, war **4** vary **5** brawl, clash **6** combat,
debate, differ **7** contest, contend, dispute,

dissent, quarrel **8** conflict, disagree
12 disharmonize

disadvantage
 3 bar **4** harm, loss **6** burden, damage,
hamper **7** barrier, setback **8** drawback,
handicap, obstacle **9** detriment, hindrance,
liability, prejudice **10** impairment,
impediment, imposition, limitation **11** deprivation, obstruction

disadvantaged
 7 lacking **8** deprived **11** handicapped

disaffect
 4 wean **5** alien, repel **8** alienate, disquiet,
disunite, estrange **10** antagonize

disaffirm
 4 deny **5** annul, belie, cross **6** abjure,
impugn, negate, refute, reject **7** confute,
explode, gainsay, reverse **8** disclaim,
disprove, negative, traverse **9** repudiate
10 contradict, contravene

disagree
 4 vary **5** argue, clash **6** bicker, differ,
divide, haggle **7** contend, contest, dispute,
dissent **8** conflict

disagreeable
 4 ugly **7** peevish **8** annoying, petulant
9 offensive **10** unpleasant **11** disobliging,
distressing, ill-tempered

disagreement
 5 clash **6** debate **7** discord, dispute,
quarrel, wrangle **8** argument, conflict,
squabble, variance **9** disparity
10 contention, difference, dissension,
divergence, unlikeness **11** altercation,
controversy, discrepancy, incongruity

disallow
 4 deny, veto **5** debar **6** enjoin, forbid,
refuse, reject **7** disavow, dismiss, exclude,
rule out, shut out **8** disclaim, prohibit
9 interdict, proscribe, repudiate

disallowance
 4 veto **5** taboo **6** denial **7** refusal
9 disavowal, dismissal, exclusion, rejection
11 prohibition, repudiation **12** interdiction,
proscription

_____-disant
 3 soi

disappear
 3 die **5** clear, leave **6** depart, die out,
vanish **8** evanesce, fade away, melt away,
pass away, slip away **9** evaporate, sneak
away, steal away **13** dematerialize

disappoint
 4 dash, foil, ruin **6** baffle, defeat, thwart
7 let down **9** frustrate **10** discourage,
dishearten

disappointment
 4 blow **6** bummer, defeat, downer
7 failure, letdown **8** comedown
9 bringdown **11** frustration

disapproval
 4 veto **6** rebuke **7** censure, dislike,
obloquy, reproof **8** reproach **9** criticism,
objection, rejection
 expression of: 3 boo **4** hiss, hoot, jeer
7 catcall **9** raspberry **10** Bronx cheer

disapprove
 4 veto **6** oppose, reject **7** decline, dislike,
dismiss, frown on **8** disfavor, turn down
9 dispraise

disarm
 5 charm **6** allure **7** win over **8** sideline
9 captivate **10** neutralize

disarming
 5 silky **6** silken **7** amiable, likable, winning,
winsome **8** likeable, pleasing **9** endearing
10 convincing, persuasive, saccharine
11 deferential, insinuating **12** ingratiating

disarrange
 4 mess **5** mix up, muss up, upset
6 jumble, mess up, mislay, muddle
7 confuse, disturb **8** disorder, displace,
misplace, unsettle **10** discompose
11 disorganize

disarray
 5 chaos **6** bedlam, jumble, mess up,
muddle **7** clutter, undress **8** disorder,
shambles, unsettle **9** confusion
10 discompose, dishabille

disassemble
 6 detach **7** scatter **8** dismount, disperse,
separate, take down, tear down **9** break
down, come apart, dismantle, dismember,
take apart

disassociate
 5 sever, unfix **6** detach, sunder **7** back off
8 abstract, alienate, back down, disunite,
liberate, separate, uncouple, withdraw
9 disengage **10** disconnect

disaster
 3 woe **6** fiasco **7** debacle, failure, tragedy
8 calamity **9** cataclysm, ruination
11 catastrophe, devastation

disastrous
 4 dire **5** fatal **6** tragic **7** fateful, ruinous

8 terrible 10 calamitous, horrendous
11 cataclysmic, destructive, devastating
12 catastrophic

disavow
4 deny 6 abjure, disown, impugn, negate,
recant, reject 7 forsake, gainsay, retract
8 abnegate, disclaim, forswear, negative,
renounce 9 repudiate

disband
3 end 4 part 5 sever 6 divide, sunder
7 break up, dissect, divorce, scatter
8 disperse, dissolve, separate

disbelieve
5 doubt, scorn, scout 6 eschew, reject
7 scoff at, suspect 8 discount, distrust,
mistrust, question 9 discredit, repudiate

disbeliever
5 cynic 7 doubter, sceptic, scoffer, skeptic
9 dissenter 10 questioner 11 freethinker

disbelieving
4 wary 5 leery 6 show-me 7 cynical,
dubious 8 doubting 9 quizzical, skeptical
11 incredulous, mistrustful, questioning,
unconvinced

disburden
4 shed 6 unlade, unload, unship, unstow
7 off-load, relieve 8 disgorge 9 discharge

disburse
3 pay 5 allot, issue 6 lay out, pay out,
supply 7 deliver, dole out, furnish, provide
8 dispense, disperse 9 apportion, partition
10 distribute, measure out

disbursement
4 cost 5 funds 6 outlay 7 expense,
payment 9 allotment 11 expenditure
12 distribution

discard
4 cast, drop, dump, junk, shed, toss, waif
5 chuck, ditch, eject, let go, scrap 6 reject
7 cast off, castoff, deep-six, wash out 8 get
rid of, jettison, shuck off, throw out 9 throw
away, toss aside

discarnate
8 bodiless, ethereal, spectral 9 asomatous,
unfleshly 10 immaterial, unembodied,
unphysical, wraithlike 11 disembodied,
incorporeal, nonphysical 12 otherworldly
13 insubstantial

discern
3 see 4 know, note 5 grasp, sense
6 behold, detect, divine, notice 7 observe
8 identify, perceive 9 apprehend,
ascertain, recognize 10 comprehend,

understand 11 distinguish 12 discriminate
13 differentiate

discernible
7 visible 8 apparent, palpable 10 detectable, noticeable, observable
11 appreciable, perceivable 12 recognizable

discerning
4 keen 5 acute, aware 6 astute
7 knowing 9 clear-eyed, insighted,
observant, sagacious 10 insightful,
perceptive 12 clear-sighted 13 knowledgeable, perspicacious

discernment
6 acumen 7 insight 8 keenness, sagacity
9 intuition 10 astuteness, perception,
shrewdness 11 penetration, percipience,
recognition 12 perspicacity
13 comprehension, sagaciousness

discharge
3 can, pay 4 drop, emit, fire, free, gush
oust, quit, sack, spew, vent, void 5 annul,
clear, demob, eject, empty, expel, exude,
let go, loose, pay up, quash, salvo, shoot,
utter 6 bounce, excuse, exempt, let fly, let
off, loosen, outlet, remove, settle, unbind,
unload, vacate 7 absolve, boot out,
barrage, cashier, deliver, dismiss, exclude,
excrete, execute, fulfill, give off, kick out,
manumit, off-load, release, relieve,
removal, satisfy, unchain 8 abrogate,
aquittal, dispense, displace, dissolve,
ejection, emission, get rid of, liberate,
separate, throw off 9 acquittal, dismissal,
eliminate, explosion, expulsion, muster out,
pour forth, send forth, terminate, unshackle
10 deactivate, demobilize, emancipate,
inactivate, liberation, separation
11 exoneration, fulfillment
electrical: 5 spark 6 leader 8 streamer
9 lightning

disciple
3 fan 6 minion 7 apostle, devotee, learner
8 adherent, follower, henchman, partisan,
retainer 9 supporter 10 enthusiast

disciplinarian
8 enforcer, martinet 10 taskmaster
11 slave driver

disciplinary
8 punitive 9 punishing 10 corrective

discipline
4 curb, rule, will 5 check, drill, field, guide,
order, teach, train 6 bridle, direct, method,
punish, school,

subdue **7** chasten, conduct, control, correct, educate **8** approach, chastise, instruct, penalize, restrain, training **9** castigate, obedience, subjugate, will-power **11** castigation, self-control, self-mastery **12** chastisement **13** self-restraint

disclaim

4 deny **6** abjure, reject **7** disavow, gainsay, retract **8** disallow, forswear, renounce, traverse, repudiate **10** contradict

disclose

3 own **4** avow, tell **5** spill **6** expose, impart, relate, report, reveal, unmask, unveil **7** display, divulge, uncover **8** discover, give away, unclothe **9** make known

disclosure

6 exposé **8** exposure **10** revelation **11** declaration

discolor

3 tar **4** blot, dull, fade, smut, soil **5** smear, stain, sully, taint, tinge **6** defile, smudge **7** besmear, bestain, tarnish **8** besmirch

discoloration

4 spot **5** stain, taint **6** blotch, bruise, smudge **7** blemish **8** birthmark

discomfit

3 irk, vex **4** faze **5** abash, annoy, upset **6** baffle, bother, defeat, rattle, thwart **7** fluster, nonplus, perturb, unnerve **8** confound **9** embarrass **10** discompose, disconcert

discomfiture

5 upset **6** unease **8** disquiet **9** abashment, agitation, confusion **10** uneasiness **11** frustration **12** discomposure, perturbation **13** embarrassment, inconvenience

discomfort

3 irk, vex **4** ache, pain **5** annoy **6** bother, unease **7** malaise **8** vexation **9** annoyance **10** uneasiness **13** embarrassment

discomforting

see **uncomfortable**

discommend

5 decry **7** censure, frown on, put down **8** admonish, disfavor, object to **9** criticize, deprecate, disesteem, disparage, reprehend **10** disapprove

discommode

3 irk, vex **5** annoy, upset **6** bother, burden, flurry, put out **7** disturb, fluster, perturb, trouble **8** encumber **9** aggravate, disoblige **13** inconvenience

discompose

3 irk, vex **5** annoy, harry, upset, worry **6** bother, dismay, flurry, harass, pester, plague, ruffle, untune **7** agitate, disturb, fluster, perturb, unhinge **8** disarray, disorder, unsettle **9** embarrass **10** disarrange **11** disorganize

discomposure

5 upset, worry **6** bother, unease **8** vexation **9** abashment, agitation, annoyance, confusion **10** discomfort, irritation, perplexity, uneasiness **11** disquietude **12** discomfiture, perturbation **13** consternation, embarrassment

disconcert

4 faze **5** abash, upset, worry **6** bemuse, bother, puzzle, rattle, ruffle **7** confuse, disturb, nonplus, perplex, perturb, trouble **8** bewilder, confound, disquiet **9** discomfit, embarrass, frustrate

disconfirm

4 deny **5** rebut **6** refute, negate **7** gainsay **8** abnegate, confound, disclaim, disprove **10** contradict, controvert

disconnect

3 cut, gap **4** break, sever, unfix **6** cut off, detach **7** disjoin **8** separate, uncouple **9** disengage **10** dissociate

disconnected

7 muddled **8** detached, separate **10** disjointed, incoherent, unattached **11** fragmentary, unorganized **13** discontinuous

disconsolate

3 low, sad **4** blue, down **5** bleak, drear **6** abject, dreary, gloomy, woeful **7** doleful, forlorn, joyless, unhappy **8** dejected, downcast, wretched **9** cheerless, depressed, miserable, sorrowful, woebegone **10** dispirited, melancholy **11** comfortless, crestfallen, downhearted

discontent

4 envy **9** dysphoria **10** depression, inquietude, uneasiness **11** displeasure **12** disaffection, restlessness

discontented

5 upset **6** uneasy **7** annoyed, fretful, unhappy **8** restless **9** disturbed, irritated, perturbed 10 displeased 11 complaining, disgruntled, ungratified, unsatisfied 12 dissatisfied

discontinuation
3 end 4 stop 5 cease, close, pause 6 ending, finish 7 closing 8 abeyance 9 cessation 10 conclusion, desistance, moratorium, suspension 12 postponement

discontinue
3 end 4 halt, quit, stay, stop 5 cease, close, sever 6 desist, give up, wind up, wrap up 8 break off, close out, conclude, knock off, leave off, shut down, surcease 9 terminate

discontinuity
3 gap 4 hole, rent, rift 5 break, cleft, crack, split 6 breach, lacuna 7 fissure, opening, rupture

discontinuous
6 fitful 7 muddled 8 discrete, separate 9 spasmodic 10 incoherent, incohesive 11 unconnected 12 disconnected, intermittent 13 nonsequential

discord
5 clash 6 enmity, rancor, strife 7 rupture 8 conflict, contrast, disunity, division, friction, mismatch, variance 9 animosity, antipathy, hostility 10 antagonism, contention, difference, dissension, dissidence, dissonance, opposition 12 inconsonance, polarization 13 inconsistency
goddess: 3 Ate 4 Eris

discordant
5 harsh 6 at odds 7 jarring 8 clashing, contrary, jangling, strident 9 dissonant 10 cacophonic, unpleasant 11 cacophonous, conflicting, disagreeing, inconsonant, quarrelsome, unmelodious 12 unharmonious

discotheque
6 bistro, nitery 7 hot spot 9 dance club, nightclub, night spot

discount
5 doubt, lower 6 deduct, ignore, reduce, slight 7 neglect, take off 8 belittle, derogate, decrease, diminish, knock off, mark down, markdown, minimize, overlook, roll back, rollback, subtract, take away 9 abatement, deduction, disregard, reduction, substract, underrate 13 underestimate

discountenance
4 faze 5 abash 6 rattle 7 frown on 8 confound, disfavor 9 deprecate,

discomfit, embarrass 10 disapprove, disconcert, discourage

discourage
4 damp 5 daunt, check, chill, deter 6 dampen, deject, divert, hinder, impede 7 depress, inhibit, trouble 8 disfavor, dissuade, suppress 10 demoralize, dishearten

discouraging
5 bleak 7 unhappy 8 daunting 9 deterring, troubling 10 depressing 11 unfavorable, unpromising 12 unpropitious 13 disappointing, disheartening

discourse
4 talk 5 argue, essay, orate, speak, spiel, voice 6 sermon, speech, thesis 7 amplify, descant, enlarge, explain, expound, lecture 8 converse, harangue, perorate, rhetoric, speaking, treatise 9 expatiate, monograph, sermonize, utterance 10 expression 11 interchange 12 conversation 13 verbalization
art of: 8 rhetoric
religious: 6 homily, sermon

discourteous
4 rude 6 unkind 7 boorish, brusque, ill-bred, uncivil, uncouth 8 impolite 10 ungracious, unmannerly 11 ill-mannered, impertinent 13 disrespectful

discover
4 espy, find, spot 5 learn 6 betray, detect, expose, reveal, unmask 7 divulge, find out, observe, unearth 8 come upon, perceive, proclaim, unshroud 9 ascertain, determine, encounter, make known 10 come across

discovery
4 find 5 trove 6 espial, strike 7 finding 8 locating, sighting 9 detection 10 revelation, unearthing

discredit
4 slur, ruin 5 doubt, shame 6 defame, malign, show up 7 asperse, degrade, put down, run down, slander, traduce 8 disgrace, ignominy 9 disparage, disrepute 10 disbelieve, opprobrium

discreditable
5 shady 6 shabby, shoddy 8 shameful, unworthy 9 degrading 10 inglorious 11 blameworthy, disgraceful, ignominious 12 contemptible, dishonorable, disreputable

discreet
4 wary 5 chary, muted, plain 6 modest, simple 7 careful, guarded, prudent, tactful

8 cautious, moderate 9 unadorned
10 controlled, reasonable, restrained
11 circumspect, considerate, unelaborate,
unobtrusive 12 unnoticeable 13 unpretentious

discrepancy

3 gap 8 alterity, conflict, variance
9 disparity, otherness, variation
10 difference, divergence, divergency,
unlikeness 12 disagreement
13 inconsistency

discrepant

6 unlike 7 diverse, varying 8 contrary
9 different, differing, disparate, divergent
11 conflicting, disagreeing
12 incompatible, inconsistent 13 contradictory

discrete

8 detached, distinct, separate 9 countable,
different 12 disconnected
13 discontinuous, noncontinuous

discretion

4 care, tact 7 caution, reserve 8 delicacy,
judgment, prudence, wariness
9 canniness, chariness, restraint
13 judiciousness

discriminate

5 judge 6 assess 7 compare, discern,
make out 8 contrast, disfavor, evaluate,
perceive, separate 9 segregate, tell apart
11 distinguish 13 differentiate

discriminating

6 choosy, select 7 finical, finicky 8 eclectic
9 judicious, selective 10 discerning
11 prejudicial

discrimination

5 taste 6 acumen 7 bigotry 8 inequity,
insight, judgment 9 prejudice
10 astuteness, favoritism, partiality,
perception 11 discernment, intolerance,
penetration

discriminatory

6 biased 7 partial, unequal 8 partisan
9 jaundiced 10 prejudiced 11 inequitable,
predisposed

discursive

5 windy, wordy 6 chatty, prolix 7 diffuse,
logical, verbose 8 rambling, tortuous
9 desultory 10 analytical, circuitous,
digressive, long-winded, meandering
11 wide-ranging

discuss

4 moot 5 argue, weigh 6 debate, parley
7 canvass, expound 8 consider, converse,
hash over, talk over 9 elucidate, expatiate,
interpret, talk about, thrash out, ventilate
10 deliberate, toss around
business: 8 talk shop
lightly: 5 bandy
thoroughly: 7 exhaust

discussion

3 rap 4 chat, talk 6 confab, debate, parley,
powwow 7 canvass, palaver 8 argument,
colloquy 10 conference, rap session
11 bull session, ventilation
12 conversation, deliberation
13 confabulation

discus thrower

6 Alekna (Virgilijus), Marten (Maritza),
Oerter (Al) 10 discobolus 11 Rashchupkin
(Viktor)

disdain

5 abhor, scorn, scout, spurn 6 deride,
refuse, reject, slight 7 contemn, despise,
despite, hauteur, put down 8 aversion,
belittle, contempt, disprize, misprize
9 antipathy 10 repugnance, undervalue

disdainful

5 aloof, proud 6 averse, lordly, snooty,
uppity 7 haughty 8 arrogant, cavalier,
derisive, insolent, scorning, spurning,
superior, toplofty 11 overbearing
12 antipathetic, contemptuous, supercilious
13 high and mighty

disease

3 bug, ill 5 upset, virus 6 blight, malady
7 ailment, anthrax, illness, malaise,
mycosis, purpura 8 debility, disorder,
epidemic, myxedema, pandemic, sickness,
syndrome, zoonoses (plural), zoonosis
9 affection, black lung, complaint, condition,
contagion, ill health, infection, infirmity,
sclerosis 10 affliction, alteration,
blackwater, bronchitis, feebleness,
impairment, infirmness, sickliness
11 decrepitude, derangement
13 unhealthiness
animal: 5 mange, surra 6 rabies
7 bighead 8 enzootic, zoonosis
9 distemper, tularemia 10 rinderpest
blood: 8 leukemia, leukoses (plural),
leukosis
cabbage: 8 clubroot
cattle: 6 cowpox 7 foot rot, locoism,
murrain 8 blackleg, vaccinia 9 vibriosis
10 rinderpest 11 brucellosis
cereal grass: 4 bunt, smut 5 ergot
children's: 5 mumps 7 measles, rubella
10 chicken pox 13 whooping cough
citrus tree: 8 tristeza

classification: 8 nosology
combining form: 4 path 5 patho
communicable: 4 mono 5 mumps, polio 6 dengue, herpes, plague, rabies 7 cholera, leprosy, malaria, measles, rubella, tetanus, typhoid 8 impetigo 9 hepatitis, influenza 10 giardiasis 12 tuberculosis
deficiency: 6 scurvy 7 rickets 8 beriberi, pellagra
disseminator: 6 vector 7 carrier
eye: 8 glaucoma, trachoma 9 retinitis
hair follicle: 7 sycoses (plural), sycosis
heart: 11 cardiopathy
horse: 6 nagana, spavin 7 locosim, sarcoid 8 glanders 9 strangles
identification of: 9 diagnosis
industrial: 10 byssinosis
infectious: 4 mono, yaws 6 dengue, typhus 7 leprosy, malaria, tetanus, typhoid 9 tularemia, vibriosis 10 rinderpest 13 whooping cough
liver: 9 cirrhosis, hepatitis
livestock: 7 locoism 9 vibriosis 10 rinderpest
lung: 8 phthisic, phthisis 9 pneumonia 10 byssinosis 12 tuberculosis
lymph glands: 8 scrofula
metabolic: 4 gout
nervous system: 4 kuru 6 rabies 10 diphtheria
of beets: 8 heartrot
of mammals: 6 rabies 7 malaria 9 distemper 10 babesiosis, rinderpest
parasitic: 3 rot 4 smut 5 mange 7 malaria 8 hookworm, kala-azar 9 heartworm
plant: 4 rust, scab, smut, wilt 5 blast, edema, scald, scurf, stunt 6 blight, blotch, canker, mosaic, streak 7 blister, crinkle, foot rot, frogeye, red leaf, root rot 8 clubroot, curly top, fusarium, gummosis, leaf curl, leaf roll, leaf rust, leaf spot, ring spot, root knot, stem rust 9 chlorosis, crown gall, white rust 10 blackheart, leaf scorch
poultry: 8 leukosis
respiratory: 6 asthma, coryza 10 byssinosis
sheep: 3 gid 7 scrapie 9 vibriosis 10 bluetongue
skin: 4 acne, yaws 5 favus, hives, lupus, mange, pinta, tinea 6 eczema, tetter 7 leprosy, prurigo, sarcoid, scabies 8 impetigo, miliaria, pyoderma, ringworm, vitiligo 9 pemphigus, psoriasis 10 erysipelas 11 scleroderma
syphilitic: 5 tabes
throat: 5 croup

thyroid: 6 struma
tropical: 4 yaws 5 pinta, sprue, surra 6 dengue 8 kala-azar
venereal: 8 syphilis 9 chancroid, gonorrhea
viral: 3 flu 4 AIDS, noma 5 Ebola, mumps, polio 6 dengue, grippe, herpes, rabies, zoster 7 measles, rubella, rubeola, variola 8 morbilli, shingles, smallpox 9 hepatitis, influenza, varicella 13 poliomyelitis

diseased
3 ill 6 ailing, infirm, sickly, unwell 7 fevered, unsound 8 feverish, infected

disembark
4 land 6 alight 7 deplane, detrain 8 go ashore

disembarrass
3 rid 4 free 7 release, relieve 8 liberate, unburden, untangle 9 extricate 11 disencumber, disentangle

disembodied
7 ghostly 8 ethereal, spectral 9 asomatous, unfleshly 10 immaterial, unphysical, wraithlike 11 incorporeal, nonmaterial, nonphysical 13 insubstantial

disembogue
4 flow, gush, pour, spew 5 empty 7 pour out 9 discharge

disembowel
3 gut 10 eviscerate, exenterate

disenchanted
5 blasé, jaded 6 soured 7 cynical 9 jaundiced 10 undeceived 11 worldly-wise 12 disappointed, dissatisfied 13 disenthralled, disillusioned

disencumber
4 free 7 lighten, release, relieve, sort out 8 free from, liberate, unburden 9 alleviate, disburden, extricate

disengage
4 free, part 5 loose, unfix 6 detach, opt out, unbind 7 back out, drop out, release, unloose 8 cut loose, liberate, separate, uncouple, unfasten, unloosen, withdraw 10 disconnect

disentangle
5 untie 6 detach 7 resolve, sort out, unravel, unsnarl, untwine 8 separate 9 extricate 10 unscramble 11 disencumber 13 straighten out

disenthrall
4 free 7 manumit, release 8 liberate 10 emancipate

disfavor
7 dislike **8** aversion, distrust, mistrust
9 deprecate, disesteem, disregard,
disrepute **10** disrespect **11** disapproval
12 disadvantage, unpopularity

disfigure
3 mar **4** maim, scar **6** deface,
defile, deform, impair, injure, mangle
7 blemish, distort **8** mutilate

disfranchise
3 bar **7** exclude **8** take away **9** deprive of
10 disentitle

disgorge
4 barf, spew **5** belch, eject, eruct, erupt,
expel, vomit **6** give up, irrupt, spit up
7 release, throw up, upchuck **9** discharge

disgrace
5 odium, shame **6** stigma **7** attaint,
mortify, obloquy **8** black eye, contempt,
dishonor, ignominy, reproach **9** discredit,
disrepute, humiliate **10** opprobrium,
stigmatize **11** degradation, humiliation

disgraceful
7 ignoble **8** shameful **9** degrading
10 deplorable, inglorious, unbecoming
11 humiliating, ignominious, reproachful
12 dishonorable, disreputable

disgruntled
5 vexed **6** cranky, put out **7** annoyed,
beefing, griping **8** grousing **9** irritated
10 discontent, displeased, ill-humored,
malcontent **11** ungratified
12 discontented, malcontented

disguise
4 hide, mask, sham, veil **5** belie, cloak,
feign, put on **6** facade **7** conceal, falsify,
obscure **8** artifice, pretense **9** deception
10 camouflage, false front, pretension
12 misrepresent

disguised
6 masked, veiled **7** cloaked, feigned
9 incognito **10** undercover **11** camouflaged

disguisement
4 mask, veil **5** cloak, front **6** facade
8 pretense **9** deception **10** false front,
pretention

disgust
6 nausea, offend, revolt, sicken **8** aversion,
gross out, loathing, nauseate **9** antipathy,
repulsion, revulsion **10** abhorrence,
repugnance **13** squeamishness

disgusted
5 fed up **8** offended, repelled, repulsed,

revolted, sickened **9** nauseated,
squeamish **10** grossed out

disgusting
4 foul, icky, vile **5** gross, nasty, yucky
7 noisome **9** loathsome, offensive,
repellent, repugnant, repulsive, revolting,
sickening **10** nauseating

dish
4 bowl, buzz, food, talk, tray **5** plate
6 course, gossip, tureen **7** chatter,
hearsay, platter, scandal, slander
9 casserole, container **11** scuttlebutt
baked: 7 soufflé
baking: 7 cocotte, scallop **9** casserole
12 scallop shell
cheese: 6 fondue **7** ramekin, rarebit
8 raclette, ramequin
Chinese: 6 dim sum, lo mein, subgum,
wonton **8** chop suey, chow mein **10** egg
foo yong, egg foo yung **11** egg foo young
deep: 9 casserole
Hungarian: 7 goulash
Italian: 5 penne, pesto, pizza **6** scampi
7 cannoli, lasagna, polenta, ravioli
8 calamari, linguine, linguini, osso buco,
rigatoni **9** foccaccia, manicotti
10 cannelloni, scaloppine, tortellini
11 saltimbocca
Japanese: 7 sashimi, tempura **8** sukiyaki
Mexican: 4 taco **5** chili **6** fajita, flauta,
nachos, tamale **7** burrito, chalupa
8 frijoles **9** enchilada, guacamole **10** carne
asada **11** chimichanga **12** refried beans
13 chili con carne
Middle Eastern: 5 halva, kebab, kibbe,
kibbi **6** halvah, hummus, kibbeh
7 baklava, falafel **8** couscous, moussaka
10 shish kebab **11** baba ghanouj **12** baba
ghanoush
principal: 6 entrée
rice: 7 risotto
rice and meat: 5 pilaf
Scottish: 5 brose **6** haggis
shallow: 6 saucer
Thai: 7 pad thai

disharmonize
3 jar, war **5** clash **6** jangle **7** discord
8 conflict, mismatch **9** disaccord

disharmony
6 strife **7** discord **8** conflict, disunion,
disunity, friction, variance **9** cacophony
10 contention, difference, dissension,
dissonance

dishearten
3 cow **5** chill, crush, daunt, shake
6 dampen, deject, dismay, sadden
7 depress, dispirit, unnerve **8** distress
10 demoralize, discourage, intimidate

disheartening
8 daunting **9** dismaying, saddening **10** depressing **11** dispiriting **12** demoralizing, discouraging, intimidating

dishes
4 ware
clay: 7 pottery
porcelain: 5 china

dishevel
5 touse **6** muss up, rumple, tousle **8** disarray, disorder **10** disarrange, discompose

disheveled
5 messy **7** ruffled, rumpled, tousled, unkempt **8** ill-kempt, mussed up, uncombed **10** disarrayed, disordered **11** discomposed

dishonest
5 false, lying, rogue, snide, unfair **6** tricky **7** corrupt, crooked, knavish **8** cheating, cozening, two-faced **9** deceitful, deceiving, deceptive, swindling **10** defrauding, fraudulent, mendacious, untruthful **13** double-dealing, untrustworthy

dishonesty
5 fraud, guile **6** deceit **7** falsity, knavery, roguery **8** flimflam, pretense, trickery **9** chicanery, deception, duplicity, falsehood, hypocrisy **10** corruption **11** crookedness **13** double-dealing

dishonor
see **disgrace**

dishonorable
see **disgraceful**

dish out
5 ladle, serve **6** pile on, supply **7** deliver, present, serve up **8** allocate, disburse, dispense **10** distribute

disillusioned
see **disenchanted**

disinclination
7 dislike **8** aversion, distaste **9** antipathy, objection **10** reluctance **13** indisposition, unwillingness

disinclined
5 loath **6** averse **7** balking, opposed **8** boggling, hesitant **9** reluctant, resistant, unwilling **10** hesitating, indisposed **12** antipathetic **13** unsympathetic

disinfect
6 purify **8** sanitize **9** autoclave, sterilize **13** decontaminate

disingenuous
3 sly **4** foxy, wily **5** false **6** artful, crafty, tricky **7** cunning, devious, feigned **8** delusive, guileful, indirect, specious **9** deceitful, deceiving, deceptive, dishonest, insidious, insincere, sophistic **10** misleading **11** calculating, casuistical, sophistical

disinherit
6 cut off **7** bereave, exclude **9** deprive of, repudiate **10** dispossess

disintegrate
3 rot **4** turn **5** break, burst, decay, spoil, taint **6** molder **7** crumble, scatter, shatter **8** splinter **9** break down, decompose, fall apart **10** deliquesce

disinter
5 dig up **6** exhume, unbury **7** unearth **8** exhumate **9** resurrect

disinterest
6 apathy **7** neglect **8** coolness, lethargy **9** aloofness, disregard, unconcern **10** detachment, dispassion, neutrality **11** impassivity, inattention, insouciance, nonchalance, objectivity **12** indifference

disinterested
4 fair, just **5** aloof **6** candid **7** neutral **8** detached, unbiased **9** impartial, impassive, incurious, objective **10** evenhanded, impersonal, neglectful, nonchalant **11** inattentive, indifferent, unconcerned

disjoin
4 part **5** sever, unfix **6** detach, divide, sunder, unlink **7** break up, divorce **8** disunite, separate, uncouple, unfasten **9** disengage, take apart **10** dissociate **12** disaffiliate, disassociate

disjointed
7 jumbled, muddled **8** confused, inchoate, rambling **9** displaced **10** disordered, incoherent, incohesive **11** unconnected, unorganized **13** discontinuous

disk
4 puck **5** wafer **6** record
metal: 4 slug
ornamental: 6 bangle, sequin

dislike
4 hate, shun **5** abhor, scorn, spurn **6** animus, detest, loathe, oppose, reject, resent **7** deplore, despise, frown on **8** aversion, disfavor, distaste, execrate **9** animosity, antipathy **10** alienation, disapprove, repugnance **11** detestation, disapproval **13** indisposition

dislimn
3 dim 5 bedim 6 darken 7 becloud, obscure 9 obfuscate

dislocate
5 break 7 disrupt, unhinge 9 disengage 10 disconnect 13 disarticulate

dislodge
4 oust 5 eject, evict, expel 6 remove, uproot 8 displace, drive out, force out

disloyal
5 false 6 untrue 8 apostate, recreant 9 alienated, faithless 10 perfidious, traitorous, unfaithful 11 disaffected, treacherous

disloyalty
7 falsity, perfidy, treason 8 apostasy 9 falseness, recreancy, treachery 10 alienation, infidelity 12 disaffection 13 faithlessness

dismal
5 bleak 6 dreary, gloomy, horrid, somber, sombre 7 joyless 8 desolate, dreadful, funereal, lowering 9 atrocious, cheerless, depressed, tenebrous 10 depressing, depressive 11 dispiriting 12 discouraging 13 disheartening

dismantle
4 raze, undo 5 strip, unrig, wreck 6 denude, divest 7 break up, destroy 8 demolish, pull down, take down 9 break down, knock down, take apart 11 disassemble

dismay
4 faze, fear 5 abash, alarm, daunt, dread, panic, scare, shake, upset 6 appall, fright, horror, rattle 7 agitate, fluster, horrify, perturb, unnerve 8 affright, bewilder, confound, dispirit, distress, frighten 9 discomfit, disconcert, dumbfound, embarrass 10 discompose, discourage, dishearten 11 trepidation 12 perturbation 13 consternation

dismayed
5 upset 6 afraid, aghast, scared, shaken 7 fearful, shocked 9 disturbed

dismember
4 maim 7 disjoin 8 mutilate 9 dismantle, take apart

dismiss
3 axe, can 4 drop, fire, oust, sack, shed 5 chuck, deride, eject, evict, let go, scorn, spurn 6 bounce, depose, lay off, reject, remove, retire, shelve, unseat 7 boot out,

cashier, contemn, decline, disband, kick out, kiss off, turn off 8 displace, furlough, pooh-pooh, ridicule, throw out, turn away, turn down 9 discharge, repudiate, terminate 11 send packing

dismissal
5 congé 6 firing, layoff, ouster 7 removal 8 brush-off, bum's rush 9 discharge, expulsion 10 cashiering

dismount
6 alight, debark, get off 7 deplane, detrain 9 disembark 10 alight from 11 descend from

Disney, Walt
10 cartoonist
character: 4 Gyro, Huey, Lady 5 Ariel, Bambi, Daisy, Dewey, Dumbo, Goofy, Louie, Mulan, Pluto, Simba, Tramp 6 Beauty, Donald, Mickey, Minnie, Mowgli 7 Aladdin, Scrooge 9 Gladstone, Pinocchio 10 Beagle Boys, Clarabelle, Pocahontas
classic: 5 Bambi, Dumbo 8 Fantasia 9 Pinocchio 10 Jungle Book (The) 15 Lady and the Tramp

disobedient
6 unruly 7 naughty, wayward, willful 8 contrary 10 headstrong, ill-behaved, misbehaving, rebellious, refractory, uncompliant 12 contumacious, noncompliant, obstreperous, recalcitrant 13 insubordinate

disoblige
5 annoy 6 bother, offend, put out 7 affront, disturb, trouble 9 displease, incommode 10 discommode 13 inconvenience

disorder
3 ill 4 mess, riot 5 chaos, mix up, snarl, upset 6 ataxia, hubbub, jumble, malady, mess up, muddle, muss up, ruckus, rumple, tumble, tumult, unrest, uproar 7 ailment, anarchy, clutter, confuse, disease, embroil, illness, misdeed, shuffle, turmoil 8 disarray, sickness, syndrome, unsettle, upheaval 9 affection, agitation, commotion, complaint, confusion, infirmity 10 affliction, turbulence, untidiness
mental: 5 mania 8 delirium, insanity, neurosis, paranoia 9 psychosis 11 psychopathy 13 schizophrenia

disordered
6 roiled 7 jumbled, muddled 8 confused, inchoate, shuffled 9 displaced 10 disjointed, dislocated, incoherent, incohesive 11 disarranged, unconnected, unorganized 13 discontinuous

disorderly
5 rowdy 6 unruly, untidy 7 jumbled, raucous, unkempt 8 confused 9 cluttered, offensive, turbulent 10 boisterous, topsy-turvy, tumultuous 12 disorganized, rambunctious, unsystematic

disorganize
5 upset 6 jumble, mess up 7 break up, confuse, derange, disband, disrupt 8 disorder, disperse, unsettle 10 disarrange

disoriented
4 lost 7 mixed up 8 confused 9 displaced, perplexed, unsettled 10 bewildered

disown
4 deny, dump 6 desert, reject 7 cast off, disavow 8 disclaim, renounce 9 repudiate

disparage
5 decry 6 defame, slight 7 condemn, degrade, devalue, dismiss, put down, run down 8 bad-mouth, belittle, derogate, discount, downplay, minimize, pooh-pooh 9 denigrate, deprecate, discredit, dispraise, downgrade, underrate 10 demoralize, depreciate, undervalue 11 detract from

disparagement
5 scorn 7 calumny, censure, despite, scandal, slander 8 contempt, despisal, reproach 9 aspersion, discredit, stricture 10 backbiting, defamation, derogation, detraction, diminution 11 degradation 12 backstabbing, depreciation 13 animadversion

disparate
6 at odds, divers, unlike, varied 7 diverse, unalike, unequal, various, varying 8 discrete, distinct, separate 9 different, divergent, unsimilar 10 dissimilar 11 distinctive, incongruous, inconsonant 12 incompatible, inconsistent

disparity
3 gap 8 contrast 9 imbalance 10 difference, divergence, divergency, inequality 11 discrepancy 13 disproportion, dissimilarity

dispassionate
4 calm, fair, just 7 neutral 8 composed, detached, unbiased 9 equitable, impartial, objective, unruffled 10 impersonal 11 unemotional 12 unprejudiced 13 disinterested

dispatch
4 kill, send, ship, slay 5 haste, hurry, scrag, speed 6 defeat, murder 7 bump off, execute, forward, killing, message, put away 8 alacrity, get rid of, shipment, transmit 9 dispose of, eliminate, swiftness 10 expedition, put to death, speediness 11 assassinate, promptitude

dispel
6 banish 7 cast out, scatter 8 disperse 9 clear away, dissipate, drive away

dispensable
5 minor 7 trivial 8 needless, unneeded 10 disposable, expendable, unrequired 11 superfluous, unessential, unimportant, unnecessary 12 nonessential

dispensary
6 clinic

dispensation
4 plan 5 favor, share 7 license, portion, service 8 bestowal, courtesy, kindness, ordering 9 allotment, exception, exemption, privilege, remission 10 indulgence, management 12 disbursement, distribution 13 apportionment, authorization

dispense
5 allot, apply, wield 6 assign, divide, excuse, exempt, ration, supply 7 absolve, deal out, deliver, dish out, dole out, furnish, give out, mete out, portion, provide, release 8 allocate, carry out, disburse, share out, transfer 9 apportion, discharge, partition 10 administer, distribute, measure out, portion out

disperse
3 sow 5 spray, strew 6 dispel, divide, spread, vanish 7 break up, diffuse, disband, radiate, scatter 9 broadcast, dissipate, partition, propagate 10 distribute

dispersion
6 spread 7 breakup, colloid 9 diffusion, spreading 10 scattering 11 dissipation 12 distribution 13 dissemination

dispirit
3 cow 5 chill, daunt 6 deject, dismay, sadden 7 depress, oppress 8 distress 10 demoralize, discourage, dishearten

dispirited
3 low, sad 4 blue, down, glum 5 cowed 6 morose 7 daunted 8 cast down, dejected, dismayed, downcast, saddened 9 bummed out, depressed, oppressed, woebegone 10 distressed, melancholy 11 crestfallen, demoralized, discouraged,

downhearted **12** disconsolate, disheartened

dispiriting
4 blue **6** dismal, dreary, gloomy
8 daunting, dolorous, funereal **9** cheerless, dismaying, saddening **10** depressing, oppressive **12** demoralizing, disconsolate, discouraging **13** disheartening

displace
4 oust, sack **5** exile, expel, usurp
6 banish, deport, depose, remove
7 succeed **8** dethrone, supplant
9 supersede, transport **10** expatriate, substitute

display
4 pomp, show **5** array, model **6** evince, expose, flaunt, lay out, parade, reveal, spread, unfold, unfurl, unveil **7** exhibit, panoply, present, showing, show off, trot out, uncover **8** brandish, evidence, manifest, showcase **9** showiness, spectacle **10** exhibiting, exhibition **11** demonstrate, ostentation **13** demonstration, manifestation

displeasing
6 vexing **7** irksome **8** annoying
10 bothersome, unpleasant **12** disagreeable **13** objectionable

displeasure
8 aversion, disfavor, vexation **9** annoyance
10 discomfort, discontent, irritation, uneasiness **11** indignation, unhappiness
13 indisposition

disport
4 show **5** amuse **6** acquit, behave, divert, expose, flaunt, frolic, parade **7** conduct, display, exhibit, show off, trot out
9 entertain

disposal
5 order **7** removal **8** bestowal, chucking, jettison, ordering, transfer **9** clearance
10 allocation, assignment, demolition, discarding, regulation, relegation
11 arrangement, consignment, destruction, disposition **12** distribution, transference

dispose
4 bend, bias, rank **5** array, order, range
6 settle **7** arrange, incline, marshal, prepare **8** organize, regulate **9** make ready **11** systematize
of: 4 dump, junk, sell **5** chuck, scrap
6 finish, handle, unload **7** deep-six,

destroy, discard **8** deal with, throw out, transfer **9** eighty-six, eliminate
10 distribute

disposed
3 apt **4** fain, game **5** prone, ready
6 biased, minded **7** partial, willing
8 arranged, inclined **9** persuaded

disposition
4 bent, cast, mood, tone, type, vein
5 being, order, stamp **6** makeup, nature, temper **7** control, leaning, mind-set
8 ordering, penchant, riddance, sequence, tendency, transfer **9** character, direction
10 management, proclivity, propensity, settlement **11** arrangement, inclination, personality, temperament **12** constitution, predilection **13** individuality
favorable: 8 optimism
unfavorable: 9 pessimism

dispossess
3 rob **4** oust **5** eject, strip **6** divest
7 bereave, deprive

dispossession
4 loss **6** ouster **7** seizure **9** privation
10 divestment **11** deprivation, divestiture
13 expropriation

dispraise
3 pan **5** decry **6** censor, deride, dump on
7 put down, run down **8** bad-mouth, belittle, derogate **9** criticize, deprecate, discredit, disparage **10** depreciate, disapprove **11** detract from
12 depreciation

disproportion
8 imparity, mismatch **9** disparity
10 inequality, unevenness **12** lopsidedness

disproportionate
6 uneven **7** unequal **8** lopsided
10 unbalanced

disprove
5 belie, rebut **6** refute, negate **7** confute, explode **8** confound, overturn, puncture, traverse **9** discredit, overthrow
10 invalidate

disputable
4 iffy, moot **7** dubious **8** arguable, doubtful
9 debatable, uncertain, unsettled
10 unresolved **11** problematic
12 questionable **13** controversial

disputation
6 debate **8** argument, forensic, polemics
9 dialectic **11** controversy
13 argumentation

dispute

4 buck, duel, moot, tiff **5** argue, fight, rebut, repel **6** bicker, combat, debate, hassle, impugn, negate, oppose, refute, resist, rumpus, strife **7** confute, contend, contest, discuss, gainsay, quarrel, quibble, wrangle **8** argument, conflict, question, squabble **9** bickering, challenge, thrash out, withstand **10** contention, controvert, falling-out **11** altercation, controversy, embroilment

disputed

7 debated **8** arguable **9** contested, uncertain **12** questionable **13** controversial

disqualified

5 unfit **8** unfitted **10** ineligible, unequipped

disqualify

3 bar **5** debar **6** except **7** exclude, rule out, suspend **9** eliminate
as judge: 6 recuse

disquiet

5 alarm, angst, upset, worry **6** bother, flurry, unease, unrest **9** agitate, anxiety, concern, disturb, ferment, fluster, perturb, trouble, turmoil **10** discompose, uneasiness **11** disturbance, restiveness **12** restlessness **13** Sturm und Drang

disquietude

4 care **5** worry **6** unease, unrest **7** anxiety, concern, ferment, turmoil **8** agitation, misgiving **10** foreboding, uneasiness **11** nervousness, restiveness **12** apprehension, restlessness **13** Sturm und Drang

Disraeli, Benjamin

novel: 5 Sybil **7** Lothair, Tancred **8** Endymion **9** Coningsby
opponent: 4 Peel (Robert) **9** Gladstone (William)
queen: 8 Victoria

disregard

6 forget, ignore, slight **7** neglect, tune out **8** overlook **9** unconcern **12** heedlessness, indifference

disregardful

3 lax **5** slack **6** remiss **8** careless, derelict, heedless **9** forgetful, unheeding, negligent, unmindful **10** neglectful, regardless, unthinking **11** indifferent, unconcerned **12** absent-minded

disremember

6 forget

disreputable

4 base **5** dingy, seamy, seedy, shady **6** scurvy, shabby, shoddy, sordid **7** run-down **8** decrepit, infamous, shameful **10** inglorious **11** dilapidated, disgraceful, ignominious **12** contemptible, unprincipled **13** discreditable, unrespectable

disrepute

5 odium, shame **7** obloquy **8** disfavor, disgrace, dishonor, ignominy **9** disesteem **10** opprobrium

disrespect

6 insult **7** disdain **8** boldness, contempt, rudeness **9** disregard, flippancy, impudence, insolence **10** incivility **11** discourtesy, presumption **12** impertinence, impoliteness

disrespectful

4 flip, rude **5** sassy, saucy **7** ill-bred, uncivil **8** flippant, impolite, impudent, insolent **10** ungracious **11** ill-mannered, impertinent **12** contemptuous, discourteous

disrobe

4 bare, peel **5** strip **6** denude, divest **7** undress **8** unclothe

disrupt

5 upset **6** mess up **7** break up, rupture **8** disorder, unsettle

dissatisfaction

6 dismay **9** annoyance, complaint **10** discontent, irritation, uneasiness **11** displeasure, frustration

dissatisfied

5 irked, vexed **7** annoyed **8** bothered **10** begrudging, discontent, displeased, malcontent **11** complaining, disaffected, unfulfilled **12** disappointed, discontented, malcontented

dissect

5 probe, study **7** analyze, examine, inspect **9** anatomize, break down, take apart **10** scrutinize

dissection

7 autopsy **8** analysis, necropsy
of animals: 7 zootomy

dissemble

4 hide, mask **5** cloak, feign **7** conceal, cover up, dress up, falsify **8** disguise, simulate **9** whitewash **10** camouflage **11** counterfeit

dissembler
4 fake 5 faker, fraud, phony 8 deceiver, imposter, impostor, pharisee 9 hypocrite, pretender

disseminate
3 sow 4 strew 6 blazon, spread 7 bestrew, diffuse, publish, scatter, send out 8 announce, disperse, proclaim 9 advertise, broadcast, circulate, propagate, publicize 10 promulgate

dissension
5 fight 6 strife 7 discord, dispute, faction, quarrel, wrangle 8 argument, clashing, conflict, disunity, friction, variance 9 bickering 10 contention, difference, quarreling 11 altercation, controversy 12 disagreement

dissent
5 demur 6 differ, heresy, object 8 conflict, variance 9 misbelief 10 contention, difference, heterodoxy, opposition, resistance 11 unorthodoxy 12 nonagreement 13 nonconformism, nonconformity

dissenter
7 heretic 8 apostate, defector, deserter, partisan, recreant 10 schismatic, separatist 11 misbeliever, schismatist 13 nonconformist

dissertation
6 thesis 8 tractate, treatise 9 discourse, monograph 10 commentary, exposition 11 disputation 12 disquisition 13 argumentation

disservice
4 harm 6 damage, injury, insult 8 disfavor, meanness, mischief 9 detriment 10 misfortune

dissever
3 cut, hew 4 hack, part 5 carve, slice, split 6 cleave, detach, divide, sunder 7 disjoin, divorce 8 disjoint, disunite, separate, uncouple 10 disconnect

dissidence
6 heresy, schism, strife 7 discord, dispute, dissent, faction 8 conflict, friction, variance 10 contention, disharmony, dissension, heterodoxy, opposition 11 discordance, unorthodoxy 12 disagreement 13 nonconformism, nonconformity

dissident
7 heretic 8 partisan, recusant 9 differing, dissenter, heretical, heterodox, protestor 10 schismatic, separatist, unorthodox

11 contentious, disagreeing, misbeliever, nonbeliever, quarrelsome, schismatist 12 disputatious, unharmonious 13 nonconformist

dissimilar
6 unlike 7 diverse, unalike, unequal, various 8 distinct 9 different, disparate, divergent 13 heterogeneous

dissimilarity
8 contrast, variance 9 disparity, diversity, variation 10 difference, divergence, divergency, unlikeness 11 incongruity 13 heterogeneity, inconsistency

dissimulate
see **dissemble**

dissimulation
5 fraud, guile, lying 6 deceit 7 cunning 8 artifice, flimflam, pretense 9 deception, duplicity, hypocrisy, mendacity, sophistry 10 craftiness, pharisaism 11 beguilement, smoke screen

dissipate
4 blow 5 use up, waste 6 burn up, spread, vanish 7 break up, scatter 8 disperse, evanesce, melt away, misspend, squander 9 evaporate, throw away 11 fritter away

dissipated
6 rakish, wanton, wasted 8 depraved 9 debauched, reprobate 10 degenerate, licentious, profligate 11 intemperate

dissociate
4 part 5 unfix 6 cut off, detach 7 disband, disjoin 8 alienate, disunite, estrange, separate, uncouple 9 disengage 10 disconnect

dissolute
3 lax 4 fast, wild 5 loose, slack 6 rakish, wanton 7 raffish, wayward 8 decadent, depraved 9 abandoned, debauched, indulgent, reprobate 10 degenerate, dissipated, licentious, profligate 12 unprincipled, unrestrained

dissolution
5 death, decay, split 6 demise 7 breakup, divorce, rupture, split-up 8 division 9 dispersal, partition 10 detachment, disbanding, profligacy 11 evaporation 12 liquefaction

dissolvable
7 soluble 8 meltable

dissolve
3 end 4 flux, melt, thaw, undo, void

5 annul, quash **6** recess, vacate, vanish **7** adjourn, break up, destroy, diffuse, disband, liquefy, resolve, shatter, unravel **8** abrogate, demolish, disperse, evanesce, fade away, get rid of, melt away, prorogue, separate **9** decompose, dissipate, evaporate, prorogate, terminate, waste away **10** deliquesce, do away with **12** disintegrate

dissonance

6 strife **7** discord **8** clashing, conflict **9** cacophony, harshness **10** contention, difference, disharmony **11** incongruity **12** disagreement **13** inconsistency

dissonant

5 harsh **7** grating, jarring, raucous **8** strident **9** unmusical **10** cacophonic, discordant, inharmonic **11** cacophonous, conflicting, incongruous **12** incompatible, inharmonious

dissuade

5 deter **7** turn off **10** discourage, disincline

distaff

6 female **8** maternal

distance

4 area **5** ambit, lapse, orbit, range, reach, scope, space, sweep **6** course, degree, extent, length, radius, remove, spread **7** breadth, compass, expanse, horizon, mileage, reserve, spacing, stretch **8** coldness, interval **9** amplitude, disparity, expansion, extension **10** divergence, divergency, remoteness, separation **11** distinction, perspective **13** dissimilarity
angular: 8 latitude **9** longitude
between levels: 4 drop
between rails: 4 gage
between supports: 4 span
from bottom to top: 6 height
geometric: 8 altitude
greatest perpendicular: 6 camber
measuring instrument: 8 odometer **9** pedometer, telemeter **11** range finder
minute: 4 hair
perpendicular: 5 depth
shortest: 7 beeline **12** straight line
the wind blows: 5 fetch

distant

3 far, shy **4** afar, cold, cool **5** aloof, apart **6** absent, far-off, remote **7** faraway, haughty, obscure, removed, spacial, spatial **8** far-flung, isolated, outlying, reserved, secluded, solitary **9** separated, unsimilar, withdrawn **10** unsociable **11** out-of-the-way, sequestered, standoffish

combining form: 3 tel **4** tele, telo

distaste

7 disgust, dislike **8** aversion, loathing **9** antipathy, hostility, revulsion **10** abhorrence, repugnance **13** indisposition

distasteful

8 unsavory **9** loathsome, obnoxious, offensive, repellent, repugnant, repulsive **10** abominable, unpleasant **11** displeasing, unpalatable **12** disagreeable, unappetizing **13** objectionable

distemper

6 malady **7** ailment, disease **8** disorder **9** contagion, strangles **10** affliction **11** derangement **13** panleucopenia

distend

5 bloat, bulge, swell, widen **6** dilate, expand, extend, puff up **7** amplify, augment, enlarge, inflate, stretch **8** increase, lengthen **10** stretch out

distill

6 refine **7** extract **8** boil down **11** concentrate, precipitate

distinct

4 sole **5** clear, lucid, plain **6** marked, patent, single, unique **7** audible, defined, diverse, evident, express, notable, obvious, special, unusual **8** apparent, clear-cut, definite, discrete, especial, explicit, manifest, palpable, peculiar, separate, specific **9** different, divergent **10** individual, noticeable, particular **11** categorical, unambiguous, unequivocal **12** unmistakable

distinction

4 bays, rank **5** award, badge, grade, honor, kudos **6** nicety, renown **7** laurels **8** accolade, eminence, prestige **10** difference, divergence, divergency, prominence, unlikeness **11** differentia, peculiarity, preeminence, recognition **12** significance **13** dissimilarity

distinctive

6 proper, single, unique **7** special **8** peculiar, separate, singular **10** individual **13** idiosyncratic

distingué

6 classy, urbane **7** courtly, elegant, eminent, genteel, refined **8** cultured, decorous, highbrow, mannerly, polished, well-bred **9** dignified, high-class **10** cultivated **13** sophisticated

distinguish
4 mark, note, spot, view 5 honor, place
6 descry, notice, set off 7 dignify, make
out, mark off, observe, pick out 8 classify,
identify, perceive, separate 9 recognize,
single out 10 categorize 12 characterize,
discriminate 13 differentiate, individualize

distinguished
5 famed, noted 6 famous 7 eminent,
notable, stately 8 esteemed, imposing,
renowned 9 dignified, prominent
10 celebrated 11 illustrious

distort
4 bend, warp, wind 5 alter, color, twist
6 deform, garble 7 contort, falsify, pervert,
torture 8 misstate 11 misconstrue
12 misinterpret, misrepresent

distortion
8 twisting 9 deformity

distract
5 addle, mix up 6 ball up, bemuse, divert,
perplex, puzzle 7 confuse, fluster, mislead
8 befuddle, bewilder, confound, throw off
9 sidetrack, unbalance

distracted
8 confused, deranged, maddened, troubled
9 oblivious 10 nonplussed 11 disoriented,
inattentive, preoccupied 12 absent-minded

distraction
5 upset 9 agitation, amusement,
confusion, diversion 10 perplexity
12 interruption 13 entertainment

distrait
5 upset 7 anxious, bemused, faraway,
worried 8 confused, deranged, harassed,
maddened, troubled 9 tormented,
withdrawn 10 abstracted, distracted,
distraught 11 inattentive, preoccupied
12 absentminded, apprehensive

distraught
5 upset 6 addled, crazed 7 anxious,
frantic, muddled, rattled, shook up,
unglued, worried 8 agitated, confused,
demented, deranged, frenzied, harassed,
troubled, worked up 9 flustered, perturbed,
tormented, wigged-out 10 distressed,
bewildered, freaked out, nonplussed
11 overwrought

distress
3 ail, irk, mar, try, vex, woe 4 ache, care,
hurt, pain, pang, rack 5 agony, annoy,
cross, dolor, grief, rigor, throe, trial, upset,
worry 6 bother, grieve, harass, misery,
pester, plague, sorrow, strain, strait, twinge

7 afflict, anguish, anxiety, exhaust, torment,
torture, trouble 8 aggrieve, calamity,
exigency, hardship 9 adversity, constrain,
hard times, suffering 10 affliction, difficulty,
heartbreak, misfortune, visitation
11 tribulation, vicissitude
call: 6 Mayday
signal: 3 SOS 5 alarm

distressing
4 dire 6 woeful 8 alarming, grievous,
shocking 9 offensive 10 deplorable,
lamentable 11 dispiriting, regrettable,
unfortunate 13 heartbreaking

distribute
4 deal, mete 5 allot, place, strew 6 assign,
assort, divide, donate, parcel, ration,
spread 7 deal out, deliver, diffuse, dish out,
divvy up, dole out, dribble, give out, hand
out, mete out, prorate, radiate, scatter, slice
up 8 allocate, classify, disburse, dispense,
position, separate 9 apportion, circulate,
partition, propagate, spread out
10 administer, measure out
11 disseminate
in a tournament: 4 seed

distribution
7 density 8 delivery, dividend, grouping,
ordering, sequence 9 allotment, allotting,
diffusion, dispersal, marketing, placement,
spreading 10 dispersion, scattering
11 arrangement, probability, propagation
12 apportioning, dispensation
13 apportionment, dissemination

distributor
5 agent 6 broker, jobber 7 carrier
10 wholesaler 12 intermediate

district
4 area, ward 5 tract 6 barrio, locale,
parcel, region, sector 7 borough, quarter,
section 8 division, locality, precinct,
vicinage, vicinity 11 subdivision
12 neighborhood
ecclesiastical: 5 synod 6 parish
7 diocese
Greek: 4 deme
Indian: 6 tahsil
judicial: 7 circuit
London: 4 Soho 7 Chelsea, Mayfair
9 Docklands, Greenwich, Southwark
10 Kensington, Piccadilly 11 Canary
Wharf, Notting Hill 13 Knightsbridge
New York: 4 Soho 7 Chelsea, Tribeca
theater: 6 rialto

District of Columbia
college, university: 6 Howard

8 American, Catholic 9 Gallaudet
10 Georgetown
motto: 13 E Pluribus Unum
official bird: 10 wood thrush
official flower: 18 American Beauty rose

distrust
5 doubt 7 suspect 8 question, wariness
9 disbelief, discredit, misgiving, suspicion
10 disbelieve

distrustful
4 wary 5 chary, leery 7 cynical, dubious,
jealous 8 doubtful, doubting 10 suspicious
12 questionable

distrusting
4 wary 5 chary, leery 7 cynical, dubious,
jealous 8 doubtful, doubting 10 suspicious

disturb
4 faze 5 alarm, daunt, rouse, upset, worry
6 bother, harass, meddle, mess up, pester,
stir up 7 agitate, break up, disrupt, fluster,
perplex, trouble, unnerve 8 bewilder,
distress, unsettle 9 incommode, interrupt
10 discompose, disconcert, tamper with
13 inconvenience, interfere with

disturbance
4 flap, fuss, stir, to-do 5 stink 6 clamor,
hubbub, rumpus, tumult, unrest, uproar
7 bobbery, turmoil 9 agitation, commotion,
confusion, disorder 10 alteration,
disruption, turbulence 11 derangement,
distraction 12 interruption
atmospheric: 5 storm 7 cyclone, tornado
9 hurricane
mental: 6 frenzy 8 delirium, neurosis
9 psychosis
oceanic: 7 tsunami

disturbed
5 upset 6 insane, shaken 7 anxious,
puzzled, rattled, worried 8 bothered,
demented, deranged, troubled 9 concerned, psychotic, unsettled 10 distracted,
distressed 12 disconcerted

disunion
7 divorce, rupture, split-up 8 division,
severing, variance 9 partition
10 detachment, difference, separation
13 disconnection

disunite
4 part 6 divide, sunder 7 break up, disjoin,
divorce, split up 8 dissever, separate,
uncouple 9 disengage, fall apart
10 disconnect 12 disaffiliate

disunity
6 strife, schism 7 discord 8 conflict,
division, variance 10 alienation,
contention, disharmony, dissension

12 disaffection, disagreement,
estrangement

disused
5 passé 8 obsolete, outdated, outmoded
9 abandoned, discarded 10 antiquated,
superseded

ditch
3 dig, pit 4 drop, dump, foss, junk, moat
5 chuck, fosse, leave, scrap, swale
6 reject, trench, trough 7 abandon, cashier,
discard, dismiss, forsake, foxhole
8 jettison, throw out 9 crash-land, dispose
of, throw away 10 excavation

dither
4 fuss, stew 5 quake, shake, tizzy, waver
6 falter, flurry, quaver, shiver 7 flutter,
tremble, twitter, whiffle 8 hesitate
9 agitation, commotion, confusion, vacillate
10 excitement, turbulence 12 shilly-shally

dithyramb
4 hymn, poem 5 chant

dithyrambic
6 ardent, fervid 9 perfervid, rhapsodic
10 boisterous, passionate 11 impassioned

ditto
4 copy, same 5 clone, me too, Xerox
6 carbon, repeat 7 replica, reprint, similar
9 duplicate, facsimile, photocopy
10 carbon copy, mimeograph
11 replication 12 reproduction
13 reduplication

ditty
3 air, lay 4 song, tune 5 carol, chant
6 ballad

diurnal
5 daily 7 daytime 8 daylight 9 circadian,
ephemeral, quotidian

diva
7 goddess 10 prima donna 11 leading
lady

divagate
4 turn, veer 5 drift, stray 6 depart, ramble,
wander 7 deviate, digress, diverge

divan
4 sofa 5 couch 6 settee 7 chamber,
council 9 davenport 12 chesterfield

dive
3 bar, pub 4 dash, dump, hole, jump, leap
5 joint, lunge, pitch, sound, swoop
6 header, lounge, plunge, saloon, tavern
7 barroom, decline, descend, descent,
hangout, plummet, taproom 8 submerge
9 honky-tonk, roadhouse 10 cannonball

type: 4 pike, swan, tuck 6 gainer
7 cutaway 9 belly flop, jackknife

diver
4 loon

diverge
4 part, vary 5 stray 6 depart, differ, swerve
7 deflect, deviate, digress 8 disagree,
separate 9 bifurcate, branch off, draw
apart

divergence
7 parting 9 departure, deviation, differing
10 aberration, deflection, difference,
digression, separation 11 disagreeing,
discrepancy, distinction 12 disagreement

divergent
6 unlike 8 aberrant, abnormal, atypical
9 anomalous, different, differing, disparate,
irregular 10 dissimilar

divers
6 sundry 7 several, various 8 assorted
9 different, disparate 13 miscellaneous

diverse
5 mixed 6 motley, sundry, unlike, varied
7 several, unalike, unequal, various,
varying 8 assorted, discrete, distinct,
manifold, separate 9 different, differing,
disparate, multiform, multiplex, unsimilar
10 contrasted, dissimilar 11 contrasting,
contrastive 12 multifarious
13 contradictory, miscellaneous
meanings: 8 polysemy

diversion
5 sport 7 pastime, turning 8 pleasure,
sideshow 9 amusement, deviation,
enjoyment 10 aberration, deflection,
recreation, red herring 11 distraction
13 entertainment

diversity
7 variety 10 assortment, difference,
unlikeness 11 variegation 12 multiformity
13 dissimilarity, heterogeneity

divert
4 turn, veer 5 amuse 6 regale, swerve
7 beguile, deflect, delight, deviate, digress
8 distract, redirect 9 entertain, turn aside

divest
3 rid, rob 4 free 5 spoil, strip 6 denude
7 bereave, deprive, despoil, disrobe,
undress 8 take away 9 dismantle
10 disinherit, dispossess

divide
3 cut 4 fork, part 5 allot, cut up, sever,
share 6 assign, cleave, parcel, ration,
sunder 7 break up, dissect, divorce, dole
out, isolate, prorate, quarter, share in, split
up 8 allocate, classify, dispense, disunite,
separate 9 apportion, branch out, partition,
watershed 10 distribute, measure out
11 dichotomize, distinguish
into four parts: 7 quarter
into three parts: 7 trisect
into two parts: 5 halve 6 bisect
9 bifurcate

divided
4 rent 5 riven, split 6 cloven 7 asunder,
partite 8 ruptured

dividend
5 bonus, share 6 return, reward 7 benefit,
guerdon, portion, premium 9 allotment
12 dispensation

divider
6 border, screen 9 partition

divination
6 augury 7 insight 8 prophecy
11 foretelling, soothsaying
by communication with the dead:
10 necromancy
by figures: 8 geomancy
by lots: 9 sortilege
by numbers: 10 numerology
by rods: 7 dowsing 11 rhabdomancy
by stars: 9 astrology

divine
4 holy 5 clerk, godly, infer 6 cleric,
deduce, deific, parson, priest, sacred,
superb 7 foresee, godlike, intuit 8 clerical,
foreknow, heavenly, luscious, minister,
preacher, prophesy, reverend
9 apprehend, churchman, clergyman,
marvelous, religious, visualize
10 anticipate, conjecture, sanctified,
superhuman, theologian 11 scrumptious
12 ecclesiastic

diviner
4 seer 5 augur, sibyl 6 oracle 7 palmist,
prophet 8 haruspex 10 forecaster,
prophetess, soothsayer

divinity
3 god 5 deity, fudge 7 goddess, godhead,
godhood 8 theology

division
3 cut 4 part, unit 5 class, piece, slice, split
6 branch, moiety, parcel, schism, sector
7 breakup, discord, dissent, divorce,
parting, portion, rupture, section, segment,
split-up 8 category, conflict, district,
disunion, disunity, variance 9 partition
10 detachment, difference, disharmony,
dissidence, separation 11 dissolution
12 disagreement 13 apportionment

Bible: 5 verse
book: 7 chapter
British territorial: 5 shire
building: 4 wing
cell: 7 meiosis, mitosis
city: 4 ward 7 borough 8 precinct
contest: 4 heat 6 inning, period
corolla: 5 petal
country: 5 state 6 canton 8 province
10 department, prefecture
family: 4 side 6 branch
geologic time: 3 eon, era 5 epoch
6 period
hospital: 4 ward, wing
into two: 9 bisection 11 bifurcation,
bipartition
meal: 6 course
music: 3 bar 4 beat 7 measure
8 movement
opera, play: 3 act 5 scena, scene
poem: 5 canto, verse 6 stanza
population: 7 segment, stratum
race: 3 lap 4 heat
social: 5 caste, class, tribe
state: 6 county, parish
term: 8 quotient
time: 3 day, eon 4 week, year 5 month
6 decade, minute, moment, second
7 century, weekend 9 fortnight
10 millennium
tribal: 4 clan
word: 8 syllable
zodiac: 4 sign

divisive
8 factious 11 disunifying

divorce
4 part 5 sever, split 6 divide, sunder
7 break up, breakup, disjoin, rupture
8 disjoint, dissever, disunion, disunite,
separate 9 partition, severance
10 detachment, separation 11 dissolution

divot
3 sod 4 turf 5 clump

divulge
4 blab, leak, tell 5 spill 6 betray, expose,
gossip, reveal, tattle 7 let slip, uncover
8 disclose, give away

Dixie composer
6 Emmett (Daniel D.)

dizziness
7 vertigo 9 giddiness

dizzy
5 addle, dazed, giddy, mix up, silly, tipsy
6 addled 7 confuse, dazzled, flighty,

foolish, fuddled, muddled, puzzled, reeling
8 confused, swimming, whirling
9 befuddled, confusing 10 bewildered,
confounded, distracted, exorbitant,
immoderate, inordinate 11 extravagant,
light-headed, vertiginous

Djibouti
capital: 8 Djibouti
language: 6 Arabic, French
monetary unit: 5 franc
neighbor: 7 Eritrea, Somalia 8 Ethiopia
sea: 3 Red

DNA
component: 7 adenine, guanine, thymine
8 cytosine 10 nucleotide 11 deoxyribose
segment: 7 cistron

doable
8 feasible, possible, workable 9 realistic
10 achievable, attainable 11 performable

do away with
3 end, nix, zap 4 kill, slay 5 annul, erase,
whack 6 cancel, finish, murder, remove,
repeal, revoke, rub out 7 abolish, bump off,
deep-six, destroy, discard, expunge,
rescind, squelch, wipe out 8 abrogate,
blow away, demolish, dispatch, dissolve,
massacre, stamp out 9 dispose of,
eliminate, eradicate, extirpate, finish off,
liquidate, slaughter 10 extinguish,
obliterate 11 discontinue, exterminate

docent
5 guide 6 leader 7 teacher 8 lecturer
10 instructor

docile
4 tame 5 pliant 7 ductile, pliable
8 amenable, biddable, obedient, yielding
9 adaptable, compliant, teachable,
tractable 10 submissive 11 acquiescent

dock
3 bob, cut 4 crop, fine, pier, quay, rump,
slip 5 berth, jetty, levee, tie up, wharf
6 anchor, hangar, lessen, marina, reduce
7 abridge, landing, shorten 8 cut short,
platform, truncate
worker: 6 lumper 9 stevedore
12 longshoreman

docket
4 card 6 agenda, lineup, record 7 program
8 abstract, calendar, caseload, register,
schedule 9 timetable

doctor
3 fix, vet 4 mend 5 adapt, alter, medic,
treat 6 medico, repair 7 croaker, dentist,
falsify, scholar, surgeon 8 sawbones

9 clinician, internist, physician
10 adulterate, recondition, reconstruct 11 medicine man,
animal: 3 vet 12 veterinarian
children's: 12 pediatrician
famous: 4 Koop (C. Everett) 5 Galen, Spock (Benjamin) 6 Atkins (Robert), Chopra (Deepak), Ornish (Dean) 9 Kevorkian (Jack) 10 Schweitzer (Albert) 11 Hippocrates, Livingstone (David)
foot: 10 podiatrist 11 chiropodist
heart: 12 cardiologist
teeth: 7 dentist
women's: 12 gynecologist

Doctor of the Church
5 Basil 6 Jerome 7 Ambrose, Gregory 9 Augustine 10 Athanasius

Doctorow novel
7 Ragtime 9 City of God (The) 10 Waterworks, World's Fair 12 Book of Daniel (The) 13 Billy Bathgate 18 Welcome to Hard Times

doctrinaire
5 rigid 8 dogmatic 9 obstinate 10 unyielding 11 domineering, magisterial 13 authoritarian

doctrine
3 ism 5 axiom, basic, canon, credo, creed, dogma, faith, tenet 7 precept 8 teaching 9 principle 11 fundamental

document
4 deed 5 paper 6 record 8 evidence, monument 9 testimony 10 instrument 11 certificate
travel: 8 passport

dodder
4 limp 5 shake 6 falter, hobble, totter 7 shamble, shuffle, stagger, tremble 12 morning glory

doddering
5 shaky 6 doting, feeble, senile 7 fragile 8 unsteady, weakened 9 faltering

dodge
4 duck, jink, ruse, slip 5 avoid, elude, evade, fence, parry, shirk, skirt, slide, trick 6 escape, scheme, weasel 7 evasion 8 sidestep 9 avoidance, deception, expedient

Dodger
5 Davis (Tommy) 6 Garvey (Steve), Karros (Eric), Koufax (Sandy), Piazza (Michael), Snider (Duke), Sutton (Don) 8 Newcombe (Don), Robinson (Jackie) 9 Hershiser (Orel) 10 Campanella (Roy)
field: 7 Ebbetts
manager: 6 Alston (Walter) 7 Lasorda (Tommy)

dodger
6 outlaw, screen 7 escapee 8 circular, deceiver, deserter, fugitive, handbill, runagate 9 throwaway

dodgy
4 iffy 5 fishy, vague 6 tricky 7 cryptic, obscure 8 doubtful, unproven 9 ambiguous, enigmatic, uncertain 10 indefinite, problematic, suspicious, unreliable 12 questionable 13 controversial

dodo
3 oaf 4 bird, boob, clod, dolt, dope, goof, yo-yo 5 chump, dummy, dunce, idiot, moron, ninny, noddy, stupe 6 dimwit, dum-dum, nitwit 7 airhead, dullard, pinhead 8 bonehead, dumbbell, imbecile, lunkhead, meathead, numskull 9 birdbrain, blockhead, ignoramus, lamebrain, nincompoop, numbskull, simpleton 10 dunderhead 11 chowderhead, chucklehead

doe
4 deer 6 female, rabbit 8 kangaroo

doff
4 shed 6 remove 7 take off

dog
3 cur, pug, pup, tag 4 bird, chow, fice, mutt, peke, puli, tail, tyke 5 Akita, boxer, feist, frank, hound, husky, lemon, pooch, puppy, spitz, trail 6 Afghan, beagle, bowwow, briard, canine, collie, detent, poodle, pursue, rascal, saluki, setter, shadow, vizsla, wiener, wretch 7 andiron, Maltese, mastiff, mongrel, pointer, Samoyed, spaniel, terrier, whippet 8 Airedale, Brittany, inferior, keeshond, papillon, Pekinese, pinscher, spurious, wirehair 9 Chihuahua, dachshund, dalmation, Great Dane, greyhound, Pekingese, retriever, schnauzer 10 bloodhound, Pomeranian, rottweiler, Weimaraner 11 bullmastiff, frankfurter, wienerwurst 12 Newfoundland, Saint Bernard 13 cocker spaniel
Alaskan: 8 malamute, malemute
Australian: 5 dingo
barkless: 7 basenji
bird: 6 setter 7 pointer, spaniel 9 retriever
Bush's: 6 Millie
Buster Brown's: 4 Tige

Charlie Brown's: 6 Snoopy
command: 3 sit 4 heel, stay
Dorothy's: 4 Toto
Eskimo: 5 husky
family: 7 Canidae
FDR's: 4 Fala
fictional: 4 Buck 5 Astro, Pluto 6 Big Red
8 McBarker 9 Marmaduke, Old Yeller,
Scooby-Doo, White Fang
"Garfield": 4 Odie
genus: 5 Canis
Hungarian: 6 vizsla
hunting: 5 hound 6 beagle, borzoi, saluki,
setter, Talbot, vizsla 7 harrier, pointer,
redbone 8 elkhound, foxhound
9 wolfhound 10 bloodhound 11 basset
hound
Indian: 5 dhole
L.B.J.'s: 3 Her
long-bodied: 9 dachshund
movie: 4 Asta, Toto 5 Benji, Tramp
6 Lassie 9 Beethoven, Old Yeller, Rin Tin
Tin
name: 4 Fido, Spot 5 Rover 6 Bowser
Nixon's: 8 Checkers
Odysseus's: 5 Argos
of Hades: 8 Cerberus
Orphan Annie's: 5 Sandy
powerful: 11 bullmastiff
Roy Rogers's: 6 Bullet
Russian: 6 borzoi 7 Samoyed
shaggy-coated: 8 komondor, sheepdog
9 deerhound
short-legged: 5 corgi
small: 3 pom, pug, pup 4 peke
8 Pekinese 9 Chihuahua, Pekingese
10 Pomeranian
space traveler: 5 Laika
Steinbeck's: 7 Charley
television: 4 King 5 Eddie, Tramp
6 Lassie, Murray 8 Wishbone 9 Rin Tin
Tin
terrier: 7 Scottie
three-headed: 8 Cerberus
Tibetan: 9 Lhasa apso
tiny: 9 Chihuahua
tooth: 4 fang
tracking: 10 bloodhound
two-headed: 6 Orthos
Wallace's: 6 Gromit
Welsh: 5 corgi
Wendy's: 4 Nana
wild: 5 dingo
young: 3 pup 5 puppy, whelp

dog days
9 canicular

dogfight
3 row 4 fray 5 brawl, broil, melee, set-to
6 fracas, ruckus 7 ruction 10 donnybrook,
free-for-all

dogfish
6 bowfin, burbot 8 mud puppy

dogged
7 adamant 8 obdurate, resolute, stubborn
9 insistent, steadfast, obstinate, tenacious,
unbending 10 bullheaded, hardheaded,
persistent, persisting, unshakable,
unyielding 11 persevering, unremitting
12 pertinacious

doggone
4 damn, dang, darn, rank 5 utter 6 cursed,
damned, darned 7 blasted, blessed,
dratted 8 absolute, accursed, infernal,
outright 9 out-and-out 10 confounded
11 unmitigated 13 blankety-blank

dogma
4 code, rule 5 canon, credo, creed, tenet
6 belief, gospel 7 precept 8 doctrine,
ideology 9 orthodoxy, postulate, teachings
10 conviction, persuasion

dogmatic
8 oracular, orthodox 9 assertive, canonical,
doctrinal 11 dictatorial, doctrinaire,
magisterial 13 authoritarian, authoritative

Dog of Flanders author
5 Ouida

dog-paddle
4 swim

dog's age
3 eon 4 aeon 8 blue moon, eternity

Dog Star
6 Sirius

dogwood
6 cornel, Cornus 8 red osier

do in
4 kill, ruin, slay 5 cheat, wreck 6 defeat,
finish, murder, rub out 7 blot out, bump off,
destroy, execute, exhaust, frazzle, take out,
wear out 8 dispatch, knock off, knock out,
wipe out 9 eliminate, liquidate, prostrate,
run ragged, shipwreck 11 assassinate

doing
3 act 6 action 8 activity
good: 10 beneficent
evil: 10 maleficent

doit
3 bit, jot 4 coin, damn, dram, drop, hoot,
iota, mite, whit 6 trifle 8 particle

doldrums
5 blahs, blues, dumps, ennui, gloom, slump
6 apathy, tedium, torpor 7 boredom
9 dejection 10 depression, inactivity,
quiescence, stagnation 12 listlessness

doleful
3 sad 4 down 7 forlorn, ruthful 8 cast
down, dejected, dolorous, downcast,
grieving, mournful, mourning 9 afflicted,
cheerless, depressed, miserable, plaintive,
sorrowful, sorrowing, woebegone
10 dispirited, lamentable, lugubrious,
melancholy 11 crestfallen, downhearted
12 disconsolate

dole out
4 deal 5 allot 6 divide, parcel, ration
7 divvy up 8 disburse, dispense, disperse
9 apportion, partition 10 administer,
distribute

doll
3 Ken 6 Barbie, figure, Kewpie, puppet
10 Betsy Wetsy, Raggedy Ann
11 Raggedy Andy
grotesque: 8 golliwog

dollar
3 one 4 bill, buck, clam, oner, peso 5 taler
6 single 7 ringgit, smacker 8 simoleon
9 cartwheel, greenback

dollop
4 blob, glob, lump 7 portion

Doll's House, A
author: 5 Ibsen (Henrik)
heroine: 4 Nora

dolly
4 cart 7 stirrer 8 platform 10 locomotive

dolomite
6 marble 9 limestone

dolor
5 agony, grief 6 misery, sorrow 7 anguish,
passion 8 distress 9 suffering 10 affliction

dolorous
6 rueful, woeful 7 ruthful 8 grievous,
mournful, wretched 9 afflicted, anguished,
miserable, plaintive, sorrowful
10 lamentable, lugubrious, melancholy
13 heartbreaking

dolphin
5 whale 7 bollard 8 porpoise

dolt
3 ass, oaf 4 boob, clod, dodo, dork, fool,
goof, goon, lout, yo-yo 5 booby, chump,
dunce, idiot 6 nitwit 7 dullard, fathead,
halfwit, jughead, saphead, schnook
8 bonehead, dumbbell, dummkopf,
imbecile, lunkhead, meathead, numskull
9 blockhead, lamebrain, numbskull,
simpleton

doltish
4 dull, dumb 5 dense, thick 6 oafish,
obtuse, stupid 7 idiotic, moronic
8 ignorant, mindless 9 dim-witted,
fatheaded, imbecilic

domain
4 land, rule, turf 5 field, realm 6 estate,
sphere 7 kingdom, terrain 8 dominion,
province 9 bailiwick, territory

dome
4 head, hill, roof 5 mound 6 cupola
7 ceiling 8 mountain

domestic
4 help, home, tame 6 family, native
7 servant 8 houseboy, internal, national
9 charwoman, household 10 indigenous
11 chambermaid

domesticate
4 tame 5 adapt, adopt, train 10 housebreak

domicile
3 pad 4 home 5 abode, house, lodge, put
up 6 bestow, billet, harbor 7 quarter
8 dwelling, quarters 9 residence, residency
10 habitation

domiciliate
4 bunk, tame 5 house, lodge, put up
6 billet, harbor, reside 7 quarter

dominance
4 rule, sway 5 power 7 command, control
7 mastery 9 supremacy 10 ascendancy,
prepotency 11 preeminence, sovereignty

dominant
4 main 5 chief, first, major 6 ruling
7 leading, supreme 8 foremost, powerful,
reigning 9 ascendant, governing, number-
one, paramount, prevalent, principal
10 commanding, preeminent, prevailing,
successful, surpassing 11 controlling,
outweighing, overbearing 12 preponderant

dominate
4 rule 5 reign 6 direct, govern, obsess
7 control, prevail, repress 8 bestride, hold
sway, look down, loom over, overlook
9 subjugate, tower over, tyrannize
10 tower above

domination
4 rule, sway 5 might, power 7 command,
control, mastery 9 authority, supremacy

dominator

10 ascendancy, prepotency, suzerainty
11 preeminence, sovereignty
13 preponderancy

dominator
4 boss, head 5 chief, ruler 6 honcho,
leader, master, top dog 7 headman
8 director, hierarch, kingfish 9 chieftain,
commander

domineer
5 bully 6 hector 7 swagger 8 browbeat,
bulldoze 9 tyrannize 10 intimidate

domineering
5 bossy 6 lordly 8 arrogant, despotic
9 imperious, masterful 10 autocratic, high-
handed, oppressive, tyrannical
11 dictatorial, magisterial, overbearing

Dominica
capital: 6 Roseau
discoverer: 8 Columbus (Christopher)
language: 7 English
location: 10 West Indies
monetary unit: 6 dollar
sea: 9 Caribbean

Dominican Republic
capital: 12 Santo Domingo
island: 10 Hispaniola
language: 7 Spanish
location: 10 West Indies
monetary unit: 4 peso
mountain: 6 Duarte
neighbor: 5 Haiti
sea: 9 Caribbean

dominion
3 raj 4 rule, sway, turf 5 realm, power
6 domain, empery, empire, regnum, sphere
7 demesne, kingdom, terrain 8 province
9 ascendant, ownership, supremacy,
territory 10 ascendancy, possession
11 preeminence, sovereignty

domino
4 mask 5 amice, cloak, visor 6 vizard
8 disguise
spot: 3 pip

don
3 sir 4 lord 5 get on, put on, tutor
6 assume, fellow, take on 9 professor,
undertake

Donalbain
brother: 7 Malcolm
father: 6 Duncan

donate
4 give 5 grant 6 chip in, supply 7 dish out,
hand out, present, provide 8 give away,
shell out, transfer 10 contribute

donation
3 aid 4 alms, gift 5 grant 7 bequest,
handout 8 offering 9 endowment
11 benefaction, beneficence 12 contribution, philanthropy

Don Carlos
author: 8 Schiller (Friedrich von)
composer: 5 Verdi (Giuseppe)
father: 6 Philip

done
4 over 5 all in, ended, ready, spent
6 bushed, decent, doomed, gone by,
proper, used up 7 correct, drained,
dressed, far-gone, settled, through, worn-
out 8 becoming, complete, depleted,
finished, washed-up 9 befitting, completed,
concluded, exhausted 10 terminated
12 accomplished
poetic: 3 o'er

donee
7 grantee 8 receiver 9 recipient
11 beneficiary

done for
4 gone, sunk 5 kaput 6 beaten, doomed,
ruined 7 wrecked 8 finished, stricken

done in
5 spent 6 effete, used up 7 far gone, worn
out 8 depleted 9 exhausted, washed out

Don Giovanni composer
6 Mozart (Wolfgang Amadeus)

Donizetti, Gaetano
hero: 7 Roberto (Devereux)
opera: 5 Lucia (di Lammermoor) 10 Anna
Bolena, La Favorita 11 Don Pasquale
12 Maria Stuarda

Don Juan
4 rake, roué, wolf 5 Romeo 6 chaser,
masher 7 amorist, gallant, playboy,
seducer 8 Casanova, lothario, paramour
9 ladies' man, libertine, womanizer
10 lady-killer, profligate 11 philanderer
drama: 10 Stone Guest (The)
home: 7 Seville
mother: 4 Inez
poet: 5 Byron (Lord) 7 Pushkin
(Alexander)

donkey
3 ass 4 mule 5 burro 7 jackass
female: 5 jenny

donkeywork
4 moil, toil 5 grind, labor 7 travail
8 drudgery

donnybrook
3 row 4 fray 5 brawl, broil, fight, melee,

set-to **6** fracas, ruckus, rumpus, tumult, uproar **7** dispute, quarrel, rhubarb, ruction **10** free-for-all **11** altercation

donor
5 giver **6** patron **7** granter, grantor **8** bestower **9** conferrer, presenter **10** benefactor **11** contributor

do-nothing
3 bum **4** slug **5** idler **6** loafer, slouch **7** goof-off, slacker **8** deadbeat, fainéant, layabout, slugabed, sluggard **9** lazybones, vegetable **11** couch potato

Don Pasquale composer
9 Donizetti (Gaetano)

Don Quixote
author: 9 Cervantes (Miguel de)
beloved: 8 Dulcinea
companion (squire): 11 Sancho Panza
giant: 8 windmill
home: 8 La Mancha
horse: 9 Rocinante, Rosinante, Rozinante

doodad
5 gizmo, thing **6** bauble, dingus, entity, gadget, gewgaw, jigger, widget **7** trinket, whatsit **8** gimcrack **9** doohickey, thingummy **10** attachment, decoration, knickknack **11** thingamabob, thingamajig, thingumajig

doodle
6 dabble, dawdle, fiddle, potter, putter, sketch, tinker, trifle **7** cartoon, drawing **8** scribble **10** mess around

doodlebug
7 ant lion, missile **8** buzz bomb

doohickey
see **doodad**

doom
4 damn, fate, ruin **5** death **6** decree, demise, kismet **7** condemn, destiny, tragedy **8** calamity, disaster, judgment, sentence **11** catastrophe **12** annihilation, last judgment

doomful
4 dire **7** baleful, baneful, direful, fateful, malefic, ominous, unlucky **8** dreadful, ill-fated, sinister **10** foreboding, portentous **11** apocalyptic

doomsayer
7 killjoy **9** Cassandra, defeatist, Gloomy Gus, pessimist

_____ Doone
5 Lorna

door
3 way **4** adit, exit **5** entry **6** access, egress, entrée, portal **7** gateway, ingress, opening **8** entrance, entryway **9** admission **10** admittance **11** entranceway
rear: 7 postern

doorkeeper
6 porter

doorway
5 entry **6** portal **8** entrance, entryway **11** entranceway

doozy
3 ace, pip **5** dandy **7** paragon **8** standout **10** phenomenon **11** crackerjack

dope
3 oaf **4** clod, dodo, dolt, drug, goof, news, yo-yo **5** chump, drugs, dummy, dunce, facts, idiot, moron, ninny, noddy, stupe **6** dimwit, dum-dum, heroin, nitwit, opiate, sedate, skinny **7** airhead, cocaine, details, dullard, lowdown, pinhead **8** bonehead, dumbbell, imbecile, lunkhead, meathead, narcotic, numskull **9** birdbrain, blockhead, ignoramus, lamebrain, marijuana, narcotize, nincompoop, numbskull, simpleton **10** dunderhead **11** anesthetize, chowderhead, chucklehead, information, preparation

doped
4 high **5** dazed **6** stoned, zonked **7** drugged **8** hopped-up, tripping, tuned-in, turned on, wiped out **9** spaced-out, strung out, stupefied **10** narcotized

dopey
4 dumb **5** silly **6** dulled, stupid, torpid **7** fatuous, fuddled, muddled **8** comatose, sluggish **9** lethargic, senseless, stupefied

Doris
brother: 6 Nereus
daughters: 7 Nereids
father: 7 Oceanus
husband: 6 Nereus

dormancy
5 sleep **6** repose **7** latency, slumber **8** abeyance, diapause, doldrums, downtime **9** torpidity **10** inactivity, quiescence, suspension **11** cold storage **12** intermission, interruption

dormant
5 inert **6** asleep, drowsy, fallow, latent, torpid **7** abeyant **8** comatose, inactive, sluggish **9** lethargic, potential, quiescent, suspended **10** slow-moving, slumbering

dormer
3 bay 4 nook 5 niche 6 window

dorsal
6 aboral 7 abaxial

_____ d'Orsay
4 Quai

dorsum
4 back

Dorus
brother: 6 Aeolus
father: 6 Hellen

dory
4 bark, boat 5 craft, skiff 6 barque, bateau
7 shallop 8 lifeboat

dose
3 fix, hit 4 dram, shot, slug 7 measure,
portion 8 medicate, quantity

Dos Passos trilogy
3 U.S.A.

dossier
4 file 6 folder 9 portfolio

dot
4 mark, mote, stud 5 dower, dowry, point,
speck 6 bestud, pepper, period 7 freckle,
speckle, stipple 8 flyspeck, sprinkle
9 bespeckle 12 decimal point

dotage
8 senility 11 decrepitude, senectitude

dote on
5 adore, enjoy, fancy, prize 7 cherish,
idolize 8 treasure 9 delight in

doting
4 dear, fond 6 loving 7 adoring, devoted
12 affectionate

dotted
6 spotty 8 punctate, stippled

dotty
4 gaga 5 crazy, loony, wacky 6 absurd,
insane 7 foolish, smitten 8 enamored
9 eccentric 10 captivated, enraptured,
infatuated 12 preposterous

double
4 copy, dual, fold, mate, tack, twin 5 clone,
duple, image, match, twice 6 bifold, binary,
duplex, paired, ringer 7 dualize, enlarge,
magnify, replica, twofold 8 alter ego,
geminate, increase 9 companion, dualistic,
duplicate, look-alike, replicate 10 dead

ringer, reciprocal, simulacrum, understudy
13 spitting image

double-barreled
4 dual 5 duple 6 bifold, binary, duplex,
paired 7 twofold 9 dualistic

double bass
10 bull fiddle

double-cross
3 con 4 dupe 5 cheat, trick 6 betray,
delude, humbug, juggle, take in 7 beguile,
deceive, sell out, two-time 8 flimflam,
hoodwink 9 four-flush

double dagger
6 diesis

double-dealer
3 gyp 5 cheat, knave 6 con man
7 cozener, diddler, sharper 8 deceiver,
swindler 9 defrauder 11 flimflammer
13 confidence man

double-dealing
5 fraud 6 deceit 7 chicane 8 flimflam,
trickery 9 chicanery, deceitful, deception,
duplicity, two-timing 10 hanky-panky
11 duplicitous

double-dome
7 egghead 8 Einstein, highbrow 10 pointy-
head 12 intellectual

double-faced
9 deceitful, deceptive, equivocal, insincere
10 reversible 12 hypocritical
13 untrustworthy

doublet
3 duo 4 dyad, pair, span 5 brace
6 couple, jacket 7 twosome

double-talk
4 bosh, bunk 5 hokum, hooey 6 babble,
bunkum, drivel, jabber 7 blather, hogwash,
twaddle 8 flimflam, nonsense 9 gibberish,
poppycock 10 balderdash 12 gobbledygook

double vision
8 diplopia

doubt
5 qualm 7 concern, dispute, dubiety,
suspect 8 distrust, mistrust, question
9 challenge, disbelief, misgiving, suspicion
10 skepticism 11 dubiousness, incertitude,
incredulity, uncertainty

doubtable
4 hazy, iffy, moot 7 dubious, suspect
8 arguable 9 ambiguous, debatable,

equivocal, uncertain, undecided
10 disputable, borderline, indefinite
11 problematic **12** questionable

doubter
5 cynic **6** Thomas **7** skeptic **8** agnostic
10 Pyrrhonist, questioner, unbeliever
11 freethinker

doubtful
4 hazy, iffy, moot **5** fishy, shady, shaky
6 chancy, unsure **7** clouded, dubious,
obscure, suspect, unclear **8** arguable,
unlikely **9** ambiguous, debatable,
dubitable, equivocal, uncertain, undecided,
unsettled **10** borderline, disputable,
improbable **11** problematic, speculative
12 questionable

doubtfulness
7 concern, dubiety **8** mistrust **9** ambiguity,
misgiving, suspicion **10** indecision,
skepticism, uneasiness **11** dubiousness,
incertitude, uncertainty **13** indeterminacy

doubting Thomas
see **doubter**

doubtless
6 likely, surely **7** certain, clearly **8** of
course, probably **10** absolutely, definitely,
positively, presumably **11** indubitably
12 indisputably **13** presumptively,
unequivocally

douceur
3 tip **4** gift **5** bribe **7** present **8** gratuity

dough
4 cash **5** bread, money **6** dinero, moolah
7 cabbage, lettuce, scratch **8** currency
11 legal tender
inflator: 5 yeast

doughboy
7 dogface **11** infantryman

doughty
4 bold **5** brave, gutsy, manly, stout
6 daring, heroic, plucky, spunky, strong
7 gallant, valiant **8** fearless, intrepid,
resolved, stalwart, unafraid, valorous
9 dauntless, undaunted **10** courageous
12 stouthearted

doughy
3 wan **4** pale **5** pasty, waxen **6** pallid
8 blanched **9** colorless

do up
3 can, fix **4** mend, wash, wrap **5** clean,
patch **6** clothe, doctor, fasten, repair,
revamp **7** exhaust, festoon, launder,

package, prepare, rebuild, wear out
8 decorate, gift wrap, ornament, overhaul
9 embellish **11** recondition, reconstruct

dour
4 glum, grim **5** bleak, harsh, rigid, stern,
surly **6** gloomy, morose, severe, strict,
sullen **7** austere, crabbed, peevish
9 obstinate, saturnine, stringent
10 forbidding, unyielding

douse
3 sop **4** duck, dunk, soak **5** bathe, drown,
plash, slosh, souse **6** drench, put out,
quench, splash, strike **7** immerse, slacken
8 inundate, saturate, snuff out, submerge,
submerse **10** extinguish

dove
6 culver, pigeon **8** pacifist
call: 3 coo
genus: 7 Columba

dovecote
6 aviary **9** birdhouse

dovetail
3 fit **4** jibe, mesh **5** agree, match, tally
6 accord, splice, square **7** comport,
conform **8** check out **9** harmonize,
interlock, intermesh **10** correspond

dovish
4 mild **6** gentle **7** antiwar, pacific **8** pacifist
9 peaceable **10** nonviolent, pacifistic
11 peace-loving **12** conciliatory

dowager
4 dame **5** widow **6** matron **9** matriarch
10 grande dame **11** grandmother

dowdy
4 drab **5** dated, frump, passé, seedy, tacky
6 blowsy, bygone, démodé, frowsy, frowzy,
frumpy, old hat, shabby **7** rundown,
unkempt **8** frumpish, outdated, outmoded,
slattern, slovenly **9** out-of-date, unstylish
10 antiquated, bedraggled, slatternly
11 draggle-tail **12** old-fashioned
13 draggletailed

dowel
3 bar, peg, pin, rod **5** stick

dower
4 gift **5** endow, endue **6** legacy, talent
8 bequeath

dowitcher
5 snipe **9** sandpiper

do without
5 forgo, waive **6** abjure, eschew, give up,
pass up **8** renounce

down

down

3 eat, fur, ill, low, off, sad 4 blue, fell, fuzz, lint, pile, sick 5 below, ended, floor, floss, fluff, level, lower, under 6 defeat, fallen, finish, lay low, nether 7 conquer, consume, destroy, flatten, swallow, unhappy 8 bowl over, complete, defeated, dejected, dispatch, feathers, finished, inferior, overcome, sluggish, surmount 9 completed, concluded, depressed, earthward, miserable 10 dispirited, groundward

down-and-out

5 broke, needy 6 hard-up, ruined 8 beggared, derelict, homeless 9 destitute, penniless, penurious 12 impoverished

down-and-outer

3 bum 6 beggar, pauper, wretch 7 have-not 9 mendicant 10 supplicant

down-at-heels

4 mean 5 dingy, ratty, seedy, tacky 6 ragged, ragtag, shabby, shoddy 7 ignoble, run-down, worn-out 8 decrepit, tattered 10 bedraggled, threadbare 11 dilapidated 12 deteriorated, disreputable

downbeat

3 low, sad 4 blue, glum 6 droopy, gloomy, morose 7 decline, doleful 8 dejected 9 depressed 10 dispirited, melancholy 11 discouraged, pessimistic 12 disconsolate, disheartened, heavyhearted

downcast

3 low, sad 4 blue, glum, sunk 5 moody, mopey 6 droopy, gloomy, morose 7 doleful, forlorn, unhappy 8 dejected, dismayed, listless, soul-sick, troubled 9 depressed, heartsick, heartsore, miserable, oppressed, woebegone 10 chapfallen, despondent, dispirited, distressed, melancholy, spiritless 11 crestfallen, discouraged, low-spirited 12 disconsolate, disheartened

downfall

4 bane, ruin 6 demise 7 decline, undoing 8 collapse, Waterloo 9 ruination 10 devolution 11 declination, destruction 12 degeneration, dégringolade 13 deterioration

downgrade

4 bump, bust 5 abase, lower 6 demote 7 decline, demerit, descent, devalue 8 belittle, diminish, discount, minimize, relegate 9 denigrate, deprecate, devaluate, discredit, disparage, humiliate 10 depreciate, undervalue 12 degeneration, dégringolade 13 deterioration

downhearted

see **downcast**

down-in-the-mouth

see **downcast**

down payment

5 token 6 pledge 7 advance, deposit, earnest

downplay

8 belittle, discount, minimize, pooh-pooh 11 de-emphasize

downpour

6 deluge 7 monsoon 8 drencher 9 drenching, rainstorm 10 cloudburst, inundation 11 gully washer

downright

5 blunt, gross, total, truly, utter 7 blatant, flat-out 8 absolute, complete, explicit, positive, thorough 9 out-and-out 10 absolutely, sure-enough 11 indubitable, unequivocal, unmitigated, unqualified 13 thoroughgoing

downslide

3 dip, sag 4 drop, slip 5 slump 7 decline, drop-off, falloff 8 decrease 9 declivity, reduction

downstairs

6 cellar 8 basement

down-to-earth

8 rational 9 practical, pragmatic, realistic 10 hard-boiled, hardheaded, no-nonsense, reasonable 11 common-sense, plain-spoken 12 matter-of-fact 13 unpretentious, unsentimental

downtrend

see **downslide**

downtrodden

6 abject, abused 9 oppressed 10 maltreated, mistreated, persecuted, tyrannized

downturn

see **downslide**

downward

8 dropping 9 declining 10 descending

downy

4 soft 5 fuzzy 6 fleecy, fluffy 7 velvety 8 feathery
filler: 5 eider

dowry
4 gift 6 talent
French: 3 dot

doxy
4 moll, tart 5 wench 6 floozy, harlot
7 trollop 8 mistress 10 prostitute

doyen
4 dean, head 5 chief, maven 6 expert,
leader, master, wizard 7 maestro
8 virtuoso 9 authority, patriarch 10 past
master

Doyle's detective
6 Holmes (Sherlock)

D'Oyly Carte offering
8 operetta

doze
3 nap 5 sleep 6 catnap, drowse, nod off,
snooze 7 drop off, slumber 8 drift off
10 forty winks

dozy
see **drowsy**

DP
5 exile 6 émigré 7 evacuee, outcast,
refugee 8 deportee, emigrant, fugitive
10 expatriate

drab
4 dull, flat 5 bleak, brown, dingy, faded,
mousy, muddy, olive, vapid 6 dismal,
dreary, mousey 7 subfusc 8 lifeless
9 cheerless, colorless 10 lackluster
11 dispiriting

draconian
5 cruel, harsh, rigid 6 severe, strict
7 callous 8 ironclad, rigorous, ruthless
9 merciless, stringent 10 inflexible,
ironfisted, ironhanded

Dracula author
6 Stoker (Bram)

draft
3 tap 4 dose, haul, plan, plot, pull, pump,
swig 5 check, claim, drink, frame, press,
swill 6 breeze, call up, demand, design,
devise, enlist, enroll, induct, potion,
scheme, select, siphon, sketch
7 compose, concoct, current, outline,
portion, prepare, project, recruit 8 block
out, contrive, rough out, skeleton, traction
9 adumbrate, allowance, blueprint,
conscribe, conscript, fabricate, formulate,
muster out 11 delineation, skeletonize
avoider: 6 dodger
of a law: 4 bill

drag
3 lug, tow, tug 4 bore, haul, puff, pull, swig
5 dally, delay, draft, tarry, trail 6 burden,
dawdle, harrow, loiter, schlep, search,
sledge 7 schlepp 8 friction, straggle 9 lag
behind 13 procrastinate

dragging
4 beat, long 5 all in, spent, weary
6 pooped 7 drained, lengthy, tedious
8 drawn-out, extended, fatigued, overlong,
sluggish, wiped out 9 exhausted, lethargic,
long-drawn, pooped out, prolonged,
washed-out, wearisome 10 protracted,
slow-moving 12 interminable, long-drawn-
out

draggle
3 lag 4 rove 5 stray, trail 8 straggle, trail
off 10 fall behind

draggle-tail
4 bawd, drab, slut 5 wench, whore
6 harlot 8 slattern 10 prostitute
11 nightwalker 12 streetwalker

draggletailed
6 blowsy, frowsy, frowzy, sordid, untidy
8 slattern, sluttish 10 slatternly

dragnet
4 trap 5 snare, trawl 7 network

drag off
4 cart, haul

dragon
5 beast 8 basilisk 10 cockatrice
biblical: 5 Rahab
Canaanite: 3 Yam 4 Yamm 5 Lotan
Chinese: 4 lung
French: 8 Tarasque
genus: 5 Draco
Greek: 5 Ladon 9 Eurythion
slayer: 4 Baal, Enki, Zeus 5 Indra
6 Cadmus, George (St.), Marduk, Sigurd
7 Beowulf, Jupiter, Michael (St.), Ninurta,
Perseus 8 Margaret (St.)
Sumerian: 3 Kur
Wagnerian: 6 Fafnir

dragoon
3 cow 5 bully 6 badger, coerce, harass,
hector 8 bludgeon, browbeat, bulldoze,
bullyrag, threaten 9 persecute, strong-arm,
terrorize 10 cavalryman, intimidate

drain
3 dry, tap 4 pump, sink, sump, swig, tire,
vent, wear 5 bleed, draft, drink, empty,
leech, sewer, swill, use up, weary
6 burden, gutter, siphon, trench 7 conduit,

culvert, deplete, dwindle, draw off, exhaust, fatigue, outflow **8** bankrupt, draw down, wear down **9** discharge **10** impoverish **11** watercourse

drain away
3 ebb **4** drop, sink, wane **5** abate **6** lessen, reduce, remove **7** draw off, dwindle, retreat, subside **8** decrease, diminish, draw back, taper off, withdraw

drained
4 beat **5** all-in, spent, weary **6** bleary, pooped, used up **7** far-gone, worn-out **8** depleted, dragging, weakened, wiped out, worn out **9** exhausted, pooped out, washed-out

drainpipe
4 duct **5** sewer, spout **7** conduit **9** downspout

dram
3 bit, dab, nip, tot **4** atom, dash, drop, iota, jolt, mite, shot, slug, spot, swig, whit **5** crumb, grain, ounce, pinch, scrap, shred, snort, speck, morsel, sliver **7** modicum, smidgen, snifter, snippet, soupçon **8** particle

drama
4 play **7** pageant, theater, theatre, tragedy
award: 4 Tony
former English: 6 masque
Japanese: 3 Noh
main part: 8 epitasis
musical: 5 opera **8** operetta
suspenseful: 11 cliff-hanger

dramatic
5 vivid **8** striking, thespian **10** histrionic, theatrical
conflict: 4 agon

dramatis personae
4 cast **5** parts, roles **6** actors, troupe **7** company **10** characters

dramatist
10 playwright
American: 4 Hart (Moss), Inge (William), Odets (Clifford), Rabe (David), Rice (Elmer), Uhry (Alfred) **5** Albee (Edward), Foote (Horton), Guare (John), Hecht (Ben), Mamet (David), Odets (Clifford), Parks (Suzan-Lori), Payne (John Howard), Simon (Neil) **6** Ferber (Edna), Gurney (A. R.), Henley (Beth), Miller (Arthur), Norman (Marsha), O'Neill (Eugene), Thomas (Augustus), Wilder (Thornton), Wilson (August, Lanford, Robert) **7** Hellman (Lillian), Kaufman (George S.), Kushner (Tony), Shanley (John Patrick), Shepard (Sam) **8** Anderson (Maxwell, Robert), Caldwell (Erskine), Connolly (Marc), Sherwood (Robert), Williams (Tennessee) **9** Chayefsky (Paddy), Fierstein (Harvey), Hansberry (Lorraine) **11** Hammerstein (Oscar), Wasserstein (Wendy)
Austrian: 10 Schnitzler (Arthur)
Belgian: 11 Maeterlinck (Maurice)
Czech: 5 Havel (Vaclav)
English: 3 Fry (Christopher), Gay (John) **4** Hare (David), Rowe (Nicholas), Tate (Nahum) **5** Frayn (Michael), Milne (A. A.), Orton (Joe), Peele (George), Wilde (Oscar) **6** Barrie (James), Coward (Nöel), Dryden (John), Jonson (Ben), Pinero (Arthur Wing), Pinter (Harold), Steele (Richard), Storey (David) **7** Delaney (Shelagh), Marlowe (Christopher), Marston (John), Osborne (John), Shaffer (Anthony, Peter), Webster (John) **8** Congreve (William), Rattigan (Terrence), Shadwell (Thomas), Stoppard (Tom), Tourneur (Cyril), Vanbrugh (John), Zangwill (Israel) **9** Ayckbourn (Alan), Churchill (Caryl), Goldsmith (Oliver), Middleton (Thomas), Wycherley (William) **11** Shakespeare (William)
French: 5 Camus (Albert), Genet (Jean) **6** Musset (Alfred de), Racine (Jean), Sardou (Victorien), Sartre (Jean-Paul), Scribe (Eugène) **7** Anouilh (Jean), Ionesco (Eugène), Labiche (Eugène), Molière, Rostand (Edmond) **8** Marivaux (Pierre) **9** Corneille (Pierre), Crébillon, Giraudoux (Jean) **12** Beaumarchais (P. A. Caron de)
German: 5 Weiss (Peter) **6** Brecht (Bertolt), Goethe (Johann Wolfgang von), Kleist (Heinrich von) **8** Schiller (Friedrich von) **9** Hauptmann (Gerhart), Zuckmayer (Carl)
Greek: 8 Menander **9** Aeschylus, Euripides, Sophocles **12** Aristophanes
Hindu: 8 Kalidasa
Irish: 4 Shaw (George Bernard) **5** Behan (Brendan), Friel (Brian), Synge (John Millington), Yeats (William Butler) **6** O'Casey (Sean) **7** Beckett (Samuel), Gregory (Lady Augusta) **8** Sheridan (Richard Brinsley)
Italian: 5 Gozzi (Carlo), Verga (Giovanni) **7** Alfieri (Vittorio), Ariosto (Ludovico), Giacosa (Giuseppe), Goldoni (Carlo) **8** Trissino (Gian Giorgio) **9** D'Annunzio (Gabriele) **10** Metastasio (Pietro), Pirandello (Luigi)
Japanese: 5 Zeami
Nigerian: 7 Soyinka (Wole)

Norwegian: 5 Ibsen (Henrik) 8 Bjornson (Bjornstjerne)
Roman: 6 Seneca 7 Plautus, Terence
Romanian: 7 Ionesco (Eugene)
Russian: 7 Chekhov (Anton) 8 Zamyatin (Yevgeny)
South African: 6 Fugard (Athol)
Spanish: 4 Vega (Lope de) 5 Lorca (Federico García) 7 Alberti (Rafael), Arrabal (Fernando) 8 Quintero (Serafín, Joaquín) 9 Benavente (Jacinto) 11 García Lorca (Federico), Valle-Inclán (R. M. del)
Swedish: 5 Sachs (Nelly) 10 Strindberg (August)
Swiss: 6 Frisch (Max)

drape
4 fold, hang, roll 5 adorn, array, cloak, clothe, cover 6 enfold, enwrap, swathe, wrap up 7 curtain, swaddle 8 enswathe, envelope, swathe in

drapery
7 curtain, hanging 8 curtains, hangings

drastic
4 dire 5 harsh 6 severe 7 extreme, radical 9 desperate 10 exorbitant

draw
3 gut, tie, tow, tug 4 etch, haul, limn, lure, puff, pull, pump 5 draft, drain, infer, judge, trace 6 allure, appeal, deduce, depict, derive, elicit, entice, extend, gather, indite, inhale, pencil, siphon, sketch 7 attract, deplete, exhaust, extract, outline, portray, prolong, spin out, win over 8 conclude, contract, convince, dead heat, deadlock, lengthen, protract, standoff 9 delineate, formulate, represent, stalemate 10 allurement, attraction, disembowel, eviscerate, exenterate
forth: 5 educe 6 elicit 7 extract
from: 4 milk, pump 5 bleed
together: 3 tie 4 join, lace

draw back
4 duck 5 cower, quail, wince 6 blench, flinch, recoil, shrink 7 back off, retreat, take off 9 turn aside

drawback
4 flaw, snag 5 fault, hitch 6 defect, refund 7 failing, trouble 8 weakness 9 detriment, hindrance 10 deficiency, difficulty, impediment 12 disadvantage, shortcoming 13 inconvenience

draw down
4 milk 5 drain, spend, use up 6 expend, reduce 7 deplete, exhaust 8 decrease, diminish 9 reduction, siphon off

drawer
9 draftsman
for money: 4 till

drawers
5 pants 6 undies 8 trousers 10 underpants

draw in
6 enmesh, entice, induce, prompt 7 involve, retract, win over 8 convince, persuade, pull back 9 prevail on 11 bring around, prevail upon

drawing
6 doodle, sketch 7 cartoon, outline

drawing power
4 lure, pull 6 appeal 9 magnetism 10 attraction

drawn
4 taut, worn 6 peaked 7 fraught, haggard, pinched 8 careworn, fatigued, pictured, strained, stressed 9 attracted 10 delineated

drawn-out
4 long 7 lengthy, tedious 8 extended, overlong 9 prolonged 10 protracted

draw off
3 tap 4 pump 5 bleed, draft, drain 6 siphon

draw out
6 extend 7 prolong, stretch 8 elongate, lengthen, protract

draw up
4 balk, halt, lift, make, stop 5 array, draft, frame, order, raise, write 6 deploy, map out 7 compose, concoct, dispose, marshal, prepare, set down 8 organize, write out 9 formulate

dray
4 cart, drag 5 wagon 6 barrow, sledge 7 travois 9 stoneboat

dread
4 fear 5 alarm, panic 6 dismay, fright, horror, phobia, terror 7 anxiety 10 foreboding 11 trepidation 12 apprehension 13 consternation

dreadful
5 awful 6 tragic 7 awesome, extreme, fearful, ghastly, hideous, ominous 8 alarming, horrible, horrific, shocking, terrible 9 appalling, frightful, revolting 11 distressing, frightening

dreadfully
7 awfully **8** horribly **9** decidedly, extremely, fearfully, hideously, seriously, tragically **10** strikingly **11** appallingly, exceedingly, frightfully

dreadnought
10 battleship

dream
4 ache, long, wish **5** crave, fancy, ideal **6** bubble, desire, hanker, vision **7** chimera, fantasy, imagine, rainbow, reverie, specter, spectre **8** ambition, delusion, illusion, phantasm, phantasy **9** fantasize, nightmare **10** aspiration
divination by: **11** oneiromancy
god: **8** Morpheus

dreamer
7 utopian **8** idealist **9** visionary **10** Don Quixote, lotus-eater **13** castle-builder

dreamlike
5 ideal, vague **6** unreal **7** shadowy, surreal **8** fanciful, illusory, nebulous **9** imaginary, visionary **12** otherworldly

Dream of Gerontius composer
5 Elgar (Edward)

dream up
5 frame, hatch **6** cook up, create, devise, invent **7** concoct, imagine **8** conceive, contrive, envisage, envision **9** formulate, visualize

dreamy
7 pensive **9** unworldly, visionary **10** idealistic **11** impractical **12** otherworldly **13** introspective

dreary
4 blah, drab, dull **5** bleak **6** boring, dismal, gloomy, somber, sombre **7** forlorn, humdrum, joyless, tedious **8** banausic, tiresome, wretched **9** cheerless **10** depressing, depressive, monotonous, oppressive, pedestrian **11** dispiriting **12** discouraging

dreck
3 mud **4** junk, muck, slop **5** offal, swill, trash, waste **6** litter, refuse, sewage **7** garbage, rubbish **9** sweepings

dredge
3 dig **5** barge, scoop **6** deepen, dig out, gather **8** excavate, scoop out **9** hollow out, scrape out

dregs
4 lees, scum **5** trash **6** grouts **7** deposit,
grounds, remains, residue **8** sediment **9** settlings **11** precipitate

drei
5 three

dreidel
3 top

Dreiser, Theodore
character: **5** Clyde (Griffiths) **6** Carrie (Meeber), Eugene (Witla), Sondra (Finchley) **7** Roberta (Alden) **9** Hurstwood (George) **10** Cowperwood (Frank)
novel: **5** Stoic (The), Titan (The) **6** Genius (The) **9** Financier (The) **12** Sister Carrie **14** Jennie Gerhardt **15** American Tragedy (An)

drench
3 sop **4** dunk, soak **5** douse, souse, steep, swill **6** deluge, seethe **7** immerse **8** inundate, saturate, submerge, waterlog

dress
3 gut **4** bind, clad, deck, doll, duds, garb, gown, sack, togs **5** adorn, align, array, frock, getup, guise, habit, smock, weeds **6** attire, bedeck, caftan, clothe, dirndl, enrobe, outfit, sacque **7** apparel, bandage, bedizen, chemise, clothes, costume, garment, garnish, raiment, threads, turnout, uniform **8** beautify, clothing, covering, decorate, ensemble, ornament, wardrobe **9** embellish, make ready **11** habiliments
a wound: **7** bandage
designer: **4** Dior (Christian), Erté, Head (Edith) **5** Blass (Bill), Bohan (Marc), Karan (Donna), Klein (Calvin), Pucci (Emilio), Quant (Mary), Worth (Charles Frederick) **6** Armani (Giorgio), Cardin (Pierre), Jacobs (Marc), Lauren (Ralph), Miyake (Issey), Poiret (Paul) **7** Balmain (Pierre), Cassini (Oleg), Halston, Lacroix (Christian), Mizrahi (Isaac), Versace (Gianni) **8** Galliano (John), Givenchy (Hubert) **9** Courrèges (André), de la Renta (Oscar), Gernreich (Rudi), Lagerfeld (Karl), Valentino **10** Balenciaga (Cristóbal) **12** Saint-Laurent (Yves), Schiaparelli (Elsa)
finically: **5** primp
hair: **4** coif **6** barber
line: **3** hem
mode of: **5** habit
oriental: **9** cheongsam
part: **5** skirt **6** bodice
South Seas: **6** sarong
with the beak: **5** preen
with vulgarity: **7** bedizen

dress down
5 chide, scold **6** berate, rail at, rebuke,

revile **7** bawl out, reprove, tell off, upbraid **8** admonish, chastise, reproach **9** castigate, reprimand **10** tongue-lash

dresser
5 chest **6** bureau **7** commode, highboy **10** chiffonier
gaudy: 9 butterfly

dressing
5 sauce **6** catsup **7** bandage, catchup, ketchup **8** stuffing
salad: 6 French, ranch **7** Italian, Russian **10** blue cheese **11** vinaigrette **12** green goddess

dressing room
6 vestry **8** vestiary

dressmaker
7 modiste **9** couturier **10** couturiere, seamstress

dress up
6 attire, clothe, rig out, tog out **7** apparel, deck out **8** beautify, disguise, prettify, trick out **9** embellish **10** camouflage

dressy
4 chic **5** showy, smart **6** classy, formal, frilly, ornate **7** duded up, elegant, stylish **9** rigged out

Dreyfus's defender
4 Zola (Emile)

dribble
4 drip, leak, weep **5** drool **6** bounce, drivel, slaver **7** distill, drizzle, slobber, trickle **8** salivate, sprinkle

driblet
4 drop **6** gobbet **7** globule, smidgen **8** particle, pittance

dried grape
6 raisin

dried meat
5 jerky

dried plum
5 prune

drift
3 bat, gad **4** flow, flux, gist, roam, sail, skim, tide, waft, wash **5** amble, coast, creep, float, mosey, range, slide, stray, trend **6** bummel, linger, ramble, stream, stroll, wander **7** current, maunder, meander, meaning, saunter **8** movement, penchant, sideslip, tendency **9** deviation **10** propensity **11** disposition, inclination, progression **12** predilection

drifter
3 bum, vag **4** hobo **5** gypsy, nomad, tramp **7** floater, migrant, vagrant **8** derelict, vagabond **9** transient **11** beachcomber **12** rolling stone

drill
3 bit, dig **4** bore **5** auger, borer, punch, train **6** pierce, trepan, wimble **7** routine, wildcat, workout **8** exercise, practice, practise, rehearse **9** penetrate, rehearsal **10** discipline
command: 6 at ease **8** left face **9** about face, attention, right face

drink
3 ade, lap, nip, sea, sip, tea **4** belt, brew, deep, down, grog, gulp, soak, swig, tope, toss **5** booze, draft, drain, ocean, quaff, slurp, swill, toast **6** absorb, brandy, cognac, guzzle, imbibe, jigger, liquid, liquor, pledge, potion, tank up, tipple **7** consume, potable, schnaps, spirits, swallow, swizzle, toss off **8** aperitif, beverage, libation, liquor up, schnapps **9** aqua vitae
after-dinner: 6 frappé **7** cordial, liqueur
drugged: 6 Mickey **10** Mickey Finn
honey: 4 mead
hot: 5 negus, toddy
liquor: 5 booze, hooch **6** red-eye **9** firewater, moonshine
mixed: 3 nog **5** julep **6** Gibson, gimlet, mai tai, mimosa, mojito, rickey, Rob Roy, zombie **7** gin fizz, martini, sidecar, stinger **8** daiquiri, pink lady **9** alexander, Cuba libre, manhattan, margarita, mint julep, rusty nail **10** Bloody Mary, piña colada, Tom Collins **11** gin and tonic, grasshopper, screwdriver, whiskey sour **12** black Russian, old-fashioned
mixer: 7 swirler
noisily: 5 slurp
of liquor: 4 dram, shot, slug **5** snort **8** highball
of the gods: 6 nectar
soft: 3 pop **4** cola, soda **5** tonic **7** soda pop **8** root beer **9** ginger ale **12** sarsaparilla
stimulating: 6 bracer
(see also **beverage**)

drinkable
6 liquor **7** potable **8** beverage, libation, potation

drinking
8 potation
fountain: 7 bubbler
horn: 6 rhyton
spree: 3 jag **4** tear, toot **5** binge, spree **6** bender **7** carouse **8** carousal

drip

4 leak, plop, weep 7 dribble, droplet, trickle
8 sprinkle

dripping

3 wet 5 runny, soppy 6 soaked, soused
7 drizzly, soaking, sopping 8 drenched
9 saturated 11 wringing-wet

drippy

5 mushy, rainy, sappy, sobby, soppy, soupy,
teary, weepy 6 slushy, syrupy 7 drizzly,
maudlin, mawkish, soaking, sopping, tearful
9 schmaltzy 11 sentimental

drive

3 pep, ram 4 goad, herd, push, spur, taxi,
trip, urge 5 chase, force, guide, impel,
jaunt, lunge, motor, moxie, oomph, pilot,
pound, spunk, steer, surge, vigor
6 compel, convey, exhort, hammer, outing,
plunge, propel, strike, thrust 7 actuate,
impetus, operate, produce 8 ambition,
mobilize, momentum, navigate, shepherd,
vitality 9 chauffeur, excursion, urge along
10 enterprise, get-up-and-go, initiative,
motivation
away: 4 shoo 5 exile 6 aroint
back: 5 repel 6 defend 7 repulse
off: 6 dispel
out: 8 exorcise

drivel

3 rot 4 bosh, bunk 5 drool, hokum, hooey,
prate 6 babble, bunkum, gabble, jabber,
slaver 7 baloney, blabber, blather, dribble,
hogwash, prattle, rubbish, slobber, twaddle
8 claptrap, flimflam, nonsense, salivate
9 gibberish, poppycock 10 balderdash,
double-talk, flapdoodle 12 blatherskite,
gobbledygook

driver

4 jehu 5 cabby 6 cabbie, cabman, hackie,
mallet 7 hackman 8 coachman, motorist,
muleteer, operator 9 chauffeur, dowitcher
10 taskmaster 11 tamping iron
of an elephant: 6 mahout
Roman: 10 charioteer
truck: 8 teamster

driving

7 dynamic, powered 8 forceful, vigorous
9 energetic, inspiring 10 compelling

drizzle

4 mist, rain 7 dribble, spatter 8 droplets,
sprinkle 10 sprinkling 13 precipitation

Dr. Jekyll and Mr. ___

4 Hyde

droll

3 odd 5 comic, funny, nutty, witty
7 comical, risible 8 farcical, humorous
9 eccentric, laughable, ludicrous, whimsical

drollery

5 humor 6 comedy, joking, whimsy
7 jesting

dromedary

5 camel

drone

3 bee, hum 4 buzz, idle, laze, loaf, loll
5 idler 6 drudge, loiter, lounge, murmur
7 bagpipe 8 aircraft, parasite 9 bombinate
10 pedal point

drool

4 gush, rave 5 froth 6 dote on, drivel,
saliva, slaver 7 blather, dribble, enthuse,
slobber 8 salivate 10 rhapsodize

droop

3 sag 4 fall, flag, hang, loll, sink, swag, wilt
5 slump 6 dangle, slouch, weaken
7 decline, let down, subside 8 languish

droopy

4 blue, down, weak 5 baggy 6 gloomy
7 doleful, languid, sagging, slouchy, wilting
8 cast down, dejected, downcast
9 depressed 10 dispirited 11 downhearted

drop

3 dip, nip, sag, tot 4 down, drib, dump, fall,
fell, jolt, lose, slip, slug, tear, 5 cease,
depth, lapse, lower, pitch, plump, scrub,
slide, snort, speck, spend 6 cancel, cave
in, demise, depart, expire, fumble, give up,
go down, ground, plunge, reduce, smitch,
topple, unload, vanish 7 abandon,
decease, decline, deposit, descend,
descent, distill, dribble, driblet, fall off,
forfeit, give out, globule, pendant, plummet,
trickle 8 bowl over, break off, collapse,
comedown, downturn, keel over, nose-dive
9 declivity, discharge, downslide,
downswing, downtrend, prostrate,
reduction, terminate 10 depository

drop by

4 call 5 pop in, visit 6 stop in 8 come over

droplet

4 drib, tear 7 globule

drop off

3 sag 4 doze, fall, slip 5 slide, slump
6 catnap, drowse, lessen, snooze
7 decline, deliver, deposit, slacken
8 diminish, fall away, hand over 10 fall
asleep

dropsical
5 puffy, tumid 6 turgid 7 swollen 8 inflated
9 edematous, tumescent

dropsy
5 edema 8 anasarca

dross
4 junk, scum, slag 5 dregs, offal, waste
6 debris, scoria 7 remains, residue,
schlock 8 detritus, impurity, leavings

drossy
4 base 6 impure, scummy 7 trivial
8 inferior, unworthy 9 worthless

drought
4 lack, need, want 6 dearth 7 aridity,
dryness 8 scarcity, shortage 10 deficiency

droughty
3 dry 4 arid, sere 7 bone-dry, dried up,
parched, thirsty 10 desiccated

drove
3 mob 4 army, herd, host, mass, pack
5 crowd, flock, horde, troop 6 myriad,
pushed, school, throng 7 phalanx
9 multitude

drover
6 cowboy 8 shepherd

drown
4 sink, soak 5 douse, flood, souse, swamp
6 deluge, drench, engulf 7 immerse,
repress, smother 8 inundate, submerge
9 overpower, overwhelm, suffocate
10 asphyxiate, extinguish

drowse
3 nod 4 doze 5 sleep 6 catnap, snooze
7 doze off, drop off, shut-eye, slumber
10 forty winks

drowsy
4 dozy 5 dopey 6 droopy, sleepy, torpid
7 languid 8 indolent, sluggish 9 lethargic,
somnolent, soporific 10 slumberous
13 lackadaisical

Dr. Seuss
6 Geisel (Theodor Seuss)
book: 11 Cat in the Hat (The) 15 Green
Eggs and Ham, Yertle the Turtle 19 Horton
Hatches the Egg 26 How the Grinch Stole
Christmas

drub
3 tan, wax, zap 4 bash, beat, club, deck,
drum, flay, flog, lash, lick, mash, maul, pelt,
trim, whip 5 baste, cream, crush, paste,
pound, score, slash, smash, smear, spank,
stamp, thresh, thump, wreck 6 batter,
berate, bruise, buffet, deface, hammer,
master, pummel, punish, revile, scorch,
thrash, wallop 7 belabor, blister, censure,
clobber, cripple, lambast, scourge, shatter,
shellac, trounce 8 bulldoze, lambaste, lash
into, outclass, outshine 9 castigate,
excoriate, overwhelm

drubbing
4 loss, rout 6 defeat 7 setback
10 defeasance 11 shellacking

drudge
4 grub, hack, moil, peon, plod, slog
5 grind, slave 6 menial, slavey 7 grubber,
plodder 8 dogsbody

drudgery
4 moil, toil 5 chore, grind 7 travail 9 grunt
work 10 donkeywork 11 backbreaker

drudging
6 boring, tiring 7 irksome, tedious
8 dragging, tiresome 9 fatiguing, laborious,
wearisome 10 monotonous

drug
4 dope, lull 5 sulfa 6 downer, ipecac,
opiate, physic, poison, potion, remedy,
statin 7 fen-phen, generic, stupefy
8 biologic, medicine, narcotic, nepenthe,
relaxant, sedative 9 ibuprofen, medicinal,
methadone 10 antibiotic, medicament,
medication 11 thalidomide
addict: 6 junkie
agent: 4 narc
calming: 8 sedative
experience: 4 trip
illicit: 3 ice, kif, LSD, pot 4 acid, coke,
dope, hash, meth, scag, snow, weed
5 crack, grass, opium, smack, speed
6 heroin, peyote 7 cocaine, crystal,
hashish 8 cannabis, goofball 9 mescaline
10 methadrine, psilocybin
seller: 10 pharmacist
sleep-inducing: 8 hypnotic 9 soporific
11 barbiturate

drugged
4 high 5 dazed, doped, dopey 6 flying,
loaded, stoned, zonked 8 benumbed,
hopped-up, turned on 9 spaced-out,
stupefied 10 narcotized

druggist
7 chemist 10 apothecary, pharmacist

drugstore
8 pharmacy 10 apothecary

druid
4 Celt 6 priest 7 prophet
sacred object: 3 oak 9 mistletoe

drum

3 keg, vat 4 beat, cask 5 conga, tabor
6 barrel, tom-tom, tympan 7 tambour,
timpani (plural), tympani (plural) 8 cylinder
Indian: 5 tabla 8 mridanga
Irish: 7 bodhran
large: 4 bass 7 timbale
small: 5 bongo, tabor 7 timbrel
string: 5 snare

drumbeat

4 flam, roll, tuck 6 ruffle, tattoo 7 booming,
pit-a-pat, rat-a-tat 8 rataplan

drumfire

5 salvo 6 volley 7 barrage, booming
9 broadside, cannonade, fusillade
11 bombardment

drumhead

4 skin 7 summary

drummer

4 Rich (Buddy) 5 Krupa (Gene), Roach
(Max), Starr (Ringo), Watts (Charlie)
6 Blakey (Art), hawker, Puente (Tito),
vendor 7 peddler 8 pitchman, salesman

drum up

6 invent 7 canvass, solicit 9 originate
interest: 8 ballyhoo

drunk

3 lit, sot 4 lush, soak, wino 5 lit up, souse,
tight, tipsy 6 blotto, boozer, juiced, soused,
stewed, stinko, tiddly, wasted, zonked
7 crocked, guzzler, pie-eyed, sloshed,
squiffy, tippler 8 squiffed 9 inebriate,
plastered 10 boozehound, inebriated
11 intoxicated

drunkard

3 sot 4 lush, soak, wino 5 rummy, souse,
stiff, toper 6 bibber, boozer, soaker
7 guzzler, swiller, tippler, tosspot
9 alcoholic, inebriate, juicehead
10 boozehound 11 dipsomaniac

Drusilla

brother: 8 Caligula
father: 5 Herod 10 Germanicus
husband: 5 Felix
mother: 9 Agrippina
sister: 8 Berenice 9 Agrippina

dry

3 set 4 arid, brut, dull, sere, sour, tart
5 baked, dusty, parch, stale, wizen
6 barren, desert, harden, stolid, thirst,
wither 7 congeal, deadpan, parched,
shrivel, sterile, thirsty 8 rainless, solidify,
tearless, teetotal, withered 9 anhydrous,
dehydrate, desiccate, evaporate,
unwatered 10 dehydrated, desiccated
11 unemotional 12 matter-of-fact
13 uninteresting
biscuit: 7 cracker 8 hardtack
goods: 6 linens, napery 8 clothing,
textiles
out: 5 sober 8 soberize
period: 7 drought
wine: 3 sec 4 brut

dryasdust

4 arid, dull 5 banal, inane, vapid 6 boring,
stodgy 7 insipid, prosaic, tedious
9 wearisome 10 uninspired
13 uninteresting

dry measure

4 peck, pint 5 quart 6 bushel

Dryope

form: 5 lotus
husband: 9 Andraemon
sister: 4 Iole

dry up

4 wilt 5 wizen 6 wither 7 deplete,
exhaust, mummify, shrivel 9 desiccate,
disappear, evaporate

dual

3 two 4 twin 5 duple 6 bifold, binary,
double, duplex, paired 7 coupled,
matched, twofold 8 matching 9 duplicate

dualistic

5 duple 6 bifold, binary, double, duplex,
paired 7 twofold 9 Manichean
10 Manichaean

dualize

4 copy, dupe 5 clone 6 double
9 duplicate, replicate, reproduce

dub

4 call, name, term, trim 5 style, title
6 duffer 7 baptize, bungler, entitle, fumbler
8 christen, nickname, rerecord 9 blunderer,
designate 10 denominate

dubiety

5 doubt 7 concern 8 mistrust 9 confusion,
suspicion 10 skepticism 11 incertitude,
incredulity, uncertainty 12 doubtfulness

dubious

4 iffy 5 fishy 6 unsure 7 suspect, unclear
8 doubtful, hesitant, unlikely 9 equivocal,
skeptical, uncertain, undecided
10 improbable, unreliable 11 mistrustful,
problematic, questioning, unconvinced,
unpromising 12 questionable,
undependable, undetermined

dubitable
5 fishy 7 suspect 8 doubtful, marginal
9 ambiguous, uncertain, unsettled
10 borderline 11 problematic
13 indeterminate

duce
5 ruler 6 despot, leader, tyrant 8 dictator
9 Mussolini (Benito), oppressor, strongman

duck
3 bob, bow, dip, shy 4 bend, dive, dunk,
shun 5 avoid, dodge, douse, elude, evade,
fence, parry, shirk, stoop 6 escape, plunge
7 back out, immerse 8 sidestep,
submerge, submerse 10 canvasback
Asian: 5 Pekin 8 mandarin
dabbling: 7 gadwall, mallard
diving: 4 smew 7 pochard 9 merganser
10 bufflehead
Eurasian: 4 smew
European: 8 shelduck
genus: 4 Anas
group: 4 team 5 brace, flock, skein
6 flight
hunter's screen: 5 blind
male: 5 drake
red-wattled: 7 Muscovy
river: 4 teal 6 wigeon 7 pintail, widgeon
scaup: 8 bluebill
sea: 5 eider, scaup 6 scoter

duckbill
8 platypus 9 hadrosaur, monotreme

duck soup
4 easy, snap 5 cinch 6 breeze, picnic,
simple 8 kid stuff, painless, pushover
10 child's play 11 piece of cake

ducky
4 cute 5 swell 6 lovely, peachy 7 darling
9 hunky-dory 10 peachy-keen

duct
4 pipe, tube 5 canal 6 course, runway
7 channel, conduit 11 watercourse
anatomical: 3 vas 4 vasa (plural)

ductile
6 pliant, supple 7 plastic, pliable 8 flexible,
moldable 9 adaptable, compliant,
malleable, tractable
metal: 4 wire

ductless gland
see **endocrine gland**

dud
3 dog 4 bomb, bust, flop 5 lemon, loser
6 bummer, misfit, turkey 7 debacle, failure,
washout 8 abortion 9 valueless
11 ineffective

dude
3 fop, guy 4 beau, buck, rake 5 blood,
dandy 6 fellow 7 coxcomb 8 macaroni
9 exquisite 12 Beau Brummell, lounge
lizard

dudgeon
3 ire 4 fury, huff, miff, rage 5 anger, pique,
wrath 7 chagrin, offense, outrage,
umbrage 8 vexation 10 resentment
11 indignation 12 exasperation

duds
3 rig 4 garb, gear, rags, togs 5 dress,
getup, weeds 6 attire, things 7 apparel,
clothes, raiment, threads, toggery
8 clothing, garments 9 trappings,
vestments 11 habiliments

due
4 debt, just, owed 5 lumps, owing, right
6 direct, earned, lawful, proper, unpaid
7 arrears, condign, deserts, exactly,
merited, payable, payment, regular
8 adequate, deserved, directly, expected,
rightful, suitable 9 deserving, equitable,
liability, requisite, scheduled 10 ascribable,
obligatory, receivable, satisfying, sufficient
11 appropriate, outstanding
12 compensation, satisfaction

duel
4 tilt 5 fight, joust 6 combat 7 contest,
dispute 8 conflict

duenna
8 chaperon 9 chaperone, companion,
governess

duet
dancer's: 9 pas de deux

due to
4 over 7 owing to, through 9 because of
11 considering

duff
3 can 4 buns, butt, rear, rump, tail, tush
5 fanny, slack 6 bottom 7 keister, pudding,
rear end 8 backside, buttocks, coal dust,
derriere, fine coal

duffer
4 boob, clod, dolt, dope, yo-yo 5 chump,
dunce, klutz 6 dimwit, dum-dum, lubber,
nitwit 7 dullard, fumbler, peddler, pinhead
8 bonehead, dumbbell, lunkhead, numskull
9 blockhead, ignoramus, numbskull,
simpleton 10 nincompoop, stumblebum
11 incompetent

dugout
5 canoe 6 trench 7 piragua, pirogue, shelter

duiker
8 antelope

dukedom
5 duchy 6 domain

dulcet
5 sweet 7 melodic, tuneful 8 charming, cheerful, engaging, euphonic, pleasant, pleasing, soothing 9 agreeable, melodious 10 euphonious 11 mellifluous

dulcimer
6 zither 8 psaltery
Hungarian: 8 cimbalom
Persian: 6 santir 7 santour

dull
3 dim, dun, mat 4 arid, blah, blur, drab, flat, numb 5 blunt, dense, dusty, faded, ho-hum, inert, matte, muddy, muted 6 benumb, blurry, boring, deaden, dreary, gloomy, leaden, obtuse, stodgy, stupid 7 blunted, humdrum, insipid, muffled, prosaic, stupefy, subdued, tarnish, tedious 8 banausic, bromidic, deadened, discolor, lifeless, listless, monotone, plodding, sluggish 9 bloodless, colorless, dim-witted, dryasdust, insensate, ponderous, wearisome 10 dispirited, indistinct, insensible, lackluster, lusterless, monotonous, pedestrian 11 commonplace, desensitize, insensitive, thickheaded, thick-witted, unsharpened 12 simpleminded 13 uninteresting

dullard
3 oaf 4 bird, boob, clod, dolt, dope, yo-yo 5 chump, dummy, dunce, idiot, moron, ninny, noddy, stupe 6 dimwit, dum-dum, nitwit 7 airhead, pinhead 8 bonehead, dumbbell, imbecile, lunkhead, meathead, numskull 9 birdbrain, blockhead, ignoramus, lamebrain, numbskull, simpleton 10 dunderhead 11 chowderhead, chucklehead

dullness
5 ennui 6 apathy, stupor, tedium, torpor 7 boredom, languor 8 hebetude, lethargy, monotony 9 bluntness, denseness, lassitude, stupidity, torpidity 12 indifference, listlessness, sluggishness

duly
8 properly, suitably 9 correctly, regularly 12 sufficiently 13 appropriately

duma
7 council 8 assembly, congress 11 legislature

Dumas character
5 Athos 6 Aramis, Dantès (Edmond) 7 Camille, Porthos 9 D'Artagnan

dumb
3 mum 4 dull, mute 5 dense, quiet, thick 6 deaden, obtuse, silent, stupid 7 doltish, foolish, idiotic, moronic 8 duncical, ignorant, taciturn, wordless 9 dim-witted, fatheaded, voiceless 10 speechless, tongue-tied 11 blockheaded, thick-witted, tight-lipped 12 closemouthed, inarticulate, simple-minded, tight-mouthed, unresponsive

dumbbell
see **dullard**

dumbfound
5 amaze 6 boggle, puzzle 7 astound, nonplus, perplex, stagger 8 astonish, bewilder, bowl over, confound, distract, surprise 9 take aback 11 flabbergast

dumbfounded
5 agape 6 amazed 7 puzzled, shocked 8 startled 9 astounded, perplexed, staggered, surprised 10 astonished, bewildered, bowled over, confounded, distracted, nonplussed, taken aback 13 thunderstruck

dummkopf
3 oaf 4 boob, clod, dodo, dolt, dope, fool, goof, jerk, mutt, simp, yo-yo 5 chump, dummy, dunce, idiot, moron, ninny, noddy, stupe 6 dimwit, donkey, dum-dum, nitwit, noodle 7 airhead, dullard, pinhead, schnook 8 bonehead, clodpoll, dumbbell, dumbhead, imbecile, lunkhead, meathead, numskull 9 birdbrain, blockhead, ignoramus, lamebrain, numbskull, simpleton, thickhead 10 dunderhead, hammerhead, nincompoop 11 chowderhead, chucklehead, knucklehead

dummy
4 boob, clod, dodo, dolt, mock, sham, yo-yo 5 chump, dunce, false, idiot, model, moron, ninny, noddy, stupe 6 dimwit, dum-dum, effigy, ersatz, layout, mock-up, nitwit, puppet, stooge 7 airhead, dullard, manikin, pinhead, stand-in 8 bonehead, dumbbell, imbecile, lunkhead, mannekin, meathead, numskull 9 birdbrain, blockhead, ignoramus, imitation, lamebrain, numbskull, simpleton, simulated 10 artificial,

dunderhead, fictitious, nincompoop,
substitute **11** chowderhead, chucklehead

dump
4 drop, junk **5** chuck, depot, ditch, scrap
6 armory, pigpen, pigsty, plunge
7 abandon, arsenal, deep-six, discard
8 jettison, magazine, throw out **9** stockpile,
throw away **10** depository

dumpling
5 dough **8** quenelle **10** butterball

dumps
4 funk **5** blues, dolor, gloom, mopes, slump
7 sadness **8** doldrums **9** dejection
10 depression, gloominess, melancholy
11 despondency, unhappiness
12 mournfulness

dumpy
5 dingy, seedy, squat, stout **6** chubby,
chunky, shabby, slummy, stocky, stubby,
stumpy **7** run-down **8** heavyset, thickset
9 shapeless **10** broken-down
11 dilapidated, thick-bodied

dun
3 dim, fly **4** dull, drab, gray **5** annoy,
brown, dusky, horse, murky, press
6 demand, gloomy, mayfly, needle, pester,
plague, somber, sombre **9** ephemerid,
importune

Duncan's slayer
7 Macbeth

dunce
3 oaf **4** boob, clod, dodo, dolt, dope, goof,
mutt, simp, yo-yo **5** booby, chump, dummy,
idiot, moron, ninny, noddy, stupe **6** dimwit,
donkey, duffer, dum-dum, nitwit, noodle,
stupid **7** airhead, dullard, fathead, pinhead
8 bonehead, clodpoll, dumbbell, imbecile,
lunkhead, numskull **9** birdbrain, blockhead,
ignoramus, lamebrain, nincompoop,
numbskull, simpleton **10** dunderhead,
hammerhead, nincompoop
11 chowderhead, chucklehead,
knucklehead

Dunciad author
4 Pope (Alexander)

dundrearies
9 burnsides, sideburns **11** muttonchops
12 side-whiskers

dune
8 sandbank
area: 3 erg

dung
4 muck **6** manure, ordure **9** excrement

beetle: 6 scarab **9** tumblebug

dungeon
4 jail **5** vault **6** prison **9** black hole,
oubliette

dunghill
6 midden

dunk
3 dip, sop **4** soak **5** douse, drown, souse
6 drench **7** immerse **8** saturate,
submerge, submerse

dunlin
9 sandpiper

duo
4 duet, dyad, pair **5** brace **6** couple
7 doublet, twosome

dupe
3 con, kid, sap **4** butt, fool, gull, hoax, mark
5 cheat, chump, cozen, patsy, spoof, trick
6 befool, delude, double, outwit, pigeon,
sucker **7** chicane, deceive, defraud,
mislead **8** flimflam, hoodwink
9 bamboozle, victimize **11** double-cross,
hornswoggle

dupery
3 con **4** scam, sham **5** cheat, fraud
6 deceit, humbug, hustle **7** chicane
8 cheating, flimflam, trickery **9** chicanery,
deception, duplicity, imposture, swindling
10 dishonesty, hanky-panky **13** double-
dealing, hoodwinking, sharp practice

duple
4 dual, twin **6** bifold, binary, double,
duplex, paired **7** coupled, doubled, twofold
9 dualistic

duplex
see **duple**

duplicate
4 copy, fake, mate, redo, same, twin
5 clone, ditto, equal, match, mimeo, repro
6 carbon, double **7** dualize, imitate, replica
8 knockoff **9** companion, facsimile,
identical, imitation, look-alike, replicate,
reproduce **10** carbon copy, dead ringer,
equivalent, reciprocal **11** counterfeit,
counterpart, replication **12** reproduction

duplicitous
5 phony **6** shifty, sneaky **7** devious
8 delusive, guileful, scheming, sneaking,
two-faced **9** deceitful, deceiving,
deceptive, dishonest, underhand
10 fraudulent **11** underhanded
12 disingenuous **13** double-dealing

duplicity
5 fraud, guile 6 deceit 7 cunning, perfidy
8 scheming, trickery 9 chicanery,
deception, treachery 10 dishonesty,
doubleness 11 skulduggery
12 dissemblance, skullduggery
13 dissimulation, double-dealing

durability
4 wear 8 firmness 9 endurance, longevity,
stability 10 permanence

durable
5 stout 6 stable, strong, sturdy 7 lasting
8 enduring 9 permanent, tenacious
10 dependable 11 long-lasting

durance
7 bondage 9 captivity, detention, restraint
11 confinement 12 enthrallment,
imprisonment 13 incarceration

duration
3 run 4 term, time 6 extent, period
7 interim 8 interval 11 persistence

duress
5 force 6 menace, threat 8 bullying,
coercion, menacing, pressure 9 restraint
10 compulsion, constraint 11 restriction
12 intimidation

during
4 amid 10 throughout

durra
7 sorghum 12 grain sorghum

durum
5 wheat

dusk
4 dark 7 evening 8 darkness, eventide,
gloaming, twilight 9 nightfall
12 semidarkness

dusky
3 dim 4 dark 5 murky, swart 6 brunet,
gloomy, opaque, twilit 7 obscure, shadowy,
swarthy 8 funereal, nubilous, overcast,
twilight 9 tenebrous 10 caliginous
11 dark-skinned

dust
4 grit, sand, sift, soot 5 ashes, grime
6 powder 8 sprinkle 10 besprinkle,
sprinkling

dustbowl victim
4 Okie

dustup
3 row 4 spat 5 fight, melee, run-in, set-to
6 battle, fracas, hassle, tussle 7 dispute,
quarrel, rhubarb, scuffle, skirmish
8 argument 9 bickering, brannigan
10 falling-out 11 altercation

dusty
3 dry 4 arid, dull 5 stale 7 parched,
powdery, tedious, unswept

Dutch
7 trouble 8 hot water
African: 9 Afrikaans
ceramics: 5 delft
cheese: 4 Edam 5 Gouda
dog breed: 7 griffon 8 keeshond
painter: 3 Dou (Gerrit, Gerard) 4 Cuyp
(Aelbert Jacobsz), Gogh (Vincent van),
Hals (Frans) 5 Bosch (Hieronymus),
Hooch (Pieter de), Steen (Jan) 7 de Hooch
(Pieter), Hobbema (Meindert), van Gogh
(Vincent), Vermeer (Jan) 8 Mondrian
(Piet), Ruysdael (Jacob van, Salomon van),
Terborch (Gerard) 9 de Kooning (Willem),
Honthorst (Gerrit van), Rembrandt (van
Rijn)
philosopher: 7 Spinoza (Benedict de)
scholar: 7 Erasmus (Desiderius)

Dutch South African
4 Boer

dutiful
7 devoted 8 faithful 9 compliant
10 respectful 13 conscientious

duty
3 job, tax, use 4 levy, onus, role, task,
work 5 chare, chore, stint 6 burden,
charge, devoir, impost, office, tariff
7 respect, service 8 function
10 allegiance, assessment, assignment,
commitment,
dedication, obligation

dwarf
4 runt 5 gnome, pygmy, stunt, troll
6 midget, peewee 7 manikin 8 Tom
Thumb 9 miniature 10 diminutive,
homunculus 11 hop-o'-my-thumb,
lilliputian
in Snow White: 3 Doc 5 Dopey, Happy
6 Grumpy, Sleepy, Sneezy 7 Bashful
Scottish: 7 blastie

dwarfish
5 pygmy, small 6 midget 7 minikin,
stunted 8 inferior, pint-size 9 miniature,
pint-sized 10 diminutive, undersized
11 lilliputian

dweeb
4 dork, drip, geek, nerd, wimp, wuss
5 loser 7 nebbish

dwell
3 lie 4 bide, live, stay 5 abide, exist
6 locate, remain, repose, reside, settle
7 hang out

dweller
7 citizen, denizen, settler 8 habitant,
occupant, resident 10 inhabitant

dwelling
3 pad 4 casa, digs, home, nest 5 abode,
haunt, house 7 address, habitat, lodging
8 domicile, quarters 9 residence
10 brownstone, habitation
American Indian: 4 tipi 5 hogan, tepee
6 pueblo, teepee, wigwam
clergyman's: 5 manse 7 rectory
8 vicarage 9 parsonage
crude: 3 hut 4 camp 5 cabin, hovel,
shack 6 cabana, shanty 7 barrack
8 barracks
Eskimo: 5 igloo
grand: 5 manor, manse, villa 6 palace
7 château, mansion
Hindu: 6 ashram
Navajo: 5 hogan
Russian: 5 dacha
small: 3 cot, hut 5 hovel 7 cottage
8 bungalow

dwindle
3 ebb 4 fade, fall, wane 5 abate, taper
6 lessen, recede, reduce, shrink, weaken,
wither 7 decline, die away, die down,
shrivel, slacken, subside 8 decrease,
diminish, taper off 9 attenuate, drain away

dyad
3 duo, two 4 pair, yoke 5 brace, twins
6 couple 7 doublet, twosome

dye
4 tint 5 color, stain, tinge 7 pigment
8 colorant, pyronine, tincture
blue: 4 woad 6 indigo 7 cyanine
for hair: 5 henna
plant: 4 woad 5 sumac 6 madder
red: 5 eosin, henna 6 kermes, ruddle
7 cudbear, fuchsin, magenta 8 alizarin,
fuchsine, amaranth, safranin 9 cochineal,
rhodamine, safranine 10 erythrosin
violet: 6 archil
yellow: 7 flavine 8 orpiment
yellowish red: 7 annatto

dyed-in-the-wool
5 loyal, sworn 7 devoted, die-hard, old-
line, settled, staunch 8 faithful, hard-core,
orthodox, standpat, true-blue 9 confirmed,
hard-shell, steadfast 10 deep-rooted,
deep-seated, entrenched, inveterate,
unwavering 11 established 13 bred-in-the-
bone, thoroughgoing

dyewood
6 fustic 10 brazilwood

dying
6 demise 7 done for, quietus 8 moribund
9 departure 10 extinction, in extremis
12 annihilation

dynamic
7 driving, intense 8 forceful, forcible,
powerful, vigorous 9 energetic, strenuous
10 compelling, energizing

dynamite
4 raze 5 blast 6 blow up 7 destroy,
explode, shatter 8 demolish 9 explosive
10 annihilate
inventor: 5 Nobel (Alfred)

dynamo
8 go-getter, live wire 9 generator 10 ball of
fire 11 self-starter

dysentery
4 flux 6 scours 8 diarrhea

dyslogistic
7 adverse 10 derogatory, pejorative
11 deleterious, disparaging, prejudicial,
unfavorable

dyspepsia
5 gloom 6 dismay 7 chagrin, pyrosis
8 glumness 9 dejection, heartburn
10 gloominess 11 frustration, indigestion

dyspeptic
5 cross, surly 6 crabby, morose, ornery
9 irritable 10 ill-humored, ill-natured
11 disgruntled, ill-tempered

dysphoria
4 funk 5 blues, dumps, gloom, mopes
6 sorrow 7 sadness 9 dejection
10 depression, gloominess, melancholy
11 unhappiness 12 mournfulness,
wretchedness 13 cheerlessness

E

each
3 all, per 4 a pop 5 every 6 apiece
8 everyone 9 per capita, everybody

eager
3 hot 4 agog, avid, keen, wild 5 antsy,
hyper, itchy, pushy, ready, vital 6 ardent,
fervid, gung ho, heated, hungry, intent,
pining, raring 7 anxious, athirst, burning,
craving, earnest, fervent, longing, restive,
thirsty, wishful 8 appetent, aspiring,
covetous, desirous, restless, striving,
vehement, yearning 9 ambitious,
energetic, hankering, impatient, voracious
10 breathless, solicitous 11 impassioned
12 enthusiastic

eagerness
4 push, urge, zeal, zest, zing 5 ardor,
gusto 6 desire, fervor, hunger, spirit, thirst
7 avidity, craving, itching, longing, passion
8 alacrity, ambition, appetite, fervency,
vitality, yearning 9 intensity, quickness,
vehemence 10 enthusiasm, impatience,
resolution

eagle
4 hawk 9 accipiter
nest: 4 aery 5 aerie, eyrie
North American: 4 bald 6 golden
sea: 4 erne 6 osprey

eagle-eyed
8 vigilant, watchful 9 attentive, observant
10 perceptive 12 sharp-sighted

ear
6 notice 7 auricle 9 attention
bone: 5 anvil, incus 6 hammer, stapes
7 malleus, stirrup
canal: 5 scala
combining form: 3 aur, oto 4 auri, otic
doctor: 9 otologist
inner: 9 labyrinth
middle: 8 tympanum
outer: 5 pinna
part: 4 drum, lobe 5 canal 6 tragus
7 cochlea

relating to: 5 aural 9 auricular
science: 7 otology

eardrum
8 tympanum

 Earhart
6 Amelia

earl
4 lord, peer 5 count, noble 8 nobleman,
seigneur 9 patrician 10 aristocrat

earlier
3 ere, yet 4 once 5 as yet, so far
6 before, sooner 7 already, thus far
8 formerly, hitherto, previous 9 erstwhile,
preceding 10 beforehand, heretofore,
previously

earlier than
3 pre 6 before

earliest
5 first, prime 6 maiden, primal 7 initial,
pioneer, primary 8 original, primeval,
pristine 10 aboriginal, primordial

earlike projection
3 lug

early
3 old 5 first, prior 6 primal, timely
7 ancient, betimes 8 original, previous,
primeval, pristine, untimely 9 preceding,
premature, primitive 10 antecedent,
antiquated, precocious, primordial
11 prematurely
prefix: 5 paleo

earn
3 bag, get, net, win 4 gain, make, rate,
reap 5 amass, clear, gross, merit, score
6 attain, come by, obtain, pick up, rack up,
secure, wangle 7 acquire, bring in, collect,
deserve, harvest, procure, produce, realize,
receive 8 pull down 9 bring home, knock
down

earnest

4 bond, busy, firm, keen, pawn, true, vow, warm 5 grave, sober, token 6 active, ardent, intent, pledge, solemn, somber, surety 7 deposit, genuine, intense, serious, sincere, up front, warrant, zealous 8 contract, covenant, diligent, interest, security, sedulous, studious 9 assiduous, heartfelt 10 determined, no-nonsense, passionate, sobersided, thoughtful, unaffected 11 industrious 12 enthusiastic, wholehearted

earnestly

5 madly 7 for real, like mad

earnestness

6 fervor 7 gravity, honesty, passion, resolve 8 sobriety 9 sincerity 10 absorption, doggedness 11 engrossment, persistence 12 perseverance 13 concentration, determination

earnings

3 net, pay 4 gain 5 lucre, wages 6 income, profit, return, salary 7 profits 8 proceeds, take-home 9 emolument 10 bottom line

ear shell

see **abalone**

earshot

5 range, sound 7 hearing

earsplitting

4 loud 6 shrill 7 blaring, grating, raucous, roaring, strident 8 piercing 9 deafening, dissonant 10 screeching, stentorian 11 fullmouthed

earth

3 orb, sod 4 dirt, land, soil, turf 5 globe, world 6 ground, planet, sphere 7 dry land, terrain 10 creation 10 terra firma
prefix: 3 geo
core: 12 centrosphere
god: 3 Geb, Keb, Seb 5 Dagan
goddess: 4 Erda, Gaea 5 Ceres, Nintu 6 Kishar 7 Demeter, Nerthus
relating to: 8 telluric 9 planetary 11 terrestrial
satellite: 4 moon
science: 7 geology 9 geography

earthenware

4 clay 5 china, delft 7 biscuit, faience, pottery 8 clayware, crockery, majolica 9 porcelain, stoneware 10 terra-cotta

earthlike

11 terrestrial

earthly

6 likely, mortal 7 mundane, worldly 8 feasible, material, physical, possible, probable, temporal 9 corporeal, potential, practical 10 imaginable 11 conceivable, terrestrial, unspiritual

earthquake

5 shake, shock 6 tremor 7 temblor
measuring device: 11 seismograph, seismometer
relating to: 7 seismic
science: 10 seismology 11 seismometry

earthwork

4 bank, wall 7 bulwark, rampart 10 embankment 13 fortification

earthworm

7 annelid 12 night crawler

earthy

3 low 4 base, real 5 crude, dirty, dusty, gross, muddy, sandy 6 clayey, coarse, common, simple 7 mundane, worldly 8 temporal 9 corporeal, inelegant, practical, pragmatic, realistic, unrefined 10 hard-boiled, hardheaded, indelicate, uncultured, unpolished 11 down-to-earth, terrestrial 12 matter-of-fact 13 materialistic, unsentimental

earwax

7 cerumen

ease

3 aid 4 bate, calm, dull, free, help, rest 5 allay, loose, peace, poise, relax, slack 6 assist, deaden, loosen, relief, repose, soften 7 assuage, comfort, fluency, improve, leisure, lighten, mollify, relieve, slacken 8 calmness, deftness, diminish, dispatch, facility, idleness, mitigate, moderate, pleasure, security, serenity 9 abundance, affluence, alleviate, expertise, reduction, untighten, well-being 10 ameliorate, artfulness, contentment, efficiency, expertness, facilitate, inactivity, mitigation, moderation, prosperity, relaxation, smoothness 11 alleviation, nonchalance, spontaneity, tranquility 12 satisfaction, skillfulness, tranquillity
off: 3 ebb 4 bate, fade, fall, flag, wane 5 abate, let up, loose, relax, slack 6 lessen, loosen, relent, unbend, unwind 7 die away, die down, slacken, subside 8 diminish, loosen up, moderate 9 untighten

easel

4 desk 5 frame, stand 7 support 9 workbench, worktable

easement
6 relief **7** comfort **10** mitigation, palliative
11 alleviation, consolation, restorative
13 mollification

easily
6 simply **7** handily, lightly, readily
8 facilely, smoothly **11** dexterously,
efficiently **12** effortlessly

East
4 Asia **6** Levant, Orient

Easter
5 Pasch
relating to: 7 paschal
symbol: 3 egg **4** lamb **5** bunny **6** rabbit

eastern
8 oriental **9** Levantine
countries: 6 Orient

East Indian country
8 Malaysia **9** Indonesia, Singapore

East Timor
capital: 4 Dili
monetary unit: 6 dollar
neighbor: 9 Indonesia

easy
3 lax **4** calm, cozy, glib, mild, soft, snug
5 basic, clear, comfy, cushy, light, loose,
naive, plain, suave **6** breezy, facile, fluent,
kindly, placid, poised, polite, secure,
serene, simple, smooth, urbane **7** amiable,
courtly, cursive, evident, flowing, lenient,
obvious, patient, relaxed **8** apparent,
composed, familiar, graceful, gullible, in
clover, informal, manifest, merciful,
obliging, peaceful, pleasant, sociable,
tolerant, tranquil, trusting **9** collected,
credulous, forgiving, indulgent, possessed
10 charitable, diplomatic, effortless,
elementary, forbearing, gregarious,
permissive **11** comfortable, complaisant,
good-humored, good-natured, susceptible,
sympathetic, unconcerned **12** good-
tempered **13** compassionate,
mollycoddling, self-possessed,
uncomplicated

easygoing
3 lax **4** calm, cool, lazy **5** quiet **6** breezy,
casual, dégagé, folksy, placid, poised,
sedate, serene **7** affable, offhand, patient,
relaxed, unfussy **8** amenable, carefree,
composed, down home, fainéant, flexible,
indolent, informal, laid-back, slothful,
together, tranquil **9** apathetic, indulgent,
offhanded, unhurried **10** nonchalant,
permissive, unaffected **11** comfortable,
complaisant, indifferent, low-pressure,
pococurante, unconcerned, unflappable,
uninhibited **12** devil-may-care, even-
tempered, happy-go-lucky, lighthearted
13 self-possessed, unconstrained

easy mark
3 sap **4** butt, dupe, fool, gull **5** chump,
patsy, sport **6** pigeon, softie, sucker,
turkey, victim **7** fall guy **8** pushover **9** soft
touch **11** sitting duck

eat
3 sup, vex **4** bite, chow, dine, gnaw, meal,
pick, take, wolf **5** annoy, erode, feast,
gorge, graze, hound, lunch, mouth, munch,
scarf, scoff, scour, snack, use up **6** devour,
feed on, gobble, harass, hassle, ingest,
inhale, nibble, pester, pick at, pig out,
plague, take in **7** banquet, bother,
consume, corrode, exhaust, gorge on,
swallow, torment **8** chow down, dissolve,
take food, wear away **9** breakfast,
decompose, masticate, partake of, polish
off **10** break bread, gormandize, nibble
away

eatable
6 edible **8** esculent, harmless, palatable
10 comestible, digestible

eatery
4 café **5** diner, grill **10** coffee shop,
restaurant **11** greasy spoon **12** luncheonette

eating place
3 pub **4** café, mess **5** diner, grill, joint
6 bistro, tavern **7** automat, beanery,
canteen, dinette, tearoom **8** cookshop,
messroom, pizzeria, snack bar
9 brasserie, cafeteria, chophouse, hash
house, lunchroom, trattoria **10** coffee shop,
restaurant, steak house **11** greasy spoon
12 luncheonette

eavesdrop
3 bug, tap **4** lurk **7** monitor **8** listen in,
overhear

ebb
4 drop, fade, fall, flag, tide, wane **5** abate,
droop, let up **6** lessen, recede, reduce,
relent, shrink, wither **7** decline, descent,
die away, die down, ease off, retreat,
slacken, subside **8** decrease, diminish,
languish, moderate, withdraw
10 retrograde

Eblis
5 Satan
son: 3 Tir **4** Awar **5** Dasim **8** Zalambur

ebon, ebony
3 jet 4 inky 5 black, jetty, raven, sable
6 brunet 8 brunette, jet-black 9 pitch-dark
10 pitch-black

ebullience
3 vim, zip 4 brio, élan, zing 6 gaiety, gusto
7 abandon, elation 8 buoyancy, vitality,
vivacity 9 animation 10 enthusiasm,
excitement, exuberance, liveliness 11 high
spirits 12 exhilaration, spiritedness 13 effervescence

ebullient
3 mad 4 gaga 5 brash, zingy, zippy
6 bouncy, bubbly, elated, frothy, geeked,
pumped, raring 7 boiling, chipper, excited,
gleeful, gushing, vibrant 8 hopped-up,
sprightly 9 vivacious 11 exhilarated
12 enthusiastic, high-spirited 13 irrepressible

eccentric
3 odd, nut 4 coot, kook 5 crank, crazy,
droll, flaky, freak, goofy, kooky, nutty, queer,
wacky, weird 6 far out, funky, funny, oddity,
quaint, quirky, screwy, weirdo, whacko,
whacky 7 bizarre, curious, deviant, erratic,
heretic, oddball, offbeat, strange, unusual
8 aberrant, abnormal, bohemian, cockeyed,
crackpot, goofball, maverick, original,
peculiar, singular, uncommon
9 anomalous, character, deviating,
fantastic, fruitcake, grotesque, irregular, off-
center, screwball, unnatural, whimsical
10 elliptical, off-balance, unbalanced,
uncentered 11 exceptional 13 idiosyncratic, nonconformist

eccentricity
4 kink 5 quirk, twist 8 crotchet, quiddity
9 deviation, weirdness 10 aberration
11 strangeness 12 idiosyncrasy

ecclesiastic
see **clergyman**

ecclesiastical
4 holy 5 papal 6 church, sacred
8 churchly, clerical, pastoral, priestly
9 apostolic, canonical, episcopal, spiritual,
synagogal 10 churchlike, pontifical,
rabbinical, sacerdotal 11 ministerial,
patriarchal, theological 12 episcopalian,
evangelistic, tabernacular

ecdysiast
see **stripteaser**

echelon
3 row 4 file, line, rank, tier 5 grade, group,
level, order, queue 6 string 7 chevron
9 formation

echidna
8 anteater 9 monotreme 13 spiny anteater

Echidna
father: 7 Phorcys 8 Chrysaor
mother: 4 Ceto 10 Callirrhoë
offspring: 5 Hydra 6 dragon, Orthus,
Sphinx 7 Chimera 8 Cerberus, Chimaera

echinoderm
6 urchin 7 crinoid, sea star 8 starfish
9 coelomate, sea urchin 11 sea cucumber

echo
3 ape 4 mime, ring 5 evoke, mimic, trace
6 mirror, parrot, repeat, result, reverb,
second 7 imitate, iterate, reflect, resound,
revoice, vestige 8 resonate, response
9 duplicate, imitation, reiterate
10 reflection, repetition 11 reverberate
12 repercussion 13 reverberation

Echo
5 nymph, oread
beloved: 9 Narcissus

echoic
7 mimetic 9 imitative 10 derivative
12 onomatopoeic 13 onomatopoetic

éclat
4 bang, dash, fame, pomp 5 glory, honor,
kudos 6 luster, lustre, praise, renown,
repute 7 acclaim, display, laurels, stardom,
success 8 applause, eminence, prestige,
standing 9 celebrity, notoriety, publicity
10 brilliance, brilliancy, exaltation,
prominence, reputation 11 distinction,
ostentation

eclectic
5 broad, fussy, mixed, picky 6 choosy,
select, varied 7 diverse, finicky, mingled
8 assorted, catholic, elective 9 inclusive,
selective 10 discerning, fastidious,
particular 11 diversified 12 dilettantish,
multifarious 13 heterogeneous

eclipse
3 dim 5 bedim, cloud, cover, excel, outdo,
shade 6 darken, exceed, shadow
7 becloud, decline, obscure, surpass
8 downfall, outshine 9 adumbrate,
obfuscate, overcloud 10 extinguish,
overshadow

eclogue
3 ode 4 idyl, poem 5 idyll, lyric 8 pastoral

ecological
5 green 8 bionomic
community: 5 biome

ecology
9 bionomics 11 environment

economic
6 fiscal 8 material, monetary 9 budgetary, financial, pecuniary 10 mercantile, profitable
doctrine: 12 laissez-faire
system: 9 communism, socialism
10 capitalism 11 syndicalism 12 mercantilism

economical
4 mean 5 canny, close, spare 6 frugal, saving, stingy 7 careful, miserly, prudent, sparing, thrifty 8 skimping 9 efficient, niggardly, penny-wise, penurious, provident, scrimping 10 unwasteful
12 cheeseparing, parsimonious 13 penny-pinching

economist
American: 5 Arrow (Kenneth), Simon (Herbert, Julian), Solow (Robert), Tobin (James) 6 Becker (Gary), George (Henry), Thurow (Lester), Veblen (Thorstein), Walker (Amasa), Weaver (Robert) 7 Krugman (Paul), Kuznets (Simon), Stigler (George), Volcker (Paul) 8 Friedman (Milton), Stiglitz (Joseph) 9 Galbraith (John Kenneth), Greenspan (Alan), Samuelson (Paul) 10 Schumpeter (Joseph)
Austrian: 5 Hayek (Friedrich von), Mises (Ludwig von)
Canadian: 7 Leacock (Stephen)
Dutch: 9 Tinbergen (Jan)
English: 3 Sen (Amartya) 4 Mill (John Stuart) 5 Coase (Ronald), Hayek (Friedrich von), Pigou (Arthur) 6 Engels (Friedrich), Keynes (John Maynard) 7 Bagehot (Walter), Malthus (Thomas), Ricardo (David)
French: 3 Say (Jean-Baptiste) 6 Monnet (Jean), Turgot (Anne-Robert-Jacques), Walras (Léon) 7 Quesnay (François)
German: 4 Marx (Karl) 5 Weber (Max) 6 Engels (Friedrich) 7 Schacht (Hjalmar)
Indian: 3 Sen (Amartya)
Scottish: 4 Mill (James) 5 Smith (Adam)
Swedish: 6 Myrdal (Gunnar)
Swiss: 8 Sismondi (Simonde de)

economize
4 save 5 skimp, stint 6 manage, scrimp 7 husband 8 conserve 10 cut corners 12 pinch pennies

economy
6 saving, thrift 8 prudence, skimping 9 concision, frugality, husbandry, parsimony, restraint, scrimping 10 discretion, efficiency, providence, stinginess 11 carefulness, conciseness, miserliness, thriftiness 13 niggardliness

Eco novel
13 Name of the Rose (The) 17 Foucault's Pendulum

ecru
see beige

ecstasy
3 joy 5 bliss 6 frenzy, heaven, trance 7 delight, elation, madness, rapture 8 euphoria, paradise, rhapsody 9 beatitude, transport 10 exaltation, joyfulness 11 blessedness, derangement, enchantment, high spirits, inspiration 12 blissfulness, exhilaration, intoxication 13 seventh heaven

ecstatic
6 elated, joyful 7 gleeful 8 euphoric, exultant, jubilant, thrilled 9 delirious, delighted, entranced, overjoyed, rapturous 11 exhilarated, transported

Ecuador
capital: 5 Quito
city: 6 Ambato, Cuenca 7 Machala 9 Guayaquil
Indian people: 7 Quechua
island group: 9 Galápagos
language: 7 Spanish
monetary unit: 5 sucre 6 dollar
mountain range: 5 Andes
neighbor: 4 Peru 8 Colombia
volcano: 6 Sangay 7 Cayambe 8 Cotopaxi 10 Chimborazo

ecumenical
6 cosmic, global 7 general, generic 8 catholic 9 inclusive, planetary, universal, worldwide 12 all-inclusive, cosmopolitan 13 comprehensive

ecumenical council
4 Lyon 5 Basel, Lyons, Trent 6 Nicene 7 Ephesus, Ferrara, Lateran, Vatican 8 Florence 9 Chalcedon, Constance

eczema
6 tetter

edacious
see voracious

eddy
4 purl 5 swirl, twirl, whirl, whorl 6 vortex 8 backwash 9 backwater, maelstrom, whirlpool 11 counterflow

edema
5 croup, tumor 6 dropsy 8 anasarca, swelling

Eden
6 heaven, utopia 7 arcadia, elysium 8 paradise
river: 5 Gihon 6 Pishon 8 Hiddekel 9 Euphrates

edentate
5 sloth 8 aardvark, anteater, pangolin 9 armadillo, toothless

Edessa's king
5 Abgar

edge
3 cut, end, hem, lip, rim 4 bank, bite, brim, cusp, draw, ease, hone, inch, lead, limb, line, pink, side, whet, worm 5 arris, bound, brink, bulge, force, ledge, picot, point, ridge, sidle, skirt, sting, strop, verge 6 border, fringe, margin, nosing 7 acidity, contour, chamfer, outline, serrate, sharpen, vantage 8 acerbity, acridity, boundary, emborder, handicap, keenness, surround, thinness 9 acuteness, advantage, extremity, harshness, head start, perimeter, periphery, sharpness, threshold, upper hand 10 causticity, shrillness, stringency 11 astringency 12 incisiveness 13 effectiveness

edge city
5 exurb 6 suburb

edged
4 acid, tart 5 acute, sharp, strong 7 cutting 8 incisive, piercing

edge in
6 inject 9 interject, interpose, insinuate 10 infiltrate 11 interpolate

edging
3 hem 4 lace 5 braid, frill, limit, margin 6 border, flounce, fringe, lacing, piping 7 selvage 8 rickrack, selvedge, trimming

edgy
3 hip 5 funky, nervy, sharp, tense, testy 6 daring, touchy, uneasy 7 excited, keyed up, offbeat, restive, uptight 8 Bohemian, out-there, renegade, restless, skittery, skittish, volatile 9 excitable, impatient, irascible, irritable 10 high-strung, outlandish 11 provocative

edible
8 esculent 9 palatable 10 comestible
root: 3 oca, yam 4 beet, taro, yuca 6 carrot, daikon, ginger, jicama, potato, radish, turnip, wasabi 7 burdock, cassava, ginseng, malanga, parsnip, salsify 8 celeriac, galangal, kohlrabi, rutabaga 11 horseradish, sweet potato
seed: 3 nut, pea 4 bean 6 peanut

edibles
4 chow, eats, feed, food, grub 6 viands 7 aliment, goodies, nurture 8 victuals 9 provender 10 provisions, sustenance 11 comestibles

edict
3 law 4 bull, fiat, rule 5 canon, order, ukase 6 decree, dictum, ruling 7 command, dictate, mandate, precept, statute 9 directive, manifesto, ordinance, prescript 10 injunction, regulation 12 proclamation 13 pronouncement
Islamic: 5 fatwa
papal: 4 bull 8 decretal

Edict of _____
5 Milan, Worms 6 Nantes

edifice
4 pile 8 building, erection 9 structure

edify
5 teach 6 better, fill in, illume, inform, update, uplift 7 educate, elevate, enhance, improve 8 illumine, instruct 9 elucidate, enlighten 10 illuminate

edit
3 cut 4 cull, omit 5 adapt, alter, amend, emend, fix up 6 delete, doctor, excise, polish, redact, refine, review, revise, reword, select 7 abridge, compile, correct, rewrite 8 annotate, assemble, condense, copyread, fine-tune 9 proofread, rearrange 10 blue-pencil, bowdlerize

edition
4 copy, form 5 issue, print 7 reissue, reprint, version 8 printing, variorum 10 impression, reprinting 12 reproduction

editor
8 redactor 9 scrivener, wordsmith 10 copyreader 11 proofreader

Edomite's ancestor
4 Esau

educate
4 rear 5 brief, coach, drill, edify, nurse, teach, train, tutor 6 inform, school 7 explain, nurture 8 instruct 9 brainwash, enlighten 10 discipline 12 indoctrinate

education
7 culture, tuition 8 breeding, coaching, guidance, learning, literacy, pedagogy, teaching, training, tutelage, tutorage,

tutoring 9 erudition, knowledge, schooling, tutorship 11 instruction, learnedness, scholarship 13 enlightenment

educational
11 informative, instructive 13 informational, instructional
institution: 6 school 7 academy, college 10 university 12 conservatory

educator
5 tutor 7 teacher 9 professor 10 instructor
American: 4 Mann (Horace) 5 Dewey (John) 6 Butler (Nicholas Murray), Conant (James Bryant), Harris (William Torrey) 7 Barnard (Henry), Beecher (Catharine), Peabody (Elizabeth) 8 Hutchins (Robert Maynard), McGuffey (William) 10 Washington (Booker T.)
Czech: 8 Comenius (John Amos)
English: 6 Arnold (Thomas) 7 Spencer (Herbert)
German: 7 Froebel (Friedrich), Herbart (Johann)
Italian: 10 Montessori (Maria)
Swiss: 10 Pestalozzi (Johann Heinrich)

educe
4 drag, draw, milk, pull 5 evoke, wrest, wring 6 derive, elicit, evince, evolve, extort, obtain, secure 7 distill, draw out, extract, procure 8 bring out 10 excogitate

eel
5 moray, siren 6 conger 7 hagfish, lamprey, sniggle
young: 5 elver

eelpout
6 blenny, burbot 10 muttonfish

eely
5 slimy 6 slippy, wiggly 7 elusive, wriggly 8 slippery, slithery 9 wriggling

eerie
5 scary, weird 6 creepy, spooky 7 bizarre, chilling, strange, uncanny 8 spectral 9 fantastic, grotesque, unearthly 10 mysterious 11 frightening, hair-raising 12 otherworldly

efface
4 dele, x out 5 annul, erase 6 cancel, delete, rub out 7 blot out, destroy, expunge, scratch, wipe out 8 black out, wear away 9 eliminate, eradicate, extirpate 10 obliterate

effect
3 end 4 make 5 cause, enact, event, fruit 6 create, draw on, induce, intent, invoke, render, result, secure, sequel, upshot 7 achieve, bring on, enforce, execute, fulfill, outcome, perform, produce, purport, realize, turn out 8 bring off, carry out, complete, conceive, generate, sequence 9 actualize, aftermath, corollary, discharge, implement, influence, operation, outgrowth, pursuance 10 accomplish, appearance, bring about, conclusion, consummate, denouement, effectuate 11 consequence, development, eventuality, precipitate 12 carry through, ramification, repercussion

effective
4 able 5 sound, valid 6 causal, cogent, direct, potent, useful 7 capable 8 adequate 9 competent, operative 10 compelling, convincing, productive

effectiveness
5 clout, force, point, power, vigor, weight 7 cogency, potency 8 strength, validity 10 capability

effects
4 gear 5 goods, stuff 6 things 8 chattels, movables, property 9 equipment, moveables, trappings 10 belongings 11 impedimenta, possessions 13 accoutrements

effectual
5 sound, valid 6 potent, strong, useful 7 capable 8 decisive, powerful, workable 10 conclusive, fulfilling, productive 11 influential, practicable 13 authoritative, determinative

effectuate
see **effect**

effeminate
5 sappy, sissy 6 chichi, prissy 7 epicene, foppish 8 delicate, overnice, precious 9 sissified 10 old-maidish 11 overrefined

effervescence
5 giddy 7 fizzing, foaming, sparkle 8 bubbling, buoyancy, vivacity 9 animation 10 ebullience, ebullition, exuberance, exuberancy, liveliness 12 exhilaration

effervescent
3 gay 4 airy 5 jolly 6 bouncy, bubbly, lively 7 boiling, buoyant, excited 8 animated, mirthful, volatile 9 sparkling, sprightly, vivacious 10 carbonated 12 high-spirited 13 irrepressible

effete
4 soft, weak 5 frail, spent 6 barren, sickly 7 decayed, drained, sterile, worn-out 8 decadent, decaying, delicate,

depleted, fatigued, pampered 9 declining,
dissolute, enfeebled, exhausted, infertile,
washedout 10 degenerate, unfruitful
11 debilitated

efficacious
6 active, potent, strong 8 forceful,
powerful, puissant 9 operative
10 productive 11 influential

efficacy
see **effectiveness**

efficiency
see **effectiveness**

efficient
4 able 5 adept 6 expert 7 capable, skilled
8 economic, masterly, skillful 9 competent
10 economical, productive

effigy
3 guy 4 icon, idol 5 dummy, image
6 figure 7 waxwork 8 likeness

effloresce
4 blow 5 bloom, burst, sprout 6 flower
7 blossom, burgeon 9 bear fruit

effluvium
3 air 4 odor, reek 5 smell, vapor, waste
6 miasma 7 exhaust 8 effusion, emission
9 by-product, discharge, emanation
10 exhalation

efflux
see **effluvium**

effort
3 job, try 4 feat, push, task, toil, work
5 chore, essay, force, labor, might, nisus,
pains, sweat, while 6 energy, strain
7 attempt, travail, trouble, venture
8 endeavor, exertion, industry, struggle
11 application, elbow grease

effortful
4 hard 6 tiring, uphill 7 arduous, labored,
operose 8 exacting, toilsome 9 ambitious,
difficult, laborious, strenuous
11 challenging

effortless
4 easy 5 adept, light, ready 6 expert,
facile, fluent, simple, smooth 8 masterly,
skillful 10 proficient 11 undemanding

effrontery
4 face, gall 5 brass, cheek, nerve
8 audacity, boldness, chutzpah, temerity
9 arrogance, assurance, brashness,
hardihood, impudence, insolence
10 brazenness 11 presumption
12 impertinence

effulgence
4 glow 5 blaze, glory 6 luster, lustre
8 radiance, splendor 9 splendour
10 brightness, brilliance, brilliancy,
luminosity

effulgent
5 vivid 6 bright, lucent 7 beaming,
glowing, lambent, radiant, shining
8 dazzling, glorious, luminous, lustrous,
splendid 9 brilliant 11 resplendent
12 incandescent

effuse
4 flow, gush, pour, shed 5 exude, issue
6 stream 7 emanate, enthuse, flow out,
radiate

effusive
5 gushy 6 lavish, sloppy, smarmy
7 cloying, fulsome, gushing, profuse,
verbose 9 expansive, exuberant
10 loquacious, outpouring, unreserved
11 extravagant 12 enthusiastic,
unrestrained 13 demonstrative,
unconstrained

eft
4 newt 6 triton 10 salamander

e.g.
10 for example 13 exempli gratia

egad
6 zounds 7 criminy 8 gadzooks 11 odds
bodkins

egg
3 ova (plural) 4 ovum, seed 5 ovule
case: 5 shell 7 ootheca
dish: 6 omelet 8 omelette
fertilized: 6 zygote 7 oospore
fish: 3 roe 6 caviar
French: 4 oeuf
immature: 6 oocyte
part: 4 yolk 5 glair, shell, white
7 albumen 8 blastodisc
shaped: 5 ovate, ovoid
white: 5 glair 7 albumen

egghead
6 pundit 8 highbrow 10 double-dome
12 intellectual

egg on
4 goad, prod, spur, urge 5 prick, rally
6 arouse, exhort, excite, incite, prompt, stir
up 7 agitate 9 instigate, stimulate

eggplant
6 purple 9 aubergine 10 nightshade

egg-shaped
4 oval 5 ovate, ovoid 7 oviform

Eglah
husband: 5 David
son: 7 Ithream

eglantine
7 dog rose 10 sweetbriar, sweetbrier

Eglantine
father: 5 Pepin
husband: 9 Valentine

Eglon
king: 5 Debir
slayer: 4 Ehud

ego
4 self 5 pride 6 vanity 7 conceit 10 self-esteem

egocentric
7 selfish 9 conceited 10 self-loving
11 self-seeking 12 narcissistic, self-absorbed, self-affected, self-centered, self-involved, vainglorious 13 individualist, self-conceited, self-concerned, self-indulgent

egoism
5 pride 6 vanity 7 conceit 8 self-love
9 self-glory, self-pride, vainglory
10 narcissism, self-regard 11 selfishness, self-opinion

egoistic
4 smug, vain 7 selfish 9 conceited
12 self-absorbed, self-centered 13 self-concerned, self-contented, self-satisfied

egomaniacal
12 self-exalting, vainglorious

egotism
5 pride 6 vanity 7 conceit 8 boasting, bragging, self-love, vainness, vaunting
9 arrogance, pomposity, self-glory, self-pride, vainglory 10 narcissism, self-esteem
11 megalomania, self-opinion 12 boastfulness 13 conceitedness

egotistic
4 vain 5 cocky, proud 7 selfish, stuck-up
8 arrogant, boastful, inflated, puffed-up
9 conceited 11 pretentious, self-serving
12 self-absorbed, self-centered, self-involved 13 self-concerned, self-satisfied

egregious
4 rank 5 gross, stark 6 arrant, brazen
7 blatant, glaring, heinous 8 flagrant, infamous, outright, shocking 9 atrocious,
notorious, shameless 10 deplorable, outrageous 11 conspicuous

egress, egression
4 door, exit 5 issue, leave 6 depart, escape, exodus, outlet 7 doorway, exiting, opening, passage 9 departure, emergence

egret
5 heron, wader

Egypt
ancient city: 6 Thebes 7 Memphis
capital: 5 Cairo
city: 4 Giza 8 Port Said 10 Alexandria
dam: 5 Aswan
desert: 6 Libyan 7 Arabian, Western
gulf: 4 Suez 5 Aqaba
lake: 6 Nasser
language: 6 Arabic
leader: 5 Sadat (Anwar el-) 6 Nasser (Gamal Abdul) 7 Mubarak (Hosni)
monetary unit: 5 pound
neighbor: 5 Libya, Sudan 6 Israel
oasis: 4 Siwa 5 Dakhla, Kharga
7 Farafra
peninsula: 5 Sinai
river: 4 Nile
sea: 3 Red 13 Mediterranean

Egyptian
burial jar: 7 canopic
Christian: 4 Copt
cross: 4 ankh
dam: 5 Aswan
dynasty: 5 Saite, Xoite 6 Hyksos, Tanite, Theban 7 Persian, Thinite 8 Memphite
9 Bubastite, Ethiopian 10 Diospolite
god:
  chief: 6 Amen-Ra
  crocodile-headed: 5 Sebek
  falcon-headed: 4 Ment 5 Horus, Mentu
  6 Sokari 7 Sokaris
  ibis-headed: 5 Thoth 6 Dhouti
  jackal-headed: 6 Anubis
  of creation: 4 Ptah 5 Phtha
  of day: 5 Horus
  of earth: 3 Geb, Keb, Seb
  of evil: 3 Set 4 Seth 5 Sebek
  of life: 4 Amen, Amon 5 Ammon
  of magic: 5 Thoth 6 Dhouti
  of Memphis: 4 Ptah 5 Phtha 6 Sokari
  7 Sokaris
  of the heavens: 5 Horus
  of the morning sun: 5 Horus 7 Khepera
  of the sun: 6 Amen-Ra
  of Thebes: 4 Amen 6 Khensu, Khonsu
  of the underworld: 6 Osiris
  of war: 4 Ment 5 Mentu
  of wisdom: 5 Thoth 6 Dhouti

ram-headed: 4 Amen, Amon 5 Ammon,
Khnum 6 Khnemu
snake: 4 Apep 5 Apepi
goddess:
cat-headed: 4 Bast 5 Pakht
cow-headed: 5 Athor 6 Hathor
lioness-headed: 4 Bast 5 Pakht
6 Sekhet
of fertility: 4 Isis
of love and mirth: 5 Athor 6 Hathor
of motherhood: 4 Apet, Isis
of Thebes: 3 Mut
of the heavens: 3 Nut
queen of the gods: 4 Sati
vulture-headed: 3 Mut 7 Nekhebt
8 Nekhebet
king:
(see **king** entry)
language: 6 Arabic, Coptic
native: 4 Arab, Copt 5 Nilot
president: 5 Sadat 6 Nasser 7 Mubarak
queen: 9 Cleopatra, Nefertiti
sacred bird: 4 ibis
solar disk: 4 Aten
sultan: 7 Saladin
talisman: 6 scarab
underworld: 4 Aaru, Duat 6 Amenti
wind: 7 khamsin, sirocco

eider
4 down, duck 7 sea duck

eidetic
5 exact, vivid 7 perfect, precise
8 absolute, lifelike

eidolon
4 icon 5 ghost, ideal, image, model, shade
6 mirage, vision, wraith 7 epitome, fantasm,
figment, paragon, phantom, specter,
spectre 8 exemplar, illusion, paradigm,
phantasm 9 archetype, prototype
10 apparition

eight
group of: 5 octet 6 octave

eight bells
4 noon

eighth note
6 quaver

eighty-six
4 boot, toss 5 chuck, eject, evict, scrap
6 bounce 7 discard, kick out 8 get rid of,
jettison, throw out

Einstein, Albert
birthplace: 3 Ulm
theory: 10 relativity

Eire
see **Ireland**

eject
4 boot, bump, dump, fire, oust, sack
5 chuck, evict, expel 6 banish, bounce
7 boot out, cast out, dismiss, kick out
8 disgorge, throw out 9 discharge

eke out
6 extend 7 augment, enhance, fill out,
squeeze, stretch 8 increase
10 supplement

elaborate
4 busy 5 fancy, showy 6 daedal, dressy,
evolve, expand, knotty, minute, ornate,
refine, unfold 7 amplify, build up, careful,
clarify, comment, complex, develop,
discuss, elegant, enlarge, explain,
expound, profuse, work out 8 detailed,
involved, overdone, thorough 9 Byzantine,
decorated, embellish, extensive, interpret,
intricate 10 overworked 11 complicated,
embellished, extravagant, painstaking
12 labyrinthine

Elaine
father: 6 Pelles
lover: 8 Lancelot 9 Launcelot
son: 7 Galahad

Elam
capital: 4 Susa 7 Shushan
father: 4 Shem
king: 12 Chedorlaomer

élan
3 pep, vim, zip 4 brio, dash, fire, life, zeal,
zest, zing 5 ardor, flair, gusto, oomph,
verve, vigor 6 energy, esprit, fervor, spirit
7 impetus 8 vivacity 9 animation,
eagerness, intensity 10 enthusiasm

élan vital
4 soul 5 anima 6 animus, pneuma,
psyche, spirit

elapse
4 go by, pass 6 expire, run out, slip by
8 pass away

elastic
6 bouncy, limber, pliant, rubber, supple
7 ductile, pliable, rubbery, springy
8 animated, flexible, moldable, stretchy,
volatile 9 adaptable, expansive, malleable,
resilient 10 extendable, extensible, rubber
band, rubberlike 11 stretchable

elate
4 buoy 5 cheer, exalt, flush, set up
6 excite, perk up, uplift 7 cheer up, delight,
enliven, gladden, gratify, hearten, inspire,

elated
overjoy **8** brighten, embolden, inspirit, spirit up **9** encourage **10** exhilarate, invigorate

elated
4 glad, high **5** happy **7** exalted, excited **8** ecstatic, euphoric, exultant, gladsome, jubilant **9** overjoyed **10** enraptured **11** exhilarated, intoxicated **12** high-spirited

elation
3 joy **4** glee **7** delight, ecstasy, rapture **8** buoyancy, euphoria **9** happiness, transport **10** exaltation, excitement, jubilation **12** exhilaration, intoxication

Elbe tributary
4 Eger, Iser, Ohre **5** Saale **6** Moldau, Vltava

elbow
4 push **5** joint, nudge, shove **6** hustle, jostle

eld
4 yore **6** old age **8** old times

elder
6 senior **8** old-timer **9** patriarch, presbyter **10** golden-ager

elderliness
3 age **6** old age **8** caducity **10** senescence **11** senectitude

elderly
3 old **4** aged, gray **5** aging, hoary **7** ancient **9** declining, venerable

eldritch
5 eerie, weird **7** uncanny

Eleanor's husband
7 Henry II **8** Franklin

elect
3 opt, tap **4** name, pick **5** co-opt, saved **6** choice, choose, chosen, decide, opt for, ordain, picked, vote in **7** resolve, vote for **8** destined, nominate, ordained, redeemed **9** delivered, designate, determine, exclusive, single out **10** designated, singled out

election
6 ballot, choice, voting **7** primary **8** choosing, decision **9** balloting **10** preference, referendum **11** alternative

electioneer
5 stump **7** canvass **8** campaign, politick **9** barnstorm

elective
6 chosen **8** optional **9** voluntary

11 sympathetic **13** discretionary, noncompulsory, nonobligatory

Electra
brother: 7 Orestes
father: 9 Agamemnon
husband: 7 Pylades
mother: 12 Clytemnestra
sister: 9 Iphigenia
victim: 9 Aegisthus **12** Clytemnestra

electric
appliance: 3 fan **4** iron, oven **5** clock, drier, dryer, mixer, range, stove **6** stereo, washer **7** blender, freezer, toaster **10** dishwasher, television **12** refrigerator
coil: 5 tesla **8** solenoid
device: 4 coil, fuse, plug **6** dynamo, magnet, switch **7** battery **8** resistor, rheostat, varistor **9** amplifier, capacitor, condenser, generator **11** transformer
generator: 6 dynamo
particle: 3 ion
unit: 3 amp, ohm **4** volt, watt **5** farad, henry, joule **6** ampere **7** coulomb, faraday **8** kilowatt

electric current
kind: 6 direct **11** alternating
power: 7 wattage
strength: 8 amperage

electricity
5 juice, spark **7** current **9** galvanism, lightning
kind: 6 static **7** current

electrify
3 jar **4** jolt, stun **5** amaze, power, shock **6** charge, excite, thrill **7** astound, enthuse, inflame, provoke, stagger, startle **8** astonish, energize

electrode
6 dynode
negative: 7 cathode
positive: 5 anode

electron
3 ion **7** polaron
stream: 10 cathode ray
tube: 6 triode **7** tetrode **8** dynatron, klystron

Electryon
brother: 6 Mestor
daughter: 7 Alcmene
father: 7 Perseus
mother: 9 Andromeda
wife: 5 Anaxo

eleemosynary
6 humane **8** generous **10** altruistic,

beneficent, benevolent, charitable, munificent, openhanded **12** humanitarian **13** philanthropic

elegance
4 chic, pomp, tone **5** charm, grace, style, taste **6** luxury, polish **7** culture, dignity **8** chicness, poshness, richness, splendor, urbanity **9** gentility, precision **10** ornateness, refinement **11** cultivation **12** magnificence, tastefulness **13** sumptuousness

elegant
4 chic, fine, posh **5** fancy, grand, noble, swank **6** choice, classy, dainty, lovely, modish, ornate, swanky, urbane **7** courtly, genteel, opulent, refined, stately, stylish **8** cultured, polished, splendid, tasteful **9** exquisite, luxurious, recherché, sumptuous **10** cultivated **11** fashionable

elegiac
7 pensive **8** dactylic **9** lamenting, sorrowful **10** melancholy

elegy
4 poem, song **5** dirge **6** lament, monody **8** threnody

_____ eleison
5 Kyrie

Elektra composer
7 Strauss (Richard)

element
4 item, part **5** basic, facet, piece, point **6** aspect, detail, factor, member, sector **7** article, feature, portion, section **8** division, particle, rudiment **9** component, essential, principle **10** ingredient, particular **11** constituent, fundamental
chemical: 3 tin **4** gold, iron, lead, neon, zinc **5** argon, boron, radon, xenon **6** barium, carbon, cerium, cesium, cobalt, copper, curium, erbium, helium, indium, iodine, nickel, osmium, oxygen, radium, silver, sodium **7** arsenic, bismuth, bohrium, bromine, cadmium, calcium, dubnium, fermium, gallium, hafnium, hassium, holmium, iridium, krypton, lithium, mercury, niobium, rhenium, rhodium, silicon, sulphur, terbium, thorium, thulium, uranium, yttrium **8** actinium, aluminum, antimony, astatine, chlorine, chromium, europium, fluorine, hydrogen, illinium, lutecium, masurium, nitrogen, nobelium, platinum, polonium, rubidium, samarium, scandium, selenium, tantalum, thallium, titanium, tungsten, vanadium **9** americium, berkelium, beryllium, columbium, germanium, lanthanum, magnesium, manganese, neodymium, neptunium, palladium, plutonium, potassium, ruthenium, strontium, tellurium, virginium, ytterbium, zirconium **10** dysprosium, gadolinium, lawrencium, meitnerium, molybdenum, seaborgium **11** californium, einsteinium, mendelevium, phosphorous **12** darmstadtium, praseodymium **13** rutherfordium, protoactinium

elemental
3 key **4** pure **5** basal, basic, crude, prime **6** inborn, innate, primal, simple **7** central, connate, primary, radical **8** cardinal, inherent, integral, intimate, simplest **9** beginning, essential, ingrained, intrinsic, primitive **10** deep-seated, primordial, underlying **11** fundamental **13** un-complicated

elementary
4 easy **5** basal, basic **6** simple **7** initial **9** beginning, essential, primitive **10** rudimental, underlying **11** fundamental, preliminary, rudimentary **12** introductory

elemi
5 resin **9** oleoresin

elephant
6 tusker **9** pachyderm
boy: 4 Sabu
driver: 6 mahout
enclosure: 6 kraal
extinct: 7 mammoth **8** mastodon
female: 3 cow
group: 4 herd
keeper: 6 mahout
male: 4 bull
maverick: 5 rogue
nose: 5 trunk **9** proboscis
seat: 6 howdah
sound: 6 bellow **7** trumpet
tooth: 4 tusk
tusk: 5 ivory
young: 4 calf

elephant-headed god
6 Ganesa **7** Ganesha

elephantine
4 huge **6** clumsy **7** awkward, hulking, mammoth, massive **8** colossal, enormous, gigantic **9** graceless, humongous, monstrous, ponderous **10** gargantuan, mastodonic, prodigious, ungraceful **11** heavy-footed

Elephant Man
7 Merrick (Joseph)

elevate
4 lift, rear, rise **5** boost, elate, erect, exalt, hoist, raise **6** buoy up, jack up, lift up, pick up, uplift **7** advance, dignify, ennoble, glorify, hearten, improve, inspire, promote, upgrade **8** heighten **10** exhilarate

elevated
4 high **5** grand, lofty, moral, noble **6** aerial, formal, superb **7** ethical, refined, soaring, stately, sublime **8** eloquent, majestic, virtuous **9** dignified, grandiose, high-flown, honorable, righteous **10** high-minded, upstanding **13** grandiloquent

elevation
4 hill, rise **5** boost **6** ascent, height, uplift **7** advance, raising **8** altitude, mountain **9** acclivity, promotion, upgrading **10** apotheosis, preference, preferment **11** advancement, ennoblement
indication: 9 benchmark

elevator
4 cage, lift, silo **5** hoist
maker: 4 Otis

elf
3 fay, imp **4** peri, puck **5** fairy, gnome, pixie, troll **6** goblin, sprite **7** brownie, gremlin **10** leprechaun

elfin
5 antic **6** frisky, impish **7** implike, playful, puckish **8** pixieish **11** mischievous

Elgin _____
7 Marbles

Eli
4 Yale **5** Yalie

Eli _____
4 Yale **5** Lilly **7** Whitney

Elia
4 Lamb (Charles)

Eliab
brother: 5 David
daughter: 7 Abihail
father: 5 Helon, Pallu
son: 6 Abiram, Dathan

Eliada
father: 5 David
son: 5 Rezon

Eliam's daughter
9 Bathsheba

elicit
5 educe, evoke **6** derive, evince, extort **7** extract, provoke **8** bring out **9** call forth, draw forth

elide
4 fail, omit, skip **6** excise, forget, ignore, remove, slight **7** abridge, curtail, neglect **8** condense, cross out, discount, overlook, pass over, suppress **9** disregard

eligible
3 fit **6** fitted, likely, nubile, seemly, suited, worthy **7** capable **8** entitled, suitable **9** desirable, qualified **10** acceptable **11** appropriate **12** marriageable

Elihu _____
4 Root, Yale

Elijah
5 Elias **7** prophet **8** Tishbite
father: 5 Harim **7** Jeroham

Elimelech's wife
5 Naomi

eliminate
3 bar **4** bate, drop, oust, void **5** debar, eject, erase, evict, expel, purge **6** delete, except, remove **7** discard, dismiss, exclude, expunge, obviate, rule out, take out **8** count out **9** clear away, eradicate, liquidate **11** exterminate

Eliot, George
lover: 5 Lewes (George Henry)
novel: 6 Romola **8** Adam Bede **11** Middlemarch, Silas Marner **13** Daniel Deronda **14** Mill on the Floss (The)
pseudonym of: 5 Evans (Mary Ann)

Eliot, T.S.
play: 13 Cocktail Party (The)
poem: 9 Gerontion, Hollow Men (The), Waste Land (The) **12** Ash Wednesday, Four Quartets

Eliphaz
father: 4 Esau
mother: 4 Adah
son: 5 Teman

Elisabeth
husband: 9 Zacharias
son: 4 John (the Baptist)

Elisha
father: 7 Shaphat
servant: 6 Gehazi

Elisheba
brother: 7 Nahshon
father: 9 Amminadab
husband: 5 Aaron
son: 5 Abihu, Nadab **7** Eleazar, Ithamar

elite
3 top **4** best, pick **5** cream, elect, pride, prime, prize **6** choice, flower, gentry, select **7** quality, society **9** exclusive, gentility,

patrician **10** upper class, upper crust
11 aristocracy **12** aristocratic

elixir
4 balm, cure **6** potion **7** arcanum, cure-all,
nostrum, panacea, philter **10** catholicon

Elizabeth I, name for
6 Oriana **8** Gloriana

elk
4 deer **5** moose **6** sambar, wapiti **7** red
deer

ell
3 arm **4** wing **5** annex, elbow, joint
8 addition **9** extension

ellipse
4 oval **5** curve, orbit

elliptical
5 brief, ovate, short **6** gnomic **7** concise,
cryptic, laconic, obscure, summary
9 condensed, enigmatic **11** abbreviated

elm
5 wahoo

elocution
7 diction, oratory **8** delivery, rhetoric
11 declamation, speechcraft

elongate
4 draw **6** extend **7** draw out, lengthy, spin
out, stretch **8** extended, lengthen
10 lengthened

elope
4 flee **6** escape, run off **7** abscond, run
away **9** steal away

eloquence
5 force, power **6** fervor, spirit **7** fluency,
oratory, passion **8** rhetoric **10** expression
12 expressivity, forcefulness

eloquent
5 lofty **6** ardent, fervid, fluent, moving
7 fervent, voluble **8** elevated, forceful,
powerful, stirring **9** affecting **10** articulate,
expressive, impressive, meaningful,
passionate, persuasive, rhetorical
11 impassioned, sententious **12** smooth-
spoken **13** silver-tongued

El Salvador
capital: 11 San Salvador
city: 8 Santa Ana **9** San Miguel
ethnic group: 5 Pipil
lake: 8 Ilopango
language: 7 Spanish
monetary unit: 5 colón **6** dollar
neighbor: 8 Honduras **9** Guatemala
river: 5 Lempa

else
5 if not **7** besides, further **9** otherwise
10 additional **11** differently **12** additionally

elucidate
7 clarify, clear up, explain, expound
8 annotate, spell out **9** exemplify,
explicate, interpret **10** illuminate, illustrate

elude
4 defy, duck, flee, foil **5** avert, avoid,
dodge, evade **6** baffle, escape, outwit,
thwart **8** confound **9** frustrate
10 circumvent

elusive
6 subtle, tricky **7** evasive, phantom
8 baffling, fleeting, fugitive, slippery
10 evanescent, intangible, mysterious
13 insubstantial

elute
7 extract

elver
3 eel

elvish
see elfin

Elysium
5 bliss **6** heaven **7** nirvana **8** empyrean,
paradise

elytron
4 wing

emaciated
4 bony, lean, thin **5** gaunt **6** skinny,
wasted **7** scrawny, starved, wizened
8 skeletal, underfed **10** cadaverous

emaciation
5 tabes **7** atrophy **8** marasmus
10 starvation **11** attenuation

emanate
4 emit, flow, rise, stem **5** arise, exude,
issue **6** derive, emerge, spring **7** come
out, give off, give out, proceed, radiate
9 originate **10** derive from

emanation
4 aura, flow **6** efflux **8** effusion, emission
9 effluence

emancipate
4 free **5** let go, loose **6** loosen, redeem,
unbind **7** manumit, release, set free,
unchain **8** liberate, unfetter **9** discharge,
unshackle **11** enfranchise

emancipation
7 release **10** liberation **11** deliverance

emancipator
5 Moses 7 Lincoln (Abraham) 9 deliverer, liberator

emasculate
3 fix 4 geld 5 alter, unman 6 neuter, soften, weaken 7 unnerve 8 castrate, enervate, unstring 10 debilitate, devitalize

embalm
7 mummify, perfume 8 preserve

embankment
4 berm, bund, dike, quay 5 levee, mound

embargo
3 ban, bar 5 edict, order 8 blockade, stoppage 10 impediment 11 prohibition

embark
5 board, enter, start 6 set out 7 set sail 8 commence

embarrass
4 faze 5 abash, upset 6 flurry, hamper, hinder, impede, rattle 7 confuse, flummox, fluster, mortify, nonplus, perturb 8 confound, distress 9 discomfit, humiliate 10 complicate, discomfort, discompose, disconcert

embarrassment
5 shame, upset 7 chagrin 8 distress 9 confusion 10 discomfort 11 humiliation 12 discomfiture, perturbation 13 mortification

embassy
5 envoy 7 mission 8 legation 10 ambassador, delegation, deputation

embay
4 trap 5 catch, seize 7 capture 8 encircle, surround

embed
3 fix, set 4 bury, root 5 infix, inlay, lodge 7 implant, ingrain 8 entrench

embellish
3 pad 4 deck, gild, trim 5 adorn, color 6 bedeck, blazon, emboss, enrich 7 amplify, dress up, enhance, festoon, garnish 8 beautify, decorate, ornament 9 elaborate, embroider 10 exaggerate 11 romanticize

embellishment
7 garnish, gilding, melisma, mordent 8 coloring, ornament 9 fioritura, floridity, hyperbole 10 decoration 11 elaboration 12 embroidering, exaggeration 13 ornamentation

ember
3 ash 6 cinder

embezzle
4 loot 5 filch, steal 6 pilfer 7 purloin 8 peculate 9 defalcate

embitter
4 sour 6 poison 7 envenom 9 acidulate

emblazon
4 laud 5 extol 7 glorify 8 inscribe 9 celebrate

emblem
4 arms, flag, logo, mace, seal, sign 5 badge, brand, crest, image, token 6 banner, device, symbol 7 pennant 8 colophon, hallmark, insignia, monogram, standard 9 attribute, trademark 10 coat of arms

emblematic
8 symbolic 10 figurative, indicative 11 allegorical 12 illustrative, metaphorical

embodiment
6 avatar 7 epitome 8 exemplar 9 archetype 11 incarnation 13 manifestation

embody
5 reify 6 evince, mirror, typify 7 compose, contain, exhibit, realize, subsume 8 manifest 9 actualize, encompass, epitomize, exemplify, incarnate, integrate, objectify, personify, represent, symbolize 10 constitute, illustrate 11 emblematize, externalize, hypostatize, incorporate, materialize 12 substantiate

embolden
5 steel 7 fortify, hearten, inspire 8 inspirit 9 encourage 10 strengthen

embolus
4 clog, clot

embosom
3 hug 7 embrace, enclose, envelop, shelter

embouchure
10 mouthpiece

embowel
3 gut 4 draw 10 eviscerate, exenterate

embrace
3 hug 4 hold, lock, love, wrap 5 admit, adopt, clasp, cling, press 6 accept, cradle, cuddle, embody, enfold, fondle, nuzzle, take in, take on, take up 7 cherish, contain, embosom, enclose, entwine, envelop, espouse, include, receive, snuggle,

squeeze, subsume, welcome **8** comprise, encircle **9** encompass **10** comprehend **11** accommodate, incorporate **12** encirclement

embrangle
see **embroil**

embrocation
5 salve **7** unguent **8** liniment

embroider
3 pad, sew, tat **4** gild **5** color **6** expand, overdo, play up, stitch **7** amplify, build up, enhance, garnish, magnify, stretch **8** decorate, ornament **9** dramatize, elaborate, embellish **10** exaggerate **11** hyperbolize, romanticize

embroidery
6 crewel **7** cutwork, orphrey **8** bargello, couching, smocking, tapestry **10** crewelwork, needlework **11** needlepoint

embroil
4 mire **6** tangle **7** confuse, ensnare, involve **8** disorder, entangle **9** implicate

embroilment
4 tiff **6** fracas **7** dispute, quarrel, wrangle **8** squabble **9** bickering **10** falling-out **11** altercation, controversy

embryo
3 bud **4** germ, seed **5** fetus, spark **7** nucleus **8** blastula, gastrula

emend
4 edit **5** alter, right **6** polish, revise **7** correct, improve, rectify, retouch

emerald
3 gem **5** beryl, green, stone **8** gemstone

Emerald Isle
4 Eire, Erin **7** Ireland

emerge
4 flow, loom, rise, stem **5** arise, issue **6** appear, derive, evolve, spring **7** come out, develop, emanate, proceed, surface **9** originate **11** come to light, materialize, transpire

emergency
3 fix **4** hole, pass **5** pinch **6** climax, clutch, crisis, crunch, strait **7** squeeze **8** accident, exigency

emeritus
7 retired

Emerson, Ralph Waldo
essay: 12 Self-Reliance
forte: 5 essay
home: 7 Concord
friend: 7 Thoreau (Henry David)

emery
6 powder **8** abrasive, corundum

emetic
8 vomitive **9** cathartic, purgative

émeute
4 riot **6** mutiny, revolt, tumult **8** outbreak, upheaval, uprising **9** rebellion **12** insurrection

emigrant
7 pioneer, settler **8** colonist **10** expatriate

émigré
5 alien, exile, expat **7** evacuee, migrant, refugee **8** colonist **10** expatriate

Emilia
husband: 4 Iago **7** Palamon
slayer: 4 Iago

eminence
3 VIP **4** fame, peak, rise **5** honor, power **6** bigwig, esteem, height, leader, renown, repute **7** dignity, notable **8** altitude, bigtimer, luminary, prestige, standing **9** authority, dignitary, elevation, greatness, loftiness **10** importance, projection, prominence, promontory, reputation **11** distinction, superiority

eminent
4 high **5** famed, grand, great, large, lofty, noble, noted **6** august, famous **7** exalted, notable **8** esteemed, renowned, towering **9** important, well-known **10** celebrated, noteworthy, projecting **11** conspicuous, illustrious, outstanding, prestigious **13** distinguished

eminently
4 very **6** highly **7** notably **9** extremely **10** remarkably, strikingly **11** exceedingly **12** surpassingly **13** exceptionally

emir
5 chief, ruler, sheik, title **6** sheikh **9** chieftain, commander

emissary
see **envoy**

emission
4 flow **7** venting **9** discharge, effluvium, emanation, radiation

emit
4 beam, glow, ooze, pour, shed, spew, vent, void **5** eject, expel, exude, issue, loose, utter **6** exhale, let out **7** emanate, excrete, extrude, give off, give out, radiate, release, secrete, send out **8** evacuate, throw off **9** circulate, discharge

emmer
5 grain, spelt, wheat

emmet
3 ant 7 pismire

emollient
4 balm 5 salve 7 lenient 8 lenitive,
liniment, sedative, softening, soothing
9 analgesic 10 mollifying

emolument
3 fee, pay 4 wage 5 wages 6 income,
reward, salary 7 guerdon, stipend
8 earnings 10 recompense 11 pay
envelope 12 compensation

emotion
3 ire, joy 4 fear, glee, hate, love 5 agony,
ardor, grief, shame 6 affect, hatred, relief,
sorrow, warmth 7 ardency, despair,
disgust, ecstasy, feeling, passion, sadness
8 jealousy, surprise 9 affection, agitation,
happiness, sentiment 11 affectivity,
sensibility, sensitivity 12 excitability

emotional
4 warm 6 ardent, fervid, heated, moving
7 feeling, fervent, intense, soulful, zealous
8 effusive, stirring, touching, vehement
9 affecting, affective, excitable, heartfelt,
impetuous, rhapsodic, sensitive 10 hysterical, passionate 11 impassioned,
overwrought, rhapsodical, softhearted,
susceptible, sympathetic

emotionless
3 icy 4 cold, cool 5 chill, staid, stoic, stony
6 frigid, remote, torpid 7 callous, deadpan,
distant, glacial 8 detached, reserved
9 apathetic, immovable, impassive,
unfeeling 10 impersonal 11 cold-blooded,
indifferent 12 matter-of-fact 13 dispassionate, unimpassioned

empathy
4 pity 6 lenity, warmth 7 rapport 8 affinity,
sympathy 9 communion 10 compassion
12 congeniality 13 compatibility,
comprehension, fellow feeling,
understanding

emperor
4 czar, shah, tsar, tzar 5 ruler 6 caesar,
kaiser 7 monarch 8 autocrat, dictator
9 potentate, sovereign
French: 8 Napoleon (Bonaparte)
9 Bonaparte (Napoleon) 11 Charlemagne
Indian: 5 Babur
Japanese: 6 mikado 7 Akihito 8 Hirohito
Mexican: 8 Iturbide (Agustín de)
10 Maximilian
Roman: 4 Nero 5 Galba, Nerva, Titus
6 Decius, Julian, Trajan 7 Gratian,
Hadrian, Severus 8 Augustus, Aurelian,
Caligula, Claudius, Commodus, Domitian,
Honorius, Tiberius, Valerian 9 Antoninus,
Caracalla, Justinian 10 Diocletian,
Elagabalus 11 Constantine

emphasis
5 focus, force 6 accent, stress, weight
9 attention 10 insistence, intensity,
prominence 12 accentuation

emphasize
6 accent, play up, stress 7 feature
8 pinpoint 9 highlight, italicize, spotlight,
underline 10 accentuate, underscore

emphatic
4 firm 6 marked 7 decided, earnest,
pointed 8 accented, decisive, forceful,
positive, stressed, vigorous 9 assertive,
energetic, insistent 10 resounding,
underlined 11 accentuated

empire
5 realm 6 domain 7 demesne, kingdom
8 dominion
ancient:
(see ancient empire)

Empire State
7 New York

empirical
7 factual 9 fact-based, pragmatic
12 experiential, experimental 13 ob-
servational

emplacement
7 battery 8 position

employ
3 job, use 4 busy, hire, work 5 apply, avail
6 devote, engage, occupy, retain, secure,
take on 7 exploit, utilize 8 exercise,
practice 9 make use of 10 occupation

employee
4 hand, help 5 agent 6 worker 7 servant
8 factotum 9 underling
bank: 5 clerk, guard 6 teller
hotel: 7 bellboy, bellhop, doorman
9 concierge, desk clerk 11 chambermaid

employer
4 boss 6 master 10 supervisor

employment
3 job, use 4 line, post, task, toil, work
5 trade, usage 6 hiring, métier, office
7 calling, mission, purpose, pursuit
8 business, exercise, function, position,
vocation 9 appliance, operation, situation
10 engagement, occupation
11 application, recruitment, utilization
12 exploitation

emporium
4 mall, mart, shop 5 store 6 bazaar, market 8 exchange 11 marketplace

empower
5 endow 6 charge, enable, invest 7 entitle, entrust, license 8 accredit, delegate, deputize, sanction 9 authorize, privilege 10 commission

empress
5 queen
Byzantine: 3 Zoe
French: 7 Eugénie 9 Josephine
Japanese: 5 Suiko
of India: 8 Victoria
Mexican: 7 Carlota
Roman: 6 Fausta
Russian: 4 Anna 7 czarina, tsarina, tzarina 9 Alexandra, Catherine, Elizabeth

empressement
6 fervor, warmth 10 cordiality

emprise
4 feat, gest 5 geste 7 exploit, venture 9 adventure 11 undertaking

emptiness
4 void 5 blank 6 hunger, vacuum 7 inanity, vacancy, vacuity

emptor
5 buyer 6 vendee 8 consumer, customer 9 purchaser

_____ emptor
6 caveat

empty
3 rid 4 bare, dump, pour, vain, void 5 blank, clear, drain 6 barren, devoid, hollow, unload, vacant, vacate 7 deplete, drained, exhaust, vacated, vacuous 8 depleted, deserted, evacuate, forsaken 9 abandoned, destitute 10 unoccupied, untenanted
Scottish: 4 toom

empty-headed
6 simple, vacant 7 vacuous, witless 8 ignorant, untaught 9 benighted, brainless, frivolous 10 illiterate, uneducated, unlettered, unschooled 11 know-nothing 12 uninstructed 13 rattlebrained

empyreal
4 airy, holy 6 aerial, divine 7 sublime 8 beatific, ethereal, heavenly 9 celestial, spiritual, unearthly 12 transcendent

empyrean
3 sky 4 Zion 5 bliss, ether 6 heaven,

welkin 7 Elysium, heavens, nirvana 8 paradise 9 firmament

emu
4 bird, rhea 6 ratite 9 cassowary

emulate
3 ape 4 copy 5 equal, mimic, rival 6 follow, mirror 7 compete, imitate 9 challenge

emulation
7 rivalry 8 striving, tug-of-war 9 imitation 10 contention 11 competition

emulous
5 vying 8 aspiring, striving, vaulting 9 ambitious 11 competitive

emulsifier
4 soap 5 algin

enable
3 fit, let 5 allow, ready 6 permit 7 empower, entitle, license, prepare, qualify 8 accredit, sanction 9 authorize, condition 10 commission, facilitate 12 make possible

enact
4 pass, play 6 decree, depict, effect, ordain, ratify 7 execute, perform, portray 8 proclaim 9 authorize, discourse, establish, institute, legislate, represent 10 accomplish, bring about, constitute, effectuate 11 impersonate

enactment
3 law 6 action, decree 7 statute 9 depiction, ordinance, portrayal 11 legislation, performance 12 ratification

enamel
5 glaze, gloss, japan, paint 7 lacquer

enamored
4 fond 6 loving 7 devoted, smitten 8 besotted 9 bewitched, enchanted, entranced, infatuate 10 captivated, infatuated

encamp
4 tent 6 settle 7 bivouac

encampment
6 billet, laager 7 bivouac, hutment

encase
3 box 4 pack 7 confine, enclose, envelop, sheathe

enceinte
6 gravid 8 pregnant 9 expectant, expecting 10 parturient

enchain
4 bind 6 fetter 7 manacle, shackle

enchant
3 hex 4 lure, wile 5 charm, spell, witch
6 allure, enamor, seduce, thrill, voodoo
7 attract, beguile, bewitch, delight
8 ensorcel, enthrall 9 captivate, enrapture,
ensorcell, fascinate, hypnotize, magnetize,
mesmerize, spellbind

enchanter
4 mage 5 magus 6 wizard 7 charmer,
warlock 8 conjurer, conjuror, magician,
sorcerer 11 necromancer, spellbinder

enchanting
5 siren 9 glamorous, seductive
10 attractive, delectable, delightful,
intriguing

enchantment
3 hex 5 charm, magic, spell 6 allure
7 glamour, sorcery 8 witchery, wizardry
9 conjuring, seduction 10 necromancy,
witchcraft 11 incantation

enchantress
3 hex 5 bruja, Circe, lamia, Medea, siren,
witch 9 sorceress

enchiridion
4 text 5 guide 6 manual 8 Baedeker,
handbook 9 guidebook, vade mecum

encipher
4 code

encircle
3 hem 4 band, gird, halo, hoop, ring
5 girth 6 begird, engird, enlace, girdle
7 compass, embrace, enclose, environ,
wreathe 8 surround 9 encompass
12 circumscribe

enclave
6 colony, ghetto, sector 7 quarter
8 district, homeland

enclose
3 box, hem, mew, pen, rim 4 cage, coop,
mure, wall, wrap 5 bound, fence, hedge,
limit 6 circle, closet, corral, hold in,
immure, shroud, shut in, wall in
7 compass, confine, contain, embosom,
include 8 fence off, imprison, surround
9 capsulize 12 circumscribe

enclosed
6 obtect

enclosure
3 box, mew, pen, sty 4 cage, camp, cell,
coop, cote, fold, jail, pale, quad, tank, trap,
wall, weir, yard 5 court, fence, kraal,
pound, stall 6 aviary, corral, cowpen,
kennel, paling, prison 7 chamber, paddock
8 cloister, stockade 9 courtyard
10 quadrangle

encomiast
7 praiser 8 eulogist 10 panegyrist

encomiastic
9 adulatory, laudative, laudatory
10 eulogistic 11 panegyrical

encomium
4 laud 5 kudos, paean 6 eulogy, homage,
praise 7 acclaim, plaudit, tribute
8 accolade, citation, plaudits 9 laudation,
panegyric 10 compliment, salutation
11 acclamation 12 commendation

encompass
3 hem 4 belt, gird, ring 5 bound 6 begird,
circle, girdle, take in 7 contain, embrace,
enclose, include, subsume 8 encircle,
surround 10 accomplish, bring about,
comprehend

encore
6 recall, repeat, return 10 repetition

encounter
4 face, find, fray, meet 5 brush, clash,
fight, run-in, scrap, set-to 6 battle, engage,
take on 7 collide, contest, meeting,
quarrel, run into 8 argument, bump into,
come upon, conflict, confront, meet with,
skirmish, struggle 10 contention,
experience

encourage
4 abet, back, buoy, push, spur, stir, urge
5 boost, cheer, egg on, rally, rouse, serve,
steel 6 assist, assure, buck up, excite,
foster, incite, induce, praise 7 advance,
animate, approve, bolster, cheer up,
endorse, fortify, further, hearten, improve,
inspire, promote, provoke, quicken,
support, sustain 8 advocate, embolden,
energize, inspirit, reassure, sanction
9 enhearten, galvanize, instigate,
patronize, reinforce, stimulate, subsidize
10 invigorate, strengthen

encouragement
4 lift, push 5 boost 7 backing, support
8 approval 11 inspiration

encouraging
4 rosy 6 bright, likely 7 hopeful
9 favorable, promising 10 auspicious,
propitious

encroach
5 poach 6 invade, meddle, trench

7 impinge, intrude 8 entrench, infringe, overstep, trespass

encrypt
4 code 6 cipher, encode 7 convert 8 disguise, encipher

encumber
4 lade, load 6 burden, charge, fetter, hamper, hinder, impede, saddle, weight 7 freight, oppress 8 handicap, obstruct, overload 9 weigh down 10 overburden 13 inconvenience

encumbrance
4 lien, load, onus 5 claim 6 burden 7 baggage 8 handicap, mortgage 9 albatross, millstone 10 impediment

encyclical
6 letter 7 general 8 circular

encyclopedic
5 broad 7 general 8 complete, thorough 9 extensive, inclusive, universal 11 compendious, wide-ranging 12 all-embracing, all-inclusive 13 comprehensive

encyclopedist
7 Diderot (Denis)

end
3 aim, tip 4 coda, doom, goal, halt, quit, stop, tail, term 5 cease, close, death, finis, limit 6 demise, expire, finale, finish, object, period, result, scotch, windup, wrap up 7 abolish, closing, closure, extreme, lineman, outcome, purpose 8 boundary, complete, conclude, confines, curtains, finality, surcease, terminal, terminus 9 cessation, extremity, objective, terminate 10 borderline, completion, conclusion, denouement, expiration, extinction, limitation 11 culmination, discontinue, termination 12 consummation

endanger
4 risk 5 peril 6 expose 7 imperil 8 threaten 10 compromise, jeopardize

endeavor
3 aim, try 4 push, seek, toil, work 5 assay, essay, labor, trial 6 effort, intend, strain, strive 7 attempt, purpose, travail, venture 8 exertion, striving, struggle 9 determine, undertake 10 enterprise 11 undertaking

ended
4 done, over, past 7 through 8 complete

endemic
5 local 6 innate, native 8 homebred, inherent, primeval 9 homegrown, prevalent 10 aboriginal, indigenous, native-born

ending
4 stop 5 close 6 finale, finish, period, windup 7 closing, closure 8 terminus 9 cessation 10 completion, conclusion, denouement 11 termination

endive
7 lettuce, witloof 8 escarole

endless
7 eternal, undying 8 constant, enduring, immortal, infinite, unending 9 ceaseless, continual, incessant, limitless, perpetual, unbounded, unceasing, unlimited 10 continuous, indefinite, unmeasured 11 everlasting, illimitable, measureless 12 immeasurable, interminable

endmost
4 last 5 final 8 farthest, furthest, ultimate 10 concluding

endocrine gland
5 gonad, ovary 6 pineal, testis, thymus 7 adrenal, thyroid 8 pancreas 9 pituitary 11 parathyroid 12 hypothalamus

endomorphic
5 beefy, heavy, husky, stout 6 portly, pyknic, rotund

endorse
4 back, okay, sign 5 bless, vouch 6 attest, ratify, second, uphold 7 approve, certify, command, confirm, stand by, support, witness 8 accredit, advocate, champion, inscribe, make over, notarize, sanction 9 autograph, recommend 10 underwrite 12 authenticate

endorsement
7 backing, support 8 approval, sanction 9 signature 12 confirmation, ratification 13 authorization

endow
4 back, fund 5 found 6 bestow, confer, enrich, supply 7 empower, enhance, finance, furnish, promote, provide, sponsor, support 8 bequeath 9 subsidize

endowment
4 fund, gift 5 award, dower, dowry, grant, power, skill 6 legacy, talent 7 ability, bequest 8 appanage, aptitude, bestowal, capacity, donation 11 benefaction

end product
5 fruit, issue 6 effect, payoff, result, upshot 7 outcome 11 consequence

endue
3 don 4 vest 5 dower, equip, imbue, put

on **6** clothe, invest, outfit **7** furnish, provide **8** accouter **9** crown with, transfuse

endurance
4 grit, guts, wind **5** moxie, pluck **6** mettle **7** stamina **8** patience, strength, tenacity **9** fortitude **10** permanence, resolution **11** persistence **12** perseverance

endure
4 bear, bide, go on, last **5** abide, brook, stand **6** accept, hold on, linger, pocket, remain, suffer **7** carry on, persist, stomach, survive, sustain, swallow, undergo, weather **8** continue, ride out, submit to, tolerate, tough out **9** withstand

enduring
3 old **4** fast, firm, sure **6** steady **7** abiding, durable, eternal, lasting, staunch **8** constant, lifelong **9** long-lived, perennial, permanent, steadfast **10** continuing, inveterate, persistent **11** long-lasting, unfaltering **12** never-failing

Endymion
father: 8 Aethlius
lover: 5 Diana **6** Selene
author: 5 Keats (John)

enemy
3 foe **5** rival **8** attacker, opponent **9** adversary, assailant **10** antagonist, competitor

energetic
4 spry **5** brisk, fresh, hardy, lusty, peppy, zippy **6** active, lively **7** driving, dynamic, vibrant **8** spirited, tireless, vigorous **9** sprightly, strenuous, vivacious **13** indefatigable

energize
3 pep **4** fuel, stir **5** liven, pep up, rouse, spark **6** enable, excite, stir up, turn on **7** empower, enliven, fortify, inspire, juice up **8** activate, inspirit, vitalize **9** electrify, galvanize, stimulate **10** invigorate, strengthen

energy
3 pep, vim, zip **4** dash, life, tuck **5** drive, force, juice, moxie, pluck, power, sinew, steam, verve, vigor **6** effort, muscle, spirit **7** current, potency, stamina, voltage **8** activity, dynamism, efficacy, exertion, strength, vitality **9** animation, intensity, puissance **10** enterprise, get-up-and-go, initiative **11** application
unit: 3 erg **4** dyne, volt **5** joule **7** quantum **10** horsepower

enervate
3 sap **4** jade, tire **5** weary **6** soften, weaken **7** disable, exhaust, fatigue, unnerve **8** enfeeble, unstring **10** debilitate, devitalize

enfant terrible
3 imp **5** scamp **6** urchin **9** skeezicks

enfeeble
3 sap **6** soften, weaken **7** deplete, disable, exhaust, fatigue **8** enervate **9** attenuate, undermine **10** debilitate, devitalize

enfold
3 hug **4** wrap **5** clasp, cover, press **6** shroud, swathe **7** contain, embrace, squeeze **8** surround

enforce
5 exact, impel **6** compel, effect, impose, invoke, oblige **7** execute, fulfill **8** carry out **9** constrain, discharge, implement, prosecute **10** accomplish, administer, strengthen

enfranchise
4 free **6** rescue **7** deliver, manumit, release, set free **8** liberate **10** emancipate

engage
4 bind, grip, hire, mesh **5** fight, troth **6** absorb, arrest, attack, battle, commit, employ, enlist, occupy, pledge, take on **7** assault, betroth, engross, immerse, involve, promise **8** affiance, enthrall, interact **9** captivate, encounter, fascinate, interlace, interlock, intermesh, interplay, preoccupy, undertake

engaged
4 busy, rapt **6** intent **7** working **8** absorbed, employed, immersed, intended, occupied, plighted **9** affianced, betrothed, committed, engrossed, wrapped up **10** contracted **11** preoccupied
person: 6 fiancé **7** fiancée

engage in
4 wage **5** enter **6** pursue, tackle, take up **7** conduct **8** embark on, practice **9** prosecute, undertake

engagement
3 gig **4** date, fray, word **5** fight, troth, tryst **6** action, battle, combat, hiring, pledge, plight **7** booking, meeting, promise **8** espousal, skirmish **9** betrothal, encounter **10** commitment, employment, rendezvous **11** appointment, assignation

engaging
7 likable, winning, winsome **8** charming,

pleasant, pleasing 9 appealing
10 attractive 13 prepossessing

engender
4 sire, stir 5 beget, breed, cause, hatch,
rouse, spawn 6 arouse, create, excite,
father, induce, lead to, work up 7 develop,
produce, provoke 8 generate 9 originate,
procreate, stimulate

engine
5 motor, turbo 7 turbine 10 locomotive
kind: 3 gas, jet 5 steam 6 diesel
7 turbine 8 gasoline 9 hydraulic
jet: 8 turbofan, turbojet
part: 3 cam, rod 4 gear, plug, pump
5 choke 6 filter, piston, tappet 8 cylinder,
manifold, throttle 9 condenser, crankcase
10 carburetor 12 transmission
siege: 3 ram 6 onager 8 ballista, catapult
9 trebuchet 12 battering ram
sound: 4 chug, roar 6 rattle

engineer
4 plan, plot 5 set up, swing 6 devise,
driver, manage, scheme, wangle
7 arrange, finagle 8 contrive, intrigue,
maneuver, motorman 9 machinate,
negotiate 10 manipulate, mastermind
11 orchestrate
kind: 5 civil 6 mining 8 chemical, sanitary
10 electrical, mechanical 12 aeronautical
military: 6 sapper

engineers' group
abbreviation: 4 IEEE

England
6 Albion 7 Britain 9 Britannia 12 Great
Britain
see also **United Kingdom**

English
7 British
cathedral city: 3 Ely 4 York 5 Wells
6 Durham, Exeter 7 Lincoln, Norwich
8 Coventry, Hereford 9 Salisbury,
Worcester 10 Canterbury, Winchester
coin: 5 crown, groat, pence 6 florin,
guinea 8 farthing, shilling, sixpence,
twopence 9 fourpence, half crown,
halfpenny, sovereign 10 threepence
combining form: 5 Anglo
farm: 5 croft
forest: 5 Arden 8 Sherwood
letter: 3 zed
measure: 3 rod, tun 4 gill, hand, peck,
span 5 chain 6 barrel, bushel, fathom,
firkin 7 furlong 8 hogshead 10 barleycorn
military college: 9 Sandhurst
patron saint: 6 George
person: 4 chap, mate 5 bloke 6 Briton
pirate: 4 Kidd (Capt. William) 5 Avery

(Henry), Teach (Edward) 6 Morgan (Henry)
7 Dampier (William) 10 Blackbeard
prince: 5 Harry 6 Andrew, Edward, Philip
7 Charles, William
princess: 4 Anne 5 Diana 8 Margaret
professor: 3 don
royal family: 5 Tudor 6 Stuart 7 Hanover,
Windsor
saint: 7 Dunstan 8 Cuthbert
spa: 4 Bath
sport: 5 rugby 7 cricket
tavern: 3 pub
university: 5 Leeds 6 Oxford
9 Cambridge
weight: 5 stone 6 firkin 7 quintal
8 quartern

English Channel swimmer
6 Ederle (Gertrude)

engrave
3 cut, fix 4 etch 5 carve, chase 6 incise,
scrive 7 instill 8 inscribe

engraver
6 chaser, etcher
German: 5 Dürer (Albrecht)
10 Schongauer (Martin)
Italian: 8 Raimondi (Marcantonio)

engraving
7 etching, linecut, woodcut 8 drypoint,
intaglio 9 xylograph

engross
4 bury, busy, copy, grip 5 apply, write
6 absorb, engage, indite, occupy, scribe
7 consume, immerse, involve 8 enthrall,
inscribe 9 captivate, preoccupy
10 transcribe

engrosser
6 scribe 7 copyist 9 scrivener
12 calligrapher 13 calligraphist

engulf
4 bury 5 drown, flood, swamp, whelm
6 deluge, devour 7 immerse, overrun,
swallow 8 flow over, inundate, overflow,
submerge 9 overwhelm, swallow up

enhance
4 lift 5 add to, adorn, exalt, raise 6 deepen
7 amplify, augment, build up, elevate,
enlarge, flatter, improve, magnify
8 beautify, heighten, increase 9 aggravate,
embellish, embroider, intensify, reinforce
10 exaggerate, strengthen

enigma
4 crux, knot 5 poser, rebus 6 puzzle,
riddle, sphinx, teaser 7 mystery, problem,
puzzler 9 conundrum 10 closed book,

perplexity, puzzlement **12** question mark **13** Chinese puzzle, mystification

enigmatic

6 mystic **7** cryptic, Delphic, obscure **8** Delphian, oracular, puzzling **9** ambiguous **10** mysterious, mystifying, perplexing **11** inscrutable

enisle

6 cut off **7** isolate **8** insulate, separate **9** segregate, sequester

enjoin

3 ban, bid **4** deny, rule, tell, urge, warn **5** order, taboo **6** adjure, charge, decree, direct, forbid, impose, outlaw **7** caution, command, counsel, dictate, inhibit **8** admonish, disallow, forewarn, instruct, prohibit **9** interdict, prescribe, proscribe

enjoy

4 like, love **5** eat up, fancy, savor **6** relish **9** delight in **10** appreciate

enjoyable

3 fun **8** pleasant, pleasing **9** agreeable **10** delightful, satisfying **11** pleasurable **12** entertaining

enjoyment

4 zest **5** gusto, savor **6** relish **7** benefit, delight **8** felicity, fruition, pleasure **9** diversion **10** indulgence, recreation, relaxation **11** delectation **12** satisfaction **13** gratification

Enki

consort: 5 Nintu
son: 6 Ninsar

enkindle

4 fire **5** flame, light **6** ignite **7** inflame **8** touch off **9** set fire to

enlarge

3 wax **4** grow, rise **5** add to, boost, build, mount, widen **6** beef up, dilate, expand, extend **7** amplify, augment, broaden, develop, greaten, inflate, magnify, stretch **8** heighten, increase, multiply **9** elaborate, embroider **10** exaggerate

enlargement

4 node **5** tumor **6** blowup, growth, nodule **7** buildup **8** addition, increase, swelling **9** accretion, expansion, extension **12** augmentation **13** amplification

enlighten

5 edify, guide, teach **6** advise, illume,

inform, uplift **7** educate, improve **8** illumine, instruct **10** illuminate

enlist

4 join **5** draft, enter **6** employ, enroll, join up, muster, sign on, sign up **7** attract, recruit **8** register **9** volunteer **11** participate

enliven

3 pep **4** buoy, fire, warm **5** amuse, cheer, pep up, renew, rouse **6** excite, jazz up, perk up, vivify, wake up **7** animate, cheer up, inspire, quicken, refresh, restore, spice up **8** energize, recreate **9** entertain, galvanize, stimulate **10** exhilarate, invigorate, rejuvenate

en masse

5 as one **6** bodily **8** together **12** collectively

enmesh

4 hook, mire, trap **5** catch, snare **6** draw in, tangle **7** embroil, ensnarl, involve, trammel **8** drag into, entangle **9** embrangle, implicate

enmity

4 hate **6** animus, hatred, rancor, spleen **7** ill will **8** aversion, bad blood, loathing **9** animosity, antipathy, hostility **10** abhorrence, antagonism **11** detestation

ennoble

5 exalt, honor, raise **6** uplift, uprear **7** dignify, elevate, glorify, magnify, sublime **10** aggrandize **11** distinguish

ennui

6 apathy, tedium **7** boredom, fatigue, languor **8** doldrums, dullness, lethargy **9** jadedness, lassitude, tiredness, weariness **11** languidness **12** listlessness

Enoch

father: 4 Cain
son: 10 Methuselah

Enoch Arden author

8 Tennyson (Alfred)

enormity

6 infamy **7** outrage **8** atrocity, hugeness, rankness, savagery, vastness **9** barbarity, depravity, flagrancy, graveness, greatness, grossness, immensity, magnitude **11** abomination, heinousness, massiveness, monstrosity, seriousness, weightiness

enormous

4 huge, vast **5** great **7** immense, mammoth, massive, titanic **8** colossal, gigantic **9** humongous, monstrous **10** astronomic, gargantuan, prodigious, stupendous, tremendous **12** astronomical

Enos
father: 4 Seth
grandfather: 4 Adam
grandmother: 3 Eve
uncle: 4 Abel, Cain

enough
5 ample **6** fairly, plenty **8** adequate, decently, passably **9** competent, tolerably **10** acceptably, adequately, sufficient **11** comfortable, sufficiency **12** satisfactory, sufficiently
poetic: 4 enow

enounce
3 say **5** state, utter **6** intone **8** proclaim, set forth **10** articulate

enrage
3 ire **4** rile **5** anger **6** madden **7** incense, inflame, steam up **9** infuriate

enrapture
5 charm, elate **6** ravish, trance **7** delight, enchant, rejoice **8** enthrall, entrance **9** captivate, transport

enraptured
6 elated **7** charmed **8** ecstatic, thrilled **9** bewitched, delighted, enchanted, entranced **10** captivated, enthralled, mesmerized, spellbound **11** transported

enrich
5 adorn, endow **6** fatten **7** enhance, improve, join up **9** embellish, fertilize **10** supplement

enroll
4 book, file, join, list **5** draft, enter **6** enlist, induct, join up, muster, record, sign on, sign up, wrap up **7** catalog, engross, recruit **8** inscribe, register **9** conscript, subscribe **10** transcribe **11** matriculate

ensconce
4 bury, hide **5** cache, cover, place, plant, stash **6** hole up, locate, settle **7** conceal, install, secrete, shelter **9** establish

ensemble
3 duo **4** band, crew, suit, trio **5** choir, combo, decor, group, suite, troop, whole **6** chorus, outfit, septet, sextet, troupe **7** chorale, company, costume, en masse, quartet, quintet **8** together **9** aggregate, orchestra

enshrine
6 hallow, revere **7** cherish **8** dedicate, preserve, sanctify, treasure **10** consecrate **11** memorialize

enshroud
4 hide, veil, wrap **5** cloak **6** clothe, enfold, enwrap, invest **7** blanket, conceal, envelop, obscure

ensign
4 flag, jack, sign **5** badge, crest **6** banner, colors, emblem, pennon **7** officer, pennant **8** gonfalon, insignia, standard, streamer **9** oriflamme

enslave
4 yoke **5** chain **6** fetter, thrall **7** enchain, oppress, shackle, subject **8** dominate, enthrall, indenture, subjugate **12** disfranchise

enslavement
4 yoke **6** thrall **7** bondage, helotry, peonage, serfdom, slavery **9** servitude, thralldom

ensnare
3 bag, net **4** hook, lure, mesh, snag, trap **5** benet, catch, decoy **6** enmesh, entrap, tangle **7** capture **8** entangle, inveigle

ensnarl
4 mire **6** enmesh, tangle **7** embroil, perplex, trammel **8** entangle **9** embrangle

ensorcell
3 hex **5** charm, spell, witch **6** allure, voodoo **7** beguile, bewitch, enchant **8** enthrall **9** captivate, enrapture, hypnotize, magnetize, mesmerize, spellbind

ensorcellment
5 magic **7** sorcery **8** witchery, wizardry **9** conjuring **10** necromancy, witchcraft **11** bewitchment, enchantment

ensphere
4 ball **8** conglobe **10** conglobate

ensue
4 stem **5** issue **6** attend, derive, follow, result **7** emanate, proceed, succeed **9** supervene

ensuing
4 next **5** later **9** resultant **10** consequent, subsequent, succeeding

ensure
5 cinch **6** clinch, secure **7** certify, confirm, warrant **9** establish, guarantee

enswathe
4 roll, wrap 5 cloak, drape 6 bundle,
enwrap, shroud, wrap up 7 envelop,
swaddle

entail
5 imply 6 assign, confer, demand, impose,
lead to 7 call for, involve, require
8 occasion, restrict, result in, transmit
11 necessitate

entangle
4 mesh, mire, trap 5 catch, ravel, snare,
snarl, tie up, twist 6 enmesh, entrap
7 capture, catch up, embroil, ensnare,
ensnarl, involve, perplex, trammel
10 complicate, intertwine, interweave

entanglement
3 web 4 knot, mesh, mess, toil 5 skein,
snare 6 affair, cobweb, muddle 8 intrigue
9 confusion, imbroglio 11 embroilment,
involvement 12 complication

entente
4 pact 6 league, treaty 7 compact
8 alliance, covenant 9 agreement,
coalition, concordat 13 understanding

enter
4 go in, join, list, open 5 admit, begin, start
6 come in, enlist, enroll, go into, insert, join
up, muster, record, sign on, sign up
7 intrude 8 come into, embark on, inscribe,
register 9 introduce, penetrate 10 embark
upon

enterprise
4 deed, feat, firm, push, task 5 cause, drive,
pluck, vigor 6 action, daring, effort, energy,
hustle, outfit, scheme 7 attempt, company,
concern, courage, exploit, project, pursuit,
venture 8 activity, ambition, audacity,
boldness, business, campaign, endeavor,
gumption, industry 9 adventure, eagerness
10 enthusiasm, get-up-and-go, initiative
11 corporation, undertaking
12 organization, self-reliance
13 establishment

enterprising
4 bold 5 eager 6 daring, hungry 7 driving,
go-ahead 8 aspiring, hustling 9 ambitious,
audacious, energetic 10 aggressive
11 adventurous, hardworking, industrious,
up-and-coming, venturesome

entertain
4 host 5 amuse 6 divert, regale 7 delight,
receive 8 consider

entertainer
4 mime 5 actor, clown, comic 6 busker,
dancer, jester, singer 7 actress, artiste,

diseuse, trouper 8 comedian, minstrel
10 comedienne

entertaining
6 lively 7 amusing 8 engaging 9 diverting,
enjoyable

entertainment
4 fete, play, show, skit 5 revue, sport
6 circus 7 banquet, concert, pastime,
ridotto 8 pleasure 9 amusement,
diversion, enjoyment 10 recreation
11 distraction, performance

enthrall
4 grip 5 charm 6 absorb, subdue
7 beguile, bewitch, enchant, engross,
enslave 9 fascinate, hypnotize,
mesmerize, spellbind, subjugate

enthralling
8 exciting, gripping, riveting 9 absorbing,
arresting 10 enchanting, engrossing,
entrancing 11 captivating, charismatic,
provocative 12 spellbinding

enthuse
4 gush, rave 6 excite, thrill 7 animate,
delight, inspire 8 energize 10 rhapsodize

enthusiasm
4 élan, fire, zeal, zest 5 ardor, craze, fever,
mania, verve 6 fervor, spirit 7 ardency,
passion, rapture 9 eagerness, intensity
10 ebullience, excitement, fanaticism

enthusiast
3 bug, fan, nut 4 buff 5 fiend, freak, lover,
maven 6 addict, junkie, maniac, votary,
zealot 7 booster, devotee, fanatic, groupie,
habitué 8 believer, partisan 9 extremist
10 aficionado

enthusiastic
4 avid, gaga, keen 5 eager, rabid
6 ardent, fervid, gung ho, hearty, hipped,
raring 7 devoted, excited, fervent, intense,
zealous 8 hopped-up, obsessed, spirited,
vascular 9 fanatical 10 passionate

entice
4 bait, coax, draw, lure, toll, wile 5 charm,
decoy, tempt 6 allure, cajole, entrap, invite,
lead on, seduce 7 attract, wheedle
8 inveigle, persuade

enticement
4 bait, lure, trap 5 decoy, snare 6 come-on
9 seduction 10 allurement, attraction,
seducement, temptation 12 blandishment,
inveiglement

enticer
4 bait, vamp 5 Circe, decoy, siren
7 Lorelei 9 attractor, temptress
10 attraction, seductress 11 enchantress,
femme fatale

enticing
5 siren 8 fetching, witching 9 seductive
10 attractive, bewitching, intriguing
11 captivating, fascinating

entire
3 all 4 full 5 gross, total, whole 6 intact
7 perfect, plenary, unified 8 complete,
integral, outright 10 integrated
12 consolidated

entirely
5 fully, quite 6 wholly 7 utterly 9 perfectly
10 altogether, completely, thoroughly
11 exclusively

entirety
3 sum 5 total, whole 8 sum total, totality
9 aggregate, wholeness 10 everything
12 completeness, universality

entitle
3 dub, let 4 call, name, term 5 allow
6 enable, permit 7 baptize, empower,
license, qualify 8 christen 9 authorize,
designate 10 denominate

entity
3 sum 4 body, item, unit 5 being, thing,
whole 6 object 7 article, integer
8 quiddity, totality 9 existence, something,
substance 10 individual

entomb
4 bury 5 inter 6 inhume, shrine
7 mummify 8 enshrine 9 sepulcher,
sepulchre

entombment
6 burial 7 obsequy 9 obsequies, sepulture
10 inhumation

entourage
5 staff, suite, train 6 escort, milieu
7 cortege, coterie, retinue 8 henchmen
9 courtiers, followers, following, hangers-
on, retainers 10 associates, attendants
12 surroundings

entr'acte
8 interval 9 interlude 12 intermission

entrails
4 guts 5 pluck, tripe 6 bowels, tripes, vitals
7 giblets, innards, insides, viscera
8 stuffing 10 intestines

entrance
4 adit, door, gate, port 5 charm, foyer, inlet,
lobby, mouth 6 access, portal, ravish
7 arrival, attract, bewitch, delight, doorway,
enchant, gateway, ingress, opening
8 aperture, enthrall, open door 9 admission, captivate, enrapture, fascinate,
hypnotize, mesmerize, spellbind, threshold,
transport, vestibule 10 admittance,
ingression 11 penetration

entrant
7 starter 10 competitor, contestant
11 participant

entrap
3 bag, net 4 bait, lure, toll 5 catch, decoy,
snare, tempt 6 allure, ambush, entice,
entoil, lead on, seduce, tangle 7 beguile,
catch up, ensnare 8 entangle, inveigle

entre _____
4 nous

entreat
3 ask, beg, bid 4 pray, urge 5 crave,
plead, press 6 adjure, appeal 7 beseech,
implore, wheedle 8 blandish 9 importune
10 supplicate

entreaty
4 plea, suit 6 appeal, orison, prayer
7 request 8 petition 11 application,
importunity 12 supplication

entrechat
4 leap

entrée
6 access 7 ingress 8 main dish
9 admission 10 admittance, main course

entrench
3 fix 4 root 5 embed, lodge 6 define,
furrow, ground, hole up, invade, settle
7 confirm, impinge, implant, intrude
8 encroach, ensconce, infringe, trespass
9 establish 10 strengthen

entrenched
3 set 4 firm 5 rigid, sworn 8 accepted,
deep-dyed 9 hard-shell 10 deep-rooted,
deep-seated, inveterate 13 bred-in-the-
bone, dyed-in-the-wool

entrepôt
3 hub 4 mart 5 depot 6 bazaar, market
8 emporium, exchange 9 concourse,
warehouse 10 depository, storehouse
11 marketplace

entrepreneur
10 capitalist, contractor, impresario

entresol
9 mezzanine

entropy
5 chaos, decay 7 decline 8 disorder
10 randomness 11 degradation

entrust
4 give 5 allot, leave 6 assign, charge,
commit, confer, impose 7 commend,
confide, consign, deliver, deposit
8 allocate, delegate, hand over, relegate,
turn over

entry
3 way 4 adit, door, gate, item, port 5 debit,
foyer, inlet, lobby 6 access, credit, portal,
record 7 doorway, ingress, opening
8 headword 9 admission, threshold,
vestibule 10 admittance, enlistment,
enrollment, ingression

entryway
4 door, gate 5 foyer, lobby 6 portal
7 ingress, narthex, portico 9 vestibule

entwine
4 coil, wind 5 braid, plait, twist 6 enmesh
7 wreathe 8 entangle 9 interlace
10 interweave

enumerate
3 sum, tot 4 cite, list, tell, tote 5 add up,
count, tally, total, tot up 6 detail, number,
recite, reckon, tote up 7 compute, itemize,
recount, specify, tick off 8 identify
9 calculate, inventory 13 particularize

enunciate
3 say 5 speak, state, utter, voice 6 affirm,
intone 7 declare, express, lay down
8 announce, proclaim, propound, vocalize
9 formulate, postulate, pronounce,
verbalize 10 articulate

envelop
3 hem 4 hide, roll, veil, wrap 5 cloak,
cover, drape 6 cocoon, enfold, engulf,
enwrap, invest, sheath, shield, shroud,
swathe, wrap up 7 blanket, embrace,
enclose, swaddle 8 encircle, enshroud,
enswathe, surround 10 circumfuse

envenom
6 poison 8 embitter 10 exacerbate

envious
7 jealous 8 coveting, covetous, grudging
9 green-eyed, invidious, resentful
10 begrudging

environment
6 medium, milieu 7 ambient, climate,
context, habitat, setting, terrain
8 ambiance, ambience, backdrop
9 situation 10 atmosphere, background,
mise-en-scène 12 surroundings
science: 7 ecology

environmentalist
4 Muir (John) 6 Brower (David), Carson
(Rachel), Nelson (Gaylord), Wilson
(Edward O.) 7 Ehrlich (Paul), Thoreau
(Henry David) 8 Commoner (Barry),
Cousteau (Jacques-Yves) 9 ecologist,
Roosevelt (Theodore)

environs
6 bounds, limits 7 compass, fringes,
suburbs 8 boundary, confines, locality,
purlieus, vicinity 9 districts, outskirts,
precincts 12 neighborhood, surroundings

envisage
4 view 5 dream, fancy, grasp, image, think
6 regard, vision 7 dream up, feature,
foresee, imagine, picture, realize
8 conceive, look upon, summon up
9 conjure up, objectify, visualize

envoy
5 agent 6 bearer, consul, deputy, legate,
nuncio 7 attaché, carrier, courier
8 diplomat, emissary, minister
9 messenger 10 ambassador
11 internuncio 12 intermediary

envy
5 covet 6 grudge 8 begrudge, grudging,
jealousy 10 resentment 12 covetousness
13 invidiousness

enwrap
4 roll, veil 5 clasp, drape 6 enfold, invest,
shroud, swathe 7 enclose, engross,
envelop, sheathe, swaddle 8 enshroud,
enswathe

enzyme
3 ase 5 ficin, lyase, renin, urase 6 kinase,
ligase, lipase, mutase, papain, pepsin,
rennin, urease, zymase 7 amidase,
amylase, cyclase, enolase, guanase,
hydrase, inulase, isozyme, lactase,
maltase, oxidase, pectase, pepsine,
plasmin, ptyalin, rennase, sucrase, trypsin,
zymogen 8 aldolase, diastase, elastase,
esterase, fumarase, lyzozyme, nuclease,
protease, steapsin, thrombin, zymogene
9 cellulase, invertase

eon
see **aeon**

Eos
see **Aurora**

épée
5 sword

epergne
5 stand 11 centerpiece

ephemeral
5 brief, short 7 passing 8 episodic,
fleeting, fugitive, volatile 9 fugacious,
momentary, temporary, transient
10 evanescent, short-lived, transitory
11 impermanent

Ephialtes
5 giant
brother: 4 Otus
father: 6 Aloeus 8 Poseidon
mother: 9 Iphimedia
slayer: 6 Apollo

Ephraim
brother: 8 Manasseh
father: 6 Joseph
grandfather: 5 Jacob
mother: 7 Asenath

epic
4 poem, saga 5 grand, Iliad 6 Aeneid,
heroic 7 Beowulf, Odyssey 8 imposing,
sweeping 9 Gilgamesh, narrative
12 Heimskringla

epicene
10 effeminate 11 intersexual 13 her-
maphrodite

epicure
7 gourmet 8 aesthete, hedonist, sybarite
9 bon vivant 10 gastronome
11 connoisseur 12 gastronomist

epicurean
7 gourmet, sensual 8 aesthete, hedonist,
sensuous, sybarite 9 bon vivant, luxurious
10 gastronome, voluptuous
11 connoisseur 12 gastronomist,
sensualistic

epidemic
3 flu 4 rash, wave 6 plague 7 rampant,
scourge 8 catching, outbreak 9 contagion,
prevalent 10 contagious, pestilence

epidermis
4 skin 7 cuticle 10 integument

epigram
3 saw 4 poem 5 adage, axiom, maxim
6 bon mot, dictum, saying, truism
7 proverb 8 aphorism, apothegm

epigrammatic
5 meaty, pithy, terse, witty 6 cogent
7 compact, concise, marrowy, piquant,
pointed

epigraph
5 motto 9 quotation 11 inscription

epilogue
4 coda 5 close 6 ending, finale, windup
7 closing 8 postlude 9 afterword
10 conclusion, postscript

Epimetheus
brother: 10 Prometheus
father: 7 Iapetus
wife: 7 Pandora

epiphany
6 aperçu, vision 7 insight 9 discovery,
intuition 10 appearance, disclosure,
revelation 11 inspiration, realization
13 manifestation

episode
5 event, phase 7 passage 8 incident,
occasion 9 happening, interlude
10 occurrence 12 circumstance

episodic
5 brief 7 passing 8 fleeting, sporadic
9 ephemeral, irregular, temporary, transient
10 evanescent, occasional, short-lived
12 intermittent

epistaxis
9 nosebleed

epistle
4 note 6 letter 7 lection, missive
13 communication

epitaph
3 R.I.P. 5 elegy 6 eulogy 8 hic jacet
11 inscription

epithet
4 name 5 label, title 7 agnomen, moniker
8 cognomen, nickname 9 sobriquet
11 appellation

epitome
3 sum 4 acme, type 5 brief, short
6 digest, précis, résumé 7 essence,
example, outline, summary 8 abstract,
breviary, exemplar, synopsis, ultimate
9 archetype, summation, summing-up
10 abridgment, apotheosis, conspectus,
embodiment 11 abridgement
12 condensation, quintessence

epitomize
5 sum up 6 digest, embody, mirror, typify
7 abridge, outline, summate 8 abstract,
boil down, condense, manifest, tabulate

epoch

9 capsulize, exemplify, incarnate, inventory, objectify, personify, represent, summarize, symbolize, synopsize 10 abbreviate, illustrate 11 concentrate, emblematize, incorporate, personalize

epoch

3 age, eon, era 4 aeon, term, time
6 period 8 interval, time span

equable

4 calm, even, just 6 serene, stable, steady
7 orderly, regular, stabile, uniform
8 composed, constant 9 immutable, temperate, unvarying 10 consistent, invariable, unchanging 12 unchangeable

equal

3 tie 4 even, fair, like, mate, peer, same, twin 5 agree, alike, match 7 uniform
8 alter ego, amount to, parallel 9 duplicate, identical, impartial, objective 10 fifty-fifty
11 counterpart, symmetrical 12 commensurate, correspond to, proportional
13 commensurable, proportionate
combining form: 3 iso 4 equi, pari
French: 4 égal

equality

3 par 6 equity, parity 7 balance, égalité
8 evenness, fairness, sameness
10 uniformity

Equality State

7 Wyoming

equalize

4 even 5 level 6 square 7 balance
9 harmonize

equalizer

3 gun 6 pistol 8 handicap 10 tying score

equally

10 fifty-fifty 11 impartially

equanimity

4 calm, cool 5 poise 6 aplomb, phlegm
7 balance 8 calmness, coolness, evenness, serenity 9 assurance, composure, equipoise, placidity, sangfroid
10 detachment, steadiness 11 tranquility
12 tranquillity

equate

4 even 5 liken, match, treat 6 adjust, regard, relate, square 7 compare
8 consider, equalize, parallel 10 assimilate

Equatorial Guinea

capital: 6 Malabo
island, island group: 5 Bioko 6 Elobey, Pagulu 7 Corisco
language: 5 Bantu 6 French 7 Spanish

mainland: 5 Mbini 7 Río Muni
monetary unit: 5 franc
neighbor: 5 Gabon 8 Cameroon

equestrian

5 rider 6 horsey 8 horseman, knightly
10 horsewoman

equidistant

3 mid 6 medial, median, middle, midway
7 central, halfway, midmost

equilibrium

5 poise 6 aplomb, stasis 7 balance
8 evenness 9 composure, stability, symmetry 10 steadiness 12 counterpoise
13 stabilization

equine

4 colt, mare 5 filly, horse, steed 6 horsey
8 stallion 9 horselike

equip

3 arm, fit, rig 5 array, dress, endow, rig up
6 attire, fit out, outfit, rig out, supply
7 appoint, furnish, prepare, provide
8 accouter, accoutre 9 provision

equipment

3 rig 4 gear 5 traps 6 attire, outfit, tackle, things 7 baggage, panoply 8 fittings, material, matériel, ordnance, supplies, tackling 9 apparatus, endowment, machinery, trappings 10 provisions 11 accessories, attachments, habiliments, impedimenta 12 accouterment, accoutrement, provisioning 13 accouterments, accoutrements, appurtenances, paraphernalia

equitable

4 even, fair, just 5 level 6 proper, square
7 condign 8 balanced, deserved, unbiased
9 identical, impartial, objective, uncolored
10 evenhanded, impersonal 12 unprejudiced 13 dispassionate

equity

3 law 7 justice 8 equality, interest, justness

equivalence

3 par 6 parity, simile 7 analogy 8 equality, identity, likeness, sameness 10 conformity
11 correlation

equivalent

4 akin, copy, like, peer, same, twin 5 alike, match 6 agnate 7 identic, similar
8 parallel 9 analogous, duplicate, identical
10 comparable, homologous, substitute, tantamount 11 convertible, correlative, counterpart 12 commensurate 13 corresponding, proportionate

equivocal
4 hazy 5 fishy, vague 6 unsure 7 clouded, dubious, obscure, suspect, unclear
8 doubtful 9 ambiguous, debatable, enigmatic, uncertain, undecided
10 ambivalent, indecisive, indistinct, irresolute, unresolved 11 problematic
12 disreputable, inconclusive, questionable
13 indeterminate

equivocate
3 fib, lie 5 cavil, dodge, evade, fudge, hedge 6 palter, waffle, weasel 7 shuffle
8 sidestep 9 pussyfoot 11 prevaricate
12 tergiversate

equivocation
3 fib 7 evasion, fibbing, hedging, sophism
8 waffling 9 ambiguity, casuistry, duplicity, sophistry 12 speciousness

equivoque
3 pun 8 wordplay

era
3 age, day 4 date, term, time 5 epoch, stage 6 period

eradicate
4 dele, raze 5 abate, erase, purge
6 delete, efface, remove, uproot 7 abolish, blot out, destroy, expunge, root out, weed out, wipe out 8 demolish, stamp out
9 eliminate, extirpate, liquidate
10 annihilate, do away with, extinguish, obliterate 11 exterminate

erase
4 dele, void, x out 6 cancel, delete, efface, excise, remove, rub out 7 abolish, blot out, expunge, nullify, scratch, take out, wipe out
8 black out, blank out, cross off, cross out
9 eliminate, extirpate, sponge out, strike out 10 obliterate

Erato
see **Muse**

Erbin
father: 9 Custennin
nephew: 6 Arthur
son: 7 Geraint

ere
6 before

Erebus
daughter: 3 Day 6 Hemera
father: 5 Chaos
home: 5 Hades
sister, wife: 3 Nox, Nyx
son: 6 Aether, Charon

Erec et _____
5 Enide

Erechteus
daughter: 8 Chthonia
father: 6 Vulcan 10 Hephaestus
mother: 4 Gaea
slayer: 4 Zeus 7 Jupiter

erect
4 form 5 build, put up, raise, set up
6 create, raised 7 build up, stand-up, upright 8 assemble, elevated, standing, straight, vertical 9 construct, establish
10 upstanding 13 perpendicular

eremite
6 hermit 7 ascetic, recluse, stylite
9 anchoress, anchorite

Erewhon
6 utopia 7 nowhere
author: 6 Butler (Samuel)

ergo
4 then, thus 5 hence 9 therefore
11 accordingly 12 consequently

Erichthonius
father: 8 Dardanus
son: 4 Tros

Eridanus star
8 Achernar

Erin
see **Eire**

Erinyes
6 Alecto, Furies 7 Megaera 9 Eumenides, Tisiphone

Eris
brother: 4 Ares, Mars
daughter: 3 Ate
fruit: 5 apple
goddess of: 6 strife 7 discord
mother: 3 Nox, Nyx

Eritrea
archipelago: 6 Dahlak
capital: 6 Asmara
island: 5 Zuqar
monetary unit: 5 nakfa
neighbor: 5 Sudan 8 Djibouti, Ethiopia
river: 6 Baraka
sea: 3 Red

ermine
3 fur 5 stoat 6 weasel

erode
3 eat, rub 4 wear 5 decay, scour
6 abrade, rub off 7 consume, corrade, crumble, eat away, rub away 8 wear away
9 scrape off 10 scrape away
11 deteriorate 12 disintegrate

Eroica composer
9 Beethoven (Ludwig van)

Eros
see **Cupid**

erose
6 jagged, uneven 9 irregular

erotic
4 lewd, racy, sexy 5 bawdy, spicy
6 carnal, earthy, ribald, risqué 7 fleshly,
obscene, profane, sensual 8 off-color,
prurient, sensuous 9 salacious
10 voluptuous 11 aphrodisiac, titillating

err
3 sin 4 goof, slip, trip 5 lapse, stray
6 bungle, foul up, mess up, slip up
7 blunder, deviate, screw up, stumble
8 trespass 10 transgress

errand
3 job 4 task 5 chore 7 mission
10 assignment

errand boy
4 page 5 gofer 7 bellboy, bellhop, courier
9 go-between

errant
5 stray 6 fickle, roving 7 aimless, deviant,
erratic, naughty, ranging, roaming,
wayward, willful 8 drifting, fallible,
rambling, shifting, straying 9 deviating,
itinerant, traveling, wandering
10 meandering, unreliable 11 mischievous

erratic
5 flaky 6 fitful 7 wayward 8 freakish,
shifting, unstable, variable, volatile
9 arbitrary, desultory, eccentric, fluctuant,
irregular, mercurial, spasmodic, uncertain,
wandering, whimsical 10 capricious,
changeable, inconstant, meandering 12 inconsistent 13 idiosyncratic, unpredictable

erring
see **errant**

erroneous
3 off 4 awry 5 amiss, askew, false, wrong
6 untrue 7 unsound 8 mistaken, specious,
spurious 9 defective, incorrect, misguided
10 fallacious, inaccurate, misleading

error
4 flub, goof, muff, slip, trip 5 boner, botch,
fault, fluff, gaffe, lapse 6 boo-boo, bungle,
fumble, howler, miscue, slipup 7 blooper,
blunder, fallacy, falsity, faux pas, misstep,
mistake, screwup, stumble, untruth 8 delusion, illusion, screamer 9 falsehood,
indecorum, oversight 10 inaccuracy,
misreading 11 impropriety, misjudgment
printing: 4 typo 6 errata (plural)
7 erratum

ersatz
4 copy, fake, sham 5 bogus, dummy,
faked, false, phony 6 pseudo 8 spurious
9 imitation, simulated, synthetic
10 artificial, factitious, simulacrum,
substitute 11 counterfeit

Erse
5 Irish 6 Celtic, Gaelic

erstwhile
3 old 4 late, once, past 5 prior 6 before,
bygone, former, whilom 7 already, earlier,
onetime, quondam 8 formerly, previous
10 heretofore, previously

eruct
4 burp, emit, gush, spew 5 belch, eject,
expel 7 explode 8 detonate, disgorge

erudite
7 bookish, learned 8 lettered, literate,
studious, well-read 9 scholarly
10 scholastic

erudition
7 culture 8 learning, literacy 9 knowledge
11 bookishness, cultivation, learnedness,
scholarship 12 studiousness
13 scholarliness

erupt
3 jet 4 spew 5 belch, burst, eject, expel,
go off, spout, spurt 7 explode 8 break out,
burst out, detonate 9 discharge 10 break
forth, burst forth

eruption
4 gust, rush 5 blast, burst, flare, sally
6 access 7 flare-up 8 outbreak, outburst
9 commotion, explosion
skin: 3 zit 4 rash 6 pimple

Esau
brother: 5 Jacob
country: 4 Edom
descendant: 7 Edomite
father: 5 Isaac
father-in-law: 4 Elon
grandson: 6 Amalek
mother: 7 Rebekah
new name: 4 Edom
son: 5 Korha, Reuel 7 Eliphaz
wife: 4 Adah 10 Aholibamah

escalade
5 climb, mount, scale 6 ascend 7 scaling

escalate
4 grow, rise, soar 5 boost, climb, mount, widen 6 expand, extend, spread, step up 7 amplify, augment, broaden, enlarge, inflate 8 heighten, increase, multiply 9 intensify 11 proliferate

escapade
4 lark, romp 5 antic, caper, fling, folly, prank, spree, stunt 6 frolic, vagary 7 roguery, rollick 8 mischief 9 adventure

escape
3 fly, lam 4 bolt, duck, flee, shun, skip, slip 5 avoid, break, dodge, elude, evade, shake 6 bypass, depart, eschew, flight, hegira, outlet 7 abscond, duck out, evasion, get away, make off, release, run away, skip out 8 breakout 9 avoidance, desertion, disappear, steal away 10 circumvent, liberation 11 deliverance, evasiveness
artist: 7 Houdini (Harry)
narrow: 9 close call 10 close shave

escargot
5 snail

escarole
6 endive

escarpment
5 bluff, cliff, slope

eschar
4 scab 5 crust 6 lesion

eschew
4 shun 5 avoid, elude, evade, forgo, spurn 6 abjure, forego, pass up, refuse, reject 7 decline 8 turn down

eschewal
7 elusion, evasion, refusal 8 shunning, spurning 9 avoidance, rejection

escort
4 beau, date, lead, show 5 guard, guide, pilot, steer, usher 6 attend, convoy, direct, gigolo, squire 7 company, conduct, consort, retinue 8 cavalier, chaperon, henchman, shepherd 9 accompany, bodyguard, chaperone, companion, entourage, safeguard 13 accompaniment

escritoire
4 desk 9 secretary 11 writing desk

escrow
4 bond, deed, fund 7 deposit

esculent
6 edible 7 eatable 10 comestible, digestible

escutcheon
6 flange, shield

Eshcol
ally: 7 Abraham
brother: 4 Aner 5 Mamre

esker
4 kame 5 mound, ridge

Eskimo
4 Inuk 5 Aleut, Inuit
boat: 5 kayak, umiak
boot: 6 mukluk
dog: 5 husky 8 malamute
dwelling: 5 igloo
outer garment: 5 parka 6 anorak
sledge: 7 komatik

esophagus
6 gullet

esoteric
5 inner 6 arcane, mystic, occult, orphic, secret 7 cryptic, private 8 abstruse, hermetic, profound 9 recondite 10 cabalistic, mysterious 12 confidential

ESP
9 telepathy 10 sixth sense 12 clairvoyance, precognition

espadrille
4 shoe 6 sandal

espalier
7 lattice, railing, trellis

esparto
5 grass

especial
4 main 5 close 7 express, notable, unusual 8 dominant, intimate, peculiar, singular, specific, uncommon 9 paramount 10 individual, particular 11 exceptional

especially
7 notably 8 markedly 9 expressly, primarily, unusually 10 peculiarly, remarkably, singularly 11 principally 12 particularly, specifically 13 distinctively, exceptionally

espial
6 notice 9 detection, discovery 11 observation

espionage
6 spying 9 sleuthing 12 surveillance

espousal
5 troth, union 6 mating 7 embrace, support, wedding 8 adoption, advocacy, approval, ceremony, marriage 9 betrothal,

embracing, matrimony, promotion
10 acceptance

espouse
3 wed 4 back 5 adopt, marry 6 accept,
take on, take up 7 approve, embrace,
support 8 advocate

esprit
3 vim, wit 4 brio, dash, élan, zest, zing
5 oomph, verve, vigor 6 fervor, gaiety,
mettle, morale, spirit 7 courage, loyalty,
panache, passion, sparkle 8 devotion,
vibrancy, vitality 9 animation
10 brightness, enthusiasm, fellowship
11 camaraderie

esprit de corps
see **morale**

espy
3 see 4 mark, spot 5 sight 6 descry,
detect, notice 7 discern, make out
9 recognize

_____ es Salaam
3 Dar

essay
3 try 4 seek, test 5 labor, paper, piece,
study, theme, tract, trial 6 effort, strive,
thesis 7 article, attempt, venture
8 endeavor, treatise 9 undertake
10 discussion, exposition 11 composition,
undertaking 12 dissertation

essayist
American: 4 Agee (James), Will (George)
5 Baker (Russell), Cooke (Alistair), Gould
(Stephen Jay), White (E. B.) 6 Brooks
(Cleanth), Fisher (M. F. K.), Holmes (Oliver
Wendell), Lowell (James Russell), Sontag
(Susan), Thomas (Lewis) 7 Buckley
(William F.), Cousins (Norman), Emerson
(Ralph Waldo), Mencken (Henry Louis),
Thoreau (Henry David) 8 Benchley
(Robert), Lippmann (Walter), Repplier
(Agnes) 10 Crèvecoeur (Jean de)
English: 4 Elia, Lamb (Charles) 5 Bacon
(Francis), Cecil (Lord David), Pater
(Walter), Smith (Sydney) 6 Arnold
(Matthew), Cowley (Abraham), Morris
(Jan), Ruskin (John), Steele (Richard)
7 Addison (Joseph), Hazlitt (William)
8 Beerbohm (Max) 9 De Quincey
(Thomas) 12 Chesterfield (Lord)
French: 9 Montaigne (Michel de)
Scottish: 7 Carlyle (Thomas)

essence
3 nub 4 base, core, crux, gist, odor, pith,
root, soul 5 basis, being, fiber, fibre, point,
spirit, stuff 6 center, entity, kernel, marrow,

nature, spirit 7 extract, perfume, quality
9 substance 10 distillate 12 distillation,
significance

essential
4 main, must 5 basal, basic, chief, prime,
vital 6 inborn, inbred, innate, primal
7 connate, crucial, element, primary
8 cardinal, foremost, inherent, required,
rudiment 9 condition, elemental, intrinsic,
necessary, necessity, principal, requisite,
substance 10 congenital, deep-seated,
elementary, idiopathic, imperative, sine qua
non, underlying 11 fundamental,
requirement 12 precondition, prerequisite
13 indispensable, part and parcel

essentially
6 almost, au fond, really 7 largely
8 actually, as good as, as much as, well-
nigh 9 basically, virtually 11 practically
13 fundamentally, substantially

essonite
6 garnet 13 cinnamon stone

establish
3 fix, lay, put, set 4 base, form, root, show
5 build, enact, endow, erect, found, place,
prove, set up, start 6 attest, create,
decree, effect, ground, impose, secure,
settle, verify 7 build up, certify, clarify,
confirm, find out, implant, install, instill,
provide, set down 8 document, ensconce,
organize 9 authorize, construct, determine,
formulate, institute, legislate, originate,
prescribe 10 bring about, constitute,
inaugurate 11 corroborate, demonstrate
12 authenticate, substantiate

establishment
4 firm 6 outfit 7 company, concern
8 business, old guard 9 institute,
workplace 10 enterprise, foundation
11 institution, ruling class

estate
4 farm, land 5 manor, ranch, villa
6 domain, legacy, quinta 7 demesne
8 dominion, hacienda, property
10 plantation
feudal: 4 fief 7 fiefdom
first: 6 clergy
fourth: 5 press
manager: 7 steward 8 executor, guardian
second: 6 nobles 8 nobility
third: 7 commons

esteem
4 deem 5 favor, honor, prize, think, value
6 admire, liking, regard, revere 7 account,
believe, cherish, idolize, respect, worship

8 approval, consider, treasure, venerate
9 valuation 10 admiration, appreciate
12 appreciation 13 consideration

ester
6 oleate 7 acetate 8 compound
9 phosphate

Esther
cousin: 8 Mordecai
enemy: 5 Haman
father: 7 Abihail
festival: 5 Purim
Hebrew name: 8 Hadassah
husband: 6 Xerxes 9 Ahasuerus

estimable
5 noble 6 august, valued, worthy
7 admired 8 laudable, sterling
9 admirable, deserving, honorable,
reputable, respected, venerable
10 creditable 11 commendable,
meritorious, respectable 12 praiseworthy

estimate
3 put 4 call, rank, rate 5 assay, gauge,
guess, infer, judge, price, set at, value
6 assess, deduce, figure, rating, reckon,
survey 7 imagine, opinion, project,
suppose, surmise 8 appraise, conclude,
discover, evaluate, forecast, judgment,
round off 9 appraisal, calculate, determine,
reckoning, valuation 10 assessment,
conjecture, evaluation, impression,
projection 11 approximate, calculation,
measurement

estimation
4 fame 5 favor, honor, stock 6 esteem,
regard 7 account, opinion, respect
8 figuring, judgment 9 appraisal,
reckoning, valuation 10 admiration,
assessment, evaluation, impression
11 calculation 13 consideration

Estonia
capital: 7 Tallinn
city: 5 Tartu
gulf: 4 Riga 7 Finland
island: 4 Muhu 6 Vormsi 7 Hiiumaa
8 Saaremaa
lake: 6 Peipus, Pskov 9 Vorts-Jarv
monetary unit: 5 kroon
neighbor: 6 Latvia, Russia
river: 5 Narva, Pärnu 6 Kasari
sea: 6 Baltic

estop
3 bar 6 enjoin, forbid 7 prevent
8 disallow, preclude, prohibit, restrain

estrange
4 part 5 split 7 break up, divorce
8 alienate, disunite, separate 9 disaffect

estrangement
4 rift 5 split 6 breach, schism 7 breakup,
cooling, divorce, rupture 8 disunity, division
10 alienation, falling-out, withdrawal
12 disaffection

estuary
5 firth, frith, mouth 10 tidal river

esurient
4 avid 6 greedy, hungry 8 covetous,
grasping, ravening, ravenous 9 rapacious,
voracious 10 avaricious, gluttonous
11 acquisitive

étagère
7 cabinet, whatnot

Etats-_____
4 Unis

etch
3 cut 5 carve, stamp 6 depict, incise
7 engrave, impress, imprint, portray
8 inscribe 9 delineate, represent

etcher
American: 7 Pennell (Joseph) 8 Whistler
(James McNeil)
Dutch: 9 Rembrandt (van Rijn)
French: 5 Redon (Odilon) 6 Villon
(Jacques)
Italian: 8 Piranesi (Giambattista)
Spanish: 6 Ribera (José)
Swiss: 4 Zorn (Anders)

Eteocles
brother: 9 Polynices
father: 7 Oedipus
mother: 7 Jocasta
slayer: 9 Polynices

eternal
7 abiding, ageless, endless, lasting,
undying 8 constant, enduring, immortal,
infinite, timeless, unending 9 ceaseless,
continual, deathless, immutable, incessant,
permanent, perpetual, unceasing 10 immemorial, unchanging 11 amaranthine,
everlasting, illimitable, inalterable, never-
ending, unalterable, unremitting
12 imperishable, interminable

Eternal City
4 Rome

eternally
3 e'er 4 ever 6 always 7 forever

8 evermore, for keeps 11 forevermore, in
perpetuum 12 in perpetuity

eternity
3 age, eon 4 aeon 7 dog's age 8 blue
moon, coon's age, infinity 9 afterlife
10 infinitude, perpetuity 11 endlessness,
immortality 12 infiniteness, timelessness

Etesian
4 wind 6 annual

Ethan _____
5 Allen, Brand, Frome

Ethbaal's daughter
7 Jezebel

ether
3 air, gas, sky 6 heaven 7 heavens
8 airwaves, empyrean 10 anesthetic,
atmosphere

ethereal
4 aery, airy 5 filmy, light 6 aerial 7 fragile
8 delicate, empyreal, empyrean, gossamer,
heavenly, rarefied, vaporous 9 celestial,
spiritual, unearthly, unworldly 10 immaterial, intangible 13 unsubstantial

ethical
4 good 5 moral, noble 6 decent 7 upright,
virtual 8 elevated, virtuous 9 righteous
10 principled, upstanding 11 right-minded
13 conscientious

ethics
5 mores 6 morals, values 8 morality
9 moral code, standards 10 principles

Ethiopia
battle site: 5 Adowa
biblical name: 4 Cush
capital: 10 Addis Ababa
city: 6 Gonder 8 Dire Dawa
desert: 4 Haud 7 Danakil
emperor: 7 Menelik, Menilek 8 Selassie
9 Ras Tafari 13 Haile Selassie
former name: 9 Abyssinia
language: 5 Oromo 7 Amharic
monetary unit: 4 birr
mountain: 9 Ras Dashen
neighbor: 5 Kenya, Sudan 7 Eritrea,
Somalia 8 Djibouti
region: 5 Tigre 6 Ogaden, Tigray
7 Danakil
river: 4 Abay 5 Awash 6 Tekeze 8 Blue
Nile

ethnic
6 racial, tribal 8 minority

etiolate
4 fade, pale 6 bleach, weaken 7 lighten,
wash out 8 enfeeble

etiquette
4 code, form 5 mores 7 conduct, customs,
decency, decorum, manners 8 behavior,
protocol 9 amenities, propriety
10 civilities, convention, deportment,
seemliness 11 conventions, formalities,
proprieties

Etruscan
city, town: 4 Roma, Veii 5 Caere, Vulci
6 Arezzo 7 Clusium, Felsina, Perugia
8 Volsinii 9 Florentia, Tarquinia, Vetulonia
deity: 3 Tin, Tiv, Uni 4 Turm, Usil 5 Tinia,
Turan, Turms 6 Menfra, Menrva, Nethun,
Trithn 7 Velchan 8 Sethlans, Voltumna
king: 7 Porsena, Tarquin 10 Tarquinius
11 Lars Porsena
kingdom: 7 Etruria

étude
5 study 8 exercise 11 composition

etui
4 case

etymology
11 word history

etymon
4 root 5 radix 6 source 8 morpheme

eucalyptus eater
5 koala

Eucharist
container: 3 pyx
plate: 5 paten
service: 4 Mass 9 Communion
vessel: 8 ciborium
wafer: 4 host 8 viaticum

Euclid
subject: 8 geometry
work: 8 Elements

_____ **Eulenspiegel**
4 Till, Tyll

eulogistic
9 adulatory, laudative, laudatory
11 encomiastic, panegyrical 12 commendatory 13 complimentary

eulogize
4 hymn, laud 5 cry up, exalt, extol 6 praise
7 acclaim, applaud, commend, glorify,
magnify 9 celebrate 10 panegyrize

eulogy
5 paean 6 praise 7 oration, tribute
8 accolade, citation, encomium

9 laudation, panegyric **10** salutation
12 commendation **13** glorification

Eumenides
see **Erinyes**

eunuch
7 gelding **8** castrate, castrato

euphony
7 harmony **8** lyricism **9** sweetness
10 consonance

euphoria
3 joy **4** glee **5** bliss **7** ecstasy, elation,
rapture **9** transport **10** exaltation, jubilation
11 high spirits **12** exhilaration, intoxication

Euphrosyne
see **Graces**

euphuistic
5 fancy, tumid **6** florid, ornate, prolix,
purple, turgid **7** elegant, flowery, fustian,
orotund, verbose **8** colorful, elevated,
sonorous **9** bombastic, elaborate, high-
flown, inflated, overblown **10** figurative,
flamboyant, rhetorical **11** highfalutin,
overwrought **12** magniloquent
13 grandiloquent

eureka
3 aha

Euridice's husband
7 Orpheus

Euripides play
3 Ion **5** Helen, Medea **6** Hecuba
7 Bacchae (The), Cyclops, Electra, Orestes
8 Alcestis **10** Andromache, Hippolytus,
Suppliants (The) **11** Trojan Women (The)

Europa
brother: 6 Cadmus
father: 6 Agenor **7** Phoenix
husband: 8 Asterius
son: 5 Minos **8** Sarpedon

Europe
9 continent
country: 4 Eire **5** Italy, Malta, Spain
6 France, Greece, Latvia, Monaco, Norway,
Poland, Russia, Sweden, Turkey
7 Albania, Andorra, Armenia, Austria,
Belarus, Belgium, Croatia, Denmark,
Estonia, Finland, Georgia, Germany,
Hungary, Iceland, Ireland, Moldova,
Romania, Rumania, Ukraine **8** Bulgaria,
Portugal, Slovakia, Slovenia **9** Lithuania,
Macedonia, San Marino **10** Azerbaijan,
Luxembourg, Yugoslavia **11** Netherlands,
Switzerland, Vatican City **13** Czech
Republic, Liechtenstein, United Kingdom

ethnic group: 4 Celt, Finn, Lapp, Lett,
Pole, Serb, Sorb, Turk, Wend **5** Croat,
Czech, Dutch, Greek, Gypsy, Irish, Latin,
Swede, Swiss, Welsh **6** Basque, Celtic,
French, German, Magyar, Polish, Scotch,
Slovak **7** Bosnian, Catalan, English,
Finnish, Fleming, Italian, Lettish, Maltese,
Russian, Slovene, Spanish, Swedish,
Walloon **8** Albanian, Andorran, Armenian,
Croatian, Romanian **9** Belarusan,
Bulgarian, Hungarian, Ukrainian
10 Belarusian, Macedonian, Monegasque,
Phoenician **11** Belarussian **12** Byelorus-
sian, Scandinavian
language: 4 Lapp **5** Czech, Dutch, Greek,
Irish, Latin, Welsh **6** Basque, Breton,
Danish, French, Gaelic, German, Magyar,
Polish, Slovak **7** Catalan, English, Finnish,
Flemish, Italian, Maltese, Romansh,
Russian, Serbian, Slovene, Spanish,
Swedish, Turkish, Wendish **8** Albanian,
Croatian, Lusatian, Romanian, Rumanian
9 Bulgarian, Hungarian, Icelandic,
Norwegian **10** Macedonian, Portuguese
13 Serbo-Croatian
mountain range: 4 Alps **8** Pyrenees
11 Carpathians

Euryale
see **Gorgon**

Eurytus
daughter: 4 Iole
slayer: 8 Hercules

Euterpe
see **Muse**

evacuate
4 exit, void **5** clear, empty, expel, leave
6 decamp, depart, remove, vacate
7 abandon, excrete, exhaust, pull out,
retreat **8** clear out, pull back, withdraw
9 eliminate

evacuee
6 émigré **7** refugee **8** fugitive

evade
4 duck, flee, foil **5** avoid, dodge, elude,
hedge, parry, shirk **6** baffle, bypass,
double, escape, eschew, outwit, thwart,
weasel **7** shuffle **8** sidestep, slip away
9 pussyfoot, turn aside **10** circumvent,
equivocate **11** prevaricate **12** tergiversate

evaluate
4 rank, rate **5** assay, class, gauge, grade,
set at, weigh **6** assess, figure, reckon, size
up, survey **7** eyeball **8** appraise, classify,
estimate **9** calculate, criticize

evaluation
6 rating 7 judging, opinion 8 estimate, judgment 9 appraisal 10 assessment 12 appreciation

Evander
father: 6 Hermes 7 Mercury
mother: 8 Carmenta 9 Carmentis
son: 6 Pallas

evanesce
4 fade 5 clear 6 vanish 7 scatter 8 disperse, dissolve, melt away 9 disappear, dissipate, evaporate 13 dematerialize

evanescent
6 fading 7 elusive, melting, passing 8 fleeting, fugitive, volatile 9 ephemeral, fugacious, momentary, transient, vanishing 10 dissolving, short-lived, transitory 12 disappearing

evangelical
6 ardent, fervid 7 fanatic, fervent, zealous 8 militant 9 crusading 10 missionary 13 proselytizing

Evangeline
author: 10 Longfellow (Henry Wadsworth)
beloved: 7 Gabriel
home: 7 Acadia

evangelist
4 John, Luke, Mark 5 Moody (Dwight) 6 Bakker (Jim, Tammy Faye), Graham (Billy, Franklin), Sunday (Billy), Wesley (John) 7 apostle, Edwards (Jonathan), Falwell (Jerry), Matthew, Roberts (Oral) 8 Schuller (Robert), Swaggart (Jimmy) 9 McPherson (Aimee Semple), missioner, Robertson (Pat) 10 colporteur, missionary, revivalist, Whitefield (George)

evangelistic
9 crusading, reforming 10 missionary, revivalist 13 proselytizing

evangelize
6 preach 7 convert 9 sermonize

evaporate
4 fade, melt 5 clear 6 vanish 8 diminish, disperse, dissolve, evanesce, melt away, vaporize 9 disappear, dissipate

evasion
5 dodge, fudge 6 escape, excuse 7 dodging, elusion, fudging 8 escaping 9 avoidance 13 circumvention

evasive
3 sly 5 cagey, dodgy, vague 6 shifty 7 elusive 8 slippery 9 ambiguous, equivocal

Eve
home: 4 Eden
husband: 4 Adam
son: 4 Abel, Cain, Seth
temptation: 5 apple, fruit

even
3 tie 4 fair, flat, just, same, tied 5 align, equal, exact, flush, grade, level, plane, still, truly 6 as well, equate, smooth, square, stable, steady 7 balance, equable, flatten, uniform 8 balanced, constant, equalize, smoothen, straight 9 equitable, expressly, identical, precisely, unvarying 10 absolutely, comparable, consistent, continuous, fifty-fifty, unchanging 13 fair and square, proportionate

evening
4 dusk 6 soiree, sunset 7 sundown 8 gloaming, twilight 9 nightfall
French: 4 soir
Italian: 4 sera
service: 7 vespers
star: 5 Venus 6 Vesper 8 Hesperus

evenness
6 equity, parity 7 balance 8 equality 9 stability 10 equanimity, uniformity 11 consistency, equilibrium

event
3 act 4 case, deed, fact, feat, meet 5 issue, match 6 action, affair, chance, effect, result, upshot 7 contest, episode, outcome, product 8 accident, function, incident, occasion 9 aftermath, happening 10 occurrence, phenomenon 11 achievement, competition, consequence, eventuality 12 circumstance, happenstance

eventful
4 busy 6 lively 9 important, momentous

eventual
4 last 5 final 6 ending 7 closing, endmost, ensuing 8 terminal, ultimate 9 resulting 10 concluding, consequent, inevitable, succeeding

eventuality
4 case 6 effect, result 7 outcome 11 consequence, contingency, possibility

eventually
6 at last, one day 7 finally, someday 8 sometime 9 hereafter 10 ultimately 13 sooner or later

eventuate
5 ensue, occur 6 befall, follow, happen, result 9 come about, take place

ever
4 once 5 at all 6 always 7 forever 9 at any time, eternally, regularly 10 constantly, invariably 11 perpetually 12 consistently, continuously

evergreen
3 fir, ivy, yew 4 ilex, pine, tree 5 cedar, holly, savin 6 laurel, myrtle, spruce 7 conifer, cypress, hemlock, juniper, lasting, redwood, sequoia, undying, unfading 8 magnolia, mangrove, timeless 9 mistletoe, perennial 10 arborvitae 12 rhododendron

Evergreen State
10 Washington

everlasting
7 abiding, endless, eternal, forever, lasting, undying 8 constant, immortal, infinite, termless, timeless, unending 9 boundless, ceaseless, continual, deathless, limitless, permanent, perpetual, unceasing 10 continuous, perdurable 11 amaranthine, never-ending, unremitting 12 imperishable

evermore
6 always 7 for good 8 for keeps 9 eternally 12 in perpetuity

every
3 all 4 each
prefix: 3 pan

everybody
3 all 4 each

everyday
5 banal, plain, usual 6 common, normal 7 mundane, prosaic, routine 8 familiar, habitual, ordinary 9 customary, quotidian 11 commonplace 12 conventional, run-of-the-mill, unremarkable

everything
3 all
French: 4 tout
German: 5 alles

everywhere
7 all over, overall 8 all round, wherever 9 all around 10 far and near, far and wide, high and low, throughout

evict
3 out 4 oust 5 eject, expel 6 bounce, put out 7 boot out, dismiss, extrude, kick out 8 dislodge, force out, throw out 10 dispossess

evidence
4 clue, mark, show, sign 5 goods, proof, prove 6 attest, evince, expose, reveal 7 confirm, display, exhibit, symptom, testify, witness 8 indicate 9 testament, testimony 10 indication, smoking gun 11 attestation, demonstrate, testimonial 12 confirmation 13 documentation

evident
5 clear, overt, plain 6 marked, patent 7 obvious, visible 8 apparent, distinct, manifest, palpable, tangible 9 prominent 10 noticeable, pronounced 11 conspicuous, perceptible, unambiguous

evidently
9 outwardly, seemingly 10 officially, ostensibly

evil
3 bad, sin 4 foul, vice, vile 5 black 6 infamy, malice, sinful, wicked 7 badness, baleful, baneful, devilry, hateful, heinous, malefic, satanic, vicious 8 damnable, iniquity, satanism, villainy 9 atrocious, diablerie, diabolism, execrable, loathsome, malicious, malignant, nefarious 10 flagitious, iniquitous, maleficent, malevolent, pernicious, sinfulness, wickedness 11 maleficence
combining form: 3 mal

evildoer
6 sinner 7 villain 8 criminal 9 miscreant 10 malefactor

evil spirit
3 imp 5 demon, devil, fiend, Satan 6 daemon

evince
4 mark, show 5 educe, evoke, prove 6 attest, betray, elicit, expose, reveal 7 bespeak, betoken, confirm, display, exhibit, signify 8 evidence, indicate, manifest, proclaim 10 illustrate 11 demonstrate

eviscerate
3 gut 4 draw 5 bowel 7 embowel 8 protrude 10 disembowel, exenterate

evocative
6 moving 8 redolent, stirring 9 affecting, emotional, nostalgic 10 expressive, meaningful, suggestive 11 stimulating

evoke
4 cite, stir 5 educe, raise, waken 6 arouse, awaken, call up, elicit, evince, excite, induce, recall 7 conjure 8 recreate,

evolution

summon up **9** call forth, conjure up, stimulate **11** summon forth

evolution

6 change, growth **8** progress, upgrowth **9** flowering, phylogeny, unfolding **10** biogenesis, maturation **11** development, progression

evolve

4 grow **5** educe, ripen **6** change, derive, emerge, mature, open up, unfold **7** advance, develop, work out **8** progress **9** elaborate

ewe

5 sheep

ewer

3 jug **4** vase **7** pitcher

ex

4 from, past **5** prior **6** former **7** earlier, without **9** erstwhile

exacerbate

6 worsen **7** envenom, inflame, provoke **8** embitter, heighten **9** aggravate, intensify

exact

4 levy, true **5** claim, force, gouge, pinch, screw, wrest, wring **6** coerce, compel, dead-on, demand, extort, spot-on, strict **7** correct, extract, literal, precise, require, solicit, squeeze **8** accurate, rigorous, selfsame **9** identical, postulate, shake down **10** meticulous, scrupulous **11** painstaking, punctilious, requisition

exacting

5 fussy, rigid, stern, tough **6** severe, strict, taxing, trying **7** exigent, finicky, onerous **8** critical, rigorous **9** demanding, stringent **10** fastidious, nitpicking, particular, scrupulous **11** persnickety **13** hypercritical

exactitude

5 rigor **8** accuracy **9** precision **10** definitude **11** correctness, preciseness **12** definiteness

exactly

4 bang, just **5** quite, right, sharp, spang **6** bang on, square, to a tee, wholly **7** totally, utterly **8** entirely, smack-dab, squarely **9** on the nose, precisely **10** absolutely, accurately, altogether, completely, positively **12** specifically

exaggerate

6 overdo **7** amplify, enlarge, inflate, magnify, overact, romance **8** overdraw, overrate **9** embellish, embroider, overstate **11** hyperbolize **13** overemphasize

exaggeration

8 travesty **9** hyperbole **10** caricature, stretching **11** enlargement, overdrawing **12** embroidering **13** embellishment, overstatement

exalt

4 fete, laud, lift **5** boost, elate, extol, honor, raise **6** praise, uplift **7** acclaim, adulate, build up, dignify, elevate, enhance, ennoble, glorify, inspire, magnify, promote **8** eulogize, heighten, inspirit **9** intensify **10** aggrandize **11** apotheosize

exaltation

3 joy **5** bliss, glory **6** homage, praise **7** delight, ecstasy, elation, rapture, transport, tribute **8** euphoria, rhapsody **9** panegyric, uplifting **10** apotheosis, jubilation **11** deification **12** exhilaration, intoxication **13** glorification

exalted

4 high **5** grand, lofty, noble **6** august **7** eminent, highest, sublime **9** venerable **11** high-ranking, illustrious, outstanding, prestigious

examination

4 quiz, scan, test **5** assay, probe, trial **6** review, survey **7** canvass, checkup, hearing, inquest, inquiry, perusal, sifting, testing **8** analysis, scrutiny **9** breakdown, check-over, diagnosis **10** dissection, inspection **11** inquisition **13** catechization, investigation, perlustration
kind: 4 oral **5** final **7** medical, midterm **8** physical
of accounts: 5 audit
of a corpse: 7 autopsy **10** postmortem

examine

3 con, vet **4** pump, quiz, scan, sift, test **5** audit, check, grill, probe, query, study **6** go over, look at, peruse, survey **7** canvass, check up, inquire, inspect, observe **8** check out, look into, look over, question **9** catechize, check over **10** scrutinize **11** interrogate, investigate

examiner

6 censor **7** auditor, coroner **9** inspector **10** inquisitor, prosecutor **12** investigator

example

4 case **5** ideal, model **7** paragon, pattern **8** instance, paradigm, specimen, standard **9** archetype, precedent, prototype **11** case history **12** illustration

exanimate
4 dead 5 inert 8 lifeless, listless, sluggish, stagnant 9 lethargic 10 spiritless

exasperate
3 irk, vex 4 gall, rile, roil 5 anger, annoy, peeve, pique, upset 6 enrage, madden, nettle, rankle 7 agitate, incense, inflame, provoke 8 irritate 9 aggravate, infuriate

exasperation
8 vexation 9 annoyance 10 irritation 11 aggravation

ex cathedra
8 official 9 ex officio 13 authoritative

excavate
3 dig 4 grub 5 scoop, spade 6 dig out, dredge, expose, hollow, quarry, shovel 7 unearth 8 gouge out, scoop out 9 hollow out, scrape out

excavation
3 dig, pit 4 hole, mine 5 ditch, stope 6 dugout, hollow, quarry, trench, trough

exceed
3 cap, top 4 beat, best, pass 5 break, excel, outdo 6 better, outrun, overdo 7 eclipse, outpace, overrun, surpass 8 go beyond, outreach, outshine, outstrip, outweigh, overstep, overtake 9 overreach, transcend

exceedingly
4 very 6 hugely, vastly 7 awfully, notably, vitally 9 extremely 10 remarkably, strikingly 12 surpassingly 13 exceptionally **prefix:** 5 ultra

excel
3 cap, top 4 beat, best, pass 5 outdo, shine 6 better, exceed, outrun, overdo 7 eclipse, outpace, overrun, surpass 8 go beyond, outclass, outreach, outshine, outstrip, outweigh, overstep, overtake 9 overreach, transcend

excellence
5 class, merit, value, worth 6 virtue 7 quality 8 fineness 9 greatness 10 perfection 11 distinction, superiority

excellent
3 top 4 fine 5 bully, prime 6 bang-up, banner, famous, Grade A, superb, tip-top 7 capital, premium, supreme 8 champion, five-star, splendid, stunning, superior, terrific, top-notch 9 classical, first-rate, high-class, high-grade, marvelous, number one, wonderful 10 blue-ribbon, first-class 11 exceptional, magnificent, meritorious, sensational, superlative, unsurpassed 12 incomparable

except
3 bar, but, yet 4 omit, only, save 6 beside, exempt, object, reject, unless 7 barring, besides, exclude, however, outside, rule out, suspend 8 pass over 9 apart from, aside from, eliminate, excluding, outside of 11 exclusive of

exception
5 demur 7 anomaly, dissent 8 question 9 allowance, deviation, exclusion, objection 10 aberration

exceptionable
8 unwanted 9 unwelcome 10 unsuitable 11 regrettable, undesirable 12 unacceptable 13 objectionable

exceptional
4 rare 6 scarce, unique 7 notable, special, unusual 8 abnormal, atypical, distinct, singular, superior, uncommon, unwonted 9 anomalous, excellent, marvelous, wonderful 10 infrequent, noteworthy, phenomenal, remarkable 11 outstanding, uncustomary 13 extraordinary

exceptionally
4 very 6 hugely 7 notably 9 extremely 10 especially, remarkably, strikingly 11 exceedingly 12 particularly, stupendously

excerpt
4 cite, cull, pick 5 glean, quote 6 choose, sample, select 7 extract, passage, pick out, portion, snippet 8 fragment 9 quotation

excess
3 fat 4 glut, rest 5 extra, flood, spare, waste 7 nimiety, overage, surfeit, surplus 8 leavings, leftover, overflow, overkill, overmuch 9 indulgent, overstock, redundant, remainder 10 oversupply, surplusage 11 dissipation, prodigality, superfluity, superfluous, unessential 12 extravagance, immoderation, intemperance 13 overabundance, supernumerary

excessive
4 over 5 dizzy, steep, super, undue 6 too-too 7 extreme, sky-high 8 overmuch, prodigal 10 exorbitant, immoderate, inordinate, profligate 11 extravagant, intemperate, overweening, superfluous 12 supernatural, unrestrained

excessively

excessively
3 too 6 overly, unduly 8 overmuch
prefix: 5 hyper

exchange
4 swap, swop 5 bandy, trade, truck
6 barter, market, switch 7 bargain,
commute, convert, pay back, replace,
traffic 8 displace 9 transpose 10 conversion, substitute 11 reciprocate

exchequer
5 funds 8 treasury

excise
3 fee, tax 4 toll 5 elide, slash 6 cut out,
delete, remove, resect 9 expurgate,
extirpate, strike out, surcharge

excision
3 cut 7 removal, surgery 8 deletion
9 resection 11 extirpation

excitable
4 rash 8 volatile 9 impetuous 10 highstrung

excite
4 fire, goad, move, spur, stir 5 elate,
evoke, key up, pique, prime, rouse, waken
6 appeal, arouse, elicit, fire up, induce,
kindle, stir up, thrill, turn on 7 agitate,
animate, commove, inflame, inspire,
provoke, quicken 8 activate, charge up,
energize, motivate 9 galvanize, impassion,
innervate, stimulate 10 exhilarate

excited
3 hot 4 avid 5 eager 6 aflame 7 fevered
8 aflutter, worked up 10 passionate
12 enthusiastic

excitement
3 ado 4 buzz, stir, to-do 5 fever, furor
6 flurry, frenzy, furore, hubbub, thrill
7 turmoil 8 delirium, hysteria 9 agitation,
commotion 10 enthusiasm, hullabaloo
11 disturbance, pandemonium
12 exhilaration

exclaim
4 blat, bolt 5 blurt 6 cry out 8 blurt out,
burst out 9 ejaculate

exclamation
3 aah, aha, bah, boo, cry, eek, feh, fie, gee,
hah, hey, huh, oho, ooh, pah, tsk, tut, ugh,
wow 4 ahem, alas, amen, damn, dang,
darn, drat, egad, gosh, heck, hell, oops,
ouch, phew, pish, posh, rats, whew, yell
5 alack, bravo, faugh, golly, humph, pshaw,
shout 6 clamor, hurrah, indeed, outcry,
phooey, shucks 7 doggone, gee whiz,
hosanna, jeepers, whoopee 9 expletive
10 hallelujah 12 interjection
of disappointment: 4 damn, darn, rats
of disapproval: 3 tsk 6 tsk-tsk
of disgust: 3 bah, boo, feh, fie, ugh
4 yech, yuck 5 faugh, yecch 6 phooey
of dismay: 4 oh no, uh-oh 5 yikes
of enthusiasm: 4 whee 5 wahoo
7 whoopie
of fear: 3 eek
of pain: 4 ouch
of relief: 4 phew
of sorrow: 3 woe 4 alas 5 alack
of surprise: 3 wow 4 gosh 5 golly
of triumph: 3 aha, hah 5 yahoo 6 eureka
(see also **interjection**)

exclude
3 ban, bar 4 oust 5 block, debar 6 banish,
disbar, reject 7 keep out, lock out, obviate,
prevent, rule out, shut out, suspend
8 count out, preclude, prohibit 9 blackball,
blacklist, eliminate, ostracize

excluding
3 bar, but 4 less, save 6 except 7 barring,
besides 9 apart from, aside from, other
than, outside of

exclusion
3 bar 6 ouster 7 barring, lockout, removal
8 ejection, eviction, omission 9 blackball,
expulsion, ostracism 10 banishment
12 blackballing, nonadmission

exclusive
4 lone, only, sole 5 elect, elite, prime,
scoop, smart, swank, swish 6 choice,
chosen, picked, select, single 7 cliquey,
high-hat, stylish 8 clannish, cliquish,
selected, snobbish 9 preferred, undivided
10 privileged 11 fashionable, prohibitive,
restrictive 12 aristocratic, concentrated,
preferential

exclusively
4 only 5 alone 6 wholly 8 entirely
10 completely 12 particularly

excogitate
6 derive, devise, invent 7 develop, think up
8 contrive, think out

excommunicate
7 cast out 8 unchurch

excoriate
4 flay, lash, skin 5 roast, slash 6 abrade,
scathe, scorch 7 blister, censure, scarify,
scourge 8 chastise, lambaste, lash into
9 castigate

excrement
6 ordure
of animals: 4 dung, muck 6 manure
of sea birds: 5 guano

excrescence
4 blot, lump, mole, wart 5 tumor 6 growth, nodule, pimple 7 blemish, process 9 by-product, outgrowth

excrete
4 emit, spew 5 eject, expel, exude 9 discharge

excruciate
4 rack 6 martyr 7 afflict, crucify, torment, torture 9 martyrize

excruciating
5 acute, sharp 6 severe 7 extreme, intense 8 piercing, shooting, stabbing 9 agonizing, harrowing, torturous 10 unbearable 11 unendurable

exculpate
4 free 5 clear, remit 6 acquit, excuse, let off, pardon 7 absolve, amnesty, condone, forgive, justify 9 exonerate, vindicate 11 rationalize

excursion
4 ride, tour, trek, trip, walk 5 aside, drive, jaunt, paseo, sally, tramp 6 cruise, junket, outing, ramble, safari 7 day trip, journey 9 round trip 10 digression, divagation, expedition 11 parenthesis 12 pleasure trip

excusable
6 venial

excuse
3 out 4 plea 5 alibi, clear, remit 6 acquit, cop-out, defend, exempt, let off, pardon, reason, wink at 7 absolve, apology, condone, defense, forgive, justify, pretext, regrets, relieve 8 mitigate, overlook, palliate, pass over, shrug off, tolerate 9 discharge, exculpate, exonerate, extenuate, gloss over, makeshift, vindicate, whitewash 10 substitute 11 explanation, rationalize 13 justification

execrable
4 base, foul, vile 7 heinous 8 accursed, damnable, horrific, infernal, wretched 9 abhorrent, atrocious, loathsome, monstrous, repulsive, revolting 10 abominable, deplorable, despicable, detestable, horrifying

execrate
4 damn, hate 5 abhor, curse 6 detest, loathe, revile, vilify 7 censure, condemn, despise 8 denounce 9 abominate, imprecate 12 anathematize

execute
3 act 4 do in, kill, play, slay 5 cause, lynch 6 effect, finish, murder, render 7 achieve, bump off, conduct, enforce, fulfill, perform, realize 8 carry out, complete, dispatch, knock off, transact 9 discharge, eliminate, implement, liquidate 10 accomplish, administer, bring about, put through, put to death 11 assassinate 12 administrate

execution
6 murder 7 killing 11 performance

executioner
7 hangman, headman 8 headsman

executive
4 dean 6 leader 7 manager 8 director, governor 9 president 10 supervisor 13 administrator

exegesis
5 gloss 8 analysis 9 construal 10 commentary, exposition 11 elucidation, explanation, explication 12 construction

exemplar
4 copy 5 ideal, model 7 epitome, paragon, pattern 8 instance, paradigm, specimen, standard 9 archetype, criterion, prototype 12 illustration

exemplary
4 pure 5 ideal, model 7 classic, typical 8 laudable, monitory, virtuous 9 admirable, blameless, classical, estimable, faultless, honorable, righteous 10 impeccable, inculpable, prototypal 11 commendable, meritorious 12 illustrative, paradigmatic, praiseworthy, prototypical

exemplify
4 copy 6 embody, mirror, typify 7 clarify 9 enlighten, epitomize, personify, represent, symbolize 10 concretize, illuminate, illustrate

exempt
4 free 5 spare 6 except, excuse, let off, spared 7 absolve, excused, relieve 8 dispense 9 discharge

exemption
7 freedom, release 8 immunity, impunity 9 discharge, exception

exenterate
3 gut 4 draw 7 embowel 10 disembowel, eviscerate

exercise

3 use, vex 4 fret, gall, hone 5 alarm, annoy, apply, drill, étude, exert, sit-up, train, upset, wield 6 crunch, employ, pull-up, push-up 7 agitate, chin-up, develop, exploit, improve, prepare, problem, provoke, utilize, work out 8 activity, maneuver, practice, rehearse 9 athletics, condition, cultivate, discharge, operation 10 employment 11 application 12 calisthenics

exert

3 use 5 apply, wield 6 employ, expend, put out, strain 8 exercise, put forth

exertion

4 toil, work 5 labor, pains 6 effort, strain 7 trouble 8 activity, exercise, striving 11 application, elbow grease

exfoliate

4 peel, shed 5 scale 7 cast off, leaf out 8 flake off 10 desquamate

exhalation

6 breath 8 emission 9 breathing, effluvium, emanation

exhale

4 blow, emit 6 expire, let out 7 breathe, respire 10 breathe out

exhaust

3 fag, sap 4 do in, tire 5 drain, eat up, empty, spend, use up, weary 6 expend, finish, tucker, wash up, weaken 7 burn out, consume, deplete, fatigue, frazzle, tire out, wear out 8 draw down, enervate, squander, wear down 9 discharge, dissipate, prostrate, tucker out 10 debilitate, overextend, run through

exhausted

4 beat, limp, weak 5 all in, spent, tired 6 bushed 7 run-down, worn out 8 dog-tired

exhaustion

7 burnout, fatigue 8 collapse 9 lassitude, tiredness, weariness 11 prostration

exhaustive

8 complete, sweeping, thorough 9 full-blown, full-scale, intensive 10 scrupulous 11 painstaking 13 comprehensive, thoroughgoing

exhibit

4 fair, show 6 evince, expose, flaunt, parade, reveal 7 display, feature, show off 8 evidence, manifest, proclaim, showcase 10 exposition 11 demonstrate

exhibition

4 fair, show 7 display, pageant, showing 12 presentation 13 demonstration, manifestation

exhibitionist

3 fop 4 toff 6 hot dog 7 peacock, show-off 8 showboat 12 grandstander

exhilarate

4 buoy, lift 5 boost, cheer, elate, exalt, pep up 6 buck up, excite, thrill, uplift 7 animate, cheer up, commove, delight, enliven, gladden, inspire, refresh 8 inspirit, vitalize 9 stimulate 10 invigorate

exhilaration

3 joy 4 glee 7 ecstasy, elation 8 euphoria, gladness 10 exaltation, excitement 11 inspiration 12 vitalization, vivification 13 galvanization

exhort

4 goad, prod, spur, urge, warn 5 egg on, plead, press, prick 6 adjure, call on, incite, prompt, propel 7 beseech, entreat 8 admonish, call upon 9 stimulate

exhortation

4 plea 6 urging 7 advice, caution, warning 8 entreaty, jeremiad 10 admonition, incitement 11 injunction, inspiration 13 encouragement

exhume

5 dig up 6 redeem 7 reclaim, recover, unearth 8 disinter 9 resurrect

exigency

3 fix, jam 4 need, pass 5 pinch, rigor 6 crisis, demand, pickle, plight, strait 7 urgency 8 juncture, pressure, zero hour 9 extremity, necessity 10 compulsion, constraint, crossroads, difficulty, insistence 11 predicament, requirement

exigent

5 acute, vital 6 crying, taxing 7 burning, clamant, instant, onerous 8 exacting, grievous, pressing 9 clamorous, demanding, insistent, necessary 10 burdensome, imperative 11 importunate

exiguous

4 poor, puny, thin, tiny 5 scant, spare, token 6 meager, meagre, measly, paltry, scanty, shabby, skimpy, slight, sparse 7 minimal, scrimpy 9 miserable 10 inadequate, straitened

exile

4 oust 5 eject, expel 6 banish, deport,

emigré **7** cast out, outcast, refugee
8 diaspora, displace, drive out, evacuate, expellee **9** exclusion, expulsion, extradite, migration, ostracism, ostracize
10 banishment, dispossess, expatriate, scattering **11** deportation, extradition
12 displacement, expatriation
place of: **4** Elba **7** Siberia

exist
3 are, lie **4** live **5** occur

existence
4 life **5** being **7** reality **8** duration
9 actuality

existent
4 live, real **5** being, thing **6** actual, entity, extant, living **7** current, instant, present
10 present-day **12** contemporary

existentialist writer
5 Buber (Martin), Camus (Albert) **6** Marcel (Gabriel), Sartre (Jean-Paul) **7** Jaspers (Karl) **8** Beauvoir (Simone de)
9 Heidegger (Martin), Nietzsche (Friedrich)
11 Kierkegaard (Søren)

existing
5 alive, being, ontic **6** extant, living
from birth: **6** innate **10** congenital
Latin: **6** in esse

exit
3 die **4** door, gate, quit **5** death, going, leave, scram, split **6** depart, egress, escape, outlet, portal, retire **7** doorway, get away, off-ramp **8** withdraw **9** departure, egression **10** withdrawal

_____ ex machina
4 deus

exodus
6 flight **9** migration **10** emigration

Exodus author
4 Uris (Leon)

exonerate
4 free **5** clear, remit **6** acquit, excuse, exempt, let off, pardon **7** absolve
8 reprieve **9** exculpate, vindicate

exorbitant
5 undue **7** extreme **9** excessive
10 immoderate, inordinate, outrageous
11 extravagant, unwarranted
12 preposterous

exordium
5 intro, proem **6** lead-in **7** opening, preface, prelude **8** foreword, overture, preamble, prologue **12** introduction, prolegomenon

exotic
4 rare **5** alien **7** bizarre, foreign, strange, unusual **8** alluring, enticing, imported, romantic **9** different, glamorous, nonnative
10 introduced, mysterious **11** fascinating

expand
3 wax **4** grow, open, rise **5** boost, mount, swell, widen **6** beef up, bulk up, dilate, pad out, spread, unfold **7** amplify, augment, bolster, develop, distend, enlarge, inflate, magnify, prolong, stretch **8** escalate, increase, lengthen, multiply, mushroom, protract **9** discourse, elaborate, expatiate, spread out

expanse
4 area, room **5** field, ocean, range, reach, scope, space, sweep, tract **6** domain, extent, sphere, spread **7** breadth, stretch
8 distance **9** territory

expansion
6 growth, spread **8** increase **9** unfolding
11 enlargement **12** augmentation

expansive
3 big **4** wide **5** ample, broad, large, roomy
6 lavish **7** buoyant, elastic, liberal, sizable
8 effusive, extended, generous, outgoing, spacious **9** capacious, garrulous, talkative
10 gregarious, openhanded, unreserved
11 extroverted **13** demonstrative

expatiate
6 ramble, wander **7** dissert, enlarge
8 dilate on, perorate **9** discourse, elaborate, sermonize **10** dilate upon, dissertate

expatriate
5 exile, expel **6** banish, deport, émigré
8 displace, expellee, relegate

expect
4 feel, hope, take **5** await, sense, think, trust **6** assume, divine, gather, look to
7 believe, count on, foresee, imagine, look for, predict, presume, suppose, surmise
8 forecast, foreknow **9** apprehend, count upon **10** anticipate, presuppose

expectant
5 alert **6** gravid **7** anxious, hopeful
8 enceinte, pregnant, vigilant, watchful
10 breathless, parturient **12** anticipatory, apprehensive

expectation
4 hope **5** hunch **8** prospect **9** assurance,

intuition **10** assumption, likelihood
11 presumption, probability **12** anticipation,
presentiment

expectorate
4 spit

expediency
5 means **6** resort, tactic **7** aptness, fitness,
measure, stopgap **8** meetness, recourse,
resource, strategy **9** makeshift, propriety,
rightness **11** opportunism, suitability
12 appositeness, practicality, suitableness

expedient
3 fit **5** ad hoc, means, shift **6** resort, timely,
useful **7** fitting, politic, pragmatic, prudent,
stopgap, suitable **8** feasible, recourse,
resource, suitable, tactical **9** advisable,
judicious, makeshift, opportune, practical,
well-timed **10** convenient **11** appropriate,
practicable, utilitarian **12** advantageous

expedite
4 send **5** hurry, issue, speed **6** hasten
7 quicken, speed up **8** dispatch
10 accelerate, facilitate

expedition
4 trek, trip **5** hurry, speed **6** voyage
7 journey **8** campaign, dispatch, efficiency
9 excursion, swiftness **10** speediness
11 punctuality

expeditious
4 fast **5** brisk, quick, rapid, swift **6** prompt,
speedy **9** efficient **11** efficacious

expeditiousness
5 hurry, speed **6** hustle **8** dispatch

expel
4 boot, oust, spew **5** eject, evict, exile
6 banish, bounce, deport, disbar **7** cast
out, dismiss, drum out, kick out, turn out
8 disgorge, displace, throw out
9 discharge, eliminate **10** expatriate

expellee
5 exile **6** émigré **7** outcast **8** deportee,
emigrant

expend
3 pay, sap **4** blow **5** drain, pay out, spend,
use up, waste **6** lay out, outlay
7 consume, deplete, dig into, dole out,
exhaust, fork out, utilize **8** disburse,
dispense, shell out, squander **9** dissipate
10 run through

expendable
10 disposable **11** dispensable, inessential,
replaceable **12** nonessential

expenditure
4 cost **6** outlay, payoff, payout
12 disbursement

expense
4 cost, loss, toll **5** debit, price **6** burden,
charge, outlay **7** forfeit, payment
8 overhead **9** decrement, sacrifice
10 forfeiture **12** disbursement

expensive
4 dear, high, posh **5** fancy, ritzy, steep, stiff
6 costly, deluxe, lavish, pricey **7** upscale
8 precious, valuable **9** big-ticket, luxurious,
wasteful **10** exorbitant, high-priced,
overpriced **11** extravagant
12 uneconomical

experience
4 know, live **5** event, savor, skill, trial
6 ordeal, suffer, wisdom **7** episode, know-
how, sustain, undergo **8** incident, practice
9 encounter, go through **10** background
11 familiarity, savoir faire
anew: 6 relive

experienced
4 wise **6** mature, versed **7** old-line,
veteran, worldly **8** broken in, seasoned
9 practiced, qualified **12** accomplished

experiential
see **empirical**

experiment
3 try **4** test **5** assay, probe, trial **6** try out
7 test out **8** research, trial run **13** trial and
error

experimental
9 empirical, tentative **10** innovative
11 exploratory, preliminary, preparatory,
provisional **13** developmental, trial-and-
error

experimentation
4 test **5** trial **7** testing **8** research, trial run
13 trial and error

expert
3 ace, pro, wiz **4** deft, whiz **5** adept, crack,
doyen, maven **6** adroit, master, wizard
7 skilled **8** masterly, skillful, virtuoso
9 authority, dexterous, masterful, virtuosic
10 past master, proficient, specialist
11 crackerjack **12** passed master,
professional

expertise
5 craft, skill **7** ability, command, know-how,
mastery **8** facility **10** adroitness,
competence **11** proficiency **12** skillfulness

expertness
see **expertise**

expiate
6 offset, pay for, redeem 7 redress
8 atone for

expiation
9 atonement, indemnity 10 recompense,
reparation 11 restitution 12 satisfaction

expiatory
7 atoning, lustral 9 purgative 11 penitential, purgatorial 12 propitiatory

expiration
3 end 5 death 10 exhalation 11 termination

expire
3 die, end 4 pass 5 lapse 6 elapse,
exhale, pass on, perish, run out 7 decease
8 pass away 9 terminate 10 breathe out

explain
5 gloss, solve 7 analyze, clarify, clear up,
condone, expound, justify, resolve, unravel
8 construe, decipher, spell out, unriddle,
untangle 9 break down, elucidate, interpret
10 account for, illuminate, illustrate,
unscramble 11 disentangle, rationalize

explain away
6 excuse 7 justify 8 minimize 9 extenuate
10 account for 11 rationalize

explanation
3 key 5 gloss 6 excuse, motive, reason
7 account, example, grounds, meaning
8 exegesis 9 construal, rationale
11 elucidation 12 significance
13 clarification

explanatory
10 discursive, exegetical 12 enlightening,
illuminating, illustrative, interpretive

expletive
4 cuss, oath 5 curse, swear 8 cussword
9 swearword 12 interjection
(see also **exclamation**)

explicate
7 amplify, develop, explain, expound
8 construe, spell out 9 elucidate, interpret

explication
5 gloss 8 exegesis 9 construal
10 commentary 11 development

explicative
10 discursive, exegetical, scholastic
12 interpretive 13 hermeneutical

explicit
4 open, sure 5 clear, exact, frank, lucid,
overt, plain 7 certain, correct, express,
obvious, precise 8 clear-cut, definite,
distinct, specific 10 definitive
11 categorical, perspicuous, unambiguous,
unequivocal

explode
3 pop 4 fire 5 blast, burst, erupt, go off
6 blow up, debunk, negate, refute
7 burgeon, deflate 8 break out, burst out,
detonate, disprove, dynamite, mushroom,
puncture 9 discharge, discredit 10 burst
forth 11 proliferate

exploit
3 act, use 4 coup, deed, feat, gest, play
5 abuse, geste, stunt 6 bestow, effort,
employ, parlay, play on 7 emprise, utilize,
venture 8 escapade, exercise
9 adventure, cultivate 10 enterprise,
manipulate 11 achievement, performance,
tour de force

explore
5 probe, scout 6 burrow, go into, search
7 dig into, examine 8 look into, prospect,
traverse 9 delve into 11 inquire into,
investigate

explorer
African: 3 Cam, Cão (Diogo) 4 Park
(Mungo) 5 Grant (James), Laird
(Macgregor), Speke (John Hanning)
6 Akeley (Carl, Mary), Burton (Richard),
Lander (John, Richard) 7 Covilhã (Pero
da), Stanley (Henry) 8 Covilhão (Pero da)
10 Clapperton (Hugh) 11 Livingstone
(David)
American: 4 Byrd (Richard), Hall (Charles
Francis), Kane (Elisha Kent), Pike
(Zebulon) 5 Beebe (Charles William),
Clark (William), Lewis (Meriwether), Peary
(Robert) 6 Henson (Matthew), Powell
(John Wesley), Wilkes (Charles) 7 Frémont
(John Charles)
Antarctic: 4 Byrd (Richard), Cook
(Frederick), Ross (James Clark) 5 Fuchs
(Vivian), Ronne (Finn), Scott (Robert
Falcon) 6 Palmer (Nathaniel), Rymill (John
Riddoch), Wilkes (Charles) 7 Weddell
(James), Wilkins (George) 8 Amundsen
(Roald), d'Urville (Dumont) 9 Ellsworth
(Lincoln) 10 Shackleton (Ernest)
Arctic: 3 Rae (John) 4 Byrd (Richard),
Cook (Frederick) 5 Davis (John), Peary
(Robert) 6 Baffin (William), Bering (Vitus),
Henson (Matthew), Hudson (Henry),
Nansen (Fridtjof), Nobile (Umberto)
7 Barents (Willem), Bennett (Floyd), Wilkins
(George), Wrangel (Ferdinand von)
8 Amundsen (Roald) 9 Mackenzie
(Alexander), MacMillan (Donald)
10 Stefansson (Vilhjalmur)

Australian: 7 Wilkins (George)
Austrian: 9 Weyprecht (Carl)
Canadian: 9 Mackenzie (Alexander)
10 Stefansson (Vilhjalmur)
Danish: 9 Rasmussen (Knud)
Dutch: 6 Tasman (Abel Janszoon)
English: 4 Cook (James) 5 Cabot (John,
Sebastian), Drake (Francis), Scott (Robert
Falcon), Smith (John) 6 Baffin (William),
Burton (Richard), Hudson (Henry)
7 Raleigh (Walter), Stanley (Henry)
9 Vancouver (George) 10 Shackleton
(Ernest) 12 Younghusband (Francis)
French: 7 Cartier (Jacques), La Salle
(Sieur de), Nicolet (Jean) 8 Cousteau
(Jacques-Yves) 9 Champlain (Samuel de),
La Perouse (Comte de), Marquette
(Jacques)
French Canadian: 6 Joliet (Louis)
7 Jolliet (Louis) 9 Iberville (Sieur d')
German: 6 Peters (Carl) 8 Humboldt
(Alexander von)
Italian: 5 Cabot (John) 6 Nobile
(Umberto) 8 Vespucci (Amerigo)
New Zealand: 7 Hillary (Edmund)
Norwegian: 6 Nansen (Fridtjof)
8 Amundsen (Roald), Sverdrup (Otto)
9 Heyerdahl (Thor)
Portuguese: 4 Gama (Vasco da)
5 Cunha (Tristão da) 6 Cabral (Pedro)
8 Cabrilho (João Rodrigues), Magellan
(Ferdinand)
Scottish: 3 Rae (John) 4 Park (Mungo),
Ross (James Clark) 7 Thomson (Joseph)
11 Livingstone (David)
Spanish: 6 Balboa (Vasco Núñez de),
Cortés (Hernán, Hernando), de Soto
(Hernando), Pinzón (Martín Alonso, Vicente
Yáñez) 7 Mendoza (Pedro de), Pizarro
(Francisco) 8 Bastidas (Rodrigo de),
Coronado (Francisco de) 11 Ponce de
León (Juan)

explosion
3 pop, pow 4 bang, boom, clap 5 blast,
burst, crack, crash, sally, salvo, storm
6 report, volley 7 barrage, blowout, torrent
8 eruption, outburst, paroxysm 9 discharge
10 detonation

explosive
3 TNT 5 nitro, tense 6 charge, petard,
powder 7 cordite, violent 8 dynamite
9 gunpowder 13 nitroglycerin
device: 3 cap 4 bomb, mine 5 shell
6 petard 7 grenade 8 firework
expert: 5 Maxim (Hudson), Nobel (Alfred)
sound: 3 pop, pow 4 bang, boom 5 crack

exponent
6 backer 7 booster 8 advocate, champion,
defender, partisan, promoter, upholder
9 supporter 12 practitioner

expose
3 air 4 bare, open, show 5 dig up, flash
6 debunk, flaunt, parade, reveal, show up,
unmask, unveil 7 abandon, display, exhibit,
lay open, publish, show off, subject,
uncover, undress 8 brandish, disclose,
discover, endanger, unclothe

exposé
10 disclosure, revelation, uncovering

exposed
4 bare, open 5 naked 6 liable 7 evident,
subject, visible 8 manifest, stripped,
unhidden 9 uncovered 11 susceptible,
unconcealed, unprotected

exposition
4 fair, show 6 bazaar 7 display, exhibit

expostulate
5 argue 6 debate, reason 7 discuss,
dispute

exposure
4 risk 5 peril 6 airing, baring, danger
8 betrayal, jeopardy, openness 9 liability,
publicity 10 revelation 12 helplessness
13 vulnerability

expound
5 state 6 defend 7 clarify, comment,
explain, present 8 construe, set forth, spell
out 9 discourse, explicate, interpret

expounder
7 teacher 8 advocate, champion, defender,
promoter 9 proponent, supporter

express
3 air, say 4 mean, tell, vent 5 couch,
crush, frame, state, utter 6 broach, convey,
denote, impart, intend, voiced 7 connote,
declare, signify, special, uttered
8 announce, clear-cut, definite, disclose,
explicit, intended, proclaim, specific
9 enunciate, formulate, high-speed,
pronounce, symbolize, ventilate 10 definitive, particular 11 categorical,
communicate, intentional, unambiguous
gratitude: 5 thank
regret: 9 apologize

expression
4 cast, face, form, look, mien, sign, vent,
word 5 idiom, issue, motto, token, voice
6 symbol, visage 7 diction, gesture
8 locution 9 eloquence, statement,

utterance, verbalism, vividness
10 embodiment, indication
11 countenance, enunciation, observation
13 demonstration, manifestation
facial: 4 grin, phiz, pout **5** frown, scowl, smile, smirk, sneer, wince **7** grimace
of assent: 3 aye, nod, yea, yes **4** okay
of sorrow: 4 alas, tear
trite: 6 cliché **7** bromide **8** banality
witty: 4 quip **5** sally **6** bon mot

expressionless
5 blank **6** stolid, vacant, wooden
7 deadpan **9** impassive **10** poker-faced
11 inscrutable

expressive
5 vivid **7** graphic **8** eloquent **9** revealing
10 meaningful, passionate

expressly
9 precisely, purposely **10** explicitly
12 particularly, specifically **13** intentionally

expressway
4 road **7** freeway, highway, parkway
8 turnpike **12** thoroughfare

expropriate
4 take **5** annex, seize **7** impound, preempt
8 arrogate **9** sequester **10** commandeer, confiscate, dispossess

expulse
see **expel**

expulsion
5 exile, purge **6** ouster **7** ousting, removal
8 ejection, eviction **9** ostracism
10 banishment, relegation **11** deportation
12 displacement

expunge
4 dele, x out **5** annul, erase **6** cancel, delete, efface **7** blot out, destroy, exclude, wipe out **8** black out **9** eliminate, eradicate, strike out **10** annihilate, obliterate

expurgate
4 blip **5** bleep, purge **6** censor, purify, screen **7** cleanse **8** sanitize
10 bowdlerize

expurgation
8 ablution **9** catharsis, cleansing
10 lustration **12** purification

exquisite
3 fop **4** fine, keen, rare **5** acute, dandy
6 choice, dainty, select, superb
7 coxcomb, elegant, extreme, intense, refined **8** delicate, finished, flawless,

macaroni **9** recherché **10** fastidious, immaculate, impeccable

exsiccate
3 dry **4** sear **5** parch

extant
4 live **5** alive **6** actual, living **7** current, present **9** surviving **10** present-day
12 contemporary

extemporaneous
5 ad-lib, ad-libbed **6** casual **7** offhand
8 informal **9** impromptu, impulsive, makeshift, unplanned **10** improvised, unprepared, unscripted **11** spontaneous, unrehearsed **12** unthought-out

extempore
see **extemporaneous**

extemporize
5 ad-lib **7** dash off, toss off **8** knock off
9 improvise

extend
4 draw, span, vary **5** award, grant, offer, range, reach **6** accord, attain, bestow, spread, tender, unbend, unfold **7** advance, amplify, augment, broaden, drag out, draw out, enlarge, further, hold out, present, proceed, proffer, project, prolong, spin out, stretch **8** continue, elongate, increase, lengthen, multiply, protract **10** outstretch, stretch out

extension
3 arm, ell **4** wing **5** annex, delay, range, reach, scope, sweep **6** radius, spread
7 adjunct, compass, purview **8** addition, increase **9** appendage, magnitude
10 broadening, elongation
11 enlargement, lengthening, protraction
12 augmentation, continuation, postponement, prolongation

extensity
5 ambit, orbit, range, reach, scope, sweep
6 radius **7** compass, purview

extensive
3 big **4** long, vast, wide **5** broad, large, major **6** general, immense, lengthy, sizable
8 far-flung, sizeable, spacious, sweeping, thorough **9** wholesale **10** large-scale, widespread **11** far-reaching, wide-ranging
12 considerable

extent
4 size **5** ambit, limit, orbit, range, reach, scope, sweep, width **6** amount, degree, domain, radius **7** breadth, compass,

measure, purview **8** vicinity **9** magnitude **10** dimensions, proportion

extenuate
6 dilute, excuse, lessen, soften, temper, weaken **7** explain, justify, qualify, varnish **8** diminish, enervate, mitigate, moderate, palliate **9** gloss over **11** rationalize

exterior
4 skin **5** outer, shell **6** facade **7** outmost, outside, outward, surface **8** apparent **9** outermost **11** superficial

exterminate
4 kill **6** rub out **7** destroy, wipe out **8** massacre **9** eliminate, eradicate, finish off, liquidate, slaughter **10** annihilate, extinguish, obliterate

external
3 out **4** over **5** outer **7** foreign, outside, outward, surface **9** outermost **10** peripheral **11** superficial

externalize
4 show **6** embody, evince, excuse, expose, reveal **7** exhibit, justify **8** manifest **9** extenuate, incarnate, objectify, personify **11** rationalize **12** substantiate

extinct
4 cold, dead, gone, late **5** passé **6** bygone **7** archaic, defunct **8** deceased, departed, obsolete, perished, vanished **10** superseded

extinction
3 end **4** doom **5** death **6** demise **11** destruction, eradication, liquidation **12** annihilation, obliteration **13** disappearance, extermination

extinguish
3 end **5** crush, douse, erase, quash, quell **6** put out, quench, squash, stifle **7** abolish, blot out, destroy, eclipse, expunge, nullify, put down, wipe out **8** snuff out, stamp out, suppress **9** eliminate, eradicate, extirpate **10** annihilate, obliterate

extirpate
5 erase **6** cut out, efface, excise, resect, uproot **7** abolish, blot out, destroy, expunge, kill off, root out, wipe out **8** demolish **9** eliminate, eradicate **10** annihilate, deracinate, extinguish

extol
4 hymn, laud **5** cry up, exalt **6** praise **7** acclaim, applaud, commend, glorify, magnify **8** eulogize **9** celebrate **10** panegyrize

extort
5 wrest, wring **7** extract

extortion
8 exaction **9** blackmail

extra
3 odd **4** more, over **5** added, spare **6** de trop, rarely **7** reserve, surplus **8** leftover **9** lagniappe, redundant, unusually **10** additional, especially **11** superfluous **12** particularly, supplemental **13** supernumerary, supplementary

extract
4 pull, yank **5** evoke, glean, quote, wring **6** derive, eke out, elicit, remove **7** abridge, distill, essence, excerpt, passage, pull out, squeeze, take out **8** citation, condense, infusion **9** quotation, selection **11** concentrate

extraction
5 birth, blood, stock **6** origin **7** descent, essence, lineage **8** ancestry, pedigree **9** parentage **10** derivation **12** distillation

extraneous
5 alien, outer **6** exotic **7** foreign, outside **8** external **9** unrelated **10** immaterial, inappos, incidental, irrelevant, peripheral **11** impertinent, inessential, superfluous, unessential **12** adventitious, inapplicable, nonessential

extraordinary
3 odd **4** rare **6** unique **7** amazing, notable, special, unusual **8** abnormal, atypical, singular, terrific, uncommon, unwonted **9** wonderful **10** noteworthy, phenomenal, remarkable, stupendous, tremendous **11** exceptional, outstanding

extravagance
5 frill, waste **6** excess, luxury **9** hyperbole, profusion **10** indulgence, lavishness **11** ostentation, prodigality, superfluity **12** immoderation, wastefulness

extravagant
4 wild **5** outré, undue **6** lavish **7** bizarre, elaborate, extreme, profuse **8** overdone, prodigal, reckless, wasteful **9** excessive, fantastic, grandiose, overblown **10** exorbitant, hyperbolic, immoderate, inordinate, profligate **11** exaggerated, implausible, intemperate, nonsensical **12** ostentatious, preposterous, unrestrained

extreme
3 top **4** apex, dire, last, peak, wild **5** crown, final, limit, ultra, undue **6** climax, excess, height, summit, utmost, zenith **7** drastic, fanatic, intense, maximal,

maximum, outmost, radical, violent
8 farthest, furthest, pinnacle, remotest,
ultimate 9 desperate, excessive,
outermost, uttermost 10 immoderate, inordinate, outlandish, outrageous
11 culmination, furthermost, unwarranted
12 unmeasurable, unreasonable
13 revolutionary
degree: 3 nth

extremely
4 very 5 ultra 6 highly, hugely, mighty,
overly, plenty 7 acutely, awfully, greatly,
utterly 8 severely, terribly 9 immensely,
seriously, unusually 10 remarkably,
strikingly 11 exceedingly 12 terrifically

extremist
5 rabid, ultra 6 zealot 7 die-hard, fanatic,
radical 8 militant, ultraist 9 fanatical
10 monomaniac, ultraistic 11 reactionary
13 revolutionary

extremity
3 arm, end, leg, tip 4 acme, apex, foot,
hand, tail 5 limit, verge 6 apogee, vertex,
zenith 8 terminal, terminus

extricate
4 free 5 loose 6 detach, redeem, rescue
7 bail out, deliver, resolve, set free, untwine
8 liberate, untangle 9 disengage
11 disencumber, disentangle, distinguish,
individuate 12 discriminate, disembarrass
13 differentiate

extrinsic
5 alien, outer 6 exotic 7 foreign, outside,
outward 8 exterior, external, imported
10 incidental, extraneous

extrude
4 spew 5 eject 7 push out 8 press out
10 squeeze out

exuberance
4 glee, life, zest 5 ardor 6 gaiety, spirit
7 abandon 8 buoyancy, hilarity, vivacity
9 profusion 10 ebullience, enthusiasm,
friskiness, liveliness 11 flamboyance, high
spirits, zestfulness 12 exhilaration 13 effervescence, sprightliness

exuberant
3 gay 4 lush, rank 5 happy 6 bouncy,
elated, fecund, lavish, lively 7 buoyant,
profuse, rampant, riotous, zestful 8 fruitful,
prodigal, prolific, spirited 9 ebullient,
luxuriant, sprightly, vivacious
10 flamboyant 11 exhilarated
12 effervescent, enthusiastic, high-spirited

exude
4 emit, leak, ooze, seep, shed 5 issue

7 diffuse, display, emanate, excrete,
exhibit, give off, ooze out, radiate, secrete
9 discharge

exult
4 crow 5 cheer, gloat, glory, revel
7 delight, rejoice 8 jubilate 9 celebrate

exultant
6 elated, joyful, joyous 7 gleeful 8 ecstatic,
euphoric, jubilant 9 cock-a-hoop,
overjoyed, rejoicing, triumphal
10 triumphant

exultation
3 joy 4 glee 7 delight, ecstasy, elation,
rapture, triumph 8 euphoria, gloating
9 jubilance, rejoicing 10 jubilation

eye
3 orb 4 lamp, ogle, scan, view 5 sight,
watch 6 behold, goggle, look at, ocular,
oculus, peeper, regard, size up, vision
7 inspect 8 check out, consider, gaze
upon, scrutiny 9 headlight 10 scrutinize
defect: 6 myopia 9 hyperopia
10 emmetropia, presbyopia 11 astig-
matism
disease: 8 cataract, glaucoma, trachoma
doctor: 7 oculist 11 optometrist
opening: 5 pupil
part: 4 iris, lens, uvea 5 pupil 6 cornea,
retina, sclera
relating to: 5 optic 7 optical
socket: 5 orbit
Spanish: 3 ojo

eyeball
4 scan 5 check, study 6 go over, look at,
peruse, survey 7 examine, inspect,
observe 8 appraise, check out, evaluate,
pore over 10 scrutinize

eye-catching
4 bold 5 gaudy, showy 6 flashy 7 salient
8 striking 9 arresting, prominent
10 noticeable, remarkable 11 conspicuous

eyeful
6 looker 7 stunner 8 knockout

eyeglass
7 monocle

eyeglasses
5 specs 6 lenses 7 lorgnon 8 bifocals,
pince-nez 9 lorgnette 10 spectacles

eyelash
6 cilium 11 hairbreadth

eyelet
4 hole 7 grommet 8 loophole, peephole

eyepiece
4 lens 6 ocular

eye-popping
7 amazing 8 exciting, stirring 9 thrilling
10 astounding 11 astonishing, mind-
blowing, spectacular 12 breathtaking

eyesore
4 blot, dump, mess 6 blight 7 blemish
8 atrocity 11 monstrosity

eyespot
6 blight, fungus 7 ocellus

eyetooth
6 canine

eyewash
3 rot 4 bunk 5 bilge, hooey, tripe
6 bunkum 7 baloney, garbage, hogwash,
rubbish, twaddle 8 malarkey, nonsense
9 poppycock 10 balderdash
13 horsefeathers

eyewitness
8 observer, onlooker 9 bystander,
spectator

eyrie
see **aerie**

F

Fabergé product
  3 egg 9 Easter egg

Fabian
  4 Shaw (George Bernard), Webb (Beatrice, Sidney) 8 cautious 9 socialist, politic 11 circumspect, calculating

fable
  4 myth, tale, yarn 5 story 6 legend 7 fantasy, fiction, figment, parable 8 allegory
  animal: 8 bestiary

fabled
  5 famed 6 famous, unreal 7 storied 8 fanciful, mythical, renowned 9 fictional, imaginary, legendary, pretended 10 fictitious 11 make-believe 12 mythological

fabric
  3 aba, rep, web 4 lamé, repp 5 cloth, fiber, grain 7 texture 8 building, material, shirting 9 structure
  coarse: 5 crash, gunny 6 burlap, linsey, ratiné 7 cheviot, hopsack 8 homespun
  corded: 3 rep 4 repp 5 piqué 6 calico, moreen, poplin 7 pinwale 8 corduroy, paduasoy 9 bengaline
  cotton: 4 jean, leno 5 baize, chino, domet, drill, scrim, wigan 6 chintz, dimity, faille, madras, muslin 7 etamine, gingham, nankeen, percale, ticking 8 chambray, dungaree, nainsook, tarlatan
  cotton and linen: 4 huck 7 fustian 9 huckaback
  crepe: 8 marocain
  dealer: 6 draper, mercer
  durable: 4 huck, jean 5 chino, denim, drill 6 frieze, moreen 7 lasting, ticking 8 cretonne, dungaree
  embroidered: 9 baldachin 10 baldachino
  finishing process: 8 lustring 9 mercerize
  flag material: 7 bunting
  glazed: 6 chintz 7 cambric, holland
  knitted: 6 tricot 10 balbriggan

linen: 7 cambric, lockram
looped: 6 bouclé
lustrous: 4 silk 5 moiré, satin, surah 7 taffeta 12 brilliantine
metallic: 4 lamé
net: 5 tulle 8 bobbinet, illusion
openwork: 4 lace 8 filigree
ornamental: 4 lace 5 braid 6 ribbon 7 bunting
pebbly-surface: 8 barathea
pile-surface: 5 panne, plush, terry 6 velour, velvet 7 duvetyn, velours 8 chenille, moleskin 9 velveteen
plaid: 6 tartan
printed: 5 batik, toile 6 calico, chintz, damask 7 allover, challis 8 cretonne, jacquard 11 toile de Jouy
puckered: 6 plissé
raised pattern: 4 lamé 7 brocade 10 brocatelle
satin weave: 5 panne
sheer: 4 lawn, mull 5 gauze, ninon, voile 6 dimity 7 batiste, chiffon, organdy, organza, tiffany 8 tarlatan
silk: 6 faille, pongee, samite 7 foulard, grogram 8 paduasoy, sarcenet, sarsenet, shantung 9 bombazine
striped: 3 aba 6 ticking 8 bayadere
synthetic: 5 ninon, nylon, Orlon, rayon 6 Dacron
twill: 4 jean 5 chino, drill, serge 7 foulard, nankeen, ticking 8 dungaree, shalloon 9 bombazine 10 broadcloth
unfinished: 6 greige
waterproof: 7 oilskin
wool: 5 baize, loden, tweed 6 alpaca, caddis, camlet, duffel, duffle, melton, merino, wadmal, wadmel, wadmol, woolen 7 woollen 8 mackinaw, prunella 9 cassimere
wool, poor quality: 5 mungo 6 shoddy
wool mixture: 6 saxony 7 drugget, ratteen 8 moquette, shalloon, zibeline 9 zibelline
woven: 4 weft 7 textile

fabricate

4 form, make **5** build, erect, frame, set up, shape **6** cook up, create, devise, invent, make up **7** concoct, dream up, fashion, produce, think up **8** assemble, contrive **9** construct, structure **11** manufacture, put together

fabrication

3 fib, lie **4** bull, jive **6** canard, deceit **7** fiction, figment, hogwash, product, untruth **8** assembly, building, creation **9** deception, fairy tale, falsehood, invention **10** concoction, production **11** manufacture **12** construction

fabulist

French: **10** La Fontaine (Jean de)
Greek: **5** Aesop
Roman: **8** Phaedrus
Russian: **6** Krylov (Ivan)

fabulous

5 super **7** amazing **8** mythical, terrific, wondrous **9** fantastic, legendary, marvelous, wonderful **10** astounding, fictitious, incredible, outrageous, phenomenal, prodigious, remarkable, stupendous **11** astonishing, extravagant, spectacular **12** mythological
animal: **6** dragon **7** centaur, unicorn
bird: **3** roc
serpent: **8** basilisk **10** cockatrice

facade

4 face, mask **5** color, front, guise, put-on **6** veneer **8** disguise, exterior, frontage, pretense **10** appearance, camouflage, false front

face

3 mug, pan **4** dare, defy, dial, meet, phiz, puss, show, side **5** abide, brave, front, guise, honor, image, nerve **6** endure, facade, kisser, makeup, mazard, oppose, resist, suffer, take on, visage **7** compete, contend, dignity, surface **8** confront, cope with, deal with, disguise, features, prestige, war paint **9** assurance, encounter, lineament, semblance, withstand **10** appearance, confidence, experience, expression, maquillage, reputation **11** countenance, self-respect

face-off

5 clash, set-to **13** confrontation

facet

4 edge, item, part, side **5** angle, bezel, front, phase, plane, point, trait **6** aspect, detail **7** element, feature, surface

9 attribute, component **10** appearance, particular

facetious

4 flip **5** comic, droll, smart, witty **6** blithe, joking **7** amusing, comical, jesting, jocular, joshing, kidding, risible, waggish **8** flippant, humorous **9** ludicrous, unserious, whimsical **10** irreverent, ridiculous **12** wisecracking **13** tongue-in-cheek

face-to-face

6 direct **7** contact, present, vis-à-vis **8** directly, in person, personal **10** personally

facile

4 deft, easy, glib, snap **5** light, quick, ready **6** adroit, expert, fluent, poised, simple, smooth **7** assured, cursory, offhand, shallow, voluble **8** skillful, untaxing **9** dexterous **10** effortless, simplistic **13** uncomplicated

facilitate

3 aid **4** abet, ease, help **6** assist, enable, smooth **7** advance, forward, further, promote **8** expedite, make easy, simplify

facility

3 aid, wit **4** bent, ease **5** knack, privy, skill **6** talent, toilet **7** ability, amenity, comfort, fluency, leaning **8** aptitude, bathroom, building, capacity, lavatory, washroom **9** advantage, dexterity **10** adroitness, competence, smoothness **11** convenience, institution, proficiency **12** installation **13** accommodation, establishment

facing

5 front, panel **6** contra, lining, toward, veneer **7** surface, vis-à-vis **8** covering, opposite, paneling **11** over against
down: **5** prone
up: **6** supine

facsimile

4 copy, dupe, fake, twin **5** clone, ditto, match, repro **6** carbon, double **7** replica **8** knockoff, likeness **9** duplicate, imitation, photocopy **10** carbon copy, dead ringer **11** counterpart, duplication, replication, similitude **12** reproduction

fact

4 dope **5** datum, event, truth **6** detail, gospel, truism, verity **7** episode, reality **8** evidence, incident **9** actuality **10** occurrence, particular, phenomenon **11** information **12** circumstance, intelligence

faction

4 band, bloc, camp, part, ring, sect, side,

wing 5 cabal, group, party 6 caucus, circle, clique, sector, strife 7 combine, coterie, discord, machine, section 8 alliance, disunity, splinter 10 contingent, disharmony

factious
7 warring 8 contrary, divisive, partisan 9 dissident, insurgent, sectarian, seditious, turbulent 10 contending, malcontent 11 contentious, disaffected, dissentious, quarrelsome 12 disputatious 13 troublemaking

factitious
4 sham 5 bogus, false, phony 6 ersatz, forced, made-up, unreal 7 assumed, created, feigned, man-made, shammed 8 affected, invented, spurious 9 concocted, contrived, fashioned, pretended, simulated, synthetic, unnatural 10 artificial, fabricated 11 constructed, counterfeit 12 manufactured 13 counterfeited

_____ facto
4 ipso 6 ex post

factor
4 gene, item 5 agent, cause, proxy 6 broker, lender, number, symbol 7 divisor, element, exclude, include, resolve 8 attorney, emissary, quantity 9 component, majordomo, substance 10 antecedent, ingredient multiplier 11 determinant 12 intermediary

factory
4 mill, shop 5 plant, works 8 workshop 9 sweatshop 11 machine shop

factotum
4 grub 5 gofer 6 drudge 7 servant 9 assistant, operative 11 functionary

factual
4 real, true 5 exact, valid 6 actual 7 certain, genuine, literal 8 absolute, positive 9 authentic, undoubted 10 undisputed 12 indisputable

faculty
4 bent, body, gift 5 flair, knack, power 6 talent 7 ability, college 8 aptitude, capacity, facility, function, instinct 9 educators, lecturers 10 department, professors 11 instructors

fad
4 chic, kick, mode, rage, whim 5 craze, furor, style, trend 6 furore, latest, whimsy 7 caprice, fashion 9 bandwagon 10 dernier cri

faddish
3 hot 4 chic 5 today 6 modish, red-hot, trendy, with-it 7 stylish, voguish 8 contempo 9 au courant 11 cutting-edge, fashionable

fade
3 die, dim, ebb 4 fail, pale, wane, wilt 6 lessen, vanish, weaken, wither 7 decline, lighten, wash out 8 decrease, discolor, diminish 9 disappear, evaporate

faded
3 dim, wan 4 drab, dull, pale 6 pallid 8 bleached, vanished, withered 9 etiolated, washed-out

Faerie Queene, The
author: 7 Spenser (Edmund)
character: 3 Ate, Una 4 Alma 5 Guyon, Talus 6 Abessa, Amavia, Amoret, Arthur, Cambel, Duessa, Palmer 7 Artegal, Corceca, Fidessa, Maleger, Sansloy 8 Calidore, Florimel, Fradubio, Gloriana, Lucifera, Orgoglio, Satyrane 9 Archimago, Britomart 11 Britomartis

Fafnir
6 dragon
brother: 5 Regin 6 Fasolt, Reginn
father: 8 Hreidmar
slayer: 6 Sigurd 9 Siegfried
victim: 6 Fasolt 8 Hreidmar

fag
4 do in, moil, tire, toil 5 serve, smoke, stick, weary 6 drudge, overdo, tucker 7 exhaust, fatigue, servant, wear out 8 drudgery, knock out 9 cigarette

fag end
4 butt, edge, fray 7 remnant

faience
11 earthenware

fail
3 die, end 4 bomb, fade, lack, lose, miss, sink, slip, stop, wane 5 break, flunk 6 fizzle, forget, ignore, lessen, weaken 7 decline, default, founder, give out, go under, neglect 8 fall flat, languish, miscarry 9 break down, fall short 10 disappoint, go bankrupt 11 deteriorate

failing
4 flaw, vice 5 fault 6 defect 8 weakness 9 weak point 10 deficiency 11 shortcoming 12 imperfection

failure
3 bum, dud 4 bomb, bust, flop, miss 5 decay, loser 6 fiasco, fizzle, no-good, outage 7 default, washout 8 collapse,

fracture, omission **9** breakdown, cessation, oversight, unconcern **10** bankruptcy, deficiency, insolvency, negligence **11** defalcation, dysfunction, miscarriage **12** interruption **13** deterioration

fain

3 apt **5** eager, prone, ready **6** gladly, minded **7** willing **8** amenable, inclined **9** agreeable

fainéant

3 bum **4** idle, lazy **5** idler, sloth **6** loafer, torpid **7** goof-off, slacker **8** deadbeat, inactive, indolent, layabout, slothful, sluggard, sluggish **9** do-nothing, lazybones, shiftless **11** couch potato, ineffectual **13** lackadaisical

faint

3 dim, low, wan **4** hazy, pale, soft, weak, wilt **5** dizzy, light, swoon, vague, woozy **6** feeble **7** conk out, obscure, pass out, shadowy, syncope, unclear **8** black out, collapse, keel over **9** undefined **10** ill-defined, indistinct

fair

3 due **4** even, expo, fine, join, just, mild, okay, open, so-so **5** ample, blond, bonny, clear, equal, fresh, light, sunny **6** bazaar, blonde, comely, decent, honest, kermis, lovely, market, pretty, square **7** cricket **8** adequate, all right, balanced, carnival, festival, mediocre, middling, pleasant, pleasing, rainless, rational, sunshiny, unbiased **9** beautiful, cloudless, equitable, favorable, fortunate, impartial, objective, tolerable, unclouded **10** aboveboard, acceptable, attractive, evenhanded, exhibition, exposition, open-minded, reasonable **11** good-looking, indifferent, nonpartisan, respectable, sportsmanly **12** satisfactory, unprejudiced **13** disinterested, dispassionate, sports-manlike

fair food

10 candy apple, candy floss, fried dough, funnel cake **11** cotton candy, elephant ear

fair-haired

3 pet **5** blond **6** blonde **7** beloved, darling, favored **8** favorite **9** fortunate

fairly

5 quite **6** nearly, rather **7** plainly **8** passably, properly, somewhat **9** tolerably **10** acceptably, deservedly, distinctly, moderately, reasonably **11** practically

fairness

6 candor **7** honesty **8** justness **9** good faith **12** impartiality

fairy

3 elf, imp, nix **4** puck **5** elfin, nixie, nymph, pixie, sylph **6** goblin, kobold, sprite **7** brownie, gremlin **10** leprechaun
king: **6** Oberon
queen: **3** Mab **7** Titania **8** Gloriana
shoemaker: **10** leprechaun

fairy tale

author: **4** Lang (Andrew) **5** Grimm (Jacob, Wilhelm), Wilde (Oscar) **7** Kipling (Rudyard) **8** Andersen (Hans Christian), Perrault (Charles)
character: **4** Jack, Puck **6** Gretel, Hansel **8** Rapunzel, Tom Thumb **9** Snow White **10** Cinderella, Goldilocks, Thumbelina

faith

4 cult, sect **5** credo, creed, stock, troth, trust **6** belief, church, credit **8** credence, reliance, religion **9** certainty, certitude, communion, credulity **10** confidence, persuasion **12** denomination
article of: **5** tenet

faithful

4 fast, just, true **5** liege, loyal, pious, tried **6** steady, trusty **7** devoted, dutiful, staunch **8** constant, follower, reliable, resolute, true-blue **9** religious, steadfast **10** dependable, scrupulous, unwavering **11** truehearted, trustworthy

faithfulness

5 piety, troth **6** fealty **7** loyalty **8** devotion, fidelity **9** adherence, constancy **10** allegiance, attachment

faithless

5 false, Punic **6** fickle, untrue **8** disloyal, recreant **10** perfidious, traitorous **11** treacherous **13** untrustworthy

faithlessness

7 perfidy, treason **8** betrayal **9** falseness, treachery **10** disloyalty, infidelity

fake

3 act, gyp **4** hoax, mock, sham **5** bluff, bogus, false, feign, fraud, phony, put on, spoof **6** affect, doctor, ersatz, forged, framed, humbug, pseudo **7** falsify, pretend **8** impostor, invented, simulate, spurious **9** brummagem, charlatan, concocted, fabricate, imitation, imposture, pinchbeck, pretended, simulated **10** artificial, fabricated, fictitious, fraudulent, simulation **11** counterfeit
combining form: **5** pseud **6** pseudo

faker

4 sham **5** fraud, phony, quack **6** con man, hoaxer **8** deceiver, impostor **9** charlatan, con artist, pretender **10** mountebank

11 four-flusher 12 double-dealer
13 confidence man

fakir
7 ascetic, dervish 9 mendicant

falcon
4 hawk 5 hobby, saker 6 lanner, merlin
7 kestrel 9 peregrine
eye cover: 4 seel
male: 4 jack 6 tercel 7 tiercel 8 lanneret
mature: 7 haggard
young: 4 eyas

falcon-headed god
see at **Egyptian**

falconry
7 hawking
equipment: 4 bell, hood, jess, lure
procedure: 3 imp 4 cope, seel

Falkland Islands
capital: 7 Stanley
colony of: 7 Britain

fall
3 dip, ebb, sag 4 dive, drip, drop, dump,
hang, plop, sink, slip, trip, wane 5 abate,
crash, lapse, slide, slump, spill 6 autumn,
drowse, give up, go down, header, plunge,
sprawl, tumble 7 cascade, decline,
descend, descent, devolve, go under,
plummet, scatter, stumble, subside
8 collapse, decrease, diminish, keel over,
nose-dive 9 hairpiece 10 depreciate
11 precipitate

fallacious
6 untrue 7 invalid 8 delusive, delusory
9 deceitful, deceptive, erroneous, sophistic
10 fraudulent

fallacy
5 error 6 canard 7 falsity, sophism, untruth
8 delusion 9 falsehood 11 non sequitur
13 misconception

fall apart
6 lose it 7 crumble 9 break down,
decompose 10 go to pieces 11 come
unglued, deteriorate 12 disintegrate

fall back
6 recede, recoil, retire 7 retract, retreat
8 withdraw 9 disengage, retrocede
10 retrograde

fall behind
3 lag 4 drag 5 delay, tarry, trail 6 dawdle,
linger, loiter

fall flat
4 bomb, fail, flop, miss 6 fizzle

fall guy
4 dupe, fool, goat, gull 5 chump, front,
patsy 6 stooge, sucker 8 front man
9 scapegoat 11 whipping boy

fallible
4 iffy, weak 5 dicey, frail, human 6 errant,
erring, faulty 9 imperfect 10 unreliable

falling-out
3 row 4 beef, feud, fuss, spat, tiff 5 break,
run-in, words 6 bicker, fracas, hassle
7 dispute, quarrel, rhubarb, wrangle
8 argument, conflict, squabble 9 brannigan
11 altercation, controversy 12 disagreement, estrangement

falloff
3 sag 4 drop, slip 5 slump 7 decline
8 downturn 9 downslide, downswing,
downtrend 13 deterioration

fall out
5 argue, break, leave, occur 6 bicker
7 brabble, quarrel, wrangle 8 disagree,
squabble

fallow
4 idle 5 inert 6 unsown 7 dormant, resting
8 inactive, unseeded, untilled 9 neglected,
quiescent, unplanted 12 uncultivated

false
4 fake, mock, sham 5 bogus, dummy,
hokey, lying, phony, wrong 6 ersatz,
forged, hollow, pseudo, untrue 7 crooked,
devious, feigned, seeming, unloyal
8 apostate, apparent, deluding, delusive,
delusory, disloyal, recreant, specious,
spurious 9 brummagem, deceitful,
deceiving, deceptive, dishonest, distorted,
erroneous, faithless, illogical, imitation,
incorrect, pinchbeck, simulated
10 artificial, fictitious, fraudulent,
inaccurate, misleading, perfidious,
traitorous, unfaithful, untruthful
11 counterfeit, treacherous
combining form: 5 pseud 6 pseudo

falsehood
3 fib, lie 5 fable 6 canard 7 fallacy,
untruth, whopper 8 roorback 9 mendacity
11 fabrication 12 misstatement
13 prevarication

falseness
7 fallacy, perfidy 8 apostasy 9 treachery
10 disloyalty, infidelity 11 insincerity

false teeth
8 dentures

falsify
3 fib, lie 4 cook, deny 5 belie, fudge, slant

falsity

6 doctor, refute 7 deceive, disprove, distort, mislead 8 misstate 10 contradict 11 prevaricate 12 misrepresent

falsity

3 fib, lie 4 tale, yarn 5 fable 6 canard 7 untruth, whopper 9 falsehood, mendacity 11 fabrication 13 prevarication

Falstaff

companion: 3 Nym 4 Peto 6 Pistol 8 Bardolph
composer: 5 Verdi (Giuseppe)
creator: 11 Shakespeare (William)
play: 7 Henry IV
prince: 3 Hal
tavern: 9 Boar's Head

Falstaffian

3 fat 6 jovial 7 roguish 8 boastful 9 convivial, dissolute

falter

4 halt, limp, reel, sway, trip 5 quail, waver 6 flinch, teeter, totter, wobble 7 give way, stagger, stammer, stumble 8 hesitate 9 vacillate 12 shilly-shally

fame

4 note 5 éclat, glory, honor, kudos 6 esteem, regard, renown, repute 7 acclaim, stardom 8 standing 9 celebrity, notoriety 10 popularity, prominence, reputation 11 acclamation, immortality, recognition

famed

5 noted 6 marked 7 eminent, notable 8 renowned 9 notorious, prominent, well-known 10 celebrated 11 illustrious 13 distinguished

familiar

4 cozy 6 common, folksy 8 domestic, everyday, frequent, informal, intimate, standard 10 accustomed 11 comfortable, commonplace 12 conventional, recognizable 13 garden-variety

familiarity

4 ease 8 intimacy 9 closeness, knowledge 11 informality 12 acquaintance

family

3 kin 4 clan, folk, home, line, race 5 brood, folks, house, issue, stirp, stock, tribe 6 ménage, strain 7 dynasty, kindred, lineage, progeny 8 pedigree 9 bloodline, household, offspring
branch: 5 stirp
lineage: 4 tree 6 stemma 8 pedigree 9 genealogy

famine

4 want 6 dearth, hunger 10 starvation

famished

6 hungry 7 starved 8 ravenous, starving

famous

5 famed, noble, noted 6 fabled 7 eminent, notable, popular 8 historic, renowned 9 legendary, notorious, prominent, well-known 10 celebrated 11 illustrious, prestigious, redoubtable

fan

3 bug, nut 4 blow, buff, open, wind 5 lover, rouse 6 addict, arouse, expand, extend, kindle, rooter, ruffle, spread, stir up, unfold, votary, whip up, winnow 7 admirer, devotee, habitué 8 adherent, enkindle, follower, railbird 9 stimulate 10 aficionado, enthusiast
horseracing: 7 turfman
India: 6 punkah
movie: 7 cineast 8 cineaste

fanatic

3 bug, nut 4 buff 5 fiend, freak, rabid 6 addict, maniac, votary, zealot 7 devotee, die-hard, habitué 10 aficionado, enthusiast

fanatical

5 fiery, rabid 6 ardent, fervid 7 extreme, fervent, zealous 8 frenetic, frenzied, maniacal, obsessed 9 perfervid 10 passionate 11 impassioned

fanaticism

4 zeal 5 mania 6 frenzy 8 zealotry 9 extremism, monomania

fancier

6 grower 7 amateur, admirer, breeder, devotee

fanciful

6 absurd, unreal 7 bizarre, fictive 8 fabulous, illusory, imagined, mythical, notional, romantic 9 fantastic, fictional, grotesque, imaginary 10 chimerical, fictitious 11 fantastical 12 preposterous

fancy

3 bee 4 posh, whim 5 dream, ritzy, shine, smart, taste 6 liking, megrim, notion, relish, snazzy, swanky, vision, whimsy 7 caprice, chimera, conceit, concept, dream up, elegant, fantasy, feature, imagine, picture 8 conceive, daydream, envision, fondness, judgment, velleity 9 capriccio, elaborate, intricate, inventive, visualize, whimsical 10 decorative, ornamental, partiality,

propensity **11** extravagant, highfalutin, imagination, inclination

fandango
5 dance **9** malaguena

fanfare
4 pomp, show **5** array **7** display, panoply **8** flourish
trumpet: **6** tucket

fanlike
7 plicate

fanny
3 bum, can **4** buns, butt, duff, moon, rear, rump, seat, tail, tush **5** booty, nates **6** behind, bottom, breech, heinie **7** caboose, hind end, keister, rear end, tail end **8** backside, buttocks, derriere **9** fundament, posterior

fantasia
6 vision **8** daydream, illusion, rhapsody **9** fairyland **10** apparition

fantasize
4 moon **5** dream, fancy **7** imagine **8** daydream **10** woolgather

fantastic
3 odd **4** wild **6** absurd, unreal **7** bizarre, surreal **8** fanciful, singular **9** eccentric, grotesque, imaginary, marvelous, monstrous, unearthly, whimsical **10** chimerical, far-fetched, improbable, incredible, outlandish, outrageous, prodigious, stupendous, tremendous **11** implausible, nonsensical, sensational, superlative **12** preposterous, unbelievable

fantasy
4 moon, whim **5** dream, fancy, freak **6** vagary, vision, whimsy **7** caprice, chimera, fiction, reverie **8** daydream, delusion, phantasm **9** imagining, invention, pipe dream **10** bizarrerie **11** imagination **12** grotesquerie

far
4 long **6** remote **7** distant **8** outlying
combining form: **3** tel **4** tele, telo

far and wide
7 all over **10** everyplace, everywhere, throughout

faraway
4 lost **5** moony **6** absent, dreamy, remote **7** distant, removed **8** outlying **9** oblivious, unheeding **10** abstracted, distracted **11** preoccupied, inattentive **12** absentminded

farce
6 comedy, satire **7** mockery **8** travesty **9** burlesque, slapstick **10** caricature

farceur
5 clown, cutup, joker **7** buffoon

farcical
5 comic **6** absurd **7** comical, foolish, risible **9** laughable, ludicrous **10** ridiculous **12** preposterous

fare
4 diet, dine, food, pass, rate toll **5** get on, price, track **6** manage, travel **7** come off, journey, make out, proceed, succeed **8** get along, progress, victuals **9** passenger, surcharge **10** provisions **11** comestibles

farewell
3 ave, bye **4** ta-ta **5** adieu, adios, aloha, congé **6** bye-bye, pip-pip, shalom, so long **7** aloha oe, cheerio, good-bye **8** swan song **9** bon voyage, departure **11** arriverderci, leave-taking, valediction, valedictory

far-fetched
5 fishy **6** absurd **7** dubious **8** doubtful, strained, unlikely **10** improbable, incredible **11** implausible, unrealistic **12** preposterous, unbelievable

far-flung
6 remote **7** distant, removed **8** outlying **10** widespread

farinaceous
5 mealy **6** floury **7** starchy
food: **4** meal **5** flour, grits **6** cereal, hominy **7** polenta, pudding, tapioca

farm
4 till **5** croft, ranch **6** grange, rancho **7** hennery **8** estancia, hacienda, hatchery **9** cultivate, farmstead **10** plantation
building: **4** barn, shed, silo
Dutch: **6** bowery
Israeli collective: **7** kibbutz
Russian: **7** kolkhoz, sovkhoz

farmer
6 grower, tiller, yeoman **7** granger, planter, rancher **8** ranchero, ranchman **13** agriculturist
Russian: **5** kulak
South African: **4** Boer
tenant: **6** cottar, cotter **7** crofter **12** sharecropper

farming
7 tillage **8** agronomy **9** husbandry **11** agriculture, cultivation

faro

faro
  5 monte
  bet: 7 sleeper
  card: 4 case, hock, soda

far-off
  6 remote **7** distant, removed **8** outlying

far-out
  3 rad **4** cool **5** outré, weird **6** groovy
  7 bizarre, offbeat, radical **9** eccentric
  10 avant-garde, off-the-wall, outlandish

farrago
  4 hash, mess, olio **5** gumbo **6** jumble,
  medley, muddle **7** goulash, mélange,
  mixture **8** mishmash, shambles
  9 potpourri **10** hodgepodge, miscellany

far-reaching
  5 broad **8** sweeping **9** extensive,
  momentous, pervasive **10** portentous,
  widespread **11** significant, wide-ranging
  13 comprehensive, consequential

farrier
  5 smith **10** blacksmith, horseshoer

farsighted
  4 sage, wise **9** hyperopic, prescient,
  sagacious **10** discerning

farthest
  6 utmost **7** apogean, extreme, outmost
  8 remotest, ultimate **9** outermost,
  uttermost

Fasching
  8 carnival

fascinate
  4 draw, wile **5** charm **6** allure, enamor,
  entice, please **7** attract, beguile, bewitch,
  enchant **8** enthrall, intrigue, transfix
  9 captivate, enrapture, magnetize,
  mesmerize, spellbind

fascination
  5 charm **6** allure, appeal **7** glamour
  8 charisma **9** magnetism **10** attraction,
  witchcraft **11** enchantment
  12 enthrallment

Fascist
  4 Nazi **6** despot, Hitler (Adolf), tyrant
  8 autocrat **9** Falangist, Mussolini (Benito)
  10 Blackshirt

fashion
  3 fad, fit, ton, way **4** chic, form, mode,
  mold, suit, tone, vein, wear **5** craze, shape,
  style, trend, usage, vogue **6** create,
  custom, design, devise, manner, method,
  sculpt, tailor **7** compose, costume, pattern
  8 contrive **9** bandwagon, construct,
  fabricate **10** dernier cri **12** haute couture

fashionable
  3 hip **4** chic, cool, posh, tony **5** fresh, ritzy,
  sharp, smart, swank, swish **6** chichi, du
  jour, modish, trendy, with-it **7** à la mode,
  current, dashing, faddish, popular, stylish,
  voguish **8** up-to-date **9** au courant,
  exclusive, happening **12** silk-stocking

fashion designer
  American: 4 Head (Edith) **5** Beene
  (Geoffrey), Blass (Bill), Dache (Lilly), Ellis
  (Perry), Karan (Donna), Klein (Anne,
  Calvin) **6** Jacobs (Marc), Lauren (Ralph),
  Mackie (Bob) **7** Galanos (James), Halston,
  Mizrahi (Isaac) **8** Galliano (John), Hilfiger
  (Tommy) **9** Claiborne (Liz), de la Renta
  (Oscar), Gernreich (Rudi)
  Anglo-French: 5 Worth (Charles
  Frederick)
  Dominican: 9 de la Renta (Oscar)
  English: 5 Quant (Mary) **8** Westwood
  (Vivienne)
  French: 4 Dior (Christian) **5** Bohan (Marc)
  6 Cardin (Pierre), Chanel (Coco), Poiret
  (Paul) **6** Ungaro (Emanuel) **7** Balmain
  (Pierre), Lacroix (Christian), Montana
  (Claude) **8** Givenchy (Hubert de)
  9 Courrèges (André), Lagerfeld (Karl)
  12 Saint-Laurent (Yves), Schiaparelli (Elsa)
  German: 9 Lagerfeld (Karl)
  Israeli: 7 Mizrahi (Isaac)
  Italian: 5 Pucci (Emilio), Ricci (Nina)
  6 Armani (Giorgio) **7** Cassini (Oleg),
  Versace (Gianni) **12** Schiaparelli (Elsa)
  Japanese: 6 Miyake (Issey)
  Spanish: 10 Balenciaga (Cristóbal)

fast
  3 set **4** diet, easy, firm, Lent, soon, sure,
  true, wild **5** fixed, fleet, hasty, hitch, loose,
  loyal, quick, rapid, swift **6** firmly, prompt,
  snappy, speedy, stable **7** abstain, hastily,
  hurried, quickly, rapidly, staunch,
  swiftly **8** chop-chop, constant, faithful, full
  tilt, immobile, promptly, resolute, speedily
  9 breakneck, dissolute, immovable,
  libertine **10** abstinence, profligate,
  recklessly, stationary **11** expeditious,
  promiscuous **12** lickety-split
  13 expeditiously

fasten
  3 fix, peg, pin, set, sew, tie, zip **4** bind, bolt,
  clip, hook, join, lace, lash, link, lock, moor,
  nail, seal, shut, weld **5** affix, cable, catch,
  chain, cinch, clamp, clasp, close, cramp,
  dowel, girth, hitch, latch, rivet, screw, stake,

stick, strap, tie up, truss **6** anchor, attach, batten, buckle, button, couple, secure, skewer, solder, staple, tether **7** connect, mortise **8** buckle up

fastener
3 nut, peg, pin, tie **4** bolt, brad, clip, cord, frog, hasp, link, lock, nail, rope, snap, stud, tack, tape **5** catch, clamp, clasp, dowel, girth, hinge, hitch, latch, rivet, screw, spike, stake, strap **6** buckle, button, cotter, skewer, staple, tether, toggle, zipper **7** grommet, padlock, netsuke, shackle **8** coupling, cuff link, handcuff, seat belt, shoelace **9** connector, cotter pin, safety pin, thumbtack **10** clothespin

fastidious
5 fussy, picky **6** choosy, dainty, queasy **7** choosey, finical, finicky, refined **8** exacting **9** demanding, squeamish **10** meticulous, particular, pernickety **11** persnickety

fastness
4 fort, hold, keep **6** bunker, castle, refuge **7** alcazar, bastion, citadel, crannog, redoubt, sanctum **8** casemate, fortress, presidio **10** stronghold, tower house **11** strongpoint

fast-talking
4 glib **5** slick **6** facile **8** slippery **13** silver-tongued

fat
3 big, oil **4** flab, lard, suet, wide **5** beefy, broad, bulky, burly, cream, dumpy, gross, heavy, husky, large, lipid, obese, plump, pudgy, round, stout, thick, tubby **6** chunky, excess, fleshy, grease, portly, rotund, stocky, stubby, tallow **7** adipose, blubber, paunchy, porcine, surfeit, surplus, weighty **8** heavyset, oversize, thickset **9** corpulent **10** full-bodied, overweight, potbellied **11** superfluity

fatal
6 deadly, lethal, mortal **7** deathly, ruinous **8** terminal **9** incurable, pestilent **10** pernicious **12** pestilential

fatality
4 doom **5** death **8** casualty **10** deadliness

fata morgana
6 mirage **8** illusion

fat cat
5 mogul, nabob **6** big gun, bigwig, tycoon **7** big shot, magnate, pooh-bah **8** big wheel **9** moneybags, plutocrat **11** muckety-muck **13** high-muck-a-muck

fate
3 end, lot **4** doom, luck, ruin **5** death, karma **6** chance, kismet, upshot **7** destiny, fortune, outcome, portion **13** inevitability

fateful
6 deadly **7** ominous, ruinous **8** decisive **9** momentous, prophetic **10** portentous

Fates
see at **Greek; Norse; Roman**

fathead
3 ass, oaf **4** boob, clod, dodo, dope, dolt, gawk, goof, goon, jerk, lump, mutt, yo-yo **5** cluck, clunk, dummy, dunce, idiot, moron, stock, stupe, yahoo **6** cretin, dimwit, donkey, doofus, dum-dum, nitwit, noodle, schlub, turkey **7** buffoon, dullard, jackass, schnook **8** dumbbell, imbecile, numskull **9** birdbrain, ignoramus, lamebrain, numbskull, simpleton

fatheaded
4 dull, dumb **5** dense, dopey, thick **6** obtuse, simple, stupid **7** doltish, idiotic **8** gormless **9** brainless, dim-witted, imbecilic **10** numskulled **11** numbskulled, thick-witted

father
3 dad, pop **4** dada, papa, père, sire **5** beget, breed, daddy, hatch, padre, pappy, pater, poppa, spawn **6** author, create, old man, parent, priest **7** builder, creator, founder, produce **8** ancestor, engender, generate, inventor, producer **9** architect, initiator, originate, patriarch, procreate **10** originator, prime mover
combining form: 4 patr **5** patri, pat.o

Father Brown creator
10 Chesterton (Gilbert Keith)

fatherland
4 home, soil **7** country

Father Time's implement
6 scythe

fathom
4 know **5** probe, sound **7** discern, explore, measure **9** apprehend, figure out, penetrate **10** comprehend, understand **11** investigate

fathomless
7 abysmal, abyssal **8** profound **12** immeasurable

fatidic
5 vatic **6** mantic **7** Delphic, sibylic **8** Delphian, oracular, sibyllic **9** prophetic, prescient, sibylline, vaticinal **10** divinatory, predictive

fatigue

3 fag 4 poop, tire, wear 5 drain, weary
6 tucker 7 deplete, burn out, exhaust,
frazzle, wear out 8 drudgery, wear down
9 tiredness, weariness 10 enervation,
exhaustion
combat: 7 frazzle 10 shell shock

Fatima

father: 8 Mohammed, Muhammad
husband: 9 Bluebeard
son: 5 Hasan 6 Husayn
stepbrother: 3 Ali

fatness

7 obesity 9 adiposity 10 corpulence,
overweight

fatty

4 oily, rich 6 greasy 7 adipose 8 unctuous
10 oleaginous
combining form: 4 lipo 5 adipo

fatuous

4 dumb, fond 5 inane, sappy, silly
6 jejune, simple 7 asinine, foolish, puerile,
witless

faucet

3 tap 4 bung, cock, gate 5 valve 6 spigot
7 hydrant, petcock 8 stopcock

Faulkner, William

character: 3 Ike (Snopes), Joe
(Christmas) 4 Eula (Varner Snopes), Flem
(Snopes), Mink (Snopes) 5 Benjy
(Compson), Caddy (Compson), Gavin
(Stevens), Henry (Sutpen), Jason
(Compson), Lucas (Beauchamp) 6 Dilsey,
Temple (Drake) 7 Candace (Compson),
Quentin (Compson) 8 Benjamin
(Compson)
county: 13 Yoknapatawpha
family: 6 Benbow, Snopes, Sutpen
7 Compson 8 McCaslin, Sartoris
9 Beauchamp
novel: 4 Town (The) 6 Hamlet (The)
7 Mansion (The), Reivers (The) 8 Sartoris
9 Sanctuary, Wild Palms (The) 11 As I Lay
Dying 13 Light in August 14 Absalom,
Absalom 15 Sound and the Fury (The)
17 Intruder in the Dust

fault

3 err, nag, sin 4 flaw, rift, slip, spot, vice,
want 5 blame, break, knock, error, scold
6 accuse, defect, foible, miscue 7 censure,
demerit, failing, fissure, frailty, mistake,
upbraid 8 fracture, weakness 9 criticize,
infirmity 10 San Andreas 11 culpability,
dereliction, shortcoming 12 imperfection

line:

4 rift 5 split 6 breach 7 fissure
8 crevasse

faultfinder

4 crab 5 grump 6 critic, griper, grouch,
nagger, whiner 7 grouser 8 grumbler
10 bellyacher, complainer, criticizer,
crosspatch

faultfinding

7 carping 8 captious, critical, nitpicky
9 criticism 10 censorious, nit-picking,
pernickety 11 persnickety 12 overcritical
13 hypercritical

faultless

4 pure 7 perfect 8 innocent, unerring
9 guiltless 10 immaculate, impeccable,
inculpable

faulty

4 awry 5 amiss, wrong 6 flawed, marred
7 botched, damaged, defaced, inexact,
unsound 8 fallible, specious 9 blemished,
defective, deficient, erroneous, imperfect,
incorrect 10 fallacious, inaccurate
prefix: 3 dys

faun

5 satyr

fauna

7 animals

Faunus

grandfather: 6 Saturn
son: 4 Acis 7 Latinus

Faust

author: 6 Goethe (Johann Wolfgang von)
beloved: 8 Gretchen
composer: 6 Gounod (Charles)

faux

4 fake, sham 5 bogus, false, phony
6 ersatz 9 imitation, pretended, simulated,
synthetic 10 substitute

faux pas

4 flub, goof, slip 5 boner, error, gaffe
6 boo-boo, howler, miscue, slipup
7 blooper, blunder, misstep, mistake,
stumble 8 pratfall, solecism 9 gaucherie
11 impropriety

favor

4 baby, back, bias, boon, gift, okay
5 bless, bribe, grace, mercy, token, value
6 accept, behalf, choose, oblige, pamper,
prefer, regard 7 indulge, present, support,
sustain 8 courtesy, goodwill, interest,
keepsake, kindness, resemble, sanction,
sympathy 9 attention, patronage, privilege,
take after 10 admiration, facilitate,

indulgence, partiality **11** approbation, benevolence, countenance

favorable
4 fair **5** lucky **6** benign, biased, golden, timely, toward, useful **7** helpful, partial **8** pleasant, pleasing, positive **9** agreeable, benignant, fortunate, promising **10** auspicious, benevolent, propitious, prosperous **11** affirmative **12** advantageous **13** complimentary

favoring
4 rosy **6** timely, toward, useful **7** helpful **9** opportune **10** auspicious, beneficial, propitious **12** advantageous
prefix: 3 pro

favorite
3 pet **7** dearest, popular, special **8** precious **9** preferred, well-liked **10** fair-haired, preference **11** front-runner, teacher's pet, white-haired

favoritism
4 bias **8** cronyism, nepotism **10** partiality **12** one-sidedness

fawn
3 kid **4** deer, ecru **5** beige, toady **6** bister, grovel, kowtow **7** flatter, truckle, wheedle **8** blandish, bootlick **9** sweet-talk **11** apple-polish

fawning
6 smarmy **8** unctuous **9** parasitic **10** obsequious **11** sycophantic

fay
3 elf **4** puck **5** elfin, fairy, pixie **6** elfish, goblin, sprite **7** brownie **10** leprechaun

faze
3 cow **5** abash, daunt, throw **6** dismay, rattle **7** confuse, disturb, nonplus, perturb **8** befuddle, bewilder, confound, unsettle **9** discomfit, dumbfound, embarrass **10** disconcert **11** flabbergast

FBI director
5 Freeh (Louis) **6** Hoover (J. Edgar) **7** Mueller (Robert)

fealty
5 faith, troth **7** loyalty **8** devotion, fidelity **9** adherence, constancy, vassalage **10** allegiance, attachment **11** devotedness **12** faithfulness

fear
3 awe **5** alarm, angst, dread, panic, qualm, scare, worry **6** dismay, fright, horror, phobia, terror **7** anxiety, jitters **8** cold feet, disquiet, timidity **9** agitation, cowardice,

misgiving **10** foreboding **11** disquietude, trepidation **12** apprehension, cowardliness, perturbation, presentiment, timorousness
of animals: 9 zoophobia
of being buried alive: 11 taphephobia
of cats: 12 ailurophobia
of crowds: 11 ochlophobia
of darkness: 11 nyctophobia
of dirt: 10 mysophobia
of fire: 10 pyrophobia
of heights: 10 acrophobia
of men: 11 androphobia
of new things: 9 neophobia
of open areas: 11 agoraphobia
of pain: 10 algophobia
of strangers: 10 xenophobia
of thunder: 12 brontophobia
of water: 11 hydrophobia
of women: 10 gynophobia

fearful
5 timid **6** afraid, aghast, scared, trepid **7** alarmed, anxious, jittery, panicky **8** alarmist, paranoid, timorous **9** terrified, tremulous **12** apprehensive

fearless
4 bold **5** brave **6** daring **7** gallant, valiant **8** intrepid, unafraid **9** dauntless **10** courageous **11** lionhearted **12** greathearted, stouthearted

Fear of Flying author
4 Jong (Erica)

fearsome
3 shy **5** scary, timid **6** afraid **7** extreme, intense **8** daunting, timorous **9** frightful **10** terrifying **11** frightening **12** intimidating

feasible
6 doable, likely, viable **8** possible, suitable, workable **10** reasonable **11** practicable **12** tried-and-true

feast
3 eat **4** dine, meal **5** gorge **6** dinner, regale, repast, spread **7** banquet, indulge **8** potlatch
Hawaiian: 4 luau
Scottish: 3 foy

Feast of Lights
8 Hanukkah

Feast of Lots
5 Purim

Feast of Tabernacles
6 Sukkot **7** Sukkoth

feat
3 act **4** deed, gest **5** stunt, trick **6** action

7 exploit 11 achievement, performance, tour de force

feather

3 ilk 4 down, kind, sort, type 5 breed, order, pinna, plume, quill 6 fledge, fletch, pinion 7 species, variety
kind: 4 down 6 covert 7 contour, plumule, rectrix 8 scapular
part: 3 web 4 barb, vane 5 shaft 7 barbule, calamus 8 barbicel

featherbrained

5 dizzy, giddy, silly 7 flighty, foolish 8 heedless 9 frivolous 11 light-headed, thoughtless

feathered

7 plumose

feathers

4 down 7 plumage

feature

4 item, mark, part 5 add-on, trait 6 aspect, detail, factor 7 article, element, fixture, gimmick, quality 8 hallmark, property 9 attribute, component, lineament 10 attraction, ingredient 11 drawing card, peculiarity

febrile

3 hot 5 fiery 7 fevered, pyretic 8 feverish

feckless

4 weak 7 useless 8 carefree, impotent 11 incompetent, ineffective, ineffectual 12 undependable 13 irresponsible

fecund

4 rich 7 fertile 8 fruitful, prolific 9 inventive 10 productive

fecundity

9 abundance, fertility 11 prodigality 12 fruitfulness, productivity

Federalist writer

3 Jay (John) 7 Madison (James) 8 Hamilton (Alexander)

federation

5 union 6 league, nation 7 council 8 alliance 10 government 11 confederacy

fed up

4 sick 9 disgusted 11 exasperated

fee

3 cut, pay, tax 4 bill, cost, dues, hire, toll, wage 5 price 6 charge 7 expense, payment, rake-off, stipend, tuition 8 retainer 9 emolument 10 commission, recompense
minting: 10 seignorage 11 seigniorage
wharf: 7 quayage

feeble

4 puny, weak 5 frail 6 infirm, sickly, weakly 7 doddery 8 decrepit 9 doddering, unhealthy 10 inadequate

feebleminded

4 daft, dull, slow 5 dense, thick 6 stupid 7 doltish, foolish, idiotic, moronic, witless 8 imbecile, retarded 9 brainless, dim-witted, imbecilic 10 half-witted, slow-witted 11 harebrained, thickheaded

feebleness

7 frailty 8 debility 9 fragility, infirmity 10 enervation, inadequacy 11 decrepitude

feed

3 eat 4 grub, hand, meal 5 feast, gorge, graze, stuff 6 browse, devour, fatten, fodder, ingest, regale, repast, supply, viands 7 banquet, consume, deliver, dish out, edibles, furnish, nourish, nurture, provide, sustain 8 dispense, hand over, victuals 9 partake of, provender, provision, refection 10 provisions

feedback

8 critique, reaction, response 9 criticism 10 evaluation

feed the kitty

4 ante

feel

5 grope, sense, touch 6 caress, fondle, handle, stroke 7 palpate

feeler

4 palp 5 probe 6 palpus 7 antenna 8 proposal, tentacle 12 trial balloon

feeling

3 air 4 aura, mood 5 hunch, sense, touch 6 notion, temper 7 emotion, inkling, opinion, outlook, passion, sensate 8 attitude, instinct, sentient 9 affection, emotional, intuition, semblance, sensation, sentiment, suspicion 10 atmosphere, impression, persuasion 11 affectivity, palpability, sensibility, sensitivity, tangibility

feign

3 act 4 fake, play, sham 5 bluff, put on 6 affect, assume 7 pretend 8 simulate 9 dissemble 11 counterfeit, make believe

feigned

4 fake, sham 5 false, phony, put-on 7 assumed 8 imagined 9 imitation, insincere, pretended, simulated 10 fabricated, fictitious 11 counterfeit

feint
4 fake, hoax, play, ploy, ruse, sham, wile
5 trick 6 gambit 8 maneuver 9 stratagem
hockey: 4 deke

feisty
6 frisky, plucky, spunky, touchy 7 bristly,
fidgety 8 petulant, snappish, spirited
9 fractious, irascible 10 aggressive
11 quarrelsome

feldspar
6 albite 8 andesine 9 anorthite,
moonstone 10 microcline, orthoclase
11 plagioclase
clay: 6 kaolin

felicitate
6 salute 7 commend 10 compliment
12 congratulate

felicitous
3 apt, fit 4 meet 5 happy 6 proper, timely
7 apropos, fitting 8 apposite, pleasant,
suitable 9 agreeable 10 delightful
11 appropriate

feline
3 cat, sly, tom 4 lion, lynx, pard, puma,
puss 5 catty, felid, pussy, sleek, tiger
6 bobcat, cougar, jaguar, margay, ocelot,
serval, slinky, sneaky, tomcat 7 caracal,
catlike, cheetah, furtive, leonine, leopard,
lioness, panther, tigress, wildcat
8 pussycat, stealthy
hybrid: 5 liger, tigon 6 tiglon

fell
3 cut, hew, mow 4 down, drop, kill, raze
5 floor 6 poleax 7 cut down, flatten
8 knock off 9 bring down, knock down

Fellini film
8 Amarcord, Casanova, La Strada
9 Satyricon 10 I Vitelloni 11 La Dolce Vita
15 Nights of Cabiria 18 Juliet of the Spirits

fellow
3 bub, guy, joe, lad, man 4 buck, chap,
dude, gent, mate, peer, twin 5 bloke,
match 6 codger, cohort, hombre, person
7 comrade, consort, partner 8 confrere
9 associate, companion, copartner,
gentleman 10 coordinate, reciprocal

fellow feeling
5 agape 7 concern, empathy, rapport
8 affinity, kindness, sympathy 9 affection
10 compassion, kindliness 11 consolation
13 understanding

fellowship
4 club 5 guild 6 league 7 coterie, society,

stipend 8 sodality 9 communion,
community 10 fraternity 11 association,
brotherhood

felon
3 con 7 convict, whitlow 8 criminal
10 malefactor

felt
6 groped, sensed

felt hat
3 fez 5 derby, terai 6 fedora, trilby
7 homburg, stetson 8 snap-brim
9 wideawake

female
4 girl 5 woman 7 girlish, womanly
8 feminine
suffix: 3 ess 4 ette, trix

Feminine Mystique author
7 Friedan (Betty)

feminist
10 suffragist

femme fatale
5 siren 7 Lorelei 8 Mata Hari 9 temptress
10 seductress 11 enchantress

femur
9 thighbone

fen
3 bog 4 mire, quag, wash 5 marsh,
swamp 6 morass, muskeg, slough
9 marshland

fence
3 bar, pen 4 cage, rail, pale, weir 5 hedge,
parry 6 corral, paling, picket 7 barrier,
enclose, railing 8 backstop, boundary,
hoarding, palisade, receiver, sidestep,
stockade 9 barricade, stone wall

fencer
7 duelist, épéeist 8 foilsman 9 swordsman

fencing
9 swordplay
attack: 5 lunge 6 thrust 7 reprise, riposte
cry: 6 touché
defense: 5 parry
movement: 4 volt
term: 4 jury 5 forte, lunge 6 flèche, foible,
touché
touch: 3 cut, hit
weapon: 4 épée, foil 5 blade, guard,
saber, sabre 6 pommel

fender
4 skid 5 guard 6 buffer, bumper, shield
7 cushion, railing 8 mudguard

fennec
3 fox

Fenrir
chain: 8 Gleipnir
father: 4 Loki
form: 4 wolf
mother: 9 Angerboda 10 Angerbotha
slayer: 5 Vidar 6 Vithar
victim: 4 Odin

Fenway Park site
6 Boston

feral
4 wild 5 brute 6 brutal, savage 7 beastly,
bestial, brutish, inhuman, untamed

Ferber novel
5 Giant, So Big 8 Cimarron, Show Boat
9 Ice Palace 13 Saratoga Trunk

Ferdinand
beloved: 7 Miranda
father: 6 Alonso

Ferdinand, King
conquest: 7 Granada
daughter: 6 Joanna
wife: 8 Germaine, Isabella

fermata
4 hold 5 pause

ferment
4 boil, brew, stir 5 rouse, sweat 6 clamor,
enzyme, excite, incite, leaven, seethe,
simmer, unrest, work up 7 smolder, turmoil
9 agitation, commotion 12 restlessness

fermentation
7 zymosis 13 bioconversion

fern
4 tree 5 brake, holly, royal 6 Boston
7 bracken 8 polypody 10 maidenhair,
spleenwort
leaf: 5 frond

ferocious
4 fell, grim, wild 5 brute, cruel 6 brutal,
fierce, savage 7 bestial, extreme,
inhuman, intense, vicious, violent
8 barbaric, inhumane, ruthless
9 barbarous, rapacious, truculent

ferret out
4 find 5 dig up, flush 6 elicit 7 unearth
8 discover 9 ascertain

ferrule
3 cap, tip 4 band, ring, virl 6 collet

ferry
5 carry 6 convey 7 shuttle 9 transport

ferryman
6 Charon 9 gondolier

fertile
4 lush, rich 6 fecund 8 abundant, creative,
fruitful, pregnant, prolific 9 bountiful,
ingenious, inventive, luxuriant, plenteous
10 productive 12 reproductive

fertilize
5 beget, breed 6 enrich 8 generate
9 fecundate, pollinate 10 impregnate,
inseminate

fertilizer
4 dung 5 guano, mulch 6 manure
7 compost 9 plant food

ferule
3 rod 5 stick

fervent
3 hot 4 keen 5 eager, fiery 6 ardent,
devout, gung-ho 7 blazing, burning,
earnest, glowing, intense, zealous
8 vehement 9 heartfelt 10 hot-blooded,
passionate 11 impassioned, warm-blooded
12 enthusiastic, wholehearted

fervor
4 fire, heat, zeal 5 ardor 6 warmth
7 passion 8 devotion, violence
9 vehemence 10 devoutness, enthusiasm

fescennine
7 obscene 10 scurrilous

fess up
3 own 5 admit 9 come clean

fester
3 rot 6 rankle 7 inflame, putrefy
8 ulcerate 9 suppurate

festina ____
5 lente

festival
4 fair, fete, gala 5 feast 6 fiesta 7 jubilee
8 carnival, jamboree 11 celebration,
merrymaking

festive
3 gay 4 gala 5 jolly, merry 6 joyful, joyous
7 gleeful 8 mirthful 11 celebratory

festivity
4 bash, fair, fete, gala 5 feast, party, revel
6 affair, frolic, gaiety 7 blowout, revelry,
whoopee 8 carnival, jamboree 9 rejoicing,
merriment 11 celebration, merrymaking

festoon
4 deck, hang 5 adorn 6 bedeck 7 garland
8 decorate, ornament 9 embellish

fetch
3 get 4 draw, earn 5 bring, yield 6 take in
7 attract, bring in, realize 8 retrieve

fetching
4 fair 6 comely, lovely, pretty 7 winsome
8 alluring, charming, enticing, engaging,
handsome, pleasing 9 appealing
10 attractive

fete
4 ball, bash, fair, gala 5 feast, honor, party
6 affair, fiesta, soiree 7 banquet, jubilee,
shindig 8 carnival, festival, jamboree,
wingding 9 celebrate, entertain
11 celebration, commemorate
13 entertainment

fetid
4 foul, high, rank 5 funky 6 putrid, rancid,
smelly, strong 8 mephitic, stinking
10 malodorous

fetish
4 idol, juju, luck 5 charm 6 amulet
7 periapt 8 fixation, gris-gris, talisman
10 phylactery

fetor
4 odor, reek 5 stink 6 stench

fetter
3 tie 4 bind, bond, gyve 5 chain, check,
irons 6 hobble, hog-tie, impede 7 enchain,
manacle, shackle, trammel 8 handcuff,
restrain 9 restraint

fettle
5 shape 6 health 7 fitness 9 condition
12 constitution

feud
6 enmity, strife 7 dispute, quarrel
8 argument, vendetta 9 hostility
11 controversy

feudal
estate: 3 fee 4 feud, fief
jurisdiction: 4 soke
laborer: 4 serf
lord: 5 laird, liege, thane 8 suzerain
status: 9 vassalage
tax: 7 tallage
tenant: 6 vassal 7 homager, socager,
vavasor 8 vavasour
tenure of land: 6 socage
tribute: 6 heriot

feuilleton
5 essay

fever
4 ague, fire, heat 5 flush, Lassa 6 dengue,

frenzy 7 ferment, passion, pyrexia
8 delirium 9 calenture
recurrent: 7 malaria, quartan, tertian

fevered
6 crazed, heated 7 burning, febrile, flushed
8 agitated, frenetic, restless 9 delirious
10 distracted, overheated 11 overwrought

feverish
3 hot 5 fiery 6 hectic 7 burning, febrile,
flushed, pyretic 8 frenetic, frenzied
10 passionate 11 overwrought

fever tree
6 acacia 8 blue gum

few
4 rare 6 meager, meagre, scant, scarce,
sparse 7 handful, limited, scanty, smatter,
spatter 8 sporadic, uncommon 9 scattered
10 infrequent, occasional, scattering,
smattering, spattering, sprinkling

fey
4 daft 5 campy, crazy, vatic 7 touched
8 oracular, precious 9 pixilated, prophetic,
sibylline, visionary 11 clairvoyant
12 otherworldly

———-fi
3 sci

fiasco
3 dud 4 bomb, flop 5 farce, flask 6 bottle,
defeat 7 blunder, debacle, failure, washout
8 abortion, disaster 11 miscarriage
13 embarrassment

fiat
5 edict, order 6 decree 7 command,
dictate, mandate, warrant 8 sanction
11 endorsement 12 proclamation
13 authorization

fib
3 lie 4 tale 5 story 7 falsify, falsity, untruth
9 falsehood, mendacity 10 taradiddle
11 fabrication, prevaricate

fiber
3 web 4 noil, pita 5 grain, istle 6 fabric,
strand, thread 7 texture
basketry: 5 istle
brain: 4 pons
coarse: 4 jute 8 piassava
coconut husk: 4 coir
rope: 4 bast, hemp 5 sisal 8 henequen
silky: 5 kapok
small: 6 fibril
substructure: 7 micelle, spongin
synthetic: 5 nylon, Orlon, rayon, saran,
vinal 6 Dacron 7 spandex

woody: 4 bast
woollike: 7 lanital

fibrous
4 ropy, wiry 5 tough, woody 6 sinewy
7 stringy

fibula
4 bone 5 clasp

fichu
5 scarf

fickle
7 flighty 8 unstable, variable, volatile
9 mercurial 10 capricious, changeable,
inconstant, unfaithful, unreliable
12 undependable 13 temperamental,
unpredictable

fiction
4 tale, yarn 5 fable, story 7 fantasy,
figment 8 pretense 9 fish story, invention,
narrative 10 concoction 11 fabrication

fictional
6 made-up, unreal 8 notional 9 imaginary
11 make-believe 12 suppositious

fictitious
4 fake, mock, sham 5 bogus, faked, false,
phony 6 ersatz, made-up, unreal, untrue
7 assumed, created 8 cooked-up, fanciful,
illusory, imagined, invented, mythical,
spurious 9 concocted, fantastic, imaginary,
simulated, trumped-up 10 apocryphal,
artificial, chimerical, fabricated 11 make-
believe 12 suppositious

fiddle
3 toy 4 play, rack 5 alter, cheat 6 dawdle,
diddle, doodle, finger, meddle, monkey,
potter, putter, tamper, tinker, trifle, violin
7 swindle 9 interfere 10 fool around,
manipulate, mess around

fiddle-faddle
3 rot 4 bosh, bull, bunk, nuts 5 fudge,
drool, hooey 6 bunkum, drivel, hokum,
hoodoo, humbug, piffle 7 baloney, blarney,
hogwash, rubbish, twaddle 8 nonsense,
pishposh, tommyrot 9 poppycock
10 applesauce, balderdash, flapdoodle

_____ Fideles
6 Adeste, Semper

Fidelio
composer: 9 Beethoven (Ludwig van)
hero: 9 Florestan
heroine: 7 Leonora

fidelity
5 ardor, piety, troth 6 fealty 7 loyalty
8 devotion 9 adherence, constancy

10 allegiance, attachment 11 staunchness
12 faithfulness 13 dependability,
steadfastness

fidget
6 fantod, fiddle, jitter, squirm, twitch
7 wriggle

fidgety
5 antsy, jumpy 6 uneasy 7 jittery, nervous,
restive, squirmy, twitchy 8 restless

field
3 lea 4 area, mead, turf 5 green, milpa,
orbit, range 6 domain, meadow, métier,
region, sphere 7 demesne, pasture,
purview, terrain 8 dominion, gridiron,
precinct, vocation 9 bailiwick, champaign,
specialty, territory 10 department,
discipline, occupation

field crop
3 hay 4 corn, oats 5 grain, wheat 6 cotton
7 alfalfa 8 soybeans

field deity
3 Pan 4 Faun 5 Fauna 6 Faunus

field glasses
10 binoculars

field hand
4 hoer 5 sower 6 picker 7 laborer, planter

Fielding novel
6 Amelia 8 Tom Jones 13 Joseph
Andrews

field marshal
Austrian: 8 Radetzky (Joseph)
British: 6 Napier (Robert), Raglan
(Baron), Wavell (Archibald), Wilson (Henry)
7 Roberts (Frederick) 8 Wolseley (Garnet)
9 Kitchener (Horatio) 10 Montgomery
(Bernard)
French: 4 Foch (Ferdinand) 6 Joffre
(Joseph-Jacques-Césaire), Pétain
(Philippe)
German: 6 Keitel (Wilhelm), Paulus
(Friedrich), Rommel (Erwin), Rupert
(Prince) 9 Mackensen (August von),
Rundstedt (Karl von), Waldersee (Alfred
von) 10 Kesselring (Albert)
Japanese: 8 Sugiyama (Hajime)
Prussian: 6 Moltke (Helmuth von)
Russian: 7 Kutuzov (Mikhail), Suvorov
(Aleksandr) 8 Potemkin (Grigory)

field mouse
4 vole

field officer
5 major 7 colonel

fiend

3 bug, imp, nut 5 demon, devil, freak, Satan 6 addict, Belial, diablo, maniac, zealot 7 devotee, fanatic, habitué, Lucifer, monster, Old Nick, serpent 8 Apollyon, succubus 9 Beelzebub 10 enthusiast, Old Scratch 13 Old Gooseberry

fiendish

3 bad 4 evil 5 cruel 6 malign, savage, wicked 7 baleful, demonic, hellish, inhuman, malefic, satanic, vicious 8 demoniac, devilish, diabolic, infernal, sinister 9 barbarous, difficult, ferocious, malicious, malignant 10 diabolical

fierce

4 fell, grim, wild 5 cruel 6 brutal, savage 7 brutish, hostile, inhuman, intense, vicious, violent, wicked, wolfish 8 inhumane, pitiless, ruthless, terrible, vehement 9 barbarous, bellicose, ferocious, merciless, truculent 10 aggressive, determined

fiery

3 hot, red 5 afire 6 ablaze, aflame, ardent, fervid, fierce, heated, red-hot, torrid 7 burning, febrile, fervent, flaming, flaring, igneous, intense, peppery 8 broiling, feverish, spirited, vehement, white-hot 9 flammable, hotheaded, irritable, perfervid 10 mettlesome, passionate 11 combustible, inflammable, impassioned

fiesta

4 fete 5 party 6 frolic 8 carnival, festival, jamboree 9 merriment

fife

4 pipe 5 flute

fifth

combining form: 5 quint

fig

genus: 5 Ficus
sacred: 5 pipal
variety: 5 elemi 6 Smyrna

fight

3 row, war 4 bout, buck, duel, feud, fray, spat, tiff 5 brawl, broil, clash, joust, match, melee, repel, scrap, set-to 6 affray, attack, battle, combat, fracas, oppose, oppugn, resist, rumble, tussle 7 contend, contest, dispute, quarrel, scuffle, wrangle, wrestle 8 conflict, skirmish, slugfest, squabble, struggle, traverse 10 aggression, donnybrook, free-for-all 11 altercation

fighter

3 pug 5 boxer 7 brawler, soldier, warrior 8 champion, gladiator, pugilist, scrapper 9 combatant, man-at-arms, mercenary 11 interceptor

fighter plane

3 MiG, Roc 4 Zero 5 Sabre 6 bomber, Fokker, Hawker, Mirage, Voodoo 7 Corsair, Harrier 8 Spitfire 11 interceptor

fighting fish

5 betta

figment

5 dream, fable, fancy 7 chimera, fiction 8 daydream, illusion, phantasm 9 invention, unreality 11 contrivance, fabrication

figure

3 add, sum, tot 4 cast, form, mold, rule, tote 5 count, digit, frame, image, model, motif, shape, total 6 cipher, decide, design, device, effigy, motive, number, reckon, settle, symbol 7 compute, integer, numeral, outline, pattern, resolve 8 conclude, estimate, physique 9 calculate, character, determine, enumerate
geometric: 4 cone, cube 5 rhomb 6 circle, isogon, square 7 decagon, ellipse, hexagon, nonagon, octagon, polygon, rhombus 8 pentacle, pentagon, rhomboid, tetragon, triangle 9 rectangle 10 hexahedron, octahedron 11 icosahedron 12 dodecahedron, rhombohedron
human: 4 nude 5 atlas 7 telamon 8 caryatid
ornamental: 6 statue 8 gargoyle

figurehead

4 pawn, tool 5 front 6 minion, puppet 7 cat's-paw 8 creature 10 instrument, mouthpiece

figure of speech

5 trope 6 aporia, simile 7 litotes 8 metaphor, metonymy 10 synecdoche

figure out

5 crack, learn, solve 6 decide, decode, fathom 7 resolve, unravel 8 decipher, discover, unriddle 9 ascertain, determine

figure skating

jump: 4 axel, loop, lutz 5 split 6 rocker 7 bracket, counter, salchow 11 spreadeagle
spin: 5 camel

figurine

9 statuette

Fiji

capital: 4 Suva

explorer: 4 Cook (Capt. James)
6 Tasman (Abel)
island: 3 Gau 4 Koro 6 Ovalau 8 Viti
Levu 9 Vanua Levu
island group: 3 Lau 6 Yasawa
language: 6 Fijian 7 English
monetary unit: 6 dollar
neighbor: 5 Samoa 7 Vanuatu

filch
3 cop, nip 4 crib, lift, take 5 boost, pinch,
steal, swipe 6 pilfer, snitch 7 purloin

file
3 row, rub 4 line, rank, rasp, tier 5 lodge,
march, place, queue 6 smooth 7 archive,
arrange, corrupt, dossier 10 emery board

filial
5 sonly 7 duteous, dutiful

filibuster
5 delay, stall 10 adventurer

filigree
4 lace 6 design 7 pattern 8 fretwork,
openwork, ornament 10 decoration
13 embellishment, ornamentation

fill
3 jam 4 clog, cloy, cram, glut, heap, lade,
load, pack, pile, plug, sate, stop 5 block,
choke, close, gorge, stock, stuff 6 charge,
stodge 7 congest, engorge, inflate,
occlude, pervade, satiate, satisfy, stopper,
surfeit 8 permeate
interstices: 4 calk 5 caulk, chink, putty

filled
5 awash, flush, sated 6 packed 7 replete
9 saturated

filler
5 squib 7 packing, padding, stuffing,
tobacco, wadding

fillet
4 band 5 slice, snood, strip 6 ribbon, stripe
7 bandeau, banding 8 headband
anatomical: 9 lemniscus
architectural: 6 listel, reglet, taenia
meat: 10 tenderloin

fill in
3 sub 4 clew, clue, post 6 advise, detail,
insert, notify 7 apprise 8 acquaint,
complete 10 substitute

fill-in
3 sub 4 temp 6 backup 7 stopgap
9 alternate, expedient, makeshift,
surrogate, temporary 10 substitute
11 locum tenens, pinch hitter, replacement,
succedaneum

fillip
3 tap 4 goad, kick, spur 5 boost, tonic
6 buffet, strike 7 impetus, wrinkle
8 catalyst, stimulus 9 incentive, stimulant,
stimulate 10 inducement, motivation
13 embellishment

film
4 coat, scum, show, skim, skin 5 flick,
glaze, layer, movie, Mylar, shoot 6 cinema,
lamina, patina 7 tarnish 8 membrane,
pellicle 9 celluloid, photoplay 11 picture
show 13 motion picture, moving picture

filmy
4 hazy 5 gauzy, misty, sheer, wispy
6 dainty 8 delicate, gossamer
10 diaphanous 11 transparent

fils
3 son

filter
4 sift 5 clean, leach, sieve 6 purify, refine,
screen, strain 7 clarify, cleanse
9 percolate

filth
4 crud, dirt, dung, muck, slop, smut
5 dreck, grime, slime, trash 6 ordure,
refuse, sludge 7 squalor 9 obscenity

filthy
4 base, foul, vile 5 black, dirty, grimy,
gross, gunky, mucky, muddy, nasty
6 coarse, cruddy, grubby, ribald, scuzzy,
skanky, smutty, sordid 7 obscene, raunchy,
squalid, unclean 8 indecent 9 loathsome,
offensive, repulsive, revolting
12 scatological

filthy lucre
4 cash, loot, pelf 5 bread, bucks, dough,
money, moola 6 boodle, riches, moolah,
wampum 7 cabbage, scratch 8 currency

fin
3 arm 4 bill 5 fiver, pinna 7 airfoil, flipper
type: 6 caudal, dorsal 7 ventral
8 pectoral

finagle
5 cheat, trick 6 wangle 7 snaffle, swindle,
wheedle 8 fast-talk, maneuver, scrounge
9 bamboozle, machinate

final
3 end 4 last 6 ending, latest 7 closing
8 hindmost, terminal, ultimate
10 concluding, conclusive, definitive
11 examination

finale
3 end 4 coda 5 close, finis 6 capper,

climax, ending, payoff, windup, wrap-up **7** closing **10** conclusion, denouement **11** culmination, termination

finalize
3 end **5** close, sew up, tie up **6** decide, finish, wind up, wrap up **7** approve **8** complete, conclude, solidify **9** terminate **10** consummate

finally
6 at last, lastly **7** someday **8** at length **9** belatedly **10** at long last, eventually, ultimately **12** subsequently

finance
4 back, bank, fund **5** endow, funds, money, stake **6** credit **7** banking, promote, revenue, sponsor, support **8** bankroll **9** grubstake, patronize, subsidize **10** capitalize, investment, underwrite

financial
6 fiscal, pocket **8** business, economic, monetary **9** pecuniary **10** commercial
plan: **6** budget
statement: **12** balance sheet

financier
American: **4** Hill (James Jerome), Ryan (Thomas Fortune), Sage (Russell) **5** Astor (John Jacob), Baker (George Fisher), Eaton (Cyrus), Field (Cyrus West), Gould (Jay), Grace (William Russell), Green (Hetty) **6** Biddle (Nicholas), Boesky (Ivan), Girard (Stephen), Mellon (Andrew), Morgan (John Pierpont, Junius Spencer), Morris (Robert), Rogers (Henry Huttleston), Yerkes (Charles Tyson) **7** Peabody (George) **10** Vanderbilt (Cornelius, William)
British: **6** Baring (Alexander), Rhodes (Cecil) **7** Gresham (Thomas)
French: **6** Necker (Jacques) **7** Colbert (Jean-Baptiste)
German: **7** Schacht (Hjalmar) **10** Rothschild (Amschel, Jakob, Karl, Mayer, Nathan, Salomon)

finch
4 pape **5** junco, serin, zebra **6** canary, linnet, siskin, towhee **7** bunting, chewink, redpoll, sparrow **8** cardinal, grosbeak, longspur **9** crossbill, seedeater

find
3 gem **4** gain, meet, spot **5** catch, dig up, hit on, reach, sight **6** attain, detect, locate, supply, turn up **7** discern, furnish, scare up, uncover, unearth **8** bump into, come upon, discover, meet with, perceive,

treasure **9** determine, discovery, encounter **10** experience **13** treasure trove

find out
4 hear **5** catch, learn **6** detect **7** catch on **8** discover, perceive **9** ascertain, determine

fine
3 end, top **4** fair, keen, levy, pure, thin **5** bonny, close, clear, dandy, mulct, sheer **6** amerce, choice, minute, ornate, punish, purify, subtle **7** clarion, damages, elegant, forfeit, penalty **8** all right, delicate, penalize, pleasant, splendid, superior **9** beautiful, enjoyable, excellent, first-rate **10** punishment, reparation

finery
5 array **6** attire **7** apparel, regalia **8** clothing, frippery, glad rags, ornament **9** caparison, full dress, trappings, trimmings **10** decoration, Sunday best

finesse
5 dodge, evade, skill, skirt **6** jockey **7** beguile, cunning, exploit **8** maneuver, subtlety **9** dexterity **10** adroitness, artfulness, manipulate

Fingal's Cave island
6 Staffa

finger
5 blame, digit, index, pinky, strum, touch **6** accuse, pinkie **7** palpate **8** identify, pinpoint
bone: **7** phalanx **9** phalanges (plural)

finicky
5 fussy, picky **6** choosy, dainty, prissy **7** choosey **8** exacting **9** squeamish **10** fastidious, meticulous, particular, pernickety **11** persnickety

finis
3 end **5** close **6** finale **10** completion, conclusion

finish
3 end **4** do in, kill, slay, stop **5** cease, close, glaze, use up **6** cut off, ending, finale, murder, patina, polish, windup, wrap up **7** closing, consume, destroy, execute, exhaust, surface **8** complete, conclude, dispatch, finalize, terminus **9** cessation, liquidate, terminate **10** completion, conclusion, denouement, run through **11** termination
dull: **3** mat **4** matt **5** matte
second: **5** place
third: **4** show

finished
4 done, over, ripe 5 ideal 7 done for, perfect, refined, through 8 achieved, complete, over with, polished, washed-up 9 perfected 10 consummate

finite
5 bound, fixed 7 bounded, limited, precise 9 definable 10 restricted 12 determinable

fink
3 rat 5 Judas 6 betray, snitch, squeal 7 traitor 8 betrayer, informer, quisling, snitcher 11 backstabber 13 strikebreaker

Finland
5 Suomi
Arctic region: 7 Lapland
capital: 8 Helsinki
city: 5 Turku 6 Espoo, Vantaa 7 Tampere
ethnic group: 4 Lapp, Sami
gulf: 7 Bothnia
invader: 9 Alexander
island: 5 Karlö 6 Kimito 9 Vallgrund
island group: 5 Åland
lake: 5 Inari 6 Saimaa 7 Keitele
8 Pielinen
language: 7 Finnish, Swedish
monetary unit: 4 euro
monetary unit, former: 6 markka
neighbor: 6 Norway, Russia, Sweden

Finlandia composer
8 Sibelius (Jean)

Finnigans Wake author
5 Joyce (James)

Finnish
bath: 5 sauna
epic: 8 Kalevala
god: 6 Jumala

fir
4 pine 6 balsam, Fraser 7 conifer, Douglas 9 evergreen
genus: 5 Abies

fire
3 can, pep, vim, zip 4 bake, brio, burn, cast, dash, hurl, sack, stir, toss, zeal, zest, zing 5 ardor, blaze, drive, flame, flare, fling, glare, ingle, light, pitch, rouse, salvo, shoot, spark, throw, torch, verve, vigor 6 arouse, energy, excite, fervor, flames, ignite, kindle, spirit 7 animate, boot out, dismiss, enthuse, inferno, inflame, inspire, kick out, passion, provoke 8 enkindle 9 calenture, discharge, holocaust, terminate 10 combustion, enthusiasm, liveliness 13 conflagration
combining form: 3 pyr 4 igni, pyro

god:
4 Agni, Loki 6 Vulcan 10 Hephaestus

firearm
see **gun**

firebrand
8 agitator 10 incendiary, instigator

firebug
5 torch 8 arsonist 10 incendiary, pyromaniac

firecracker
5 squib 6 banger 9 explosive 10 cherry bomb, noisemaker

firedog
7 andiron

firedrake
6 dragon

firefly
12 lightning bug

fire opal
7 girasol

fireplace
5 grate, ingle
equipment: 6 fender, screen 7 andiron
part: 3 hob 6 hearth, mantel

fireplug
7 hydrant

fire up
5 anger, annoy, rouse, spark 6 excite, ignite, incite, kindle 7 enliven, inflame, inspire, provoke 8 enkindle, irritate

firework
6 petard, rocket 8 pinwheel, sparkler 11 pyrotechnic, Roman candle
cluster: 9 girandole

firkin
3 keg, tun, vat 4 butt, cask, pipe 6 barrel, vessel 8 hogshead

firm
3 set 4 fast, hard, sure 5 fixed, rigid, solid, sound, stiff, tight, tough 6 harden, outfit, secure, settle, stable, steady, strong, sturdy 7 abiding, adamant, certain, company, concern, improve, settled, staunch, unmoved 8 business, constant, definite, enduring, faithful, resolute, specific, vigorous 9 steadfast, tenacious 10 determined, enterprise, inflexible, stipulated, strengthen, unwavering, unyielding 11 established, partnership, substantial, unfaltering, well-founded 13 establishment

firmament
3 sky 5 vault 6 welkin 7 expanse, heavens, sphere 8 empyrean

firmness
7 resolve 8 decision, security, solidity, strength, tenacity 9 constancy, stability 10 durability, resolution 13 determination

first
4 arch, head 5 alpha, chief, prime 6 maiden, primal 7 highest, initial, leading, lead-off, opening, pioneer, premier, primary, supreme 8 champion, dominant, earliest, foremost, headmost, original 9 inaugural, initially, paramount, principal, sovereign 10 aboriginal, preeminent, primordial **prefix:** 4 prot 5 proto

firstborn
4 heir 6 eldest, oldest

first-class
3 top 4 A-one, best, fine 5 prime 6 tip-top 7 capital, supreme 8 five-star, superior, top-notch 9 excellent, top-drawer

firsthand
6 direct 7 primary 9 immediate

first man in space
7 Gagarin (Yury)

first showing
5 debut 7 opening 8 premiere

First State
8 Delaware

firth
3 arm, bay 4 cove, gulf 5 inlet 6 harbor, slough 7 estuary

fiscal
8 monetary 9 budgetary, financial

fish
3 bob, net 4 cast, gill, hint 5 angle, seine, trawl, troll 7 gillnet, sniggle
angler: 9 goosefish
aquarium: 4 barb 5 betta, danio, guppy, platy, tetra 7 cichlid, gourami, rasbora 8 goldfish 9 angelfish
basket: 5 creel
catfish: 8 bullhead, hornpout
cod: 4 cusk, hake, ling 6 burbot, tomcod 7 pollack, pollock
croaker: 4 drum 7 corbina 8 kingfish, sea trout, weakfish 10 squeteague
eellike: 5 moray 6 conger 7 hagfish, lamprey

eggs: 3 roe 5 spawn
electric: 7 torpedo 9 stargazer
flatfish: 3 dab 4 butt, dace, sole 5 bream, brill, fluke 6 plaice, turbot 7 halibut 8 flounder
food: 3 cod, eel 4 bass, carp, cero, hake, ling, scup, shad, sole, tuna 5 jurel, perch, scrod, skate, smelt, trout 6 bonito, caviar, kipper, mullet, plaice, pompon, salmon, tautog, wrasse 7 alewife, catfish, cavalla, escolar, grouper, haddock, halibut, herring, pollack, pollock, pompano, sardine, sea carp, snapper 8 brisling, crevalle, flounder, mackerel 9 barracuda
game: 4 bass, pike, tuna 5 cobia, perch, trout 6 grilse, marlin, salmon, tarpon 8 pickerel 9 swordfish
grunt: 7 pigfish
herring: 4 shad, sild 5 sprat 7 alewife, sardine 8 brisling, pilchard
kind: 3 gar, ray 4 bass, cero, chub, dory, goby, jack, opah, pike, rudd, scup, tuna 5 bream, cisco, loach, perch, porgy, shark, skate, smelt, snook, tench, tuna, wahoo 6 blenny, bonito, dorado, marlin, minnow, mullet, permit, puffer, remora, sauger, sucker, tarpon, tautog, warsaw, wrasse 7 anchovy, buffalo, capelin, cavalla, chimera, cowfish, crappie, dolphin, grunion, haddock, hogfish, jewfish, mudfish, oarfish, piranha, pupfish, sardine, sawfish, sculpin, snapper, sunfish, tilapia, whiting 8 albacore, blowfish, bluefish, bluegill, bonefish, chimaera, filefish, gambusia, grayling, halfbeak, ladyfish, lookdown, lumpfish, lungfish, mackerel, menhaden, moonfish, pickerel, pipefish, rockfish, sailfish, seahorse, skipjack, stingray, sturgeon, tilefish, warmouth, wolffish 9 amberjack, barracuda, greenling, jacksmelt, killifish, mummichog, pilotfish, spadefish, swordfish, topminnow, trunkfish, whitebait, whitefish 10 butterfish, flying fish, needlefish, parrotfish, silverside, tripletail, yellowtail 11 muskellunge, pumpkinseed, stickleback, triggerfish 12 schoolmaster
luminescent: 11 hatchetfish, lanternfish
minnow: 3 koi 4 carp, chub, dace 6 shiner
pan: 5 bream, perch, trout 7 crappie, sunfish 8 bluegill, rock bass 11 pumpkinseed
porgy: 4 scup 7 pinfish 10 sheepshead
relating to: 7 piscine
rockfish: 8 bocaccio, lionfish, rosefish
salmon: 3 dog 4 chum, coho 6 sebago 7 chinook, sockeye
spear: 3 gig 7 harpoon, trident

stew: 8 cioppino, matelote 13 bouillabaisse
trap: 4 weir
trout: 4 char 5 charr 7 rainbow 9 cutthroat 11 Dolly Varden
voracious: 6 caribe 7 piranha
young: 3 fry 4 parr 5 larva, smolt 6 alevin, grilse

fisherman
6 angler

fish hawk
6 osprey

fishhook
adjunct: 5 snell
part: 4 barb 5 shank

fishing line
4 trot 7 setline 8 longline, trotline
float: 3 bob 5 quill
leader: 5 snell

fishing lure
3 fly 4 bait 5 spoon 7 spinner

fishing net
5 seine, trawl

fishlike mammal
4 orca 5 whale 6 dugong, sea cow 7 dolphin, grampus, manatee, narwhal 8 cetacean, porpoise

fish story
3 fib, lie 4 bunk, yarn 11 fabrication 12 exaggeration 13 overstatement

fishwife
5 harpy, scold, shrew, vixen 6 virago 9 termagant, Xanthippe

fishy
7 dubious, suspect 8 doubtful, unlikely 9 ambiguous, dubitable, equivocal, uncertain 10 suspicious 11 problematic 12 questionable

fission element
7 uranium 9 plutonium

fissure
3 gap 4 gash, hole, part, rent, rift 5 break, chasm, chink, cleft, crack, split 6 breach, cleave, discord, divide, schism 7 crevice, opening, rupture 8 crevasse, fracture 10 disharmony, separation

fist
4 duke, grip, hand 5 clamp, grasp 6 clench, clinch, clutch

fit
3 apt, set 4 hale, jibe, just, sane, suit, turn 5 adapt, agree, frame, ready, sound, spasm, spell, tally, throe 6 access, accord, adjust, attack, become, belong, decent, go with, proper, seemly, square, tailor, useful 7 capable, conform, healthy, prepare, qualify, seizure, tantrum 8 assemble, decorous, dovetail, eligible, paroxysm, suitable 9 agree with, congruous, consonant, harmonize, reconcile 10 applicable, convenient, correspond, felicitous, go together 11 accommodate, appropriate

fitful
6 random, spotty 7 erratic 8 periodic, sporadic, variable 9 haphazard, hit-or-miss, irregular, spasmodic, uncertain 10 changeable, convulsive, herky-jerky, inconstant 12 intermittent

fitness
4 trim 5 order, shape 6 fettle, health, kilter, repair 7 account, decorum, service, utility 8 capacity 9 condition, propriety, relevance 11 eligibility, suitability 13 applicability

fit out
3 arm, rig 5 equip 6 outfit 7 appoint, furnish 8 accouter, accoutre

fitting
3 apt, due 4 able, just, meet, part, true 5 happy 6 proper, right, seemly 7 apropos, germane 8 apposite, relevant, suitable 9 accessory, befitting, pertinent, qualified 10 applicable, attachment, felicitous, harmonious 11 appropriate

fit together
4 hook, join, mesh 6 hook up 7 connect 8 dovetail 9 integrate

Fitzgerald novel
10 Last Tycoon (The) 11 Great Gatsby (The) 16 Tender Is the Night 17 Tales of the Jazz Age 18 This Side of Paradise 17 All the Sad Young Men 21 Beautiful and the Damned (The)

five
combining form: 4 pent 5 penta 6 quinqu 7 quinque
group of: 6 pentad 7 quintet

five-dollar bill
3 fin

fivefold
9 quintuple

Five Nations
8 Iroquois
member: 7 Cayugas, Mohawks, Oneidas, Senecas 9 Onondagas

five-sided figure
8 pentagon

five-star
6 deluxe, superb 8 superior, top-notch
9 excellent, first-rate 10 first-class
11 outstanding

five-year period
6 luster, lustre 7 lustrum

fix
3 jam, rig, set 4 cook, cure, geld, mend, mess, moor, root, spay, spot, work 5 affix, alter, catch, patch, ready, renew, rivet, solve, state, stick 6 adjust, anchor, assign, attach, change, decide, doctor, fasten, neuter, pickle, plight, repair, revamp, scrape, secure, settle, square, steady
7 appoint, arrange, correct, dilemma, resolve, restore, specify, work out
8 castrate, discover, overhaul, position, renovate, solution 9 condition, establish, stabilize, sterilize 11 predicament

fixation
5 craze, mania 6 fetish 9 obsession
11 fascination, infatuation

_____ fixe
4 idée, prix

fixed
3 pat, set 4 fast, firm, sure 6 frozen, secure, stable, stated, steady 7 abiding, certain, limited, precise, settled 8 constant, definite, enduring, immobile, resolute
9 exclusive, immovable, immutable, permanent, steadfast, tenacious
10 inflexible, invariable, restricted, stationary, stipulated, unswerving, unwavering 11 determinate, unalterable
12 concentrated, unchangeable 13 circumscribed

fizz
4 buzz, foam, hiss 5 froth 6 bubble, spirit
7 bubbles, sparkle, sputter 10 effervesce, liveliness 13 effervescence

fizzle
4 bomb, fail, flop 6 fiasco 7 failure, misfire
8 miscarry, peter out 10 effervesce 11 fall through

fjord
Baffin Island: 9 Admiralty

Denmark: 3 Ise, Lim 5 Lamme
Iceland: 4 Axar, Eyja 5 Horna, Skaga, Vopna
Norway: 3 Tys 4 Bokn, Nord, Salt, Stor, Tana, Vest 5 Lakse, Ranen, Sogne
9 Stavanger, Trondheim
Spitsbergen: 3 Ice
Svalbard: 4 Stor

flab
3 fat 4 bulk, lard 5 flesh 7 blubber, fatness 9 cellulite 10 corpulence 11 love handles

flabbergast
3 awe 4 stun 5 amaze, shock, throw
7 astound, nonplus 8 astonish, bowl over, surprise 9 dumbfound, overwhelm

flabby
see **flaccid**

flaccid
4 limp, soft, weak 6 feeble, flabby, flexible, floppy

flag
3 ebb, lag, sag, tag 4 fade, fail, hail, iris, jack, sign, swag, tail, tire, waft, wane, wave, wilt 5 abate, color, droop, stone
6 banner, burgee, colors, ensign, guidon, pennon, signal, weaken 7 bunting, decline, pendant, pennant 8 bannerol, gonfalon, languish, Old Glory, penalize, registry, standard, streamer, tricolor 9 banderole, blue peter, oriflamme, Union Jack 10 Jolly Roger 11 deteriorate, Stars and Bars

flagellate
4 beat, flog, hide, lash, whip 5 whale
6 larrup, lather, stripe, switch, thrash
7 scourge 9 horsewhip

flagitious
4 evil 6 sinful, wicked 7 corrupt, vicious
8 criminal, depraved, infamous, perverse, shameful 9 miscreant, nefarious, perverted
10 degenerate, scandalous, villainous
11 disgraceful

flagon
3 jug 4 ewer 5 stoup 6 vessel 7 tankard

flagpole
4 mast 5 staff
rope: 7 halyard

flagrant
4 bold, rank 5 gross 6 wanton 7 blatant, glaring, heinous, obvious 8 striking
9 atrocious, egregious, monstrous
10 outrageous 11 conspicuous

flagstone
5 shale, slate

flag-waver
7 patriot 8 jingoist, loyalist 10 chauvinist
11 nationalist 12 superpatriot

flail
4 club, beat, flog, whip 6 strike, thrash,
thresh 7 scourge 8 flounder, thresher

flair
4 bent, chic, élan, gift 5 knack, style
6 genius, talent 7 ability, aptness, faculty
8 aptitude, tendency 10 proclivity
11 inclination

flak
4 fire 5 abuse 6 shells 7 censure, vitriol
9 brickbats, criticism, hostility
10 opposition 11 disapproval 12 condemnation, fault-finding

flake
3 bit 4 chip, kook, peel 5 scale 6 lamina
7 oddball 8 crackpot, fragment 9 eccentric

flake off
4 chip, peel 5 scale 9 exfoliate
10 desquamate

flaky
3 odd 5 goofy, nutty, wacky, weird 6 fickle,
screwy 7 bizarre, erratic, offbeat
9 eccentric

flambé
6 ablaze, aflame, alight 7 blazing, flaming

flamboyant
4 loud 5 gaudy, showy 6 flashy, florid,
ornate, rococo 7 baroque, splashy
8 colorful, luscious 10 over-the-top
12 ostentatious

flame
4 beau, dear, fire, glow, love 5 ardor,
blaze, flare, flash, honey, light, lover
7 beloved, darling, passion, sweetie
8 ladylove, truelove 9 boyfriend,
inamorata, inamorato 10 brilliance,
brightness, girlfriend, heartthrob,
sweetheart

flamen
6 priest

flaming
5 afire, fiery 6 ablaze, alight, ardent, red-
hot 7 blazing, burning, fervent, flaring,
ignited, intense 10 hot-blooded,
passionate 11 conflagrant, impassioned

flammable
8 burnable 9 ignitable 10 incendiary
11 combustible
liquid: 3 gas, oil 7 acetone, alcohol,
ethanol 8 gasoline, kerosene 9 petroleum
10 turpentine

Flanders
capital: 5 Lille
language: 7 Flemish

flaneur
12 boulevardier, man-about-town

flank
4 abut, side 6 adjoin, border

flap
3 tab, tap 4 beat, flog, fold, slap, stew,
wave, wing 5 fling, panel 6 crisis, dither,
lather, pother, tumult, uproar 7 aileron,
flutter, turmoil 9 agitation, commotion,
confusion

flapdoodle
3 rot 4 bosh, bull, nuts 5 drool, fudge,
hokum, hooey 6 bunkum, drivel 7 baloney,
blarney, hogwash, rubbish 8 malarkey,
nonsense, tommyrot 9 poppycock
10 applesauce, balderdash
12 blatherskite, fiddle-faddle, fiddlesticks

flapjack
7 hotcake, pancake 11 griddle cake

flare
4 burn 5 blaze, burst, flame, flash 6 signal
7 flicker 8 outburst

flare-up
5 blaze, burst, flame, flash, surge
8 eruption, outburst 9 explosion

flaring
5 afire, fiery 6 ablaze, aflame, alight
7 blazing, burning 11 conflagrant

flash
3 ray 4 beam, rush, snap, show 5 blaze,
blink, crack, flame, flare, glare, gleam, glint,
jiffy, shake, shine, showy, spark, speed
6 dazzle, expose, flaunt, glance, minute,
moment, second 7 display, disport, exhibit,
flicker, glamour, glimmer, glisten, glitter,
instant, pizzazz, shimmer, show off,
spangle, sparkle, twinkle 8 brandish
9 coruscate 11 coruscation, scintillate, split
second 13 scintillation

flashy
4 loud 5 gaudy, jazzy, showy 6 brazen,
florid, garish, glitzy, ornate, snazzy, sporty,
tawdry, tinsel 7 blatant, chintzy, glaring,

insipid **9** sparkling **10** flamboyant, glittering **12** meretricious, ostentatious

flask
6 bottle, fiasco, flacon **7** ampulla, canteen, costrel, thermos

flat
3 dim, mat **4** dead, drab, dull, even **5** banal, bland, exact, fixed, flush, level, muted, plane, prone, rooms, stale, vapid **7** insipid, prosaic **8** lodgings, tenement, unsavory **9** apartment, colorless, innocuous **10** flavorless, lackluster, monotonous

flatfish
see at **fish**

flatland
4 mesa **5** plain **6** steppe, tundra **7** plateau **9** tableland

flat-out
8 absolute **9** downright **10** absolutely

flatten
4 deck, down, dull, even, fell, raze **5** crush, floor, level **6** smooth, squash **9** knock down, prostrate

flattened at the poles
6 oblate

flatter
4 coax, suit **5** toady **6** become, cajole, praise, stroke **7** adulate, blarney, gratify, wheedle **8** blandish, bootlick, butter up, soft-soap **9** sweet-talk

flattery
5 smarm **6** praise **7** blarney, butter **8** cajolery, soft soap, toadyism **9** adulation, sweet talk **10** sycophancy **11** compliments **12** blandishment, ingratiation, unctuousness

Flaubert, Gustave
birthplace: 5 Rouen
heroine: 4 Emma (Bovary)
novel: 8 Salammbô **12** Madame Bovary

flaunt
4 show, wave **5** flash, flout, vaunt **6** expose, parade **7** display, disport, exhibit, show off **8** brandish, flourish

flavor
4 race, tang, zest, zing **5** smack, spice, taste, tinge **6** relish, season **7** variety, version

flavorless
4 flat **5** bland, stale **7** insipid **8** unsavory **11** unpalatable

flavorsome
5 sapid, tasty, yummy **6** savory **9** delicious, palatable **10** appetizing, delectable **11** good-tasting

flaw
3 gap, rip, sin **4** blot, chip, tear, vice **5** crack, fault **6** defect **7** blemish **9** deformity, weakness **12** imperfection

flawed
5 amiss **6** faulty, marred **7** damaged, spoiled **8** impaired **9** defective, imperfect

flawless
4 pure **5** ideal, model **6** intact **7** perfect **8** seamless, unmarred **9** exquisite **10** immaculate, impeccable **11** unblemished

flax
5 linen
fiber: 3 tow
prepare: 3 ret **4** card **5** dress **6** hackle, scutch

flaxen
4 fair **5** blond, straw **6** blonde, golden, yellow **7** towhead

flay
4 beat, lash, peel, skin **7** blister, censure, lambast, upbraid **8** lambaste **9** castigate, criticize, excoriate

flea
6 chigoe, jigger **7** chigger
water: 7 daphnid

Fleance's father
6 Banquo

flèche
5 spire

fleck
3 dot **4** mark, mote, spot **5** flake, speck **6** dapple, mottle, streak, stripe **7** spatter, speckle, stipple **8** particle **9** bespeckle

Fledermaus, Die
3 bat
character: 5 Adele, Falke, Frank **6** Alfred **9** Rosalinde **10** Eisenstein
composer: 7 Strauss (Johann)

fledge
4 rear **7** feather

fledgling
4 colt, tyro **6** novice, rookie **8** beginner, freshman, neophyte, newcomer **10** apprentice

flee
3 fly, lam, run 4 bolt, scat, skip 5 elude, scoot, scram, skirr, steal 6 decamp, escape 7 abscond, make off, run away, scamper, vamoose 8 stampede, turn tail 9 skedaddle 10 make tracks

fleece
3 rob 4 bilk, clip, gaff, milk, rook, skin, soak, wool 5 bleed, cheat, cozen, mulct, shear, stick, sweat 6 extort, hustle, rip off 7 defraud, swindle 8 flimflam 10 overcharge

fleecy
5 downy 6 fluffy, pilose, woolly 7 hirsute 9 whiskered 10 flocculent

fleer
4 gibe, gird, jeer, jest, mock, quip 5 flout, laugh, scoff, scout, sneer, taunt

fleet
4 fast, navy, spry 5 agile, brisk, group, hasty, quick, rapid, swift 6 argosy, armada, nimble, speedy 8 flotilla 9 breakneck 10 harefooted

fleeting
5 brief 7 passing 8 fugitive, volatile 9 ephemeral, fugacious, momentary, temporary, transient 10 evanescent, short-lived, transitory

Fleming, Ian
hero: 9 James Bond
novel: 4 Dr. No 9 Moonraker 10 Goldfinger 11 Thunderball 12 Casino Royale, Live and Let Die 16 You Only Live Twice 18 From Russia with Love

flesh
4 beef, meat, skin 5 stock 7 kindred 9 offspring, relatives, substance

fleshly
5 obese 6 animal, bodily, carnal 7 lustful, profane, secular, sensual 8 corporal, physical, sensuous, temporal 9 corporeal, epicurean, luxurious, sybaritic 10 voluptuous

fleshy
3 fat 5 ample, beefy, burly, gross, heavy, hefty, husky, meaty, obese, plump, pudgy, stout, tubby 6 chubby, chunky, portly, rotund 7 porcine, weighty 9 corpulent 10 overweight, well-padded
fruit: 4 pome 5 berry, drupe

Fletcher's partner
8 Beaumont (Francis)

fleur-de-lis
4 iris

flex
4 bend 5 tense

flexible
5 lithe, loose 6 docile, floppy, limber, pliant, supple 7 elastic, pliable, springy, willowy 8 amenable, bendable, stretchy, yielding 9 adaptable, compliant, malleable, tractable

flexion
3 bow 4 bend, fold, turn 5 angle

flexuous
5 fluid, lithe, snaky 7 sinuous, winding 8 tortuous 10 circuitous, convoluted, meandering, serpentine 11 anfractuous

flick
4 film, show 5 movie 13 motion picture, moving picture

flicker
4 bird, film, flit, hint 5 flash, gleam, glint, movie, waver 6 quiver 7 twinkle 10 woodpecker 13 motion picture, moving picture

flickering
7 lambent 8 unsteady

flier
3 ace 5 pilot 6 airman 7 aviator, birdman, handout 8 aviatrix, brochure, circular 9 throwaway

flight
3 hop, lam 4 rout, soar, slip, wing 5 flock, floor, flush, flyby, story 6 escape, flying, series 7 getaway 8 breakout

flighty
5 dizzy, giddy, silly, swift 7 foolish 8 freakish, skittish, unstable, volatile 9 frivolous, mercurial, transient 10 capricious, changeable, inconstant 11 empty-headed, harebrained 13 irresponsible

flimflam
3 con, gyp 4 bilk, dupe, fake, fool, gull, hoax, jazz, sham 5 cheat, cozen, fraud, hokum, trick 6 chouse, deceit, diddle, humbug 7 chicane, deceive, defraud, swindle 8 hoodwink, trickery 9 bamboozle, deception, moonshine 10 balderdash, double-talk 11 hornswoggle

flimflammer
3 gyp 5 cheat 6 con man 7 diddler, sharper 8 swindler 9 defrauder 11 four-flusher 12 double-dealer

flimsy
4 limp, weak 5 cheap, filmy, frail, gauzy, sheer, slight 6 feeble, flabby, sleazy, slight,

spindly **7** flaccid, fragile, rickety, tenuous, unsound **8** decrepit, delicate, gossamer **10** diaphanous, improbable **11** implausible, transparent **12** unconvincing **13** insubstantial

flinch
5 quail, start, wince **6** blench, cringe, recoil, shrink

fling
3 peg **4** cast, emit, fire, flap, hurl, plop, rush, shot, slap, stab, tear, toss **5** binge, chuck, heave, pitch, shoot, spree, throw **6** affair, charge, hurtle, launch **7** splurge **8** catapult

flip
4 glib, leaf, pert, riff, toss, wise **6** breezy, riffle, ruffle **8** turn over **10** somersault **11** impertinent, smart-alecky

flip-flop
5 U-turn, waver **6** sandal, switch, waffle **7** reverse **8** reversal **9** about-face, turnabout, vacillate, volte-face **10** turnaround **11** vacillation

flippancy
5 cheek **6** levity **8** archness, pertness **9** cockiness, freshness, frivolity **10** cheekiness, impishness **11** roguishness

flippant
4 glib, pert **5** sassy, saucy **6** breezy, cheeky **11** impertinent, smart-alecky **13** disrespectful

flirt
3 toy **4** flit, fool, minx, ogle, vamp **5** dally, tease **6** coquet, trifle, wanton **8** coquette **10** experiment, mess around

flit
3 fly, zip **4** dart, pass, rush, sail, scud, whiz, wing **5** flash, hurry, scoot, speed **7** flicker, flutter, twinkle

flitter
4 dart, flap, wing **5** hover, waver **6** quiver **7** skitter **9** fluctuate

flivver
6 jalopy **9** tin lizzie

float
3 bob, fly **4** buoy, cork, hang, raft, ride, sail, scud, swim, waft **5** drift, hover **7** pontoon, propose, wander **8** levitate **9** negotiate

floater
3 bum, vag **4** hobo, raft **5** tramp **7** drifter, vagrant **8** derelict, vagabond **10** roustabout

floating
5 fluid, loose **6** adrift **7** buoyant, movable **8** moveable, shifting, variable **10** adjustable **11** fluctuating

flocculent
5 flaky **6** fleecy, fluffy, woolly

flock
3 mob **4** army, bevy, herd, host, mass, pack, rout **5** brood, bunch, cloud, covey, crowd, drove, group **6** flight, gaggle, gather, legion, scores, throng **8** assemble, assembly, converge **9** multitude **11** aggregation **12** congregation

floe
3 ice **4** berg **7** glacier, iceberg **8** ice field

flog
3 tan **4** beat, cane, flap, hide, lash, slog, whip **5** birch, drive, flail, whale **6** larrup, lather, stripe, switch, thrash **7** cowhide, leather, scourge **10** flagellate

flood
4 fill, flow, flux, glut, pour, rush, tide **5** burst, drown, float, spate, swamp **6** deluge, engulf, stream **7** current, freshet, immerse, Niagara, torrent **8** alluvion, cataract, inundate, overflow, submerge **9** avalanche, cataclysm, overwhelm **10** inundation, outpouring

floor
4 base, down, drop, fell **5** amaze, level, shock, story **6** ground **7** astound, flatten **8** astonish, audience, bowl down, bowl over, surprise **9** dumbfound, knock down **11** flabbergast

flop
3 dud **4** bomb, bust, fail, fall **5** lemon, loser **6** bummer, fizzle, turkey **7** clinker, failure

floppy
4 limp **6** flimsy **7** flaccid **8** diskette, flexible

flora
6 plants **10** vegetation

flora and fauna
5 biota

Florence
bridge: **12** Ponte Vecchio
cathedral: **5** Duomo
family: **6** Medici
museum: **6** Uffizi **8** Bargello
palace: **5** Pitti
river: **4** Arno

florid
3 red **5** flush, gaudy, ruddy, showy

6 ornate, rococo **7** baroque, flowery,
flushed, glowing **8** rubicund, sanguine,
sonorous **9** bombastic, elaborate,
overblown **10** euphuistic, flamboyant,
rhetorical **11** declamatory
12 magniloquent **13** grandiloquent

Florida
capital: 11 Tallahassee
city: 5 Miami, Tampa **6** Naples, Venice
7 Hialeah, Key West, Orlando **8** Sarasota
9 Palm Beach **11** St. Augustine
12 Jacksonville, St. Petersburg
college, university: 7 Rollins, Stetson
key: 4 Long, Vaca, West **5** Largo **7** Big
Pine **9** Matecumbe, Sugarloaf
lake: 9 Kissimmee **10** Okeechobee
nickname: 8 Sunshine (State)
park: 10 Everglades
river: 6 Indian **7** St. Johns **8** Suwannee
12 Apalachicola
state bird: 11 mockingbird
state flower: 13 orange blossom
state tree: 9 sabal palm

florilegium
5 album **7** garland, omnibus, reader
8 analects **9** anthology **10** collection,
miscellany

Florimel's husband
7 Marinel

floss
4 down, fuzz, lint **5** fluff **6** thread

flotilla
5 fleet **6** argosy, armada

Flotow opera
5 Indra **6** L'Ombre, Martha

flotsam
6 debris, jetsam **7** remains **8** wreckage
9 driftwood

flounce
5 frill, mince, strut, waltz **6** bounce, prance,
ruffle, sashay

flounder
3 dab **5** slosh **6** fumble, muddle, splash,
thrash, wallow **7** blunder, flounce
8 flatfish, struggle

flour
4 meal **6** pinole, powder
beetle: 6 weevil

flourish
3 wax **4** grow, wave **5** adorn, bloom
6 flower, stroke, thrive **7** blossom,
burgeon, develop, fanfare, prosper,

succeed **8** brandish, curlicue, ornament
13 embellishment, ornamentation

flout
4 defy, mock **5** scorn, spurn **6** deride,
insult, scoff at

flow
4 emit, flux, gush, ooze, pour, rill, rise, rush,
stem, tide, well **5** arise, drift, flood, issue,
spate, spill, surge, swarm **6** course,
deluge, onrush, sluice, spring, stream
7 cascade, current, emanate, give off,
outflow, proceed **8** inundate, sequence
9 discharge, originate **10** continuity,
inundation, succession **11** progression
12 continuation

flower
4 best, blow, pick, posy **5** bloom, cream,
elite, pride, prime, prize **6** choice, thrive
7 blossom, burgeon, develop **10** effloresce
13 inflorescence
buttonhole: 11 boutonniere
cluster: 4 cyme **5** spike, umbel
6 corymb, floret, raceme, spadix **7** panicle
8 spikelet **9** capitulum, dichasium,
glomerule **11** monochasium
13 inflorescence
cup: 5 calyx
garden: 4 iris, lily, pink, rose **5** aster,
canna, daisy, pansy, peony, phlox, poppy,
tulip **6** azalea, cosmos, crocus, dahlia,
orchid, violet **7** jonquil, petunia **8** camellia,
daffodil, gardenia, geranium, gloxinia,
hyacinth, larkspur, marigold, primrose
9 carnation, gladiolus, narcissus
10 delphinium, heliotrope **13** chrysanthemum
opening: 8 anthesis
part: 5 bract, calyx, ovary, ovule, petal,
sepal, style **6** anther, pistil, spathe,
stamen, stigma **7** corolla, nectary, pedicel,
petiole **8** calyptra, filament, peduncle,
perianth
spike: 5 ament **6** catkin, spadix
stalk: 7 pedicel **8** peduncle
type: 3 ray **4** disk **6** annual, simple
9 composite, perennial
wild: 4 flag **5** bluet, daisy, vetch **6** lupine
7 anemone, arbutus, cowslip, gentian,
vervain **8** bluebell, hepatica, trillium
9 buttercup, columbine, dandelion,
saxifrage **10** cinquefoil **12** lady's slipper

flower arranging
7 ikebana

flowering
6 growth **8** progress **9** evolution
11 development, florescence, progression

flowerless plant
4 fern, moss 6 lichen 9 liverwort

flowery
5 wordy 6 florid, ornate, prolix 7 aureate,
diffuse, verbose 8 sonorous 9 overblown
10 euphuistic, rhetorical 11 declamatory
12 magniloquent 13 grandiloquent

Flowery Kingdom
5 China

flowing
4 easy 5 fluid 6 fluent, liquid, smooth
7 cursive, running 10 effortless
back: 6 reflux 8 refluent
in: 6 influx 8 influent
together: 7 conflux 9 confluent

flow regulator
4 cock, gate 5 valve 8 throttle

flub
4 goof, mess, muff, slip 5 boner, botch,
error, fluff, gaffe, lapse, snarl 6 bollix,
bungle, foul up, goof up, mess up
7 blunder, faux pas, louse up

fluctuate
4 sway, yo-yo 5 swing, waver 6 seesaw
8 undulate 9 alternate, oscillate, vacillate

flue
4 pipe, vent 6 funnel, uptake 7 channel,
chimney, outtake

fluent
4 easy, glib 5 fluid 6 facile, liquid, smooth
7 cursive, flowing, supple, voluble
8 eloquent, polished 10 articulate,
effortless

fluff
4 down, flub, fuzz, goof, lint, mess, muff,
slip, trip 5 boner, botch, error, floss, gaffe,
lapse, whisk 6 bobble, bollix, bungle, goof
up, mess up 7 blooper, blunder, faux pas,
louse up, mistake

fluffy
5 downy 6 flossy 7 cursory, shallow
8 puffed up 10 flocculent 11 superficial
13 unsubstantial

fluid
4 free 5 lymph, water 6 liquid, mobile,
molten, serous, watery 7 mutable, protean
8 flexible, shifting, unstable, unsteady,
variable 9 adaptable, changeful, unsettled
10 changeable
excessive: 5 edema

fluke
3 hap 4 lobe, worm 5 quirk 6 chance
8 flatfish, fortuity 9 trematode

fluky
3 odd 6 casual, chance, chancy, random
9 arbitrary 10 accidental, fortuitous

flume
5 chute 6 sluice, stream 7 channel
8 aqueduct 11 watercourse

flummox
5 abash, addle 6 baffle, rattle, stymie
7 confuse, fluster, perplex 8 befuddle,
bewilder, confound 9 discomfit, embarrass
10 disconcert

flunk
4 fail

flunky
4 peon 5 gofer, toady 6 drudge, lackey,
stooge, yes-man 7 footman, servant,
steward 8 factotum, follower

flurry
3 ado, fit 4 fuss, gust, spit, stir, to-do
5 haste, whirl 6 bother, bustle, furore,
pother, tumult 7 barrage, flutter, turmoil
8 snowfall 9 agitation, commotion,
confusion, whirlpool, whirlwind
10 excitement, turbulence

flush
4 even, flat, glow, pink, rich, rose, wash
5 bloom, color, level, plane, raise, rinse,
rouge, sluice 6 florid, filled, mantle, redden
7 cleanse, crimson, glowing, inflame,
opulent, suffuse, wealthy 8 abundant,
abutting, irrigate, rubicund, sanguine,
squarely 9 turn color

fluster
5 addle, dizzy, shake, upset 6 ball up,
bother, fuddle, muddle, rattle, ruffle
7 agitate, confuse, disturb, nonplus,
perturb, unhinge 8 befuddle, bewilder,
confound, disquiet, distract 10 discompose

flustered
5 upset 7 abashed, anxious, rattled
8 agitated, confused, troubled 9 chagrined,
disturbed, flummoxed, perplexed,
perturbed 10 bewildered, disquieted,
distracted, distraught, distressed,
nonplussed 11 discomposed, embarrassed
12 disconcerted

flute
4 fife, roll 5 pleat 6 goffer, groove
7 chamfer, channel, piccolo 8 recorder
9 wineglass

flutist

Japanese: 10 shakuhachi
player: 5 piper **7** flutist **8** flautist

flutist

American: 5 Baker (Julius), Baron (Samuel) **7** Robison (Paula) **8** Zukerman (Eugenia)
British: 6 Galway (James)
French: 6 Rampal (Jean-Pierre)

flutter

4 beat, flap, flit **5** hover, quake, shake **6** flurry, quaver, quiver, wobble **7** flicker, flitter, pulsate, tremble, vibrate **9** agitation, commotion, confusion, palpitate, vibration **11** fluctuation

flu type

5 Asian, swine

flux

3 run **4** flow, fuse, melt, rush, thaw, tide **5** drift, flood, spate **6** change, stream **7** current, flowing, outflow **8** dissolve

fly

3 zip **4** bolt, dart, dash, flee, flit, lure, scud, skip, soar, whiz, wing **5** fleet, float, glide, hover, hurry, pilot, scoot, shoot, skirr, sweep, whish, whisk **6** aviate, escape, hasten, hustle **7** abscond, flutter
insect: 4 gnat **5** midge **6** botfly, gadfly, mayfly, tsetse **7** deerfly, sandfly **8** blackfly, dipteron, horsefly, housefly, tachinid **10** bluebottle
larva: 6 maggot

fly-by-night

5 shady **7** passing **9** transient **10** transitory, unreliable **12** disreputable, undependable **13** untrustworthy

flycatcher

5 pewee **6** phoebe, tyrant **8** bellbird, kingbird **9** passerine

flying

5 aloft **6** volant **8** airborne

Flying Dutchman, The

composer: 6 Wagner (Richard)
heroine: 5 Senta

flying fish

7 gurnard

flying fox

3 bat **8** fruit bat

flying horse

7 Pegasus **10** hippogriff

flying island

6 Laputa

flying lemur

6 colugo

flying mammal

3 bat

flying saucer

3 UFO

fly in the ointment

5 catch **8** drawback

foam

4 head, scud, scum, suds, surf **5** churn, froth, spume **6** bubble, lather, seethe **7** bubbles **10** effervesce

fob

4 seal **5** chain **6** pocket, ribbon **8** ornament

fob off

5 foist **6** put off **7** palm off, pass off

focus

3 fix, hub **4** zoom **5** heart, rivet **6** adjust, center, fixate, home in **8** converge, emphasis, meditate, polestar **9** concenter, epicenter **10** hypocenter **11** concentrate, nerve center

fodder

4 feed, food **6** forage, silage **9** provender
crop: 3 hay, oat, rye **4** corn **5** maize, vetch, wheat **6** barley, clover, millet **7** alfalfa, sorghum
storage structure: 4 silo
store: 6 ensile

foe

5 enemy, rival **8** opponent **9** adversary **10** antagonist

fog

4 blur, daze, foam, haze, mist, murk, soup **5** brume, cloud, vapor **6** miasma, muddle **7** pea soup, pogonip

foggy

4 hazy **5** dirty, grimy, misty, murky, soupy, vague **7** brumous, muddled, obscure, tenuous **8** confused, pea soupy, vaporous

fogy

6 fossil, square **7** diehard **8** mossback **10** fuddy-duddy **12** antediluvian, conservative **11** standpatter **13** stick-in-the-mud

fogyish

7 old-line **8** outmoded, standpat **9** hidebound, out-of-date **10** antiquated, fuddy-duddy, mossbacked **11** reactionary **12** conservative, old-fashioned

foible
4 vice 5 fault 6 defect 7 failing, frailty
8 weakness 11 shortcoming
12 imperfection

foil
4 balk, beat, curb, dash, faze 5 check,
sword 6 baffle, defeat, rattle, thwart
7 buffalo 8 contrast, restrain 9 discomfit,
embarrass, frustrate 10 circumvent,
disappoint, disconcert 11 straight man

foist
6 fob off 7 palm off, pass off

fold
3 pen, ply 4 bend, fail, tuck 5 drape, flock,
pleat, plica, ridge 6 crease, double, furrow,
pucker 7 flexure, plicate 9 plication
11 corrugation
skin: 4 ruga 5 plica, rugae (plural)
6 dewlap, plicae (plural)

folder
4 file 6 binder 9 portfolio

foliage
6 growth, leaves 7 verdure 8 greenery,
lushness 10 vegetation

folk
4 race 6 people 9 community

folklore
4 myth, tale 5 fable 6 belief, custom,
legend, mythos, wisdom 9 mythology,
tradition 12 superstition

folks
6 family 7 parents 9 relatives

folksinger
4 Baez (Joan), Ives (Burl) 5 Dylan (Bob),
Niles (John Jacob), White (Josh) 6 Odetta,
Seeger (Pete) 7 Collins (Judy), Guthrie
(Arlo, Woody), Robeson (Paul) 9 Belafonte
(Harry), Ledbetter (Huddie)

folksy
5 homey 6 casual, earthy, mellow, rustic,
simple 7 natural 8 down-home, familiar,
informal, laid-back, sociable 9 easygoing,
ingenuous 10 unaffected, unpolished
13 unpretentious

folktale
4 myth 5 fable 6 legend 7 märchen

follow
3 dog, spy, tag 4 hunt, keep, obey, seek,
tail, walk 5 catch, chase, ensue, grasp,
hound, trace, track, trail 6 accept, comply,
convoy, pursue, search, shadow, travel
7 conform, imitate, proceed, replace,

succeed 8 postdate, practice, supplant
9 accompany, supersede 10 comprehend,
understand

follower
3 fan 5 toady 6 addict, cohort, minion,
sequel, votary 7 apostle, devotee, groupie,
habitué, sectary, trailer 8 adherent,
advocate, disciple, faithful, hanger-on,
henchman, myrmidon, parasite, partisan,
tagalong 9 dependent, satellite, supporter,
sycophant 10 aficionado

following
4 next 5 after, below, later, since 6 behind,
public 7 ensuing, retinue 8 audience,
believers, partisans 9 adherents,
afterward, disciples, entourage
10 afterwards, sequential, supporters,
subsequent, succeeding, successive
12 subsequently, subsequent to

follow-up
6 sequel

folly
4 whim 6 lunacy, vanity 7 fatuity, foolery,
inanity, madness 8 insanity, nonsense
9 absurdity, craziness, dottiness, silliness,
stupidity 10 indulgence 11 foolishness
12 extravagance

foment
3 sow 4 brew, goad, spur 5 rouse, set on
6 arouse, excite, foster, incite, stir up, whip
up 7 agitate, nurture, provoke 9 cultivate,
encourage, instigate

fond
4 dear, warm 5 silly 6 doting, loving,
tender 7 devoted, fatuous, foolish, partial
8 desirous, enamored, romantic
9 indulgent 10 infatuated 11 sentimental
12 affectionate

fondle
3 paw, pet 5 grope, touch 6 caress,
cosset, dandle, stroke 7 embrace
8 canoodle

fondness
4 love 5 fancy, taste 6 liking, relish
8 appetite, devotion, penchant, soft spot,
weakness 9 affection, tendresse
10 attachment, partiality, preference,
propensity 11 inclination 12 predilection

font
4 root, type 6 origin, source 8 fountain
10 receptacle

food
3 pap 4 chow, diet, eats, fare, grub, meal,

meat **5** bread, manna **6** fodder, viands
7 aliment, cuisine, edibles, nurture,
pabulum, vittles **8** delicacy, victuals
9 nutriment, provender **10** provisions,
sustenance **11** comestibles, nourishment
disorder: 7 bulimia **8** anorexia
divine: 8 ambrosia
element: 5 fiber, fibre, sugar **6** starch
7 mineral, protein, vitamin **12** carbohydrate
from heaven: 5 manna
lover: 7 epicure, gourmet **8** gourmand
provision: 4 mess **6** ration **7** serving
scarcity: 6 famine
waste: 7 garbage

foofaraw

3 ado **4** fuss, stir, to-do **5** stink **6** bother,
finery, frills, furore, hurrah, ruckus, rumpus
8 brouhaha, disturbance **9** commotion

fool

3 ass, kid, oaf, rag, rib, sap, toy **4** boob,
butt, clod, dolt, dope, dupe, fish, gull, hoax,
jerk, jest, joke, josh, zany **5** chump, clown,
comic, dally, dummy, dunce, goose, idiot,
loser, moron, ninny, patsy, schmo, trick
6 banter, cretin, delude, dimwit, doodle,
galoot, gammon, jester, lead on, meddle,
monkey, motley, nitwit, pigeon, schmoe,
stooge, sucker, tamper, trifle, victim
7 beguile, buffoon, chicane, dawdle,
deceive, diddle, fake out, fall guy, fritter,
half-wit, jackass, mislead, pinhead,
saphead, schmuck **8** bonehead,
comedian, dumbbell, flimflam, hoodwink,
imbecile, lunkhead, numskull, pushover
9 bamboozle, birdbrain, blockhead,
interfere, simpleton **10** nincompoop
11 hornswoggle, merry-andrew, string
along **13** laughingstock
around: 4 futz, idle, laze, loaf, loll **5** flirt
6 dawdle, diddle, lounge **8** lollygag,
womanize **9** philander

foolhardy

4 bold, rash **6** daring, madcap **8** headlong,
reckless **9** audacious, daredevil,
impetuous **11** precipitate, temerarious

foolish

3 mad **4** daft, gaga, rash, zany **5** balmy,
batty, crazy, dippy, dizzy, dorky, dotty,
goofy, inane, inept, kooky, loony, loopy,
nutty, sappy, silly, wacky **6** absurd, insane,
simple, stupid, unwise **7** asinine, doltish,
fatuous, idiotic, lunatic, meshuga, moronic,
witless **8** clueless, fatuous, reckless, trifling
9 half-baked, brainless, fantastic, frivolous,
half-baked, imbecilic, insensate, laughable,
ludicrous, senseless **10** cockamamie,
feebleminded, half-cocked, half-witted,

irrational, ridiculous **11** harebrained,
nonsensical

foolishness

4 bull, bunk **5** folly, fudge **6** bêtise,
bunkum, lunacy **7** fatuity, inanity, rubbish
8 claptrap, drollery, insanity, nonsense,
tommyrot **9** absurdity, craziness, silliness,
stupidity **10** imbecility, imprudence
12 fiddle-faddle **13** horsefeathers

fool's gold

6 pyrite

foot

3 paw **4** hoof
ailment: 4 corn **6** bunion, callus
animal: 3 pad, paw **4** hoof **7** fetlock,
flipper, pastern, trotter
bones of: 5 talus, tarsi (plural) **6** cuboid,
tarsal, tarsus **7** phalanx **9** calcaneus,
cuneiform, navicular, phalanges (plural)
10 metatarsal
doctor: 10 podiatrist **11** chiropodist
metric: 4 iamb **5** arsis **6** dactyl, thesis
7 anapest, pyrrhic, spondee, trochee
part: 3 toe **4** arch, ball, claw, nail **5** ankle,
digit, talon **6** hallux, instep

football

5 rugby **6** rugger, soccer **7** pigskin
field: 8 gridiron
foul: 7 holding, offside **8** clipping
12 interference
official: 6 umpire **7** referee **8** linesman
9 back judge, line judge **10** field judge
play: 4 dive, trap **5** sneak, sweep
6 option, screen **7** audible, counter,
handoff, rollout, runback **8** dropback
9 crossbuck, off-tackle **10** buttonhook
player position: 3 end **4** back **5** guard
6 center, safety, tackle **7** flanker, lineman,
wideout **8** fullback, halfback, slotback, split
end, tailback, tight end, wingback **9** noseguard **10** cornerback, linebacker, nose
tackle **11** quarterback **12** defensive end,
wide receiver
scoring: 6 safety **9** field goal, touchdown
10 conversion
starting play: 7 kickoff
team: 6 eleven
term: 4 down, kick, pass, punt, rush, snap
5 blitz, block, squad **6** fumble, huddle,
onside, option, safety, spiral **7** end zone,
handoff, kickoff, offside, pigskin, quarter,
spinner, yardage **8** clipping, crossbar, goal
line, goalpost, gridiron, halftime
9 backfield, defensive, field goal, intercept,
offensive, placekick, scrimmage,

touchback, touchdown **11** broken field
12 interception

footballer
3 end **4** half, Kemp (Jack), Long (Howie),
Lott (Ronnie), Levy (Marv), Monk (Art),
Moon (Warren), Reed (Andre), Rice (Jerry),
wing **5** Allen (Marcus), Baugh (Sammy),
Berry (Raymond), Brady (Tom), Brown
(Bob, Jim), Clark (Gary), Ditka (Mike),
Elway (John), Eller (Carl), Favre (Brett),
Gibbs (Joe), Groza (Lou), guard, Jones
(Bert, Deacon), Kelly (Jim), Kosar (Bernie),
Leahy (Pat), Lomax (Neil), Muñoz
(Anthony), Shula (Don), Simms (Phil),
Smith (Emmitt), Starr (Bart), Stram (Hank),
Swann (Lynn), Young (Steve) **6** Aikman
(Troy), Blanda (George), Butkus (Dick),
Carter (Chris, Ki-Jana), center, Csonka
(Larry), Dawson (Len), Ellard (Henry),
Graham (Otto), Grange (Red), Greene
(Joe), Harris (Franco), Jaeger (Jeff), Joiner
(Charlie), kicker, Lofton (James), Lowery
(Nick), Marino (Dan), Murray (Eddie),
Namath (Joe), Payton (Walter), player,
Rypien (Mark), safety, Sayers (Gale), Slater
(Jackie), tackle, Taylor (Lawrence), Thorpe
(Jim), Tittle (Y. A.), Turner (Jim), Unitas
(Johnny), Walker (Herschel) **7** Bledsoe
(Drew), Dorsett (Tony), Esiason (Boomer),
flanker, Gifford (Frank), Hornung (Paul),
Johnson (Norm), Largent (Steve), lineman,
Luckman (Sid), Manning (Peyton),
Montana (Joe), Newsome (Ozzie), Riggins
(John), Sanders (Barry, Deion), Simpson
(O. J.), Stabler (Ken), Thurman (Thomas),
tweener **8** Andersen (Morten), Anderson
(Gary, Ottis), Bradshaw (Terry), defender,
fullback, halfback, linesman, Nagurski
(Bronko), Plunkett (Jim), receiver,
scatback, split end, Staubach (Roger),
tailback, tight end, wingback **9** Dickerson
(Eric), Jurgensen (Sonny), Hostetler (Jeff),
noseguard, Tarkenton (Fran)
10 cornerback, linebacker, Stallworth
(John), Singletary (Mike), Stephenson
(Dwight), Youngblood (Jack) **11** ballcarrier,
placekicker, quarterback, running back,
snapper-back **12** strong safety, triple
threat, wide receiver

Foote play
15 Trip to Bountiful (The) **19** Young Man
from Atlanta (The)

footfall
4 step **5** tread

footing
4 base, rank, seat, term **5** basis, place,
state **6** bottom, ground, status **7** bedrock,
seating, station, warrant **8** basement,

capacity, pedestal, position, standing
9 character, situation **10** foundation,
groundwork, substratum **12** underpinning

footless
4 dull, dumb **5** crass, dense, inept, unfit
6 stupid **7** foolish

foot lever
5 pedal **7** treadle

footman
7 servant **10** pedestrian **11** infantryman

footpad
5 thief **6** mugger, robber **8** criminal
10 highwayman, pickpocket

footprint
3 pug **4** sign, step **5** spoor, trace, track,
tract **7** pugmark, vestige

footslog
4 plod, slop, toil, tramp, tromp **6** trudge

footstone
6 ledger, marker **8** monument **11** grave
marker

footstool
7 cricket, hassock, ottoman

fop
3 jay **4** beau **5** blade, blood, dandy, spark,
swell **7** coxcomb, gallant **8** cavalier,
macaroni, popinjay **9** exquisite, ladies'
man, pretty boy **10** lady-killer **11** Beau
Brummel, petit-maître **12** fashion plate,
lounge lizard

foppish
6 chichi **8** dandyish, peacocky
10 peacockish

for
3 pro

forage
4 beat, comb, grub, prog, raid, rake, sack
5 scour **6** browse, fodder, ravage, rustle,
search **7** plunder, ransack, rummage
8 finecomb, scrounge **9** pasturage
(see also **fodder**)

foray
4 raid **6** inroad, sortie **8** invasion
9 incursion, irruption

forbear
4 shun **5** avoid, forgo, spare **6** endure,
eschew, resist, suffer **7** abstain, decline,
refrain **8** hold back, restrain, tolerate

forbearance
5 grace, mercy **6** lenity **7** charity
8 clemency, lenience, leniency, mildness,

patience **9** restraint, tolerance
10 abstinence, toleration **13** consideration

forbearing
4 easy, kind, mild **6** gentle **7** clement,
lenient, patient **8** merciful, tolerant
9 indulgent **10** charitable, magnanimous,
thoughtful **11** considerate

Forbes hero
8 Tremaine (Johnny)

forbid
3 ban, bar, nix **4** curb, deny, halt, stop,
veto **5** block, check, debar **6** enjoin,
hinder, impede, outlaw, refuse **7** inhibit,
prevent, rule out, shut out **8** disallow,
obstruct, preclude, prohibit, restrain
9 interdict, proscribe

forbidden
5 taboo **6** banned **7** illegal, illicit
8 verboten **10** prohibited

Forbidden City
5 Lhasa **6** Gu Gong **7** Beijing

forbidding
4 grim **5** drear, harsh **6** dreary, severe
8 daunting, menacing, sinister **9** repellent
10 formidable **11** threatening

force
3 jam **4** cram, push **5** drive, foist, impel,
might, power, press, vigor, wreak, wreck,
wrest **6** coerce, compel, demand, duress,
effort, energy, extort, impose, legion,
muscle, oblige **7** command, impetus,
inflict, potency, require, sandbag
8 coercion, manpower, momentum,
obligate, pressure, shoehorn, strength,
violence **9** constrain, intensity, puissance,
strong-arm **10** compulsion, constraint
apart: 5 wedge
unit: 4 dyne

forced
8 strained **9** contrived, unnatural
10 artificial, compulsory **11** involuntary

forceful
5 stiff, stout **6** mighty, potent, punchy,
strong, virile **7** dynamic **8** emphatic,
powerful, puissant, vigorous **9** assertive
10 compelling

forceless
4 lame, weak **5** wimpy **6** feeble
8 impotent, nugatory, powerless
10 inadequate **11** ineffective, ineffectual

force out
see **expel**

forcible
8 coercive **9** compelled **10** compulsory,
obligatory, peremptory

ford
5 cross

Ford's folly
5 Edsel

for each
3 per **6** apiece

forearm bone
4 ulna **6** radius

forebear
8 ancestor **9** precursor **10** antecedent,
progenitor **11** predecessor
12 primogenitor

forebode
5 augur **7** betoken, portend, predict,
presage **8** foretell, prophesy, soothsay
13 prognosticate

foreboding
4 omen, sign **5** dread **6** augury **7** anxiety,
portent, presage, warning **10** prediction,
prognostic **11** premonition
12 apprehension, presentiment

forecast
5 augur **6** divine **7** foresee, portend,
predict, presage **8** estimate, foretell,
indicate, prophecy, prophesy **9** adumbrate,
calculate, prevision, prognosis
10 prediction **13** prognosticate

forecaster
4 seer **5** augur **6** oracle **7** diviner, prophet
8 haruspex **9** predictor **10** prophesier,
soothsayer, weatherman **11** Nostradamus
13 meteorologist, weatherperson

foreclose
3 bar **5** debar **6** cut off, hinder **7** prevent,
shut out **8** preclude

forefather
see **forebear**

forefeel
6 divine **9** apprehend, prevision

forefinger
5 index

forefront
3 van **4** lead **8** vanguard **10** avant-garde,
firing line **11** cutting edge

foregoer
6 herald **8** ancestor, forebear **9** harbinger,
precursor, prototype **10** antecedent,

antecessor, forerunner, progenitor
11 predecessor **12** primogenitor

foregoing
5 prior **6** former **7** earlier **8** anterior, previous **9** precedent, preceding
10 antecedent

forehanded
7 prudent, thrifty **8** well-to-do **9** provident
10 prosperous

forehead
4 brow **5** frons, front **8** sinciput **9** sincipita (plural)

foreign
5 alien **6** exotic **7** strange **8** external, offshore, overseas **9** extrinsic, nonnative
10 accidental, extraneous, immaterial, irrelevant **11** incongruous **12** adventitious, inapplicable, incompatible, inconsistent
13 inappropriate
prefix: 4 xeno

foreigner
5 alien **8** outsider, stranger **9** outlander
10 tramontane

foreknow
6 divine **9** apprehend, prevision
10 anticipate

foreland
4 beak, cape, head, ness **5** point
10 promontory

forelock
5 bangs, quiff

foreman
4 boss **5** chief **6** gaffer, ganger, honcho, leader **7** captain, manager, steward
8 overseer **10** supervisor

foremost
4 arch, head, high, main **5** chief, first, front, grand **7** leading, premier, supreme
9 number one, paramount, principal
10 preeminent **11** cutting-edge, outstanding

forenoon
4 morn **7** morning **12** ante meridiem

forensic
8 judicial **9** debatable **10** rhetorical
13 argumentative

foreordain
4 doom, fate **9** determine **10** predestine
12 predetermine

forerunner
4 omen, sign **5** envoy **6** augury, herald

7 pioneer, portent, presage, symptom, warning **8** ancestor, exemplar, outrider
9 announcer, harbinger, initiator, messenger **10** antecedent, originator, prognostic **11** anticipator, predecessor

foresee
6 divine **7** predict, presage **8** perceive, prophesy **9** apprehend, prefigure, prevision **10** anticipate **13** prognosticate

foreseer
5 augur **6** auspex, oracle **7** diviner, prophet **8** haruspex **9** predictor
10 soothsayer **11** Nostradamus

foreshadow
4 bode, hint **5** augur **6** herald **7** betoken, portend, predict, presage, promise, suggest
8 forecast, intimate **9** adumbrate, prefigure
13 prognosticate

foresight
6 vision **7** caution **8** prudence, sagacity
10 discretion, perception, precaution, prescience, providence

forest
4 bosk, wood **5** copse, grove, weald, woods **6** bosque **7** coppice, thicket, woodlot **8** wildwood, woodland
10 timberland, wilderness
deity: 5 dryad **6** sylvan **8** Sylvanus
English: 5 Arden **8** Sherwood
opening: 5 glade
relating to: 6 sylvan
subarctic: 5 taiga
tropical: 5 selva **6** jungle

forestall
5 avert, block, deter **6** hinder **7** obviate, preempt, prevent, rule out, ward off
8 preclude, stave off **10** anticipate

Forester, C. S.
hero: 10 Hornblower (Horatio)
novel: 12 African Queen (The)

foretell
4 bode, warn **5** augur **6** divine **7** portend, predict, presage, promise **8** proclaim, prophesy, soothsay **9** adumbrate, apprehend, prefigure **10** anticipate, vaticinate **13** prognosticate

forethought
8 judgment, planning, prudence
10 discretion, precaution **12** deliberation
13 premeditation

foretoken
4 bode, hint, omen, sign, warn **5** augur
6 augury, herald **7** portend, portent,

presage, promise, symptom, warning
8 forecast **9** harbinger, precursor
10 intimation

forever
3 aye **6** always **7** endless **8** eternity,
evermore **9** endlessly, eternally **10** in
aeternum **11** ad infinitum, ceaselessly,
continually, everlasting, incessantly,
permanently, perpetually, unceasingly **12** in
perpetuity **13** everlastingly

forewarning
6 caveat, tip-off **7** caution **8** monition
11 premonition

foreword
5 intro, proem **7** preface, prelude
8 exordium, overture, preamble, prologue
12 introduction, prolegomenon

for example
6 such as

for fear that
4 lest

forfeit
4 fine, lose **5** mulct **6** give up **7** penalty
9 sacrifice **10** amercement

forfend
4 ward **5** avert, deter **6** secure **7** obviate,
prevent, protect, rule out, ward off
8 preclude, preserve, stave off

forge
4 copy, fake, form, make **5** pound, shape
6 smithy **7** advance, continue, fashion,
imitate, produce, turn out **9** construct,
fabricate **11** counterfeit, manufacture

forget
4 fail, omit **6** ignore, slight **7** neglect
8 discount, overlook, pass over
9 disregard

forgetful
3 lax **5** slack **6** absent, remiss **7** amnesic
8 amnesiac, careless, heedless
9 negligent, oblivious, unwitting
10 abstracted, neglectful **11** inattentive,
thoughtless **12** absentminded

forgetfulness
5 lethe **7** amnesia **8** oblivion **10** negligence **11** inattention

forgivable
6 venial **10** remissible

forgive
5 remit **6** excuse, pardon **7** absolve,
condone **8** overlook

forgiveness
6 pardon **7** amnesty **9** remission
10 absolution

forgo
3 bag **5** leave, waive, yield **6** eschew, give
up, resign **7** abandon **8** abnegate, jettison,
renounce **9** sacrifice, surrender
10 relinquish

fork
6 bisect, branch, crotch **7** diverge, utensil
9 branch off
prong: 4 tine

fork out
3 pay **5** spend **10** contribute

forlorn
5 alone **6** bereft, futile, lonely **8** desolate,
forsaken, hopeless, lonesome, solitary,
wretched **9** abandoned, depressed,
destitute, miserable **10** despairing,
despondent **12** disconsolate

form
3 way **4** body, cast, make, mode, mold
5 build, forge, found, frame, image, model,
shape, style **6** create, design, devise,
figure, make up, manner **7** compose,
contour, develop, fashion, outline, process,
produce, profile **8** comprise, organize,
practice **9** construct, establish, fabricate,
framework, procedure, structure, take
shape **10** constitute, convention, regulation
11 materialize **13** configuration
combining form: 5 morph

formal
3 set **4** prim **5** exact, legal, rigid, stiff
6 dressy, lawful, proper, seemly, solemn
7 distant, orderly, regular, stately, starchy,
stilted **8** abstract, black-tie, decorous,
elevated, official, reserved **10** ceremonial,
methodical, systematic **11** ceremonious,
syntactical **12** conventional

formality
4 form, rite **6** ritual **7** liturgy, service
8 ceremony, insignia **10** ceremonial,
convention, observance

formalize
6 codify **9** establish, normalize
10 regularize **11** standardize

format
4 plan, size **5** shape, style **6** makeup,
method **11** arrangement **12** organization

formation
4 rank **6** design, makeup **9** structure
11 arrangement, composition, development
12 architecture, construction

former
3 old 4 late, once, past 5 prior 6 bygone, whilom 7 earlier, onetime, quondam 8 anterior, previous, sometime 9 erstwhile, precedent, preceding 10 antecedent

formerly
4 erst, once 6 before, whilom 7 already, earlier 9 erstwhile 10 heretofore, previously

formidable
8 daunting 9 difficult 10 impressive 11 redoubtable

formless
5 vague 7 chaotic, obscure, unclear 8 inchoate, nebulous, unshaped 9 amorphous, undefined, unordered 10 immaterial, indefinite, indistinct 11 unorganized

Formosa
6 Taiwan
capital: 6 Taipei

formula
4 rite, rule 5 canon, maxim, tenet 6 method, recipe, ritual 7 precept, theorem 8 equation 9 algorithm, blueprint, principle, yardstick 10 touchstone 12 prescription

formulate
5 couch, draft, frame, hatch 6 codify, devise, invent, make up, phrase 7 concoct, dream up, express, prepare, work out 8 contrive

forsake
4 quit 5 avoid, leave, spurn 6 defect, depart, desert, give up, reject, resign 7 abandon 8 abdicate, renounce 9 throw over 10 relinquish

forsaken
4 lorn 6 bereft 7 forlorn 8 derelict, deserted, desolate, solitary 9 abandoned

Forseti
father: 6 Balder
palace: 7 Glitnir

forswear
4 deny 5 unsay 6 abjure, recall, recant, reject 7 perjure, retract 8 renounce, take back, withdraw

fort
6 castle 7 bastion, bulwark, citadel, redoubt 8 fastness, fortress, garrison, martello, stockade 10 stronghold
Baltimore: 7 McHenry
California: 3 Ord
New Jersey: 3 Dix

New York: 7 Niagara, Stanwix 8 Schuyler 11 Ticonderoga
Ontario: 9 Frontenac
San Antonio: 5 Alamo
South Carolina: 6 Sumter
Spanish: 7 alcazar 8 presidio

forte
3 bag 4 loud 5 thing 6 métier 8 long suit, strength 9 specialty 10 strong suit 11 strong point

forthcoming
8 imminent, pending 9 impending, proximate 10 responsive 11 approaching

for the most part
9 generally, typically 10 on the whole

for the time being
3 now 6 pro tem 9 at present, currently, presently 10 pro tempore

forthright
4 open 5 blunt, frank, plain 6 candid, direct 7 up-front 8 straight 10 aboveboard, foursquare 11 openhearted, straight-out, undisguised, unvarnished

forthwith
3 now 6 at once 8 directly 9 instantly, right away, thereupon 11 immediately, straightway 12 straightaway

fortification
4 moat, wall 6 abatis, buffer, glacis 7 barrier, bastion, bulwark, citadel, parapet, rampart, redoubt 8 barbican, enceinte, fastness, garrison, palisade, presidio, stockade 9 barricade, earthwork 10 breastwork, stronghold
part: 7 salient

fortify
3 arm 4 gird, stir 5 brace, rally, ready, renew, rouse, steel 6 enrich, secure 7 hearten, prepare, protect, refresh, restore 8 embolden, energize 9 encourage, reinforce 10 invigorate, strengthen

fortitude
4 grit, guts, pith 5 fiber, heart, nerve, pluck, spunk, valor 6 mettle, phlegm, spirit 7 bravery, courage, stamina 8 backbone, boldness, strength, tenacity 9 constancy, endurance, tolerance 10 resolution 11 intrepidity 12 fearlessness, perseverance, resoluteness, staying power 13 dauntlessness, determination

fortress
see fort

fortuitous
 5 fluky, lucky 6 casual, chance, happy
 10 accidental, auspicious 12 providential

fortuity
 3 hap 4 luck 5 fluke 6 chance 8 accident
 9 happening 10 occurrence

Fortuna
 5 Tyche
 symbol: 5 wheel 6 rudder

fortunate
 5 happy, lucky 9 favorable 10 auspicious,
 propitious 12 providential

Fortunate Islands
 8 Canaries

fortune
 3 lot, pot, wad 4 doom, fate, luck, mint,
 pile, ship 5 worth 6 boodle, bundle,
 chance, happen, hazard, packet, riches,
 wealth 7 destiny, success, weather
 8 property 9 resources

Fortune founder
 4 Luce (Henry)

fortune-teller
 4 seer 5 augur, sibyl 7 diviner, palmist
 9 wisewoman 10 soothsayer
 (see also **foreteller**)

fortune-telling
 see **divination**

forty winks
 3 nap 6 catnap, siesta, snooze 7 shut-eye

forum
 5 court, panel 6 medium 8 congress,
 tribunal 9 symposium 10 colloquium,
 conference, roundtable 11 convocation,
 marketplace

forward
 3 aid 4 abet, bold, send, ship 5 ahead,
 brash, eager, pushy, ready, relay, remit,
 sassy, saucy 6 cheeky, foster, onward,
 uphold 7 address, advance, consign,
 further, promote, support 8 advanced,
 champion, dispatch, impudent, transmit
 9 encourage, in advance 11 smart-alecky
 12 presumptuous 13 self-assertive
 prefix: 4 ante

For Whom the Bell Tolls
 author: 9 Hemingway (Ernest)
 character: 5 Maria, Pablo, Pilar 6 Jordan

Forza del Destino composer
 5 Verdi (Giuseppe)

fossa
 3 pit 5 fovea 6 cavity, groove
 10 depression

fosse
 4 dike, moat 5 canal, ditch 6 trench
 7 acequia, channel

fossil
 4 fogy 5 amber, relic 7 antique
 8 calamite, conodont, mossback
 10 antiquated, fuddy-duddy 12 antediluvian 13 stick-in-the-mud
 fuel: 3 gas, oil 4 coal, peat 9 petroleum
 10 natural gas

foster
 4 back, help, rear, tend 5 nurse 6 assist,
 harbor, parent 7 advance, bring up,
 nourish, nurture, promote, support, sustain
 8 champion 9 cultivate, encourage

fou
 5 crazy, drunk

foul
 4 base, rank, soil, vile 5 botch, dirty, fetid,
 funky, muddy, nasty, yucky 6 coarse,
 defile, filthy, grubby, horrid, impure, odious,
 putrid, rotten, scuzzy, smutty, stormy,
 turbid, vulgar, wicked 7 abusive, noisome,
 obscene, pollute, profane, raunchy, squalid,
 tarnish, unclean 8 indecent, obstruct,
 polluted, stinking, wretched 9 collision,
 loathsome, obnoxious, offensive, repellent,
 repugnant, repulsive, revolting
 10 abominable, detestable, disgusting,
 malodorous 11 contaminate, treacherous
 12 dishonorable, scatological

foul play
 3 hit 5 blood 6 murder 7 killing, outrage
 8 homicide, violence 12 manslaughter

found
 4 base, cast, rear 5 begin, erect, raise, set
 up, start 6 bottom, create, invent
 7 fashion, support 8 commence, initiate,
 organize 9 establish, institute, originate,
 predicate

foundation
 3 bed 4 base, rock 5 basis 6 bottom,
 corset, makeup 7 bedding, footing, support
 8 pedestal 9 endowment 10 groundwork,
 substratum 11 institution 12 organization,
 substructure, underpinning

foundational
 5 basic 6 bottom 7 primary 10 supportive,
 underlying 11 fundamental

founder
 4 fail, sink 5 wreck 6 author, father, go

down **7** creator **8** collapse, inventor, submerge, submerse **9** architect, generator, patriarch, shipwreck **10** originator

fountain
3 jet **4** head, root **5** spout **6** geyser, origin, source, spring **7** bubbler **8** wellhead **9** inception, reservoir **10** wellspring
nymph: 6 Egeria

four
6 tetrad **7** quartet **10** quaternion
bagger: 5 homer **7** home run
combining form: 4 tetr **5** quadr, tetra **6** quadri, quadru, quater, tessar **7** tessara, tessera
gills: 4 pint
hundred: 5 elite **10** upper crust
inches: 4 hand
pecks: 6 bushel
quarts: 6 gallon

four-flush
4 dupe **5** bluff **6** betray, delude, humbug, take in **7** beguile, deceive **11** doublecross

four-footed animal
8 tetrapod **9** quadruped

Four Horsemen
3 War **5** Death **6** Famine **8** Conquest **10** Pestilence

four-in-hand
3 tie **5** coach **7** necktie

fourpence
5 groat

four-poster
3 bed

fourscore
6 eighty

four-sided figure
5 rhomb **6** square **7** rhombus **9** rectangle **13** quadrilateral, parallelogram

foursquare
8 straight **10** forthright **13** quadrilateral

fourteen pounds
5 stone

fourth
7 quarter **8** quadrant, quartern
combining form: 5 quadr, quart **6** quadri, quadru

fowl
3 hen **4** bird, cock, duck **5** chick, goose, poult **6** bantam, pullet **7** chicken, rooster, turkey
(see also **chicken; poultry**)

Fowles novel
5 Magus (The) **9** Collector (The)
22 French Lieutenant's Woman (The)

fox
4 fool **5** trick **6** baffle, outwit **7** confuse, reynard **8** bewilder
African: 4 asse
female: 5 vixen
kind: 3 kit, red **5** swift **6** arctic, fennec, silver **8** bat-eared
Scottish: 3 tod
young: 3 cub

foxglove
9 digitalis

fox grape
9 muscadine **11** scuppernong

foxiness
4 wile **5** craft, guile **7** cunning, slyness **8** wiliness **10** artfulness, craftiness, cleverness

foxlike
7 vulpine

foxy
3 sly **4** wily **5** canny, slick **6** artful, astute, clever, crafty, shrewd, tricky **7** cunning, vulpine **8** guileful **9** insidious

foyer
5 lobby **8** anteroom, entrance **9** vestibule

fracas
3 row **4** feud, fray **5** brawl, broil, fight, melee, run-in, set-to **6** affray, hassle, shindy, uproar **7** dispute, quarrel, ruction **8** squabble **9** bickering **10** donnybrook, free-for-all **11** altercation

fraction
3 bit, cut **4** part **5** piece, scrap **6** divide, little **7** portion, section **8** fragment

fractious
4 wild **6** unruly **7** peevish, pettish, willful **8** contrary **9** bellicose, irritable **10** headstrong, pugnacious, refractory **11** belligerent, contentious, intractable, quarrelsome **12** recalcitrant, ungovernable, unmanageable

fracture
4 rent, rift, tear **5** break, cleft, crack, split **6** breach, schism **7** rupture

Fra Diavolo composer
5 Auber (Esprit)

fragile
4 weak **5** frail **6** feeble, flimsy, infirm **7** brittle, friable, tenuous, unsound **8** decrepit, delicate **9** breakable, frangible

fragment
3 bit **4** chip, iota, part, rive **5** burst, crumb, flake, grain, piece, scrap, shard, shred, smash **6** morsel, shiver, sliver **7** break up, flinder, shatter **8** fraction, particle, splinter **9** fall apart **12** disintegrate

fragmentary
6 broken **7** partial **10** fractional, incomplete, unfinished

fragrance
4 musk, nose, odor **5** aroma, attar, scent, smell, spice **7** bouquet, cologne, incense, perfume **9** redolence **11** eau de parfum, toilet water **13** eau de toilette

fragrant
7 odorous, scented **8** aromatic, perfumed, redolent **11** odoriferous

frail
4 puny, slim, thin, weak **5** petty, reedy, wispy **6** feeble, flimsy, infirm, sickly, slight **7** brittle, fragile, slender, spindly, tenuous, unsound **8** decrepit, delicate **9** breakable, frangible

frailty
4 vice **5** fault **6** foible **7** failing **8** delicacy, weakness **9** infirmity **10** feebleness **11** tenuousness **12** imperfection

frame
4 body, form, mold, plan, sash **5** build, draft, erect, forge, mount, shape, shell **6** border, casing, cook up, devise, draw up, figure, invent, make up, sketch, system **7** arrange, chassis, concoct, fashion, imagine, prepare **8** assemble, casement, conceive, contrive, regulate, skeleton **9** cartouche, construct, fabricate, formulate, structure
part: 4 sill, stud **5** joist, plate

framework
4 rack **5** shell, truss **7** trestle **8** cribbing, cribwork, scaffold, skeleton, studding, studwork, trussing **9** bare bones, structure
of crossed strips: 7 lattice, trellis

France
bay: 6 Biscay
capital: 5 Paris
channel: 6 Manche (La) **7** English
city: 4 Caen, Lyon, Metz, Nice **5** Brest, Lyons **6** Amiens, Calais, Nantes, Rennes **8** Bordeaux, Grenoble, Toulouse **9** Marseille **10** Marseilles, Strasbourg, Versailles **11** Montpellier
conqueror: 6 Caesar (Julius)
emperor: 5 Pepin (III, the Short)
8 Napoleon (Bonaparte) **11** Charlemagne
enclave: 6 Monaco
former name: 4 Gaul **6** Gallia
historic province: 4 Foix **5** Anjou, Aunis, Bearn, Berry, Maine **6** Alsace, Artois, Marche, Poitou, Vendée **7** Gascony, Guyenne, Picardy **8** Auvergne, Bretagne, Brittany, Burgundy, Dauphine, Flanders, Gascogne, Limousin, Lorraine, Lyonnais, Normandy, Picardie, Provence, Touraine **9** Angoumois, Bourgogne, Champagne, Languedoc, Nivernois, Orléanais, Saintonge, Venaissin **10** Roussillon **11** Bourbonnais, Île-de-France **12** Franche-Comté
island: 3 Yeu **6** Hyères, Oléron, Ushant **7** Corsica **8** Belle-Île **11** Noirmoutier
monarch: 5 Henri, Henry, Louis **6** Philip **7** Charles **8** Philippe
monetary unit: 4 euro
monetary unit, former: 3 sou **5** franc
mountain, range: 4 Alps, Jura **6** Vosges **8** Auvergne, Pyrenees **9** Mont Blanc
neighbor: 5 Italy, Spain **7** Andorra, Belgium, Germany **10** Luxembourg **11** Switzerland
president: 8 de Gaulle (Charles) **10** Mitterrand (François)
region: 5 Corse **6** Alsace, Centre **7** Corsica, Picardy **8** Auvergne, Bourgogne, Bretagne, Brittany, Burgundy, Limousin, Normandy, Picardie **9** Aquitaine, Champagne, Languedoc, Normandie **10** Rhône-Alpes **11** Île-de-France **12** Franche-Comté, Midi-Pyrénées
river: 4 Aire, Aude, Oise **5** Adour, Isère, Loire, Marne, Rhone, Saône, Seine, Somme, Yonne **7** Garonne
sea: 13 Mediterranean
strait: 5 Dover

Francesca's lover
5 Paolo

franchise
4 vote **6** ballot **7** freedom, license **8** suffrage **9** privilege

frangible
7 brittle, fragile, friable **8** delicate **9** breakable

frank
3 dog **4** fair, free, open **5** blunt, plain **6** candid, direct, honest, hot dog, weenie, wiener, wienie **7** upright **8** man-to-man, out-front, straight **9** barefaced, outspoken **10** forthright, scrupulous, unreserved **11** openhearted, plainspoken, transparent, unconcealed, undisguised, uninhibited, unvarnished, wienerwurst **12** heart-to-heart, unmistakable

Frankenstein author
7 Shelley (Mary)

frankfurter
3 dog 6 hot dog, weenie, wiener, wienie
11 wienerwurst

Frankie's lover
6 Johnny

Frankish hero
6 Roland

Franklin, Benjamin
birthplace: 6 Boston
invention: 5 stove 8 bifocals
pen name: 11 Poor Richard

frankness
6 candor 7 honesty

frantic
3 mad 4 wild 5 upset, wired 7 fraught,
shook up, unglued 8 feverish, frenetic,
frenzied, maniacal, worked up
10 distraught 11 overwrought

Franzen novel
11 Corrections (The)

frappe
7 chilled, liqueur 9 milk shake

fraternal
6 clubby 8 sociable 9 brotherly,
comradely, dizygotic 10 like-minded

fraternal society
3 FOE 4 Elks 5 Lions, Moose 6 Eagles,
Masons 7 Woodmen (of the World)
8 Shriners 10 Freemasons, Hibernians,
Odd Fellows

fraternity
4 club 5 guild, order, union 6 league
7 company 8 sodality 10 fellowship
11 association, brotherhood 13 brother-
liness

fraud
3 gyp 4 fake, gaff, hoax, sham 5 cheat,
faker, phony, quack, trick 6 deceit, dupery,
humbug, hustle 7 chicane, swindle
8 cozenage, flimflam, impostor,
mountebank, operator, trickery 9 charlatan,
chicanery, deception, imposture, pretender,
shell game, trickster 10 dishonesty,
subterfuge 11 counterfeit 12 double-
dealer 13 double-dealing, sharp practice

fraudulence
6 quackery, trickery 9 chicanery,
deception, phoniness 10 dishonesty

fraudulent
4 fake 5 false, phony 7 crooked

8 cheating, guileful 9 deceitful, deceptive,
dishonest 10 fallacious 11 duplicitous

fraught
4 full 5 laden, tense 6 filled, uneasy
7 charged, replete, stuffed 8 pregnant
9 stressful

fräulein
4 maid, Miss 6 maiden 9 governess
12 mademoiselle

fray
3 row 4 fret 5 brawl, broil, brush, clash,
fight, melee, ravel, shred 6 combat, fracas,
strain, strife 7 dispute, frazzle, ruction,
scuffle, struggle 8 irritate, skirmish
9 commotion, scrimmage 10 donnybrook
11 disturbance

frayed
4 worn 6 ragged, shabby 8 tattered
9 moth-eaten 10 threadbare

frazzle
4 do in, fray, poop, tire, wear 5 upset
6 tucker 7 exhaust, fatigue, wear out

frazzled
4 beat 5 upset 6 bushed, sapped
7 drained, rattled 8 agitated, confused,
fatigued, tired out 9 exhausted, fagged out,
unsettled 10 distressed 11 overwrought
12 disconcerted

freak
3 bug, nut 4 buff, geek, whim 5 go ape,
fancy, fiend, maven 6 addict, hippie,
maniac, megrim, oddity, vagary, weirdo,
whimsy, zealot 7 anomaly, caprice,
chimera, conceit, deviate, fanatic, monster
8 crotchet, flimflam 9 androgyne, curiosity
10 aberration, enthusiast 11 abnormality,
monstrosity 12 lusus naturae,
malformation

freakish
3 odd 5 kooky, outré, weird 6 far-out,
quirky 7 bizarre, erratic, oddball, strange
8 aberrant, abnormal 9 arbitrary, eccentric,
grotesque, whimsical 10 capricious,
outlandish

freckle
3 dot 4 mole, spot 5 fleck 7 speckle,
stipple

free
3 rid 4 comp, frank, open 5 loose, untie
6 acquit, exempt, gratis, loosen, unbind,
untied 7 absolve, at large, liberal,
manumit, movable, release, unbound,
unchain, unleash, unloose 8 detached,

generous, liberate, relieved, separate, unburden, unfasten, unloosen **9** at liberty, discharge, exculpate, exonerate, extricate, sovereign, unchained, unchecked, unimpeded, unshackle, unsparing **10** autonomous, democratic, emancipate, gratuitous, unconfined, unfastened, unfettered, unhampered, unshackled, voluntary **11** disentangle, emancipated, independent, spontaneous, untrammeled **12** unrestrained, unrestricted **13** complimentary, self-directing, self-governing, unconstrained

freebie
4 gift, pass **7** present **8** giveaway

freebooter
5 rover **6** bandit, pirate, raider **7** brigand, corsair, marauder, picaroon, pillager, rapparee, sea rover **9** buccaneer, pickaroon, plunderer, ransacker

freedom
5 right **7** liberty, license, release **8** autonomy, immunity, latitude **9** exemption, franchise, privilege **11** prerogative **12** emancipation, independence **13** outspokenness

free-for-all
4 fray **5** brawl, broil, melee **6** affray, fracas, rumble **7** ruction **10** donnybrook

freehanded
7 liberal **8** generous **9** bounteous, bountiful **10** munificent

freeloader
3 bum **5** leech **6** sponge **7** moocher **8** barnacle, hanger-on, parasite **11** bloodsucker

Free State
8 Maryland

free ticket
4 pass **11** Annie Oakley

freeze
4 halt, stop **5** chill, stall **6** benumb **7** congeal **8** glaciate, solidify, stoppage **10** immobilize

freezing
3 icy **4** cold **5** chill, gelid, nippy, polar **6** arctic, bitter, chilly, frigid, frosty, wintry **9** glacial, shivery
combining form: 4 cryo, kryo

freight
4 haul, lade, load **5** cargo **6** burden, charge, lading **7** payload **9** transport

freighter
4 scow, ship **7** carrier, shipper

Freischütz composer
5 Weber (Carl Maria von)

French
article: 3 les, une
attendant: 9 concierge
back: 3 dos
bed: 3 lit **6** couche
boy: 6 garçon
brother: 5 frère
cap: 5 beret
cardinal: 7 Mazarin (Jules) **9** Richelieu (Duc de)
castle: 7 château
cathedral city: 4 Albi **5** Paris, Reims, Rouen **6** Amiens, Nantes, Rheims **8** Chartres
clergyman: 4 abbé, curé, père
coin: 3 ecu
combining form: 5 Gallo **6** Franco
conjunction: 4 mais
daughter: 5 fille
day: 5 jeudi, lundi, mardi **6** samedi **8** dimanche, mercredi, vendredi
dear: 5 cher
department head: 7 prefect
direction: 3 est, sud **4** nord **5** ouest
down with: 4 à bas
dream: 4 rêve
drink: 5 boire
dynasty: 5 Capet **6** Valois **7** Bourbon
egg: 4 oeuf
emblem: 10 fleur-de-lis
empress: 7 Eugénie **9** Joséphine
evening: 4 soir
exclamation: 3 zut **4** eheu, hein **9** sacrebleu
farewell: 5 adieu **8** au revoir
father: 4 père
forest: 7 Argonne, Belleau
friend: 3 ami **4** amie
game: 3 jeu **4** jeux (plural)
God: 4 dieu
good: 3 bon **5** bonne
hat: 7 chapeau
here: 3 ici
income: 5 rente
king: 3 roi
language: 9 Provençal
month: 3 mai **4** août, juin, mars, mois **5** avril **7** février, janvier, juillet
mother: 4 mère
national anthem: 12 Marseillaise (La)
opera: 5 Faust, Lakmé, Manon, Thaïs **6** Carmen, Mignon **7** Werther
pancake: 5 crêpe
pastry: 6 éclair **8** napoleon

policeman: 4 flic 8 gendarme
porcelain: 6 Sèvres 7 Limoges
preposition: 3 par, sur 4 avec, dans, pour, sans, sous
pretty: 4 joli 5 jolie
prison: 8 Bastille
pronoun: 3 eux, ils, mes, moi, toi, une 4 elle, nous, vous
Protestant: 6 Calvin (John) 8 Huguenot
pupil: 5 élève
queen: 5 reine
rabbit: 5 lapin
railroad station: 4 gare
resort: 3 Pau 4 Nice 5 Vichy 6 Cannes, Menton 7 Antibes 8 Biarritz
resort area: 7 Riviera
restaurant: 6 bistro
revolutionist: 5 Marat (Jean-Paul) 6 Danton (Georges) 11 Robespierre (Maximilien)
Revolution party: 7 Gironde, Jacobin 8 Mountain
Revolution song: 5 Ça Ira
saint: 4 Joan (of Arc) 5 Denis 6 Martin (of Tours) 7 Thérèse (of Lisieux)
school: 5 école, lycée
sea: 3 mer
season: 3 été 5 hiver 7 automne 9 printemps
servant: 5 valet
shop: 8 boutique
shrine: 7 Lourdes
singer: 4 Piaf (Edith) 8 chanteur 9 chanteuse
sister: 5 soeur
small: 5 petit 6 petite
soldier: 5 poilu 6 soldat, Zouave 8 chasseur
son: 4 fils
song: 7 chanson
soup: 6 potage
star: 6 étoile
state: 4 état
stock exchange: 6 bourse
street: 3 rue
subway: 5 metro
there!: 5 voilà
too much: 4 trop
very: 4 très
wartime capital: 5 Vichy
water: 3 eau
well: 4 bien
wineshop: 6 bistro
wood: 4 bois
yesterday: 4 hier

French Guiana
capital: 7 Cayenne
department of: 6 France

ethnic group: 6 Creole
island: 6 Devil's
mountain range: 10 Tumac-Humac
neighbor: 6 Brazil 8 Suriname
river: 4 Mana 6 Maroni 7 Oyapock

French Polynesia
archipelago 7 Tuamotu
capital: 7 Papeete
island, island group: 6 Tahiti 7 Austral, Gambier, Society 9 Marquesas
territory of: 6 France

frenetic
3 mad 4 loco, wild 5 crazy, wired 6 crazed, hectic 7 berserk, frantic 8 agitated, feverish, frenzied, maniacal 9 delirious, orgiastic 10 corybantic

frenzied
see **frenetic**

frenzy
4 amok, fury, rage 5 amuck, craze, furor, mania 6 madden 7 derange, madness, unhinge 8 delirium, distract, hysteria, insanity, paroxysm 9 unbalance 11 derangement

frequency unit
5 hertz 7 fresnel 9 gigahertz

frequent
5 haunt, often, usual, visit 6 common, hourly 7 regular 8 everyday, familiar, habitual 9 customary

frequenter
7 denizen, habitué, haunter

frequently
5 often 8 commonly 9 routinely 10 oftentimes, repeatedly 11 customarily, recurrently

fresh
3 new, raw 4 rude 5 green, naive, novel, sassy, saucy, smart 6 callow, cheeky, recent, unused, vernal, virgin 8 brand-new, impudent, insolent, original 9 unspoiled 11 impertinent, smart-alecky 12 invigorating 13 inexperienced

freshet
5 flood, spate 6 influx

freshman
4 tyro 5 frosh, plebe 6 novice, rookie 8 beginner, neophyte, newcomer 10 apprentice, tenderfoot 13 underclassman

fret

fret
4 fume, fuss, stew 5 brood, chafe, worry
6 dither, pother

fretful
5 angry, cross 6 crabby, cranky 7 carping,
chafing, peevish, pettish, whining
8 captious, caviling, critical, perverse,
petulant, restless, snappish 9 fractious,
impatient, irascible, irritable, querulous

Frey
father: 5 Njörd 6 Njörth
god of: 3 sun 4 rain 5 peace 9 fertility
sister: 5 Freya
wife: 4 Gerd 5 Gerda, Gerth

Freya
brother: 4 Frey
domain: 9 Folkvangr
father: 5 Njörd 6 Njörth
husband: 4 Odin

friable
5 mealy 7 brittle, crumbly, fragile
9 frangible

friar
7 brother 8 cenobite 9 mendicant

fribble
3 toy 5 dally, flirt 6 coquet, trifle 7 trifler
8 trifling 9 dalliance, frivolity 10 dillydally,
fool around

friction
4 drag 7 discord, rubbing 8 abrasion
9 animosity, attrition 10 disharmony,
dissension, resistance 12 disagreement

friction match
5 vesta 7 lucifer 8 vesuvian

Friday's rescuer
6 Crusoe (Robinson)

friend
3 pal 4 ally, chum, mate 5 buddy, crony,
matey, serve 6 cohort 7 comrade, partner
8 alter ego, compadre, confrere, familiar,
intimate, playmate, sidekick 9 associate,
colleague, companion, confidant
10 confidante 11 cater-cousin
12 acquaintance
French: 3 ami 4 amie
Spanish: 5 amiga, amigo

Friend
6 Quaker
founder: 3 Fox (George)

friendly
5 happy 6 amical, chummy, folksy, genial
7 affable, amiable, cordial 8 amicable,
cheerful, familiar, sociable 9 congenial,
favorable 10 buddy-buddy, compatible,

hospitable, neighborly 12 affectionate,
well-disposed 13 accommodating

Friendly Islands
5 Tonga

friends and neighbors
4 kith

friendship
5 amity 6 accord, comity 7 concord,
empathy, harmony 8 affinity, alliance,
goodwill

frigate bird
3 ioa, iwa 8 alcatras 11 man-o'-war bird
genus: 7 Fregata

Frigga, Frigg
husband: 4 Odin
son: 6 Balder

fright
4 fear 5 alarm, dread, panic, scare, shock
6 dismay, horror, terror 11 trepidation

frighten
3 cow 5 alarm, daunt, scare, shock, spook
6 appall, bully, dismay 7 horrify, perturb,
scarify, startle, terrify, unnerve 9 terrorize
10 intimidate

frightful
4 ugly 5 awful, scary 6 horrid 7 fearful,
ghastly, hideous 8 alarming, dreadful,
fearsome, horrible, horrific, shocking,
terrible, terrific 9 appalling, startling
10 formidable, horrendous, terrifying

frigid
3 icy 4 cold 5 chill 6 arctic, chilly, frosty
7 glacial 8 freezing 11 emotionless,
indifferent, passionless, unemotional
12 unresponsive

frijoles
5 beans

frill
4 ruff 5 jabot, ruche 6 doodad, luxury,
ruffle 7 flounce, ruching 8 furbelow
11 affectation, superfluity 12 extravagance

fringe
3 hem, rim 4 brim, ruff 5 bound, brink,
skirt, thrum, verge 6 border, edging,
margin 7 fimbria 8 penumbra, trimming
9 perimeter, periphery 10 borderland

frippery
6 finery, frills, tawdry 7 regalia 8 foofaraw,
trumpery 9 trappings 11 ostentation

frisée
6 endive 7 lettuce

frisk
4 leap, play, romp, skip 5 caper, dance
6 cavort, frolic, gambol, search 7 disport,
pat down, rollick

frisky
3 gay 5 antic 6 feisty, lively 7 coltish,
playful 8 animated, gamesome, sportive
9 sprightly, vivacious 10 frolicsome

fritter away
4 blow 5 spend, waste 7 consume
8 squander 9 dissipate

frivolity
3 fun 4 play 6 gaiety, levity, whimsy
8 nonsense 12 childishness

frivolous
3 gay 5 dizzy, giddy, light, silly 6 frothy,
yeasty 7 flighty, playful, shallow, trivial
8 carefree, careless, heedless, trifling
11 light-headed, superficial

frizzy
5 kinky 6 coiled, curled 7 twisted

frock
4 gown 5 dress, habit 6 jersey, mantle

frog
4 toad 5 ranid 6 anuran 7 croaker
9 amphibian 10 batrachian
family: 7 Ranidae
genus: 4 Rana
kind: 4 hyla 6 peeper 7 leopard
8 bullfrog, tree toad
larva: 7 tadpole

frolic
3 fun 4 lark, play, romp 5 antic, caper,
dance, frisk, party, prank, revel, sport,
spree 6 cavort, didoes, gaiety, gambol,
prance 7 disport, skylark 8 escapade,
hilarity 9 festivity, merriment
10 shenanigan, tomfoolery

frolicsome
3 gay 5 antic 6 frisky, impish 7 coltish,
jocular, playful, roguish, sportful 8 sportive
9 sprightly 10 rollicking 11 mischievous

from
German: 3 von
Scottish: 4 frae

From Here to Eternity author
5 Jones (James)

frondeur
5 rebel 8 mutineer, renegade 9 anarchist,
dissident, insurgent 10 malcontent

front
3 bow, van 4 face, fore, lend, look, mask,
prow 5 beard 6 facade, facing 7 forward
8 anterior, disguise 9 challenge, encounter
10 appearance, figurehead
11 countenance

frontier
5 bound, field, march 6 border 8 backland,
backwash, boundary 9 up-country
10 borderland, hinterland 11 backcountry

frontiersman
5 Boone (Daniel), Clark (George Rogers,
William) 6 Carson (Kit) 7 pioneer, settler
8 Crockett (Davy) 10 bushranger

fronton game
7 jai alai

frontward
8 anterior

frost
4 hoar, rime 6 freeze

frostfish
5 smelt 6 tomcod

frost heave
5 pingo

frosting
5 icing 7 topping 8 trimming

Frost poem
11 Mending Wall 12 Road Not Taken (The)
18 Death of the Hired Man (The)
30 Stopping By Woods on a Snowy
Evening

frosty
3 icy 4 cold, rimy 5 chill, frore, hoary,
nippy 6 chilly, frigid 7 glacial 8 freezing
10 unfriendly

froth
4 foam, head, suds 5 cream, spume, yeast
6 lather 8 airiness 9 frivolity, lightness

froufrou
6 frills 8 rustling

froward
5 balky 6 mulish, ornery 7 peevish, restive
8 contrary, perverse, petulant, stubborn
9 obstinate 10 headstrong, refractory
11 disobedient

frown
4 pout, sulk 5 glare, lower, scowl 6 glower

frowsy
5 dowdy, funky, fusty, messy, musty, stale
6 shabby, smelly, sordid, untidy 7 squalid,
unkempt 8 slattern, slovenly
10 disheveled, disordered, slatternly
13 draggletailed

frozen
4 cold, hard **5** fixed, frore, rigid, stiff
6 frigid, numbed **7** chilled **8** benumbed,
immobile **9** congealed, petrified

frugal
4 mean **5** canny, scant, spare **6** Scotch
7 careful, prudent, scrimpy, sparing, stingy,
thrifty **8** discreet, stinting **9** niggardly,
penurious, provident **10** economical,
unwasteful **12** cheeseparing, parsimonious
13 penny-pinching

frugality
6 thrift **7** economy **8** prudence
9 husbandry **10** providence **11** thriftiness

fruit
5 issue, young **6** result **7** outcome,
progeny **9** offspring
citrus: 4 lime **5** lemon **6** citron, orange,
pomelo **7** kumquat, tangelo **8** bergamot,
mandarin, shaddock **9** tangerine
10 calamondin, grapefruit
dried: 5 prune **6** raisin
drink: 3 ade **5** juice, punch
fleshy: 7 syconia (plural) **8** syconium
hard-shelled: 3 nut **4** seed **5** gourd
7 coconut
residue: 4 marc **6** pomace
seed: 3 pip
study of: 8 pomology **9** carpology
subtropical: 3 fig **4** date, lime **5** lemon,
olive **6** citron, orange **7** avocado, kumquat
9 tangerine **10** grapefruit
sugar: 7 glucose **8** fructose, levulose
temperate-zone: 4 pear, plum, sloe
5 apple, grape, melon, papaw, peach,
prune **6** casaba, cherry, loquat, pawpaw,
quince **7** apricot, currant **8** dewberry
9 blueberry, cranberry, muskmelon,
nectarine, raspberry **10** blackberry,
gooseberry, loganberry, strawberry **11** boy-
senberry, huckleberry, pomegranate
tropical: 5 guava, mango **6** banana,
papaya **7** acerola **8** rambutan, tamarind
9 cherimoya, persimmon, pineapple
10 calamondin, mangosteen
type: 3 nut **4** pepo, pome **5** berry, drupe
6 achene, legume, loment, samara
7 capsule, silique, utricle **11** hesperidium
undeveloped: 6 nubbin

fruitful
6 fecund **7** copious, fertile **8** abundant,
prolific **9** bountiful, fructuous, plenteous,
plentiful **10** productive **11** proliferant

fruition
7 delight **8** pleasure **9** enjoyment

10 attainment, conclusion **11** achievement,
delectation, fulfillment, realization

fruitless
4 vain **6** barren, futile **7** sterile, useless
8 abortive **10** unavailing **11** ineffective,
ineffectual **12** unproductive, unsuccessful

frumpy
4 drab, dull **5** dated, dowdy, tacky
6 stodgy **8** outmoded **9** out-of-date,
unstylish **12** old-fashioned

frustrate
4 balk, bilk, dash, foil, halt **5** block, check,
stump **6** arrest, baffle, defeat, hinder,
impede, stymie, thwart **7** inhibit, prevent
8 confound, obstruct, preclude, prohibit
9 discomfit, forestall, interrupt
10 disappoint

frustration
6 defeat, dismay **7** chagrin, letdown
8 vexation **9** annoyance, hindrance
10 impediment, irritation **11** displeasure,
obstruction

fry
4 burn, sear **5** frizz, grill, sauté **6** fishes,
picnic **7** frizzle **11** electrocute

frying pan
6 spider **7** griddle, skillet

fuddle
5 befog, booze **6** ball up, jumble, tipple
7 confuse, fluster, stupefy **8** bewilder
10 intoxicate

fuddy-duddy
4 fogy **6** fossil, square, stodgy
8 mossback, outdated, outmoded
12 antediluvian, Colonel Blimp, old-
fashioned, stuffed shirt **13** stick-in-the-mud

fudge
3 pad **4** blur, bosh, fake **5** candy, cheat,
color, dodge, hedge, hooey, welsh
6 bunkum **7** distort, falsify, hogwash,
penuche **8** contrive, divinity, nonsense
9 embellish, embroider, overstate,
poppycock **10** equivocate, flapdoodle
11 foolishness

fuel
3 gas, oil **4** coal, coke, fire, peat, wood
5 stoke **6** biogas, diesel, petrol **7** ethanol,
gasohol, inflame, propane **8** charcoal,
gasoline, kerosene **9** petroleum, stimulate
10 natural gas **13** reinforcement

fugacious
7 brittle, fugitive, passing **8** fleeting, volatile

9 ephemeral, momentary, transient
10 evanescent, short-lived, transitory

fugitive
5 exile 6 outlaw 7 escapee, lamster, nomadic, passing, refugee, runaway 8 deserter, fleeting, runagate, vagabond 9 ephemeral, fugacious, momentary, transient, wandering 10 evanescent, short-lived, transitory

fugue master
4 Bach (Johann Sebastian)

Führer, der
6 Hitler (Adolf)

fulcrum
3 hub 4 axis, prop 5 hinge, nexus, pivot 7 support

fulfill
4 meet 5 honor 6 effect, finish, redeem 7 achieve, execute, perform, satisfy 8 complete 9 discharge, implement 10 accomplish

fulgent
6 bright 7 beaming, glowing, radiant, shining 8 luminous, lustrous 9 brilliant

fuliginous
4 dark 5 dingy, dusky, grimy, murky, sooty 7 obscure

full
5 sated, total, whole 6 entire, gorged, jammed, loaded, packed, utmost 7 crammed, crowded, glutted, maximum, plenary, replete, stuffed 8 brimming, complete, satiated 9 jam-packed, plentiful, surfeited 11 chockablock

full-blooded
4 rich 5 flush, ruddy 6 ardent, florid 7 flushed, genuine, glowing 8 forceful, purebred, rubicund, sanguine 9 pedigreed, pureblood 10 compelling 12 thoroughbred

full-blown
4 lush, ripe 5 adult, total 6 all-out, mature 7 grown-up

full-bodied
4 rich 5 husky, lusty, stout 6 potent, robust, strong 9 corpulent 10 meaningful 11 significant, substantial

full dress
6 finery 7 regalia 8 frippery, glad rags 10 Sunday best

full-figured
5 ample, buxom, plump 6 zaftig

10 curvaceous, Rubenesque, statuesque, voluptuous

full-fledged
4 ripe 5 adult, grown, total 6 mature 7 genuine, grown-up 8 complete 9 full-blown

full-grown
4 ripe 5 adult 6 mature

fullness
6 plenty 7 satiety 9 abundance, amplitude, repletion 10 perfection 12 completeness

full-scale
5 total 6 all-out 8 complete, life-size 9 unlimited

full tilt
7 flat-out, rapidly, swiftly 8 pell-mell, speedily 9 posthaste 12 lickety-split

fulminate
4 boil, burn, foam, fume, rage, rave 5 curse, flare 7 bluster, explode, inveigh

fulsome
4 oily 5 plump, slick, soapy, suave 6 lavish, smarmy, smooth 7 buttery, cloying, copious, generous, profuse 8 abundant, effusive, overdone, unctuous 9 excessive 10 flattering, oleaginous 11 extravagant, pharisaical 12 ingratiating, Pecksniffian

Fulton's steamboat
8 Clermont

fumarole
4 vent

fumble
3 bob, paw 4 feel, flub, mess, muff 5 botch, grope 6 bobble, bollix, bungle, muddle 7 blunder, misplay 8 flounder

fume
3 gas 4 boil, burn, odor, rage, rant, rave, reek, snit, stew 5 smoke, vapor 6 seethe, swivet 7 sputter

fun
4 play 5 sport 6 frolic, gaiety 7 amusing, jollity, pastime, whoopee 8 hilarity, pleasant, ridicule, frivolity, horseplay, jocundity, joviality, merriment 10 pleasantry 12 entertaining 13 entertainment

function
3 act, job, run, use 4 duty, goal, mark, role, task, work 5 party, power, react, serve 6 affair, behave, object, office, target

7 concern, faculty, operate, perform, purpose, service 8 activity, behavior, business, capacity, ceremony, occasion, province 9 objective, officiate, operation, reception
trigonometric: 4 sine 6 cosine, secant 7 tangent 8 cosecant 9 cotangent

functional
5 handy, utile 6 useful 7 working 9 practical 11 practicable, serviceable, utilitarian 12 occupational

functioning
6 active 7 dynamic 9 operative

fund
4 bank, pool 5 endow, stake, stock, store 6 coffer, supply 7 capital, finance, reserve 8 bankroll, treasury 9 inventory, subsidize 10 accumulate, capitalize

fundament
4 butt, rear, rump, seat 5 basis, fanny 6 behind, bottom 8 backside, buttocks, derriere 9 posterior, principle 10 foundation, groundwork

fundamental
3 key 5 axiom, basal, basic, prime, vital 6 bottom, factor, primal, simple 7 bedrock, organic, primary, radical, theorem 8 absolute, cardinal, dominant, ultimate 9 component, essential, important, necessary, paramount, primitive, principal, principle, requisite 10 deep-rooted, elementary, grassroots, nitty-gritty, primordial, rock-bottom, underlying 11 constituent, irreducible 12 constitutive, foundational

fund-raiser
8 telethon

funeral
6 burial 7 obsequy 9 obsequies
car: 6 hearse
director: 9 mortician 10 undertaker
oration: 6 eulogy 8 encomium 9 panegyric
procession: 7 cortege
service: 7 requiem 9 obsequies
song: 5 dirge, elegy 8 threnody

funereal
3 sad 4 dark 5 black, bleak, grave 6 dismal, dreary, gloomy, solemn, somber, sombre 7 elegiac 8 mournful 9 deathlike, sorrowful 10 depressing, depressive, lugubrious, oppressive, sepulchral

fungus
4 conk, mold, rust, smut 5 ergot, yeast 6 agaric, dry rot, mildew 7 candida, truffle

8 mushroom, puffball 9 earthstar, stinkhorn, toadstool
combining form: 4 myco 5 myces, mycet 6 mycete, myceto
part: 3 cap 4 gill 5 ascus, hypha, stipe, volva 7 annulus 8 basidium, conidium, mycelium

fungus disease
3 rot 4 mold, rust, scab, smut 5 ergot, tinea 6 blight, mildew, thrush 7 mycosis 8 lumpy jaw, ringworm 12 athlete's foot

funk
4 odor, reek 5 blues, dolor, dumps, ennui, gloom, smell, stink, slump 6 recoil, stench 7 sadness 9 dejection 10 depression, melancholy

funky
3 hip, odd 4 foul, rank 5 fetid, reeky 6 earthy, frowsy, grungy, quaint, quirky, smelly 7 natural, noisome, oddball, offbeat, stinky 8 down-home 10 malodorous

funnel
4 flue, pipe 5 stack 6 hopper 7 channel, conduct, tundish 8 transmit 10 smokestack

funny
3 odd 4 joke, zany 5 antic, comic, droll, fishy, queer 7 amusing, bizarre, comical, jocular, risible, strange 8 farcical, humorous, peculiar 9 facetious, fantastic, hilarious, laughable, ludicrous 10 ridiculous

Funny Girl
5 Brice (Fanny)
composer: 5 Styne (Jule)

funnyman
3 wag, wit 5 clown, comic, cutup, droll, joker 6 gagman, jester 8 comedian, humorist, jokester, quipster 10 comedienne

fur
4 down, hide, pelt, pile 5 floss, fluff, stole 6 pelage, peltry
kind: 3 fox 4 mink, seal 5 fitch, otter, sable 6 ermine, fisher, marten, nutria, tanuki 7 raccoon 10 chinchilla
lamb: 7 caracul, karakul 9 broadtail
medieval: 4 vair 7 miniver

furbelow
5 frill 7 flounce

furbish
4 buff 5 fix up, renew, shine 6 polish, revive 7 burnish, refresh, restore 8 renovate

Furies
6 Alecto 7 Erinyes, Megaera 9 Eumenides, Tisiphone

furious
3 mad 4 wild 5 angry, livid, irate, rabid, upset 6 crazed, fierce, insane, raging, stormy 7 enraged, excited, extreme, frantic, intense, violent 8 feverish, frenetic, frenzied, incensed, maddened, vehement, wrathful 9 impetuous, turbulent 10 boisterous, corybantic

furl
4 curl, fold, roll, wrap 6 take in

furlough
4 pass 5 leave 6 lay off 7 liberty 10 shore leave 13 authorization

furnace
4 kiln, oven 5 forge, stove 6 heater 7 smelter 8 tryworks 11 incinerator
part: 4 port, vent 6 tuyere
tender: 6 stoker

furnish
3 arm, rig 4 give, hand, lend 5 endow, endue, equip 6 fit out, outfit, supply 7 apparel, appoint, deliver, provide, turn out 8 accouter, accoutre, dispense, hand over, transfer 9 provision 10 contribute

furnishings
4 gear 5 decor 9 equipment, trappings 10 housewares 11 appointment 13 accouterments, accoutrements, paraphernalia

furniture designer
American: 5 Eames (Charles, Ray), Phyfe (Duncan) 7 Goddard (John, Stephen, Thomas), Haldane (William) 8 Stickley (Gustav)
British: 6 Morris (William) 7 Gibbons (Grinling), Shearer (Thomas) 8 Sheraton (Thomas) 11 Chippendale (Thomas), Hepplewhite (George)
French: 5 Marot (Daniel) 6 Boulle (André-Charles)
German: 6 Breuer (Marcel)
Scottish: 4 Adam (James, Robert)

furniture style
4 Adam 6 Empire, Shaker 7 Bauhaus, Federal, Mission 8 Colonial, Georgian, Jacobean, Sheraton, Stickley 9 Queen Anne 11 chinoiserie, Chippendale, Duncan Phyfe, Hepplewhite 13 Arts and Crafts

furor
3 ado, cry, fad, wax 4 chic, mode, rage, stir, to-do 5 anger, craze, mania, style, vogue 6 flurry, frenzy, pother, ruckus, rumpus, uproar 7 fashion, madness 8 foofaraw 10 commotion 10 dernier cri, excitement 11 controversy

furrow
3 rut 4 ruck 5 plica, ridge, sulci (plural) 6 course, crease, groove, sulcus, trench 7 channel, crinkle, wrinkle 8 entrench 9 corrugate 11 corrugation

furrowed
5 lined 6 rugose 7 grooved, sulcate 8 wrinkled 10 corrugated

further
4 abet, also, help 5 again, fresh 6 beyond 7 advance, besides, forward, promote 8 engender, moreover 9 encourage, propagate 10 additional, in addition 12 additionally

furthermore
3 and, too 4 also 6 as well, withal 7 besides 8 likewise, moreover 9 what's more 12 additionally

furthermost
4 last 7 extreme 8 farthest, remotest, ultimate

furtive
3 sly 4 foxy, wary, wily 6 artful, covert, crafty, feline, masked, secret, shifty, sneaky, stolen, tricky 7 catlike, cunning, evasive, sub-rosa 8 guileful, hush-hush, scheming, stealthy 9 disguised, insidious 11 circumspect, clandestine 12 hugger-mugger 13 surreptitious, under-the-table
look: 4 peek, peep

fur trader
8 voyageur

furuncle
4 boil 7 abscess

fury
3 ire 4 burn, rage 5 anger, furor, wrath 6 frenzy 7 madness, passion 8 violence 9 vehemence 10 fierceness

furze
4 whin 5 gorse
genus: 4 Ulex 7 Genista

fuse
3 mix 4 flux, meld, melt, weld 5 blend, merge, smelt, unify, unite 6 anneal, solder 7 liquefy 8 coalesce, conflate, dissolve, intermix 9 commingle, integrate 10 amalgamate 11 consolidate, incorporate

fusillade
4 hail 5 burst, salvo 6 shower, volley

7 barrage 8 drumfire, outburst
9 broadside, cannonade 11 bombardment

fusion
5 alloy, blend, union 6 merger 7 amalgam, mixture 8 compound 9 coalition, immixture, synthesis

fuss
3 ado, nag, row 4 beef, crab, flap, fret, miff, stew, stir, to-do, wail 5 gripe, stink, upset, whine, worry 6 bother, bustle, hassle, hurrah, pother, ruckus, rumpus, squawk 7 protest, quarrel 8 complain, foofaraw, squabble 9 commotion, complaint, kerfuffle, objection 10 excitement 11 controversy 12 perturbation

fussbudget
3 hen 6 granny 8 stickler 10 fuddy-duddy 13 perfectionist

fusspot
8 stickler 9 nitpicker, worrywart

fussy
5 picky 6 cranky, dainty, ornate 7 careful, finicky, fretful 9 crotchety, irritable, querulous 10 fastidious, meticulous, particular, pernickety, scrupulous 11 painstaking, persnickety, punctilious 13 conscientious

fustian
4 rant 7 bombast, pompous 8 affected, inflated 9 high-flown 11 exaggerated, highfalutin, pretentious 13 grandiloquent

fusty
4 rank 5 close, dated, fetid, moldy, passé, stale 6 bygone, old-hat, smelly 7 archaic 8 outdated 10 antiquated, malodorous 11 reactionary 12 old-fashioned 13 superannuated

futile
4 idle, vain 5 empty 6 hollow, otiose 7 useless 8 abortive, bootless, hopeless, nugatory 9 fruitless, worthless 10 unavailing 11 ineffective, ineffectual 12 unproductive, unsuccessful

future
5 later 6 offing, to come 7 by-and-by 8 oncoming, tomorrow 9 hereafter

Futurism
founder: 9 Marinetti (Filippo Tommaso)
painter: 5 Balla (Giacomo), Carra (Carlo) 7 Russolo (Luigi) 8 Boccioni (Umberto), Severini (Gino)
sculptor: 8 Boccioni (Umberto)

fuzz
3 cop 4 down, lint 6 police

fuzzy
3 dim 5 faint, gauzy, linty, vague, woozy 6 bleary, blurry 7 blurred, muddled, obscure, shadowy, unclear 8 confused 9 distorted, undefined 10 ill-defined, incoherent, indefinite, indistinct

fylfot
8 swastika

G

gab
3 jaw, rap, yak **4** blab, chat, talk **5** clack, drool, prate, speak **6** babble, drivel, gibber, gossip, jabber, natter, yammer **7** blabber, blather, chatter, palaver, prattle, twaddle **8** chitchat, converse, idle talk **9** gibberish, small talk

gabber
6 gossip, magpie **7** blabber **9** chatterer **10** chatterbox **12** blabbermouth, gossipmonger

gabby
4 glib **5** talky, windy **6** chatty **7** voluble **8** effusive **9** garrulous, talkative **10** long-winded, loquacious **11** loose-lipped **12** loose-tongued

gaberdine
4 coat, suit **5** cloak, cloth **6** capote, fabric **7** garment, manteau **8** material

gable
4 wall **8** pediment
ornament: 6 finial

Gabon
capital: 10 Libreville
city: 10 Port-Gentil
ethnic group: 4 Fang **5** Bantu
language: 6 French
monetary unit: 5 franc
neighbor: 5 Congo **8** Cameroon
river: 6 Ogooué

gad
3 bat **4** flit, roam, rove **5** amble, drift, mooch, range, stray, tramp **6** chisel, ramble, wander **7** maunder, meander, traipse **9** gallivant

Gad
brother: 5 Asher
father: 5 Jacob
mother: 6 Zilpah
son: 3 Eri **5** Ezbon, Haggi

Gaddis novel
12 Recognitions (The) **14** Frolic of His Own (A) **16** Carpenter's Gothic

gadfly
3 nag **4** pest, pill **6** bother, critic, insect, nudnik **8** nuisance

gadget
4 tool **5** gizmo, thing **6** device, dingus, doodad, hickey, jigger, widget **7** concern, gimmick, utensil **9** apparatus, appliance, doohickey, implement, mechanism **10** instrument **11** contraption, thingamabob, thingamajig, thingumajig

gadwall
4 bird, duck, fowl **9** waterfowl

gadzooks
4 drat, egad **6** crikey, zounds

Gaea
husband: 6 Uranus
offspring: 6 Furies, Giants, Titans, Typhon, Uranus **7** Erinyes **8** Cyclopes **9** Eumenides
parent: 5 Chaos

Gaelic
4 Erse **5** Irish **6** Celtic **8** Scottish
god: 3 Ler **5** Dagda
hero: 5 Oisin **6** Ossian **11** Finn MacCool
king: 9 Conchobar, Conchobor
language: 4 Manx
poet: 4 bard **6** Ossian
queen: 4 Medb
soldier: 4 kern **6** Fenian
spirit: 7 banshee

gaff
3 fix, rig **4** hoax, hook, spar, spur **5** abuse, fraud, spear, trick **6** fleece, ordeal **7** deceive, gimmick **8** raillery **12** climbing iron

gaffe
4 flub, goof, muff **5** boner, bungle, error, fault, fluff, foul-up, lapse **6** bollix, boo-boo, howler, slipup **7** blooper, blunder, clinker,

gag

faux pas, misstep, mistake **8** solecism
9 gaucherie **11** impropriety, misjudgment
12 indiscretion

gag

4 balk, gasp, hoax, jape, jest, joke, quip
5 choke, crack, heave, prank, retch, trick
6 muffle, muzzle, shtick, stifle, strain
7 repress, silence, squelch **8** throttle
9 restraint, wisecrack, witticism

gaga

4 agog, wild **5** crazy, giddy, nutty, wacky
6 doting, fervid, gung ho **7** foolish,
gushing, excited, smitten **8** animated,
enamored, obsessed, thrilled **9** ebullient,
exuberant **10** captivated, infatuated
12 enthusiastic

gage

3 vow **4** bond **5** token **6** pledge, surety
8 gauntlet, security
(see also **gauge**)

gaggle

4 crew, gang, pack **5** array, bunch, flock,
group **6** clutch, number **7** cluster
10 assemblage, collection **11** aggregation

Gaheris

brother: **6** Gareth, Gawain
father: **3** Lot
mother: **8** Margawse, Morgause
uncle: **6** Arthur
victim: **8** Margawse, Morgause

gaiety

3 fun, joy **4** glee **5** mirth, revel **6** finery,
frolic, hoopla **7** elation, jollity, revelry,
whoopee **8** elegance, hilarity, reveling,
vivacity **9** animation, festivity, happiness,
joviality, merriment **10** ebullience,
exuberance, hullabaloo, joyousness,
jubilation, liveliness **11** high spirits,
merrymaking **12** conviviality

gain

3 get, net, win **4** earn, land, make, reap
5 clear, cover, lucre, reach, score **6** attain,
expand, obtain, pick up, profit, rack up,
return, secure **7** achieve, acquire,
advance, attract, augment, benefit, bring in,
enlarge, procure **8** draw down, earnings,
increase, overtake, persuade, proceeds,
traverse, windfall **10** accomplish **11** move
forward

gainful

6 paying **8** fruitful, generous **9** lucrative,
rewarding **10** beneficial, productive,
profitable, well-paying, worthwhile
12 advantageous, remunerative

gainsay

4 buck, defy, deny **6** impugn, negate,
oppose, refute, resist **7** dispute **8** disclaim,
disprove, negative, traverse **9** disaffirm,
repudiate, withstand **10** contradict,
contravene, controvert

Gainsborough painting

7 Blue Boy

gait

3 air, run **4** clip, dash, lope, pace, rate,
step, trot, walk **5** amble, speed, strut, train,
tread **6** canter, gallop, stride **7** bearing
8 demeanor

gaiter

4 boot, shoe, spat **7** legging **8** overshoe

gal

4 babe, doll **5** chick

gala

4 ball, bash, fete, prom **5** merry, party
6 lively **7** festive, jubilee, pageant, shindig
8 festival, jamboree, wingding **9** festivity,
spectacle **11** celebration **13** entertainment

galago

5 lemur **8** bush baby

Galahad

father: **8** Lancelot **9** Launcelot
mother: **6** Elaine
quest: **5** Grail **9** Holy Grail

Galatea

father: **6** Nereus
husband: **9** Pygmalion
lover: **4** Acis
mother: **5** Doris

galaxy

6 nebula **8** Milky Way, universe

Galba

predecessor: **4** Nero
successor: **4** Otho

gale

4 blow, gust, wind **5** blast, storm **6** squall
7 cyclone, tempest, typhoon **8** outburst
9 hurricane

galena

3 ore

Galen's forte

7 healing **8** medicine

galilee

5 porch **6** chapel

Galilee town

4 Cana **7** Gergesa **8** Nazareth, Tiberias
9 Bethsaida, Capernaum

Galileo's birthplace
4 Pisa 5 Italy 7 Tuscany

gall
3 irk, nag, rub, vex 4 bile, fray, fret, rile, roil, sore, wear 5 annoy, brass, chafe, cheek, erode, grate, graze, nerve 6 abrade, bother, burn up, harass, pester, plague, rancor, ruffle, scrape 7 conceit, disturb, frazzle, inflame, provoke, scratch, torment 8 audacity, boldness, chutzpah, irritate, temerity 9 aggravate, arrogance, brashness, impudence, insolence 10 bitterness, effrontery

gallant
3 fop 4 beau, bold, buck, dude, hero 5 blade, blood, brave, civil, dandy, lover, manly, Romeo, showy, suave, swain, wooer 6 daring, heroic, suitor, urbane 7 courtly, coxcomb, dashing, Don Juan, stately, valiant 8 Casanova, gracious, lothario, paramour, spirited, valorous 9 attentive, courteous, dauntless, ladies' man 10 chivalrous, courageous

gallantry
5 honor, poise, valor 6 daring, mettle, spirit 7 amenity, bravery, courage, heroism, prowess, suavity 8 boldness, chivalry, courtesy, urbanity, valiance, valiancy 9 attention, manliness 10 resolution 11 courtliness 12 fearlessness

galleon
7 warship 12 square-rigger

gallery
5 patio, porch, salon 6 arcade, loggia, museum, piazza 7 balcony, passage, portico, veranda 8 audience, corridor, showroom 9 colonnade, onlookers, promenade
ancient Greek: 4 stoa

galley
3 gig 4 boat, mess, ship, tray 5 cuddy, proof 6 bireme 7 canteen, kitchen, trireme, warship 8 scullery 9 cookhouse

Gallic
6 French

gallimaufry
3 mix 4 hash, mess, olio, stew 5 chaos 6 jumble, medley 7 clutter, goulash, mélange, mixture, variety 8 mishmash, pastiche 9 patchwork, potpourri 10 assortment, hodgepodge, hotchpotch, miscellany, salmagundi

gallinaceous bird
3 hen 5 quail 6 grouse, turkey 7 chicken, hoatzin, peacock 8 curassow, pheasant 9 partridge 10 guinea fowl

galling
6 bitter, vexing 8 rankling 9 upsetting, vexatious 10 afflictive, irritating, nettlesome 11 aggravating, distressing, troublesome 12 exasperating

gallivant
3 bat, bum, gad 4 flit, roam, rove 5 amble, drift, jaunt, mooch, range, stray 6 cruise, ramble, travel, wander 7 meander, traipse 8 vagabond 10 knock about

gallop
4 dash, race 6 sprint

gallows
6 gibbet
bird: 7 villain 8 criminal

galore
4 full, lush, rich 5 ample, great 6 lavish 7 aplenty, copious, endless, profuse 8 abundant, generous 9 bountiful, expansive, plentiful 11 overflowing

galosh
4 boot, shoe 6 rubber 8 overshoe

Galsworthy work
7 Justice 11 Forsyte Saga (The)

galumph
4 plod 5 barge, clomp, clump, stomp, stump, tramp 6 lumber, trudge

galvanize
3 jar, zap 4 coat, fire, jolt, stir, spur, stun 5 pep up, pique, prime, react, rouse, shock 6 arouse, excite, perk up, thrill 7 animate, enliven, immerse, inspire, provoke, quicken 8 activate, astonish, energize, motivate, vitalize 9 electrify, innervate, magnetize, stimulate 10 invigorate

gam
3 leg, pin, pod, rap 4 chat, flap, limb, talk 5 visit 6 confab 9 drumstick 12 conversation

Gambia
capital: 6 Banjul
city: 9 Serekunda
language: 7 English
monetary unit: 6 dalasi
neighbor: 7 Senegal

gambit
3 con, jig 4 move, play, ploy, ruse, wile 5 dodge, topic, trick 6 design, device, remark, tactic 7 gimmick 8 artifice, maneuver, trickery 9 expedient, stratagem 10 subterfuge

gamble

3 bet, lay, set **4** dare, game, play, punt, risk
5 put on, stake, wager **6** chance, hazard,
plunge, raffle **7** imperil, lottery, venture
8 cast lots, long shot **9** crapshoot,
speculate **10** jeopardize

gambler

5 dicer, shark, sharp **7** sharper
9 cardsharp **10** cardplayer **11** cardsharper

gambling place

3 den **4** club, dive, Reno **5** joint, Vegas
6 casino **8** Las Vegas, pool hall
9 roadhouse **10** Monte Carlo **12** Atlantic
City, betting house

gambol

3 hop **4** jump, lark, leap, romp, skip
5 bound, caper, frisk, revel, sport **6** cavort,
frolic, prance, spring **7** carry on, roister,
rollick

Gambrinus' invention

3 ale **4** beer **5** lager

game

3 bet, fun, lay **4** bold, jest, joke, lark, play,
prey, romp **5** brave, chase, eager, hardy,
sport, stake, trick, wager **6** gamble, quarry,
spunky **7** contest, pastime, valiant, willing
8 fearless, intrepid, resolute, unafraid,
valorous **9** amusement, dauntless,
diversion, undaunted **10** courageous,
recreation

ball: 4 golf, polo, pool **5** fives, rogue,
rugby **6** hockey, pelota, soccer, squash,
tennis **7** cricket, croquet, jai alai
8 baseball, football, handball, hardball,
lacrosse, racquets, rounders, softball
9 billiards **10** basketball, volleyball **11** racquetball

Basque: 6 pelota **7** jai alai

bird: 4 duck **5** quail **6** chukar, turkey
7 bustard **8** bobwhite, pheasant
9 partridge

board: 5 chess **7** pachisi **8** checkers,
Scrabble **9** crokinole, Parcheesi
10 backgammon

card: 3 gin, loo, Uno, war **4** faro, fish,
skat, solo **5** monte, ombre, pitch, poker,
rummy, whist **6** Boston, bridge, casino,
écarté, euchre, fan-tan, hearts, piquet
7 auction, bezique, canasta, cooncan, old
maid, primero **8** baccarat, Canfield,
conquian, cribbage, gin rummy, pinochle
9 blackjack, solitaire, twenty-one, vingt-et-
un **11** chemin de fer

child's: 3 tag **5** jacks **7** marbles
8 leapfrog, peekaboo **9** hopscotch

confidence: 4 scam **5** bunco, bunko,
sting

court: 5 roque **6** pelota, squash, tennis
7 jai alai **8** handball, racquets **9** badminton
10 basketball, volleyball **11** racquetball

electric: 7 pinball

English: 5 rugby **7** cricket **8** draughts

Irish: 7 hurling

of chance: 4 faro, keno **5** beano, bingo,
boule, craps, lotto, rondo **6** fan-tan,
hazard, policy, raffle **7** lottery, rondeau
8 roulette

parlor: 8 charades

racket: 6 squash, tennis **8** lacrosse, ping-
pong, racquets **9** badminton
11 racquetball, table tennis

roulette-like: 5 boule

rule maker: 5 Hoyle (Edmond)

string: 10 cat's cradle

table: 4 pool **5** craps **7** mah-jong,
snooker **8** dominoes, mah-jongg, ping-
pong, roulette **9** bagatelle, billiards
11 table tennis

word: 5 rebus **6** crambo **7** anagram,
hangman **8** acrostic, charades, Scrabble
9 crossword, logogriph

game plan

6 scheme, tactic **8** scenario, strategy
9 blueprint **10** big picture

gamete

3 egg **4** ovum **5** sperm **8** germ cell

gamin

3 elf, imp, tad **4** brat, tyke, waif **5** scamp
6 monkey, rascal, urchin **11** guttersnipe
12 street urchin

gamine

3 elf, imp **4** brat, waif **5** scamp **6** hoyden,
rascal, tomboy, urchin **11** guttersnipe
12 street urchin

gaming cubes

4 dice **5** bones

gammon

3 ham **4** dupe, fool, rook **5** bacon, feign
6 delude, fleece, humbug **7** deceive,
pretend, swindle **8** flimflam, hoodwink
9 bamboozle **11** hornswoggle

gamut

5 range, scale, scope, sweep **6** extent,
series, spread **7** compass **8** diapason,
spectrum

gamy

3 off **4** foul, racy, rank, vile **5** brave, fetid,
funky, plucky, putrid, rancid, rotten,
smelly, sordid, stinky, strong **7** corrupt,
decayed, noisome, noxious, reeking

10 decomposed, malodorous, scandalous
12 disagreeable, disreputable

gander
4 look, peek **5** goose **6** glance **7** glimpse
9 simpleton, waterfowl

_____ Gandhi
5 Rajiv **6** Indira **7** Mahatma **8** Mohandas

gandy dancer
10 railroader, tracklayer

ganef
5 thief **6** rascal **9** scoundrel

Ganesa, Ganesh
father: 4 Siva **5** Shiva
head: 8 elephant
mother: 7 Parvati

gang
3 lot, mob, set **4** band, clan, club, crew,
pack, ring, team **5** bunch, crowd, group,
horde **6** circle, clique, outfit **7** arrange,
cluster, collect, combine, company, coterie
8 assemble **10** accumulate, assemblage
11 combination

gangling
4 bony, lean, slim **5** gaunt, lanky, rangy
6 meager, meagre, skinny **7** angular,
scrawny, slender, spindly **8** rawboned **9** spindling

ganglion
5 tumor **7** nucleus

gangrene
3 rot **5** decay **7** mortify, putrefy **8** necrosis
9 decompose

gangster
4 goon, hood, thug **5** rough, thief, tough
6 bandit, gunman **7** hoodlum, mafioso,
mobster, ruffian **8** criminal **9** cutthroat,
racketeer
girlfriend: 4 moll

gangway
4 hall, path **5** aisle **7** passage, walkway
8 corridor **10** passageway

ganja
3 kef, kif, pot, tea **4** hemp, herb, weed
5 grass, smoke **7** hashish **8** cannabis,
Mary Jane **9** marijuana

gannet
4 bird **5** booby **7** seabird

ganoid fish
3 gar **6** beluga, bowfin **7** dogfish, garfish,
teleost **8** billfish, sturgeon **10** paddlefish

Ganymede
abductor: 4 Zeus **7** Jupiter
brother: 4 Ilus
father: 4 Tros
function: 9 cupbearer

gaol
3 jug, pen **4** jail **5** clink, joint, pokey
6 cooler, lockup, prison **7** slammer
8 bastille **9** calaboose, jailhouse
12 penitentiary

gap
3 cut, pit **4** gash, gulf, hole, lull, pass, rent,
rift, skip, slit, slot, tear, vent, void, yawn
5 abyss, blank, break, chasm, chink, cleft,
clove, crack, gorge, gulch, gully, pause,
recess, space, split **6** arroyo, breach,
canyon, cavity, cranny, divide, hiatus,
hollow, lacuna, ravine, schism, vacuum
7 caesura, crevice, fissure, interim,
opening, orifice, rupture, vacancy, vacuity
8 aperture, cleavage, division, fracture,
interval **9** disparity, interlude **10** deficiency,
difference, interstice, separation **12** intermission, interruption **13** discontinuity

gape
3 eye, yaw **4** bore, gawk, gawp, gaze,
glom, leer, look, ogle, open, part, peer,
yawn **5** crack, glare, gloat, space, split,
stare **6** glance, goggle **7** eyeball
10 rubberneck

gaping
4 huge, open, vast, wide **5** broad, great
7 chasmal **9** cavernous

gar
4 fish, pike **8** billfish **10** needlefish

garage
4 shop **7** cabinet, car park, carport, shelter

Garand
5 rifle

garb
4 clad, duds **5** array, cover, dress, getup,
style **6** attire, clothe, outfit **7** apparel,
clothes, garment, raiment, threads
9 trappings **10** appearance

garbage
4 junk, muck, slop **5** dreck, dregs, filth,
offal, trash, waste **6** debris, litter, refuse,
sewage **7** rubbish **8** detritus, riffraff
heap: 6 midden

garble
4 sift, warp **5** alter, belie, color, twist
6 jumble, mangle, muddle **7** becloud,
confuse, contort, distort, falsify, obscure,

garçon
pervert 8 miscolor, misstate, mutilate
9 obfuscate 10 impurities 12 misrepresent

garçon
3 boy 6 waiter 7 servant

garden
4 Eden, park 7 nursery
shelter: 5 arbor 6 arbour

gardener
6 grower 7 yardman 9 topiarist

garden house
6 alcove, gazebo 9 belvedere

Garden State
9 New Jersey

garden tool
3 hoe 4 claw, fork, rake 5 mower, spade
6 dibble, pruner, scythe, shears, shovel,
sickle, trowel, weeder 8 clippers

Gardner character
10 Perry Mason

Gareth
brother: 6 Gawain 7 Gaheris
father: 3 Lot
mother: 8 Margawse, Morgause
slayer: 8 Lancelot 9 Launcelot
uncle: 6 Arthur
wife: 6 Liones

Gargamelle's son
9 Gargantua

Gargantua
abbey: 7 Thélème
author: 8 Rabelais (François)
father: 12 Grandgousier
first word: 5 drink
mother: 10 Gargamelle
son: 10 Pantagruel

gargantuan
see gigantic

Garibaldi follower
8 redshirt

garish
4 loud 5 gaudy, showy, vivid 6 brassy,
brazen, flashy, tawdry, tinsel, vulgar
7 blatant, chintzy, glaring, raffish
12 meretricious

garland
3 ana, lei 5 album, crown 6 anadem,
digest, laurel, wreath 7 chaplet, coronal,
coronet, laurels, omnibus 8 analects
9 anthology, selection 10 collection,
compendium, miscellany 11 florilegium

garlic
4 moly, ramp 5 clove 6 allium

garment
4 garb, gear 5 array, habit 6 attire
7 apparel, raiment 8 clothing, vestment
10 habiliment
African: 6 kaross 7 dashiki
Arab: 3 aba 4 haik
British: 10 mackintosh
clergy's: 3 alb 4 cope 7 cassock,
soutane 8 vestment
close-fitting: 6 girdle, tights 7 leotard
for sleeping: 6 pajama 7 nightie
9 nightgown
Greek: 5 tunic 6 chiton, peplos
7 chlamys 8 himation
Hindu: 4 sari
hooded: 8 djellaba
Japanese: 6 kimono
lace: 10 chemisette
Malay: 6 sarong
men's: 3 tie 4 vest 5 pants, shirt, socks
6 jacket, slacks 7 drawers 8 trousers
outer: 4 cape, coat, robe, wrap 5 cloak,
parka, shawl, smock, stole 6 capote,
jacket, kimono, poncho, sarong, ulster,
wammus 7 overall, pelisse, surtout,
sweater, topcoat 8 overcoat, pinafore,
pullover, scapular 9 coveralls, gaberdine,
polonaise
Polynesian: 5 pareo, pareu
rain: 6 poncho 7 oilskin, slicker
Roman: 4 toga 5 tunic
Scottish: 4 jupe, kilt 7 sporran
sleeveless: 3 aba 4 cape 6 mantle,
tabard
Turkish: 6 dolman
women's: 4 gown 5 dress, skirt 6 blouse,
vestee 7 blouson, nightie, partlet
8 negligee, peignoir, pelerine

garner
4 cull, earn, hive, reap 5 amass, glean,
hoard, lay up, store 6 gather, pick up, roll
up 7 collect, extract, harvest, store up
8 cumulate, ingather 9 stockpile
10 accumulate

garnet
5 jewel, stone 6 pyrope 8 essonite
9 hessonite
black: 8 melanite
red: 9 almandine, almandite

garnish
4 deck, trim 5 adorn 6 bedeck 7 dress up,
enhance 8 beautify, decorate, ornament
9 embellish

garret
4 loft, room 5 attic 8 cockloft

garrison
4 camp, fort, post 6 assign, billet, occupy,
troops 7 station 8 fortress 10 stronghold

garrote
5 choke 8 strangle, throttle 11 strangulate

garrulous
see **gabby**

garter
4 band, belt 5 strap 7 support 9 supporter

garth
4 yard 5 close 9 enclosure

gas
4 fuel, fume 5 fumes, steam, vapor
6 petrol 8 gasoline 9 petroleum
atmospheric: 4 neon 5 argon, oxide,
ozone, xenon 6 helium, oxygen 7 krypton
methane 8 hydrogen, nitrogen
flammable: 6 butane, ethane, ethyne
7 methane, propane, propene 8 ethylene
inert: 4 neon 5 argon, radon, xenon
6 helium 7 krypton
mine: 8 firedamp 9 black damp
oxygen: 5 ozone
toxic: 5 sarin, soman, tabun 6 arsine,
ketene 7 mustard 8 phosgene
9 phosphine

gasconade
4 brag 7 bravado 8 boasting, bragging
11 braggadocio

gash
3 cut, rip 4 rend, slit, tear 5 carve, cleft,
gouge, slash, slice, split 6 incise 8 lacerate
10 depression, laceration

gasket
4 ring, seal 5 O-ring 6 sealer

gasoline
4 fuel 6 petrol
rating: 6 octane

gasp
4 blow, huff, pant, puff 5 heave 6 wheeze
11 exclamation

Gaspar
companion: 8 Melchior 9 Balthazar
gift: 12 frankincense

gassy
5 windy 7 verbose 8 inflated, vaporous
9 flatulent

gastronome
7 epicure, gourmet 8 gourmand 9 bon
vivant 11 connoisseur

gastropod
4 slug 5 conch, murex, snail, whelk
6 cowrie, limpet, volute 7 abalone,
mollusc, mollusk, sea slug 8 pteropod,
univalve 10 periwinkle

gat
3 gun 6 pistol, roscoe 7 channel, firearm,
handgun, passage 8 revolver

gate
3 tap 4 cock, door, exit, port 5 entry,
hatch, toril, valve 6 faucet, portal, spigot,
switch, wicket 7 hydrant, opening, petcock
8 entrance, entryway, stopcock 9 turnstile
10 attendance

gâteau
4 cake

gatefold
6 insert 7 foldout

Gates of Hercules
9 Gibraltar 12 promontories

gateway
4 arch, door, exit 5 pylon, toril 6 portal
7 archway, doorway, opening 8 entrance

gather
4 brew, cull, gain, grow, heap, herd, loom,
mass, meet, pick, pile, pool, reap 5 amass,
bunch, flock, glean, group, horde, infer,
judge, pluck, shirr, swarm 6 assume,
deduce, derive, expect, garner muster, pick
up, pucker, summon, take in 7 cluster,
collect, convene, extract, harvest, marshal,
round up, suppose, surmise, suspect
8 assemble, conclude, converge, increase
9 aggregate, intensify 10 accumulate,
congregate, understand 11 concentrate

gathering
4 bevy, crew, gang, herd, mass, ruck
5 bunch, crowd, crush, drove, flock, group,
horde, party, press, rally, swarm 6 caucus,
klatch, muster, throng 7 company, harvest,
klatsch, meeting, reunion, turnout 8 assembly, congress, junction 9 concourse,
congeries 10 assemblage, collection,
conference, confluence 11 aggregation,
get-together 12 congregation

Gath's giant
7 Goliath 10 Philistine

gauche
5 crude, gawky, inept 6 clumsy
7 awkward, halting, loutish, uncouth
8 bumbling, tactless 9 graceless, ham-
handed, inelegant, maladroit 10 blundering

gaucho
6 cowboy 8 herdsman
weapon: 4 bola 5 bolas 7 machete

gaudeamus ____
6 igitur

gaudy
4 loud 5 showy 6 brassy, brazen, coarse, flashy, garish, tawdry, tinsel, vulgar 7 blatant, chintzy, glaring 9 brummagem, tasteless 10 outlandish 12 meretricious, ostentatious

Gaugamela
loser: 6 Darius, Persia
victor: 9 Alexander (the Great)

gauge
4 bore, rule, size 5 check, judge, meter, scale, weigh, width 6 assess, degree 7 compute, measure 8 diameter, estimate, evaluate, quantify, standard 9 benchmark, criterion, dimension, thickness, yardstick 10 instrument, touchstone 11 measurement

Gauguin's island
6 Tahiti

Gaul
4 Celt 6 France 9 Frenchman

Gaulish
6 French
god: 4 Esus 7 Taranis
goddess: 8 Belisama
priest: 5 druid

gaunt
4 bare, bony, grim, lank, lean, thin 5 harsh, lanky, spare 6 barren, gangly, skinny, wasted 7 angular, scraggy, scrawny 8 gangling, rawboned, skeletal 9 emaciated 10 cadaverous

gauntlet
4 dare, test 5 glove, trial 6 attack, ordeal 9 challenge, onslaught

Gautama
6 Buddha 10 Siddhartha
mother: 4 Maya 8 Mahamaya
son: 6 Rahula
wife: 9 Yasodhara

gauze
4 film, haze, leno, mesh, mist 5 cloth, crepe, tulle 6 fabric, tissue 7 bandage, chiffon, tiffany 8 compress, dressing 11 cheesecloth

gauzy
4 thin 5 filmy, fuzzy, sheer, vague 6 flimsy 8 delicate, gossamery, pellucid 10 diaphanous 11 transparent

gavel
6 hammer, mallet

gavial
7 gharial, reptile 9 crocodile

gavotte
4 tune 5 dance

Gawain
brother: 6 Gareth 7 Gaheris
father: 3 Lot
mother: 8 Margawse, Morgause
slayer: 8 Lancelot 9 Launcelot
uncle: 6 Arthur
victim: 6 Uwayne 7 Lamerok 9 Pellinore

gawk
3 oaf 4 bore, gape, gaze, hick, look, lout, lump, peer, rube 5 churl, glare, gloat, klutz, looby, stare, yokel 6 goggle, lubber

gawky
5 inept, splay 6 clumsy, coarse, gauche, oafish 7 awkward, loutish, lumpish, uncouth 8 bumbling, bungling, lubberly, ungainly 9 graceless, ham-handed, lumbering, maladroit

gay
4 glad, keen, wild 5 bonny, brash, happy, jolly, merry, queer, showy, sunny, vivid 6 blithe, bouncy, bright, cheery, festal, frisky, jocund, jovial, joyful, joyous, lively, rakish, sporty 7 animate, chipper, excited, festive, forward, gleeful, lesbian, playful, raffish 8 animated, cheerful, colorful, mirthful, rakehell, spirited, sportive 9 brilliant, exuberant, homophile, sparkling, sprightly, vivacious 10 blithesome, frolicsome, homoerotic, homosexual, insouciant, licentious, nonchalant 12 light-hearted

_____ Gay
4 John 5 Enola

Gaza victor
7 Allenby (Edmund)

gaze
3 eye 4 bore, gape, gawk, leer, look, ogle, peer, pore, scan, view 5 glare, gloat, stare, watch 6 goggle 7 eyeball, observe 8 consider 10 rubberneck 11 contemplate

gazebo
6 alcove 8 pavilion 9 belvedere 11 garden house, summerhouse

gazelle
4 kudu, oryx 5 eland, nyala 7 gemsbok 8 antelope

gazette
5 paper 6 record 7 journal, publish

9 newspaper 10 periodical 11 publication
12 announcement

gazetteer
5 atlas, guide, index

Ge
see Gaea

gear
3 cam, cog, rig 5 dress, goods, shift, stuff,
wheel 6 adjust, tackle, things 7 apparel,
harness, rigging 8 clothing, cogwheel,
garments, materiel, property, sprocket,
tackling, trapping 9 apparatus, equipment,
machinery 10 belongings 11 accessories,
habiliments, possessions
13 accouterments, accoutrements,
paraphernalia

Geats
king: 7 Hygelac
prince: 7 Beowulf

Geb
daughter: 4 Isis 8 Nephthys
father: 3 Shu
mother: 6 Tefnut
sister: 3 Nut
son: 3 Set 6 Osiris
wife: 3 Nut

gecko
6 lizard 7 reptile

Gedaliah
father: 6 Ahikam 7 Pashhur 8 Jeduthun
slayer: 7 Ishmael

gee
3 wow 4 gosh, turn 5 golly, right
8 goodness, gracious 9 turn right

geek
4 buff, guru, nerd, whiz 5 carny, fiend,
freak 6 carney, carnie, expert, pundit,
weirdo 7 devotee, egghead, fanatic,
oddball 9 authority, eccentric
10 enthusiast 12 intellectual

Gehenna
3 pit 4 hell 5 abyss, hades, Sheol
6 Tophet 7 inferno 8 Tartarus 9 perdition
10 underworld 11 netherworld

Geisel pseudonym
7 Dr. Seuss

geisha wear
3 obi 6 kimono

gel
3 dry, set 4 clot 6 harden, mousse

7 colloid, congeal, thicken 8 solidify
9 coagulate

gelatin
3 jam 4 agar 5 jelly 7 sericin

geld
3 cut, fix, tax 5 alter, desex, unsex
6 change, neuter 7 deprive 8 castrate,
mutilate 9 sterilize 10 emasculate
11 desexualize

gelid
3 icy 4 cold 5 chill, nippy, polar 6 arctic,
chilly, frigid, frosty, frozen, steely 7 glacial
8 freezing

gelt
5 money

gem
3 jet 4 jade, onyx, opal, rock, ruby, sard
5 agate, amber, beryl, bijou, coral, jewel,
pearl, stone, topaz 6 amulet, garnet,
jasper, scarab, sphene, spinel, zircon
7 bejewel, corundum, diopside, fluorite,
emerald, enjewel, olivine, peridot
8 amethyst, corundum, diopside, fluorite,
intaglio, lazurite, obsidian, sapphire,
sardonyx, sparkler, tigereye 9 carnelian,
moonstone, phenakite, scapolite, spodu-
mene, tiger's-eye, turquoise 10 aquamarine, cordierite, tourmaline
11 alexandrite, chrysoberyl, chrysoprase,
lapis lazuli, masterpiece
blue: 6 zircon 8 sapphire 9 turquoise
10 aquamarine 11 lapis lazuli
carved: 8 intaglio
changeable: 9 chatoyant
cut: 7 marquis 8 baguette, cabochon,
marquise 9 brilliant
face: 5 facet
green: 4 jade 7 emerald, peridot,
smaragd 10 chrysolite 11 chrysoprase
red: 4 ruby, sard 6 garnet, pyrope, spinel
9 carnelian
support: 7 setting
weight: 5 carat
yellow: 5 amber, topaz 6 sphene 7 citrine

Gemini star
6 Castor, Pollux

gemmule
3 bud

gemsbok
4 oryx 8 antelope

Gem State
5 Idaho

gemütlich
see **genial**

gendarme

3 cop **5** bobby **7** officer, soldier **8** flatfoot
9 constable, patrolman, policeman

gender

3 sex **4** kind, male, sort, type **5** class
6 female, neuter **8** feminine **9** masculine

genealogy

5 roots, stirp, stock **6** origin, stemma
7 descent, history, lineage **8** ancestry,
heredity, pedigree **9** bloodline **10** family
tree

general

4 wide **5** broad, usual, vague **6** common,
global, normal, public **7** blanket, generic,
overall, regular, routine, typical **8** catholic,
everyday, sweeping **9** all-around, inclusive,
prevalent, universal **10** collective,
prevailing, unspecific, widespread **11** com-
monplace **13** comprehensive
American: 3 Lee (Robert E.) **4** Haig
(Alexander), Pike (Zebulon), Wood
(Leonard) **5** Clark (Mark, Wesley, William),
Grant (Ulysses S.), Meade (George), Scott
(Charles, Hugh, Winfield), Smith (Andrew
Jackson, Giles, Holland, Morgan, Samuel,
Walter, Bedell), Stark (John), Worth
(William) **6** Abrams (Creighton), Custer
(George Armstrong), Franks (Tommy),
Hooker (Joseph), Kearny (Philip, Stephen),
Patton (George S.), Porter (Fitz-John),
Powell (Colin), Slocum (Henry), Spaatz
(Carl), Taylor (Maxwell, Richard, Zachary)
7 Bradley (Omar), Frémont (John Charles),
Houston (Samuel), Jackson (Andrew,
Thomas "Stonewall"), Lejeune (John),
Ridgway (Matthew B.), Sherman (William
Tecumseh), Twining (Nathaniel), Wallace
(Lewis), Wheeler (Joseph) **8** Burnside
(Ambrose), Goethals (George Washington),
Marshall (George), Mitchell (Billy), Pershing
(John J.), Sheridan (Philip), Stilwell
(Joseph) **9** MacArthur (Arthur, Douglas),
McClellan (George), Rosecrans (William),
Schofield (John), Wilkinson (James)
10 Beauregard (P. G. T.), Eisenhower
(Dwight D.), Vandegrift (Alexander),
Wainwright (Jonathan) **11** Schwarzkopf
(Norman) **12** Westmoreland (William)
American Revolutionary: 4 Knox
(Henry), Ward (Artemas) **5** Gates
(Horatio), Wayne ("Mad Anthony") **6** de
Kalb (Baron), Greene (Nathanael), Morgan
(Daniel), Putnam (Israel, Rufus) **8** Moultrie
(William), Sullivan (John) **10** Washington
(George)
Austrian: 11 Wallenstein (Albrecht von)
British: 4 Gage (Thomas), Howe (William)

5 Clive (Robert), Monck (George), Wolfe
(James) **6** Rupert (Prince) **7** Amherst
(Jeffery), Wingate (Orde Charles, Reginald)
8 Burgoyne (John), Cromwell (Oliver)
10 Abercromby (Ralph, Robert), Cornwallis
(Charles), Wellington (Duke of)
Carthaginian: 8 Hamilcar, Hannibal
9 Hasdrubal
Chinese: 3 Yan (Xishan), Yen (Hsi-shan)
4 Feng (Guozhang, Kuo-chang, Yü-hsiang,
Yuxiang) **5** Chang (Tso-lin), Zhang (Zuolin)
Confederate: 3 Lee (Robert E.) **4** Hill
(Ambrose), Hood (John Bell) **5** Bragg
(Braxton), Ewell (Richard Stoddart), Price
(Sterling), Smith (Edmund Kirby) **6** Morgan
(John Hunt), Stuart (Jeb) **7** Forrest (Na-
than Bedford), Hampton (Wade), Jackson
(Thomas "Stonewall"), Pickett (George)
8 Johnston (Albert Sidney, Joseph
Eggleston) **9** Pemberton (John)
10 Beauregard (Pierre G. T.), Longstreet
(James)
French: 3 Ney (Michel) **4** Foch
(Ferdinand) **6** Moreau (Victor), Pétain
(Philippe) **7** Weygand (Maxime) **8** de
Gaulle (Charles), Lefebvre (Pierre),
Montcalm (Marquis de), Saint-Cyr (Laurent
de Gouvion-) **9** Frontenac (Comte de)
10 Rochambeau (Comte de)
German: 4 Jodl (Alfred) **6** Kleist (Paul
Ludwig von), Rommel (Erwin) **9** Rundstedt
(Gerd von) **10** Kesselring (Albert),
Ludendorff (Erich)
Greek: 6 Nicias **9** Miltiades **10** Alcibiades
12 Themistocles
Japanese: 4 Tojo (Hideki) **5** Koiso
(Kuniaki) **6** Yasuda (Yoshisada)
8 Yamagata (Aritomo) **9** Yamashita
(Tomoyuki)
Mexican: 9 Santa Anna (Antonio López
de)
Prussian: 11 Scharnhorst (Gerhard von)
Roman: 5 Sulla (Lucius Cornelius)
6 Caesar (Julius), Fabius (Quintus), Marius
(Gaius), Pompey (the Great), Scipio
(Gnaeus Cornelius, Publius Cornelius)
7 Regulus (Marcus Atilius), Ricimer
(Flavius) **8** Agricola (Gnaeus Julius),
Lucullus (Lucius Licinius), Stilicho (Flavius)
9 Marcellus (Marcus Claudius), Sertorius
(Quintus) **10** Theodosius (the Great)
11 Cincinnatus (Lucius Quinctius)
Russian: 6 Zhukov (Georgy) **7** Kutuzov
(Mikhail), Trotsky (Leon), Wrangel (Pyotr),
Zhdanov (Andrey) **9** Yeremenko (Andrey)
Spanish: 4 Alba (Duke of), Alva (Duke of)
6 Franco (Francisco)
Swedish: 7 Wrangel (Karl Gustav)

general assembly
4 diet 6 plenum 8 congress 10 parliament
11 legislature

generalize
5 infer, widen 6 derive, extend, induce,
spread 7 broaden 8 conclude
12 universalize

generally
6 mainly, mostly, widely 7 all told, as a rule,
broadly, chiefly, en masse, largely, overall,
usually 8 all in all, commonly, normally
9 on average, primarily, typically
10 altogether, by and large, frequently, on
the whole, ordinarily 11 customarily,
principally 12 almost always
13 predominantly

generate
4 bear, make, sire 5 beget, breed, cause,
get up, hatch, spawn, yield 6 create, effect,
father, induce, whip up, work up 7 achieve,
develop, produce, provoke 8 engender,
initiate, multiply, muster up 9 originate,
procreate, propagate, reproduce 10 bring
about, bring forth

generic
5 broad 6 common, global 7 blanket
9 inclusive, unbranded, universal
10 indistinct 12 nonexclusive

_____ generis
3 sui

generosity
7 charity 8 altruism, kindness, largesse
9 abundance 10 liberality 11 beneficence,
benevolence, magnanimity, munificence
12 philanthropy 13 unselfishness

generous
4 free, kind 5 ample 6 lavish 7 copious,
helpful, liberal, profuse, willing 8 abundant
9 bounteous, bountiful, plenteous, plentiful,
unselfish, unsparing 10 altruistic,
benevolent, bighearted, charitable,
munificent, openhanded, ungrudging,
unstinting 11 considerate, kindhearted,
magnanimous, overflowing
12 greathearted

genesis
4 dawn, root 5 alpha, birth, start 6 origin,
outset, source 7 dawning, opening
8 creation 9 beginning, formation,
inception 10 provenance
12 commencement

genetic
10 congenital, hereditary

material: 3 DNA, RNA 7 cistron
9 chromatid 10 chromosome
term: 8 synapsis 9 backcross

genial
4 kind, warm 5 jolly, merry 6 benign,
blithe, hearty, jocund, jovial, kindly, mellow,
social 7 affable, amiable, cordial
8 amicable, friendly, gracious, pleasant,
sociable 9 agreeable, congenial, convivial,
easygoing 10 neighborly 11 good-
humored, good-natured, warmhearted

genie
3 imp 4 jinn, puck 5 afrit 6 afreet, spirit,
sprite 7 servant

geniture
4 dawn 5 birth, start 6 origin 8 nativity
9 beginning, inception

genius
4 bent, gift, head, turn 5 flair, jinni, knack
6 acumen, brains, master, spirit, talent,
wizard 7 aptness, faculty, prodigy
8 aptitude, capacity, penchant 9 ingenuity,
intellect 10 brilliance, creativity,
mastermind, propensity 12 intelligence
13 inventiveness

Genoa's liberator
5 Doria (Andrea)

genre
3 ilk 4 kind, sort, type 5 class, style
6 family, stripe 7 species, variety
8 category, division

gens
3 kin 4 clan 5 group 6 family, people
7 kinfolk 9 relations, relatives

Genseric's subjects
7 Vandals

genteel
4 nice, prim 5 civil 6 formal, la-di-da,
polite, prissy, strict, stuffy, urbane 7 courtly,
elegant, prudish, refined, stilted, stylish
8 affected, cultured, graceful, ladylike,
mannerly, polished, precious, priggish, well-
bred 9 courteous, gracious 10 artificial,
cultivated 11 fashionable, gentlemanly,
pretentious, straitlaced, well-behaved
12 aristocratic, well-mannered
13 distinguished

gentile
3 goy 5 pagan 7 heathen 9 Christian,
non-Jewish

gentility
5 elite 6 gentry 7 decorum, manners,
quality, society 8 breeding, courtesy,
nobility 9 blue blood 10 aristocrat,

gentle

refinement, upper class, upper crust
11 aristocracy

gentle

4 calm, easy, kind, meek, mild, soft, tame
5 balmy, bland, quiet, tamed 6 benign,
docile, genial, kindly, mellow, placid,
serene, smooth, tender 7 amiable, lenient
8 delicate, merciful, peaceful, pleasant,
pleasing, soothing, tranquil 9 agreeable
11 softhearted, sympathetic, warmhearted
13 compassionate
creature: 4 lamb

gentleman

3 sir 6 aristo, fellow, mister 8 cavalier
9 blue blood, chevalier, patrician
10 aristocrat
English: 6 milord
French: 8 monsieur
Hindu: 4 babu
Spanish: 3 don 5 señor

gentleman friend

4 beau 5 lover, swain 6 fiancé, squire,
suitor 7 gallant

gentlemanly

5 civil, noble, suave 6 polite, urbane
7 elegant, gallant, genteel, refined
8 mannerly, well-bred 9 courteous,
honorable 10 chivalrous, cultivated
11 considerate

gentry

5 elite, folks 7 quality, society 8 nobility
9 gentility, patrician 10 gentlefolk,
patriciate, upper class, upper crust
11 aristocracy, high society, ruling class

genuflect

3 bow 4 fawn 5 kneel 6 kowtow

genuine

4 pure, real, true 5 plain, pukka, valid
6 actual, dinkum, honest, tested 7 factual,
natural, sincere 8 absolute, bona fide,
positive, trueborn 9 authentic, certified,
unalloyed, undoubted, unfeigned, veritable
10 sure-enough, unaffected

genus

3 ilk 4 kind, mode, sort, type 5 class,
group, order 6 family 7 species, variety
8 category

geode

4 rock 5 stone 6 cavity, nodule

geoduck

4 clam

geographer

American: 10 Huntington (Ellsworth)
Flemish: 8 Mercator (Gerardus)
German: 6 Ratzel (Friedrich)
Greek: 6 Strabo 7 Ptolemy
Italian: 8 Vespucci (Amerigo)

geologic period

5 azoic 6 Eocene, Hadean 7 Archean,
Miocene, Permian 8 Cambrian, Cenozoic,
Devonian, Holocene, Jurassic, Mesozoic,
Pliocene, Silurian, Triassic 9 Oligocene,
Paleocene, Paleozoic 10 Cretaceous,
Ordovician 11 Phanerozoic, Pleistocene,
Precambrian, Proterozoic
13 Mississippian, Pennsylvanian

geometer

6 Euclid 13 mathematician

geometric

coordinate: 8 abscissa, ordinate
curve: 3 arc 6 spiral 7 ellipse, evolute
8 parabola
figure: 5 rhomb 6 circle, oblong, square
7 ellipse, hexagon, octagon, polygon,
rhombus 8 heptagon, pentagon, rhomboid,
triangle 9 rectangle
solid: 4 cone, cube 5 prism 6 sphere
7 pyramid 8 cylinder, spheroid, spherule
surface: 5 nappe, torus 6 toroid

geometry letters

3 QED

geophagy

4 pica

Georgia

capital: 7 Atlanta
city: 5 Macon 6 Albany, Athens
7 Augusta 8 Columbus, Savannah
college, university: 5 Clark, Emory
6 Mercer 7 Spelman 8 Valdosta
9 Morehouse
founder: 10 Oglethorpe (James)
nickname: 5 Peach (State) 21 Empire
State of the South
river: 8 Ocmulgee 13 Chattahoochee
state bird: 13 brown thrasher
state flower: 12 Cherokee rose
state tree: 7 live oak
swamp: 10 Okefenokee

Georgia, Republic of

ancient kingdom: 6 Iberia 7 Colchis
capital: 6 Tiflis 7 Tbilisi
city: 7 Kutaisi, Rustavi
includes: 6 Ajaria 8 Abkhazia, Adzharia
12 South Ossetia

monarch: 6 Tamara (Queen)
monetary unit: 4 lari
mountain range: 8 Caucasus
neighbor: 6 Russia, Turkey 7 Armenia
10 Azerbaijan
river: 4 Kura 5 Rioni
sea: 5 Black

Georgics author
6 Virgil

Geraint's wife
4 Enid

Gerda's husband
4 Frey

geriatric
3 old 4 aged 5 aging 6 senior 7 elderly
8 outmoded 12 old-fashioned
13 superannuated

germ
3 bud, bug 4 seed 5 spark, spore, virus
6 embryo, origin, source 7 microbe,
nucleus 8 pathogen 9 bacterium
cell: 3 egg 4 ovum 5 sperm

German
3 Hun 4 Goth 6 Teuton
article: 3 das, der, des, die
bomber: 5 Gotha, Stuka
child: 4 Kind
coin: 4 Mark 5 Taler 6 Thaler 7 Pfennig
empire: 5 Reich
head: 4 Kopf
highway: 8 Autobahn
leader: 6 Führer, Kaiser
measles: 7 rubella
mister: 4 Herr
no: 4 nein
nobleman: 6 Junker
pronoun: 3 ich, sie, wir
rifle: 6 Mauser
weight: 3 Lot 5 Pfund, Stein 8 Vierling
woman: 4 Frau 8 Fräulein

germane
3 apt 5 ad rem 7 apropos, fitting, related
8 material, relevant 9 pertinent
10 applicable 11 appropriate

Germany
11 Deutschland
capital: 6 Berlin
city: 3 Ulm 4 Bonn, Jena, Kiel 5 Essen,
Mainz 6 Bremen, Erfurt, Lübeck, Munich
7 Cologne, Dresden, Hamburg, Hanover,
Leipzig, München, Potsdam 8 Augsburg,
Dortmund, Duisburg, Freiburg, Hannover,
Schwerin 9 Frankfurt, Nuremberg,
Stuttgart, Wiesbaden 10 Baden Baden,
Düsseldorf
leader: 4 Kohl (Helmut) 6 Brandt (Willy),
Hitler (Adolf) 7 Schmidt (Helmut), Wilhelm
(Kaiser) 8 Bismarck (Otto)
monetary unit: 4 euro
monetary unit, former: 4 mark 5 taler
6 thaler 12 deutsche mark
mountain, range: 4 Harz 7 Brocken
neighbor: 6 France, Poland 7 Austria,
Belgium, Denmark 10 Luxembourg
11 Netherlands, Switzerland 13 Czech
Republic
region: 4 Ruhr 6 Saxony 7 Bavaria
11 Black Forest
river: 4 Eder, Elbe, Isar, Main, Oder, Ruhr
5 Rhein, Rhine 6 Danube 7 Moselle
sea: 5 North 6 Baltic
state: 5 Hesse 6 Saxony 7 Bavaria
8 Saarland 9 Thuringia 11 Brandenburg

germinate
3 bud 6 evolve, spring, sprout 7 blossom,
develop 9 originate, pullulate

Gerontion poet
5 Eliot (T. S.)

Gershom, Gershon
father: 4 Levi
son: 5 Libni 6 Shimei

Gershwin
3 Ira 6 George
opera: 12 Porgy and Bess
piece: 14 Rhapsody in Blue 15 American
in Paris (An)
show: 5 Oh Kay 9 Funny Face, Girl Crazy
10 Lady Be Good 11 Of Thee I Sing
15 Strike Up the Band
song: 10 I Got Rhythm, Summertime

Gertrude
husband: 8 Claudius
son: 6 Hamlet

Gervaise's daughter
4 Nana

Geryon
dog: 6 Orthus
father: 8 Chrysaor
mother: 10 Callirrhoë
slayer: 8 Hercules

gestalt
4 form 5 shape 6 figure 7 pattern
9 structure 13 configuration

Gestapo chief
7 Himmler (Heinrich)

geste
4 deed, feat 7 emprise, exploit, romance, venture 9 adventure 10 enterprise 11 undertaking

gesticulate
3 nod 4 move, wave 6 beckon, motion, signal

gesticulation
4 wave 6 motion 7 gesture 8 high sign 9 pantomime 12 body language, sign language

gesture
3 nod 4 sign, wave 5 shrug, token 6 motion, salute, signal 8 reminder 9 signalize 10 expression, indication
graceful: 9 beau geste

get
3 bag 4 draw, earn, gain, land 5 catch, cause, seize 6 access, attain, become, elicit, extort, obtain, pick up, secure 7 achieve, acquire, bring in, capture, chalk up, deliver, extract, procure, receive 8 contract 12 come down with

get around
4 roam, rove, tour, trek, walk 5 avoid, dodge, elude, evade, skirt 6 cruise, detour, escape, ramble, travel, wander 8 ambulate, outflank, sidestep 10 circumvent

get away
see **get out**

getaway
3 lam 4 exit, slip 6 escape, flight 7 retreat 8 breakout, vacation

get back
6 go home, recoup, regain, return, revert 7 recover, reclaim, revenge, revisit 8 retrieve 9 repossess, retaliate

get by
4 cope, fare 5 slide 6 eke out, endure, manage, survive 7 carry on 8 maintain

get off
4 walk 5 leave 6 alight, depart, go free, launch 7 pull out 8 dismount 9 disembark 10 beat the rap

get out
4 exit, kite, leak 5 break, issue, leave, scram, split 6 alight, beat it, begone, decamp, depart, egress, escape 7 buzz off, publish, skiddoo, take off, vamoose

8 dispatch, hightail 9 circulate, skedaddle 10 make tracks

Gettysburg general
3 Lee (Robert E.) 5 Meade (George)

get up
4 gain 5 arise, breed, cause, dress, hatch, mount, raise, stand 6 create, induce, summon 7 acquire, prepare, produce 8 engender, generate 12 rise and shine

getup
3 rig 4 duds, garb, togs 5 array, dress, guise 6 outfit 7 costume, threads

get-up-and-go
3 pep, vim, zip 4 bang, push, snap, zeal, zest 5 drive, moxie, oomph, punch, spunk, steam, verve, vigor 6 energy, spirit, starch 8 ambition 10 enterprise, initiative

gewgaw
3 toy 4 dido 5 bijou, curio 6 bangle, bauble, doodad, trifle 7 bibelot, novelty, trinket, whatnot 8 gimcrack, kickshaw 9 bagatelle, objet d'art 10 knickknack

geyser
3 jet 5 fount, spout, spurt 6 gusher, spring 8 fountain 10 wellspring 11 Old Faithful

Ghana
capital: 5 Accra
city: 4 Tema 6 Kumasi, Tamale
ethnic group: 4 Akan 5 Mossi
former name: 9 Gold Coast
gulf: 6 Guinea
lake: 5 Volta
language: 7 English
monetary unit: 4 cedi
neighbor: 4 Togo 10 Ivory Coast 11 Burkina Faso
river: 5 Volta

ghastly
4 grim, pale 5 awful, lurid 6 grisly, horrid, pallid 7 ghostly, hideous, macabre 8 dreadful, ghoulish, gruesome, horrible, shocking, spectral, terrible 9 appalling, deathlike, frightful, ghostlike, repulsive, sickening 10 cadaverous, corpselike, disgustful, disgusting, horrifying, nauseating, terrifying 11 frightening

ghee
3 fat 6 butter

gherkin
4 vine 6 pickle 8 cucumber

ghetto
4 slum

ghost
4 soul 5 demon, haunt, shade, spook, trace 6 kelpie, shadow, spirit, wraith, zombie 7 eidolon, phantom, specter 8 phantasm 10 apparition 11 poltergeist

ghostly
5 eerie, scary 6 spooky 7 shadowy 8 ethereal, spectral 9 deathlike, spiritual, unearthly, unworldly 10 cadaverous, corpselike, phantasmal 12 supernatural

Ghosts author
5 Ibsen (Henrik)

ghoul
4 ogre 5 fiend 7 monster 11 grave robber

GI
5 grunt 7 dogface, fighter, soldier, warrior 8 doughboy 9 man-at-arms 10 serviceman

Gianni Schicchi composer
7 Puccini (Giacomo)

giant
4 huge, hulk, ogre, Otus, vast 5 gross, Gyges, Hymir, jumbo, titan, whale 6 Cottus, Typhon 7 Aloadae (plural), Antaeus, Cyclops, Goliath, mammoth, monster, titanic, whopper 8 behemoth, Briareus, colossal, colossus, enormous, gigantic, immense, Orgoglio 9 cyclopean, Enceladus, Ephialtes, Gargantua, Herculean, humongous, leviathan, monstrous 10 gargantuan, prodigious 11 elephantine
biblical: 4 Anak 7 Goliath
cactus: 7 saguaro
killer: 4 Jack 5 David
one-eyed: 5 Arges 7 Cyclops 10 Polyphemus
100-armed: 9 Enceladus
100-eyed: 5 Argus
rime-cold: 4 Ymer, Ymir
sea god: 5 Aegir

Giant author
6 Ferber (Edna)

giaour
7 infidel 10 unbeliever 11 nonbeliever

gib
6 tomcat

gibber
3 gab, yak 4 blab 5 prate 6 babble, drivel, gabble, jabber, yammer 7 blabber, blather, chatter, palaver, prattle, twaddle

gibberish
3 gab 5 Greek, hokum 6 babble, bunkum,
burble, drivel, gabble, jabber, yammer 7 blabber, blather, chatter, palaver, prattle, twaddle 8 claptrap, flimflam, nonsense 10 balderdash, double-talk, hocus-pocus, mumbo jumbo 11 abracadabra, jabberwocky 12 gobbledygook

gibbet
4 hang 5 lynch, noose, scrag 7 execute, gallows 8 string up

gibbon
3 ape 7 primate, siamang 10 anthropoid

gibbous
6 arched, convex, humped 7 bulging, rounded, swollen 10 humpbacked 11 protuberant

gibe
4 gird, jeer, jest, mock, quip, rail 5 fleer, flout, scoff, scorn, scout, sneer, taunt, tease 6 deride, insult 8 ridicule

Gibraltar
colony of: 7 Britain, England
conqueror: 5 Tarik, Tariq
neighbor: 5 Spain
opposite: 5 Ceuta

giddy
4 gaga 5 dizzy, inane, light, silly, woozy 6 elated, yeasty 7 flighty, foolish, vacuous 8 euphoric 9 frivolous, slaphappy 10 hoity-toity 11 empty-headed, harebrained, light-headed, vertiginous 12 bubbleheaded 13 rattlebrained

_____ Gide
5 André

Gideon
father: 5 Joash
servant: 5 Purah
son: 9 Abimelech

gift
3 set, tip 4 alms, bent, boon, head, turn 5 award, bonus, endow, favor, flair, grant, knack 6 genius, legacy, reward, talent 7 ability, aptness, cumshaw, faculty, freebie, handout, present, subsidy 8 apti-tude, bestowal, capacity, donation, gratuity, largesse, oblation, offering 9 endowment, lagniappe 11 benefaction, benevolence 12 contribution, presentation

gifted
4 able 5 smart 6 expert 7 hotshot, skilled 8 masterly, skillful, talented 9 ingenious, masterful

gig
3 jab, job, top 4 boat, fool, goad, prod,

spur **5** annoy, freak, rotor, spear **6** chaise, harass **7** demerit, provoke, rowboat **8** carriage **10** engagement

gigantic
4 huge, vast **5** giant, jumbo **7** hulking, immense, mammoth, massive, titanic **8** behemoth, colossal, enormous, whopping **9** cyclopean, humongous, king-size, monstrous, walloping **10** gargantuan, king-sized, prodigious, stupendous **11** elephantine

giggle
5 laugh **6** guffaw, hee-haw, titter **7** chortle, chuckle, snicker, snigger, twitter

Gigi author
7 Colette

Gilbert and Sullivan opera
6 Mikado (The) **8** Iolanthe, Patience, Sorcerer (The) **9** Grand Duke (The), Ruddigore **10** Gondoliers (The) **11** H.M.S. Pinafore, Princess Ida, Trial by Jury

Gil Blas author
6 Lesage (Alain-René)

gild
4 coat, deck **5** adorn, bedeck, cover, tinge **6** tinsel **7** enhance, overlay **8** brighten, ornament **9** embellish, embroider

Gilda's father
9 Rigoletto

Gilead
father: **6** Machir
grandfather: **8** Manasseh
son: **7** Jephtha **8** Jephthah

Gilgamesh
4 epic
companion: **6** Eabani, Enkidu
home: **4** Uruk **5** Erech
mother: **6** Ninsun
victim: **6** Huwawa **7** Humbaba

gill
4 race **5** brook, creek **6** runnel, stream, wattle **7** rivulet
relating to: **9** branchial

gillyflower
4 pink **9** carnation, clove pink

Gilroy play
15 Subject Was Roses (The)

gilt
3 hog, pig, sow **4** bond, gold **5** swine **6** gilded, golden **10** brilliance

gimcrack
5 cheap **6** bauble, gewgaw, shoddy, trifle **7** bibelot, chintzy, trinket **8** kickshaw **10** knickknack

gimlet
4 tool **5** drill, drink **8** cocktail
ingredient: **3** gin **5** vodka **9** lime juice

gimmick
3 con **4** ploy, ruse, wile **5** angle, catch, dodge, feint, gizmo, trick **6** device, gadget, gambit, jigger, scheme, widget **8** artifice, maneuver **9** stratagem **10** subterfuge

gimp
3 vim **4** cord, halt **5** braid, hitch **6** dodder, falter, hobble, spirit **7** cripple **8** lameness

gimpy
4 game, halt, lame **7** hobbled, limping **8** crippled

gin
3 net **4** sloe, trap **5** catch, rummy, snare **6** device, liquor **7** springe **8** beverage, generate, separate

ginger
3 fig, pep, vim, zip **4** herb, stir, zing **5** liven, spice, verve, vigor **6** energy, mettle, revive, spirit **7** sparkle
cookie: **4** snap

gingerly
4 safe, wary **5** canny, chary **7** careful, guarded **8** cautious, delicate, discreet

gingery
4 tart **5** fiery, peppy, sharp, spicy, tangy, zesty **6** snappy, spunky **7** peppery, piquant, pungent **8** spirited **10** mettlesome **12** high-spirited

gingham
5 cloth **6** fabric **7** textile **8** material

gingiva
3 gum

gin mill
3 bar, pub **4** dive **5** joint **6** saloon, tavern **7** barroom, taproom **8** alehouse **9** roadhouse **11** public house **12** watering hole

Ginsberg poem
4 Howl **7** Kaddish

ginseng
4 herb, root

Gioconda, La
8 Mona Lisa
composer: **10** Ponchielli (Amilcare)

painter: **7** da Vinci (Leonardo)

giraffe
8 ruminant **9** quadruped **10** camelopard

girandole
7 earring **10** candelabra **11** candelabrum, candlestick, composition

girasol
3 gem **4** opal **5** jewel, stone **7** mineral **8** fire opal **9** artichoke

gird
3 hem **4** band, belt, bind, ring, wrap **5** brace, equip, hem in, ready, round, steel **6** circle **7** bolster, enclose, fortify, prepare, provide, shore up, wreathe **8** buttress, cincture, encircle, surround **9** encompass, reinforce **10** strengthen

girder
4 beam **5** brace **7** support **8** crossbar **9** crossbeam **10** crosspiece, transverse

girdle
4 band, belt, ring, sash **6** cestus, circle **8** ceinture, cincture, encircle, surround **9** encompass, waistband
of Aphrodite: 6 cestus

girl
4 babe, bird, coed, doll, lass, maid, miss **5** chick, filly, missy, wench **6** damsel, lassie, maiden **8** daughter **10** sweetheart

girth
4 band, belt, bind, size **5** brace, cinch, strap **6** circle, fasten, girdle **7** measure **8** cincture, encircle, surround **9** thickness **10** dimensions **13** circumference

Giselle composer
4 Adam (Adolphe)

gist
3 nub, sum **4** core, meat, pith **5** sense **6** burden, ground, kernel, marrow, matter, thrust, upshot **7** essence **9** main point, substance

give
3 pay **4** deal, hand **5** allot, allow, award, grant, issue, offer, remit **6** accord, afford, assign, bestow, commit, confer, convey, devote, direct, donate, extend, market, pony up, render, supply, tender **7** deliver, dish out, display, dole out, fall out, fork out, furnish, hand out, mete out, present, produce, proffer, provide **8** allocate, bequeath, disburse, dispense, give away, hand over, shell out, turn over **9** apportion,

sacrifice **10** administer, contribute, distribute

give-and-take
6 banter **8** exchange, repartee, trade-off **10** compromise **11** cooperation, reciprocity

give away
4 blab, leak **5** award, grant, spill **6** bestow, betray, confer, devote, donate, expose, reveal, tattle **7** deliver, divulge, hand out, let slip, present **8** bequeath, disclose

giveaway
4 deal, gift, leak **5** steal, value **6** tip-off **7** bargain, freebee, freebie, premium, present, sellout **8** betrayal, exposure **10** disclosure, revelation

give back
6 refund, retire, return **7** replace, restore, retreat **8** withdraw **9** reinstate

give in
4 fold, quit, stop **5** yield **6** assent, comply, desist, relent, submit **7** concede, deliver, indulge, succumb **8** back down, cry uncle **9** surrender **10** relinquish

given
5 prone **6** donnée **7** assumed, granted **8** inclined **9** presented, specified **10** particular **11** considering, susceptible

give off
4 beam, emit, flow, vent **5** exude, issue **6** effuse **7** emanate, radiate, release **9** discharge

give out
4 deal, dole, emit, fail, mete, vent **5** issue **6** cave in **7** declare, release, succumb **8** collapse, throw off **9** break down **10** distribute

giver
5 donor **7** donator, grantor

give up
4 cede, quit **5** allow, cease, forgo, waive, yield **6** abjure, devote, resign, vacate **7** abandon, despair **8** abdicate, hand over, renounce, withdraw **9** sacrifice, surrender **10** relinquish

give way
5 yield **6** buckle, cave in **7** retreat, succumb **8** collapse **9** surrender

gizmo
see **gadget**

glabrous
4 bald, bare **6** shaven, smooth **8** hairless

9 beardless 10 bald-headed 12 smooth-shaven

glacial
3 icy, raw 5 chill, gelid, nippy, polar 6 arctic, biting, chilly, frigid, frosty, frozen, wintry 8 freezing

glacier
3 ice 6 ice cap 8 ice field, ice sheet
Alaska: 4 Muir, Taku 6 Bering 10 Mendenhall
Antarctica: 9 Beardmore
deposit: 4 kame 5 esker 6 placer 7 moraine
fissure: 8 crevasse
fragment: 4 berg 7 iceberg
Greenland: 8 Humboldt
hill: 7 drumlin
Karakoram: 5 Biafo 7 Baltoro
New Zealand: 6 Tasman
pinnacle: 5 serac

glacis
5 grade, slope 7 incline 10 buffer zone 11 buffer state

glad
3 gay 4 fain 5 happy, jolly, merry 6 blithe, bright, cheery, genial, jocund, jovial, joyful, joyous 7 beaming, gleeful, pleased, radiant, tickled, willing 8 cheerful, mirthful, pleasant, rejoiced 9 delighted, gratified, overjoyed 11 exhilarated 12 lighthearted

gladden
4 buoy 5 cheer, elate 6 buck up, perk up, please, uplift 7 cheer up, delight, gratify, hearten

glade
6 meadow 8 clearing 9 open space

gladiator
7 fighter 9 combatant, Spartacus

gladly
4 fain, lief 6 freely 7 happily, readily 8 heartily 9 willingly 10 cheerfully, with relish 12 with pleasure

gladness
3 joy 4 glee 5 bliss, cheer, gaiety, mirth 7 delight, jollity 9 happiness, merriment

gladstone
3 bag 8 suitcase

glamorous
7 elegant 8 alluring, charming, dazzling, enticing, magnetic 9 seductive 10 attractive, bewitching, enchanting 11 captivating, fascinating 13 sophisticated

glamour
5 charm, magic, spell 6 allure, appeal 7 romance 8 charisma, witchery 9 magnetism, sex appeal 10 attraction, witchcraft 11 fascination 12 razzle-dazzle

glance
4 peek, peep, skim, skip 5 brush, carom, flash, glaze, graze, shine 6 bounce, careen 7 glimpse 8 ricochet
lascivious: 4 leer

gland
5 gonad, liver, organ 6 pineal, thymus 7 adrenal, mammary, parotid, thyroid 8 exocrine, pancreas, prostate, salivary 9 endocrine, pituitary 11 parathyroid
secretion: 7 hormone
swelling: 4 bubo

glare
4 gaze, glow, peer 5 blaze, flame, flash, frown, gleam, light, lower, scowl, shine, stare 6 dazzle, glower 7 obtrude 8 stand out 10 garishness

glaring
4 loud, rank 5 gaudy, plain, vivid 6 brazen, flashy, garish, tawdry, tinsel 7 blatant, obvious 8 blinding, flagrant 9 audacious, egregious, obtrusive 10 noticeable 11 conspicuous, outstanding 12 ostentatious

Glasgow's patron saint
5 Mungo 9 Kentigern

glass
4 lens, pane 5 image, lense, prism 6 mirror 7 reflect 9 barometer, telescope
combining form: 5 vitro
container: 3 jar 6 beaker, bottle
decorative: 7 schmelz 8 schmelze
drinking: 4 pony 5 flute 6 goblet, jigger, rummer, seidel 7 snifter, tumbler 8 schooner
gem: 5 paste 6 strass
magnifying: 5 loupe
milky: 7 opaline
volcanic: 7 perlite 8 obsidian

glasses
5 specs 6 shades 7 goggles 8 bifocals, tumblers 9 lorgnette, pince-nez, trifocals 10 spectacles

glass-like
5 clear 6 glazed, limpid, smooth 8 pellucid, vitreous 9 vitrified 11 translucent, transparent

glassmaker
6 Blenko (William) 7 Lalique (René), Tiffany (Louis Comfort) 9 Waterford

glassmaking tool
5 punty 6 pontil 8 blowpipe

Glass Menagerie author
8 Williams (Tennessee)

glassy
5 blank, dazed, shiny 6 glazed, smooth, vacant 7 hyaloid 8 polished, vitreous 9 burnished

glaucous
4 waxy 7 frosted, powdery

Glaucus
beloved: 6 Scylla
father: 5 Minos 8 Sisyphus
mother: 6 Merope 8 Pasiphaë
son: 11 Bellerophon

glaze
3 rub 4 buff, coat, film 5 cover, glint, gloss, sheen, shine 6 enamel, finish, luster, patina, polish 7 burnish, coating, furbish, lacquer, overlay

glazed
5 blank 6 glassy

gleam
3 ray 4 beam, burn, glow 5 flare, flash, glint, sheen, shine 6 glance 7 glimmer, glisten, glitter, radiate, shimmer, sparkle, twinkle 8 radiance 11 coruscation, scintillate 13 scintillation

gleaming
5 aglow, shiny 6 glossy, sheeny 7 beaming, burning, glowing, lambent, radiant, shining 8 flashing, luminous, lustrous, polished 9 brilliant, burnished, refulgent, sparkling, twinkling 10 glimmering, glistening, glittering, shimmering 13 scintillating

glean
4 cull, reap, sift 5 amass, learn 6 garner, gather, pick up 7 extract, find out, harvest

glebe
4 land 5 field, tract 7 acreage 8 cropland, farmland

glee
3 joy 5 mirth 6 gaiety, levity 7 delight, elation, jollity 8 gladness, hilarity, part-song 9 enjoyment, festivity, good cheer, happiness, jocundity, joviality, merriment 10 exuberance, joyfulness, jubilation 12 exhilaration

gleeful
3 gay 5 jolly, merry 6 blithe, elated, jocund, jovial, joyous 8 cheerful, exultant, jubilant, mirthful 9 exuberant 12 lighthearted

glen
4 dale, vale 5 swale 6 dingle, valley
deep: 5 gorge 6 ravine

glengarry
3 cap 6 bonnet

glib
4 easy 5 slick 6 facile, fluent, smooth 7 offhand, shallow, voluble 8 eloquent, flippant 10 articulate, nonchalant 11 superficial

glide
3 fly 4 flow, sail, skim, slip, soar, waft 5 coast, creep, drift, float, skate, skirr, skulk, slide, slink, sneak, steal 7 descend, slither 8 glissade, volplane 10 portamento

glimmer
4 glow, hint 5 blink, flash, gleam, glint, shine, spark, trace 6 glance 7 flicker, glisten, glitter, inkling, shimmer, sparkle, twinkle 9 coruscate 10 suggestion 11 coruscation, scintillate 13 scintillation

glimpse
4 peek, peep 5 flash, glint, stime 6 glance

glint
3 ray 5 flash, glaze, gleam, sheen, shine, trace 6 glance, luster 7 glimmer, glisten, glitter, shimmer, sparkle, twinkle 9 coruscate 11 coruscation, scintillate 13 scintillation

glissade
4 skim, slip 5 glide, slide

glissando
3 run 5 slide 7 gliding, sliding

glisten
4 glow 5 flash, gleam, glint, shine 6 glance 7 flicker, glimmer, glitter, shimmer, spangle, sparkle, twinkle 9 coruscate 11 coruscation, scintillate 13 scintillation

glitch
3 bug 4 flaw, snag 5 fault 6 defect 7 failing, failure, gremlin, problem 8 obstacle 10 difficulty 11 malfunction

glitter
5 flash, gleam, glint, shine 7 glimmer, glisten, shimmer, spangle, sparkle, twinkle

glittering

9 coruscate **11** coruscation, scintillate
13 scintillation

glittering
5 gaudy, shiny, showy **6** flashy **7** fulgent
9 brilliant, clinquant, coruscant, effulgent
11 spectacular

gloaming
3 eve **4** dusk **5** gloom **7** evening
8 eventide, twilight **9** nightfall

gloat
4 crow **5** exult, revel, vaunt **6** relish
7 triumph **9** celebrate

glob
4 clot, lump **6** dollop

global
5 grand **6** cosmic **7** blanket, general,
overall **8** all-round, catholic **9** inclusive,
planetary, spherical, universal, worldwide
12 encyclopedic **13** comprehensive

globe
3 orb **4** ball **5** earth, round, world
6 planet, sphere **7** rondure
half: **10** hemisphere

globule
4 ball, bead, drip, drop **6** gobbet, pellet
7 driblet, droplet **8** spherule

gloom
3 dim **4** dusk, funk, loom, murk **5** bedim,
blues, cloud, dumps, frown, lower, mopes,
scowl **6** darken, glower, shadow
7 becloud, despair, dimness, obscure,
sadness **8** darkness, overcast, twilight
9 adumbrate, bleakness, dejection **10** blue
devils, depression, melancholy,
overshadow **11** despondency,
unhappiness **12** mournfulness

gloomy
3 dim, dun, sad **4** cold, dark, dour, down,
drab, dull, glum **5** black, bleak, drear,
dusky, mopey, murky, muzzy, sulky, surly
6 dismal, dreary, morose, solemn, somber,
sullen **7** forlorn, joyless, obscure, stygian,
unhappy **8** dejected, desolate, downcast,
funereal, mournful **9** cheerless, depressed,
mirthless, oppressed, saturnine, tenebrous,
woebegone **10** caliginous, chapfallen,
depressing, depressive, dispirited,
despondent, forbidding, lugubrious,
melancholy, oppressive, tenebrific
11 dispiriting, pessimistic **12** disconsolate,
discouraging

glorify
4 hymn, laud **5** bless, cry up, erect, exalt,
extol, honor **6** admire, praise, revere
7 acclaim, dignify, elevate, ennoble, light
up, lionize, magnify, sublime, worship

8 eulogize, venerate **9** celebrate
10 aggrandize

glorious
5 grand, great, noble, proud **6** august,
divine, superb **7** eminent, exalted, radiant,
sublime **8** esteemed, gorgeous, lustrous,
majestic, renowned, splendid, stunning
9 beautiful, brilliant, effulgent, excellent,
marvelous, ravishing, wonderful
11 illustrious, magnificent, resplendent,
splendorous

glory
4 crow, fame, halo, pomp **5** exalt, exult,
gloat, honor, revel **6** heaven, praise, relish,
renown **7** acclaim, aureole, delight,
majesty, rejoice, triumph **8** eminence,
eternity, grandeur, jubilate, radiance,
splendor **9** greatness, hereafter
10 effulgence, exaltation, exultation
11 distinction **12** magnificence,
resplendence

gloss
4 buff **5** glaze, glint, sheen, shine **6** define,
enamel, facade, finish, luster, patina,
polish, veneer **7** burnish, comment,
explain, furbish, varnish **8** annotate
9 interpret, sleekness, slickness, translate
10 annotation, appearance, brilliance,
commentary, definition **11** elucidation,
explanation, translation

glossary
7 lexicon **8** wordbook **9** word-hoard
10 dictionary, vocabulary

gloss over
4 mask **5** slant **6** veneer **7** conceal, cover
up, distort, falsify, varnish **8** disguise,
palliate **9** dissemble, extenuate, sugarcoat,
whitewash **10** camouflage

glossy
5 shiny, sleek, slick **7** shining **8** gleaming,
lustrous, polished **9** burnished
10 glistening
fabric: **4** silk **5** satin
paint: **6** enamel

glove
4 gage, mitt **5** catch, cover **6** mitten,
sheath **8** covering, gauntlet

glow
4 burn, pink, rose **5** bloom, blush, flush,
gleam, rouge, shine **6** mantle, redden
7 blossom, crimson, fox fire, glisten, glitter,
radiate **8** brighten, radiance **10** brilliance,
luminosity **13** incandescence

glower
5 frown, scowl, stare **11** look daggers

glowing
3 hot, red 4 avid 5 flush, ruddy, shiny
6 ardent, fervid, florid, heated 7 beaming,
burning, fervent, flushed, lambent, radiant,
red-hot, vibrant 8 blushing, dazzling,
gleaming, luminous, lustrous, rubicund,
sanguine, suffused 9 brilliant 10 candes-
cent, hot-blooded, passionate
11 impassioned 12 enthusiastic,
incandescent

Gluck opera
5 Orfeo 6 Armide 7 Alceste

glucose
5 sugar, syrup

glue
3 fix, gum 4 bind, join 5 epoxy, paste, stick
6 adhere, attach, cement, fasten 7 plaster,
stickum 8 adhesive, mucilage

gluey
5 gummy, tacky 6 sticky, viscid 7 viscous
8 adhesive 12 mucilaginous

glum
3 sad 4 blue, dour, down 5 moody, sulky,
surly 6 dismal, dreary, gloomy, morose,
sullen, woeful 7 crabbed 8 brooding,
dejected, downcast, taciturn 9 depressed,
oppressed, saturnine, sorrowful,
woebegone 10 despondent, dispirited,
melancholy 11 downhearted, melancholic

glut
4 clog, cloy, cram, fill, pack, pall, sate
5 feast, flood, gorge, stuff 6 deluge,
excess, stodge 7 satiate, surfeit, surplus,
swallow 8 saturate 10 oversupply
13 overabundance

glutinous
4 ropy 5 gluey, gooey, gummy, pasty,
tacky, thick 6 sticky, viscid 7 viscous
10 gelatinous 12 mucilaginous

glutton
3 hog, pig 8 gourmand 9 chowhound,
wolverine 11 gormandizer

gluttonous
7 hoggish, piggish 8 edacious, ravening,
ravenous 9 dissolute, indulgent, rapacious,
voracious 10 insatiable 11 intemperate
13 overindulgent

gluttony
6 excess 7 edacity 8 gulosity, rapacity,
voracity 11 piggishness

glyph
6 figure, groove, symbol 7 graphic
9 character

G-man
3 fed 4 narc, Ness (Eliot) 5 agent
6 Hoover (J. Edgar)

gnarl
4 bend, knot, warp 5 growl, snarl, twist
6 deform 7 contort, distort

gnash
4 bite 5 grind

gnat
3 bug, fly 4 pest 5 midge 6 insect 7 no-
see-um

gnaw
3 eat, nag, vex 4 bite, chaw, chew
5 annoy, chomp, erode, munch, scour,
tease, worry 6 bother, crunch, nibble,
pester, plague, rankle 7 bedevil, corrode,
eat away 8 irritate, wear away 9 masticate

gnome
3 elf, saw 4 rule 5 adage, axiom, dwarf,
maxim, moral, troll, truth 6 dictum, goblin,
saying, truism 7 proverb 8 aphorism,
apothegm 10 shibboleth

gnostic
6 occult, secret 8 abstruse 10 mysterious

gnu
10 wildebeest

go
against: 4 defy 5 fight 6 oppose, resist
7 counter, protest 10 contradict
ahead: 4 lead 7 precede, proceed
8 continue, progress
along: 5 agree, yield 6 accede, comply,
concur 7 consent 9 acquiesce
around: 5 avoid, skirt 6 bypass, detour
7 compass 8 outflank,
sidestep 10 circumvent
at: 6 assail, attack, tackle 7 assault
away: 3 git 4 exit, scat, shoo 5 leave,
scram, split 6 beat it, begone, cut out,
depart, move on, retire 7 buzz off, get lost,
pull out, take off 8 clear out, run along,
shove off, withdraw 9 skedaddle
back: 6 recede, return, revert 7 regress
retreat
back on: 6 betray, renege 7 abandon
8 abrogate
back over: 6 rehash, review, rework
7 recheck, retrace
before: 4 lead 7 precede, predate
8 antedate
beyond: 4 pass 5 excel, outdo 6 exceed,
outrun 7 eclipse, surpass 8 outshine,
outstrip, overtake 9 transcend
forward: 6 move on, push on 7 advance,
press on, proceed 8 continue, progress
in: 5 enter 9 penetrate
out: 4 exit 5 leave 6 expire

Scottish: 3 gae
through: 4 bear **5** audit, brave, check, spend **6** endure, suffer **7** consume, deplete, examine, exhaust, ride out, survive, sustain, undergo **8** squander **9** penetrate, withstand **10** experience
together: 3 fit **4** date, jibe, suit **5** agree, match, tally **6** accord, square **7** conform **8** dovetail **9** accompany, harmonize **10** correspond
with: 4 suit **5** befit, match **9** accompany

goad
3 egg, rod, sic **4** prod, push, spur, urge **5** drive, egg on, impel, prick, thorn **6** coerce, exhort, incite, motive, needle, prompt, propel **7** impetus, impulse **8** catalyst, motivate, stimulus **9** encourage, impulsion, incentive, stimulant, stimulate **10** inducement

go-ahead
4 okay **7** consent **8** spirited **9** ambitious, authority, clearance, energetic **10** green light, permission **11** progressive, up-and-coming **12** enterprising **13** authorization

goal
3 aim, end, use **4** duty, hope, mark **5** score **6** design, intent, object, target **7** mission, purpose **8** ambition, function **9** intention, objective

goat
3 kid, ram **4** lech **5** billy, letch, nanny **6** alpaca, angora, lecher, Saanen **8** cashmere **10** Toggenburg
female: 3 doe **5** nanny
genus: 5 Capra
Himalayan: 4 tahr
male: 4 buck **5** billy
neutered: 6 wether
relating to: 7 caprine
wild: 4 ibex
wool: 6 mohair **8** pashmina

goat antelope
5 serow **7** chamois

goatee
5 beard **7** Vandyke **8** imperial, whiskers

goatfish
6 mullet

goatish
3 hot **4** lewd **6** carnal **7** caprine, lustful, satyric **8** prurient **9** indulgent, lecherous, lickerish **10** lascivious, libidinous, passionate **12** concupiscent

goat-man deity
3 Pan

goat nut
6 jojoba, pignut

gob
3 wad **4** blob, clod, glob, hunk, lump, mass **5** chunk, mouth **6** nugget, sailor **7** extract

gobbet
4 drib, drip, drop, hunk, lump, mass **5** chunk, piece **7** driblet, droplet, globule, portion **8** fragment

gobble
3 eat **4** bolt, cram, grab, glut, gulp, slop, wolf **5** gorge **6** devour, guzzle **7** swallow **11** ingurgitate

gobbledygook
see **gibberish**

go-between
5 agent, envoy, proxy **6** broker, deputy, factor **7** liaison **8** emissary, mediator, procurer **9** middleman **10** arbitrator, interagent, interceder, matchmaker, negotiator, procurator **11** intercessor **12** intermediary, intermediate

goblet
3 cup **5** glass, grail **6** vessel **7** chalice

goblin
3 elf, fay, hob, imp **4** puck **5** bogey, bogle, fairy, ghost, gnome **6** sprite **7** brownie, bugbear **8** bogeyman

_____ go bragh
4 Erin

gobs
4 lots, tons, wads **5** heaps, loads, lumps, piles, rafts, reams, scads **6** oodles **8** slathers **10** quantities

god
4 idol **5** deity **7** creator **8** Almighty, divinity, immortal
combining form: 4 theo
false: 4 baal
French: 4 dieu
Hebrew: 6 Elohim, Yahweh
Latin: 4 deus
Spanish: 4 dios
(see specific entries (as **Greek; Roman**) for names of specific gods and goddesses)

god-awful
4 foul **6** horrid, rotten **7** beastly **8** dreadful, horrible, shameful, shocking, terrible, wretched **9** appalling, atrocious, miserable **10** abominable, deplorable, despicable, detestable, disgusting, outrageous

God Bless America composer
6 Berlin (Irving)

goddess
4 idol 5 deity 8 divinity, immortal
Latin: 3 dea
(see note at **god**)

godfather
3 don 4 boss, capo 6 leader 7 sponsor

Godfather, The
8 Corleone (Don)
actor: 6 Brando (Marlon), De Niro
(Robert), Pacino (Al)
author: 4 Puzo (Mario)
director: 7 Coppola (Francis Ford)

God-fearing
5 pious 6 devout 8 faithful, reverent
9 pietistic, religious, righteous

godforsaken
4 bare 5 bleak 6 barren, dismal, gloomy,
remote 7 pitiful 8 deserted, desolate,
pitiable, wretched 9 miserable, neglected
11 unfortunate

Godiva's husband
7 Leofric

godless
5 pagan 6 unholy, wicked 7 heathen,
impious, infidel, profane 8 agnostic
9 atheistic 11 irreligious, unreligious

godlike
4 holy 6 divine 7 blessed, supreme
8 almighty, immortal 10 omniscient 11 all-
powerful

godliness
5 piety 6 purity 8 devotion, divinity,
holiness, sanctity 9 beatitude, reverence
10 devoutness, sacredness 11 religiosity,
saintliness 12 spirituality, virtuousness
13 righteousness

godly
4 holy 5 pious 6 devout, divine 7 angelic,
blessed, saintly, supreme 8 almighty,
hallowed, immortal, virtuous 9 pietistic,
prayerful, religious 10 omniscient 11 all-
powerful

go down
3 dip, set 4 drop, fall, fold, lose, sink
5 ensue, lower, occur, pitch, slide, slump
6 cave in, happen, plunge, settle, topple,
tumble 7 crumple, decline, descend,
founder, succumb 8 collapse, keel over,
submerge, submerse 9 surrender, take
place

God's acre
8 boneyard, catacomb, cemetery
9 graveyard 10 churchyard, necropolis
12 burial ground, memorial park, potter's
field

godsend
4 boon, gift, good 5 manna 7 benefit
8 blessing, windfall 9 advantage
11 benevolence, serendipity

Goethe work
5 Faust 6 Egmont, Stella 7 Clavigo
10 Prometheus

gofer
4 aide, peon 5 flunky, menial, toady
6 drudge, helper, lackey 7 courier, servant
8 factotum 9 assistant, attendant

goffer
5 crimp, flute, pinch, plait, pleat

go-getter
6 dynamo 7 hustler, rustler 8 live wire
10 ball of fire, powerhouse 11 self-starter

goggle
3 eye 4 bore, gape, gawk, gaze, look,
ogle, peer 5 glare, gloat, stare
10 rubberneck

goggles
5 specs 7 glasses 10 eyeglasses,
spectacles

go-go
5 hyper 6 hectic 7 frantic 8 frenetic,
frenzied

Gogol novel
novel: 9 Dead Souls
story: 8 Overcoat (The) 10 Taras Bulba
14 Diary of a Madman

goiter
6 struma 8 swelling

Golconda
see **gold mine**

gold
4 gilt 5 money 6 riches, wealth, yellow
7 bullion 8 treasure
bar: 5 ingot
combining form: 4 auri, auro 5 chrys
6 chryso
fool's: 6 pyrite
imitation: 6 ormolu
measure: 5 carat, karat
Spanish: 3 oro

goldbrick
3 bum 4 idle, laze, lazy, loaf, loll 5 cheat,

dally, idler, shirk, slack **6** dawdle, loafer, loiter, lounge **7** lounger, shirker, slacker, swindle **8** lollygag, malinger, sluggard **9** lazybones **10** dillydally, malingerer

Gold Bug author
3 Poe (Edgar Allan)

gold cloth
4 lamé

gold-covered
4 gilt **6** gilded

golden
4 gilt, rich **5** auric, blond, shiny, straw **6** blonde, flaxen, gilded, mellow, superb, yellow **7** aureate, honeyed, shining **8** lustrous, resonant **9** favorable, glorious **10** auspicious, prosperous **11** flourishing

golden-ager
5 elder **6** senior **7** ancient, oldster, retiree **8** old-timer **13** senior citizen

golden-apples guardian
5 Ithun **6** Ithunn

golden bough
9 mistletoe

Golden Bough author
6 Frazer (James George)

Golden Boy playwright
5 Odets (Clifford)

golden-crowned accentor
7 warbler **8** ovenbird

goldeneye
3 bug **4** duck, fowl **6** insect **8** lacewing

Golden Fleece seeker
5 Jason **8** Argonaut

Golden Hind captain
5 Drake (Francis)

Golden Horde
6 Tatars **7** Mongols
leader: 4 Batu

golden horse
7 Trigger **8** palomino

golden shiner
4 dace, fish

Golden State
10 California

goldfinch
4 bird **8** songbird **12** yellowhammer

gold mine
7 bonanza, pay dirt **8** El Dorado, Golconda, treasure, treasury **13** treasure trove

golem
3 oaf **4** clod, dolt, dope **5** dunce, idiot, robot **6** nitwit **7** halfwit, machine **8** imbecile **9** automaton, blockhead **10** nincompoop **11** blunderhead

golf
assistant: 5 caddy **6** caddie
club: 4 iron, wood **5** billy, spoon, wedge **6** driver, putter **7** niblick, pitcher **9** metal wood, sand wedge
club part: 3 toe **4** face, grip, head, heel, neck, sole **5** hosel, shaft **6** socket
course: 5 links
cup: 5 Ryder **6** Curtis, Walker
hazard: 4 trap **6** bunker **8** sand trap
mound: 3 tee
score: 3 ace, par **5** bogey, eagle **6** birdie
stroke: 4 baff, chip, draw, fade, hook, putt **5** drive, pitch, shank, slice **7** sclaff
target: 3 cup, par, pin **4** flag **5** green **7** fairway
term: 3 lie **4** club, fore, hole, loft **5** divot, rough, swing **6** hazard, marker, stance, stroke **8** foursome, handicap **9** backswing, downswing, flagstick

golfer
8 linksman
man: 3 Els (Ernie) **4** Daly (John), Ford (Doug), Kite (Tom), Lyle (Sandy), Mize (Larry), Tway (Bob) **5** Boros (Julius), Faldo (Nick), Floyd (Ray), Grady (Wayne), Green (Hubert), Hagen (Walter), Hogan (Ben), Jones (Bobby), Irwin (Hale), North (Andy), Pavin (Corey), Price (Nick), Shute (Denny), Singh (Vijay), Snead (Sam), Woods (Tiger) **6** Casper (Billy), Graham (David), Janzen (Lee), Langer (Bernhard), Miller (Johnny), Nelson (Byron), Norman (Greg), Ouimet (Francis), Palmer (Arnold), Player (Gary), Sluman (Jeff), Sutton (Hal), Vardon (Harry), Watson (Tom) **7** Azinger (Paul), Couples (Fred), Guldahl (Ralph), Mayfair (Billy), Sarazen (Gene), Simpson (Scott), Stewart (Payne), Strange (Curtis), Trevino (Lee), Woosnam (Ian), Zoeller (Fuzzy) **8** Crenshaw (Ben), Nicklaus (Jack), Olazabal (José), Weiskopf (Tom) **9** Rodriguez (Chi Chi), Elkington (Steve) **10** Middlecoff (Cary) **11** Ballesteros (Seve)
woman: 4 Berg (Patty), King (Betsy) **5** Baker (Kathy), Lopez (Nancy), Rawls (Betsy), Stacy (Hollis), Suggs (Louise) **6** Alcott (Amy), Carner (Joanne), Daniel (Beth), Davies (Laura), Geddes (Jane), Mallon (Meg), Merten (Lauri), Wright (Mickey) **7** Bradley (Pat), Inkster (Juli), Mochrie (Dottie), Sheehan (Patty) **8** Zaharias (Babe) **9** Didrikson (Babe),

Sorenstam (Annika), Whitworth (Kathy)
10 Stephenson (Jan)

Golgotha
7 Calvary

Goliath
5 giant **10** Philistine
deathplace: 4 Elah
home: 4 Gath
slayer: 5 David

Gollum creator
7 Tolkien (J. R. R.)

gonad
5 gland, ovary **6** testis **8** testicle

gondola
3 car **4** boat **7** ski lift **11** railroad car

gone
4 away, dead, left, lost, past **5** flown
6 absent **7** defunct, extinct, lacking,
missing **8** departed, vanished

gonef
see **ganef**

goner
8 dead duck **9** lost cause

Goneril
father: 4 Lear (King)
husband: 6 Albany
sister: 5 Regan **8** Cordelia
victim: 5 Regan

Gone with the Wind
author: 8 Mitchell (Margaret)
character: 5 Rhett (Butler) **6** Ashley
(Wilkes) **7** Melanie (Wilkes) **8** Scarlett
(O'Hara)
plantation: 4 Tara

gonfalon
4 flag, jack **6** banner, ensign **7** pendant,
pennant **8** banderol, standard **9** banderole

gong
6 cymbal, tam-tam

gonzo
6 far-out **7** bizarre, offbeat **9** wigged-out
10 outrageous

goo
4 crud, glop, guck, gunk, muck **5** slime

goober
6 peanut

good
4 pure **5** right, sound, whole **6** decent,
humane, kindly, toward, worthy **7** benefit,
healthy, upright, welfare **8** innocent,

virtuous **9** admirable, advantage,
blameless, exemplary, favorable, healthful,
honorable, righteous, well-being,
wholesome **10** altruistic, beneficent,
beneficial, benevolent, charitable,
worthwhile **11** respectable, well-behaved
12 humanitarian **13** philanthropic
French: 3 bon **5** bonne
German: 3 gut
Spanish: 5 bueno

good-bye
4 ciao, ta-ta **5** adieu, congé, later **6** so
long **7** cheerio, parting, send-off, toodles
8 farewell, toodle-oo **9** departing,
departure **11** leave-taking, valediction,
valedictory
French: 5 adieu **8** au revoir **9** bon
voyage
German: 8 lebe wohl
Italian: 11 arrivederci
Japanese: 8 sayonara
Spanish: 5 adios **12** hasta la vista

Good Earth author
4 Buck (Pearl S.)

good-for-nothing
3 bum **6** rascal, waster **7** inutile, rounder,
useless, wastrel **8** feckless, rascally,
unworthy **9** dissolute, scoundrel, valueless,
worthless **10** ne'er-do-well, profligate,
scapegrace **11** purposeless

good-looking
4 cute, fair, foxy **5** bonny, dishy, hunky
6 comely, lovely, pretty **8** alluring, drop-
dead, fetching, handsome **9** beauteous,
beautiful, bodacious, ravishing
10 attractive

goodly
4 fair, tidy **5** ample, hefty, large **7** sizable
8 generous **9** bountiful, plentiful
11 significant, substantial **12** considerable

good-natured
4 easy, kind, mild, warm **6** genial, jovial,
mellow **7** affable, amiable, cordial, lenient
8 cheerful, friendly, laid-back, obliging,
pleasing, sanguine **9** agreeable, congenial,
easygoing, gemütlich, pleasant
10 altruistic, benevolent, charitable
11 complaisant

goodness
5 honor, merit, worth **6** purity, virtue
7 decency, honesty, probity **8** morality,
quality **9** integrity, rectitude
11 benevolence

goods
4 gear **5** cargo, stock, stuff, wares

7 effects 8 chattels, movables, property
9 vendibles 10 belongings
11 commodities, merchandise,
possessions 13 paraphernalia
smuggled: 10 contraband
stolen: 4 loot, swag 5 booty 6 boodle,
spoils 7 plunder
thrown overboard: 5 lagan 6 jetsam

good-tasting

5 sapid, yummy 6 delish, savory, toothy
8 luscious 9 delicious, palatable, relishing,
toothsome 10 appetizing, delectable,
flavorsome 11 scrumptious
13 mouthwatering

goodwill

5 amity, favor 6 comity 7 charity, rapport
8 altruism, kindness, sympathy 9 tolerance
10 compassion, friendship, generosity,
kindliness 11 benevolence, helpfulness
12 friendliness

goody

5 candy, treat 6 bonbon, dainty, morsel,
tidbit 8 delicacy, kickshaw

goody-goody

4 prig 5 prude 6 Grundy 7 prudish,
puritan, uptight 8 bluenose, Comstock,
priggish 9 Mrs. Grundy, nice-nelly
11 puritanical

gooey

5 gluey, gummy, mushy, sappy, soupy
6 cloggy, drippy, slushy, sticky, viscid
7 maudlin, viscous 8 adhesive 9 glutinous
11 sentimental 12 mucilaginous

goof

3 err, kid 4 boob, dolt, flub, fool, mess,
muff 5 boner, booby, botch, chump, dunce,
error, fluff, gaffe, gum up, idiot, put on
6 bobble, boggle, bollix, bumble, bungle,
fumble, mess up 7 blooper, blunder,
fathead, louse up, mistake, slip-up
8 dolthead, lunkhead 9 blockhead

go off

4 blow 5 blast, burst, erupt, leave, sound
6 blow up, depart 7 explode 8 detonate

goofy

5 balmy, batty, crazy, daffy, dippy, loony,
nutty, potty, silly 6 simple, stupid 7 foolish,
idiotic 9 ludicrous 10 ridiculous
11 harebrained

gook

4 crud, glop, gunk, muck 5 gumbo, slime
6 debris, sludge

go on

4 last, stay 5 occur 6 endure, happen,
keep up 7 persist, proceed 8 continue
9 persevere

goon

3 oaf, sap 4 boob, dodo, dolt, dope, fool,
hood, thug 5 dummy, idiot 6 dimwit, hit
man, nitwit 7 hoodlum 8 dumbbell,
enforcer 10 triggerman

gooney

7 seabird 9 albatross

goop

4 crud, gunk, muck 5 gumbo, tripe

Goops author

7 Burgess (Gelett)

goose

4 poke, spur 9 stimulate
cry: 4 honk 5 clang
flock: 3 vee 5 skein 6 gaggle
genus: 5 Anser
Hawaiian: 4 nene
male: 6 gander
wild: 5 brant 7 greylag 8 barnacle
young: 7 gosling

gooseberry

7 currant

Goosebumps author

5 Stine (R. L.)

goose egg

3 nil, zip 4 nada, zero 5 aught, zilch
6 cipher, naught, nought 7 no score,
nothing

gooseflesh

5 bumps 7 pimples

go over

4 scan, skim 5 study 6 peruse, review
7 examine, inspect

gopher

6 rodent 8 tortoise

Gopher State

9 Minnesota

Gordian knot cutter

9 Alexander

Gordius' son

5 Midas

gore

3 jab 4 stab 5 blood, slime, wound
6 gusset, pierce 7 carnage 12 grue-
someness

gorge

3 gap 4 cloy, fill, glut, jade, pall, sate
5 abyss, chasm, cleft, clove, flume, gulch,
stuff 6 arroyo, canyon, clough, defile, pig

out, ravine **7** couloir, overeat, satiate,
surfeit **11** overindulge
Arizona: 11 Grand Canyon
Colorado: 5 Royal

gorgeous
5 grand, plush **6** comely, lavish, lovely,
pretty, superb **7** opulent, sublime
8 alluring, dazzling, glorious, splendid
9 beautiful, brilliant, exquisite, luxurious,
sumptuous **10** attractive, glittering
11 magnificent, resplendent, splendorous

gorgon
3 hag **5** crone, harpy, witch **6** Medusa,
ogress, virago **8** battle-ax, fishwife,
harridan, slattern **9** battle-axe, termagant
father: 7 Phorcus, Phorcys
mother: 4 Ceto

gorilla
3 ape **4** goon, hood, thug **5** tough
6 simian **7** primate **8** gangster
10 anthropoid

Gorky drama
11 Lower Depths (The)

gormless
4 dumb, slow **6** stupid

gorse
4 whin **5** furze, shrub **6** legume

gory
5 lurid **6** bloody, grisly **8** gruesome,
sanguine **10** sanguinary **11** ensanguined,
sanguineous, sensational **12** bloodstained
13 bloodcurdling

gosh
3 gee, wow **4** dang, darn, drat, egad, geez,
heck **5** golly **6** crikey, cripes, shucks
7 doggone **8** goodness, gracious

gospel
5 truth **6** truism **7** message **8** doctrine
9 scripture **11** evangelical

gossamer
4 airy, film, fine, webs **5** filmy, gauzy, sheer
6 flimsy **7** cobwebs, tenuous **8** delicate
10 diaphanous **11** transparent

gossip
4 blab, buzz, chat, dirt, talk **5** clack, prate,
rumor **6** babble, rumble, tattle **7** babbler,
chatter, hearsay, prattle, tattler **8** bigmouth,
busybody, informer, prattler, quidnunc,
telltale **10** talebearer **11** rumormonger,
scandalizer, scuttlebutt **12** blatherskite

gossipy
5 gabby, talky **6** chatty **8** babbling,
blabbing **9** garrulous, talkative

Gotham
7 New York (City)

Gothic
4 dark, wild **5** crude **6** brutal, coarse,
savage uncouth **8** barbaric, Germanic,
medieval, Teutonic **9** barbarian, barbarous,
sans serif **11** black letter, uncivilized

Götterdämmerung composer
6 Wagner (Richard)

Gouda
6 cheese

gouge
3 dig **4** milk, ream, tool **5** cheat, coerce,
exact, pinch, screw, wrest, wring **6** chisel,
extort, groove, wrench **7** squeeze **8** scoop
out **9** blackmail, extortion, shake down
10 overcharge

goulash
4 stew **6** jumble, medley **7** mélange
8 mishmash **9** potpourri **10** bridge hand,
hodgepodge, salmagundi **11** gallimaufry

go under
4 fall, flop, fold, lose, sink **5** drown, plunge
6 submit **7** founder, immerse, succumb
8 collapse, submerge, submerse
9 surrender **10** capitulate

Gounod work
5 Faust **8** Ave Maria

gourd
4 pepo **5** fruit, melon **6** bottle, squash,
vessel **7** chayote, gherkin, pumpkin
8 calabash, cucumber, cucurbit
instrument: 6 maraca

gourmand
see **glutton; gourmet**

gourmet
7 epicure **9** bon vivant **10** gastronome
11 connoisseur **12** gastronomist

gout
4 blob, clot, gush **5** spurt **6** splash
7 disease, podagra **8** eruption, swelling

govern
4 head, lead, rule **5** guide, order, reign,
steer **6** direct, manage, master
7 command, conduct, control, execute,
oversee **8** dominate, hold sway, regulate
9 supervise **10** administer **11** superintend

governess
5 nanny, nurse **6** duenna **8** mistress

9 nursemaid **10** babysitter **11** Mary Poppins

government

4 rule **5** power **6** polity, regime **7** regency, regimen **8** monarchy, republic, Uncle Sam **9** authority, autocracy, democracy, hierarchy, oligarchy **10** Big Brother **11** aristocracy, sovereignty
autocratic: 7 czarism, fascism, tyranny **9** despotism **10** absolutism **12** dictatorship
by a few: 9 oligarchy
by eight: 8 octarchy
by one: 8 monarchy
by three: 8 triarchy **11** triumvirate
by women: 8 gynarchy
official: 10 bureaucrat, functionary
without: 7 anarchy

government agency

3 ATF, BIA, BLM, CDC, CIA, DEA, EPA, FAA, FBI, FCC, FDA, FEC, FHA, GAO, GPO, HUD, ICC, INS, IRS, NBS, NEA, NIH, NRC, TVA **4** FDIC, FEMA, FEPC, NASA, NOAA, NTSB, OSHA

governor

3 bey **4** head **5** chief, nabob, ruler **6** leader, regent **7** manager, viceroy **8** director, executive, regulator **10** commandant, magistrate
Chinese: 6 tuchun
of a fort: 7 alcaide, alcayde **9** castellan, chatelain
Persian: 6 satrap

gown

4 robe, toga **5** dress, frock, habit, tunic **6** camise, kimono, kirtle, mantua **7** cassock, chemise **8** peignoir
dressing: 8 bathrobe
hospital: 6 johnny

goy

7 gentile, non-Jew

grab

3 nab **4** glom, grip, snag, take **5** catch, clasp, grasp, pluck, seize **6** clutch, collar, snatch, tackle **7** capture, grapple, seizure

grabby

6 greedy **8** covetous, desirous, grasping, rapacious **10** avaricious, prehensile **11** acquisitive

grace

4 ease **5** adorn, charm, favor, mercy, poise **6** allure, lenity, pardon, polish, prayer, thanks, virtue **7** charity, dignify, dignity, enhance **8** approval, blessing, clemency, easiness, elegance, goodness, kindness, leniency, petition, reprieve **9** embellish, privilege **10** indulgence, invocation, refinement **11** benediction, forbearance **12** thanksgiving

graceful

4 airy, deft, easy **5** agile, lithe **6** nimble, poised, seemly, smooth, urbane **7** elegant, flowing, genteel, refined **8** debonair, elegance, pleasing, polished

graceless

4 rude **5** crude, gawky, inept **6** clumsy, coarse, gauche, klutzy, vulgar **7** awkward, boorish, uncouth **8** barbaric, ungainly **9** barbarian, barbarous **10** outlandish, unmannered **12** infelicitous

Graces

6 Charis **8** Charites (plural)
brilliance: 6 Aglaia
bloom: 6 Thalia
joy: 10 Euphrosyne
mother: 5 Aegle

gracious

4 kind **5** suave **6** benign, genial, kindly, urbane **7** affable, amiable, cordial, courtly, gallant, stately, tactful **8** charming, generous, mannered, merciful, obliging, sociable **9** congenial, courteous **11** complaisant, good-natured **13** compassionate

grackle

5 mynah **7** jackdaw **8** starling **9** blackbird

gradation

4 rank, step **5** order, range, scale, shade, stage **6** ablaut, change, degree, nuance, series **7** ordering, position, spectrum **9** continuum, variation **10** difference, succession

grade

3 peg **4** cant, form, kind, lean, mark, rank, rate, rung, sort, step, tier, tilt **5** blend, class, group, level, notch, order, pitch, place, slant, slope, stage **6** assess, degree, league, rating **7** arrange, caliber, echelon, incline, leaning, quality **8** appraise, category, classify, division, evaluate, grouping, position, standard **10** categorize **11** inclination

Grade A

3 ace, top **4** best, boss, fine, tops **5** grand, great, prime, primo, super **6** choice **7** capital, supreme, tip-top **8** five-star, superior, top-notch **9** excellent, first-rate, nonpareil, number one, top-drawer **10** first-class **11** outstanding **13** par excellence

gradient
4 lean, ramp, rise, tilt 5 angle, pitch, slant, slope 7 incline, leaning 9 acclivity, declivity 11 inclination

gradual
4 even, slow 6 Psalms, steady 7 ongoing 8 bit-by-bit, creeping 9 piecemeal, prolonged 10 continuous, developing, protracted, step-by-step 11 progressive

gradually
6 slowly 7 by steps 8 bit by bit 9 by degrees, piecemeal 10 step by step 12 deliberately 13 imperceptibly, incrementally

graduate
4 alum
female: 6 alumna 7 alumnae (plural)
male: 6 alumni (plural) 7 alumnus

Graeae, Graiae
4 Enyo 5 Deino 8 Pephredo
father: 7 Phorcus, Phorcys
mother: 4 Ceto
sisters: 7 Gorgons

graft
4 join, mend, scam, skim 5 affix, crime, fraud, scion, unite 6 attach, boodle, fasten, payola, splice 7 implant, swindle, topwork 8 kickback 10 corruption

Grafton, Sue
character: 8 Millhone (Kinsey)
novel: 11 A Is for Alibi

Grahame, Kenneth
character: 3 Rat 4 Toad, Mole 6 Badger
novel: 16 Wind in the Willows (The)

grail
3 cup, end 4 goal 6 goblet, object, target 7 chalice 9 objective

grain
3 bit, jot, rye 4 corn, flax, iota, meal, mito, oats, rice 5 crumb, fiber, kamut, maize, speck, spelt, trace, wheat 6 barley, cereal, millet, quinoa, tittle 7 granule, smidgen, sorghum, texture 8 amaranth, molecule, particle 9 buckwheat, triticale
bundle: 4 bale 5 sheaf
chute: 6 hopper
ear: 5 spike
elevator: 4 silo
mixture: 6 fodder
row: 5 swath 7 windrow

grainy
5 rough 6 coarse 8 granular 10 un-finished, unpolished

grammarian
Roman: 7 Donatus (Aelius)

grammatical case
6 dative 7 oblique 8 ablative, genitive, locative, vocative 9 objective 10 accusative, nominative, possessive, subjective

grampus
5 whale 7 dolphin 8 cetacean, porpoise, scorpion 9 blackfish 12 whip scorpion

Granada
building: 8 Alhambra
citadel: 8 Alcazaba
last Moorish king: 7 Boabdil

granary
3 bin 4 silo 9 grain area 10 repository, storehouse

grand
3 fab 4 epic, fine, huge, vast 5 gaudy, lofty, noble, regal, royal, showy, super 6 august, flashy, garish, lavish, lordly, mighty, ornate, superb 7 exalted, opulent, pompous, stately, sublime 8 baronial, elevated, foremost, gorgeous, imposing, majestic, princely, splendid 9 first-rate, inclusive, luxurious, principal, sumptuous, wonderful 10 first-class, impressive, monumental, prodigious, stupendous, tremendous 11 magnificent 12 ostentatious 13 comprehensive

Grand Canyon
explorer: 6 Powell (John Wesley)
state: 7 Arizona

grande dame
5 queen 6 matron 7 dowager 9 matriarch

grandee
4 duke, earl, king, lord, peer 5 baron, noble, pasha 6 bashaw, prince 8 mandarin, marquess, nobleman, viscount 11 muckety-muck

grandeur
4 pomp 5 glory 7 dignity, majesty 8 nobility, opulence, splendor, vastness 9 greatness, immensity, largeness, loftiness, nobleness, sublimity 10 augustness 11 stateliness 12 magnificence

grandiloquent
5 lofty 7 aureate, bloated, fustian, pompous 8 inflated 9 bombastic, flatulent, high-flown, overblown 10 histrionic, portentous 11 declamatory, highfalutin, pretentious 12 magniloquent

grand inquisitor
Spanish: 10 Torquemada (Tomás de)

grandiose
4 epic, vast 5 lofty, noble, regal, royal, showy 6 august, cosmic, lavish, lordly 7 pompous, stately, sublime, utopian 8 affected, imposing, majestic, princely, splendid 9 ambitious, high-flown 11 extravagant, highfalutin, magnificent, pretentious 12 ostentatious

grand mal
7 seizure 8 epilepsy

grandmother
Russian: 8 babushka

grange
4 farm 9 farmhouse, farmstead

granite
3 ore 4 rock 5 stone 6 aplite 7 mineral 11 igneous rock

Granite State
12 New Hampshire

grant
3 aid 4 alms, avow, cede, dole, gift, give 5 admit, allow, award, endow yield 6 accord, assert, assign, assume, bestow, confer, convey, donate, permit 7 charity, concede, consent, entitle, handout, present, property, subsidy, suppose 8 bequeath, donation, transfer 9 endowment, vouchsafe 10 assistance, concession, relinquish, subvention 11 acknowledge, benefaction 12 contribution 13 appropriation

granular
5 rough, sandy 6 coarse, grainy 7 powdery 8 powdered 10 unfinished, unpolished

granule
3 bit, jot 4 iota, pill, spot 5 grain 6 pellet 8 fragment, particle

grape
3 fox, uva 4 Bual 5 Gamay, Pinot, Syrah 6 Arinto, Burger, Gentil, merlot, muscat, Shiraz 7 Albillo, Aligote, Barbera, Catawba, Concord, Furmint, Niagara, sultana 8 Aleatico, Cabernet, Charbono, Delaware, Friularo, Grenache, Isabella, malvasia, muscadel, Muscadet, Nebbiolo, Riesling, Semillon, Sylvaner, Thompson, Traminer, vinifera, Viognier 9 Carmenère, Chasselas, Lambrusco, Malvoisie, muscadine, Pinot Gris, pinot noir, Sauvignon, Trebbiano, zinfandel 10 chardonnay, Grignolino, muscadelle, pinot blanc, Sangiovese, Verdicchio 11 Chenin Blanc, Petite Sirah, pinot grigio, scuppernong
disease: 4 esca
dried: 6 raisin
drink: 4 wine
pulp: 4 rape 6 pomace
residue: 4 marc

grapefruit
6 pomelo

Grapes of Wrath, The
author: 9 Steinbeck (John)
family: 4 Joad
people: 5 Okies

grapevine
4 buzz 5 rumor 6 gossip 7 hearsay 9 rumor mill 11 scuttlebutt

graph
3 map 4 plot 5 chart 6 sketch 7 diagram, outline 8 nomogram, pie chart

graphic
3 map 5 clear, lucid, photo, vivid 6 cogent, visual 7 picture, precise, telling, written 8 clear-cut, definite, detailed, explicit, incisive, striking 9 pictorial, realistic 10 compelling, photograph 11 descriptive, picturesque

graphite
4 lead 6 carbon 8 plumbago

grapnel
4 hook 6 anchor

grappa
6 brandy

grapple
3 nab 4 bind, cope, grab, grip, hold 5 catch, clamp, clasp, fight, grasp, seize 6 battle, bucket, clench, clinch, clutch, fasten, tackle, tussle 7 contest, scuffle, wrestle 8 struggle

grasp
3 dig, ken, see 4 glom, grip, hold, know, take 5 catch, clamp, clasp, seize 6 accept, clench, clinch, clutch, fathom, follow, handle, take in, tenure 7 cognize, compass, control, embrace, grapple, realize 8 envisage, perceive 9 apprehend, awareness 10 appreciate, comprehend, take hold of, understand 12 apprehension 13 comprehension, understanding

graspable
5 clear, lucid 6 lucent 8 coherent,

knowable, palpable **10** fathomable
11 perspicuous **12** intelligible
13 apprehensible

grasping
4 avid **6** grabby, greedy **8** covetous,
desirous **9** rapacious **10** avaricious,
prehensile **11** acquisitive

grass
3 pot, sod, tea **4** lawn, reed, turf, weed
6 redtop **7** herbage, panicum, pasture
8 cannabis, Mary Jane **9** cocksfoot,
marijuana
African: 6 imphee
annual: 6 darnel **8** teosinte
Asian: 7 vetiver, whangee
Australian: 8 spinifex
beach: 6 marram
cereal: 3 oat, rye **4** milo, teff **5** kafir,
maize, proso, sorgo, wheat **6** millet
7 sorghum **8** triticum
clump: 4 tuft **7** tussock
dried: 3 hay **5** straw
European: 7 Bermuda, timothy
fiber: 4 flax
fragrant: 10 citronella
pasture: 5 Bahia, grama
perennial: 6 fescue, quitch, zoysia
7 esparto, galleta
prairie: 8 bluestem
second growth: 5 rowen
tropical: 5 cogon **6** bamboo

grasshopper
6 locust **7** katydid **8** cocktail

grassland
3 lea **5** field **6** meadow **7** pasture, prairie
African: 4 veld **5** veldt
flat: 7 savanna **8** savannah
South American: 5 pampa **6** pampas

Grass novel
7 Tin Drum (The)

grate
3 irk, jar, rub, vex **4** file, fray, fret, gall,
rasp, rile **5** annoy, chafe, gnash, grind,
peeve, pique **6** abrade, grille, nettle,
rankle, scrape **7** provoke, scratch **8** irritate
9 aggravate, fireplace

grateful
7 obliged, pleased, restful, welcome
8 beholden, indebted, pleasant, pleasing,
thankful **9** agreeable, congenial, favorable
10 refreshing **11** restorative
12 appreciative

Gratiano
brother: 9 Brabantio

friend: 7 Antonio **8** Bassanio
niece: 9 Desdemona
wife: 7 Nerissa

gratify
4 baby, sate **5** favor, humor, spoil
6 coddle, oblige, pamper, pander, please
7 appease, cater to, content, delight,
gladden, indulge, satisfy

gratin
5 crust

grating
3 dry **4** grid, rasp **5** grill, harsh, rough
6 grille, hoarse **7** irksome, jarring, lattice,
rasping, raucous **8** gridiron, strident
9 vexatious **10** stridulous

gratis
4 comp, free **6** comped **8** costless
10 chargeless **13** complimentary, without
charge

gratitude
6 thanks **12** appreciation, gratefulness,
thankfulness

gratuitous
6 wanton **8** baseless **9** unfounded,
voluntary **10** groundless, reasonless,
ungrounded **11** uncalled-for, unnecessary,
unwarranted **12** indefensible

gratuity
3 tip **4** gift, perk **5** bonus **6** reward
7 cumshaw, douceur **8** donation, largesse,
offering **9** baksheesh, lagniappe, pourboire
10 perquisite **11** benefaction
12 contribution

grave
3 pit, sad **4** dire, dour, fell, grim, tomb
5 acute, awful, crypt, fatal, heavy, major,
sober, staid, vault **6** burial, deadly, gloomy,
sedate, severe, solemn, somber, sombre,
urgent **7** austere, ghastly, ominous,
ossuary, serious, subdued, weighty
8 catacomb, critical, dreadful, perilous,
pressing, terrible **9** dangerous,
mausoleum, momentous, ponderous,
saturnine, sepulcher, sepulchre, sepulture,
unsmiling
marker: 5 stela, stele **8** memorial,
monument **9** footstone, headstone,
tombstone **11** sarcophagus
mound: 6 barrow **7** tumulus
robber: 5 ghoul

gravel
4 dirt, grit, sand
ridge: 5 esker

gravelly
5 raspy, rough 6 gritty, hoarse 7 rasping,
grating 8 abrasive, granular, guttural,
scratchy

graven image
4 icon, idol

graver
4 tool 5 burin 8 sculptor

graveyard
8 boot hill, catacomb, cemetery, God's acre
10 necropolis 12 burial ground, memorial
park, potter's field

gravid
5 heavy 8 enceinte, pregnant 9 expectant,
expecting, with child 10 parturient
12 childbearing

gravity
5 force 6 weight 7 dignity, urgency
8 sobriety 9 heaviness, solemnity
10 importance, somberness 11 consequence, seriousness 12 significance

gravlax
3 lox 6 salmon

gravy
4 perk 5 bonus, bribe, graft, juice, sauce
6 payola 8 dressing, windfall
French: 3 jus

gray
3 ash, old 4 aged, ashy, blah, drab, dull
5 ashen, bleak, color, hoary, slate, slaty
6 dismal, gloomy, leaden 7 elderly, grizzly,
neutral 8 grizzled, gunmetal, overcast
9 cinereous, colorless
brownish: 5 taupe 7 fuscous

gray duck
7 gadwall, pintail

grayfish
5 shark 7 dogfish

gray matter
3 wit 4 head, mind 5 brain 6 brains,
noddle, noggin, noodle 8 cerebrum
9 intellect 10 encephalon 12 intelligence,
neural tissue

graze
3 eat, rub 4 feed, gall, kiss, skim, skip,
wear 5 brush, chafe, erode, shave, touch
6 abrade, browse, bruise, forage, glance,
scrape 7 contuse, corrade, pasture
8 abrasion, ricochet

grazier
7 rancher

grease
3 fat, oil 4 lard 5 smear 6 smooth
7 lanolin 9 lubricant, lubricate
combining form: 4 sebi, sebo

greasy
4 oily 5 fatty, slick 8 slippery, unctuous
10 lubricious, oleaginous

greasy spoon
4 café 5 diner, grill 6 eatery 7 beanery,
hashery 9 chophouse, hash house,
lunchroom 10 coffee shop
12 luncheonette

great
3 big, fat 4 huge, vast 5 famed, grand,
jumbo, large, noble 6 famous, heroic
7 eminent, exalted, extreme, immense,
mammoth, notable, sublime, supreme,
titanic 8 colossal, enormous, gigantic,
glorious, oversize, renowned, terrific,
towering 9 excellent, fantastic,
humongous, paramount, prominent,
wonderful 10 celebrated, impressive, noteworthy, prodigious, remarkable,
stupendous, surpassing, tremendous,
voluminous 11 illustrious, magnificent,
outstanding, superlative 13 distinguished
combining form: 4 mega 6 megalo

Great Bear
9 Big Dipper, Ursa Major 13 constellation

Great Britain
see **England**

Great Commoner, the
4 Pitt (William) 5 Bryan (William Jennings)
7 Lincoln (Abraham)

Great Emancipator, the
7 Lincoln (Abraham)

greater
4 more 5 metro 6 better, bigger, higher,
larger 8 superior 9 exceeding
10 surpassing 12 metropolitan

greatest
4 best, most 6 utmost 7 maximum,
supreme 8 foremost

Great Expectations
author: 7 Dickens (Charles)
character: 3 Joe (Gargery), Pip 5 Biddy
7 Estella, Jaggers 8 Havisham (Miss),
Magwitch (Abel)

greathearted
4 bold, kind 5 brave, lofty, noble 6 heroic
7 gallant 8 fearless, generous, princely
10 benevolent, chivalrous, courageous
11 considerate, high-minded,
magnanimous

Great Lake
  4 Erie 5 Huron 7 Ontario 8 Michigan,
  Superior
  acronym: 5 HOMES

Great Lake State
  8 Michigan

greave
  7 legging

grebe
  4 bird, fowl 8 dabchick 10 diving bird

Greece
  ancient city-state: 5 Argos 6 Athens,
  Sparta, Thebes 7 Corinth
  capital: 6 Athens
  city: 6 Patras 7 Larissa, Piraeus
  8 Salonika 12 Thessaloníki
  conqueror: 6 Philip (of Macedonia)
  9 Alexander (the Great)
  island, island group: 5 Crete 6 Aegean,
  Euboea, Ionian 8 Cyclades, Sporades
  monetary unit: 4 euro
  mountain, range: 3 Ida 4 Ossa 6 Pindus
  7 Olympus 9 Parnassus
  neighbor: 6 Turkey 7 Albania 8 Bulgaria,
  Macedonia
  part of: 7 Balkans
  peninsula: 6 Balkan 10 Chalcidice
  11 Peloponnese
  region: 6 Epirus, Thrace 8 Thessaly
  sea: 6 Aegean, Ionian 13 Mediterranean

greed
  6 excess, hunger 7 avarice, avidity,
  craving 7 edacity, longing 8 cupidity,
  gluttony, rapacity, voracity 12 covetousness, ravenousness

greedy
  4 avid 5 itchy 6 grabby 7 hoggish,
  miserly, selfish 8 covetous, desirous,
  edacious, esurient, grasping 10 avaricious,
  gluttonous 11 acquisitive

Greek
  6 babble, drivel, jabber 7 Achaean
  8 Hellenic, nonsense 9 gibberish
  assembly: 5 agora, boule
  coin: 4 obol 6 lepton, stater
  column: 5 Doric, Ionic 10 Corinthian
  contest: 4 agon
  counselor: 6 Nestor
  dictator: 7 Metaxas (Ioannis)
  dragon: 9 Eurythion
  drink: 4 ouzo
  epic: 5 Iliad 7 Odyssey
  Fates: 6 Clotho, Moirae 7 Atropos
  8 Lachesis
  god:
    chief: 4 Zeus

messenger: 6 Hermes
  of agriculture: 6 Cronus
  of death: 8 Thanatos
  of dreams: 8 Morpheus
  of fire: 10 Hephaestus
  of healing: 9 Asclepius 11 Aesculapius
  of love: 4 Eros
  of marriage: 5 Hymen
  of the sun: 6 Apollo
  of physicians: 6 Hermes
  of the sea: 6 Nereus, Triton 7 Oceanus
  8 Poseidon
  of the sun: 6 Helios
  of the underworld: 5 Pluto
  of the winds: 5 Eurus, Notus 6 Aeolus,
  Boreas 8 Zephyrus
  of war: 4 Ares
  of wine: 8 Dionysus
  of woods: 3 Pan
  goddess:
    of agriculture: 7 Demeter
    of beauty: 9 Aphrodite
    of dawn: 3 Eos
    of discord: 4 Eris
    of fertility: 6 Cybele
    of flowers: 7 Chloris
    of harvests: 4 Rhea
    of hunting: 7 Artemis
    of justice: 7 Astraea
    of love: 9 Aphrodite
    of marriage: 4 Hera
    of night: 3 Nyx
    of peace: 5 Irene
    of retribution: 7 Nemesis
    of ruin: 3 Ate
    of the earth: 4 Gaea, Gaia
    of the hearth: 6 Hestia
    of magic: 6 Hecate, Hekate
    of the moon: 6 Hecate, Hekate, Selena,
    Selene 7 Artemis, Astarte
    of the rainbow: 4 Iris
    of the seasons: 5 Horae
    of the underworld: 6 Hecate, Hekate
    10 Persephone
    of vengeance: 7 Nemesis
    of victory: 4 Nike
    of wisdom: 6 Athena
    of witchcraft: 6 Hecate, Hekate
    of womanhood: 4 Hera
    of youth: 4 Hebe
  hero: 4 Aias, Ajax 5 Jason 7 Theseus
  8 Achilles, Argonaut, Heracles, Hercules,
  Odysseus 9 Achilleus
  historian: 8 Xenophon 9 Herodotus
  10 Thucydides
  lawgiver: 5 Draco, Solon
  leader: 9 Agamemnon
  letter: 3 chi, eta, phi, psi, rho, tau 4 beta,

iota, zeta **5** alpha, delta, gamma, kappa, omega, sigma, theta **6** lambda **7** epsilon, omicron, upsilon
magistrate: 6 archon
marketplace: 5 agora
porch: 4 stoa
sandwich: 4 gyro
soldier: 7 hoplite
theater: 5 odeon, odeum
underworld: 5 Hades
war cry: 5 alala
warrior: 4 Ajax **7** Ulysses **8** Achilles, Diomedes, Odysseus **9** Agamemnon, Palamedes
wine: 7 retsina

green
3 raw **4** jade, lime, moss **5** alive, fresh, kelly, leafy, naive, virid, young **6** callow, forest, unripe **7** avocado, celadon, emerald, untried, verdant **8** immature, juvenile, unversed, youthful **9** unfledged **10** unseasoned **11** unpracticed **13** inexperienced
bluish: 8 glaucous
combining form: 4 verd **6** chloro
grayish: 5 olive
yellowish: 7 luteous **10** chartreuse

greenbacks
4 cash, jack, loot **5** bread, bucks, dough, lucre, money, moola **6** moolah, wampum **7** dollars, scratch **8** currency, smackers **11** legal tender

greenery
7 foliage, leafage **8** verdancy

green-eyed
7 envious, jealous **9** invidious
monster: 8 jealousy

greenfly
5 aphid

greengage
4 plum

greenhead
3 fly **8** horsefly

greenheart
6 laurel **9** evergreen

greenhorn
4 babe, hick, jake, naif, rube, tyro **5** clown **6** newbie, novice, rookie **7** bumpkin, ingenue **8** beginner, newcomer **10** clodhopper, provincial

greenhouse
7 nursery **12** conservatory

Greenland
capital: 4 Nuuk **7** Godthåb
city: 5 Thule
ethnic group: 5 Inuit **6** Eskimo
explorer: 4 Eric (the Red), Erik (the Red), Leif (Eriksson) **9** Rasmussen (Knud)
language: 6 Danish
monetary unit: 5 krone
possession of: 7 Denmark

green light
3 nod **4** okay **5** leave **6** assent **7** consent, go-ahead, mandate **8** approval, blessing, sanction **9** authority, clearance, thumbs-up **10** permission **11** endorsement **13** authorization

Green Mansions
author: 6 Hudson (W. H.)
character: 4 Rima

green monkey
6 guenon, simian, vervet

Green Mountain State
7 Vermont

greenness
5 youth **6** spring **7** puberty **8** verdancy, viridity **9** youthhood **10** immaturity, juvenility, pubescence, springtide, springtime **11** adolescence **12** inexperience

green osier
6 willow **7** dogwood

green plover
7 lapwing **9** shorebird

greenroom
6 lounge

greenstone
4 jade **7** diabase **8** nephrite **9** tremolite **10** actinolite

greet
3 bow **4** hail, meet **6** accost, call to, salaam, salute **7** address, react to, receive, welcome

greeting
3 ave, bow, nod **4** ciao, hail **5** aloha, hello, howdy **6** salaam, salute **7** address, welcome **9** handshake, reception **10** salutation

gregarious
6 clubby, genial, social **7** affable **8** outgoing, sociable **9** clubbable, congenial, convivial **11** extroverted **13** companionable

gremlin
3 bug, elf, imp 5 dwarf, gnome 6 defect, glitch 7 brownie

Grenada
capital: 9 St. George's
discoverer: 8 Columbus (Christopher)
former name: 10 Concepción
language: 7 English
location: 10 West Indies
nickname: 11 Isle of Spice

grenade
4 bomb 5 shell 7 missile 9 explosive, pineapple

grenadier
7 rattail, soldier

grenadine
4 pink, yarn 5 syrup 6 fabric 9 carnation

Grendel's slayer
7 Beowulf

Gretchen's lover
5 Faust

greylag
5 goose

Grey's forte
7 Western

grid
3 net 5 grate, grill 6 grille 7 grating, lattice, network, trellis

griddle
3 pan 5 grill

griddle cake
7 hotcake, pancake 8 flapjack

gridiron
3 net 5 field, grate, grill 7 grating, network

grief
3 rue, woe 4 care 5 agony, dolor, gloom, tears 6 mishap, regret, sorrow 7 anguish, chagrin, sadness, trouble 8 disaster, distress, hardship 9 adversity, heartache, suffering 10 affliction, heartbreak, misfortune 11 despondency

Grieg work
8 Peer Gynt

grievance
4 beef 5 cross, gripe, trial, wrong 6 burden, grouse, injury, squawk 8 hardship, jeremiad 9 complaint, injustice 10 affliction, allegation, unfairness 11 tribulation

grieve
3 cry 4 ache, keen, moan, wail, weep 5 mourn 6 burden, lament, sadden, sorrow, suffer 7 afflict, agonize 8 distress

grievous
3 sad 4 dire, fell, sore 5 cruel, grave, great, major 6 bitter, severe, taxing, tragic, woeful 7 galling, heinous, onerous, painful, serious, weighty 9 egregious 10 abominable, burdensome, calamitous, deplorable, lamentable, oppressive 11 distressing, regrettable, troublesome, unfortunate 12 heartrending

grift
3 con, gyp 4 bilk, rook 7 defraud, swindle 8 flimflam

grifter
3 gyp 5 cheat, crook, thief 6 con man, gouger 7 cheater, scammer, sharper, slicker 8 swindler 9 defrauder, trickster 13 confidence man

grill
3 fry, vex 4 cook, grid, pump, quiz 5 broil, grate, sauté, toast 6 eatery 7 afflict, debrief, grating, griddle, torment 8 gridiron, question 10 restaurant 11 interrogate 12 cross-examine

grilse
6 salmon

grim
3 set 4 cold, dour, fell, firm, hard 5 bleak, cruel, fixed, grave, harsh, rigid, stern 6 dismal, dogged, dreary, fierce, grisly, intent, savage, severe, somber 7 adamant, austere, inhuman, ominous 8 gruesome, inhumane, obdurate, resolute, ruthless, stubborn 9 merciless, offensive, truculent 10 determined, forbidding, implacable, inevitable, inexorable, inflexible, melancholy, relentless, unyielding, vindictive 11 unforgiving, unrelenting

grimace
3 mow, mug 4 face, moue, pout, scowl 5 frown, lower, mouth, sneer

grimalkin
3 cat 5 tabby 6 feline 9 female cat

grime
4 crud, dirt, gunk, muck, smut, soot 5 filth

grim reaper
5 death

grimy
5 dingy, dirty 6 filthy, grubby, grungy, soiled, scuzzy, smutty 10 besmirched

grim

grin
4 beam 5 smile, smirk

grind
3 rut, vex 4 chew, grub, mill, moil, pace, plod, plug, rote, slog, toil, whet 5 crank, crush, gnash, grate, labor, slave, sweat 6 abrade, crunch, drudge, groove, harass, kibble, powder, rotate 7 oppress, routine, travail 8 drudgery, monotony, wear down 9 pulverize, treadmill 10 donkeywork

grinder
3 sub 4 gyro, hero 5 molar, tooth 6 hoagie 8 sandwich 9 submarine

grinding
5 harsh 6 severe 7 arduous, grating, wearing 9 fatiguing, strenuous
stone: 4 mano 6 mortar, muller, pestle

griot
11 storyteller

grip
4 glom, hold, take 5 clamp, clasp, grasp, seize 6 clench, clinch, clutch, handle, tenure, valise 7 grapple 8 enthrall, suitcase 9 fascinate, mesmerize, restraint, spellbind, stagehand 10 constraint

gripe
3 bug, vex 4 beef, carp, crab, fuss, yawp 5 annoy, bitch, bleat, cavil, croak, groan, whine 6 bother, grouch, grouse, kvetch, murmur, mutter, object, squawk, yammer 7 afflict, grumble 8 complain, distress, irritate 9 bellyache, complaint, grievance, objection

griper
see **grumbler**

grippe
3 flu 9 influenza

gripper
4 clip, hand, vise 5 clamp, clasp, tongs 6 pliers

gris-gris
5 charm, spell 6 amulet, fetish 8 talisman 11 incantation

Grisham novel
4 Firm (The) 6 Broker (The), Client (The) 7 Chamber (The), Partner (The) 8 Brethren (The) 12 Pelican Brief (The)

grisly
4 gory, grim 5 awful, lurid 6 horrid 7 ghastly, hideous, macabre 8 fearsome, gruesome, horrible, terrible 9 frightful, god-awful, repellent, repulsive, sickening 10 disgusting, horrifying, terrifying

grist
3 lot 5 grain, input, stint 6 amount, output 7 product 8 quantity

gristle
9 cartilage

grit
4 guts, sand 5 grate, grind, heart, moxie, nerve, pluck, spunk 6 gravel, mettle, powder, smooth, spirit 7 bravery, courage, granule 8 backbone, tenacity 9 fortitude 10 doggedness 13 determination

gritty
4 game 5 dirty, gutsy, rough, sandy 6 dogged, plucky, spunky 8 abrasive, gravelly, resolute, spirited 9 steadfast, tenacious 10 courageous, determined

groan
4 beef, carp, moan 5 cavil, creak, gripe 6 bemoan, grouse, lament, object, repine 7 grumble 8 complain 9 bellyache

grocery
5 store 11 supermarket
Spanish: 6 bodega

grog
3 rum 5 booze, drink, hooch, juice, sauce 6 liquor, tipple 7 alcohol, spirits 9 firewater

groggy
4 dull, hazy, logy, weak 5 dazed, dopey, foggy, muzzy, tired, woozy 6 dulled, sleepy 7 muddled 8 befogged, confused, sluggish 9 befuddled, slaphappy, stupefied 10 punch-drunk

groin
4 fold 6 crotch

grok
6 intuit

grommet
6 eyelet 7 cringle

groom
4 comb, tend, tidy 5 brush, clean, curry, primp, ready, shave 6 neaten, ostler, polish 7 hostler, prepare, servant 8 benedict 9 attendant
Indian: 4 syce

groove
3 rut 4 pace, rote, slot 5 canal, flute, glyph, gouge, grind, niche, score, stria 6 furrow, gutter, hollow, rabbet, rhythm 7 chamfer, channel, routine, top form 8 monotony 10 depression

groovy
3 hip 4 cool, neat 5 ducky, great, nifty, sharp, slick, super, swell 6 choice, gnarly,

peachy 7 right-on **8** smashing **9** copacetic, excellent, hunky-dory, marvelous, wonderful **10** delightful, marvellous, peachy keen

grope
  4 feel, grub, poke, root **6** fondle, fumble, search **7** grabble **8** scrabble

grosbeak
  5 finch **8** hawfinch, songbird

gross
  3 fat, raw, sum **4** earn, foul, mass, rude **5** brute, bulky, crude, obese, rough, utter, whole **6** carnal, coarse, entire, vulgar **7** blatant, boorish, capital, extreme, glaring, hulking, obscene, overall, porcine, uncouth **8** absolute, complete, flagrant, ignorant, improper, indecent, outright, sum total, tangible, totality **9** aggregate, before tax, corporeal, corpulent, downright, egregious, excessive, loathsome, offensive, out-and-out, repulsive, revolting, unrefined **10** disgusting, exorbitant, immoderate **11** twelve dozen

grotesque
  6 absurd, rococo, unreal **7** baroque, bizarre, extreme **8** aberrant, abnormal, deformed, fanciful, freakish **9** distorted, fantastic, ludicrous, misshapen, monstrous **11** incongruous

grotto
  4 cave, hole **5** crypt, vault **6** cavern
  Capri: 4 Blue

grouch
  4 beef, carp, crab, kick, sulk, yawp **5** crank, croak, growl, grump, pique, whiner **6** carper, griper, grouse, grudge, kicker, kvetch, murmur, mutter, repine, squawk, whiner, yawper **7** crabber, grouser, growler, grumble **8** complain, grumbler, kvetcher, sorehead, sourpuss, squawker **9** bellyache, complaint **10** bellyacher, complainer, crosspatch, malcontent

ground
  3 bed, sod **4** dirt, land, root, seat, soil, turf **5** basis, cause, earth, floor, proof **6** bottom, reason **7** bedrock, dry land, footing, support, sustain, terrain **8** argument, buttress, evidence **9** establish, testimony **10** foundation, terra firma

groundbreaking
  10 innovative, innovatory, pioneering **11** cutting-edge, leading-edge

grounded
  6 stable **7** beached **8** marooned, sensible, stranded **9** realistic **13** unpretentious

groundhog
  6 marmot **9** woodchuck

grounding
  8 practice, training, tutelage **11** instruction, preparation

groundless
  4 idle **5** empty, false **6** hollow **8** baseless **9** causeless, unfounded **10** gratuitous **11** uncalled-for, unjustified, unwarranted

groundwork
  3 bed **4** base, foot, root **5** basis **6** bottom **7** bedrock, footing, support **8** basement **10** foundation, substratum **11** cornerstone, preparation **12** substruction, substructure, underpinning

ground zero
  5 focus, get-go **6** center, outset, target **8** bull's-eye **9** epicenter, square one

group
  3 lot, set **4** band, bevy, body, club, crew, gang, pack, push, ruck, sect, team, tier **5** array, batch, bunch, class, clump, covey, crowd, grade, horde, squad, suite, troop **6** adjust, assort, bundle, cartel, circle, clique, clutch, gather, huddle, league, passel **7** battery, brigade, cluster, combine, company, coterie, council, dispose, echelon, platoon **8** assemble, assembly, category, classify, ensemble, organize **9** congeries, gathering, syndicate **10** assemblage, categorize, collection
  of angels: 4 host
  of ants: 6 colony
  of bees: 4 hive **5** swarm
  of birds: 6 flight
  of cats: 7 clowder, clutter
  of cattle: 5 drove
  of chicks: 5 brood **6** clutch
  of clams: 3 bed
  of crows: 6 murder
  of ducks: 5 brace
  of eight: 5 octet
  of elephants: 4 herd
  of elks: 4 gang
  of fish: 5 shoal **6** school
  of five: 5 quint **6** pentad **7** quintet
  of four: 7 tetrad **9** quartet
  of foxes: 5 leash, skulk
  of geese: 5 flock, skein **6** gaggle
  of gnats: 5 cloud, horde
  of goats: 5 tribe
  of gorillas: 4 band
  of greyhounds: 5 leash
  of grouse: 5 covey
  of hares: 4 down, husk

of hawks: 4 cast
of hounds: 3 cry 4 mute, pack
of kangaroos: 3 mob 5 troop
of kittens: 6 litter
of larks: 10 exaltation
of lions: 5 pride
of locusts: 6 plague
of monkeys: 5 troop
of mules: 4 span
of nine: 5 nonet
of oysters: 3 bed
of partridges: 4 covey
of peacocks: 6 muster
of pheasants: 4 nest
of plovers: 4 wing 12 congregation
of quail: 4 bevy 5 covey
of seals: 3 pod 5 patch
of seven: 6 pleiad, septet
of sheep: 5 drove, flock
of six: 6 sextet
of swans: 4 bevy
of teals: 6 spring
of three: 4 trio 5 triad 7 ternary, trinity, triplet
of vipers: 4 nest
of whales: 3 gam, pod
of wolves: 4 pack

grouper
8 rockfish

grouse
4 beef, carp 5 croak, gripe, quail, scold
6 mutter, yammer 7 grumble 8 complain
9 bellyache, blackcock,
ptarmigan 12 capercaillie
extinct: 8 heath hen
red: 8 moorfowl
strut: 3 lek

grout
4 lees, lute 5 dregs 6 cement, filler, mortar
7 grounds, plaster 8 concrete

grove
4 holt, wood 5 copse 7 boscage, coppice, orchard, thicket

grovel
4 fawn 5 abase, cower, crawl, creep, toady
6 cajole, cringe, kowtow, snivel, wallow
7 eat dirt, truckle 8 blandish, bootlick
9 brownnose 10 curry favor, ingratiate
11 apple-polish

grow
3 age, wax 4 flow, gain, rise, tend
5 amass, breed, nurse, raise, ripen, swell
6 abound, become, expand, foster, mature, sprout, thrive 7 burgeon, care for, develop, enlarge, gestate, nurture, produce
8 escalate, flourish, increase, multiply,
mushroom, spring up 9 cultivate, propagate

growl
4 beef, carp, crab, fuss, roar 5 bitch, gripe, groan, snarl 6 grouse, kvetch, mutter, repine, rumble, yammer 7 grumble
8 complain 9 bellyache

growler
3 can 4 crab, floe 5 crank, grump
6 grouch, vessel 7 ice floe, iceberg, pitcher
8 sorehead, sourpuss 9 container
10 crosspatch, malcontent 11 faultfinder

grown-up
5 adult 6 mature 8 seasoned 9 developed
11 full-fledged

grow old
3 age 4 wane 5 ripen, wizen 6 mature, mellow

growth
4 gain, rise 5 surge, swell, tumor 7 buildup
8 increase, progress, swelling 9 accretion, evolution, expansion, flowering, unfolding
11 development, enlargement, progression
malignant: 6 cancer
skin: 3 tag, wen 4 corn, cyst, mole, wart
5 nevus 6 bunion, callus, keloid 7 verruca

grow up
3 age 5 ripen 6 evolve, mature, mellow
7 advance, develop 8 maturate 9 come of age

grub
3 dig 4 chow, comb, eats, feed, food, hack, moil, plod, poke, rake, root, slog, toil
5 grind, larva, scour, slave, spade, stump
6 burrow, drudge, forage, menial, shovel, slavey, uproot, viands 7 edibles, ransack, rummage, unearth, vittles 8 excavate, hireling, victuals 9 provender
11 comestibles

grubby
4 foul 5 dirty, grimy, messy, seedy 6 filthy, frowsy, frowzy, grungy, scuzzy, shabby, sloppy, soiled 7 scruffy, squalid, unclean, unkempt 8 slovenly, unwashed

grubstake
3 aid 4 back, fund, help, loan 5 funds
6 assist 7 backing, capital, finance, support 8 bankroll 9 financing
10 assistance, capitalize, underwrite

grudge
4 deny, envy 5 spite 6 refuse, spleen 7 ill will 9 grievance 10 resentment 12 hard feelings, spitefulness

gruel
4 mush 5 atole, kasha 6 burgoo, congee, sowens 8 flummery, loblolly, porridge 9 stirabout

gruesome
see **grisly**

gruff
4 curt, dour 5 bluff, blunt, cross, harsh, husky, stern, surly 6 abrupt, crabby, crusty, hoarse, morose, sullen 7 bearish, brusque, crabbed, grating, grouchy 8 churlish, croaking, snappish, snippety 9 saturnine 10 ill-natured 11 bad-tempered

grumble
4 beef, carp, crab, fuss, moan, yawp 5 bitch, croak, gripe, groan, growl, snarl, whine 6 bemoan, grouch, grouse, murmur, mutter, repine, squawk 8 complain 9 bellyache

grumbler
4 crab 5 crank, grump 6 grouch 8 sorehead 10 crosspatch, malcontent

grump
3 pet 4 beef, carp, crab, pout, sulk 5 crank, gripe, growl 6 griper, grouch 7 growler, grumble 8 complain, sorehead, sourpuss 9 bellyache 10 bellyacher, malcontent

grumpy
4 dour, sour 5 cross, moody, sulky, surly, testy 6 crabby, cranky, sullen 7 crabbed, peevish 8 petulant, vinegary 9 crotchety, irascible 11 bad-tempered, ill-tempered 12 cantankerous

grunion
10 silverside

grunt
5 groan, growl, snort 7 dogface, draftee, soldier

guacharo
7 oilbird

Guadeloupe
capital: 10 Basse-Terre
department of: 6 France
dependency: 8 Désirade, St. Martin 12 Marie-Galante, St. Barthélemy
discoverer: 8 Columbus (Christopher)
island: 10 Basse-Terre 11 Grande-Terre
location: 10 West Indies
volcano: 9 Soufrière

Guam
capital: 5 Agana
ethnic group: 8 Chamorro

island group: 7 Mariana

guanaco
5 llama 6 alpaca
kin: 5 camel

guano
6 manure 9 excrement

guarantee
3 vow 4 bail, bond, oath, seal, word 5 token, vouch 6 assert, assure, ensure, insure, pledge, surety 7 certify, earnest, promise, warrant 8 security, warranty 9 agreement, assurance, insurance, undertake 11 stand behind, undertaking

guarantor
5 angel 6 backer, patron, surety 7 ensurer, insurer, sponsor 8 bondsman 11 underwriter

guard
4 fend, mind, tend, ward 5 aegis, alert, armor, cover, watch 6 convoy, defend, escort, jailer, keeper, minder, patrol, picket, police, screen, secure, sentry, shield, warden, warder 7 bulwark, defense, lookout, oversee, protect, turnkey 8 chaperon, overseer, preserve, security, sentinel, shepherd, watchdog, watchman 9 chaperone, custodian, look after, patrolman, protector, watch over 10 protection

guarded
4 safe, wary 5 cagey, chary, leery 7 careful, politic, prudent 8 cautious, discreet, gingerly, reserved 11 circumspect, considerate

guardhouse
4 brig, jail, keep 5 clink 6 lockup, prison 8 stockade

guardian
6 escort, keeper, patron, warden, warder 7 curator, trustee 8 Cerberus, defender, overseer, watchdog 9 custodian, protector 11 conservator

guardianship
4 care, keep, ward 5 aegis, trust 6 charge 7 custody, keeping 8 auspices 10 protection 11 safekeeping

Guare play
17 House of Blue Leaves (The) 22 Six Degrees of Separation

Guatemala
capital: 9 Guatemala (City)
ethnic group: 4 Maya 5 Mayan
lake: 6 Izabal 7 Atitlán 9 Petén Itzá
language: 7 Spanish

monetary unit: 7 quetzal
mountain, range: 6 Tacaná 9 Tajumulco
10 Acatenango, Santa María 11 Sierra
Madre
neighbor: 6 Belize, Mexico 8 Honduras
10 El Salvador
peninsula: 7 Yucatán
river: 7 Motagua 8 Polochic, Sarstoon
10 Usumacinta

guck
3 bog, goo, mud 4 clay, crud, dirt, glop,
goop, mire, ooze, smut 5 filth, slime
7 stickum

gudgeon
3 pin 4 fish 5 pivot 6 socket 7 journal

Gudrun
brother: 6 Gunnar 7 Gunther
father: 5 Hetel
husband: 4 Atli 5 Etzel 6 Sigurd
9 Siegfried

guerrilla
8 partisan 9 irregular
Greek: 6 klepht

guess
4 call, shot, stab 5 fancy, hunch, infer
7 believe, predict, presume, suppose,
surmise 8 estimate 9 speculate
10 conjecture, prediction 11 presumption,
supposition, speculation

guest
6 caller, lodger, roomer 7 boarder,
company, visitor 9 sojourner

guff
3 jaw, lip 4 bosh, sass 5 bilge, cheek,
hokum, hooey, mouth, sauce, trash
6 bunkum, drivel, hot air, humbug
7 baloney, hogwash, palaver, twaddle
8 back talk, claptrap, malarkey, nonsense,
tommyrot 9 poppycock 10 balderdash
13 horsefeathers

guffaw
6 cackle, hee-haw 7 chortle

guidance
6 advice 7 control, counsel 8 handling
9 direction, oversight 10 leadership,
management 11 instruction, supervision

guide
4 dean, guru, help, lead, show 5 doyen,
pilot, route, steer, usher 6 beacon, convoy,
direct, docent, escort, handle, leader,
manage, manual, mentor 7 adviser,
conduct, control, marshal, oversee 8 Baedeker, chaperon, director, handbook,
instruct, maneuver, navigate, shepherd,
signpost 9 accompany, chaperone,

conductor, vade mecum, Sacagawea
10 bellwether, compendium, instructor,
pathfinder 11 enchiridion

guidebook
6 Fodor's, manual 8 Baedeker, Frommer's,
handbook, Michelin 9 itinerary, vade
mecum 10 compendium 11 enchiridion

guided missile
3 ABM 4 Hawk, ICBM, IRBM, Nike, Thor,
Zuni 5 Atlas, drone, Snark, Titan
6 Bomarc, cruise, Exocet, Falcon, Navaho,
rocket 7 Bullpup, Matador, Polaris,
Regulus, Terrier 8 Redstone, Tomahawk
9 Minuteman 10 projectile, Sidewinder

Guiderius
brother: 9 Arviragus
father: 9 Cymbeline

guidon
4 flag 6 banner, burgee, ensign, pennon

guild
4 club 5 lodge, order, union 6 cartel,
league 7 society 8 sodality 10 fellowship,
fraternity 11 association, brotherhood
medieval: 5 Hansa, Hanse

guile
4 wile 5 craft, fraud 6 deceit 7 cunning
8 artifice, trickery, wiliness 9 deception,
duplicity, stratagem 10 cleverness
13 dissimulation

guileful
3 sly 4 foxy, wily 5 cagey, canny, slick
6 artful, astute, crafty, shifty, shrewd,
sneaky, tricky 7 cunning, devious
8 indirect, slippery, sneaking 9 designing,
insidious, underhand 11 calculating,
duplicitous, underhanded

guileless
4 open 5 frank, naive 6 candid, direct,
honest 7 genuine, natural, sincere, up-
front 8 innocent, truthful 9 ingenuous
10 aboveboard, forthright

guillemot
3 auk 5 murre 7 seabird

guillotine
6 behead 9 decollate 10 decapitate

guilt
4 onus 5 blame, fault, shame 6 regret,
stigma 7 offense, remorse 10 contrition
11 culpability 12 self-reproach

guiltless
4 pure 5 clean 6 chaste 8 innocent,
virtuous 9 blameless, exemplary, faultless,

righteous, stainless **10** immaculate, inculpable

guilty
6 liable, rueful, sinful **7** ashamed, at fault **8** blamable, contrite, culpable, indicted, penitent **9** impeached, regretful **10** answerable, remorseful **11** accountable, blameworthy, responsible

guimpe
6 blouse

Guinea
capital: 7 Conakry
city: 4 Labé **6** Kankan, Kindia
ethnic group: 6 Fulani **7** Malinke
island, island group: 3 Los **5** Tombo
language: 6 French
monetary unit: 5 franc
mountain: 5 Nimba
neighbor: 4 Mali **7** Liberia, Senegal
10 Ivory Coast **11** Sierra Leone
12 Guinea-Bissau
river: 5 Niger **6** Gambia **7** Senegal

Guinea-Bissau
archipelago: 7 Bijagós
capital: 6 Bissau
ethnic group: 6 Fulani **7** Malinke
8 Mandyako
language: 10 Portuguese
monetary unit: 5 franc
neighbor: 6 Guinea **7** Senegal
river: 4 Gêba

guinea fowl
genus: 6 Numida
young: 4 keet

guinea pig
4 cavy **6** rodent
genus: 5 Cavia

Guinevere
court: 7 Camelot
husband: 6 Arthur
lover: 8 Lancelot **9** Launcelot

guise
4 mask **5** cloak, cover, dress, getup **6** aspect, facade, outfit, veneer **7** costume, pretext **8** coloring, pretense **9** posturing, semblance **10** appearance, false front

guitar
accessory: 4 capo
Mexican: 5 tiple **6** cuatro **8** charango
part: 3 nut, peg **4** fret, neck **5** brace
6 bridge, string **7** peghead
small: 3 uke **7** ukulele
tool: 4 pick **8** plectrum

guitarist
American: 4 Byrd (Charlie), King (B. B., Freddie), Page (Jimmy), Pass (Joe) **5** Ellis (Herb), Isbin (Sharon) **6** Kessel (Barney), Kottke (Leo), Watson (Doc) **7** Burrell (Kenny), Hendrix (Jimi), Metheny (Pat), Vaughan (Stevie Ray) **9** Christian (Charlie), Parkening (Christopher) **10** Montgomery (Wes), Pizzarelli (Bucky, John)
Australian: 8 Williams (John)
British: 4 Beck (Jeff) **5** Bream (Julian)
8 Richards (Keith)
French: 9 Reinhardt (Django)
Italian: 7 Ghiglia (Oscar)
Spanish: 5 Yepes (Narciso) **6** Romero (Celedonio) **7** Segovia (Andrés)

guitarlike instrument
3 uke **4** lute, vina **5** banjo, sitar **7** bandore, pandora, samisen, ukulele **8** mandolin, shamisen

gulch
3 gap **4** glen **5** gorge, gully **6** arroyo, canyon, coulee, hollow, ravine, valley **7** couloir

gules
3 red

gulf
3 bay, pit **4** cove **5** abysm, abyss, bayou, bight, chasm, firth, gorge, gulch, inlet **6** cavity, harbor, hollow, ravine, slough **8** crevasse
Adriatic Sea: 6 Venice
Aegean Sea: 7 Saronic **8** Salonika
Africa: 6 Guinea
Arabian Sea: 4 Oman **7** Persian
Australia: 9 Van Diemen **11** Carpentaria
Baltic Sea: 4 Riga **6** Danzig, Gdansk
7 Bothnia, Finland
Bering Sea: 6 Anadyr
Canada: 13 Saint Lawrence
Central America: 7 Fonseca
Djibouti: 6 Tajura **8** Tadjoura
Europe: 7 Bothnia, Gascony **8** Gascogne
Greece: 7 Corinth, Lepanto
Indian Ocean: 4 Aden
Ionian Sea: 4 Arta **7** Taranto
Iran: 7 Arabian
Italy: 5 Genoa
Mediterranean Sea: 5 Sidra, Tunis
8 Valencia **10** Khalij Surt **11** Syrtis Major
New Guinea: 5 Papua **7** McCluer
New Zealand: 7 Hauraki
North America: 6 Mexico
Northwest Territories: 7 Boothia
8 Amundsen **9** Queen Maud

Gulf State

508

Philippines: 4 Asid 5 Davao, Leyte, Panay, Ragay
Red Sea: 4 Suez 5 Aqaba 11 Aelaniticus
Russia: 8 Sakhalin
Solomon Sea: 4 Huon, Kula 5 Vella
South China Sea: 4 Siam 7 Tonkin 8 Lingayen
Tyrrhenian Sea: 7 Paestum
Yellow Sea: 6 Chihli

Gulf State
5 Texas 7 Alabama, Florida 9 Louisiana 11 Mississippi

gull
3 con, mew, sap 4 bird, dupe, fool, hoax, scam 5 chump, cozen 6 fleece, pigeon, stooge, sucker, take in 7 chicane, fall guy 8 flimflam, hoodwink 9 bamboozle 11 hornswoggle

gullet
3 maw 4 crop, tube 6 dewlap, throat 7 channel 9 esophagus

gullible
4 easy 5 green, naive 8 innocent, trusting 9 believing, credulous 11 susceptible 12 unsuspecting

Gulliver's Travels
author: 5 Swift (Jonathan)
horses: 10 Houyhnhnms
land: 6 Laputa 8 Lilliput 11 Brobdingnag
people: 6 Yahoos

gully
3 gap 4 glen 5 gorge, gulch 6 arroyo, coulee, hollow, ravine, valley 7 couloir

gulp
4 bolt, chug, cram, glut, slop, swig, wolf 5 gorge, scarf, scoff, stuff, swill 6 devour, gobble, guzzle, quaff 7 swallow 8 mouthful 11 ingurgitate

gum
4 chew 5 botch 6 bobble, bollix, bungle, chicle, gluten, goof up, tupelo 7 exudate, gingiva, louse up 8 adhesive, mucilage 9 sapodilla 10 eucalyptus
kind: 6 acacia, Arabic, balata, bubble 7 chewing, dextrin
resin: 5 myrrh 7 gamboge 8 ammoniac, galbanum, scammony 9 asafetida 10 asafoetida 12 frankincense

gumbo
3 mud 4 okra, soil, soup 6 creole 7 mélange, mixture

gummy
5 gooey, pasty 6 cloggy, sticky, viscid 7 viscous 8 adhesive 9 glutinous 10 gelatinous 12 mucilaginous

gumption
5 drive, nerve, savvy 6 energy 8 industry 10 enterprise, get-up-and-go, initiative

gumshoe
3 cop 4 bull, dick, fuzz, G-man, heat, narc 6 copper, peeler, shamus, sleuth 7 officer 8 flatfoot, hawkshaw, Sherlock 9 detective, policeman 10 bloodhound, private eye 12 investigator

gun
3 gat, rod 4 Colt 5 rev up, rifle 6 cannon, Garand, heater, mortar, musket, pistol, weapon 7 bazooka, carbine, firearm 8 Browning, howitzer, revolver 9 derringer, Remington 10 Winchester
antiaircraft: 6 ack-ack, Bofors
Austrian: 5 Glock
British: 4 Sten
French: 8 arquebus 9 harquebus
German: 5 Glock, Luger
Italian: 7 Beretta
mount: 6 turret
part: 3 pin 4 bolt, bore, butt, lock 5 sight, stock 6 barrel, breech, hammer, muzzle, safety 7 chamber, trigger 8 cylinder, magazine 9 buttstock

gunfire
4 shot 5 blast, salvo 6 volley 7 barrage 9 broadside, discharge, fusillade

gung ho
4 avid, keen 6 ardent, fervid, raring 7 fervent, zealous 9 exuberant 11 impassioned 12 enthusiastic

Guni's father
8 Naphtali

gunk
3 goo 4 crud, glop, gook, goop, muck 5 slime

gunman
5 bravo 6 hit man, killer 7 shooter, torpedo 8 assassin, enforcer

Gunnar
brother-in-law: 6 Sigurd
father: 5 Hetel
sister: 6 Gudrun
wife: 8 Brunhild, Brynhild

gunner
6 sniper 7 shooter 8 marksman, rifleman 9 musketeer 11 infantryman 12 artilleryman

Gunther
sister: 7 Gutrune 9 Kriemhild
slayer: 5 Hagen
uncle: 5 Hagen
wife: 8 Brunhild 9 Brynhilde

gurgle
3 lap 4 flow, purl, wash 5 plash, slosh, swash 6 babble, bubble, burble, ripple

Gurkha knife
5 kukri

gurney
3 cot 9 stretcher

guru
4 sage 5 guide, swami, tutor 6 expert, leader, master, mentor 7 teacher 9 maharishi

gush
3 jet 4 emit, flow, pour, rave, roll, rush, spew, teem, well 5 burst, flood, flush, issue, spout, spurt, surge 6 babble, effuse, sluice, spring, stream 7 cascade, emanate 10 effervesce, outpouring

gushy
5 gooey, mushy, sappy, soppy 6 sloppy, slushy, sticky 7 cloying, maudlin, mawkish, tearful 8 bathetic, effusive 9 schmaltzy, sickening 10 nauseating, saccharine 11 sentimental

gusset
4 fold, gore, tuck 5 armor, plate, pleat 6 insert 7 bracket

gussy up
5 adorn 6 bedeck 7 furbish 8 decorate, renovate

gust
3 fit 4 blow, gale, rush, wind 5 blast, burst, draft, sally, surge, whiff 6 breeze, flurry, squall 7 bluster, flare-up 8 eruption, outburst, paroxysm

gusto
3 vim 4 brio, élan, zeal, zest 5 ardor, heart, oomph, taste, verve 6 fervor, palate, relish, spirit 7 delight, passion 9 enjoyment 10 enthusiasm

gusty
5 blowy, windy 6 breezy 8 blustery

gut
4 draw, loot 5 belly, bowel, dress, empty, tummy 6 bowels, paunch 7 abdomen, ransack, stomach 8 clean out, entrails, visceral 9 intestine 10 disembowel, eviscerate, exenterate, intestines 11 instinctive

Gutenberg, Johannes
city: 5 Mainz
invention: 11 movable type
partner: 4 Fust (Johann)

gutless
5 sissy, wimpy, wussy 6 coward, craven, yellow 7 chicken, unmanly 8 cowardly, timorous 9 spineless, spunkless, weak-kneed 11 lily-livered, poltroonish 12 fainthearted 13 pusillanimous

guts
4 grit, sand 5 bowel, heart, moxie, nerve, pluck, spunk, tripe 6 bowels, mettle, spirit 7 bravery, courage, innards, insides, stamina, viscera 8 backbone, entrails, stuffing 9 fortitude, intestine 10 intestines, resolution

gutsy
4 bold 5 brave 6 plucky, spunky 7 valiant 8 intrepid, resolute 10 courageous, determined, mettlesome

gutter
5 chase, ditch, flume, gully 6 furrow, groove, trench, trough 7 channel, conduit

guttersnipe
3 bum 4 hobo, scum, waif 5 gamin 6 beggar, gamine, urchin 7 outcast, vagrant, wastrel 8 derelict, riffraff, vagabond 10 ragamuffin

guttural
4 deep 5 gruff, harsh, husky, rough, velar 6 croaky, hoarse 7 grating, palatal, rasping, throaty 8 gravelly

guy
3 cat, lad, man 4 buck, chap, dude, male, rope, stud, wire 5 bloke, brace, chain, guide 6 effigy, fellow, steady 7 support

Guyana
capital: 10 Georgetown
language: 7 English
monetary unit: 6 dollar
mountain range: 9 Pacaraima
neighbor: 6 Brazil 8 Suriname 9 Venezuela
river: 9 Essequibo

Guys and Dolls
author: 6 Runyon (Damon)
composer: 7 Loesser (Frank)

guzzle
4 belt, gulp, slop, soak, swig, toss, tope 5 booze, drink, quaff, slosh, swill 6 imbibe, tank up, tipple 7 consume, swizzle

Gwendolen's husband
7 Locrine

gymnast
7 acrobat, athlete, tumbler
American: 4 Hamm (Paul) 5 Rigby (Cathy) 6 Conner (Bart), Miller (Shannon), Retton (Mary Lou), Thomas (Kurt)
Romanian: 8 Comaneci (Nadia)
Russian: 3 Kim (Nelly) 6 Korbut (Olga)

gymnastics
5 sport 8 exercise, tumbling 9 athletics
10 acrobatics 12 calisthenics
apparatus: 3 bar 4 bars, beam, buck,
ring, rope 5 horse 11 balance beam
feat: 3 kip 4 flip 5 vault 6 tumble
9 handstand, headstand 10 handspring,
headspring, somersault

gyp
3 con 4 bilk, dupe, fake, hoax, rook, scam,
sham 5 bunco, cheat, cozen, cross, fraud,
spoof, trick 6 chisel, chouse, con man,
diddle, fleece, humbug, rip off 7 cheater,
deceive, defraud, diddler, finagle, rip-off,
sharper, swindle 8 chiseler, hoodwink,
swindler 9 bamboozle, defrauder,
imposture, trickster 10 mountebank
11 double-cross, flimflammer 12 double-
dealer

gypsum
7 drywall, mineral 8 selenite 9 alabaster,
wallboard

gypsy
3 Rom 5 caird, nomad, rover 6 roamer,
Romany, tinker 7 drifter, tzigane
8 Bohemian, vagabond, wanderer
Spanish: 6 gitano

gyrate
4 coil, purl, roll, spin, turn, wind 5 orbit,
twirl, whirl 6 circle, rotate 7 revolve
9 oscillate, pirouette

gyration
4 coil, turn 5 cycle, orbit, twirl, wheel, whirl
6 circle 7 circuit, turning 8 rotation
10 revolution

gyre
4 coil, gird, ring, spin, wind 5 cycle, orbit,
twirl, whirl 6 circle, girdle, rotate, spiral,
vortex 7 circuit, revolve 8 rotation
10 revolution

gyro
8 sandwich

gyve
4 bond, iron 5 chain 6 fetter 7 shackle
8 restrain 9 restraint

H

Habakkuk
7 prophet

habeas corpus
4 writ 5 right 7 mandate

habiliments
4 gear 5 dress 6 attire, outfit 7 apparel,
clothes 8 clothing 9 apparatus,
equipment, trappings

habilitate
5 dress 6 clothe 7 qualify

habit
3 rut 4 bent, form, garb, mode, rote, wont
5 dress, quirk, style, usage 6 attire, clothe,
custom, groove, manner, outfit 7 costume,
fashion, pattern, routine 8 behavior,
clothing, practice, tendency 9 addiction,
mannerism 10 consuetude, convention,
proclivity 11 disposition, inclination
riding: 8 jodhpurs
wearer: 3 nun 5 rider

habitable
7 livable

habitant
5 liver 7 denizen, dweller, resider
8 occupant, resident

habitat
4 home, site, turf 5 abode, haunt, range
6 locale, milieu 7 terrain 8 domicile
9 territory 11 environment 12 surroundings

habitation
3 pad 4 digs, flat, home, nest, seat
5 abode, haunt, haven, house, place, roost
7 housing, lodging, tenancy 8 domicile,
dwelling, lodgment, quarters 9 homestead,
residence, residency 10 settlement

habitual
3 set 5 fixed, usual 6 addict, inborn,
native, normal, steady, wonted 7 chronic,
regular, routine, settled 8 accepted,
addicted, constant, familiar, frequent,
inherent 9 automatic, confirmed, continual,

customary, ingrained 10 accustomed,
inveterate, persistent 11 established,
instinctive, involuntary

habitually
8 commonly, normally, wontedly
9 generally, regularly, routinely
10 ordinarily 11 customarily 12 consistently

habituate
4 bear 5 inure, train 6 addict, adjust,
endure, harden, school, season, take to
7 break in, prepare, support 8 accustom,
tolerate 9 acclimate, condition
11 familiarize

habitué
3 fan 4 buff, user 5 hound, lover 6 addict,
patron 7 denizen, devotee, haunter
8 adherent, customer 10 enthusiast,
frequenter

hacienda
4 farm 5 manor, ranch, villa 6 estate,
quinta 8 dwelling 9 residence
10 plantation

hack
3 cab, cut, hew, try, vex 4 blow, chip, chop,
dull, gash, grub, jade, loaf, mean, ride, taxi
5 annoy, cabby, cough, grind, horse, petty,
sever, slave, usual 6 cabbie, cliché,
drudge, lackey, mangle, stroke, writer
7 clichéd, grating, machine, plodder,
taxicab, trivial, vehicle 8 inferior, low grade,
mediocre, tolerate 9 cabdriver, mercenary,
potboiler 10 second-rate, uninspired
11 commonplace

hacker
4 geek, nerd 6 duffer

hackney
3 cab 4 taxi 5 horse 6 jitney 7 taxicab
8 carriage

hackneyed
3 old 4 dull, worn 5 banal, corny, stale,

stock, tired, trite **6** cliché, common, old hat,
old saw **7** archaic, clichéd, worn-out
8 everyday, obsolete, outdated, overused,
outmoded, timeworn **9** out-of-date
10 antiquated, overworked, pedestrian
11 commonplace, meaningless

Hadad
father: **5** Bedad **7** Ishmael
victim: **6** Midian

Hades
4 Hell **5** Pluto, Sheol **6** blazes, Tophet
7 Gehenna, inferno **8** Tartarus **9** perdition
10 underworld **11** netherworld
Babylonian: **5** Aralu
god: **3** Dis **5** Orcus, Pluto
goddess: **10** Persephone
guard: **8** Cerberus
lake: **7** Avernus
river: **4** Styx **5** Lethe **7** Acheron, Cocytus
10 Phlegethon

haft
4 grip, hilt, knob **5** helve **6** handle

hag
3 hex **5** biddy, crone, harpy, shrew, vixen,
witch **6** beldam, gorgon, virago **8** battle-
ax, fishwife, harridan, slattern **9** hobgoblin

Hagar
9 concubine
lover: **7** Abraham
son: **7** Ishmael

Hagar's son
7 Ishmael

Hagen
father: **8** Alberich
nephew: **7** Gunther
slayer: **9** Kriemhild
victim: **9** Siegfried

haggard
3 wan **4** hawk, lank, pale, thin, weak, wild,
worn **5** ashen, drawn, faded, gaunt, tired
6 fagged, pallid, skinny, wasted **7** angular,
pinched, scraggy, scrawny, starved,
wearied **8** careworn, fatigued, shrunken,
worn-down **9** emaciated, exhausted

Haggard, H. Rider
novel: **3** She **17** King Solomon's Mines

Haggith
husband: **5** David
son: **8** Adonijah

haggle
4 deal **5** argue, cavil, trade **6** barter,
bicker, dicker **7** bargain, dispute, quibble,

stickle, wrangle **8** squabble **10** horse-
trade

hagiography subject
5 saint

hail
3 ave **4** ahoy, call **5** greet, salvo, shout,
storm **6** accost, call to, holler, praise,
salute, shower, volley **7** acclaim, address,
applaud, barrage, call out, commend
8 greeting **9** broadside, cannonade,
fusillade, originate, recommend
10 salutation **11** acclamation,
bombardment

Haile Selassie
follower: **11** Rastafarian
nation: **8** Ethiopia

hair
3 bit, jot **4** hint, mite, wool **5** cilia (plural),
pilus, trace **6** cilium, trifle **7** eyelash,
whisker **8** fraction, particle
animal: **3** fur **4** mane, pelt, wool
8 vibrissa **9** vibrissae (plural)
braid: **5** queue **7** pigtail
clip: **8** barrette
coarse: **7** bristle
covering of: **3** wig
cream: **6** pomade **7** pomatum
12 brilliantine
facial: **5** beard, patch **6** goatee
7 Vandyke **8** mustache, whiskers
9 burnsides, handlebar, moustache,
sideburns, soul patch **11** muttonchops
fine: **6** lanugo
fringe: **4** bang
head of: **9** chevelure
knot: **3** bun
lock of: **4** curl **5** tress **7** cowlick
loose roll: **4** pouf
matted: **6** dreads **10** dreadlocks
ornament: **7** topknot
preparation: **3** gel **6** mousse, pomade
12 brilliantine
root: **6** fibril
set: **4** perm
stiff: **4** seta **5** setae (plural)
style: **4** flip, pomp, shag **5** butch, taper,
wedge **6** Caesar, mullet **7** bowl cut, buzz
cut, crew cut, flattop, pageboy **8** ducktail
9 pompadour
tangled: **7** elflock
tuft of: **7** fetlock
unruly: **3** mop
without: **4** bald

haircutter
6 barber **7** stylist **8** coiffeur **9** coiffeuse

hairdo
3 bob, bun **4** afro, bangs, flip, perm, trim
5 braid **6** Mohawk, mullet **7** beehive, bowl
cut, buzz cut, chignon, crew cut, flattop,
pageboy **8** brush cut, coiffure, cornrows,
ducktail, permanent, pigtails, ponytail, razor
cut **9** pompadour **10** dreadlocks

hairdresser
see **haircutter**

hair-raising
5 eerie, scary **6** spooky **7** amazing,
awesome **8** exciting **9** thrilling
10 terrifying **11** astonishing, frightening

hairsplitting
7 finicky **8** exacting **9** quibbling **10** nit-
picking **12** overcritical **13** hypercritical

hairstyle
see **hairdo**

hairy
5 bushy, downy, furry, fuzzy, nappy, risky,
rough **6** chancy, fleecy, fluffy, shaggy,
tufted, woolly **7** bristly, hirsute, scraggy,
unshorn, villous **8** perilous, strigose
9 dangerous, difficult, hazardous,
tomentose, whiskered **11** treacherous

Haiti
capital: 12 Port-au-Prince
island: 7 Tortuga **10** Hispaniola
language: 6 Creole, French
leader: 8 Aristide (Jean-Bertrand),
Duvalier (François, Jean-Claude)
location: 10 West Indies
monetary unit: 6 gourde
passage: 8 Windward
peninsula: 7 Tiburon
river: 10 Artibonite

hake
4 fish, ling **7** codling, whiting
relative: 3 cod

halcyon
4 calm **5** happy, lucky, quiet, still **6** golden,
hushed, placid, serene **8** affluent,
peaceful, tranquil **9** favorable
10 auspicious, felicitous, kingfisher,
prosperous, untroubled

Halcyone
father: 6 Aeolus
husband: 4 Ceyx

hale
3 fit **4** sane, well **5** sound, stout **6** hearty,
robust **7** healthy **8** vigorous **9** strapping,
wholesome

Hale character
5 Nolan (Philip)

Haley epic
5 Roots

half
6 moiety
prefix: 4 demi, hemi, semi

half-baked
8 slapdash, slipshod **9** imbecilic,
senseless, underdone **11** harebrained,
impractical, nonsensical, unrealistic **12** ill-
conceived, shortsighted **13** irresponsible

half-cocked
4 rash **5** brash **8** reckless **9** foolhardy,
imprudent, impulsive, misguided,
premature **10** incautious, unprepared
11 precipitate

halfhearted
4 weak **5** tepid **6** feeble **8** lukewarm
12 uninterested

half-moon
4 arch **5** curve **6** lunule **8** crescent

halfway
3 mid **6** center, medial, median, middle
7 midmost **10** centermost **11** equidistant,
intermediate

half-wit
4 dolt, dope, fool **5** dunce, idiot, moron
6 cretin **8** imbecile **9** blockhead, simpleton

half-witted
4 dull, slow **7** moronic **8** backward,
imbecile **9** imbecilic **12** feebleminded,
simpleminded

hall
4 dorm **5** foyer, lobby **6** lyceum
7 passage **8** corridor **9** dormitory
10 auditorium, passageway
exhibition: 5 salon
Salvation Army: 7 citadel

Halley's _____
5 comet

hallmark
4 logo, seal, sign **5** badge, stamp, trait
6 device, emblem, symbol, virtue
7 feature, imprint, quality **8** logotype,
property **9** attribute **11** distinction
13 certification

hallow
5 bless, honor **6** anoint, devote, revere
8 dedicate, make holy, sanctify, venerate
10 consecrate

hallowed
4 holy 6 sacred

hallucination
4 trip 5 ghost 6 mirage, vision, wraith
7 fantasy, phantom, specter 8 delusion,
illusion, phantasm 10 apparition 11 fata
morgana, ignis fatuus

hallucinogen
3 LSD 9 mescaline 10 psilocybin
11 scopolamine

halo
4 aura 5 nimbi (plural) 6 corona, nimbus
7 aureole

halogen
6 iodine 7 bromine, element 8 astatine,
chlorine, fluorine

halt
3 bar, end 4 lame, limp, quit, stay, stop
5 cease, check, close, hitch, lapse, stall,
waver 6 arrest, desist, dither, falter, finish,
pull up 7 adjourn, bring up, stagger,
suspend 8 conclude, cut short, hesitate,
knock off, leave off 9 determine, interrupt,
terminate, vacillate 10 standstill
11 discontinue

halter
3 bit 4 hang, rope 5 noose 6 blouse,
bridle, hamper 8 restrain, trammels
9 hackamore, headstall, restraint

ham
4 hock 5 bacon, emote, thigh 7 buttock,
overact 8 overplay, strutter 10 scene-eater
13 exhibitionist

Ham
brother: 4 Shem 7 Japheth
father: 4 Noah
son: 4 Cush, Phut 6 Canaan 7 Mizraim

Haman's adversary
6 Esther

ham-handed
5 inept 6 clumsy, gauche 8 bumbling 9 all
thumbs, graceless, inelegant, maladroit
10 blundering, unskillful

Hamilcar
conquest: 5 Spain
home: 8 Carthage
son: 8 Hannibal
surname: 5 Barca

hamlet
7 village
Irish, Scottish: 7 clachan

Hamlet
author: 11 Shakespeare (William)
beloved: 7 Ophelia
castle: 8 Elsinore
country: 7 Denmark
friend: 7 Horatio
mother: 8 Gertrude
slayer: 7 Laertes
uncle: 8 Claudius
victim: 7 Laertes 8 Claudius, Polonius

Hamlet, The
author: 8 Faulkner (William)
family: 6 Snopes

hammer
4 drub, maul, peen 5 forge, gavel, pound
6 batter, mallet, pummel, sledge 7 malleus
8 lambaste
type: 3 air 4 claw, maul 6 sledge 8 ball-
peen 9 pneumatic

hammerhead
4 dolt, dope, fool 5 dunce, idiot, shark
8 clodpoll, numskull 9 numbskull
10 thickskull

hamper
3 bin, tie 4 balk, curb, snag 5 block,
check, cramp, crimp, leash, limit 6 baffle,
basket, fetter, hinder, hobble, hold up,
impede, pannier, retard, stymie, thwart
7 inhibit, manacle, prevent, trammel
8 encumber, handicap, obstacle, obstruct,
restrain, restrict, slow down 9 frustrate

hamstring
4 lame 6 muscle, tendon 7 cripple, disable
10 immobilize 12 incapacitate

Hamutal
father: 8 Jeremiah
husband: 6 Josiah
son: 8 Jehoahaz, Zedekiah

hand
3 aid, paw 4 fist, pass 5 manus 6 script,
worker 7 deliver, dish out, laborer,
workman 8 employee, transfer
10 assistance, penmanship 11 calligraphy,
chirography
clenched: 4 fist
counting zero: 8 baccarat
covering: 5 glove 6 mitten
down: 8 bequeath
gesture: 5 mudra
make: 5 craft
on hip: 6 akimbo
part: 4 palm 5 thumb 6 finger
poker: 5 flush 8 straight 9 full house
protector: 5 glove 7 gantlet 8 gauntlet

handbag
4 grip 5 purse 6 clutch 8 reticule, suitcase
10 pocketbook

handbill
5 flier, flyer **6** poster **7** affiche, leaflet, placard **9** circular

handbook
5 guide **6** manual **8** Baedeker **9** vade mecum **10** compendium **11** enchiridion
religious: **9** catechism

handcuff
6 fetter **7** manacle, shackle
British: **7** darbies (plural)

hand down
4 will **6** bestow, pass on **7** deliver
8 bequeath, transmit

Handel, George Frideric
aria: **5** Largo
birthplace: **5** Halle **7** Germany
opera: **4** Nero **5** Serse **6** Admeto, Alcina, Almira, Ottone, Xerxes **7** Arminio, Orlando, Rinaldo, Rodrigo **8** Berenice **9** Agrippina, Ariodante **12** Giulio Cesare, Julius Caesar
oratorio: **4** Saul **6** Esther, Joshua, Samson, Semele **7** Athalia, Deborah, Jephtha, Messiah, Solomon **8** Theodora

handicap
4 edge, load, odds **6** burden, hamper, hinder, impede **8** drawback, encumber, restrict **9** advantage, allowance, detriment, head start, hindrance **10** disability, limitation **11** encumbrance
12 disadvantage

handicraft
5 skill **8** artefact, artifact

hand in
6 submit, tender **7** deliver, present

handkerchief
5 hanky **6** hankie **7** bandana **8** bandanna, mouchoir **9** accessory

handle
3 paw, use **4** feel, grip, haft, hilt, knob, name, test **5** crank, touch, trade, treat, wield **6** manage **7** control, moniker, operate **8** deal with, doorknob, exercise, maneuver, nickname **10** manipulate
scythe: **5** snath **6** snathe

handling
4 care **6** charge **9** packaging, treatment
partner: **8** shipping

hand out
4 give, mete **6** bestow, donate **7** deliver, present, provide **8** disburse, dispense, give away **10** administer, distribute

hand over
4 cede, feed, give **5** leave, yield **6** commit, donate, fork up, give up, supply
7 commend, confide, consign, deliver, entrust, present **8** dispense, give back, relegate, transfer **9** deliver up, surrender
10 relinquish

handrail
8 banister

handsome
4 buff, cute, fair **5** ample, hunky, noble
6 comely, lavish **7** dashing, liberal, sizable, stately, stylish **8** abundant, generous, gracious, majestic **9** beautiful, bounteous, bountiful **10** attractive, munificent
11 fashionable, good-looking **12** considerable

handspring
6 tumble
lateral: **9** cartwheel

handwriting
6 script **8** longhand **10** autography, manuscript, penmanship **11** calligraphy, chirography
bad: **10** cacography
study of: **10** graphology

handy
4 able, deft, near **5** adept, close, utile
6 adroit, clever, nearby, nimble, useful
7 close-by, skilled **8** adjacent, skillful
9 adaptable, available, dexterous
10 accessible, convenient, proficient
11 practicable, within reach

handyman
6 helper **7** go-to guy **8** factotum

hang
3 jut, sag **4** hook, idle, loll **5** cling, drape, droop, float, hoist, knack, lynch, sling, swing **6** dangle, depend **7** suspend
back: **3** lag **4** drag, poke **5** trail
6 dawdle, schlep **7** schlepp **8** straggle
loosely: **3** sag **6** dangle

hang around
4 stay, wait **5** abide, dally, tarry **6** dawdle, linger, loiter **7** goof off **8** frequent

hangdog
3 sad **4** blue, glum **5** cowed **6** guilty
7 ashamed, pitiful, unhappy **8** dejected, sheepish **9** chagrined, depressed
11 embarrassed

hanger-on
5 leech **6** sponge, sucker **7** sponger
8 barnacle, follower, parasite **9** sycophant
10 freeloader **11** bloodsucker

hanging
5 arras, slope 7 curtain, drapery, pendant, pendent 8 covering, tapestry 9 declivity, execution, pendulous, suspended

Hanging Gardens
7 Babylon

hang on
4 grip 5 grasp 6 clutch, endure, remain 7 persist, survive 8 continue, hold fast 9 persevere

hang out
4 idle, loaf 5 chill, dally, relax 6 loiter, lounge 7 goof off

hangout
5 haunt, joint 6 resort 7 purlieu, retreat 10 rendezvous 12 watering hole

hang up
4 mire, snag 5 delay 6 detain, impede, retard 7 bog down, set back, suspend 8 slow down

hang-up
5 block 7 dilemma, problem 9 obsession 10 difficulty, inhibition

hank
4 clip, coil, loop, ring 6 bundle

hanker
3 yen 4 ache, itch, long, lust, want, wish 5 covet, crave, yearn 6 desire, hunger, thirst

hankering
3 yen 4 ache, itch, lust, urge 5 ardor 6 desire, hunger, pining, thirst 7 craving, longing, passion 8 appetite, yearning

hanky-panky
5 fraud, trick 7 chicane 8 mischief, trickery 9 chicanery, dalliance, deception 13 double-dealing, sharp practice

Hannibal
defeat: 4 Zama
father: 8 Hamilcar
home: 8 Carthage
surname: 5 Barca
vanquisher: 6 Scipio
victory: 6 Cannae

Hansa
5 guild 6 league

Hans Brinker author
5 Dodge (Mary Mapes)

Hanseatic League city
6 Bremen, Lübeck, Wismar 7 Cologne, Hamburg, Rostock

Hänsel und Gretel composer
11 Humperdinck (Engelbert)

Hansen's disease
7 leprosy

hansom
5 coach 8 carriage

haole
5 white

haphazard
6 casual, chance, random 7 aimless 8 at random, careless, slipshod, willy-nilly 9 desultory, hit-or-miss, irregular, unplanned 10 accidental 11 unorganized 12 unsystematic 13 helter-skelter

hapless
4 poor 6 woeful 7 unhappy, unlucky 8 ill-fated, wretched 9 miserable 10 ill-starred 11 star-crossed, unfortunate

happen
4 pass 5 occur 6 befall, betide 7 develop, fall out, turn out 8 bechance 9 transpire
again: 5 recur
together: 6 concur 8 coincide

happening
3 new 5 event, scene, thing 7 episode 8 incident, occasion 9 adventure 10 experience, occurrence, phenomenon 12 circumstance, fashionable

happen on
4 find 8 bump into, discover

happenstance
5 event 6 chance 8 incident, occasion 9 condition, situation 11 coincidence

happiness
3 joy 4 glee 5 bliss, cheer, mirth 6 gaiety 7 aptness, content, delight, elation, jollity 8 felicity, gladness, pleasure 9 enjoyment, well-being 11 contentment 12 satisfaction

happy
4 glad 5 jolly, lucky, merry 6 joyful, joyous, upbeat 7 blessed, content, pleased 8 friendly, jubilant 9 contented, favorable, satisfied 12 enthusiastic, lighthearted

happy-go-lucky
4 easy 6 blithe, breezy, casual 8 carefree, careless, cheerful, heedless, laid-back, reckless 9 easygoing, unworried 10 insouciant, nonchalant 11 unconcerned 12 devil-may-care, light-hearted

hara-kiri
7 seppuku, suicide 8 felo-de-se

Haran
brother: **7** Abraham
daughter: **5** Iscah **6** Milcah
father: **5** Terah **6** Shimei
son: **3** Lot

harangue
4 rant, rave **5** orate, spiel **6** exhort, hassle,
tirade **7** declaim, lecture, oration
8 bloviate, diatribe, jeremiad **9** discourse,
philippic **11** declamation, exhortation

harass
3 irk, vex **4** bait, bully, raid, ride **5** annoy,
beset, chivy, harry, hound, tease, worry
6 badger, hassle, heckle, hector, pester,
plague, stress **7** bedevil, exhaust, fatigue,
torment, trouble **8** bullyrag, distress **9** beleaguer, persecute

harbinger
4 omen, sign **5** augur **6** augury, herald
7 apostle, portent **9** messenger, precursor
10 forerunner, indication

harbor
3 bay **4** cove, port **5** haven, inlet, lodge,
put up **6** billet, refuge, shield, take in
7 nurture, protect, seaport, shelter
9 anchorage, safeguard, sanctuary
Hawaii: **5** Pearl

hard
4 firm, iron **5** cruel, harsh, solid, tough
6 brutal, knotty, packed, rugged, tiring,
trying **7** arduous, callous, onerous
8 absolute, concrete, exacting, granitic,
grinding, indurate, pitiless, rigorous **9** demanding, difficult, fatiguing, intensely,
intensive, laborious, unfeeling
10 adamantine, exhausting, spirituous,
thoroughly, vigorously **11** complicated,
intensively, intractable, troublesome,
unrelenting, unremitting **12** backbreaking
to please: **7** finicky

hard-boiled
4 grim **5** rough, stoic, tough **6** coarse
7 callous **8** seasoned **9** impassive,
pragmatic, unfeeling **11** insensitive,
unemotional **12** stonyhearted, thick-
skinned **13** unsympathetic

harden
3 dry, set **5** inure, steel **6** anneal, freeze,
ossify, season, temper **7** calcify, compact,
congeal, densify, lithify, petrify, stiffen,
toughen **8** solidify **9** acclimate, fossilize,
habituate **10** strengthen

hardfisted
4 mean **5** close, tight **6** stingy, strict
13 penny-pinching

hardheaded
5 sober, tough **6** mulish, shrewd **7** willful
8 obdurate, perverse, stubborn
9 obstinate, practical, pragmatic, realistic
10 determined **11** down-to-earth,
intractable

hardhearted
4 cold **8** pitiless, uncaring **9** merciless,
unfeeling

hard-hitting
6 strong **8** emphatic, forceful, powerful
9 effective

hardihood
3 pop **4** gall, grit, guts **5** cheek, moxie,
nerve, pluck, vigor **6** daring **7** courage
8 audacity, boldness, temerity
9 assurance, brashness, cockiness,
fortitude, impudence, insolence
10 brazenness, robustness

hard-line
4 firm **5** fixed, rigid, tough **8** obdurate
9 obstinate, unbending **10** inflexible,
unyielding **11** stiff-necked **12** intransigent

hardness
5 rigor **7** density **8** rigidity, severity
10 difficulty, resistance

hardscrabble
6 barren **8** marginal **9** infertile, unbearing,
unfertile **12** impoverished, unproductive

hardship
4 need, toil **5** rigor, trial **6** burden **7** travail
8 asperity, distress, drudgery **9** adversity,
privation, suffering **10** affliction, difficulty,
discomfort, misfortune **11** tribulation

Hard Times author
7 Dickens (Charles)

hard up
4 poor **5** broke, needy **6** bad off
8 beggared, bankrupt, deprived, indigent,
strapped **9** desperate, destitute, penniless
10 down-and-out **11** necessitous
12 impoverished

hardy
4 bold, hale **5** brave, tough **6** daring,
robust, rugged, strong **7** healthy
8 intrepid, resolute **9** audacious

Hardy, Thomas
character: **3** Sue (Brideshead) **4** Alec
(D'Urberville), Clym (Yeobright), Jude

(Fawley), Tess (Durbeyfield) **5** Angel
(Clare) **7** Gabriel (Oak) **8** Arabella (Donn),
Eustacia (Vye), Henchard (Michael)
9 Bathsheba (Everdene)
novel: 11 Woodlanders (The) **14** Jude the
Obscure **17** Return of the Native (The)
19 Mayor of Casterbridge (The) **21** Tess of
the D'Urbervilles **22** Far from the Madding
Crowd
setting: 6 Wessex

hare
5 lapin **6** rabbit
female: 3 doe
genus: 5 Lepus
male: 4 buck
tail: 4 scut
young: 7 leveret

harebrained
5 crazy, loony, silly, wacky **6** absurd,
insane, stupid **7** asinine, foolish **9** frivolous
10 ridiculous **12** preposterous

harem
5 serai **6** zenana **8** seraglio
concubine: 9 odalisque

haricot
3 pod **4** bean **10** kidney bean

hark
4 hear, heed, mind, note **6** attend, listen,
notice

harlequin
5 clown, joker **6** jester, mottle **7** buffoon
9 prankster

Harlequin
beloved: 9 Columbine
rival: 7 Pierrot

harm
3 mar **4** hurt, maim, ruin **5** abuse, spoil,
wound, wrong **6** damage, ill-use, impair,
injure, injury, misuse, molest **7** tarnish
8 ill-treat, maltreat, mischief, mistreat
9 undermine **10** disservice, misfortune

harmful
3 bad **4** evil **5** risky, toxic **6** malign, unsafe
7 noisome, noxious **8** damaging
9 dangerous, hazardous, injurious,
malignant, unhealthy **10** pernicious
11 deleterious, detrimental, unhealthful

harmless
4 safe **6** benign **8** innocent, nontoxic
9 innocuous **11** inoffensive

Harmonia
daughter: 3 Ino **5** Agave **6** Semele
7 Autonoë
father: 4 Ares, Mars
husband: 6 Cadmus

mother: 5 Venus **9** Aphrodite
son: 9 Polydorus

harmonious
5 sweet **7** chiming, chordal, musical,
pacific **8** blending, friendly, in accord,
peaceful, pleasing **9** agreeable, congenial,
congruous, consonant, symphonic
10 compatible, concordant **11** cooperative,
symmetrical, sympathetic

harmonize
3 fit **4** jibe, sing **5** agree, blend, match
6 accord, attune **7** arrange, concert,
conform **8** coincide, dovetail **9** integrate
10 coordinate, correspond, synthesize
11 orchestrate

harmony
5 grace, peace, unity **6** accord **7** balance,
concert, concord, oneness, rapport
8 affinity, sonority, symmetry **9** agreement,
congruity, polyphony **10** accordance,
concinnity, conformity, consonance,
proportion **11** concordance, consistency,
cooperation
lack of: 7 discord **10** dissonance
of movement: 8 eurythmy

harness
4 curb, gear, yoke **5** hitch, leash **6** bridle,
tackle **7** utilize **11** domesticate
part: 3 bit **4** rein **5** girth, trace **6** collar
7 blinder, crupper **9** bellyband, breeching,
checkrein **12** breast collar
ring: 6 terret

harp
4 lyre **9** harmonica
Greek: 7 cithara, kithara

harpsichord
7 cembalo **8** clavecin

harpsichordist
American: 6 Fuller (Albert, David), Kipnis
(Igor), Newman (Anthony) **7** Marlowe
(Sylvia), Pinkham (Daniel), Pinnock
(Trevor), Valenti (Fernando) **11** Kirkpatrick
(Ralph)
English: 7 Malcolm (George)
German: 7 Richter (Karl) **9** Leonhardt
(Gustav)
Italian: 7 Sgrizzi (Luciano)
Polish: 9 Landowska (Wanda)

harpy
3 nag **5** leech, scold, shrew, vixen
6 virago **8** fishwife, harridan **9** termagant

Harpy
5 Aello **7** Celaeno, Ocypete
father: 7 Thaumas
mother: 7 Electra
sister: 4 Iris

harridan
3 hag **4** fury **5** biddy, harpy, shrew, vixen, witch **6** dragon, gorgon, ogress, virago **7** hellcat **8** battle-ax, fishwife **9** battle-axe, termagant

harrier
3 dog **4** hawk **6** hector, runner **10** persecutor

harrow
3 try, vex **4** bait, rack **5** devil, tease **6** badger, heckle, hector, needle, pester, suffer **7** afflict, bedevil, torment, torture, trouble **8** distress, irritate **9** cultivate **10** excruciate

harry
3 dog, irk, vex **4** gnaw, raid, sack **5** annoy, tease, upset, worry **6** attack, badger, harass, hassle, pester, plague, ravage **7** assault, bedevil, despoil, perturb, pillage, plunder, torment **8** desolate, maltreat **9** beleaguer, depredate

harsh
5 cruel, gruff, rough, stern **6** biting, brutal, coarse, severe, uneven, unkind **7** austere, caustic, grating, jarring, painful, pungent, raucous, stubbly **8** exacting, grinding, jangling, scraping, scratchy, strident, unsmooth **9** dissonant, inclement **10** discordant, irritating, unpleasant

hart
4 deer, stag **7** red deer
mate: **4** hind

hartebeest
8 antelope
family: **7** Bovidae

Harte story
17 Luck of Roaring Camp (The) **19** Outcasts of Poker Flat (The)

Hartford
college: **7** Trinity
specialty: **9** insurance

Hart, Moss
autobiography: **6** Act One
collaborator: **7** Kaufman (George S.)
musical: **13** Lady in the Dark
play: **15** Once in a Lifetime **18** Man Who Came to Dinner (The) **20** You Can't Take It with You

haruspex
5 augur **7** diviner, prophet **8** foreseer **9** predictor **10** forecaster, foreteller, soothsayer

harvest
4 crop, pick, reap **5** amass, cache, glean, hoard, stash, yield **6** garner, gather

7 collect, reaping, store up, vintage **8** ingather, squirrel, stow away **9** garnering, gathering
bug: **4** mite **7** chigger
fly: **6** cicada
festival: **6** Lammas **7** Cerelia **10** Michaelmas **12** Thanksgiving
god, goddess: **3** Ops **5** Ceres **6** Consus **7** Demeter

harvester
7 gleaner
grain: **6** header
of grapes: **8** vintager

Harvey
5 pooka **6** rabbit
author: **5** Chase (Mary)
character: **6** Elwood (P. Dowd)

hash
4 chop, mess, stew **5** botch, mince, mix-up **6** jumble, medley, muddle, review **7** clutter, confuse, mélange, mixture **8** consider, shambles **9** patchwork **10** assortment, hodgepodge, miscellany

hash house
4 café **5** diner **6** bistro, eatery **7** pit stop **10** coffee shop **12** luncheonette

hashish
5 bhang, ganja **6** charas **8** cannabis, narcotic
plant: **4** hemp

hash out
6 review **7** discuss **8** talk over **9** talk about

hasp
5 catch **6** fasten **8** fastener **9** fastening

hassle
3 row **4** beef, to-do **5** annoy, argue, brawl, fight, run-in **6** bicker, clamor, harass, hubbub, tumult, uproar **7** dispute, problem, quarrel, rhubarb, turmoil, wrangle **8** argument, squabble, struggle **9** commotion **11** altercation, controversy

hassock
4 pouf **7** cushion, kneeler, ottoman **9** footstool

haste
3 run **4** dash, rush **5** hurry, speed **6** barrel, bustle, flurry, hustle **7** beeline, hotfoot **8** celerity, dispatch, rapidity, velocity **9** fleetness, quickness, swiftness **10** speediness **11** hurriedness, impetuosity

hasten
3 fly, hie, run **4** rush, urge **5** hurry, press, speed **6** barrel, hustle, step up, urge on

7 hurry up, quicken, speed up 8 expedite
10 accelerate

hasty
4 fast, rash 5 brisk, eager, fleet, quick,
rapid, swift 6 abrupt, rushed, speedy,
sudden 7 cursory, hurried, rushing
8 careless, fleeting, headlong, heedless,
reckless, slapdash 9 hotheaded, impatient,
impetuous, irritable, quickened 10 ill-
advised, incautious 11 expeditious,
perfunctory, precipitate, precipitous,
superficial, thoughtless

hat
5 derby, tuque 6 boater, cloche, fedora,
panama, topper 7 bicorne, chapeau,
homburg, porkpie, Stetson, tricorn
8 sombrero, tricorne 9 headpiece
11 deerstalker
ancient Greek: 7 petasos, petasus
brimless: 7 pillbox
close-fitting: 4 kufi 5 toque, tuque
6 cloche, turban
felt: 5 busby, derby 6 bowler, trilby
fur: 5 busby 6 castor
helmetlike: 4 topi 5 topee
maker: 7 modiste 8 milliner
Middle Eastern: 3 fez
military: 4 kepi 5 busby, shako
Muslim: 3 fez 6 turban 8 tarboosh
sheepskin: 6 calpac 7 calpack
soft: 5 toque
straw: 6 boater, panama, sailor
7 bangkok, leghorn, skimmer 8 sombrero
sun: 5 terai
tall: 9 stovepipe
waterproof: 9 sou'wester
woman's: 4 coif 5 toque 6 bonnet
7 pillbox

hatch
4 door, plan, plot 5 breed, brood, cover,
inlay, spawn 6 cook up, create, design,
devise, emerge, invent, make up, work up
7 concoct, dream up, opening, produce,
think up 8 contrive, engender, generate,
incubate, occasion 9 floodgate, formulate,
give birth, give forth, originate, procreate
11 compartment

hatchet
3 axe 8 tomahawk

hatchet man
6 killer 7 torpedo 8 assassin, enforcer,
murderer 9 attack dog, cutthroat
10 eliminator

hate
5 abhor, scorn, spite 6 animus, detest,
enmity, horror, loathe, malice, rancor

7 despise, disgust 8 aversion, execrate,
loathing 9 abominate, animosity, antipathy,
deprecate, repulsion, revulsion
10 abhorrence, repugnance
11 abomination, detestation

hateful
4 evil, foul, mean, vile 5 nasty 6 horrid,
malign, odious, scurvy 7 vicious
8 accursed, damnable, infamous
9 abhorrent, execrable, malicious,
obnoxious, repellent, repulsive
10 abominable, despicable, detestable,
malevolent 11 blasphemous, opprobrious,
unspeakable 13 reprehensible

Hatfields vs. _____
6 McCoys

hatred
5 odium, spite 6 animus, enmity, rancor
7 dislike 8 aversion, loathing 9 animosity,
antipathy, hostility, repulsion, revulsion
10 abhorrence, repugnance
11 abomination, detestation, malevolence
of change: 9 misoneism
of humankind: 11 misanthropy
of marriage: 8 misogamy
of men: 8 misandry
of women: 8 misogyny

hats
9 millinery

hauberk
5 armor 9 chain mail, habergeon

haughtiness
4 airs 5 pride, scorn 7 conceit, disdain,
hauteur 9 arrogance, insolence, pomposity
12 snobbishness

haughty
5 aloof, proud 6 lordly, sniffy 7 distant
8 arrogant, cavalier, scornful, snobbish,
superior 9 egotistic 10 disdainful
11 overbearing 12 contemptuous,
supercilious

haul
3 lug, tow, tug 4 cart, drag, draw, hump,
lift, load, loot, pull, swag, take, tote
5 boost, booty, cargo, hoist, raise, truck
6 burden, lading, schlep, spoils 7 freight,
payload, schlepp
with a tackle: 5 bowse

haul up
5 hoise, hoist
with a rope: 5 trice

haunch
3 hip 11 hindquarter

haunches
4 rump 7 hind end, rear end 8 backside, buttocks 9 posterior 12 hindquarters

haunt
4 site 5 spook 6 obsess, prey on 7 habitat, hang out, inhabit, torment, trouble 8 frequent 9 preoccupy 10 hang around, rendezvous, stay around, visit often

haunter
5 ghost 7 denizen, habitué

hautbois
4 oboe

hauteur
see **haughtiness**

haut monde
5 elite 6 jet set 7 society, who's who 10 glitterati, upper crust 11 aristocracy, high society 13 carriage trade

have
3 own 4 hold 7 contain, include, possess

haven
4 port, roof 5 house 6 asylum, harbor, refuge 7 retreat, shelter 9 anchorage, sanctuary

haversack
3 bag 4 pack 8 backpack

havoc
4 loss, ruin, sack 5 chaos, waste 6 mayhem 8 calamity, disorder, ravaging 9 confusion, ruination 11 catastrophe, destruction, devastation, pandemonium

haw
4 left, tree 5 berry, fruit, shrub 8 turn left 10 equivocate

Hawaii
author: 8 Michener (James A.)
capital: 8 Honolulu
city: 4 Hilo
coast: 4 Kona
discoverer: 4 Cook (Capt. James)
island: 4 Maui, Oahu 5 Kauai, Lanai 6 Niihau 7 Molokai
mountain: 7 Kilauea 8 Mauna Kea, Mauna Loa
nickname: 5 Aloha (State)
park: 9 Haleakala
state bird: 4 nene
state flower: 8 hibiscus
state tree: 5 kukui 9 candlenut

Hawaiian
dance: 4 hula

feast: 4 luau
food: 3 poi
god: 4 Kane, Lono 5 Wakea 7 Kanaloa
goddess: 4 Pele
goose: 4 nene
instrument: 3 uke 7 ukulele
neckwear: 3 lei
nonnative: 5 haole 8 malihini
resident: 8 kamaaina
shaman: 6 kahuna
soup: 6 saimin
tree: 3 koa

hawk
4 kite, sell, vend 5 buteo 6 falcon, monger, osprey, peddle 7 Cooper's, goshawk, haggard, harrier, tiercel 8 caracara, huckster, roughleg 9 accipiter, red-tailed, warmonger 10 militarist 11 ferruginous, rough-legged
young: 4 eyas

hawker
6 coster, monger, seller, vendor 7 packman, peddler 8 pitchman 12 costermonger

hawkeyed
11 keen-sighted 12 sharp-sighted

Hawkeye State
4 Iowa

hawkish
7 martial, warlike 9 combative 10 aggressive 11 belligerent 12 militaristic

_____ Hawley Tariff
5 Smoot

Hawthorne, Nathaniel
birthplace: 5 Salem
character: 6 Hester (Prynne) 8 Clifford (Pyncheon), Hepzibah (Pyncheon), Pyncheon (Judge) 10 Dimmesdale (Rev. Arthur) 13 Chillingworth (Roger)
novel: 10 Marble Faun (The) 13 Scarlet Letter (The) 21 House of the Seven Gables (The)

hay
3 bed 4 feed 5 grass 6 fodder, reward 7 herbage
crops: 6 clover 7 alfalfa, timothy

Haydn oratorio
7 Seasons (The) 8 Creation (The)

hay fever
7 allergy 10 pollenosis, pollinosis
cause: 6 pollen 7 ragweed

haying machine

haying machine
5 baler

haymaker
3 box 4 blow, sock 5 clout, punch
6 wallop

hayseed
see **hick**

haywire
4 amok, awry 5 amuck, crazy, faulty, upset
8 confused 10 out of order 12 out of
control

hazard
3 bet, try 4 dare, game, luck, risk 5 peril,
shoal, wager 6 chance, danger, gamble,
menace 7 fortune, imperil, venture
8 accident, endanger, jeopardy, obstacle

hazardous
5 hairy, risky 6 chancy, unsafe 7 unsound
8 perilous 9 dangerous, unhealthy
10 precarious

haze
3 fog 4 film, mist, murk, smog 5 brume,
cloud, drive, smoke, vapor 6 harass
7 dimness, obscure 8 dullness, initiate,
overcast 9 mistiness, murkiness,
vagueness 10 cloudiness

hazel
4 wood 5 birch, shrub 7 filbert

hazy
3 dim 5 faint, filmy, foggy, fuzzy, misty,
murky, smoky, vague 6 cloudy, unsure
7 blurred, clouded, obscure, unclear
8 nebulous, vaporous 9 uncertain
10 indefinite, indistinct

head
3 nut 4 boss, john, main, pate, poll
5 brain, caput, chief, first, privy, scalp, skull
6 climax, honcho, leader, master, noggin,
noodle, prime, set out, talent, toilet
7 cranium, faculty, latrine, leading, premier,
proceed, supreme 8 director, foremost,
lavatory, light out 9 chieftain, principal,
strike out 10 promontory
area: 5 crown 6 temple
back part: 7 occiput
bone: 5 skull 7 cranium 8 parietal
combining form: 6 cranio 7 cephalo
covering: 3 cap, hat 6 bonnet 8 kerchief
monastery: 4 dean 5 abbot 8 superior
nunnery: 6 abbess 8 superior
of hair: 4 mane 6 fleece 9 chevelure
relating to: 8 cephalic
shaving of: 7 tonsure
skin: 5 scalp
top: 4 pate 5 crown

headache
4 pain 5 worry 6 bother, megrim
7 problem 8 migraine, nuisance, vexation
9 annoyance 10 irritation

headband
7 bandeau, circlet, coronal
ancient Greek: 6 taenia 7 taeniae (plural)

headdress
7 topknot
American Indian: 9 warbonnet
Arab: 8 kaffiyeh
bishop's: 5 miter, mitre
medieval: 4 barb
Eastern: 6 turban
nobleman's: 7 coronet
royal: 5 crown, tiara 6 diadem
Spanish women's: 8 mantilla
women's: 6 bonnet
(see also **hat**)

headland
4 cape 5 point 10 promontory

headline
6 banner 7 feature, promote 8 screamer
9 emphasize, publicize, spotlight
10 noteworthy

headlong
4 rash 5 hasty 6 abrupt, daring, rashly,
sudden 7 hurried, rushing 8 heedless,
reckless 9 foolhardy, impetuous, impulsive
10 heedlessly, recklessly 11 precipitate,
precipitous

headmaster
6 leader 9 principal

head off
4 stop 5 avert, block 6 thwart 7 deflect,
obviate, prevent, ward off 8 stave off, turn
back 9 forestall, intercept

headquarters
3 hub 4 base, seat 6 center

head start
4 edge, jump, lead, odds 5 boost
7 advance, vantage 8 handicap
9 advantage, allowance

headstone
8 memorial, monument 11 grave marker

headstrong
6 dogged, mulish, unruly 7 willful
8 contrary, perverse, stubborn 9 obstinate
10 bullheaded, refractory, self-willed
11 intractable, stiff-necked

heads-up
5 alarm, alert 6 signal, tip-off 7 warning
8 high sign 11 resourceful

headway
4 gain 6 growth 7 advance 8 anabasis,
progress 11 advancement, improvement

heady
4 rash, rich 5 giddy 6 elated, potent
7 willful 8 exciting 9 impetuous
11 exhilarated, intoxicated 12 intoxicating

heal
3 fix 4 cure, mend 5 sew up, treat
6 cement, remedy, repair 7 patch up,
restore 8 make well

healer
6 doctor, shaman

healing
8 curative, remedial, salutary, sanative
9 vulnerary, wholesome 10 salubrious
11 restorative, therapeutic
12 convalescent
goddess of: 3 Eir

health
7 fitness, welfare 8 haleness, vitality,
wellness 9 soundness, well-being,
wholeness
club: 3 gym, spa

healthful
8 curative, hygienic, remedial, salutary
9 favorable, wholesome 10 beneficial,
corrective, profitable, salubrious
11 restorative

healthy
3 fit 4 hale, spry, well 5 sound, tonic
6 benign, robust, strong, sturdy 7 chipper
8 blooming, hygienic, positive, salutary,
thriving, vigorous 9 wholesome 10 able-
bodied, beneficial, prosperous, salubrious
11 flourishing

heap
3 lot 4 cock, fill, gobs, hill, load, lump,
mass, much, pack, pile, rick, scad
5 amass, bunch, clump, crate, loads,
mound, shock, stack, wreck 6 barrel,
charge, gather, jalopy, junker, lumber,
oodles 7 clunker, collect, deposit, jillion
8 assemble, mountain, slathers
9 abundance, great deal, profusion,
stockpile 10 quantities
combustible: 4 pyre

hear
4 heed 5 learn 8 listen to, perceive
9 apprehend

hearing
4 test 5 trial 6 tryout 7 earshot, inquiry
8 audience, audition 9 interview
10 conference, discussion
distance: 7 earshot

hearken
4 heed, mind, note 6 attend, listen, notice
7 observe

hearsay
4 buzz, news, talk 5 rumor 6 gossip,
report 7 account, chatter 9 grapevine
11 scuttlebutt

heart
3 hub 4 core, crux, gist, guts, love, pith,
root, seat, soul, zest 5 ardor, bosom,
focus, gusto, moxie, pluck, spunk 6 breast,
center, kernel, mettle, relish, spirit, ticker
7 courage, resolve 8 feelings, sympathy
9 character, fortitude 10 affections,
compassion, conscience, enthusiasm
combining form: 6 cardio
contraction: 7 systole
dilation: 8 diastole
part: 5 valve 6 atrium, septum 9 ventricle

heartache
3 rue, woe 4 care, pain, pang 5 grief
6 regret, sorrow 7 anguish, sadness
8 distress 10 affliction

heartbeat
5 flash, jiffy, pulse, throb, trice 6 moment,
second 9 pulsation
irregular: 10 arrhythmia

heartbreak
3 rue, woe 5 agony, grief 6 misery, regret,
sorrow 7 anguish, despair, torment, torture
9 suffering 10 desolation 12 wretchedness

heartbreaking
6 bitter, tragic 8 grievous 9 agonizing
10 calamitous, deplorable, lamentable
11 devastating, distressing

heartbroken
7 crushed, grieved 8 mournful, overcome,
wretched 9 sorrowful 10 despairing,
despondent 12 disconsolate

heartburn
7 pyrosis

hearten
4 buoy, stir 5 cheer, rally, rouse 6 arouse,
buck up, buoy up, perk up 7 animate,

cheer up, enliven, inspire **8** embolden, energize, inspirit **9** encourage

heartfelt
4 deep, true **6** honest **7** earnest, fervent, genuine, sincere **8** profound **9** unfeigned

hearth
4 home **5** abode **8** domicile, dwelling, fireside **9** fireplace, residence

heartily
6 wholly **9** sincerely, with gusto, zestfully **10** completely, thoroughly

heartless
4 cold, hard **5** cruel **6** unkind **7** callous **8** uncaring **9** unfeeling **10** hard-boiled **11** insensitive, unemotional **13** unsympathetic

Heart of Dixie
7 Alabama

heartsease
5 pansy, viola **6** violet **11** peace of mind, tranquility **12** johnny-jump-up, tranquillity

heart-shaped
7 cordate

heartsick
4 blue, down **8** dejected, desolate, dismayed, downcast **9** depressed **10** despondent, dispirited **11** demoralized **12** disconsolate

heartthrob
4 idol, love **5** flame, honey, sweet **7** beloved, darling, passion **10** sweetheart

heart-to-heart
4 open, talk **5** frank **6** candid, honest **7** sincere **8** truthful **12** conversation

hearty
4 hale, warm **5** ample **6** jovial, robust, sailor, strong **7** cordial, healthy, profuse, sincere **8** abundant, vehement, vigorous **9** approving, energetic, exuberant, flavorful, unfeigned **12** enthusiastic, unrestrained

heat
4 cook, rage, warm, zeal **5** ardor, fever **6** fervor, simmer, warmth **7** caloric, inflame, passion, swelter **8** pyrolyze
combining form: 4 pyro **6** calori, thermo **7** thermia
measuring device: 11 calorimeter, thermometer
quantity: 3 BTU

heated
3 hot, mad **5** angry, fiery, irate **6** ardent,

fervid, fierce, ireful, raging, steamy **7** boiling, burning, fevered, furious **8** broiling, feverish, scalding, sizzling, vehement, wrathful **9** indignant, scorching **10** passionate **11** acrimonious

heater
3 gun, rod **5** stove **6** boiler, pistol **7** furnace **8** fastball, radiator

heath
4 moor **5** shrub **9** wasteland

heathen
5 pagan **7** infidel **8** barbaric **11** irreligious, uncivilized

heat-producing
9 calorific

heave
3 lob **4** cast, draw, fire, gasp, haul, heft, huff, hurl, lift, pant, puff, pull, push, toss **5** fling, hoist, labor, pitch, raise, retch, sling, surge, throw, vomit **6** launch

heave-ho
4 boot **6** ouster **8** bum's rush **9** dismissal

heaven
3 God **4** Zion **5** bliss, glory **6** utopia **7** arcadia, delight, ecstasy, elysium, nirvana, rapture **8** empyrean, eternity, paradise **9** firmament, Shangri-la **10** wonderland **11** immortality, kingdom come **12** promised land

heavenly
4 lush **6** divine, sacred **7** blessed **8** beatific, empyreal, empyrean, ethereal **9** ambrosial, celestial, delicious **10** delectable, delightful, enchanting

heavy
3 big, fat **4** rich **5** beefy, bulky, gross, hefty, obese, stout **6** bad guy, chunky, drowsy, fleshy, gravid, leaden, portly **7** arduous, intense, labored, massive, porcine, villain, weighty **8** burdened, cumbrous, enceinte, pregnant, sluggish, unwieldy **9** corpulent, expectant, laborious, lumbering, ponderous, strenuous **10** burdensome, cumbersome, formidable, oppressive, overweight

heavy-handed
5 crude, harsh, inept **6** clumsy, gauche, klutzy **7** awkward **8** bumbling, despotic **9** maladroit **10** oppressive **11** domineering, overbearing

heavyhearted
3 sad **4** glum **5** sorry **7** unhappy **8** dejected, downcast, mournful, saddened

9 depressed, miserable, sorrowful
10 despondent, dispirited, melancholy

heavyset
5 beefy, husky, stout, thick **6** chunky, portly, stocky **11** thick-bodied

heavyweight
3 VIP **4** lion **5** boxer, chief **6** big gun, bigwig, leader **7** big shot, notable **8** big-timer

Hebe
father: **4** Zeus **7** Jupiter
husband: **8** Hercules
mother: **4** Hera, Juno
successor: **8** Ganymede

hebetude
6 stupor, torpor **7** languor **8** dullness, lethargy **9** lassitude, torpidity **10** drowsiness

hebetudinous
4 dull, logy **5** dopey **6** drowsy, stupid, torpid **8** listless, sluggish **9** lethargic

Hebrew
3 Jew **6** Jewish
coin: **6** lepton, shekel
festival: **5** Purim **6** Pesach, Sukkot **7** Hanukah, Sukkoth **8** Chanukah, Lag b'Omer, Passover, Shabuoth **9** Tishah-b'Ab, Yom Kippur **12** Rosh Hashanah, Simchas Torah
God: **6** Adonai, Elohim, Yahweh **7** Jehovah
judge: **6** Gideon
lawgiver: **5** Moses
letter:
(see at **alphabet**)
measure: **5** cubit, ephah
month: **4** Adar, Elul, Iyar **5** Nisan, Sivan, Tebet **6** Kislev, Shebat, Tammuz, Tishri **6** Veadar (in leap year) **7** Heshvan
patriarch: **3** Dan, Gad **4** Cain, Levi, Seth **5** Asher, David, Isaac, Jacob, Judah **6** Joseph, Reuben, Simeon **7** Abraham, Zebulun **8** Benjamin, Issachar, Naphtali
sacred city: **5** Safad, Safed **6** Hebron **8** Tiberias **9** Jerusalem
(see also **Jewish**)

Hebrides island
4 Eigg, Rhum, Skye, Uist **5** Lewis **6** Harris

Hecate
father: **6** Perses
goddess of: **5** night **10** underworld, witchcraft
mother: **7** Asteria

hecatomb
7 killing, slaying **8** butchery **9** bloodbath, sacrifice, slaughter

heck
4 darn, drat, geez, gosh, hell, jeez **5** golly **6** shucks

heckle
3 nag **4** bait, faze, gibe, ride **5** annoy, chivy, hound, tease, worry **6** badger, bother, harass, hassle, hector, molest, needle, pester, plague, rattle **7** disrupt, disturb, torment **9** interrupt **10** disconcert

hectic
3 red **6** fervid **7** burning, excited, fevered, flushed **8** confused, exciting, feverish, frenetic, restless **9** turbulent **10** persistent

hector
3 cow, nag **4** bait, ride **5** bully, chivy, harass, hound **6** badger, lean on **7** bedevil, swagger **8** browbeat, bullyrag, domineer **10** intimidate

Hector
brother: **5** Paris **7** Helenus, Troilus **9** Deiphobus, Polydorus
father: **5** Priam
mother: **6** Hecuba
sister: **6** Creusa **8** Polyxena **9** Cassandra
slayer: **8** Achilles
victim: **9** Patroclus
wife: **10** Andromache

Hecuba
daughter: **6** Creusa **8** Polyxena **9** Cassandra
father: **5** Dymas
husband: **5** Priam
son: **5** Paris **6** Hector **7** Helenus, Troilus **9** Deiphobus, Polydorus
victim: **11** Polymnestor

hedge
4 trim **5** avoid, evade, fence, guard, hem in, limit **7** barrier, defense, enclose, evasion, protect **8** boundary, encircle, restrict, shrubbery **10** protection

hedgehog
9 porcupine **10** stronghold

hedonist
4 rake **7** epicure, gourmet **8** gourmand, sybarite **9** bon vivant, epicurean, libertine **10** sensualist, voluptuary

heebie-jeebies
5 jumps **6** creeps, nerves, shakes **7** jitters, shivers, willies **11** nervousness

heed
4 care, hark, mark, mind, note, obey

heedful

5 watch 6 attend, be aware, harken, listen, notice, regard, remark 7 concern, hearing, hearken, observe, respect 8 consider, interest 9 attention 10 observance

heedful
5 alert, aware 7 on guard 8 vigilant 9 attentive, observant, observing 10 interested, meticulous, scrupulous 13 conscientious

heedless
9 negligent, oblivious, unmindful 10 unthinking 11 inadvertent, inattentive, unobservant 12 unreflective 13 inconsiderate

heedlessness
7 neglect 9 disregard, unconcern 11 disinterest, inattention, insouciance 12 indifference

hee-haw
4 bray 5 laugh 6 guffaw 10 horse laugh

heel
3 bum, cad, tip 4 cant, hock, lean, list, tilt 5 creep, knave, louse, rogue, skunk, slope 6 rascal, rotter 7 incline, lowlife, villain 9 scoundrel
bone: 8 calcanea (plural), calcanei (plural) 9 calcaneum, calcaneus

heft
4 lift, load 5 hoist, raise, weigh 6 weight 7 heave up 9 heaviness, influence 10 importance

hefty
3 big 5 beefy, burly, bulky, heavy, husky, large, major 6 brawny, mighty, rugged, strong 7 massive, sizable 8 imposing, powerful 9 extensive, good-sized, plentiful, ponderous, strapping 11 substantial

hegira
6 escape, exodus, flight 7 journey 10 emigration, evacuation 11 deliverance

Heidi
author: 5 Spyri (Johanna)
goatherd: 5 Peter
setting: 4 Alps

heifer
4 calf

_____ Heifetz
6 Jascha

height
3 top 4 acme, apex, cusp, peak, rise 6 apogee, climax, heyday, summit, vertex, zenith 7 stature 8 altitude, pinnacle 9 elevation, loftiness 10 prominence

combining form: 4 acro

heighten
3 wax 5 boost, mount, raise 6 beef up, expand, extend 7 amplify, augment, build up, elevate, enhance, enlarge, improve, magnify 8 increase 9 highlight, intensify 10 aggrandize

heinie
3 bum 4 butt, rear, rump 5 fanny 6 bottom 7 rear end 8 backside

heinous
4 evil 6 odious 7 hateful 8 infamous, shocking 9 abhorrent, atrocious, execrable, monstrous 10 abominable, detestable, outrageous

heinousness
4 evil 6 horror, infamy 8 atrocity, enormity 13 monstrousness

heir
5 scion 7 grantee, heritor, legatee 9 inheritor, successor 11 beneficiary
joint: 8 parcener 10 coparcener

heist
3 cop, rob 4 lift, loot 5 boost, caper, filch, pinch, steal, swipe, theft 6 holdup, rip off 7 larceny, purloin, robbery 8 burglary 9 strong-arm

Helen of Troy
abductor: 5 Paris
husband: 8 Menelaus

Helenus
brother: 5 Paris 6 Hector 7 Troilus 9 Deiphobus, Polydorus
father: 5 Priam
mother: 6 Hecuba
sister: 6 Creusa 8 Polyxena 9 Cassandra
wife: 10 Andromache

Hel, Hela
father: 4 Loki
hall: 7 Niflhel 8 Niflheim
mother: 9 Angerboda

helical
6 spiral

helicopter
7 chopper 9 eggbeater 10 whirlybird
armed: 7 gunship
blade: 5 rotor

Helios
6 Apollo
daughter: 5 Circe 8 Pasiphaë
father: 8 Hyperion
mother: 5 Theia
sister: 3 Eos 6 Aurora, Selene

son: 8 Phaethon

heliotrope
4 herb 5 shrub 6 borage 10 bloodstone

hell
5 hades, Sheol 6 blazes, Tophet
7 Gehenna, inferno 9 perdition

hell-bent
6 driven, intent 8 obsessed, resolved
10 determined

Hellen
father: 9 Deucalion
mother: 6 Pyrrha
son: 5 Dorus 6 Aeolus, Xuthus

hellhole
3 pit 8 dystopia, snake pit 9 mare's nest

hellion
3 elf, imp 4 puck, punk 5 demon, rogue,
scamp 6 rascal 7 gremlin

hellish
6 horrid 7 ghastly, hideous, satanic,
stygian 8 damnable, diabolic, dreadful,
gruesome, horrible, infernal, terrible
9 appalling, frightful, monstrous, plutonian
10 diabolical

Hellman play
11 Little Foxes (The) 13 Children's Hour
(The) 15 Watch on the Rhine

hello
3 hey 4 ciao, hail 5 aloha, howdy 7 hi
there, welcome 8 greeting 9 greetings

helm
5 wheel 7 cockpit 8 controls

helmet
6 casque, sallet, tin hat 7 morrion
8 burgonet, headgear
medieval: 6 sallet 7 basinet
part: 7 ventail 8 aventail
sun: 4 topi 5 topee

helmsman
5 pilot

Heloïse
husband: 7 Abelard (Peter)
son: 9 Astrolabe

helot
4 peon, serf 5 slave 6 vassal 7 laborer,
peasant, servant

helotry
4 yoke 6 thrall 7 bondage, peonage,
serfdom, slavery 9 servitude, thralldom
11 enslavement

help
3 aid 4 abet, back, mend 5 avail, boost,
guide, serve 6 assist, relief, remedy,
succor 7 advance, benefit, bolster, further,
promote, relieve, secours, service, support
8 mitigate, palliate 9 alleviate, meliorate
10 ameliorate, assistance, facilitate
11 cooperation
forward: 7 further
hired: 5 labor

helper
4 aide 6 deputy, server 7 ancilla, servant
8 employee 9 assistant, associate,
attendant, auxiliary 10 apprentice
11 subordinate

helpful
5 of use 6 usable, useful 8 salutary,
valuable 9 effective, favorable, practical
10 beneficial, profitable, propitious
11 encouraging 12 advantageous,
constructive

helping
4 dose 5 share 7 portion, serving
9 auxiliary

helpless
4 weak 6 feeble, futile, unable 7 forlorn
8 desolate 9 abandoned, dependent
11 unprotected

helter-skelter
6 anyhow 7 anywise, flighty, hastily turmoil
8 at random, disorder, pell-mell, randomly
9 confusion, haphazard, hit-or-miss 11 any
which way, haphazardly, in confusion,
precipitate

helve
4 haft 6 handle

Helvetian
5 Swiss

hem
3 pen, rim 4 brim, edge, gird, ring, seam,
shut 5 bound, brink, fence, hedge, skirt,
verge 6 border, circle, corral, edging,
fringe, immure, margin, stitch 7 close in,
enclose, selvage, shorten 8 encircle,
surround 9 encompass, perimeter,
periphery
turned-back: 4 cuff

Heman
father: 4 Joel
grandfather: 6 Samuel

hematite
3 ore 7 mineral 12 black diamond

Hemingway, Ernest
novel: 9 In Our Time (The) 12 Sun Also Rises
13 Moveable Feast (A) 14 Farewell
to Arms (A) 15 Old Man and the Sea (The)
16 To Have and Have Not 18 Islands in the
Stream, Snows of Kilimanjaro (The) 19 For
Whom the Bell Tolls
sobriquet: 4 Papa

hemlock
4 drug, herb, tree, wood 6 poison

hemophiliac
7 bleeder

hemp
3 kef, kif 7 hashish 8 cannabis
9 marijuana
fiber: 5 oakum
kind: 4 aloe

hen
5 biddy
broody: 6 sitter
spayed: 8 poularde
young: 6 pullet

hence
4 away, ergo, thus 5 since 9 as a result,
from now on, therefore, thereupon
11 accordingly 12 consequently

henceforth
9 from now on, hereafter

henchman
6 cohort, lackey, minion, stooge 7 abettor
8 adherent, disciple, follower, partisan,
retainer 9 attendant, supporter
10 accomplice

Henley poem
8 Invictus

henpeck
3 nag 4 carp, fuss 5 annoy 6 badger,
carp at, harass, hector 8 domineer 9 find
fault

Henry II
adversary: 6 Becket (Thomas à)
son: 7 Richard (Lionheart)
surname: 5 Anjou 11 Plantagenet
wife: 7 Eleanor

Henry IV
surname: 9 Lancaster
victim: 10 Richard III

Henry VIII
archbishop: 7 Cranmer (Thomas)
10 Thomas More
daughter: 9 Elizabeth
son: 6 Edward
surname: 5 Tudor

victim: 4 Anne (Boleyn) 9 Catherine
(Howard) 10 Thomas More
wife: 4 Anne (Boleyn, of Cleves), Jane
(Seymour) 9 Catherine (Howard, of
Aragon, Parr)

hepatic
9 liverwort

Hephaestus
6 Vulcan
father: 4 Zeus 7 Jupiter
mother: 4 Hera, Juno
wife: 5 Venus 6 Charis 9 Aphrodite

Hephzibah
husband: 8 Hezekiah
son: 8 Manasseh

hepped up
5 eager 7 excited, fervent 12 enthusiastic

Hera
4 Juno
father: 6 Cronus, Saturn
husband: 4 Zeus 7 Jupiter
messenger: 4 Iris
mother: 4 Rhea

Heracles
beloved: 4 Iole
brother: 8 Iphicles
charioteer: 6 Iolaus
father: 4 Zeus 7 Jupiter
mother: 7 Alcmene
son: 6 Hyllus
victim: 5 Hydra, Ladon 6 Geryon,
Megara, Orthus 10 Nemean lion
wife: 4 Hebe 6 Megara 8 Deianira

herald
4 hail, tout 5 crier, greet 6 signal
7 courier, declare, portend, precede,
presage, proclaim, trumpet 8 announce,
ballyhoo, exponent, outrider 9 advertise,
harbinger, messenger, precursor, publicize,
spokesman 10 forerunner, foreshadow

heraldic
border: 7 bordure
cross: 6 fleury, formée, moline, pommée
8 fourchée
term: 4 bend, fess, orle, pale, seme, vert
5 crest, flank, gules 6 argent, blazon,
canton, charge, device, dexter, emblem,
impale, manche, sejant, voided, volant
7 chevron, nombril, passant, purpure,
rampant, saltire, statant 8 guardant,
sinister, tincture 9 regardant
10 escutcheon

heraldry
6 armory 9 pageantry

herb

3 oca 4 dill, flax, forb, hemp, leek, mint, nard, sage, wort 5 basil, chive, tansy, thyme 6 allium, arnica, borage, catnip, endive, eryngo, fennel, garlic, hyssop, lovage, orpine, salsify, squill, yarrow 7 boneset, caraway, catmint, chervil, chicory, comfrey, episcia, ginseng, milfoil, mullein, oregano, parsley, pinesap, pussley, sanicle 8 angelica, camomile, capsicum, cardamom, centaury, cilantro, costmary, feverfew, freewort, hepatica, lungwort, mandrake, marjoram, origanum, pokeweed, purslane, rapeseed, selfheal, tarragon, turmeric, euphrasy, valerian, woodruff, wormwood 9 birthwort, bush basil, chamomile, patchouli, spikenard 10 basil thyme 12 balm of Gilead
mythical: 4 moly
poisonous: 7 aconite, dogbane, hemlock, henbane 8 veratrum 9 hellebore

herbicide

6 dioxin, diquat, diuron 7 monuron 8 picloram, simazine 11 Agent Orange

Herculean

4 huge, vast 5 giant 7 arduous, immense, mammoth, titanic 8 colossal, enormous, gigantic, powerful 10 formidable, superhuman

Hercules

see **Heracles**

herd

3 mob 4 bevy, lead 5 covey, crowd, drive, drove, flock, swarm 6 gather, throng 9 associate, multitude

herdsman

6 Boötes, cowboy 7 breeder 8 shepherd

here and there

6 passim 7 at times 9 sometimes 11 irregularly

hereditary

6 inborn, inbred, innate, lineal 7 genetic 9 ancestral, inherited 10 congenital 11 traditional, transmitted

heredity

7 lineage 8 ancestry 9 tradition 11 inheritance
unit: 4 gene

heresy

6 schism 7 dissent, fallacy, impiety 9 defection, deviation, misbelief 10 dissidence, heterodoxy, infidelity, radicalism 11 revisionism, unorthodoxy 13 nonconformism, nonconformity

heretic

7 infidel 8 apostate, defector, recusant, renegade 9 dissenter, dissident 10 iconoclast, schismatic, separatist, unbeliever 11 misbeliever, nonbeliever, revisionist 13 nonconformist

heretical

7 infidel 8 apostate 9 dissident, heterodox, miscreant, sectarian 10 dissenting, schismatic, unorthodox 11 revisionist 12 misbelieving 13 nonconformist

heritage

6 legacy 7 bequest 9 patrimony, tradition 10 birthright

Hermes

7 Mercury
attribute: 7 petasos, petasus 8 caduceus
father: 4 Zeus 7 Jupiter
mother: 4 Maia

hermetic

6 closed, occult, secret 7 recluse 8 abstruse, airtight, profound, secluded, solitary 9 recondite 10 cloistered, impervious 11 sequestered

Hermia

beloved: 8 Lysander
father: 5 Egeus

Hermione

father: 8 Menelaus
husband: 7 Orestes, Pyrrhus 11 Neoptolemus
mother: 5 Helen

hermit

5 loner 6 cookie 7 eremite, recluse 8 solitary 9 anchorite

hermitage

7 retreat 8 cloister, hideaway 9 monastery

hernia

6 breach 7 rupture 10 protrusion
support: 5 truss
type: 6 cystic, hiatal 7 femoral 9 umbilical 10 incisional

hero

4 idol 6 knight 7 demigod, paladin 8 champion 11 protagonist
American: 6 Bunyan (Paul) 8 Superman
Armenian: 10 Skanderbeg
Babylonian: 9 Gilgamesh
Celtic-French: 7 Tristan 8 Tristram
Crusades: 7 Tancred 8 Tancredi
English: 6 Arthur 7 Beowulf 9 Robin Hood

French: 6 Roland 11 Charlemagne
German: 5 Etzel 8 Arminius 9 Siegfried
Greek: 4 Ajax 5 Jason 7 Perseus, Ulysses 8 Achilles, Heracles, Hercules, Leonidas, Odysseus 11 Bellerophon
Hebrew: 5 David 6 Daniel, Samson
Hungarian: 5 Arpad 7 Hunyadi (János)
Irish: 9 Cuchulain, Cuchulinn, Cuchullin
Italian: 7 Orlando
Roman: 7 Romulus 8 Horatius
Scandinavian: 6 Sigurd 9 Siegfried
Scottish: 5 Bruce (Robert) 6 Rob Roy
Spanish: 5 El Cid
Spartan: 8 Leonidas
Trojan: 6 Aeneas, Hector

Herod
daughter: 6 Salome
father: 7 Antipas 9 Antipater
kingdom: 5 Judea 6 Judaea
mother: 6 Cyprus
son: 5 Herod (Antipas) 6 Joseph 7 Pheroas 9 Phasaelus

Herodias
daughter: 6 Salome
father: 11 Aristobulus
husband: 5 Herod (Antipas)

heroic
4 bold, huge 5 brave, daring, noble 6 mighty 7 drastic, extreme, radical, valiant 8 colossal, enormous, fearless, gigantic, intrepid, unafraid, valorous 9 dauntless, Herculean, undaunted 10 courageous

heroin
4 gear, skag 5 horse, smack 8 narcotic 11 diamorphine

heroism
5 valor 6 daring, spirit 7 bravery, courage, prowess 8 boldness, chivalry, nobility, valiance 9 gallantry 11 intrepidity

heron relative
5 egret 7 bittern

Hero's lover
7 Leander

herring
7 sardine 8 brisling, pilchard
smoked: 7 bloater

Herse
father: 7 Cecrops
sister: 8 Aglauros
son: 8 Cephalus

Hersey
novel: 4 Wall (The) 12 Bell for Adano (A)

town: 5 Adano

Hesione
brother: 5 Priam
father: 8 Laomedon
husband: 7 Telamon
rescuer: 8 Heracles, Hercules
son: 6 Teucer

hesitant
4 slow 5 chary, loath, timid 6 afraid, averse, unsure 7 halting, uneager 9 faltering, reluctant, tentative, uncertain, unwilling 10 irresolute 11 disinclined, vacillating

hesitate
4 balk 5 delay, demur, hedge, pause, stall, stick, waver 6 dawdle, dither, falter, waffle 7 stammer, stutter 8 hang back, hold back 9 temporize, vacillate 12 shilly-shally

Hesperides
6 nymphs

Hesperus
5 Venus 11 evening star
father: 8 Astraeus
mother: 3 Eos

Hesse novel
6 Demian 10 Siddhartha 11 Steppenwolf 12 Magister Ludi

Hestia
5 Vesta
father: 6 Cronus, Saturn
mother: 4 Rhea

heterodox
9 dissident, heretical, sectarian 10 schismatic, unorthodox 13 non-conformist

heterodoxy
6 heresy, schism 7 dissent 9 misbelief 10 dissidence 13 nonconformism, nonconformity

heterogeneous
5 mixed 6 motley, sundry, varied 7 diverse, various 8 assorted 9 disparate 12 conglomerate

het up
5 irate, upset 7 excited 8 agitated

hew
3 axe, cut 4 chop, fell, form 5 shape, stick 6 adhere 7 conform, cut down

hex
4 jinx 5 charm, curse, spell, witch 6 voodoo, whammy 7 bad luck, bewitch,

enchant 9 sorceress **11** enchantment, enchantress

heyday
4 acme, peak **5** prime **6** height, zenith **9** high point

Hezekiah
father: 4 Ahaz **7** Neariah
mother: 3 Abi
son: 8 Manasseh
wife: 9 Hephzibah

hiatus
3 gap **5** break, space **6** breach, lacuna **7** interim **8** aperture, downtime, interval **10** suspension **12** interruption **13** discontinuity

Hiawatha
author: 10 Longfellow (Henry Wadsworth)
grandmother: 7 Nokomis
mother: 7 Wenonah
tribe: 6 Ojibwa, Ojibwe **7** Ojibway
wife: 9 Minnehaha

hibernal
6 wintry **8** winterly

Hibernia
4 Eire, Erin **7** Ireland

hick
4 rube **5** yokel **6** rustic **7** bumpkin, hayseed **8** cornball **10** clodhopper, provincial

hidden
5 privy **6** buried, covert, occult, secret, veiled **7** obscure **8** obscured, shrouded, ulterior **9** concealed **11** undisclosed
combining form: 6 crypto, krypto

hide
3 fur **4** bury, lurk, mask, pelt, skin, veil **5** cache, cloak, cover, inter, shade, stash **6** harbor, lie low, screen, shroud **7** conceal, cover up, leather, obscure, seclude, secrete, shelter **8** ensconce

hideaway
see **hideout**

hidebound
8 obdurate **9** parochial **10** inflexible, provincial **11** reactionary, straitlaced **12** conservative, narrow-minded **13** straightlaced

hideous
4 ugly **5** awful, gross, lurid, nasty **6** grisly, horrid **7** ghastly, hateful **8** gruesome, horrible, shocking, terrible **9** appalling, dismaying, frightful, loathsome, monstrous, offensive, repellent, repugnant, repulsive,
revolting, sickening **10** disgusting, horrifying

hideout
3 den **4** lair **5** cache, haven **6** covert, refuge **7** retreat, shelter **9** hermitage, safe house, sanctuary

hie
3 run **4** dash, push, trot **5** scoot **6** hasten, hurry, hustle

hierarch
4 boss, head **5** chief **6** honcho, leader, master **7** headman **9** chieftain **10** high priest

hierarchy
5 group, order, ranks **6** ladder, system **7** pyramid **9** food chain, structure **11** bureaucracy **12** pecking order

hieratic
6 formal **8** priestly, stylized **10** priestlike, sacerdotal

high
4 tall **5** drunk, giddy, grand, lofty, noble, tipsy **6** elated, raised, stoned, treble, zonked **7** drugged, keyed up, soaring, supreme **8** abstruse, elevated, eloquent, euphoric, hopped-up, piercing, towering **9** climactic, delirious, prominent, spaced-out **11** extravagant, intoxicated
combining form: 4 alti

high ___
3 hat, tea **4** five, noon, road, sign, tech, tide, time **5** chair, heels, jinks **6** priest, roller, school

high-and-mighty
5 bossy, proud **6** lordly **7** haughty **8** arrogant, cavalier, insolent, superior **9** imperious **10** disdainful **11** domineering, overbearing **12** supercilious

highball
3 fly, run **4** dash, rush, whiz **5** hurry, speed **6** barrel, hustle, signal **7** hotfoot **8** cocktail

highboy
5 chest **6** bureau **7** dresser **9** furniture

highbrow
4 snob **7** egghead **8** cerebral, cultured, educated **9** intellect **12** intellectual

high-class
7 elegant **8** five-star, superior **9** exclusive, exquisite, first-rate, patrician **11** fashionable **12** aristocratic **13** sophisticated

highest
3 top **5** chief **6** apical, upmost **7** exalted,

supreme, topmost **9** top-drawer, uppermost **10** top-ranking
point: 4 acme, apex **5** crest **6** summit, zenith **8** pinnacle

highfalutin
5 fancy, windy **6** florid **7** aureate, flowery, fustian, orotund, pompous **8** affected **9** bombastic, grandiose, overblown, rhapsodic **10** oratorical, rhetorical **11** declamatory, pretentious

high-flown
5 showy, tumid, windy **6** turgid **7** aureate, flowery, fustian, orotund, pompous, swollen **8** elevated, inflated, sonorous **9** bombastic, grandiose, overblown **10** flamboyant **11** declamatory, pretentious **12** magniloquent, ostentatious **13** grandiloquent

high-handed
5 bossy **8** dogmatic, imperial **9** arbitrary, imperious **10** autocratic, disdainful, imperative, peremptory **11** dictatorial, domineering, magisterial, overbearing

high-hat
4 snub **6** slight, snobby, snooty **7** disdain, haughty **8** arrogant, snobbish **9** conceited, disregard **11** pretentious **12** supercilious

high jinks
3 fun **6** antics **7** fooling, revelry **9** horseplay, rowdiness, whoop-de-do

Highlander
4 Gael, Scot

highlight
4 mark **5** focus **6** accent, stress **7** feature **8** point out **9** emphasize, underline **10** accentuate, focal point

high-minded
5 lofty, moral, noble **7** ethical, upright **8** elevated **10** principled

high-muck-a-muck
3 VIP **5** nabob **6** bigwig **7** big shot, notable

high-pitched
6 shrill **7** excited **8** agitated, feverish, frenetic, piercing

high point
3 top **4** acme, peak **6** apogee, summit, zenith **8** best part, pinnacle

high-powered
6 driven, strong **7** dynamic **8** animated, forceful, vigorous **9** energetic, strenuous **10** aggressive, compelling **12** enterprising

high-pressure
8 forceful **9** insistent, stressful **10** aggressive

high roller
7 gambler, spender, wastrel **8** prodigal **10** big spender, profligate, squanderer **11** spendthrift

high sign
3 nod, tip **4** wink **5** alarm **6** signal, tipoff **7** gesture, warning

Highsmith novel
11 Ripley's Game **16** Talented Mr. Ripley (The)

high-sounding
7 pompous **8** affected, imposing, inflated, puffed-up **9** grandiose, overblown **11** pretentious

high-spirited
4 bold **5** brash, fiery, jolly, merry **6** bubbly, daring, joyful, lively, plucky, spunky **7** excited, gleeful **9** ebullient, energetic, exuberant, vivacious **12** effervescent, lighthearted

high-strung
4 edgy, taut **5** hyper, jumpy, nervy, tense, tight, wired **6** touchy **7** fidgety, jittery, keyed up, nervous, uptight **8** restless **9** excitable, sensitive

hightail it
3 run **4** bolt, dash, flee **5** scoot, scram **6** get out, run off **7** take off **8** clear out **9** skedaddle

highway
4 pike, road **5** track **6** artery **8** corridor, turnpike **10** interstate **12** thoroughfare
German: 8 autobahn
Italian: 10 autostrada

highwayman
5 thief **6** bandit, robber **7** brigand

hijack
5 seize, steal **6** abduct, kidnap **8** take over **10** commandeer **11** appropriate

hike
4 jump, rove, snap, trek, walk **5** boost, raise, tramp, tromp **6** jack up, rise up, travel **7** journey, traipse, upgrade **8** backpack, increase

hilarious
5 funny, merry **7** comical **8** humorous, mirthful **9** laughable, priceless **10** rollicking

hilarity
4 glee **5** cheer, mirth **6** gaiety **7** delight
8 jocosity, laughter **9** merriment
12 cheerfulness

hill
4 bank, bump, cock, dune, heap, knob,
pile, rick, rise **5** bluff, butte, knoll, mound,
ridge, shock, slope, stack **6** cuesta, height
7 hummock, incline **8** mountain
9 elevation, monadnock
African veld: **5** kopje **6** koppie
Boston: **6** Bunker
craggy: **3** tor
Cuba: **7** San Juan
D.C.: **7** Capitol
elongate: **7** drumlin
level-topped: **4** mesa **5** butte
of stratified drift: **4** kame
rounded: **5** swell
sand: **4** dune
small: **5** knoll, kopje, mound **6** koppie
surrounded by ice: **7** nunatak

hillbilly
4 rube **5** yokel **6** rustic **7** bumpkin,
hayseed **10** clodhopper **12** backwoodsman

hillock
4 rise **5** knoll, mound

hillside
5 slope
Scottish: **4** brae

hilt
4 grip, haft **6** handle **8** handgrip

Himalayan country
5 Nepal **6** Bhutan

hind
3 doe **4** back, deer, rear **5** after **7** grouper
9 posterior
mate: **4** hart

hinder
4 balk, curb, mire **5** block, check, delay,
deter **6** baffle, burden, fetter, hamper, hold
up, impede, retard, thwart **7** inhibit,
prevent, shackle, trammel **8** handicap,
hold back, obstruct, restrain **9** frustrate,
hamstring, interfere, interrupt

hindmost
3 end **4** back, last, rear **5** after, final
6 latter **7** closing **8** farthest, terminal,
ultimate **9** posterior **10** concluding

hindquarters
8 haunches

hindrance
3 bar **4** snag **8** obstacle **9** impedance
10 impediment **11** obstruction

Hindu
age: **4** yuga
ascetic: **4** yogi **5** fakir, swami
caste (varna): **5** Sudra **6** Vaisya
7 Brahman **9** Kshatriya
class: **5** caste, varna
community: **6** ashram
demon: **4** Rahu **6** Ravana
essence: **5** atman
force: **5** karma
garment: **4** sari
gentleman: **4** babu
god: **4** deva, Siva **5** Shiva **6** Brahma,
Vishnu
goddess: **4** devi
goddess of beauty: **7** Lakshmi
goddess of destruction: **4** Kali
god of destruction: **4** Siva **5** Shiva
god of fire: **4** Agni
god of love: **4** Kama
god of the heavens: **7** Krishna
god of war: **5** Skanda **6** Karttikeya
god of wisdom: **6** Ganesa, Ganesh
hell: **6** Naraka
holy man: **5** sadhu
instrument: **5** sitar, tabla
leader: **6** Gandhi (Mahatma)
lowest caste: **5** Sudra
nobleman: **4** raja **5** rajah
philosophy: **7** Vedanta
precept: **5** sutra
prince: **4** raja **5** rajah **8** maharaja
9 maharajah
queen: **4** rani **5** ranee **8** maharani
9 maharanee
salvation: **7** nirvana
scripture: **4** Veda **6** Purana **12** Bhagavad
Gita
social group: **5** caste, varna
teacher: **4** guru **5** swami **9** maharishi
term of respect: **5** sahib
title: **3** sri
treatise: **9** Upanishad
twice-born: **6** Vaisya **7** Brahman
9 Kshatriya

hinge
4 pawl **5** joint, mount **12** turning point
kind: **4** butt **5** piano **10** hook-and-eye

hint
3 cue, tip **4** clue, dash, sign, wisp **5** imply,
taste, tinge, touch, trace **6** allude, notion,
shadow, tipoff **7** inkling, soupçon, suggest
8 allusion, indicate, innuendo, intimate
9 insinuate, scintilla, suspicion

10 indication, intimation, suggestion
11 implication, insinuation

hinterland
4 bush 6 sticks 8 frontier, interior
9 backwater, backwoods, boondocks, up-
country 10 wilderness 11 backcountry

hip
3 hot 4 chic, coxa 5 aware, savvy
6 haunch, trendy, with-it 7 tuned in
11 fashionable
bone: 5 ilium, pubis 6 pelvis 7 ischium
cattle: 5 thurl
disorder: 8 sciatica

hippie
8 bohemian, longhair 11 flower child
13 nonconformist

Hippocratic _____
4 oath

Hippodamia
father: 8 Oenomaus
husband: 6 Pelops 9 Pirithous
10 Peirithous
son: 6 Atreus 8 Thyestes

Hippolytus
father: 7 Theseus
mother: 7 Antiope 9 Hippolyte
stepmother: 7 Phaedra

hire
3 fee, pay 4 rent, wage 5 lease, wages
6 employ, engage, retain, sign on, take on
7 charter, payment, recruit 8 contract
10 employment 11 contract for

hireling
4 hack 6 worker 7 servant 8 employee
9 mercenary

Hirschfeld's daughter
4 Nina

hirsute
5 hairy 6 shaggy, woolly 9 whiskered

Hispania
6 Iberia 9 peninsula
part: 5 Spain 8 Portugal

Hispaniola country
5 Haiti

hiss
3 boo 4 hoot, jeer 5 decry 6 deride,
revile, sizzle, wheeze 7 catcall, whisper,
whistle 8 sibilate

historian
8 annalist 10 chronicler
American: 4 Webb (Charles Richard)
5 Adams (Brooks, Charles Kendall,
Hannah, Henry, Herbert Baxter), Beard
(Charles, Mary), Foote (Shelby) 6 Brooks
(Van Wyck), Catton (Bruce), DeVoto
(Bernard), Durant (Ariel, Will), Malone
(Dumas), Miller (Perry), Muzzey (David),
Nevins (Allen), Sarton (George Alfred),
Shirer (William), Sparks (Jared), Turner
(Frederick Jackson) 7 Ambrose (Stephen),
Morison (Samuel Eliot), Parkman (Francis),
Ridpath (John Clark), Tuchman (Barbara),
Woodson (Carter G.) 8 Bancroft (George),
Boorstin (Daniel), Channing (Edward),
Commager (Henry Steele), Prescott
(William H.), Robinson (James Harvey),
Woodward (C. Vann) 10 McCullough
(David) 11 Schlesinger (Arthur)
Arab: 10 Ibn Khaldun
Danish: 4 Saxo (Grammaticus)
Dutch: 8 Huizinga (Johan)
English: 4 Bede (Venerable), Stow (John),
Ward (Adolphus) 5 Acton (Lord), Grote
(George), Wells (Herbert George)
6 Camden (William), Gibbon (Edward),
Keegan (John), Namier (Lewis Bernstein),
Stubbs (William), Taylor (A. J. P.) 7 Hakluyt
(Richard), Raleigh (Walter), Toynbee
(Arnold), Whewell (William) 8 Geoffrey (of
Monmouth), Macaulay (Thomas Babington)
9 Holinshed (Raphael), Trevelyan (George)
French: 5 Bloch (Marc), Renan (Ernest),
Taine (Hippolyte) 6 Guizot (François),
Thiers (Louis-Adolphe), Volney (Comte de)
7 Braudel (Ferdinand) 8 Hanotaux
(Gabriel), Michelet (Jules)
German: 5 Ranke (Leopold von)
7 Mommsen (Theodor), Niebuhr (Barthold
Georg) 8 Spengler (Oswald)
Greek: 8 Plutarch, Polybius, Xenophon
9 Dionysius, Herodotus 10 Thucydides
Italian: 4 Vico (Giovanni) 5 Croce
(Benedetto) 8 Salvemini (Gaetano)
Jewish: 8 Josephus (Flavius)
Roman: 4 Livy 7 Sallust, Tacitus
(Cornelius) 9 Suetonius
Scottish: 7 Carlyle (Thomas)
9 Robertson (William)
Swiss: 6 Müller (Johannes von)
Welsh: 7 Nennius

historical period
3 age, era 5 epoch

history
4 past, saga 5 diary 6 annals, memoir,
record 7 account, done for, journal
9 chronicle, narrative, treatment
10 chronology

histrionic
5 showy, stagy 6 staged 8 affected, dramatic 10 artificial, theatrical

hit
3 bop, jab, rap 4 bang, bash, bean, biff, blow, bump, bunt, butt, conk, cuff, ding, lick, slap, slug, sock, swat 5 clout, knock, paste, pound, punch, smack, smash, smite, swipe, whack 6 batter, buffet, chance, larrup, strike, stroke, thwack, wallop 7 clobber, sellout, success 8 bludgeon, lambaste 9 collision, sensation
baseball: 5 homer, liner 6 double, single, triple 7 home run 9 line drive
golf ball: 5 shank

hitch
4 jerk, join, halt, hook, knot, lift, limp, snag, yoke 5 delay, thumb, unite 6 attach, couple, fasten, hobble, tether 7 connect, harness 8 make fast, stoppage 10 connection, difficulty, impediment 11 obstruction 12 entanglement

Hitchcock, Alfred
film: 4 Rope 5 Birds (The), Topaz 6 Frenzy, Marnie, Psycho 7 Rebecca, Vertigo 8 Lifeboat, Sabotage 9 Notorious, Suspicion 10 Rear Window, Spellbound 12 Lady Vanishes (The) 13 To Catch a Thief 14 Shadow of a Doubt 16 North by Northwest
forte: 8 suspense

hitchhike
5 thumb

hither
4 here 6 nearer 11 to this place

hitherto
5 as yet, so far 7 earlier, thus far, till now 8 formerly, until now 10 previously

Hitler, Adolf
follower: 4 Nazi
title: 6 Führer 7 Fuehrer
wife: 5 Braun (Eva)

hit man
5 bravo 6 killer 7 torpedo 8 assassin, enforcer 9 cutthroat, murderer

hit-or-miss
6 casual, chance, random 7 aimless, erratic 8 careless 9 desultory, haphazard, irregular, unplanned

hive
6 apiary, colony 7 cluster 9 stockpile

HMS Pinafore
composer: 8 Sullivan (Arthur)
librettist: 7 Gilbert (W. S.)

hoagie
3 sub 4 hero 5 po'boy 7 grinder, torpedo 8 sandwich 9 submarine

hoar
4 rime 5 frost

hoard
4 save 5 amass, cache, lay by, lay up, stash, stock, store, trove 6 supply 7 collect, lay away, nest egg, reserve 8 squirrel, treasure 9 stockpile 10 accumulate, collection, cumulation 11 aggregation 12 accumulation

hoarder
5 miser 7 scrooge

hoarse
5 gruff, husky, rough, thick 6 croaky 7 grating, rasping, raucous, throaty 8 croaking, gravelly, guttural

hoary
3 old 4 aged 5 stale 6 age-old 7 ancient, antique 8 timeworn 9 venerable

hoax
3 con 4 dupe, fake, fool, gull, sham 5 fraud, phony, trick 6 befool, delude, humbug, take in 7 deceive, mislead 8 flimflam, hoodwink, trickery 9 bamboozle, deception, imposture

Hobbit creator
7 Tolkien (J. R. R.)

hobble
4 lame, limp 6 fetter, hamper, hinder, hogtie, impede 7 cripple, trammel 8 handicap

hobby
6 falcon 7 pastime, pursuit 8 activity, sideline 9 avocation, diversion

hobgoblin
5 bogey 7 bugaboo

hobnob
3 mix 5 mingle 7 consort 9 associate, rub elbows, socialize 10 fraternize 11 get together

hobo
3 bum 5 gypsy, tramp 7 drifter, floater, swagman, vagrant 8 derelict, vagabond

hock
4 debt, pawn 5 ankle 6 prison

hockey

6 shinny
arena: **4** rink
cup: **7** Stanley
implement: **4** puck **5** stick
official: **7** referee **8** linesman
player: **3** Orr (Bobby), Roy (Patrick)
4 Bure (Pavel), Fuhr (Grant), Howe
(Gordie), Hull (Bobby, Brett), Jagr
(Jaromir), wing **5** Bossy (Mike), Bucyk
(John), Hasek (Dominik), Kurri (Jari), Maruk
(Dennis), Sakic (Joe), Shore (Eddie), Shutt
(Steve) **6** center, Clarke (Bobby), Coffey
(Paul), Dionne (Marcel), Dryden (Ken),
goalie, Forsberg (Peter), Harvey (Doug),
Juneau (Joe), Kariya (Paul), Leetch (Brian),
Mikita (Stan), Morenz (Howie), Parent
(Bernie), Potvin (Denis), Recchi (Mark),
Savard (Denis), Sundin (Mats) **7** Belfour
(Ed), Bourque (Ray), Brodeur (Martin),
Chelios (Chris), Fedorov (Sergei), forward,
Francis (Ron), Gretzky (Wayne), Lafleur
(Guy), Lemieux (Claude, Mario), Lindros
(Eric), Messier (Mark), Mogilny (Alexander),
Richard (Maurice), Richter (Mike), Selanne
(Teemu), Stastny (Peter), Yzerman (Steve)
8 Beliveau (Jean), Esposito (Phil, Tony),
Nicholls (Bernie), pointman, Shanahan
(Brendan), Trottier (Bryan), Ysebaert (Paul)
9 Hawerchuk (Dale) **10** Carbonneau
(Guy), defenseman, goalkeeper
team: **4** Jets **5** Blues, Kings, Stars
6 Bruins, Devils, Flames, Flyers, Oilers,
Sabres, Sharks **7** Canucks, Rangers,
Whalers **8** Capitals, Panthers, Penguins,
Red Wings, Senators **9** Canadiens,
Islanders, Lightning, Nordiques **10** Black
Hawks, Maple Leafs, North Stars
11 Mighty Ducks
term: **3** box **4** cage, goal, puck, rink
5 bandy, bench, check, icing, stick
6 charge, crease, shinny **7** face-off, offside
8 blue line **9** back-check, body-check
10 center line, penalty box
variation of: **9** broomball

hocus-pocus

4 sham **8** artifice, nonsense, trickery
9 conjuring, deception, imposture
10 mumbo jumbo **11** abracadabra,
incantation, legerdemain **13** sleight of
hand

hod

4 tray **6** trough **7** scuttle **11** coal scuttle

Hoder, Hoth

brother: **6** Balder
slayer: **4** Vali
victim: **6** Balder

hodgepodge

4 hash **6** jumble, medley **7** mélange,
mixture **8** mishmash, mixed bag
9 patchwork, potpourri **10** assortment,
miscellany **11** gallimaufry

hoe

4 till, weed **6** tiller, weeder **9** cultivate

hoedown

9 barn dance **11** contra dance, square
dance

hog

3 pig, sow **4** boar **5** swine
family: **6** Suidae
female: **3** sow **4** gilt
genus: **3** Sus
red: **5** duroc
young: **5** shoat

hogback

5 crest, ridge

hogshead

3 keg, tun **4** butt, cask **6** barrel
9 container

hog-tie

4 bind **6** fetter **7** shackle, trammel

hogwash

3 rot **4** bunk, slop **5** bilge, hokum, hooey,
swill **6** piffle **7** baloney, garbage, rubbish
8 nonsense **9** moonshine, poppycock
10 applesauce, balderdash, flapdoodle,
taradiddle **12** gobbledygook

hog wild

5 crazy **6** crazed, madcap **7** berserk

ho-hum

4 dull **5** bored **6** boring **7** tedious
8 tiresome **10** unexciting **11** indifferent

hoi polloi

3 mob **5** horde **6** masses **8** populace
9 multitude **10** lower class **11** proletariat

hoist

4 lift **5** drink, raise, winch **6** lift up, pick up,
take up **7** derrick, elevate **8** windlass

hoity-toity

4 smug **5** dizzy, giddy, silly **7** flighty,
pompous **9** conceited, frivolous
11 highfalutin

hokey

4 fake, mock, sham **5** banal, bogus, corny,
hammy, phony, stale, stagy, trite **6** ersatz,
pseudo **7** clichéd **8** cornball, outdated
9 contrived, hackneyed **12** melodramatic

hokum

4 bosh 5 hooey 7 baloney, hogwash
8 malarkey, nonsense 9 moonshine,
poppycock 10 applesauce, balderdash,
flapdoodle, taradiddle 11 foolishness
12 gobbledygook

hold

3 own 4 bear, deem, grab, grip, keep
5 carry, clamp, clasp, cling, grasp, gripe,
judge, sense, think, value 6 arrest, clench,
clinch, clutch, detain, harbor, regard, retain
7 contain, convene, convoke, fermata,
grapple, keep out, possess, reserve,
support, sustain 8 keep back, maintain,
preserve, restrict
close: 6 cuddle
dear: 7 cherish
in check: 7 repress
in common: 5 share
out: 4 last 6 endure
together: 4 bond 5 clamp 6 fasten
wrestling: 6 nelson 8 headlock, scissors
10 full nelson, half nelson

hold back

4 curb, keep, stop 5 check, delay 6 bridle,
detain, impede, retain 7 inhibit, keep out,
prevent, refrain, reserve 8 restrain,
suppress, withhold 9 constrain

hold forth

4 rant 5 orate, speak, spout 7 declaim,
expound, lecture 8 harangue, proclaim
9 expatiate 10 dilate upon

hold off

4 stay, wait 5 defer, delay, pause, repel
6 rebuff, resist 7 abstain, adjourn, repulse,
suspend 8 hesitate, postpone, prorogue
9 withstand 11 discontinue

hold up

3 rob 4 halt, lift, stay 5 check, defer, delay,
raise 6 hinder, impede, put off, retard
7 support, suspend 8 postpone, prorogue,
slow down

hole

3 den, gap, jam, pit 4 cave, flaw, lair, rent,
spot, void 5 fault, niche 6 breach, burrow,
cavity, cranny, defect, eyelet, lacuna, outlet
7 dilemma, opening, orifice 8 aperture,
weakness 9 perforate 10 excavation,
interstice 11 perforation, predicament

hole in one

3 ace

holiday

5 leave 6 May Day 7 Flag Day 8 Labor
Day, New Year's, vacation 9 Christmas,
Halloween 10 Father's Day, Mother's

Day 11 Memorial Day, Veterans Day
12 All Saints' Day, Groundhog Day,
Thanksgiving 13 Presidents' Day, St.
Patrick's Day, Valentine's Day
British: 9 Boxing Day
Canadian: 11 Dominion Day, Victoria Day
Jewish: 8 Passover

holiness

5 piety 6 purity 8 devotion, divinity,
sanctity 9 beatitude 11 religiosity
12 consecration, spirituality

Holland

see **Netherlands**

holler

3 cry 4 call, yell 5 shout 6 bellow, clamor,
cry out, outcry 7 call out 8 complain
9 complaint

hollow

3 dip, sag 4 void 5 basin, empty, false
6 cavity, ravine, sunken, vacant 7 concave,
echoing, sinkage 8 sinkhole, thorough
9 cavernous, concavity 10 depression,
sepulchral
out: 3 dig, gut 4 mine 5 gouge
8 excavate

holly

4 tree 5 shrub
genus: 4 Ilex

holocaust

4 fire 7 inferno 8 genocide 9 sacrifice
10 mass murder 11 destruction
13 conflagration

Holofernes' slayer

6 Judith

holy

6 adored, divine, sacred 7 angelic,
blessed, revered, sainted, saintly, sublime
8 hallowed 9 glorified, religious, spiritual,
venerated, worshiped 10 reverenced,
sacrosanct, sanctified 11 consecrated
combining form: 5 hagio, hiero
communion: 9 Eucharist
oil: 6 chrism
person: 5 saint 6 zaddik 7 tzaddik
Spirit: 9 Paraclete
vessel: 5 grail 7 chalice 8 ciborium

holy place

6 church, shrine, temple 7 sanctum
9 sanctuary

Holy Roman Emperor

4 Karl, Otto 5 Adolf, Franz, Henry, Louis
6 Albert, Arnulf, Conrad, Joseph, Lothar,
Ludwig, Philip, Rudolf, Rupert, Wenzel
7 Charles, Francis, Leopold, Lothair

Holy Thursday
8 Heinrich 9 Ferdinand, Frederick,
Friedrich, Sigismund 10 Maximilian
11 Charlemagne

Holy Thursday
6 Maundy (Thursday) 9 Ascension (Day)

holy writ
5 Bible 9 Scripture

homage
5 honor 6 praise 7 respect, tribute
9 deference, obeisance, reverence

hombre
3 cat, guy, lad, man 4 buck, chap, dude,
gent, stud 6 fellow, honcho 7 comrade

home
4 digs, land, site 5 abode, haunt, house,
range 6 family, hearth 7 country, habitat,
housing 8 domicile, dwelling, locality
9 household, residence 10 fatherland,
habitation, motherland 12 headquarters
country: 5 cabin 7 cottage 8 bungalow

homeless
5 stray 6 exiled 7 outcast, vagrant
8 derelict 9 abandoned, displaced,
wandering 12 dispossessed

homely
4 cozy 5 plain 6 direct, modest, simple
7 natural 8 familiar, ordinary
11 comfortable, commonplace
12 unattractive 13 unpretentious

Homer epic
5 Iliad 7 Odyssey

homesickness
7 longing 9 nostalgia

homespun
5 plain 6 fabric, folksy, simple 8 ordinary
9 practical 13 unpretentious

Home, Sweet Home
music: 6 Bishop (Henry)
words: 5 Payne (John Howard)

homicidal
6 bloody 8 sanguine 9 murdering,
murderous 10 sanguinary 11 sanguineous
12 bloodthirsty

homicide
5 blood 6 killer, murder, slayer 7 killing
8 foul play, murderer 9 manslayer
12 manslaughter

homily
6 sermon 7 lecture 9 discourse

homogeneous
7 uniform 10 consistent

Homo sapiens
3 man 7 mankind 8 humanity
9 humankind, human race

homunculus
5 dwarf, pygmy 6 midget, peewee
7 manikin 8 Tom Thumb

honcho
4 boss, head 5 chief 6 leader, master
7 big shot, foreman, headman 8 hierarch,
overseer 9 chieftain

Honduras
capital: 11 Tegucigalpa
city: 7 La Ceiba 9 Choluteca 10 El
Progreso 12 San Pedro Sula
coast: 8 Mosquito
discoverer: 8 Columbus (Christopher)
Indian people: 4 Maya 5 Mayan
language: 7 Spanish
monetary unit: 7 lempira
neighbor: 9 Guatemala, Nicaragua 10 El
Salvador
river: 4 Coco, Ulúa 5 Aguán 6 Patuca
sea: 9 Caribbean

hone
4 edge, whet 6 finish, polish, refine,
smooth 7 perfect, sharpen 9 whetstone

honest
4 fair, just, open, real, true 5 frank, plain
6 candid, simple 7 genuine, sincere,
upright 8 innocent, reliable, truthful
9 objective, reputable, unfeigned, veracious
10 creditable, forthright, legitimate,
scrupulous 11 respectable
12 praiseworthy 13 conscientious,
dispassionate, unimpeachable

honesty
4 herb 5 honor 6 candor, virtue 7 probity
8 fairness, goodness, justness, veracity
9 integrity, rectitude, sincerity
11 uprightness 12 truthfulness

honey
combining form: 4 meli, mell 5 melli
drink: 4 mead

honeybee genus
4 Apis

honeycomb
3 pit 4 fill, fret 5 cells 6 impair, infest,
riddle, weaken 7 subvert 9 perforate

honeydew
5 melon

honeyed
5 sweet 6 golden, liquid, mellow
9 sweetened 10 flattering 11 mellifluous

honeysuckle
6 azalea **9** columbine **13** pinxter flower

honk
4 blow, toot **5** blare, blast **7** trumpet

honky-tonk
4 dive **5** joint **7** hangout **9** juke joint, roadhouse **11** barrelhouse

honor
4 fete, laud **5** adorn, asset, award, badge, exalt, glory, kudos, medal **6** credit, esteem, homage, praise, purity, regard, trophy **7** commend, dignify, ennoble, fulfill, glorify, laurels, respect **8** accolade, approval, carry out, chastity, decorate, devotion, good name **9** adulation, deference, integrity, privilege, recognize, reverence **10** admiration, decoration, reputation, veneration **11** distinction, distinguish, recognition **12** commendation

honorable
4 just, true **5** moral, right **6** honest, worthy **7** ethical, upright **8** laudable **9** dignified **10** creditable, scrupulous **11** illustrious **13** conscientious

honorarium
7 payment **8** gratuity **10** recompense **12** compensation **13** consideration

hooch
6 liquor, rotgut **7** bootleg **8** dwelling, home brew **9** firewater, moonshine **10** bathtub gin

hood
4 cowl, thug **5** tough **6** bonnet, helmet **7** capuche **8** covering, gangster, hooligan **10** delinquent

hoodlum
4 punk, thug **5** bully **7** mobster, ruffian **8** criminal, gangster, hooligan **10** delinquent

hoodoo
3 hex **4** jinx, juju, rock **5** curse, haunt, hokum, magic, spell, spook **6** harass, voodoo, whammy **7** bewitch, evil eye, sorcery, terrify, torment **8** nonsense **9** conjuring **10** black magic, hocus-pocus, mumbo jumbo, witchcraft

hoodwink
3 con **4** dupe, fool, gull, hoax **5** trick **6** befool **7** deceive, mislead **8** flimflam **9** bamboozle

hooey
3 rot **4** bunk **5** bilge **6** bunkum **7** baloney, hogwash **8** claptrap, malarkey, nonsense

hoof
4 foot, walk **5** troop **7** traipse **8** ambulate
cloven: 5 cloot

hoofer
6 dancer **7** danseur **8** coryphée, danseuse, tap dancer **9** ballerina

hooflike
6 ungual

hook
3 nab, nip **4** gore, hasp **5** catch, curve, hitch, pinch, steal **6** anchor, fasten, pilfer **7** hamulus **8** crotchet
a fish: 4 gaff, snag
for keys: 10 chatelaine

hooklike
7 falcate **8** unciform, uncinate
part: 5 uncus **7** hamulus

hookup
7 circuit, linkage **8** alliance **10** assemblage, connection **11** affiliation, association, combination, conjunction, partnership

hooky
6 truant **7** truancy **8** truantry

hooligan
see **hoodlum**

hoop
4 band, ring **6** circle **7** circlet

hoopla
4 bash, fuss, stir, to-do **5** bustle, frolic **7** revelry, shindig, whoopee **8** ballyhoo, wingding **9** commotion, festivity, merriment, promotion **13** entertainment

hoops
5 b-ball **10** basketball

hooray
3 rah, yay **5** cheer, huzza **6** huzzah, yippee **7** acclaim **10** hallelujah

hoosegow
3 jug, pen **4** brig, cage, coop, jail, keep, stir **5** clink, pokey **6** cooler, lockup, prison **7** slammer **8** bastille, big house **9** calaboose, jailhouse **12** penitentiary

Hoosier State
7 Indiana

hoot
3 bit, boo, jot **4** hiss, iota, jeer, whit **5** laugh, scrap, shout, whoop **6** assail, deride, heckle **7** catcall, modicum **8** particle

hooter
 3 owl 5 owlet

Hoover Dam lake
 4 Mead

hop
 4 jump, leap, trip, vine 5 bound, dance
 6 bounce, spring, wait on 7 rebound
 8 jump over

hope
 4 goal, wish 5 await, dream, faith, trust
 6 aspire, desire, expect 7 count on,
 longing, promise 8 ambition, optimism,
 prospect 9 count upon 10 anticipate,
 aspiration, confidence
 loss of: 7 despair

hopeful
 4 rosy 5 eager, sunny 6 bright, cheery,
 golden, seeker, upbeat 7 assured
 8 aspirant, aspiring 9 candidate, confident,
 expectant, promising 10 auspicious,
 contestant, optimistic, propitious
 11 encouraging 12 advantageous

hopeless
 4 glum, lost, vain 6 futile, gloomy, morose
 7 forlorn 8 downcast 9 desperate,
 incurable, insoluble 10 despairing,
 despondent, impossible 11 ineffectual,
 irreparable, pessimistic 12 incorrigible,
 irredeemable, irremediable

hoper
 7 truster 8 optimist 9 expectant, Pollyanna

hopped-up
 4 high 5 giddy 6 stoned, zonked
 7 drugged, excited 9 delirious
 12 enthusiastic

hopper
 3 box, mix 4 frog, hare, tank, toad
 5 bunny, chute 6 rabbit 7 cricket
 10 freight car, receptacle

_____ Hopper
 5 Grace (Murray), Hedda 6 Edward

hopping
 4 busy 5 irate, livid 6 lively 7 furious
 9 extremely, violently 10 infuriated

Horae
 4 Dike 6 Eirene 7 Eunomia, seasons

Horam
 kingdom: 5 Gezer
 slayer: 6 Joshua

horde
 3 mob 4 army 5 crowd, crush, drove,
 press, swarm 6 throng 9 multitude

horizon
 4 goal 5 limit, range, reach, scope, vista
 6 extent 7 purview, skyline 8 prospect
 11 perspective

horizontal
 4 flat 5 level 8 parallel

hormone
 4 ACTH 5 kinin 6 estrin 7 estriol, estrone,
 gastrin, insulin, relaxin 8 autacoid,
 estrogen, glucagon, kallidin, secretin
 female: 8 estrogen
 insect: 8 ecdysone
 pituitary: 8 oxytocin

horn
 4 toot 5 cornu 6 antler, klaxon, shofar
 7 trumpet 10 cornucopia, projection
 ancient Greek: 5 rhyta (plural) 6 rhyton
 animal: 6 antler

_____ Hornblower
 7 Horatio

horn in
 6 meddle 7 intrude, obtrude 9 insinuate,
 interfere, interlope, interrupt

hornlike
 8 corneous 10 keratinous

hornswoggle
 3 con 4 dupe, fool, gull, hoax 5 trick
 7 deceive 8 flimflam, hoodwink
 9 bamboozle

horrendous
 5 awful 7 fearful, ghastly, heinous, hideous
 8 alarming, dreadful, gruesome, horrible,
 horrific, shocking, terrible 9 abhorrent,
 appalling, execrable, frightful, repugnant,
 revolting 11 distressing, unspeakable

horrible
 4 grim 5 awful, lurid 6 grisly 7 fearful,
 ghastly, hateful, hellish, hideous
 8 dreadful, gruesome, shocking
 9 abhorrent, appalling, frightful, loathsome,
 repellent, repugnant, repulsive, revolting
 10 abominable, disgusting, terrifying

horrid
 5 nasty 7 noisome 8 shocking
 9 loathsome, offensive, repulsive, sickening
 10 detestable, disgusting

horrific
 5 awful 7 fearful 8 dreadful, shocking,
 terrible 9 appalling, dismaying, frightful,
 harrowing

horrify
5 daunt, shock 6 appall, dismay 7 disgust

horrifying
4 grim 5 awful, lurid 6 grisly 7 ghastly, hideous 8 gruesome, terrible 9 appalling, atrocious

horror
4 fear, hate, pain 5 alarm, dread, panic, shock 6 dismay, fright, hatred, terror 7 disgust 8 aversion, loathing 9 repulsion, revulsion 10 abhorrence, repugnance 11 abomination, detestation, trepidation

hors d'oeuvre
4 whet 6 canape 7 crudité 9 antipasto, appetizer

horse
4 buck, roan 5 bronc, pacer, steed 6 bronco, brumby, equine 7 cavalry, palfrey, sawbuck, trestle, trotter 8 footrope, jackstay, palomino, skewbald, stallion, traveler
Australian-bred: 5 waler
battle: 7 charger
breed: 5 pinto 6 Morgan 7 Arabian, Belgian, Iceland 8 Palomino, Shetland 9 Appaloosa, Percheron 10 Lippizaner 12 standardbred, Thoroughbred
champion: 7 Man o' War 8 Affirmed, Citation 10 Seabiscuit 11 Seattle Slew, Secretariat, Smarty Jones
collar part: 4 hame
color: 3 bay 6 sorrel 8 chestnut
covering: 8 trapping
draft: 10 Clydesdale
extinct: 8 eohippus
farm: 6 dobbin
female: 4 mare 5 filly
foot part: 7 pastern
gait: 4 trot 6 canter, gallop
gear: 3 bit 4 rein 6 saddle 7 harness 9 checkrein
leg joint: 7 fetlock
leg part: 6 gaskin 7 gambrel
male: 4 colt 8 stallion
mark: 5 blaze
naturalized: 7 mustang
of the movies: 4 Fury 6 Flicka, Silver 7 Trigger 8 Champion 11 Black Beauty
race: 5 Ascot, derby 7 Belmont 9 Preakness
rump: 7 crupper
small: 4 pony 6 garron, jennet
spotted: 5 pinto 7 piebald
tan: 8 palomino
thoroughbred: 8 hotblood
war: 8 destrier
wild: 7 mustang

horsefeathers
3 rot 4 bull, bunk 5 bilge, hokum, hooey, trash 6 bunkum, drivel, piffle 7 baloney, garbage, hogwash, rubbish, twaddle 8 claptrap, flimflam, nonsense, tommyrot 9 poppycock 10 applesauce, balderdash

horseman
5 rider 6 cowboy 7 vaquero 8 cavalier 9 caballero, chevalier 10 equestrian

horsemanship
6 manège 10 equitation

horse opera
5 oater 7 western

horseplay
7 fooling 8 clowning, rowdyism 9 high jinks, rowdiness 10 buffoonery, roughhouse 11 shenanigans 12 roughhousing

horseshoer
6 smithy 10 blacksmith

hortative
8 advisory 9 exhorting, homiletic

horticulturist
7 Burbank (Luther)

Horus
brother: 6 Anubis
father: 6 Osiris
mother: 4 Isis
victim: 3 Set 4 Seth

hose
4 sock, tube, wash 5 cheat, spray, trick, water 6 tights 8 stocking

hoser
6 barfly, boozer 7 redneck

hospice
see **hostel**

hospitable
4 kind, open 6 social 7 cordial 8 friendly, generous, gracious 9 convivial, receptive, welcoming 10 gregarious

hospital
6 clinic 7 lazaret 9 infirmary, lazaretto
attendant: 7 orderly
ship's: 7 sickbay

Hospitallers' island
5 Malta 6 Rhodes

host
4 army 5 array, cloud, crowd, emcee, flock, horde 6 angels, legion, myriad, scores, server 7 present, receive 8 assemble 9 innkeeper, introduce, moderator, multitude, presenter

hostage
4 pawn 5 token 6 pledge, surety
7 captive, earnest 8 guaranty, prisoner,
security 9 guarantee

hostel
3 inn 4 stay 5 lodge 6 tavern, travel
7 auberge, lodging 11 caravansary, public
house

hostile
4 anti, mean 5 enemy 6 bitter, fierce
7 adverse, opposed, warlike 8 contrary,
inimical, opposite 9 bellicose, combative,
resistant, resisting 10 malevolent,
pugnacious, unfriendly 11 belligerent,
contentious 12 antagonistic 13 argumentative

hostility
3 war 6 animus, enmity, hatred, rancor
7 ill will 8 conflict 9 antipathy
10 aggression, antagonism, opposition,
resistance 12 belligerence

hot
3 new 4 fast, heat, sexy 5 angry, close,
eager, fiery, lucky, spicy 6 ardent, baking,
banned, heated, hectic, on fire, raging,
stolen, sultry, torrid, urgent 7 boiling,
burning, excited, fevered, illicit, lustful,
peppery, popular, pungent, zealous
8 broiling, feverish, in demand, scalding,
sizzling, tropical, vehement 9 energized,
lecherous, scorching 10 blistering,
contraband, passionate, sweltering
11 radioactive

hot air
4 bosh 6 bunkum 7 blather, prattle,
twaddle 8 malarkey, nonsense 9 empty
talk, poppycock 10 double-talk

hotbed
3 hub 4 core, seat 5 heart 6 center
7 nucleus 10 focal point 11 nerve center

hot-blooded
5 fiery 6 ardent 7 burning, fervent, flaming
9 excitable, impetuous, impulsive
10 passionate 11 impassioned 12 high-
spirited

hotchpotch
see hodgepodge

hot dog
5 frank 6 weenie, wiener, wienie
7 sausage, show-off 11 frankfurter,
wienerwurst

hotel
3 inn 5 lodge 6 tavern 7 auberge,
hospice, pension 8 motor inn 11 public
house 12 lodging house, rooming house
13 boardinghouse
chain: 5 Hyatt 6 Hilton, Ramada, Westin
7 Days Inn 8 Marriott, Radisson, Sheraton,
Stouffer 10 Holiday Inn 11 Best Western,
Four Seasons
inferior: 7 fleabag 9 flophouse

hothead
5 rebel 7 fanatic, inciter, radical 8 agitator
9 demagogue, firebrand 10 incendiary
12 rabble-rouser, troublemaker
13 revolutionary

hotheaded
4 rash 5 brash, fiery, hasty 6 madcap
8 reckless 9 excitable, impetuous,
imprudent, impulsive, irritable

hotshot
3 ace 4 star, whiz 5 comer 6 expert,
master, wizard 8 virtuoso 10 powerhouse
11 heavyweight

hot-tempered
see quick-tempered

hot water
3 box, fix, jam 4 bind, hole 6 corner, pickle
7 dilemma, problem, trouble 9 tight spot
10 difficulty 11 predicament

_____ Houdini
5 Harry

hound
3 dog, fan 4 bait, buff, ride 5 chivy
6 badger, basset, beagle, bowwow, canine,
harass, hassle, heckle, hector, pester,
pursue, Talbot 7 devotee 8 bullyrag
9 dachshund, persecute 10 aficionado
Russian: 6 borzoi

hourglass
5 timer

house
3 cot, hut, ken 4 home, shed 5 abode,
board, cabin, dwell, hovel, lodge, put up,
shack 6 billet, chalet, harbor, shanty
7 contain, cottage, enclose, mansion,
quarter, saltbox, shelter, theater
8 audience, bungalow, domicile, dwelling,
quarters 9 residence
clergyman's: 5 manse 7 rectory
9 parsonage
country: 5 manor 7 cottage 8 bungalow
dog: 6 kennel
earth: 5 adobe
Eskimo: 5 igloo
mean: 5 hovel, shack

of prostitution: 4 crib **6** bagnio **7** brothel
8 bordello
religious: 5 abbey **6** priory **7** convent,
nunnery **9** monastery
rooming: 5 lodge
Russian: 5 dacha
small: 4 camp **5** cabin, shack **6** shanty
7 cottage **8** bungalow
Spanish: 4 casa

housebreaker
4 yegg **5** thief **7** burglar, prowler
8 picklock

household
4 home **5** folks **6** family, ménage
8 domestic, familiar
gods (Roman): 5 lares **7** penates

house of worship
6 bethel, chapel, church, mosque, pagoda,
shrine, temple **7** chantry, minster, oratory
8 basilica **9** cathedral, sanctuary,
synagogue **10** tabernacle **11** conventicle

housing
4 case, room **7** shelter **8** barracks,
quarters **9** enclosure

hovel
3 hut, sty **4** dump, shed **5** hutch, shack
6 burrow, pigpen, pigsty, shanty **7** shelter

hover
4 flit, hang **5** dance, drift, float, poise,
waver **7** flitter, flutter, suspend **9** fluctuate,
hang about

howbeit
3 yet **4** when **5** still, while **6** even if, much
as, though **7** whereas **8** after all, although
11 nonetheless **12** nevertheless

however
3 but, yet **4** only **5** still **6** except, though
8 after all **11** nonetheless

howl
3 bay, cry **4** bark, keen, wail, yell, yelp
6 cry out **9** caterwaul

howler
4 flub, gaff, goof **5** boner, fluff, gaffe
6 boo-boo **7** blooper, blunder

huarache
6 sandal

hub
4 axis, core **5** focus, heart, pivot **6** center
8 polestar **10** focal point **11** nerve center
opposite: 3 rim

hubbub
3 din **4** fuss, stir, to-do **5** babel, furor, hoo-

ha, noise **6** clamor, furore, hassle, jangle,
racket, rumpus, tumult, uproar **7** turmoil
8 brouhaha, foofaraw **9** commotion,
confusion **10** hullabaloo, hurly-burly
11 disturbance, pandemonium

hubris
3 ego, gall **5** brass, cheek, nerve, pride
7 conceit, hauteur, swagger **8** audacity,
chutzpah **9** arrogance, cockiness,
vainglory **11** braggadocio

hubristic
4 vain **5** cocky, proud **7** haughty
8 arrogant, insolent, superior **11** overbearing, overweening **13** overconfident

Huckleberry Finn
author: 5 Twain (Mark) **7** Clemens
(Samuel)
character: 3 Jim, Tom (Sawyer) **4** Duke,
King
river: 11 Mississippi

huckster
4 hawk, plug, vend **5** pitch **6** dicker,
haggle, hawker, peddle, vendor **7** bargain,
chaffer, haggler, packman, peddler,
promote **8** pitchman

huddle
4 lump, mass **5** bunch, crowd, group,
hunch **6** confab, confer, crouch, curl up,
gather, parley, powwow **7** cluster, consult,
meeting **8** assemble **10** conference,
discussion

Hudson's ship
8 Half Moon

hue
4 cast, tint, tone **5** color, shade, shape,
tinge, value **6** aspect, manner **8** coloring,
tincture **10** coloration, complexion

huff
3 pet **4** blow, gasp, pant, rile, roil, snap,
snit, tiff **5** annoy, grate, heave, peeve,
pique, storm **6** nettle, put out **7** bluster,
inflate **8** irritate

huffy
5 angry, proud, testy **6** piqued, touchy
7 annoyed, fretful, haughty, peevish,
prickly, waspish **8** arrogant, petulant,
snappish **9** irritable, irritated, querulous

hug
4 hold **5** clasp, press, prize, value **6** clinch,
clutch, cuddle, enfold **7** cherish, embrace,
envelop, squeeze **8** hold fast, hold onto
12 congratulate

huge

4 vast, wide 5 bulky, giant, grand, great, jumbo 6 heroic, mighty, untold 7 immense, mammoth, massive, titanic 8 colossal, enormous, extensive, gigantic, whopping 9 extensive, monstrous 10 monumental, prodigious, stupendous, tremendous 11 magnificent, mountainous

hugeness

8 enormity 9 immensity, magnitude

hugger-mugger

4 hash 6 jumble, muddle, secret, tangle 7 clutter, furtive, jumbled, secrecy 8 confused, covertly, disorder secretly 9 by stealth, confusion, furtively 10 disordered, disorderly, stealthily, undercover 11 clandestine 13 clandestinely

Hugo, Victor

character: 6 Javert (Inspector) 7 Cosette, Fantine, Valjean (Jean) 9 Esmeralda, Quasimodo
novel: 13 Les Misérables 20 Hunchback of Notre Dame (The)

Huguenot

10 Protestant
leader: 5 Condé (Prince de), Rohan (Henri) 6 Mornay (Philippe) 7 Coligny (Gaspard II de)

Huguenots composer

9 Meyerbeer (Giacomo)

hulk

4 body, loom, ship 5 shell, wreck 8 skeleton 9 shipwreck

hulking

4 huge 5 beefy, bulky, burly, husky 7 immense, mammoth, massive 8 colossal, enormous, gigantic, oversize 9 humongous, lumbering, monstrous, ponderous, strapping 11 heavyweight

hull

3 pod 4 bark, body, case, husk, peel, rind, skin 5 chaff, frame, shell, shuck 6 casing 8 covering 11 decorticate

hullabaloo

3 din 4 to-do 5 hoo-ha, noise 6 clamor, hubbub, jangle, racket, tumult, uproar 8 ballyhoo, foofaraw 9 commotion, hue and cry 11 pandemonium

hum

4 buzz, purr, sing, zing 5 drone 6 murmur 7 vibrate

human

5 being, party 6 mortal, person 7 hominid 8 hominoid 10 individual
race: 7 mankind

Human Comedy author

6 Balzac (Honoré de) 7 Saroyan (William)

humane

4 kind 6 gentle, kindly, tender 8 merciful 10 altruistic, benevolent, charitable 11 considerate, kindhearted, soft-hearted, sympathetic, warmhearted 13 compassionate, philanthropic

humanitarian

5 giver 8 generous 10 altruistic, benefactor, beneficent, benevolent, charitable 13 compassionate, philanthropic

humanity

6 people 7 mankind 8 kindness, sympathy 10 compassion, generosity 11 benevolence, Homo sapiens

humble

3 low 4 meek 5 abash, crush, lowly, quiet 6 demean, modest, simple 7 chagrin, deflate, degrade, subdued 8 cast down, disgrace, ordinary 9 compliant, diffident, discomfit, embarrass, humiliate 10 submissive, unassuming 11 acquiescent, deferential 13 insignificant, unpretentious

humbug

3 con, rot 4 fake, fool, hoax, sham 5 faker, fraud, hokum, phony, spoof, trick 6 bunkum, delude, drivel, take in 7 beguile, deceive, mislead 8 flimflam, impostor, malarkey, nonsense, pretense, quackery 9 deception, hypocrite, imposture, pretender, trickster 10 balderdash

humdinger

3 gem 5 beaut, dandy, dilly, doozy, jewel, prize 6 doozie 8 jim-dandy 11 crackerjack

humdrum

4 blah, dull, flat 6 boring, dreary, stodgy 7 prosaic, tedious 8 monotone, monotony, plodding, unvaried, workaday 10 monotonous, uneventful 13 uninteresting

humid

3 wet 4 damp, dank 5 close, moist, muggy, soggy 6 clammy, sodden, steamy, sticky, stuffy 10 oppressive

humidify

6 dampen 7 moisten

humiliate
5 abase, crush, lower, shame **6** bemean, debase, demean, humble **7** chagrin, degrade, mortify **8** belittle, cast down, disgrace **9** embarrass

humiliation
5 shame **7** chagrin, put-down **8** disgrace, ignominy, reproach **9** abasement, disrepute, indignity **11** degradation **13** embarrassment, mortification

humility
7 modesty, shyness **8** meekness **9** abasement, lowliness **10** diffidence, submission **12** subservience **13** self-abasement

humming
4 busy **5** brisk **6** active, lively **8** bustling, hustling **9** energetic

hummock
5 couch, hump, knoll, mound **7** hillock

humongous
4 huge, vast **5** giant, jumbo **7** immense, mammoth, massive, titanic **8** colossal, enormous, gigantic **9** monstrous **10** gargantuan, prodigious, tremendous

humor
3 wit **4** baby, bent, mind, mood, tone, vein, whim **5** fancy, fluid, spoil, yield **6** banter, coddle, comedy, cosset, esprit, joking, levity, nature, pamper, temper **7** caprice, cater to, conceit, gratify, indulge, jesting, kidding **8** crotchet, drollery, jocosity, repartee **9** character, drollness, flippancy, funniness, witticism, wittiness **10** complexion, jocularity, pleasantry **11** disposition, temperament

humorist
3 Ade (George), wag, wit **4** card, Nash (Ogden), Shaw (Henry Wheeler), Ward (Artemus, Edward) **5** Adams (Franklin Pierce), Allen (Fred), Barry (Dave), clown, comic, cutup, droll, Dunne (Finley Peter), joker, Twain (Mark), White (E. B.) **6** Blount (Roy), Browne (Charles Farrar), Diller (Phyllis), gagman, jester, kidder, Parker (Dorothy), Rogers (Will), Rourke (P. J.), Runyon (Damon), Thorpe (Thomas Bangs) **7** buffoon, Bombeck (Erma), Burgess (Gelett), Clemens (Samuel Langhorne), gagster, Hubbard (Kin), Keillor (Garrison), Marquis (Don), punster, Sedaris (David), Thurber (James), Trillin (Calvin) **8** Aleichem (Shalom), Benchley (Robert), comedian, funnyman, jokester, Perelman

(S. J.), quipster **9** jokesmith, prankster, Wodehouse (P. G.)
Canadian: 7 Leacock (Stephen)

humorous
5 comic, droll, funny, jokey, merry, witty **6** jocose **7** amusing, comical, jocular, risible, waggish **8** mirthful **9** facetious, laughable, whimsical

hump
3 lug **4** bump, carry, race, tote **5** bulge, carry, hunch, mound, range **6** hustle, schlep **7** hummock, schlepp **8** mountain, obstacle, swelling **9** transport **10** protrusion

humpback
5 whale **8** kyphosis **10** pink salmon

humpbacked
6 convex, curved **7** gibbous

Humperdinck opera
15 Hansel and Gretel

humus
3 mor **4** mull, soil **7** compost **8** material

hunch
4 arch, clod, idea, lump, hump, push **5** chunk, clump, crook, squat, stoop **6** crouch, curl up, huddle, jostle, notion, nugget **7** feeling, inkling **9** intuition

Hunchback of Notre Dame
author: 4 Hugo (Victor)
character: 9 Esmeralda, Quasimodo

hundred
combining form: 5 centi, hecto

Hungary
capital: 8 Budapest
city: 4 Pécs **6** Szeged **7** Miskolc **8** Debrecen
ethnic group: 6 Magyar
lake: 7 Balaton
monetary unit: 6 forint
mountain range: 10 Carpathian
national hero: 5 Árpád
neighbor: 6 Serbia **7** Austria, Croatia, Romania, Ukraine **8** Slovakia, Slovenia
plain: 11 Great Alföld
river: 5 Tisza **6** Danube

hunger
3 yen **4** ache, itch, long, lust, need, pine, want **5** crave, greed, yearn **6** desire, hanker, thirst **7** craving, longing

hungry
4 avid, keen, poor **5** eager **6** barren **7** craving, starved, thirsty **8** desirous,

hunk

famished, ravenous, starving, underfed, yearning 9 hankering, motivated

hunk
3 gob, wad 4 clod, lump 5 chunk, clump, piece, wedge 6 nugget 7 portion

hunker down
5 dig in, squat 6 crouch 8 settle in

hunky
4 buff 5 burly 6 buffed 8 athletic, muscular 9 strapping, well-built

hunky-dory
4 fine, okay 5 dandy, ducky, nifty, swell 6 peachy 10 peachy keen 12 satisfactory

Hunnish
4 rude, wild 6 savage 7 fearful, uncivil 9 barbarian, barbarous, ferocious 11 uncivilized

hunt
3 dog, run 4 hawk, seek 5 chase, hound, prowl, quest, shoot, snare, stalk, track, trail 6 battue, course, dig out, prey on, pursue, safari, search 7 explore, pursuit, rummage 9 ferret out, search for, search out
birds: 4 fowl
illegally: 5 poach

hunter
6 jaeger, nimrod 8 predator
biblical: 6 Nimrod
cap: 7 montero
constellation: 5 Orion
mythological: 5 Orion 7 Actaeon

hunting
5 chase 6 venery 7 gunning, hawking 8 coursing, falconry 9 predatory 10 predacious
bird: 6 falcon
call: 7 recheat
cry: 6 yoicks 7 tallyho 10 view halloo
dog: 5 hound 6 basset, beagle, borzoi, saluki, setter, vizsla 7 harrier, pointer, spaniel 9 ridgeback, wolfhound 10 bloodhound
expedition: 6 safari
horn: 5 bugle

huntress
5 Diana 7 Artemis 8 Atalanta

hurdle
3 bar 4 leap, snag 5 bound, clear, vault 6 hamper, spring 7 barrier 8 leap over, obstacle, overcome, overleap, surmount, traverse 9 negotiate 10 difficulty, impediment 11 obstruction

hurl
4 cast, fire 5 chuck, fling, heave, pitch, sling, throw, vomit 6 launch, thrust 8 catapult

hurly-burly
3 din 4 riot, to-do 5 melee 6 clamor, furore, hassle, hubbub, racket, rumpus, tumult, uproar 7 turmoil 8 confused 9 commotion, confusion

hurrah
4 fuss, to-do, zeal 5 cheer 6 fervor, rumpus 7 fanfare, ovation 8 approval 9 commotion 10 enthusiasm 11 acclamation

hurricane
7 typhoon

hurried
4 fast, sped 5 hasty, quick, swift 6 abrupt, rushed, sudden 7 cursory, rushing 8 headlong 9 impetuous 11 precipitant, precipitate

hurry
3 fly, hie, jog, run, zip 4 post, prod, push, rush 5 fleet, haste, scoot, speed, whirl, whish, whisk 6 barrel, breeze, bullet, bustle, hasten, hustle, rocket, rustle, step up, tumult 7 beeline, hotfoot, quicken, shake up, skelter, speed up, swiften 8 celerity, dispatch, expedite, highball, make time 9 commotion, make haste, swiftness 10 accelerate, speediness

hurt
3 mar 4 ache, blow, harm, pain 5 wound, wrong 6 damage, grieve, hamper, harmed, impair, injure, injury, in pain, misuse, offend, pained, suffer 7 afflict, anguish, blemish, damaged, wounded 8 aggrieve, distress, mischief, mistreat 9 constrain, detriment, prejudice, resentful, suffering 10 resentment

hurtful
4 mean, sore 6 aching, unkind 7 harmful, painful 8 damaging, wounding 9 injurious 11 deleterious, destructive, detrimental, distressing, prejudicial

hurtle
3 fly 4 race, rush, tear 5 fling, shoot, speed, throw 6 charge, plunge, rocket

husband
3 man 4 mate, save 6 manage, mister, spouse 7 consort, partner 8 conserve, helpmate, helpmeet 9 economize, other half 10 bridegroom

husbandry
6 thrift 7 control, economy, farming
8 prudence 9 frugality 10 management
11 agriculture, thriftiness 12 conservation,
preservation

hush
4 calm 5 quell, quiet 6 shut up, stifle
7 cover up, mollify, secrecy, silence
8 choke off, suppress 9 cessation,
quietness, stillness

hush-hush
6 covert, secret 7 private, sub-rosa 9 top
secret 11 clandestine 12 confidential
13 surreptitious, under-the-table

husk
3 pod 4 case, peel, rind, skin 5 shell,
shuck, strip 6 casing

husky
3 big, dog 5 beefy, burly, great, hefty,
large, rough, stout 6 brawny, croaky,
hoarse, mighty, robust, strong, sturdy
7 throaty 8 muscular, oversize, stalwart,
thickset 9 strapping

hustings
5 stump

hustle
3 fly, rob, run, sell 4 earn, move, push,
rush, urge, work 5 cheat, elbow, fraud,
haste, hurry, press, shove, speed 6 hasten
7 hotfoot, promote, solicit, swindle
8 bulldoze, deception, dispatch 9 swiftness

hustler
4 doer 6 dynamo, vendor 8 go-getter, live
wire 10 powerhouse

hustling
4 busy 5 eager 6 active, lively, speedy
7 hopping, humming 9 energetic
10 aggressive

hut
3 cot 4 camp, crib, shed 5 cabin, dacha,
hooch, hovel, hutch, jacal, lodge, roost,
shack 6 cabana, chalet, lean-to, shanty
7 cottage 8 bungalow
American Indian: 6 wigwam 7 wickiup
Scottish: 5 bothy, shiel 8 shieling

hutch
3 bin, pen 4 cage, coop 5 chest, shack
6 locker, shanty 8 cupboard 9 enclosure

Huxley novel
8 Antic Hay 11 Crome Yellow 13 Brave
New World, Eyeless in Gaza

Hyacinthus
father: 7 Amyclas
slayer: 6 Apollo

hybrid
5 blend, cross, mixed 7 amalgam, mixture
8 combined, compound 9 composite,
crossbred 10 crossbreed 11 combination

hybridize
4 join 5 blend, cross 7 combine
10 crossbreed, interbreed, intercross

Hydra
5 polyp 6 plague 7 monster, serpent
13 constellation
father: 6 Typhon
mother: 7 Echidna
slayer: 8 Heracles, Hercules

hydrant
3 tap 4 pipe 5 valve 6 faucet, spigot
7 petcock 8 fireplug

hydraulic device
3 ram 4 jack, lift, pump 5 brake, press
8 elevator

hydrocarbon
5 xylol 6 dioxin, ethane, xylene
7 benzene, methane, styrene, toluene
8 biphenyl, butylene, ethylene
liquid: 6 octane 7 retinol, styrene
8 menthene

hydroid
5 polyp 6 medusa, obelia 9 jellyfish

hydrometer scale
4 Brix 5 Baumé

hydrophobia
5 lyssa 6 rabies

hyena
5 dingo 6 jackal 9 scavenger

Hygeia
5 Salus
father: 9 Asclepius 11 Aesculapius
goddess of: 6 health

hygiene
6 health 10 sanitation 11 cleanliness

hygienic
5 clean 7 aseptic, healthy, sterile
8 sanitary 9 healthful 10 antiseptic,
unpolluted

Hyllus' father
8 Heracles, Hercules

hymeneal
6 bridal, wedded 7 marital, married,

hymn

nuptial, spousal **8** conjugal **9** connubial
11 matrimonial

hymn

4 laud, song **5** bless, carol, chant, extol,
paean, psalm **6** anthem, choral, praise
7 chorale, glorify **8** canticle, doxology,
eulogize

hype

4 plug, tout **5** boost, thump **7** acclaim,
enliven, glorify, promote, puffery, trumpet
8 ballyhoo, increase **9** advertise, excellent,
publicity, publicize, stimulate
11 advertising

hyper

4 edgy **5** antsy, jumpy, wired **6** on edge
7 anxious, frantic **8** agitated, frenetic,
hopped-up **9** excitable **10** high-strung,
overactive **11** overwrought

hyperbole

6 excess **12** embroidering, exaggeration
13 embellishment, overstatement

hypercritical

6 severe **7** carping **8** captious, exacting
10 censorious, nit-picking **12** faultfinding

Hyperion

daughter: 3 Eos **6** Aurora, Selene
father: 6 Uranus
mother: 4 Gaea
son: 6 Helios
wife: 5 Theia

hypnotic

6 opiate, sleepy **8** mesmeric, narcotic,
sedative **9** somnolent, soporific
11 mesmerizing, somniferous
12 somnifacient, spellbinding

hypnotize

4 drug **5** charm **6** dazzle, trance
8 enthrall, entrance, overcome **9** captivate,
mesmerize, overpower, spellbind

hypocorism

7 pet name **8** nickname **9** sobriquet

hypocrisy

4 cant, sham **6** deceit, humbug **7** falsity,
pietism **8** quackery **9** deception, duplicity,
phoniness **10** sanctimony **11** insincerity,
religiosity

hypocrite

4 fake, sham **5** actor, faker, fraud, phony,
poser **6** humbug, poseur **7** bluffer, pietist
8 deceiver, impostor, pharisee **9** charlatan,
pretender **10** dissembler **11** masquerader
12 dissimulator

hypocritical

5 false **7** canting **8** affected, specious,

two-faced **9** deceitful, insincere, pietistic
10 Janus-faced **11** dissembling, double-
faced, duplicitous **12** mealymouthed,
pecksniffian **13** sanctimonious

hypothesis

6 belief, theory **7** premise **8** position,
supposal **9** condition, inference
10 antecedent, assumption, conjecture
11 explanation, speculation, supposition

hypothetical

7 assumed **8** abstract, academic,
supposed **10** assumptive **11** conditional,
conjectural, suppositous, theoretical
12 suppositious **13** suppositional

hyrax

4 cony **5** coney **6** dassie, mammal
8 ungulate

hysteria

4 fear **5** craze, furor, mania, panic
6 excess, frenzy **7** madness **8** delirium

hysterical

5 rabid **6** crazed, madcap, raving
7 berserk, frantic **8** agitated, frenzied,
neurotic **9** delirious, disturbed, hilarious,
impetuous **10** convulsive, distraught,
uproarious **11** impassioned, overexcited,
overwrought **13** side-splitting

I

Iago
general: **7** Othello
victim: **6** Cassio, Emilia **7** Othello **9** Desdemona
wife: **6** Emilia

Iapetus
father: **6** Uranus
mother: **4** Gaea
son: **5** Atlas **9** Menoetius **10** Epimetheus, Prometheus
wife: **7** Clymene

Iasion
brother: **8** Dardanus
father: **4** Zeus **7** Jupiter
lover: **5** Ceres **7** Demeter
mother: **7** Electra
son: **6** Plutus

ibex
4 tahr **8** wild goat
family: **7** Bovidae
genus: **5** Capra

Ibhar's father
5 David

ibis-headed god
5 Thoth

ibis relative
5 heron, stork

Ibsen, Henrik
character: **3** Ase **4** Nora (Helmer) **5** Brack (Judge), Brand, Hedda (Gabler), Helen (Alving), Werle (Gergers) **6** Ejlert (Lovberg), Hedvig (Ekdal), Jorgen (Tesman), Oswald (Alving) **7** Solness (Halvard), Solveig, Torvald (Helmer) **8** Peer Gynt **9** Stockmann (Thomas)
country: **6** Norway
play: **6** Ghosts **8** Peer Gynt, Wild Duck (The) **10** Doll's House (A) **11** Hedda Gabler, Little Eyolf, Rosmersholm **13** Master Builder (The) **16** Enemy of the People (An)

Icarus' father
8 Daedalus

ice
area: **4** rink
dessert: **6** sorbet **7** sherbet
floating: **4** berg, floe
hanging: **6** icicle
pinnacle: **5** serac

icebox
6 cooler, fridge **12** refrigerator

ice cream
7 spumoni, tortoni
dish: **6** sundae **11** baked Alaska
drink: **4** soda **6** frappe

iced
5 glacé **6** glazed **7** chilled

ice field
4 floe **7** glacier

ice game
6 hockey **7** curling

ice house
5 igloo

Iceland
capital: **9** Reykjavik
monetary unit: **5** krona
sea: **9** Norwegian
snowfield: **11** Vatnajökull
strait: **7** Denmark
volcano: **5** Hekla

Icelandic
epic: **4** Edda, saga
hero: **5** Njáll **6** Gunnar **7** Grettir

Ichabod Crane's beloved
7 Katrina

icing
7 topping **8** frosting

icky
4 vile **5** awful, gross, nasty **9** loathsome,

icon   550

offensive, repellent, repulsive, revolting,
sickening 10 disgusting 11 distasteful

icon
4 idol, sign 5 image 6 emblem, symbol

iconoclastic
9 dissident, heretical 10 rebellious,
unorthodox 13 nonconformist

icy
4 cold 5 gelid, polar 6 arctic, chilly, frigid,
frosty, steely 7 glacial 8 freezing
11 emotionless, unemotional

Idaho:
capital: 5 Boise
city: 6 Moscow 9 Pocatello, Twin Falls
10 Idaho Falls 11 Coeur d'Alene
mountain: 5 Borah (Peak)
nickname: 3 Gem (State)
river: 5 Snake 6 Salmon
state bird: 8 bluebird
state flower: 7 syringa
state tree: 9 white pine

Idas
brother: 7 Lynceus
father: 8 Aphareus
slayer: 4 Zeus
victim: 6 Castor
wife: 8 Marpessa

idea
4 whim 5 fancy, guess, motif 6 belief,
notion, theory, thesis, vagary 7 caprice,
conceit, concept, inkling, meaning, opinion,
subject, surmise, thought 8 estimate
9 sentiment, suspicion 10 assumption,
brainstorm, conception, conclusion,
conjecture, conviction, estimation,
hypothesis, impression, perception,
reflection 11 abstraction, formulation,
supposition

ideal
4 best, goal 5 model 7 chimera, classic,
epitome, paragon, perfect, utopian
8 absolute, ensample, exemplar, flawless,
nonesuch, paradigm, standard, ultimate
9 archetype, classical, exemplary, nonpareil
10 archetypal, conceptual, consummate
11 theoretical

idealist
7 dreamer, quixote, utopian 9 ideologue,
visionary

idealistic
6 dreamy 7 utopian 8 poetical, quixotic,
romantic 9 visionary 10 starry-eyed
11 impractical, unrealistic

idealize
5 deify, exalt, extol 7 elevate, ennoble,
glorify, worship 8 venerate

ideate
5 think 7 imagine 8 conceive, envisage,
envision

idée fixe
5 mania 6 fetish, phobia 7 complex
8 fixation 9 obsession 13 preoccupation

identical
3 one 4 like, same, very 5 alike, equal,
exact 8 selfsame 9 duplicate
10 equivalent, synonymous

identification mark
4 logo 5 badge, brand, label 6 emblem

identify
3 tag 4 mark, name, spot 5 brand, place
6 finger, select 7 make out, pick out
8 pinpoint 9 determine, recognize
11 distinguish

identity
4 name, self 7 oneness 8 sameness,
selfhood 9 character 10 congruence,
uniformity, uniqueness 11 personality,
singularity 13 individuality, particularity

ideological
8 notional 10 conceptual, ideational
11 speculative 13 philosophical

ideologue
8 believer, idealist, partisan, theorist

ideology
3 ism 5 credo, creed 7 beliefs 8 doctrine
10 philosophy, principles

idiocy
7 fatuity 9 cretinism, stupidity 10 imbecility
11 foolishness

idiomatic
7 demotic 8 peculiar 9 dialectal
10 colloquial, vernacular

idiosyncrasy
5 quirk 6 oddity 7 anomaly 11 peculiarity,
singularity 12 eccentricity

idiosyncratic
3 odd 5 kooky, queer, weird 6 quirky
7 erratic, oddball, offbeat, unusual
8 peculiar, singular 9 eccentric
11 distinctive

idiot
3 ass 4 dolt, fool, jerk, simp 5 dummy,
dunce, moron, ninny 6 cretin, nitwit, stupid
7 airhead, dullard, half-wit, jackass, natural,
tomfool 8 dumbbell, imbecile, numskull

9 ignoramus, numbskull, simpleton **10** nincompoop

idiotic
5 dopey **6** stupid **7** foolish, moronic
8 ignorant **9** brainless, imbecilic, senseless

idle
3 bum **4** laze, lazy, loaf, loll, rest, vain
5 dally, drone, empty, inert, slack, tarry
6 asleep, dawdle, diddle, fallow, futile, inactive, linger, loiter, lounge, otiose, unused, vacant **7** aimless, dormant, passive **8** inactive, indolent, slothful
9 shiftless **10** unoccupied

idleness
4 ease **5** sloth **6** vanity **7** leisure, loafing
8 lethargy **9** indolence **10** inactivity

idler
3 bum **4** slug **5** drone **6** loafer, slouch
7 dawdler **8** deadbeat, fainéant, loiterer, slugabed, sluggard **9** do-nothing, lazybones **11** couch potato

Idmon
daughter: **7** Arachne
father: **6** Apollo
mother: **6** Cyrene

idol
3 god **4** hero, icon, star **5** deity, image, totem **6** fetish, minion, symbol **8** likeness
Chinese: **4** joss

idolatry
7 worship **8** devotion **9** adoration
10 exaltation, veneration **11** deification
13 glorification

idolize
5 adore, deify, exalt **6** revere **7** glorify, worship **8** venerate

Idomeneo composer
6 Mozart (Wolfgang Amadeus)

idyllic
5 ideal **6** rustic **7** bucolic, halcyon, perfect, utopian **8** arcadian, heavenly, pastoral, peaceful, romantic **9** idealized, unspoiled
11 picturesque, sentimental

Idylls of the King
author: **8** Tennyson (Alfred)
character: **4** Enid **6** Arthur, Elaine, Gareth, Merlin, Vivien **7** Geraint, Lynette
8 Lancelot

iffy
5 dicey, risky **6** chancy, unsure **7** dubious, erratic **8** doubtful **9** uncertain

10 unreliable **12** inconsistent
13 unpredictable

igneous rock
4 lava **5** magma **6** basalt, gabbro
7 diabase, granite **8** porphyry

ignis fatuus
6 mirage **7** chimera **8** delusion, illusion, phantasm **9** pipe dream **12** will-o'-the-wisp
13 hallucination

ignitable
8 burnable **9** excitable, flammable
10 incendiary **11** combustible, inflammable

ignite
4 fire **5** light, spark **6** excite, kindle
7 inflame **8** enkindle, touch off

ignited
3 lit **5** afire, fiery **6** ablaze, aflame, alight
7 blazing, burning, flaming, flaring
11 conflagrant

ignoble
3 low **4** base, mean, poor, vile **5** lowly
6 abject, coarse, common, scurvy, sordid, vulgar **7** lowborn, servile **8** baseborn, indecent, inferior, plebeian, shameful, unwashed, wretched **10** despicable, inglorious **11** disgraceful **12** contemptible, dishonorable

ignominious
6 odious **8** infamous, shameful
9 degrading **10** despicable, inglorious
11 disgraceful, humiliating, opprobrious
12 contemptible, dishonorable, disreputable **13** discreditable, unrespectable

ignominy
5 odium, shame **6** infamy **7** obloquy, scandal **8** disgrace, dishonor **9** discredit, disesteem, disrepute **10** opprobrium
11 humiliation **13** mortification

ignoramus
4 dolt **5** dummy, dunce, idiot, moron
6 dimwit, nitwit, stupid **7** airhead, dullard, half-wit **8** dumbbell, imbecile, numskull
9 numbskull, simpleton

ignorance
7 naiveté **9** innocence, nescience, stupidity
10 illiteracy, simpleness, simplicity
11 unawareness **12** incognizance

ignorant
5 naive **6** simple **7** unaware **8** nescient, untaught **9** benighted, ingenuous, oblivious, unknowing, unlearned, untutored, unwitting **10** illiterate, uncultured,

uneducated, uninformed, unlettered, unschooled **11** incognizant, know-nothing **12** uninstructed **13** unenlightened

ignore
4 omit, snub **5** avoid **6** forget, reject, slight **7** neglect **8** overlook **9** disregard

Igraine
husband: 5 Uther **7** Gorlois
son: 6 Arthur

iguana
5 anole **6** lizard **8** basilisk **10** chuckwalla

ilex
4 maté **5** holly **6** yaupon **7** holm oak **8** inkberry

Iliad
4 epic
author: 5 Homer
character: 4 Ajax **5** Helen, Paris, Priam **6** Aeneas, Hector **8** Achilles, Diomedes, Odysseus **9** Agamemnon, Patroclus
city: 4 Troy

Ilium
4 Troy

ilk
4 kind, sort, type **5** breed, class, genre **6** family, kidney, nature, stripe **7** variety

ill
4 sick **6** ailing, infirm, laid up, malady, peaked, queasy, unwell **7** ailment, disease, trouble, unlucky **8** diseased, disorder, distress, feverish, nauseous, scarcely, sickness, syndrome **9** afflicted, infirmity, nauseated, unhealthy **10** misfortune

ill-adapted
8 unfitted, unsuited **10** unsuitable

ill-advised
4 rash **5** brash, hasty **6** madcap, unwise **7** foolish **8** careless, heedless, reckless **9** foolhardy, impolitic, imprudent **10** incautious, indiscreet, unthinking **11** inexpedient, injudicious, thoughtless

ill at ease
3 shy **4** edgy **6** on edge **7** anxious, awkward, fidgety, nervous **8** insecure, restless **9** unsettled **11** discomfited **12** apprehensive **13** self-conscious, uncomfortable

ill-boding
4 dire **7** baleful, doomful, fateful, ominous, unlucky **8** sinister **10** portentous **11** apocalyptic **12** inauspicious, unpropitious

ill-bred
4 rude **5** crude **7** boorish, loutish, uncivil, uncouth **8** impolite **9** unrefined **10** uncultured, ungracious, unmannered, unmannerly, unpolished **11** uncivilized **12** discourteous

ill-defined
5 faint, fuzzy, vague **7** shadowy **10** indistinct

illegal
3 hot **6** banned **7** bootleg, illicit, lawless **8** criminal, outlawed, unlawful, wrongful **9** felonious, forbidden **10** actionable, prohibited, proscribed, unlicensed **12** illegitimate
act: 5 crime **6** felony
scheme: 4 scam

illegible
8 scrawled **10** unreadable **11** inscrutable

illegitimacy
8 bastardy **11** bar sinister **12** unlawfulness

illegitimate
7 bastard, bootleg, erratic, invalid, lawless, natural **8** criminal, improper, spurious, unlawful **11** misbegotten **12** unauthorized

ill-fated
6 cursed, doomed **7** unhappy, unlucky **8** accursed, luckless, untoward **10** disastrous **11** star-crossed, unfortunate

ill-favored
4 ugly **5** plain **6** homely **12** unattractive

ill-humored
4 dour, sour **5** cross, surly, testy **6** crabby, cranky, crusty, grumpy, morose, ornery, sullen, tetchy, touchy **7** crabbed, grouchy, peevish, prickly **8** choleric, churlish, snappish **9** dyspeptic, irascible, irritable, saturnine, splenetic **12** cantankerous, disagreeable, misanthropic

illiberal
6 biased, narrow **7** bigoted, insular **9** hidebound, parochial, penurious **10** intolerant, prejudiced, provincial **11** reactionary, small-minded **12** conservative, narrow-minded, uncharitable

illicit
7 bootleg, crooked, lawless **8** criminal, unlawful **9** forbidden **10** contraband, prohibited **11** black-market, clandestine **12** unauthorized

illimitable
  7 endless 8 infinite, unending 9 boundless
  11 measureless

Illinois
  capital: 11 Springfield
  city: 6 Aurora, Cicero, Joliet, Peoria
  7 Chicago 8 Rockford
  college, university: 4 Knox 6 DePaul
  7 Wheaton 12 Northwestern
  nickname: 7 Prairie (State)
  river: 6 Wabash
  state bird: 8 cardinal
  state flower: 6 violet
  state tree: 8 white oak

illiterate
  6 unread 8 untaught 9 untutored
  10 uneducated, unlettered, unschooled

ill-mannered
  4 rude 6 coarse 7 boorish, loutish, uncivil,
  uncouth 8 churlish, impolite 10 ungracious
  12 discourteous

ill-natured
  4 sour 5 cross, huffy, surly, testy 6 bitchy,
  crabby, grumpy, ornery, tetchy 7 grouchy,
  peevish, waspish 8 choleric, churlish,
  snappish, spiteful 9 dyspeptic, fractious,
  irascible, irritable 10 malevolent 11 belligerent, contentious, quarrelsome 12 cantankerous, disagreeable

illness
  6 malady 7 ailment, disease, malaise
  8 cachexia, disorder, sickness 9 infirmity
  10 affliction 13 indisposition

illogical
  6 absurd 7 invalid, unsound 8 specious
  9 plausible, senseless, sophistic
  10 fallacious, irrational, unreasoned
  11 nonrational 12 preposterous,
  unreasonable

ill-starred
  6 cursed, doomed, malign 7 fateful,
  ominous, unhappy, unlucky 8 luckless,
  untoward 10 disastrous, foreboding,
  portentous 11 unfavorable, unfortunate,
  unpromising 12 inauspicious, unpropitious

ill-tempered
  4 sour 5 cross, huffy, surly 6 crabby,
  bitchy, grumpy, ornery, snippy 7 grouchy,
  peevish, waspish 8 choleric, churlish,
  petulant, shrewish, snappish, spiteful
  9 dyspeptic, fractious, irascible, irritable
  11 belligerent, contentious, quarrelsome
  12 cantankerous, disagreeable

ill-timed
  11 inopportune 12 unseasonable

ill-treat
  4 harm, hurt 5 abuse 6 injure, misuse,
  molest 7 torment 8 aggrieve
  10 traumatize

illuminate
  5 clear, edify, exalt, gloss, light 6 uplift
  7 clarify, clear up, explain, lighten
  8 brighten, decorate 9 elucidate,
  embellish, enlighten, highlight, irradiate,
  spotlight

illuminati
  5 elite 7 clerisy, scholar 8 academic
  11 academician 13 intellectuals

illumination
  8 lighting
  unit of: 3 lux 4 phot 5 lumen 6 candle
  7 candela 10 footcandle

illusion
  4 myth 5 dream, fancy, ghost 6 facade,
  mirage 7 chimera, fantasy 8 phantasm,
  phantasy 9 invention, pipe dream,
  semblance 11 ignis fatuus 12 will-o'-the-
  wisp 13 hallucination

illusionist
  8 conjurer, magician 9 trickster

illusive
  see **illusory**

illusory
  4 sham 6 unreal 7 seeming 8 apparent,
  fanciful 9 deceptive, fictional, imaginary,
  visionary 10 chimerical, fallacious,
  fictitious, misleading, ostensible

illustrate
  4 mark, show 6 depict, evince, expose,
  reveal 7 clarify, display, exhibit, explain,
  picture, portray 8 decorate, describe,
  evidence, instance, manifest 9 elucidate,
  epitomize, exemplify 11 demonstrate

illustration
  4 case 6 sample 7 diagram, drawing,
  example, picture, problem 8 instance

illustrative
  7 graphic 9 pictorial 10 clarifying
  11 descriptive 12 iconographic

illustrator
  American: 4 Kent (Rockwell), Pyle
  (Howard) 5 Abbey (Edwin Austin), Flagg
  (James Montgomery), Smith (Jessie
  Willcox), Wyeth (Newell Convers)
  6 Gibson (Charles Dana) 7 Burgess

(Gelett), Parrish (Maxwell) 8 Rockwell
(Norman) 9 Remington (Frederic)
English: 5 Crane (Walter) 6 Morris
(William), Potter (Beatrix) 7 Nielsen (Kay),
Rackham (Arthur), Tenniel (John)
9 Beardsley (Aubrey), Caldecott
(Randolph), du Maurier (George),
Greenaway (Kate)
French: 4 Doré (Gustave) 5 Dulac
(Edmund)
German: 5 Dürer (Albrecht)

illustrious
5 famed, great, lofty, noted 6 famous
7 eminent, exalted, notable, sublime
8 glorious, renowned, splendid
9 acclaimed, prominent 10 celebrated,
preeminent 11 outstanding, prestigious
13 distinguished

illustriousness
4 fame 5 glory 6 renown 8 eminence,
prestige 9 celebrity 10 prominence
11 distinction, preeminence

ill will
5 spite, venom 6 animus, enmity, malice,
rancor, spleen 7 despite, dislike
8 acrimony, aversion, bad blood
9 animosity, antipathy, hostility, malignity
10 resentment 11 malevolence
12 spitefulness 13 maliciousness

Ilus
father: 4 Tros
grandson: 5 Priam
mother: 10 Callirrhoë
son: 8 Laomedon

image
4 copy, form, icon, idea, idol 5 equal,
match 6 double, effigy, figure, mirror,
notion, ringer, vision 7 concept, fantasm,
feature, picture 8 likeness, phantasm,
portrait 9 facsimile, semblance
10 conception, equivalent, impression,
reflection, simulacrum 12 illustration
Polynesian: 4 tiki
Semitic: 6 teraph 8 teraphim (plural)

imaginary
5 ideal 6 made-up, unreal 7 fancied,
fictive 8 abstract, fabulous, fanciful,
illusive, illusory, notional, quixotic
9 dreamlike, fantastic, fictional, legendary,
visionary 10 apocryphal, chimerical,
fictitious, phantasmal 11 make-believe
12 hypothetical, suppositious

imagination
5 fancy 7 fantasy 8 phantasy 9 invention

10 creativity 11 inspiration
13 inventiveness

imaginative
5 false 7 blue-sky, fictive 8 artistic,
creative, fanciful, original, poetical
9 ingenious, inventive, visionary, whimsical
11 resourceful 12 enterprising

imagine
5 dream, fancy 6 assume, invent, make up
7 dream up, feature, picture, suspect
8 conceive, envisage, envision 9 fabricate,
visualize 10 conjecture

imbecile
4 dodo, dolt, dull, fool, jerk 5 dunce, idiot,
moron, ninny 6 cretin, dimwit, nitwit 7 half-
wit, jackass, moronic, pinhead, tomfool
8 numskull 9 birdbrain, blockhead,
numbskull 10 dunderhead, nincompoop

imbibe
3 sip, sup 4 chug, soak, swig, toss
5 booze, drink, quaff, swill 6 absorb,
guzzle, tipple 7 consume, swallow, swizzle
10 assimilate

imbricate
3 lap 7 overlap, shingle 11 overlapping

imbroglio
3 row 4 maze, mess, spat, to-do 5 brawl,
mix-up 6 fracas, muddle, tangle 7 dispute,
quarrel, rhubarb, scandal, wrangle
8 argument, disorder, squabble
9 confusion, intricacy 10 falling-out
11 altercation, predicament
12 complication, entanglement

imbrue
4 soil 5 stain 8 discolor

imbue
3 dye 4 soak 5 bathe, endow, steep, tinge
6 infuse, invest, leaven 7 ingrain, instill,
pervade, suffuse 8 permeate, saturate
9 influence, inoculate

imitate
3 ape 4 copy, echo, mime, mock 5 forge,
mimic, spoof 6 parody 7 emulate, take off
8 resemble, simulate, travesty
9 burlesque, duplicate, replicate, reproduce
11 counterfeit, impersonate

imitation
4 copy, fake, mock, sham 5 clone, ditto,
dummy, false, match, phony 6 ersatz,
parody, ringer 7 forgery, replica
8 likeness, parallel, spurious, travesty
9 duplicate, semblance, simulated
10 artificial, simulacrum, simulation,

substitute **11** counterfeit, counterpart
12 reproduction, substitution

imitative
4 mock **5** apish **6** echoic **7** copycat,
mimetic, parodic, slavish **11** counterfeit
12 onomatopoeic **13** onomatopoetic

immaculate
4 pure **5** clean **6** chaste, virgin **7** cleanly,
perfect, sinless **8** flawless, spotless,
unsoiled, virtuous **9** stainless, undefiled,
unsullied **11** spic-and-span, unblemished
12 spick-and-span

immaterial
7 trivial **8** bodiless, ethereal **10** extraneous, inapposite, intangible, irrelevant
11 disembodied, incorporeal, nonphysical,
unimportant **12** inapplicable
13 insignificant, insubstantial, unsubstantial

immature
3 raw **5** crude, green, young **6** callow,
infant, unripe **7** puerile **8** childish, juvenile,
youthful **9** infantile, primitive, unfledged
10 unfinished **11** undeveloped

immaturity
6 nonage **7** infancy **8** minority
9 childhood, salad days **11** adolescence
12 juvenescence

immeasurable
4 vast **6** untold **7** endless **8** infinite
9 boundless, extensive, limitless,
unbounded, unlimited **11** illimitable,
inestimable, uncountable **12** incalculable,
unfathomable

immediate
4 next, nigh **5** close **6** at hand, direct,
nearby, urgent **7** current, instant, ongoing,
primary **9** firsthand, proximate
10 unmediated **12** straightaway
13 instantaneous

immediately
3 now, PDQ **4** anon, stat **6** at once,
presto, pronto **8** directly, promptly
9 forthwith, instanter, instantly, right away
11 straightway **12** straightaway

immense
4 huge, vast **5** great, large **6** mighty
7 mammoth, massive, titanic **8** colossal,
enormous, gigantic **9** humongous,
monstrous **10** gargantuan, monumental,
prodigious, tremendous **11** elephantine

immensely
4 a lot **8** terribly **9** extremely **11** exceedingly **12** inordinately

immensity
8 enormity, hugeness, vastness
9 greatness **12** enormousness

immerse
3 dip **4** duck, dunk, sink, soak **5** bathe,
douse **6** drench, engage, plunge
7 baptize, engross, involve **8** saturate,
submerge

immigrant
5 alien **7** settler **8** newcomer
10 transplant
Japanese: 5 issei

imminent
6 at hand **6** coming **7** brewing, nearing,
ominous, pending **8** upcoming
9 gathering, proximate **11** approaching,
overhanging

immobile
3 set **5** fixed, inert, still **6** frozen, stable,
static **9** unmovable **10** motionless,
stationary

immobilize
5 still **7** cripple, disable **8** paralyze
9 hamstring **12** incapacitate

immoderate
5 undue **7** extreme **9** excessive
10 exorbitant, inordinate, untempered
11 extravagant, intemperate
12 unreasonable, unrestrained
13 extraordinary, overindulgent

immoderation
6 excess **11** exorbitance, prodigality
12 extravagance, intemperance

immodest
4 lewd, vain **7** stuck-up **8** arrogant,
boastful, indecent, puffed-up, unchaste
9 conceited, egotistic **11** pretentious

immolate
4 burn, kill **7** destroy **9** sacrifice

immoral
4 evil, vile **5** dirty, wrong **6** sinful, wanton,
wicked **7** corrupt, unclean, vicious
8 depraved, indecent, unchaste
9 dissolute, reprobate, uncleanly
10 degenerate, iniquitous, licentious

immorality
3 sin **4** vice **8** iniquity **9** depravity
10 corruption, unchastity, wickedness

immortal
7 endless, eternal, godlike, undying
8 timeless, unending **9** ceaseless,
deathless, perpetual **11** amaranthine,
everlasting, sempiternal

immotile
5 fixed, inert 6 rooted, static 9 paralyzed
10 stationary

immovable
3 pat, set 4 fast, firm 5 fixed, rigid
6 rooted, stable 7 adamant 8 constant,
obdurate, stubborn 9 steadfast
10 inflexible, invariable, stationary,
unyielding

immune
4 free, safe 6 exempt, secure 9 protected
10 impervious 12 invulnerable,
unassailable

immunity
7 defense, freedom 9 exemption, privilege
10 protection

immure
3 pen 4 cage, coop, jail, wall 6 entomb,
intern, shut in 7 confine, enclose
8 imprison 11 incarcerate

immutable
4 firm 5 fixed 8 constant 9 permanent,
steadfast 10 changeless, inflexible,
invariable, unchanging 11 inalterable,
unalterable 12 unchangeable

Imogen
father: 9 Cymbeline
husband: 9 Posthumus

imp
3 elf 4 brat, puck 5 demon, devil, fiend,
gamin, gnome, pixie, scamp 6 goblin,
kobold, sprite, urchin 7 gremlin
9 hobgoblin

impact
3 hit, jar, rap 4 blow, bump, jolt, rock, slam,
slap 5 brunt, embed, pound, punch, shock,
smash, smite 6 affect, buffet, strike, wallop
9 collision, influence 10 concussion,
percussion

impair
3 mar, sap 4 harm, hurt 5 spoil
6 damage, injure, lessen, weaken, worsen
7 cripple, tarnish, vitiate 8 enfeeble
9 prejudice, undermine 10 debilitate

impala
8 antelope

impale
4 gore, spit, stab 5 lance, prick, spear,
spike, stick 6 pierce, skewer 8 puncture,
transfix 11 transpierce

impalpable
4 fine 7 powdery 8 ethereal 10 intangible

11 disembodied, incorporeal
12 imponderable 13 imperceptible,
indiscernible

impart
4 cede, give, lend, tell 5 grant, share, yield
6 afford, bestow, confer, convey, pass on,
relate, render 8 disclose, transmit
11 communicate
knowledge: 5 teach 6 inform 7 educate
8 instruct

impartial
4 even, fair, just 5 equal 7 neutral
8 detached, unbiased 9 equitable,
objective, uncolored 10 evenhanded
12 unprejudiced 13 disinterested,
dispassionate

impassable
6 closed 7 blocked 10 obstructed
12 impenetrable

impasse
3 box, fix, jam 6 aporia, corner, logjam,
pickle, pocket 7 catch-22, dead end,
dilemma 8 cul-de-sac, deadlock, standoff
9 stalemate 10 blind alley, bottleneck

impassioned
3 hot 5 fiery 6 ardent, fervid, fierce,
heated, red-hot, torrid 7 blazing, burning,
fervent, flaming, intense, violent, zealous
8 feverish, romantic, vehement, white-hot
9 emotional, perfervid 10 hot-blooded,
overheated 11 dithyrambic 12 melodramatic 13 overemotional

impassive
4 calm, cold, cool 5 stoic 6 stolid, vacant
7 deadpan 8 composed, hardened,
reserved, reticent, taciturn 9 heartless
10 insensible, insentient, phlegmatic,
poker-faced 11 cold-blooded, emotionless,
insensitive, passionless, unconcerned,
unemotional, unexcitable, unflappable
12 inexpressive, unexpressive,
unresponsive 13 dispassionate, self-
possessed, unsusceptible

impassivity
6 apathy, phlegm 8 stoicism 9 stolidity
12 indifference 13 insensibility

impatient
4 edgy 5 antsy, eager, hasty 7 anxious,
fretful, restive 8 restless 9 irascible,
irritable 10 intolerant

impeach
5 blame, doubt 6 accuse, charge, indict

7 censure 9 inculpate, reprehend
11 incriminate

impeccable
4 pure 5 exact 7 perfect, precise
8 absolute, accurate, flawless, unerring
9 blameless, errorless, faultless, guiltless
10 infallible 11 unblemished

impecunious
4 poor 5 broke, needy 7 pinched
8 bankrupt, beggarly, indigent 9 destitute,
insolvent, penniless, penurious 10 down-
and-out 11 necessitous

impecuniousness
4 need, want 6 penury 7 poverty
9 indigence, neediness, pauperism,
privation 11 destitution

impedance
3 bar 4 clog 5 block 8 blockage, obstacle
9 hindrance 10 opposition 11 obstruction

impede
3 bar, dam 4 clog, slow 5 block, check,
debar, delay, deter, stall 6 hinder, hang up,
hold up, stymie, thwart 7 bog down
8 encumber, obstruct 9 embarrass,
interfere, stonewall

impediment
3 bar 4 clog, snag 5 block, hitch 6 hurdle
7 barrier 8 obstacle 9 barricade,
hindrance, roadblock 10 difficulty
11 encumbrance, obstruction

impel
4 goad, prod, push, spur, urge 5 drive,
force, rouse 6 excite, incite, prompt
7 actuate, inspire 8 mobilize, motivate
9 instigate, stimulate

impend
4 loom, near 6 menace 8 approach,
overhang, threaten

impenetrable
5 dense 6 arcane 7 obscure 9 enigmatic,
recondite 10 impervious, invincible,
mysterious, unknowable 11 impermeable,
bulletproof, inscrutable, ungraspable
12 unfathomable

imperative
4 duty, need, rule, writ 5 acute, vital
6 crying, urgent 7 burning, clamant,
command, crucial, exigent 8 critical,
pressing, required 9 clamorous, essential,
insistent, mandatory, necessary, necessity,
requisite 10 compulsory, obligation,
obligatory 11 fundamental, necessitous
12 prerequisite

imperceptible
3 dim 5 faint, vague 6 slight, subtle
7 gradual 9 invisible 10 impalpable,
indistinct, insensible, intangible,
unapparent 12 undetectable, unnoticeable,
unobservable 13 inappreciable,
inconspicuous, indiscernible

imperceptive
4 dull 7 shallow, unaware 11 inattentive,
insensitive

imperfect
6 faulty, flawed 9 defective, deficient,
irregular 10 defeasible, inadequate

imperfection
3 sin 4 flaw, wart 5 fault 6 defect, foible
7 blemish, demerit, failing, frailty
8 weakness 10 deficiency 11 shortcoming

imperial
5 regal, royal 6 kingly, lordly 7 haughty
8 absolute, majestic 9 masterful, sovereign
10 high-handed, peremptory 11 domineering, magisterial, monarchical

imperil
4 risk 6 hazard, menace 7 venture
8 endanger, threaten 10 jeopardize

imperious
5 bossy 6 urgent 7 haughty 8 absolute,
arrogant, despotic, dominant 9 arbitrary,
masterful 10 autocratic, commanding,
high-handed, oppressive, peremptory,
tyrannical 11 dictatorial, domineering,
heavy-handed, magisterial, overbearing

impermanent
7 passing 8 fleeting, fugitive 9 ephemeral,
fugacious, momentary, temporary, transient
10 evanescent, short-lived, transitory

impersonal
4 cold 5 aloof 8 abstract, detached
11 cold-blooded, emotionlesst
13 dispassionate, unimpassioned

impersonate
3 ape 4 play 5 mimic 6 act out 7 imitate,
playact, portray 9 represent 11 counterfeit

impersonator
4 mime 5 actor, mimic 6 mummer, player,
ringer 7 actress, copycat 8 thespian

impertinence
3 lip 4 gall, guff, sass 5 brass, cheek
8 audacity, boldness, chutzpah, rudeness,
temerity 9 brashness, impudence,
insolence 10 brazenness, effrontery,
incivility 11 discourtesy, irrelevance

impertinent

4 bold, busy, rude 5 brash, fresh, sassy, saucy 6 brazen, cheeky 7 uncivil
8 insolent, meddling 9 audacious, intrusive, obtrusive, officious
10 inapposite, irrelative, irrelevant, meddlesome 11 ill-mannered
12 discourteous, inapplicable, presumptuous

imperturbability

5 poise 6 aplomb, phlegm 8 calmness, coolness, serenity, stoicism 9 composure, placidity, sangfroid 10 dispassion, equanimity, tranquility 11 equilibrium, nonchalance, tranquillity

imperturbable

4 calm, cool 5 stoic 6 placid, poised, serene, smooth, steady, stolid 7 unmoved
8 composed, tranquil 9 collected, unruffled
10 nonchalant, phlegmatic, unaffected
11 unflappable

impervious

4 safe 6 immune 8 hardened
10 inviolable 12 inaccessible, invulnerable

impetuous

3 hot 4 rash, wild 5 fiery, hasty 6 ardent, fervid, madcap, sudden 8 headlong, vehement, volatile 9 hotheaded, mercurial
10 irrational, passionate 11 precipitant, precipitate, precipitous, spontaneous
13 temperamental

impetus

4 goad, push, spur 5 force, motive
8 catalyst, momentum, stimulus
9 incentive, stimulant 10 incitement, motivation 13 encouragement

impinge

5 press 6 border 7 intrude, obtrude
8 encroach

impious

6 sinful, unholy, wicked 7 godless, infidel, profane, secular, ungodly 8 agnostic, apostate 9 atheistic 10 irreverent, unfaithful, unhallowed 11 blasphemous, irreligious, unrighteous 12 iconoclastic, sacrilegious 13 unconsecrated

impish

4 arch 5 elfin 6 elvish 7 playful, puckish, roguish, waggish 11 mischievous

impishness

7 devilry, roguery, waggery 8 deviltry, mischief 9 devilment 11 roguishness, waggishness

implacable

4 grim 8 ruthless 9 merciless
10 inexorable, unyielding 11 intractable
12 unappeasable

implant

3 fix 4 root 5 embed, graft, infix 6 enroot, infuse, insert 7 ingrain, inspire, instill
9 establish, inculcate, inoculate, introduce
10 inseminate 12 augmentation

implausible

5 fishy 6 flimsy 7 dubious, fanciful, suspect 8 doubtful, unlikely 10 far-fetched, incredible 12 questionable, unbelievable, unconvincing

implement

4 tool 6 device, effect, enable, gadget
7 enforce, execute, fulfill, perform, realize, utensil 8 carry out, complete, make good
9 actualize, apparatus, appliance
10 accomplish, instrument, supplement
11 contraption, contrivance
carpentry: 3 die, saw 4 file 5 brace, clamp, drill, punch, tongs 6 chisel, hammer, pliers, reamer, sander, wrench
7 hacksaw, scraper 9 blowtorch
11 screwdriver
cleaning: 3 mop 5 broom, brush, whisk
6 duster, vacuum 7 sweeper
10 whiskbroom
cutting: 5 knife, mower, razor 6 scythe, shears, sickle 8 scissors
digging: 5 spade 6 dibber, dibble, shovel
drawing: 3 pen 6 eraser, pencil
7 compass 8 template
eating: 4 fork 5 knife, spoon
engraving: 5 burin 6 graver
farm: 4 plow 6 binder, harrow, plough, scythe, seeder, sickle 8 gangplow, reaphook, spreader, thresher 9 pitchfork
10 cultivator
fireplace: 5 poker, tongs 7 andiron
fishing: 3 rod 4 hook, lure, reel 6 sinker
7 harpoon, trident
garden: 3 hoe 4 rake 5 spade 6 dibber, dibble, digger, tiller, trowel 7 mattock
11 wheelbarrow
grooming: 4 comb, file 5 brush, razor
7 clipper 8 clippers, nail file, tweezers
10 toothbrush
kitchen: 3 pan, pot 4 mold 5 mixer, whisk
6 grater, kettle, mortar, pestle 7 blender, skillet, spatula 8 colander, saucepan, stockpot
logging: 5 peavy 6 peavey 8 cant hook
measuring: 3 cup 4 gage, rule 5 gauge,

ruler, scale **7** caliper, divider, trammel, T-square **10** micrometer, protractor
stone: 5 burin **7** neolith **9** paleolith

implicate
4 link, mire **5** blame **6** tangle **7** concern, embroil, entwine, include, involve
8 entangle, intimate **11** incriminate

implication
4 hint **8** allusion, overtone **9** inference, undertone **10** connection, intimation, suggestion **11** association, connotation
12 significance

implicit
5 tacit **6** unsaid **8** inherent, unspoken **9** doubtless, potential, unuttered
10 undeclared, understood
11 unexpressed **13** unquestioning

implied
5 tacit **6** unsaid **8** unspoken **9** suggested
10 undeclared, understood
11 unexpressed

implore
3 ask, beg **4** coax, pray **5** crave, plead **6** adjure, appeal **7** beseech, entreat, solicit
10 supplicate

imply
4 hint, mean **7** connote, include, involve, signify, suggest **8** indicate, intimate
9 insinuate

impolite
4 rude **5** crude **7** ill-bred, uncivil, uncouth
10 ungracious, unladylike, unmannered, unmannerly **11** ill-mannered
12 discourteous **13** ungentlemanly

impolitic
5 brash **6** unwise **8** tactless **9** imprudent, maladroit, untactful **10** ill-advised, indiscreet **11** inadvisable, inexpedient, injudicious **12** shortsighted, undiplomatic

import
4 bear, gist, mean, pith **5** sense, value, worth **6** convey, denote, intend, intent, matter, moment, stress, thrust, weight
7 concern, connote, express, meaning, message, purpose, signify **8** emphasis, indicate, transfer **9** magnitude, substance
10 intendment **11** acceptation, consequence **12** significance
13 signification

importance
4 mark, note, pith **5** value, worth
6 moment, weight **7** account, gravity

8 eminence, priority, salience, standing
9 greatness, magnitude, substance
10 prominence, worthiness
11 consequence, distinction, seriousness, weightiness **12** significance

important
3 big **5** chief, grave, great, heavy, major, noted, vital **6** famous, marked, potent, urgent, worthy **7** big-time, capital, crucial, eminent, fateful, notable, salient, serious, telling, weighty **8** critical, eventful, foremost, material, powerful, pressing, valuable **9** essential, estimable, imperious, memorable, momentous, prominent
10 meaningful, noteworthy, preeminent, worthwhile **11** outstanding, significant, substantial **12** considerable
13 consequential, distinguished, indispensable

importune
3 beg **4** pray, urge **5** annoy, plead, worry **6** appeal, invoke, plague **7** beseech, besiege, entreat, solicit, trouble **8** petition

impose
3 fob **4** lade, levy **5** abuse, enact, exact, foist, force, order, place, put on, visit, wreak
6 assess, burden, charge, compel, decree, demand, enjoin, fob off, ordain, saddle
7 command, dictate, exploit, inflict, intrude, lay down, obtrude, palm off, pass off, require **8** encroach, encumber, infringe, trespass **9** authorize, constrain, establish

imposing
4 huge **5** grand, noble, regal, royal
6 august **7** awesome, massive, pompous, stately **8** baronial, majestic, towering
9 dignified **10** commanding, monumental
11 magnificent, outstanding **12** high-sounding **13** distinguished

imposition
3 tax **4** duty, fine, levy **6** burden, demand **7** penalty **9** deception **13** inconvenience

impossible
6 absurd **8** hopeless **10** infeasible, unfeasible, unworkable **11** unthinkable
12 preposterous, unacceptable, unattainable, unbelievable, unimaginable, unrealizable, unreasonable
13 inconceivable

impost
3 fee, tax **4** duty, levy, toll **6** charge, tariff **7** tribute **9** surcharge **10** assessment

impostor
4 fake, sham **5** actor, cheat, faker, fraud,

mimic, phony, poser, quack **6** humbug,
poseur **8** deceiver **9** charlatan, con artist,
hypocrite, pretender **10** dissembler,
mountebank **11** masquerader
12 impersonator

imposture
4 fake, hoax, sell, sham, wile **5** cheat, fraud
6 deceit, humbug **8** flimflam **9** deception,
mare's nest, stratagem **11** counterfeit

impotence
8 weakness **9** sterility **10** inadequacy
12 helplessness **13** powerlessness

impotent
4 lame, weak **6** effete, feeble **7** sterile
8 helpless **9** forceless, incapable,
powerless **11** ineffective, ineffectual
12 invertebrate

impound
5 seize **6** immure, lock up **7** confine,
enclose, put away **8** imprison **10** confiscate

impoverish
4 bust, ruin **5** break **6** beggar **8** bankrupt
9 pauperize

impoverished
4 poor **5** broke, needy **8** bankrupt,
indigent **9** destitute, penniless, penurious

impoverishment
4 need, want **6** penury **9** indigence,
neediness, privation **11** destitution

impracticable
8 unusable **10** infeasible, unfeasible,
unworkable **11** insuperable, unrealistic
12 inaccessible, unattainable

impractical
7 utopian **8** quixotic, romantic, unusable
9 visionary **10** idealistic, infeasible, ivory-
tower, starry-eyed, unfeasible, unworkable
11 theoretical, unrealistic

imprecation
3 hex **4** cuss **5** curse **7** malison
8 anathema **11** malediction

imprecise
5 rough, vague **7** inexact **9** estimated
10 indefinite **11** approximate, unspecified

impregnable
4 safe **6** immune, secure **9** protected
10 invincible, inviolable, unbeatable
11 indomitable, insuperable
12 unassailable **13** unconquerable

impregnate
3 sop **4** fill, soak **5** imbue, souse, steep

6 drench, infuse **7** pervade **8** conceive,
permeate, saturate **9** fecundate, fertilize,
penetrate, transfuse **10** inseminate

impresario
4 Bing (Rudolf) **5** Carte (Richard D'Oyly),
Hurok (Sol) **6** Pastor (Tony) **7** manager
8 director, Kirstein (Lincoln), producer,
promoter **9** Diaghilev (Sergei) **10** D'Oyly
Carte (Richard)

impress
3 fix, set **4** dent, etch, mark, move, seal,
sway **5** brand, carry, drive, exert, force,
grave, infix, print, stamp, touch **6** affect,
effect, excite, strike **7** engrave, ingrain,
inspire **8** inscribe, transfer, transmit
9 establish, influence, stimulate

impressible
8 gullible, immature, moldable **9** malleable,
receptive, sensitive **10** affectable,
susceptive, vulnerable **11** persuadable,
suggestible, susceptible

impression
4 dent, idea, mark, sign **5** image, print,
stamp, trace, track **6** effect, hollow, notion
7 concept, edition, feeling, reissue, thought,
vestige **8** printing, reaction **9** influence

impressionable
8 sensible, sentient **9** malleable, receptive,
sensitive **10** responsive **11** suggestible,
susceptible

impressionist
composer: 5 Ravel (Maurice) **7** Debussy
(Claude)
mimic: 6 Carvey (Dana), Little (Rich)
painter: 5 Degas (Edgar), Manet
(Edouard), Monet (Claude) **6** Renoir
(Auguste), Sisley (Alfred) **7** Cassatt
(Mary), Morisot (Berthe) **8** Pissarro
(Camille)
(see also **postimpressionist**)

impressive
5 grand, noble **6** moving, superb
7 amazing, awesome, notable, stately,
sublime **8** dazzling, dramatic, gorgeous,
majestic, powerful, splendid, stirring,
striking, touching **9** admirable, affecting,
arresting, inspiring **11** magnificent

imprimatur
6 permit **7** license **8** approval, sanction
10 permission **13** authorization

imprint
3 fix **4** dent, etch, mark **5** grave, press,
stamp **6** dimple, effect **7** engrave

8 inscribe 9 engraving, influence
10 depression 11 indentation, inscription

imprison
3 jug 4 cage, jail 6 coop up, detain,
immure, intern, send up 7 confine, enclose
8 restrain, restrict, stockade 9 constrain
11 incarcerate

improbable
5 fishy 7 dubious 8 doubtful, fanciful,
unlikely 10 far-fetched 11 implausible

impromptu
5 ad-lib 7 offhand 9 extempore, makeshift,
unplanned, unstudied 10 off-the-cuff,
unprepared, unscripted 11 extemporary,
spontaneous, unrehearsed

improper
5 inapt, inept, outré, undue, wrong
6 gauche, risqué 7 illicit, naughty 8 ill-
timed, indecent, tactless, unseemly,
untimely, untoward 9 incorrect, unethical,
unfitting 10 inaccurate, inapposite,
indecorous, indelicate, malapropos,
unbecoming, undecorous, unsuitable
11 impertinent, unbefitting 12 illegitimate,
inadmissible, inapplicable, infelicitous,
unseasonable 13 inappropriate

impropriety
5 gaffe 7 blooper, blunder, faux pas
8 solecism 9 barbarism, gaucherie,
indecorum, vulgarism 12 unseemliness
13 incorrectness

improve
4 edit, help, mend 5 amend, better, boost,
edify, emend, raise 6 better, enrich, look
up, perk up, refine, reform, remedy, revise,
revive, uplift 7 advance, amplify, augment,
build up, correct, develop, enhance,
enlarge, further, perfect, recover, rectify,
upgrade 8 increase, progress 9 cultivate,
intensify, meliorate 10 aggrandize,
ameliorate, recuperate, strengthen

improvident
4 rash 5 lavish 8 careless, feckless,
heedless, prodigal, reckless, wasteful
9 impetuous, negligent, unthrifty
10 profligate 11 extravagant, spendthrift
12 shortsighted, uneconomical

improvise
5 ad-lib 6 cook up, invent, make up
7 concoct 8 contrive 9 fabricate
11 extemporize

improvised
7 offhand 9 extempore, unstudied 10 off-

the-cuff, unprepared, unscripted
11 extemporary, unrehearsed

imprudent
4 rash 6 unwise 7 foolish 8 reckless
9 foolhardy 10 ill-advised, incautious,
indiscreet 11 inadvisable, inexpedient,
injudicious 12 shortsighted

impudence
4 gall 5 brass, cheek, nerve 8 audacity,
boldness, chutzpah, temerity 9 brashness,
cockiness, hardihood, insolence, nerviness
10 disrespect, effrontery 11 presumption

impudent
4 bold, flip, pert, wise 5 brash, cocky,
fresh, nervy, sassy, saucy 6 brassy,
brazen, cheeky 7 blatant, forward
8 flippant, insolent, overbold 9 audacious,
barefaced, bold-faced 11 brazen-faced,
smart-alecky 12 contumelious
13 disrespectful

impugn
5 cross 6 assail, attack, defame, malign,
oppose, vilify 7 asperse, gainsay, impeach
8 chastise, reproach, traverse 9 castigate,
denigrate, deprecate, disparage, reprehend
9 criticize, denigrate

impugnable
5 fishy, shady 6 guilty 7 suspect
8 doubtful 9 equivocal, uncertain
10 assailable, suspicious 11 problematic
12 disreputable

impulse
4 goad, push, spur, urge, whim 5 drive,
force 6 motive, thrust, whimsy 7 caprice,
passion 8 catalyst, excitant, stimulus
9 actuation, incentive, stimulant
10 incitation, incitement, motivation
11 inspiration, instigation

impulsive
4 rash 5 hasty 6 abrupt, fickle, sudden
7 erratic, flighty, offhand 8 headlong,
volatile 9 automatic, extempore, mercurial,
unplanned, capricious, whimsical
11 instinctive, involuntary, precipitate,
spontaneous

impunity
7 freedom, liberty, license 8 immunity
9 exception, exemption, indemnity, privilege
10 absolution, protection 12 dispensation

impure
3 raw 5 mixed 6 soiled, sordid, unholy
7 alloyed, defiled, profane, sullied, unclean
8 indecent, polluted, unchaste 9 uncleanly,
unrefined 10 desecrated, unhallowed
11 adulterated

impute

3 lay 4 cite 5 blame, refer 6 accuse,
adduce, assign, charge, credit, indict
7 ascribe 8 accredit 9 attribute, implicate

inaccessible

5 aloof 6 arcane, closed, far-off, remote
7 cryptic, distant, faraway, obscure
8 abstruse, esoteric, hermetic 9 recondite
11 unavailable, unreachable
12 unattainable, unobtainable

inaccurate

5 false, wrong 6 all wet, faulty, untrue
7 unsound 8 specious 9 distorted,
erroneous 10 fictitious

inaction

6 repose 7 latency 8 dormancy, idleness,
lethargy 9 indolence, passivity, slackness,
torpidity 10 quiescence 12 slothfulness

inactive

4 idle, lazy 5 inert, quiet, slack, still
6 asleep, latent, sleepy, static, torpid
7 abeyant, dormant, passive, resting
8 slothful, sluggish 9 do-nothing, lethargic,
quiescent, sedentary

in addition

4 also 6 as well, to boot, withal 7 besides,
further 8 moreover 11 furthermore

inadequacy

4 lack, want 6 dearth 7 deficit, failure,
paucity 8 shortage, weakness
9 impotence 10 deficiency, scantiness
11 shortcoming

inadequate

3 shy 5 scant, short 6 meager, scanty,
scarce, skimpy 7 lacking, scrimpy, wanting
8 impotent 9 defective, deficient
10 emasculate

inadmissible

5 unapt, unfit 8 unusable, unworthy
9 unwelcome 10 unsuitable 11 unqualified
12 unacceptable

inadvertent

8 careless, heedless 9 negligent,
unmindful, unplanned, unwitting
10 accidental, unintended, unthinking
13 unintentional

inadvisable

4 rash 6 unwise 7 foolish 8 careless,
reckless 9 foolhardy, impolitic, imprudent,
pointless 10 ill-advised 11 harebrained

inalterable

5 fixed 6 stable 8 constant 9 immovable,
immutable, steadfast, unmovable,
unvarying 12 unchangeable

inamorata, inamorato

4 beau, dear 5 flame, honey, lover
6 steady 7 beloved, darling, squeeze,
sweetie 8 ladylove, mistress, paramour,
truelove 9 boyfriend 10 girlfriend,
heartthrob, sweetheart

inane

4 flat, idle, vain 5 blank, dotty, empty, silly,
vapid 6 absurd, hollow, jejune, vacant
7 asinine, fatuous, foolish, idiotic, insipid,
lunatic, trivial, vacuous, witless 8 mindless
9 frivolous, pointless, senseless

inanimate

4 dead, dull 5 inert 6 still 6 asleep, torpid
7 dormant 8 immotile, lifeless 9 quiescent
10 motionless 11 unconscious

inanity

5 folly 6 idiocy, lunacy 7 fatuity, vacuity
8 vapidity 9 absurdity, dottiness,
emptiness, silliness 10 hollowness
11 foolishness, vacuousness, witlessness
13 senselessness

inappreciable

6 meager, scanty, skimpy, slight
10 impalpable, unapparent 13 imperceptible

inappropriate

5 amiss, undue, unfit 6 unmeet
8 improper, unseemly, untimely, untoward
9 ill-suited 10 malapropos, unsuitable
11 impertinent

inapt

5 unfit 6 clumsy, gauche, jejune, unmeet
7 awkward, unhandy 8 improper, unfitted,
unsuited, untimely 9 maladroit, unfitting,
unskilled 10 amateurish, irrelevant,
malapropos, unskillful, unsuitable

inarticulate

4 dumb, mute 5 tacit 6 silent 7 halting,
unvocal 8 mumbling, unspoken, wordless
9 voiceless 10 maundering, speechless,
tongue-tied, undeclared 11 unexpressed

inasmuch as

5 since 7 because, whereas 11 considering

inattentive

6 absent, remiss 8 distrait, heedless
9 forgetful, negligent, unheeding, unmindful
10 abstracted, distracted, unthinking
12 absentminded

inaugural
5 first 6 maiden, speech 7 address, initial, leading, opening, premier 8 foremost 9 beginning

inaugurate
5 begin, set up, start 6 launch 7 kick off 8 commence, dedicate, initiate 9 establish, institute, originate 10 consecrate

inauspicious
4 dire 7 adverse, baleful, direful, fateful, ominous, unlucky 8 sinister 9 ill-boding 11 threatening, unfavorable, unpromising 12 unpropitious

inborn
6 innate, native 7 connate, natural 8 inherent, intrinsic 10 congenital, connatural, hereditary, unacquired

inbred
7 connate, genetic, natural 8 inherent 9 intrinsic 10 congenital, connatural, deep-seated, hereditary

Inca
capital: 5 Cuzco
conqueror: 7 Pizarro (Francisco)
god: 4 Inti 9 Viracocha 10 Pachacamac
language: 7 Quechua
record: 5 quipu
ruler: 9 Atahualpa, Pachacuti 10 Ata-huallpa

incalculable
4 huge, iffy, vast 6 untold 8 enormous 9 boundless, countless, limitless, uncertain 10 tremendous, unnumbered 11 illimitable, measureless, uncountable 12 immeasurable, unmeasurable 13 unpredictable

in camera
7 privily, sub rosa 8 covertly, secretly 9 furtively, privately 10 stealthily 13 clandestinely

incandescent
3 hot 5 lucid 6 ardent, bright, lucent 7 beaming, fulgent, glowing, intense, lambent, radiant 8 dazzling, luminous 9 brilliant, effulgent, refulgent 11 resplendent

incantation
3 hex 4 rune 5 chant, charm, magic, spell 10 hocus-pocus, mumbo-jumbo, necromancy 11 abracadabra, conjuration, enchantment
Buddhist, Hindu: 6 mantra

incapable
5 unfit 6 unable 8 impotent, unexpert, unfitted 9 powerless, unskilled 10 unequipped, unskillful 11 unqualified 12 disqualified

incapacitate
6 disarm 7 cripple, disable 8 paralyze 10 debilitate, devitalize, disqualify, immobilize

incapacity
9 impotence, unfitness 10 impairment 11 disablement 12 fecklessness

incarcerate
3 jug 4 jail 6 coop up, immure, intern, send up 7 confine, enclose, impound 8 imprison

incarnadine
3 red 4 rosy 5 ruddy 6 redden 7 pinkish 8 bloodred

incarnate
5 human, reify 6 embody 7 realize 8 embodied, manifest 9 actualize, corporeal, personify 11 materialize, personalize 12 substantiate

incarnation
6 avatar 10 embodiment 11 reification
of Christ: 7 kenosis

incautious
4 rash 5 brash, hasty 6 daring, madcap, unwary 8 careless, heedless, reckless 9 daredevil, foolhardy, impetuous, imprudent, negligent, unmindful 10 ill-advised, neglectful, regardless 11 precipitate, thoughtless

incendiary
5 fiery, torch 7 firebug 8 agitator, arsonist, arsonous 9 explosive, firebrand, ignitable 10 pyromaniac 12 pyromaniacal

incense
3 ire, mad, oil 4 balm, burn, rile 5 anger, aroma, scent, spice 6 arouse, enrage, homage, incite, madden 7 inflame, provoke 8 irritate 9 infuriate
vessel: 6 censer 8 thurible

incentive
4 goad, spur 5 spark 6 motive 7 impetus, impulse 8 catalyst, stimulus 9 stimulant 10 inducement, motivation 11 provocation 13 encouragement

inception
4 root 5 birth, start 6 origin, outset, source 7 genesis, kickoff, opening 9 beginning

10 derivation, provenance **11** provenience
12 commencement

inceptive

7 initial, leadoff, nascent **9** beginning
10 initiatory

incertitude

5 doubt **7** dubiety **8** mistrust **9** suspicion
10 skepticism **11** dubiousness, uncertainty,
vacillation **12** irresolution

incessant

6 steady **7** endless, eternal, nonstop
8 constant **9** ceaseless, continual,
perpetual, unceasing **10** continuous
11 everlasting, unremitting **12** interminable
13 uninterrupted

inch

3 bit **5** crawl, creep **7** modicum

inchoate

8 formless, immature, unformed, unshaped
9 amorphous, embryonic, incipient,
potential, shapeless **10** disjointed,
incoherent **11** rudimentary, unorganized
12 disconnected

incident

5 event **6** moment **7** episode **8** occasion
9 ancillary, attendant, happening, satellite
10 affiliated, collateral, consequent,
occurrence **11** concomitant, subordinate
12 circumstance

incidental

5 fluky, minor **6** casual, chance
9 accessory **10** contingent, fortuitous
11 subordinate **12** nonessential

incidentally

7 by the by **8** by the bye, by the way,
casually **12** fortuitously

incinerate

4 burn **7** cremate

incipient

7 nascent **9** beginning, embryonic
10 commencing

incipit

5 start **7** opening **9** beginning

incise

3 cut **4** etch, gash, kerf, slit **5** carve, slash,
slice **6** chisel, pierce **7** engrave

incision

3 cut **4** gash, slit **5** blaze, notch
10 laceration

incisive

4 keen **5** acute, crisp, sharp, terse **6** direct
7 cutting, mordant **8** clear-cut, piercing,

slashing, succinct **9** trenchant
11 penetrating **13** perspicacious

incite

3 egg **4** abet, goad, prod, spur, urge **5** egg
on, raise, rouse, set on **6** arouse, exhort,
foment, kindle, set off, spur on, stir up, whip
up **7** actuate, agitate, provoke, trigger
8 motivate **9** instigate, stimulate

incitement

see **incentive**

inclement

3 raw **5** harsh, rough **6** bitter, brutal,
severe, stormy **8** rigorous

inclination

3 bow, nod **4** bent, bias, lean, tilt, will
5 fancy, grade, pitch, slant, slope, taste,
trend **6** ascent, liking **7** descent, incline,
leaning **8** affinity, appetite, fondness,
gradient, penchant, soft spot, tendency,
velleity, weakness **9** affection **10** attachment, partiality, proclivity, propensity
11 disposition **12** predilection

incline

3 tip **4** bend, bias, cant, cast, heel, lean,
list, sway, tend, tilt, turn **5** grade, impel,
slant, slide, slope **6** affect, induce
7 dispose, leaning **8** gradient, persuade
9 influence, prejudice

inclined

3 apt **5** given, prone, raked **6** liable, likely,
minded **7** dipping, leaning, oblique,
sloping, tilting, willing **8** diagonal, pitching
11 predisposed
way: 4 ramp

include

5 admit, bound, cover **6** enfold, number,
take in **7** confine, contain, embrace,
enclose, receive, subsume **8** comprise,
encircle **9** encompass **10** comprehend
11 accommodate

inclusive

5 broad **6** global **7** general, overall
8 complete, sweeping **9** all-around,
embracive **11** compendious **12** encompassing, encyclopedic **13** comprehensive

incognito

6 veiled **7** cloaked **9** anonymous,
disguised **11** camouflaged

incognizant

7 unaware **8** ignorant **9** oblivious,
unknowing, unmindful, unwitting
10 unfamiliar, uninformed **11** unconscious
12 unacquainted

incoherent
5 loose 6 broken, raving 7 muddled,
unclear 8 confused 9 illogical
10 disjointed, disordered, irrational,
maundering, tongue-tied 11 unconnected,
unorganized 12 disconnected,
disorganized 13 discontinuous

incombustible
9 fireproof 10 unburnable 12 nonflam-
mable

income
4 gain, take 5 wages 6 profit 7 revenue
8 entrance, proceeds, receipts
9 emolument

incommode
3 irk, vex 5 annoy, upset 6 bother, burden,
hinder, plague, put out 7 disturb, perturb,
trouble 8 disquiet, distress, irritate
9 disoblige 10 disconcert

incommodious
7 awkward, cramped, crowded 8 confined
9 congested

incommunicable
8 reserved, taciturn 9 ineffable, withdrawn
11 unspeakable, unutterable
13 undescribable, unexpressible

incomparable
6 unique 7 supreme 8 peerless, singular,
ultimate 9 matchless, nonpareil,
paramount, unequaled, unmatched,
unrivaled 10 preeminent, surpassing,
unequalled, unrivalled 11 outstanding,
superlative, unequalable, unmatchable
12 transcendent, unparalleled 13 unsurpassable

incompatible
7 adverse, counter 8 contrary, opposite
9 dissonant, unmixable 10 discordant,
discrepant 11 conflicting, disagreeing,
uncongenial, unfavorable 12 antagonistic,
antithetical 13 contradictory,
unsympathetic

incompetence
9 unfitness 10 disability, ineptitude
12 fecklessness

incompetent
5 inept, unfit 6 clumsy 8 helpless,
inexpert, unfitted 9 incapable, maladroit,
unskilled 10 unequipped 11 inefficient,
unqualified

incomplete
4 part 5 short 6 broken, undone 7 partial,
sketchy 8 abridged, immature 9 truncated
10 unfinished 11 fragmentary

incompliant
5 rigid, stiff 6 mulish 7 defiant 8 perverse,
stubborn 9 obstinate, pigheaded, resistant,
unbending 10 bullheaded, headstrong,
inflexible, self-willed, unyielding 11 intractable 12 pertinacious, recalcitrant

incomprehensible
7 cryptic, obscure, unclear 8 abstruse,
baffling, esoteric 9 fantastic
10 fathomless, mysterious, mystifying,
unknowable 11 ungraspable
12 impenetrable, unfathomable,
unimaginable

inconceivable
10 improbable, unknowable 11 implausible, unthinkable 12 unbelievable,
unconvincing, unimaginable

in conclusion
6 lastly 7 finally

inconclusive
4 open 9 equivocal, uncertain, undecided,
unsettled 10 unfinished

incongruous
5 alien 6 absurd 7 foreign, variant
9 anomalous, dissonant 10 discordant,
discrepant, unsuitable 11 conflicting,
disagreeing 12 disconsonant

inconsequential
5 petty, small 6 measly, paltry 7 trivial
8 picayune, trifling 9 illogical, small-time
10 immaterial, irrelevant, negligible
11 impertinent, superficial, unimportant

inconsiderable
4 puny 5 minor, petty 6 meager, meagre,
paltry, scanty, skimpy, slight 7 scrimpy,
trivial 8 picayune, trifling 9 frivolous, small-
beer 10 negligible 11 unimportant

inconsiderate
4 rash 5 brash, hasty 6 unkind
8 careless, heedless, impolite, reckless
9 hotheaded, impulsive 10 ill-advised,
ungracious 11 precipitate, thoughtless
12 discourteous, uncharitable

inconsistent
6 fickle 8 contrary 9 dissonant, illogical,
mercurial 10 capricious, changeable,
discordant, discrepant 11 conflicting
13 contradictory

inconsolable
7 forlorn 8 desolate 9 heartsick
11 comfortless, heartbroken

inconspicuous
6 hidden, subtle 7 obscure 9 concealed
11 unobtrusive 12 unnoticeable

inconstant

6 fickle, untrue 7 erratic, mutable, protean, vagrant 8 unstable, unsteady, variable, volatile, wavering 9 changeful, faithless, fluctuant, irregular, mercurial, uncertain, unsettled 10 capricious, changeable, irresolute, perfidious, unfaithful 11 chameleonic, vacillating 13 temperamental

incontestable

4 sure 7 certain 8 absolute, clear-cut, ironclad, positive 9 apodictic, undoubted 10 conclusive, inarguable, undeniable 11 irrefutable, unequivocal 12 unassailable, undisputable 13 unimpeachable

incontinent

5 loose 6 wanton 9 dissolute 10 licentious, profligate 12 unrestrained

incontrovertible

4 sure 7 certain 8 absolute, clear-cut, definite, positive 10 conclusive, undeniable 11 irrefutable, unequivocal 12 undisputable

inconvenience

3 irk, vex 5 annoy 6 bother, meddle, put out 7 disrupt, disturb, trouble 8 handicap, vexation 9 aggravate, annoyance, disoblige 10 discomfort, discommode, disruption, exasperate 11 aggravation, awkwardness 12 disadvantage, discomfiture, exasperation 13 embarrassment

inconvenient

7 awkward, unhandy 8 annoying 10 bothersome, unsuitable 11 pestiferous, troublesome

incorporate

3 mix 4 form, fuse, join 5 blend, merge, unite 6 absorb, embody, imbibe, mingle 7 combine 8 organize 9 establish 10 amalgamate, assimilate

incorporeal

8 bodiless, formless 9 spiritual 10 discarnate, immaterial, unphysical 11 disembodied, nonmaterial, nonphysical 12 metaphysical 13 unsubstantial

incorrect

5 false, wrong 6 faulty, untrue 7 unsound 8 improper, specious 9 erroneous, imprecise 10 fallacious, inaccurate, unbecoming

incorrigible

6 unruly 8 depraved 9 incurable

10 delinquent, inveterate 11 unalterable 12 irredeemable

increase

3 add, eke, wax 4 gain, grow, hike, jump, plus, push, rise, teem 5 boost, build, mount, put up, raise, run up, surge, swarm, swell 6 accrue, amount, beef up, dilate, expand, extend, gather, growth, jack up, markup 7 accrual, advance, amplify, augment, burgeon, distend, enhance, enlarge, inflate, magnify, prolong, upsurge 8 addition, compound, escalate, flourish, heighten, lengthen, manifold, multiply, protract, snowball 9 accession, accretion, aggravate, expansion, extension, increment, inflation, intensify, pullulate, reinforce 10 accelerate, accumulate, aggrandize, appreciate, strengthen 11 enlargement 12 augmentation, breakthrough 13 amplification

incredible

7 amazing, awesome 8 unlikely 9 cockamamy, fantastic 10 astounding, cockamamie, far-fetched, impossible, improbable, outlandish, phenomenal, remarkable 11 astonishing, implausible 12 preposterous, unbelievable, unconvincing, unimaginable 13 extraordinary

incredulity

7 unfaith 8 distrust, mistrust, unbelief 9 disbelief, nonbelief, suspicion 10 skepticism

incredulous

6 show-me 7 dubious 8 doubting 9 quizzical, skeptical 10 suspicious 11 distrustful, mistrustful, questioning, unbelieving, unconvinced 12 disbelieving

increment

4 gain, hike, rise, step 5 raise 6 degree, growth 7 quantum 8 addition 9 accession, accretion 11 enlargement 12 augmentation

incriminate

6 accuse, charge 7 arraign, impeach 9 implicate

incrustation

4 film, rime, scab 5 scale 6 tartar 7 coating

incubus

5 demon, fiend 9 nightmare

inculcate

5 teach, train 6 impart 7 educate, implant, impress, instill

inculpable
4 pure 5 clean 8 innocent, spotless, virtuous 9 blameless, guiltless, righteous 10 impeccable

incumbent
7 leaning, resting 8 occupant, required 9 overlying 10 obligatory 12 officeholder

incur
7 acquire, bring on 8 contract

incurable
5 fatal 6 deadly, lethal 8 hopeless, terminal 9 immutable 11 immedicable, irreparable 12 irremediable, unchangeable 13 uncorrectable

incursion
4 raid 5 blitz, foray, sally 6 attack, sortie 7 assault 9 irruption

incus
4 bone 5 anvil

indebted
5 bound 7 obliged 8 beholden 9 obligated

indebtedness
3 due, IOU 7 arrears 9 arrearage, gratitude, liability 10 obligation 11 delinquency 12 thankfulness

indecent
4 blue, foul, lewd, racy 5 bawdy, dirty, gross, nasty 6 coarse, filthy, impure, risqué, smutty, vulgar 7 obscene, profane, raunchy 8 immodest, improper, off-color, unseemly, untoward 9 offensive 10 malodorous, scurrilous 12 scatological 13 objectionable

indecision
5 doubt 8 wavering 9 hesitancy 11 ambivalence, uncertainty, vacillation 12 equivocation, irresolution, shilly-shally

indecisive
5 vague 6 unsure 7 dubious, unclear 8 wavering 9 equivocal, tentative, uncertain, undecided, unsettled 10 irresolute 11 problematic, vacillating

indecorous
4 rude 5 gross, rough 6 coarse, vulgar 7 uncivil 8 impolite, improper, unseemly, untoward 9 graceless, irregular, offensive, tasteless, unrefined 10 unbecoming 11 ill-mannered, undignified 12 discourteous

indecorum
5 gaffe 6 breach 7 blooper, blunder, faux pas, offense 8 solecism 11 impropriety

indeed
4 amen 5 truly 6 really, surely, verily 8 forsooth, honestly 9 assuredly, certainly 10 positively, undeniably 11 doubtlessly, undoubtedly 13 unequivocally

indefatigable
6 dogged 8 tireless, untiring, vigorous 9 energetic, tenacious 10 persistent, relentless, unflagging, unwearying 11 unrelenting

indefensible
9 unguarded, untenable 10 assailable, vulnerable 11 unprotected 12 unforgivable, unpardonable 13 unjustifiable

indefinable
5 vague 7 elusive 9 uncertain 11 unspeakable, unutterable 13 undescribable

indefinite
4 wide 5 broad, loose, vague 7 endless, general, inexact, obscure, unclear, unfixed 8 infinite 9 ambiguous, boundless, imprecise, limitless, unbounded, uncertain, undefined, unlimited 10 indistinct, inexplicit, unmeasured, unspecific 12 inconclusive 13 indeterminate
pronoun: 3 all, any, few 4 each, many, most, none, some 6 anyone, nobody 7 anybody, several, someone 8 everyone, somebody 9 everybody

indehiscent fruit
3 key, nut 4 pepo 5 berry, grain, grape, melon 6 achene, loment, samara, squash 7 pumpkin 8 cucumber 9 caryopsis 10 schizocarp

indelible
4 fast 5 fixed 7 lasting 8 enduring 9 memorable, permanent 13 unforgettable

indelicate
3 raw 4 lewd, rude 5 crude, gross, rough 6 coarse, vulgar 7 uncouth 8 impolite, improper, tactless, unseemly, untoward 9 unrefined 10 unbecoming

indemnify
5 repay 6 secure 7 redress, requite 9 reimburse 10 compensate, recompense, remunerate

indemnity
6 amends 7 redress 8 requital, security 9 exemption, quittance, reprisals 10 protection, recompense, reparation 11 restitution 12 compensation, remuneration 13 fee-for-service

indentation
4 dent, nick 5 notch 6 dimple, recess
10 depression

indenture
4 nick 5 notch 8 contract 9 agreement
11 certificate

indentured
5 bound 10 controlled 11 apprenticed

independent
4 free 8 absolute, autarkic, separate
9 autarchic, sovereign 10 autonomous
11 self-reliant 13 self-contained

indescribable
11 unspeakable, unutterable 13 unexplainable

indestructible
7 lasting 8 enduring, immortal
9 permanent 12 imperishable,
irrefragable, unperishable

indeterminate
5 vague 9 imprecise, uncertain, unlimited

index
4 list, mark, sign 5 ratio, table 7 catalog,
symptom 8 classify, evidence, regulate
9 catalogue 11 systematize

India
bay: 6 Bengal
capital: 8 New Delhi
city: 5 Delhi 6 Bombay, Kanpur, Madras,
Mumbai, Nagpur 7 Chennai, Kolkata,
Lucknow 8 Calcutta 9 Ahmadabad,
Bangalore, Hyderabad
coast: 7 Malabar 10 Coromandel
European discoverer: 4 Gama (Vasco
da)
language: 5 Hindi
leader: 5 Nehru (Jawaharlal) 6 Gandhi
(Indira, Mohandas, Rajiv)
monetary unit: 5 rupee
mountain range: 7 Vindhya 9 Himalayas
neighbor: 5 Burma, China, Nepal
6 Bhutan 7 Myanmar 8 Pakistan
10 Bangladesh
pass: 5 Bolan, Gumal 6 Khyber
plateau: 6 Deccan
river: 5 Indus 6 Ganges, Yamuna
7 Krishna 11 Brahmaputra
sea: 7 Arabian

Indian
bread: 3 nan 4 naan 7 chapati
butter: 3 ghi 4 ghee
caste: 5 Sudra 6 Vaisya 7 Brahman
9 Kshatriya
female dancer: 8 bayadere
groom: 4 syce

harem: 6 zenana
instrument: 4 vina 5 sarod, sitar, tabla
7 tambura
lady: 4 bibi 5 begum 8 memsahib
nurse: 4 amah, ayah
outcast: 6 pariah
prince: 4 raja, rana 5 rajah 8 maharaja
9 maharajah
princess: 4 rani 5 begum, ranee
scholar: 6 pandit, pundit
screen: 6 purdah
seal, stamp: 4 chop
soldier: 4 peon 5 sepoy
teacher: 4 guru
viceroy: 5 nabob, nawab
weight unit: 3 ser 4 cash, dhan, pank,
pice, powe, rati, tank, tola 5 adpao, fanam,
hubba, masha, maund, pally, pouah, ratti
6 dhurra, pagoda, pollam 7 chinnam,
chittak

Indiana
capital: 12 Indianapolis
city: 4 Gary 6 Muncie 9 Fort Wayne,
South Bend 10 Evansville, Terre Haute
11 Bloomington
college, university: 6 DePauw, Purdue
9 Ball State, Notre Dame
nickname: 7 Hoosier (State)
river: 5 White 6 Wabash
state bird: 8 cardinal
state flower: 5 peony
state tree: 5 tulip

Indian, American
baby: 7 papoose
ball game: 8 lacrosse
carrier: 7 travois
Central and South American: 3 Ona
4 Cuna, Inca, Maya 5 Arara, Aztec, Carib,
Huave, Olmec, Yagua 6 Arawak, Aymara,
Jivaro, Omagua, Toltec, Yahgan
7 Chibcha, Quechua, Zapotec 8 Tarascan,
Yanomamo 10 Araucanian 11 Tupi-
Guaraní
food: 4 samp 6 maize 8 pemmican
home: 5 hogan, lodge, tepee 6 pueblo,
teepee, wigwam 7 wickiup
leader: 4 Popé 6 Wovoka 7 Cochise,
Osceola, Pontiac, Sequoia, Sequoya
8 Geronimo, Hiawatha, Powhatan,
Sequoyah, Tecumseh 9 Black Hawk,
Massasoit 10 Crazy Horse
11 Cornplanter, Sitting Bull
money: 6 wampum
North American: 3 Oto, Sac, Ute 4 Cree,
Crow, Erie, Hopi, Hupa, Iowa, Otoe, Pima,
Pomo, Sauk, Taos, Yuma, Zuni 5 Aleut,
Caddo, Creek, Haida, Huron, Kansa,
Kiowa, Maidu, Miami, Modoc, Omaha,
Osage, Sioux, Uinta 6 Apache, Cayuga,

Dakota, Lenape, Mandan, Micmac, Mohawk, Munsee, Navaho, Navajo, Nootka, Oglala, Ojibwa, Oneida, Paiute, Pawnee, Pueblo, Quapaw, Salish, Santee, Seneca, Siwash **7** Anasazi, Arapaho, Arikara, Bannock, Chilkat, Chinook, Choctaw, Dakotah, Esselen, Klamath, Kutenai, Mohican, Naskapi, Natchez, Ojibway, Pontiac, Shawnee, Tlingit **8** Cherokee, Cheyenne, Chippewa, Comanche, Delaware, Illinois, Iroquois, Kickapoo, Kwakiutl, Nez Percé, Onondaga, Powhatan, Seminole, Shoshoni **9** Blackfoot, Chickasaw, Menominee, Tsimshian, Tuscarora, Wampanoag, Winnebago **10** Assiniboin, Chiricahua, Gros Ventre, Potawatomi **11** Massachuset, Narraganset
pipe: 7 calumet
spirit: 5 totem **6** manitu **7** kachina, manitou

Indian paintbrush
8 hawkweed **10** painted cup

indicate
4 bode, hint, mark, mean, show **5** augur, imply, point, prove **6** attest, convey, denote, evince, import, reveal **7** bespeak, betoken, connote, display, exhibit, express, presage, signify, suggest **8** disclose, evidence, foretell, manifest, register **9** designate **10** foreshadow, illustrate **11** demonstrate

indication
3 cue **4** clue, hint, mark, sign **5** proof, token, trace **6** augury, signal **7** gesture, inkling, portent, symptom **8** evidence, reminder, telltale **9** testimony **10** expression, suggestion **13** fore-shadowing, manifestation

indicative
10 expressive, suggestive **11** evidentiary, symptomatic **12** illustrative **13** demonstrative

indicia
5 marks, signs **8** imprints, markings

indict
5 blame **6** accuse, charge **7** arraign, censure, impeach **9** criticize

indifference
6 apathy **9** aloofness, unconcern **10** detachment, dispassion **11** disinterest **12** carelessness, impartiality

indifferent
4 cold, cool, numb, so-so **5** aloof, blasé, stoic **6** casual, remote **7** average, neutral **8** careless, detached, mediocre, middling, moderate, ordinary, passable, unbiased, uncaring **9** apathetic, impartial, impassive, objective **10** nonchalant, unaffected **11** unconcerned, unemotional **12** uninterested, unprejudiced **13** disinterested, dispassionate

indigence
4 need, want **6** penury **7** poverty **9** neediness, pauperism, privation **11** deprivation, destitution

indigene
6 native **9** aborigine **10** aboriginal

indigenous
6 native **7** endemic, natural **10** aboriginal, congenital, connatural, unacquired **13** autochthonous

indigent
4 poor **5** broke, needy **9** destitute, penniless **11** impecunious, necessitous **12** impoverished

indigestion
9 dyspepsia, heartburn

indignant
3 mad **5** irate, riled, upset, vexed **6** galled, heated **7** annoyed **8** offended, outraged, provoked **9** affronted, irritated, resentful

indignation
5 pique **7** dudgeon **10** irritation, resentment

indignity
3 cut **4** slap **6** injury, insult, slight **7** affront, outrage **9** contumely, grievance **10** disrespect **11** humiliation **13** disparagement, embarrassment

indigo
4 blue **8** deep blue

indigo bird
5 finch **7** bunting

Indira's father
5 Nehru (Jawaharlal)

indirect
7 devious, oblique, vagrant, winding **8** circular, sidelong, tortuous **9** deceitful, underhand, wandering **10** backhanded, circuitous, collateral, meandering, roundabout **11** duplicitous, underhanded

indiscreet
5 gabby **6** unwise **7** foolish, gossipy **8** tactless **9** impolitic, imprudent, untactful **10** ill-advised **11** loose-lipped

indiscretion
4 slip **5** folly, gaffe, lapse **7** blunder, faux

pas, mistake, misstep 8 solecism
10 imprudence 11 impropriety

indiscriminate
5 mixed 6 hybrid, motley, random, varied
7 aimless, jumbled, vagrant 8 assorted,
careless 9 arbitrary, desultory, haphazard,
hit-or-miss, unplanned, wholesale
10 uncritical 11 promiscuous
12 conglomerate, multifarious, unrestrained
13 heterogeneous, miscellaneous

indispensable
5 basic, vital 6 needed 7 crucial, needful,
pivotal 8 cardinal, critical 9 essential,
necessary, requisite 10 imperative,
obligatory 11 fundamental

indisposed
3 ill 4 down, sick 5 loath 6 ailing, averse,
poorly, sickly, unwell 7 uneager 8 hesitant
9 reluctant, resistant, unwilling
11 disinclined

indisposition
6 malady 7 ailment, dislike, illness,
malaise 8 aversion, disfavor, distaste,
sickness, unhealth 10 affliction, reluctance

indisputable
4 sure, true 7 certain, evident, obvious
8 absolute, ironclad, positive 9 apodictic
10 undeniable 11 irrefutable, unequivocal
12 irrefragable, unassailable

indistinct
3 dim 4 hazy 5 faint, foggy, misty, murky,
vague 6 bleary, blurry, cloudy 7 blurred,
obscure, shadowy, unclear 8 confused
9 uncertain, undefined 12 undetermined

indistinguishable
4 same 5 alike, equal, vague 7 unclear
9 duplicate, identical 10 equivalent

indite
3 pen 5 write 6 record, scribe 7 compose,
engross 10 transcribe

individual
3 one 4 body, lone, self, sole, soul, unit
5 being, human, party, thing 6 entity,
mortal, person, proper, single 7 special
8 creature, discrete, distinct, peculiar,
personal, separate, singular, solitary,
specific 10 particular, respective
11 distinctive 13 idiosyncratic
combining form: 4 idio

individualist
5 loner 6 hermit 8 lone wolf, maverick
13 nonconformist

individuality
4 self 7 essence, oneness 8 identity,

selfhood 9 character 10 uniqueness
11 personality, singularity 12 idiosyncrasy,
separateness

individualize
4 mark 7 specify 9 customize
10 specialize 11 distinguish, personalize,
singularize 12 characterize
13 differentiate, particularize

Indochinese country
4 Laos 5 Burma 7 Myanmar, Vietnam
8 Cambodia, Thailand 9 Kampuchea

indoctrinate
5 teach, tutor 7 educate, program
8 convince, persuade 9 brainwash,
inculcate

indolence
4 laze 5 sloth 7 inertia, languor
8 idleness, laziness, lethargy 9 torpidity
12 slothfulness, sluggishness
13 shiftlessness

indolent
4 idle, lazy 6 torpid 8 fainéant, slothful,
sluggish 9 lethargic, shiftless

indomitable
7 staunch 9 steadfast 10 invincible,
unbeatable 11 impregnable 13 unconquerable

Indonesia
archipelago: 5 Malay
capital: 7 Jakarta 8 Djakarta
city: 5 Medan 7 Bandung, Cilacap
8 Semarang, Surabaja, Surabaya
9 Palembang
island group: 5 Sunda 8 Moluccas
language: 6 Bahasa
leader: 7 Suharto, Sukarno
monetary unit: 6 rupiah
regions: 4 Bali, Java 5 Ceram, Timor
6 Bangka, Borneo, Flores, Lombok,
Madura 7 Celebes, Sumatra 8 Sulawesi
9 Irian Jaya
volcano: 8 Krakatau, Krakatoa

indubitable
4 sure 6 patent 7 certain, evident, obvious
8 definite, ironclad, positive 9 apodictic,
veritable 10 undeniable 11 irrefutable,
self-evident, unequivocal 12 irrefragable

induce
5 cause 6 effect, elicit, prompt 7 actuate,
procure 8 convince, engender, generate,
motivate, occasion, persuade 9 encourage

inducement
4 bait, lure 6 come-on, motive
10 attraction, motivation 13 consideration

induct
4 lead 5 admit 6 enlist, enroll 7 appoint, install

inductance unit
5 henry

induction
8 entrance 9 accession, reasoning
10 enlistment 11 appointment
13 ratiocination

inductive
7 logical 9 prefatory, prelusive 11 a posteriori

indulge
3 pet 4 baby, bask 5 allow, favor, humor, spoil 6 cocker, coddle, cosset, oblige, pamper, permit, please, wallow 7 cater to, delight, gratify, satisfy 9 luxuriate
11 mollycoddle

indulgence
5 favor, mercy, treat 6 luxury 7 charity
8 clemency, courtesy, kindness, lenience, leniency 9 allowance, remission, tolerance
10 compassion, kindliness, permission, toleration 11 forbearance, forgiveness
12 dispensation, mercifulness 13 gratification

indulgence seller
5 Tezel (Johann) 6 Tetzel (Johann)

indulgent
4 easy, kind 7 clement, lenient
8 generous, merciful, tolerant 9 forgiving
10 charitable, permissive

indurate
6 harden 7 callous, confirm, congeal
8 hardened, solidify, stubborn 9 unfeeling
11 hard-hearted

industrialist
6 tycoon 7 magnate 12 manufacturer

industrious
4 busy 8 diligent, sedulous 9 assiduous, laborious

industry
4 work 5 labor 8 business, commerce
9 assiduity, diligence 10 enterprise

inebriant
see **intoxicant**

inebriate
3 sot 4 lush, soak 5 drunk, souse, tight, tipsy, toper 6 bibber, boozer 7 stupefy, tippler, tosspot 8 drunkard 10 intoxicate

inebriated
3 lit 5 drunk, lit up, oiled, stiff, tipsy
6 blotto, juiced, loaded, plowed, potted, soused, stewed, tanked, wasted
7 crocked, pickled, pie-eyed, sloshed, smashed 8 polluted 9 plastered

inedible
9 poisonous 12 unappetizing

ineffable
5 taboo 9 forbidden 11 unspeakable, unutterable 13 undescribable

ineffaceable
7 lasting 8 enduring 9 indelible, permanent

ineffective
4 vain, weak 6 futile 7 useless 8 abortive, bootless, feckless, impotent, useless
9 fruitless, powerless 10 emasculate, unavailing 12 unproductive, unsuccessful

ineffectiveness
8 futility 9 impotence

ineffectual
see **ineffective**

inefficient
5 slack 6 clumsy 8 careless, slipshod, wasteful 9 negligent

inelastic
5 rigid, stiff 7 brittle 9 unbending
10 unyielding

inelegant
5 crass, crude, gross, rough 6 coarse, gauche, vulgar 7 awkward, uncouth
9 graceless, unrefined 10 uncultured, ungraceful 12 uncultivated

ineligible
5 unfit 8 unfitted, unworthy 10 unequipped, unsuitable 11 unqualified
12 disqualified

ineluctable
4 sure 5 bound, fated 6 doomed 7 certain
8 destined 9 necessary 10 inevitable, unevadable 11 unavoidable, unescapable
13 unpreventable

inept
5 unfit 6 clumsy, gauche, klutzy 7 artless, awkward, foolish, halting, unhandy
8 bumbling, bungling 9 all thumbs, ham-handed, maladroit, unskilled
10 malapropos, unskillful, unsuitable
11 heavy-handed, undexterous, unfortunate

inequality
8 imparity **9** disparity **10** unevenness
12 irregularity, variableness
13 disproportion, heterogeneity

inequitable
6 biased, unfair, unjust **7** partial
10 prejudiced **11** unjustified, unrighteous

inequity
4 bias **5** wrong **9** prejudice **10** unfairness, unjustness

ineradicable
6 innate **7** chronic **8** constant, inherent, stubborn **9** ingrained **10** deep-rooted, deep-seated, entrenched, inveterate
11 established, ever-present, never-ending

inert
4 calm, dead, idle **5** quiet, still **6** asleep, sleepy **7** dormant, passive **8** immobile, lifeless, sluggish **9** apathetic, lethargic
10 motionless

inert gas
4 neon **5** argon, radon, xenon **6** helium
7 krypton

inertia
5 sloth **6** apathy, stupor, torpor **7** languor
8 idleness, laziness, lethargy **9** indolence, inertness, lassitude, passivity, torpidity
10 immobility, inactivity **11** disinterest
12 listlessness, sluggishness

inescapable
see **inevitable**

inessential
see **unessential**

inestimable
9 priceless **11** measureless **12** immeasurable, unmeasurable, unfathomable

inevitable
4 sure **5** bound, fated **6** doomed **7** certain
8 destined **9** necessary **11** unavoidable, unescapable **12** foreordained
13 unpreventable

inevitably
8 perforce **10** willy-nilly **11** like it or not, unavoidably

inexcusable
6 guilty **8** blamable, culpable **9** untenable
10 censurable **11** blameworthy, condemnable **12** criticizable, unforgivable, unpardonable **13** reprehensible, unjustifiable

inexhaustible
8 tireless, untiring **9** unfailing, weariless
10 bottomless, unflagging **13** indefatigable

inexorable
5 rigid **6** strict **7** adamant **8** immobile, obdurate, stubborn **9** immovable, unbending **10** relentless, unyielding
11 unrelenting

inexpensive
3 low **5** cheap **7** cut-rate **8** moderate
10 reasonable

inexperience
7 naïveté, rawness **8** verdancy
9 freshness, greenness **10** callowness

inexperienced
3 raw **5** fresh, green, naive, young
6 callow **7** untried **8** unversed **9** unskilled, untrained, unworldly **10** amateurish, unseasoned

inexpert
9 maladroit, unskilled, untrained
10 amateurish

inexplicable
6 arcane, obtuse, opaque **7** cryptic
9 enigmatic **10** mysterious, mystifying, unsolvable **11** undefinable
12 impenetrable, unfathomable
13 unaccountable, unexplainable

inexpressible
8 nameless **11** unspeakable, unutterable
13 undescribable, unexplainable

inexpressive
5 blank, stoic **6** stolid, vacant, wooden
7 deadpan **9** impassive **10** poker-faced
13 straight-faced

inextricable
9 insoluble **10** unsolvable

infallible
4 sure **5** exact **6** trusty **7** certain, correct, perfect **8** absolute, accurate, flawless, surefire, unerring **9** errorless, unfailing
10 dependable, impeccable **11** trustworthy
12 tried-and-true **13** unimpeachable

infamous
4 evil, vile **6** odious **7** hateful, heinous
8 flagrant, shameful **9** abhorrent, miscreant, nefarious, notorious
10 abominable, despicable, detestable, flagitious, scandalous, villainous
11 disgraceful, ignominious, opprobrious
12 contemptible, disreputable

infamy
5 odium, shame **7** obloquy **8** disgrace, dishonor, ignominy **9** disrepute, notoriety
10 opprobrium

infancy
8 babyhood   9 childhood

infant
4 babe, baby   5 bairn, child, green
7 bambino, neonate, newborn, papoose,
toddler   8 bantling, immature, nursling
9 unfledged
bed: 4 crib   6 cradle   8 bassinet
food: 3 pap   4 milk   7 pabulum
room: 7 nursery

infanta
8 princess

infantile
7 babyish, puerile   8 childish, immature

infantryman
7 dogface   8 doughboy   11 foot soldier
Algerian: 6 Zouave

infatuated
5 dotty, silly   7 foolish   8 besotted,
enamored, obsessed   9 bewitched,
rapturous   10 captivated, passionate

infatuation
4 rage   5 ardor, craze, crush, folly
7 passion, rapture   8 devotion
9 obsession, puppy love   11 fascination

infect
5 taint   6 defile, poison   7 corrupt, pollute
11 contaminate

infection
3 bug   6 sepses (plural), sepsis
fungous: 8 mycetoma

infectious
8 catching, epidemic, virulent   9 pestilent
10 contagious, corrupting
12 communicable   13 contaminating,
transmittable

infelicitous
5 unapt, unfit   6 unmeet   7 awkward,
unhappy   8 improper   9 imperfect
10 malapropos, unsuitable   11 regrettable,
unfortunate

infer
5 judge   6 deduce, deduct, derive, gather,
reason   7 collect, make out, suppose,
surmise   8 conclude, construe
10 conjecture   11 hypothesize

inference
7 surmise   8 illation, sequitur   9 deduction
10 assumption, conclusion, conjecture,
derivation   11 presumption, supposition

inferior
3 low   4 base, fair, hack, mean, poor, puny
5 cheap, lousy, lower, minor, petty, scrub,
sorry, under, worse   6 common, deputy,
feeble, impure, junior, lesser, nether, no-
good, paltry, satrap, shoddy, sleazy, tawdry,
tinpot, vassal   7 average, subject, unequal
8 declassé, low-grade, mediocre, middling,
ordinary, unworthy, wretched   9 attendant,
auxiliary, no-account, satellite, secondary,
subaltern, subjacent, underling, worthless
10 inadequate, second-rate
11 substandard
prefix: 3 sub   4 demi   5 infra

infernal
6 Hadean   7 hellish, satanic   8 chthonic,
damnable, demoniac, devilish, diabolic,
plutonic   9 chthonian, plutonian, Tartarean
10 diabolical, sulphurous

inferno
3 pit   4 fire, hell   5 Hades, Sheol   6 blazes,
Tophet   7 Gehenna   9 holocaust, perdition
10 underworld   11 netherworld
13 conflagration

Inferno
division: 5 canto
poet: 5 Dante (Alighieri)
verse form: 9 terza rima

infertile
6 barren, effete   7 sterile   8 impotent
10 unfruitful   12 hardscrabble, unproductive

infest
4 teem   5 beset, swarm   6 plague
7 overrun   10 parasitize

infidel
5 pagan   7 atheist, heathen, heretic,
skeptic   8 agnostic   10 unbeliever

infidelity
7 perfidy, treason   8 adultery, betrayal,
cheating   9 disbelief, treachery
10 disloyalty   13 faithlessness

infinite
4 vast   7 endless, eternal, immense
8 unending   9 boundless, countless,
limitless, perpetual, unlimited   11 everlasting, illimitable, measureless,
sempiternal   12 immeasurable

infinity
8 eternity   10 perpetuity   11 endlessness
12 sempiternity   13 boundlessness,
limitlessness

infirm
4 lame, sick, weak   5 frail   6 ailing, feeble,

sickly **7** failing, fragile, unsound
8 decrepit, unstable **9** doddering
11 debilitated

infirmity
3 ill **4** flaw **5** decay **6** malady **7** ailment,
disease, frailty, illness, malaise **8** debility,
disorder, sickness, syndrome, weakness
9 complaint, condition **10** affliction,
feebleness, sickliness **11** decrepitude
12 debilitation, enfeeblement

infix
4 root **5** embed, lodge **6** fasten, pierce
7 engrave, implant, impress

inflame
4 fire, gall, goad, rile, roil **5** anger, light,
rouse **6** arouse, enrage, excite, foment,
ignite, kindle, madden, redden, stir up
7 provoke **8** enkindle, irritate **9** aggravate
10 exacerbate, exasperate

inflammable
5 fiery **6** ardent **8** burnable, volatile
9 excitable, ignitable, irascible **11** combustible

inflammation
4 gout, sore **6** otitis, quinsy **7** catarrh,
colitis **8** adenitis, bursitis, cystitis, neuritis,
pleurisy, rachitis, swelling **9** arthritis,
chilblain, gastritis, laryngitis, nephritis,
phlebitis **10** bronchitis, cellulitis,
combustion, dermatitis, gingivitis, tendinitis
12 encephalitis **13** poliomyelitis
eye: 6 iritis **7** pinkeye **9** keratitis
horse: 7 fistula, quittor
intestines: 7 ileitis **9** enteritis
suffix: 4 itis

inflammatory
8 exciting **9** explosive, seditious
11 provocative **13** rabble-rousing,
revolutionary

inflate
4 fill **5** bloat, elate, swell **6** expand
7 amplify, distend **10** aggrandize

inflated
5 tumid, windy **6** turgid **7** bloated, swollen,
verbose **9** bombastic, distended, dropsical,
flatulent, overblown **10** heightened
11 exaggerated, pretentious

inflection
4 bend, tone **5** curve, pitch **6** accent,
change, stress, timbre **8** emphasis, tonality
9 accidence **10** modulation

inflexible
3 set **4** grim, hard, iron **5** fixed, rigid, stiff

6 strict **7** adamant, die-hard **8** granitic,
hard-line, immobile, ironclad, obdurate,
stubborn **9** immovable, immutable,
obstinate, steadfast, unbending
10 adamantine, brassbound, implacable,
rock-ribbed, unbendable, unyielding
11 unalterable, unrelenting
12 unchangeable **13** dyed-in-the-wool

inflict
5 visit, wreak **7** mete out, subject
8 dispense **10** administer

inflow
4 rush **7** arrival

influence
4 move, pull, sway **5** alter, bribe, clout,
force, impel, lobby, touch **6** affect, compel,
impact, modify, moment, strike, weight
7 command, control, impress, mastery
8 dominate, militate, persuade, prestige
9 authority, dominance

influenceable
8 gullible **9** malleable, receptive, tractable
11 persuadable, persuasible, suggestible

influential
6 potent **8** forceful, powerful **9** effective
10 persuasive **13** authoritative

influx
7 arrival **8** entrance, invasion **9** accession

inform
3 rat **4** blab, clue, leak, post, tell, warn
5 brief, edify, endow, endue, imbue, teach
6 advise, betray, fill in, impart, leaven,
notify, reveal, snitch, squeal, tattle, turn in,
update **7** animate, apprise, caution,
educate **8** acquaint, disclose, forewarn
9 advertise, enlighten **10** illuminate
11 familiarize

informal
6 casual, dégagé, folksy **7** natural,
offhand, relaxed **8** down-home, familiar,
laid-back **9** easygoing **10** colloquial,
unofficial **13** unceremonious

information
4 data, fact, lore, news, poop, word
5 scoop **6** advice, notice, skinny, wisdom
7 lowdown, tidings **9** knowledge
12 intelligence
secondhand: 7 hearsay

information bureau
abbreviation: 4 USIA, USIS

informative
8 edifying, exegetic **10** exegetical

11 educational, elucidative, explanatory
12 enlightening, illuminating

informed
4 wise 5 aware 6 au fait, versed
7 abreast, knowing 8 apprised, educated
9 au courant, cognizant 10 acquainted,
conversant 11 enlightened
13 knowledgeable

informer
3 rat, spy 4 fink, mole 5 stool 6 canary,
gossip, snitch 7 rat fink, stoolie, tattler,
tipster 8 squealer, telltale 10 deep throat,
talebearer, tattletale 11 stool pigeon
13 whistle-blower

infra
5 after, below, later, under 7 beneath

infract
3 sin 6 breach, offend 7 violate
8 trespass 10 contravene, transgress

infraction
3 sin 4 foul 5 crime, error 6 breach
7 faux pas, misdeed, offense 8 trespass
9 violation 12 encroachment
13 contravention, transgression

infrastructure
4 base 5 basis 9 framework 10 foundation,
groundwork, substratum 12 underpinning

infrequent
3 odd 4 rare 6 scarce, seldom 7 unusual
8 isolated, sporadic, uncommon, unwonted
10 occasional 11 exceptional

infringe
6 breach, impose, meddle, offend
7 disturb, obtrude, violate 8 encroach,
entrench, trespass 10 transgress

infuriate
3 ire, mad 4 rile 5 anger, pique 6 enrage,
madden, rankle 7 incense, inflame,
outrage, provoke, steam up

infuse
4 fill, soak 5 imbue, steep 6 leaven
7 animate, implant, pervade, suffuse
8 permeate, saturate 10 impregnate

ingenious
5 acute, canny, sharp, smart 6 adroit,
clever, crafty 7 cunning, fertile 8 creative,
original 11 imaginative, resourceful

ingenuity
5 knack, savvy, skill 6 acumen, smarts,
talent 7 know-how, mastery 8 deftness,
keenness 9 adeptness, handiness
10 adroitness, capability, cleverness,

perception, shrewdness 11 proficiency
12 intelligence, skillfulness
13 inventiveness

ingenuous
4 open 5 naive 6 simple 7 artless, natural
8 innocent 9 childlike, guileless, unstudied
10 unaffected

ingest
3 eat 4 feed 6 devour 7 consume,
partake, swallow

Inge work
6 Picnic 7 Bus Stop 18 Splendor in the
Grass 19 Come Back Little Sheba

inglorious
8 shameful 11 disgraceful, ignominious,
opprobrious 12 dishonorable, disreputable
13 discreditable, unrespectable

ingot
3 bar, rod 4 mold 6 billet

ingrained
6 innate 8 inherent 9 essential
10 congenital, deep-rooted, deep-seated

ingratiating
5 silky 6 silken, smarmy 7 fawning
8 pleasing, unctuous 9 adulatory
10 flattering 11 sycophantic

ingredient
4 part 5 piece 6 factor 7 element
9 component 11 constituent

ingress
4 door 5 entry 6 access, entrée, portal
7 doorway, passage 8 entrance, entryway
9 admission, vestibule 10 admittance
11 entranceway

ingurgitate
4 bolt, cram, gulp, slop, wolf 5 gorge, scarf,
stuff, swill 6 devour, gobble, guzzle
7 swallow

inhabit
4 live 5 dwell, haunt 6 occupy, people,
settle, tenant 8 populate

inhabitant
5 liver 6 inmate, native 7 citizen, denizen,
dweller, resider 8 indigene, resident
9 aborigine 10 autochthon
foreign: 5 alien
indigenous: 6 native 9 aborigine

inhale
7 breathe, consume, respire, swallow

inharmonious
6 atonal 7 jarring 9 dissonant, unmusical
10 discordant 11 cacophonous, conflicting,

conflictive, disagreeing, quarrelsome,
uncongenial 12 antagonistic

inhere
3 lie 5 dwell 6 belong, reside

inherent
4 born 5 basic 6 native 7 built-in,
connate, natural 8 immanent 9 elemental,
essential 10 congenital, deep-seated
11 fundamental

inherit
7 acquire, receive, succeed

inheritance
3 DNA 4 gene, gift 6 devise, estate,
legacy 7 bequest 8 heirloom, heritage
9 patrimony, tradition 10 birthright
13 primogeniture

inherited
6 native 7 connate, genetic, natural
10 bequeathed, congenital, connatural,
handed-down, hand-me-down

inheritor
4 heir 7 heiress, legatee 11 beneficiary

inhibit
4 curb, slow 5 check 6 arrest, bridle,
enjoin, fetter, hamper, hinder, hobble,
impede 7 prevent, repress, trammel
8 hold back, obstruct, restrain, suppress,
withhold 9 constrain 10 discourage

inhibition
4 curb 5 taboo 6 hang-up 7 barrier
9 hindrance, restraint, stricture
10 impediment, repression 11 suppression

inhuman
5 cruel, feral 6 brutal, savage 7 beastly,
bestial, brutish 8 fiendish 9 barbarous,
monstrous 10 diabolical

inhumane
4 fell, grim 5 cruel 6 brutal, fierce, malign,
savage 8 ruthless, sadistic 9 barbarous,
ferocious, heartless, merciless, truculent

inhumation
6 burial 9 interment, sepulture
10 entombment

inhume
4 bury 5 plant 6 entomb 7 put away 9 lay
to rest

inimical
7 adverse, harmful, hostile 10 malevolent,
unfriendly 11 belligerent, contentious
12 antagonistic, antipathetic

iniquitous
3 bad 4 base, evil, vile 5 wrong 6 sinful,
unjust, wicked 7 immoral, vicious
9 nefarious

iniquity
3 sin 4 evil 5 crime, wrong 7 offense
9 turpitude 8 trespass 10 immorality,
wickedness, wrongdoing 13 transgression

initial
5 first, prime 6 anlage, letter, maiden
7 approve, engrave, leading, opening,
primary 8 earliest, foremost, monogram,
original 9 beginning

initiate
4 open 5 begin, enter, set up, start
6 enroll, get off, induct, invest, launch, take
up 7 install, kick off, usher in 8 commence
9 originate 10 inaugurate

initiation
5 debut 7 baptism 9 admission, beginning,
induction 10 admittance 11 investiture,
origination 12 commencement,
introduction

initiative
4 push 5 drive, spunk 6 energy
8 ambition, aptitude, gumption 9 beginning
10 enterprise, get-up-and-go

inject
3 add 6 insert 7 implant, instill
9 inoculate, introduce, vaccinate

injection
3 fix 4 hypo, shot 5 serum 7 booster,
vaccine 10 hypodermic 11 inoculation,
vaccination

injudicious
4 rash 5 hasty 6 unwise 8 heedless,
reckless 9 ill-judged, impolitic, imprudent
10 ill-advised, indiscreet 11 inexpedient
12 shortsighted

injunction
3 ban, bar 4 writ 5 order 6 behest, charge
7 bidding, command, dictate, mandate
9 direction 11 prohibition

injure
3 mar 4 foul, harm, hurt, maim, pain
5 spoil, wound, wrong 6 blight, bruise,
damage, deface, deform, foul up, impair,
mangle 7 afflict, contort, cripple, disable,
torture 8 distress, maltreat, mutilate 9 disfigure 12 incapacitate

injurious
6 nocent 7 abusive, adverse, harmful,

hurtful **8** damaging **9** offensive
10 defamatory **11** detrimental

injury
3 ill **4** harm, hurt **5** wound, wrong
6 bruise, damage, trauma **8** distress
9 detriment

injustice
4 tort **5** crime, wrong **6** breach, damage
7 outrage **8** inequity, trespass
9 grievance, violation **10** favoritism,
wrongdoing

ink
3 dye, pen **4** sign **8** inscribe **9** autograph,
signature, subscribe

inkling
3 cue, tip **4** clue, hint, idea, lead, wind
5 hunch **6** notion, tip-off **8** telltale
9 suspicion **10** indication, intimation,
suggestion

inky
3 jet **4** ebon **5** black, ebony, jetty, raven,
sable **9** Cimmerian, pitch-dark **10** pitch-
black

inlaid
5 piqué **6** boolle **7** hatched **8** enchased,
nielloed **9** damascene, incrusted

Inland Empire
8 Illinois

inlet
3 arm, bay **4** cove, gulf **5** bayou, bight,
creek, fiord, firth, fjord, sound **6** harbor,
slough, strait **7** estuary
Admiralties: 4 Kali
Adriatic Sea: 5 Vlorë
Aegean Sea: 7 Saronic
Africa: 6 Walvis
Alaska: 4 Cook **5** Cross, Taiya **7** Glacier
8 Chilkoot
Aleutians: 5 Holtz, Nazan
Angola: 5 Bengo, Tiger **6** Tigres
Antarctica: 3 Ice **7** McMurdo
8 Amundsen **10** Shackleton
Arabian Sea: 4 Qamr **5** Kamar
Australia: 4 King **6** Botany **9** Discovery
10 Broad Sound
Baffin Bay: 8 Melville
Baffin Island: 9 Admiralty
Baltic Sea: 4 Hano **6** Danzig, Gdansk
9 Pomerania **10** Pomeranian
Barents Sea: 4 Kola **7** Pechora
Beaufort Sea: 7 Prudhoe **9** Mackenzie
Bismarck Sea: 5 Kimbe
Brazil: 9 Guanabara
Bristol Channal: 10 Carmarthen

California: 5 Morro **8** Monterey
Canada: 5 Fundy **9** Howe Sound
Cape Breton Island: 4 Mira
Caribbean Sea: 5 Limón
Central America: 7 Fonseca
Chile: 5 Otway
Crete: 4 Suda **5** Canea
Denmark: 4 Ise
Djibouti: 6 Tajura **8** Tadjoura
East River: 8 Flushing
Ecuador: 5 Manta
Eire: 4 Clew **7** Brandon
English Channel: 3 Tor
Florida: 5 Biscayne **10** Saint Lucie
Georgia: 8 Altamaha
Greenland: 6 Baffin
Gulf of Alaska: 3 Icy **5** Woman
12 Resurrection
Gulf of Mexico: 7 Aransas **8** Suwannee
9 Matagorda, Pensacola **10** Terrebonne
11 Atchafalaya **12** Apalachicola
Gulf of St. Lawrence: 5 Bonne
Hawaii: 11 Pearl Harbor
Honshu: 3 Ise **5** Owari **6** Atsuta
Hudson Bay: 7 Repulse
Iceland: 4 Axar, Eyja, Huna **5** Horna,
Skaga, Vopna **8** Hunafloi
Indonesia: 4 Bima **5** Saleh
Ionian Sea: 7 Taranto
Irish Sea: 4 Luce **7** Dundalk
Japan: 4 Tosa
Java: 4 Lada **5** Peper
Java Sea: 7 Batavia
Kara Sea: 6 Enisei **7** Yenisei
Labrador: 8 Hamilton
Lake Erie: 8 Put-in-Bay, Sandusky
Lake Huron: 7 Saginaw, Thunder
Lake Ontario: 11 Irondequoit
Lake Superior: 5 Huron **8** Keweenaw
9 Whitefish
Long Island: 8 Rockaway
Long Island Sound: 6 Oyster
Madagascar: 8 Antongil
Maine: 5 Casco **7** Machias
Maryland-Virginia: 10 Chesapeake
Massachusetts: 8 Buzzards, Plymouth
9 Annisquam
Massachusetts Bay: 10 Lynn Harbor
Mediterranean Sea: 8 Valencia
9 Famagusta **10** Khalij Surt **11** Syrtis Major
Mozambique: 5 Memba, Pemba
Nantucket Sound: 5 Lewis
Newfoundland: 4 Hare **5** White
7 Fortune
New Guinea: 3 Oro **5** Berau, Hansa
11 McCluer Gulf
New Jersey: 7 Raritan **8** Barnegat
9 Little Egg
New Zealand: 5 Hawke **6** Tasman

North Carolina: 9 Albemarle
Northern Ireland: 12 Belfast Lough
North Sea: 4 Lyse 9 Hardanger
Northwest Territories: 5 Wager
8 Bathurst, Franklin 9 Frobisher 12 Prince Albert
Norway: 3 Tys 4 Bokn, Tana 5 Lakse, Sogne
Norwegian Sea: 4 Nord, Salt, Stor, Vest
5 Ranen 8 Scoresby 9 Trondheim
Ontario: 4 Owen
Oregon: 4 Coos
Philippines: 5 Baler, Pilar, Sogod
6 Butuan 9 Davao Gulf, Leyte Gulf, Panay Gulf
Puget Sound: 4 Carr, Case
Quebec: 6 Ungava
Red Sea: 4 Foul
Rhode Island: 12 Narragansett
Russia: 5 Chaun 8 Sakhalin
Santo Cruz Islands: 8 Basilisk
Solomon Islands: 4 Deep 8 Huon Gulf
South Africa: 5 Table
South Carolina: 4 Bull
South China Sea: 4 Bias, Datu, Siam, Taya 5 Dasol, Subic, Subig 6 Brunei, Paluan 7 Camranh 8 Lingayen
Spain: 5 Cádiz
Spitsbergen: 3 Ice 4 Bell 5 Kings
Sumatra: 5 Bajur 10 Koninginne
Tyrrhenian Sea: 6 Naples 7 Paestum
Wales: 5 Burry
Washington: 5 Dabob 6 Skagit 11 Grays Harbor

inmate
7 convict 8 occupant, prisoner, resident
10 inhabitant

inmost part
4 core, pith 5 heart 6 center, depths, kernel, marrow 7 nucleus

inn
5 hotel, lodge, motel, serai 6 hostel, tavern
7 auberge, hospice, pension 8 hostelry
9 roadhouse 11 caravansary, public house
12 caravansarai 13 boardinghouse
German: 7 Gasthof 8 Gasthaus
Spanish: 5 fonda 6 posada 7 parador
Turkish: 6 imaret

innards
4 guts 5 belly 6 bowels, tripes 7 viscera
8 entrails, stuffing 10 intestines

innate
see **inherent**

inner
3 gut 5 focal 6 hidden, middle, secret
7 central, nuclear, private 8 familiar, interior, internal, personal, visceral
9 concealed, essential

innervate
4 jolt, move 5 pique, rouse 6 excite
7 animate, provoke, quicken 8 motivate, vitalize 9 electrify, galvanize, stimulate

Innisfail
4 Eire, Erin 7 Ireland

innkeeper
4 host 8 boniface, hosteler, hotelier, landlord, publican

innocence
6 purity 7 naiveté 8 chastity 10 simplicity
11 artlessness, sinlessness

innocent
4 good, lamb, naïf, pure, void 5 clean, legal, licit, naive 6 chaste, devoid, lawful
7 artless, natural, unaware 8 harmless, ignorant, virtuous 9 blameless, childlike, exemplary, faultless, guileless, guiltless, ingenuous, innocuous, righteous, stainless, unstained, unsullied, untainted
10 inculpable, legitimate 12 unsuspecting

innocuous
5 banal, bland 6 pallid 7 insipid
8 harmless 11 inoffensive, unoffending
13 insignificant

innovation
6 change 7 novelty

innovative
3 new 5 novel 8 creative, original
9 inventive 10 newfangled, trailblazing
11 cutting-edge, leading-edge

innovator
9 architect, developer 10 originator
11 trailblazer 13 revolutionary

innuendo
4 clue, hint, slur 7 calumny 8 allusion
9 aspersion 10 backbiting, intimation
11 implication, insinuation

innumerable
4 many 6 legion, myriad, untold
7 umpteen 9 countless, uncounted
10 numberless 13 multitudinous

Ino
brother: 9 Polydorus
father: 6 Cadmus
grandfather: 6 Agenor
husband: 7 Athamas
mother: 8 Harmonia
sister: 5 Agave 6 Semele 7 Autonoë
son: 8 Learchus, Palaemon 10 Melicertes

inobtrusive
5 muted, quiet 6 modest 7 subdued
8 discreet, tasteful 10 restrained

inoculate
5 imbue, shoot, steep 6 infuse 7 implant,
suffuse 9 vaccinate

inoffensive
5 bland 7 neutral 8 harmless
9 innocuous, peaceable

inopportune
8 ill-timed, mistimed, untimely 12 unseasonable

inordinate
5 undue 6 wanton 7 extreme 8 overmuch
9 excessive 10 exorbitant, gratuitous,
immoderate, irrational 11 extravagant,
intemperate, superfluous, uncalled-for
12 unreasonable 13 extraordinary

inorganic
7 mineral 10 artificial

in passing
5 aside 6 obiter 7 by the by 8 by the bye,
by the way 12 incidentally

in perpetuum
4 ever 6 always 7 forever, for good
8 evermore, for keeps 9 eternally
10 enduringly 11 forevermore

input
4 data 6 advice, energy 7 comment,
counsel, opinion 8 feedback, guidance,
material, stimulus 11 information

inquest
5 probe 7 hearing, inquiry 11 examination
13 investigation

inquietude
5 angst 6 unease, unrest 7 anxiety,
ferment, turmoil 8 distress 10 uneasiness
11 restiveness 12 restlessness 13 Sturm
und Drang

inquire
3 ask, pry 4 seek 5 probe, query
7 examine 8 question 9 catechize
11 interrogate, investigate

inquiry
5 audit, probe, query 7 hearing 8 grilling,
question, research, scrutiny
11 examination, questioning 13 investigation

inquisition
4 hunt 5 probe, quest, trial 6 search
7 inquiry 8 grilling, research 11 examination 13 interrogation, investigation

inquisitive
4 nosy 6 prying, snoopy 7 curious
8 meddling, snooping 9 intrusive
10 meddlesome 11 questioning

inquisitor
10 Torquemada (Tomás de)

in re
4 as to 5 about, as for 7 apropos 9 as
regards, regarding 10 as respects,
concerning, respecting 12 with regard to
13 with respect to

in respect to
see **in re**

inroad
4 raid 5 foray 7 advance 8 invasion
9 incursion 12 encroachment

ins and outs
5 ropes 6 quirks 7 details 8 minutiae,
oddities 11 incidentals, particulars 12 lay
of the land 13 peculiarities, ramifications

insane
3 mad, off 4 daft, nuts 5 batty, crazy, daffy,
dotty, loony, manic, nutsy, nutty, rabid, silly,
wacky 6 absurd, crazed, cuckoo, maniac,
raving, schizo, screwy, teched 7 berserk,
bonkers, cracked, haywire, lunatic, tetched,
touched, unsound 8 demented, deranged,
unhinged 9 eccentric, psychotic
10 disordered, irrational, moonstruck,
unbalanced 11 harebrained 12 crackbrained, preposterous, unreasonable

insane asylum
6 bedlam 8 loony bin, madhouse,
nuthouse, snake pit 10 sanatorium,
sanitarium

insanity
5 folly, mania 6 frenzy, lunacy 7 madness
8 delirium, delusion, dementia, hysteria,
illusion 9 craziness, dottiness, psychosis
11 derangement, psychopathy

insatiable
6 crying, greedy, urgent 7 exigent
8 pressing, ravenous 9 clamorous,
demanding, voracious 10 quenchless
11 importunate 12 unappeasable,
unquenchable

inscribe
4 etch, list 5 carve, enter, print, write
6 enroll, record 7 engrave, engross,
impress, imprint 8 dedicate, enscroll,
register

inscription
5 title 6 legend 7 epigram, epitaph,
heading 8 epigraph 10 dedication

inscrutable
6 arcane 7 deadpan 10 mysterious, poker-faced, sphinxlike, unknowable, unreadable 12 impenetrable, unfathomable

insect
3 bee, bug, fly 6 beetle
adult: 5 imago
antenna: 4 palp 6 feeler, palpus
butterfly:
(see **butterfly** entry)
covering: 6 chitin
immature: 4 grub, pupa 5 larva, nymph 6 larvae (plural), maggot 8 wriggler 9 chrysalis 11 caterpillar
kind: 3 ant, bee 4 flea, moth, wasp 5 aphid, scale 6 bedbug, beefly, beetle, cicada, earwig, hornet, mantid, mantis, mayfly 7 ant lion, cricket, firefly, June bug, katydid, ladybug, termite 8 honeybee, horsefly, housefly, lacewing, mosquito, stinkbug 9 bumblebee, butterfly, damselfly, dragonfly 10 silverfish, springtail 11 grasshopper 12 walkingstick
luminous: 5 firefly 8 glowworm
molt: 7 ecdysis
moth: 4 luna 5 gypsy 6 miller, sphinx 7 noctuid, pyralid, tortrix, tussock 8 cecropia, cinnabar, forester, sphingid 9 clearwing, geometrid, saturniid, tortricid 10 Polyphemus
multi-legged: 8 diplopod 9 centipede, millipede
part: 4 palp 5 cerci (plural) 6 cercus, labium, labrum, ocelli (plural), palpus, thorax 7 antenna, maxilla, ocellus 8 antennae (plural), mandible, maxillae (plural) 9 proboscis, spiracles 10 ovipositor 11 exoskeleton
pest: 4 flea, lice (plural), mite 5 louse, midge, scale 7 blowfly, termite 8 horsefly, housefly, mealybug 9 cockroach, gypsy moth 10 boll weevil, Hessian fly, silverfish
science: 10 entomology
winged: 5 alate
wingless: 4 flea, lice (plural) 5 louse 8 firebrat 10 silverfish, springtail 11 bristletail

insecticide
3 DDT 5 mirex, naled 6 aldrin, endrin 7 lindane, phorate 8 carbaryl, dieldrin, rotenone 9 chlordane, malathion, parathion 10 permethrin

insecure
5 shaky 6 unsafe, unsure, wobbly 7 anxious 8 unstable 9 uncertain 10 precarious 11 unconfident 12 apprehensive

inseminate
7 implant, instill 9 fertilize, pollinate 10 impregnate

insensate
4 dull, hard, numb 5 stony 6 brutal, numbed 7 callous 8 comatose 9 bloodless, heartless, impassive, unfeeling

insensibility
4 coma 6 apathy, torpor 8 lethargy, stoicism 12 indifference

insensible
4 cold, dead, dull, hard, numb, rapt 5 stoic 6 asleep, intent, numbed, obtuse, stolid 7 callous 8 absorbed, comatose, deadened, hardened, obdurate 9 apathetic, bloodless, engrossed, impassive, unfeeling 11 unconscious 12 anesthetized

insensitive
4 dull, hard, numb, rude 5 crass 6 numbed, obtuse, unkind 7 callous 8 benumbed, deadened, hardened, tactless, uncaring 9 bloodless, heartless, unfeeling 10 anesthetic, impassible 11 indifferent, unconcerned 12 anesthetized, unresponsive

insert
5 enter 7 implant, obtrude 9 interpose 10 interleave 11 intercalate, interpolate

insertion
8 addendum, addition 11 interpolation

in short
7 briefly, tersely 9 concisely 10 succinctly

inside
6 closet, secret, within 7 private 8 hush-hush, interior 12 confidential
combining form: 4 endo

insidious
3 sly 4 foxy, wily 6 artful, crafty, subtle, tricky 7 cunning, gradual 8 creeping, guileful 9 deceitful 13 surreptitious

insight
6 acumen, aperçu, wisdom 8 sagacity, sapience 9 intuition 11 discernment, penetration 13 understanding

insightful
4 keen, sage, wise 7 gnostic, knowing 9 intuitive, sagacious 10 discerning, perceptive 11 penetrating

insignia
4 mark, sign 5 badge 6 emblem
8 brassard 10 decoration

insignificant
4 puny 5 dinky, minor, petty, small
6 casual, little, minute, paltry 7 minimal,
trivial, nugatory, trifling 9 secondary,
small-time 10 negligible 11 minor-league,
unimportant

insincere
5 false, lying, phony 6 double, forced,
hollow, shifty, tricky 7 feigned 8 mala fide,
slippery, spurious 9 deceitful, deceptive,
dishonest, pretended, simulated 10 left-
handed, mendacious, untruthful 11 dissembling, double-faced 12 hypocritical

insinuate
4 hint 5 imply 6 inject, insert, work in,
worm in 7 implant, instill, suggest
9 introduce

insipid
3 dry 4 arid, dull, flat, mild, pale, thin, weak
5 banal, bland, vapid 6 jejune, watery
7 mundane, prosaic, subdued, tedious
8 bromidic, lifeless, ordinary 9 innocuous,
tasteless 10 flavorless, monotonous,
namby-pamby, wishy-washy 11 commonplace

insist
4 hold 5 argue, claim, swear 6 affirm,
assert, demand, stress 7 certify, contend,
declare, require, testify 8 maintain

insistent
6 crying, dogged, urgent 7 adamant,
burning, clamant, exigent 8 emphatic,
forceful, pressing, resolute 9 assertive,
clamorous, obtrusive 10 determined,
imperative, relentless 11 persevering

insolence
4 gall, guff, sass 5 brass, cheek, nerve
8 audacity, boldness, chutzpah, contempt,
rudeness 9 arrogance, impudence
10 brazenness, disrespect, effrontery
11 haughtiness, presumption
12 impertinence

insolent
4 bold, flip, pert, rude 5 cocky, lofty, sassy,
saucy 6 brazen, cheeky 7 haughty, uncivil
8 arrogant, cavalier, flippant, impolite,
impudent, superior 9 audacious,
barefaced, bold-faced 10 disdainful,
peremptory 11 impertinent, overbearing
12 contumelious, discourteous,
supercilious 13 high-and-mighty

insouciance
6 aplomb 9 disregard, unconcern
10 breeziness 11 disinterest, nonchalance
12 carelessness, heedlessness,
indifference

insouciant
4 airy, flip 6 blithe, breezy, casual, jaunty
8 carefree, flippant, heedless 9 easygoing
10 nonchalant, untroubled 11 indifferent,
thoughtless, unconcerned 12 devil-may-
care, happy-go-lucky, lighthearted

inspect
3 con, vet 4 scan, view 5 audit, check,
probe, study 6 review, size up, survey
7 canvass, examine, observe 8 appraise,
check out, look over, question 9 check
over 10 scrutinize 11 investigate

inspiration
4 muse 6 animus, genius, vision 7 insight
8 afflatus 9 brainwave, influence
10 brainchild, brainstorm, creativity
13 enlightenment

inspire
4 fire, stir 5 elate, exalt, imbue, rouse
6 arouse, excite, foment, incite, prompt,
strike 7 animate, enliven, impress, instill,
quicken 8 motivate 9 encourage,
galvanize, influence, stimulate
10 exhilarate

inspiring
6 moving 7 awesome, rousing 8 exalting
stirring 9 animating, uplifting 10 vitalizing

inspirit
4 fire, lift, spur, stir 5 cheer, exalt, excite,
liven, rally, rouse, spark, steel 6 arouse,
incite, kindle, revive, uplift, vivify
7 animate, comfort, console, delight,
enliven, gladden, hearten, nourish,
quicken, refresh, restore 8 activate,
embolden, energize, revivify, vitalize
9 encourage, stimulate 10 invigorate,
strengthen

instability
8 fluidity 9 shakiness 10 insecurity,
volatility 11 inconstancy 12 unsteadiness

install
4 seat, vest 5 put in, set up 6 induct,
invest 8 ensconce, enthrone, entrench
9 establish

instance
4 case, cite, item 6 detail, ground, reason,
sample 7 example 8 specimen
10 particular 12 illustration

instant
3 sec 4 wink 5 flash, jiffy, point, shake, trice 6 moment, second, urgent 7 current, exigent, present 8 existent, occasion, pressing 9 heartbeat, immediate, insistent, twinkling 10 imperative, present-day

instantaneous
4 fast 5 quick, rapid 9 immediate, ligntning, momentary 11 hair-trigger, split-second

instanter
3 now 6 at once 8 directly 9 forthwith, right away 11 immediately

instantly
3 now 6 at once 8 directly 9 forthwith, right away 11 immediately

instead
4 else 6 in lieu, rather 11 alternately 13 alternatively

instigate
4 abet, fire, goad, plan, plot, prod, spur, urge 5 egg on, impel, raise 6 excite, foment, incite, stir up, whip up 7 provoke, suggest 8 motivate 9 stimulate 10 bring about

instill
5 imbue 6 impart, infuse, inject 7 implant, suffuse 8 engender 9 inculcate, introduce

instinct
4 nose 5 hunch, sense 7 feeling, impulse 8 aptitude, behavior 9 intuition 10 proclivity, sixth sense 11 gut reaction

instinctive
3 gut 6 inborn, innate, normal 7 natural 8 habitual, inherent, visceral 9 automatic, ingrained, intrinsic, intuitive, reflexive, unlearned 10 congenital, unprompted 11 involuntary, spontaneous, unmeditated

instinctual
6 reflex 7 natural, routine 8 habitual, knee-jerk, untaught 9 automatic, impulsive, intuitive, reflexive 10 mechanical, unthinking 11 involuntary, spontaneous, unconscious

institute
5 begin, found, set up, start 6 decree, launch, ordain 7 academy, pioneer, usher in 8 initiate, organize 9 establish, introduce, originate 10 inaugurate 12 organization

institution
4 firm, rite 5 habit 6 custom 9 enactment 10 foundation 13 establishment

kind:
6 asylum, school 7 academy, college 8 hospital 10 sanatorium, sanitarium, sanitorium, university

instruct
4 show 5 coach, drill, guide, order, steer, teach, train, tutor 6 direct, enjoin, inform, school 7 apprise, command, counsel, educate, lecture 9 enlighten, prescribe

instruction
5 drill 6 advice, lesson 7 precept 8 coaching, guidance, teaching, training, tutelage 9 catechism, education, schooling 10 directions
place of: 6 school 7 academe, academy, college 10 university

instructive
8 didactic, edifying, pedantic 9 pedagogic 11 educational, explanatory, explicative, informative 12 enlightening

instructor
3 don 4 guru 5 coach, guide, swami, tutor 6 mentor 7 teacher, trainer 8 educator, lecturer 9 pedagogue, preceptor

instrument
4 deed, gear, mean, tool 5 agent, means, organ 6 agency, device, gadget, medium 7 utensil, vehicle 9 apparatus, appliance, machinery, mechanism 11 contraption, contrivance 13 paraphernalia
aircraft: 5 radar, radio 7 compass 9 altimeter, gyroscope 10 altazimuth, tachometer 11 transponder
calculating: 6 abacus 8 computer 9 slide rule
graphic: 6 camera 8 otoscope 9 telescope 10 binoculars, microscope 11 fluoroscope, stethoscope, stroboscope 12 bronchoscope, oscilloscope, spectrograph, spectroscope
measuring: 4 gage 5 clock, gauge, radar, scale, sonar 7 alidade, ammeter, balance, caliper, sextant, transit 8 quadrant 9 altimeter, astrolabe, barometer, bolometer, manometer, pedometer, sonometer, voltmeter 10 anemometer, Fathometer, hydrometer, hygrometer, micrometer, radiometer, radiosonde, spirometer, tachometer, theodolite 11 chronometer, lie detector, range finder, seismograph, speedometer, thermometer 12 electroscope, galvanometer, oscillograph, oscilloscope 13 Geiger counter, potentiometer
medical: 6 lancet, trocar 7 curette, forceps, specula (plural) 8 tenacula (plural) 9 tenaculum

radiation-producing: **5** laser, maser
(see also **implement; musical
instrument; tool**)

instrumental
5 vital **6** useful **7** crucial, helpful
9 conducive, essential, necessary, requisite
10 imperative **13** indispensable

instrumentality
5 agent, force, means, organ **6** agency,
energy, medium **7** channel, vehicle
8 ministry **9** mechanism

insubordinate
6 unruly **8** factious, mutinous **9** fractious,
seditious **10** headstrong, rebellious,
refractory **11** disobedient, intractable,
uncompliant **12** contumacious, recalcitrant,
ungovernable

insubstantial
4 airy, weak **5** frail **6** feeble, flimsy
7 fragile, tenuous **8** bodiless, ethereal
9 imaginary, unfleshly **10** intangible
11 disembodied **12** apparitional

insufferable
10 unbearable **11** intolerable, unendurable
13 insupportable

insufficiency
4 lack **6** dearth **7** paucity, poverty
8 scarcity, shortage **10** deficiency,
inadequacy, scantiness, scarceness
11 defalcation

insufficient
5 scant **6** scanty, scarce, skimpy
7 lacking, wanting **10** inadequate,
incomplete

insular
5 local **6** narrow **7** bigoted, limited
8 confined, isolated, secluded **9** illiberal,
parochial, sectarian, small-town
10 prejudiced, provincial, restricted

insulate
6 cut off, enisle **7** isolate **8** close off
9 segregate, sequester

insult
4 gibe, jeer, mock, slap, slur **5** abuse, fleer,
scoff, scorn, shame, sneer, taunt
6 debase, deride, offend, revile **7** affront,
disdain, obloquy, offense, outrage
8 derision, disgrace, ignominy, ridicule
9 contumely, humiliate **10** opprobrium
12 vituperation

insurance
8 guaranty, warranty **10** protection

agency: **7** actuary **8** adjuster
11 underwriter
term: **6** policy **7** annuity **8** coverage
9 bordereau **11** beneficiary

insure
5 cinch, guard **6** shield **7** confirm, protect
9 guarantee, safeguard **10** underwrite

insurgent
5 rebel **6** anarch **8** factious, frondeur,
mutineer, mutinous, revolter **9** anarchist,
seditious **10** incendiary, rebellious
12 contumacious **13** insubordinate,
revolutionary

insurrection
4 coup **6** mutiny, putsch, revolt, rising
8 uprising **9** rebellion

insurrectionist
5 rebel **6** anarch **8** frondeur, mutineer,
revolter **10** malcontent

insusceptible
6 exempt, immune **9** resistant
10 impervious **11** unreceptive

intact
5 sound, whole **6** entire, unhurt, virgin
7 perfect **8** complete, unbroken, unmarred,
virginal **9** undamaged, uninjured,
untouched **10** unimpaired

intangible
4 airy **5** vague **7** elusive, ghostly
8 ethereal **10** evanescent, immaterial,
impalpable **11** incorporeal

integer
4 unit **5** digit **6** entity, figure, number
7 numeral **11** whole number

integral
4 full **5** whole **6** entire **7** perfect
8 complete, inherent **9** composite,
elemental, essential, necessary, requisite
11 constituent **13** indispensable

integrate
3 mix **4** fuse, join, link **5** blend, merge,
unify, unite **6** embody, mingle **7** combine,
conjoin **8** coalesce **9** harmonize, reconcile
10 amalgamate, assimilate, coordinate,
synthesize **11** consolidate, desegregate

integrity
5 honor **6** virtue **7** honesty, probity
8 cohesion **9** coherence, constancy,
rectitude, soundness, wholeness
12 completeness

integument
4 coat **5** testa **7** coating, cuticle
8 covering, envelope

intellect

intellect
3 wit 4 mind 5 brain 6 acumen, brains,
genius, reason, smarts 9 intuition,
mentality 12 intelligence
13 comprehension, understanding

intellectual
5 brain 6 brainy, mental, pundit 7 bookish,
egghead, erudite, psychic, thinker
8 academic, cerebral, highbrow, longhair
9 scholarly

intelligence
3 wit 4 dope, info, mind, news, word
5 brain, savvy, sense 6 acuity, acumen,
brains, notice, reason, smarts, wisdom
7 hearsay, tidings 8 aptitude, judgment,
learning, sagacity 9 knowledge, mentality,
mother wit 10 brainpower, shrewdness

intelligent
4 keen, wise 5 acute, alert, aware, quick,
sharp, smart, sound 6 adroit, astute,
brainy, bright, clever, shrewd 7 cunning,
knowing, logical 8 rational, sensible
9 brilliant, ingenious, sagacious
10 reasonable 11 quick-witted, ready-
witted 13 perspicacious

intelligentsia
7 clerisy 8 literati, vanguard 10 avant-
garde, illuminati

intelligible
5 clear, lucid, plain

intemperance
6 excess 7 license 9 depravity
10 debauchery, profligacy 11 dissipation,
drunkenness 12 immoderation,
incontinence

intemperate
5 harsh 6 bitter, brutal, severe 7 drunken,
extreme, violent 8 bibulous 9 crapulous,
dissipated, dissolute, excessive
10 exorbitant, gluttonous, immoderate,
inordinate, profligate 12 unrestrained
13 overindulgent

intend
3 aim, try 4 mean, plan 5 essay, spell
6 assign, denote, design, scheme, strive
7 attempt, connote, propose, purpose,
signify 8 endeavor 9 designate

intended
6 fiancé 7 engaged, fiancée 8 destined,
plighted, promised, proposed 9 affianced,
betrothed 10 calculated, deliberate

intense
4 keen 5 acute, vivid 6 ardent, fervid,
fierce, severe, strong 7 extreme, fervent,
furious, violent, zealous 8 powerful,
vehement 9 assiduous, excessive,
exquisite 10 heightened 12 concentrated

intensify
4 rise 5 mount, rouse 6 accent, heat up,
stress 7 enhance, sharpen 8 escalate,
heighten, increase, redouble 9 aggravate,
emphasize 10 accentuate, aggrandize,
exacerbate 11 concentrate

intensity
6 energy, fervor 7 passion 8 emphasis,
ferocity, fervency, loudness 9 vehemence

intensive
6 all-out 7 zealous 8 sweeping, thorough
10 exhaustive 12 concentrated
pronoun: 6 itself, myself 7 herself,
himself 8 yourself 9 ourselves
10 themselves, yourselves

intent
3 aim, set 4 goal, plan, rapt, will 5 eager,
fixed 6 design, import, object 7 decided,
earnest, engaged, meaning, purport,
purpose, riveted, wrapped 8 absorbed,
conation, decisive, diligent, immersed,
resolute, resolved, sedulous, volition
9 engrossed, objective, wrapped up
10 determined

intention
3 aim, end 4 goal, hope, plan, wish
6 design, desire, object 7 meaning,
purpose 8 ambition 9 objective
10 aspiration

intentional
5 meant 7 advised, studied, willful, willing,
witting 8 designed, proposed 9 voluntary
10 considered, deliberate 12 premeditated

intentionally
9 on purpose, purposely

inter
4 bury 5 plant 6 entomb, inhume 9 lay to
rest

interact
9 cooperate 11 collaborate

interbreed
5 cross 9 hybridize 10 mongrelize

intercede
6 step in 7 mediate 9 arbitrate

intercept
4 grab 5 catch, seize, steal 6 cut off,
hijack

intercessor
5 agent 6 broker 8 advocate, mediator
9 go-between, middleman

interconnect
4 join, link 5 unite 6 couple, hook up, link
up

intercourse
5 trade, truck 7 contact, dealing, traffic
8 business, commerce, dealings
9 communion 10 connection, networking
11 give-and-take 12 conversation
13 communication

intercross
9 hybridize 10 mongrelize

interdict
3 ban, bar 4 veto 5 block, taboo 6 cut off,
enjoin, forbid, outlaw 7 censure, condemn,
embargo 8 disallow, prohibit, sanction
9 proscribe 11 prohibition

interest
4 gain, grab, hook, lure, pull 5 pique,
stake, tempt 6 appeal, arouse, behalf,
engage, profit, regard 7 attract, concern,
engross, involve, welfare 8 appeal to,
intrigue 9 attention, curiosity, fascinate,
tantalize, well-being 10 prosperity

interested
4 rapt 5 drawn 7 curious, partial
8 invested, partisan 9 attentive

interface
3 GUI 6 border 8 boundary 9 cooperate
11 communicate

interfere
6 butt in, horn in, meddle, step in 7 barge
in, intrude

interim
3 gap 5 break, pause 6 acting, breach,
hiatus, lacuna, pro tem 7 stopgap, time-out
8 downtime, meantime 9 makeshift,
temporary 10 pro tempore 11 provisional

interior
3 gut 4 pith 5 belly, bosom, heart, inner
6 center, inland, inside, inward, marrow
8 visceral 9 heartland 10 hinterland

interject
3 add 6 fill in, insert 7 throw in

interjection
agreement: 4 amen 5 roger 6 righto
7 right on
attention-getter: 3 hey 4 ahem, ahoy,
psst 6 yoo-hoo
calling pigs: 5 sooey

cheer: 3 rah 5 wahoo 6 hooray, hurrah,
hurray
contempt: 4 pooh 5 pshaw
disappointment: 4 rats 5 shoot 6 shucks
disapproval: 3 boo, fie
disbelief: 3 huh
disgust: 3 bah, boo, pah, ugh 4 rats, yuck
5 faugh, yecch 6 phooey
dismay: 4 oh no, uh-oh
dismissal: 3 git 4 shoo
farewell: 3 bye 4 ciao 5 adios 6 bye-
bye, so long 7 cheerio
greeting: 4 ciao 5 aloha, hello, howdy
in golf: 4 fore
in hunting: 6 yoicks
in marching: 3 hup, hut
joy: 4 whee 6 hooray, hurrah, hurray,
yippee 7 hosanna, whoopee 8 alleluia
10 hallelujah
mild apology: 4 oops 6 whoops
mild oath: 3 gad 4 darn, drat, egad, geez,
gosh, heck, jeez 5 egads, golly, zooks
6 jiminy, zounds 7 begorra, gee whiz,
jeepers 8 gadzooks 13 gee whillikers
O.K.: 5 roger, wilco
pain: 4 ouch
peace: 6 shalom
regret: 3 woe 4 alas 5 alack 8 lackaday
relief: 4 phew
request: 7 prithee
silence: 3 shh
sneeze: 5 achoo 6 atchoo 7 kerchoo
sorrow: 4 alas 5 alack 8 lackaday
stop: 4 whoa
surprise: 3 aha, huh, oho, wow 4 gosh,
oops 5 blimy, yikes, yipes, zowie 6 blimey
to a horse: 4 whoa 7 giddyap
toast: 5 salud, skoal 6 cheers, prosit
6 l'chaim 7 l'chayim
triumph: 3 aha, hah 6 eureka
(see also **exclamation**)

interlace
3 mix 5 braid, plait, twine, weave
7 entwine 9 alternate

interlard
3 mix 6 mingle

interlocuter
4 host 5 emcee

interlope
6 butt in, horn in, meddle 7 intrude
8 encroach, infringe 9 interfere

interlude
4 halt, lull, rest 5 break, idyll, letup, pause,
spell 6 recess 7 episode, respite
8 breather, entr'acte, meantime, stoppage
9 meanwhile 10 suspension

intermediary
3 mid 4 mean 5 agent, envoy, organ
6 agency, broker, center, medium, middle,
midway 7 central, channel, vehicle
8 delegate, emissary, mediator, ministry
9 go-between, middleman

intermediate
3 mid 4 fair, mean, so-so 6 broker, center,
medium, middle, midway, step in
7 average, between, central 8 middling
9 arbitrate, go-between, middleman

intermediator
6 broker 7 liaison, referee 9 go-between,
middleman

interment
6 burial 9 sepulture 10 inhumation

intermesh
4 lock 6 engage 8 dovetail

interminable
7 endless, eternal, lasting 8 constant,
infinite, unending 9 boundless, ceaseless,
continual, limitless, permanent, perpetual,
unceasing 10 protracted 11 everlasting,
never-ending

intermission
4 lull, rest, stop 5 break, pause, spell
6 recess 7 latency, respite, time-out
8 abeyance, dormancy, interval
10 quiescence, suspension 11 parenthesis

intermit
4 halt, stay 5 break, defer, delay 6 arrest,
hold up, put off 7 suspend 8 postpone,
prorogue 9 interrupt 11 discontinue

intermittent
6 broken, cyclic, fitful, serial 8 cyclical,
metrical, periodic, seasonal, sporadic
9 irregular, recurrent, recurring, spasmodic,
stop-and-go 10 occasional

intermix
4 meld 5 blend 6 mingle 8 comingle,
compound 9 commingle, integrate
10 amalgamate 11 intermingle

intermixture
4 brew 5 blend 7 amalgam 8 compound
9 composite, synthesis 12 amalgamation
13 miscegenation

intern
4 jail 6 immure 7 confine, impound, put
away, trainee 8 imprison 11 incarcerate

internal
6 native 7 private 8 visceral 10 subjective
prefix: 5 intra

internal organs
4 guts 6 bowels, vitals 7 innards, viscera
8 entrails 10 intestines, penetralia

international organization
3 FAO, IAM, ICJ, IFC, ILO, ITO, ITU, OAS,
WHO, WMO, WTO 4 IAAF, IABA, IAEA,
IARU, IATA, ICAO, IFIP, IMCO, NATO
5 ICFTU, SEATO 6 UNESCO, UNICEF

internuncio
5 envoy 6 bearer, legate 7 carrier, courier
8 delegate, emissary 9 go-between,
messenger, middleman

interpolate
3 add 5 admit, annex, enter 6 append, fill
in, inject, insert 7 throw in 9 introduce

interpose
6 butt in, fill in, insert, meddle, step in
7 intrude, mediate, obtrude, throw in
8 moderate 9 arbitrate, insinuate,
introduce, negotiate 11 come between

interpret
5 gloss 6 decode 7 explain, expound
8 annotate, construe 9 elucidate, explicate
10 paraphrase

interpretation
5 gloss 7 meaning, reading, version
8 exegesis 9 construal, rendering
11 explanation, translation

interpretive
8 exegetic 10 diagnostic, exegetical,
expository 11 explanatory, explicatory

interregnum
5 break, lapse, pause 6 hiatus 7 time-out

interrogate
3 ask 4 pump, quiz 5 grill, query
7 examine 8 question 9 catechize
12 cross-examine

interrupt
4 halt, stay, stop 5 abort, break, cut in
7 break in, chime in, suspend 8 cut short

interruption
3 gap 4 halt 5 break, cutoff, pause, split
6 breach, hiatus, lacuna, recess 7 caesura
8 stoppage

intersect
4 meet 5 cross 9 decussate 10 crisscross

intersection
8 crossing, junction 10 crossroads

intersperse
7 diffuse, scatter 8 sprinkle

interstice
3 gap 4 slit, slot, vent 5 chink, cleft, crack, space 6 breach, cavity, cranny 7 crevice, fissure, opening, orifice 8 aperture

intertwine
4 mesh 5 braid, plait, twist, weave
7 network 9 convolute 10 crisscross

interval
3 gap 4 lull, wait 5 break, comma, delay, letup, pause, space 6 breach, hiatus, lacuna 7 caesura, interim, respite, time-out 8 downtime 9 pausation
11 parenthesis
music: 4 rest

intervene
6 butt in, meddle, step in 7 intrude, mediate, obtrude

interweave
3 mix 4 fuse, join, knit, link, mesh 5 blend, plait, twine 6 enmesh 7 entwine, wreathe

intestinal fortitude
4 grit, guts 5 nerve, pluck, spunk 6 mettle, spirit 7 courage 8 backbone 10 resolution

intestine
3 gut 4 tube 5 bowel, canal 7 viscera (plural)
combining form: 4 coli, colo 6 entero
part: 5 cecum, colon, ileum 6 jejunum
8 duodenum

in the same place
6 ibidem

intimacy
9 closeness 11 familiarity 12 ac-quaintance

intimate
3 gut 4 cozy, dear, fond, hint 5 amigo, close, crony, imply, inner, privy 6 attest, friend, impart, loving, secret 7 comrade, connote, devoted, nearest, suggest
8 familiar, inherent 9 close-knit, companion, confidant, ingrained, insinuate, intrinsic 12 confidential

intimation
3 cue 4 clue, hint 5 shade, tinge, trace
6 breath 7 inkling 8 telltale 10 suggestion

intimidate
3 awe, cow 4 bait 5 bully, chivy, daunt, scare 6 badger, coerce, hector 7 buffalo, overawe 8 browbeat, bulldoze, bullyrag
9 strong-arm, terrorize

intolerable
10 unbearable 11 unendurable
12 insufferable 13 insupportable

intolerant
6 narrow 7 bigoted 8 dogmatic
9 hidebound, illiberal 10 inflexible, prejudiced 11 small-minded 12 narrow-minded

intonation
5 chant, pitch 6 accent, timbre 7 cadence
8 chanting 10 inflection, modulation, recitation

intone
5 chant, croon, drone 10 cantillate

in toto
3 all 6 wholly 7 all told, en masse
10 altogether

intoxicant
5 booze, drink, hooch, sauce 6 hootch, liquor, rotgut 7 alcohol, spirits 9 aqua vitae, firewater, moonshine

intoxicated
3 lit, wet 4 high 5 blind, drunk, fried, giddy, lit up, oiled, stiff, tight, tipsy 6 blotto, bombed, canned, elated, juiced, loaded, looped, potted, sodden, soused, stewed, stoned, tanked, tiddly, zonked 7 blitzed, crocked, drunken, excited, maudlin, muddled, pickled, pie-eyed, sloshed, smashed, sozzled 8 cockeyed, polluted, squiffed 9 crapulous, plastered
11 exhilarated

intoxication
3 joy 5 bliss 6 frenzy 7 ecstasy, elation, rapture 8 delirium, euphoria 9 transport
10 exaltation 11 drunkenness, inebriation

intractable
4 wild 5 balky 6 mulish, ornery, unruly
7 froward, willful 8 mutinous, obdurate, perverse, stubborn 9 fractious, obstinate, pigheaded, unbending 10 bullheaded, headstrong, inflexible, rebellious, refractory, unyielding 12 pertinacious, recalcitrant, ungovernable 13 undisciplined

intransigent
5 rigid, tough 7 willful 8 obdurate, resolute, stubborn 9 obstinate, unbending, unpliable 10 refractory, self-willed, unyielding 12 contumacious, pertinacious

intrepid
4 bold, game 5 brave, gutsy, hardy
6 daring, heroic 7 doughty, gallant, valiant
8 fearless, resolute, stalwart, unafraid, valorous 9 audacious, dauntless, undaunted 10 courageous
11 adventurous, temerarious

intricate
4 mazy 6 daedal, knotty 7 complex, gordian, tangled 8 abstruse, involved, tortuous 9 Byzantine, elaborate 10 circuitous, convoluted 11 complicated 12 labyrinthine 13 sophisticated

intrigue
4 plot, wile 5 amour, cabal, cheat, pique, trick 6 affair, appeal, excite, scheme 7 attract, beguile, collude, connive, liaison, romance 8 cogitate, conspire, contrive, interest 9 machinate 10 conspiracy 11 machination

intriguing
8 enticing 9 absorbing, beguiling 10 engrossing, entrancing 11 captivating, fascinating, stimulating

intrinsic
see **inherent**

intrinsically
5 per se 6 as such 7 at heart 10 inherently

introduce
5 begin, enter, found, set up 6 broach, fill in, insert, launch, unveil, work in 7 bring up, implant, install, instill, pioneer, precede, preface, present, throw in, usher in 8 initiate, innovate, organize 9 establish, insinuate, institute, interject, interpose, originate

introduction
5 debut, proem 6 lead-in 7 introit, opening, preface, prelude 8 entrance, exordium, foreword, overture, preamble, prologue, protases (plural), protasis 12 prolegomenon

introductory
5 basic 7 initial, nascent, opening 8 proemial 9 beginning, prefatory 10 elementary 11 preliminary, preparatory

intrude
5 cut in 6 butt in, horn in, impose, invade, meddle 7 barge in, burst in, presume 8 encroach, infringe, trespass 9 interfere, interlope, interrupt

intrusive
4 busy, nosy 5 nosey 6 prying, snoopy 7 curious 8 meddling, snooping 9 officious 10 meddlesome 11 impertinent

in truth
6 indeed, really, verily 8 actually, candidly 9 veritably

intuit
5 infer, sense 6 deduce, divine 7 surmise

intuition
5 hunch 7 feeling, inkling, insight 8 instinct 10 sixth sense 11 second sight 12 presentiment

intuitive
6 innate 7 natural 8 unwilled, visceral 10 unthinking 11 instinctive, instinctual, involuntary, spontaneous, unconscious

Inuit
6 Eskimo

inundate
4 glut 5 drown, flood, swamp, whelm 6 deluge, engulf 7 overrun 8 overflow, submerge 9 overwhelm

inundation
5 flood, spate 6 deluge 7 Niagara, torrent 8 cataract, flooding, overflow 9 avalanche, cataclysm, landslide 10 cloudburst

inure
5 steel, train 6 harden, season 7 prepare, toughen 8 accustom 9 acclimate, habituate 10 discipline 11 familiarize

inutile
6 no-good 7 useless 8 unusable 9 valueless, worthless

invade
4 loot, raid 6 breach, occupy, ravage 7 overrun, pillage, plunder 8 encroach, infringe, trespass 9 penetrate

invader
8 intruder 10 encroacher, interloper, trespasser 11 infiltrator

invalid
3 bad 4 null, sick, void 5 false 6 ailing, infirm, shut-in, sickly 7 unsound 8 baseless, disabled 9 bedridden, illogical, sophistic 10 fallacious, irrational 11 null and void 12 convalescent

invalidate
4 undo, void 5 annul, quash 6 cancel, offset, vacate 7 abolish, nullify 9 discredit, repudiate 10 counteract, disqualify, neutralize

invaluable
7 crucial 8 precious 9 essential, priceless 11 beyond price, inestimable 13 irreplaceable

invariable
4 same 5 fixed 6 static, steady 7 uniform

8 constant 9 continual, immovable, immutable, unfailing, unvarying 10 changeless, consistent, unchanging 11 inalterable, unalterable 12 unchangeable

invariably
4 ever 6 always 7 forever

invasion
4 raid 5 foray 6 attack, inroad 7 assault, offense 8 trespass 9 incursion, intrusion, offensive, onslaught 12 encroachment

invective
5 abuse 6 tirade 7 abusive, obloquy 8 diatribe, jeremiad 9 contumely, philippic, truculent 10 opprobrium, scurrility, scurrilous 11 opprobrious 12 billingsgate, contumelious, vituperation, vituperative

inveigh
4 kick, rail, rant 6 object 7 protest 8 complain 9 fulminate 11 expostulate, remonstrate

inveigle
4 coax, lure 5 decoy, snare, tempt 6 allure, cajole, entice, entrap, lead on, rope in, seduce, wangle 7 blarney, win over 8 blandish, butter up, maneuver, persuade

invent
4 coin, mint 6 cook up, create, design, devise, make up, patent, vamp up 7 concoct, dream up, fashion, hatch up, pioneer, think up 8 conceive, contrive, discover, engineer, envision 9 fabricate, formulate, originate

invention
7 coinage, fiction 8 creation 10 brainchild, innovation 11 contrivance

inventive
7 fertile, teeming 8 creative, fruitful, original 9 demiurgic, ingenious 10 innovative, innovatory 11 imaginative

inventor
5 maker 6 author, father, mother 7 creator, founder 8 engineer 9 architect, generator, innovator 10 discoverer, introducer, originator
air brake: 12 Westinghouse (George)
air conditioning: 7 Carrier (Willis)
automobile: 7 Daimler (Gottlieb)
ballpoint pen: 4 Loud (John)
barbed wire: 7 Glidden (Joseph Farwell)
barometer: 10 Torricelli (Evangelista)
bifocal lens: 8 Franklin (Benjamin)

camera: 7 Eastman (George)
cash register: 5 Ritty (James)
cotton gin: 7 Whitney (Eli)
cylinder lock: 4 Yale (Linus)
dirigible: 8 Zeppelin (Ferdinand von)
dynamite: 5 Nobel (Alfred)
electric battery: 5 Volta (Alessandro)
electric fan: 7 Wheeler (George)
electric organ: 7 Hammond (Laurens)
electric razor: 6 Schick (Jacob)
electric stove: 7 Hadaway (W. S.)
elevator: 4 Otis (Elisha)
fountain pen: 8 Waterman (Lewis)
friction match: 6 Walker (John)
gyrocompass: 6 Sperry (Elmer)
helicopter: 8 Sikorsky (Igor)
hot-air balloon: 11 Montgolfier (Jacques, Joseph)
incandescent lamp: 6 Edison (Thomas Alva)
induction motor: 5 Tesla (Nikola)
lawn mower: 5 Hills (Amariah)
Linotype: 12 Mergenthaler (Ottmar)
logarithm: 6 Napier (John)
machine gun: 7 Gatling (Richard)
microphone: 8 Berliner (Emile)
microwave oven: 7 Spencer (Percy)
movable type: 9 Gutenberg (Johannes)
parachute: 9 Blanchard (Jean-Pierre)
pendulum clock: 7 Huygens (Christiaan)
phonograph: 6 Edison (Thomas Alva)
photography: 6 Niepce (Nicéphore), Talbot (W. H. Fox) 8 Daguerre (Louis)
piano: 10 Cristofori (Bartolomeo)
radio: 7 Marconi (Guglielmo)
reaper: 9 McCormick (Cyrus)
revolver: 4 Colt (Samuel)
rocket engine: 7 Goddard (Robert)
safety pin: 4 Hunt (Walter)
safety razor: 8 Gillette (King)
sewing machine: 4 Howe (Elias)
sleeping car: 7 Pullman (George)
spinning jenny: 10 Hargreaves (James)
steamboat: 5 Fitch (John) 6 Fulton (Robert), Miller (Patrick), Rumsey (James) 8 Jouffroy (Claude de)
steam engine: 4 Watt (James)
steam locomotive: 10 Stephenson (George)
stethoscope: 7 Laënnec (René)
submarine: 7 Holland (John Philip)
synthesizer: 4 Moog (Robert)
tank: 7 Swinton (Ernest)
telegraph: 5 Morse (Samuel F. B.)
telephone: 4 Bell (Alexander Graham)
telescope: 10 Lippershey (Hans)
television: 5 Baird (John) 6 Nipkow (Paul) 8 Zworykin (Vladimir) 10 Farnsworth (Philo)

thermometer: 7 Galileo (Galilei)
torpedo: 9 Whitehead (Robert)
tractor: 5 Deere (John)
transistor: 7 Bardeen (John) 8 Brattain (Walter), Shockley (William)
vulcanized rubber: 8 Goodyear (Charles)
writing for the blind: 7 Braille (Louis)
zipper: 6 Judson (Whitcomb)

inventory
3 sum 4 fund, list 5 hoard, stock, store, tally 6 assets, digest, record, supply, survey 7 account, backlog, catalog, itemize, reserve, specify, summary 8 register, tabulate 9 catalogue, checklist, enumerate, reservoir, stockpile, summarize, synopsize

inverse
8 contrary, opposite

inversion
7 reverse 8 flipping, reversal, upending 9 about-face, turnabout, volte-face

invert
4 flip 5 upend 7 reverse 8 overturn, turn over 9 transpose

invertebrate
4 weak 5 timid 7 chicken, doormat, milksop 8 boneless, impotent, weakling 9 jellyfish, spineless 10 namby-pamby 11 ineffectual, milquetoast
kind: 4 worm 6 insect, sponge 7 mollusc, mollusk 8 arachnid 9 arthropod 12 coelenterate

invest
4 gird, veil, wrap 5 adorn, array, dress, endow, imbue 6 clothe, confer, enfold, induct, infuse, ordain 7 empower, enclose, envelop, ingrain, install, suffuse

investigate
3 pry 4 sift 5 audit, probe, study 6 go into, search 7 dig into, examine, explore, inquire, inspect 8 check out, look into, muckrake, prospect, research 9 delve into 10 scrutinize 11 inquire into

investigation
5 audit, probe 6 survey 7 inquest, inquiry 8 research, scrutiny 11 fact-finding, inquisition

investigator
3 spy 4 dick 5 hound 6 shamus, sleuth 7 gumshoe 8 hawkshaw, sherlock 9 detective

investiture
9 inaugural, induction 10 initiation, ordination 12 inauguration, installation, ratification

inveterate
3 old, set 5 fixed, sworn 6 rooted 7 abiding, chronic, settled 8 deep-dyed, enduring, habitual, hard-core, hardened, lifelong 9 confirmed, ingrained, perennial 10 continuing, deep-rooted, deep-seated, entrenched, habituated, persistent, persisting 11 established 12 incorrigible 13 dyed-in-the-wool

Invictus author
6 Henley (William Ernest)

invidious
7 envious, envying, jealous 9 green-eyed, obnoxious, resentful

invigorate
4 stir 5 brace, pep up, rally, renew, rouse 6 vivify 7 animate, brace up, enliven, fortify, juice up, perk up, refresh, restore 8 energize, vitalize 9 reinforce, stimulate 10 rejuvenate, revitalize, strengthen

invincible
10 inviolable, unbeatable 11 impregnable, indomitable, insuperable 12 invulnerable, unassailable, undefeatable 13 unconquerable

in vino _____
7 veritas

inviolable
4 safe 6 secure 10 impervious, sacrosanct 11 consecrated, impregnable 12 unassailable 13 incorruptible

invisible
6 hidden 9 concealed 10 intangible 12 unnoticeable 13 imperceptible

Invisible Man
author: 5 Wells (H. G.) 7 Ellison (Ralph)
character: 7 Griffin

Invisible Man, The
author: 5 Wells (Herbert George)
character: 7 Griffin (Herbert)

invitation
4 call, lure 6 come-on 7 bidding, proffer 8 entreaty, proposal 10 enticement 11 proposition 12 solicitation

invite
3 ask, bid 4 call, lure 5 tempt 6 allure, call in, entice, summon 7 propose, request, solicit

inviting
8 engaging, enticing, tempting

9 appealing, beguiling, seductive
10 attractive, intriguing

invocation
6 appeal, prayer 8 entreaty, petition
11 conjuration, incantation 12 supplication

invoice
3 tab 4 bill, list 5 score 7 account
8 manifest 9 reckoning, statement
11 consignment

invoke
3 beg 4 pray 5 crave, plead 6 appeal, call
on, effect 7 beseech, conjure, enforce,
entreat, implore, solicit 8 call upon, petition
9 call forth, conjure up, implement,
importune 10 supplicate

involuntary
6 forced, reflex 8 knee-jerk 9 automatic,
impulsive, reflexive, unwitting
10 compulsory, unintended, unprompted
11 instinctive, spontaneous, unconscious,
unmeditated 13 unintentional

involve
4 mire 6 affect, embody, engage, entail,
take in 7 call for, concern, contain,
embrace, embroil, include, require,
subsume 8 comprise, entangle
9 encompass, implicate 10 complicate,
comprehend 11 necessitate

involved
6 daedal, knotty 7 complex, gordian
8 confused 9 Byzantine, elaborate,
intricate 10 convoluted 11 complicated
12 labyrinthine

invulnerable
6 immune, secure 10 impervious,
invincible, unbeatable 11 impregnable,
indomitable 12 unassailable

Io
father: 7 Inachus
guard: 5 Argus
son: 7 Epaphus

iodine source
4 kelp

Iolanthe
composer: 8 Sullivan (Arthur)
librettist: 7 Gilbert (W. S.)

Iolcus king
5 Aeson 6 Pelias

Iole
captor: 8 Heracles, Hercules
father: 7 Eurytus
husband: 6 Hyllus

ion
6 ligand
kind: 5 anion 6 cation 8 thermion

Ion
father: 6 Apollo
mother: 6 Creusa
stepfather: 6 Xuthus

Ionesco, Eugène
play: 6 Chairs (The), Lesson (The)
10 Rhinoceros 11 Bald Soprano (The)

iota
3 bit, jot, ray 4 atom, hint, mite, whit
5 crumb, grain, ounce, scrap, shred, speck,
trace 6 tittle 7 smidgen 8 molecule,
particle 9 scintilla

IOU
4 chit, debt
part: 3 owe, you

Iowa
capital: 9 Des Moines
city: 4 Ames 7 Dubuque 8 Waterloo
9 Davenport, Sioux City 11 Cedar Rapids
13 Council Bluffs
college, university: 5 Drake 8 Grinnell
nickname: 7 Hawkeye (State)
river: 9 Des Moines
state bird: 9 goldfinch
state flower: 15 wild prairie rose
state tree: 3 oak

Iphicles
brother: 8 Heracles, Hercules
mother: 7 Alcmene
son: 6 Iolaus

Iphigenia
avenger: 12 Clytemnestra
brother: 7 Orestes
father: 9 Agamemnon
mother: 12 Clytemnestra
sister: 7 Electra

Iran
ancient civilization: 4 Elam 5 Medes,
Media 6 Persia
capital: 6 Tehran 7 Teheran
city: 3 Qom, Qum 6 Shiraz, Tabriz
7 Esfahan, Isfahan, Mashhad
conqueror: 9 Alexander (the Great)
gulf: 4 Oman 7 Persian
island: 5 Qeshm
language: 5 Farsi 7 Persian
leader: 7 Pahlavi (Mohammad Reza,
Reza Shah) 8 Khomeini (Ayatollah
Ruholla)
monetary unit: 4 rial
mountain, range: 6 Elburz, Zagros
8 Damavand 9 Hindu Kush
neighbor: 4 Iraq 6 Turkey 7 Armenia

8 Pakistan 10 Azerbaijan 11 Afghanistan
12 Turkmenistan
river: 5 Atrek, Karun, Safid 7 Karkheh
sea: 7 Caspian
strait: 6 Hormuz

Iranian
7 Persian
parliament: 6 Majlis
religious movement: 5 Baha'i
sect: 4 Shia
sect member: 6 Shiite

Iraq
ancient civilization: 5 Akkad, Sumer
8 Akkadian, Sumerian 9 Babylonia
10 Babylonian
ancient name: 11 Mesopotamia
capital: 7 Baghdad
city: 5 Basra, Mosul, Najaf 6 Kirkuk
7 Falluja, Karbala 8 Fallujah
conqueror: 9 Alexander (the Great)
desert: 6 Syrian
gulf: 7 Persian
leader: 6 Faisal 7 Hussein (Saddam)
monetary unit: 5 dinar
neighbor: 4 Iran 5 Syria 6 Jordan,
Kuwait, Turkey 11 Saudi Arabia
river: 6 Tigris 9 Euphrates

irascible
4 tart 5 huffy, surly, testy 6 crabby, cranky,
feisty, tetchy, touchy 7 bristly, grouchy,
peevish, peppery, prickly 8 choleric,
petulant, snappish 9 crotchety, fractious,
irritable, querulous, splenetic 11 hot-
tempered 12 cantankerous 13 quick-
tempered

irate
3 mad 5 angry, livid, riled, vexed, wroth
6 fuming 7 enraged, furious, steamed
8 choleric, incensed, provoked, wrathful
9 indignant 10 infuriated

ire
4 fury, rage, rile 5 anger, wrath 6 choler,
enrage, madden, temper 7 incense, steam
up, umbrage 9 infuriate 10 exasperate
11 indignation 12 exasperation

Ireland
4 Eire, Erin 8 Hibernia
capital: 6 Dublin
city: 4 Cork 5 Kerry, Louth, Meath, Sligo
6 Galway 7 Donegal, Kildare, Wexford,
Wicklow 8 Kilkenny, Limerick 9 Waterford
12 Dun Laoghaire
county: 4 Mayo 5 Clare 6 Galway
8 Limerick
island group: 4 Aran 8 Hibernia
lake: 3 Ree (Lough) 4 Derg (Lough)
5 Neagh (Lough) 6 Corrib (Lough)

language: 5 Irish 6 Gaelic 7 English
monetary unit: 4 euro
monetary unit, former: 5 pound
nickname: 11 Emerald Isle
river: 6 Barrow, Liffey 7 Shannon

Irene
3 Pax
father: 4 Zeus 7 Jupiter
mother: 6 Themis

irenic
4 calm 7 pacific 8 pacifist 9 peaceable,
placative, placatory 10 nonviolent
12 conciliatory, propitiatory

Iris
father: 7 Thaumas
mother: 7 Electra

Irish
4 Erse 6 Celtic, Gaelic
accent: 6 brogue
cattle: 5 Kerry
clan: 4 sept
combining form: 7 Hiberno
coronation stone: 7 Lia Fail
cudgel: 10 shillelagh
death spirit: 7 banshee
dog: 6 setter 7 terrier
elf: 10 leprechaun
flag color: 5 green, white 6 orange
flower: 8 shamrock
girl: 4 lass 6 lassie 7 colleen
god: 3 Ler 5 Dagda 6 Aengus
goddess: 4 Badb, Bodb 6 Brigit
8 Morrigan
hero: 9 Cuchulain 10 Cú Chulainn
heroine: 7 Deirdre
king: 9 Brian Boru
lake: 5 lough
language: 6 Gaelic
legislature: 4 Dail
militant force: 3 IRA
nationalist: 4 Tone (Wolfe) 6 Pearse
(Padraig) 7 Collins (Michael), Parnell
(Charles) 8 De Valera (Eamon), O'Connell
(Daniel) 9 Sarsfield (Patrick)
nationalist society: 8 Sinn Fein
patron saint: 7 Patrick
theater: 5 Abbey
writing system: 4 ogam 5 ogham
(see also **Gaelic; Celtic**)

Irish moss
7 seaweed 9 carrageen

irk
3 try, vex 4 fret, gall, pain, rile 5 annoy,
peeve, pique, upset 6 abrade, bother,
harass, nettle, ruffle, strain, stress

7 provoke, trouble 8 exercise, irritate
10 exasperate

irksome
6 vexing 7 tedious 8 annoying, rankling
9 provoking, upsetting, vexatious
10 bothersome, irritating, nettlesome,
unpleasant 11 aggravating, troublesome,
unpalatable

iron
4 firm, gyve, hard 5 press, rigid 6 fetter,
strong 7 adamant, manacle, shackle
8 handcuff, obdurate 9 unbending
10 inexorable, inflexible, relentless,
unyielding
German: 5 Eisen
relating to: 6 ferric 7 ferrous

ironbound
5 harsh, rocky, rough, stern 6 craggy,
jagged, rugged, severe, strict, uneven
7 scraggy 8 asperous, exacting, rigorous,
scabrous 9 stringent 10 inflexible

Iron City
10 Pittsburgh

ironclad
5 fixed 7 binding 8 constant 9 immovable,
immutable 10 inflexible, invariable
11 inalterable, irrefutable, unalterable
12 indisputable, irrefragable, unchangeable
13 unimpeachable

ironfisted
4 grim, hard, mean 5 harsh 6 brutal,
severe, stingy 7 callous, miserly 8 pitiless,
ruthless 9 merciless 10 implacable,
unmerciful 11 hard-hearted, intractable,
remorseless 12 unappeasable

ironhanded
5 harsh, rigid 6 severe, strict 8 despotic,
rigorous 9 draconian, stringent
10 tyrannical 11 unpermissive

ironhearted
5 stony 7 callous 8 hardened, obdurate,
ruthless 9 merciless, unfeeling 10 hard-
boiled 11 cold-blooded 13 unsympathetic

iron horse
10 locomotive

ironic
3 wry 6 biting 7 caustic, cutting, cynical,
mordant, satiric 8 sardonic 9 sarcastic,
trenchant

iron ore
8 goethite, hematite, limonite, siderite,
taconite 9 magnetite

Iron Pants
6 Patton (George)

irons
5 bonds, gyves 6 chains 7 bilboes,
darbies, fetters 8 manacles, shackles

Iroquois tribe
6 Cayuga, Mohawk, Oneida, Seneca
8 Onondaga 9 Tuscarora

irradiate
4 beam, glow 5 edify, light, shine 6 uplift
7 light up 8 illumine 9 enlighten
10 illuminate

irrational
3 mad 5 crazy 6 absurd, insane 7 invalid
8 demented 9 illogical, senseless,
sophistic 10 cockamamie, fallacious,
ridiculous 12 preposterous, unreasonable

irrefutable
4 sure 6 proven 7 certain 8 airtight,
ironclad, positive 9 apodictic, veracious
10 conclusive, inarguable 11 indubitable
12 indisputable 13 incontestable

irregular
3 odd 5 queer 6 fitful, patchy, random,
spotty, uneven 7 aimless, erratic, unequal
8 aberrant, abnormal, atypical, informal,
lopsided, peculiar, singular, sporadic,
unstable, unsteady, variable 9 anomalous,
desultory, divergent, eccentric, guerrilla,
haphazard, hit-or-miss, spasmodic,
unregular, unsettled 10 asymmetric,
capricious, changeable, inconstant, off-
balance, unbalanced, unofficial
11 exceptional, fluctuating 12 intermittent,
unsystematic

irregularity
5 freak, quirk 6 oddity 7 anomaly
8 deviance 9 deviation, roughness
10 aberration, inequality, unevenness
11 abnormality

irrelevant
5 inapt 9 unrelated 10 extraneous,
immaterial, inapposite, peripheral
11 inessential, unessential, unimportant
12 inapplicable 13 insignificant

irreligious
6 unholy 7 godless, impious, profane,
ungodly 11 blasphemous

irreparable
8 cureless, hopeless 9 incurable
11 immedicable 12 irredeemable,
irremediable 13 irretrievable,
unrecoverable

irreproachable
4 pure **8** flawless, innocent, spotless, virtuous **9** blameless, errorless, exemplary, faultless, guiltless, righteous **10** immaculate, impeccable, inculpable, unblamable

irresolute
5 shaky **6** fickle, unsure, wobbly **7** halting **8** doubtful, hesitant, unstable, waffling, wavering **9** equivocal, faltering, tentative, uncertain, undecided **10** ambivalent, changeable, inconstant, wishy-washy **11** fluctuating, half-hearted, vacillating

irresponsible
4 rash, wild **8** carefree, careless, feckless, reckless **10** incautious, unreliable **12** undependable **13** unaccountable, untrustworthy

irreverent
4 flip **7** impious, profane, ungodly **8** flippant **9** satirical **11** blasphemous **12** sacrilegious

irrevocable
4 firm **5** final **9** immutable **11** unalterable **12** irreversible, unchangeable **13** nonreversible

irrigation ditch
5 flume **6** sluice **7** acequia

irritability
5 pique **6** choler **8** edginess **9** petulance **10** crabbiness, impatience **11** fretfulness, peevishness
abnormal: 8 erethism

irritable
4 edgy, sour **5** cross, huffy, testy, waspy, whiny **6** crabby, cranky, crusty, grumpy, ornery, snappy, tetchy, touchy **7** fretful, grouchy, peevish, pettish, prickly, waspish **8** captious, choleric, petulant, snappish **9** crotchety, fractious, impatient, irascible, querulous, splenetic **12** cantankerous, disagreeable

irritant
4 itch, pest **5** nudge **6** bother, gadfly, noodge, nudnik, pester, plague **8** headache, nuisance, vexation **9** annoyance **11** botheration

irritate
3 bug, irk, rub, vex **4** fret, gall, goad, rile, roil **5** anger, annoy, chafe, grate, peeve, pique, spite **6** abrade, badger, bother, burn up, harass, hector, madden, needle, nettle, offend, ruffle **7** inflame, provoke

9 aggravate, stimulate **10** exacerbate, exasperate

irritated
5 irate, testy **7** fretful, peevish **8** choleric **9** impatient, irascible

irritation
4 itch, pest, rash, sore **6** bother, plague **7** chagrin **8** nuisance, vexation **9** annoyance

irrupt
5 belch, eruct, surge **6** invade **7** intrude

irruption
4 raid **5** foray **6** inroad **7** upsurge **8** invasion **9** incursion, intrusion

I.R.S. employee
7 auditor **10** accountant

Irving novel
15 Cider House Rules (The) **17** Hotel New Hampshire (The) **20** World According to Garp (The)

Isaac
father: 7 Abraham
mother: 5 Sarah
son: 4 Esau **5** Jacob
wife: 7 Rebekah

Isabella I
country: 5 Spain
home: 7 Castile
husband: 9 Ferdinand

Isaiah
7 prophet
father: 4 Amoz

Iscah
brother: 3 Lot
father: 5 Haran
sister: 6 Milcah

Iseult, Isolde
beloved: 7 Tristan **8** Tristram
husband: 4 Mark

Ishbak
father: 7 Abraham
mother: 7 Keturah

Ishbosheth's father
4 Saul

Ishmael
6 pariah **7** outcast **8** castaway, outsider **11** untouchable
father: 7 Abraham
mother: 5 Hagar

Ishtar
brother: 7 Shamash
father: 3 Anu, Sin

lover: 6 Tammuz

Ishui's father
    4 Saul 5 Asher

Isis
  brother: 6 Osiris
  father: 3 Geb
  husband: 6 Osiris
  mother: 3 Nut
  son: 4 Sept 5 Horus

Islam
  adherent: 6 Moslem, Muslim
  founder: 8 Mohammed, Muhammad
  god: 5 Allah
  holy city: 5 Mecca
  holy month: 7 Ramadan
  law: 6 Sharia
  place of worship: 6 mosque
  priest: 4 imam
  scriptures: 5 Koran, Quran
  sect: 4 Shia, Sufi 5 Sunni 6 Shiite,
  Sufism 7 Ismaili, Wahhabi
  (see also **Muslim**)

island
  3 ait, cay, key 4 holm 5 atoll, oasis
  6 skerry 7 crannog
  Admiralty group: 6 Manus
  Adriatic Sea: 3 Vis 4 Brac, Cres, Hvar
  5 Brach, Ciovo, Mljet, Solta 6 Lesina,
  Pharus
  Aegean Sea: 4 Scio 5 Chios, Khios,
  Samos, Thira 6 Ikaria, Lemnos, Lesbos,
  Limnos 7 Nikaria 8 Mitilini, Mytilene,
  Santorin 10 Sakis-Adasi, Susam-Adasi
  Alaska: 4 Adak, Atka, Attu, Kuiu
  8 Wrangell
  Aleutian group: 3 Rat 4 Adak, Akun, Attu
  5 Amlia, Kiska, Umnak 6 Kanaga, Tanaga,
  Unimak 8 Amchitka, Unalaska
  American Samoa: 3 Ofu, Tau 4 Rose
  6 Swains
  Andaman Sea: 4 Mali 5 Tavoy
  Antarctica: 5 Scott, Young
  Apostle group: 3 Oak 4 Long, Sand
  5 Outer 8 Madeline, Michigan, Stockton
  Arafura Sea: 5 Dolak
  Arctic Archipelago: 6 Baffin 8 Victoria
  Arctic Ocean: 5 Senja
  Australian: 5 Cocos 8 Tasmania
  Azores: 4 Pico 5 Corvo, Faial
  Bahamas: 3 Cat, Rum 4 Long 5 Abaco,
  Exuma 6 Andros, Inagua 7 Acklins,
  Crooked 8 Watlings 9 Eleuthera,
  Mayaguana 11 San Salvador
  Bahrain: 5 Sitra 8 Muharraq
  Balearic group: 5 Ibiza 7 Majorca,
  Menorca, Minorca 8 Mallorca

Baltic Sea: 4 Moon, Muhu 5 Faron,
Mukhu, Rugen, Worms 6 Vormsi
7 Gotland 8 Bornholm, Gothland, Gottland
Barents Sea: 4 Bear
Bay of Naples: 5 Capri
Bay of Panama: 4 Naos
Bering Sea: 5 Medny 7 Nunivak 10 Big
Diomede 13 Little Diomede
Bismarck Archipelago: 5 Lihir 10 New
Britain
Bristol Channel: 5 Lundy
Buzzards Bay: 9 Cuttyhunk
Canadian: 5 Banks, Devon 6 Baffin
8 Bathurst, Melville, Somerset, Victoria
9 Anticosti, Ellesmere 10 Cape Breton
11 Axel Heiberg, Southampton
12 Newfoundland, Prince Edward
Canaries: 6 Gomera 7 La Palma
8 Tenerife 9 Lanzarote
Cape Verde: 4 Fogo, Maio, Mayo
5 Brava, Rombo
Caribbean Sea: 4 Cuba 5 Aruba, Utila,
Vache 6 Tobago 7 Antigua, Curaçao,
Jamaica 8 Barbados, Dominica, Trinidad
10 Guadeloupe, Martinique, Puerto Rico
(see also **Virgin group**)
Carolines: 5 Sorol 6 Ponape
9 Ascension
Chagos Archipelago: 11 Diego Garcia
Channel group: 4 Herm, Sark 5 Lihou,
Sercq 6 Jersey 8 Guernsey
Chesapeake Bay: 4 Deal, Kent 5 Smith,
Watts
Chukchi Sea: 6 Herald
Comoro group: 7 Mayotte
Congo River: 4 Bamu
Cook group: 4 Atiu 5 Mauke
Croatia: 3 Krk, Pag, Rab 5 Susak, Unije
Cyclades: 3 Ios, Kea, Nio 4 Keos, Keos,
Milo 5 Delos, Melos, Milos, Naxos, Paros,
Siros, Syros 6 Andros, Dhilos 7 Amorgos,
Cythnos, Kithnos, Kythnos, Mykonos
Denmark: 3 Als, Fyn, Mon 4 Aero, Fano,
Moen, Mors 5 Alsen, Funen, Moers,
Samso 8 Bornholm 13 Fanum Fortunae
D'Entrecasteaux group: 8 Kaluwawa
9 Fergusson
Dodecanese group: 3 Coo, Cos, Kos
4 Caso, Lero, Simi, Syme 5 Kasos, Leros,
Lipso, Lisso, Patmo, Telos 6 Calino,
Lipsos, Nisiro, Patmos 7 Calimno, Nisiros,
Nisyros 8 Kalymnos
East River: 5 Ward's 7 Welfare
9 Roosevelt
England's: 7 Britain 8 Britannia 12 Great
Britain
English Channel: 5 Wight
Faeroes: 4 Vago 5 Bordo, Sando
Fiji: 4 Koro 5 Mango, Vatoa

Florida Keys: 4 Long, Vaca, West
5 Largo 7 Big Pine 9 Matecumbe, Sugarloaf
Fox group: 5 Umnak 6 Akutan, Unimak
8 Unalaska
French: 7 Corsica 12 New Caledonia
French Polynesia: 4 Rapa, Reao, Ua Pu
5 Ua Pau
Frisian group: 3 Rom 4 Föhr, Sylt
5 Amrum, Juist, Mando, Texel 6 Borkum
7 Ameland, Langeoog, Pellworm, Vlieland 9 Helgoland, Norderney
Futunas: 5 Alofi
Galápagos: 5 Pinta 7 Chatham, Isabela
8 Abingdon 10 Albermarle
Georgia: 5 Tybee
Germany: 4 Fohr 7 Fehmarn
9 Helgoland 10 Heligoland
Greater Antilles: 4 Cuba 7 Jamaica
10 Hispaniola, Puerto Rico
Greece: 4 Milo, Rodi 5 Creta, Crete, Hydra, Idhra, Kriti, Rodos, Tenos, Tinos
6 Euboea, Evvoia, Hydrea, Lesbos, Rhodes, Rhodus 9 Negropont
10 Negroponte
Grenadines: 5 Union
Gulf of Alaska: 6 Kodiak
Gulf of Bothnia: 5 Karlö
Gulf of Carpentaria: 5 Maria 6 Groote
7 Eylandt
Gulf of Guinea: 7 Sao Tomé 8 Príncipe, Sao Thomé 11 Saint Thomas
Gulf of Mexico: 3 Cat 5 Lobos
Gulf of Panama: 3 Rey
Gulf of St. Lawrence: 5 Brion
Gulf of Thailand: 3 Kut 5 Samui
Haiti: 6 Gonâve
Hawaii: 4 Maui, Oahu 5 Kauai, Lanai
6 Niihau 7 Molokai 9 Kahoolawe
Hudson Bay: 5 Coats
Indian Ocean: 4 Mahé, Nias 5 Heard, Pemba 7 La Dique, Praslin, Réunion 8 Sri Lanka, Zanzibar 9 Mauritius
10 Madagascar
Indonesia: 4 Bali, Biak, Java, Maja, Muna, Nias, Rhio, Riau, Roma, Roti, Savu, Sawu
5 Batam, Boano, Buton, Djawa, Japen, Lakor, Moena, Riouw, Rotti, Rupat, Sawoe, Solor, Sumba, Wetar, Wokam 6 Butung, Flores, Jappen, Lombok, Madura, Padang, Roepat, Romang, Soemba 7 Celebes, Madoera, Sumatra, Sumbawa 8 Boetoeng, Soembawa, Sulawesi 10 Bandanaira, Banda Neira, Sandalwood
Inner Hebrides: 4 Coll, Eigg, Iona, Jura, Muck, Mull, Skye 5 Canna, Gigha, Islay, Tiree, Tyree
Ionian group: 5 Corfu, Paxos, Zante
6 Cerigo, Ithaca, Leukas, Levkas 10 Santa Maura

Iran: 5 Shahi
Ireland: 4 Aran
Irish Sea: 3 Man
Italy: 4 Elba 6 Sicily 8 Sardinia
Japan: 3 Iki, Uku 4 Naru, Yezo 5 Awaji, Fukae, Fukue, Hondo, Shodo 6 Honshu, Kyushu 7 Shikoku 8 Hokkaido
10 Shodoshima
Java Sea: 4 Laut
Kiribati: 6 Tarawa
Kuril group: 4 Urup 5 Ketoi, Matua
6 Iturup 7 Etorofu, Matsuwa 8 Kunashir
9 Kunashiri
Lake Champlain: 5 Grand
Lake Erie: 9 North Bass, South Bass
10 Middle Bass
Lake Huron: 8 Drummond 10 Manitoulin
Lake Michigan: 3 Hog 4 High 6 Beaver
Lake Ontario: 5 Wolfe
Lake Superior: 4 Sand 6 Royale
7 Manitou
Lake Winnipeg: 5 Hecla
largest: 9 Greenland
Leeward group: 5 Nevis 7 Antigua, Barbuda, Redonda 8 Anguilla, Sombrero
10 Montserrat, Saint Kitts 13 St. Christopher
legendary: 7 Cipango
Lesser Sundas: 4 Alor 5 Ombai
Leti group: 3 Moa 5 Lakor
Line group: 5 Flint 6 Malden, Vostok
7 Fanning, Palmyra 8 Starbuck
9 Christmas
Long Island Sound: 4 City, Hart
5 Goose, Harts
Loyalty group: 3 Uea 4 Lifu, Maré, Uvea
5 Lifou
Malay Archipelago: 5 Kisar, Larat, Timor
6 Borneo 9 New Guinea
Malaysia: 6 Penang, Pinang 13 Prince of Wales
Malta: 4 Gozo
Marianas: 4 Maug, Rota 5 Pagan
6 Saipan
Marquesas group: 4 Eiào, Ua Pu
6 Hatutu, Hiva Oa, Ua Huka 7 Tahuata
8 Fatu Hiva, Nuku Hiva
Marshall group: 5 Wotho, Wotje
8 Eniwetok 9 Kwajalein
Massachusetts: 9 Nantucket
Mediterranean Sea: 4 Elba 5 Corfu, Crete, Malta 6 Cyprus, Euboea, Rhodes, Sicily 7 Corsica 8 Sardinia
Midway group: 4 Sand 8 Eastern
Moluccas: 4 Buru 5 Ambon, Ceram, Seram 6 Boeroe
Mozambique channel: 10 Juan de Nova
Myanmar: 5 Daung, Kadan, Lanbi
Narragansett Bay: 5 Rhode 8 Prudence
9 Aquidneck, Conanicut

Netherlands: 5 Texel **7** Ameland **8** Vlieland
Netherlands Antilles: 7 Curaçao
New York: 4 Fire, Long **9** Gardiners, Roosevelt
New York Bay: 5 Ellis **6** Staten **7** Liberty **9** Governors, Manhattan
New Zealand: 5 South, White **7** Chatham, Stewart **8** D'Urville
Niagara River: 4 Goat
Nile River: 4 Argo, Roda, Ruda **5** Rhoda **6** Rawdah **11** Elephantine
North Channel: 3 Mew
Northern Cook group: 7 Penrhyn **8** Manihiki **9** Tongareva
North Pacific: 4 Wake
Northwest Territories: 5 Banks, Bylot, Devon **8** Bathurst, Melville **9** Ellesmere **10** Cornwallis, Resolution **13** Prince of Wales
Norwegian: 8 Jan Mayen
Norwegian Sea: 5 Donna, Smola, Vikna
Nova Scotia: 5 Sable **10** Cape Breton
off Alaska: 4 Dall **5** Kayak
off Albania: 5 Sazan **6** Saseno
off Australia: 4 Dunk
off Belize: 9 Ambergris
off Brazil: 4 Apeu **5** Rocas
off British Columbia: 4 King, Pitt **9** Vancouver
off Cape Cod: 8 Muskeget **9** Nantucket
off Chile: 5 Guafo, Mocha
off China: 5 Amoy **5** Ma-tsu **6** Hainan, Quemoy, Taiwan
off Crete: 3 Dia
off Ecuador: 4 Puna
off England: 3 Man **5** Wight **6** Walney
off Florida: 3 Dog **4** Pine **6** Amelia **7** Pelican, Sanibel **9** Anastasia
off French Guiana: 6 Devil's
off Georgia: 10 Cumberland **11** Saint Simons
off Germany: 4 Sylt
off Greenland: 5 Disko
off Guinea: 5 Tombo
off Hispaniola: 5 Beata
off Honduras: 5 Tigre
off Iceland: 4 Surtsey
off India: 5 Sagar
off Ireland: 4 Tory **5** Clare, Clear
off Kenya: 5 Lamu
off Long Island: 7 Fishers
off Louisiana: 5 Marsh
off Maine: 4 Deer, Orrs **5** Swans **8** Monhegan **11** Mount Desert
off Malay Peninsula: 6 Phuket **9** Singapore
off Maryland: 10 Assateague
off Massachusetts: 4 Plum **7** Naushon
off Mexico: 7 Cozumel

off Mississippi: 4 Horn, Ship
off Mozambique: 3 Ibo
off New Brunswick: 10 Campobello
off Newfoundland: 4 Bell
off Nigeria: 5 Lagos
off North Carolina: 5 Bodie
off Norway: 5 Bomlo, Froya, Hitra, Sotra, Stord, Vardo **8** Hitteren
off Panama: 5 Coiba **6** Parida
off Poland: 5 Wolin **6** Wollin
off Puerto Rico: 4 Crab **7** Culebra, Vieques
off Rhode Island: 5 Block
off Scotland: 4 Bute **5** Arran
off South Carolina: 5 North **6** Parris **10** Hilton Head
off Sri Lanka: 5 Delft
off Staten Island: 7 Hoffman
off Sumatra: 3 Weh
off Sweden: 5 Graso, Oland, Vaddo
off Syria: 5 Arvad, Arwad, Rouad **6** Aradus
off Tanzania: 5 Mafia, Pemba
off Tasmania: 5 Bruni, Bruny
off Tunisia: 5 Jerba **6** Djerba, Meninx
off Venezuela: 5 Aruba **7** Bonaire **8** Buen Aire
off Virginia: 5 Wreck
off Wales: 5 Caldy **6** Caldey
Okinawa group: 4 Kume
Orkneys: 3 Hoy
Outer Hebrides: 5 Barra, Scarp
Palmer Archipelago: 6 Anvers **7** Antwerp, Brabant
Pearl Harbor: 4 Ford
Persian Gulf: 4 Qeys **5** Kharg, Khark
Philippines: 4 Buad, Cebu, Fuga, Ilin, Poro, Sulu **5** Balut, Batan, Bohol, Coron, Daram, Leyte, Luzon, Panay, Samal, Samar, Sugbu, Talim, Ticao, Verde **6** Negros **7** Masbate, Mindoro, Palawan, Paragua **8** Limasawa, Mindanao **10** Corregidor
Phoenix group: 4 Hull, Mary **6** Birnie, Canton **9** Enderbury
Puerto Rico: 4 Mona
Quebec: 4 Alma
Queen Charlotte group: 7 Moresby
Red Sea: 5 Tiran, Zugur, Zuqar
Russia: 7 Wrangel
Ryukyu group: 7 Okinawa
St. Lawrence River: 4 Hare **5** Jesus **8** Montreal
San Francisco Bay: 5 Angel
Santa Cruz: 5 Anuda, Ndeni **6** Cherry
Sea of Japan: 4 Sado **5** Rebun
Sea of Marmara: 4 Avsa
second largest: 9 New Guinea
Senegal: 5 Gorée
Seychelles: 4 Mahé **7** La Digue, Praslin

Shetland archipelago: 4 Unst, Yell **5** Foula

Shumagin group: 4 Unga

Sierra Leone: 5 Tasso

Society group: 5 Eimeo, Tahaa, Tahao, Taiti **6** Moorea, Tahiti **8** Otaheite

Solomon group: 4 Buka, Gizo, Savo **7** Malaita **11** Guadalcanal **12** Bougainville

South Atlantic: 5 Qeshm, Gough **6** Gough's **11** Saint Helena

South Korea: 5 Cheju

South of Tokyo: 3 Iwo **7** Iwo Jima, Naka Iwo

South Orkneys: 10 Coronation

South Pacific: 3 Hiu **4** Niue **5** Raoul **6** Savage, Sunday **7** Norfolk **8** Pitcairn

Spitsbergen archipelago: 4 Edge

Strait of Hormuz: 5 Qeshm, Qishm

Sulu Archipelago: 4 Jolo **5** Lapac

Svalbard: 4 Hope

Sverdrup: 11 Axel Heiberg **12** Amund Ringnes

Swedish: 3 Ven **4** Hven **5** Hveen, Orust

Tanzania: 8 Zanzibar

Texas: 5 Padre

Thames River: 7 Sheppey

third largest: 6 Borneo

Tierra del Fuego: 5 Hoste

Tonga: 3 Eua, Foa **4** Uiha **5** Haano

Treasury group: 5 Mono

Truk group: 3 Tol **4** Haru, Moen, Udot, Uman **5** Fefan

Tuamotu Archipelago: 4 Anaa **5** Chain

Turkish: 5 Imroz **6** Imbros

Tuvalu: 7 Nanumea **9** Nukufetau

Tyrrhenian Sea: 6 Ischia **11** Montecristo

Vanuatu: 4 Api, Epi, Oba **5** Aoba, Gaua, Tana, Vate **5** Efate, Maewo, Tanna

Venezuelan: 5 Patos **9** La Tortuga

Virgin group, American: 9 Saint John **10** Saint Croix **11** Saint Thomas

Virgin group, British: 5 Peter **6** Norman **7** Anegada, Tortola **11** Jost Van Dyke

volcanic: 5 Tofua **7** Iwo Jima

Wales: 4 Anglesea, Anglesey, Holyhead

Weddell Sea: 4 Ross **6** Hearst

Western Samoa: 5 Upolu **6** Savaii

West Indies: 4 Mona, Saba, Salt **5** Nevis, Peter, Saona **6** Tobago, Tortue **7** Grenada, Tortuga **8** Trinidad **9** Santa Cruz **10** Concepción, Hispaniola, Montserrat, Saint Croix

(see also **Bahamas; Greater Antilles; Leeward group; Virgin group; Windward group**)

West of England: 7 Ireland

West Pacific: 5 Dyaul, Fauro, Ocean **6** Banaba, Marcus **7** Iwo Jima, Kita Iwo **9** Minami Iwo

Windward group: 10 Martinique **with former penitentiary: 8** Alcatraz

island group

Alaska: 3 Rat **8** Aleutian, Pribilof **9** Andreanof, Catherine

Aleutians: 4 Near

American Samoa: 5 Manua

Arabian Sea: 9 Laccadive

Arctic Archipelago: 8 Sverdrup

Arctic Ocean: 8 Svalbard **12** Novaya Zemlya

Bahamas: 5 Berry, Exuma **6** Bimini

Banda Sea: 5 Damar

Bangladesh: 5 Hatia, Hatya

Bay of Bengal: 7 Andaman, Nicobar

between England and France: 7 Channel

Bismarck Archipelago: 4 Feni **5** Tabar, Tanga

Bismarck Sea: 4 Vitu

British: 7 Bermuda

Caribbean Sea: 4 Swan **5** Pearl **6** Cayman, Perlas, Pigeon **8** Pichones **10** Grenadines, West Indies

Carolines: 3 Uap, Yap **4** Truk **5** Nomoi **7** Hogoleu

Central Pacific Ocean: 4 Line **5** Samoa, Union **6** Danger, Midway **7** Phoenix, Tokelau **8** Manihiki **9** Polynesia **12** Northern Cook

Coral Sea: 4 Huon

Cuba: 8 Camagüey

east of Philippines: 10 Micronesia

East Siberian Sea: 4 Bear **8** Medvezhi

Ecuador: 6 Colón **9** Galápagos

England: 5 Farne

Fiji: 3 Lau **7** Eastern

Formosa Strait: 4 Hoko **6** Peng hu **10** Pescadores

French: 5 Salut **6** Safety **9** Kerguelen

French Polynesia: 3 Low **6** Tubuai **7** Austral, Paumotu, Société, Society, Tuamotu **9** Marquesas, Touamotou

Germany: 8 Halligen

Greece: 6 Aegean, Ionian **8** Cyclades **10** Dodecanese **11** Dodecanesus

Hudson Bay: 7 Belcher

Indian Ocean: 7 Aldabra

Indonesia: 4 Asia, Batu, Pagi, Sula **5** Babar, Batoe, Pagai, Pageh, Penju, Spice, Wakde **6** Maluku

Ireland: 4 Aran

Japan: 5 Osumi

largest: 5 Malay **8** Malaysia

Lesser Antilles: 8 Windward

Malay Archipelago: 5 Sunda **6** Soenda

Mediterranean Sea: 8 Baleares, Balearic

Moluccas: 3 Kai, Kei, Obi 4 Leti
5 Banda, Letti 8 Tanimbar 9 Timorlaut
New Caledonia: 7 Loyalty 9 Loyalties
north of Australia: 9 Melanesia
north of British Isles: 5 Faroe 7 Faeroes
north off Fiji: 5 Hoorn 6 Futuna
north of Madagascar: 7 Aldabra
8 Farquhar
north of New Caledonia: 5 Belep
north of New Guinea: 8 Bismarck
9 Admiralty 11 Admiralties
Northwest Territories: 5 Parry
off Alaska: 3 Fox
off Alaska Peninsula: 8 Shumagin
off Cape Cod: 9 Elizabeth
off eastern Asia: 5 Kuril 6 Kurile
off England: 6 Scilly
off Florida: 11 Dry Tortugas
off Guinea: 3 Los 4 Loos
off Honduras: 5 Bahia
off Morocco: 7 Madeira
off New Guinea: 3 Aru 4 Aroe
off Nicaragua: 4 Corn
off northern Africa: 6 Canary 8 Canaries
off northern Australia: 6 Wessel
7 Dampier
off Sicily: 5 Egadi 8 Aegadian
Outer Hebrides: 4 Uist
Papua New Guinea: 5 Green
Persian Gulf: 4 Tunb
Philippines: 4 Cuyo 5 Tapul 6 Lubang
7 Basilan, Bisayas, Visayan
Portuguese: 6 Azores
Quebec: 8 Magdalen 9 Madeleine
Ryukyus: 5 Amami
St. Lawrence River: 8 Thousand
Sea of Japan: 3 Oki
Sea of Marmara: 5 Kizil 7 Princes
11 Kizil Adalar
South Atlantic Ocean: 8 Falkland,
Malvinas
South China Sea: 6 Hirata 7 Paracel,
Spratly
south of New Zealand: 8 Auckland
South Pacific: 11 Austronesia
Sulu Sea: 7 Cagayan 9 Cagayanes
Tonga: 5 Vavau
Tyrrhenian Sea: 5 Ponza
Venezuelan: 4 Aves, Bird 9 Los Roques
West Europe: 12 British Isles
West Indies: 6 Virgin 10 Guadeloupe
west of French Polynesia: 4 Cook
west of Scotland: 7 Western 8 Hebrides
west Pacific Ocean: 4 Duff 5 Bonin,
Mapia, Palau, Pelew 7 Ladrone, Mariana,
Solomon, Vanuatu 8 Marshall, Treasury
9 Ogasawara 10 Saint David

island nation
   Atlantic Ocean: 9 Cape Verde
   Indian Ocean: 8 Malagasy, Malgache, Sri
   Lanka 9 Mauritius 10 Madagascar,
   Seychelles
   Mediterranean Sea: 6 Cyprus
   Mozambique Channel: 6 Comoro
   7 Comores
   off southern China: 6 Taiwan
   south of Greenland: 7 Iceland
   West Indies: 4 Cuba 7 Jamaica
   8 Barbados 10 Saint Lucia
   West Pacific Ocean: 5 Nauru
   Windward group: 8 Dominica

island province
   12 Prince Edward

island state
   6 Hawaii

isle
   see **island**

Ismene
   brother: 9 Polynices
   father: 7 Oedipus
   mother: 7 Jocasta
   sister: 8 Antigone
   uncle: 5 Creon

isochronous
   7 regular 8 cyclical, periodic, rhythmic
   9 recurrent, recurring 10 periodical
   12 intermittent

isolate
   6 cut off, detach, enisle 7 seclude 8 close
   off, insulate, pinpoint, separate, set apart
   9 segregate, sequester 10 quarantine

isolated
   5 alone 6 random, remote, unique
   7 unusual 8 solitary, sporadic 9 separated,
   withdrawn 11 exceptional, quarantined

Isolde
   see **Iseult**

Israel
   ancient name: 4 Zion 5 Judea
   6 Canaan, Judaea 9 Palestine
   capital: 9 Jerusalem
   city: 4 Acre 5 Haifa, Jaffa 7 Tel Aviv
   9 Beersheba
   desert: 5 Negeb, Negev
   gulf: 5 Aqaba
   lake: 8 Tiberias 12 Sea of Galilee
   language: 6 Arabic, Hebrew
   monetary unit: 6 shekel
   neighbor: 5 Egypt, Syria 6 Jordan
   7 Lebanon
   plain: 9 Esdraelon

Israeli
river: 6 Jordan
sea: 4 Dead 13 Mediterranean

Israeli
5 Sabra

Israelite
see **Hebrew; Jewish**

Issachar
father: 5 Jacob
mother: 4 Leah

issue
4 emit, flow, gush, pour, rise, seed, stem, vent 5 arise, birth, brood, child, fruit, scion, topic 6 affair, appear, effect, emerge, get out, matter, put out, result, scions, sequel, source, spring, upshot 7 concern, descent, edition, emanate, give off, give out, outcome, problem, proceed, progeny, publish, release, subject 8 bulletin, children, question, throw off 9 come forth, offspring, originate, posterity 10 derive from, distribute, end product, promulgate 11 consequence, descendants, progeniture, publication

Istanbul
ancient name: 9 Byzantium
business section: 6 Galata
country: 6 Turkey
foreign quarter: 4 Pera 7 Beyoglu
park: 8 Seraglio
residential section: 7 Uskudar

isthmus
Africa-Asia: 4 Suez
Greece: 7 Corinth
North America-South America:
6 Panama

Italian
automobile: 4 Fiat 6 Lancia 7 Ferrari 8 Maserati 9 Alfa Romeo 11 Lamborghini
cathedral: 5 duomo
dialect: 6 Tuscan 8 Sicilian
dictator: 9 Mussolini (Benito)
family: 4 Este 5 Cenci, Savoy 6 Borgia, Medici, Orsini, Pepoli, Savoia, Sforza 7 Colonna, Gonzaga, Spinola 8 Visconti
fascist: 10 Blackshirt
game: 5 bocce, bocci 6 boccie
gentleman: 6 signor 7 signore
highway: 10 autostrada
lady: 5 donna 7 signora 9 signorina
magistrate: 7 podestà
meat: 6 salami 8 pancetta 9 pepperoni, salsiccia 10 mortadella, prosciutto
opera house: 7 La Scala
patriot: 6 Cavour (Conte di), Rienzo (Cola di) 7 Mazzini (Giuseppe) 9 Garibaldi (Giuseppe)
religious reformer: 10 Savonarola (Girolamo)
resort: 4 Lido 5 Abano, Capri 8 Sorrento, Taormina
road: 6 strada
soup: 10 minestrone
square: 6 piazza
street: 3 via 5 corso
weight: 5 libra, oncia

Italy
bay: 6 Naples
capital: 4 Rome
city: 4 Asti, Bari, Pisa 5 Aosta, Genoa, Milan, Padua, Parma, Siena, Turin 6 Genova, Mantua, Milano, Modena, Naples, Napoli, Padova, Torino, Venice, Verona 7 Bergamo, Bologna, Bolzano, Catania, Cremona, Firenze, Leghorn, Livorno, Mantova, Palermo, Perugia, Ravenna, Salerno, Taranto, Trieste, Venezia 8 Florence, Siracusa, Syracuse
enclave: 9 San Marino 11 Vatican City
gulf: 5 Gaeta 7 Salerno, Taranto 11 Sant' Eufemia
island, island group: 4 Elba 5 Capri 6 Ischia, Lipari, Sicily 7 Aeolian, Capraia 8 Sardinia
lake: 4 Como 5 Garda 7 Bolsena 8 Maggiore 9 Bracciano
leader: 9 Mussolini (Benito)
monetary unit: 4 euro
monetary unit, former: 4 lira
mountain, range: 4 Alps, Etna 9 Apennines, Mont Blanc, Monte Rosa 10 Monte Corno
neighbor: 6 France 7 Austria 8 Slovenia 11 Switzerland
peninsula: 9 Salentina
river: 4 Arno, Liri 5 Adige, Piave, Tiber 6 Isonzo, Tevere 8 Volturno
sea: 6 Ionian 8 Adriatic, Ligurian 10 Tyrrhenian 13 Mediterranean
strait: 7 Messina, Otranto
volcano: 4 Etna 8 Vesuvius
wine region: 4 Asti

itch
3 yen 4 ache, long, lust, pine 5 crave, yearn 6 desire, hanker, hunger, thirst 7 craving, longing 8 appetite, pruritus, yearning 9 hankering

itchy
4 avid, edgy, keen 5 antsy, eager, jumpy 7 fidgety, restive 8 desirous, prurient, restless 9 impatient

item
  3 bit **5** entry, point, scrap, story, thing, topic
  6 detail, matter **7** account, article, element,
  feature, product **8** clipping **9** commodity
  10 particular

itemize
  4 list **5** count, tally **6** number **7** catalog,
  run down, specify, tick off **8** document,
  spell out **9** catalogue, enumerate,
  inventory

iterate
  5 drill, recap, renew **6** rehash, repeat,
  replay, retell **7** reprise, restate
  12 recapitulate

Ithaca king
  8 Odysseus

Ithamar's father
  5 Aaron

itinerant
  5 gypsy, nomad **6** roving **7** migrant,
  nomadic, roaming, vagrant **8** drifting,
  rambling, traveler, vagabond, wanderer
  9 migratory, transient, unsettled,
  wandering, wayfaring **11** peripatetic

itty-bitty
  3 wee **4** tiny **5** teeny, weeny **6** teensy
  10 teeny-weeny **12** teensy-weensy

Ivanhoe
  author: **5** Scott (Walter)
  character: **5** Isaac **6** Cedric, Rowena,
  Ulrica **7** Rebecca, Wilfred **9** Robin Hood

Ivory Coast
  11 Côte d'Ivoire
  capital: **7** Abidjan **12** Yamoussoukro
  city: **6** Bouaké
  language: **6** French
  monetary unit: **5** franc
  mountain: **5** Nimba
  neighbor: **4** Mali **5** Ghana **6** Guinea
  7 Liberia **11** Burkina Faso
  river: **7** Bandama **9** Sassandra

ivory-tower
  8 academic **11** conjectural, impractical,
  theoretical, unrealistic

J

jab
  3 hit **4** blow, poke, prod, sock, stab
5 nudge, prick, punch **6** pierce, strike,
thrust **8** puncture

jabber
  3 gab, jaw, yak **6** babble, drivel, gabble
7 blather, chatter, prattle **8** nonsense
9 gibberish

jabberer
  6 gabber, magpie **7** babbler, blabber,
gabbler **8** prattler **9** chatterer **10** chatterbox

Jabberwocky author
  7 Carroll (Lewis)

jabot
  4 fall **5** frill **6** ruffle

_____ jacet
  3 hic

jack
  3 tar **4** bird, card, fish, flag, hike, lift, move,
salt **5** boost, brace, bread, dough, knave,
knife, money, put up, raise **6** brandy,
cheese, device, donkey, rabbit, sailor,
seaman **7** laborer, mariner, servant **8** increase, standard **9** criticize, mechanism
10 take to task

jackal
  4 dupe, pawn **5** agent, canid, patsy
6 canine, flunky, lackey, minion, stooge
7 cat's-paw **9** accessory, auxiliary
10 accomplice **11** stool pigeon
  god: 4 Anpu **6** Anubis

jackanapes
  3 ape **4** brat, fool **6** monkey

jackass
  4 dolt, dope, fool, jerk **5** burro, dunce, idiot,
schmo **6** donkey, nitwit **7** nebbish
8 bonehead, imbecile, numskull
9 blockhead, numbskull **10** nincompoop
  deer: 3 kob **8** antelope

jackdaw
  7 grackle **9** blackbird

jacket
  4 Eton **5** parka, tunic **6** anorak, blazer,
bolero, jerkin, reefer, sacque, tuxedo
7 doublet, Norfolk, peacoat, spencer
8 camisole **10** roundabout
  armored: 7 hauberk **9** habergeon
  sleeveless: 4 vest **6** bolero, jerkin
9 waistcoat

jackhammer
  5 drill **9** rock drill

jackknife
  4 dive **6** barlow
  game: 11 mumblety-peg

jackleg
  6 make-do, novice **7** amateur, shyster,
stopgap **9** dishonest, greenhorn,
makeshift, temporary, unskilled
10 substitute **11** pettifogger
12 unscrupulous

jack-of-all-trades
  6 tinker **7** go-to guy **8** factotum, handyman

jack-o'-lantern
  6 fungus **7** pumpkin

jackpot
  3 sum **4** pool **5** award, kitty, prize
6 reward, stakes **7** bonanza, success
8 windfall

jackrabbit
  4 hare

jackstay
  3 bar, rod **4** rope **7** rigging, support

Jacob
  brother: 4 Esau
  daughter: 5 Dinah
  father: 5 Isaac
  father-in-law: 5 Laban
  mother: 7 Rebekah
  new name: 6 Israel
  son: 3 Dan, Gad **4** Levi **5** Asher, Judah

6 Joseph, Reuben, Simeon 7 Zebulun
8 Benjamin, Issachar, Naphtali
variant: 5 James
wife: 4 Leah 6 Rachel

Jacobin
7 radical 9 Dominican, extremist

Jacob's ladder
4 herb 5 phlox 9 perennial

jade
3 gem, nag 4 bore, cloy, dull, minx, pall,
tire, wear 5 color, drain, flirt, green, hussy,
jewel, stone, tramp, weary, wench
6 wanton 7 fatigue, jezebel, mineral,
trollop, wear out 8 gemstone, nephrite,
strumpet, wear down

jaded
4 worn 5 blasé, bored, sated, tired, weary
6 dulled 7 cynical, wearied, worn-out
8 fatigued, satiated, worn down
9 apathetic, exhausted, surfeited
10 overworked

jaeger
4 skua 6 hunter 8 huntsman

Jael
husband: 5 Heber
victim: 6 Sisera

jag
3 cut 4 barb, jerk, load, pink, tear 5 binge,
notch, prick, spell, spree 6 bender, indent,
thrill, thrust 7 serrate

jagged
5 harsh, rough, sharp 6 broken, craggy,
rugged, spiked, uneven 7 scraggy
8 serrated, unsmooth 9 irregular

_____ Jagger
4 Mick

jai alai
6 pelota
basket: 5 cesta
court: 6 cancha 7 fronton

jail
3 can, jug, pen 4 coop, gaol, poky 5 clink
6 cooler, lockup, pokey, prison 7 confine,
freezer, slammer 8 hoosegow, imprison,
stockade 9 constrain 11 confinement,
incarcerate

jailbird
3 con 5 felon, loser 7 convict 8 criminal,
prisoner, repeater 10 recidivist

jailer
5 guard, screw 6 keeper, warden
7 turnkey 8 overseer

jakes
5 privy 8 outhouse 9 backhouse

jalopy
3 car 4 auto, heap 5 crate, wreck
6 beater, junker 7 clunker, vehicle
10 automobile, rattletrap

jalousie
5 blind 6 window 7 shutter

jam
3 box, fix 4 bind, clog, cram, dunk, pack,
push 5 block, crowd, crush, force, jelly,
press, stuff, wedge 6 bruise, impede,
plight, scrape, squash, squish 7 dilemma,
squeeze 8 compress, conserve, preserve
9 confiture, obstacle, preserves
10 difficulty 11 predicament

Jamaica
capital: 8 Kingston
cay: 5 Pedro 6 Morant
city: 10 Montego Bay 11 Spanish Town
discoverer: 8 Columbus (Christopher)
language: 7 English
location: 10 West Indies
mountain range: 4 Blue 10 Dry Harbour
sea: 9 Caribbean

Jamaican
export: 3 rum 5 sugar
hair style: 10 dreadlocks
music: 3 dub, ska 6 reggae
musician: 5 Cliff (Jimmy) 6 Marley (Bob,
Ziggy) 7 Wailers
nationalist: 6 Garvey (Marcus)

jambalaya
4 olio 5 gumbo 7 mélange, mixture
8 mishmash

jamboree
4 gala 5 revel 6 fiesta, frolic 7 carouse,
shindig 8 carnival, festival, wingding
9 merriment 11 celebration
13 entertainment

James
brother: 4 John 5 Jesus, Joses
cousin: 5 Jesus
father: 7 Zebedee 8 Alphaeus
mother: 4 Mary 6 Salome

James novel
8 American (The) 9 Europeans (The)
10 Bostonians (The), Confidence, Golden
Bowl (The), Tragic Muse (The)
11 Ambassadors (The), Daisy Miller
14 Turn of the Screw (The), Wings of the
Dove (The) 15 Portrait of a Lady (The)
16 Washington Square

Jammu and ____
7 Kashmir

Jane Eyre
author: 6 Brontë (Charlotte)
lover: 9 Rochester

jangle
3 jar 4 ring 5 babel, clash 6 clamor,
excite, hubbub 7 discord, quarrel 8 conflict
11 discordance, discordancy
12 disharmonize

jangling
5 harsh, noisy, tense 7 grating 9 dissonant
10 discordant, quarreling

janitor
5 super 6 porter 7 cleaner 9 caretaker,
concierge, custodian 10 doorkeeper

japan
4 coat 7 coating, varnish 11 lacquerware

Japan
5 Nihon 6 Nippon
capital: 3 Edo 5 Tokyo
city: 4 Kobe 5 Kyoto, Osaka, Otaru
6 Nagoya 7 Fukuoka, Okinawa, Sapporo
8 Kawasaki, Nagasaki, Yokohama
9 Hiroshima
island: 6 Honshu, Kyushu 7 Shikoku
8 Hokkaido
lake: 4 Biwa 8 Chuzenji
monetary unit: 3 yen
mountain: 4 Fuji 8 Fujiyama

Japanese
aborigine: 4 Ainu
art: 6 bonsai 7 ukiyo-e
baron: 6 daimyo
battle cry: 6 banzai
Buddha: 5 Amida, Amita
cartoons: 5 anime
comics: 5 manga
dancing girl: 6 geisha
dish: 4 miso, soba 5 gyoza, katsu,
kombu, sushi 7 sashimi, tempura
8 sukiyaki, teriyaki
drama: 3 Noh 6 Bugaku, Kabuki
7 Bunraku
drink: 4 sake, saki
emperor: 6 Mikado 7 Akihito 8 Hirohito
fencing: 5 kendo
festival: 3 Bon
fish: 4 fugu
flower arrangement: 7 ikebana
garment: 6 kimono
gateway: 5 torii
god: 5 Ebisu, Hotei 7 Daikoku, Jurojin
8 Bishamon

goddess: 6 Benten 9 Amaterasu
governor: 6 shogun
grill: 7 hibachi
immigrant: 5 issei
instrument: 4 biwa, koto 7 samisen
8 shamisen 10 shakuhachi
martial art: 4 judo 5 kendo 6 aikido,
karate 7 jujitsu
martial artist: 5 ninja
money: 3 sen, yen
plum: 6 loquat
poem: 5 haiku, tanka
porcelain: 5 imari
pottery: 4 raku 7 satsuma
radish: 6 daikon
religion: 6 Shinto 8 Buddhism
9 Shintoism
rice wine: 4 sake, saki
robe: 6 kimono
samurai clan: 5 Taira 8 Minamoto
sash: 3 obi
song: 3 uta
suicide: 7 seppuku 8 hara-kiri, kamikaze
theater: 3 Noh 6 Bugaku, Kabuki
7 Bunraku
tidal wave: 7 tsunami
vehicle: 8 rickshaw
warrior: 7 samurai
warrior code: 7 bushido
wrestling: 4 sumo
writing: 4 kana 8 hiragana, katakana
zither: 4 koto

Japanese-American
5 Issei, Nisei
second-generation: 6 Sansei

jape
3 gag, kid, rib 4 gibe, jest, jibe, joke, mock,
quip 5 crack, laugh, prank, tease
7 waggery 8 drollery 9 wisecrack,
witticism

Japheth
brother: 3 Ham 4 Shem
father: 4 Noah
son: 5 Gomer, Javan, Madai, Magog,
Tiras, Tubal 7 Meshech

jar
4 bump, jolt, olla 5 cruse, quake, shake,
shock, upset 6 jangle, jounce 7 tremble,
vibrate 8 mismatch 9 container
ancient: 6 krater 7 amphora
Egyptian: 7 canopic

jardiniere
5 stand 6 holder 7 garnish

jargon
4 cant 5 argot, idiom, lingo, slang 6 patois,
pidgin 7 dialect, lexicon, palaver

8 language 9 gibberish 10 mumbo-jumbo, vernacular, vocabulary 11 terminology
lawyer's: 8 legalese

jarl
4 earl 5 noble 8 nobleman 12 Scandinavian

jarring
5 harsh, rough 6 hoarse, jangly 7 grating, rasping, raucous 8 strident 9 dissonant 10 discordant, unsettling

jasmine
3 tea 4 vine 5 shrub 6 flower, yellow 7 perfume

Jason
father: 5 Aeson
helper: 5 Medea
lover: 6 Creusa, Glauce, Glauke
quest: 6 Fleece 12 Golden Fleece
ship: 4 Argo
shipmate: 8 Argonaut
teacher: 6 Chiron 7 Cheiron
uncle: 6 Pelias
wife: 5 Medea

jasper
6 morlop, quartz 9 stoneware 10 chalcedony

jaundice
4 bias 7 disease, icterus 9 prejudice

jaundiced
6 biased, warped, yellow 7 colored, cynical, envious, hostile, jealous 9 distorted 10 suspicious

jaunt
4 ride, trip 5 drive, sally 6 junket, outing, ramble 7 journey 9 excursion

jaunty
4 airy, pert 5 fresh, light, peppy, perky 6 breezy, lively 7 buoyant 8 debonair 9 sprightly 10 nonchalant

java
6 coffee

Java
almond: 7 talisay
cotton: 5 kapok
jute: 5 kenaf
plum: 5 jaman 6 jambul 7 jambool

Javanese
civet: 5 rasse
orchestra: 7 gamelan
tree: 4 upas

Javan squirrel
8 jelerang

javelin
5 lance, shaft, spear 6 weapon 7 assagai, assegai, harpoon

Javert's prey
7 Valjean (Jean)

jaw
3 gab, yak 4 chat, rail, talk 5 clack, prate 6 babble, gabble 7 chatter, prattle 9 yakety-yak

jawbone
7 maxilla 8 arm-twist, mandible, persuade, talk into

jawbreaker
9 hard candy

jay
4 bird, blue, hick, rube 5 dandy 6 rustic 7 bumpkin, hayseed 9 chatterer, greenhorn

Jayhawker
9 guerrilla
State: 6 Kansas 8 Missouri

jazz
3 bop 4 guff, jive 5 bebop, stuff, swing 6 boogie 7 ragtime 8 malarkey, nonsense
up: 5 rouse 6 vivify 7 animate, enliven 9 stimulate

jazz musician
4 Cole (Nat "King"), Getz (Stan), Hirt (Al), Monk (Thelonious), O'Day (Anita), Rich (Buddy), Shaw (Artie) 5 Baker (Chet), Basie (Count), Brown (Clifford), Corea (Chick), Davis (Miles), Evans (Bill, Gil), Hines (Earl "Fatha"), Jones (Hank), Krall (Diana), Krupa (Gene), McRae (Carmen), Roach (Max), Smith (Jimmy), Sun Ra, Tatum (Art), Tormé (Mel), Young (Lester) 6 Bechet (Sidney), Blakey (Art), Burton (Gary), Carter (Benny), Dorsey (Jimmy, Tommy), Farmer (Art), Garner (Erroll), Gordon (Dexter), Herman (Woody), Jordan (Louis), Kenton (Stan), Mingus (Charles), Morton (Jelly Roll), Oliver (King), Parker (Charlie), Pepper (Art), Powell (Bud), Puente (Tito), Silver (Horace), Waller (Fats) 7 Brubeck (Dave), Coleman (Ornette), Connick (Harry), Goodman (Benny), Hampton (Lionel), Hancock (Herbie), Hawkins (Coleman), Holiday (Billie), Jarrett (Keith), Metheny (Pat), Rollins (Sonny), Rushing (Jimmy), Shorter (Wayne), Vaughan (Sarah), Webster (Ben)

8 Adderley (Cannonball), Calloway (Cab), Coltrane (John), Eldridge (Roy), Marsalis (Wynton), Mulligan (Gerry), Peterson (Oscar), Williams (Mary Lou) 9 Armstrong (Louis), Ellington (Duke), Gillespie (Dizzy), Reinhardt (Django) 10 Fitzgerald (Ella), Montgomery (Wes), Washington (Dinah) 11 Beiderbecke (Bix)

jazzy
5 gaudy 6 brassy, flashy, glitzy, lively, rakish 7 raffish, splashy 8 animated, colorful, exciting, spirited 9 vivacious 10 flamboyant

jealous
5 green 7 envious, hostile 8 doubting, vigilant 9 demanding, green-eyed, invidious, resentful 10 intolerant, possessive, suspicious 11 distrustful, mistrustful

jeer
4 gibe, jibe, mock 5 fleer, flout, scoff, scorn, sneer, taunt 6 deride, heckle, hector, insult 7 contemn, laugh at, mockery 8 derision, ridicule

Jeeves
creator: 9 Wodehouse (P. G.)
employer: 7 Wooster (Bertie)
position: 5 valet 6 butler

jeez
4 gosh, heck 5 golly, shoot 6 shucks 7 jeepers

jefe
4 boss, head, lord 5 chief, ruler 6 honcho, leader 9 chieftain, commander

Jefferson, Thomas
home: 10 Monticello
lover: 5 Sally (Hemings)
state: 8 Virginia

Jehoram
brother: 7 Ahaziah
father: 4 Ahab 11 Jehoshaphat
kingdom: 5 Judah
slayer: 4 Jehu
wife: 8 Athaliah

Jehoshaphat
father: 3 Asa 6 Ahilud, Nimshi, Paruah
father-in-law: 4 Ahab
son: 4 Jehu 7 Jehoram
wife: 8 Athaliah

Jehovah
3 God 6 Adonai, Elohim, Yahweh

Jehu
6 driver
father: 6 Hanani 11 Jehoshaphat
grandfather: 6 Nimshi
son: 8 Jehoahaz
victim: 5 Joram 7 Jehoram

jejune
4 dull, flat 5 banal, bland, empty, inane, silly, trite, vapid 7 insipid, puerile 8 childish, juvenile, lifeless 9 colorless, innocuous 10 spiritless 13 uninteresting

Jekyll's alter ego
4 Hyde (Mr.)

jell
3 set 4 form 6 cohere, gelate 7 congeal, thicken 8 coalesce 9 coagulate, take shape

jelly
3 set 4 mass 5 aspic 6 spread 7 congeal, thicken 9 coagulate

jellyfish
6 coward, medusa 7 doormat, medusan 8 medusoid, pushover, weakling 10 ctenophore 12 coelenterate, invertebrate, siphonophore

je ne _____ quoi
4 sais

jennet
3 ass 5 hinny, horse 6 donkey

jenny
4 bird 6 donkey, female 7 machine

jeopardize
4 risk 5 peril 6 chance, expose, hazard 7 imperil 8 endanger

jeopardy
4 risk 5 peril 6 danger, hazard, menace 8 exposure 9 liability 12 endangerment

jeremiad
6 lament, tirade 7 lecture 8 diatribe, harangue 9 complaint, philippic 11 declamation, lamentation

Jeremiah
scribe: 6 Baruch

Jericho's conqueror
6 Joshua

jerk
3 ass, lug, tic, tug 4 dolt, dope, fool, jolt, pull, push, snap, thrust, twit, yank 5 brute, idiot, lurch, ninny, spasm, twist, wrest

6 bounce, nitwit, twitch, wrench **7** jackass
8 preserve **10** nincompoop

jerkin
6 jacket

jerky
4 meat **5** inane **6** abrupt, stupid, sudden
7 foolish, idiotic, jolting **8** saccadic
9 senseless

Jerome's Bible
7 Vulgate

jersey
3 cow **6** fabric **7** garment, sweater
8 pullover

Jerusalem
4 Sion, Zion **5** Salem **8** Holy City
hill: **4** Sion, Zion **6** Moriah
mosque: **4** Omar **6** Al-Aqsa **13** Dome of
the Rock
pool: **6** Siloam **8** Bethesda

Jerusalem artichoke
5 tuber **8** girasole **9** sunflower

Jerusalem thorn
5 shrub **9** horsebean

jess
5 strap

Jesse
daughter: **7** Abigail, Zeruiah
father: **4** Obed
grandfather: **4** Boaz
son: **4** Ozem **5** David, Eliab, Elihu
6 Raddai **7** Shammah **8** Abinadab,
Nethanel
youngest son: **5** David

Jessica
father: **7** Shylock
husband: **7** Lorenzo

jest
3 fun, gag, kid, rag, rib **4** butt, game, gibe,
jape, jeer, joke, josh, mock, quip, razz
5 crack, fleer, flout, humor, prank, scoff,
sneer, spoof, sport, tease **6** banter, gaiety
7 mockery, waggery **8** derision, drollery,
ridicule **9** merriment, wisecrack, witticism

jester
3 wag, wit **4** fool **5** actor, clown, comic,
joker **7** buffoon **8** comedian, funnyman,
humorist, jokester, quipster **9** prankster
11 entertainer

Jesuit
founder: **6** Loyola (Ignatius)
leader: **6** Xavier (St. Francis)

jet
4 coal, ebon, emit, gush, inky, rush
5 black, ebony, plane, spew, spout, spurt
6 engine, nozzle, squirt, stream, travel
7 current, jewelry **8** airplane **9** pitch-dark
10 pitch-black

Jethro
daughter: **8** Zipporah
son-in-law: **5** Moses

jetsam
7 flotsam **8** wreckage **9** driftwood

jet set
5 A-list, elite **9** beau monde, haut monde
10 glitterati

jettison
4 drop, dump, junk, omit **5** eject, forgo,
scrap **6** reject, remove **7** deep-six, discard
8 disposal, get rid of, throw out **9** sacrifice,
throw away

jetty
4 dock, ebon, inky, pier, quay **5** black,
ebony, groin, wharf **7** project **9** pitch-dark
10 pitch-black

Jew
6 Essene, Hebrew, Semite **7** Israeli,
Judaist **9** Israelite

jewel
3 gem **5** adorn, bijou, ideal, prize, rock,
stone **7** bearing **8** gemstone, ornament,
treasure **9** embellish

jeweler
8 lapidary
famous: **7** Tiffany (Charles Lewis)

jewelry
10 bijouterie
artificial: **5** glass, paste **6** strass
7 costume
piece: **3** pin **4** ring **6** brooch **7** earring
8 bracelet, cufflink, necklace, tieclasp
9 lavaliere
set: **6** parure

Jewish
bread: **5** matzo **6** matzoh
ceremony: **4** bris **8** havdalah **10** bar
mitzvah, bas mitzvah
combining form: **5** Judeo **6** Judaeo
credo: **5** shema
doctrine: **6** Mishna **7** Mishnah
New Year: **12** Rosh Hashanah
organization: **8** Hadassah **9** B'nai B'rith
prayer: **7** kaddish, kiddush
prayer book: **6** siddur
sabbath: **8** Saturday
scripture: **5** Torah **6** Talmud

synagogue: 4 shul
teacher: 5 rabbi, rebbe 6 Hillel
village: 6 shtetl
(see also **Hebrew**)

Jezebel
4 slut 5 hussy, tramp, trull, wench
6 wanton 7 trollop 8 slattern, strumpet
father: 7 Ethbaal
home: 5 Sidon
husband: 4 Ahab
slayer: 4 Jehu
victim: 6 Naboth

jib
3 arm, shy 4 balk, boom, sail, stop
5 demur 6 refuse 9 stop short

jibe
5 agree, fit in, match, shift, tally 6 accord,
concur, square 7 conform 8 dovetail
9 harmonize 10 correspond, go together
12 change course

jiffy
3 sec 4 tick, wink 5 flash, hurry, shake,
trice 6 minute, moment, second 7 instant
11 split second

jig
4 fish, game, hoax, hook, jerk, play, ploy,
ruse, sham, wile 5 catch, dance, feint, trick
6 device, gambit 7 gimmick 9 deception

jigger
4 jerk, mold, sail 5 alter, gizmo 6 device,
dingus, doodad, gadget, widget 7 gimmick,
machine, measure 9 doohickey, shot
glass, thingummy 10 manipulate,
rearrange

jiggle
4 jerk 5 shake 7 agitate 9 oscillate

jigsaw
3 cut 4 tool 6 puzzle 7 arrange, machine

jihad
3 war 6 strife 7 crusade, holy war
8 campaign, struggle

jilt
4 drop 5 ditch, leave 6 desert, reject
7 abandon, cast off, discard

jim-dandy
5 great, ideal, nifty, super 7 perfect
8 knockout 9 excellent, first-rate,
humdinger 11 outstanding

jimmy
3 bar, pry 4 open 5 crack, force, lever
7 crowbar 9 break open, force open

jimsonweed
6 datura 10 thorn apple

jingle
4 call, ring, song 5 clink, rhyme, sound,
verse 6 tinkle

jingoistic
7 hawkish 11 belligerent 12 chauvinistic,
militaristic 13 nationalistic

jinn
5 afrit, genie 6 afreet, spirit

jinx
3 hex 5 charm, curse, plague, spell
6 whammy 7 bad luck, evil eye
8 foredoom 10 affliction, misfortune

jitters
5 jumps, panic 6 nerves, shakes
7 anxiety, shivers, willies 9 whim-whams
11 nervousness, stage fright 13 heebie-
jeebies

jittery
5 jumpy, nervy 6 goosey, spooky
7 anxious, fearful, fidgety, nervous, panicky
10 high-strung

jive
3 kid 4 fool, jazz, talk 5 dance, music,
swing, tease 6 cajole, hot air, jargon

Joab
brother: 6 Asahel 7 Abishai
father: 7 Seraiah, Zeruiah
slayer: 7 Benaiah
uncle: 5 David
victim: 5 Abner, Amasa

Joan of Arc
birthplace: 7 Domremy
epithet: 7 Pucelle (La) 13 Maid of
Orléans
king: 10 Charles VII
victory: 7 Orléans

Joan's husband
5 Darby

Joash
father: 4 Ahab 7 Ahaziah 8 Jehoahaz
son: 6 Gideon 7 Amaziah 8 Jeroboam
victim: 9 Zechariah

job
4 duty, hire, item, post, role, spot, task,
work 5 chore, stint, trade 6 effort, office
7 calling, deprive, posting, pursuit, robbery
8 business, function, penalize, position,
vocation 9 situation, speculate, victimize
10 assignment, difficulty, employment,
engagement, livelihood, occupation,
profession 11 undertaking

Job
daughter: 6 Keziah 7 Jemimah
father: 8 Issachar
friend: 6 Bildad, Zophar 7 Eliphaz

jobber
6 broker, dealer, seller, trader 8 merchant
10 contractor, wholesaler

job-safety agency
4 OSHA

job-training program
4 CETA

Jocasta
daughter: 6 Ismene 8 Antigone
husband: 5 Laius 7 Oedipus
son: 7 Oedipus 8 Eteocles 9 Polynices

jock
5 pilot 7 athlete

jockey
4 play 5 rider, trick 7 beguile, exploit,
finesse 8 maneuver 10 manipulate
famous: 5 Baeza (Braulio) 6 Arcaro
(Eddie), Bailey (Jerry), Murphy (Isaac),
Pincay (Laffit) 7 Cauthen (Steve), Cordero
(Angel), Hartack (Bill), Longden (Johnny),
Stevens (Gary) 8 McCarron (Chris), Mc-
Hargue (Darrel), Turcotte (Ron) 9 Shoe-
maker (Willie)

jocular
5 comic, funny, jolly, merry, witty 6 jocose,
jocund, jovial, lively 7 amusing, comical,
jesting, playful 8 cheerful, humorous
9 facetious

jocularity
3 fun, wit 4 glee 5 humor, mirth 6 gaiety
7 jollity 8 hilarity 9 jocundity, joviality,
merriment 11 high spirits, playfulness

jocund
3 gay 5 happy, jolly, merry 6 elated, jovial,
lively 7 festive, gleeful, playful 8 mirthful
12 lighthearted

joe
3 guy 4 java 6 coffee, fellow

jog
3 dig, jab, run 4 lope, move, pace, poke,
prod, push, ride, stir, trot 5 nudge, punch,
rouse, shake 6 bounce, change, jounce,
prompt, remind

joggle
4 join, trot 5 dowel, joint, notch, shake,
tooth 6 jostle

john
4 head 5 privy 6 toilet 7 latrine

8 bathroom, lavatory 11 water closet

John Hancock
9 autograph, signature

Johnson, Samuel
biographer: 7 Boswell (James)
work: 8 Rasselas 10 dictionary

John the Baptist
father: 9 Zacharias
mother: 9 Elisabeth

John the Evangelist
brother: 5 James
father: 7 Zebedee
mother: 6 Salome

join
3 tie, wed 4 abut, ally, bind, bond, fuse,
line, link, mate, yoke 5 affix, align, blend,
marry, merge, piece, touch, unify, union,
unite 6 attach, border, couple, engage,
enlist, enroll, sign on, sign up, splice
7 combine, connect 8 compound, side with
9 affiliate, associate, integrate 12 come
together

joint
3 bar, ell, hip, tie 4 butt, crux, dive, knee,
link, node, seam 5 ankle, elbow, hinge,
nexus, union, wrist 6 common, mutual,
public, shared, suture, united 7 hangout,
knuckle, shiplap 8 abutment, combined,
communal, conjunct, coupling, junction,
juncture, shoulder 9 concerted, honky-tonk
10 collective, connection 11 cooperative
12 articulation
combining form: 5 arthr 6 arthro, condyl
7 condylo
disease: 9 arthritis 10 rheumatism

joist
4 beam 6 rafter, timber 7 support

joke
3 gag, kid, pun, rag, rib, yak 4 fool, jape,
jest, josh, quip, razz 5 crack, humor, prank,
sally 6 banter, corker, parody 7 mockery,
sarcasm, waggery 8 drollery, one-liner
9 burlesque, wisecrack, witticism 11 monkeyshine
stale: 8 chestnut

joker
3 guy, wag, wit 4 card, fool 5 catch, clown,
comic, cutup 6 fellow, jester, kicker
7 proviso 8 comedian, humorist
9 condition 10 limitation 11 stipulation

jollity
3 fun, joy 4 glee 5 cheer, mirth 6 gaiety,
revels 7 revelry, whoopee 8 hilarity

9 festivity, jocundity, joviality, merriment
10 ebullience, jocularity, liveliness 11 high
spirits, merrymaking 12 cheerfulness,
conviviality

jolly

3 fun, gay, kid 4 glad, jest, josh, very
5 humor, merry 6 banter, blithe, jocund,
jovial, joyful, joyous 7 festive, gleeful,
jocular, playful, roguish, waggish
8 cheerful, mirthful, splendid 9 convivial
10 frolicsome 12 lighthearted

Jolly Roger

4 flag 6 ensign
user: 6 pirate

jolt

3 hit, jar 4 blow, bump, jerk, shot, slug,
stun 5 check, clash, crash, knock, lurch,
shake, shock, snort, upset 6 impact,
jounce, rattle 7 disturb, reverse, shake up,
startle 8 astonish, surprise 9 collision

Jonah

7 prophet
swallower: 4 fish 5 whale

Jonathan

brother: 7 Johanan
father: 4 Saul
friend: 5 David

Jones, John Paul

ship: 15 Bonhomme Richard
victim: 7 Serapis

Jones novel

11 Thin Red Line (The) 15 Some Came
Running 18 From Here to Eternity

jongleur

4 bard 6 singer 7 juggler 8 minstrel
10 troubadour 11 entertainer

jonquil

8 daffodil 9 narcissus, perennial

Jonson play

7 Volpone 9 Alchemist (The) 15 Bartholomew Fair

Joplin creation

3 rag 7 ragtime

Joram

brother: 7 Ahaziah
father: 3 Toi 4 Ahab 11 Jehoshaphat
slayer: 4 Jehu
son: 7 Ahaziah

Jordan

capital: 5 Amman
city: 5 Irbid, Zarqa
gulf: 5 Aqaba
language: 6 Arabic

monarch: 7 Hussein
monetary unit: 5 dinar
mountain: 4 Ramm
neighbor: 4 Iraq 5 Syria 6 Israel
11 Saudi Arabia
river: 6 Jordan
sea: 4 Dead

jorum

3 cup, jug 6 vessel

Joseph

brother:
(see **Jacob** son)
buyer: 8 Potiphar
father: 5 Asaph, Jacob 9 Zacharias
10 Mattathias
mother: 6 Rachel
son: 5 Jesus 7 Ephraim 8 Manasseh
wife: 4 Mary 7 Asenath

josh

3 kid, rag, rib 4 jest, joke, razz 5 chaff,
jolly, tease 6 banter

Joshua's victory

7 Jericho

Joshua tree

5 yucca

joss

4 idol 5 image

Jo's sister

3 Amy, Meg 4 Beth

jostle

3 jar, jog 4 bump, push 5 crowd, elbow,
nudge, press, shove 7 agitate, collide,
compete, contend, vie with 8 shoulder

jot

3 bit 4 atom, iota, note, whit 5 grain,
minim, speck, write 6 tittle 7 smidgen
8 particle

joule component

3 erg

jounce

3 bob, jar, jog 4 bump, jolt 5 shake, shock,
thump 6 impact

journal

3 log 5 diary, organ, paper 6 ledger,
record, review 7 account, gazette, minutes
8 magazine, register 9 chronicle,
newspaper 10 periodical

journalist

3 Bly (Nellie) 4 Dowd (Maureen), Drew
(Elizabeth), King (Larry), Pyle (Ernie), Reed
(John), Rose (Charlie), Will (George F.),
Zahn (Paula) 5 Baker (Russell), Brown

(George), Cooke (Alistair), Dunne (Finley
Peter), Evans (Rowland), Hersh (Seymour),
Novak (Robert), Rowan (Carl), Royko
(Mike), Safer (Morley), Smith (Hedrick),
Stahl (Lesley), Stone (I. F.), Szulc (Tad),
White (William Allen), Wolfe (Tom) **6** Arnett
(Peter), Bierce (Ambrose), Broder (David),
Brokaw (Tom), Ephron (Nora), Koppel
(Ted), Kuralt (Charles), Lehrer (Jim),
Moyers (Bill), Murrow (Edward R.), Osgood
(Charles), Rather (Dan), Reston (James),
Reuter (Paul Julius), Rivera (Geraldo),
Runyon (Damon), Safire (William), Shirer
(William L.), Thomas (Helen, Lowell),
Zenger (John Peter) **7** Blitzer (Wolf), Brad-
lee (Benjamin), Breslin (Jimmy), Cousins
(Norman), Greeley (Horace), Gunther
(John), Huntley (Chet), Kempton (Murray),
McGrory (Mary), Mencken (H. L.), Pearson
(Drew), Royster (Vermont), Russert (Tim),
Tarbell (Ida), Trillin (Calvin), Wallace (Chris,
Mike), Walters (Barbara) **8** Amanpour
(Christiane), Anderson (Jack, Terry),
Atkinson (Brooks), Brinkley (David),
Cronkite (Walter), Garrison (William Lloyd),
Jennings (Peter), Lippmann (Walter),
Pulitzer (Joseph), Salinger (Pierre),
Sevareid (Eric), Steffens (Lincoln),
Thompson (Dorothy, Hunter), Winchell
(Walter), Woodward (Bob) **9** Bernstein
(Carl), Donaldson (Sam), Frederick (Pau-
line), Salisbury (Harrison), Schieffer (Bob)

journey
3 hie **4** hike, roam, tour, trek, trip **5** jaunt,
quest **6** cruise, junket, push on, safari,
travel, voyage **7** caravan, odyssey,
proceed, travels **8** progress **9** excursion
10 expedition, pilgrimage
route: **9** itinerary
stage: **3** leg

joust
4 duel, feud, spar, tilt **5** clash, fight
6 combat **7** contest **8** conflict **10** tournament
arena: **5** lists **8** tiltyard

Jove
see **Jupiter**

jovial
5 happy, jolly, merry **6** cheery **7** amiable
8 cheerful **9** convivial **11** good-humored,
good-natured

jowl
3 jaw **5** cheek **6** dewlap, wattle
8 mandible

joy
4 glee **5** bliss, mirth **6** gaiety **7** delight,
elation **8** felicity, fruition, gladness,
pleasure **9** enjoyment, happiness,
merriment **11** delectation

Joyce, James
birthplace: **6** Dublin
character: **5** Bloom (Leopold), Bloom
(Molly) **7** Dedalus (Stephen)
work: **6** Exiles **7** Ulysses **9** Dubliners
13 Finnegans Wake

joyful
3 gay **4** glad **5** happy, jolly, merry
6 elated, jocund **7** buoyant, festive, gleeful,
pleased **8** ecstatic, jubilant, mirthful
9 delighted, rapturous **12** lighthearted

jubilant
5 happy **6** elated, joyful, joyous
8 euphoric, exultant, exulting **9** cock-a-
hoop, delighted, overjoyed, triumphal
10 triumphant

jubilate
5 exult, glory **7** delight, rejoice **9** celebrate

jubilation
3 joy **4** glee **7** ecstasy, rapture
8 euphoria, rhapsody, transport **9** rejoicing
10 exaltation, exultation, joyfulness,
joyousness **11** celebration **12** exhilaration

jubilee
6 flambé **8** festival **9** festivity **10** indulgence **11** anniversary, celebration
13 commemoration

Judah
brother:
(see **Jacob** son)
father: **5** Jacob
king: **3** Asa **4** Ahaz, Amon **5** Joash
6 Abijam, Josiah, Jotham, Uzziah
7 Ahaziah, Amaziah, Jehoram **8** Hezekiah,
Jehoahaz, Manasseh, Rehoboam,
Zedekiah **9** Jehoiakim **10** Jehoiachin
11 Jehoshaphat
mother: **4** Leah
son: **4** Onan **6** Shelah

Judas
7 traitor **8** informer, turncoat
father: **5** Simon **7** Chalphi **10** Mattathias
replacement: **8** Matthias
suicide place: **8** Aceldama, Akeldama

judge
3 ref, try, ump **4** call, deem, rule, test
5 infer **6** critic, decide, deduce, jurist,
reckon, settle, umpire **7** arbiter, justice,
mediate, referee **8** assessor, critique,

estimate, mediator **9** arbitrate, criticize, determine, moderator **10** adjudicate, arbitrator, chancellor, magistrate, negotiator **11** conciliator **12** intermediary
bench: 4 banc
chamber: 6 camera
in Hades: 5 Minos **6** Aeacus **12** Rhadamanthus
mallet: 5 gavel
Muslim: 5 mufti

judgment
5 award, sense **6** acumen, decree, ruling, result, wisdom **7** finding, insight, opinion, verdict **8** decision, sagacity, sentence **9** appraisal, deduction, good sense, inference **10** assessment, conclusion, discretion, estimation, evaluation, horse sense, punishment **11** common sense, discernment **13** determination

judgmental
7 carping **8** captious, critical **10** belittling, censorious, derogatory **11** disparaging, reproachful **12** disapproving, faultfinding **13** hypercritical

Judgment Day
8 doomsday

_____ **judicata**
3 res

judicial
assembly: 5 court
document: 4 writ

judicious
3 apt **4** fair, just, sage, sane, wise **5** right, sound **6** astute **7** careful, prudent, sapient **8** accurate, discreet, rational, sensible **9** equitable, objective, sagacious **10** discerning, reasonable

Judith
father: 5 Beeri
home: 8 Bethulia
husband: 4 Esau
victim: 10 Holofernes

judo
10 martial art
teacher: 6 sensei

Judy's husband
5 Punch

jug
3 jar, pen **4** coop, ewer, gaol, jail, stew, stir, toby **5** pokey **6** cooler, flagon, immure, intern, lockup, prison, vessel **7** confine, pitcher, slammer **8** demijohn, imprison **9** constrain, container **11** incarcerate

jug-band instrument
5 kazoo **6** bottle **7** washtub **9** stovepipe, washboard

juggernaut
11 steamroller

juggle
3 fix **4** fool, toss **5** bluff, trick **6** change, delude, doctor, handle, humbug, take in **7** balance, beguile, deceive, mislead, shuffle **9** rearrange **10** manipulate

juice
3 sap **4** fuel, must **5** fluid **7** current, essence **8** vitality **10** succulence **11** electricity
fermented: 4 wine **5** cider, perry

juicy
3 fat **4** racy, rich **5** lusty, vital **7** piquant **8** colorful, dripping, exciting **9** delicious, rewarding, succulent **10** profitable **11** fascinating, sensational

juju
4 luck **5** charm, magic **6** amulet, fetish, mascot **8** talisman **10** lucky charm

jujube
4 tree **5** fruit **7** gumdrop, lozenge

julep
5 drink

Juliet
betrothed: 5 Paris
father: 7 Capulet
lover: 5 Romeo

July 14
11 Bastille Day

jumble
3 mix **4** cake, hash, mess, olio **5** chaos, mix up, shake **6** cookie, medley, mess up, muddle, muss up **7** clutter, confuse, disturb, mélange, rummage, shuffle **8** disarray, disorder, mishmash, pastiche, scramble **9** confusion, patchwork, potpourri **10** assortment, hodgepodge, hotchpotch, miscellany

jumbo
4 huge, vast **5** giant **6** mighty **7** immense, mammoth, massive **8** colossal, enormous, gigantic, oversize **9** oversized **10** prodigious **11** elephantine

jump
3 hop **4** bolt, hike, leap, move, trip **5** avoid, begin, boost, bound, clear, flush, hurry, leave, put up, raise, shift, start, vault **6** attack, bounce, bustle, change, hurdle, hustle, jack up, pounce, spring **7** bail out,

elevate, startle **8** increase, leap over
9 advantage

jumper
4 sled **5** dress, horse, smock **6** blouse,
jacket

jumping-frog county
9 Calaveras

jumpy
6 on edge **7** anxious, jittery, nervous
9 excitable, high-strung

junction
4 seam **5** joint, union **7** joining, meeting
8 coupling **9** interface **10** confluence,
connection, crossroads **12** intersection

juncture
4 seam **5** joint, point, union **6** crisis,
moment **7** instant, joining **8** coupling
10 connection, crossroads **11** concurrence, convergence **12** turning point

jungle
3 web, zoo **4** hash, mash, maze **5** snarl
6 jumble, morass, muddle, tangle **7** clutter,
thicket **8** mishmash **9** labyrinth

Jungle Books, The
  author: **7** Kipling (Rudyard)
  bear: **5** Baloo
  boy: **6** Mowgli
  panther: **8** Bagheera
  python: **3** Kaa
  tiger: **9** Shere Khan
  wolf: **5** Akela

Jungle, The
  author: **8** Sinclair (Upton)
  locale: **7** Chicago **10** stockyards

junior
3 son **5** lower, minor, sonny, youth
6 lesser **7** student, younger **8** inferior,
young man, youthful **9** secondary,
youngster **11** subordinate

juniper
4 cone **5** cedar, fruit, savin, shrub
7 conifer **9** evergreen

junk
4 boat, dope, drug, ship **5** scrap, trash,
waste **6** debris, heroin, litter, refuse, reject
7 cashier, clutter, discard, rubbish,
rummage **8** get rid of, jettison, throw out
9 narcotics, throw away

junker
4 heap **5** crate, wreck **6** jalopy

junket
4 trip **5** feast, jaunt, spree **6** outing, picnic
7 banquet, dessert, journey **9** excursion

junk mail
4 spam

Juno
  bird: **7** peacock
  epithet: **6** Moneta
  Greek equivalent: **4** Hera
  husband: **7** Jupiter
  (see also **Hera**)

Junoesque
7 stately **10** curvaceous, statuesque

junta
5 cabal, group **7** council, faction
9 committee

Jupiter
4 Jove, Zeus
  angel: **7** Zadkiel
  cupbearer: **8** Ganymede
  daughter: **5** Venus **7** Minerva
  epithet: **6** Fidius, Fulgur, Stator, Tonans
  7 Pluvius
  father: **6** Saturn
  lover: **6** Europa **8** Callisto
  mother: **3** Ops
  satellite: **6** Europa **8** Callisto, Ganymede
  son: **5** Arcas **6** Castor, Pollux
  temple: **7** Capitol
  wife: **4** Juno

Jurgen
  author: **6** Cabell (James Branch)
  trade: **10** pawnbroker

juridical
5 legal **6** lawful **8** juristic **10** legalistic

jurisdiction
3 law, see **4** sway, zone **5** might, orbit,
power, range, reach, scope, venue
6 county, domain, parish, sphere **7** circuit,
command, compass, control, diocese,
mastery, purview **8** dominion, hegemony,
province **9** authority, bailiwick, supervision,
territory **10** domination

jurisprudence
3 law

jurist
5 judge

jury
5 panel
  decision: **7** verdict

jury-rigged
6 make-do **7** stopgap **9** makeshift,

temporary **10** improvised

just

3 apt, due, fit **4** even, fair, good, meet, only, true, very **5** equal, legal, quite, right **6** barely, hardly, honest, lawful, nearly, proper, simply, square **7** correct, ethical, exactly, fitting, merited, perhaps, precise, totally, upright **8** accurate, deserved, directly, possibly, recently, rightful, scarcely, squarely, suitable, unbiased **9** equitable, expressly, honorable, impartial, justified, objective, precisely, requisite, righteous **10** accurately, completely, legitimate, reasonable, scrupulous **11** appropriate, immediately, well-founded **12** unprejudiced **13** conscientious

justice

3 law **5** court, judge, right **6** equity **7** honesty **8** evenness, fairness, fair play **10** lawfulness, magistrate **11** correctness **12** impartiality

justification

6 excuse, reason **7** account, apology, defense, grounds **8** apologia **9** rationale **10** validation **11** explanation, vindication

justify

5 argue, claim, prove **6** assert, defend, uphold, verify **7** account, bear out, confirm, contend, explain, support, warrant **8** maintain, make even, validate **9** vindicate **10** legitimate, legitimize **11** corroborate, rationalize **12** authenticate, legitimatize, substantiate

jut

4 hang, poke **5** bulge, pouch **6** beetle, thrust **7** project **8** extend up, overhang, protrude, stand out, stick out **9** extend out, extension **10** projection, protrusion **12** protuberance

jute

5 gunny **6** burlap **7** sacking

Juvenal

4 poet **5** Roman
forte: 6 satire

juvenile

3 kid **5** actor, child, green, young, youth **6** callow, jejune, junior, moppet **7** preteen, puerile **8** childish, immature, youthful **9** childlike, fledgling, youngling, youngster **11** undeveloped

juvenility

5 youth **9** childhood, greenness **10** immaturity, springtide, springtime **12** youthfulness

juxtaposed

4 next **8** abutting, adjacent, neighbor, proximal, touching **9** adjoining, bordering **10** appositive, contiguous, side-by-side **11** coterminous, neighboring **12** conterminous

K

kabob
see **kebab**

kachina
4 doll 6 spirit 12 impersonator

kaddish
6 prayer

Kafka, Franz
character: 4 Olga 6 Gregor (Samsa),
Joseph (K.)
novel: 5 Trial (The) 6 Castle (The)
7 Amerika
story: 8 Judgment (The) 12 Hunger Artist
(A) 13 Metamorphosis (The)

kaiser
5 ruler 7 emperor, monarch 8 autocrat
9 sovereign

kaka
6 parrot

kale
4 cash, cole 5 bucks, money, moola
6 moolah 7 cabbage 8 colewort

kaleidoscopic
8 changing, colorful 10 variegated

Kali
aspect: 5 Durga 7 Parvati
husband: 4 Siva 5 Shiva

Kama
god of: 4 love
mount: 6 parrot 7 sparrow
wife: 4 Rati

kamikaze
7 suicide 8 suicidal

kampong
6 hamlet 7 village

Kampuchea
see **Cambodia**

kangaroo
6 leaper 7 wallaby 8 wallaroo 9 marsupial
herd: 3 mob
young: 4 joey

Kansas
capital: 6 Topeka
city: 6 Olathe, Salina, Topeka 7 Abilene,
Emporia, Shawnee, Wichita 8 Lawrence
nickname: 9 Jayhawker (State),
Sunflower (State)
prison: 11 Leavenworth
river: 8 Arkansas
state bird: 10 meadowlark
state flower: 9 sunflower
state tree: 10 cottonwood

kaolin
4 clay

kaput
5 spent 6 ruined 7 done for, useless
8 defeated, finished, outmoded
9 destroyed

karakul
5 sheep 9 broadtail

karma
4 fate 9 emanation

kaross
3 rug 7 garment

kasha
5 grain 8 porridge 9 buckwheat

Katharina
father: 8 Baptista
suitor: 9 Petruchio

Katrina's suitor
9 Brom Bones 12 Ichabod Crane

katydid
3 bug 6 insect 11 grasshopper

katzenjammer
3 din 5 noise 6 clamor, hubbub, racket
8 distress, hangover, headache
9 commotion

kava

kava
5 shrub 6 pepper 8 beverage

kayo
6 defeat, finish 8 knockout 9 finish off
11 coup de grace

Kazakhstan
capital: 6 Akmola, Astana
city: 5 Semey 8 Pavlodar, Shymkent
lake: 6 Tengiz 8 Balkhash
language: 6 Kazakh 7 Russian
monetary unit: 5 tenge
mountain: 10 Khan-Tengri
neighbor: 5 China 6 Russia 10 Kyrgyzstan, Uzbekistan 12 Turkmenistan
river: 4 Ural 6 Irtysh 8 Syr Dar'ya
sea: 4 Aral 7 Caspian

Kazantzakis hero
5 Zorba (Alexis)

kea
6 parrot

Keats poem
5 Lamia 8 Endymion, Hyperion, Isabella,
To Autumn 11 Ode to Psyche 12 Eve of
St. Agnes (The) 16 Ode on a Grecian Urn
17 Ode to a Nightingale

kebab
8 shashlik

kedge
6 anchor

keel
4 boat, lean, ship 5 barge, pitch, ridge,
slump 6 carina 7 capsize 8 overturn
11 centerboard

keen
4 avid, fine, wail, yowl 5 acute, alert,
eager, honed, mourn, sharp, smart
6 ardent, astute, bewail, bright, clever,
gung ho, intent, lament, shrewd 7 anxious,
fervent, intense, whetted, zealous
8 animated, spirited 9 fine-edged,
impatient, sensitive, wonderful
10 perceptive, razor-sharp 11 lamentation,
penetrating, quick-witted, sharp-witted
12 enthusiastic, sharp-sighted

keenness
3 wit 4 edge, zeal 6 acuity, acumen
10 enthusiasm 11 discernment,
penetration 12 incisiveness, perspicacity

keep
3 own 4 hold, jail, mind, obey, save, stay,
tend 5 lodge, stock 6 castle, comply,
detain, living, lockup, manage, prison,
retain 7 abstain, conduct, confine, forbear,
fulfill, possess, refrain, reserve 8 conserve,
fortress, maintain, preserve, withhold

9 constrain 10 livelihood, sustenance
11 maintenance, subsistence

keep back
3 bar, dam 4 curb, hold, save, stay
6 detain, retain, retard, stifle 7 contain,
inhibit, repress, reserve 8 restrain, restrict,
suppress, withhold

keeper
5 guard 6 warden 7 big fish, curator
8 Cerberus, guardian, watchdog
9 custodian, protector

keeping
4 care, ward 5 aegis, trust 6 charge
7 custody, support 8 wardship 9 provision
10 caretaking, conformity, observance
11 maintenance 12 conservation,
guardianship

keep on
4 last 5 abide 6 endure 7 persist
8 continue 9 hang tough, persevere

keep out
3 ban, bar 4 hold, stop 5 block, check,
debar 6 forbid 7 embargo, exclude
8 prohibit, turn back 9 blackball

keepsake
5 token 6 trophy 7 memento 8 memorial,
reminder, souvenir 11 remembrance

keep up
7 persist, prolong, sustain 8 continue,
maintain, preserve 9 persevere

kef
4 hash, hemp 7 hashish 10 dreaminess
12 tranquillity

keg
3 tun 4 butt, cask, pipe 6 barrel, firkin,
vessel 8 hogshead 9 container

kegler
6 bowler

keister
3 bum, end 4 buns, duff, rear, rump, seat,
tail, tush 5 fanny 6 behind, bottom
8 backside, buttocks, derriere 9 posterior

keloid
4 scar

kelp
4 alga 7 seaweed

kelpie
3 dog 5 naiad, nixie 6 sprite

ken
4 view 5 grasp, range, reach, scope, sight
7 horizon, purview 9 knowledge

10 perception 13 comprehension, understanding

kenaf
5 fiber, plant 8 hibiscus

Kenilworth author
5 Scott (Walter)

Kennedy novel
8 Ironweed

kennel
4 pack 5 board 6 gutter 7 shelter
9 enclosure

keno
4 game
similar to: 5 beano, bingo, lotto

Kentucky
capital: 9 Frankfort
city: 9 Lexington 10 Louisville
12 Bowling Green
nickname: 9 Bluegrass (State)
park: 11 Mammoth Cave
racecourse: 14 Churchill Downs
river: 4 Ohio
state bird: 8 cardinal
state flower: 9 goldenrod
state tree: 11 tulip poplar

Kentucky bluegrass
3 Poa

Kenya
capital: 7 Nairobi
city: 6 Kisumu, Nakuru 7 Mombasa
lake: 7 Turkana 8 Victoria
language: 7 English, Swahili
monetary unit: 8 shilling
mountain: 5 Elgon, Kenya
neighbor: 5 Sudan 6 Uganda 7 Somalia
8 Ethiopia, Tanzania
river: 4 Tana

kepi
3 cap

kerchief
6 hankie 7 bandana 8 babushka,
bandanna, kaffiyeh
Scottish: 5 curch

kerf
3 cut 4 nick, slit 5 cleft, notch 6 groove

kerfuffle
3 ado, row 4 flap, fuss, stir, to-do 5 hoo-ha
6 dust-up, ruckus, rumpus 7 turmoil
8 foofaraw 11 disturbance

kermis
4 fair 8 carnival, festival

kernel
3 nub, nut 4 core, crux, gist, meat, pith,
seed 5 grain 6 nubbin, upshot 7 essence,
nucleus 9 substance

Kerouac novel
6 Big Sur 9 On the Road 10 Dharma
Bums (The) 13 Subterraneans (The)

Kesey novel
21 Sometimes a Great Notion 25 One
Flew over the Cuckoo's Nest

kestrel
4 bird, hawk 6 falcon 9 windhover

ketch
4 boat 6 vessel 8 sailboat 10 watercraft

ketone
7 acetone, camphor

kettle
3 pot 6 hollow, vessel 7 caldron, marmite,
pothole 8 cauldron

kettledrum
5 naker 7 timpani (plural), timpano

key
4 clue, isle, reef 5 basic, islet, vital
6 cotter, island, legend, master, opener,
samara, spline, ticket, tip-off 7 central,
crucial, digital, pivotal 8 critical, essential,
passport, password, skeleton, solution,
tonality 9 important 10 open sesame
11 fundamental
combining form: 5 clavi, clavo
notch: 4 ward

keyboard
6 manual 7 clavier

key fruit
6 samara

key man
5 chief 7 kingpin 9 locksmith

keynote
4 core, crux, gist, pith, tone 5 theme, tonic

keynoter
6 orator 7 speaker

Keystone State
12 Pennsylvania

khaki
3 tan 5 brown, cloth, color 7 garment,
uniform

khamsin
4 wind

khan
5 chief, ruler 9 chieftain, sovereign
11 caravansary

khedive
5 ruler 7 viceroy

Khomeini
4 imam 9 ayatollah

Ki
mother: 5 Nammu
son: 5 Enlil

kiang
3 ass

kibble
4 meal 5 grain, grind 9 pulverize

kibbutz
4 co-op, farm 7 commune 10 collective,
settlement 11 cooperative

kibe
4 heel, sore 8 swelling 9 chilblain

kibitz
4 chat 6 banter, butt in, meddle
7 comment, intrude, obtrude 9 interfere

kibitzer
7 meddler 8 busybody, observer
9 buttinsky, spectator 10 rubberneck

kibosh
3 hex 4 jinx, stop 5 check, curse

kick
4 bang, boot, carp, fuss, punt, wail 5 gripe,
rebel, whine 6 object, recoil, repine, resist,
thrill, wallop 7 grumble, protest 8 complain

kicker
5 catch 6 clause, punter 9 condition, fine
print

kick in
3 die, pay 4 give 5 begin, put up, start
6 donate, pony up 7 cough up, fork out
8 fork over, hand over 10 contribute

kick off
3 die 4 open 5 begin, croak, start
6 launch 7 cough up 8 commence, drop dead, embark
on, initiate 10 inaugurate

kick out
3 axe, can 4 fire, oust, sack 5 eject, evict
6 bounce 7 boot out, cashier, dismiss
8 throw out 9 discharge

kickshaw
5 goody, treat 6 bauble, dainty, gewgaw,
morsel, tidbit, trifle 7 bibelot, trinket
8 delicacy 9 bagatelle

kid
3 guy, rag, rib 4 dupe, fool, gull, hoax, jest,
joke, josh, razz 5 child, jolly, trick, youth
6 banter, befool, moppet, nipper 7 deceive,
younger 8 flimflam, hoodwink, juvenile
9 bamboozle, youngling, youngster

kidnap
6 abduct, snatch 8 shanghai

kidney
5 gland, organ
combining form: 4 reni, reno 5 nephr
6 nephro

kidney-shaped
8 reniform

kielbasa
7 sausage

kilderkin
3 keg 4 cask 6 barrel 9 container

kilim
3 mat, rug 6 carpet

kill
3 end, off, zap 4 do in, prey, slay, stop,
veto 5 creek, croak, scrag, snuff, waste
6 defeat, delete, finish, murder, quarry,
stifle 7 bump off, butcher, channel, destroy,
execute 8 blow away, carry off, dispatch,
knock off, massacre 9 sacrifice, slaughter
10 annihilate 11 assassinate, exterminate

killer
6 gunman, hit man 7 butcher, torpedo
8 assassin, homicide
combining form: 4 cide

Killer Angels author
6 Shaara (Michael)

killer whale
4 orca 8 cetacean

killing
5 blood, fatal 6 deadly, lethal, mortal,
murder 7 carnage 8 butchery, foul play,
homicide 9 bloodbath, bloodshed,
slaughter 12 manslaughter
of a race: 8 genocide
of bacteria: 11 bactericide
of a brother: 10 fratricide
of a father: 9 patricide
of a king: 8 regicide
of a mother: 9 matricide
of a relative: 9 parricide
of a sister: 10 sororicide
of oneself: 7 suicide
of plants: 9 herbicide

killjoy
6 downer, grinch, grouch 7 spoiler
8 doomster, sourpuss 9 Cassandra,
defeatist, doomsayer, gloomy Gus,
pessimist, worrywart 10 spoilsport, wet
blanket

Kilmer poem
5 Trees

kiln
4 oast, oven 7 furnace

kilt
5 skirt
accessory: 7 sporran
fabric: 5 plaid 6 tartan

kilter
4 trim 5 order, shape 6 fettle, repair
7 fitness 9 condition

kimono
4 gown, robe
sash: 3 obi

kin
3 sib 4 clan, folk, sept 5 blood, flesh,
house, stock, tribe 6 family 7 lineage,
related 8 relation, relative

kind
3 ilk 4 good, like, sort, type, warm
5 breed, class, genre 6 benign, genial,
gentle, humane, loving, nature, stripe,
tender 7 affable, amiable, clement,
essence, feather, helpful, lenient, quality,
species, variety 8 category, merciful,
tolerant 9 character 10 altruistic,
benevolent, charitable, forbearing,
responsive 11 considerate, description,
good-hearted, good-humored, good-
natured, openhearted, softhearted,
sympathetic, warmhearted 12 affectionate,
good-tempered, humanitarian
13 compassionate, philanthropic

kindle
4 bear, fire, stir, wake, whet 5 light, rally,
rouse, spark, start, waken 6 arouse,
awaken, bestir, excite, foment, ignite, incite
7 inflame, provoke 8 activate 9 instigate,
stimulate 10 illuminate

kindliness
8 goodwill, sympathy 9 affection
10 solicitude 11 benevolence

kindly
6 benign, gentle 7 benefic 8 friendly,
generous, gracious, pleasant 9 agreeable,
attentive, benignant 10 beneficent,
beneficial, neighborly 11 considerate,
good-hearted, sympathetic

kindness
5 favor, mercy 7 service 8 clemency,
courtesy, goodwill, sympathy 10 compassion, generosity, indulgence
11 benevolence 13 consideration

kind of
5 quite 6 fairly, pretty, rather 8 passably,
somewhat 9 tolerably 10 more or less,
reasonably, relatively

kindred
3 sib 4 clan, folk, like, sept 5 alike, blood,
flesh, house, stock, tribe 6 agnate, allied,
family 7 cognate, connate, lineage,
related, similar 9 relatives 10 affiliated,
connatural 11 consanguine

king
3 rex 4 czar, tsar 5 mogul, ruler 6 tycoon
7 magnate, monarch 9 sovereign
Albanian: 3 Zog 7 William
Assyrian: 6 Sargon 11 Sennacherib,
Shalmaneser
Babylonian: 6 Sargon 9 Hammurabi
10 Belshazzar
Belgian: 6 Albert 7 Leopold 8 Baudouin
Bohemian: 9 Wenceslas 10 Wenceslaus
Bulgarian: 5 Boris 6 Simeon
Damascus: 8 Benhadad
Danish: 4 Abel, Eric, Gorm, Hans, John,
Olaf 5 Sweyn 6 Canute, Harold, Magnus
8 Nicholas, Waldemar 9 Christian,
Frederick 11 Christopher
Dutch: 7 William
Egyptian: 3 Tut 4 Pepi, Seti 5 Khufu,
Menes, Necho 6 Cheops, Ramses
7 Harmhab, Osorkon, Psamtik, Ptolemy
8 Ikhnaton, Thothmes, Thutmose
9 Amenhotep, Sesostris 11 Tutankhamen
English: 4 John 5 Henry, James 6 Alfred,
Canute, Edmund, Edward, Egbert, George,
Harold 7 Charles, Richard, Stephen,
William 8 Ethelred 9 Athelstan, Ethelbald,
Ethelbert
French: 3 Odo, roi 4 Jean, John 5 Henri,
Henry, Louis, Pepin, Raoul 6 Philip,
Robert, Rudolf 7 Charles, Francis, Lothair
8 François 9 Hugh Capet
11 Charlemagne
German: 4 Carl, Karl 5 König, Louis
6 Lothar, Ludwig 7 Charles, Lothair
Greek (modern): 4 Paul 6 George
9 Alexander 11 Constantine
Hawaiian: 10 Kamehameha
Hungarian: 6 Attila
Indian: 4 raja 5 rajah
Irish: 9 Brian Boru
Italian: 7 Humbert, Umberto
Jordanian: 5 Talal 7 Hussein 8 Abdullah
Judah:
(see at **Judah**)
Judean: 5 Herod
Lydian: 5 Gyges 7 Croesus 8 Alyattes
Norwegian: 4 Eric, Erik, Inge, Olaf

5 Sweyn 6 Haakon, Harald, Harold,
Magnus, Sigurd, Sverre
Ostrogothic: 9 Theodoric
Persian: 5 Cyrus 6 Darius, Xerxes
Portuguese: 4 John 5 Henry, Louis, Peter
6 Carlos, Edward, Manuel, Sancho
7 Alfonso 9 Ferdinand, Sebastian
Prussian: 7 Wilhelm, William 9 Frederick,
Friedrich
relating to: 5 regal, royal
Saudi Arabian: 4 Saud 6 Faisal 9 Abdul-
Aziz
Scottish: 4 John 5 David, Edgar, James
6 Duncan 7 Macbeth, Malcolm, William
9 Alexander, Donalbane 10 David Bruce
11 Robert Bruce
Spanish: 3 rey 5 Louis 6 Philip
7 Alfonso, Amadeus, Charles 9 Ferdinand
10 Juan Carlos
Spartan: 8 Leonidas
Swedish: 4 Eric, John 5 Oscar 6 Birger,
Gustav, Haakon, Magnus 7 Charles
8 Gustavus, Waldemar 9 Frederick,
Sigismund, Sten Sture
Visigothic: 6 Alaric

King Arthur

birthplace: 8 Tintagel
chronicler: 8 Geoffrey (of Monmouth)
court site: 7 Camelot 8 Caerleon
deathplace: 6 Camlan
father: 5 Uther
father-in-law: 9 Laodogant, Leodegran
11 Leodegrance
foster father: 5 Ector
jester: 7 Dagonet
knight: 3 Kay 4 Bors 5 Balan, Balin
6 Gareth, Gawain, Modred 7 Galahad,
Geraint, Lamerok, Mordred, Tristan
8 Bedivere, Lancelot, Parsifal, Percival,
Tristram 9 Launcelot
lance: 3 Ron
last abode: 6 Avalon
last name: 9 Pendragon
magician: 6 Merlin
mother: 6 Ygerne 7 Igraine
nephew: 6 Gareth, Modred 7 Mordred
queen: 9 Guinevere
shield: 7 Pridwin
sister: 7 Morgain 11 Morgan le Fay
slayer: 6 Modred 7 Mordred
son: 6 Modred 7 Mordred
steward: 3 Kay
sword: 9 Excalibur
victim: 6 Modred 7 Mordred
wife: 9 Guinevere

king crab

7 limulus

kingdom

5 realm 6 domain, empire 7 demesne
8 monarchy

kingdom come

4 Zion 6 heaven 8 paradise 9 hereafter
10 afterworld

kingfish

4 boss 6 bigwig, honcho, master 7 big
shot, croaker 8 mackerel

kingfisher

7 halcyon 10 kookaburra

kingly

5 regal, royal 6 august, lordly, regnal
7 exalted 8 imperial, majestic 9 imperious,
masterful, monarchal, sovereign
10 monarchial 11 monarchical

King novel

6 Carrie, Shining (The) 8 Dead Zone (The)
9 Dark Tower (The), Green Mile (The),
Salem's Lot 11 Firestarter, Pet Sematary

King Philip

9 Metacomet

kingpin

4 boss, guru, head 5 chief, mogul
6 bigwig, top dog 7 magnate 9 top banana
10 mastermind

Kings Peak range

5 Uinta

Kingu

consort: 6 Tiamat
slayer: 6 Marduk

kink

4 bend, curl, knot, whim 5 cramp, crick,
quirk, snarl, spasm, twist 6 tangle
11 peculiarity 12 eccentricity, imperfection

kinky

3 odd 4 bent 5 curly, outré, ultra, weird
6 curled, far-out, frizzy, quirky 7 bizarre,
deviant, knotted, strange, twisted
9 eccentric 10 outlandish

kiosk

5 booth 8 pavilion 9 newsstand
11 summerhouse

kip

3 bed, nap 4 hide, pelt, skin 5 sleep

Kipling, Rudyard

work: 3 Kim 6 L'Envoi 8 Gunga Din,
Mandalay 10 Fuzzy Wuzzy 11 Jungle
Books (The), Recessional 13 Just So
Stories, Soldiers Three 15 Light That

Failed (The), Puck of Pook's Hill
18 Captains Courageous

Kiribati
capital: 6 Tarawa
island, island group: 4 Line **6** Banaba
7 Gilbert, Phoenix
language: 7 English
location: 7 Oceania
monetary unit: 6 dollar

kirk
6 church

kirsch
6 brandy, liquor

kirtle
4 coat, gown **5** dress, tunic **7** garment

Kish
father: 3 Ner **4** Abdi **5** Abiel, Jeiel
6 Jehiel
son: 4 Saul

kismet
3 lot **4** doom, fate, luck **5** weird **6** Moirai
7 destiny, fortune

kiss
4 buss, neck, peck **5** graze, smack
6 cookie, glance, smooch **7** lip-lock
8 osculate, pucker up **10** osculation

kisser
3 mug **4** face, lips **5** mouth

Kiss sculptor
5 Rodin (Auguste)

kit
3 set **4** gear, pelt **5** group **6** outfit, tackle,
violin **7** package **8** caboodle **9** container
10 collection

kitchen
4 mess **6** galley **7** cuisine **8** scullery
appliance:
(see at **appliance**)
boss: 4 chef
(see also **cooking**)

kite
4 hawk, sail, soar **5** check, glede, hurry,
mosey **7** saunter, take off **8** clear out,
hightail, predator **9** spinnaker

kith
3 kin, sib **4** clan, folk **6** family **7** friends,
kindred, kinfolk **9** neighbors, relatives

kitsch
4 camp, junk **9** vulgarity

kittenish
3 coy **6** elvish, frisky, impish **7** coltish,
playful **10** frolicsome **11** mischievous

kitty
3 cat, pot **4** fund, pool, puss **5** pussy
6 feline, stakes **7** jackpot

kiwi
4 bird **5** fruit **7** Apteryx **12** New Zealander

klatch
5 bunch, group **7** meeting **9** gathering
11 get-together

kleptomaniac
5 thief **7** booster **10** shoplifter

klutz
3 oaf **4** boob, clod, gawk, lout, lump
5 looby **6** lubber, lummox **7** bungler,
palooka **8** shlemiel **9** schlemiel
10 stumblebum

klutzy
5 inept **6** clumsy **7** awkward **9** all thumbs,
maladroit **10** blundering

knack
4 bent, gift, head **5** flair, forte, skill, trick
6 genius, talent **7** ability, aptness,
command, faculty, know-how, mastery
8 aptitude, capacity, facility **9** dexterity,
expertise, stratagem **10** expertness

knapsack
4 pack **8** backpack

knave
4 heel, jack **5** fraud, rogue, scamp
6 rascal, varlet **7** lowlife, villain
8 scalawag, swindler **9** scoundrel
10 blackguard **11** rapscallion

knavery
5 fraud **6** deceit **8** mischief, trickery,
villainy **9** chicanery, deception, rascality
10 dishonesty

knavish
5 lying **6** shifty, tricky **7** devious, roguish
8 rascally **9** deceitful, deceptive, dishonest
10 mendacious **12** unscrupulous

knead
4 form, mold, work **5** press, shape
7 massage **10** manipulate

knee
5 joint
bend: 9 genuflect **12** genuflection
bone: 7 patella

kneeler
5 stool **7** cushion **8** prie-dieu **9** footstool

knell
4 bong, peal, ring, toll **5** chime **6** summon
7 warning **8** announce, proclaim

knickknack
3 toy **4** dido **5** curio **6** bauble, gadget,
gewgaw, trifle **7** bibelot, novelty, trinket,
whatnot, whatsit **8** gimcrack, ornament,
souvenir **9** bagatelle, bric-a-brac, objet
d'art

knife
4 bolo, shiv, snee **5** blade, bowie, panga,
shank, sword **6** barong, cutter, dagger,
parang, sickle **7** cleaver, machete, scalpel
8 stiletto, yataghan **11** switchblade
case: 6 sheath
handle: 4 haft, hilt
maker: 6 cutler **7** grinder

knifelike
4 keen **5** acute, sharp **7** cutting
8 piercing, stabbing **11** penetrating

knight
3 dub, sir **5** eques **8** cavalier, chessman,
horseman **9** caballero, chevalier
code: 8 chivalry
competition: 7 listing, tilting **8** jousting
10 tournament
German: 6 Ritter
servant: 4 page **5** valet **6** squire
title: 3 sir
wife: 4 lady

knighthood
8 chivalry

knightly
4 bold **5** brave, noble **6** heroic **7** gallant,
valiant **10** chivalrous

Knight of the Round Table
see **King Arthur**

Knight of the Rueful Countenance
10 Don Quixote

knit
4 bind, heal, join, link, mend, purl **5** plait,
unite, weave **6** fabric, stitch **7** conjoin,
crochet **8** contract **9** interlace
10 intertwine

knitting
material: 4 yarn
stitch: 3 rib **4** purl **6** garter
tool: 6 needle

knob
3 bun, bur, nub **4** bump, burl, burr, dial, hill,
hump, lump, node, umbo **5** bulge, gnarl,
knoll, mound **6** button, finial, handle,
nubble, pommel **7** hillock **12** protuberance

knobkerrie
3 bat **4** club, mace **5** billy **6** cudgel,
weapon **7** war club **8** bludgeon **9** billy
club, truncheon

knock
3 bob, hit, rap, tap **4** bash, blow, bump,
cuff, lick, swat **5** blame, clout, fault, pound,
swipe, thump **6** strike **7** censure,
condemn, setback **8** denounce, reversal
9 criticize **10** denunciate

knock down
4 drop, earn, fell, gain, raze **5** floor, level,
lower **6** lay low, reduce **7** acquire, bring in,
flatten **9** dismantle **11** disassemble

knocker
6 carper, critic **7** caviler **8** quibbler
10 complainer, criticizer **11** fault-finder

knock off
3 rob **4** copy, do in, halt, kill, quit, slay, stop
5 cease **6** deduct, defeat, desist, finish,
murder **7** execute, imitate, take out
8 discount, overcome, subtract **9** liquidate
11 assassinate, call it quits, counterfeit

knockout
4 kayo **5** dandy, final **6** beauty, eyeful,
looker, lovely **7** stunner **8** decisive, jim-
dandy, striking, stunning **9** deathblow,
finishing, humdinger **10** attractive **11** coup
de grace, crackerjack

knock over
3 rob **4** down, drop, fell **5** amaze, floor,
steal, upset **6** boggle, hijack, hold up, lay
low, topple **7** flatten, stick up **9** bring
down, eliminate, overpower, overthrow,
overwhelm, prostrate

knoll
4 hill, knob **5** mound **7** hillock

knot
3 bow, tie **4** bond, burr, link, loop, lump,
node **5** bunch, gnarl, hitch, nexus
6 jungle, tangle **8** ligament, ligature,
vinculum
in fiber: 3 nep
kind: 4 bend, loop, slip **5** hitch **6** granny,
splice, square **7** bowline **9** sheet bend
10 clove hitch, sheepshank

knotty
4 hard **6** sticky **7** complex, gnarled,
Gordian **8** involved **9** byzantine, difficult,
elaborate, intricate **10** formidable
11 complicated, problematic

knout
4 flog, lash, whip **7** scourge

know
3 wot 5 grasp 6 fathom, intuit 7 discern, realize 9 apprehend, recognize
10 appreciate, comprehend, experience, understand
Scottish: 3 ken

knowable
9 graspable 10 cognizable, fathomable
12 intelligible 13 apprehensible

know-how
5 craft, knack, skill 6 talent 7 ability, cunning, faculty, mastery 8 aptitude
9 dexterity, expertise 10 adroitness, expertness 11 proficiency

knowing
3 hep, hip 4 sage, wise 5 aware, blasé, canny, smart 6 bright, clever 7 witting, worldly 8 sentient 9 cognizant, conscious, sagacious 10 conversant, discerning, insightful, perceptive 11 worldly-wise
13 sophisticated

know-it-all
6 smarty 7 wise guy 8 wiseacre 10 smart aleck 11 smarty-pants, wisenheimer

knowledge
3 ken 4 lore, news 5 facts 6 wisdom
7 science 8 learning 9 cognition, education, erudition 10 cognizance
11 information, scholarship 12 intelligence
13 enlightenment
lack of: 9 ignorance
mystical: 6 gnosis

knowledgeable
5 savvy 8 educated, informed

know-nothing
4 dolt, dope, fool 5 dummy, dunce, idiot, yahoo 6 dimwit 7 pinhead 8 agnostic, ignorant, numskull 9 benighted, blockhead, brainless, ignoramus, lamebrain, numbskull
10 illiterate, uneducated 11 empty-headed

knuckle
5 joint
combining form: 6 condyl 7 condylo

knucklehead
4 dolt, dope, fool 5 dummy, dunce, idiot, yahoo 6 dimwit 8 clodpole, numskull
9 ignoramus, lamebrain, numbskull

knuckle under
3 bow 4 cave 5 yield 6 cave in, give in, submit 7 succumb 8 say uncle
9 surrender 10 capitulate

knurl
3 nub 4 bead, knob 5 ridge 12 protuberance

KO
4 kayo 8 knockout

koan
7 paradox

kobold
5 dwarf, gnome 6 goblin, spirit, sprite

Kohinoor
3 gem 7 diamond

kohlrabi
7 cabbage

kola
3 nut 4 tree

komatik
4 sled 6 sledge

kook
3 nut 5 crank, loony, wacko 6 cuckoo, weirdo 7 dingbat, lunatic, oddball
8 crackpot 9 ding-a-ling, fruitcake, screwball 10 crackbrain

kooky
4 daft, nuts 5 batty, crazy, daffy, dotty, flaky, loony, nutty, silly, wacky, weird
6 freaky, fruity, insane, screwy 7 bizarre, idiotic, lunatic, offbeat, touched
8 demented 9 eccentric, fantastic
10 flipped out, freaked-out, off-the-wall, outlandish

kopeck
4 coin
one hundred: 5 ruble

Koran
chapter: 4 sura
revealer of: 7 Gabriel
scholar: 5 ulama, ulema

Korea
see **North Korea; South Korea**

Korean
dynasty:
national dish: 6 kimchi

Korea, North
capital: 9 P'yongyang
city: 7 Hamhung 8 Ch'ongjin
leader: 9 Kim Il-sung, Kim Jong Il 10 Kim Chong-Il
monetary unit: 3 won
mountain: 6 Paektu
neighbor: 5 China 6 Russia 10 South Korea
sea: 6 Yellow

Korea, South
captial: 5 Seoul
city: 5 Pusan, Taegu 6 Inch'on, Taejon 7 Kwangju
island: 5 Cheju
monetary unit: 3 won
neighbor: 10 North Korea
river: 3 Han 7 Naktong
sea: 5 Japan 6 Yellow

kosher
3 fit 4 pure 5 clean 6 proper 10 acceptable, legitimate, sanctioned 12 satisfactory

Kosinski novel
5 Steps 10 Being There 11 Painted Bird (The)

Koussevitzky
5 Serge 6 Sergei 9 conductor

kowtow
3 bow 4 fawn 5 cower, defer, kneel, toady 6 cringe, grovel 7 honey up, truckle 8 bootlick 11 apple-polish

kraal
3 pen 6 corral 7 village 9 enclosure

kraken
5 squid 9 leviathan 10 giant squid, sea monster

krater
3 jar 4 vase 6 vessel

Kriemhild
brother: 7 Gunther
husband: 5 Etzel 6 Attila 9 Siegfried
slayer: 10 Hildebrand
victim: 5 Hagen

kris
6 dagger

Krishna
avatar of: 6 Vishnu
brother: 8 Balarama
father: 8 Vasudeva
mother: 6 Devaki
uncle: 5 Kansa
victim: 5 Kansa

Krupp works site
5 Essen

kudos
4 bays, fame 5 award, glory, honor 6 honors, praise, renown 7 acclaim, bouquet, laurels 8 accolade, bouquets 10 compliment 11 distinction, recognition

kudu
8 antelope

kukri
5 sword

kumquat
5 fruit
kin: 6 orange

Kushner play
15 Angels in America

Kuwait
capital: 6 Kuwait
gulf: 7 Persian
island: 7 Bubiyan 8 Faylakah
language: 6 Arabic 7 Persian
monetary unit: 5 dinar
neighbor: 4 Iraq 11 Saudi Arabia
oasis: 8 Al-Jahrah

kvass
4 beer

kvetch
4 beef, crab, fret, fuss 5 gripe, whine 6 grouch, grouse 7 grumble 8 complain 9 bellyache

_____ kwon do
3 tae

kyphosis
8 humpback 9 curvature, hunchback

Kyrgyzstan
capital: 7 Bishkek
city: 3 Osh
conqueror: 9 Jöchi Khan
lake: 8 Issyk-Kul
language: 6 Kyrgyz 7 Russian
monetary unit: 3 som
mountain, range: 4 Alai 6 Pobedy 7 Victory 8 Tian Shan 10 Khan-Tengri 11 Kok Shaal-Tau
neighbor: 5 China 10 Kazakhstan, Tajikistan, Uzbekistan
river: 5 Naryn

L

Laadah
father: 6 Shelah
grandfather: 5 Judah

laager
4 camp 6 encamp 7 bivouac

lab
13 proving ground

Laban
daughter: 4 Leah 6 Rachel
father: 7 Bethuel
grandfather: 5 Nahor
sister: 7 Rebekah

label
3 tag 4 band, mark 6 marker, ticket
7 epithet, hallmark, sticker 8 classify,
identify, insignia

labium
3 lip

labor
4 moil, task, toil, work 5 chore, grind,
sweat 6 drudge, effort, strain, strive
7 slavery, travail 8 drudgery, endeavor,
exertion, struggle 10 birth pangs,
childbirth, donkeywork 12 childbearing
group: 3 AFL, CIO 5 ILGWU, union
6 AFL-CIO
leader: 5 Hoffa (James, Jimmy), Lewis
(John L.), Meany (George) 6 Chavez
(Cesar) 7 Gompers (Samuel), Reuther
(Walter), Sweeney (John J.) 8 Kirkland
(Lane), Randolph (A. Philip)

laboratory
device: 5 flask 6 beaker, mortar, pestle,
retort 7 burette, pipette 8 crucible, test
tube 12 Bunsen burner

labored
4 hard 6 forced, taxing, tiring 7 arduous
8 strained 9 difficult, effortful, fatiguing,
strenuous

laborer
4 hack, hand, peon 5 grind, navvy

6 coolie, menial 7 workman 10 roustabout,
workingman
Mexican: 7 bracero

laborious
4 hard 6 tiring, uphill 7 arduous, onerous,
operose 8 diligent, grueling, sedulous,
toilsome 9 assiduous, difficult, effortful,
strenuous 10 burdensome, unflagging
11 hardworking, industrious, persevering
12 backbreaking

La Brea
4 pits 7 tar pits
fossil: 7 mammoth 8 mastodon
10 saber-tooth

labyrinth
3 web 4 coil, knot, maze, mesh 5 skein,
snarl 6 jungle, morass, tangle
builder: 8 Daedalus
hero: 7 Theseus
monster: 8 Minotaur

labyrinthine
4 mazy 6 daedal, knotty 7 complex,
gordian 8 involved, mazelike, tortuous
9 Byzantine, elaborate, intricate
10 convoluted, perplexing 11 bewildering,
complicated

lace
3 net, tat, tie 4 cord, trim 5 adorn, braid,
frill, plait, twine 6 fasten, string 7 entwine,
netting, tatting 8 filigree, openwork
9 embroider 10 embroidery, intertwine
11 needlepoint
edge: 5 picot
ground: 6 reseau
into: 5 abuse 6 attack 7 condemn
kind: 6 bobbin 7 Alençon, guipure,
macramé, Maltese, Mechlin, torchon
8 Brussels, Venetian 9 Chantilly
11 needlepoint 12 Valenciennes
make: 3 tat
pattern: 5 toilé

Lacedaemon
6 Sparta

lacerate

lacerate
3 cut, rip 4 gash, rend, tear 5 slash, wound 6 mangle, pierce 7 afflict, mangled, torment 8 distress

lachrymose
3 sad 5 teary, weepy 7 doleful, tearful, weeping 8 dolorous, mournful 11 tear-jerking

lack
4 need, want 6 dearth, defect 7 absence, default, deficit, failure, paucity, poverty, require 8 scarcity, shortage 9 privation 10 deficiency, inadequacy, scantiness 13 insufficiency

lackadaisical
4 idle, lazy, limp, slow 5 moony 6 dreamy 7 languid, passive 8 fainéant, indolent, listless, slothful 9 apathetic, enervated 10 languorous, spiritless 11 daydreaming, halfhearted, languishing

lackey
5 toady 6 fawner, flunky, minion, vassal 7 footman, servant 8 truckler 9 attendant, sycophant

lacking
3 shy 4 sans 5 minus, short 6 absent, flawed, needed 7 missing, needing, omitted, wanting, without 8 devoid of, impaired 9 defective, deficient 10 deprived of, inadequate, incomplete 11 halfhearted 12 insufficient

lackluster
3 dim 4 arid, blah, drab, dull, flat 5 blind, ho-hum, matte, muted, prosy, rusty, vapid 6 boring, leaden 7 prosaic 8 lifeless, mediocre 9 colorless, tarnished, wearisome 10 uninspired 13 unimaginative

Laconian
7 Spartan
king: 5 Lelex, Myles 8 Menelaus

laconic
4 curt 5 bluff, blunt, brief, pithy, short, terse 7 brusque, concise 8 succinct

lacquer
5 glaze, gloss 6 enamel, finish 7 shellac, varnish

lacrosse
related game: 7 jai alai
term: 5 clamp 6 crease, crosse, pocket 7 face-off
team: 3 ten

lactate
4 salt 5 ester, nurse 6 suckle 7 secrete 8 wet-nurse 10 breast-feed

lacteal
5 milky 6 cloudy, pearly

lacuna
3 gap, pit 4 void 5 blank, break, space 6 breach, cavity, hiatus 7 caesura 10 deficiency 12 interruption 13 discontinuity

lacy
5 meshy 6 dainty 7 netlike 8 delicate, gossamer 9 filigreed

lad
3 boy, son, tad 5 youth 6 shaver 9 shaveling, stripling
Irish: 4 boyo 5 bucko
Scottish: 5 chiel 7 callant

ladder
3 run 5 ranks, scale 6 series 7 ranking 9 hierarchy
adjunct: 4 rung 6 rundle

ladderlike
6 scalar, scaled 7 stepped 11 scalariform

lade
3 dip, tax 4 bail, load, pack, ship, stow 5 ladle, scoop 6 burden, saddle, weight 8 encumber

la-di-dah
6 too-too 7 elegant, genteel, stuck-up 8 affected, snobbish 9 conceited, grandiose, high-flown 10 hoity-toity 11 pretentious

lading
4 haul, load 5 cargo, goods 6 burden 7 bailing, dipping, freight, loading, payload 8 shipment 11 consignment

ladle
3 dip 4 bail 5 scoop, spoon 6 dipper

Ladon
6 dragon
father: 7 Phorcus, Phorcys
mother: 4 Ceto
slayer: 8 Heracles, Hercules

lady
4 dame 5 madam, woman 6 female, matron
French: 4 dame
German: 4 Frau
Italian: 5 donna 7 signora
Muslim: 5 begum
Spanish: 4 doña 6 señora

lady _____
   4 luck 5 apple 6 beetle, chapel

ladybug
   6 beetle
   Australian: 7 vedalia

Lady Chatterley's Lover
   author: 8 Lawrence (David Herbert)
   character: 6 Connie 7 Mellors (Oliver)
   9 Constance

lady-killer
   4 dude, hunk, roué, stud 7 playboy,
   seducer 8 Casanova, lothario
   10 heartbreaker

Lady of the Lake, The
   5 Ellen (Douglas), Nimue 6 Vivien
   author: 5 Scott (Walter)

Lady Windermere's Fan
   author: 5 Wilde (Oscar)

Laertes
   father: 8 Acrisius, Polonius
   sister: 7 Ophelia
   son: 7 Ulysses 8 Odysseus
   victim: 6 Hamlet
   wife: 8 Anticlea

La Fontaine's forte
   5 fable

lag
   4 drag, flag, last, poke, slow, tire 5 dally,
   delay, tarry, trail 6 dawdle, linger, loiter
   7 slacken 8 hang back, hindmost, interval
   10 dillydally 13 procrastinate

lager
   4 beer, brew, malt, suds 7 brewski

laggard
   3 lax 4 slow 5 tardy 6 loafer 7 dawdler
   8 dallying, dawdling, delaying, dilatory,
   flagging, lingerer, loiterer, slowpoke,
   sluggish, tarrying 9 apathetic, lazybones,
   lethargic, loitering, straggler
   10 behindhand

La Gioconda
   8 Mona Lisa
   composer: 10 Ponchielli (Amilcare)
   painter: 7 da Vinci (Leonardo)
   8 Leonardo (da Vinci)

lagniappe
   3 tip 4 gift, perk 5 bonus 7 cumshaw,
   largess 8 dividend, gratuity 9 baksheesh,
   pourboire 10 perquisite

lagomorph
   4 hare, pika 6 rabbit

lagoon
   4 pond, pool 5 bayou, sound 6 strait
   7 channel, narrows

_____ **La Guardia**
   8 Fiorello

Lahmi
   brother: 7 Goliath
   slayer: 7 Elhanan

laid-back
   4 cool 6 breezy, casual 7 relaxed
   8 carefree, informal 9 easygoing, hang-
   loose 10 nonchalant

lair
   3 den 4 cave 5 haunt, lodge 6 burrow,
   refuge 7 hideout, retreat 8 hideaway
   9 sanctuary

Laius
   father: 8 Labdacus
   slayer, son: 7 Oedipus
   wife: 7 Jocasta

lake
   4 loch, mere, pond, pool, tarn 5 lough
   6 lagoon
   Adriatic: 6 Varano
   Alberta: 6 Louise
   Algeria: 5 Hodna
   Alps: 6 Annecy
   Arizona-Nevada: 4 Mead
   Armenia: 5 Sevan 6 Gokcha, Sevang
   9 Lychnitis
   Aswan's: 6 Nasser
   Australia: 4 Eyre 5 Carey, Cowan,
   Frome, Wells 6 Barlee 7 Amadeus,
   Everard, Torrens 8 Gairdner
   Austria: 5 Atter, Traun 6 Kammer
   8 Attersee 9 Kammersee
   Bolivia: 5 Poopó
   Botswana: 5 Ngami
   British Columbia: 4 Pitt 5 Atlin
   California: 4 Mono, Tule 5 Clear, Eagle,
   Honey
   Cambodia: 8 Tonle Sap
   Canada: 4 Dyke 8 Manitoba
   central Africa: 4 Kivu 5 Mweru 6 Albert
   Central America: 5 Guija
   central Europe: 5 Leman 6 Geneva,
   Lugano 7 Ceresio 8 Bodensee
   9 Constance
   central North America: 5 Rainy
   Chile: 4 Laja 5 Ranco
   China: 6 Poyang 8 Dongting
   Colorado: 5 Grand
   Denmark: 5 Esrum
   east Africa: 6 Rudolf 7 Turkana
   east Asia: 6 Khanka 7 Xingkai
   8 Hsingkai

east central Africa: 8 Victoria 10 Tanganyika
east China: 3 Tai 5 Dalai, Hulun
Ethiopia: 4 Tana, Zwai 5 Abaya, Shala, Shamo, Tsana 8 Stefanie 9 Chew Bahir
Finland: 5 Inari
Florida: 5 Worth 10 Okeechobee
Germany: 5 Ammer, Chiem 8 Ammersee, Chiemsee
Ghana: 5 Volta
Great: 4 Erie 5 Huron 7 Ontario 8 Michigan, Superior
Greece: 5 Bolbe, Volvi
Guatemala: 7 Atitlán
Honduras: 5 Yojoa
Honshu: 3 Omi 4 Biwa, Suwa, Yodo
Hungary: 7 Balaton 10 Plattensee
Idaho: 4 Waha 5 Grays 6 Priest 11 Coeur d'Alene, Pend Oreille
India: 3 Dal 5 Wular 6 Chilka
Indonesia: 4 Poso, Toba 5 Ranau
Iowa: 5 Storm
Iran: 5 Niriz, Shahi, Urmia 8 Matianus, Urumiyeh 9 Bakhtigan
Ireland: 3 Gur, Ree 4 Conn, Derg, Mask 5 Allen, Arrow, Leane
Israel: 12 Bahr Tabariya, Sea of Galilee
Israel-Jordan: 7 Dead Sea
Italy: 4 Como, Iseo, Nemi 5 Garda 6 Albano 7 Bolsena, Perugia 8 Maggiore 9 Trasimene
Japan: 4 Imba 8 Imbanuma
Kazakhstan: 7 Balqash 8 Balkhash
Louisiana: 4 Soda 9 Catahoula 13 Pontchartrain
Maine: 7 Sebago 9 Moosehead
Mali: 4 Debo
Manitoba: 4 Gods 5 Cedar, Moose 8 Winnipeg
Mexico: 7 Chapala
Michigan: 4 Burt
Minnesota: 3 Red 4 Cass, Gull, Swan 5 Leech 6 Itasca 9 Mille Lacs 10 Minnetonka, of the Woods 11 Lac qui Parle
Minnesota-Wisconsin: 5 Pepin
Mongolian: 3 Har 5 Har Us, Khara 8 Khara Usu
Montana: 8 Medicine
mountain: 4 tarn
Myanmar: 4 Inle
Nevada: 4 Ruby 7 Pyramid
New Hampshire: 5 Squam 13 Winnipesaukee
New Jersey: 5 Union
New York: 4 Long 5 Chazy, Keuka 6 Cayuga, George, Oneida, Otsego, Owasco, Placid, Seneca 7 Crooked, Saranac 8 Onondaga, Saratoga

10 Chautauqua 11 Canandaigua, Skaneateles
New Zealand: 4 Ohau 5 Hawea, Taupo 6 Pukaki, Wanaka 8 Wakatipu
Nicaragua: 7 Managua
North Africa: 4 Chad
Northern Ireland: 5 Neagh
Northwest Territories: 4 Gras 5 Baker, Garry, Pelly 8 Great Bear 10 Great Slave
Norway: 5 Mjosa
Nova Scotia: 7 Bras d'Or
Ontario: 4 Rice, Seul 5 Trout
Oregon: 5 Abert 6 Crater 7 Malheur, Wallowa
Paraguay: 4 Ypoá
Peru: 5 Junín 13 Chinchaycocha
Philippines: 4 Bato, Taal 5 Lanao 6 Bombon
Poland: 5 Mamry, Mauer
Quebec: 5 Minto, Payne
Russia: 3 Seg 5 Chany, Ilmen, Lacha, Onega 6 Baikal, Ladoga 7 Rybinsk 10 Eltonskoye 11 Ladozhskoye
Saskatchewan: 4 Cree 5 Ronge
Scotland: 3 Ard, Awe 4 Doon, Earn, Ness, Oich, Shin, Sloy 5 Leven, Lochy, Maree, Morar, Shiel 6 Lomond
Siberia: 6 Baikal, Baykal
South Africa: 4 Kosi
South America: 5 Merin, Mirim 8 Titicaca
South Carolina: 7 Wateree
South Dakota: 5 Andes
southeast Africa: 5 Nyasa 6 Nyassa
southwest Europe: 5 Ohrid 7 Okhrida
Sweden: 5 Asnen, Roxen 6 Siljan, Vänern, Vetter 7 Malaren, Vattern
Switzerland: 3 Zug 4 Biel, Joux 5 Zuger 6 Bieler, Bienne, Brienz, Sarnen, Sarner, Zurich 7 Lucerne, Lungern 8 Brienzer, Züricher 9 Neuchâtel, Zürichsee
Tajikistan: 7 Karakul
Tanzania: 5 Rukwa
Texas-Louisiana: 5 Caddo
Tibet: 4 Na-mu 6 Nam Tso, Tengri
Turkey: 3 Tuz, Van 4 Bafa, Nice 5 Iznik, Sugla 6 Nicaea
Uganda: 5 Kyoga
Utah: 6 Powell, Sevier 9 Great Salt
Wales: 4 Bala
Washington: 4 Omak 5 Moses 6 Chelan 9 Wenatchee
western China: 4 Ai-pi 6 Ebinur
western United States: 4 Bear 5 Tahoe
Wisconsin: 5 Green 9 Winnebago
Yellowstone National Park: 5 Heart, Lewis 8 Shoshone
Zaire: 5 Tumba
Zambia: 9 Bangweolo, Bangweulu

lake group
  central North America: 5 Great
  Connecticut: 4 Twin
  Egypt: 5 Balah
  Maine: 8 Rangeley
  New Hampshire: 11 Connecticut
  New York: 6 Finger
  Saskatchewan: 5 Quill
  Twin: 8 Washinee **9** Washining
  Wisconsin: 4 Four

lake herring
  5 cisco

Lake poet
  7 Southey (Robert) **9** Coleridge (Samuel
  Taylor) **10** Wordsworth (William)

Lake Wobegon Days author
  7 Keillor (Garrison)

Lakmé
  aria: 8 Bell Song
  composer: 7 Delibes (Léo)

Lakshmi
  husband: 6 Vishnu
  son: 4 Kama

lam
  3 hit **4** beat, blow, bolt, drub, flay, flee, flog,
  pelt, skip, whip **5** baste, paste, pound,
  scram, smack, split, whale **6** batter, beat it,
  buffet, cut out, decamp, escape, flight,
  hammer, pummel, strike, thrash, wallop
  lop **7** getaway, take off, vamoose **8** breakout, escaping **9** skedaddle

La Mancha's knight
  10 Don Quixote

lamb
  4 cade **5** sheep **6** cosset **8** yeanling
  leg of: 5 gigot

lambaste
  3 pan **4** beat, drub, flay, flog, lash, lick,
  pelt, slam, slap, trim, whip **5** paste, pound,
  roast, scold, score, slash, smear **6** assail,
  attack, berate, cudgel, hammer, pummel,
  scathe, scorch, thrash, wallop **7** assault,
  blister, censure, clobber, reprove, scourge,
  shellac, upbraid **8** bludgeon, denounce,
  harangue, lash into **9** castigate, criticize,
  excoriate **10** tongue-lash

lambent
  5 aglow, ardent **6** bright, lucent
  7 beaming, glowing, radiant, shining
  8 gleaming, luminous, lustrous **9** brilliant,
  effulgent, refulgent, twinkling **10** flickering,
  glittering, shimmering **12** incandescent

lamblike
  4 meek **6** docile

lamb of God
  5 Jesus **6** Christ **8** Agnus Dei

Lamb's pseudonym
  4 Elia

lame
  4 gimp, halt, limp **5** gimpy, stiff **6** feeble,
  flimsy **7** cripple, disable, halting, limping
  8 crippled, disabled, hobbling, inferior
  10 inadequate **11** ineffectual
  12 contemptible, unconvincing
  13 incapacitated

lamebrain
  3 oaf **4** dolt, dope, goof, mutt, simp, yo-yo
  5 chump, dummy, dunce, idiot, moron,
  ninny, noddy, stupe **6** dimwit, donkey, dum-
  dum, nitwit, noodle **7** airhead, dullard,
  pinhead, schnook **8** bonehead, clodpoll,
  dumbbell, dumbhead, imbecile, lunkhead,
  meathead, numskull **9** blockhead,
  ignoramus, numbskull, simpleton,
  thickhead **10** dunderhead, hammerhead,
  nincompoop **11** chowderhead,
  chucklehead, knucklehead

Lamech
  daughter: 6 Naamah
  father: 10 Methuselah
  son: 4 Noah **5** Jabal, Jubal **9** Tubalcain
  wife: 4 Adah **6** Zillah

lament
  3 cry, rue **4** keen, moan, pine, wail, weep
  5 dirge, elegy, mourn **6** bemoan, bewail,
  grieve, plaint, regret, repent, sorrow
  7 deplore, elegize, wailing **8** jeremiad,
  threnody **9** complaint, ululation

lamentable
  6 rueful, woeful **7** doleful, pitiful
  8 dolorous, grievous, mournful **9** plaintive,
  sorrowful **10** afflictive, deplorable,
  lugubrious, melancholy **11** distressing,
  regrettable, unfortunate **13** heartbreaking

lamentation
  5 elegy, grief **7** anguish, remorse, wailing
  8 grieving, mourning, threnody
  9 sorrowing, ululation **13** mortification

Lamerok
  father: 9 Pellinore
  lover: 8 Margawse
  slayer: 6 Gawain

lamia
3 hag, hex **5** witch **7** hellcat, vampire
9 sorceress **11** enchantress, necromancer

Lamia
country: 5 Libya
form: 7 serpent
lover: 4 Zeus

lamina
5 blade, flake, layer, plate, scale

lamp
3 arc **4** bulb **5** klieg, light, torch **7** lantern
10 candelabra **11** candelabrum
floor: 8 torchère **9** torchiere
hanging: 10 chandelier

lampblack
4 soot **6** carbon

Lampetia
father: 6 Apollo, Helios
husband: 9 Asclepius
mother: 6 Neaera
sister: 9 Phaethusa

lampoon
4 mock **5** roast, spoof, squib **6** parody,
satire, send-up **7** take off **8** ridicule,
satirize **9** burlesque **10** caricature,
pasquinade

lamprey
3 eel

lanai
5 patio, porch **6** piazza **7** terrace, veranda

lance
4 gash, hurl **5** slash, spear **6** impale,
pierce, skewer **7** javelin **8** transfix

Lancelot, Launcelot
father: 3 Ban
lover: 6 Elaine **9** Guinevere
son: 7 Galahad
victim: 6 Gawain

lancer
10 cavalryman
Prussian: 5 uhlan

lancet
4 arch **5** blade, knife **6** cutter, window
7 scalpel

land
4 dirt, dock, gain, soil **5** acres, berth, earth,
light, manor, shore, terra, tract **6** alight,
estate, ground, obtain, pick up, secure
7 acquire, acreage, country, expanse,
grounds, procure, set down, terrain, terrene
9 touch down **10** terra firma
alluvial: 5 delta

barren: 5 waste **6** desert
cultivated: 4 farm **5** tilth **7** tillage
for grazing: 3 lea, ley **5** range **6** meadow
7 pasture
high: 4 hill, mesa **7** plateau **8** mountain
level: 4 mesa **5** plain **7** plateau
low: 4 vale **6** valley **9** intervale
measure: 3 rod **4** acre
open: 3 lea **5** field, green, plain
6 meadow **7** pasture
piece: 3 lot **4** plot **5** tract **6** estate, parcel
reclaimed: 6 polder
sloping: 6 cuesta
strip: 7 isthmus
wet: 3 bog, fen **5** marsh, swamp
6 marish

land east of Eden
3 Nod

landed
4 alit

landlord
6 lessor, squire **9** innkeeper **10** freeholder

landmark
5 cairn, guide **9** benchmark, milestone,
watershed **11** achievement
12 breakthrough, turning point

Land of Enchantment
9 New Mexico

Land of Lakes
8 Michigan

Land of Opportunity
3 USA **8** Arkansas **12** United States

Land of the Midnight Sun
6 Norway

landowner
6 squire, yeoman
Anglo-Saxon: 5 thane, thegn
Dutch: 7 patroon
Scottish: 5 laird

landscape
5 scene, vista **7** scenery, setting, terrain
8 backdrop, prospect

lane
3 way **4** path, road **5** aisle, alley, byway,
track **6** street **7** pathway, roadway
8 footpath **10** passageway

lang syne
4 past, yore **10** yesteryear

language
4 cant **5** argot, idiom, lingo, prose, slang
6 jargon, patois, speech, tongue **7** dialect,

lexicon, palaver **10** vernacular, vocabulary
11 terminology
ambiguous: 8 newspeak **10** double-talk
ancient: 5 Greek, Latin **6** Hebrew
8 Etruscan, Sanskrit
artificial: 3 Ido **7** Volapük **9** Esperanto
classical: 5 Greek, Latin
combining form: 5 gloss, glott **6** glosso,
glotto
expert: 8 linguist
informal: 4 jive **5** lingo, slang
meaningless: 6 babble, jabber **7** blather
9 gibberish **10** mumbo-jumbo
mixed: 6 creole, pidgin
pretentious: 7 bombast, fustian
8 claptrap
regional: 7 dialect
relating to: 10 linguistic
Romance: 6 French **7** Catalan, Italian,
Spanish **8** Romanian, Rumanian
10 Portuguese
secret: 4 cant, code **5** argot
structure: 6 syntax **7** grammar
suffix: 3 ese
written: 5 prose

languid
4 lazy, limp **5** inert **6** draggy, supine, torpid
8 drooping, flagging, inactive, listless,
slothful, sluggish **9** apa-
thetic, enervated, impassive, lethargic
10 languorous, phlegmatic, spiritless
13 lackadaisical

languish
4 fade, fail, pine, tire, wilt **5** brood, droop
6 weaken **7** decline **9** waste away

languishing
4 limp, weak **6** feeble, pining **7** languid
8 fainéant, indolent, listless, weakened
9 depressed, enervated, enfeebled
10 dispirited, languorous, spiritless
11 debilitated, devitalized **13** lackadaisical

languor
3 kef, kif **5** ennui **6** stupor, tedium, torpor
7 fatigue **8** doldrums, dullness, hebetude,
lethargy **9** heaviness, inertness, lassitude,
torpidity, weariness **10** exhaustion

languorous
4 lazy, limp **5** inert **6** draggy, supine, torpid
7 laggard, languid, passive, relaxed
8 dilatory, drooping, fainéant, flagging,
inactive, indolent, indulged, laggard,
languid, listless, pampered, slothful,
sluggard **9** apathetic, enervated,
impassive, lethargic **10** phlegmatic,
spiritless **11** languishing **13** lackadaisical

lank
4 bony, lean, thin **5** rangy, spare **6** gangly
7 angular, scraggy, slender **8** gangling
10 attenuated

lanky
4 lean, thin **5** gaunt, spare **6** gangly
7 scrawny **8** gangling, rawboned

lanyard
4 cord, line, rope **7** cordage

Laocoön
city: 4 Troy
killer: 8 serpents

Laodamia
father: 7 Acastus
husband: 11 Protesilaus

Laomedon
daughter: 7 Hesione
father: 4 Ilus
kingdom: 4 Troy
mother: 8 Eurydice
slayer: 8 Heracles, Hercules
son: 5 Priam **8** Tithonus

Laos
capital: 9 Vientiane
city: 11 Savannakhet
ethnic group: 5 Hmong
monetary unit: 3 kip
neighbor: 5 Burma, China **7** Myanmar,
Vietnam **8** Cambodia, Thailand
9 Kampuchea
river: 6 Mekong

lap
3 sip **4** fold, join, wind **6** cuddle, splash,
swathe **7** circuit, control, custody, shingle
9 imbricate

lapidary
6 cutter **7** elegant, jeweler **8** engraver,
polisher

lapillus
4 lava **6** cinder

lapin
6 rabbit

Lapiths
foes: 8 centaurs
king: 5 Ixion

lappet
4 flap, fold **5** lapel

Lapsang
3 tea **6** Fujian

lapse

3 err, gap, sin **4** fall, flub, goof, sink, slip, vice **5** boner, cease, error, fluff, gaffe, slide **6** breach, bungle, expire, foible, miscue **7** blooper, blunder, decline, descend, failing, failure, faux pas, forfeit, frailty, mistake, screwup, subside **8** apostasy, interval, trespass **9** backslide, deviation, oversight, violation **10** apostatize **11** backsliding, impropriety **12** indiscretion, interruption **13** retrogression, transgression

lapsed

4 sunk **5** ended **6** ceased **7** expired **8** obsolete **9** forfeited

Laputan

6 absurd **9** visionary

Lar

3 god **6** spirit

larboard

4 left, port **8** leftward

larcenist

5 thief **6** bandit, robber **7** burglar, filcher, stealer **8** pilferer **9** embezzler, plunderer, purloiner **10** pickpocket, shoplifter

larcenous

7 robbing **8** thieving **9** pilfering **10** plunderous **13** light-fingered

larceny

5 theft **7** looting, robbery **8** burglary, stealing, thievery, thieving
kind: **5** grand, petty

lard

3 fat **6** fatten, grease **10** shortening

larder

6 pantry

large

3 big, fat **4** bull, huge, vast **5** ample, bulky, giant, grand, great, gross, hefty, husky, jumbo, major **6** goodly **7** copious, extreme, immense, mammoth, massive, outsize, sizable **8** colossal, enormous, gigantic, king-size, oversize, spacious, whopping **9** capacious, excessive, extensive, humongous, monstrous **10** exorbitant, immoderate, inordinate, large-scale, monumental, prodigious, stupendous, tremendous, voluminous **11** extravagant, substantial
combining form: **4** macr, mega **5** macro **6** megalo

largesse

4 alms, gift **6** bounty **7** bequest, charity, cumshaw, gifting, present **8** donation, gratuity **9** endowment, pourboire **10** almsgiving, generosity, liberality **11** benefaction, benevolence, benificence, magnanimity, munificence **12** philanthropy

largo

4 slow **5** broad, tempo

lariat

4 rope **5** lasso, noose, reata, riata
user: **6** cowboy, drover **10** cowpuncher

lark

4 bird, dido, romp **5** antic, caper, prank, shine, stunt, trick **6** frolic **7** rollick **8** escapade, songbird **9** diversion **10** tomfoolery **11** distraction, shenanigans **12** monkeyshines

larrup

3 tan **4** beat, cane, drub, dust, flay, flog, hide, lash, lick, whip, whup **5** pound, spank, whale **6** cudgel, lather, paddle, thrash, wallop **7** clobber, scourge, shellac, trounce **8** lambaste **10** flagellate

larva

3 bot **4** grub, worm **6** dobson, maggot **8** cercaria, hornworm, mealworm **10** casebearer **11** caterpillar **12** hellgrammite
amphibian: **7** tadpole
crustacean: **4** zoea
flatworm: **5** redia
free-swimming: **7** planula
mollusk: **7** veliger
moth: **8** leafworm
tapeworm: **6** measle

larynx

7 trachea **8** voice box

lasagna

5 pasta **7** noodles

lascivious

4 lewd **5** bawdy, loose, randy **6** carnal, coarse, rakish, wanton **7** fleshly, goatish, immoral, lustful, satyric **8** depraved, prurient **9** lecherous, libertine, lickerish, salacious **10** libidinous, licentious, lubricious, profligate **12** concupiscent

lash

4 beat, bind, dash, flay, flog, hide, whip **5** baste, birch, fling, pound, scold, slash, whale **6** assail, berate, buffet, pummel, scathe, strike, stripe, switch, thrash **7** blister, scarify, scourge, upbraid

8 lambaste **9** castigate, excoriate, horsewhip **10** flagellate

lass
3 gal **4** girl, maid **5** wench **6** damsel, maiden **7** colleen

lassitude
5 ennui, sloth **6** apathy, stupor, tedium, torpor **7** fatigue, languor **8** debility, doldrums, dullness, hebetude, laziness, lethargy **9** indolence, tiredness, torpidity, weariness **10** exhaustion **11** disinterest, insouciance **12** heedlessness, indifference, listlessness, sluggishness

lasso
see **lariat**

last
3 end, lag **5** abide, final **6** endure, latest, latter, utmost **7** closing, extreme, perdure, persist **8** continue, crowning, eventual, farthest, furthest, hindmost, rearmost, remotest, terminal, ultimate **9** umpteenth, uttermost **10** concluding, conclusive **11** terminating
French: 7 dernier
next to: 6 penult **11** penultimate

last-ditch
5 final **7** defiant **8** ultimate **9** desperate **10** concluding

lasting
6 stable **7** abiding, durable, undying **8** enduring, lifelong, long-term, longtime **9** continual, indelible, perennial, permanent, unceasing **10** continuing, continuous, perdurable, persisting **12** indissoluble, long-standing

Last of the Mohicans, The
5 Uncas
author: 6 Cooper (James Fenimore)
character: 4 Cora **5** Alice, Magua, Uncas **11** Natty Bumppo **12** Chingachgook

Last Supper, The
painter: 7 da Vinci (Leonardo)

latch
4 bolt, hasp, hook **5** catch **6** fasten, secure **8** fastener
British: 5 sneck

latchet
4 band, cord, lace **5** strap, thong **8** shoelace

late
4 dead, past, slow **5** tardy **6** former, recent, whilom **7** defunct, delayed, onetime, overdue, quondam **8** deceased, departed, sometime **9** preceding

Late George Apley, The
author: 8 Marquand (John P.)

latent
4 idle **5** inert **6** covert, fallow, hidden, innate, unripe **7** abeyant, dormant, lurking **8** immature, inactive, inherent **9** concealed, intrinsic, potential, quiescent

later
4 anon, soon **5** after, infra **6** behind **7** by and by, ensuing **9** afterward, following, posterior **10** subsequent, succeeding **12** subsequently

lateral
4 pass, side **6** branch **8** crabwise, flanking, sidelong, sideward, sideways, sidewise

laterally
8 crabwise, sideward, sideways, sidewise

latest
6 newest, red-hot **7** current **8** contempo **9** au courant **10** dernier cri **13** up-to-the-minute

latex
6 balata **8** emulsion
product: 5 paint **6** chicle, rubber

lath
4 slat **5** board, frame, stave, stick, strip

lather
4 flap, flog, foam, hide, lash, soap, stew, suds, whip **5** froth, spume, tizzy, yeast **6** dither, hoopla, pother, thrash, welter **7** scourge, turmoil **8** soapsuds

Latin
5 Roman **7** Italian **8** Hispanic
after: 4 post
always: 6 semper
before: 4 ante, prae
book: 5 liber
boy: 4 puer
brother: 6 frater
but: 3 sed
day: 4 dies
dog: 5 canis
foot: 3 pes
friend: 6 amicus
god: 4 deus
goddess: 3 dea
grammarian: 7 Donatus (Aelius)
hand: 5 manus
is: 3 est

law: 3 ius, jus, lex
light: 3 lux
love: 3 amo 4 amas, amat, amor
peace: 3 pax
pronoun: 3 ego, nos, vos
road: 3 via
see: 4 vide
that is: 5 id est
thing: 3 res
this: 3 hic, hoc 4 haec
thus: 3 sic
war: 6 bellum
wife: 4 uxor
woman: 6 femina
year: 5 annus

Latin American

country: 4 Cuba, Peru 5 Chile 6 Belize, Brazil, Guyana, Mexico, Panama 7 Bolivia, Ecuador, Uruguay 8 Colombia, Honduras, Paraguay, Suriname 9 Argentina, Costa Rica, Guatemala, Nicaragua, Venezuela 10 El Salvador
revolutionary: 6 Castro (Fidel) 7 Bolívar (Simón), Guevara (Ché), Hidalgo (Father Miguel) 8 O'Higgins (Bernardo) 9 San Martín (José de)

Latinus

daughter: 7 Lavinia
father: 6 Faunus 8 Odysseus
son-in-law: 6 Aeneas
wife: 5 Amata

latitude

4 play, room 5 range, scope, space, width 6 leeway, margin 7 breadth, compass, freedom, liberty, license 9 elbowroom 10 discretion 12 independence

latke

7 pancake 13 potato pancake

Latona

4 Leto
daughter: 5 Diana 7 Artemis
father: 5 Coeus
mother: 6 Phoebe
son: 6 Apollo

Latter-day Saint

6 Mormon

lattice

4 grid, mesh 5 grate, grill 7 grating, network, trellis 12 reticulation

Latvia

capital: 4 Riga
city: 7 Liepaja 10 Daugavpils
gulf: 4 Riga
monetary unit: 3 lat

neighbor: 6 Russia 7 Belarus, Estonia 9 Lithuania
river: 7 Daugava 12 Western Dvina
sea: 6 Baltic

Latvian

4 Lett 7 Lettish

laud

5 adore, bless, cry up, extol, glory, honor 6 admire, praise, revere 7 acclaim, flatter, glorify, magnify, worship 8 eulogize, venerate 9 celebrate, reverence

laudable

6 worthy 9 admirable, deserving, estimable 11 commendable, meritorious, thankworthy 12 praiseworthy

laudatory

7 glowing 9 adulatory, approving 10 eulogistic, flattering 11 approbative, encomiastic, panegyrical 12 commendary 13 complimentary

laugh

3 yuk 4 ha-ha, roar, yuck 5 tehee, whoop 6 cackle, giggle, guffaw, hee-haw, titter 7 chortle, chuckle, snicker 10 cachinnate

laughable

4 rich 5 comic, droll, funny, goofy, witty 6 absurd, jocose 7 amusing, comical, jocular, mocking, risible 8 derisive, derisory, farcical, humorous 9 ludicrous 10 ridiculous

laughing

5 merry, riant 6 blithe 8 mirthful 9 sparkling

laughingstock

4 butt, dupe, fool, jest, joke, mark, mock 5 sport 6 target 7 mockery 8 derision

launch

4 boat, cast, fire, hurl 5 begin, debut, fling, heave, pitch, sling, start, throw 6 get off, set afloat 7 jump off, kick off, lift off, release, take off, usher in 8 blast off, catapult, commence, embark on, initiate 9 inception, institute, introduce, motorboat 10 inaugurate, initiation 12 inauguration

launder

4 wash 5 clean 6 trough 7 cleanse 8 sanitize, transfer

Laura's lover

8 Petrarch

laurels

4 bays, fame 5 award, honor, kudos, prize 6 awards, badges, honors, prizes, renown

7 acclaim **8** accolade, citation
9 accolades, citations **10** decoration,
reputation **11** decorations, distinction
12 achievements, distinctions

laurel-tree nymph
  6 Daphne

lava
  4 slag **5** magma **6** scoria **8** andesite,
trachyte
  fragment: 8 lapillus
  stream: 4 flow **6** coulee

lavalava
  5 cloth, skirt

lavaliere
  7 pendant **8** necklace

lavatory
  4 head, john **5** basin, potty, privy **6** johnny,
toilet **7** latrine **8** bathroom, restroom,
washroom **11** water closet

lave
  4 pour, wash **5** bathe

Lavinia
  father: 7 Latinus
  husband: 6 Aeneas
  mother: 5 Amata

Lavinium's founder
  6 Aeneas

lavish
  4 lush, pour **5** plush, spend, waste
6 swanky **7** liberal, opulent, profuse
8 effusive, prodigal, splendid, squander
9 bountiful, excessive, exuberant, luxuriant,
luxurious, sumptuous **10** immoderate,
inordinate, munificent **11** extravagant

law
  3 act, lex **4** bill, code, rule **5** axiom, canon,
edict, Torah **6** assize, decree, equity
7 dictate, justice, mandate, precept,
statute, theorem **8** exigency **9** enactment,
ordinance, principle **10** principium,
regulation **11** commandment, fundamental
12 prescription
  body of: 4 code **7** pandect **12** constitution
  degree: 3 LLB, LLD
  expert: 5 judge **6** jurist **7** justice
  practitioner: 6 lawyer **7** counsel
8 attorney **9** barrister, solicitor
  relating to: 5 jural, legal **7** canonic
8 forensic, juristic **9** judiciary
  violation of: 4 tort **5** crime **6** felony
11 misdemeanor

law-abiding
  6 decent **7** duteous, dutiful, orderly, upright
8 obedient, obliging, straight **9** compliant,
peaceable **10** forthright, respectful, well-
behaved **11** respectable

lawbreaker
  3 con **4** hood, thug **5** crook, felon
6 outlaw, sinner **7** convict, hoodlum,
mobster **8** criminal, gangster, hooligan,
jailbird, offender, scofflaw, violator
9 desperado, wrongdoer **10** malefactor,
trespasser **12** transgressor

lawful
  3 due **4** just **5** legal, legit, licit, valid
6 kosher **7** condign **8** bona fide, innocent,
mandated, ordained **9** allowable,
canonical, juridical, legalized
10 authorized, legitimate **11** permissible

lawgiver
  5 Draco, Moses, solon **7** senator
8 alderman **10** councilman, legislator
11 congressman

lawlessness
  5 chaos **6** strife **7** anarchy, discord,
misrule, turmoil **8** conflict, disorder
9 mobocracy **10** illegality, misconduct,
ochlocracy, unruliness, wrongdoing
11 criminality, pandemonium

lawman
  7 marshal, officer, sheriff **9** policeman

Lawrence novel
  7 Rainbow (The) **8** Kangaroo, Lost Girl
(The) **9** Aaron's Rod **11** Women in Love
13 Sons and Lovers

lawsuit
  4 case **5** cause, claim **6** action **8** replevin
9 assumpsit **10** litigation, proceeding
11 presentment, prosecution

lawyer
  6 jurist, legist **7** counsel, pleader
8 advocate, attorney **9** barrister, counselor,
solicitor
  dishonest: 7 shyster **11** pettifogger
  fictional: 7 Matlock (Ben) **10** Perry
Mason
  French: 6 avocat

lax
  5 loose, slack **6** casual, remiss, sloppy
7 lenient **8** careless, derelict, lacrosse
9 deficient, forgetful, negligent
10 neglectful **11** inattentive

lay
  3 bet, put, set **5** apply, hatch, place, wager

lay by

6 assert, assign, ballad, charge, credit, devise, impute, settle, spread **7** amateur, arrange, ascribe, concoct, deposit, prepare, present **11** nonclerical

lay by

4 keep, save **5** amass, hoard, store **7** deposit, discard, store up **8** preserve, salt away, set aside **10** accumulate

lay down

3 set **4** rule **5** order, store, yield **6** assert, decree, define, give up, impose, ordain, record, resign **7** abandon, command, dictate, specify **8** hand over, preserve, proclaim **9** establish, prescribe, surrender **10** relinquish

layer

3 hen, ply **4** coat, film, seam, tier **5** paver, sheet **6** folium, lamina, veneer **7** coating, stratum **8** covering, laminate, membrane, sandwich, stratify
inner: 6 lining
of skin: 6 dermis **9** epidermis
outer: 4 skin **6** veneer

lay for

6 ambush **8** surprise

lay in

see **lay by**

layman

6 novice **7** amateur, secular **11** parishioner

lay off

4 halt, quit, stop **5** avoid, cease, let go, lie by **6** desist **7** dismiss, measure, release **9** discharge, terminate **10** inactivity **11** discontinue

lay out

3 pay **4** give, plan **5** chart, dummy, place, spend **6** design, expend **7** arrange, display, exhibit, prepare **8** disburse

lay waste

4 ruin **6** ravage **7** destroy **8** desolate **9** devastate

lazar

5 leper

Lazarus' sister

4 Mary **6** Martha

laze

3 bum, lag **4** bask, hang, idle, loaf, loll **5** chill **6** dawdle, loiter, lounge, slouch **7** goof off, hang out **8** chill out **9** goldbrick **10** hang around

laziness

5 sloth **6** torpor **7** inertia, languor, laxness, loafing **8** idleness, lethargy, otiosity **9** indolence, lassitude, loitering, slackness **10** inactivity **11** languidness **12** listlessness

lazy

3 lax **4** idle **5** inert, slack **6** droopy, remiss, supine, torpid **7** languid, loafing, passive **8** fainéant, inactive, indolent, listless, slothful, sluggish **9** lethargic, negligent, shiftless, slowgoing **10** languorous

lazy Susan

4 tray **9** turntable

leach

4 drip, leak, ooze, perk, seep, suck, weep **5** bleed, drain, exude, issue **7** draw out, dribble, trickle **8** filtrate, perspire **9** discharge, lixiviate, percolate

lead

3 tip **4** head, hint, show, star **5** guide, metal, plumb, route, steer, trace, usher **6** bullet, ceruse, direct, escort, leader **7** captain, conduct, precede, preface **8** graphite, persuade, shepherd **10** bellwether
combining form: 5 plumb **6** plumbo
ore: 6 galena **9** anglesite
oxide: 6 sinter
sounding: 5 plumb **7** plummet

lead astray

6 seduce **7** corrupt

leaden

4 drab, dull, flat, gray **5** heavy, inert **6** gloomy, somber **7** languid, weighty **8** dragging, lifeless, sluggish **9** ponderous

leader

4 boss, dean, duce, guru, head, jefe, lord **5** chief, guide, pilot **6** despot, honcho, rector **7** captain, foreman, general, headman, manager, warlord **8** chairman, director, hierarch, superior **9** chieftain, commander, conductor, demagogue, harbinger, precursor, president, principal, straw boss **10** bellwether, forerunner, pacesetter
authoritarian: 10 Big Brother
Cossack: 6 ataman, hetman
German: 6 führer **7** fuehrer
Japanese: 6 shogun
military: 7 admiral, general, warlord **9** commander **12** field marshal

Muslim: 3 aga **4** agha, emir **6** caliph, mullah
national: 7 premier **9** president **12** chief of state

leading
4 arch, head, main **5** chief, first, major **6** famous, master **7** premier, primary **8** champion, foremost, headmost, peerless **9** paramount, principal, prominent, well-known **10** preeminent

lead on
3 con **4** bait, dupe, fool, gull, hoax, lure, scam, tole, toll, wile **5** cozen, flirt, tempt **6** allure, betray, cajole, coquet, delude, entice, entrap, humbug, seduce, suck in, take in, trifle **7** beguile, deceive, toy with **8** coquette, hoodwink, inveigle **9** bamboozle **11** string along

leaf
4 flip, foil, page, riff, scan, skim **5** blade, bract, folio, frond, petal, scale, sepal, thumb **6** browse, glance, riffle, spathe
aperture: 5 stoma
axis: 6 rachis
combining form: 5 phyll **6** phyllo **7** phyllum
edge: 9 crenation
lily: 3 pad
part: 4 lobe, vein **5** blade, costa, stoma **7** petiole, stipule, tendril
pine: 6 needle
vein: 5 costa

leafage
7 foliage, umbrage, verdure

leaflet
5 flier, flyer, pinna, sheet, tract **6** folder **8** circular, handbill, handout, pamphlet

leafy
4 lush **5** green, shady **6** shaded, wooded **7** foliate, verdant **8** foliated, laminate **9** verdurous

league
4 band, bond, club, crew **5** class, grade, group, guild, order, union, unite **6** circle **7** circuit, combine, society **8** alliance, category, division, grouping, sodality **9** coalition **10** conference, consortium, federation, fellowship, fraternity **11** association, brotherhood, confederacy **13** confederation

Leah
daughter: 5 Dinah
father: 5 Laban
husband: 5 Jacob

sister: 6 Rachel
son: 4 Levi **5** Judah **6** Reuben, Simeon **7** Zebulun **8** Issachar

leak
4 drip, ooze, seep **5** break, crack, spill **6** escape, get out, reveal, source **7** come out, divulge, seepage **8** disclose **9** discharge **10** make public

leaky
6 broken, faulty, porous **7** cracked, damaged

lea, ley
4 veld **5** field, veldt **6** fallow, meadow **7** pasture **9** grassland, pasturage

lean
3 sag, tip **4** bend, bony, cant, heel, lank, list, slim, thin, tilt **5** gaunt, lanky, shift, slant, slope, spare **6** meager, meagre, skinny, slight, wasted **7** angular, deviate, haggard, incline, pinched, scraggy, scrawny, slender, stringy, wizened **8** gradient, rawboned **9** deficient **11** inclination

Leander's beloved
4 Hero

Leaning Tower site
4 Pisa

lean-to
3 hut **4** shed **5** shack **6** shanty **7** bivouac, shelter

leap
3 hop **4** buck, jump, loup, rise, soar **5** bound, caper, clear, mount, vault **6** ascend, gambol, hurdle, spring **7** saltate **8** capriole, surmount
ballet: 4 jeté **9** entrechat
by a horse: 7 gambado

Lear, King
daughter: 5 Regan **7** Goneril **8** Cordelia
servant: 4 Kent

learn
3 con **4** hear **5** grasp, study **6** attain, detect, master, pick up **7** acquire, catch on, discern, find out, realize, uncover, unearth **8** discover, memorize **9** ascertain, determine **10** comprehend, understand **11** stumble onto

learned
4 sage, wise **6** expert, versed **7** bookish, erudite, sapient, studied **8** abstruse, academic, cultured, educated, esoteric, highbrow, lettered, pedantic, well-read

learner (continued)
9 recondite, scholarly 10 cultivated, scholastic 12 intellectual

learner
4 tyro 5 pupil 6 novice, rookie 7 student, trainee 8 beginner, disciple, initiate, neophyte 9 greenhorn, postulant 10 apprentice, catechumen 11 abecedarian

learning
4 lore 6 wisdom 7 science, tuition 8 booklore, pedantry 9 education, erudition, knowledge 11 scholarship
person of: 7 egghead, scholar 9 professor 12 intellectual

lease
3 let 4 hire, rent 6 sublet 7 charter, compact 8 contract, covenant, document 11 continuance

leash
3 tie 4 bind, cord, curb, rein, rope 5 strap 6 bridle, fetter, hamper, tether 7 shackle, trammel 8 restrain 9 entrammel

least
6 fewest 7 minimal, minimum 8 smallest

leather
3 tan 4 hide, skin, whip 6 thrash
kind: 3 kid, kip, oak 4 bock, buff, calf, roan 5 crown, grain, mocha, strap, suede, whang 6 castor, latigo, oxhide, patent, roller, saddle, skiver 7 buffalo, chamois, morocco, ostrich, peccary 8 capeskin, cordovan, cordwain, shagreen
maker: 5 tawer 6 tanner 7 tannery
piece: 4 welt 5 strap, thong
prepare: 3 tan, taw 5 curry
soft: 5 mocha, suede 8 cabretta

leatherneck
6 marine

Leatherstocking Tales, The
author: 6 Cooper (James Fenimore)
hero: 5 Natty (Bumppo)
title: 7 Prairie (The) 8 Pioneers (The) 10 Deerslayer (The), Pathfinder (The) 17 Last of the Mohicans (The)

leave
3 fly, let 4 blow, cede, exit, flee, move, part, quit, will 5 allow, scram, split 6 assent, assign, beat it, commit, cut out, decamp, depart, desert, devise, escape, get off, legate, permit, resign, retire, set out, vacate 7 abandon, abscond, absence, consent, consign, entrust, forsake, get away, liberty, pull out, take off, vamoose 8 bequeath, clear out, farewell, furlough, hand down, transmit, vacation, withdraw 9 departure, disappear, surrender, terminate 10 permission, relinquish, sabbatical 13 authorization

leaved
5 green 7 foliate, verdant 8 foliated

leaven
5 imbue, steep, yeast 6 infuse, invest, modify, temper, vivify 7 enliven, ingrain, lighten, suffuse 8 moderate 9 alleviate, inoculate, sourdough 12 baking powder

leave of absence
8 furlough

leave off
3 end 4 halt, quit, stop 5 cease 6 desist, give up 7 abstain 8 give over, surcease 9 terminate 11 discontinue

leave out
4 omit, skip 5 elide 7 exclude

Leaves of Grass author
7 Whitman (Walt)

leavings
4 lees, orts, rest 5 dregs, scrap 6 debris, grouts 7 balance, remains, remnant, residue, rubbish 8 discards, oddments, remnants, residual, residuum 9 fragments, leftovers, remainder

Lebanon
capital: 6 Beirut
city: 4 Tyre 5 Sidon 6 Zahlah 7 Tripoli
language: 6 Arabic, French
monetary unit: 5 pound
mountain: 6 Hermon
neighbor: 5 Syria 6 Israel
river: 6 Litani 7 Orontes
sea: 13 Mediterranean
valley: 5 Bekáa

Le Carré, John
character: 6 Smiley (George)
novel: 11 Russia House (The) 17 Little Drummer Girl (The) 22 Tinker, Tailor, Soldier, Spy 23 Spy Who Came in from the Cold (The)

lecher
4 rake, roué, wolf 7 Don Juan, seducer 8 Casanova, lothario 9 debauchee, reprobate, libertine, womanizer 10 degenerate, profligate, voluptuary 11 philanderer

lecherous
4 lewd 5 bawdy, loose, randy 6 carnal, coarse, rakish, wanton 7 fleshly, goatish, immoral, lustful, satyric 8 depraved,

prurient, scabrous **9** debauched, libertine, lickerish, salacious **10** lascivious, libidinous, licentious, lubricious, profligate **11** promiscuous **12** concupiscent

lectern
4 desk **5** stand

lecture
4 talk **5** chide, scold, speak **6** berate, preach, rebuke, sermon, speech **7** address, declaim, expound, oration, reproof, reprove, upbraid **8** admonish, briefing, harangue, scolding **9** chalk talk, criticism, criticize, discourse, hold forth, reprimand, talking-to **10** allocution **12** disquisition, dressing-down

lecturer
3 don **6** docent, fellow, master, orator, reader **7** scholar, speaker, teacher, trainer **9** pedagogue, preceptor, professor **10** instructor **11** academician

Leda
daughter: **5** Helen **12** Clytemnestra
father: **8** Thestius
husband: **9** Tyndareus
lover: **4** swan, Zeus
son: **6** Castor, Pollux

ledge
3 bar, rim **4** berm, lode, reef, sill, vein **5** bench, ridge, shelf **6** mantle **7** bedrock, molding **10** projection

ledger
4 book **5** tally **6** record **7** account, balance **8** register **9** reckoning

lee
5 haven **7** shelter **9** protected, sheltered

leech
4 milk, worm **5** bleed, drain **6** sponge, sucker **7** exhaust, sponger **8** barnacle, hanger-on, parasite **10** freeloader **11** bloodsucker **12** lounge lizard

leer
3 eye **4** ogle **5** fleer, gloat, smirk, sneer, stare **6** glance, goggle, squint **7** grimace

leery
4 wary **5** chary **6** unsure **7** dubious, guarded **8** cautious, doubtful, doubting **10** suspicious **11** circumspect, distrustful, mistrustful

lees
5 dregs **6** grouts, refuse **7** deposit, grounds, residue **8** leavings, residual, residuum, sediment **9** settlings **11** precipitate

leeward
8 downwind
opposite: **8** windward

leeway
4 play, room **5** scope, space **6** margin **7** breadth, compass, freedom, liberty **8** latitude **9** elbowroom, tolerance

left
4 port **7** liberal, radical **8** departed, deserted, larboard, residual, sinister **9** abandoned, discarded, remaining, sinistral

left-handed
5 inept **6** clumsy, gauche **7** awkward, dubious **8** fumbling, southpaw **9** ambiguous, equivocal, insincere, maladroit **10** morganatic

left-hand page
5 verso

leftover
5 extra, spare **6** excess, unused **7** remnant, reserve, residue, surplus, uneaten, vestige **8** residual, unneeded **9** redundant, remainder, remaining **10** unconsumed **11** superfluous

leftovers
see **leavings**

leftward
4 levo **5** aport
go: **3** haw

leg
3 gam **4** limb **5** shank **7** support, upright **8** cabriole **9** appendage, drumstick
bone: **4** shin **5** femur, tibia **6** fibula **7** patella
part: **4** calf, crus, foot, knee, shin **5** ankle, thigh

legacy
4 gift **5** trust **6** devise, estate **7** bequest **8** heirloom, heritage **9** endowment, patrimony, tradition **10** birthright **11** benefaction, inheritance

legal
5 legit, licit **6** lawful **7** allowed **8** innocent **9** juridical, statutory **10** legitimate, sanctioned
matter: **3** res **4** case, suit
order: **4** writ **7** summons **8** subpoena
party: **6** suitor **8** litigant **9** defendant, plaintiff
restraint: **8** estoppel

legal tender
3 wad 4 cash 5 bread, dough, money,
moola, notes 6 moolah, specie 7 coinage
8 banknote, currency 9 long green

legate
4 will 5 endow, envoy, grant, leave
6 bestow, commit, devise, deputy, devise,
pass on 7 entrust, leave to 8 bequeath,
delegate, emissary, hand down, transmit
10 ambassador

legatee
4 heir 7 devisee 9 inheritor

legato
5 fluid 6 smooth 7 flowing

legend
3 key 4 lore, myth, saga, tale, yarn
5 fable, motto, story 6 mythos 7 caption,
fiction 8 epigraph, folklore, folktale
9 mythology, tradition 11 inscription

legendary
5 famed 6 fabled, famous, mythic
7 fabular, fancied, fictive, storied
8 fabulous, mythical, renowned, supposed
9 well-known 10 apocryphal, celebrated
11 illustrious, traditional 12 mythological

legerdemain
5 magic 8 trickery 9 chicanery, conjuring,
deception 13 sleight of hand

leggings
5 chaps 7 puttees 9 gambadoes

leghorn
3 hat 4 fowl 5 straw 7 chicken

legible
5 clear 8 distinct, readable 12 decipherable, intelligible

legion
4 army, host, many, mass, rout 5 cloud,
crowd, drove, flock, horde 6 myriad,
scores, sundry, throng 7 phalanx, various
8 numerous, populous 9 countless,
multitude 10 numberless

legislate
5 enact, order 6 codify, decree, ordain,
permit, ratify 7 empower, mandate
8 legalize, regulate, sanction 9 establish

legislation
3 act, law 4 acts, bill, code, laws 5 bills,
codes, rules 6 edicts 7 statute 8 charters,
dictates, statutes 9 enactment, lawmaking
10 enactments, ordinances, regulation
11 regulations 12 codification

legislator
5 solon 7 senator 8 alderman, lawgiver,
lawmaker 10 councilman
11 assemblyman, congressman

legislature
4 diet 5 house, junta 6 senate 7 council
8 assembly, congress 10 parliament
Communist: 6 soviet 9 politburo,
presidium
czarist Russian: 4 duma
Danish: 9 Folketing
Finnish: 9 Eduskunta
German: 9 Bundesrat, Bundestag
Iceland: 7 Althing
Israel: 7 Knesset
Norway: 8 Storting
one-house: 10 unicameral
Poland: 4 Sejm
Spain: 6 Cortes
Sweden: 7 Riksdag
two-house: 9 bicameral

legitimate
4 fair, just, true 5 legal, licit, sound, usual,
valid 6 kosher, lawful, normal, proper
7 genuine, regular, typical 8 accepted,
innocent, orthodox, rightful 9 allowable,
authentic, canonical, customary
10 admissable, authorized, reasonable,
recognized 11 justifiable, well-founded

Le Guin novel
7 Telling (The) 18 Left Hand of Darkness
(The)

legume
3 pea, pod 4 bean, guar, seed 5 pulse
6 clover, lentil 7 soybean

leg up
3 aid 4 edge, lift 5 boost 6 assist
9 advantage, head start

lei
6 wreath 7 garland 8 necklace

Leibniz's invention
8 calculus

Leif Eriksson
discovery: 7 Vinland
father: 4 Eric, Erik (the Red)

leisure
4 ease, rest, time 6 casual, chance,
repose 7 freedom, liberty 10 relaxation
11 opportunity

leisurely
4 easy, slow 6 lazily, slowly 7 relaxed,
restful 8 laid-back 9 unhurried

leitmotiv
4 idea 5 theme, topic 6 burden, motive, thesis 7 subject

lemma
5 bract, theme 7 heading, premise, theorem 8 argument 11 proposition

lemon
3 dud 4 bomb, bust, flop 5 fruit, loser, scent 6 flavor, yellow 7 failure

lemur
5 indri, loris, potto 6 aye-aye, colugo, galago 7 tarsier 8 bush baby

lend
4 give, loan 5 allow, grant 6 afford, oblige, supply 7 advance, furnish, provide 11 accommodate

length
4 span 5 ambit, range, reach, realm, scope 6 extent, radius 7 compass, expanse, measure, purview, section, stretch, yardage 8 distance, duration

lengthen
6 expand, extend, let out 7 draw out, prolong, spin out, stretch 8 elongate, increase, protract 9 string out
Scottish: 3 eke

lengthy
4 long 8 dragging, drawn-out, extended, overlong 9 elongated, prolonged 10 long-winded, protracted, voluminous 12 interminable

leniency
5 mercy 7 quarter 8 clemency 9 tolerance 10 indulgence, toleration 11 forbearance

lenient
4 easy, kind, mild, soft 6 benign, gentle, kindly 7 amiable, clement 8 merciful, obliging, tolerant 9 benignant, forgiving, indulgent 10 forbearing, permissive

lenity
5 mercy 7 quarter 8 clemency 9 tolerance 10 humaneness, indulgence 11 forbearance

lens
5 glass 6 lentil 8 meniscus
kind: 5 toric 6 convex 7 bifocal, concave 8 trifocal

lento
4 slow 5 tempo

Leofric's wife
6 Godiva

Leoncavallo opera
9 Pagliacci (I) 10 Chatterton

leonine
8 lionlike

Leonora
7 heroine
alias: 7 Fidelio
husband: 9 Florestan

leopard
3 cat 4 pard 5 ounce 7 panther

leper
6 pariah 7 Ishmael, outcast 8 castaway, derelict 9 incurable 10 Ishmaelite 11 untouchable

Leper Priest
6 Damien (Father)

lepers' hospital
9 lazaretto

lepers' island
7 Molokai

lepidoptera
5 moths 8 skippers 11 butterflies 12 caterpillars

Leporello's master
11 Don Giovanni

leprechaun
3 elf 5 fairy 6 dwarf, sprite 7 brownie
trade: 8 cobbling

Lesage hero
7 Gil Blas

Lesbos poet
6 Sappho 7 Alcaeus

_____ LeShan
3 Eda

lesion
3 cut 4 boil, flaw, harm, sore 5 ulcer, wound 6 injury 7 blister

Lesotho
capital: 6 Maseru
ethnic group: 5 Sotho
former name: 10 Basutoland
language: 5 Sotho
monetary unit: 4 loti
mountain: 9 Ntlenyana
neighbor: 11 South Africa
river: 6 Orange 7 Caledon

lessen
3 cut 4 clip, crop, ease, thin, wane 5 abate, erode, lower, taper 6 dilute, impair, minify, recede, reduce, shrink, weaken 7 abridge, assuage, curtail, degrade, dwindle, lighten, relieve, subside 8 decrease, diminish, minimize, mitigate, taper off 9 attenuate

lessening
4 drop, fall 5 letup 8 decrease, slowdown
9 abatement, reduction 10 curtailing,
diminution 11 degradation

lesser
5 lower, minor 7 smaller 8 inferior
9 secondary, small-time, subjacent
11 minor-league, subordinate 13 insignificant

lesson
4 text 5 chide, moral, study 6 rebuke
7 example, lecture, reading, reprove,
warning 8 admonish, exercise, homework,
reproach 9 reprimand 10 admonition,
assignment 11 instruction

lessor
8 landlady, landlord 9 landowner
10 freeholder

let
4 make, rent 5 allow, grant, lease, leave
6 assign, permit, suffer 9 authorize
11 obstruction

letdown
5 slump 7 decline, defeat, descent, failure,
reverse, setback 10 anticlimax,
depression, misfortune 11 frustration

let go
3 can 4 boot, fire, free, sack 5 remit
6 unhand 7 dismiss, neglect, release, set
free 8 liberate 9 discharge, terminate

lethal
4 fell 5 fatal 6 deadly, mortal, poison
7 baleful, deathly 8 poisoned, virulent
9 murderous, poisonous 11 destructive,
devastating

lethargic
4 dull, idle, slow 5 dopey, heavy, inert
6 draggy, supine, torpid 7 dormant,
laggard, languid, passive 8 comatose,
dilatory, inactive, listless, slothful, sluggish
9 apathetic, impassive 10 languorous,
phlegmatic, spiritless 11 indifferent
12 hebetudinous 13 lackadaisical

lethargy
5 sloth 6 apathy, phlegm, stupor, torpor
7 inertia, languor, slumber 8 dullness,
hebetude, idleness, laziness 9 disregard,
inanition, indolence, inertness, lassitude,
torpidity 10 inactivity, supineness
11 impassivity, passiveness 12 listlessness

lethe
7 amnesia 8 oblivion 13 forgetfulness

Leto
see **Latona**

let off
5 spare 6 excuse, exempt 7 absolve,
relieve 8 dispense 9 discharge

let on
3 own 5 admit, allow, grant, own up, spill
6 betray, fess up, reveal 7 concede,
confess, confirm, divulge, pretend
8 disclose, give away

let out
5 blurt, loose 6 exhale 7 release, set free,
unloose 8 lengthen, liberate, set loose
9 discharge, turn loose

letter
3 bee, cee, cue, dee, ess, gee, jay, kay,
pee, tee, vee, wye, zed, zee 4 line, mail,
memo, note, rune 5 aitch, print, vowel
6 report, screed, symbol 7 epistle,
message, missive 8 dispatch, inscribe
9 consonant
airmail: 8 aerogram
Anglo-Saxon:
(see **Anglo-Saxon**)
Arabic:
(see **alphabet**)
Greek:
(see **alphabet**)
Hebrew:
(see **alphabet**)
kind: 5 chain, roman 6 italic, uncial
8 Dear John
large: 7 capital 9 majuscule, uppercase
small: 9 lowercase, minuscule

lettuce
3 cos 4 Bibb, head 6 Boston 7 iceberg,
romaine, Simpson 10 butterweed

let up
3 ebb 4 fall, stop, wane 5 abate, cease
6 lessen, relent 7 die away, die down,
ease off, slacken, subside 8 decrease,
diminish, moderate, taper off

letup
4 lull 5 break, pause 7 respite
9 abatement, cessation, lessening,
reduction 10 slackening

levee
4 dike, dock, pier, quay 5 jetty, ridge, wharf
7 seawall 8 assembly, function 9 reception
10 breakwater, embankment, riverfront

level
3 aim, lay, par 4 calm, even, flat, raze, same, tier 5 equal, floor, flush, grade, plane 6 direct, ground, smooth, status, steady 7 aligned, flatten, mow down 8 balanced, bulldoze, demolish, equalize, parallel, smoothen, standing 9 bring down, intensity, knock down, magnitude 10 equivalent, horizontal, reasonable 11 equilibrium

lever
3 bar, pry 4 jack, tool 5 jimmy, peavy, prize 6 peavey, tappet 7 crowbar

leverage
5 clout, power 7 exploit 9 advantage, dominance, influence 11 superiority 13 effectiveness

leveret
4 hare

Levi
father: 5 Jacob
mother: 4 Leah
son: 6 Kohath, Merari 7 Gershon

leviathan
4 huge 5 giant, jumbo, large, titan, whale 6 Goliath, immense, mammoth, massive, monster, titanic 8 behemoth, colossal, colossus, enormous, gigantic 9 cyclopean, monstrous 10 formidable, gargantuan 11 elephantine, monstrosity

Leviathan author
6 Hobbes (Thomas)

levitate
4 lift, rise 5 float, raise 7 elevate, suspend

levity
5 folly, humor 8 buoyancy 9 absurdity, flippancy, frivolity, giddiness, lightness, silliness 10 jocularity, volatility

levy
3 tax 4 duty, toll, wage 5 exact, lay on 6 assess, charge, custom, enlist, impose, impost, tariff 7 carry on, collect 9 conscript 10 assessment, enlistment 12 conscription

lewd
5 bawdy, gross 6 coarse, ribald, smutty, vulgar 7 fleshly, goatish, lustful, obscene, satyric 8 depraved, improper, indecent, prurient, unchaste 9 debauched, lecherous, libertine, lickerish, salacious 10 indelicate, lascivious, libidinous, licentious, lubricious

Lewis and Clark interpreter
9 Sacagawea

Lewis novel
7 Babbitt 9 Dodsworth 10 Arrowsmith, Main Street 11 Elmer Gantry

Lewis work
18 Chronicles of Narnia (The)

lexicographer
8 compiler
American: 6 Porter (Noah) 7 Webster (Noah) 9 Worcester (Joseph)
English: 4 Wyld (Henry) 6 Fowler (Francis, Henry), Murray (James), Onions (Charles) 7 Craigie (William), Johnson (Samuel) 9 Partridge (Eric)
French: 6 Littré (Paul-Emile) 8 Larousse (Pierre)
German: 5 Grimm (Jakob, Wilhelm)

lexicon
4 cant 6 jargon 8 glossary, language, wordbook 9 inventory, word-hoard 10 dictionary, repertoire, vocabulary 11 terminology

liable
3 apt 4 open 5 given, prone 6 likely 7 exposed, subject 8 inclined 9 sensitive 10 answerable, assailable, vulnerable 11 accountable, responsible, susceptible

liaison
4 bond, link 5 amour, fixer 6 affair, broker, hookup 7 contact, romance 8 intrigue 9 go-between 10 connection 12 entanglement, intermediary, relationship 13 communication

liana
4 vine

liar
6 fibber 7 Ananias 8 fabulist, perjurer 9 falsifier 12 prevaricator
female: 8 Sapphira

libation
5 drink 6 liquid, liquor 7 potable 8 beverage, oblation, offering, potation

libel
4 slur 5 smear 6 defame, malign, vilify 7 asperse, calumny, obloquy, slander, traduce 8 bad-mouth, tear down 9 aspersion, denigrate 10 calumniate, defamation, scandalize 11 denigration

libelous
6 untrue 9 injurious, invidious, maligning, traducing, vilifying 10 backbiting,

calumnious, defamatory, derogative,
derogatory, detracting, detractive,
malevolent, pejorative, scandalous,
slanderous

liberal
4 full, open **5** ample, broad, loose **6** lavish
7 copious, profuse, radical **8** abundant,
generous, prodigal, tolerant **9** bounteous,
bountiful, indulgent, plentiful, unsparing
10 benevolent, bighearted, charitable,
freehanded, munificent, openhanded,
permissive, unorthodox **11** broad-minded

liberate
4 free **5** loose **7** manumit, release,
unchain **9** discharge, unshackle
10 commandeer, emancipate **11** appropriate, expropriate

liberator
6 savior **7** messiah **9** deliverer
of Argentina: **9** San Martín (José de)
of Chile: **8** O'Higgins (Bernardo)
of Ecuador: **5** Sucre (Antonio José de)
of Scotland: **5** Bruce (Robert the)
of South America: **7** Bolívar (Simón)

Liberia
capital: **8** Monrovia
coast: **3** Kru **5** Grain
language: **7** English
neighbor: **6** Guinea **10** Ivory Coast
11 Sierra Leone

Liberian
language: **3** Kwa
native: **3** Kru, Vai **4** Gola, Toma **5** Bassa,
Grebo **6** Kruman

libertine
4 lewd, rake, roué **5** bawdy, loose, randy
6 carnal, rakish, wanton **7** lustful, raffish,
satyric **8** debauched, debauchee,
dissolute, lecherous, salacious
10 degenerate, dissipated, lascivious,
libidinous, licentious, profligate
11 promiscuous

liberty
4 risk **5** leave **6** chance **7** freedom,
license **8** autonomy **9** franchise, privilege
10 permission **11** familiarity
12 emancipation, independence

libidinous
4 lewd **5** bawdy, loose, randy **6** carnal,
rakish, wanton **7** fleshly, goatish, lustful,
satyric **8** depraved, prurient **9** debauched,
lecherous, libertine, lickerish, salacious
10 lascivious, licentious, lubricious,
profligate **11** promiscuous **12** concupiscent

librarian
5 Dewey (Melvil)

library
7 archive **8** atheneum **9** athenaeum
11 bibliotheca
desk: **6** carrel

Libya
capital: **7** Tripoli
city: **8** Benghazi
desert: **6** Sahara
gulf: **5** Sidra
language: **6** Arabic **7** Hamitic
leader: **7** Gadhafi, Qaddafi (Mu'ammar)
monetary unit: **5** dinar
neighbor: **4** Chad **5** Egypt, Niger, Sudan
7 Algeria, Tunisia
sea: **12** Mediterranean

lice
7 cooties

license
3 let, tag **5** allow, grant, leave **6** enable,
laxity, permit, suffer, ticket **7** certify,
empower, freedom, go-ahead, liberty
8 accredit, document, sanction, variance
9 authority, authorize, slackness
10 permission, profligacy **11** certificate,
impropriety **12** carte blanche **13** authorization

licentious
4 lewd **5** bawdy, loose, randy **6** amoral,
carnal, rakish, wanton **7** fleshly, goatish,
immoral, lustful, satyric **8** depraved,
prurient, scabrous **9** abandoned,
debauched, dissolute, lecherous, libertine,
lubricious, salacious **10** lascivious,
libidinous, lubricious, profligate
11 promiscuous **12** concupiscent

lichen
4 moss **6** archil, litmus **7** oakmoss
genus: **5** Usnea

licit
5 legal, okay **6** lawful **7** allowed
8 approved, innocent, licensed
9 allowable, permitted **10** admissible,
authorized, legitimate, sanctioned
11 permissible

lick
3 bit, dab, dig, hit, lap, rap, tan **4** beat,
dash, deck, down, drub, hint, swat, whip,
wipe **5** cream, pinch, pound, smack,
smear, spank, taste, touch, trace, whiff
6 defeat, master, punish, thrash, tongue,
wallop **7** clobber, conquer, shellac, trounce
8 lambaste, outstrip, overcome, surmount
9 overwhelm

lickerish
see **libidinous**

lickety-split
4 fast **5** apace **6** presto, pronto **7** flat out,
hastily, quickly, rapidly, swiftly **8** chop-
chop, full tilt, headlong, pell-mell, speedily
9 posthaste **13** expeditiously, precipitately

licorice
4 root **5** candy
pill: 6 cachou

lid
3 cap, top **5** cover **8** covering
moss: 9 operculium

lie
3 fib **4** rest, tale **5** exist, fable, libel
6 belong, canard, covert, delude, extend,
inhere, remain, repose, reside **7** consist,
falsify, falsity, perjure, recline, untruth
8 misspeak, misstate **9** dissemble,
falsehood, fish story, mendacity
10 inaccuracy, taradiddle **11** prevaricate
12 misstatement

Liechtenstein
capital: 5 Vaduz
language: 6 German
monetary unit: 4 euro
mountain range: 4 Alps
neighbor: 7 Austria **11** Switzerland
river: 5 Rhein, Rhine

lied
4 song **7** art song

lief
4 fain, soon **6** freely, gladly **7** happily,
readily **9** willingly **11** contentedly

liege
4 lord, true **5** loyal **6** ardent, master,
vassal **7** abiding, staunch **8** constant,
enduring, faithful, reliable, resolute, stalwart
9 dedicated, steadfast **10** dependable

lien
5 claim **6** charge, demand **8** interest,
mortgage **10** imposition

lieu
5 place, stead

lieutenant
4 aide **6** backup, deputy **7** officer
9 assistant, coadjutor **10** aide-de-camp,
coadjutant **11** subordinate

life
3 vim **4** brio, dash, élan, soul **5** verve
6 energy, esprit, spirit **8** vitality
9 animation, existence
animal: 5 fauna
animal and plant: 5 biota
combining form: 3 bio

plant: 5 flora
relating to: 5 vital **8** biologic **10** biological
science: 7 biology

life jacket
7 Mae West

lifeless
4 dead, drab, dull **5** inert **6** asleep, barren,
torpid, wasted **7** defunct, extinct
8 comatose, deceased, departed
9 inanimate, inorganic, insensate
10 lackluster

lifelike
5 exact **7** natural, precise **8** accurate,
faithful, veristic **9** realistic

life of _____
5 Riley **8** the party

Life with Father author
3 Day (Clarence)

lift
4 heft, hike, jack, load, rear, rise **5** boost,
exalt, filch, heave, hoist, pinch, raise, steal,
swipe, theft **6** assist, pick up, pilfer, repeal,
revoke, snitch, take up **7** elevate, purloin,
rescind, reverse, support **8** levitate,
stealing, thievery **10** plagiarize

lift-off
6 ascent, launch **7** takeoff **9** launching

ligament
3 tie **4** band, bond, link, yoke **5** nexus
8 ligature, vinculum **10** connection

ligature
see **ligament**

Ligeia author
3 Poe (Edgar Allan)

light
4 airy, dawn, deft, easy, fair, fire, lamp,
land, luck, neon **5** blond, flash, minor,
perch, roost, sunny, torch **6** beacon, blithe,
bright, candle, casual, facile, flimsy, fluffy,
ignite, kindle, settle, simple, slight, strobe
7 lantern, sunrise, trivial **8** cheerful,
daybreak, enkindle, illumine, luminous,
trifling **9** frivolous, touch down
10 chandelier, effortless, illuminate
combining form: 4 luci, phos, phot
5 lumin, photo **6** lumini, lumino
measure: 3 lux **4** phot **5** lumen **6** candle
7 candela
refractor: 5 prism
relating to: 6 photic
ring: 4 halo **6** corona **7** aureole, aureola
science: 6 optics
source: 3 sun **4** lamp

light-emitting
6 lucent **7** fulgent, lambent, shining
8 luminous **9** effulgent, refulgent

lighten
4 dawn, ease, fade **5** allay, cheer
6 bleach, lessen, reduce **7** assuage,
gladden, hearten, mollify, relieve
8 decrease, mitigate, unburden **9** alleviate,
attenuate, extenuate **11** disencumber

light-headed
5 dizzy, faint, giddy, silly **6** swimmy
7 flighty **9** frivolous, slaphappy
10 unbalanced **11** disoriented, vertiginous

lighthearted
3 gay **4** glad **5** happy, jolly, merry, sunny
6 blithe, jocund, jovial, joyful, joyous, lively,
upbeat **7** buoyant, festive, gleeful, playful,
winsome **8** carefree, cheerful, mirthful,
spirited, volatile **9** easygoing, expansive,
resilient, sprightly, vivacious **10** blithesome, insouciant **12** effervescent, happy-
go-lucky, high-spirited

lighthouse
6 beacon **7** warning

lightless
4 dark **5** unlit **7** aphotic, stygian
9 tenebrous, pitch-dark **10** caliginous,
pitch-black **11** unillumined

lightness
6 bounce, gaiety, levity **8** buoyancy,
vivacity **9** animation, frivolity **10** cheer-
iness, liveliness, resiliency, volatility
12 cheerfulness **13** effervescence

lightning bug
7 firefly

lignite
4 coal **9** brown coal

likable
4 nice **6** genial **7** affable, amiable, popular,
winning, winsome **8** charming, engaging,
friendly, pleasant, pleasing **9** agreeable,
appealing, congenial **10** attractive,
personable **11** good-natured

like
3 à la, dig **4** akin, same, such **5** close,
enjoy, equal, match **6** admire, agnate,
allied, prefer, relish **7** approve, cognate,
kindred, related, similar, uniform **8** parallel,
selfsame **9** analogous, consonant,
identical **10** appreciate, comparable,
comprehend, equivalent, resembling

likelihood
6 chance **8** prospect **11** eventuality,
possibility, presumption, probability

likely
3 apt **5** given, odds-on, prone **6** liable
7 assumed **8** credible, inclined, possible,
presumed, probable, probably, reliable,
suitable **9** doubtless, plausible, promising
10 achievable, attractive, believable,
presumably

liken
5 match **6** equate **7** compare **8** parallel
10 assimilate

likeness
4 copy, twin **5** clone, image **6** double,
effigy **7** analogy, picture, replica **8** affinity,
portrait, sameness **9** depiction, facsimile,
look-alike, semblance **10** appearance,
photograph, similarity, similitude, uniformity
11 resemblance

likewise
3 and, too **4** also **6** as well, withal
7 besides **8** moreover **9** similarly **10** in
addition **11** furthermore

liking
4 bent **5** fancy, taste **6** desire **8** affinity,
appetite, fondness, penchant, pleasure,
soft spot, weakness **9** affection
10 attraction, partiality **11** inclination
12 appreciation, predilection

Lilith
husband: 4 Adam
successor: 3 Eve

lilliputian
3 wee **4** runt, tiny **5** dwarf, little, petty,
pygmy, small **6** bantam, midget, peanut,
peewee, shrimp **7** manikin **8** pint-size,
Tom Thumb **9** miniature, pint-sized,
undersize **10** diminutive, homunculus

lilt
3 air **4** flow, purl, sing, song, tune **5** carol,
pulse, swing, tempo **6** melody, rhythm
7 cadence **8** buoyancy

lily
3 pad **4** aloe, sego **5** calla, tiger, yucca
6 flower **7** leopard **8** mariposa

lily-livered
5 sissy, wimpy **6** craven, yellow **7** caitiff,
chicken, fearful, gutless **8** cowardly,
cowering, poltroon, recreant, timorous
9 spineless, spunkless, weak-kneed

12 fainthearted, poor-spirited **13** pusillanimous

lily-white
4 pure **7** upright **8** innocent, virtuous
9 blameless, estimable, exclusive,
exemplary, guiltless, righteous, untainted
10 inculpable **11** uncorrupted

limb
3 arm, fin, gam, leg **4** lobe, twig, wing
5 bough, shoot, spray, sprig **6** branch,
member, pinion **7** flipper **8** offshoot
9 appendage, dismember, extremity

limber
4 spry **5** agile, lithe, loose **6** nimble, pliant,
supple **7** elastic, lissome, pliable, springy
8 flexible **9** lithesome, resilient

limbo
5 dance **7** neglect **8** oblivion **9** detention,
purgatory **11** confinement, uncertainty

lime
4 tree **5** color, fruit, green **6** citrus, linden
7 calcium

limen
8 doorsill, doorstep **9** threshold

limerick
4 poem **5** verse
writer: **4** Lear (Edward)

limestone
4 tufa, tuff **5** chalk **6** marble, oolite
7 coquina **10** travertine

lime tree
6 linden

limit
3 bar, cap, end, fix, set **4** curb **5** check,
quota **6** border, bounds, curfew, define,
extent, hinder, lessen **7** confine, curtail,
enclose, extreme, mark out, measure
8 boundary, deadline, restrain, restrict
9 constrict, demarcate, determine,
extremity, prescribe **12** circumscribe

limitless
4 vast **7** endless **8** infinite, wipen
9 boundless, unbounded **10** indefinite
11 illimitable, innumerable, measureless
12 immeasurable, incalculable
13 inexhaustible

limn
4 draw **5** image, paint **6** depict, render,
sketch **7** outline, picture, portray
8 describe **9** delineate, interpret, represent

Limoges product
9 porcelain

limp
3 lax **4** bent, halt, lame, wilt **5** hitch, loose,
slack, spent, weary **6** dodder, droopy,
falter, hobble **7** flaccid, languid, shamble,
shuffle, slumped **8** drooping **9** enervated,
exhausted **10** spiritless

limpid
4 pure **5** clear, lucid **6** glassy, serene
8 pellucid **10** see-through, untroubled
11 crystalline, translucent, transparent,
unambiguous **12** crystal clear

limping
4 halt, lame **5** gimpy **7** halting **8** hobbling,
lameness **9** faltering **12** claudication

linchpin
8 backbone, mainstay

Lincoln
assassin: **5** Booth (John Wilkes)
biographer: **8** Sandburg (Carl)
debater: **7** Douglas (Stephen)
law partner: **7** Herndon (William)
mother: **5** Nancy (Hanks)
nickname: **9** Honest Abe **12** Railsplitter
photographer: **5** Brady (Mathew)
secretary of state: **6** Seward (William)
secretary of war: **7** Stanton (Edwin)
wife: **8** Mary Todd

line
3 row **4** file, rank, rope **5** array, goods,
queue, route **6** border, column, series,
strain, string **7** contour, descent
8 business, pedigree, sequence
10 employment, occupation, succession
curved: **3** arc
mathematical: **6** vector
metrical: **5** verse **6** verset **8** versicle
weather map: **6** isobar

lineage
3 kin **4** clan, folk, race **5** birth, blood,
breed, house, stirp, stock, tribe **6** family,
origin, strain **7** descent, kindred
8 ancestry, breeding, pedigree
9 forebears, genealogy **10** derivation,
extraction, succession **11** forefathers,
progenitors

lineal
6 direct **8** familial **9** ancestral, inherited
10 bequeathed, hereditary

lineament
4 form **6** figure, relief **7** contour, feature,
outline, profile **10** figuration, silhouette

lined
5 drawn, ruled **7** aligned, striate, striped
8 streaked, wrinkled

linen

linen
4 lawn 5 cloth, toile 6 byssus, damask, fabric, napery, sheets 7 batiste, bedding, cambric, taffeta 8 cretonne, lingerie
fiber: 3 tow
source: 4 flax

linger
3 lag 4 bide, drag, loll, mope, poke, stay, wait 5 abide, dally, delay, mosey, tarry 6 dawdle, loiter, put off, remain 7 saunter 10 dillydally 11 stick around 13 procrastinate

lingerie
8 negligee

lingo
4 cant 5 argot, idiom, slang 6 jargon, patois, patter, speech, tongue 7 dialect 10 vernacular, vocabulary

linguist
8 polyglot 11 philologist

linguistics
9 philology

liniment
3 oil 4 aloe, balm 5 salve 6 lotion 7 anodyne, unction, unguent 8 aloe vera, lenitive, ointment 9 demulcent 11 embrocation

lining
6 facing, insert 8 wainscot

link
3 tie 4 bind, bond, join, knot, ring, yoke 5 hitch, nexus, unite 6 attach, copula, couple, hookup, relate, splice 7 bracket, combine, conjoin, connect, contact, joining 8 catenate, division, vinculum 9 associate, conjugate 10 attachment, connection 11 association 12 relationship

linksman
6 golfer

linnet
5 finch

lint
3 fur, nap 4 down, fuzz, pile 5 floss, fluff 9 ravelings

lion
3 cat 4 puma 6 cougar 7 notable 8 eminence, luminary 9 carnivore, personage
group: 5 pride
young: 3 cub

lionhearted
4 bold 5 brave 6 heroic 7 valiant 8 fearless, intrepid, stalwart, unafraid, valorous 9 dauntless 10 courageous

lionize
4 fete 5 exalt, extol, honor 7 glorify 8 venerate 9 celebrate

lion monkey
7 tamarin 8 marmoset

Lion of Judah
8 Selassie (Haile)

lip
3 rim 4 brim, edge, guff, sass 6 labium, labrum, margin 8 back talk
relating to: 6 labial

lipid
3 fat, wax

lipped
7 labiate 9 bilabiate

liquefy
3 run 4 flux, melt, thaw 5 smelt 6 render 8 dissolve 10 deliquesce

liqueur
4 arak, ouzo, raki 5 crème 6 brandy, Kahlua, kirsch, kummel, pastis, Pernod 7 cordial, curaçao, ratafia, sambuca, sloe gin 8 absinthe, amaretto, anisette, Drambuie, Galliano 10 Chartreuse, pousse-café

liquid
5 drink, fluid, sauce, water 6 watery 7 flowing 8 beverage, emulsion 11 mellifluous
container: 3 cup, jug, keg, mug 4 vial 5 glass 6 bottle, goblet 7 pitcher, tumbler
flammable: 3 gas, oil 5 ether, furan 6 butane, toluol 7 alcohol, toluene 8 gasoline, pyridine
measure: 3 cup, gal 4 pint 5 liter, ounce, quart 6 gallon
thick: 5 syrup 8 molasses

liquidate
3 pay 4 do in, kill 5 pay up, purge 6 murder, remove, rub out, settle, square 7 bump off, convert, gun down, satisfy 8 amortize, dispatch, dissolve, knock off 9 eliminate, terminate 10 annihilate 11 assassinate

liquor
5 booze, drink, hooch 7 alcohol, potable, spirits 8 potation 9 firewater, inebriant 10 intoxicant
add: 4 lace 5 spike
Asian: 4 arak 6 arrack
homemade: 9 moonshine 10 bathtub gin
inferior: 5 hooch 6 red-eye, rotgut
Japanese: 4 sake, saki
kind: 3 gin, rum, rye 5 vodka 6 brandy,

geneva, scotch **7** aquavit, bourbon, schnaps, whiskey **8** schnapps, vermouth **9** aqua vitae **10** barley-bree
malt: 3 ale **4** beer **5** nappy, stout **6** porter
measure: 4 dram, shot **6** jigger **7** shooter
Mexican: 5 sotol **6** mescal **7** tequila

lissome
5 agile, lithe **6** limber, nimble, supple, svelte **7** slender **8** flexible, graceful

list
3 tip **4** book, cant, file, heel, lean, menu, note, post, roll, tilt **5** arena, count, index, slant, slate, slope, tally **6** agenda, census, docket, lineup, record, roster **7** catalog, incline, itemize, specify **8** calendar, glossary, manifest, register, roll call, schedule, tabulate **9** chronicle, enumerate, inventory **13** particularize

listen
4 hark, hear, heed, note **5** audit **6** attend, harken **7** hearken, monitor **8** overhear **9** eavesdrop

listeners
8 audience

listless
4 dull, limp, weak **5** inert, slack **6** torpid, vacant **7** languid **8** indolent, sluggish **9** apathetic, enervated, lethargic, lymphatic **10** languorous, phlegmatic, spiritless **11** indifferent, languishing **13** lackadaisical

listlessness
6 apathy, stupor, torpor **7** fatigue, inertia, languor **8** doldrums, lethargy **9** indolence, lassitude, torpidity **10** enervation

litany
4 list **5** chant **6** prayer **7** account, listing, recital, refrain **8** petition, rogation **9** catalogue **10** invocation, recitation **11** enumeration **12** supplication

literal
4 bald, bare **5** blunt, exact, stark **6** actual, simple, strict **7** precise **8** accurate, bona fide, faithful, verbatim **9** authentic **11** unvarnished, word-for-word **13** unembellished

literally
5 truly **6** direct, indeed, openly, simply **7** plainly, totally, utterly **8** candidly, directly, verbatim **9** genuinely, virtually **11** word for word

literary
7 bookish, erudite, learned **8** lettered, well-read **9** authorial, scholarly **12** belletristic

literary work
4 book, opus, play, poem **5** drama, essay, novel **10** short story

literature
5 prose **6** poetry **7** fiction **13** belles-lettres

lithe
4 lean, slim **5** agile, spare **6** limber, supple, svelte **7** lissome, pliable, slender **8** flexible, graceful

lithographer
4 Ives (James Merritt) **7** Currier (Nathaniel)

Lithuania
capital: 7 Vilnius
city: 6 Kaunas **8** Klaipeda
monetary unit: 5 litas
neighbor: 6 Latvia, Poland, Russia **7** Belarus
river: 5 Neman, Venta **7** Lielupe
sea: 6 Baltic

litigant
4 suer **6** suitor **9** defendant, disputant, plaintiff

litigate
3 sue **6** indict **7** arraign, contest, dispute **9** prosecute

litigation
4 case, suit **7** lawsuit **11** prosecution, proceedings

litter
3 bed **4** cubs, junk **5** brood, couch, issue, strew, trash, waste, young **6** clutch, debris, refuse **7** bedding, clutter, garbage, kittens, piglets, progeny, puppies, rubbish, scatter **8** detritus **9** offspring, stretcher **10** scattering

little
3 bit, dab, toy, wee **4** dash, hint, mean, puny, tiny **5** brief, dinky, minor, petty, pinch, short, small, taste, trace, young **6** bantam, meager, meagre, minute, narrow, paltry, petite, skimpy **7** limited, trivial **8** dwarfish, slightly, smallish, trifling **9** miniature, small-beer **10** diminutive, short-lived, undersized **11** microscopic, unimportant

Little Bighorn
state: 7 Montana
victim: 6 Custer (George Armstrong)
victor: 11 Sitting Bull

little by little
6 slowly **8** inchmeal, steadily **9** gradually, piecemeal

Little Dipper
constellation: 9 Ursa Minor
star: 5 North 7 Polaris

Little Women
author: 6 Alcott (Louisa May)
character: 3 Amy, Meg 4 Beth 6 Laurie, Marmee
surname: 5 March

littoral
5 beach, coast, shore 6 strand 7 coastal, seaside 8 seaboard, sea front, seashore 9 shoreline 10 oceanfront

liturgy
4 rite 6 ritual 7 service 8 ceremony 9 sacrament 10 ceremonial, observance, repertoire

livable
6 viable 8 adequate, bearable, passable 9 endurable, habitable, tolerable 11 inhabitable, supportable

live
4 fare, stay 5 abide, dwell, exist, vital, vivid 6 actual, reside, thrive 7 breathe, current, subsist, survive

livelihood
3 job 4 game, keep, work 5 craft, trade 7 support 8 business, vocation 10 employment, handicraft, occupation, profession, sustenance 11 subsistence

liveliness
3 pep, zip 4 brio, élan, zing 5 verve, vigor 6 energy, hustle, spirit 8 dispatch, vibrance, vibrancy, vitality, vivacity 9 animation

lively
3 gay 4 busy, keen, pert, spry, yare 5 agile, alert, brisk, fresh, jazzy, jolly, merry, peppy, zippy 6 active, bouncy, bright, chirpy, frisky, jocund, nimble 7 animate, buoyant, chipper, intense, rousing 8 animated, bustling, hustling, spirited, vigorous, volatile 9 energetic, resilient, sparkling, sprightly, vivacious 11 stimulating

liven
5 pep up 6 jazz up, vivify 7 animate, freshen, quicken 8 energize, inspirit, vitalize 10 invigorate

liver
7 denizen 8 habitant, occupant, resident 10 inhabitant
combining form: 5 hepat 6 hepato
disease: 9 cirrhosis, hepatitis

French: 4 foie
lobster's: 8 tomalley

liverwort
8 hepatica 9 bryophyte

livestock
4 cows, hogs, pigs 5 bulls, goats, sheep 6 beasts, calves, cattle 7 animals
feed: 6 silage 8 ensilage

live wire
6 dynamo 7 hustler, rustler 8 go-getter, promoter 9 energizer, generator 11 self-starter

livid
3 hot, mad, wan 4 ashy, pale 5 ashen, lurid, waxen 6 fuming, leaden, pallid, sultry 7 boiling, bruised, enraged, furious, reddish 8 blanched, contused, incensed 9 colorless 10 discolored, infuriated 12 black-and-blue 13 beside oneself

living
5 means, vital 6 extant, income 8 animated, existent 10 livelihood, sustenance

living room
6 parlor 10 lebensraum

lizard
3 eft 4 gila, newt 5 anole, gecko, skink, teiid 6 dragon, goanna, iguana 7 monitor, reptile, saurian 8 basilisk, mosasaur, slowworm, squamate, whiptail 9 alligator, blindworm, chameleon, crocodile 10 chuckwalla, salamander
combining form: 4 saur 5 saura, sauro

llama
6 alpaca, vicuña 7 camelid, guanaco
country: 4 Peru
habitat: 5 Andes

Lloyd's business
9 insurance

lo
4 hark, heed, look, mark, mind 6 attend 7 observe

load
3 tax 4 bias, copy, fill, haul, heap, lade, onus, pack, pile, task 5 cargo, laden, swamp, weigh 6 burden, debase, doctor, dope up, eyeful, lading, saddle, weight 7 freight 8 encumber, shipment, transfer 9 liability, millstone, transport 11 consignment, encumbrance

loaded
4 full, high, rich 5 awash, doped 6 aboard, biased, filled, packed, stoned 7 boarded,

brimful, crowded, wealthy **8** affluent, brimming, chockful, tripping, turned on **9** chock-full

loaf
3 bum, bun **4** idle, laze, lazy, loll **5** bread, dough **6** dawdle, lounge **7** goof off **8** lollygag **9** bum around, goldbrick **10** fool around

loafer
3 bum **4** shoe, slug **5** idler **6** slouch **7** goof-off, lounger **8** deadbeat, dolittle, fainéant, slugabed, sluggard **9** do-nothing, goldbrick, lazybones **11** beachcomber, lollygagger

loam
4 clay, dirt, sand, silt, soil **7** topsoil
deposit: 5 loess

loan
3 pay **4** lend **6** credit **7** advance, imprest **9** grubstake

loan shark
6 lender, usurer **7** Shylock **10** pawnbroker **11** moneylender

loath
6 afraid, averse **8** hesitant **9** reluctant, unwilling **10** indisposed **11** disinclined **12** antipathetic

loathe
4 hate **5** abhor, scorn, spurn **6** detest, refuse, reject **7** despise **8** execrate **9** abominate

loathsome
4 foul, ugly, vile **5** gross, nasty **6** odious **7** beastly, hateful, hideous **8** horrible **9** abhorrent, execrable, obnoxious, offensive, repellent, repugnant, repulsive, revolting **10** abominable, deplorable, detestable, disgusting, nauseating

lob
4 loft, toss **5** chuck, fling, heave, pitch, sling, throw **6** propel

lobby
4 hall **5** foyer **7** promote **8** anteroom, corridor **9** influence, vestibule **10** passageway **11** waiting room

lobe
4 flap **7** pendant

lobo
4 wolf **8** gray wolf **10** timber wolf

lobster
8 crawfish **10** crustacean

claw: 5 chela **6** pincer
female: 3 hen
male: 4 cock
trap: 3 pot **5** creel

local
6 native **7** endemic, insular, topical **9** parochial **10** provincial

locale
4 area, belt, site, turf, ward **5** place, scene, venue **6** milieu, parish, region, sector **7** commune, quarter, setting **8** district, precinct, vicinage, vicinity **9** community, territory **11** mise-en-scène **12** neighborhood

locality
4 area, belt, city, site, turf, zone **5** block, county, field, haunt, place, tract **6** domain, hamlet, region, sector, sphere, square **7** habitat, section **8** district, environs, precinct, province, purlieus, township, vicinage, vicinity **9** bailiwick, situation, territory **12** neighborhood

localize
4 mass **5** amass, focus **7** cluster, collect **8** coalesce, pinpoint **10** accumulate **11** concentrate, consolidate **12** conglomerate

locate
3 fix, spy **4** espy, find, site, spot **5** dwell, place, trace **6** detect, reside, settle **7** nose out, situate, station, uncover **8** come upon, discover, pinpoint, position **9** establish, ferret out, search out **10** come across

location
4 area, site, post, spot **5** locus, place, point, scene, venue, where **7** bearing, habitat, setting **8** position **9** situation **11** mise-en-scène, whereabouts

loch
3 bay **4** lake

lock
4 bolt, curl, hank, hold, tuft **5** latch, tress **6** fasten, secure **7** ringlet **8** fastener **9** enclosure, fastening

lockjaw
7 tetanus, trismus

lockup
3 jug, pen **4** brig, cell, coop, jail, stir, tank **5** clink, pokey, pound **6** cooler, prison **7** slammer **8** bastille

loco
3 ape, mad 4 nuts 5 balmy, batty, crazy, kooky, loony, nutty 6 crazed, insane, screwy 7 bananas, berserk, bonkers, cracked, flipped, lunatic 8 demented, deranged, frenzied, unhinged 10 flipped out

locomotive
5 cheer, dolly, train 6 engine
small: 5 dinky 6 dinkey
type: 5 steam 6 diesel 8 electric

locum tenens
3 sub 5 proxy 6 backup, fill-in, supply 7 stand-in 9 alternate, auxiliary, surrogate 10 substitute 11 pinch hitter, replacement, succedaneum

locus
3 hub 4 seat, site 5 focus, heart, stage 6 center 7 setting 8 cynosure, location, polestar 10 focal point 11 nerve center 12 headquarters

locust
4 tree, wood 5 carob 6 cicada, insect 11 grasshopper

locution
4 word 5 argot, idiom, lingo 6 jargon, patois, phrase 7 dialect 8 parlance, phrasing 9 utterance 10 expression 11 phraseology

lode
4 seam, vein 5 store 6 source, supply 7 deposit

lodestar
4 guru 5 gauge, guide, ideal, model 6 beacon, leader, mentor 7 epitome 8 exemplar, paradigm 9 archetype, guidepost 11 inspiration

lodestone
6 magnet 9 magnetite

lodge
3 den, fix, inn 4 bunk, camp, club, file, lair, nest, root, stay 5 abide, abode, board, cabin, couch, dwell, embed, guild, hotel, house, motel, order, put up 6 billet, burrow, hostel, league, remain, shanty, tavern, wigwam 7 auberge, contain, cottage, deposit, hospice, quarter, receive, shelter 8 domicile, hostelry, sodality 9 gatehouse 10 fellowship 11 accommodate, brotherhood, caravansary, public house

lodger
5 guest 6 renter, roomer, tenant 7 boarder, resider

lodging
3 inn, pad 4 dorm, room 5 abode, hotel, motel, place 7 shelter 8 chambers, diggings, domicile, dwelling, quarters 9 apartment, residence 10 pied-à-terre 13 accommodation

loess
4 clay, loam, marl 7 deposit

loft
4 rise 5 attic, raise 6 dormer, garret, propel 7 gallery

loftiness
5 pride 6 height 7 disdain, hauteur, stature 8 altitude, eminence 9 aloofness, arrogance, elevation, pomposity, sublimity 11 haughtiness, superiority 13 condescension

lofty
4 airy, epic, high, tall 5 grand, noble, proud 6 aerial, august, raised, remote, superb 7 exalted, haughty, soaring, stately, sublime, utopian 8 arrogant, cavalier, elevated, eloquent, imposing, insolent, majestic, superior, towering 9 ambitious, grandiose, visionary 10 disdainful 11 overbearing, pretentious, skyscraping 12 supercilious

log
5 diary, tally 6 record, timber 7 journal 8 register
mover: 5 peavy 6 peavey 7 cant dog

loge
3 box 5 booth, stall 7 balcony 9 mezzanine

logger
9 lumberman 10 lumberjack, woodcutter
legendary: 10 Paul Bunyan

loggerhead
6 shrike, turtle

loggia
6 arcade 7 balcony, gallery, veranda

logic
6 reason 9 reasoning 10 syntactics
specious: 7 sophism 9 sophistry

logical
5 sound, valid 6 cogent 8 analytic, sensible 9 deducible, deductive, plausible 10 analytical, compelling, convincing, diagnostic, reasonable, scientific, systematic

logjam
5 crowd 7 impasse 8 blockage, deadlock, stoppage 11 obstruction

logo
5 badge, brand, motto 6 cipher, device, emblem, symbol 8 colophon, hallmark, monogram 9 trademark

logogriph
6 puzzle 7 anagram

logroll
4 birl

logy
4 dull, slow 5 dopey, heavy 6 drowsy, groggy, torpid 8 listless, sluggish

Lohengrin
composer: 6 Wagner (Richard)
father: 8 Parsifal, Parzival
wife: 4 Elsa

loincloth
5 dhoti 11 breechcloth, breechclout

Loire city
5 Blois, Tours 6 Nantes 7 Orléans

loiter
3 bum, lag 4 drag, idle, laze, lazy, loaf, loll, poke 5 dally, delay, tarry, trail 6 dawdle, diddle, linger, lounge, put off, putter 8 lollygag 10 dillydally, fool around, hang around 11 screw around 13 procrastinate

Loki
father: 8 Farbauti
mother: 3 Nal 6 Laufey
offspring: 3 Hel 4 Hela 6 Fenris 7 Midgard
slayer: 8 Heimdall
victim: 6 Balder
wife: 5 Sigyn 9 Angurboda

Lolita author
7 Nabokov (Vladimir)

loll
3 bum, lag 4 drag, idle, laze, lazy, loaf, poke 5 chill, dally, delay, droop, slump, tarry, trail 6 dawdle, diddle, linger, lounge, putter, slouch 8 chill out 10 dillydally, fool around, hang around 13 procrastinate

Lollards' leader
8 Wycliffe (John)

lollygag
4 idle, loaf, loll, poke, drag 6 dawdle, diddle, loiter, piddle, putter 10 dilly-dally, fool around 11 horse around 12 monkey around

Lombard
6 banker 11 moneylender
king: 5 Cleph 6 Alboin, Audoin 7 Aistulf, Aripert, Authari 9 Liudprand

London
borough: 5 Brent 6 Barnet, Bexley, Ealing, Harrow, Sutton 7 Barking, Bromley, Chelsea, Croydon, Enfield, Hackney, Lambeth 8 Haringey, Havering, Hounslow, Lewisham 9 Greenwich, Islington, Redbridge 10 Kensington 11 Westminster
cathedral: 7 St. Paul's
clock: 6 Big Ben
district: 4 Soho 5 Acton 7 Chelsea, Mayfair 9 Belgravia, Southwark
gallery: 4 Tate
policeman: 5 bobby
prison: 7 Newgate
river: 6 Thames
square: 9 Leicester, Trafalgar
street: 4 Bond 5 Fleet 6 Strand 7 Downing, Whitehall 10 Piccadilly
subway: 4 tube

London novel
7 Sea Wolf (The) 8 Iron Heel (The) 9 White Fang 10 Martin Eden 13 Call of the Wild (The)

lone
4 only, sole, solo 5 alone 6 single, unique 8 deserted, forsaken, isolated, secluded, separate, singular, solitary 13 unaccompanied

lonely
4 left, lorn 5 alone 7 forlorn 8 deserted, forsaken, homesick, lonesome, rejected, solitary 9 abandoned

loneness
8 solitude 9 isolation 10 detachment 12 separateness, solitariness

loner
6 hermit 7 isolate, outcast, recluse 8 outsider, solitary 13 individualist

Lone Ranger, The
creator: 7 Striker (Fran)
companion: 5 Tonto
horse: 6 Silver
trademark: 4 mask 12 silver bullet

Lone Star State
5 Texas

long
3 far, yen 4 ache, itch, lust, pine, sigh, tall 5 large, wordy, yearn 6 hanker, hunger, prolix, strong, thirst 7 endless, lengthy,

tedious **8** dragging, drawn-out, extended, unending **9** extensive **10** full-length, protracted

long-drawn-out
7 endless, lengthy **8** dragging, unending **10** protracted **12** interminable

Longfellow poem
8 Christus, Hiawatha, Hyperion, Kavanagh **10** Evangeline **11** My Lost Youth, Psalm of Life (A)

long for
4 want **5** covet, crave, mourn **6** desire **8** aspire to

longing
3 yen **4** itch, lust, urge, wish **5** greed **6** desire, hunger, thirst **7** avidity, craving, passion **8** appetite

longshoreman
9 stevedore **10** roustabout

long-suffering
7 patient, stoical **8** enduring, resigned **9** compliant **10** forbearing, submissive **13** accommodating, uncomplaining

long suit
3 bag **4** gift **5** forte, thing **6** métier, talent **8** strength **9** specialty

long-winded
5 wordy **6** prolix **7** diffuse, lengthy, verbose **8** rambling **9** garrulous, redundant **10** loquacious

look
3 air, eye **4** gape, gawk, leer, mien, ogle, peek, peep, peer, seem, view **5** glare, stare, watch **6** admire, appear, aspect, behold, expect, eyeful, glance, glower, goggle, regard, squint, survey, visage **7** bearing, examine, eyeball, glimpse, observe **8** demeanor, once-over **10** appearance, expression, rubberneck **11** countenance, physiognomy

look after
4 mind, tend **5** nurse, serve, watch **6** attend, wait on **7** care for, husband **8** wait upon **9** watch over **10** provide for

look-alike
4 twin **5** clone **6** double **7** similar **8** matching **9** duplicate

look at
3 eye, see **4** face, ogle, scan, view **5** check **6** behold, ponder **7** examine, inspect **8** confront, consider **11** investigate

look back
6 recall, review **7** reflect **8** remember **9** reminisce

look down on
5 abhor, scorn, scout, spurn **7** contemn, despise, disdain **8** dominate **9** tower over **10** tower above

looker
6 beauty, eyeful, lovely, vision **7** stunner, witness **8** knockout, ornament **9** bystander, sightseer, spectator **10** eyewitness

looker-on
5 gaper **6** viewer **7** watcher, witness **8** beholder, observer **9** bystander, spectator **10** eyewitness **12** rubbernecker

look for
4 seek **5** await **6** expect, plan on **9** search out **10** anticipate

looking glass
6 mirror **9** reflector

look into
5 check, probe, study **6** pursue, survey **7** examine, explore, inspect **8** check out, question, research **10** scrutinize **11** investigate

look out
4 mind **6** beware

lookout
4 view **5** guard, scout, tower, vista, watch **6** affair, cupola, picket, sentry **7** spotter **8** panorama, prospect, sentinel, watchman **9** belvedere, crow's nest, firetower **10** watchtower, widow's walk **11** observatory, perspective

look over
3 vet **4** read **5** check **6** review, size up **7** examine, inspect **8** appraise, evaluate

loom
4 brew, bulk, near, rear **5** hover, mount, tower **6** appear, come on, emerge, gather, impend, portend **8** approach, overhang, stand out, threaten **9** take shape
part: **6** heddle **7** harness, shuttle, treadle, trundle

loon
3 nut, oaf **4** bird, clod, dodo, dolt, goof, lout, yo-yo **5** chump, dummy, dunce, ninny, noddy, stupe, yokel **6** dimwit, dum-dum, nitwit **7** airhead, buffoon, dullard, pinhead **8** bonehead, dumbbell, crackpot, imbecile, lunkhead, meathead, numskull **9** birdbrain, blockhead, ignoramus, lamebrain,

numbskull, simpleton **10** dunderhead, nincompoop **11** chowderhead, chucklehead

loony

3 nut **5** balmy, batty, crazy, daffy, dippy, goofy, inane, nutty, silly, wacky **6** absurd, insane, madman, maniac, screwy **7** fatuous, foolish, idiotic, lunatic **8** demented, reckless **9** bedlamite, half-baked, ludicrous, senseless **10** ridiculous **11** harebrained **12** preposterous

loony bin

6 asylum, bedlam **8** bughouse, madhouse, nuthouse **9** funny farm **10** booby hatch, crazy house

loop

3 arc, eye **4** ring **5** curve, noose, picot **6** circle, eyelet, league, staple **7** circlet, circuit **13** circumference

looped

4 high **5** bowed, drunk, stiff **6** blotto, bombed, curved, juiced, loaded, potted, stewed, tanked, zonked **7** crocked, pickled, pie-eyed, sloshed, smashed **9** plastered **10** inebriated **11** curvilinear, intoxicated

loophole

3 out **6** escape, outlet **7** opening

loopy

4 daft, nuts, wavy **5** arced, batty, bowed, crazy, daffy, dotty, flaky, nutty, silly, snaky, wacky **6** arched, curved, freaky, fruity, screwy, swirly **7** bizarre, idiotic, lunatic, offbeat, sinuous, touched **8** demented **9** eccentric **10** flipped out, off-the-wall, outlandish

loose

3 lax **4** easy, fast, free, lewd, limp **5** baggy, slack, vague **6** flabby, wanton **7** flaccid, relaxed **8** flexible **9** debauched, desultory, dissolute, imprecise **10** disjointed, dissipated, ill-defined, licentious, unattached, unconfined **12** disconnected, unrestrained

loose end

6 detail **8** fragment

loose-lipped

see **loquacious**

loosen

4 ease, free, undo **5** relax, slack, untie **6** unbind **7** ease off, manumit, release, slacken, unchain **8** liberate, unbuckle, unfasten **10** emancipate

loosen up

5 relax **6** unbend, unwind **7** ease off, stretch

loot

3 rob **4** haul, lift, pelf, raid, sack, swag **5** boost, booty, dough, lucre, money, moola, reave, rifle, spoil **6** boodle, moolah, ravish, spoils **7** despoil, pillage, plunder, ransack, stick up **9** knock over

looter

5 thief **7** brigand **8** marauder

lop

3 cut **4** chop, clip, crop, trim **5** prune, sever **6** excise **8** amputate, truncate **9** dismember **10** guillotine

lope

3 jog, run **4** gait, romp, trot **5** amble **6** canter

lopsided

4 awry **5** askew **6** uneven **7** crooked, leaning, tilting **8** top-heavy **10** asymmetric, off-balance, unbalanced **12** asymmetrical **13** unsymmetrical

loquacious

5 gabby, talky, wordy **6** chatty, mouthy, prolix **7** verbose, voluble, yakking **8** babbling **9** garrulous, jabbering, talkative **10** blathering, chattering, long-winded **11** loose-lipped **12** motormouthed

lord

3 sir **4** boss, duke, earl, peer **5** noble, ruler **6** master **7** marquis **8** governor, marquess, nobleman, viscount **9** sovereign, tyrannize **11** liege **8** seigneur, suzerain
feudal: **5** liege
Muslim: **6** sayyid

Lord High Executioner

4 Koko

Lord Jim author

6 Conrad (Joseph)

lordly

5 grand, lofty, noble, proud **6** august, uppity **7** exalted, haughty, pompous, stately, swollen **8** affected, arrogant, cavalier, gracious, imposing, insolent, majestic, princely, snobbish, superior **9** dignified, egotistic, grandiose **10** disdainful, high-handed **11** dictatorial, magisterial, magnificent, overbearing, patronizing **12** aristocratic, supercilious **13** authoritarian, high-and-mighty

Lord of the Flies author

author: 7 Golding (William)

character: 4 Jack 5 Piggy, Ralph

Lord's Prayer
9 Our Father 11 Paternoster

lore
6 mythos, wisdom 7 history 8 folkways, learning 9 knowledge, mythology, tradition 11 information 12 superstition

Lorelei
5 siren 9 temptress 10 seductress 11 femme fatale
poet: 5 Heine (Heinrich)
river: 5 Rhein, Rhine
victim: 6 sailor 7 mariner

lorgnette
10 eyeglasses, spectacles 12 opera glasses

Lorna Doone
author: 9 Blackmore (Richard)
hero: 4 Ridd (John)

_____ Lorraine
6 Alsace

lorry
3 rig, van 4 semi 5 truck

lose
4 miss 5 evade, shake, waste, yield 6 escape, give up, mislay 7 destroy, forfeit, succumb 8 misplace, shake off, throw off 9 sacrifice, surrender

lose it
7 crack up, flip out, go crazy 8 freak out

loser
3 dud 4 bomb, bust, flop 5 lemon 6 bummer, fiasco, misfit, turkey 7 also-ran, debacle, failure, washout 8 deadbeat 11 incompetent

loss
4 harm, ruin 5 waste 6 damage, defeat, injury 7 deficit, failure, forfeit 8 casualty, decrease, fatality 9 depletion, privation, sacrifice, shrinkage 10 divestment, forfeiture, misfortune, misplacing 11 bereavement, deprivation, destruction 13 disappearance

lost
4 dead, gone, rapt 6 absent, astray, bygone, damned, doomed, futile, hidden, wasted 7 defunct, faraway, lacking, mislaid, missing 8 absorbed, departed, distrait, helpless, hopeless, vanished 9 condemned, desperate, destroyed 10 abstracted, insensible, overlooked

11 irrevocable, preoccupied 12 irredeemable, unregenerate

Lost Horizon
author: 6 Hilton (James)
character: 6 Conway (Hugh)
land: 9 Shangri-La

lot
3 cut, ilk, set 4 doom, fate, give, heap, kind, mass, part, plat, sort, type, yard 5 allow, batch, block, bunch, field, group, moira, patch, quota, share, slice, tract, weird 6 assign, barrel, bundle, clutch, kismet, parcel, stripe 7 acreage, cluster, destiny, fortune, mete out, portion, species 8 allocate, clearing, frontage 9 aggregate, allowance, apportion

Lot
father: 5 Haran
sister: 5 Iscah 6 Milcah
son: 4 Moab 5 Ammon
uncle: 7 Abraham

lothario
4 stud, wolf 5 letch, Romeo 6 lecher, tomcat 7 amorist, Don Juan, gallant, seducer 8 Casanova, paramour 9 debaucher, womanizer 10 lady-killer 11 philanderer

lotion
3 oil 4 balm 5 cream, salve 6 cerate 7 unguent 8 ablution, cosmetic, lenitive, liniment, ointment 9 demulcent 11 embrocation

lottery
6 raffle 7 drawing 11 sweepstakes

lotus-eater
7 dreamer 8 escapist, romantic 10 daydreamer 13 castle-builder

loud
5 forte, gaudy, noisy, showy 6 brassy, brazen, flashy, garish, glitzy, tawdry, vulgar 7 blaring, blatant, booming, chintzy, glaring, pealing, raucous, roaring 8 piercing, resonant, sonorous, strident 9 clamorous, deafening, obnoxious, obtrusive, offensive, tasteless 10 bigmouthed, boisterous, flamboyant, resounding, stentorian, thunderous, vociferous 12 earsplitting

loudmouth
6 ranter 7 stentor 8 blowhard, braggart 9 blusterer

loudspeaker
6 woofer 7 tweeter 9 amplifier

Louisiana
  capital: 10 Baton Rouge
  city: 10 New Orleans, Shreveport
  college, university: 6 Tulane
  county: 6 parish
  lake: 13 Pontchartrain
  nickname: 7 Pelican (State)
  river: 11 Mississippi
  state bird: 12 brown pelican
  state flower: 8 magnolia
  state tree: 11 bald cypress

lounge
  3 bar, bum, lie, pub, tap 4 idle, laze, loaf,
  loll, sofa 5 couch, dally, drift, lobby, relax
  6 dawdle, loiter, parlor, repose, saloon
  7 barroom, goof off, lie down, recline,
  taproom 8 restroom, kill time 10 living
  room

lounge lizard
  3 fop 4 rake, toff 5 blade, dandy, leech
  6 gigolo, sponge 9 ladies' man

Lourdes saint
  10 Bernadette

louse
  3 cur, dog, rat 4 toad 5 aphid, creep,
  skunk, snake 6 cootie, psylla, rotter, slater,
  wretch 7 stinker
  egg: 3 nit

louse up
  4 blow, flub, muff, ruin 5 botch, spoil,
  wreck 6 bobble, bollix, bumble, bungle,
  fumble

lousy
  3 ill 4 poor, rife 5 awful 6 shoddy,
  7 replete, teeming 8 crawling, horrible,
  inferior, infested, terrible 9 miserable,
  repulsive 10 despicable 12 contemptible

lout
  3 oaf 4 boob, boor, dolt, gawk, hick, rube
  5 brute, chuff, churl, klutz, looby, scorn,
  yokel 6 galoot, lubber, lummox, rustic
  7 bumpkin, hayseed, palooka 9 simpleton
  10 clodhopper

Louvre masterpiece
  8 Mona Lisa 11 Venus de Milo

lovable
  4 dear 5 sweet 6 cuddly 7 winning,
  winsome 8 adorable 9 appealing,
  endearing 11 embraceable

love
  4 zeal 5 adore, ardor, crush, Cupid, exalt,
  prize, value 6 desire, dote on, fervor,
  revere 7 adulate, cherish, idolize, passion,

romance, worship 8 devotion, fondness,
idolatry, treasure, venerate, yearning
9 adoration, adulation, affection, delight in,
sentiment 10 allegiance, appreciate,
attachment, enthusiasm 11 amorousness,
infatuation
  combining form: 5 phily 6 philia
  French: 5 amour
  Italian: 5 amore

love apple
  6 tomato

lovebird
  6 budgie, parrot 10 budgerigar

love feast
  5 agape

love god
  4 Amor, Eros, Kama 5 Bhaga, Cupid

love goddess
  5 Athor, Freya, Venus 6 Hathor, Inanna,
  Ishtar 7 Astarte 9 Aphrodite, Ashtoreth

love letter
  8 mash note 9 valentine 10 billet-doux

lovely
  4 fair 5 sweet, swell 6 comely, dainty,
  pretty 7 elegant 8 adorable, alluring,
  charming, delicate, engaging, graceful,
  knockout 9 beauteous, beautiful, exquisite
  10 attractive, delightful, enchanting,
  entrancing 11 captivating, good-looking

love potion
  7 philter, philtre 11 aphrodisiac

lover
  3 fan 4 beau, buff 5 flame, leman, Romeo,
  swain 6 addict, steady, suitor, votary
  7 amorist, darling, devotee, Don Juan,
  gallant, habitué, squeeze 8 fancy man,
  lothario, mistress, paramour 9 boyfriend,
  inamorata, inamorato 10 aficionado,
  girlfriend, sweetheart

lovey-dovey
  5 mushy 6 doting 7 amorous
  12 affectionate

loving
  4 dear, fond 6 ardent, erotic, tender
  7 amatory, amorous, cordial, devoted,
  fervent 8 attached, enamored, faithful
  10 benevolent, in-
  fatuated, passionate, solicitous 11 impassioned 12 affectionate

low
  3 moo 4 base, blue, dead, deep, down,
  flat, mean, neap, poor, weak 5 cheap,
  short 6 abject, ailing, humble, hushed,

lesser, nether, poorly, sickly, sordid, sparse, unwell **7** cut-rate, reduced, scrubby **8** cast down, dejected, depleted, downcast, inferior, mediocre, wretched **9** declining, depressed, miserable, subnormal, woebegone **10** economical, inadequate, indisposed, marked down, spiritless **11** crestfallen, downhearted, substandard, unfavorable

lowbred
4 base, rude **6** coarse, oafish, vulgar **7** boorish, brutish, loutish, uncouth **8** churlish, cloddish, lubberly **11** uncivilized

low-cost
5 cheap **6** budget, cheapo **7** bargain, cut-rate **10** affordable, reasonable **11** inexpensive

low-down
4 base, mean, ugly, vile **6** odious, scurvy **7** ignoble **8** shameful, wretched **9** abhorrent, worthless **10** despicable, disgusting **11** ignominious **12** contemptible

lowdown
4 dope, info **5** facts, scoop, specs **6** skinny **8** briefing **11** information

lower
3 cut **4** clip, drop, fall, sink **5** frown, gloom, scowl, shave, slash, under **6** debase, demean, demote, humble, lesser, menace, nether, reduce **7** cut down, deflate, degrade, demerit, depress, descend, devalue, let down **8** inferior, mark down, overcast, submerge, threaten **9** devaluate, downgrade
prefix: 5 infra

Lower Depths author
5 Gorki, Gorky (Maksim, Maxim)

lowest point
5 nadir
in the U.S.: 11 Death Valley
on earth: 7 Dead Sea

low-grade
4 hack **5** junky, lousy **6** cheesy, cruddy, shabby, shoddy, sleazy, tawdry **8** below par, déclassé, inferior, mediocre **9** deficient **10** second-rate **11** second-class, substandard **12** second-drawer

low-key
4 soft **5** muted, quiet **7** relaxed, subdued **8** laid-back, softened, tasteful **9** easygoing, minimized, temperate, toned down **10** played down, restrained **11** understated

lowland
4 flat, sump, vale **5** basin **6** bottom, slough, valley **7** bottoms
Scottish: 6 lallan **7** lalland

lowlife
4 fink, heel **5** knave, rogue **6** no-good, outlaw, rascal, wretch **7** hoodlum, ruffian, villain **9** miscreant, reprobate, scoundrel **10** blackguard, black sheep, sleazeball **11** rapscallion, slimebucket **12** bottom-feeder

lowly
4 base, mean, meek **6** abject, humble, menial, modest **7** ignoble, mundane, obscure, prosaic, servile **8** baseborn, plebeian, unwashed

low-pressure
4 calm **6** casual, dégagé, folksy, mellow **7** relaxed **8** flexible, informal, laid-back **9** easygoing **10** nonchalant

low-spirited
3 sad **4** blue, down, glum **6** abject, droopy, gloomy, morose **7** doleful **8** cast down, dejected, downcast, saddened **9** bummed out, cheerless, depressed, woebegone **10** dispirited, melancholy **11** discouraged, downhearted **12** disheartened, heavyhearted

low tide
3 ebb **4** neap

loyal
4 firm, true **5** liege **6** ardent, trusty **7** devoted, dutiful, staunch **8** constant, faithful, resolute, true-blue **9** allegiant, steadfast, unfailing **10** dependable **11** trustworthy

loyalist
4 Tory **7** patriot **8** partisan **10** countryman **11** nationalist

loyalty
6 fealty **8** adhesion, devotion, fidelity **9** adherence, constancy **10** allegiance, attachment, dedication **11** staunchness **12** faithfulness **13** dependability, steadfastness

lozenge
4 pill **6** troche **7** diamond, rhombus **8** pastille

LSD
4 acid
user: 8 acidhead

lubricate
3 oil **6** grease, smooth **7** moisten

lubricious
4 lewd, oily 5 slick 6 carnal, greasy, slippy, wanton 8 prurient, slippery, slithery, ticklish 9 lecherous, salacious 10 lascivious, libidinous 12 concupiscent

lucent
5 clear 6 bright, limpid 7 beaming, crystal, glowing, lambent, radiant, shining 8 clear-cut, luminous, pellucid 9 brilliant, effulgent, refulgent 11 unambiguous

Lucia di Lammermoor
character: 7 Edgardo
composer: 9 Donizetti (Gaetano)
novelist: 5 Scott (Walter)

lucid
4 sane 5 clear 6 bright, limpid 7 crystal, lambent, radiant 8 clear-cut, knowable, luminous 9 brilliant, effulgent, graspable, refulgent, unblurred 10 articulate, fathomable 11 translucent, transparent, unambiguous 12 compos mentis, incandescent, intelligible, transpicuous 13 apprehensible

lucidity
6 acumen, sanity 7 clarity 8 sagacity, saneness 9 clearness, plainness, soundness 10 cognizance, perception 12 clairvoyance

Lucifer
5 devil, fiend, Satan, Venus 7 Old Nick 8 Apollyon 9 archfiend, Beelzebub 10 Old Scratch 13 Old Gooseberry

Lucinde
beloved: 7 Leandre 9 Clitandre
father: 7 Geronte 10 Sganarelle

luck
3 hap, hit 4 juju, meet 5 fluke, light 6 chance, happen, hazard, kismet 7 fortune, godsend, stumble 8 fortuity, occasion, windfall 9 advantage 11 opportunity
token: 5 charm 6 amulet, clover, fetish, mascot 8 talisman 9 horseshoe 11 rabbit's foot

luckless
7 adverse, hapless, unhappy 8 ill-fated, untoward, wretched 9 miserable 10 ill-starred 11 star-crossed, unfavorable, unfortunate 12 misfortunate, unpropitious

lucky
6 golden, timely 7 favored 9 favorable, fortunate 10 auspicious, beneficial, felicitous, fortuitous, propitious 12 advantageous, providential 13 serendipitous
Scottish: 5 canny

Lucky Jim author
4 Amis (Kingsley)

lucrative
6 paying 7 gainful 8 fruitful 10 high-income, productive, profitable, well-paying, worthwhile 11 moneymaking 12 advantageous, remunerative

lucre
3 pay 4 cash, gain, jack, loot 5 dough, green, money, moola 6 dinero, do-re-mi, moolah, profit, wampum 7 cabbage, revenue 9 long green 10 greenbacks

Lucrezia _____
6 Borgia

ludicrous
4 zany 5 antic, comic, droll, funny, goofy, nutty, silly 6 absurd 7 amusing, bizarre, comical, foolish, risible 8 farcical 9 fantastic, grotesque, laughable 10 off-the-wall, outlandish, ridiculous 11 incongruous 12 preposterous

Ludlum novel
14 Bourne Identity (The) 15 Bourne Supremacy (The) 16 Holcroft Covenant (The) 19 Prometheus Deception (The)

lug
3 nut, oaf, tow, tug 4 bear, buck, drag, draw, haul, hump, jerk, pull, tote 5 carry, ferry, shlep 6 convey, schlep 9 transport

luggage
4 bags, gear 7 baggage

lugubrious
3 sad 4 blue, dour, down, glum 5 bleak 6 dismal, dreary, gloomy, morose, rueful, somber, sullen, woeful 7 doleful, joyless 8 cast down, dejected, dolesome, downcast, mournful 9 cheerless, depressed, plaintive, saturnine, sorrowful, woebegone 10 depressing, despondent, lamentable, melancholy, oppressive 11 discouraged, dispiriting, downhearted 12 disconsolate

lukewarm
5 blasé, tepid 7 dubious, offhand 8 hesitant 9 uncertain, undecided 10 wishy-washy 11 halfhearted, indifferent

lull
3 ebb 4 balm, calm, hush, wane 5 letup, pause, quiet, still 6 becalm, pacify, soothe, temper 7 compose, decline, ease off, slacken 8 abeyance, interval 9 stillness 10 quiescence 11 tranquilize

lullaby
8 berceuse 10 cradlesong

lulu

3 ace **5** dandy, doozy, dream **6** doozie, wonder **7** delight **8** knockout **9** sensation

lumber

3 tax **4** clog, lade, load, logs, plod, slog, wood **5** barge, clump, stump, weigh **6** burden, charge, rumble, saddle, timber, trudge **8** encumber

lumberjack

see **logger**

luminance

10 brightness

luminary

3 sun, VIP **4** lion, name, star **5** celeb, light, nabob **6** leader, worthy **7** big name, notable **8** big-timer, eminence, somebody **9** celebrity, dignitary, superstar **10** notability **12** leading light

luminous

5 clear, lucid **6** bright, lucent **7** beaming, crystal, fulgent, lambent, radiant, shining **8** clear-cut, lustrous, pellucid **9** brilliant, effulgent, refulgent **11** illustrious, translucent, transparent **12** enlightening, incandescent

lummox

3 oaf **4** boor, clod, gawk, lout **5** klutz, looby **6** lubber **7** palooka

lump

3 gob, lot, oaf, wad **4** blob, bulk, chip, clod, gawk, glob, heap, hunk, lout, mass, pile, welt **5** abide, batch, block, brook, bulge, bunch, chunk, hunch, klutz, knurl, looby, piece, scrap, stand, tumor **6** digest, endure, entire, lubber, morsel, nugget **7** handful, palooka, portion, stomach, swallow **8** swelling, totality **9** aggregate **10** protrusion, tumescence **12** protuberance

lumpy

5 crude, gawky, rough **6** choppy, clumsy, coarse, oafish **8** clumpish, unformed **9** roughhewn

lunacy

5 folly, mania **6** idiocy **7** fatuity, foolery, inanity, madness **8** delirium, dementia, insanity **9** absurdity, craziness, silliness, stupidity **10** imbecility **11** derangement, foolishness **13** senselessness

lunar

dark area: 4 mare **5** maria (plural)
valley: 4 rill **5** rille

lunatic

3 mad, nut **4** daft, kook, loco, yo-yo, zany **5** balmy, batty, crank, crazy, nutty, raver, wacko, wacky **6** absurd, crazed, cuckoo, insane, madman, maniac, nitwit, psycho, screwy **7** bonkers, cracked, foolish **8** crackpot, demented, demoniac, deranged, frenzied, maniacal, paranoid, schizoid, unhinged **9** bedlamite, ding-a-ling, fruitcake, harebrain, screwball **10** crackbrain **11** nonsensical

lunch

3 eat **4** meal, nosh **5** snack

luncheonette

4 café **5** diner **6** bistro, eatery **7** beanery, canteen, tearoom **8** snack bar **9** cafeteria **10** coffee shop, restaurant **11** greasy spoon

lune

3 bow **5** curve **6** sickle **8** crescent, meniscus

lung

combining form: 5 pneum, pulmo **6** pneumo, pulmon
disease: 9 emphysema, pneumonia **10** byssinosis **12** tuberculosis

lunge

3 jab **4** dash, dive, stab **5** bound, drive, pitch, surge **6** charge, plunge, pounce, thrust

lunkhead

3 oaf **4** boob, clod, dodo, dolt, goof, yo-yo **5** booby, chump, dummy, dunce, idiot, moron, ninny, noddy, stupe **6** dimwit, dum-dum, nitwit **7** dullard **8** dumbbell, imbecile, numskull **9** birdbrain, ignoramus, lamebrain, numbskull, simpleton **10** nincompoop

lupine

5 feral **6** brutal, fierce **7** wolfish **8** ravening **9** predatory, rapacious **10** bluebonnet, sanguinary

lurch

3 bob, yaw **4** jerk, lean, list, reel, rock, roll, sway, tilt, toss **5** heave, pitch, slide, swing **6** bumble, careen, falter, plunge, seesaw, swerve, teeter, totter **7** blunder, stagger, stumble **8** flounder

lure

3 bag **4** bait, call, draw, fake, hook, pull, rope, toll, trap, wile **5** blind, catch, charm, decoy, snare, tempt, trick **6** appeal, cajole, come-on, draw in, draw on, entice, entrap, invite, lead on, seduce **7** attract, beguile,

bewitch, capture, con game, enchant, ensnare, gimmick, wheedle **9** blandish, delusion, illusion, inveigle **9** captivate, fascinate, incentive, seduction, siren song **10** attraction, camouflage, enticement, inducement, seduceunce, temptation
fishing: 3 fly **4** worm **5** spoon **6** minnow **8** bucktail

lurid
3 wan **4** ashy, gory, gray, grim, pale **5** ashen, fiery, gross, livid, waxen **6** doughy, grisly, malign, sultry, yellow **7** baleful, ghastly, graphic, hideous, macabre, malefic, tabloid **8** blanched, gruesome, horrible, shocking, sinister, terrible **9** colorless **10** horrifying, maleficent, terrifying **11** sensational **12** melodramatic

Lurie novel
14 Foreign Affairs **18** War Between the Tates (The)

lurk
4 hide, slip **5** creep, prowl, skulk, slide, slink, sneak, snoop, steal **9** pussyfoot

luscious
4 rich, sexy **5** sapid, sweet, tasty, yummy **6** delish, divine, ornate, savory **7** opulent, piquant, sensual **8** sensuous **9** ambrosial, epicurean, exquisite, flavorful, luxurious, seductive, sumptuous, toothsome **10** delectable, delightful, flamboyant, flavorsome, voluptuous **11** scrumptious **13** mouthwatering

lush
3 sot **4** rank, rich, wino **5** dense, drink, drunk, yummy **6** bibber, boozer, deluxe, lavish, savory **7** fertile, opulent, profuse, sensual, teeming, tippler **8** abundant, drunkard, palatial, prodigal, sensuous, thriving **9** ambrosial, delicious, epicurean, exuberant, inebriate, luxuriant, luxurious, plentiful, sumptuous, toothsome **10** boozehound, delectable, delightful, profitable, prosperous, voluptuous **11** extravagant, flourishing

Lusitania
8 Portugal

lust
3 rut, yen **4** ache, itch, pine, urge, wish, zeal, zest **5** ardor, crave, drive, greed, letch, yearn **6** desire, fervor, hanker, hunger, libido **7** avidity, craving, lechery, longing, passion **8** appetite, coveting, cupidity, lewdness, priapism, salacity,

satyrism, yearning **9** carnality, eagerness, eroticism, lubricity, prurience, pruriency **10** enthusiasm, excitement, satyriasis, wantonness **11** nymphomania **13** concupiscence, lecherousness, salaciousness

luster
4 glow **5** glaze, gleam, glint, gloss, sheen, shine **6** polish **7** burnish, shimmer **8** lambency, radiance **9** afterglow **10** brightness, brilliance, brilliancy, effulgence, luminosity, refulgence **11** candescence, iridescence

lusterless
3 dim, wan **4** blah, drab, dull, flat, gray, matt **5** brown, dingy, dusky, faded, matte, muddy, muted, vapid **6** boring **10** uninspired

lustful
3 hot **4** lewd **5** bawdy, horny **6** carnal, erotic, wanton **7** burning, goatish, itching, ruttish, satyric **8** prurient **9** debauched, lecherous, libertine, lickerish, salacious **10** hot-blooded, lascivious, libidinous, licentious, lubricious, passionate **12** concupiscent

lustrate
5 purge **6** purify **7** cleanse

lustration
6 ritual **8** ablution **9** catharsis, cleansing, purgation **10** sprinkling **12** purification

lustrous
5 nitid, shiny **6** bright, gleamy, glossy, sheeny **7** fulgent, glowing, lambent, radiant, shining **8** gleaming, luminous, polished, splendid **9** brilliant, burnished, effulgent, refulgent **10** glimmering, glistening **11** resplendent **12** incandescent

lusty
4 hale **5** hardy, vital **6** brawny, hearty, mighty, potent, robust, strong, virile **7** dynamic, healthy, rousing **8** vigorous **9** energetic, strapping, strenuous **10** prodigious, red-blooded **12** enthusiastic

lute
4 clay, seal **5** grout **6** cement **7** bandora **8** mandolin **10** chitarrone, instrument
Arabic: 3 oud
two-necked: 7 theorbo

lutenist
5 Bream (Julian) **7** Dowland (John) **8** Gaultier (Denis)

Lutetia
5 Paris

Luxembourg
capital: 10 Luxembourg
monetary unit: 4 euro
mountain range: 8 Ardennes
neighbor: 6 France 7 Belgium, Germany
river: 4 Sûre 7 Alzette

luxuriant
4 lush, rank, rich 5 dense 6 fecund, lavish
7 copious, fertile, opulent, profuse,
rampant, riotous, teeming 8 abundant,
fruitful, luscious, prodigal, prolific
9 excessive, exuberant, sumptuous

luxuriate
4 bask 5 bloom, enjoy, feast, revel
6 abound, relish, thrive, wallow 7 delight,
indulge 8 flourish

luxurious
4 lush, posh, rich 5 fancy, grand, plush,
ritzy, showy 6 costly, deluxe, lavish, plushy
7 opulent, sensual, stately 8 imposing,
majestic, palatial, splendid 9 elaborate,
epicurean, expensive, grandiose,
sumptuous 10 impressive 11 extravagant,
magnificent
situation: 7 fat city 10 bed of roses, easy
street

luxury
5 frill, treat 6 dainty 7 amenity, comfort
8 delicacy, opulence 9 abundance,
affluence 10 indulgence 11 superfluity
12 extravagance

lycée
6 school 10 high school

lyceum
4 hall 6 school 7 academy, chamber
9 institute

Lycidas author
6 Milton (John)

Lycomedes
daughter: 8 Deidamia
victim: 7 Theseus

Lycus
brother: 7 Nycteus
father: 7 Pandion
slayer: 6 Zethus 7 Amphion
wife: 5 Dirce

Lydian
king: 5 Gyges 7 Croesus 8 Alyattes
queen: 7 Omphale

lye
7 caustic 9 hydroxide

lynch
4 hang 5 scrag 6 gibbet, murder
7 execute, string up

Lynette
see **Line**

lynx
4 puma 6 bobcat, cougar 7 caracal,
wildcat 9 catamount

Lyra star
4 Vega

lyre
4 harp

lyric
3 ode 4 odic, poem 5 melic, verse
6 poetic 7 melodic, musical 8 operatic
9 exuberant, rhapsodic

lyrical
7 lilting, melodic, musical, songful, tuneful
8 operatic

lyricist
4 poet 10 librettist

Lysander's beloved
6 Hermia

M

Maacah
   father: 5 Nahor 6 Talmai 7 Absalom
   husband: 5 David 6 Jehiel, Machir
   8 Rehoboam
   son: 5 Hanan 6 Abijam, Achish
   7 Absalom 10 Shephatiah

macabre
   4 grim 5 lurid 6 grisly, horrid, morbid
   7 deathly, ghastly, hideous 8 ghoulish,
   gruesome, horrible 9 deathlike
   10 horrifying

macadam
   3 tar 7 asphalt, roadway 8 pavement

macaque
   6 monkey, rhesus

macaroni
   3 fop 4 beau, buck, dude, toff 5 dandy,
   pasta, swell 7 coxcomb, gallant

macaw
   6 parrot

Macbeth
   character: 4 Ross 5 Angus 6 Hecate,
   Lennox 7 Fleance
   slayer: 7 Macduff
   successor: 7 Malcolm
   title: 5 thane
   victim: 6 Banquo, Duncan

mace
   4 club 5 baton, staff 6 cudgel, nutmeg
   8 bludgeon

Macedonia
   capital: 6 Skopje
   city: 6 Tetovo
   monetary unit: 5 denar
   neighbor: 6 Greece, Serbia 7 Albania
   8 Bulgaria
   part of: 7 Balkans
   peninsula: 6 Balkan

macerate
   4 soak 5 steep 6 drench, soften
   7 immerse, suffuse 8 saturate

machete
   4 bolo 5 knife 6 scythe

Machiavellian
   4 wily 6 shrewd 7 cunning, devious
   8 guileful, scheming 9 conniving, deceitful,
   insidious 10 conspiring 11 duplicitous,
   treacherous 12 unscrupulous

Machiavelli work
   6 Prince (The) 8 Mandrake (The)
   10 Mandragola (La)

machinate
   4 plot 6 scheme 7 connive, finagle
   8 conspire, intrigue, maneuver

machination
   4 plot, ploy, ruse 5 cabal, dodge 6 gambit,
   scheme 8 artifice, in-
   trigue, maneuver, scheming, trickery
   9 chicanery, collusion, deception, dirty
   work, expedient, stratagem 10 hanky-
   panky, subterfuge 11 contrivance,
   skulduggery 12 gamesmanship,
   skullduggery

machine
   6 device, engine, gadget 9 apparatus,
   appliance, automaton 11 contraption

machine-gun
   4 rake 6 strafe 8 enfilade 9 rapid-fire

machine-gun inventor
   7 Gatling (Richard)

machinery
   5 works 9 apparatus, equipment,
   mechanism

machismo
   7 swagger 8 virility 9 manliness
   11 masculinity

macho
   5 manly 6 virile 9 masculine

Machu Picchu resident
4 Inca

mackinaw
4 coat   5 cover, trout   7 blanket

mackintosh
7 slicker   8 raincoat

macrocosm
5 world   6 cosmos   8 creation, universe

mad
4 daft, nuts, rash, sore, wild   5 angry, crazy, irate, irked, kooky, livid, loony, nutty, rabid, wacky   6 absurd, crazed, cuckoo, heated, insane, ireful, screwy   7 berserk, bonkers, cracked, enraged, foolish, frantic, furious, lunatic   8 choleric, demented, deranged, frenetic, frenzied, incensed, offended, outraged, unhinged, worked up, wrathful   9 delirious, fanatical, fantastic, hilarious, illogical, senseless   10 distracted, infuriated, irrational, unbalanced

Madagascar
capital: 12 Antananarivo
channel: 10 Mozambique
city: 9 Mahajanga, Toamasina
language: 6 French   8 Malagasy
monetary unit: 5 franc
mountain range: 9 Ankaratra

madame
3 Mrs.   4 wife   6 milady, missus

Madame Bovary
author: 8 Flaubert (Gustave)
character: 4 Emma (Bovary)   7 Charles (Bovary)   8 Rodolphe

Madame Butterfly
character: 9 Cho-Cho-San, Cio-Cio-San, Pinkerton, Sharpless
composer: 7 Puccini (Giacomo)

madcap
4 rash, wild   7 foolish   8 reckless   9 frivolous, hotheaded   10 capricious, incautious

Mad Cavalier
6 Rupert (Prince)

madden
3 ire, vex   4 goad   5 anger, craze   6 enrage   7 derange, incense, inflame, outrage, possess, steam up, unhinge   9 infuriate, unbalance

Madeira Islands
capital: 7 Funchal
export: 4 wine
part of: 8 Portugal

mademoiselle
4 girl, Miss   6 maiden   9 governess   10 yellowtail   11 silver perch

made-to-order
6 custom   7 bespoke   10 customized   11 custom-built

made-up
5 bogus, false   7 painted   8 invented, mythical   9 fictional, imaginary, pretended, specious, trumped-up   10 fabricated, fictitious   11 make-believe   12 cosmeticized

madhouse
6 asylum, bedlam   8 loony bin   9 funny farm   10 booby hatch

madman
3 nut   4 kook, loon   5 loony, raver   6 cuckoo, maniac, psycho   7 lunatic, nutcase   9 bedlamite, psychotic, fruitcake

madness
4 rage   5 folly   6 lunacy   8 insanity   9 psychosis   11 derangement

Madonna initials
3 BVM

Madras
9 Tamil Nadu
founder: 3 Day (Francis)

Madrid museum
5 Prado

madrigal
4 glee, poem, song   8 part-song

madrigalist
English: 4 Byrd (William)   6 Morley (Thomas), Wilbye (John)   7 Tomkins (Thomas), Weelkes (Thomas)
Flemish: 8 Willaert (Adriaan)
Italian: 8 Marenzio (Luca)   10 Monteverdi (Claudio)

maelstrom
4 eddy   5 whirl   6 vortex   7 turmoil   9 whirlpool

maenad
9 bacchante, priestess

maestro
see **conductor**

Mafia
3 mob   4 ring   6 clique   7 rackets   8 gangland   9 Black Hand, syndicate   10 Cosa Nostra, underworld

mafioso
4 goon   6 hit man   7 mobster   8 gangster   9 racketeer

magazine
4 dump 5 cache, depot, organ, store
6 armory, digest, review, weekly 7 arsenal,
gazette, journal, monthly 8 biweekly
9 bimonthly, quarterly, warehouse
10 depository, periodical, repository,
storehouse 11 publication

mage
6 priest 8 magician, sorcerer

maggot
4 grub, whim 5 fancy, larva 6 vagary
7 caprice, conceit

Magi
6 Caspar, Gaspar 8 Melchior 9 Balthasar,
Balthazar
gift: 4 gold 5 myrrh 7 incense
12 frankincense

Magian
see **magus**

magic
4 juju 5 wicca 6 hoodoo, voodoo
7 alchemy, devilry, sorcery 8 satanism,
witchery, witching, wizardry 9 conjuring,
diablerie, diabolism, occultism, sortilege
10 hocus-pocus, mumbo jumbo,
necromancy, witchcraft 11 abracadabra,
bewitchment, enchantment, legerdemain,
thaumaturgy

magical
6 occult 8 wizardly 10 bewitching,
entrancing 11 necromantic 12 thaumaturgic

Magic Flute composer
6 Mozart (Wolfgang Amadeus)

magician
5 brujo, witch 6 shaman, wizard
7 Houdini, warlock 8 conjurer, satanist,
sorcerer 9 diabolist, enchanter, trickster,
voodooist 11 medicine man, necromancer,
thaumaturge
Arthurian: 6 Merlin
Shakespearean: 8 Prospero
stage: 5 Randi (James) 11 Copperfield
(David), illusionist
Tolkien's: 7 Gandalf

Magic Mountain, The
author: 4 Mann (Thomas)
character: 7 Castorp (Hans)

magisterial
6 lordly 7 pompous 8 dogmatic
9 imperious, masterful 10 high-handed
11 doctrinaire, domineering, overbearing
13 authoritative, self-important

Magister Ludi author
5 Hesse (Hermann)

magistrate
5 court, judge 7 bencher, justice 8 official
ancient Greek: 5 ephor 6 archon
ancient Roman: 6 aedile 7 duumvir,
praetor, questor 8 quaestor
Italian: 7 podesta
Scottish: 6 bailie

Magna Carta
king: 4 John
place signed: 9 Runnymede

magnanimous
5 noble 7 liberal 8 generous, princely
9 forgiving, unselfish 10 benevolent,
bighearted, charitable, chivalrous, high-
minded, munificent

magnate
5 baron, mogul, nabob 6 fat cat, prince,
tycoon 9 personage, plutocrat

magnet
9 lodestone 10 attraction

magnetic
8 alluring 9 appealing, seductive
10 attractive 11 captivating, charismatic,
fascinating 12 irresistible
substance: 4 iron 7 ferrite

magnetism
4 draw, lure, pull 5 charm 6 allure, appeal
7 glamour 8 charisma 10 attraction
11 fascination

magnetize
4 draw, lure, wile 5 charm 7 attract,
bewitch, enchant 9 captivate, fascinate

magnification unit
8 diameter

magnificence
4 pomp 7 majesty 8 grandeur, splendor
9 pageantry 13 sumptuousness

magnificent
5 grand, noble, regal, royal 6 august,
lavish, lordly, superb 7 exalted, opulent,
stately, sublime 8 glorious, imposing,
majestic, palatial, princely, splendid
9 brilliant, grandiose, luxurious, sumptuous
11 extravagant, resplendent, splendorous
13 splendiferous

magnifier
4 lens 9 telescope
jeweler's: 5 loupe

magnify
4 hymn, laud 5 add to, boost, cry up, exalt,

extol, honor, swell **6** expand, extend, praise **7** amplify, augment, enhance, enlarge, ennoble, glorify, inflate **8** eulogize, heighten, increase, maximize, multiply, overplay **9** aggravate, celebrate, embellish, embroider, intensify, overstate **10** aggrandize, exaggerate, panegyrize **13** overemphasize

magniloquent

5 tumid, windy **6** florid, turgid **7** aureate, flowery, fustian, orotund, pompous, swollen **8** sonorous **9** bombastic, high-flown, overblown, rhapsodic **10** euphuistic, rhetorical **11** declamatory

magnitude

4 size **5** order, range **6** extent, import, number, volume **7** bigness, caliber, measure, quality **8** enormity, hugeness, quantity, vastness **9** greatness, immensity, largeness **10** dimensions, importance, proportion **11** consequence

Magnolia State

11 Mississippi

magnum opus

7 classic **10** masterwork **11** chef d'oeuvre, masterpiece, tour de force

Magog's king

3 Gog

magpie

3 jay **4** bird **6** gabber, prater **7** blabber, hoarder **8** jabberer, prattler **9** chatterer, collector **10** chatterbox **12** blabbermouth

maguey

5 agave, fiber **7** cantala
relative: 4 aloe

magus

6 wizard **7** diviner, warlock **8** conjurer, sorcerer **9** enchanter **10** astrologer **11** necromancer

Magyar

9 Hungarian

Mahalath

father: 7 Ishmael **8** Jerimoth
husband: 4 Esau **8** Rehoboam

mah-jongg piece

4 tile

Mahlon

father: 9 Elimelech
mother: 5 Naomi
wife: 4 Ruth

Maia

father: 5 Atlas
mother: 7 Pleione
sisters: 8 Pleiades
son: 6 Hermes **7** Mercury

maid

4 girl, lass, miss **5** biddy, bonne, wench **6** au pair, damsel, lassie, live-in, virgin **7** servant **8** domestic **9** charwoman, hired girl **10** au pair girl
Indian: 4 ayah
lady's: 7 abigail
stage: 9 soubrette

maiden

3 gal **4** girl, lass, miss **5** first, fresh, missy, prime, wench **6** damsel, lassie, unused, virgin **7** initial, pioneer, primary **8** earliest, original, spinster, virginal **10** spinsterly
Norse mythological: 8 valkyrie

maidenhair tree

6 ginkgo

maidenhead

5 hymen **6** purity **9** virginity

maidenhood

9 virginity

Maid of Astolat

6 Elaine

Maid of Orleans, The

4 Joan (of Arc) **7** Pucelle (La)
author: 8 Schiller (Friedrich von)

mail

4 post **5** armor **7** hauberk, letters **8** messages

_____ mail

3 air **5** chain

maim

4 maul **6** mangle **7** cripple, disable **8** mutilate, paralyze **9** disfigure

main

3 sea **5** chief, great, major, ocean, prime, trunk, vital **7** central, high sea, leading, premier, primary **8** cardinal, foremost, high seas **9** essential, paramount, principal **10** preeminent, prevailing **11** fundamental, outstanding, predominant

Maine

capital: 7 Augusta
city: 6 Bangor **8** Lewiston, Portland
college, university: 5 Bates, Colby **7** Bowdoin
lake: 6 Sebago
motto: 6 Dirigo

mountain: 8 Cadillac, Katahdin
nickname: 8 Pine Tree (State)
park: 6 Acadia
river: 8 Kennebec 9 Penobscot
state bird: 9 chickadee
state flower: 22 white pine cone and tassel
state tree: 9 white pine

mainly

6 mostly 7 chiefly, largely 8 above all
9 primarily 10 especially 11 principally
13 predominantly

mainstay

4 prop 5 brace 6 pillar 7 bulwark,
standby, support 8 backbone, buttress
9 supporter, sustainer

Main Street author

5 Lewis (Sinclair)

maintain

4 aver, avow 5 argue, claim 6 affirm,
allege, assert, back up, defend, insist, keep
up, manage, stress, uphold 7 care for,
carry on, contend, declare, justify, persist,
profess, support, sustain, warrant
8 continue, preserve 9 cultivate,
emphasize, look after 10 provide for

maintenance

4 care, keep 6 living, upkeep 7 alimony,
support 8 livelihood 11 subsistence
12 alimentation
worker: 7 janitor 9 custodian

maize

4 corn, milo 10 Indian corn

majestic

5 grand, noble, regal, royal 6 august,
kingly, lordly, superb 7 exalted, stately
8 elevated, imperial, imposing, princely,
splendid 9 dignified, grandiose, sumptuous
11 ceremonious, magnificent

majesty

4 pomp 5 glory 8 eminence, grandeur,
splendor 9 greatness, loftiness
11 stateliness 12 magnificence

major

3 big 4 main, star 5 chief, grave, large
6 higher, larger 7 capital, greater, notable,
primary, serious, sizable 8 sizeable,
superior 9 principal, prominent 10 large-
scale, preeminent 11 outstanding,
predominant, significant 12 considerable

Major Barbara author

4 Shaw (George Bernard)

majority

4 bulk, edge 6 margin 13 preponderance

make

3 act, net, set 4 earn, form, gain, mold
5 build, cause, erect, forge, frame, hatch,
shape, spawn 6 compel, create, derive,
draw up, effect, output, parent 7 achieve,
bring in, compose, fashion, prepare,
produce 8 comprise, conclude, draw down,
generate 9 construct, establish, fabricate,
originate 10 constitute 11 manufacture,
put together
amends: 5 atone
believe: 7 pretend
certain: 6 assure 8 convince
fast: 3 fix 4 gird 6 secure
good: 7 succeed 9 indemnify
known: 3 air 6 expose, reveal, spread
7 declare, divulge, uncover 8 announce,
disclose, proclaim
use of: 6 employ

make-believe

4 mock, sham 7 charade, feigned, fiction
8 disguise, pretense 9 fictional, imaginary,
insincere, pretended, simulated
10 fictitious

make do

4 cope 5 get by, get on, shift 6 endure,
fake it, manage, wing it 7 survive 8 get
along 9 improvise 11 extemporize
13 muddle through

make off

3 fly, run 4 flee, skip 5 leave, scoot, scram
6 decamp, depart, escape 7 abscond, run
away 9 skedaddle

make out

3 see 4 fare, neck 5 grasp, infer 6 accept,
deduce, derive, follow, gather, manage,
take in, thrive 7 discern, prosper, succeed
8 conclude, flourish, get along, perceive
9 apprehend, determine, establish,
interpret 10 comprehend, understand

make over

4 cede, deed 6 assign, convey, reform
7 remodel 8 renovate, transfer

maker

7 builder, creator 8 borrower, designer,
inventor, producer 10 originator
11 constructor 12 manufacturer

makeshift

6 resort 7 stopgap 8 recourse, resource
9 expedient, temporary 10 expediency,
substitute 11 provisional 13 quick-and-
dirty, rough-and-ready

make up

4 form **5** atone **6** devise, invent
7 arrange, compile, compose, concoct,
fashion, prepare **8** comprise, contrive
9 apologize, construct, fabricate, formulate,
improvise, reconcile **10** compensate

makeup

4 cast, form, kohl, mold **5** blush, fiber,
gloss, grain, paint, rouge, shape, stamp,
style **6** design, nature, powder, stripe,
temper **7** blusher, mascara **8** lip gloss, war
paint **9** character, formation
10 complexion, maquillage **11** arrangement, composition, disposition,
greasepaint, personality, temperament
12 architecture, constitution, construction,
organization

maladroit

5 inept **6** clumsy, gauche, klutzy
7 awkward, unhandy **8** bumbling, bungling,
tactless **9** ham-handed, impolitic
10 blundering, ungraceful **11** heavy-
handed **12** undiplomatic

malady

3 ill **7** ailment, disease, illness **8** disorder,
sickness, syndrome **9** complaint, condition,
infirmity **10** affliction

malaise

4 funk **5** dumps, ennui **8** debility, doldrums
10 enervation

Malamud, Bernard

novel: **5** Fixer (The) **7** Natural (The)
9 Assistant (The)
story: **11** Magic Barrel (The)

malapert

4 rude **5** brash, fresh, nervy, sassy, saucy,
smart **6** brassy, brazen, cheeky **7** forward
8 impudent, insolent **12** presumptuous

Malaprop creator

8 Sheridan (Richard Brinsley)

malapropos

5 inapt, undue **8** improper, unseemly,
untimely **10** unsuitable **11** inopportune
13 inappropriate, inopportunely

malaria

4 ague **6** miasma
medicine: **7** quinine **8** cinchona
mosquito: **9** anopheles

malarkey

4 guff **5** bilge, hokum, hooey, tripe
6 bunkum, drivel **7** hogwash, rubbish,
twaddle **8** nonsense **9** poppycock
10 balderdash **12** blatherskite

Malawi

capital: **8** Lilongwe
city: **8** Blantyre
explorer: **11** Livingstone (David)
former name: **9** Nyasaland
lake: **5** Nyasa **6** Malawi
language: **7** English **8** Chichewa
monetary unit: **6** kwacha
neighbor: **6** Zambia **8** Tanzania
10 Mozambique
river: **5** Shire

Malaysia

capital: **11** Kuala Lumpur
city: **4** Ipoh **6** Penang **11** Johor Baharu
island: **6** Borneo
monetary unit: **7** ringgit
neighbor: **8** Thailand **9** Indonesia
peninsula: **5** Malay
sea: **10** South China
strait: **7** Malacca

malcontent

5 rebel **6** griper, grouch, unruly **8** agitator,
factious, frondeur, grumbler, mutinous,
restless **9** alienated **10** bellyacher,
complainer, rebellious **11** disaffected,
disgruntled, disobedient, ungratified
12 contumacious, dissatisfied

mal de mer

6 nausea **8** vomiting **10** queasiness
11 seasickness

Maldives

capital: **4** Male
language: **6** Divehi
monetary unit: **7** rufiyaa

male

3 guy, tom **4** gent **5** macho, manly
6 manful, virile **7** manlike **9** masculine,
staminate

malediction

4 jinx, oath **5** curse **7** malison
8 anathema **10** execration **11** imprecation

malefactor

5 felon, knave, rogue **6** sinner **8** criminal,
evildoer, offender **9** miscreant, reprobate,
scoundrel, wrongdoer **10** blackguard,
lawbreaker

maleficent

4 evil, vile **5** toxic, wicked **6** malign, sinful
7 baleful, baneful, beastly, harmful,
noxious, vicious **8** damnable, sinister,
virulent **9** execrable, injurious, nefarious,
repugnant **10** pernicious, villainous **11** destructive

malevolence
4 evil 5 spite 6 grudge, malice, spleen
7 ill will 9 hostility, malignity
12 spitefulness 13 maliciousness

malevolent
4 evil 6 malign, wicked 7 baleful, hateful,
hurtful, vicious 8 sinister, spiteful,
venomous 9 injurious, malicious,
malignant, poisonous

malfunction
6 glitch 7 misfire

Mali
capital: 6 Bamako
city: 5 Mopti, Ségou 7 Sikasso
8 Timbuktu 10 Tombouctou
desert: 6 Sahara
former name: 11 French Sudan
language: 6 French
monetary unit: 5 franc
neighbor: 5 Niger 6 Guinea 7 Algeria,
Senegal 10 Ivory Coast, Mauritania
11 Burkina Faso
river: 5 Niger

malice
4 bile, hate 5 spite, venom 6 animus,
enmity, grudge, hatred, poison, spleen 7 ill
will 8 meanness 9 animosity, antipathy
10 bitterness, resentment 11 hatefulness,
malevolence 12 spitefulness 13 invidiousness

malicious
4 evil, mean 5 nasty, petty 6 wicked
7 baneful, hateful, heinous, jealous
8 spiteful, vengeful, venomous, virulent
9 poisonous, poison-pen, rancorous
10 malevolent

maliciousness
see **malevolence**

malign
4 evil, soil 5 abuse, decry, libel, smear,
stain, sully, taint 6 befoul, defame, defile,
revile, smirch, vilify, wicked 7 asperse,
baleful, baneful, blacken, detract, hateful,
hostile, noxious, slander, tarnish, traduce,
vicious 8 besmirch, derogate, inimical,
sinister, spiteful, tear down, virulent
9 denigrate, disparage, injurious, rancorous
10 calumniate, depreciate, maleficent,
malevolent, pernicious, scandalize,
vituperate 11 deleterious, opprobriate
12 antagonistic, antipathetic

malignant
4 evil 5 fatal 6 deadly, lethal, wicked
7 baleful, hateful, vicious 8 devilish,

fiendish, spiteful 9 injurious, rancorous
10 diabolical, malevolent

malison
5 curse 8 anathema 11 commination,
imprecation, malediction

mall
4 lane 5 alley, plaza, strip 7 passage
9 concourse, esplanade, promenade
10 passageway 11 median strip

malleable
6 pliant, supple 7 ductile, plastic, pliable
8 flexible 9 adaptable

mallet
6 hammer

malodorous
4 foul, gamy, rank 5 fetid, fuggy, funky,
fusty, musty, stale 6 frowsy, putrid, rancid,
rotten, smelly, stinky 7 noisome, noxious,
reeking, spoiled 8 mephitic, stinking
9 offensive 10 nauseating 11 ill-smelling
12 pestilential

Malta
capital: 8 Valletta
city: 5 Qormi 10 Birkirkara
island: 4 Gozo 6 Comino
language: 6 French 7 Maltese
monetary unit: 4 lira
sea: 13 Mediterranean

Maltese Falcon, The
actor: 5 Astor (Mary), Lorre (Peter)
6 Bogart (Humphrey) 11 Greenstreet
(Sydney)
author: 7 Hammett (Dashiell)
detective: 5 Spade (Sam)
director: 6 Huston (John)

maltreat
5 abuse 6 ill-use, misuse, molest

mama
4 dame, doll, wife 5 broad, femme, hussy,
madam, woman 6 matron, mother

Mamet play
7 Oleanna 14 Boston Marriage
15 American Buffalo 17 Glengarry Glen
Ross

mammal
3 ass 5 camel, hippo, hyrax 6 alpaca,
colugo, dassie, rabbit 7 primate
8 elephant 12 hippopotamus
African: 5 okapi, zebra 8 aardvark,
aardwolf
aquatic: 6 dugong, sea cow 7 cowfish,
manatee, narwhal, platypi (plural)
8 cetacean, platypus, porpoise, sirenian

arboreal: 5 lemur 6 sifaka 7 opossum 8 kinkajou
Australian: 5 koala 8 kangaroo
burrowing: 8 starnose
carnivorous: 3 cat, dog, fox 4 bear, lion, mink, seal, wolf 5 genet, hyena, otter, panda, ratel, sable, tiger 6 badger, grison, marten, racoon, walrus 7 linsang, polecat, raccoon 8 mongoose
catlike: 5 civet
doglike: 4 jackal
extinct: 6 quagga 8 mastodon, stegodon
feline: 4 lion 5 tiger, tigon 6 ocelot, tiglon 7 leopard, lioness, tigress
flying: 3 bat
gnawing: 3 rat 6 beaver, rodent 8 squirrel
goatlike: 4 tahr 5 takin
harelike: 5 hyrax 7 hyraces (plural)
hoofed: 3 cow, pig 4 deer, goat, oxen (plural) 5 camel, sheep, tapir 6 alpaca 7 peccary 8 ruminant, ungulate 12 hippopotamus
horned: 4 goat
insect-eating: 4 mole 5 shrew 6 tenrec 8 hedgehog
long-necked: 7 giraffe
marine: 4 orca 6 walrus 7 dolphin, grampus
marsupial: 9 bandicoot
nocturnal: 6 wombat
raccoon-like: 10 cacomistle
ruminant: 4 deer 5 llama, moose, sheep 6 vicuña
small: 4 pika 8 hedgehog, hedgepig
South American: 7 guanaco
toothless: 5 sloth 8 edentate, pangolin 9 armadillo
tropical: 5 coati
unweaned: 8 suckling
with flippers: 8 pinniped
wolflike: 5 hyena

mammon
4 pelf 5 lucre 6 riches, wealth 8 treasure 9 abundance, affluence 10 prosperity 11 possessions

mammoth
4 huge, vast 5 giant, jumbo 6 mighty 7 immense, massive, monster, titanic 8 colossal, enormous, gigantic 9 leviathan, monstrous 10 gargantuan, mastodonic, monumental 11 elephantine

man
3 guy 4 buck, chap, cuss, dude, gent 5 being, bloke 6 fellow, mister, mortal, person 7 husband 8 creature, paramour 9 boyfriend, mortality, personage 10 individual 11 Homo sapiens

castrated: 6 eunuch
combining form: 4 andr 5 andro, homin 6 homini
French: 5 homme
Italian: 4 uomo
Latin: 3 vir 4 homo
old: 6 codger, geezer
Spanish: 6 hombre
Yiddish: 6 mensch
young: 3 boy, lad 6 shaver 9 stripling

manage
3 run 4 cope, fare, head, keep 5 get by, get on, guide, shift 6 afford, direct, effect, govern, handle 7 achieve, carry on, conduct, control, execute, finagle, operate, oversee, succeed 8 carry out, contrive, cope with, deal with, dominate, engineer, get along, maintain 9 cultivate, supervise 10 accomplish, administer, bring about 11 superintend

manageable
6 docile 8 amenable, bearable, biddable, passable 9 agreeable, compliant, endurable, tractable 10 responsive 11 cooperative, supportable, sustainable 13 accommodating

management
4 care 5 brass 6 charge 7 conduct, control, running 8 guidance, handling 9 direction, oversight 10 conducting 11 front office, supervising, supervision

manager
4 boss, exec 6 gerent 7 handler, officer 8 director, official, overseer, producer 9 conductor, executive 10 impresario, supervisor 13 administrator
museum: 7 curator

mañana
7 someday 8 sometime, tomorrow

Man and Superman author
4 Shaw (George Bernard)

Manassas battle
7 Bull Run

Manasseh, Manasses
brother: 7 Ephraim
father: 6 Hashum, Joseph 8 Hezekiah 10 Pahathmoab
grandfather: 5 Jacob
grandson: 6 Gilead
mother: 7 Asenath
son: 6 Machir

man-at-arms
7 fighter, soldier, warrior 10 serviceman

Mandalay author
7 Kipling (Rudyard)

mandarin
5 elder 6 orange 8 official 9 tangerine
10 bureaucrat, panjandrum

mandate
4 fiat, word 5 edict, order, ukase 6 behest,
charge, decree 7 bidding, command,
dictate 9 authority, directive 10 imperative,
injunction 13 authorization

mandatory
6 forced 7 binding 8 required 9 de
rigueur, necessary, requisite
10 compulsory, imperative, obligatory
11 involuntary

mandible
3 jaw 8 lower jaw

man-eater
4 lion, ogre 5 shark, tiger 8 cannibal
13 mackerel shark

Manette's daughter
5 Lucie

maneuver
3 ply 4 move, plan, plot, ploy, step 5 feint,
trick, wield 6 design, device, gambit,
handle, jockey, scheme, tactic, wangle
7 exploit, finagle, finesse 8 artifice,
démarche, engineer, exercise, intrigue,
movement, navigate 9 machinate,
procedure, stratagem 10 manipulate,
proceeding, subterfuge 11 contrivance,
machination 12 manipulation

maneuvering room
8 latitude

Man for All Seasons, A
author: 4 Bolt (Robert)
subject: 4 More (Thomas)

manganese
ore: 10 pyrolusite

manger
4 rack 6 cratch, feeder, trough

mangle
3 mar 4 iron, maim, maul 5 press
6 damage, deface, deform, impair, injure
7 butcher, contort, distort 8 lacerate,
mutilate 9 disfigure

mangy
5 seedy 6 ragtag, shabby 7 scruffy,
squalid 8 decrepit, tattered 9 moth-eaten
10 down-at-heel, threadbare

manhandle
5 abuse 6 batter 7 rough up 8 maltreat,
mistreat 10 push around, slap around

Manhattan
building: 11 Empire State
district: 4 Soho 6 Harlem 7 Chelsea,
Tribeca
entertainment district: 11 Times Square
financial district: 10 Wall Street
museum: 7 Whitney 10 Guggenheim
12 Metropolitan
opera house: 12 Metropolitan
purchaser: 6 Minuit (Peter)
river: 4 East 6 Hudson
school: 3 NYU 8 Columbia 9 Juilliard

mania
4 rage, zeal 5 craze, fancy 6 frenzy,
lunacy 7 madness, passion 8 fixation,
idée fixe, insanity 9 cacoëthes, obsession
10 compulsion, enthusiasm 11 infatuation

maniac
3 bug, nut 4 loon 5 fiend, freak
6 madman, psycho, zealot 7 fanatic,
lunatic, nutcase 8 crackpot 9 bedlamite
10 enthusiast

manifest
4 show 5 clear, overt, plain, shown, utter,
voice 6 appear, embody, evince, expose,
patent, reveal 7 display, evident, evinced,
exhibit, express, invoice, obvious, visible
8 apparent, distinct, evidence, palpable,
proclaim, revealed 9 evidenced, incarnate,
objectify, prominent 10 illustrate,
noticeable, observable 11 demonstrate,
exteriorize, externalize, perceptible,
unambiguous

manifestation
4 show, sign 5 proof 7 display, symptom
8 epiphany 10 appearance, revelation

manifesto
4 fiat, rule, writ 5 credo, creed, edict,
ukase 6 decree, dictum, gospel, notice,
policy, ruling 7 mandate, statute
8 doctrine, document, platform 9 affidavit,
directive, statement, testament, testimony,
ultimatum 10 deposition, indictment,
injunction, regulation, resolution
11 declaration 12 announcement,
denunciation, notification, proclamation
13 pronouncement

manifold
7 diverse, various 8 compound, multiple,
multiply, numerous 9 multiform, multiplex
10 multiphase 12 multifarious

manikin

4 runt 5 dummy, dwarf, gnome, model, pygmy 6 midget, peewee 8 Tom Thumb
10 homunculus

Manila

founder: 7 Legazpi (Miguel López de)
site: 11 Phillipines
victor: 5 Dewey (George)

manipulate

3 ply, rig 4 play 5 steer, swing, wield
6 direct, doctor, handle, jockey, juggle, manage 7 beguile, conduct, control, exploit, finagle, finesse, massage
8 engineer, maneuver 9 machinate
10 tamper with

Man, Isle of

capital: 7 Douglas
cat: 4 Manx
possession of: 7 Britain
sea: 5 Irish

Manitoba

capital: 8 Winnipeg
lake: 8 Winnipeg 12 Winnipegosis
mountain: 5 Baldy
provincial flower: 13 prairie crocus
river: 6 Nelson 9 Churchill

mankind

6 humans, people 8 humanity 11 Homo sapiens

manlike

4 male 6 virile 8 hominoid, humanoid
9 masculine 10 anthropoid

manly

4 male 5 macho 6 virile 9 masculine

man-made

9 synthetic 10 artificial, factitious
object: 8 artefact, artifact

Mann character

6 Joseph 8 Aschenbach (Gustav von), Felix Krull 11 Hans Castorp, Tonio Kröger

manner

3 air, use, way 4 form, kind, look, mien, mode, sort, vein, wont 5 habit, modus, style, usage 6 aspect, custom, method
7 bearing, conduct, fashion 8 behavior, demeanor, habitude, practice, presence
9 demeanour, etiquette, technique
10 consuetude, deportment 11 affectation, comportment, peculiarity 12 idiosyncrasy

mannered

7 stilted 8 affected 10 artificial 13 self-conscious

mannerism

3 tic 4 pose 5 quirk 10 preciosity
11 affectation, peculiarity, singularity
12 eccentricity, idiosyncrasy 13 artificiality

mannerless

4 rude 6 coarse 7 boorish, ill-bred, uncivil, uncouth 8 impolite 12 discourteous

mannerly

5 civil 6 polite 7 genteel, refined, well-bred
8 decorous, gracious 9 civilized, courteous
10 respectful

Manon composer

8 Massenet (Jules)

Manon Lescaut

author: 7 Prévost (Abbé)
composer: 7 Puccini (Giacomo)
8 Massenet (Jules)
lover: 9 des Grieux

manor

5 villa 6 estate, quinta 7 château, demesne 12 landed estate

manservant

5 valet 6 butler

mansion

4 hall 5 villa 6 palace 7 château

manslayer

6 killer 8 homicide, murderer

manta

3 ray 5 cloak, cloth, shawl 7 blanket

manteau

4 coat, robe, wrap 5 cloak 6 capote, mantle, tabard

mantic

5 vatic 7 Delphic, fatidic 8 Delphian, oracular 9 prophetic, sibylline, vaticinal
10 divinatory

mantilla

4 cape, wrap 5 cloak, fichu, scarf, shawl

mantle

4 cope, glow, pink, robe, rose 5 blush, cloak, color, cover, flush, rouge 6 capote, casing, pinken, redden 7 crimson

man-to-man

4 open 5 frank, plain 6 candid, direct, honest 10 forthright, unreserved
11 openhearted

mantra

5 chant, motto 6 prayer, slogan
9 watchword 10 invocation 11 incantation

manual

4 text 5 guide 6 primer 8 Baedeker,

handbook, hornbook, textbook
9 guidebook, vade mecum **10** compendium **11** abecedarium, enchiridion
religious: 9 catechism
worker: 6 menial **7** laborer

manufacture
4 form, make **6** create, invent **7** fashion, produce **8** assemble **9** fabricate **11** put together

manumit
4 free **6** unbind **7** release, set free, unchain **8** liberate **9** unshackle
10 emancipate

manure
4 dung **6** ordure **7** excreta **9** excrement
10 fertilizer

manuscript
4 hand **6** scrawl **8** longhand **9** autograph
10 penmanship **11** calligraphy, handwriting
ancient: 5 codex **6** scroll **7** codices (plural)
red part: 6 rubric

Man Without a Country, The
author: 4 Hale (Edward Everett)
character: 5 Nolan

many
5 scads **6** divers, legion, myriad, sundry
7 copious, diverse, umpteen, various
8 abundant, manifold, multiple, numerous
9 abounding, bounteous, bountiful, countless, multitude, plentiful
12 multifarious **13** multitudinous
combining form: 4 poly **5** multi, pluri

many-sided
7 diverse **8** all-round, talented **9** all-around, versatile **10** variegated
11 diversified **12** multifaceted, multifarious
13 comprehensive

Mao's successor
3 Hua (Guofeng, Kuo-feng) **4** Deng (Xiaoping), Teng (Hsiao-p'ing)

map
4 plan, plat **5** chart, draft, globe, graph
6 design, lay out, set out, sketch, survey
7 arrange, diagram, drawing, outline, tracing **9** delineate
collection: 5 atlas
line: 6 isobar **7** contour, isogram, isohyet
8 isogloss, isogonic, isopleth, isotherm
maker: 12 cartographer
making: 11 cartography

maple
genus: 4 Acer
product: 5 syrup

type: 3 red **5** sugar **8** box elder

map projection
5 conic **8** Mercator **9** polyconic
10 sinusoidal **12** orthographic
13 stereographic

maquillage
6 makeup

mar
4 ding, harm, hurt, scar, warp **5** spoil, stain
6 bruise, damage, deface, deform, impair, injure **7** blemish, scratch, tarnish, vitiate
9 disfigure

marabou
5 stork

Marat/Sade author
5 Weiss (Peter)

Marat, Jean-Paul
colleague: 6 Danton (Georges)
11 Robespierre (Maximilien)
slayer: 6 Corday (Charlotte)

maraud
4 loot, raid, sack **5** foray, harry **6** harass, ravage, ravish **7** despoil, pillage, plunder, ransack

marauder
6 bandit, pirate **7** brigand, spoiler, wrecker
9 buccaneer, desperado **10** freebooter

marble
3 mib, mig, taw **4** immy, migg **5** agate, aggie, alley, rance **6** blotch, miggle, mottle, streak **7** cipolin, glassie, steelie
9 limestone

marbled
6 veined **7** dappled, flecked, mottled
8 speckled, streaked

Marble Faun, The
author: 9 Hawthorne (Nathaniel)
character: 5 Hilda **6** Kenyon, Miriam
9 Donatello
setting: 4 Rome

marcel
4 wave

march
3 hem, rim **4** abut, file, line **5** skirt
6 adjoin, border, parade **7** advance, headway, proceed **8** anabasis, boundary, frontier, outlands, progress, traverse
9 periphery **10** borderland

March
date: 4 ides
mother: 6 Marmee
sisters: 3 Amy, Meg **4** Beth

March Hare creator
7 Carroll (Lewis)

March King
5 Sousa (John Philip)

Mardi Gras
8 carnival 10 Fat Tuesday
city: 10 New Orleans

Marduk
city: 7 Babylon
consort: 8 Zarbanit, Zarpanit
victim: 5 Kingu 6 Tiamat

mare
3 sea 5 horse 6 equine

mare's nest
3 con, din 4 hoax, scam 5 babel, cheat,
fraud, put-on, spoof 6 bedlam, clamor,
hubbub, humbug, racket, ruckus, tumult,
uproar 7 swindle, turmoil 8 brouhaha,
flimflam, illusion 9 confusion, imposture
10 hullabaloo 11 pandemonium

margarine
4 oleo

margin
3 hem, rim 4 brim, edge, join, line, play,
room, side 5 bound, brink, frame, scope,
shore, skirt, verge 6 border, fringe, leeway
7 minimum, outline, selvage 8 boundary,
latitude, selvedge, surround, trimming
9 elbowroom, perimeter, periphery
13 circumference
tiny: 4 hair

marginal
5 minor 7 limited, minimal 9 bordering
10 borderline, negligible, peripheral,
subsidiary 13 insignificant

Marguerite's lover
5 Faust

Maria ____
5 Elena 7 Stuarda

Marianas
discoverer: 8 Magellan (Ferdinand)
island: 4 Guam, Rota 5 Pagan
6 Guguan, Saipan, Tinian 7 Agrihan,
Aguijan

marijuana
3 pot 4 hash, hemp, weed 5 bhang, grass
6 reefer 7 hashish 8 cannabis

marina
4 dock, pier, quay 5 basin, berth, wharf
8 boatyard

marinate
4 soak 5 steep 6 drench, pickle
7 immerse 8 macerate

marine
5 naval 7 abyssal, aquatic, deep-sea,
oceanic, pelagic 8 nautical, seagoing
9 seafaring, thalassic 10 oceangoing
12 hydrographic 13 oceanographic
crustacean: 6 shrimp 7 lobster
8 barnacle
deposit: 5 coral
plant: 4 kelp, nori 5 dulse 6 wakame
7 seaweed

mariner
3 gob, tar 4 jack, salt, swab 5 limey
6 hearty, rating, sailor, sea dog, seaman
7 jack-tar, old salt, swabbie 8 seafarer
9 sailorman, shellback, tarpaulin
10 bluejacket

marital
6 wedded 7 married, nuptial, spousal
8 conjugal, hymeneal 9 connubial

maritime
7 oceanic, pelagic 8 nautical 9 thalassic
12 navigational

mark
3 aim, jot, sap 4 butt, dupe, fool, goal, gull,
heed, look, nick, note, pick, show, sign,
view 5 blaze, bound, brand, chart, chump,
elect, grade, label, notch, stamp, token,
trait 6 behold, choose, denote, evince, lay
off, notice, object, opt for, rating, record,
select, sucker, target, victim, virtue
7 betoken, delimit, discern, exhibit, fall guy,
feature, gudgeon, indicia, initial, measure,
observe, qualify, scratch, signify, symptom
8 function, indicate, perceive, register
9 attribute, character, designate, objective,
single out 10 indication 11 differentia,
distinction, distinguish 12 characterize
distinctive: 7 indicia 8 indicium
identifying: 4 logo, seal 6 emblem,
signet, symbol 8 colophon, logotype
of insertion: 5 caret
of omission: 8 ellipsis 10 apostrophe
over a vowel: 5 breve 6 accent, macron
over n: 5 tilde
punctuation: 4 dash 5 brace, colon,
comma, slant, slash 6 hyphen, period
7 bracket, solidus 9 backslash, guillemet,
semicolon 10 apostrophe
under a letter: 7 cedilla

Mark
6 Gospel
cousin: 8 Barnabas

mother: 4 Mary

mark down
3 cut 4 pare 5 shave, slash 6 reduce
7 devalue 8 discount 9 devaluate
10 depreciate, undervalue

marked
5 noted 6 patent, signal 7 evident,
notable, obvious, pointed, salient
8 distinct, manifest, striking 9 arresting,
prominent 10 noticeable, remarkable
11 conspicuous, outstanding
12 considerable 13 distinguished
man: 4 Cain

market
4 fair, mall, sell, shop, vend 5 store
6 bazaar, outlet, retail 8 emporium,
exchange, showroom 9 advertise, traffic in,
wholesale 11 merchandise
kind: 4 flea 5 money, stock

marketable
5 sound 7 salable 8 vendible 10 commercial

marketplace
4 mall, souk 5 agora 6 bazaar, rialto
8 emporium

marksman
4 shot 7 deadeye, shooter 12 sharpshooter

marl
4 clay, silt

marlin
8 billfish 9 spearfish

Marlowe play
8 Edward II 9 Dr. Faustus 10 Jew of Malta
(The) 11 Tamburlaine 13 Doctor Faustus

marmot
6 rodent 9 woodchuck 10 prairie dog

maroon
3 red 6 claret, desert, strand 7 abandon,
crimson, forsake, isolate, outcast
8 burgundy, castaway

Marquand character
4 Gray (Charles), Moto (Mr.) 5 Apley
(George), Wayde (Willis) 6 Pulham (H.M.)
7 Goodwin (Melville)

Marquis, Don
cat: 9 Mehitabel
cockroach: 5 Archy

marriage
5 match, union 6 bridal 7 nuptial, spousal,
wedding, wedlock 8 coupling, espousal,
monogamy, nuptials, polygamy
9 matrimony 11 conjugality
12 connubiality
combining form: 4 gamy 6 gamous
notice: 5 banns
outside a group: 7 exogamy
within a group: 8 endogamy

marriageable
6 nubile 8 eligible

marriage broker
9 go-between 10 matchmaker

Marriage of Figaro composer
6 Mozart (Wolfgang Amadeus)

marrow
4 core, meat, pith, soul 5 heart, stuff
6 kernel 7 essence 12 quintessence

marry
3 tie, wed 4 join, link, mate, wive, yoke
5 hitch, merge, unite 6 couple, splice,
spouse 7 combine, conjoin, espouse
9 conjugate

Mars
4 Ares 6 planet
lover: 5 Venus
mission: 6 Viking 7 Mariner 10 Pathfinder
moon: 6 Deimos, Phobos
relating to: 7 martian
(see also **Ares**)

Marseillaise composer
13 Rouget de Lisle (Claude-Joseph)

marsh
3 bog, fen 4 mire, ooze, quag 5 bayou,
glade, swale, swamp 6 morass, muskeg,
slough 7 wetland 8 quagmire
9 swampland

marshal
5 align, array, guide, order, rally, usher
6 deploy, direct, escort, muster 7 arrange,
officer, round up 8 assemble, mobilize,
organize, shepherd 9 methodize,
systemize

Marshall Islands
atoll: 6 Bikini 8 Enewetak 9 Kwajalein
capital: 6 Majuro
ethnic group: 11 Micronesian
island chain: 5 Ralik, Ratak 6 Sunset
7 Sunrise
language: 7 English 11 Marshallese
monetary unit: 6 dollar

marsupial
5 koala 6 possum, wombat 7 opossum
8 kangaroo 9 bandicoot

marten
6 fisher, weasel

Martha
brother: 7 Lazarus
sister: 4 Mary

martial
7 warlike 8 militant, military, spirited
9 bellicose, combative, soldierly
11 belligerent 12 militaristic

martial art
4 judo 5 kendo 6 aikido, karate, kung fu,
tai chi 7 shaolin 8 capoeira, jiujitsu 9 tae
kwon do 11 tai chi chuan
school: 4 dojo

Martial's forte
7 epigram

Martin Chuzzlewit author
7 Dickens (Charles)

Martinique
capital: 12 Fort-de-France
department of: 6 France
discoverer: 8 Columbus (Christopher)
island group: 8 Windward
location: 10 West Indies
neighbor: 10 Dominica, Saint Lucia
volcano: 5 Pelée

martyr
4 Paul, rack 5 Agnes, Alban, James, Peter,
saint, wring 6 George, harrow, Justin
7 afflict, agonize, Clement, crucify, Cyprian,
Stephen, torment, torture 8 Ignatius,
Lawrence, Polycarp, sufferer 9 Joan of
Arc, Sebastian 10 excruciate, Thomas
More
Protestant: 6 Ridley (Nicholas)
7 Cranmer (Thomas), Latimer (Hugh)

marvel
4 gape 6 wonder 7 miracle, portent,
prodigy, stunner 9 curiosity, sensation
10 phenomenon 12 astonishment

marvelous
5 super, swell 6 divine 7 amazing,
awesome, ripping 8 glorious, striking,
stunning, superior, terrific, wondrous
9 excellent, wonderful 10 astounding,
incredible, miraculous, phenomenal,
prodigious, remarkable, staggering,
stupendous, surprising 11 astonishing,
exceptional, sensational, spectacular
12 awe-inspiring, supernatural 13 extraordinary

Marx brother
5 Chico, Harpo, Zeppo 7 Groucho

Marxist
9 socialist 9 communist

Marx, Karl
book: 7 Kapital (Das)
collaborator: 6 Engels (Friedrich)

Mary
husband: 6 Clopas, Joseph 8 Alphaeus
kinswoman: 9 Elisabeth
son: 4 Mark 5 James, Jesus

Maryland
bay: 10 Chesapeake
capital: 9 Annapolis
city: 9 Baltimore, Frederick
college, university: 6 Towson 7 Goucher
9 Annapolis 12 Johns Hopkins 12 Naval
Academy (U.S.)
fort: 7 McHenry
nickname: 7 Old Line (State)
river: 7 Potomac 8 Patuxent
state bird: 15 Baltimore oriole
state flower: 14 black-eyed Susan
state tree: 8 white oak

mascot
4 juju 5 charm 6 amulet, fetish, symbol
8 talisman

masculine
4 male 5 macho, manly 6 manful, virile
7 manlike

masculinity
8 machismo, virility 9 manliness

mash
4 pulp 5 crush, smash 6 squish
8 macerate 9 pulverize

masher
4 wolf 5 flirt 6 chaser 7 Don Juan,
seducer 8 Casanova 9 ladies' man,
womanizer 10 lady-killer 11 philanderer

mash note
10 billet-doux, love letter

mask
4 hide, pose, sham, veil 5 cover, front,
guard, guise, visor 6 facade, screen,
vizard 7 dress up, frisket, pretext
8 coloring, disguise, pretense 9 dissemble,
semblance 10 appearance, camouflage,
false front, simulation 11 dissimulate
13 dissimulation

masonry
9 brickwork, stonework
in a frame: 7 nogging

masquerade
4 pose 6 facade 7 costume, posture
8 carnival, disguise 10 camouflage,
masked ball 11 costume ball

mass
3 lot, sum, wad 4 bank, body, bulk, clot,
core, glob, heap, hill, lump, pack, peck, pile
5 clump, group, mound 6 corpus, volume
7 expanse, globule, wadding 8 assemble
9 aggregate, great deal, stockpile,
substance 11 aggregation 12 conglomerate
for the dead: 7 requiem
of individuals: 3 mob 4 host 5 crowd,
crush, flock, horde, swarm 6 throng
12 congregation 13 agglomeration
part: 6 proper 8 ordinary

Massachusetts
cape: 3 Ann, Cod
capital: 6 Boston
city: 6 Lowell, Quincy 9 Cambridge,
Worcester 10 New Bedford 11 Springfield
college, university: 3 MIT 5 Clark, Smith,
Tufts 6 Boston 7 Amherst, Berklee,
Harvard 8 Brandeis, Williams
9 Hampshire, Radcliffe, Wellesley
12 Mount Holyoke, Northeastern
island: 9 Nantucket 15 Martha's Vineyard
mountain, range: 8 Greylock 9 Berkshire
nickname: 3 Bay (State) 9 Old Colony
(State)
river: 11 Connecticut
state bird: 9 chickadee
state flower: 9 mayflower
state tree: 3 elm (American)

massacre
4 kill 6 mangle, murder, pogrom 7 butcher,
carnage 8 butchery, decimate, genocide,
mangling, mutilate 9 bloodbath,
bloodshed, slaughter 10 annihilate, blood
purge, decimation, mutilation 11 exterminate 12 annihilation

massage
3 rub 5 knead 7 flatter, rubdown
8 blandish 10 manipulate

Massenet opera
5 Le Cid, Manon, Sapho, Thaïs 7 Werther

massive
4 huge, vast 5 bulky, giant, jumbo, solid
6 mighty 7 hulking, immense, mammoth,
weighty 8 colossal, cumbrous, enormous,
gigantic, towering 9 humongous,

monstrous 10 gargantuan, monumental,
prodigious, stupendous, tremendous
11 elephantine, mountainous

master
4 best, boss, guru, head, lick, rule, tame
5 adept, bwana, chief, crack, learn, ruler,
sahib, tutor 6 artist, expert, genius,
honcho, leader, subdue, victor 7 captain,
conquer, headman, maestro, padrone,
prevail, skilled, triumph 8 dominant,
dominate, employer, governor, overcome,
overlord, overseer, regulate, skeleton,
skillful, superior, surmount, virtuoso
9 authority, chieftain, conqueror, dominator,
paramount, principal, sovereign
10 proficient 11 predominant

masterful
4 deft 5 adept, bossy 6 adroit, expert
7 skilled 8 despotic, skillful 9 imperious
10 autocratic, high-handed, proficient,
tyrannical 11 dictatorial, domineering,
magisterial, overbearing 13 authoritarian,
authoritative, high-and-mighty

masterly
5 adept, crack 6 adroit, expert 7 skilled
8 skillful 9 dexterous 10 proficient
11 crackerjack 12 accomplished

Master of Ballantrae, The
6 Durrie
author: 9 Stevenson (Robert Louis)

masterpiece
7 classic 10 magnum opus 11 chef
d'oeuvre, tour de force

mastery
5 knack, skill 7 ability, command, control,
know-how, prowess 8 dominion
9 authority, expertise 10 ascendancy,
domination, expertness, virtuosity
11 proficiency, superiority

masticate
4 chaw, chew, pulp 5 champ, chomp,
crush, munch 6 crunch 7 scrunch
8 macerate, ruminate 9 break down

mat
3 rug 4 felt 6 border, carpet

matador
6 torero 8 toreador 11 bullfighter
adjunct: 6 muleta
move: 4 pase 5 faena 8 veronica

Mata Hari
3 spy

match

3 pit 4 bout, game, like, meet, peer, suit,
twin 5 array, equal, liken, rival, touch,
union 6 double, equate, oppose
7 compare, compeer, contest, counter,
opposer, paragon, play off 8 alliance,
analogue, marriage, opponent, parallel
9 adversary, correlate, duplicate,
encounter, measure up, partake of 10 antagonist, complement, coordinate,
engagement, equivalent, reciprocal,
supplement, tournament 11 counterpart
12 correspond to 13 correspondent,
harmonize with
a bet: 3 see
friction: 7 lucifer

matchless

6 unique 7 supreme 8 peerless, singular
9 nonpareil, unequaled, unrivaled
10 inimitable 12 incomparable,
unparalleled

matchmaker

see **marriage broker**

mate

3 pal, tie, wed 4 chum, pair, twin 5 amigo,
breed, buddy, crony, equal, hitch, marry
6 cohort, couple, double, fellow, friend,
helper, splice, spouse 7 compeer,
comrade, consort, partner 8 confrere,
sidekick 9 associate, companion,
copartner, duplicate, procreate
10 complement, equivalent, reciprocal
11 concomitant

maté

3 tea 5 holly 8 beverage

mater

3 mom, mum 6 mother 9 matriarch

_____ mater

4 alma

material

4 real, true 5 cloth, stuff 6 actual, fabric,
matter, object 7 earthly, element, germane,
worldly 8 apposite, palpable, physical,
relevant, sensible, tangible 9 component,
corporeal, equipment, essential, important,
objective, pertinent, substance
10 applicable, individual, ingredient,
meaningful, phenomenal 11 appreciable,
constituent, fundamental, perceptible,
significant, substantial 12 considerable
13 consequential
building: 5 adobe, brick 6 stucco
7 lagging, plaster, plywood, shingle
8 concrete

materialistic

7 secular, worldly 11 acquisitive

materialize

4 loom, rise 5 arise, issue, reify 6 appear,
embody, emerge, evolve, show up, typify
7 develop, surface 8 manifest 9 come
about, incarnate, objectify, take shape
11 exteriorize 12 substantiate

matériel

4 gear 5 stock 8 supplies 9 apparatus,
equipment, machinery 10 provisions
13 accouterments, accoutrements,
paraphernalia

maternal

8 motherly

matey

5 pally, tight 6 clubby 7 affable
8 amicable, familiar, friendly, intimate,
sociable 9 congenial

mathematician

American: 5 Wiles (Andrew) 6 Peirce
(Charles S.), Veblen (Oswald), Wiener
(Norbert)
Austrian: 5 Gödel (Kurt)
British: 6 Stokes (George)
Dutch: 7 Huygens (Christiaan)
English: 6 Newton (Isaac), Taylor (Brook),
Turing (Alan), Wallis (John) 7 Pearson
(Karl), Russell (Bertrand) 8 Hamilton
(James Rowan) 9 Sylvester (James
Joseph), Whitehead (Alfred North, Henry)
French: 5 Borel (Emile), Comte (Auguste),
Viète (François) 6 Galois (Evariste),
Pascal (Blaise), Picard (Charles-Emile)
7 Fourier (Jean-Baptiste), Laplace (Marquis
de), Vernier (Pierre) 8 Painlevé (Paul),
Poincaré (Jules-Henri) 9 Descartes (René)
German: 5 Gauss (Carl), Wolff (Freiherr
von) 6 Staudt (Karl von) 7 Leibniz
(Gottfried Wilhelm), Riemann (Georg)
11 Weierstrass (Karl)
Greek: 6 Euclid 10 Archimedes,
Pythagoras
Hungarian: 5 Erdos (Paul)
Italian: 8 Volterra (Vito) 10 Torricelli
(Evangelista)
Norwegian: 7 Stormer (Fredrik)
Russian: 11 Lobachevsky (Nikolay)
Scottish: 4 Tait (Peter) 6 Napier (John)
8 Stirling (James)
Swiss: 5 Euler (Leonhard), Sturm
(Jacques) 7 Steiner (Jakob)

mathematics

branch: 4 trig 7 algebra 8 calculus,
geometry, topology 10 arithmetic, statistics
12 trigonometry

proven statement in: 7 theorem

_____ **Mather**
6 Cotton 7 Richard 8 Increase

matriarch
4 dame 6 mother 7 dowager 10 grande dame

matriculate
4 join 5 enter 6 enroll, sign on 8 register

matrimonial
6 bridal, wedded 7 marital, married, nuptial, spousal 8 conjugal, hymeneal 9 connubial 11 epithalamic

matrimony
7 wedlock 8 marriage 11 conjugality 12 connubiality

matrix
3 die, net, web 4 grid, mesh 5 array 6 cradle, gangue 7 complex, network 10 groundmass, truth table

matron
4 dame 7 dowager 8 chaperon 9 chaperone 10 grande dame

Mattathias
father: 5 Simon 6 Ananos 7 Absalom, Boethus 10 Theophilus
son: 8 Josephus

matter
4 body, core, gist, meat, pith, text 5 being, cause, order, point, sense, stuff, theme, thing, topic, value, weigh 6 affair, amount, burden, entity, import, object 7 concern, signify, subject 8 argument, material 9 grievance, magnitude, substance 11 constituent 12 circumstance

matter-of-fact
3 dry 5 plain, prose, prosy, sober, stoic 6 stolid 7 prosaic 9 impassive, objective, practical, pragmatic, realistic 10 hard-boiled, hardheaded, impersonal, phlegmatic, unaffected 11 cold-blooded, down-to-earth, emotionless 13 unimpassioned, unsentimental

mattress
3 pad 4 sack
case: 4 tick
fabric: 7 ticking
straw: 6 pallet

mature
3 age, due 4 grow, ripe 5 adult, grown, owing, ready, ripen 6 flower, grow up, mellow, season, unpaid 7 advance, blossom, decline, develop, grown-up,

overdue, payable, ripened 8 progress 9 developed, full-blown, full-grown 11 full-fledged

maudlin
5 gushy, mushy, silly, sappy, soppy 6 slushy, sticky 7 cloying, gushing, mawkish 8 bathetic 11 sentimental, tear-jerking

Maugham character
4 Kear, Liza 5 Carey, Rosie, Sadie 7 Mildred 8 Ashenden, Craddock 10 Strickland

maul
4 bang, bash, beat, club, drub, flog, whip 5 abuse, flail, pound 6 batter, bruise, buffet, cudgel, hammer, injure, mangle, molest, pummel, sledge, thrash 7 clobber, rough up 8 bludgeon, lambaste, maltreat 9 manhandle

Mauna _____
3 Kea, Loa

maunder
3 bat, gad 4 rove 5 drift, mooch, range 6 mumble, mutter, ramble, wander 7 blather, digress, traipse 8 divagate

Mauritania
capital: 10 Nouakchott
desert: 6 Sahara
language: 5 Wolof 6 Arabic, Fulani 7 Soninke
monetary unit: 7 ouguiya
neighbor: 4 Mali 6 Guinea 7 Senegal 7 Algeria 13 Western Sahara
river: 7 Senegal

Mauritius
capital: 9 Port Louis
island group: 9 Mascarene
language: 6 Creole 7 English
monetary unit: 5 rupee

Maurois biographee
4 Hugo (Victor), Sand (George) 5 Byron (Lord), Dumas (Alexandre) 6 Balzac (Honoré de), Proust (Marcel) 7 Shelley (Percy Bysshe) 8 Disraeli (Benjamin)

mauve
5 lilac 6 purple, violet

maven
3 ace 4 buff, whiz 5 adept, freak, shark 6 addict, expert, master, savant 7 devotee, fanatic, hotshot 8 virtuoso 9 authority 10 enthusiast 11 connoisseur

maverick

5 stray 7 heretic 8 unmarked 9 dissident, unbranded 10 iconoclast 11 independent 13 nonconformist

maw

4 crop 5 chasm, mouth 6 cavity, gullet 7 stomach

mawkish

5 gushy, mushy, sappy, soppy 6 sloppy, slushy, sticky, syrupy 7 cloying, gushing, insipid, maudlin 8 bathetic, romantic 9 schmaltzy, sickening 10 lovey-dovey, nauseating 11 sentimental, tear-jerking

maxilla

3 jaw 4 bone

maxim

3 law, saw 4 rule 5 adage, axiom, gnome, moral, motto, tenet, truth 6 byword, dictum, saying, truism 7 precept, proverb, theorem 8 aphorism, apothegm 9 platitude, prescript, principle 11 commonplace

maximal

3 top 6 utmost 7 highest, largest, supreme, topmost 8 complete, greatest, ultimate 9 paramount

maximum

3 top 6 utmost 7 highest, largest, supreme, topmost 8 extremum, greatest, ultimate 9 paramount

may

5 might, shrub 6 spirea 8 hawthorn

maybe

7 perhaps 8 possibly 9 perchance 11 conceivably, uncertainty

Mayflower

document: 7 Compact
passengers: 8 Pilgrims

mayhem

4 maim, riot 5 chaos, havoc 7 cripple, dislimb 8 mutilate 9 dismember 10 mutilation

mayor

11 burgomaster
Chicago (former): 5 Daley (Richard)
New York (former): 4 Koch (Edward) 6 Walker (Jimmy) 7 Lindsay (John) 8 Giuliani (Rudolph) 9 La Guardia (Fiorello)
Spanish: 7 alcalde

Mayor of Casterbridge, The

author: 5 Hardy (Thomas)
character: 8 Henchard (Michael)

maze

3 web 4 knot, mesh 5 skein, snarl 6 jungle, morass, tangle 7 confuse, network, perplex 8 bewilder, mishmash 9 labyrinth

Mazel _____!

3 tov

McCarthy novel

8 Crossing (The) 16 Cities of the Plain 18 All the Pretty Horses

McCullers, Carson

novel: 18 Ballad of the Sad Cafe (The) 18 Member of the Wedding (The) 20 Heart Is a Lonely Hunter (The) 23 Reflections in a Golden Eye

McCullough novel

10 Thorn Birds (The)

McMurtry novel

12 Buffalo Girls, Lonesome Dove 14 Horseman Pass By 15 Last Picture Show (The) 17 Terms of Endearment

McTeague author

6 Norris (Frank)

MD

3 doc 6 doctor, medico 8 sawbones 9 physician

mea culpa

5 error, fault 7 apology 9 admission 10 concession, confession

meadow

3 lea, ley 5 green 7 pasture 9 grassland
historic: 9 Runnymede
low-lying: 5 haugh

meadow mushroom

6 agaric

meager

4 bare, bony, lean, mere, thin 5 gaunt, lanky, scant, short, spare 6 paltry, scanty, shabby, skimpy, skinny, slight, sparse 7 angular, minimum, scraggy, scrawny, scrimpy 8 exiguous, rawboned 9 deficient, miserable 10 inadequate 12 insufficient

meal

4 chow, fare, feed, grub 5 board, feast, lunch, snack 6 brunch, dinner, farina, picnic, repast, spread, supper 7 high tea, nooning 8 victuals 9 breakfast, collation, refection
army: 4 mess

mealy

6 spotty, uneven 11 farinaceous

mean

3 low, mid, par 4 base, fair, hint, norm, poor, want, wish 5 cheap, cruel, imply, lousy, lowly, mingy, petty, rough, small, snide, spell, tight, weigh 6 attest, center, common, denote, design, humble, intend, matter, medial, medium, middle, paltry, scummy, scurvy, shabby, shoddy, sleazy, stingy, unwell 7 average, betoken, connote, express, lowborn, miserly, pitiful, portend, propose, purport, signify, suggest, vicious 8 déclassé, indicate, inferior, lmediocre, middling, midpoint, moderate, ordinary, pitiable, plebeian, stand for 9 designate, penurious, represent, symbolize 10 despicable, second-rate 11 closefisted, tightfisted 12 contemptible, intermediary, intermediate

meander

4 roam, rove, turn, wind 5 amble, drift, range, snake, stray, twist 6 ramble, wander 7 traipse, winding 8 vagabond 9 gallivant, labyrinth

meandering

5 snaky 7 sinuous 8 flexuous, tortuous 10 convoluted, serpentine 11 anfractuous

meaning

3 aim 4 gist, pith 5 drift, force, point, sense 6 effect, import, intent 7 essence, message, purport 8 intention, substance 10 definition, denotation, intimation 11 connotation, implication 12 significance 13 signification

meaningful

5 valid 7 pointed, serious, weighty 8 eloquent, material 9 important, momentous 10 expressive 11 sententious, significant, substantial 13 consequential

meaningless

5 empty, inane 6 absurd, futile, hollow 7 trivial 8 nugatory 11 nonsensical 13 insignificant

meanings

diverse: 8 polysemy
study of: 9 semantics

means

5 funds, money 6 agency, assets, avenue, income 7 backing, capital 8 finances, holdings, property, reserves 9 apparatus, equipment, resources, substance 10 instrument 11 wherewithal

meantime

7 interim 8 interval

measly

4 poor, puny 5 petty, scant 6 meager, meagre, paltry, scanty 7 pitiful, trivial 8 niggling, pathetic, picayune, piddling, trifling 9 miserable 10 picayunish 13 insignificant

measure

3 bar 4 bill, size, step, test 5 bound, gauge, index, quota, scale, share, shift, weigh 6 amount, bounds, degree, effort, extent, figure, ration, reckon, resort, size up, survey 7 caliper, compute, delimit, mark out, portion, stopgap 8 calliper, estimate, regulate, resource, standard 9 allotment, benchmark, calculate, calibrate, criterion, demarcate, determine, expedient, magnitude, yardstick 10 dimensions, indication, proceeding, proportion, touchstone 11 proposition 13 apportionment

area: 4 acre 7 hectare
capacity: 4 gill, peck, pint 5 liter, minim, quart 6 bushel, gallon 8 fluidram 9 fluid dram 10 fluid ounce, milliliter
cloth: 3 ell
combining form: 6 metric 8 metrical
depth: 5 plumb, sound
dry: 4 peck 6 bushel
electrical: 3 amp 4 watt 6 ampere 7 coulomb
horse height: 4 hand
interstellar space: 6 parsec
length: 3 rod 4 foot, inch, link, mile, yard 5 chain, cubit, meter 6 league 7 furlong 9 kilometer 10 centimeter
liquid: 4 gill, pint 5 minim, quart 6 gallon
mixed drinks: 6 jigger
of comparison: 8 standard
paper: 4 ream
printer's: 4 pica 5 point
radioactive decay: 8 halflife
rotation: 5 angle
strength of solution: 7 titrate
surface: 3 are
thermodynamic: 7 entropy 8 enthalpy

measured

7 regular, stately 8 metrical 9 regulated, temperate, unhurried 10 calculated, controlled, deliberate, restrained 13 proportionate

Measure for Measure

character: 6 Angelo, Juliet 7 Claudio, Mariana 8 Isabella 9 Vincentio
setting: 6 Vienna

measurement

4 area 6 degree 8 capacity, quantity

9 dimension, magnitude   11 calibration, mensuration

measure up to
3 tie 4 meet 5 equal, match, rival, touch
7 emulate 10 qualify for

measuring device
4 gage 5 buret, gauge, scale 7 burette, caliper, sextant, venturi 8 calipers
8 dipstick 9 altimeter, barometer, dosimeter, pedometer 11 tensiometer, velocimeter

meat
4 core, food, gist, pith, pork, veal 5 flesh, jerky, steak 6 thrust, upshot 7 edibles
8 victuals 8 foodstuff, provender, substance 10 provisions 11 comestibles
broth: 8 bouillon
cake: 6 burger 9 hamburger
cured: 7 biltong
cut: 3 rib 4 loin, rump 5 chuck, flank, plate, round, shank 7 brisket, sirloin 8 rib roast 9 club steak, rump roast, short loin, short ribs 10 blade roast, flank steak, round steak, T-bone steak 12 boneless neck, pinbone steak, sirloin steak 13 blade rib roast, crosscut shank
dealer: 7 butcher
deer: 7 venison
dried: 5 jerky
fastening pin: 6 skewer
holding rod: 4 spit 10 rotisserie
juices: 5 gravy
packer: 5 Swift 6 Armour
raw: 6 gobbet
roasted: 8 barbecue
roasting shop: 10 rotisserie
seasoned: 7 sausage 8 pastrami, scrapple
sheep: 6 mutton
side: 8 sowbelly
skewered: 5 kebab, kebob
slice: 6 cutlet, rasher
small portion: 6 collop
tough part: 7 gristle

meat-eating
11 carnivorous

meathead
3 lug, oaf 4 clod, dodo, dolt, gawk, goon, lout 5 chump, klutz, looby 6 dimwit, lubber
7 bungler, palooka 8 dumbbell, numskull
9 birdbrain, ignoramus, lamebrain, numbskull 10 nincompoop

Mebd
husband: 6 Ailill
victim: 10 Cuchulainn

Mecca
4 goal
country: 11 Saudi Arabia
pilgrimage: 4 hadj, hajj
port: 5 Jedda, Jidda 6 Jeddah, Jiddah
shrine: 5 Kaaba

mechanic
7 artisan 9 machinist

mechanical
4 cold 7 cursory, robotic 8 lifeless
9 automated, automatic, unfeeling
10 impersonal 11 emotionless, instinctive, involuntary, perfunctory, unemotional

mechanism
4 gear 5 gizmo, means, works 6 agency, doodad, jigger, medium, widget 7 whatsit
8 dohickey 9 apparatus, appliance, procedure, technique, thingummy
10 instrument 11 contraption, contrivance, thingamabob, thingamajig, thingumajig

medal
5 badge, honor, prize 6 reward 7 laurels
8 accolade 10 decoration
13 commemoration

meddle
3 pry 4 fool, nose 5 snoop 6 butt in, dabble, horn in, kibitz, monkey, putter, tamper, tinker 7 intrude, obtrude
8 trespass 9 interfere, interlope, intervene
10 mess around

meddler
5 snoop, yenta 7 snooper 8 busybody, intruder, kibitzer 9 buttinsky
12 troublemaker

meddlesome
4 busy, nosy 6 prying 9 intrusive, obtrusive, officious 11 impertinent, interfering

Medea
5 witch 9 sorceress 11 enchantress
aunt: 5 Circe
brother: 8 Absyrtus
father: 6 Aeëtes
husband: 5 Jason 6 Aegeus
sister: 5 Circe
son: 6 Medeus
victim: 6 Creusa, Glauce, Glauke

medial
3 mid 4 mean 6 center, middle 7 average, central, halfway, midmost 8 middling, moderate 10 centermost, middlemost
11 equidistant 12 intermediary, intermediate

median
see **medial**

mediate
5 judge 6 broker, convey, liaise, settle, step in, umpire 7 adjudge, referee, resolve 8 moderate, transmit 9 arbitrate, intercede, interfere, interpose, intervene, negotiate 10 conciliate

mediator
5 judge 6 broker, umpire 7 arbiter, liaison, referee 9 go-between, middleman 10 interceder, negotiator, peacemaker 11 intercessor

medical instrument
6 needle 7 forceps, scalpel, scanner, speculum, syringe 8 otoscope 9 endoscope 11 cardiograph, stethoscope

medical practitioner
3 doc 5 nurse 6 doctor, intern 7 surgeon 9 physician

medicament
4 cure, pill 6 elixir, physic, remedy 7 nostrum 8 antidote, curative 10 palliative
inert: 7 placebo

medicate
4 cure, dose, drug, heal 5 treat

medicinal
8 curative, remedial, salutary, sanative 9 healthful 12 health-giving, pharmaceutic

medicine
4 cure, pill 5 bromo 6 physic, remedy 7 anodyne, nostrum 8 busulfan, poultice 11 antipyretic
bottle: 4 vial
branch: 7 surgery 8 oncology 9 neurology, pathology 10 bariatrics, cardiology, geriatrics, gynecology, nephrology, obstetrics, pediatrics, psychiatry
cathartic: 8 evacuant 9 purgative
combining form: 5 iatro 8 pharmaco
quantity of: 4 dose 6 dosage
shell: 7 capsule
soothing: 7 anodyne 8 lenitive, narcotic, sedative 9 calmative, soporific

medicine man
6 doctor, kahuna, shaman 9 curandero

medieval study
5 logic 7 grammar, trivium 8 rhetoric 10 quadrivium

mediocre
4 dull, fair, hack, so-so 6 common 7 average, fairish 8 inferior, middling, moderate, ordinary, passable 9 tolerable 10 pedestrian, uninspired 11 commonplace, indifferent 12 run-of-the-mill, unexceptional

meditate
4 mull, muse 5 weigh 6 intend, ponder 7 purpose, reflect, revolve 8 cogitate, consider, mull over, ruminate, turn over 9 reflect on 10 deliberate 11 contemplate

meditative
6 broody 7 pensive 8 brooding 10 reflective, ruminative, thoughtful

meditator
4 yogi

Mediterranean
11 Mare Nostrum 12 Mare Internum
coastal region: 7 Riviera
eastern shores: 6 Levant
island:
(see at **island**)
wind: 7 mistral, sirocco

medium
3 par 4 fair, mean, so-so 5 agent, organ 6 agency, métier, milieu, normal 7 ambient, average, channel, climate, culture, neutral, vehicle 8 ambience, middling, moderate, passable, standard 9 tolerable 10 atmosphere 11 clairvoyant, environment 12 run-of-the-mill
of exchange: 5 money 8 currency 11 legal tender

medley
4 brew, olio 5 combo, gumbo 6 jumble, ragout 7 farrago, mélange, mixture 8 mishmash, pastiche 9 pasticcio, patchwork, potpourri 10 assortment, hodgepodge, miscellany, salmagundi 11 gallimaufry

Medusa
6 Gorgon
father: 7 Phorcus, Phorcys
hair: 6 snakes
mother: 4 Ceto
offspring: 7 Pegasus 8 Chrysaor
sister: 6 Stheno 7 Euryale
slayer: 7 Perseus

medusa
9 jellyfish

meed
3 due 4 part 5 quota, share 6 amount, desert, ration, return, reward 7 guerdon, measure, portion 8 dividend 9 allotment, allowance 10 recompense 13 apportionment

meek
3 shy 4 mild, tame 5 lowly, timid 6 docile, gentle, humble, modest 7 patient 8 tolerant 10 submissive, unassuming 11 deferential 13 long-suffering

meerschaum
4 pipe 9 sepiolite

meet
3 apt, fit 4 face, fair, fill, find, join, just, open, spot 5 cross, event, hit on, match, right, touch, unite 6 answer, chance, engage, oppose, proper, settle, take on, useful 7 contest, convene, fitting, fulfill, hit upon, satisfy, stumble, undergo 8 approach, assemble, come upon, concours, conflict, confront, converge, suitable 9 encounter, impinge on, measure up 10 congregate, provide for 11 appropriate, competition
a bet: 3 see
a need: 7 suffice
athletic: 8 gymkhana 10 tournament
by appointment: 10 rendezvous

meeting
4 moot, talk 5 tryst 6 huddle, parley, powwow 7 session 8 assembly, conclave, concours, congress, junction 9 concourse, encounter, gathering, rencontre 10 conference, confluence, convention, get-together, rendezvous 11 competition, convocation 12 intersection
Anglo-Saxon: 5 gemot 6 gemote
place: 5 forum
spiritual: 6 séance

Mefistofele composer
5 Boito (Arrigo)

Megaera
see **Erinyes**

megaphone
8 bullhorn 10 mouthpiece

Megara
father: 5 Creon
husband: 8 Heracles, Hercules
king: 5 Nisus

megillah
5 story 7 account

megrim
4 urge, whim 5 fancy, freak, humor 6 notion, vagary, whimsy 7 caprice, conceit, impulse, vertigo 8 crotchet, migraine 9 dizziness

Mehitabel
3 cat
creator: 7 Marquis (Don)

friend: 5 Archy

Mein Kampf author
6 Hitler (Adolf)

meiosis
7 litotes 12 cell division

Meissen
5 china 8 ceramics 9 porcelain

Meistersinger
5 Sachs (Hans) 9 Frauenlob

Meistersinger, Die
beloved: 3 Eva
composer: 6 Wagner (Richard)
hero: 6 Walter
mentor: 5 Sachs (Hans)

melancholia
5 gloom 6 sorrow 7 despair, sadness 9 dejection, morbidity 10 depression, desolation, gloominess 11 despondency, dolefulness

melancholic
3 low, sad 4 blue, glum 6 gloomy, morose, triste 7 joyless 8 dejected, downcast, mournful 9 depressed, saddening 10 depressing, despondent, dispirited

melancholy
3 low, sad 4 blue, funk, glum 5 blues, dumps, ennui, gloom 6 dismal, dreary, gloomy, misery, morose, rueful, somber, tedium, triste, woeful 7 boredom, despair, doleful, joyless, pensive, sadness, unhappy 8 dejected, dolorous, downcast, funereal, mournful, saddened 9 black bile, dejection, depressed, plaintive, saddening, sorrowful 10 depressing, depression, despondent, dispirited, lachrymose, lamentable, lugubrious, reflective, thoughtful 11 despondency, unhappiness 12 heavyhearted, wretchedness

mélange
see **medley**

Melanippus
father: 7 Theseus
slayer: 10 Amphiaraus
victim: 6 Tydeus

Melchior
companion: 6 Caspar, Gaspar 9 Balthasar, Balthazar
gift: 4 gold

Melchizedek's kingdom
5 Salem

meld
3 mix 4 fuse 5 blend, merge 6 mingle 7 combine, mixture 8 compound

9 commingle, interfuse 10 amalgamate
11 intermingle

Meleager
beloved: 8 Atalanta
father: 6 Oeneus
mother: 7 Althaea
victim: 4 boar

melee
3 row 4 fray, riot 5 brawl, broil, clash, fight
6 affray, fracas, ruckus, rumpus 7 scuffle
8 skirmish 9 scrimmage 10 donnybrook,
free-for-all

meliorate
4 help 5 amend 6 better, soften
7 improve 8 mitigate, palliate

Mélisande's lover
7 Pelléas

melisma
7 cadenza, descant

mellifluous
5 sweet 6 dulcet, fluent, golden, liquid,
smooth 7 flowing, honeyed, silvery
8 euphonic, soothing 10 euphonious
13 silver-tongued

mellow
3 age 4 aged, ripe 5 ripen 6 genial,
golden, grow up, mature, season, smooth
7 honeyed, matured, ripened 8 laid-back,
pleasant, seasoned 9 agreeable

melodic
5 sweet 6 dulcet 7 musical, songful,
tuneful 8 canorous, euphonic
10 euphonious

melodious
5 lyric, sweet 6 dulcet 7 musical, songful,
tuneful 8 euphonic 9 cantabile
10 euphonious

melody
3 air, lay 4 aria, song, tune 5 canto, music,
theme 6 chorus, strain, warble 7 descant,
refrain 11 tunefulness

melon
4 pepo 5 gourd 6 casaba, profit
8 crenshaw, honeydew, windfall
10 cantaloupe

Melpomene
see **Muse**

melt
3 run 4 flux, fuse, thaw 6 relent, soften
7 liquefy 8 dissolve, liquesce, unfreeze
9 disappear 10 deliquesce
down: 6 render

together: 4 fuse

Melville, Herman
character: 3 Pip 4 Ahab, Toby 5 Bembo,
Chase 6 Cereno (Benito), Jermin, Pierre
7 Fayaway, Ishmael 8 Bartleby, Queequeg,
Starbuck
work: 4 Omoo 5 Mardi, Typee 6 Pierre
7 Redburn 8 Moby Dick 11 White-Jacket
12 Benito Cereno 13 Confidence-Man
(The)

member
3 cut 4 part 5 piece 6 clause, parcel
7 portion, section, segment 8 division
9 appendage, component 10 ingredient
political party: 4 Tory, Whig 7 Liberal
8 Democrat, Laborite 9 Labourite
10 Republican 12 Conservative
service club: 4 Lion 8 Kiwanian, Rotarian

membrane
4 film 6 pleura 7 pleurae (plural)
bodily: 6 serosa
brain: 3 pia
diffusion through: 7 osmosis
dividing: 5 septa (plural) 6 septum
ear: 8 tympanum
enclosing: 8 indusium
thin: 6 lamina 7 lamella, laminae (plural)
8 lamellae (plural)
wing: 8 patagium

memento
5 relic, token, trace 6 trophy 7 vestige
8 keepsake, reminder, souvenir
11 remembrance

Memnon
father: 8 Tithonus
mother: 3 Eos 6 Aurora
slayer: 8 Achilles

memoir
3 bio 4 life 5 diary 6 record, report, thesis
7 account, journal 8 anecdote 9 biography
11 confessions 12 recollection,
reminiscence 13 autobiography

memoirist
7 Boswell, diarist 10 biographer

memorable
7 lasting, notable 8 historic 9 deathless,
indelible, momentous, red-letter
10 noteworthy 11 significant 13 distinguished

memorandum
4 chit, note 6 minute, notice, record
7 tickler 8 notation, reminder 12 announcement

memorial
4 note **5** relic, token, trace **6** record, trophy **7** relique **8** keepsake, monument, reminder, souvenir **10** dedicatory **11** celebrative, remembrance **12** consecrative, remembrancer **13** commemoration, commemorative
mound: **5** cairn

memorial park
see **cemetery**

memorize
3 con, get **6** retain **8** remember

memory
6 recall **8** mind's eye, souvenir **9** anamnesis, awareness, flashback, retention **10** reflection **11** remembrance **12** recollection, reminiscence **13** retentiveness, retrospection
assisting: **8** mnemonic
loss: **7** amnesia

menace
4 risk **5** alarm, peril, scare **6** danger, hazard, threat **7** imperil, jeopard, torment **8** endanger, frighten, jeopardy, threaten **9** terrorize **10** intimidate, jeopardize

ménage
4 clan **5** house **6** family **8** quarters **9** household **12** housekeeping

menagerie
3 zoo **7** mixture

mend
3 fix, sew **4** cure, darn, heal **5** patch, renew **6** cobble, doctor, look up, perk up, reform, remedy, repair, revamp **7** correct, improve, patch up, rebuild, rectify, redress, restore **8** overhaul, renovate **9** condition, refurbish **10** ameliorate, convalesce, recuperate **11** recondition, reconstruct

mendacious
5 false, lying **6** shifty **7** fibbing **9** deceitful, deceptive, dishonest, paltering **10** untruthful **11** dissembling **13** prevaricating

mendacity
3 lie **6** deceit **9** deception, duplicity, falsehood **10** dishonesty **12** equivocation **13** truthlessness

mendicancy
7 beggary, begging, bumming, cadging **8** mooching, sponging **11** panhandling

mendicant
5 friar **6** beggar **7** begging

Mending Wall author
5 Frost (Robert)

Menelaus
brother: **9** Agamemnon
father: **6** Atreus
kingdom: **6** Sparta
mother: **6** Aerope
wife: **5** Helen

menial
4 dull **5** lowly **6** humble **7** servant, servile, slavish **8** obeisant, retainer **9** unskilled **10** obsequious **11** subservient, undignified

meniscus
4 lens **9** cartilage

Menlo Park inventor
6 Edison (Thomas Alva)

menopause
11 climacteric **12** change of life

menorah
10 candelabra

Menotti, Gian Carlo
character: **5** Amahl
opera: **6** Consul (The), Medium (The) **9** Telephone (The)

men's store
12 haberdashery

mental
5 inner **7** psychic **8** cerebral, rational, thinking **9** reasoning, spiritual **10** immaterial, telepathic **11** intelligent **12** intellective, intellectual **13** psychological
faculty: **6** memory

mentality
3 wit **5** sense **6** brains **7** mindset, outlook **9** intellect, mother wit **10** brainpower **12** intelligence

mention
4 cite, name, note **7** refer to, specify **8** advert to, allude to, citation, instance **9** reference

mentor
4 guru **5** coach, guide, tutor **7** teacher **9** counselor **10** counsellor

Mentor's pupil
10 Telemachus

menu
4 card, diet **5** carte **10** bill of fare **11** carte du jour
item: **4** soup **5** salad **6** entrée **7** dessert **9** appetizer

Mephibosheth
father: 4 Saul 8 Jonathan
mother: 6 Rizpah

Mephistophelian
7 satanic 8 devilish, diabolic 10 diabolical

mephitic
4 rank 5 fetid, funky, musty 6 putrid,
smelly 7 noisome, noxious, reeking
8 stinking 9 poisonous 10 malodorous

Merab
father: 4 Saul
husband: 6 Adriel

mercenary
4 hack 5 venal 6 greedy 7 corrupt, soldier
8 hireling

merchandise
4 line, sell 5 cargo, goods, stock, trade,
wares 6 deal in, job lot, market, retail
7 effects, promote, staples, traffic
8 products 9 publicize, vendibles
11 commodities

merchandiser
6 dealer, trader, vendor 8 retailer
9 tradesman 10 wholesaler 11 businessman 13 businesswoman

merchant
5 buyer 6 dealer, jobber, seller, trader,
vendor 7 peddler 8 purveyor, retailer
9 tradesman 10 trafficker, wholesaler
11 businessman, storekeeper
guild: 5 Hansa, Hanse
League: 9 Hanseatic
ship: 5 oiler 6 argosy, coaler, galiot,
packet, tanker, trader 7 collier, galliot,
steamer 8 Indiaman 9 freighter
wine: 7 vintner

Merchant of Venice, The
7 Antonio
character: 6 Portia 7 Jessica, Lorenzo,
Nerissa, Shylock 8 Bassanio

merciful
4 kind 6 benign, humane, kindly
7 clement, lenient 8 tolerant 9 forgiving,
indulgent 10 charitable, forbearing
11 softhearted 13 compassionate

merciless
4 grim 5 cruel, harsh 6 brutal, savage,
wanton 9 cutthroat, ferocious, unfeeling
10 gratuitous, implacable, ironfisted,
unyielding 11 hardhearted, unrelenting
12 unappeasable

mercurial
5 flaky 6 fickle, mobile 7 erratic

8 unstable, variable, volatile 9 impulsive
10 capricious, changeable, inconstant
13 temperamental, unpredictable

mercury
5 azoth 11 quicksilver
ore: 8 cinnabar

Mercury
6 planet
(see also **Hermes**)

Mercutio
friend: 5 Romeo
slayer: 6 Tybalt

mercy
4 pity, ruth 5 grace 6 lenity 7 caritas,
charity 8 clemency, goodwill, kindness,
leniency 9 benignity, tolerance
10 compassion, generosity, kindliness
11 benevolence, forbearance
13 commiseration
petition for: 5 kyrie 8 miserere

mere
4 bare, lake, pool, pure 8 boundary,
landmark 9 undiluted

merely
4 just, only 6 simply, solely, wholly

meretricious
4 loud, sham 5 gaudy, phony, showy
6 flashy, garish, glitzy, sleazy, tawdry, tinsel,
trashy 7 chintzy 8 delusive, delusory,
illusory 9 contrived, deceptive
10 misleading 11 counterfeit, pretentious

merganser
4 duck, smew

merge
3 mix 4 fuse, join 5 blend, unify, unite
6 mingle 7 combine 8 coalesce,
compound 9 commingle, interfuse
10 amalgamate, assimilate 11 consolidate,
intermingle

merger
5 union 6 fusion 7 melding 8 alliance,
takeover 9 coalition 10 absorption
11 combination, unification
12 amalgamation 13 consolidation

meridian
4 acme, apex, peak 6 apogee, climax,
summit, zenith 8 pinnacle

merit
3 due 4 earn, rate 5 arete, value, worth
6 virtue 7 caliber, deserts, deserve, entitle,
justify, quality, stature, warrant

10 excellence, perfection, recompense
11 achievement

merited

3 due 4 fair, just 5 right 7 condign, fitting
8 deserved, rightful, suitable 9 justified,
requisite 11 appropriate

meritorious

6 worthy 8 laudable 9 admirable,
deserving, estimable, honorable
10 creditable 11 commendable,
thankworthy 12 praiseworthy

Merlin

4 seer 5 augur, magus 6 shaman, wizard
7 prophet 8 magician 10 soothsayer
11 necromancer, thaumaturge

merlin

6 falcon 10 pigeon hawk

mermaid

3 nix 5 Ariel, nixie 7 manatee 8 sirenian
10 water nymph 11 water sprite

Merope

father: 5 Atlas 8 Oenopion
husband: 7 Polybus 8 Sisyphus
11 Cresphontes
lover: 5 Orion
mother: 7 Pleione
sisters: 8 Pleiades
son: 7 Aepytus, Glaucus

merriment

4 glee 5 mirth, revel 6 gaiety 7 jollity,
revelry, whoopee 8 hilarity, reveling
9 festivity, jocundity, joviality 10 jocularity,
jubilation 13 entertainment

merry

3 gay 4 glad 5 happy, jolly 6 blithe,
jocund, jovial, joyful, joyous, lively
7 festive, gleeful 8 animated, cheerful,
mirthful 9 hilarious, sprightly, vivacious
12 high-spirited, lighthearted

merry-andrew

4 fool, zany 5 clown, joker 6 jester,
madcap 7 buffoon 9 harlequin
10 mountebank

merrymaker

7 partyer, reveler 8 carouser

merrymaking

5 party, revel 6 frolic, gaiety 7 jollity,
revelry, whoopee 8 hilarity 9 festivity
12 conviviality

Merry Widow composer

5 Lehár (Franz)

Merry Wives of Windsor, The

character: 3 Nym 4 Ford, Page 5 Caius
6 Fenton, Pistol 7 Slender 8 Falstaff

mesa

5 bench, butte 7 plateau 9 tableland

mescal

5 agave 6 cactus, liquor, maguey, peyote

mesh

3 net, web 4 jibe, maze 5 skein, snare,
snarl 6 engage, morass, tangle 7 netting,
network 8 dovetail, entangle 9 harmonize,
interlock, labyrinth 10 coordinate 12 reticulation

meshuga

3 mad 4 nuts 5 crazy, goofy, kooky, loony,
nutty, wacky 6 insane, screwy 7 foolish

mesmeric

8 alluring, hypnotic 9 glamorous
10 bewitching, enchanting 11 captivating

mesmerize

4 vamp 6 dazzle, seduce 7 bewitch
8 ensorcel, enthrall, entrance 9 captivate,
ensorcell, fascinate, hypnotize, spellbind

Mesopotamia

4 Iraq
civilization: 4 Elam 5 Akkad, Sumer
7 Assyria, Elamite 8 Akkadian, Assyrian,
Sumerian 9 Babylonia 10 Babylonian
river: 6 Tigris 9 Euphrates

mess

4 hash 5 botch, snafu 6 fright, jumble,
muddle 7 eyesore 8 botchery, disarray,
disorder, shambles, wreckage 9 confusion
10 hodgepodge, miscellany
around: 4 idle 5 chill, dally 6 dawdle,
doodle, fiddle, potter, putter 7 goof off,
hang out 8 chill out, lollygag 10 dilly-dally
up: 4 blow, flub, muff, ruin 5 botch, fluff,
fudge, spoil, touse 6 bungle, fumble, tousle
7 butcher

message

4 note 5 sense, theme 6 letter, report
7 epistle, meaning, mission, missive,
purport 8 bulletin, dispatch, telegram
9 directive, telegraph 10 communiqué
12 significance 13 communication,
signification

Messalina's husband

8 Claudius

mess around

4 fool, idle 5 flirt 6 dabble, dawdle, fiddle,
meddle, monkey, potter, putter, tamper,

tinker **8** womanize **9** associate, interfere, interlope, philander

messenger
4 post **5** envoy **6** herald, runner
7 apostle, courier **8** emissary **9** go-between, harbinger **10** ambassador
11 internuncio **12** intermediary
God's: 5 angel
of the gods: 6 Hermes **7** Mercury
Turkish: 6 chiaus

messiah
6 savior **7** saviour **8** defender **9** deliverer, liberator

Messiah composer
6 Handel (George Frideric)

messy
6 frowsy, frowzy, sloppy, unneat, untidy
7 chaotic, rumpled, unkempt **8** careless, confused, ill-kempt, slapdash, slipshod, slovenly **9** disheveled, disorderly
11 dishevelled
abode: 3 sty **6** pigpen, pigsty

mestizo
6 ladino, métis **10** mixed-blood

Mestor
father: 7 Perseus
mother: 9 Andromeda

metal
4 gold, iron **5** steel **6** bronze
alloy:
(see **alloy**)
casting mold: 5 ingot
corrosion: 4 rust
fuse: 6 solder
in mass: 7 bullion
layer: 7 plating
lump: 6 nugget
magnetic: 4 iron
refuse: 4 slag **5** dross **6** scoria
sheath: 5 armor
thin: 4 foil, leaf **5** plate
worker: 5 smith **10** blacksmith

metallic element
3 tin **4** gold, iron, lead, zinc **6** barium, cobalt, copper, nickel, radium, silver, sodium **7** arsenic, bismuth, cadmium, calcium, lithium, mercury, uranium
8 aluminum, chromium, platinum, titanium, tungsten, vanadium **9** magnesium, manganese, potassium, strontium
10 molybdenum

metamere
6 somite **7** segment

metamorphic rock
5 slate **6** gneiss, marble, schist
9 quartzite, soapstone

metamorphose
6 change, mutate **7** convert, develop
9 transform, translate, transmute
11 transfigure **12** transmogrify

metamorphosis
6 change **8** changing, mutation
9 evolution, sea change **10** changeover
13 transmutation

Metamorphosis author
5 Kafka (Franz)

_____ me tangere
4 noli

metaphor
5 trope **6** simile, symbol **7** analogy
8 allegory **10** comparison, similitude

metaphorical compound
7 kenning

metaphysical
8 bodiless, numinous **9** unearthly, unfleshly **10** immaterial, suprahuman
12 supermundane, supramundane, supranatural, transcendent
13 preternatural
poet: 5 Donne (John) **6** Cowley (Abraham) **7** Crashaw (Richard), Herbert (George), Marvell (Andrew), Vaughan (Henry) **9** Cleveland (John)

mete
4 deal, dole, give **5** allot, bound **6** border, parcel, ration **7** portion **8** allocate, boundary, disburse, dispense **9** apportion
10 distribute

meteor
8 fireball **12** shooting star
exploding: 6 bolide
shower: 5 Lyrid **6** Leonid, Taurid
7 Aquarid, Geminid, Orionid, Perseid
10 Quadrantid

meteorite
8 aerolite **10** siderolite

meter
4 beat, scan **6** rhythm **7** cadence, measure, pattern

metheglin
4 mead **8** beverage
ingredient: 5 honey

method
3 way **4** mode, modi (plural), plan

5 means, modus, order, style 6 course, design, manner, schema, scheme, system 7 fashion, formula, pattern, process, routine, wrinkle 8 practice 9 procedure, technique 11 orderliness 13 modus operandi
careful: 8 strategy
of employing troops: 6 tactic 7 tactics
of procedure: 4 game

methodical
5 exact 7 careful, logical, orderly, precise, regular 9 efficient, organized 10 deliberate, scrupulous, systematic, systemized 12 systematized

Methuselah
father: 5 Enoch
grandson: 4 Noah
son: 6 Lamech

meticulous
5 exact, fussy, picky 6 strict 7 careful, finicky, precise 8 detailed, thorough 10 fastidious, nitpicking, pernickety, scrupulous 11 microscopic, painstaking, persnickety, punctilious 13 conscientious

métier
4 work 5 craft, field, forte, trade 7 calling, pursuit 8 business, strength, vocation 9 specialty 10 employment, occupation, profession

metrical foot
4 iamb 5 ionic, paeon 6 cretic, dactyl, iambic, iambus 7 anapest, pyrrhic, pyrrhus, spondee, triseme, trochee 8 bacchius, choriamb, dactylic, spondaic, tribrach, trochaic 9 anapestic 10 tribrachic

metric unit
area: 3 are 7 hectare
capacity: 5 liter, litre 9 decaliter, deciliter, kiloliter 10 centiliter, hectoliter, milliliter
length: 5 meter 9 decameter, decimeter, dekameter, kilometer 10 centimeter, hectometer, millimeter
mass and weight: 4 gram 7 quintal 8 decagram, decigram, dekagram, kilogram 9 centigram, hectogram, metric ton, milligram

metro
4 tube 6 subway 11 underground

metropolis
4 city 7 capital

metropolitan
5 urban 6 urbane 7 primate 9 municipal 10 archbishop

mettle
4 fire, grit, guts 5 heart, moxie, nerve,

pluck, spunk, steel, valor, vigor 6 daring, spirit, starch, temper 7 cojones, courage, resolve, stamina 8 backbone, boldness, tenacity, vitality 9 fortitude 10 resolution

mettlesome
4 bold, game 5 brave, fiery, gutsy 6 plucky, spunky 7 staunch, valiant 8 intrepid, resolute, spirited, vigorous 9 tenacious 10 courageous, determined

mew
3 hem, pen 4 cage, coop, gull 5 alley, fence 6 corral, immure, shut in, stable 7 enclose 8 hideaway

mewl
4 moan, pule 5 whine 6 snivel 7 whimper

Mexican
crop: 5 sisal
estate: 8 hacienda
food: 4 masa, taco 5 chili, salsa 6 tamale 7 burrito, panocha, penuche, tostada 8 frijoles, tortilla 9 enchilada, guacamole 10 quesadilla 11 chimichanga
house: 5 jacal
liquor: 7 tequila

Mexico
ancient city: 12 Tenochtitlán
ancient culture: 4 Maya 5 Aztec, Mayan, Olmec 6 Toltec
bay: 8 Campeche
capital: 10 Mexico City
city: 4 León 6 Juárez, Mérida, Oaxaca, Puebla 7 Nogales, Tijuana 8 Acapulco, Mexicali, Saltillo 9 Chihuahua, Matamoros, Monterrey 10 Cuernavaca 11 Guadalajara 12 Ciudad Juárez
conqueror: 6 Cortés (Hernán, Hernando)
discoverer: 7 Córdoba (Fernández de)
emperor: 10 Maximilian
gulf: 10 California
island: 7 Cozumel
island group: 13 Revillagigedo
lake: 7 Chapala, Cuitzeo, Texcoco 9 Pátzcuaro
language: 7 Spanish
leader: 4 Díaz (Porfirio) 6 Juárez (Benito) 8 Carranza (Venustiano)
monetary unit: 4 peso
mountain, range: 8 Malinche 11 Sierra Madre
neighbor: 6 Belize 9 Guatemala
peninsula: 4 Baja 7 Yucatán
port: 7 Tampico 8 Ensenada, Mazatlán, Veracruz
resort:Cancún 8 Acapulco
revolutionist: 5 Villa (Pancho) 7 Hidalgo (Padre Miguel), Zapata (Emiliano)
river: 4 Mayo 5 Bravo, Yaquí 6 Balsas, Grande, Pánuco 7 Conchos 8 Grijalva,

Río Bravo, Santiago **9** Rio Grande
10 Usumacinta
ruined city: 5 Uxmal **7** Mayapán
8 Palenque **11** Chichén Itzá
sea: 9 Caribbean
volcano: 6 Colima **9** Paricutín
11 Ixtacihuatl **12** Citlaltépetl, Ixtaccíhuatl,
Popocatépetl

mezzanine
5 story **7** balcony **8** entresol

mezzo
4 half **6** singer **7** soprano

mezzo-soprano
American: 5 Elias (Rosalind), Horne
(Marilyn), Jones (Sissieretta) **6** Bumbry
(Grace), Graves (Denyce) **7** Stevens
(Risë), Verrett (Shirley) **8** Troyanos
(Tatiana), von Stade (Frederica)
Austrian: 6 Ludwig (Christa)
English: 5 Baker (Janet)
Italian: 7 Bartoli (Cecilia) **8** Cossotto
(Fiorenza)

Miami
bowl: 6 Orange
chief: 12 Little Turtle
county: 4 Dade
stadium: 9 Joe Robbie
team: 4 Heat **7** Marlins **8** Dolphins,
Panthers

miasma
3 fog **4** haze, mist, murk, smog **5** brume,
vapor **9** effluvium

mica
7 biotite **8** silicate **9** isinglass, muscovite

Michelangelo Buonarotti
painting: 10 Holy Family (The) **12** Last
Judgment (The)
statue: 5 David, Moses, Pietà **7** Bacchus

Michener novel
5 Space, Texas **6** Hawaii, Poland, Source
(The) **8** Caravans, Covenant (The),
Drifters (The), Sayonara **10** Centennial,
Chesapeake **13** Fires of Spring (The)
15 Bridges at Toko-Ri (The)

Michigan
capital: 7 Lansing
city: 5 Flint **7** Detroit, Lansing, Pontiac
8 Ann Arbor, Dearborn **9** Kalamazoo
11 Grand Rapids **13** Sault Ste. Marie
16 Sault Sainte Marie
college, university: 6 Calvin
9 Kalamazoo **10** Wayne State
lake: 4 Erie **5** Huron **8** Michigan,
Superior

nickname: 9 Wolverine (State) **10** Great
Lakes (State)
state bird: 5 robin
state flower: 12 apple blossom
state tree: 9 white pine

mickey
5 flask, split

microbe
3 bug **4** germ **5** virus **8** bacillus, pathogen
9 bacterium **13** microorganism

microfilm sheet
5 fiche

Micronesia
capital: 7 Palikir
island, island group: 3 Yap **5** Chuuk
6 Kosrae **7** Pohnpei **8** Caroline
language: 7 English

microorganism
4 germ **5** virus **6** aerobe **7** bacilli (plural),
microbe, protist **8** bacillus, bacteria
(plural), pathogen, protozoa (plural)
9 bacterium, protozoan, protozoon

microphone
3 bug **4** mike
shield: 4 gobo

microscope
9 magnifier
inventor: 11 Leeuwenhoek (Antoni van)
part: 5 stage **6** mirror **8** eyepiece
9 objective

microscopic
4 tiny **5** small **6** minute

Mid-Atlantic state
7 New York **8** Delaware, Maryland, Virginia
9 New Jersey **12** Pennsylvania, West
Virginia

midday
4 noon, sext **8** high noon, noontide,
noontime

middle
4 core, mean **5** mesne, waist **6** center,
medial, median **7** average, central, halfway
8 interior **10** centermost **11** equidistant,
intervening **12** intermediary, intermediate

Middle American country
4 Cuba **5** Haiti **6** Belize, Mexico, Panama
7 Bahamas, Grenada, Jamaica
8 Barbados, Dominica, Honduras **9** Costa
Rica, Guatemala, Nicaragua **10** El
Salvador

middlebrow
7 Babbitt

middle class
11 bourgeoisie

middle-class
9 bourgeois

middle ear
bone: 5 incus 6 stapes 7 malleus
membrane: 7 eardrum 8 tympanum

Middle Eastern country
4 Iran, Iraq, Oman 5 Egypt, Qatar, Sudan, Syria, Yemen 6 Cyprus, Israel, Jordan, Kuwait, Turkey 7 Bahrain, Lebanon 11 Saudi Arabia

Middle Kingdom
5 China

middleman
5 agent 6 broker 8 mediator 9 go-between 11 intercessor 12 intermediary, intermediate

Middlemarch author
5 Eliot (George), Evans (Mary Ann)

middle-of-the-road
7 neutral 8 moderate 9 impartial 11 nonpartisan

middling
4 fair, okay, so-so 5 fairly, medium, rather 7 average, fairish, typical 8 adequate, mediocre, moderate, ordinary, passable 9 tolerable 10 moderately, second-rate 11 indifferent 12 intermediate, run-of-the-mill

midge
3 fly 6 punkie 7 no-see-um 8 dipteran 10 chironomid
larva: 9 bloodworm

midget
4 runt 5 dwarf, pygmy 6 bantam, peewee 7 manikin 8 Tom Thumb 10 homunculus 11 hop-o'-my-thumb, Lilliputian

Midian
father: 7 Abraham
mother: 7 Keturah

midpoint
3 par 4 mean, norm 6 center, median, middle 7 average, centrum, halfway 8 bull's-eye, standard

midwife
6 granny, Lucina 10 accoucheur

mien
3 air, set 4 look 6 aspect, manner 7 address, bearing 8 carriage, demeanor, presence 9 mannerism 10 appearance, deportment, expression 11 comportment

miff
3 fit, irk, vex 4 beef, flap, spat 5 annoy, pique, run-in, upset 6 bother, fracas, nettle, offend, put out 7 dispute, provoke, quarrel, rhubarb 8 irritate, squabble 10 conniption, falling-out 11 altercation

might
3 may 4 sway 5 brawn, clout, force, means, power 6 energy, muscle 7 ability, command, control, mastery, potency 8 capacity, strength 9 authority, resources 12 forcefulness

mighty
4 huge, very 5 grand, great 6 heroic, potent, strong 7 eminent, immense, massive, titanic 8 enormous, forceful, gigantic, imposing, powerful, puissant 10 impressive, monumental, prodigious, stupendous, tremendous 11 illustrious 13 extraordinary

Mignon composer
6 Thomas (Ambroise)

mignonette
4 herb 5 sauce 6 annual 6 reseda

migrant
5 exile, mover, nomad 7 drifter, nomadic, refugee 8 traveler, wanderer 9 itinerant, transient 10 expatriate

migrate
4 move, trek 5 drift, range, shift 6 wander 8 transfer

migration
6 exodus 8 diaspora
of professionals: 10 brain drain

migratory
5 nomad 6 errant, mobile, moving, roving 7 nomadic, ranging 9 wandering

Mikado, The
composer: 8 Sullivan (Arthur)
librettist: 7 Gilbert (W. S.)

milady
6 madame 10 noblewoman 11 gentlewoman

Milan
family: 6 Sforza 8 Visconti
opera house: 7 La Scala

Milcah
brother: 3 Lot
father: 5 Haran 10 Zelophehad
husband: 5 Nahor

son: 7 Bethuel

mild
4 calm, easy, meek, soft, tame 5 balmy, bland, faint, tepid 6 benign, docile, gentle, placid, serene, smooth, tender 7 amiable, clement, equable, insipid, lenient, patient, subdued 8 moderate, obliging 9 benignant, temperate 10 forbearing, submissive

mildew
4 mold, rust 6 fungus, growth

_____ mile
7 statute 8 nautical

mileage recorder
8 odometer

milestone
5 event 6 marker 8 landmark, occasion

milieu
5 scene 6 medium, sphere 7 ambient, climate, setting 8 ambience 10 atmosphere, background 11 environment, mise-en-scène 12 surroundings

militant
7 fighter, martial, warlike, warrior 8 activist, fighting 9 assertive, bellicose, combatant, combative, truculent 10 aggressive, pugnacious 11 belligerent, contentious, quarrelsome 12 gladiatorial

military
5 troop 6 forces, troops 7 martial, warlike 8 soldiery 9 soldierly 10 servicemen 11 armed forces, soldierlike
alliance: 4 NATO
base: 4 camp, fort, post 5 depot, field 6 billet 8 barracks, garrison, quarters 10 encampment
officer: 5 major 7 captain, colonel, general 9 brigadier 10 lieutenant
prisoner: 3 POW
school: 3 OCS, OTS 4 ROTC, USMA 9 Annapolis, West Point
sector: 10 combat zone, front lines 11 battlefront
store: 10 commissary
storehouse: 5 depot 6 armory 7 arsenal
supplies: 8 matériel, ordnance
unit: 5 corps, squad, troop 7 company, platoon 8 division, regiment 9 battalion 11 battle group
vehicle: 4 jeep, tank 6 Abrams, Humvee 7 Bradley 9 Blackhawk, half-track

militate
4 tell 5 count, weigh 6 matter 11 carry weight

militia
7 reserve

milk
4 pump, rook, suck 5 drain, educe, empty, evoke, exact, mulct, nurse, wring 6 elicit, extort, fleece 7 exhaust, exploit, extract
coagulated: 4 curd
combining form: 4 lact 5 lacti, lacto
curdled: 7 clabber
fermented: 5 kefir 6 kumiss, yogurt 7 koumiss, yoghurt
liquid part: 4 whey
store: 5 dairy
sugar: 7 lactose

milk shake
6 frappe 7 frosted

milky
4 fair, meek, mild, pale, tame 5 white 6 chalky, cloudy, gentle 7 lacteal, whitish 8 timorous

mill
5 grind, plant, shape, works 7 factory, machine 9 circulate, pulverize 11 manufactory

millenary
8 thousand

Miller, Arthur
film: 7 Misfits (The)
play: 5 Price (The) 9 All My Sons 8 Crucible (The) 12 After the Fall 16 Death of a Salesman 17 View from the Bridge (A)
salesman: 5 Loman (Willy)

milliner
6 hatter

million
combining form: 3 meg 4 mega

millionth
combining form: 4 micr 5 micro

Mill on the Floss author
5 Eliot (George), Evans (Mary Ann)

millstone
4 duty, load, onus 6 burden, charge, weight 9 albatross 10 affliction, deadweight

Milne bear
4 Pooh

milord
8 nobleman 9 gentleman, patrician 10 aristocrat 12 silk stocking

Milquetoast, Caspar
creator: 7 Webster (Harold Tucker)

(see also **milksop**)

Miltiades' victory
8 Marathon

Milton work
5 Comus 7 Lycidas 8 L'Allegro
12 Areopagitica, Paradise Lost

mime
3 act 5 actor 6 act out 7 Marceau
(Marcel) 9 performer, represent
11 impersonate 12 impersonator

mimic
3 act, ape 4 copy, mock, play 5 actor,
enact 6 mummer, parody, parrot, player
7 copycat, imitate 8 resemble, simulate,
travesty 9 burlesque, pantomime 11 impersonate 12 impersonator

mimicry
4 echo 6 parody 8 travesty 9 imitation,
parroting 10 caricature 13 impersonation

minatory
4 dire, grim 7 baleful, baneful, direful,
hostile, malefic, ominous 8 menacing,
sinister 9 ill-boding 10 forbidding,
foreboding, maleficent 11 frightening,
threatening 12 intimidating

mince
4 chop, dice, hash 5 cut up, strut
6 prance, sashay, soften 8 moderate,
restrain, tone down 9 euphemize

mincing
5 fussy 6 dainty, la-di-da, too-too 7 finical,
finicky, stilted 8 affected, delicate
10 fastidious, pernickety 11 persnickety

mind
3 wit 4 mood, obey, soul, tend, will, wits
5 brain, fancy, watch, weigh 6 attend,
belief, beware, brains, follow, memory,
notice, psyche, reason, senses, spirit
7 care for, discern, dislike, feeling, observe,
opinion, oversee, purpose 8 consider,
remember 9 intellect, intention, mentality,
sentiment, supervise 10 brainpower, gray
matter 11 disposition, temperament
12 intelligence 13 consciousness

mindful
5 alert, awake, aware 7 knowing
8 sensible, vigilant 9 attentive, cognizant,
conscious, observant 10 conversant
13 conscientious

mindless
4 rash 5 silly 6 simple, stupid 7 asinine,
foolish, unaware, vacuous 9 nitwitted,

oblivious 10 irrational, unthinking
13 unintelligent

mine
3 dig, pit, sap 4 fund, lode, vein, well
5 delve, drill, hoard, stock, store 6 burrow,
quarry, spring 7 bonanza, deposit, extract
8 eldorado, excavate, Golconda
10 excavation, wellspring 13 treasure trove
coal: 8 colliery
entrance: 4 adit

miner
6 pitman 7 collier

mineral
5 beryl, topaz, trona 6 augite, barite,
garnet, iolite, pinite, rutile, sphene, spinel,
sulfur, zircon 7 apatite, azurite, bornite,
calcite, citrine, coesite, cyanite, jadeite,
kernite, kunzite, olivine, zeolite 8 boracite,
cinnabar, dolomite, epsomite, fayalite,
feldspar, fluorite, hematite, lazulite, lazurite,
siderite, sodalite, stibnite, triplite, wellsite
9 aragonite, celestite, cerussite, danburite,
fosterite, kaolinite, lawsonite, magnetite,
malachite, muscovite, phenakite, scapolite,
tridymite, turquoise, wulfenite
10 chalcedony, orthoclase, pyrrhotite,
tourmaline 11 alexandrite, chrysoberyl,
melanterite 12 brazilianite, chalcopyrite,
tincalconite 13 rhodochrosite
flaky: 4 mica
greasy: 4 talc 10 serpentine
hard: 6 spinel 7 diamond 8 corundum
iridescent: 4 opal
nonmetallic: 5 boron 6 gypsum, halite
8 asbestos, graphite
shiny: 4 gold 6 galena, pyrite, silver
soft: 4 talc 6 gypsum 8 graphite
transparent: 6 quartz

mineral water
7 seltzer 8 club soda

Minerva
see **Athena**

mingle
3 mix 4 meld 5 blend, merge 6 commix
7 combine 8 intermix 9 associate,
socialize

mingy
4 mean 5 cheap, tight 6 stingy 7 chintzy,
miserly, scrimpy 8 grudging, ungiving
9 niggardly, penurious 10 pinchpenny
11 closefisted, tightfisted

miniature
3 wee 4 tiny 5 small, teeny, weeny 6 little,
minute, petite, teensy 9 itsy-bitsy, itty-bitty

10 diminutive, small-scale, teeny-weeny
11 Lilliputian 12 illumination

minify
4 trim 6 lessen, shrink 7 abridge, curtail
8 decrease, diminish 10 abbreviate

minim
3 bit, jot 4 atom, iota 5 grain, speck
7 modicum, smidgen 8 particle
music: 8 half note

minimal
5 basic, least, token 6 lowest 7 nominal
8 littlest, smallest 9 slightest

minimize
5 decry 6 reduce 7 run down 8 belittle,
derogate, discount, downplay, play down
9 disparage, soft-pedal, underrate
10 depreciate 13 underestimate

minimum
3 dab, jot 4 iota, whit 5 least, speck
6 lowest, margin 7 smidgen 8 particle,
pittance, smallest

minion
4 idol 5 toady 6 flunky, lackey, vassal,
yes-man 7 darling, devotee, spaniel
8 creature, favorite, follower, parasite,
truckler 9 sycophant, toadeater, underling
10 bootlicker 11 lickspittle, subordinate

minister
4 tend 5 agent, clerk, serve 6 cleric,
curate, divine, parson 8 clerical, preacher,
reverend 9 churchman, clergyman
10 ambassador 12 ecclesiastic
of state: 10 chancellor
plenipotentiary: 5 envoy 6 consul
8 diplomat, emissary

ministry
5 agent, organ 6 agency, clergy, medium
7 cabinet 10 department, instrument
11 bureaucracy

Minnehaha's husband
8 Hiawatha

Minnesota
capital: 6 St. Paul
city: 5 Edina 6 Duluth 9 Rochester
11 Minneapolis
college, university: 8 Carleton 9 Saint
Olaf 10 Macalester
nickname: 6 Gopher (State) 9 North Star
(State)
park: 9 Voyageurs
river: 7 St. Croix 9 Minnesota
11 Mississippi
state bird: 4 loon (common)
state flower: 12 lady's slipper

state tree: 7 red pine

minor
5 lower, petty, small, youth 6 casual,
lesser, little, paltry, slight 7 trivial 8 inferior,
mediocre, piddling, small-fry, trifling,
underage 9 dependent, secondary, small-
beer, small-time 10 bush-league, second-
rate, shoestring 11 indifferent, unimportant
13 insignificant

minority
5 youth 6 nonage 7 infancy 9 childhood
10 immaturity

minor-league
5 small 6 lesser 9 secondary, small-time
11 unimportant

Minos
daughter: 7 Ariadne, Phaedra
father: 4 Zeus 7 Jupiter
kingdom: 5 Crete
monster: 8 Minotaur
mother: 6 Europa
son: 9 Androgeos
wife: 8 Pasiphaë

Minotaur
father: 4 bull
home: 9 labyrinth
mother: 8 Pasiphaë
slayer: 7 Theseus

minstrel
4 bard, wait 6 harper, singer 7 gleeman
8 jongleur 9 balladist 10 troubadour
end man: 5 Bones (Mr.), Tambo (Mr.)
instrument: 4 lute, lyre 5 rebec, shawm,
tabor 8 crumhorn, psaltery 9 krummhorn
10 tambourine

mint
3 pot 4 cast, coin, heap, pile, sage 5 basil,
bugle, forge, issue, stamp, trove 6 boodle,
bundle, create, intact, packet, savory,
strike, unused 7 fortune, like-new, menthol,
perfect, produce 8 brand-new, lavender,
marjoram, original 9 blue curls,
bugleweed, undamaged

Minuit's purchase
9 Manhattan

minus
4 flaw, lack, less, sans 6 absent, defect
7 lacking, missing, wanting, without
8 drawback, negative, subtract
10 deficiency

minuscule
4 tiny 5 small 6 letter, little, minute
7 trivial 9 lowercase, miniature

10 negligible, small-scale 11 meaningless, microscopic 13 imperceptible, inappreciable, insignificant

minute
3 wee 4 jiff, memo, note, tiny 5 draft, flash, jiffy, small, teeny, weeny 6 little, moment, record, teensy 7 careful, instant, precise, trivial 8 detailed, itemized, thorough, trifling 9 itsy-bitsy, itty-bitty, miniature, minuscule 10 diminutive, memorandum, meticulous, scrupulous, teeny-weeny 11 Lilliputian, punctilious 13 infinitesimal

minutes
3 log 6 annals, record 7 summary 10 transcript 11 proceedings

minutiae
6 trivia 7 details 10 fine points, triviality 11 particulars

minx
4 bawd, moll, slut, tart 5 bimbo, tramp, wench, whore 6 floozy, harlot, hooker 7 hustler, trollop 8 strumpet 10 prostitute

miracle
4 boon, feat 6 marvel, wonder 7 godsend, portent, prodigy, stunner, windfall 9 sensation 10 phenomenon

miraculous
7 amazing 8 wondrous 9 marvelous, unearthly, wonderful 10 astounding, prodigious, superhuman 11 astonishing, spectacular 12 inexplicable, supernatural 13 preternatural

mirage
6 vision, wraith 8 delusion, illusion, phantasm 11 fata morgana, ignis fatuus 13 hallucination

Miranda
father: 8 Prospero
lover: 9 Ferdinand

mire
3 bog, fen, mud 4 muck, ooze, sink, trap 5 delay, marsh, slush, swamp 6 detain, enmesh, entrap, hang up, morass, slough, tangle 7 bog down, embroil, ensnare, involve, set back 8 entangle 9 imbroglio, implicate, quicksand

Miriam's brother
5 Aaron, Moses

mirror
5 glass 6 embody, typify 7 reflect 8 speculum 9 exemplify, personify, reflector, represent 10 illustrate 11 cheval glass 12 looking glass

signaling: 10 heliograph

mirth
3 fun, joy 4 glee 5 cheer 6 gaiety, levity 7 jollity 8 gladness, hilarity, revelry 9 festivity, frivolity, happiness, jocundity, joviality, merriment 10 jocularity 11 merrymaking 12 cheerfulness

mirthful
3 gay 5 jolly, merry, riant 6 jocund, jovial 7 festive 9 exuberant, hilarious 12 lighthearted

miry
4 oozy 5 boggy, mucky, muddy 6 marshy, slushy, swampy

misadventure
4 slip 5 boner, error, lapse 6 howler, mishap 7 blunder, faux pas 8 accident, calamity, casualty, disaster 9 cataclysm 10 misfortune 11 catastrophe

misanthrope
5 cynic, grump, loner 6 grinch 7 killjoy, recluse, scoffer 10 curmudgeon

misanthropic
7 cynical 10 antisocial

misappropriate
5 filch, steal 6 pilfer 7 purloin 8 embezzle, peculate 9 defalcate

misbegotten
7 bastard, illicit, natural 8 baseborn, deformed, spurious 10 fatherless, unfathered 12 contemptible, disreputable, ill-conceived, illegitimate

misbehave
5 act up, cut up, lapse, rebel, stray 6 act out, offend 7 carry on, disobey 8 trespass 10 roughhouse, transgress

misbehavior
7 misdeed 8 rudeness 9 high jinks 10 misconduct, wrongdoing 11 de-linquency, dereliction, naughtiness, transgression

miscalculate
3 err 8 miscount, misgauge

miscarry
4 fail, flop 5 abort 6 fizzle 7 go wrong

miscellaneous
3 odd 5 mixed 6 motley, sundry, varied 7 diverse 8 assorted 9 different, disparate, scrambled 13 heterogeneous

miscellany
3 ana 4 hash, olio, stew 5 salad 6 jumble,

medley, motley, muddle **7** farrago, mélange, mixture, omnibus **8** mixed bag, pastiche **9** anthology, congeries, pasticcio, patchwork, potpourri **10** assortment, hodgepodge, hotchpotch, salmagundi **11** aggregation, gallimaufry, odds and ends, olla podrida, smorgasbord

mischance

6 mishap **7** bad luck, tragedy **8** accident, casualty **9** adversity **10** misfortune **11** contretemps

mischief

3 ill **4** evil, harm **5** prank **6** damage, strife **7** devilry, roguery, trouble, waggery **8** deviltry, sabotage **9** devilment, diablerie, vandalism **10** wrongdoing **11** naughtiness, shenanigans **12** monkeyshines

mischief-maker

3 imp **4** puck **5** devil, knave, rogue, scamp **6** rascal **7** villain **8** agitator, scalawag **9** prankster, trickster **11** rapscallion **12** rabble-rouser

mischievous

3 sly **4** arch, foxy **5** antic, saucy **6** artful, bratty, impish, tricky, vexing **7** harmful, irksome, larkish, naughty, playful, puckish, roguish, tricksy, waggish **8** annoying, damaging, perverse, prankish, rascally, sportive **9** injurious, malicious **10** bothersome, frolicsome, ill-behaved

misconception

5 error **7** fallacy, mistake **8** delusion, illusion

misconduct

8 adultery **10** wrongdoing **11** dereliction, impropriety, malfeasance, malpractice, misbehavior, transgression **12** malversation

miscreant

4 heel **5** felon, knave, rogue **6** outlaw, rascal, sinner, wretch **7** corrupt, culprit, heretic, hoodlum, infidel, lowlife, vicious, villain **8** apostate, criminal, depraved, infamous, perverse **9** heretical, nefarious, scoundrel, unhealthy, wrongdoer **10** blackguard, degenerate, delinquent, unbeliever, villainous

miscue

4 goof, miss, slip, trip **5** error, fluff, lapse **6** slipup **7** blooper, blunder, mistake

misdeed

3 sin **5** crime, wrong **6** breach **7** offense **9** violation **10** infraction **13** transgression

misdoubt

4 fear **5** dread **7** suspect

mise-en-scène

3 set **4** site **6** locale, medium, milieu **7** ambient, climate, context, scenery, setting **8** ambience, stage set **10** atmosphere, background **11** environment **12** stage setting, surroundings

miser

5 piker **7** hoarder, niggard, scrooge **8** tightwad **9** skinflint **10** cheapskate, pinchpenny

miserable

6 gloomy, meager, meagre, paltry, rueful, sordid, woeful **7** doleful, forlorn, piteous, pitiful, squalid **8** desolate, dolorous, downcast, hopeless, shameful, tortured, wretched **9** afflicted, destitute, sorrowful, worthless **10** despairing, despondent, melancholy **12** contemptible

Miserables, Les

author: **4** Hugo (Victor)
character: **6** Javert (Inspector) **7** Cosette, Fantine, Valjean (Jean)

miserly

4 mean **5** close, tight **6** greedy, stingy **7** scrimpy **8** covetous, grasping **9** niggardly, penurious, scrimping **10** avaricious **11** closefisted, tightfisted **12** cheeseparing, parsimonious **13** penny-pinching

misery

3 woe **5** agony, dolor, grief **6** sorrow **7** anguish, squalor **8** calamity, distress **9** adversity, dejection, suffering **10** affliction, depression, desolation **11** despondency **12** wretchedness

misfit

6 oddity, weirdo, zombie **7** oddball **8** maverick **9** eccentric, screwball

misfortune

3 woe **4** blow, harm, loss **5** cross, trial **7** reverse, setback, tragedy, trouble **8** accident, calamity, casualty, disaster, hardship **9** adversity, cataclysm **10** affliction, visitation **11** catastrophe, contretemps, tribulation

misgiving

4 fear **5** doubt, dread, qualm **6** unease **7** anxiety **8** distrust **9** suspicion **10** foreboding **11** premonition, trepidation **12** apprehension, presentiment

misguided
5 wrong **9** erroneous **10** ill-advised
11 injudicious **12** short-sighted

mishandle
4 flub **5** abuse, botch **6** bungle, fumble,
mess up **7** rough up **8** maltreat **10** knock
about, slap around

mishap
7 bad luck, tragedy **8** accident, casualty
9 adversity **11** contretemps

mishmash
6 jumble, litter, medley, muddle **7** clutter,
mélange, mixture, rummage **8** pastiche,
scramble **9** pasticcio, patchwork, potpourri
10 hodgepodge, hotchpotch

misidentify
5 mix up **7** confuse **8** confound

misinterpret
7 confuse, misread

mislay
4 lose

mislead
4 dupe, fool, gull, lure **5** bluff, cheat
6 betray, delude, entice, seduce, take in
8 beguile, deceive **8** hoodwink, inveigle
11 double-cross

misleading
5 false, wrong **8** delusive, delusory,
specious **9** deceitful, deceptive
10 fallacious, inaccurate **11** casuistical,
sophistical

mismatch
3 jar **5** clash **6** jangle **7** discord **8** conflict

misplace
4 lose

misprint
4 typo

misprision
5 scorn **7** despite, disdain, neglect
8 contempt, sedition **9** contumely,
disregard **10** misconduct, negligence
11 concealment, dereliction, impropriety,
malpractice

misrepresent
4 warp **5** twist **6** garble **7** distort, falsify,
varnish **8** disguise **9** embellish, embroider
10 camouflage **11** counterfeit

misrepresentation
3 fib, lie **4** tale **5** story **6** canard **7** falsity,
untruth **9** falsehood **10** distortion

miss
3 err, gal **4** fail, girl, lass, maid, omit, skip
5 avoid **6** damsel, escape, forget, ignore,
lassie, maiden **7** failure, misfire, neglect
8 discount, leave out, overlook **9** disregard

Missa Solemnis composer
9 Beethoven (Ludwig van)

misshape
4 warp **6** deform **7** contort, distort, torture
9 disfigure

missile
4 bolt, dart **5** arrow, shell, spear **6** bullet,
rocket **10** cannonball, projectile
underwater: 7 torpedo
(see also **guided missile**)

missing
4 AWOL **6** absent

mission
3 aim, job **4** duty, goal, task **5** quest
6 charge, errand, object **7** calling,
embassy, purpose **8** legation, lifework,
ministry, vocation **9** objective
10 assignment

missionary
7 apostle **8** emissary **10** evangelist,
revivalist **12** propagandist, proselytizer

Mississippi
capital: 7 Jackson
city: 6 Biloxi **8** Gulfport **10** Greenville
college, university: 12 Jackson State
8 Millsaps
nickname: 8 Magnolia (State)
river: 5 Pearl **11** Mississippi
state bird: 11 mockingbird
state flower: 8 magnolia
state tree: 8 magnolia

missive
4 memo, note **6** letter, report **7** epistle,
message **8** dispatch

Miss Julie author
10 Strindberg (August)

Miss Lonelyhearts author
4 West (Nathanael)

Missouri
capital: 13 Jefferson City
city: 7 St. Louis **10** Kansas City
11 Springfield **12** Independence
college, university: 10 Washington
lake: 15 Lake of the Ozarks
nickname: 8 Show Me (State)
river: 8 Missouri **11** Mississippi
state bird: 8 bluebird

state flower: 8 hawthorn
state tree: 7 dogwood

misstate
4 warp 5 color, twist 6 garble 7 distort, falsify

misstatement
3 fib, lie 4 tale 7 falsity, untruth
9 falsehood 13 prevarication

misstep
4 flub, goof, slip 5 boner, error, fluff, gaffe, lapse 6 slipup 7 blooper, blunder, faux pas

mist
3 dim, fog 4 blur, film, haze, murk 5 befog, brume, cloud 7 becloud, obscure

mistake
4 flub, slip 5 boner, error, fluff, folly, gaffe, lapse 6 boo-boo, bungle, howler, slipup
7 blooper, blunder, confuse, faux pas, take for 8 confound 10 inaccuracy

mistaken
5 false, wrong 6 all wet, faulty, flawed, untrue 7 invalid 8 specious 9 defective, incorrect, misguided, unfounded
10 fallacious, fraudulent, inaccurate
11 misinformed

mister
3 sir 7 husband
French: 8 monsieur
German: 4 Herr
Italian: 6 signor
Spanish: 5 señor

Mister Roberts author
6 Heggen (Thomas)

mistreat
5 abuse 6 ill-use, molest 7 rough up
9 brutalize, manhandle

mistress
4 doxy, moll 5 lover, woman 7 hetaira
8 dulcinea, ladylove, paramour
9 concubine, courtesan, inamorata, kept woman 10 chatelaine, girl friend
of Charles II: 4 Gwyn (Nell) 8 Villiers (Barbara)
of Edward III: 7 Perrers (Alice)
of Henry II (England): 8 Clifford (Rosamund)
of Henry II (France): 9 de Poiters (Diane)
of Louis XV: 9 Pompadour (Madame de)

mistrust
5 doubt 7 concern, dispute, dubiety, surmise, suspect 8 wariness 9 apprehend, misgiving, suspicion 10 foreboding,

skepticism 11 incertitude, uncertainty
12 apprehension

mistrustful
4 wary 5 leery 6 uneasy 7 dubious, jealous 8 doubting 9 skeptical
10 disquieted, suspicious 12 apprehensive

misty
3 dim 4 hazy 5 foggy, vague 6 cloudy, vapory 7 blurred, obscure, tearful, unclear
8 confused, nebulous, vaporous
10 indistinct

misunderstanding
4 rift, spat, tiff 5 mix-up 6 breach
7 dispute, quarrel, rupture 8 squabble
10 falling-out 12 disagreement

misuse
5 waste
of a word: 8 malaprop 11 malapropism

mite
3 bit, jot 4 atom, iota 5 grain, minim, ounce, speck 6 acarid, tittle 7 chigger, modicum, smidgen 8 molecule, particle
family: 8 oribatid

miter
5 crown, joint 9 headdress

mitigate
4 ease 5 abate, allay, relax, slake
6 lessen, soften, subdue, temper
7 assuage, lighten, mollify, relieve
8 palliate, moderate, tone down 9 alleviate, extenuate, meliorate

mitigation
4 ease 6 relief 8 easement

mitosis
12 cell division, karyokinesis
stage: 8 anaphase, prophase
9 metaphase, telophase

mix
4 fuse, link, lump, meld, stir 5 blend, merge, unite 6 fusion, jumble, mingle, tangle, work in 7 amalgam, combine, concoct, confuse, conjoin 8 coalesce, compound, confound 9 associate, commingle, interfuse 10 amalgamate, crossbreed 11 intermingle 12 amalgamation

mixed
6 hybrid, impure, motley, sundry, varied
7 diluted, diverse, mongrel 8 assorted, compound 9 composite, interbred, irregular 12 multifarious
13 heterogeneous, miscellaneous

mixed bag
4 olio **5** salad **6** jumble, medley
7 mélange **8** mishmash, pastiche
9 potpourri **10** assortment, hodgepodge,
miscellany **11** gallimaufry

mixed-up
5 fazed **7** jumbled **8** confused **9** flustered,
perplexed **10** bewildered, disjointed,
distracted, incoherent, nonplussed
12 disconcerted

mixologist
6 barman **7** tapster **9** barkeeper,
bartender

mixture
4 brew, hash, olio, stew **5** alloy, blend
6 fusion, hybrid, jumble, medley
7 amalgam, farrago, mélange
8 compound, mishmash, solution
9 composite, potpourri **10** concoction,
confection, miscellany, salmagundi
11 combination **12** amalgamation

mix up
5 addle **6** fuddle, jumble, muddle
7 confuse, fluster, mistake **8** befuddle,
bewilder, confound **10** disarrange,
discompose **11** disorganize, misidentify

mix-up
4 hash, mess, muss **5** botch, chaos, error,
melee **6** muddle, tangle **7** mistake
8 shambles **9** commotion, confusion

mks unit
3 lux, ohm **4** mole, volt, watt **5** farad,
henry, hertz, joule, lumen, meter, metre,
tesla, weber **6** ampere, kelvin, newton,
pascal, second **7** candela, coulomb,
siemens **8** kilogram

Mnemosyne
6 Memory
daughters: 5 Muses
father: 6 Uranus
lover: 4 Zeus
mother: 4 Gaea

Moabite
city: 3 Kir
god: 7 Chemosh
king: 5 Eglon, Mesha

Moab's father
3 Lot

moan
4 wail, weep **5** gripe, groan, whine
6 bewail, grieve, grouse, lament **7** deplore
8 complain

mob
3 jam **4** clan, gang, herd, pack, push, ring,
riot **5** crowd, crush, horde, mafia, press,
swarm **6** jostle, masses, rabble, throng
8 canaille, riffraff **9** hoi polloi, multitude
11 proletariat

mobile
5 fluid **6** moving **7** migrant, movable,
protean **8** cellular, moveable, unstable,
unsteady, variable **9** adaptable, changeful,
itinerant, mercurial, migratory, unsettled,
versatile **10** ambulatory, capricious,
changeable, inconstant **11** peripatetic

mobile home
6 camper **7** trailer **9** Airstream

mobile-phone area
4 cell

mobilize
5 drive, impel, rally, ready, rouse **6** arouse,
call up, muster, prompt, propel **7** actuate,
animate, marshal **8** activate, assemble,
organize **9** circulate

mobster
4 goon, thug **6** hit man **7** mafioso
8 criminal, gangster **9** godfather, racketeer

Moby Dick
5 whale **10** white whale
author: 8 Melville (Herman)
character: 3 Pip **6** Daggoo, Parsee
7 Ishmael **8** Queequeg, Starbuck,
Tashtego
pursuer: 4 Ahab
ship: 6 Pequod

moccasin
6 loafer **7** slipper **8** larrigan

mock
3 ape **4** defy, fake, gibe, jape, jeer, razz,
twit **5** bogus, chaff, dummy, false, feign,
mimic, phony, quasi, sneer, taunt, tease
6 deride, ersatz, parody, pseudo, send up
7 deceive, feigned, imitate, lampoon,
mislead, ridicule, satirize, so-called,
spurious **9** imitation, simulated **10** artificial
11 counterfeit

mockery
4 sham **5** farce, scorn, sport **6** japery,
parody, satire **7** take-off **8** contempt,
derision, raillery, ridicule, travesty
9 burlesque, imitation **10** caricature
13 laughingstock

mocking
8 derisive, sardonic, scornful **9** sarcastic

mode
3 fad, way 4 chic, rage 5 state, style, vogue 6 custom, manner, method, status, system 7 fashion 9 condition, procedure, situation, technique 10 convention, dernier cri

model
4 copy, type 5 dummy, ideal, shape 6 design, effigy, mirror, mockup, symbol 7 classic, epitome, example, imitate, manikin, maquette, paragon, pattern, perfect, replica, typical 8 ensample, exemplar, flawless, mannikin, nonesuch, paradigm, standard 9 archetype, beau ideal, blueprint, classical, criterion, exemplary, miniature, nonpareil 10 apotheosis, embodiment, prototypal, touchstone 12 paradigmatic, prototypical, reproduction

moderate
3 ebb 4 calm, cool, curb, even, fair, mild, slow, so-so, wane 5 abate, bland, let up, sober 6 gentle, lessen, medium, paltry, reduce, relent, slight, soften, steady, subdue, temper 7 average, chasten, control, cushion, die away, die down, ease off, equable, lighten, limited, neutral, relieve, slacken, subside, trivial 8 centrist, constant, decrease, diminish, discreet, mediocre, middling, mitigate, restrain 9 alleviate, constrain, temperate 10 abstemious, controlled, reasonable, restrained 11 indifferent 12 conservative

moderation
7 control, measure 9 restraint 10 abstinence, constraint, limitation, temperance 13 temperateness

moderator
5 judge 7 arbiter 8 chairman, examiner, governor, mediator 10 peacemaker 11 chairperson

modern
3 new 5 fresh, novel 6 recent 7 current 8 neoteric, up-to-date 10 newfangled, present-day 12 contemporary

modernize
5 renew 6 update 8 renovate 9 refurbish 10 rejuvenate

modest
3 coy, shy 4 meek, prim 5 lowly, plain, timid 6 decent, demure, humble, prissy, proper, seemly, simple 7 bashful, prudish 8 decorous, discreet, moderate, priggish, reserved, reticent, retiring 9 diffident 10 unassuming 11 puritanical, straitlaced,

unassertive, unelaborate 12 self-effacing, unornamented 13 unembellished, unpretentious

Modest Proposal author
5 Swift (Jonathan)

modesty
7 decency, reserve 8 chastity, humility, timidity 9 propriety, reticence 10 diffidence

modicum
3 bit, jot 4 atom, iota, mite, whit 5 grain, minim, ounce, pinch, scrap, speck, trace 7 smidgen, soupçon 8 particle

modify
4 vary 5 adapt, alter, amend, limit, tweak 6 adjust, change, mutate, revise, rework, temper 7 qualify 8 mitigate, moderate, restrain 9 refashion

modish
4 chic 5 smart, swank 6 chichi, trendy, with-it 7 dashing, stylish 11 fashionable

Modred
father: 6 Arthur
mother: 8 Margawse
slayer, victim: 6 Arthur

modulate
4 vary 5 tweak 6 adjust, attune, temper 8 fine-tune, regulate, restrain

modus ____
7 vivendi 8 operandi

modus operandi
5 style 6 custom, manner, method, system 7 process, program, routine 8 approach, practice, strategy 9 procedure, technique

mogul
4 czar, king, lord 5 baron, nabob, ruler 6 bigwig, prince, sachem, tycoon 7 kingpin, magnate 9 plutocrat, potentate

Mohammed
see **Muhammad**

Mohawk chief
5 Brant (Joseph) 8 Hiawatha

Mohican chief
5 Uncas

moiety
3 cut 4 half, part 5 piece 7 element, portion, section, segment 8 division 9 component

moil
3 tug, wet 4 grub, to-do, work 5 churn, dirty, drive, grind, labor, swirl 6 bustle,

clamor, drudge, hubbub, lather, seethe, strain, strive, uproar **7** ferment, travail, trouble, wrangle **8** drudgery **9** agitation, commotion, confusion **10** hurly-burly, turbulence

moist
3 wet **4** damp, dank, dewy **5** humid **6** clammy, steamy, sticky **7** dampish, maudlin, tearful, wettish

moisten
3 wet **6** dampen **8** humidify, saturate

moisture
4 damp **5** vapor **7** wetness **8** humidity **13** precipitation

mojo
3 hex **4** jinx **5** charm, magic, power, spell **6** hoodoo, whammy

molar
5 tooth **7** grinder
neighbor: 6 canine

molasses
7 treacle **10** blackstrap

mold
3 die **4** cast, form, sort, type **5** forge, knead, shape, stamp **6** design, fungus **7** fashion, pattern **8** template **9** construct **11** description

moldable
6 pliant, supple **7** ductile, plastic, pliable **9** adaptable, malleable

molder
3 rot **5** decay, waste **7** crumble **9** break down, decompose **11** deteriorate **12** disintegrate

molding
4 bead, ogee **5** congé, ogive, talon, torus **6** reglet **7** annulet, beading, cavetto, cornice, reeding **8** cincture **9** baseboard
compound: 4 beak, cyma, ogie **10** serpentine
edge: 5 arris
flat: 5 bevel, splay **6** fascia, fillet, listel, regula **7** chamfer
simple curve: 4 roll **5** flute, ovolo, torus **6** scotia **8** astragal

Moldova
capital: 8 Chisinau, Kishinev
former name: 8 Moldavia
language: 8 Romanian
monetary unit: 3 leu
neighbor: 7 Romania, Ukraine
river: 8 Dniester

moldy
5 dated, fusty, musty, passé **6** bygone, old hat **7** ancient, antique, archaic, outworn **8** mildewed, outdated **9** crumbling, moth-eaten **10** antiquated **12** old-fashioned

mole
3 spy **4** pier, quay **5** jetty, nevus **6** burrow, tunnel **9** birthmark **10** breakwater

molecule
3 bit, jot **4** iota **5** minim, speck **7** modicum **8** particle

molest
3 vex **4** bait **5** abuse, annoy, harry, tease **6** badger, bother, harass, heckle, hector, pester, plague **7** disturb, torment, trouble **9** persecute

Moll Flanders author
5 Defoe (Daniel)

mollify
4 calm, ease **5** allay **6** pacify, soften, soothe, temper **7** appease, assuage, lighten, placate, relieve, sweeten **8** mitigate **9** alleviate **10** ameliorate, conciliate, propitiate

mollusk
6 chiton
bivalve: 4 clam **6** cockle, mussel, oyster, teredo **7** geoduck, scallop **8** shipworm
cephalopod: 5 squid **7** octopus **8** argonaut, nautilus **10** cuttlefish
part: 6 mantle, radula, siphon
tooth shell: 9 dentalium
univalve: 4 slug **5** conch, cowry, murex, snail, whelk **6** cowrie, limpet, triton **7** abalone **10** nudibranch, periwinkle

Molly _____
7 Maguire, Pitcher

mollycoddle
3 pet **4** baby **5** humor, spoil **6** cocker, cosset, dandle, pamper **7** cater to, indulge

Moloch's pit
6 Tophet

molt
4 cast, shed, slip **6** change, slough **7** cast off, discard, ecdysis **9** slough off

molted skins
7 exuviae

molten
6 melted **7** glowing **9** liquefied

molten rock
4 lava **5** magma

moment
5 flash, jiffy, point, shake, trice 6 import, minute, second 7 instant 8 juncture, occasion 9 magnitude 10 importance 11 consequence, split second 12 significance

momentary
5 brief, quick 8 fleeting, fugitive 9 ephemeral, fugacious, transient 10 evanescent, short-lived, transitory

momentous
5 grave 7 epochal, fateful, serious, weighty 9 important 10 meaningful 11 significant, substantial 12 considerable 13 consequential

momentousness
6 import, weight 9 magnitude 10 importance 11 consequence, weightiness 12 significance

momentum
5 drive 6 energy, thrust 7 impetus, impulse 10 propulsion

Momo author
4 Ende (Michael)

momus
6 carper, critic, mocker 7 caviler 8 caviller 9 detractor 11 faultfinder

Monaco
commune: 10 Monte Carlo
language: 6 French
monetary unit: 4 euro
neighbor: 6 France
prince: 7 Rainier
princess: 5 Grace

monad
3 one 4 atom, unit 8 zoospore 9 protozoan

Mona Lisa
10 La Gioconda
painter: 7 da Vinci (Leonardo)
8 Leonardo (da Vinci)

monarch
4 czar, king, raja, tsar, tzar 5 queen, rajah, ruler 6 kaiser, prince 7 emperor, empress, majesty 9 butterfly, potentate, sovereign

monarchical
5 regal, royal 6 kingly 8 imperial, kinglike, majestic 9 sovereign

monarch's daughter
8 princess
Portuguese, Spanish: 7 infanta

monarch's son
6 prince
French: 7 dauphin
Portuguese, Spanish: 7 infante

monarchy
4 rule 5 realm, reign 7 kingdom 8 kingship 9 autocracy, monocracy 11 sovereignty

monastery
5 abbey 6 friary, priory 7 convent, nunnery 8 cloister
Buddhist: 8 lamasery
Eastern Orthodox: 5 laura
head: 5 abbot, prior

monastic
4 abbé, monk 7 ascetic, brother 8 isolated, secluded 9 reclusive 10 cloistered 11 sequestered

_____ Mondrian
4 Piet

monetary
6 fiscal 9 financial, pecuniary 10 numismatic

monetary rate
7 millage

monetary unit
see at individual countries

money
4 cash, coin, gelt, kale, loot, pelf, swag 5 bread, chips, dough, funds, lucre, moola, rhino 6 boodle, change, dinero, do-re-mi, mammon, moolah, riches, specie, wampum, wealth 7 cabbage, capital, coinage, lettuce, needful, scratch, stipend 8 bankroll, currency, finances, treasure 9 resources 10 greenbacks 11 filthy lucre, legal tender

moneyed
4 rich 5 flush 6 loaded 7 opulent, wealthy, well-off 8 affluent, well-to-do 10 prosperous, well-heeled

money-grubber
5 miser 7 hoarder, niggard, scrooge 8 tightwad 9 skinflint 10 cheapskate 12 penny-pincher

moneymaking
6 paying 7 gainful 9 lucrative 10 profitable, well-paying, worthwhile 12 advantageous, remunerative

monger
4 hawk, sell, vend 6 broker, dealer,

hawker, peddle, trader, vendor **7** higgler, packman, peddler **8** huckster

Mongol conqueror
9 Tamerlane **10** Kublai Khan **11** Genghis Khan, Tamburlaine

Mongolia
capital: 9 Ulan Bator **11** Ulaanbaatar
conqueror: 6 Ögödei **11** Genghis Khan
desert: 4 Gobi
lake: 6 Baikal
monetary unit: 6 tugrik
mountain range: 5 Altai, Altay **6** Kentai **7** Hentiyn **9** Altai Shan, Altay Shan
neighbor: 5 China **6** Russia
river: 5 Orhun **7** Selenga

mongrel
3 cur **4** mule, mutt **5** cross **6** hybrid **7** bastard, mixture **8** half-bred **9** crossbred, half blood, half-breed **10** crossbreed

moniker
3 tag **4** name **6** handle **8** cognomen, nickname **9** sobriquet **11** appellation, designation

monish
4 warn

monition
6 caveat **7** caution, portent, warning **11** forewarning

monitor
4 test **5** check, watch **6** screen **7** adviser, observe, oversee **8** watchdog **11** keep track of

Monitor
designer: 8 Ericsson (John)
opponent: 8 Virginia **9** Merrimack

monitory
7 warning **8** advisory **10** cautionary

monk
4 abbé **5** friar **7** brother **8** cenobite, monastic **9** anchorite
Buddhist: 4 lama **5** bonze
Hindu: 8 sannyasi
Roman Catholic: 8 Capuchin, Salesian, Trappist **9** Carmelite, Dominican **10** Carthusian, Cistercian, Franciscan **11** Augustinian
room: 4 cell
shaven crown: 7 tonsure
title: 3 Dom, Fra **5** Padre

monkey
3 imp **4** mess **5** gamin **6** meddle, simian,

tamper, urchin **8** busybody **9** interfere, interlope
New World: 4 titi **6** howler, spider, uakari, woolly **7** sapajou, tamarin **8** capuchin, marmoset, squirrel **11** douroucouli
Old World: 5 Diana, drill **6** guenon, langur, rhesus, vervet **7** colobus, hanuman, macaque **8** mandrill, mangabey **9** proboscis **10** Barbary ape

monkeyshine
3 gag **4** dido, jape, lark **5** antic, caper, prank, stunt, trick **6** frolic **10** shenanigan, tomfoolery

monocratic
8 absolute, despotic **9** arbitrary, autarchic, tyrannous **10** autocratic, tyrannical

monogram
8 initials

monograph
5 study **6** thesis **8** tractate, treatise **9** discourse **12** disquisition, dissertation

monopolize
3 hog **5** sew up **6** absorb, corner **7** control, engross **8** dominate, take over

monopoly
5 trust **6** cartel, corner **7** control **9** ownership, syndicate **10** consortium, domination **11** exclusivity

monotone
5 drone

monotonous
4 blah, dull **6** boring, dreary **7** droning, humdrum, one-note, uniform **8** singsong, unvaried **9** unvarying **10** pedestrian, repetitive **11** repetitious

monotony
6 tedium **7** humdrum **8** flatness, sameness **10** uniformity

monsoon
6 deluge **8** downpour **9** rainstorm **10** cloudburst

monster
4 ogre **5** beast, freak, giant, whale **6** mutant, ogress **8** behemoth, bogeyman, colossus, giantess **9** hellhound, leviathan, manticore
biblical: 5 Rehab **8** Behemoth **9** Leviathan
female: 6 Gorgon, Medusa, Scylla
fire-breathing: 6 dragon, Typhon **7** Chimera **8** Chimaera
fowl-dragon: 10 cockatrice
French: 8 Tarasque

horse-fish: 11 hippocampus
hundred-armed: 9 Enceladus
hundred-eyed: 5 Argus
hundred-handed: 8 Briareus
lion-eagle: 7 griffin
serpent-headed: 6 gorgon
study of: 10 teratology
three-bodied: 6 Geryon
three-headed dog: 6 Cerberus
two-headed dog: 6 Orthos
water: 6 kraken
woman-bird: 5 Harpy
woman-lion: 6 Sphinx
woman-serpent: 7 Echidna
(see also **dragon**)

_____ monster
4 Gila

monstrosity
4 mess 5 freak 6 fright, horror 7 eyesore,
outrage, prodigy 8 atrocity, enormity
11 abomination 12 malformation

monstrous
4 huge, vast 5 awful, giant, large
7 glaring, heinous, hellish, hideous,
immense, mammoth, massive, titanic
8 aberrant, abnormal, colossal, deformed,
dreadful, enormous, fiendish, freakish,
gigantic, god-awful, gruesome, horrible,
infamous, shocking, towering 9 atrocious,
egregious, fantastic, frightful, grotesque,
loathsome, malformed, unnatural
10 diabolical, flagitious, gargantuan,
horrendous, impressive, monumental,
outrageous, prodigious, scandalous,
stupendous, tremendous 11 elephantine

montage
6 jumble, medley 7 mélange, mixture
9 composite, patchwork, potpourri
10 assortment, miscellany
12 conglomerate

Montagues' enemies
8 Capulets

Montaigne's forte
5 essay

Montana
capital: 6 Helena
city: 5 Butte 7 Bozeman 8 Billings,
Missoula 10 Great Falls
lake: 8 Flathead
motto: 9 Oro y plata
mountain: 7 Granite (Peak)
nickname: 8 Treasure (State)
park: 7 Glacier
river: 8 Missouri 11 Yellowstone
state bird: 10 meadowlark

state flower: 10 bitterroot
state tree: 13 ponderosa pine

Monteverdi opera
5 Orfeo 7 Arianna

Montezuma
capital: 12 Tenochtitlán
conqueror: 6 Cortés, Cortéz (Hernán,
Hernando)
people: 6 Aztecs
revenge: 8 diarrhea

month
Hindu: 3 Pus 4 Asin, Jeth, Magh
5 Aghan, Chait, Sawan 6 Asargh, Bhadon,
Kartik, Phagun 7 Baisakh
Jewish: 4 Adar, Elul, Iyar 5 Nisan, Sivan,
Tebet 6 Kislev, Shebat, Tammuz, Tishri
7 Heshvan
Muslim: 4 Rabi 5 Rajab, Safar
6 Jumada, Sha'ban 7 Ramadan, Shawwal
8 Muharram 9 Dhu'l-Hijja, Dhu'l-Qa'dah

Montmartre church
10 Sacré Coeur

Montserrat
capital: 8 Plymouth
discoverer: 8 Columbus (Christopher)
location: 10 West Indies
territory of: 7 Britain
volcano: 9 Soufrière

monument
5 cairn, stela, stupa 7 memento, tribute
8 archives, cenotaph, document, memorial
9 footstone, headstone, tombstone
10 gravestone 11 grave marker,
testimonial
prehistoric: 6 dolmen, menhir
8 cromlech, megalith

monumental
4 huge, vast 6 mighty, mortal 7 awesome,
immense, mammoth, massive
8 enormous, gigantic, historic, majestic,
towering 9 monstrous 10 prodigious,
stupendous, tremendous 11 mountainous,
outstanding 12 overwhelming

mooch
3 bat, beg, bum 4 grub, roam, rove
5 amble, cadge, drift, range, slink, sneak,
steal, stray 6 ramble, sponge, wander
7 maunder, meander, saunter 8 freeload,
scrounge 9 panhandle

mooching
7 beggary 9 mendicity 10 mendicancy

mood
3 air 4 aura, feel, tone, whim 5 fancy,
humor 6 spirit, temper, vagary 7 caprice,

emotion, feeling, mind-set **8** ambiance,
ambience **9** character, semblance
10 atmosphere **11** disposition, personality,
temperament

moody

4 glum **5** mopey **6** fickle, gloomy
7 pensive **8** unstable **9** mercurial,
whimsical **10** capricious, changeable,
depressive, inconstant, melancholy
13 temperamental

moola

4 cash, coin, pelf, swag **5** bread, dough,
money **6** dinero, specie, wampum
7 cabbage, scratch **9** long green

moon

4 gape, mope **5** dream **6** dawdle
8 languish **9** satellite
dark area: 4 mare **5** maria (plural)
7 farside
god: 3 Sin **5** Nanna **6** Meztli
goddess: 4 Luna **5** Diana, Tanit
6 Hecate, Hekate, Selena, Selene, Tanith
7 Artemis, Astarte
valley: 4 rill
vehicle: 3 LEM
(see also **satellite**)

Moon and Sixpence author

7 Maugham (W. Somerset)

mooncalf

4 dolt, fool **5** dunce, ninny **7** jackass,
tomfool **9** simpleton

Moon River composer

7 Mancini (Henry)

moonshine

4 bosh, jake **5** hokum **6** bunkum, humbug
7 bootleg, eyewash, hogwash
8 homebrew, malarkey, nonsense,
tommyrot **9** poppycock **10** balderdash,
bathtub gin, contraband, flapdoodle
11 mountain dew **12** blatherskite

Moonstone, The

author: 7 Collins (Wilkie)
detective: 4 Cuff

moonstruck

4 daft, nuts **5** batty, corny, flaky, kooky,
mushy, nutty, sappy, wacko, wacky
6 crazed, cuckoo, fruity, insane, screwy
7 berserk, bonkers, lunatic, maudlin,
touched **8** romantic **9** nostalgic, schmaltzy
10 lovey-dovey, saccharine, unbalanced
11 sentimental

moor

3 bog, fen **4** dock, fell **5** berth, catch, tie
up **6** anchor, Berber, fasten, Muslim,
secure, tether **7** peat bog **8** make fast,
Moroccan
fictional: 7 Othello

moose

6 cervid
female: 3 cow
male: 4 bull
relative: 3 elk **4** deer

moot

5 argue, plead **6** broach, debate **7** agitate,
bring up, canvass, discuss, dispute,
dubious, suggest, suspect **8** abstract,
academic, arguable, disputed, doubtful
9 debatable, introduce, thrash out,
uncertain, unsettled, ventilate **10** disputable, unresolved **11** problematic
12 questionable **13** controversial

mop

4 swab, wipe

mope

4 fret, idle, moon, pine, pout, sigh, stew,
sulk **5** brood, drift, mosey **6** dawdle, linger
7 maunder, meander, saunter **8** languish

mopes

4 funk **5** blues, dumps, ennui, slump
7 dismals, malaise, sadness **8** dolefuls
9 depression, melancholy
11 unhappiness

mopey

3 low **4** blue, down, glum **6** broody,
droopy, morose **7** doleful **8** cast down,
dejected, downcast **9** depressed
10 dispirited, melancholy, spiritless

moppet

3 kid, tot **4** tyke **5** chick, child **7** toddler
8 juvenile **9** youngster

mop up

4 beat, drub, dust, lick, whip **6** absorb,
garner, gather **7** shellac, trounce
8 complete, lambaste **9** overwhelm

moral

3 saw **4** good, just, pure, rule **5** adage,
axiom, gnome, maxim, noble, right
6 chaste, decent, dictum, honest, lesson,
proper, saying, truism **7** epigram, ethical,
preachy, precept, proverb, upright, virtual
8 aphorism, apothegm, didactic, elevated,
sermonic, virtuous **9** honorable, righteous
10 high-minded, principled, scrupulous,
upstanding **11** right-minded
13 conscientious

morale

4 mood **5** heart **6** esprit, mettle, spirit,

temper **7** resolve **10** confidence **13** esprit de corps

moralistic
5 noble, pious **7** canting, ethical
8 didactic, virtuous **9** righteous
10 principled **11** pharisaical, right-minded
13 sanctimonious

morality
5 ethic, honor, mores **6** purity, virtue
7 decency, probity **8** goodness **9** integrity,
rectitude, rightness **11** saintliness,
uprightness **13** righteousness

moralize
6 preach **7** lecture **9** preachify, sermonize
11 pontificate

morals
5 mores **6** ethics, ideals **8** scruples
9 integrity, standards **10** principles

morass
3 bog, fen, web **4** knot, maze, mesh, mire,
quag, trap **5** marsh, skein, snarl, swamp
6 jungle, muddle, tangle **8** quagmire
9 imbroglio

moratorium
3 ban **5** delay **8** interval **10** suspension

moray
3 eel

morbid
4 dark, sick **5** moody **6** gloomy, grisly,
morose, sickly, sullen **7** unsound
8 diseased, gruesome, saturnine,
unhealthy **11** melancholic, unwholesome
12 pathological

mordancy
7 acidity **8** acerbity, acridity, acrimony,
asperity, pungency **9** harshness,
sharpness **10** causticity, trenchancy
11 astringency, sardonicism
12 incisiveness

mordant
4 keen **5** acrid, salty, sharp **6** biting
7 burning, caustic, cutting, pungent
8 incisive, sardonic, scathing **9** sarcastic,
trenchant

Mordecai
cousin: **6** Esther
father: **4** Jair
mother: **6** Esther

more
3 new, too **4** also, else, plus **5** added,
again, along, extra, fresh, older, other,
spare **6** as well, better, nearer, withal

7 another, besides, farther, further, greater
8 likewise, moreover **9** increased
10 additional

More book
6 Utopia

more or less
5 about **7** roughly **13** approximately

moreover
3 and, too **4** also **6** as well, withal
7 besides, further **8** likewise **10** in addition
11 furthermore **12** additionally

mores
5 ethics, habits, values **7** beliefs, customs,
manners **8** folkways **9** amenities, etiquette
10 civilities **11** proprieties

Morgana's brother
6 Arthur

Morgan le Fay
9 sorceress
brother: **6** Arthur (King)

moribund
5 dying **6** ebbing, fading **7** dormant,
outworn **8** decaying, expiring, inactive
9 declining **11** obsolescent
13 deteriorating

Mormon Church
administrative unit: **4** ward **5** stake
founder: **5** Smith (Joseph)
leader: **5** Young (Brigham)
priest: **5** elder

Mormon State
4 Utah

morning
4 dawn **5** sunup **6** aurora **7** dawning,
sunrise **8** cockcrow, daybreak, daylight,
forenoon
moisture: **3** dew **8** dewdrops
song: **6** aubade

Morocco
capital: **5** Rabat
city: **3** Fès **6** Meknès **9** Marrakech,
Marrakesh **10** Casablanca
coast: **7** Barbary
language: **6** Arabic, Berber
monetary unit: **6** dirham
mountain: **7** Toubkal
mountain range: **3** Rif **5** Atlas
neighbor: **5** Spain **7** Algeria **13** Western
Sahara
sea: **13** Mediterranean

moron
4 dodo, dolt, dope, fool **5** dummy, dunce,
idiot **6** cretin, dimwit, stupid **7** dullard, half-

wit **8** dumbbell, imbecile, numskull **9** ignoramus, lamebrain, numbskull, simpleton

moronic
4 dull, dumb **6** simple, stupid **8** backward, retarded **9** brainless, dim-witted, imbecilic **10** half-witted, slow-witted **12** feebleminded, simpleminded

morose
4 dour, glum, sour **5** moody, sulky **6** cranky, crusty, gloomy, morbid, sullen **7** crabbed, unhappy **9** depressed, saturnine **10** depressive, ill-humored, melancholy

morph
6 change, mutate **7** convert **9** transform, transmute **12** metamorphose, transmogrify

Morpheus
father: **6** Hypnos
god of: **5** sleep

Morrison novel
4 Jazz, Love, Sula **7** Beloved **9** Bluest Eye (The) **13** Song of Solomon

Morse code
dash: **3** dah
dot: **3** dit

morsel
3 bit **4** bite **5** crumb, goody, piece, scrap, snack, taste, treat **6** dainty, nibble, tidbit **7** soupçon **8** delicacy, fragment, kickshaw, mouthful

mortal
3 man **5** awful, being, fatal, frail, human, party **6** deadly, lethal, person **7** deathly, earthly, extreme, fleshly, tedious, worldly **8** creature, ruthless, temporal **9** merciless, personage **10** implacable, individual, perishable **11** conceivable

mortality
5 flesh **7** mankind **8** fatality, humanity **9** death rate, humankind, lethality **10** deadliness

mortar
5 grout **6** binder, cannon, cement, vessel **7** plaster, sealant **8** howitzer, ordnance

Morte d'Arthur author
6 Malory (Thomas)

mortgage
4 hock, lien, pawn **6** pledge **10** obligation

mortician
8 embalmer **10** undertaker

mortified
6 shamed **7** ascetic, ashamed, austere **8** red-faced **9** chagrined **10** humiliated, shamefaced **11** embarrassed

mortify
5 abash, shame **6** dismay **7** chagrin, perturb **8** disgrace **9** discomfit, embarrass, humiliate

mortuary
8 funereal **10** sepulchral **11** funeral home

mosaic
5 inlay **7** chimera **8** terrazzo **9** composite, patchwork **12** tessellation
piece: **6** smalto **7** tessera **8** tesserae (plural)

Moscow
cathedral: **11** Saint Basil's
citadel: **7** Kremlin
resident: **9** Muscovite

Moses
brother: **5** Aaron
brother-in-law: **5** Hobab
deathplace: **4** Nebo
father-in-law: **6** Jethro
sister: **6** Miriam
son: **7** Eliezer, Gershom
spy: **5** Caleb
successor: **6** Joshua
wife: **8** Zipporah

mosey
4 mope **5** amble, drift **6** dawdle, linger, ramble, stroll, wander **7** maunder, meander, saunter

mosh
4 slam **9** slam-dance

Moslem
see **Muslim**

mosque
6 masjid
niche: **6** mihrab
prayer caller: **7** muezzin
turret: **7** minaret

mosquito
5 culex
genus: **5** Aëdes, Culex **9** Anopheles

moss
9 bryophyte
kind: **4** peat **8** sphagnum
part: **4** seta **7** capsule, rhizoid
study of: **8** bryology

mossback
4 fogy **6** fossil **10** fuddy-duddy

11 reactionary 12 antediluvian,
conservative 13 stick-in-the-mud

mostly
6 mainly 7 chiefly, largely, overall, usually
9 generally, primarily 11 principally
13 predominantly

mote
3 bit, dot, jot 4 iota, whit 5 grain, point,
speck, trace 8 flyspeck, particle

moth
immature: 5 larva 6 larvae (plural)
11 caterpillar
kind: 4 luna 7 codling, tussock
8 Cecropia, silkworm 9 browntail
order: 11 Lepidoptera

moth-eaten
4 worn 5 dated, dingy, faded, mangy,
moldy, musty, passé, ratty, seedy
6 bygone, old hat, patchy, shabby
7 antique, archaic, raggedy, run-down,
unkempt 8 decrepit, outdated, outmoded,
tattered, timeworn 10 antiquated, down-at-
heel, threadbare 11 dilapidated

mother
3 dam, mom 4 mama, root 5 fount,
mammy, mater, momma, mommy, mummy,
nurse 6 origin, source 7 care for, nurture
9 prototype, rootstock 10 provenance,
wellspring
combining form: 4 matr 5 matri, matro

mother country
8 homeland 10 fatherland

Mother Courage author
6 Brecht (Bertolt)

motherly
8 maternal 9 nurturing 10 protective

mother-of-pearl
5 nacre

Mother of Presidents
8 Virginia

Mother of the Gods
3 Ops 4 Rhea 6 Cybele

motif
4 idea, text 5 point, theme, topic 6 design,
device, figure, matter 7 pattern, subject
13 subject matter

motion
4 stir, sway 6 signal 7 gesture
8 movement, proposal, stirring 9 agitation

motionless
4 fixed, inert, still 6 frozen, static 7 stalled
8 becalmed, immobile, stagnant, unmoving

9 immovable, steadfas 10 stationary,
stock-still

motion picture
see **movie**

motivate
4 fire, goad, move, spur 5 impel, pique,
rouse 6 arouse, excite, incite, induce,
prompt 7 actuate, inspire, provoke,
quicken, trigger 8 inspirit, persuade
9 galvanize, influence, stimulate

motivation
4 spur 5 drive 7 impetus, impulse
8 ambition, catalyst, stimulus 9 impulsion,
incentive, stimulant 10 incitation,
incitement 11 inspiration, instigation,
provocation

motive
3 aim, end 4 spur 5 cause, point, theme,
topic 6 design, device, figure, intent,
matter, object, reason, spring 7 impulse,
pattern, purpose, subject 8 stimulus
9 incentive, intention, rationale
10 incitement, inducement 11 inspiration

motley
5 mixed, salad 6 jumble, medley, varied
7 dappled, diverse, piebald 8 assorted,
pastiche 9 disparate, multihued
10 assortment, hodgepodge, miscellany,
multicolor, variegated 11 gallimaufry,
varicolored 12 conglomerate, multicolored,
multifarious, parti-colored 13 heterogeneous, miscellaneous, polychromatic

motor
3 car 4 auto, ride 5 buggy, drive 6 cruise,
engine 7 machine 10 automobile

motorboat
6 launch 7 cruiser, inboard 8 outboard,
runabout 12 cabin cruiser

motorcycle
7 chopper 8 minibike 9 trail bike
adjunct: 7 sidecar

Motown
7 Detroit

mottle
4 spot 5 fleck 6 blotch, dapple, marble
7 spatter, speckle, stipple, splotch

mottled
5 tabby 7 blotchy, dappled, flecked,
spotted 8 blotched, brindled, speckled
9 checkered 10 variegated

motto
3 cry 5 adage, axiom, maxim 6 byword,

saying, slogan, war cry **7** precept, proverb **8** aphorism **9** battle cry, catchword, watchword **10** shibboleth **11** catchphrase

moue
3 mow, mug **4** face, pout **7** grimace

mound
4 bank, cock, heap, hill, hump, mass, pile **5** cairn, drift, knoll, shock, stack **6** barrow, tumuli (plural) **7** bulwark, hillock, rampart, tumulus **9** elevation **10** embankment
Buddhist: 5 stupa
burial, Eastern Europe: 6 kurgan
of detritus: 4 kame
of sand: 4 dune
of stones: 5 cairn

mount
3 alp, wax **4** lift, peak, rise, show, soar **5** arise, build, climb, frame, horse, put on, raise, rouse, scale, set up, stage, steed, swell **6** ascend, aspire, deepen, expand, launch, uprear **7** advance, augment, display, enhance, enlarge, install, magnify, produce, support, upsurge **8** bestride, escalade, escalate, heighten, increase, multiply, redouble **9** aggravate, intensify **10** promontory

mountain
3 alp, lot **4** bank, crag, dome, heap, hill, hulk, lump, mass, mesa, much, peak, pile, slew **5** bluff, butte, drift, mound, shock, stack **6** height
Alaska: 4 Bona **6** Denali **7** Foraker, Sanford **8** McKinley, Wrangell
Alberta: 6 Castle **10** Eisenhower
Alps: 4 Rosa (Monte) **5** Blanc, Eiger **8** Jungfrau **10** Matterhorn
Angola: 4 Moco
Antarctica: 4 Mohl **6** Vinson (Massif) **7** Gardner **9** Elizabeth
Appalachians: 8 Mitchell **10** Kittatinny **10** Washington **13** Clingmans Dome
Argentina: 9 Aconcagua
Australia: 4 Ziel **5** Bruce **6** Cradle **9** Kosciusko
biblical: 5 Horeb, Tabor **6** Hermon **8** Har Tavor
Black Hills: 6 Harney (Peak)
Bolivia: 6 Sorata **8** Illimani
Borneo: 8 Kinabalu, Kinabulu
California: 5 Guyot **6** Shasta, Sonora (Peak) **7** Palomar, Whitney **8** Tuolumne **10** Buena Vista, Stanislaus
Canada: 5 Logan
China: 4 Emei, Song
Colorado: 5 Pikes (Peak) **9** Purgatory (Peak)
Costa Rica: 6 Blanco **14** Chirripó Grande

Cyprus: 7 Olympus, Troodos
depression: 3 col
Dominican Republic: 6 Duarte **8** Trujillo
Egypt: 4 Musa **5** Sinai
Fiji: 8 Victoria **9** Tomaniivi
foot: 8 piedmont
France: 5 Blanc (Mont)
Gabon: 8 Iboundji
Georgia: 8 Springer **10** Oglethorpe
Germany: 7 Zollern **11** Fichtelberg, Zugspitze
Greece: 3 Ida **5** Athos, Levka **7** Helicon, Olympus **9** Parnassus, Psiloriti **10** Pendelikon, Pentelicus
Greenland: 9 Gunnbjorn
Himalayas: 6 Lhotse **7** Everest **9** Annapurna
India: 5 Japvo
Indonesia: 4 Lawu **5** Kwoka, Lawoe, Raung **6** Raoeng, Semeru **7** Kerinci
Israel: 5 Meron **6** Carmel
Ivory Coast: 5 Nimba
Japan: 4 Fuji **5** Iwate **7** Fujisan **8** Fujiyama
Java: 5 Liman
Jordan: 3 Hor **5** Hārūn
Maine: 8 Katahdin
Malaysia: 5 Ophir, Tahan **6** Ledang
Mediterranean entrance: 5 Calpe **9** Gibraltar
Mexico: 7 Orizaba (Pico de)
New York: 4 Bear **5** Marcy
North America's highest: 6 Denali **8** McKinley
North Carolina: 8 Mitchell
Oman: 5 Sham
Oregon: 4 Hood
Pakistan: 9 Tirich Mir
Papua New Guinea: 7 Wilhelm
Pennine Alps: 4 Rosa (Monte)
Philippines: 3 Apo, Iba **4** Labo **5** Silay **6** arête, crest **7** sawbuck
ridge: 4 spur **6** arête, crest **7** sawbuck
Romania: 11 Moldoveanul
South America: 7 Roraima **9** Aconcagua
South Dakota: 6 Custer (Peak)
Switzerland: 3 Dom **4** Rosa (Monte) **5** Eiger **8** Jungfrau **10** Matterhorn
Syria: 4 Druz **5** Duruz
Tanzania: 11 Kilimanjaro
Tasmania: 4 Ossa
Tennessee: 13 Clingmans Dome
Togo: 4 Agou
Utah: 5 Kings
Vermont: 9 Mansfield
Vietnam: 5 Ngoo Linh
Virginia: 6 Rogers
Western Hemisphere's highest: 9 Aconcagua
world's highest: 7 Everest

Wyoming: 5 Cloud 7 Gannett (Peak)
(see also **peak**)

mountain climbing
equipment: 3 axe, nut 5 piton 7 crampon
9 carabiner
maneuver: 6 rappel 10 rappelling

mountain dew
see **moonshine**

mountain formation
7 orogeny 10 orogenesis

mountainous
4 huge, vast 5 alpine, mighty 7 immense,
mammoth, massive 8 enormous, gigantic,
towering 10 monumental, prodigious

mountain pass
3 col
Afghanistan-Pakistan: 6 Khyber
Alps: 5 Gries
California: 4 Muir 6 Sonora
China-Myanmar: 5 Namni
Colorado: 3 Ute 5 Mosca, Muddy, Music,
Raton
Europe: 8 Moravian
Greece: 5 Rupel
Hindu Kush Mts.: 5 Dorah, Durah
Pakistan: 5 Bolan, Gomal, Gumal
Sierra Nevada: 4 Mono
Switzerland: 5 Furka, Gemmi 7 Grimsel
8 Lötschen
Tunisia: 4 Faïd
Ukrainian: 5 Uzhok
Wyoming: 5 Union

mountain range
Asia: 5 Altai, Altay 8 Himalaya, Tien Shan
9 Altai Shan, Altay Shan, Himalayan,
Himalayas, Hindu Kush
Australia: 8 Flinders
Europe: 4 Alps 10 Carpathian
Germany: 4 Harz 5 Hartz
Greece: 4 Oeta
India: 5 Ghats
Iran: 6 Zagros
Italy: 9 Apennines
Mexico: 11 Sierra Madre
North Africa: 5 Atlas
North America: 5 Rocky 7 Rockies
11 Appalachian
Russia: 4 Ural
Scotland: 9 Grampians
Sinai: 9 Gebel Musa
Slovakia: 5 Tatra, Tatry 9 High Tatra
South America: 5 Andes
Turkey: 6 Taurus
United States: 5 Rocky, White 6 Brooks
7 Cascade, Olympic, Rockies, Sawatch,
Wasatch 8 Absaroka, Aleutian, Catskill,

Wrangell 9 Blue Ridge, Wind River
10 Adirondack, Bitterroot, Black Hills,
Clearwater, Grand Teton
Zimbabwe: 6 Matopo (Hills) 7 Matoppo
(Hills)

Mountain State
7 Montana 12 West Virginia

mountebank
5 quack 6 con man 8 swindler
9 charlatan 11 flimflammer, quacksalver
13 confidence man

Mount St. Helens
7 volcano

mourn
3 rue 6 bemoan, bewail, grieve, lament,
sorrow 7 deplore, protest

mournful
3 sad 6 dismal, gloomy, rueful, somber,
triste, woeful 7 doleful, forlorn, joyless,
unhappy 8 dejected, desolate, dolorous,
funereal, grievous, wretched 9 dirgelike,
plaintive 10 depressing, despondent,
dispirited, lugubrious, melancholy
11 distressing, melancholic, regrettable,
unfortunate 12 heavyhearted

mournfulness
5 blues, dumps, gloom 7 dismals, sadness
9 dejection 10 depression, melancholy

mourning
5 grief 7 keening, remorse, wailing,
weeping 8 grieving 9 lamenting, morbidity,
sorrowing, ululation 10 heartbreak
11 bereavement, lamentation

Mourning Becomes Electra
author: 6 O'Neill (Eugene)

mourning period, Jewish
5 shiva 6 shivah

mourning symbol
7 armband

mouse
6 rodent, shiner 8 black eye

mousy
3 shy 4 drab, dull 5 plain, quiet, timid
7 bashful 8 retiring, timorous 9 colorless,
diffident, shrinking 11 unassertive 12 self-
effacing

mouth
3 gob 4 trap 5 chops 6 kisser 8 entrance
10 embouchure

mouthlike opening
5 stoma 7 stomata (plural)

mouthpiece

5 organ 6 puppet 7 speaker 8 front man
9 spokesman 10 figurehead
11 spokeswoman 12 spokesperson

mouthwatering

5 sapid, tasty, yummy 6 savory, toothy
8 tasteful 9 delicious, palatable, succulent,
toothsome 10 appetizing, delectable
11 good-tasting

mouthy

4 glib 5 gabby, talky, windy 7 verbose,
voluble 8 effusive 9 bombastic, garrulous,
talkative

movable

5 loose 6 mobile, motile, roving 8 portable
10 changeable

movables

5 goods 7 effects 8 chattels 10 belongings 11 furnishings

move

3 act 4 lead, spur, stir, sway 5 bring,
budge, carry, drive, impel, leave, march,
rouse, shift, start, touch 6 affect, convey,
depart, excite, incite, induce, kindle,
prompt, propel 7 actuate, advance,
animate, conduct, impress, inspire,
migrate, proceed, propose, provoke,
request, suggest 8 activate, dislodge,
displace, evacuate, get along, maneuver,
motivate, persuade, progress, relocate,
resettle, transfer, withdraw 9 dislocate,
galvanize, influence, instigate, stimulate,
transport

movement

4 flow, stir 5 tempo, trend 6 action, motion
7 crusade 8 activity, campaign, dynamism,
maneuver, progress, stirring, tendency,
velocity 9 migration
music: 4 moto
reflex: 5 taxis
stimulated: 7 kinesis

movie

4 cine, film, show 5 flick 6 cinema, talkie
7 picture 9 photoplay 11 picture show
13 motion picture
cowboy: 5 oater 7 western
short: 4 clip 8 newsreel

movie director

American: 3 Lee (Spike), Ray (Nicholas)
4 Coen (Joel), Ford (John), Hill (George
Roy), Mann (Anthony), Penn (Arthur), Ritt
(Martin), Ross (Herbert), Sirk (Douglas),
Wise (Robert) 5 Allen (Woody), Ashby
(Hal), Brown (Clarence), Capra (Frank),
Cukor (George), Demme (Jonathan),
Donen (Stanley), Fosse (Bob), Hawks
(Howard), Ivory (James), Jonze (Spike),
Kazan (Elia), LeRoy (Mervyn), Logan
(Joshua), Lucas (George), Lumet (Sidney),
Lynch (David), Moore (Michael), Roach
(Hal), Stone (Oliver), Vidor (King), Walsh
(Raoul), Whale (James), Wyler (William),
Zwick (Ed) 6 Altman (Robert), Beatty
(Warren), Benton (Robert), Brooks
(Richard), Burton (Tim), Cimino (Michael),
Curtiz (Michael), Fuller (Samuel), Gibson
(Mel), Hanson (Curtis), Howard (Ron),
Huston (John), Kramer (Stanley), Malick
(Terrence), Parker (Alan), Welles (Orson),
Wilder (Billy) 7 Borzage (Frank), Cameron
(James), Chaplin (Charlie), Coppola
(Francis Ford, Sofia), Costner (Kevin), De
Mille (Cecil B.), De Palma (Brian), Fleming
(Victor), Gilliam (Terry), Jewison (Norman),
Kubrick (Stanley), McCarey (Leo), Mulligan
(Robert), Nichols (Mike), Pakula(Alan),
Pollack (Sydney), Redford (Robert),
Siodmak (Robert), Stevens (George),
Sturges (Preston), Van Sant (Gus),
Wellman (William) 8 Avildsen (John),
Eastwood (Clint), Flaherty (Robert),
Friedkin (William), Griffith (David Wark),
Jarmusch (Jim), Levinson (Barry), Lubitsch
(Ernst), Marshall (Penny), Minnelli
(Vincente), Preminger (Otto), Scorsese
(Martin), Zemeckis (Robert) 9 Hitchcock
(Alfred), Milestone (Lewis), Peckinpah
(Sam), Preminger (Otto), Spielberg
(Steven), Sternberg (Josef von), Streisand
(Barbra), Tarantino (Quentin), Zinnemann
(Fred) 10 Cassavetes (John), Heckerling
(Amy), Mankiewicz (Joseph), Soderbergh
(Steven) 11 Bogdanovich (Peter)
13 Frankenheimer (John)
Australian: 4 Weir (Peter) 6 Noonan
(Chris) 9 Armstrong (Gillian), Beresford
(Bruce)
Austrian: 4 Lang (Fritz) 8 Stroheim (Erich
von) 9 Sternberg (Josef von)
British: 4 Lean (David), Reed (Carol)
5 Leigh (Mike), Losey (Joseph), Reisz
(Karel), Scott (Ridley) 6 Figgis (Mike),
Frears (Stephen), Jordan (Neil), Newell
(Mike), Parker (Alan), Powell (Michael)
7 Boorman (John), Branagh (Kenneth),
Forsyth (Bill) 8 Anderson (Lindsay)
9 Hitchcock (Alfred) 10 Richardson (Tony)
11 Schlesinger (John)
Chinese: 3 Lee (Ang) 4 Chen (Kaige)
5 Zhang (Yimou)
French: 4 Demy (Jacques), Tati
(Jacques), Vigo (Jean) 5 Malle (Louis)
6 Godard (Jean-Luc), Ophüls (Marcel),
Renoir (Jean), Rohmer (Eric) 7 Bresson
(Robert), Chabrol (Claude), Cocteau

(Jean), Resnais (Alain), Rivette (Jacques)
8 Truffaut (François)
German: 6 Herzog (Werner), Ophüls
(Max) 7 Winders (Wim) 8 Petersen
(Wolfgang) 10 Fassbinder (Rainer Werner)
11 Riefenstahl (Leni), Schlöndorff (Volker)
Italian: 5 Leone (Sergio) 6 De Sica
(Vittorio) 7 Fellini (Federico) 8 Pasolini
(Pier Paolo), Visconti (Luchino) 9 Antonioni
(Michelangelo) 10 Bertolucci (Bernardo),
Rossellini (Roberto), Wertmüller (Lina),
Zeffirelli (Franco)
Japanese: 3 Ozu (Yasujiru) 5 Itami (Juzo)
8 Kurosawa (Akira), Miyazaki (Hayao)
9 Mizoguchi (Kenji)
New Zealand: 7 Campion (Jane)
Polish 5 Wajda (Ardrzej) 7 Holland
(Agnieszka) 8 Polanski (Roman)
Russian: 9 Tarkovsky (Andrei)
10 Eisenstein (Sergei)
Spanish: 6 Buñuel (Luis) 9 Almodóvar
(Pedro)
Swedish: 7 Bergman (Ingmar)
10 Zetterling (Mai)

movie producer
American: 3 Fox (William) 4 Cohn (Jack)
5 Lasky (Jesse), Mayer (Louis B.), Zukor
(Adolph) 6 Warner (Jack L.), Zanuck
(Darryl, Richard) 7 Goldwyn (Samuel),
Laemmle (Carl) 8 Selznick (David O.)
Austrian: 9 Reinhardt (Max)

moving
5 astir 6 mobile 7 emotive, rousing
8 arousing, exciting, gripping, pathetic,
poignant, stirring, touching 9 affecting,
emotional, inspiring, transient
11 stimulating

moving stairs
9 escalator

mow
3 cut 4 clip, crop, fell, heap, moue, pile,
raze, rick 5 level, shave, shear, stack
7 grimace 9 knock down

moxie
3 pep, vim, zip 4 grit, guts 5 brass, heart,
nerve, oomph, pluck, savvy, spunk, vigor
6 energy, mettle, spirit, starch 7 cojones,
courage, know-how 8 backbone
9 fortitude 10 get-up-and-go, resolution
13 determination

Mozambique
capital: 6 Maputo
language: 8 Bantu 7 Swahili 10 Portuguese
monetary unit: 7 metical

neighbor: 6 Malawi, Zambia 8 Tanzania
9 Swaziland, Zimbabwe 11 South Africa
river: 6 Ruvuma 7 Limpopo, Zambezi

Mozart, Wolfgang Amadeus
birthplace: 8 Salzburg
cataloger: 6 Köchel (Ludwig)
deathplace: 6 Vienna
opera: 8 Idomeneo 10 Magic Flute (The)
11 Don Giovanni, Il Rè Pastore 12 Cosí
Fan Tutte 16 Marriage of Figaro (The)

MP's prey
4 AWOL 8 deserter

Mr. Moto star
5 Lorre (Peter)

Mrs. Grundy
4 prig 5 prude 7 puritan 8 bluenose

much
3 oft 4 long, many, most 5 often 6 highly,
hugely, plenty 7 greatly, notably
8 abundant 9 eminently, extremely, great
deal 10 frequently, oftentimes, repeatedly
combining form: 4 poly 5 multi

Much Ado About Nothing
character: 4 Hero 7 Claudio, Don John
8 Beatrice, Benedick, Dogberry

muck
3 goo, mud 4 crap, crud, dirt, dung, gook,
goop, grub, gunk, junk, mess, mire, murk,
plod, slog, slop, soil, toil 5 dirty, dreck, filth,
grime, gumbo, slave, slime, swill, trash,
waste 6 drudge, litter, manure, meddle,
putter, sleaze, sludge, smirch, tinker
7 garbage, rubbish 8 nonsense 9 interfere

muckety-muck
3 VIP 5 nabob 6 bigwig, fat cat 7 big
shot, kingpin, notable 8 kingfish,
somebody 9 dignitary

mucky
4 foul 5 dirty, grimy, muddy, muggy, murky,
nasty, soggy 6 cruddy, filthy, grubby,
grungy 8 squalid, unclean

mucous
5 slimy 6 viscid

mud
4 dirt, mire, muck, ooze 5 dregs, slime
6 depths, sludge

muddle
3 mix 4 hash, mess, muck, rile, roil
5 addle, botch, mix up, snarl 6 ataxia,
bungle, drivel, foul up, fumble, jumble,
jungle, litter, mess up, tangle, tumble
7 clutter, confuse, fluster, perplex,
rummage, shuffle, snarl up, stumble,

muddled

stupefy **8** befuddle, bewilder, confound, disarray, disorder, distract, entangle, mishmash, scramble, shambles, throw off, unsettle **9** confusion, throw away **10** complicate, disarrange, discompose **11** disorganize

muddled
5 drunk, tight, tipsy, vague **7** mixed-up **8** inchoate **10** disjointed, disordered, incoherent, inebriated **11** intoxicated, unorganized

muddle through
4 cope, fare **5** get by, get on **6** manage **7** carry on, make out **8** get along

muddy
3 dim, fog **4** base, blur, drab, dull, fade, foul, hazy, oozy, roil, soil **5** befog, cloud, dingy, dirty, grime, grimy, murky **6** cloudy, gloomy, grubby, sordid, turbid **7** becloud, begrime, confuse, obscure, squalid, tarnish, unclean, unclear **8** confused

muff
4 blow, flub **5** botch, fluff **6** bobble, bollix, bungle, fumble, goof up, mess up **7** louse up, misplay, screw up **9** mishandle

muffle
4 dull, mute, veil **5** shush **6** dampen, deaden, lessen, shroud, soften, stifle, subdue, wrap up **7** envelop, repress, silence, smother, squelch **8** bundle up, suppress, tone down

muffled
5 muted **6** dulled **7** stifled, subdued **8** deadened, obscured, silenced **9** distorted, enveloped **10** indistinct, suppressed

muffler
4 mask, veil **5** cloak, scarf

mug
3 cup, ham, mop, mow, rob **4** boob, dolt, dope, face, fool, moue, phiz, punk, puss, thug **5** dunce, idiot, mouth, rowdy, stein, tough **6** ambush, dimwit **7** assault, grimace, tankard **8** bullyboy, dumbbell, features, numskull **9** blockhead, bushwhack, ignoramus, roughneck

mugger
4 thug **6** robber **9** assailant, crocodile

muggy
4 damp **5** humid, moist **6** sticky, sultry **7** dampish

Muhammad
adopted son: 3 Ali
birthplace: 5 Mecca
camel: 5 Kaswa
daughter: 6 Fatima
deathplace: 6 Medina
deity: 5 Allah
father: 8 Abdallah, Abdullah
father-in-law: 7 Abu Bakr
flight: 6 hegira, hejira
follower: 6 Moslem, Muslim
horse: 5 Buraq 7 Alborak
religion: 5 Islam
son: 7 Ibrahim
son-in-law: 3 Ali
successor: 6 caliph 7 Abu Bakr
tribe: 7 Koreish, Quraysh
uncle: 8 Abu Talib
wife: 5 Aisha 6 Ayesha 7 Khadija

mulatto
5 métis, mixed **7** mestizo **9** half-breed, half-caste **10** crossbreed

mulberry
3 fig **10** breadfruit
type: 6 banyan 11 India rubber, osage orange

mulct
4 fine, milk, rook **5** bleed, cheat, gouge **6** extort, fleece **7** deceive, defraud, forfeit, penalty, swindle **8** penalize **9** blackmail

mule
5 cross, scuff **6** bagman, hybrid **7** bastard, courier, mongrel **8** smuggler **9** crossbred, half blood, half-breed **10** crossbreed

mulish
8 contrary, perverse, stubborn **9** obstinate, pigheaded **10** bullheaded, headstrong, inflexible, refractory, unyielding **11** stiff-necked

mull
4 hash, muse **5** brood, think, weigh **6** ponder **7** reflect **8** cogitate, consider, meditate, ruminate, turn over **9** pulverize **10** deliberate **11** contemplate

multicolored
4 pied **6** motley **7** dappled **9** prismatic **10** variegated **13** polychromatic

multifarious
5 mixed **6** motley, sundry, varied **7** diverse, various **8** assorted, manifold **13** heterogeneous, miscellaneous

multiform
6 sundry, varied **7** diverse, various

8 assorted, manifold 9 disparate
12 multifarious

multilateral
9 many-sided

multiple
4 many 6 shared, sundry 7 diverse,
several, various 8 assorted, manifold,
numerous 9 composite

multiplicity
3 lot 4 heap, load, mass, peck 5 flood,
hoard, horde 6 barrel 7 variety
8 mountain, plethora 9 diversity, great
deal, profusion

multiply
3 wax 4 rise 5 boost, breed, build, mount
6 expand, extend, spread 7 amplify,
augment, enlarge, magnify 8 generate,
heighten, increase 9 procreate, propagate,
reproduce 10 aggrandize 11 proliferate

multitude
3 mob 4 army, herd, host, mass, slew
5 crowd, crush, drove, flock, horde, swarm
6 legion, myriad, public, throng 9 populace

multitudinous
4 many 6 legion, myriad, sundry
7 copious, various 8 abundant, manifold,
numerous, populous 9 countless
10 numberless, voluminous
11 innumerable

mum
4 dumb, mute 5 quiet 6 silent 8 wordless
10 speechless, tongue-tied

mumble
6 murmur, mutter 7 maunder

mumbo jumbo
4 juju 6 fetish 9 gibberish 10 hocus-pocus
11 abracadabra 12 gobbledygook,
superstition

mummer
4 mime 5 actor, mimic 12 impersonator

mummify
5 dry up, wizen 6 embalm, wither 7 shrivel
9 desiccate

munch
3 eat 4 chaw, chew 5 champ, chomp,
snack 6 crunch 9 masticate

mundane
5 lowly 6 earthy, normal 7 earthly,
humdrum, prosaic, routine, terrene, worldly

8 banausic, day-to-day, everyday, familiar,
ordinary, telluric, workaday 9 practical,
sublunary, tellurian 11 commonplace,
terrestrial, uncelestial 13 materialistic

municipal
5 civic, local, urban 12 metropolitan

munificent
6 lavish 7 liberal 8 generous, handsome
9 bounteous, bountiful 10 benevolent,
freehanded, openhanded
11 magnanimous 13 philanthropic

munitions maker
5 Krupp

muralist
4 Sert (José María) 6 Benton (Thomas
Hart), Giotto, Orozco (José Clemente),
Rivera (Diego) 7 La Farge (John)
9 Siqueiros (David Alfaro) 12 Michelangelo
(Buonarotti)

murder
3 hit, off 4 do in, kill, slay 5 blood, lynch,
scrag, snuff, waste 6 rub out 7 bump off,
execute, garrote, killing, smother, take out
8 foul play, homicide, knock off, strangle
9 eradicate, liquidate, slaughter
10 annihilate, asphyxiate, decapitate,
extinguish 11 assassinate, electrocute,
exterminate 12 manslaughter
brother: 10 fratricide
father: 9 patricide
king: 8 regicide
mother: 9 matricide
parent: 9 parricide
sister: 10 sororicide

murderer
6 hit man, killer, slayer 7 butcher
8 assassin, homicide 9 cutthroat,
manslayer 11 slaughterer

Murder in the Cathedral
author: 5 Eliot (Thomas Stearns)
character: 5 Henry (II) 6 Becket (Thomas
à)

murderous
6 deadly, lethal 10 sanguinary
12 bloodthirsty

murk
3 fog 4 haze, mist 5 brume, gloom
6 miasma 8 darkness 9 obscurity

murky
3 dim 4 dark, dull, foul, gray 5 dirty, dusky,
foggy, misty, muddy, roily, vague 6 cloudy,
gloomy, opaque, somber, turbid 7 obscure

8 nebulous 9 ambiguous, equivocal, tenebrous 10 caliginous

murmur

3 hum 4 buzz, purr 5 drone, rumor
6 grouch, grouse, mumble, mutter, rumble
7 grumble, whisper 8 complain
9 grumbling, undertone 11 scuttlebutt, susurration

Muscat sultanate

4 Oman

muscle

4 beef, thew 5 brawn, force, might, power, sinew 6 energy 7 potency 8 strength
9 strong arm
abdomen: 7 abdomen
arm: 6 biceps 7 triceps
back: 9 trapezius
calf: 6 soleus
chest: 10 pectoralis
jaw: 8 masseter
kind: 6 flexor, tensor 7 dilator, evertor, levator, rotator 8 abductor, adductor, extensor
loin: 5 psoas
neck: 8 platysma
shoulder: 7 deltoid 10 deltoideus
study of: 7 myology
thigh: 8 gracilis 9 sartorius

muscle-bound

5 rigid, stiff 6 wooden

muscular

4 ropy 5 beefy, burly, husky 6 brawny, mighty, robust, sinewy, strong, sturdy
8 athletic, forceful, powerful, resolute, stalwart, vigorous 9 Herculean, strapping, well-built

muse

5 angel, brood, guide, think 6 genius, ponder, trance 7 reflect, reverie 8 cogitate, meditate, mull over, ruminate, turn over
10 deliberate 11 contemplate

Muse

father: 4 Zeus 7 Jupiter
mother: 9 Mnemosyne
of astronomy: 6 Urania
of choral song: 11 Terpsichore
of comedy: 6 Thalia
of dancing: 11 Terpsichore
of epic poetry: 8 Calliope
of history: 4 Clio
of love poetry: 5 Erato
of lyric poetry: 5 Erato
of music: 7 Euterpe
of pastoral poetry: 6 Thalia
of sacred poetry: 8 Polymnia
10 Polyhymnia
of tragedy: 9 Melpomene

museum

5 salon 7 archive, exhibit, gallery
8 atheneum 10 collection, repository

mush

4 slop 5 grits, gruel, hokum 6 bathos, drivel, hominy 8 porridge, schmaltz

mushroom

4 grow 6 expand, spread 7 burgeon, explode, inflate 8 snowball 11 proliferate
combining form: 3 myc 4 myco 5 mycet
6 myceto
edible: 5 enoki, morel 6 bolete 7 cremini, crimini, porcini 8 shiitake 9 mousseron
10 champignon, portabella, portabello, portobello 11 chanterelle
kind: 6 agaric, bolete 7 inky cap, russula
part: 3 cap 4 gill, ring 5 stipe, volva
6 pileus 7 annulus 8 mycelium
poisonous: 7 amanita 8 death cap 9 fly agaric, toadstool

mushy

4 soft 5 pulpy, soppy, vague 6 quaggy, spongy 7 amorous, maudlin, mawkish, squashy, squishy 8 bathetic, effusive, romantic, squooshy 9 schmaltzy 10 lovey-dovey, saccharine 11 sentimental

music

abbreviation: 3 fff, ppp, sfz 5 cresc
bass staff lines: 5 GBDFA
bass staff spaces: 4 ACEG
characteristic phrase: 9 leitmotif, leitmotiv
chord: 5 major, minor, tonic 7 harmony
8 dominant 9 augmented 10 diminished
embellishment: 3 run 4 turn 5 trill
7 cadenza, mordent, roulade 8 arpeggio, flourish 9 grace note
for eight: 5 octet
for five: 7 quintet
for four: 7 quartet
for nine: 5 nonet
for one: 4 solo
for seven: 6 septet
for six: 6 sextet
for three: 4 trio
for two: 3 duo 4 duet
god: 6 Apollo
hall: 7 cabaret, theater
instrumental form: 3 jig 4 jazz, reel
5 étude, fugue, gigue, march, polka, rondo, suite, swing, waltz 6 minuet, pavane, sonata 7 bourrée, gavotte, mazurka, prelude, ragtime, toccata 8 chaconne,

concerto, courante, fantasia, galliard, nocturne, overture, rhapsody, ricercar, saraband, serenade, symphony, tone poem **9** allemande, polonaise **11** rock and roll
medley: 4 olio
morning: 6 aubade
Muse: 7 Euterpe
night: 8 nocturne, serenade
note: 4 half **5** breve, minim, neume, whole **6** eighth, quaver **7** quarter **8** crotchet **9** sixteenth **10** semiquaver
patron saint: 7 Cecilia
period: 6 Modern, Rococo **7** Baroque **8** Medieval, Romantic **9** Classical
symbol: 3 bar, key **4** clef, flat, note, rest, slur, turn **5** sharp, staff **7** fermata, mordent **9** alla breve **10** accidental
treble staff lines: 5 EGBDF
treble staff spaces: 4 FACE
vocal form: 3 air **4** aria, hymn, lied, mass, song **5** chant, motet, opera, round **6** anthem, ballad **7** cantata, chanson, chorale **8** cavatina, madrigal, operetta, oratorio, serenade **9** cabaletta

musical
4 show **5** revue **6** choral **7** lyrical, melodic, songful, tuneful **8** harmonic, operetta, zarzuela **9** melodious, symphonic **10** euphonious, harmonious

musical composition
4 aria, hymn, lied, opus, song, trio **5** chant, canon, carol, étude, fugue, march, motet, opera, rondo, suite **6** anthem, ballad, sextet, sonata **7** cantata, chanson, chorale, prelude, quartet, quintet, requiem, scherzo, toccata **8** concerto, fantasia, madrigal, nocturne, operetta, oratorio, overture, postlude, serenade, sonatina, symphony **9** bagatelle, cabaletta, interlude **10** intermezzo, recitative

musical direction
accented: 7 marcato **8** sforzato **9** sforzando
all: 5 tutti
brisk: 4 vivo **6** vivace **7** allegro, animato
connected: 6 legato
detached: 8 spiccato, staccato
dignified: 8 maestoso
disconnected: 8 staccato
emotional: 12 appassionato
emphatic: 7 marcato
excited: 7 agitato
fast: 4 vite, vivo **6** presto, veloce, vivace **7** allegro
faster: 7 stretto **11** accelerando
fluctuating tempo: 6 rubato
forcefully: 7 furioso

freely: 9 ad libitum
gay: 7 giocoso
gentle: 5 dolce **7** amabile, amoroso **10** affettuoso
graceful: 8 grazioso
half: 5 mezzo
heavy: 7 pesante
held firmly: 6 tenuto
less: 4 meno
little: 4 poco
little by little: 9 poco a poco
lively: 4 vite **6** vivace **7** allegro, animato, giocoso
loud: 5 forte
louder: 9 crescendo
majestic: 8 maestoso
moderate: 7 andante **8** moderato
moderately loud: 10 mezzo forte
moderately soft: 10 mezzo piano
playful: 10 scherzando
plucked: 9 pizzicato
quick: 4 vite, vivo **6** presto, veloce, vivace **7** allegro
quickening: 11 affrettando
repeat: 3 bis **6** da capo
run: 8 arpeggio **9** glissando
sad: 7 dolente **8** doloroso
separate: 6 divisi
silent: 5 tacet
singing: 9 cantabile
sliding: 9 glissando
slow: 5 grave, largo **6** adagio **7** andante **9** larghetto
slowing: 3 rit **6** ritard **10** ritardando **11** rallentando
smooth: 6 legato
soft: 5 dolce, piano
softening: 10 diminuendo **11** decrescendo
solemn: 5 grave
spirited: 4 vivo **6** vivace **7** animato **9** spiritoso
stately: 7 pomposo **8** maestoso
sustained: 6 tenuto **9** sostenuto
sweet: 5 dolce
tender: 7 amabile, amoroso **10** affettuoso
together: 4 a due **5** tutti
very: 5 assai
very fast: 11 prestissimo
very loud: 10 fortissimo
very soft: 10 pianissimo

musical drama
5 opera **8** operetta, zarzuela **9** singspiel

musical group
4 band, trio **5** choir, combo **6** chorus, sextet **7** quartet, quintet **8** ensemble, glee club **9** orchestra

musical instrument

African: 5 mbira 7 kalimba
ancient: 4 lyre, rote 5 crwth 6 syrinx
7 cithara, kithara, panpipe, sistrum
Arabic: 3 oud
bagpipe: 7 musette, pibroch
biblical: 6 cymbal 7 timbrel 8 psaltery
brass: 4 horn, tuba 5 bugle 6 cornet
7 althorn, clarion, helicon, saxhorn, trumpet
8 trombone 10 French horn
Indian: 4 vina 5 sarod, sitar, tabla
Japanese: 4 biwa, koto 7 samisen
8 shamisen 10 shakuhachi
keyboard: 5 organ, piano 6 spinet
7 celesta, cembalo, clavier 8 calliope,
melodeon, virginal 9 accordion
10 clavichord, concertina, pianoforte
11 harpsichord
medieval: 4 lute 5 naker, rebab, rebec,
shawm, tabor 7 gittern, mandola, panpipe
8 cornetto, dulcimer, gemshorn, hornpipe,
Jew's harp, oliphant, recorder 9 mono-
chord 10 clavichord, hurdy-gurdy
percussion: 4 bell, drum 5 anvil, güiro,
piano 6 cymbal, maraca 7 marimba,
timbrel, timpani, tympani 8 bass drum,
castanet, triangle 9 snare drum, xylophone
10 kettledrum, tambourine, vibraphone
Persian: 6 santir
pipe: 6 syrinx 7 bagpipe, musette,
panpipe
reed: 4 oboe 7 bassoon 8 clarinet
9 harmonica, saxophone 11 English horn
Renaissance: 4 viol 5 regal, shawm
6 curtal, spinet 7 bagpipe, bandora, cittern,
rackett, sackbut, serpent, theorbo, vihuela,
violone 8 crumhorn, recorder, virginal
10 chitarrone, colascione 11 harpsichord
Russian: 9 balalaika
stringed: 3 oud 4 harp, lute, lyre, vina,
viol 5 banjo, cello, piano, rebec, sitar, viola
6 fiddle, guitar, violin, zither 7 bandora,
cittern, gittern, kantele, pandura, ukulele
8 autoharp, dulcimer, mandolin
10 contrabass, double bass 11 harpsichord, violoncello
toy: 5 kazoo 7 ocarina
two-necked: 7 theorbo
woodwind: 4 oboe 5 flute 7 bassoon,
piccolo 9 flageolet, saxophone 11 English
horn

musical interval

5 fifth, major, minor, sixth, third 6 fourth,
octave, second 7 perfect, seventh, tritone

musical syllable

3 sol

musician

4 bard 5 piper 6 player 7 jazzman,
maestro 8 minstrel, virtuoso 9 performer
10 troubadour

muskeg

3 bog, fen 4 mire, quag 5 marsh, swamp
6 morass, slough 8 quagmire

musket

5 fusil 9 flintlock, matchlock 12 muzzle-
loader

Musketeer

5 Athos 6 Aramis 7 Porthos
author: 5 Dumas (Alexandre)
friend: 9 d'Artagnan

muskmelon

10 cantaloupe

Muslim

ascetic: 4 Sufi 5 fakir 7 dervish
8 marabout
body of scholars: 5 ulama, ulema
branch: 4 Shia 5 Sunni 6 Shiite
caller to prayer: 7 muezzin
decree: 5 fatwa, irade
devil: 5 Iblis
garment: 6 chador
god: 5 Allah
holy city: 5 Mecca 6 Medina
holy war: 5 jihad
judge: 5 mufti
leader: 3 aga 4 agha, amir, emir 5 ameer
mendicant: 5 fakir
messiah: 5 Mahdi
month:
(see at **month**)
month of fasting: 7 Ramadan
mosque: 6 masjid
mystic: 4 Sufi
pilgrim: 5 hajji
pilgrimage: 4 hajj
prayer: 5 salat
priest: 4 imam
prophet: 8 Mohammed, Muhammad
religion: 5 Islam
scripture: 5 Koran, Quran
shrine: 5 Kaaba
temple: 6 mosque
title: 3 aga 4 emir 6 caliph
tradition: 5 sunna
(see also **mosque; Muhammad**)

muss

3 row 4 mess 5 botch, chaos, mix-up,
upset 6 jumble, mess-up, muddle, rumple,
tousle 7 disrupt, rummage 8 disarray,
dishevel, disorder, shambles 9 confusion
10 disarrange 11 disorganize

mussel

5 naiad
genus: 4 Unio 7 Mytilus 8 Anodonta

larva: 9 blackhead

Mussolini, Benito
4 Duce (Il)
son-in-law: 5 Ciano (Galeazzo)

mussy
6 sloppy, untidy 7 tousled, unkempt
8 slovenly 9 cluttered 10 disheveled

must
4 duty, mold, need, want 5 juice, ought
6 devoir, should 9 condition, essential,
necessity, requisite 10 obligation, sine qua
non 11 requirement 12 precondition, prerequisite

muster
4 call, roll 5 crowd, group, raise, rally,
rouse 6 enlist, enroll, gather, induce,
invoke, join up, roster, sample, sign on,
sign up, summon, work up 7 collect,
convene, develop, include, marshal,
produce 8 assemble, assembly, comprise,
congress, generate, mobilize, organize, roll
call, specimen 9 gathering, inventory, nose
count 10 accumulate, assemblage,
collection, congregate, rendezvous
12 accumulation, congregation

muster out
5 demob, let go 9 discharge 10 demobilize

musty
4 dank, dull, sour 5 funky, moldy, stale,
tired, trite 6 frowsy, frowzy, old hat, smelly
7 airless, antique, mildewy, squalid
8 shopworn, timeworn 10 antiquated,
malodorous, threadbare

Mut
husband: 4 Amen, Amon
son: 5 Chons 6 Chonsu, Khonsu

mutable
5 fluid 6 fickle, mobile, shifty 7 erratic,
protean 8 slippery, unstable, unsteady,
variable, volatile, wavering 9 changeful,
mercurial, unsettled 10 capricious,
changeable, inconstant 11 fluctuating,
vacillating 12 inconsistent

mutate
4 vary 5 alter, morph 6 change, modify
9 refashion, transform, transmute
11 transfigure 12 metamorphose,
transmogrify

mutation
5 sport 6 change 7 novelty 9 deviation,
variation 10 alteration 11 vicissitude
12 modification 13 metamorphosis

mute
3 mum 4 dumb 5 quiet 6 dampen,
deaden, muffle, muzzle, reduce, silent,
soften, stifle, subdue 7 silence 8 silencer,
wordless 9 voiceless 10 speechless,
tongue-tied

muted
3 dim, mat 4 dull 6 low-key, silent
10 speechless

mutilate
3 mar 4 maim 6 damage, deface, injure,
mangle 7 cripple 9 disfigure, dismember

mutineer
5 rebel

mutinous
6 unruly 8 factious 9 insurgent, seditious,
turbulent 10 rebellious 12 contumacious
13 insubordinate

mutiny
5 rebel 6 revolt, rise up 8 uprising
9 rebellion 12 insurrection

mutt
3 cur, dog 4 mule 5 cross 6 hybrid
7 mixture, mongrel 9 half blood, half-breed
10 crossbreed

Mutt and _____
4 Jeff

mutter
5 growl 6 grouch, grouse, mumble,
murmur 7 grumble 9 undertone

muttonchops
9 burnsides, sideburns 10 sideboards
11 dundrearies 12 side-whiskers

mutual
5 joint 6 common, public, shared, united
7 related 8 communal, conjoint, conjunct
9 bilateral, connected 10 associated,
reciprocal, respective
prefix: 5 inter

muumuu
6 caftan

muzzle
3 gag 4 hush, mute, nose, phiz 5 snout
7 silence, squelch

muzzy
3 dim 4 dull, hazy 5 faint, vague 6 blurry,
gloomy 7 blurred, muddled, unclear
8 confused, nebulous 9 imprecise

myalgia
4 ache, pain 5 cramp 6 strain 8 soreness

Myanmar
5 Burma

bay: 6 Bengal
capital: 6 Yangon 7 Rangoon
monetary unit: 4 kyat
neighbor: 4 Laos 5 China, India
8 Thailand 10 Bangladesh
peninsula: 9 Indochina
river: 7 Salween 9 Irrawaddy
sea: 7 Andaman

My Antonia author
6 Cather (Willa)

My Last Duchess author
8 Browning (Robert)

My Lost Youth author
10 Longfellow (Henry Wadsworth)

Myra Breckenridge author
5 Vidal (Gore)

myriad
3 lot 4 heap, host, raft, slew 5 flood,
horde, swarm 6 throng 9 countless,
multitude 10 infinitude, numberless
11 innumerable 12 incalculable
13 multitudinous

myrmecology subject
3 ant 4 ants

myrmidon
6 minion 8 follower, retainer 9 attendant,
underling 11 subordinate

Myron's statue
10 Discobolos, Discobolus 13 Discus
Thrower (The)

Myrrha's son
6 Adonis

mysterious
6 arcane, mystic, occult, secret 7 cryptic,
obscure, strange 8 abstruse, esoteric,
numinous 9 ambiguous, enigmatic,
equivocal, recondite 10 cabalistic,
unknowable 11 inscrutable
12 impenetrable, inexplicable,
unfathomable 13 unaccountable

mystery
5 poser 6 enigma, puzzle, riddle, secret
7 arcanum, problem, stumper 8 whodunit
9 conundrum 10 closed book, perplexity,
puzzlement 13 Chinese puzzle

mystic
4 seer 6 arcane, medium, occult, oracle,
secret 7 obscure 8 anagogic, esoteric,
hermetic, numinous 9 enigmatic, visionary
10 cabalistic, unknowable 11 inscrutable,
necromantic 12 impenetrable, thaumaturgic 13 unaccountable

mystical
4 holy 6 arcane, covert, divine, occult,
orphic, sacred, secret 7 cryptic, sub-rosa
8 anagocic, esoteric, hermetic, oracular,
profound 9 recondite, spiritual
10 miraculous, symbolical 11 clandestine
12 supernatural, supranatural

mysticism
7 Orphism 8 cabalism, quietism
11 hermeticism

mystify
6 baffle, puzzle 7 confuse, obscure,
perplex 8 befuddle, bewilder, confound
9 obfuscate

mystifying
7 cryptic, delphic 8 Delphian 9 enigmatic

mystique
5 charm, magic 7 glamour 8 charisma
9 magnetism

myth
4 lore, saga, tale 5 fable, story 6 legend
7 fiction, figment, parable 8 allegory,
folklore 9 tradition 11 fabrication

mythical
6 fabled, made-up, unreal 7 created, fictive
8 fabulous, fanciful, invented 9 fantastic,
fictional, imaginary, legendary
10 apocryphal, fictitious

mythologist
4 Jung (Carl Gustav), Ovid 5 Tylor
(Edward Burnett) 6 Eliade (Mircea), Frazer
(James George), Müller (Friedrich Max)
8 Campbell (Joseph) 9 Euhemerus
10 Malinowski (Bronislaw)

mythology
see **myth**

N

Naamah
- brother: **9** Tubalcain
- father: **6** Lamech
- husband: **7** Solomon
- mother: **6** Zillah
- son: **8** Rehoboam

nab
4 grab **5** catch, pinch, run in, seize **6** arrest, clutch, collar, pick up, pull in, snatch **7** capture **9** apprehend

nabob
3 VIP **5** mogul, noble **6** bigwig, fat cat, tycoon **7** big shot, magnate, notable **8** big chief, eminence, governor **9** big cheese, dignitary, personage **10** notability

Nabokov novel
3 Ada **4** Gift (The), Pnin **6** Lolita **7** Defense (The), Despair **8** Pale Fire **14** King Queen Knave

nacre
13 mother-of-pearl

nada
3 nil, zip **5** zilch **6** naught **7** nothing, nullity **11** nothingness

nadir
4 base, foot **5** depth **6** bottom **8** low point
- opposite: **6** zenith

nag
3 irk, vex **4** bait, carp, goad, ride **5** annoy, chivy, harry, horse, hound, worry **6** badger, bother, carp at, harass, heckle, hector, needle, peck at, pester, plague **7** henpeck, torment **8** complain, harangue, irritate

naiad
5 nymph

naïf
7 ingenue

nail
3 bag, get, nab **4** brad, grab, stud, tack, trap **5** catch, clone, spike, sprig **6** arrest, collar, secure **7** capture **9** apprehend

naive
6 simple **7** artless, natural **8** gullible, innocent, wide-eyed **9** childlike, credulous, guileless, ingenuous, unstudied **10** self-taught, unaffected, unschooled **11** susceptible

naked
3 raw **4** bald, bare, mere, nude, pure **5** clear, sheer **6** peeled, scanty, simple, unclad **7** denuded, evident, exposed, obvious **8** revealed, stripped **9** au naturel, disclosed, unclothed, uncovered, undressed
- combining form: **4** gymn **5** gymno

Naked and the Dead author
6 Mailer (Norman)

namby-pamby
4 weak **5** banal, bland, inane, sissy, vapid **6** effete, jejune **7** insipid **8** nebbishy, weakling **9** spineless **10** effeminate, indecisive, pantywaist, wishy-washy **12** milk-and-water **13** characterless

name
3 dub, nom, tab, tag, tap **4** call, cite, race, term **5** alias, label, nomen, quote, state, style, title **6** byword, finger, handle, report, repute, rubric **7** appoint, baptize, declare, entitle, epithet, mention, moniker, publish, specify **8** announce, christen, identify, instance, nominate **9** advertise, character, designate, incognito, recognize, sobriquet, stipulate **10** denominate, reputation **11** appellation, appellative, designation
- ancient Rome: **6** agnomen **8** prenomen
- assumed: **5** alias **9** sobriquet
- family: **8** cognomen
- fictitious: **9** pseudonym
- giver: **6** eponym

nameless
6 unsung **7** obscure, unknown **9** anonymous **11** indefinable, unutterable

namely

12 uncelebrated, unidentified

namely
3 viz. 5 to wit 6 that is 8 scilicet
9 expressly, specially, videlicet
10 especially 12 particularly, specifically

Namibia
capital: 8 Windhoek
city: 8 Oshakati, Rehoboth
desert: 5 Namib 8 Kalahari
language: 5 Bantu 6 German 9 Afrikaans
neighbor: 6 Angola 8 Botswana
11 South Africa
river: 6 Cunene, Orange 8 Okavango

nana
7 grandma 11 grandmother

Nana
author: 4 Zola (Emile)
mother: 6 Gervaise

Nanna
brother: 6 Nergal, Ninazu
father: 5 Enlil
husband: 6 Balder
mother: 6 Ninlil
son: 3 Utu
wife: 6 Ningal

nanny
5 nurse 9 caregiver, governess, nursemaid

Naomi
4 Mara
daughter-in-law: 4 Ruth 5 Orpah
husband: 9 Elimelech
son: 6 Mahlon 7 Chilion

nap
4 doze, pile, rest, shag, wale, warp, weft,
woof 5 sleep, weave 6 drowse, nod off,
siesta, snooze 7 drop off, surface 10 forty
winks

nape
6 scruff

Naphtali
brother: 3 Dan
father: 5 Jacob
mother: 6 Bilhah
son: 4 Guni 5 Jezer 7 Jahzeel, Jahziel,
Shallum

naphtha
7 solvent 9 petroleum

napkin
5 cloth, doily, towel 9 serviette

napoleon
4 boot 6 pastry 8 card game 9 solitaire

bid: 7 blucher 10 wellington

Napoleon
adversary: 6 Nelson (Horatio) 7 Kutuzov
(Mikhail) 10 Wellington (Duke of)
birthplace: 7 Ajaccio, Corsica
brother: 5 Louis 6 Jérome, Joseph,
Lucien
brother-in-law: 5 Murat (Joachim)
deathplace: 8 St. Helena
defeat: 7 Leipzig 8 Waterloo 9 Trafalgar
father: 5 Carlo
island of exile: 4 Elba 8 St. Helena
marshal: 3 Ney (Michel) 5 Murat
(Joachim), Soult (Nicolas-Jean) 6 Suchet
(Louis-Gabriel)
sister: 5 Maria 8 Carlotta, Carolina
victory: 3 Ulm 4 Jena, Lodi 5 Ligny
6 Abukir, Abu Qir, Arcole, Wagram
7 Bautzen, Dresden, Marengo 8 Borodino
10 Austerlitz
wife: 9 Josephine 11 Marie Louise

narcissism
6 egoism, vanity 7 conceit, egotism 8 self-
love, vainness 9 vainglory
11 egocentrism, self-conceit 13 conceitedness

narcissistic
4 vain 7 stuck-up 9 conceited, egotistic
10 self-loving 11 egotistical 12 self-
absorbed, self-admiring, self-centered,
vainglorious

Narcissus
admirer: 4 Echo
father: 9 Cephissus
mother: 7 Liriope

narcotic
3 hop 4 dope, drug, junk 5 opium
6 heroin, opiate 7 anodyne, cocaine,
hashish 8 hypnotic, morphine, nepenthe
9 somnolent, soporific 10 somnorific
11 somniferous
peddler: 6 dealer, pusher

narrate
4 tell 5 state 6 depict, detail, recite, relate,
report 7 express, outline, portray, recount
8 describe, rehearse 9 chronicle, delineate

narrative
4 epic, myth, saga, tale, yarn 5 fable, story
6 legend, report 7 account, history, recital,
version 8 anecdote 9 chronicle
medieval French: 5 roman 7 romance
prose: 5 novel 7 novella

narrator
6 teller 7 reciter 8 reporter 9 describer,
performer 10 chronicler

narrow

5 close, small, taper 6 lessen, strait
7 bigoted, limited, precise, slender
8 contract, decrease, straiten 9 confining,
constrict, hidebound, illiberal
10 brassbound, inflexible, intolerant,
prejudiced, restricted

narrowly

6 barely 7 closely 8 scarcely, strictly

narrow-minded

5 petty 7 bigoted, insular 9 hidebound,
illiberal 10 brassbound, intolerant,
prejudiced, provincial

nasal

6 rhinal, twangy 9 nosepiece
combining form: 4 rhin 5 rhino

nascency

5 birth 6 origin 7 genesis 8 birthing,
creation, nativity 9 inception 11 parturition

nascent

7 budding, growing, newborn 8 emergent
9 beginning, embryonic, fledgling, incipient,
sprouting 10 blossoming, burgeoning,
initiative, initiatory

Naseby victor

7 Fairfax (Thomas) 8 Cromwell (Oliver)

Nastase

4 Ilie

nasty

4 evil, foul, icky, mean, vile 5 awful, dirty,
gross, snide 6 coarse, filthy, grubby, horrid,
malign, odious, wicked 7 beastly, harmful,
hateful, ill-bred, painful, raunchy, squalid,
vicious 8 god-awful, improper, indecent,
spiteful 9 hazardous, loathsome,
malicious, malignant, obnoxious, offensive,
repugnant, repulsive, vexatious
10 disgusting, malevolent 11 distasteful
12 disagreeable

natant

8 floating, swimming

Nathan

father: 4 Bani 5 Attai, David
son: 5 Zabad

nation

4 race 5 realm, state, tribe 6 domain,
people, polity 7 country, kingdom, society
8 dominion, populace, republic
11 sovereignty 12 commonwealth,
principality

national

6 native 7 citizen, federal, subject
8 resident 10 countryman 11 countrywide

National Basketball Association

Atlanta: 5 Hawks
Boston: 7 Celtics
Charlotte: 7 Hornets
Chicago: 5 Bulls
Cleveland: 9 Cavaliers
Dallas: 9 Mavericks
Denver: 7 Nuggets
Detroit: 7 Pistons
Golden State: 8 Warriors
Houston: 7 Rockets
Indiana: 6 Pacers
Los Angeles: 6 Lakers 8 Clippers
Miami: 4 Heat
Milwaukee: 5 Bucks
Minnesota: 12 Timberwolves
New Jersey: 4 Nets
New York: 6 Knicks
Orlando: 5 Magic
Phoenix: 4 Suns
Portland: 12 Trail Blazers
Sacramento: 5 Kings
San Antonio: 5 Spurs
Seattle: 11 SuperSonics
Toronto: 7 Raptors
Utah: 4 Jazz
Vancouver: 9 Grizzlies
Washington: 7 Bullets

National Football League

Arizona: 9 Cardinals
Atlanta: 7 Falcons
Baltimore: 6 Ravens
Buffalo: 5 Bills
Carolina: 8 Panthers
Chicago: 5 Bears
Cincinnati: 7 Bengals
Cleveland: 6 Browns
Dallas: 7 Cowboys
Denver: 7 Broncos
Detroit: 5 Lions
Green Bay: 7 Packers
Houston: 6 Oilers
Indianapolis: 5 Colts
Jacksonville: 7 Jaguars
Kansas City: 6 Chiefs
Miami: 8 Dolphins
Minnesota: 7 Vikings
New England: 8 Patriots
New Orleans: 6 Saints
New York: 4 Jets 6 Giants
Oakland: 7 Raiders
Philadelphia: 6 Eagles
Pittsburgh: 8 Steelers
St. Louis: 4 Rams
San Diego: 8 Chargers
Seattle: 8 Seahawks
Tampa Bay: 4 Bucs 10 Buccaneers

Tennessee: 6 Oilers
Washington: 8 Redskins

national historical park
Alaska: 5 Sitka
Idaho: 8 Nez Percé
Kentucky-Tennessee: 13 Cumberland Gap
Maryland-West Virginia: 12 Harpers Ferry
Massachusetts: 9 Minute Man
New York: 8 Saratoga

National Hockey League
Anaheim: 11 Mighty Ducks
Atlanta: 9 Thrashers
Boston: 6 Bruins
Buffalo: 6 Sabres
Calgary: 6 Flames
Carolina: 10 Hurricanes
Chicago: 10 Blackhawks
Colorado: 9 Avalanche
Columbus: 11 Blue Jackets
Dallas: 5 Stars
Detroit: 8 Red Wings
Edmonton: 6 Oilers
Florida: 8 Panthers
Los Angeles: 5 Kings
Minnesota: 4 Wild
Montreal: 9 Canadiens
Nashville: 9 Predators
New Jersey: 6 Devils
New York: 7 Rangers 9 Islanders
Ottawa: 8 Senators
Philadelphia: 6 Flyers
Phoenix: 7 Coyotes
St. Louis: 5 Blues
San Jose: 6 Sharks
Tampa Bay: 9 Lightning
Toronto: 10 Maple Leafs
Vancouver: 6 Canucks
Washington: 8 Capitals

nationalism
8 jingoism 10 chauvinism, patriotism

National League
Arizona: 12 Diamondbacks
Atlanta: 6 Braves
Chicago: 4 Cubs
Cincinnati: 4 Reds
Colorado: 7 Rockies
Florida: 7 Marlins
Houston: 6 Astros
Los Angeles: 7 Dodgers
Milwaukee: 7 Brewers
New York: 4 Mets
Philadelphia: 8 Phillies
Pittsburgh: 7 Pirates

St. Louis: 9 Cardinals
San Diego: 6 Padres
San Francisco: 6 Giants
Washington: 9 Nationals

national military park
Alabama: 13 Horseshoe Bend
Arkansas: 8 Pea Ridge
Mississippi: 9 Vicksburg
Pennsylvania: 10 Gettysburg
South Carolina: 13 Kings Mountain
Tennessee: 6 Shiloh

national monument
Alabama: 11 Russell Cave
Alaska: 9 Aniakchak
Arizona: 5 Tonto 6 Navajo 7 Saguaro, Wupatki 8 Tuzigoot 10 Chiricahua, Pipe Spring, Tumacacori 11 Hohokam Pima 12 Sunset Crater, Walnut Canyon
California: 8 Cabrillo, Lava Beds 9 Muir Woods, Pinnacles 10 Joshua Tree 11 Death Valley
Colorado: 10 Yucca House
Colorado-Utah: 8 Dinosaur 9 Hoven-weep
Florida: 12 Fort Matanzas 13 Fort Jefferson
Georgia: 8 Ocmulgee 11 Fort Pulaski 13 Fort Frederica
Iowa: 12 Effigy Mounds
Louisiana: 12 Poverty Point
Maryland: 11 Fort McHenry
Minnesota: 9 Pipestone 12 Grand Portage
Nebraska: 9 Homestead 11 Scotts Bluff
New Mexico: 5 Pecos 7 El Morro 9 Bandelier, El Malpais, Fort Union 10 Aztec Ruins, White Sands
New York: 11 Fort Stanwix 13 Castle Clinton
South Carolina: 10 Fort Sumter 13 Congaree Swamp
South Dakota: 9 Jewel Cave
Utah: 11 Cedar Breaks 13 Rainbow Bridge
Wyoming: 11 Devils Tower, Fossil Butte

national park
Alaska: 6 Denali, Katmai 9 Lake Clark 10 Glacier Bay 11 Kenai Fjords, Kobuk Valley
Angola: 4 Iona, Mupa
Arizona: 11 Grand Canyon
Arkansas: 10 Hot Springs
Botswana: 5 Chobe
California: 7 Redwood, Sequoia 8 Yosemite 11 King's Canyon
Chad: 5 Manda

Colombia: 5 Uraba
Colorado: 9 Mesa Verde 13 Rocky Mountain
eastern Africa: 10 Mount Kenya
Florida: 8 Biscayne 10 Everglades
Hawaii: 9 Haleakala
India: 5 Kanha
Japan: 5 Nikko
Kentucky: 11 Mammoth Cave
Kenya: 4 Meru 5 Tsavo 10 Royal Tsavo
Lake Superior: 10 Isle Royale
Maine: 6 Acadia
Malaysia: 8 Kinabalu
Minnesota: 9 Voyageurs
Montana: 7 Glacier
Nevada: 6 Great Basin
Oregon: 10 Crater Lake
Poland: 5 Ojcow, Tatra
South Africa: 6 Kruger
South Dakota: 8 Badlands, Wind Cave
Sri Lanka: 4 Yala
Sweden: 5 Sarek
Tanzania: 5 Ruaha 9 Serengeti
Texas: 7 Big Bend
Utah: 4 Zion 6 Arches 11 Bryce Canyon, Canyonlands, Capitol Reef
Virginia: 10 Shenandoah
Washington: 7 Olympic 12 Mount Rainier 13 North Cascades
Wyoming: 10 Grand Teton
Wyoming-Idaho-Montana: 11 Yellowstone
Zambia: 5 Kafue
Zimbabwe: 13 Rhodes Inyanga, Victoria Falls

native

3 raw 4 wild 5 local 6 inborn, innate 7 connate, endemic, natural 8 domestic, indigene, inherent, internal, national 9 inherited 10 aboriginal, congenital, connatural, indigenous, unacquired
Acadian Louisiana: 6 Cajun
China: 3 Han 9 Celestial
India: 5 sepoy
Japan: 9 Nipponese
London: 7 Cockney
New England: 4 Yank 6 Yankee
New York: 13 Knickerbocker

Native Son author

6 Wright (Richard)

Nativity

4 Noel, Xmas, yule 8 yuletide 9 Christmas

nativity

5 birth, start 6 origin, outset 7 genesis 8 delivery 9 beginning, horoscope, inception 11 parturition

natter

3 gab, jaw, yak, yap 4 blab, buzz, chat, go on 5 prate, run on 6 babble, gabble, gossip, tattle 7 chatter, prattle, twaddle 8 chitchat, converse

natty

4 neat, tidy, trim 5 doggy, sassy, smart, spiffy, swank 6 classy, dapper, jaunty, snazzy, spiffy, spruce, sprucy, swanky 7 bandbox, doggish, stylish 9 turned out 11 well-groomed

natural

4 pure, wild 5 naive, usual 6 candid, inborn, innate, native, normal, simple 7 artless, connate, organic 8 homespun, inherent, innocent 9 childlike, ingenuous, ingrained, primitive 10 congenital, indigenous, legitimate, unaffected 11 commonplace, instinctive, spontaneous

naturalist

American: 4 Muir (John) 5 Hyatt (Alpheus) 7 Audubon (John James), Verrill (Addison, Alpheus)
English: 3 Ray (John) 5 White (Gilbert) 6 Darwin (Charles) 7 Wallace (Alfred) 10 Williamson (William)
French: 5 Fabre (Jean-Henri) 7 Lamarck (Chevalier de), Réaumur (René-Antoine)
Scottish: 6 Wilson (Alexander) 10 Richardson (John)

nature

3 ilk, way 4 kind, sort, type 6 makeup, manner, stripe, temper 7 essence, scenery 8 creation, tendency, universe 9 character, landscape 10 complexion 11 description, disposition, personality, temperament 12 constitution

naught

3 nil, zip 4 love, nada, zero 5 zilch 6 cipher 7 nothing, nullity 8 goose egg 11 nothingness

naughty

3 bad 4 lewd 5 bawdy 6 unruly, ribald, risqué, smutty, vulgar 7 froward, obscene, raunchy, wayward, willful 8 contrary, improper, perverse, rascally 10 ill-behaved 11 disobedient, mischievous 12 obstreperous, recalcitrant

Nauru

capital: 5 Yaren
former name: 8 Pleasant (Island)
monetary unit: 6 dollar

nauseate
5 repel 6 offend, sicken 7 disgust, repulse

nauseated
6 queasy 7 carsick 8 qualmish
9 disgusted, squeamish 10 grossed out

nauseating
6 putrid 7 noisome 9 loathsome,
offensive, repellant, repugnant, repulsive,
revolting, sickening 10 disgusting

Nausicaa
father: 8 Alcinous
mother: 5 Arete

nautical
5 naval 6 marine 7 oceanic 8 maritime
12 navigational
instrument: 3 aba 7 compass, pelorus,
sextant

Navajo dwelling
5 hogan

naval hero
5 Jones (John Paul), Perry (Matthew),
Oliver Hazard) 8 Farragut (David, George),
Lawrence (James)

navel
6 middle 7 nombril 9 umbilicus 11 belly
button
combining form: 6 omphal 7 omphalo

navigate
4 helm, plot, sail 5 guide, pilot, steer
6 cruise 8 maneuver, traverse

navigation
8 piloting 10 seamanship 12 helms-
manship

navigational system
5 loran

navigator
5 flyer, pilot 6 airman 7 copilot
Danish: 6 Bering (Vitus)
Dutch: 6 Tasman (Abel) 7 Barents
(Willem)
English: 4 Cook (Captain James)
5 Cabot (John, Sebastian), Drake (Francis)
6 Hudson (Henry) 7 Gilbert (Humphrey),
Raleigh (Walter) 9 Vancouver (George)
French: 7 Cartier (Jacques) 9 La Perouse
(Comte de)
Italian: 6 Caboto (Giovanni) 8 Columbus
(Christopher), Vespucci (Amerigo)
9 Verrazano (Giovanni) 10 Verrazzano
(Giovanni)
Norwegian: 4 Eric (the Red) 8 Ericsson
(Leif) 12 Leif Ericsson, Leif Eriksson
Portuguese: 4 Dias (Bartolomeu, Dinis)

6 Cabral (Pedro Alvares), da Gama (Vasco)
8 Magellan (Ferdinand)
Spanish: 9 Fernández (Juan)

navy
4 blue 5 fleet 6 argosy, armada 8 flotilla

Nazi
9 Hitlerite 10 brownshirt
admiral: 6 Dönitz (Karl), Raeder (Erich)
7 Doenitz (Karl)
air force: 9 Luftwaffe
armed forces: 9 Wehrmacht
collaborator: 5 Laval (Pierre) 8 Quisling
(Vidkun)
concentration camp: 6 Belsen, Dachau
9 Auschwitz, Treblinka 10 Buchenwald,
Nordhausen
field marshal: 5 Model (Walter) 6 Keitel
(Wilhelm), Paulus (Friedrich), Rommel
(Erwin) 9 Rundstedt (Karl von)
10 Kesselring (Albert)
greeting: 4 heil
leader: 3 Ley (Robert) 4 Hess (Rudolf),
Röhm (Ernst) 5 Roehm (Ernst) 6 Führer,
Göring (Hermann), Hitler (Adolf) 7 Fuehrer,
Goering (Hermann), Himmler (Heinrich)
8 Goebbels (Joseph), Heydrich (Reinhard)
9 Rosenberg (Alfred)
police: 7 Gestapo
propagandist: 8 Goebbels (Joseph)
submarine: 6 U-boat
surrender signer: 4 Jodl (Alfred) 6 Keitel
(Wilhelm)
symbol: 6 fylfot 8 swastika
tactic: 10 blitzkrieg
tank: 6 Panzer

NCO
3 cpl, sgt 8 corporal, sergeant

neap
3 low 4 tide

near
4 nigh 5 about, circa, close, round
6 almost, around 7 close by, close on
8 adjacent, approach 9 immediate,
proximate 11 approximate

nearby
4 nigh 5 about, aside, close, handy
6 around, beside 8 adjacent 9 adjoining,
proximate 10 contiguous, convenient
11 neighboring

nearest
4 next 7 closest 8 adjacent, proximal
9 proximate 10 contiguous

nearsighted
6 myopic

neat
4 deft, nice, prim, snug, tidy, trig, trim
5 clean, clear, kempt 6 clever, smooth,
spruce 7 orderly, precise, unmixed
8 straight, well-kept 9 shipshape, undiluted
10 methodical, systematic 11 spic-and-
span, uncluttered, well-groomed 12 spick-
and-span 13 unadulterated

neb
3 tip 4 beak, bill, nose, prow 5 snoot, snout
6 proboscis

Nebraska
   capital: 7 Lincoln
   city: 5 Omaha
   college, university: 9 Creighton
   nickname: 10 Cornhusker (State)
   river: 6 Platte 8 Missouri
   state bird: 10 meadowlark
   state flower: 9 goldenrod
   state tree: 10 cottonwood

nebula
6 galaxy

nebulous
4 hazy 5 vague 6 cloudy, turbid
7 clouded, obscure, unclear 9 ambiguous,
amorphous, uncertain 10 indefinite,
indistinct 13 indeterminate

necessary
5 basic, vital 6 needed 7 crucial, needful
8 cardinal, integral, required 9 de rigueur,
essential, mandatory, requisite
10 compulsory, imperative, inevitable,
obligatory, undeniable 11 fundamental,
ineluctable, inescapable, unavoidable
12 all-important, prerequisite 13 indispensable

necessitate
5 cause, exact, force 6 compel, demand,
entail 7 call for, involve, require
8 occasion

necessity
4 must, need 6 crisis, duress 7 poverty
8 exigency 9 essential, privation, requisite
10 compulsion, imperative, obligation, sine
qua non 11 dire straits, needfulness,
requirement 12 precondition, prerequisite

neck
3 pet 4 kiss 6 fondle, smooch
   back of: 4 nape 5 nucha 6 scruff
   ornament: 6 gorget, torque

necklace
5 chain 6 choker 7 rivière 8 carcanet

necktie
5 ascot 6 cravat 10 four-in-hand

necrology
4 obit 8 obituary

necromancy
4 juju 5 magic, vodun 6 hoodoo, voodoo
7 devilry, sorcery 8 witchery, wizardry
9 conjuring, diabolism, magicking 10 black
magic, witchcraft 11 bewitchment,
conjuration, enchantment, incantation,
thaumaturgy

necropolis
8 boneyard, boot hill, cemetery, God's acre
9 graveyard 10 churchyard 12 memorial
park, potter's field

necropsy
7 anatomy, autopsy 10 dissection,
postmortem

née
4 born 10 originally

need
3 use 4 call, duty, lack, must, want 5 crave
6 demand, devoir, hunger, penury, thirst
7 poverty, require 8 distress, exigency,
occasion, shortage 9 indigence, necessity,
privation, requisite 10 compulsion,
deficiency, obligation 11 deprivation,
destitution, requirement

neediness
4 want 6 penury 7 poverty 9 indigence,
privation 11 deprivation, destitution
13 insufficiency

needle
3 rib 5 annoy, tease 6 harass, pester,
plague 7 bedevil, hagride, obelisk, pricker,
syringe 10 hypodermic
   case: 4 etui
   hole: 3 eye

needlefish
3 gar 8 pipefish

needlelike
7 styloid 8 belonoid
   part: 7 acicula

needlepoint
4 lace 7 alençon, crochet, tatting
8 bargello 10 embroidery 11 cross-stitch

needlework
4 lace 6 sewing 7 alençon, crochet,
sampler, tatting 8 bargello, knitting
9 stitching 10 crocheting, embroidery
11 cross-stitch

needy
4 poor 5 broke 6 hard up 8 beggared,
dirt-poor, indigent, strapped 9 destitute,
penniless, penurious 10 down-and-out
11 impecunious, necessitous
12 impoverished

ne'er-do-well
3 bum, dud 5 loser 6 loafer, no-good
7 failure, wastrel 8 derelict 9 shiftless
10 profligate, scapegrace

nefarious
4 evil, vile 6 savage, wicked 7 heinous,
impious, noxious 8 depraved, dreadful,
flagrant, infamous, perverse 9 execrable,
miscreant, monstrous, offensive
10 abominable, degenerate, detestable,
iniquitous, outrageous, villainous
11 opprobrious 13 reprehensible

negate
4 deny, undo, void 5 annul, cancel, quash,
rebut 6 impugn, refute, vacate 7 abolish,
gainsay, nullify, redress, vitiate 8 abrogate,
disallow, disprove, overturn, traverse
9 cancel out, disaffirm, repudiate 10 contradict, contravene, counteract, invalidate,
neutralize 12 countercheck

negative
3 nix 4 deny, kill, veto 5 annul, cross,
minus 6 impugn 7 adverse, gainsay,
nullify, redress, refusal 8 abrogate,
disprove, traverse 9 cancel out, frustrate
10 contradict, contravene, counteract,
invalidate, neutralize 11 detrimental,
unfavorable
battery terminal: 5 anode
ion: 5 anion
Scottish: 3 nae
sign: 5 minus

neglect
4 fail, omit 5 let go, shirk 6 forget, ignore,
laxity, slight 7 failure, laxness 8 omission,
overlook, overpass, pass over
9 avoidance, disregard, oversight, pretermit
10 negligence 11 dereliction, inattention
12 carelessness 13 pretermission

neglectful
see **negligent**

negligee
4 gown 5 teddy 7 chemise, nightie
8 camisole, peignoir 9 nightgown

negligent
3 lax 5 slack 6 remiss 8 careless,
derelict, heedless 9 forgetful, imprudent
10 delinquent, neglectful, nonchalant,
regardless, unthinking 11 inattentive,
pococurante, unconcerned 12 disregardful
13 irresponsible, lackadaisical

negligible
4 puny, slim 5 minor, petty, small
6 meager, meagre, minute, remote, paltry,
skimpy, slight 7 minimal, slender, trivial
8 nugatory, picayune, trifling 9 minuscule
11 meaningless, unimportant
13 imperceptible, insignificant

negotiable
8 passable 11 convertible 12 transferable

negotiate
4 cash 6 confer, dicker, hurdle, manage,
parley, settle 7 arrange, bargain, develop,
mediate, work out, wrangle 8 contract,
covenant, moderate, surmount, transact,
transfer 9 arbitrate 10 horse-trade

neigh
6 nicker, whinny

neighbor
4 abut 5 flank, frame, skirt 6 adjoin, border
7 abutter 8 border on

neighborhood
4 area, turf, ward 5 block, range 6 parish
8 district, locality, precinct, purlieus,
vicinage, vicinity 9 community, proximity

neighborly
6 genial 7 amiable, cordial, helpful
8 amicable, friendly, obliging, sociable
9 congenial 10 gregarious, hospitable
11 considerate, cooperative, good-natured
13 accommodating

nematode
4 worm 7 eelworm 9 roundworm

Nemean predator
4 lion

nemesis
4 bane, doom 5 curse, enemy, rival
8 opponent 9 bête noire 11 retribution

neologism
7 coinage, new word

neophyte
see **newcomer**

Neoptolemus
7 Pyrrhus
father: 8 Achilles
slayer: 7 Orestes
victim: 5 Priam
wife: 8 Hermione

neoteric
6 modern, recent

Nepal
capital: 8 Katmandu 9 Kathmandu

city: 7 Pokhara 8 Lalitpur
monetary unit: 5 rupee
mountain, range: 7 Everest 8 Himalaya
9 Himalayan, Himalayas 10 Dhaulagiri
11 Gauri Sankar 12 Kanchenjunga
neighbor: 5 China, India
river: 6 Ganges

nepenthe
6 opiate, potion 7 anodyne 8 lenitive,
narcotic 9 analgesic 10 anesthetic,
painkiller

Nephthys
brother, husband: 3 Set 4 Seth

nepotism
10 favoritism, partiality

Neptune
6 planet
satellite: 6 Nereid, Triton
(see also **Poseidon**)

nerd
4 drip, geek 6 misfit 7 egghead, nebbish,
oddball 10 pointy-head

Nereid
6 Thetis 7 Galatea 10 Amphitrite
father: 6 Nereus
mother: 5 Doris

Nereus
daughters: 8 Nereides
emblem: 7 trident
father: 6 Pontus
mother: 4 Gaea
wife: 5 Doris

Nergal
brother: 5 Nanna 6 Ninazu
father: 5 Enlil
mother: 6 Ninlil

Nero
birthplace: 4 Rome
mother: 9 Agrippina
successor: 5 Galba
tutor: 6 Seneca
victim: 5 Lucan 6 Seneca 7 Octavia,
Poppaea 9 Agrippina
wife: 7 Octavia, Poppaea

Nero Wolfe creator
5 Stout (Rex)

nerve
4 face, gall, grit, guts 5 brass, cheek,
crust, heart, moxie, spunk 6 daring
7 sciatic 8 audacity, backbone, boldness,
chutzpah, temerity 9 assurance,
brashness, fortitude, hardihood, hardiness
10 confidence, effrontery 11 presumption
cell: 6 neuron
cell group: 7 ganglia (plural) 8 ganglion

combining form: 4 neur 5 neura, neuro
cranial: 4 vagi (plural) 5 optic, vagus
8 abducens
ending: 8 receptor
lesion: 8 neuritis

nerve center
3 hub 4 core, seat 5 focus, heart, locus
7 capital 8 cynosure, polestar
10 crossroads, focal point 12 headquarters

nerve gas
5 sarin, soman, tabun

nervous
4 edgy 5 jerky, jumpy, tense, timid 6 fitful,
goosey, on edge, spooky, uneasy 7 erratic,
fidgety, fretful, jittery, restive, twitchy,
uptight 8 aflutter, agitated, forcible, skittery,
skittish, spirited, twittery, unsteady,
vigorous, volatile 9 excitable, irregular,
irritable 10 high-strung 12 apprehensive

nervy
4 bold, edgy, pert 5 brash, cocky, fresh,
jerky, jumpy, sassy, tense 6 brassy,
cheeky, goosey, plucky, spooky, uneasy
7 fidgety, forward, jittery, restive, twitchy,
uptight 8 impudent, intrepid, twittery
9 excitable 10 high-strung 11 smart-
alecky

ness
4 cape 8 foreland, headland 9 peninsula
10 promontory

Nessus' victim
8 Heracles, Hercules

nest
3 den 4 aery, home, lair, nidi (plural)
5 aerie, eyrie, nidus 7 hangout, shelter
11 aggregation
eagle's: 4 aery 5 aerie, eyrie
wasp's: 8 vespiary

nest egg
5 cache, funds, hoard, kitty, stash 6 assets
7 reserve

nestle
4 snug 6 bundle, burrow, cuddle, huddle,
nuzzle 7 snuggle

Nestor
father: 6 Neleus
kingdom: 5 Pylos

net
4 gain, gist, mesh 5 basic, catch, clear,
seine, tulle, yield 6 maline 7 clean up,
essence, malines
conical: 5 trawl
fishing: 5 seine

Nethanel

hair: 5 snood

Nethanel
brother: 5 David
father: 5 Jesse 7 Pashhur 8 Obededom
son: 8 Shemaiah

nether
3 low 4 down 5 below, lower, under
6 lesser 8 chthonic, inferior 9 subjacent
10 underworld 11 underground
12 subterranean

Netherlands
7 Holland
capital: 9 Amsterdam
city: 5 Hague (The) 7 Utrecht 8 The
Hague 9 Rotterdam
former inlet: 9 Zuider Zee
island group: 11 West Frisian
lake: 10 IJsselmeer
language: 5 Dutch
monetary unit: 4 euro
monetary unit, former: 7 guilder
neighbor: 7 Belgium, Germany
river: 4 Maas 5 Meuse, Rhein, Rhine
7 Scheldt
sea: 5 North

Netherlands Antilles
capital: 10 Willemstad
discoverer: 8 Columbus (Christopher)
former name: 7 Curaçao
island: 4 Saba 7 Bonaire 7 Curaçao
location: 10 West Indies
part of: 11 Netherlands

netherworld
3 pit 4 hell 5 abyss, hades, Sheol
6 blazes, Tophet 7 Gehenna, inferno
8 hellfire 9 perdition 10 no-man's-land,
underworld 11 underground

netlike
9 reticular 10 reticulate

nettle
3 nag, vex 4 gall, huff, rile, roil 5 annoy,
chafe, peeve, pique, upset 6 abrade,
badger, harass, incite, put out, pester,
ruffle, stir up 7 agitate, disturb, perturb,
provoke 8 irritate 10 exasperate

nettle rash
5 hives 9 urticaria

nettlesome
5 pesky 6 vexing 7 galling, irksome,
prickly 8 annoying, rankling 9 irritable,
upsetting, vexatious 10 irritating

network
3 web 4 mesh 8 gridiron 9 reticulum

anatomical: 4 rete 5 retia (plural)

neurotic
6 phobic, touchy 7 anxious 8 abnormal,
unstable 9 disturbed, obsessive
10 compulsive, disordered

neuter
3 fix 4 geld, spay 5 alter, unsex 7 sexless
8 castrate, mutilate 9 sterilize
11 desexualize 12 intransitive

neutral
7 hueless 8 detached, middling, unbiased
9 colorless, impartial, unaligned
10 achromatic, disengaged, even-handed,
impersonal, nonaligned, pokerfaced
11 indifferent, nonpartisan
13 disinterested, dispassionate

neutralize
4 undo 5 annul 6 negate, offset
7 balance, nullify, redress, reverse
9 cancel out 10 counteract, invalidate
11 countervail 12 countercheck,
counterpoise

Nevada
capital: 10 Carson City
city: 4 Elko, Reno 8 Las Vegas
dam: 6 Hoover 7 Boulder
lake: 4 Mead 5 Tahoe
mountain: 8 Boundary (Peak)
nickname: 6 Silver (State)
river: 8 Humboldt
state bird: 8 bluebird (mountain)
state flower: 9 sagebrush
state tree: 5 piñon 6 pinyon 15 bristlecone pine

névé
4 firn, snow

never-ending
7 eternal 8 immortal 9 ceaseless
11 everlasting

Never-Ending Story author
4 Ende (Michael)

nevertheless
3 but, yet 5 still 6 anyhow, anyway,
though, withal 7 howbeit, however 8 after
all 10 regardless 11 nonetheless, still and
all

nevus
4 mole 9 birthmark

new
5 fresh, novel 6 modern, recent 7 another,
revived 8 neoteric, pristine 10 additional,
unfamiliar 11 modernistic
12 contemporary

combining form: 3 neo, nov 4 novo
word: 7 coinage 9 neologism

New Brunswick
capital: 11 Fredericton
city: 6 St. John 7 Moncton
mountain: 8 Carleton
provincial flower: 12 purple violet
river: 9 Miramichi, Saint John
10 Nepisiguit 11 Restigouche

New Caledonia
capital: 6 Nouméa
department of: 6 France
discoverer: 4 Cook (Capt. James)
island: 7 Loyalty, Walpole 11 Isle of Pines

newcomer
4 colt, tyro 6 novice, rookie 8 beginner,
freshman, initiate, neophyte 9 greenhorn,
immigrant, novitiate 10 apprentice,
tenderfoot

New Deal agency
3 CCC, NRA, SEC, TVA, WPA 4 FDIC,
NLRB

Newfoundland and Labrador
capital: 7 St. John's
mountain: 8 Caubvick
provincial flower: 12 pitcher plant
river: 6 Gander 8 Exploits 9 Churchill

New Hampshire
capital: 7 Concord
city: 6 Nashua 10 Manchester,
Portsmouth
college, university: 9 Dartmouth
motto: 13 Live Free or Die
mountain, range: 5 White 10 Washington
nickname: 7 Granite (State)
river: 9 Merrimack 11 Connecticut
state bird: 11 purple finch
state flower: 11 purple lilac
state tree: 10 white birch

New Jersey
capital: 7 Trenton
city: 6 Camden, Newark 7 Cape May
8 Paterson 9 Elizabeth 10 Jersey City
college, university: 4 Drew 7 Rutgers
9 Princeton, Seton Hall 18 Fairleigh
Dickinson
nickname: 6 Garden (State)
river: 6 Hudson 7 Raritan 8 Delaware
state bird: 9 goldfinch
state flower: 6 violet
state tree: 6 red oak

New Mexico
capital: 7 Santa Fe
caverns: 8 Carlsbad
city: 4 Taos 7 Roswell 9 Las Cruces, Los
Alamos 10 Farmington 11 Albuquerque

mountain, range: 7 Wheeler (Peak)
14 Sangre de Cristo
nickname: 17 Land of Enchantment
river: 5 Pecos 9 Rio Grande
state bird: 10 roadrunner
state flower: 5 yucca
state tree: 5 piñon 6 pinyon

news
4 dope, poop, word 5 rumor 6 advice,
gossip, report, tattle 7 lowdown, tidings
9 knowledge, speerings 11 information,
scuttlebutt 12 announcement, intelligence
4 TASS 7 Reuters 8 ITAR-TASS

newspaper
5 daily, organ 6 review 7 journal, tabloid
8 magazine 10 periodical
publisher: 6 Hearst (William Randolph)
7 Murdoch (Rupert) 11 Beaverbrook (Lord)

newt
3 eft 6 triton
green: 5 ebbet

New Testament
see at **Bible**

New York
capital: 6 Albany
city: 4 Rome, Troy 5 Utica 6 Elmira,
Ithaca 7 Buffalo, Yonkers 8 Saratoga,
Syracuse 9 Rochester 11 New York City
college, university: 3 RPI 4 Pace, CUNY,
SUNY 5 Pratt, Siena 6 CW Post, Hunter,
Vassar 7 Adelphi, Barnard, Colgate,
Cornell, Fordham, Hofstra, St. Johns,
Yeshiva 8 Columbia, Skidmore, Syracuse
9 Juilliard, West Point 13 Sarah Lawrence
island: 4 Long, Fire
lake, lake group: 4 Erie 6 Cayuga,
Finger, Oneida 7 Saranac 9 Champlain
motto: 9 Excelsior
mountain, range: 5 Marcy 8 Catskill
10 Adirondack
nickname: 6 Empire (State)
river: 6 Hudson 7 Niagara 10 St.
Lawrence
state bird: 8 bluebird
state flower: 4 rose
state tree: 10 sugar maple

New York City
6 Gotham 9 Big Apple
borough: 5 Bronx 6 Queens 8 Brooklyn,
Richmond 9 Manhattan 12 Staten Island

New Zealand
capital: 10 Wellington
city: 8 Auckland 12 Christchurch
ethnic group: 5 Maori
explorer: 4 Cook (Capt. James)
6 Tasman (Abel)

island: 5 North, South 7 Chatham, Stewart
island group: 4 Cook 8 Manihiki 12 Northern Cook
lake: 5 Taupo
language: 5 Maori 7 English
monetary unit: 6 dollar
mountain, range: 4 Cook 6 Egmont 12 Southern Alps
native: 4 Kiwi
strait: 4 Cook
volcano: 7 Ruapehu 9 Ngauruhoe

next
4 then 5 after, later 6 behind, beside, second 7 closest, ensuing, nearest 8 abutting, adjacent, touching 9 adjoining, afterward, alongside, following, proximate 10 contiguous, subsequent, succeeding 11 neighboring

next to
4 near 6 almost, beside 7 abreast, close by 8 abutting, adjacent, opposite, touching 9 adjoining, alongside, bordering 11 neighboring

nexus
3 tie 4 bond, knot, link, yoke 5 focus 6 center 8 ligament, ligature, vinculum 10 connection

Nez Percé chief
6 Joseph

Niagara
5 flood, spate 6 deluge 7 torrent 8 alluvion, cataract, flooding, overflow 9 cataclysm, waterfall 10 inundation

nib
3 neb, tip 4 beak, bill, nose, prow 5 prong, snoot, snout, tooth 8 pen point 9 proboscis

nibble
3 eat, nip 4 bite, chew, crop, gnaw, nosh, peck, pick 5 graze, munch, snack, taste 6 morsel, tidbit

Nicaragua
capital: 7 Managua
city: 4 León 6 Masaya
coast: 8 Mosquito
ethnic group: 4 Maya 5 Mayan
discoverer: 8 Columbus (Christopher)
language: 7 Spanish
monetary unit: 7 córdoba
neighbor: 8 Honduras 9 Costa Rica
sea: 9 Caribbean

nice
4 fine, good, kind, mild, neat 5 right 6 benign, comely, dainty, decent, polite, proper, seemly 7 affable, clement, cordial,

correct, fitting, refined 8 becoming, charming, decorous, obliging, pleasant, pleasing, suitable, virtuous, well-bred 9 admirable, agreeable, courteous, congenial, enjoyable, favorable, judicious 10 attractive, personable 11 appropriate, respectable

niche
4 nook 6 alcove, corner, cranny, recess 7 calling 8 vocation 9 cubbyhole 11 compartment

Nicholas Nickleby author
7 Dickens (Charles)

nick
3 cut 4 chip, gash 5 cheat, notch, score 6 groove, record 10 overcharge 11 indentation

nickname
3 tag 5 label 6 byword, handle 7 agnomen, epithet, moniker 8 cognomen 9 sobriquet 10 diminutive, hypocorism

Nicomede
conquest: 10 Cappadocia
dramatist: 9 Corneille (Pierre)
half-brother: 6 Attale
stepmother: 7 Arsinoë

nictitate
3 bat 4 wink 5 blink 7 flutter, twinkle

nifty
4 cool, keen, neat 5 dandy, ducky, super, swell 6 clever, groovy, peachy 7 stylish 8 jim-dandy, splendid, terrific 9 ingenious

Niger
capital: 6 Niamey
city: 6 Maradi, Zinder
desert: 5 Sahel 6 Sahara
ethnic group: 5 Hausa
language: 5 Hausa 6 Arabic, French
monetary unit: 5 franc
neighbor: 4 Chad, Mali 5 Benin, Libya 7 Algeria, Nigeria 11 Burkina Faso
river: 5 Niger

Nigeria
capital: 5 Abuja, Lagos
city: 4 Kano 6 Ibadan, Ilorin 7 Oshogbo 9 Ogbomosho
ethnic group: 4 Igbo 5 Hausa 6 Fulani, Yoruba
gulf: 6 Guinea
lake: 4 Chad
language: 5 Hausa 7 English
monetary unit: 5 naira
neighbor: 4 Chad 5 Benin, Niger 8 Cameroon
river: 5 Benue, Niger 6 Kaduna

niggard
5 churl, miser, piker, screw 7 hoarder,
scrooge 8 tightwad 9 skinflint
10 cheapskate, curmudgeon 12 money-
grubber, penny-pincher

niggardly
5 tight 6 scanty, stingy 7 chintzy, miserly
9 penurious 10 begrudging 11 closefisted,
tightfisted 12 cheeseparing, parsimonious
13 penny-pinching

niggling
5 minor, petty 6 measly, paltry, two-bit
7 trivial 8 picayune, piddling, tiresome,
trifling 9 small-time 10 bothersome,
picayunish 11 small-minded

nigh
4 near 5 about, close, round 6 all but,
almost, around, beside, nearby, nearly
7 close to 8 approach 9 immediate, just
about, proximate, virtually 10 near at hand,
pretty much 11 practically

night blindness
10 nyctalopia

nightclub
5 disco 6 bistro, casino 7 cabaret
9 honky-tonk, speakeasy 11 discotheque

nightfall
3 eve 4 dusk, even 6 sunset 7 evening,
sundown 8 eventide, gloaming, twilight

nighthawk
6 petrel 7 bullbat 10 goatsucker

nightjar
9 nighthawk 10 goatsucker 12 whip-poor-
will

nightly
9 nocturnal

nightmare
5 dream, fancy, fright, worry 6 horror,
ordeal, vision 7 bugbear, fantasy, incubus,
torment 8 phantasm, phantasy, succubus
12 apprehension 13 hallucination

nightshade
6 tomato 7 henbane 10 belladonna
11 bittersweet

nightstick
3 bat 4 club, mace 5 baton, billy, staff
6 cudgel 8 bludgeon 9 billy club,
blackjack, truncheon 10 shillelagh

Nike
father: 6 Pallas
goddess of: 7 victory
mother: 4 Styx

nil
3 nix, zip 4 love, wind, zero 5 zilch
6 naught 7 nothing

Nile
6 Al-Bahr
dam: 5 Aswan 6 Makwar 10 Gebel Aulia
explorer: 5 Baker (Sir Samuel), Bruce
(James), Grant (James Augustus), Speke
(John Hanning)
queen: 4 Cleo 9 Cleopatra
section: 4 Abay 5 Abbai

nilgai
8 antelope

nimble
4 deft, spry, yare 5 agile, alert, fleet, handy,
light, quick, zippy 6 adroit, limber, lively
7 lissome 9 dexterous, sprightly
10 responsive 11 quick-witted

Nimrod
6 hunter
father: 4 Cush

Ninazu
brother: 5 Nanna 6 Nergal
father: 5 Enlil
mother: 6 Ninlil

nincompoop
3 oaf 4 boob, clod, dodo, fool, goof, mutt,
simp, yo-yo 5 chump, dummy, dunce, idiot,
moron, ninny, noddy, stupe 6 dimwit,
donkey, dum-dum, nitwit 7 airhead,
dullard, pinhead, schnook, tomfool
8 bonehead, clodpoll, dumbbell,
dumbhead, imbecile, lunkhead, meathead,
numskull 9 birdbrain, blockhead,
ignoramus, lamebrain, numbskull,
simpleton, thickhead 10 dunderhead,
hammerhead 11 chowderhead,
chucklehead, knucklehead

nine
12 baseball team
combining form: 3 non 4 nona
goddesses: 5 Muses
group: 6 ennead
inches: 4 span
instruments: 5 nonet

Nine Worlds
3 Hel 6 Asgard 7 Alfheim, Midgard
8 Niflheim, Vanaheim 10 Jotunnheim
12 Muspellsheim 13 Svartalfaheim

ninny
see **nincompoop**

Ninsum's son
9 Gilgamesh

Nintu
consort: 4 Enki
son: 6 Ninsar

Ninurta
father: 5 Enlil
victim: 3 Kur

Ninus
father: 5 Belus
wife: 9 Semiramis

Niobe
brother: 6 Pelops
father: 8 Tantalus
husband: 7 Amphion
sister-in-law: 5 Aedon

nip
3 bit, nab, sip 4 bite, dart, dash, dram,
drop, jolt, peck, shot, slug, swig 5 chill,
clamp, hurry, pinch, sever, snort, steal
6 imbibe, snatch, thwart, tipple 7 cabbage,
snifter, swallow 9 frustrate

nipper
3 kid 4 tyke 5 child 6 moppet, shaver
7 pincers 8 young one 9 youngling,
youngster

nipple
3 pap 4 teat

Nippon
5 Japan

nippy
3 icy, raw 4 cold, cool 5 algid, chill, crisp,
sharp 6 arctic, biting, bitter, chilly, frosty,
wintry 7 caustic, glacial, numbing, shivery
8 chilling, freezing

nirvana
5 bliss, dream 6 heaven 7 elysium
8 empyrean, oblivion, paradise 9 Shangri-
la

Nisus
betrayer, daughter: 6 Scylla
father: 7 Pandion

nitid
6 bright, glossy, lucent 7 fulgent, glowing,
shining 8 gleaming, glinting, luminous,
lustrous, polished 9 burnished

nitpick
4 carp 5 cavil 7 quibble 10 split hairs

nitrogen
5 azote
combining form: 3 azo

nitwit
3 oaf 4 boob, clod, dodo, dolt, dope, goof,
mutt, simp 5 chump, cluck, dummy, dunce,
idiot, moron, ninny, noddy, stupe 6 donkey,
dum-dum 7 airhead, dullard, pinhead,
schnook 8 bonehead, clodpoll, dumbbell,
imbecile, lunkhead, meathead, numskull
9 birdbrain, blockhead, ignoramus,
lamebrain, numbskull, simpleton, thickhead
10 dunderhead, hammerhead, nincompoop
11 chowderhead, chucklehead,
knucklehead

nix
3 nay, zap 4 kill, nope, veto 5 quash
6 cancel, naught, reject, scotch, sprite
7 call off, nothing, nullify

Njord, Njorth
daughter: 5 Freya
son: 4 Frey
wife: 6 Skadhi, Skathi

no
3 nay, nix 6 denial 7 refusal 8 negative
10 thumbs-down
German: 4 nein

no-account
see **no-good**

Noachian
3 old 4 aged 5 fusty, hoary 6 age-old
7 ancient, antique, archaic 8 timeworn
9 venerable 10 antiquated, oldfangled
12 antediluvian, old-fashioned
13 superannuated

Noah
father: 6 Lamech 10 Zelophehad
grandson: 4 Aram 6 Canaan
great-grandson: 3 Hul
landing place: 6 Ararat
son: 3 Ham 4 Shem 6 Canaan
7 Japheth

Nobel Prize winner
chemistry:
1901: 8 van't Hoff (Jacobus)
1902: 7 Fischer (Emil)
1903: 9 Arrhenius (Svante)
1904: 6 Ramsay (William)
1905: 9 von Baeyer (Adolf)
1906: 7 Moissan (Henri)
1907: 7 Buchner (Eduard)
1908: 10 Rutherford (Ernest)
1909: 7 Ostwald (Wilhelm)
1910: 7 Wallach (Otto)
1911: 5 Curie (Marie)
1912: 8 Grignard (François), Sabatier
(Paul)
1913: 6 Werner (Alfred)
1914: 8 Richards (Theodore)
1915: 11 Willstatter (Richard)

1918: 5 Haber (Fritz)
1920: 6 Nernst (Walther)
1921: 5 Soddy (Frederick)
1922: 5 Aston (Francis)
1923: 5 Pregl (Fritz)
1925: 9 Zsigmondy (Richard)
1926: 8 Svedberg (Theodor)
1927: 7 Wieland (Heinrich)
1928: 7 Windaus (Adolf)
1929: 6 Harden (Athur) 12 Euler-Chelpin (Hans von)
1930: 7 Fischer (Hans)
1931: 5 Bosch (Karl) 7 Bergius (Friedrich)
1932: 8 Langmuir (Irving)
1934: 4 Urey (Harold)
1935: 11 Joliot-Curie (Frédéric, Irene)
1936: 5 Debye (Peter)
1937: 6 Karrer (Paul) 7 Haworth (Walter)
1938: 4 Kuhn (Richard)
1939: 7 Ruzicka (Leopold) 9 Butenandt (Adolf)
1943: 6 Hevesy (Georg de)
1944: 4 Hahn (Otto)
1945: 8 Virtanen (Artturi)
1946: 6 Sumner (James) 7 Stanley (Wendell) 8 Northrop (John Howard)
1947: 8 Robinson (Robert)
1948: 8 Tiselius (Arne)
1949: 7 Giauque (William)
1950: 5 Alder (Kurt), Diels (Otto)
1951: 7 Seaborg (Glenn) 8 McMillan (Edwin)
1952: 5 Synge (Richard) 6 Martin (Archer)
1953: 10 Staudinger (Hermann)
1954: 7 Pauling (Linus)
1955: 10 du Vigneaud (Vincent)
1956: 7 Semenov (Nikolay) 11 Hinshelwood (Cyril)
1957: 4 Todd (Alexander)
1958: 6 Sanger (Frederick)
1959: 9 Heyrovsky (Jaroslav)
1960: 5 Libby (Willard)
1961: 5 Calvin (Melvin)
1962: 5 Perutz (Max) 7 Kendrew (John)
1963: 5 Natta (Giulio) 7 Ziegler (Karl)
1964: 7 Hodgkin (Dorothy) 8 Woodward (Robert)
1966: 8 Mulliken (Robert)
1967: 5 Eigen (Manfred) 6 Porter (George) 7 Norrish (Ronald)
1968: 7 Onsager (Lars)
1969: 6 Barton (Derek), Hassel (Odd)
1970: 6 Leloir (Luis)
1971: 8 Herzberg (Gerhard)
1972: 7 Moore (Stanford), Stein (William) 8 Anfinsen (Christian)
1973: 7 Fischer (Ernst) 9 Wilkinson

(Geoffrey)
1974: 5 Flory (Paul)
1975: 6 Prelog (Vladimir) 9 Cornforth (John)
1976: 8 Lipscomb (William)
1977: 9 Prigogine (Ilya)
1978: 8 Mitchell (Peter)
1979: 5 Brown (Herbert) 6 Wittig (Georg)
1980: 4 Berg (Paul) 6 Sanger (Frederick) 7 Gilbert (Walter)
1981: 5 Fukui (Kenichi) 8 Hoffmann (Roald)
1982: 4 Klug (Aaron)
1983: 5 Taube (Henry)
1984: 10 Merrifield (R. Bruce)
1985: 5 Karle (Jerome) 8 Hauptman (Herbert)
1986: 3 Lee (Yuan) 7 Polanyi (John) 10 Herschbach (Dudley)
1987: 4 Cram (Donald), Lehn (Jean-Marie) 8 Pedersen (Charles)
1988: 5 Huber (Robert) 6 Michel (Hartmut) 11 Deisenhofer (Johann)
1989: 4 Cech (Thomas) 6 Altman (Sidney)
1990: 5 Corey (Elias)
1991: 5 Ernst (Richard)
1992: 6 Marcus (Rudolph)
1993: 5 Smith (Michael) 6 Mullis (Kary)
1994: 4 Olah (George)
1995: 6 Molina (Mario) 7 Crutzen (Paul), Rowland (F. Sherwood)
1996: 4 Curl (Robert) 5 Kroto (Harold) 7 Smalley (Richard)
1997 4 Skou (Jens) 5 Boyer (Paul) 6 Walker (John)
1998: 4 Kohn (Walter) 5 Pople (John)
1999: 6 Zewail (Ahmed)
2000: 6 Heeger (Alan) 9 Shirakawa (Hideki) 10 MacDiarmid (Alan)
2001: 6 Noyori (Ryoji) 7 Knowles (William) 9 Sharpless (K. Barry)
2002: 4 Fenn (John) 6 Tanaka (Koichi) 8 Wüthrich (Kurt)
2003: 4 Agre (Peter) 9 MacKinnon (Roderick)
2004: 4 Rose (Irwin) 7 Hershko (Avram) 11 Ciechanover (Aaron)
economics:
1969: 6 Frisch (Ragnar) 9 Tinbergen (Jan)
1970: 9 Samuelson (Paul)
1971: 7 Kuznets (Simon)
1972: 5 Arrow (Kenneth), Hicks (John)
1973: 8 Leontief (Wassily)
1974: 5 Hayek (Friedrich von) 6 Myrdal (Gunnar)
1975: 8 Koopmans (Tjalling)

11 Kantorovich (Leonid)
1976: 8 Friedman (Milton)
1977: 5 Meade (James), Ohlin (Bertil)
1978: 5 Simon (Herbert)
1979: 5 Lewis (Arthur) 7 Schultz (Theodore)
1980: 5 Klein (Lawrence)
1981: 5 Tobin (James)
1982: 7 Stigler (George)
1983: 6 Debreu (Gerard)
1984: 5 Stone (Richard)
1985: 10 Modigliani (Franco)
1986: 8 Buchanan (James)
1987: 5 Solow (Robert)
1988: 6 Allais (Maurice)
1989: 8 Haavelmo (Trygve)
1990: 6 Miller (Merton), Sharpe (William) 9 Markowitz (Harry)
1991: 5 Coase (Ronald)
1992: 6 Becker (Gary)
1993: 5 Fogel (Robert), North (Douglass)
1994: 4 Nash (John) 6 Selten (Reinhard) 8 Harsanyi (John)
1995: 5 Lucas (Robert)
1996: 7 Vickrey (William) 8 Mirrlees (James)
1998: 3 Sen (Amartya)
1999: 7 Mundell (Robert)
2000: 7 Heckman (James) 8 McFadden (Daniel)
2001: 6 Spence (Michael) 7 Akerlof (George) 8 Stiglitz (Joseph)
2002: 5 Smith (Vernon) 8 Kahneman (Daniel)
2003: 5 Engle (Robert) 7 Granger (Clive)
2004: 7 Kydland (Finn) 8 Prescott (Edward)
literature:
1901: 9 Prudhomme (Sully)
1902: 7 Mommsen (Theodor)
1903: 8 Bjornson (Bjornstjerne)
1904: 7 Mistral (Frédéric) 9 Echegaray (José)
1905: 11 Sienkiewicz (Henryk)
1906: 8 Carducci (Giosue)
1907: 7 Kipling (Rudyard)
1908: 6 Eucken (Rudolf)
1909: 8 Lagerlof (Selma)
1910: 5 Heyse (Paul)
1911: 11 Maeterlinck (Maurice)
1912: 7 Hauptmann (Gerhart)
1913: 6 Tagore (Rabindranath)
1915: 7 Rolland (Romain)
1916: 10 Heidenstam (Verner von)
1917: 9 Gjellerup (Karl) 11 Pontoppidan (Henrik)
1919: 9 Spitteler (Carl)
1920: 6 Hamsun (Knut)
1921: 6 France (Anatole)

1922: 9 Benavente (Jacinto)
1923: 5 Yeats (William Butler)
1924: 7 Reymont (Wladyslaw)
1925: 4 Shaw (George Bernard)
1926: 7 Deledda (Grazia)
1927: 7 Bergson (Henri)
1928: 6 Undset (Sigrid)
1929: 4 Mann (Thomas)
1930: 5 Lewis (Sinclair)
1931: 9 Karlfeldt (Erik Axel)
1932: 10 Galsworthy (John)
1933: 5 Bunin (Ivan)
1934: 10 Pirandello (Luigi)
1936: 6 O'Neill (Eugene)
1937: 12 Martin du Gard (Roger)
1938: 4 Buck (Pearl)
1939: 9 Sillanpää (Frans Eemil)
1944: 6 Jensen (Johannes)
1945: 7 Mistral (Gabriela)
1946: 5 Hesse (Hermann)
1947: 4 Gide (André)
1948: 5 Eliot (Thomas Stearns)
1949: 8 Faulkner (William)
1950: 7 Russell (Bertrand)
1951: 10 Lagerkvist (Pär)
1952: 7 Mauriac (François)
1953: 9 Churchill (Winston)
1954: 7 Hemingway (Ernest)
1955: 7 Laxness (Halldór)
1956: 7 Jiménez (Juan Ramón)
1957: 5 Camus (Albert)
1958: 9 Pasternak (Boris)
1959: 9 Quasimodo (Salvatore)
1960: 7 Perse (Saint-John)
1961: 6 Andric (Ivo)
1962: 9 Steinbeck (John)
1963: 7 Seferis (George)
1964: 6 Sartre (Jean-Paul)
1965: 9 Sholokhov (Mikhail)
1966: 5 Agnon (Shmuel Yosef), Sachs (Nelly)
1967: 8 Asturias (Miguel Angel)
1968: 8 Kawabata (Yasunari)
1969: 7 Beckett (Samuel)
1970: 12 Solzhenitsyn (Alexander)
1971: 6 Neruda (Pablo)
1972: 4 Böll (Heinrich)
1973: 5 White (Patrick)
1974: 7 Johnson (Eyvind) 9 Martinson (Edmund)
1975: 7 Montale (Eugenio)
1976: 6 Bellow (Saul)
1977: 10 Aleixandre (Vicente)
1978: 6 Singer (Isaac Bashevis)
1979: 6 Elytis (Odysseus)
1980: 6 Milosz (Czeslaw)
1981: 7 Canetti (Elias)
1982: 13 García Márquez (Gabriel)
1983: 7 Golding (William)
1984: 7 Seifert (Jaroslav)

1985: 5 Simon (Claude)
1986: 7 Soyinka (Wole)
1987: 7 Brodsky (Joseph)
1988: 7 Mahfouz (Naguib)
1989: 4 Cela (Camilo José)
1990: 3 Paz (Octavio)
1991: 8 Gordimer (Nadine)
1992: 7 Walcott (Derek)
1993: 8 Morrison (Toni)
1994: 2 Oe (Kenzaburo)
1995: 6 Heaney (Seamus)
1996: 10 Szymborska (Wislawa)
1997: 2 Fo (Dario)
1998: 8 Saramago (José)
1999: 5 Grass (Günter)
2000: 3 Gao (Xingjian) 11 Gao Xingjian
2001: 7 Naipaul (V. S.)
2002: 7 Kertész (Imre)
2003: 7 Coetzee (J. M.)
2004: 7 Jelinek (Elfriede)

peace:
1901: 5 Passy (Frédéric) 6 Dunant
(Jean-Henri)
1902: 7 Gobat (Charles Albert)
8 Ducommun (Elie)
1903: 6 Cremer (William)
1905: 7 Suttner (Bertha von)
1906: 9 Roosevelt (Theodore)
1907: 6 Moneta (Ernesto) 7 Renault
(Louis)
1908: 5 Bajer (Fredrik) 9 Arnoldson
(Klas Pontus)
1909: 7 Beernaert (Auguste)
13 d'Estournelles (Paul)
1911: 5 Asser (Tobias), Fried (Alfred)
1912: 4 Root (Elihu)
1913: 10 La Fontaine (Henri)
1919: 6 Wilson (Woodrow)
1920: 6 Bourgeois (Léon)
1921: 5 Lange (Christian Louis)
8 Branting (Karl Hjalmar)
1922: 6 Nansen (Fridtjof)
1925: 6 Dawes (Charles) 11 Chamberlain
(Austen)
1926: 6 Briand (Aristide) 10 Stresemann
(Gustav)
1927: 6 Quidde (Ludwig) 7 Buisson
(Ferdinand)
1929: 7 Kellogg (Frank)
1930: 9 Soderblom (Nathan)
1931: 6 Addams (Jane), Butler (Nicholas
Murray)
1933: 6 Angell (Norman)
1934: 7 Henderson (Arthur)
1935: 9 Ossietzky (Carl von)
1936: 13 Saavedra Lamas (Carlos de)
1937: 5 Cecil (Robert)
1945: 4 Hull (Cordell)
1946: 4 Mott (John) 5 Balch (Emily
Greene)

1949: 3 Orr (John Boyd)
1950: 6 Bunche (Ralph)
1951: 7 Jouhaux (Léon)
1952: 10 Schweitzer (Albert)
1953: 8 Marshall (George)
1957: 7 Pearson (Lester)
1958: 4 Pire (Dominique Georges)
1959: 9 Noel-Baker (Philip)
1960: 7 Luthuli (Albert John)
1961: 12 Hammarskjold (Dag)
1962: 7 Pauling (Linus)
1964: 4 King (Martin Luther)
1968: 7 Cassin (René)
1970: 7 Borlaug (Norman)
1971: 6 Brandt (Willy)
1973: 8 Le Duc Tho 9 Kissinger (Henry)
1974: 4 Sato (Eisaku) 8 MacBride
(Sean)
1975: 8 Sakharov (Andrey)
1976: 8 Corrigan (Mairead), Williams
(Betty)
1978: 5 Begin (Menachem), Sadat
(Anwar el-)
1979: 12 Mother Teresa
1980: 8 Esquivel (Adolfo Pérez)
1982: 6 Myrdal (Alva) 12 García Robles
(Alfonso)
1983: 6 Walesa (Lech)
1984: 4 Tutu (Desmond)
1986: 6 Wiesel (Elie)
1987: 12 Arias Sánchez (Oscar)
1989: 9 Dalai Lama
1990: 9 Gorbachev (Mikhail)
1991: 13 Aung San Suu Kyi
1992: 6 Menchú (Rigoberta)
1993: 7 de Klerk (F. W.), Mandela
(Nelson)
1994: 5 Peres (Shimon), Rabin (Yitzhak)
6 Arafat (Yasir)
1995: 7 Rotblat (Joseph)
1996: 10 Ramos-Horta (José)
11 Ximenes Belo (Carlos Felipe)
1997: 8 Williams (Jody)
1998: 4 Hume (John) 7 Trimble (David)
2000: 3 Kim (Dae-jung) 10 Kim Dae-
jung
2001: 5 Annan (Kofi)
2002: 6 Carter (Jimmy)
2003: 5 Ebadi (Shirin)
2004: 7 Maathai (Wangari)

physics:
1901: 8 Roentgen (Wilhelm)
1902: 6 Zeeman (Pieter) 7 Lorentz
(Hendrik Antoon)
1903: 5 Curie (Marie, Pierre)
9 Becquerel (Antoine-Henri)
1904: 6 Strutt (John) 8 Rayleigh (Lord)
1905: 6 Lenard (Philipp von)
1906: 7 Thomson (Joseph)
1907: 9 Michelson (Albert)

1908: 8 Lippmann (Gabriel)
1909: 5 Braun (Karl) 7 Marconi (Guglielmo)
1910: 11 van der Waals (Johannes)
1911: 4 Wien (Wilhelm)
1912: 5 Dalen (Nils)
1914: 4 Laue (Max von)
1915: 5 Bragg (William)
1917: 6 Barkla (Charles)
1918: 6 Planck (Max)
1919: 5 Stark (Johannes)
1920: 9 Guillaume (Charles)
1921: 8 Einstein (Albert)
1922: 4 Bohr (Niels)
1923: 8 Millikan (Robert)
1924: 8 Siegbahn (Karl)
1925: 5 Hertz (Gustav) 6 Franck (James)
1926: 6 Perrin (Jean-Baptiste)
1927: 6 Wilson (Charles) 7 Compton (Arthur)
1928: 10 Richardson (Owen)
1929: 7 Broglie (Louis-Victor de)
1930: 5 Raman (Chandrasekhara)
1932: 10 Heisenberg (Werner)
1933: 5 Dirac (Paul) 11 Schrödinger (Erwin)
1935: 8 Chadwick (James)
1936: 4 Hess (Victor) 8 Anderson (Carl)
1937: 7 Thomson (George) 8 Davisson (Clinton)
1938: 5 Fermi (Enrico)
1939: 8 Lawrence (Ernest)
1943: 5 Stern (Otto)
1944: 4 Rabi (Isidor Isaac)
1945: 5 Pauli (Wolfgang)
1946: 8 Bridgman (Percy)
1947: 8 Appleton (Edward)
1948: 8 Blackett (Patrick)
1949: 6 Yukawa (Hideki)
1950: 6 Powell (Cecil)
1951: 6 Walton (Ernest) 9 Cockcroft (John)
1952: 5 Bloch (Felix) 7 Purcell (Edward)
1953: 7 Zernike (Frits)
1954: 4 Born (Max) 5 Bothe (Walther)
1955: 4 Lamb (Willis) 5 Kusch (Polykarp)
1956: 7 Bardeen (John) 8 Brattain (Walter), Shockley (William)
1957: 3 Lee (Tsung Dao) 4 Yang (Chen Ning)
1958: 4 Tamm (Igor) 5 Frank (Ilya) 9 Cherenkov (Pavel)
1959: 5 Segrè (Emilio) 11 Chamberlain (Owen)
1960: 6 Glaser (Donald)
1961: 4 Mossbauer (Rudolf) 10 Hofstadter (Robert)

1962: 6 Landau (Lev)
1963: 5 Mayer (Maria) 6 Jensen (J. Hans), Wigner (Eugene)
1964: 5 Basov (Nikolay) 6 Townes (Charles) 9 Prochorov (Alexander)
1965: 7 Feynman (Richard) 8 Tomonaga (Shinichiro) 9 Schwinger (Julian)
1966: 7 Kastler (Alfred)
1967: 5 Bethe (Hans)
1968: 7 Alvarez (Luis)
1969: 8 Gell-Mann (Murray)
1970: 4 Néel (Louis) 6 Alfven (Hannes)
1971: 5 Gabor (Dennis)
1972: 6 Cooper (Leon) 7 Bardeen (John) 10 Schrieffer (John)
1973: 5 Esaki (Leo) 7 Giaever (Ivar) 9 Josephson (Brian)
1974: 7 Ryle (Martin) 6 Hewish (Antony)
1975: 4 Bohr (Aage) 9 Mottelson (Ben), Rainwater (L. James)
1976: 4 Ting (Samuel) 7 Richter (Burton)
1977: 4 Mott (Nevill) 8 Anderson (Philip), Van Vleck (John)
1978: 6 Wilson (Robert) 7 Kapitsa (Pyotr), Penzias (Arno)
1979: 5 Salam (Abdus) 7 Glashow (Sheldon) 8 Weinberg (Steven)
1980: 5 Fitch (Val) 6 Cronin (James)
1981: 8 Schawlow (Arthur), Siegbahn (Kai) 11 Bloembergen (Nicholaas)
1982: 7 Wilson (Kenneth)
1983: 6 Fowler (William) 13 Chandrasekhar (Subrahmanyan)
1984: 6 Rubbia (Carlo) 11 van der Meere (Simon)
1985: 8 Klitzing (Klaus von)
1986: 5 Ruska (Ernst) 6 Binnig (Gerd), Rohrer (Heinrich)
1987: 6 Müller (K. Alex) 7 Bednorz (J. Georg)
1988: 8 Lederman (Leon), Schwartz (Melvin) 11 Steinberger (Jack)
1989: 4 Paul (Wolfgang) 6 Ramsey (Norman) 7 Dehmelt (Hans)
1990: 6 Taylor (Richard) 7 Kendall (Henry) 8 Friedman (Jerome)
1991: 8 De Gennes (Pierre-Gilles)
1992: 7 Charpak (Georges)
1993: 5 Hulse (Russell) 6 Taylor (Joseph)
1994: 5 Shull (Clifford) 10 Brockhouse (Bertram)
1995: 4 Perl (Martin) 6 Reines (Frederick)
1996: 3 Lee (David) 8 Osheroff (Douglas) 10 Richardson (Robert) 3 Chu (Steven) 8 Phillips (William) 14 Cohen-Tannoudji (Claude)
1998: 4 Tsui (Daniel) 7 Störmer (Horst)

    8 Laughlin (Robert)

1999: 6 't Hooft (Gerardus) **7** Veltman (Martinus)

2000: 5 Kilby (Jack) **7** Alferev (Zhores), Kroemer (Herbert)

2001: 6 Wieman (Carl) **7** Cornell (Eric) **8** Ketterle (Wolfgang)

2002: 5 Davis (Raymond) **7** Koshiba (Masatoshi) **8** Giacconi (Riccardo)

2003: 7 Leggett (Anthony) **8** Ginzburg (Vitaly) **9** Abrikosov (Alexei)

2004: 5 Gross (David) **7** Wilczek (Frank) **8** Politzer (David)

physiology or medicine:

1901: 7 Behring (Emil von)

1902: 4 Ross (Ronald)

1903: 6 Finsen (Niels Ryberg)

1904: 6 Pavlov (Ivan)

1905: 4 Koch (Robert)

1906: 5 Golgi (Camillo) **11** Ramón y Cajal (Santiago)

1907: 7 Laveran (Alphonse)

1908: 7 Ehrlich (Paul) **11** Metchnikoff (Elie)

1909: 6 Kocher (Emil)

1910: 6 Kossel (Albrecht)

1911: 10 Gullstrand (Allvar)

1912: 6 Carrel (Alexis)

1913: 6 Richet (Charles)

1914: 6 Barany (Robert)

1919: 6 Bordet (Jules)

1920: 5 Krogh (August)

1922: 4 Hill (Archibald) **8** Meyerhof (Otto)

1923: 7 Banting (Frederick), Macleod (John)

1924: 9 Einthoven (Willem)

1926: 7 Fibiger (Johannes)

1927: 13 Wagner-Jauregg (Julius)

1928: 7 Nicolle (Charles)

1929: 7 Eijkman (Christiaan), Hopkins (Frederick)

1930: 11 Landsteiner (Karl)

1931: 7 Warburg (Otto)

1932: 6 Adrian (Edgar) **11** Sherrington (Charles)

1933: 6 Morgan (Thomas)

1934: 5 Minot (George) **6** Murphy (William) **7** Whipple (George)

1935: 7 Spemann (Hans)

1936: 4 Dale (Henry) **5** Loewi (Otto)

1937: 12 Szent-Györgyi (Albert)

1938: 7 Heymans (Corneille)

1939: 6 Domagk (Gerhard)

1943: 4 Dam (Henrik) **5** Doisy (Edward)

1944: 6 Gasser (Herbert) **8** Erlanger (Joseph)

1945: 5 Chain (Ernst) **6** Florey (Howard) **7** Fleming (Alexander)

1946: 6 Muller (Hermann)

1947: 4 Cori (Carl, Gerty) **7** Houssay (Bernardo)

1948: 7 Mueller (Paul)

1949: 4 Hess (Walter) **5** Moniz (Antonio)

1950: 5 Hench (Philip) **7** Kendall (Edward) **10** Reichstein (Tadeus)

1951: 7 Theiler (Max)

1952: 7 Waksman (Selman)

1953: 5 Krebs (Hans) **7** Lipmann (Fritz)

1954: 6 Enders (John), Weller (Thomas) **7** Robbins (Frederick)

1955: 8 Theorell (Hugo)

1956: 8 Cournand (André), Richards (Dickinson) **9** Forssmann (Werner)

1957: 5 Bovet (Daniel)

1958: 5 Tatum (Edward) **6** Beadle (George) **9** Lederberg (Joshua)

1959: 5 Ochoa (Severo) **8** Kornberg (Arthur)

1960: 6 Burnet (Macfarlane) **7** Medawar (Peter)

1961: 6 Bekesy (Georg von)

1962: 6 Crick (Francis) **7** Watson (James) **7** Wilkins (Maurice)

1963: 6 Eccles (John), Huxley (Andrew) **7** Hodgkin (Alan)

1964: 5 Bloch (Konrad), Lynen (Feodor)

1965: 5 Jacob (Francois), Monod (Jacques) **5** Lwoff (André)

1966: 4 Rous (Francis) **6** Huggins (Charles)

1967: 4 Wald (George) **6** Granit (Ragnar) **8** Hartline (H. Keffer)

1968: 6 Holley (Robert) **7** Khorana (H. Gobind) **9** Nirenberg (Marshall)

1969: 5 Luria (Salvador) **7** Hershey (Alfred) **8** Delbruck (Max)

1970: 4 Katz (Bernard) **5** Euler (Ulf von) **7** Axelrod (Julius)

1971: 10 Sutherland (Earl)

1972: 6 Porter (Rodney) **7** Edelman (Gerald)

1973: 6 Frisch (Karl von), Lorenz (Konrad) **9** Tinbergen (Nikolaas)

1974: 4 Duve (Christian) **6** Claude (Albert), Palade (George)

1975: 5 Temin (Howard) **8** Dulbecco (Renato) **9** Baltimore (David)

1976: 8 Blumberg (Baruch), Gajdusek (D. Carleton)

1977: 5 Yalow (Rosalyn) **7** Schally (Andrew) **9** Guillemin (Roger)

1978: 8 Arber (Werner), Smith (Hamilton) **7** Nathans (Daniel)

1979: 7 Cormack (Allan) **10** Hounsfield (Godfrey)

1980: 5 Snell (George) **7** Dausset (Jean) **10** Benacerraf (Baruj)

1981: 5 Hubel (David) 6 Sperry (Roger), Wiesel (Torsten)

1982: 4 Vane (John) 9 Bergstrom (Sune) 10 Samuelsson (Bengt)

1983: 10 McClintock (Barbara)

1984: 5 Jerne (Niels) 7 Koehler (Georges) 8 Milstein (Cesar)

1985: 5 Brown (Michael) 9 Goldstein (Joseph)

1986: 5 Cohen (Stanley) 14 Levi-Montalcini (Rita)

1987: 8 Tonegawa (Susumu)

1988: 5 Black (James), Elion (Gertrude) 9 Hitchings (George)

1989: 6 Bishop (J. Michael), Varmus (Harold)

1990: 6 Murray (Joseph), Thomas (E. Donnall)

1991: 5 Neher (Erwin) 7 Sakmann (Bert)

1992: 5 Krebs (Edwin) 7 Fischer (Edmond)

1993: 5 Sharp (Phillip) 7 Roberts (Richard)

1994: 6 Gilman (Alfred) 7 Rodbell (Martin)

1995: 5 Lewis (Edward) 9 Wieschaus (Eric) 15 Nüsslein-Volhard (Christiane)

1996: 7 Doherty (Peter) 11 Zinkernagel (Rolf)

1997: 8 Prusiner (Stanley)

1998: 5 Murad (Ferid) 7 Ignarro (Louis) 9 Furchgott (Robert)

1999: 6 Blobel (Günter)

2000: 6 Kandel (Eric) 8 Carlsson (Arvid) 9 Greengard (Paul)

2001: 4 Hunt (Tim) 5 Nurse (Paul) 8 Hartwell (Leland)

2002: 7 Brenner (Sydney), Horvitz (Robert), Sulston (John)

2003: 9 Lauterbur (Paul), Mansfield (Peter) 4 Axel (Richard), Buck (Linda)

Nobel's invention
8 dynamite

nobility
6 virtue 7 dignity, peerage, royalty 8 eminence, noblesse 9 loftiness 10 exaltation, excellence, worthiness 11 aristocracy, superiority, uprightness

noble
4 peer 5 grand, lofty, moral 6 august, lordly, titled, worthy 7 courtly, eminent, exalted, notable, princely, stately, sublime, upright 8 baronial, elevated, generous, gracious, heroical, highborn, highbred, imposing, magnific, majestic, princely, sterling, virtuous, wellborn 9 dignified, estimable, excellent, grandiose, honorable,

righteous 10 high-minded, impressive, principled 11 illustrious, magnanimous, magnificent, outstanding, right-minded 12 aristocratic

nobleman
4 duke, earl, peer 5 baron, count 6 prince 7 baronet, marquis 8 marquess, viscount
French: 5 comte 7 vicomte
German: 4 Graf 8 margrave 9 landgrave
Indian: 6 sardar, sirdar 8 maharaja 9 maharajah
Italian: 8 marchese
Japanese (former): 6 daimyo
Scandinavian: 4 jarl
Spanish: 7 hidalgo

noblewoman
4 lady 7 baronne, duchess, peeress 8 baroness, countess, princess 11 marchioness, viscountess
French: 8 marquise
Italian: 8 marchesa

nobody
4 zero 6 cipher 7 nothing, nullity, upstart 9 nonentity 11 lightweight, small potato

nocturnal
7 nightly 9 nighttime

nocuous
3 bad 6 nocent 7 harmful, hurtful 8 damaging 9 injurious 11 deleterious, destructive, detrimental, mischievous

nod
3 bob, err 4 doze, okay 5 agree, droop, slump 6 assent, invite, signal 7 approve 8 approval 10 acceptance

nodding
6 casual, slight 7 passing 8 drooping 9 pendulous 11 superficial

noddle
3 nob, nut 4 bean, head, pate, poll 6 noggin

noddy
3 oaf 4 boob, clod, dodo, dolt, dope, fool, goof, mutt, simp, yo-yo 5 chump, dummy, dunce, moron, ninny, stupe 6 dimwit, donkey, dum-dum 7 airhead, dullard, pinhead, schnook 8 bonehead, clodpoll, dumbbell, dumbhead, imbecile, lunkhead, meathead, numskull 9 birdbrain, blockhead, ignoramus, lamebrain, numbskull, simpleton, thickhead 10 dunderhead, hammerhead, nincompoop 11 chowderhead, chucklehead,

knucklehead

node
4 bump, burl, knob, knot, lump, mass
5 bulge, point 6 growth, vertex 8 swelling
11 enlargement, predicament
12 entanglement, protuberance

Noel
4 Xmas 5 carol 9 Christmas

nog
3 ale 4 beer, brew, malt, suds 5 lager,
stout

noggin
3 cup, mug, nip, nob, nut 4 bean, gill,
head, pate, poll 6 noddle, noodle

no-good
3 bum, dud 4 base, vile, worm 5 loser
6 scurvy, wretch 7 dirtbag, inutile, lowlife,
rounder, wastrel 8 deadbeat, shameful,
unworthy, wretched 9 no-account,
valueless, worthless 10 ne'er-do-well, profligate, scapegrace 11 ignominious
12 contemptible, disreputable
13 reprehensible

noise
3 din 4 blab, talk 5 babel, rumor, sound
6 clamor, gossip, hubbub, racket, ruckus,
rumpus, tattle, uproar 7 ruction, sonance,
stridor 8 resonant 11 pandemonium

noiseless
4 hush, mute 5 muted, quiet, still, whist
6 hushed, silent, stilly 9 soundless

noisemaker
4 horn 6 rattle 7 clapper

noisome
4 foul, rank, vile 5 fetid, funky, fusty, musty,
nasty 6 filthy, horrid, putrid, rancid smelly
7 harmful, noxious, squalid 8 stinking
9 obnoxious, offensive, repulsive, revolting,
sickening 10 disgusting, malodorous,
nauseating

noisy
4 loud 5 rowdy 7 blatant, booming,
clamant, rackety, raucous, squeaky
8 clattery, strident 9 clamorous, deafening,
turbulent 10 boisterous, chattering,
clangorous, tumultuous, uproarious,
vociferous 11 conspicuous 12 earsplitting,
obstreperous

nomad
5 gypsy, rover 7 migrant, rambler
8 vagabond, wanderer
Arabic: 7 bedouin

nomadic
5 gypsy 6 roving 7 roaming, vagrant
8 drifting, vagabond 9 itinerant, migratory,
wandering, wayfaring 11 peripatetic
13 perambulatory

nom de plume
see **pen name**

nomen
4 name 7 moniker 11 appellation,
designation

nomenclature
4 list, name 7 catalog 8 glossary,
taxonomy 11 appellation, designation,
phraseology, terminology 12 codification

nominal
3 low 5 given, named, rated, small
6 formal, puppet 7 alleged, minimal,
seeming, titular 8 apparent, so-called,
trifling 9 pretended, professed
10 ostensible 11 approximate, inexpensive
12 satisfactory, substantial
13 insignificant

nominate
3 tap 4 call, name 5 offer, put up
7 appoint, propose suggest 9 designate,
recommend

nominee
6 choice 8 aspirant 9 candidate,
contender 10 contestant

nonage
5 youth 7 infancy 8 minority 9 childhood
10 immaturity, juvenility

nonchalant
4 cool, easy 5 blase 6 casual, mellow,
serene 7 offhand 8 carefree, careless,
cheerful, composed, laid-back 9 collected,
easygoing, incurious, unruffled
10 effortless, insouciant, untroubled
11 indifferent, unconcerned, unflappable,
unperturbed 12 lighthearted 13 dispassionate, imperturbable, lackadaisical

noncommittal
7 neutral 8 reserved 9 impassive
10 disengaged

nonconformist
5 rebel 7 beatnik, heretic, oddball, offbeat,
radical 8 bohemian, maverick 9 dissenter,
dissident, eccentric, heretical, heterodox,
protester, sectarian 10 schismatic,
separatist, unorthodox 11 misbeliever,
schismatist

nonconformity

6 heresy, schism 7 dissent 9 misbelief, recusancy 10 dissidence, heterodoxy, opposition 11 unorthodoxy 12 disaffection 13 individualism, noncompliance

nonentity

4 zero 5 aught, zilch 6 cipher, nobody 7 nothing, nullity, whiffet 8 unperson 10 figurehead, mouthpiece

nonesuch

5 ideal 7 epitome, paragon, pattern 8 exemplar, paradigm, standard 9 archetype, matchless, nonpareil, unequaled, unrivaled

nonetheless

3 yet 5 still 6 anyway, though, withal 7 howbeit, however 8 although, after all 10 regardless 11 still and all

nonexistence

4 nada, void 7 nullity, vacuity 11 nothingness

nonflammable

9 fireproof 10 unburnable 13 incombustible

non-Hawaiian

5 haole

non-Jewish

3 goy 6 goyish 7 gentile

non-Muslim

6 giaour

no-nonsense

5 grave, sober 6 solemn 7 earnest, serious 8 resolute 9 pragmatic, realistic 10 determined, hardheaded, plainspoken, sobersided 12 businesslike 13 unsentimental

nonpareil

see nonesuch

nonpartisan

7 neutral 8 unbiased 9 equitable, impartial, objective, uncolored 10 nonaligned 11 independent 12 unprejudiced

nonplus

4 faze 5 stump 6 baffle, boggle, muddle, puzzle, rattle, stymie 7 buffalo, confuse, dilemma, flummox, fluster, mystify, perplex, stagger 8 bewilder, confound, distract, overcome, paralyze, quandary 9 discomfit, dumbfound, frustrate 10 disconcert

nonresistant

6 docile, pliant 7 passive, pliable 8 resigned, yielding 9 complying, tractable 10 conforming, submissive 11 acquiescent, conformable 13 accommodating

nonsense

3 rot 4 blah, bosh, bull, bunk, crap, gook, guff, jazz, punk, tosh 5 bilge, crock, drool, folly, fudge, Greek, hokum, hooey, trash 6 babble, blague, bunkum, drivel, hot air, humbug, jabber, piffle 7 baloney, blather, eyewash, flubdub, foolery, fooling, hogwash, inanity, rubbish, trifles, twaddle 8 buncombe, claptrap, falderal, folderol, flimflam, malarkey, pishposh, slipslop, tommyrot, trumpery 9 gibberish, moonshine, poppycock 10 applesauce, balderdash, double-talk, flapdoodle, tomfoolery 11 jabberwocky 12 blatherskite, fiddle-faddle, fiddlesticks 13 horsefeathers
British: 10 codswallop

nonsensical

5 crazy, daffy, flaky, goofy, inane, kooky, loony, nutty, silly, wacky 6 absurd, screwy 7 foolish, idiotic, risible 9 illogical, laughable, ludicrous, senseless 10 irrational 12 preposterous, unreasonable

nonviolent

6 irenic 7 pacific 8 pacifist 9 peaceable 10 pacifistic

noodle

3 oaf 4 bean, boob, clod, dodo, dope, goof, head, mutt, poll, simp, yo-yo 5 chump, dummy, dunce, idiot, moron, ninny, noddy, stupe 6 dimwit, donkey, dumdum, nitwit, noggin 7 airhead, dullard, pinhead, schnook 8 bonehead, clodpoll, dumbbell, dumbhead, imbecile, lunkhead, meathead, numskull 9 birdbrain, blockhead, ignoramus, lamebrain, numbskull, simpleton 10 dunderhead, hammerhead, nincompoop 11 chowderhead, chucklehead, knucklehead

nook

3 bay 4 cove 5 hutch, niche 6 alcove, cavity, corner, cranny, recess 9 cubbyhole 11 compartment

noose

3 tie 4 bait, bind, hang, loop, lure, trap 5 lasso, snare 6 entrap, secure

norm
3 par **4** mean, rule, type **5** gauge, maxim, model **6** median **7** average, measure, pattern **8** paradigm, standard **9** benchmark, criterion **10** touchstone

Norma
composer: **7** Bellini (Vincenzo)
librettist: **6** Romani (Felice)

normal
4 sane **5** usual **6** common **7** average, general, natural, regular, typical **8** ordinary, standard **9** customary, prevalent **11** commonplace, traditional **12** conventional **13** perpendicular

Normandy's capital
5 Rouen

Norns
5 fates, Skuld, Urdur **9** Verthandi

Norris novel
3 Pit (The) **4** Blix **7** Octopus (The) **8** McTeague

Norse
abode of the dead: **8** Niflheim
alphabet: **5** Runic
archer: **4** Egil
bard: **5** scald, skald
chieftain: **4** jarl, Rolf **5** Rollo
demon: **4** Mara, Surt **5** Surtr
dragon: **6** Fafnir **8** Nithhogg
epic: **4** Edda
explorer: **4** Erik, Leif **8** Ericsson (Leif), Eriksson (Leif)
first man: **3** Ask **4** Askr
first woman: **5** Embla
giant: **4** Egil, Wade, Wate, Ymer, Ymir **5** Aegir, Egill, Hymir, Jotun, Mimir **6** Fafnir, Jotunn
giantess: **4** Egia, Norn, Nott
god: **3** Asa, Ass **4** Surt, Vali, Vili **5** Aesir (plural), Surtr, Vanir (plural) **6** Hoenir, Vithar **7** Vitharr
blind: **4** Hoth **5** Hoder, Hodur, Hothr
chief: **4** Odin **5** Othin, Wodan, Woden, Wotan
guardian: **7** Heimdal **8** Heimdall **9** Heimdallr
messenger: **6** Hermod **7** Hermodr
of beauty: **5** Baldr **6** Balder, Baldur
of evil: **4** Loke, Loki
of fertility: **4** Frey **5** Freyr
of justice: **7** Forsete, Forseti
of light: **3** Dag
of peace: **5** Baldr **6** Balder, Baldur
of poetry: **5** Brage, Bragi
of the hunt: **3** Ull **4** Ullr

of the seas: **5** Njord **6** Njoerd, Njorth **4** Hler **5** Aegir, Gymir
of the sky: **4** Odin **5** Othin
of thunder: **4** Thor **5** Donar
of war: **3** Tiu, Tiw, Tyr, Zio, Ziu
wolf: **6** Fenrir
goddess: **3** dis **4** Saga **5** disir (plural) **7** Asynjur
of fate: **3** Urd **4** Norn, Urth, Wyrd **5** Skuld **9** Verthandi
of healing: **3** Eir
of love: **5** Freya
of marriage: **5** Frigg **6** Frigga
of night: **4** Natt, Nott
of storms: **3** Ran
of the earth: **5** Joerd, Jorth
of the moon: **5** Nanna
of the sea: **3** Ran
of the sky: **5** Frigg **6** Frigga
of the underworld: **3** Hel **4** Hela
of youth: **4** Idun **6** Ithun, Ithunn
gods' abode: **6** Asgard
hall of heroes: **8** Valhalla
king: **4** Atli, Olaf
nobleman: **4** jarl
patron saint: **4** Olaf
poem: **4** rune
poet: **5** scald, skald
rainbow bridge: **7** Bifrost
sea serpent: **4** Wade, Wate **6** kraken **7** Midgard
smith: **6** Völund
tale: **4** saga
toast: **5** skoal
watchdog: **4** Garm **5** Garmr
world's destruction: **8** Ragnarok
world tree: **8** Ygdrasil **10** Yggdrasill

north
combining form: **4** arct **5** arcto

North African
country: **5** Egypt, Libya **7** Algeria, Morocco, Tunisia
fruit: **3** fig **4** date
garment: **4** haik
grass: **4** alfa **7** esparto
jackal: **4** dieb
language: **6** Arabic, Berber
Muslim sect: **6** Sanusi **7** Senussi
people: **6** Berber, Hamite **7** bedouin
seaport: **4** Oran, Sfax **6** Annaba **7** Tangier **10** Casablanca

North America
country: **6** Canada, Mexico, Panama **8** Honduras **9** Costa Rica, Guatemala, Nicaragua **10** El Salvador **12** United States

North Carolina
capital: 7 Raleigh
city: 6 Durham 9 Asheville, Charlotte
10 Greensboro 12 Winston-Salem
college, university: 4 Duke, Elon
10 Wake Forest
mountain, range: 8 Mitchell 9 Blue Ridge
10 Great Smoky
nickname: 7 Tar Heel (State)
state bird: 8 cardinal
state flower: 7 dogwood
state tree: 4 pine

North Dakota
capital: 8 Bismarck
city: 5 Fargo, Minot 10 Grand Forks
nickname: 5 Sioux (State) 11 Flickertail
(State)
river: 3 Red 8 Missouri
state bird: 10 meadowlark
state flower: 11 prairie rose
state tree: 3 elm (American)

northern
4 pike 6 boreal 11 hyperborean

Northern Mariana Islands
commonwealth of: 12 United States
discoverer: 8 Magellan (Ferdinand)
island: 4 Rota 6 Saipan, Tinian

North Star State
9 Minnesota

Northwest Passage author
7 Roberts (Kenneth)

Northwest Territories
capital: 11 Yellowknife
gulf: 8 Amundsen
island: 5 Banks 8 Victoria
lake: 9 Great Bear 10 Great Slave
river: 9 Mackenzie
sea: 8 Beaufort

north wind
see at **wind**

Norway
Arctic region: 7 Lapland
cape: 7 Nordkyn
capital: 4 Oslo
city: 6 Bergen 9 Stavanger, Trondheim
inlet: 9 Skagerrak
island: 5 Senja 6 Sørøya 8 Magerøya,
Steinsøy 10 Nord-Kvaløy, Ringvassøy
island group: 7 Lofoten 10 Vesterålen
lake: 5 Mjøsa
monetary unit: 5 krone
mountain range: 6 Kjølen 11 Jotun-
heimen
neighbor: 6 Russia, Sweden 7 Finland
part of: 11 Scandinavia

port: 5 Vardø 6 Tromsø 8 Kirkenes
10 Hammerfest
river: 4 Tana 5 Glåma, Lågen
9 Dramselva
sea: 5 North

Norwegian
goblin: 5 nisse
language: 5 Norse 6 Bokmal 7 Bokmaal,
Nynorsk, Riksmal 8 Landsmal, Riksmaal
9 Landsmaal

nose
3 pry 4 beak, bent, bump, gift, head, poke
5 aroma, flair, knack, scent, smell, sniff,
snift, snoop, snoot, snout, snuff 6 genius,
muzzle, nuzzle, talent 7 aptness, faculty,
smeller, sneezer 8 smell out 9 olfaction,
proboscis, schnozzle
French: 3 nez
kind: 3 pug 5 Roman 8 aquiline
lengthener: 3 lie
opening: 7 nostril

nosebleed
9 epistaxis

nosedive
4 drop, fall 6 header, plunge 7 plummet

nosegay
4 posy 6 flower 7 bouquet, corsage
11 boutonniere

nosh
4 bite 5 graze, munch, snack 6 nibble

Nostradamus
7 prophet

Nostromo author
6 Conrad (Joseph)

nostrum
4 cure 6 elixir, remedy 7 cure-all, panacea
8 antidote, medicine 10 catholicon,
corrective 11 restorative

nosy
6 prying, snoopy 7 curious, peeping
8 snooping 9 intrusive 11 inquisitive,
inquisitory

notability
3 VIP 4 lion, star 5 celeb, chief 6 leader,
worthy 7 big name, big shot 8 big-timer,
eminence, luminary, presence, somebody
9 celebrity, chieftain, dignitary, personage,
superstar 11 personality

notable
3 VIP 4 star 5 celeb, chief, famed, mogul,
nabob, power 6 big boy, biggie, big gun,
bigwig, famous, fat cat, leader, prince 7 big

name, big shot, eminent, magnate, pooh-bah **8** big chief, big-timer, big wheel, eminence, luminary, renowned, somebody, striking **9** big cheese, celebrity, character, dignitary, distingué, personage, prominent, superstar **10** celebrated, celebrious, noteworthy, remarkable **11** conspicuous, heavyweight, illustrious, muckety-muck, personality **13** distinguished, high-muck-a-muck

notarize
7 certify, endorse **8** validate **12** authenticate

notch
3 cut, gap, jag **4** gash, mark, nick, nock, rung, slit, step **5** cleft, grade, score, stage **6** degree, groove, indent, rabbet, record **7** achieve, scratch **8** incision, undercut **11** indentation

note
3 jot **4** bond, chit, heed, mark, memo, show, sign, tone **5** catch, sound, token **6** letter, notice, record, regard **7** comment, discern, jotting, missive, observe, promise, set down **8** eminence, indicate, perceive, reminder **9** attention, knowledge **10** cognizance, commentary, memorandum, observance, reputation **11** distinction, distinguish, observation

notebook
3 log **5** diary **7** journal

noted
6 famous **7** eminent, leading, popular **8** esteemed, renowned, striking **9** acclaimed, prominent, well-known **10** celebrated, recognized, remarkable **11** illustrious **13** distinguished

noteworthy
7 salient **8** singular, striking **9** arresting, bodacious, memorable, prominent, red-letter **10** impressive, meaningful, remarkable **11** conspicuous, exceptional, high-profile, major-league, outstanding, significant **12** considerable **13** extraordinary

nothing
3 nil, nix **4** zero **5** aught, nihil, zilch **6** cipher, naught, nobody, nought, trifle **7** nullity, whiffet **8** goose egg, whipster **9** no-account, nonentity
French: 4 rien
German: 6 nichts
Latin: 5 nihil
Spanish: 4 nada

nothingness
4 nada, void **5** death **6** vacuum **7** nullity, vacuity **9** emptiness **12** nonexistence

notice
3 see **4** espy, heed, mark, memo **5** catch, sight **6** descry, regard, review **7** discern, observe, respect **8** handbill, perceive **9** attention, directive, recognize **10** cognizance, evaluation **11** declaration, information, observation **12** announcement, proclamation **13** communication

noticeable
6 marked, patent, signal **7** evident, obvious, pointed, salient **8** apparent, manifest, striking **9** arresting, prominent **10** noteworthy, observable, remarkable **11** appreciable, conspicuous, eye-catching, outstanding, perceptible, significant **12** unmistakable

notify
3 cue **4** tell, warn **5** alert, brief **6** advise, clue in, fill in, inform **7** apprise **8** acquaint **9** enlighten

notion
4 clue, hint, idea, whim **5** fancy **6** belief, maggot, theory, vagary **7** caprice, conceit, concept, inkling, thought **8** crotchet **10** conception, impression, intimation, perception **11** inclination

notional
5 ideal **6** unreal **7** fancied, fictive **8** fanciful, illusory, imagined **9** imaginary, visionary, whimsical **10** capricious, conceptual **11** speculative, theoretical **12** hypothetical

notoriety
4 fame **6** infamy, renown **7** obloquy **9** disrepute **10** opprobrium, prominence **11** recognition

notorious
5 noted **6** famous **8** ill-famed, infamous **9** prominent, well-known **10** outrageous, scandalous **12** disreputable

Notus
6 Auster
brother: 5 Eurus **6** Boreas **8** Zephyrus
father: 6 Aeolus **8** Astraeus
mother: 3 Eos

noun
4 name **7** nominal **11** substantive
inflectional form: 4 case
verbal: 6 gerund

nourish
4 feed, rear 5 nurse, raise 6 foster 7 bring up, build up, nurture, promote, support 8 maintain 9 cultivate, encourage 10 provide for, strengthen

nourishment
3 pap 4 diet, eats, feed, food, grub 6 viands 7 aliment, pabulum, vittles 8 victuals 9 nutriment, provender 10 sustenance

_____ nous
5 entre

nouveau riche
7 parvenu, upstart 9 arriviste

Nova Scotia
capital: 7 Halifax
city: 9 Dartmouth
island: 10 Cape Breton
lake: 7 Bras D'Or
provincial flower: 9 mayflower

novel
3 new, odd 5 fresh 6 unique 7 offbeat, unusual 8 atypical, original, peculiar, singular, uncommon 9 different, narrative 10 avant-garde, innovative, newfangled

novelist
see author

novelty
5 curio 6 bauble, gewgaw, oddity, trifle 7 bibelot, gimmick, newness, trinket, whatnot 8 gimcrack, souvenir 9 bagatelle, curiosity, objet d'art 10 innovation, knickknack

novice
3 cub 4 colt, punk, tyro 6 rookie 7 amateur, learner, recruit, student, trainee 8 aspirant, beginner, freshman, neophyte, newcomer, prentice 9 fledgling, greenhorn, novitiate, postulant 10 apprentice, tenderfoot 11 probationer

Novum Organum author
5 Bacon (Francis)

now
3 PDQ 4 soon 5 today 6 at once, pronto 7 anymore, present 8 directly, first off, promptly 9 forthwith, instanter, instantly, presently, right away, sometimes 11 immediately, straightway 12 straightaway

now and then
7 at times, betimes 9 sometimes 12 infrequently, occasionally, periodically, sporadically

Nox
brother: 6 Erebus
daughter: 3 Day 4 Eris 5 Light
father: 5 Chaos
husband: 6 Erebus
son: 6 Charon, Hypnos 8 Thanatos

noxious
4 foul 5 fetid, toxic 6 deadly, putrid 7 baneful, harmful, noisome 8 stinking 9 dangerous, pestilent, poisonous, unhealthy 10 corrupting, pernicious 11 deleterious, destructive, detrimental, pestiferous 12 disagreeable, pestilential

nozzle
4 nose, vent 5 spout 7 channel

nuance
4 hint 5 shade, tinge, touch, trace 6 nicety 7 shading, soupçon 8 overtone, subtlety 9 gradation, suspicion 10 refinement, suggestion 11 distinction

nub
4 core, crux, gist, knob, knot, lump, meat, node, pith 5 bulge, point, short 6 kernel, upshot 8 swelling 9 substance 10 projection 12 protuberance

Nubian
5 Mahas 6 Birked, Kenuzi, Midobi 7 Dongola 8 Cushitic 9 Chari-Nile

nubile
4 ripe 10 attractive 12 marriageable

nuchal
4 nape

nuclear agency
3 AEC, NRC

nuclear particle
5 meson 6 proton 7 neutron

nucleus
3 bud 4 core, germ, head, kern, ring, seed 5 focus, spark 6 embryo
material: 8 karyotin

nude
3 raw 4 bald, bare 5 naked, stark 6 barren, peeled, unclad 8 disrobed, stripped 9 au naturel, buck naked, unattired, unclothed, uncovered, undressed 10 stark naked

nudge
3 dig, jab, jog 4 near, poke, prod, push 5 elbow, punch, shove 8 approach

nudnik
4 bore, drip, pill, twit 8 nuisance

nugatory
4 idle, vain 5 empty, inane, vapid 6 futile, hollow, otiose 7 invalid, vacuous 8 trifling 9 fruitless, worthless 11 inoperative, meaningless

nugget
3 gob, wad 4 hunk, lump, plum 5 chunk 6 tidbit

nuisance
4 pain, pest, pill 6 bother, nudnik 8 headache, irritant, pesterer, vexation 11 botheration

nuke
4 bomb 5 crush, smash 6 attack 7 destroy 8 demolish 9 eradicate, microwave 10 annihilate 11 exterminate

null
4 void, zero 5 annul, empty 6 futile 7 invalid, useless 8 nugatory 9 worthless 10 invalidate, obliterate, unavailing 11 ineffective, ineffectual, inoperative

nullify
3 zap 4 undo, veto, void 5 abate, annul, limit, quash, scrub, trash 6 cancel, efface, negate, offset, repeal, revoke, squash 7 abolish, rescind, scratch, take out, wipe out 8 abrogate 10 annihilate, compensate, counteract, invalidate, neutralize 11 countervail

nullity
4 nada, zero 5 zilch 6 cipher, nobody 7 nothing, vacuity, whiffet 9 annulment, nonentity 11 nothingness 12 nonexistence

numb
5 chill, dazed 6 deaden, freeze 7 callous 8 deadened, detached 9 insensate, paralyzed, stupefied, unfeeling 10 insensible, insentient 11 desensitize, indifferent 12 anesthetized, desensitized

number
5 add up, count, digit, run to, sum to, tally, total 6 amount, cipher, come to, figure 7 chiffer, include, integer, numeral, ordinal, run into, several, sum into 8 cardinal, numerate, paginate 9 aggregate, enumerate
added to another: 6 augend
resulting from division: 8 quotient
resulting from multiplication: 7 product
resulting from subtraction: 10 difference
science: 11 mathematics

number one
4 best, main 5 chief, major 6 finest, Grade A, top dog 7 capital, highest, leading, primary, stellar 8 dominant, five-star, foremost, superior 9 excellent, first-rate, front-rank, numero uno, principal, top-drawer 10 blue-ribbon, first-class, preeminent 11 first-string, outstanding, predominant

numbness
5 shock 6 stupor 10 anesthesia 12 stupefaction
combining form: 4 narc 5 narco

numeral
5 digit 6 cipher, figure, number 7 integer 11 whole number

numerate
4 list 5 count, tally 6 number 7 compute, itemize, tick off 8 tabulate 9 calculate

numerous
4 many 6 legion 7 profuse, umpteen 8 abundant, populous 9 plentiful 10 voluminous 13 multitudinous

Numitor
brother: 7 Amulius
daughter: 9 Rea Silvia 10 Rhea Silvia
grandson: 5 Remus 7 Romulus

numskull
3 oaf 4 boob, clod, dodo, dolt, dope, goof, mutt, simp 5 chump, dummy, dunce, idiot, moron, ninny, noddy, stupe 6 dimwit, donkey, dum-dum, nitwit 7 airhead, dullard, pinhead, schnook 8 bonehead, clodpate, clodpoll, dumbbell, dumbhead, imbecile, lunkhead, meathead 9 birdbrain, blockhead, ignoramus, lamebrain, simpleton, thickhead 10 dunderhead, hammerhead, nincompoop 11 chowderhead, chucklehead, knucklehead

nun
6 sister
headcloth: 6 wimple

Nunavut
capital: 7 Iqaluit
island: 5 Devon 6 Baffin 9 Ellesmere 11 Southampton
mountain: 7 Barbeau (Peak)
peninsula: 7 Boothia 8 Melville
provincial flower: 11 Arctic poppy

nunnery
7 convent 10 sisterhood
head: 8 superior

nuptial
6 bridal, wedded 7 marital, married, spousal, wedding 8 conjugal, espousal, hymeneal, marriage 9 connubial 11 matrimonial

nurse
4 feed, nana, rear, suck 5 nanny, serve 6 attend, foster, pamper, suckle 7 care for, cherish, nourish, nurture 9 cultivate 10 minister to
children's: 5 nanny
English: 11 Nightingale (Florence)
Indian: 4 ayah
Chinese: 4 amah

nursemaid
4 nana 5 nanny 6 minder, sitter 9 governess 10 babysitter
Indian: 4 ayah
Chinese: 4 amah

nursery
6 crèche 7 brooder 8 hothouse 9 fosterage 10 greenhouse 12 conservatory

nurture
4 care, feed, rear, tend 5 nurse, raise, train 6 cradle, foster 7 bring up, care for, develop, educate, nourish, rearing 8 breeding, instruct, training, tutelage 9 cultivate 10 upbringing

nut
3 bug 4 kook, loon 5 acorn, crank, fiend, freak, loony, pecan 6 almond, cashew, cuckoo, madman, maniac, zealot 7 fanatic, filbert, hickory, lunatic 8 crackpot 9 bedlamite, ding-a-ling, macadamia, pistachio, screwball 10 enthusiast, Tom o' Bedlam
of a violin bow: 4 frog, heel

Nut
consort: 3 Geb, Keb
daughter: 4 Isis 8 Nephthys
son: 6 Osiris

nuthouse
6 asylum, bedlam 8 loony bin 9 funny farm 10 booby hatch 11 institution 12 insane asylum

Nutmeg State
11 Connecticut

nutria
5 coypu

nutriment
4 diet, fare, food, grub, keep 6 viands 7 aliment, pabulum 8 victuals 9 provender 10 provisions, sustenance 11 comestibles, nourishment, subsistence

nutrition
4 diet 7 vittles 8 victuals 10 sustenance 11 nourishment

nutritious
9 healthful, wholesome 10 alimentary, nourishing

nuts
3 mad 4 daft, keen, wild 5 batty, crazy, kooky, loony, rabid, wacky 6 absurd, cuckoo, insane, screwy 7 bonkers, cracked, excited, foolish, idiotic 8 animated, demented, deranged 9 exuberant, fanatical, screwballl 10 passionate, unbalanced 12 enthusiastic

nutty
see **nuts**

nuzzle
3 rub 4 root, snug 5 nudge 6 burrow, cuddle, nestle 7 snuggle

Nycteus
brother: 5 Lycus
daughter: 7 Antiope

nymph
3 nix 5 dryad, larva, naiad, nixie, sylph 6 kelpie, maiden, sprite 7 mermaid
changed into a bear: 8 Callisto
changed into a laurel: 6 Daphne
changed into a rock: 4 Echo
mountain: 5 oread
sea: 6 Nereid 7 Calypso
water: 5 naiad 6 undine
wood: 5 dryad

Nyx
see **Nox**

O

oaf
4 boob, boor, bull, clod, dodo, dolt, goof, goon, hulk, lout, lump, slob **5** booby, chump, clown, dummy, dunce, klutz **6** dum-dum, galoot, lubber, lummox **7** fathead, palooka **8** bonehead, lunkhead, meathead **9** blockhead, blunderer, lamebrain, simpleton

oafish
5 dense **6** clumsy, klutzy, rustic **7** boorish, doltish, loutish **8** bungling, churlish, clownish, lubberly

oak
African: 7 turtosa
fruit: 5 acorn
genus: 7 Quercus
kind: 3 bur, pin, red **4** bear, cork, holm, ilex, live **5** black, holly, roble, white **6** barren, cerris, encina **7** durmast, English, moss-cup, valonia **9** blackjack
Mexican: 8 chaparro
young: 8 flittern

oar
3 row **4** pole, pull **5** rower, scull **6** paddle **7** paddler
part: 4 loom, palm **5** blade, shaft **6** button, collar
pin: 5 thole

oarsman
3 bow **5** rower **6** stroke **7** sculler
director: 3 cox **8** coxswain

oasis
3 spa **4** wadi **6** refuge, relief
ancient: 4 Merv
Egypt: 4 Siwa **5** Gafsa **6** Dakhla **7** Farafra **8** Ammonium
Libya: 5 Mizda, Sebha **6** Sabhah **7** Gadames **8** Ghudamis
Niger: 5 Bilma
Saudi Arabia: 5 Hofuf, Taima **7** Al-Hufuf

oast
4 kiln, oven

oat
5 grain, grass **6** cereal
genus: 5 Avena
Scottish: 3 ait

oater
7 western **10** horse opera

oath
3 vow **4** cuss **5** curse, swear **6** pledge **7** promise **8** cussword **9** expletive, profanity, swearword
mild: 3 gee **4** darn, drat, egad, geez, gosh, jeez **5** golly **6** jiminy **7** gee whiz

oatmeal
5 gruel **6** burgoo **8** porridge
Scottish: 8 drammock

obdurate
3 set **4** firm, hard **5** harsh, rigid, stony **6** dogged, mulish **7** adamant, callous **8** stubborn **9** heartless, immovable, unbending, unfeeling **10** hard-boiled, inflexible, insensitive, unshakable, unyielding **11** coldhearted, hardhearted, unemotional **12** intransigent, stonyhearted **13** unsympathetic

obeah
5 charm, magic

Obed
father: 4 Boaz **6** Ephlal **8** Shemaiah
mother: 4 Ruth
son: 5 Jesse **7** Azariah

obedient
5 loyal **6** docile **7** devoted, duteous, dutiful, willing **8** amenable, biddable, obliging, yielding **9** compliant, tractable **10** law-abiding, manageable, respectful, submissive **11** acquiescent, cooperative, deferential, subservient

obeisance
3 bow **5** honor **6** curtsy, esteem, fealty, homage, kowtow, salaam **7** gesture,

loyalty, respect **9** deference, reverence
10 allegiance, submission

obelisk
6 dagger, pillar, symbol

Oberon
messenger: 4 Puck
wife: 7 Titania

Oberto composer
5 Verdi (Giuseppe)

obese
3 fat **5** bulky, gross, heavy **6** fleshy, tubby
7 adipose, outsize, porcine **9** corpulent
10 overweight

obey
3 bow **4** heed, keep, mind **5** agree, defer,
serve, yield **6** accede, accept, assent,
comply, follow, regard, submit **7** abide by,
conform, execute, fulfill, observe, satisfy
8 adhere to, carry out **9** acquiesce

obfuscate
4 blur **5** cloud, muddy **6** darken
7 becloud, conceal, confuse, cover up,
obscure **9** adumbrate

obi
4 sash

obiter dictum
4 note **6** remark **7** comment, opinion
10 commentary, incidental **11** observation

obituary
9 necrology **11** death notice

object
3 aim, end, use **4** goal, idea, item, kick,
view, wish **5** being, cause, demur, focus,
frown, point, thing **6** design, entity, except,
intent, matter, motive, oppose, target
7 article, dissent, protest, purpose
8 complain, disagree, function, material
9 criticize, intention, something
10 disapprove

objection
5 demur **7** protest **8** argument, demurral,
demurrer, question **9** challenge, complaint,
exception **10** difficulty, opposition
11 disapproval **12** disagreement,
remonstrance **13** remonstration

objectionable
5 unfit **8** unwanted **9** abhorrent, invidious,
loathsome, obnoxious, offensive, repellent,
repugnant, repulsive, revolting, unwelcome
10 ill-favored, unpleasant **11** displeasing,
distasteful, undesirable **12** disagreeable

objective
3 aim, end **4** fair, goal, just, lens, mark
6 actual, design, intent, target **7** mission,
purpose **8** ambition, function, material,
physical, sensible, unbiased **9** corporeal,
equitable, impartial, intention **10** impersonal **11** independent, substantial
12 unprejudiced **13** dispassionate

objet d'art
5 curio, virtu (plural) **7** bibelot, novelty
10 knickknack

objurgate
5 chide, decry, scold **6** rebuke **7** censure,
reprove, upbraid **8** admonish, reproach
9 castigate, reprimand

oblate
7 lay monk **9** flattened, religious

oblation
4 gift **6** corban **8** holy gift, offering
9 sacrifice **12** presentation

obligate
4 bind **7** require **8** encumber, restrict
9 constrain

obligated
5 bound, owing **6** liable **8** beholden,
indebted **11** accountable, responsible

obligation
3 IOU, vow **4** bond, call, debt, dues, duty,
need, oath **5** cause **6** burden, charge,
pledge **7** promise **8** business, contract
9 committal, liability, necessity, restraint
10 commitment, compulsion, constraint
11 requirement **12** indebtedness

obligatory
7 binding **8** required **9** essential,
mandatory, necessary, requisite
10 compulsory, imperative **11** unavoidable

oblige
3 aid **4** bind, help, make **5** avail, favor,
force **6** assist, coerce, command, compel,
please, profit **7** benefit, gratify, require
9 constrain **10** contribute
11 accommodate, necessitate

obliged
4 made **5** bound **6** forced **8** beholden,
grateful, indebted, thankful **11** constrained
12 appreciative

obliging
4 kind **5** civil **7** amiable, helpful, willing
8 friendly, pleasant **11** complaisant,
considerate, cooperative, good-humored,
good-natured **12** good-tempered

oblique
6 sloped, tilted 7 devious, leaning, obscure, sloping, tilting 8 inclined, indirect 9 inclining 10 roundabout

obliterate
4 raze, x out 5 erase 6 cancel, delete, efface, remove, rub out 7 blot out, destroy, expunge, wipe out 8 black out, cross out 10 annihilate

oblivion
5 lethe, limbo 7 amnesia, nirvana, nowhere 9 emptiness 11 nothingness 13 forgetfulness, insensibility

oblivious
4 lost 5 blind 7 unaware 8 absorbed, heedless, ignorant 9 forgetful, unknowing, unmindful, unwitting 10 unfamiliar, uninformed 11 inattentive, incognizant, unconscious

oblong
4 oval 5 ovate 7 ellipse 8 elongate 9 elongated, rectangle 11 rectangular

obloquy
4 slam, slur 5 abuse, odium, shame 6 infamy, rebuke 7 calumny, censure 8 disgrace, dishonor, ignominy 9 aspersion, contumely, discredit, disrepute, invective, stricture 10 defamation, disapproval, opprobrium, scurrility 12 billingsgate, condemnation, vituperation

obnoxious
4 vile 5 awful 6 odious, rotten 7 hateful 9 abhorrent, invidious, loathsome, offensive, repellent, repugnant, revulsive, sickening 10 abominable, detestable, disgusting

oboe
4 reed 7 hautboy 8 hautbois, woodwind 10 double reed
early: 5 shawm
relative: 7 bassoon 11 English horn

O'Brian character
6 Aubrey (Jack) 7 Maturin (Stephen)

obscene
4 foul, lewd, rank, vile 5 bawdy, crass, crude, dirty, gross, lurid, taboo 6 coarse, filthy, impure, ribald, risqué, smutty, vulgar 7 immoral, noisome, profane, raunchy 8 indecent, scabrous 9 abhorrent, appalling, excessive, offensive, repellent, repugnant, repulsive, salacious 10 disgusting, lascivious, scurrilous

11 foulmouthed, unprintable 12 pornographic, scatological

obscure
3 dim 4 blur, hide, mask, veil 5 blind, cloak, cloud, cover, dusky, faint, minor, murky, shade, shady, vague 6 cloudy, darken, hidden, opaque, remote, screen, secret, shadow, shroud, veiled 7 clouded, conceal, cryptic, eclipse, removed, shadowy, unclear, unknown, unnoted 8 disguise, nameless, overcast, puzzling, secluded, shrouded 9 ambiguous, enigmatic, tenebrous, uncertain, undefined 10 camouflage, ill-defined, indefinite, indistinct, mysterious, overshadow 11 out-of-the-way, unimportant 12 inaccessible, unnoticeable 13 inconspicuous

obscurity
3 fog 4 haze, mist, murk 5 gloom 6 enigma, miasma, puzzle 7 dimness, mystery, shadows 8 darkness 9 ambiguity

obsequies
4 rite 5 rites 7 funeral 10 burial rite

obsequious
4 oily 6 abject 7 fawning, servile, slavish 8 obedient, obeisant, toadying, unctuous 9 parasitic 10 flattering, submissive 11 deferential, subservient, sycophantic

observance
4 rite, rule 6 custom, notice, regard, ritual 7 liturgy, service 8 ceremony, practice 9 adherence, attention, formality 10 ceremonial

observant
4 keen 5 alert, awake, aware, sharp 7 heedful, mindful 8 watchful 9 advertent, attentive 10 perceptive

observation
4 note 6 notice, record, regard, remark 7 comment, finding, opinion 8 judgment, notation 9 attention, inference 10 commentary 12 obiter dictum

observatory
5 tower 7 lookout, outlook 8 overlook
famous: 4 Lick 6 Wilson, Yerkes 7 Palomar
instrument: 9 telescope

observe
3 see 4 espy, keep, look, mark, mind, note, obey, twig, view 5 honor, opine, sight, state, study, watch 6 behold, comply, follow, look at, notice, remark 7 abide by, comment, conform, discern, respect

8 perceive 9 celebrate, solemnize
10 comply with 11 commemorate

obsess
5 beset, haunt, hound, rivet 6 absorb,
plague 7 consume, possess 9 captivate,
preoccupy

obsessed
6 dogged, driven, hipped, hooked
7 gripped, haunted, plagued 8 overcome,
troubled 9 dominated, possessed
11 preoccupied 12 prepossessed

obsession
5 craze, mania 6 fetish, hang-up
8 fixation, idée fixe 11 infatuation
13 preoccupation

obsessive
5 rabid 8 frenetic, maniacal, neurotic
9 fanatical, possessed 10 passionate
11 preoccupied

obsolete
3 old 5 dated, passé, stale 6 old hat
7 disused, worn-out 8 outmoded, timeworn 9 out-of-date 10 antiquated,
superseded 12 antediluvian, old-fashioned

obstacle
3 bar 4 bump, clog, snag 5 block, catch,
check, crimp, hitch 6 hurdle 7 barrier
8 handicap, hardship 9 hindrance,
impedance, roadblock 10 difficulty,
impediment 11 encumbrance, vicissitude
12 interference

obstinate
4 deaf, firm 5 balky, fixed 6 dogged,
mulish 7 staunch, willful 8 obdurate,
perverse, resolute, stubborn 9 pigheaded,
resistant, unbudging, immovable
10 hardheaded, headstrong, inflexible,
persistent, refractory, unyielding
11 intractable, opinionated, stiff-necked,
wrongheaded 12 intransigent,
pertinacious, recalcitrant

obstreperous
4 loud 5 noisy, rowdy 6 unruly 7 blatant,
raucous 8 strident 9 clamorous, insistent
10 boisterous, disorderly, vociferant,
vociferous 11 disobedient, loudmouthed
12 rambunctious

obstruct
3 bar, dam 4 clog, hide, plug, stop 5 block,
check, choke, close 6 cut off, hamper,
hinder, impede, stymie, thwart 7 congest,
occlude, prevent, shut off, shut out,
trammel 9 interfere

obstruction
3 bar 4 snag 5 hitch 6 hamper, hurdle
7 barrier 8 blockage, obstacle, stoppage
9 hindrance, impedance 10 impediment

obtain
3 buy, get, win 4 earn, gain, have, reap
5 annex, reach 6 pick up, secure
7 achieve, acquire, chalk up, procure
8 purchase

obtrude
5 cut in 6 butt in, horn in, impose, meddle
7 presume, push out 8 chisel in, infringe
9 interfere, thrust out

obtrusive
4 nosy 5 pushy 6 prying 7 forward
8 meddling 9 bumptious, officious
10 meddlesome, protruding 11 impertinent, interfering

obtuse
4 dull, dumb, slow 5 blunt, dense, thick
6 stupid 7 rounded, unclear 11 insensitive

obverse
4 face, side 5 front 8 opposite 9 other
side 10 complement 11 counterpart

obviate
4 ward 5 avert, deter, block 7 forfend,
prevent, rule out 8 preclude, stave off
9 forestall, interfere, interpose, intervene
10 anticipate

obvious
5 clear, overt, plain 6 patent, simple
7 blatant, evident, glaring 8 apparent,
clear-cut, distinct, manifest, palpable
10 undeniable 11 conspicuous, self-
evident, transparent, unambiguous,
unequivocal

oca
5 tuber 6 sorrel

O'Casey, Sean
9 dramatist 10 playwright
plays: 17 Juno and the Paycock, Plough
and the Stars (The)

occasion
4 call, need, shot, show, time 5 basis,
break, cause, event 6 chance, demand,
effect, excuse, ground, lead to, moment,
reason 7 episode, instant, opening,
produce 8 ceremony, incident, instance
9 condition, happening, necessity 10 bring
about, foundation, obligation, occurrence
11 celebration, determinant, opportunity
12 circumstance 13 justification

occasional
3 few, odd   4 rare   6 casual, random, scarce, seldom   7 special, unusual   8 specific, sporadic, uncommon   9 irregular   10 incidental, infrequent

Occidental
7 Western   8 European   9 Westerner

occlude
4 clog, fill, hide, plug, stop   5 block, choke, close, cover   6 screen   7 close up, conceal, congest, stop up   8 block off, obstruct

occult
5 eerie, magic   6 arcane, orphic, secret   8 abstruse, esoteric, hermetic, mystical   9 recondite, unearthly   10 cabalistic, mysterious   12 supernatural

occupant
5 liver   6 inmate, tenant   7 denizen, dweller, resider   8 habitant, resident   10 inhabitant

occupation
3 job, use   4 line, work   5 trade   6 career, métier, office   7 calling, control, pursuit, seizure   8 activity, business, position, vocation   9 occupancy, residence   10 employment, habitation, settlement   11 possession

occupy
3 use   4 busy, fill, hold, take   5 seize, tie up   6 absorb, employ, engage, live in, people, take up, tenant   7 control, engross, immerse, inhabit, involve, possess   8 populate, reside in, take over

occur
3 hap   4 pass   5 arise, ensue, pop up   6 appear, befall, betide, chance, dawn on, happen, result, strike   7 come off, develop   9 take place, transpire

occurrence
3 hap   4 pass   5 event, state   7 episode   8 exigency, incident, juncture, occasion   9 adventure, condition, emergency, happening, situation

ocean
3 sea   4 blue, deep, main   5 brine, drink   6 Arctic, Indian   7 Pacific   8 Atlantic   9 Antarctic
movement: 4 tide, wave

Oceania
country: 4 Fiji   5 Belau, Nauru, Palau, Samoa, Tonga   6 Tuvalu   7 Vanuatu   8 Kiribati   9 Australia   10 New Zealand

territory: 7 Tokelau   12 New Caledonia   13 American Samoa
ethnic group: 6 Fijian, Papuan, Samoan   10 Melanesian, Polynesian   11 Micronesian
language: 5 Maori   6 Fijian, Papuan, Pidgin, Samoan   10 Melanesian

oceanic
4 huge, vast   5 great   6 marine   7 immense, pelagic   8 enormous, maritime   9 saltwater, thalassic

Ocean State
11 Rhode Island

Oceanus
daughter: 5 Doris   7 Oceanid   8 Eurynome
father: 6 Uranus
mother: 4 Gaea
sister: 6 Tethys
son: 6 Peneus   7 Alpheus
wife: 6 Tethys

ocellus
3 eye   7 eyespot

ocelot
3 cat   7 wildcat

octave
5 eight, scale   6 eighth, stanza   8 interval

Octavia
brother: 8 Augustus
grandson: 8 Caligula
husband: 4 Nero   6 Antony

octopus
7 mollusc, mollusk   9 devilfish   10 cephalopod
arm: 8 tentacle
genus: 7 Polypus
kin: 5 squid   10 cuttlefish

ocular
4 seen   5 optic   6 visual   7 eyelike, optical, visible   8 eyepiece, viewable   9 perceived

Odalisque painter
6 Ingres (Jean-Auguste-Dominique)   7 Matisse (Henri)

odd
4 lone, rare   5 extra, fluky, queer, rummy, weird   6 casual, chance, single, uneven   7 curious, erratic, strange, unusual   8 peculiar, singular   9 eccentric, unmatched   13 idiosyncratic

oddball
4 kook   5 kooky, weird   6 weirdo   7 bizarre, curious, offbeat, strange, unusual

oddity

8 original, peculiar 9 character, eccentric
10 outlandish 13 idiosyncratic

oddity

5 freak, quirk 6 weirdo 7 anomaly
9 character, curiosity, departure, deviation,
eccentric, weirdness 10 aberration,
difference, strangeness 11 abnormality,
peculiarity 12 eccentricity, idiosyncrasy,
irregularity

odds

4 edge 5 favor, ratio 7 benefit, chances
8 handicap, variance 9 advantage,
allowance, disparity 10 difference,
likelihood, partiality, probability
12 disagreement

odds and ends

4 bits, olio 6 jumble, medley, motley,
scraps 7 mélange, mixture 8 remnants,
sundries 9 etceteras, leftovers, potpourri
10 assortment, hodgepodge, miscellany
13 paraphernalia

ode

4 hymn, poem 5 lyric, psalm, verse
part: 5 epode 7 strophe 11 antistrophe

Odets play

9 Golden Boy 11 Country Girl (The)
12 Awake and Sing 15 Waiting for Lefty

odeum

4 hall 7 theater 11 concert hall

Odin

brother: 4 Vili
daughter-in-law: 5 Nanna
father: 3 Bor
hall: 8 Valhalla
horse: 8 Sleipnir
maiden: 8 Valkyrie
mansion: 9 Gladsheim
mother: 6 Bestla
raven: 5 Hugin, Munin
ring: 8 Draupnir
son: 3 Tyr 4 Thor, Vali 6 Balder
spear: 7 Gungnir
sword: 4 Gram
wife: 4 Fria, Rind 5 Frigg 6 Frigga
wolf: 4 Geri 5 Freki

odious

4 foul, vile 6 horrid 7 hateful 8 horrible
9 abhorrent, execrable, invidious,
loathsome, malicious, repellent, repugnant
10 abominable, despicable, detestable

odium

4 hate, onus 5 shame 6 hatred, infamy,
stigma 7 censure, obloquy 8 contempt,
disgrace, dishonor, ignominy, loathing

9 disrepute 10 abhorrence, opprobrium
11 detestation 12 condemnation

odor

4 funk 5 aroma, scent, smell, stink, whiff
6 stench 7 bouquet, perfume 9 fragrance,
redolence

odorous

5 heady, sweet 6 smelly, strong
7 pungent, scented 8 aromatic, fragrant,
perfumed, redolent, unsavory 9 offensive

Odysseus

7 Ulysses
dog: 5 Argos
enchantress: 5 Circe
father: 7 Laertes
friend: 6 Mentor
harasser: 8 Poseidon
herb: 4 moly
kingdom: 6 Ithaca
mother: 8 Anticlea
son: 9 Telegonus 10 Telemachus
swineherd: 7 Eumaeus
voyage: 7 odyssey
wife: 8 Penelope

odyssey

4 trek 5 quest 6 voyage 7 journey
9 wandering 13 peregrination

Odyssey author

5 Homer

Oedipus

brother-in-law: 5 Creon
daughter: 6 Ismene 8 Antigone
father: 5 Laius
foster father: 7 Polybus
foster mother: 8 Periboea
kingdom: 6 Thebes
mother: 7 Jocasta
son: 8 Eteocles 9 Polynices 10 Polyneices
victim: 5 Laius
wife: 7 Jocasta

Oeneus

kingdom: 7 Calydon
son: 8 Meleager
wife: 7 Althaea

Oenomaus

charioteer: 8 Myrtilus
daughter: 10 Hippodamia
kingdom: 4 Pisa
slayer: 6 Pelops

Oenone

husband: 5 Paris
rival: 5 Helen

oeuvre
4 work 6 corpus, output 8 lifework
10 collection 11 compilation

of
German: 3 aus, von
Italian: 5 degli, della, delle

off
4 away, kill 5 aside 6 depart, murder,
remote, slight 7 seaward, spoiled
9 eccentric, incorrect

offal
4 guts 4 junk 5 gurry, trash, waste
6 debris, litter, refuse, spilth 7 carrion,
garbage, innards, rubbish, viscera
8 entrails 9 sweepings 10 intestines

offbeat
3 odd 5 fresh, outré, weird 6 way out
7 bizarre, oddball, strange, unusual
8 bohemian, peculiar, singular, uncommon
9 different, eccentric, whimsical
10 outlandish, unorthodox 11 distinctive
13 idiosyncratic

off-color
3 ill, low 4 blue, racy 5 bawdy, broad,
salty, shady 6 ailing, peaked, poorly,
risqué, sickly, unwell 7 dubious, naughty
8 improper, indecent 10 indisposed,
suggestive

offend
3 sin, vex 4 gall, hurt, miff, pain 5 anger,
annoy, pique, repel, shock, upset 6 appall,
breach, insult, nettle 7 affront, disturb,
provoke, violate 8 aggrieve, distress,
irritate 9 displease 10 antagonize,
transgress

offender
5 felon 6 sinner 7 culprit 8 criminal,
violator 9 wrongdoer 10 lawbreaker,
malefactor 12 transgressor

offense
3 sin 4 huff, hurt, miff, tort, vice 5 crime,
fault, pique, wrong 6 attack, breach, felony,
injury, insult 7 affront, assault, dudgeon,
misdeed, mistake, outrage, umbrage
9 indignity, onslaught, violation
10 aggression, infraction, resentment
11 displeasure, indignation, misdemeanor

offensive
3 bad 4 foul, rank, vile 5 drive, onset
6 attack, odious 7 assault, noisome,
obscene, painful 8 nauseous, unsavory
9 loathsome, obnoxious, onslaught,
repellent, repugnant, repulsive, sickening
10 aggression, aggressive, disgusting,
nauseating, unpleasant 11 uncongenial,
unpalatable, unwholesome
12 disagreeable, unappetizing
13 objectionable

offer
3 bid, try 4 seek, show 5 assay, essay,
pitch, put up 6 afford, extend, submit,
tender 7 advance, attempt, display, exhibit,
hold out, present, propose, provide,
suggest 8 endeavor, proposal, threaten
9 sacrifice 10 submission 11 proposition

offering
4 alms, gift 5 grant 6 course, corban
7 charity, present 8 donation, oblation
9 sacrifice 10 benefaction, beneficence
12 contribution

offhand
5 ad-lib 6 blithe, breezy, casual 8 informal
9 extempore, impromptu, unstudied
10 improvised, nonchalant, unprepared
11 extemporary, spontaneous, unrehearsed

office
3 job 4 duty 5 berth, suite 6 agency, billet,
bureau 7 station 8 business, cube farm,
function, province 9 situation, workplace
10 department
head: 4 boss 7 manager
machine: 3 fax 6 copier 7 printer
8 computer 10 calculator, fax machine
11 photocopier
seeker: 9 candidate 10 politician
worker: 5 clerk 6 typist 9 file clerk,
secretary 10 bookkeeper

officer
3 cop 4 exec 6 noncom, police 7 John
Law, manager 8 official 9 executive
abbreviation: 3 Adm., Col., Ens., Gen.,
Maj. 4 Capt., Cmdr. 5 Comdr., Lieut.
army: 5 major 7 captain, colonel, general
10 lieutenant
British: 9 brigadier
court: 7 bailiff
king's: 11 chamberlain
law-enforcement: 3 cop 6 deputy, police
7 marshal, sheriff 9 constable, patrolman,
policeman
naval: 4 mate 6 ensign 7 admiral, captain
9 commander, commodore 10 lieutenant
noncommissioned: 5 sarge 8 corporal,
sergeant
petty: 5 bosun 6 yeoman 9 boatswain
prison: 5 guard 6 warden

official
4 exec 7 cleared, manager 8 approved,

bona fide, endorsed **9** authentic,
canonical, cathedral, certified, executive
10 accredited, authorized, ex cathedra,
magistrate, sanctioned **13** administrator,
authoritative
city or town: 5 mayor **8** alderman
9 councilor, selectman **10** councillor
diplomatic: 5 envoy **6** consul **7** attaché
10 ambassador
governmental: 6 syndic
parish: 6 beadle
sports: 3 ref, ump **6** umpire **7** referee
8 linesman
university: 4 dean **6** bursar **7** provost
9 registrar **10** chancellor

officiate
5 chair, serve **6** direct, umpire **7** conduct,
oversee, preside, referee **9** supervise
11 superintend

officious
4 busy, nosy **5** pushy **7** forward
8 meddling **9** assertive, intrusive, obtrusive
10 meddlesome **11** impertinent **13** self-
important

offing
6 future **7** by-and-by **9** aftertime, hereafter
10 near future

off-key
3 odd **4** sour **7** jarring **9** anomalous,
dissonant, unnatural **10** discordant
12 inharmonious

off-putting
8 daunting **9** dismaying, offensive,
repellent **10** forbidding, foreboding
11 distasteful **12** disagreeable,
discouraging **13** disconcerting,
disheartening, objectionable

offscouring
5 trash **6** pariah, refuse, reject **7** outcast
8 castaway, derelict **11** untouchable

offset
6 square **7** balance **8** equalize
10 balance out, compensate, neutralize
11 counterpose, countervail
12 counterpoise, displacement

offshoot
5 scion **6** branch **7** product, spin-off
9 affiliate, by-product, outgrowth
10 derivative, descendant

offspring
3 kid **4** kids, seed **5** brood, child, hatch,
issue, scion, spawn, swarm, young
7 produce, product, progeny **8** children
9 posterity **10** descendant **11** progeniture

off-the-wall
3 odd **5** kooky, weird **6** far-out, oddball,
way-out **7** bizarre, oddball, unusual
8 freakish **9** eccentric, fantastic, grotesque
10 outlandish

off-white
4 bone **5** cream, ivory **6** oyster, vellum
9 parchment

Of Human Bondage author
7 Maugham (W. Somerset)

Of Mice and Men
author: 9 Steinbeck (John)
character: 6 George (Milton), Lennie
(Small)

often
9 generally **10** frequently, habitually,
repeatedly **11** recurrently

ogee
3 ess **4** arch **5** curve **7** molding

Ogier the _____
4 Dane

ogive
3 rib **4** arch **5** graph

ogle
3 eye **4** gape, gaze, leer, look **5** stare
6 goggle **10** rubberneck

ogre
5 bogey, giant **7** bugbear, monster
8 bogeyman **9** boogeyman
Algonquian: 7 windigo

ogress
5 harpy, scold, shrew, vixen **6** amazon,
virago **8** fishwife **9** termagant, Xanthippe

O'Hara novel
7 Pal Joey **12** Butterfield 8 **17** Ten North
Frederick

Ohio
capital: 8 Columbus
city: 5 Akron, Xenia **6** Canton, Dayton,
Toledo **9** Cleveland **10** Cincinnati
college, university: 5 Miami **6** Kenyon
7 Antioch, Denison, Oberlin **9** Kent State
12 Bowling Green
nickname: 7 Buckeye (State)
river: 4 Ohio **6** Maumee **8** Sandusky
state bird: 8 cardinal
state flower: 16 scarlet carnation
state tree: 7 buckeye

Oholibamah
father: 4 Anah
husband: 4 Esau

oil
3 fat, gas 4 balm, fuel, lube, oleo 5 oleum, slick 6 anoint, grease, pomade 7 blarney, incense, lanolin 8 flattery, soft soap 9 adulation, lubricant, lubricate, petroleum
combining form: 3 ole 4 olei, oleo
consecrated: 6 chrism
fragrant: 5 attar 6 neroli
fuel: 3 gas 6 petrol 8 gasoline, kerosene
relating to: 5 oleic
ship: 6 tanker
source: 5 olive, shale
well: 6 gusher

Oil! author
8 Sinclair (Upton)

oilbird
8 guacharo

oily
5 fatty, slick, soapy, suave 6 greasy, smarmy, smooth 7 fulsome 8 slippery, unctuous 10 lubricious, obsequious, oleaginous

ointment
4 balm 5 cream, salve 6 lotion 7 unction, unguent 8 calamine, liniment 9 emollient 11 embrocation

Okinawa capital
4 Naha

Oklahoma
capital: 12 Oklahoma City
city: 3 Ada 4 Enid 5 Tulsa 6 Norman
college, university: 11 Oral Roberts
mountain: 9 Black Mesa
nickname: 6 Sooner (State)
river: 3 Red 8 Arkansas, Canadian
state bird: 10 flycatcher
state flower: 9 mistletoe
state tree: 6 redbud

OK, okay
3 aye, yea, yes 4 fine, good, safe, well 5 agree, allow, favor 6 agreed, assent, decent, permit 7 approve, certify, endorse, support 8 accredit, adequate, all right, approval, blessing, high sign, passable, sanction, thumbs-up 9 authorize, hunky-dory 10 acceptable, permission 11 endorsement 12 satisfactory

okra
4 herb, soup 5 gumbo 6 mallow

old
4 aged, gray, late, past 5 dated, hoary, passé, stale 6 bygone, démodé, former, mature, senior, whilom 7 ancient, antique, archaic, elderly, lasting, onetime, overage, quondam, veteran 8 enduring, lifelong, Noachian, outmoded, timeworn 9 erstwhile, geriatric, long-lived, perennial, perpetual, primitive, venerable 10 antiquated, inveterate 13 superannuated
Scottish: 4 auld

old age
6 dotage 8 caducity 10 senescence 11 decrepitude, elderliness, senectitude

Old Bailey
5 court

Old Colony State
13 Massachusetts

Old Curiosity Shop author
7 Dickens (Charles)

Old Dominion State
8 Virginia

Old Faithful
6 geyser

old-fashioned
4 aged 5 dated, dowdy, fusty, moldy, passé, stale, tired 6 bygone, démodé, quaint, stodgy 7 ancient, antique, archaic, outworn, vintage 8 cocktail, obsolete, outdated, outmoded 9 out-of-date, unstylish 10 antiquated

old hand
3 pro, vet 6 expert, master 7 veteran 9 authority 10 past master, specialist

old hat
5 dated, passé, stale, tired, trite 6 démodé 7 antique, clichéd, vintage 8 outmoded, timeworn, well-worn 9 hackneyed, out-of-date 10 antiquated

Old Ironsides
12 Constitution (U.S.S.)
poet: 6 Holmes (Oliver Wendell)

Old Line State
8 Maryland

old maid
6 fusser 7 fusspot 8 card game, spinster 10 fussbudget

Old North State
13 North Carolina

Old Rough and Ready
6 Taylor (Zachary)

Olds' car
3 Reo

old-time
5 dated **6** bygone **7** antique, vintage
10 antiquated **12** long-standing

old-timer
3 vet **5** elder **6** senior **7** ancient, antique,
veteran

Old World
6 Europe

oleaginous
see **oily**

oleaster
5 shrub **12** Russian olive

olecranon
9 funny bone

oleo
9 margarine

oleoresin
10 turpentine

oleum
3 oil

olfaction
5 sense, smell **8** smelling

olid
4 rank **5** fetid **6** putrid, rancid, rotten
7 stenchy **8** stinking **9** offensive
10 malodorous

olio
3 mix **4** stew **5** umble **6** medley
7 mélange, mixture **8** mishmash, mixed
bag **9** potpourri **10** assortment, collection,
hodgepodge, miscellany

Oliver Twist
author: **7** Dickens (Charles)
character: **5** Fagin, Nancy, Sikes (Bill)
6 Bumble (Mr.) **12** Artful Dodger

Ollie's partner
4 Stan

Olympian
3 god **5** lofty, noble **6** lordly **7** athlete,
exalted, godlike **8** majestic, superior
10 competitor

Olympics
5 games **6** sports **9** athletics
place of origin: **6** Greece
symbol: **5** flame, torch

Oman
capital: **6** Masqat, Muscat
language: **6** Arabic **7** Baluchi
monetary unit: **4** rial
mountain range: **7** Al-Hajar

neighbor: **5** Yemen **11** Saudi Arabia
peninsula: **7** Arabian
sea: **7** Arabian

Omar
4 poet **7** Khayyém
country: **6** Persia
father: **7** Eliphaz
poem: **8** Rubaiyat

omega
3 end **6** ending, finale, letter
kin: **3** zed, zee

omen
4 sign **5** augur, token **6** augury, boding
7 auspice, portent, presage, warning
8 bodement, prophecy **9** foretoken
10 foreboding, prediction, prognostic

ominous
4 dark, dire, grim **6** dismal **7** baleful,
direful, doomful, fateful **8** alarming,
lowering, menacing, sinister **9** ill-boding,
prophetic **10** forbidding, foreboding,
portentous **11** frightening, threatening
12 inauspicious, unpropitious

omission
3 cut, gap **4** lack, skip, slip **5** blank, break,
chasm, error, lapse **6** hiatus, lacuna
7 elision, failure **8** eclipsis, ellipsis,
overlook **9** exclusion
mark: **5** caret **8** ellipsis **10** apostrophe

omit
4 drop, fail, skip **5** elide **6** except, forget,
ignore, slight **7** exclude, neglect **8** leave
out, overlook, pass over **11** leave undone

omnibus
3 ana **4** posy **5** album **7** garland
8 analects, treasury **9** anthology
10 miscellany **11** florilegium

omnipotent
6 divine **7** godlike, supreme **8** almighty
9 unlimited **11** all-powerful

omnipresent
7 allover, endless **8** infinite, unending
9 boundless, limitless, universal
10 ubiquitous

omniscient
4 wise **7** learned **9** know-it-all **10** all-
knowing

omnium-gatherum
see **olio**

Omphale
domain: **5** Lydia
slave: **8** Heracles, Hercules

omphalos
3 hub 5 navel 9 umbilicus 10 focal point

on
4 atop, over 5 above, along 7 working
9 operating 11 functioning

onager
3 ass 5 kiang 8 catapult

Onan's father
5 Judah

once
4 ever, late, past 5 at all 6 before, bygone,
former, whilom 7 already, earlier, long ago,
onetime, quondam 8 formerly, sometime

once-over
4 look 5 check 6 gander, glance, survey
10 inspection 11 examination

one
4 lone, only, sole, unit 5 monad 6 single,
unique 7 numeral 8 separate, singular,
solitary 9 undivided 10 individual,
particular
combining form: 4 mono
French: 3 une
German: 3 ein 4 eine
prefix: 3 uni
Scottish: 3 ane
Spanish: 3 una, uno

one and a half
combining form: 6 sesqui

one-eyed giant
7 Cyclops 10 Polyphemus

one-handed god
3 Tiu, Tyr

one-horse town
4 burg 6 hamlet, Podunk 11 whistle-stop

one hundred
6 centum
years: 7 century

O'Neill, Eugene
heroine: 4 Anna, Nina
play: 3 Ile 4 Gold 8 Hairy Ape (The)
12 Ah Wilderness, Anna Christie, Emperor
Jones, Iceman Cometh (The) 13 Great
God Brown (The), Marco Millions
16 Strange Interlude 18 Desire Under the
Elms 22 Mourning Becomes Electra
24 Long Day's Journey into Night

oneiric
6 dreamy 8 anagogic 9 dreamlike

oneness
3 all 5 union, unity, whole 7 harmony

8 entirety, identity, sameness, totality
9 integrity, unanimity 10 singleness,
uniformity 11 singularity, unification
13 individuality

onerous
4 hard 5 heavy, tough 6 taxing, trying
7 arduous, exigent, wearing, weighty
8 exacting, grievous, imposing, pressing,
toilsome 9 demanding, difficult, laborious
10 burdensome, cumbersome, oppressive
11 troublesome

one-sided
6 biased, uneven 7 colored, partial,
unequal 8 inclined, partisan, weighted
10 prejudiced, unbalanced, unilateral

onetime
3 old 4 once, past 6 bygone, former,
whilom 7 quondam 8 previous 9 erstwhile

ongoing
7 current, growing 8 evolving 9 advancing,
in process 10 continuing, continuous,
developing, in progress, unfinished
11 progressing

on hand
4 here 5 ready 6 nearby 7 pending,
present 9 available

onion
4 bulb 7 shallot
bulb: 3 set
genus: 6 Allium
kin: 4 leek 6 garlic
kind: 7 Bermuda, Danvers, Spanish
roll: 5 bialy
young: 8 scallion

online
5 wired 9 connected
business: 5 e-tail
guffaw: 3 LOL
system: 3 Web 8 Internet

onlooker
6 viewer 7 watcher, witness 8 beholder,
kibitzer, observer 9 bystander, spectator
10 eyewitness 12 rubbernecker

only
3 but, few, one, yet 4 just, lone, mere,
save, sole, solo 5 alone 6 and yet, at
most, except, merely, simply, single, solely,
unique 7 however, utterly 8 entirely,
singular, solitary 11 exclusively

onomasticon
7 lexicon 8 wordbook

onomatopoeic
5 mimic **6** echoic **7** mimetic **9** emulative, imitative **10** simulative

onset
4 dawn, rush **5** birth, start **6** attack, coming, origin **7** arrival, assault, dawning, offense, opening **8** invasion **9** beginning, inception, offensive **10** aggression **12** commencement

onslaught
5 blitz **6** attack, charge, deluge **7** assault, barrage, offense, torrent **8** invasion **9** offensive **10** aggression

on-target
5 exact, right **7** correct, perfect, precise **8** accurate **11** appropriate

Ontario
bay: **8** Georgian
capital: **7** Toronto
city: **4** York **6** London, Ottawa **7** Markham, Windsor **8** Hamilton **9** Etobicoke, Kitchener, North York **10** Thunder Bay **11** Mississauga, Scarborough **13** Sault Ste. Marie
lake: **4** Erie **5** Huron **7** Nipigon, Ontario **8** Superior
provincial flower: **13** white trillium
river: **5** Moose **6** Albany, Severn, Winisk

on the house
4 free **6** gratis **13** complimentary

on the nose
5 bingo **6** dead-on, spot-on **7** exactly **8** accurate **9** precisely **10** accurately

on the other hand
3 but **7** however

on the rocks
4 iced **7** with ice, wrecked

on the whole
6 mainly, mostly **7** usually **8** all in all **9** generally, in general, typically **10** altogether, by and large

onus
3 tax **4** duty, load, task **5** blame, brand, fault, guilt, odium, stain **6** burden, charge, stigma, weight **8** black eye **9** liability **10** obligation, oppression

onward
5 ahead, along, forth **7** forward **9** advancing

onyx
5 agate **10** chalcedony

oodles
4 gobs, lots, tons **5** heaps, loads, rafts, scads **6** plenty

oolong
3 tea

oomph
3 pep, vim, zip **4** brio, dash, élan, life, push, zest, zing **5** charm, drive, punch, verve, vigor **6** esprit, pizazz, spirit **7** glamour, pizzazz **8** strength, vitality **9** magnetism, sex appeal

ooze
3 goo, mud **4** emit, goop, leak, seep, weep **5** bleed, exude, issue, marsh, slime, sweat **7** secrete, seepage **8** transude

opacity
8 dullness **9** murkiness, obscurity **10** obtuseness

opal
3 gem **5** jewel, stone **6** silica **7** girasol, hyalite, mineral **8** gemstone

opaque
3 dim **4** dull, hazy **5** dense, filmy, murky, vague **6** cloudy **7** clouded, obscure, unclear **8** abstruse

OPEC nation
3 UAE **4** Iran, Iraq **5** Libya, Qatar **6** Kuwait **7** Algeria, Nigeria **9** Indonesia, Venezuela **11** Saudi Arabia

open
4 ajar, bare, free, wide **5** frank, naked, overt **6** broach, candid, expand, expose, public, reveal, spread, unfold, unlock, unseal, unveil **7** convene, outdoor, uncover, unlatch **8** disclose, outdoors, stripped, unclothe, unlocked, unsealed **9** available, uncovered **10** out-of-doors, unfastened **11** susceptible, unconcealed, undisguised **12** unrestricted

open-air
7 outdoor, outside **8** alfresco, outdoors **9** out-of-door **10** out-of-doors

open-and-shut
4 easy **5** clear, plain **6** patent, simple **7** evident, obvious

openhanded
6 giving, lavish **7** liberal **8** generous **9** bounteous, bountiful, unselfish, unsparing **10** beneficent, bighearted, charitable, munificent **11** magnanimous

openhearted
4 kind, warm **5** frank, plain **6** candid,

honest **8** generous **10** responsive
11 sympathetic

opening
3 gap **4** dawn, door, gate, hole, pass, pore,
slit, slot, vent **5** break, chasm, chink, cleft,
crack, debut, mouth, onset, start, stoma
6 breach, chance, lacuna, outlet, outse
7 crevice, dawning, fissure, orifice, pinhole
8 aperture, overture **9** beginning
11 opportunity
ship's: 5 hatch **8** hatchway, porthole

open-minded
7 liberal **8** tolerant, unbiased **9** receptive
12 freethinking, unprejudiced

openmouthed
4 agog, awed, rapt **5** agape **6** amazed,
gaping **7** stunned **9** astounded, surprised
10 astonished, speechless

open sesame
3 key **5** charm **6** ticket **8** passport,
password

open up
4 fire, talk **5** shoot **6** reveal **7** cut into,
divulge **8** disclose **9** make plain, spread
out **11** communicate

opera
comic: 5 buffa **6** bouffe
glasses: 9 lorgnette
kind: 4 soap **5** comic, grand, horse,
space
part: 3 act **4** aria **5** scena
solo: 4 aria
star: 4 diva **10** prima donna
text: 8 libretto
(see also individual titles and composers)

operant
8 behavior **9** effective **10** measurable,
observable, productive **12** conditioning

operate
3 act, cut, run, use **4** work **5** drive, exert,
steer **6** behave, direct, effect, handle,
manage **7** carry on, conduct, control,
perform, produce **8** function, maneuver
9 influence **10** bring about, manipulate

operation
3 use **4** step **6** action **7** concern, mission,
process, surgery **8** activity, business,
exercise, exertion, function, maneuver
9 procedure **10** employment, engagement,
enterprise, transaction **11** performance

operative
3 key **4** hand, live, open **5** agent, alive

6 active, artisan, moving, usable, worker
7 dynamic, in force, laborer, running,
working, workman **8** mechanic, relevant
9 effective, essential, important
10 functional **11** efficacious, influential,
secret agent, significant

operator
5 agent, fixer, pilot **6** doctor, driver
7 schemer, surgeon **9** conductor

operculum
3 lid **4** flap **8** covering

operetta composer
5 Friml (Rudolf), Lehár (Franz), Suppé
(Franz von) **6** Straus (Oscar) **7** Gilbert
(William S.), Herbert (Victor), Romberg
(Sigmund), Strauss (Johann) **8** Sullivan
(Arthur) **9** Offenbach (Jacques)

operose
4 dull **6** boring, tiring **7** tedious
8 tiresome, toilsome, weariful **9** difficult,
laborious, wearisome

Ophelia
beloved: 6 Hamlet
brother: 7 Laertes
father: 8 Polonius

ophidian
5 snake **9** snakelike

opiate
4 dope, drug **7** anodyne **8** hypnotic,
narcotic, nepenthe, sedative **9** analgesic,
soporific **10** anesthetic, painkiller
11 somnifacient **12** somnifacient,
tranquilizer
type: 7 codeine **8** morphine

opine
4 deem, hold, view **5** judge, state, think
6 advise, assert **7** believe, express,
suppose **8** point out **9** recommend

opinion
4 idea, view **5** tenet **6** belief, notion, theory
7 feeling, thought **8** attitude, estimate,
judgment, reaction **9** sentiment
10 assumption, conclusion, conjecture,
conviction, estimation, hypothesis,
persuasion **11** speculation, supposition
express an: 4 vote **5** judge **9** criticize

opium
4 dope, drug **8** narcotic
derivative: 6 heroin **7** codeine
8 laudanum, morphine **9** paregoric
source: 5 poppy

opossum
9 marsupial

kin: 8 kangaroo

opponent
3 con, foe 4 anti 5 enemy, muscle, rival
7 nemesis 9 adversary, assailant,
combatant 10 antagonist, challenger,
competitor 12 counteragent

opportune
3 apt, fit 6 timely 8 suitable 9 favorable,
well-timed 10 auspicious, convenient,
felicitous, propitious 11 appropriate

opportunity
4 turn 5 break, space, spell 6 chance
7 opening 8 juncture, occasion, prospect
12 circumstance

oppose
4 buck, defy, deny, duel 5 cross, fight,
repel 6 attack, combat, debate, differ,
object, refute, resist 7 assault, contest,
counter, dispute, prevent, protest
8 confront, contrast, disagree, obstruct
9 withstand 10 contradict, contravene,
controvert, disapprove

opposite
4 foil 5 polar 6 contra, facing 7 antonym,
counter, inverse, obverse, opposed,
reverse 8 antipode, antipole, contrary,
contrast, converse 9 antipodal, diametric
10 antipodean, antithesis 11 contrasting,
counterpole 12 antithetical, counterpoint
13 contradictory
prefix: 3 dis 5 retro 6 contra 7 counter

opposition
3 con, foe 5 enemy 7 rivalry 8 conflict,
defiance 9 adversary, animosity, hostility,
other side 10 antagonism, antithesis,
resistance 11 contrariety, disapproval

oppress
5 abuse, crush, wrong 6 burden, injure,
sadden, subdue 7 afflict, torment, torture,
trouble 8 aggrieve, distress, overload
9 persecute, subjugate, weigh down

oppressive
5 harsh, heavy 6 brutal, dismal, gloomy,
severe, somber, sombre, taxing 7 exigent,
onerous, weighty 8 crushing, exacting,
grievous, stifling 9 demanding 10 burdensome, depressing, tyrannical 11 dispiriting,
overbearing, suffocating 12 discouraging,
overwhelming

oppressive force
4 onus, yoke 6 burden, weight

oppressor
5 bully 6 despot, tyrant 8 autocrat, dictator
9 strongman

opprobrious
4 evil, vile 6 odious, vulgar 7 abusive,
hateful 8 infamous 9 notorious, truculent
10 despicable, scurrilous 11 ignominious
12 contemptible, contumelious, disgraceful,
vituperative

opprobrium
5 abuse, blame, odium, scorn, shame
6 infamy 7 obloquy 8 contempt, disgrace,
dishonor, ignominy, reproach 9 discredit,
disesteem, disrepute 10 scurrility
12 vituperation

oppugn
5 argue, fight 6 battle, combat 7 contend,
contest, dispute 8 question

Ops
4 Rhea
consort: 6 Cronus, Saturn
daughter: 5 Ceres 7 Demeter

opt
3 tap 4 pick 5 elect, favor 6 choose,
decide, prefer, select

optical
6 ocular, visual 8 visional
instrument: 4 lens 5 scope 7 transit
9 magnifier, periscope, telescope
10 microscope

optimal
4 best 5 ideal 6 choice, finest 7 perfect
8 choicest, superior

optimist
5 hoper 7 dreamer 8 idealist, Micawber
9 Pollyanna 10 positivist

optimistic
4 rosy 5 happy, merry, sunny 6 bright,
hoping, upbeat 7 assured, buoyant,
hopeful 8 cheerful, positive, sanguine,
trusting 9 confident, promising 11 rose-
colored 12 Pollyannaish

option
4 pick 5 claim, extra, grant, right 6 choice
7 license 8 contract, election 9 accessory,
privilege, selection 10 preference 11 alternative, prerogative

optional
4 free 5 extra 8 elective 9 voluntary
11 alternative 13 discretionary
item: 5 add-on, extra

opulence
6 bounty, luxury, plenty, riches, wealth
7 fortune 9 abundance, affluence,
plenitude, profusion

opulent
4 lush, rich 5 plush, showy, swank
6 deluxe, lavish 7 moneyed, profuse,
wealthy 8 affluent, palatial 9 luxuriant,
luxurious, plentiful, sumptuous
11 extravagant 12 ostentatious

opuntia
6 cactus

opus
4 work 5 piece 6 oeuvre 7 product
8 creation 11 composition

or
4 else, gold 6 golden, yellow 9 otherwise

oracle
4 sage, seer 5 augur, sibyl 6 augury,
medium, Pythia, vision 7 prophet
8 haruspex, prophecy 10 apocalypse,
revelation, soothsayer
site: 6 Claros, Delphi, Didyma, Dodona
7 Olympia 9 Epidaurus

oracular
5 vatic 6 mantic, orphic 7 cryptic, Delphic,
fatidic, obscure 8 Delphian, dogmatic
9 ambiguous, arbitrary, prophetic, sibylline,
vaticinal

oral
4 exam 5 vocal 6 spoken, verbal, voiced
8 narrated, viva voce 9 unwritten
11 examination

orange
6 citrus
brownish: 6 Titian
deep: 11 bittersweet
genus: 6 Citrus
kin: 4 lime 5 lemon 7 kumquat, satsuma
8 mandarin 9 tangerine 10 grapefruit
kind: 4 sour 5 blood, chino, navel, Osage,
sweet 7 Seville 8 bergamot, mandarin,
Valencia
oil: 6 neroli
seed: 3 pip
skin: 4 rind

orangutan
3 ape 6 pongid 7 primate 10 anthropoid

orate
4 rant 5 mouth, speak, spiel 6 preach
7 address, declaim, lecture 8 bloviate,
harangue, perorate 9 discourse,
sermonize, speechify 11 pontificate

oration
6 homily, sermon, speech 7 address,
lecture 9 discourse
funeral: 6 eulogy

orator
7 speaker
American: 4 Clay (Henry) 5 Bryan
(William Jennings), Henry (Patrick)
7 Calhoun (John C.), Douglas (Stephen),
Webster (Daniel)
British: 5 Burke (Edmund) 8 Disraeli
(Benjamin) 9 Churchill (Winston),
Gladstone (William)
French: 8 Mirabeau (Comte de)
Greek: 5 Corax 8 Pericles 11 Demo-
sthenes
Roman: 6 Cicero

oratory
6 chapel, speech 7 bombast 8 rhetoric
9 discourse, elocution, eloquence
10 expression 11 exhortation, speechcraft

orb
3 eye 4 ball 5 globe, round 6 circle,
sphere

orbit
4 path 5 ambit, range, reach, scope,
sweep, track 6 extent, radius 7 ellipse
farthest point: 5 apsis 6 apogee
8 aphelion
nearest point: 5 apsis 7 perigee
10 perihelion

orchard
5 trees 10 plantation

orchestra
4 band 7 gamelan 8 ensemble, symphony
12 philharmonic
leader: 9 conductor
section: 5 brass 6 string 7 brasses,
strings 8 woodwind 9 woodwinds
10 percussion

orchestrate
5 blend, score, unify 6 manage 7 arrange,
compose 8 organize 9 harmonize,
integrate 10 coordinate

orchid
kind: 7 calypso, pogonia 8 cattleya,
oncidium 9 cymbidium 11 cypripedium
petal: 3 lip 8 labellum
product: 5 salep
tuber: 5 salep

ordain
4 will 5 enact, order 6 decree, direct,
impose, invest 7 appoint, command,
conduct, destine, dictate, install, lay down

9 establish, prescribe, pronounce
10 predestine

ordeal
4 test 5 agony, cross, trial 7 calvary,
torment, trouble 8 crucible 9 suffering
10 affliction, difficulty, visitation
11 tribulation

order
4 book, rank 5 array, caste, class, genre,
range 6 decree, lineup, method, scheme,
series, system 7 command, harmony,
mandate, marshal, pattern, reserve
8 classify, neatness, position, shipment,
tidiness 9 directive, hierarchy, procedure,
structure 10 injunction, regularity
11 progression
lack of: 5 chaos 6 ataxia 7 anarchy,
clutter 9 confusion 11 pandemonium
of business: 6 agenda, docket
of preference: 8 priority

orderly
4 aide, calm, neat, tidy, trim 6 batman
7 correct, precise, regular, soldier, uniform
8 methodic, peaceful 9 attendant,
organized, peaceable, regulated,
shipshape 10 methodical, systematic
11 uncluttered, well-behaved
12 businesslike

ordinance
3 law 4 code, rule 5 edict 6 decree
7 precept, statute 9 direction, prescript
10 regulation

ordinary
4 so-so 5 banal, cheap, judge, plain, trite,
usual 6 common, normal 7 average,
humdrum, mundane, natural, popular,
prelate, prosaic, regular, routine, typical
8 everyday, familiar, inferior, mediocre,
workaday 9 clergyman, customary,
quotidian 10 uneventful, unoriginal
11 commonplace 12 unnoteworthy

ordnance
4 arms, guns 6 cannon 7 weapons
8 armament, supplies, weaponry 9 artillery,
munitions 10 ammunition

ore
4 gold, rock 5 metal 6 copper, silver
7 mineral 8 platinum
analysis: 5 assay
deposit: 4 lode, vein
excavation: 5 stope
iron: 5 ocher, ochre 8 goethite, hematite,
limonite
lead: 6 galena
process: 8 leaching, smelting

refuse: 4 slag 5 dross, matte 6 scoria
smelted: 7 regulus

oread
5 nymph

Oregon
capital: 5 Salem
city: 4 Bend 6 Eugene 7 Coos Bay,
Medford 8 Portland
college, university: 4 Reed
lake: 6 Crater
mountain, range: 4 Hood 7 Cascade
nickname: 6 Beaver (State)
river: 5 Snake 8 Columbia
state bird: 10 meadowlark
state flower: 11 Oregon grape
state tree: 10 Douglas fir

Orestes
father: 9 Agamemnon
friend: 7 Pylades
mother: 12 Clytemnestra
sister: 7 Electra 9 Iphigenia
victim: 9 Aegisthus 12 Clytemnestra
wife: 8 Hermione

organ
5 agent, means 6 agency, medium, review
7 channel, journal, vehicle 8 magazine,
ministry 9 newspaper 10 instrument,
periodical
ancient: 9 hydraulus
barrel: 10 hurdy-gurdy
bodily: 3 ear, eye 4 lung, nose, skin
5 gland, heart, liver 6 kidney, larynx,
spleen, tongue, tonsil, viscus 9 intestine
mouth: 9 harmonica
part: 4 pipe, reed, stop 5 pedal, valve
6 blower 7 console, tremolo 8 keyboard
9 wind chest
reed: 8 melodeon 9 harmonium
stop: 4 oboe, sext 5 gamba, quint, viola
6 dulcet 7 bassoon, celesta, melodia,
subbass, tertian 8 carillon, diapason,
dulciana, gemshorn
tactile: 6 feeler 8 tentacle

organ cactus
7 saguaro

organic
5 basic 6 innate 7 natural, primary
8 inherent, integral 9 essential
10 structural 11 fundamental

organism
5 being, plant 6 animal
disease-producing: 4 germ 5 virus
8 pathogen 9 bacterium
single-celled: 5 monad 6 amoeba
9 protozoan

organist
American: 3 Fox (Virgil) 5 Biggs (E. Power) 6 Newman (Anthony)
Dutch: 9 Sweelinck (Jan)
English: 6 Wesley (Samuel) 7 Gibbons (Christopher), Edward, Ellis, Orlando)
French: 5 Alain (Marie-Claire), Widor (Charles) 6 Franck (César) 8 Messiaen (Olivier)
German: 4 Bach (Johann Sebastian) 6 Handel (George Frideric), Walcha (Helmut) 7 Richter (Anton, Ernst, Ferdinand, Johann, Karl)
Swiss: 4 Rogg (Lionel)

organization
4 body, club, unit 5 group, guild, setup 6 agency, system 7 pattern 9 framework, structure 11 arrangement, association, corporation, institution 13 establishment
college: 4 frat 8 sorority 10 fraternity
criminal: 4 gang 5 Mafia
fraternal:
(see **fraternal society**)
government:
(see **government agency**)
lack of: 5 chaos
political: 4 bloc 5 party 7 apparat, machine

organize
4 form 5 array, group, order, rally, set up, start 6 create, line up 7 arrange 8 classify, unionize 9 construct, establish, institute, integrate 10 constitute, coordinate 11 put together

orgulous
5 proud

orgy
4 rite 5 binge, revel, spree 7 blowout, carouse, debauch, rampage, revelry, splurge 8 carousal 9 bacchanal 10 indulgence, saturnalia 11 bacchanalia

oriel
3 bay 6 window

orient
3 set 4 face 5 adapt, align, pearl, sheen 6 adjust, direct, inform, locate, luster 7 arrange 8 acquaint, lustrous 9 sparkling 11 accommodate, familiarize

Orient
4 Asia, East 7 Far East

Oriental
3 rug 5 Asian 6 carpet 7 Eastern 10 Far Eastern

orientation
7 bearing 8 location, position 9 alignment, direction 10 adjustment 11 arrangement

orifice
see **opening**

oriflamme
4 flag 5 ideal 6 banner, pennon, symbol 7 pendant, pennant 8 standard, streamer

origami
12 paper folding
bird: 5 crane

origin
4 root, seed, well 5 birth, blood, start 6 source 7 descent, genesis, lineage 8 ancestry, fountain, pedigree 9 beginning, inception, maternity, parentage, paternity 10 derivation, extraction, provenance, wellspring

original
3 new 5 first, model, novel, prime 6 native, unique 7 initial, pattern, pioneer, primary 8 creative, earliest 9 archetype, ingenious, innovator, inventive, precursor, primitive, prototype 10 archetypal, forerunner, innovative

originally
5 first 7 at first 8 formerly 9 initially, primarily

originate
4 coin, flow, hail, make, rise, stem 5 arise, begin, found, hatch, issue, set up, start 6 create, derive, invent, launch, spring 7 emanate, proceed, produce, think up 8 commence, generate, initiate, innovate 9 institute, introduce

originator
5 maker 6 author 7 creator, founder, planner 8 inventor, producer 9 initiator, innovator 10 institutor, introducer

oriole
4 bird 8 troupial
European: 6 loriot
genus: 7 Icterus
golden: 6 loriot
kind: 6 golden 7 orchard 8 Bullock's 9 Baltimore

Orion
6 hunter 13 constellation
beloved: 3 Eos
belt: 7 Ellwand
father: 7 Hyrieus 8 Poseidon
slayer: 5 Diana 7 Artemis
star: 5 Rigel 9 Bellatrix 10 Betelgeuse

orison
6 prayer 8 entreaty, petition 12 supplication

Orithyia
lover: 6 Boreas
son: 5 Zetes 6 Calais

Orlando author
5 Woolf (Virginia)

Orlando Furioso author
7 Ariosto (Ludovico)

Orléans heroine
9 Joan of Arc

orlop
4 deck

ormolu
5 brass 6 bronze

ornament
3 gem 4 bead, deck, trim 5 adorn, jewel
6 bedeck, finial, tassel 7 dress up, garnish,
jewelry, pendant, whatnot 8 beautify,
decorate, filigree 9 embellish, embroider,
lavaliere
Christmas tree: 4 bulb 5 angel 6 tinsel
lip: 6 labret
shoulder: 7 epaulet

ornamental case
4 etui

ornate
4 lush, rich 5 fancy, gaudy, showy 6 florid,
frilly, gilded, glitzy, rococo 7 baroque,
flowery, opulent 8 overdone 9 elaborate,
luxuriant, sumptuous 10 flamboyant

ornery
5 balky, cross, testy 6 crabby, cranky,
crusty, grumpy 7 bearish, froward, grouchy
8 contrary, perverse, stubborn, vinegary
9 crotchety, difficult, irascible, irritable
10 inflexible, vinegarish 12 cantankerous

ornithic
5 avian 8 birdlike

ornithologist
American: 4 Bond (James) 7 Audubon
(John James), Bartram (William)
8 Peterson (Roger Tory)
English: 5 Gould (John)
Scottish: 6 Wilson (Alexander)

orotund
4 full, loud 5 round 7 flowery, pompous,
ringing 8 resonant, sonorous 9 bombastic,
high-flown, overblown 10 euphuistic,
oratorical, resounding, rhetorical, stentorian
11 declamatory 12 magniloquent
13 grandiloquent

Orpah
husband: 7 Chilion
sister-in-law: 4 Ruth

orphan
4 waif 5 Annie, gamin, stray 6 bereft,
gamine, urchin 7 cast-off, ignored
8 forsaken, homeless 9 abandoned,
foundling, neglected 10 motherless,
parentless

Orpheus
father: 6 Apollo 7 Oeagrus
home: 6 Thrace
instrument: 4 lyre
mother: 8 Calliope
wife: 8 Euridice

orphic
6 arcane, mystic, occult 7 cryptic, Delphic,
obscure 8 abstruse, Delphian, esoteric,
hermetic, mystical, oracular, profound
9 enigmatic, recondite

ort
3 bit 4 bite 5 crumb, piece, scrap
6 morsel 7 remnant 8 leftover

orthodox
6 proper 8 accepted, approved, official,
received, standard 9 canonical, customary
10 conformist, recognized, sanctioned
11 established, traditional
12 acknowledged, conservative,
conventional 13 authoritative

orthography
7 writing 8 spelling

ortolan
7 bunting

Orwell novel
10 Animal Farm 18 Nineteen Eighty-four

oryx
7 gemsbok 8 antelope

os
3 ora (plural) 4 bone, ossa (plural)
5 mouth 7 orifice

Osborne play
15 Look Back in Anger

oscillate
4 sway, vary 5 swing, waver 6 change,
seesaw 7 vibrate 9 alternate, fluctuate

oscillation
4 sway 5 swing 9 variation, vibration
10 undulation 11 fluctuation, periodicity

osculate
3 lip 4 buss, kiss, peck 5 smack
6 smooch

osier
3 rod 6 willow 7 dogwood

Osiris
brother: 3 Set 4 Seth
father: 3 Geb, Keb, Seb
mother: 3 Nut
scribe: 5 Thoth
sister: 4 Isis
slayer: 3 Set 4 Seth
son: 5 Horus 6 Anubis
wife: 4 Isis

osmosis
4 flow 8 transfer 9 diffusion 10 absorption
12 assimilation 13 incorporation

osprey
4 hawk 8 fish hawk

osseous
4 bony 8 bonelike

ossicle
4 bone 5 incus 6 stapes 7 malleus

ossify
3 set 6 harden 7 stiffen 8 solidify
9 fossilize

osso _____
4 buco

ossuary
4 tomb 5 vault 8 boneyard, cemetery
9 sepulcher, sepulchre

ostensible
6 stated 7 alleged, seeming 8 apparent,
asserted, illusive, illusory, so-called,
supposed 9 pretended, professed,
purported, semblable 11 superficial

ostentation
4 show 5 flash, swank 7 display
9 pomposity, showiness, vainglory
10 flashiness, pretension 11 flamboyance

ostentatious
4 loud 5 gaudy, showy, swank 6 flashy,
garish, swanky 7 pompous, splashy
8 overdone, peacocky 10 flamboyant,
peacockish 11 pretentious, vainglorious

ostiole
4 pore 7 orifice 8 aperture

ostracism
5 exile 7 removal 9 exclusion
10 banishment, relegation 11 deportation

ostracize
3 bar, cut 4 shun, snub 5 exile 6 banish,
deport 7 exclude, keep out, shut out
8 throw out 9 blackball 10 expatriate
12 cold-shoulder

ostrich
6 ratite

Ostrogoth king
9 Theodoric

otalgia
7 earache

Otello composer
5 Verdi (Giuseppe) 7 Rossini (Gioacchino)

O tempora! O _____!
5 mores

Othello
author: 11 Shakespeare (William)
ensign: 4 Iago
lieutenant: 6 Cassio
maid: 6 Emilia
victim, wife: 9 Desdemona

others
4 rest 9 remainder
and: 4 et al 6 et alia, et alii 7 et aliae

other than
3 but 4 save 6 except 7 besides 9 apart
from, aside from, except for, excepting,
excluding

otherwise
3 not 5 if not 6 or else 7 changed
9 different 11 differently 12 anything else
13 alternatively

otic
5 aural 8 auditory 9 auricular

otiose
4 idle, vain 5 empty 6 futile, hollow
7 surplus, useless 8 nugatory 9 fruitless,
pointless, worthless 11 ineffective,
purposeless, superfluous 12 functionless
13 supernumerary

Ottawa chief
7 Pontiac

ottoman
4 seat 5 couch 6 fabric 9 footstool

Ottoman
4 Turk 7 Turkish
ruler: 5 Osman, Selim 8 Suleiman,
Süleyman

Otus
5 giant

brother: 9 Ephialtes
father: 6 Aloeus 8 Poseidon
mother: 9 Iphimedia
slayer: 6 Apollo

ouch

3 cry 5 bezel, jewel 6 brooch, buckle
7 setting 8 ornament 11 exclamation

ounce

3 bit, cat 4 dram 5 scrap, shred
6 amount, pinch, splash, weight
7 measure, modicum, smidgen 8 fraction,
particle 11 snow leopard

our

French: 5 notre
Italian: 6 nostra

Our Town author

6 Wilder (Thornton)

oust

4 fire, sack 5 eject, evict, expel 6 banish,
deport, remove, topple, unseat 7 boot out,
cast out, deprive, dismiss, kick out
8 displace, drive out, force out, relegate,
supplant, take away, throw out
10 dispossess

ouster

7 removal 8 ejection, eviction 9 discharge,
dismissal, expulsion 10 banishment

out

4 away, exit 5 forth, loose 6 absent,
excuse
of control: 4 wild 7 chaotic
of gas: 5 tired 7 drained 9 exhausted
of line: 4 awry, rude 5 askew, fresh
of place: 13 inappropriate
of sorts: 5 cross 7 grouchy, peevish
9 irritable
of the ordinary: 3 odd 7 bizarre, strange,
unusual

outage

4 loss 5 break 7 failure 8 blackout
12 interruption

out-and-out

5 gross, sheer, total, utter 7 perfect
8 absolute, complete, positive 9 downright
10 consummate 11 unmitigated,
unqualified 13 thoroughgoing

outback

4 bush 6 sticks 7 boonies 9 boondocks
10 hinterland, wilderness

outboard

4 boat 5 motor 6 engine

outbreak

4 rash, rise, rush 5 burst, flare, spike,
surge 6 attack, blowup, plague, revolt
7 flare-up 8 epidemic, eruption, increase,
uprising 9 rebellion 12 insurrection

outburst

3 fit 4 gush, gust 5 flare, sally, scene,
spasm, storm, surge 6 frenzy, tirade
7 flare-up, tantrum, torrent 8 eruption,
paroxysm, upheaval 9 explosion

outcast

4 hobo 5 exile, leper, tramp 6 pariah
7 Ishmael, vagrant 8 castaway, derelict,
vagabond 9 reprobate 10 expatriate,
Ishmaelite 11 offscouring, untouchable

outclass

3 top 4 best 5 excel 6 exceed 7 surpass

outcome

3 end 5 event, fruit, issue 6 effect, result,
sequel, upshot 9 aftermath 10 conclusion
11 aftereffect, consequence, development

outcrop

4 rock 5 ledge 6 appear 7 project
8 protrude 10 projection, protrusion
12 protuberance

outcry

4 yell 5 noise, shout 6 clamor, tumult,
uproar 7 auction, ferment, protest
8 upheaval 9 commotion, objection
11 exclamation

outdated

3 old 5 passé 6 démodé, old hat
7 antique 12 old-fashioned

outdistance

3 top 4 beat, best, pass 5 trump 6 better
7 eclipse, surpass

outdo

3 top 4 beat, best 5 excel, trump 6 better,
defeat, exceed 7 eclipse, surpass, triumph
8 overcome 9 transcend

outdoor

7 open-air 8 alfresco

outer

6 remote 7 surface 8 exoteric, exterior,
external 9 extrinsic 10 extraneous
11 superficial

outermost

4 last 5 final 6 far-off 7 distant, extreme
8 farthest, furthest, remotest

outfit

3 kit, rig, set 4 band, firm, gear, suit, team,
togs, unit 5 corps, dress, equip, getup,
group, squad, troop 6 clothe, supply,
tackle, troupe 7 appoint, company,

concern, costume, furnish **8** accouter,
accoutre, business, clothing, ensemble,
matériel, tackling **9** equipment, provision
10 enterprise **12** organization
13 accouterments, accoutrements,
establishment

outflank
5 evade **6** bypass **9** get around
10 circumvent

outflow
6 efflux **8** drainage, effluent **9** effluence

out-front
4 open **5** frank **6** candid, honest
10 forthright

outgoing
4 open **7** affable **8** friendly, sociable
9 departing, expansive **10** gregarious,
responsive **11** extroverted

outgrowth
6 effect, result **7** product, spin-off
8 offshoot **9** by-product, offspring
10 derivative **11** aftereffect, consequence

outhouse
5 jakes, privy **7** latrine

outing
4 spin, trip **5** drive, jaunt, sally **6** junket,
picnic **9** excursion **10** appearance,
disclosure

outlandish
3 odd **4** wild **5** alien, outré, ultra, weird
6 exotic, quaint, remote, vulgar **7** bizarre,
curious, extreme, foreign, offbeat, strange,
uncouth, unusual **8** peculiar, singular **9** eccentric, fantastic, tasteless **10** ridiculous,
unorthodox **11** extravagant

outlast
6 endure **7** survive, weather **9** withstand

outlaw
3 ban, con **4** wild **5** crook **6** bandit,
banned, enjoin, forbid, illegal **7** exclude
8 criminal, disallow, fugitive, prohibit,
renegade, restrict **9** desperado, illegalize,
interdict, proscribe **10** rebellious

outlay
3 pay, tab **4** cost, give **5** spend **6** amount,
expend **7** expense, payment **8** disburse
11 expenditure **12** disbursement

outlet
4 exit, hole, mart, shop, vent **5** issue, store
6 avenue, egress, escape, market
7 channel, opening, passage, release
8 aperture **10** discounter, receptacle

outline
4 edge, form, limn, plan **5** brief, draft,
shape, trace **6** bounds, border, précis,
schema, sketch **7** contour, profile,
summary **8** abstract, boundary, skeleton,
syllabus, synopsis **9** delineate, summarize
10 figuration, silhouette **11** skeletonize

outlive
7 survive, weather

outlook
4 side, view **5** angle, scope, sight, slant,
vista **6** aspect, future **7** promise
8 attitude, forecast, position, prospect
9 direction, viewpoint **10** standpoint
11 expectation, observatory, perspective,
point of view

outlying
3 far **6** far-off, remote **7** distant, faraway,
removed **8** far-flung

outmoded
4 dead **5** dated, passé, tired **8** obsolete
9 moth-eaten, unstylish **10** oldfangled
11 obsolescent **12** old-fashioned

Out of Africa author
7 Dinesen (Isak)

out-of-date
3 old **4** past **5** passé, square **6** démodé,
old hat **7** antique, archaic, old-time,
vintage **8** obsolete **9** unstylish
10 antiquated **12** old-fashioned

out of it
4 lost **5** dazed **7** muddled **8** confused
10 bewildered

out-of-the-way
4 rare **6** remote **7** distant, obscure,
removed, unusual **8** secluded, uncommon

outpost
4 base **6** branch, colony **8** foothold
10 detachment, settlement

outpouring
4 flow, gush, rush **5** burst, flood, spate,
spurt **6** deluge, stream **7** torrent
8 effusion

output
4 crop, gain, take **5** power, yield
6 amount, profit **7** harvest, produce,
product **10** production **11** achievement,
information

outrage
4 fury, rape **5** abuse, shock, wrong
6 injury, insult, offend **7** affront, incense,
violate **8** aggrieve, atrocity, ill-treat,

outrageous

mischief, violence 9 brutality, infuriate
10 resentment, scandalize

outrageous

5 awful, gross 6 horrid, insane, odious,
unholy, wicked 7 beastly, ghastly, heinous,
ignoble, obscene 8 dreadful, flagrant,
horrible, shocking, terrible 9 atrocious,
egregious excessive, fantastic
10 abominable, inordinate, scandalous
11 intolerable

outré

3 odd 5 ultra 6 far-out 7 bizarre, extreme,
off-beat, strange 8 peculiar 9 eccentric

outrigger

4 boat, beam, spar prau, proa

outright

4 pure 5 total, utter, whole 6 entire
7 perfect 8 absolute, complete, entirely,
positive 9 on the spot 10 completely,
consummate 11 unequivocal, unmitigated,
unqualified 13 thoroughgoing

outrun

3 top 4 beat, pass 6 exceed 7 surpass

outset

4 dawn 5 birth, start 7 opening
9 beginning, inception 12 commencement

outshine

3 top 4 beat, best 5 excel 6 exceed
7 surpass

outside

5 alien 7 foreign, open-air 8 alfresco,
exterior, external

outsider

5 alien 7 inconnu 8 newcomer, stranger
9 foreigner

outsmart

see **outwit**

outspoken

4 free, open 5 blunt, frank, plain, vocal
6 candid, direct, honest 7 up front
8 explicit 10 forthright, point-blank,
unreserved 11 unequivocal

outstanding

3 due 4 star 5 noted, owing 6 signal,
superb, unpaid 7 capital, eminent, notable,
salient, stellar 8 dominant, striking,
superior 9 arresting, excellent, prominent,
unsettled 10 noticeable, preeminent,
remarkable 11 conspicuous, distinctive,
exceptional, magnificent, superlative,
uncollected, unresolved 13 extraordinary

outstrip

3 top 4 beat, best, pass 5 excel 6 better,
exceed 7 surpass 8 distance, go beyond,
overtake 9 transcend 11 leave behind

outward

5 overt 7 evident, visible 8 apparent,
exterior, external 10 noticeable, ostensible
11 superficial

outweigh

6 exceed 8 overbear 10 overshadow
11 overbalance 12 preponderate

outworn

see **outmoded**

ouzel

6 dipper, thrush 9 blackbird

oval

5 track 6 oblong 7 ellipse 8 elliptic 9 egg-
shaped, racetrack 10 elliptical
11 ellipsoidal

ovation

5 kudos 6 homage, praise 7 acclaim,
plaudits, tribute 8 applause, approval,
cheering, clapping 11 acclamation

oven

4 kiln, oast 5 range, stove

over

4 anew, atop, done, past, upon 5 above,
again, aloft, ended 6 across, beyond
8 finished, once more
French: 3 sur
German: 4 über
prefix: 3 epi, sur 5 extra, hyper, super,
supra
Spanish: 5 sobre

overabundance

4 glut 6 excess 7 surfeit, surplus
8 plethora 10 surplusage 11 superfluity

overact

3 ham, mug 4 rant 5 emote 10 exaggerate

overage

6 excess 7 surplus

overall

5 smock, total 6 global, mainly, mostly
7 chiefly, general, largely 8 as a whole,
sweeping 9 generally, inclusive, in general,
primarily 10 far and wide 11 principally
13 comprehensive, predominantly

overalls

5 pants 8 trousers

over and above
4 also 6 as well, beyond 7 besides 8 as well as 10 in addition

over and over
3 oft 5 often 8 ofttimes 10 frequently, oftentimes, repeatedly 11 continually, recurrently

overbearing
5 bossy 6 lordly 7 haughty, pompous 8 absolute, arrogant, despotic, dogmatic, dominant, imperial, insolent, scornful, superior 9 imperious, tyrannous 10 autocratic, disdainful, dominating, high-handed, oppressive, peremptory, tyrannical 11 dictatorial, domineering, magisterial 12 supercilious 13 high-and-mighty

overblown
6 turgid 7 flowery, hyped up, orotund, pompous 8 bombastic, excessive, high-flown 10 euphuistic, oratorical, rhetorical 11 declamatory, exaggerated, pretentious 12 magniloquent 13 grandiloquent

overcast
3 sew 4 dull, gray, hazy 5 cloud, cover 6 cloudy, darken, shadow 7 becloud, blanket, clouded, obscure 8 covering, lowering 9 adumbrate

overcharge
3 pad 4 bilk, clip, skin, soak 5 cheat, stick 6 fleece 7 inflate

overcoat
5 paint 6 capote, raglan, ulster 7 surtout 9 balmacaan, outerwear 12 chesterfield

overcome
4 beat, best, lick 5 drown, throw 6 defeat, hurdle, master 7 conquer, prevail, triumph 8 surmount 9 prostrate

overconfident
4 rash 5 brash, cocky, pushy 8 arrogant, cocksure, reckless 9 hubristic, presuming 12 presumptuous

overdo
7 exhaust, fatigue, wear out 9 embellish 10 exaggerate

overdue
4 late 5 owing, tardy 6 behind, unpaid 7 belated, delayed, payable 8 dilatory 9 unsettled 10 behindhand, delinquent, unpunctual 11 outstanding

overemphasize
7 magnify 8 heighten 9 dramatize, embellish 10 exaggerate

overflow
4 pour 5 cover, drown, flood, slosh, spate, spill, swamp 6 deluge, engulf, excess, outlet 7 surfeit, surplus, torrent 8 flooding, inundate, spillage, submerge 10 inundation, surplusage 11 superfluity

overgrown
4 lush 5 dense, thick 6 brushy 7 hulking 8 ungainly 9 excessive, ponderous 10 junglelike

overhang
3 jut 4 loom 5 bulge 6 beetle, extend, impend 7 project 8 protrude, stick out, threaten 10 projection

overhaul
3 fix 4 mend, redo 5 patch, renew 6 doctor, remake, repair, revamp, revise 7 rebuild, restore 8 renovate 11 recondition, reconstruct

overhead
4 atop 5 above, aloft, smash 7 ceiling, expense 8 expenses

overheated
5 fiery 7 fervent 8 inflated 9 perfervid 11 impassioned

overindulgence
6 excess 7 surfeit 8 gluttony 11 dissipation 12 immoderation, intemperance

overjoyed
6 elated 7 gleeful 8 ecstatic, euphoric, exultant, jubilant, thrilled 9 rapturous 11 transported

overkill
4 glut 6 excess 7 surfeit, surplus, too much 8 plethora 10 obliterate, redundancy, surplusage 11 superfluity

overlap
7 shingle 9 imbricate

overlay
3 cap 4 coat 5 cover, glaze 6 finish, veneer 7 blanket, coating, lacquer, varnish 8 covering 11 superimpose 12 transparency

overload
4 glut 5 stuff 6 burden, excess, pile on, strain 7 surfeit

overlook
4 fail, miss, omit, skip 5 check, let go

overlord

6 excuse, forget, ignore, pass by, slight, slip up, survey, wink at 7 blink at, condone, forgive, inspect, let pass, neglect 8 discount, dominate, surmount 9 disregard, supervise 11 superintend

overlord

4 czar, tsar, tzar 5 chief, mogul, ruler 6 tycoon 7 magnate 8 suzerain 9 potentate, sovereign

overly

3 too 6 unduly 11 exceedingly, excessively 12 immoderately, inordinately

overpass

5 cross 6 bridge 8 crossing, traverse 9 traversal 11 interchange

overplay

4 hype 6 expand 7 enlarge, inflate, magnify, point up, stretch 8 maximize 9 dramatize 10 exaggerate 11 hyperbolize

overpower

4 rout 5 crush, swamp, whelm 6 defeat, master, subdue 7 conquer 8 vanquish 9 prostrate, subjugate

overreach

3 con 4 beat, bilk 5 cheat, outdo 6 defeat, outfox, outwit 7 defraud 8 flimflam, outsmart 10 exaggerate 11 outmaneuver

override

4 veto 5 annul 6 cancel 7 nullify 10 counteract, neutralize

overriding

3 key 4 main 5 chief, major, prime, vital 7 central, crucial, pivotal, primary, supreme 8 cardinal, dominant, foremost 9 paramount, principal

overrule

4 undo, veto 5 upset 6 negate, revoke 7 reverse 8 set aside 11 countermand

overrun

4 beat, raid, teem, whip 5 swamp, swarm 6 defeat, excess, infest, invade, occupy, ravage, spread, thrash 7 clobber, conquer

overseas

6 abroad 11 transmarine, transoceanic, ultramarine

oversee

3 run 4 boss 5 watch 6 direct, manage, survey 7 command, examine, inspect 9 supervise 11 superintend

overseer

4 boss, exec, head 5 chief 7 foreman, manager 8 director 9 executive 10 supervisor 13 administrator

overshadow

4 veil 5 cloud, dwarf, shade 6 darken, exceed 7 becloud, eclipse, obscure, surpass 8 dominate, outshine, outweigh 9 adumbrate

overshoe

4 boot 6 arctic, galosh, patten, rubber

oversight

4 care, slip 5 aegis, check, error, lapse 6 charge, slip-up 7 control, failure, mistake, neglect 8 omission 10 intendance, management 11 supervision

overspread

3 cap 5 beset, cover, flood, swarm 6 infest, invade 7 blanket, obscure, pervade 8 permeate

overstate

3 pad 7 amplify, enlarge, magnify 9 embellish, embroider 10 exaggerate

overstep

6 exceed, offend 7 surpass, violate 8 infringe, trespass 10 transgress

overstock

4 glut 5 extra 6 excess 7 surplus 9 remainder 10 surplusage

overstress

7 magnify 8 maximize 10 exaggerate

overt

4 open 5 clear 6 patent 7 evident, obvious, outward, visible 8 apparent, manifest 10 observable

overtake

4 pass 5 catch 6 pass by 7 outpace, surpass 8 come upon, outstrip 11 outdistance

Over the Rainbow

composer: 5 Arlen (Harold) 7 Harburg (E. Y.)

singer: 7 Garland (Judy)

over there

3 yon 6 yonder

over-the-top

7 extreme 8 reckless 9 egregious, excessive 10 exorbitant, flamboyant, outrageous 11 extravagant

overthrow

4 fell, oust, rout 5 purge, upset 6 defeat, depose, remove, topple, unseat 7 conquer 8 dethrone, downfall 9 bring down

overtone
4 hint 5 sense 8 coloring, harmonic
9 inference 10 suggestion 11 association,
connotation, implication 12 undercurrent

overture
3 bid 5 proem 7 advance, preface,
prelude, present 8 approach, foreword,
preamble, prologue, proposal 9 prelusion
10 initiative 11 proposition 12 introduction,
presentation

overturn
3 tip 4 flip, void 5 upend, upset 6 topple,
tumble 7 capsize, nullify, reverse 8 set
aside 10 invalidate

overused
5 stale, tired, trite 7 clichéd, worn-out
9 hackneyed

overview
6 aperçu, précis, survey 7 epitome,
summary 10 conspectus

overweening
5 brash, pushy 6 lordly, uppish, uppity
7 forward 8 arrogant 9 conceited,
presuming 10 immoderate
11 exaggerated 12 presumptuous

overweight
3 fat 5 beefy, burly, dumpy, gross, heavy,
husky, obese, plump, pudgy, stout
6 chubby, chunky, flabby, fleshy, outsize,
portly, rotund 8 heavyset, thickset
9 corpulent

overwhelm
4 beat, bury, rout, ruin, sink, whip 5 crush,
drown, flood, swamp, upset, wreck
6 defeat, deluge, engulf, thrash 7 conquer,
destroy, oppress, shatter, shellac, smother
8 inundate, submerge 9 devastate,
prostrate 10 demoralize 11 subordinate

overwhelmed
6 aghast, touched 7 shocked, stunned
8 defeated, helpless 10 distressed
13 thunderstruck

overwhelming
4 huge 5 great 7 extreme 8 numerous

overwrought
5 hyper, upset 7 anxious, frantic, wound up
8 agitated, frenetic, stressed, troubled
9 disturbed, emotional 10 distracted,
freaked out, high-strung, hysterical 11 discomposed

Ovid work
5 Fasti 6 Amores 7 Tristia 8 Heroides
13 Metamorphoses

ovine
5 sheep 9 sheeplike

ovoid
4 oval 5 ovate 9 egg-shaped

ovule
3 egg
fertilized: 4 seed

ovum
3 egg 6 gamete 7 egg cell 11 macro-
gamete

owing
3 due 6 in debt, mature, unpaid
7 overdue, payable 9 unsettled
11 outstanding

owing to
4 over 7 through 9 because of 10 by
reason of 11 on account of

owl
cry: 4 hoot
genus: 4 Otus
kind: 3 elf 4 barn, gray, lulu 5 eagle,
gnome, madge, pygmy, snowy 6 barred,
horned 7 saw-whet, screech 9 long-eared
10 short-eared 11 great horned

Owl and the Pussycat author
4 Lear (Edward)

own
4 avow, have, hold 5 admit, allow, enjoy,
grant, let on 6 accept, fess up, retain
7 concede, confess, possess 8 disclose
9 recognize 11 acknowledge

owner
6 holder 8 landlady, landlord 9 possessor,
purchaser 10 proprietor

ownership
4 hand 5 title 8 dominion, property
10 possession 11 proprietary
perpetual: 8 mortmain

ox
3 yak 4 anoa, gaur, musk, zebu 5 bison,
steer 6 bovine 7 banteng, buffalo
Asian: 4 zebu
attachment: 4 yoke
extinct: 4 urus 7 aurochs
family: 7 Bovidae
relating to: 6 bovine
wild: 4 anoa, gaur 7 banteng

oxeye
5 daisy 6 flower

oxford
 4 shoe 5 cloth, sheep 6 cotton, fabric

oxide
 calcium: 4 lime 9 quicklime
 ferric: 4 rust
 sodium: 4 soda

oxidize
 4 rust

oxygen
 3 air, gas 5 ozone 7 element
 discoverer: 9 Lavoisier (Antoine)
 form: 5 ozone
 liquid: 3 lox

oyster
 7 bivalve, mollusc, mollusk
 bed: 4 park 6 claire, cultch
 eggs: 5 spawn
 genus: 6 Ostrea
 Long Island: 9 bluepoint
 product: 5 pearl
 shell: 4 test 5 shuck
 young: 4 spat

oyster plant
 7 salsify

Oz
 creator: 4 Baum (L. Frank)
 inhabitant: 8 Munchkin
 princess: 4 Ozma

Ozark State
 8 Missouri

Ozem
 brother: 5 David
 father: 5 Jesse 9 Jerahmeel

Ozymandias author
 7 Shelley (Percy Bysshe)

P

pabulum
3 pap 4 food 7 aliment 8 nutrient
9 blandness, nutriment 10 insipidity,
sustenance 11 nourishment

paca
4 cavy

pace
3 set 4 beat, clip, gait, lead, rate, step,
time, walk 5 speed, tempo, tread, troop
6 motion, stride, timing 7 example, fluency,
measure, precede, proceed, routine, step
off 8 ambulate, antecede, movement,
progress, regulate

pachyderm
8 elephant

pacific
4 calm, mild 6 gentle, irenic, placid, serene
8 dovelike, peaceful, soothing, tranquil
9 peaceable, temperate 12 conciliatory

Pacificator, Great
4 Clay (Henry)

Pacific nation
5 Belau, Japan, Nauru, Palau, Tonga 6 Tuvalu 7 Vanuatu 8 Kiribati

Pacific Ocean discoverer
6 Balboa (Vasco Núñez de)

pacifist
4 dove 6 irenic 8 appeaser, peaceful,
peacenik 9 peaceable 10 nonviolent
11 peacemonger

pacify
4 calm, cool, ease, lull 5 allay, quell, quiet,
still 6 disarm, settle, soften, soothe,
subdue, temper 7 appease, assuage,
mollify, placate 9 subjugate 10 conciliate,
propitiate

pack
3 jam, kit, lot, lug, ram, set, wad 4 band,
bear, cram, deck, fill, gang, heap, load,
lump, mass, pile, stow, tamp, tote, unit
5 bunch, carry, cover, crowd, ferry, group,
store, stuff, troop 6 bundle, charge, clique,
convey, depart, gather 7 possess
8 assemble, compress, knapsack
9 container, equipment, influence, transport
10 collection, congregate

package
3 box 4 deal, unit, wrap 5 array, combo,
whole 6 bundle, parcel 7 enclose, present,
wrapper 8 shipment 9 container
10 collection 11 combination

pack animal
3 ass 4 mule 5 burro, camel, horse, llama
6 donkey 7 jackass 13 beast of burden

packed
4 full 5 awash, dense, flush 6 filled,
jammed 7 brimful, crowded, stuffed
8 brimming 9 chock-full 10 compressed

packet
3 wad 4 boat, mass, pile 5 group
6 bundle, parcel 7 cluster

pact
4 bond, deal 6 treaty 7 bargain, concord
8 alliance, contract, covenant 9 agreement

pad
3 bed, mat, wad 4 foot, mute 5 fudge,
guard, paper, stuff 6 buffer, expand, muffle,
shield, tablet 7 augment, bolster, cushion,
stretch 8 dressing, increase 9 embellish,
embroider, overstate 10 exaggerate,
overcharge

paddle
3 oar, row 4 beat, stir 5 spank 6 propel,
thrash

paddock
5 field 7 pasture 9 enclosure

paddy wagon
10 Black Maria

padre

3 Fra 6 father, priest 8 chaplain, minister
9 clergyman, confessor

paean

4 hymn, song 6 anthem, eulogy, praise
7 tribute 8 accolade, encomium
9 panegyric

page

4 book, call, leaf 5 folio, sheet 6 locate,
summon 7 bellhop, equerry
left-hand: 5 verso
right-hand: 5 recto

pageant

4 sham, show 7 charade, display, tableau
8 pretense 9 spectacle 10 exhibition

pageantry

4 pomp, show 7 display, panoply
8 flourish, splendor 9 spectacle
10 exhibition 11 flamboyance, ostentation
12 magnificence

Pagliacci, I

character: 5 Canio, Nedda, Tonio 6 Silvio
composer: 11 Leoncavallo (Ruggero)

pagoda

6 temple

pail

6 bucket, piggin, vessel

pain

3 irk 4 ache, care, hurt, pang 5 agony,
cramp, grief, throe, upset 6 grieve, harass,
stitch, twinge 7 afflict, anguish, torture,
travail, trouble 8 aggrieve, distress 9 suffering 10 affliction, discomfort
back: 7 lumbago
muscular: 7 myalgia

painful

3 raw 4 hard, sore 5 acute, sharp
6 aching, trying 7 arduous 8 annoying,
piercing, shooting, stabbing, stinging
9 agonizing, difficult, laborious, torturous,
upsetting, vexatious 10 afflictive,
tormenting

painkiller

4 drug 6 opiate 7 anodyne, codeine
8 morphine, narcotic 9 analgesic
10 anesthetic

painstaking

5 exact 7 careful, heedful 8 diligent,
exacting, thorough 9 assiduous, diligence,
laborious 10 meticulous, scrupulous
11 punctilious

paint

4 coat, daub, limn, swab, tint 5 adorn,
brush, color, cover, horse, pinto, rouge,
stain 6 depict, makeup 7 coating, pigment,
portray, produce, touch up 8 cosmetic,
decorate 9 delineate, represent
10 maquillage

painter

6 artist
American: 4 Cole (Thomas), Haas
(Richard), West (Benjamin), Wood (Grant)
5 Abbey (Edwin Austin), Davis (Stuart),
Gorky (Arshile), Grosz (George), Henri
(Robert), Hicks (Edward), Homer
(Winslow), Johns (Jasper), Kline (Franz),
Kroll (Leon), Marin (John), Marsh
(Reginald), Moses (Grandma), Peale
(Anna, Charles Willson, James, Raphaelle,
Rembrandt, Sarah, Titian), Ryder (Albert
Pinkham), Shahn (Ben), Sloan (Eric, John),
Weber (Max), Wyeth (Andrew, Jamie,
Newell Convers) 6 Albers (Josef), Benton
(Thomas Hart), Catlin (George), Church
(Frederick Edwin), Coburn (Alvin Langdon),
Copley (John Singleton), Durand (Asher),
Eakins (Thomas), Hassam (Childe),
Hopper (Edward), Inness (George), Leutze
(Emanuel), Martin (Agnes, Homer),
Newman (Barnett), Rivers (Larry), Rothko
(Mark), Stella (Frank), Stuart (Gilbert),
Tanguy (Yves), Thorpe (Thomas), Warhol
(Andy) 7 Allston (Washington), Bearden
(Romare), Bellows (George), Bingham
(George Caleb), Cassatt (Mary), Duchamp
(Marcel), Harnett (William), Hartley
(Marsden), Kinkade (Thomas), La Farge
(John), O'Keeffe (Georgia), Parrish
(Maxfield), Pollock (Jackson), Sargent
(John Singer), Sheeler (Charles), Tiffany
(Louis Comfort), Tworkov (Jack), Wiggins
(Carleton) 8 Melchers (Gari), Rockwell
(Norman), Sullivan (Patrick), Trumbull
(John), Whistler (James McNeill)
9 Bierstadt (Albert), de Kooning (Willem),
Feininger (Lyonel), Reinhardt (Ad),
Remington (Frederic), Twachtman (John
Henry), Vanderlyn (John) 10 Motherwell
(Robert), Whittredge (Thomas) 12 Lichten-
stein (Roy), Rauschenberg (Robert)
Austrian: 5 Klimt (Gustav) 9 Kokoschka
(Oskar)
Belgian: 5 Ensor (James) 6 Campin
(Robert) 8 Magritte (René)
Canadian: 4 Kane (Paul) 6 Harris
(Lawren), Watson (Homer) 7 Jackson
(Alexander Young), Thomson (Tom)
9 MacDonald (James Edward Hervey)
Chinese: 4 Wu Li 6 Ma Yüan 7 Wang
Wei 8 Yen Li-pen
Dutch: 3 Dou (Gerrit) 4 Hals (Frans), Lely
(Peter), Maas (Nicolas) 5 Bosch

(Hieronymus), Hooch (Pieter de), Steen (Jan) **6** Potter (Paul) **7** de Hooch (Pieter), de Witte (Emanuel de), Hobbema (Meindert), van Gogh (Vincent), Vermeer (Jan) **8** Mondrian (Piet), Ruisdael (Jacob van, Salomon), Ruysdael (Salomon), Terborch (Gerard) **9** de Kooning (Willem), Rembrandt (van Rijn), Wouwerman (Philips) **11** Terbrugghen (Hendrik)
English: 4 John (Augustus), Lear (Edward) **5** Bacon (Francis), Blake (William), Brown (Ford Madox), Lewis (Wyndham), Watts (George Frederick) **6** Romney (George), Turner (Joseph Mallord William), Wilson (Richard) **7** Hogarth (William), Kneller (Godfrey), Millais (John) **8** Lawrence (Thomas), Reynolds (Joshua), Rossetti (Dante Gabriel) **9** Constable (John), Nicholson (Ben, William) **12** Gainsborough (Thomas)
Finnish: 9 Järnefelt (Edvard)
Flemish: 4 Eyck (Hubert van, Jan van), Goes (Hugo van der) **6** Rubens (Peter Paul), Weyden (Rogier van der) **7** Memling (Hams), Teniers (David), Van Dyck (Anthony), van Eyck (Hubert, Jan) **8** Breughel, Brueghel (Abraham, Ambrose, Jan, Pieter)
French: 4 Doré (Gustave), Dufy (Raoul), Erté **5** Corot (Camille), David (Jacques-Louis), Degas (Edgar), Léger (Fernand), Manet (Edouard), Monet (Claude), Redon (Odilon), Vouet (Simon) **6** Braque (Georges), Breton (André), Claude (of Lorrain), Clouet (François, Jean) Gérôme (Jean-Léon), Greuze (Jean-Baptiste), Ingres (Jean-Auguste-Dominique), Le Brun (Charles), Le Nain (Antoine, Louis, Mathieu), Millet (Jean-François), Renoir (Pierre-Auguste), Seurat (Georges), Sisley (Alfred), Tanguy (Yves), Vernet (Carle, Horace, Joseph) **7** Balthus, Bonheur (Rosa), Bonnard (Pierre), Boucher (François), Cézanne (Paul), Chardin (Jean-Baptiste), Courbet (Gustave), Daumier (Honoré), Duchamp (Gaston, Marcel), Gauguin (Paul), Matisse (Henri), Morisot (Berthe), Poussin (Nicolas), Rouault (Georges), Utrillo (Maurice), Watteau (Antoine) **8** Dubuffet (Jean), Magritte (René) Pissarro (Camille), Rousseau (Henri, Théodore), Vlaminck (Maurice de), Vuillard (Edouard) **9** Delacroix (Eugène), Fragonard (Jean-Honoré), Géricault (Théodore), Laurencin (Marie) **10** Bouguereau (William), Meissonier (Jean-Louis) **11** Caillebotte (Gustave) **13** Claude Lorrain
German: 5 Dürer (Albrecht), Ernst (Max),

Grosz (George), Nolde (Emil) **6** Albers (Josef), Müller (Friedrich "Maler") **7** Cranach (Lucas), Holbein (Hans), Lochner (Stefan), Schwind (Moritz von), Zoffany (Johann) **8** Kirchner (Ernst), Kollwitz (Käthe) **9** Grünewald (Matthias), Kandinsky (Wassily) **10** Schongauer (Martin), Wohlgemuth (Michael)
Greek: 6 Zeuxis **7** Apelles **10** Polygnotus
Irish: 5 Yeats (Jack, John Butler)
Italian: 4 Reni (Guido), Rosa (Salvator), Tura (Cosme) **5** Campi (Antonio, Bernardino, Giulio, Vincenzo), Lippi (Fra Filippo, Filippino, Lorenzo), Piero (della Francesca, di Cosimo), Sarto (Andrea del) **6** Andrea (del Sarto), Cosimo (Agnolo di, Piero di), Giotto, Romano (Giulio), Sodoma (Il), Titian, Vasari (Giorgio) **7** Bellini (Gentile, Giovanni, Jacopo), Chirico (Giorgio De), Cimabue, da Vinci (Leonardo), Fiesole (Giovanni da), Martini (Simone), Orcagna, Peruzzi (Baldassare), Raphael, Tiepolo (Giovanni), Uccello (Paolo), Zuccari (Taddeo) **8** del Sarto (Andrea), Fabriano (Gentile da), Giordano (Luca), Leonardo (da Vinci), Mantegna (Andrea), Masaccio, Montagna (Bartolommeo), Perugino, Pontorno (Jacopo da), Severini (Gino), Veronese (Paolo), Vivarini (Alvise, Antonio, Bartolomeo) **9** Carpaccio (Vittore), Correggio, Francesca (Piero della) **10** Caravaggio, Modigliani (Amedeo), Signorelli (Luca), Tintoretto, Verrocchio (Andrea del), Zuccarelli (Francesco) **11** Ghirlandaio (Domenico), Ghirlandajo (Domenico) **12** Michelangelo (Buonarotti), Parmigianino
Japanese: 5 Korin **6** Sesshu
Lithuanian: 7 Soutine (Chaim)
Mexican: 6 Orozco (Jose), Rivera (Diego), Tamayo (Rufino) **9** Siqueiros (David)
Norwegian: 5 Munch (Edvard)
Russian: 7 Chagall (Marc), Roerich (Nikolay) **9** Kandinsky (Wassily)
Scottish: 6 Ramsay (Allan) **7** Nasmyth (Alexander), Raeburn (Henry)
Spanish: 4 Dalí (Salvador), Goya (Francisco), Gris (Juan), Miró (Joan), Sert (José Maria) **6** Ribera (José), Rincón (Antonio del), Tapiés (Antonio) **7** El Greco, Herrera (Francisco de), Murillo (Bartolomé Esteban), Picasso (Pablo), Zuloaga (Ignacio) **8** Zurbarán (Francisco de) **9** Velázquez (Diego)
Swedish: 4 Zorn (Anders) **6** Roslin (Alexander)
Swiss: 4 Klee (Paul), Witz (Konrad)

painting

3 oil **7** acrylic, picture **10** watercolor
circular: **5** tondo
one-color: **8** monotint **10** monochrome
plaster: **5** secco **6** fresco
style: **4** Dada **5** fauve **6** cubism, cubist, Gothic, pop art, rococo **7** baroque, Bauhaus, dadaism, fauvism, fauvist, realism, realist **8** Barbizon, futurism, futurist, romantic **9** Byzantine, geometric, mannerism, mannerist **10** classicism, classicist, surrealism, surrealist **11** romanticism **13** expressionism, expressionist, impressionism, impressionist
technique: **3** oil **6** fresco, pastel **7** gouache, polymer, tempera **9** encaustic **10** watercolor
tool: **5** brush, easel, knife, paint **6** canvas **7** palette
wall: **5** mural

pair

3 duo, two **4** dyad, join, mate, span, team, twin, yoke **5** brace, match, twins, unite **6** couple **7** doublet, twosome **8** geminate

Pakistan

capital: **9** Islamabad
city: **6** Lahore, Multan **7** Karachi **9** Hyderabad **10** Faisalabad, Rawalpindi
language: **4** Urdu
leader: **6** Bhutto (Benazir)
monetary unit: **5** rupee
mountain, range: **8** Himalaya **9** Himalayan, Himalayas **11** Nanga Parbat
neighbor: **4** Iran **5** China, India **11** Afghanistan
sea: **7** Arabian

pal

4 chum, mate **5** amigo, buddy, crony **6** comate, friend **7** comrade, partner **9** companion

palace

5 court, manor, manse **6** castle **7** alcazar, château, mansion

paladin

6 leader **8** advocate, champion, defender, official

Palamedes

brother: **6** Sforza **8** Achilles
father: **8** Nauplius
slayer: **7** Corinda, Ulysses **8** Odysseus

palatable

5 sapid, tasty **6** savory **8** pleasing, savorous, tasteful **9** agreeable, appealing, delicious, toothsome **10** acceptable, appetizing **12** satisfactory

palate

5 taste **6** liking **6** relish

palatial

4 rich **5** grand, large, noble, plush, regal **6** deluxe, ornate **7** opulent, stately **8** imposing, majestic, splendid **9** grandiose, luxuriant, luxurious, sumptuous **10** impressive **11** magnificent

Palau

capital: **5** Koror
former name: **5** Pelew
island: **5** Koror **6** Angaur **7** Eli Malk **10** Babelthuap, Urukthapel
language: **7** English, Palauan

palaver

3 gas, yak **4** blab, cant, chat, guff, talk **6** babble, cajole, hot air, jargon, parley, powwow, speech **7** chatter, prattle **8** colloquy, converse, dialogue **10** conference, discussion, rap session **12** conversation

pale

3 dim, wan **4** area, ashy, dull, fade, sick, weak **5** ashen, faded, faint, fence, field, light, livid, pasty, stake, waxen **6** anemic, blanch, chalky, doughy, feeble, pallid, picket, sallow, sickly, weaken, whiten **7** enclose, ghastly, insipid **8** blanched, district, encircle **9** bloodless, colorless, enclosure

palinode

10 retraction **11** recantation

pall

4 bore, cloy, damp, jade, sate, tire **5** cloak, cloth, cloud, drape, ennui, gloom, weary **6** coffin, damper, mantle, shadow **7** dwindle, satiate, surfeit **8** covering

palladium

9 safeguard

Pallas

6 Athena
brother: **6** Aegeus
father: **7** Pandion
slayer: **7** Theseus
wife: **4** Styx
(see also **Athena**)

palliate

4 ease, help **5** cover, salve **6** excuse, lessen, reduce, soften, soothe, temper **7** assuage, cover up, lighten **8** mitigate, moderate **9** alleviate, sugarcoat, whitewash **10** ameliorate

pallid
3 wan 4 ashy, dull, pale, weak 5 ashen,
pasty, waxen 6 anemic, doughy, sickly
8 blanched, lifeless 9 bloodless, colorless

pallor
8 lividity, paleness 9 pastiness, whiteness
10 etiolation 12 glaucousness

pally
4 cozy 5 close, matey 6 chummy
7 devoted 8 familiar, friendly, intimate

palm
5 prize, steal, swipe 6 trophy 7 conceal,
triumph, victory
beverage: 4 nipa
fiber: 4 bass, bast 8 piassava
fruit: 4 date 7 coconut 11 coquilla nut
kind: 3 fan, wax 4 coco, date, doom,
hemp, nipa, sago 5 areca, betel, ivory,
royal 6 raffia, rattan 7 cabbage, feather,
palmyra 8 carnauba, palmetto, piassava
12 Washingtonia
leaf: 4 olla 5 frond
starch: 4 sago
vine: 6 rattan

palmer
7 pilgrim

Palmetto State
13 South Carolina

palmistry
6 augury 8 prophecy 10 divination
11 soothsaying

palm off
5 foist 7 deceive, pretend 8 disguise

palmy
6 golden 7 booming, halcyon, opulent
8 affluent, thriving 10 prospering,
prosperous 11 flourishing

Palmyra's queen
7 Zenobia

palooka
3 oaf 4 boob, dolt, goon, lout, lump
5 boxer, klutz 6 baboon, galoot, lummox
7 bruiser

palpable
4 real, sure 5 clear, plain 6 patent
7 certain, concrete, evident, obvious, tactile
8 apparent, definite, distinct, manifest,
material, positive, tangible 10 noticeable
11 discernible, perceptible, unequivocal

palpate
4 feel 5 touch 6 finger 7 examine

palpitate
4 beat 5 pulse, throb 6 quiver 7 flutter,
pulsate 12 pitter-patter

palsy-walsy
4 cozy 5 close, thick, tight 6 chummy
8 intimate 10 buddy-buddy

palter
3 fib, lie 5 evade 6 dicker, haggle
7 bargain, chaffer, deceive, falsify, wrangle
10 equivocate 11 prevaricate
12 misrepresent

paltry
3 low 4 base, mean, poor, puny, vile
5 cheap, petty, tatty 6 meager, measly,
narrow, shabby, shoddy, sleazy, trashy
7 low-down, pitiful, trivial 8 beggarly,
inferior, picayune, piddling, rubbishy, trifling
9 worthless 10 despicable, picayunish
11 unimportant 12 contemptible 13 insignificant

paludal place
3 fen 5 marsh

Pamela author
10 Richardson (Samuel)

pampa
5 plain 7 prairie 9 grassland

pamper
3 pet 4 baby 5 humor, spoil 6 caress,
cocker, coddle, cosset, cuddle, dandle,
fondle 7 cater to, cherish, gratify, indulge
9 spoon-feed 11 mollycoddle

pamphlet
5 flier, flyer, tract 6 folder 7 leaflet
8 brochure, circular 9 throwaway
10 broadsheet

pan
3 pot, rap 4 slam, wash 5 basin, knock,
roast, trash 6 attack, vessel 7 censure,
condemn, skillet 8 denounce, ridicule
9 betel leaf, container, criticism, criticize
10 receptacle

Pan
5 Inuus 6 Faunus
father: 6 Hermes
invention: 6 syrinx
lower part: 4 goat
mother: 8 Penelope
pipe: 6 syrinx
seat of worship: 7 Arcadia
son: 7 Silenus

panacea
4 cure 6 remedy 7 cure-all, nostrum
10 catholicon

Panacea's father
9 Asclepius 11 Aesculapius

panache
4 brio, dash, élan, tuft, zest 5 ardor, crest, flair, style, verve, vigor 6 esprit, polish, spirit 8 aigrette, flourish, vivacity
11 flamboyance

panama
3 hat

Panama
capital: 10 Panama City
discoverer: 6 Balboa (Vasco Núñez de) 8 Columbus (Christopher)
gulf: 7 San Blas 8 Mosquito
language: 7 Spanish
leader: 7 Noriega (Manuel)
monetary unit: 6 balboa
neighbor: 8 Colombia 9 Costa Rica
peninsula: 6 Azuero
sea: 9 Caribbean
volcano: 8 Chiriquí

pancake
8 flapjack, slapjack
French: 5 crepe
Jewish: 5 latke 6 blintz 7 blintze
Russian: 5 blini

Pandarus
6 archer 8 procuror
father: 6 Lycaon
slayer: 8 Diomedes

pandect
4 code, laws 8 treatise 10 compendium
11 compilation

pandemic
4 rife 7 general, rampant 9 contagion, extensive, prevalent 10 contagious, widespread 11 wide-ranging

pandemonium
3 din 5 babel, chaos, furor 6 bedlam, clamor, hubbub, tumult, uproar 7 anarchy, discord, inferno, misrule, turmoil 8 disorder 9 confusion 10 hullabaloo

pander
4 pimp 5 cater 9 exploiter, go-between

Pandion
daughter: 6 Procne 9 Philomela
son: 6 Pallas

Pandora
creator: 10 Hephaestus
husband: 10 Epimetheus

pane
4 side 5 sheet 7 section

panegyric
6 eulogy, praise 7 tribute 8 citation, encomium 9 laudation 10 compliment
12 commendation

panegyrical
8 praising 9 laudative, laudatory
10 eulogistic 11 encomiastic 12 commendatory 13 complimentary

panel
4 jury 5 board, frame 6 hurdle 7 section 9 dashboard

panfry
5 sauté

pang
4 ache, pain, stab 5 agony, prick, spasm, throe 6 stitch, twinge 7 anguish, torment 8 distress

Pangloss's pupil
7 Candide

panhandle
3 beg, bum, tap 5 cadge, hit up, touch 6 hustle 7 solicit

panhandler
6 beggar

panic
4 fear, riot, rush 5 alarm, scare 6 dismay, frenzy, fright, horror, terror 7 anxiety, terrify 8 frighten, hysteria, stampede

pannier
4 hoop, pack 6 basket, hamper 9 overskirt

panoply
4 pomp, show 5 armor, array 6 attire 7 display, fanfare 9 trappings

panorama
4 view 5 range, reach, scene, scope, sweep, vista 7 display, expanse, picture, purview 12 presentation

panoramic
8 sweeping, synoptic 12 all-inclusive, unobstructed 13 comprehensive

pan out
4 work 5 click, prove, score 7 come off, succeed

pant
4 blow, gasp, gulp, huff, puff 5 chuff, heave 6 wheeze

Pantagruel
5 giant
companion: 7 Panurge

father: 9 Gargantua
mother: 7 Badebec

pantaloon
7 buffoon, trouser

Pantaloon's daughter
9 Columbine

pantheon
4 gods 5 Aesir 6 temple 9 hierarchy
10 hall of fame

panther
4 pard, puma 6 cougar, jaguar 7 leopard
12 mountain lion

pantomime
5 drama, mimic 6 act out, ballet, dancer
7 charade 12 harlequinade
clown: 7 Pierrot

pantry
6 closet, larder 7 buttery 9 storeroom

pants
5 jeans 6 slacks 7 drawers, garment
8 breeches, britches, knickers, trousers

Panurge's companion
10 Pantagruel

Paolo's lover
9 Francesca

pap
4 food, mash, mush 7 aliment, pabulum
8 soft food 9 blandness, nutriment
10 sustenance 11 nourishment

papal
8 pontific 9 apostolic 10 pontifical
court: 5 Curia
decree: 8 decretal
envoy: 6 nuncio
letter: 4 bull 10 encyclical

paper
5 essay, sheet, theme 6 letter, report
7 article 8 document 9 monograph,
newsprint 10 memorandum 11 composition, publication 12 dissertation
measure: 4 ream 5 quire
roll: 6 scroll
scrap: 4 chad
size: 3 cap 5 atlas, crown, folio, legal,
royal, sexto, sixmo 6 octavo, quarto
7 emperor 8 elephant, foolscap, imperial
stiff: 7 bristol 9 cardboard 12 bristol
board
strong: 5 kraft 6 manila
thin: 6 tissue 9 onionskin
transparent: 8 glassine
writing: 3 rag 6 vellum 9 parchment

paper folding
7 origami

paperwork
7 red tape

papillon
7 spaniel 9 butterfly

Papua New Guinea
archipelago: 8 Bismarck
capital: 11 Port Moresby
city: 3 Lae
island: 12 Bougainville
language: 4 Motu 8 Tok Pisin
monetary unit: 4 kina
neighbor: 9 Indonesia, Irian Jaya

par
4 mean, norm 5 equal, score, usual
6 median, normal 7 average, typical
8 equality, standard

parable
4 myth, tale 5 fable, moral, story
7 example 8 allegory

parachute
7 bailout, skydive
part: 5 riser 6 canopy 7 harness, ripcord

Paraclete
9 Holy Ghost 10 Holy Spirit

parade
4 brag, pomp, show 5 array, boast, flash,
march, shine, strut 6 expose, flaunt,
ground, reveal, review 7 display, disport,
exhibit, fanfare, marshal, panoply, show off,
trot out 8 brandish, ceremony, movement,
proclaim 9 advertise, cavalcade,
pageantry, promenade 10 exhibition,
masquerade, procession 11 demonstrate

paradigm
5 ideal, model 6 mirror 7 example, pattern
8 exemplar, standard 9 archetype, beau
ideal, framework, prototype

paradise
4 Eden, Zion 5 bliss 6 heaven, utopia
7 arcadia, elysium, nirvana 8 empyrean
9 Shangri-la 10 wonderland 12 New
Jerusalem, promised land

Paradise Lost author
6 Milton (John)

paragon
3 gem 4 tops 5 champ, cream, ideal,
jewel, match, model, peach, saint 6 beauty
7 compare, epitome 8 champion,
exemplar, last word, nonesuch, parallel,
ultimate 9 archetype, beau ideal, nonpareil
10 apotheosis

Paraguay
capital: 8 Asunción
lake: 4 Ypoá
language: 7 Guarani, Spanish
monetary unit: 7 guarani
neighbor: 6 Brazil 7 Bolivia 9 Argentina
river: 9 Pilcomayo

parallel
4 akin, copy, even, like 5 agree, align, alike, along, equal, liken, match 6 double, equate, line up 7 aligned, compare, similar 8 analogue 9 alongside, analogous, companion, consonant, corollary, correlate, duplicate 10 comparable, comparison, correspond, equivalent, similarity 11 coextensive, counterpart, duplication, resemblance 13 correspondent, corresponding

parallelogram
5 rhomb 6 oblong, square 7 rhombus 8 rhomboid 9 rectangle 13 quadrilateral

paralysis
5 palsy 7 inertia 9 impotence

paralyze
3 awe 4 daze, numb, stun 6 benumb, deaden, dismay 7 cripple, disable, nonplus, petrify, stupefy 8 shut down 10 immobilize 12 incapacitate

paramount
5 chief, ruler 6 master 7 capital, leading, primary, regnant, supreme 8 cardinal, crowning, dominant, foremost, headmost, superior 9 principal, sovereign, uppermost 10 commanding, preeminent 11 predominant

paramour
5 lover, Romeo 7 Don Juan, gallant 8 Casanova, lothario, mistress 9 courtesan, inamorata, inamorato

parapet
4 wall 7 bastion, bulwark, rampart 10 battlement, breastwork
part: 6 merlon 12 crenellation

paraphernalia
4 gear 5 items 6 outfit, tackle 7 effects 8 property 9 equipment, trappings 10 belongings 11 accessories, furnishings 13 accouterments, accoutrements, appurtenances

paraphrase
6 reword 7 restate, version 9 interpret, rendering, translate 11 restatement, translation

parasite
5 leech, toady 6 sponge, sucker 7 sponger 8 barnacle, deadbeat, hanger-on 9 dependent, exploiter, sycophant 10 freeloader, self-seeker 11 bloodsucker

parasitic
8 sponging, toadying 9 leech-like 11 freeloading, sycophantic 12 bloodsucking

parasol
8 umbrella

_____ paratus
6 semper

Parcae
5 Fates, Norns 6 Moirai
name: 4 Nona 5 Morta 6 Decuma

parcel
3 box, cut, lot 4 body, deal, land, mete, pack, part, plot, wrap 5 allot, array, batch, bunch, group, piece, share, tract 6 assign, bundle, divide, packet, ration 7 package, partial, portion, prorate, section, segment 8 allocate, disburse, disperse, division, part-time 9 apportion, partition 10 distribute

parch
3 dry 4 burn, sear 5 dry up, roast, toast 6 dry out, scorch 7 shrivel 9 dehydrate, desiccate

parched
3 dry 4 arid, sere 5 dusty 7 bone-dry, thirsty 8 scorched, withered 9 shriveled, waterless 10 dehydrated

parchment
4 skin 5 paper 6 vellum 7 diploma 8 document

pardon
4 free 5 remit, spare 6 excuse, let off 7 absolve, amnesty, condone, forgive, release 8 liberate, reprieve, tolerate 9 acquittal, exculpate, indemnity, remission 10 absolution, indulgence 11 exculpation, exoneration, forgiveness

pardonable
6 venial 9 allowable, excusable 11 permissible

pare
3 cut 4 clip, crop, peel, trim 5 lower, prune, shave 6 reduce, remove 7 curtail, cut back, cut down, trim off, whittle 8 diminish

parent
4 make, rear 5 beget, cause, hatch, raise, spawn 6 author, create, father, mother, origin 7 bring up, care for, produce 8 begetter, generate 9 originate, procreate 10 progenitor

parenthetically
7 by the by 8 by the bye, by the way 9 in passing 12 incidentally

parentless
6 orphan 8 orphaned

par excellence
3 top 5 prime 7 premier, supreme 8 foremost, peerless, superior 9 number one, unmatched 10 first-class, preeminent 11 outstanding

pariah
5 leper 7 Ishmael, outcast 8 castaway 10 Ishmaelite 11 offscouring, untouchable
Japanese: 3 eta

Paris
ancient name: 7 Lutetia
avenue: 13 Champs-Elysées
basilica: 10 Sacré Coeur
cathedral: 9 Notre Dame
city hall: 12 Hôtel de Ville
college: 8 Sorbonne
garden: 9 Tuileries 10 Luxembourg
island: 11 Île de la Cité
museum: 5 Cluny 6 Louvre
palace: 6 Louvre 7 Bourbon
patron saint: 9 Geneviève
racecourse: 7 Auteuil
river: 5 Seine
section: 8 Left Bank 9 Right Bank 10 Montmartre 12 Latin Quarter
stock exchange: 6 Bourse
subway: 5 Métro
tower: 6 Eiffel

Paris
beloved: 5 Helen
betrothed: 6 Juliet
father: 5 Priam
mother: 6 Hecuba
slayer: 11 Philoctetes
wife: 6 Oenone

parish
6 county 8 district 9 community 12 congregation, neighborhood

Parisina
author: 5 Byron (Lord)
husband: 3 Azo
lover: 4 Hugo
slayer: 3 Azo

parity
8 equality, sameness, symmetry 10 similarity, similitude 11 equivalence, equivalency, parallelism

park
4 stop 5 green, plaza 7 deposit, funfair, reserve 8 carnival, preserve 9 esplanade 11 reservation

parka
6 anorak, jacket 7 garment 8 pullover 9 outerwear

park designer
4 Vaux (Calvert) 6 Paxton (Joseph) 7 Alphand (Jean), Le Nôtre (André), Olmsted (Frederick Law)

parlance
4 talk 5 idiom, style, usage 6 phrase, speech 7 wording 8 language, locution, phrasing 9 verbalism 11 phraseology

parlay
3 bet 4 risk 5 bid up, boost, stake, wager 6 expand, extend, hazard 7 build up, enhance, enlarge, exploit, venture 8 increase, leverage 9 transform

parley
4 talk 5 speak 6 confab, confer, huddle, powwow 7 discuss, meeting 8 colloquy, converse, dialogue 9 discourse, negotiate 10 conference, discussion 11 confabulate 12 conversation 13 confabulation

parliament
see **legislature**

parlor
4 room 5 salon 11 drawing room 13 reception room

parlous
5 hairy, risky 6 chancy, unsafe 8 critical 9 dangerous, hazardous 10 precarious

Parnassian
4 poet 6 poetic

parochial
5 local 6 narrow 7 insular, limited 9 sectarian, small-town 10 provincial, restricted

parody
3 rib 4 mock 5 mimic, spoof 6 satire 7 imitate, lampoon, mockery, takeoff 8 ridicule, travesty 9 burlesque, imitation 10 caricature

parole
4 free, word 6 let out, pledge 7 promise,

release **9** discharge, probation, watchword **11** performance

paronomasia
3 pun **11** play on words

paroxysm
3 fit **4** bout **5** spasm, throe **6** attack, frenzy **7** flare-up, seizure **8** eruption, outbreak, outburst **9** explosion **10** conniption, convulsion

parrot
3 ape **4** aper, copy, echo **5** mimic **6** repeat **7** chatter, copycat, imitate
kind: 3 ara, kea **4** kaka, lory **5** macaw **6** Amazon, budgie, kakapo **8** cockatoo, lorikeet, lovebird, parakeet **9** cockatiel **10** budgerigar

parrot fever
11 psittacosis

parry
4 duck, fend **5** avert, avoid, block, dodge, elude, evade **7** counter, deflect, evasion, fend off, prevent, respond, ward off **8** sidestep, stave off **9** turn aside **10** circumvent

parse
4 scan **7** analyze, dissect, examine, resolve **8** construe **9** anatomize, explicate, interpret

Parsi
11 Zoroastrian

Parsifal
composer: 6 Wagner (Richard)
magician: 8 Klingsor
quest: 5 Grail
son: 9 Lohengrin
temptress: 6 Kundry

parsimonious
4 mean **5** cheap, close, tight **6** frugal, stingy **7** chintzy, miserly, sparing, thrifty **9** penurious **10** restrained **11** closefisted, tightfisted **13** penny-pinching

parsley
4 herb **7** garnish
family: 6 carrot
piece: 5 sprig

parson
6 cleric, pastor, rector **8** clerical, minister, preacher, reverend **9** clergyman **12** ecclesiastic

parsonage
5 manse **7** rectory

part
3 bit, cut **4** chip, unit **5** chunk, piece, quota, scrap, sever, slice **6** detail, divide, member, moiety, ration, sector **7** element, measure, portion, quantum, quarter, section, segment **8** division, fraction, fragment, function, separate **9** component

partake
3 eat **5** savor, share **6** accept, sample **7** acquire, consume, receive **9** enter into **11** participate

Parthenon
sculptor: 7 Phidias **8** Pheidias
sculpture: 6 frieze
site: 9 Acropolis

partial
6 biased, unfair, warped **7** colored, halfway **8** inclined, one-sided **9** jaundiced **10** fractional, incomplete, prejudiced **11** fragmentary, predisposed

partiality
4 bent, bias **5** favor, taste **6** liking **7** leaning **8** affinity, fondness, tendency **10** favoritism, preference **11** inclination **12** one-sidedness, predilection

participant
5 party **6** fellow, member, player, sharer **7** partner, sharing **11** contributor, shareholder

participate
4 join, play **5** share **6** engage, join in **7** partake **8** take part

particle
3 ace, bit, dot, jot, tad **4** atom, doit, dram, drop, hint, hoot, iota, mite, mote, spot, whit **5** atomy, crumb, fleck, grain, minim, ounce, scrap, shred, speck **6** morsel, tittle **7** granule, modicum, smidgen, soupçon **8** fragment **9** scintilla
atomic: 3 ion **5** anion **6** cation
elementary: 3 psi, tau **4** kaon, muon, pion **5** boson, meson **6** baryon, hadron, lambda, lepton, photon, proton **7** fermion, hyperon, neutron, nucleon, upsilon **8** electron, mesotron, neutrino, positron
hypothetical: 5 gluon, quark **6** parton **8** graviton
virus: 6 virion
with negative charge: 8 electron
with positive charge: 6 proton **8** positron

particular
3 one **4** fact, full, item, lone **5** exact, fussy, picky, point, thing **6** detail, marked, minute,

single, unique **7** careful, correct, element, feature, finicky, notable, precise, several, special, unusual **8** accurate, concrete, detailed, distinct, especial, exacting, itemized, separate, solitary, specific, uncommon **10** blow-by-blow, fastidious, individual, meticulous, pernickety, scrupulous **11** distinctive, exceptional, persnickety, punctilious **12** circumstance

particularize
4 list **6** detail **7** catalog, itemize, specify **8** spell out **9** enumerate, inventory **13** individualize

parting
4 last **5** adieu, break, congé, final **6** good-by **7** good-bye **8** division, farewell **10** divergence, separation **11** leave-taking, valedictory

partisan
6 backer, biased, warped **7** devotee, die-hard, fanatic, patriot, sectary **8** adherent, advocate, disciple, follower, one-sided, stalwart, upholder **9** factional, guerrilla, irregular, satellite, sectarian, supporter

partition
4 wall **6** divide, screen **7** divider, section, wall off **8** disunion, division, fence off, separate **10** separation

partner
4 ally, chum, mate **5** buddy, crony **6** cohort, fellow **7** comrade **8** confrere, sidekick **9** assistant, associate, colleague, companion **10** accomplice **11** confederate

partnership
4 firm **5** union **7** cahoots, company, sharing **8** alliance, business, marriage, relation **11** affiliation, association, combination **12** consociation, togetherness **13** participation

parturient
6 gravid, parous **8** enceinte, pregnant **9** expecting

parturition
5 birth **8** delivery **10** childbirth **12** childbearing

party
4 ball, band, bash, bevy, bloc, crew, fete, gala, orgy, side **5** actor, corps, covey, feast, group, revel, troop **6** fiesta, frolic, kegger, mortal, person, social, soiree, troupe **7** blowout, carouse, faction, roister, shindig **8** carousal, litigant, wingding **9** bacchanal, gathering, make merry, raise

hell **10** detachment, individual, saturnalia **11** bacchanalia, celebration, participant

parvenu
7 upstart **9** arriviste **12** nouveau riche

Pascal essay
6 Pensée

Pasiphaë
daughter: 7 Ariadne, Phaedra
husband: 5 Minos
son: 8 Minotaur

pass
3 die, end **4** fare, hand **5** cease, lapse, occur, relay, spend, while **6** crisis, depart, elapse, exceed, expire, hand on, happen, permit, push on, slight, slip by, strait **7** come off, develop, journey, proceed, succumb **8** bequeath, fork over, hand down, juncture, outshine, outstrip, transmit **9** while away
Afghanistan: 5 Murgh
Afghanistan-Pakistan: 6 Khyber
Alaska: 5 White
Alps: 3 col **5** Cenis, Loibl **7** Brenner, Ljubelj, Simplon **9** St. Bernard
California: 5 Cajon
China-India: 9 Karakoram
Colorado: 3 Ute
Pakistan: 5 Kilik
Russian: 12 Caspian Gates
Tennessee: 10 Cumberland
Turkey: 13 Cilician Gates

passable
4 okay, open, so-so **6** decent **8** adequate, all right **9** tolerable, unblocked **10** accessible, good enough **12** satisfactory

passably
6 enough **8** all right, somewhat **10** moderately

passage
3 way **4** exit, fare, hall, path, text **5** route, shift **6** access, arcade, avenue, course, egress, strait, travel, tunnel, voyage **7** channel, excerpt, hallway, journey, transit **8** corridor, transfer, traverse **9** enactment, quotation **10** transition **11** transmittal **12** transference, transmission
air: 7 windway
arched: 6 arcade
Atlantic-Pacific: 9 Northwest
roofed: 6 arcade **9** breezeway

Passage to India author
7 Forster (E. M.)

pass away
3 die, end 6 demise, depart, elapse, expire, perish 7 decease, succumb 9 disappear

pass by
4 miss, omit 6 forget, ignore 7 neglect 8 overlook 9 disregard

passé
4 dead 5 dated, stale 6 démodé, old hat 7 demoded, disused, extinct, outworn 8 obsolete, outdated, outmoded 9 out-of-date 10 antiquated, superseded 12 old-fashioned

passel
3 lot 4 heap, pack 5 bunch 6 bundle 9 multitude

passing
5 brief, death, quick 6 demise, highly 7 cursory, decease 8 fleeting 9 ephemeral, fugacious, extremely, momentary, transient 10 evanescent, short-lived, transitory 11 exceedingly, superficial 12 satisfactory

passion
4 fire, fury, heat, itch, love, lust, rage, urge, zeal 5 agony, amour, anger, ardor, craze, crush, drive 6 desire, fervor, hunger 7 avidity, craving, ecstasy, emotion, feeling, rapture 8 appetite, devotion, outburst, yearning 9 affection, eagerness, suffering, transport 10 enthusiasm, excitement, heartthrob 11 amorousness, infatuation

passionate
3 hot 5 angry, fiery 6 ardent, fervid, heated 7 amorous, aroused, blazing, burning, excited, fervent, furious, intense 8 incensed, vehement 9 impetuous, steamed up 10 hot-blooded, stimulated 11 hot-tempered 12 enthusiastic 13 quick-tempered

passive
4 idle 5 inert 6 docile, latent 8 enduring, immobile, inactive, listless, resigned, yielding 9 apathetic, compliant, lethargic, quiescent 10 motionless, nonviolent, phlegmatic, submissive 11 acquiescent, complaisant, indifferent, unresistant

pass out
3 die 5 faint, swoon 7 divvy up 8 disburse, keel over 10 distribute

pass over
4 miss, omit, skip 6 forget, ignore

7 dismiss, neglect 8 discount, leave out 9 disregard

Passover
5 Pasch 6 Pesach
bread: 5 matzo 6 matzoh
meal: 5 seder

pass up
5 forgo 6 refuse, reject 7 decline

past
3 ago, old 4 gone, late, once, yore 5 above, after, prior 6 beyond, bygone, former, whilom 7 onetime, quondam 8 anterior, foretime, lang syne, previous, sometime 9 antiquity, erstwhile, foregoing, precedent, preceding, yesterday 10 antecedent, yesteryear

pasta
5 dough
kind: 4 ziti 7 gnocchi, lasagna, ravioli 8 linguine, linguini, macaroni, rigatoni 9 canneloni, fettucine, fettucini, manicotti, spaghetti 10 cannelloni, fettuccine, fettuccini, tortellini, vermicelli 11 cappelletti

paste
3 fix, hit 4 beat, clay, drub, food, glue, sock 5 affix, dough, pound, stick, stuff 6 adhere, attach, cement, defeat, fasten, thrash, wallop 7 trounce 8 adhesive, material

Pasternak hero
7 Zhivago (Dr.)

pastiche
4 olio 6 jumble, medley 7 farrago, mélange, mixture 8 mishmash 9 potpourri 10 assortment, hodgepodge, hotchpotch, miscellany, salmagundi 11 gallimaufry

pastime
4 game 5 hobby, sport 9 amusement, diversion 10 recreation 13 entertainment

past master
4 whiz 5 adept, maven 6 expert, wizard 9 authority

pastor
5 padre 6 cleric, parson 8 minister, preacher, reverend, sky pilot 9 clergyman

pastoral
5 idyll, rural 6 rustic 7 bucolic, country, crosier, idyllic 8 agrarian, clerical, innocent, peaceful 10 campestral

pastor's assistant
6 curate

pastry
  3 bun, pie 4 baba, cake, flan, tart 5 torte
  6 cornet, Danish, éclair, gâteau, pirogi
  7 baklava, beignet, bouchée, dariole, fritter,
  gâteaux (plural), palmier, savarin, strudel,
  tartlet 8 napoleon, papillon, pirozhki,
  pirozhki, turnover 9 barquette, cream puff,
  madeleine, petit four, vol-au-vent
  10 cheesecake 11 profiterole
  12 millefeuille
  kind: 4 filo, puff 5 flaky 6 phyllo
  shell: 7 timbale 8 meringue

pasture
  3 lea, ley 4 feed, land 5 field, grass, graze
  6 browse, meadow 9 grassland

pasty
  3 wan 4 pale 6 doughy, pallid, sickly
  7 meat pie 8 turnover 9 unhealthy

pat
  3 apt, dab, set 4 firm 5 fixed, slice, stiff,
  trite 6 dead-on 7 apropos, fitting
  8 apposite, standard, suitable 9 contrived,
  pertinent, rehearsed

patch
  3 bit, fix 4 area, fill, mend, plot 5 cover,
  piece, scrap, spell 6 doctor, emblem, fill
  up, repair, shield 7 connect, plaster
  8 material 10 connection

patchwork
  4 olio 5 quilt 6 jumble 7 mixture
  8 covering, mishmash, mixed bag
  10 assortment, hodgepodge, hotchpotch,
  miscellany, salmagundi

patchy
  6 fitful, random, spotty, uneven 7 erratic
  8 sporadic 9 haphazard, hit-or-miss,
  irregular 12 intermittent

pate
  4 bean, dome, head, poll 5 brain, crown
  6 noddle, noggin, noodle

pâté de _____
  8 foie gras

patella
  7 kneecap, kneepan

patent
  4 open 5 clear, plain, right 6 secure
  7 evident, license, obvious, visible
  8 apparent, distinct, manifest, unclosed
  9 exclusive, privilege, prominent, protected
  11 proprietary 12 intelligible, unobstructed

paternal
  8 fatherly

relative: 6 agnate

paternity
  7 lineage 8 ancestry 10 fatherhood,
  provenance 11 progenitors

Pater Noster
  9 Our Father

path
  3 way 4 lane, line, road, tack, walk
  5 byway, orbit, route, track, trail 6 avenue,
  bridle, course 7 passage, walkway
  9 direction 10 trajectory

pathetic
  3 sad 4 poor 5 sorry 6 absurd, moving,
  paltry, rueful 7 piteous, pitiful, risible,
  useless 8 inferior, pitiable, poignant,
  touching 9 affecting, laughable, miserable
  10 inadequate, lamentable, ridiculous

Pathfinder
  author: 6 Cooper (James Fenimore)
  hero: 6 Bumppo (Natty)

pathogen
  4 germ 5 virus 9 bacterium

pathological
  7 deviant 8 aberrant, abnormal, diseased,
  maniacal, schizoid 9 psychotic

pathos
  4 pity 7 emotion 8 sympathy 9 poi-
  gnance, poignancy

pathway
  4 line, walk 5 route, track, trail 6 course
  7 channel, conduit, network, passage

patience
  4 cool 8 calmness, stoicism 9 composure,
  endurance 10 equanimity, sufferance
  11 forbearance, resignation, self-control

Patience
  composer: 8 Sullivan (Arthur)
  librettist: 7 Gilbert (W. S.)

patient
  4 case, meek 8 enduring 9 easygoing
  10 persistent 11 susceptible 13 long-
  suffering
  man: 3 Job

patina
  4 aura, coat, film 6 finish, polish 7 coating
  8 covering 10 appearance, coloration

patio
  5 court 6 atrium 7 terrace 9 courtyard

patois
  4 cant 5 argot, lingo, slang 6 jargon
  7 dialect 10 colloquial, vernacular

patriarch
4 sire 6 father 7 creator, founder
9 architect, graybeard
biblical: 5 David, Isaac, Jacob 7 Abraham

patrician
5 noble 6 aristo 9 blue blood, gentleman
10 aristocrat, upper-class

patriciate
5 elite 6 gentry 9 blue blood, gentility
10 upper crust 11 aristocracy

patrimony
6 estate, legacy 8 heritage 9 endowment
10 birthright 11 inheritance

patriot
5 jingo 8 jingoist, loyalist 9 flag-waver
10 chauvinist 11 nationalist

patriotism
8 jingoism 10 chauvinism 11 nationalism

Patroclus
friend: 8 Achilles
slayer: 6 Hector

patrol
5 guard, round, scout, troop, watch
7 protect 8 sentinel 9 keep watch

patrolman
3 cop 5 guard 6 police 7 officer

patrol wagon
see **paddy wagon**

patron
5 angel 6 backer, client 7 sponsor
8 customer, guardian 9 protector,
supporter 10 benefactor

patronage
4 help 5 aegis, trade 6 custom 7 backing,
subsidy, support, traffic 8 activity,
advocacy, auspices, business, cronyism
9 clientage, clientele, influence 10 pork
barrel, protection 11 benefaction,
sponsorship 12 guardianship

patronize
3 aid, use 4 back 5 deign, favor 6 assist,
shop at 7 protect, support 8 frequent
10 condescend

patron saint
of beggars, cripples: 5 Giles
of children: 8 Nicholas
of England: 6 George
of fishermen: 5 Peter
of France: 5 Denis
of Ireland: 7 Patrick
of lawyers: 4 Ives
of musicians: 7 Cecilia
of Norway: 4 Olaf

of physicians: 4 Luke
of sailors: 4 Elmo 8 Nicholas
of Scotland: 6 Andrew
of shoemakers: 7 Crispin
of Spain: 5 James 8 Santiago
of Wales: 5 David
of winegrowers: 7 Vincent
of workers: 6 Joseph

patsy
3 sap 4 dupe, fool, mark 5 chump
6 pigeon, sucker, victim 8 easy mark,
pushover

patter
4 cant 5 argot, lingo, slang, spiel 6 babble,
jargon, patois 7 chatter, prattle

pattern
4 copy, form, plan 5 guide, ideal, model,
motif, order, shape 6 design, figure, follow,
method, mirror, system 7 diagram,
emulate, example, imitate 8 exemplar,
grouping, paradigm, standard, template
9 archetype, incidence, prototype 10 flight
path 11 arrangement, orderliness 12 distribution 13 configuration

paucity
4 lack, want 6 dearth 7 poverty 8 scarcity,
shortage 9 scantness, smallness
10 deficiency, meagerness, meagreness
13 insufficiency

_____ Paulo
3 São

Paul the Apostle
birthplace: 6 Tarsus
companion: 5 Silas, Titus 7 Artemas,
Timothy 8 Barnabas
original name: 4 Saul
place of conversion: 8 Damascus
prosecutor: 9 Tertullus
teacher: 8 Gamaliel
tribe: 8 Benjamin

paunch
3 gut, pot 5 belly, tummy 7 abdomen,
stomach 8 potbelly 9 bay window, beer
belly 11 breadbasket

paunchy
3 fat 5 beefy, plump, tubby 6 chunky,
portly, rotund 8 thickset 10 overweight,
potbellied

pauper
6 beggar 7 have-not 8 bankrupt, indigent
9 mendicant

pauperism
4 need, ruin, want 6 penury 7 beggary,

poverty 9 indigence, neediness, privation
11 destitution

pause
3 gap 4 halt, hush, lull, rest, stop, wait
5 break, comma, delay, lapse, letup
6 hiatus, linger, recess 7 caesura, respite,
time out 8 breather, hesitate, inaction,
interval, take five 9 cessation, interlude
10 hesitation, suspension 12 intermission,
interruption

pave
3 lay, tar 5 cover 7 asphalt, surface
8 blacktop, concrete

pavement
6 tarmac 7 asphalt, macadam, surface
8 concrete, sidewalk

pavilion
4 tent 5 kiosk 6 canopy, gazebo
9 belvedere 11 summerhouse

paw
4 feel, foot, grab, hand 5 grope, touch
6 fondle, handle, molest, scrape

pawn
4 hock, tool 6 pledge, puppet, stooge,
victim 7 deposit, hostage, warrant
8 guaranty, security 9 guarantee 10 chess
piece, instrument

pax
5 peace 6 tablet

Pax _____
3 Dei 6 Romana 10 Britannica

pay
3 fee 4 wage 5 clear, offer, remit, serve,
spend 6 answer, defray, employ, expend,
kick in, lay out, pony up, profit, render,
return, salary, settle, square, tender, reward
7 benefit, bring in, cough up, forfeit, fork
out, requite, satisfy, stipend 8 defrayal,
disburse, earnings, shell out 9 discharge,
emolument, indemnify, liquidate, reimburse
10 compensate, recompense, remunerate
12 compensation, remuneration

payable
3 due 4 owed 5 owing 6 mature, unpaid
7 overdue 9 unsettled 10 obligatory
11 outstanding, uncollected

paycheck
5 wages 6 salary

payload
4 haul 5 cargo, goods 6 burden, lading,
weight 7 freight, tonnage 8 shipment

payment
3 fee 4 dues 5 award, money 6 amends,
outlay, return, reward 7 penance

8 defrayal, requital 11 restitution
12 compensation, remuneration,
satisfaction

payoff
3 fix 5 bribe 6 climax, profit, result,
reward, upshot 7 outcome 8 clincher,
decisive 10 conclusion, conclusive,
denouement 11 retribution

payola
5 bribe

PDQ
4 ASAP 6 at once, pronto 8 directly, right
now, right off 9 forthwith, instanter,
instantly, right away 11 immediately,
straightway 12 straightaway

peace
3 pax 4 calm, ease, pact 5 amity, order,
quiet 6 accord, repose 7 concord,
harmony, silence 8 serenity 11 tranquility
12 tranquillity

peaceable
6 dovish, irenic 7 amiable, pacific
8 amicable, friendly, pacifist, tranquil
10 nonviolent 11 complaisant
12 conciliatory

peaceful
4 calm 5 still, quiet 6 irenic, placid, serene
7 equable, pacific 8 composed, tranquil
9 unruffled 10 harmonious, nonviolent,
untroubled

peacemaker
7 arbiter 8 mediator, pacifier, placater
10 arbitrator, negotiator 11 conciliator,
pacificator

peace officer
3 cop 6 police 9 policeman 11 police-
woman

peach
3 rat 4 blab, tree 5 fruit 6 betray, inform,
reveal, snitch, squeal 9 freestone,
humdinger, nectarine 10 clingstone
11 crackerjack
family: 4 rose

Peach State
7 Georgia

peachy
4 fine, good, nice 5 dandy, nifty, super,
swell 8 pleasant, pleasing 9 excellent,
hunky-dory, marvelous, wonderful

peacockish
5 showy, swank 6 chichi, flashy, swanky
7 splashy 8 show-offy 10 flamboyant
11 pretentious 12 ostentatious

peak
3 alp, top, tor 4 acme, apex, bill, crag, roof
5 crest, crown, mount, visor 6 apogee,
summit, vertex, zenith 8 capsheaf,
capstone, meridian, mountain, pinnacle
Adirondack: 9 Whiteface
Africa's highest: 4 Kibo
Alaska-Canada: 12 Mt. Saint Elias
Andes: 4 Ruiz 5 Torrá
Apennines: 5 Amaro
Argentina: 4 Azul 5 Negra, Payún
Bavaria: 5 Arber
Berkshires: 8 Greylock
Black Hills: 8 Rushmore
Bolivia: 5 Cuzco, Tahua, Ubina 6 Sajama
Borneo: 4 Raja
California: 6 Shasta, Sonora 7 Palomar
8 Half Dome 9 Excelsior, Whitney
Canada: 5 Keele
Canaries: 5 Teide 8 Tenerife
Carpathian: 4 Rysy
Cascades: 7 Rainier
Catskill: 6 Pisgah
Caucasus: 5 Ushba 6 Elbrus
Chile: 4 Mayo, Pili 5 Paine, Pular
Colombia: 4 Tama 5 Neiva
Colorado: 3 Ute 5 Pikes 9 Purgatory
Cuba: 8 Turquino
Ecuador: 10 Chimborazo
England: 11 Scafell Pike
Ethiopia: 4 Guna 5 Holla
France: 5 Pilat
French Guiana: 5 Amana
Georgia: 8 Springer
Glacier National Park: 8 Kootenai
Greece: 4 Ossa 5 Pelion
Himalayas: 3 Api 5 Kamet 6 Lhotse
10 Gasherbrum
Honshū: 4 Yari 10 Yarigatake
Idaho: 11 Pend Oreille
Iran: 8 Damavand
Italy: 4 Etna 8 Vesuvius
Japan: 4 Sobo 5 Oyama 7 Sobozan
Java: 6 Slamet
Jordan: 6 Gilead
Karakoram Range: 7 Dapsang
10 Masherbrum 12 Godwin Austen
Maine: 8 Katahdin 10 Saddleback
Montana: 8 Gallatin
Nevada: 3 Ely
Newfoundland: 9 Gros Morne
New Hampshire: 9 Monadnock
New Zealand: 3 Una 4 Cook 7 Aorangi
8 Aspiring
Oahu: 5 Kaala
Oregon: 4 Hood
Papua New Guinea: 8 Victoria
Pennine Alps: 10 Matterhorn, Mont
Cervin

Philippines: 4 High
Pyrenees: 11 de Vignemale
Russia's highest: 6 Elbrus
Scotland: 8 Ben Nevis
Sicily: 4 Etna
Spain: 5 Yelmo 8 Mulhacén
Switzerland: 3 Dom 4 Dôle, Tödi
5 Eiger, Mönch 6 La Dôle, Rusein
7 Pilatus 8 Jungfrau
Tanzania: 11 Kilimanjaro
Utah: 5 Kings
Venezuela: 5 Icutú
Vermont: 8 Haystack, Stratton
8 Ascutney 9 Mansfield
Washington: 7 Olympus, Rainier
11 Saint Helens
White Mts.: 10 Washington
Wyoming: 3 Elk 10 Grand Teton
Yukon: 4 King 5 Logan

peaked
3 ill, wan 4 ashy, pale, sick 5 acute,
ashen, drawn, sharp 6 ailing, pallid, sickly
7 pointed 9 emaciated

peal
4 bell, bong, ring, toll 5 chime, knell, sound
7 ringing 8 ding-dong

peanut
6 goober, legume 10 foam pellet

pear
4 Bosc 5 Anjou, Hardy 6 Comice, Garber,
Seckel 7 Kieffer, LeConte 8 Bartlett
cider: 5 perry

pearl
3 gem 4 dear 5 jewel 7 paragon
8 treasure

Pearl Mosque site
4 Agra

pearly
8 lustrous, nacreous, precious
10 iridescent, opalescent

pear-shaped
8 pyriform

peasant
4 carl, kern, peon, serf 5 churl 6 rustic
7 bumpkin, hayseed, villein
Arab: 6 fellah
Latin-American: 9 campesino
Russian: 6 muzhik

peccary
8 javelina
genus: 7 Tayassu

peck
3 lot, nag 4 buss, carp, fuss, heap, kiss,

load, mess, pile, poke **6** carp at, nibble, pick at, pick up, pierce, strike **8** quantity

pecking order
6 ladder **7** pyramid **9** food chain, hierarchy

peculate
5 steal **8** embezzle **9** defalcate
11 appropriate

peculiar
3 odd **4** rare **5** queer, weird **6** unique
7 bizarre, curious, oddball, offbeat, special, strange, unusual **8** abnormal, singular, specific, uncommon **9** eccentric
10 individual, particular **11** distinctive

peculiarity
4 mark **5** quirk, trait **6** oddity **7** feature, quality **8** property **9** attribute, character, mannerism **12** eccentricity, idiosyncrasy

pecuniary
6 fiscal **8** economic, monetary **9** financial

pedagogue
5 tutor **6** pedant **7** teacher **8** educator
12 schoolmaster

pedagogy
8 teaching **9** education

pedal
5 lever **7** bicycle, treadle
digit: 3 toe

pedant
7 teacher **9** formalist **10** schoolmarm
12 precisionist

pedantic
3 dry **4** arid, dull **6** stodgy **7** bookish, donnish, erudite, learned, tedious
8 academic, didactic, priggish **9** ponderous
10 pedestrian, scholastic **11** pedagogical
13 unimaginative

peddle
4 hawk, push, sell, vend **5** pitch **6** monger
8 huckster

peddler
6 coster, dealer, hawker, monger, vendor
8 huckster, merchant, promoter
9 tradesman **12** costermonger

pedestal
4 base, foot **5** stand **7** footing, support
10 foundation **12** underpinning
part: 4 dado **6** plinth **7** subbase

pedestrian
4 blah, dull **5** banal **6** dreary, stodgy, walker **7** humdrum, mundane, prosaic

8 everyday, ordinary **11** commonplace
13 unimaginative

pedigree
6 origin, purity **7** descent, history, lineage
8 ancestry, purebred **9** bloodline, genealogy **10** background, extraction, family tree

peduncle
4 stem **5** stalk **7** pedicel

peek
3 spy **4** look **6** glance **7** glimpse

peel
4 bark, pare, rind, skin **5** flake, scale, strip
7 take off **8** flake off **9** break away, exfoliate

peeled
4 bare, open **5** naked **7** denuded, exposed **8** stripped **9** uncovered

peep
3 see, spy **4** look **5** chirp, tweet, watch
6 glance, squeak **7** glimpse, twitter
9 sandpiper

Peeping Tom
5 snoop **6** voyeur **7** prowler, snooper

peer
3 pry **4** gaze, lord **5** equal, glare, noble, stare **6** goggle, squint **9** associate
British: 4 duke, earl **5** baron **7** marquis
8 marquess, viscount

Peer Gynt
author: 5 Ibsen (Henrik)
beloved: 7 Solveig
composer: 5 Grieg (Edvard)
mother: 3 Ase **4** Aase

peerless
4 best **6** unique **7** perfect, supreme
8 superior **9** matchless, nonpareil, paramount, unequaled, unmatched, unrivaled **12** incomparable, unparalleled

peeve
3 bug, irk, vex **4** miff, rile **5** anger, annoy, pique **6** bother, nettle, put out **7** disturb, provoke **8** irritate, nuisance, vexation
9 aggravate, annoyance, grievance
10 exasperate **11** aggravation

peevish
4 sour **5** cross, testy **6** cranky, grumpy, ornery **7** fretful, whining **8** petulant
9 fractious, irritable, obstinate, querulous
11 ill-tempered

peewee
4 runt, tyke **5** dwarf, pygmy, small, squirt

Peewee _____
6 midget, shaver, shrimp 9 miniature
10 diminutive, flycatcher 11 lilliputian

Peewee _____
5 Reese

peg
3 fix, pin 4 hold, mark, plod, plug, step,
work 5 dowel, place, prong, stake, throw
6 attach, degree, fasten, hustle, marker,
reason 7 pin down, pretext, support
8 identify, restrict

Pegasus
5 horse, steed
rider: 11 Bellerophon

pejorative
7 adverse 8 critical, debasing 9 slighting
10 belittling, derogatory, detractive
11 denigrating, deprecatory, disparaging,
opprobrious, unfavorable 12 depreciatory

pelagic
6 marine 7 oceanic 8 maritime

Peleus
brother: 7 Telamon
father: 6 Aeacus
half brother: 8 Phocus
son: 8 Achilles
victim: 8 Eurytion
wife: 6 Thetis

pelf
4 loot, swag 5 booty, money, moola
6 boodle, moolah, riches, spoils 7 plunder

Pelias
country: 6 Iolcus
father: 8 Poseidon
half brother: 5 Aeson
son: 7 Acastus

Pelican State
9 Louisiana

Pelléas
beloved: 9 Mélisande
brother, slayer: 6 Golaud

Pelles
daughter: 6 Elaine
grandson: 7 Galahad

pellet
3 wad 4 ball, shot 6 sphere 10 projectile

Pellinore
slayer: 6 Gawain
son: 5 Torre 6 Dornar 7 Lamerok
8 Percival 9 Agglovale

pell-mell
5 chaos, snarl 6 muddle, rashly 7 chaotic,
clutter, hastily 8 confused, disarray,
disorder, headlong, reckless 9 confusion,
haphazard, hurriedly 10 carelessly,
heedlessly 11 hurry-scurry 13 helter-
skelter

pellucid
5 clear, plain, sheer 6 limpid 7 crystal,
evident, obvious 8 clear-cut, luminous
9 unblurred 10 see-through 11 crystalline,
transparent

Pelops
father: 8 Tantalus
son: 6 Atreus 8 Pittheus, Thyestes
wife: 10 Hippodamia

pelota
4 ball 7 jai alai

pelt
3 fur, run 4 beat, blow, dash, drub, hide,
hurl, rush, skin, whop 5 hurry, pound,
scoot, speed, strip, throw, whack 6 assail,
batter, pepper, pummel, strike, wallop
7 bombard, hotfoot

pen
3 sty 4 cage, coop, jail, swan 5 pound,
quill, write 6 cooler, corral, indite, prison,
shut in, stylus, writer 7 close in, confine,
enclose, fence in 9 ballpoint, enclosure

penal
8 punitive 12 correctional, disciplinary

penalize
4 dock, fine 5 mulct 6 punish 7 deprive
8 handicap 10 discipline 12 disadvantage

penalty
4 fine, loss 5 mulct 7 damages, forfeit
8 hardship 10 amercement, forfeiture,
punishment 12 disadvantage

penance
4 rite 7 penalty 8 hardship 9 atonement
10 punishment

penchant
4 bent 5 taste 6 liking 7 leaning 8 affinity,
fondness, tendency 9 inclining
10 partiality, proclivity, propensity
11 inclination 12 predilection

pendant
4 flag, jack, rope 7 fixture 8 ornament
10 supplement

pendent
7 hanging 9 suspended, undecided,
unsettled 11 overhanging 12 undetermined

pending
6 during 8 awaiting, imminent 9 undecided, unsettled 12 undetermined

_____ **Pendragon**
5 Uther

pendulous
7 hanging 8 dangling, drooping, wavering 9 faltering, suspended, tentative, uncertain 10 hesitating, indecisive 11 vacillating

Penelope
father: 7 Icarius
father-in-law: 7 Laertes
husband: 7 Ulysses 8 Odysseus
mother: 8 Periboea
son: 10 Telemachus
suitor: 7 Agelaus

penetrable
6 porous 8 pervious 9 permeable

penetrate
3 jab 4 bore, go in, stab 5 break, drive, enter, probe, touch 6 affect, charge, invade, pierce 7 pervade 8 discover, encroach, perceive, permeate, puncture, saturate 9 percolate, perforate 10 understand

penetrating
4 keen 5 acute, sharp 6 astute, shrewd 8 incisive, piercing 9 trenchant 10 discerning, insightful, perceptive 11 quick-witted, sharp-witted 12 sharp-sighted

Peneus
daughter: 6 Daphne
father: 7 Oceanus
mother: 6 Tethys

penguin type
6 Adélie

_____ **Penh**
5 Phnom

peninsula
4 neck 10 chersonese
Alaska: 5 Kenai 6 Seward
Australia: 6 Tasman
Barents Sea: 5 Kanin
British colony: 9 Gibraltar
Canada: 8 Labrador
Chile: 5 Swett
Costa Rica: 3 Osa
Croatia: 6 Istria
Denmark: 7 Jutland
eastern United States: 8 Delmarva
Estonia: 5 Sorve
Florida: 8 Pinellas 9 Canaveral
France: 5 Giens

Greece: 4 Acte 10 Chalcidice 11 Peloponnese 12 Peloponnesus
Guam: 5 Orote
Hong Kong: 7 Kowloon
Honshu: 3 Izu 5 Miura
Massachusetts: 7 Cape Ann, Cape Cod
Mexico: 7 Yucatan 14 Baja California
Michigan: 8 Keweenaw
Middle East: 5 Sinai
New Guinea: 4 Huon
New Jersey: 9 Sandy Hook
New Zealand: 5 Banks, Mahia
Nunavut: 7 Boothia 8 Melville
Ontario: 5 Bruce
Persian Gulf: 9 Ras Tanura
Quebec: 5 Gaspé
Russia: 4 Kola 5 Taman, Yamal 6 Kolski, Taimyr 9 Kamchatka
Scotland: 7 Kintyre
South Australia: 4 Eyre 5 Yorke
Southeast Asia: 5 Malay 9 Indochina
southeastern Europe: 6 Balkan
southwestern Asia: 6 Arabia 7 Arabian
southwestern Europe: 7 Iberian
Texas: 9 Matagorda
Tierra del Fuego: 5 Mitre
Turkey: 8 Anatolia 9 Asia Minor
Ukraine: 5 Kerch
Wales: 5 Gower, Lleyn
Washington: 7 Olympic
Wisconsin: 4 Door

Peninsular State
7 Florida

penitence
3 rue 4 ruth 6 regret, sorrow 7 anguish, remorse 8 distress, humbling 10 contrition, repentance 11 compunction, self-reproof 12 self-reproach

penitent
5 sorry 6 rueful 8 contrite 9 regretful, repentant 10 apologetic, remorseful

penitentiary
see **prison**

penman
5 clerk 6 author, scribe, writer 7 copyist 9 scrivener 12 calligrapher

penmanship
4 hand 5 style 6 script 7 writing 11 calligraphy, chirography, handwriting

pen name
6 anonym 9 pseudonym 10 nom de plume
Addison, Joseph: 4 Clio
Arouet, François-Marie: 8 Voltaire
Beyle, Marie-Henri: 8 Stendhal
Blair, Eric: 12 George Orwell

Brontë, Anne: 9 Acton Bell
Brontë, Charlotte: 10 Currer Bell
Brontë, Emily: 9 Ellis Bell
Clemens, Samuel: 9 Mark Twain
Dickens, Charles: 3 Boz
Dodgson, Charles Lutwidge: 12 Lewis Carroll
Dupin, Amandine-Aurore: 10 George Sand
Evans, Mary Ann: 11 George Eliot
Faust, Frederick: 8 Max Brand
Franklin, Benjamin: 11 Poor Richard
Geisel, Theodore: 7 Dr. Seuss
Glidden, Frederick: 9 Luke Short
Lamb, Charles: 8 Elia
Munro, Hector Hugh: 4 Saki
Poquelin, Jean-Baptiste: 7 Molière
Porter, William Sidney: 6 O. Henry
Ramé, Maria Louise: 5 Ouida
Thibault, Jacques-Anatole-François: 13 Anatole France
Viaud, Louis-Marie-Julien: 10 Pierre Loti

pennant
4 flag, jack 5 color 6 banner, ensign 8 standard, streamer 9 banderole 12 championship

penniless
4 poor 5 broke, needy 8 bankrupt, indigent 9 destitute, insolvent 11 impecunious

pennon
4 flag, jack, wing 5 color 6 banner, ensign 8 bannerol, gonfalon, streamer 9 banderole, oriflamme

Pennsylvania
capital: 10 Harrisburg
city: 4 Erie 7 Reading 8 Scranton 9 Allentown 10 Pittsburgh 12 Philadelphia
college, university: 6 Drexel, Lehigh, Temple 7 LaSalle 8 Bryn Mawr, Bucknell 9 Dickinson, Lafayette, Penn State, Villanova 10 Swarthmore 14 Carnegie Mellon
mountain range: 6 Pocono
nickname: 8 Keystone (State)
river: 9 Allegheny 10 Schuylkill 11 Monongahela, Susquehanna
state bird: 12 ruffed grouse
state flower: 14 mountain laurel
state tree: 7 hemlock

penny-pincher
5 miser 7 niggard, scrooge 8 tightwad 9 skinflint 10 cheapskate

penny-pinching
4 mean 6 frugal, stingy, thrift 7 miserly, thrifty 9 frugality, niggardly, parsimony, penurious 11 tightfisted 12 cheeseparing, parsimonious

penny-wise
5 canny, tight 6 frugal, stingy 7 prudent, sparing, thrifty 9 provident 10 economical 12 parsimonious

pen point
3 neb, nib

pension
3 inn 5 hotel, lodge 6 hostel, reward 7 annuity, auberge, payment, stipend 8 gratuity 9 allowance 12 room and board, roominghouse 13 boardinghouse

pensioner
7 retiree

pensive
3 sad 6 dreamy, musing 7 wistful 10 meditative, melancholy, reflective, ruminative, thoughtful 11 preoccupied 13 contemplative

Pentateuch
5 Torah
books: 6 Exodus 7 Genesis, Numbers 9 Leviticus 11 Deuteronomy

Penthesilea
queen of: 7 Amazons
slayer: 8 Achilles

Pentheus
grandfather: 6 Cadmus
king of: 6 Thebes
mother: 5 Agave

penumbra
4 veil 5 cover, shade 6 fringe, screen, shadow, shroud 7 curtain

penurious
4 mean, poor 5 needy, tight 6 frugal, stingy 7 miserly 8 indigent 9 destitute, niggardly, stinting 11 impecunious, tightfisted 12 impoverished, parsimonious 13 penny-pinching

penury
4 need, want 7 beggary, distress, poverty 9 indigence, privation, pauperism 11 destitution, needfulness

peon
4 serf 5 slave 6 drudge, toiler 7 laborer, peasant 11 galley slave
Anglo-Saxon: 4 esne

peonage
4 yoke 6 thrall 7 bondage, helotry, serfdom, slavery 9 servitude, thralldom, villenage 11 enslavement

people
  3 kin 4 folk 5 plebs 6 public 7 society
8 populace 9 commoners, community,
plebeians 10 commonalty 11 inhabitants,
rank and file, third estate

pep
  3 vim 4 brio, dash 5 moxie, punch, verve,
vigor 6 energy 7 sparkle 8 vitality, vivacity
10 get-up-and-go, liveliness 11 high spirits

pepo
  5 gourd, melon 6 squash 7 pumpkin
8 cucumber

pepper
  4 pelt 5 chili 6 season, shower
7 cayenne, paprika, pimento, tabasco
8 capsicum, cascabel, chipotle, habanero,
jalapeño, pimiento, sprinkle 9 condiment,
seasoning 12 Scotch bonnet

peppery
  3 hot 5 cross, fiery, sharp, spicy, testy,
zesty 6 biting, lively, snappy, touchy
7 piquant, pungent 8 choleric, poignant,
seasoned, stinging 9 irascible, irritable
11 hot-tempered 13 quick-tempered

peppy
  5 alert, perky 6 active, bright, lively
7 vibrant 8 animated, spirited, vigorous
9 energetic, sprightly, vivacious

_____ **Pepys**
  6 Samuel

Pequod
  cabin boy: 3 Pip
  captain: 4 Ahab
  harpooner: 6 Daggoo 8 Queequeg,
Tashtego
  mate: 8 Starbuck

per
  3 via 4 a pop, each, with 6 apiece 7 by
way of, for each, through 9 by means of
12 individually

perambulate
  4 walk 6 ramble, stroll 8 traverse
9 promenade

per capita
  4 each 6 apiece, by each 7 equally, for
each

perceive
  3 see 4 espy, feel, know, mark, note
5 grasp, seize, sense 6 detect, notice,
remark 7 discern, observe, realize
8 identify 9 apprehend, recognize
10 comprehend, understand

percentage
  3 cut 4 part 5 piece, share, slice 6 profit

7 portion 9 advantage 10 commission,
proportion 11 probability

perceptible
  5 clear 6 marked 7 visible 8 apparent,
definite, distinct, palpable, sensible,
tangible 10 detectable, noticeable,
observable 11 appreciable, discernible
12 recognizable

perception
  4 idea 5 grasp, image 6 acumen, notion
7 concept, feeling, insight, thought
9 awareness, cognition 10 impression
11 discernment, observation
12 appreciation 13 understanding

perceptive
  4 keen, sage, wise 5 acute, alert, aware,
sharp 7 knowing 9 intuitive, observant,
sagacious, sensitive 10 discerning,
insightful, responsive 13 understanding

perch
  3 bar, peg, set 4 fish, land, rest, seat
5 light, roost, sit on 6 alight, settle 7 set
down, sit atop, sit down

perchance
  5 maybe 7 perhaps 8 possibly
11 conceivably

percipience
  6 acumen 8 keenness 9 cognition,
intuition 10 astuteness 11 discernment
12 appreciation, perspicacity
13 comprehension

percolate
  4 drip, ooze, seep 5 exude 6 charge, filter,
simmer, spread 7 pervade, trickle
9 penetrate

percussion
  3 jar 4 bump, jolt 5 clash, crash, shock
6 impact 8 collision 10 concussion
  instrument:
(see at **musical instrument**)

Perdita
  father: 7 Leontes
  mother: 8 Hermione

perdition
  4 hell 5 hades 7 inferno 9 damnation
10 underworld 11 netherworld

Père Goriot author
  6 Balzac (Honoré de)

peregrination
  4 trek, trip, walk 7 journey, travels
9 traversal 10 expedition

peremptory

5 bossy, final 7 haughty 8 absolute,
arrogant, decisive, dogmatic, imperial
9 imperious, masterful 10 autocratic,
commanding, disdainful, high-handed,
imperative 11 dictatorial, domineering,
magisterial, overbearing

perennial

7 durable 8 constant, enduring, lifelong
9 continual, long-lived, permanent,
perpetual, recurrent, unceasing
10 continuing, persistent, persisting,
unchanging 11 long-lasting

Perez

brother: 5 Zerah
father: 5 Judah
mother: 5 Tamar

perfect

4 full, pure 5 exact, ideal, model, right,
sound, total, utter, whole 6 entire, expert,
intact, polish, proper, refine 7 correct,
improve, precise 8 absolute, accurate,
complete, finished, flawless, outright,
peerless, spotless, unbroken, unflawed
9 downright, excellent, faultless, matchless,
stainless, unalloyed, undamaged, undiluted
10 consummate, impeccable, proficient
11 unequivocal, unmitigated, unqualified

perfection

4 acme 5 ideal 6 purity, virtue 7 paragon
9 integrity, wholeness 10 excellence,
excellency, saintliness 12 completeness,
flawlessness, transcendence
13 faultlessness

perfectly

5 fully, quite 6 wholly 7 to a turn, utterly
8 entirely 10 altogether, completely,
thoroughly

perfidious

5 false 6 untrue 8 disloyal 9 deceitful,
dishonest, faithless 10 treasonous,
traitorous, unfaithful, unreliable
11 treacherous

perfidy

6 deceit 7 falsity, sellout, treason
8 betrayal 9 falseness, treachery
10 disloyalty, infidelity 13 faithlessness

perforate

3 pit 4 bore 5 drill, prick, punch 6 pierce
8 puncture 9 penetrate

perform

3 act 4 play, work 5 enact 6 behave,
comply, effect 7 achieve, execute, fulfill,
operate, playact, present, satisfy 8 bring
off, carry out, complete, function
9 discharge, entertain, implement
10 accomplish

performance

3 act 4 deed, feat, show, work 6 acting,
action 7 conduct, display 8 behavior,
efficacy, exercise 9 discharge, execution,
operation 10 efficiency, exhibition
11 achievement, fulfillment 12 presentation

performer

4 doer, mime 5 actor, mimic 6 mummer,
player 7 actress, artiste, trouper
8 thespian 9 playactor 12 impersonator

perfume

4 balm 5 aroma, cense, scent, smell, spice
6 sachet 7 bouquet, incense, odorize
9 aromatize, fragrance, redolence
source: 4 musk 5 attar, myrrh, orris
8 bergamot

perfumer

6 Chanel (Coco)

perfunctory

7 cursory, routine 8 careless 9 automatic
10 impersonal, mechanical 11 superficial

pergola

5 arbor, bower 7 trellis

perhaps

5 maybe 8 feasibly, possibly 9 perchance
11 conceivably

periapt

see **amulet**

Pericles

father: 10 Xanthippus
mistress: 7 Aspasia
mother: 8 Agariste

peril

4 risk 6 danger, hazard, menace
8 exposure, jeopardy 9 liability
12 endangerment

perilous

5 hairy, risky 6 chancy, unsafe 7 unsound
9 dangerous, desperate, hazardous,
uncertain 11 treacherous

_____ Perilous

5 Siege

perimeter

4 edge 5 limit, verge 6 border, bounds,
margin 8 boundary

period

3 age, end, era 4 span, stop, term, time
5 cycle, phase, point, spell, stage 6 extent
8 division, duration, interval, sentence

periodic
6 cyclic, fitful 7 regular 8 cyclical, repeated, sporadic 9 cyclical, recurring 10 occasional 11 fluctuating 12 intermittent

periodical
5 organ 6 cyclic, review 7 journal 8 cyclical, magazine 9 alternate, newspaper, recurrent, recurring 10 isochronal 11 isochronous, publication 12 intermittent

peripatetic
6 moving, roving 7 nomadic, walking 8 ambulant, vagabond 9 itinerant, traveling, wayfaring 10 ambulatory, pedestrian, travelling 13 perambulatory

peripheral
6 remote 7 lateral, surface 8 far-flung, marginal, outlying 9 auxiliary, secondary 10 borderline, tangential 11 out-of-the-way 13 supplementary

perish
3 die, end 4 pass 5 cease 6 be lost, demise, depart, expire, vanish 7 decease, decline, go under, succumb 8 collapse, pass away 9 disappear

perjure
3 lie 6 delude 7 deceive, distort, falsify, mislead 8 forswear 9 misinform 10 equivocate 11 prevaricate

perk
4 gain, mend, plus 5 cheer, extra 7 benefit, freshen, improve, refresh, smarten 8 brighten

perky
5 alert, cocky, happy 6 bouncy, bubbly, cheery, chirpy, frisky, jaunty, lively, upbeat 7 buoyant, chipper 8 animated, cheerful, spirited, sportive 9 energetic, sparkling, sprightly, vivacious 12 effervescent, high-spirited

permanent
5 fixed 6 stable 7 abiding, durable, lasting 8 constant, enduring, hair wave 9 continual, perennial 10 changeless, invariable, unchanging 11 established, everlasting 12 imperishable

permeable
6 porous, spongy 8 pervious 9 diffusive 10 penetrable

permeate
6 drench, imbrue, infuse, spread 7 diffuse, pervade, suffuse 8 saturate 9 penetrate, percolate 10 impregnate, infiltrate 11 pass through

permissible
4 okay 5 legal 7 allowed 8 approved 9 allowable, tolerable, tolerated 10 acceptable, authorized, sanctioned

permission
5 leave 6 assent, permit 7 consent, license 8 approval, sanction 9 agreement, allowance 11 approbation, endorsement 12 acquiescence 13 authorization

permissive
3 lax 4 open 7 lenient, liberal 8 tolerant 9 easygoing, forgiving, indulgent 10 forbearing 11 acquiescent, complaisant

permit
3 let 4 okay, pass 5 agree, allow, grant, leave 6 accede, enable, say yes, suffer 7 consent, license, warrant 8 sanction, tolerate 9 allowance, authorize, give leave 10 permission 13 authorization

permutation
6 change 7 variety, version 9 variation 10 alteration, innovation 11 arrangement, vicissitude 12 modification

pernicious
4 evil 5 fatal, toxic 6 deadly, lethal, malign, wicked 7 baleful, baneful, harmful, hurtful, killing, malefic, noxious, ruinous 8 damaging, sinister, virulent 9 injurious, malignant, offensive, poisonous 10 maleficent 11 deleterious, destructive, detrimental, devastating

Pernod flavor
5 anise 8 licorice

perorate
5 speak 7 declaim, lecture 8 bloviate, harangue, proclaim 9 hold forth

perpend
5 study, weigh 6 ponder 7 examine, reflect 8 consider, think out 9 reflect on, think over 10 excogitate, think about 11 contemplate

perpendicular
5 plumb, sheer, steep 7 upright 8 straight, vertical 11 precipitate, precipitous

perpetrate
6 commit, effect 7 inflict, execute, perform 8 carry out 10 bring about

perpetual
7 endless, eternal, undying 8 constant,

unending **9** ceaseless, continual, incessant, perennial, recurrent, unceasing **10** continuous **11** everlasting, unremitting

perpetuate
7 sustain **8** conserve, continue, eternize, maintain, preserve **9** keep alive **10** eternalize **11** immortalize

perplex
5 befog, mix up, stump **6** baffle, bemuse, muddle, puzzle **7** buffalo, confuse, mystify, nonplus, perturb **8** befuddle, bewilder, confound, distract, entangle **9** dumbfound **10** discompose

perquisite
3 tip **4** gain **5** right **6** profit **7** benefit, payment **8** gratuity **9** privilege

per se
6 as such, solely **8** in itself **11** essentially **13** intrinsically

persecute
4 bait, ride **5** annoy, harry, hound, worry, wrong **6** badger, harass, hector, injure, molest, pester, pick on, plague, punish, pursue **7** afflict, oppress, torment, torture **8** aggrieve

Persephone
4 Kore **10** Proserpina
father: **4** Zeus **7** Jupiter
husband: **5** Hades, Pluto
mother: **5** Ceres **7** Demeter

Perseus
father: **4** Zeus **7** Jupiter
grandfather: **8** Acrisius
mother: **5** Danaë
victim: **6** Medusa **8** Acrisius
wife: **9** Andromeda

perseverance
8 tenacity **9** diligence, endurance **10** dedication **11** persistence **13** steadfastness

persevere
see **persist**

Persia
4 Iran

Persian
ancient: **4** Mede
fairy: **4** peri
governor: **6** satrap
language: **5** Parsi
mystic: **4** sufi
poet: **5** Hafez, Hafiz **7** Firdusi

8 Ferdowsi, Firdausi, Firdawsi, Firdousi **11** Omar Khayyám
prophet: **9** Zoroaster
robe: **6** caftan
sacred books: **6** Avesta
sun-god: **7** Mithras
title: **4** shah
writing: **9** cuneiform

persiflage
6 banter, joking **7** jesting, kidding, ribbing **8** badinage, raillery, repartee

persist
4 go on, last **5** abide **6** endure, hang on, keep on, linger **7** carry on, prevail **8** continue **9** persevere

persistence
8 duration **9** endurance **10** continuity **11** continuance **12** continuation

persistent
6 dogged **7** lasting **8** enduring, obdurate, stubborn **9** continual, steadfast, tenacious **10** continuing, determined, relentless, unshakable **11** persevering, unremitting

persnickety
5 fussy, picky **6** choosy **7** finicky **8** exacting **10** fastidious, particular

person
3 guy **4** self, soul **5** being, human **6** entity, mensch, mortal **8** creature, specimen **10** individual

personable
4 nice **6** genial **7** affable, amiable **8** charming, friendly, pleasant, pleasing **9** appealing, congenial **10** attractive

personage
3 VIP **5** human **6** bigwig, figure **7** big shot, notable **8** creature, luminary, somebody **9** celebrity, character, dignitary **10** individual

personal
3 own **5** privy **7** private, special **8** peculiar **10** individual, particular

personal effects
5 stuff **10** belongings **11** possessions

personality
3 ego, VIP **4** self **6** makeup, nature, temper, traits **7** notable **8** identity, selfhood, selfness **9** celebrity, character, dignitary **10** complexion, qualities **11** disposition, singularity, temperament **13** individualism, individuality

personate
3 act **4** play **5** enact **6** embody, typify

7 perform 9 epitomize, exemplify,
represent 10 illustrate

personify
6 embody, typify 8 stand for 9 actualize,
epitomize, exemplify, incarnate, represent,
symbolize 11 emblematize

perspective
4 view 5 angle, scene, slant, vista
7 outlook 8 position, prospect 9 viewpoint
10 standpoint 11 point of view

perspicacious
4 keen 5 acute, quick, savvy, sharp
6 astute, clever, shrewd 9 observant,
sagacious 10 discerning, insightful,
perceptive 11 penetrating

perspicacity
6 acumen 7 insight 8 keenness
10 astuteness, shrewdness 11 discernment, penetration, percipience

perspicuous
5 clear, lucid, plain 6 lucent, simple
7 crystal, precise 8 clear-cut, pellucid
11 unambiguous

perspiration
5 sweat

perspire
see **sweat**

persuadable
4 open 7 willing 9 receptive 11 suggestible, susceptible

persuade
3 win 4 coax, lead, sell, sway, urge
5 argue 6 entice, induce, prompt
7 convert, impress, win over 8 convince
9 influence, prevail on 11 bring around

persuasion
4 kind, mind, sort, type, view 5 group
6 belief, school 7 faction, opinion
8 argument 9 character, prejudice,
sentiment 10 connection, conviction
11 affiliation, description

Persuasion author
6 Austen (Jane)

persuasive
6 cogent 7 telling, winning 8 credible
10 compelling, convincing 11 influential

pert
4 bold, chic, flip, trim 5 alert, cocky, fresh,
sassy, saucy, smart 6 brazen, bright,
cheeky, jaunty, lively 7 forward
8 animated, flippant, spirited 9 audacious,
sprightly, vivacious

pertain
5 apply, refer 6 affect, bear on, belong,
regard, relate 7 concern 8 bear upon
9 touch upon

pertinacious
4 firm 5 fixed 6 dogged, mulish 7 willful
8 resolute, stubborn 9 obstinate, tenacious
10 inflexible, persistent, unshakable,
unyielding

pertinent
3 apt, fit 5 ad rem 7 apropos, fitting,
germane 8 apposite, material, relevant
10 applicable 11 appropriate

perturb
5 upset, worry 6 bother 7 agitate, disturb,
fluster, trouble 8 disorder, disquiet, unsettle
10 discompose, disconcert

Peru
  ancient civilization: 4 Inca
  capital: 4 Lima
  city: 5 Cusco, Cuzco 6 Callao
  7 Arequipa, Trujillo
  conqueror: 7 Pizarro (Francisco)
  ethnic group: 7 Quechua
  lake: 8 Titicaca
  language: 6 Aymara 7 Quechua, Spanish
  leader: 8 Fujimori (Alberto)
  monetary unit: 3 sol
  mountain, range: 5 Andes 9 Huascarán
  neighbor: 5 Chile 6 Brazil 7 Bolivia,
  Ecuador 8 Colombia
  river: 6 Amazon 7 Marañón
  volcano: 5 Misti 7 El Misti 8 Yucamani

peruse
4 read, scan 5 study 6 survey 7 examine
8 consider, look over, pore over

pervade
5 imbue 6 spread 7 diffuse 8 permeate,
saturate 9 penetrate, percolate, transfuse
10 impregnate

perverse
5 balky 6 cranky, mulish, ornery 7 corrupt,
deviant, froward, peevish, wayward, willful
8 contrary, depraved, improper, stubborn
9 incorrect, irritable, obstinate 10 degenerate, headstrong, refractory 11 stiff-
necked, wrongheaded 12 cross-grained,
unreasonable

pervert
4 ruin, skew, warp 5 abuse, twist
6 debase, divert, garble, misuse 7 corrupt,
debauch, deprave, distort, deviant, falsify,
vitiate 8 misstate, mistreat 9 misdirect
11 misconstrue 12 misinterpret,
misrepresent

pervious
4 open 6 porous 9 permeable
10 accessible, penetrable

pesky
6 vexing 7 irksome 8 annoying
9 vexatious 10 bothersome 11 troublesome

pessimist
5 cynic 9 Cassandra, defeatist, doomsayer, worrywart 11 misanthrope

pessimistic
6 gloomy, morose 7 cynical 10 despairing
11 distrustful 12 misanthropic

pest
4 bane 5 trial, worry 6 bother, plague, vermin 7 nudnick, trouble 8 irritant, nuisance, vexation 9 annoyance, tormentor

pester
3 bug, irk, nag 4 ride 5 annoy, harry, hassle, tease, worry 6 badger, bother, harass, plague 7 bedevil, disturb, torment 8 irritate

pestiferous
7 baneful, noxious 8 annoying, infected
9 infective, pestilent 10 pernicious
11 troublesome 12 pestilential

pestilence
5 curse 6 plague 7 scourge

pestilential
5 fatal 6 deadly, lethal, vexing 7 baneful, deathly, noxious, ruinous 8 annoying
10 pernicious

pestle
4 mano 6 muller
vessel: 6 mortar

pet
3 hug 4 dear, kiss, love, neck, pout, sulk
5 loved 6 caress, cosset, dandle, fondle, pamper, stroke 7 beloved, cherish, darling, indulge 8 favorite, treasure 9 cherished, endearing, sulkiness

petcock
3 tap 5 valve 6 faucet, spigot

Peter Grimes composer
7 Britten (Benjamin)

peter out
4 fade, wane 5 abate, cease 6 lessen, recede, run dry 7 dwindle 8 decrease, diminish, taper off 9 drain away

Peter Pan
author: 6 Barrie (James)

character: 5 Wendy 7 Michael 9 Tiger Lily 10 Tinker Bell
dog: 4 Nana
pirate: 4 Hook, Smee

Peter the Apostle
brother: 6 Andrew
father: 5 Jonah
original name: 5 Simon

Peter the Great
father: 6 Alexis
wife: 7 Eudoxia 9 Catherine

petite
5 small 6 little 8 smallish 10 diminutive

petition
3 ask 4 plea 5 plead 6 appeal
7 beseech, entreat, implore, request, solicit
8 entreaty 10 supplicate 11 application
12 supplication

Petrarch's beloved
5 Laura

Petrified Forest author
8 Sherwood (Robert)

petrify
4 daze, numb, stun 5 chill, scare
6 benumb, deaden, harden 7 startle
8 confound, frighten, paralyze

Petruchio's wife
9 Katharina, Katharine

pettifogger
7 shyster 8 quibbler 9 nitpicker

petty
4 mean 5 minor, small 6 measly, narrow, paltry 7 trivial 8 niggling, picayune, piddling, trifling 9 frivolous, secondary
10 irrelevant, negligible 11 small-minded, subordinate, unimportant 13 insignificant

petty officer
6 noncom

petulant
5 huffy, moody, sulky, testy, whiny 6 touchy
7 grouchy, peevish 8 snappish 9 irascible, irritable, querulous 10 ill-humored

pew
3 row 4 seat 5 bench

peyote
6 cactus, mescal
drug: 9 mescaline

Phaedra
father: 5 Minos
husband: 7 Theseus
mother: 8 Pasiphaë
sister: 7 Ariadne

stepson: 10 Hippolytus

Phaëthon's father
6 Helios 7 Phoebus

phalanx
4 army, host, mass 5 horde 6 myriad,
throng 6 troops

phantasm
5 dream, fancy, ghost 6 spirit, vision
7 fantasy, fiction, figment, specter, spectre
8 daydream, delusion, illusion 9 invention
10 apparition 11 fabrication
13 hallucination

phantom
5 dummy, ghost, shade, spook 6 goblin,
shadow, spirit, vision 7 bugbear, chimera,
eidolon, specter, spectre 8 illusory
9 imaginary 10 apparition, fictitious
12 will-o'-the-wisp

pharaoh
3 Tut 4 Seti 5 Menes, ruler 6 Ahmose,
Ramses, tyrant 7 Harmhab 8 Ikhnaton,
Thutmose 9 Amenhotep, Merneptah
11 Tutankhamen

pharisee
9 hypocrite

pharmacist
8 druggist 10 apothecary
British: 7 chemist

pharos
6 beacon 10 lighthouse

Pharsalus, battle of
vanquished: 6 Pompey
victor: 6 Caesar (Julius)

phase
4 part, side, view 5 point, stage, state
6 adjust, aspect 7 conduct 8 carry out,
position 9 condition, situation, viewpoint
10 appearance

PhD exam
5 orals

Phèdre author
6 Racine (Jean)

phenomenal
6 actual 7 unusual 8 material, physical,
sensible, singular, tangible, uncommon
9 corporeal, fantastic, objective
10 remarkable 11 exceptional,
outstanding, perceivable, perceptible,
substantial 13 extraordinary

phenomenon
4 fact 5 event 6 marvel, object, rarity,

wonder 7 miracle, reality 9 actuality,
sensation 10 experience, uniqueness
11 peculiarity, singularity

Phi _____ Kappa
4 Beta

philander
8 womanize

philanthropic
6 giving, humane 8 generous 10 altruistic,
benevolent, bighearted, charitable
11 magnanimous 12 eleemosynary,
humanitarian

philanthropist
American: 5 Gates (Bill) 6 Cooper
(Peter), Girard (Stephen), Mellon (Andrew)
7 Cornell (Ezra), Eastman (George),
Packard (David), Whitney (Gertrude
Vanderbilt) 8 Carnegie (Andrew), Stanford
(Leland) 9 Rosenwald (Julius)
10 Vanderbilt (Cornelius) 11 Rockefeller
(J. D.)
English: 11 Wilberforce (William)
Swedish: 5 Nobel (Alfred)

Philemon's wife
6 Baucis

philharmonic
8 symphony 9 orchestra, symphonic

Philip of Macedonia
father: 7 Amyntas
son: 9 Alexander

philippic
6 tirade 8 diatribe, harangue, jeremiad
12 condemnation

Philippics author
6 Cicero

Philippines
capital: 6 Manila
city: 4 Cebu 5 Davao 10 Quezon City
discoverer: 8 Magellan (Ferdinand)
island: 4 Cebu 5 Leyte, Luzon, Panay,
Samar 6 Negros 7 Masbate, Mindoro,
Palawan 8 Mindanao
language: 7 Ilocano, Tagalog 8 Filipino,
Pilipino
leader: 6 Aquino (Corazon), Marcos
(Ferdinand)
liberator: 9 MacArthur (Douglas)
patriot: 5 Rizal (José)
monetary unit: 4 peso
sea: 4 Sulu 5 Samar 7 Celebes, Sibuyan,
Visayan 8 Mindanao 10 Philippine, South
China
volcano: 4 Taal 5 Mayon

Philippi victor
6 Antony (Marc, Mark) 8 Octavian

Philip the Tetrarch
father: 5 Herod
mother: 9 Cleopatra

philistine
4 boob 7 Babbitt 9 bourgeois, vulgarian
10 capitalist 11 materialist

Philistine
champion: 7 Goliath
city: 4 Gath, Gaza 5 Ekron 6 Ashdod
8 Ashkelon
foe: 5 David 6 Samson
god: 5 Dagon

Philoctetes
father: 5 Poeas
victim: 5 Paris

Philomela
11 nightingale
father: 7 Pandion
ravisher: 6 Tereus
sister: 6 Procne

philosopher
American: 5 Adler (Mortimer), Dewey
(John), James (William), Quine (Willard),
Rorty (Richard), Royce (Josiah) 6 Langer
(Susanne), Peirce (C. S.) 7 Marcuse
(Herbert), Mumford (Lewis), Strauss (Leo)
9 Santayana (George)
Arab: 8 Averroës, Avicenna
Austrian: 6 Popper (Karl) 12 Wittgenstein
(Ludwig)
Chinese: 5 Laoxi 6 Lao-tsu 7 Dai Zhen,
Mencius, Tai Chen 9 Confucius
Danish: 11 Kierkegaard (Soren)
Dutch: 7 Erasmus (Desiderius), Spinoza
(Baruch de)
English: 4 Ayer (A. J.), Mill (John Stuart),
More (Henry, Thomas), Watt (James)
5 Bacon (Francis), Burke (Edmund), Locke
(John), Moore (G. E.), Occam (William of),
Paine (Thomas) 6 Berlin (Isaiah), Hobbes
(Thomas), Huxley (Thomas), Ockham
(William), Popper (Karl) 7 Bentham
(Jeremy), Russell (Bertrand), Spencer
(Herbert), Whewell (William) 9 Whitehead
(Alfred North) 12 Wittgenstein (Ludwig)
Finnish: 11 Westermarck (Edward)
French: 4 Weil (Simone) 5 Comte
(Auguste), Taine (Hippolyte) 6 Pascal
(Blaise), Sartre (Jean-Paul), Valéry (Paul)
7 Abelard (Peter), Bergson (Henri), Derrida
(Jacques), Diderot (Denis), Fourier
(Charles) 8 Foucault (Michel), Maritain
(Jacques), Rousseau (Jean-Jacques),
Voltaire 9 Descartes (René), Montaigne
(Michel de) 10 Saint-Simon (Comte de)
11 Montesquieu (Baron de) 12 Merleau-
Ponty (Maurice)
German: 4 Kant (Immanuel), Marx (Karl)
5 Frege (Gottlob), Hegel (Georg Wilhelm
Friedrich), Wolff (Christian von) 6 Carnap
(Rudolf), Fichte (Immanuel, Johann),
Herder (Johann von) 7 Husserl (Edmund),
Jaspers (Karl), Leibniz (Gottfried)
8 Spengler (Oswald) 9 Heidegger (Martin),
Nietzsche (Friedrich), Schelling (Friedrich
von) 12 Schopenhauer (Arthur)
14 Albertus Magnus
Greek: 4 Zeno 5 Plato, Timon 6 Thales
7 Gorgias, Proclus 8 Diogenes, Epicurus,
Longinus, Socrates 9 Aristotle, Epictetus
10 Anaxagoras, Democritus, Empedocles,
Heraclitus, Parmenides, Protagoras,
Pythagoras, Xenocrates, Xenophanes
11 Anaximander 12 Theophrastus
Irish: 8 Berkeley (George)
Italian: 5 Croce (Benedetto) 6 Ficino
(Marsilio) 11 Machiavelli (Niccolo)
Jewish: 5 Buber (Martin), Philo
10 Maimonides (Moses) 12 Philo Judaeus
Roman: 5 Seneca (Lucias Annaeus)
8 Boethius (Anicius), Plotinus 9 Lucretius
Scottish: 4 Hume (David), Mill (James),
Reid (Thomas) 7 Stewart (Dugald)
Spanish: 6 Suárez (Francisco)
7 Unamuno (Miguel de) 13 Ortega y
Gasset (José)
Swedish: 10 Swedenborg (Emanuel)

philosopher's stone
3 key 6 elixir

philosophical
4 calm 7 stoical 8 composed, rational,
resigned 9 unruffled 10 thoughtful

philosophy
6 system, theory, values 7 beliefs, inquiry
8 attitude, calmness 10 discipline
component: 5 logic 6 ethics
10 aesthetics 11 metaphysics
12 epistemology

philter
4 drug 5 charm, tonic 6 potion 9 stimulant
10 love potion 11 aphrodisiac, restorative

Phineas
beloved: 9 Andromeda
tormentors: 7 Harpies
wife: 9 Cleopatra

phlegm
5 humor, mucus 6 apathy 8 calmness,
coolness, dullness 9 composure, sangfroid

10 equanimity **11** impassivity, nonchalance
12 indifference

phlegmatic
4 calm, cool, dull **5** aloof, stoic **6** stolid
8 detached **9** apathetic, impassive,
lethargic **11** indifferent, unconcerned

Phlegyas
daughter: 7 Coronis
father: 4 Ares, Mars
son: 5 Ixion

phobia
see **fear**

Phobos
4 moon **9** satellite
brother: 6 Deimos
father: 4 Ares, Mars

Phocus
father: 6 Aeacus **8** Ornytion
half brother: 6 Peleus **7** Telamon
mother: 8 Psamathe
slayer: 6 Peleus **7** Telamon
wife: 7 Antiope

Phoebe
5 Diana **7** Artemis
daughter: 4 Leto
father: 9 Leucippus
mother: 4 Gaea

Phoebus
see **Apollo**

Phoenician
city: 4 Acre, Tyre **5** Sidon
colony: 8 Carthage
god: 4 Baal **6** Eshmun
goddess: 6 Baltis **7** Astarte

Phoenix
pupil: 8 Achilles
sister: 6 Europa
team: 4 Suns **7** Coyotes **9** Cardinals
12 Diamondbacks

phony
4 fake, sham **5** bogus, cheat, faker, false,
fraud **6** humbug, pseudo **8** impostor,
specious, spurious **9** charlatan, dishonest,
pretender **10** ficticious, suspicious
11 counterfeit **12** hypocritical

photograph
3 pic **4** film, snap **5** shoot **6** glossy
7 picture, tintype **8** snapshot
three-dimensional: 8 hologram

photographer
8 photoist **9** cameraman **10** shutterbug
famous: 3 Ray (Man) **4** Capa (Cornell,
Robert), Haas (Ernst), Hine (Lewis), Penn
(Irving), Riis (Jacob) **5** Adams (Ansel),

Arbus (Diane), Atget (Eugène), Brady
(Mathew), Evans (Frederick, Walker), Horst
(Horst Peter), Karsh (Yousuf), Lange
(Dorothea), Model (Lisette), Nadar, Parks
(Gordon), Ritts (Herb), Smith (W. Eugene),
Weber (Bruce), White (Clarence, Minor)
6 Abbott (Berenice), Avedon (Richard),
Beaton (Cecil), Brandt (Bill), Coburn (Alvin),
Curtis (Edward S.), Newton (Helmut),
Porter (Eliot), Rowell (Galen), Siegel (Eliot),
Strand (Paul), Talbot (William Henry Fox),
Weegee, Wegman (William), Weston
(Brett, Edward) **7** Brassaï, Cameron (Julia
Margaret), Emerson (Peter), Halsman
(Philippe), Jackson (William Henry),
Kertész (André), Salomon (Erich), Siskind
(Aaron), Snowdon (Earl of), Thomson
(John), Watkins (Carleton) **8** Callahan
(Harry), Cosindas (Marie), Daguerre (Louis-
Jacques-Mandé), Kasebier (Gertrude),
Scavullo (Francesco), Steichen (Edward),
Steinert (Otto) **9** Caponigro (Paul),
Feininger (Andreas), Leibovitz (Annie),
Meyrowitz (Joel), Muybridge (Eadweard),
O'Sullivan (Timothy), Rejlander (Oscar),
Rothstein (Arthur), Stieglitz (Alfred),
Winogrand (Garry) **10** Cunningham
(Imogen), Heartfield (John), Moholy-Nagy
(Laszlo) **11** Bourke-White (Margaret),
Eisenstaedt (Alfred) **12** Mapplethorpe
(Robert)

photographic
5 exact, vivid **7** graphic **8** accurate,
detailed **9** pictorial **11** picturesque
solution: 4 hypo **5** fixer, toner **7** reducer
9 developer

phrase
5 couch, frame, idiom **6** slogan **7** diction,
express, styling, wording **8** locution,
verbiage **9** catchword, formulate,
verbalism, watchword **10** expression

Phrygian
god: 4 Atys **5** Attis
goddess: 6 Cybele
king: 5 Midas **7** Gordius

phylactery
5 charm **6** amulet **7** periapt **8** talisman

physic
4 cure, heal **5** purge **6** remedy
8 medicine **9** cathartic, purgative
10 medication

physical
4 real **5** lusty, rough **6** actual, bodily,
carnal, sexual **7** fleshly, natural, somatic
8 concrete, corporal, material, sensible,
tangible **9** corporeal, objective

10 phenomenal **11** perceivable, perceptible, substantial

physician
3 doc **5** medic **6** doctor, medico
7 surgeon **8** sawbones
American: 4 Rush (Benjamin), Salk (Jonas) **5** Minot (George), Spock (Benjamin), Still (Andrew) **6** Jarvik (Robert), Murphy (John), Weller (Thomas) **7** Huggins (Charles), Robbins (Frederick), Theiler (Max) **8** Richards (Dickinson) **9** Sternberg (George Miller)
Arab: 8 Avicenna
Canadian: 5 Osler (William)
English: 4 Ross (Ronald) **6** Harvey (William), Jenner (Edward, William), Willis (Thomas) **8** Sydenham (Thomas)
French: 5 Widal (Fernand) **7** Laveran (Charles) **10** Schweitzer (Albert)
German: 7 Sylvius (Franciscus)
Greek: 5 Galen **11** Hippocrates
Italian: 7 Galvani (Luigi)
South African: 7 Barnard (Christiaan)
Swiss: 10 Paracelsus
(see also **Nobel Prize winner physiology or medicine; surgeon**)

physicist
American: 4 Rabi (I. I.), Ting (Samuel) **5** Fermi (Enrico), Gibbs (J. Willard), Kusch (Polykarp), Mayer (Maria-Goeppert), Pauli (Wolfgang), Pupin (Michael), Segré (Emilio), Smyth (Henry DeWolf), Stern (Otto) **6** Teller (Edward), Townes (Charles), Wigner (Eugene) **7** Alvarez (Luis), Feynman (Richard), Goddard (Robert), Purcell (Edward) **8** Einstein (Albert), Gell-Mann (Murray), McMillan (Edwin), Millikan (Clark, Robert), Mulliken (Robert), Shockley (William), Van Allen (James) **9** Michelson (Albert), Schwinger (Julian) **11** Oppenheimer (J. Robert)
Austrian: 4 Mach (Ernst) **7** Doppler (Christian) **11** Schrödinger (Erwin)
British: 6 Stokes (George) **7** Tyndall (John) **8** Thompson (Benjamin, Silvanus)
Chinese: 4 Yang (Chen-ing)
Danish: 4 Bohr (Aage, Niels)
Dutch: 6 Zeeman (Pieter) **7** Huygens (Christian), Lorentz (Hendrik), Zernike (Frits) **11** Van der Waals (Johannes)
English: 4 Snow (C. P.) **5** Jeans (James), Joule (James) **6** Dalton (John), Kelvin (Baron), Newton (Isaac), Powell (Cecil) **7** Faraday (Michael), Hodgkin (Dorothy), Thomson (George, Joseph, William) **8** Rayleigh (Lord), Robinson (Robert) **9** Wollaston (William) **10** Richardson

(Owen), Rutherford (Ernest), Wheatstone (Charles)
French: 4 Néel (Louis) **5** Arago (François) **6** Ampère (André-Marie), Perrin (Jean-Baptiste) **7** Coulomb (Charles-Augustin de), Kastler (Alfred), Réaumur (René-Antoine de) **8** Lippmann (Gabriel)
German: 3 Ohm (Georg) **4** Laue (Max von), Wien (Wilhelm) **5** Hertz (Gustav, Heinrich), Stark (Johannes) **6** Jensen (Hans), Lenard (Philipp), Nernst (Walther), Planck (Max) **7** Meitner (Lise) **8** Roentgen (Wilhelm) **9** Helmholtz (Hermann von), Kirchhoff (Gustav), Mossbauer (Rudolf) **10** Fahrenheit (Daniel), Hofstadter (Robert)
Indian: 5 Raman (Chandrasekhara)
Irish: 6 Walton (Ernest)
Italian: 5 Rossi (Bruno), Volta (Alessandro) **7** Galileo (Galilei), Galvani (Luigi) **10** Torricelli (Evangelista)
Japanese: 7 Yukawa (Hideki) **8** Tomonaga (Shinichiro)
Mexican: 8 Vallarta (Manuel)
Russian: 4 Tamm (Igor) **6** Landau (Lev) **9** Prokhorov (Aleksandr)
Scottish: 4 Tait (Peter) **6** Wilson (Charles) **7** Maxwell (James Clerk)
Swedish: 7 Rydberg (Johannes) **8** Angstrom (Anders), Siegbahn (Kai, Karl)
Swiss: 6 Zwicky (Fritz) **7** Piccard (Auguste)
(see also **Nobel Prize winner physics**)

physiognomy
3 mug **4** face **5** front **6** aspect, visage **7** profile **8** features **9** character **10** lineaments **11** countenance, temperament

physiologist
English: 8 Starling (Ernest)
German: 5 Weber (Ernst), Wundt (Wilhelm) **7** Schwann (Theodor) **9** Helmholtz (Hermann von)
Italian: 11 Spallanzani (Lazzaro)
(see also **Nobel Prize winner physiology or medicine**)

physique
4 body, form **5** build, shape **6** figure, makeup **7** anatomy **9** structure **12** constitution

pianist
American: 4 Nero (Peter), Wild (Earl) **5** Arrau (Claudio), Janis (Byron), Watts (André) **6** Duchin (Peter), Joplin (Scott), Serkin (Peter, Rudolf) **7** Cliburn (Van), Istomin (Eugene), Ohlsson (Garrick), Perahia (Murray), Winston (George) **8** Graffman (Gary), Horowitz (Vladimir),

Pennario (Leonard) **9** Fleischer (Leon)
10 Johannesen (Grant), Rubinstein (Arthur)
Argentinian: 8 Argerich (Martha)
Austrian: 6 Czerny (Karl) **7** Brendel
(Alfred) **8** Schnabel (Artur)
Bulgarian: 11 Weissenberg (Alexis)
Canadian: 5 Gould (Glenn)
Cuban: 5 Bolet (Jorge)
English: 4 Hess (Myra) **5** Ogdon (John)
6 Curzon (Clifford)
French: 6 Cortot (Alfred) **7** Cziffra
(Gyorgy) **9** Casadesus (Robert),
Entremont (Philippe) **10** Saint-Saëns
(Camille)
German: 6 Kempff (Wilhelm)
8 Schumann (Clara) **9** Gieseking (Walter)
Hungarian: 5 Liszt (Franz) **7** Cziffra
(Gyorgy)
Italian: 6 Busoni (Ferruccio) **7** Pollini
(Maurizio) **8** Clementi (Muzio)
Japanese: 6 Uchida (Mitsuko)
Polish: 5 Chopin (Frédéric) **7** Hofmann
(Josef) **10** Paderewski (Ignacy),
Rubinstein (Arthur)
Romanian: 4 Lupu (Radu) **7** Lipatti (Dinu)
Russian: 6 Berman (Lazar), Gilels (Emil),
Kissin (Evgeny) **7** Richter (Sviatoslav)
8 Horowitz (Vladimir), Pachmann (Vladimir
von) **9** Ashkenazy (Vladimir)
10 Rubinstein (Anton) **12** Rachmaninoff
(Sergey)
Spanish: 6 Iturbi (José) **8** Granados
(Enrique) **10** de Larrocha (Alicia)
Swiss: 4 Anda (Geza)

piano
5 grand **6** softly, spinet **7** quietly, upright
9 baby grand
builder: 5 Knabe (William), Stein
(Johann), Zumpe (Johann) **7** Baldwin
(Dwight) **8** Steinway (Henry) **9** Bechstein
(Friedrich) **10** Chickering (Jonas),
Silbermann (Johann)
inventor: 10 Cristofori (Bartolomeo)
pedal: 6 damper **8** sostenuto

piazza
5 patio, plaza, porch, square **7** balcony,
gallery, portico, terrace, veranda
9 courtyard

picaroon
5 rogue, rover, thief **6** pirate **7** brigand,
corsair **8** sea rover **9** buccaneer
10 freebooter

picayune
5 petty **6** measly, paltry, trifle **7** trivial
8 piddling **11** small-minded **13** insignificant

pick
3 rob, tap **4** best, carp, cull, open, pilfer,
pull, take, tool **5** elect, pluck, probe, prize
6 choice, choose, chosen, option, pierce,
remove, select, unlock **7** harvest, provoke
8 selected **9** exclusive, single out

picket
4 pale, post **5** fence, guard, stake, watch
6 sentry, tether **7** enclose, lookout, protest
8 palisade, sentinel, watchman
11 demonstrate

pickle
3 fix, jam **4** dill, spot **5** brine, treat
6 plight, scrape **7** dilemma, gherkin,
trouble **8** marinate, preserve **10** difficulty
11 predicament

pick on
5 bully, harry, taunt, tease **6** hector, pester
9 criticize, single out

pick out
4 espy, name, spot **6** choose, descry,
detect, select, take in **7** discern **8** identify,
perceive **9** apprehend, ascertain,
recognize **11** distinguish

pickpocket
3 dip **5** thief **6** dipper **8** cutpurse

pick up
3 buy, get **4** cull, gain, earn, land, lift, tidy
5 catch, glean, hoist, learn, raise, run in
6 arrest, detain, gather, notice, obtain, pull
in, resume, revive **7** acquire, clean up,
collect, restart **8** perceive **9** apprehend
10 appreciate, understand

pickup
5 truck **9** detention **10** hitchhiker
11 improvement **12** acceleration

picky
5 fussy **6** choosy **7** finicky **10** fastidious,
particular, pernickety **11** persnickety

picnic
4 snap **5** cinch **6** breeze, outing
7 cookout **8** cakewalk **11** piece of cake

picture
4 limn, show **5** image, photo, pinup
7 drawing, tableau **8** describe, painting,
portrait **9** depiction, portrayal
10 simulacrum **11** delineation, description
13 spitting image
stand: 5 easel

picturesque
5 vivid **6** quaint, scenic **8** artistic, charming

piddling
4 puny 5 petty 6 meager, meagre, measly, paltry 7 trivial 8 picayune, trifling 11 Mickey Mouse, unimportant 13 insignificant

pie
4 flan, tart 5 pasty 6 pastry 7 cobbler, dessert 8 turnover

piebald
5 mixed 6 motley 7 mottled 10 multicolor

piece
4 part 5 patch, slice 6 member, parcel 7 firearm, portion, section, segment 8 division, fraction, fragment 9 allotment 10 allocation

pièce de résistance
8 main dish 9 showpiece 11 centerpiece, chef d'oeuvre, masterpiece

piecemeal
5 apart 7 gradual, slowly 8 bit by bit 9 by degrees, gradually 11 fragmentary

pied
6 motley 7 blotchy, brindle, dappled, mottled 8 brindled, speckled 9 multihued 10 variegated 11 varicolored 12 parti-colored

pier
4 anta, dock, quay, slip 5 berth, jetty, levee, wharf 6 column, pillar 8 pilaster
architectural: 4 anta

pierce
3 cut 4 stab 5 probe, spear 6 impale, incise, skewer 8 puncture 9 penetrate, perforate 10 run through

piercing
4 high, keen 5 acute, sharp 6 piping, shrill 8 shooting, stabbing, strident 9 knifelike 12 earsplitting
tool: 3 awl

piety
6 fealty 7 loyalty 8 devotion, fidelity, sanctity 9 reverence 10 allegiance, dedication, devoutness 12 faithfulness

piffle
4 bosh, bunk 5 hooey 6 drivel 7 baloney, rubbish, twaddle 8 malarkey, nonsense 10 balderdash

pig
3 hog 4 slob 5 shoat, swine 6 farrow, piglet, porker 7 casting, glutton
breed: 5 Duroc 8 Tamworth 9 Berkshire, Hampshire, Yorkshire
female: 3 sow 4 gilt

feral: 9 razorback
litter: 6 farrow
male: 4 boar 6 barrow
meat: 3 ham 4 pork 5 bacon 7 sausage 8 chitlins 12 chitterlings
wild: 7 peccary, warthog 8 babirusa

pigeon
3 sap 4 dupe, fool, gull, mark 5 chump, decoy, patsy 6 culver, stooge, sucker 7 fall guy 8 rock dove
genus: 7 Columba
house: 4 cote, loft
kind: 4 barb, rock 5 homer 6 homing, pouter, roller 7 carrier, crowned, fantail, tumbler
relative: 4 dove
young: 5 squab

pigeon hawk
6 merlin

pigeonhole
4 slot, sort 5 class, cubby, grade, group, niche, recess 6 shelve 7 catalog 8 category, classify, grouping 10 categorize 11 compartment

piggish
6 greedy 7 selfish, swinish 10 gluttonous

pigheaded
5 rigid 6 dogged, mulish 7 willful 8 contrary, perverse, stubborn 9 obstinate 10 inflexible, unyielding

piglet
5 shoat

pigment
3 dye 4 tint 5 color, paint, stain 8 colorant, dyestuff, tincture
black: 9 lampblack
blue: 4 cyan 5 azure, smalt 6 indigo 7 cyanine 8 cerulean 9 verdigris 11 ultramarine
brown: 5 sepia
umber: 6 bister, sienna
combining form: 5 chrom 6 chromo
dark: 7 melanin
green: 5 celadon 8 viridian 10 biliverdin
orange: 7 realgar 8 carotene
red: 4 lake
toxic: 8 gossypol
yellow: 5 ocher, ochre 6 flavin, lutein 7 flavine, xanthin

pigpen
3 sty 4 dump, mess 5 hovel

pigskin
6 saddle 8 football

pike
4 dive, fish 5 spear 7 highway 8 pickerel

piker
5 miser 7 scrooge 8 tightwad 9 skinflint
10 cheapskate 12 penny-pincher

pilaster
4 pier 6 column, pillar

pilchard
7 herring, sardine

pile
3 fur, lot, nap 4 coat, fill, heap, hill, load,
mass, much, pack, peck, pyre 5 amass,
crowd, drive, stack 6 bundle, column,
jumble 7 collect, fortune, reactor
8 quantity 9 great deal 10 assemblage,
collection 11 aggregation 12 accumulation

pileup
4 mass 5 crash, smash 8 accident
9 collision 12 accumulation

pilfer
3 rob 4 lift, take 5 filch, pinch, steal, swipe
6 finger, snitch, thieve 7 purloin
11 appropriate

pilgarlic
4 butt 8 baldhead 13 laughingstock

Pilgrim
5 Alden (John) 6 Carver (John) 7 Puritan,
Winslow (Edward) 8 Bradford (William),
Brewster (William), Standish (Myles)

pilgrim
5 hadji, hajji 6 palmer 8 traveler,
wanderer, wayfarer

pilgrimage
4 hajj, trip 7 journey

Pilgrims' interpreter
7 Squanto

Pilgrim's Progress
8 allegory
author: 6 Bunyan (John)
hero: 9 Christian

pill
4 ball, bore, pain, pest 5 bolus 6 pellet
7 capsule, lozenge 8 medicine, nuisance
9 annoyance

pillage
4 lift, loot, sack 5 booty, prize, spoil, steal
6 maraud, ravage, thieve 7 despoil,
plunder, purloin 8 spoliate 9 depredate,
desecrate

pillar
4 pier, post, prop 5 pylon, shaft, stela, stele
6 column, stelae (plural) 7 obelisk,
support, upright 8 backbone, mainstay,
pedestal, pilaster

pillory
6 stocks

pillow
3 pad 4 rest 7 bolster, cushion, support

pilot
4 lead, show, tool 5 drive, flier, guide, steer
6 airman, direct, leader 7 aviator, conduct,
guiding, tracing 8 aviatrix, helmsman,
shepherd

pimple
3 dot, zit 4 acne, boil, spot, stud 6 papule
7 blemish, blister, pustule, speckle
8 sprinkle, swelling

pin
3 leg, peg 4 clip, hold, join 5 affix, blame,
stake 6 attach, broach, brooch, cotter,
emblem, fasten, secure, trifle 8 fastener,
hold down, ornament, restrain

pinafore
5 apron, dress, frock

pinch
3 bit, nab, nip 4 dash, lift, pain, take
5 filch, press, prune, run in, skimp, steal,
swipe, taper, theft, tweak 6 arrest, crisis,
narrow, pilfer, snatch, stress 7 confine,
deficit, larceny, squeeze, straits
8 compress, exigency, hardship, juncture,
pressure, stealing, straiten 9 apprehend,
constrict, emergency, privation, tight spot
10 substitute

pinchbeck
4 fake, sham 5 alloy, bogus, false, phony
6 pseudo 8 spurious 9 brummagem
11 counterfeit

pinch hitter
3 sub 6 backup, fill-in, relief 7 stand-in
9 alternate, surrogate 10 substitute
11 alternative, replacement

pinchpenny
4 mean 5 cheap, close, mingy, tight
6 stingy 7 chintzy, costive, miserly, scrimpy
9 niggardly, penurious 11 closefisted,
tightfisted 12 parsimonious

Pindar
home: 6 Thebes
poem: 3 ode

pine
4 ache, long, mope, sigh, tree, wish, wood
5 brood, crave, dream, yearn 6 desire,
grieve, hanker, hunger, lament, thirst
7 conifer 8 languish 9 evergreen

Pine Tree State
5 Maine

pinhead
4 dolt, dope, fool 5 dunce 6 dimwit, nitwit
7 dullard 8 dumbbell 9 birdbrain

pinion
3 cog 4 bind, gear, wing 5 quill, tie up,
truss 6 fetter, tether 7 disable, feather,
shackle 8 cogwheel, restrain 9 hamstring

pink
3 cut 4 best, peak, stab 5 blush 6 flower,
height, pierce 7 excited, paragon
9 perforate

pinna
3 ear, fin 4 wing 7 feather, leaflet

pinnacle
4 top, tor 4 acme, apex, peak 5 crest,
crown, serac, spire 6 apogee, climax,
height, summit, zenith 7 steeple
8 capsheaf, meridian 11 culmination

pinniped
4 seal 6 walrus

Pinocchio author
7 Collodi (Carlo) 9 Lorenzini (Carlo)

pinochle
card: 3 ace, ten 4 jack, king, nine
5 queen
term: 4 meld 5 widow 7 auction
two-handed: 7 goulash

pinpoint
3 aim, fix 4 spot, tiny 5 exact, place
6 locate 7 precise 8 identify, stand out
9 determine, highlight, recognize
11 distinguish

Pinter play
8 Betrayal 9 Caretaker (The) 10 Home-
coming (The)

pinto
4 pied, pony 5 horse, paint 7 mottled,
piebald 8 skewbald

pint-size
3 wee 5 dwarf, small 6 midget, pocket
9 miniature 10 diminutive

pioneer
5 first, prime 6 maiden 7 explore, founder,
initial, primary, settler 8 colonist, earliest,
explorer, original 9 innovator 10 avant-
garde, pathfinder 11 trailblazer
12 frontiersman
famous: 5 Boone (Daniel), Bowie (Jim),
Clark (William), Lewis (Meriwether)
6 Carson (Kit), Colter (John) 7 Bridger
(Jim), Chapman (John), Frémont (John C.),
Whitman (Marcus) 8 Crockett (Davy)

pious
4 holy 5 godly 6 devout, worthy
7 devoted, dutiful 8 reverent, virtuous
9 hypocrite, pietistic, prayerful, religious
10 devotional 12 hypocritical

pip
3 dot 4 blip, peep, seed, spot 5 speck
9 break open

pipe
3 keg, tun 4 butt, cask, duct, hose, tube
6 barrel, convey, funnel, siphon 7 channel,
conduct, conduit 8 aqueduct, hogshead
ceremonial: 7 calumet
part: 4 bowl, stem

pipe down
4 hush 5 dry up, quiet 6 shut up 7 be
quiet

pipe dream
4 wish 7 chimera, fantasy 8 illusion

pipeline
5 works 6 system 7 channel, conduit,
process 8 activity, supplier 10 connection

pipsqueak
6 shaver, squirt 7 tadpole 8 half-pint, small
fry

piquant
4 tart 5 sharp, spicy, tangy, zesty 6 biting,
lively, savory, snappy 7 peppery, pungent
8 poignant, spirited 9 flavorful, sparkling
10 appetizing 11 provocative, stimulating

pique
3 irk, vex 4 huff, miff, move 5 anger,
annoy, peeve, pride, rouse 6 arouse,
excite, nettle, offend, put out 7 dudgeon,
offense, provoke, quicken 8 irritate,
motivate, vexation 9 aggravate,
annoyance, challenge, stimulate
10 exasperate, irritation, resentment

piracy
5 theft 7 lifting, looting, pillage, plunder,
robbery 8 stealing, thievery 10 plagiarism

piranha
6 caribe

pirate
5 rover 6 looter, raider, robber, sea dog 7 brigand, corsair, sea wolf 8 marauder, picaroon, pillager, sea rover 9 buccaneer, plunderer, privateer, sea robber 10 freebooter
English: 4 Read (Mary) 5 Bonny (Anne), Teach (Edward) 6 Morgan (Henry) 7 Dampier (William) 10 Blackbeard
flag: 10 Jolly Roger
French: 7 Laffite (Jean), Lafitte (Jean)
Scottish: 4 Kidd (William)

Pirates of Penzance, The
composer: 8 Sullivan (Arthur)
librettist: 7 Gilbert (W. S.)

pirogue
5 canoe 6 dugout

pirouette
4 spin, turn 5 twirl, whirl

piscator
6 angler 9 fisherman

pismire
3 ant

pistol
3 gat, rod 4 Colt 5 Glock, Luger 6 Magnum, Mauser, roscoe 7 bulldog, handgun 8 revolver, small arm 9 derringer, pepperbox
case: 7 holster

pit
3 vie 4 dent, hell, hole, scar 5 arena, hades, match, shaft, stone 6 cavity, hollow, oppose 7 counter, play off 8 pockmark 11 indentation

Pit and the Pendulum author
3 Poe (Edgar Allan)

pitch
3 dip, set 4 buck, dive, drop, fall, hurl, line, play, plug, tilt, tone, toss 5 erect, fling, heave, lurch, put up, resin, slant, sling, slope, spiel, throw 6 encamp, go down, plunge 7 discard, incline, present, promote 8 distance 9 advertise, declivity 13 advertisement

pitch-dark
3 jet 4 ebon, inky 5 black, ebony, jetty

pitcher
4 ewer, olla, toby 5 cruse 6 beaker, flagon 7 creamer
area: 5 mound
handle: 3 ear 4 ansa
see also **baseballer**

pitch in
3 aid 4 help 5 begin, set to, start 6 fall to 8 commence, get going, start off 9 subscribe, volunteer 10 contribute

piteous
3 sad 4 poor 8 pathetic 9 affecting 10 lamentable 11 distressing

pitfall
4 risk, snag, trap 5 catch, peril, snare 6 danger, hazard 9 booby trap 10 difficulty 12 entanglement

pith
3 nub 4 core, kill, meat, pulp 5 focus, heart 6 center, import, kernel 7 essence, nucleus 9 substance 10 importance 12 significance

pith helmet
5 topee

pithy
5 brief, crisp, meaty, short, terse 6 cogent 7 compact, concise, pointed 8 succinct 12 epigrammatic 13 short and sweet

pitiable
4 poor 5 cheap, sorry 8 shameful 10 deplorable, lamentable 12 contemptible

pitiful
3 sad 4 mean, poor 5 cheap, sorry 6 meager, meagre, paltry, shabby 7 forlorn 8 beggarly, pathetic, wretched 9 miserable 10 despicable, inadequate 12 contemptible 13 heartbreaking

pitiless
4 cold, hard 5 cruel, harsh, stony 6 brutal 8 inhumane, uncaring 9 barbarous, unfeeling 10 unmerciful 11 coldhearted, hardhearted

pittance
4 wage 5 scrap, trace 6 trifle 7 modicum, peanuts 9 allowance

pity
3 rue 4 ache, ruth 5 mercy 6 regret, sorrow 7 empathy, feel for, sadness 8 distress, sympathy 10 compassion, condolence, sympathize 11 commiserate 13 commiseration

pivot
3 pin 4 turn 5 hinge, shaft, swing, wheel 6 center, swivel

pivotal
3 key 5 chief, vital 7 central, crucial 8 critical, decisive 9 essential, important

pixie

3 elf, fay, imp 5 antic, fairy, scamp
6 elvish, impish, rascal, sprite 7 brownie,
coltish, playful, puckish 8 prankish
11 mischievous

pixilated

3 fey \ 7 bemused, erratic, flighty,
muddled, touched 9 eccentric, whimsical
10 capricious

Pizarro, Francisco

brother: 7 Gonzalo
city founded: 4 Lima
conquest: 4 Peru
victims: 5 Incas 9 Atahualpa
10 Atahuallpa

pizzazz

3 pep, vim, zip 4 bang, brio, snap, zest,
zing 5 éclat, flair, flash, gusto, moxie,
oomph, punch, verve 6 dazzle, energy,
hoopla, sizzle, spirit 7 glamour, panache
8 vitality 10 excitement

placard

4 bill, post 6 notice, plaque, poster
7 affiche 8 handbill

placate

4 calm, ease 6 pacify, soothe 7 appease,
assuage, comfort, mollify, satisfy, sweeten,
win over 9 conciliate, propitiate

place

3 lay, put, set 4 area, lieu, loci (plural),
post, rank, site, spot, zone 5 locus, point,
stead, tract 6 region, status 7 situate,
station 8 district, identify, locality, location,
pinpoint, position, standing 9 establish,
recognize
combining form: 3 top 4 loco, topo, topy

placid

4 calm, easy, mild 5 quiet, still 6 gentle,
serene 7 halcyon 8 composed, peaceful,
tranquil, waveless, windless 9 unruffled
10 complacent, unagitated, undisturbed,
untroubled 13 imperturbable

plagiarize

4 copy, crib 5 steal 6 pirate 11 appropriate

plague

3 vex 4 bane, evil, pest 5 annoy, beset,
curse, harry, hound, smite, trial, worry
6 blight, bother, infest, harass, hassle,
hector, pester 7 afflict, bedevil, disease,
disturb, scourge, torment, trouble
8 calamity, distress, epidemic, invasion,
irritant, irritate, nuisance, outbreak,
pandemic 9 annoyance, beleaguer
10 affliction, black death, pestilence
11 infestation

plaid

6 tartan

plain

3 lea 4 bald, bare, open, pure 5 blunt,
clear, field, frank, usual 6 candid, common,
homely, modest, patent, severe, simple,
tundra 7 expanse, evident, obvious,
prairie, savanna 8 apparent, distinct,
everyday, homespun, manifest, ordinary,
straight 9 outspoken, unadorned
10 absolutely, forthright, unaffected
11 undecorated, unvarnished 13 uncomplicated

plainclothesman

4 dick 6 shamus, sleuth 7 gumshoe
8 hawkshaw 9 detective 12 investigator

_____ Plaines

3 Des

plainness

6 candor, purity 7 clarity, honesty 8 lucidity
10 simplicity

plainsong

5 chant 12 cantus firmus

plainspoken

4 open 5 frank 6 candid, direct, honest
8 straight, truthful 10 forthright
11 undisguised, unvarnished

plaintive

3 sad 4 glum 6 woeful 7 doleful, piteous,
pitiful 8 dolorous, downcast, mournful
9 sorrowful 10 dispirited, lamentable,
lugubrious, melancholy

plait

4 fold 5 braid, pleat, weave 7 pigtail
10 intertwine, interweave

plan

3 aim, map, way 4 cast, goal, idea, mean,
plot 5 chart, frame 6 design, devise,
intend, intent, lay out, map out, method,
scheme, set out 7 arrange, diagram,
drawing, outline, pattern, program, project,
propose, purpose, work out 8 contrive,
engineer, organize, strategy, think out
9 blueprint, formulate, intention, procedure
11 arrangement, formulation

plane

3 fly, jet 4 even, flat, tool, tree 5 flush,
level 6 smooth 8 aircraft, airliner

planet

4 Mars 5 Earth, Pluto, Venus 6 Saturn,
Uranus 7 Jupiter, Mercury, Neptune
path: 5 orbit
satellite: 4 moon

shadow: 5 umbra
small: 8 asteroid

planetary
4 vast 6 global 7 erratic, immense
8 colossal, enormous 9 universal,
wandering, worldwide 11 terrestrial

plangent
7 orotund, ringing, vibrant 8 resonant,
sonorous 9 consonant, plaintive
10 expressive, resounding 11 reverberant

plank
4 item, wood 5 board, floor 6 lumber,
timber 7 article, support

plant
3 fix, pot, set, sow 4 bury, grow, hide, mill,
park, root, seed, tomb 5 cache, cover,
imbed, inter, place, plunk, put in, stash,
works 6 entomb, inhume, occult, screen
7 conceal, factory, install, lay away, put
away, secrete 8 colonize, populate 9 cultivate
angiosperm: 5 dicot 7 monocot
aquatic: 4 reed 5 lotus, sedge 7 awlwort,
cattail, fanwort, papyrus 8 duckweed,
eelgrass, hornwort, pondweed 9 water lily
10 watercress 11 bladderwort 12 pickerel-
weed
Australian: 6 mallee 7 banksia
8 blackboy 10 eucalyptus
body: 4 stem 7 thallus
bulbous: 4 lily 5 camas, onion, tulip
7 jonquil 8 hyacinth 9 narcissus
carnivorous: 6 sundew 10 butterwort
12 pitcher plant, Venus flytrap 13 Venus's-
flytrap
cell layer: 7 phellem
climbing: 3 ivy 4 vine 5 betel, liana,
vetch 6 bryony, derris, smilax 7 creeper,
jasmine 8 bignonia, fumitory, moonseed,
scammony, wisteria 12 morning glory
coloring agent: 8 carotene 11 chlorophyll, xanthophyll
cone-bearing: 3 fir, yew 4 pine 5 cedar,
cycad 6 ginkgo, spruce 7 conifer, cypress,
redwood 8 arborvitae, gymnosperm
desert: 4 aloe 5 agave 6 cactus, cholla
8 mesquite, ocotillo 9 paloverde
11 brittlebush
disease: 3 rot 4 gall, mold, rust, scab,
smut, wilt 5 ergot 6 blight, mildew, mosaic
7 blister 8 clubroot 9 black spot 10 black
heart
extinct: 8 calamite
flowerless: 4 alga, fern, kelp, moss
5 algae (plural), fungi (plural) 6 fungus,
lichen 7 seaweed 8 clubmoss
9 bryophyte, equisetum, horsetail, liverwort
fluid: 3 gum, sap 4 milk 5 latex, resin

gland: 7 nectary
hallucinogenic: 4 hemp 5 poppy
6 mescal 8 cannabis 9 marijuana
largest: 7 sequoia
life: 5 flora
marine: 4 kelp, nori 5 dulse, fucus
6 wakame 7 seaweed 8 gulfweed 10 sea
lettuce
marsh: 4 reed 5 carex, sedge
7 bogbean, bulrush, calamus, cattail 8 red
maple, sphagnum 11 loosestrife
medicinal: 4 aloe, sage 5 poppy, senna,
tansy 6 catnip, fennel, garlic, hyssop,
ipecac, nettle 7 aconite, boneset, burdock,
camphor, comfrey, ginseng, hemlock,
henbane, juniper, lobelia, mullein, mustard,
parsley 8 camomile, capsicum, cinchona,
feverfew, licorice, pilewort, plantain,
wormwood 9 asafetida, chamomile,
dandelion, echinacea, fenugreek,
monkshood 10 asafoetida, goldenseal,
peppermint
microscopic: 4 mold 6 diatom 7 euglena
8 bacteria (plural) 9 bacterium
oldest: 11 bristlecone
onion-like: 4 leek 5 chive 7 shallot
8 scallion
opening: 5 stoma 7 stomata (plural)
parasitic: 6 dodder, fungus 7 pinesap
8 gerardia 9 broomrape, mistletoe,
rafflesia, witchweed 10 beechdrops
part: 3 bud, nut, sap 4 bark, bulb, cell,
cone, corm, leaf, pome, root, seed, stem,
wood 5 drupe, fruit, grain, spore, thorn,
tuber, xylem 6 catkin, flower, nectar,
phloem, raceme 7 rhizome 8 lenticel
9 cellulose, cotyledon 11 chlorophyll,
chloroplast 13 inflorescence
pest: 5 aphid, scale 6 chafer, thrips,
weevil 7 cutworm 8 fruit fly, wireworm
9 gypsy moth 10 cankerworm, leafhopper,
phylloxera 11 codling moth
poisonous: 4 poke, upas 5 sumac
6 castor, croton, datura 7 amanita,
cassava, cowbane, henbane, lobelia,
tobacco 8 foxglove, larkspur, locoweed,
mayapple, oleander, pokeweed
9 baneberry, monkshood 10 belladonna,
jimsonweed, manchineel, nightshade
saprophytic: 5 fungi (plural) 6 fungus
7 pinesap 9 pinedrops, snow plant
10 beechdrops, Indian pipe
succulent: 4 aloe 5 agave 6 cactus
10 bitterroot
thorny: 4 rose 5 briar 6 cactus, nettle,
teasel 7 caltrop, thistle 9 cocklebur
tissue: 5 xylem 6 phloem 7 cambium,
medulla 9 meristem
young: 5 scion, shoot 6 sprout 7 cutting
8 seedling

plantain
5 fruit 6 banana

plantation
5 manor 6 colony, estate, quinta
7 acreage, demesne 8 hacienda
10 encampment, habitation, settlement

plant louse
5 aphid

plaque
4 film 5 badge, patch 6 brooch, lesion,
tablet 7 tribute 8 bacteria, memorial
13 commemoration

plaster
3 dab 4 coat 5 affix, cover, gesso
6 stucco 7 coating, conceal, overlay
8 dressing
of paris: 5 gesso 6 gypsum

plastered
3 lit 4 high 5 drunk, lit up, oiled 6 bashed,
blotto, bombed, juiced, potted, soaked,
soused, stewed, stoned, tanked, wasted,
zonked 7 crocked, drunken, pickled, pie-
eyed, sloshed, smashed, sottish
10 inebriated, liquored up 11 intoxicated

plastic
4 soft 5 vinyl 6 pliant, supple 7 ductile,
pliable 8 creative, flexible, moldable,
workable 9 adaptable, formative,
malleable, synthetic 10 artificial, credit
card, sculptural

plat
3 lot, map 4 plan 5 chart, tract 6 parcel
7 quadrat

plate
4 base, coat, disc, dish, disk, gild, tile
5 layer, paten, scute, slice 6 enamel,
fascia, lamina, plaque 7 anodize, lamella,
overlay

plateau
4 mesa 5 table 6 upland 9 altiplano,
tableland
arid: 4 puna
barren: 5 field 6 paramo
dry: 5 karoo 6 karroo

platform
3 map 4 bank, base, dais, deck, plan
5 bimah, forum, ledge, riser, shelf, stage,
stump 6 design, perron, podium, pulpit,
scheme 7 balcony, pattern, rostrum
8 hustings, scaffold 9 banquette, manifesto
11 declaration
temporary: 7 staging 8 scaffold
wooden: 9 boardwalk

Plath, Sylvia
novel: 7 Bell Jar (The)
poem: 5 Ariel, Daddy

platitude
6 cliché, truism 7 bromide 8 banality,
prosaism 10 shibboleth

Plato
father: 7 Ariston
literary form: 6 dialog 8 dialogue
original name: 10 Aristocles
school: 7 Academy
work: 3 Ion 4 Meno 5 Crito, Lysis
6 Laches, Phaedo 7 Apology, Gorgias
8 Phaedrus, Republic (The) 9 Charmides,
Symposium

platter
5 plate 6 record 8 trencher

platypus
8 duckbill

plaudits
5 kudos 6 cheers, praise 7 acclaim,
ovation 8 applause, approval, encomium
9 accolades 11 acclamation

plausible
8 credible, specious 10 believable,
convincing, creditable, persuasive,
reasonable

play
3 act, fun 4 game, jest, joke, romp
5 drama, feint, serve, sport, treat, trick,
wager 6 cavort, comedy, fiddle, frolic,
gambit, gambol, leeway, margin 7 delight,
disport, perform, twiddle 8 latitude,
maneuver, pleasure 9 amusement,
diversion, enjoyment, stratagem 10 manipulate, recreation
kind: 5 farce 6 comedy 7 musical,
tragedy 8 one-acter 9 melodrama,
pantomime
part: 3 act 5 scene 8 epilogue, prologue

playact
5 put on 7 perform, posture, pretend
9 personate 11 impersonate, make believe

playboy
4 rake, roué 8 hedonist 9 bon vivant

play down
8 minimize 9 deprecate, soft-pedal,
underrate 11 de-emphasize

player
5 actor 6 mummer 7 actress, athlete,
trouper 8 musician, thespian 9 contender,
performer 10 competitor, contestant
11 participant

playful
5 antic, jolly, merry, pixie 6 elvish, frisky, impish, jocund, joking, jovial, lively
7 coltish, jocular, puckish, waggish
8 humorous, , sportive 9 kittenish, sprightly
10 frolicsome

play off
3 pit, vie 5 match 6 oppose 7 counter
8 contrast

plaything
3 toy

play up
6 stress 7 feature 9 dramatize, emphasize, highlight, overstate, underline
10 accentuate, exaggerate, underscore

playwright
9 dramatist 10 dramaturge
(see also **dramatist**)

plaza
6 circus, common, square, zocalo
9 carrefour 11 marketplace

plea
4 suit 5 alibi 6 appeal, excuse, orison, prayer 7 apology, defense, pretext, request
8 entreaty, overture, petition
11 application, imploration 12 supplication
defendant's: 4 nolo 6 guilty 8 innocent
9 not guilty

plead
3 beg 4 pray 5 argue 6 allege, answer, appeal 7 beseech, entreat, implore
8 advocate, maintain 9 importune
10 supplicate

pleasant
4 fair, fine, good, nice 5 clear, sunny, sweet 6 cheery, genial, pretty 7 amiable, clarion, likable, welcome 8 amicable, charming, cheerful, engaging, gracious, grateful, likeable, pleasing, sunshine, sunshiny 9 agreeable, appealing, cloudless, congenial, convivial, enjoyable, favorable, unclouded 10 delightful, gratifying

pleasantry
3 fun 4 jest, joke 6 banter, levity
8 badinage, repartee 9 wittiness
10 jocularity

please
4 like, suit, wish 5 agree, amuse, enjoy, serve 6 choose 7 content, delight, gladden, gratify, indulge, satisfy
French: 12 s'il vous plait
German: 5 bitte

Spanish: 8 por favor

pleasing
4 good, nice 6 pretty 7 welcome
8 suitable 9 agreeable, congenial, favorable, palatable 10 attractive, delightful, gratifying 12 satisfactory

pleasure
3 fun, joy 4 will 5 bliss, fancy 6 desire, liking, relish 7 delight, gladden, gratify
8 felicity, gladness, hedonism
9 amusement, diversion, enjoyment, happiness, merriment 11 inclination

pleat
4 fold 5 crimp 6 crease

plebe
5 frosh 8 freshman

plebeian
3 low 4 base 5 crude, lowly 6 coarse, common, humble, menial 8 commoner, everyday, ordinary 10 lower-class

plectrum
4 pick

pledge
3 vow 4 bail, bind, bond, gage, hock, oath, pawn, seal, sign, word 5 drink, swear, toast, token 6 parole, plight, surety
7 chattel, earnest, promise, warrant
8 bailment, contract, covenant, guaranty, security, warranty 9 agreement, assurance, certainty, guarantee, undertake

pledget
3 pad 8 compress

Pleiades
4 Maia 6 Merope 7 Alcyone, Celaeno, Electra, Sterope, Taygeta 8 Asterope
brightest star: 7 Alcyone

plenary
4 full 5 whole 6 entire 7 general
8 absolute, complete 9 inclusive
11 unqualified 12 unrestricted

plenitude
4 glut 6 excess 7 satiety, surfeit 8 fullness
9 abundance, profusion, repletion
11 copiousness, sufficiency, superfluity
12 completeness

plenteous
7 fertile 8 abundant, fruitful, prolific
9 abounding 10 productive

plentiful
4 full, rich 5 ample, flush 7 copious, profuse 8 abundant, affluent, generous

plenty
9 abounding, bounteous, unstinted
10 sufficient

plenty
3 lot 4 heap, pack, peck, pile 6 stacks, wealth 8 adequacy, fullness, mountain 9 abundance, affluence, great deal 10 cornucopia

pleonasm
8 verbiage 9 prolixity, tautology, verbosity, wordiness 10 redundancy 11 periphrasis, superfluity

plethora
4 glut 5 flood 6 excess 7 overrun, surfeit, surplus 8 fullness, overflow 9 abundance, profusion, repletion 11 superfluity 13 overabundance

plexus
4 rete 7 network

pliable
6 supple 7 plastic 9 adaptable 10 adjustable, complaisant 11 manipulable

pliant
5 lithe 6 limber, supple 7 ductile, plastic, springy 8 flexible, moldable, workable, yielding 9 adaptable, malleable, tractable 10 manageable

plica
4 fold 6 crease, groove

plight
3 fix, jam, vow 4 hole, spot, word 5 swear 6 engage, pickle, pledge, scrape 7 betroth, dilemma, promise 8 quandary 9 betrothal 10 difficulty, engagement 11 predicament

plod
4 slog, toil 5 grind, slave, tramp, tread, tromp 6 drudge, lumber, trudge 8 plug away

plot
3 map 4 area, land, mark, note, plan 5 cabal, chart, story, tract 6 design, devise, invent, lay out, locate, parcel, scheme 7 collude, compact, connive, diagram, outline 8 conspire, contrive, intrigue, scenario 9 collusion, conniving, machinate 10 complicity, connivance, conspiracy 11 machination

plover
5 pewit, stilt 6 peewit 7 lapwing 8 dotterel, killdeer
relative: 9 sandpiper, turnstone

plow
3 dig 4 till, turn 5 break 6 furrow, harrow, trench 8 turn over 9 cultivate

part: 4 beam, frog 5 share 7 coulter 8 landside 9 moldboard

ploy
4 ruse, scam, wile 5 feint, trick 6 device, frolic, gambit, tactic 7 gimmick 8 artifice, escapade, maneuver 9 stratagem 11 contrivance

pluck
3 rob, tug 4 grit, guts, pick, pull, yank 5 cheek, grasp, heart, moxie, nerve, spunk 6 daring, fleece, mettle, remove, snatch, spirit, tweeze 7 bravery, courage, pull out 8 gameness 10 resolution

plucky
4 bold, game 5 brave 6 feisty, spunky 7 doughty 8 fearless, spirited, unafraid 9 dauntless 10 courageous

plug
3 tap 4 bung, clog, core, cork, fill, hype, pack, push, stop, tout 5 block, blurb, boost, choke, close, cry up, shoot 6 device, remedy 7 congest, fitting, hydrant, promote, stopper 8 obstruct 9 advertise, publicity, publicize 10 connection

plug-ugly
4 thug 5 bully, rowdy, tough 7 hoodlum, ruffian 9 roughneck

plum
5 prize 6 purple, reward 7 guerdon, premium 8 dividend
dried: 5 prune
kind: 6 damson 7 bullace 9 greengage
spiny: 10 blackthorn

plumage
8 feathers
early: 4 down

plumb
5 delve, probe, sound 6 fathom, weight 7 exactly, examine, explore, install, measure 8 absolute, complete, thorough, vertical 10 absolutely, vertically 11 immediately 13 perpendicular

plume
4 tail 5 array, preen, pride, prize 6 column 7 feather 8 aigrette

plummet
4 dive, drop, fall 5 crash 6 plunge, tumble 8 collapse, nose-dive 11 precipitate

plump
3 fat 4 drop, fall, full 5 ample, buxom, favor, pudgy, round, stout, tubby 6 chubby, portly, rotund 7 rounded, support 8 abundant, directly, roly-poly, Rubenesque

plumply
7 frankly, plainly 8 candidly 12 forthrightly

plunder
3 rob 4 loot, sack, swag, take 5 booty, prize, seize, spoil, steal, strip 6 boodle, rapine, spoils 7 despoil, pillage, ransack, relieve, stick up 9 pillaging

plunge
3 bet, ram, run 4 dive, drop, fall, jump, rush, sink, stab, swim 5 drive, lunge, pitch, stick 6 charge, gamble, hasten, hurtle, thrust, topple, tumble 7 descend, immerse, plummet 8 nose-dive, submerge 9 penetrate

plus
3 and 4 more, perk 5 added, asset, bonus, boost, extra 6 excess 7 benefit 8 addition, increase, positive

plush
4 full, rich 6 deluxe, fabric, lavish, velvet 7 opulent 8 luscious, palatial 9 expensive, luxuriant, luxurious, sumptuous

Pluto
3 Dis 5 Hades
brother: 4 Zeus 7 Jupiter, Neptune 8 Poseidon
father: 6 Cronus, Saturn
mother: 3 Ops 4 Rhea
wife: 10 Persephone, Proserpina

plutocrat
5 mogul 6 fat cat, tycoon 7 magnate 9 financier, moneybags 10 capitalist

plutonian
8 infernal 10 underworld

Plutus
father: 6 Iasion
god of: 6 riches, wealth
mother: 5 Ceres 7 Demeter

ply
3 use 4 bias, sail 5 apply, exert, layer, wield 6 employ, handle, strand, supply, travel, voyage 7 furnish, perform 8 maneuver, practice 11 inclination

pneuma
4 soul 5 anima 6 psyche, spirit

pneumatic
4 airy 5 ample, buxom, plump 6 aerial, zaftig 9 spiritual 10 curvaceous 11 atmospheric

poach
4 cook 5 steal 6 coddle, simmer 7 intrude

8 encroach, trespass 9 interlope 11 appropriate

Pocahontas
father: 8 Powhatan
husband: 5 Rolfe (John)

pock
3 pit 4 hole, spot 7 pustule

pocket
3 bag 4 lift, sack 5 filch, pinch, pouch, purse, steal, swipe 6 cavity 7 capsule, dead end, impasse 8 cul-de-sac 9 condensed 10 blind alley
billiards: 4 pool

pocketbook
3 bag 4 poke 5 purse 6 clutch, income, wallet 7 handbag 8 billfold 9 clutch bag

pocket bread
4 pita

pocket money
6 change 9 petty cash 11 small change

pocket-size
4 tiny 5 small 9 miniature 10 diminutive

pod
3 bag, gam, sac 4 boll, case, hull, husk, skin 5 shell, shuck 6 cocoon 7 capsule, silique 8 seedcase
plant: 3 pea 4 bean, okra 5 chili, gumbo 6 cassia, cowpea, legume, lentil, peanut, pepper 8 capsicum, mesquite, milkweed 9 lespedeza

pod-bearing tree
5 carob 6 locust 7 catalpa

podiatry
9 chiropody

podium
4 dais 6 pulpit 7 lectern, rostrum 8 platform

_____ podrida
4 olla

Poe, Edgar Allan
detective: 5 Dupin (C. Auguste)
poem: 5 Bells (The), Raven (The) 6 Lenore 7 Israfel, To Helen, Ulalume 8 Eldorado, For Annie 10 Annabel Lee
tale: 6 Ligeia, Shadow 7 Gold-Bug (The), Morella, Silence 8 Black Cat (The) 11 Tell-tale Heart (The) 15 Purloined Letter (The) 17 Cask of Amontillado (The), Pit and the Pendulum (The) 19 Masque of the Red Death (The) 21 Fall of the House of Usher (The)

poem

3 ode **4** epic, epos, idyl, rime, rune, song
5 ditty, elegy, epode, idyll, lyric, rhyme,
verse **6** ballad, epopee, jingle, rondel,
sonnet **7** eclogue, rondeau **8** limerick,
madrigal
  closing: 5 envoi, envoy
  division: 4 foot, line **5** canto, epode,
stich, verse **6** stanza **7** refrain **8** epilogue,
prologue
  Japanese: 5 haiku, tanka
  of eight lines: 6 octave **7** triolet
  of four lines: 8 quatrain
  of fourteen lines: 6 sonnet
  of three lines: 7 triplet
  pastoral: 7 eclogue, georgic
  short: 5 ditty **7** epigram

poet

4 bard, muse, scop **5** skald **6** lyrist
7 elegist **8** idyllist, lyricist **9** balladist,
sonneteer **10** Parnassian
  American: 3 Poe (Edgar Allan) **4** Dove
(Rita), Hass (Robert), Nash (Ogden), Read
(Thomas), Rich (Adrienne), Tabb (John
Banister), Tate (Allen) **5** Auden (Wystan
Hugh), Benét (Stephen Vincent), Crane
(Hart), Field (Eugene), Frost (Robert),
Guest (Edgar), Moore (Marianne), Plath
(Sylvia), Pound (Ezra), Riley (James
Whitcomb), Wylie (Elinor) **6** Barlow (Joel),
Bishop (Elizabeth), Brooks (Gwendolyn),
Bryant (William Cullen), Ciardi (John),
Dickey (James), Dunbar (Paul Laurence),
Hughes (Langston), Kilmer (Joyce), Lanier
(Sidney), Lowell (Amy, James Russell,
Robert), McKuen (Rod), Millay (Edna St.
Vincent), Pinsky (Robert), Ransom (John
Crowe), Seeger (Alan), Strand (Mark),
Taylor (Edward), Warren (Robert Penn),
Wilbur (Richard) **7** Angelou (Maya),
Ashbery (John), Emerson (Ralph Waldo),
Freneau (Philip), Halleck (Fitz-Greene),
Jeffers (Robinson), Lindsay (Vachel),
Markham (Edwin), Merrill (James),
Nemerov (Howard), Roethke (Theodore),
Shapiro (Karl), Stevens (Wallace), Whitman
(Walt) **8** Berryman (John), Cummings (E.
E.), Ginsberg (Allen), MacLeish (Archibald),
Robinson (Edwin Arlington), Sandburg
(Carl), Teasdale (Sara), Wheatley (Phillis),
Whittier (John Greenleaf), Williams (C. K.,
William Carlos) **9** Dickinson (Emily),
Santayana (George) **10** Bradstreet (Anne),
Longfellow (Henry Wadsworth)
12 Wigglesworth (Michael)
  Anglo-Saxon: 7 Caedmon, Cynwulf
8 Cynewulf, Kynewulf
  Arab: 5 Jarir **6** Hariri **8** al-Hariri
  Australian: 8 Paterson (Andrew Barton)

  Belgian: 11 Maeterlinck (Maurice)
  Canadian: 5 Pratt (Edwin John) **6** Hébert
(Anne) **7** Roberts (Charles G. D.), Service
(Robert) **8** Drummond (William Henry)
9 Fréchette (Louis-Honoré)
  Chilean: 6 Neruda (Pablo) **7** Mistral
(Gabriela)
  Chinese: 4 Li Po, Tu Fu **7** Wang Wei
  Danish: 4 Rode (Helge) **5** Ewald
(Johannes)
  English: 3 Gay (John) **4** Gray (Thomas),
Owen (Wilfred), Pope (Alexander), Rowe
(Nicholas), Tate (Nahum), Wyat (Thomas)
5 Blake (William), Byron (Lord), Carew
(Thomas), Clare (John), Donne (John),
Eliot (Thomas Stearns), Gower (John),
Hardy (Thomas), Keats (John), Noyes
(Alfred), Wilde (Oscar), Wyatt (Thomas),
Young (Edward) **6** Arnold (Matthew),
Austin (Alfred), Belloc (Hilaire), Brooke
(Rupert), Butler (Samuel), Clough (Arthur
Hugh), Cowper (William), Dryden (John),
Graves (Robert), Larkin (Philip), Milton
(John), Savage (Richard), Sidney (Philip),
Surrey (Earl of), Symons (Arthur), Waller
(Edmund), Warton (Thomas), Watson
(William), Wotton (Henry) **7** Bridges
(Robert), Campion (Thomas), Chaucer
(Geoffrey), Gilbert (W. S.), Herbert
(George), Herrick (Robert), Hopkins
(Gerard Manley), Housman (A. E.), Kipling
(Rudyard), Layamon, Marvell (Andrew),
Patmore (Coventry), Quarles (Francis),
Shelley (Percy Bysshe), Skelton (John),
Southey (Robert), Spender (Stephen),
Spenser (Edmund) **8** Betjeman (John),
Browning (Elizabeth Barrett, Robert), de la
Mare (Walter), Langland (William),
Lovelace (Richard), Meredith (George),
Rossetti (Christina, Dante Gabriel),
Suckling (John), Tennyson (Alfred Lord),
Thompson (Francis) **9** Coleridge (Samuel
Taylor), Masefield (John), Swinburne
(Algernon Charles) **10** Chatterton
(Thomas), FitzGerald (Edward),
Wordsworth (William) **11** Shakespeare
(William)
  Finnish: 8 Runeberg (Johan Ludvig)
  French: 5 Marot (Clément) **6** Musset
(Alfred de), Valéry (Paul), Villon (François)
7 Bourget (Paul), Chénier (André de,
Marie-Joseph), Gautier (Théophile),
Rimbaud (Arthur), Ronsard (Pierre de)
8 Malherbe (François de), Mallarmé
(Stéphane), Verlaine (Paul) **9** Lamartine
(Alphonse de) **10** Baudelaire (Charles)
11 Apollinaire (Guillaume)
  German: 5 Heine (Heinrich), Rilke (Rainer
Maria), Sachs (Hans), Storm (Theodor)
6 Brecht (Bertolt), Goethe (Johann

Wolfgang von), Uhland (Ludwig) **7** Walther
(von der Vogelweide), Wolfram (von
Eschenbach) **8** Schiller (Friedrich von)
9 Klopstock (Friedrich Gottlieb)
Greek: **5** Arion, Homer **6** Elytis
(Odysseus), Erinna, Hesiod, Pindar, Ritsos
(Yannis), Sappho **7** Agathon, Alcaeus,
Orpheus, Seferis (George), Thespis
8 Anacreon **9** Simonides **10** Apollonius,
Theocritus
Hindu: **5** Naidu (Sarojini) **6** Tagore
(Rabindranath) **8** Kalidasa, Tulsidas
Hungarian: **6** Petofi (Sandor), Zrinyi
(Miklos)
Irish: **5** Moore (Thomas), Wolfe (Charles),
Yeats (William Butler) **6** Heaney (Seamus)
7 Dunsany (Lord) **8** Drummond (William
Henry), MacNeice (Louis)
Italian: **4** Rosa (Salvator), Vida (Marco)
5 Dante (Alighieri), Tasso (Torquato)
7 Ariosto (Ludovico), Manzoni
(Alessandro), Montale (Eugenio)
8 Carducci (Giosuè), Leopardi (Giacomo),
Petrarch **9** Boccaccio (Giovanni),
D'Annunzio (Gabriele), Marinetti (Filippo
Tommaso), Quasimodo (Salvatore),
Ungaretti (Giuseppe)
Japanese: **5** Basho **6** Matsuo
medieval: **8** minstrel, trouvère
10 troubadour
Mexican: **3** Paz (Octavio)
nonsense: **4** Lear (Edward)
Norwegian: **5** Bjornson (Bjornstjerne),
Welhaven (Johan) **9** Wergeland (Henrik)
Persian: **4** Sadi **5** Attar, Hafez, Hafiz
11 Omar Khayyám
Roman: **4** Ovid **6** Horace, Vergil, Virgil
7 Juvenal, Martial, Statius **8** Catullus,
Tibullus **9** Lucretius
Russian: **4** Blok (Aleksandr) **7** Brodsky
(Joseph), Pushkin (Aleksandr), Yesenin
(Sergey) **9** Akhmatova (Anna), Kheraskov
(Mikhail), Pasternak (Boris), Tsvetaeva
(Marina) **10** Mandelstam (Osip), Maya-
kovsky (Vladimir) **11** Yevtushenko
(Yevgeny)
Saint Lucian: **7** Walcott (Derek)
Scottish: **4** Hogg (James), Muir (Edwin)
5 Burns (Robert), Scott (Alexander, Walter)
6 Dunbar (William), Ramsay (Allan)
7 Thomson (James) **10** MacDiarmid
(Hugh)
Spanish: **5** Lorca (Federico García)
7 Jiménez (Juan Ramón) **8** Figueroa
(Francisco) **10** Aleixandre (Vicente)
11 García Lorca (Federico)
Swedish: **5** Sachs (Nelly) **6** Tegner
(Esaias) **8** Snoilsky (Carl Johan)
9 Karlfeldt (Erik Axel)

Swiss: **5** Amiel (Henri Frédéric)
9 Spitteler (Carl)
Welsh: **6** Thomas (Dylan) **7** Aneurin,
Watkins (Vernon)

poetic
5 lyric **6** dreamy **8** romantic **9** aesthetic,
beautiful

poet laureate
British: **3** Pye (Henry) **4** Rowe (Nicholas),
Tate (Nahum) **6** Austin (Alfred), Cibber
(Colley), Dryden (John), Hughes (Ted),
Jonson (Ben), Motion (Andrew) **7** Bridges
(Robert), Southey (Robert) **8** Betjeman
(John), Davenant (William), Day-Lewis
(Cecil), Shadwell (Thomas), Tennyson
(Alfred) **9** Masefield (John), Whitehead
(William) **10** Wordsworth (William)
American: **4** Dove (Rita), Hass (Robert)
5 Glück (Louise) **6** Kunitz (Stanley),
Merwin (W. S.), Pinsky (Robert), Strand
(Mark), Warren (Robert Penn), Wilbur
(Richard) **7** Brodsky (Joseph), Collins
(Billy), Nemerov (Howard), Van Duyn
(Mona)

Pogo creator
5 Kelly (Walt)

poi
4 taro

poignancy
6 pathos **7** emotion, sadness **9** sentiment

poignant
3 sad **4** keen **5** acute, biting, sharp
6 moving **7** painful, piquant, pointed,
pungent **8** incisive, piercing, stirring,
touching **9** affecting, emotional
11 penetrating, stimulating

point
3 aim, bit, dot, end, jag, nib, tip **4** apex,
barb, crux, goal, item, mark, show, site,
spot, step, tine, turn, unit **5** brink, motif,
place, stage, theme, topic, trace, verge
6 credit, detail, direct, intent, moment,
motive, object, period, reason **7** cogency,
decimal, element, essence, feature, instant,
meaning, purpose, sharpen, subject
8 headland, juncture, locality, location,
particle, position **9** direction, emphasize,
punctuate **10** promontory **12** significance

Point Counter Point author
6 Huxley (Aldous)

pointed
5 acute, sharp **6** barbed, marked, signal
7 salient **8** incisive, striking **9** arresting,

pointer

pertinent, prominent **11** conspicuous, penetrating

pointer

3 dog, tip **4** clue, hint **5** arrow, guide **6** gundog **9** indicator **10** suggestion

pointillist

6 Seurat (Georges), Signac (Paul) **8** Pissarro (Camille)

pointless

4 idle, vain **5** inane, silly **6** futile **7** useless **8** bootless **9** fruitless, senseless, worthless **10** immaterial, irrelevant, unavailing, unfruitful **11** meaningless **12** unprofitable

point of view

5 angle, slant **7** outlook **8** position, prospect **11** perspective

poise

4 ease, hang, tact **5** brace, grace, hover, skill **6** aplomb, steady **7** address, balance, bearing, dignity, support, suspend **8** calmness, carriage, elegance, serenity **9** assurance, composure, diplomacy **10** confidence, equanimity **11** delicatesse, equilibrium, savoir faire, tactfulness

poised

4 calm **6** at ease, serene, steady **7** assured, equable **8** composed, tranquil **9** collected, confident **13** self-possessed

poison

4 bane, upas **5** toxin, venom **6** toxoid **7** arsenic, botulin, cyanide, envenom **8** toxicant **9** botulinum, contagion **10** strychnine **13** contamination **arrow:** **4** inée, upas **6** curare **7** ouabain **combining form:** **3** tox **4** toxi, toxo **6** toxico

poisoning

food: **8** botulism **lead:** **8** plumbism

poisonous

5 toxic **7** baneful, miasmal, nocuous, noxious **8** mephitic, venomous, virulent **9** pestilent **10** pernicious

poke

3 dig, hit, jab, jut, lag, pry **4** cuff, nose, prod, push, sock, stab, stir, urge **5** bulge, dally, delay, elbow, nudge, punch, snoop, tarry **6** dawdle, meddle, pierce, putter, thrust **7** intrude, project, rummage **8** stick out **9** interfere, interject, interpose

poker

bet total: **3** pot **form:** **4** stud

hand: **4** pair **5** flush **8** straight **9** full house **10** royal flush **13** straight flush **stake:** **4** ante **term:** **3** see **4** call, draw, open **5** raise **token:** **4** chip

poker-faced

5 blank, staid **7** deadpan, neutral **9** impassive **11** inscrutable, noncommital **12** inexpressive

pokey

3 can, jug, pen **4** brig, coop, jail, stir **5** clink **6** cooler, prison **7** slammer **9** calaboose

poky

4 slow **5** dingy, seedy **6** dreary, shabby **7** cramped, laggard, run-down **8** dilatory, plodding, sluggish

Poland

capital: **6** Warsaw **city:** **4** Lódz **6** Gdansk, Kraków, Poznan **7** Wroclaw **8** Katowice, Szczecin **leader:** **6** Walesa (Lech) **monetary unit:** **5** zloty **mountain range:** **10** Carpathian **national hero:** **10** Kosciuszko (Thaddeus) **neighbor:** **6** Russia **7** Belarus, Germany, Ukraine **8** Slovakia **9** Lithuania **13** Czech Republic **river:** **4** Oder **7** Vistula **sea:** **6** Baltic

polar

6 arctic **7** pivotal **8** opposite **9** diametric

pole

4 punt, spar **5** shaft, staff, stick, stilt **Indian:** **5** totem **Scottish:** **5** caber

polecat

5 fitch, skunk **6** ferret **7** fitchet

polemic

6 attack, debate, screed, tirade **7** defense, dispute **8** argument, diatribe, harangue, jeremiad **9** assertion, philippic **10** contention, refutation **11** controversy, disputation **12** denunciation, remonstrance

polemical

7 scrappy **10** pugnacious **11** contentious, opinionated **12** disputatious **13** argumentative, controversial

polestar

3 hub **5** focus, guide **10** focal point

police

3 cop, law, man **4** fuzz, heat **6** copper,

govern, lawman, patrol **7** control, monitor, trooper **8** bluecoat, flatfoot, gendarme, regulate **9** patrolman **12** peace officer

police officer
3 cop **4** fuzz, heat **5** bobby **6** copper, peeler **7** John Law, sheriff, trooper **8** bluecoat, Dogberry, flatfoot, gendarme **9** constable, patrolman
Italian: **11** carabiniere
Parisian: **4** flic **8** gendarme

policy
4 plan **6** course, method, number **7** lottery, program **8** contract, practice **9** procedure **10** management

polio vaccine developer
4 Salk (Jonas) **5** Sabin (Albert)

polish
3 rub, wax **4** buff **5** glaze, glint, gloss, sheen, shine **6** luster, refine, smooth, soften **7** burnish, culture, enhance, improve, perfect, touch up **8** brighten **10** refinement

Polish
dumpling: **7** pierogi
leader: **6** Walesa (Lech)
patriot: **9** Kosciusko (Thaddeus)
pope: **8** John Paul
sausage: **8** kielbasa
soldier: **7** Pulaski (Casimir)

polish off
5 eat up **6** devour **7** consume, put away **8** dispatch **9** dispose of

polite
5 civil **7** courtly, genteel, refined **8** cultured, mannerly, polished, well-bred **9** attentive, courteous **10** thoughtful **11** considerate **12** well-mannered

politeness
7 manners **8** civility, courtesy **10** refinement

politic
4 wise **5** suave **6** adroit, shrewd, smooth **7** prudent, tactful **8** tactical **9** advisable, expedient, judicious, sagacious **10** diplomatic

political
meeting: **6** caucus
party: **3** GOP **10** Democratic, Republican
system: **7** fascism **9** communism, democracy, socialism

poll
4 cast, clip, crop, head, nape **5** count,

shear, tally, votes **6** record, sample, survey **7** canvass, pollard **8** question **9** interview **10** canvassing

pollack
4 fish **6** saithe **8** bluefish
family: **3** cod

pollard
3 top **4** crop, tree **7** cut back

pollen-producing organ
6 stamen

pollex
5 thumb

_____ polloi
3 hoi

pollster
5 Zogby (John) **6** Gallup (George), Harris (Lou)

pollute
4 foul, soil **5** dirty, spoil, stain, sully, taint **6** befoul, damage, debase, defile **7** corrupt, profane **10** adulterate **11** contaminate

pollution
4 smog **5** abuse **8** impurity **10** defilement

Pollux
10 Polydeuces
brother: **6** Castor
father: **4** Zeus
mother: **4** Leda
sister: **5** Helen **12** Clytemnestra

Pollyanna
8 optimist
author: **6** Porter (Eleanor)

Pollyannaish
6 blithe, cheery, upbeat **8** cheerful, positive **10** optimistic **11** rose-colored

pollywog
7 tadpole

Polonius
daughter: **7** Ophelia
slayer: **6** Hamlet
son: **7** Laertes

poltergeist
5 ghost **6** spirit

poltroon
6 coward, craven, yellow **7** chicken, dastard, gutless **8** cowardly **9** dastardly **11** lily-livered

Polydorus
father: **5** Priam **6** Cadmus
mother: **6** Hecuba **8** Harmonia

slayer: 8 Achilles 10 Polymestor 11 Polymnestor

polygon
eight-sided: 7 octagon
five-sided: 8 pentagon
four-sided: 8 tetragon
nine-sided: 7 nonagon
seven-sided: 8 heptagon
six-sided: 7 hexagon
ten-sided: 7 decagon
three-sided: 8 triangle
twelve-sided: 9 dodecagon

Polyhymnia
4 Muse
invention: 4 lyre

Polynesian
5 Maori 6 Samoan, Tongan 8 Hawaiian, Tahitian 9 Marquesan

Polynices
brother: 8 Eteocles
father: 7 Oedipus
mother: 7 Jocasta
wife: 5 Argia 6 Argeia

polyp
5 tumor, zooid 6 growth 7 hydroid
freshwater: 5 hydra

Polyphemus
7 Cyclops
beloved: 7 Galatea
father: 8 Poseidon
victim: 4 Acis

pome
4 pear 5 apple, fruit

pommel
4 knob 6 handle

pomp
4 show 5 array 6 parade, ritual 7 display, fanfare, panoply 8 ceremony, grandeur, splendor 9 pageantry, vainglory 11 ostentation

pompano
4 fish 8 carangid 10 butterfish

Pompeii's volcano
8 Vesuvius

pompous
4 vain 5 proud, showy 6 ornate, stuffy 7 stuck-up 8 arrogant, boastful, inflated, lordly 9 bombastic, conceited, important, overblown 10 egocentric, flamboyant pontifical 11 magisterial, pretentious 12 ostentatious, vainglorious

pond
4 mere, pool, tarn 5 stank 6 lagoon

ponder
4 mull, muse 5 study, think, weigh 6 reason 7 examine, perpend, reflect 8 appraise, cogitate, consider, evaluate, meditate, mull over, ruminate 9 reflect on, speculate 10 deliberate, think about 11 contemplate

ponderous
4 dull 5 heavy 6 clumsy, dreary, stodgy, wooden 7 labored, massive, weighty 8 cumbrous, lifeless, plodding, unwieldy 9 lumbering 10 burdensome, cumbersome, oppressive

poniard
6 dagger

Ponte Vecchio
city: 8 Florence
river: 4 Arno

Pontiac
5 chief
tribe: 6 Ottawa

pontiff
4 pope

pontifical
7 pompous 8 dogmatic 9 episcopal 11 magisterial

pony
4 crib, trot 5 horse 6 bronco, cayuse 7 mustang
breed: 6 Exmoor 8 Shetland

pony up
3 pay 6 lay out, pay out 7 dish out, dole out, fork out 8 hand over, shell out, turn over 10 compensate, remunerate

pooch
3 dog, pup 4 tyke 5 hound, puppy 6 bowwow, canine

Pooh
creator: 5 Milne (A. A.)
illustrator: 7 Shepard (Ernest)

pooh-bah
3 VIP 4 czar, king, star, tsar, tzar 5 baron, heavy, mogul 6 big gun, bigwig, honcho, kahuna, prince, worthy 7 big name, big shot, kingpin, magnate, notable 8 big wheel, eminence, luminary 9 big cheese, personage, superstar 11 heavyweight

pooh-pooh
5 scorn 6 deride 7 disdain, dismiss, sneer at 8 minimize, play down

pool
3 pot 4 mere, pond, tarn 5 chain, group, kitty, merge, trust 6 cartel, lagoon, laguna, puddle 7 combine, jackpot 9 syndicate **player:** 7 Mosconi (Willie) 13 Minnesota Fats

poop
4 dirt, info, tire 7 fatigue

poor
4 base, mean 5 broke, needy, scant, skimp, spare 6 humble, meager, meagre, paltry, scanty, skimpy, sparse 8 bankrupt, beggarly, indigentstrapped 9 destitute, insolvent, penniless, penurious 10 down-and-out, pauperized, stone-broke 11 impecunious, necessitous

poorly
3 ill, low 4 sick 5 badly 6 ailing, sickly, unwell 10 indisposed 11 imperfectly

pop
3 dad, dot, gun, hit, try 4 dada, dart, ding, shot, slap, slog, sock, soda 5 catch, crack, daddy, drink, fling, shoot, whack, whirl 6 attack, bug out, effort, father, strike 7 assault, attempt, explode 8 backfire

pop artist
5 Blake (Peter), Johns (Jasper) 6 Warhol (Andy) 7 Hockney (David), Indiana (Robert) 9 Oldenburg (Claes), Wesselman (Tom) 10 Rosenquist (James) 12 Lichtenstein (Roy)

pope
3 Leo 4 John, Mark, Paul, Pius 5 Caius, Conon, Donus, Felix, Gaius, Lando, Linus, Peter, Soter, Urban 6 Adrian, Agatho, Fabian, Julius, Lucius, Martin, Sixtus, Victor 7 Anterus, Clement, Damasus, Gregory, Hadrian, Hyginus, Marinus, Paschal, Pontian, Romanus, Sergius, Stephen, Zosimus 8 Agapetus, Anicetus, Benedict, Boniface, Calixtus, Eugenius, Eusebius, Formosis, Gelasius, Hilarius, Honorius, Innocent, John Paul, Liberius, Nicholas, Pelagius, Siricius, Theodore, Vigilius, Vitalian 9 Adeodatus, Alexander, Anacletus, Callistus, Celestine, Cornelius, Densdedit, Dionysius, Eutychian, Evaristus, Hormisdas, Marcellus, Miltiades, Severinus, Silverius, Silvester, Sisinnius, Sylvester, Symmachus, Valentine, Zacharias 10 Anastasius, Melchiades, Sabinianus, Simplicius, Zephyrinus 11 Christopher, Constantine, Eleutherius, Eutychianus, Marcellinus, Telesphorus

Pope poem
7 Dunciad (The) 10 Essay on Man (An) 13 Rape of the Lock (The)

Popeye
accessory: 4 pipe
baby: 7 Swee'Pea 8 Sweet Pea
energizer: 7 spinach
friend: 5 Wimpy 8 Olive Oyl
occupation: 6 sailor
rival: 5 Bluto

pop in
4 call 5 visit 6 drop by, look up, stop by 8 come over

popinjay
3 fop 4 toff 5 dandy, swell 7 peacock 8 macaroni

poplar
5 abele, alamo, aspen 6 balsam 9 tulip tree 10 cottonwood 12 balm of Gilead

Poppaea's husband
4 Nero

poppycock
3 rot 4 bosh, bunk, guff 5 bilge, hokum 6 bunkum 7 baloney 8 malarkey, nonsense 10 balderdash

populace
5 plebs 6 masses, people, public 9 citizenry, commonage, commoners, plebeians 10 commonalty 11 commonality, rank and file, third estate

popular
5 cheap, noted 6 common, famous 7 admired, current, favored, general, leading 8 accepted, approved, favorite, ordinary 9 preferred, prevalent, prominent, well-known, well-liked 10 democratic, prevailing, widespread 11 inexpensive

populate
6 occupy, people, settle 7 inhabit

populous
6 packed 7 crowded, teeming 8 numerous 9 congested 13 multitudinous

porcelain
Chinese: 9 Lowestoft
English: 3 Bow 5 Derby, Spode 6 Minton 7 Aynsley, Belleek, Bristol, Chelsea 8 Caughley, Wedgwood
French: 6 Sèvres 7 Limoges
German: 7 Dresden, Meissen
ingredient: 6 kaolin
Italian: 6 Doccia
Japanese: 5 Imari

porch
4 deck 5 lanai 6 piazza 7 gallery, veranda
8 verandah

porcupine
8 hedgehog

pore
6 outlet 7 opening, orifice, reflect
8 meditate 10 interstice

pore over
4 read, scan 5 study 6 peruse
10 scrutinize

porgy
4 fish, scup 6 sparid 8 menhaden

Porgy and Bess
composer: 8 Gershwin (George)
librettist: 7 Heyward (DuBose)
8 Gershwin (Ira)

Po River city
5 Milan, Padua, Turin 6 Milano, Padova,
Torino, Verona 7 Brescia

pork
3 ham, pig 5 bacon, swine 8 sowbelly
cut: 3 ham 4 jowl, loin, side 7 fatback
8 forefoot, hind foot, spare rib 9 picnic ham
10 Boston butt

pork-barreling
9 patronage

pornographic
7 obscene

porous
5 leaky 6 spongy 8 pervious 9 permeable
10 penetrable

porpoise
5 whale 7 dolphin

porridge
4 mush 5 gruel, kasha 6 burgoo, cereal,
congee, pablum, sowens 7 oatmeal,
pabulum 8 flummery, loblolly 9 stirabout

port
4 hole, jack, left, wine 5 cover, haven
6 harbor, refuge 7 bearing, opening,
retreat, shelter 8 larboard, left side
9 anchorage, harborage, roadstead,
sanctuary 11 comportment
opposite: 9 starboard

portable
5 handy 6 mobile, wieldy

portal
4 door, gate 5 entry 7 doorway, gateway
8 approach, entrance, entryway

portcullis
4 gate 7 grating, lattice

portend
4 bode 5 augur 6 signal 7 betoken,
predict, presage, promise, signify
8 forebode, forecast, foretell, indicate,
prophesy 9 adumbrate, foretoken
10 foreshadow, vaticinate

portent
4 omen, sign 6 augury, boding 7 presage,
prodigy 9 foretoken, sensation
10 foreboding, indication 11 premonition

portentous
5 grave 6 solemn 7 ominous, pompous,
serious, weighty 8 inflated 9 marvelous,
momentous, ponderous 10 prodigious

porter
5 hamal, stout 6 bearer, redcap, skycap
7 bellboy, bellhop, carrier 9 transport
10 doorkeeper

Portia
6 lawyer
husband: 6 Brutus 8 Bassanio
maid: 7 Nerissa

portico
4 stoa 9 colonnade

portion
3 cut, lot 4 bite, part 5 dower, moira,
piece, quota, share, slice 6 moiety, parcel
7 measure, quantum, segment 8 division
largest: 10 lion's share
unused: 8 leftover

portly
3 fat 5 bulky, heavy, large, stout 6 fleshy
7 rotound, stately, weighty 8 imposing
9 corpulent 10 overweight

portmanteau
8 carryall, suitcase

portrait
4 bust 5 image 6 figure, statue 7 picture
8 painting 9 depiction

portray
4 draw, limn, play 5 enact, paint 6 depict,
render 7 picture 8 describe 9 delineate,
interpret, represent

portrayal
5 image 7 account, picture 8 likeness,
painting 9 depiction 11 delineation,
description, performance 12 illustration

Portugal
capital: 6 Lisbon

city: 5 Porto **6** Oporto **7** Amadora
former name: 9 Lusitania
island group: 6 Azores **7** Madeira
leader: 7 Salazar (Antonio de)
monetary unit: 4 euro
monetary unit, former: 6 escudo
neighbor: 5 Spain
peninsula: 7 Iberian
river: 5 Tagus

pose
3 act, air, ask, set, sit **4** airs, fake, role,
sham **5** feign, front, offer, place, stand,
state, strut **6** affect, assume, pass as,
stance **7** pass for, pass off, present,
pretend, show off, suggest **8** attitude,
pretense, set forth **9** mannerism
10 pretension **11** affectation

Poseidon
7 Neptune
brother: 4 Zeus **5** Hades, Pluto **7** Jupiter
consort: 4 Tyro **6** Medusa **7** Demeter
father: 6 Cronus
mother: 4 Rhea
offspring: 7 Pegasus
son: 5 Orion **6** Neleus, Pelias, Triton
7 Antaeus **10** Polyphemus
weapon: 7 trident
wife: 10 Amphitrite

poser
6 puzzle, riddle **7** problem **9** conundrum
11 brainteaser

poseur
4 fake **5** bluff, decoy, fraud, phony, quack
7 bluffer **8** deceiver, imposter **9** charlatan,
hypocrite, pretender **10** mountebank
11 masquerader **12** impersonator

posh
4 chic, rich, tony **5** fancy, grand, smart,
swank **7** elegant, stylish **9** exclusive,
expensive, luxurious **11** fashionable,
highfalutin, pretentious

posit
3 fix **5** offer **6** affirm, assert, assume
7 premise, present, presume, propose,
suggest **9** postulate

position
3 job **4** rank, site, spot **5** locus, place,
point, situs, stand, state **6** belief, locate,
stance **7** emplace, footing, stature
8 attitude, capacity, location, prestige,
standing **10** standpoint

positive
4 firm, real, sure **5** clear, sound **6** actual,
useful **7** assured, certain, decided, factual,

genuine, helpful, reality **8** absolute,
complete, constant, definite, forceful,
outright **9** confident, doubtless, downright,
effective, favorable, realistic **10** beneficial,
inarguable, optimistic, prescribed,
undeniable **11** categorical, irrefutable,
unequivocal, unmitigated, unqualified
12 indisputable, unmistakable
13 incontestable

possess
3 own **4** have, hold, keep **5** carry **6** retain
7 acquire, control

possessed
3 mad **6** crazed, hooked **8** frenzied
9 bewitched

possession
7 control **8** property **9** occupancy,
ownership **10** occupation

possessive
7 jealous **8** watchful **10** protective
11 proprietary

possibility
4 odds **6** chance **8** instance **9** potential
10 likelihood **11** contingency, feasibility

possible
6 doable, likely, viable **7** earthly **8** feasible
9 expedient, potential **10** imaginable,
realizable **11** practicable

possibly
5 maybe **7** perhaps **8** by chance
9 perchance **11** conceivably

post
3 set **4** camp, mail, pole, ride, spot, task
5 affix, hurry, newel, place, score, stage,
stake **6** advise, column, fill in, inform,
notify, office, pillar, put up **7** apprise,
express, placard, publish, station **8** announce, denounce, position **9** advertise
10 assignment

poster
4 bill, sign **6** notice **7** affiche, placard
9 broadside, signboard **12** announcement
13 advertisement

posterior
4 back, hind, rear, rump, seat, tail **5** after,
fanny, later **6** behind, caudal, dorsal,
hinder **7** ensuing, rear end, tail end
8 backside, buttocks, derriere, hindmost,
rearward **9** following **10** subsequent

posterity
6 future **7** progeny **8** children **9** offspring
11 descendants

posthaste
4 fast 6 at once, pronto 7 fleetly, quickly, rapidly, swiftly 8 promptly, speedily 11 immediately

Postimpressionist painter
6 Seurat (Georges) 7 Cezanne (Paul), Gauguin (Paul), Van Gogh (Vincent) 8 Pissarro (Camille), Rousseau (Henri)

postmortem
7 autopsy 8 necropsy

postpone
5 defer, delay, table 6 hold up, put off, shelve 7 hold off, lay over, suspend 8 hold over, prorogue

postulate
5 axiom, claim 6 assert, assume, demand, thesis 7 premise, suppose 10 assumption, hypothesis, presuppose 11 hypothesize, presumption, supposition

posture
4 mode, pose 5 state 6 affect, assume, manner, stance, status 7 bearing, outlook 8 attitude, carriage, position 9 condition, situation 12 attitudinize

posy
5 bloom 6 flower 7 blossom, bouquet, corsage, nosegay 9 sentiment

pot
3 bet, pan, wad 4 ante, hemp, olla 5 grass, kitty, stake, wager 6 boodle, bundle, pipkin 8 cannabis 9 marijuana

potable
5 clean, drink, fresh 6 liquid, liquor 8 beverage 9 drinkable

potassium ore
7 sylvite

potato
3 yam 4 spud 5 tater
bud: 3 eye

pot-au-_____
3 feu

potbelly
3 gut 5 stove 6 paunch 9 bay window, spare tire

potency
3 pep 5 force, might, power, vigor 6 energy, muscle 8 strength 9 influence, puissance 10 capability 13 effectiveness

potent
4 rich 6 mighty, robust, strong, virile 7 dynamic 8 forceful, forcible, powerful 9 effective 10 persuasive 11 influential

potential
6 latent, likely 7 ability, promise 8 capacity, possible 9 plausible, promising 10 imaginable 11 conceivable, possibility

pother
3 ado 4 flap, fret, fuss, stir, to-do 5 furor, whirl, worry 6 bustle, flurry, fluster, furore, hassle, hubbub, tumult, uproar 7 turmoil 9 agitation, annoyance, commotion, confusion

potion
6 liquid 7 mixture, philter, philtre 8 medicine 10 concoction

Potiphar's slave
6 Joseph

Potiphera
daughter: 7 Asenath
son-in-law: 6 Joseph

Potok novel
6 Chosen (The) 16 My Name Is Asher Lev

potpourri
4 olio 5 blend 6 medley 7 grab bag, mélange, variety 8 mishmash, pastiche 10 assortment, collection, hodgepodge, miscellany, salmagundi

potshot
3 cut, dig 4 gibe, jibe 5 crack, shoot, swipe 6 attack, insult 9 criticism

potter
see **putter**

Potter character
5 Mopsy, Mr. Tod 6 Flopsy, Jemima (Puddleduck) 10 Cotton-tail, Hunca Munca 11 Peter Rabbit 12 Jeremy Fisher

potter's field
8 cemetery, God's acre 9 graveyard

pottery
4 raku 5 delft 7 redware 8 ceramics, clayware, slipware 10 lusterware, terracotta, yellowware 11 earthenware

pouch
3 bag, sac 4 sack 5 bulge, bursa, burse 6 pocket 7 saccule 8 sacculus

pouf
5 quilt 7 ottoman 9 comforter

poultry
4 fowl
type: 4 duck, swan 5 goose, quail 6 grouse, pigeon, turkey 7 chicken, ostrich, peacock 8 pheasant 9 partridge

pounce
5 seize, swoop, talon 6 attack, powder
7 assault, stencil

pound
4 bang, bash, beat, slam, slug, sock
5 drive, money, stamp, throb, thump, tramp
6 batter, buffet, hammer, pummel, strike,
thrash, wallop 7 belabor, impress, pulsate
9 enclosure

Pound work
6 Cantos (The)

poupée
4 doll

pour
4 flow, gush, rain, rill, rush, teem 5 flood,
issue, skink, spate, surge, swarm
6 decant, deluge, drench, sluice, spring,
stream 7 cascade, torrent 8 inundate,
overflow

pourboire
3 tip 7 cumshaw 8 gratuity

pout
3 pet 4 fish, moue, sulk 5 grump
8 protrude 10 expression, protrusion

poverty
4 need, want 6 dearth, penury 7 beggary,
paucity 8 hardship, poorness, scarcity,
shortage 9 indigence, neediness,
pauperism, privation 10 mendicancy,
scarceness 11 destitution
13 pennilessness

POW camp
6 stalag

powder
4 bray, dust, talc 5 crush 6 talcum
8 sprinkle 9 comminute, pulverize, triturate
10 besprinkle

power
3 vis 4 sway 5 force, might, sinew, steam,
vigor, vires (plural) 6 energy, muscle
7 command, ability, control, potency,
voltage 8 dominion, dynamism, imperium,
strength 9 authority, influence, privilege,
puissance, strong arm 10 ascendancy,
domination 11 prerogative, sovereignty,
superiority 12 jurisdiction, potentiality
combining form: 5 dynam 6 dynamo
unit: 4 watt

powerful
5 great 6 mighty, potent, strong 7 dynamic
8 dominant, puissant, vigorous
9 energetic, strenuous 10 convincing,
impressive, invincible, persuasive
11 efficacious, influential, prestigious
13 authoritative

powerless
4 weak 5 inert 6 feeble, unable 7 passive
8 impotent 9 incapable 11 incompetent,
ineffective

powwow
4 chat, talk 6 confab, confer, huddle,
parley 7 discuss, meeting 8 ceremony
9 gathering 10 discussion 11 confabulate,
get-together

practicable
5 utile 6 doable, likely, usable, useful
8 feasible, possible 9 operative
10 functional

practical
5 handy, utile 6 active, useful, versed
7 applied, skilled, trained, virtual 8 sensible
9 pragmatic, realistic 10 functional
11 down-to-earth, experienced
12 businesslike

practically
5 about 6 all but, almost, near to, nearly
7 close to 8 in effect 9 in essence, just
about

practice
3 use, way 4 form, mode, wont 5 drill,
habit, usage 6 custom, manner, method,
repeat, system, tryout, warm up 7 perform,
process 8 drilling, engage in, exercise,
habitude, rehearse 9 procedure, rehearsal
10 convention

pragmatic
7 factual, logical 8 rational 9 practical,
realistic 11 down-to-earth

prairie
4 veld 5 plain, veldt 7 plateau 9 grassland

prairie chicken
6 grouse

prairie wolf
6 coyote

praise
4 hail, hymn, laud, puff 5 bravo, cry up,
exalt, extol, honor, kudos 6 belaud, kudize
7 acclaim, adulate, applaud, commend,
enhance, flatter, glorify, hosanna, magnify,
ovation, plaudit, puffery, sublime
8 accolade, applause, approval, citation,
encomium, eulogize, flattery 9 celebrate,
laudation, panegyric, recommend

praiseworthy
10 aggrandize, compliment, panegyrize
11 acclamation 12 commendation

praiseworthy
8 laudable 9 admirable, deserving, estimable 11 commendable, meritorious

prance
4 step 5 mince, strut 6 sashay, spring 8 cakewalk

prank
3 gag 4 deck, dido, lark, whim 5 adorn, antic, caper, fancy, spiff, sport, trick 6 doll up, frolic, gambol, levity, shavie, vagary, whimsy 7 caprice, deck out, doll out, dress up, garnish, rollick, spiff up 8 beautify, decorate, escapade, ornament, spruce up 9 embellish, frivolity, horseplay, smarten up 10 shenanigan, tomfoolery
11 monkeyshine

prankster
3 wag 5 cutup, joker

prate
3 gab, jaw, yak 4 blab, chat, go on 5 run on 6 babble, gabble, jabber 7 blabber, blather, chatter 9 yakety-yak

prater
6 gossip, magpie 10 chatterbox
12 blabbermouth

pratfall
6 mishap, tumble 7 blunder, stumble
11 humiliation

prawn
6 shrimp 11 langoustine
French: 8 crevette

praxis
5 habit 6 action, custom, manner
7 conduct 8 exercise, habitude, practice

Praxiteles statue
5 Satyr 6 Hermes 9 Aphrodite

pray
3 ask, beg 5 plead 6 appeal 7 beseech, entreat, implore, request 8 petition
10 supplicate

prayer
4 plea, suit 6 appeal, litany, orison 7 angelus, begging, worship 8 blessing, devotion, entreaty, petition, pleading, rogation 9 adoration 11 application, imploration, imprecation 12 supplication
beads: 6 rosary
ending: 4 amen
for the dead: 7 requiem
Jewish: 7 kaddish, kiddush

period: 6 novena 7 triduum
shawl: 7 tallith

prayer book
6 missal, siddur 8 breviary

prayerful
4 holy 5 godly, pious 6 devout 7 earnest, sincere

preach
4 urge 6 exhort 7 address, deliver, lecture 8 admonish, advocate, moralize
9 sermonize 10 evangelize

preacher
5 padre 6 cleric, divine, parson, pastor 8 chaplain, clerical, minister, reverend 9 churchman, clergyman 10 evangelist, sermonizer 12 ecclesiastic

preaching friar
9 Dominican

preachy
4 smug 7 donnish 8 didactic, sermonic, unctuous 9 homiletic, hortative, pedagogic, pietistic 10 moralizing 11 exhortative, sermonizing 13 sanctimonious, self-righteous

preamble
5 intro, proem 8 exordium, foreword, overture, prologue 12 introduction

precarious
4 iffy 5 dicey, risky, shaky 6 chancy, touchy, tricky, unsafe 7 dubious 8 delicate, doubtful, insecure, ticklish, unstable 9 dangerous, hazardous, sensitive, uncertain 10 unreliable

precaution
4 care 8 prudence 9 foresight, insurance, provision, safeguard 11 forethought

precede
4 lead, rank 5 usher 6 herald 7 forerun, outrank, surpass 8 announce, antedate, go before 9 introduce

precedence
5 order 8 priority 9 seniority

precedent
4 past, rule 5 model, prior 6 former 7 earlier, example 8 anterior 9 foregoing 10 convention

preceding
4 past 5 prior 6 before, former 7 ahead of, prior to 8 anterior, hitherto 9 erstwhile 10 heretofore 11 in advance of
prefix: 4 ante

precept
3 law 4 rule 5 axiom, edict, order, tenet
6 behest, decree 7 bidding, command
8 doctrine 9 principle 10 injunction,
regulation 11 fundamental

preceptive
8 didactic

preceptor
4 head 5 tutor 7 teacher 9 principal
10 headmaster

precinct
4 area 6 domain, region, sector, sphere
7 quarter, section 8 district, division,
township 9 bailiwick, enclosure

precious
3 pet 4 dear, nice, rare, rich, very 5 fussy,
great, loved, showy 6 adored, choice,
costly, la-di-da, prized 7 beloved, darling
8 affected, esteemed, favorite, valuable
9 cherished, exquisite, extremely, priceless
10 invaluable

precipice
5 brink, cliff 8 overhang

precipitancy
4 rush 5 haste, hurry 9 hastiness
10 abruptness, suddenness 11 hurriedness

precipitate
4 fall, hurl 5 hasty, sheer, steep, throw
6 abrupt, madcap, result, sudden, upshot
7 bring on, deposit, falling, flowing,
grounds, hurried, outcome, product
8 condense, headlong, sediment, separate
9 breakneck, impatient, impetuous,
impulsive 10 unexpected, unforeseen
11 consequence

precipitation
4 hail, mist, rain, snow 5 sleet 7 deposit
8 sediment

precipitous
4 rash 5 hasty, sheer, steep 6 abrupt,
sudden 7 hurried, rushing 8 headlong,
heedless, plunging 9 breakneck
13 perpendicular

précis
6 digest, survey 7 summary 8 abstract,
overview, syllabus 10 abridgment,
compendium 11 abridgement
12 condensation

precise
4 nice 5 exact, fixed, right 6 narrow, strict
7 correct, limited 8 accurate, clear-cut,
definite, rigorous, specific 9 clocklike,
stringent 10 particular

precisely
4 just 5 right 7 exactly 8 strictly

precision
4 care 5 rigor 8 accuracy 9 exactness
10 exactitude, refinement 11 correctness

preclude
5 avert, deter 7 forfend, obviate, prevent,
rule out 8 prohibit, stave off 9 forestall

precocious
5 smart 6 brainy, bright, mature 7 forward
8 advanced

precondition
4 must, need 7 proviso 9 essential,
necessity, provision, requisite 10 sine qua
non, stipulation 11 requirement

precursor
6 herald 8 ancestor, forebear 9 harbinger,
indicator, prototype 10 antecedent,
forerunner

predator
6 hunter, preyer, raptor 7 stalker
8 devourer 9 destroyer 10 bird of prey

predatory
6 greedy 9 pillaging, rapacious
10 plundering 12 exploitative

predecessor
8 ancestor, forebear 9 precursor, prototype
10 antecedent, forerunner

predicament
3 fix, jam 4 bind, hole, spot 5 pinch, state
6 corner, muddle, pickle, plight, puzzle,
scrape, strait 7 dilemma, impasse, trouble
8 hardship, nuisance, quagmire
9 condition, situation 10 difficulty

predicate
4 aver, avow, base, imply, rest 5 found
6 affirm, assert, avouch 7 declare, profess
9 establish

predict
5 augur, guess, infer 6 expect 7 forbode,
foresee, portend, surmise 8 announce,
conclude, forebode, forecast, foretell,
indicate, prophesy, soothsay
10 conjecture, vaticinate 13 prognosticate

prediction
6 augury 8 forecast, prophecy 9 prognosis
10 expectancy 11 expectation

predilection
4 bent, bias 5 fancy, taste 6 liking

predispose
7 leaning 8 fondness, penchant, tendency
9 inclining 10 proclivity, propensity
11 inclination, partiality

predispose
4 bend, bias, tend, sway 5 prime 6 affect
7 incline 9 influence

predisposed
5 prone, ready 6 biased 7 partial, willing
8 inclined 11 susceptible

predisposition
4 bent, bias 7 leaning 8 penchant,
tendency 9 inclining 10 partiality,
proclivity, propensity 11 inclination

predominant
4 main 5 chief, major, ruling 6 master
7 capital, general, leading, primary
8 reigning, superior 9 number one,
paramount, principal, sovereign
10 prevailing 11 outstanding

predominate
4 rule 5 reign 6 govern, master
7 command, control, prevail 8 outweigh

preeminence
6 renown 7 primacy 8 dominion, prestige
9 supremacy 10 ascendancy, domination,
excellence, importance 11 distinction,
superiority

preeminent
4 main 5 chief 7 capital, stellar, supreme
8 dominant, foremost, peerless, towering,
ultimate 9 matchless, number-one,
paramount, principal, unrivaled
10 surpassing, unrivalled 11 outstanding,
unmatchable 12 incomparable,
transcendent
prefix: 4 arch

preempt
4 bump, take 5 annex, seize, usurp
6 assume 7 acquire, replace 8 arrogate
9 forestall 10 confiscate, substitute
11 appropriate, expropriate

preen
5 gloat, groom, pride, primp, swell
6 smooth

preface
4 lead, open 5 begin, proem, usher
6 herald 8 exordium, foreword, overture,
preamble, prologue 9 introduce
11 preliminary 12 introduction

prefatory
7 opening 8 proemial 12 introductory

prefect
7 head boy, monitor 8 head girl
10 magistrate

prefer
5 elect, favor 6 choose, opt for, select
7 advance, elevate, promote, upgrade

preferable
5 finer 6 better 8 superior, worthier

preference
4 pick 6 choice, option 8 election, priority
9 advantage, elevation, promotion,
selection, upgrading 10 favoritism,
partiality

prefigure
4 hint 7 foresee 8 indicate 9 adumbrate
10 foreshadow

pregnancy
9 gestation, gravidity

pregnant
4 full, rich 5 heavy 6 gravid, parous
7 teeming, weighty 8 eloquent, enceinte,
profound 9 expectant, expecting,
gestating, inventive, momentous, with child
10 expressive, meaningful, parturient
11 significant

prehensile
8 grasping

prejudice
3 mar 4 bias, harm, hurt, sway 5 color,
favor 6 damage, injure, injury, racism,
sexism 7 bigotry, leaning 8 aversion
9 antipathy, hostility, influence 10 partiality
11 intolerance 12 one-sidedness

prejudicial
6 biased 7 bigoted 8 damaging
9 injurious 11 deleterious, detrimental

prelate
5 abbot 6 bishop 7 primate 8 cardinal,
diocesan 9 patriarch 10 archbishop
12 ecclesiastic

preliminary
4 heat 5 basic, match, trial 7 initial,
opening 8 proemial 9 beginning
10 qualifying 11 fundamental 12 introductory

prelude
5 intro, proem 8 exordium, foreword,
overture, prologue 12 introduction,
prolegomenon

premature
5 early 8 untimely 10 beforehand

premeditated
5 set up 7 planned, studied, willful
8 designed, intended 9 conscious
10 calculated, considered, deliberate,
thought-out 11 intentional

premier
4 head, main 5 chief, first 7 leading, primary 8 earliest, foremost, original 9 principal 13 prime minister

premiere
5 debut 7 opening 8 earliest, original 9 beginning 10 first night

premise
4 base 5 posit 6 assume, thesis 8 building, property, set forth 9 postulate 10 assumption 11 postulation, proposition, supposition

premium
5 bonus, extra, prize 6 reward 8 dividend, superior 9 excellent 10 recompense 11 exceptional

premonition
4 omen 9 misgiving, suspicion 10 foreboding 11 forewarning 12 apprehension, presentiment

preoccupied
4 deep, lost, rapt 6 absent, intent 7 engaged, faraway, worried 8 absorbed, immersed 9 concerned, engrossed, wrapped up 10 abstracted, distracted 11 inattentive 12 absentminded

prep
5 basic, coach, drill, equip, groom, prime, ready, train, trial 8 get ready 11 preliminary 12 introductory

preparation
4 base, plan 5 study 7 fitness, measure 8 compound, medicine, training 9 alertness, foresight, readiness 10 background, concoction

preparatory
5 basic 11 preliminary, rudimentary 12 introductory

prepare
3 fit, fix 4 gird 5 draft, prime, ready, train 6 draw up, make up, outfit 7 fortify, furnish 9 formulate

prepared
3 set 4 up on 5 fixed, ready 6 primed 7 treated 9 processed

preponderance
4 bulk 8 dominion, majority, main part 9 ascendant, dominance, supremacy 10 ascendancy, domination 11 superiority

preponderant
7 supreme 8 dominant, superior 9 paramount 10 prevailing

preponderate
4 rule 5 reign 6 exceed 7 command, dictate, outrank, prevail 8 dominate, outweigh

prepossess
4 bias, sway 5 favor 6 absorb, engage, occupy 7 engross, immerse, involve 9 influence

prepossessing
7 likable 9 appealing 10 attractive

preposterous
4 wild 5 crazy, wacky 6 absurd, insane 7 asinine, foolish, idiotic 9 fantastic, laughable, senseless 10 irrational, ridiculous 11 harebrained 12 unreasonable

prerequisite
4 must, need 5 vital 8 required 9 condition, essential, mandatory, necessary, necessity 10 imperative, sine qua non 11 requirement 13 indispensable

prerogative
5 power, right 8 appanage, immunity 9 authority, exemption, privilege 10 birthright, perquisite

presage
4 bode, omen, warn 5 augur, sense 6 augury, boding, herald, intuit 7 portend, portent, predict, promise, warning 8 announce, forebode, forecast, foretell, forewarn, indicate, prophesy, soothsay 9 foretoken, harbinger, intuition, misgiving 10 foreboding, foreshadow, prediction, prognostic, vaticinate

presbyter
5 elder 6 priest

prescience
9 foresight 12 anticipation, clairvoyance 13 foreknowledge

prescribe
3 fix, set 4 rule 5 guide, order 6 assign, choose, decide, decree, define, direct, impose, ordain, select 7 dictate, lay down, pick out, require, specify 9 designate, determine, stipulate

prescript
3 law 4 rule 5 edict, order 6 decree 10 regulation

prescription
4 drug, rule 5 claim, right, title 6 custom, remedy 8 medicine 9 direction 10 medication

presence
3 air 4 look, mien 5 poise 6 aspect, spirit

7 address, bearing 8 carriage, demeanor 9 composure

present

3 act, aim, now 4 boon, gift, give, here, pose, show 5 award, bring, favor, offer, point, stage, tense, today 6 at hand, bestow, confer, convey, direct, donate, extend, in view, modern, submit, tender 7 hand out, largess, perform, proffer 8 existing, nominate 9 introduce 12 contemporary

presentable

3 fit 6 decent, proper 8 becoming 9 befitting 10 acceptable 11 appropriate 12 satisfactory

present-day

6 living, recent 7 current, ongoing, popular, topical 8 contempo, existent, existing, pressing, up-to-date 9 prevalent, surviving 10 prevailing 12 contemporary

presently

3 now 4 anon, soon 5 today 6 in time, one day 7 by and by 9 forthwith, these days 10 before long

preservation

4 care 6 saving, shield 7 defense, keeping 8 pickling 10 husbanding, protection 11 conservancy, maintenance, safekeeping

preserve

3 can, jam 4 save 5 jelly, put up 6 keep up, pickle 7 protect, shelter, sustain 8 keep safe, maintain 9 confiture

preside

3 run 4 head, lead 5 chair 6 direct, handle, manage 7 conduct, control, operate, oversee 8 moderate 9 officiate

president

United States: 4 Bush (George, George W.), Ford (Gerald R.), Polk (James K.), Taft (William H.) 5 Adams (John, John Quincy), Grant (Ulysses S.), Hayes (Rutherford B.), Nixon (Richard M.), Tyler (John) 6 Arthur (Chester A.), Carter (Jimmy), Hoover (Herbert), Monroe (James), Pierce (Franklin), Reagan (Ronald), Taylor (Zachary), Truman (Harry S.), Wilson (Woodrow) 7 Clinton (Bill), Harding (Warren), Jackson (Andrew), Johnson (Andrew, Lyndon), Kennedy (John F.), Lincoln (Abraham), Madison (James) 8 Buchanan (James), Coolidge (Calvin), Fillmore (Millard), Garfield (James), Harrison (Benjamin, William Henry), McKinley (William), Van Buren (Martin)

9 Cleveland (Grover), Jefferson (Thomas), Roosevelt (Franklin D., Theodore) 10 Eisenhower (Dwight D.), Washington (George)

presidio

4 fort 7 bastion, citadel 8 fastness, fortress, garrison 10 stronghold 13 fortification

press

3 hug, jam, ram 4 cram, iron, mass, pack, pile, push, rush, urge 5 clasp, crowd, crush, drive, force, horde, hurry, media, shove 6 demand, hustle, insist, jostle, propel, squash, stress, throng, thrust 7 beseech, entreat, imprint, printer, squeeze 9 constrain, influence, multitude

pressing

5 acute, vital 6 urgent 7 crucial, earnest, exigent, serious 8 critical 9 immediate, important, insistent 10 compelling, imperative

pressure

4 push, rush 5 drive, impel 6 burden, strain, stress 7 tension 10 constraint **combining form:** 5 piezo **instrument:** 9 barometer **unit:** 3 bar 6 pascal

prestige

4 fame, rank, sway 5 power 6 cachet, credit, esteem, regard, renown, repute, status, weight 7 dignity, stature 8 eminence, position, standing 9 authority, influence 10 importance, prominence 11 consequence, distinction

prestigious

5 famed, great 6 famous 7 eminent, honored, notable 8 esteemed, renowned 9 prominent, respected 10 celebrated 11 influential 13 distinguished

presto

4 fast 7 hastily, quickly, rapidly 8 suddenly 9 posthaste 11 immediately

presumably

6 likely, surely 8 probably 9 doubtless

presume

4 dare 5 guess, imply, infer, think, trust 6 expect, gather, impose, reason 7 believe, intrude, suppose, surmise, venture 8 infringe 9 postulate 10 conjecture

presumption

4 gall 5 brass, cheek, nerve 6 belief, daring, ground, reason, thesis 7 conceit

presumptuous
8 audacity, chutzpah, evidence
9 brashness, inference, postulate
10 confidence, effrontery

presumptuous
4 bold, smug 5 brash, fresh, pushy
6 cheeky, uppity 7 forward 8 arrogant
9 audacious, confident 11 overweening,
self-assured

presuppose
5 posit 6 assume, expect 7 imagine,
require, surmise 9 postulate

pretend
3 act 4 fake, pose, sham 5 bluff, claim,
false, feign, guess, put on 6 affect,
assume, delude, invent 7 deceive, imitate,
mislead, playact, profess, purport,
suppose, surmise 8 simulate 9 imaginary
11 counterfeit, make-believe

pretender
4 fake, sham 5 actor, faker, fraud, phony
6 humbug 8 claimant, impostor
9 hypocrite

pretense
3 act, air 4 face, fake, mask, pose, sham
5 claim, cloak, cover, front, guise 6 deceit,
facade, humbug 7 charade, fiction
8 disguise 9 deception, false show,
imposture 10 masquerade, ostentation,
simulation 11 affectation, make-believe

pretension
5 claim, right 6 vanity 8 ambition
10 allegation, aspiration 11 affectation

pretentious
5 lofty, put-on, showy 6 chichi, la-di-da,
too-too 7 pompous, stilted 8 affected,
inflated, puffed up, snobbish, specious
9 bombastic, conceited, grandiose,
overblown 10 euphuistic, rhetorical
11 highfalutin 12 high-sounding,
magniloquent, vainglorious

preternatural
7 psychic, unusual 8 abnormal, atypical
9 anomalous, unearthly, untypical
10 mysterious 12 inexplicable,
supernatural 13 extraordinary

pretext
4 mask, ploy 5 alibi, cloak, cover, front,
guise 6 device, excuse 7 apology
10 subterfuge

pretty
3 apt, pat 4 cute, fair, nice, some 5 bonny,
quite 6 adroit, artful, clever, comely, fairly,
kind of, lovely, mainly, rather, seemly, sort
of 7 cunning, darling 8 graceful,
handsome, pleasant, pleasing, skillful,
somewhat 9 appealing, beautiful
10 attractive, moderately, more or less
11 good-looking 12 considerable

prevail
4 beat, rule 5 reign 6 master 7 conquer,
impress, persist, triumph 8 convince,
dominate, domineer, overcome, override,
persuade 9 influence

prevalent
4 rife 6 ruling 7 favored, popular, regnant
8 accepted, dominant, superior
9 ascendant, customary, paramount,
sovereign 10 accustomed, widespread

prevaricate
3 fib, lie 5 avoid, evade 6 palter
7 confuse, deceive, distort, falsify, quibble
12 misrepresent

prevarication
3 fib, lie 4 tale 5 lying, story 6 canard,
deceit 7 falsity 9 deception, falsehood

prevent
3 bar, dam 4 balk, foil, ward 5 avert,
avoid, block, check, debar, deter 6 arrest,
baffle, forbid, hinder, impede, thwart
7 forfend, head off, inhibit, obviate
8 obstruct, prohibit, stave off 9 forestall,
frustrate, interdict 10 anticipate

previous
4 fore, past 5 early, prior 6 before, former
7 earlier, onetime 8 anterior 9 erstwhile,
foregoing, in advance 10 antecedent,
beforehand

previously
4 once 5 afore, ahead 6 before 7 already,
earlier 8 formerly 9 erstwhile
10 heretofore

prewar
10 antebellum

prey
4 feed, game, mark 5 chase 6 quarry,
target, victim 8 casualty, distress

Priam
daughter: 6 Creusa 8 Polyxena
9 Cassandra
father: 8 Laomedon
grandfather: 4 Ilus
kingdom: 4 Troy
slayer: 7 Pyrrhus 11 Neoptolemus
son: 5 Paris 6 Hector, Lycaon 7 Helenus,
Troilus 9 Deiphobus, Polydorus
wife: 6 Arisbe, Hecuba

Priapus
 father: **7** Bacchus **8** Dionysus
 mother: **5** Venus **9** Aphrodite

price
 3 fee, fix, tab **4** cost, fare, rate, toll
 6 amount, assess, charge, figure, outlay,
 reward, tariff **7** expense, payment
 8 appraise

priceless
 4 rare, rich **5** droll, funny, witty **6** absurd,
 costly, prized, valued **7** amusing
 8 precious, valuable **9** cherished,
 treasured **10** invaluable

pricey
 4 dear **5** steep **6** costly **9** expensive

prick
 3 jab **4** goad, mark, prod, spur, urge **5** egg
 on, point, sting, thorn **6** affect, excite,
 exhort, pierce, prompt **7** pinhole
 8 puncture **9** perforate

prickly
 5 burry, sharp, spiny **6** briary, thorny, tingly,
 touchy, trying **7** brambly, waspish
 8 annoying, nettling, snappish, stinging
 9 difficult, fractious, irritable, vexatious
 10 bothersome, irritating, nettlesome
 11 troublesome

pride
 3 ego, top **4** best, brag, pack, pick
 5 boast, cream, elite, exult, group, preen,
 prime, prize, vaunt **6** choice, egoism,
 vanity **7** conceit, delight, elation, dignity,
 disdain, egotism **8** smugness, treasure
 9 arrogance, cockiness, vainglory **10** self-
 esteem, self-regard **11** self-respect
 12 congratulate

Pride and Prejudice author
 6 Austen (Jane)

prideful
 6 elated **7** haughty **8** exultant
 10 disdainful

prier
 5 snoop **7** meddler **8** busybody, quidnunc
 9 buttinsky

priest
 6 cleric, divine, rector **8** chaplain
 9 clergyman, presbyter
 ancient Roman: **6** flamen **8** pontifex
 Buddhist: **4** lama
 Celtic: **5** druid
 French: **4** abbé, curé
 Muslim: **4** imam
 tribal: **6** shaman

priestly
 8 clerical, hieratic **10** sacerdotal

prig
 5 prude, thief **6** pedant **8** bluenose **9** Mrs.
 Grundy **10** goody-goody

priggish
 5 fussy **6** stuffy **7** genteel, pompous,
 prudish **8** affected, pedantic
 11 puritanical, straitlaced

prim
 4 neat, nice, snug, tidy, trig **5** stiff **6** formal,
 proper, strict, stuffy, wooden **7** correct,
 genteel, orderly, precise, prudish
 8 decorous, priggish **11** straitlaced

prima donna
 4 diva, snob, star **7** artiste **9** chanteuse
 10 narcissist **11** leading lady

prima facie
 4 true **5** valid **8** apparent **11** self-evident

primal
 5 basic **6** age-old **7** ancient, premier
 8 cardinal, original **9** atavistic, paramount,
 primitive **10** preeminent **11** prehistoric

primary
 4 main **5** basal, basic, chief, first **6** direct
 7 initial, pioneer, radical **8** cardinal,
 earliest, original **9** elemental, essential,
 firsthand, immediate, number-one,
 paramount, principal **10** aboriginal,
 underlying **11** fundamental, rudimentary
 12 foundational, introductory
 combining form: **4** prot **5** proto
 prefix: **4** arch **5** archi

primate
 3 ape, man **5** human, lemur, loris **6** aye-
 aye, bonobo, monkey **7** gorilla
 10 anthropoid, chimpanzee, human being
 11 Homo sapiens
 nocturnal: **5** loris **7** tarsier
 small: **6** galago

prime
 3 top **4** best, dawn, fill, load, morn, peak,
 pick, rate **5** coach, cream, elite, first, paint,
 sunup, tonic, youth **6** choice, excite,
 height, spring, symbol **7** capital, highest,
 initial, morning, prepare, provoke, quicken
 8 earliest, motivate, original, superior
 9 excellent, first-rate, principal, stimulate
 10 first-class

primer
 4 book **5** guide **6** manual, reader
 8 hornbook

primeval
7 ancient 8 earliest, original 10 aboriginal

primitive
3 raw 4 rude 5 basic, crude, early
6 savage 7 archaic, Spartan 8 barbaric,
original, primeval 9 atavistic, barbarian,
barbarous, elemental, essential, unevolved
10 elementary, primordial, underlying
11 fundamental, preliterate, uncivilized,
undeveloped 12 uncultivated
combining form: 5 palae, paleo
6 archae, archeo, palaeo 7 archaeo
prefix: 4 arch 5 arche, archi

primogenitor
8 ancestor, forebear 9 precursor
10 forefather

primordial
5 basic, early, first 7 ancient 8 earliest,
original

primp
4 fuss 5 adorn, dress, fix up, preen
7 dress up

prince
Anglo-Saxon: 8 atheling
Arab: 4 amir, emir
Austrian: 8 archduke
Ethiopian: 3 ras
Indian: 4 raja 5 rajah
of demons: 9 Beelzebub
of Monaco: 7 Rainier
of the church: 8 cardinal
of Wales: 7 Charles

Prince and the Pauper author
5 Twain (Mark) 7 Clemens (Samuel)

Prince _____ Coast, Antarctica
4 Olav

Prince Edward Island
capital: 13 Charlottetown
provincial flower: 12 lady's slipper

Prince Igor composer
7 Borodin (Aleksandr)

princely
5 grand, noble, royal 8 generous,
imposing, majestic 9 dignified
11 magnificent

princess
7 infanta
mythical: 3 Ino
of Monaco: 5 Grace

Prince Valiant
artist: 6 Foster (Hal)
son: 3 Arn
wife: 5 Aleta

principal
4 arch, dean, head, main, star 5 chief, first,
major, prime 6 assets 7 capital, leading,
premier, primary, stellar 8 cardinal,
champion, dominant, foremost
9 paramount 10 headmaster, preeminent
11 outstanding, predominant
combining form: 4 prot 5 proto
prefix: 4 arch 5 archi

principium
3 law 5 axiom, basis 7 element, theorem
10 foundation 11 fundamental

principle
3 law 4 code, form, rule 5 axiom, basis,
canon, ethic, tenet 6 ground, origin, source
7 conduct, faculty, precept 8 doctrine,
polestar, rudiment 10 assumption,
convention, foundation 11 fundamental

principled
5 moral, noble 6 honest 7 ethical, upright
8 virtuous 9 righteous 10 moralistic

print
4 type 5 issue, litho, stamp, write
7 engrave, impress, publish, typeset
10 impression
style: 4 bold 5 roman 6 italic 7 cursive
8 boldface

printer
English: 6 Caxton (William)
German: 9 Gutenberg (Johann,
Johannes)
Italian: 6 Bodoni (Giambattista)
8 Manutius (Aldus)

printing
7 edition, reissue 10 impression
measure: 4 pica 5 agate
process: 4 roto 7 gravure

priority
4 lead 5 order 8 ordering 9 supremacy
10 importance, precedence, preference

prison
3 can, pen 4 brig, coop, jail, keep 5 clink
6 cooler, lockup 7 dungeon, slammer
8 bastille, big house, stockade
9 calaboose 11 reformatory
12 penitentiary
California: 8 Alcatraz 10 San Quentin
New York: 6 Attica 8 Sing Sing 12 Rikers
Island
Northern Ireland: 4 Maze
resident: 6 inmate 7 convict 8 jailbird

prisoner
7 captive, convict, hostage 8 criminal, detainee, jailbird

prissy
5 picky 7 finicky, precise 8 exacting, prudish 10 fastidious, particular 11 straitlaced

pristine
4 pure 5 clean, fresh 8 earliest, original 9 unspoiled

privacy
6 secret 7 retreat, secrecy 9 seclusion 11 concealment

private
5 inner 6 secret 7 soldier 8 eyes-only, hush-hush, intimate, personal 9 concealed 10 closed-door, restricted, unofficial 11 independent, sequestered 12 confidential

privateer
4 ship 7 gunship 9 mercenary

private eye
3 spy 4 G-man, tail 6 sleuth, shamus 7 gumshoe 9 detective 12 investigator

privately
7 sub rosa 8 covertly, in camera, in secret, secretly

privation
4 lack, loss, need, want 6 dearth, penury 7 absence, poverty 8 distress 9 indigence, neediness, suffering

privilege
4 boon 5 favor, grant, right 7 license 8 appanage 9 allowance, exemption 10 birthright, concession, perquisite 11 entitlement, opportunity, prerogative
pope-granted: 6 indult

privy
3 can, loo 4 head, john 5 jakes 6 secret, toilet 7 latrine 8 bathroom, informed, lavatory, outhouse, personal 9 concealed, withdrawn 11 water closet

prize
3 pry, top 4 best, loot, pick, plum, rate, swag 5 award, booty, cream, elite, force, lever, spoil, value 6 choice, esteem, reward, spoils, trophy 7 capture, cherish, jackpot, plunder, premium 8 treasure 10 appreciate 11 outstanding

prizefighting
6 boxing 8 pugilism

pro
3 for 6 expert, master 8 skillful 9 authority, in favor of 11 affirmative

probable
6 likely 7 seeming 8 apparent, credible, expected, feasible, rational, reliable 10 reasonable

probe
4 poke, quiz, test 5 query, study 6 search 7 dig into, examine, explore, feel out, inquest, inquire, inquiry 8 check out, look into, research, sound out 9 delve into, penetrate 11 exploration, investigate, reconnoiter 13 investigation

probity
5 honor 6 virtue 7 honesty 8 fairness, goodness 9 integrity, rectitude 11 uprightness

problem
4 mess 5 hitch, issue, poser 6 enigma, puzzle, riddle 7 dilemma, example, mystery, puzzler, trouble 8 hardship, headache, question 10 difficulty

problematic
4 iffy, moot, open 7 dubious 8 arguable, doubtful 9 debatable, uncertain, unsettled 10 precarious 12 questionable

proboscis
4 beak, nose 5 snoot, snout, trunk

procedure
4 plan, step 6 course, custom, method, policy, system 7 formula, measure, routine 8 protocol 9 operation 11 instruction

proceed
4 flow, move, rise, stem, wend 5 arise, get on, issue, segue 6 emerge, push on, spring, travel 7 advance, carry on, emanate, journey 8 continue, get along 9 originate 10 derive from

proceedings
8 goings-on
recorded: 4 acta 6 annals 7 minutes

proceeds
4 gain, take 5 yield 6 profit, result, return 8 earnings

process
3 way 4 mode, wise 5 modus, treat 6 handle, manner, method, refine, system 7 fashion, prepare, recycle, routine 8 workings 9 evolution, operation, outgrowth, procedure, technique 11 development

procession
5 march, order, train 6 parade, series, string 7 caravan, cortege 8 sequence 9 cavalcade, march-past, motorcade 11 consecution

proclaim
5 extol 6 assert, insist 7 declare, exhibit, glorify, publish 8 announce, evidence, manifest 9 advertise, broadcast, make known 10 annunciate, bruit about

proclivity
4 bent 6 liking 7 leaning 8 penchant 9 proneness 11 inclination

Procne
father: 7 Pandion
husband: 6 Tereus
sister: 9 Philomela
son: 4 Itys

procrastinate
5 dally, delay 6 dawdle

procreate
5 beget, breed 7 produce 8 conceive, generate, multiply 9 reproduce

Procris' husband
8 Cephalus

Procrustean _____
3 bed

proctor
7 monitor, oversee 9 supervise 10 supervisor

procure
3 buy, get 4 gain 6 obtain, pick up 7 achieve, acquire 8 purchase 10 bring about

prod
3 dig, jab, jog, stir 4 goad, poke, push, spur, urge 5 elbow, nudge, point, prick, rouse 6 excite, exhort, incite, thrust 8 motivate 9 stimulate 10 incitement

prodigal
4 lush 6 lavish 7 opulent, profuse, riotous, spender, wastrel 8 reckless, wasteful 9 exuberant, luxuriant 10 profligate, squanderer 11 extravagant, spendthrift

prodigious
4 huge, vast 6 mighty, unreal 7 amazing, immense, mammoth, massive, strange, unusual 8 colossal, enormous, gigantic 9 fantastic, marvelous, wonderful 10 astounding, impressive, monumental, phenomenal, remarkable, staggering, stupendous, surprising 11 astonishing 13 extraordinary

produce
4 bear, form, grow, make, show, sire 5 beget, breed, build, cause, erect, frame, hatch, mount, put on, raise, spawn, stage, yield 6 create, effect, father, output, parent, secure, work up 7 deliver, fashion, turn out 8 engender, generate, multiply 9 construct, fabricate, originate, procreate, propagate 10 bring about 11 manufacture, put together

product
5 fruit, issue, yield 6 effect, legacy, output, result, upshot 7 harvest, outcome, turnout 8 artifact, creation, multiple, offshoot 9 handiwork, outgrowth 11 consequence, manufacture

production
5 fruit, yield 6 output 7 staging, turnout 8 artifact, assembly, creation 9 execution, handiwork, rendering 11 achievement, manufacture, realization

productive
4 rich 6 fecund, useful 7 fertile 8 abundant, fruitful, prolific 9 rewarding 10 beneficial

proem
7 preface, prelude 8 exordium, foreword, overture, prologue 11 preliminary

profane
3 lay 4 damn, foul 5 abuse, dirty, pagan 6 coarse, debase, defile, filthy, impure, unholy, vulgar 7 impious, obscene, secular 8 indecent, temporal, unsacred 9 desecrate 10 irreverent, unhallowed 11 blasphemous, irreligious 12 sacrilegious, unsanctified

profanity
4 oath 5 abuse, curse 7 cursing, cussing 8 swearing 9 blasphemy, sacrilege 10 execration 11 imprecation, irreverence

profess
4 aver, avow 5 claim, teach 6 affirm, allege, assert, avouch 7 declare, pretend, protest, purport 8 maintain, practice

profession
3 art, job, vow 5 craft, trade 6 avowal, career, métier 7 calling 8 business, vocation 9 assertion, specialty, statement, testimony 10 handicraft, occupation 11 affirmation

professional
4 paid 6 expert, master 7 learned, skilled
9 authority 10 proficient, specialist
11 experienced 12 businesslike

professor
3 don 6 expert 7 teacher 8 academic,
educator

proffer
4 give, pose 6 extend, submit, tender
7 hold out, present, suggest 10 invitation,
suggestion

proficiency
5 savvy, skill 7 ability, advance 8 progress
9 adeptness, expertise, knowledge
10 competence

proficient
4 able 5 adept 6 expert 7 capable, skilled
8 advanced, masterly, skillful 9 authority,
competent, effective, masterful, qualified
11 crackerjack, experienced
12 accomplished

profile
5 chart 6 sketch, survey 7 contour,
diagram, outline 8 exposure, portrait, side
view 9 biography 10 silhouette
11 description

profit
3 net 4 gain, take 5 serve, yield 6 excess,
income, payoff, return 7 benefit, receipt
8 earnings, proceeds 10 percentage
12 compensation

profitable
6 paying, useful 7 gainful 8 fruitful
9 lucrative, rewarding 10 beneficial, well-
paying, worthwhile 11 moneymaking
12 advantageous, remunerative

profligate
4 wild 6 waster 7 immoral, spender,
wastrel 8 prodigal, reckless, wasteful
9 abandoned, dissipated, dissolute,
indulgent, reprobate 10 immoderate,
licentious, squanderer 11 extravagant,
promiscuous, spendthrift 13 self-indulgent

profound
4 deep, wise 5 heavy, total, utter
7 abysmal, intense 8 absolute, abstruse,
complete, esoteric, thorough 9 intensive
10 deep-seated, insightful

profundity
5 depth 6 wisdom 7 insight 8 deepness
12 abstruseness

profuse
4 lush 6 lavish 7 copious, fulsome, liberal,
opulent 8 abundant, generous, prodigal

9 abounding, bounteous, bountiful,
excessive, exuberant, luxuriant, plentiful
10 munificent 11 extravagant

profusion
4 glut, riot 5 flood, spate, surge 6 bounty,
deluge, excess, wealth 7 nimiety, satiety,
surfeit, surplus, torrent 8 overflow,
overload, plethora 9 abundance, plenitude
10 lavishness, luxuriance, oversupply,
plentitude, redundancy 11 copiousness,
prodigality, sufficiency, superfluity
12 extravagance 13 overabundance

progenitor
4 sire 6 author, father, mother 8 ancestor,
forebear 9 initiator, precursor
10 antecessor, forefather, forerunner,
originator 11 predecessor

progeny
4 line 5 issue 6 litter, result, scions
7 outcome, product 8 children 9 offspring,
posterity 11 descendants

prognosis
8 estimate, forecast, prophecy 9 prevision
10 estimation, prediction 11 expectation
12 anticipation

prognostic
4 omen, sign 6 augury 7 portent, presage
10 foreboding, indication

prognosticate
6 divine 7 foresee, predict, presage
8 forecast, foretell, prophesy

program
4 bill, book, plan, show 5 plans, slate
6 agenda, course, docket, lineup, policy
7 listing 8 calendar, playbill, schedule,
syllabus 9 broadcast, procedure, timetable
10 bill of fare, curriculum

progress
4 fare, gain, grow 5 get on, march
6 course, growth 7 advance, headway,
passage, proceed 8 anabasis, get along,
momentum 9 evolution, flowering,
unfolding 11 advancement, development,
improvement
planned: 7 telesis

progressing
5 afoot 7 en route 8 under way

progression
5 chain 6 course, growth, series
7 advance 8 sequence 9 evolution,
unfolding 11 development

progressive
6 modern 7 growing, liberal, radical

8 advanced, tolerant 9 advancing
10 developing, increasing

prohibit
3 ban, bar 4 stop 5 block, debar 6 enjoin,
forbid, outlaw 7 prevent 8 preclude
9 interdict

prohibited
5 taboo 6 banned, barred 7 illegal, illicit
8 verboten 9 forbidden

prohibition
3 ban, bar 5 taboo 7 embargo 8 sanction
9 interdict 10 constraint, forbidding,
injunction 12 disallowance, interdiction,
proscription

prohibitive
5 steep 6 costly 7 sky-high 9 excessive
10 exorbitant, forbidding 11 restrictive

project
3 jut 4 cast, feat, plan 5 bulge 6 affair,
design, devise, extend, intend, scheme,
vision 7 arrange, concern, emprise,
exploit, feature, imagine, propose, purpose,
venture 8 business, conceive, envisage,
envision, game plan, overhang, protrude,
stand out, stick out, strategy 9 blueprint,
visualize 10 enterprise 11 proposition,
undertaking

projection
3 jut 4 bump, knob, view 5 bulge
7 display 8 estimate, forecast, overhang,
scheming, swelling 9 extension, jutting
out, perception 11 expectation

proletariat
6 masses 7 workers 8 laborers
9 commoners, hoi polloi 12 working class

prolific
4 rich 6 fecund, gifted, lavish 7 fertile
8 abundant, fruitful 9 abounding, bountiful,
creative, inventive 10 generating,
generative 11 reproducing
12 reproductive

prolix
4 long 5 windy, wordy 7 diffuse, lengthy,
tedious, verbose 8 drawn out, rambling,
tiresome 9 redundant, wearisome 10 long-
winded

prologue
7 opening, preface, prelude 8 exordium,
foreword, overture, preamble 9 beginning
12 introduction

prolong
6 extend 7 drag out, draw out, spin out,
stretch 8 continue, elongate, lengthen

prolonged
7 lasting, lengthy 8 drawn-out 9 lingering
10 continuing, persistent, persisting

prom
4 ball, fete, gala 5 dance 6 formal

promenade
4 deck, walk 6 parade, stroll 9 boardwalk

Prometheus
brother: 5 Atlas 9 Menoetius
10 Epimetheus
creation: 3 man 7 mankind
father: 7 Iapetus
gift: 4 fire
mother: 7 Clymene
rescuer: 8 Heracles, Hercules
tormentor: 5 eagle

prominence
4 crag, fame, rise, spur 5 bulge 6 height,
renown, status 8 eminence, headland,
prestige, salience, standing 9 celebrity,
elevation 10 importance, projection
11 distinction

prominent
5 famed, great, noted 6 famous, marked,
signal 7 eminent, jutting, leading, notable,
popular, salient 8 renowned, striking
9 arresting, notorious, well-known
10 celebrated, noticeable, pronounced,
remarkable 11 conspicuous, eye-catching,
illustrious, outstanding 13 distinguished
person: 3 VIP 4 BMOC, lion 5 mogul,
nabob 6 bigwig, honcho 7 big shot,
grandee 8 luminary, mandarin, somebody
9 dignitary 13 high-muck-a-muck

promiscuous
5 mixed 6 casual, random, varied
7 immoral 8 careless 9 haphazard, hit-or-
miss, irregular 10 licentious
11 unselective 12 unrestrained

promise
3 vow 4 bode, bond, oath 5 agree, augur,
swear, vouch 6 assure, engage, ensure,
expect, insure, parole, pledge, plight
7 betroth, compact, consent, declare,
outlook, portend, presage, suggest 8 contract, covenant, indicate 9 assurance,
betrothal, potential, undertake
11 declaration, expectation

promised land
4 Zion 6 Canaan, heaven 8 paradise
11 kingdom come

promising
6 likely 7 hopeful 9 favorable
10 auspicious 11 encouraging

promissory note
3 IOU

promontory
4 beak, bill, cape, head, ness 5 bulge, point
8 foreland, headland

promote
3 aid 4 help, plug, puff, push, sell, tout
5 boost, favor, raise 6 foster, launch, prefer
7 advance, build up, elevate, endorse,
forward, further, nurture, present, support
8 advocate, champion 9 advertise,
encourage, publicize, recommend

promotion
6 step up 7 advance, buildup, puffery
9 elevation, publicity, upgrading
10 preference, preferment 11 advancement, advertising, improvement
13 advertisement

prompt
3 apt, cue, jog 4 fast, goad, help, hint,
move, spur, urge 5 alert, quick, rapid,
ready 6 assist, incite, induce, on time,
remind, speedy, stir up, timely 7 suggest
8 convince, persuade, punctual, reminder
10 responsive

promulgate
5 issue 7 declare, decree, publish
8 announce, proclaim 9 advertise,
broadcast 10 annunciate 11 disseminate

prone
3 apt 4 flat, open 5 given, level 6 liable,
likely, supine 7 subject, tending, willing
8 disposed, facedown, inclined 9 lying
down, reclining, recumbent 10 horizontal
11 predisposed, susceptible

prong
4 barb, fang, fork, spur, stab, tine 5 point,
thorn 6 pierce

pronghorn
8 antelope

_____ pro nobis
3 ora

pronoun
archaic: 3 thy 4 thou 5 thine
demonstrative: 4 that, this 5 these, those
indefinite: 3 all, any, few, one 4 both,
each, none, some 5 no one, other
6 anyone, either, nobody 7 another,
anybody, neither, nothing, someone
8 anything, somebody 9 everybody,
something 10 everything
personal: 3 her, him, she, you 4 them,
they
possessive: 3 her, his, its, our 4 hers,
mine, ours, your 5 their, yours 6 theirs
reflexive: 6 itself, myself 7 herself,
himself, oneself, ourself 8 yourself
9 ourselves 10 themselves, yourselves
relative: 3 who 4 that, what, whom
5 which, whose, whoso 6 whomso
7 whoever 8 whatever, whomever
9 whichever, whosoever 10 whatsoever,
whomsoever 11 whichsoever

pronounce
3 say 5 judge, sound, speak, utter
6 affirm, assert, decree, recite 7 declare
9 enunciate 10 articulate

pronounced
5 clear 6 marked, strong 7 assured,
decided, evident, obvious 8 clear-cut,
definite, distinct 12 unmistakable

pronouncement
5 edict 6 decree 9 manifesto, statement
11 declaration, publication 12 notification

pronto
3 now, PDQ 4 ASAP, fast, stat 6 at once
7 quickly 9 directly 9 forthwith, posthaste,
right away 11 immediately

pronunciation
distinctive: 4 burr, lilt 5 drawl, twang
6 accent, brogue
study: 8 orthoepy 9 phonetics

proof
4 test 5 facts, goods 6 galley 8 argument,
evidence 9 testament, testimony
10 impression 11 attestation
12 confirmation

proofreaders' mark
4 dele, stet 5 caret

prop
4 stay 5 brace, shore 6 buoy up, hold up
7 bolster, shore up, support, sustain
8 buttress 10 strengthen 12 underpinning

propaganda
4 hype 8 agitprop, lobbying

propagandize
4 tout 5 boost, extol 7 advance, promote,
trumpet 9 brainwash, catechize, inculcate
10 promulgate 11 proselytize
12 indoctrinate

propagate
5 beget, breed, raise, strew 6 extend,

spread **7** diffuse, publish, radiate
8 disperse, generate, increase, multiply,
transmit **9** circulate, cultivate, publicize,
reproduce **10** distribute **11** disseminate

propel
4 goad, move, push, spur, urge **5** drive,
egg on, power, shoot, shove **6** exhort,
launch, thrust **7** actuate **8** activate

propellant
3 gas **4** fuel, spur **7** impetus, impulse
8 catalyst, stimulus **9** explosive, incentive,
stimulant **10** motivation

propensity
7 leaning **8** penchant **10** preference
11 inclination

proper
3 apt, due, fit **4** good, just, meet, nice,
prim, true **5** exact, happy, right **6** au fait,
decent, prissy, seemly, useful **7** correct,
desired, fitting, genteel, precise
8 accurate, becoming, decorous, peculiar,
priggish, rightful, rigorous, suitable
9 befitting **10** applicable, convenient,
felicitous, individual **11** appropriate,
comme il faut, distinctive
combining form: 4 orth **5** ortho

property
4 land, mark **5** acres, trait, worth **6** assets,
estate, realty, riches, virtue, wealth
7 acreage, chattel, effects, feature, fortune,
quality **8** chattels, dominion, hallmark,
holdings, premises **9** attribute, ownership,
resources, substance **10** belongings,
possession, real estate
conveyor: 7 alienor
recipient: 7 alienee
seller: 7 Realtor
transfer: 8 alienate

prophecy
6 vision **8** forecast **10** divination,
prediction **11** foretelling

prophesy
5 augur **6** divine, preach **7** foresee,
portend, predict, presage **8** forecast,
foretell, instruct, soothsay **9** adumbrate,
prefigure **10** vaticinate **13** prognosticate

prophet
4 seer **5** augur, sibyl **6** auspex, oracle
7 diviner, seeress **8** foreseer, haruspex
9 predictor **10** forecaster, foreteller,
prophesier, soothsayer **11** Nostradamus
13 fortune-teller
Arthurian: 6 Merlin
Major: 6 Daniel, Isaiah **7** Ezekiel
8 Jeremiah

Minor: 4 Amos, Joel **5** Hosea, Jonah,
Micah, Nahum **6** Haggai **7** Malachi,
Obadiah **8** Habakkuk **9** Zechariah,
Zephaniah

Prophet author
6 Gibran (Khalil)

prophetess
5 sibyl **7** Deborah **9** Cassandra

prophetic
5 vatic **6** orphic **7** Delphic **8** Delphian,
oracular **9** presaging, prescient, sibylline,
vaticinal **10** predictive, revelatory
11 apocalyptic, foretelling

propinquity
7 kinship **8** nearness **9** closeness,
proximity **10** contiguity

propitiate
5 adapt, atone **6** adjust, pacify, soothe
7 appease, assuage, gratify, mollify,
placate, satisfy **9** intercede, reconcile
10 conciliate

propitious
4 good, rosy **5** lucky **6** benign, bright
7 benefic, helpful **8** favoring **9** favorable,
fortunate, opportune, promising
10 auspicious, beneficent, beneficial,
benevolent **12** advantageous

proponent
6 backer **8** advocate, champion, defender
9 expounder, supporter **10** enthusiast

proportion
4 rate, size **5** allot, ratio, quota, share
6 adjust, divide **7** balance, conform,
harmony **8** symmetry **9** dimension
10 percentage **12** relationship

proportional
5 scale **7** in scale **8** relative **9** equalized
10 contingent, equivalent, reciprocal
11 correlative, symmetrical
12 commensurate **13** commensurable,
corresponding

proposal
3 bid **4** idea, plan **6** motion, scheme
7 outline, proffer, project **8** scenario
10 invitation, suggestion **11** proposition
final: 9 ultimatum

propose
3 aim, ask, put **4** name, plan, pose **5** offer
6 design, intend, submit, tender
7 advance, move for, present, request,
solicit, suggest **8** nominate, put forth, set

forth, theorize **9** recommend **10** put forward

proposition
4 plan **5** offer **6** scheme, thesis **7** premise, suggest, theorem **10** invitation, suggestion

propound
3 put **4** pose **5** offer **7** present, suggest **8** put forth

proprietor
5 owner **8** landlord **9** possessor

propriety
7 aptness, decency, decorum, manners **8** behavior, civility, good form **9** etiquette, rightness **10** seemliness **11** correctness, fittingness, suitability **12** decorousness

propulsion
4 fuel, push **5** drive, force, power **6** energy, thrust

prorate
5 allot, divvy, quota, share, split **6** assess, divide, parcel, ration **8** divvy up, portion **9** apportion, partition **10** distribute

prorogue
3 end **4** rise, stay **5** defer, delay **6** hold up, put off, recess, shelve **7** adjourn, hold off, suspend **8** dissolve, hold over, postpone **9** terminate

prosaic
4 dull, flat **5** banal, prose, prosy, trite, vapid **6** boring, common **7** factual, literal, mundane, tedious **8** everyday, lifeless, ordinary, workaday **9** colorless **10** lackluster, uneventful **11** commonplace **13** unimaginative

proscenium
5 frame, stage **9** forestage **10** foreground

proscribe
3 ban **4** damn **6** enjoin, forbid, outlaw **7** condemn **8** prohibit, sentence **9** interdict

proscription
3 ban **5** taboo **11** prohibition **12** condemnation, interdiction

prosecute
3 sue **4** wage **5** press **6** charge, indict, pursue **7** carry on, perform **8** continue **9** bring suit, persevere

proselyte
7 convert, recruit **8** neophyte

proselytize
5 draft **6** enlist, enroll, sign up **7** convert,

recruit, win over **8** convince **9** brainwash, catechize **11** prevail upon **12** indoctrinate

_____ prosequi
5 nolle

prospect
4 mine, view **5** scene, vista **6** chance, survey, vision **7** dig into, explore, lookout, outlook **8** customer, exposure **9** candidate **10** expectancy **11** expectation, possibility **12** anticipation

prospective
6 coming, future, likely **7** awaited, ensuing, nearing, pending, planned, would-be **8** destined, eventual, expected, hoped-for, intended, proposed, soon-to-be **9** impending, looked-for, potential, scheduled **10** consequent, succeeding **11** anticipated, approaching, predestined, forthcoming

prospectus
4 list, plan **6** design, layout, précis **7** epitome, outline, program, summary **8** bulletin, synopsis **9** catalogue, timetable **10** projection **11** description **12** announcement

prosper
5 score, yield **6** arrive, do well, thrive **7** make out, produce, succeed, turn out **8** flourish, grow rich

prosperity
4 ease **6** riches, wealth **7** success **8** thriving **9** abundance, advantage, affluence, well-being

Prospero
daughter: **7** Miranda
servant: **5** Ariel
slave: **7** Caliban

prosperous
4 rich, well **5** happy, lucky **6** robust, strong **7** booming, halcyon, opulent, wealthy, well-off **8** affluent, thriving, well-to-do **9** desirable, favorable, fortunate, promising, well-fixed **10** auspicious, successful, well-heeled **11** comfortable, flourishing

prostitute
4 bawd, doxy, drab, moll **5** abuse, B-girl, madam, quean, whore **6** callet, debase, floozy, harlot, hooker, misuse, wanton **7** chippie, cocotte, corrupt, cyprian, floozie, hustler, Paphian **8** call girl, meretrix, strumpet **9** courtesan, party girl **11** fille de joie, nightwalker **12** camp follower, streetwalker
reformed: **8** magdalen **9** magdalene

prostitution
8 harlotry, whoredom 13 streetwalking
house of: 4 crib, stew 6 bagnio 7 brothel,
lupanar 8 bordello, cathouse 10 bawdy
house 13 sporting house

prostrate
4 fell, flat 5 abase, level, prone 6 humble,
lay low, submit, supine 7 exhaust, wear out
8 helpless, overcome 9 decumbent,
exhausted, overpower, overwhelm,
powerless, recumbent 10 procumbent,
submissive

protagonist
5 hero, lead, star 5 actor 6 leader
7 heroine, sponsor 8 advocate, champion
9 principal

protean
6 mobile, varied 7 diverse, mutable
8 variable 9 adaptable, versatile
10 changeable

protect
4 save 5 cover, guard 6 defend, screen,
secure, shield 7 shelter 8 preserve,
restrict 9 safeguard

protection
4 care 5 aegis, armor, bribe, graft, guard
6 safety, shield 7 bulwark, defense,
shelter, support 8 armament, coverage,
immunity, security 9 extortion, insurance,
safeguard 11 supervision

protector
5 armor, guard 6 patron, regent, shield
8 guardian 9 caretaker

protégé
4 ward 5 pupil 7 student, trainee
8 disciple

protein
4 zein 5 actin, opsin 6 avidin, enzyme,
fibrin, globin 7 albumin, elastin, fibroin,
histone, keratin, legumin, sericin
8 creatine, globulin, glutelin, prolamin,
protamin, proteose, vitellin
complex: 6 mucoid
derivative: 7 peptone
poisonous: 5 abrin, ricin

pro tem
6 acting 7 interim 9 ad interim, temporary

protest
4 aver, avow, beef 6 affirm, assert, avouch,
except, object, oppose, picket, resist
7 declare, profess 8 maintain 9 challenge,
complaint, objection 10 disapprove
11 demonstrate, disapproval
13 demonstration

Protestant
5 Amish 6 Mormon, Quaker, Shaker
7 Baptist, Lollard, Pilgrim, Puritan
8 Anglican, Lutheran, Moravian
9 Adventist, Mennonite, Methodist,
Unitarian 11 Pentecostal 12 Episcopalian,
Presbyterian
Bohemian: 7 Hussite
French: 8 Huguenot

protocol
4 code, form, rule 6 custom, ritual
7 compact, conduct, decorum, manners
8 courtesy 9 concordat, etiquette,
politesse, propriety 11 conventions,
formalities

prototype
4 norm 5 model 6 design 7 example,
pattern 8 original, paradigm, standard

prototypical
5 ideal, model 7 classic 9 classical,
exemplary 10 archetypal

protozoan
4 cell 5 ameba 6 amoeba 7 ciliate,
stentor 10 flagellate, paramecium

protract
6 drag on, extend 7 drag out, draw out,
prolong, stretch 8 continue

protrude
3 jut 4 poke, pout 5 bulge 6 jut out
7 project 8 overhang, stand out, stick out

protrusion
3 jut, nub 4 bump 5 bulge 8 swelling
10 projection

protuberant
5 bulgy 7 bulging 9 prominent
11 conspicuous

proud
4 vain 5 huffy, lofty, noble 6 lordly, stuffy,
superb 7 haughty, pleased, pompous,
stuck-up, stately 8 arrogant, exultant,
glorious, scornful, snobbish, spirited,
splendid, superior, vigorous 9 conceited,
delighted, imperious 10 disdainful, high-
handed 11 magnificent, pretentious,
resplendent 12 ostentatious, supercilious

Proulx novel
9 Postcards 12 Shipping News (The)

prove
3 try 4 show, test 5 argue, check 6 attest,
pan out, verify 7 bear out, certify, confirm,
examine, explain, turn out 8 document,
indicate, validate 9 determine, establish

11 corroborate, demonstrate 12 substantiate

provenance
4 root, well 6 origin, source 7 history
9 inception 10 derivation

provender
4 feed, food 8 victuals 10 provisions

proverb
3 saw 5 adage, axiom, maxim 6 byword,
saying 7 epigram 8 aphorism

provide
4 give, hand 5 endow, equip, serve, state
6 afford, outfit, supply 7 deliver, furnish,
prepare, specify, support 8 dispense, hand
over, maintain, stipulate

provided
5 given 6 if only 8 equipped, supplied

providence
4 care 6 thrift 7 caution, economy
8 prudence 9 foresight, frugality
11 forethought, thriftiness

provident
5 canny, chary 6 frugal, saving 7 careful,
prudent, sparing, thrifty 8 prepared
10 economical, unwasteful 11 foresighted

providential
5 happy, lucky 9 benignant, fortunate
10 auspicious, fortuitous

province
4 area, duty, role, work 5 field, shire
6 canton, county, domain, office, region,
sphere 7 demesne, pursuit, terrain
8 district, dominion, function 9 bailiwick,
champaign, territory 10 department
12 jurisdiction

provincial
5 local, rural 6 narrow, rustic, simple
7 country, insular, limited 8 pastoral
9 parochial, sectarian, small-town
11 countrified

provision
5 stock, store 6 supply 9 condition
11 preparation, requirement, reservation,
stipulation

provisional
5 stamp 6 acting, pro tem 9 temporary
10 contingent 11 conditional

provisions
4 feed, food, grub 5 stock 6 viands
7 aliment, edibles, nurture, vittles

8 supplies, victuals 9 provender
10 sustenance 11 comestibles
dealer: 8 chandler

proviso
6 clause 7 article 9 condition
11 stipulation

provocation
5 cause, wrong 7 offense 8 stimulus,
vexation 9 annoyance, incentive
10 incitement 11 instigation

provocative
5 heady 8 alluring, annoying, arousing,
exciting 9 offensive 10 intriguing
11 challenging, stimulating

provoke
3 bug, irk, vex 4 abet, rile, stir, wake
5 anger, annoy, cause, evoke, pique, rouse,
upset, waken 6 arouse, awaken, bother,
excite, foment, harass, incite, induce,
kindle, nettle, stir up, whip up 7 incense,
inflame, inspire, outrage, quicken
8 generate, irritate, motivate, occasion
9 challenge, galvanize, instigate, stimulate

provost
4 head 6 keeper 7 marshal 8 director
10 magistrate 13 administrator

prow
3 bow 4 stem 5 front 10 projection

prowess
5 skill, valor 7 bravery, command, courage,
heroism, mastery 9 expertise, gallantry
10 excellence

prowl
4 hunt, roam 5 skulk, slink, sneak, steal
6 search, wander

proximate
4 near, next 5 close 6 nearby 8 adjacent,
imminent 9 following, immediate,
preceding 10 near-at-hand 11 forthcoming

proximity
8 nearness, vicinity 9 adjacency,
closeness, immediacy 10 contiguity
11 propinquity

proxy
5 agent 6 deputy 7 stand-in 8 attorney
9 surrogate 10 substitute

pro _____
3 tem 4 bono, rata 5 forma 7 tempore

prude
4 prig 7 old maid, Puritan 8 bluenose
9 Mrs. Grundy

prudence
4 care **5** skill **6** acumen, reason, thrift, wisdom **7** caution, economy **8** sagacity **9** foresight, frugality **10** astuteness, discretion, expediency, precaution, providence, shrewdness **11** calculation, forethought, thriftiness

prudent
4 sage, sane, wary, wise **5** canny, chary **6** frugal **7** careful, politic **8** cautious, discreet, sensible **9** expedient, judicious **11** circumspect

prudish
4 prim **5** stern **6** narrow, prissy, proper, severe, strict, stuffy **7** austere, genteel **8** affected, decorous, priggish **11** puritanical, straitlaced

prune
3 cut, lop **4** clip, crop, pare, plum, thin, trim **5** shear **6** cut off, reduce, remove **7** cut away, cut back, shorten **8** pare down, truncate

prurience
4 lust **6** desire, libido **7** lechery, passion **8** cupidity **9** carnality, eroticism **11** lustfulness **13** concupiscence

prurient
4 lewd **5** bawdy **6** erotic **7** goatish, lustful, satyric, sensual **9** lickerish **10** lascivious, libidinous, passionate **12** concupiscent

pruritic
5 itchy

Prussian
aristocrat: 6 Junker **12** Hohenzollern
prime minister: 8 Bismarck (Otto von)
ruler: 7 Wilhelm **9** Frederick (the Great)

pry
4 nose, open, poke **5** jimmy, lever, snoop **6** meddle **7** inquire **9** interfere

prying
4 nosy **6** snoopy **7** curious **8** meddling, snooping **9** intrusive, obtrusive, officious **10** meddlesome **11** impertinent, inquisitive

psalm
3 ode **4** hymn, poem, song **5** paean
book: 7 psalter
selection: 6 Hallel
word: 5 selah

psalmist
4 poet **5** Asaph, David **6** cantor

pseudo
4 fake, mock, sham **5** bogus, false, phony **7** pretend **8** spurious **9** imitation **10** artificial **11** counterfeit

pseudonym
5 alias **7** pen name **9** false name, stage name **10** nom de plume **11** nom de guerre

psyche
4 mind, soul **5** anima **6** animus, pneuma, spirit
part: 3 ego **8** superego

Psyche's beloved
4 Eros **5** Cupid

psychiatrist
6 shrink
American: 3 May (Rollo) **5** Reich (Wilhelm) **6** Rogers (Carl) **7** Erikson (Erik) **8** Sullivan (Harry Stack) **9** Menninger (Karl) **10** Bettelheim (Bruno)
Austrian: 4 Rank (Otto) **5** Adler (Alfred), Freud (Anna, Sigmund), Reich (Wilhelm) **10** Bettelheim (Bruno)
French: 5 Lacan (Jacques)
German: 5 Fromm (Erich) **6** Horney (Karen)
Swiss: 4 Jung (Carl) **9** Rorschach (Hermann)

psychic
4 seer **6** medium, mental, occult **8** cerebral **9** mentalist, prophetic, spiritual **10** mind reader, telepathic **11** clairvoyant, telekinetic **12** intellectual, supersensory
American: 5 Cayce (Edgar), Dixon (Jeane) **10** Montgomery (Ruth)
power: 3 ESP

psycho
3 nut **5** crazy, sicko, wacko **6** madman, maniac, mental, schizo, weirdo **7** berserk, haywire, lunatic, nutcase **8** crackpot, demented, deranged, head case **9** fruitcake, screwball, sociopath

psychoanalyst
4 Jung (Carl Gustav), Rank (Otto) **5** Adler (Alfred), Freud (Sigmund), Fromm (Erich), Klein (Melanie), Kohut (Heinz), Lacan (Jacques) **6** Horney (Karen) **7** Erikson (Erik) **8** Ferenczi (Sandor)

psychologist
6 shrink **9** therapist
American: 5 James (William) **6** Terman (Lewis), Watson (John), Yerkes (Robert) **7** Skinner (B. F.) **9** Thorndike (Edward L.)
English: 4 Ward (James) **8** Spearman (Charles), Tichener (Edward)

German: 5 Wundt (Wilhelm) 6 Müller (Georg), Stumpf (Carl) 10 Wertheimer (Max)

psychotic
3 mad 5 crazy 6 insane 8 demented, deranged, schizoid 13 schizophrenic

ptarmigan
6 grouse

ptomaine
6 poison

pub
3 bar, inn 4 dive 5 joint 6 tavern 7 barroom, gin mill, taproom 8 grogshop 9 roadhouse 11 rathskeller

puberty
11 adolescence

public
4 open 5 civic, civil, state 6 common, mutual, people, shared, social 7 general, popular, society 8 communal, national, populace 9 community, municipal, universal 10 accessible, government

publican
7 barkeep 8 landlord, licensee, taverner 9 bartender, collector, innkeeper 12 tax collector

publication
4 book 7 article, journal 8 magazine, pamphlet 9 broadside, newspaper 10 periodical
list: 12 bibliography

public house
3 bar, inn 6 hostel, saloon, tavern 7 auberge, hospice 8 hostelry

publicity
3 ink 4 hype, plug 5 blurb, press, promo 6 hoopla, notice 7 billing, write-up 8 ballyhoo 9 attention, promotion 11 advertising 12 announcement 13 advertisement

publicize
4 bill, hype, plug, puff, push, tout 5 boost 7 promote, trumpet 8 announce 9 advertise, broadcast 10 press-agent, promulgate

publish
3 air 5 issue, print 6 get out, inform, put out, report 7 release 8 announce, bring out, proclaim 9 advertise, broadcast, make known 10 distribute, promulgate 11 disseminate

Puccini, Giacomo
opera: 5 Tosca 7 Le Villi 8 La Bohème, Turandot 12 Manon Lescaut 15 Madame Butterfly

puck
3 elf, imp 4 disk 5 fairy 6 spirit, sprite 9 hobgoblin, prankster

pucker
4 fold 5 purse 6 cockle, crease 7 wrinkle 8 compress, contract 9 constrict

puckish
5 antic, elfin, larky, pixie 6 elvish, impish 7 playful 8 prankish 9 whimsical 11 mischievous

Puck's master
6 Oberon

pudding
4 duff 6 burgoo 7 custard, tapioca
baked: 5 kugel 10 brown Betty

pudgy
3 fat 5 plump, round, stout, tubby 6 chubby, chunky, flabby, rotund 8 plumpish, roly-poly

pueblo
4 town 7 village 8 dwelling
ceremonial room: 4 kiva

puerile
5 inane, silly 6 jejune 7 foolish 8 childish, immature, juvenile

Puerto Rico
capital: 7 San Juan
city: 5 Ponce 7 Bayamon 8 Mayagüez
discoverer: 8 Columbus (Christopher)
language: 7 Spanish
location: 10 West Indies

puff
3 pad 4 blow, brag, crow, drag, emit, huff, pant, plug, pouf, push, tout, waft 5 blurb, boast, boost, elate, expel, quilt, swell, vaunt, whiff 6 exhale, pastry, praise 7 flatter, inflate 8 swelling 9 advertise, comforter, publicize 10 exaggerate

puffer
8 blowfish 9 globefish, swellfish

puffery
4 hype, plug 9 promotion, publicity 11 advertising 12 exaggeration, press-agentry

puffin
4 bird 7 seabird 9 sea parrot 10 shearwater
cousin: 3 auk

puffy
7 swollen 8 inflated

pug
  3 bun, dog 4 nose 5 boxer, track
  9 footprint

pugilism
  6 boxing 13 prizefighting

pugilist
  5 boxer 7 fighter 12 prizefighter

pugnacious
  7 defiant, scrappy 8 brawling, fighting,
  militant 9 bellicose, combative, truculent
  10 aggressive, rebellious 11 belligerent,
  contentious, quarrelsome 13 argumentative

pugnacity
  9 hostility 10 aggression, truculence,
  truculency 12 belligerence 13 combativeness

puisne
  6 junior 8 inferior

puissance
  5 force, might, power 6 energy 7 potency
  8 strength

puissant
  6 mighty, potent, strong 8 forceful,
  powerful

pukka
  4 real, tops 7 genuine 8 bona fide
  9 authentic 10 first-class

pule
  3 cry 4 mewl 5 whine 7 whimper

Pulitzer Prize fiction winner
  1918: 5 Poole (Ernest)
  1919: 10 Tarkington (Booth)
  1921: 7 Wharton (Edith)
  1922: 10 Tarkington (Booth)
  1923: 6 Cather (Willa)
  1924: 6 Wilson (Margaret)
  1925: 6 Ferber (Edna)
  1926: 5 Lewis (Sinclair)
  1927: 9 Bromfield (Louis)
  1928: 6 Wilder (Thornton)
  1929: 8 Peterkin (Julia)
  1930: 8 La Farge (Oliver)
  1931: 6 Barnes (Margaret)
  1932: 4 Buck (Pearl)
  1933: 9 Stribling (T. S.)
  1934: 6 Miller (Caroline)
  1935: 7 Johnson (Josephine)
  1936: 5 Davis (Harold)
  1937: 8 Mitchell (Margaret)
  1938: 8 Marquand (John)
  1939: 9 Rawlings (Marjorie Kinnan)
  1940: 9 Steinbeck (John)
  1942: 7 Glasgow (Ellen)

  1943: 8 Sinclair (Upton)
  1944: 6 Flavin (Martin)
  1945: 6 Hersey (John)
  1947: 6 Warren (Robert Penn)
  1948: 8 Michener (James)
  1949: 7 Cozzens (James Gould)
  1950: 7 Guthrie (A. B.)
  1951: 7 Richter (Conrad)
  1952: 5 Wouk (Herman)
  1953: 9 Hemingway (Ernest)
  1955: 8 Faulkner (William)
  1956: 6 Kantor (MacKinlay)
  1958: 4 Agee (James)
  1959: 6 Taylor (Robert Lewis)
  1960: 5 Drury (Allen)
  1961: 3 Lee (Harper)
  1962: 7 O'Connor (Edwin)
  1963: 8 Faulkner (William)
  1965: 4 Grau (Shirley Ann)
  1966: 6 Porter (Katherine Anne)
  1967: 7 Malamud (Bernard)
  1968: 6 Styron (William)
  1969: 7 Momaday (N. Scott)
  1970: 8 Stafford (Jean)
  1972: 7 Stegner (Wallace)
  1973: 5 Welty (Eudora)
  1975: 6 Shaara (Michael)
  1976: 6 Bellow (Saul)
  1978: 9 McPherson (James Alan)
  1979: 7 Cheever (John)
  1980: 6 Mailer (Norman)
  1981: 5 Toole (John Kennedy)
  1982: 6 Updike (John)
  1983: 6 Walker (Alice)
  1984: 7 Kennedy (William)
  1985: 5 Lurie (Alison)
  1986: 8 McMurtry (Larry)
  1987: 6 Taylor (Peter)
  1988: 8 Morrison (Toni)
  1989: 5 Tyler (Anne)
  1990: 8 Hijuelos (Oscar)
  1991: 6 Updike (John)
  1992: 6 Smiley (Jane)
  1993: 6 Butler (Robert Olen)
  1994: 6 Proulx (E. Annie)
  1995: 7 Shields (Carol)
  1996: 4 Ford (Richard)
  1997: 10 Millhauser (Steven)
  1998: 4 Roth (Philip)
  1999: 10 Cunningham (Michael)
  2000: 6 Lahiri (Jhumpa)
  2001: 6 Chabon (Michael)
  2002: 5 Russo (Richard)
  2003: 9 Eugenides (Jeffrey)
  2004: 5 Jones (Edward P.)

pull
  3 oar, row, tow, tug 4 drag, draw, haul,
  lure, root, yank 5 clout, draft, drive, force,

pull back

pluck, put on **6** appeal, assume, entice **7** attract, draw out, extract, stretch **9** advantage, influence **10** attraction

pull back

6 rein in **7** retreat **8** withdraw

pull down

4 draw, earn, raze, ruin **5** lower, wreck **6** reduce **7** depress, destroy **8** demolish, overcome **9** dismantle

pullet

3 hen **5** chick **7** chicken

pulley

5 wheel **6** sheave
watch's: 5 fusee

pull in

3 nab **4** stop **5** check, pinch **6** arrest, arrive, collar, detain, pick up **7** inhibit **8** hold back, restrain **9** apprehend

pulling

6 towage **7** draught, haulage **8** traction
cable: 7 towline

Pullman

3 car **7** sleeper **8** suitcase **11** railroad car

pull off

6 attain, manage **7** achieve, succeed **8** carry out **10** accomplish

pull out

4 exit, quit **5** leave **6** depart **7** abandon, retreat, take off **8** shove off, withdraw

pull through

5 rally **7** get over, recover, ride out, survive, weather **9** get better

pullulate

4 teem **5** breed, crawl, swarm **6** abound, sprout **7** produce **9** germinate

pull up

4 halt, stop **5** check **6** rebuke **8** draw even **9** reprimand

pulp

4 mash, pith **5** crush **6** bruise, squash **8** soft part, tabloid

pulpit

4 ambo, dais **6** podium **7** lectern, rostrum **8** ministry, platform

pulpy

4 soft **5** cheap, juicy, lurid, mushy **6** spongy **11** sensational

pulsate

4 beat, pump **5** pound, throb **7** vibrate **9** oscillate, palpitate

pulse

4 beat **5** throb **6** rhythm

pulverize

4 beat, ruin **5** crush, grind, smash, wreck **6** crunch, powder **7** atomize, destroy **8** demolish **9** micronize **10** annihilate

puma

3 cat **6** cougar **7** panther **12** mountain lion

pumice

5 glass, stone **8** polisher

pummel

3 hit **4** beat, drub **5** pound, punch **6** batter, buffet, hammer, thrash, wallop **7** belabor

pump

4 draw, shoe, quiz **5** exert, grill, heart, raise **6** device, elicit **7** operate **8** energize, question

pumpernickel

3 rye **5** bread

pumpkin

4 pepo **6** orange, squash **12** jack-o'-lantern
family: 5 gourd

pump up

4 fill **6** excite, expand **7** enthuse, inflate **8** energize, increase, motivate **9** stimulate

pun

4 joke **11** paronomasia, play on words **13** double meaning

punch

3 box, cut, die, dig, hit, jab, jog, pep **4** bang, blow, cuff, poke, prod, push, snap, sock **5** clout, drive, notch, smack, vigor **6** buffet, emboss, energy, impact, pummel, strike, thrust **8** uppercut, vitality **9** emphasize, perforate

punch bowl

8 monteith

punch-drunk

5 dazed, dizzy, woozy **6** addled, groggy **8** unsteady **9** befuddled, slaphappy **10** staggering **11** disoriented

puncheon

3 log **4** cask, slab, tool **6** timber

puncher

5 boxer **6** cowboy

Punch's wife

4 Judy

punchy
5 dazed, dizzy, vivid 6 addled, lively
7 dynamic, vibrant 8 forceful, spirited,
vigorous 9 befuddled, energetic,
slaphappy 11 light-headed

punctilious
5 exact, fussy 7 careful, precise
9 attentive, observant, particular
10 meticulous, scrupulous 11 painstaking

punctual
5 ready 6 on time, prompt, timely

punctuate
4 mark 5 point 6 accent, divide, stress
8 separate 9 emphasize, interrupt
10 accentuate

punctuation mark
4 dash 5 brace, colon, comma, slant, slash
6 hyphen, parens, period 7 bracket,
solidus, virgule 8 diagonal, ellipsis
9 backslash, guillemet, semicolon
10 apostrophe 11 parenthesis

puncture
3 jab 4 bore, flat, hole, stab 5 burst, drill,
prick, punch 6 blow up, debunk, riddle
7 deflate, explode 9 disprove 9 discredit,
perforate 11 perforation

pundit
4 guru, sage 5 maven, swami 6 critic,
expert 7 teacher, wise man 9 authority

pungency
4 bite 5 sting 8 piquancy 9 intensity,
sharpness

pungent
5 acrid, acute, harsh, sharp, spicy, tangy,
zesty 6 barbed, biting 7 caustic, cutting,
intense, mordant, painful, peppery, piquant,
pointed 8 exciting, incisive, poignant,
stinging 9 trenchant 10 irritating 11 provocative, stimulating

punish
4 fine, hurt 5 mulct, spank 6 amerce,
avenge 7 chasten, correct, put down,
reprove, revenge, scourge, torture
8 chastise, penalize 9 castigate, criticize
10 discipline

punishment
3 rod 4 fine 5 lumps, mulct 7 penalty,
reproof 10 amercement, chastening,
correction, discipline 11 castigation,
comeuppance, just deserts
12 chastisement

punitive
5 penal 11 castigating, vindicative
12 correctional, disciplinary

punk
4 hood, thug 5 rowdy, tough 6 novice,
rookie, tinder 7 hoodlum, ruffian, toughie
8 beginner, gangster, inferior 9 roughneck
10 delinquent

punkah
3 fan

punt
4 boat, boot, kick, play 6 gamble, propel

Punta del _____
4 Este

puny
4 weak 5 dinky, petty, small 6 feeble, little,
measly, paltry, slight 7 trivial 8 inferior,
niggling, picayune, piddling, trifling

pupa
9 chrysalid, chrysalis

pupil
5 cadet, tutee 7 learner, scholar, student
8 disciple 9 schoolboy 10 apprentice,
schoolgirl
French: 5 élève

puppet
4 doll, dupe, pawn, tool 6 figure, stooge
10 figurehead, marionette

puppy
3 dog 5 whelp

Purcell opera
13 Dido and Aeneas

purchase
3 buy 4 hold 6 obtain, pay for 7 acquire,
procure 9 advantage 11 acquisition

pure
5 clean, fresh, plain, sheer, total, utter
6 chaste, decent 7 a priori, genuine,
perfect, unmixed 8 absolute, abstract,
innocent, spotless, virtuous 9 authentic,
continent, exemplary, inviolate, stainless,
unalloyed, undiluted, untainted
10 immaculate 11 theoretical,
unblemished, unmitigated, unqualified
13 unadulterated

purebred
8 pedigree 9 full-blood, pedigreed
10 registered 11 full-blooded

puree
4 soup 5 paste

purely
4 just 5 quite 6 merely, simply, wholly
7 exactly, totally, utterly 8 entirely
10 altogether, completely 11 exclusively

purfle
4 trim 6 border 8 decorate, ornament

purgation
9 catharsis, cleansing 10 lustration

purgative
5 jalap 7 lustral 9 cathartic

purge
3 rid 4 oust 5 clear, expel 6 purify,
remove 7 cleanse, wipe out 8 get rid of,
lustrate 9 eliminate, liquidate

purification
8 ablution 9 catharsis, cleansing,
expiation, purgation 10 absolution,
lustration 11 expurgation 12 regeneration
sacrament: 7 baptism

purify
5 clean, purge 6 filter, refine 7 clarify,
cleanse

Purim
11 Feast of Lots
queen: 6 Esther

puritan
4 prig 5 prude 8 bluenose 9 Mrs. Grundy

puritanical
4 prim 5 rigid 6 severe, strict 7 ascetic,
austere, prudish 8 priggish 9 bluenosed
11 straitlaced

purity
8 chastity 9 innocence

purl
4 eddy, edge, knit 5 swirl, whirl 6 border,
murmur, stitch 9 embroider

purlieu
5 haunt 7 hangout

purlieus
6 bounds, limits 7 suburbs 8 boundary,
confines, environs 9 outskirts, precincts
12 neighborhood

purloin
3 nip 4 lift, take 5 filch, pinch, steal, swipe
6 pilfer, remove, rip off, snitch
11 appropriate

purloiner
5 crook, thief 8 larcener 9 larcenist

purple
4 plum, robe 5 cloth, grape, lilac, mauve,
regal 6 florid, maroon, orchid, ornate,
turgid, violet 7 flowery, pigment, pompous
8 imperial, lavender 9 bombastic, high-
flown, overblown 10 rhetorical

Purple Heart
5 award, medal 10 decoration

purport
4 gist, mean 5 claim, drift, sense, tenor
6 allege, intend, thrust 7 meaning,
message, profess, purpose 8 maintain
9 substance 11 connotation, implication
12 significance, significancy

purported
7 alleged, reputed, seeming 8 apparent,
so-called, supposed 9 professed
10 ostensible

purpose
3 aim, end, use 4 goal, plan 5 point
6 action, design, intent, object 7 meaning,
mission, resolve, subject 8 ambition,
function, proposal 9 direction, intention,
objective 10 aspiration, resolution
13 determination

purposeful
6 driven, intent 7 earnest, planned,
studied, willful 8 resolute 9 conscious,
dedicated 10 calculated, considered,
deliberate, determined 11 intentional
12 premeditated

purposeless
6 random 9 desultory, haphazard, hit-or-
miss, irregular, unplanned

purposely
9 expressly 10 explicitly 12 deliberately
13 intentionally

purr
3 hum 6 murmur

purse
3 bag, sum 4 knit 5 money, pouch, prize
6 pucker, wallet 7 handbag 8 reticule
9 clutch bag 10 pocketbook, prize money
Scottish: 7 sporran

pursue
3 woo 4 hunt, seek 5 chase, haunt,
hound, stalk, track, trail 6 badger, follow
7 afflict, go after, proceed 8 continue,
engage in 9 persecute, persevere

pursuit
3 job 4 hunt, work 5 chase, quest, trade
6 search 8 activity, business, vocation

9 avocation, following **10** employment, occupation, profession

purvey
6 obtain, peddle, supply **7** furnish, provide **9** provision

purview
3 ken **5** ambit, limit, orbit, range, reach, scope, sweep **6** extent **8** boundary

push
3 pep **4** goad, plug, prod, sell, spur, urge **5** boost, drive, elbow, exert, force, impel, press, punch, shove, vigor **6** attack, effort, energy, expand, peddle, propel, throng, thrust **7** advance, assault, impetus, promote **8** ambition, pressure, vitality **9** incentive, influence, offensive **10** enterprise, get-up-and-go, initiative

Pushkin, Alexander
novel: **12** Eugene Onegin
play: **10** Stone Guest (The) **12** Boris Godunov
story: **13** Queen of Spades (The)

push off
4 exit **5** leave, start **6** depart, set out

push on
6 travel **7** advance, journey, proceed **8** continue, progress

pushover
4 snap **5** chump, cinch, softy **6** breeze, picnic, stooge, sucker **9** soft touch

pushy
4 bold **5** brash, nervy **7** forward **8** forceful **9** assertive, obnoxious **10** aggressive **12** presumptuous

pusillanimous
5 timid **6** coward, craven **7** chicken, gutless **8** cowardly, poltroon, timorous **9** spineless **11** lily-livered

puss
3 cat, mug **4** face **6** kisser, kitten

pussycat
5 sissy, softy **6** softie **8** pushover, weakling **9** soft touch **10** namby-pamby **13** bleeding heart

pussyfoot
5 creep, dodge, evade, glide, skulk, slink, sneak, steal **6** tiptoe **10** equivocate

pustule
4 boil **6** pimple **7** abscess, blister **8** furuncle **9** carbuncle

put
3 lay, set **4** park **5** place **8** position

putative
7 assumed, reputed **8** accepted, believed, presumed, supposed **11** conjectural **12** hypothetical

put away
3 eat **4** stow **5** eat up, swill **6** commit, devour, lock up **7** confine, consume **9** polish off **11** incarcerate

put by
4 save **5** lay in, store **7** lay away **8** lay aside, salt away

put down
5 crush, quash, quell **6** demean, demote, depose, squash, subdue **7** squelch **8** belittle, suppress **9** criticize, disparage, downgrade, humiliate

put forth
5 issue **6** assert **7** present, propose

put off
5 defer, delay **7** suspend **8** hold over, postpone

put on
3 act, don, kid **4** fake **5** apply, bluff, feign, mount, stage **6** affect, assume **7** mislead, perform, pretend, produce

put-on
3 act **4** fake, sham, show **5** faked, phony, spoof **6** parody **7** assumed, feigned **8** affected, disguise **9** pretended **10** artificial, false front

put out
3 vex **4** gall **5** annoy, douse, issue, upset **6** bother, quench **7** disturb, produce, publish, trouble **8** irritate **9** aggravate, displease, embarrass **10** disconcert, exasperate, extinguish **13** inconvenience

putrefy
3 rot **5** decay, spoil, taint **6** molder **7** corrupt **9** break down, decompose

putrid
4 foul **5** fetid **6** rancid, rotten **7** corrupt, decayed, noisome, spoiled

putsch
4 coup **6** revolt **8** takeover, uprising **9** coup d'état, overthrow, rebellion **10** usurpation

putter
4 club, idle 6 fiddle, golfer, tinker 8 golf club

putting area
5 green

putto
6 cherub 8 amoretto

put together
4 form, join, make 5 build, unite 7 combine, connect, fashion, produce 8 assemble, construct, fabricate

putty
3 mud 4 clay 6 cement

put up
4 bunk 5 board, build, erect, house, lodge, raise 6 billet, harbor 7 quarter 8 domicile 9 construct

put up with
4 bear 5 stand 6 endure 8 tolerate

Puzo novel
6 Omerta 7 Last Don (The) 8 Fools Die, Sicilian (The) 9 Godfather (The)

puzzle
3 why 4 foil 5 poser, rebus 6 baffle, enigma, fuddle, muddle, riddle 7 anagram, confuse, mystery, mystify, nonplus, perplex, problem, tangram 8 acrostic, befuddle, bewilder, confound 9 conundrum, crossword, dumbfound, frustrate 10 disconcert 11 brainteaser

puzzle out
5 solve 6 answer, decode 7 clarify, clear up, explain, unravel 8 decipher, unriddle

puzzling
6 knotty 7 cryptic 8 baffling 9 confusing, difficult, enigmatic 10 mystifying, perplexing 11 bewildering, paradoxical 12 inexplicable

Pygmalion
beloved: 7 Galatea
father: 5 Belus
playwright: 4 Shaw (George Bernard)
sister: 4 Dido
victim: 8 Sichaeus

pygmy
4 tiny 5 dwarf 6 bantam, little, midget 8 dwarfish 10 diminutive, homunculus 11 lilliputian

Pylades
companion: 7 Orestes

father: 9 Strophius
wife: 7 Electra

pylon
4 post 5 tower 6 marker 7 gateway

Pym's creator
3 Poe (Edgar Allan)

Pynchon novel
15 Gravity's Rainbow

pyramid builder
5 Khufu 6 Cheops

Pyramus' beloved
6 Thisbe

pyre
4 heap, pile

pyretic
3 hot 7 burning, febrile, fevered 8 feverish

pyromaniac
5 torch 8 arsonist 10 incendiary

pyrosis
9 heartburn

pyrotechnics
7 display 9 fireworks, spectacle

Pyrrha's husband
9 Deucalion

Pyrrhonist
7 doubter, skeptic 10 unbeliever

Pyrrhus
kingdom: 6 Epirus
victory: 7 Asculum

Pythias' friend
5 Damon

python
3 boa 5 snake
slayer: 6 Apollo

pyx
3 box 4 case 6 vessel 9 container 10 receptacle

Q

Qatar
capital: 4 Doha
gulf: 7 Persian
language: 6 Arabic
monetary unit: 5 riyal
neighbor: 11 Saudi Arabia
peninsula: 7 Arabian

QED word
4 erat, quod 13 demonstrandum

q.t., on the
8 covertly, secretly 13 under the table

quack
3 cry 4 honk, sham 6 con man, humbug
7 shammer 9 charlatan 10 mountebank
12 saltimbanque

quackery
4 hoax, scam 5 fraud, hokum 6 deceit
8 flimflam, pretense 9 deception, duplicity,
imposture 11 dissembling

quad
see **quadrangle**

quadrangle
4 yard 5 close, court, patio 6 square
7 polygon 9 courtyard, curtilage, enclosure

quadrant
3 arc 6 fourth 10 instrument, one-fourth

quadratic
4 boxy 6 square 7 boxlike 10 foursquare

quadriga
7 chariot

quadrille
5 dance, ombre 8 card game

quadrivium subject
5 music 8 geometry 9 astronomy
10 arithmetic

quaestor
6 bursar 8 official 9 paymaster, treasurer

quaff
3 sip 4 swig, toss 5 drink, sup up
6 guzzle, imbibe, sup off 7 carouse,
swallow

quagga
3 ass

quaggy
4 soft 5 boggy, mushy, pulpy 6 flabby,
marshy, spongy 7 flaccid, squashy,
squishy 8 squooshy, yielding

quagmire
3 bog, fen, fix, jam 4 mire 5 marsh, pinch,
swamp 6 morass, pickle, plight, scrape,
slough 7 dilemma 8 quandary
9 imbroglio, marshland, swampland
11 predicament

quahog
4 clam 7 mollusc, mollusk 9 shellfish
11 cherrystone

quail
5 cower, wince 6 blanch, blench, cringe,
flinch, recoil, shrink 7 shudder, squinch,
tremble 8 bobwhite
flock of: 4 bevy

quaint
3 odd 5 funny, queer 7 antique, archaic,
curious, oddball, strange, unusual
8 peculiar, singular 9 different, eccentric,
whimsical 10 antiquated, unfamiliar
12 old-fashioned

quake
5 shake, waver 6 dither, quaver, quiver,
shiver, tremor 7 shudder, temblor, tremble,
twitter, vibrate 8 trembler

Quaker
6 Friend
city: 12 Philadelphia
colonizer: 4 Penn (William)
founder: 3 Fox (George)
poet: 6 Barton (Bernard) 8 Whittier (John
Greenleaf)
State: 12 Pennsylvania

qualification
6 caveat 7 ability, fitness 8 adequacy, aptitude, capacity, condition, criterion, standard 10 capability, competence 11 requirement, restriction, stipulation

qualified
3 fit 4 able 6 au fait, proper, proved, proven, tested 7 capable, limited, partial, skilled, trained 8 eligible, modified, reserved 9 competent 10 restricted 11 conditional 12 accomplished

qualify
3 fit 5 limit 6 lessen, modify, reduce, soften, temper 7 certify, entitle, license, mollify, prepare 8 describe, mitigate, moderate 9 authorize 12 characterize

quality
4 rank 5 class, elite, grade, merit, prime, savor, state, trait, value, worth 6 factor, flower, gentry, status, virtue 7 caliber, element, feature, stature 8 position, property, standing 9 attribute, blue blood, character, gentility, parameter 10 excellence, patriciate, perfection

qualm
4 fear 5 demur, doubt 6 nausea, unease 7 illness, scruple 8 mistrust 9 faintness, misgiving, objection 10 conscience, foreboding, reluctance, uneasiness 11 compunction, nervousness, uncertainty 12 apprehension, remonstrance 13 unwillingness

qualmish
3 ill 4 sick 6 queasy, uneasy, unwell 8 hesitant, nauseous 9 nauseated, reluctant, squeamish, uncertain 10 scrupulous 12 apprehensive

quandary
3 fix, jam 4 bind, hole, spot 5 pinch 6 pickle, plight, scrape 7 dilemma 8 quagmire 10 difficulty 11 predicament

quantity
4 body, bulk, dose 5 total 6 amount, degree, volume 9 abundance, aggregate, magnitude
fixed: 8 constant
small: 3 bit 7 modicum, smidgen

Quantrill's _____
7 Raiders

quantum
5 quota, share, total 6 amount, budget, ration 7 measure, portion 9 aggregate, allotment, allowance, increment 13 apportionment
of gravity: 8 graviton

of radiant energy: 6 photon
of vibrational energy: 6 phonon
theory originator: 6 Planck (Max)

quarantine
6 detain 7 confine, isolate 8 restrain 9 isolation, restraint 10 detainment 11 confinement

quarrel
3 row 4 beef, bolt, dust, feud, fray, fuss, miff, spar, spat, tiff 5 argue, arrow, brawl, broil, clash, fight, melee, run-in, scrap, set-to 6 affray, battle, bicker, differ, dustup, fracas, ruckus, squall, strife 7 brabble, discord, dispute, dissent, fall out, rhubarb, ruction, scuffle, wrangle 8 argument, catfight, conflict, disagree, skirmish, squabble 9 altercate, bickering, brannigan, disaccord, lock horns, imbroglio, scrimmage 10 contention, difference, dissension, donnybrook, falling-out, free-for-all 11 altercation, battle royal, embroilment 12 disagreement

quarrelsome
6 brawly 7 adverse, counter, hostile, scrappy, warlike 8 brawling, choleric, inimical, militant 9 bellicose, combative, irascible, irritable, rancorous, truculent 10 pugnacious 11 bad-tempered, belligerent, contentious 12 cantankerous, disputatious 13 argumentative

quarry
3 dig, pit 4 game, mine, pane, prey 5 chase, delve 6 source, victim 8 excavate 10 excavation

quarter
4 area, bunk, part 5 board, house, lodge, mercy, put up 6 barrio, billet, canton, fourth, ghetto, harbor, sector 7 barrack, section, shelter 8 clemency, district, division, locality, precinct, quadrant
circle: 8 quadrant
note: 8 crotchet
pint: 4 gill
ship's: 6 fo'c'sle 10 forecastle

quarterback
4 boss, head, lead 6 direct, leader, player 7 athlete, oversee 8 director, overseer 9 supervise 10 footballer, supervisor

quartet
4 four 5 group 6 tetrad 8 ensemble, foursome 10 quadruplet, quaternion 11 composition

quart, metric
5 liter, litre

quartz
4 onyx, sard 5 agate 6 jasper 7 citrine, mineral 8 amethyst, sardonyx 9 cairngorm, carnelian 10 chalcedony

quash
4 undo, void 5 annul, crush, quell 6 defeat, negate, quench, stifle, subdue 7 abolish, nullify, put down, repress, smother, squelch 8 abrogate, dissolve, suppress 10 extinguish, invalidate

quasi
6 almost 7 nominal, seeming, virtual 8 apparent

Quasimodo
9 hunchback
creator: 4 Hugo (Victor)
occupation: 10 bell ringer
residence: 9 Notre Dame

quaver
4 note 5 quake, shake, trill, waver 6 dither, shiver, tremor 7 shudder, tremble, twitter 10 eighth note

quay
4 dock, pier, slip 5 berth, jetty, levee, wharf 6 marina 7 moorage

quean
4 bawd, slut, tart 5 tramp, wench, whore 6 harlot, hooker 7 chippie, hustler 8 strumpet 9 courtesan 10 prostitute 12 streetwalker

queasy
3 ill 4 sick 6 qualmy, uneasy, unwell 7 dubious 8 delicate, doubtful, hesitant, nauseous, qualmish, troubled 9 hazardous, nauseated, reluctant, squeamish

Quebec province
capital: 6 Quebec
city: 5 Laval 8 Montreal 9 Longueuil
island: 9 Anticosti
mountain: 9 Tremblant 10 D'Iberville
peninsula: 5 Gaspé
provincial flower: 10 fleur-de-lys 11 madonna lily
river: 10 St. Lawrence

Queeg's ship
5 Caine

queen
Austria-Hungary: 12 Maria Theresa
Belgian: 6 Astrid
Danish: 8 Margaret, Margrete
Egyptian: 9 Cleopatra 10 Hatshepsut
English: 4 Anne, Mary 8 Victoria 9 Elizabeth
French and English: 7 Eleanor

Netherlands: 7 Beatrix, Juliana 10 Wilhelmina
of heaven: 4 Mary, moon 7 Astarte
of Isles: 6 Albion
of Ithaca: 8 Penelope
of Navarre: 8 Margaret
of Scots: 4 Mary
of Sheba: 6 Balkis
of the Adriatic: 6 Venice
of the Antilles: 4 Cuba
of the East: 7 Zenobia
of the fairies: 3 Mab 7 Titania
of the gods: 4 Hera, Juno, Sati
of the Nile: 9 Cleopatra
of the North: 9 Edinburgh
of the underworld: 3 Hel 4 Hela 10 Persephone, Proserpina
Spanish: 8 Isabella
Swedish: 9 Christina

Queen Anne's lace
6 carrot 10 wild carrot

Queen of Spades
author: 7 Pushkin (Alexander)
composer: 11 Tchaikovsky (Peter Ilyich)

Queensland
capital: 8 Brisbane
explorer: 4 Cook (Captain James)

queer
3 odd 4 ruin 5 bogus, droll, funny, spoil, weird 6 qualmy, queasy, unwell 7 bizarre, curious, dubious, oddball, strange, touched, unusual 8 doubtful, obsessed, peculiar, qualmish, singular 9 eccentric, squeamish, worthless 10 outlandish, suspicious 11 counterfeit 12 questionable

quell
4 calm, stop 5 check, crush, quash, quiet 6 pacify, quench, squash, subdue 7 conquer, put down, squelch 8 overcome, suppress, vanquish 9 overwhelm, subjugate 10 extinguish

Quemoy's neighbor
4 Amoy 5 Matsu

quench
4 sate 5 allay, douse, quash, quell, slake 6 lessen, put out, reduce 7 appease, assuage, gratify, lighten, put down, relieve, satiate, satisfy 8 mitigate, suppress 9 alleviate, eliminate 10 extinguish

quenelle
8 dumpling, meatball 9 forcemeat

quern
4 mill

querulous
5 whiny 7 fretful, peevish, pettish, whining

query

8 petulant 9 lamenting 10 whimpering
11 complaining

query

3 ask 4 quiz 5 doubt, grill 7 dubiety,
inquire, inquiry 8 question 9 catechize
11 interrogate 13 interrogation

quest

4 hunt 5 probe 6 pursue, search
7 delving, inquire, inquiry, probing, pursuit,
seeking 8 research 9 pursuance
11 inquisition 13 investigation

question

3 ask, pry 4 poll, pump, quiz 5 doubt, grill,
issue, probe, query 6 chance, matter
7 debrief, dispute, examine, inquire, inquiry,
problem, suspect 8 distrust, mistrust
9 catechize, challenge, objection
10 difficulty, puzzle over 11 interrogate,
possibility 13 interrogation, interrogatory

questionable

4 iffy, moot 5 shady, vague 6 unsure
7 dubious, obscure, suspect 8 arguable,
doubtful, unproven 9 debatable, equivocal,
refutable, uncertain 10 disputable, fly-by-
night, improbable, unreliable 11 problematic 12 undependable

questioning

5 probe, query 6 show-me 7 delving,
dubious, inquiry, probing 8 doubtful, grilling
9 inquiring, quizzical, skeptical, uncertain
11 incredulous, inquisitive, unbelieving
12 disbelieving 13 interrogation,
interrogatory, investigative

quetzal

4 bird, coin 6 trogon

queue

3 row 4 file, line, rank, wait 5 braid
6 column 8 sequence

quibble

4 carp 5 argue, cavil 6 argufy, bicker,
niggle, object 7 dispute, evasion, nitpick,
wrangle 8 squabble 9 criticism, criticize,
objection 10 split hairs

quick

4 core, deft, fast, keen, pith, root 5 acute,
agile, brisk, fleet, hasty, rapid, sharp, smart,
swift 6 abrupt, clever, nimble, prompt,
speedy, sudden 7 hurried 9 breakneck,
impetuous 10 harefooted 11 expeditious
12 lickety-split
combining form: 5 tachy

quick bread

6 muffin 7 biscuit

quicken

4 goad, grow, move, spur, stir, wake
5 hurry, liven, pique, rouse, speed
6 arouse, awaken, excite, hasten, incite,
induce, kindle, revive, step up, vivify
7 actuate, animate, enliven, provoke, shake
up, sharpen, speed up 8 activate,
energize, motivate, vitalize 9 galvanize,
stimulate 10 accelerate, exhilarate,
invigorate

quickly

5 apace 6 at once, pronto 9 forthwith,
posthaste 12 straightaway

quickness

5 haste, speed 8 alacrity, celerity, dispatch,
legerity, rapidity, velocity 9 fleetness,
rapidness, swiftness 10 promptness

quicksand

3 bog 4 mire 6 morass

quicksilver

7 mercury 9 mercurial 10 inconstant

quick-tempered

5 cross, fiery, ratty, testy 6 cranky, touchy
7 peppery 8 choleric, petulant 9 irascible,
irritable, splenetic 10 passionate

quick-witted

3 apt 4 keen 5 acute, agile, alert, canny,
ready, sharp, smart 6 astute, brainy, bright,
clever, prompt 9 brilliant 10 perceptive
11 intelligent, penetrating

quid

3 cut, wad 4 chew, coin 5 money, pound
9 sovereign

quiddity

3 nub 4 gist, meat, pith 6 trifle 7 essence,
quibble 8 crotchet 12 eccentricity,
quintessence

quidnunc

see **rumormonger**

quiescent

4 calm 5 quiet, still 6 benign, hushed,
latent, placid, serene, stilly 7 abeyant,
dormant, halcyon, lurking 8 inactive,
tranquil 10 untroubled

quiet

4 calm, hush, idle, lull, mute, stop 5 abate,
allay, inert, muted, shush, still, whist
6 asleep, becalm, gentle, hushed, lessen,
placid, serene, settle, silent, sleepy, soothe,
subdue 7 compose, halcyon, pacific,
passive, restful, silence, subdued
8 decrease, easygoing, inactive, peaceful,

reserved, secluded, taciturn, tranquil
9 cessation, noiseless, soundless, stillness,
unruffled 10 restrained, untroubled
11 tranquility, tranquilize, unobtrusive
12 tranquillity

quietus
3 end 5 death, finish, sleep 6 damper,
demise 7 decease, passing, silence
8 curtains 10 inactivity, settlement
11 termination

quill
3 pen 5 float, shaft, spine, spool 6 bobbin
7 feather, spindle

quilt
4 pouf, puff 5 duvet 8 coverlet
9 comforter, eiderdown 11 counterpane
design: 8 trapunto

quintessence
4 gist, meat, pith, soul 5 ideal, model, stuff
6 marrow 7 epitome 8 exemplar, last
word, quiddity, ultimate 9 substance
10 apotheosis 12 essentiality

quintessential
5 ideal, model 7 classic, typical 8 ultimate
9 classical, exemplary 10 archetypal,
consummate, prototypal 12 prototypical

quintuple
8 fivefold

quip
3 dig, gag, kid 4 gibe, gird, jape, jeer, jest,
jibe, joke 5 crack, fleer, sally, scoff, sneer,
tease 6 banter, oddity, retort 7 quibble
8 drollery, repartee 9 wisecrack, witticism
12 equivocation

quipster
3 wag, wit 4 card 5 clown, comic, droll,
joker 6 jester 8 comedian, funnyman,
humorist, jokester 11 wisecracker

quirk
3 tic 4 bend, kink, quip, whim 5 crook,
curve, twist 6 groove, oddity, vagary
7 caprice 8 accident, crotchet
9 mannerism 11 peculiarity
12 idiosyncrasy

quirky
3 odd 7 erratic, offbeat 8 peculiar
9 eccentric, irregular, whimsical
10 capricious 13 idiosyncratic

quirt
4 lash, whip

quisling
5 Judas, rebel 7 traitor 8 apostate,
betrayer, defector, turncoat 10 copperhead
11 backstabber 12 collaborator

quit
3 end, pay 4 drop, free, halt, stop 5 cease,
chuck, leave 6 depart, desert, desist, give
up, resign, retire, settle 7 abandon, drop
out, forsake, release, relieve, satisfy
8 knock off, leave off, released, renounce,
withdraw 9 discharge, liquidate, surrender,
terminate 10 relinquish 11 discontinue

quite
3 all 4 just, very, well 5 fully, in all 6 in
toto, purely, rather, wholly 7 exactly, totally,
utterly 8 entirely 9 perfectly 10 absolutely,
altogether, completely, positively,
thoroughly 12 considerably

quittance
6 amends 7 redress 8 reprisal, requital
9 atonement, discharge, expiation,
repayment 10 recompense, reparation
11 restitution 12 compensation

quitter
4 funk 6 coward, craven 7 chicken,
dastard 8 poltroon, recreant 9 defeatist
11 yellowbelly

quiver
4 beat, case 5 pulse, quake, shake, throb,
waver 6 arrows, dither, jitter, quaver,
shiver, tremor 7 pulsate, shudder, tremble,
twitter, vibrate 9 palpitate, vibration

Quixote
see **Don Quixote**

quixotic
7 foolish 8 fanciful, illusory, romantic
9 fantastic, imaginary, visionary
10 capricious, chimerical, idealistic
11 impractical 13 unpredictable

quiz
3 ask 4 exam, test 5 grill, query
7 examine, inquire 8 question 9 catechize
11 interrogate 12 cross-examine

quizzical
3 odd 5 queer 6 quaint, show-me
7 curious, dubious, mocking, probing,
puzzled, teasing 8 doubtful, doubting,
sardonic 9 inquiring, skeptical
11 incredulous, inquisitive, questioning,
unbelieving 12 disbelieving

quodlibet
5 issue, point 6 debate, medley

7 mélange 8 fantasia, question
11 disputation

quoin
5 angle, block, wedge 6 corner
8 keystone, voussoir

quoit
4 game, ring 6 circle

quoits peg
3 hob

quondam
4 late, once, past 6 bygone, former,
whilom 7 defunct, onetime 8 sometime
9 erstwhile 10 occasional

quorum
4 body 5 group 7 council 8 majority

quota
3 cut, lot 4 bite, meed, part 5 share, slice,
whack 6 amount, parcel, ration
7 measure, portion, quantum 9 allotment,
allowance 10 allocation, percentage,
proportion

quotation
3 bid 5 offer, price 7 excerpt, extract,
passage 8 citation

quotation mark, French
9 guillemet

quote
3 bid 4 cite, list 5 offer, price, refer
6 adduce, borrow, repeat 7 excerpt,
extract, passage 8 citation

quotidian
5 daily, plain, usual 6 common 7 average,
diurnal, prosaic, regular, routine, vanilla
8 day-to-day, everyday, ordinary, workaday
9 circadian 11 commonplace
12 unremarkable

quotient
5 ratio, share 7 caliber, portion
9 allotment, magnitude 10 percentage,
proportion

Quo Vadis
author: 11 Sienkiewicz (Henryk)
character: 4 Nero 5 Lygia, Peter
8 Vinicius 9 Petronius

R

Ra
son: **6** Khonsu
wife: **3** Mut

Raamah
father: **4** Cush
son: **5** Dedan, Sheba

Rabbi Ben Ezra author
8 Browning (Robert)

rabbit
4 cony, hare **5** bunny, coney
female: **3** doe
fictional: **5** Fiver, Hazel, Mopsy, Peter
6 Flopsy, Harvey **7** Thumper **8** Crusader,
Ricochet **9** Bugs Bunny **10** Cotton-tail
11 Easter Bunny
food: **5** salad **6** carrot **7** lettuce
neutered: **5** lapin
tail: **4** scut

rabble
3 mob **4** mass, rout **5** crush, horde
6 masses **8** canaille, populace, riffraff,
unwashed **9** hoi polloi **10** lower class
11 proletariat, rank and file

rabble-rouser
7 inciter **8** agitator, fomenter **9** demagogue **10** incendiary **12** troublemaker

Rabelais character
7 Panurge **9** Gargantua **10** Pantagruel

rabid
3 mad **4** wild **5** crazy, ultra **6** crazed,
insane **7** extreme, fanatic, frantic, furious,
radical, zealous **8** demented, deranged,
frenetic, frenzied, obsessed, ultraist
9 delirious, extremist **10** corybantic
11 hydrophobic

rabies
11 hydrophobia

raccoon
8 ringtail
dog: **6** tanuki

relative: 5 civet, coati, panda **8** civet cat,
kinkajou **10** cacomistle, coatimundi

race
4 bolt, dart, dash, gill, lash, meet, rush,
tear, type **5** brook, chase, creek, fling,
hurry, match, rally, relay, shoot, speed,
spurt **6** charge, course, gallop, runnel,
scurry, sprint, stream **7** channel, contest,
rivalry, rivulet, scamper **8** marathon
9 grand prix **11** competition, watercourse

racecourse
4 oval, turf **5** track

racehorse
5 Alsab, Kelso **6** Forego **7** Assault, Man O'
War **8** Affirmed, Citation **9** Riva Ridge,
War Emblem, stream **10** War Admiral **11** Forward
Pass, Seattle Slew, Secretariat, Smarty
Jones **12** Native Dancer

Rachel
father: **5** Laban
husband: **5** Jacob
servant: **6** Bilhah
sister: **4** Leah
son: **6** Joseph **8** Benjamin

rachis
4 back **5** chine, spine **8** backbone
12 spinal column

rachitic
5 shaky **6** wobbly **7** rackety, rickety,
tenuous **9** tremulous **10** ramshackle,
rattletrap

_____ Rachmaninoff
6 Sergei, Sergey

racing enthusiast
8 railbird

racism
7 bigotry, jim crow **9** apartheid, prejudice
11 segregation

racist
4 nazi 5 bigot 7 bigoted 10 intolerant, prejudiced 11 supremacist

rack
3 bed 4 buck, bunk, pace, pain, sack, scud 5 frame, wring 6 harass, harrow, martyr, strain, wrench 7 afflict, agonize, antlers, crucify, ratchet, sawbuck, stretch, torment, torture 8 distress, sawhorse 9 framework, persecute 10 excruciate

racket
3 con, din 5 babel, fraud, game, hoo-ha, noise 6 clamor, hubbub, rattle, scheme, tumult, uproar 7 pursuit, swindle 8 ballyhoo, brouhaha, foofaraw 10 hullabaloo 11 pandemonium

racketeer
7 mafioso, mobster 8 extorter, gangster 9 godfather

rack up
3 win 4 gain 5 reach, score 6 attain 7 achieve, realize 10 accomplish

raconteur
11 storyteller

racy
4 blue, gamy 5 bawdy, broad, juicy, salty, spicy, vampy, zesty 6 purple, risqué, smutty, snappy, vulgar, wicked 7 piquant, pungent 8 indecent, off-color, vigorous 10 suggestive

Radames' beloved
4 Aïda

radar image
3 pip 4 blip, spot 5 trace

Raddai
brother: 5 David
father: 5 Jesse

radiance
3 ray 4 glow 5 glory, shine 6 luster 7 aureola, aureole 8 splendor 10 brightness, brilliance

radiant
4 glad 5 beamy, shiny 6 bright, cheery, lucent 7 beaming, fulgent, glowing, lambent 8 cheerful, luminous, lustrous 9 brilliant, effulgent 10 effulgence 12 incandescent

radiate
4 beam 5 gleam, glow, shine, strew 6 spread 7 diverge 8 illumine 10 illuminate

radiation unit
3 rad, rem, rep 7 langley, sievert 8 roentgen

radiator
6 cooler, heater 9 convector 11 transmitter 13 heat exchanger

radical
4 acyl, root 5 basal, basic, rebel, ultra 7 extreme, fanatic, primary 8 agitator, cardinal, inherent, militant, ultraist 9 anarchist, essential, extremist, intrinsic 10 subversive, underlying 11 fundamental 12 foundational, iconoclastic 13 revolutionary
mathematical: 4 surd

radicle
4 root 5 radix 9 hypocotyl

radio
8 wireless
frequency range: 8 waveband

radioactive
3 hot 7 nuclear

radius
5 ambit, orbit, range, reach, sweep 6 extent 7 compass, purview 9 extension

radix
4 base, root 6 source

raffish
6 coarse, jaunty, rakish, sporty, vulgar 9 dissolute 12 devil-may-care

raffle
7 drawing, lottery

raft
3 lot, ton 4 heap, mess, pile, scad, slew 5 balsa, float 6 bundle

rafter
4 balk, beam, viga

rag
3 jaw, kid, rib 4 bait, jive, josh, rail, razz, rock 5 baste, berate, cloth, scold, tease 6 harass, hector, needle, pester 7 tabloid, torment 9 newspaper

ragamuffin
3 bum 4 hobo, waif 5 gamin, tramp, urchin 6 beggar, gamine, orphan 7 wastrel 8 vagabond 9 scarecrow 11 guttersnipe

rage
3 cry, fad, ire, mad, wax 4 chic, fume, fury, mode, rant 5 anger, craze, fancy, furor, mania, storm, style, vogue, wrath 6 blow

up, frenzy, furore, seethe **7** fashion, madness, passion **8** boil over, hysteria, violence **10** dernier cri **11** indignation

ragged
4 rent, torn **5** seedy **6** frayed, jagged, shabby, uneven **7** unkempt, worn-out **8** frazzled, straggly, tattered **10** threadbare

raging
4 wild **6** stormy **7** furious, extreme, intense, violent **8** blustery **9** ferocious, turbulent **10** blustering **11** tempestuous

ragout
4 stew **5** salmi **6** burgoo, jumble, medley **7** farrago, goulash, mélange, mixture **8** mishmash **9** potpourri **10** hodgepodge, salmagundi **11** gallimaufry

rags
4 duds, garb **5** dress **6** attire, shreds **7** apparel, clothes, raiment, threads **8** clothing **10** attirement **11** habiliments

ragtag
see **rabble**

ragwort
7 senecio **9** cineraria, groundsel **10** butterweed

raid
4 bust, loot, sack **5** foray, harry **6** attack, forage, harass, inroad, invade, maraud, ravage, sortie **7** assault, despoil, overrun, plunder **8** invasion, spoliate **9** incursion, onslaught

raider
6 pirate **10** freebooter

rail
3 bar, jaw **5** fence, scold, track **6** berate, revile **7** barrier, inveigh, upbraid **8** banister **10** tongue-lash, vituperate

rail bird
4 sora **5** crake **7** clapper **8** marsh hen, water hen

railing
8 banister **10** balustrade
part: 8 baluster

raillery
5 scorn **6** banter **7** mockery, taunting, teasing **8** badinage, derision, ridicule **10** lampoonery, persiflage

railroad
branch: 6 siding
car: 5 coach, diner, stock **6** hopper **8** caboose, gondola, Pullman
engine: 10 locomotive

locomotive: 9 iron horse
station: 5 depot
underground: 4 tube **5** metro **6** subway
worker: 6 porter **7** fireman **8** brakeman, engineer **9** conductor **11** gandy dancer

raiment
4 duds, garb, gear, togs **5** array, dress **6** attire **7** apparel, clothes, threads, vesture **8** clothing, garments, glad rags, vestiary **9** caparison **10** attirement **11** habiliments

rain
6 deluge, mizzle, shower **7** drizzle **8** downpour, sprinkle **10** cloudburst **13** precipitation

rainbow
3 arc **4** iris **5** array, gamut **7** fantasy **8** illusion, spectrum **9** pipe dream
bridge: 7 Bifrost
chaser: 9 visionary
goddess: 4 Iris

rainbow fish
5 guppy, trout **6** wrasse

raincoat
3 mac **4** mack **6** poncho, trench **7** oilskin, slicker **10** mackintosh

rain leader
9 downspout

rain tree
9 monkeypod

raise
4 ante, grow, hike, jack, jump, lift, pump, rear **5** boost, breed, erect, exalt, hoist, put up **6** foment, incite, jack up, muster **7** augment, bring up, collect, elevate, enhance, inflate, produce **8** heighten, increase **9** construct, cultivate, increment, propagate

raisin
5 grape **7** currant, sultana **10** dried grape

Raisin in the Sun author
9 Hansberry (Lorraine)

raison d'_____
4 état, être

raja
4 king **5** chief, ruler **6** prince **9** dignitary

rake
3 rip **4** comb, roué **5** angle, blood, lecher, pitch, rifle, scamp, scour, slope **6** forage, glance, rascal, scrape, search, strafe **7** incline, playboy, ransack, rummage, scratch **8** enfilade, lothario **9** debauchee, libertine **10** profligate

rakehell

rakehell
4 fast, wild 5 blood 6 rascal, sporty
7 playboy, raffish 8 lothario, rascally
9 debauchee, dissolute, lecherous, libertine
10 licentious, profligate

rake-off
3 cut 4 bite, take 5 chunk, share 7 portion
9 baksheesh, lagniappe 10 commission,
percentage

rake's look
4 leer, ogle

Rake's Progress artist
7 Hogarth (William)

rakish
see **rakehell**

rally
4 race, stir, wake 5 harry, renew, rouse,
waken 6 arouse, awaken, bestir, kindle,
muster, perk up, pick up, repair, volley
7 convene, enliven, marshal, rebound,
recover 8 assemble, clambake, comeback,
mobilize, re-collect, recovery 9 challenge
10 invigorate, reorganize

rallying cry
5 motto 6 byword, slogan 9 watchword
10 shibboleth 11 catchphrase

ram
5 Aries, crash, crowd, drive, pound, sheep,
stuff 6 batter, plunge, strike, thrust
7 warship

Rama's wife
4 Sita

ramble
3 gad 4 roam, rove 5 drift, range, stray,
troll 6 stroll, wander 7 blather, digress,
diverge, maunder, meander, saunter,
traipse 8 divagate, straggle 9 gallivant

rambler
4 rose 5 gypsy, hiker, nomad, rover
6 roamer, walker 7 drifter, vagrant
8 stroller, vagabond, wanderer 9 itinerant
10 ranch house

rambunctious
5 rowdy 6 unruly 7 raucous, willful
10 boisterous, headstrong 11 intractable,
recalcitrant 12 ungovernable

ramification
5 shoot 6 branch, offset 8 offshoot
9 outgrowth, offspring 11 consequence

ramify
6 branch, divide, extend 7 develop, radiate
9 branch out, propagate 11 proliferate

Ramona author
7 Jackson (Helen Hunt)

ramose
8 branched

ramp
5 apron 7 incline

rampage
4 rage, riot, tear 5 binge, fling, spree,
storm

rampageous
4 wild 6 unruly 7 riotous

rampant
4 rank, rife, wild 7 rearing, regnant
9 prevalent, unbridled 10 widespread
12 uncontrolled, unrestrained

rampart
4 wall 5 ridge 7 bulwark, parapet
9 barricade 10 breastwork

ramshackle
6 flimsy 7 rickety, run-down 8 decrepit
10 tumbledown 11 dilapidated

ram's mate
3 ewe

ranch
5 finca 8 estancia, hacienda
worker: 6 cowboy, gaucho 7 cowgirl,
cowhand, cowpoke 10 cowpuncher

rancher
6 cowboy 7 breeder 9 cattleman

rancid
4 high, rank, sour 5 fetid 6 putrid, skunky,
smelly 7 noisome, spoiled 8 stinking
9 offensive 10 malodorous

rancor
4 gall 6 animus, enmity, hatred 7 ill will
9 animosity, antipathy, hostility
10 antagonism, bitterness

rancorous
6 bitter 7 hateful, hostile 8 spiteful,
venomous 9 malicious, malignant, vitriolic
10 malevolent 11 acrimonious
12 antagonistic

Rand, Ayn
novel: 6 Anthem 12 Fountainhead (The)
13 Atlas Shrugged

random
6 casual 7 aimless 8 slapdash 9 arbitrary,
desultory, haphazard, hit-or-miss,
unplanned 10 accidental, contingent, hit-
and-miss, incidental 11 purposeless

randy
4 lewd 5 bawdy, lusty 7 lustful, satyric
9 lecherous, libertine, lickerish, salacious
10 lascivious, libidinous, licentious

range
3 row, run 4 area, band, roam, rove, shot,
site, sort, span, vary 5 align, ambit, carry,
drift, field, gamut, orbit, order, reach, realm,
ridge, scale, scope, space, stove, stray,
sweep, width 6 assort, domain, extent,
length, limits, ramble, sierra, sphere,
spread, wander 7 compass, distance,
earshot, expanse, eyeshot, habitat,
meander, purview, panorama, province,
stovetop, traverse, vicinity 9 amplitude,
extension, gallivant, magnitude, territory
12 distribution

range finder
9 telemeter

ranger
3 spy 4 scout 6 lawman, patrol, warden
8 overseer 9 caretaker, protector

rangy
4 lean 5 lanky 6 gangly 7 spindly
8 gangling

rani's mate
4 raja 5 rajah

rank
3 row 4 file, foul, lush, rate, sort, tier
5 class, fetid, funky, grade, gross, humid,
order, place, queue 6 assort, cachet,
coarse, filthy, lavish, putrid, rancid, rating,
smelly, status 7 arrange, dignity, echelon,
footing, noisome, perfect, profuse,
rampant, reeking, station, stature
8 absolute, classify, evaluate, flagrant,
outright, position, standing, stinking
9 downright, egregious, loathsome, luxuriant, overgrown, repulsive 10 consummate, malodorous 11 conspicuous,
outstanding, unmitigated

rank and file
5 plebs 6 people, plebes 8 populace
9 commonage, commoners, plebeians
10 commonalty 11 enlisted men

rankle
3 irk, vex 4 rile 5 annoy 6 bother, fester,
nettle, seethe 8 embitter, irritate
9 aggravate 10 exasperate

ransack
3 rob 4 comb, grub, loot, rake 5 rifle,
scour 6 forage, ravage 7 plunder,
rummage

Ran's husband
5 Aegir

ransom
3 buy 4 free 6 redeem, regain 7 deliver,
recover, rescue 8 liberate
13 consideration

rant
3 jaw, rag 4 huff, rage, rail, rate, rave
5 mouth, scold 7 bluster, bombast,
declaim, fustian 8 bloviate, harangue,
perorate 10 vituperate 11 rodomontade

ranula
4 cyst

rap
3 hit, tap 4 blow, chat, swat, talk, wipe
5 blame, chide, knock, swipe 6 charge,
patter 7 censure, condemn, reproof
8 causerie, denounce, reproach, sentence
9 criticize, criticism, reprehend, reprimand,
reprobate 10 discussion 12 conversation

rapacious
6 greedy 8 covetous, grasping, ravening,
ravenous 9 predatory, raptorial, voracious
10 gluttonous, predaceous

rapacity
5 greed 7 avarice, avidity 8 cupidity,
voracity 10 greediness 12 covetousness,
ravenousness

rape
4 ruin 5 colza, force, spoil 6 canola, defile,
ravage, ravish 7 assault, debauch, despoil,
outrage, plunder, violate 9 violation
10 ravishment, spoliation

Rape of the Lock, The
author: 4 Pope (Alexander)
heroine: 7 Belinda

Raphael
birthplace: 6 Urbino
subject: 7 Madonna
teacher: 8 Perugino

rapid
4 fast 5 brisk, chute, fleet, hasty, quick,
swift 6 speedy 7 hurried 9 breakneck
11 expeditious

rapidity
5 haste, hurry, speed 8 celerity, velocity

rapids
5 chute 8 cataract 10 white water

rapine
4 loot, swag 5 booty, prize, spoil 6 boodle, spoils 7 pillage, plunder 10 spoliation

Rappaccini's Daughter
8 Beatrice
author: 9 Hawthorne (Nathaniel)

rapport
5 unity 6 accord 7 concord, harmony 8 affinity, rapport 9 communion 13 communication

rapscallion
see **rascal**

rap session
6 confab, parley 7 palaver 8 colloquy 10 discussion

rapt
6 intent 7 engaged 8 absorbed, immersed 9 engrossed 11 carried away, preoccupied, transported

raptor
3 owl 4 hawk 5 eagle 6 condor, falcon, merlin, osprey 7 kestrel, vulture 9 gyrfalcon 10 bird of prey 11 deinonychus

rapture
5 swoon 6 heaven 7 delight, ecstasy, nirvana 9 transport 10 exaltation 13 seventh heaven

rara ____
4 avis

rare
3 few, red 4 pink, thin 6 choice, dainty, exotic, scarce, seldom, select 7 elegant, unusual 8 delicate, singular, sporadic, superior, uncommon, unwonted 9 exquisite, recherché, underdone 10 infrequent, occasional 11 distinctive, exceptional 13 extraordinary

rarefied
4 fine, thin 7 tenuous 8 esoteric 10 attenuated

rarefy
4 thin 6 refine 9 attenuate

rarely
6 little, seldom 9 extremely, unusually 12 infrequently

raring
4 avid, keen 5 eager 6 gung-ho 12 enthusiastic

rarity
5 curio 6 oddity 7 curiosa 8 scarcity 9 curiosity 10 aberration 11 collectible

rascal
4 rake 5 devil, knave, rogue, scamp 7 lowlife, villain, wastrel 8 scalawag 9 miscreant, reprobate, scoundrel, skeezicks 10 blackguard 11 rapscallion
Irish: 8 spalpeen

rash
5 hasty, heady 6 abrupt, daring, madcap, plague, sudden, unwary, unwise 7 foolish 8 careless, epidemic, eruption, headlong, heedless, outbreak, reckless 9 audacious, daredevil, foolhardy, hotheaded, impetuous, imprudent, impulsive 10 ill-advised, incautious, indiscreet, unthinking 11 injudicious, precipitate, temerarious, thoughtless

rasp
4 file, fret 5 annoy, chafe, grate 6 abrade, scrape 7 scratch 8 irritate

raspberry
7 catcall 8 blackcap 10 Bronx cheer

raspy
3 dry 5 harsh, rough 6 hoarse 7 grating, jarring, raucous 8 scrabbly, scratchy

rat
4 fink, heel, scab 5 louse 6 defect, desert, inform, rodent, snitch, squeak, squeal, tattle 7 stoolie 8 apostate, defector, informer, recreant, renegade, squealer, turncoat 9 bandicoot, repudiate, turnabout 11 stool pigeon 12 tergiversate
female: 3 doe

rate
3 fee, set, tab 4 cost, earn, rank 5 assay, class, grade, merit, price, scale, set at, value 6 amount, assess, charge, degree, esteem, regard, survey, tariff 7 apprize, deserve, valuate 8 appraise, classify, consider, estimate, evaluate, price tag 9 valuation 10 proportion

rather
4 a bit 5 quite 6 fairly, in lieu, kind of, pretty, sort of 7 instead 8 somewhat 9 tolerably 10 moderately, more or less, preferably 11 alternately 12 considerably 13 alternatively

rathskeller
3 bar, inn, pub 4 dive 6 saloon, tavern 7 barroom, taproom 8 alehouse, basement

ratify
4 seal 5 enact 7 approve, certify, confirm, endorse, license 8 accredit, sanction, validate

rating
4 mark, rank 5 class, grade 6 number 8 estimate, standing

ratio
5 scale 7 percent 8 fraction, quotient 10 percentage, proportion

ratiocination
8 judgment, sequitur 9 inference, reasoning 10 conclusion

ration
4 dole, food, meal, mete 5 allot, divvy, quota, share 6 divide, parcel 7 measure, mete out, prorate 8 allocate 9 allotment, allowance 10 provisions 13 apportionment

rational
4 calm, cool, sane 5 lucid, sober, sound 6 stable 7 logical, prudent 8 sensible, thinking 9 judicious 10 consequent, reasonable 11 circumspect, intelligent, level-headed 12 intellectual

rationale
5 basis, logic 6 reason 7 grounds 9 reasoning 11 explanation 13 justification

rationalize
7 explain, justify 10 account for 11 externalize

ratite
3 emu, moa 4 kiwi, rhea 7 ostrich

rattail
3 cod 9 grenadier

rattan
4 cane, palm 6 switch 7 malacca

Rattigan play
10 Winslow Boy (The) 14 Separate Tables

rattle
3 gab, jaw, yak 4 chat, faze 5 abash, addle, clack, noise, rouse, run on, upset 6 babble, gabble, jangle, racket 7 chatter, clatter, confuse, disturb, flummox, perplex 8 bewilder, confound, distract 9 discomfit, embarrass 10 noisemaker

rattlebrained
5 dizzy, giddy, silly 7 flighty 8 skittish 9 frivolous

rattling
4 very 5 brisk, quick 6 damned, lively, mighty 8 whacking, whopping 9 energetic, extremely 11 exceedingly

ratty
5 dowdy, dumpy, mean, tacky 6 cheesy, scurvy, shabby 7 unkempt 8 slovenly 10 despicable 11 treacherous 12 contemptible

raucous
4 loud 5 harsh, noisy, rough, rowdy 6 hoarse, unruly 7 grating, jarring, squawky 8 rowdyish, strident 9 termagant, turbulent 10 boisterous, disorderly, stridulent, stridulous, tumultuous 11 cacophonous 12 rambunctious

raunchy
4 foul 5 dirty, nasty 6 coarse, filthy, sloppy, smutty, vulgar 7 obscene 8 indecent 9 salacious

ravage
4 loot, raze, ruin, sack 5 foray, harry, spoil, strip, waste, wreck 6 forage, invade, ravish 7 despoil, overrun, pillage, plunder, ransack, scourge 8 desolate, spoliate 9 depredate, desecrate, devastate

rave
4 gush, rant 5 storm 6 babble, jabber 7 enthuse 10 rhapsodize

ravel
3 run 4 fray 5 snarl 6 muddle, tangle 7 perplex, untwine 8 entangle 9 extricate 10 complicate 11 disentangle

ravelings
4 lint 7 threads

Ravel work
6 Boléro 7 La Valse 14 Daphnis et Chloé 17 Rapsodie espagnole

raven
3 jet 4 ebon, inky, prey 5 black, ebony, jetty, sable 7 despoil, plunder 9 pitch-dark 10 pitch-black
relative: 3 jay 4 crow 6 magpie 7 blue jay

Raven, The
author: 3 Poe (Edgar Allan)
lost love: 6 Lenore
refrain: 9 Nevermore

ravenous
6 greedy, hungry 7 starved 8 edacious,

famished, starving **9** rapacious, voracious
10 gluttonous

ravine
3 cut, gap **4** gulf, pass **5** abyss, chasm,
cleft, clove, flume, gorge, gulch, gully, notch
6 arroyo, canyon, clough, coulee, defile,
gutter, nullah **7** crevice, fissure
8 barranca, crevasse
Mt. Washington's: 9 Tuckerman

raving
3 mad **5** manic, rabid, upset **6** crazed
7 frantic, lunatic, unglued **8** demented,
deranged, frenetic, frenzied, maniacal,
obsessed, unhinged, worked up
9 ravishing **10** distraught, flipped out,
hysterical, irrational **11** overwrought

ravish
4 rape **5** force, spoil **6** defile **7** assault,
despoil, outrage, pillage, plunder, violate
8 deflower, entrance, overcome
9 enrapture, transport

raw
4 cold, nude, rude **5** bleak, chill, crass,
crude, fresh, green, naked, rough, young
6 callow, coarse, impure, native, unclad,
unripe, vulgar **7** uncouth **8** immature,
uncooked, unformed **9** au naturel,
inelegant, irritated, run-of-mine, unbridled,
unclothed, undressed, unrefined
10 unfinished, unpolished **13** inexperienced

rawboned
4 bony, lank, lean **5** gaunt, gawky, lanky,
spare **6** skinny **7** angular, scraggy,
scrawny

ray
4 beam **5** gleam, manta, shaft, skate, trace
6 radius, streak, stream **7** radiate, sawfish,
sunbeam, torpedo **8** moonbeam
9 devilfish, guitarfish, thornback

raze
4 ruin **5** level **7** destroy **8** demolish, pull
down, tear down

razor
6 shaver

razz
3 rag, rib **4** bait, josh, mock, twit **5** scout,
taunt **6** badger, banter, deride, heckle,
hector **8** ridicule
(see also **raspberry**)

RBI
11 run batted in **12** runs batted in

re
4 as to **5** as for **7** apropos **9** apropos of, as

regards, regarding **10** as respects,
concerning, relating to, respecting **12** with
regard to **13** with respect to

reach
4 beat, gain, pass, span, tack **5** carry, get
at, get to, grasp, level, range, scope,
sweep, touch **6** arrive, attain, extend,
extent, rack up **7** achieve, horizon, project,
stretch, thrust **9** encompass, influence
10 accomplish, get through

_____ reaction
4 dark **5** alarm, chain, light **7** nuclear
8 chemical

reactivate
5 renew **6** revive **8** rekindle, revivify
9 resurrect **10** revitalize **11** resuscitate

read
4 scan, skim **6** peruse **8** pore over
inability to: 8 dyslexia

readable
7 legible

reader
6 lector, primer **7** proofer, scanner
8 bookworm **9** anthology

readily
4 well **6** easily, freely **7** lightly **9** willingly
12 effortlessly

readiness
4 ease **5** skill **7** aptness **8** alacrity,
dispatch, facility **9** dexterity, quickness
10 promptness **11** inclination, promptitude
12 preparedness

reading
6 lesson **7** lection, version, vulgate
9 rendition **10** recitation

ready
3 set **4** prep, ripe **5** equip **6** active, gear
up, make up, primed **7** prepare, prompt
8 prepared, available, inclined

real
4 true, very **5** pukka, sound, valid **6** actual,
honest **7** certain, genuine, sincere **8** bona
fide, concrete, existent, tangible
9 authentic, undoubted, veridical **10** sure-
enough, undeniable **11** substantive
12 indisputable

realism
6 verism **7** verismo **10** naturalism,
pragmatism **11** objectivism, objectivity

realistic
4 sane **5** sober, sound **7** genuine, natural
8 lifelike, rational, sensible, veristic

9 practical, pragmatic 10 bottom-line, hard-boiled, hardheaded, reasonable, unromantic 11 down-to-earth 12 matter-of-fact 13 unsentimental

reality
4 fact, true 5 being, sooth, truth 9 actuality, existence, substance 13 flesh and blood

realize
4 gain 5 grasp, reach, score 6 attain, rack up 7 achieve, feature, imagine, reflect 8 conceive, envisage, envision 9 actualize, recognize 10 accomplish, comprehend

really
4 very 5 truly 6 indeed, verily 7 awfully, clearly 8 actually, honestly 9 assuredly, certainly, decidedly, genuinely 10 definitely, positively 11 exceedingly, indubitably, undoubtedly 12 unmistakably

realm
5 orbit, range, scope, sweep 6 domain, empire, estate, extent, radius, sphere 7 compass, demesne, kingdom, purview 8 dominion

ream
4 load, scad 5 widen 7 enlarge 11 countersink

reanimation
7 rebirth, revival 10 renascence, resurgence 11 reawakening, renaissance 12 risorgimento

reap
3 cut 4 earn, gain 5 glean, shear 6 garner, gather, obtain, sickle, thresh 7 harvest

rear
3 aft 4 back, butt, hind, lift, ramp, rump, seat, tail 5 after, breed, build, erect, fanny, hoist, nurse, put up, raise, set up 6 behind, bottom, fledge, foster, uphold 7 bring up, caboose, elevate, nurture 8 backside, buttocks, hindmost 9 construct, posterior

rear end
3 bum, bun, can, duff 4 moon, rump, seat, tail, tush 5 booty, fanny 6 behind, bottom, heinie 7 caboose, keister, tail end 8 backside, buttocks, derriere 9 posterior

rearmost
3 end 4 last 5 final 8 terminal, ultimate

rearrange
see **readjust**

rearward
3 aft 4 back 6 behind 8 backward 9 posterior 10 retrograde

Rea Silvia
father: 7 Numitor
son: 5 Remus 7 Romulus

reason
3 why, wit 4 mind, nous 5 basis, cause, infer, proof, think 6 excuse, ground, motive, sanity, senses 7 account, reflect 8 argument, cogitate, conceive, persuade 9 inference, intellect, rationale, soundness, speculate, wherefore 10 antecedent, deliberate 11 determinant, explanation 12 intelligence 13 consideration, justification, ratiocination, understanding

reasonable
4 fair, just 5 cheap, level, sound 6 modest 7 logical, low-cost, tenable 8 credible, feasible, moderate, rational, sensible 9 equitable, plausible 10 acceptable, affordable, restrained 11 inexpensive, intelligent

reasoning
4 case 5 logic 8 argument 9 deduction

reasonless
7 invalid 8 baseless 9 illogical, senseless, unfounded 10 fallacious, groundless, irrational 11 meaningless, purposeless

reawaken
5 renew 6 revive 7 refresh 8 revivify 9 reanimate 10 regenerate 12 reinvigorate

rebate
6 lessen, refund, return 8 decrease, diminish, give back 9 deduction, reduction

Rebecca
beloved: 7 Ivanhoe
father: 5 Isaac

Rebekah
brother: 5 Laban
father: 7 Bethuel
husband: 5 Isaac
nurse: 7 Deborah
son: 4 Esau 5 Jacob

rebel
6 anarch, mutiny, resist, revolt 7 disobey 8 frondeur, mutineer 9 insurgent 10 malcontent 13 revolutionary, revolutionist

rebellion
6 émeute, mutiny, revolt, rising 8 defiance, intifada, sedition, uprising 9 insurgence, insurgency, resistance, revolution 12 insurrection

rebellious
6 unruly 8 mutinous, stubborn 9 insurgent 10 refractory 11 disaffected, disobedient

rebirth

12 contumacious, unmanageable
13 insubordinate

rebirth
7 revival 9 awakening 10 conversion, renascence, resurgence 11 reanimation, reawakening, renaissance 12 resurrection, risorgimento

rebound
5 rally 6 bounce, reecho, recoil 7 recover, repeat 8 comeback, recovery, ricochet, snap back 10 convalesce

rebozo
5 scarf, shawl

rebuff
4 slap, snub 5 repel 6 reject 7 fend off, repulse, ward off 8 turn away

rebuild
6 repair, revamp 7 remodel, restore 8 overhaul, renovate, retrofit 9 modernize, refurbish 11 recondition, reconstruct 12 rehabilitate

rebuke
3 rap 4 snub 5 chide, scold, scorn 6 berate, earful, lesson, rebuff 7 lecture, reproof, reprove 8 admonish, bawl out, call down, reproach, scolding 9 reprimand, talking-to 10 tongue-lash 11 comeuppance, objurgation 12 admonishment, dressing-down 13 tongue-lashing

rebut
5 repel 6 refute, reject 7 confute, fend off, repulse, ward off 8 confound, disprove, stave off 10 controvert, disconfirm

rebuttal
5 reply 6 answer, retort 7 defense, riposte 8 argument, comeback, response 9 rejoinder 10 refutation 11 repudiation

recalcitrant
6 unruly 7 froward, willful 8 contrary, perverse, stubborn, untoward 9 fractious, obstinate, resistant 10 headstrong 11 intractable 12 ungovernable, unmanageable

recall
4 stir 5 evoke, renew, rouse, waken 6 arouse, awaken, cancel, memory, remind, repeal, revive, revoke 7 bethink, rescind, restore, retract, reverse 8 callback, represent, remember, resemble, take back, withdraw 9 anamnesis, recollect, reinstate, reminisce, reproduce 10 revocation 11 bring to mind, countermand

recant
5 unsay 6 abjure 7 retract, revoke 8 forswear, renounce, take back, withdraw 9 backtrack, repudiate

recap
5 sum up 6 précis, résumé 7 reprise, retread, summary 8 overview, summarize 10 retrograde

recapitulate
5 sum up 6 resume 9 summarize 10 retrograde

recapitulation
5 sum-up 6 précis, résumé 7 epitome, reprise, summary 9 summing-up

recede
3 ebb 4 back 5 abate, taper 6 lessen, reduce, retire 7 dwindle, regress, retract, retreat 8 decrease, diminish, fall back, withdraw 10 retrograde, retrogress

receipts
4 gate, take 5 sales 6 income, takings 7 revenue 8 earnings, proceeds

receive
4 host 5 admit, catch, greet 6 accept, endure, suffer, take in 7 acquire, sustain, welcome 10 experience

received
5 plain, sound 6 common 7 popular 8 accepted, familiar, ordinary, orthodox 12 acknowledged, conventional

receiver
4 dish 5 donee, fence, pager 6 aerial 7 antenna, catcher, scanner 9 recipient, treasurer

recent
3 new 4 late 5 fresh, novel 6 latest, modern 8 neoteric

receptacle
6 hamper, holder, hopper, trough, vessel 9 container 10 repository

receptive
4 open 7 passive 8 amenable 9 sensitive 10 accessible, hospitable, open-minded, responsive 11 persuadable, persuasible, suggestible, susceptible

recess
4 cove, nook 5 break, cleft, niche 6 alcove, grotto, hiatus 7 adjourn

recollection, remembrance, reminiscence
12 recollection, remembrance, reminiscence

8 prorogue 9 prorogate, terminate
11 indentation

Recessional author
7 Kipling (Rudyard)

recessive
3 shy 8 retiring 9 reclusive, withdrawn
10 unsociable

recherché
4 rare 5 novel 6 choice, dainty, exotic,
select 7 elegant, unusual 8 affected,
delicate, original, superior, uncommon
9 exquisite 11 pretentious

recipe
7 formula 9 procedure 12 prescription

reciprocal
4 mate, twin 5 match 6 double, fellow,
mutual 8 requited 9 companion, duplicate
10 coordinate 11 interactive
prefix: 5 inter

reciprocate
5 repay 6 retort, return 7 requite
8 exchange 9 retaliate 10 compensate,
recompense 11 interchange

recital
5 story 6 soiree 7 concert, reading
9 discourse, narration 10 recounting
11 enumeration, performance

recite
4 tell 5 chant, count, state 6 detail,
number, relate, repeat, report, set out
7 declaim, narrate, recount, reel off
8 describe, rehearse 9 pronounce

reckless
4 rash, wild 5 brash, hasty 6 daring,
madcap 8 carefree, heedless 9 audacious, daredevil, foolhardy, hotheaded
10 ill-advised, incautious 11 harebrained,
temerarious, thoughtless 12 devil-may-
care 13 irresponsible

reckon
3 sum 5 count, gauge, guess, judge, tally,
total 6 cipher, figure, number, regard
7 account, compute, suppose, surmise
8 consider, estimate 9 calculate,
enumerate 10 conjecture 11 approximate

reckoning
3 tab 4 bill 5 tally, score 7 account,
invoice 9 statement 10 arithmetic,
estimation 11 calculation, computation

reclaim
4 save, tame 6 redeem, reform, rescue
7 deliver, recover, restore 9 restitute
11 recondition, reconstruct 12 rehabilitate

recline
3 lie 4 rest, tilt 5 couch, slant, slope
6 lounge, repose 7 lie down 10 stretch out

reclining
4 flat 5 prone 6 supine 9 decumbent,
prostrate, recumbent

recluse
5 loner 6 hermit, shut-in 7 eremite
8 cenobite, solitary 9 anchorite
female: 7 ancress 9 anchoress

reclusive
8 eremitic, hermetic, reserved, solitary
9 withdrawn 10 antisocial, eremitical,
unsociable 12 misanthropic

recognition
6 credit, esteem, notice 9 attention,
awareness, gratitude 10 cognizance,
perception 11 realization 12 appreciation

recognize
4 note, spot 5 admit 6 notice 7 observe,
realize 8 diagnose, identify 9 apprehend
10 appreciate 11 acknowledge,
determinate, distinguish

recoil
4 balk, kick 5 cower, dodge, quail, start,
wince 6 blench, cringe, flinch, shrink
7 rebound, retract, squinch 8 reaction

recollect
5 evoke 6 recall, remind, revive 7 bethink
8 remember 9 reminisce

recollection
6 memory, recall 9 anamnesis, flashback
11 remembrance 12 reminiscence

recommence
5 renew 6 pick up, reopen, resume, take
up 7 restart 8 continue

recommend
4 tout 6 advise, priase, prefer 7 acclaim,
commend, counsel, endorse, entrust,
propose, suggest 8 advocate

recommendation
4 plug 5 pitch 6 advice 7 counsel
11 endorsement, testimonial

recompense
3 pay 4 wage 5 repay 6 amends, reward
7 guerdon, premium, redress, requite
8 gratuity, requital 9 indemnify, indemnity,
quittance, reimburse, repayment
10 compensate, remunerate, reparation
11 reciprocate, restitution, retribution

reconcile

12 compensation, remuneration
13 consideration, gratification

reconcile

4 suit, tune 5 adapt 6 accept, accord, adjust, attune, resign, settle, square, submit, tailor 7 conform, get over, make up, resolve 9 harmonize, integrate 10 conciliate, coordinate 11 accommodate

recondite

4 deep 6 hidden, mystic, occult, orphic, secret 7 cryptic, erudite, learned, obscure 8 abstruse, academic, esoteric, hermetic, profound 9 concealed, difficult, enigmatic, scholarly

recondition

3 fix 4 mend 6 doctor, repair, revamp 7 rebuild, restore 8 make over, overhaul, retrofit 9 restitute 10 rejuvenate 12 rehabilitate

reconnoiter

5 scout 6 survey

reconsider

6 review, revise 7 rethink, reweigh 8 reassess 9 reexamine 10 reevaluate 13 think better of

reconstruct

6 recast, re-form, remake, revamp 7 rebuild, reclaim, remodel, restore 8 make over, overhaul, readjust, renovate 9 refashion, restitute 10 reassemble, reorganize

record

4 disc, disk 5 album 6 annals, enroll 7 archive, journal, platter 8 archives, document, register 9 chronicle 10 transcript
of a meeting: 7 minutes
of proceedings: 4 acta
ship's: 3 log 7 logbook

recorder

5 flute 9 registrar
flight: 8 black box

record player

5 phono 8 Victrola 9 turntable 10 gramophone, phonograph

recount

4 tell 5 state 6 recite, relate, report, retail 7 narrate 8 describe, rehearse 9 enumerate

recoup

6 regain 7 get back, reclaim, recover 8 retrieve 9 repossess

recourse

6 backup, refuge, resort 7 standby, stopgap, support 8 resource 9 expedient, makeshift

recover

4 heal, mend 5 evict, rally, renew 6 recoup, recycle, redeem, regain, revive 7 get back, get over, improve, rebound, reclaim, restore 8 retrieve, snap back 9 come round, reacquire, recapture, re-collect, repossess, restitute 10 bounce back, convalesce, recuperate

recreant

3 rat 5 false 6 coward, craven, untrue 7 chicken, dastard, unloyal 8 apostate, cowardly, defector, deserter, disloyal, poltroon, renegade, turncoat 9 dastardly, faithless, turnabout 10 perfidious, traitorous, unfaithful 13 pusillanimous

recreate

4 play 5 evoke, renew 7 freshen, refresh, restore 11 reconstruct

recreation

4 play 5 hobby, sport 7 leisure, pastime 8 activity, avocation, diversion 10 relaxation 13 entertainment

recrudesce

5 recur 6 return, revert, revive 7 reoccur 8 break out

recruit

4 boot, hire 5 raise 6 engage, enlist, enroll, muster, novice, rookie 7 draftee 8 beginner, enlistee, freshman, headhunt, neophyte, newcomer 9 conscript, fledgling, reinforce, replenish 10 apprentice, tenderfoot

rectifier

4 tube 5 diode 8 detector, ignitron

rectify

3 fix 4 mend 5 amend, emend 6 adjust, remedy, repair 7 correct

rectitude

6 virtue 7 honesty, probity 8 morality 9 rightness 11 uprightness 13 righteousness

rector

6 parson, pastor, priest 9 clergyman 10 headmaster

rectory

5 manse 8 benefice 9 parsonage

recumbent

4 flat 5 prone 6 supine 7 leaning, resting

8 reposing 9 lying down, prostrate, reclining

recuperate
4 heal, mend 5 rally 6 regain, revive
7 rebound, recover 8 snap back
10 convalesce

recur
5 cycle, haunt 6 repeat, resort, return
7 iterate, revolve 8 turn back

recurring
7 chronic 8 periodic 10 continuous, isochronal, periodical, persistent
11 isochronous 12 intermittent

red
4 puce, ruby 5 coral, gules, rouge, ruddy
6 cerise, claret, florid, maroon 7 carmine, crimson, flushed, glowing, magenta, oxblood, scarlet, vermeil 8 burgundy, sanguine 9 carnation, vermilion

Red
6 Bolshy, commie 7 Bolshie, comrade
9 Bolshevik, Communist

redact
4 edit 6 censor, revise

Red and the Black author
8 Stendhal

red ape
9 orangutan

red arsenic
7 realgar

red-backed sandpiper
6 dunlin

Red Badge of Courage
author: 5 Crane (Stephen)
hero: 7 Fleming (Henry)

red-bellied snipe
9 dowitcher

redbird
7 tanager 8 cardinal 13 summer tanager

red blood cell
11 erythrocyte

red-blooded
5 juicy, lusty, manly 6 hearty, robust, virile
8 vigorous 9 energetic

redbreast
4 knot 5 robin 7 sunfish

red-breasted snipe
9 dowitcher

Redburn author
8 Melville (Herman)

red carp
8 goldfish

red cobalt
9 erythrite

red copper ore
7 cuprite

Red Cross
founder: 6 Barton (Clara)
Knight: 6 George

redden
5 blush, color, flush, rouge 6 mantle, ruddle 11 incarnadine

red dog
5 blitz

redecorate
4 redo 5 fix up 9 refurbish

redeem
4 free, save 5 atone, loose, renew
6 offset, pay off, ransom, reform, rescue
7 expiate, reclaim, recover, restore
9 exonerate

redeemer
5 Jesus 6 Christ, savior 7 messiah, saviour

redemption
6 ransom 7 release 9 atonement, expiation, salvation 11 deliverance

red-eye
5 hooch 6 flight, rotgut 7 whiskey 8 rock bass 9 moonshine

red-faced
5 ruddy 6 florid, shamed 7 abashed, flushed, glowing 8 blushing, rubicund, sanguine, sheepish 9 mortified
11 embarrassed

redfish
4 bass, drum 5 perch 6 salmon 10 ocean perch 11 channel bass

red hickory
6 pignut

red-hot
5 fiery 6 ardent, fervid 7 blazing, boiling, burning, fervent, flaming, glowing 8 brand-new, scalding, sizzling 9 scorching
10 blistering, passionate, sweltering
11 impassioned

red Indian paint
9 bloodroot 11 sanguinaria

red ink
7 arrears, deficit 8 shortage

red inkberry
8 pokeweed

red ironbark
8 eucalypt 10 eucalyptus

red iron ore
5 ocher, ochre 8 hematite

red lauan
8 mahogany

red-legged crow
6 chough

red-legged sandpiper
9 turnstone

red-letter
7 notable 8 historic 9 important,
memorable 10 noteworthy, observable,
remarkable 11 significant

red-light district
5 stews 10 tenderloin

red mite
7 chigger

redneck
4 clod, hick, rube 5 Bubba, yahoo, yokel
6 rustic 7 bumpkin, hayseed 9 hillbilly
10 clodhopper, good old boy, good ole boy

redo
5 renew 6 repeat, revamp 7 remodel,
restyle 8 make over, overhaul, refinish,
renovate 9 refurbish 10 redecorate

red ocher
8 hematite

redolence
4 balm, odor 5 aroma, attar, scent, spice
7 bouquet, incense, perfume 9 fragrance

redolent
5 balmy, spicy, sweet 7 odorous, scented
8 aromatic, fragrant, perfumed
9 ambrosial, evocative 10 suggestive
11 reminiscent

redouble
4 dupe 7 dualize, enhance, magnify
8 heighten 9 duplicate, intensify, reinforce
10 strengthen

redoubt
4 fort 7 bastion, citadel 8 fastness,
fortress 10 stronghold

redoubtable
5 famed, great 6 famous, mighty

7 awesome, eminent 8 imposing,
renowned 9 prominent, puissant
10 celebrated, formidable, impressive
11 illustrious 12 intimidating, overwhelming
13 distinguished

redound
6 accrue, recoil 7 conduce, reflect
10 contribute

red pigment
5 ocher, ochre 6 ruddle

Red Planet
4 Mars

redpoll
5 finch 6 linnet

redraft
6 revamp, revise, rework 7 restyle, rewrite
8 make over, overhaul, rescript, revision,
work over 9 recension

redress
4 heal 6 amends, avenge, negate, offset,
relief, remedy 7 correct, requital 8 reprisal
9 cancel out, indemnity, quittance, vindicate
10 compensate, counteract, correction,
neutralize, recompense, reparation
11 restitution, retribution 12 compensation

red roe
5 coral 6 caviar

redroot
7 alkanet, pigweed 9 bloodroot 12 New
Jersey tea

red sable
8 kolinsky

red silver ore
9 proustite

red squirrel
9 chickaree

reduce
3 cut 4 cull, diet, melt, pare 5 abate, force,
lower, shade, shave, slash, smelt
6 humble, lessen, recede, weaken
7 abridge, curtail, cut back, cut down,
dwindle, liquefy, squeeze 8 boil down,
compress, contract, decrease, diminish,
discount, mark down, minimize, simplify,
taper off 10 depreciate, slenderize 11 consolidate

reductio ad _____
8 absurdum

reduction
6 digest, précis, rebate 7 cutback,

cutdown, epitome, summary **8** abstract, discount, markdown, synopsis **9** abatement **10** shortening **11** curtailment **12** condensation

redundancy
6 excess **7** nimiety, surfeit **8** pleonasm **9** abundance, profusion, prolixity, tautology **10** repetition **11** periphrasis, reiteration, superfluity **13** supernumerary

redundant
5 extra, spare, windy, wordy **6** prolix **7** surplus, verbose **9** duplicate, excessive, iterative **11** duplicative, reiterative, repetitious, superfluous, tautologous **13** supernumerary

redux
7 revived **8** restored

redwing
6 thrush **9** blackbird

redwood
7 amboyna, sequoia **8** mahogany

reed
4 pipe **5** arrow, grass

reedy
4 thin **6** skinny, spindly, stalky, twiggy

reef
3 bar, cay, key **4** lode, vein **5** atoll, ledge **6** reduce, skerry **7** sandbar

reek
4 funk **5** fetor, smell, stink **6** stench **9** effluvium

reeking
4 rank **5** fetid, funky, fusty **6** putrid, rancid, smelly, stinky **7** noisome, stenchy **10** malodorous

reel
4 spin, sway, turn **5** lurch, spool, weave, whirl **6** bobbin, careen, teeter, totter, waggle, wobble **7** stagger, stumble **8** fall back

reestablish
5 renew **6** revive **7** restore **9** reinstate **10** reinscribe **11** reintroduce

reevaluate
6 review **7** rethink, reweigh **8** reassess **9** reexamine **10** reconsider

reeve
4 ruff **6** thread **9** sandpiper **10** magistrate

reexamine
see **reevaluate**

refashion
5 alter **6** change, modify, recast, remake, revamp **7** remodel **8** make over, overhaul **9** transmute

refection
4 feed, meal **6** repast **11** nourishment, refreshment

refectory
10 dining hall

refer
6 advert, allude, assign, relate, submit **7** ascribe **9** attribute

referee
3 ump **5** judge **6** umpire **7** adjudge, arbiter, mediate **8** mediator **9** arbitrate, officiate **10** adjudicate, arbitrator

reference
5 atlas **6** credit, source **7** almanac, meaning, mention **8** allusion, citation, innuendo, relation, resource **9** directory **10** dictionary **11** testimonial **12** encyclopedia

reference book
5 atlas, bible, guide **6** manual **7** almanac **8** handbook **9** guidebook **10** dictionary **11** enchiridion **12** encyclopedia

reference guide
5 index **12** bibliography

referendum
4 poll, vote **10** plebiscite

refine
5 smelt **6** polish, prune, purify, smooth **7** elevate, improve, perfect, process **8** civilize **9** cultivate

refined
4 pure **6** subtle, urbane **7** elegant, genteel, raffiné **8** cultured, elevated, ladylike, raffinée, well-bred **9** civilized **10** cultivated, fastidious **13** sophisticated

refinement
5 couth, grace, taste **6** finish, polish **7** culture, finesse, suavity **8** breeding, civility, courtesy, elegance, subtlety, urbanity **9** politesse **10** politeness **11** cultivation **12** civilization, distillation, purification **13** clarification

reflect
4 echo, pore, show **5** weigh **6** bounce, mirror, ponder, reason, return **7** redound **8** chew over, cogitate, consider, ruminate **9** cerebrate **10** deliberate, retrospect **11** contemplate, demonstrate

reflection
4 slur 5 image 6 musing 7 replica,
thought 8 reproach 9 aspersion
10 cogitation, meditation, rumination,
simulacrum 11 cerebration 12 deliberation, reproduction 13 animadversion,
consideration, contemplation

reflective
7 pensive 9 reflexive 10 cogitative,
indicative, meditative, ruminative,
thoughtful 12 deliberative 13 contemplative

reflux
3 ebb 4 GERD 8 backflow

reform
5 amend, emend 6 redeem, revise
7 correct, improve, reclaim, shape up
8 make over 10 correction, houseclean,
regenerate

Reformation leader
4 Knox (John) 6 Calvin (John), Luther
(Martin) 7 Zwingli (Huldrych)

reformatory
3 pen 6 prison 7 borstal 8 big house,
remedial 10 corrective 12 penitentiary

refractory
6 mulish, unruly 7 froward, restive
8 contrary, perverse, stubborn 9 obstinate
10 bullheaded, headstrong, rebellious,
unyielding 11 intractable, stiff-necked
12 unmanageable

refrain
4 keep, stop 6 burden, chorus, shrink
7 abstain, forbear 8 hold back

refresh
5 renew 6 revive 7 animate, enliven,
quicken, restore 8 irrigate, recreate,
renovate 9 replenish, stimulate
10 rejuvenate

refresher
5 drink, tonic 6 bracer 8 reminder
9 stimulant 11 restorative

refreshing
5 brisk, tonic 7 bracing 8 reviving
9 analeptic, animating 10 delightful,
energizing 11 restorative, stimulating
12 invigorating, rejuvenating

refrigerant
3 ice 5 freon 7 coolant, cryogen
12 fluorocarbon 13 sulfur dioxide

refrigerator
6 cooler, fridge, icebox, walk-in
9 condenser 10 Frigidaire

refuge
4 lair, port 5 cover, haven 6 asylum,
covert, harbor, resort 7 hideout, protect,
retreat, shelter 8 hideaway, recourse,
resource 9 expedient, harborage,
sanctuary, safe house

refugee
5 exile 6 émigré 7 evacuee 8 emigrant,
fugitive 10 boat person, expatriate

refulgent
6 bright 7 glowing, radiant 8 luminous
9 brilliant

refund
5 repay 6 rebate 8 give back
9 reimburse, repayment, restitute
11 restitution

refurbish
4 redo 5 fix up, renew 6 revamp 7 restore
8 make over, overhaul, renovate
10 redecorate, rejuvenate 11 recondition

refusal
4 veto 6 denial 7 regrets 8 negative,
negation 9 disavowal 10 abnegation
11 declination, repudiation

refuse
3 jib, nix 4 deny, junk, scum 5 dreck,
dross, offal, spurn, swill, trash, waste
6 debris, litter, reject, scraps, spilth
7 decline, garbage, residue, rubbish
8 disallow, leavings, remnants, turn down,
withhold 9 reprobate, repudiate,
sweepings 10 disapprove

refutation
8 disproof, elenchus, rebuttal

refute
4 deny 5 rebut 7 confute 8 confound,
disprove 10 controvert, disconfirm

regain
6 recoup 7 get back, recover 8 reoccupy,
retrieve 9 recapture, repossess
possession: 7 replevy 8 replevin

regal
5 grand 6 august, kingly, purple 7 queenly,
stately, sublime 8 glorious, imperial,
imposing, kinglike, majestic, princely,
splendid 9 monarchal, sovereign
10 monarchial 11 magnificent,
monarchical, resplendent

regale
4 feed 5 amuse, feast 6 dinner, divert, spread 7 banquet 9 entertain

regalia
5 array 6 finery 8 frippery, insignia 9 caparison, full dress, trappings 10 decoration 11 habiliments

Regan
father: 4 Lear
husband: 8 Cornwall
sister: 7 Goneril 8 Cordelia

regard
4 deem, heed, mark, note, rate, view 5 assay, favor, honor, judge, value 6 admire, assess, esteem, homage, liking, notice, reckon, repute 7 account, concern, respect 8 approval, consider, devotion, estimate, fondness 9 attention 10 admiration, cognizance, estimation, observance, solicitude 11 approbation, contemplate, observation 12 appreciation, satisfaction 13 consideration

regardful
7 heedful 8 watchful 9 advertent, attentive, observant 10 perceptive, respectful

regarding
4 as to, in re 5 about, anent, as for 7 apropos 8 touching 9 apropos of, in respect to 10 as respects, concerning, relative to, respecting 13 with respect to

regatta
4 race

regenerate
5 renew 6 reform, revive 7 rebirth, restore 8 recreate 9 reproduce

regent
5 ruler 6 warden 8 governor 9 protector

regicide's victim
4 king

regime
4 rule, term 5 reign 6 empire, tenure 7 dynasty 10 government, leadership

regimen
4 diet, plan, rule 6 course 10 government

region
4 area, belt, part, zone 5 field, tract 6 domain, locale, sector, sphere 7 demesne, terrain 8 locality, province, vicinity 9 bailiwick, territory 12 neighborhood

regional
5 local 9 localized, sectional 10 provincial 11 territorial

register
4 file, list, note, roll, till 5 enter, range, tally 6 annals, docket, enroll, ledger, record, roster 7 catalog, check in, express 8 indicate 9 catalogue

regnant
4 rife 6 ruling 7 current, popular 8 dominant, reigning 9 paramount, prevalent, sovereign 10 prevailing, widespread

regress
6 revert 9 backslide 10 retrograde

regret
3 rue, woe 4 care 5 grief, mourn 6 bemoan, bewail, excuse, grieve, lament, repent, sorrow 7 anguish, apology, deplore, remorse 9 heartache, penitence 10 contrition, heartbreak 11 compunction

regretful
5 sorry 6 rueful 8 contrite, mournful, penitent 9 repentant, sorrowful 10 apologetic, remorseful 11 penitential

regrettable
3 sad 6 too bad, woeful 8 grievous 10 lamentable 11 distressing, unfortunate 13 heartbreaking

regular
3 due, set 4 even 5 fixed, usual 6 common, normal, steady 7 average, equable, general, natural, orderly, typical, uniform 8 complete, constant, everyday, methodic, ordinary, standard 9 clocklike, customary, prevalent 10 methodical, systematic 11 commonplace 12 run-of-the-mill

regulate
5 order, scale 6 adjust, direct, govern, police, square, temper 7 arrange, control 8 organize 9 methodize, systemize 11 systematize

regulation
3 law 4 rule 5 canon, edict, order 6 decree 7 precept, statute 9 ordinance, prescript 11 restriction 12 codification

regulator
8 governor

rehabilitate
4 cure, heal 7 reclaim, recover, restore

8 renovate 9 reeducate, restitute
11 recondition

rehash
5 reuse 6 repeat, review, rework 7 restate,
version 8 chew over, rehearse, talk over
9 rendering, rendition, rewording
11 restatement 12 recapitulate

rehearse
5 drill, train 6 repeat 7 run over
8 exercise, practice 10 run through

Rehoboam
father: 7 Solomon
kingdom: 5 Judah 6 Israel
mother: 6 Naamah

reign
4 rule, sway 6 govern 7 prevail
8 dominate, dominion 11 predominate,
sovereignty

reimburse
3 pay 5 repay 6 recoup, refund 7 requite
9 indemnify 10 compensate, remunerate

rein
4 curb, stem 5 check 6 bridle 7 compose,
control, repress 8 hold back, restrain,
suppress

reinforce
4 prop 5 brace 7 augment, bolster,
enlarge, fortify, recruit, sustain 8 buttress,
increase, redouble 10 invigorate,
strengthen

reinstate
6 recall 7 restore 11 reestablish,
reintroduce 12 rehabilitate

reintroduce
6 recall, revive 7 restore 9 reinstate
11 reestablish

reinvestment
4 DRIP 8 plowback

reiterate
5 renew, resay 6 repeat, resume, retell
7 reprise

reject
3 nix 4 jilt, junk, shed 5 debar, scorn,
scrap, spurn 6 abjure, pariah, pass up,
rebuff, refuse 7 cashier, castoff, decline,
discard, dismiss, exclude, repulse,
shut out 8 castaway, jettison, throw out,
turn away, turn down 9 eliminate,
repudiate, shoot down, throw away 10 disapprove

rejoice
5 cheer, exult, glory 7 delight, gladden
8 jubilate

rejoinder
5 reply 6 answer, retort 8 comeback,
rebuttal, repartee, response

rejuvenate
5 green, renew 7 refresh 8 renovate
9 modernize 10 revitalize

rekindle
5 renew 6 revive 7 restart 8 reawaken,
reignite, revivify 10 reactivate, revitalize

relate
4 link, tell 5 apply, refer 6 assign, detail,
recite, report 7 connect, express, pertain,
recount 8 describe, disclose, interact,
rehearse 9 appertain, chronicle

related
4 akin 5 alike, enate 6 agnate, allied
7 cognate, connate, germane, kindred
8 incident 9 analogous, connected,
identical, pertinent 10 associated,
connatural, homologous 11 consanguine

relation
3 kin 6 agnate 7 hinship, kinsman
8 affinity 9 kinswoman, reference
11 propinquity

relationship
3 tie 4 bond, link 5 ratio, tie-in, union
6 affair 7 analogy, contact, liaison
8 affinity, alliance 10 connection
11 affiliation, association 13 confederation,
consanguinity

relative
3 mom, sib, sis, son 4 aunt, mama, papa
5 blood, madre, mamma, momma, niece,
pappy, pater, poppa, uncle 6 agnate,
cousin, father, mother, nephew, parent,
sister 7 apropos, brother, cognate,
germane, kinsman, sibling 8 ancestor,
daughter, grandson, relation, relevant
9 ascendant, dependent, kinswoman,
pertinent 10 applicable, collateral,
descendant, grandchild 11 comparative,
conditional, grandfather, grandmother,
grandparent 13 granddaughter

relatives
3 kin 4 kith 5 folks 7 kindred, kinfolk
8 kinfolks, relations

relax
4 bask, ease, loll, rest 5 chill, let go, loose,
remit 6 loosen, lounge, modify, unkink,
unwind 7 slacken 8 chill out, kick back,

relaxation
3 fun 4 ease, rest 5 hobby 6 repose
7 leisure, pastime 9 amusement, diversion,
enjoyment 10 recreation

relaxed
5 loose, slack 6 casual, dégagé, mellow
8 informal 9 easygoing 11 low-pressure

release
4 emit, free, vent 5 issue, loose, untie,
yield 6 acquit, loosen, pardon, ransom,
unbind, uncage 7 give off, give out,
manumit, set free, unchain, unleash
8 liberate, unfetter 9 acquittal, discharge,
exculpate, exonerate, surrender
10 emancipate 11 manumission
12 emancipation
conditional: 6 parole

relegate
5 exile, expel 6 assign, banish, charge,
commit, demote, resign 7 commend,
confide, consign, entrust 8 delegate, hand
over, transfer, turn over

relent
3 ebb 4 cave, wane 5 abate, ease, let up,
yield 6 give in, submit 7 die away, die
down, ease off, slacken, subside
8 moderate 9 acquiesce 10 capitulate

relentless
5 cruel, rigid, stern 6 dogged 7 adamant,
nonstop 8 constant, obdurate, rigorous,
unabated 9 ferocious, incessant, stringent
10 implacable, inexorable, inflexible,
unyielding 11 remorseless, unfaltering

relevant
3 apt, fit 5 ad rem 6 cogent 7 apropos,
germane 8 apposite, material, relative
9 pertinent 10 admissible, applicable
11 applicative, appropriate 12 proportional

reliable
4 safe, sure 5 solid, sound, tried, valid
6 proven, secure, trusty 7 bedrock, certain
8 constant, verified 9 foolproof, validated
10 dependable 11 trustworthy 12 tried-
and-true

reliance
4 hope 5 faith, stock, trust 10 dependence

relic
6 token 6 corpse 7 antique, memento,
remains, remnant, vestige 8 artifact,
fragment, keepsake, memorial, reminder,
souvenir 11 remembrance

relict
5 widow 8 survivor

relief
3 aid 4 ease, fret, hand, help, lift 5 break,
cameo 6 assist, raised, remedy, succor
7 comfort, redress, respite, support, welfare
8 breather, fretwork, repoussé
9 abatement, diversion 10 assistance,
mitigation 11 alleviation, deliverance
pitcher: 6 closer 7 fireman, stopper

relieve
3 rid 4 calm, ease, free, help, quit, vent
5 allay, assist, relax, spell 6 exempt,
lessen, loosen, reduce, remedy, soften,
solace, soothe, succor, supply 7 absolve,
assuage, comfort, deprive, lighten, mollify,
release 8 diminish, dispense, mitigate,
moderate, palliate, unburden 9 alleviate

religion
4 cult, sect 5 cause, creed, dogma, faith
6 belief, church 8 devotion, doctrine

religious
3 nun 4 holy, monk 5 friar, godly, pious
6 devout, priest, sacred, votary 7 staunch,
upright 8 cenobite, faithful, monastic,
priestly, reverent 9 pietistic, prayerful,
spiritual, steadfast 10 scriptural,
scrupulous, worshipful

relinquish
4 cede, quit, shed 5 forgo, leave, waive,
yield 6 desert, give up, resign 7 abandon,
discard, lay down, release 8 abdicate,
hand over, renounce 9 quitclaim, sacrifice,
surrender

relish
4 like, tang, zest 5 enjoy, fancy, flair, gusto,
savor, taste 6 flavor, liking, palate
7 delight 8 fondness, penchant, pleasure,
sapidity 9 appetizer, condiment, enjoyment
10 appreciate 11 delectation, hors
d'oeuvre

relucent
6 bright 7 glaring, radiant, shining
10 reflecting

reluctant
3 shy 4 wary 5 chary, loath 6 afraid,
averse 8 cautious, grudging, hesitant
9 unwilling 10 indisposed 11 disinclined
prophet: 5 Jonah

rely
3 bet 4 bank, plan 5 count 6 depend,
gamble, reckon

rely on
5 trust 6 expect 10 anticipate

remain
4 bide, last, live, stay, wait **5** abide, tarry
6 endure, linger, loiter **7** persist, survive
8 continue **10** hang around **11** stick
around

remainder
4 rest **5** dregs, trace **6** excess **7** balance,
residue, remnant, surplus, vestige
8 leavings, leftover, residual, residuum

remains
4 body **5** ashes, bones, ruins **6** corpse,
debris, relics **7** balance, cadaver, carcass,
flotsam **8** leavings, remnants **9** reliquiae

remand
8 send back

remark
4 gibe, note **5** aside, crack **7** comment,
mention **9** utterance, wisecrack, witticism
10 annotation **11** observation **12** obiter
dictum

remarkable
4 rare **5** great **6** signal, unique **7** salient,
strange, unusual **8** singular, striking,
uncommon **9** arresting, bodacious,
momentous, prominent **10** impressive,
noteworthy, noticeable **11** conspicuous,
exceptional, outstanding, significant
13 extraordinary

_____ Remarque
5 Erich (Maria)

remedial
8 curative, salutary, sanative **9** medicinal
10 corrective **11** restorative, therapeutic
12 recuperative

remedy
3 fix **4** cure, drug, heal **5** salve, solve
6 elixir, relief, repair **7** correct, cure-all,
nostrum, panacea, rectify, redress, relieve
8 antidote, medicine, specific **9** alleviate,
treatment **10** corrective, medicament,
medication

remember
5 educe, evoke **6** recall, record, relive,
retain, reward **7** bethink **9** flash back,
recollect, reminisce **10** bear in mind
11 commemorate, memorialize

remembrance
4 gift **5** favor, recall, relic, token **6** memory,
recall, trophy **7** memento, present, thought
8 keepsake, memorial, reminder, souvenir
9 anamnesis, flashback **12** recollection,
reminiscence

remind
6 advise, prompt **7** bethink **8** admonish

reminder
4 hint, memo **5** relic, token **6** prompt,
trophy **7** memento **8** keepsake, memorial,
monument, souvenir **9** refresher
10 admonition, memorandum
11 remembrance

reminisce
see **remember**

reminiscence
6 memory, recall **8** anecdote **9** anamnesis, flashback **11** remembrance
12 recollection

remise
4 cede, deed **5** alien, grant **6** assign,
convey **8** make over, transfer **9** quitclaim

remiss
3 lax **4** lazy **5** slack **8** careless, derelict,
heedless, indolent, slothful **9** negligent,
slatternly **10** delinquent, neglectful
11 inattentive

remit
4 send, ship, stay, stop **5** abate, defer,
delay, relax **6** desist, hold up, pardon, put
off, remand, shelve **7** condone, consign,
forgive, forward, hold off **8** dispatch,
moderate, postpone

remnant
3 end **4** heel, husk, part, rest, rump **5** relic,
trace, wrack **6** fag end, relict **7** balance,
oddment, residue **8** leavings, leftover,
residuum **9** remainder

remodel
4 redo **6** recast, revamp **8** make over,
overhaul, redesign **9** refashion
11 reconstruct

remonstrance
5 demur **7** protest **8** demurral, demurrer
9 challenge, objection

remonstrate
5 argue, demur, plead **6** combat, object,
oppose, reason **7** protest **9** challenge

remora
4 clog, drag **6** sucker **9** hindrance
10 impediment **11** encumbrance, shark
sucker

remorse
3 rue **4** ruth **5** guilt, smart **6** regret, sorrow
9 penitence **10** contrition, repentance
11 compunction **12** self-reproach

remorseful
see **regretful**

remote
3 far, off   4 slim   5 aloof   6 far-off, slight
7 distant, faraway, obscure, outside,
slender   8 detached, far-flung, frontier,
isolated, lonesome, off-lying, outlying,
secluded   9 backwoods, withdrawn
10 negligible   11 godforsaken, out-of-the-
way
combining form: 3 tel   4 tele

remotest
6 utmost   7 extreme, outmost   8 farthest
9 outermost, uttermost   11 furthermost

remove
4 doff, skim   5 purge   6 unseat   7 extract,
take off, take out   8 dislodge, evacuate,
take away, withdraw   9 clear away,
eliminate
from office: 6 depose
hair: 8 depilate
surgically: 6 resect

removed
5 aloof, apart   6 far-off, remote   7 devious,
distant, faraway, obscure   8 detached, far-
flung, isolated, outlying, separate
10 distracted   11 unconnected

remunerate
3 pay   5 repay   7 requite   9 indemnify,
reimburse   10 compensate, recompense

remunerative
6 paying   7 gainful, payable   9 lucrative,
productive   10 profitable   11 moneymaking

Remus
brother: 7 Romulus
father: 4 Mars
mother: 9 Rea Silvia   10 Rhea Silvia
slayer: 7 Romulus

renaissance
see **rebirth**

renal
7 nephric   9 nephritic

rend
3 rip   4 rive, tear   5 split   6 cleave, divide

render
3 pay   4 cede, limn   5 yield   6 depict, give
up, impart, return, submit   7 deliver,
execute, pay back, picture, portray, provide,
restore   8 carry out, describe, hand over,
turn over   9 delineate, interpret, represent,
translate, transpose   10 administer,
relinquish   12 administrate

rendering
4 copy   7 version   9 depiction   10 paraphrase   11 description, performance,
restatement, translation   12 reproduction

rendezvous
4 date   5 haunt, tryst   6 gather, muster
7 collect, hangout, meeting   8 assemble
10 congregate, engagement
11 appointment, assignation, get-together

rendition
7 reading, version   10 adaptation
11 performance, translation

renegade
3 rat   5 rebel   6 outlaw   7 heretic
8 apostate, defector, deserter, maverick,
recreant, turncoat   9 turnabout
10 schismatic

renege
4 deny   5 welsh   6 cry off, recall, recant,
revoke   7 back off, back out, retract
8 renounce, withdraw   9 backpedal

renew
6 redeem, reform, revamp, revive   7
freshen, refresh, remodel   8 make over,
overhaul, recharge, recreate, rekindle,
renovate, revivify   9 refurbish, resurrect
10 reactivate, recommence, regenerate,
rejuvenate, revitalize

rennet
8 abomasum

renounce
4 deny, quit   5 demit   6 abjure, defect,
desert, give up, recant, renege, resign
7 abandon, decline, forsake, put away,
retract   8 abdicate, abnegate, disclaim,
forswear, swear off   9 repudiate, sacrifice
10 apostatize

renovate
4 redo   5 renew   6 remake, repair, revamp,
revive   7 furbish, refresh, restore
8 overhaul, revivify   9 modernize, refurbish,
resurrect   10 rejuvenate, revitalize
12 rehabilitate

renown
4 fame   5 éclat, glory, kudos   6 repute
7 acclaim   8 eminence, prestige
9 celebrity, notoriety   10 prominence,
reputation   11 distinction

renowned
5 famed, great, noted   6 fabled, famous
7 eminent, notable   8 extolled   9 acclaimed,
legendary, notorious, prominent, well-

known **10** celebrated **11** illustrious, outstanding **13** distinguished

rent
3 let, rip **4** hire, rift, tear, torn **5** lease, split **6** breach, sublet **7** charter, fissure, rupture **8** fracture

rental
4 hire **7** tenancy

renter
6 lessee, tenant **11** leaseholder

renunciation
6 denial **7** refusal **8** apostasy, eschewal, forgoing **9** disavowal, sacrifice, surrender **10** abdication, abnegation, disclaimer, self-denial **11** abandonment, forswearing, repudiation, resignation

reorder
5 shift **7** permute **9** rearrange, reshuffle

reorganization
7 shake-up **8** turnover

repair
3 fix **4** mend **5** patch **6** cobble, doctor **7** fitness, service **8** overhaul **9** condition **11** recondition

reparations
6 amends **7** redress **9** indemnity, quittance **10** recompense, settlement **11** restitution **12** satisfaction

repartee
4 quip **6** banter, retort **7** riposte **8** backchat, badinage, comeback **9** cross talk, rejoinder **10** persiflage

repast
3 eat **4** feed, meal **5** feast **9** refection

repay
6 offset, return, reward **7** requite **9** indemnify, reimburse **10** compensate, recompense, remunerate **11** get even with

repeal
4 lift, void **5** annul **6** recall, revoke **7** abandon, abolish, abrogate, nullify, rescind, reverse **8** renounce

repeat
4 copy, echo **5** recap, recur, rerun, resay **6** go over, parrot, reecho, recite, rehash, relate, retell **7** imitate, iterate, reprise, restate **9** duplicate, reiterate, replicate **11** reduplicate **12** recapitulate

repeater
7 firearm **10** recidivist

repeating
7 iterant **9** perennial, recurrent **11** reiterative, repetitious

repel
5 rebut **6** rebuff, reject, revolt, sicken **7** disgust, fend off, hold off, repulse, ward off **8** nauseate, stave off

repellent
4 foul, vile **5** nasty **7** noisome **8** aversive **9** abhorrent, loathsome, obnoxious, offensive, repulsive, revolting **10** forbidding, disgusting, off-putting **11** rebarbative

repent
3 rue **6** regret

repentance
3 rue **4** ruth **6** sorrow **7** remorse **10** contrition **11** compunction

repentant
see **regretful**

repetition
4 copy, echo **5** rerun **7** recital, reprise **11** duplication

rephrase
6 recast, reword **7** restate

repine
4 beef, fuss, kick, long, moan, wail **5** gripe, yearn **6** grouse, hanker, murmur **7** grumble **8** complain

replace
7 put back, restore **8** exchange, supplant **9** supersede **10** substitute

replacement
3 sub **6** fill-in, makeup **7** stand-in **9** alternate, surrogate, temporary **10** substitute **11** locum tenens, pinch hitter, succedaneum

replenish
4 fill **5** renew, stock **6** refill **7** refresh, restore

replete
4 full, rife **5** awash, lousy **7** brimful, crammed, stuffed **8** brimming **9** chock-full **11** overflowing

replica
4 copy, dupe, fake **5** clone, ditto **6** carbon **9** duplicate, facsimile, imitation **10** carbon copy, simulacrum **12** reproduction

replicate
4 copy **5** clone **6** repeat **9** reproduce

reply
4 echo 6 answer, rejoin, retort 7 respond
8 comeback, repartee, response
9 rejoinder

report
4 bang, boom, news, tell 5 crack, relay,
rumor, study 6 record, relate, return,
review, show up 7 account, article, check
in, hearsay, narrate, recount, rundown
8 advisory, bulletin, describe, dispatch
9 broadcast, chronicle, narrative, statement
11 compte rendu

reporter
7 newsman 8 pressman 9 newshound,
newswoman 10 journalist
inexperienced: 3 cub

repose
3 lie 4 calm, rest 5 peace, poise, quiet,
sleep 7 lie down, recline 8 quietude
9 composure, stillness 10 inactivity,
quiescence, relaxation 11 restfulness,
tranquility 12 tranquillity

repository
3 ark 5 depot, store 7 archive, arsenal
8 magazine, treasury 10 storehouse

repossess
see regain

reprehend
3 rap 4 rate, skin 5 blame, chide, fault,
knock, scold 6 berate, rebuke 7 censure,
condemn, upbraid 8 admonish, denounce
9 criticize 10 denunciate

reprehensible
4 base, evil 6 guilty, sinful, unholy, wicked
8 blamable, criminal, culpable
10 censurable 11 blameworthy, disgraceful

represent
3 act 6 denote, depict, embody, mirror,
relate, render, sketch, typify 7 display,
exhibit, express, hold out, imitate, make
out, narrate, outline, picture, portray,
present, protest, realize, recall, signify,
suggest 8 describe, stand for 9 delineate,
epitomize, exemplify, interpret, personify,
symbolize 10 constitute, illustrate,
substitute 11 emblematize, impersonate

representation
5 draft, image 6 effigy, symbol 7 picture
8 likeness 9 portrayal, statement
10 caricature, delegation

representative
5 agent, envoy, model, proxy 6 deputy,
sample 7 burgess, example, typical
8 delegate, emissary, sampling, specimen
9 exemplary, spokesman 10 ambassador,
legislator, prototypal, substitute 11 congressman 12 illustrative, prototypical
13 congresswoman

repress
4 curb 5 check, sit on 6 bridle, muffle,
stifle, subdue 7 smother, squelch, swallow
8 keep down, restrain, suppress

repression
4 curb 7 amnesia, control 8 stifling
9 clampdown, crackdown, restraint
10 constraint

reprieve
4 stay 5 grace 7 respite, suspend

reprimand
3 rap 4 rate, ream, task 5 chide, scold
6 rebuke 7 bawl out, censure, chew out,
reproof, reprove 8 admonish, call down,
reproach, scolding 9 reprimand, talking-to
10 admonition 12 admonishment,
dressing-down 13 tongue-lashing

reprisal
7 redress, revenge 8 revanche
9 vengeance 11 counterblow, retaliation,
retribution

reprise
5 recap 6 repeat 9 reiterate 10 recurrence, repetition

reproach
3 rap 4 rail 5 blame, chide, scold
6 berate, rebuke 7 bawl out, censure,
chew out, remorse, reprove, upbraid
8 admonish, call down 9 reprimand
10 admonition, opprobrium
12 admonishment

reprobate
3 rap 4 skin 5 blame, scamp, spurn
6 refuse, reject, sinner 7 censure,
condemn, lowlife, villain 8 denounce,
scalawag 9 miscreant, scoundrel
10 blackguard, degenerate

reproduce
4 bear, copy 5 beget, breed, spore
7 imitate 8 multiply 9 duplicate, procreate,
propagate, replicate 10 regenerate
11 reduplicate

reproduction
see replica

reproductive cell
3 egg 4 ovum 5 sperm, spore 6 gamete
12 spermatozoid, spermatozoon

reproof
3 rap 6 rebuke 7 censure, lecture

reprove
8 scolding 9 criticism, reprimand
10 admonition 11 castigation 12 admonishment, reprehension 13 remonstration

reprove
5 chide, scold 6 rebuke 7 censure, chasten 8 admonish, call down, dress down, lambaste, reproach 9 criticize, reprimand

reptile
5 snake 6 caiman, cayman, gavial, iguana, lizard, turtle 7 tuatara 8 tortoise 9 alligator, crocodile, sphenodon
combining form: 6 herpet 7 herpeto
extinct: 8 dinosaur

republic
5 state 6 nation 9 democracy

Republican Party
3 GOP
mascot: 8 elephant

Republic author
5 Plato

repudiate
4 deny 5 spurn 6 abjure, disown, recant, refuse, reject 7 decline, disavow, dismiss 8 disclaim, renounce 9 disaffirm 10 apostatize, disapprove

repugnance
6 horror 7 disgust 8 aversion, loathing 9 repulsion, revulsion 10 abhorrence, antagonism, odiousness 11 abomination, detestation

repugnant
4 foul, vile 5 nasty, yucky 6 creepy, horrid, skanky 8 noisome 8 aversive, gruesome 9 abhorrent, loathsome, obnoxious, offensive, repulsive, revolting 10 disgusting

repulse
5 rebut, repel, spurn 6 rebuff, reject, revolt, sicken 7 disgust, fend off, hold off, ward off 8 nauseate, stave off

repulsion
see **repugnance**

repulsive
see **repugnant**

reputable
7 eminent, upright 8 esteemed 9 estimable, honorable 10 creditable, legitimate, recognized, sanctioned 11 respectable, trustworthy 13 well-thought-of

reputation
4 fame, name, note 5 éclat, honor 6 esteem, renown, report 8 position, prestige, standing 9 celebrity, character, notoriety

reputed
6 honest 7 alleged 8 putative, supposed 9 estimable, purported 10 creditable, ostensible 11 respectable 12 hypothetical

request
3 ask, dun, sue 4 pray, seek 5 plead, press 6 appeal, demand, invite 7 entreat, solicit 8 entreaty, petition 10 invitation

Requiem for a Nun author
8 Faulkner (William)

require
3 ask, beg 4 lack, need, want 5 claim, crave 6 demand, desire 7 call for, dictate, mandate, solicit 11 necessitate

required
3 due 5 vital 7 crucial 9 essential, mandatory, necessary, requisite 10 compulsory, obligatory 11 fundamental

requirement
4 must, need, want 5 claim 6 charge, demand 9 condition, essential, necessity, requisite 10 imperative, sine qua non 11 stipulation

requisite
3 due 4 must 5 vital 7 crucial, needful 8 cardinal 9 condition, essential, necessity 10 imperative, sine qua non 11 fundamental 12 precondition 13 indispensable

requisition
4 call 5 claim, exact 6 demand 7 solicit 11 application

requite
3 pay 5 repay 6 return 7 revenge, satisfy 9 indemnify, reimburse 10 compensate, recompense, remunerate 11 reciprocate

reredos
6 screen 9 partition

rescind
4 lift 5 annul 6 cancel, recall, repeal, revoke 7 retract, reverse 8 roll back, take back

rescue
4 free, save 6 ransom, reclaim, redeem 7 bailout, deliver, recover, release, salvage 8 liberate, preserve 9 extricate 11 deliverance

rescuer
6 savior 7 saviour

research
5 probe, study 7 inquest, inquiry 8 look into 9 delve into 10 experiment 11 examination, inquisition, investigate 13 investigation

resect
6 cut out, excise 8 amputate 9 extirpate

resemblance
7 analogy 8 likeness 9 alikeness 10 comparison, similarity, similitude 11 parallelism

resemble
5 favor 6 recall 8 look like, simulate 9 take after 11 approximate

resembling
4 like 6 akin to

resentful
4 sore 6 bitter, piqued, sullen 7 envious

resentment
5 pique 6 animus, grudge, malice, rancor 7 dudgeon, offense, umbrage 9 animosity 11 indignation

reservation
5 doubt 7 booking, proviso 8 homeland, preserve 9 condition, misgiving, sanctuary 10 limitation

reserve
4 book, fund, hold, keep 5 hoard, put by, stash, stock, store, tract 6 retain, supply 7 nest egg, savings, standby 8 contract, distance, fallback, hold back, postpone, set aside, squirrel, withhold 9 inventory, restraint, reticence, stockpile 10 constraint, discretion, diffidence 13 qualification

reserved
4 cool 5 aloof, remote, stiff 6 demure, formal 7 distant 8 reticent, retiring, taciturn 9 diffident, reclusive, secretive, withdrawn 10 unsociable 11 tight-lipped 12 closemouthed 13 self-contained

reservoir
5 hoard, stock, store 6 supply 7 nest egg 9 inventory, stockpile

reside
3 lie 4 live, stay 5 dwell, exist 6 inhere 7 consist

residence
4 home, stay 5 abode, house 7 address 8 domicile, dwelling 9 occupancy 10 habitation

resident
5 liver 6 lodger, native, tenant 7 citizen, denizen, dweller, present 8 inherent, inmate, occupant 10 inhabitant 11 householder

residential area
9 community 12 neighborhood

residual
7 balance, payment, remnant 8 leavings, leftover 9 remainder

residue
3 ash 4 heel, lees, rest, silt, slag 5 ashes, dregs, grout 6 debris, excess, scraps 7 balance, grounds, remains, remnant, surplus 8 leavings, remnants, residuum 9 leftovers, remainder, scourings

resign
4 cede, quit 5 demit, leave, yield 6 give up, retire, submit 7 abandon, consign 8 abdicate, hand over, relegate, renounce, step down 9 reconcile, surrender 10 relinquish

resignation
8 meekness 9 demission, surrender 10 abdication, compliance, submission 12 acquiescence, renunciation

resigned
9 compliant 10 submissive 11 acquiescent, complaisant

resile
6 recede, recoil, spring 7 rebound, retract, retreat 8 draw back, snap back

resilient
6 bouncy, supple, whippy 7 buoyant, elastic, springy 8 flexible, stretchy 9 adaptable

resin
4 balm 5 copal, damar, roset 6 dammar 7 acrylic, copaiba
aromatic: 6 balsam, mastic 8 sandarac
fragrant: 5 elemi 6 storax, styrax 7 ladanum 8 labdanum
gum: 5 myrrh 7 benzoin
medicinal: 6 guaiac 8 guaiacum
of an insect: 3 lac
synthetic: 8 phenolic
used by bees: 8 propolis

resist
4 buck, defy, kick 5 rebel 6 baffle, combat, oppose, revolt 7 contest, counter, gainsay 8 traverse 10 contradict, contravene

resistance
7 dissent 8 defiance, variance 10

dissension, dissidence, opposition **11**
contrariety, obstruction

resistance unit
3 ohm

resistor
8 rheostat, varistor **10** thermistor

resolute
3 set **4** bent, bold, fast, firm, true **6** intent,
steady, sturdy **7** decided, staunch **8**
constant, decisive, faithful, intrepid,
stubborn **9** obstinate, steadfast, tenacious,
undaunted **10** determined, persistent **12**
pertinacious, single-minded

resolution
4 guts **5** heart, nerve, pluck, spunk **6**
mettle, spirit **7** courage, outcome **8**
decision, firmness, tenacity **10** conclusion
12 perseverance **13** determination,
steadfastness

resolve
5 clear, crack **6** decide, settle **7** clear up,
iron out, unravel, work out **8** boldness,
conclude, decipher, firmness **9** breakdown,
determine, intention, reconcile **10**
unscramble **13** determination,
steadfastness

resonant
4 deep, full, rich **6** silver **7** booming,
echoing, orotund, vibrant **8** powerful,
sonorous **11** reverberant

resonate
4 echo, peal, ring **7** resound, vibrate **11**
reverberate

resort
3 spa **5** haven, hotel, lodge, shift **6** harbor,
refuge **7** retreat, riviera, stopgap **8**
recourse **9** expedient, makeshift **10**
substitute

resound
4 boom, echo, peal, ring **11** reverberate

resounding
7 booming, echoing, orotund, vibrant **8**
emphatic, sonorous **10** clangorous,
resonating, thunderous **11** unequivocal

resource
3 aid **5** asset, means, shift **6** supply **7**
standby

resourceful
5 adept **6** adroit, artful, clever, shrewd **7**
capable, cunning **8** creative, skillful **9**
ingenious, inventive **10** innovative **11**
imaginative **12** enterprising

resources
5 funds, means, purse **6** assets, riches,
wealth **7** capital, fortune, reserve **8**
bankroll, finances, property, reserves **9**
substance **11** wherewithal

respect
3 awe **5** favor, honor, props **6** admire,
detail, devoir, esteem, homage, regard,
revere **7** account, concern **8** venerate **9**
deference **10** admiration, estimation,
particular, veneration

respectable
4 fair **5** ample **6** decent, proper, worthy **8**
adequate **9** admirable, estimable,
honorable **10** sufficient **11** appropriate,
presentable **12** satisfactory **13** well-
thought-of

respectful
5 civil **6** polite **8** obeisant, reverent **9**
courteous **11** deferential, reverential

respecting
3 per **4** as to, in re **5** about **7** apropos **9**
as regards, regarding, relating to **10** as
concerns, concerning **11** considering

respire
7 breathe

respite
4 lull, rest **5** break, delay, pause, spell,
truce **6** hiatus, recess, relief **8** breather,
reprieve, surcease **12** intermission

resplendent
5 regal **7** glowing, shining **8** glorious,
gorgeous **9** brilliant, refulgent **11**
magnificent

respond
5 react, reply **6** answer, rejoin, retort **8**
come back

response
5 reply **6** answer, retort, return **7** riposte **8**
antiphon, comeback,
reaction **9** rejoinder
involuntary: 6 reflex **7** tropism

responsibility
4 buck, duty, onus **5** blame, brief, fault **6**
burden, charge, devoir **10** obligation **11**
reliability

responsible
6 liable **8** amenable, reliable **10**
answerable, chargeable, dependable **11**
accountable, trustworthy

responsive
4 open 8 sentient 9 sensitive 11 susceptible, sympathetic

rest
3 sit 4 calm, ease, loaf, loll, lull, stay 5 let up, pause, peace, quiet, relax, spell 6 depend, excess, lounge, repose 7 balance, leisure, lie down, recline, remains, remnant, surplus 8 breather, interlude, leavings, vacation 9 predicate, remainder

restate
4 echo 6 reword 8 rephrase 9 translate 10 paraphrase 12 recapitulate

restatement
10 paraphrase 11 translation

restaurant
4 café 5 diner 6 eatery 7 beanery 9 brasserie, cafeteria 10 coffee shop 11 coffeehouse, greasy spoon
price: 8 à la carte, prix fixe 10 table d'hôte
worker: 4 chef, cook 6 busboy, server, waiter 7 maître d', waitron 8 waitress 10 dishwasher, headwaiter, waitperson 12 maître d'hôtel

_____ Restaurant
6 Alice's

restful
4 calm 5 quiet 6 placid 8 peaceful, tranquil

restitute
6 refund, return 7 reclaim, recover, restore 8 give back 11 recondition, reconstruct 12 rehabilitate

restitution
6 amends, refund, return 7 redress 8 reprisal 9 indemnity, quittance 10 recompense, reparation 11 restoration 12 remuneration, satisfaction

restive
4 edgy 5 balky, nervy, tense 6 ornery, uneasy 7 fidgety, froward, uptight, wayward 8 contrary, perverse, skittish

restiveness
7 anxiety, ferment, turmoil 8 disquiet 9 balkiness 10 inquietude, perversity 11 contrariety, disquietude, waywardness 12 contrariness

restless
5 antsy, itchy, jumpy 6 fitful, uneasy 7 anxious, fidgety, fretful, jittery, nervous, unquiet 8 agitated, troubled 9 disturbed, perturbed, unsettled 12 discontented, dissatisfied

restorative
4 balm 5 tonic 7 healing 8 curative, remedial, sanative 12 recuperative

restore
4 cure, heal, mend 5 amend, remit, renew, right 6 recall, recoup, reform, remedy, render, repair, return, revive 7 get back, improve, reclaim, recover, rectify, refresh, replace 8 give back, recreate, renovate, revivify 9 refurbish, reinstate, replenish, restitute 10 regenerate, rejuvenate 11 recondition, reestablish 12 rehabilitate

restrain
3 bit, gag 4 curb, rein 5 check, leash 6 arrest, bridle, halter, hamper, hinder, hold in, impede, muzzle, temper 7 collect, control, harness, inhibit, repress 8 hold back, hold down, moderate, suppress
trade: 7 embargo

restrained
4 cool 6 low-key 5 canny, quiet 6 modest 7 subdued 8 discreet, reserved, reticent, retiring, tasteful 9 contained, inhibited, temperate 10 controlled, reasonable

restraint
6 bridle 7 durance, embargo, reserve 8 estoppel, pullback 9 hindrance 10 deterrence, inhibition, limitation, moderation 11 confinement, forbearance 12 straitjacket

restrict
3 bar, tie 4 bind, curb 5 hem in, limit 6 hamper, hobble, impede, narrow, shrink 7 confine, curtail, delimit, inhibit, trammel 8 hold back, prelimit 10 delimitate 12 circumscribe
a will: 6 entail

restriction
4 curb 5 check, limit, stint 7 control 9 restraint 10 constraint, limitation, regulation 11 confinement, prohibition, proscription 13 qualification

restyle
4 redo 6 revamp, revise, rework 8 make over

result
3 end 4 flow, stem 5 close, ensue, fruit, issue 6 effect, emerge, finish, follow, payoff, sequel, upshot 7 outcome, product 8 sequence, solution 9 aftermath, come about, eventuate 10 conclusion, denouement, production 11 aftereffect, consequence, eventuality
incidental: 7 spinoff

resume
4 go on 5 renew 6 pick up, reopen 7 carry on, proceed, restart 8 continue 10 recommence

résumé
4 vita 5 sum-up 7 summary 9 summation, summing-up

resurgence
5 rally 7 rebirth, revival 8 comeback, recovery 10 renascence 11 renaissance 12 risorgimento

resurrect
5 raise, renew 6 come to, revive 8 retrieve, revivify 10 reactivate

resurrection
7 rebirth, revival 10 renascence 11 renaissance 12 risorgimento

resuscitate
see **resurrect**

retail
4 sell, tell, vend 6 market 7 narrate 11 merchandise

retailer
6 dealer, seller, trader, vendor 8 merchant 9 tradesman 10 shopkeeper 11 storekeeper 12 merchandiser

retain
3 own 4 hire, hold, keep 6 detain 7 reserve 8 hold over, preserve, remember, withhold

retainer
3 fee 6 lackey, menial, minion, yeoman 7 deposit, servant 8 employee, follower 9 bite plate, dependent, pensioner

retaliate
7 get back, get even

retaliation
see **reprisal**

retaliatory
8 punitive, vengeful 10 vindictive

retard
4 clog, mire, slow 5 delay, stunt 6 detain, fetter, hamper, hang up, hinder, impede, slow up 7 set back, slacken 8 decrease, hold back, restrain 10 decelerate

retarded
3 dim 4 dull, dumb, slow 6 opaque, simple, stupid 8 backward 9 dim-witted 10 half-witted, slow-witted 11 exceptional

retch
3 gag 4 barf, hurl, puke, spew 5 heave,

vomit 6 spit up 7 bring up, throw up, upchuck 8 disgorge

retention
6 memory 7 storage

reticent
see **reserved**

reticulate
4 vein 5 veiny 6 meshed, netted 7 netlike 10 crisscross

retinue
4 band, tail 5 suite, train 6 livery 7 company, cortege 9 entourage, following

retire
4 exit, quit 5 leave, yield 6 bow out, depart, recede, resign, turn in 7 dismiss, pension 8 step down, withdraw 9 discharge, strike out, terminate 10 relinquish

retired person
7 emerita 8 emeritus 9 pensioner

retiree
9 pensioner 10 golden-ager 13 senior citizen

retirement allowance
3 SEP 7 pension

retiring
3 shy 5 mousy, timid 6 demure, modest 7 bashful 8 reserved 9 diffident, withdrawn 11 unassertive

retool
7 reequip 10 reengineer

retort
5 reply, sally 6 answer, rejoin 7 counter, respond, riposte 8 comeback, repartee, response 9 rejoinder, retaliate, wisecrack

retouch
5 alter, emend, renew 6 repair 7 correct, enhance, improve, restore

retract
4 deny 5 unsay 6 abjure, recall, recant, recede, renege, resile, revoke 7 disavow, rescind, retreat, swallow 8 forswear, renounce, take back, withdraw

retreat
3 den, ebb 4 flee, quit 5 cover, haven, leave 6 ashram, asylum, bow out, covert, decamp, depart, escape, recede, recoil, refuge, shrink, vacate 7 abandon, back off, back out, pull out, shelter 8 back down, draw back, evacuate, fall back, hideaway,

withdraw **9** backtrack, climb down, sanctuary **10** give ground, withdrawal

retrench
3 cut **4** pare **5** slash **6** excise, lessen, reduce **7** abridge, curtail **9** economize

retribution
6 return, reward **7** deserts, revenge **8** avenging, reprisal, requital, revanche **9** vengeance **10** punishment, recompense **11** counterblow, retaliation
goddess of: 3 Ate **4** Fury **7** Nemesis

retrieve
5 fetch **6** recall, recoup, redeem, rescue **7** get back, recover, restore, salvage **9** resurrect

retro
7 antique, revival, vintage **9** nostalgic **12** old-fashioned

retrograde
4 back **7** inverse, reverse **8** backward, inverted, rearward

retrogress
see **revert**

retrospect
9 hindsight **12** recollection **13** re-examination

retrospective
6 review **8** backward **10** exhibition, reflective, ruminative

return
5 recur, repay, reply, yield **6** answer, rebate, regain, rejoin, render, repeat, retort, revert **7** bring in, get back, rebound, recover, reprise, requite, respond, reverse, riposte **8** comeback, dividend, earnings, give back, proceeds, reappear, response **9** rejoinder, repayment, reversion **10** recompense, recurrence **11** reciprocate, restitution

Return of the Native
author: 5 Hardy (Thomas)
character: 4 Clym **8** Eustacia

Reuben
brother: 6 Joseph
father: 5 Jacob
mother: 4 Leah
son: 5 Carmi **6** Hanoch, Hezron, Phallu

Réunion
capital: 7 St.-Denis
city: 6 St.-Paul **7** St.-Louis **8** St.-Pierre
department of: 6 France
ethnic group: 6 Creole

former name: 7 Bourbon **9** Bonaparte
island group: 9 Mascarene

revamp
4 redo **5** renew **6** remake, repair, revise, rework **7** remodel, restyle, rewrite **8** make over, overhaul, redesign, renovate **9** refurbish **11** recondition

reveal
4 bare, blab, jamb, leak, open, show, tell **5** admit, let on, peach, spill **6** betray, evince, expose, impart, unmask, unveil **7** confess, declare, display, divulge, exhibit, publish, uncover, undress **8** announce, decipher, disclose, discover, give away, unclothe **9** broadcast **11** acknowledge, communicate **12** bring to light

revel
4 bask, orgy, riot **5** binge, feast, party, spree **6** boogie, frolic, gaiety, hoopla, wallow **7** carouse, delight, indulge, jollity, roister, rollick, wassail, whoopla **8** carnival, carousal, festival **9** bacchanal, celebrate, festivity, luxuriate, merriment, whoop-de-do **11** bacchanalia, celebration, merrymaking

revelation
6 kicker **8** epiphany, giveaway, prophecy, surprise **9** discovery **10** apocalypse, disclosure **13** manifestation

reveler
7 orgiast **8** bacchant, carouser **9** bacchante, wassailer **10** merrymaker

revelry
4 orgy, riot **6** gaiety **7** carouse, jollity, wassail, whoopee, whoopla **8** carousal, partying **9** festivity, high jinks, merriment, whoop-de-do **10** whoop-de-doo **11** merrymaking

revenant
5 ghost, haunt, shade, spook **6** shadow, spirit, wraith, zombie **7** phantom, specter, spectre **8** phantasm, prodigal, visitant **10** apparition

revenge
5 right **6** defend **7** get back, get even, redress, requite **8** reprisal, requital, revanche **9** retaliate, vindicate **11** retaliation, retribution

revenue
4 rent **5** gains, issue, yield **6** income, profit, return **7** comings **8** earnings, interest, proceeds, receipts, taxation

reverberant
6 hollow 7 booming, echoing 8 resonant 10 resounding

reverberate
4 echo, ring 6 reecho 7 resound

revere
4 laud 5 adore, exalt, extol, honor, prize, value 6 admire, esteem, regard 7 cherish, magnify, respect, worship 8 treasure, venerate 10 appreciate

revered
9 venerable

reverence
3 awe 5 adore, dread, honor, piety 6 esteem, fealty, homage 7 loyalty, respect, worship 8 devotion, venerate 9 deference, obeisance, solemnity 10 veneration
gesture of: 3 bow 6 kotow 8 kneeling 12 genuflection

reverend
4 abbé, holy 5 clerk, vicar 6 clergy, cleric, deacon, divine, parson, rector 8 chaplain, clerical, minister, preacher 9 churchman, clergyman 11 clergywoman 12 ecclesiastic

reverent
5 godly 6 devout 7 dutiful 9 prayerful 10 God-fearing, respectful, worshipful

reverie
4 muse 5 dream 6 trance, vision 7 fantasy 8 daydream 10 absorption, brown study, meditation 11 abstraction 13 woolgathering

reversal
4 turn 5 U-turn 6 double, switch 7 setback, undoing 8 backfire, flip-flop 9 about-face, inversion, turnabout, volte-face 10 switcheroo 12 solarization 13 change of heart

reverse
4 lift 6 change, contra, defeat, invert, recall, repeal, revoke 7 capsize, counter, rescind, setback 8 antipode, backward, contrary, disaster, exchange, opposite, overrule, overturn 9 about-face, backwards, diametric, overthrow, transpose, turnabout, volte-face 10 antithesis, misfortune

reversion
4 turn 5 lapse 6 return 7 atavism, escheat 9 about-face, throwback, turnabout, volte-face 10 regression, succession

revert
4 turn 6 return 7 decline, devolve, escheat, inverse, regress 8 turn back 9 backslide 10 degenerate, retrograde, retrogress

revetment
6 bunker, riprap 9 barricade, earthwork 10 embankment

review
4 scan 5 audit, recap, study 6 assess, go over, parade, report, revise, survey 7 analyze, journal, rethink 8 analysis, critique, magazine, revision, scrutiny, talk over 9 criticism, reexamine, refresher 10 evaluation, inspection, periodical, reconsider, reevaluate 11 examination 13 reexamination, retrospective

revile
4 rail, rate 5 abuse, scold 6 attack, berate, defame, malign, vilify 7 asperse, bawl out, chew out, upbraid 8 belittle, disgrace, execrate 9 blaspheme 10 tongue-lash, vituperate

revise
4 edit 5 alter, amend, emend, proof, renew 6 change, polish, redraw, reform, retool, revamp, rework 7 correct, improve, redraft, restore, restyle, rewrite 8 overhaul, redesign, work over 9 red-pencil 10 blue-pencil

revision
6 change, revamp, update 7 redraft 8 facelift, overhaul, updating 10 alteration, correction, emendation 11 overhauling 12 modification

revitalize
see **revive**

revival
7 rebirth, renewal 8 comeback 10 renascence, resurgence 11 reanimation, renaissance, restoration 12 regeneration, rejuvenation, resurrection, risorgimento 13 recrudescence, resuscitation

revive
4 wake 5 rally, renew, rouse 6 arouse, awaken, come to, recall 7 bring to, enliven, freshen, quicken, refresh, restore 8 reawaken, rekindle, renovate, retrieve 9 reanimate, resurrect 10 reactivate, recuperate, regenerate, rejuvenate 11 bring around, reintroduce, resuscitate 12 reinvigorate

revoke
4 lift, void 5 annul, erase 6 abjure, cancel, recall, recant, renege, repeal 7 abolish, nullify, rescind, retract, reverse 8 abrogate, call back 10 invalidate 11 countermand

revolt
4 riot 5 rebel, repel, shock 6 mutiny, resist, sicken 7 disgust, repulse 8 nauseate, outbreak, uprising 9 jacquerie, rebellion 10 insurgence, insurgency 12 insurrection

revolter
5 rebel 6 anarch 8 frondeur, mutineer 9 anarchist, insurgent 10 malcontent

revolting
4 foul, ugly, vile 5 nasty 6 horrid 7 hideous, noisome, obscene 8 shocking 9 atrocious, loathsome, repellent, repugnant, repulsive 10 disgusting, nauseating

revolution
4 gyre, reel, riot, roll, spin, turn 5 cycle, orbit, twirl, wheel, whirl 6 mutiny 7 circuit 8 gyration, rotation, uprising 9 pirouette, rebellion 10 barrel roll, changeover, somersault 12 insurrection

revolutionary
5 rebel, ultra 7 extreme, radical 8 mutineer, rotating, ultraist 9 extremist, insurgent
American: 4 Reed (John) 5 Shays (Daniel)
French: 5 Marat (Jean-Paul) 6 Danton (Georges) 8 Mirabeau (Comte de) 9 Saint-Just (Louis) 11 Robespierre (Maximilien)
Irish: 4 Tone (Wolfe) 6 Pearse (Padraig, Patrick) 7 Collins (Michael), Parnell (Charles Stewart) 8 Casement (Roger), de Valera (Eamon), Griffith (Arthur), O'Connell (Daniel)
Mexican: 5 Villa (Pancho) 6 Zapata (Emiliano) 7 Hidalgo (Padre Miguel)
Russian: 5 Kirov (Sergey), Lenin (Vladimir Ilyich) 7 Trotsky (Leon) 8 Kerensky (Aleksandr) 9 Kropotkin (Pyotr)

revolutionize
9 transform 11 transfigure

revolve
4 spin, turn 5 twirl, wheel, whirl 6 circle, gyrate, rotate

revolver
3 gun, rod 4 Colt 5 Glock, Luger, Ruger 6 Magnum, pistol, six-gun 7 firearm, handgun, shooter, sidearm 10 six-shooter

revue
4 show 9 burlesque 10 production, vaudeville 13 entertainment

revulsion
4 hate 6 hatred, horror 7 disgust 8 aversion, loathing 10 abhorrence, repugnance 11 abomination, detestation

reward
5 bonus, booty, crown, medal, price, prize 6 bounty, carrot, payoff, trophy 7 guerdon, jackpot, premium 8 dividend 10 compensate, honorarium, recompense, remunerate 12 compensation, remuneration

rewarding
7 gainful 8 edifying, fruitful, valuable 9 lucrative 10 beneficial, fulfilling, gratifying, productive, profitable, satisfying, worthwhile 12 advantageous, remunerative

reword
see **restate**

rework
6 revamp, revise 7 restyle, rewrite

Reynard
3 fox

rhadamanthine
3 due 4 just 5 right 6 strict 7 condign, fitting, merited 8 deserved, rigorous, rightful, suitable 9 requisite, stringent 11 appropriate

Rhadamanthus
5 judge
brother: 5 Minos
father: 4 Zeus 7 Jupiter
mother: 6 Europa

rhapsodic
5 lyric 8 ecstatic, effusive 9 emotional, exuberant

rhapsodize
4 gush, rave 5 drool 6 effuse 7 enthuse

Rhea
3 Ops
daughter: 4 Hera, Juno 5 Ceres, Vesta 6 Hestia 7 Demeter
father: 6 Uranus
husband: 6 Cronus, Saturn
mother: 4 Gaea
son: 4 Zeus 5 Hades, Pluto 7 Jupiter, Neptune 8 Poseidon

Rheingold, Das
character: 4 Loki 5 Freya, Wotan 6 Fafner, Fafnir, Fasolt 8 Alberich

composer: 6 Wagner (Richard)

rheostat
8 resistor

rhesus
6 monkey 7 macaque

rhetoric
4 rant 6 speech 7 bombast, fustian, oratory 8 rhapsody 9 elocution, eloquence, verbosity 11 rodomontade, speechcraft
term: 5 aporia, simile 7 litotes 8 metaphor 10 apostrophe, digression 12 alliteration, onomatopoeia

rhetorical
4 glib 5 gassy, grand, tumid, windy 6 florid, fluent, ornate, purple, turgid 7 aureate, flowery, orotund, pompous, stilted 8 eloquent, forensic, inflated, overdone, sonorous 9 bombastic, grandiose, high-flown, overblown, tumescent 10 euphuistical, flamboyant, oratorical 11 declamatory, highfalutin, overwrought, pretentious 12 high-sounding, magniloquent 13 grandiloquent

rhetorician
6 orator, writer 7 speaker
Roman: 10 Quintillian

Rhine River
city: 4 Bonn, Köln 5 Basel, Mainz 7 Coblenz, Cologne, Koblenz 8 Duisburg, Mannheim 9 Rotterdam, Weisbaden 10 Düsseldorf
nymph: 7 Lorelei
tributary: 3 Aar, Ill, Lek 4 Aare, Lahn, Main, Ruhr, Waal

rhizome
4 root 5 tuber

Rhode Island
bay: 12 Narragansett
capital: 10 Providence
city: 7 Newport, Warwick 9 Pawtucket
college, university: 4 RISD 5 Brown
island: 5 Block
nickname: 5 Ocean (State) 11 Little Rhody
river: 8 Pawtuxet
state bird: 14 Rhode Island red
state flower: 6 violet
state tree: 8 red maple

Rhodesia
8 Zimbabwe

rhombus
7 diamond, lozenge 13 parallelogram

rhonchus
5 snore

Rhône River
city: 4 Lyon 5 Arles, Lyons 6 Geneva 7 Avignon
lake: 6 Geneva
mountain range: 4 Jura
tributary: 5 Isère, Saône

rhubarb
3 row 4 flap 5 run-in 6 tangle 7 dispute, quarrel, ruckus, wrangle 8 argument, pieplant 11 altercation, controversy

rhyme
4 poem, song 5 agree, ditty, verse 6 accord, jingle, poetry 7 conform 8 dovetail 9 harmonize 10 coordinate, correspond

rhymer
4 bard, poet 5 odist 7 metrist 9 poetaster, rhymester, sonneteer, versifier

rhythm
4 beat, flow, lilt, time 5 meter, pulse, swing 6 accent, groove 7 cadence, measure, pattern 8 sequence

rhythmic
7 pulsing, regular 8 measured, metrical

rialto
6 market 8 district, exchange 11 marketplace

riant
3 gay 5 jolly, merry 6 blithe, bright, jocund, jovial 7 buoyant, gleeful 8 cheerful, mirthful 10 blithesome

riata
4 rope 5 lasso 6 lariat

rib
3 fun, kid, rag 4 band, bone, dike, fool, jape, jest, joke, josh, purl, razz, stay, wale 5 chaff, costa, ridge, tease 6 banter, costae (plural), lierne, needle

ribald
3 raw 4 blue, racy, rude 5 bawdy, crude, dirty 6 coarse, earthy, filthy, purple, risqué, smutty, vulgar 7 obscene, profane, raunchy 8 indecent, off-color 9 offensive, reprobate 10 suggestive

ribbon
3 bow 4 band, tape 5 braid, shred, strip 6 cordon, fillet, stripe, tatter 7 bandeau

rice
7 arborio, risotto
dish: 5 pilaf 6 congee 7 risotto 9 jambalaya
drink: 4 sake, saki 5 mirin 6 arrack

field: 5 paddy
husk: 5 lemma

rich

4 dear, lush, oily, posh 5 ample, fatty, flush, grand, heavy, plush, swank, vivid 6 costly, creamy, deluxe, fecund, gilded, lavish, loaded, monied, ornate, potent, rococo 7 baroque, copious, elegant, fertile, filling, moneyed, opulent, orotund, profuse, wealthy, well-off 8 abundant, affluent, eloquent, fruitful, palatial, well-to-do 9 abounding, bountiful, elaborate, luxuriant, luxurious, plentiful, sumptuous, well-fixed 10 productive, prosperous, well-heeled 11 extravagant
person: 5 Midas, mogul, nabob 6 fat cat 7 Croesus, magnate 9 moneybags, plutocrat

Richardson work

6 Pamela 8 Clarissa

Richelieu's successor

7 Mazarin

riches

4 gold, pelf 5 booty, lucre, worth 6 mammon, wealth 7 fortune 8 opulence, property, treasure 9 resources
demon of: 6 Mammon

rick

4 cock, heap, pile 5 shock, stack

rickety

4 weak 5 shaky 6 wobbly 7 unsound 8 decrepit, insecure, rachitic, unstable, unsteady 10 ramshackle, rattletrap

ricochet

4 ping, skim, skip 5 carom 6 bounce, glance 7 rebound 9 boomerang

rid

6 divest 7 relieve 8 unburden 11 disencumber

riddle

5 rebus 6 enigma, puzzle 7 mystery, perplex, problem 9 conundrum, perforate 10 closed book, puzzlement 11 brainteaser

ride

4 spin, tour, trip 5 drive, jaunt, mount 7 journey 8 carousel 9 excursion

ride out

6 endure 7 outlast, survive, weather 9 withstand

rider

6 clause, cowboy, jockey 7 codicil 8 addendum, addition, appendix, horseman, reinsman 9 amendment 10 equestrian, horsewoman, supplement

ridge

3 rib, top 4 bank, brow, fold, keel, reef, roll, ruck, seam, wave 5 arête, arris, chine, crest, knurl, plica, spine 6 crease, divide, furrow, rimple, saddle, summit 7 annulet, breaker, crinkle, hogback, wrinkle 8 shoulder 9 razorback 11 corrugation
gravelly: 5 esker
on the skin: 4 welt
sharp: 7 hogback

ridicule

3 pan 4 gibe, haze, jape, jeer, mock, razz, ride, twit 5 chaff, flout, mimic, roast, scoff, scout, sneer, squib, taunt 6 deride, satire 7 lampoon, mockery, pillory, sarcasm 8 derision, raillery, satirize, travesty 9 burlesque 10 caricature
god of: 5 Momus
object of: 4 butt 13 laughingstock

ridiculous

5 comic, daffy, dotty, goofy, silly, wacky 6 absurd, insane 7 bizarre, comical, foolish, risible 8 derisory, farcical 9 cockamamy, fantastic, grotesque, laughable, ludicrous, monstrous 10 cockamamie, outrageous 11 for the birds, harebrained 12 preposterous, unbelievable

riding

academy: 6 manège
costume: 5 habit
pants: 8 jodhpurs
whip: 4 crop 5 quirt

Rienzi composer

6 Wagner (Richard)

rife

4 full 5 flush 6 common 7 replete, teeming 8 abundant, swarming 9 abounding, plentiful, prevalent 10 widespread 11 overflowing

riff

4 flip, leaf, scan, skim 5 thumb 6 browse

riffle

4 flip, leaf, fret, scan, skim, wave 5 shoal, sluice, thumb 6 browse 7 shallow, shuffle 10 interstice

riffraff

3 mob 5 trash, waste 6 debris, kelter, litter, masses, rabble, refuse 7 garbage, rubbish 8 canaille, unwashed 11 proletariat

rifle

3 arm, gun, rob 4 loot, sack 5 steal 6 burgle, groove, weapon 7 carbine, despoil, firearm, pillage, plunder, ransack, rummage 9 chassepot
accessory: 6 ramrod

kind: 6 Garand, Mauser 7 Enfield 8 Browning 9 Remington 10 Winchester 11 Springfield

rift
3 gap 4 rent 5 break, chasm, chink, cleft, crack, fault, space, split 6 breach, cleave, divide, hiatus, schism 7 fissure, opening, rupture 8 crevasse, division, fracture, interval 9 fault line 10 separation 12 estrangement

rig
3 arm, fit, fix 4 fake, gear 5 dress, equip, getup, trick 6 adjust, clothe, doctor, outfit, tackle 7 apparel, arrange, costume, derrick, furnish, turn out 8 accouter, accoutre, clothing, equipage 9 apparatus, construct, equipment 10 manipulate

rigging
3 net 4 duds, gear, togs 5 dress, lines, ropes 6 attire, chains, tackle, things 7 apparel, clothes, raiment 8 clothing 9 apparatus, equipment

right
3 apt, due, fit 4 fair, just, sane, true, well 5 amend, amply, claim, droit, emend, exact, sound, title 6 at once, common, decent, dexter, direct, equity, honest, lawful, proper, square, strict 7 condign, correct, exactly, fitting, freedom, genuine, healthy, liberty, license, merited, old-line, rectify, redress 8 accurate, becoming, bona fide, decorous, easement, faithful, interest, orthodox, smack-dab, straight, suffrage, suitable 9 authentic, befitting, equitable, forthwith, honorable, privilege, requisite, veracious, veritable 10 altogether, applicable, felicitous, perquisite, scrupulous 11 appropriate, correctness, prerogative
combining form: 4 orth, rect 5 dextr, ortho, recti 6 dextro
feudal: 4 soke
legal: 5 droit 8 usufruct
royal: 7 regalia (plural)

right away
3 now 6 at once, pronto 8 directly, promptly 9 forthwith, instanter, instantly 11 immediately, straight off, straightway 12 then and there

righteous
4 good, holy, just, pure 5 godly, moral, noble, pious 6 devout, worthy 7 ethical, genuine, sinless, up-right 8 innocent, virtuous 9 blameless, guiltless 10 inculpable, principled

righteousness
6 equity, virtue 7 justice, probity 8 holiness, morality 9 rectitude

rightful
3 apt, due, fit 4 fair, just, true 5 legal 6 honest, lawful, proper 7 condign, fitting 8 deserved, suitable 9 befitting, equitable, impartial 10 applicable, legitimate 11 appropriate

right-handed
6 dexter 7 dextral 9 clockwise

right-hand page
5 recto

rightist
4 tory 11 reactionary 12 conservative

right-minded
5 moral, noble 6 decent, honest 7 ethical 8 virtuous 10 upstanding

Rights of Man author
5 Paine (Thomas)

rigid
3 set 4 firm, hard, taut 5 fixed, stiff, tense 6 severe, strict 7 austere, precise, hard-set 8 cast-iron, ironclad, obdurate, rigorous 9 draconian, immovable, inelastic, rockbound, stringent, unbending 10 adamantine, brassbound, inflexible, relentless, unyielding 11 unbudgeable 13 rhadamanthine

rigidity
6 turgor 7 buckram 8 hardness 9 stiffness
muscular: 8 myotonia

rigmarole
6 bunkum, drivel, ramble 8 nonsense 9 gibberish, procedure 10 balderdash, mumbo jumbo

Rigoletto
composer: 5 Verdi (Giuseppe)
daughter: 5 Gilda

rigor
7 cruelty 8 asperity, hardness, hardship, severity 9 austerity, exactness, harshness, roughness, sharpness, sternness 10 affliction, difficulty, exactitude, strictness 11 tribulation 13 inflexibility

rigorous
5 exact, harsh, rigid, rough, stern, stiff 6 bitter, brutal, proper, rugged, severe, strict 7 ascetic, drastic, onerous, precise 8 accurate, exacting 9 draconian, ironbound, stringent 10 burdensome, inflexible, ironhanded, oppressive 13 rhadamanthine

rile
3 bug, rub, vex 4 roil 5 anger, annoy, grate, muddy, peeve, pique, upset 6 muddle, nettle, put out, rankle 7 agitate, disturb, fluster, inflame, perturb, provoke 8 disorder, disquiet, irritate 9 aggravate 10 discompose, exasperate

rill
3 run 4 burn, purl 5 bourn, brook, creek 6 runnel, stream, valley 7 freshet, rivulet 8 brooklet 9 streamlet 11 watercourse

rim
3 hem, lip 4 bank, boss, brim, edge, ring 5 bezel, bezil, bound, brink, skirt, verge 6 border, flange, fringe, margin, shield 7 annulus, horizon, outline 8 boundary, surround 9 perimeter, periphery
of a basket: 4 hoop
of a cask: 5 chime
of an insect's wing: 6 termen
of a spoked wheel: 5 felly 6 felloe

rime
3 ice 4 hoar 5 crust, frost 7 coating, encrust 9 hoarfrost, Jack Frost 12 incrustation

Rinaldo
beloved: 8 Angelica
cousin: 7 Orlando
father: 5 Aymon
horse: 6 Bayard
mother: 3 Aya
sister: 10 Bradamante
uncle: 11 Charlemagne

rind
4 bark, husk, peel, skin 5 crust 9 crackling

ring
3 eye, hem, rim 4 band, bloc, bong, echo, gird, gyre, hoop, loop, peal, toll 5 arena, bezel, cabal, chime, clang, cycle, group, knell, knoll, round, sound 6 circle, clique, collar, girdle, staple 7 annulus, clangor, combine, compass, resound, vibrate 8 bracelet, cincture, encircle, surround 9 coalition, encompass 11 combination, reverberate
around sun or moon: 6 corona
curtain: 3 eye
for a compass: 6 gimbal
harness: 3 dee 6 button, terret
heraldic: 7 annulet
in a hinge: 7 gudgeon
of chain: 4 link
of color: 8 stocking
of leaves or flowers: 6 wreath 7 garland

of light: 4 halo 5 glory 6 corona, nimbus 7 aureole 8 halation
of rope or metal: 4 hank 6 becket 7 garland, grommet, thimble
of two hoops: 6 gimmal
relating to: 7 annular
used as a valve or diaphragm: 5 wafer
wedding: 4 band

Ring and the Book author
8 Browning (Robert)

ringed
8 annulate, bordered 9 encircled 10 surrounded

ringer
4 fake, spit 5 clone, image 6 double 7 clapper, picture 8 impostor, portrait 10 simulacrum 13 spitting image

ringing
7 orotund, vibrant 8 decisive, emphatic, plangent, resonant, sonorous 10 clangorous, resounding, unequivocal 11 reverberant

ringleader
4 boss 5 chief 6 honcho 7 kingpin 9 godfather 10 head honcho, instigator, mastermind

ringlet
4 curl, lock 5 crimp, tress 7 circlet, earlock, tendril

Ring of the Nibelung composer
6 Wagner (Richard)

rinse
4 dunk, lave, wash 5 bathe, douse, swill 6 shower, sluice 7 cleanse
the mouth: 6 gargle

riot
5 brawl, melee, revel, spree 6 bedlam, émeute, jumble, revolt, tumult, uproar 7 carouse, debauch, rampage, revelry, roister, wassail 8 carousal, disorder, uprising 9 commotion 10 debauchery, donnybrook, revolution 11 disturbance

riotous
4 lush, wild 6 stormy, unruly, wanton 7 bacchic, profuse 8 abundant, clamorous 9 abounding, exuberant, luxuriant, plentiful, turbulent 10 boisterous 11 saturnalian, tempestuous 12 unrestrained

rip
4 gash, hole, rend, rent, rive, spit, tear 5 shred, slash, split 6 attack, cleave 7 current, sputter 8 lacerate, undertow 9 criticize, disparage 12 undercurrent

into: 5 go for 6 assail, attack 8 lambaste
off: 3 con, rob 4 copy 5 cheat, steal, theft 7 defraud, imitate, swindle 9 imitation

ripe
4 aged, full, late 5 adult, grown, ready, ruddy, plump, smelly 6 mature, mellow, timely 7 grown-up 8 prepared, suitable 9 developed, full-blown, full-grown, offensive, opportune 10 seasonable 11 appropriate, full-fledged

ripen
3 age 4 cure, grow 6 better, grow up, mature, mellow, season 7 develop, enhance, improve, perfect 8 heighten, maturate

riposte
5 parry, reply 6 retort, return, thrust 8 back talk, comeback, repartee 13 counterattack

ripping
4 fine 5 grand, nifty, super, swell 6 divine, peachy 7 capital 8 glorious, splendid, terrific 9 admirable, delicious, excellent, fantastic, marvelous, wonderful 10 delightful, delectable, remarkable 11 scrumptious, sensational

ripple
3 lap 4 curl, fret, riff, wave 6 cockle, dimple, lipper, popple, ruffle, spread, wimple 7 crinkle, wavelet, wrinkle 8 undulate

rip-roaring
5 noisy 6 lively 8 exciting 9 hilarious 10 boisterous, rollicking, uproarious

ripsnorter
5 dandy 6 hummer 8 jim-dandy 9 humdinger 11 crackerjack

riptide
7 current 8 undertow 12 undercurrent

Rip Van Winkle
author: 6 Irving (Washington)
dog: 4 Wolf

rise
3 wax 4 flow, grow, lift, rear, soar, stem, well 5 awake, begin, climb, get up, issue, mount, rouse, stand, surge, swell, tower 6 ascend, ascent, awaken, emerge, expand, growth, spring, thrive, uprear 7 advance, augment, develop, emanate, enhance, enlarge, stand up, succeed, surface, upsurge 8 eminence, heighten, increase 9 ascension, increment, intensify, originate, terminate
above: 8 surmount
again: 7 resurge 9 resurrect

against: 5 rebel 6 mutiny, revolt
and fall: 4 tide 5 heave 6 welter
and shine: 5 get up
gradually: 4 loom

Rise and Fall of the Third Reich author
6 Shirer (William)

Rise of Silas Lapham author
7 Howells (William Dean)

riser
4 step 8 platform

risible
4 rich 5 comic, droll, funny, jokey 6 absurd 7 comical 8 farcical 9 laughable, ludicrous 10 ridiculous

risk
4 ante, dare, defy 5 peril, stake, throw, wager 6 chance, danger, gamble, hazard, menace 7 imperil, jeopard, stakes, venture 8 endanger, exposure, jeopardy 9 adventure, encounter, liability 10 jeopardize

risky
4 bold 5 dicey, hairy 6 chancy, daring, touchy, tricky 7 parlous, unsound 8 delicate, perilous, ticklish 9 dangerous, hazardous, unhealthy 10 jeopardous, precarious 11 adventurous, speculative, treacherous

risqué
4 blue, lewd, racy, sexy 5 broad, crude, dirty, salty, spicy, vampy 6 coarse, daring, earthy, purple, ribald, vulgar 7 naughty, obscene, raunchy 8 indecent, off-color, scabrous 9 salacious 10 indecorous, indelicate, suggestive

rite
6 office 7 liturgy, mystery, service 8 ceremony 9 formality, ordinance, sacrament, solemnity 10 ceremonial, initiation, observance 11 celebration, sacramental
funeral: 6 exequy 7 obsequy 8 exequies 9 obsequies
Jewish: 4 bris
of initiation or purification: 7 baptism
of knighthood: 8 accolade
(see also **sacrament**)

ritual
see **rite**

ritzy
4 posh 5 fancy, swank 6 chichi, classy, modish, snazzy, swanky 7 elegant, high-hat, stylish 9 au courant, exclusive,

expensive, luxurious **11** fashionable **12** ostentatious

rival
3 tie, try, vie **4** even, peer, side **5** equal, match **6** strive **7** attempt, compete, contend, contest, emulate **8** approach, opponent **9** adversary, competing, contender, measure up **10** antagonist, competitor, contending, contestant **11** comparative, competition

rivalry
6 strife **7** contest, warfare **8** conflict, jealousy, tug-of-war **9** emulation **10** contention, opposition **11** competition

rive
3 rip **4** rend, tear **5** break, burst, crack, sever, smash, split **6** cleave, divide, shiver, sunder **7** fissure, shatter **8** fracture, fragment, lacerate, separate, splinter

river
Africa: 4 Bomu, Juba **5** Chari, Congo, Shari, Tsavo, Zaire **6** Atbara, Mbomou, Songwe, Ubangi **8** Aruwimi, Limpopo, Zambesi, Zambezi **9** Astaboras, Crocodile
Alabama: 5 Coosa **6** Mobile **7** Conecuh, Perdido **9** Tombigbee **10** Tallapoosa
Alaska: 5 Kobuk **6** Copper, Noatak, Tanana **7** Koyukuk, Susitna **9** Kuskokwim
Albania: 4 Drin **5** Drini
Argentina: 5 Negro **6** Paraná **7** Matanza
arm: 6 branch **9** tributary
Asia: 3 Ili **4** Amur, Oxus **5** Indus **6** Jayhun, Sutlej **7** Oedanes **8** Amu Darya **9** Dyardanes **11** Brahmaputra
Australia: 4 Daly **5** Roper, Yarra **6** Barwon, Culgoa, Dawson, DeGrey, Murray **7** Darling, Fitzroy, Lachlan **8** Victoria **10** Yarra Yarra
Austria: 4 Enns
bank: 5 levee
Belgium: 5 Rupel, Senne, Weser **6** Dender, Dindar, Ourthe **8** Visurgis
Bolivia: 4 Beni **5** Abuná **6** Mamoré
Borneo: 5 Kajan
bottom: 3 bed
Brazil: 3 Ica **4** Pará, Paru **5** Negro, Xingu **6** Paraná **7** Madeira, Tapajos, Tapajoz
British Columbia: 6 Skeena **10** Bella Coola
California: 3 Eel, Pit **4** Kern, Yuba **6** Merced **7** Feather, Salinas, Trinity **8** Tuolumne
Cambodia: 8 Tonle Sap
Canada: 3 Bow **4** Back **5** Moose, Peace, Slave **6** Beaver, Fraser, Nelson **8** Gatineau, Saguenay **9** Athabasca, Great Fish, Mackenzie, Richelieu **11** Assiniboine
Carolinas: 7 Catawba

central United States: 3 Fox **5** Grand **6** Neosho, Platte, Wabash **8** Keya Paha, Missouri, Niobrara **9** Tennessee, Verdigris **10** Republican, Saint Croix **11** Mississippi
channel: 6 alveus
Chile: 3 Loa **5** Itata, Maule **6** Bío-Bío **8** Valdivia
China: 3 Bei, Hun, Wei **4** Dong **5** Baihe, Chang, Huang, Tarim **6** Yellow **7** Kashgar, Yangtze
China-North Korea: 4 Yalu
Colombia: 4 Tomo **6** Atrato **9** Magdalena
Colorado: 5 Yampa **8** Gunnison
Connecticut: 6 Thames **7** Niantic, Shepaug **9** Naugatuck **10** Farmington, Housatonic, Quinnipiac **11** Willimantic
crossing: 4 ford
current: 4 eddy **6** rapids
Czech Republic: 4 Iser **6** Jizera, Moldau, Vltava
dam: 4 weir
Denmark: 4 Stor
dried bed: 4 wadi
East Asia: 4 Yalu **5** Amnok **7** Oryokko
Ecuador: 4 Napo **10** Esmeraldas
England: 3 Esk, Exe, Nen, Ure **4** Aire, Avon, Eden, Nene, Ouse, Tees, Tyne, Wear, Yare **5** Swale, Trent **6** Mersey, Ribble, Thames
Ethiopia: 3 Omo **4** Baro, Dawa
Europe: 4 Eger, Elbe, Labe, Oder, Ohre **5** Albis, Saale **6** Danube, Ticino
Florida: 6 Indian **9** Kissimmee **10** Saint Johns **12** Apalachicola
France: 3 Ain, Lot, Var **4** Aire, Aude, Cher, Eure, Gers, Loir, Oise, Orne, Saar, Tarn, Yser **5** Adour, Aisne, Drôme, Indre, Isère, Loire, Marne, Rhône, Saare, Sâone, Seine, Somme, Yonne **6** Allier, Ariège, Scarpe, Vienne **7** Durance, Garonne, La Riège **8** Charente, Dordogne
Georgia: 6 Etowah, Oconee **8** Altamaha, Ocmulgee **13** Chattahoochee
Germany: 3 Ems, Rur **4** Eder, Eger, Elbe, Isar, Main, Rems, Ruhr **5** Hunte, Lippe, Rhine, Spree, Werra, Weser **6** Neckar
Germany-Poland: 4 Oder
Ghana: 5 Volta
god: 7 Alpheus, Inachus **8** Achelous
Greece: 3 Iri **4** Arta **5** Lerna, Lerne **7** Alpheus, Eurotas **8** Achelous **9** Arakhthos
Honduras: 4 Ulúa **5** Aguán **6** Patuca
Iberian: 5 Douro, Duero
Idaho: 5 Lemhi
Illinois: 8 Mackinaw
India: 4 Sind **5** Sindh, Tapti **6** Chenab, Ganges, Jhelum, Kaveri, Kistna **7** Cauvery, Krishna **8** Acesines, Godavari
inlet: 5 bayou **6** slough

Iran: 3 Kor 4 Mand, Mund 5 Karun 8 Safid Rud, Sefid Rud
Ireland: 3 Lee 4 Deel, Erne, Suir 5 Boyne, Clare, Foyle 6 Barrow, Liffey 7 Shannon
Italy: 4 Adda, Arno, Liri, Nera 5 Adige, Arnus, Etsch, Liris, Oglio, Padus, Piave, Tiber 6 Ollius, Rapido, Tevere, Trebia 7 Athesis, Rubicon, Secchia, Tiberis, Trebbia 8 Rubicone, Volturno
Kansas: 6 Pawnee
Kazakhstan-Russia: 4 Ural 5 Tobol 6 Irtysh
Kenya: 4 Athi, Tana
Kubla Khan's: 4 Alph
land: 4 holm 5 flats 7 bottoms
Latvia: 5 Gauja
Latvia-Lithuania: 7 Lielupe
Lebanon: 6 Litani
Little Rock's: 8 Arkansas
living on the bank of: 8 riparian
longest: 4 Nile
Louisiana: 11 Atchafalaya
Maine: 8 Kennebec 9 Aroostook, Penobscot
Malaysia: 9 Trengganu
Maryland: 8 Monocacy, Patapsco, Patuxent 9 Nanticoke
Massachusetts: 7 Charles, Taunton 9 Westfield 10 Housatonic
Mexico: 6 Pánuco, Sonora 7 Tabasco 8 Grijalva
Michigan: 4 Cass 5 Huron 7 Saginaw 8 Manistee, Muskegon 9 Cheboygan, Kalamazoo 10 Michigamme, Shiawassee
Mississippi: 5 Pearl, Yazoo 10 Pascagoula
Moldova-Ukraine: 8 Dneister
Missouri: 5 Osage
mouth: 5 delta
Myanmar (Burma): 4 Pegu 8 Chindwin, Irrawady
Nebraska: 4 Loup 6 Nemaha, Platte 7 Elkhorn
Netherlands: 4 Waal 5 Issel, Yssel 6 IJssel 7 Vahalis
New England: 4 Saco 6 Nashua 9 Merrimack 10 Blackstone 11 Connecticut 12 Androscoggin
New Jersey: 6 Rahway 7 Passaic, Raritan 8 Tuckahoe
New York: 5 Tioga 6 Hudson, Mohawk, Oneida, Oswego, Seneca 7 Chemung, Niagara 8 Chenango
New Zealand: 7 Waikato
Nicaragua: 4 Coco 7 Segovia
Nigeria: 5 Benin
North Carolina: 3 Haw, Tar 5 Neuse 6 Chowan 8 Alamance

northeast United States: 4 Ohio 6 Hoosic 7 Genesee, Hocking 8 Delaware, Mahoning 9 Allegheny 11 Monongahela, Susquehanna
Northern Ireland: 4 Bann 6 Mourne
North Korea: 5 Daido 7 Taedong
northwest United States: 5 Snake 7 Klamath 8 Columbia 11 Pend Oreille
Norway: 4 Tana, Teno
nymph: 5 naiad
of fire: 10 Phlegethon
of forgetfulness: 5 Lethe
of ice: 7 glacier
of woe: 7 Acheron
Ohio: 5 Miami 8 Cuyahoga, Sandusky 9 Muskingum 10 Tuscarawas
Oklahoma: 8 Cimarron
Oregon: 5 Rogue 6 Owyhee 7 Malheur 8 McKenzie 9 Clackamas, Deschutes 10 Willamette
Panama: 5 Tuira 7 Chagres
Papua New Guinea: 3 Fly 5 Sepik
Paraguay: 3 Apa 9 Pilcomayo
Pennsylvania: 6 Lehigh 10 Schuylkill
Peru: 5 Rímac, Santa 7 Marañón 8 Apurímac, Huallaga, Urubamba
Philippines: 4 Abra, Agno 5 Pasig 7 Cagayan 8 Cotabato, Mindanao, Pampanga
Poland: 3 San 7 Vistula
Portugal: 4 Sado 7 Mondego
relating to: 7 fluvial
Rhode Island: 7 Seekonk 8 Sakonnet 10 Providence
Romania: 5 Arges
Russia: 3 Don, Oka, Ufa, Usa 4 Kama, Kara, Lena, Msta, Neva, Sura, Svir 5 Onega, Terek, Volga 6 Anadyr, Angara, Belaya, Kolima, Kolyma, Ussuri, Vyatka 7 Dnieper, Pechora, Yenisey 8 Barguzin, Kostroma, Voronezh, Vychegda
Russia-Ukraine: 6 Donets
sacred: 6 Ganges
Scotland: 3 Dee, Don, Esk, Tay 4 Doon, Nith, Spey, Tyne 5 Afton, Annan, Clyde, Forth, Tweed 6 Teviot 7 Deveron 8 Findhorn
Shanghai's: 7 Huangpu, Hwang Pu
Sicily: 5 Salso 6 Simeto
siren: 7 Lorelei
Slovakia: 3 Vag, Vah 4 Gran, Hron, Waag 5 Garam, Nitra 6 Neutra, Nyitra
South Africa: 4 Vaal 6 Orange
South America: 3 Apa 6 Amazon 8 Amazonas, Orellana 9 Pilcomayo
South Carolina: 6 Saluda, Santee 7 Wateree 8 Congaree
South Dakota: 3 Bad

Southeast Asia: 6 Dza-chu, Mekong 7 Salween 8 Lan-ts'ang
southeast United States: 6 Pee Dee 7 Noxubee, Washita 8 Escambia, Ouachita, Suwannee 10 Okanoxubee
southern United States: 6 Sabine
South Korea: 3 Kum
southwest United States: 4 Gila, Zuni 5 Pecos 8 Colorado
Spain: 4 Ebro 6 Aragon 12 Guadalquivir
Sweden: 4 Göta 5 Kalix
Switzerland: 3 Aar 4 Aare 5 Reuss
Syria: 6 Khabur 7 Orontes
Tasmania: 4 Huon
Tbilisi's: 4 Kura
Texas: 5 Llano 6 Brazos, Nueces 7 San Saba, Trinity 9 Guadalupe
Texas-Mexico: 8 Rio Bravo 9 Rio Grande
tidal: 7 estuary
Tokyo's: 6 Sumida
Turkey: 4 Aras 5 Araks 6 Seihun, Seyhan
Ukrainian: 3 Bug 4 Alma
underworld: 4 Styx 5 Lethe 6 Acheron, Cocytus 10 Phlegethon
Uruguay: 5 Negro
Utah: 5 Provo, Uinta, Weber 6 Jordan, Sevier
valley: 6 strath
Venezuela: 5 Apure, Caura 6 Caroní 7 Orinoco
Vermont: 3 Mad 5 Onion, White 8 Wlnooski
Virginia: 3 Dan 5 James 7 Rapidan 9 Nansemond 10 Appomattox, Shenandoah 12 Chickahominy, Rappahannock
wailing: 7 Cocytus
Wales: 4 Dyfi 5 Clwyd, Dovey, Teifi
Washington: 6 Skagit, Yakima 9 Klickitat, Snohomish, Wenatchee
West Africa: 5 Niger 6 Gambia 7 Senegal
western United States: 7 Laramie 8 Columbia, Flathead 11 Yellowstone
West Virginia: 7 Kanawha
Wisconsin: 8 Kickapoo 9 Menominee
Wyoming: 8 Shoshone 10 Gros Ventre 11 Medicine Bow

_____ **Rivera**
5 Diego

river duck
4 teal 6 wigeon 7 dabbler, mallard, widgeon 8 shoveler 9 greenwing

river horse
5 hippo 12 hippopotamus

riverine
8 riparian

river island
3 ait

rivet
3 fix, pin 4 bolt, brad, stud 5 affix 6 absorb, attach, clinch, fasten 7 engross 8 fastener

Riviera city
4 Nice 6 Cannes, Monaco 7 Antibes, San Remo 8 St. Tropez 10 Monte Carlo

rivulet
3 run 4 beck, burn, gill, race, rill 5 bourn, brook, creek 6 runlet, runnel, stream 9 streamlet

Rizpah
father: 4 Aiah
lover: 4 Saul
son: 6 Armoni 12 Mephibosheth

roach
3 hog 6 shiner 7 sunfish

road
3 way 4 fare, lane, line, path 5 drive, going, route, track 6 artery, avenue, career, causey, course, street 7 highway, journey, passage 8 causeway, chaussée, crossway, high-road, pavement, speedway, turnpike 9 boulevard 12 thoroughfare
along a cliff: 8 corniche
around a city: 6 bypass 7 beltway
bend: 7 hairpin
edge: 4 berm 8 shoulder
French: 6 chemin
Irish: 6 boreen
machine: 5 paver 6 grader 9 bulldozer
Roman: 3 via 4 iter
side: 6 branch 8 shunpike
Spanish: 6 camino
surface: 3 tar 6 gravel 7 macadam 8 pavement

roadblock
7 barrier 8 blockade 9 barricade 11 obstruction

road book
3 map 5 atlas 9 gazetteer, itinerary

roadhouse
3 bar, inn 4 dive 5 hotel, lodge 6 tavern 9 nightclub

roadrunner
6 cuckoo 13 chaparral cock

road rut
6 kettle 7 pothole 9 chuckhole

roam
3 bat, bum, gad, run 4 rove, walk 5 drift,

prowl, range, stray **6** ramble, stroll, travel, wander **7** meander, traipse **8** straggle, vagabond **9** gallivant

roamer
3 bum **5** gipsy, gypsy, nomad, rover **6** ranger, walker **7** drifter, prowler, rambler, vagrant **8** marauder, stroller, traveler, vagabond, wanderer **11** nightwalker

roar
3 din **4** bawl, bell, boom, bray, howl, yell **5** shout **6** bellow, clamor, outcry **7** bluster **10** vociferate
bullring: 3 olé

roast
4 bake, grill, mock, rack, sear **5** broil, joint, parch **6** scathe, scorch **7** banquet, blister, mockery, swelter **8** barbecue, ridicule **9** criticize

rob
3 cop, mug **4** lift, loot, nick, raid, roll, sack **5** boost, filch, heist, pinch, pluck, reave, steal **6** burgle, fleece, hijack, hold up, pilfer, rip off, snitch, thieve **7** defraud, deprive, despoil, pillage, plunder, purloin, ransack, stick up, swindle **8** knock off **9** knock over **10** burglarize

robber
4 yegg **5** crook, thief **6** bandit, looter, mugger, pirate, reiver **7** brigand, burglar, footpad, rustler **8** hijacker, swindler **9** holdup man **10** cat burglar, highwayman, sandbagger, stickup man **12** housebreaker
grave: 5 ghoul

robbery
5 heist, theft **6** holdup, piracy **7** larceny, mugging, stickup **8** banditry

robe
3 aba **4** cape, gown, wrap **5** cloak, habit **6** caftan, mantle **7** garment, manteau **8** covering, dalmatic, vestment
baptismal: 7 chrisom
bishop's: 7 chimere
of Roman emperors: 6 purple
Turkish: 6 dolman

Robinson Crusoe
author: 5 Defoe (Daniel)
character: 6 Friday

robot
5 golem **7** android **8** automata (plural) **9** automaton

Rob Roy author
5 Scott (Walter)

robust
4 hale, rude **5** hardy, husky, lusty, rough, sound, stout **6** hearty, potent, rugged, sinewy, strong, sturdy **7** healthy **8** athletic, muscular, vigorous **9** strapping **10** boisterous, red-blooded, full-bodied, prosperous

robustious
4 rude **5** lusty, rough, rowdy **6** rugged, wooly **7** boorish, ill-bred, loutish **8** churlish, clownish **9** unrefined **10** boisterous, unpolished

rock
4 crag, reel, roll, sway, toss **5** geode, pitch, quake, shake, swing **6** totter **7** boulder, breccia **8** astonish, convulse, undulate **9** oscillate
basaltic: 5 wacke
cavity: 3 vug
combining form: 4 lite, lith, lyte, petr **5** clast, petri, petro
decomposed: 6 gossan
fissile: 5 shale
formation: 5 nappe **6** pluton **7** rimrock, terrane **8** isocline, syncline
fragment: 8 xenolith
igneous: 4 lava **6** basalt, gabbro, pumice **7** diabase, diorite, granite **8** eruptive, felstone, obsidian, porphyry, traprock **10** travertine
layer: 10 mantlerock
mass: 5 scree **9** batholith
metamorphic: 5 slate **6** gneiss, marble, schist **9** quartzite, soapstone
molten: 4 lava
sedimentary: 4 clay, coal **5** chalk, chert, coral, flint, shale **8** mudstone **9** limestone, sandstone, siltstone
volcanic: 4 tuff **6** basalt

rock bass
7 sunfish

rock-bottom
4 root **6** lowest **8** cheapest **9** lowermost **11** fundamental

rocket
3 fly, zip **4** soar, whiz, zoom **5** mount **6** ascend, bullet **7** missile, shoot up **8** firework, starship **10** projectile
landing: 7 reentry **10** splashdown
launcher: 7 bazooka
launching: 7 liftoff **8** blastoff
scientist: 5 Braun (Wernher von) **7** Goddard (Robert)

rockfish
4 cony, hind **5** coney **7** grouper, jewfish,

sea bass **8** bocaccio **10** scorpaenid **11** striped bass

Rockies resort
4 Vail **5** Aspen **8** Snowmass **9** Telluride

_____ Rockne
5 Knute

rock rabbit
4 cony, pika **5** coney, hyrax **6** dassie

rock-ribbed
5 rigid **8** dogmatic, obdurate **9** unbending **10** inflexible, unyielding

rockweed
5 algae, fucus **7** seaweed **12** bladder wrack

rocky hill
3 tor **5** kopje

rococo
4 busy **5** showy **6** florid, frilly, ornate **7** baroque, elegant, opulent **9** elaborate, intricate **10** decorative, flamboyant **11** overwrought

rod
3 bar **4** cane, pole, wand **5** baton, dowel, spoke, staff, stave, stick **6** pistol **7** scepter **8** revolver **10** correction, discipline, punishment **11** castigation **12** chastisement
bundle of: 6 fasces

rodent
3 rat **4** cavy, cony, mole, paca, pika, vole **5** cavie, coney, coypu, mouse, shrew **6** agouti, beaver, gerbil, gopher, jerboa, marmot, murine, nutria, rabbit **7** hamster, lemming, leveret, muskrat **8** capybara, chipmunk, dormouse, squirrel, tuco tuco, viscacha, vizcacha, water rat **9** guinea pig, porcupine **10** chinchilla, field mouse, prairie dog **11** kangaroo rat, meadow mouse, pocket mouse **12** pocket gopher
aquatic: 5 coypu **6** beaver, nutria **7** muskrat **8** musquash
burrowing: 6 gerbil, gopher **7** hamster **8** viscacha, vizcacha
family: 5 murid **6** murine **7** sciurid
genus: 3 Mus **5** Lepus

rodeo
7 contest, roundup **9** enclosure **10** exhibition **11** competition
animal: 5 horse, steer **10** Brahma bull
event: 10 calf roping **11** bulldogging **12** bronco riding
performer: 5 clown **6** cowboy

_____ Rodin
7 Auguste

rodomontade
4 blow, brag, rant **5** boast, swash, vaunt **7** bluster, swagger **9** gasconade **11** braggadocio

Rodomonte
beloved: 8 Doralice
slayer: 8 Ruggiero

Rodrigo Díaz de Bivar
5 El Cid

rod-shaped
7 virgate **8** bacillar **9** bacillary

roe
4 deer, eggs **6** beluga, caviar, osetra **7** sevruga

Roentgen's discovery
4 X-ray

rogation
6 litany, prayer **8** entreaty, petition **10** beseeching **12** supplication

_____ Rogers
3 Roy **4** Carl, Fred, Will **6** Ginger, Robert

rogue
5 cheat, gypsy, knave, scamp **6** rascal **7** lowlife, sharper, villain **8** picaroon, scalawag, swindler **9** defrauder, miscreant, reprobate, scoundrel, skeezicks, trickster **10** blackguard, mountebank **11** rapscallion
relating to: 10 picaresque

roguery
5 fraud **7** devilry, knavery, waggery **8** deviltry, mischief, trickery **9** devilment, diablerie **11** waggishness **12** sportiveness

roguish
3 sly **4** arch **6** impish, wicked **7** knavish **8** devilish, espiègle, scampish **10** picaresque **11** mischievous

roil
3 mud, vex **4** foul, rile, romp **5** annoy, dirty, grate, muddy, peeve, upset **6** befoul, muddle, nettle, stir up **7** agitate, disturb **8** disorder, irritate **9** aggravate **10** exasperate

roily
5 muddy, riley **6** turbid **9** turbulent

roister
4 riot **5** revel **6** frolic **7** carouse, reveler, wassail **9** wassailer

Roland
7 Orlando

beloved: 4 Aude
betrayer: 4 Gano 7 Ganelon
friend: 6 Oliver 7 Olivier
horn: 7 Olivant
sword: 8 Durandal, Durendal
uncle: 11 Charlemagne

role
3 bit 4 duty, lead, part, pose 5 cameo, cloak, guise, guide 6 aspect, office 7 quality 8 capacity, function, position 9 character 13 impersonation

roll
3 bun, rob 4 bolt, coil, flow, furl, gyre, list, pour, rock, toss, turn, wind, wrap 5 heave, pitch, surge 6 bundle, roster, rotate, stream, swathe, wallow, wrap up 7 biscuit, brioche, envelop, revolve, swaddle, trundle 8 involute, register, schedule, turn over

roll about
6 wallow, welter

roll back
5 lower 6 reduce, repeal 7 curtail, rescind

roller
3 rod 4 bowl, drum, wave 6 canary, caster, platen 7 breaker, carrier, tumbler 8 cylinder

Roller-Derby round
3 jam

rollick
4 lark, play, romp 5 caper, frisk, party, revel, sport 6 cavort, frolic, gambol 7 disport, skylark 8 escapade 9 merriment

rollicking
4 wild 5 antic, merry 6 frisky, lively 8 sportive 10 boisterous, frolicsome 12 high-spirited

rolling stock
4 cars 7 coaches, engines 8 cabooses, Pullmans, sleepers, trailers 11 locomotives

rolling stone
5 rover 6 roamer 7 drifter, rambler, vagrant 8 wanderer, vagabond

roly-poly
see **rotund**

Roman
5 Latin 7 Italian
amphitheater: 9 Colosseum
assembly: 5 forum 6 senate 7 comitia
building: 5 Forum 6 Circus 8 basilica, Pantheon
clan: 4 gens
comedy writer: 7 Plautus (Titus), Terence

conspirator: 6 Brutus (Marcus Junius) 7 Cassius (Gaius) 8 Catiline
date: 4 Ides 7 calends, kalends
emperor: 4 Nero, Otho 5 Galba (Servius Sulpicius), Nerva (Marcus Cocceius), Titus, Verus (Lucius Aurelius) 6 Julian, Trajan 7 Hadrian, Maximus (Magnus Clemens, Marcus Clodius, Petronius), Severus (Lucius Septimius) 8 Augustus, Caligula, Claudius, Commodus (Lucius Aelius), Domitian, Tiberius, Valerian 9 Caracalla, Vespasian 10 Diocletian, Theodosius 11 Constantine, Valentinian
entrance hall: 5 atria (plural) 6 atrium
epic: 6 Aeneid
epigrammatist: 7 Martial
family: 7 Gracchi
Fates: 4 Nona 5 Morta 6 Decuma, Parcae
founder: 5 Remus 7 Romulus
fountain: 5 Trevi
garment: 4 toga 5 tunic
general: 5 Sulla (Lucius Cornelius), Titus 8 Antony (Marc), Marius (Gaius), Scipio (Publius Cornelius) 8 Agricola (Gnaeus Julius)
god: 4 deus
  blind: 6 Plutus
  chief: 4 Jove 7 Jupiter
  messenger: 7 Mercury
  of agriculture: 6 Saturn
  of animals: 6 Faunus
  of death: 4 Mors
  of dreams: 8 Morpheus
  of fire: 6 Vulcan
  of gates and doors: 5 Janus
  of healing: 9 Asclepius 11 Aesculapius
  of heaven: 6 Uranus
  of households: 5 Lares 7 Penates
  of love: 4 Amor 5 Cupid
  of medicine: 9 Asclepius 11 Aesculapius
  of mirth: 5 Comus
  of regeneration: 7 Priapus
  of sleep: 6 Somnus
  of the sea: 6 Pontus 7 Neptune, Proteus
  of the sun: 3 Sol 6 Apollo
  of the underworld: 3 Dis 5 Orcus, Pluto 8 Dispater
  of the wind: 5 Eurus, Notus 6 Aeolus, Aquilo, Auster, Boreas 8 Favonius, Zephyrus
  of war: 4 Mars 8 Quirinus
  of wealth: 6 Plutus
  of wine: 7 Bacchus
  of woods: 6 Faunus
  two-faced: 5 Janus
goddess: 3 dea

of agriculture: 5 Ceres
of beauty: 5 Venus
of dawn: 6 Aurora
of flowers: 5 Flora
of handicrafts: 7 Minerva
of harvests: 3 Ops
of health: 7 Minerva
of hope: 4 Spes
of hunting: 5 Diana
of justice: 7 Astraea
of love: 5 Venus
of marriage: 4 Juno
of night: 3 Nox
of peace: 3 Pax
of springs: 7 Juturna
of strife: 9 Discordia
of the earth: 6 Tellus
of the hearth: 5 Vesta
of the moon: 4 Luna
of the sea: 10 Amphitrite
of the underworld: 10 Proserpina
of victory: 6 Vacuna
of war: 7 Bellona
of wisdom: 7 Minerva
of womanhood: 4 Juno
greeting: 3 ave
hero: 6 Caesar (Julius) 11 Cincinnatus
(Lucius Quinctius)
hill: 7 Caelian, Viminal 8 Aventine,
Palatine, Quirinal 9 Esquiline 10
Capitoline
historian: 4 Livy 5 Nepos 7 Sallust,
Tacitus 8 Suetonius
king: 7 Romulus, Servius, Tullius 12
Ancus Martius 13 Numa Pompilius
marketplace: 5 agora
military formation: 3 ala 6 alares (plural)
7 phalanx
military unit: 6 cohort, legion 7 maniple
officer: 9 centurion
official: 5 augur, edile 6 aedile, censor,
consul, lictor 7 praetor, prefect, tribune 8
quaestor
people: 5 Laeti, plebs 6 populi (plural) 7
populus, Sabines 9 plebeians
philosopher: 4 Cato 6 Seneca 8
Apuleius 9 Epictetus, Lucretius
physician: 5 Asclepius 11 Aesculapius
port: 5 Ostia
procurator: 6 Pilate (Pontius)
racecourse: 6 circus
road: 4 iter
slave: 9 Spartacus
statesman: 4 Cato 5 Pliny 6 Caesar,
Cicero, Pompey, Seneca 7 Agrippa 8
Augustus, Gracchus, Maecenas 9
Flaminius
symbol of authority: 6 fasces

roman à _____
4 clef

romance
3 woo 4 gest, love 5 amour, court, fling,
geste, novel 6 affair 7 fantasy, fiction 8
stardust 10 love affair 12 bodice ripper

Romance language
6 French 7 Catalan, Italian, Spanish 8
Romanian, Rumanian 9 Sardinian 10
Portuguese

Romania
capital: 9 Bucharest
city: 4 Iasi 6 Brasov, Galati 7 Craiova 9
Constanta, Timisoara
monetary unit: 3 leu
mountain range: 10 Carpathian
neighbor: 6 Serbia 7 Hungary, Moldova,
Ukraine 8 Bulgaria
part of: 7 Balkans
peninsula: 6 Balkan
river: 5 Tisza 6 Danube
sea: 5 Black

romantic
5 gauzy, ideal, idyll, mushy 6 ardent,
dreamy, exotic, gothic, poetic, unreal 7
amorous, maudlin, mawkish 8 fanciful,
quixotic 9 fantastic, imaginary, visionary
10 idealistic, lovey-dovey 11 sentimental

Romany
5 Gipsy, Gypsy

Romeo
7 amorist, Don Juan, gallant 8 Casanova,
lothario, paramour
beloved: 6 Juliet
enemy: 6 Tybalt
father: 8 Montague
friend: 8 Mercutio

Rommel, Erwin
9 Desert Fox

romp
4 lark, play 5 caper, frisk, sport 6 cavort,
frolic, gambol, hoyden 7 rollick, runaway,
skylark 8 escapade

Romulus
brother: 5 Remus
father: 4 Mars
mother: 9 Rea Silvia 10 Rhea Silvia
victim: 5 Remus

rondure
3 arc, orb 4 arch, ball, ring 5 curve, globe,
round 6 circle, sphere 9 curvature

rood
5 cross 8 crucifix

roof

3 hip, top 4 apex, peak 5 cover, crest, crown 6 summit 7 ceiling 8 covering, housetop
material: 3 tar, tin 4 tile 5 slate, straw, terne 6 copper, thatch 7 shingle
of a cavern: 4 dome
of the mouth: 6 palate
part: 3 hip 4 eave
structure: 9 penthouse
type: 5 gable 7 gambrel, mansard 9 butterfly
vaulted: 4 dome

roofer

5 tiler

rook

4 bilk, colt, crow, scam, tyro 5 cheat, mulct, raven, stick 6 castle, fleece, novice 7 amateur, defraud, recruit, swindle, trainee 8 beginner, freshman, neophyte, newcomer 10 apprentice, flimflam, tenderfoot

rookery

5 roost 6 colony

rookie

4 colt, tyro 6 novice 7 amateur, recruit, trainee 8 beginner, freshman, neophyte, newcomer 10 apprentice, tenderfoot

room

3 den 4 cell, hall, play, rein 5 divan, house, lodge, put up, salon, scope, space 6 alcove, billet, leeway, margin, reside, studio 7 chamber, cubicle, expanse, gallery, lodging 9 clearance
ancient Roman: 5 atria (plural) 6 atrium
eating: 4 nook 5 alcove 7 commons, kitchen 8 mess hall 9 refectory
food storage: 6 larder, pantry
for paintings: 7 gallery
in a monastery: 4 cell 9 refectory 11 calefactory
in a prison: 4 cell
on a ship: 4 cabin 6 galley
round: 7 rotunda

roomer

5 guest 6 lodger, renter, tenant 7 boarder

roomy

4 wide 5 ample, broad, large 8 spacious 9 capacious 10 commodious

Roosevelt, Franklin D.

birthplace: 8 Hyde Park
dog: 4 Fala
message: 12 fireside chat
mother: 4 Sara
predecessor: 6 Hoover (Herbert)
program: 7 New Deal
successor: 6 Truman (Harry)
wife: 7 Eleanor

roost

3 sit 4 land, nest, rest 5 perch 6 alight, settle 7 rookery 8 dovecote

rooster

4 cock 5 capon 8 cockerel, gamecock 10 cockalorum 11 chanticleer

root

3 dig, fix 4 base, bulb, core, grub, pith, stem, well 5 basis, cheer, embed, grout, lodge, plant, radix, tuber 6 bottom, etymon, ground, marrow, origin, settle, source 7 applaud, bedrock, essence, footing, radical 8 radicate 9 beginning, establish, inception 10 foundation
aromatic: 7 ginseng
edible: 3 oca, yam 4 beet 6 carrot, daikon, ginger, jicama, potato, radish, turnip 7 burdock, parsnip, salsify 8 celeriac, kohlrabi, rutabaga, tuckahoe 11 horseradish
fragrant: 5 orris 7 vetiver
main: 7 taproot
medicinal: 5 jalap 7 ginseng
relating to: 7 radical
starch: 4 arum
tropical: 4 taro
word: 6 etymon

rootlet

7 radicle, rhizoid

root out

4 grub 9 eradicate, extirpate 10 deracinate

Roots author

5 Haley (Alex)

rope

3 guy, tie 4 bind, cord, line, stay 5 belay, bight, brace, cable, chord, lasso, riata, sheet 6 binder, fasten, halter, hawser, lariat, marlin, shroud, strand, string, tether 7 halyard, lashing, marline, painter, towline 8 buntline, lifeline
loop: 7 cringle
mooring: 6 hawser
ship's: 6 marlin, parral, parrel 7 lanyard, marline, ratline

ropedancer

11 funambulist

rope off

6 cordon

ropes
10 ins and outs, procedures, techniques

ropy
4 wiry 6 sinewy 7 stringy, viscous 8 muscular

roque
7 croquet

rorqual
5 whale 7 finback 8 fin whale 11 baleen whale

Rosalind's beloved
7 Orlando

rosary
5 beads 7 chaplet 8 beadroll, devotion 11 prayer beads

rose
4 glow, pink 5 blush, color, flush, rouge 6 mantle, pinken, redden 7 crimson 10 erysipelas
Chinese: 8 Cherokee
cotton: 7 cudweed
feature: 5 thorn
kind: 4 moss 5 Peace, Vogue 6 Circus, damask 7 Fashion, Granada, Iceberg, New Dawn, Pascali, Tiffany 8 Rubaiyat 9 Floradora, Montezuma, polyantha, Tropicana 10 Floribunda 11 grandiflora, Mount Shasta 12 Crimson Glory

roseate
3 red 4 pink 6 bright, sunny, upbeat 7 beamish 8 cheerful, sanguine 10 optimistic

rose-colored
see **roseate**

Rosenkavalier composer
7 Strauss (Richard)

rose of ____
6 Sharon

rose oil
5 attar

Rose Tattoo author
8 Williams (Tennessee)

rosette
7 cockade 8 ornament

Rosinante's master
7 Quixote (Don)

Rosmersholm author
5 Ibsen (Henrik)

____ **Rossetti**
5 Dante (Gabriel) 9 Christina
work: 8 Sing-Song 11 Annus Domini, House of Life (The), Seek and Find, Sister Helen 12 Beata Beatrix, Goblin Market

Rossini opera
6 Otello 8 Tancredi 11 Cenerentola (La), William Tell 14 Siege of Corinth (The) 15 Barber of Seville (The)

Rostand hero
6 Cyrano (de Bergerac)

roster
4 list, roll, rota 5 slate 6 muster, scroll 8 register, roll call, schedule 9 honor roll 10 muster roll 11 waiting list

rostrum
4 dais 5 bimah 6 pulpit 7 lectern, tribune 8 platform

rosy
see **roseate**

rot
4 bosh, bull, mold 5 decay, hooey, spoil, taint, trash 6 fester, molder 7 corrupt, crapola, crumble, garbage, hogwash, putrefy, rubbish 8 gangrene, nonsense 9 break down, decompose, poppycock 10 balderdash, degenerate 11 deteriorate, putrescence 12 disintegrate, putrefaction 13 decomposition

rotary
6 circle 8 gyratory, spinning, whirling 10 roundabout 11 vertiginous 13 traffic circle

rotate
4 gyre, roll, spin, turn 5 pivot, twirl, wheel, whirl 6 gyrate, swivel 7 revolve, trundle 9 alternate, pirouette
a log: 4 birl

rotation
4 gyre, loop, turn 5 cycle, orbit, pivot, round, wheel, whirl 7 circuit, turning 8 gyration 10 revolution, succession

rote
5 crowd, grind 6 custom, groove, memory 7 routine 8 practice 9 automatic, treadmill 10 mechanical, repetition 12 memorization

Roth novel
11 Call It Sleep 15 Goodbye Columbus 16 American Pastoral 17 Portnoy's Complaint

rotten
4 foul 5 fetid, lousy 6 crummy, putrid 7 corrupt, decayed, spoiled, tainted 9 nefarious, offensive, putrified 10 decomposed, degenerate, putrescent

rotter
3 cad, cur 4 lout 5 creep, louse 7 bounder 9 scoundrel 10 blackguard

rotund
3 fat 5 obese, plump, podgy, pudgy, round, stout, thick, tubby 6 chubby, chunky, portly, stocky 7 rounded 8 heavyset, roly-poly, thickset 9 corpulent 10 potbellied

roué
4 lech, rake, wolf 6 lecher 7 Don Juan, seducer, swinger 8 Casanova, lothario, sybarite 9 bon vivant, debauchee, libertine, womanizer 10 sensualist, voluptuary 11 philanderer

rouge
3 red 4 glow, pink, rose 5 blush, color, flush 6 mantle, pinken, redden 7 crimson

rough
3 raw 4 rude, wild 5 brute, bumpy, crass, crude, hairy, harsh, raspy, rowdy, yahoo 6 choppy, coarse, craggy, crusty, hoarse, jagged, rugged, stormy, uneven 7 cragged, grating, jarring, rasping, raucous, ruffian, scraggy, uncivil, uncouth 8 bullyboy, churlish, impolite, scabrous, unformed 9 difficult, imperfect, strenuous, turbulent, unrefined 10 boisterous, tumultuous, unfinished, unpolished 11 approximate, tempestuous

rough-and-ready
5 crude 6 make-do 7 stopgap 8 slapdash 9 expedient, impromptu, makeshift 10 improvised, quick-and-dirty 11 provisional

rough-hewn
4 rude 5 crude, plain 10 unfinished, unpolished 12 uncultivated

roughly
5 about 9 virtually 10 more or less 13 approximately

roughneck
see **ruffian**

rough out
5 block, chalk, draft 6 sketch 7 outline 9 adumbrate 11 skeletonize

rough up
4 beat, maul 6 batter, pummel 8 maltreat 9 brutalize, manhandle 10 slap around

round
4 gyre, tour, turn 5 bowed, cycle, globe, wheel 6 circle, curved, rotund 7 annular, circuit 8 circular, globular, roly-poly, rotation 9 orbicular, spherical 10 conglobate

roundabout
6 circle, detour, rotary 7 circuit, compass, curving, devious, oblique, winding 8 circular, indirect 10 circuitous, meandering 13 traffic circle

rounded
5 bowed, plump 6 arched, convex, curved, zaftig 7 concave 9 developed 10 curvaceous, Rubenesque 13 well-developed

rounder
4 rake, roué, waif 6 no-good, waster 7 wastrel 8 vagabond 9 libertine 10 profligate

roundly
4 well 5 fully, quite 6 widely, wholly 7 bluntly, sharply, smartly, utterly 8 candidly, entirely 9 brusquely 10 altogether, completely, rigorously, scathingly, thoroughly, vigorously

round off
3 cap, top 5 crown 6 climax, finish 8 conclude 9 culminate

round-robin
6 appeal, letter, series 7 protest 8 petition, sequence 9 statement 10 tournament

round trip
4 tour 7 circuit 9 excursion

round up
4 herd 5 drive, group 6 gather 7 cluster, collect 8 assemble

rouse
3 jog 4 call, goad, rock, stir, wake, whet 5 alarm, awake, pique, rally, roust, waken 6 awaken, bestir, excite, foment, incite, kindle, muster, rattle, recall, revive, vivify, work up 7 agitate, animate, commove, disturb, enliven, provoke, quicken 8 motivate 9 aggravate, challenge, galvanize, instigate, stimulate

rousing
5 brisk, peppy 6 lively 8 animated, exciting, spirited, stirring 9 inspiring 11 stimulating 12 exhilarating, intoxicating

Rousseau work
5 Émile

roustabout
4 hand 6 worker 7 laborer, workman 8 deckhand 10 workingman 12 longshoreman, troublemaker

route
3 way 4 path, road, send, ship 5 guide,

pilot, steer, track, trail **6** avenue, bypass, course, detour, direct, divert, escort, flyway, seaway, skyway **7** channel, circuit, conduct, consign, forward, highway, journey, passage, portage, sea-lane **8** corridor, dispatch, transmit, traverse **9** direction, itinerary

routine
3 act, bit, rut **4** dull, pace, rote **5** chore, drill, grind, habit, ho-hum, plain, round, trial, usual **6** course, groove, improv, wonted **7** chronic, formula, program, regular, shtick, utility **8** accepted, everyday, habitual, ordinary, standard, workaday **9** customary, procedure, quotidian, treadmill **10** accustomed, donkeywork, mechanical, monologue **11** commonplace, cut-and-dried, housekeeping, perfunctory **12** unremarkable

rove
3 gad **4** roam **5** drift, range, stray **6** ramble, wander **7** meander, traipse **8** straggle, vagabond **9** gallivant

rover
5 stray **6** pirate, roamer, viking **7** corsair, drifter, floater, rambler, vagrant **8** picaroon, runabout, traveler, wanderer **9** buccaneer, meanderer **10** freebooter **12** rolling stone

roving
6 errant, mobile, movable **7** nomadic, vagrant **8** straying, vagabond **9** itinerant, migratory, wayfaring **11** peripatetic

row
3 oar, way **4** bank, crew, file, fray, fuss, line, muss, rank, spat, tier, tiff **5** align, brawl, broil, chain, fight, melee, order, queue, run-in, scrap, scull, strip, swath **6** bicker, clamor, column, dustup, fracas, kickup, paddle, propel, range, ruckus, serles, string, stroke **7** brabble, dispute, quarrel, rhubarb, wrangle **8** argument, diagonal, sequence, squabble **9** commotion **10** falling-out, single file, succession **11** altercation, disturbance, progression

rowdy
4 punk, rude **5** bully, crude, rough, yahoo **6** unruly **7** hoodlum, rackety, raffish, raucous, ruffian **8** bullyboy, hooligan **9** roughneck **10** boisterous, disorderly, robustious **11** rumbustious **12** rambunctious

Rowena
father: **7** Hengist
guardian: **6** Cedric
husband: **7** Ivanhoe **9** Vortigern

Rowling character
11 Harry Potter

Roxana
husband: **9** Alexander
rival: **7** Statira

royal
5 grand, noble, regal **6** kingly, lordly **7** stately **8** glorious, imperial, imposing, majestic, princely, splendid **9** grandiose, monarchal, sovereign **10** monarchial **11** magnificent, monarchical

rub
4 buff **5** chafe, grate, shine **6** abrade, polish, smooth, stroke **7** burnish, massage

Rubaiyat author
4 Omar (Khayyám)

rubber
4 buna **5** crepe **6** eraser **10** caoutchouc
basis: **5** latex
hard: **7** ebonite
synthetic: **8** neoprene
tree: **4** Para

Rubber City
5 Akron

rubberneck
3 eye **4** gape, gawk, gaze **5** snoop, stare **6** goggle **8** sightsee

rubber-stamp
7 approve, certify, endorse **9** authorize

rubbish
3 rot **4** bosh, crap, crud, junk, muck, slop **5** bilge, dreck, hooey, offal, trash, truck, waste **6** debris, litter, refuse, raffle, rubble, spilth **7** crapola, garbage, hogwash **8** nonsense, riffraff, tommyrot **9** poppycock, sweepings **11** foolishness

rubbishy
5 cheap, tatty **6** paltry, shoddy, sleazy, trashy **9** worthless

rubble
5 ruins, scree **6** debris, litter **8** detritus, wreckage

rube
4 boor, hick, naïf **5** churl, cluck, swain, yahoo, yokel **6** rustic **7** bumpkin, hayseed, redneck **9** greenhorn, hillbilly **10** clodhopper **11** apple-knocker, backwoodsman

rubicund
3 red **5** flush, ruddy **6** florid, reddish **7** glowing **8** sanguine **11** full-blooded, incarnadine

____ Rubik
4 Erno

rub out
3 ice, off, zap 4 do in, kill, slay 5 erase,
smoke, waste, whack 6 finish, murder 7
bump off, destroy, put away 8 dispatch,
knock off 9 liquidate, terminate 10
extinguish, obliterate 11 assassinate

rubric
4 name, rule 5 canon, class, gloss, style,
title 6 custom 7 concept, heading 8
category, headline 9 tradition 11
appellation, designation 13 interpolation

ruck
3 mob 4 fold, heap, mass, pile 5 crimp,
crowd, group, purse, ridge 6 cockle,
crease, furrow, gather, jumble, pucker,
rumple 7 crinkle, crumple, scrunch, wrinkle
10 generality 11 corrugation

rucksack
4 pack 6 kit bag 7 musette 8 backpack

ruckus
3 row 4 fuss, to-do 5 brawl, melee, scrap
6 fracas, furore, hassle, rumpus, shindy,
uproar 7 dispute, quarrel, rhubarb, shindig,
wrangle 8 squabble 9 commotion 10
falling-out 11 altercation, controversy,
disturbance

ruddle
see **redden**

ruddy
3 red 4 ripe, rosy 5 flush 6 blowsy, florid
7 flushed, glowing 8 rubicund, sanguine
11 full-blooded, incarnadine

rude
3 raw 4 curt 5 crass, gross, gruff, harsh,
rough, rowdy, surly 6 abrupt, callow,
clumsy, coarse, crusty, robust, rugged,
rustic, sturdy, unhewn, vulgar 7 boorish,
brusque, ill-bred, loutish, lowbred, uncivil,
uncouth 8 arrogant, churlish, clownish,
impolite, tactless 9 barbarian, barbarous,
elemental, inelegant, primitive, roughhewn, unrefined 10 ungracious,
unmannered, unmannerly, unpolished 11
ill-mannered, impertinent, uncivilized 12
discourteous, uncultivated 13 disrespectful

rudimentary
5 basal, basic 6 simple 7 initial, primary 8
simplest 9 beginning, elemental, vestigial
10 elementary 11 fundamental,
undeveloped 12 introductory

rudiments
6 basics 10 essentials 12 fundamentals

rue
3 woe 4 pity, ruth 5 dolor, grief, mourn,
prick 6 grieve, lament, regret, repent,
sorrow 7 anguish, deplore, remorse 8
sympathy 9 heartache, penitence 10
affliction, compassion, contrition,
heartbreak, repentance 11 compunction

rueful
5 sorry 6 woeful 8 contrite, penitent 9
regretful, sorrowful 10 remorseful

ruff
5 frill, perch, trump 6 collar, fringe 9
sandpiper 11 pumpkinseed
female: 5 reeve

ruffian
4 goon, hood, punk, thug 5 beast, brute,
bully, rowdy, tough, yahoo 6 Apache,
hector 7 gorilla, hoodlum 8 bullyboy,
hooligan 9 muscleman, roughneck,
swaggerer

ruffle
3 bug, irk, rub, vex 4 fret, gall, wear 5
annoy, brawl, chafe, frill, graze, jabot, pleat,
ruche 6 abrade, bother, nettle, ripple 7
agitate, bristle, disturb, flounce, provoke,
trouble, wrinkle 8 drumbeat, furbelow,
irritate, skirmish 9 commotion

rug
3 mat 6 carpet, runner 7 laprobe
kind: 3 rag, rya 6 hooked 7 braided,
dhurrie, flokati, Persian 8 Aubusson,
bearskin, Oriental 10 Savonnerie

rugby
formation: 5 scrum 9 scrummage
goal: 7 dropped, penalty
period: 4 half
player: 6 center, hooker, winger 8
standoff 9 scrum half
scoring: 3 try 4 goal 10 conversion
team: 7 fifteen
term: 4 heel 5 match 7 convert, dribble,
hand off, knock on 9 fair catch
time-out: 8 stoppage
version: 5 union 6 league

rugged
5 burly, hardy, harsh, heavy, husky, rough,
tough 6 brawny, coarse, craggy, jagged,
robust, severe, stable, stormy, strong,
sturdy, uneven 7 arduous, austere,
scraggy 8 leathery, muscular, rigorous,
scabrous, stalwart, vigorous 9 difficult,

inclement, strenuous, unrefined, weathered **10** formidable, unpolished **11** tempestuous

Ruggiero
guardian: **7** Atlante
sister: **7** Marfisa
slayer: **11** Tisaphernes
wife: **10** Bradamante

rug rat
3 tot **4** tyke **6** moppet **7** toddler

Ruhr industrial city
5 Essen

ruin
4 bane, bust, dash, do in, doom, fall, loss, rape, raze, sack, undo **5** decay, havoc, smash, spoil, use up, waste, wrack, wreck **6** beggar, finish, pauper, perish, ravage, trash **7** corrupt, deplete, despoil, destroy, exhaust, failure, nemesis, pillage, shatter, undoing, wipe out **8** bankrupt, collapse, decimate, demolish, downfall, spoliate **9** depredate, devastate, disrepair, overthrow, pauperize, shipwreck **10** desolation, impoverish **11** destruction, devastation, dissolution **12** degeneration **13** deterioration

ruination
4 bane, loss, rack **5** havoc **7** undoing **8** calamity, disaster, downfall **10** decimation **11** destruction, devastation

ruinous
5 fatal **7** baneful **10** calamitous, disastrous, pernicious **11** destructive **12** catastrophic

rule
3 law **4** lead, sway **5** axiom, bylaw, canon, edict, habit, judge, maxim, moral, order, reign **6** assize, custom, decree, deduce, dictum, direct, govern, regime, truism **7** brocard, command, control, precept, prevail, regency, regimen, resolve, statute **8** decretum, doctrine, dominate, domineer, dominion **9** authority, determine, etiquette, ordinance, principle, procedure **10** regulation
absolute: **7** autarky **8** autarchy
by a god: **8** theonomy

Rule Britannia composer
4 Arne (Thomas)

rule out
3 bar **5** block, debar **6** forbid, refuse, reject **7** exclude, forfend, head off, obviate, prevent **8** preclude, prohibit, stave off **9** eliminate

ruler
4 king, lord **5** queen **6** archon, dynast, ferule, gerent, prince, regent, satrap, sultan **7** emperor, monarch, viceroy **8** governor, hierarch, oligarch, pentarch, princess, theocrat **9** dominator, imperator, matriarch, patriarch, potentate, sovereign **12** straightedge
absolute: **6** despot, tyrant **8** autocrat, dictator, overlord
Arab: **4** amir, emir **5** sheik **6** sharif, sheikh, sultan
Asian: **4** khan
Byzantine Empire: **6** exarch
Egyptian: **7** pharaoh
family: **7** dynasty
Iranian: **4** shah
one of four: **8** tetrarch
one of seven: **8** heptarch
one of three: **7** triarch **8** triumvir
Persian: **6** satrap
Russian: **4** czar, tsar, tzar
Turkish: **3** bey, dey

ruling
3 law **4** call **5** chief, edict, order, ukase **6** decree **7** current, finding, popular, regnant, verdict **8** decision, judgment **9** directive, judgement, prevalent, statement **10** prevailing, widespread **11** predominant **12** adjudication

Rumania
see **Romania**

rumble
4 buzz, roar, roll **5** brawl, drone, fight, growl, rumor **6** murmur, report **7** hearsay, quarrel, resound, thunder **8** feedback **9** complaint **11** altercation, disturbance, reverberate, scuttlebutt

ruminant
3 cow, yak **4** deer, goat, tahr **5** bison, camel, okapi, serow, sheep, takin **6** alpaca, cattle, musk ox, vicuña **7** buffalo, chamois, chewing, giraffe, guanaco **8** antelope
stomach: **5** rumen **6** omasum **8** abomasum **9** reticulum

ruminate
4 chew, mull, muse **5** champ, chomp, weigh **6** ponder **7** reflect **8** cogitate, consider, meditate **9** masticate **10** deliberate **11** contemplate

ruminative
7 pensive **8** thinking **9** pondering **10** cogitative, meditative, reflective, thoughtful

11 speculative 13 contemplative, introspective

rummage
4 comb, fish, grub, hash, hunt, poke, rake, rout, seek 5 delve, scour 6 ferret, forage, jumble, litter, search 7 clutter, ransack 8 mishmash 9 potpourri 10 hodgepodge, hotchpotch, miscellany

rummy
3 gin, odd, sot 4 lush, soak, wino 5 drunk, souse, toper 6 boozer 7 bizarre, canasta, curious, guzzler, strange, swiller, tippler, tosspot 8 drunkard, peculiar 9 eccentric, inebriate 10 boozehound

rumor
4 blab, buzz, talk 5 bruit, story 6 canard, gossip, murmur, mutter, report, rumble, tattle 7 hearsay, tidings, whisper 9 grapevine 11 scuttlebutt, susurration

rumormonger
6 gossip 8 gossiper, informer, quidnunc, telltale 9 whisperer 10 talebearer, tattletale

rump
3 can 4 beam, butt, duff, hind, rear, tush 5 fanny 6 behind, bottom, breech, heinie 7 keister, rear end 8 backside, buttocks, derriere, haunches 9 posterior

rumple
4 fold, muss, ruck 5 crimp, screw, touse 6 pucker, tousle 7 crimple, crinkle, scrunch, wrinkle 8 dishevel, disorder

rumpus
see **ruckus**

run
3 fly, hie, jog 4 bolt, dart, dash, flee, flow, race, rush, scud, tear 5 chase, haste, hurry, scoot, skirr, speed 6 career, gallop, hasten, scurry, sprint, streak, stream 7 scamper, scuttle, smuggle 9 skedaddle

run across
4 meet 8 bump into, discover 9 encounter, stumble on

runagate
4 hobo 5 tramp 6 outlaw 7 drifter, floater, lamster, vagrant, wastrel 8 bohemian, fugitive, rapparee, vagabond, wanderer 11 guttersnipe

run along
5 leave, scram 6 beat it, begone, cut out, depart 7 get lost, skiddoo, take off, vamoose 8 shove off 9 skedaddle 10 make tracks

runaround
4 duck, slip 5 dodge 7 elusion, evasion

run away
4 bolt, flee, skip 5 elope, leave, scram, skirr, split, steal 6 depart, desert, escape 7 abscond, clear out, make off 8 light out, stampede 9 skedaddle 10 make tracks

runaway
4 wild 5 loose 6 outlaw 7 escapee, lamster 8 deserter, fugitive 10 delinquent 12 uncontrolled

run down
3 hit, ram, tag 5 catch, knock, trace 6 pursue 7 decline 8 belittle, derogate, diminish 9 apprehend, disparage 10 depreciate 11 catch up with

run-down
5 dingy, seedy, tacky, tired 6 beat-up, bushed, shabby 7 rickety, ruinous, worn-out 8 decrepit, tattered, untended 9 exhausted, neglected 10 bedraggled, burned-out, down-at-heel, ramshackle, uncared-for 11 dilapidated

rundown
4 dope, poop 5 recap, scoop 6 report, review, skinny, update 7 outline, summary 8 briefing, synopsis

runes
5 ogham 7 futhark 10 characters

rung
3 bar 4 step 5 grade, notch, round, spoke, staff, stage, stair, tread 6 degree, rundle 10 crosspiece

run-in
3 row 4 tiff 5 brush, fight, scrape, set-to 6 hassle, tangle 7 dispute, quarrel, rhubarb, wrangle 8 skirmish, squabble 9 encounter 10 falling-out 11 altercation

run into
3 hit, ram 4 meet 9 encounter, stumble on 11 collide with

runner
3 rug 5 miler, racer 6 carpet, stolon 7 carrier, courier 8 smuggler, sprinter 9 go-between, messenger 10 marathoner 11 ballcarrier

running
6 active, fluent 7 cursive, dynamic, flowing, working 9 operative 10 continuous 11 functioning

run-of-the-mill
4 dull, so-so 5 usual 6 common, normal 7 average, humdrum, regular, typical 8

everyday, familiar, mediocre, middling, moderate, ordinary **9** prevalent **10** monotonous **11** commonplace, indifferent **12** intermediate **13** unexceptional

run on
3 gab, yak **4** blab **5** clack **6** babble, cackle, gabble, jabber, rattle **7** chatter, prattle **8** continue

run out of
5 use up **6** finish **7** exhaust

run over
5 spill **6** exceed, repeat **7** examine **8** overfill, overflow, rehearse

runt
5 dwarf, pygmy **6** midget, peanut, peewee, shrimp, squirt **7** manikin **8** Tom Thumb **10** homunculus **11** hop-o'-my-thumb, lilliputian

run through
3 jab **4** blow, gore, read, scan, stab **5** spend, use up, waste **6** expend, finish, impale, pierce **7** consume, examine, exhaust **8** rehearse, squander, transfix

runty
3 wee **4** puny **6** peewee **7** stunted **8** dwarfish **10** diminutive, undersized

run up
5 build, erect, mount **6** expand **7** augment, enlarge **8** increase, multiply **9** construct **10** accumulate

runway
4 duct, path **5** strip, track, trail **6** sluice, tarmac **7** channel, conduit **8** airstrip, platform

rupture
4 rend, rent, rift, rive **5** break, burst, cleft, sever, split **6** breach, cleave, hernia, schism, sunder **7** blowout, break up, disrupt, divorce, fissure, parting, split-up **8** division, fracture, separate **9** partition **10** separation **11** dissolution **12** estrangement

R.U.R.
  author: 5 Capek (Karel)
  character: 5 robot

rural
6 rustic **7** bucolic, country, idyllic **8** agrarian, arcadian, down-home, pastoral **10** campestral **11** countrified

ruse
3 con, jig **4** hoax, ploy, wile **5** dodge, feint, fraud, stall, trick **6** deceit, gambit **7** gimmick, swindle **8** artifice, maneuver,

trickery **9** deception, stratagem **10** subterfuge **13** double-dealing

rush
3 fly, rip, run **4** boil, bolt, dart, dash, flit, flow, hurl, lash, race, roar, scud, tear, tide, whiz **5** blitz, break, carry, chase, court, daily, flash, haste, hurry, lunge, onset, sally, scoot, shoot, spate, speed, storm, streak, surge **6** attack, barrel, beat it, bustle, career, charge, course, hasten, hurtle, hustle, irrupt, plunge, stream, thrill, whoosh **7** assault, cattail, current, rampage, torrent **8** stampede **9** whirlwind, wire grass **13** precipitation

Rushdie novel
5 Shame **13** Satanic Verses (The) **17** Midnight's Children

rushing
5 hasty **6** abrupt, sudden **7** hurried **8** headlong **9** impetuous **11** precipitate, precipitous

rusk
7 biscuit **8** biscotto

Russia
  capital: 6 Moscow
  city: 3 Ufa **4** Omsk, Perm' **5** Kazan', Kursk, Samara **6** Grozny **7** Groznyy, Izhevsk, Ivanovo **8** Murmansk **9** Leningrad, Volgograd **10** Stalingrad **11** Chelyabinsk, Novosibirsk, Vladivostok **12** St. Petersburg **13** Yekaterinburg
  emperor: 5 Boris (Godunov), Peter (the Great) **7** Godunov (Boris), Michael (Romanov), Romanov (Michael) **8** Nicholas
  empress: 4 Anna (Ivanovna) **9** Catherine (the Great), Elizabeth (Petrovna)
  ethnic group: 7 Cossack
  island: 8 Sakhalin
  island group: 5 Kuril **6** Kurile
  lake: 5 Il'men', Onega **6** Baikal, Ladoga
  leader: 5 Lenin (Vladimir), Putin (Vladimir) **6** Stalin (Joseph) **7** Trotsky (Leon) **8** Brezhnev (Leonid) **10** Khrushchev (Nikita)
  monetary unit: 5 ruble
  mountain, range: 4 Ural **5** Altai, Altay, Sayan **6** Elbrus, Kolyma, Koryak **8** Caucasus, Stanovoy
  neighbor: 5 China **6** Latvia, Norway **7** Belarus, Estonia, Finland, Georgia, Ukraine **8** Mongolia **9** Kazakstan **10** Azerbaijan, Kazakhstan, North Korea
  peninsula: 4 Kola **5** Gydan, Kanin, Yamal **6** Taymyr **7** Chukchi **9** Kamchatka
  region: 7 Siberia **9** Circassia **11** Golden Horde

Russian

revolution: 9 Bolshevik
river: 3 Don **4** Amur, Lena, Ural **5** Desna, Dvina, Vitim, Volga **6** Belaya, Kolyma, Vilyui, Vilyuy **7** Pechora, Yenisey **9** Indigirka
sea: 4 Azov, Kara **5** Black, White **6** Laptev, Okhotsk **7** Barents, Caspian, Chukchi
strait: 6 Bering

Russian
aristocrat: 5 boyar
family: 7 Romanov **9** Stroganov
grandmother: 8 babushka
monk: 8 Rasputin
peasant: 5 kulak, mujik **6** moujik, muzhik
ruler:
(see **czar**)
saint: 15 Alexander Nevsky
urn: 7 samovar
vehicle: 6 troika
villa: 5 dacha

rustic
4 hick, rube, rude **5** churl, clown, plain, rough, rural, swain, yokel **6** farmer **7** bucolic, bumpkin, country, granger, hayseed, peasant, plowboy, plowman, redneck, uncouth **8** agrarian, pastoral **9** chawbacon, hillbilly **10** campestral, clodhopper, countryman, husbandman **11** countrified **12** apple-knocker, backwoodsman

rustle
5 haste, hurry, speed, steal, swish **6** forage, swoosh **7** crackle, crinkle **8** susurrus

rustler
5 thief **6** duffer, robber **7** forager **8** marauder

Rustum's son
6 Sohrab

rusty
4 slow **6** bygone, creaky **7** outworn **8** outdated, outmoded **10** antiquated, discolored **12** old-fashioned

rut
5 gouge, grind, track **6** furrow, groove **7** channel, routine **9** treadmill

rutabaga
5 swede **6** turnip

ruth
3 rue, woe **4** pity **5** grief, mercy **6** regret, sorrow **7** anguish, remorse, sadness **8** distress, sympathy **9** attrition, penitence **10** compassion, contrition, repentance **11** compunction **13** commiseration

Ruth
husband: 4 Boaz **6** Mahlon
mother-in-law: 5 Naomi
son: 4 Obed

ruthful
6 woeful **7** doleful **8** dolorous, wretched **9** miserable, sorrowful

ruthless
4 hard **5** cruel, harsh **6** brutal, savage **7** inhuman **8** pitiless **9** barbarous, cutthroat, dog-eat-dog, ferocious, heartless, merciless, unsparing **10** implacable, ironfisted

ruttish
4 lewd **5** lusty, randy **6** wanton **7** goatish, lustful, satyric **9** lecherous, lickerish, salacious **10** lascivious, libidinous **12** concupiscent

Rwanda
city: 6 Kigali
ethnic group: 4 Hutu **5** Tutsi
language: 6 French, Rwanda
monetary unit: 5 franc
neighbor: 5 Congo **6** Uganda **7** Burundi **8** Tanzania

S

_____ Saarinen
4 Eero 5 Eliel

Sabatini novel
11 Scaramouche 12 Captain Blood

sabbatical
4 rest 5 leave 7 time off 8 vacation

saber
5 sword 7 cutlass 8 scimitar

sabertooth
3 cat 5 tiger

sable
3 fur 4 dark, inky 5 black, ebony, raven 6 gloomy, somber, sombre, weasel 8 mourning

sabot
4 clog, shoe 10 wooden shoe

sabotage
5 wreck 6 damage, hamper, hinder 7 cripple, disable, subvert, torpedo 8 obstruct, wreckage, wrecking 9 frustrate, undermine, vandalize 10 subversion 11 undermining

Sabra
father: 7 Ptolemy
rescuer: 8 St. George
son: 3 Guy 5 David 9 Alexander

sac
4 caul, cyst 5 pouch 7 vesicle

saccharine
5 mushy, sweet 6 sugary, syrupy 7 candied, cloying, honeyed, maudlin, mawkish, sugared 9 oversweet, schmaltzy 11 sentimental, sugar-coated 12 ingratiating

sacerdotal
8 hieratic, pastoral, priestly 10 priestlike 11 ministerial

sachem
4 boss 5 chief 6 leader

sachet
3 bag 6 powder 7 perfume 9 potpourri

sack
3 bag, bed, can 4 bunk, drop, fire, loot, raid, wine 5 expel, pouch, strip, waste 6 pocket, ravage 7 boot out, cashier, despoil, dismiss, hammock, kick out, pillage, plunder 8 desolate, spoliate 9 container, depredate, desecrate, devastate, white wine

sackbut
8 trombone

sacque
6 jacket

sacrament
4 rite 6 ritual 7 baptism, penance 8 ceremony, marriage 9 Communion, Eucharist, matrimony 10 holy orders 12 confirmation

sacrarium
6 chapel, shrine 7 oratory, piscina 8 sacristy 9 sanctuary

sacred
4 holy 5 godly 6 divine, immune 7 angelic, blessed, saintly 8 hallowed, numinous 9 inviolate, spiritual 10 inviolable, sacrosanct, sanctified 11 consecrated, sacramental
combining form: 4 hagi, hier, sacr 5 hagio, hiero, sacro
monkey: 6 baboon, rhesus 7 hanuman
place: 7 sanctum
weed: 7 vervain

sacrifice
4 bunt, cede, lose, loss 5 forgo, yield 6 devote, donate, eschew, give up, martyr, victim 7 forfeit, offer up 8 dedicate,

hecatomb, immolate, oblation, offering **12** renunciation

sacrilege
6 heresy **7** impiety, offense **9** blasphemy, violation **11** desecration, irreverence, profanation

sacrilegious
7 impious, profane, ungodly **10** irreverent **11** blasphemous

sacristan
6 sexton

sacristy
6 vestry

sacrosanct
9 inviolate **10** inviolable

sad
4 blue, down **5** sorry **6** dismal, dreary, gloomy, morose, triste, woeful **7** doleful, joyless, piteous, pitiful, unhappy **8** dejected, desolate, dolorous, downbeat, downcast, grieving, mournful, pathetic, pitiable **9** depressed, sorrowful, woebegone **10** depressing, dispirited, lamentable, melancholy **11** melancholic **12** heavyhearted

sadden
7 depress, oppress, trouble **8** aggrieve, dispirit **9** weigh down **10** discourage

saddle
3 tax **4** lade, load, task **5** weigh **6** burden, charge, hamper, impede, impose, weight **7** aparejo, inflict **8** encumber, restrict
adjunct: 7 stirrup
part: 6 cantle, pommel
strap: 5 cinch, girth **6** latigo **7** harness

sadness
3 woe **4** funk **5** blues, dolor, dumps, gloom, grief, mopes **6** misery, sorrow **7** dismals, megrims **8** doldrums, glumness, mourning **9** dejection, dysphoria, heartache **10** blue devils, depression, desolation, melancholy **11** despondency, melancholia, unhappiness

safari
4 hunt, trek, trip **7** caravan, journey **10** expedition

safe
4 snug, wary **5** chary **6** secure, unhurt **7** careful, guarded **8** cautious, defended, shielded, unharmed **9** innocuous, protected, sheltered, uninjured, unscathed **10** inviolable, sheltering **11** impregnable **12** invulnerable, unassailable

safecracker
4 yegg **8** picklock **9** cracksman

safeguard
4 ward **6** convoy, defend, escort, shield, surety **7** bulwark, defense, protect **8** armament, preserve **10** precaution, protection

safety
6 asylum, refuge **7** defense, shelter **8** immunity, security **9** assurance, sanctuary **10** protection **13** inviolability

sag
3 dip **4** bend, drop, flag, flap, flop, hang, sink, slip, wilt **5** droop, slide, slump **6** dangle, hollow, slouch **7** decline, drop off, falloff, sinkage, sinking **8** downturn, settling, sinkhole **9** concavity, downswing **10** depression

saga
4 edda, epic, myth, tale **5** story **6** legend **9** chronicle, narrative **12** Heimskringla

sagacious
4 keen, wise **5** acute, smart **6** astute, clever, shrewd **7** knowing, prudent, sapient **8** critical **9** far-seeing, judicious **10** discerning, insightful, perceptive **11** intelligent **13** perspicacious

sagacity
5 grasp **6** acuity, acumen, wisdom **7** insight **8** judgment, keenness, prudence, sapience **10** perception, shrewdness **11** discernment, penetration, percipience, perspicuity **12** perspicacity **13** comprehension, judiciousness, understanding

sagamore
5 chief **6** sachem

Sagan work
6 Cosmos **16** Bonjour tristesse

sage
4 guru, mint, wise **6** expert, master, nestor, pundit, savant, shrewd **7** gnostic, knowing, learned, prudent, sapient, scholar, wise man **8** polymath, profound, sensible **9** judicious **10** discerning, insightful, perceptive **11** penetrating, philosophic
Hindu: 6 pandit **7** mahatma

Sage
of Chelsea: 7 Carlyle (Thomas)
of Concord: 7 Emerson (Ralph Waldo)
of Emporia: 5 White (William Allen)
of Ferney: 8 Voltaire
of Monticello: 9 Jefferson (Thomas)
of Pylos: 6 Nestor

Sagebrush State
6 Nevada

Sagittarius
6 archer 7 centaur 13 constellation

sago
4 palm 6 starch

saguaro
6 cactus

sahib
3 sir 6 master 9 gentleman

sail
3 fly 4 dart, flit, scud, skim, wing 5 fleet,
float, shoot, skirr, sweep 6 cruise, mizzen
7 spencer 9 spinnaker
triangular: 3 jib 5 genoa

sailboat
4 bark, yawl 5 ketch, skiff, sloop, yacht 6
dinghy 8 schooner, skipjack

sailing vessel
4 bark, brig 5 xebec 6 barque 7 frigate,
galleon 8 schooner 10 barkentine,
brigantine 11 barquentine

sailor
3 gob, tar 4 jack, mate, salt, swab 6
hearty, sea dog, seaman 7 jack-tar,
mariner, matelot, old salt, swabbie 8
flatfoot, seafarer, shipmate, water dog 9
shellback, tarpaulin, yachtsman 10
bluejacket
British: 5 limey
fictional: 6 Sinbad
patron saint: 4 Elmo
song: 6 chanty 7 chantey 9 barcarole

saint
7 paragon
biography: 11 hagiography
list: 9 hagiology
(see also **patron saint**)

Saint, The
12 Simon Templar
creator: 9 Charteris (Leslie)

Saint Anthony's cross
3 tau

Saint Elmo's Fire
9 corposant

Saint Helena
capital: 9 Jamestown
colony of: 7 Britain
island: 9 Ascension

Saint Joan author
4 Shaw (George Bernard)

Saint John's bread
5 carob

Saint Kitts and Nevis
capital: 10 Basseterre
island group: 7 Leeward
language: 7 English
location: 10 West Indies
monetary unit: 6 dollar

Saint Lucia
capital: 8 Castries
island group: 8 Windward
language: 6 French 7 English
location: 10 West Indies
monetary unit: 6 dollar
volcano: 8 Quilabou

saintly
4 holy, pure 5 godly, pious 6 devout,
worthy 7 angelic, blessed, upright 8
beatific, seraphic, virtuous 9 righteous

Saint Paul's architect
4 Wren (Christopher)

Saint Peter's Basilica
architect: 7 Bernini (Gian Lorenzo) 12
Michelangelo (Buonarotti)
sculpture: 5 Pietà

Saint-Pierre and Miquelon
capital: 8 St.-Pierre
department of: 6 France

Saint Vincent and the Grenadines
capital: 9 Kingstown
island group: 8 Windward
language: 6 French 7 English
location: 10 West Indies
monetary unit: 6 dollar
volcano: 9 Soufrière

Saint Vitus' dance
6 chorea

sake
3 end 4 good 5 drink 7 benefit, purpose,
welfare

Saki
5 Munro (H. H.)

salaam
3 bow 6 kowtow 8 greeting 9 obeisance

salacious
4 fast, lewd 5 bawdy 6 erotic, ribald,
risqué 7 lustful, satyric 8 indecent, prurient
9 lecherous, libertine 10 lascivious,
libidinous, licentious

salad
item: 3 egg 4 bean, cuke, herb 5 cress,
olive, onion 6 carrot, celery, cheese,
endive, pepper, potato, radish, tomato 7

anchovy, cabbage, crouton, lettuce, parsley, spinach **8** chickpea, coleslaw, cucumber, garbanzo, mushroom, scallion **10** watercress
type: **5** chef's **6** Caesar

salamander
3 eft **4** newt **7** urodele **8** mud puppy, water dog **10** hellbender
Mexican: **7** axolotl

salary
3 pay **4** take, wage **6** income **7** stipend **8** earnings **9** emolument **10** recompense **12** compensation, remuneration

sale
6 bazaar, demand **7** auction **8** closeout, disposal, transfer **9** clearance **11** transaction

salient
6 marked, signal **7** obvious, weighty **8** striking **9** arresting, important, obtrusive, pertinent, prominent **10** impressive, noticeable, projecting, pronounced, remarkable **11** conspicuous, outstanding, significant

saline
5 briny, salty **8** brackish

Salinger, J. D.
character: **4** Esmé **6** Holden (Caulfield)
novel: **14** Franny and Zooey **15** Catcher in the Rye

saliva
4 spit **6** slaver, sputum **7** spittle

salivate
5 drool **6** drivel, slaver **7** slobber

_____ Salk
5 Jonas

sallow
3 wan **4** pale, waxy **5** pasty **6** pallid, sickly, willow, yellow **7** bilious **9** jaundiced

sally
3 gag **4** gust, jape, jest, joke, quip **5** blast, burst, crack, jaunt **6** depart, junket, outing, set out, sortie, volley **7** barrage, flare-up **8** drollery, eruption, outbreak, outburst, paroxysm **9** discharge, excursion, explosion, wisecrack, witticism

salmagundi
see **hodgepodge**

salmon
4 parr, pink **5** smolt **6** grilse **7** sockeye brandling
cured: **7** gravlax **8** gravlaks

male: **6** kipper
smoked: **3** lox

Salome
composer: **7** Strauss (Richard)
father: **5** Herod
husband: **6** Philip **7** Zebedee **11** Aristobulus
mother: **8** Herodias
son: **4** John **5** James
victim: **4** John (the Baptist)

salon
4 hall, shop **5** suite **6** parlor **7** gallery **9** apartment, reception **10** exhibition

saloon
3 bar, pub **6** tavern **7** barroom, cantina, gin mill, taproom **9** beer joint **12** watering hole

salt
3 tar **4** jack, keep, NaCl **5** brine **6** sailor, saline, seaman **7** jack-tar, mariner **8** salinize **9** sailorman

salt away
4 bank, save **5** hoard, lay by, lay up, put by, stash, store **7** deposit **8** lay aside, squirrel

saltpeter
5 niter, nitre

salty
4 blue, racy **5** briny, crude, spicy, tangy **6** earthy, purple, risqué, saline **7** caustic, mordant, pungent **8** brackish, off-color, scathing **9** trenchant

salubrious
5 tonic **6** bracing, healthy **8** hygienic, salutary **9** healthful, wholesome **10** beneficial **11** restorative **12** invigorating

Salus
see **Hygeia**

salutary
5 tonic **6** benign **7** bracing, healing **8** curative, remedial, sanative **9** analeptic, healthful, vulnerary, wholesome **10** beneficial, salubrious **11** restorative, therapeutic **12** advantageous, health-giving

salutation
4 hail **5** hello, howdy **7** welcome **8** greeting
Arab: **6** salaam
French: **5** salut
Hawaiian: **5** aloha
Italian: **4** ciao
Latin: **3** ave

Spanish: 4 hola

salute
4 hail 5 greet, honor 6 praise 7 address, commend 8 greeting 12 congratulate

salvage
4 save 6 ransom, recoup, redeem, regain, rescue 7 deliver, reclaim, recover 8 retrieve

salvation
6 saving 7 keeping 10 redemption 11 deliverance 12 conservation, preservation

Salvation Army founder
5 Booth (General William)

salve
4 balm 5 cream, quiet 6 cerate, chrism, lotion, remedy 7 assuage, unction, unguent 8 ointment 9 emollient

salver
4 tray

salvo
4 hail 5 burst, spray, storm 6 attack, shower, volley 7 barrage, proviso 9 broadside, cannonade, discharge, fusillade 11 bombardment

Samaritan
6 helper 10 benefactor

same
4 idem, like, very 5 equal, exact 7 coequal, similar 8 constant 9 duplicate, identical, unvarying 10 consistent, equivalent, invariable, unchanging

Samoa
capital: 4 Apia
island: 5 Upolu 6 Savai'i
language: 6 Samoan 7 English
monetary unit: 4 tala

samovar
3 urn

samp
6 cereal, hominy

sampan
4 boat 5 skiff

sample
3 try 4 case, part, test, unit 5 piece, taste 7 element, example, excerpt, portion, segment 8 fragment, instance, specimen 10 indication 11 case history, constituent 12 illustration

Samson
betrayer: 7 Delilah

birthplace: 5 Zorah
deathplace: 4 Gaza
father: 6 Manoah
tribe: 3 Dan

Samson Agonistes author
6 Milton (John)

Samuel
father: 7 Elkanah
grandson: 5 Heman
mother: 6 Hannah

samurai code
7 Bushido

San Antonio
team: 5 Spurs
landmark: 5 Alamo

sanatorium
3 spa 8 hospital, rest home

sanctify
5 bless 6 hallow, ordain, purify 8 dedicate 10 consecrate

sanctimonious
5 pious 7 canting, preachy 8 unctuous 9 pharisaic 11 pharisaical 12 hypocritical, Pecksniffian 13 self-righteous

sanction
4 fiat, okay 5 bless, leave 6 assent, decree, permit, ratify 7 approve, backing, boycott, certify, consent, embargo, endorse, license, penalty, support 8 accredit, approval 9 allowance, authorize 10 commission, permission, sufferance 11 approbation, endorsement 12 confirmation, ratification 13 authorization, encouragement

sanctity
8 holiness 9 godliness 11 saintliness, uprightness 13 inviolability, righteousness

sanctuary
5 haven, oasis 6 asylum, covert, harbor, refuge, shrine, temple 7 reserve, retreat, shelter 8 preserve 9 holy place

sanctum
4 lair 6 shrine 7 retreat, shelter 9 holy place, sanctuary

sand
3 tan 4 buff, ecru, fawn, grit 5 beach, beige, camel, grind, khaki, scour, shore 6 gravel, polish, smooth 7 burnish 8 granules

sandal
4 clog, zori 5 sabot, thong 6 patten 8 flip-flop, huarache 10 espadrille

sandbag
6 ambush, waylay

sandbar
4 reef, spit 7 tombolo

Sand County Almanac author
7 Leopold (Aldo)

sandpiper
4 knot, ruff 5 reeve 6 dunlin 9 shorebird

sandstone deposit
6 flysch

sandwich
3 BLT, sub 4 club, gyro, roti 5 butty,
Cuban 6 Denver, hoagie, Reuben 7
grinder, Western 9 submarine 10
muffuletta
shop: 4 deli

sandy
4 fair 5 blond 6 blonde, grainy, gritty

sane
3 fit 4 good, hale, sage, well, wise 5 lucid,
right, sober, sound 6 cogent, normal 7
healthy, logical, prudent, sapient 8 all
there, balanced, oriented, rational, sensible
9 judicious, wholesome 10 reasonable 11
levelheaded 12 compos mentis

San Francisco
hill: 3 Nob 7 Russian
tower: 4 Coit

sangfroid
4 calm 5 poise 6 aplomb, phlegm 9
composure 10 equanimity 11 self-control

sanguinary
4 gory 6 bloody 9 homicidal, murdering,
murderous 12 bloodstained, bloodthirsty

sanguine
4 gory 5 flush, ruddy 6 bloody, florid,
secure, upbeat 7 assured, buoyant,
flushed, glowing, hopeful 8 bloodred,
cheerful, rubicund 9 confident, homicidal,
murdering, murderous 10 optimistic 11
self-assured 12 blood-stained, bloodthirsty,
Pollyannaish 13 self-confident

sanitary
5 clean 7 sterile 8 hygienic 9 healthful 10
antiseptic, salubrious

sanitize
5 clean, purge 6 bleach, censor, purify 7
cleanse, launder 8 black out 9 disinfect,
expurgate, sterilize 10 bowdlerize

sanity
6 health, reason 7 balance 8 lucidity,
prudence 9 normality, soundness, stability

San Marino
capital: 9 San Marino
monetary unit: 4 euro
monetary unit, former: 4 lira
neighbor: 5 Italy

sans
7 lacking, missing, wanting, without

Sanskrit
dialect: 4 Pali
epic: 8 Ramayana
Scripture: 4 Veda

Santa Lucia composer
5 Denza (Luigi)

São Tomé and Príncipe
capital: 7 São Tomé
language: 10 Portuguese
location: 12 Gulf of Guinea
monetary unit: 5 dobra

sap
4 dupe, fool, gull, mark 5 chump, drain 6
pigeon, sucker, weaken 7 cripple, deplete,
disable, exhaust, fall guy 8 enervate,
enfeeble 9 attenuate, schlemiel,
undermine 10 debilitate

sapid
5 tasty 6 savory 9 delicious, flavorful,
palatable, toothsome 10 appetizing 11
scrumptious

sapience
see **sagacity**

sapient
see **sagacious**

sapling
4 tree 5 child, youth 9 youngster

Sapphira's husband
7 Ananias

Sappho
forte: 6 poetry
island: 6 Lesbos

sappy
5 ditzy, flaky, mushy, silly, soupy 6 drippy,
slushy, sticky, syrupy 7 cloying, foolish,
maudlin, mawkish 8 bathetic 11
sentimental

Saracen hero
9 Rodomonte

Sarah
husband: 7 Abraham
maid: 5 Hagar
son: 5 Isaac

sarcasm
3 wit 4 gibe 5 irony, scorn 6 satire 7 mockery 8 acerbity, mordancy, ridicule, sneering 10 causticity

sarcastic
4 acid, tart 5 acerb, sharp 6 biting, ironic 7 acerbic, caustic, cutting, cynical, jeering, mocking, mordant, satiric 8 sardonic, scathing, scornful, stinging 9 corrosive

sarcophagus
4 tomb 6 coffin

sardine
4 sild 7 anchovy, herring 8 pilchard

Sardinia's capital
8 Cagliari

sardonic
3 wry 6 ironic 7 caustic, cynical, jeering, mocking, satiric 8 derisive, scornful, sneering 9 corrosive, sarcastic 10 disdainful 12 contemptuous

sarong
5 skirt 7 garment

Sarpedon
brother: 5 Minos 12 Rhadamanthus
father: 4 Zeus 7 Jupiter
mother: 6 Europa 8 Laodamia

Sartor _____
8 Resartus

Sartre work
4 Wall (The) 5 Flies (The) 6 Nausea, No Exit 8 Huis Clos 10 Saint Genet

sash
4 belt 6 girdle 8 ceinture, cincture 9 waistband 10 cummerbund

sashay
5 mince, strut 6 prance 7 flounce, saunter, swagger

Saskatchewan
capital: 6 Regina
city: 8 Moose Jaw 9 Saskatoon 12 Prince Albert
mountain range: 12 Cypress Hills
provincial flower: 7 red lily 11 prairie lily
river: 9 Churchill 11 Assiniboine

sass
3 lip 4 guff 5 brass, cheek, mouth, sauce 8 back talk 9 impudence, insolence 12 impertinence

sassy
4 bold, flip, pert, wise 5 fresh, lippy, nervy, smart 6 brazen, cheeky 7 forward 8 flippant, impudent, insolent, malapert 9 audacious, unabashed 11 smart-alecky

Satan
5 demon, devil, fiend 6 diablo 7 Lucifer, Old Nick, serpent, villain 9 archfiend, Beelzebub 10 Old Scratch

satanic
4 evil 6 wicked 7 demonic, hellish 8 demoniac, devilish, diabolic, fiendish, infernal

satanism
9 diabolism

satchel
3 bag 4 case, tote 5 pouch 6 valise 7 handbag 9 briefcase

sate
4 cloy, fill, glut, jade, pall 5 gorge, stuff 6 stodge 7 appease, overeat, placate, surfeit 8 overfill 9 overstuff 10 conciliate

sated
4 full 6 filled, gorged 7 glutted, overfed, replete, stuffed 8 appeased, chockful 9 chock-full, surfeited

satellite
4 moon 5 toady 6 cohort, minion 7 Sputnik 8 adherent, disciple, follower, henchman, partisan 9 attendant, supporter, sycophant, tributary
of Jupiter: 6 Europa 8 Callisto, Ganymede
of Mars: 6 Deimos, Phobos
of Neptune: 6 Nereid, Triton
of Saturn: 4 Rhea 5 Dione, Janus, Mimas, Titan 6 Phoebe, Tethys 7 Iapetus 8 Hyperion 9 Enceladus
of Uranus: 5 Ariel 6 Oberon 7 Miranda, Titania, Umbriel

satiate
see **sate**

satire
3 wit 5 irony, spoof, squib 6 parody 7 lampoon, mockery, takeoff 8 raillery, ridicule, spoofery, travesty 9 burlesque 10 caricature, lampoonery, pasquinade, persiflage

satiric
6 ironic 7 mocking 8 farcical, ironical

satirist
English: 5 Swift (Jonathan) 7 Marston (John)
French: 8 Rabelais (François), Voltaire
Greek: 8 Menippus
Italian: 7 Aretino (Pietro)

satirize

Roman: 6 Horace 7 Juvenal, Martial, Persius 9 Petronius

satirize
4 mock 5 spoof 6 parody, send up 7 lampoon 8 ridicule 10 caricature

satisfaction
6 amends 7 redress 8 pleasure, serenity 9 atonement 10 reparation 11 contentment, fulfillment, restitution, vindication 12 propitiation 13 gratification

satisfactory
4 fair, good, okay 5 sound 6 decent 8 adequate, all right, passable 9 competent, tolerable 10 acceptable, sufficient 13 unexceptional

satisfy
3 pay 4 fill, meet, sate, suit 5 clear, humor, pay up, serve 6 answer, assure, dispel, pacify, please, settle, square 7 appease, content, fulfill, gladden, gratify, indulge, placate, satiate, suffice, win over 8 convince, persuade 9 conform to, discharge, indemnify 10 comply with

satori
12 illumination 13 enlightenment

satrap
5 ruler 6 cohort 7 viceroy 8 governor, henchman, sidekick 11 subordinate

saturate
3 sop, wet 4 fill, soak 5 bathe, douse, imbue, souse, steep 6 charge, drench, infuse 7 pervade, suffuse 8 permeate, waterlog 9 transfuse

Saturn
moon: 4 Rhea 5 Dione, Janus, Mimas, Titan 6 Phoebe, Tethys 7 Iapetus 8 Hyperion 9 Enceladus
see also **Cronus**

saturnalia
4 orgy 5 party, revel 6 excess 7 debauch 9 bacchanal 11 bacchanalia, dissipation

saturnine
4 dour, glum, grim 5 sulky, surly 6 gloomy, moping, morose, somber, sombre, sullen 7 crabbed 8 funereal, sardonic

satyr
4 goat, rake, wolf 6 lecher 9 butterfly

satyric
4 lewd 5 randy 6 wanton 7 goatish, lustful 8 prurient 9 lecherous, libertine, lickerish, salacious 10 lascivious, libidinous, licentious, lubricious 11 promiscuous 12 concupiscent

sauce
4 guff, sass 5 mouth 6 relish 7 topping 8 back talk 9 condiment, impudence
kind: 3 soy 4 hard, mole 5 chili, curry, gravy, melba, pesto, salsa 6 Mornay, panada, tamari, tartar 7 chutney, marengo, Newburg, piquant, soubise, tartare, velouté 8 béchamel, duxelles, marinara, matelote, noisette, normande 9 béarnaise, lyonnaise, rémoulade 10 bordelaise, Provençale 11 hollandaise, vinaigrette

saucy
see **sassy**

Saudi Arabia
capital: 6 Riyadh
city: 5 Jedda, Jidda, Mecca 6 Jeddah, Jiddah, Medina
desert: 7 Arabian 10 Rub Al-Khali 12 Empty Quarter
gulf: 7 Persian
monetary unit: 5 riyal
neighbor: 3 UAE 4 Iraq, Oman 5 Qatar, Yemen 6 Jordan
peninsula: 7 Arabian
sea: 3 Red

Saul
concubine: 6 Rizpah
cousin: 5 Abner
daughter: 5 Merab 6 Michal
father: 4 Kish
son: 8 Jonathan
successor: 5 David
uncle: 3 Ner
wife: 7 Ahinoam

saunter
4 mope, roam, rove 5 amble, drift, mosey 6 loiter, ramble, sashay, stroll, wander 7 meander, traipse

sausage
5 wurst 6 banger, kishke, salami, Vienna, wiener 7 baloney, bologna, boloney, chorizo, saveloy 8 cervelat, kielbasa 9 andouille, bratwurst, frankfurt, pepperoni, Thuringer 10 knackwurst, knockwurst, liverwurst, mortadella 11 frankfurter

sauté
3 fry 4 sear 5 brown, grill 6 sizzle 7 frizzle

savage
4 grim, wild 5 brute, cruel, feral 6 bloody, brutal, fierce, Gothic, rugged 7 bestial, brutish, inhuman, untamed, vicious, wolfish 8 barbaric, inhumane, primeval, ravenous, unbroken 9 barbarian, barbarous, ferocious, heartless, murderous, primitive, rapacious, truculent, voracious 10 implacable, relentless 11 uncivilized 12

bloodthirsty, uncontrolled, uncultivated, unsocialized

savagery
7 cruelty 8 atrocity 9 barbarity, brutality, depravity 10 bestiality, inhumanity 11 abomination, monstrosity, viciousness 12 ruthlessness

savanna
5 plain 9 grassland

savant
4 sage 7 scholar, thinker, wise man

save
3 bar, but, yet 4 bank, keep, only, stow 5 amass, avoid, cache, guard, hoard, lay by, lay in, lay up, put by, set by, skimp, spare, store 6 defend, except, gather, keep up, manage, ransom, redeem, rescue, scrimp, shield, unless 7 barring, besides, collect, deliver, deposit, however, husband, lay away, protect, reclaim, reserve, salvage, set free, store up 8 conserve, lay aside, liberate, maintain, preserve, salt away, set aside, squirrel 9 aside from, economize, excluding, safeguard, stash away, stockpile 10 accumulate

savior
7 messiah, paladin, rescuer 8 defender 9 deliverer, liberator, preserver, protector, salvation 11 white knight

savoir faire
4 tact 5 grace, poise 6 aplomb 7 address, dignity, finesse, manners 8 urbanity 10 confidence, refinement 13 self-assurance

savor
4 odor, tang 5 enjoy, scent, smack, smell, spice, taste, tinge 6 flavor, relish, season 8 sapidity

savory
5 sapid, spicy, tangy, tasty 7 piquant 9 flavorful, palatable, toothsome 10 appetizing

savvy
4 deft 5 adept, craft, handy, knack, skill 6 clever, talent 7 ability, know-how, skilled 8 deftness 9 adeptness, expertise, handiness, ingenuity 10 capability, cleverness, competence

saw
3 cut, hew 5 adage, axiom, maxim 6 byword, cliché, saying 7 precept, proverb 8 aphorism, apothegm

_____ saw
3 bow, jig, pit, rip 4 band, buck, buzz, fret,

hack, whip 5 chain, crown, saber 6 coping, scroll 7 compass, keyhole 8 circular, crosscut

sawbones
3 doc 6 doctor 7 surgeon 9 physician

sawbuck
6 tenner 7 trestle

sawhorse
see **sawbuck**

saw-toothed
7 serrate, serried 8 serrated 11 denticulate

Saxon
assembly: 4 moot 5 gemot 6 gemote
nobleman: 8 atheling
serf: 4 esne
warrior: 5 thane

say
4 talk, tell 5 mouth, speak, state, utter, voice 6 affirm, assert, assume, recite, remark 7 comment, declare, express 8 announce, proclaim 9 enunciate, pronounce 10 articulate

Sayers character
6 Wimsey (Lord Peter)

saying
3 mot, saw 5 adage, axiom, maxim 6 byword, dictum, truism 7 precept, proverb 8 apothegm

scab
5 crust 6 eschar 13 strikebreaker

scabbard
6 sheath

scabrous
4 lewd 5 harsh, rough, salty, scaly 6 craggy, grubby, jagged, knobby, knotty, rugged, scabby, scurfy, sordid, uneven 7 bristly, prickly, scraggy, squalid 8 indecent 10 scandalous

scads
4 gobs, lots, wads 5 loads, piles, reams 6 oodles 8 slathers 10 quantities

scaffold
5 stage, truss 7 staging 8 platform 9 framework

Scala, La
city: 5 Milan
production: 5 opera

scalawag
see **scamp**

scald
4 boil, burn 6 scorch

scale
4 peel, rate, skin 5 climb, flake, gamut, gauge, mount, ratio, scute, strip 6 ascend, degree, extent, ladder, lamina, scutum, squama 7 measure, ranking 8 escalade, flake off, spall off 9 exfoliate, hierarchy 10 desquamate, proportion 11 decorticate
auxiliary: 7 vernier
earthquake: 7 Richter
temperature: 6 Kelvin 7 Celsius 10 centigrade, Fahrenheit
wind: 8 Beaufort

scallion
4 leek 5 onion 7 shallot 10 green onion

scalp
4 flay, skin 5 cheat 6 resell, trophy

scam
3 con, gyp 4 bilk, dupe, fool, hoax 5 cheat, fraud, stick, trick 6 delude, diddle, take in 7 beguile, deceive, defraud, swindle 8 flimflam, hoodwink 11 double-cross

scamp
3 imp 4 brat, rake, tyke 5 devil, joker, knave, rogue 6 rascal, urchin 7 hellion 8 scalawag, slyboots 9 prankster, skeezicks 11 rapscallion

scamper
3 run 4 dash, skip 5 scoot 6 scurry 7 scuttle

scan
3 eye 4 skim, view 5 audit, check 6 browse, review, survey 7 examine, eyeball, inspect 8 glance at 10 run through, scrutinize

scandal
5 rumor 6 gossip, infamy 7 calumny, obloquy, offense, slander 8 disgrace, dishonor, reproach 9 aspersion, discredit, disrepute 10 backbiting, defamation, detraction, opprobrium

scandalize
5 libel, shock, smear 6 defame, malign 7 asperse, slander 9 denigrate 10 calumniate

scandalmonger
6 gossip 8 busybody, gossiper, quidnunc, telltale 9 backbiter, muckraker 10 talebearer

scandalous
7 heinous 8 infamous, libelous, shameful, shocking 9 notorious, offensive 10 defamatory, outrageous, scurrilous 11 disgraceful

Scandinavian
see **Norse**

Scandinavian country
6 Norway, Sweden 7 Denmark, Finland, Iceland

scant
5 short, skimp, spare, stint, tight 6 meager, meagre, paltry, scarce, scrimp, skimpy, slight, sparse 7 scrimpy, wanting 8 exiguous 10 inadequate 12 insufficient

scantiness
4 lack 6 dearth 7 deficit, paucity 8 scarcity, shortage, sparsity 10 deficiency, inadequacy, scarceness, sparseness 13 insufficiency

scanty
see **scant**

scapegoat
6 target, victim 7 fall guy 9 sacrifice 11 whipping boy

scapegrace
5 knave, rogue, scamp 6 bad egg, rascal 7 ruffian, varmint, villain 8 hooligan, recreant, scalawag 9 miscreant, reprobate, scoundrel 10 blackguard, black sheep, delinquent 11 rapscallion

Scapin
5 rogue, valet 6 rascal
author: 7 Molière
employer: 7 Léandre

scar
3 mar 4 flaw 5 score 6 deface, defect, keloid 7 blemish, scratch 8 cicatrix, pockmark 9 cicatrize, disfigure
on a seed: 5 hilum

scarab
6 beetle

scaramouch
see **scamp**

scarce
3 few 4 rare 5 scant 6 barely, hardly, scanty, sparse 7 limited, wanting 8 sporadic, uncommon 9 deficient 10 inadequate, infrequent, occasional 12 insufficient

scarcity
see **scantiness**

scare
 5 alarm, panic, spook 6 fright 7 horrify,
 petrify, shake up, startle, terrify 8 frighten,
 paralyze 9 terrorize

scaredy-cat
 4 wimp, wuss 5 mouse, sissy 6 coward 7
 chicken, dastard 8 alarmist, poltroon 11
 milquetoast, yellowbelly

scare up
 4 find, snag 5 rally 6 corral, gather, locate,
 obtain, secure 7 acquire, collect, procure,
 unearth 8 smoke out 9 ferret out, track
 down

scarf
 4 gulp, wolf 5 ascot, fichu, plaid, shawl,
 stole 6 cravat, devour, gobble, inhale 8
 babushka, liripipe, mantilla, puggaree 10
 lambrequin
 Mexican: 6 rebozo

Scarlet Letter, The
 author: 9 Hawthorne (Nathaniel)
 character: 5 Pearl 6 Hester (Prynne) 10
 Dimmesdale (Arthur) 13 Chillingworth
 (Roger)

Scarlet Pimpernel author
 5 Orczy (Baroness Emmuska)

Scarlett's home
 4 Tara

scary
 6 creepy, spooky 8 chilling 9 frightful

scathe
 4 burn, flay, flog, harm, lash, sear 5 roast,
 slash 6 assail, berate, scorch, thrash 7
 blister, scarify, scourge, upbraid 8
 lambaste 9 castigate, excoriate

scathing
 6 biting, brutal 7 caustic, mordant 8
 stinging 9 trenchant

scatter
 3 sow 4 cast, part, shed 5 strew 6 divide,
 spread 7 bestrew, break up, diffuse,
 disband, diverge 8 disperse, sprinkle 9
 broadcast, dissipate 10 besprinkle,
 distribute 11 disseminate

scatterbrained
 5 dizzy, giddy, silly 7 flighty, foolish 8
 heedless 9 frivolous

scattering
 8 diaspora 10 dispersion

scavenger
 5 hyena 6 jackal 7 vulture

scenario
 4 plot 6 script 7 outline 8 libretto,
 synopsis 10 screenplay

scene
 3 row, set 4 fuss, site, spot, view 5 arena,
 field, place, sight, vista 6 locale, milieu,
 sphere 7 episode, outlook, setting,
 tableau, tantrum 8 backdrop, locality,
 location, stage set 9 commotion,
 landscape, situation 10 background 11
 environment 12 stage setting

scenery
 3 set 5 decor, props 7 setting 8 stage set
 10 properties 11 furnishings 12 stage
 setting

scent
 4 nose, odor 5 aroma, smell, sniff, snuff,
 whiff 7 bouquet, essence, incense,
 odorize, perfume 9 aromatize, fragrance,
 redolence

scepter
 4 mace 5 baton, staff 11 sovereignty

schedule
 4 list, roll 5 chart, slate, table 6 agenda,
 docket, record, roster 7 catalog, program,
 reserve 8 calendar, register, roll call 9
 catalogue, timetable

scheme
 4 plan, plot, ploy, ruse 5 cabal, order 6
 design, device, devise 7 collude, connive,
 diagram, program, project 8 cogitate,
 conspire, contrive, game plan, intrigue,
 proposal, strategy 9 blueprint, expedient,
 machinate 10 conspiracy 11 arrangement,
 contrivance, machination

schism
 4 rent, rift 5 break, chasm, cleft, split 6
 breach, heresy 7 discord, dissent, fissure,
 rupture 8 cleavage, division, fracture 10
 disharmony, dissidence, divergence, falling-
 out, heterodoxy, separation 11
 unorthodoxy 12 estrangement

schlemiel
 4 fool 5 chump, klutz 7 bungler

schlep
 3 lug, tow 4 drag, haul, hump, plod, pull,
 slog, tote 5 carry, truck 6 trudge 7
 shamble, shuffle 8 straggle

schlock
 4 junk, mean 5 cheap, dreck, gaudy, junky,
 tacky, tatty 6 cheesy, common, kitsch,

shoddy, sleazy, tawdry, trashy **8** inferior, low-grade **11** second-class, substandard

schmaltzy
5 mushy, soppy **6** drippy **7** maudlin, mawkish **11** sentimental

schmo
4 dolt, dope, dork, fool, goof, jerk, mutt, simp, twit, yo-yo **5** brute, chump, idiot, moron, ninny, noddy, scamp **6** dimwit, donkey, dum-dum, nitwit, noodle, nudnik, rascal **7** dullard, halfwit, jackass, schmuck, schnook **8** bonehead, clodpoll, imbecile, lunkhead, meathead, numskull **9** birdbrain, blockhead, ignoramus, lamebrain, numbskull, thickhead **10** dunderhead, hammerhead, nincompoop **11** chowderhead, chucklehead, knucklehead

schmooze
3 gab, yak **4** chat **6** chat up **8** converse

schnoz
4 beak, nose **6** honker

scholar
4 sage, wonk **5** pupil **6** savant **7** bookman, egghead, student, wise man **8** bookworm, polymath **12** intellectual
Hindu: 6 pandit, pundit
Muslim: 5 ulama, ulema

scholarly
7 bookish, erudite, learned **8** academic, educated, studious **10** scholastic **12** intellectual

scholarship
5 award, grant **7** stipend **8** learning **9** education, erudition, knowledge **11** learnedness

scholastic
7 bookish, erudite, learned **8** academic, lettered, literary, pedantic **9** scholarly
life: 8 academia

school
3 gam, pad **5** shoal, teach, train, tutor **7** academy, borstal, college, educate **8** instruct **9** alma mater, institute **10** discipline, university
French: 5 école, lycée
grounds: 6 campus
Jewish: 5 heder **7** yeshiva
judo: 4 dojo
organization: 3 PTA, PTO
religious: 8 seminary
term: 7 quarter **8** semester **9** trimester

schoolbook
4 text **6** primer, reader **7** speller

School for Scandal author
8 Sheridan (Richard Brinsley)

schooner
4 ship **5** stoup **6** goblet, seidel **7** tumbler **8** sailboat

Schubert forte
4 lied, song

science
of agriculture: 8 agronomy
of animals: 7 zoology
of armorial bearings: 8 heraldry
of criminal punishment: 8 penology
of environment: 7 ecology
of fermentation: 8 zymology
of health: 7 hygiene **9** hygienics
of heredity: 8 genetics
of human behavior: 10 psychology
of measuring time: 8 horology **11** chronometry
of motion: 8 kinetics
of mountains: 7 orology
of plants: 6 botany
of projectiles: 10 ballistics
of the earth: 7 geology

scientific classification
8 taxonomy

sci-fi writer
3 Lem (Stanislaw) **4** Card (Orson Scott), Dick (Philip K.), Pohl (Frederik) **5** Disch (Thomas M.), Lewis (C. S.), Niven (Larry), Verne (Jules), Wells (H. G.) **6** Aldiss (Brian), Asimov (Isaac), Bester (Alfred), Bishop (Michael), Butler (Octavia), Clarke (Arthur C.), Delany (Samuel), Farmer (Philip José), Gibson (William), Le Guin (Ursula), Leiber (Fritz), Miller (Walter) **7** Ballard (J. G.), Clement (Hal), Ellison (Harlan), Herbert (Frank), Hubbard (L. Ron), Van Vogt (A. E.), Zelazny (Roger) **8** Anderson (Poul), Bradbury (Ray), Heinlein (Robert A.), Sterling (Bruce), Sturgeon (Theodore), Vonnegut (Kurt) **9** Gernsback (Hugo), Kornbluth (C. M.) **10** Silverberg (Robert)

scimitar
5 saber, sabre, sword **7** cutlass

scintilla
3 bit, jot **4** iota, whit **5** grain, spark, speck, trace **8** particle

scintillate
5 flash, gleam, glint, spark **6** glance **7** glimmer, glisten, glitter, shimmer, sparkle, twinkle **9** coruscate

scion
4 heir **5** child, graft, issue **7** progeny **8**

offshoot **9** inheritor, offspring, successor
10 descendant

scoff at
4 mock, twit **5** fleer, scorn **6** deride **7**
contemn, disdain **8** belittle, pooh-pooh,
ridicule

scold
3 rag **4** chew, lash, rail, rant **5** baste,
blame, chide, grill, harpy, hound, shrew,
vixen **6** berate, grouch, grouse, harass,
murmur, mutter, rebuke, revile, virago **7**
bawl out, blister, censure, chasten, chew
out, grumble, lecture, reprove, tell off,
upbraid **8** admonish, execrate, fishwife,
lambaste, reproach, Xantippe **9** criticize,
dress down, excoriate, objurgate,
reprehend, reprimand, termagant,
Xanthippe **10** tongue-lash, vituperate

scoop
3 dig, dip **4** bail, beat, lift **5** gouge, ladle,
spade **6** dig out, pick up, shovel **8**
excavate **9** exclusive

scoot
3 fly, run, zip **4** dash, flee, race, rush, skip
5 hurry, scram, skirr, slide **6** hustle, scurry,
sprint **7** scamper **9** skedaddle

scope
4 area, room **5** ambit, gamut, orbit, range,
reach, sweep **6** extent, leeway, margin,
radius **7** breadth, compass, purview **8**
capacity, fullness, latitude **9** amplitude,
extension

Scopes trial lawyer
5 Bryan (William Jennings) **6** Darrow
(Clarence)

scorch
4 bake, burn, char, flay, sear **5** broil, roast,
singe **6** scathe **7** blacken, blister, scarify,
scourge, swelter **8** lambaste **9** castigate,
excoriate

score
3 cut, tab, win **4** bill, gain, goal, line, mark,
nick, slit **5** cleft, count, notch, tally,
total **6** attain, furrow, groove, grudge, rack
up, record, thrive, twenty **7** account,
achieve, invoice, prosper, scratch, succeed
8 flourish **9** reckoning **10** accomplish

scorn
4 gibe, jeer, mock **5** abhor, flout, scoff,
spurn, taunt **6** deride **7** contemn, despise,
despite, disdain, jeering, mockery **8**
contempt, derision, ridicule, scoffing,
taunting **9** contumely

Scorpius star
7 Antares

Scotch cocktail
6 Rob Roy **9** Rusty Nail

scoter
7 sea coot, sea duck

Scotland
capital: 9 Edinburgh
city: 6 Dundee **7** Glasgow **8** Aberdeen **9**
Inverness **11** Dunfermline
firth: 5 Clyde, Forth, Moray **6** Solway
former capital: 5 Perth
island, island group: 4 Iona, Jura, Mull,
Skye, Uist **5** Arran, Islay **7** Orkneys **9**
Shetlands **8** Hebrides
lake: 8 Loch Ness **10** Loch Lomond
mountain, range: 8 Ben Nevis **9**
Grampians
patron saint: 6 Andrew
river: 3 Dee, Esk

Scott, Sir Walter
novel: 5 Abbot (The) **6** Rob Roy **7**
Ivanhoe **8** Talisman (The), Waverley **9**
Woodstock **10** Kenilworth **11** Redgauntlet
12 Old Mortality **14** Quentin Durward
poem: 7 Marmion **13** Lady of the Lake
(The)

_____ Scott case
4 Dred

Scottish
cap: 3 tam **9** glengarry **11** tam-o'-shanter
child: 5 bairn
dance: 4 reel **5** fling **10** strathspey
guide: 6 gillie
hero: 6 Bruce (Robert) **7** Wallace
(William)
hill: 4 brae
lake: 4 loch
landowner: 5 laird
outlaw: 6 Rob Roy
patron saint: 6 Andrew
plaid: 6 tartan
pudding: 6 haggis
skirt: 4 kilt
spirit: 6 kelpie **7** banshee
sword: 8 claymore
trousers: 5 trews

scoundrel
see **scamp**

scour
4 comb, rake **5** erode, purge, range, scrub
6 forage, search **7** corrode, eat away,
ransack, rummage **8** wear away **9** ferret
out

scourge
4 bane, flay, flog, hide, lash, whip, whop 5 curse, flail, slash, whale 6 plague, ravage, scathe, stripe, thrash 7 afflict, blister, despoil, pillage, scarify 8 chastise, lambaste 9 castigate, depredate, desecrate, devastate, excoriate 10 affliction, flagellate, pestilence

Scourge of God
6 Attila

scout
3 spy 6 ranger, survey 7 explore, lookout 8 searcher, watchman 11 investigate, reconnoiter

scouting group
3 BSA, GSA

scow
3 hoy 5 barge 6 garvey 7 lighter

scowl
5 frown, glare, lower 6 glower

scrabble
5 grope 6 scrawl 7 clamber 8 flounder

scraggly
6 ragged, shaggy, uneven 7 unkempt 9 irregular

scraggy
4 bony, lank, lean 5 gaunt, harsh, lanky, rocky, rough 6 jagged, rugged, skinny, uneven 7 angular, scrawny, spindly, unlevel 8 gangling, rawboned, scabrous

scram
5 scoot, split 6 beat it, get out 7 buzz off, get lost, skiddoo, take off, vamoose 8 clear out 9 skedaddle

scramble
4 hash 6 jumble, jungle, muddle, scurry, tumble 7 clamber, clutter, rummage, scuttle, shuffle 8 mishmash, scrabble, straggle 9 confusion

scrambled
7 chaotic, jumbled, mixed-up 8 confused 9 corrupted 10 disordered, disorderly

scrap
3 bit, jot, row 4 chip, dump, fray, junk, spat, tiff, whit 5 brawl, chuck, crumb, fight, melee, piece, set-to, shred, speck 6 bicker, fracas, reject, sliver, tittle 7 brabble, cutting, discard, fall out, quarrel, scuffle, smidgen, wrangle 8 fragment, jettison, leftover, particle, squabble, throw out 9 throw away

scrape
3 fix, jam, rub 4 mess, rasp, spot 5 chafe, fight, grate, graze, pinch, scour, scuff, shave, skimp, spare, stint 6 abrade, pickle, plight, scrimp 7 dilemma, scratch, trouble 8 abrasion, struggle 11 predicament

scrappy
6 feisty 8 brawling 9 combative, truculent 10 pugnacious 11 belligerent, contentious, quarrelsome

scratch
4 claw, rake, rasp 5 grate, score, scrup 6 scotch, scrape, scrawl 7 call off 8 scrabble, scribble

scratchy
5 rough 6 gritty 7 itching, prickly, rasping 8 abrasive, granular, tingling 10 irritating

scrawl
6 doodle 7 scratch 8 scrabble, scribble

scrawny
4 bony, lank, lean 5 gaunt, lanky 6 skinny 7 scraggy 8 rawboned

scream
3 cry 4 yell, yowl 5 shout 6 screak, shriek, shrill, squeal 7 screech

screech
6 screak, scream, shriek, shrill, squeal

screed
5 level, spiel 6 letter, tirade 8 diatribe, harangue, jeremiad 9 discourse, philippic 11 disputation 12 disquisition

screen
4 cull, sift, veil 5 blind, sieve 6 facade, filter, movies, shroud, winnow 7 conceal, obscure, pick out 9 partition 10 camouflage
Japanese: 5 shoji

screw
9 propeller

screwball
3 nut, wag 4 kook, zany 5 clown, crazy, cutup, flake, flaky, freak, gonzo, joker, kooky, loony, nutty, silly, wacko, wacky 6 madcap, weirdo 7 buffoon, dingbat, farceur 8 crackpot, jokester 9 ding-a-ling, eccentric, fruitcake, whimsical

Screwtape Letters author
5 Lewis (C. S.)

screwy
3 mad 4 daft, nuts 5 batty, crazy, goofy, loony, nutty, wacky 6 absurd, insane 7 bizarre, cracked, lunatic 9 eccentric 10 unbalanced

scribble
5 write 6 scrawl 7 scratch 8 squiggle

scribe
5 clerk, write 6 author, writer 7 copyist 9 scrivener, secretary

scrimmage
4 fray 5 brawl, broil, clash, fight, melee, scrap, set-to 6 battle, fracas, ruckus, rumpus 7 scuffle 8 skirmish 10 donnybrook, free-for-all

scrimp
4 save 5 stint 6 save up, scrape 8 conserve 9 economize

script
4 hand, text 5 write 8 longhand, scenario 10 penmanship, screenplay 11 calligraphy, chirography, handwriting, orchestrate

scrivener
6 notary, scribe, writer 7 copyist

scrooge
5 miser 7 niggard 8 tightwad 9 skinflint 10 cheapskate 12 moneygrubber

scrounge
3 beg, bum, tap 4 grub, hunt, loot 5 cadge, filch, mooch, pinch, steal, swipe, touch 6 forage, hustle, pilfer, snitch, sponge, thieve 7 finagle, solicit, wheedle 8 freeload 9 panhandle

scroungy
5 dirty, seedy 6 grubby, grungy, scruffy, scurvy, scuzzy, shabby, sleazy, sordid 7 squalid, unkempt 8 slovenly 10 slatternly

scrub
3 rub 4 buff, drop, wash 5 abort, brush, scour 6 cancel, mallee, maquis, polish 7 abandon, call off, cleanse, scratch 9 chaparral, eliminate

scrubby
4 drab, mean 5 dingy, dowdy, runty 6 paltry, ragged, shabby, shoddy 7 rundown, runtish, stunted 8 inferior 9 neglected 10 bedraggled, broken-down

scruff
4 nape, neck

scruffy
5 mangy, seedy, tacky 6 frowsy, frowzy, shabby, shaggy 7 run-down, scrubby, unkempt 8 slovenly, tattered 10 down-at-heel, threadbare

scrumptious
5 tasty, yummy 8 heavenly, luscious 9 ambrosial, delicious, succulent, toothsome 10 delectable, delightful 13 mouthwatering

scruple
3 bit, jot 4 balk, iota 5 demur, doubt, grain, qualm, scrap, shred, worry 7 concern, modicum 8 particle, question 9 hesitancy 11 compunction

scrupulous
5 exact, fussy 6 honest, minute, strict 7 careful, heedful, upright 8 critical, punctual, rigorous 9 honorable 10 fair-minded, fastidious, meticulous, principled, upstanding 11 painstaking, punctilious 12 conscionable 13 conscientious

scrutinize
4 comb, scan 5 audit, probe, study 6 peruse 7 analyze, canvass, dig into, dissect, examine, eyeball, inspect 8 look over, pore over 9 check over 11 contemplate, investigate

scrutiny
4 scan 5 audit 6 review, survey 7 perusal 8 analysis 10 inspection 11 examination 12 surveillance

scuba diver
7 frogman 8 aquanaut

scud
3 fly 4 race, rain, rush, sail, skim 5 brume, froth, scoot, speed, spray, spume 6 clouds, scurry, shower

scuff
6 scrape 7 scratch, shamble, shuffle

scuffle
3 row 4 fray 5 brawl, broil, fight, scrap, set-to 6 affray, fracas, hubbub, tussle 7 bobbery, grapple, shamble, shuffle, wrestle 10 roughhouse

scull
3 oar, row 4 boat 5 shell 6 propel

sculpt
3 hew 5 carve, shape 6 chisel

sculptor
American: 3 Lin (Maya) 4 Gabo (Naum), Taft (Lorado) 5 Andre (Carl), Koons (Jeff), Pratt (Bela), Segal (George), Serra (Richard), Smith (David), Story (William) 6 Aitkin (Robert), Calder (Alexander), French (Daniel Chester), Powers (Hiram), Zorach (William) 7 Borglum (Gutzon), Cornell (Joseph), Noguchi (Isamu) 8 Lachaise (Gaston), Lipchitz (Jacques), Nadelman (Elie), Nevelson (Louise) 9 Bourgeois

(Louise), Mestrovic (Ivan), Oldenburg (Claes), Remington (Frederic) **12** Saint-Gaudens (Augustus)
Czech: 6 Stursa (Jan)
Danish: 11 Thorvaldsen (Bertel), Thorwaldsen (Bertel)
Dutch: 6 Sluter (Claus)
English: 5 Moore (Henry), Watts (George) **7** Epstein (Jacob), Flaxman (John) **8** Hepworth (Barbara)
French: 3 Arp (Hans, Jean) **4** Bloc (André) **5** Rodin (Auguste) **6** Dubois (Paul), Houdon (Jean-Antoine) **7** Maillol (Aristide), Pevsner (Antoine) **9** Bartholdi (Frédéric-Auguste), Roubillac (Louis-François)
Greek: 5 Myron **7** Phidias **8** Pheidias **10** Polyclitus, Praxiteles **11** Polycleitus
Italian: 5 Leoni (Leone), Salvi (Niccolò, Nicola) **6** Canova (Antonio), Pisano (Andrea, Nino), Robbia (Andrea, Giovanni, Girolamo, Luca della) **7** Bernini (Gian Lorenzo), Cellini (Benvenuto), da Vinci (Leonardo), Orcagna, Quercia (Jacopo della) **8** Ghiberti (Lorenzo), Leonardo (da Vinci), Vittoria (Alessandro) **9** Donatello, Sansovino (Jacopo) **10** Verrocchio (Andrea del) **12** Michelangelo (Buonarroti)
Rhodian: 9 Polydorus
Romanian: 8 Brancusi (Constantin)
Russian: 7 Zadkine (Ossip)
Swedish: 6 Milles (Carl) **9** Oldenburg (Claes)
Swiss: 10 Giacometti (Alberto)

scum
5 algae, dregs, dross **6** refuse, vermin **8** riffraff

scummy
3 low **4** base, mean, vile **5** dirty, mucky, slimy **6** grubby, odious, sleazy, sordid **7** squalid **10** despicable **12** contemptible

scurrilous
4 foul **5** dirty, gross, nasty **6** coarse, filthy, vulgar **7** abusive, obscene, profane **8** indecent **9** insulting, offensive **10** outrageous **11** opprobrious **12** contumelious, vituperative

scurry
3 run **4** dart, dash **5** scoot, shoot **6** bustle **7** scamper, scuffle, scuttle

scurvy
see **scummy**

scut
4 tail

scuttlebutt
4 buzz, talk **5** rumor **6** gossip, report **7** chatter, hearsay **9** grapevine

Scylla
4 rock
counterpart: 9 Charybdis
father: 5 Nisus
lover: 5 Minos

scythe handle
5 snath **6** snathe

sea
4 blue, deep, main **5** brine, drink, ocean
Antarctica: 4 Ross **5** Davis **7** Weddell **8** Amundsen
Arctic: 4 Kara **7** Chukchi **8** Beaufort, Karskoye **9** Chuckchee, Norwegian **11** Chukotskoye **12** East Siberian
Asia-Europe: 5 Black
Asia Minor: 7 Icarian
Atlantic: 5 North **7** Weddell **9** Caribbean
Australia-Indonesia: 7 Arafura
Balkan Peninsula-Italy: 8 Adriatic
Bay of Bengal: 7 Andaman
China-Korea: 5 Huang, Hwang **6** Yellow
combining form: 3 mer **4** mari **5** pelag **6** pelago **7** thalass **8** thalasso
Corsica-Italy: 10 Tyrrhenian
Denmark-Norway: 9 Skagerrak
Denmark-Sweden: 8 Kattegat
England-Ireland: 5 Irish
Fiji: 4 Koro
France-Italy: 8 Ligurian
Greece: 5 Crete
Greece-Italy: 6 Ionian
Greece-Turkey: 6 Aegean **8** Thracian
Honshu: 6 Sagami
Indian Ocean: 5 Timor **7** Arabian
Indonesia: 4 Bali **6** Flores
inland: 3 Red **4** Aral **7** Caspian
Japan: 3 Suo **6** Inland
Malay Archipelago: 5 Banda
Mexico: 6 Cortés
Netherlands: 6 Wadden
North Atlantic: 8 Sargasso
Northern Europe: 6 Baltic, Ostsee **8** Suevicum
North Pacific: 6 Bering
off Scotland: 8 Hebrides
off Sweden: 5 Aland
Pacific: 4 Java **5** China, Coral **6** Maluku **7** Celebes, Eastern, Molucca, Solomon **9** East China **10** South China
Philippine: 4 Sulu
Russia: 5 White **7** Okhotsk
Russia-Ukraine: 4 Azov
South Pacific: 4 Ross **6** Tasman **8** Amundsen
Turkey: 7 Marmara **9** Propontis

West Pacific: **5** Ceram, Japan **8**
Bismarck **10** Philippine

sea anemone
  5 polyp

seabird
  see **bird aquatic**

seacoast
  5 beach, coast, shore **6** strand **8** littoral **9**
  shoreline

sea cucumber
  7 trepang **11** holothurian

sea dog
  see **sailor**

sea duck
  5 eider, scaup **6** scoter **9** merganser

sea eagle
  4 erne **6** osprey **8** fish hawk

seafarer
  3 tar **4** salt **6** sailor **7** jack-tar, mariner

seafood dish
  4 clam, crab **5** clams, squid **6** mussel,
  oyster, shrimp **7** lobster, mussels, oysters,
  scallop **8** calamari, scallops

seagoing
  8 maritime, nautical

seal
  5 sigil, stamp **6** cachet, signet **7** sticker
  female: 3 cow
  herd: 3 pod **5** patch
  young: 5 pup

sealant
  4 lute **5** caulk, grout **6** luting, mastic **8**
  caulking

sea lily
  7 crinoid

seam
  4 bond **5** joint, union **8** coupling, juncture
  10 connection

seaman
  see **sailor**

sea monster
  3 Orc **6** kraken **9** leviathan

seamount
  5 guyot

seamy
  5 dirty, rough, seedy **6** sordid **7** squalid
  12 disreputable

séance
  7 meeting, session, sitting
  holder: 6 medium

seaport
  Alaska: 6 Juneau **9** Anchorage
  Albania: 5 Vlorë **6** Durres, Valona
  Algeria: 4 Bône, Oran **6** Annaba
  Angola: 6 Lobito, Luanda **7** Cabinda **8**
  Benguela
  Argentina: 11 Buenos Aires, Mar del Plata
  Australia: 4 Eden **5** Bowen, Perth **6**
  Darwin, Hobart, Sydney **8** Brisbane **9**
  Melbourne **10** Wollongong
  Azores: 5 Horta
  Balearic: 5 Ibiza
  Belgium: 6 Ostend **7** Antwerp
  Benin: 7 Cotonou **9** Porto-Novo
  Black Sea: 5 Varna **6** Burgas, Odessa **9**
  Constanta
  Brazil: 3 Rio **4** Pará **5** Bahia, Belém,
  Natal **6** Recife, Santos **7** Vitoria **8**
  Salvador **9** Fortaleza **10** Pernambuco **11**
  Pôrto Alegre, São Salvador **12** Rio de
  Janeiro
  Bulgaria: 5 Varna **6** Burgas
  Cameroon: 6 Douala
  Canaries: 8 Arrecife **9** Las Palmas
  Chile: 5 Arica **8** Coquimbo **10** Valparaíso
  China: 4 Amoy **6** Dalian, Fuzhou, Lüshun,
  Xiamen **7** Foochow, Hsia-men, Qingdao,
  Tianjin **8** Shanghai, Tientsin, Tsingtao **9**
  Guangzhou, Zhenjiang **10** Chen-chiang,
  Port Arthur
  Colombia: 6 Lorica **9** Cartagena **12**
  Barranquilla
  Corsica: 5 Calvi **7** Ajaccio
  Costa Rica: 5 Limón **10** Puntarenas
  Crimean: 5 Kerch, Yalta **10** Sebastopol,
  Sevastopol
  Croatia: 5 Rieka, Split **6** Rijeka **9**
  Dubrovnik
  Cuba: 6 Havana **8** Matanzas, Santiago
  Cyprus: 9 Famagusta
  Denmark: 5 Arhus **6** Aarhus, Alborg **7**
  Aalborg **8** Elsinore **10** Copenhagen
  Ecuador: 9 Guayaquil
  Egypt: 4 Said **10** Alexandria
  England: 4 Hull **5** Dover **9** Liverpool **10**
  Portsmouth **11** Southampton
  Equatorial Guinea: 4 Bata
  Eritrea: 4 Aseb
  Estonia: 5 Pärnu **7** Tallinn
  Finland: 3 Abo **4** Kemi, Oulu, Pori, Vasa
  5 Hango, Kotka, Rauma, Turku, Vaasa **6**
  Vyborg
  Florida: 5 Miami, Tampa **9** Pensacola **12**
  Apalachicola, Jacksonville
  France: 4 Nice **5** Brest, Havre **6** Calais,
  Cannes, Toulon **7** Dunkirk, Le Havre **8**
  Bordeaux, Boulogne **9** Cherbourg,
  Dunkerque, Marseille **10** Marseilles
  French Polynesia: 7 Papeete
  Georgia: 8 Savannah **9** Brunswick

Georgia, Republic of: 4 Pot'i
Germany: 4 Kiel 5 Emden 6 Bremen,
Lübeck, Wismar 7 Hamburg, Rostock 8
Cuxhaven 11 Bremerhaven
Ghana: 4 Tema 5 Accra
Greece: 5 Pylos, Syros, Volos 7 Piraeus
Guatemala: 7 San José 10 Livingston
Haiti: 5 Cayes 10 Cap Haitien
Honduras: 7 La Ceiba 8 Trujillo
India: 3 Goa 4 Puri 5 Marud 6 Bombay,
Madras, Mumbai, Old Goa 7 Calicut,
Chennai 8 Calcutta 9 Jagannath 10
Trivandrum
Iran: 4 Jask 7 Bushehr
Iraq: 5 Basra
Ireland: 4 Cork 5 Sligo 6 Dingle, Dublin,
Galway, Tralee 8 Drogheda, Limerick 9
Waterford 10 Balbriggan
Israel: 4 Acre, Akko, Elat, Yafo 5 Accho,
Eilat, Haifa, Jaffa, Joppa 6 Ashdod 8
Ashqelon
Italy: 4 Bari 5 Anzio, Gaeta, Genoa 6
Naples, Pesaro, Rimini, Venice 7 Leghorn,
Livorno, Marsala, Messina, Rapallo,
Salerno, Taranto, Trieste 8 Brindisi,
Sorrento, Syracuse
Ivory Coast: 5 Tabou 7 Abidjan
Jamaica: 8 Kingston 10 Montego Bay
Japan: 4 Kobe 5 Kochi, Osaka, Rumoi,
Ujina, Uraga 6 Sasebo 7 Fukuoka 8
Nagasaki, Yokohama 9 Hiroshima
Jordan: 5 Aqaba, Elath 6 Aelana
Latvia: 4 Riga
Lebanon: 4 Tyre 5 Saida, Sidon 6 Beirut
7 Tripoli
Libya: 6 Tobruk 7 Tripoli 8 Benghazi
Lithuania: 5 Memel 6 Klaipeda
Madagascar: 8 Tamatave
Maine: 7 Belfast 8 Portland
Malaysia: 4 Miri, Weld 5 Pekan 6
Melaka, Pinang 7 Malacca 10 George
Town
Massachusetts: 6 Boston 9 Fall River
10 New Bedford
Mauritius: 9 Port Louis
Mediterranean: 4 Gaza, Oran 5 Genoa,
Haifa, Jaffa 6 Beirut, Naples, Venice 7
Algiers, Bizerte, Catania, Palermo, Piraeus,
Tripoli 8 Benghazi, Port Said 9 Barcelona,
Marseille 10 Alexandria, Marseilles
Mexico: 7 Tampico 8 Acapulco, Mazatlán,
Veracruz
Minorca: 5 Mahón
Moluccas: 5 Ambon
Montenegro: 5 Kotor
Morocco: 4 Safi, Salé 5 Ceuta 6 Agadir
7 Tangier, Tétouan 10 Casablanca

Mozambique: 5 Beira, Pemba 6 Amelia,
Maputo, Xai Xai 11 Porto Amelia
New Hampshire: 10 Portsmouth
New Zealand: 8 Auckland 10 Wellington
Nicaragua: 5 Brito
Nigeria: 5 Lagos 8 Harcourt
Niger mouth: 5 Bonny
North Korea: 4 Yuki 5 Nampo, Unggi 6
Wonsan
Norway: 4 Bodo, Moss 5 Vadso 6
Bergen, Tromso 9 Stavanger, Trondheim
11 Fredrikstad
Oman: 6 Masqat, Muscat
Pakistan: 5 Pasni 6 Gwadar 7 Karachi
Papua New Guinea: 3 Lea
Peru: 3 Ilo 4 Eten 5 Paita, Pisco 6
Callao
Philippines: 4 Cebu 5 Davao, Laoag 6
Aparri, Cavite, Iloilo, Manila 7 Legaspi 8
Tacloban 9 Zamboanga
Poland: 6 Danzig, Gdansk, Gdynia 7
Stettin 8 Szczecin
Portugal: 4 Faro 5 Porto 6 Oporto 7
Funchal
Puerto Rico: 5 Ponce 7 Arecibo, San
Juan 8 Mayagüez
Russia: 6 Vyborg 8 Murmansk 11
Kaliningrad, Vladivostok
Ryukyu: 4 Naha, Nawa
Sakhalin Island: 8 Korsakov
Saudi Arabia: 5 Jedda, Jidda, Yanbu,
Yenbo 6 Jeddah, Jiddah
Scotland: 3 Ayr 5 Leith, Leven 6 Dundee
7 Glasgow 8 Aberdeen
Sicily: 7 Catania, Marsala, Messina,
Palermo 8 Syracuse
Slovenia: 5 Kopar, Koper, Piran
Somalia: 7 Berbera 9 Mogadishu
South Africa: 5 Natal 6 Durban 8 Cape
Town
South Carolina: 8 Savannah 10
Charleston
South Korea: 5 Masan, Mokpo, Pusan 6
Inchon 7 Incheon, Masampo
Spain: 5 Cádiz, Gijón 6 Abdera, Málaga
8 Alicante 9 Algeciras, Barcelona,
Cartagena, Las Palmas
Sri Lanka: 7 Colombo 10 Batticaloa
Sumatra: 5 Medan 6 Padang 9 Banda
Aceh
Sweden: 4 Umea 5 Gavle, Lulea, Malmö,
Pitea, Ystad 8 Göteborg 9 Stockholm 10
Gothenburg 11 Helsingborg
Tanzania: 5 Lindi, Tanga 8 Zanzibar 11
Dar es Salaam
Thailand: 4 Trat 8 Bang Phra
Tunisia: 4 Sfax 5 Gabès 6 Sousse 7
Bizerta, Bizerte

Turkey: 4 Rize 5 Izmir, Sinop 6 Samsun, Smyrna 7 Antalya 8 Istanbul
Ukraine: 5 Kerch, Yalta 6 Odessa 7 Kherson
Vanuatu: 4 Vila 8 Port-Vila
Vietnam: 3 Hue 6 Da Nang 7 Tourane 8 Haiphong, Nha Trang
Virginia: 7 Norfolk 10 Portsmouth
Yemen: 4 Aden 5 Mocha

seaport capital
4 Aden, Apia, Dili, Lomé, Suva 5 Accra, Adana, Dakar, Lagos 6 Banjul, Belize, Bissau, Dublin, Havana, Kuwait, Lisbon, Maputo, Masqat, Muscat, Roseau 7 Algiers, Batavia, Colombo, Jakarta, Moresby, San Juan 8 Castries, Djakarta, Freetown, Hamilton, Helsinki, Honolulu, Kingston, Monrovia, Valletta 9 Mogadishu, Nuku'alofa, Porto-Novo, Reykjavík, Singapore 10 Bridgetown, Daressalem, Libreville, Mogadiscio, Paramaribo 11 Dar es Salaam, Port of Spain 12 Port-au-Prince

sear
3 dry 5 parch, singe 6 burn up, scorch, sizzle 7 shrivel 9 cauterize, dehydrate, desiccate

search
4 beat, comb, grub, hunt, scan, seek 5 chase, check, delve, frisk, grope, quest, rifle, scour 6 ferret, forage 7 fossick, hunting, manhunt, pursuit, ransack, rummage, run down 8 finecomb, scavenge, scout out 9 cast about, ferret out 10 scrutinize

searing
3 hot 5 harsh 6 severe 7 blazing, burning, intense 8 scathing 9 agonizing, scorching 10 blistering 12 excruciating

sea robber
5 rover 6 pirate 7 corsair 8 picaroon 9 buccaneer 10 freebooter

seasickness
6 nausea 8 mal de mer

season
3 fit 4 fall, term, time 5 spice, train, treat 6 autumn, harden, pepper, period, school, spring, summer, winter 7 prepare, toughen 8 marinade, marinate 9 acclimate 10 case-harden, discipline 11 acclimatize

seasonable
3 apt 6 timely 7 welcome 9 favorable, opportune, pertinent, well-timed 10 auspicious, convenient, propitious 11 appropriate

seasoned
6 inured, mature, tested, versed 7 adapted, matured, veteran 8 flavored, hardened 9 flavorful, practiced 10 acclimated, habituated 11 experienced 12 acclimatized, accomplished

seasoning
3 bay 4 dill, herb, mace, sage, salt 5 anise, basil, chili, clove, cumin, spice, thyme 6 cloves, fennel, garlic, ginger, nutmeg, pepper, savory 7 cayenne, chervil, mustard, oregano, paprika, parsley, saffron 8 allspice, cardamom, cinnamon, rosemary, tarragon, turmeric 9 condiment, coriander

seat
3 hub 4 base, beam, duff, rear, rest, rump 5 basis, chair, place, usher 6 behind, bottom, center, settee 7 fulcrum 8 backside, buttocks, derriere 9 fundament, posterior 10 foundation
church: 7 pew
on a camel or elephant: 6 howdah
upholstered: 9 banquette

sea urchin
7 echinus 8 echinoid

seaweed
4 kelp, nori, ulva 5 dulse, fucus, kombu 6 fucoid, wakame 8 sargasso 9 carrageen, Irish moss 12 bladder wrack

Sea Wolf, The
author: 6 London (Jack)
captain: 10 Wolf Larsen
ship: 5 Ghost

Sebastian
brother: 6 Alonso
sister: 5 Viola

secco
3 dry 8 painting, staccato

secede
4 quit 5 leave 8 separate, withdraw

seclude
4 hide 6 closet, immure, retire, screen 7 confine, enclose, isolate, shut off 8 cloister, separate, withdraw 9 sequester

secluded
6 hidden, remote 7 private, recluse, shut off 8 hermetic, isolated, screened, solitary 9 concealed, reclusive, withdrawn 10 cloistered, tucked away 11 out-of-the-way, quarantined, sequestered

seclusion

7 privacy 8 solitude 9 isolation 10 separation, withdrawal

second

4 wink 5 flash, jiffy, trice 6 moment 7 endorse, instant, support 9 twinkling

secondary

3 sub 6 lesser 7 derived 8 borrowed, inferior 9 resultant, tributary 10 collateral, derivative, subsequent 11 subordinate, subservient

second-class

6 common 8 déclassé, inferior, low-grade, mediocre

secondhand

4 used, worn 7 derived 8 borrowed 10 derivative

second-string

3 sub 6 backup 9 alternate 10 substitute

secrecy

7 silence, stealth 10 covertness, subterfuge 11 concealment, furtiveness

secret

5 sneak 6 arcane, closet, covert, hidden, occult 7 cryptic, furtive, obscure, sub-rosa 8 abstruse, backdoor, discreet, hermetic, hush-hush, stealthy 9 concealed, recondite 10 classified, restricted, undercover 11 clandestine, out-of-the-way, underhanded 12 confidential, hugger-mugger 13 surreptitious, under-the-table
combining form: 5 crypt, krypt 6 crypto, krypto

secret agent

3 spy 8 emissary

secretary

4 aide, desk 5 clerk 6 scribe 9 assistant 10 amanuensis, escritoire
king's: 10 chancellor

secrete

4 bury, emit, hide 5 cache, exude, plant, stash 6 screen 7 conceal, deposit, emanate

secretive

7 furtive 8 reticent, taciturn 10 backstairs, buttoned-up 11 tight-lipped 12 close-mouthed 13 unforthcoming

secretly

7 sub rosa 9 furtively 10 stealthily

secret society

3 KKK 4 tong 5 cabal, Mafia, Triad 6 Mau Mau, Yakuza 7 camorra 9 camarilla, Carbonari 10 Cosa Nostra, Freemasons, Ku Klux Klan

sect

4 cult 5 creed, party 7 faction 8 division, religion 12 denomination

sectarian

5 local 8 splinter 9 dissident, heretical, heterodox, parochial 10 provincial, schismatic, unorthodox 13 nonconformist

sectary

5 rebel 7 heretic 8 adherent, disciple, follower, partisan 9 dissenter, dissident 10 schismatic, separatist 13 nonconformist, revolutionary

section

3 cut 4 area, belt, part, zone 5 chunk, piece, slice, tract 6 member, moiety, parcel, region, sector, sphere 7 portion, quarter, segment 8 district, division, locality, precinct 11 subdivision

sector

4 area, zone 7 quarter, section 8 district, precinct 11 subdivision

secular

3 lay 7 earthly, profane, worldly 8 temporal, unsacred 11 nonclerical, terrestrial 12 nonreligious

secure

3 fix 4 bind, fast, firm, gain, land, lock, moor, nail, safe 5 catch, cinch, clamp, cover, fixed, guard, solid, sound, tried 6 anchor, assure, cement, clinch, defend, effect, ensure, fasten, insure, obtain, shield, stable 7 acquire, assured, capture, procure, protect, tie down 8 reliable, sanguine 9 confident, safeguard 10 batten down, bring about 11 established, impregnable

security

4 bail, bond, pawn 5 guard, token 6 pledge, safety, shield, surety 7 defense, earnest, warrant 8 guaranty, immunity, warranty 9 assurance, guarantee, safeguard, soundness, stability 10 collateral, protection, steadiness 13 certification

sedate

4 calm 5 grave, sober, staid 6 placid, proper, seemly, serene, steady 7 earnest, serious 8 composed, decorous, tranquil 9 collected, dignified, unruffled 10 sobersided 13 dispassionate, imperturbable

sedative
4 balm 6 downer, Valium 7 calmant, Librium, Miltown, Seconal 8 barbital, hyoscine, Nembutal 9 calmative 10 depressant 11 barbiturate 12 sleeping pill, tranquilizer

sedentary
4 lazy 6 seated 7 settled, sitting 8 inactive 10 stationary

sediment
4 lees, silt 5 dregs, dross 7 bottoms, deposit, grounds, heeltap, residue 8 residuum 9 settlings 11 precipitate
layer: 5 varve

sedition
4 coup 6 mutiny, putsch, revolt, strike 7 protest, treason 8 intrigue, uprising 9 coup d'état, rebellion 10 revolution 12 insurrection

seditious
8 disloyal, factious, mutinous 9 dissident, insurgent 10 rebellious, traitorous 11 treacherous

seduce
4 bait, coax, lure 5 decoy, tempt 6 allure, betray, delude, entice, entrap, lead on, ravish 7 corrupt, debauch, deceive 8 entrance, inveigle

seducer
4 roué, vamp 7 Don Juan, playboy 8 lothario 9 libertine

seduction
4 lure 8 conquest 9 siren song allurement, attraction, ravishment, temptation

seductive
5 siren 8 alluring, magnetic, tempting 9 beguiling 10 attractive, bewitching, enchanting 11 captivating

seductress
5 siren 7 Lorelei 9 temptress 11 femme fatale

sedulous
8 diligent, tireless 9 assiduous, laborious 10 persistent 11 industrious, persevering, unremitting

see
4 call, date, espy, gape, gaze, look, mark, peer, scan, view 5 grasp, sight, visit, watch 6 behold, come by, descry, divine, drop by, drop in, go with, look in, notice, stop by, stop in, take in 7 discern, examine, find out, glimpse, imagine, make out, observe, realize 8 conceive, consider, envisage, envision, perceive 9 apprehend, ascertain, determine, recognize, visualize 10 comprehend, scrutinize, understand

seed
3 sow 4 core, germ 5 brood, grain, issue, ovule, plant, spark, spawn 6 embryo, kernel, notion 7 concept, nucleus, progeny 8 children 9 offspring 11 descendants
aromatic: 6 fennel
coating: 5 testa 6 testae (plural)
covering: 4 aril
of a bean: 7 haricot
of a vine: 6 peanut
poisonous: 10 castor bean
vessel: 3 pod 5 fruit, pyxis 7 silicle, silique

seedcase
3 pod

seedy
5 dingy, faded, mangy, ratty, tired 6 droopy, frowsy, frowzy, shabby, used up, wilted 7 run-down, scruffy, squalid, unkempt, wilting 8 decaying, decrepit, drooping, flagging, inferior, slovenly, tattered 9 neglected, overgrown 10 bedraggled, down-at-heel, threadbare 12 disreputable

seek
3 try 4 fish, hunt, root 5 assay, delve, essay, offer, quest, sniff 6 pursue, strive 7 attempt, inquire, look for, request 8 endeavor, smell out 9 search for, search out, undertake

seem
3 act 4 look 5 imply 6 appear, behave 7 suggest 8 resemble

seemly
3 fit 6 decent, proper, suited 7 apropos, correct, fitting 8 becoming, decorous, suitable 9 befitting, congenial, congruous 10 compatible, conforming 11 appropriate, comme il faut

seep
4 drip, leak, ooze, weep 5 bleed, exude, leech, sweat 6 filter, strain 7 diffuse, dribble, trickle 8 transude 9 percolate

seer
5 augur, sibyl 6 oracle 7 diviner, prophet 8 foreseer, haruspex 9 predictor 10 forecaster, foreteller, soothsayer 11 clairvoyant, Nostradamus

seesaw
3 yaw 4 rock, veer 5 lurch, pitch, swing 6 teeter 7 bascule 9 alternate, flip-flop, fluctuate, oscillate 11 teeterboard

seethe
3 sop 4 boil, burn, foam, fret, fume, rage,

soak, stew **5** churn, erupt, froth, souse, steam, steep **6** bubble, drench, simmer, sizzle **7** bristle, ferment, parboil, smolder **8** saturate, smoulder, waterlog

see-through
5 clear **6** limpid **8** pellucid **11** translucent, transparent

segment
3 cut **4** part **5** piece **6** divide, member, moiety **7** portion, section **8** division, separate **10** categorize

sego
4 lily

segregate
6 enisle, select **7** isolate **8** separate **9** sequester **10** disconnect

segregation
9 apartheid, isolation **10** jim crowism, separatism **13** ghettoization

segue
7 proceed **8** continue **10** transition **11** progression

seidel
5 stoup **8** schooner

seine
3 net **5** trawl

Seine tributary
4 Oise **5** Marne, Yonne

seismologist
7 Richter (Charles)

seize
3 bag, nab **4** grab, take **5** annex, catch, clasp, grasp, usurp **6** abduct, arrest, clinch, clutch, kidnap, occupy, secure, snatch **7** capture, grapple, impound **8** arrogate, carry off **9** apprehend, sequester **10** commandeer, confiscate **11** appropriate, expropriate

seizure
3 fit **4** turn **5** spasm, spell, throe **6** access, attack, taking **7** capture **8** paroxysm, takeover **9** breakdown **10** annexation, convulsion, usurpation **12** confiscation

seldom
6 hardly, rarely **8** scarcely **10** hardly ever **12** infrequently, occasionally, sporadically

select
4 best, cull, fine, pick, rare **5** cream, elite, prime **6** choice, choose, chosen, culled, opt for, picked **7** favored, pick out **8**

screened, superior **9** exclusive, exquisite, preferred, recherché, single out

selection
6 choice **7** culling, excerpt, picking **8** choosing **10** assortment, preference

selective
5 fussy, picky **6** choosy **7** choosey, finicky **8** specific **10** discerning, particular, scrupulous **11** persnickety

Selene
4 Luna **6** Hecate **7** Artemis
beloved: 8 Endymion
brother: 6 Helios
father: 8 Hyperion
mother: 4 Thea

self
3 ego
combining form: 3 aut **4** auto

self-absorbed
4 smug **8** egoistic **9** conceited, egotistic **10** complacent, egocentric **11** egotistical, introverted **12** narcissistic **13** inner-directed

self-acting
9 automatic

self-assertive
4 bold **5** brash, pushy **6** cheeky **7** forward **8** cocksure, militant **9** audacious, obtrusive, officious **10** aggressive **11** impertinent, overweening **12** presumptuous

self-assurance
5 poise **6** aplomb **8** coolness **9** composure, sangfroid **10** confidence, equanimity **13** collectedness

self-assured
4 smug **6** poised **8** sanguine **9** confident

self-centered
9 conceited, egotistic **10** egocentric **11** egotistical **12** narcissistic

self-composed
4 calm **6** poised, serene **7** assured **9** collected, confident, possessed **10** controlled

self-confidence
5 poise **6** aplomb **9** assurance

self-confident
5 cocky **6** jaunty, poised **7** assured **8** sanguine

self-conscious
4 prim **5** stiff **6** formal, uneasy **7** awkward,

stilted, studied **8** affected, mannered **9** contrived, ill at ease **10** artificial

self-contained
6 closed, formal **7** built-in **8** composed, enclosed, reserved, reticent **9** exclusive **10** restrained **11** independent

self-control
7 balance, dignity, reserve **9** restraint, stability, willpower **10** abstinence, constraint, discipline, temperance **11** forbearance

self-defense art
4 judo **6** aikido, karate, kung fu **7** jujitsu **9** tai kwan do

self-destruction
7 suicide **8** felo-de-se, hara-kiri

self-discipline
4 will **8** stoicism **9** willpower **10** abstinence

self-educated
12 autodidactic

self-effacing
3 shy **5** timid **6** modest **7** bashful **8** retiring, sheepish **9** diffident, unassured **11** unassertive

self-esteem
5 pride **6** vanity **7** conceit, dignity, egotism **10** narcissism **11** amour propre

self-evident
5 clear, plain **6** patent **7** obvious **8** manifest, palpable **10** prima facie, undeniable **12** demonstrable, unmistakable

self-explanatory
5 clear, plain **7** evident, obvious **8** manifest **11** perspicuous, transparent

self-governing
7 popular **9** sovereign **10** autonomous, democratic

self-importance
3 ego **5** pride **6** egoism, hubris **7** conceit, egotism **9** arrogance, pomposity, vainglory

self-important
4 smug, vain **6** lordly **7** bloated, haughty, pompous **8** arrogant **9** conceited, egotistic **10** pontifical **11** magisterial, pretentious

self-indulgent
9 libertine, sybaritic **10** hedonistic

self-interest
6 egoism

selfish
6 stingy **8** egoistic **9** egotistic **10** egocentric, ungenerous **11** egomaniacal **12** self-centered **13** self-indulgent

selfless
8 generous **10** altruistic, benevolent, charitable

self-love
6 egoism, vanity **7** conceit, egotism **8** vainness **9** vainglory **10** narcissism **11** amour propre **13** conceitedness

self-possessed
4 calm **6** poised, serene **8** composed, equable, sanguine **9** collected, unruffled **11** unflappable **13** imperturbable

self-proclaimed
8 so-called **9** soi-disant **10** self-styled

Self-Reliance author
7 Emerson (Ralph Waldo)

self-respect
5 pride **7** dignity **11** amour propre

self-restraint
8 chastity, sobriety **9** willpower **10** abnegation, abstention, abstinence, continence, discipline **11** forbearance

self-righteous
5 pious **7** canting, preachy **8** unctuous **9** pharisaic **10** complacent, goody-goody **11** pharisaical **12** hypocritical, pecksniffian **13** sanctimonious

self-sacrificing
8 generous, selfless **9** unselfish

self-satisfied
4 smug **8** priggish **10** complacent

self-seeking
6 greedy **7** selfish **8** egoistic **9** egotistic **10** egocentric **11** egotistical

self-serving
see **self-seeking**

self-starter
7 hustler **8** go-getter

self-styled
7 nominal, would-be **8** so-called **9** soi-disant

self-taught
12 autodidactic

sell
4 hawk, vend **5** trade **6** barter, deal in, hustle, market, peddle, retail, unload **7** auction **8** exchange

sell out
4 dump, move 6 betray, turn in, unload 7 deceive 8 inform on 11 double-cross

selvage, selvedge
3 hem 4 edge 6 border

semblance
3 air 4 face, look, mask, pose, show, veil 5 front, guise, image 6 aspect, facade, simile, veneer 7 analogy, feeling, modicum 8 affinity, disguise, likeness, pretense 10 apparition, appearance, comparison, false front, masquerade, similarity, similitude, simulacrum 11 countenance

Semele
father: 6 Cadmus
mother: 8 Harmonia
sister: 3 Ino 5 Agave 7 Autonoë
son: 7 Bacchus 8 Dionysus

semi
3 rig 4 demi, half, hemi 5 truck 6 partly

seminar
5 forum 8 colloquy 10 colloquium, conference, roundtable

Seminole chief
7 Osceola

Semiramis
husband: 5 Ninus
kingdom: 7 Babylon

Semite
3 Jew 4 Arab 6 Hebrew 7 Moabite 8 Akkadian, Assyrian 9 Canaanite 10 Babylonian, Phoenician

Senapo
daughter: 8 Clorinda
kingdom: 8 Ethiopia

senate
7 chamber, council 8 assembly 11 legislature

senator
5 solon 8 lawmaker 10 legislator

send
4 mail, post, ship 5 relay, remit, route 6 commit, export, launch 7 address, advance, airmail, consign, forward, traject 8 dispatch, transmit
back: 6 remand

Sendak book
17 In the Night Kitchen 21 Where the Wild Things Are

send in
6 submit

send-up
5 roast, spoof 6 parody, satire 7 lampoon, takeoff 9 burlesque 10 caricature, pasquinade

Senegal
capital: 5 Dakar
enclave: 6 Gambia
ethnic group: 5 Wolof 6 Fulani 7 Malinke
language: 6 French
monetary unit: 5 franc
neighbor: 4 Mali 6 Guinea 10 Mauritania 12 Guinea-Bissau
river: 6 Gambia 7 Senegal

senescence
6 old age 8 caducity 11 elderliness, senectitude

senior
5 doyen, elder, older, prior 7 ancient, doyenne, oldster 8 higher-up, old-timer, superior 10 golden-ager

Sennacherib
domain: 7 Assyria
father: 6 Sargon
kingdom: 7 Assyria
slayer, son: 8 Sharezer 11 Adrammelech

sensation
4 bomb 6 marvel, tingle, wonder 7 feeling, miracle, prodigy, stunner 8 response 9 bombshell 10 impression, perception, phenomenon 13 consciousness

sensational
3 hot 5 boffo, juicy, lurid 6 purple, vulgar 7 tabloid 8 dramatic, exciting, fabulous, glorious, slambang, smashing, stunning 9 hunky-dory, marvelous, thrilling 10 astounding, impressive, incredible, remarkable, scandalous 11 astonishing, extravagant, outstanding, spectacular 12 electrifying

sense
3 wit 4 feel 5 sight, smell, taste, touch 6 divine, intuit, pick up 7 believe, discern, feeling, hearing, meaning, message, realize 8 consider, judgment, perceive, prudence 9 awareness, foresight, intuition 10 anticipate, cognizance, discretion, perception 12 intelligence, significance 13 comprehension, consciousness, understanding
sixth: 3 ESP

Sense and Sensibility author
6 Austen (Jane)

senseless
4 cold, numb 5 silly 6 absurd, numbed, simple, stupid 7 fatuous, foolish, idiotic,

moronic, trivial, witless **8** benumbed, comatose, deadened, mindless **9** brainless, pointless **10** irrational **11** meaningless, purposeless, unconscious

senselessness
5 folly **7** inanity **8** insanity **9** absurdity, stupidity **12** illogicality

sense organ
3 ear, eye **4** nose, skin **6** tongue **8** receptor

sensibility
5 taste **7** emotion, feeling, insight **8** judgment, keenness **9** affection, awareness, sensation **11** discernment, penetration **12** appreciation

sensible
4 sage, sane, wise **5** solid, sound **6** astute, shrewd **7** logical, prudent, sapient **8** rational **9** judicious, objective, sagacious **10** reasonable

sensitive
4 keen, sore **5** aware, prone **6** liable, tender, touchy, tricky **7** feeling, nervous **8** delicate, sensible, sentient, ticklish **9** emotional **10** high-strung, perceptive, precarious, responsive **11** susceptible **13** understanding

sensitive plant
6 mimosa
family: 3 pea

sensual
4 lush **6** animal, carnal, earthy **7** fleshly, mundane, worldly **8** temporal **9** epicurean, luxurious, sybaritic **10** hedonistic, voluptuous **11** irreligious, unspiritual

sensuality
4 lust **6** desire, luxury **7** lechery, license **8** hedonism, lewdness, pleasure **9** carnality, depravity, eroticism, prurience **10** debauchery, degeneracy, dissipation, immorality, indulgence, perversion, profligacy, sybaritism **12** incontinence **13** dissoluteness, gratification, salaciousness

sensuous
4 lush **6** carnal **7** fleshly **8** luscious **9** epicurean, luxurious, sybaritic **10** hedonistic, voluptuous **13** self-indulgent

sentence
3 rap **4** damn, doom **5** blame, judge **6** dictum, ordain, punish **7** adjudge, condemn, convict, verdict **8** decision, denounce, judgment, penalize **10** adjudicate, punishment

sententious
5 crisp, pithy, terse **7** concise, piquant, pointed **8** eloquent, pregnant, succinct **10** aphoristic, expressive, meaningful, moralistic, moralizing

sentient
5 alert, aware, savvy **7** knowing **8** sensible **9** attentive, cognizant, conscious, receptive, sensitive **10** conversant, discerning, perceptive, percipient, responsive **12** appreciative

sentiment
4 view **6** belief **7** emotion, feeling, leaning, opinion, passion, posture **8** penchant, position, tendency **9** affection, inclining, sensation **10** conception, conviction, partiality, persuasion, propensity **11** disposition, inclination, sensibility

sentimental
4 soft **5** corny, gooey, gushy, mushy, sappy, soupy, sweet **6** dreamy, drippy, slushy, sticky, sugary, syrupy, tender **7** cloying, gushing, insipid, maudlin, mawkish **8** bathetic, effusive, romantic **9** misty-eyed, nostalgic, schmaltzy **10** idealistic, lovey-dovey, moonstruck, namby-pamby, saccharine, soft-boiled **11** tear-jerking **12** affectionate

sentimentality
4 mush **8** schmaltz

sentinel
see **sentry**

sentry
5 guard, watch **6** picket **7** lookout **8** sentinel, watchman

separate
4 comb, only, part, sift, sole, sort **5** apart, sever, split **6** cut off, detach, divide, single, sunder, unique, winnow **7** asunder, disjoin, diverse, divided, divorce, isolate, several, split up, unravel, various **8** alienate, detached, discrete, disjoint, disperse, distinct, insulate, isolated, solitary, splinter, uncouple **9** different, divergent, extricate, segregate, sequester **11** compartment, distinctive, distinguish, independent, unconnected **12** disconnected, discriminate **13** differentiate

separation
3 gap **4** rift **5** break, split **6** schism **7** breakup, divorce, parting, rupture, split-up **8** disunion, disunity, division **9** apartheid, dichotomy, partition **11** disjunction, dissolution, segregation **12** dissociation, estrangement **13** disconnection, sequestration

separatism
  9 apartheid 11 segregation

separatist
  10 schismatic 12 secessionist

sepia
  3 ink 5 brown, umber 6 sienna

sepulchral
  4 grim 5 bleak, grave 6 dismal, gloomy,
  solemn, somber 7 doleful, macabre 8
  funereal, ghoulish, mortuary 9 tenebrous

sepulchre
  4 tomb 5 grave, vault 9 mausoleum

sequel
  3 end 5 close 6 effect, ending, finish,
  result, upshot 7 closing, outcome 8
  epilogue 9 aftermath 10 succession 11
  aftereffect, consequence, development,
  eventuality, progression, termination 12
  continuation

sequence
  3 row, run, set 4 flow 5 chain, order, train
  6 course, series, string 8 disposal,
  ordering 9 placement 10 procession,
  succession 11 arrangement, disposition,
  progression 12 distribution

sequential
  6 serial 9 succedent 10 continuous,
  succeeding, successive 11 consecutive
  12 successional 13 chronological

sequester
  4 hide, take 5 annex, seize 6 attach, cut
  off, enisle 7 impound, isolate, preempt,
  seclude, secrete 8 accroach, arrogate,
  cloister, close off, insulate, separate, set
  apart, withdraw 9 segregate 10
  commandeer, confiscate, dispossess 11
  appropriate, expropriate

sequoia
  7 big tree, redwood 12 coast redwood

seraglio
  5 harem

serape
  5 shawl

seraph
  5 angel 8 guardian 9 messenger

seraphic
  4 pure 7 angelic, sublime 8 beatific,
  cherubic, ethereal

Serbia and Montenegro
  capital: 8 Belgrade

city: 3 Bar 5 Kotar, Tivat 7 Novi Sad,
  Pancevo 9 Podgorica 11 Pristinauzi
monetary unit: 4 euro 5 dinar
neighbor: 6 Bosnia, Kosovo 7 Albania,
  Croatia, Hungary, Romania 8 Bulgaria 9
  Macedonia
part of: 7 Balkans
peninsula: 6 Balkan
province: 9 Vojvodina
province, former: 6 Kosovo
river: 4 Sava 6 Danube
sea: 8 Adriatic

sere
  3 dry 5 dried 7 parched, thirsty 8 withered
  9 shriveled, unwatered

serenade
  7 lullaby 8 shivaree 9 charivari

serene
  4 calm 5 quiet, still 6 limpid, placid,
  poised, sedate 7 halcyon 8 composed,
  tranquil 9 unruffled 10 untroubled

serenity
  4 calm 5 peace 8 calmness, quietude 9
  composure, placidity, stillness 10
  equanimity 11 contentment, tranquility 12
  peacefulness, tranquillity

serf
  4 esne, peon 5 churl, helot, slave 6 thrall
  7 bondman, villein
  freeborn: 7 colonus

serial
  10 sequential, successive 11 consecutive,
  installment

series
  3 row, run, set 4 list, tier 5 chain, range,
  scale, train 6 catena, column, parade,
  sequel, string 8 sequence 9 cavalcade,
  gradation 10 procession, succession 11
  progression 12 continuation

serious
  4 grim, hard 5 grave, heavy, major, sober,
  staid, stern, tough 6 intent, sedate, severe,
  solemn, somber, sombre, steady 7
  austere, earnest, intense, pensive, sincere,
  unfunny, weighty 8 funereal, menacing,
  resolute, sobering 9 difficult, humorless,
  important, laborious, strenuous, unamusing
  10 determined, formidable, meditative, no-
  nonsense, poker-faced, purposeful,
  reflective, sobersided, thoughtful,
  unhumorous 11 significant, threatening 12
  businesslike 13 contemplative

sermon
  6 homily, speech, tirade 7 address, lecture,

oration 8 harangue 9 preaching 10
preachment 11 exhortation

sermonize

5 orate 6 dilate, exhort, preach 7 dissert,
lecture 8 moralize 9 discourse, expatiate,
preachify 10 dissertate, evangelize 11
pontificate

serpent

5 fiend, Satan, snake
fabled: 8 basilisk
mythical: 10 cockatrice
sound: 4 hiss

serpentine

4 rock, wily 5 snaky 7 cunning, devious,
mineral, sinuous, winding 8 flexuous,
tempting, tortuous 9 snakelike 10
circuitous, convoluted, meandering

serrated

7 notched, toothed 8 saw-edged, sawtooth
10 saw-toothed 11 denticulate

servant

4 maid, peon 5 slave, valet 6 butler,
flunky, helper, lackey, menial 7 famulus,
footman 8 domestic, handmaid, hireling,
houseboy 9 attendant 11 chamberlain,
chambermaid
India: 4 syce
kitchen: 8 scullion
Wodehouse: 6 Jeeves

serve

3 act, fit, use 4 help, make, play, suit, work
5 nurse, spend, treat 6 foster, handle, wait
on 7 advance, benefit, care for, present,
promote, provide, satisfy, suffice, work for
8 deal with, function 9 encourage, officiate
10 minister to

service

3 use 4 duty, help, rite 5 favor 6 employ,
repair, ritual 7 account, benefit, fitness,
liturgy 8 ceremony, courtesy, disposal,
maintain 10 active duty, assistance,
ceremonial, observance, usefulness 11
maintenance 12 dispensation

serviceable

5 handy, utile 6 decent, usable, useful 7
durable, helpful 8 adequate, suitable 9
efficient, practical 10 acceptable,
beneficial, convenient, dependable,
functional 11 utilitarian 12 satisfactory

servile

6 abject, craven, humble, menial 7
fawning, slavish 8 obedient, obeisant 9
groveling 10 obsequious, submissive 11
subservient

servility

7 bondage, helotry, peonage, serfdom,
slavery 9 thralldom 11 enslavement

serving

6 dollop 7 helping, portion

servitude

5 labor 6 corvée, thrall 7 bondage, helotry,
peonage, serfdom, slavery 9 captivity,
indenture, thralldom, villenage 10
subjection 11 enslavement 12
enthrallment

sesame

3 til
grass: 4 gama

sessile

5 fixed 6 rooted 7 settled 8 attached 11
established

session

6 assize, séance 7 meeting, sitting

set

3 aim, dry, fix, gel, lay, lot, put 4 firm, jell 5
array, batch, bunch, fixed, group, place, put
on, ready, rigid, scene 6 belong, harden,
impose, placed, rooted, secure, stated 7
arrange, certain, cluster, congeal, decided,
deposit, dictate, jellify, lay down, located,
prepare, scenery, situate, specify, station 8
prepared, resolute, resolved, situated,
solidify, specific 9 confirmed, designate,
establish, prescribe, specified, stipulate,
tenacious 10 assortment, determined,
gelatinize, inflexible, positioned, prescribed,
stipulated 11 established, mise-en-scène
a gem: 6 collet
right: 7 redress

set aside

4 void 5 annul 7 discard, dismiss, reserve
8 overrule

set back

4 mire 5 delay 6 detain, hang up, hinder,
retard, slow up

setback

5 check, hitch 6 defeat, rebuff 7 reverse 8
obstacle, reversal 9 hindrance 10
impediment, regression

set down

4 land 5 light, perch, roost 6 alight, record
9 establish, touch down

set fire to

4 burn 6 ignite 7 emblaze, inflame 8
enkindle, touch off

set forth
4 cite 5 state 6 adduce, affirm, allege, avouch, depart, embark, launch, submit 7 advance, declare, express, present, proffer, propose, take off 8 proclaim, spell out 9 introduce 10 account for

set free
5 loose 6 redeem, rescue, unbind 7 deliver, manumit, unchain, unloose 8 liberate, unloosen 9 unshackle 10 emancipate

Seth
brother: 4 Abel, Cain
father: 4 Adam
mother: 3 Eve
son: 4 Enos

set out
5 start 6 embark, intend 7 take off 9 undertake

Set's victim
6 Osiris

settee
4 seat, sofa 5 bench, divan 6 lounge

setting
5 scene 7 context, scenery 8 ambience 10 background 11 mise-en-scène
for a stone: 4 ouch

settle
3 fix, lay, pay, put 4 calm 5 allay, judge, light, pay up, perch, place, quiet, roost, still 6 alight, clinch, decide, soothe, square, verify, wind up 7 arrange, compose, confirm, dispose, install, mediate, resolve, satisfy, work out 8 colonize, conclude, ensconce, nail down 9 determine, discharge, establish, negotiate, reconcile, touch down

settlement
4 deal 6 colony, hamlet 7 outpost, quietus, village 8 decision 9 agreement 10 conclusion, encampment, habitation, resolution 11 arrangement 13 determination
Israeli: 6 moshav

settler
7 pioneer 8 colonist, squatter 9 colonizer

set-to
3 row 4 fray, spat 5 brawl, broil, brush, fight, run-in, scrap 6 affray, blowup, fracas, tussle 7 dispute, quarrel, rhubarb, scuffle 8 argument, skirmish 9 encounter 10 falling-out 11 altercation

set up
4 open 5 erect, found, raise, start 6 create, launch 7 arrange, install 8 assemble, generate, initiate, organize 9 construct, establish, institute, originate

setup
4 plan 5 array, trick 6 layout, scheme, shoo-in 7 pattern, project, setting 8 assembly, carriage, position, slam dunk 9 alignment, apparatus, structure, sure thing 11 arrangement, preparation 12 constitution

seven
combining form: 4 hept, sept 5 hepta, septi
group of: 6 heptad 8 hebdomad

seventeenth century
8 seicento

sever
3 cut, lop 4 part, rend 5 slice, split 6 cleave, cut off, detach, divide, sunder 7 break up, divorce 8 amputate, disjoint, separate

several
4 a few, many, some 6 divers, plural, sundry, varied 7 certain, diverse, various 8 assorted, discrete, distinct, manifold, numerous, separate, specific 9 different 10 respective

severe
4 dour, grim, hard 5 acute, grave, harsh, heavy, rigid, sober, stern, tough 6 bitter, brutal, rugged, strict 7 arduous, ascetic, austere, extreme, intense, onerous, serious, weighty 8 exacting, pitiless, rigorous 9 demanding, difficult, laborious, strenuous, stringent, unbending 10 forbidding, implacable, inflexible, iron-willed, oppressive, unyielding 11 disciplined, heavy-handed

severity
5 rigor 7 gravity, urgency 8 exigency, grimness, obduracy, rigidity 9 austerity, harshness, intensity, plainness, privation, restraint, spareness, starkness, sternness 10 strictness, stringency 11 seriousness

sew
4 darn, mend, seam 5 baste 6 needle, stitch, suture

sewer
4 duct 5 ditch, drain 6 tailor 7 cesspit, conduit 8 cesspool, stitcher

sewing
aid: 7 thimble
case: 4 etui

kit: 9 housewife

sewing-machine inventor
4 Howe (Elias)

sexless
6 neuter 7 epicene 8 neutered

sex manual
9 Kama-sutra

sexton
6 deacon 9 custodian, sacristan

sexual
4 blue, lewd, racy 6 carnal, erotic, ribald, risqué, smutty 7 obscene 8 venereal 9 salacious 12 pornographic

sexual desire
4 eros, lust 6 libido

sexy
4 blue, racy 5 bawdy, spicy 6 erotic, purple, ribald, risqué, steamy, sultry 7 naughty 8 alluring, off-color, sensuous 9 appealing, salacious, seductive 10 attractive, suggestive

Seychelles
capital: 8 Victoria
island: 4 Mahé 7 La Digue, Praslin
language: 6 Creole, French
monetary unit: 5 rupee

Sganarelle
brother: 6 Ariste
daughter: 7 Lucinde
ward: 7 Leonore 8 Isabelle
wife: 7 Martine

shabby
5 dingy, dowdy, faded, mangy, ratty, seedy, sorry, tacky, tired 6 frayed, scurvy, shoddy, sleazy, sordid 7 outworn, rickety, run-down, scrubby, scruffy, squalid, worn-out 8 beggarly, decaying, decrepit, dog-eared, tattered 9 miserable, moth-eaten, neglected, worm-eaten 10 bedraggled, down-at-heel, ramshackle, threadbare 11 dilapidated 12 deteriorated, disreputable 13 deteriorating, unrespectable

shack
3 cot, hut 4 camp, shed 5 cabin, hovel, lodge 6 shanty 7 cottage

shackle
4 gyve 5 bilbo, chain, leash, strap 6 fetter, hobble, hog-tie, impede, pinion, secure 7 enchain, leg-iron, manacle, trammel 8 handcuff 9 entrammel

shad
7 clupeid, herring

shade
3 hue 4 cast, tint, tone, veil 5 ghost, tinge, trace, umbra 6 awning, darken, nuance, screen 7 dimness, eclipse, phantom, shelter, specter, spectre, umbrage 8 darkness, penumbra, phantasm, tincture 9 gradation, intensity, obscurity 10 apparition 11 distinction

shadow
3 dim, dog, tag 4 haze, hint, tail 5 cloud, shade, tinge, touch, trace, trail, umbra 6 screen, spirit, wraith 7 eidolon, obscure, phantom, specter, umbrage, vestige 8 overcast, penumbra, phantasm, revenant, tincture 9 inumbrate, overcloud, suspicion 10 apparition, intimation, suggestion 11 adumbration

shadowy
3 dim 4 dark 5 dusky, faint, murky, vague 6 gloomy, shaded 7 ghostly, obscure 9 tenebrous 10 indistinct

shady
4 dark 5 bosky, dusky, fishy 6 purple, shabby, shoddy 7 clouded, dubious, suspect 8 doubtful, screened 9 equivocal, sheltered, uncertain 10 suggestive, suspicious, umbrageous, unreliable 12 disreputable

Shaffer play
5 Equus 7 Amadeus

shaft
3 jab, ray, rod 4 axle, barb, beam, dart, pole, stem 5 arrow, lance, shoot, spear, stalk, thill 6 thrust 7 chimney, spindle 8 short end

shag
3 nap, rug 4 pile 5 chase, fetch 7 thicket, tobacco 9 cormorant

shaggy
5 bushy 7 unkempt 8 uncombed

shake
3 jar, jog, rid 4 deal, jerk, jolt, lose, rock, roil, sway 5 avoid, churn, daunt, elude, jiffy, quail, quake, shock, upset, waver, worry 6 escape, frappe, jiggle, joggle, outwit, quaver, quiver, rattle, ruffle, shimmy, shiver, stir up, tremor 7 agitate, chatter, disturb, perturb, shingle, shudder, temblor, tremble, unnerve, vibrate 8 brandish, convulse, throw off, unsettle 9 oscillate, palpitate 10 earthquake

shake down
5 frisk, gouge, screw, wrest, wring 6 coerce, extort, fleece, search 7 squeeze 9 blackmail

shakedown

3 bed 4 test 5 dance, trial 6 pallet,
search, tryout 7 pursuit, testing 8 exaction
9 blackmail, extortion 10 inspection

Shakers leader

3 Lee (Ann) 9 Mother Ann

Shakespearean actor

4 Kean (Edmund) 5 Booth (Edwin), Dench
(Judi), Evans (Maurice), Terry (Ellen) 6
Irving (Henry) 7 Branagh (Kenneth),
Burbage (Richard), Garrick (David),
Gielgud (John), Olivier (Laurence), Siddons
(Sarah) 8 Ashcroft (Peggy), Macready
(William), Redgrave (Michael), Scofield
(Paul) 9 Barrymore (Ethel, John, Lionel,
Maurice) 10 Richardson (Ralph)

Shakespeare, William

mother: 9 Mary Arden
play: 6 Hamlet, Henry V 7 Henry IV,
Henry VI, Macbeth, Othello, Tempest (The)
8 King John, King Lear, Pericles 9
Cymbeline, Henry VIII, Richard II 10
Coriolanus, Richard III 11 As You Like It,
Winter's Tale (The) 12 Julius Caesar,
Twelfth Night 13 Timon of Athens 14
Comedy of Errors (The), Romeo and Juliet
16 Love's Labour's Lost, Merchant of
Venice (The), Taming of the Shrew (The)
17 Measure for Measure 18 Antony and
Cleopatra 19 Much Ado About Nothing 20
All's Well That Ends Well, Midsummer
Night's Dream (A)
theater: 5 Globe
wife: 12 Anne Hathaway

shaky

4 weak 6 infirm, unsure, wobbly 7 aquiver,
dubious, jittery, quaking, rackety, rickety,
suspect, trembly, unsound 8 doubtful,
insecure, rachitic, unstable, unsteady,
wavering 9 quivering, tottering, trembling,
tremulous, uncertain, unsettled 10
indecisive, precarious, rattletrap, unreliable
11 problematic, vacillating

shale

4 rock 5 slate

shallot

4 herb 5 onion 10 green onion

shallow

4 idle, vain 5 petty, shoal 7 cursory,
sketchy, trivial 8 trifling 9 depthless,
frivolous 11 perfunctory, superficial

shallows

6 lagoon, shoals

Shallum

father: 5 Shaul, Zadok 6 Jabesh, Josiah,
Sismai, Tikvah 8 Colhozeh, Naphtali 9
Hallohesh
mother: 6 Bilhah
nephew: 8 Jeremiah
slayer: 7 Menahem
son: 6 Mibsam 7 Hilkiah 8 Maaseiah
victim: 9 Zechariah

shalom

5 peace

sham

3 act, ape 4 fake, hoax, mock 5 bluff,
bogus, bunco, cheat, dummy, false, farce,
feign, fraud, phony, put on, spoof 6 deceit,
ersatz, facade, fakery, forged, invent,
pseudo 7 assumed, feigned, forgery,
imitate, mislead, mockery, pretend 8
affected, flimflam, simulate, spurious,
travesty 9 brummagem, burlesque,
deception, hypocrisy, imitation, imposture,
pinchbeck, simulated 10 artificial,
caricature, false front, fictitious, fraudulent,
sanctimony, substitute 11 counterfeit,
make-believe 12 pecksniffery
combining form: 5 pseud 6 pseudo

shaman

6 healer, priest, wizard 7 diviner 8
conjurer, conjuror, magician, sorcerer 9
enchanter, priestess 10 high priest,
soothsayer 11 faith healer, necromancer,
thaumaturge, witch doctor

Shamash

6 sun-god
father: 3 Sin
sister: 6 Ishtar
wife: 3 Aya

shamble

see **shuffle**

shambles

4 mess 5 chaos 6 jumble, muddle 8
disarray, disorder, wreckage 9 confusion

shame

4 pity 5 abash, guilt, odium 6 infamy,
stigma 7 chagrin, mortify, obloquy,
remorse, scandal 8 disgrace, dishonor,
ignominy 9 disrepute, embarrass,
humiliate, ill repute 11 opprobrium 12
humiliation 12 self-reproach 13
embarrassment, mortification

shamefaced

7 abashed 8 blushing, sheepish 9
mortified 10 humiliated 11 crestfallen,
embarrassed

shameless

6 arrant, brazen, wanton 7 blatant,

immoral **8** depraved, flagrant, immodest, impudent **9** abandoned, bald-faced, barefaced, dissolute, unabashed **10** outrageous, profligate, unblushing **11** brazen-faced, disgraceful **12** presumptuous

Shammah
brother: 5 David
father: 4 Agee **5** Jesse, Reuel
grandfather: 4 Esau **7** Ishmael
son: 7 Jonadab **8** Jonathan

Shammua
father: 5 David, Galal **6** Bilgah, Zaccur
mother: 9 Bathsheba
son: 4 Abda

shamus
3 cop **4** dick, tail **6** copper, shadow, sleuth **7** gumshoe **8** flatfoot, sherlock **9** constable, detective, operative, policeman **10** private eye **12** investigator **13** police officer

shanghai
6 abduct, hijack, kidnap

Shangri-la
5 Tibet **6** utopia **7** arcadia **8** paradise **9** Cockaigne, fairyland **10** wonderland

shank
3 leg **4** shin, stem **5** stalk, tibia

shanty
3 cot, hut **4** camp, shed **5** cabin, hovel, lodge, shack **7** cottage

shape
3 fit **4** case, cast, form, mold, plan, trim **5** forge, frame, state, whack **6** aspect, devise, fettle, figure, kilter, repair, sculpt, tailor, work up **7** contour, fitness, outline, pattern, profile **8** assemble **9** condition, construct, fabricate, semblance **10** appearance, silhouette **12** conformation **13** configuration
combining form: 5 morph **6** morpho

shapeable
6 pliant, supple **7** ductile, plastic, pliable **8** flexible **9** tractable

shapeless
8 inchoate, unformed **9** amorphous

shapely
4 trim **5** buxom **9** Junoesque **10** curvaceous, statuesque, well-turned **11** clean-limbed

shard
4 chip **5** chunk, scale, scrap, shell **6** sliver **7** elytron **8** carapace, fragment

share
3 cut, lot **4** part **5** chunk, claim, quota, slice, stake **6** divide, parcel, ration **7** dole out, give out, helping, partake, portion, prorate, quantum **8** dispense, fraction, interest, quotient **9** allotment, allowance, apportion **10** experience, percentage, proportion **11** participate

shared
5 joint **6** common, mutual, public **8** communal, conjoint, conjunct **9** concerted **10** collective **11** cooperative

Sharezer
father, victim: 11 Sennacherib

shark
5 cheat **8** swindler
kind: 4 mako, sand, tope **5** nurse, tiger **7** basking, dogfish, leopard **8** mackerel, man-eater, thresher **9** porbeagle **10** great white, hammerhead
skin: 8 shagreen

sharp
3 sly **4** acid, keen, tony, trig **5** acrid, acute, alert, canny, crisp, honed, quick, slick, smart, swank **6** biting, bitter, brainy, bright, clever, jagged, nimble, peaked, shrewd, shrill, snappy **7** caustic, dashing, intense, pointed, prickly, stylish, whetted **8** clean-cut, clear-cut, incisive, piercing, shooting, stabbing, stinging **9** agonizing, brilliant, ingenious, knifelike, vitriolic **10** astringent, perceptive **11** intelligent, penetrating, quick-witted, resourceful **12** excruciating, nimble-witted

sharpen
4 edge, file, hone, whet **5** grind, strop

sharper
6 con man **7** diddler **8** chiseler, swindler **9** defrauder, trickster **10** mountebank **12** double-dealer

sharp-eyed
4 keen **5** alert **8** vigilant, watchful **9** attentive, observant **10** discerning, perceptive

sharpie
see **sharper**

sharpness
4 edge **6** acumen **9** precision

sharpshooter
8 marksman

sharp-sighted
8 hawk-eyed, lynx-eyed 9 eagle-eyed

sharp-witted
4 keen 5 acute, canny, quick, smart 6 astute, clever, shrewd 11 intelligent

shatter
4 dash 5 break, burst, crush, smash 6 shiver 8 demolish, fragment, splinter 9 pulverize 10 annihilate 11 fragmentize 12 disintegrate

shatterable
7 brittle, fragile 9 breakable, frangible

shave
3 cut 4 clip, crop, pare, peel, skim, trim 5 lower, prune, shear, skive 6 barber, cut off, deduct, reduce, scrape, sliver 7 cut back, whittle 8 mark down

shaveling
3 boy, kid, lad, tad 6 laddie, squirt 9 stripling, youngster

shaver
3 boy, kid, lad, tad 5 child, razor 6 barber, laddie, squirt 9 stripling, youngster

shawl
4 wrap 5 fichu, manta 6 chador, serape 7 tallith 8 mantilla

shawm's descendant
4 oboe

Shawnee chief
8 Tecumseh, Tecumtha 9 Cornstalk

Shaw play
6 Geneva 7 Candida 9 Pygmalion, Saint Joan 11 Misalliance 12 Major Barbara 13 Arms and the Man

shay
6 chaise 8 carriage

shear
3 cut, mow 4 clip, crop, pare, snip, trim 5 prune, shave, skive 6 barber

shears
8 scissors

shearwater
4 bird 6 petrel 7 skimmer

sheath
4 case, skin 5 cover 7 holster 8 scabbard

sheathe
4 case, clad, face, side, skin, wrap 5 cover, panel 6 encase, jacket

Sheba
father: 6 Bichri

queen: 6 Balkis

shebang
4 mess 6 affair 7 schmear 8 business, caboodle 9 ball of wax, enchilada

shed
3 hut 4 cast, doff, drop, emit, molt 5 exude, hovel, hutch, scrap, shack, stall 6 divest, lean-to, reject, slough 7 cast off, diffuse, discard, radiate, take off 8 jettison, throw out 9 throw away

sheen
5 glaze, gleam, glint, gloss, shine 6 finish, luster, lustre, polish 7 burnish, glitter, shimmer 8 radiance 9 shininess 10 brightness

sheeny
see **shiny**

sheep
5 ovine
breed: 5 Tunis 6 Dorper, Dorset, Merino, Navajo, No-Tail, Oxford, Panama, Romney 7 Cheviot, Colbred, Karakul, Lincoln, Ryeland, Suffolk 8 Columbia, Cotswold, Polwarth 9 Hampshire, Leicester, Montadale, Southdown 10 Corriedale, Debouillet 11 Rambouillet
coat: 4 wool 6 fleece
disease: 3 gid
female: 3 ewe
male: 3 ram 6 wether
meat: 6 mutton
relating to: 5 ovine
Scottish: 9 blackface
sound: 5 bleat
tender: 8 shepherd
wild: 5 urial 6 aoudad, argali, bharal 7 bighorn, mouflon
young: 4 lamb

sheepish
4 meek 5 timid 7 abashed, ashamed, bashful 8 timorous 9 diffident 10 shamefaced 11 embarrassed

sheepskin
4 roan 6 mouton 7 diploma 9 parchment
prepare: 3 taw

sheer
4 pure, skew, thin, turn, veer 5 filmy, gauzy, steep, utter 6 abrupt, arrant, flimsy, simple, swerve 7 chiffon, deflect, deviate, perfect, unmixed 8 absolute, complete, gossamer, outright 9 out-and-out, unalloyed, undiluted 10 diaphanous, see-through 11 precipitate, precipitous, transparent, unmitigated

sheet
3 ply 4 film, leaf, page, sail, slab 5 cover, linen, paper 6 lamina, veneer 8 membrane 9 newspaper

sheet _____
3 ice 4 film 5 glass, metal, music 6 anchor

shelf
3 hob 4 bank, edge, reef, sill 5 ledge, shoal 6 mantel 7 counter 8 sandbank

shell
3 pod 4 boat, bomb, case, hull, husk, rake, skin 5 blitz, conch, shuck 6 pepper 7 bombard, capsule, grenade, mollusc, mollusk 8 carapace 9 cannonade, cartridge
defective: 3 dud
explosive: 4 bomb
layer: 5 nacre
ornamental: 6 cowrie
study: 10 conchology

shellac
4 beat, drub, flay, lick, rout, trim, whap, whip, whop, whup 5 resin, smear, whomp 6 defeat, thrash 7 clobber, smother, trounce 8 lambaste, vanquish

Shelley, Percy Bysshe
poem: 5 Cloud (The) 7 Adonais, Alastor 8 Queen Mab 10 Ozymandias, To a Skylark 16 Ode to the West Wind

shellfish
4 clam, crab 5 conch, cowry, prawn, snail, whelk 6 cockle, limpet, mussel, oyster, quahog, triton 7 abalone, crawdad, geoduck, lobster, mollusc, mollusk, scallop 8 barnacle, crayfish, escargot 10 crustacean, periwinkle

shell out
3 pay 4 give 5 spend 8 fork over, hand over

shell-shaped
6 spiral 9 cochleate

shelter
3 den, hut, lee 4 cote, fold, hide, port, roof, shed, tent 5 arbor, bower, cloak, cover, haven, house, shack, tower 6 asylum, burrow, covert, defend, harbor, refuge, shield 7 chamber, defense, foxhole, hideout, hospice, housing, lodging, pergola, pillbox, protect, retreat 8 hideaway, hidy-hole, security 9 dwellings, hermitage, hidey-hole, sanctuary 10 retirement
for aircraft: 6 hangar

for cows: 4 barn, byre
toward: 4 alee

shelve
4 dish, drop, stay, tilt 5 defer, delay, slope, stock, waive 6 freeze, give up, hold up, put off 7 hold off, suspend 8 hold over, mothball, postpone, prorogue, set aside

Shem
brother: 3 Ham 7 Japheth
father: 4 Noah

Shema's father
4 Joel 6 Hebron

Shemida's father
6 Gilead

shenanigan
4 dido, lark 5 antic, caper, prank, stunt, trick 6 frolic 8 escapade, mischief 10 tomfoolery 11 monkeyshine

Sheol
see **hades**

shepherd
4 lead, show, tend 5 guide, pilot, route, steer, watch 6 direct, escort, leader 7 conduct 8 guardian
dog: 6 collie 12 border collie
stick: 5 crook, staff

Sheridan play
6 Critic (The), Rivals (The) 7 Pizarro 16 School for Scandal (The)

sheriff
5 reeve 6 lawman 7 marshal, officer
aide: 6 deputy

sherlock
4 dick, tail 5 snoop 6 shadow, shamus, sleuth 7 gumshoe 8 hawkshaw 9 detective 10 private eye 12 investigator

Sherlock Holmes
creator: 5 Doyle (Arthur Conan)
sidekick: 6 Watson (Dr.)

sherry
4 fino, wine 7 oloroso 10 manzanilla 11 amontillado

Sherwood play
10 Road to Rome (The) 13 Idiot's Delight 14 Waterloo Bridge 15 Petrified Forest (The)

shibboleth
3 saw, tag 5 axiom, maxim 6 byword, cliché, phrase, saying, slogan, truism 7 bromide 8 banality, chestnut, password,

prosaism **9** catchword, platitude, watchword **11** catchphrase, commonplace

shield
4 fend, roof, ward **5** aegis, armor, cover, guard, haven, house **6** buffer, defend, harbor, screen, secure **7** buckler, bulwark, defense, protect, shelter **8** defilade **9** safeguard **10** escutcheon
band: 4 fess
bullfighter's: 9 burladero
light: 5 targe
part: 4 boss, umbo **7** bordure
Roman: 7 testudo

shield-like
7 peltate

shift
3 yaw **4** bend, bout, move, stir, tack, time, tour, turn, vary, veer **5** alter, budge, get by, spell, stint, trick **6** change, make do, manage, remove, resort, swerve **7** deviate, replace, shuffle, stopgap **8** get along, relocate, resource, transfer **9** deviation, expedient, fluctuate **10** alteration, changeover, conversion, transition **11** fluctuation

shiftless
4 idle, lazy **5** inept **8** feckless, indolent, slothful **11** inefficient

shifty
3 sly **4** foxy, wily **5** cagey, lying, shady, slick **6** crafty, sneaky, tricky **7** cunning, devious, elusive, evasive, furtive **8** guileful, slippery, sneaking **9** conniving, deceitful, deceptive, dishonest, insidious, underhand **10** inconstant, untruthful **11** duplicitous, underhanded **12** equivocating

shill
5 blind, decoy, pitch **6** capper **8** promoter **10** accomplice, sales pitch

shillelagh
3 bat **4** club, cosh, mace **5** baton, billy, stick **6** cudgel **8** bludgeon **9** bastinado, billy club, blackjack, truncheon **10** nightstick

shilling
3 bob

shilly-shally
5 fudge, hedge, stall, waver **6** dawdle, dither, waffle **7** whiffle **8** hesitate **9** temporize, vacillate **11** prevaricate **12** tergiversate

Shimea
brother: 5 David

father: 5 David, Jesse
son: 7 Jonadab **8** Jonathan

shimmer
5 flash, gleam, glint, sheen **6** luster, lustre **7** glimmer, glisten, glitter, spangle, sparkle, twinkle **9** coruscate **11** coruscation, scintillate **13** scintillation

shimmy
5 dance, shake **6** quiver, shiver, tremor **7** chemise, shudder, tremble, vibrate **9** vibration

shin
3 run **4** dash **5** scoot, tibia **6** scurry, sprint **7** scamper

shindig
4 ball, bash, fête, gala **5** binge, dance, party, revel **6** affair, frolic **7** blowout **8** wingding

shine
3 ray, rub **4** beam, buff, burn, glow **5** blaze, flare, flash, glare, glaze, gleam, glint, gloss, sheen **6** luster, lustre, polish **7** burnish, glimmer, glisten, glitter, radiate, shimmer, sparkle, twinkle **9** luminesce **10** incandesce

shiner
4 fish **8** black eye, cyprinid

shingle
5 beach, coast, shore **7** haircut, overlap, overlay **8** detritus **9** signboard

shiny
6 bright, glossy **7** fulgent, radiant **8** dazzling, gleaming, lustrous, polished **9** burnished, effulgent **10** glistening

ship
4 boat, send **5** remit, route **6** export **7** consign, forward, freight **8** dispatch, transfer, transmit
ancient: 6 galley **7** galleon, trireme
attendant: 7 steward
beam: 7 keelson
berth: 4 dock, slip
boat: 6 dinghy
body: 4 hull
cabin: 9 stateroom
commercial: 5 liner, oiler **6** argosy, tanker, trader **9** freighter
crew member: 4 hand, mate **6** sailor
deck: 4 boat, main, poop **5** orlop **6** bridge **10** forecastle
fishing: 6 lugger **7** trawler
fleet: 6 armada
floor: 4 deck

front: 3 bow 4 prow, stem 8 cutwater
hoister: 4 boom 5 davit 7 capstan
kitchen: 6 galley
left side: 4 port 8 larboard
military: 6 cutter, PT boat 7 carrier, cruiser 9 destroyer, submarine
officer: 4 mate 5 bosun 6 purser 7 captain, steward 9 boatswain
part: 3 bow 4 beam, deck, helm, hold, hull, keel, mast, stem 5 bilge, hatch, stern 6 bridge, rudder 7 scupper
partition: 7 bulwark 8 bulkhead
personnel: 4 crew
platform: 9 crow's nest, gangboard, gangplank
post: 4 mast 7 bollard
prison: 4 brig
projection: 7 sponson
rear: 5 stern
record: 3 log
right side: 9 starboard
room: 4 brig 5 cabin 6 galley
rope: 4 line 5 sheet 7 halyard
sailing: 4 brig, dhow, prau, proa, yawl 5 ketch, sloop, xebec, yacht 6 lugger 7 caravel, galleon 8 schooner
steerer: 4 helm 6 tiller
storage area: 4 hold
to the rear of: 3 aft 5 abaft 6 astern
valve: 7 seacock
window: 4 port 8 porthole

shipment
5 cargo 6 lading 7 freight, payload 8 delivery 11 consignment

Ship of Fools author
6 Porter (Katherine Anne)

Shipping News author
6 Proulx (Annie)

ships, group of
4 navy 5 fleet, flota 6 armada 8 flotilla

shipshape
4 neat, snug, tidy, trig, trim 7 orderly 11 spic-and-span, uncluttered 12 spick-and-span

shipworm
6 teredo

shire
5 horse 6 county 8 district 10 draft horse

shirk
4 duck, lurk, shun 5 avoid, creep, dodge, elude, evade, skulk, slink, sneak, steal 8 sidestep

shirker
see **slacker**

shirt
4 polo, sark 5 dress, kurta, sport 6 blouse, jersey 9 guayabera

shirty
3 mad 5 angry, cross, irate 6 heated, ireful 7 annoyed 8 choleric, incensed, offended 9 indignant, irritated

shiv
5 blade, knife, shank 6 dagger 8 stiletto

Shiva
consort: 3 Uma 4 Devi, Kali 5 Durga, Gauri 6 Ambika, Chandi 7 Parvati 9 Haimavati
son: 6 Ganesa, Skanda 7 Ganesha 10 Karttikeya

shiver
5 burst, quake, shake, smash 6 quaver, quiver, tremor 7 shatter, shudder, tremble, twitter 8 fragment, splinter, splitter

shoal
3 bar 4 bank, hook, reef, spit 6 school 7 barrier, sandbar, shallow, tombolo 8 sandbank, sand reef

shoat
3 hog, pig 5 swine 6 porker

Shobab
father: 5 Caleb, David
mother: 6 Azubah 9 Bathsheba

shock
3 jar 4 blow, bump, daze, jolt, pile, rick, stun 5 amaze, clash, crash, mound, quake, shake, sheaf 6 appall, dismay, impact, insult, offend, trauma, tremor 7 astound, disgust, horrify, outrage, stagger, startle, stupefy, temblor 8 astonish, surprise 9 collision, electrify 10 concussion, earthquake, percussion, scandalize, traumatize 11 flabbergast 12 stupefaction

shock absorber
6 spring 7 dashpot, snubber

shocker
4 blow 7 stunner 8 surprise, thriller 9 bombshell, eye-opener, sensation 11 showstopper

shocking
5 awful, lurid 6 horrid 7 glaring, heinous 8 dreadful, horrible, horrific, shameful, terrible 9 appalling, atrocious, frightful, monstrous,

revolting **10** outrageous, scandalous **11** disgraceful, distressing, unspeakable

shoddy
4 base, mean, poor **5** cheap, dingy, gaudy, junky, seedy, tacky, tatty **6** cheesy, common, paltry, shabby, sleazy, tawdry, trashy **7** run-down, scruffy **8** inferior, rubbishy, shameful **9** makeshift **10** broken-down, down-at-heel **11** dilapidated, disgraceful, ignominious, pretentious **12** dishonorable, disreputable **13** discreditable

shoe
4 boot, clog, geta, mule, pump **5** sabot, wedge **6** brogan, brogue, buskin, gaiter, galosh, gillie, loafer, oxford, patten, sandal **7** chopine, ghillie, slipper, sneaker **8** balmoral, moccasin, platform, plimsoll **10** clodhopper, espadrille
armored: **8** solleret
athlete's: **7** sneaker
form: **4** last, tree
kind: **8** elevator, open-toed **10** high-heeled
part: **3** tip, toe **4** arch, heel, lace, lift, sole, vamp **5** shank, upper **6** box toe, collar, foxing, insole, lining, throat, tongue **7** counter, outsole **8** backstay
protective: **6** galosh, rubber
shiner: **6** polish **9** bootblack
wooden: **5** sabot **7** chopine

shoelace tip
5 aglet

shoeless
6 unshod **8** barefoot **9** discalced

shoemaker
7 cobbler
patron saint: **7** Crispin
Scottish: **6** souter

Shogun author
7 Clavell (James)

Sholem Aleichem character
5 Tevye

shoo
4 scat **5** drive, leave, scare, scram, split **6** beat it, begone, bug off, skidoo **7** buzz off, get lost, skiddoo, vamoose **8** clear out **9** skedaddle, take a hike **10** hit the road

shoo-in
6 winner **7** sure bet **8** slam dunk **9** sure thing

shoot
3 bud, fly, gun, ray **4** beam, bolt, dart, dash, fire, lash, race, rush, sail, scud, skim, spew, tear **5** blast, chase, fling, photo, shaft, skirr, snipe, spurt **6** branch **7** project **9** discharge **10** photograph

shoot down
3 pan, rap **4** bash, kill, slam **5** blast, decry, knock, scorn, trash **6** assail, deride, dump on, reject, squash **7** deflate, squelch, torpedo **8** bad-mouth, belittle, derogate, discount, disprove, puncture, ridicule **9** discredit

shooting
4 keen **5** acute, sharp **7** gunplay **8** piercing, stabbing

shooting star
6 meteor **8** fireball

shoot up
4 soar **6** inject, rocket **7** burgeon **8** mushroom **9** skyrocket

shop
4 hunt **5** store **6** browse, market, outlet, search **8** boutique, emporium, showroom

shoplift
3 bag, cop **4** lift, palm **5** filch, pinch, steal, swipe **6** pilfer, rip off, snitch

shop owner
8 merchant, retailer **9** tradesman **10** proprietor

shopworn
5 banal, faded, stale, tired, trite **6** cliché, soiled **7** clichéd **8** overused **9** hackneyed **10** threadbare

shore
4 bank, prop, stay **5** beach, brace, brink, coast **6** bear up, strand, uphold **7** bolster, shingle, support, sustain **8** buttress, littoral, seacoast **9** coastland, coastline, riverbank, riverside, waterside **10** embankment, waterfront

shorebird
see at **bird**

short
3 shy **4** curt **5** blunt, brief, crisp, scant, skimp, spare, squat, stint, terse **6** abrupt, meager, meagre, scanty, scarce, skimpy, stubby **7** brusque, compact, concise, lacking, laconic, stunted, wanting **8** abridged, succinct **9** deficient **10** inadequate **11** abbreviated **12** insufficient

shortage
4 lack **5** pinch **6** dearth, ullage **7** deficit, paucity **8** scarcity **10** deficiency, inadequacy, scantiness

shortcoming
3 bug, sin 4 flaw, lack 5 fault, lapse 6 defect 7 demerit, failing 8 weakness 9 weak point 10 deficiency 12 imperfection

shortcut
6 bypass, cutoff

shorten
3 bob, cut 4 clip, dock 5 elide, slash 6 lessen, reduce, shrink 7 abridge, curtail, cut back, cut down, excerpt 8 boil down, compress, condense, contract, decrease, diminish, minimize, truncate 10 abbreviate

shorthand
11 stenography
method: 5 Gregg 6 Pitman

shorthanded
7 wanting 11 undermanned 12 understaffed

short-lived
5 brief 7 passing 8 fleeting 9 ephemeral, fugacious, momentary, temporary 10 evanescent, transitory

shortly
4 anon, soon 6 pronto 7 briefly, by and by, in brief, quickly, tersely 8 directly 9 concisely, presently 10 succinctly 11 laconically

shortness
7 brevity 9 concision

shortsighted
6 myopic 8 heedless, reckless 10 astigmatic

short-spoken
4 curt 5 bluff, blunt, brief, gruff, terse 6 abrupt, crusty, snippy 7 brusque 8 snippety

short-tempered
5 testy 6 touchy 7 prickly 8 snappish 9 irascible, irritable

Shoshone chief
8 Washakie 9 Pocatello

shot
3 nip, pop, try 4 dose, dram, drop, jolt, stab 5 blast, break, carom, crack, fling, guess, ounce, photo, range, reach, snort, swipe, whack, whirl 6 chance, effort, stroke 7 attempt, snifter 8 marksman, occasion 9 discharge 11 opportunity

shoulder
4 bear, edge, push, side 5 elbow, press,

shove 6 assume, hustle, jostle, take on 8 bulldoze
bone: 7 scapula 8 clavicle
covering: 6 tippet 8 scapular
muscle: 7 deltoid
relating to: 7 humeral 8 scapular

shoulder blade
7 scapula

shout
3 cry 4 bark, bawl, bray, call, roar, yell 5 blare, whoop 6 bellow, clamor, holler, scream 7 exclaim 10 vociferate

shove
3 dig, jab, jam 4 cram, prod, push 5 crowd, drive, elbow, press 6 jostle, propel, thrust 8 bulldoze, shoulder

shovel
3 dig 4 grub 5 delve, scoop, spade 6 dig out, dredge, trowel 8 excavate

shoveler
4 duck 9 broadbill

shove off
3 git 4 blow, exit 5 leave, scoot, scram, split 6 beat it, cut out, decamp, depart, move on 7 move out, pull out, vamoose 8 clear out, run along

show
4 fair, film, lead, pomp, sham 5 array, flick, front, guide, mount, movie, offer, prove, revue, sport, stage 6 appear, arrive, direct, effect, evince, expose, flaunt, lay out, parade, reveal, set out, submit, unveil 7 conduct, display, divulge, exhibit, explain, fanfare, panoply, picture, present, produce, project, trot out 8 brandish, disclose, evidence, illusion, indicate, instruct, manifest, proclaim 9 determine, establish, pageantry, represent, semblance, spectacle 10 appearance, exhibition, exposition, illustrate, production 11 demonstrate, materialize, performance 13 demonstration, manifestation

Show Boat
author: 6 Ferber (Edna)
composer: 4 Kern (Jerome)
lyricist: 11 Hammerstein (Oscar)

showcase
6 flaunt, parade 7 cabinet, exhibit, feature, vitrine

shower
4 hail, rain, wash 5 bathe, burst, party, salvo, spray, storm 6 deluge, lavish, volley

7 barrage, cascade, shatter, spatter 8 cataract, downpour, fountain, rainfall 9 broadside, cannonade, fusillade 10 cloudburst 11 bombardment

showman

8 producer, promoter 10 impresario
famous: 4 Cody (William F.) 6 Barnum (Phineas T.)

Show Me State

8 Missouri

show off

4 brag 5 boast, flash, model, vaunt 6 expose, flaunt, hotdog, parade 7 display, exhibit, swagger, trot out 8 brandish 10 grandstand

show-off

3 ham 5 hotdog 7 boaster, hotshot, peacock 8 blowhard, braggart 9 swaggerer 13 exhibitionist

showpiece

3 gem 5 jewel, prize 10 magnum opus, masterwork 11 chef d'oeuvre, masterpiece

show up

4 come 6 appear, arrive, debunk, expose, reveal, unmask 8 discover 9 discredit, embarrass 10 invalidate 11 materialize

showy

4 loud 5 gaudy, jazzy 6 flashy, garish, ornate, sporty, tawdry 7 opulent, splashy 8 gorgeous, overdone, striking 9 luxurious, sumptuous 10 flamboyant 11 overwrought, pretentious, resplendent, sensational 12 meretricious, orchidaceous, ostentatious

shred

3 bit, dag, jot, rag 4 iota, whit 5 crumb, grain, grate, ounce, scrap, shave, speck, trace 6 sliver, tatter 7 modicum, smidgen, snippet 8 demolish, fragment, particle 9 scintilla

shrew

3 nag 4 mole 5 harpy, scold, vixen, witch 6 dragon, gorgon, ogress, rodent, virago 7 hellcat 8 battle-ax, fishwife, harridan, she-devil, spitfire, Xantippe 9 battle-axe, termagant, Xanthippe

shrewd

3 sly 4 foxy, keen, wily, wise 5 acute, cagey, canny, savvy, sharp, slick, smart 6 artful, astute, clever, crafty, smooth 7 knowing, prudent 8 sensible 9 ingenious, judicious, sagacious 10 discerning 11 intelligent, penetrating, quick-witted 13 perspicacious

shrewish

5 cross, testy 6 cranky, snappy 7 peevish, peppery 8 choleric, petulant 9 crotchety, fractious, irascible, splenetic 10 ill-natured 11 contentious, intractable, quarrelsome 12 disputatious 13 quick-tempered, short-tempered

shriek

3 cry 4 yell 6 screak, scream, shrill, squawk, squeal 7 screech

shrill

4 keen 5 acute, sharp 6 piping 8 piercing, strident 9 deafening 12 earsplitting

shrimp

4 runt 5 prawn 6 peanut, scampi 10 crustacean

shrine

5 altar 6 temple 7 sanctum 9 reliquary, sacrarium, sanctuary
Buddhist: 5 stupa 7 chorten

shrink

3 shy 4 wane 5 cower, quail, slink, start, wince 6 blench, boggle, cringe, flinch, huddle, recede, recoil, wither 7 analyst, dwindle, refrain 8 compress, condense, contract, draw back, withdraw 9 constrict, shrivel up, therapist, waste away 12 psychiatrist, psychologist

shrinking

3 shy 5 mousy, timid 7 bashful 8 retiring, skittish 9 withdrawn

shrive

5 purge 6 pardon, purify 7 absolve, confess, expiate, lustrate

shrivel

4 wilt 5 dry up, parch, wizen 6 shrink, wither 7 dwindle, wrinkle 9 dehydrate, desiccate

Shropshire Lad author

7 Housman (A. E.)

shroud

4 hide, rope, veil, wrap 5 cloak, cover, shade 6 enfold, enwrap, screen 7 conceal, enclose, envelop, obscure 8 cerement, obstruct 9 cerecloth 12 winding-sheet

shrouded

5 privy 6 covert, hidden, secret 7 obscure 10 mysterious

shrub

4 bush 5 elder, erica, hazel 6 muskit, privet 7 arboret, dyeweed, guayule 8 barberry, bluewood, boxthorn, inkberry, ironweed, rosebush 9 bearberry 10 bladdernut

Asian: 4 bago 6 kerria 8 caragana, japonica
desert: 7 ephedra
dwarf: 6 bonsai
East Indian: 3 aal 4 sunn
European: 4 cade 8 woodbine
evergreen: 3 box, kat, yew 4 ilex, khat, titi 5 furze, heath, holly, pyxie, savin, taxus 6 kalmia, laurel, myrtle, nandin, protea, sabine, savine 7 boxwood, heather, jasmine, juniper, rosebay 8 lambkill, oleander, rosemary, tamarisk
flowering: 5 ribes, tiara, wahoo 6 daphne, laurel, myrtle, spirea 7 chamise, chamiso, mahonia, maybush, rhodora, spiraea, weigela 8 magnolia, mezereon, nineback, oleander, oleaster, shadblow, shadbush, snowball, snowbush, tornillo, viburnum, wisteria
genus: 4 Inga, Itea 7 Solanum 8 Euonymus
hardwood: 6 cornel
Mexican: 8 ocotillo
ornamental: 6 privet 7 syringa 9 bluebeard
pasture: 8 cowberry
prickly: 5 briar, chico, furze, gorse 7 bramble 8 hawthorn, mesquite 9 buckthorn
thicket: 6 maquis 7 macchia 9 chaparral
tropical: 4 kava 5 henna 7 lantana 8 buddleia 10 frangipani
West Indian: 4 anil 7 acerola

shrug off

8 belittle, downplay, minimize

shtick

3 act, bag, bit 5 spiel 6 number 7 routine 9 specialty 11 performance

Shuah

father: 7 Abraham
mother: 7 Keturah

shuck

3 pod 4 case, cast, hull, husk, junk, peel, shed, skin 5 ditch, scrap, shell, strip 6 reject, remove, slough 7 discard, peel off, take off 8 jettison 11 decorticate

shudder

5 quake, shake 6 quaver, quiver, shimmy, shiver, tremor 7 frisson, tremble, twitter, vibrate

shuffle

3 mix 4 hash 5 dodge, evade, hedge, scuff, shift 6 jumble, mess up, muddle, weasel 7 clutter, reorder, rummage, shamble 8 disarray, disorder, intermix, mishmash 9 rearrange 10 disarrange, equivocate 11 disorganize

shun

3 cut 4 duck, snub 5 avoid, dodge, elude, evade, scorn 6 escape, eschew, refuse, reject 7 decline, disdain

shunt

4 turn 5 avert, shift 6 change, divert, switch 7 deflect, shuttle 8 transfer 9 sidetrack

shush

4 hush 5 quiet, still 6 muffle, muzzle, shut up, stifle 7 repress, silence, squelch 8 suppress

shut

3 bar 4 lock, seal, slam 5 close 6 fasten 9 close down 10 batten down

Shute novel

10 On the Beach

shut in

3 hem, mew, pen 4 cage, coop, wall 5 fence 6 coop up, immure 7 confine, enclose 8 imprison

shut-in

7 invalid 8 confined 9 withdrawn 12 convalescent

shut out

3 bar 6 screen 7 exclude 9 ostracize

shutter

5 blind 6 screen

shuttle

5 ferry, shunt 6 bobbin 7 commute, spindle 9 alternate

shuttlecock

4 bird 5 bandy

shut up

3 gag, mew, pen 4 cage, hush, jail, mute 5 burke, choke, quiet, shush, still 6 muzzle, stifle 7 confine, enclose, impound, silence, squelch 8 choke off, imprison, pipe down, suppress 9 quiet down 11 incarcerate

shy

3 coy 4 balk, duck, meek, shun, wary 5 avoid, chary, elude, evade, mousy, quail, scant, short, timid 6 averse, blench, demure, modest, recoil, scanty, scarce, shrink 7 bashful, fearful, lacking, wanting

8 hesitant, reserved, reticent, retiring, sheepish, timorous 9 diffident 11 introverted, unassertive 12 apprehensive, insufficient, self-effacing 13 self-conscious

Shylock
6 usurer 9 loan shark
daughter: 7 Jessica

shyster
11 pettifogger

Siam
see **Thailand**

sib
3 bro, kin, sis 4 akin 6 sister 7 brother, kindred, kinsman, related 8 relation, relative 9 relatives

Sibelius composition
9 Finlandia 11 Valse Triste

Siberian
dog: 5 husky 7 Samoyed
native: 5 Tatar, Yakut 6 Tartar, Tungus 7 Chukchi 9 Mongolian
plain: 6 steppe
tent: 4 yurt

sibilate
4 buzz, fizz, hiss, whiz 6 fizzle, sizzle 7 whisper

sibling
3 bro, sis 6 sister 7 brother

sibyl
4 seer 6 oracle 7 prophet 10 prophetess, soothsayer 13 fortune-teller

sic
3 set 4 thus 5 chase 6 attack

Sicilian
secret organization: 5 Mafia
volcano: 4 Etna

Sicily
capital: 7 Palermo
city: 7 Catania, Messina 8 Siracusa, Syracuse, Taormina
volcano: 4 Etna

sick
3 ill 5 fed up, tired, weary 6 ailing, laid up, morbid, peaked, rotten, unwell, wobbly 7 fevered, invalid 8 confined, diseased 9 bedridden, defective, disgusted, unhealthy 10 indisposed 11 debilitated

sicken
5 upset 7 afflict, disgust, fall ill 8 nauseate

sickle
5 blade, mower 6 scythe 8 crescent

sickle-shaped
7 falcate

sickly
3 ill, low, wan 4 puny, weak 5 frail 6 ailing, anemic, feeble, infirm, morbid, peaked, poorly, unwell 8 delicate, diseased 9 unhealthy 10 indisposed 11 unhealthful, unwholesome 12 insalubrious

sickness
3 bug 6 malady 7 ailment, disease, illness 8 disorder, syndrome 9 complaint, condition, infirmity 10 affliction 13 indisposition

sic transit gloria _____
5 mundi

side
4 clad, team 5 angle, facet, flank 6 aspect 9 direction 10 standpoint
combining form: 5 later 6 lateri, latero
exposed: 8 windward
sheltered: 3 lee

sideboard
5 table 6 buffet 8 credence, credenza
for wine: 8 cellaret 10 cellarette

sideburns
9 burnsides 10 sideboards 11 dundrearies, muttonchops

sidekick
3 pal 4 chun 5 buddy, crony 7 partner 9 assistant, companion 10 accomplice

sideline
5 eject, hobby 6 injure 7 disable, pastime, take out 9 avocation, diversion 10 recreation 11 distraction 12 incapacitate

sidereal
6 astral, starry 7 stellar

side road
5 byway 8 bystreet, shunpike

sideshow
9 diversion 11 distraction

sidestep
4 duck 5 avoid, burke, dodge, evade, hedge, skirt 6 bypass, swerve, weasel 10 circumvent, equivocate 12 tergiversate

sideswipe
5 brush, carom, graze, shave 6 glance, scrape

sidetrack
5 shunt 6 divert, switch 7 deflect

sidewhiskers
see **sideburns**

side with
4 back 5 favor 6 second, uphold 7
endorse, support 8 backstop, champion

sidle
4 edge, slip

siege
4 bout 5 spell 6 attack 7 assault, seizure
8 blockade 9 onslaught

Siegfried
composer: 6 Wagner (Richard)
lover: 8 Brunhild
mother: 9 Sieglinde
slayer: 5 Hagen
sword: 7 Balmung
vulnerable spot: 4 back 8 shoulder
wife: 9 Kriemhild

Sienkiewicz novel
8 Quo Vadis

sierra
3 saw 4 fish 5 range 8 mackerel 13
mountain range

Sierra Leone
capital: 8 Freetown
ethnic group: 5 Mende, Temne
language: 4 Krio 7 English
monetary unit: 5 leone
neighbor: 6 Guinea 7 Liberia

Sierra Nevada lake
5 Tahoe

Sierra _____
5 Ancha, Leone, Madre 6 Blanca, Nevada

siesta
3 nap 4 doze 5 sleep 6 catnap, snooze
10 forty winks

sieve
4 sift 6 filter, screen, winnow 8 colander,
filtrate, strainer

Sif's husband
4 Thor

sift
3 pan 4 comb, cull, sort 5 glean, sieve 6
filter, screen, strain, winnow 8 filtrate,
separate

sigh
3 sob 4 gasp, long, moan, pine 5 groan,
sough, whine, yearn 6 exhale, grieve,
hanker, murmur 7 breathe, respire, suspire

sight
3 aim, eye, spy 4 espy, view 5 scene, vista
6 notice, vision 7 make out, outlook

relating to: 5 optic 6 ocular, visual 7
optical

sightseer
7 tourist 10 rubberneck 12 rubbernecker

sign
3 cue, ink 4 flag, hint, mark, omen 5
index, proof, token, trace 6 motion, signal,
symbol 7 endorse, gesture, indicia, initial,
symptom, vestige, warning 8 evidence,
exponent, reminder 9 autograph, indicator
10 expression, indication, suggestion
directional: 5 arrow
of the zodiac:
(see **zodiac sign**)

signal
3 cue, nod 4 flag 5 alarm, alert 6 beckon,
wigwag 7 gesture 8 high sign 9 indicator
distress: 3 SOS 6 Mayday

signature
4 name 9 autograph 11 John Hancock
flourish: 6 paraph

signet
4 ring, seal 5 stamp 6 device 8 hallmark,
intaglio

significance
4 pith 5 merit, point, sense 6 credit,
import, moment, weight 7 gravity, meaning
9 authority, magnitude 10 importance 11
consequence, weightiness

significant
5 sound, valid 7 notable, telling, weighty 8
material, powerful 9 important, momentous
10 compelling, convincing, meaningful,
noteworthy 11 substantial 12 considerable
13 consequential

signification
4 gist 5 point, sense 6 import 7 essence,
meaning, message, purport 9 substance
10 intendment 11 implication 12
notification 13 understanding

signify
4 mean, show 5 count, imply, spell, weigh
6 convey, denote, intend, matter 7 add up
to, bespeak, connote, express, purport,
suggest 8 indicate

sign on
4 book, hire, join 5 draft 6 engage, enlist,
enroll, induct, join up, retain, secure 7
recruit 9 conscript

sign over
4 cede, deed 5 alien, grant 6 assign,
convey, remise 7 consign 8 alienate,
transfer

sign up
4 join 5 enter 6 enlist, enroll, muster

Sigurd
horse: 5 Grani
slayer: 5 Hogni
victim: 6 Fafner, Fafnir
wife: 6 Gudrun

Sigyn's husband
4 Loki

Sikhism
deity: 4 Akal
founder: 5 Nanak 9 Guru Nanak
leader: 5 Arjan 9 Guru Arjan 11 Gobind Singh
scripture: 9 Adi Granth
shrine: 12 Golden Temple

silage
6 fodder

silence
3 gag 4 calm, hush, lull, mute 5 quash, quell, quiet, shush, still 6 dampen, deaden, muffle, muzzle, shut up, squash, stifle 7 secrecy, squelch 8 choke off, muteness, quietude, reticence, stillness

silent
3 mum 4 dumb, mute 5 muted, quiet, still, tacit, whist 6 hushed, stilly 8 reticent, taciturn, unspoken, wordless 9 noiseless, soundless, voiceless 10 speechless 11 close-lipped, tight-lipped 12 closemouthed, tight-mouthed

silhouette
6 shadow 7 contour, outline, profile 9 lineament, lineation 10 figuration 11 delineation

Silicon Valley city
8 Palo Alto

silk
5 fiber 7 foulard 8 sarcenet, sarsenet
fabric: 4 gros 5 caffa, ninon, Pekin, satin, surah, tulle 6 mantua, pongee, samite, sendal, tussah 7 taffeta
factory: 8 filature
hat: 6 topper
maker: 4 worm
raw: 6 greige
source: 6 cocoon
waste: 4 noil 5 floss
wild: 6 tussah

sill
5 bench, ledge, shelf 9 threshold

silliness
5 folly 6 idiocy 7 inanity 9 absurdity, stupidity

silly
4 daft 5 balmy, crazy, daffy, dippy, dizzy, funny, giddy, inane, loony, sappy, wacky 6 absurd, simple 7 asinine, fatuous, flighty, foolish, idiotic, vacuous, witless 9 brainless, frivolous, ludicrous, nitwitted, senseless 10 irrational, ridiculous, weak-minded 11 empty-headed, harebrained, light-headed 12 preposterous, simpleminded 13 rattlebrained

silt
5 dregs 7 deposit, residue 8 alluvium, sediment

silver
4 coin 5 money, shiny 6 argent, dulcet 7 bullion, element 8 flatware, lustrous, sterling 9 argentine, tableware
relating to: 9 argentine

silverfish
6 insect, tarpon

silversmith
6 Revere (Paul) 11 metalworker

silver-tongued
4 glib 6 fluent 7 voluble 8 eloquent

silvery
6 argent 7 shining 9 argentine, brilliant 10 glittering, shimmering

Silvia's beloved
9 Valentine

_____ Simbel
3 Abu

Simenon character
7 Maigret (Inspector)

Simeon
father: 5 Jacob
mother: 4 Leah
son: 4 Ohad 6 Nemuel

simian
3 ape 5 chimp, lemur, loris 6 bonobo, galago, monkey 7 apelike, baboon, gorilla, primate, tarsier 9 orangutan 10 anthropoid, chimpanzee, monkeylike

similar
4 akin, like 5 alike 6 agnate 7 uniform 8 parallel, suchlike 9 analogous, consonant 10 comparable, reciprocal 11 correlative 13 complementary, corresponding

similarity
6 parity **7** analogy, harmony, kinship **8** affinity, likeness, parallel, sameness **9** alikeness, closeness, congruity, semblance **10** conformity, congruence **11** coincidence, correlation, homogeneity, parallelism, resemblance

similarly
8 likewise

simile
7 analogy **8** affinity, likeness, metaphor **9** alikeness, semblance **10** comparison **11** correlation, resemblance
word: 4 like

similitude
4 copy **5** image **6** double **7** analogy, kinship, replica **8** affinity, likeness, metaphor, relation, sameness **9** alikeness, congruity, semblance **10** comparison, similarity **11** correlation, counterpart, equivalence, resemblance

simmer
4 boil, fret, fume, stew, stir **5** churn **6** bubble, seethe **7** ferment, smolder

simmer down
5 relax

Simon
brother: 5 Jesus **6** Andrew
father: 5 Jonah
new name: 5 Peter
son: 5 Judas, Rufus **9** Alexander

Simon _____
5 Magus **6** Legree **8** of Cyrene **9** the Zealot

Simon Maccabaeus
father: 10 Mattathias
nickname: 6 Thassi
slayer: 7 Ptolemy

Simon play
9 Odd Couple (The) **10** Chapter Two, Plaza Suite **11** Biloxi Blues **13** Lost in Yonkers, Sunshine Boys (The) **16** Come Blow Your Horn **17** Barefoot in the Park **20** Brighton Beach Memoirs **21** Last of the Red Hot Lovers **22** Prisoner of Second Avenue (The)

simp
4 dope **5** dunce, idiot, moron **6** dimwit, nitwit **7** pinhead **8** bonehead, imbecile, lunkhead, numskull **9** blockhead, lamebrain, numbskull **10** nincompoop

simple
4 easy, mere, pure **5** basic, lucid, naive, plain, sheer **6** modest **7** artless, natural, unmixed **8** absolute, trusting **9** childlike, credulous, ingenuous, unadorned **10** effortless, elementary, unaffected **11** fundamental, undecorated, unelaborate **13** unpretentious
combining form: 4 hapl **5** haplo

simpleminded
4 dull, slow **5** naive **6** stupid **7** foolish, idiotic, moronic **8** gullible, retarded **9** dim-witted, imbecilic **10** half-witted, slow-witted

simpleton
4 dolt, dope, fool **5** dummy, dunce, idiot, moron **6** cretin, dimwit, nitwit **7** dullard, half-wit, pinhead **8** bonehead, dumbbell, imbecile, lunkhead **9** blockhead, ignoramus, lambrain **10** nincompoop

simplify
4 ease **7** clarify, clear up **8** boil down **10** facilitate, streamline, unscramble **11** disentangle **13** straighten out

simply
4 just, only **6** merely

simulacrum
4 copy **5** clone, ditto, guise, image, trace **6** double, ersatz, mirror, ringer **7** picture, replica **8** likeness, portrait **9** facsimile, imitation, semblance **10** appearance **12** reproduction **13** impersonation, spitting image

simulate
3 ape **4** fake, sham, feign, mimic **6** embody, mirror, parody, parrot **7** imitate **8** resemble **9** incarnate **11** counterfeit

simulated
4 fake, mock, sham **5** bogus, dummy, false, phony **6** ersatz **8** spurious **9** imitation, insincere, pretended **10** artificial, fictitious, substitute **11** counterfeit

simultaneous
6 coeval **10** coexistent, coexisting, coincident, coinciding, concurrent, synchronic **11** synchronous **12** contemporary

simultaneously
6 at once **7** jointly **8** together **9** meanwhile

sin
3 err **4** debt, evil, tort, vice **5** crime, fault, guilt, lapse, stray, wrong **6** offend **7** demerit, misdeed, offense **8** hamartia, iniquity, trespass **10** deficiency, peccadillo, transgress, wickedness, wrongdoing **11** shortcoming **12** imperfection

deadly: 4 envy, lust 5 anger, greed, pride, sloth 8 gluttony 12 covetousness

Sin
7 moon-god
daughter: 6 Ishtar
son: 7 Shamash
wife: 6 Ningal

since
3 ago 5 after 6 behind 7 because, whereas 8 as long as 9 following 10 inasmuch as 11 considering
Scottish: 4 syne

sincere
4 real, true 5 frank, plain 6 actual, candid, devout, honest 7 artless, earnest, genuine, serious 8 bona fide, truthful 9 authentic, heartfelt, ingenuous, unfeigned 10 aboveboard, forthright 12 wholehearted 13 unpretentious

sincerity
6 candor 7 honesty 8 goodwill, openness 9 frankness, good faith 11 artlessness, earnestness

sine qua non
4 must 9 condition, essential, necessity, requisite 11 requirement 12 precondition, prerequisite

sinew
6 tendon

sinewy
4 ropy, wiry 5 tough 6 brawny 7 fibrous, stringy 8 muscular

sinful
3 bad 4 base, evil, vile 5 wrong 6 guilty, unholy, wicked 7 immoral, peccant, vicious 8 blamable, culpable, damnable, depraved, shameful 9 reprobate 10 iniquitous 11 blameworthy, disgraceful 13 reprehensible

sing
3 rat 4 fink, hymn 5 carol, chant, chirp, croon, troll, yodel 6 inform, intone, snitch, squeal, warble 7 confess, descant, lullaby 8 serenade, vocalize 10 cantillate

Singapore
capital: 9 Singapore
language: 5 Malay, Tamil 8 Mandarin
monetary unit: 6 dollar

singe
4 burn, char, sear 6 scorch

singer
4 alto, bass 5 mezzo, tenor 6 canary 7 crooner, soloist, soprano 8 baritone, choirboy, songbird, songster, vocalist

balladeer, chorister, contralto 10 troubadour
cabaret: 11 chansonnier
female: 9 chanteuse
opera: 4 diva 10 cantatrice
religious: 6 cantor

singing
exercise: 7 solfège
group: 3 duo 4 trio 5 choir 6 chorus 7 chorale, quartet, quintet
voice: 4 alto, bass 5 mezzo, tenor 7 soprano 8 baritone 9 contralto 12 mezzo-soprano

single
3 hit, odd, one 4 free, lone, only, sole 5 unwed 6 maiden, unique 7 base hit, unitary 8 distinct, isolated, separate, solitary, specific 9 exclusive, unmarried 10 individual, particular, unattached
combining form: 3 mon 4 hapl, mono 5 haplo
prefix: 3 uni

single-minded
5 rigid 6 dogged, driven, intent 7 adamant, devoted, diehard, hell-bent 8 obdurate, resolute, resolved, stubborn 9 dedicated, steadfast, unbending 10 brassbound, determined, inexorable, inflexible, purposeful, relentless, unyielding

single out
4 cull, mark, pick 5 elect, favor 6 choose, opt for, select 9 designate 11 distinguish

singular
3 odd 4 lone, only, rare, sole, solo 5 weird 6 unique 7 bizarre, oddball, strange, unusual 8 peculiar, solitary, uncommon 9 exclusive 10 individual, outlandish, particular, unexampled 11 exceptional 13 extraordinary

singularity
5 quirk, unity 6 oddity 7 anomaly, oneness 8 identity 9 exception 11 peculiarity, personality 12 idiosyncrasy 13 individuality, particularity

singularize
4 mark 11 distinguish, individuate 12 characterize 13 differentiate, individualize

sinister
4 dark, dire, evil, left 6 creepy, malign 7 baleful, fateful, malefic, ominous 8 lowering, menacing 9 ill-omened, malicious 10 foreboding, maleficent, portentous 11 apocalyptic, threatening 12 inauspicious, unpropitious

sink
3 dip, pit, sag 4 bore, bury, dive, drop, fall, sump, wane 5 basin, drill, droop, lower, sewer, slope, slump, stoop, swamp 6 hollow, invest, plunge, settle, thrust, worsen 7 capsize, cesspit, decline, depress, descend, founder, go under, immerse, let down, scuttle, subside, torpedo 8 cesspool, hellhole, submerge, submerse 9 concavity, disappear 10 depression

sinker
3 bob 5 plumb 6 weight 8 doughnut, fastball, plumb bob

sinkhole
3 dip, sag 4 bowl 5 basin 6 hollow 8 cesspool 9 concavity 10 depression

sinless
4 pure 6 chaste 8 innocent 9 righteous 10 impeccable

sinner
5 rogue, scamp 6 bad egg, outlaw, rascal, wretch 7 lowlife, villain 8 criminal, evildoer, offender 9 libertine, miscreant, reprobate, scoundrel, wrongdoer 10 black sheep, delinquent, profligate, malefactor 11 rapscallion

Sinn _____
4 Fein

sinuous
4 wavy 5 lithe, snaky 7 winding 8 flexuous, tortuous 10 convoluted, meandering, serpentine 11 anfractuous, snake-shaped

sinus
6 cavity, hollow, recess

Sioux
6 Dakota
chief: 8 Red Cloud 10 Crazy Horse 11 Sitting Bull
people: 3 Ofo 4 Crow 6 Biloxi, Tutelo 7 Catawba, Hidatsa 9 Winnebago

sip
5 drink, savor, taste 6 imbibe

siphon
3 tap 4 draw, pipe, pump 5 draft, drain 6 convoy, divert, funnel 7 channel, conduct, draw off 8 transmit

sir
4 lord 5 title 6 knight, mister 9 gentleman

sire
4 lord 5 beget, breed, hatch, spawn 6 father, parent 7 founder 8 engender 9 patriarch, procreate, propagate 10 forefather

siren
4 vamp 5 alarm 7 Lorelei 9 temptress 10 seductress 11 femme fatale
film: 4 Bara (Theda)

Siren
5 Ligea 8 Leucosia 10 Parthenope
German: 7 Lorelei

sirenian
6 dugong, sea cow 7 manatee

siren song
4 lure 5 decoy, snare 6 come-on 10 allurement, enticement, temptation

Sirius
7 Dog Star

sister
3 nun 7 sibling
French: 5 soeur
Latin: 5 soror
Spanish: 7 hermana

Sister Carrie author
7 Dreiser (Theodore)

sisterly
7 sororal

Sisyphus
brother: 7 Athamas 9 Salmoneus
father: 6 Aeolus
mother: 7 Enarete
son: 7 Glaucus

sit
4 pose 5 perch, roost

Sita
abductor: 6 Ravana
husband, rescuer: 4 Rama

sitarist
7 Shankar (Ravi)

site
3 dig 4 home, spot 5 haunt, locus, place, point, scene, venue 6 locale 7 station 8 locality, location, position

sit-in
7 protest

sitting
6 séance 7 session
prolonged: 8 sederunt

Sitting Bull's tribe
5 Sioux

sitting duck
4 butt, mark 6 target

situate
  3 put, set 5 place 6 locate 7 install 8 position

situation
  3 job 4 post, rank 5 point, state 6 plight, status 7 footing, setting, station 8 location, position, standing 9 condition 13 circumstances

situs
  5 place, venue 6 locale

Siva
  see **Shiva**

six
  combining form: 3 hex, sex 4 hexa, sexi 5 sexti
  group of: 6 sestet, sextet 7 sextuplet
  relating to: 6 senary

sixfold
  8 sextuple

six-shooter
  3 gun 6 pistol 8 revolver

sixth sense
  3 ESP 7 insight 9 intuition, telepathy 12 clairvoyance

sizable
  3 big 5 ample, hefty, large, major, roomy 8 spacious 9 capacious, extensive 10 commodious, large-scale 11 substantial 12 considerable

size
  4 area, bulk, mass 5 range, scope, width 6 extent, height, length, spread, volume 7 bigness, breadth, caliber, expanse, measure, stature 9 amplitude, dimension, extension, greatness, largeness, magnitude 10 dimensions, proportion 11 measurement, proportions

size up
  3 peg 4 rate, read 5 assay, gauge, judge, value 6 assess, review, survey 7 adjudge, dope out 8 appraise, estimate, evaluate 9 figure out

sizzle
  3 fry 4 buzz, fizz, hiss, whiz 5 grill 6 hoopla, seethe 7 pizzazz 8 sibilate 10 excitement

sizzling
  3 hot 6 red-hot, torrid 7 burning 8 scalding, white-hot 9 scorching

skald
  4 bard, poet

Skanda
  6 war-god
  brother: 6 Ganesa 7 Ganesha
  father: 4 Siva 5 Shiva

skate
  3 nag, ray 4 skid, skim 5 glide, skirr, slide 8 glissade 11 Rollerblade
  blade: 6 runner
  kind: 6 figure, hockey

skating site
  3 ice 4 rink

skedaddle
  3 run 4 bolt, flee, skip 5 scoot, scram, split 6 beat it, begone, bug off, cut out, decamp, get out 7 make off, run away, scamper, skiddoo, take off, vamoose 8 clear out 10 make tracks

skein
  4 coil 5 flock, snarl, twist 6 tangle 12 entanglement

skeletal
  4 bony 5 gaunt 6 wasted 7 angular, scraggy, starved 8 rawboned 9 emaciated 10 cadaverous

skeleton
  5 bones, draft, frame 6 sketch 7 diagram, outline 9 bare bones, framework
  marine: 5 coral, shell

skeptic
  5 cynic 7 doubter, scoffer 8 agnostic 10 Pyrrhonist, questioner, unbeliever 11 disbeliever

skeptical
  4 wary 5 leery 6 show-me 7 cynical, dubious 8 doubtful, doubting 9 quizzical 10 dissenting, suspicious 11 mistrustful, questioning, unbelieving 12 disbelieving, freethinking

skepticism
  5 doubt 7 dubiety 8 distrust, mistrust, wariness 9 dubiosity, misgiving, suspicion 11 incertitude, uncertainty

skerry
  4 isle, reef 6 island

sketch
  4 draw, plot 5 draft, rough, trace 6 depict, design, doodle, lay out, map out, précis 7 develop, diagram, outline, portray 8 block out, chalk out, rough out 9 blueprint, delineate 12 characterize

sketchy
  4 iffy 5 crude, rough, vague 6 skimpy, slight

7 cursory, shallow 8 skeletal 10 incomplete 11 preliminary, superficial 12 questionable

skew
4 bias, veer 5 angle, fudge, slant, slide 6 swerve 7 distort

skewer
3 rod 4 spit 5 lance, spear, spike 6 impale, pierce 8 puncture, ridicule, transfix 9 brochette, criticize

ski
5 glide, slide
lift: 4 J-bar, T-bar 5 chair 7 gondola

skid
5 glide, skate, slide 6 pallet, runner 7 spinout 8 sideslip

skiddoo
4 scat 5 leave, scram, split 6 beat it, begone, bug off, decamp, depart, vacate 7 buzz off, take off, vamoose 8 clear out, shove off 9 skedaddle, take a hike 10 hit the road, make tracks

skid row
6 bowery

skier
American: 3 Moe (Tommy) 4 Kidd (Billy) 5 Mahre (Phil, Steve) 6 Miller (Bode) 7 Johnson (Bill)
Austrian: 5 Maier (Hermann) 6 Proell (Annemarie), Sailer (Toni) 7 Klammer (Franz), Schranz (Karl) 10 Girardelli (Marc) 11 Moser-Proell (Annemarie)
French: 5 Killy (Jean-Claude)
Italian: 5 Tomba (Alberto) 6 Thoeni (Gustavo)
Luxembourg: 10 Girardelli (Marc)
Swedish: 8 Stenmark (Ingemar)
Swiss: 10 Zurbriggen (Pirmin)

skiff
4 boat 7 rowboat

skiing
area: 3 run 5 slope
cross-country: 7 touring
event: 6 schuss, slalom 8 downhill 11 giant slalom
horse-drawn: 9 skijoring
kind: 6 Alpine, Nordic
position: 7 vorlage
technique: 6 wedeln 8 snowplow, traverse
turn: 7 christy 8 christie

skill
3 art 5 craft, knack 7 ability, address,

command, cunning, finesse, know-how, mastery, prowess, sleight 8 deftness, facility 9 dexterity, expertise, ingenuity, readiness, technique 10 adroitness, competence 11 proficiency

skilled
3 apt 4 able 5 adept 6 expert 7 capable, trained 8 masterly, talented 9 competent, masterful, practiced 10 proficient 12 accomplished

skillet
3 pan 6 spider 9 frying pan

skillful
4 deft 5 adept, crack, handy 6 adroit, clever, daedal, expert 7 skilled 8 masterly 9 competent, dexterous, masterful, practiced, workmanly 10 proficient 11 crackerjack, workmanlike 12 accomplished

skim
4 sail, scan, scud, skip 5 brush, carom, glide, graze, skirr 6 browse 8 embezzle, ricochet

skimp
4 save 5 pinch, scant, spare, stint 6 meager, scanty, scrape, sparse 7 slender 8 begrudge, conserve, retrench, withhold 9 economize

skimpy
5 scant, spare 6 meager, meagre, paltry, scanty, scarce, sparse 7 limited, wanting 8 exiguous 9 deficient 10 inadequate 12 insufficient

skim through
4 scan 6 browse

skin
3 fur, gyp, pod, rap 4 clad, clip, husk, hide, pare, peel, pelt, rind, soak 5 blame, cheat, cover, scale, shell, stiff, strip 6 fleece, sheath, sheathe 7 censure, condemn, sheathe 8 denounce 9 epidermis, sheathing 10 integument, overcharge 11 decorticate
animal: 4 coat, hide, pelt 6 hackle, peltry
combining form: 3 cut 4 cuti, derm 5 derma, dermo, dermy 6 dermat, dermia, dermis 7 cutaneo, dermata (plural), dermato, epiderm 8 epidermo
depression: 6 dimple
disease: 4 acne 5 hives, mange 6 eczema 10 dermatitis
dry: 5 scurf
fold: 5 plica

layer: 5 derma 6 corium, dermis 7 cuticle 9 epidermis
opening: 4 pore
protuberance: 3 tag, wen 4 mole, wart 6 pimple
rabbit: 5 coney
relating to: 6 dermal 9 cuticular, epidermal
spot: 7 freckle

skin-deep
7 shallow, trivial 11 superficial

skinflint
5 miser 7 niggard, scrooge 8 tightwad 10 cheapskate, pinchpenny

skin game
3 con 4 scam 5 bunco, bunko, cheat, fraud, sting, trick 6 hustle, racket 7 swindle 8 flimflam

skink
6 lizard

skinny
4 bony, dope, info, lank, lean, thin 5 gaunt, lanky, scoop, spare, weedy 6 twiggy 7 angular, lowdown, scraggy, scrawny 8 rawboned, skeletal 9 emaciated

Skin of Our Teeth author
6 Wilder (Thornton)

skip
3 hop, run 4 flee, jump, leap, omit, trip 5 bound, caper, carom, frisk, leave, scoot, skirr 6 cavort, gambol, pass up, spring 7 misfire, scamper, skitter 8 leave out, overlook, pass over, ricochet 9 skedaddle

skipjack
4 boat, fish, tuna 8 bluefish, ladyfish, sailboat

skipper
5 pilot 6 leader 7 captain 9 butterfly, commander

skirmish
3 row 4 fray 5 broil, brush, clash, melee, run-in, scrap, set-to 6 affray, battle, fracas 7 assault, dispute 8 conflict, struggle 9 encounter, scrimmage

skirr
3 run 4 bolt, flee, sail, scud, skim, skip 5 float, scoot, shoot 7 make off, scamper 9 skedaddle

skirt
3 hem, rim 4 brim, duck, edge 5 avoid, bound, brink, burke, dodge, elude, evade, hedge, verge 6 border, bypass, define, detour, escape, fringe, ignore, margin 8 sidestep, surround 9 perimeter, periphery 10 circumvent
ballet: 4 tutu
feature: 3 hem 4 slit
long: 4 maxi
Scottish: 4 kilt
short: 4 mini
style: 5 A-line 6 sheath

skit
6 shtick, sketch 9 burlesque

skitter
3 hop 4 flit, skip, trip 6 scurry, spring 7 scamper

skittery
see **skittish**

skittish
3 coy, shy 4 edgy, wary 5 chary, dizzy, jumpy, leery 6 fickle 7 bashful, fidgety, flighty, nervous, rabbity, restive 8 unstable, volatile 9 excitable, frivolous, impulsive, mercurial, whimsical 10 capricious, unreliable

skive
4 pare 5 carve, shave, slice

skivvies
9 underwear

skoal
5 toast 6 health

skua
4 bird 6 jaeger 7 seabird

skulduggery
5 fraud 8 foul play, trickery 9 chicanery, duplicity 10 hanky-panky

skulk
4 lurk, slip 5 creep, prowl, shirk, slink, sneak, steal

skull
4 head, mind 5 brain 7 cranium 8 brainpan 9 braincase
back of: 7 occiput
bone: 5 vomer 6 zygoma 7 ethmoid, frontal 8 parietal, sphenoid, temporal
jawless: 9 calvarium
joint: 6 suture
part: 3 jaw 5 inion

skullcap
6 beanie, pileus 7 calotte 8 yarmulke 9 calvarium, zucchetto

skunk
4 beat, drub, lick, scum, whip, whup 6 thrash, wallop 7 clobber, polecat, shellac,

stinker, trounce **8** civet cat, lambaste **9**
overwhelm, slaughter
genus: 8 Mephitis

sky
5 azure **6** heaven, welkin **7** heavens **8**
empyrean **9** firmament

sky-blue
5 azure **8** cerulean

skylarking
5 revel **7** revelry, whoopee **9** high jinks,
horseplay, rowdiness, whoop-de-do **10**
roughhouse **12** roughhousing

skylight
6 window

skyline
7 horizon, outline

sky pilot
5 padre **6** cleric, parson, pastor **8**
chaplain, minister, preacher **9** churchman,
clergyman

skyrocket
4 rise, soar **7** shoot up **8** catapult

sky sighting
3 UFO

slab
5 block, chunk, slice, strip **8** pavement

slack
3 lax **4** lazy, slow, soft **5** inert, loose, relax
6 remiss **7** ease off, laggard, passive,
relaxed **8** careless, derelict, dilatory,
inactive, indolent, slothful, sluggish,
stagnant **9** leisurely, lethargic, negligent
10 neglectful

slacken
3 ebb, lax **4** ease, slow, wane **5** abate, let
up, loose, relax **6** detain, ease up, lessen,
loosen, relent, retard, slow up **7** die down,
dwindle, ease off, subside **8** diminish,
moderate, slow down **9** untighten **10**
decelerate

slacker
3 bum **4** slug **5** idler, sloth **6** loafer **7**
goof-off, shirker, wastrel **8** deadbeat,
layabout, slugabed, sluggard **9** goldbrick,
lazybones **10** delinquent **11** couch potato

slag
4 lava **5** dross **6** cinder, debris, scoria

slake
5 allay **6** deaden, quench **7** crumble,
hydrate, relieve, satisfy **9** alleviate

slam
3 bat, hit, jab, pan, rap **4** bang, bash, beat,
belt, blow, boom, dash, drub, flay, slug, slur,
swat, wham **5** blast, crack, crash, fling,
knock, pound, slash, smack, smash, swipe,
whack **6** batter, cudgel, hammer, scathe,
strike, thwack, wallop **7** clobber, potshot **8**
lambaste **9** castigate

slam-dance
4 mosh

slam dunk
5 cinch, setup **6** shoo-in **7** safe bet **9**
certainty, sure thing

slammer
3 can, jug, pen **4** brig, coop, jail, stir **5**
clink, pokey **6** cooler, lockup, prison **9**
calaboose **12** penitentiary

slander
4 slur, tale **5** libel, slime, smear, sully **6**
defame, malign, smirch, vilify **7** calumny,
scandal, tarnish, traduce **8** besmirch **9**
denigrate **10** backbiting, calumniate,
defamation, detraction, scandalize **11**
mud-slinging **12** back-stabbing

slang
4 cant, jive **5** argot, lingo **6** jargon, patois,
patter **7** dialect **10** vernacular

slant
3 tip **4** bank, bias, cant, heel, lean, list,
skew, tilt, veer, warp **5** angle, aside, bevel,
grade, slope, splay **7** distort, incline,
leaning, outlook **8** gradient **9** prejudice,
viewpoint **10** standpoint **11** inclination **12**
predilection
combining form: 4 clin **5** clino

slap
3 hit, pop **4** bash, blow, cuff, shot, slam,
swat **5** clout, smack, spank, whack **6**
buffet, insult, rebuff, strike **7** affront,
putdown **8** brickbat, lambaste, penalize **9**
castigate

slapdash
5 hasty, messy **6** random, sloppy **7**
cursory **8** careless, slipshod **9** half-baked,
haphazard, hit-or-miss, makeshift

slap down
5 quell **6** kibosh **7** squelch **8** prohibit,
suppress

slaphappy
5 dazed, dizzy, woozy **6** punchy **10**
punch-drunk

slash
3 cut **4** clip, gash, hack, pare, slit **5** lower,

slat

shave, slice **6** reduce, scathe, scorch **7** abridge, blister, curtail, cut back, cut down, scarify, scourge, shorten **8** lacerate, lambaste, mark down **9** castigate, excoriate **10** abbreviate

slat

4 lath **5** board, stave, strip **6** louver, louvre **7** airfoil

slate

4 gray, list, rock, tile **6** lineup, record, tablet, ticket **7** shingle **8** schedule **9** designate

slather

5 smear **6** spread **8** squander

slattern

4 bawd, moll, slut, tart **5** hussy, tramp, wench **6** floozy, harlot **7** chippie, jezebel, trollop **8** strumpet **10** prostitute **11** painted lady **12** scarlet woman, streetwalker

slaughter

4 kill, slay **6** murder **7** butcher, carnage, killing, wipe out **8** butchery, decimate, demolish, hecatomb, massacre **9** bloodbath, bloodshed, exterminate, liquidate **10** annihilate, butchering **11** destruction, exterminate, liquidation **12** annihilation

slaughterhouse

8 abattoir

Slav

4 Pole, Serb, Sorb, Wend **5** Croat, Czech **6** Bulgar, Slovak **7** Russian, Serbian, Slovene **8** Bohemian, Croatian, Moravian **9** Bulgarian, Ruthenian, Ukrainian

slave

4 grub, help, peon, plod, serf, slog, toil **5** grind, helot, swink **6** drudge, menial, thrall, toiler, vassal **7** bondman, chattel, servant
feudal: **4** serf
harem: **9** odalisque
liberated: **8** freedman
Muslim: **6** Mamluk **8** Mameluke
Spartan: **5** helot

slave driver

6 tyrant **7** foreman **8** martinet, overseer **10** taskmaster **11** Simon Legree

slaver

4 spit **5** drool, froth **6** drivel, saliva **7** dribble, slobber, spittle **8** salivate

slavery

6 thrall **7** bondage, helotry, peonage, serfdom **9** indenture, servitude, thralldom **11** subjugation

Slavic apostle

5 Cyril **9** Methodius

slavish

6 abject, menial **7** servile **8** obeisant, wretched **9** groveling, imitative, laborious **10** obsequious, unoriginal **11** subservient

slay

4 do in, kill **6** murder **7** bump off, butcher, execute, put away **8** dispatch, knock off **9** liquidate, slaughter **11** assassinate

slayer

7 butcher **11** executioner

sleazy

3 low **5** cheap, dingy, seedy, tacky, tatty **6** cheesy, flimsy, shabby, shoddy, trashy **7** run-down, squalid **8** gimcrack **10** down-at-heel **11** dilapidated **12** disreputable

sled

4 luge, pung **6** sleigh **7** coaster, travois **8** toboggan
Russian: **6** troika

sled dog

5 husky **8** malamute

sledge

4 maul **6** hammer, sleigh
Eskimo: **7** komatik

sleek

4 oily **6** glassy, glossy, smooth **7** elegant, stylish **8** lustrous, polished **10** glistening

sleep

3 nap **4** doze, rest **6** catnap, repose, siesta, snooze **7** shut-eye, slumber **11** slumberland
bringer: **7** sandman
combining form: **4** hypn, narc **5** hypno, narco, somni
god: **6** Hypnos, Somnus

sleeper

4 beam, mole **7** Pullman **8** long shot **11** double agent, stringpiece

sleeping

7 dormant **8** comatose
disease: **10** narcolepsy

sleepless

7 wakeful **8** vigilant **9** insomniac

sleeplessness

8 insomnia

sleepwalker

12 somnambulist

sleepy
4 dozy 6 drowsy 7 nodding 9 somnolent 10 slumberous

sleigh
4 pung 6 sledge

sleight
4 ploy, ruse, wile 5 skill, trick 7 gimmick, prowess 8 artifice, deftness, maneuver 9 dexterity, stratagem 10 adroitness

sleight of hand
11 legerdemain

slender
4 lean, slim, thin, trim 5 lithe, reedy, spare 6 skinny, slight, svelte, twiggy 7 spindly, willowy

sleuth
4 dick, Drew (Nancy) 5 Brown (Encyclopedia, Father), Kojak, Morse, Queen (Ellery), Saint (The), snoop, Spade (Sam), Tracy (Dick), Wolfe (Nero) 6 Hammer (Mike), Holmes (Sherlock), Marple (Miss), Poirot (Hercule), shamus, Wimsey (Peter) 7 Cadfael (Brother), Columbo, Fansler (Kate), gumshoe, Maigret, Marlowe (Philip) 8 hawkshaw, Millhone (Kinsey), Rockford (Jim), sherlock 9 Dalgliesh (Adam), detective, Scarpetta (Kay) 10 private eye 12 investigator

slew
3 lot, mob, ton 4 army, heap, host, load, mess, pile, raft, skid, turn, veer 5 batch, bunch, crowd, flock, pivot, twist 6 myriad, passel, swerve, throng 9 abundance, multitude

slice
3 cut 4 gash, slit 5 allot, carve, divvy, quota, sever, share, slash, split, wedge 6 cleave, divide, incise, sample 7 dissect, portion, segment 8 allocate 9 allotment, allowance

slick
4 film, glib, oily, slip, wily 5 sharp, sleek, soapy 6 crafty, glossy, greasy, shrewd, smarmy, smooth, tricky 7 cunning 8 slippery, slithery, unctuous 10 lubricious, oleaginous

slicker
4 dude 5 dandy, shark 6 con man 7 cheater, diddler, grifter, oilskin, sharper 8 raincoat, swindler 9 trickster 11 flimflammer

slide
3 dip, sag 4 flow, ramp, skid, slip 5 chute, coast, chute, drift, glide, skate, slump, spill

6 scooch, stream 7 decline, slither 8 downturn 9 downswing, downtrend 12 transparency

slight
4 omit, skip, slim, snub, thin 5 frail, reedy, scorn, small 6 flimsy, ignore, meager, meagre, modest, offend, paltry, remote, skinny 7 contemn, neglect, outside, put-down, slender, tenuous, trivial 8 brush-off, delicate, discount, overlook, smallish, trifling 9 disregard, pint-sized 10 disrespect, negligible

slim
4 thin 5 lithe, reedy, small, spare 6 meager, meagre, minute, narrow, paltry, remote, skinny, slight, svelte, twiggy 7 lissome, outside, slender, tenuous 9 lithesome 10 negligible

slim down
4 diet, fast 6 reduce 10 slenderize

slime
3 goo, mud 4 glop, gunk, muck, ooze, scum 5 filth 6 sleaze, sludge 7 slander

slimy
4 oozy 6 mucous 7 viscous

sling
3 lob 4 cast, fire, hang, hurl, sock, toss 5 chuck, heave, march, pitch, throw 6 dangle, launch 7 suspend 8 catapult

slink
4 lurk 5 creep, prowl, skulk, slide, sneak, steal 7 gumshoe

slinky
4 sexy 5 lithe, sleek 6 svelte 7 furtive, lissome, sinuous, slender, willowy 8 graceful, sensuous, stealthy

slip
3 sag 4 dock, drop, fall, flow, flub, goof, lurk, shed, sink, skid 5 berth, boner, creep, error, fluff, gaffe, glide, lapse, slide, slink, slump, sneak, steal 6 escape 7 blooper, blunder, decline, drop off, fall off, faux pas, mistake, slither 8 downturn, throw off 9 downswing, downtrend

slipper
4 mule, shoe 5 scuff 6 bootee, bootie, sandal 8 flip-flop, pantofle

slippery
3 icy 4 eely, oily 5 slick 6 greasy, shifty, smooth 7 devious, evasive 8 illusive, slithery 10 lubricious

slipshod

6 blowsy, blowzy, frowsy, frowzy, shabby, shoddy, sloppy, untidy **7** rumpled, scrubby, scruffy, unkempt **8** careless, ill-kempt, slapdash, slovenly, tattered **9** haphazard, negligent **10** bedraggled, disheveled, down-at-heel

slipup

4 goof **5** boner, error, fluff, lapse **6** bungle, glitch, miscue, mishap **7** blooper, blunder, faux pas, misstep, mistake, setback, stumble **8** accident **9** mischance, oversight **10** misfortune **11** misjudgment

slit

3 cut, gap **4** gash, rent **5** chink, crack, slash, slice **6** cranny, incise **7** crevice, fissure, opening

slither

4 slip **5** creep, glide, sidle, slide, slink, snake, sneak, steal **7** wriggle **8** undulate

slithery

see **slippery**

sliver

5 scrap, shard, shave, shred, slice **6** paring **7** shaving, snippet **8** splinter

slob

3 oaf **4** boor, clod, goon, lout **6** galoot, sloven

slobber

4 gush **5** drool, froth **6** drivel, effuse, slaver **7** dribble, enthuse **8** salivate

sloe

4 plum **10** blackthorn

slog

4 grub, moil, plod, plug, toil **5** chore, grind, labor, slave, sweat **6** drudge, schlep, trudge **7** schlepp

slogan

5 motto **6** byword **9** catchword, watchword **10** shibboleth **11** catchphrase

sloop

4 boat **8** sailboat

slop

3 mud, pap **4** gush, muck **5** douse, dreck, dregs, offal, slosh, slush, spill, swill **6** guzzle, pablum, refuse, splash, sludge **7** garbage, pabulum, rubbish **8** splatter

slope

3 tip **4** bend, cant, heel, lean, list, rise, skew, swag, sway, tilt **5** grade, pitch, scarp, slant **6** ascent, glacis **7** descent, incline, leaning, recline **8** gradient **9** acclivity, declivity, obliquity **11** inclination **combining form: 5** cline **6** clinal

sloppy

5 dowdy, gushy, messy **6** slushy, untidy **7** gushing, unkempt **8** careless, effusive, ill-kempt, slapdash, slipshod, slovenly **10** bedraggled, disheveled **11** dishevelled

slosh

4 gush, slop, wash **5** churn, swash **6** gurgle, splash **8** flounder, splatter

slot

4 vent **5** niche, notch **6** groove, keyway **7** keyhole, opening, passage **8** aperture **10** pigeonhole

sloth

4 laze **5** idler **6** acedia, apathy, idling, lazing, loafer, slouch, torpor **7** goof-off, languor, loafing, slacker **8** idleness, laziness, lethargy **9** heaviness, indolence, lassitude, lazybones, torpidity **11** couch potato **12** listlessness, sluggishness **13** shiftlessness

slothful

4 idle, lazy **8** fainéant, indolent **9** shiftless

slouch

3 bum, oaf, sag **4** laze, loaf, loll, lout, mope, slug **5** droop, idler, sloth, slump, stoop **6** loafer, loiter, lounge **7** saunter, shamble, shuffle **8** fainéant, slugabed, sluggard **9** do-nothing, lazybones

slough

3 bog, fen **4** cast, mire, molt, quag, shed, sump **5** inlet, marsh, scrap, swamp **6** morass, reject **7** discard **8** jettison, quagmire, throw out **9** backwater, marshland, swampland, throw away

Slovakia

capital: 10 Bratislava
city: 6 Kosice
monetary unit: 6 koruna
mountain range: 10 Carpathian
neighbor: 7 Austria, Hungary, Poland, Ukraine **13** Czech Republic
river: 3 Váh **4** Hron **6** Danube, Morava

Slovenia

capital: 9 Ljubljana
city: 7 Maribor
monetary unit: 5 tolar
neighbor: 5 Italy **7** Austria, Croatia, Hungary
part of: 7 Balkans
peninsula: 6 Balkan

slovenly

5 dingy, messy, mussy, seedy, slack **6**

frowsy, frowzy, grubby, grungy, scuzzy, shabby, skanky, sleazy, sloppy, untidy **7** squalid, unkempt **8** careless, slapdash, slipshod **10** bedraggled, slatternly

slow
4 late, poky **5** brake, check, lento, tardy **6** adagio, hinder, impede, leaden, retard, torpid **7** halting, lagging, slacken **8** dilatory, dragging, plodding, sluggish, stagnant **9** leisurely, snaillike, unhurried **10** decelerate, snail-paced, straggling

slowpoke
5 snail **6** lagger **7** dawdler, laggard **8** lingerer, loiterer **9** straggler

sludge
3 mud **4** crud, gunk, mire, muck, ooze, slop **5** slime **6** sewage **8** sediment

slug
3 bum, hit, nip, tot **4** bash, belt, dram, drop, jolt, shot, slam, swat **5** blast, clout, idler, larva, pound, punch, smack, smash, snail, snort, thump **6** buffet, loafer, slouch, thwack, wallop **7** clobber, goof-off, slacker **8** fainéant, toothful **9** do-nothing, lazybones **11** couch potato
genus: 5 Limax

slugfest
4 bout **5** brawl, set-to **6** rumble **8** dogfight **10** donnybrook, prizefight

sluggard
3 bum **5** idler **6** loafer, slouch **7** dawdler, goof-off, laggard, shirker, slacker **8** deadbeat, fainéant, slowpoke, slugabed **9** do-nothing, goldbrick, lazybones

slugger
5 boxer **6** batter, hitter **7** palooka

sluggish
4 lazy, logy, slow **5** inert, slack **6** draggy, leaden, stupid, torpid **7** lumpish **8** dragging, indolent, listless, slothful **9** apathetic, lethargic

sluice
4 duct, flow, gush, pour, race, wash **5** flush, surge **6** trough **7** channel **8** spillway **9** floodgate

slum
6 ghetto **7** skid row

slumber
3 nap **4** doze **5** sleep **6** catnap, drowse, snooze, stupor, torpor **8** dormancy, hebetude, lethargy **9** lassitude, torpidity

slumberous
see **sleepy**

slumgullion
4 stew **6** burgoo, ragout **7** goulash

slump
3 dip, sag **4** drop, fall, flag, funk, loll, sink, slip **5** droop, hunch, slide **6** slouch, trough **7** decline, drop off, falloff **8** collapse, downturn **9** downslide, downswing, downtrend, recession **10** depression, stagnation

slur
4 blot, blur, lisp, onus, slam, spot **5** brand, knock, libel, odium, smear, stain **6** befoul, defame, insult, malign, stigma, vilify **7** blacken, calumny, obloquy, obscure, slander, spatter, traduce **8** black eye, brickbat, innuendo, tear down **9** aspersion, bespatter, denigrate, discredit, disparage **10** accusation, calumniate

slurp
3 lap **4** gulp, suck **5** lap up, swill **6** guzzle

slush
3 mud **4** mire, muck, slop **6** drivel **8** schmaltz

sly
4 foxy, wily **5** cagey, saucy, shady, slick **6** artful, clever, crafty, shrewd, smooth, sneaky, subtle, tricky **7** cunning, devious, furtive, roguish, vulpine **8** guileful, scheming, slippery, stealthy **9** designing, insidious, underhand **11** mischievous, underhanded

slyboots
see **scamp**

slyness
4 wile **5** guile **7** cunning **8** caginess, foxiness, wiliness **9** canniness **10** craftiness

smack
3 bat, bop, box **4** bang, bash, belt, biff, blow, buss, chop, clip, cuff, dash, hint, kiss, peck, reek, slam, slap, sock, tang, whop **5** clout, crack, plumb, punch, right, savor, smell, spank, stink, taste, tinge, trace, whack **6** buffet, heroin, relish, smooch, square, strike, thwack **7** clobber, soupçon

smack-dab
4 bang, just **5** plumb, right **7** exactly **8** squarely **9** perfectly, precisely

small
3 wee **4** mean, mini, puny, tiny **5** bitty, dinky, dwarf, micro, minor, petty, runty,

short, teeny **6** bantam, little, meager, meagre, minute, monkey, narrow, paltry, petite, slight, teensy **7** cramped, stunted, trivial **8** picayune, piddling, pint-size, trifling **9** miniature, minuscule, pint-sized **10** diminutive, negligible, undersized **11** ineffectual, unimportant **13** insignificant

small fry
4 kids, tots **8** children **10** youngsters

small-minded
4 mean **5** petty **6** narrow **7** bigoted **9** hidebound, illiberal, parochial **10** brassbound, intolerant, provincial

smallpox
7 variola

small talk
4 chat **6** banter **7** chatter, palaver, prattle **8** badinage, chitchat, raillery, repartee **10** persiflage

small-time
5 minor, petty **6** paltry, two-bit **7** trivial **8** picayune, piddling, trifling **9** bush-league, negligible, shoestring **11** minor-league, unimportant **13** insignificant

smalt
4 blue

smarmy
4 glib, oily **5** slick **6** sleazy **7** buttery, fawning, fulsome **8** unctuous **10** obsequious, oleaginous **12** ingratiating

smart
3 apt **4** ache, chic, keen **5** acute, alert, canny, fresh, natty, quick, sassy, saucy, sharp, slick, sting, swank, throb **6** brainy, bright, cheeky, clever, dapper, shrewd, spruce, suffer **7** dashing, stylish **8** impudent **9** fashionable, intelligent, quick-witted, ready-witted, sharp-witted

smart aleck
7 show-off, wise guy **8** wiseacre **9** know-it-all **11** wisecracker, wisenheimer

smart-alecky
4 wise **5** fresh, sassy, saucy **6** cheeky **8** impudent, insolent **9** bold-faced **11** impertinent

smart set
5 elect, elite **6** bon ton, gentry **7** in crowd, quality, society, who's who **9** beau monde, haut monde **10** blue bloods, upper crust **11** aristocracy, Four Hundred, high society

smarty-pants
7 wise guy **9** know-it-all, swellhead **11** wisenheimer

smash
3 hit, jar **4** bang, bash, belt, blow, boom, clap, jolt, raze, ruin, slam, slug, sock, wham, whop **5** blast, burst, clash, crack, crash, crush, pound, shock, whack, wreck **6** batter, impact, pileup, shiver, wallop **7** clobber, crack-up, debacle, destroy, shatter, smashup, success **8** collapse, decimate, demolish, fragment, knockout, overhand, splinter, tear down **9** breakdown, collision, pulverize, sensation, succès fou **10** annihilate **12** disintegrate

smashup
5 crash, wreck **6** fiasco, pileup **7** crack-up, debacle **8** accident, collapse, disaster **9** breakdown, collision

smattering
3 few **7** handful **10** sprinkling

smear
3 dab, tar **4** beat, coat, daub, drub, lick, slur, soil, whip **5** cover, libel, stain, sully, taint **6** befoul, defame, defile, malign, smirch, smudge, spread, thrash, vilify **7** asperse, blacken, calumny, plaster, shellac, slander, tarnish, traduce **8** besmirch, bespatter, denigrate **10** calumniate

smell
4 funk, nose, odor, reek **5** aroma, scent, sense, smack, sniff, snuff, stink, trace, whiff **6** detect, stench **7** bouquet, perfume **9** fragrance, redolence

smell, sense of
9 olfaction

smelly
4 rank **5** fetid, funky, reeky **6** foetid, putrid, rancid, stinky **7** noisome, reeking, stenchy **8** mephitic, stinking **10** malodorous

smelt
4 flux, fuse, slag **6** reduce, refine, tomcod **8** sparling **9** sand lance, whitebait

smidgen
see **particle**

smile
4 beam, grin **5** smirk **6** simper

smirch
see **smudge**

smirk
4 grin, leer **5** fleer, sneer **6** simper **7** grimace

smite
3 hit **4** belt, kill, sock **5** clout, whack **6**

assail, attack, strike **7** afflict, assault, clobber, torment

smithereens
4 bits **6** pieces **9** fragments, particles

smitten
5 taken **6** hooked **8** besotted, enamored **9** enamoured, enchanted, entranced **10** captivated, enraptured, infatuated **11** intoxicated

smock
5 apron, dress, frock **8** pinafore

smoke
4 cure, fume **5** fumes, vapor **8** fastball, fumigate **9** cigarette

smoky
4 fumy, gray, hazy **5** murky, sooty **6** turbid **7** reeking **10** caliginous, smoldering

smolder
4 glow **5** churn **6** bubble, seethe, simmer **7** ferment **9** fulminate

smooch
4 buss, kiss, neck, peck **5** smack **8** osculate

smooth
4 easy, even, flat **5** fluid, flush, level, plane, sleek, slick, suave **6** facile, fluent, glassy, glossy, polish, urbane **7** cursive, flatten, flowing, running **8** glabrous, hairless, soothing, unbroken **10** effortless, unwrinkled

smooth-spoken
4 glib **6** fluent **8** eloquent **10** articulate **13** silver-tongued

smorgasbord
4 hash, olio **6** buffet, jumble, medley **7** farrago, mélange **8** mishmash, mixed bag, pastiche **9** potpourri **10** hodgepodge, miscellany, salmagundi **11** gallimaufry

smother
5 choke, douse, quell **6** hush up, muffle, quench, stifle **7** blanket, repress, squelch **8** inundate, restrain, suppress **9** overwhelm, suffocate **10** asphyxiate

smudge
3 dab **4** blot, blur, daub, foul, soil **5** dirty, smear, stain, sully, taint **6** bedaub, blotch, defile, smirch **7** begrime, besmear, blacken, blemish, splotch, tarnish **8** besmirch

smug
8 priggish **9** conceited **10** complacent **13** self-satisfied

smuggle
3 run **7** bootleg

smut
4 porn **5** filth **9** obscenity **11** pornography

smutty
4 blue, foul, lewd, racy **5** bawdy, dirty, nasty, sooty **6** coarse, filthy, risqué, vulgar **7** obscene, raunchy **8** indecent, off-color, prurient **9** salacious **12** pornographic, scatological

Smyrna
5 Izmir

snack
3 tea **4** bite, nosh, tapa **6** morsel, nibble **11** refreshment

snaffle
3 bit, cop **4** lift **5** filch, pinch, swipe **6** pilfer, pocket **7** purloin

snafu
5 botch, error, mix-up, snarl **6** bungle, foul up, mess up, muddle **7** chaotic, screwup **9** confusion

snag
3 nab **4** curb, grab, hook, nail, tear **5** catch, hitch **6** glitch, holdup, hurdle, obtain, secure **7** capture **8** drawback, obstacle **9** apprehend **10** impediment **11** obstruction

snail
5 whelk **6** limpet **7** mollusc, mollusk **8** escargot, ramshorn, slowpoke **9** gastropod **10** periwinkle

snake
3 boa **4** fink **5** crawl, creep, racer, slide **6** python, writhe **7** hognose, serpent, slither **8** anaconda, ophidian, undulate
poisonous: 3 asp **5** adder, cobra, coral, krait, mamba, viper **6** elapid, taipan **7** rattler **8** pit viper **10** bushmaster, copperhead, fer-de-lance **11** cottonmouth **13** water moccasin

snakebird
6 darter **7** anhinga

snake-eater
8 mongoose **13** secretary bird

snakelike
7 sinuous **8** ophidian **10** serpentine

snakeroot
7 bugbane **10** wild ginger **11** blazing star

snakeweed
7 bistort 13 poison hemlock

snaky
7 sinuous, winding 8 flexuous, tortuous 10 convoluted, meandering, serpentine 11 anfractuous

snap
4 bang, bark 5 break, cinch, crack 6 breeze, picnic 7 crackle 8 duck soup, kid stuff, pushover 10 child's play

snap back
6 revive 7 rebound, recover 10 convalesce, recuperate

snappy
4 edgy, fast, tart 5 brisk, hasty, huffy, natty, quick, rapid, sharp, smart, swank, swift, testy 6 lively, prompt, speedy, touchy 7 dashing, stylish, waspish 8 animated, petulant, vigorous 9 breakneck, fractious, irritable, vivacious

snare
3 bag 4 bait, hook, lure, trap 5 catch, decoy, tempt 6 come-on, enmesh, entice, entrap, seduce, tangle 7 capture, catch up, chicane, embroil, ensnare, ensnarl, involve, pitfall, trammel 8 entangle, inveigle 9 chicanery, deception 10 enticement, temptation

snarl
3 jam, web 4 bark, knot, maze, mesh 5 chaos, growl, ravel, skein 6 jungle, morass, muddle, tangle 7 perplex 8 disarray, disorder, entangle, mishmash 9 confusion, labyrinth 10 complexity, complicate 12 complication, entanglement

snatch
3 bit, nab 4 grab, jerk, take, yank 5 catch, pluck, seize, swipe 6 abduct, clutch, kidnap, wrench 8 fragment

snazzy
4 chic 5 fancy, gaudy, jazzy, nobby, ritzy, sassy, sharp, smart, showy, swank 6 chichi, classy, flashy, garish, glitzy, jaunty, spiffy, swanky 7 elegant

sneak
3 cur, pad 4 lurk, slip, worm 5 crawl, creep, glide, mooch, prowl, shirk, skulk, skunk, slide, slink, steal 6 covert, secret, tiptoe, weasel 7 furtive, gumshoe, slither, smuggle 8 hush-hush, slyboots, stealthy 9 pussyfoot, scoundrel 10 undercover 11 clandestine

sneaky
4 foxy 6 shifty, tricky 7 devious, furtive 8 guileful, indirect, slippery, stealthy 9 underhand 11 duplicitous, underhanded

sneer
4 gibe, jeer 5 fleer, scoff, smirk 7 grimace, snigger

snicker
5 laugh 6 giggle, titter 7 chortle, chuckle

snide
4 mean 5 nasty 8 spiteful 9 malicious 11 insinuating

sniff
4 jeer, nose 5 scent, scoff, smell, snoop 6 inhale

sniffy
4 smug 5 aloof, lofty 6 lordly, snooty, uppity 7 haughty, pompous, stuck-up 8 scornful, superior 10 disdainful, hoity-toity 12 contemptuous, supercilious

snifter
3 nip, sip, tot 4 dram, drop, jolt, shot, slug 5 glass, snort 6 finger, goblet

snip
3 bit, cut 4 clip, crop, trim 5 notch, scrap 8 fragment

snipe
4 carp 9 sandpiper

sniper
6 gunman, killer 7 shooter 8 marksman, rifleman 12 sharpshooter

snippety
see **snippy**

snippy
4 curt 5 bluff, blunt, brief, gruff, short, terse 6 abrupt, crusty 7 brusque 8 snappish

snit
3 fit 4 flap, fume, huff, stew 5 panic, pique, sweat, tizzy 6 dither, frenzy, lather, pother, swivet 10 conniption

snitch
3 cop, nip, rat 4 beak, fink, hook, lift, palm, sing, tell 5 filch, peach, pinch, spill, steal, swipe 6 inform, pilfer, pocket, squeal, tattle 7 purloin, rat fink, tattler, tipster 8 betrayer, informer, squealer 11 stool pigeon

snivel
3 sob 4 weep 5 cower, whine 6 cringe, whinge 7 blubber, snuffle, whimper

snob
6 poseur 7 parvenu, tinhorn, upstart

snobbish
6 snooty, uppity 7 haughty, high-hat, stuck-up 10 hoity-toity 11 patronizing, pretentious 12 supercilious 13 condescending

snook
5 cobia 6 robalo 12 sergeant fish

snooker
3 con 4 dupe, fool, hoax, pool 5 trick 6 delude 7 beguile, deceive, defraud 8 flimflam, hoodwink 9 bamboozle 11 hornswoggle

snoop
3 pry, spy 4 nose, peek, peep, peer, poke 5 prier, pryer 6 ferret, meddle, sleuth 7 gumshoe, intrude, meddler 8 busybody, quidnunc 9 detective, inspector, interfere 10 rubberneck

snooper
3 spy 9 detective, inspector 12 investigator

snoopy
4 nosy 6 prying 7 curious 8 meddling 9 intrusive 10 meddlesome 11 inquisitive

snoot
see **snout**

snooty
see **snobbish**

snooze
3 kip, nap 4 doze 5 sleep 6 catnap, drowse, nod off, siesta 7 drop off, slumber 10 forty winks

snore
8 rhonchus

snort
3 nip, tot 4 dram, drop, jolt, shot, slug 5 scoff, snarl 6 exhale, inhale 7 snifter

snout
4 beak, nose 6 muzzle 9 proboscis

snow
glacial: 4 firn, névé
melted: 5 slush
pellet: 7 graupel
ridge: 8 sastruga

snow apple
8 mushroom

snowball
5 mount, run up 6 expand 7 augment, burgeon, explode, inflate 8 increase, multiply, mushroom, viburnum 10 accumulate 11 proliferate

snowbird
5 finch, junco 6 thrush 7 bunting 9 fieldfare, ivory gull

Snow-Bound author
8 Whittier (John Greenleaf)

snow finch
9 brambling

snow grouse
9 ptarmigan

snow leopard
5 ounce

Snow Leopard author
11 Matthiessen (Peter)

snowstorm
8 blizzard

snub
3 cut 4 shun 5 blunt, scorn, spite, spurn 6 rebuff, rebuke, slight, stubby 7 put down 9 ostracize, repudiate 12 cold-shoulder

snuff
3 ice, off 4 kill, nose 5 pinch, scent, smell 6 murder, rappee 7 execute 10 extinguish 11 exterminate

snug
4 cozy, neat, taut, tidy, trim 5 comfy, cushy, tight 6 burrow, cuddle, nestle, nuzzle, secure 7 orderly 9 sheltered, shipshape 11 comfortable

snuggle
5 spoon 6 burrow, cuddle, curl up, huddle, nestle, nuzzle

so
3 sae 4 ergo, then, thus 5 hence 6 indeed 9 similarly, therefore 11 accordingly 12 consequently

soak
3 sot, wet 4 bilk, clip, lush, skin, swig, wino 5 douse, drink, gouge, imbue, souse, steep 6 boozer, drench, fleece, infuse, seethe 7 drinker, guzzler, immerse 8 drunkard, permeate, saturate, submerge 9 alcoholic, penetrate 10 boozehound, impregnate, overcharge
flax: 3 ret

soap
4 suds 6 stroke 7 flatter, wheedle 8 blandish, butter up, inveigle 9 sweet-talk
hard: 7 castile
ingredient: 3 lye

soapbox

soapbox
4 dais 6 podium 7 rostrum 8 hustings, platform, scaffold

soap plant
5 amole

soapstone
8 steatite

soapwort
7 cowherd 11 bouncing bet

soar
3 fly 4 lift, rise 5 arise, climb, glide, hover, mount, shoot 6 ascend, rocket 7 shoot up 8 increase 9 skyrocket

sob
3 cry 4 bawl, blub, wail, weep 7 blubber, whimper

sober
4 calm, cool 5 grave, staid 6 low-key, proper, sedate, serene, solemn 7 austere, earnest, serious, subdued 8 composed, decorous, low-keyed, moderate, rational, reserved 9 abstinent, collected, practical, pragmatic, realistic, temperate 10 abstaining, abstemious, controlled, forbearing, hardheaded, no-nonsense, reasonable, restrained 11 disciplined, down-to-earth 12 matter-of-fact 13 imperturbable, self-possessed, unimpassioned

sobriety
7 gravity 10 abstinence, continence, sedateness, temperance 11 seriousness

sobriquet
3 tag 5 alias 6 byname 7 epithet, moniker 8 cognomen, nickname 10 hypocorism

so-called
6 formal 7 alleged, nominal, titular 8 supposed 9 pretended, professed, purported 10 ostensible, self-styled

soccer
cup: 5 World
official: 7 referee 8 linesman
player: 6 booter, goalie, kicker, winger 7 forward, link man, striker, sweeper 8 defender, fullback, halfback 10 goalkeeper
star: 4 Hamm (Mia), Pelé 5 Akers (Michelle) 7 Beckham (David), Ronaldo 8 Maradona (Diego) 11 Beckenbauer (Franz)
term: 3 net 4 boot, chip, kick, trap 6 corner, header, tackle, volley 7 dribble, kickoff, throw-in 8 back-heel, free kick, goal kick, goal line 9 touchline 10 center

spot, corner flag, corner kick 11 dropped ball, halfway line, penalty kick, penalty spot

sociable
5 close 6 genial 7 affable, amiable, cordial 8 familiar, gracious 9 clubbable, congenial, convivial 10 gregarious, hospitable 11 good-natured

social
5 civic, civil 8 communal 9 clubbable, convivial 10 collective, gregarious, hospitable 13 extroverted 13 companionable
class: 5 caste

Social Contract author
8 Rousseau (Jean-Jacques)

socialist
American: 4 Debs (Eugene) 6 Ripley (George), Thomas (Norman)
British: 4 Owen (Robert, Robert Dale), Webb (Beatrice, Sidney) 6 Morris (William)
French: 7 Fourier (Charles), Viviani (René) 10 Saint-Simon (Henri de)
German: 4 Marx (Karl) 6 Engels (Friedrich) 9 Luxemburg (Rosa) 10 Liebknecht (Wilhelm)

socialize
3 mix 5 party 6 hobnob, mingle 7 consort 9 associate 10 fraternize

social worker
4 Riis (Jacob), Wald (Lillian D.) 6 Addams (Jane) 7 Alinsky (Saul), Lathrop (Julia C.)

society
4 club 5 elite, guild 6 gentry, league, people, public 7 company, quality, who's who 8 populace, sodality 9 beau monde, community, haut monde 10 fellowship, fraternity, upper class, upper crust 11 aristocracy, association, brotherhood 13 companionship

sociologist
American: 4 Bell (Daniel), Ward (Lester Frank) 5 Balch (Emily Green), Whyte (William H.) 6 Du Bois (W. E. B.), Glazer (Nathan), Sumner (William Graham) 7 Johnson (Charles Spurgeon), Riesman (David)
English: 7 Spencer (Herbert)
French: 8 Durkheim (Emile)
German: 5 Weber (Max)
Italian: 6 Pareto (Vilfredo)
Swedish: 6 Myrdal (Alva, Gunnar)

sock
3 bop, box, hit 4 bash, belt, blow, chop, cuff, ding, slap, slog 5 clout, punch, smack, smash, whack 6 argyle, buffet, strike, thwack 8 stocking

sock away
  4 bank, save, stow 5 cache, hoard, lay by, put by, stash 8 lay aside

socks
  4 hose 7 hosiery

Socrates
  birthplace: 6 Athens
  poison: 7 hemlock
  pupil: 5 Plato
  wife: 8 Xantippe 9 Xanthippe

Socratic
  8 maieutic

sod
  4 land, peat, turf 5 earth, grass 6 ground

soda
  3 pop 4 cola 5 tonic 7 seltzer

sodality
  4 club 5 guild, lodge, order, union 6 league 7 society 9 community 10 fellowship, fraternity 11 association, brotherhood

sodden
  3 wet 5 soggy, soppy 6 soaked, soused 7 soaking, sopping 8 drenched, dripping 9 saturated 11 waterlogged, wringing-wet

Sodom and _____
  8 Gomorrah

sofa
  5 couch, divan 7 ottoman 9 banquette, davenport

so far
  3 yet 5 as yet, still 6 to date 7 till now 8 hitherto, until now 10 heretofore

Sofia native
  6 Bulgar 9 Bulgarian

soft
  4 cozy, easy, mild, snug 5 balmy, comfy, cushy, downy, faint, mushy, silky 6 doughy, flabby, gentle, low-key, pliant, satiny, silken, simple, smooth, spongy, tender 7 cottony, lenient, pillowy, pliable, squashy, squishy, subdued, velvety 8 cushiony, workable, yielding 9 malleable 11 comfortable

softcover
  9 paperback

soften
  4 ease, tame 5 abate, allay, blunt, relax 6 dampen, lessen, mellow, soothe, subdue, temper, weaken 7 assuage, lighten, mollify 8 diminish, enfeeble, mitigate, moderate, palliate, tone down, turn down 9 alleviate

soft hail
  7 graupel

softhearted
  4 kind, warm 6 humane, kindly, tender 7 lenient 10 responsive 11 sympathetic 13 compassionate

soft palate
  5 velum

soft-pedal
  4 mute 6 dampen, hush up, muffle, subdue 8 minimize, play down, suppress, tone down 9 underplay 11 de-emphasize

soft-soap
  3 con 4 coax 6 cajole, soothe, wangle 7 blarney, flatter, wheedle 8 blandish, butter up, inveigle 9 sweet-talk

soggy
  3 wet 6 doughy, soaked, sodden 7 soaking, sopping 8 drenched, dripping 9 saturated 10 bedraggled 11 waterlogged

Sohrab and Rustum author
  6 Arnold (Matthew)

soi-disant
  7 alleged 8 putative, so-called, supposed 9 pretended, professed, purported 10 ostensible, self-styled

soil
  3 mud, tar 4 daub, dirt, foul, land, loam, mess, muck, murk 5 dirty, earth, grime, muddy, smear, stain, sully, taint 6 defile, ground, smirch, smudge 7 blacken, country, pollute, tarnish 8 besmirch, discolor, homeland 10 fatherland, motherland, terra firma 11 contaminate
  aggregate: 3 ped
  clay: 5 gault
  dark: 9 chernozem
  deposit: 5 loess 7 eluvium
  infertile: 6 podzol
  layer: 4 gley, sola (plural) 5 solum
  rich: 6 hotbed
  tropical: 7 latosol

soiree
  4 fete, gala 5 party 6 affair, social 7 shindig 8 function 9 festivity, reception 11 celebration 13 entertainment

sojourn
  4 bide, stay, stop 5 abide, lodge, tarry, visit 6 linger 7 layover 8 stopover

Sol
  3 sun 7 daystar, phoebus
  horse: 4 Eous 5 Ethon 9 Erythreos
  (see also **Helios**)

solace
  5 allay, amuse, cheer 6 buck up 7

comfort, console, hearten **8** inspirit **10** condolence

solar disk
4 Aten, Aton

solarium
7 sunroom

solder
4 fuse, weld **5** braze

soldier
5 grunt, sepoy **7** dogface, draftee, fighter, private, recruit, trooper, veteran, warrior **8** bluecoat, doughboy, fusilier, rifleman **9** free lance, guerrilla, man-at-arms, mercenary **10** carabineer, carabinier, serviceman **11** condottiere, infantryman
ancient Greece: 7 hoplite
British: 5 Tommy **7** redcoat
cavalry: 6 hussar **8** chasseur
Confederate: 3 reb
French: 5 poilu **6** Zouave
German: 5 jerry
irregular: 8 guerila **9** guerrilla
Prussian: 5 uhlan
Turkish: 9 janissary

sole
3 one **4** lone, only **5** alone **6** bottom, single, unique **8** flatfish, singular **9** exclusive

solecism
4 goof, slip **5** boner, error, gaffe, lapse **6** misuse **7** blooper, blunder, faux pas, mistake **9** barbarism, indecorum, vulgarism **11** impropriety

solemn
5 grand, grave, sober, staid, stern **6** august, formal, ritual, sedate, somber, sombre **7** earnest, plenary, serious, stately, weighty **8** funereal, imposing, majestic **9** dignified **10** ceremonial, impressive, no-nonsense, sobersided **11** ceremonious, magnificent

solemnize
4 keep **5** bless, honor **6** hallow **7** dignify, observe **8** venerate **9** celebrate, ritualize **10** consecrate **11** commemorate

solicit
3 ask, beg **4** lure, tout, urge **5** apply **6** demand, drum up, entice **7** beseech, bespeak, canvass, entreat, implore, request **8** petition **9** importune **11** proposition, requisition

solicitor
6 jurist, lawyer, suitor **7** pleader **8** advocate, attorney **9** counselor

solicitous
4 avid, keen **5** eager, fussy **6** ardent, tender **7** anxious, careful, devoted, fearful, finicky, worried **8** rigorous **9** assiduous, attentive, concerned, impatient **10** fastidious, meticulous, scrupulous **11** considerate, punctilious, sympathetic **12** apprehensive **13** conscientious

solicitude
4 care, heed **5** qualm, worry **6** unease **7** anxiety, concern, scruple **8** attention, vigilance **10** uneasiness **11** compunction **12** watchfulness **13** consideration

solid
4 firm, hard **5** dense, sound, valid **6** cogent, secure, stable, sturdy, united **7** compact **8** reliable, unbroken **9** steadfast, unanimous, undivided **10** convincing **11** substantial

solidarity
5 union, unity **6** esprit **7** concord, oneness **8** cohesion **9** integrity **10** singleness **12** cohesiveness, togetherness **13** esprit de corps

solidify
3 dry, fix, gel, set **4** cake, jell **6** freeze, harden, secure **7** compact, congeal **8** compress, contract, indurate **11** consolidate

solitary
4 lone, lorn, only, solo **5** alone **6** hermit, lonely, single, unique **7** recluse **8** derelict, deserted, desolate, eremitic, forsaken, isolated, lonesome, separate, singular **9** abandoned, reclusive, withdrawn **10** antisocial, particular, unsociable **11** standoffish **12** misanthropic **13** unaccompanied

solitude
7 privacy **8** loneness **9** aloneness, isolation, seclusion **10** detachment, loneliness, quarantine, retirement, withdrawal **11** confinement **12** separateness

solo
4 lone **5** alone **6** single **7** unaided **8** solitary **13** independently, unaccompanied

Solomon
brother: 8 Adonijah
daughter: 7 Taphath **8** Basemath
father: 5 David

kingdom: 6 Israel
mother: 9 Bathsheba
son, successor: 8 Rehoboam
victim: 4 Joab 8 Adonijah

Solomon Islands
capital: 7 Honiara
ethnic group: 10 Melanesian
island: 7 Florida, Malaita, Rennell 8 Choiseul 11 Guadalcanal 12 San Cristóbal, Santa Isabel
language: 5 Pijin 7 English
monetary unit: 6 dollar

solon
8 lawgiver 10 legislator

so long
4 by-by, ciao, ta-ta 5 adieu, adios 6 bye-bye 7 cheerio, farewell, goodbye, toodles 8 farewell, Godspeed, toodle-oo

solution
6 answer, result
salt: 6 saline

solve
3 fix 5 break, crack 6 decode, reveal, settle 7 clarify, clear up, dope out, explain, unravel, work out 8 construe, decipher, unriddle, untangle 9 elucidate, figure out, interpret, puzzle out 11 disentangle

Somalia
capital: 9 Mogadishu
gulf: 4 Aden
language: 6 Arabic, Somali
location: 12 Horn of Africa
monetary unit: 8 shilling
neighbor: 5 Kenya 8 Djibouti, Ethiopia

somatic
6 bodily, carnal 7 fleshly 8 corporal, parietal, physical 9 corporeal

somber
3 dim 4 dark, drab, dull, grim 5 bleak, dusky, grave, heavy, murky, staid 6 dismal, dreary, gloomy, sedate, solemn 7 doleful, joyless, obscure, serious, weighty 8 funereal, mournful 9 tenebrous 10 caliginous, depressing, depressive, lugubrious, melancholy, sepulchral, sobersided, tenebrific 11 dispiriting

somewhat
5 quite 6 fairly, kind of, rather, sort of 7 a little 8 slightly 9 partially, tolerably 10 moderately

sommelier's offering
4 wine

somniferous
see **sleepy**

somnolent
see **sleepy**

Somnus
brother: 4 Mors
god of: 5 sleep
mother: 3 Nox

son
French: 4 fils
Italian: 6 figlio
Spanish: 4 hijo

song
3 air, lay 4 aria, glee, hymn, lied, tune 5 carol, chant, ditty, lyric, paean 6 ballad, melody, number 7 chanson 8 madrigal
biblical: 8 canticle
boat: 9 barcarole 10 barcarolle
French: 7 chanson
German: 4 lied 6 lieder (plural)
lamentation: 5 dirge 8 threnode, threnody
medieval: 8 sirvente 9 sirventes
morning: 6 aubade
of joy: 5 paean
operatic: 4 aria 8 cavatina 9 cabaletta
Portuguese: 4 fado
sacred: 5 psalm
sailor's: 6 chanty, shanty 7 chantey
short: 8 canzonet
wedding: 8 hymeneal

song and dance
5 pitch, spiel

songbird
see at **bird**

Song of Myself author
7 Whitman (Walt)

Song of Solomon
9 Canticles

songwriter
8 composer, lyricist

Sonja ___
5 Henie

Sonnambula composer
7 Bellini (Vincenzo)

sonnet
developer: 8 Petrarch
part: 5 octet 6 octave, sestet

sonorous
7 ringing, vibrant 8 resonant 10 oratorical, resounding, rhetorical 11 declamatory 12 magniloquent 13 grandiloquent

Sontag novel
9 In America 12 Volcano Lover (The)

soon
4 anon 6 any day, pronto 7 betimes, quickly, rapidly, shortly 8 directly, promptly, speedily 9 forthwith, presently, right away 10 before long

Sooner State
8 Oklahoma

soothe
4 balm, calm, ease, hush, lull 5 allay, quiet, salve, still 6 becalm, pacify, settle, solace, subdue 7 appease, assuage, comfort, compose, console, massage, mollify, placate, relieve 8 calm down, reassure 9 alleviate 10 conciliate, propitiate 11 tranquilize

soothsay
5 augur 8 prophesy 9 adumbrate 10 vaticinate 13 prognosticate

soothsayer
4 seer 5 sibyl 6 oracle 7 diviner, prophet 8 foreseer 9 predictor 10 forecaster, foreteller
ancient Roman: 5 augur 6 auspex 8 haruspex
blind: 8 Tiresias
(see also **prophet**)

sop
3 wet 4 gift, soak 5 bribe, douse, goody, souse, steep 6 deluge, drench, reward, seethe 7 douceur 8 gratuity, saturate, waterlog 9 incentive, lagniappe, sweetener 10 enticement

sophism
see **sophistry**

sophistic
5 false, phony 7 invalid, seeming, unsound 8 delusive, illusory, spurious 9 beguiling, casuistic, deceptive, plausible 10 fallacious, fraudulent, misleading, ostensible

sophisticated
5 blasé, jaded, suave 6 smooth, svelte, urbane 7 complex, knowing, refined, worldly 8 cultured, involved, schooled, seasoned 9 Byzantine, elaborate, intricate, practiced 10 world-weary 11 complicated, experienced, worldly-wise 12 cosmopolitan

sophistry
9 casuistry 12 equivocation 13 dissimulation, prevarication

Sophocles play
4 Ajax 7 Electra 8 Antigone 10 Oedipus Rex

Sophonisba
brother: 8 Hannibal
father: 9 Hasdrubal
husband: 6 Syphax

soporific
4 dozy 5 drowsy, opiate, sleepy 7 anodyne, calming, numbing 8 hypnotic, narcotic, sedative 9 calmative, deadening, somnolent 10 anesthetic, slumberous 11 somniferous 12 somnifacient 13 tranquilizing

soprano
American: 4 Pons (Lily) 5 Costa (Mary), Gluck (Alma), Moffo (Anna), Moore (Grace), Price (Leontyne), Sills (Beverly) 6 Arroyo (Martina), Battle (Kathleen), Callas (Maria), Curtin (Phyllis), Donath (Helen), Farrar (Geraldine), Garden (Mary), Munsel (Patrice), Norman (Jessye), Peters (Roberta), Piazza (Marguerite), Resnik (Regina) 7 Farrell (Eileen), Fleming (Renée), Kirsten (Dorothy), Stevens (Risë), Traubel (Helen) 8 Ponselle (Rosa)
Australian: 5 Melba (Nellie) 10 Sutherland (Joan)
Austrian: 4 Popp (Lucia) 7 Rysanek (Leonie) 8 Sembrich (Marcella)
Canadian: 7 Stratas (Teresa)
French: 7 Crespin (Régine)
German: 6 Leider (Frida) 7 Lehmann (Lilli, Lotte) 11 Schwarzkopf (Elisabeth)
Italian: 5 Freni (Mirella), Grisi (Giuditta, Giulia), Patti (Adelina) 6 Scotto (Renata) 7 Bartoli (Cecilia), Tebaldi (Renata) 10 Tetrazzini (Luisa) 11 Ricciarelli (Katia)
Korean: 6 Sumi Jo
Mexican: 8 Cruz-Romo (Gilda)
New Zealand: 8 Te Kanawa (Kiri)
Norwegian: 8 Flagstad (Kirsten)
Romanian: 8 Cotrubas (Ileana)
Spanish: 7 Caballé (Montserrat) 8 Berganza (Teresa) 12 de los Angeles (Victoria)
Swedish: 4 Lind (Jenny) 7 Nilsson (Birgit)
(see also **mezzo-soprano**)

sorcerer
4 mage 5 magus 6 wizard 7 warlock 8 conjurer, conjuror, magician 9 enchanter 11 necromancer, thaumaturge 13 thaumaturgist

sorceress
3 hag, hex 5 Circe, witch

sorcery
5 magic 8 diablery, wizardry 9 conjuring
10 necromancy, witchcraft 11
bewitchment, enchantment, thaumaturgy
West Indian: 5 obeah

sordid
3 low 4 base, foul, mean, vile 5 dirty,
nasty, seamy, shady, venal 6 blowsy,
blowzy, filthy, frowsy, frowzy, grubby,
scurvy, shabby, sleazy 7 ignoble, low-
down, squalid, unclean 8 degraded,
shameful, wretched 9 loathsome,
mercenary 10 despicable, disgraceful,
scandalous, slatternly 12 contemptible,
disreputable, reprehensible

sore
3 raw 4 boil 5 angry, irked, ulcer, upset,
vexed 6 aching, bitter, canker, peeved,
tender 7 abscess, chancre, hurting, painful
8 inflamed, smarting 9 chilblain, irritated,
rancorous, resentful, sensitive 10 affliction

sorehead
4 crab 5 grump 6 griper, grouch 7
grouser 8 grumbler, sourpuss 10
bellyacher, complainer, crosspatch,
malcontent

sorrel
4 dock 8 chestnut, sourwood

sorrow
3 rue, sob, woe 4 moan, ruth 5 dolor,
grief, mourn 6 grieve, lament, misery,
regret 7 anguish, remorse, sadness 8
distress, grieving, mourning 9 dejection,
heartache, suffering 10 affliction,
heartbreak, melancholy 11 lamentation,
unhappiness 12 mournfulness

sorrowful
3 sad 6 rueful, triste, woeful 7 doleful,
forlorn, ruthful, unhappy 8 dolorous,
downcast, grieving, mournful, piteous,
tristful, wretched 9 afflicted, miserable,
plaintive, woebegone 10 lamentable,
lugubrious, melancholy 11 heartbroken 12
disconsolate

sorry
3 bad, sad 4 mean, poor 5 cheap 6
cheesy, paltry, scummy, scurvy, shabby,
shoddy 7 scruffy, unhappy 8 beggarly,
contrite, mournful, penitent, pitiable,
saddened, trifling, wretched 9 miserable,
regretful, repentant 10 apologetic,
despicable, inadequate, melancholy,
remorseful 11 disgraceful, penitential 12
contemptible, heavyhearted

sort
3 ilk, lot, set 4 comb, cull, kind, pick, sift,
type 5 class, order 6 choose, screen,
select, stripe, winnow 7 arrange, catalog,
species, variety 8 classify, separate 9
catalogue, character 10 categorize,
pigeonhole

sortie
4 dash, raid 5 foray, sally 7 assault,
mission 9 excursion 10 expedition

sortilege
6 augury 7 sorcery 8 divining, witchery 10
divination, necromancy, witchcraft 11
thaumaturgy

so-so
4 fair, okay 6 decent, enough, fairly,
medium, rather 7 average, fairish 8
adequate, mediocre, middling, moderate,
passable, passably 9 tolerably 10
moderately 11 indifferent 12 run-of-the-
mill

sot
4 lush, wino 5 drunk, souse 6 bibber,
boozer 7 guzzler, tippler 8 drunkard 9
alcoholic, inebriate 10 boozehound

sotto voce
3 low 5 aside 6 softly 7 faintly, mutedly,
quietly 9 privately

souchong
3 tea

sough
4 sigh 7 suspire, whisper

soul
4 pith 5 anima, being, heart, stuff 6
animus, breast, marrow, pneuma, psyche,
spirit 7 essence 9 élan vital, substance
10 conscience, vital force 12 quintessence
combining form: 5 psych 6 psycho

soulful
6 moving, tender 7 emotive, fervent 8
poignant, stirring, touching 9 affecting,
emotional 11 impassioned, sentimental

soul singer
4 Gaye (Marvin) 5 Bland (Bobby), Brown
(James), Cooke (Sam), Flack (Roberta),
Green (Al), Hayes (Isaac) 6 Butler (Jerry),
Knight (Gladys), Sledge (Percy) 7 Charles
(Ray), Pickett (Wilson), Redding (Otis) 8
Franklin (Aretha), Mayfield (Curtis)

sound
3 fit 4 firm, hale, safe, sane 5 audio, legit,
noise, plumb, probe, right, sober, solid,

valid, whole **6** cogent, fathom, intact,
secure, stable, sturdy, unhurt **7** correct,
earshot, healthy, logical, prudent **8**
rational, reliable, sensible, unharmed **9**
judicious, resonance, undamaged,
vibration, wholesome **10** convincing,
reasonable **11** well-founded **12** satisfactory, well-grounded **13** reverberation
combining form: 3 son **4** phon, soni,
sono **5** audio, audit, phone, phony **6**
audito, phonia
high-pitched: 4 ping, ting
pleasant: 7 euphony
quality: 6 timbre
repeating: 7 rat-a-tat **8** rataplan **10** rat-a-
tat-tat
science: 6 sonics **7** phonics **9** acoustics

Sound

Alaska: 5 Cross
Antarctica: 7 McMurdo
Australia: 4 King **5** Broad
Bahamas: 5 Exuma
Canada: 4 Howe **6** Nansen
Connecticut-New York: 10 Long Island
English Channel: 8 Plymouth
Georgia: 8 Altamaha
Greenland: 5 Smith
Gulf of Mexico: 8 Suwannee **11**
Mississippi
Massachusetts: 8 Vineyard **9** Nantucket
New England: 11 Block Island
North Carolina: 4 Core **5** Bogue **7**
Pamlico, Roanoke **9** Albemarle, Currituck
Northwest Territories: 4 Peel **8** Melville
9 Lancaster **12** Prince Albert
Norwegian Sea: 8 Scoresby
Ontario: 4 Owen
Scotland: 3 Hoy **4** Jura, Mull **5** Inner
Spitsbergen: 4 Bell
Washington: 5 Puget

Sound and the Fury, The

author: 8 Faulkner (William)
character: 5 Benjy (Compson), Caddy
(Compson), Jason (Compson) **6** Dilsey **7**
Quentin (Compson)

soundness

6 health, sanity **7** balance **8** lucidity,
prudence, security, solidity, strength **9**
integrity, stability **11** reliability **12**
practicality

sound off

7 speak up **8** speak out

soup

beet: 6 borsch **7** borscht
bowl: 6 tureen

clear: 5 broth **8** bouillon, consommé,
julienne
cold: 8 gazpacho **11** vichyssoise
curry: 12 mulligatawny
okra: 5 gumbo
seafood: 7 chowder
thick: 5 gumbo, puree **6** bisque, burgoo
vegetable: 10 minestrone

soupçon

see **particle**

soupy

5 foggy, gooey, gushy, murky, mushy **6**
drippy, slushy, smoggy **7** cloying, cornball,
maudlin, mawkish **9** schmaltzy **10**
saccharine **11** sentimental, tear-jerking

sour

4 acid, dour, tart **5** acerb, acrid, tangy,
testy **6** acidic, bitter, crabby, cranky, curdle,
grumpy, morose, rancid, rotten, sullen,
turned **7** acerbic, grouchy, peevish, prickly,
spoiled, unhappy **8** embitter, vinegary **9**
acidulous, fermented **12** disagreeable

source

4 font, root, well **5** basis, cause, fount,
model, onset, start **6** mother, origin, spring
7 dawning, genesis **8** begetter, fountain,
wellhead **9** beginning, inception, informant,
precursor, prototype, reference, rootstock
10 antecedent, authorship, birthplace,
derivation, originator, progenitor,
provenance, wellspring **11** origination,
provenience **12** fountainhead

sourness

7 acidity **8** acerbity, asperity

sourpuss

4 crab **5** crank, grump **6** griper, grouch **7**
grouser, killjoy **8** grumbler, sorehead **10**
bellyacher, complainer, crosspatch,
curmudgeon **11** misanthrope

souse

3 dip, sop, sot **4** lush, soak, wino **5** binge,
drown, steep **6** boozer, drench, pickle,
plunge, seethe **7** immerse **8** drunkard,
inundate, marinate, preserve, saturate,
submerge, submerse **9** alcoholic,
immersion, inebriate **10** boozehound,
intoxicate **11** dipsomaniac

soused

3 lit **4** high **5** drunk, lit up, oiled **6** bashed,
blotto, bombed, juiced, potted, soaked,
soused, stewed, stoned, tanked, wasted,
zonked **7** crocked, drunken, pickled, pie-
eyed, sloshed, smashed, sottish **8** polluted
9 plastered **10** inebriated, liquored up **11**
intoxicated

south
combining form: 5 austr 6 austro
French: 3 sud
Spanish: 3 sur

South Africa
capital: 8 Cape Town, Pretoria 12 Bloemfontein
city: 6 Durban 12 Johannesburg
desert: 8 Kalahari
enclave: 7 Lesotho
grassland: 4 veld, veldt
language: 5 Bantu 7 English 9 Afrikaans
monetary unit: 4 rand
mountain range: 11 Drakensberg
neighbor: 7 Namibia 8 Botswana 9 Swaziland, Zimbabwe 10 Mozambique
plateau: 5 Karoo 6 Karroo
river: 6 Molopo, Orange
settlers: 5 Boers

South America
country: 4 Peru 5 Chile 6 Brazil, Guyana 7 Bolivia, Ecuador, Uruguay 8 Colombia, Paraguay, Suriname 9 Argentina, Venezuela
ethnic group: 6 Aymara, Creole, Indian 7 mestizo, mulatto, Quechua, Spanish 10 Amerindian, Portuguese
language: 6 Aymara 7 Guaraní, Quechua, Spanish 10 Portuguese

South Carolina
capital: 8 Columbia
city: 10 Charleston, Greenville
college, university: 7 Citadel, Clemson
fort: 6 Sumter
island, island group: 3 Sea 6 Edisto, Parris 10 Hilton Head
nickname: 8 Palmetto (State)
river: 6 Edisto, Pee Dee, Santee 7 Tugaloo 8 Savannah
state bird: 12 Carolina wren
state flower: 13 yellow jasmine
state tree: 8 palmetto

South Dakota
capital: 6 Pierre
city: 9 Rapid City 10 Sioux Falls
mountain: 6 Harney (Peak) 8 Rushmore 10 Black Hills
nickname: 6 Coyote (State) 10 Mt. Rushmore (State)
park: 8 Badlands, Wind Cave
river: 8 Missouri 11 Belle Forche
state bird: 18 ring-necked pheasant
state flower: 12 pasqueflower
state tree: 6 spruce

southerly
7 austral

South-West Africa
7 Namibia

south wind
see at **wind**

souvenir
5 relic, token 6 trophy 7 memento 8 keepsake, memorial, reminder 11 remembrance

sovereign
4 coin, czar, free, king, tsar 5 queen, regal, royal, ruler 6 kingly, ruling 7 emperor, empress, highest, monarch, regnant, supreme 8 absolute, autarkic, autocrat, dominant, imperial, kinglike, majestic 9 ascendant, autarchic, monarchal, number one, paramount, potentate 10 autonomous, monarchial 11 independent, monarchical, predominant 12 self-governed

soviet
7 council 9 committee

sow
4 seed, toss 5 drill, fling, plant, strew 7 bestrew, scatter 9 broadcast 11 disseminate

spa
5 baths, hydro, wells 6 hot tub, resort, spring, waters 7 springs 13 watering place
Czech: 6 Bilina 8 Karlsbad
English: 4 Bath 6 Buxton 9 Harrogate
French: 3 Dax 5 Evian
German: 3 Ems 5 Baden 6 Bad Ems 9 Kissingen

space
3 gap 4 area, room 5 blank, scope 6 cavity, extent, spread, volume 7 breadth, expanse, stretch 8 capacity, distance, interval, universe 9 amplitude, expansion

spaced-out
4 high 5 doped 6 stoned, zonked 7 drugged 8 hopped-up, turned on

spacious
3 big 4 vast, wide 5 ample, large, roomy 7 immense 8 enormous, extended 9 boundless, capacious, cavernous, expansive, extensive 10 commodious, voluminous

spade
3 dig 4 grub 5 dig up, scoop 6 dig out, shovel 8 excavate

Spade, Sam
4 dick 6 shamus, sleuth 7 gumshoe 9 detective 10 private eye

creator: 7 Hammett (Dashiell)
novel: 13 Maltese Falcon (The)

Spain

ancient name: 8 Hispania
capital: 6 Madrid
city: 6 Málaga 7 Seville 8 Valencia, Zaragoza 9 Barcelona, Saragossa
island group: 6 Canary 8 Balearic
king: 10 Juan Carlos
leader: 6 Franco (Francisco)
monetary unit: 4 euro
monetary unit, former: 4 real 6 peseta
mountain: 8 Mulhacén 11 Pico de Aneto
mountain range: 8 Pyrenees
neighbor: 6 France 8 Portugal
peninsula: 7 Iberian
region: 8 Valencia 9 Catalonia
river: 4 Ebro 12 Guadalquivir
sea: 13 Mediterranean
strait: 9 Gibraltar

spall
4 chip 5 flake 7 shaving 8 fragment 9 exfoliate

spam
8 junk mail

span
4 arch, term, time 5 cross, reach 6 extent, length, period, spread 7 compass, measure, stretch 8 duration, interval, lifetime, straddle, traverse

spangle
4 trim 5 flash, gleam 6 sequin 7 glitter, shimmer, sparkle, twinkle 9 coruscate 11 scintillate

Spaniard
9 Castilian

Spanish
boss: 7 cacique
chaperone: 6 duenna
combining form: 7 hispano
dictator: 8 caudillo
folksong: 6 tonada
fortress: 7 alcazar
garrison: 8 presidio
hors d'oeuvre: 4 tapa
inn: 6 posada
mayor: 7 alcalde
national hero: 3 Cid (El) 5 El Cid
nobleman: 7 grandee
operetta: 8 zarzuela
penal settlement: 8 presidio
plain: 5 llano, pampa
plantation: 8 hacienda
princess: 7 infanta
ranch: 5 finca 8 estancia

saint: 7 Dominic 8 Ignatius
scarf: 8 mantilla
shawl: 6 serape
title: 3 don 4 doña 5 señor 6 señora 8 señorita
wine: 4 sack 6 sherry

Spanish fly
9 cantharis

spank
4 cane, flog, lash, slap 5 smack 6 larrup, paddle, punish, thrash 7 scourge 8 chastise

spar
3 box, vie 4 pole 5 joust, stall 7 dispute, wrangle 8 longeron
ship's: 4 boom, gaff, mast, yard 7 yardarm 8 bowsprit

spare
4 lank, lean, pity, save, slim 5 avoid, extra, gaunt, lanky 6 backup, excess, excuse, exempt, let off, meager, meagre, pardon, scanty, scrape, scrimp, skimpy, skinny, slight, surplus, unused 7 absolve, relieve, reserve, scrawny, scrimpy, surplus 8 leftover 10 additional 11 superfluous

sparing
4 bare, wary 5 canny, chary, tight 6 frugal, meager, meagre, saving, stingy 7 prudent, thrifty 9 provident 10 economical, restrained, unwasteful 11 tightfisted 12 parsimonious

spark
3 woo 5 court, ember, glint 6 foment, incite, kindle, set off 7 provoke, trigger 8 activate, touch off 9 instigate, scintilla

sparkle
4 zing 5 flash, gleam, glint, verve 7 glimmer, glisten, glitter, shimmer, twinkle 8 vivacity 9 animation, coruscate 10 effervesce, liveliness 11 coruscation, scintillate 13 scintillation

sparkling
6 bubbly, lively 8 animated, bubbling 9 brilliant 12 effervescent

Spark novel
11 Memento Mori 21 Prime of Miss Jean Brodie (The)

sparse
4 rare, thin 5 scant 6 meager, meagre, scanty, scarce, skimpy 7 limited, scrimpy 8 exiguous, sporadic, uncommon 9 dispersed, scattered 10 inadequate, infrequent, occasional 12 insufficient

Sparta
10 Lacedaemon
country: 7 Laconia
king: 8 Leonidas
opponent: 6 Athens

Spartacus
author: 4 Fast (Howard)
slayer: 7 Crassus

spasm
3 fit, tic 4 pang 5 burst, crick, throe 6 twitch 8 paroxysm 10 convulsion
muscular: 6 clonus

spasmodic
5 jerky 6 fitful, spotty 7 erratic 8 sporadic 9 desultory, excitable 10 convulsive 12 intermittent

spat
3 row 4 flap, miff, tiff 5 fight, scene, scrap 6 bicker, gaiter, hassle, oyster 7 brabble, dispute, fall out, quarrel, rhubarb, wrangle 8 argument, outburst, squabble 10 falling-out 11 altercation

spate
4 flow, flux, gush, pour, rain, rush, tide 5 flood, river, spurt, surge 6 deluge, series, shower, stream 7 current, freshet, torrent 8 cataract, outburst, overflow 10 inundation, outpouring

spatter
4 slop, slur, spit 5 douse, fleck, plash, slosh, smear, spray, spurt, swash 6 befoul, defame, malign, splash, splosh, vilify 7 asperse, blacken, handful, slander, speckle, splurge, stipple, traduce 8 besmirch, sprinkle 9 denigrate, disparage

spawn
4 eggs, sire 5 beget, breed, brood, hatch, issue 6 create, father, parent 7 produce, product, progeny, provoke 8 engender, generate 9 offspring, originate, procreate, propagate, reproduce, stimulate

speak
3 gab, jaw, say, yak 4 blab, chat, chin, talk 5 blurt, drawl, mouth, orate, spiel, spout, utter, voice 6 assert, convey, intone, mumble, murmur, mutter, parley 7 address, declaim, declare, lecture, phonate, whisper 8 converse, dilate on, perorate, vocalize 9 discourse, enunciate, expatiate, hold forth, verbalize
confusedly: 7 stammer, stutter 8 splutter
for: 7 testify

speaker
5 voice 9 spokesman 10 mouthpiece 12 spokesperson

spear
3 gig 4 pike, spit 5 gouge, lance, spike 6 impale, pierce, skewer 7 harpoon, leister, trident 8 puncture, transfix 9 penetrate

special
4 rare 6 unique 7 express, notable, unusual 8 peculiar, uncommon 10 designated, individual, noteworthy, particular 11 distinctive, exceptional, outstanding

species
4 kind, sort, type 5 breed, class, order

specific
3 set 5 exact 6 strict, unique 7 express, limited, precise, special 8 clean-cut, clear-cut, definite, distinct, especial, explicit 10 individual, particular 11 categorical, unambiguous

specify
3 fix, set 4 cite, list, name 6 detail 7 itemize, mention, pin down, tick off 8 instance, spell out 9 determine, enumerate, establish, inventory, stipulate 13 particularize

specimen
4 case, sort, type 6 sample 7 example, neotype, variety 8 exemplar, holotype, instance, sampling 12 illustration

specious
5 empty, false 6 hollow 8 spurious 9 casuistic, plausible, sophistic 10 misleading, ostensible 11 sophistical

speciousness
7 sophism 9 casuistry, sophistry

speck
3 bit, dot, jot 4 atom, iota, mite, mote, spot, tick, whit 5 crumb, flock, grain, point, shred, trace 7 freckle, smidgen 8 molecule, particle, pinpoint

speckle
3 dot 4 spot 5 flake, fleck 6 dapple, pepper 7 stipple 8 sprinkle

spectacle
4 pomp, show 5 drama, sight 6 parade 7 display, pageant, panoply, tableau 10 exhibition, exposition 12 extravaganza

spectacular
5 stagy 7 amazing, pageant 8 dazzling, dramatic, striking, wondrous 9 marvelous, thrilling, wonderful 10 astounding, eye-

popping, histrionic, miraculous, phenomenal, prodigious, staggering, stupefying, stupendous, theatrical **11** astonishing, sensational **12** extravaganza

spectator
5 gazer **6** viewer **7** watcher, witness **8** beholder, observer, onlooker **9** bystander **10** eyewitness

Spectator author
6 Steele (Richard) **7** Addison (Joseph)

specter
5 ghost, shade **6** shadow, spirit, wraith **7** eidolon, phantom **8** phantasm, revenant, visitant **10** apparition

spectral
6 spooky **7** ghastly, ghostly, phantom **9** ghostlike, unearthly **10** shadowlike **11** disembodied, phantomlike

spectrum
5 ambit, gamut, range, scale, sweep **7** compass **8** diapason **9** continuum

speculate
4 muse **5** study, think, weigh **6** ponder, reason, review, wonder **7** reflect **8** cogitate, consider, meditate, ruminate, theorize **9** cerebrate **10** conjecture, deliberate **11** contemplate

speculation
5 guess, hunch **6** gamble, review, theory **7** surmise **9** brainwork **10** conjecture

speculative
7 curious, pensive **8** academic **10** thoughtful **11** conjectural, theoretical **12** hypothetical

speech
4 talk **5** idiom, spiel, voice **6** debate, homily, parley, sermon, tirade, tongue **7** address, dialect, diction, lecture, oration, palaver **8** dialogue, diatribe, harangue, language, parlance, rhetoric **9** discourse, monologue, utterance **10** allocution, expression, vernacular **11** declamation **12** articulation, disquisition, vocalization **13** verbalization
defect: 4 lisp **7** stutter

speechcraft
7 oratory **8** rhetoric **9** elocution

speechless
3 mum **4** dumb, mute **6** silent **7** aphonic **10** dumbstruck, tongue-tied

speed
3 fly, run, zip **4** clip, gait, pace, race, rush, tear, whiz **5** chase, haste, hurry, tempo **6** barrel, burn up, career, hasten, hustle, whoosh **7** quicken **8** alacrity, celerity, dispatch, expedite, highball, legerity, momentum, rapidity, velocity **9** fleetness, quickness, swiftness **10** accelerate, cannonball, facilitate, promptness

speedway
5 track **8** turnpike **9** racetrack **10** racecourse

speedy
4 fast **5** brisk, fleet, hasty, quick, rapid, swift **6** nimble, prompt **8** headlong **9** breakneck **11** expeditious

spell
3 hex **4** bout, jinx, time, tour, turn **5** charm, hitch, shift, stint, throe, while **6** attack, period, streak, voodoo **7** relieve, stretch **11** conjuration, incantation

spellbind
3 hex **4** grip, vamp **5** charm **7** bewitch, catch up, enchant **8** enthrall, entrance **9** enrapture, fascinate, hypnotize, mesmerize

spelling
11 orthography
bad: 10 cacography

spell out
7 clarify, explain, expound **8** construe, set forth **9** elucidate, explicate, interpret

spend
3 pay **4** blow, drop, pass **5** use up, waste **6** lavish, lay out, outlay **7** consume, exhaust, fork out, hand out, splurge **8** disburse, shell out, squander **9** dissipate, go through, throw away, while away **10** contribute, run through

spender
7 wastrel **8** prodigal **10** high roller, profligate, squanderer **11** scattergood

spendthrift
see **spender**

spent
4 shot **5** all in **6** effete, pooped, used-up, wasted **7** drained, worn-out **8** burnt out, consumed, depleted, washed-up **9** exhausted, washed-out

spew
4 gush, ooze **5** belch, eject, eruct, erupt, expel, exude, flood, heave, shoot, spray, vomit **6** irrupt, spit up, squirt **7** throw up, upchuck **8** disgorge

sphagnum
4 moss

sphere
3 orb 4 area, ball, star, turf, zone 5 field, globe, range, realm, round, scope 6 circle, domain, planet 7 demesne, rondure, terrain 8 dominion, province 9 bailiwick, territory 12 jurisdiction

spherical
5 round 6 global 7 globose 8 globular 9 orbicular

Sphinx
builder: 6 Khafre
father: 6 Typhon
mother: 7 Echidna
query: 6 riddle
site: 4 Giza 6 Thebes

spice
3 pep, zip 4 kick, mace, tang, zest 5 anise, aroma, clove, cumin, poppy, savor, scent, smack, smell, taste 6 cloves, fennel, ginger, nutmeg, pepper, relish, sesame 7 bouquet, caraway, perfume 8 cardamom, cinnamon, piquancy 9 fragrance, redolence, seasoning

Spice Islands
8 Moluccas

spick-and-span
3 new 4 mint, neat, snug, tidy, trig, trim 5 clean, fresh 6 spruce 7 orderly 8 brand-new, spotless 9 shipshape 10 immaculate 11 well-groomed

spicy
3 hot 4 racy 5 bawdy, fiery, salty, tangy, zesty 6 lively, purple, ribald, risqué, savory, snappy, wicked 7 gingery, peppery, piquant, pungent, scented, zestful 8 aromatic, fragrant, off-color, perfumed, redolent, seasoned, spirited 9 flavorful, salacious 10 scandalous, suggestive 11 titillating

spider
6 frypan 7 skillet 8 arachnid 9 frying pan 10 black widow

spiel
4 jive, line 5 pitch 6 patter 12 song and dance

spieler
4 tout 6 barker, hawker, talker 8 huckster

spigot
3 tap 4 cock, gate 5 valve 6 faucet 7 hydrant, petcock, shutoff 8 stopcock

spike
3 pin 4 heel, nail 5 lance, piton, spear 6 antler, impale, needle, skewer 7 spindle 8 increase, mackerel, puncture, transfix

spile
4 bung 5 spout

spill
4 blab, drip, drop, fall, flow, slop, tell 5 spray 6 betray, inform, reveal, splash, squeal, tattle 7 divulge, dribble, run over, spatter 8 disclose, overflow

Spillane detective
10 Mike Hammer

spilth
5 dregs, dross, swill, trash, waste 6 debris, refuse, scraps 7 garbage, rubbish 8 leavings

spin
4 gyre, reel, ride, swim, turn 5 dizzy, swirl, twirl, wheel, whirl 6 gyrate, rotate 7 revolve 8 rotation 9 pirouette, whirligig 10 revolution
a log: 4 birl
out: 4 draw 6 extend 7 prolong, stretch 8 elongate, lengthen, protract 10 prolongate

spinal column
5 chine 6 rachis
curvature: 8 lordosis
part: 8 vertebra
(see also **spine**)

spindle
3 pin, rod 5 newel, shaft, spike 6 impale, rachis

spindly
5 frail, lanky, rangy, shaky, weedy 6 flimsy, gangly, skinny, twiggy, wobbly 7 fragile, rickety, tottery 8 gangling, skeletal, unsteady 9 emaciated 10 jerry-built

spine
4 back 6 rachis 7 spicule 8 backbone 9 vertebrae

spineless
5 timid 8 cowardly, timorous 9 weak-kneed 10 weak-willed 12 invertebrate

spin-off
8 offshoot 9 by-product, outgrowth 10 derivative, descendant

_____ Spinoza
6 Baruch

spinster
7 old maid 10 maiden lady

spiny
6 barbed, thorny 7 prickly 8 echinate 10 nettlesome

spiral
4 coil, curl, wind 5 helix, twine, twist 6

volute **7** helical, helices (plural) **8** gyroidal, volution **9** cochleate, corkscrew
combining form: 3 gyr **4** gyro **5** helic **8** helico

spire
4 coil **5** twist, whorl **7** steeple **8** pinnacle

spirit
3 pep, vim, zip **4** brio, dash, élan, gimp, grit, guts, life, mood, snap, soul, zeal, zest, zing **5** anima, ardor, drive, force, heart, moxie, oomph, pluck, shade, spunk, tenor, verve, vigor **6** animus, daimon, energy, esprit, fervor, ginger, mettle, morale, pneuma, psyche, starch, temper, wraith **7** passion, phantom, specter, spectre **8** phantasm, revenant, vitality **9** animation, élan vital, substance **10** apparition, enthusiasm, get-up-and-go, liveliness
away: 6 abduct, kidnap, snatch
evil: 5 afrit, demon **6** afreet **7** erlking, shaitan
female: 5 nymph **7** banshee
Hopi: 7 kachina
Persian: 4 peri

spirited
4 bold, game, keen **5** eager, fiery, peppy **6** ardent, gritty, lively, plucky, spunky **7** chipper, fervent, gingery, peppery, valiant, zealous **8** animated, cheerful, intrepid, resolute **9** audacious, dauntless, energetic, sprightly, vivacious **10** courageous, mettlesome, passionate **12** enthusiastic

spirits
5 booze, drink **6** liquor, tipple **9** aqua vitae, firewater
low: 5 blues, dumps, ennui **8** doldrums **10** blue devils, depression, melancholy

spiritual
6 sacred **7** saintly **8** churchly, mystical, numinous, platonic **9** religious **10** high-minded, immaterial, unphysical **11** disembodied, incorporeal, nonmaterial, nonphysical **12** metaphysical, supernatural, transcendent

spiritualist
6 medium, mystic **7** psychic

spit
5 spear **6** impale, saliva, skewer, slaver, sputum **7** spatter, sputter **8** splutter **9** brochette **11** expectorate

spite
5 venom **6** grudge, malice, rancor, spleen **7** ill will, revenge **9** pettiness, vengeance **11** malevolence **13** maliciousness

spiteful
4 mean **5** catty, nasty, snide **6** malign, wicked **7** vicious, waspish **8** venomous **9** malicious, malignant, rancorous **10** malevolent, vindictive

spitfire
4 fury **5** harpy, shrew, vixen **6** dragon, virago **7** hellcat, tigress **8** fishwife, harridan **9** termagant

spitting image
4 twin **5** clone **6** double, ringer **9** duplicate **10** carbon copy, dead ringer, simulacrum

spittoon
8 cuspidor

splash
3 sop, wet **4** slop, soak **5** douse, slosh, spray, swash **6** drench **7** spatter **8** sprinkle

splashy
5 gaudy, jazzy, showy **6** flashy, garish, glitzy, tawdry **7** blatant, dashing **8** colorful, dazzling, striking **10** flamboyant, theatrical **11** sensational **12** meretricious, ostentatious

splatter
4 slop **5** douse, plash, slosh, spray, swash **6** splash **8** sprinkle

splay
4 cant, tilt **5** angle, bevel, gawky, slant, slope **6** clumsy, extend, spread **7** awkward, incline **8** ungainly **9** expansion **11** inclination

spleen
see **spite**

splendid
4 fine **5** grand, showy **6** superb **7** shining **8** glorious, gorgeous **9** brilliant, excellent, marvelous, wonderful **10** first-class, impressive **11** illustrious, magnificent, outstanding **12** transcendent

splendor
4 pomp **5** glory **6** dazzle **7** panoply **8** grandeur, richness **9** pageantry, spectacle **10** brilliance, brilliancy **12** magnificence

splenetic
5 cross, surly **6** fuming **8** incensed, spiteful **9** malicious **10** ill-natured, malevolent **11** ill-tempered

splice
3 tie 4 join, mate, mesh 5 braid, graft, plait, unite

splint
5 brace, strip 7 support 10 immobilize

splinter
4 rive 5 burst, smash 6 shiver, sliver 7 faction, shatter 8 fragment 12 disintegrate

split
3 rip 4 part, rend, rent, rift, rima, rime, rive, tear 5 break, carve, chasm, chink, cleft, crack, sever, slice 6 breach, cleave, cloven, divide, schism, sunder 7 break up, disjoin, dissect, diverge, divorce, divvy up, fission, fissure, rupture 8 cleavage, dissever, fracture, separate 11 dichotomize
combining form: 5 schiz 6 schizo 7 schisto

splotch
4 blob, blot, spot 5 fleck, stain 6 smudge

splurge
4 orgy 5 binge, fling, spree 7 blowout, rampage 10 indulgence 12 extravagance

splutter
4 spit 6 babble, jabber 7 stammer

spoil
3 mar, rob, rot 4 baby, harm, prey, ruin, sack 5 decay, humor, taint, waste, wreck 6 coddle, cosset, curdle, damage, defile, impair, molder, pamper, ravish 7 blemish, cater to, destroy, indulge, pillage, putrefy, tarnish, vitiate 8 demolish 9 break down, decompose 11 mollycoddle

spoiled
4 rank, sour 6 putrid, rancid, rotten, ruined 7 coddled, decayed 8 impaired, indulged, pampered 9 indulgent

spoils
4 haul, loot, swag 5 booty 7 pillage, plunder

spoilsport
7 killjoy

spoken
4 oral, said, told 6 verbal, voiced 7 uttered 8 phonetic, viva voce 9 delivered, unwritten 11 articulated

sponge
4 grub 5 cadge, leech, mooch 7 moocher 8 freeload, parasite, scrounge 10 freeloader
material: 8 mesoglea

opening: 6 oscula (plural) 7 osculum, ostiole

sponger
5 leech 7 moocher 8 parasite 10 freeloader

spongy
4 soft 5 mushy, pulpy 6 porous, quaggy 7 squashy, squishy 9 absorbent

sponsor
4 back, fund 5 angel, stake 6 backer, patron, surety 7 endorse, finance 8 advocate, bankroll, champion, Maecenas, mainstay, promoter, vouch for 9 grubstake, guarantee, guarantor, patronize, subsidize, supporter 10 benefactor, underwrite 11 underwriter

sponsorship
5 aegis 7 backing, support 8 advocacy, auspices 9 patronage

spontaneous
5 ad-lib 7 natural, offhand 8 ad-libbed, unforced 9 automatic, extempore, impromptu, impulsive, unstudied 10 improvised, off-the-cuff, unprompted 11 instinctive, unmeditated 13 unconstrained

spontoon
4 pike 5 lance, spear

spoof
4 sham 5 farce, put-on 6 parody, satire, send-up 7 lampoon, takeoff 8 travesty

spook
3 spy 5 agent, alarm, ghost, haunt, scare 7 specter, spectre, startle, terrify 8 frighten

spooky
5 eerie, weird 6 creepy 7 ghostly, ominous, uncanny 9 unearthly

spool
4 wind 6 bobbin

spoon
3 pet, woo 4 neck 5 court, ladle, scoop 6 cuddle

spoonbill
4 ibis 8 shoveler 9 ruddy duck 10 paddlefish

Spoon River poet
7 Masters (Edgar Lee)

spoony
5 mushy, silly 6 simple, slushy, syrupy 7 fatuous, foolish, mawkish, smitten, witless 9 schmaltzy 10 saccharine 11 sentimental

spoor
5 scent, trace, track, tract, trail 7 vestige 8 footstep 9 droppings, footprint

sporadic
4 rare 6 catchy, fitful, random, scarce, sparse, spotty 8 episodic, erratic, isolated, uncommon 9 desultory, irregular, scattered, spasmodic 10 infrequent, occasional

sport
3 fun 4 game, jest, joke, mock, play 6 frolic, racing, trifle 7 mockery, show off 9 diversion, high jinks, horseplay 10 recreation
indoor: 6 boxing, hockey, squash 7 bowling 8 handball 9 wrestling 10 acrobatics, basketball, gymnastics 11 racquetball, table tennis
Olympic: 4 judo 6 boxing, diving, hockey, rowing 7 archery, cycling, fencing, shot put 8 canoeing, football, high jump, long jump, marathon, shooting, swimming, yachting 9 decathlon, pole vault, water polo, wrestling 10 basketball, gymnastics, pentathlon, triple jump, volleyball 11 discus throw, hammer throw 12 javelin throw, steeplechase 13 weightlifting
water: 6 diving, rowing 7 sailing, surfing 8 canoeing, swimming, yachting
winter: 4 luge 6 hockey, skiing 7 curling, lugeing, skating 8 biathlon, sledding 10 ski jumping 11 bobsledding, tobogganing

sporting house
6 bagnio 7 brothel 8 bordello

sportive
5 antic 6 frisky, impish 7 playful, roguish, waggish 10 frolicsome 11 mischievous

sportiveness
7 devilry, roguery, waggery 8 deviltry, mischief 9 devilment, rascality

sporty
4 fast 5 peppy 6 breezy, casual, jaunty, lively 7 dashing, relaxed 8 debonair, informal 10 insouciant 11 streamlined

spot
3 fix, jam, nip, see 4 espy, post, site 5 fleck, hit on, locus, place, point, speck 6 blotch, detect, pickle, plight, scrape 7 dilemma, smidgen, spatter, speckle 8 diagnose, flyspeck, identify, location, pinpoint, position 9 recognize, situation 11 predicament

spotless
4 pure 5 clean 6 chaste 8 hygienic, sanitary, unsoiled 9 undefiled, unstained, unsullied 10 immaculate 11 unblemished

spotlight
5 focus 6 notice 7 feature, point up 8 interest, point out 9 attention, emphasize, public eye, publicity 10 illuminate 12 illumination

spotted
4 seen 6 motley 7 brindle, dappled, piebald 8 brindled, speckled, stippled

spouse
4 mate, wife 5 bride, groom, hubby 7 consort, husband

spout
3 jet 4 gush 5 chute, eject, spray, spurt 6 nozzle, squirt

sprain
4 pull, tear, turn 5 twist 6 wrench 7 stretch

sprawl
4 flop, loll 5 drape, slump 6 extend, lounge, slouch, spread 7 stretch 11 spread-eagle

spray
3 fog 4 hose, mist 6 shower, spritz 7 aerosol, atomize, diffuse, spatter 8 atomizer, droplets, fumigate, nebulize 9 spindrift

spread
3 jam, lay, set, sow 4 deal, oleo, open, pâté, push 5 apply, feast, jelly, space, splay, strew, sweep 6 butter, expand, extend, fan out, pass on, retail 7 banquet, breadth, diffuse, expanse, overrun, pervade, radiate, scatter, slather, stretch, suffuse 8 bedcover, coverlet, dispense, disperse, mushroom, permeate 9 amplitude, broadcast, circulate, diffusion, dissipate, expansion, extension, profusion, propagate, radiation 10 dispersion, distribute, outstretch 11 counterpane, disseminate 12 transmission 13 proliferation

spree
3 jag 4 bash, bust, lark, orgy, riot, tear 5 binge, drunk, fling, revel 6 bender, frolic 7 blowout, carouse, rampage, splurge 8 carousal, wingding 10 indulgence 11 bacchanalia

sprig
4 brad, heir, twig 5 scion, shoot 7 pintail 9 ruddy duck

sprightly
3 gay 4 keen, spry, yare 5 agile, alert, antic, brisk, peppy, perky, zesty, zingy, zippy 6 active, breezy, chirpy, frisky, jaunty, lively, nimble 7 animate, chipper, coltish,

piquant, playful, pungent **8** animated, cheerful, spirited, sportive **9** energetic, vivacious **10** frolicsome, rollicking **13** scintillating

spring

3 hop **4** flow, jump, leap, lope, rise, root, skip, stem, trip, well **5** arise, begin, bound, cause, fount, issue, start **6** appear, bounce, emerge, hurdle, reason, source, uncoil, vernal **7** come out, emanate, proceed, rebound, startle **8** commence, fountain, stimulus, wellhead **9** originate **10** incitement, resilience **12** fountainhead
back: 6 resile

springe

4 trap **5** noose, snare **7** pitfall **9** booby trap

springlike

6 vernal

springy

6 supple **7** elastic **8** flexible, stretchy **9** recoiling, resilient

sprinkle

3 dot **4** rain, spot **5** shake, speck, spray, strew **6** pepper, powder, spritz **7** asperse, drizzle, freckle, scatter, speckle, stipple **9** bespeckle

sprint

3 run **4** dart, dash, race, shin, tear **5** scoot **6** gallop, hurtle, scurry **7** scamper

sprite

3 elf, fay, nix **4** puck **5** dryad, fairy, naiad, nixie, nymph, pixie, sylph **6** kelpie **7** brownie **9** hamadryad

spritz

3 jet **4** spray, spurt **6** shower, squirt

sprout

3 bud **4** grow **5** scion, shoot **6** ratoon, sucker **7** burgeon **8** offshoot **9** germinate

spruce

4 trim **5** natty, sassy, spiff **6** dapper, spiffy **11** well-groomed

spry

4 yare **5** agile, brisk, sound, zesty, zippy **6** active, lively, nimble, robust **7** healthy **8** animated, spirited, vigorous **9** energetic, vivacious

spud

6 potato

___ Spumante

4 Asti

spume

4 fizz, foam, head, scum, suds **5** froth, spray, yeast **6** lather

spunk

4 grit, guts **5** heart, moxie, nerve, pluck **6** mettle, spirit, tinder **7** cojones, courage **8** backbone, gumption **9** fortitude, toughness **10** liveliness, resolution

spunky

4 bold **5** brave, fiery **6** daring **7** doughty, gingery, peppery **8** fearless, spirited **9** dauntless **10** courageous, mettlesome **12** high-spirited

spur

4 goad, prod, stir, urge **5** egg on, impel, prick, rally, rouse, spine **6** arouse, branch, exhort, motive, prompt, propel **7** impetus, impulse **8** buttress, catalyst, excitant, stimulus **9** actuation, incentive, instigate, stimulant, stimulate **10** incitement, inducement, motivation, projection
part: 5 rowel

spurious

4 fake, mock, sham **5** bogus, dummy, false, phony, put-on **6** ersatz, pseudo **7** assumed, feigned, pretend **8** affected **9** brummagem, imitation, pinchbeck, pretended, simulated **10** apocryphal, artificial, substitute **11** counterfeit, make-believe **12** illegitimate
combining form: 5 pseud **6** pseudo

spurn

4 snub **5** flout, scoff, scorn, scout, sneer **6** rebuff, refuse, reject **7** contemn, decline, despise, disdain, dismiss, repulse **8** turn down **9** disregard, reprobate, repudiate **10** disapprove **12** cold-shoulder

spurt

3 jet **4** gush, jump **5** burst, expel, spout, surge **6** shower, spritz, squirt **7** upsurge **8** eruption, increase **9** discharge

sputter

4 fizz, fume, rage, rant, rave, spew, spit **6** gibber, jabber **7** bluster, stammer

spy

5 agent, scout, snoop, spook **6** beagle, sleuth **7** gumshoe **8** informer, saboteur **9** detective **12** investigator **13** undercover man
name: 4 Ames (Aldrich), Boyd (Belle), Hari (Mata) **5** André (John), Blunt (Anthony), Fuchs (Klaus) **6** Philby (Kim), Smiley (George) **7** Burgess (Guy), Hanssen (Robert), Maclean (Donald), Pollard (Jonathan)

spyglass
9 telescope

spying
9 espionage

Spyri's heroine
5 Heidi

squab
5 couch 6 pigeon 7 cushion

squabble
see **spat**

squalid
3 low 4 base, foul, mean, vile 5 dingy, dirty, nasty, seedy 6 filthy, frowsy, frowzy, grubby, scurvy, shabby, shoddy, sleazy, sordid 7 ignoble, low-down, run-down, scrubby, unclean, unkempt 8 slovenly, wretched 10 despicable, disheveled 11 dilapidated 12 disreputable

squall
3 caw, row, yap, yip 4 bark, bawl, beef, feud, fuss, gust, howl, roar, tiff, wail, yawp, yell, yelp, yowl 5 brawl, fight, hoo-ha, shout 6 bellow, clamor, flurry, fracas, hubbub, ruckus, rumpus, scream, shriek, squeal, yammer 7 dispute, flare-up, quarrel, rhubarb, screech 8 brouhaha, squabble 9 bickering, caterwaul, commotion 10 falling-out, hullabaloo 11 altercation

squalor
5 filth 6 misery 7 neglect, poverty 8 baseness, iniquity 9 depravity, dirtiness 10 sordidness 11 degradation 12 wretchedness

squander
4 blow 5 spend, waste 7 consume, exhaust, fritter, scatter 9 dissipate, throw away 10 trifle away 11 fritter away

squanderer
see **spender**

square
3 fit, fix 4 bang, boxy, even, fair, jibe, just, tied 5 adapt, agree, align, clear, equal, exact, fit in, match, pay up, plaza, right, sharp, spang, tally 6 accord, adjust, settle 7 balance, conform, exactly, satisfy, settled 8 check out, coincide, dovetail, orthodox, quadrate, smack-dab, straight, unbiased 9 discharge, equitable, harmonize, impartial, liquidate, objective, precisely, quadratic, reconcile, rectangle 10 accurately, correspond

squash
3 jam 4 cram, mash, pepo, pulp 5 crush, gourd, press, quell 7 flatten, put down, squeeze, squelch 8 suppress
variety: 5 acorn 6 cushaw, Sibley, turban 7 Hubbard, scallop 8 pattypan, zucchini 9 butternut, crookneck 10 Marblehead

squat
3 low 5 dumpy, hunch, stoop, stout, thick 6 chunky, crouch, hunker, stocky, stubby 8 heavyset, thickset 10 hunker down 11 thick-bodied

squawfish
4 chub 8 cyprinid 10 pikeminnow

squawk
3 caw, yap, yip 4 beef, crab, fuss, yawp 5 bleat, gripe 6 yammer 7 protest, screech 8 complain 9 bellyache, complaint

squeak
3 rat 4 blab, fink, peep, pipe, sing 5 cheep, creak 6 escape, inform, snitch, tattle 10 tattletale

squeal
3 rat, yip 4 blab, howl, sing, yell, yelp, yowl 5 bleat, creak, grate, gripe, peach 6 inform, screak, scream, shriek, shrill, snitch, squawk, tattle 7 protest, screech 8 complain 10 tattletale

squealer
3 rat 4 fink 6 canary, snitch, weasel 7 ratfink, stoolie, tattler, tipster 8 betrayer, informer 10 talebearer, tattletale 11 stool pigeon

squeamish
5 fussy, upset 6 queasy 7 finical, finicky 8 nauseous 9 nauseated 10 fastidious, particular, pernickety 11 persnickety

squeeze
3 hug, jam 4 bind, cram, grip, milk, pack, push 5 clasp, crowd, crush, exact, gouge, juice, pinch, press, screw, wring 6 clutch, coerce, compel, crunch, eke out, enfold, extort, jostle, squash, squish 7 dilemma, embrace, extract 8 compress, contract, pressure, quandary 9 shake down 11 compression, predicament

squelch
5 quell, shush, sit on 6 muffle, muzzle, squash, squish, stifle, subdue 7 repress, silence, smother 8 strangle, suppress 10 extinguish

squib
4 fire 6 filler 7 lampoon 8 shoot off 9 detonator 11 firecracker

squid
7 mollusc, mollusk 8 calamari, calamary 10 cephalopod
kin: 7 octopus 10 cuttlefish

squiggle
4 worm 6 doodle, scrawl, squirm, writhe 7 scratch 8 curlicue, scrabble, scribble

squinch
5 quail, start, wince 6 blench, crouch, recoil, shrink

squint
4 peek, peep, peer 10 hagioscope, strabismus

squire
6 attend, escort, lawyer 7 consort, gallant 8 cavalier, chaperon 9 accompany, landowner

squirm
4 worm 6 fidget, wiggle, writhe 7 wriggle

squirrel
4 stow 5 cache, hoard, stash 7 secrete
red: 9 chickaree

squirt
3 jet, kid, pup, tot 4 brat, tyke 5 sprat, spray, spurt, twerp 6 shaver, shrimp, splurt, spritz 7 spatter

squish
3 jam 4 cram, mash, mush, pack, push 5 crush, press, quash, smash 7 flatten, scrunch, squeeze, squelch, trample

squishy
4 soft 6 flabby, quaggy, slushy, spongy

Sri Lanka
bay: 6 Bengal
capital: 7 Colombo
city: 8 Moratuwa
ethnic group: 9 Sinhalese
former name: 6 Ceylon
language: 5 Tamil 9 Sinhalese
monetary unit: 5 rupee
shoals: 11 Adam's Bridge
strait: 4 Palk

SRO
7 sellout

SS chief
7 Himmler (Heinrich)

S-shaped
7 sigmoid

stab
3 dig, pop, try 4 pang, poke, shot 5 crack, drive, fling, prick, spear, stick, whack, whirl 6 effort, pierce, thrust, twinge 7 attempt 8 puncture 9 penetrate

Stabat ____
5 Mater

stabile
6 steady 9 sculpture 10 stationary

stabilize
3 fix, set 4 prop 5 brace, poise 6 cement, firm up, fixate, prop up, secure, settle, steady 7 balance, ballast, support, sustain 8 solidify 9 reinforce

stable
3 set 4 barn, fast, firm, mews, safe, sure 5 fixed, solid, sound 6 secure, steady, sturdy 7 abiding, durable, lasting, staunch 8 balanced, constant, enduring, resolute 9 immutable, permanent, steadfast, unvarying 10 perdurable, stationary, unchanging, unshakable

stack
4 cock, heap, hill, load, mass, pile, pipe 5 mound, sheaf 7 chimney, pyramid

stack up
3 add 5 equal, total 6 equate, gather 7 compare, measure

stadium
4 bowl, rink, ring 5 arena 6 garden 8 coliseum 10 hippodrome 12 amphitheater

staff
3 rod 4 club, prop, rung, team, wand 5 baton, billy 6 cudgel 7 faculty, support 9 personnel
bishop's: 7 crosier, crozier
medical: 8 caduceus

stage
3 lot 4 play, rung, show, step 5 grade, level, mount, notch, phase, put on 6 degree, period, status 7 execute, perform, present, produce
direction: 4 exit 5 enter 6 exeunt
scenery: 3 set 8 backdrop
show: 4 play 5 drama, revue 7 musical 9 burlesque 10 vaudeville
signal: 3 cue
whisper: 5 aside

stage set
5 decor, scene 7 scenery 8 backdrop 11 mise-en-scène

stagger
4 daze, reel, stun, sway 5 amaze, floor, lurch, pitch, stump, waver, weave 6 boggle, careen, dither, falter, teeter, topple, totter, wobble, zigzag 7 astound, nonplus, perplex, shatter, stumble, stupefy 8 astonish, bowl over 9 dumbfound, overwhelm, vacillate 11 flabbergast

stagnant
5 musty, stale 6 static 8 immobile, unmoving 10 motionless, stationary

stagnate
4 idle 5 stall 6 fester 8 languish, stultify, vegetate

stagy
10 artificial, histrionic, theatrical 11 pretentious 12 melodramatic

staid
5 grave, sober 6 formal, sedate, solemn, somber, sombre, stuffy 7 earnest, serious, starchy 8 composed, decorous, priggish 9 dignified

stain
3 dye, tar 4 blot, daub, onus, slur, soil, spot 5 brand, color, odium, shame, smear, sully, taint, tinge 6 blotch, defile, embrue, imbrue, smirch, smudge, stigma 7 blemish, pigment, tarnish 8 besmirch, colorant, discolor, dishonor, dyestuff, tincture

staircase
handrail: 8 banister
outdoor: 6 perron
post: 5 newel 8 baluster

stake
3 bet, lay, pot, set 4 ante, back, game, pale, play, post, risk 5 claim, put on, share, wager 6 gamble, paling, picket, pledge, tether 7 finance 8 bankroll, interest 10 capitalize, investment

stalag
7 POW camp 10 prison camp

stale
5 banal, dusty, faded, fusty, moldy, musty, passé, tired, trite 7 clichéd, tedious, worn-out 8 overused, shopworn, timeworn 9 hackneyed, tasteless 11 commonplace, stereotyped

stalemate
3 tie 4 draw 7 impasse 8 deadlock, gridlock, standoff

stalk
4 hunt, prey 5 chase, track 6 ambush, follow, pursue, stride 8 flush out
flower: 8 peduncle
leaf: 7 petiole
short: 5 stipe

stall
3 bay, pew 4 halt 5 booth, brake, check, delay, hedge, kiosk, stand 6 arrest, put off 7 conk out, counter, hold off 8 obstruct 9 stonewall 10 filibuster 11 compartment, prevaricate

stalwart
4 bold 5 brave, gutsy, husky, stout, tough 6 brawny, robust, sinewy, strong, sturdy 7 valiant 8 fearless, intrepid, unafraid, valorous, vigorous 9 dauntless, tenacious, undaunted 10 courageous

stamen part
6 anther 8 filament

stamina
8 tenacity 9 endurance, fortitude, tolerance 11 persistence 12 staying power

stammer
6 gibber, jabber 7 sputter, stutter 8 hesitate, splutter

stamp
3 ilk, lot 4 etch, kind, mark, mint, mold, seal, sort, type 5 clomp, clump, pound, print, tromp 6 hammer, stripe 7 impress, imprint, trample 8 hallmark, inscribe 9 character 10 impression 12 characterize

stampede
4 bolt, dash, rout, rush, tear 5 crush, panic, rodeo 6 charge

stamps
7 postage

stance
4 pose 7 bearing, posture 8 attitude, carriage, position 10 deportment

stanch
4 stem, stop 5 check 6 stop up 8 hold back

stanchion
4 post, prop 5 brace 7 support

stand
4 bear 5 abide, booth, brook, kiosk, stall, treat 6 endure, handle, suffer 7 counter, stomach, swallow, weather 8 attitude, platform, position, tolerate
artist's: 5 easel
three-legged: 6 tripod, trivet
ornamental: 7 étagère

standard
3 law, par 4 flag, jack, mean, norm, rule 5

color, gauge, ideal, model, stock, usual **6** banner, belief, common, ensign, median, normal, pennon **7** average, classic, example, general, measure, pattern, pennant, regular, typical, uniform **8** accepted, everyday, exemplar, familiar, ordinary, orthodox, paradigm **9** archetype, benchmark, criterion, customary, principle, yardstick **10** definitive, prevailing, recognized, regulation, touchstone **11** established, fundamental

standardize
6 adjust **7** conform **8** regulate **9** reconcile

stand for
4 bear, mean **5** allow **6** denote, permit **7** signify **8** indicate, tolerate **9** put up with, represent, symbolize

stand-in
3 sub **5** proxy **6** backup, second **9** alternate, surrogate **10** substitute, understudy **11** pinch hitter, replacement **12** impersonator

standing
4 rank, term **5** erect, fixed, place **6** cachet, credit, repute, status **7** dignity, footing, station, stature, upright **8** capacity, duration, eminence, position, prestige, stagnant **9** character, permanent, situation **10** estimation, reputation **11** consequence, established

standoff
see **stalemate**

standoffish
5 aloof **6** chilly **7** distant, haughty **8** detached, reserved **9** reclusive, withdrawn **10** unfriendly, unsociable **12** misanthropic

stand out
3 jut **4** bulk, loom **5** bulge **7** project **8** protrude

standpatter
4 fogy, tory **7** diehard **8** mossback **11** bitter-ender **12** conservative

standpoint
4 side **5** angle, slant **7** outlook **9** direction **11** perspective

standstill
4 halt, stop **5** check, pause **7** impasse **8** deadlock, dead stop **9** cessation, stalemate

Stanford site
8 Palo Alto

Stanley Kowalski's wife
6 Stella

Stanleys' car
7 steamer

Stan's partner
5 Ollie

stanza
7 strophe
combining form: 5 stich
of eight lines: 6 octave
of four lines: 6 ballad **8** quatrain
of six lines: 6 sestet
of three lines: 6 tercet **7** triplet
Persian: 8 rubaiyat

star
4 icon, idol, lead, main, nova **5** actor, chief, major **6** étoile **7** actress, capital **8** asterisk, dominant, luminary **9** celebrity, headliner, principal **10** preeminent **11** outstanding
bright: 4 Vega **5** Deneb, Rigel, Spica **6** Altair, Pollux, Sirius **7** Antares, Canopus, Capella, Procyon **8** Arcturus **9** Aldebaran, Archernar, Fomalhaut **10** Beta Crucis, Betelgeuse **11** Alpha Crucis **12** Beta Centauri **13** Alpha Centauri
combining form: 4 astr **5** aster, astro **6** astero, sidero
five-pointed: 8 pentacle **9** pentagram
giant: 10 Betelgeuse
six-pointed: 8 hexagram

starch
3 pep **4** push, snap **5** drive, moxie, punch, spunk, vigor **7** stiffen **8** gumption, vitality **9** formality
combining form: 4 amyl **5** amylo

starchy
4 prim **5** aloof, stiff **6** doughy, formal, wooden **7** stilted

star-crossed
6 doomed **7** hapless, unlucky **8** ill-fated, luckless **10** ill-starred **11** unfortunate **12** misfortunate

Stardust composer
10 Carmichael (Hoagy)

stare
3 eye **4** gape, gawk, gaze, ogle, peer **6** goggle **10** rubberneck

stark
3 raw **4** bare, nude, pure **5** bleak, blunt, clear, harsh, naked, quite, rigid, sheer, utter **6** barren, strict, unclad, vacant, wholly **8**

absolute, complete, desolate, stripped **9**
au naturel, out-and-out **10** absolutely

starry
6 astral **7** stellar **8** sidereal

starry-eyed
6 dreamy, unreal **7** utopian **8** ecstatic **9**
rapturous, visionary **11** impractical,
unrealistic **13** impracticable

Star-Spangled Banner writer
3 Key (Francis Scott)

start
4 bolt, dawn, draw **5** arise, begin, crank,
found, issue, onset, quail, react, set up,
wince **6** blench, create, embark, flinch,
launch, outset, recoil, shrink, spring, take
up **7** actuate, genesis, infancy, kickoff,
opening, trigger **8** activate, commence,
embark on, initiate, organize, reaction **9**
beginning, establish, institute, originate **10**
inaugurate **12** commencement

startle
4 jolt, jump **5** alarm, scare, shock, spook **8**
astonish, frighten, surprise

starved
6 hungry **8** famished, ravenous, underfed

stash
4 bury, hide **5** cache, hoard, plant, store **7**
conceal, lay away, nest egg, secrete **8** lay
aside, sock away, squirrel **9** stockpile

stasis
7 balance, inertia **9** equipoise **10**
immobility, stagnation **11** equilibrium

state
3 air, put, say **4** aver, mode, rank, tell, vent
5 utter **6** affirm, assert, recite, relate, report
7 declare, dignity, explain, expound,
express, posture, recount **8** attitude,
capacity, describe, position, set forth,
standing **9** condition, enunciate, situation,
ventilate
subdivison: 6 county

state
easternmost: 5 Maine
largest: 6 Alaska
smallest: 11 Rhode Island
southernmost: 6 Hawaii

state abbreviation
Alabama: 3 Ala.
Alaska: 4 Alas.
Arizona: 4 Ariz.
Arkansas: 3 Ark.
California: 3 Cal. **5** Calif.
Colorado: 3 Col. **4** Colo

Connecticut: 4 Conn.
Delaware: 3 Del.
Florida: 3 Fla.
Idaho: 3 Ida.
Illinois: 3 Ill.
Indiana: 3 Ind.
Kansas: 3 Kan. **4** Kans.
Kentucky: 3 Ken.
Massachusetts: 4 Mass.
Michigan: 4 Mich.
Minnesota: 4 Minn.
Mississippi: 4 Miss.
Montana: 4 Mont.
Nebraska: 3 Neb. **4** Nebr.
Nevada: 3 Nev.
New Mexico: 4 N. Mex.
North Carolina: 4 N. Car.
North Dakota: 4 N. Dak.
Oklahoma: 4 Okla.
Oregon: 3 Ore. **4** Oreg.
Pennsylvania: 4 Penn. **5** Penna.
South Carolina: 4 S. Car.
South Dakota: 4 S. Dak.
Tennessee: 4 Tenn.
Texas: 3 Tex.
Vermont: 4 Verm.
Virginia: 4 Virg.
Washington: 4 Wash.
West Virginia: 3 W. Va.
Wisconsin: 3 Wis. **4** Wisc.
Wyoming: 3 Wyo.

stately
5 grand, lofty, noble, regal, royal **6** august,
formal, kingly, lordly, solemn **7** courtly,
elegant, gallant, haughty **8** gracious,
imperial, imposing, majestic, palatial,
princely **9** dignified **10** ceremonial,
impressive, monumental **11** ceremonious,
magnificent

statement
3 tab **4** bill **5** score **6** avowal, charge,
dictum, remark, report **7** account,
comment, invoice, recital **8** averment **9**
affidavit, assertion, manifesto, narrative,
reckoning, testimony, utterance **10**
deposition, expression **11** description
introductory: 7 preface **8** foreword,
prologue

stateroom
5 cabin

statesman
10 politician
American: 3 Hay (John Milton) **4** Clay
(Henry), Hull (Cordell), Otis (James), Root
(Elihu) **5** Adams (Samuel), Henry (Patrick),
Lodge (Henry Cabot), Vance (Cyrus) **6**
Bunche (Ralph), Bunker (Ellsworth), Dulles

(John Foster), Kennan (George F.), Morris (Gouverneur), Powell (Colin), Sumner (Charles) **7** Acheson (Dean), Hancock (John), Kellogg (Frank B.), Lansing (Robert), Sherman (John, Roger), Stimson (Henry L.), Webster (Daniel) **8** Franklin (Benjamin), Hamilton (Alexander), Harriman (Averell), Pinckney (Charles, Thomas), Randolph (Edmund Jennings, John, Payton), Rutledge (John), Stevenson (Adlai), Trumbull (Jonathan, Joseph) **9** Kissinger (Henry) **10** Stettinius (Edward Reilly)
Australian: 9 Wentworth (William Charles)
Austrian: 6 Renner (Karl) **7** Kaunitz (Wenzel von) **8** Dollfuss (Engelbert) **10** Metternich (Klemens von) **13** Schwarzenberg (Felix zu)
Canadian: 4 King (W. L. Mackenzie) **7** Laurier (Wilfrid) **8** Thompson (John Sparrow) **9** Macdonald (John Alexander, John Sandfield), Mackenzie (Alexander, William Lyon)
Chinese: 3 Yen (Hsishan) **4** Deng (Xiaoping), Kung (Hsiang-hsi), Teng (Hsiaop'ing), Wang (Anshih, Chingwei), Yuan (Shih-kai) **9** Sun Yat-Sen
Dutch: 6 de Witt (Johan de) **7** Grotius (Hugo), Stikker (Dirk)
East German: 8 Ulbricht (Walter)
English: 3 Fox (Charles, Henry) **4** Eden (Anthony, George, William), More (Thomas), Peel (Arthur, Robert, William), Pitt (William), Vane (Henry) **5** Cecil (Robert, William), North (Francis, Frederick, Roger) **6** Morley (John), Sidney (Algernon, Henry, Philip, Robert), Temple (Henry, William), Wolsey (Thomas) **7** Halifax (Earl of), Reading (Marquis of), Russell (John, William), Stanley (Edward George, Edward Henry), Stewart (Robert), Warwick (Earl of) **8** Cromwell (Oliver, Thomas), Disraeli (Benjamin), Robinson (George Frederick Samuel), Villiers (George) **9** Cavendish (Spencer, WIllIam), Churchill (Randolph, Winston), Gladstone (William), Salisbury (Earl, Marquis of), Strafford (Earl of), Wellesley (Arthur, Richard Colley) **10** Palmerston (Lord), Rockingham (Marquis of), Sunderland (Earl of), Walsingham (Francis), Wellington (Duke of) **11** Chamberlain (Austen, Joseph, Neville), Shaftesbury (Earl of) **12** Chesterfield (Earl of)
Finnish: 9 Stahlberg (Kaarlo Juho)
French: 5 Sully (Duc de) **6** Guizot (François-Pierre-Guillaume), Thiers (Louis-Adolphe), Turgot (Anne-Robert-Jacques) **7** Herriot (Edouard), Mazarin (Jules),

Schuman (Robert), Viviani (René) **8** Hanotaux (Gabriel) **9** Lafayette (Marquis de), Millerand (Alexandre), Richelieu (Duc de) **10** Clemenceau (Georges) **11** Tocqueville (Alexis de)
German: 5 Wirth (Joseph) **10** Stresemann (Gustav)
German-Danish: 9 Struensee (Johann Friedrich)
Greek: 6 Zaimis (Alexandros) **8** Pericles **9** Aristides **11** Cleisthenes, Demosthenes **12** Themistocles
Israeli: 4 Eban (Abba) **5** Begin (Menachem), Dayan (Moshe)
Italian: 6 Cavour (Conte di), Crispi (Francesco) **7** Orlando (Vittorio Emanuele) **11** Machiavelli (Niccolo)
Japanese: 5 genro, Kanoe **6** Kanoye
Norwegian: 6 Nansen (Fridtjof)
Polish: 7 Zaleski (August) **9** Pilsudski (Jozef) **10** Paderewski (Ignacy)
Prussian: 5 Stein (Karl)
Roman: 4 Cato (Marcus Porcius) **6** Cicero (Marcus Tullius), Pompey, Seneca (Lucius Annaeus) **7** Agrippa (Marcus Vipsanius) **8** Gracchus (Gaius, Tiberius), Maecenas (Gaius) **9** Symmachus (Quintus Aurelius)
Russian: 5 Witte (Sergey) **7** Molotov (Vyacheslav) **8** Potemkin (Grigory) **9** Vyshinsky (Andrey)
Scottish: 4 Knox (John)
South American: 7 Bolívar (Simón) **9** San Martín (José de)
Swiss: 4 Ador (Gustave) **5** Welti (Emil)

static

5 fixed, inert **6** stable, steady **7** stabile, stalled, stopped **8** constant, immobile, inactive, stagnant, unmoving **9** immovable, unvarying **10** changeless, unchanging

station

4 post, rank, site, spot **5** depot, locus, place, point **6** assign **7** footing **8** capacity, standing **9** character **10** whIte noIse

stationary

5 fixed **6** static **8** immobile, stagnant, unmoving **9** immovable **10** motionless, stock-still

statue

base: 6 plinth **8** pedestal
gigantic: 8 Colossus
Greek: 5 atlas **7** telamon **8** caryatid
religious: 5 Pietà
small: 8 figurine

stature

see **status**

status

4 rank 5 merit, place, worth 6 cachet, rating, renown 7 caliber, dignity, footing, posture, quality 8 capacity, eminence, position, prestige, standing 9 character, condition, situation 10 prominence 11 consequence, distinction

statute

3 act, law 4 bill 5 canon, edict 9 enactment, ordinance

staunch

4 fast, firm, sure, true 5 liege, loyal, solid, sound 6 secure, stable, strong, trusty 8 constant, faithful, reliable, resolute, stalwart 9 steadfast 10 dependable 11 substantial, trustworthy

stave off

4 foil 5 avert, block, deter, dodge, elude, parry, rebut, repel 6 rebuff, thwart 7 forfend, obviate, prevent, repulse 8 preclude 9 forestall 10 circumvent

stay

3 guy, lag 4 bide, halt, prop, rest, stop, wait 5 abide, brace, check, defer, delay, dwell, lodge, tarry, visit 6 linger, put off, remain 7 sojourn, support, suspend 8 hold over, postpone, stop over 9 interrupt 10 suspension 11 stick around

steadfast

4 firm, sure, true 5 fixed, liege, loyal 7 abiding, adamant, patient, staunch 8 constant, enduring, faithful, immobile, reliable, resolute, stubborn 9 immovable, unbending, unmovable 10 dependable, unwavering, unyielding 11 unfaltering, unflinching 12 never-failing, single-minded, wholehearted 13 unquestioning

steady

3 set 4 even, fast, firm, sure 5 fixed, liege, loyal, sober 6 stable, static 7 abiding, ballast, certain, durable, equable, nonstop, regular, stabile, staunch, uniform 8 constant, enduring, faithful, habitual, reliable, resolute, unbroken, unshaken 9 ceaseless, incessant, stabilize, unvarying 10 changeless, consistent, continuous, dependable, persistent, sweetheart, unchanging, unswerving, unwavering 11 unfaltering 12 unchangeable, wholehearted

steak

4 club, cube, loin 5 chuck, flank, round, T-bone 6 rib eye 7 brisket, sirloin 9 Delmonico, hamburger, Salisbury 10

tenderloin 11 filet mignon, London broil, porterhouse 13 chateaubriand

steal

3 bag, cop, nab, nip, rob 4 grab, hook, kite, lift, loot, lurk, slip, take 5 creep, filch, glide, heist, pinch, poach, prowl, seize, shirk, sidle, skulk, slide, slink, sneak, swipe 6 burgle, fleece, hijack, pilfer, pocket, snatch, snitch, thieve, tiptoe 7 bargain, pillage, plunder, purloin 8 embezzle, shanghai, shoplift 9 pussyfoot 10 burglarize, plagiarize 11 appropriate
a vehicle: 6 hijack 8 highjack

stealing

5 theft 6 piracy 7 larceny, robbery 8 burglary

stealthy

3 sly 4 wily 6 covert, crafty, feline, secret, shifty, silent, slinky, sneaky 7 catlike, cunning, furtive, sub-rosa 8 hush-hush, skulking, slinking, sneaking 9 noiseless 10 undercover 11 clandestine 13 surreptitious

steam bath

5 sauna

steamboat structure

5 texas

steamer

4 boat, clam, ship

steam organ

8 calliope

steed

5 horse, mount 7 charger

steel

4 gird 5 brace, nerve, rally 6 buck up, harden 7 fortify, hearten, stiffen 8 embolden, inspirit 9 reinforce 10 strengthen

steep

3 sop 4 high, soak 5 bathe, dizzy, imbue, sheer 6 abrupt, drench, infuse 7 arduous, extreme, immerse, suffuse 8 elevated, marinate, saturate 9 excessive 10 exorbitant, immoderate, impregnate, inordinate 11 precipitate, precipitous

steeple

5 spire, tower 6 flèche

steer

4 helm, lead 5 guide, pilot, point, route 6 direct, escort, tip-off 7 channel, conduct, skipper 8 shepherd
a ship: 4 conn, helm, luff

Stegner novel
13 Angle of Repose, Spectator Bird (The)
20 Big Rock Candy Mountain (The)

stein
3 mug 5 stoup 6 goblet 7 tankard

Steinbeck novel
5 Pearl (The) 10 Cannery Row, East of
Eden 12 Of Mice and Men, Tortilla Flat 13
Grapes of Wrath (The)

Stein's companion
6 Toklas (Alice B.)

Steinway product
5 piano

stellar
6 astral, starry 7 leading, shining 8
sidereal, standout, starlike 10 preeminent
11 outstanding, predominant, superlative

stem
4 flow, head, rise, stop 5 arise, check,
issue 6 arrest, derive, spring, stanch 7
control, develop, emanate, proceed 8
peduncle 9 originate
plant: 5 haulm
underground: 5 tuber 7 rhizome

stench
4 funk, reek 5 smell, stink

stentorian
4 loud 7 blaring, booming, orotund,
raucous, roaring 8 sonorous, strident 9
clamorous, deafening 10 thundering 12
earsplitting

step
4 hoof, pace, rung, walk 5 grade, level,
notch, stage, stair, track, tread 6 degree 7
measure, traipse 8 footfall 9 gradation
dance: 3 pas

step-by-step
7 gradual 9 piecemeal

steppe
5 plain 6 tundra

Steppenwolf author
5 Hesse (Hermann)

stereotype
4 mold 7 pattern 10 categorize,
pigeonhole 11 standardize

stereotypical
4 hack 5 banal, stale, trite 7 clichéd 8
shopworn, timeworn 9 hackneyed 11
commonplace

sterile
4 arid, bare, vain 6 barren, fallow 7
aseptic, worn-out 8 desolate, hygienic,
impotent, lifeless, sanitary 9 fruitless,
infertile 10 antiseptic, unfruitful, uninspired
11 disinfected 12 unproductive

sterilize
3 fix 4 geld, spay 5 alter 6 neuter, purify
7 cleanse 8 sanitize 9 disinfect 10
emasculate

sterilized
7 aseptic

sterling
4 pure, true 5 noble 6 worthy 8 virtuous
9 estimable, exemplary, honorable

stern
4 grim 5 harsh, rigid, sober, stony 6
gloomy, severe, strict 7 ascetic, austere 8
obdurate 10 forbidding, implacable,
inexorable, inflexible 11 unrelenting

sternward
3 aft

Sterope
father: 5 Atlas
mother: 7 Pleione
sisters: 8 Pleiades

Stevenson novel
9 Kidnapped

stew
4 boil, brew, flap, fret, fume, fuss, hash,
olio, olla, snit 5 daube, salmi, sweat, tizzy,
worry 6 burgoo, dither, jumble, lather,
medley, pother, ragout, seethe, simmer,
swivet, tumult 7 brothel, goulash, mélange,
mixture, parboil, swelter, turmoil 8 bordello,
mishmash, mulligan, pot-au-feu 9
Brunswick, cassoulet, commotion,
confusion, pasticcio, potpourri 10
hodgepodge, hotchpotch, miscellany,
turbulence 11 olla podrida, ratatouille,
slumgullion 13 bouillabaisse

steward
6 manage 7 manager 8 overseer 10
supervisor

stewed
3 lit 4 high 5 drunk, lit up, oiled 6 bashed,
blotto, bombed, cooked, juiced, potted,
soaked, soused, stewed, stoned, tanked,
wasted, zonked 7 crocked, drunken,
pickled, pie-eyed, sloshed, smashed,
sottish 8 simmered 9 plastered 10
inebriated, liquored up 11 intoxicated

Stheno
see **Gorgon**

stick
3 put, rod 4 glue, pole, stab 5 affix, baton, cling 6 adhere, attach, cleave, cohere, fasten 7 scruple 10 overcharge

stick around
4 bide, stay, wait 5 abide, dally, tarry 6 linger, remain

sticker
3 pin 4 barb, seal, shiv, spur 5 point, prong, shank, spike, spine, stamp 6 dagger 8 stiletto

stick-in-the-mud
4 fogy 6 fossil 8 mossback 10 fuddy-duddy

stick out
3 jut 5 bulge 6 beetle 7 project 8 overhang, protrude

stick up
3 mug, rob 6 waylay 7 project 8 protrude

sticky
5 gluey, gooey, gummy, humid, muggy, mushy, soggy, tacky 6 clammy, knotty, slushy, sultry, thorny, viscid 7 awkward, cloying, maudlin, mawkish, viscous 8 adhesive, bathetic, clinging, romantic 9 difficult 11 problematic, sentimental, tear-jerking

stiff
3 guy, lit, set 4 body, firm, hard, lush 5 cheat, drunk, harsh, oiled, proud, rigid, stark, steep, stick, tense, tight, tipsy 6 buzzed, corpse, frozen, jelled, juiced, person, plowed, potent, potted, severe, soused, stewed, wooden 7 cadaver, carcass, sloshed, starchy, stilted 8 hardened, reserved, stubborn 9 cardboard, excessive, inelastic, obstinate, petrified, plastered, unbending 10 exorbitant, inebriated, inflexible, mechanical, unyielding 11 intoxicated, intractable

stiffen
5 tense 6 harden 7 thicken 8 rigidify, solidify 9 stabilize 10 immobilize

stifle
3 gag 4 hush, mute 5 burke, choke, deter 6 dampen, deaden, hush up, muffle, muzzle 7 repress, silence, smother, squelch 8 stultify, suppress 9 suffocate 10 asphyxiate, discourage

stigma
4 blot, onus, spot 5 brand, odium, shame, stain, taint 6 smudge, smutch 8 black eye, disgrace, dishonor, petechia, tainting

stigmatize
5 brand, label, stamp

still
3 yet 4 calm, even, hush, lull 5 allay, inert, quiet, shush, whist 6 becalm, hushed, placid, serene, settle, silent, though, withal 7 halcyon, however, silence 8 after all, likewise, peaceful, stagnant, tranquil 9 noiseless, quietness, soundless 10 motionless, stationary 11 furthermore, nonetheless, tranquility 12 nevertheless

stilt
4 bird, pile, pole 8 longlegs 9 shorebird

stilted
4 prim 5 stiff 6 formal, wooden 7 pompous, starchy 8 affected 9 cardboard

stilt-like bird
6 avocet

stimulant
4 goad, spur 5 tonic 7 impetus, impulse 8 caffeine, catalyst, excitant 9 analeptic, energizer, incentive 10 incitement, motivation

stimulate
4 fire, goad, move, prod, spur, urge, whet 5 impel, pique, rouse, set up, spark 6 arouse, excite, fire up, foment, incite, prompt, vivify, work up 7 agitate, enliven, inspire, provoke, quicken, trigger 8 activate, energize, motivate, vitalize 9 galvanize 10 exhilarate

stimulus
4 goad, kick, push, spur 5 boost, cause 6 charge, motive 7 impetus, impulse 8 catalyst 9 incentive 10 incitement, inducement, motivation 11 instigation, provocation 13 encouragement

sting
3 con 4 trap 5 cheat, prick, smart, snare 6 hustle, tingle 7 con game 8 skin game

stinging
8 aculeate

stingy
4 mean 5 close, tight 6 frugal, narrow, paltry, skimpy 7 chintzy, costive, miserly, niggard, scrimpy, sparing, thrifty 8 grudging 9 niggardly, penny-wise, penurious 10 economical, ironfisted, pinchpenny, ungenerous 11 tightfisted 12 cheeseparing, parsimonious 13 penny-pinching

stink
4 flap, funk, fuss, reek 5 smell 6 stench

stinker
3 dog, dud 4 bomb, bust, flop 5 lemon, skunk 6 petrel

stinking
see **smelly**

stinky
see **smelly**

stint
3 job 4 bout, task, time, tour, turn 5 chore, cramp, pinch, scant, share, shift, skimp, spare, spell 6 amount, scrape, scrimp 8 quantity, restrict 9 allotment, stricture 10 assignment, limitation 11 restriction

stipend
3 fee, pay 4 hire, wage 5 award 6 salary 7 payment 9 allowance, emolument 13 consideration

stipple
3 dot 5 fleck, speck 6 pepper 7 freckle, speckle 8 sprinkle

stipulate
5 state 6 detail 7 specify 8 contract, spell out 13 particularize

stipulation
5 limit, terms 7 proviso, strings 9 condition, provision 11 requirement

stir
3 ado, din, mix 4 beat, fuss, rout, wake, whet 5 awake, blend, budge, churn, evoke, impel, raise, rally, rouse, roust, set on, spark, waken, whirl 6 arouse, awaken, bustle, excite, flurry, foment, hubbub, incite, kindle, pother, seethe, simmer, tumult, whip up 7 actuate, agitate, disturb, ferment, inspire, provoke, quicken 8 activate, activity, energize 9 agitation, commotion, galvanize, stimulate 11 disturbance

stirrup
6 stapes 8 footrest

stithy
5 anvil

stoat
6 ermine, weasel

stock
4 butt, fund, hope, race 5 brace, carry, faith, goods, hoard, store, trunk, trust 6 family, supply 7 furnish, lineage 8 pedigree, reliance 9 inventory, selection 10 confidence, dependence 11 merchandise

stockade
4 jail 5 fence 6 paling, prison 8 palisade 9 enclosure, guardroom

stock exchange
6 bourse

stockings
4 hose 5 socks 7 hosiery

stockpile
4 bank, heap, mass 5 amass, cache, hoard, lay up, store 6 garner, supply 7 backlog, collect, nest egg, reserve, store up 9 inventory, reservoir 10 accumulate, repository

stocky
3 fat 5 beefy, burly, dumpy, husky, plump, pudgy, squat, stout, thick 6 chunky, stubby, stumpy 8 heavyset, thickset 9 corpulent

stodge
4 fill, sate 5 gorge, stuff 7 overeat, surfeit

stodgy
5 fusty 6 stuffy 9 hidebound, out-of-date 12 old-fashioned

stogie
4 shoe 5 cigar 6 brogan

stoic
6 stolid 7 Spartan 9 apathetic, impassive 10 phlegmatic 11 indifferent, unconcerned

stoicism
9 stolidity 11 impassivity
founder: 4 Zeno

stoke
3 fan 4 feed, fuel, poke, stir, tend 6 supply

Stoker novel
7 Dracula

stolid
3 dry 4 dull, flat 5 stoic 6 wooden 8 rocklike 9 apathetic, impassive, unruffled 10 phlegmatic 11 unemotional

stomach
3 gut 4 bear, craw 5 abide, belly, brook, stand, taste, tummy 6 digest, endure, paunch, venter 7 abdomen, swallow 8 appetite, tolerate
combining form: 5 gastr 6 gastro, ventri, ventro
enzyme: 6 pepsin, rennin
muscle: 7 pylorus
ruminant: 6 omasum 8 abomasum 9 reticulum
Scottish: 4 kyte

stomachache
5 colic, gripe 12 collywobbles

stomp
5 clomp, clump, pound, tramp, tromp 7 trample

stone
3 gem 4 rock 5 lapis 6 pebble 7 boulder
base: 6 plinth
block of: 8 monolith
chip: 5 spall
combining form: 4 lite, lith, lyte
cosmic: 6 meteor 9 chondrite, meteorite
for grinding grains: 6 metate
fruit: 5 drupe
memorial: 7 obelisk
monument: 8 megalith
of a fruit: 3 pit

_____ Stone
7 Blarney, Rosetta

Stone novel
11 Lust for Life 18 Agony and the Ecstasy (The)

stonecrop
5 sedum

stoned
3 lit 4 high 5 boozy, doped, drunk, fried, oiled, tight, tipsy 6 buzzed, canned, juiced, loaded, plowed, potted, soused, stewed, tanked, wasted, zonked 7 crocked, drugged, muddled, pickled, pie-eyed, sloshed, smashed 8 hopped-up, strung out, turned on, wiped out 9 pixilated, plastered, spaced-out 10 inebriated, tripped out 11 intoxicated

stooge
3 act, sap 4 dupe, foil, gull, mark, pawn, tool 5 chump, dummy, patsy, proxy 6 puppet, sucker, victim 7 fall guy 8 sidekick 9 represent 11 stool pigeon, straight man 12 second banana

Stooge
3 Moe (Howard) 5 Curly (Howard), Larry (Fine)

stool pigeon
3 rat 4 fink, nark 5 decoy 6 canary, snitchl 7 ratfink, tipster 8 informer

stoop
3 dip 4 bend, duck, sink 5 deign, hunch, porch, slump 6 resort, slouch 7 descend, portico, veranda 8 stairway 10 condescend

stop
3 bar, can, dam, end 4 clog, fill, halt, plug, quit, stay, stem 5 block, brake, cease, check, close, stall, tarry 6 arrest, cut off, desist, draw up, ending, kibosh, stanch 7 disrupt, occlude, prevent, shut off, sojourn, suspend, turn off 8 knock off, leave off, obstruct 9 cessation, interrupt, terminate 10 conclusion, standstill 11 discontinue, refrain from, termination
up: 4 cork, plug 7 occlude

stopgap
5 shift 6 resort 8 recourse, resource 9 expedient, makeshift 10 expediency, substitute

stopover
4 stay 5 visit 7 sojourn

stoppage
4 halt 6 cutoff, strike 7 walkout 8 shutdown 10 standstill 11 obstruction

stopper
4 bung, cork, fill, plug 5 close

store
3 bin 4 fund, mart, pack, shop, tank 5 amass, cache, depot, hoard, lay up, stash 6 ensile, garner, market, outlet, shoppe, supply 7 arsenal, backlog, bootery, deposit, reserve 8 boutique, emporium, mothball, showroom, squirrel 9 abundance, chandlery, inventory, reservoir, stockpile, warehouse 10 accumulate, depository, five-and-ten, repository 11 five-and-dime 12 accumulation

storehouse
5 depot 7 arsenal, granary 8 magazine 9 stockpile 10 depository, repository

storekeeper
8 merchant, retailer 9 tradesman

storeroom
6 larder, pantry 7 buttery

storm
3 row 4 fury, gale, hail, rage, rant, rave, roar, rush, to-do 5 beset, blast, blitz, burst, furor, onset, salvo 6 assail, attack, charge, clamor, fall on, flurry, furore, hubbub, outcry, pother, racket, rumpus, shower, squall, strike, tumult, volley 7 assault, barrage, bluster, cyclone, monsoon, ruction, tempest, thunder, tornado, turmoil, twister, typhoon 8 blizzard, downpour, drumfire, fall upon, outbreak, outburst, paroxysm, upheaval 9 broadside, cannonade, commotion, discharge, fusillade, hurricane, nor'easter, onslaught 10 blitzkrieg, cloudburst, hurly-burly 11 bombardment, northeaster, northwester

storm trooper
10 brownshirt

stormy
4 foul 5 rainy, rough 6 raging 7 furious 8 blustery 9 turbulent 10 tumultuous 11 tempestuous, threatening

story
3 fib, lie 4 epic, saga, tale, yarn 5 conte, fable 6 canard, legend, report 7 account, fiction, märchen, parable, version 8 allegory, anecdote, folktale, megillah, tall tale 9 chronicle, fairy tale, narration, narrative 11 description, fabrication

storyteller
4 liar 6 fibber 8 fabulist 9 raconteur

stoup
4 font 5 basin 6 flagon, goblet 7 chalice, tankard

stout
3 ale, fat 4 brew 5 beefy, bulky, burly, heavy, husky, obese, plump, thick 6 fleshy, portly, strong, sturdy 9 corpulent 10 overweight

Stout detective
5 Wolfe (Nero)

stouthearted
4 bold, game 5 brave, gutsy 7 doughty, valiant 8 fearless, intrepid, resolute, stalwart, stubborn, unafraid 9 audacious, dauntless, undaunted 10 courageous

stove
4 kiln, oven 5 range 8 Franklin, potbelly

stow
4 load, pack 5 stash, store 7 deposit

stower
9 stevedore

Stowe work
4 Dred

strabismus
6 squint

straddle
4 span 6 sprawl 8 bestride 11 spread-eagle

strafe
4 rake 6 attack 8 enfilade 10 machine-gun

straggle
3 lag 4 poke, roam, rove 5 drift, range, stray 6 dawdle, loiter, ramble, wander 7 maunder, meander 8 trail off 9 string out

straight
4 even, fair, neat, pure, true 5 erect, plain, plumb, right 6 at once, candid, direct, honest, linear, square 7 unmixed, upright 8 orthodox 9 bourgeois, forthwith, undiluted 10 aboveboard, button-down, forthright 12 conventional 13 unadulterated
combining form: 4 orth, rect 5 ortho, recti

straightaway
3 now 6 at once 7 stretch 8 directly, first off, promptly 9 forthwith, instanter 11 immediately

straighten
4 even, tidy 5 align 6 neaten, unbend, uncurl 7 rectify

straightforward
5 frank, lucid 6 candid, direct, honest 7 genuine, precise, sincere 8 clear-cut 9 outspoken 10 forthright 11 undeviating

strain
3 air, tax, try 4 hint, kind, pull, sort, toil, tune, vein 5 exert, stock, sweat, tinge, touch, trace, twist 6 filter, melody, screen, streak, stress, strive, wrench 7 lineage, overtax, tension, trouble 8 ancestry, exertion, overwork, pedigree, pressure, struggle 9 overexert

strait
4 bind, pass 5 pinch 6 crisis, plight 7 channel, dilemma, narrows, squeeze 8 exigency, hardship, juncture 9 crossroad, emergency 10 difficulty 11 contingency
Adriatic Sea-Ionian Sea: 7 Otranto
Alaska: 3 Icy
Alaska-Russia: 6 Bering
Albania-Greece: 5 Corfu
Asia-Europe: 11 Dardanelles
Atlantic-Baffin Island: 5 Davis
Atlantic-Mediterranean: 9 Gibraltar
Atlantic-Nantucket Sound: 8 Muskeget
Atlantic-North Sea: 7 English
Atlantic-Pacific: 5 Drake 8 Magellan
Atlantic-Saint Lawrence: 5 Cabot
Baffin Island-Quebec: 6 Hudson
Bering Sea-Sea of Okhotsk: 5 Kuril 6 Kurile
Bismarck Sea-Solomon Sea: 6 Vitiaz
Canada: 3 Rae 5 Dease
East China Sea: 5 Korea 8 Tsushima
East China-South China: 6 Taiwan 7 Formosa
England-France: 5 Dover
Flores Sea-Indian Ocean: 4 Sape

Flores Sea-Savu Sea: 4 Alor
Indian Ocean-Java Sea: 5 Sunda
India-Sri Lanka: 4 Palk
Indonesia: 4 Alas, Alor, Bali **5** Tioro **6** Lombok **7** Dampier **8** Macassar, Makassar, Surabaya
Inner Hebrides: 5 Tiree
Iran-Oman: 6 Hormuz
Italy: 7 Messina
Japan: 4 Yura **5** Bungo, Kitan **7** Hayasui
Japan-Sakhalin Island: 4 Soya
Lake Huron: 10 Mississagi
Lake Huron-Lake Michigan: 8 Mackinac
Malay Archipelago: 5 Wetar
Malaysia-Singapore: 6 Johore
Malay-Sumatra: 7 Malacca
New Jersey-Staten Island: 7 van Kull
New South Wales-Tasmania: 4 Bass
New Zealand: 4 Cook
Northwest Territories: 6 Barrow **8** Franklin, Victoria **13** Prince of Wales
Nova Scotia: 5 Canso
Pacific-San Francisco Bay: 10 Golden Gate
Pacific-South China Sea: 5 Luzon
Philippines: 5 Bohol, Tanon **6** Iloilo **7** Basilan
Russia: 4 Kara
Suvu Sea-Timor Sea: 4 Roti
Sea of Azov-Black Sea: 5 Kerch **7** Enikale
Sea of Japan: 5 Tatar
Solomon Islands: 12 Bougainville
South China Sea: 7 Mindoro **9** Singapore
Turkey: 8 Bosporus **9** Bosphorus, Karadeniz
Vancouver-Washington: 10 Juan de Fuca
Wales: 5 Menai
Washington Sound: 4 Haro

straitened
7 lacking, pinched, wanting **8** deprived, strapped **9** deficient, destitute, distressed **10** inadequate **12** impoverished

straitlaced
4 prim **5** staid, stiff **6** formal, narrow, prissy, strict, stuffy **7** genteel, prudish, starchy, stilted **8** priggish **9** hidebound, Victorian **11** puritanical

strand
4 bank **5** beach, coast, fiber, leave, shore, wreck **6** desert, maroon, thread **7** abandon, shingle **8** cast away, littoral, seacoast, seashore **9** shipwreck **10** run aground, waterfront

strange
3 odd **5** alien, crazy, fishy, funny, kinky, kooky, nutty, outré, queer, weird **6** exotic, far-out, freaky **7** bizarre, curious, oddball, offbeat, uncanny, unknown, unusual **8** aberrant, abnormal, atypical, peculiar, singular, wondrous **9** eccentric, fantastic, grotesque **10** mysterious, off-the-wall, outlandish, surprising, unfamiliar **11** exceptional **12** unaccustomed

Strange Interlude author
6 O'Neill (Eugene)

stranger
5 alien, guest **7** visitor **8** newcomer, outsider, wanderer **9** auslander, foreigner, immigrant, transient

strangle
5 burke, choke, shush **6** muffle, quelch, stifle **7** garotte, garrote **8** suppress, throttle **10** asphyxiate

strap
4 band, beat, belt, bind **5** leash **6** attach, punish, secure, suffer **7** binding, leather **8** distress **9** constrict

strapping
5 beefy, burly, hardy, husky **6** brawny, robust, rugged, sturdy **8** muscular, vigorous **10** able-bodied

stratagem
4 play, plot, ploy, ruse, wile **5** feint, trick **6** device, gambit, scheme, tactic **8** artifice, intrigue, maneuver **10** conspiracy, subterfuge **11** machination

strategy
4 plan **6** design, method, scheme **7** project, tactics **8** game plan **9** blueprint

stratum
3 bed **4** rank **5** class, grade, layer, level

Strauss, Richard
opera: 6 Salome **7** Elektra **13** Rosenkavalier (Der) **15** Ariadne auf Naxos **16** Frau ohne Schatten (Der)
tone poem: 7 Don Juan **10** Don Quixote **11** Heldenleben (Ein) **20** Thus Spake Zarathustra **23** Death and Transfiguration

straw
3 hay **5** blond **6** flaxen, golden, thatch
braided: 6 sennit
mat: 6 tatami
plaited: 7 leghorn

stray
3 err, gad **4** lost, roam, rove, waif **5** drift, range **6** depart, errant, ramble, random,

wander **7** deviate, digress, diverge, erratic, meander, runaway, traipse, vagrant **8** divagate, homeless, sporadic **9** gallivant

streak
4 hint, vein **5** fleck, tinge, trace **6** dapple, marble, mottle, strain, stripe **7** striate **8** tincture **9** suspicion, variegate **10** intimation, suggestion

streaked
5 upset **7** brindle, marbled, striped **8** brindled, grizzled **9** disturbed

stream
3 run **4** beck, burn, flow, flux, gill, gush, pour, race, rill, rush, sike, tide **5** bourn, brook, creek, spate, surge **6** bourne, branch, rindle, runnel, sluice **7** current, freshet, rivulet, torrent **8** affluent

streamer
4 flag, jack **6** banner, burgee, ensign, pennon **7** pennant **8** banderol, bannerol, standard **9** banderole

streamline
7 contour **8** organize, simplify **9** modernize

street
3 way **4** drag, road, wynd **5** alley, drive **6** artery, avenue **7** roadway **9** boulevard **12** thoroughfare
border: 4 curb **7** curbing
material: 6 cobble **7** asphalt, macadam **11** cobblestone

streetcar
4 tram **7** trolley

Streetcar Named Desire, A
author: 8 Williams (Tennessee)
character: 6 Stella (Kowalski) **7** Blanche (DuBois), Stanley (Kowalski)

Street Scene author
4 Rice (Elmer)

strength
5 brawn, force, might, power, sinew, vigor **6** energy, muscle **7** potency **8** firmness, security **9** fortitude, intensity, soundness, stability, toughness **10** steadiness, sturdiness

strengthen
4 gird **5** brace, steel **6** anneal, harden, prop up **7** bolster, enhance, fortify, support, toughen **8** buttress, embolden, energize **9** intensify, reinforce, undergird **10** invigorate, rejuvenate

strenuous
4 hard **5** tough **6** taxing, uphill **7** arduous, operose **8** demanding, difficult, effortful, Herculean, laborious **12** backbreaking

Strephon
8 shepherd
beloved: 5 Chloe **6** Urania

stress
6 accent, burden, import, play up, strain, weight **7** anxiety, feature, tension, trouble, urgency **8** emphasis, pressure **9** emphasize, italicize, underline **10** accentuate, underscore **12** accentuation
in poetry: 5 ictus

stretch
4 area, draw, time range, reach, scope, space, spell, sweep, tract, while **6** extend, extent, length, limber, region, spread **7** breadth, compass, draw out, expanse, magnify, prolong, purview, spin out, tighten **8** distance, elongate, lengthen, protract **9** embellish, embroider, expansion, overstate **10** exaggerate
on a frame: 6 tenter
out: 6 sprawl **7** lie down, recline

stretchable
7 ductile, elastic, tensile

stretched
4 taut

stretcher
4 yarn **6** gurney, litter **8** tall tale

strew
3 sow **4** dust **5** cover **6** pepper, spread **7** scatter **8** disperse, sprinkle **9** broadcast, circulate, propagate **10** distribute **11** disseminate

stricken
3 hit, ill **4** hurt, sick **7** injured, wounded **9** afflicted **11** overwhelmed

strict
4 firm **5** exact, harsh, rigid, stern, tough **6** narrow, severe **7** precise **8** exacting, faithful, rigorous **9** draconian, stringent, unsparing **10** inflexible, ironhanded, meticulous, scrupulous **11** punctilious

stricture
5 cramp, stint **7** censure, reproof **8** reproach **9** aspersion, criticism, reprimand **10** constraint, limitation **11** restriction **13** animadversion

stride
  4 gait, pace, step 5 march, stalk 7 advance 8 straddle

strident
  4 loud 5 harsh 6 shrill 7 grating, jarring, rasping, raucous, squawky 8 piercing 9 clamorous, insistent, obtrusive 10 boisterous, discordant, stentorian, vociferous 11 loudmouthed 12 earsplitting, obstreperous

strife
  4 fray 5 broil, fight 6 battle, combat 7 discord, dispute, dissent, quarrel, rivalry, warfare, wrangle 8 argument, conflict, disunity, friction, struggle, tug-of-war 10 contention, difference, dissension, dissidence 11 altercation, competition, controversy

strike
  3 hit, pop, rap 4 bash, beat, find, poke, slam, slap, slug, sock, swat, whap, whop 5 clout, knock, punch, smack, smite, swipe, thump, whack 6 affect, assail, attack, cudgel, delete, hammer, pummel, thrash 7 assault, impress, inflict, inspire 8 discover, stoppage

striking
  5 showy, vivid 6 cogent, marked, signal 7 salient, telling 8 forceful 9 arresting, prominent 10 compelling, noticeable, remarkable 11 conspicuous, outstanding

Strindberg play
  6 Easter, Father (The) 8 Comrades 9 Creditors (The), Dream Play (A), Miss Julie 10 Master Olaf 11 Ghost Sonata (The) 12 Dance of Death (The), Gustavus Vasa

string
  3 row 4 file, line, rank, tier 5 chain, order, queue, train, twine 6 sequel, series 7 echelon 8 recourse, resource, sequence 10 succession
  up: 4 hang 5 noose, scrag 6 gibbet

stringent
  see **strict**

stringy
  4 lean, ropy, wiry 6 sinewy 7 fibrous 8 muscular

strip
  4 band, bare, doff, flay, husk, peel, sack, skin 5 scale 6 billet, denude, divest, expose, fillet, ravage, ribbon 7 bandeau, deprive, disrobe, pillage, uncover, undress 8 unclothe
  leather: 5 thong

  of wood: 4 lath, slat
  skin: 6 flense

stripe
  3 ilk 4 band, kind, lash, sort, type 5 order 6 strake, streak, striate 7 banding, chevron, lineate, variety

stripling
  3 boy, lad 5 youth 9 youngster 10 adolescent

stripper
  6 peeler, teaser 9 ecdysiast

stripteaser
  see **stripper**

strive
  3 try, vie 4 seek 5 labor 6 strain 7 attempt, contend 8 endeavor, struggle 9 undertake

stroke
  3 fit, hit, pet, rub 4 blow, hone, whet 5 swing 6 attack, caress, fondle, soothe 7 flatter 8 apoplexy, ischemia 9 heartbeat

stroll
  4 rove, turn, walk 5 amble, drift, mosey, paseo 6 cruise, linger, ramble, wander 7 saunter, traipse 9 promenade

stroller
  4 pram 6 go-cart 8 carriage 12 baby carriage, perambulator

strong
  4 fast, firm, hard 5 burly, hardy, lusty, solid, sound, stout, tough 6 brawny, hearty, heroic, mighty, potent, robust, rugged, secure, sinewy, stable, sturdy 7 durable, intense, staunch 8 forceful, muscular, powerful, stalwart, vigorous 9 resilient, strapping, tenacious 10 able-bodied, full-bodied, spirituous 12 concentrated

strong-arm
  5 bully 6 bounce, hector, lean on 7 assault, dragoon 8 browbeat, bulldoze, bullyrag 9 terrorize 10 intimidate

strongbox
  4 safe 5 chest 6 coffer 13 treasure chest

stronghold
  4 fort 7 bastion, bulwark, citadel, redoubt 8 fastness, fortress

strong point
  5 forte 6 métier

strong suit
  see **strong point**

strophe
5 verse 6 stanza

structure
4 form 5 frame 6 format, makeup, system
7 anatomy, complex, edifice, network 8
building, erection, skeleton 9 framework
10 morphology 11 arrangement,
composition

struggle
3 try, vie 4 agon 5 trial 6 battle, effort,
hassle, strain, strife, strive, tussle 7
attempt, compete, contest, grapple, scuffle
8 endeavor, exertion, flounder, skirmish,
striving 9 undertake 11 undertaking

strumpet
4 bawd, jade, slut, tart 5 hussy, tramp, trull,
wench 6 floozy, harlot, hooker, wanton 7
jezebel, trollop 8 slattern

strut
6 flaunt, parade, prance, sashay 7 flounce,
peacock, show off, swagger

stub
3 end 4 butt, tail 5 stump 6 put out, strike
7 remnant 10 extinguish

stubborn
5 balky, rigid 6 cussed, dogged, mulish,
ornery 7 adamant, lasting, willful 8
obdurate, perverse 9 obstinate,
pigheaded, steadfast, unbending 10
bullheaded, determined, headstrong,
inexorable, inflexible, persistent, rebellious,
refractory, relentless, unyielding 11
intractable 12 cantankerous,
contumacious, pertinacious, single-minded

stubby
5 dumpy, short, squat, stout 6 stocky,
stumpy 8 heavyset, thickset

stuck
5 clung, glued 6 jammed, wedged 7
adhered, baffled, blocked, saddled,
stabbed, stopped, stumped 8 attached,
held fast 11 overcharged

stuck-up
4 vain 6 sniffy, snippy 7 haughty, snooty 8
snobbish 9 conceited 12 narcissistic,
supercilious

stud
3 guy 4 dude, hunk, male, nail, post 5
cleat 6 button, pillar 7 earring, speckle,
upright 8 sprinkle, stallion

student
5 pupil 6 novice 7 protégé, scholar 8
disciple 10 apprentice

college: 9 undergrad 13 undergraduate
female: 4 coed
first-year: 5 frosh 8 freshman
fourth-year: 6 senior
French: 5 élève 8 étudiant
military: 5 cadet, middy 10 midshipman
second-year: 9 sophomore
third-year: 6 junior
wandering: 7 goliard

studio
4 shop 7 atelier 8 workroom, workshop

studious
7 bookish, learned 9 scholarly

Studs Lonigan creator
7 Farrell (James T.)

study
3 con, den, vet 4 cram, muse 6 ponder,
survey 7 analyze, examine, inspect,
reverie 8 consider 9 attention, think over
10 excogitate, scrutinize 11 application

stuff
3 jam, ram 4 cram, fill, glut, junk, pack,
sate, tamp 5 crowd, gorge, shove 6
matter, things 7 essence, jam-pack,
squeeze, surfeit 8 material, overfill 9
substance 11 possessions

stuffy
4 dull, prim 5 close, fuggy, heavy, humid,
stale, thick 6 narrow, stodgy 7 airless,
bloated, genteel, humdrum, pompous,
prudish, stilted 8 priggish, stagnant, stifling
9 hidebound, Victorian 10 oppressive,
pontifical 11 puritanical 12 suffocating 13
narrow-minded 13 self-important, self-
righteous

stultify
4 dull 6 deaden, impair, stifle, weaken 7
inhibit, nullify, repress, smother, trammel 8
restrain, stagnate, suppress 9 suffocate
10 discourage, invalidate

stumble
3 err 4 reel, slip, trip 5 error, fluff, gaffe,
lapse, lurch 6 falter, slipup, totter 7
blunder, faux pas, mistake, muddle,
stagger, stammer 8 flounder

stump
3 end 4 beat, butt, dare, defy, plod, stub 5
barge, clomp, clump, stick 6 baffle, outwit,
puzzle, stymie, trudge 7 buffalo, flummox,
galumph, mystify, nonplus, perplex 8
bewilder, campaign, confound, politick 9
barnstorm, challenge, hustings 11
electioneer

stun

4 daze **5** amaze, floor, shock **6** dazzle **7** astound, nonplus, stagger, stupefy **8** astonish, bewilder, bowl over, knock out, paralyze **9** dumbfound **11** flabbergast

stunning

6 superb **7** amazing, awesome **8** gorgeous, striking **9** excellent, wonderful **10** astounding, impressive, remarkable, staggering, surprising **11** astonishing

stunt

4 curb, feat **5** antic, caper, check, dwarf, prank, trick **6** hinder, impair, retard **8** escapade, hold back, suppress

stupefy

4 daze, dull, faze, stun **5** addle, amaze **6** muddle, rattle **7** astound, nonplus, petrify, stagger **8** astonish, bewilder, paralyze **9** disorient, dumbfound **11** flabbergast

stupendous

7 amazing, awesome, massive, titanic **8** colossal, enormous, gigantic, stunning, towering, wondrous **9** fantastic, marvelous, monstrous, wonderful **10** astounding, miraculous, monumental, phenomenal, prodigious, staggering, tremendous **11** astonishing, spectacular **12** breathtaking, mind-boggling, overwhelming

stupid

3 dim **4** dull, dumb, slow **5** dense, dopey, inane, silly, thick **6** oafish, obtuse, simple, torpid **7** asinine, doltish, fatuous, foolish, idiotic, moronic, witless **8** backward, ignorant, mindless, retarded **9** brainless, fatheaded, imbecilic, laughable, ludicrous, pinheaded, senseless **10** half-witted, slow-witted **11** blockheaded, thickheaded, thickwitted **13** chuckleheaded

stupor

6 torpor **7** languor **8** dullness, hebetude, lethargy, narcosis **9** lassitude, torpidity **10** anesthesia, somnolence **13** insensibility
combining form: 4 narc **5** narco

sturdy

5 hardy, solid, sound, stout, tough **6** robust, rugged, secure, strong **7** durable, healthy, staunch **8** stalwart, vigorous **9** strapping

sturgeon

6 beluga
roe: 6 caviar

Sturm und Drang

5 angst **6** unease, unrest **7** anxiety, ferment, turmoil **8** disquiet **9** agitation **10** inquietude, turbulence **11** disquietude, restiveness **12** restlessness

St. Vitus' _____

5 dance

sty

3 pen **4** coop, cyst **6** pigpen **7** piggery

stygian

4 dark **6** gloomy **7** hellish, sunless **8** infernal, plutonic **9** Cimmerian, plutonian

style

3 fad, way **4** élan, mode, rage, vein **5** craze, decor, flair, trend, vogue **6** manner **7** fashion, panache **10** dernier cri **11** savoir-faire
hair: 4 coif **8** coiffure

stylish

3 mod **4** chic, posh, tony, trig **5** doggy, natty, ritzy, sassy, sharp, showy, sleek, slick, smart, swank, swell **6** chichi, dapper, dressy, modern, modish, snappy, snazzy, spiffy, trendy, with-it **7** à la mode, dashing, doggish **8** spiffing, up-to-date **10** newfangled **11** fashionable

stymie

4 stop **5** block **6** hamper, hinder, impede, thwart **7** flummox, prevent **8** confound, obstruct **9** frustrate, hamstring

Stymphalides' slayer

8 Heracles, Hercules

Styron novel

13 Sophie's Choice **22** Confessions of Nat Turner (The)

Styx

father: 7 Oceanus
ferryman: 6 Charon
location: 5 Hades
mother: 6 Tethys

Styx's counterpart

5 Lethe **7** Acheron, Cocytus **10** Phlegethon

suave

4 oily **5** slick **6** smooth, urbane **7** cordial, courtly, gallant, politic, refined, tactful, worldly **8** debonair, gracious, polished, unctuous, well-bred **9** courteous **10** cultivated, diplomatic **12** ingratiating **13** sophisticated

sub

5 below, proxy, under **6** backup, fill-in **7** stand-by, stand-in **8** pinch-hit **9** alternate, secondary, surrogate **10** understudy **11** locum tenens, pinch hitter, replacement

subaltern
8 inferior **9** secondary, underling

subdue
4 curb, tame **5** crush, quash, quell **6** defeat, master, quench **7** conquer, control, put down, repress, squelch **8** beat down, overcome, suppress, tone down, vanquish **9** overpower, overthrow, subjugate

subdued
4 soft, tame **5** muted, quiet, sober **6** low-key, mellow, subtle **7** neutral, serious **8** low-keyed, softened, tasteful, tempered **9** moderated, toned down **10** controlled, restrained, submissive **11** unobtrusive

subjacent
3 low **5** lower, under **6** lesser, nether **8** inferior

subject
3 apt **4** core, open **5** motif, point, prone, theme, topic **6** expose, liable, likely, matter, motive, vassal **7** citizen, exposed, lay open, problem **8** argument, inferior, material, question **9** dependent, leitmotif, secondary, sensitive, subjugate, substance, tributary **11** subordinate, subservient, susceptible

subjective
6 biased **10** prejudiced

subjugate
see **subdue**

sublime
4 holy **5** ideal, lofty, noble, proud **6** august, divine, sacred, superb **7** blessed, exalted **8** elevated, glorious, heavenly, majestic, splendid **9** celestial, spiritual **11** magnificent, resplendent **12** transcendent

submarine
4 hero **5** po'boy, U-boat **6** hoagie **7** grinder
detector: 5 sonar

submerge
3 dip **4** duck, dunk, sink **5** drown, flood, swamp **6** deluge, engulf, plunge **7** founder, go under, immerse **8** inundate, overflow

submerse
see **submerge**

submissive
4 meek, tame **6** abject, docile, pliant **7** servile, slavish, subdued **8** amenable,

obedient, obeisant, yielding **9** compliant, tractable **10** obsequious **11** acquiescent, deferential, subservient, unresisting **12** nonresisting

submit
3 bow **4** cave, fold, obey **5** defer, offer, yield **6** accede, comply, give in, hand in, relent, send in, tender **7** concede, deliver, go under, present, proffer, provide, subject, succumb, suggest **9** acquiesce, surrender **10** capitulate **11** buckle under **12** knuckle under

subordinate
5 minor, scrub, under **6** junior **7** adjunct, subject **8** inferior **9** accessory, ancillary, auxiliary, dependent, secondary, subaltern, tributary, underling **10** collateral, submissive, subsidiary **11** subservient

sub rosa
6 covert, secret **7** furtive, private **8** covertly, in camera, secretly, stealthy **9** by stealth, furtively, privately, secretive, underhand **10** stealthily **11** clandestine, underhanded **13** clandestinely, surreptitious

subscribe
3 ink **4** sign **5** agree **6** accede, adhere, assent, attest, pledge **7** approve, consent, endorse, support **8** sanction **9** acquiesce

subsequent
4 next **5** after, later **6** serial **7** ensuing **9** following, resultant, resulting **10** sequential, succeeding, successive **11** consecutive
prefix: 4 post

subsequently
4 next, then **5** after, later **9** afterward **10** afterwards, thereafter

subservient
6 abject, docile **7** fawning, ignoble, servile, slavish **8** adjuvant, obelsant **9** accessory, ancillary, auxiliary, compliant, truckling **10** collateral, obsequious, submissive **11** acquiescent, deferential, subordinate, sycophantic

subside
3 ebb **4** ease, fall, lull, sink, wane **5** abate, let up, taper **6** ease up, recede, settle **7** decline, descend, die away, die down, dwindle, ease off, slacken **8** decrease, diminish, moderate

subsidiary
5 minor **6** backup, branch **7** subject **8** adjuvant **9** accessory, ancillary, auxiliary,

secondary, tributary **10** collateral **11** subordinate **12** supplemental **13** supplementary

subsidize
4 back, fund **5** endow, stake **7** finance, promote, sponsor, support **8** bankroll **9** grubstake **10** underwrite

subsidy
4 gift **5** grant **6** reward **10** subvention **13** appropriation

subsistence
4 keep, salt **5** bread, means **6** income, living, support **9** resources **10** livelihood, sustenance **11** maintenance, wherewithal **12** alimentation

substance
3 nub **4** bulk, core, crux, gist, mass, meat, pith, soul **5** being, drift, focus, heart, point, sense, stuff, tenor **6** amount, burden, entity, import, kernel, marrow, matter, nubbin, object, thrust, upshot, wealth **7** essence, meaning, nucleus, purport **8** material, property, sum total **9** resources **12** essentiality, quintessence

substantial
3 big **4** full **5** ample, hefty, large, solid **6** strong, sturdy **7** massive, sizable, weighty **8** abundant, concrete, material, physical, sensible, tangible **9** corporeal, important, objective **10** meaningful, phenomenal **11** significant **12** considerable

substantiate
5 prove **6** embody, evince, verify **7** bear out, confirm, justify **8** evidence, manifest, validate **9** establish, incarnate, objectify, vindicate **11** corroborate, demonstrate **12** authenticate

substantive
4 firm, noun, real **5** solid **8** definite **9** essential

substitute
4 mock, sham, swap **5** dummy, locum, proxy, trade **6** acting, backup, deputy, double, ersatz, fill-in, refuge, resort, second, switch **7** replace, reserve, standby, stand-in, stopgap **8** exchange, recourse, resource, spurious **9** alternate, expedient, imitation, makeshift, simulated, surrogate, temporary **10** artificial, expediency, understudy **11** alternative, locum tenens, pinch hitter, replacement, succedaneum

substratum
4 base **5** basis **6** bottom, ground **7**

bedrock, footing **10** foundation, groundwork **12** underpinning

substructure
4 base, seat **5** basis **6** bottom **7** footing **10** foundation, groundwork **12** underpinning

subsume
6 embody, take in **7** contain, embrace, include, involve **8** comprise **9** encompass **10** comprehend

subterfuge
4 ploy, ruse, sham **5** cheat, feint, fraud **6** deceit, dupery **7** chicane **8** trickery **9** chicanery, deception **10** dishonesty

subterranean
11 underground

subtle
4 fine **5** faint **6** artful, astute **7** cunning, refined **8** delicate, finespun, guileful, skillful **9** insidious **10** indistinct **13** inconspicuous

subtract
6 deduct, remove **7** take off **8** discount, knock off, take away, withdraw, withhold

subtraction
6 rebate **8** discount **9** abatement, deduction **10** diminution, withdrawal
term: **7** minuend **9** remainder **10** subtrahend

suburb
8 edge city

suburbs
7 fringes **8** environs, purlieus **9** outskirts

subversion
8 sabotage **11** undermining **12** undercutting

subvert
5 upset **6** debase **7** corrupt, deprave, vitiate **8** overturn, sabotage **9** overthrow, undermine

subway
British: **4** tube **11** underground
French: **5** métro

succeed
3 win **4** boom **5** click, ensue, score **6** arrive, follow, go over, make it, pan out, thrive, win out **7** catch on, come off, make out, prevail, prosper, replace, triumph **8** displace, flourish, get ahead, make good, supplant **9** supervene

succes _____
3 fou **7** d'estime

success
3 hit **5** smash **7** arrival, fortune, killing,

triumph, victory **8** fruition **10** attainment, prosperity **11** achievement, fulfillment

successful
5 smash **7** booming **8** fruitful, thriving **9** effective, lucrative **10** prosperous, triumphant, victorious **11** flourishing

succession
3 row **5** chain, cycle, march, order, round, suite, train **6** course, sequel, series, string **8** sequence **11** progression

successive
4 next **7** ensuing **9** following **10** subsequent

successor
4 heir **8** claimant, follower **9** inheritor **11** beneficiary

succinct
4 curt **5** blunt, brief, pithy, short, terse **7** brusque, compact, concise, laconic, summary **11** compendious

succor
3 aid **4** help, lift **6** assist, relief **7** comfort, relieve, support **10** assistance, sustenance

succulent
5 juicy **8** luscious

succumb
3 bow, die **4** cave, fold, wilt **5** defer, yield **6** accede, buckle, cave in, expire, give in, perish, relent, resign, submit **7** give out, go under, knuckle **8** collapse **9** break down, surrender **10** capitulate **11** buckle under **12** knuckle under

sucker
3 con, gyp, sap **4** bilk, dupe, fool, gull, mark, rook **5** cheat, chump, patsy, shoot **6** diddle, pigeon **7** defraud, fall guy, swindle **8** hoodwink, pushover **9** bamboozle

suckle
5 nurse **7** nourish, nurture **10** breast-feed

Sudan
capital: 8 Khartoum
desert: 6 Libyan
language: 6 Arabic
monetary unit: 5 dinar
neighbor: 4 Chad **5** Congo, Egypt, Kenya, Libya **6** Uganda **7** Eritrea **8** Ethiopia
river: 4 Nile
sea: 3 Red

sudden
4 rash **5** hasty, swift **6** abrupt, prompt **7** hurried **8** headlong **9** impetuous, impromptu, impulsive **10** unexpected,

unforeseen **11** precipitant, precipitate, precipitous

suddenly
5 aback **7** hastily, shortly, unaware **8** abruptly, promptly, unawares **10** by surprise **12** unexpectedly

suds
4 beer, fizz, foam, head, soap **5** froth, spume **6** lather

sue
8 litigate

suer
8 litigant

suet
3 fat **4** lard **6** tallow

Suez Canal
builder: 7 Lesseps (Ferdinand de)
city: 8 Ismailia, Port Said

suffer
4 ache, bear, lump **5** abide, admit, allow, brook, leave, stand, yield **6** accept, endure, permit, submit **7** agonize, anguish, stomach, sustain, swallow, undergo **8** tolerate **10** experience **11** countenance

sufferer
6 victim

suffering
4 ache **5** agony, dolor **6** misery, ordeal **7** anguish, passion, torment, torture **8** distress **10** affliction, misfortune

suffice
5 avail, serve

sufficient
3 due **5** ample **6** common, decent, enough, plenty **8** adequate, all right **9** competent, tolerable **10** acceptable **11** comfortable **12** commensurate, satisfactory **13** commensurable, proportionate
poetic: 4 enow

suffocate
5 burke, choke **6** stifle **7** smother **8** snuff out, strangle **10** asphyxiate

suffrage
4 vote **5** voice **6** ballot **9** franchise

suffragist
4 Catt (Carrie Chapman), Howe (Julia Ward), Mott (Lucretia), Paul (Alice) **5** Stone (Lucy) **7** Anthony (Susan B.), Bloomer (Amelia),

Stanton (Elizabeth Cady) **8** Woodhull
(Victoria Claflin) **9** Pankhurst (Emmeline)

suffuse

4 fill **5** flush, imbue, steep **7** pervade **8**
permeate, saturate **10** impregnate

sugar

6 aldose, fucose, xylose **7** glucose,
lactose, maltose, mannose, pentose,
sorbose, sucrose, sweeten **8** fructose,
furanose, levulose **10** saccharose
combining form: 4 gluc, glyc, sucr **5**
gluco, glyco, sucro **7** sacchar **8** sacchari,
saccharo
from palm sap: 7 jaggery
Mexican: 7 panocha, penuche
source: 4 beet, cane, corn **5** maple

sugarcane refuse

7 bagasse

sugarcoat

5 candy **6** veneer **7** sweeten,
varnish **8** palliate **9** extenuate, gloss over,
gloze over, whitewash

sugary

6 syrupy **7** cloying, honeyed, mawkish **10**
saccharine **11** sentimental

suggest

4 hint **5** evoke, imply **6** submit **7** connote,
propose, signify **8** indicate, intimate **9**
adumbrate, insinuate

suggestion

3 cue **4** clue, hint **5** shade, smack, tinge,
trace **6** advice **7** inkling **8** allusion,
innuendo, overtone, proposal, reminder **9**
suspicion, undertone **10** indication,
intimation **11** implication, insinuation

suggestive

4 racy **5** salty, spicy **6** ribald, risqué **8** off-
color **9** evocative **10** indicative **11**
reminiscent

suicidal pilot

8 kamikaze

suicide

8 felo-de-se, hara-kiri **10** self-murder **13**
self-slaughter
Japanese: 7 seppuku

suit

3 fit **4** case, jibe, plea **5** adapt, agree,
befit, cause, check, serve, tally **6** accord,
action, adjust, appeal, become, go with,
please, prayer, square, tailor **7** conform,
enhance, flatter, lawsuit, request, satisfy **8**
entreaty, petition **9** agree with, reconcile
10 go together **11** accommodate,

application, imploration, imprecation **12**
solicitation, supplication
type: 4 zoot **6** monkey, vested **9** paternity
10 pin-striped **11** class-action

suitable

3 apt, due, fit **4** just, meet **5** right **6**
proper, seemly, useful **7** condign, fitting **8**
apposite, becoming, deserved, eligible **9**
pertinent, qualified, requisite **10**
acceptable, felicitous **11** appropriate

suitcase

3 bag **4** grip **6** valise **7** carry-on, holdall **8**
carryall

suite

3 lot, row, set **4** flat **5** array, group, rooms,
staff, train **6** sequel, series, string **7**
lodging, retinue **8** chambers, sequence **9**
apartment, entourage, following

suitor

4 beau **5** lover, spark, swain, wooer **7**
admirer, gallant, sparker **8** cavalier,
paramour **9** boyfriend **10** petitioner

sulfur

9 brimstone

sulk

4 mope, pout **5** brood, gloom

sulky

4 cart, dour, glum **5** moody **6** gloomy,
morose, sullen **7** crabbed **9** saturnine

sullen

4 dour, glum, mean, sour **5** moody, pouty,
surly **6** crabby, dismal, gloomy, grumpy,
morose, somber, sombre **7** crabbed,
pouting **8** lowering, scowling **9** glowering,
saturnine **10** ill-humored **11** pessimistic

Sullivan's partner

7 Gilbert (William Schwenk)

sully

3 tar **4** soil **5** dirty, shame, smear, stain,
taint **6** defame, defile, malign, vilify **7**
asperse, blacken, pollute, slander, tarnish,
traduce **8** besmirch, disgrace, dishonor **9**
denigrate

Sultan of Swat

8 Babe Ruth

sultry

3 hot **4** sexy **5** close, humid, muggy **6**
steamy, sticky, stuffy, torrid **7** airless **8**
stifling **9** seductive **10** passionate,
sweltering, voluptuous

sum

3 add, all, tot **4** mass, tote **5** gross, total,
whole **6** amount, digest, entity, figure,

resumé **7** epitome **8** entirety, integral, nutshell, totality **9** aggregate, epitomize

Sumatra
country: 9 Indonesia
highest peak: 7 Kerinci **8** Kerintji
largest city: 5 Medan
shrew: 4 tana

Sumerian
city: 4 Umma
dragon: 3 Kur
god: 3 Abu, Kur, Utu **4** Enki **5** Enlil, Lahar, Nanna, Nintu **6** Dumuzi, Nergal, Ninazu **7** Enkimdu
goddess: 6 Ningal, Ninlil

summarize
5 recap **6** digest **7** abridge, outline **8** boil down, condense **9** epitomize, synopsize **11** encapsulate **12** recapitulate

summary
5 recap **6** aperçu, digest, précis, résumé, review, wrap-up **7** compend, epitome, outline, roundup, rundown **8** abstract, overview, scenario, synopsis **9** inventory **10** abridgment, compendium, conspectus **12** condensation

summer
French: 3 été

summerhouse
6 alcove, gazebo, pagoda **9** belvedere

summery
7 estival

summit
3 top **4** acme, apex, peak, roof **5** crest, crown **6** apogee, climax, height, vertex, zenith **8** capstone, meridian, pinnacle **11** culmination

summon
3 bid **4** call, cite **5** evoke, order **6** beckon, call in, invite, muster **7** arraign, command, conjure, convene, convoke, send for **8** assemble, subpoena

sump
4 sink **8** cesspool

sumptuous
4 lush, rich **5** grand **6** costly, deluxe, lavish, superb **7** opulent **8** gorgeous, luscious, palatial, splendid **9** grandiose, luxurious **11** extravagant, resplendent **12** awe-inspiring

sun
3 orb, Sol **4** bask, star **7** daystar, phoebus **8** daylight, luminary, radiance **9** radiation

combining form: 4 heli **5** helio
disk: 4 Aten
god: 3 Lug, Sol, Tem, Utu **4** Amen, Atmu, Atum, Inti, Lleu, Llew, Lugh, Utug **5** Horus, Sunna, Surya **6** Apollo, Babbar, Helios, Marduk **7** Khepera, Ninurta, Phoebus, Shamash **8** Hyperion, Merodach

Sun Also Rises, The
author: 9 Hemingway (Ernest)
character: 6 Ashley (Brett), Barnes (Jake)

sunder
3 cut **4** rend, rive **5** break, sever, slice, split **6** cleave, divide **8** dissever, disunite, separate

sundial part
6 gnomon

sundown
4 dusk **7** evening **8** eventide, gloaming, twilight

sundries
7 notions **8** oddments **9** etceteras **11** odds and ends

sundry
4 many, some **6** varied **7** diverse, several, various **8** assorted, manifold, numerous **9** different, disparate **12** multifarious **13** miscellaneous, multitudinous

sunfish
4 opah **7** pompano **8** bluegill **11** pumpkinseed

Sunflower State
6 Kansas

sun-god
see at **sun**

Sun King
8 Louis XIV

sunny
4 fair, fine, warm **5** clear, happy **6** blithe, bright, cheery, chirpy, golden **7** beaming, clarion, radiant **8** cheerful, pleasant, rainless **9** brilliant, cloudless, unclouded **10** optimistic

sunrise
4 dawn, morn **6** aurora **7** dawning, morning **8** cockcrow, daybreak, daylight
goddess: 3 Eos **6** Aurora

sunroom
8 solarium

sunset
3 eve **4** dusk **7** evening **8** gloaming, twilight

Sunset State
6 Oregon

Sunshine State
7 Florida

sunup
see **sunrise**

sup
3 eat 4 dine 5 feast

super
4 very 5 great 8 powerful, splendid, terrific
9 excellent, extremely, fantastic, first-rate,
wonderful 11 outstanding

superannuated
4 aged 5 hoary, passé 6 bygone 7
ancient, archaic, elderly, outworn 8
obsolete, outdated, outmoded 9 out-of-
date 10 antiquated 11 obsolescent 12
old-fashioned

superb
4 rich 5 grand, lofty, noble, prime, super 7
elegant, exalted, optimal, optimum,
opulent, stately, sublime, supreme 8
glorious, gorgeous, imposing, majestic,
peerless, splendid, standout 9 excellent,
marvelous, matchless, wonderful 11
magnificent, outstanding, resplendent,
sensational, splendorous, superlative 13
splendiferous

supercilious
5 lofty 6 lordly, sniffy, snippy 7 haughty,
stuck-up 8 cavalier, snobbish, superior 10
disdainful 11 patronizing 13
condescending, high-and-mighty

superficial
5 hasty 6 casual, slight 7 cursory, shallow,
sketchy, trivial 8 external, skin-deep 9
depthless 11 perfunctory

superfluity
4 glut 5 frill 6 excess 7 nimiety, overrun,
surfeit, surplus 8 overflow, overkill,
overload, overmuch, overplus, plethora 10
oversupply, redundancy, surplusage 11
prodigality 12 extravagance 13
overabundance

superfluous
5 extra, spare 6 de trop, excess 7 surplus
8 needless 9 excessive, redundant 10
gratuitous 11 uncalled-for, unnecessary

superintend
4 boss 6 direct, manage 7 control,
oversee 10 administer

superintendence
4 care 6 charge 7 conduct, running 8
handling 9 authority, direction, oversight
10 management

superior
4 rare 5 above, lofty, major, prime, proud,
upper 6 better, choice, higher, lordly,
select, senior, sniffy, snippy, snooty 7
capital, greater, haughty, premium, stuck-
up 8 arrogant, brass hat, cavalier,
dominant, higher-up, insolent 9 excellent,
first-rate, marvelous 10 disdainful, first-
class, noteworthy, preeminent, preferable,
remarkable 11 exceptional, overbearing,
patronizing, predominant 13
condescending, high-and-mighty

superiority
9 advantage, dominance, seniority,
supremacy, upper hand 10 ascendancy

superjacent
4 over 6 higher 7 greater 9 overlying

superlative
4 best 8 peerless, standout 10
consummate 11 magnificent, outstanding

Superman
9 Clark Kent
cartoonist: 7 Shuster (Joe)
girlfriend: 8 Lois Lane

supernatural
5 magic 6 divine, mystic 7 magical,
psychic, uncanny 8 heavenly 9 celestial,
unearthly 10 miraculous, paranormal,
phenomenal 12 metaphysical,
transcendent 13 extraordinary

supernatural being
3 elf, fay, god, hob, imp, nix 4 jinn, ogre,
peri, puck 5 afrit, angel, bogle, deity,
demon, fairy, gnome, jinni, lamia, naiad,
nixie, nymph, pixie, satyr, sylph, Titan, troll
6 afreet, goblin, kelpie, seraph, spirit, sprite
7 banshee, brownie, bugbear, goddess,
incubus, silenus, vampire 8 bogeyman,
demiurge, succubus 9 hobgoblin 10
leprechaun

supernumerary
5 extra, spare 6 de trop, excess, walk-on
7 reserve, surplus 8 leftover 9 redundant

supersede
5 usurp 7 replace, succeed 8 displace,
supplant

supervene
5 ensue, occur 6 befall, follow, result 7
succeed 9 eventuate, transpire

supervise

3 run **4** boss **5** steer **6** direct, govern, manage **7** conduct, control, monitor, oversee, proctor, referee **8** chaperon, overlook **10** administer

supervision

4 care **6** charge **7** control, running **8** auspices, handling **9** direction, oversight **10** intendance, management **11** stewardship

supervisor

7 foreman, manager **8** director, overseer **13** administrator

supine

5 inert, prone, slack **7** passive **8** inactive, indolent **9** prostrate, recumbent **10** horizontal **12** outstretched

supper club

6 nitery **7** cabaret **9** night spot

supplant

4 oust **5** usurp **6** cut out, unseat **7** replace, succeed **8** crowd out, displace, force out **9** overthrow, supersede

supple

5 agile, lithe, withy **6** limber, nimble, pliant, whippy **7** ductile, elastic, lissome, plastic, pliable, springy, willowy **8** flexible, graceful, moldable **9** adaptable, malleable, resilient

supplement

3 add, pad **5** rider **6** append, beef up, enrich, extend, sequel **7** adjunct, augment, codicil, enhance, fill out, fortify **8** addendum, addition, appendix, buttress, increase **9** accessory, reinforce **10** postscript, strengthen

suppliant

5 asker **6** beggar, suitor **9** solicitor **10** petitioner

supplicant

see **suppliant**

supplicate

3 ask, beg, sue **4** pray **5** crave, plead **6** appeal, invoke **7** beseech, entreat, implore, solicit **8** petition **9** importune

supplication

4 plea, suit **6** appeal, orison, prayer **8** entreaty, petition **11** application

supplies

6 stores **8** matériel **9** equipment, materials **10** provisions

supply

3 man **4** fund, hand, help **5** cache, equip, hoard, stock, store **6** afford, outfit, purvey **7** deliver, fulfill, furnish, provide, reserve, satisfy, surplus **8** dispense, hand over, transfer, turn over **9** inventory, provision, reservoir, stockpile **10** contribute **12** accumulation

support

3 aid **4** back, base, bear, hand, help, lift, prop, root, side, stay **5** abide, adopt, boost, brace, bread, brook, carry, favor, shore, strut, truss **6** anchor, assist, bear up, buoy up, column, crutch, defend, endure, girder, pillar, second, suffer, uphold, verify **7** alimony, applaud, approve, backing, bolster, comfort, confirm, embrace, endorse, espouse, fortify, fulcrum, nourish, nurture, pull for, shore up, stiffen, sustain **8** abutment, advocate, backstop, buttress, champion, mainstay, maintain, sanction, side with, underpin **9** encourage, reinforce, underprop **10** assistance, foundation, livelihood, provide for, strengthen, sustenance **11** corroborate, maintenance, subsistence **12** underpinning

supporter

4 ally **6** patron **7** booster, sectary **8** adherent, advocate, champion, disciple, exponent, follower, henchman, partisan **9** proponent

suppose

4 deem **5** allow, guess, infer, opine, posit, think **6** assume, expect, gather, reckon **7** believe, imagine, presume, pretend, surmise, suspect **8** consider **9** postulate, speculate **10** conjecture **11** hypothesize

supposed

7 alleged, seeming **8** apparent, putative **10** ostensible

supposition

5 guess, hunch, posit **6** notion, theory, thesis **7** premise, surmise **9** postulate **10** assumption, conjecture, hypothesis **11** postulation, presumption, speculation

supposititious

6 unreal **7** dubious, fictive, reputed **8** doubtful, fanciful, illusory, putative, spurious **9** fantastic, fictional, imaginary, pretended, simulated **10** chimerical, fictitious, fraudulent **11** conjectural **12** hypothetical, illegitimate, questionable

suppress

4 curb, stop **5** burke, check, choke, crush, drown, quash, quell, shush, spike, stunt **6**

arrest, censor, cut off, hush up, muffle, muzzle, quench, retard, squash, stifle, subdue **7** abolish, collect, conceal, control, prevent, put down, silence, smother, squelch, swallow **8** prohibit, restrain, snuff out, withhold **9** overthrow **10** extinguish

suppurate
6 fester

supra
5 above

supremacy
7 control, mastery **8** dominion **9** authority, dominance **10** ascendancy, domination, mastership, prepotency **11** preeminence, sovereignty **12** predominance **13** preponderance

supreme
4 best **5** chief, final, prime **6** superb, utmost **7** highest, leading, maximum, perfect **8** absolute, cardinal, crowning, foremost, greatest, peerless, towering, ultimate **9** matchless, paramount, principal, sovereign, unequaled, unmatched, unrivaled **10** preeminent, surpassing **11** culminating, predominant, superlative, unmatchable, unsurpassed **12** incomparable, transcendent, unparalleled **13** unsurpassable

Supreme Being
3 God **5** Allah **7** creator, Jehovah **8** Almighty

surcease
3 end **4** halt, quit, rest, stay, stop **6** desist **7** refrain, respite, suspend **8** knock off, leave off, postpone, stoppage **9** cessation, remission **10** suspension **11** discontinue **12** postponement

sure
3 set **4** fast, firm, safe **5** fixed **6** indeed, secure, stable, steady, strong **7** certain, staunch **8** absolute, definite, enduring, positive, reliable, unerring **9** confident, convinced, steadfast **10** convincing, dependable, inevitable, infallible, undeniable, unshakable, unwavering **11** indubitable, trustworthy, unequivocal, unfaltering **12** indisputable **13** incontestable, unquestioning

surefire
7 assured, certain **8** reliable **10** dependable, guaranteed

sure thing
6 shoo-in, winner **9** certainty

surety
4 bail, bond **5** angel **6** backer, patron, pledge **7** sponsor **8** guaranty, security, warranty **9** certainty, certitude, guarantee, guarantor **10** confidence, conviction

surface
3 top **4** face, pave, rise, skin **5** cover **6** appear, come up, facade, facing, finish, patina, show up, veneer **7** outside **8** covering, exterior **11** superficial

surfeit
4 cloy, fill, glut, jade, pall, sate **5** gorge, stuff **6** excess **7** replete, satiate, surplus **8** overfill, overflow, overkill, overmuch, overplus, plethora **9** surplusage **11** overindulge, superfluity **13** overabundance

surge
4 flow, gush, pour, rise, roll, rush, tide, wave **5** flood, swell **6** billow, deluge, sluice, stream **7** torrent

surgeon
8 sawbones
American: 4 Mayo (Charles, William), Reed (Walter) **6** Thorek (Max) **7** Cushing (Harvey), DeBakey (Michael) **8** McDowell (Ephraim)
British: 6 Hunter (John)
English: 5 Paget (James) **6** Lister (Joseph)
French: 4 Paré (Ambroise) **5** Broca (Paul)
South African: 7 Barnard (Christiaan)
Swiss: 6 Kocher (Emil Theodor)

surgery
9 operation
instrument: 5 clamp, curet, lance, probe **6** gorget, lancet, splint, stylet, trocar **7** forceps, scalpel

surgical removal
8 ablation
combining form: 6 ectomy

Suriname
capital: 10 Paramaribo
former name: 11 Dutch Guiana
language: 5 Dutch, Hindi **6** Sranan
monetary unit: 7 guilder
mountain range: 10 Tumac-Humac
neighbor: 6 Brazil, Guyana **12** French Guiana
river: 6 Maroni **8** Suriname **10** Courantyne

surly
4 dour, glum **5** cross, gruff, sulky **6** crusty, grumpy, morose, sullen **7** bearish,

crabbed, grouchy 8 churlish, menacing, snappish 9 irritable, saturnine 10 ungracious 11 ill-mannered, threatening 12 discourteous

surmise
see **suppose**

surmount
3 cap, top 4 best, down, leap, lick 5 clear, climb, crest, crown, excel, outdo, vault 6 better, hurdle, master 7 conquer, surpass 8 outstrip, overcome, vanquish 9 negotiate, transcend

surpass
3 cap, top 4 beat, best 5 excel, outdo, trump 6 better, exceed, outrun 7 eclipse, outpace 8 go beyond, outclass, outshine, outstrip, outweigh, overstep 9 transcend 10 overshadow 11 outdistance

surplice
5 cotta, ephod 8 vestment

surplus
5 extra, spare 6 excess 7 overage, overrun, reserve, surfeit 8 leftover, overflow, overkill, overmuch, plethora 9 overstock, remainder 10 oversupply 11 superfluity, superfluous 13 overabundance, supernumerary

surprise
4 faze, stun 5 amaze, floor 6 ambush, dismay, rattle, waylay, wonder 7 astound, capture, nonplus, stagger, startle, stupefy 8 astonish, bewilder, bowl over 9 amazement, dumbfound, overpower, take aback 11 flabbergast 12 astonishment, stupefaction

surreal
5 weird 7 bizarre 9 dreamlike, fantastic 10 outlandish, unbelievable

surrender
4 cave, cede, fold 5 waive, yield 6 cave in, give in, give up, resign, submit 7 abandon, concede, succumb 8 cry uncle, hand over 10 abdication, capitulate, relinquish 11 submission 12 capitulation, renunciation sign: 7 hands up 9 white flag

surreptitious
see **stealthy**

surrogate
3 sub 5 proxy 6 acting, deputy, fill-in 7 stand-in, stopgap 9 alternate, makeshift 10 substitute 11 alternative, locum tenens, pinch hitter, replacement, succedaneum

surround
3 hem, rim 4 edge, gird, loop, ring 5 beset, bound, hem in, limit, round, skirt, verge 6 border, circle, fringe, girdle, margin 7 besiege, compass, confine, enclose, envelop, outline 8 encircle 9 encompass 12 circumscribe

surrounding
5 about 7 ambient 12 circumjacent prefix: 4 peri 6 circum

surroundings
6 milieu 7 ambient 8 ambience 11 environment, mise-en-scène

surveillance
3 eye, tab 4 tail 5 vigil, watch 7 lookout 8 scrutiny, stakeout 9 vigilance 11 supervision

survey
3 con, vet 4 case, scan, view 5 assay, audit 6 assess, précis, review, size up 7 canvass, examine, inspect, pandect, perusal, preview 8 analysis, appraise, estimate, evaluate, look over, overlook, overview, scrutiny, syllabus 9 check over 10 inspection, scrutinize 11 reconnoiter, superintend

survive
4 keep, last 6 endure 7 carry on, hold out, outlast, outlive, outwear, persist, recover, ride out, weather 8 continue, live down 9 withstand 11 come through, live through, pull through

Surya
6 sun-god son: 4 Manu, Yama 5 Karna 6 Asvins 7 Sugriva temple site: 7 Konarak

susceptible
4 open 5 naive, prone 6 liable 7 exposed, pliable, subject 8 disposed, inclined, sensible 9 malleable, receptive, sensitive 10 responsive, vulnerable 11 impressible, persuadable, predisposed 12 nonresistant

suspect
5 doubt, fishy, guess 6 assume, unsure 7 believe, dubious, imagine, suppose, surmise 8 distrust, doubtful, mistrust 9 doubtable, uncertain 10 disbelieve 11 problematic 12 questionable

suspend
3 bar 4 bate, halt, hang, stay, stop 5 debar, defer, delay, hover, sling 6 dangle,

depend, hold up, put off, shelve **7** adjourn, hold off **8** intermit, postpone, prorogue **9** eliminate **11** discontinue

suspended

6 frozen **7** hanging, pendant, pendent, stopped **8** dangling, swinging **9** pendulous

suspenders

6 braces **8** galluses

suspense

7 anxiety, mystery, tension **10** expectancy **11** expectation, uncertainty **12** apprehension

suspension

4 halt, stay, stop **5** delay, letup, pause **6** cutoff, freeze **7** latency, respite, time-out **8** abeyance, dormancy, stoppage **9** remission, moratorium, quiescence **11** cold storage, withholding **12** intermission, interruption, postponement

suspicion

4 hint **5** doubt, dread, guess, hunch, qualm, shade, smell, tinge, touch, trace, whiff **7** concern, dubiety, surmise **8** distrust, mistrust, wariness **9** chariness, misgiving **10** foreboding, intimation, skepticism, suggestion **11** incertitude, premonition, supposition, uncertainty

suspicious

4 wary **5** chary, fishy, leery **7** dubious, jealous, suspect **8** doubtful, watchful **9** doubtable, skeptical **11** distrustful, mistrustful, problematic **12** apprehensive, questionable

suspire

4 sigh **5** sough

sustain

4 bear, feed, prop, save **5** brace, carry, stand **6** bear up, buoy up, endure, foster, hold up, keep up, succor, suffer, uphold **7** bolster, confirm, nourish, nurture, prolong, relieve, shore up, support, undergo **8** buttress, preserve, tolerate **9** withstand **10** experience, strengthen

sustenance

3 pap **4** food, keep, meat **5** bread, means **6** living, viands **7** aliment, alimony, pabulum, support **8** victuals **9** nutriment, provender **10** livelihood, provisions **11** maintenance, nourishment, subsistence, wherewithal **12** alimentation

susurration

4 purr **6** mumble, murmur, mutter, rustle **7** whisper **9** undertone

suture

3 sew **4** seam **6** stitch

suzerain

5 ruler **8** overlord **9** sovereign

svelte

4 slim **5** lithe, sleek, suave **6** smooth, urbane **7** elegant, slender **8** graceful

swab

3 mop **5** clean **6** sponge

swaddle

4 roll, wrap **5** drape **6** enfold, enwrap, swathe, wrap up **7** blanket, envelop **8** enshroud, enswathe

swag

3 yaw **4** loot, tilt **5** booty, droop, lurch, money, pitch, prize **6** boodle, seesaw, spoils **7** cluster, festoon, garland, pillage, plunder, profits **10** contraband

swagger

4 brag **5** boast, bully, strut, swank, swash, swell **7** bluster, bravado, peacock, saunter **9** arrogance, cockiness, gasconade **11** braggadocio, swashbuckle

swagman

4 hobo **5** rover, tramp **7** drifter, vagrant **8** vagabond, wanderer

swain

4 beau **5** lover, spark, wooer **6** rustic, suitor **7** admirer, peasant, sparker **8** shepherd **9** boyfriend

swallow

3 buy, sip **4** bear, belt, bolt, down, gulp, swig, take, toss, wolf **5** abide, brook, drink, quaff, slurp, stand, swill **6** absorb, accept, digest, endure, guzzle, imbibe, ingest, inhale **7** believe, consume, fall for, repress, retract, stomach **8** chugalug, take back, tolerate **11** ingurgitate

swamp

3 bog, fen **4** holm, mire, moss, muck, quag **5** drown, flood, glade, marsh, whelm **6** deluge, engulf, morass, muskeg, slough **7** bottoms **8** inundate, overcome, overflow, quagmire, submerge **9** everglade, marshland, overwhelm
Everglades: 10 Big Cypress
Georgia: 10 Okefenokee
North Carolina-Virginia: 6 Dismal

Swamp Fox

6 Marion (Francis)

swan

female: 3 pen

male: 3 cob 4 cobb
young: 6 cygnet

Swanhild
father: 6 Sigurd
mother: 6 Gudrun

swank
4 posh, tony, trig 5 boast, fancy, ritzy, sharp, showy, smart, swell, swish 6 chichi, classy, dapper, deluxe, lavish, plushy, snappy, trendy 7 elegant, peacock, show off, splashy, stylish, swagger 8 peacocky 9 glamorous, luxurious 10 flamboyant, peacockish 12 orchidaceous, ostentatious

swap
5 trade, truck 6 barter, change, switch 7 bargain, traffic 8 exchange 10 substitute

swarm
3 jam, mob 4 army, bevy, herd, host, mass, pack, push, shin, teem 5 crawl, crowd, crush, drove, flock, group, horde, mount, press 6 abound, gather, myriad, throng 7 climb up, cluster, overrun 9 multitude, pullulate 10 congregate

swarthy
4 dark 5 dusky, sooty 6 brunet 8 bistered 11 dark-skinned

swash
3 lap 4 brag, dash, gush, rush, slop 5 boast, churn, douse, froth, plash, slosh 6 bubble, burble, gurgle, seethe, splash 7 bluster, channel, saunter, spatter, splurge, swagger 8 splatter

swat
3 bat, box, hit, rap 4 bash, belt, blow, cuff, lick, slap, slog, slug, sock 5 blast, clout, homer, knock, smack, smash, smite, swipe, whack 6 buffet, larrup, strike, wallop 7 clobber, home run

swath
4 belt, path 5 strip, sweep 6 stroke

swathe
see **swaddle**

sway
4 bend, bias, rock, rule 5 lurch, might, power, range, reach, reign, scope, sweep, swing, waver, weave 6 affect, direct, govern, induce, totter, wobble 7 command, control, dispose, impress, incline, mastery, stagger, win over 8 dominate, dominion, overrule, persuade, undulate 9 authority, dominance, fluctuate, influence, oscillate, prevail on, vacillate 10 domination, predispose 11 fluctuation

Swaziland
capital: 7 Lobamba, Mbabane
city: 7 Manzini
language: 5 Swazi 7 English
monetary unit: 9 lilangeni
neighbor: 10 Mozambique 11 South Africa
river: 5 Usutu 6 Komati 8 Umbeluzi

swear
3 vow 4 avow, bind, cuss, damn, oath, rail, rant 5 abuse, curse, vouch 6 adjure, affirm, assert, attest, depone, depose, pledge, plight 7 declare, promise, testify, warrant 8 covenant, maintain 9 blaspheme, imprecate 10 asseverate, vituperate

swearword
4 cuss, oath 5 curse 9 expletive, obscenity 10 scurrility

sweat
4 emit, glow, moil, ooze, seep, toil, weep 5 exude, grind, labor 6 strain, swivet 7 excrete 8 perspire, transude 12 perspiration

sweater
8 cardigan, pullover, slipover 10 turtleneck

sweaty
6 clammy, sticky 7 glowing 10 perspiring

Sweden
Arctic region: 7 Lapland
capital: 9 Stockholm
city: 5 Malmö 8 Göteborg
gulf: 7 Bothnia 8 Kattegat
island: 5 Öland 7 Gotland
lake: 6 Vänern 7 Mälaren, Vättern 9 Hjälmaren
monetary unit: 5 krona
mountain range: 5 Kölen
neighbor: 6 Norway 7 Finland
part of: 11 Scandinavia
river: 3 Dal
sea: 6 Baltic

Swedish Nightingale
4 Lind (Jenny)

sweep
3 arc, fly, mop, win 4 flit, sail, scud, skim, wing 5 ambit, broom, brush, clean, clear, curve, drive, orbit, range, reach, scope, surge, whisk 6 extent, radius, search 7 compass, purview, victory 9 extension

sweeping
5 broad 6 all-out 7 blanket, general, overall, radical 8 thorough, whole-hog 9 extensive, inclusive, out-and-out, universal,

wholesale **12** all-embracing **13**
comprehensive, thoroughgoing

sweepings
4 dust **5** trash, waste **6** debris, litter,
refuse **7** garbage, residue, rubbish **8**
detritus

sweet
5 candy, honey **6** bonbon, dulcet, lovely,
sugary, syrupy **7** angelic, cloying, dessert,
melodic, scented, sugared, winning,
winsome **8** aromatic, fragrant, heavenly,
luscious, perfumed **9** ambrosial, delicious
10 delectable, saccharine
combining form: 4 glyc **5** glyco

Sweet ____
7 Adeline, Charity **8** Caroline

sweeten
5 candy, honey, sugar **6** soften **7**
appease, assuage, enhance, mollify,
placate **9** sugarcoat, sugar over **10**
conciliate, propitiate

sweet potato
3 yam

sweet-talk
4 coax **5** charm **6** banter, cajole, wangle
7 blarney, flatter, wheedle **8** blandish,
butter up, inveigle, soft-soap

swell
4 fine, grow, keen, neat, pout, puff **5** bloat,
bulge, dandy, nifty, pouch, super, surge,
swank **6** abound, billow, blow up, dilate,
expand, groovy **7** amplify, augment,
balloon, distend, inflate, peacock, swagger,
upsurge **8** increase, terrific **9** crescendo,
marvelous, wonderful
British: 3 nob **4** toff

swelled head
5 pride **6** egoism, vanity **7** conceit,
egotism **8** smugness **9** arrogance,
vainglory **10** narcissism **11** amour propre,
self-conceit **13** conceitedness

swelling
3 sty **4** boil, bubo, bump, corn, gall, node
5 bulge, edema, tumid, tumor **6** bunion,
growth, nodule **7** gibbous **8** tubercle **9**
carbuncle, chilblain, expansion, tumescent
10 tumescence **11** excrescence **12**
inflammation, protuberance

sweltering
3 hot **5** fiery **6** baking, sultry, torrid **7**
burning, searing **8** broiling, roasting,
sizzling, tropical **9** scorching

swerve
4 skew, turn, veer **5** sheer, shift, stray,
waver **6** depart, wander **7** deflect, deviate,
digress, diverge

swift
4 fast **5** fleet, hasty, quick, rapid, ready **6**
prompt, snappy, speedy, sudden **8** full-tilt,
headlong **9** breakneck

____ Swift
3 Tom **8** Jonathan
character: 8 Gulliver

swiftness
4 gait, pace **5** haste, hurry, speed **6** hustle
8 celerity, dispatch, legerity, rapidity,
velocity **9** quickness, rapidness **10**
expedition, speediness

swig
4 belt, down, drag, gulp, pull, slug **5** booze,
draft, drain, drink, quaff, swill **6** guzzle,
imbibe, tipple **7** swallow, swizzle

swill
4 bolt, gulp, slop, swig, tope, wolf **5** booze,
draft, drink, gorge, scarf, scoff, slops, trash,
waste **6** debris, gobble, guzzle, ingest,
inhale, refuse, spilth, tank up, tipple **7**
consume, garbage, hogwash, put away,
rubbish, swizzle **8** chow down **9** polish off

swim
3 dip **4** reel, spin, turn **5** bathe, crawl,
float, swoon, whirl **9** dizziness, dog-paddle

swimmingly
6 easily **8** smoothly **10** splendidly

swimming stroke
5 crawl **7** dolphin, trudgen **9** butterfly, dog
paddle

swindle
3 con, gyp **4** bilk, clip, dupe, fake, hoax,
rook, scam, sell, sham, skin, soak **5**
bunco, bunko, cheat, cozen, fraud, gouge,
phony, rogue, shaft, skunk, sting **6** chouse,
diddle, fleece, humbug, hustle, take in **7**
defraud **8** flimflam, hoodwink **9**
bamboozle, imposture, victimize **11**
hornswoggle

swindler
5 cheat, crook, ganef, gonif, shark **6** con
man, goniff **7** sharper, shyster **8** deceiver
9 charlatan, defrauder **10** mountebank

swine
see **hog**

swing
4 sway, veer **5** flail, lurch, pivot, twirl,

waver, weave, whirl, wield **6** dangle, divert, rhythm, rotate, seesaw, stroke, swerve, switch **7** revolve, suspend **8** brandish **9** alternate, fluctuate, oscillate, vacillate

swinish
5 feral **6** animal, coarse **7** beastly, bestial, porcine

swipe
3 cop, hit, nab, rap **4** blow, clip, conk, grab, hook, lick, lift, nick, sock, swat, wipe **5** clout, filch, heist, knock, pinch, smack, steal **6** pilfer, snatch, snitch, strike, wallop

swirl
4 eddy, purl, roil **5** curve, twist, whirl, whorl **6** swoosh, vortex **9** whirlpool **11** convolution

swish
4 buzz, chic, fizz, hiss, posh, tony, whiz **5** ritzy, smart, swank, whisk **6** classy, dressy, sizzle, trendy, whoosh **7** elegant, stylish **8** sibilate **9** exclusive

Swiss Family Robinson author
4 Wyss (Johann David)

switch
3 rod, wag **4** beat, flay, flog, lash, swap, veer, wand, whip **5** shift, shunt, trade, whisk **6** change, strike, waggle **7** scourge **8** exchange, flip-flop, reversal **9** about-face, sidetrack **10** substitute **12** substitution

Switzerland
capital: 4 Bern
city: 5 Basel **6** Geneva, Zürich **8** Lausanne
lake: 6 Geneva, Wallen **7** Lucerne **9** Constance, Neuchâtel, Thunersee, Zürichsee
language: 6 French, German **7** Italian
monetary unit: 5 franc
mountain, range: 4 Alps, Jura **9** Monte Rosa
neighbor: 5 Italy **6** France **7** Austria, Germany **13** Liechtenstein
resort: 5 Davos, Vevey **7** Zermatt **8** Montreux, St. Moritz **10** Interlaken
river: 4 Aare **5** Rhine, Rhône
state: 6 canton

swivel
4 spin, turn **5** pivot, swing, twirl, whirl **6** rotate **7** revolve **9** pirouette

swivet
see **snit**

swizzle
see **swig**

swollen
5 puffy, tumid **6** turgid **7** bloated, bulbous, bulging, pompous **8** enlarged, inflated, varicose **9** bombastic, distended, tumescent **10** rhetorical **12** magniloquent **13** grandiloquent

swoon
4 coma, daze, fade **5** droop, faint **6** torpor **7** pass out, rapture, syncope **8** black out

swoosh
4 eddy, gush, purl, rush **5** swirl, whirl, whorl

sword
4 épée, foil **5** saber, sabre **6** barong, bilboa, rapier, Toledo **7** cutlass **8** claymore, falchion, scimitar, yataghan

sword of _____
8 Damocles

sword-shaped
8 ensiform

sworn
6 avowed **7** devoted **8** affirmed **9** committed, confirmed **10** deep-rooted, deep-seated, entrenched, inveterate

sybarite
7 epicure **8** hedonist **9** libertine **10** sensualist, voluptuary

sybaritic
6 carnal **7** sensual **8** sensuous **9** epicurean, libertine, luxurious **10** hedonistic, voluptuous **13** self-indulgent

sycophancy
7 fawning **8** flattery, toadying **9** truckling **11** bootlicking

sycophant
5 leech, toady **6** flunky, lackey, minion, yes-man **8** groveler, hanger-on, parasite, truckler **9** easy rider, flatterer toadeater **10** bootlicker, self-seeker **11** lickspittle **13** apple-polisher

sycophantic
7 fawning, servile, slavish **8** toadying, unctuous **9** groveling, kowtowing, parasitic, truckling **10** obsequious **11** bootlicking

Sycorax's son
7 Caliban

syllable
deletion: 7 apocope
last: 6 ultima
lengthening of: 7 ectasis
next to last: 6 penult
shortening: 7 elision, systole
stressed: 5 arsis

syllabus
6 aperçu, digest, précis, sketch, survey 7 epitome, outline, pandect, summary 8 abstract, headnote, synopsis 10 compendium

sylph
5 fairy, nymph 6 sprite

sylvan
5 bosky, woody 6 rustic, wooded
deity: 3 Pan 4 Faun 5 dryad, satyr 6 Faunus 7 Silenus 8 Arethusa, Silvanus, Sylvanus

symbol
4 logo, mark, sign 5 badge, motif, stamp, token 6 design, device, emblem, mascot 9 attribute 10 indication
chemical:
see individual element
musical: 4 clef, flat, hold, note, rest, turn 5 shake, sharp, trill 7 fermata, mordent, natural 8 arpeggio 9 crescendo 10 diminuendo 11 decrescendo

symbolic
5 token 10 emblematic 11 allegorical

symbolist poet
7 Rimbaud (Arthur) 8 Mallarmé (Stéphane), Verlaine (Paul)

symbolize
4 mean 6 embody, mirror, typify 7 signify 8 stand for 9 epitomize, exemplify, personify, represent 10 illustrate 11 emblematize

symmetrical
5 equal 7 regular 8 balanced 12 commensurate, proportional 13 commensurable

symmetry
5 order 6 parity 7 balance, harmony 8 equality, evenness 9 agreement, congruity 10 conformity, proportion, regularity 11 arrangement

sympathetic
4 kind, warm 6 benign, caring, humane, kindly, tender 8 amenable, friendly 9 agreeable, approving, benignant, congenial, congruous, consonant, favorable, receptive 10 compatible,

consistent, responsive 11 considerate, kindhearted, softhearted, warmhearted 12 well-disposed 13 compassionate, understanding

sympathize
4 pity 7 condole 11 commiserate 13 compassionate

sympathy
4 pity, ruth 5 heart 6 accord, solace, warmth 7 comfort, harmony, rapport 8 affinity, kindness 9 agreement 10 benignancy, compassion, condolence, kindliness, tenderness 11 consolation, sensitivity 13 commiseration

symphonic
10 orchestral

symphony
9 orchestra 12 philharmonic

symposium
4 forum 7 meeting, seminar 9 gathering 10 conference, discussion

symptom
4 mark, sign 5 index, token 8 evidence 10 indication

symptoms
7 indicia 8 syndrome

synagogue
6 temple

sync
4 jibe 5 agree, match 7 harmony 8 coincide 9 harmonize 10 concurrent 12 simultaneous

synchronize
5 agree 6 concur 8 coincide

synchronous
6 coeval 10 coetaneous, coexistent, coexisting, coincident, concurrent 11 concomitant 12 contemporary, simultaneous 13 geostationary

syncope
4 coma 5 faint, swoon 8 blackout

syndicate
3 mob 4 pool 5 chain, group, mafia, trust, union 6 cartel, league 7 combine 11 association, partnership 12 conglomerate, organization 13 confederation

syndrome
3 ill 6 malady 7 ailment, disease 8 disorder, sickness 9 complaint, condition, infirmity

synergic
5 joint 6 shared 8 coacting, coactive,

conjoint **9** collusive, concerted **11** cooperating, cooperative, coordinated

synod
4 body, diet **7** council, meeting **8** assembly, conclave, congress **10** conference, convention **11** convocation

synopsis
5 brief, recap **6** aperçu, digest, précis, review **7** capsule, epitome, outline, rundown, summary **8** abstract, breviary, syllabus **10** abridgment, compendium, conspectus **12** condensation

synopsize
5 recap, sum up **6** digest **7** outline, summate **8** abstract, boil down, compress, condense **9** epitomize, inventory, summarize **11** encapsulate

synthesis
5 blend, union **6** fusion, merger **7** amalgam **8** blending, compound **9** composite **11** combination **12** amalgamation **13** incorporation

synthesize
4 fuse, meld **5** blend, merge, unify **7** combine **8** compound **9** harmonize, integrate **10** amalgamate **11** incorporate

synthetic
6 ersatz **7** man-made **9** unnatural **10** artificial, fabricated **11** counterfeit

Syria
capital: **8** Damascus
city: **4** Homs **6** Aleppo
desert: **6** Syrian
language: **6** Arabic, French
monetary unit: **5** pound
mountain range: **7** Lebanon
neighbor: **4** Iraq **6** Israel, Jordan, Turkey **7** Lebanon
plain: **11** Mesopotamia
river: **9** Euphrates
sea: **13** Mediterranean

syringe
6 needle

Syrinx
5 nymph
pursuer: **3** Pan

syrinx
7 panpipe **8** panpipes

syrup
6 orgeat **9** grenadine

syrupy
5 gooey, mushy, sappy, sweet **6** drippy, dulcet, slushy, sticky, sugary **7** cloying,
maudlin, mawkish **9** schmaltzy **10** saccharine **11** sentimental

system
3 way **4** mode, plan **5** modus, order, setup **6** entity, manner, method, scheme **7** complex, network, pattern, process, regimen, routine **8** strategy **9** procedure, structure, technique **10** regularity **11** arrangement, disposition, orderliness

systematic
7 logical, ordered, orderly, regular **8** arranged **9** organized **10** analytical, methodical **12** businesslike

systematize
5 array, order **6** codify **7** arrange, catalog, dispose, marshal **8** classify, organize, regiment **9** catalogue, methodize

system of weights
4 troy **11** avoirdupois **12** apothecaries

T

tab
4 bill, cost, flap, list, loop, rate 5 check, count, price, score 6 charge, record 7 account, invoice 8 eagle eye, price tag, scrutiny 9 appendage, designate, extension, reckoning, statement 12 surveillance

tabard
4 cape, coat 5 tunic 10 coat of arms

tabby
3 cat 6 feline, cement 8 brindled

tabernacle
4 tent 5 hovel 6 church, temple

tabes
7 atrophy, wasting 12 degeneration

Tabitha's Greek name
6 Dorcas

table
4 fare, list 5 bench, board, chart, defer, stand 6 buffet, put off, record, shelve, teapoy 7 counter 8 mahogany, postpone 9 sideboard
 ornament: 7 epergne 11 centerpiece
 writing: 4 desk 9 secretary 10 escritoire

table d' ____
4 hôte

tableland
4 mesa 5 butte 6 upland 7 plateau
 Alabama-West Virginia: 10 Cumberland
 Arizona: 5 Kanab 6 Kaibob
 England: 8 Dartmoor
 India: 5 Malwa
 (see also **plateau**)

tablet
3 bar, pad 4 cake, disk, pill, slab 5 panel, slate 6 pellet, plaque, troche 7 lozenge, notepad 8 steno pad

Table Talk author
6 Selden (John)

tableware
4 cups 5 bowls, china, forks 6 dishes, knives, plates, silver, spoons 7 glasses, saucers 8 settings, utensils 9 stainless

tabloid
3 rag 5 lurid, pulpy 6 digest 7 summary 9 condensed, newspaper 11 sensational 12 scandal sheet

taboo
3 ban 4 no-no 6 banned, enjoin, forbid 7 inhibit, obscene 9 forbidden, ineffable, interdict, off-limits, restraint 10 inhibition 11 restriction, unspeakable 12 interdiction

tabor
4 drum

tabulate
4 list 5 count, order 6 codify, figure, record 7 arrange 9 enumerate 11 systematize

tabulation
4 list 5 chart, tally 6 record 7 account

tabula ____
4 rasa

tacit
6 silent, unsaid 7 assumed, implied 8 implicit, inferred, unspoken 9 intimated, suggested 10 subtextual, undeclared, underlying, understood 11 acquiescent, unexpressed 12 inarticulate

taciturn
4 dumb 6 silent 7 laconic 8 reserved, reticent, wordless 9 secretive 11 tight-lipped 12 closemouthed

Tacitus work
7 Annales 8 Dialogus, Germania 9 Historiae

tack
3 pin, yaw 4 beat, brad, gear, join, nail, stay, turn 5 baste, reach, shift 6 attach, double, stitch, swerve, turn up, zigzag 7 tangent 8 put about 9 come about,

deviation **10** alteration, deflection, digression, sea biscuit **12** pilot biscuit, ship biscuit

tackle

3 cat, rig **4** gear, sack **6** outfit, take on, take up **7** halyard, lineman, rigging **8** set about **9** apparatus, equipment, machinery, undertake **10** footballer, linebacker, plunge into **13** paraphernalia

tacky

5 cheap, crude, dingy, dowdy, gaudy, messy, seedy, ratty, tatty **6** blowsy, frowsy, frumpy, kitsch, shabby, sleazy, sloppy, sticky, frumpy, tawdry, untidy, vulgar **7** run-down, unkempt **8** adhesive, frumpish, slovenly **9** inelegant, tasteless, unstylish **10** broken-down, down-at-heel, threadbare

tact

5 poise, touch **6** acumen **7** address, finesse, suavity **8** civility, courtesy, delicacy, urbanity **9** diplomacy, politesse **10** adroitness, politeness, smoothness **11** savoir faire, sensitivity

tactful

5 civil, suave **6** adroit, urbane **7** politic **8** delicate, discreet, polished **9** courteous, sensitive **10** diplomatic, perceptive, thoughtful **11** considerate

tactical

7 politic, prudent **9** advisable, expedient, strategic

tactics

4 plan **6** method, scheme **8** maneuver, playbook, strategy **9** stratagem

tactile

8 palpable, tangible **9** touchable

taction

4 feel **5** touch **7** contact **9** palpation

tactless

4 rude **5** blunt, crude, inept **6** candid, clumsy, gauche **7** awkward **8** impolite **9** impolitic, maladroit **10** indiscreet **11** insensitive

tad

3 bit, boy, lad, son **4** lick, mite, snap, spot, whit **5** child, crumb, sonny, speck **6** laddie, nipper, shaver **7** smidgen **8** fraction

tadpole

8 polliwog, pollywog

taffy

5 candy **8** flattery

tag

3 bit, dog, end **4** cost, flag, game, logo, mark, name, tail **5** aglet, brand, label, price, trail **6** append, charge, follow, select, shadow, slogan, tatter, ticket **7** license, run down, tassel **8** graffito, identify, insignia

Tahiti

city: 7 Papeete

painter: 7 Gauguin (Paul)

tail

3 dog, end, tag **4** butt, rear **5** hound, stalk **6** follow, pursue, shadow **7** hind end, rear end **8** backside, buttocks **9** posterior

bone: 8 coccyx

relating to: 6 caudal

short: 4 scut

tailed

7 caudate

tailor

3 fit, sew **4** suit **5** alter **8** clothier, seamster **11** haberdasher

tailor-made

6 fitted, suited **7** bespoke, fitting **8** suitable **10** well-suited **11** appropriate

taint

3 rot **4** blot, blur, foul, harm, hurt, smut, soil, spot, turn, vice **5** brand, cloud, color, decay, dirty, fault, smear, spoil, stain, sully, touch **6** befoul, darken, defile, poison, smudge, smutch **7** blacken, blemish, corrupt, pollute, putrefy, tarnish **8** besmirch, discolor **9** discredit **10** adulterate, stigmatize **11** contaminate

taipan

5 snake **8** merchant **11** businessman

Taiwan

7 Formosa

capital: 6 Taipei

channel: 5 Bashi

city: 6 T'ai-nan **8** Pan-ch'iao, T'ai-chung **9** Kao-hsiung

language: 8 Mandarin

leader: 13 Chiang Kai-shek

monetary unit: 6 dollar

mountain: 6 Yü Shan

Tajikistan

capital: 8 Dushanbe

monetary unit: 5 ruble

mountain, range: 6 Pamirs **9** Communism (Peak), Trans Alai **10** Revolution (Peak)

neighbor: 5 China **10** Kyrgyzstan, Uzbekistan **11** Afghanistan

river: 8 Amu Dar'ya, Syr Dar'ya

Taj Mahal
9 mausoleum
builder: 9 Shah Jahan
site: 4 Agra

take
3 get, nab 4 grab 5 annex, catch, seize
6 gather, obtain, secure 7 capture, receive
8 proceeds, receipts
account of: 6 notice
advantage of: 5 abuse 7 exploit
after: 6 follow 8 resemble
apart: 7 analyze, dissect 9 dismantle
care: 6 beware
care of: 3 fix 4 tend 5 nurse 6 attend
exception: 6 object
five: 4 rest
from: 7 deprive, detract 8 subtract
it easy: 5 relax
on the: 7 corrupt
part: 4 join 5 share 11 participate
place: 5 occur 6 happen
to task: 5 scold 7 reprove
turns: 9 alternate
unawares: 8 surprise

take away
4 grab 5 wrest 6 arrest, commit, deduct,
detach, detain, remove 7 deprive, detract
8 diminish, discount, minimize, subtract,
withdraw

take back
5 unsay 6 abjure, recall, recant, return
7 replace, restore, retract, swallow
8 forswear, withdraw 9 repossess

take down
4 note 5 lower, record, write 6 humble,
reduce 7 deflate 8 dismount 9 dismantle
11 disassemble

take in
3 con 4 dupe, fool, furl, jail 5 admit, bluff,
board, house, trick 6 absorb, accept,
arrest, attend, betray, delude, embody
7 beguile, compass, contain, deceive,
embrace, include, involve, mislead,
observe, receive, shelter, snooker,
subsume 8 flimflam, hoodwink, perceive
9 apprehend, bamboozle, encompass,
four-flush 10 assimilate, comprehend,
understand 11 double-cross

take off
4 doff, exit, quit 5 leave, scram 6 begone,
deduct, depart, remove, set out 7 pull out,
skiddoo, vamoose 8 clear out, discount,
hightail, light out, subtract, withdraw
9 skedaddle

takeoff
5 spoof 6 launch, parody, satire, send-up

7 lampoon 8 travesty 9 burlesque
10 caricature
area: 3 pad 6 runway

take on
3 don 4 face, hire, meet 5 adopt, annex,
fight 6 accept, append, assume, attack,
battle, employ, engage, strike, tackle
7 contest, embrace, espouse, venture
8 endeavor, set about 9 encounter,
undertake

take out
4 date, kill, omit 5 loose 6 deduct, destroy,
remove 7 release, unleash 8 absorb, discount,
knock off, separate, subtract, withdraw,
withhold 9 eliminate 10 annihilate

take over
5 seize, spell, usurp 6 assume 7 capture,
relieve

take up
3 use 4 fill, open 5 adopt, begin, enter,
raise, renew, set to, start 6 absorb, accept,
assume, gather, occupy, resume, shrink,
tackle 7 embrace, espouse, kick off,
restart, shorten, tighten 8 commence,
continue, initiate 10 recommence

talc
6 powder 8 steatite 9 soapstone

tale
3 fib, lie 4 myth, saga, yarn 5 fable, rumor,
story 6 canard, legend 7 fiction
8 anecdote 9 narration, narrative

talebearer
3 rat 4 fink 6 canary, gossip, snitch 7 rat
fink, tattler 8 busybody, gossiper, informer,
quidnunc, squealer, telltale 9 informant
10 newsmonger, tattletale
11 rumormonger, stool pigeon
12 blabbermouth 13 scandalmonger

talent
4 bent, gift, head, nose 5 craft, dowry, flair,
forte, knack, skill 6 genius 7 ability,
aptness, faculty 9 endowment, expertise

talented
4 able 6 clever, expert, gifted 8 skillful

Tale of Two Cities, A
author: 7 Dickens (Charles)
character: 5 Lucie (Manette) 6 Carton
(Sidney), Darnay (Charles) 7 Defarge
(Madame), Manette (Alexander)

Tales of a Traveller author
6 Irving (Washington)

Tales of a Wayside Inn author
10 Longfellow (Henry Wadsworth)

Tales of Hoffman composer
9 Offenbach (Jacques)

talisman
4 juju, luck 5 charm 6 amulet, fetish,
mascot, scarab 7 periapt 10 phylactery

Talisman author
5 Scott (Walter)

talk
3 gab, rap, yak 4 blab, buzz, chat, chin,
yarn 5 prate, rumor, run on, speak, utter,
voice 6 babble, gabble, gossip, parley,
patter, report, speech 7 address, chatter,
declaim, hearsay, lecture, prattle
8 colloquy, converse, dialogue, harangue
9 discourse, utterance 10 discussion
12 conversation
about: 7 discuss
back: 4 sass
foolish: 4 bunk 6 babble 7 chatter,
palaver
indistinctly: 6 mumble, mutter
over: 7 discuss
slowly: 5 drawl
small: 8 chitchat
wildly: 4 rant, rave

talkative
4 glib 5 gabby, vocal 6 chatty, fluent
7 gossipy, voluble 9 garrulous
10 loquacious 13 communicative

talk over
6 debate 7 discuss, hash out 8 consider
9 thrash out 10 deliberate

talky
5 gabby, windy, wordy 6 chatty, prolix
7 verbose, voluble

tall
4 high, long 5 lanky, large, lofty, rangy
6 absurd 7 pompous 8 towering 9 high-
flown 10 far-fetched 11 skyscraping
12 altitudinous

tallow
3 fat 4 lard, suet 6 grease

tally
3 tab 4 jibe, list, tale 5 agree, count,
match, score, total 6 accord, census,
number, reckon, square 7 account,
balance, catalog, compute, conform,
itemize 8 check off, register, tabulate
9 agreement, catalogue, enumerate,
harmonize, inventory, reckoning
10 complement, correspond

talon
4 claw, hand 5 stock 6 finger

talus
5 ankle, scree, slope 9 anklebone
10 astragalus

tam
3 cap

Tamar
brother: 7 Absalom
father: 5 David 7 Absalom
father-in-law: 5 Judah
half brother: 5 Amnon
seducer: 5 Amnon
son: 5 Perez, Zerah

tamarisk
9 salt cedar

tambour
3 cup 4 drum 9 embroider 10 embroidery

Tamburlaine the Great author
7 Marlowe (Christopher)

tame
4 bust, dull, meek, mild 5 break, train,
vapid 6 bridle, docile, gentle, humble,
soften, subdue 7 harness, insipid, reclaim,
subdued 8 domestic, familiar, obedient
9 tractable 10 housebreak, submissive
11 domesticate, housebroken 12 domes-
ticated

Taming of the Shrew, The
character: 6 Bianca 8 Baptista
9 Katharina, Petruchio

Tammany boss
5 Tweed (William)

Tammuz's lover
6 Ishtar

tam-o'-shanter
3 cap

tamp
3 ram 4 pack, press 5 pound, stuff

tampion
4 plug 5 cover

tan
3 sun, taw 4 beat, ecru, flog, whip 5 beige,
brown, tawny, toast 6 bronze, darken,
thrash 7 biscuit

Tan novel
11 Joy Luck Club (The) 15 Kitchen God's
Wife (The) 19 Bonesetter's Daughter (The)

tanager
7 redbird

Tancred, Tancredi
beloved: 8 Clorinda
father: 3 Odo
mother: 4 Emma

victim: 8 Clorinda

tandem
4 pair 7 bicycle, concert 8 carriage

tang
3 nip 4 bite, fang, odor, ring, zest 5 aroma, clang, prong, sapor, savor, shank, smack, taste, trace 6 flavor, relish 8 piquancy, pungency, sapidity 9 spiciness

tangible
4 real 7 tactile 8 concrete, material, palpable, physical, sensible 9 corporeal, touchable 10 detectable, observable, phenomenal 11 appreciable, discernible, perceptible, substantial

tangle
3 mat, web 4 foul, knot, maze, mesh, shag 5 clash, ravel, skein, snare, snarl 6 entrap, foul up, hamper, jumble, jungle, morass, muddle, pileup, raffle 7 dispute, embroil, ensnare, ensnarl, involve, perplex, seaweed, thicket 8 obstruct 9 embarrass, implicate 10 complicate 11 altercation, predicament 12 bewilderment, complication

Tanglewood Tales author
9 Hawthorne (Nathaniel)

tango
5 dance 8 circuity 11 indirection 13 deceitfulness

tangy
5 sharp 6 lively 7 piquant, pungent, zestful 9 flavorful

tank
3 vat 5 basin 7 cistern 8 aquarium 9 reservoir
American: 6 Abrams 7 Bradley, Sherman
German: 6 panzer
part: 6 turret

tankard
3 mug 5 stoup 6 flagon 9 blackjack

tanked
3 lit 4 high, lost 5 drunk, gave up, lit up, oiled 6 bashed, blotto, bombed, failed, juiced, potted, soaked, soused, stewed, stoned, tanked, wasted, zonked 7 crocked, drunken, pickled, pie-eyed, sloshed, smashed, sottish 9 collapsed, plastered 10 inebriated, liquored up 11 intoxicated

tanker
4 ship 5 oiler

Tannhäuser composer
6 Wagner (Richard)

tantalize
3 rag 4 bait, lure 5 tease, tempt 6 entice, needle 7 torment 9 frustrate

Tantalus
daughter: 5 Niobe
father: 4 Zeus
son: 6 Pelops

tantamount
4 same 5 alike, equal 8 parallel, selfsame 9 duplicate, identical 10 equivalent 12 commensurate

tantara
5 blare 7 fanfare

tantivy
3 run 6 gallop

tantrum
3 fit 6 blowup 8 outburst, paroxysm 9 hysterics 10 conniption

Tanzania
capital: 6 Dodoma 11 Dar es Salaam
city: 6 Arusha
former name: 10 Tanganyika
island: 5 Mafia, Pemba 8 Zanzibar
lake: 5 Rukwa 6 Malawi 8 Victoria 10 Tanganyika
language: 7 English, Swahili
monetary unit: 8 shilling
mountain: 11 Kilimanjaro
neighbor: 5 Congo, Kenya 6 Malawi, Rwanda, Uganda, Zambia 7 Burundi 10 Mozambique
plain: 9 Serengeti
river: 6 Kagera, Rufiji, Ruvuma 7 Pangani
volcano: 6 Lengai

Taoism founder
5 Laozi 6 Lao Tzu

tap
3 hit, pat 4 cock, draw, flap, name, plug, tick 5 chuck, draft, drain, nudge, touch, valve 6 faucet, select, siphon, spigot, strike 7 appoint, draw off, hydrant, percuss, petcock 8 drumbeat, half sole, nominate, stopcock 9 designate

tape
4 band, belt, bind 5 strip 6 fillet, ribbon 7 bandage
kind: 5 inkle 6 ferret 7 masking 8 adhesive
machine: 4 deck 8 recorder

taper
4 wick 5 abate, close, draft, pinch, spire, wane 6 candle, lessen, narrow, reduce 7 dwindle, glimmer 8 decrease, diminish

tapering
5 conic, spiry 6 spired, terete 7 conical
8 ensiform, fusiform, napiform, subulate
9 acuminate, attenuate 10 lanceolate

tapestry
5 arras, kilim 6 dossal 7 curtain, Gobelin,
hanging
pattern: 7 cartoon

Taphath's father
7 Solomon

tapioca
4 yuca 5 yucca 6 manioc 7 cassava,
farinha, pudding

taproom
3 bar, pub 4 café 6 bodega, saloon, tavern
7 cantina 8 dramshop 9 roadhouse

tapster
6 barman 7 barkeep, barmaid, skinker
9 barkeeper, bartender 10 mixologist

tar
3 gob 4 jack, salt, soil, swab 5 pitch,
smear, stain, sully 6 defile, hearty,
sailor, seaman 7 asphalt, besmear,
mariner, shipman 8 besmirch, creosote,
deckhand, flatfoot 9 shellback

taradiddle
3 fib, lie 5 hooey, story, trash 6 bunkum,
canard 7 baloney, falsity 8 claptrap,
nonsense 9 falsehood 10 balderdash
13 prevarication

tarantella
5 dance

tarantula
6 spider 10 wolf spider

Taras Bulba author
5 Gogol (Nikolai)

tarboosh
3 fez, hat

tardy
4 dull, late, lazy, slow 7 belated, delayed,
laggard, overdue 8 dilatory, sluggish
10 behindhand, delinquent, unpunctual

tare
4 seed 5 vetch, weigh 6 weight
11 undesirable 13 counterweight

target
3 aim 4 butt, goal, mark, prey 5 aim at
6 object, quarry, victim 9 objective
11 sitting duck
center: 8 bull's-eye
shooter's: 10 clay pigeon

Tar Heel State
13 North Carolina

tariff
3 tax 4 cost, duty, levy, rate 5 price
6 charge, impost 7 tribute 10 assessment

Tarkington character
6 Penrod

tarn
4 lake, pool

tarnish
3 dim, mar 4 dull, foul, harm, hurt, soil
5 dirty, muddy, smear, spoil, stain, sully,
taint 6 damage, darken, defile, injure,
smirch, smudge, smutch 7 begrime,
besmear, blemish, vitiate 8 besmirch,
discolor

taro
5 aroid 6 yautia 7 dasheen, malanga
product: 3 poi

tarpaulin
3 gob 4 jack, salt, swab 5 cover, sheet
6 hearty, sailor, seaman 7 mariner,
shipman 9 shellback

tarpon
8 ladyfish 10 silverfish

tarry
3 lag 4 bide, drag, stay, wait 5 abide, dally,
delay, visit 6 dawdle, linger, loiter, pitchy,
remain 7 sojourn

tarsus
5 ankle

tart
3 pie 4 acid, bawd, moll, slut, sour
5 acerb, quean, sharp, tramp, trull, whore
6 biting, harlot, pastry 7 acerbic, chess pie,
cutting, piquant, pungent, tootsie
8 strumpet 10 prostitute

tartar
5 argol 6 plaque 8 calculus

Tartar
6 Mongol, Turkic 7 Turkish 9 Mongolian

Tartuffe author
7 Molière

Tarzan
chimpanzee: 7 Cheetah
creator: 9 Burroughs (Edgar Rice)
mate: 4 Jane

task
3 job 4 duty, lade, load, post, slog, toil,

work **5** chare, chore, detail, labor, stint
6 assign, burden, charge, devoir
7 mission, project **8** business, encumber,
function **9** challenge, dress down,
reprimand **10** assignment, commission
11 undertaking **12** dressing-down

Tasmanian
4 wolf **5** devil
capital: 6 Hobart
pine: 4 Huon

tassel
3 tag **4** tuft **5** adorn **6** fringe **7** pendant,
tzitzit **8** ornament **13** inflorescence

Tasso, Torquato
patron: 4 Este (Alfonso II d')
work: 6 Aminta **7** Rinaldo **18** Jerusalem
Delivered

taste
3 eat, sip, try **4** tang, zest **5** savor, smack
6 flavor, liking, palate, relish **7** stomach
8 appetite, elegance, fondness, sapidity,
soft spot, weakness **10** experience,
partiality, refinement **11** inclination
kind: 4 salt, sour **5** sweet **6** bitter
organ: 3 bud

tasteful
4 fine **7** elegant, genteel, refined, stylish
8 artistic, becoming **9** aesthetic

tasteless
4 dull, flat **5** bland, crass, gaudy, showy,
stale, tacky, vapid **6** vulgar **7** insipid **8** off-
color, unsavory **9** inelegant, savorless,
unrefined **10** flavorless

tasty
5 sapid, yummy **6** dainty, delish, savory
8 luscious, flavorful, palatable,
succulent, toothsome **10** appetizing,
delectable, flavorsome

tattered
4 torn **5** dingy, seedy **6** frayed, ragged,
ripped, shabby **7** raggedy, run-down, worn-
out **10** bedraggled, threadbare
11 dilapidated

tattle
3 wag, yak **4** blab, buzz, dish, talk **5** clack,
prate, rumor **6** gossip, inform, report,
snitch, squeal **7** chatter, hearsay, prattle
8 chitchat **9** grapevine **11** scuttlebutt

tattletale
see **talebearer**

tatty
5 cheap, dingy, dowdy, dumpy, seedy, tacky
6 beat-up, cheesy, paltry, scuzzy, shabby,
shoddy, sleazy, trashy **7** run-down,

scrubby **8** rubbishy **10** threadbare
11 dilapidated

taunt
3 jab **4** gibe, jeer, mock, quip, razz, skit,
twit **5** scout, tease **6** deride, insult
7 affront, provoke **8** reproach, ridicule
9 challenge

taurine
6 bovine **8** bull-like

Taurus
4 bull
star: 9 Aldebaran

taut
4 firm, snug, trim **5** rigid, tense, tight
6 corded **10** high-strung

tautology
8 iterance, pleonasm **9** iteration
10 redundancy, repetition

tavern
3 bar, inn, pub **4** café, dive **6** bistro,
bodega, saloon **7** barroom, cantina, gin
mill, taproom **8** alehouse, pothouse,
wineshop **9** roadhouse **11** public house,
rathskeller **12** watering hole **13** watering
place

taverner
7 barkeep **8** boniface, publican
9 barkeeper, bartender, innkeeper
12 saloonkeeper

taw
3 tan **6** marble **7** partner

tawdry
4 loud **5** cheap, gaudy, tacky **6** brazen,
flashy, garish, tinsel **7** chintzy, glaring,
ignoble **9** brummagem, dime-store
12 meretricious

tawny
3 tan **4** buff **5** beige, brown, sandy
6 copper, tanned

tax
4 duty, lade, levy, load, onus, scot, toll
5 drain, tithe **6** assess, burden, cumber,
impost, saddle, strain, tariff, weight
7 tribute **8** encumber **10** imposition
agency: 3 IRS
feudal: 7 scutage, tallage
kind: 4 geld **5** sales, tithe **6** excise,
income **8** property **9** surcharge
on salt: 7 gabelle
rate: 10 assessment

taxi
3 cab, car **4** hack **5** cyclo

taxing
5 tough 6 trying 7 exigent, onerous, wearing 8 exacting, grievous, grueling 9 demanding, difficult 10 burdensome, oppressive

Taygeta
father: 5 Atlas
mother: 7 Pleione
sisters: 8 Pleiades

tazza
3 cup 4 vase

Tchaikovsky, Pyotr Ilyich
ballet: 8 Swan Lake 10 Nutcracker (The) 14 Sleeping Beauty
opera: 12 Eugene Onegin 13 Queen of Spades (The)

tea
5 party 6 repast 8 beverage 9 reception
black: 5 bohea, pekoe 8 souchong
cake: 6 cookie
genus: 4 Thea
kind: 4 herb, Java 5 Assam, black, bohea, green, hyson, pekoe 6 Ceylon, congou, oolong 7 cambric 8 Earl Grey, souchong 9 sassafras 10 Darjeeling

teach
5 coach, edify, guide, train, tutor 6 impart, school 7 educate, instill, profess 8 instruct 9 enlighten, inculcate 12 indoctrinate

teacher
4 guru, prof 5 coach, guide, tutor 6 docent, master, mentor, pedant 7 maestro, trainer 8 educator 9 pedagogue, preceptor, professor 10 instructor 12 schoolmaster
Hindu: 5 swami
Jewish: 5 rabbi, rebbe
Muslim: 6 mullah
organization: 3 NEA
religious: 9 catechist 10 mystagogue

Tea for Two composer
7 Youmans (Vincent)

team
4 band, club, crew, gang, join, pair, side, yoke 5 group, squad, troop, wagon 6 stable, troupe 8 carriage
baseball: 4 nine
basketball: 4 five 7 quintet
football: 6 eleven
kind: 6 jayvee 7 varsity

teamster
6 driver 7 trucker

tear
3 cry, cut, fly, rip, run 4 bolt, claw, dash, drop, flaw, gash, hole, lash, pull, race, rend, rift, rive, rush, slit, snag, weep 5 chase, hurry, shoot, shred, slash, speed, split, spree 6 career, charge, course, fissure, sunder, tatter, wrench 7 droplet, rupture 8 lacerate 10 laceration

tear down
4 raze, ruin, slur 5 knock, smash, smear, wreck 6 defame, malign, vilify 7 asperse, traduce, destroy, shatter, slander 8 demolish 9 denigrate, disparage, take apart 10 annihilate, calumniate 11 disassemble

tearful
3 sad 5 misty, moist, watery, weepy 6 crying, woeful 7 bawling, sobbing, weeping 8 mournful, pathetic 9 lamenting, sniveling, sorrowful 10 blubbering, lachrymose

tear-jerking
5 mushy 6 drippy, sticky 7 maudlin, mawkish 8 touching 9 schmaltzy 11 sentimental

teary-eyed
5 blear, moist

tease
3 bug, kid, rag, rip 4 bait, chivy, coax, comb, gibe, jive, josh, ride, tear, twit 5 annoy, chaff, harry, shred, taunt, worry 6 cajole, harass, needle, pester, pick on, plague 7 bedevil, torment 8 ridicule 9 tantalize

teaser
5 promo 7 preview

teched
3 mad 4 daft 5 batty, crazy 6 insane 7 cracked, lunatic 8 demented

technicality
6 detail 8 loophole

technique
4 mode 5 modus 6 method, system 8 approach 9 procedure 13 modus operandi

ted
5 strew 6 spread 7 scatter

tedious
3 dry 4 dull 5 ho-hum, stale 6 boring, dreary 7 irksome, operose 8 drudging, tiresome 9 dryasdust, wearisome 10 monotonous 11 mind-numbing 13 uninteresting

tedium
4 yawn **5** ennui **7** boredom **8** doldrums, dullness, monotony, sameness

teem
4 flow, pour **5** crawl, empty, swarm **6** abound, bustle, produce **9** pullulate

teeming
4 lush, rife **5** alive **6** aswarm **7** replete **8** abundant, swarming, thronged **9** abounding **11** overflowing

teen
5 youth **10** adolescent

tee off
4 open **5** begin, drive, enter, start **8** commence, initiate

teeter
4 rock, sway **5** waver **6** falter, seesaw, wobble **9** vacillate

telamon
5 atlas
counterpart: **8** caryatid

Telamon
brother: **6** Peleus
father: **6** Aeacus
half-brother: **6** Phocus
son: **4** Ajax **6** Teucer

Telegonus
father: **7** Ulysses **8** Odysseus
mother: **5** Circe

telegraph
4 wire **5** cable **6** signal
code: **5** Morse

Telemachus
father: **7** Ulysses **8** Odysseus
mother: **8** Penelope

telephone
4 buzz, call, dial, ring **5** phone **6** ring up
inventor: **4** Bell (Alexander Graham)

Telephus
father: **8** Heracles, Hercules
mother: **4** Auge

telescope
5 glass **6** finder **7** compact **8** compress, condense, contract, refractor, spyglass **9** reflector

television
4 tube **5** video **8** boob tube, idiot box
antenna: **10** rabbit ears
award: **4** Emmy
British: **5** telly
children's: **6** kidvid

frequency: **3** UHF, VHF
interference: **4** snow
network: **3** ABC, BBC, CBS, Fox, NBC, NET, PBS
pioneer: **5** Baird (John Logie) **8** De Forest (Lee), Zworykin (Vladimir)
program: **4** news **5** rerun **6** series, sitcom **7** western **8** game show, talk show **9** broadcast, docudrama, soap opera **11** infomercial **12** infotainment
tube: **9** kinescope

tell
3 say **4** blab, clue, warn **5** break, count, crack, mound, order, spill, state, utter **6** advise, betray, fill in, inform, notify, relate, report, retail, reveal **7** confess, declare, divulge, narrate, recount, reel off **8** describe, disclose, give away **9** come clean

teller
5 clerk **6** banker **7** cashier, counter **8** informer, narrator **12** communicator

telling
5 solid, sound, valid **6** cogent **7** weighty **8** powerful **9** effective **10** convincing, expressive

tell off
4 flay, rate, ream **5** chide, scold **6** berate, rebuke, reprove **7** bawl out, chew out, upbraid **8** admonish, call down **9** dress down, excoriate, reprimand **10** take to task, tongue-lash, vituperate

tell on
6 inform, snitch, tattle

telltale
3 cue **4** clue, fink, lead, sign **5** proof **6** canary, gossip, signal, snitch, tip-off **7** rat fink, tattler **8** evidence, gossiper, informer, quidnunc, signpost, squealer **9** indicator **10** indication, newsmonger **12** blabbermouth, gossipmonger **13** scandalmonger

telluric
6 earthy **7** earthly, mundane, terrene, worldly **9** sublunary **11** terrestrial

temblor
5 quake, shake, shock **6** tremor **8** upheaval **10** aftershock, earthquake

temerarious
4 rash **6** daring **8** heedless, reckless **9** audacious, daredevil, foolhardy, venturous **11** adventurous, venturesome **13** adventuresome

temerity
4 gall 5 cheek, nerve 6 daring 8 audacity, chutzpah, rashness 9 assurance, brashness, hardihood, hardiness 10 effrontery 12 recklessness 13 foolhardiness

temper
4 heat, mean, mind, mood, tone, vein 5 admix, alloy, anger, anneal, blood, grain, humor, trend 6 anneal, attune, dander, dilute, govern, hackle, makeup, medium, season, soften, spirit, strain 7 courage, mollify, passion, quality 8 hardness, moderate, modulate, restrain, toughen 9 character, composure, condition 10 resilience, resiliency 11 disposition, personality

temperament
4 mood 5 humor 6 manner, makeup, mettle, nature 9 character 10 complexion 11 disposition, personality

temperamental
5 moody 6 ornery, touchy 7 erratic 8 contrary, ticklish, unstable, variable, volatile 9 mercurial 10 capricious, changeable, high-strung, inconstant 13 unpredictable

temperance
8 sobriety 9 austerity, restraint 10 abstinence, continence, moderation, self-denial 11 self-control
advocate of: 6 Nation (Carry) 7 Willard (Frances)

temperate
4 calm, even, mild, soft 5 balmy, sober 6 modest, steady 7 clement 8 discreet, moderate 9 abstinent, continent 10 abstemious, controlled, reasonable, restrained 11 abstentious

temperature
4 heat, mood 5 fever 6 degree, warmth 7 hotness 8 coldness 9 intensity

tempered
7 diluted, treated 8 adjusted, hardened, softened 9 mitigated, moderated, qualified 12 strengthened

tempest
3 din 4 blow, gale, rage, wind 5 furor, hurly, storm 6 hubbub, squall, tumult, uproar 8 brouhaha, foofaraw 9 commotion, hurricane 10 hullabaloo, hurly-burly

Tempest, The
character: 5 Ariel 6 Alonso 7 Caliban, Miranda 8 Prospero 9 Ferdinand

tempestuous
4 wild 5 roily, rough 6 raging, stormy 7 furious, moiling, violent 8 blustery 9 turbulent 10 tumultuous

temple
4 fane 6 church 9 synagogue 10 tabernacle
ancient: 8 pantheon
Aztec: 8 teocalli
Buddhist: 3 wat
Eastern: 6 pagoda
Greek: 9 Parthenon
sanctuary: 5 cella 6 adytum 10 penetralia

tempo
4 pace, rate, time 5 speed 6 rhythm
fast: 6 presto, vivace 7 allegro
moderate: 7 andante
slow: 5 grave, lento 6 adagio

temporal
3 lay 5 civil 6 carnal 7 earthly, mundane, profane, secular, worldly 13 chronological, synchronistic

temporary
6 acting 7 Band-Aid, interim 8 fleeting 9 ad interim, makeshift, transient 10 short-lived, substitute, transitory 11 provisional

temporize
5 delay, stall, yield 6 palter 7 draw out 8 gain time 10 equivocate 11 pervaricate

tempt
3 woo 4 bait, lure, risk, sway 5 court, decoy 6 allure, entice, entrap, invite, lead on, seduce 7 provoke 8 inveigle 9 tantalize

temptation
4 bait, lure, trap 5 decoy, siren, snare 6 allure, come-on 9 seduction 10 attraction, enticement

tempting
8 alluring 9 appealing, delicious, seductive 10 attractive, come-hither

temptress
4 vamp 5 siren 7 Lorelei 10 seductress 11 femme fatale

ten
cents: 4 dime
combining form: 3 dec, dek 4 deca, deka 5 decem
dollars: 7 sawbuck
mills: 4 cent

thousand: 6 myriad
years: 6 decade

tenable
5 sound 8 rational 10 defendable, defensible, reasonable 12 maintainable

tenacious
3 set 4 fast, firm, true 5 fixed, stout 6 dogged, secure, sturdy 8 adhesive, clinging, resolute, stalwart, stubborn 9 obstinate, steadfast 10 persistent 11 persevering

tenacity
4 grit, guts 5 moxie, pluck, spunk 6 mettle, spirit 7 courage 8 firmness 10 resolution 11 persistence 13 determination

tenant
6 holder, lessee, lodger, renter 7 boarder, dweller 8 occupant
feudal: 6 vassal

tenantable
7 livable 9 habitable 11 inhabitable

Ten Commandments
9 Decalogue

tend
4 lean, mind, till, work 5 guard, labor, nurse, serve, watch 6 foster 7 babysit, care for, conduce, incline, nurture, oversee 8 minister 9 cultivate, look after, watch over

tendency
4 bent, bias 5 drift, tenor, trend 7 current, leaning 8 penchant 10 partiality, proclivity, propensity 11 disposition 12 predilection

tendentious
6 biased 7 colored, partial 8 one-sided, partisan 10 prejudiced

tender
3 bid 4 fond, mild, soft, sore, warm 5 green, money, mushy, offer, young 6 callow, extend, gentle, humane, loving, submit, touchy 7 fragile, hold out, lenient, painful, present, proffer, propose 8 delicate, immature, proposal 9 sensitive, succulent 10 benevolent, solicitous 11 considerate, warmhearted 12 affectionate 13 compassionate

tenderfoot
4 colt, punk, tyro 6 novice, rookie 7 amateur 8 beginner, freshman, neophyte, newcomer 9 cheechako, fledgling, greenhorn, novitiate 10 apprentice

tenderhearted
6 kindly 11 sympathetic 13 compassionate

Tender Is the Night author
10 Fitzgerald (F. Scott)

tendon
4 band, cord 5 nerve, sinew 6 leader 9 hamstring

tendril
4 curl, vine 6 cirrus, spiral 7 ringlet

tenebrific
4 dark, glum, gray, grim 5 black, bleak, sable 6 dismal, dreary, gloomy, somber, sombre 8 desolate, funereal 10 depressing, oppressive 11 dispiriting

tenebrous
3 dim 4 dark, deep, dusk, hazy 5 dusky, foggy, muddy, murky, vague 6 cloudy, gloomy 7 cryptic, obscure, shadowy, unclear 9 ambiguous, lightless 10 caliginous

tenement
4 flat 6 rental, walk-up, warren 7 lodging, rookery 8 building, residence 9 apartment

tenet
3 ism 5 canon, creed, dogma 6 belief 7 paradox 8 doctrine 9 principle 10 empiricism

tenfold
7 decuple

Tennessee
capital: 9 Nashville
city: 7 Memphis 9 Knoxville 11 Chattanooga
college, university: 10 Vanderbilt
mountain, range: 7 Lookout 10 Great Smoky 13 Clingmans Dome
nickname: 9 Volunteer (State)
public works: 3 TVA 9 Norris Dam
river: 9 Tennessee 11 Mississippi
state bird: 11 mockingbird
state flower: 4 iris
state tree: 11 tulip poplar

tennis
award: 8 Davis Cup
item: 3 net 4 ball 6 racket 7 racquet
kind: 5 table 7 doubles, singles 8 platform
score: 4 love 5 deuce
serve: 3 ace
shoe: 7 sneaker
stroke: 3 cut, lob 4 chop, drop 5 serve, slice 6 volley 8 backhand, forehand

term: 3 let, set 5 court, fault 7 service
9 advantage, backcourt

tennis champ
4 Ashe (Arthur), Borg (Bjorn), Cash (Pat),
Graf (Steffi), King (Billie Jean), Noah
(Yannick), Wade (Virginia) 5 Budge (Don),
Chang (Michael), Court (Margaret Smith),
Evert (Chris), Gómez (Andres), Laver
(Rod), Lendl (Ivan), Perry (Fred), Seles
(Monica), Stich (Michael), Vilas (Guillermo),
Wills (Helen) 6 Agassi (André), Austin
(Tracy), Becker (Boris), Casals (Rosie),
Edberg (Stephan), Fraser (Neale), Gibson
(Althea), Hewitt (Lleyton), Hingis (Martina),
Kramer (Jack), Muster (Thomas), Pierce
(Mary), Stolle (Fred), Tilden (Bill)
7 Connors (Jimmy), Courier (Jim), Emerson
(Roy), Federer (Roger), Lacoste (Rene),
McEnroe (John), Nastase (Ilie), Novótna
(Jana), Sampras (Pete) 8 Connolly
(Maureen), González (Pancho), Martínez
(Conchita), Newcombe (John), Rosewall
(Ken), Sabatini (Gabriela), Wilander (Mats),
Williams (Serena, Venus) 9 Davenport
(Lindsay) 10 Mandlikova (Hana)
11 Navratilova (Martina) 14 Sánchez
Vicario (Arantxa)

Tennyson poem
4 Maud 7 Ulysses 8 Princess (The),
Tiresias 10 Enoch Arden, In Memoriam
12 Locksley Hall 23 Charge of the Light
Brigade (The)

tenor
4 mood, tone 5 drift, voice 6 singer
7 meaning, purport 8 tendency
9 substance
American: 5 Lanza (Mario) 6 Hadley
(Jerry), Peerce (Jan), Tucker (Richard)
8 Melchior (Lauritz) 9 McCormack (John),
McCracken (James)
Canadian: 7 Vickers (Jon)
Czech: 6 Slezak (Leo)
German: 10 Wunderlich (Fritz)
Italian: 5 Gigli (Beniamino) 6 Alagna
(Roberto), Caruso (Enrico) 7 Bocelli
(Andrea), Corelli (Franco) 8 Bergonzi
(Carlo) 9 del Monaco (Mario), di Stefano
(Giuseppe), Pavarotti (Luciano)
Spanish: 5 Kraus (Alfredo) 7 Domingo
(Plácido) 8 Carreras (Josá)
Swedish: 5 Gedda (Nicolai) 8 Björling
(Jussi) 9 Bjoerling (Jussi)

tenpins
7 bowling

tense
4 edgy, taut 5 nervy, rigid, tight, wired
6 uneasy 7 anxious, jittery, nervous,
restive, uptight 8 strained, stressed
10 high-strung
grammatical: 4 past 6 future 7 perfect,
present 8 preterit 9 preterite 10 pluperfect
11 progressive

tension
5 state, steam 6 nerves, strain, stress,
unease 7 anxiety, balance 8 edginess,
pressure, tautness 9 agitation, hostility,
stiffness 10 discomfort, opposition,
uneasiness 11 nervousness, uptightness

tent
4 camp 6 canopy, encamp, laager
7 bivouac, shelter
kind: 3 pup 4 yurt 5 Baker, tepee
6 wigwam 7 marquee 8 pavilion, umbrella
maker: 4 Omar
material: 6 canvas
part: 3 fly, guy, peg 4 pole

tentacle
3 arm 6 barbel, feeler

tentative
4 test 5 loath, probe, trial 6 averse, chary
7 halting 8 hesitant, insecure 9 diffident,
makeshift, reluctant, uncertain, undecided,
unsettled 10 irresolute 11 conditional,
disinclined, problematic, provisional

tenth
5 tithe
combining form: 4 deci

tenuous
4 slim, thin, weak 5 reedy, shaky 6 feeble,
flimsy, slight, stalky 7 fragile, sketchy,
slender 8 gossamer 10 precarious
11 implausible 13 insubstantial,
unsubstantial

tenure
4 term 6 estate 10 incumbency
feudal: 7 burgage

tepid
4 mild, warm 7 warmish 8 lukewarm
9 apathetic 11 halfhearted, indifferent

tequila source
5 agave

Terentia's husband
6 Cicero

Tereus
son: 4 Itys

wife: 6 Procne

tergiversate
3 haw, hem, rat 5 dodge, evade, hedge
6 defect, desert, waffle, weasel 7 abandon,
shuffle 8 renounce, sidestep 9 pussyfoot,
repudiate 10 apostatize, equivocate

term
3 dub, end 4 call, name, span, tour, word
5 label, spell, stint, title 6 detail, period,
tenure 7 quarter, session 8 duration,
semester 9 designate 10 conclusion,
denominate, expression, limitation,
particular 11 appellation, designation

termagant
5 harpy, scold, shrew, vixen 6 ogress,
virago 8 fishwife, harridan 9 Xanthippe

terminable
6 finite

terminal
3 end, lag 4 last 5 depot, fatal, final
6 finial, latest, latter, lethal 7 closing,
extreme, station 8 eventual, hindmost,
junction, ultimate 9 extremity
10 concluding
negative: 7 cathode
positive: 5 anode

terminate
3 end 4 boot, drop, fire, halt, kill, quit, sack,
stop 5 abort, cease, close, issue, leave
6 cut off, finish, wind up 7 abolish, dead-
end, dismiss 8 complete, conclude,
dissolve 9 determine, discharge 10 extinguish 11 assassinate, discontinue

terminology
4 cant 5 argot, idiom, lingo 6 jargon,
patois 7 lexicon 8 language, shoptalk
10 vernacular, vocabulary
12 nomenclature

termite
5 alate 8 white ant

ternary
5 third 6 triple 9 threefold

Terpsichore
see Muse

terrace
4 bank, deck, mesa, park, roof, step
5 bench, porch, shelf 6 street 7 balcony,
sundeck 8 platform 9 promenade

terra-cotta
4 clay 7 pottery

terra firma
4 dirt, land, soil 5 earth 6 ground

terrain
4 area, land, turf 5 field 6 domain, ground,
milieu, sphere 8 province 9 bailiwick,
territory 10 topography 11 environment

terrapin
6 turtle

terrestrial
4 land 6 earthy, ground 7 earthly,
mundane, worldly 8 everyday, ordinary,
telluric, workaday 9 earthlike, planetary,
sublunary 10 earthbound

terrible
4 dire 5 awful, dread 6 fierce, grisly,
horrid, severe 7 dreaded, fearful, furious,
ghastly, hideous, intense, macabre, vicious,
violent 8 dreadful, gruesome, horrible,
horrific, loathsome, shocking, vehement
9 abhorrent, appalling, atrocious,
desperate, frightful, harrowing, laborious,
monstrous, strenuous 10 disastrous,
formidable, horrendous, horrifying

terrier
3 dog
kind: 3 fox 4 blue, bull, Skye 5 cairn,
Irish, Welsh 6 Boston 8 Airedale,
Lakeland 9 Yorkshire

terrific
5 super, swell 6 superb 7 amazing,
awesome 8 dreadful, dynamite, glorious
9 appalling, frightful, marvelous, upsetting,
wonderful 10 formidable 11 magnificent,
sensational 13 extraordinary

terrify
5 alarm, scare 7 scarify, startle 8 affright,
frighten 10 intimidate

terrifying
4 grim 5 scary 6 grisly, horrid 7 ghastly,
hideous, macabre 8 alarming, dreadful,
fearsome, frightful, gruesome, horrible,
terrible 10 formidable, horrifying

territory
4 area, belt, land, turf, zone 5 field, route,
state, tract 6 domain, region, sphere
7 country, demesne, terrain 8 conquest,
district, dominion, province 9 bailiwick
10 borderland 12 jurisdiction

terror
4 brat, fear 5 alarm, dread, panic, worry
6 dismay, fright, horror 7 scourge
9 nightmare 11 fearfulness, trepidation

terrorize
3 cow 5 alarm, bully, scare 6 coerce, fright,
menace 7 scarify 8 browbeat, bulldoze,

frighten, threaten **9** strong-arm
10 intimidate

terry
4 loop **5** cloth **6** fabric **12** Turkish towel

terse
4 curt **5** brief, crisp, pithy, short **6** abrupt
7 brusque, compact, concise, elegant,
laconic, summary **8** polished, succinct
11 compendious, sententious, telegraphic
12 monosyllabic

tertiary
5 third

terza _____
4 rima

tessera
3 die **4** tile **6** tablet, ticket

test
3 try **4** exam, quiz **5** assay, check, essay,
final, proof, prove, shell, taste, touch, trial,
try on **6** sample, tryout, verify **7** confirm,
examine, midterm **8** evaluate, gut check,
sounding, trial run **9** benchmark, criterion
10 evaluation, experiment, touchstone
11 demonstrate, examination
12 experimental

testa
6 cupule **7** coating **8** envelope, seed coat,
tegument **10** integument

testament
4 will **5** credo, creed, proof **7** tribute,
witness **8** evidence **9** scripture
11 attestation **12** confirmation

tester
4 coin **6** canopy, prover **7** analyst, assayer
8 examiner **12** investigator

testifier
7 witness **8** deponent

testify
5 prove, swear **6** affirm, attest, depone,
depose, evince **7** certify, witness
11 certificate

testimonial
5 proof **6** salute **7** tribute, witness
8 evidence, memorial, monument
9 affidavit, character, reference
11 attestation **12** appreciation,
commendation, confirmation **13** commemoration

testimony
5 proof **6** avowal **7** witness **8** evidence
9 affidavit, authority, declaration

10 deposition, profession **11** affirmation,
attestation **12** confirmation
13 corroboration, documentation

testy
4 edgy **5** cross, fussy, hasty **6** cranky,
ornery, peevish, tetchy, touchy **7** fretful,
grouchy **8** choleric **9** crotchety, irascible,
irritable **10** ill-humored, out of sorts
12 cantankerous **13** quick-tempered

tetanus
7 lockjaw, trismus

tetchy
see **testy**

tête-à-tête
4 chat, talk **5** à deux **7** private, vis-à-vis
8 causerie **10** face-to-face
12 conversation

tether
3 tie **4** bind, rope **5** cable, chain, stake
6 fasten, fetter, lariat, picket **8** restrain
9 restraint

Tethys
daughters: 9 Oceanides
father: 6 Uranus
husband: 7 Oceanus
mother: 4 Gaea **5** Terra

tetrad
4 four **7** quartet **8** foursome **10** quaternion

Teutonic
6 German **8** Germanic
language: 5 Dutch **6** Danish, German,
Gothic **7** English, Flemish, Frisian,
Swedish **9** Afrikaans, Norwegian

Texas
capital: 6 Austin
city: 4 Waco **6** Dallas, El Paso **7** Houston
8 Amarillo **9** Arlington, Fort Worth **10** San
Antonio
college, university: 3 SMU **4** Rice
5 Lamar **6** Baylor **9** Texas Tech **15** Sam
Houston State
island: 5 Padre
mountain: 9 Guadalupe (Peak)
nickname: 8 Lone Star (State)
park: 7 Big Bend
river: 3 Red **5** Pecos **6** Brazos
8 Colorado **9** Rio Grande
state bird: 11 mockingbird
state flower: 10 bluebonnet
state tree: 5 pecan

text
6 script

textbook
6 primer

textile
5 cloth 6 fabric
dealer: 6 mercer
machine: 8 calender
shop: 7 mercery
treat: 9 mercerize

texture
3 web 4 feel, hand, wale, woof 5 weave
6 fabric

Thackeray novel
9 Pendennis 10 Vanity Fair 11 Barry
Lyndon, Henry Esmond

Thailand
capital: 7 Bangkok
city: 9 Chiang Mai
former name: 4 Siam
island: 6 Phuket
monetary unit: 4 baht
neighbor: 4 Laos 5 Burma 7 Myanmar
8 Cambodia, Malaysia
river: 10 Chao Phraya
sea: 7 Andaman

Thaïs
7 hetaera, hetaira 9 courtesan
author: 6 France (Anatole)
composer: 8 Massenet (Jules)
husband: 7 Ptolemy
lover: 9 Alexander (the Great)

thalassic
6 marine 7 oceanic 8 maritime

Thalia
see **Graces; Muse**

Thanatopsis author
6 Bryant (William Cullen)

Thanatos
5 death
brother: 6 Hypnos
mother: 3 Nyx

thankful
4 glad 8 grateful 12 appreciative

thanks
5 grace 8 blessing 9 gratitude
11 benediction 12 appreciation,
gratefulness

Thanksgiving
5 feast 7 holiday
first celebrant: 6 Indian 7 Pilgrim
food: 6 turkey

thatch
3 mop 4 hair, roof 5 cover

that is
Latin: 5 id est

Thaumas
daughter: 4 Iris 5 Aello, Harpy
7 Celaeno, Ocypete
daughters: 7 Harpies
father: 6 Pontus
mother: 4 Gaea
wife: 7 Electra

thaumaturgic
5 magic 6 Magian, mystic, witchy
7 magical 8 wizardly 9 marvelous
10 miraculous 11 necromantic
12 supernatural

thaumaturgy
5 magic 7 sorcery 8 cabbalah, kabbalah,
witchery, wizardry 10 necromancy

thaw
4 melt 5 relax 6 unbend 7 defrost, liquefy
8 dissolve, unfreeze 10 condescend,
deliquesce

the
7 article
French: 3 les
German: 3 das, der, die
Spanish: 3 las, los

Thea
daughter: 6 Selene
father: 6 Uranus
husband: 8 Hyperion
mother: 4 Gaea

theater
4 nabe 5 drama, stage 6 boards
9 playhouse 10 footlights
award: 4 Tony
district: 6 rialto
entrance: 5 foyer, lobby
Greek: 5 odeum
movie: 6 cinema 8 cineplex, megaplex
9 multiplex
outdoor: 7 drive-in
part: 3 box, pit 4 loge 5 apron, stage,
wings 7 balcony, parquet 8 parterre
9 greenroom, mezzanine, orchestra
10 proscenium

theatrical
5 stagy 6 staged 8 dramatic, thespian
10 artificial, flamboyant, histrionic
11 dramaturgic 12 melodramatic
agent: 6 Morris (William)
device: 4 prop
group: 6 troupe

Theban Eagle
6 Pindar

Thebes
founder: 6 Cadmus
king: 5 Laius 7 Oedipus
queen: 7 Jocasta

theft
5 heist, pinch 6 holdup, piracy 7 break-in, larceny, robbery 8 burglary, stealing, thievery 9 pilferage
combining form: 5 klept 6 klepto

theme
4 stem, text, tune 5 essay, lemma, motif, paper, point, topic, topos 6 burden, matter, melody, mythos, thesis 7 article, conceit, message, subject 8 argument
11 composition 12 dissertation

Themis
father: 6 Uranus
goddess of: 3 law 7 justice
husband: 4 Zeus 7 Jupiter
mother: 4 Gaea

then
4 also, anon, ergo, next, thus, when 5 again, hence, later 7 besides, further 8 moreover 9 therefore, thereupon 10 in addition 11 accordingly, furthermore 12 additionally, consequently

thence
4 away 7 thereof 9 from there, therefrom

Theogony poet
6 Hesiod

theologian
American: 6 Merton (Thomas) 7 Edwards (Jonathan), Niebuhr (Reinhold), Tillich (Paul), Walther (Carl)
Dutch: 6 Jansen (Cornelis)
English: 4 Bede (Venerable) 5 Pusey (Edward), Watts (Isaac) 6 Alcuin, Wesley (John) 7 Langton (Stephen) 8 Pelagius, Wycliffe (John)
French: 6 Calvin (John) 7 Abelard (Peter), William (of Auvergne, of Auxerre) 8 Maritain (Jacques), Sabatier (Auguste), Teilhard (de Chardin, Pierre)
German: 6 Rahner (Karl) 7 Eckhart (Meister) 8 Albertus (Magnus) 9 Niemöller (Martin) 10 Bonhoeffer (Dietrich)
Greek: 9 Zygomalas (Theodore)
Italian: 6 Thomas (Aquinas) 7 Aquinas (Thomas), Socinus (Fausto, Laelius)
Scottish: 10 Duns Scotus (John)
Spanish: 6 Suárez (Francisco) 7 Vitoria (Francisco de) 8 Servetus (Michael)
Swedish: 9 Soderblom (Nathan)
Swiss: 4 Küng (Hans) 5 Barth (Karl), Vinet (Alexandre-Rodolphe)

theological
school: 8 seminary
virtue: 4 hope 5 faith 7 charity

_____ Theologica
5 Summa

theorbo
4 lute

theorem
3 law 4 rule 5 axiom 7 formula, inverse, stencil 8 converse 9 principle
10 principium 11 fundamental, proposition

theoretical
4 pure 5 ideal 8 abstract, academic, notional, unproved 11 conjectural, speculative 12 hypothetical 13 problematical, suppositional

theorize
5 guess 6 submit 7 suggest 9 formulate, postulate, speculate 10 conjecture
11 hypothesize

theory
7 perhaps, premise, surmise 8 supposal 10 conjecture, hypothesis 11 speculation, supposition
astronomical: 7 big bang
suffix: 3 ism

therapeutic
5 tonic 7 healing, helpful 8 curative, remedial, salutary, sanative 9 healthful, medicinal, vulnerary, wholesome
10 beneficial, corrective 11 restorative
12 health-giving

therapy
9 treatment

therefore
4 ergo, then, thus 5 hence 6 thence
11 accordingly 12 consequently

therefrom
4 away 6 thence

thereupon
4 ergo, then, thus 6 at once, at that, thence 8 directly 9 right away, therefore, wherefore 11 accordingly, straightway
12 consequently

thermal unit
3 Btu 6 degree 7 calorie

thermometer
5 gauge 9 indicator
kind: 7 Celsius, Réaumur 10 centigrade, Fahrenheit

thermos
5 dewar 10 Dewar flask

Theroux work
9 Saint Jack 13 Mosquito Coast (The)
14 Half Moon Street 18 Great Railway
Bazaar (The)

Thersites' slayer
8 Achilles

thesaurus editor
5 Roget (Peter Mark)

Theseus
beloved: 7 Ariadne
father: 6 Aegeus
mother: 6 Aethra
slayer: 9 Lycomedes
son: 10 Hippolytus
victim: 6 Sciron 8 Minotaur 10 Procrustes
wife: 7 Phaedra

thesis
5 essay, point, theme 6 belief 7 premise
8 downbeat, tractate, treatise 9 discourse,
monograph, position, postulate, synthesis
10 contention, exposition 11 postulation,
proposition, supposition 12 disquisition,
dissertation

thespian
5 actor 6 mummer, player 7 actress,
trouper 8 dramatic 9 performer
10 histrionic, theatrical 11 dramaturgic
12 impersonator, melodramatic

Thespis' forte
5 drama 7 tragedy

Thessalian hero
5 Jason 8 Achilles

_____ the Terrible
4 Ivan

Thetis
6 Nereid
father: 6 Nereus
husband: 6 Peleus
mother: 5 Doris
son: 8 Achilles

theurgist
5 witch 7 warlock 8 magician, sorcerer
12 wonder-worker

thew
4 beef 5 brawn, might, power, sinew, vigor
6 muscle 8 strength, vitality

thick
3 fat 4 wide 5 broad, bulky, burly, close,
dense, dumpy, husky, squat, stout
6 chummy, chunky, packed, stocky
7 compact, crammed, crowded, viscous
8 familiar, heavyset, intimate
11 inspissated

thicken
3 set 4 blur, clot, jell 6 curdle 7 broaden,
compact, congeal 8 condense 9 coagulate
10 inspissate 11 concentrate, consolidate

thicket
4 bosk, bush, shaw, wood 5 clump, copse,
grove, hedge 6 bosket, covert, mallee,
tangle 7 boscage, bosquet, coppice,
spinney 8 hedgerow, quickset
9 brushwood, canebrake, chaparral

thickness
3 ply 4 loft 5 depth, gauge, layer, sheet
7 density 8 dullness 9 stupidity, viscosity

thickset
5 bulky, burly, husky, pudgy, stout
6 chunky, portly, stocky, sturdy 7 compact
9 corpulent

thief
3 dip 4 prig 5 ganef 6 bandit, lifter, looter,
pirate, rascal, robber 7 booster, burglar,
filcher, stealer 8 hijacker, larcener, pilferer
9 larcenist, purloiner, water rat 10 cat
burglar, highwayman, pickpocket, shoplifter
12 housebreaker

thieve
3 rob 4 hook, lift, pick, roll 5 filch, pinch,
pluck, steal, swipe 6 hijack, hold up, pilfer,
rip off, snitch 7 purloin 8 knock off
9 knock over

thievery
see **theft**

thievish
9 larcenous 13 light-fingered

thigh
3 ham 5 flank 6 gammon
bone: 5 femur
relating to: 6 crural 7 femoral

thimble
3 cup 5 cover

thin
4 fine, lank, lean, slim 5 gaunt, lanky,
reedy, scant, sharp, spare 6 dilute, flimsy,
meager, meagre, rarefy, scanty, skimpy,
skinny, slight, sparse, stalky, treble, twiggy,
watery 7 diluted, scraggy, scrawny,
slender, spindly, squinny, subtile, tenuous
8 rarefied, skeletal 9 attenuate, extenuate
10 attenuated 11 watered-down
13 unsubstantial

thing
4 item 5 being, event 6 entity, matter,
object 7 article, concern, element
8 business, incident, material, occasion

9 existence, happening 10 occurrence, phenomenon
in law: 3 res

thingamajig
5 gizmo 6 dingus, doodad, gadget, jigger, widget 7 whatsit 9 doohickey

things
4 gear 5 goods, stock, stuff 7 baggage, clothes, effects, luggage 8 chattels, clothing, matériel, movables, property, supplies 10 belongings, provisions 11 impedimenta, merchandise, paraphernalia 13 accoutrements

think
4 mull, muse 5 brood, study, weigh 6 ideate, ponder, reason 7 believe, imagine, reflect, suppose, surmise 8 cogitate, consider, meditate, ruminate 9 cerebrate, speculate 10 conjecture, deliberate, excogitate 11 contemplate

Thinker sculptor
5 Rodin (Auguste)

third
8 tertiary
combining form: 3 tri
power: 4 cube

third degree
7 torture 8 grilling 11 inquisition, questioning 13 interrogation

third estate
5 plebs 6 people, plebes 8 populace 9 commonage, commoners, plebeians 10 commonalty 11 rank and file

Third Man author
6 Greene (Graham)

Third of May painter
4 Goya (Francisco)

thirst
3 yen 4 itch, long, lust, pine 5 crave, desire, yearn 6 hanker, hunger 7 craving, dryness, longing 8 appetite

thirsty
3 dry 4 arid, avid 5 eager 6 ardent 7 anxious, bone-dry, parched 8 droughty 9 absorbent, waterless

this and that
8 oddments, sundries 9 etceteras 11 miscellanea, odds and ends

Thisbe's lover
7 Pyramus

This Side of Paradise author
10 Fitzgerald (F. Scott)

thistle
4 weed 7 caltrop
Russian: 10 tumbleweed

thistlebird
9 goldfinch

thither
3 yon 5 there 6 yonder

thole
3 peg, pin 6 endure

Thomas à _____
6 Becket, Kempis

Thomas's Greek name
7 Didymus

Thomas opera
6 Mignon

Thompson
4 Emma 5 Sadie 6 Hunter 7 Dorothy, Francis, J. Walter 8 Benjamin

thong
4 band, lace, lash, rein, zori 5 lasso, strap, strip, whang 6 sandal 7 latchet 8 flip-flop

Thor
5 Donar
father: 4 Odin 5 Wotan
god of: 7 thunder
hammer: 8 Mjollnir
mother: 5 Jordh, Jorth

thorax
5 chest, trunk 6 pereon

Thoreau, Henry David
friend: 7 Emerson (Ralph Waldo)
town: 7 Concord
work: 6 Walden

thorn
4 barb 5 briar, spike, spine 7 prickle, spinule 9 annoyance 10 irritation

thorny
5 sharp, spiny 6 briary, tricky 7 awkward, prickly, spinous, touchy 8 ticklish 9 difficult, vexatious 10 nettlesome 11 troublesome

thorough
4 full 6 minute 7 careful, in-depth 8 complete, detailed, diligent, whole-hog 9 downright 10 blow-by-blow, exhaustive, meticulous 11 painstaking 13 conscientious

thoroughbred
8 pedigree, purebred 9 pedigreed, pureblood 10 bloodstock 11 full-blooded

thoroughfare
3 way 4 road 5 track 6 artery, avenue, street 7 highway, parkway 8 corridor 9 boulevard

thoroughgoing
5 utter 6 all-out 7 extreme 8 absolute, complete, outright, whole-hog 9 out-and-out 10 consummate, exhaustive 11 straight-out, unmitigated 13 dyed-in-the-wool

thou
3 you 5 grand
French: 5 mille

though
3 yet 5 still, while 6 albeit 7 however, whereas 8 after all 11 nonetheless 12 nevertheless

thought
4 idea 6 notion, reason 7 concept, opinion 8 ideation 9 brainwork 10 cogitation, conception, meditation, reflection, rumination 11 cerebration, speculation 12 deliberation, intellection 13 contemplation

thoughtful
6 polite 7 careful, gallant, heedful, mindful, pensive, serious, studied 8 gracious, studious, thinking 9 attentive, courteous, pondering, regardful 10 cogitative, meditative, reflective, ruminative, solicitous 11 considerate 12 deliberative, intellectual 13 contemplative

thoughtless
4 rash, rude 5 brash, hasty 6 madcap 7 selfish 8 careless, feckless, heedless, impolite, reckless, uncaring 9 insensate 10 incautious, ungracious 12 discourteous 13 inconsiderate

thousand
combining form: 4 kilo
dollars: 5 grand
years: 10 millennium

thousandth
10 millesimal
combining form: 5 milli

thrall
4 peon, serf, yoke 5 helot, slave 7 bondage, bondman, helotry, peonage, serfdom, slavery, villein 9 servitude, villenage 10 absorption 11 enslavement

thrash
3 tan 4 beat, belt, drub, flog, hide, lash, lick, maul, pelt, trim, whip 5 baste, flail, pound, smear, swing, thump, whale, whang 6 batter, buffet, larrup, pummel, stripe, wallop 7 scourge, shellac, trounce 8 flounder, lambaste, work over 10 flagellate

thrash out
4 moot 5 argue 6 debate 7 discuss 10 deliberate, kick around

thread
4 line, vein, yard 5 fiber, trail, weave 6 strand, stream, string 8 filament
ball of: 4 clew
dental: 5 floss
holder: 6 bobbin
kind: 4 silk, yarn 5 floss, lisle 6 cotton 8 surgical
loose: 8 raveling 9 ravelling
surgical: 6 catgut, suture

threadbare
4 hack, worn 5 dingy, faded, seedy, stale, tacky, tatty, tired, trite 6 beat-up, cheesy, cliché, frayed, ragged, shabby, shoddy 7 clichéd, run-down, tedious, worn-out 8 shopworn, slipshod, tattered, timeworn, well-worn 9 destitute, hackneyed 10 down-at-heel 11 commonplace, dilapidated, down-at-heels, stereotyped 13 down-at-the-heel

threadlike
11 filamentous

threads
4 duds 7 clothes 8 clothing, garments

threat
6 danger, duress, menace 7 assault, warning 8 big stick, coercion 11 thunderbolt

threaten
3 cow 4 warn 5 augur 6 coerce, menace 7 caution, portend, presage 8 endanger, forebode, forewarn, overhang 10 intimidate

three
4 trey 5 crowd
combining form: 3 ter, tri

threefold
5 trine 6 thrice, treble, trinal, triple 7 triplex

Three Musicians artist
7 Picasso (Pablo)

Three Musketeers
5 Athos 6 Aramis 7 Porthos
author: 5 Dumas (Alexandre)
friend: 9 D'Artagnan

Threepenny Opera, The
author: 6 Brecht (Bertolt)

music: **5** Weill (Kurt)

threescore
5 sixty

Three Sisters, The
4 Olga **5** Irina, Masha
author: **7** Chekhov (Anton)

threesome
4 trio **5** triad, trine **6** triple, triune, troika
7 trinity **8** triangle **11** triumvirate

three-wheeler
5 cycle, trike **7** pedicab **8** tricycle
10 velocipede

threnody
5 dirge, elegy **6** lament

thresh
3 lam, tan **4** beat, belt, drub, flog, hide,
lash, lick, pelt, trim, wave, whip **5** baste,
forge, flail, pound, slate, smear, swing,
thump, whale, whang **6** batter, buffet,
larrup, pummel, strike, stripe, wallop,
winnow **7** scourge, shellac, trounce
8 lambaste, work over **10** flagellate

threshold
3 eve **4** door, edge, gate, sill **5** brink,
limen, verge **6** outset **8** boundary

thrift
6 saving **7** economy, sea pink **8** prudence
9 frugality, parsimony

thrifty
5 canny **6** frugal, saving **7** sparing
9 provident **10** economical **12** parsimonious

thrill
3 wow **4** bang, boot, kick, rush, send
5 blast, throb **6** charge, excite, shiver,
tingle, wallop **7** frisson, tremble, vibrate
9 electrify **10** excitement **11** titillation

thriller
6 gothic **7** chiller, mystery, shocker
8 whodunit **9** dime novel **10** hair-raiser
13 penny dreadful

thrive
4 boom, grow **7** advance, burgeon,
develop, prosper, succeed **8** flourish, get
ahead

throat
3 maw **4** tube **5** gorge **6** groove, gullet
7 channel, weasand
inflammation: **5** croup **6** angina, quinsy
10 laryngitis
relating to: **8** guttural
warmer: **5** scarf

throaty
5 gruff, husky, thick **6** hoarse **8** gravelly,
gutteral

throb
4 ache, beat, drum **5** pound, pulse **6** thrill
7 pulsate, vibrate **9** palpitate

throe
3 fit **4** pain, pang **5** agony, spasm **6** attack
7 seizure **9** suffering **10** convulsion
11 contraction

thrombus
4 clot **8** blockage, coagulum

throne
4 seat **5** chair, crown, power, reign
8 cathedra, dominion **11** sovereignty

throng
3 jam, mob **4** host, pack, push, rout
5 bunch, crowd, crush, drove, flock, group,
horde, press, scrum, shoal, swarm **6** resort
9 multitude **10** assemblage

throttle
3 gun **5** choke **6** throat **7** garrote, trachea
8 strangle, suppress **11** accelerator,
strangulate

through
3 per, via **4** done, past **5** due to, ended
6 direct **7** by way of, done for, nonstop,
owing to **8** by dint of, complete, finished,
washed-up **9** because of, by means of,
completed, concluded **10** by virtue of,
terminated, throughout
prefix: **3** dia, per

throughout
3 mid **4** amid **5** midst **6** during **7** all over,
overall **10** everywhere, far and near, far
and wide, high and low

Through the Looking Glass
author: **7** Carroll (Lewis)
character: **5** Alice

throve
9 burgeoned, prospered **10** flourished

throw
3 lob, peg, put **4** cast, fire, hurl, toss
5 chuck, fling, heave, pitch, sling **6** launch,
propel **7** buck off, project
in the towel: **4** quit **6** give up

throw away
4 blow, cast, junk, shed **5** scrap, waste
7 discard, fritter **8** jettison, squander

throwback
7 atavism **9** reversion

throw down the gauntlet
4 defy 8 confront 9 challenge

throw off
4 lose, shed 5 addle, shake 7 confuse, fluster 8 befuddle, bewilder, distract
the track: 6 derail 7 confuse, mislead

throw out
4 emit, junk, shed 5 chuck, eject, evict, scrap 6 reject 7 discard 8 jettison

throw up
4 barf, cast, hurl, lose, puke, quit, spew, toss 5 heave, retch, vomit 7 upchuck 8 disgorge 11 regurgitate

thrush
5 mavis, ouzel, robin, veery 6 mistle 8 bluebird 9 blackbird, fieldfare, mistletoe 11 nightingale

thrust
3 dig, jab, ram 4 barb, butt, core, cram, dash, dive, duck, gist, hurl, kick, pith, poke, prod, push, stab, tilt 5 barge, crowd, cut in, drive, force, lunge, press, punch, sense, shoot, shove, spear, stick, stuff 6 burden, extend, insert, pierce, plunge, propel, upshot 7 assault, obtrude, project, purport, riposte 8 pressure 9 substance

thud
3 jar 4 bump, jolt, plop 5 clunk, throb, thump 6 impact 10 concussion

thug
3 mug 4 goon, hood, punk 5 bully, rough, rowdy, tough 6 Apache, Capone, gunman, hit man 7 hoodlum, mobster, ruffian 8 enforcer, gangster, hooligan, plug-ugly 9 cutthroat, roughneck

thumb
4 leaf, turn 5 digit, hitch, ovolo 6 pollex, riffle 8 pollices (plural) 9 hitchhike

thumbs-up
3 AOK, nod 4 okay 7 go-ahead 10 green light

thumb through
4 scan 6 browse, riffle 7 dip into

thump
3 bop, hit 4 bash, beat, belt, blow, drub, jolt, pelt, whip 5 knock, paste, pound, punch, shock, smack, sound, whack 6 batter, buffet, impact, pummel, strike, thrash, thwack, wallop 7 clobber, endorse, promote, shellac, trounce 8 advocate

thunder
4 bang, boom, clap, peal, roar 6 rumble 7 resound 8 rumbling 9 fulminate

thunderbolt
9 lightning

thunder lizard
11 apatosaurus 12 brontosaurus

thunderstruck
5 agape 6 amazed 7 shocked, stunned 8 dismayed 9 astounded, staggered 10 astonished, bewildered, confounded 11 dumbfounded 13 flabbergasted

Thurber character
5 Mitty (Walter)

thus
3 sic 4 ergo, then 5 hence 9 therefore 11 accordingly 12 consequently
French: 5 ainsi

Thus Spake Zarathustra author
9 Nietzsche (Friedrich)

thwack
3 bop 4 belt, biff, blow, pelt, sock, whop 5 crack, pound, smack, thump, whack

thwart
4 balk, beat, dash, foil 5 bench 6 baffle, hinder, oppose, scotch, stymie 9 checkmate, frustrate 10 circumvent, contravene, disappoint

Thyestes
brother: 6 Atreus
daughter: 7 Pelopia
father: 6 Pelops
mother: 10 Hippodamia
son: 9 Aegisthus

Tiamat
husband: 4 Apsu
slayer: 6 Marduk

tiara
5 crown 6 diadem 8 headband

Tibetan
animal: 3 yak 5 takin
capital: 5 Lhasa
coin: 5 tanga
monk: 4 lama
people: 6 Bhotia, Sherpa

tibia
8 shinbone

tic
5 quirk, spasm 6 twitch 9 twitching

tick
5 check 8 arachnid, parasite 9 checkmark 11 bloodsucker

ticker
4 bomb 5 clock, heart, watch

ticket
3 key, tag 4 comp, pass, vote 6 ballot
7 receipt 8 passport, password 10 open
sesame
seller: 7 scalper

tickle
4 stir 5 amuse, tease, touch 6 arouse,
excite, please, tingle 7 delight, gratify,
provoke 9 stimulate, titillate

tickled
5 happy 6 amused 7 pleased 9 delighted

ticklish
6 tender, thorny, touchy, tricky 8 delicate,
unstable 9 sensitive 10 precarious
13 oversensitive

tick off
3 ire, irk 5 anger 6 rankle 7 incense,
provoke 9 aggravate

tidal flood
4 bore

tidbit
4 bite 5 goody, treat 6 dainty, morsel,
nugget

tide
4 flow, flux, rush 5 drift, flood, spate, surge
6 stream 7 current, holiday
type: 3 ebb, low 4 high, neap 5 flood
6 spring

tidings
4 news, word 6 advice 7 message
11 information 12 intelligence

tidy
4 fair, neat, smug, snug, trim 5 kempt
6 pick up 7 clean up, orderly, precise
9 shipshape 10 acceptable, methodical
11 respectable, spic-and-span, substantial,
uncluttered, well-groomed 12 satisfactory,
spick-and-span

tie
3 rod 4 band, bind, bond, cord, draw, gird,
join, knit, knot, lash, link, moor, rope, yoke
5 equal, leash, match, truss 6 attach,
cravat, fasten, fetter, hamper, oxford,
ribbon, secure 7 connect, harness, shackle
8 dead heat, deadlock, fastener, ligament,
ligature, restrain, shoelace, standoff,
vinculum 9 constrain, stalemate
10 attachment, four-in-hand

tied
5 bound 6 joined, united 8 attached,
fastened 9 connected

tier
3 row 4 bank, deck, file, line, rank 5 class,
grade, group, story 6 league 7 echelon
8 category, grouping

tie-up
3 jam 4 snag 5 crimp, delay, hitch 6 glitch
7 problem 8 gridlock, slowdown, stoppage
10 connection, traffic jam 11 association

tiff
3 row 4 fuss, spat 5 run-in, scrap 6 bicker
7 brabble, dispute, quarrel, wrangle
8 argument, squabble 10 falling-out
11 altercation 12 disagreement

tiffany
5 gauze 11 cheesecloth

tiger
3 cat 6 feline 9 carnivore
young: 3 cub

tight
4 fast, firm, snug, taut, trim 5 cheap, close,
drunk, fixed, tipsy 6 firmly, secure, stingy
7 compact, crowded, drunken, miserly
8 intimate 9 tenacious 10 inebriated
11 closefisted, intoxicated
12 cheeseparing, parsimonious 13 penny-
pinching

tighten
4 bind 5 choke, close, cramp, pinch, screw
6 clench, fasten, narrow, secure, shrink
8 compress, restrict 9 clamp down,
constrict

tightfisted
see **stingy**

tight-lipped
6 silent 8 reserved, reticent, taciturn
12 closemouthed

tightwad
5 miser, piker 7 niggard, scrooge
9 skinflint 10 cheapskate 12 penny-
pincher

tile
5 plate, slate 6 domino 7 tessera
8 linoleum

till
3 hoe, sow 4 disk, plow, tend, turn, up to,
work 6 before, harrow 7 prior to
9 cultivate 11 in advance of 12 cash
register

tillable
6 arable **10** cultivable **12** cultivatable

tillage
4 farm, land **5** tilth **7** culture **11** cultivation

tiller
4 helm **5** stalk **6** farmer, sprout **7** planter, steerer **9** sodbuster **10** cultivator

tilt
3 tip **4** bank, bent, bias, cant, cock, heel, lean, list, toss **5** grade, joust, level, lurch, pitch, slant, slope, speed **6** attack, charge, thrust **7** dispute, incline, leaning, recline **8** gradient **11** inclination

timbal
4 drum **10** kettledrum

timber
3 log **4** balk, beam, stud, tree, wood **5** board, joist, plank, trees, woods **6** forest, girder, lumber, rafter **8** woodland
uncut: 8 stumpage
wolf: 4 lobo

timbre
4 tone **6** temper **7** quality **9** resonance, tone color

timbrel
4 drum **10** tambourine

time
3 age, era **4** bout, date, hour, pace, span, term **5** clock, epoch, shift, space, spell, stint, tempo, while **6** moment, period, season **7** instant, stretch **8** duration, occasion **11** opportunity
combining form: 5 chron **6** chrono
gone by: 4 past **9** yesterday
long: 3 age, eon, era **4** aeon
of day: 4 dawn, dusk, noon **5** night **6** sunset **7** evening, morning, sunrise **8** daybreak, twilight **9** afternoon
olden: 4 yore **10** yesteryear
period: 3 age, day, eon, era **4** aeon, hour, week, year **5** epoch, month **6** decade, minute, moment, second **7** century, instant **9** fortnight **10** millennium
present: 3 now
relating to: 8 temporal
short: 5 jiffy **6** moment, second **7** instant
to come: 6 future **8** tomorrow
waste: 4 loaf **5** dally **6** loiter

time and again
3 oft **5** often **6** hourly **8** commonly, ofttimes **10** constantly, frequently, oftentimes, repeatedly **11** continually, over and over **12** periodically

Time founder
4 Luce (Henry R.) **6** Hadden (Briton)

timeless
7 ageless, eternal, unaging **8** unageing **9** atemporal, perpetual **11** everlasting

timely
5 early **6** prompt, proper **8** punctual, suitable **9** opportune **10** seasonable **11** appropriate

Time Machine author
5 Wells (H. G.)

Time of Your Life author
7 Saroyan (William)

time-out
4 rest **5** break, pause, recess **6** hiatus **7** respite **8** breather **9** interlude **12** interruption

timepiece
5 clock, watch **7** sundial **8** horologe **9** clepsydra, stopwatch **10** water clock **11** chronograph, chronometer

timetable
6 agenda, docket **7** program **8** calendar, schedule

timeworn
3 old **4** aged, hack **5** hoary, stale, trite **6** age-old **7** ancient **8** dog-eared, Noachian **9** hackneyed **10** threadbare

time zone
7 Central, Eastern, Pacific **8** Mountain

timid
3 shy **4** wary **5** chary, mousy **6** afraid, yellow **7** bashful, chicken, fearful, halting, nervous, panicky **8** cowardly, retiring, timorous **9** diffident, tentative, trepidant, uncertain **11** unassertive **12** apprehensive, fainthearted

timidity
4 fear **7** modesty, shyness **8** meekness **9** hesitancy, reticence **10** diffidence, hesitation

Timon's servant
7 Flavius

timorous
4 wary **5** timid **6** afraid **7** fearful **8** retiring **9** shrinking, tremulous **12** apprehensive

Timothy's associate
4 Paul

tin
3 box, can **5** metal **7** element **9** container

mining region: 8 stannary
relating to: 7 stannic **8** stannous
sheet: 6 latten

tincture
3 dye **4** cast, hint, tint **5** color, shade, smack, stain, tinge, touch, trace **6** iodine, streak **8** colorant, dyestuff, laudanum **9** paregoric **10** intimation, suggestion

tinder
4 punk **5** spunk **8** kindling

tine
5 point, prong, spike **6** branch

tinge
3 dye, hue **4** cast, hint, tint, tone **5** color, imbue, shade, stain, tinct, touch **8** tincture **10** intimation

tingle
5 sting **6** thrill **7** prickle **9** sensation

tinker
3 fix **4** mend, mess, muck, play **5** gypsy **6** adjust, diddle, fiddle, mender, potter, putter, repair **7** bungler, twiddle **9** repairman

tinkle
4 ring, ting **5** chink, clink, plink **6** jingle

tinny
4 thin **5** cheap, harsh **8** metallic

Tin Pan Alley acronym
3 BMI **5** ASCAP

tinsel
5 gaudy **6** flashy, garish, tawdry **7** chintzy, glaring, trinket **8** ornament, specious **9** clinquant **11** superficial **12** meretricious

tint
3 dye, hue **4** cast, tone, wash **5** color, shade, tinge, touch **8** tincture **10** col-oration **12** pigmentation

tiny
3 wee **5** bitsy, bitty, elfin, pygmy, teeny, weeny **6** minute, peewee, pocket, teensy, weensy **8** pint-size **9** itsy-bitsy, itty-bitty, miniature, minuscule **10** diminutive, pocket-size, teeny-weeny **11** lilliputian, microscopic **12** teensy-weensy **13** infinitesimal

tip
3 cap, cue, top **4** apex, cant, clue, cusp, heel, hint, list, peak, perk, tilt **5** point, slant, slope, steer, upset **6** advice, topple **7** cumshaw, incline **8** gratuity, overturn, turn over **9** baksheesh, lagniappe, pourboire **11** information

tip-off
4 clue, hint, sign **6** advice **7** pointer, warning **8** giveaway, jump ball **10** indication

Tippecanoe and _____ too
5 Tyler

tippet
4 cape **5** scarf **8** liripipe

tipple
3 bib, sip **4** swig, tope **5** booze, drink **6** guzzle, imbibe **7** swizzle **8** liquor up

tippler
3 sot **4** lush, soak **5** drunk, toper **6** bibber, boozer **7** tosspot **8** drunkard **9** inebriate

tipstaff
7 bailiff

tipster
4 fink **6** canary, snitch **7** adviser, rat fink, stoolie, tattler **8** informer, squealer **11** stool pigeon

tipsy
3 lit **4** high **5** askew, drunk, lit up, oiled, tight **7** drunken, fuddled **8** unsteady **10** inebriated **11** intoxicated

tiptoe
5 creep, steal **9** pussyfoot

tirade
4 rant **6** screed **8** diatribe, harangue, jeremiad **9** philippic **12** denunciation, vituperation **13** tongue-lashing

tire
3 sap **4** bore, fail, flag, jade, pall, poop, wear **5** drain, droop, ennui, weary, wheel **6** tucker, weaken **7** exhaust, fatigue, wear out **8** enervate, wear down
airless: 4 flat **7** blowout
kind: 4 bias, snow **6** radial **7** retread **9** whitewall

tired
4 worn **5** spent, weary **6** done in **7** drained, run-down, worn out **8** fatigued, flagging **9** enervated, exhausted

tiredness
7 fatigue **8** collapse **9** lassitude **10** exhaustion **11** prostration

tireless
10 unflagging **13** indefatigable, inexhaustible

Tiresias
4 seer **10** soothsayer

tiresome
4 dull, stale 6 boring 7 irksome, lumpish, operose, tedious

Tirol
capital: 9 Innsbruck
country: 7 Austria
mountains: 4 Alps

Tisiphone
see Erinyes

tissue
3 web 4 film, mesh 5 fiber, gauze, paper 6 fabric
anatomical: 4 tela 5 fiber 6 diploe 8 ganglion 10 epithelium
connective: 6 stroma, tendon 9 cartilage
kind: 3 fat 5 nerve 6 muscle 7 nervous 8 muscular 10 connective
layer: 6 dermis 7 stratum
plant: 4 bast, wood 5 xylem 6 phloem

titan
5 giant 8 colossus

Titan
father: 6 Uranus
female: 4 Rhea 6 Tethys, Themis
male: 6 Cronus 7 Iapetus, Oceanus
mother: 4 Gaea

Titan author
7 Dreiser (Theodore)

Titania's husband
6 Oberon

titanic
4 huge, vast 5 great 6 mighty 7 immense, mammoth, massive 8 colossal, enormous, gigantic 9 cyclopean, Herculean, monstrous 10 gargantuan, tremendous

tithe
3 tax 4 levy 5 tenth 12 contribution

Tithonus
beloved by: 3 Eos
father: 8 Laomedon

Titian painting
5 Danaë 8 Ecce Homo 10 Assumption (The), Holy Family (The) 12 Rape of Europa (The) 13 Maltese Knight, Medea and Venus, Venus and Cupid 14 Worship of Venus (The) 17 Bacchus and Ariadne

titillate
6 arouse, excite, stir up, thrill, tickle 9 stimulate

title
3 dub, due 4 call, deed, dibs, name, term 5 claim, merit, nomen 7 baptize, caption, heading 8 christen, cognomen, pretense 9 designate 10 denominate, pretension 11 appellation, appellative, designation 12 championship, compellation, denomination
Dutch: 7 mynheer
ecclesiastic: 8 reverend
feminine: 3 Mrs. 4 dame, lady, ma'am, miss 5 madam 6 madame, milady, missus 8 mistress
French: 6 madame 8 monsieur 12 mademoiselle
German: 4 Frau, Herr 8 Fräulein
holder: 5 noble 8 champion
Indian: 3 sri 5 sahib
Islamic: 5 hajji 6 sayyid 9 ayatollah
Italian: 5 donna 6 signor 7 signora 9 signorina
monk's: 3 fra 7 brother
of nobility: 3 sir 4 duke, earl, king, lady, lord, sire 5 baron, count, queen 6 prince 7 baronet, duchess, marquis 8 Archduke, baroness, countess, marchesa, marchese, marquise, princess, viscount 11 marchioness, viscountess
Oriental: 4 khan
Persian: 5 mirza
Portuguese: 3 dom 4 dona 6 senhor 7 senhora 9 senhorita
Spanish: 3 don 4 doña
Turkish: 3 bey

titmouse
4 bird 6 tomtit 7 bushtit 9 chickadee

Tito
4 Broz (Josip)

titter
5 laugh 6 giggle 7 chortle, chuckle, snicker, snigger

tittle
3 bit, jot 4 atom, iota, mite 5 minim, speck 7 smidgen 8 particle 9 diacritic

titular
5 legal 6 titled 7 nominal 8 so-called 11 designative

Tityus
father: 4 Zeus
slayer: 6 Apollo

Tiu
see Tyr

tizzy
4 flap, fume, snit, stew 5 sweat 6 dither, swivet, uproar

T-man
5 agent 8 revenuer

to
be sure: 6 indeed 7 granted 9 certainly
Scottish: 3 tae
wit: 3 viz 6 namely, that is 8 scilicet

toad
6 anuran, peeper 8 truckler 9 amphibian,
brownnose, sycophant 10 batrachian,
bootlicker 11 lickspittle
genus: 4 Bufo

toady
4 fawn 5 cower, leech 6 cringe, flunky,
grovel, kowtow, lackey, sponge 7 truckle
8 bootlick, parasite, truckler 9 brownnose,
sycophant 10 bootlicker 11 apple-polish,
lickspittle

toast
5 bread, drink, skoal 6 cheers, health,
l'chaim, pledge, prosit, salute 7 wassail
8 mazel tov
kind: 5 melba 6 French 8 zwieback

toastmaster
5 emcee

To a Waterfowl author
6 Bryant (William Cullen)

tobacco
4 leaf, weed
cask: 8 hogshead
chewing: 4 chaw, quid
ingredient: 3 tar 8 nicotine
juice: 6 ambeer
kind: 4 shag 5 snuff 6 burley 7 caporal,
perique, Turkish 9 broadleaf, mundungus
pipe: 4 heel 6 dottle
rolled: 5 cigar 9 cigarette
Turkish: 7 latakia

Tobacco Road author
8 Caldwell (Erskine)

to be
Latin: 4 esse

Tobias
father: 5 Tobit
son: 8 Hyrcanus

toby
3 jug, mug 7 pitcher

tocsin
3 SOS 5 alarm, alert 6 signal

today
3 now 9 currently, presently

toddler
3 tot 4 tyke

to-do
4 fuss, rout, stir 5 hoo-ha, rouse, stink,
whirl 6 bother, bustle, clamor, furore,
hubbub, hurrah, pother, ruckus, rumpus,
uproar 7 blather, turmoil 8 foofaraw
9 agitation, commotion 10 hurly-burly
11 disturbance

toe
5 digit
big: 6 hallux

toehold
7 footing

toff
3 fop 4 beau 5 blade, dandy, swell
7 coxcomb, peacock 8 macaroni, popinjay
9 exquisite 12 clotheshorse

toga
4 gown, robe, wrap

together
6 at once, joined, united 7 jointly
8 mutually 10 conjointly 11 concertedly
12 coincidently, collectively, concurrently
prefix: 3 col, com, con, cor, sym, syn

togetherness
5 union 7 cahoots 8 alliance 10 connection, solidarity 11 affiliation,
association, combination, conjunction,
partnership

toggle
3 pin 6 fasten, switch 9 alternate
10 crosspiece

Togo
capital: 4 Lomé
language: 3 Ewe 6 French
monetary unit: 5 franc
neighbor: 5 Benin, Ghana 11 Burkina
Faso

togs
3 rig 4 duds, suit 5 dress 6 attire, outfit
7 apparel, clothes, raiment, rigging
8 clothing, ensemble, garments

To His Coy Mistress author
7 Marvell (Andrew)

toil
3 fag, net, tug 4 grub, plod, plug, slog,
trap, work 5 grind, labor, slave, snare,
sweat 6 drudge 7 slavery, travail
8 drudgery

toiler
4 peon 5 slave 6 drudge, slavey
9 workhorse

toilet
3 loo 4 head, john 5 bidet, potty, privy

6 johnny 7 latrine 8 bathroom, lavatory
11 water closet

toilsome
4 hard 5 heavy 6 uphill 7 arduous,
labored 9 difficult, effortful, laborious,
strenuous

Tokay
4 wine

token
4 buck, chip, gift, mark, note, sign
5 badge, check, favor, index, piece, plume,
prize, relic, scrip 6 copper, emblem,
pledge, symbol, ticket, trophy 7 earnest,
gesture, memento, symptom, warrant
8 evidence, keepsake, memorial, reminder,
security, souvenir 9 indicator 10 expression, indication 11 perfunctory,
remembrance

To Kill a Mockingbird author
3 Lee (Harper)

Tokyo
formerly: 3 Edo
island: 6 Honshu

tolerable
4 fair 6 common, decent 7 livable
8 adequate, all right, bearable, passable
9 endurable 10 acceptable, sufferable
11 respectable 12 satisfactory

tolerably
4 so-so 5 quite 6 fairly, pretty, rather
8 passably 9 averagely 10 moderately

tolerance
6 leeway 8 patience 9 allowance,
endurance, deviation, fortitude, variation
10 indulgence, resistance, sufferance
11 forbearance, habituation

tolerant
4 easy 5 broad 7 lenient, liberal
8 placable 9 easygoing, eurytopic,
forgiving, indulgent, tractable 10 open-
minded, permissive 11 broad-minded,
progressive, sympathetic
13 understanding

tolerate
4 bear, bide, hack 5 abide, allow, brook,
stand 6 accept, endure, pardon, permit,
suffer 7 condone, stomach, swallow
8 bear with, live with 9 put up with
11 countenance

Tolkien creature
3 Ent, Orc 5 Ainur 6 Balrog, Hobbit,
Nazgul, Shelob 9 Oliphaunt

toll
3 fee, tax 4 bell, bong, cost, levy, peal, ring
5 chime, knell, price, sound 6 charge,
summon, tariff 7 expense 8 casualty
10 assessment

tollbooth
11 customhouse

Tolstoy novel
8 Cossacks (The) 11 War and Peace
12 Anna Karenina 16 Death of Ivan Ilich
(The)

tomato
9 love apple

tomb
5 crypt, grave 6 burial 9 mausoleum,
sepulcher, sepulchre, sepulture
ancient Egyptian: 7 mastaba
empty: 8 cenotaph

tomboy
6 gamine, hoyden

tombstone
4 slab 8 memorial, monument 11 grave
marker
inscription: 3 RIP 8 hic jacet

tome
4 book 6 volume

_____ Tomé and Príncipe
3 Sao

tomfool
3 ass 4 dolt, fool, jerk 5 crazy, idiot, loony,
ninny, silly, stupid, wacky 6 absurd, donkey
7 doltish, foolish, jackass 8 clodpoll,
dummkopf, imbecile 9 blockhead,
fantastic, horse's ass, thickhead
10 dunderhead, nincompoop
11 chowderhead, chucklehead,
harebrained 12 preposterous

tomfoolery
4 dido, lark 5 antic, caper, prank, shine,
trick 6 frolic 8 escapade, fandango 9 high
jinks 10 shenanigan 11 monkeyshine

Tom Jones author
8 Fielding (Henry)

tommyrot
4 bull 5 hooey, trash 7 baloney, hogwash,
rubbish 8 claptrap, nonsense
10 balderdash 13 horsefeathers

Tom o'Bedlam
3 nut 4 loon 5 loony 6 madman, maniac
7 lunatic 9 bedlamite

tomorrow
6 future, mañana

Tom Sawyer
author: 5 Twain (Mark) 7 Clemens (Samuel)
character: 5 Becky (Thatcher) 8 Huck Finn, Injun Joe 9 Aunt Polly 10 Muff Potter

Tom Thumb
4 runt 5 dwarf, pygmy 6 midget, peanut, peewee 7 manikin 8 half-pint
10 homunculus 11 lilliputian

ton
3 lot 4 chic 5 bunch, style, trend, vogue 6 bundle 7 fashion

tone
3 hue 4 cast, mode, mood, note, tint, vein 5 color, pitch, shade, style, tinge 6 accent, manner, spirit, strain, temper, timbre 7 fashion 10 inflection

toned down
4 mute, soft 5 sober 6 low-key, mellow 7 subdued 8 laid-back, low-keyed, softened

Tonga
capital: 9 Nuku'alofa
ethnic group: 10 Polynesian
explorer: 4 Cook (Capt. James) 6 Tasman (Abel)
island group: 5 Vava'u 6 Haapai 9 Tongatapu
language: 6 Tongan 7 English
monetary unit: 6 pa'anga

tongue
4 lick, pole, tang 6 glossa, lingua, speech 7 clapper, dialect, languet 8 language 10 vernacular
combining form: 4 glot 5 gloss, lingu 6 glossa, glosso, lingua, lingui, linguo 7 glossia

tongue-lash
4 lash, rail 5 chide, scold 6 berate, rebuke, revile 7 bawl out, chew out, tell off, reprove, upbraid 8 admonish, call down, reproach 9 castigate, reprimand
10 vituperate

tongue-lashing
6 rebuke, tirade 7 censure, reproof 8 scolding 9 reprimand, talking-to 11 castigation 12 dressing-down

tongue-tied
3 mum, shy 4 mute 6 silent 7 bashful 9 diffident 10 speechless 12 inarticulate

tonic
3 pop 4 cola, soda 5 brisk 7 bracing, soda pop 8 curative, salutary 10 refreshing 11 restorative, stimulating 12 exhilarating, invigorating
extract: 4 cola 9 berberine

tons
4 gobs, lots 5 heaps, loads, piles, scads

tony
4 chic, posh 5 smart, swank, swish 6 classy, modish, uptown 7 à la mode, elegant, stylish 9 exclusive 11 fashionable

too
4 also, ever, over, very 5 along 6 as well, overly, unduly, withal 7 awfully, besides, further, greatly 8 likewise, moreover, overmuch 9 extremely, immensely 10 in addition, remarkably, strikingly 11 exceedingly, excessively, furthermore 12 additionally, exorbitantly, immoderately, inordinately 13 exceptionally

tool
4 pawn 5 means 6 puppet, rimmer, stooge 7 cat's-paw, hayfork, machine, rounder, utensil 8 picklock 9 appliance, implement, mechanism 10 instrument
axlike: 4 adze
boring: 5 auger, drill
carving: 6 veiner
cleaving: 4 froe
cobbler's: 3 awl
cutting: 3 axe, saw 4 adze 5 knife 6 shears 8 billhook
digging: 4 pick 5 spade 6 shovel 7 mattock
engraving: 5 burin
farm: 6 seeder
filing: 4 rasp 7 riffler
garden: 3 hoe 4 rake 5 spade 6 trowel, weeder
grasping: 6 pincer 7 tweezer 8 tweezers
mining: 6 trepan
prehistoric: 6 eolith
pruning: 6 shears 8 secateur
rubbing: 9 burnisher
scooping: 6 router
toothed: 3 saw 7 rippler
woodworking: 3 saw 5 bevel, plane 6 chisel, hammer

toot
3 bat, jag 4 bout, bust, tear 5 binge, blast, drunk, snort, sound, souse, spree 6 bender 7 carouse

tooth
5 molar 7 incisor 8 bicuspid, premolar

toothless

combining form: 4 dent 5 denti, dento
cuspid: 6 canine 8 dogtooth, eyetooth
cutting: 10 carnassial
decay: 6 caries
doctor: 7 dentist
pointed: 4 fang 6 canine, cuspid
small: 8 denticle

toothless
7 useless 8 edentate 10 edentulous
11 ineffective, ineffectual

toothsome
5 sapid, tasty 6 delish, savory 8 luscious,
pleasant, pleasing, tasteful 9 agreeable,
delicious, palatable, succulent
10 appetizing, attractive

too-too
6 la-di-da 7 extreme 8 affected, overdone,
overmuch, precious 9 excessive 10 hoity-
toity, inordinate 11 exaggerated,
overrefined, pretentious

tootsie
3 pet 4 dear 5 honey 7 beloved, darling,
sweetie 10 sweetheart

top
3 cap, tip 4 acme, apex, best, cusp, head,
peak, pick, roof 5 cream, crest, crown,
elite, point, prime, prize 6 apical, choice,
climax, height, summit, utmost, vertex
7 capital, highest, maximal, maximum,
surface 8 five-star, loftiest, pinnacle,
superior 9 first-rate, uppermost 10 first-
class 11 culmination

tope
3 nip 4 soak 5 booze, drink, shark, stupa
6 guzzle, imbibe, tipple 7 swizzle 8 liquor
up

toper
3 sot 4 lush, soak, wino 5 drunk, rummy,
souse 6 bibber, boozer 7 tippler, tosspot
8 drunkard 9 inebriate

Tophet
4 hell 5 hades, Sheol 6 blazes
7 Gehenna, inferno 9 perdition
10 underworld

topic
4 talk, text 5 issue, motif, point, score,
theme 6 burden, matter, motive, thread
7 content, subject 8 argument
11 proposition

topical
5 local 7 current, nominal 8 regional
9 temporary 11 superficial

topmost
7 highest, leading, supreme 8 crowning,
ultimate 9 paramount, principal
10 consummate, preeminent
11 culminating

top-notch
5 prime 7 capital, choice 8 five-star,
superior 9 excellent, first-rate 10 first-
class 11 first-string

top off
3 cap 5 crown 6 climax, complete, finish,
refill 8 conclude, resupply 9 culminate

topography
7 surface, terrain 8 features

topple
3 tip 4 drop, fall 5 crash, lurch, pitch,
slump, upset 6 defeat, falter, plunge, totter,
tumble 8 collapse, keel over, overturn
9 overthrow

tops
4 best 5 primo 6 at most 7 highest
8 peerless, superior 9 at the most, first-
rate, matchless 11 outstanding

topsy-turvy
7 chaotic, jumbled, mixed-up 8 cockeyed,
confused, inverted 10 disjointed,
disordered, upside down

toque
3 cap, hat

tor
4 crag, hill, peak 5 butte, cliff, mound, talus

Torah
10 Pentateuch

torch
4 fire 5 flame, light 6 ignite 7 firebug
8 arsonist, flambeau, guidance
10 flashlight, incendiary

toreador
6 torero 7 matador 11 bullfighter

torero
7 matador 11 bullfighter

torment
3 rag, try, vex 4 bait, bane, hell, hurt, pain,
pang, rack 5 abuse, agony, curse, grill,
harry, tease, worry, wring 6 harass, harrow,
heckle, misery, molest, needle, plague
7 afflict, agonize, anguish, crucify, distort,
hagride, torture, travail, trouble 8 distress
9 persecute, tantalize 10 affliction,
excruciate

torn
4 rent 5 split 6 ragged, ripped, unsure 7 mangled 8 tattered, wrenched 9 lacerated, uncertain, undecided

tornado
6 funnel 7 cyclone, twister 9 windstorm, whirlwind

toro
4 bull

torpedo
3 gun, ray 4 mine, thug 5 blast, bravo, smash, wreck 6 gunman, gunsel, hit man, killer, weapon 7 destroy, nullify, scuttle 8 assassin, firework 9 explosive, shoot down 10 hatchet man, projectile, triggerman 11 electric ray

torpid
4 dull, lazy, numb 5 dopey, inert 6 sodden, stupid 7 dormant, inactive 8 comatose, sluggish 9 apathetic, lethargic 12 hebetudinous

torpor
4 coma, daze 5 swoon 6 apathy, stupor 7 languor 8 dopiness, dullness, hebetude, lethargy 9 lassitude, passivity, stolidity 10 stagnation 12 listlessness

torque
5 twist

torrent
4 rush 5 flood, spate 6 deluge, stream 7 cascade, Niagara 8 cataract, flooding 9 cataclysm 10 inundation, outpouring

torrid
3 hot 5 fiery 6 ardent, fervid, heated, red-hot, sultry 7 boiling, burning, flaming, parched 8 broiling, white-hot 9 scorching 10 hot-blooded, passionate, sweltering 11 impassioned

tort
5 crime, wrong 7 offense 10 wrongdoing

tortilla dish
4 taco 6 flauta 7 burrito, chalupa, tostada 9 enchilada 10 quesadilla 11 chimichanga

Tortilla Flat author
9 Steinbeck (John)

tortoise
6 turtle 8 terrapin 9 chelonian
beak: 3 neb
shell: 8 carapace

tortuous
5 snaky 6 cranky, tricky 7 crooked, devious, sinuous, winding 8 flexuous, indirect, involute, involved 9 meandrous 10 circuitous, convoluted, meandering, serpentine 11 anfractuous, labyrinthine, vermiculate

torture
4 pain, rack, warp 5 agony, wring 6 harrow, martyr 7 afflict, agonize, anguish, crucify, torment 9 martyrdom 10 excruciate 11 third degree

tortured
4 bent 6 racked, warped 7 twisted 8 deformed 9 distorted

tory
5 right 7 old-line 8 loyalist, old guard, orthodox, rightist, royalist 12 conservative

Tosca
character: 5 Mario (Cavaradossi)
7 Scarpia (Baron)
composer: 7 Puccini (Giacomo)

_____ Toscanini
6 Arturo

tosh
3 rot 4 bosh, bunk 5 bilge, hooey 6 bunkum, drivel, humbug 7 baloney, eyewash, hogwash, twaddle 8 malarkey, nonsense, tommyrot, trumpery

toss
4 cast, flap, flip, hurl, rock, roll 5 chuck, drink, fling, heave, match, pitch, quaff, sling, surge, throw, vomit 6 imbibe, tumble, welter, writhe 7 discard 9 knock back, throw away

tosspot
see **tippler**

tot
3 add, kid, nip, sum 4 dram, shot, slug, tyke 5 child, snort 6 figure, infant, nipper, shaver, squirt 7 snifter, toddler

total
3 add, all, sum 4 foot, full 5 add up, equal, gross, run to, smash, sum to, utter, whole, wreck, yield 6 all-out, amount, budget, entire, figure, number 7 crack up, destroy, full-out, overall, perfect, plenary, quantum 8 absolute, complete, demolish, entirety, outright, positive, quantity 9 aggregate, full-blown, full-scale, inclusive, out-and-out, unlimited 10 consummate, unreserved 11 unmitigated 13 comprehensive, thoroughgoing

totalitarian
8 absolute, despotic 10 autocratic
11 dictatorial 13 authoritarian

totality
3 all, sum 4 lump 5 whole 7 oneness
8 entirety 9 aggregate, wholeness
12 completeness

totalize
3 add, sum 5 sum up 6 figure 7 summate

tote
3 lug 4 cart, haul, load, pack 5 carry, ferry,
sum up 6 burden, convey, figure
7 summate 9 transport 10 pari-mutuel

totem
6 emblem, symbol

To the Lighthouse author
5 Woolf (Virginia)

totter
4 reel, sway 5 lurch, shake, waver 6 falter,
toddle, topple, wobble 7 stagger

touch
4 abut, feel, meet, move, stir 5 brush,
graze 6 adjoin, border, caress, finger,
stroke 7 contact, palpate 9 palpation,
tactility

touchable
7 tactile 8 palpable, tangible

touch down
4 land 5 light, perch, roost 6 alight, settle

touched
3 odd, off 5 batty, crazy, moved 7 stirred
8 affected 9 emotional

touching
4 as to, in re 5 about, anent, as for
6 moving, tender 7 against, apropos,
emotive, meeting, piteous, pitiful, tangent
8 abutting, adjacent, pathetic, pitiable,
poignant, stirring 9 adjoining, affecting,
apropos of, as regards, bordering,
immediate, impinging, regarding 10 as
respects, back-to-back, concerning,
contiguous, respecting, tangential
11 coterminous 12 conterminous

touch off
5 erupt, spark, start 6 ignite, incite, kindle
7 explode, inflame, provoke, trigger
8 initiate 9 instigate 11 precipitate

touchstone
4 test 5 check, gauge, proof, trial
7 measure 8 standard 9 barometer,
benchmark, criterion, yardstick

touch up
3 fix 5 patch 6 rework 7 improve, perfect

touchy
5 dicey, huffy, risky, testy 6 tender, tricky
7 peppery 8 delicate, ticklish 9 explosive,
hazardous, irascible, irritable, sensitive
10 precarious 11 inflammable,
quarrelsome, thin-skinned
13 oversensitive, temperamental,
unpredictable

tough
3 bad, mug 4 goon, hard, hood, lout, punk,
stud, thug 5 bully, hardy, harsh 6 rugged,
severe, sturdy, unruly 7 arduous, hoodlum,
onerous, ruffian 8 bullyboy, exacting,
hooligan, obdurate 9 arbitrary, demanding,
difficult, effortful, hard-nosed, hidebound,
immutable, laborious, resistant, roughneck,
strenuous 10 hard-bitten, hard-boiled,
hardheaded, inflexible, refractory,
unyielding 11 intractable, unbreakable
12 pertinacious

toughen
5 inure 6 anneal, harden, season, temper
9 acclimate, habituate 10 strengthen
11 acclimatize

toughie
4 goon, hood, lout, punk, thug 5 poser,
rowdy 7 hoodlum, ruffian, stumper
8 bullyboy, hooligan, plug-ugly
9 roughneck

toupee
3 rug, wig 6 peruke, wiglet 7 periwig
8 postiche 9 hairpiece

tour
4 bout, trip, turn 5 jaunt, round, shift, spell,
stint 6 junket, period, travel, troupe
7 circuit, journey 8 progress 9 barnstorm,
excursion 10 expedition, rubberneck

tour de force
4 deed, feat 7 classic, display, exploit
10 magnum opus, masterwork
11 achievement, chef d'oeuvre,
masterpiece

tour guide
8 cicerone

tourist
7 tripper, visitor 8 traveler 9 sightseer,
traveller 10 day-tripper, rubberneck,
vacationer 12 excursionist, globe-trotter

tournament
4 open, tilt 5 pro-am 6 jousts, series

7 contest, tourney **8** carousel **10** round-robin **11** competition **12** championship

tourney
4 meet **5** event, games, match **7** compete, concours, contest **11** competition

tousle
4 mess, muss **6** rumple **8** dishevel, disorder

tout
3 spy, tip **4** brag, laud, plug **5** watch **6** blow up, peddle, praise, talk up **7** acclaim, crack up, promote, solicit **8** ballyhoo, persuade, proclaim **9** publicize

tovarich
7 comrade

tow
3 lug, tug **4** drag, draw, haul, pull, rope, yarn **5** chain, trail **6** hawser
truck: 7 wrecker

towel word
3 his **4** hers

tower
4 loom **5** spire **6** turret **8** overlook
on a mosque: 7 minaret

towering
4 high, tall **5** grand, great, lofty **6** aerial, mighty **7** extreme, soaring, stately **8** imposing, majestic **9** excessive, grandiose **10** exorbitant, immoderate, inordinate, monumental, prodigious **11** extravagant, magnificent, skyscraping **12** altitudinous, overwhelming

towhee
5 finch **7** chewink

to wit
3 viz **6** namely **8** scilicet **9** c'est-à-dire, videlicet

town
4 burg **6** hamlet, podunk **7** borough, village
medieval: 5 bourg

town and ____
4 gown **7** country

townsman
7 burgher, citizen

town square
5 plaza
Italian: 6 piazza

toxic
6 poison **7** harmful **8** venomous, virulent **9** poisonous **10** infectious

toxin
5 venom **6** poison

toy
4 fool, play **5** antic, curio, dally, flirt, knack, mouse, tease **6** bauble, caress, coquet, diddle, fiddle, gewgaw, trifle **7** bibelot, novelty, pastime, trinket, whatnot **8** gimcrack **9** plaything **10** diminutive, knickknack

trace
3 jot, ray, run, tug **4** blip, echo, hint, iota, mark, path, scan, wisp **5** relic, shade, tinge, trail, tread **6** derive, detect, nuance, shadow, strain, streak **7** outline, remains, remnant, run down, soupçon, symptom, vestige **8** discover, tincture, traverse **9** delineate, footprint, remainder, scintilla, suspicion **10** intimation, suggestion

trachea
6 larynx, throat, vessel **7** weasand **8** throttle, windpipe

track
3 way **4** drag, path, road, sign, step, tail **5** chase, cover, print, spoor, trace, trail, tread **6** artery, follow, pursue, shadow, travel **7** footway, imprint, monitor, pathway, vestige **8** footpath, footstep **9** footprint

track-and-field event
4 dash **5** relay **6** discus **7** javelin, hurdles, shot put **8** footrace, high jump, long jump **9** broad jump, decathlon, pole vault **10** heptathlon, triple jump **11** discus throw **12** steeplechase

tract
3 lot **4** area, belt, farm, land, plat, plot, zone **5** block, claim **6** parcel, region **7** leaflet, portion, terrain **8** pamphlet, preserve **9** territory

tractable
4 tame **6** docile, gentle, pliant **7** ductile, plastic, pliable **8** amenable, biddable, flexible, obedient, workable **9** adaptable, malleable **10** manageable

tractate
5 summa **6** memoir, thesis **7** pandect **8** hornbook, monument, treatise **9** discourse, monograph **10** commentary **12** disquisition, dissertation, introduction

traction
4 drag, pull **5** force **7** drawing, tension **8** friction

tractor maker
5 Deere (John)

trade

4 deal, sell, swap 5 craft, truck 6 barter,
change, custom, market, métier, peddle,
switch 7 bargain, calling, pursuit, traffic
8 business, commerce, exchange, industry,
vocation 10 employment, occupation,
profession, substitute, transaction
11 merchandise
illicit: 11 black market

trademark

3 tag 4 logo 5 brand, label, stamp
6 patent, symbol 8 colophon, logotype
9 brand name

trader

4 ship 6 broker, dealer, vendor 8 merchant

trade route

7 sea-lane

tradition

4 lore, myth 5 habit 6 belief, custom,
legacy, legend, mythos, rubric 7 folkway
8 folklore, heredity, heritage, practice
9 mythology 10 convention 12 old wives'
tale

traditional

4 oral 5 usual 6 common, spoken, verbal
7 classic, old-line, popular 8 habitual,
orthodox 9 classical, customary, old-
school, unwritten 10 button-down
11 established 12 acknowledged,
buttoned-down, conservative, conventional

traditionalist

6 purist 12 conservative

traditionalistic

4 tory 7 die-hard, old-line 8 orthodox,
standpat 12 conservative

traduce

4 slur 5 libel, smear, wrong 6 betray,
breach, defame, malign, vilify 7 asperse,
slander, violate 8 disgrace, tear down
9 denigrate 10 calumniate

Trafalgar commander

6 Nelson (Horatio)

traffic

4 deal 5 cargo, fence, trade, truck
6 barter, custom 7 bootleg, freight
8 commerce, dealings, exchange,
movement 9 patronage, transport
11 black-market
circle: 6 rotary 10 roundabout
cone: 5 pylon
jam: 5 tie-up 6 holdup 8 gridlock
10 bottleneck

trafficker

6 dealer, trader

tragedy

3 woe 6 mishap, plague 8 calamity,
disaster 9 cataclysm, mischance
10 misfortune 11 catastrophe
12 misadventure

trail

3 dog, lag, tag 4 drag, flag, path, plod,
poke 5 chase, dally, delay, tarry, trace,
track 6 dawdle, follow, linger, pursue,
shadow 7 draggle, gumshoe, pathway,
traipse 8 footpath, footwalk 10 bridle path
emigrant: 6 Oregon
Florida: 7 Tamiami
Georgia-Maine: 11 Appalachian
Indian: 5 Great

trailer

5 truck 7 preview 9 motor home, transport
10 mobile home

trailer truck

4 semi

train

3 row 4 file, tame 5 coach, drill, teach,
track 6 convoy, course, school, sequel,
series, thread 7 caravan, column, cortege,
educate, prepare, retinue 8 exercise,
instruct, sequence 9 cultivate, entourage,
following, habituate 10 succession
11 progression

trainee

6 novice 7 learner, new hire 8 beginner
10 apprentice

training

7 tuition 8 teaching, tutelage 9 education,
schooling 11 instruction
horses: 6 manège

traipse

3 gad 4 hoof, pace, roam, rove, step, walk
5 amble, range, trail, tramp, tread
6 ramble, stroll, wander 7 maunder,
meander 8 ambulate 9 gallivant

trait

4 mark 5 point, quirk, trace 6 oddity
7 feature, quality 8 hallmark, property,
specific 9 attribute

traitor

5 Judas 8 apostate, betrayer, defector,
deserter, quisling, renegade, turncoat
9 turnabout

traitorous

5 Punic 8 apostate, disloyal, mutinous,
recreant, renegade 9 faithless

10 perfidious, rebellious, unfaithful
11 treacherous

traject
4 beam, pass, pipe, send 5 carry
6 convey, render 7 conduct, forward,
impress 8 hand down, transfer, transmit
9 broadcast, transfuse

tram
3 car 7 trolley 9 streetcar

trammel
3 tie 4 bind, curb 5 check, gauge, leash
6 fetter, hamper, hobble 7 compass,
confine, ensnare, manacle, pothook,
shackle 8 entangle, handcuff 9 restraint

tramontane
8 outsider 9 foreigner, outlander
11 transalpine

tramp
3 bum 4 hike, hobo, jade, plod, slog, stiff,
thud 5 bimbo, caird, clump, gypsy, march,
stamp, stomp, tread 6 ramble, stroll, travel,
trudge, wander 7 chippie, clochard, drifter,
floater, saunter, stroller, traipse, vagrant
8 derelict, footslog, homeless, vagabond
10 prostitute

trample
4 mash 5 crush, pound, stamp, stomp,
tread, tromp

trance
4 daze, muse 5 swoon 7 ecstasy, rapture,
reverie 8 hypnosis 9 catalepsy, enrapture
10 absorption, brown study 11 abstraction

tranquil
4 calm, easy 5 quiet, still 6 dreamy, placid,
poised, serene 7 restful 8 composed,
peaceful 10 untroubled 13 self-possessed

tranquilize
4 calm, hush, lull 5 quiet, relax, still
6 becalm, pacify, sedate, settle, soothe,
subdue 7 compose, mollify

tranquilizer
6 downer 8 diazepam, pacifier, sedative
10 depressant 11 barbiturate

tranquillity
4 calm 5 peace, quiet 8 calmness,
serenity 9 composure, placidity

transaction
4 deal 5 trade 7 bargain, dealing
8 contract, covenant 9 agreement

transcend
3 top 4 beat, best 5 excel, outdo 6 better,
exceed 7 surpass 8 outshine, outstrip,
overcome, surmount

transcendent
5 ideal 7 perfect, sublime, supreme
8 abstract, immanent 10 consummate,
surpassing

Transcendentalist
6 Alcott (Bronson), Fuller (Margaret)
7 Emerson (Ralph Waldo), Thoreau (Henry
David)

transcribe
4 copy 5 write 6 record 8 transfer
9 translate, write down 13 transliterate

transfer
4 cede, deed, hand, pass, ship 5 carry,
grant, shift 6 assign, convey, remove,
supply 7 consign, convert, deliver, devolve,
dispose 8 alienate, hand over, make over,
relocate, turn over 9 carry over
10 assignment, conveyance 11 disposition

transfix
4 spit 5 lance, spear, spike, stick 6 impale,
skewer 7 spindle 8 entrance 9 fascinate,
hypnotize, mesmerize

transform
5 alter, morph 6 change, mutate
7 commute, convert 12 metamorphose

transformation
8 reaction 10 changeover, conversion
13 metamorphosis

transfuse
5 endue, imbue 7 pervade, suffuse, traject
8 permeate, saturate 9 penetrate,
percolate 10 impregnate

transgress
3 err, sin 6 breach, exceed, offend
7 violate 8 infringe, overpass, overstep,
trespass 10 contravene

transgression
3 sin 5 crime, error, wrong 6 breach
7 misdeed, offense 9 violation 12 infringement

transient
4 hobo 5 brief, tramp 7 drifter, migrant,
passing 8 fleeting, flitting, fugitive, volatile
9 ephemeral, fugacious, momentary,
temporary 10 evanescent, fly-by-night,
short-lived 11 impermanent

transit
7 passage 8 traverse 10 conveyance

transition
5 segue, shift 6 change 7 passage
10 conversion 13 metamorphosis

transitory
see **transient**

translate
6 render 7 convert 9 interpret, reproduce
10 paraphrase

translation
9 rendition 10 conversion, paraphrase

transmarine
7 oversea 8 overseas

transmission
7 gearbox 8 handover 9 broadcast,
infection

transmit
3 air 4 beam, hand, pass, pipe, send
6 convey, hand on, impart, pass on, render,
signal 7 channel, conduct, consign,
diffuse, forward, traject 8 bequeath,
dispatch, hand down 9 broadcast

transmogrify
see **transform**

transmute
see **transform**

transoceanic message
4 wire 5 cable 9 cablegram

transparent
5 clear, filmy, gauzy, sheer 6 limpid
7 crystal 8 clear-cut, gossamer, pellucid
10 diaphanous, see-through 11 crystalline

transpire
3 hap 4 leak 5 exude, occur, sweat
6 chance, emerge, happen 7 develop
9 come about, take place 11 come to light

transplant
8 relocate, resettle

transport
3 bus, fly, lag, lug, wow, zap, zip 4 haul,
hump, lift, pack, pass, send, ship, taxi, tote
5 carry, ferry, motor, truck 6 convey, excite,
ravish, remove, thrill 7 delight, ecstasy,
freight, rapture, sealift, trundle, vehicle
8 carriage, displace, railroad, rhapsody
9 carry away, chauffeur, troopship
10 conveyance, helicopter

transportation
6 moving 7 freight, hauling, removal,
vehicle 8 carriage, carrying 10 conveyance 12 displacement

transpose
6 invert 7 convert, permute, reorder,
reverse 9 rearrange 11 interchange

transude
4 ooze, reek, seep, weep 5 bleed, sweat
7 diffuse, give off 8 permeate 9 transfuse

transverse
5 cross 6 across, thwart 8 crossbar,
crossing 9 crossbeam, crosswise
10 crosspiece

trap
3 bag, net 4 bait, snag 5 catch, decoy, set
up, snare 6 ambush, enmesh, tangle
7 ensnare, pitfall 8 birdlime, deadfall,
entangle, quagmire 9 ambuscade

trappings
4 gear 5 dress 6 finery 8 equipage,
ornament 9 adornment, caparison,
equipment 10 decoration 11 habiliments
13 accouterments, accoutrements,
embellishment, paraphernalia

Trappist
4 monk
writer: 6 Merton (Thomas)

trash
3 rag, rot 4 bosh, junk, ruin, scum, slop
5 bilge, blast, dreck, dregs, hokum, offal,
spoil, tripe, waste, wreck 6 bunkum,
debris, insult, litter, refuse, rubble 7 clutter,
destroy, garbage, hogwash, put down,
rubbish 8 claptrap, malarkey, nonsense
9 disparage, throw away, vandalize
10 balderdash 11 guttersnipe, proletariat

trash can
7 dustbin

trashy
5 bawdy, cheap, tatty 6 cruddy, shoddy,
sleazy, smutty, vulgar 8 rubbishy 9 third-
rate

trauma
4 blow, pain 5 shock, upset, wound
6 crisis, injury, stress 8 collapse
9 suffering

travail
4 grub, moil, task, toil, work 5 grind, labor,
pains 6 drudge, effort 7 slavery, torment
8 drudgery, struggle

travel
4 fare, pass, roam, tour, trek, trip, wend
5 jaunt, tramp 6 junket, push on, voyage
7 explore, journey, passage, proceed,
traffic, transit 8 movement, traverse
9 gallivant 10 hit the road

traveler
5 gypsy 7 drummer, tourist 8 salesman,

vagabond **9** itinerant, journeyman, sightseer **11** peripatetic

traveling library
10 bookmobile

traverse
4 ride, route, walk **5** cover, cross, march, trace, track **6** course, thwart, travel, voyage **7** transit **8** crossing, navigate, pass over **10** crisscross **11** perambulate, peregrinate

travesty
3 ape **4** mock, sham **5** farce, mimic, spoof **6** parody **7** imitate, lampoon, mimicry, mockery, take off **8** ridicule **9** burlesque **10** caricature, distortion
satanic: 9 Black Mass

Traviata, La
character: 7 Alfredo (Germont), Germont **8** Violetta (Valéry)
composer: 5 Verdi (Giuseppe)

trawl
3 net **4** fish **7** setline

tray
6 salver, server **7** platter **8** teaboard
revolving: 9 lazy Susan

treacherous
5 false, Punic, risky **6** chancy, tricky **7** unsound **8** disloyal, perilous, recreant **9** dangerous, deceptive, faithless, hazardous, insidious **10** perfidious, traitorous, unfaithful, unreliable

treachery
7 perfidy, treason **8** bad faith, betrayal **10** disloyalty, infidelity **11** double-cross **13** dastardliness, double-dealing, faithlessness

treacle
4 mush **5** slush, syrup **8** molasses, schmaltz **11** golden syrup

tread
4 hoof, pace, plod, step, walk **5** dance, march, stamp, stomp, trace, track, tramp, tromp, troop **6** follow, stride **7** footing, traipse, trample **8** footstep

treadle
5 lever, pedal

treadmill
3 rut **4** rote **5** chore, grind **6** groove **7** routine **8** drudgery, turnspit

treason
7 perfidy **8** betrayal, sedition **9** treachery **10** disloyalty, misprision

treasure
4 haul, save **5** adore, cache, hoard, pearl, prize, trove, value **6** esteem, revere, riches, wealth **7** apprize, cherish, idolize, worship **8** conserve, preserve, venerate **9** reverence **10** appreciate

Treasure Island
author: 9 Stevenson (Robert Louis)
character: 7 Ben Gunn **8** Long John (Silver)
narrator: 10 Jim Hawkins

treasurer
6 bursar, purser **7** curator **8** receiver **11** chamberlain

Treasure State
7 Montana

treasure trove
4 find, mine **7** bonanza, pay dirt **8** El Dorado, Golconda, gold mine

treasury
4 fisc, mine **5** cache, chest, hoard **6** argosy, coffer, museum **7** bonanza, gallery, omnibus **8** archives, El Dorado, Golconda, gold mine, war chest **9** anthology, exchequer **10** depositary, depository, repository, storehouse

treat
5 goody, nurse **6** bonbon, dainty, doctor, goodie, handle, manage, morsel, tidbit **7** care for **8** deal with, delicacy, medicate **10** minister to
animals: 3 vet
leather: 3 tan, taw **7** tanning

treatise
6 thesis **8** tractate **9** discourse, monograph **10** exposition **12** disquisition, dissertation

treatment
4 care **7** therapy

treaty
4 pact **6** accord **7** charter, compact, concord **8** alliance, contract, covenant **9** agreement, concordat **10** convention

treble
4 high **6** shrill, triple **7** descant, soprano **9** threefold **11** high-pitched

tree
African: 4 akee, cola, shea **5** limba, sassy **6** baobab **7** avodire, bubinga **8** sasswood **9** berberine
Asian: 4 dhak, upas **6** banyan, kamala
Australian: 7 blue gum **8** lacewood, quandong **9** casuarina

branch: 5 bough
Brazilian: 3 apa, ule 7 arariba, seringa, wallaba
Chinese: 4 tung 5 yulan 6 ginkgo, lychee 7 kumquat
citrus: 4 lime 5 lemon 6 orange 8 bergamot
combining form: 3 dry 4 dryo 5 dendr 6 dendra (plural), dendro
coniferous: 3 fir, yew 4 pine 5 alder, cedar, larch 6 spruce 7 cypress, hemlock, juniper, redwood, sequoia
dwarf: 8 arbuscle 10 chinquapin
East Indian: 4 neem, poon, teak, toon 6 banyan, deodar 7 deodara
elm: 4 wych
Eurasian: 5 abele, rowan 6 medlar
European: 5 osier 8 bourtree, caprifig
European oak: 7 murmast
evergreen: 3 fir, yew 4 atle, pine, titi 5 athel, carob, cedar, piñon, taxus 6 arbute, loquat, mallee, sapota 7 arbutus, camphor, conifer, inkwood, juniper, lentisk, madrona, madrone, redwood, sequoia 8 loblolly, longleaf, tamarisk 9 balsam fir 12 balm of Gilead
evergreen oak: 6 encina
fig: 5 pipal
flowering: 5 sumac 6 acacia 7 dogwood 8 sourwood
hardwood: 3 oak 5 beech, birch, ebony, maple 6 cherry, cornel, walnut 7 hickory 8 chestnut, mahogany
Japanese: 4 kaki 7 zelkova
linden: 8 basswood
mulberry: 8 sycamine
North African: 5 babul
nut-bearing: 4 cola, kola 5 hazel, pecan, piñon 6 almond, cashew 7 buckeye, filbert, hickory 9 pistachio
oak: 5 roble 8 bluejack
ornamental: 3 box 5 holly 6 ginkgo, mimosa, myrtle, redbud 8 laburnum, magnolia 9 poinciana 12 rhododendron
palm: 4 coco, nipa 5 ratan 6 pinang, raffia, rattan 7 coquito 8 carnauba
Peruvian: 8 cinchona
Philippine: 4 dita, pili 6 bataan 10 calamondin
resinous: 10 candlewood
rubber: 5 ule
shade: 3 elm, oak 5 maple 6 linden 8 sycamore 10 chinaberry
softwood: 5 alamo 6 tupelo 8 black gum, corkwood
(see also **coniferous**)
South American: 3 apa 4 ombu 7 wallaba 9 Brazil nut
swamp: 11 bald cypress

tropical: 4 akee, ohia, palm, sago, teak 5 areca, assai, balsa, cacao, ceiba, lehua, mamey 6 acajou, balata, baobab, citrus 7 genipap, logwood, majagua, palmyra, quassia, soursop 8 allspice, barbasco, mahogany, mangrove, milkwood, palmetto, rosewood, soapbark, sweetsop, tamarind 9 candlenut, jacaranda 10 breadfruit, manchineel 11 candleberry, coconut palm
trunk: 4 bole
willow: 5 osier, sauch, saugh 6 poplar
young: 7 sapling

trefoil
4 leaf 6 clover
part: 3 arc

trek
4 hike, trip 6 travel, trudge 7 journey 9 migration 10 expedition

trellis
5 arbor 6 screen 7 lattice, pergola 8 espalier 11 latticework

tremble
5 quake, shake 6 dither, quaver, quiver, shiver 7 shudder, twitter, vibrate

tremblor
see temblor

tremendous
4 huge, vast 6 mighty, raging 7 awesome, immense, massive, titanic 8 colossal, enormous, fearsome, gigantic, terrific, towering 9 fantastic, monstrous 10 formidable, gargantuan, incredible, monumental, prodigious, stupendous 13 extraordinary

tremolo
7 vibrato

tremor
5 quake, shock 6 quaver, quiver, shiver 7 shudder, temblor 10 earthquake
muscular: 8 dystaxia

tremulous
5 shaky, timid 6 afraid 7 aquiver, fearful, quaking, shivery 8 timorous 9 quivering, shivering

trench
4 sink 5 ditch, fosse, gully, verge 6 border, furrow, trough
Caribbean: 6 Cayman

trenchant
4 keen 5 crisp, sharp 6 biting 7 caustic, cutting, mordant, probing, satiric 8 clearcut, distinct, incisive, sardonic, scathing 9 sarcastic 11 penetrating

trencher
4 tray 7 platter

trencherman
7 glutton

trend
3 fad, run 4 flow, mode 5 curve, drift, shift, style, swing, tenor, vogue 6 course, temper 7 current, fashion, incline 8 approach, movement, tendency 9 direction

trendy
3 hep, hip, hot 4 cool, tony 5 faddy 6 groovy, modish, with-it 7 à la mode, faddish, stylish 8 downtown, nouvelle, up-to-date 11 fashionable, ultramodern

trepang
10 bêche-de-mer

trepidation
4 fear 5 alarm, dread 6 dismay 7 anxiety 12 apprehension 13 consternation

trespass
3 err, sin 4 debt 5 lapse, poach 6 breach, invade, offend 7 impinge, intrude 8 encroach, entrench, infringe 9 interlope, violation 10 infraction, transgress 12 encroachment, infringement 13 transgression

tress
4 curl, lock 5 braid, plait

trestle
4 buck 6 bridge 7 sawbuck 8 sawhorse

trey
5 three

triad
4 trio 5 chord 6 triple, troika 7 harmony, trinity 9 threesome 11 triumvirate

trial
3 woe 4 care, test 5 agony, cross, essay, grief, rigor, worry 6 dry run, hassle, misery, ordeal, sorrow, tryout 7 anguish, attempt, contest, trouble 8 crucible, distress, endeavor, gauntlet, hardship, struggle, vexation 9 adversity, rehearsal, suffering 10 affliction, coup d'essai, difficulty, experiment, misfortune, proceeding, temptation 11 preliminary, tribulation 12 experimental

trial balloon
6 feeler, tryout

trial run
4 test 5 essay 7 break-in 10 experiment

triangle type
5 acute, right 6 obtuse 7 scalene 9 isosceles 11 equilateral

tribal unit
6 moiety 7 phratry

tribe
4 clan, folk, race 5 house, stock 6 family 7 kindred, lineage

tribulation
3 woe 5 cross, trial 6 burden, ordeal 9 adversity 10 affliction, oppression, visitation 11 persecution

tribunal
3 bar 4 dais 5 bench, court 8 platform 10 consistory 12 court of honor

tributary
5 bayou, creek 6 branch, feeder, stream 7 subject 8 affluent, influent 9 backwater, confluent, dependent, satellite 12 contributory

tribute
5 paean 6 eulogy 8 citation, encomium 9 panegyric 10 salutation 11 recognition, testimonial 12 appreciation

trice
4 lash, wink 5 blink, flash, jiffy, shake 6 moment, second, secure 7 instant 8 eyeblink 9 twinkling 11 split second

trick
3 jig 4 dido, dupe, fool, gull, hoax, lark, play, ploy, ruse, sham 5 antic, caper, dodge, feint, fraud, prank, stunt 6 gambit, outwit, scheme 7 chicane, finagle, gimmick, sleight 8 escapade, flimflam, hoodwink 9 bamboozle, deception, stratagem, victimize 10 red herring, shenanigan, tomfoolery 11 hornswoggle, monkeyshine 13 practical joke

trickery
4 scam, wile 5 cheat, fraud 6 deceit 7 chicane, dodgery 8 jugglery 9 chicanery, deception 10 subterfuge 11 double cross 13 double-dealing, jiggery-pokery, sharp practice

trickle
4 drip, seep 5 creep, trill 7 dribble

trickster
5 cheat, shark 7 cheater, diddler, grifter, sharper 8 conjurer, deceiver, magician, swindler 9 defrauder 11 flimflammer, illusionist 12 double-dealer

tricksy
5 rough 6 trying 7 arduous 8 prankish

tricky
3 sly 4 foxy, wily 5 dodgy 6 catchy, clever,

crafty, shifty, sticky, touchy, trying
7 cunning, knavish, thorny 8 delusive,
guileful, slippery, ticklish, tortuous, unstable
9 deceptive, difficult, dishonest, ingenious,
intricate 10 misleading, nettlesome,
precarious, unreliable 11 complicated,
treacherous, troublesome
12 undependable

trident
5 spear

tried
6 proved, proven, secure, tested, trusty
7 staunch 8 approved, faithful, reliable,
true-blue 9 certified, steadfast
10 dependable 11 trustworthy

tried and true
6 proven, secure, tested, trusty 8 reliable
10 dependable 11 trustworthy

trifle
3 bob, fig, pin, toy 4 doit, fool, mess, play
5 curio, dally, flirt, sport, waste 6 bauble,
coquet, diddle, doodle, fiddle, fidget, footle,
frivol, gewgaw, monkey, niggle 7 bibelot,
conceit, fribble, fritter, novelty, trinket,
twiddle, whatnot 8 folderol, gimcrack,
kickshaw, nonsense, squander 9 bagatelle, cream puff, dalliance 10 knickknack,
triviality 11 small change

trifling
4 tiny 5 petty 6 measly, paltry 7 trivial
8 niggling, picayune, piddling 9 frivolous,
worthless 10 negligible 11 unimportant
13 insignificant

trifolium
6 clover 8 shamrock

trig
4 chic, neat, prim, snug, tidy, trim 5 sharp,
smart, swank, trick 6 classy, modish,
snappy 7 chipper, dashing, orderly,
precise, stylish 9 shipshape

trigger
4 fire 5 cause, spark, start 6 ignite, kindle,
set off 7 actuate, release 8 activate,
initiate, touch off

triggerman
3 gun 5 bravo 6 gunsel, killer 7 torpedo
8 assassin 9 cutthroat, pistolero

trigonometric function
see at **function**

trill
4 burr, drop, roll 5 chirr, shake, twirl

6 quaver, warble 7 dribble, revolve, trickle,
twitter, vibrato

trillion
  combining form: 4 tera, treg 5 trega

trillionth
  combining form: 4 pico

trim
3 cut, fit 4 clip, crop, deck, neat, pare,
snug, tidy, trig 5 adorn, order, prune,
shape, shave, shear, skive 6 barber,
dapper, fettle, kilter, repair, spruce
7 chipper, dress up, garnish, orderly,
shapely 8 clean-cut, decorate, manicure
9 shipshape 11 spic-and-span,
streamlined, well-groomed 12 spick-and-
span
  a tree: 5 prune 7 pollard

Trinidad and Tobago
  capital: 11 Port of Spain
  language: 7 English
  monetary unit: 6 dollar
  sea: 9 Caribbean

trinity
see **triad**

trinket
3 toy 5 curio, jewel 6 bauble, doodad,
gewgaw, trifle 7 bibelot, novelty, whatnot
8 gimcrack, kickshaw 9 bagatelle,
plaything, tchotchke 10 knickknack

trinkets
10 bijouterie

trio of goddesses
5 Fates 6 Furies, Graces

trip
3 hop, run 4 fall, ride, skip, slip, step, tour,
trek 5 boner, caper, dance, error, lapse
6 bungle, junket, outing, sashay, travel,
tumble, voyage 7 blooper, blunder,
journey, mistake, misstep, stumble
9 excursion 10 expedition

tripe
4 guts 5 bilge, trash 6 waffle, viscus
7 innards, viscera (plural) 8 entrails,
stuffing 9 internals

triple
4 trio 5 triad, trine 6 treble, triune, troika
7 triform, trilogy, trinity 8 trifecta
9 threefold, threesome 11 three-bagger,
triumvirate

Triple Crown winner
  1919: 9 Sir Barton
  1930: 10 Gallant Fox

tripped out
4 high 5 doped 6 stoned, zonked
7 drugged 8 hopped-up, turned on, wiped
out 9 spaced-out 10 freaked-out

Tristan's beloved
6 Iseult, Isolde

Tristan und Isolde composer
6 Wagner (Richard)

triste
3 sad 5 sorry 7 doleful, pensive, wistful
8 mournful 9 depressed, sorrowful
10 melancholy 11 melancholic

Tristram Shandy author
6 Sterne (Laurence)

trite
3 pat, set 4 dull, flat, hack 5 banal, corny,
musty, slick, stale, stock, tired, vapid
6 cliché, common, jejune, old-hat
7 prosaic, worn out 8 bathetic, bromidic,
flyblown, ordinary, shopworn, timeworn,
well-worn 9 hackneyed 10 threadbare
11 commonplace, stereotyped 13 platitudinous, stereotypical

triton
5 conch 7 mollusc, mollusk 9 shellfish

Triton
6 merman
attribute: 5 conch
father: 7 Neptune 8 Poseidon
mother: 10 Amphitrite

triturate
4 bray 5 crush, grind 6 powder
9 comminute, pulverize

triumph
3 joy, win 4 crow, palm 5 exult, glory,
vaunt 6 master 7 conquer, prevail,
succeed, success, victory 8 conquest,
overcome, surmount 10 exultation,
jubilation

triumphant
8 exultant, exulting, jubilant 10 conquering,
victorious

triumvirate
see **triad**

Triumvirate, First
member: 6 Caesar (Julius), Pompey (the
Great) 7 Crassus (Marcus Licinius)

Triumvirate, Second
member: 6 Antony (Marc) 7 Lepidus
(Marcus Aemilius) 8 Octavius (Gaius)

trivet
4 rack 5 stand 6 tripod

trivia
8 factoids, minutiae 9 small beer 11 small
change 13 small potatoes

trivial
5 light, minor, petty, small 6 casual,
measly, paltry, piddly, slight 8 picayune,
piddling, piffling, trifling 9 small-beer
10 negligible 11 Mickey Mouse,
unimportant 13 insignificant

troche
6 tablet 7 lozenge 8 pastille 9 cough drop

troglodyte
6 hermit 7 caveman, recluse 11 cave
dweller

Troilus
beloved: 8 Cressida, Criseyde
father: 5 Priam
mother: 6 Hecuba
slayer: 8 Achilles

Trojan
horse builder: 5 Epeus
king: 5 Priam
priest: 7 Laocoon
soothsayer: 7 Helenus 9 Cassandra
warrior: 5 Paris 6 Aeneas, Agenor, Hector
9 Euphorbus

Trojan Horse builder
5 Epeus 6 Epeius

troll
4 fish, lure, sing, spin 5 angle, dwarf, prowl
6 goblin, search

trolley
3 car 4 cart, tram 8 carriage 9 streetcar

Trollope novel
10 Claverings (The) 11 Ayala's Angel,
Phineas Finn 12 Phineas Redux 12 Way
We Live Now (The) 15 Eustace Diamonds
(The) 16 Barchester Towers

trombone
7 sackbut

tromp
4 beat, drub, hike, pelt, slog, walk 5 pound, stamp, stomp, stump, tramp, tread
6 batter, buffet, pummel, thrash, trudge
7 belabor, trample 8 lambaste

troop
4 army, band, crew, host, pace, step, walk
5 corps, crowd, flock, tread 6 legion, outfit
7 brigade, company, soldier, traipse
8 assembly 9 associate, battalion, gathering, multitude 10 collection

trooper
3 cop 5 actor, horse 7 soldier
9 policeman 10 cavalryman

trope
6 cliché, simile 8 metaphor, metonymy
10 synecdoche

Trophonius
brother: 8 Agamedes
temple site: 6 Delphi

trophy
3 cup 5 award, prize, relic, scalp, token
6 spoils 7 memento 8 hardware, keepsake, memorial, reminder, souvenir
9 loving cup 11 remembrance

tropical
3 hot 4 lush, warm 5 balmy, humid
6 jungly, steamy, sultry, torrid 10 equatorial

tropical storm
see typhoon

Tropic of Cancer author
6 Miller (Henry)

Tros' son
4 Ilus 8 Ganymede

trot
3 jog 4 gait, lope, pony, rack 5 amble, hurry
7 setline 11 translation

troth
6 commit, engage, pledge 7 loyalty
8 affiance, contract, espousal, fidelity
10 engagement 12 faithfulness

trot out
4 show 6 expose, parade 7 display, disport, exhibit, show off

Trotsky, Leon
associate: 5 Lenin (Vladimir)
rival: 6 Stalin (Joseph)

troubadour
4 bard, poet 6 singer 8 jongleur, minstrel, musician 9 balladist 10 folksinger

trouble
3 ado, ail, ill, irk, try, vex, woe 4 care, fret, fuss, pain 5 annoy, beset, Dutch, grief, harry, haunt, pains, trial, upset, worry
6 bother, doo-doo, effort, harass, impose, kiaugh, misery, pester, plague, put out, ruffle, strain, stress, unrest 7 afflict, agitate, ailment, bedevil, concern, disturb, oppress, perturb, torment 8 aggrieve, disquiet, distress, exertion, hardship, hot water, irritate, vexation 9 beleaguer, importune, suffering 10 difficulty, disconcert 11 disturbance, predicament

troubled
6 uneasy 7 anxious, worried 9 concerned, disturbed 10 distressed

troublemaker
7 hellion 8 agitator 9 firebrand
10 instigator 11 provocateur 12 rabble-rouser

troublesome
5 pesky 6 thorny, tricky, trying, vexing
7 carking, onerous, prickly 8 annoying, difficult 9 upsetting, vexatious
10 bothersome, burdensome, cumbersome, disturbing 11 disquieting, importunate, pestiferous

troublous
5 pesky 6 rugged, stormy 7 onerous
9 turbulent, vexatious 10 tumultuous
11 tempestuous

trough
3 hod 4 bowl, tank 5 basin, drain 6 vessel
7 channel

trounce
4 beat, drub, lick, rout, whip, whup
5 whomp 6 defeat, larrup, thrash, thresh, wallop 7 clobber, punish, shellac
9 overwhelm

troupe
4 band 5 corps, party 6 outfit 7 company

trouper
4 mime 5 actor, mimic 6 mummer, player
7 actress, artiste 8 thespian 9 performer
11 entertainer

trousers
5 pants 6 slacks 7 drawers 8 breeches, britches
tartan: 5 trews

trout
kind: 3 sea 4 char, lake 5 brook, brown, river 7 rainbow 8 speckled 9 steelhead

Trovatore, Il
character: 7 Azucena, Leonora, Manrico
11 Count di Luna
composer: 5 Verdi (Giuseppe)

trove
4 find, haul 5 hoard, store 8 treasure
10 collection 11 aggregation
12 accumulation

Troy
5 Ilium
epic of: 5 Iliad
excavator: 10 Schliemann (Heinrich)
founder: 4 Ilus
modern site: 9 Hissarlik
(see also **Trojan**)

truant
4 idle 5 shirk 7 shirker, slacker 8 shirking
10 delinquent

truce
4 lull 5 letup, pause, peace 6 accord
7 respite 9 armistice, cease-fire

truck
3 van 4 semi, swap 5 lorry, trade 6 barter,
handle, peddle, retail 7 bargain, traffic
8 commerce, dealings, exchange
military: 6 camion

Truckee River city
4 Reno

truckle
4 fawn 5 cower, defer, toady 6 cringe,
grovel, kowtow 8 bootlick 11 apple-polish

truckler
5 leech, toady 6 lackey, sponge 7 spaniel
8 parasite 9 sycophant 10 bootlicker
11 lickspittle 13 apple-polisher

truculent
4 fell, grim 5 cruel, harsh, rough, sharp
6 brutal, deadly, fierce, savage, severe
7 abusive, warlike 9 barbarous, bellicose,
combative, ferocious 10 pernicious,
pugnacious 11 belligerent, contentious,
destructive, opprobrious, quarrelsome

trudge
4 plod, slog, trek 5 march, tramp, tromp
8 footslog

true
4 real, very 5 valid 6 actual, honest, trusty
7 factual, genuine, staunch, upright
8 accurate, bona fide, constant, faithful,
resolute, rightful 9 authentic, honorable,
steadfast, undoubted, veracious, veritable
10 dependable, legitimate, undeniable
11 indubitable, trustworthy 12 indisputable
13 authoritative

true-blue
5 loyal 6 proven, steady 7 genuine
8 bona fide, constant, faithful 9 steadfast
10 unswerving

truism
3 saw 4 rule 5 adage, axiom, gnome,
maxim, moral 6 cliché, dictum, gospel,
saying, verity 8 aphorism, apothegm
9 platitude 10 shibboleth 11 commonplace

Truk Island
3 Tol 4 Moen, Udot, Uman 5 Fefan
6 Dublon

truly
4 well 6 easily, indeed, really, surely, verily
7 de facto 8 actually 9 doubtless,
genuinely, sincerely, veritably
10 absolutely, definitely, positively,
truthfully, undeniably 11 confidently,
doubtlessly, undoubtedly

Truman, Harry S
birthplace: 5 Lamar (Missouri)
predecessor: 3 FDR
successor: 3 DDE

trump
3 cap, top 4 beat, best, pass, ruff 5 excel,
outdo 6 better 7 manille, surpass
8 clincher, jew's harp, outstrip, override,
spadille
up: 6 invent 7 concoct 9 fabricate
11 manufacture

trumpery
4 bosh, junk, muck, slop, tosh 5 bilge,
cheap, dreck, hokum, trash 6 bunkum,
cheesy, common, humbug, paltry, piffle,
shoddy, trashy 7 baloney, twaddle
8 claptrap, flimflam, malarkey, nonsense,
rubbishy, tommyrot 10 double-talk

trumpet
4 horn, tout 6 herald 8 ballyhoo
call: 6 sennet
ram's horn: 6 shofar

trumpeter
4 Hirt (Al), swan 5 André (Maurice), Baker
(Chet), Brown (Clifford), Davis (Miles),
James (Harry) 6 Alpert (Herb), Bolden
(Buddy), Farmer (Art), Voisin (Roger)
7 Schwarz (Gerard) 8 advocate, Eldridge
(Roy), eulogist, Marsalis (Wynton),
Masekela (Hugh) 9 Armstrong (Louis),
encomiast, Gillespie (Dizzy), spokesman

10 mouthpiece, panegyrist, Severinsen (Doc)

truncate
3 lop, top 4 crop, trim 5 prune, shear 6 cut off 7 abridge, shorten 10 abbreviate

truncheon
3 bat 4 club 5 baton, billy 6 cudgel, warder 8 bludgeon 9 billy club 10 nightstick, shillelagh

trundle
3 bed, tub 4 cart, haul, roll, spin 5 churn, wheel 6 rotate 7 revolve 9 transport

trunk
3 box 4 body, case, stem 5 chest, torso 7 channel, circuit, luggage
elephant: 9 proboscis
tree: 4 bole 5 stump

truss
3 tie 4 band, bind 5 brace 7 bandage, bracket, support 9 framework, supporter 10 strengthen

trust
4 hope, pool, rely 5 faith, stock 6 assume, bank on, belief, cartel, charge, commit, credit, rely on 7 build on, combine, confide, consign, count on, custody, keeping, presume 8 bank upon, credence, depend on, reckon on, reliance, rely upon 9 assurance, certainty, certitude, syndicate 10 confidence, conviction, dependence, depend upon 11 safekeeping 12 conglomerate

trustee
8 guardian 9 custodian, protector 10 supervisor

trustworthy
4 sure, true 5 tried, valid 6 honest, proven, secure 8 accurate, credible, faithful, reliable 9 authentic, realistic, responsible, veracious 10 dependable 12 tried and true 13 authoritative

trusty
4 true 5 tried 6 proven, secure, stable, steady 7 certain, convict 8 faithful, reliable 9 truepenny 10 dependable 11 responsible 12 tried and true

truth
5 axiom, maxim, sooth 6 candor, gospel, verity 7 lowdown, reality, veritas 8 veracity 9 rightness 11 genuineness 12 authenticity
goddess: 4 Maat
serum: 11 scopolamine

truthful
5 frank 6 candid, honest 7 factual, sincere 8 accurate 9 realistic, veracious, veridical

truthfulness
6 candor, verity 7 honesty 8 veracity

try
3 aim, tax, vex 4 seek, shot, stab, test 5 annoy, assay, essay, judge, offer, prove, study, whack, whirl, worry 6 aspire, harass, harrow, strain, stress, strive 7 afflict, adjudge, attempt, trouble 8 endeavor, struggle 9 undertake 10 adjudicate, experiment

trying
6 taxing, thorny, tricky, vexing 7 arduous, onerous 8 annoying, exacting, grueling, vexatious 9 demanding, difficult, strenuous 10 irritating 11 aggravating, troublesome

try out
8 audition

tryst
4 date 7 meeting 10 engagement, rendezvous 11 appointment, assignation

tsunami
9 tidal wave

tub
3 vat 4 boat 9 container
hot: 3 spa 7 Jacuzzi

tuba
7 helicon 9 bombardon, euphonium 10 sousaphone

Tubalcain
father: 6 Lamech
mother: 6 Zillah

tubby
3 fat 5 plump, podgy, porky, pudgy 6 chubby, chunky, rotund 8 roly-poly

tube
4 duct, hose, pipe 5 buret 6 siphon, subway, tunnel, vessel 7 burette, conduit, cuvette, pipette, syringe 8 pipeline
anatomical: 3 vas 4 duct, vasa (plural) 7 salpinx 9 salpinges (plural)

tuber
3 set 4 bulb, corm, root, stem 6 potato 7 rhizome 10 prominence

tuberculosis
8 phthisis, scrofula 11 consumption 12 Pott's disease

tucker out
4 do in, poop, tire 5 drain, weary 7 exhaust

tuft
5 clump, mound 7 cluster
of feathers: 7 panache
ornamental: 6 pom-pom
vascular: 6 glomus

tufted
7 crested

tug
3 tow 4 drag, draw, haul, moil, pull, toil
5 labor 6 strain, strive

tug-of-war
5 match 6 strife 7 contest, grapple, rivalry
8 conflict, struggle 10 contention
11 competition

tuition
3 fee 6 charge 8 teaching, training,
tutelage 9 education, schooling
11 instruction

tumble
4 drop, fall, trip 5 upset 6 plunge, topple
8 collapse, keel over 9 bring down,
overthrow 10 somersault

tumbledown
8 decrepit 10 ramshackle 11 dilapidated

tumbler
5 glass 6 roller 7 acrobat, gymnast
11 cartwheeler

tumbrel
4 cart 5 wagon 7 tipcart

tumescent
6 turgid 7 aureate, bloated, bulging,
flowery, swollen 8 inflated, swelling
9 bombastic, dropsical, overblown
10 euphuistic, rhetorical 12 magniloquent
13 grandiloquent

tummy
3 gut 5 belly 6 paunch 7 abdomen,
stomach 8 potbelly 9 bay window
11 breadbasket

tumult
3 din 4 flap, riot, to-do 5 babel, broil, hoo-
ha, hurly, noise, whirl 6 clamor, dither,
hubbub, lather, outcry, pother, racket, strife,
uproar 7 ferment, tempest, turmoil
8 disorder, foofaraw, outburst, paroxysm,
upheaval 9 agitation, commotion,
confusion, kerfuffle, maelstrom
10 convulsion, hullabaloo, hurly-burly,
turbulence 11 disturbance, pandemonium

tumultuous
5 rowdy 6 stormy, unruly 7 raucous,
riotous 9 clamorous, turbulent
10 boisterous, disorderly 11 rumbustious,
tempestuous 12 rambunctious

tumulus
5 grave, knoll, mound 6 barrow 7 hillock

tun
3 keg, vat 4 butt, cask, pipe 6 barrel
8 hogshead, puncheon

tuna
3 ahi 4 pear 6 bigeye, bonito 7 bluefin
8 albacore, skipjack 9 scombroid,
yellowfin

tune
3 air 4 dial, lilt, song 5 theme 6 accord,
adjust, amount, attune, extent, jingle,
melody, strain, temper 7 descant
8 modulate, regulate 9 harmonize
10 coordinate, intonation
out: 6 ignore

tuneful
5 sweet 6 dulcet 7 melodic 9 melodious
10 euphonious

tungsten
7 wolfram 9 scheelite 10 wolframite

tunic
5 jupon 6 kirtle
Greek: 6 chiton

tunicate
4 salp 8 ascidian, chordate 9 sea squirt
11 urochordate

Tunisia
capital: 5 Tunis
city: 4 Sfax 6 Ariana
island: 5 Jerba
language: 6 Arabic
monetary unit: 5 dinar
neighbor: 5 Libya 7 Algeria
ruins: 8 Carthage
sea: 13 Mediterranean

tunnel
4 tube 6 burrow 7 conduit 8 crawlway
Alps: 7 Simplon
France: 4 Rove
Hudson river: 7 Holland, Lincoln
Nevada: 5 Sutro
railroad: 6 Hoosac 7 Cascade

Turandot
character: 3 Liu 5 Calaf
author: 5 Gozzi (Carlo)
composer: 6 Busoni (Ferruccio) 7 Puccini
(Giacomo)

turban
7 bandana, pugaree 8 bandanna
9 headdress

turbid
4 dark 5 dense, mucky, muddy, murky,

turbot

riley, roily, smoky, thick **6** cloudy, opaque, roiled **7** clouded, obscure

turbot
8 flatfish

turbulence
3 din **4** flap, stew **5** babel, fight, hoo-ha **6** dither, fracas, lather, pother, tumult, uproar **7** turmoil **8** foofaraw **9** agitation, commotion, confusion **11** pandemonium

turbulent
4 wild **5** bumpy, roily, rough, rowdy **6** raging, stormy, unruly **7** furious, moiling, raucous, riotous, roaring **8** agitated, blustery, brawling, mutinous, rowdyish, swirling **9** clamorous **10** boisterous, disorderly, tumultuous **11** rumbustious, tempestuous **12** rambunctious

tureen
3 pot **4** bowl **5** crock **6** vessel **9** casserole

turf
3 sod **4** area, peat **5** grass, sward, track **6** domain, region **7** terrain **9** racetrack, territory **11** horse racing **12** neighborhood

turgid
see **tumescent**

Turkey
capital: 6 Ankara
city: 5 Adana, Bursa, Izmir, Konya **8** Istanbul **9** Gaziantep
enclave: 8 Naxçivan
lake: 3 Van
leader: 7 Atatürk (Kemal)
monetary unit: 4 lira
mountain, range: 6 Ararat, Taurus
neighbor: 4 Iran, Iraq **5** Syria **6** Greece **7** Armenia, Georgia **8** Bulgaria
part of: 7 Balkans
peninsula: 6 Balkan **9** Asia Minor
river: 6 Tigris **8** Menderes **9** Euphrates **10** Kizil Irmak
sea: 6 Aegean **7** Marmara **13** Mediterranean

turkey
buzzard: 7 vulture
disease: 9 blackhead
female: 3 hen
head growth: 5 snood **7** dewbill
male: 3 tom **7** gobbler
throat pouch: 6 wattle
young: 5 poult

Turkey in the ___
5 Straw

Turkish
cavalryman: 5 spahi

empire: 7 Ottoman
governor: 4 vali
inn: 4 kahn **6** imaret
measure: 3 ohe
music: 9 janissary
soldier: 5 nizam **9** janissary
sultan: 5 Ahmed, Selim **7** Bajazet, Bayezid, Ilderim
sword: 8 yataghan
title: 3 aga, bey **4** agha **5** pasha **6** vizier **7** effendi

Turkmenistan
capital: 8 Ashgabat **9** Ashkhabad
city: 9 Chardzhou, Dashhowuz
desert: 7 Kara-Kum
monetary unit: 5 manat
neighbor: 4 Iran **10** Kazakhstan, Uzbekistan **11** Afghanistan
river: 6 Murgab **7** Murghab **8** Amu Dar'ya
sea: 7 Caspian

Turks and Caicos Islands
capital: 9 Grand Turk
location: 10 West Indies
passage: 6 Caicos **8** Mouchoir
territory of: 7 Britain

turmeric
3 dye **4** herb **5** spice **6** ginger **8** dyestuff

turmoil
4 coil, flap, moil, riot, stew, stir, to-do **5** chaos, whirl **6** clamor, dither, hassle, hubbub, lather, pother, strife, tumult, unease, unrest, uproar, welter **7** anxiety, ferment **8** disorder, disquiet, distress, upheaval **9** agitation, commotion, confusion **10** disruption, hurly-burly, inquietude, storminess, turbulence, uneasiness **11** anxiousness, disquietude, hurry-scurry, pandemonium, restiveness **12** restlessness **13** helter-skelter, Sturm und Drang

turn
3 yaw, zag, zig **4** bend, bias, bout, cast, grow, gyre, reel, spin, tack, tour, veer, whip, wind **5** angle, curve, pivot, refer, shunt, spell, stint, swirl, train, twirl, whirl **6** detour, divert, gyrate, mutate, revert, rotate, switch, swivel **7** circuit, convert, deflect, deviate, digress, diverge, reverse, revolve **8** gyration, rotation **9** about-face, deviation, pirouette, volte-face **10** deflection, revolution, tergiverse **11** changeabout **12** tergiversate
to stone: 8 lapidify

turnabout
3 rat **6** coward **7** reverse **8** apostate,

defector, recreant, renegade, reversal
9 about-face, reversion, volte-face
11 retaliation **12** merry-go-round
13 tergiversator

turn aside
4 veer, shun, sway, veer **5** avert, repel,
shunt, stave **6** divert, refuse, reject, swerve
7 deflect, deviate,
digress, dismiss, diverge, fend off, reflect,
ward off **8** alienate, estrange, separate
9 sidetrack

turncoat
3 rat, spy **5** Judas **7** traitor **8** apostate,
betrayer, defector, deserter, quisling,
recreant, renegade **9** traitress, turnabout
13 tergiversator

turn down
4 jilt, veto **5** spurn **6** rebuff, refuse, reject
7 decline, dismiss **9** repudiate
10 disapprove

turned on
4 high **5** doped **6** stoned, zonked
7 aroused, drugged, excited, tripping
8 hopped-up **9** activated, spaced-out,
zonked-out **10** passionate **12** enthusiastic

turn in
5 crash, rat on **6** betray, inform, rat out,
retire **7** deliver, produce, sack out **8** hand
over **10** hit the sack, relinquish

turning point
4 cusp **5** pivot **6** climax, crisis **8** landmark
11 climacteric

turnip
5 swede **8** rutabaga
Scottish: 4 neep

turnip-shaped
8 napiform

turnkey
6 jailer

turn left
3 haw

Turn of the Screw, The
author: 5 James (Henry)
character: 5 Flora, Miles **10** Peter Quint
composer: 7 Britten (Benjamin)

turn on
5 start **6** excite, ignite **7** start up
8 activate, motivate **9** stimulate, titillate

turn over
4 plow, roll **5** upset **6** assign, commit, give
up, rotate **7** capsize, consign, deliver,
entrust, furnish, provide, revolve

8 delegate, transfer **9** overthrow, surrender
10 relinquish

turnpike
7 highway

turn right
3 gee

turn up
4 find **6** appear, arrive, reveal **7** uncover,
unearth **8** discover **9** encounter
11 materialize

Turnus
beloved: 7 Lavinia
slayer: 6 Aeneas

Turow work
4 One L **13** Burden of Proof **14** Pleading
Guilty **16** Personal Injuries, Presumed
Innocent

turpentine
7 galipot, solvent, thinner
ingredient: 6 pinene
tree: 4 pine **9** terebinth

turret
5 tower **6** cupola, louver, louvre **7** mirador
8 bartizan **9** belvedere

turtle
8 terrapin, tortoise **9** chelonian
edible part: 7 calipee **8** calipash
sea: 6 ridley **8** hawkbill
shell: 8 carapace
shell part: 8 plastron

Tuscany
city: 4 Pisa **8** Florence
river: 4 Arno
tower: 4 Pisa
wine: 7 chianti

tusk
4 fang **5** ivory, tooth

tusker
6 dugong, walrus **7** mammoth, muntjac,
musk deer, narwhal, warthog **8** elephant
11 barking deer

tussle
4 spar **5** scrap, scrum **6** hassle, scrape
7 scuffle, wrangle, wrestle **8** argument,
skirmish, struggle **9** scrimmage
11 controversy

tussock
4 tuft **5** clump, mound **7** cluster

tutelage
see **tuition**

tutor
3 don 5 coach, teach 6 docent, mentor
7 teacher 9 pedagogue, preceptor
10 instructor

Tut's tomb discoverer
6 Carter (Howard)

tutti
3 all

Tuvalu
capital: 9 Fongafale
ethnic group: 10 Polynesian
former name: 6 Ellice (Islands)
monetary unit: 6 dollar

twaddle
3 jaw, yak 4 bosh, bull, bunk, chat, guff,
muck, talk, tosh 5 clack, drool, hooey,
prate, run on 6 babble, bunkum, burble,
chatter, drivel, gabble, hot air, humbug,
jabber, tattle 7 baloney, blabber, blarney,
blather, chatter, hogwash, prattle, rubbish
8 claptrap, malarkey, nonsense, tommyrot,
trumpery 9 poppycock 10 applesauce,
balderdash 12 blatherskite
13 horsefeathers

tweak
4 jerk, mock, pull, zing 5 annoy, pinch,
pluck 6 adjust, bother, twitch 8 fine-tune
9 poke fun at

tweet
4 call, note 5 cheep, chirp 7 chirrup,
twitter

Twelfth Night character
5 Viola 6 Olivia, Orsino (Duke) 7 Antonio,
Cesario 8 Malvolio 9 Sebastian, Toby
Belch

twelve
combining form: 5 dodec 6 dodeca

twenty
combining form: 4 icos 5 icosa, icosi

twerp
4 brat, drip, fool, jerk, nerd, twit 6 squirt

twice
3 bis 7 twofold
combining form: 3 bis
prefix: 3 dis

twice a day
3 b.i.d. 8 bis in die 11 semidiurnal

twice a year
8 biannual 10 semiannual, semiyearly

Twice-Told Tales author
9 Hawthorne (Nathaniel)

twig
5 shoot, sprig 6 branch
bundle of: 5 fagot 6 faggot

twiggy
4 slim, thin 5 reedy 6 slight, stalky
7 slender 9 sticklike

twilight
3 eve 4 dusk 5 gloam, gloom 6 sunset
7 decline 8 gloaming 9 nightfall
10 crepuscule

Twilight of the Gods
8 Ragnarok
composer: 6 Wagner (Richard)

twill
5 chino, cloth, serge, toile, tweed, weave
6 fabric 7 cheviot 8 dungaree
9 bombazine, gabardine 11 herringbone

twin
4 dual, like, mate 5 clone, match 6 bifold,
binary, double, fellow, paired 7 matched,
similar, twofold 8 matching 9 companion,
duplicate, identical 10 coordinate,
reciprocal

Twin Cities
6 St. Paul 11 Minneapolis

twine
4 coil, cord, curl, wind, wrap 5 twist, weave
6 spiral, string 7 embrace, meander,
wreathe 8 entangle 9 interlace
10 interweave

twinge
4 ache, pain, pang 5 pluck, shoot, throe,
tweak 6 stitch

twinkle
3 bat 4 flit, wink 5 blink, flash, flirt, gleam,
glint, light, shake, shine, trice 6 moment,
second, winkle 7 flicker, flutter, glimmer,
glisten, glitter, instant, shimmer, sparkle
9 coruscate, nictitate 11 coruscation,
scintillate, split second

twin stars
6 Castor, Pollux

twirl
4 coil, gyre, spin 5 pitch, trill, whirl, whorl
6 gyrate 7 revolve 9 pirouette

twist
3 wry 4 coil, curl, turn, warp, wind 5 belie,
gnarl, pivot, twine, twirl, wring 6 garble,

spiral, sprain, squirm, torque, wrench, writhe **7** contort, distort, entwine, falsify, pervert, wriggle **8** misstate **9** corkscrew **12** misrepresent

twisted
3 wry **4** awry, kinky, sick **5** askew **6** swirly, warped **9** perverted

twister
6 funnel **7** tornado **9** dust devil, whirlwind **10** waterspout

twit
4 dolt, fool, gibe, jeer, jive, josh, mock, quiz, razz **5** chide, rally, scout, taunt, tease, twerp **6** deride **8** bonehead, numskull, ridicule **9** blockhead, numbskull **10** nincompoop

twitch
3 tic **4** jerk, pull, yank **5** pluck, spasm, throe, tweak **6** quiver **10** quack grass **11** contraction

twitter
4 chat, peep **5** cheep, chirp, quake, tweet **6** cackle, giggle, jargon, quiver, shiver, titter, tremor, warble **7** chatter, chitter, chirrup, chitter, flicker, flitter, flutter, tremble **9** vibration

twittery
6 giggly **8** chattery **9** flustered, tremulous

two
3 duo **4** duet, pair **5** twain **6** couple
combining form: 3 bis, duo, dyo
divide into: 4 fork **6** bisect **9** bifurcate
prefix: 3 twi

two-faced
9 deceitful, dishonest, insincere **11** duplicitous **12** hypocritical **13** double-dealing
god: 5 Janus

twofold
4 dual, twin **5** binal, duple **6** binary, double, duplex, dyadic, paired **9** dualistic

Two Gentlemen of Verona
author: 11 Shakespeare (William)
character: 5 Julia **6** Silvia, Thurio **7** Proteus **9** Valentine

twosome
3 duo **4** dyad, pair **5** brace **6** couple **7** doublet

two-time
4 dupe **6** betray, delude, humbug, take in

7 beguile, cheat on, deceive, mislead **9** bamboozle **11** double-cross

two-wheeler
4 bike **5** cycle **7** bicycle, scooter **10** motorcycle

Two Years Before the Mast author
4 Dana (Richard Henry)

Tybalt
cousin: 6 Juliet
family: 7 Capulet
slayer: 5 Romeo
victim: 8 Mercutio

Tyche
goddess of: 7 fortune

tycoon
5 mogul, nabob **7** magnate

tyke
3 dog, kid **5** child, hound, puppy **6** canine, moppet, nipper, shaver **7** mongrel

Tyler novel
16 Breathing Lessons **17** Accidental Tourist (The) **29** Dinner at the Homesick Restaurant

tympanum
7 eardrum **9** middle ear

Tyndareus
kingdom: 6 Sparta
wife: 4 Leda

type
3 cut, ilk, lot, way **4** cast, form, kind, mold, sort **5** breed, class, genre, order, print, serif, stamp **6** kidney, nature, stripe **7** feather, species, variety **8** category **9** character **10** persuasion **11** description
bar: 4 slug
measure: 4 pica **5** point
set: 7 compose
setter: 10 compositor
size: 4 pica **5** agate, pearl
stroke: 5 serif
style: 4 bold **5** roman **6** Gothic, italic **7** Fraktur **8** boldface **9** lightface, sans serif
tray: 6 galley

Typee
author: 8 Melville (Herman)
character: 4 Toby

typewriter
part: 3 key **6** platen, spacer
type size: 4 pica **5** elite

Typhon
3 Set **7** monster **8** Typhoeus

offspring: 6 Sphinx **7** Chimera
8 Cerberus, Chimaera
wife: 7 Echidna

typhoon

7 cyclone **9** hurricane **13** tropical storm

typical

5 ideal, model, usual **6** common, normal
7 classic, general, natural, regular
8 symbolic

typify

6 embody, mirror **9** epitomize, exemplify,
personify, represent, symbolize
10 illustrate **11** emblematize
12 characterize

typo

5 error **7** erratum **8** misprint **11** cor-
rigendum

typographer

7 printer **10** compositor

Tyr

3 Tiu
brother: 4 Thor
father: 4 Odin
god of: 3 war
mother: 5 Jordh, Jorth

tyrannical

8 absolute, despotic **9** arbitrary
10 absolutist, autocratic, oppressive
11 dictatorial **12** totalitarian

tyrannize

7 oppress **8** dominate, domineer, overbear
9 terrorize

tyrannous

5 harsh **6** brutal, severe **8** absolute,
despotic **9** arbitrary, fascistic **10** autocratic
11 dictatorial **12** totalitarian

tyranny

7 cruelty, fascism **9** autocracy, despotism,
monocracy **10** absolutism, domination,
oppression **12** dictatorship

tyrant

4 czar, duce, tsar, tzar **5** ruler **6** despot,
führer **7** fuehrer, pharaoh, usurper
8 autocrat, dictator **9** oppressor,
strongman **10** absolutist **12** totalitarian

Tyrian _____

6 purple

tyro

4 punk **6** novice, rookie **7** amateur,
dabbler, student **8** beginner, freshman,
neophyte, newcomer **9** novitiate
10 apprentice, dilettante, tenderfoot
11 abecedarian

Tyrol

see **Tirol**

tzar

see **czar**

tzigane

3 Rom **5** gypsy **6** Romany

U

übermensch
8 superman

ubiquitous
7 allover 9 pervasive, universal
10 everywhere, wall-to-wall, widespread
11 omnipresent

U-boat
3 sub 7 pigboat 9 submarine

Uganda
capital: 7 Kampala
falls: 5 Ripon
lake: 5 Kyoga 6 Albert, Edward, George
8 Victoria
language: 7 English, Swahili
leader: 4 Amin (Idi)
monetary unit: 8 shilling
mountain: 5 Elgon
mountain range: 9 Ruwenzori
neighbor: 5 Congo, Kenya, Sudan
6 Rwanda 8 Tanzania
river: 4 Nile

ugly
4 vile 7 hideous 8 deformed 9 loathsome,
misshapen, offensive, repugnant, repulsive,
unsightly 10 disfigured 12 unattractive

Ugly Duckling author
8 Andersen (Hans Christian)

ukase
4 fiat 5 edict, order 6 decree, dictum,
ruling 7 command, dictate, mandate
9 directive 10 injunction 12 proclamation
13 pronouncement

Ukraine
capital: 4 Kiev
city: 4 Lviv, Lvov 5 Yalta 6 Odessa
7 Kharkiv 9 Chernobyl
ethnic group: 7 Cossack
monetary unit: 6 hryvny
mountain range: 10 Carpathian
neighbor: 6 Poland, Russia 7 Belarus,
Hungary, Moldova 8 Slovakia
peninsula: 5 Kerch 6 Crimea 7 Crimean

river: 3 Bug 5 Tisza 6 Donets 7 Dnieper
8 Dniester
sea: 4 Azov 5 Black

Ulalume author
3 Poe (Edgar Allan)

ulcer
4 sore 6 fester 7 corrupt
kind: 6 peptic 8 duodenal
mouth: 10 canker sore

ulna
7 forearm

Ulster hero
6 Fergus 7 Deirdre 9 Conchobar,
Cuchulain, Cuchullin 10 Cú Chulainn

ulterior
5 privy 6 covert, future, hidden, latent
7 further, obscure, remoter 9 ambiguous,
concealed 10 subsequent, succeeding
11 undisclosed

ultimate
3 end 4 acme, last, peak 5 basic, final
6 summit, utmost, zenith 7 closing,
epitome, extreme, maximum, primary,
supreme, topmost 8 absolute, deciding,
decisive, eventual, farthest, furthest,
greatest, original, terminal 9 elemental,
paramount 10 apotheosis, concluding,
conclusive, consummate, preeminent
11 categorical, fundamental, furthermost,
indivisible 12 incomparable, quintessence

ultimatum
5 order 6 demand, threat 7 mandate
9 challenge 12 notification

ultra
5 kinky, outré, rabid 6 beyond, far-out, too-
too 7 extreme, fanatic, radical
9 excessive, extremist, fanatical
10 outlandish 11 extravagant

ultraconservative
11 reactionary

ultraist
5 rabid 6 zealot 7 extreme, fanatic, radical
9 extremist

ultramarine
7 oversea, sea-blue 8 overseas 11 lapis
lazuli

ululate
3 bay 4 howl, wail, yowl

Ulysses
author: 5 Joyce (James)
character: 5 Bloom (Leopold), Molly
(Bloom) 6 Blazes (Boylan) 7 Dedalus
(Stephen)
(see also **Odysseus**)

umber
5 brown, sepia, shade 6 darken, shadow

umbilicus
3 hub 4 core 5 heart, hilum, navel
6 center

umbra
5 shade 6 shadow

umbrage
4 hint, huff 5 anger, pique, shade
6 shadow 7 chagrin, dudgeon, foliage,
leafage, offense 9 annoyance, suspicion
10 irritation, resentment 11 displeasure,
indignation 12 exasperation

umbrageous
5 shady 6 shaded, touchy 7 shadowy
8 shadowed 9 defensive, sensitive

umbrella
5 cover, guard, shade 6 brolly, pileus,
screen 7 parasol, protect, shelter
8 sunshade 10 protection 11 bumbershoot

umph
see **oomph**

umpire
3 ref 5 judge 6 decide, settle 7 arbiter,
referee 9 arbitrate 10 arbitrator
call: 3 out 4 balk, ball, safe 6 strike

unabashed
5 blunt, brash, frank, naked, overt 6 arrant,
brassy, brazen, candid 7 blatant, forward
8 outright 9 audacious, barefaced,
shameless, undaunted 10 unblushing
11 undisguised, unmitigated 12 unapolo-
getic

unabbreviated
see **unabridged**

unable
5 inept, unfit 8 helpless, impotent
9 incapable, maladroit, powerless, unskilled

10 unequipped 11 incompetent,
unqualified 13 incapacitated

unabridged
5 uncut, whole 6 entire, intact 8 complete
10 full-length 11 uncondensed
13 unabbreviated

unacceptable
8 unwanted 9 unwelcome 10 unsuitable
11 intolerable, undesirable 12 inadmissible
13 exceptionable, inappropriate,
insupportable, objectionable

unaccompanied
4 lone, sole, solo, stag 5 alone, apart
6 single 8 detached, solitary 9 a cappella
10 unattended, unescorted

unaccountable
6 arcane, mystic 7 strange 8 baffling,
puzzling 9 enigmatic 10 mysterious,
mystifying, unknowable, unreliable
12 impenetrable, inexplicable,
undependable, unfathomable
13 irresponsible, unexplainable

unaccustomed
3 new 5 alien, novel 6 unused 7 strange,
unusual 8 singular, uncommon, unwonted
10 unexpected, unfamiliar

unadorned
4 bald, bare 5 naked, plain, spare, stark
6 rustic, severe, simple 7 artless, austere,
natural, spartan 11 undecorated
13 unembellished, unembroidered,
unpretentious

unadulterated
4 neat, pure 5 sheer, utter 7 genuine,
unmixed 8 absolute, straight 9 unalloyed,
undiluted 11 unmitigated, unqualified

unaffected
5 naive 6 candid, simple 7 artless, callous,
genuine, natural, sincere, unmoved
9 guileless, impassive, ingenuous,
unaltered, unchanged, unstudied,
untouched 10 hard-boiled, impervious
13 unpretentious

unalloyed
4 pure 5 sheer, total 7 genuine, unmixed
8 absolute, straight 9 authentic, out-and-
out, undiluted 11 unmitigated, unqualified
13 thoroughgoing, unadulterated

unalterable
5 fixed 7 binding, bounden, certain,
decided 8 constant, required 9 immutable,
mandatory, necessary 10 compulsory,
invariable 12 unchangeable

13 predetermined

unambiguous
5 clear, lucid, plain 6 patent 7 evident, express, obvious, precise 8 apparent, clean-cut, clear-cut, decisive, definite, distinct, explicit, manifest, specific, univocal 10 definitive, forthright 11 categorical, translucent, transparent, unequivocal 12 transpicuous

unanimous
6 united 8 communal, univocal 9 unopposed 10 collective 11 uncontested 13 consentaneous

unanimously
5 as one 7 en masse, wholly 10 altogether

unanticipated
9 unplanned 11 surprising, unexpected, unforeseen 12 out of the blue

unappeasable
4 grim 7 adamant 8 obdurate, resolute 9 insatiate, unbending 10 implacable, insatiable, relentless, unyielding 11 unrelenting 12 unquenchable

unappetizing
4 icky 5 gross, yucky 7 insipid 8 unsavory 9 repugnant 11 unappealing, unpalatable 12 unattractive

unapproachable
5 aloof 6 remote, offish 7 distant 8 reserved 10 unfriendly, unsociable 11 standoffish, unreachable 12 inaccessible, unattainable

unasked
7 willing 8 unbidden, unsought, unwanted 9 uninvited, unwelcome, voluntary 10 gratuitous, unprompted 11 spontaneous, uncalled-for, unrequested, voluntarily

unassailable
6 secure 8 airtight 10 invincible, inviolable, undeniable 11 impregnable, irrefutable 12 indisputable, invulnerable 13 incontestable, unconquerable

unassertive
3 shy 4 meek 5 mousy, timid 6 modest, mousey 7 bashful 8 backward, reticent, retiring, sheepish, timorous 9 diffident, shrinking 10 submissive 12 self-effacing

unassuming
3 shy 6 humble, modest, simple 8 ordinary, retiring 9 diffident 11 unassertive 12 self-effacing 13 unpretentious

unattached
4 free 5 loose 6 single 8 separate 9 unmarried 10 unassigned 11 uncommitted, unconnected 12 disconnected, freestanding, unassociated

unattainable
7 elusive 10 impossible 12 inaccessible

unattractive
4 drab, dull, ugly 5 dowdy, plain 6 homely 8 frumpish 10 unalluring, unsuitable 11 unappealing, undesirable 12 unflattering

unauthentic
4 fake, mock, sham 5 bogus, dummy, faked, false, phony 6 ersatz, forged, pseudo 7 feigned 8 affected, spurious 9 contrived, imitation, pretended, simulated 10 apocryphal, artificial 11 counterfeit, make-believe 12 illegitimate

unavailable
4 busy 6 absent, tied up 7 missing 8 occupied

unavailing
4 idle, vain 5 empty 6 barren, futile 7 useless 8 abortive, bootless 9 fruitless, pointless 11 ineffective, ineffectual 12 unproductive

unavoidable
5 fated 7 certain 8 destined, impending 9 necessary 10 compulsory, inevitable, obligatory 11 ineluctable, inescapable

unavoidably
8 perforce 10 helplessly, inevitably, willy-nilly 11 inescapably, necessarily, whether or no

unaware, unawares
5 aback 7 unready 8 abruptly, heedless, ignorant, off guard, suddenly 9 oblivious, unknowing, unmindful, unwitting 10 by surprise, unfamiliar, uninformed, unprepared 12 unacquainted, unexpectedly

unbalance
11 destabilize

unbalanced
3 mad 4 daft 5 batty, nutty 6 crazed, insane, uneven, wobbly 7 unequal, unsound 8 demented, deranged, lopsided, unhinged, unstable 9 psychotic 10 disordered, moonstruck

unbearable
11 unendurable 12 excruciating, insufferable, intolerable

unbeautiful
4 ugly 5 plain 6 homely 8 uncomely, unlovely 9 unsightly 10 ill-favored, unbecoming, uninviting 12 unattractive

unbecoming
8 improper, unlovely, unseemly, untimely, untoward, unworthy 9 inelegant, tasteless, unfitting 10 indecorous, indelicate, malapropos, unsuitable 11 disgraceful 12 unattractive 13 inappropriate

unbelievable
7 amazing, awesome 8 fabulous 9 fantastic 10 astounding, improbable, incredible, phenomenal, staggering, stupendous 11 astonishing, implausible, spectacular 12 unconvincing, unimaginable 13 extraordinary, inconceivable

unbeliever
5 pagan 6 giaour 7 atheist, doubter, gentile, heathen, heretic, infidel, scoffer, skeptic 9 agnostic 10 Pyrrhonist 11 freethinker

unbelieving
5 leery 6 show-me 8 agnostic, apostate, doubting 9 quizzical, skeptical 10 dissenting, suspicious 11 incredulous, mistrustful, questioning

unbending
5 rigid, stern, stiff 8 hard-line, obdurate, resolute 9 inelastic 10 brassbound, inexorable, inflexible, unyielding

unbiased
4 fair, just 5 equal 7 neutral 8 detached, tolerant 9 equitable, impartial, objective, unbigoted 10 even-handed, open-minded 11 broad-minded, uncommitted 12 unprejudiced 13 disinterested, dispassionate

unbidden
7 unasked, willing 8 unsought, unwanted 9 impromptu, uninvited, unwelcome, voluntary 10 gratuitous, unprompted 11 spontaneous, unrequested

unbind
4 free, undo 5 loose, untie 6 detach, loosen 7 manumit, release, unchain, unloose 8 dissolve, liberate, unfasten, unloosen 9 discharge, disengage, unshackle 10 emancipate

unblemished
4 pure 7 perfect 8 flawless, spotless, unmarred, virtuous 9 exemplary, faultless, stainless, undefiled, unspotted, unsullied

10 immaculate 11 untarnished

unbosom
4 bare, open, tell 6 betray, expose, reveal, unveil 7 divulge, express, uncover 8 disclose

unbound
4 free 5 freed, loose 6 loosed 10 unattached, unconfined, unfastened

unbounded
4 open 6 untold 7 endless 8 infinite, unending 9 excessive, limitless, unchecked, unlimited 10 immoderate, indefinite, inordinate 11 extravagant, measureless 12 immeasurable, incalculable, uncontrolled, unrestrained

unbreakable
7 durable, lasting 10 unyielding 11 everlasting

unbridled
4 free 5 loose 6 madcap 8 reckless, uncurbed 9 dissolute, unchecked 10 immoderate, licentious, unconfined, unfettered, ungoverned 11 spontaneous, uninhibited, unrepressed 12 uncontrolled, unrestrained, unrestricted 13 unconstrained

unbroken
5 solid, sound, whole 6 entire, intact, single 8 complete, constant, enduring 9 ceaseless, steadfast, unceasing, undamaged, undivided, unsubdued, unvarying 10 continuous, unimpaired 13 uninterrupted

unburden
3 rid 4 dump, ease, lose 5 shake 6 reveal, unload 7 cast off, confess, confide, off-load, relieve 8 shake off, throw off 9 discharge 10 relinquish 11 disencumber

uncalled-for
8 baseless, needless 9 officious, unfounded 10 gratuitous, groundless 11 unessential, unjustified, unnecessary, unwarranted 13 unjustifiable

uncanny
5 eerie, weird 6 creepy, spooky 7 ghostly, strange 9 unearthly, unnatural 10 mysterious, mystifying, superhuman 11 supernormal, supranormal 12 supernatural

uncared-for
5 dingy 6 beat-up, shabby 7 rickety, run-down, worn-out 8 decrepit, derelict, deserted, desolate, forsaken, tattered,

untended **9** neglected **10** broken-down, down-at-heel, ramshackle, tumble-down **11** dilapidated

uncaring
4 cold **7** callous **9** heartless, negligent, oblivious, unfeeling, unheeding **11** coldhearted, hard-hearted, indifferent, insensitive, thoughtless, unconcerned **13** inconsiderate, unsympathetic

unceasing
7 abiding, endless, eternal, nonstop, undying **8** constant, enduring, unbroken, unending **9** continual, perennial, perpetual **10** continuous, amaranthine, everlasting, unremitting **12** imperishable, interminable **13** uninterrupted

unceremonious
4 curt, rude **5** bluff, blunt, frank, hasty, sharp, short, terse **6** abrupt, breezy, casual, sudden **7** brusque, hurried, offhand **8** familiar, informal **10** ungracious **11** precipitate, precipitous

uncertain
4 hazy, iffy, moot **5** vague **6** chancy, fitful, unsure, wobbly **7** dubious, erratic, halting, unclear **8** arguable, doubtful, insecure, slippery, unstable, unsteady, variable **9** ambiguous, debatable, undecided, unsettled **10** ambivalent, disputable, inconstant, indefinite, precarious, speculative **11** problematic **12** questionable, undependable **13** indeterminate, problematical, unforeseeable, unpredictable, untrustworthy

uncertainty
5 doubt **7** dubiety **8** distrust, mistrust **9** ambiguity, suspicion **10** indecision, perplexity, puzzlement, skepticism, uneasiness **11** ambivalence **12** doubtfulness, irresolution

unchain
4 free **5** loose **6** loosen, unbind **7** manumit, release **8** liberate, unfasten, unfetter **9** discharge, unshackle **10** emancipate **11** disenthrall

unchangeable
3 set **4** firm **5** fixed **7** settled **8** constant **9** immutable, permanent **10** continuing, inflexible, invariable **11** established, inalterable

unchanging
5 fixed **6** stable, static, steady **7** abiding, equable, eternal, settled, stabile, uniform **8** constant, enduring **9** immutable,

steadfast, unvarying **10** consistent, continuing, invariable

unchaste
4 easy, lewd **5** bawdy, loose **6** impure, vulgar, wanton **7** immoral, lustful, obscene, scarlet, unclean **8** depraved, prurient **9** debauched, dissolute, lecherous, salacious **10** adulterous, lascivious, libidinous, licentious, profligate **11** promiscuous

unchecked
5 loose **7** rampant **9** spreading, unbounded, unbridled **10** widespread **11** uninhibited **12** unrestrained, unrestricted

uncivil
4 rude **5** crass, crude **6** coarse, savage, vulgar **7** boorish, ill-bred, uncouth **8** barbaric, impolite **9** barbarous **10** indecorous, uncultured, ungracious **11** ill-mannered, uncourteous **12** discourteous **13** disrespectful

uncivilized
4 rude, wild **5** crude **6** brutal, coarse, Gothic, savage **7** boorish, Hunnish, ill-bred, loutish, lowbred, uncouth **8** barbaric, churlish **9** barbarian, barbarous, primitive, unrefined **10** mannerless, uncultured, unmannerly, unpolished **12** uncultivated **13** unenlightened

unclad
see **unclothed**

uncle
cry: **6** give up **9** surrender
Scottish: **3** eme
Spanish: **3** tío
U.S. symbol: **3** Sam

unclean
4 foul **5** dingy, dirty, grimy **6** filthy, grubby, grungy, impure, soiled, sordid **7** corrupt, defiled, immoral, obscene, squalid, stained, sullied, tainted **8** befouled, indecent, polluted, unchaste **9** tarnished **10** besmirched, desecrated **12** contaminated

unclear
3 dim **4** hazy **5** murky, vague **6** bleary, blurry, cloudy, opaque, unsure **7** clouded, cryptic, dubious, obscure, shadowy **8** doubtful, nebulous, overcast, puzzling **9** ambiguous, enigmatic, tenebrous, unsettled **10** ill-defined, indistinct, indefinite, inexplicit **13** indeterminate

Uncle Remus creator
6 Harris (Joel Chandler)

Uncle Tom's Cabin
author: 5 Stowe (Harriet Beecher)
character: 5 Eliza, Topsy 6 Legree
(Simon) 9 Little Eva

Uncle Vanya author
7 Chekhov (Anton)

unclothe
5 strip 6 denude, divest, expose, unveil
7 display, disrobe, uncloak, uncover,
undress

unclothed
4 bare, nude 5 naked 6 peeled, unclad
7 denuded, exposed 8 in the raw, stripped
9 au naturel, buck-naked, undressed
10 stark naked

unclouded
4 fair 5 clear, lucid, sunny 6 bright
7 halcyon 8 rainless, sunshiny

uncluttered
4 neat, tidy, trig, trim 7 orderly
9 organized, shipshape 11 spic-and-span,
well-ordered 12 spick-and-span

uncombed
5 messy, mussy 6 matted, mussed
7 ruffled, snarled, tangled, tousled,
unkempt 10 disheveled

uncommon
3 odd 4 rare 5 novel 6 choice, scarce,
unique 7 special, unusual 8 esoteric,
especial, singular, sporadic, unwonted
10 infrequent, noteworthy, remarkable
11 distinctive, exceptional 12 unaccustomed 13 extraordinary

uncommunicative
3 mum 4 dumb 5 aloof 6 offish, silent
7 distant, guarded, private 8 reserved,
reticent, taciturn 9 reclusive, withdrawn
10 antisocial, poker-faced, secretive,
speechless, tongue-tied, unsociable 11 inscrutable, standoffish, tight-lipped
12 closemouthed, tight-mouthed,
unresponsive 13 unforthcoming

uncompassionate
4 cold, hard 5 stony 7 callous 8 obdurate,
pitiless, uncaring 9 heartless, unfeeling
10 hard-boiled 11 coldhearted,
hardhearted, insensitive 12 stonyhearted
13 unsympathetic

uncomplicated
4 easy 5 basic, clear, plain 6 simple

8 clear-cut 10 effortless, elementary,
manageable, uninvolved

uncomplimentary
7 adverse 8 critical 9 degrading
10 belittling, derogatory, pejorative
11 deprecatory, disparaging, unfavorable
12 depreciative, depreciatory, unflattering

uncompromising
4 firm 5 rigid 8 hard-line, obdurate,
resolute, stubborn 9 hard-nosed,
immovable, insistent, unbending
10 brassbound, determined, inexorable,
inflexible, unshakable, unyielding
12 intransigent, single-minded

unconcealed
4 bald, bare, open 5 frank, naked, overt,
plain 6 candid 7 blatant, evident, exposed,
express, obvious, visible 8 apparent,
explicit, manifest, palpable 10 forthright,
transparent 11 openhearted, undisguised,
unvarnished

unconcern
6 apathy 7 neglect 9 aloofness, disregard
10 alienation, detachment, dispassion
11 disinterest, inattention, insouciance,
nonchalance 12 carelessness,
heedlessness, indifference
13 preoccupation

unconcerned
4 cool 6 remote 7 unmoved 8 careless,
detached, heedless 9 alienated, apathetic,
oblivious, unmindful, unruffled
10 insouciant, neglectful, untroubled
11 inattentive, indifferent, unperturbed
12 uninterested 13 disinterested,
dispassionate

unconditional
5 sheer, total, utter 8 absolute, definite,
explicit, outright 9 downright, out-and-out
10 unreserved 11 unequivocal, unqualified
12 unrestricted 13 thoroughgoing

unconfined
4 free, vast 5 loose 7 at large 9 at liberty
boundless, limitless, unlimited
12 unrestrained, unrestricted

uncongenial
6 at odds 8 unfitted 9 repellent,
repugnant, unlikable 10 discordant,
unsociable, unsuitable 11 conflicting,
displeasing 12 antipathetic, disagreeable,
incompatible, unattractive
13 unsympathetic

unconnected

5 alone, apart 8 discrete, detached, disjoint, disjunct, distinct, inchoate, rambling, separate 9 unrelated 10 unattached 11 independent 12 unassociated 13 discontinuous, noncontinuous

unconquerable

10 invincible, inviolable, unbeatable 11 bulletproof, impregnable, indomitable, insuperable 12 invulnerable, unassailable

unconscionable

5 undue 6 unfair, unholy, unjust, wanton, wicked 7 immoral, ungodly 8 barbaric, criminal 9 barbarous, unethical 10 exorbitant, inordinate, outrageous 11 inexcusable, uncivilized 12 unprincipled, unscrupulous

unconscious

3 out 6 asleep, chance 7 out cold, stunned, unaware 8 comatose 9 insensate, passed out, unplanned, unwitting 10 blacked out, insensible, knocked out 11 inadvertent, instinctual, involuntary 12 uncalculated 13 unintentional

unconsciousness

4 coma 5 faint 6 stupor, torpor, trance 7 syncope 13 obliviousness

unconsidered

4 rash 5 brash, hasty 6 casual 7 offhand 8 careless, reckless, slapdash 9 desultory, haphazard, hit-or-miss, hotheaded, impetuous, unplanned 10 ill-advised, incautious, unthinking 11 thoughtless

unconstrained

4 free, open 6 blithe, dégagé, wanton 7 buoyant, gushing, relaxed 8 animated, carefree, effusive, informal, outgoing 9 easygoing, expansive, liberated 10 expressive, nonchalant, unreserved

uncontrollable

4 wild 6 unruly 7 wayward, willful 9 fractious 10 headstrong, refractory, self-willed 11 intractable 12 overwhelming, recalcitrant, ungovernable, unmanageable 13 irrepressible, undisciplined

uncontrolled

4 free, wild 5 loose 6 wanton 9 automatic, excessive, unbounded, unlimited, unmanaged 10 autonomous, immoderate, licentious, ungoverned 11 independent, instinctual, involuntary, unconscious, uninhibited, unregulated 12 disorganized, unrestrained 13 self-governing

unconventional

3 odd 4 beat 5 kinky, kooky, outré 6 casual, far-out, freaky, quirky, unique, way-out, weirdo 7 bizarre, deviant, oddball, offbeat, unusual, wayward 8 aberrant, abnormal, atypical, bohemian, freakish, original, peculiar 9 anomalous, eccentric, irregular 10 avant-garde, unexpected, unorthodox 11 uncustomary 13 idiosyncratic

unconvinced

5 leery 6 unsure 7 dubious 8 doubtful 9 skeptical, undecided 10 suspicious

unconvincing

4 lame 6 feeble, flimsy, forced 7 dubious, suspect 8 doubtful, strained 10 farfetched, improbable, incredible 11 implausible, unrealistic 12 unbelievable 13 unsubstantial

uncooked

3 raw

uncouple

4 part 6 detach, divide 7 disjoin, divorce, unhitch 8 separate, unfasten 9 disengage 10 disconnect, dissociate 12 disaffiliate

uncouth

3 odd, raw 4 rude 5 crass, crude, gross, rough 6 clumsy, coarse, rugged, vulgar 7 awkward, bizarre, boorish, ill-bred, loutish, strange, uncivil 8 barbaric, clownish, impolite, ungainly 9 eccentric, graceless, inelegant, unrefined 10 outlandish, uncultured, unpolished 11 ill-mannered, uncivilized 12 discourteous, uncultivated
person: 3 oaf 4 boor, dolt, lout 5 clown 7 bumpkin 9 barbarian

uncover

4 bare 5 strip 6 betray, detect, divest, expose, remove, reveal, unmask, unveil 7 display, divulge, unearth 8 disclose

uncritical

5 naive 9 credulous 11 perfunctory

unction

3 oil 4 balm 5 cream, salve 6 balsam, cerate, chrism 7 suavity, unguent 8 liniment, ointment 9 emollient 11 embrocation

unctuous

4 oily 5 fatty, slick, soapy, suave 6 greasy, smarmy 7 cloying, fawning, fulsome 8 slippery 9 wheedling 10 flattering,

uncultivated

oleaginous, saccharine 11 sycophantic

uncultivated
4 wild 5 crass, crude, gross 6 coarse, desert, fallow, savage, vulgar 7 boorish, lowbrow, uncouth 8 barbaric, unplowed, untilled 9 barbarian, barbarous, inelegant, unrefined 10 unpolished 11 uncivilized

uncultured
3 raw 4 rude 5 crass, crude, gross, rough 6 coarse, vulgar 7 artless, boorish, ill-bred, loutish, lowbrow, lowbrow, natural, uncouth 8 barbaric, churlish, cloddish 9 barbarian, barbarous, benighted, inelegant, unrefined 10 unpolished 11 uncivilized 13 unenlightened

uncustomary
4 rare 7 special, strange, unusual 8 aberrant, abnormal, atypical, singular, uncommon 9 anomalous 10 surprising, unfamiliar, unorthodox 11 exceptional 13 extraordinary

uncut
5 whole 6 entire, intact 8 complete 9 undiluted 10 full-length, unabridged 11 uncondensed 13 unabbreviated

undamaged
5 sound, whole 6 intact, unhurt 8 unbroken, unmarred 9 uninjured, unscathed 10 unimpaired 11 unblemished

undaunted
4 bold 5 brave 6 daring, heroic 7 doughty, Spartan, valiant 8 fearless, intrepid, resolute, unafraid, valorous 9 audacious 10 courageous 11 lionhearted, unconquered, unflinching 12 stouthearted

_____ und Drang
5 Sturm

undeceive
8 disabuse 11 disillusion

undecided
4 iffy, moot, open 6 unsure 7 dubious, pending 8 doubtful, wavering 9 equivocal, tentative, uncertain, unsettled 10 ambivalent, indefinite, unresolved 12 undetermined

undeclared
5 tacit 6 unsaid 7 assumed, implied 8 accepted, implicit, inferred, presumed, unspoken, unstated 10 understood

undecorated
4 bare 5 plain, stark 6 homely, severe, simple 8 no-frills 9 unadorned

12 unornamented 13 unembellished, unembroidered

undefiled
4 pure 6 chaste, intact, vestal, virgin 8 innocent, spotless, virginal, virtuous 9 stainless, unstained, unsullied, untainted 10 immaculate 11 unblemished, untarnished

undefined
3 dim 4 hazy 5 faint, vague 6 bleary 7 obscure, shadowy, unclear 8 inchoate, nebulous, unformed 9 amorphous, shapeless 10 indistinct 12 undetermined

undemonstrative
4 calm, cold, cool 5 aloof, chill 7 aseptic, distant, laconic 8 reserved, retiring 9 contained, inhibited, shrinking, withdrawn 10 restrained, unsociable 11 emotionless, passionless, standoffish, unemotional 12 matter-of-fact, unresponsive 13 self-contained

undeniable
6 patent 7 certain, evident, genuine, obvious 8 manifest 9 veridical 10 inarguable 11 indubitable, irrefutable, unequivocal 12 indisputable 13 incontestable

undependable
6 fickle, tricky, unsafe 7 erratic 10 capricious, fly-by-night, inconstant, unreliable 12 inconsistent, questionable 13 irresponsible, unpredictable, untrustworthy

under
3 low, sub 4 down, less 5 below, lower, short 6 lesser 7 beneath, covered, subject 8 downward, inferior 9 dependent, receiving, secondary, subjacent 11 subordinate
prefix: 3 hyp, sub 4 hypo

undercarriage
5 frame 9 framework 11 landing gear

undercover
6 covert, hidden, secret 7 furtive, stealth, sub-rosa 8 hush-hush, stealthy 11 clandestine 12 confidential 13 surreptitious
person: 3 spy 4 mole 5 agent, spook 6 sleuth 9 detective, operative 10 counterspy 11 double agent, secret agent 12 counteragent

undercroft
5 crypt, vault 7 chamber 8 catacomb

undercut
7 subvert 8 sabotage

underdeveloped
4 poor 7 dwarfed, stunted 8 backward, immature 9 unevolved 10 third-world

underdog
5 loser 6 victim 7 also-ran, fall guy 9 dark horse

underdone
3 raw, red 4 rare

underestimate
6 slight 7 dismiss 8 belittle, discount, disprize, minimize 9 deprecate, disparage, sell short 10 depreciate

undergarment
3 bra 4 BVD's, slip 5 teddy 6 bikini, bodice, briefs, corset, girdle, shorts, undies 7 chemise, drawers, panties, stammel, step-ins 8 lingerie, pretties, Skivvies, woollies 9 brassiere, jockstrap, long johns, petticoat, underwear 10 foundation

undergo
4 bear, face 5 abide, brave, brook 6 endure, suffer 7 sustain, weather 8 submit to, tolerate 9 withstand 10 experience

undergraduate
4 coed 5 frosh 6 junior, senior 8 freshman 9 collegian, sophomore

underground
4 tube 5 metro, train 6 buried, hidden, nether, secret, subway 7 illegal, off-beat, railway 8 hypogeal, hypogean 10 undercover 11 alternative, clandestine 12 subterranean 13 surreptitious

underhanded
3 sly 4 wily 5 shady 6 covert, crafty, secret, shifty, sneaky, tricky 7 cunning, devious, elusive, evasive, furtive, sub-rosa 8 guileful, sneaking, stealthy 9 deceitful, deceptive 10 circuitous 11 clandestine, duplicitous 13 surreptitious

underlie
4 bear 6 prop up 7 subtend, support 8 buttress

underline
4 mark 6 play up, stress 9 emphasize, italicize 10 accentuate, underscore

underling
4 aide, peon, serf 5 gofer, scrub, slave 6 flunky, gopher, lackey, menial, minion 7 fall guy 8 inferior 9 assistant, attendant, subaltern 11 subordinate

underlying
4 root 5 basal, basic 7 primary 8 implicit 9 elemental, essential 11 fundamental

Under Milk Wood author
6 Thomas (Dylan)

undermine
3 sap 4 foil 5 blunt, erode 6 impair, thwart, weaken 7 cripple, disable, subvert 8 sabotage 9 attenuate, frustrate 10 debilitate, demoralize

undermost
6 bottom, lowest 9 lowermost 10 bottommost, nethermost, rock-bottom

underneath
4 sole 5 below, lower 6 bottom 7 covered

underpin
4 back, base, prop, root 5 brace 6 uphold 7 bolster, justify, shore up, support 8 buttress, validate 10 strengthen 11 corroborate

underpinning
4 base, prop, root, stay 5 basis, brace 7 bedrock, footing, seating, support 8 buttress 10 foundation, groundwork 12 substructure

underprivileged
4 poor 5 needy 7 hapless, unlucky 8 deprived 11 handicapped, unfortunate 13 disadvantaged

underrate
7 devalue 8 discount, mark down, minimize, write off 9 devaluate, write down 10 depreciate

underscore
6 accent, play up, stress 9 emphasize, italicize 10 accentuate

underside
4 sole 6 bottom 7 reverse

undersized
3 toy 4 baby, mini, puny 5 dinky, dwarf, pygmy, runty, short, small 6 bantam, little, pocket, slight 9 miniature 10 diminutive 11 Lilliputian

understand
3 con, ken, see 4 know 5 grasp, guess, infer, savvy, sense, think 6 accept, assume, deduce, expect, fathom, figure, follow, gather, reason, reckon, take in, take it 7 believe, discern, imagine, presume, realize, suppose, surmise, suspect 8 conceive, conclude, consider, perceive

9 apprehend, interpret 10 appreciate, comprehend, conjecture

understandable
5 clear, lucid, plain 8 clear-cut, coherent, knowable 9 excusable, graspable, plausible 10 articulate, believable, defensible, fathomable, justifiable, reasonable 11 perceivable, unambiguous 12 intelligible 13 apprehensible

understanding
3 ken, wit 4 deal, pact 5 grasp, sense 6 accord, humane, kindly 7 compact, empathy, entente, insight, mastery 8 sympathy 9 agreement, awareness, knowledge, tolerance 10 acceptance, impression, perception 11 considerate, discernment, explanation, sympathetic 12 apprehension, relationship 13 comprehension

understatement
7 litotes

understood
5 tacit 7 assumed, implied 8 accepted, implicit, inferred, unspoken

understudy
6 double, backup, fill-in, standby 7 stand-in 9 surrogate 10 substitute 11 replacement

undertake
3 try 4 dare 5 assay, begin, essay, start 6 accept, assume, pledge, strive, tackle, take on, take up 7 attempt, certify, execute, perform, promise, warrant 8 commence, contract, covenant, endeavor, set about, set forth, shoulder 9 guarantee

undertaker
8 embalmer 9 mortician

undertaking
3 job 4 task 6 affair, charge, effort 7 calling, emprise, exploit, mission, project, pursuit, venture 8 endeavor 9 adventure, guarantee, operation 10 enterprise 11 proposition, transaction

under-the-table
6 covert, hidden, secret, sneaky 7 furtive, sub-rosa 8 hush-hush, stealthy 9 concealed, underhand 10 undercover 11 clandestine 13 surreptitious

undertone
3 hue, hum 4 cast, hint, tint 5 shade 6 mumble, murmur, mutter 7 inkling 10 suggestion 11 association, connotation, implication

undertow
4 eddy 7 current, riptide, sea puss

undervalue
see **underrate**

underwater
9 submarine 10 subaquatic, subaqueous
breathing apparatus: 5 scuba
captain: 4 Nemo
chamber: 7 caisson
device: 8 paravane
missile: 7 torpedo
sound detector: 5 sonar

underwear
see **undergarment**

underwood
5 brush, copse, hedge, scrub 7 boscage, coppice, thicket 9 shrubbery

underworld
4 hell 5 hades, Sheol 6 Erebus, Tophet 7 Gehenna, inferno 8 gangland 9 antipodes 11 Pandemonium
boatman: 6 Charon
deity: 3 Dis 4 Bran 5 Pluto 6 Osiris
goddess: 6 Hecate 10 Persephone
organization: 5 Mafia
relating to: 8 chthonic
watchdog: 8 Cerberus

underwrite
4 back, fund, sign 5 endow, stake 6 assure, insure, pay for, secure 7 agree to, endorse, finance, sponsor, support 8 bankroll 9 grubstake, guarantee 11 subscribe to

undesigning
5 frank 6 candid, honest 7 artless, earnest, genuine, sincere 9 guileless, ingenuous, unfeigned 10 aboveboard, forthright

undesirable
8 annoying, unwanted 9 offensive, unwelcome 10 ill-favored, unpleasant, unsuitable 11 displeasing, inadvisable, troublesome 12 disagreeable, unacceptable, unattractive 13 inappropriate, objectionable

undesired
8 needless, unsought, unwanted 9 uninvited, unwelcome 10 gratuitous 11 uncalled-for, unnecessary 12 nonessential

undetermined
5 vague 7 dubious, obscure, pending, unclear 8 doubtful 9 ambiguous,

equivocal, uncertain, undecided, undefined, unsettled **10** ill-defined, indefinite, indistinct **12** inconclusive

undeveloped
5 crude, green, rough **6** latent
8 backward, immature, inchoate
9 embryonic, incipient, primitive, unevolved
10 unfinished

undiluted
4 neat, pure **5** sheer, utter **7** genuine, unmixed **8** absolute, straight **9** authentic, unalloyed **11** unmitigated, unqualified
13 unadulterated

undiplomatic
4 rash, rude **5** brash, cocky **6** brazen, cheeky **8** impudent, tactless **9** audacious, hotheaded, impolitic, impulsive, maladroit, untactful **10** ill-advised, indiscreet
11 impertinent, injudicious, insensitive, thoughtless **12** presumptuous

undisciplined
4 wild **6** unruly, wanton **7** froward, restive, wayward, willful **8** contrary, untoward
9 fractious **10** disorderly, rebellious, refractory **11** intractable **12** contumacious, noncompliant, obstreperous, recalcitrant, ungovernable, unmanageable

undisclosed
6 hidden, sealed, secret **7** unknown, unnamed **8** ulterior, withheld **9** anonymous **10** unreported, unrevealed **11** clandestine, unmentioned, unspecified **12** confidential, undesignated, unidentified

undisguised
4 bald, open, pure **5** frank, naked, overt, sheer, stark **6** candid, patent **7** obvious
8 apparent, explicit, manifest, palpable
9 barefaced **11** openhearted, unconcealed, unvarnished

undistinguished
5 cheap, stock **6** common **7** humdrum, obscure, routine **8** déclassé, everyday, inferior, low-grade, mediocre, middling, ordinary, workaday **10** second-rate
11 commonplace, nondescript, second-class **12** run-of-the-mill **13** insignificant

undivided
3 one **4** full **5** fixed, total, whole **6** entire, intact, united **8** complete, unbroken
9 unanimous **10** continuous, unswerving
11 indivisible **12** concentrated, undistracted

undo
4 free, open, ruin **5** annul, loose, untie, upset, wrack, wreck **6** cancel, defeat, loosen, negate, stymie, unbind, unsnap
7 abolish, destroy, nullify, release, reverse, vitiate, wipe out **8** abrogate, unfasten, unloosen **9** disengage **10** invalidate
11 disentangle, outmaneuver

undoing
4 bane, doom, ruin, slip **5** shame
7 misstep **8** downfall, reversal **9** destroyer, overthrow, ruination **10** misfortune
11 destruction, humiliation

undoubted
4 real, sure, true **7** certain, genuine
8 definite, positive **9** authentic
10 undisputed

undoubtedly
5 truly **6** indeed, really, surely **7** clearly
8 of course **9** assuredly, certainly
10 definitely, positively, presumably, undeniably **11** indubitably

undress
see **unclothe**

undressed
4 nude, rude **5** naked **6** unclad **7** exposed
8 in the raw, stripped **9** au naturel, unclothed

undue
5 inapt **7** extreme **8** ill-timed, improper, needless, untimely **9** excessive, unfitting
10 immoderate, indecorous, inordinate, unsuitable **11** extravagant, uncalled-for, unnecessary, unwarranted **12** unreasonable **13** inappropriate, unjustifiable

undulant fever
11 brucellosis

undulate
4 roll, swag, sway, wave **5** heave, snake, swell, swing **6** billow, ripple **7** slither
9 fluctuate, oscillate

unduly
3 too **6** overly **9** extremely, immensely
11 excessively **12** immoderately, inordinately, unreasonably
13 unnecessarily

undying
7 abiding, ageless, endless, eternal
8 enduring, immortal, unending
9 continual, deathless, perennial, perpetual, unceasing **10** continuing

11 amaranthine, everlasting 12 imperishable, unquenchable

unearth
4 find, show 5 dig up, learn 6 exhume, expose, reveal 7 exhibit, find out, root out, uncover 8 come upon, disclose, discover, dredge up, excavate 9 ascertain, determine 10 come across

unearthly
5 eerie, weird 6 absurd, insane, spooky 7 awesome, ghostly, uncanny, ungodly 8 abnormal, ethereal, heavenly, numinous, spectral 9 appalling, fantastic 10 miraculous, mysterious, outlandish, superhuman, suprahuman 12 preposterous, supermundane, supernatural 13 preternatural

unease
4 care, fear 5 angst, worry 6 strain, stress, unrest 7 anxiety, concern, tension 8 disquiet, distress 9 abashment, confusion, misgiving 10 discomfort, discontent, solicitude 11 disquietude, fretfulness, nervousness, uncertainty, uptightness 12 apprehension, discomfiture, discomposure 13 embarrassment

uneasy
4 edgy 5 jumpy, tense 6 afraid 7 anxious, awkward, fearful, fidgety, fretful, nervous, restive, unquiet, uptight, worried 8 agitated, doubtful, insecure, restless, unstable 9 ambiguous, concerned, difficult, disturbed, perturbed, uncertain, unsettled 10 disquieted, precarious, solicitous 11 embarrassed 12 apprehensive 13 uncomfortable

uneducated
5 crude, rough 8 ignorant, untaught 9 benighted, untutored 10 illiterate, unlettered, unschooled 12 uncultivated, uninstructed

unembellished
4 bald, bare 5 blunt, plain, spare, stark 6 severe 7 austere 9 essential, unadorned 11 undecorated, unelaborate, ungarnished, unvarnished 12 unornamented 13 unembroidered, unpretentious

unemotional
4 cold, cool 5 chill, stoic, stony 6 frigid, sedate, serene 7 deadpan, equable, glacial, stoical 8 composed, obdurate, reserved, reticent 9 apathetic, impassive 10 hard-boiled, phlegmatic 11 insensitive, passionless, unexcitable 12 intellectual, thick-skinned, unresponsive 13 dispassionate

unemployed
4 idle 5 fired 6 otiose, unused 7 jobless, laid off, loafing 8 inactive, leisured, workless 10 unoccupied

unending
7 eternal, undying 8 constant, immortal, infinite, timeless 9 boundless, ceaseless, continual, incessant, limitless, perennial, perpetual, unceasing 10 continuous 11 amaranthine, everlasting, unremitting 12 interminable 13 uninterrupted

unenlightened
5 naive 6 unread 7 heathen, unaware 8 backward, ignorant, nescient 9 benighted, unknowing 10 uneducated, uninformed 11 uninitiated 12 uncultivated

unenthusiastic
4 cool 5 tepid 8 grudging, listless, lukewarm 9 apathetic, unexcited 10 lackluster, lacklustre, spiritless 11 halfhearted, indifferent, perfunctory 12 uninterested

unequal
3 odd 6 uneven, unfair 7 diverse 8 inferior, lopsided, one-sided 9 different, disparate, divergent, irregular 10 asymmetric, dissimilar, inadequate, mismatched, off-balance 12 insufficient

unequaled
6 unique 7 supreme 8 foremost, nonesuch, peerless 9 matchless, paramount, unmatched, unrivaled 10 preeminent, surpassing 12 incomparable, transcendent, unparalleled 13 unprecedented

unequivocal
5 clear 6 direct, patent 7 certain, evident 8 apparent, definite, distinct, explicit, manifest, palpable 10 undeniable 11 categorical, indubitable, unambiguous 12 indisputable, undisputable

unerring
5 exact 6 dead-on 7 certain, correct, perfect, precise 8 accurate, reliable 9 faultless, unfailing 10 dependable, infallible 11 trustworthy

unessential
8 marginal, needless, unneeded 9 redundant 10 expendable, gratuitous, irrelevant, peripheral, unrequired 11 dispensable, superfluous, uncalled-for,

unimportant, unnecessary **13** insignificant, insubstantial

unethical
5 venal, wrong **7** corrupt, crooked, immoral **9** dishonest, reprobate **12** disreputable, unprincipled, unscrupulous

uneven
3 odd **4** wavy **5** bumpy, erose, harsh, jaggy, rough **6** craggy, jagged, patchy, ragged, random, rugged, spotty **7** scraggy, unequal, varying **8** lopsided, scabrous, scraggly, variable haphazard, hit-or-miss, irregular **10** asymmetric, imbalanced, unbalanced

unevenness
4 bump, wave **7** anomaly **8** asperity, imparity **9** disparity, imbalance, roughness, variation **10** inequality **12** irregularity, lopsidedness **13** disproportion

uneventful
5 usual **6** placid **7** humdrum, prosaic, routine **8** ordinary **10** unexciting **11** commonplace **12** unremarkable

unexampled
4 lone, only, sole, solo **5** alone **6** unique **8** singular, solitary **9** matchless, unequaled, unmatched, unrivaled **10** consummate, inimitable, sui generis, unequalled, unrivalled **12** incomparable, unparalleled **13** unprecedented

unexcited
4 calm **5** blasé, stoic **6** placid, sedate, serene **7** relaxed, stoical **8** composed, tranquil **9** apathetic, collected, unruffled **10** nonchalant **11** indifferent **12** uninterested **13** dispassionate

unexciting
4 arid, dull, tame **5** banal, bland, ho-hum **6** boring, stodgy **7** humdrum, insipid, prosaic, tedious **8** lifeless, tiresome **10** monotonous **11** commonplace **13** uninteresting

unexpected
10 surprising, unforeseen **11** unpredicted **13** unanticipated

unexpectedly
5 aback, short **6** sudden **7** unaware **8** abruptly, suddenly, unawares **9** forthwith **11** unwittingly **12** accidentally **13** inadvertently

unexpended
5 saved **7** reserve, surplus **8** left over, reserved **9** remaining

unexpired
5 valid **9** operative

unexpressed
5 tacit **6** silent, unsaid **7** assumed, implied **8** implicit, presumed, unspoken, wordless **9** unuttered **10** undeclared, understood

unfailing
4 fast, sure **7** certain, devoted **8** constant, faithful, reliable, resolute, surefire, unerring **9** steadfast, unvarying **10** consistent, dependable, infallible, invariable, persistent, unchanging, unflagging, unwavering **11** everlasting, persevering, unrelenting **12** tried-and-true **13** inexhaustible

unfair
4 foul **5** wrong **6** biased, shabby, uneven, unjust **7** unequal **8** wrongful **9** arbitrary, dishonest, unethical **10** prejudiced **11** inequitable, underhanded, unrighteous

unfaithful
5 false **6** untrue **8** cheating, disloyal, recreant, turncoat **9** faithless, two-timing **10** adulterous, inaccurate, perfidious, traitorous **11** treacherous **13** untrustworthy

unfaltering
3 set **4** firm **6** steady **7** abiding **8** constant, enduring, resolute, tireless **9** steadfast, unfailing **10** continuous, unflagging, unwavering **11** persevering **12** never-failing, wholehearted

unfamiliar
3 new **5** alien, novel **6** exotic **7** foreign, strange, unaware, unknown **8** peculiar **11** incognizant, out-of-the-way **12** unaccustomed, unacquainted

unfashionable
5 dated, dowdy, passé, stale **6** bygone, démodé, old-hat, shabby **7** outworn **8** outdated, outmoded **9** out-of-date, unstylish **10** antiquated, oldfangled

unfasten
4 free, open, undo **5** loose, unbar, unfix, unpin, untie **6** detach, loosen, unbind, unbolt, unlace, unlock, unsnap **7** release, unclasp, unhitch, unlatch, unleash, unloose, unstrap **8** unbuckle, unfetter, unloosen, untether **9** disengage

unfathomable
7 abysmal, obscure **8** profound **9** boundless, enigmatic, unplumbed **10** bottomless, fathomless, unknowable **11** inscrutable **12** immeasurable,

impenetrable

unfavorable
3 bad, ill **4** poor **6** averse, unfair, unkind
7 adverse, hostile, opposed **8** contrary,
damaging, inimical, negative **9** disliking,
troubling **11** detrimental, displeasing
12 antagonistic, disapproving, inauspicious
prefix: 3 dys

unfavorably
4 awry **5** amiss, badly **6** astray, poorly
7 wrongly **10** negatively, unsuitably
13 unfortunately

unfeasible
8 quixotic **9** visionary **10** chimerical,
impossible, unworkable **11** impractical,
speculative, theoretical, unrealistic
12 unattainable, unrealizable
13 impracticable

unfeeling
4 cold, hard, numb **5** cruel, harsh, stern,
stony **6** brutal, leaden, marble, numbed,
severe, stolid, unkind **7** callous
8 benumbed, deadened, hardened,
obdurate, pitiless, ruthless **9** apathetic,
heartless, indurated, insensate, senseless,
uncaring **10** hardboiled, insensible,
insentient **11** cold-blooded, coldhearted,
hardhearted, insensitive, unemotional
12 anesthetized **13** unsympathetic

unfeigned
4 real, true **6** actual, hearty, honest
7 artless, earnest, genuine, natural, sincere
8 innocent **9** guileless, heartfelt, ingenuous
11 undesigning **12** wholehearted

unfinished
3 raw **5** crude, rough **7** sketchy
9 imperfect, roughhewn, undressed
10 incomplete, unpolished

Unfinished Symphony composer
8 Schubert (Franz)

unfit
4 sick, weak **5** inapt, inept **6** faulty
7 deprive, disable, unsound, useless
8 disabled, improper, unsuited **9** ill-suited,
incapable, maladroit **10** disqualify, ill-
adapted, inadequate, ineligible, unsuitable
11 incompetent, unqualified
12 disqualified, incompatible
13 inappropriate, incapacitated

unfitting
5 inapt **8** improper, unseemly **9** imprudent
10 ill-advised, inapposite, malapropos,
unbecoming, unsuitable **11** inadvisable
13 inappropriate

unfix
4 part, undo **5** loose, sever **6** cut off,
detach, loosen, sunder, unbind **7** unloose
8 uncouple, unfasten, unloosen
9 disengage **10** disconnect, dissociate

unflagging
6 steady **7** staunch **8** constant, tireless,
untiring **9** unceasing, unfailing, unwearied
11 persevering, unfaltering, unrelenting,
unremitting **13** indefatigable, inexhaustible

unflappable
4 calm **6** poised, serene **7** assured,
equable **8** composed, laid-back
9 collected, unruffled **10** deliberate,
nonchalant **11** self-assured **13** imperturbable, self-possessed

unfledged
5 green, young **6** callow, jejune, unripe
7 puerile **8** immature, juvenile
10 unseasoned **11** undeveloped,
unfeathered **13** inexperienced

unflinching
4 firm, grim **6** dogged **7** doughty, staunch,
valiant **8** intrepid, resolute **9** dauntless,
steadfast **10** relentless, unwavering,
unyielding **11** unfaltering, unrelenting
12 stouthearted

unfold
4 open **6** deduce, evolve, expand, expose,
extend, flower, mature, reveal, unwrap
7 blossom, burgeon, clear up, develop,
display, dope out, exhibit, explain, resolve
8 decipher, disclose, evidence, manifest
9 elaborate, explicate, figure out, puzzle
out, transpire **10** effloresce, outstretch
11 come to light

unforced
4 easy **7** natural, willing, witting **8** elective,
optional **9** available, easygoing, voluntary
10 deliberate, volitional **11** intentional
12 unprescribed **13** discretionary,
noncompulsory

unforeseeable
9 uncertain, unplanned **10** accidental

unforeseen
6 chance **8** surprise **10** accidental,
surprising, unexpected **11** unlooked-for,
unpredicted **12** unanticipated

unforgivable
9 untenable **10** censurable, inexpiable,
outrageous **11** blameworthy, inexcusable,
intolerable **12** indefensible, unacceptable,
unpardonable **13** insupportable,
reprehensible, unjustifiable

unformed
4 rude 5 crude, rough, vague 6 callow
8 immature, inchoate, nebulous, unshaped
9 amorphous, roughhewn, shapeless
10 indefinite, unfinished, unpolished 11 undeveloped, unfashioned 12 unstructured
13 indeterminate

unfortunate
3 bad, sad 4 dire, poor 6 woeful, wretch
7 adverse, awkward, hapless, unhappy,
unlucky 8 grievous, ill-fated, luckless,
untoward, wretched 9 desperate,
graceless, ill-chosen, miserable
10 afflictive, calamitous, deplorable,
disastrous, ill-starred, lamentable,
unsuitable 11 distressing, regrettable, star-
crossed, unfavorable 12 disagreeable,
inauspicious, infelicitous, unsuccessful
13 heartbreaking

unfounded
4 idle, vain 5 false 8 baseless, spurious,
unproven 9 deceptive, dishonest,
untenable 10 fabricated, fallacious,
gratuitous, groundless, mendacious,
misleading, untruthful 11 uncalled-for,
unsupported, unwarranted

unfriendly
4 cold, cool 5 alien, aloof, chill, gruff, surly
6 chilly, frosty, remote 7 distant, grouchy,
hostile, opposed, warlike 8 inimical,
unsocial 10 antisocial, censorious,
inimicable, unsociable 11 ill-disposed,
uncongenial 12 antagonistic, disagreeable,
inhospitable, misanthropic, unneighborly
13 unsympathetic

unfruitful
4 arid, idle 5 empty, waste 6 barren,
desert, effete, fallow, futile, wasted
7 parched, sterile, useless 8 abortive,
bootless, depleted, impotent 9 infertile,
pointless 10 unavailing 11 ineffective,
ineffectual 12 impoverished, unproductive,
unprofitable

unfurl
4 open 6 expose, reveal, spread, unfold,
unroll, unwind 7 develop, display, exhibit,
uncover 8 disclose 9 elaborate, spread
out

unfurnished
4 bare 5 empty 6 vacant

unfussy
5 loose 6 breezy, casual, common,
dégagé, folksy, mellow 7 cursory, relaxed
8 familiar, informal, laid-back 9 easygoing
10 unreserved 11 low-pressure,
pococurante, unconcerned 12 unparticular
13 unceremonious, uncomplicated

ungainly
5 gawky, lanky, splay 6 clumsy, klutzy,
oafish 7 awkward, boorish, hulking, loutish,
lumpish, uncouth 8 bungling, clownish,
lubberly, unwieldy 9 lumbering, maladroit
10 blundering

ungarnished
5 plain 6 modest, simple 9 unadorned
11 undecorated, unelaborate
12 unornamented 13 unembellished,
unembroidered

ungenerous
4 mean 5 petty, tight 6 paltry, shabby,
skimpy, stingy 7 chintzy, miserly
8 grudging, picayune, ungiving 9 illiberal,
niggardly, penurious 11 closefisted,
tightfisted 12 parsimonious 13 penny-
pinching

ungodly
see **unholy**

ungovernable
4 wild 6 unruly 7 froward, lawless, willful
8 mutinous, untoward 9 fractious,
turbulent, unbridled 10 disorderly,
headstrong, rebellious, refractory,
tumultuous 11 intractable 12 recalcitrant,
uncontrolled, unmanageable
13 irrepressible, undisciplined

ungraceful
5 crude, gawky, inept, stiff 6 clumsy,
gauche, klutzy, oafish, wooden 7 artless,
awkward, halting, labored, stilted
8 bumbling, bungling, ungainly, untoward
9 all thumbs, inelegant, lumbering,
maladroit 10 blundering

ungracious
4 rude 5 gruff 6 crusty 7 brusque, uncivil
8 churlish, impolite 9 offensive
10 unmannerly 11 disobliging, ill-
mannered, impertinent, thoughtless,
uncalled-for 12 disagreeable, discourteous
13 disrespectful, inconsiderate,
unceremonious

ungraspable
6 opaque 7 obscure 8 baffling
9 enigmatic 10 unknowable 12 impenetrable, inexplicable, unfathomable

ungrateful
9 thankless

unguarded
5 frank, hasty 6 candid, direct, unwary

7 offhand **8** careless, heedless, reckless
9 impolitic, imprudent, impulsive
10 incautious, indiscreet, unthinking
11 defenseless, thoughtless, unprotected

unguent
4 balm **5** cream, salve **6** balsam, cerate, chrism, lotion **8** ointment **9** emollient, lubricant **11** embrocation

ungulate
3 hog, pig **4** deer **5** horse, tapir **6** hoofed **8** elephant **10** rhinoceros

unhallowed
4 evil **6** impure, unholy, wicked **7** immoral, impious, profane, ungodly **8** infernal **9** nefarious **10** desecrated, iniquitous, irreverent **13** unconsecrated

unhampered
4 free, open **5** frank, loose **6** direct **8** uncurbed **9** unbridled, unchecked, unimpeded, unlimited **10** unhindered **11** uninhibited, untrammeled **12** unrestrained, unrestricted, unobstructed **13** unconstrained

unhand
5 let go **7** release

unhandy
5 bulky, inept **6** clumsy, gauche, klutzy **7** awkward, halting, hulking **8** bumbling, bungling, cumbrous, unwieldy **9** all thumbs, ham-handed, maladroit, ponderous **10** cumbersome, unskillful **12** inconvenient

unhappiness
3 woe **5** blues, dolor, dumps, gloom, grief, worry **6** misery, mishap, sorrow **7** anxiety, sadness **8** distress **9** dejection **10** depression, desolation, discontent, heartbreak, melancholy **11** despondency, dolefulness **12** mournfulness, wretchedness **13** cheerlessness

unhappy
3 sad **4** down, grim **5** sorry **6** dismal, dreary, gloomy **7** joyless **8** dejected, downcast, mournful, saddened, troubled, wretched **9** cheerless, depressed, sorrowful, woebegone **10** despondent, dispirited, melancholy **11** melancholic, unfortunate **12** disconsolate, heavyhearted

unharmed
4 safe **5** sound **6** intact, secure, unhurt **8** unbroken, unmarred **9** protected, undamaged, undefiled, uninjured, unscathed **10** unimpaired **11** unblemished

unhealthiness
7 ailment, disease, illness, malaise **8** debility, sickness **9** infirmity **10** affliction, sickliness **11** decrepitude **13** indisposition

unhealthy
3 ill **4** sick **6** ailing, infirm, sickly, unwell **7** baneful, noisome, noxious, unsound **8** diseased **9** injurious **11** deleterious, unwholesome **12** insalubrious

unheard-of
3 new **6** unique **7** obscure, unknown, unnoted **8** nameless **10** phenomenal, unrenowned **12** uncelebrated **13** extraordinary, unprecedented

unhesitating
7 assured, earnest **8** decisive, positive, resolute **9** confident, immediate, unchecked **10** determined, forthright, purposeful **11** unflinching **12** wholehearted

unhinge
5 addle, craze **6** madden, ruffle **7** derange **9** unbalance

unhinged
3 mad **4** daft, loco, nuts **5** balmy, crazy, loony, wacky **6** insane **7** lunatic, unglued **8** demented, deranged **9** disturbed **10** unbalanced

unholy
4 base, evil, vile **6** impure, sinful, wicked **7** heinous, immoral, impious, profane, ungodly **8** dreadful, fiendish, god-awful, shocking **9** atheistic, barbarous **10** iniquitous, irreverent, outrageous, scandalous, unhallowed **11** irreligious, unbelieving **12** sacrilegious, unsanctified **13** reprehensible

unhorse
5 pitch, throw **6** topple, tumble, unseat **7** buck off **8** dislodge, dismount, overturn, unsaddle **9** overthrow

unhurried
4 easy, slow **7** laggard, relaxed **8** dilatory, laid-back **9** easygoing, leisurely **10** deliberate **11** low-pressure

unhurt
4 safe **5** sound, whole **6** entire, intact **7** perfect **8** unbroken, unharmed, unmarred **9** undamaged, uninjured, unscathed, untouched **10** unimpaired **11** unblemished

unification
5 union **6** fusion, hookup, merger

7 amalgam, joining, linkage, melding, merging 8 alliance, coupling 9 coalition 10 connection, federation 11 affiliation, coalescence, combination 12 amalgamation 13 confederation, consolidation

uniform
4 even, like, suit 5 alike, dress, equal, level 6 attire, outfit, stable, steady 7 ordered, orderly, regular, similar, stabile 8 constant, unvaried 9 consonant, unvarying 10 comparable, consistent, invariable, unchanging 11 homogeneous 13 unfluctuating
combining form: 3 iso
type: 5 blues, habit, khaki, whites 6 livery

uniformity
6 parity 7 oneness 8 equality, evenness, identity, monotony, sameness 9 agreement, congruity, constancy 11 consistency 13 invariability

uniformly
6 always, evenly 7 equally 8 smoothly 10 comparably 11 analogously, identically 12 equivalently

unify
3 tie, wed 4 bind, bond, fuse, knit, link, mesh 5 blend, marry, merge, unite 6 cement, couple 7 combine, conjoin 8 coalesce, compound, federate 9 integrate 10 amalgamate, centralize, synthesize 11 concatenate, consolidate

unimaginable
10 incredible, unknowable 11 unthinkable 12 mind-boggling, unbelievable 13 extraordinary, inconceivable, indescribable

unimaginative
4 dull, flat 5 banal, bland, trite, vapid 6 common 7 literal, prosaic, routine, vanilla 8 bromidic 10 derivative, pedestrian, uncreative, uninspired 11 commonplace

unimpaired
4 safe 5 sound 6 intact, unhurt 7 perfect 8 unbroken, unharmed, unmarred 9 undamaged, uninjured, unscathed 11 unblemished

unimpassioned
4 calm, cool 5 sober, stoic 6 placid, remote, stolid 7 deadpan 8 detached, lukewarm, reserved, tranquil 9 impassive, temperate 10 phlegmatic, spiritless 11 cold-blooded, emotionless 12 matter-of-fact

unimpeachable
5 valid 7 correct 8 flawless, reliable, virtuous 9 blameless, exemplary, faultless, unspotted, unsullied 10 conclusive, impeccable, undisputed 11 unblemished, untarnished 13 authoritative

unimportant
5 minor, petty 6 casual, minute, paltry 7 trivial 8 piddling 9 small-beer, worthless 10 expendable, immaterial, irrelevant, negligible 11 dispensable, meaningless, superfluous 13 insignificant

uninformed
7 unaware 8 ignorant, nescient 9 oblivious, unknowing, unwitting 10 unfamiliar 11 incognizant, superficial 12 unacquainted, undiscerning

uninhabited
5 empty, waste 6 barren, vacant 7 vacated 8 deserted, desolate, forsaken 9 abandoned, evacuated 10 unoccupied

uninhibited
3 lax 4 free 5 loose 8 uncurbed 9 expansive, fancy-free, liberated, unbridled 10 boisterous, ungoverned, unhampered, unreserved 11 spontaneous, unrepressed, untrammeled 12 unrestrained, unsuppressed 13 unconstrained

uninjured
4 safe 5 sound, whole 6 intact, unhurt 8 unharmed, unmarred 9 undamaged, undefiled, unscathed, untouched 10 unimpaired 11 unblemished

uninspired
4 blah, drab, dull 5 stock, trite, vapid 6 boring, leaden, old-hat, stodgy 7 humdrum, insipid, plastic, sterile, vanilla 8 bromidic, lifeless, ordinary 9 colorless 10 lackluster, lacklustre, pedestrian, uncreative, unoriginal 11 commonplace 13 unimaginative

unintelligent
4 dumb 6 obtuse, stupid 7 asinine, brutish, doltish, fatuous, foolish, moronic, vacuous, witless 8 mindless 9 brainless, ludicrous 10 half-witted, ill-advised, irrational, ridiculous, weak-minded 11 harebrained, lamebrained 12 feebleminded

unintentional
6 chance, random 9 haphazard, unplanned, unwitting 10 accidental, fortuitous, incidental, unexpected, unforeseen, unthinking 11 inadvertent, unconscious, unlooked-for 12 adventitious, coincidental 13 unanticipated

uninterested
5 aloof, blasé, bored, jaded 9 apathetic, incurious, unexcited 10 uninvolved 11 indifferent, unconcerned

uninteresting
3 dry 4 arid, blah, drab, dull, flat 5 banal, dusty, ho-hum, stale 6 boring, jejune 7 humdrum, insipid, tedious 8 bromidic, plodding, tiresome 9 colorless, dryasdust, wearisome 10 monotonous, pedestrian, uneventful, unexciting 11 uninspiring

uninterrupted
6 direct 7 endless, nonstop 8 constant, unbroken, unending 9 ceaseless, continual, incessant, perpetual, sustained, unceasing 10 continuous 11 undisturbed, unremitting 12 interminable

uninvited
7 unasked 8 unbidden, unsought 9 intruding 10 gratuitous 11 uncalled-for, unrequested, unsolicited 12 presumptuous

union
4 bloc, bond, club 5 alloy, group, guild, joint 6 fusion, league, merger 7 amalgam, joining, melding, merging, society 8 alliance, congress, coupling, junction, juncture, marriage, sodality 9 coalition 10 connection, federation, fellowship 11 association, brotherhood, coalescence, combination, confederacy, cooperative, unification 13 confederation, consolidation
labor: 3 AFL, CIO, UAW, UMW 5 ILGWU

Union of Soviet Socialist Republics
see U.S.S.R.

unique
3 odd, one 4 lone, only, sole, solo 5 alone, novel 6 single 8 peculiar, peerless, singular, solitary, uncommon, unwonted 9 anomalous, exclusive, matchless, unequaled, unmatched, unrivaled 10 inimitable, particular, sui generis, unequalled, unexampled, unrivalled 11 distinctive, exceptional 12 incomparable, unparalleled, unrepeatable 13 extraordinary, idiosyncratic, unprecedented

uniqueness
8 identity 10 singleness 11 singularity 13 individuality

_____-Unis
5 Etats

unit
3 arm, one 4 area, item, part, wing 5 digit, group, monad, piece, whole 6 entity 7 element, measure 8 molecule

9 component 10 individual 11 constituent
administrative: 6 agency, bureau, sector 8 district
boy scout: 5 troop
educational: 6 course
military:
(see at **military**)
of acceleration: 3 gal
of action: 7 episode
of advertising space: 4 line 6 column
of an element: 4 atom 8 molecule
of angular measure: 6 radian
of area: 3 are 4 acre 6 morgen 7 hectare 9 square rod 10 square mile, square yard
of astronomical distance: 6 parsec 9 light-year
of brightness: 7 lambert
of capacity: 3 cup, tun 4 cord, dram, gill, peck, pint 5 liter, litre, minim, ounce, quart 6 barrel, bushel, firkin, gallon
of computer information: 3 bit, gig, meg 4 byte 8 gigabyte, megabyte
of conductance: 3 mho 7 siemens
of distance: 4 mile, yard 5 meter 6 league 7 furlong
of electricity: 3 amp 4 volt, watt 6 ampere 7 coulomb
of energy: 3 erg 5 joule 7 quantum 8 watt-hour
of explosive force: 7 megaton
of fineness: 5 carat, karat
of force: 4 dyne 6 newton 7 poundal
of frequency: 5 hertz 7 fresnel
of grain: 5 sheaf
of heat: 3 BTU 5 therm 7 calorie
of illumination: 3 lux 5 lumen
of inductance: 5 henry
of length: 3 mil, rod 4 foot, hand, inch, mile, rood, yard 5 chain, fermi, meter 6 fathom, micron 7 furlong 9 kilometer
historic: 5 cubit
of loudness: 4 sone 7 decibel
of lumber: 9 board foot
of magnetic flux: 5 gamma, gauss, tesla, weber 7 maxwell
of magnetic intensity: 7 oersted
of magnetomotive force: 7 gilbert
of pressure: 3 bar 4 torr 6 pascal 10 atmosphere
of radiation: 3 rad 8 roentgen
of radioactivity: 5 curie
of resistance: 3 ohm
of solar radiation: 7 langley
of sound absorption: 5 sabin
of speech: 4 word 6 toneme 7 phoneme 8 morpheme, syllable
of speed: 3 CPS, MPH, RPM 4 knot
of temperature: 6 degree, kelvin

of time: 3 day 4 beat, bell, hour, week, year 5 month 6 minute, season, second 8 svedberg
of viscosity: 5 poise
of volume: 9 cubic foot, cubic yard 10 cubic meter
of weight: 3 cwt, ton 4 dram, gram, tael 5 carat, grain, ounce, pound, tonne 6 drachm 7 gigaton, kiloton, quintal, scruple 8 kilogram, millieme 9 metric ton, microgram, milligram
   historic: 3 tod 5 gerah, libra
   Indian: 4 tola
   Russian: 4 pood
of work: 3 erg 5 ergon, joule
social: 4 clan 5 tribe 6 family 7 chapter

unite
3 mix, tie, wed 4 ally, band, bind, bond, fuse, join, knit, link, meld, pool, weld 5 blend, graft, marry, merge, unify 6 cement, couple, gather, league, mingle, splice 7 combine, conjoin, connect 8 assemble, coadjute, coalesce, compound, federate 9 affiliate, aggregate, commingle 10 amalgamate, federalize 11 confederate, incorporate

united
3 one, wed 5 joint 6 allied, linked, merged, wedded 7 made one 8 agreeing, combined, in accord 10 harmonious

United Arab Emirates
capital: 8 Abu Dhabi
city: 5 Dubai 6 Dubayy
coast: 6 Pirate 7 Trucial
emirate: 5 Dubai 6 Dubayy 8 Abu Dhabi
former name: 13 Trucial States
gulf: 4 Oman 7 Persian
monetary unit: 6 dirham
neighbor: 4 Oman 11 Saudi Arabia
peninsula: 7 Arabian
strait: 6 Hormuz

United Kingdom
capital: 6 London
city: 3 Ely 4 Bath 5 Derby, Dover, Leeds 6 Exeter, Oxford 7 Bristol, Cardiff, Glasgow, Paisley 8 Bradford, Brighton, Coventry, Plymouth 9 Cambridge, Edinburgh, Leicester, Liverpool, Newcastle, Sheffield 10 Birmingham, Manchester, Nottingham 11 Bournemouth
colony: 8 Falkland (Islands)
component: 5 Wales 7 England 8 Scotland 12 Great Britain
conqueror: 6 Caesar (Julius) 7 William (the Conqueror)
island: 3 Man 4 Jura, Skye 5 Islay, Lewis, Wight 6 Jersey 8 Anguilla,

Guernsey, Mainland
island group: 6 Orkney 7 Channel 8 Hebrides, Shetland
language: 5 Welsh 6 Gaelic 7 English
leader: 8 Cromwell (Oliver) 9 Churchill (Winston)
monarch: 4 Anne, Mary 5 Henry, James 6 Alfred (the Great), Edward, George 7 Charles, Richard, William 8 Victoria 9 Elizabeth
monetary unit: 5 pence, penny, pound
monetary unit, former: 3 bob 5 crown, groat 6 florin, guinea 7 ha'penny 8 farthing, shilling, sixpence 9 halfpenny 10 threepence
mountain, range: 7 Scafell (Peak), Snowdon 8 Ben Nevis, Cumbrian, Grampian 12 Cheviot Hills
peninsula: 7 Kintyre
prehistoric site: 7 Avebury 9 Skara Brae 10 Stonehenge
river: 3 Dee, Exe, Wye 4 Aire, Avon, Ouse 5 Clyde 6 Mersey, Severn, Thames
sea: 5 Irish, North 6 Celtic
territory: 8 Anguilla

United Nations
secretary-general: 3 Lie (Trygve) 5 Annan (Kofi), Thant (U) 8 Waldheim (Kurt) 12 Boutros-Ghali (Boutros), Hammarskjöld (Dag) 14 Pérez de Cuéllar (Javier)

United States
desert: 6 Mojave 7 Sonoran 8 Colorado
highest point: 6 Denali (Mt.) 8 McKinley (Mt.)
island: 5 Hawaii, Kodiak, Unimak 7 Nunivak 9 Admiralty, Chichagof 10 St. Lawrence 13 Prince of Wales
island group: 3 Fox 6 Hawaii 8 Aleutian, Pribilof, Thousand
lowest point: 11 Death Valley
mountain range: 5 Coast, Green, Ozark, Rocky, White 7 Cascade, Olympic 9 Blue Ridge, Catskills 10 Adirondack, Great Smoky 11 Appalachian 12 Sierra Nevada
national park: 4 Zion 6 Denali 7 Glacier, Olympic, Redwood, Sequoia 8 Badlands, Carlsbad, Wind Cave, Yosemite 9 Mesa Verde, Mt. Rainier 10 Everglades, Grand Teton, Hot Springs, Isle Royale, Shenandoah 11 Dry Tortugas, Grand Canyon, Kenai Fjords, Mammoth Cave, Yellowstone
possession: 10 Puerto Rico
state: 4 Iowa, Ohio, Utah 5 Idaho, Maine, Texas 6 Alaska, Hawaii, Kansas, Nevada,

Oregon **7** Alabama, Arizona, Florida, Georgia, Indiana, Montana, New York, Vermont, Wyoming **8** Arkansas, Colorado, Delaware, Illinois, Kentucky, Maryland, Michigan, Missouri, Nebraska, Oklahoma, Virginia **9** Louisiana, Minnesota, New Jersey, New Mexico, Tennessee, Wisconsin **10** California, Washington **11** Connecticut, Mississippi, North Dakota, Rhode Island, South Dakota **12** New Hampshire, Pennsylvania, West Virginia **13** Massachusetts, North Carolina, South Carolina
territory: 4 Guam **13** American Samoa, Virgin Islands

unity
5 union **6** accord **7** concord, harmony, oneness **8** identity, soleness **9** agreement, consensus **10** continuity, singleness, solidarity

universal
3 all **5** broad, total, whole **6** common, cosmic, entire, global **7** general, generic **8** catholic **9** extensive, planetary, unlimited, worldwide **10** ecumenical, ubiquitous **11** omnipresent **12** all-embracing, all-inclusive, comprehensive, cosmopolitan
combining form: 4 omni

universe
3 all **5** whole, world **6** cosmos, system **8** creation **9** macrocosm

unjust
5 wrong **6** biased, shabby, unfair **7** partial, unequal **8** one-sided, improper, wrongful **9** inequable **10** prejudiced, undeserved **11** inequitable, unrighteous

unjustifiable
5 undue **7** invalid **8** baseless **9** unfounded, untenable **10** groundless **11** inexcusable, unsupported, unwarranted **12** indefensible

unkempt
5 messy **6** frowsy, frowzy, shaggy, sloppy, untidy **7** ruffled, rumpled, scruffy, tousled **8** scraggly, slipshod, slovenly, uncombed **10** bedraggled, disarrayed, disheveled, disordered, unpolished **11** disarranged

unkind
4 mean, vile **5** cruel, harsh, rough, stern **6** severe **7** callous **8** uncaring **9** inclement, malicious **10** ungenerous, ungracious **11** insensitive, thoughtless, unfavorable **12** uncharitable **13** unsympathetic

unknowable
6 arcane, hidden, mystic, occult, secret **7** cryptic **8** mystical, numinous **9** enigmatic, recondite **10** mysterious **11** inscrutable, ungraspable **12** impenetrable, unfathomable

unknowing
6 unwary **7** unaware **8** heedless, ignorant **9** oblivious, unmindful, unwitting **10** insensible, unfamiliar, uninformed **11** incognizant **12** unsuspecting

unknown
6 hidden, nobody, secret **7** obscure, strange **8** nameless **9** anonymous, incognito

unlawful
6 banned **7** bootleg, corrupt, crooked, illegal, illicit, immoral **8** criminal, outlawed, wrongful **9** forbidden, felonious, nefarious **10** contraband, flagitious, indictable, iniquitous, prohibited, proscribed, unlicensed **11** black-market **12** illegitimate, unauthorized

unlearned
5 naive **6** unread **7** unaware **8** ignorant, nescient, untaught **10** illiterate, uneducated, unlettered, unschooled **11** instinctive **13** unenlightened

unleash
4 free, vent **5** let go, loose, untie, visit, wreak **6** unbind **7** inflict, release **8** carry out, liberate **10** bring about

unless
3 but **4** save **6** except, saving **7** barring, but that, without **9** excepting, excluding

unlettered
see **uneducated**

unlikable
9 obnoxious, offensive, repellent **10** unpleasant **11** displeasing, distasteful **12** disagreeable

unlike
5 mixed **7** diverse, unequal, various **8** assorted **9** different, disparate, divergent **10** dissimilar **11** distinctive, diversified **13** heterogeneous

unlikely
5 faint, unfit **6** remote, slight **7** distant, dubious **8** doubtful **10** farfetched, improbable, unsuitable **11** implausible, unpromising **12** questionable

unlimited
4 full, vast **5** total **6** untold **7** endless,

immense **8** absolute, infinite, wide-open **9** boundless, countless, unbounded, universal **10** unconfined, unfettered **11** unqualified, untrammeled **12** immeasurable, interminable, unrestrained, unrestricted **13** comprehensive, unconditional, unconstrained

unlit
4 dark, inky **6** gloomy **9** lightless

unload
4 drop, dump, junk **5** chuck, ditch, empty **6** debark, remove **7** confess, confide, deep-six, deliver, discard, divulge, lighten, relieve **8** disclose, disgorge, jettison **9** disburden, discharge, disembark, eighty-six, stevedore **11** disencumber

unloose
4 free, undo **5** let go, relax, untie **6** detach, unbind **7** break up, manumit, release, set free, slacken **8** liberate, uncouple, unfasten **9** disengage, extricate, untighten **10** disconnect

unlucky
6 jinxed **7** hapless, ominous **8** ill-fated, untoward **9** ill-boding **10** ill-starred **11** detrimental, inopportune, regrettable, star-crossed, unfavorable, unfortunate **12** inauspicious, unpropitious

unmanageable
4 wild **5** balky, bulky **6** unruly **7** awkward **8** contrary, cumbrous, perverse, stubborn, unwieldy **9** fractious, obstinate **10** cumbersome, disorderly, headstrong, inflexible, rebellious, refractory **11** intractable **12** obstreperous, recalcitrant, ungovernable **13** uncooperative, undisciplined

unmannered
4 rude **5** crude, rough **6** coarse, gauche **7** boorish, ill-bred, loutish **8** impolite **10** indecorous, ungracious **12** discourteous **13** disrespectful

unmarred
5 sound, whole **6** intact, unhurt **7** perfect **8** pristine, unflawed, unharmed **9** undamaged, undefiled, unscathed, unstained **10** unimpaired **11** unblemished, untarnished

unmask
6 debunk, detect, expose, reveal, show up, unveil **7** deflate, uncover **8** disclose, discover, disprove **9** demystify

unmatched
3 odd **4** only **5** alone **6** unique **8** peerless, singular **9** unequaled, unrivaled **10** inimitable, unequalled, unrivalled **11** exceptional **12** incomparable, unparalleled

unmerciful
5 cruel, harsh **6** brutal **7** callous, extreme **8** inhumane, pitiless, ruthless, uncaring, vengeful **9** heartless, unfeeling, unsparing **10** relentless

unmindful
7 unaware **8** careless, heedless **9** forgetful, negligent, oblivious, unheeding, unwitting **10** abstracted, distracted, neglectful **11** inattentive

unmistakable
5 clear, frank, plain **6** patent **7** certain, decided, evident, express, obvious **8** apparent, definite, distinct, explicit, manifest, palpable **11** unambiguous, unequivocal

unmitigated
4 pure, rank **5** gross, sheer, utter **6** arrant **7** perfect, unmixed **8** absolute, clearcut, complete, outright **9** downright, out-and-out, unalloyed, undiluted **10** consummate, unmodified, unrelieved **11** straight-out, unqualified **12** unalleviated **13** thoroughgoing, unadulterated

unmixed
4 mere, neat, pure **5** plain, sheer, utter **6** simple **7** perfect, sincere **8** absolute, straight **9** unalloyed, unblended, undiluted, undivided **11** unmitigated, unqualified **13** unadulterated

unmoved
4 calm, cool, firm **5** aloof, stony **6** stolid **7** adamant, callous, stoical **8** obdurate **9** impassive, untouched **10** insensible, untroubled **11** unconcerned, unemotional, unimpressed **12** unresponsive

unnamed
5 incog **6** secret **7** obscure, unknown **9** anonymous, incognito **11** unspecified **12** unidentified

unnatural
7 uncanny **8** aberrant, abnormal **9** anomalous, contrived, irregular, synthetic **10** artificial, fabricated, factitious

unnecessary
6 excess **7** surplus **8** needless, optional, prodigal **9** redundant **10** expendable, extraneous, gratuitous, unrequired

11 dispensable, inessential, superfluous, uncalled-for, unessential 12 nonessential

unnerve
5 daunt, shake, throw, upset 6 dismay, rattle 7 agitate, fluster, perturb, unhinge 8 bewilder, confound 9 undermine 10 demoralize, disconcert, discourage, dishearten, intimidate

unobstructed
4 open 5 clear 8 passable 9 unblocked, unimpeded 10 unhampered, unhindered 12 unrestricted

unobtrusive
5 quiet 6 modest 7 subdued 8 reserved, retiring, tasteful 10 restrained 13 inconspicuous

unoccupied
4 free, idle 5 empty 6 vacant 7 jobless, vacated 8 deserted 9 abandoned, available 10 employable, unemployed 11 uninhabited

unofficial
7 pirated, private, wildcat 8 informal 9 irregular 10 unapproved, unorthodox 12 unauthorized, unsanctioned

unorganized
7 aimless, chaotic, muddled 8 confused, inchoate, nebulous, rambling, unformed 9 amorphous, arbitrary, haphazard, shapeless, unplanned 10 disjointed, disordered, incoherent, incohesive 11 spontaneous

unoriginal
5 banal, stock 6 copied, old-hat 7 clichéd, humdrum, prosaic, sterile 8 borrowed, ordinary 9 hackneyed, imitative 10 derivative, uninspired 11 commonplace, plagiarized, uninventive 12 conventional 13 unimaginative

unornamented
4 bare 5 plain, spare, stark 6 chaste, modest, severe, simple 7 austere 9 unadorned 11 unelaborate, ungarnished 13 unembellished, unembroidered

unorthodox
3 odd 5 kinky, novel, weird 6 far-out 7 strange, unusual 8 abnormal 9 different, dissident, eccentric, heretical, irregular, sectarian 10 schismatic, unexpected 13 nonconformist

unorthodoxy
6 heresy, schism 7 dissent 8 variance 9 disbelief, ingenuity, recusancy

10 contention, dissidence, innovation 13 nonconformism, nonconformity

unpaid
3 due 5 owing 6 mature 7 donated, overdue, payable, pro-bono 8 freewill, honorary, wageless 9 unsettled, voluntary, volunteer 10 delinquent, gratuitous, receivable, unsalaried 11 contributed, outstanding 13 uncompensated, unremunerated

unpalatable
8 unsavory 10 flavorless 11 distasteful 12 unappetizing

unparalleled
6 unique 8 peerless, singular 9 matchless, unequaled, unmatched, unrivaled 10 inimitable, unequalled, unrivalled 11 exceptional 12 incomparable

unplanned
5 fluky 6 chance, random 7 aimless 9 desultory, haphazard, hit-or-miss 10 accidental, unexpected, unforeseen, unintended 11 inadvertent 12 adventitious, coincidental, unconsidered 13 unintentional

unpleasant
4 sour 5 seamy 7 painful 8 annoying 9 offensive 10 disturbing, irritating, troubling 11 displeasing, distasteful, distressing 12 disagreeable 13 objectionable

unpolished
4 rude 5 crude, gruff, rough 6 crusty, unhewn, vulgar 7 brusque, uncivil, uncouth 8 homespun, unworked 9 inelegant, roughhewn, unrefined 10 amateurish, uncultured, unfinished, ungracious 11 ill-mannered, uncivilized 12 discourteous

unpredictable
4 iffy 5 dicey, fluky 6 chancy, fickle, random, touchy 7 erratic, mutable 8 unstable, variable, volatile 9 arbitrary, mercurial, uncertain, whimsical 10 capricious, changeable 13 unforeseeable

unprejudiced
4 fair, just 5 equal 8 balanced, unbiased 9 equitable, impartial, objective, unbigoted, uncolored 10 even-handed, fair-minded, open-minded 11 nonpartisan 12 un-influenced 13 disinterested, dispassionate

unpressed
7 rumpled, wrinkly 8 crinkled, puckered,

wrinkled

unpretentious
5 frank, plain **6** candid, honest, modest, simple **7** genuine **8** ordinary **9** unadorned **10** forthright, unaffected, unassuming **11** plain-spoken

unprincipled
5 venal **7** corrupt, crooked, immoral **9** deceitful, dishonest, dissolute, mercenary, reprobate, unethical **10** inconstant, iniquitous, profligate, unfaithful **11** underhanded **12** unscrupulous

unproductive
4 vain **6** barren, futile **7** sterile, useless **8** bootless, depleted, feckless, impotent **9** fruitless, infertile **10** unavailing **11** ineffectual **12** hardscrabble

unprofitable
4 idle, vain **6** barren, futile **7** useless **8** bootless **9** fruitless **10** unavailing **11** ineffective **12** unproductive, unsuccessful

unprogressive
8 orthodox **9** illiberal **11** traditional **12** conservative

unpropitious
4 grim **5** bleak **7** ominous, unlucky **9** ill-boding, ill-omened **10** foreboding **11** inopportune, threatening, unfavorable **12** discouraging **13** disheartening

unprosperous
4 poor **5** needy **8** strapped **9** penurious **11** impecunious

unprotected
6 unsafe **7** exposed **8** helpless, insecure **9** unguarded **10** endangered, undefended, unshielded, vulnerable **11** defenseless, susceptible, unsheltered

unproved
7 untried **8** untested **10** postulated **11** conjectural, preliminary, provisional, speculative, theoretical **12** experimental, hypothetical

unpunctual
4 late **5** tardy **6** remiss **7** belated, delayed, overdue **10** behindhand, delinquent

unqualified
4 firm, rank **5** sheer, total, unfit, utter **6** express **8** absolute, explicit, unfitted **9** incapable, out-and-out, steadfast, unalloyed, undiluted, unskilled

10 ineligible, unequipped, unreserved, unsuitable **11** ill-equipped, incompetent, unmitigated **12** wholehearted **13** unadulterated, unconditional

unquenchable
6 crying **7** buoyant, exigent **8** pressing, yearning **9** demanding, insatiate, insistent **10** insatiable **12** effervescent, unrestrained **13** irrepressible, unconstrained

unquestionable
4 real, sure, true **7** certain, genuine **8** absolute, bona fide **9** authentic, undoubted **10** sure-enough, undeniable **11** established, indubitable, self-evident, well-founded **12** indisputable, well-grounded **13** authoritative, incontestable, unimpeachable

unquestioning
4 firm, sure **5** fixed **6** steady **7** abiding **8** enduring, gullible, resolute, trusting, unshaken **9** accepting, believing, credulous, steadfast **10** uncritical, undoubting, unshakable, unwavering **11** unfaltering, unqualified **12** never-failing, unhesitating, unsuspecting, unsuspicious, wholehearted

unravel
5 break, solve **6** answer, decode, unknit, unwind **7** clear up, dope out, explain, resolve, unsnarl **8** decipher, dissolve, untangle **9** elucidate, extricate, figure out, interpret, puzzle out, translate **11** disentangle

unreadable
7 deadpan **9** illegible **10** poker-faced **11** inscrutable **12** hieroglyphic **13** cacographical

unreal
4 fake **5** false **6** fabled **7** fictive **8** chimeric, fanciful, illusory, mythical **9** fantastic, fictional, imaginary, imitation **10** artificial, chimerical, fictitious, improbable, incredible **11** nonexistent **12** unbelievable
combining form: 5 pseud **6** pseudo

unrealistic
7 blue-sky, idyllic, utopian **8** fanciful, quixotic, romantic **9** distorted, idealized, overblown **10** farfetched, ivory-tower, overstated, starry-eyed, unworkable **11** exaggerated, extravagant, impractical, sensational

unreasonable
5 undue **6** absurd **7** invalid **9** arbitrary, excessive, illogical, senseless, sophistic

unreasoned

10 exorbitant, fallacious, headstrong, immoderate, inordinate, irrational, peremptory, ridiculous 11 extravagant, incongruous, nonsensical, uncalled-for, unwarranted 12 preposterous 13 unjustifiable

unreasoned

7 invalid, unsound 9 deceptive, illogical, sophistic, unfounded 10 fallacious, ill-founded, irrational, misleading, ungrounded 11 nonrational

unrefined

3 raw 4 rude 5 crass, crude, rough, tacky 6 coarse, earthy, impure, vulgar 7 natural, uncouth 9 graceless, inelegant, maladroit, roughhewn 10 uncultured, unpolished 11 ill-mannered, uncivilized, unprocessed 12 uncultivated

unreflective

6 casual 7 offhand 8 careless, feckless, heedless, mindless 9 imprudent, impulsive, oblivious, unheeding 10 indiscreet, nonchalant, unthinking 11 inadvertent, perfunctory, thoughtless 13 ill-considered

unrehearsed

7 offhand 8 informal 9 extempore, impromptu, unstudied 10 improvised, off-the-cuff, unprepared 11 extemporary, spontaneous 12 extemporized

unrelated

8 discrete, separate 9 different, disparate 10 dissimilar, extraneous, irrelevant 11 independent

unrelenting

3 set 4 grim 5 stern 7 adamant, endless 8 constant, resolute, ruthless, tireless 9 ceaseless, continual, hard-nosed, incessant, tenacious, unbending, unsparing 10 continuous, determined, implacable, inexorable, inflexible, persistent, unflagging, unshakable, unwavering, unyielding 12 unappeasable

unreliable

6 fickle, shifty, tricky, unsafe 7 dubious 8 fallible, slippery, two-faced 9 deceitful, deceptive, faithless, trustless, unassured, uncertain 10 capricious, fly-by-night, inaccurate, inconstant, perfidious, unfaithful 11 vacillating 12 falsehearted, questionable, unconvincing, undependable 13 irresponsible, unpredictable, untrustworthy

unremarkable

4 so-so 5 plain, usual 6 common, decent, normal 7 average, mundane, prosaic, routine, vanilla 8 adequate, everyday, familiar, habitual, mediocre, ordinary, workaday 9 customary, quotidian, tolerable 11 commonplace, nondescript 12 run-of-the-mill 13 unexceptional

unremitting

7 abiding, chronic, endless, lasting, nonstop 8 constant, enduring, unending 9 ceaseless, continual, incessant, perennial, perpetual, sustained, unceasing 10 continuous, persistent, persisting, relentless 12 interminable 13 uninterrupted

unrepentant

10 impenitent 11 remorseless 12 unregenerate

unrepresentative

7 deviant, unusual 8 aberrant, abnormal, atypical 9 anomalous, divergent, eccentric, irregular, untypical 11 exceptional, heteroclite 13 nonconforming

unreserved

4 open 5 frank, plain 6 candid 7 sincere 8 effusive, explicit, informal, outgoing, outright 9 expansive, talkative 10 definitive 11 forthcoming, openhearted, unconcealed, undisguised, unqualified, unvarnished 13 demonstrative, unconstrained

unresolved

4 moot 7 pending 8 hesitant, wavering 9 faltering, tentative, uncertain, undecided, unsettled 10 ambivalent, hesitating, indecisive, irresolute, unanswered 11 vacillating

unrespectable

3 low 5 shady 6 shabby, shoddy 8 shameful, unworthy 10 inglorious 11 disgraceful, ignominious 12 dishonorable, disreputable 13 discreditable

unresponsive

4 cold 5 aloof, stoic 6 frigid, remote, stolid 7 distant, passive 8 detached, reserved 9 inhibited, withdrawn 10 forbidding, insentient 11 insensitive, passionless, unemotional 12 uninterested 13 insusceptible, unsusceptible

unrest

6 strife, tumult 7 anarchy, anxiety, ferment, tension, turmoil 8 disorder, disquiet, distress, edginess, upheaval 9 agitation, commotion, confusion 10 inquietude, turbulence, uneasiness 11 disquietude,

disturbance, instability **12** perturbation **13** Sturm und Drang

unrestrained
5 bluff, blunt, frank candid, wanton **7** rampant **8** outgoing, uncurbed **9** audacious, excessive, expansive, indulgent, unbridled **10** forthright, immoderate, implacable, inordinate, ungoverned, unhampered **11** extravagant, impassioned, intemperate, overwrought, plainspoken, spontaneous, uninhibited, untrammeled **12** uncontrolled **13** demonstrative, irrepressible, overindulgent

unrestricted
4 free, full, open **9** boundless, extensive, unlimited **10** accessible, unconfined, unfettered, unhampered **11** far-reaching, unqualified, wide-ranging **12** unobstructed **13** unconditional

unripe
3 raw **5** green, young **6** callow, jejune **7** untried **8** emergent, immature, juvenile, unformed, youthful **9** unfledged, untrained **10** unprepared, unseasoned **13** inexperienced, undeveloped

unrivaled
4 only, sole **5** alone **6** unique **7** leading, stellar, supreme **8** champion, foremost, greatest, peerless **9** matchless, paramount, principal, unequaled, unmatched **10** inimitable, preeminent, unequalled **11** outstanding, predominant, unsurpassed **12** incomparable, unparalleled

unroll
6 expose, extend, reveal, unfurl, unwind **7** exhibit, open out **8** disclose **9** spread out

unromantic
5 sober **8** sensible **9** practical, pragmatic, realistic **10** hard-boiled, hardheaded **11** down-to-earth, level-headed, utilitarian **12** businesslike, matter-of-fact **13** unsentimental

unruffled
4 calm, cool **6** poised, placid, serene, smooth **7** collected, unexcited **8** composed, tranquil **9** collected, unexcited **10** nonchalant, untroubled **11** unconcerned, undisturbed, unflappable **13** imperturbable, self-possessed

unruly
4 wild **5** rowdy **7** froward, naughty, raucous, wayward, willful **8** contrary, perverse, untoward **9** fractious, obstinate,

turbulent **10** boisterous, disorderly, headstrong, ill-behaved, rebellious, refractory, tumultuous **11** disobedient, indomitable, intractable **12** contumacious, incorrigible, obstreperous, rambunctious, recalcitrant, ungovernable, unmanageable **13** undisciplined

unsafe
5 risky, shaky **6** chancy **7** erratic, harmful, parlous, rickety, tottery **8** insecure, perilous, slippery, unstable **9** dangerous, hazardous, uncertain **10** precarious, ramshackle, unreliable, vulnerable **11** threatening, treacherous **12** undependable

unsaid
5 known, tacit **6** silent **7** assumed, implied **8** accepted, implicit, indirect, inferred, presumed, unspoken, unstated, wordless **9** customary, unuttered **10** insinuated, undeclared, understood **11** traditional, unexpressed

unsatisfactory
3 bum **4** lame **5** amiss **8** mediocre **9** defective, deficient **10** inadequate **11** displeasing, substandard **13** disappointing, unacceptable

unsavory
4 rank **5** gross, shady **7** insipid, rancid **9** repugnant, repulsive, sickening, tasteless **10** disgusting, flavorless **11** distasteful, ill-flavored, unpalatable **12** disagreeable, unappetizing

unsay
4 lift, void **6** abjure, cancel, disown, recall, recant, revoke **7** nullify, rescind, retract, reverse, suspend **8** abnegate, abrogate, disclaim, forswear, renounce, take back, withdraw **11** countermand

unscathed
4 safe **5** sound, whole **6** intact, unhurt **8** unharmed **9** uninjured, unscarred, untouched **11** unscratched

unscented
8 odor-free, odorless

unschooled
5 naive **7** artless, natural, vacuous **8** ignorant, untaught **9** ingenuous, unstudied, untrained, untutored **10** illiterate, unaffected, uneducated, unlettered **11** empty-headed **12** unartificial, uninstructed

unscramble
5 solve, untie 6 unwind 7 clarify, resolve, restore, sort out, unravel, untwine 8 untangle 9 extricate 11 disentangle 12 disembarrass

unscrupulous
5 shady, venal 7 corrupt, crooked, knavish 8 scheming, wrongful 9 deceitful, dishonest, mercenary, shameless, underhand, unethical 11 underhanded 12 dishonorable, exploitative, unprincipled

unseasonable
8 ill-timed, untimely 12 inconvenient

unseasoned
3 raw 4 flat 5 bland, fresh, green, young 6 callow 7 untried 8 immature 9 credulous, tasteless, unfledged, untrained 10 flavorless 11 unpracticed 13 inexperienced

unseat
3 axe, can 4 boot, buck, fire, oust, sack 5 eject, pitch, purge, throw 6 depose, recall, remove 7 buck off, dismiss, unhorse 8 dethrone, dislodge, displace 9 ostracize

unseemliness
5 gaffe 7 blunder, faux pas 8 solecism 9 barbarism, gaucherie, immodesty, impudence, indecency, vulgarity 10 coarseness, imprudence, incivility, indelicacy 11 impropriety, indiscretion

unseemly
8 improper, untoward 9 inelegant, unrefined 10 indecorous, indelicate, malapropos, unbecoming, unsuitable 11 unbefitting 13 inappropriate

unseen
6 hidden 9 concealed, invisible, unnoticed 10 overlooked, unobserved 11 unsuspected

unsentimental
see **unromantic**

unserviceable
7 useless 10 inoperable, unfeasible, unworkable 11 impractical, unrealistic 13 impracticable, nonfunctional

unsettle
3 vex 4 faze 5 spook, upset 6 bother, flurry, jumble, rattle, ruffle 7 agitate, disturb, fluster, perturb, trouble, unhinge, unnerve 8 bewilder, confound, disarray, disorder, disquiet 9 discomfit 10 disarrange, discompose, disconcert 11 disorganize

unsettled
3 due 4 open 5 fluid, owing, shaky 6 mobile, queasy, shaken, uneasy, unpaid 7 anxious, dubious, mutable, overdue, payable, pending, restive 8 agitated, bothered, doubtful, frontier, restless, troubled, unstable, unsteady, variable 9 disturbed, uncertain, undecided 10 changeable, indecisive, unbalanced, unresolved 11 outstanding, problematic 12 undetermined

unsex
3 fix 4 geld, spay 5 alter 6 change, neuter 8 castrate 9 sterilize 10 emasculate

unshackle
4 free 5 loose 6 loosen, unbind 7 manumit, release, unchain 8 liberate, unfetter 10 emancipate

unshakable
4 firm, sure 5 fixed 6 stable, steady 7 abiding, adamant, settled, staunch 8 resolute 9 steadfast, tenacious, unbending 10 determined, persistent, unwavering, unyielding 11 unfaltering, unrelenting 12 never-failing 13 unquestioning

unshaped
5 vague 7 nascent 8 formless, inchoate, unformed 9 amorphous, embryonic 11 preliminary, undeveloped 13 indeterminate

unshared
4 sole 6 single, unique 7 private 8 singular 9 exclusive, undivided 10 individual 11 distinctive

unshod
8 barefoot, shoeless 9 discalced 10 barefooted

unsightly
4 ugly 5 gross 6 grisly 7 hideous 9 repulsive 10 ill-favored 12 unattractive

unskillful
5 inept 6 clumsy, gauche 7 awkward, unhandy 8 bumbling, bungling, inexpert 9 ham-handed, incapable, maladroit, stumbling, untrained 11 unpracticed 13 unworkmanlike

unsnarl
see **untangle**

unsociable
3 shy 4 cold, cool 5 aloof, timid 6 offish, remote, shut-in 7 distant 8 reserved, secluded, solitary 9 diffident, reclusive,

unbending, withdrawn **10** unfriendly
11 introverted, standoffish **12** inaccessible, unneighborly

unsoiled
5 clean **8** spotless **9** unspotted, unstained, unsullied, untainted **10** immaculate
11 unblemished, untarnished

unsophisticated
5 corny, green, naive **6** callow, folksy, rustic, simple **7** artless, natural, sincere, uncouth **8** gullible, innocent **9** childlike, ingenuous, unrefined, unworldly

unsorted
5 mixed **6** divers, motley, sundry, varied
7 diverse, jumbled, mingled **8** ungraded
9 disparate, scrambled, unmatched, unrefined **10** variegated **11** diversified
12 multifarious **13** heterogeneous, miscellaneous

unsought
7 unasked, willing **8** unbidden, unwanted
9 undesired, uninvited, unwelcome, voluntary **10** gratuitous, unprompted
11 spontaneous, unrequested, unsolicited

unsound
3 mad **4** weak **5** false, frail, shaky, wrong
6 faulty, flawed, flimsy, infirm, insane, sickly, untrue, weakly **7** cracked, damaged, fragile, invalid **8** decrepit, demented, deranged, specious **9** defective, erroneous, imperfect, incorrect, unhealthy
13 insubstantial

unsparing
5 ample, harsh, stern, tough **6** lavish, severe, strict **7** copious, liberal, onerous, profuse **8** abundant, exacting, generous, prolific, rigorous, ruthless **9** bounteous, bountiful, demanding, plenteous **10** free-handed, munificent, openhanded, unmerciful **11** magnanimous

unspeakable
4 dire, evil **5** awful **6** grisly **7** beastly, ghastly, hateful, heinous, hideous
8 dreadful, ghoulish, gruesome, horrific, shocking **9** appalling, atrocious, execrable, frightful, loathsome, monstrous, obnoxious, repugnant, repulsive, revolting
10 abominable, detestable, disgusting, horrendous, outrageous, scandalous
11 unutterable **13** inexpressible

unspoiled
5 ideal **6** intact, virgin **7** halcyon, idyllic, perfect, untamed **8** arcadian, pastoral, pristine, virginal **9** idealized, undamaged, undefiled, untouched **10** unimpaired

11 unblemished, uncorrupted

unspoken
4 mute **5** tacit **6** hinted, silent, unsaid
7 assumed, implied **8** implicit, inferred, presumed, unstated, wordless **9** intimated, suggested, unuttered **10** undeclared, understood **11** unexpressed

unstable
5 fluid, shaky **6** fickle, shifty, tricky, wobbly
7 dubious, protean, rickety, suspect
8 insecure, rootless, slippery, ticklish, unsteady, variable, volatile, wavering
9 ambiguous, changeful, fluctuant, irregular, mercurial, teetering, uncertain, unsettled **10** capricious, inconstant, precarious **11** vacillating **13** temperamental, unpredictable

unstated
5 tacit **6** latent, unsaid **7** assumed, implied
8 implicit **10** understood

unsteady
5 rocky, shaky, tippy **6** uneven, wobbly
7 erratic, mutable, rickety, varying
8 shifting, unstable, variable **9** changeful, irregular, tottering **10** changeable, inconstant
British: 5 wonky

unstudied
5 naive **6** casual, improv, simple **7** artless, natural, offhand **8** careless, informal, unforced, unversed **9** extempore, guileless, impromptu, ingenuous, makeshift, unlabored, unlearned, unplanned, untutored **10** improvised, nonchalant, unaffected, unpolished, unschooled **11** extemporary, spontaneous, uncontrived, unrehearsed **13** improvisatory

unstylish
4 drab, dull **5** dated, dowdy, fusty, passé, ratty, tacky **6** démodé, frumpy, old-hat, shabby, stodgy **7** vintage **8** outdated, outmoded **9** inelegant, moth-eaten, out-of-date **10** antiquated, oldfangled **12** old-fashioned **13** unfashionable

unsubstantial
4 thin **5** frail, shaky **6** feeble, flimsy, infirm
7 fragile, shadowy, tenuous, unsound
8 ethereal, illusory **9** dreamlike, imaginary, spiritual, unearthly **10** immaterial, impalpable, intangible **11** implausible, incorporeal, nonmaterial, nonphysical
12 metaphysical

unsuitable
5 inapt, undue, unfit **7** awkward, jarring
8 ill-timed, improper, unfitted, unseemly,

untimely 9 ill-suited 10 ill-adapted, inadequate, inapposite, malapropos, mismatched, unbecoming 11 inadvisable, inopportune, unbefitting, unqualified 12 incompatible, infelicitous, unacceptable, unseasonable 13 inappropriate

unsullied
4 pure 5 clean 6 chaste 8 flawless, spotless, unsoiled 9 blameless, exemplary, guiltless, stainless, taintless, undefiled 10 immaculate 11 unblemished, untarnished

unsure
5 dicey, shaky 6 wobbly 7 dubious, unclear 8 doubtful, insecure, unstable, wavering 9 fluctuant, skeptical, uncertain, undecided 10 ambivalent, indecisive, irresolute, unreliable 11 unconvinced, vacillating 12 questionable, undependable 13 indeterminate, untrustworthy

unsurpassable
7 supreme 8 ultimate 9 matchless 10 consummate, preeminent 12 transcendent

unsusceptible
6 immune, inured 8 hardened 9 impassive, resistant 10 impervious 11 insensitive 12 invulnerable, unresponsive

unsuspecting
5 naive 6 unwary 8 gullible, trustful, trusting 9 confiding, credulous, imprudent 10 incautious

unswerving
see **unfaltering**

unsympathetic
4 cold, cool 5 chill, stony 6 averse 7 callous, haughty, unmoved 8 detached, lukewarm 9 apathetic, unfeeling, unpitying 10 disdainful, hard-boiled 11 coldhearted, hardhearted, indifferent, insensitive, unconcerned, uncongenial 12 contemptuous, stonyhearted, unresponsive 13 disinterested

untactful
4 flip, rash, rude 5 brash, nervy 6 brazen 8 flippant, insolent 9 audacious, impolitic, imprudent, maladroit 10 indiscreet 11 impertinent, thoughtless 12 presumptuous, undiplomatic

untamed
4 wild 5 brute, feral 6 carnal, fierce, savage 7 bestial, brutish 8 barbaric 9 primitive 11 uncivilized

untangle
5 solve 7 clear up, explain, resolve, unravel, unsnarl, untwine, untwist 9 elucidate, extricate, interpret 10 disembroil, disentwine, straighten, unscramble 11 disencumber 12 disembarrass

untaught
5 naive 7 natural 8 ignorant, nescient 9 intuitive, untrained, untutored 10 uneducated, unlettered, unschooled 11 empty-headed, instinctive, instinctual, spontaneous 12 uncultivated, uninstructed

untempered
6 wanton 7 extreme 9 excessive 10 gratuitous, immoderate, inordinate 11 extravagant 12 unrestrained

untenable
5 wrong 6 faulty, flimsy 10 inadequate 12 indefensible

untended
5 seedy 7 rickety, run-down 8 decrepit, derelict, deserted, forsaken, tattered 9 neglected 10 ramshackle, tumbledown, uncared-for 11 dilapidated

Unter den _____
6 Linden

untested
6 intact, unused 7 untried 8 unproved, unproven 11 unpracticed

unthinkable
10 impossible, incredible, outlandish 12 preposterous, unimaginable 13 extraordinary, inconceivable, unprecedented

unthinking
8 careless, feckless, habitual, heedless, knee-jerk, uncaring 9 automatic, reflexive, unheeding, unmindful 10 distracted, unintended 11 inattentive, inadvertent, instinctive, instinctual, involuntary, perfunctory, spontaneous, thoughtless 12 unreflective

unthrifty
6 lavish, wanton 7 ruinous 8 prodigal, wasteful 9 imprudent 10 profligate 11 extravagant, improvident 12 uneconomical

untidy
5 messy 6 sloppy 7 chaotic, jumbled, unkempt 8 confused, littered, slapdash, slipshod, slovenly 9 cluttered 10 disheveled, disordered, disorderly,

topsy-turvy 11 disarranged, dishevelled **12** disorganized, unsystematic

untie
5 let go **6** loosen, unbind, unknot, unlace, unlash **7** release, resolve, set free **8** unstring **9** extricate **11** disencumber, disentangle **12** disembarrass

until
4 up to **6** before **7** prior to **11** in advance of

untimely
5 early, undue **9** premature **10** malapropos **11** ill-seasoned, inopportune **12** unseasonable **13** inappropriate

untiring
7 devoted, patient **8** diligent, enduring **9** assiduous, ceaseless, dedicated, energetic, unceasing **10** determined, persistent, unflagging, unwavering, unwearying **11** persevering, unfaltering **13** indefatigable, inexhaustible

untold
4 huge, vast **7** immense **8** enormous, gigantic **9** countless **10** prodigious **11** innumerable, uncountable **12** incalculable **13** indescribable

untouchable
5 leper **6** pariah **7** outcast **8** outcaste

untouched
4 pure **5** sound, whole **6** intact, virgin **7** unmoved **8** flawless, pristine, unharmed, unmarred, untapped, virginal **9** undamaged, unspoiled **10** unaffected **11** unblemished, unconcerned, unimpressed

untoward
6 unruly **7** adverse, awkward, froward, ungodly, unhappy, unlucky **8** ill-fated, improper, indecent, luckless, unseemly **9** fractious, unfitting, vexatious **10** ill-starred, indecorous, indelicate, refractory, unbecoming **11** detrimental, intractable, star-crossed, troublesome, unfortunate **12** inconvenient, recalcitrant, ungovernable, unmanageable, unpropitious

untrained
see **unskilled**

untrammeled
8 uncurbed **9** unimpeded **10** unconfined, unfettered, ungoverned, unhampered **11** uninhibited **12** unobstructed, unrestrained, unrestricted

untried
3 raw **5** fresh, green **6** callow, rookie **8** unproved, untested **10** innovative, pioneering, unseasoned **11** unpracticed **13** inexperienced, unprecedented

untroubled
4 calm **5** still **6** blithe, placid, serene **7** halcyon **8** carefree, composed, peaceful, tranquil **9** easygoing, unruffled **10** insouciant, nonchalant **11** unconcerned, unperturbed **12** lighthearted

untrue
4 fake **5** false, wrong **7** inexact **8** disloyal, specious **9** erroneous, faithless, imprecise, incorrect **10** fictitious, inaccurate, unfaithful **combining form: 5** pseud **6** pseudo

untrustworthy
5 shady **6** shifty, unsafe, unsure **7** devious, dubious **8** disloyal, slippery, two-faced **9** deceptive, negligent, two-timing **10** fly-by-night, unreliable **11** duplicitous **12** questionable, undependable **13** double-dealing, irresponsible

untruth
3 fib, lie **4** sham **5** error **6** canard, deceit **7** blarney, fallacy, falsity, fiction, hogwash **9** deception, duplicity, falsehood, falseness, hypocrisy, mendacity **11** fabrication, insincerity **12** misstatement **13** prevarication

untruthful
4 sham **5** bogus, false, lying, phony **7** knavish **8** specious **9** deceitful, dishonest, erroneous, incorrect **10** fictitious, inaccurate, mendacious

untutored
see **unschooled**

unusable
7 outworn, useless **8** obsolete **9** worthless **10** inoperable, unavailing, unworkable **11** impractical, unrealistic **12** inapplicable **13** nonfunctional

unused
3 new **4** idle **5** fresh **6** excess **7** dormant, surplus **8** leftover, residual **9** untouched

unusual
3 odd **4** rare **6** quaint, unique **7** bizarre, curious, special, strange **8** aberrant, abnormal, peculiar, singular, uncommon, atypical, unwonted **9** anomalous, different, eccentric, irregular **11** exceptional

13 extraordinary

unusually
4 very 5 extra 6 rarely, seldom
8 markedly 9 curiously, extremely,
strangely 10 abnormally, especially,
peculiarly, remarkably, strikingly,
uncommonly 11 exceedingly 12 infrequently, particularly

unutterable
5 taboo 7 awesome 9 ineffable
11 unspeakable 13 indescribable,
inexpressible

unvaried
4 like, same 5 alike 7 uniform 9 identical
10 consistent, unchanging 11 undeviating

unvarnished
see **undisguised**

unvarying
see **unchanging**

unveil
see **uncover**

unversed
3 raw 5 fresh, green 6 callow 7 untried
8 inexpert 9 unfledged 10 unfamiliar,
unseasoned 11 uninitiated, unpracticed
12 unaccustomed 13 inexperienced

unwanted
see **unwelcome**

unwarranted
5 undue 8 baseless 9 misguided,
unfounded 10 gratuitous, groundless,
immoderate, unprovoked 11 extravagant,
inexcusable, injudicious, uncalled-for,
unjustified 12 indefensible, unreasonable
13 insupportable, unjustifiable,
unsupportable

unwary
5 brash, hasty 8 careless, gullible,
heedless, reckless 9 credulous,
impetuous, imprudent, unguarded 10 ill-
advised, incautious, indiscreet
11 thoughtless 12 unsuspecting

unwavering
see **unfaltering**

unwelcome
7 unasked 8 unsought, unwanted
9 undesired, uninvited 11 undesirable
12 unacceptable 13 objectionable

unwell
3 ill 4 sick 5 frail, shaky 6 ailing, feeble,
infirm, offish, peaked, queasy, sickly,
wobbly 8 diseased, stricken 9 afflicted,

enfeebled, unhealthy 10 indisposed
11 debilitated

unwholesome
4 foul 5 toxic 6 sickly 7 adverse, baneful,
corrupt, harmful, immoral, noisome,
noxious, obscene, ruinous, unsound
8 diseased 9 injurious, loathsome,
offensive, unhealthy 10 disgusting,
pernicious, subversive 11 deleterious,
detrimental, unhealthful 12 insalubrious

unwieldy
5 bulky 7 awkward, massive 8 cumbrous
9 ponderous 10 burdensome,
cumbersome 12 unmanageable

unwilling
5 loath 6 averse 8 grudging, hesitant
9 obstinate, reluctant 10 indisposed
11 disinclined

unwind
4 rest, undo 5 let go, relax 6 loosen,
unbend, uncoil, unfold, unreel, unroll
7 ease off, slacken, unravel 8 calm down,
kick back, loosen up

unwise
4 rash 5 silly 6 stupid 7 asinine, fatuous,
foolish, idiotic, witless 8 reckless
9 brainless, foolhardy, ill-judged, imbecilic,
impolitic, imprudent, ludicrous, misguided,
senseless 10 ill-advised, indiscreet,
ridiculous 11 impractical, injudicious,
thoughtless, undesirable, unfortunate
13 unintelligent

unwitting
6 chance 7 unaware 8 ignorant, innocent
9 haphazard, oblivious, unknowing,
unmindful, unplanned 10 unfamiliar,
uninformed, unintended 11 inadvertent
12 unacquainted

unwonted
4 rare 6 signal, unique 7 not-able, unusual
8 singular, uncommon 10 remarkable,
unexpected 11 exceptional
12 unaccustomed 13 extraordinary

unworkable
7 useless 8 quixotic 9 half-baked
10 impossible, infeasible, inoperable,
unfeasible 11 impractical, unrealistic
12 inapplicable 13 impracticable,
nonfunctional

unworldly
5 naive 6 astral, dreamy, simple 7 artless,
natural 8 ethereal, innocent, trusting
9 celestial, ingenuous, spiritual, unearthly,

visionary **11** impractical **13** inexperienced

unworthy
6 no-good **7** ignoble **8** shameful, unseemly **9** no-account, worthless **10** unbecoming **11** disgraceful, inexcusable, undeserving, unmerited

unwrap
see **uncover**

unwritten
4 oral **5** blank, tacit **6** latent, spoken, verbal **7** assumed **8** accepted, implicit **10** understood **11** traditional, word-of-mouth **12** conventional

unyielding
4 firm, grim, hard **5** fixed, rigid, stern, stiff, tough **6** dogged, mulish **7** adamant **8** hard-core, obdurate, stubborn **9** hard-nosed, insistent, obstinate, pigheaded, steadfast, unbending **10** determined, headstrong, implacable, inexorable, inflexible, persistent, relentless **11** intractable, unrelenting **12** pertinacious, single-minded, unappeasable

up
4 hike, jump, lift, rise **5** above, ahead, arise, boost, built, mount, raise, risen **6** ascend, arisen, lifted, versed **7** abreast, promote **8** familiar, increase, informed, positive **9** au courant, northward **10** acquainted, conversant
prefix: 3 ana, sur

up-and-coming
7 go-ahead, hot-shot **8** aspiring **9** promising **11** presumptive, prospective **12** enterprising

upbeat
4 rosy **6** cheery **7** buoyant, hopeful **8** cheerful, positive, sanguine **9** confidant, expectant, promising **10** heartening, optimistic **12** Pollyannaish

upbraid
4 lash, rate **5** chide, scold **6** berate, rail at, rebuke, revile, scorch **7** bawl out, censure, chasten, chew out, reprove, scourge, tell off **8** admonish, chastise, reproach **9** castigate, criticize, dress down, reprimand **10** tongue-lash, vituperate

upbringing
7 nurture, rearing **8** training **9** schooling

upchuck
4 barf, hurl, puke, spew **5** heave, retch, vomit **6** spit up **7** bring up, throw up **8** disgorge **11** regurgitate

upcoming
7 looming, nearing, pending **8** expected, foreseen, imminent **9** advancing, impending, onrushing **11** anticipated, approaching, forthcoming, prospective

up-country
4 bush **6** inland, sticks, upland **7** outback **8** backland, frontier, interior, outlying, woodland **9** backwater, backwoods, boondocks **10** hinterland, timberland

update
5 amend, brief, renew **6** inform, revamp, revise, revive **7** apprise, enhance, improve, refresh, restore, rundown, upgrade **8** renovate **9** modernize, refurbish **10** rejuvenate

upend
4 beat, best, drub, flip, lick, skin, trim, whip **5** cream, crush, upset **6** invert, subdue, thrash, topple, unseat, wallop **7** capsize, clobber, conquer, overrun, shellac, trounce **8** dethrone, lambaste, overcome, overturn, vanquish **9** overpower, overwhelm, subjugate

upgrade
4 hike, rise **5** boost, raise **6** prefer **7** advance, elevate, enhance, improve, promote **8** increase **9** promotion **10** betterment **11** advancement, improvement **12** breakthrough

upheaval
6 clamor, outcry, tumult, upturn **7** ferment, turmoil **8** churning, disaster, disorder **9** cataclysm, commotion **10** alteration, convulsion, disruption **11** catastrophe

uphill
4 hard **6** rising, rugged, taxing **7** arduous, labored, operose, tedious **8** climbing, grueling, toilsome **9** ascending, difficult, effortful, gruelling, laborious, punishing, strenuous, wearisome

uphold
3 aid **4** back, help, lift, prop **5** brace, carry, hoist, raise **6** assist, back up, bear up, buoy up, defend, second **7** bolster, elevate, justify, shore up, support, sustain **8** advocate, backstop, buttress, champion, maintain, side with **9** vindicate

upkeep
4 cost **7** expense **8** overhead **11** expenditure, maintenance

upland
4 mesa **5** table **7** plateau

uplift

4 buoy 5 cheer, hoist, raise 6 take up
7 animate, elevate, enliven, gladden,
hearten 8 brighten, embolden, inspirit
9 encourage 10 exhilarate, strengthen

upon

4 atop
prefix: 3 epi

upper class

4 rank 5 elite 6 gentry 7 peerage, quality,
society, who's who 8 affluent, nobility,
noblesse, well-to-do 9 blue blood, gentility,
haut monde 10 patricians, patriciate
11 aristocracy 13 carriage trade,
Establishment

upper hand

4 edge, sway 5 leg up 7 control, mastery
8 leverage 9 advantage, dominance
10 ascendancy 11 superiority
12 predominance

uppermost

3 top 6 apical 7 highest 8 loftiest

uppity

4 smug 5 aloof, brash 6 lordly, sniffy,
snippy, snooty, snotty 7 forward, haughty,
pompous 8 arrogant, cavalier 9 conceited,
egotistic, imperious, know-it-all, presuming
10 disdainful, high-handed 11 overweening, pretentious 12 contemptuous,
presumptuous, supercilious 13 self-
asserting, self-assertive, self-important

upright

4 fair, good, just, pure, true 5 erect, moral,
noble, piano 6 honest, raised 7 correct,
ethical 8 elevated, goalpost, standing,
vertical, virtuous 9 equitable, exemplary,
honorable, impartial 10 principled,
scrupulous 13 conscientious,
perpendicular

uprightness

5 honor 6 repute, virtue 7 honesty, probity
8 morality, nobility 9 character, integrity,
rectitude 13 righteousness

uprising

4 riot 6 mutiny, revolt 8 upheaval
9 rebellion 10 insurgence, revolution
12 insurrection

uproar

3 din, row 4 coil, fuss, to-do, riot 5 babel,
brawl, broil, chaos, furor, hoo-ha, melee,
whirl 6 bedlam, clamor, fracas, furore,
hassle, hubbub, mayhem, pother, racket,
ruckus, rumpus, shindy, tumult 7 shindig,
turmoil 8 brouhaha, disorder, foofaraw
9 commotion, confusion 10 hullabaloo,
hurly-burly, turbulence 11 pandemonium

uproarious

5 noisy, rowdy 7 comical, rackety, raucous,
riotous 8 brawling, clattery, mirthful,
strident 9 clamorous, hilarious
10 clangorous, hysterical, resounding,
rollicking, tumultuous 12 obstreperous
13 sidesplitting

uproot

4 grub, move, weed 8 displace, overturn,
supplant 9 eradicate, extirpate, overthrow,
supersede 10 annihilate, transplant
11 exterminate

upset

3 ail, ill 5 worry 6 bother, defeat, dismay,
invert, jumble, muddle, topple, tumble
7 afflict, agitate, capsize, disturb, fluster,
invalid, jittery, jumbled, muddled, perturb,
rattled, reverse, tip over, toppled, trouble,
unnerve, worried 8 agitated, bewilder,
bothered, confound, confused, disarray,
dismayed, disorder, distress, overturn,
troubled, turn over, unnerved 9 afflicted,
confusion, disturbed, flustered, knock over,
overthrow, perturbed 10 bewildered,
confounded, disconcert, disordered,
distracted, distressed, indisposed,
invalidate, overthrown, overturned, tipped
over 11 overwrought 12 apprehensive,
disconcerted

upshot

5 issue 6 burden, climax, effect, ending,
finish, result 7 outcome, purport
9 substance 10 conclusion, denouement
11 consequence, culmination, termination
12 significance

upside-down

7 chaotic, haywire, jumbled 8 backward,
confused, inverted, pell-mell, reversed
10 disordered, overturned, topsy-turvy
13 helter-skelter

upstanding

see **upright**

upstart

5 comer 7 parvenu 8 outsider 9 arriviste,
pretender 12 nouveau riche 13 social
climber

upsurge

4 gain, jump, rise, wave 5 boost, spurt
6 growth 7 advance 8 increase

uptight

4 edgy 5 riled, tense 6 uneasy 7 anxious,
nervous, restive, worried

up to
4 till 5 until 6 before 11 in advance of

up-to-date
6 modern, modish, timely, trendy
7 abreast, à la mode, current, stylish
8 advanced, brand-new, contempo 9 au
courant 10 avant-garde 11 cutting-edge,
fashionable 12 contemporary 13 state-of-
the-art

upturn
4 jump, rise 6 growth 8 increase
11 improvement

Urania
see **Muse**

Uranus
6 planet
mother, wife: 4 Gaea
offspring: 6 Titans 8 Cyclopes
overthrower, son: 6 Cronus

urban
9 municipal 12 metropolitan

urbane
5 suave 6 poised, smooth 7 elegant,
genteel, politic, refined 8 cultured,
debonair, gracious, polished 9 civilized,
distingué 10 cultivated, diplomatic
12 cosmopolitan 13 sophisticated

urbanize
6 citify

urchin
3 imp 4 brat 5 child, gamin, scamp
10 ragamuffin

Urdur
see **Norn**

urge
3 egg, sic, yen 4 coax, goad, itch, lust,
prod, push, spur, wish 5 drive, egg on,
impel, press, prick, set on, tar on 6 adjure,
cajole, compel, demand, desire, exhort,
incite, induce, needle, prompt, propel 7 beseech, conjure, craving, entreat, implore,
impulse, inspire, longing, passion, promote,
propose, provoke, solicit, wheedle
8 advocate, appetite, blandish, pressure,
yearning 9 encourage, instigate, stimulate
12 high-pressure

urgency
6 duress, stress 8 exigence, exigency,
pressure 9 necessity 10 compulsion,
insistence

urgent
5 vital 6 crying 7 burning, clamant, crucial,

driving, exigent, instant, present 8 critical,
pressing 9 clamorous, demanding,
immediate, impelling, insistent, momentous
10 compelling, imperative 11 importunate

Uriel
9 archangel

Uris novel
3 Haj (The) 5 QB VII 6 Exodus 7 Trinity
9 Battle Cry, Mitla Pass 10 Angry Hills
(The), Redemption

urn
4 vase 6 vessel 7 samovar
Greek: 7 amphora

Ursa Major
9 Great Bear 11 Great Dipper

Ursa Minor
10 Little Bear 12 Little Dipper
star: 7 Polaris 8 polestar 9 North Star

Uruguay
capital: 10 Montevideo
language: 7 Spanish
monetary unit: 4 peso
neighbor: 6 Brazil 9 Argentina
river: 7 La Plata 8 Río Negro

usable
6 liquid 7 running, working 9 adaptable,
available, operative 10 accessible,
applicable, employable, expendable,
functional, marketable, negotiable
11 exploitable, operational, serviceable

usage
3 way 4 form, mode, wont 5 habit, sense
6 action, amount, custom, manner, method,
praxis 7 process 8 habitude, practice
9 formality, procedure 10 convention

use
3 ply 4 wont, work 5 apply, avail, habit,
serve, treat, value, wield, worth 6 custom,
demand, employ, handle, liking, manage,
manner 7 benefit, exploit, operate,
purpose, service, utility, utilize 8 deal with,
exercise, exertion, function, impose on,
occasion, practice, regulate 9 advantage,
habituate, objective, relevance
10 employment, manipulate 11 application

used
8 pre-owned, shopworn 10 secondhand

used up
5 all in, spent 6 bleary, effete, sapped,
wasted 7 drained, emptied, far-gone,
worn-out 8 consumed, depleted
9 exhausted, washed-out

useful

3 fit 4 meet 5 handy, utile 7 helpful
8 fruitful, suitable, valuable 9 favorable,
practical 10 beneficial, convenient,
functional, productive, profitable, propitious,
worthwhile 11 appropriate, practicable,
serviceable, utilitarian 12 advantageous

usefulness

5 value, worth 7 fitness, service, utility
8 function 9 advantage, relevance,
substance 10 expedience, expediency
12 practicality 13 applicability

useless

4 idle, vain 5 inept 6 futile 7 inutile
8 bootless, hopeless, unusable 9 fruitless,
pointless, worthless 10 unavailing,
unworkable 11 impractical, ineffective,
ineffectual, inoperative 12 unproductive,
unprofitable 13 impracticable,
nonfunctional

user

5 buyer 6 addict 8 consumer, customer,
utilizer

use up

5 drain, spend 6 devour, expend
7 consume, deplete, exhaust 8 draw down
10 run through

usher

4 lead, seat 5 guide 6 escort 7 conduct,
precede 9 conductor 10 doorkeeper

usher in

5 begin, greet, start 6 launch 7 kick off,
trumpet, welcome 8 announce,
commence, initiate, proclaim 9 institute,
introduce, originate 10 inaugurate

usual

5 stock, typic 6 common, kosher, normal,
wonted 7 average, regular, routine, typical,
vanilla 8 accepted, everyday, expected,
familiar, habitual, ordinary, orthodox,
standard, workaday 9 customary,
prevalent, quotidian 10 accustomed,
prevailing 11 commonplace, established
12 conventional, unremarkable

usually

6 mainly, mostly 7 as a rule 8 commonly,
normally 9 generally, routinely
10 habitually, ordinarily 11 customarily

usurer

7 Shylock 9 loan shark 11 moneylender

usurp

5 wrest 6 assume 7 preempt 8 arrogate,
displace, supplant 10 commandeer
11 appropriate

Utah

capital: 12 Salt Lake City
city: 4 Orem 6 Ogden, Provo
college, university: 12 Brigham Young
lake: 6 Powell 9 Great Salt
motto: 8 Industry
mountain: 5 Kings (Peak)
nickname: 7 Beehive (State)
park: 4 Zion 5 Bryce 6 Arches
11 Canyonlands
river: 5 Green 6 Sevier
state bird: 14 California gull
state flower: 8 sego lily
state tree: 10 blue spruce

utensil

3 pan, pot 4 fork, tool 5 knife, spoon
6 device, vessel 8 saucepan, teaspoon
9 implement 10 instrument

uterus

4 womb

Uther Pendragon

son: 6 Arthur
wife: 6 Ygerne 7 Igraine

utile

5 handy 6 useful 7 working 9 available,
operative, practical 10 accessible,
convenient, dependable, functional
11 practicable, serviceable

utilitarian

6 useful 9 practical, pragmatic
10 functional
philosopher: 4 Mill (John Stuart)
7 Bentham (Jeremy)

utility

3 use 7 benefit, fitness, service 8 function
9 advantage, relevance 10 efficiency,
usefulness 12 practicality 13 applicability

utilize

3 use 5 apply, spend 6 bestow, deploy,
employ, handle, occupy 7 exploit
8 exercise 11 appropriate

utmost

3 top 4 acme, apex, best, peak 6 height,
zenith 7 extreme, highest, maximal,
maximum, supreme 8 farthest, furthest,
greatest, pinnacle, remotest, ultimate
9 damnedest, extremity

utopia

4 Eden, Zion 5 bliss 6 heaven 7 Elysium
8 paradise 9 Cockaigne, dreamland,
Shangri-la 10 dreamworld 12 promised
land 13 Elysian fields

Utopia author

4 More (Thomas)

utopian

5 ideal, lofty 6 edenic 7 dreamer
8 arcadian, fanciful, idealist, quixotic
9 grandiose, ideologue, visionary
10 chimerical, idealistic, impossible,
millennial, unfeasible 11 impractical
12 otherworldly 13 castle-builder,
impracticable

utter

3 say 4 damn, dang, darn, rank, talk, tell
5 sheer, speak, stark, state, total, voice
6 arrant, dashed, deuced, reveal 7 blasted,
blessed, declare, deliver, divulge, flat-out
8 absolute, bring out, complete, crashing,
disclose, infernal, outright, positive, throw
out 9 downright, out-and-out, pronounce,
verbalize 10 confounded, consummate
11 come out with, straight-out, unmitigated,
unqualified 13 thoroughgoing

utterance

4 rant, vent, word 5 voice 6 speech
7 oration 8 delivery, discourse, speaking
9 assertion, discourse, statement
10 expression, revelation 11 declaration
12 announcement, articulation
13 pronouncement, verbalization

utterly

4 just 5 plumb, quite 6 in toto 7 totally
8 entirely 9 perfectly 10 absolutely,
altogether, completely, thoroughly

uttermost

4 last 5 final 7 extreme, outmost
8 farthest, furthest, remotest

Utu

see **Shamash**

Uzbekistan

capital: 8 Tashkent
city: 7 Bokhara, Bukhara 9 Samarkand,
Samarqand
desert: 8 Kyzyl Kum
enclave: 10 Karakalpak
monetary unit: 3 sum
neighbor: 9 Kazakstan 10 Kazakhstan,
Kyrgyzstan, Tajikistan 11 Afghanistan
12 Turkmenistan
river: 8 Amu Dar'ya, Syr Dar'ya
9 Zeravshan
sea: 4 Aral

V

vacancy
4 void **6** vacuum **7** opening **8** idleness
9 blankness, emptiness

vacant
4 bare, free, idle, open, void **5** blank, clear,
empty, inane, stark **6** unused **7** deadpan,
vacuous **8** deserted, unfilled
9 abandoned, impassive **10** tenantless,
unoccupied **11** empty-headed
12 inexpressive

vacate
4 quit, void **5** annul, clear, empty, leave
6 bow out, give up, repeal, revoke
7 abandon, rescind, retract, reverse
8 abrogate, check out, dissolve, evacuate
9 discharge **10** relinquish

vacation
4 rest, trip **5** break, leave **6** recess
7 holiday, leisure, respite, time off
8 furlough, interval **10** sabbatical
12 intermission

vacationer
7 tourist, tripper **9** weekender
10 rubberneck **12** holidaymaker

vaccination
4 shot **7** booster **9** injection **11** inoculation

vaccine
4 shot **5** serum **9** antiserum **11** preparation
inventor: **6** Jenner (Edward)

vacillate
4 sway, yo-yo **5** waver **6** dither, falter,
teeter, waggle **7** swither, whiffle **8** hesitate
9 alternate, fluctuate, oscillate
10 equivocate **12** shilly-shally

vacillating
4 weak **6** fickle, unsure, wobbly **8** hesitant,
shifting, unstable, unsteady **9** fluctuant,
tentative, uncertain, undecided, unsettled
10 changeable, inconstant, indecisive,
irresolute **12** shilly-shally

vacillation
5 doubt **8** to-and-fro, wavering **9** hesitancy
10 fickleness, indecision **12** irresolution,
shilly-shally

vacuity
4 hole, void **6** cavity, hollow, vacuum
7 inanity **9** black hole, blankness,
ditsiness, ditziness, emptiness, stupidity
10 hollowness **11** nothingness

vacuous
4 idle, void **5** blank, empty, inane, silly,
stupid **6** stupid, vacant **7** foolish, shallow
11 birdbrained, empty-headed, superficial

vacuum
4 void **5** space **7** suction **9** emptiness
11 nothingness
bottle: **5** dewar **7** thermos

vacuum tube
5 diode **6** triode **7** tetrode
casing: **4** bulb

vade mecum
5 guide **6** manual **8** Baedeker, handbook
9 guidebook **11** enchiridion

_____ Vadis
3 Quo

vagabond
3 bum **4** hobo **5** gypsy, idler, rogue, rover,
tramp **6** picaro, roamer **7** drifter, migrant,
nomadic, vagrant, wastrel **8** bohemian,
clochard, picaroon, runabout, runagate,
traveler, wanderer **9** itinerant, transient,
wandering **11** peripatetic

vagarious
6 fickle **7** erratic, flighty, mutable, wayward
8 unstable, volatile **9** impulsive, mercurial,
whimsical **10** capricious, inconstant
13 unpredictable

vagary
3 bee **4** whim **5** crank, fancy, freak,
humor, quirk **6** megrim, whimsy **7** caprice,
fantasy **8** crotchet

vagrancy
6 roving **7** roaming **8** drifting, nomadism, rambling **9** wandering **10** itinerancy

vagrant
see **vagabond**

vague
3 dim **4** hazy **5** blear, faint, foggy, fuzzy, gauzy, misty, muddy, woozy **6** bleary, blurry, cloudy, dreamy, slight, vacant **7** inexact, obscure, shadowy, unclear **8** confused, imprecise, nebulous, vaporous **9** ambiguous, dreamlike, enigmatic, uncertain **10** diaphanous, indefinite, indistinct **13** indeterminate, unsubstantial

vain
4 idle **5** empty, proud **6** futile, hollow, otiose **7** foppish, haughty, stuck-up, trivial, useless **8** abortive, arrogant, boastful, bootless, nugatory **9** conceited, fruitless, valueless, worthless **10** egocentric, profitless, sophomoric, unavailing **11** egotistical, ineffective, ineffectual **12** narcissistic, unproductive, unprofitable, unsuccessful **13** self-important

vainglorious
8 arrogant, boastful, bragging, puffed-up, vaunting **9** conceited, egotistic **10** swaggering **11** egotistical **12** supercilious

vainglory
4 pomp **5** pride **6** egoism, vanity **7** conceit, egotism **9** arrogance **10** pretension **11** haughtiness **12** boastfulness

valance
5 drape **6** pelmet **7** curtain, drapery **10** lambrequin

vale
4 dale, dell, glen **5** combe **6** dingle, hollow, valley

valediction
5 adieu **7** good-bye **8** farewell **11** leave-taking

valedictory
see **valediction**

valentine
4 card, dear, love **7** beloved, darling, tribute **10** sweetheart

valet
7 servant **9** attendant **10** manservant

valiant
4 bold **5** brave **6** heroic, plucky **7** doughty, gallant, valiant **8** fearless, intrepid **10** chivalrous, courageous **11** lionhearted **12** greathearted, stouthearted

valid
4 just, true **5** legal, solid, sound **6** cogent, lawful, potent, proven **7** binding, in force, logical, telling **8** attested, bona fide, credible, forceful **9** effective, effectual, operative **10** acceptable, compelling, convincing, legitimate, persuasive **11** justifiable, trustworthy **12** well-grounded

validate
5 prove **6** affirm, ratify, verify **7** approve, bear out, certify, confirm, endorse, justify, probate **8** legalize, sanction **10** legitimate, legitimize **11** corroborate, rubber-stamp **12** authenticate, substantiate

validity
5 force, proof **7** cogency, potency **8** efficacy **9** soundness **10** lawfulness **13** effectiveness

valise
3 bag **4** grip **6** kit bag, suiter **7** handbag, Pullman **8** gripsack, suitcase **9** gladstone, two-suiter **10** weekend bag **11** portmanteau **12** overnight bag, traveling bag **13** traveling case

Valjean's pursuer
6 Javert

Valkyrie
6 maiden **8** Brynhild

valley
4 dale, dell, glen, vale, wadi **5** basin, combe, gulch, gully, swale **6** canyon, dingle, hollow, ravine **10** depression
Africa-Asia: 4 Rift **9** Great Rift
Alps: 11 Grindelwald
ancient Greece: 5 Nemea
Asia: 7 Fergana
California: 4 Napa **5** Death, Squaw **7** Central **8** Imperial, Yosemite **11** San Fernando
Dead Sea area: 6 Arabah
Dominican Republic: 5 Cibao
Egypt: 6 Kharga
England: 5 Doone
Germany: 4 Ruhr
Greece: 5 Tembi, Tempe
India: 4 Kulu **7** Kashmir (Vale of)
Ireland: 5 Avoca, Ovoca
Israel: 4 Elah
Lebanon: 4 Biqa **5** Bekaa
moon: 4 rill **5** rille
New York: 12 Sleepy Hollow
Pennsylvania: 7 Nittany
Scotland: 7 Glen Roy
Switzerland: 5 Hasli **8** Engadine **11** Grindelwald

Virginia: 10 Shenandoah
Washington: 11 Grand Coulee

Valmiki's epic
8 Ramayana

valor
4 guts **6** mettle, spirit, virtue **7** bravery, courage, heroism, prowess, stomach **8** chivalry, valiance, valiancy **9** fortitude, gallantry **10** resolution

valorous
see **valiant**

valse
5 waltz

valuable
4 dear **6** costly, prized, useful, worthy **8** precious **9** expensive, important, rewarding, treasured **10** satisfying, worthwhile

valuate
4 rate **5** assay, price **6** assess, survey **7** adjudge **8** appraise, estimate

valuation
4 cost, rate **5** price, worth **6** rating **7** opinion **8** estimate, judgment **9** appraisal **10** assessment, estimation **12** appreciation

value
4 cost, rate **5** assay, gauge, judge, price, prize, scale, worth **6** assess, assign, charge, esteem, figure, reckon, regard, return, survey **7** account, apprize, care for, cherish, compute, quality, respect, utility **8** appraise, estimate, evaluate, quantity, treasure **9** appraisal, principle **10** appreciate, assessment, equivalent, importance **11** market price **12** denomination

valve
3 tap **4** cock, flap, gate **6** device, faucet, poppet, spigot **7** hydrant, petcock, shutoff **8** stopcock **9** regulator
cardiac: 6 mitral **8** bicuspid

vamoose
3 git **4** scat **5** leave, scram, split **6** beat it, begone, cut out, decamp, depart, get out **7** run away, skiddoo, take off **8** clear out **9** skedaddle

vamp
3 fix **4** fake, lure, mend, wile **5** ad-lib, flirt, intro, patch, siren, tempt **6** cook up, entice, groove, lead-in, make up, repair, seduce **7** beguile, charmer, rebuild **8** inveigle **9** fabricate, formulate, improvise, refurbish,

temptress **10** gold digger, seductress **11** enchantress, extemporize, femme fatale

vampire
3 bat **5** lamia **6** undead **7** Dracula **9** Nosferatu **11** bloodsucker

van
3 car **4** head, lead, wing **5** front, truck, wagon **7** minibus **11** cutting edge, leading edge

vandal
3 Hun **5** yahoo **6** looter **8** pillager **9** despoiler, destroyer, plunderer, spoliator

vandalize
5 smash, trash, wreck **6** damage, deface, ravage, tear up **7** destroy **8** demolish, sabotage

Vandal king
8 Gaiseric, Genseric

Vandyke
5 beard **6** border, collar, edging, goatee

vane
3 web **7** feather, wind tee **8** vexillum **10** bellwether **11** weathercock

vanguard
4 lead **5** front **9** forefront **11** cutting edge, leading edge

vanilla
4 tame **5** beige, cream, plain **7** extract **8** ordinary **9** innocuous **10** white-bread **12** conventional **13** garden-variety

vanish
3 die, fly **4** fade, flee, melt **5** clear **8** dissolve, evanesce **9** disappear, dissipate, evaporate **13** dematerialize

vanity
3 ego **5** pride **6** egoism **7** conceit, egotism **8** self-love, smugness **9** vainglory **10** narcissism, pretension **13** dressing table

Vanity Fair author
9 Thackeray (William Makepeace)

vanquish
4 beat, best, drub, lick, rout **5** cream, crush, quell **6** defeat, humble, subdue, thrash **7** clobber, conquer, destroy, smother, trounce **8** surmount **9** overpower, overthrow, subjugate **10** annihilate

vantage
4 edge, odds **8** handicap **9** head start, upper hand

point: 3 POV 5 perch 7 lookout, outlook
8 position 10 watchtower

Vanuatu
capital: 8 Port-Vila
ethnic group: 10 Melanesian
explorer: 4 Cook (Capt. James)
former name: 11 New Hebrides
island: 3 Epi 5 Efate, Maéwo, Tanna
6 Ambrim 8 Aneityum, Malekula
9 Erromango, Pentecost 13 Espíritu Santo
language: 6 French
monetary unit: 4 vatu

vapid
4 dull, flat, weak 5 banal, bland, ditsy,
ditzy, inane, silly 6 jejune 7 fatuous,
insipid, sapless, vacuous 9 brainless,
colorless, innocuous 10 namby-pamby,
wishy-washy 13 uninteresting

vapor
3 fog, gas 4 brag, haze, mist, smog
5 brume, cloud, smoke, steam 6 breath,
miasma, nimbus 7 bluster 8 phantasm
condensed: 3 dew
frozen: 4 hoar, rime 5 frost 9 hoarfrost

vaporize
5 steam 6 ablate 8 disperse, dissolve,
evanesce 9 dissipate, evaporate

vaporous
4 airy, hazy 5 foggy, misty, vague, wispy
6 cloudy, unreal 7 gaseous 8 ethereal,
illusory, volatile 10 evanescent
13 unsubstantial

vaquero
5 waddy 6 cowboy, gaucho, herder,
waddie 7 cowpoke 8 buckaroo, herdsman,
wrangler 10 cowpuncher

varia
6 medley 7 mélange, mixture, omnibus
8 treasury 9 anthology 10 compendium,
miscellany 11 compilation

variable
5 fluid 6 fickle, fitful, mobile, symbol
7 mutable, protean 8 unstable, unsteady,
volatile 9 irregular, mercurial, uncertain,
unsettled, versatile 10 capricious,
changeable, inconstant 13 temperamental

variance
3 war 4 odds 6 change, strife 7 discord,
dispute, dissent 8 conflict, disunity, division
9 variation 10 contention, difference,
dissension, dissidence 11 fluctuation
12 disagreement

variation
4 riff 5 shade, shift 6 change, nuance
7 partita 8 mutation 9 disparity
10 alteration, difference, divergence
11 fluctuation, declination, discrepancy,
oscillation 12 modification 13 dissimilarity

varicolored
see **variegated**

varicose
7 bulging, dilated, swollen

varied
5 mixed 6 motley, sundry 7 diverse,
various 8 assorted 9 different, disparate,
divergent 10 dissimilar 12 multifarious
13 heterogeneous, kaleidoscopic,
miscellaneous

variegated
4 pied 5 mixed, pinto 6 calico, motley
7 checked, dappled, diverse, mottled,
piebald, spotted 8 skewbald, stippled,
streaked 9 checkered, multihued
10 multicolor, parti-color, polychrome
12 multicolored, parti-colored
13 kaleidoscopic, polychromatic

variety
3 ilk 4 kind, sort, type 5 array, breed,
mode 6 flavor, medley, nature, stripe
8 mixed bag 9 diversity, variation
10 assortment, collection, miscellany,
subspecies 12 multiformity, multiplicity

various
4 some 5 mixed 6 divers, sundry, unlike
7 diverse, several, unalike 8 assorted,
separate 9 different, disparate, divergent,
unsimilar 10 dissimilar 12 multifarious
13 heterogeneous, miscellaneous

varlet
3 cur 4 page 5 knave, rogue, skunk
6 menial, rascal, wretch 8 coistrel
9 attendant, miscreant, scoundrel
10 blackguard

varmint
4 pest 5 knave, rogue, scamp, skunk,
sneak 6 rascal 7 critter 9 scoundrel

varnish
4 coat 5 adorn, cover, glaze, gloss, japan
6 veneer 7 coating, conceal, cover up,
shellac 9 covering 9 embellish, gloss over,
sugarcoat, whitewash
component: 5 resin

vary
5 alter, range 6 change, depart, differ,

vase

modify, mutate **7** deviate, digress, diverge
8 modulate **9** diversify

vase
3 urn **5** tazza **6** crater, krater, vessel
7 amphora

Vashni's father
6 Samuel

Vashti's husband
6 Xerxes **9** Ahasuerus

vassal
4 leud, serf **5** helot, liege, slave **6** tenant
7 bondman, homager, peasant, servant,
subject **8** bondsman, liege man
9 dependent, underling **11** subordinate
12 feudal tenant
high-ranking: 7 vavasor **8** vavasour

vast
4 huge, mega **5** giant, great, jumbo
6 untold **7** immense, mammoth, oceanic,
titanic **8** colossal, enormous, gigantic,
spacious, whopping **9** boundless,
expansive, humongous **10** gargantuan,
tremendous, widespread **12** astronomical

vastness
5 sweep **8** enormity, hugeness
9 immensity, magnitude **13** expansiveness

vat
3 tub, tun **4** beck, butt, cask, kier, tank
5 keeve, kieve **6** barrel, liquor, vessel
7 cistern **8** cauldron
cheese: 7 chessel

vatic
6 mantic **7** fatidic **8** oracular **9** fatidical,
prophetic, sibylline **10** predictive
11 apocalyptic

Vatican City
10 papal state
army: 11 Swiss Guards
chapel: 7 Sistine
church: 11 Saint Peter's
ruler: 4 Pope
site: 4 Rome

vaticinal
see **vatic**

vaticinate
5 augur **6** divine **7** portend, predict,
presage **8** forebode, forecast, foretell,
prophesy, soothsay **9** adumbrate
13 prognosticate

vaudeville
5 revue **9** burlesque, music hall **11** variety
show **12** song and dance

vaudevillian
11 entertainer

vault
3 pit, sky **4** arch, cave, dome, jump, leap,
room, safe, tomb **5** bound, crypt **6** cavern,
cellar, cupola, hurdle, spring, welkin
7 archway, dungeon **8** catacomb, overleap
9 firmament **10** undercroft

vaulting
4 arch, dome **7** emulous **8** aspiring
9 ambitious **12** enthusiastic **13** opportunistic

vaunt
4 blow, brag, crow, puff, rant **5** boast, strut
6 flaunt, parade **7** bluster, display, exhibit,
show off **8** brandish **9** gasconade
11 rodomontade

veal
4 calf
cutlet: 9 schnitzel
roasted: 10 fricandeau
shank: 8 osso buco

vector
5 agent **7** carrier **9** direction **10** pollinator

Vedic religion
country: 5 India
god: 4 Agni, deva, Soma **5** Indra
6 Varuna
language: 8 Sanskrit
priest: 7 Brahman
treatise: 7 Upanishad
writing: 7 Rig Veda, Samhita

veer
3 yaw **4** cast, chop, slew, sway, turn
5 fetch, sheer, shift, trend **6** depart, swerve
7 deflect, deviate, digress, diverge

vegetable
3 pea, soy, yam **4** bean, beet, corn, kale,
leek, okra, soya, taro, wort **5** chard, chive,
cress, green, onion, plant **6** carrot, celery,
cowpea, endive, garlic, legume, lentil,
peanut, pepper, potato, radish, sorrel,
squash, tomato, turnip **7** cabbage,
chayote, dullard, lettuce, mustard, parsley,
parsnip, pumpkin, rhubarb, salsify, shallot,
soybean, spinach **8** broccoli, collards,
cucumber, eggplant, kohlrabi, lima bean,
rutabaga, scallion, snap bean **9** artichoke,
asparagus, muskmelon **10** watermelon
11 cauliflower, horseradish, sweet potato
bog: 6 muskeg
dish: 5 salad

mold: 5 humus
seller: 6 grocer 7 grocery 12 coster-monger
sponge: 5 luffa 6 loofah
spread: 4 oleo 9 margarine

vegetarian
9 herbivore 11 herbivorous

vegetate
4 idle, laze, loaf, loll 5 chill, slack 6 loiter, lounge 7 goof off, hang out 8 languish, lollygag, slack off, stagnate 9 goldbrick, hibernate

vegetation
5 flora 6 growth, plants 7 verdure 8 greenery 9 plant life
floating: 4 sudd 8 pleuston

vehement
3 hot 4 wild 5 fiery, rabid 6 ardent, bitter, fervid, fierce, heated 7 excited, fervent, vicious, violent, zealous 8 forceful, powerful 9 perfervid 10 passionate 11 impassioned 12 antagonistic

vehicle
3 ATV, bus, cab, car, SUV, van 4 auto, bike, taxi, tool 5 agent, buggy, means, organ, plane, sedan, train, truck, wagon 6 agency, binder, medium, vector 7 bicycle, carrier, channel, machine, solvent, travois 8 airplane, ministry 9 ambulance, implement, motor home, transport 10 automobile, conveyance, instrument, motorcycle
baby's: 4 pram 8 carriage, stroller 9 baby buggy
child's: 5 trike 7 scooter 8 tricycle
farm: 4 wain 7 tractor
horse-drawn: 4 cart, dray 5 buggy, lorry, sulky, wagon 6 hansom, landau, troika 7 calèche, phaeton 8 carriage 9 buckboard
military: 4 jeep, tank 6 Humvee
one-wheeled: 8 unicycle
passenger: 3 bus, cab, car 4 auto, taxi 7 ricksha 8 cable car, rickshaw
public: 3 bus 4 tram 5 train 6 subway 7 omnibus, trolley
Roman: 7 chariot
winter: 4 sled 6 sleigh 8 snowplow 10 snowmobile

veil
4 caul, hide, mask, wrap 5 cloak, cloth, cloud, cover, velum 6 mantle, screen, shield, shroud 7 conceal, cover up, curtain, obscure, secrete 8 covering, disguise, enshroud 10 camouflage, false front
Muslim: 7 yashmak

netting: 6 maline 7 malines

vein
3 bed, way 4 line, lode, mind, mode, mood, seam, tone, tube 5 style, tenor 6 manner, nature, spirit, strain, streak, vessel 7 channel, fashion, pattern, quality, stratum 8 aptitude 11 blood vessel
combining form: 3 ven 4 veni, veno
deposit: 3 ore
fluid: 5 blood
heart: 8 vena cava
leaf: 3 rib
leg: 7 saphena 9 saphenous
neck: 7 jugular
small: 6 venule
varicose: 5 varix

velar
8 guttural

veld
7 prairie 9 grassland

velleity
4 bent, wish 5 fancy 6 desire, liking 7 leaning 10 propensity 11 inclination

velocipede
4 bike 5 cycle, trike 6 tandem 7 bicycle, pedicab 8 tricycle

velocity
4 pace 5 haste, speed, tempo 7 headway 8 celerity, rapidity 9 quickness, swiftness 12 acceleration

velum
4 caul, veil 8 membrane 10 soft palate

velvet
4 gain, mild, rich, soft 5 cloth 6 fabric, profit, smooth 8 winnings 10 antler skin

velvety
4 mild, soft 5 plush 6 smooth

venal
4 paid 6 sordid 7 corrupt 8 bribable 9 mercenary, unethical 11 corruptible, purchasable 12 unprincipled, unscrupulous

vend
4 hawk, sell, toot 6 market, monger, peddle, retail 8 huckster 9 advertise, broadcast

vendee
5 buyer 6 client 8 customer 9 purchaser

vendetta
4 feud 7 rivalry 9 blood feud

vendible
7 salable 8 sellable 10 marketable 12 merchantable

vendor
6 dealer, duffer, hawker, seller 7 packman, peddler 8 huckster, merchant, retailer, salesman

vendue
4 sale 7 auction 10 public sale

veneer
3 ply 4 burl, coat, face, mask, show, veil 5 cover, front, gloss, layer, plate 6 facade, facing 7 conceal, overlay 8 disguise

venerable
3 old 4 aged 5 hoary 6 sacred 7 ancient, antique, elderly, honored, revered, stately 8 esteemed 9 admirable, dignified, estimable, honorable, respected

venerate
5 adore, honor, prize 6 admire, esteem, revere 7 cherish, idolize, respect, worship 8 treasure 9 reverence

veneration
3 awe 5 honor 6 esteem, homage 7 respect, worship 9 adoration, reverence 10 admiration 11 hero worship

venery
3 sex 4 game, prey 5 chase 7 hunting

venesection
10 phlebotomy

Venetian
boat: 7 gondola
boatman: 9 gondolier
product: 5 glass 9 glassware
ruler: 4 doge
school: 7 Bellini, Tiepolo, Titian 8 Veronese 9 Giorgione 10 Tintoretto
street: 5 canal
suburb: 6 Murano

Venezuela
capital: 7 Caracas
city: 8 Valencia 9 Maracaibo 12 Barquisimeto
island: 9 Margarita
lake: 8 Valencia 9 Maracaibo
language: 7 Spanish
monetary unit: 7 bolívar
mountain, range: 5 Andes 6 Parima (Serra, Sierra) 7 Bolívar (Pico) 9 Pacaraima 11 Pico Bolívar, Serra Parima 12 Sierra Parima
neighbor: 6 Brazil, Guyana 8 Colombia
peninsula: 9 Paraguaná
river: 7 Orinoco
sea: 9 Caribbean
waterfall: 10 Angel Falls

Venezuelan
herdsman: 7 llanero
liberator: 7 Bolívar (Simón)
people: 5 Carib 6 Timote

vengeance
6 payoff 7 payback, redress, revenge 8 reprisal, revanche 9 repayment 10 punishment 11 retaliation, retribution

vengeful
8 punitive 10 vindictive 11 retaliatory

venial
5 minor 7 trivial 8 harmless, trifling 9 allowable, excusable, tolerable 10 condonable, forgivable, pardonable, remissible, remittable 13 insignificant

Venice of the East
7 Bangkok, Udaipur

Venice of the North
6 Bruges, Brugge 9 Amsterdam, Stockholm 12 St. Petersburg

Veni, Creator _____
8 Spiritus

venison
4 deer

veni, vidi, _____
4 vici

venom
4 bane, hate 5 spite 6 malice, poison, rancor 7 ill will, vitriol 8 embitter 9 contagion, malignity, virulence 11 malevolence

venomous
5 toxic 6 deadly, malign, poison 7 baneful, malefic, noxious 8 spiteful, viperish, viperous, virulent 9 malicious, malignant, poisonous 10 malevolent, pernicious 12 vituperative

vent
3 air 4 emit, expel, flue, hole, pipe, pour, slit 5 burst, issue, loose, utter, voice 6 broach, nozzle, outlet 7 chimney, exhaust, express, give off, opening, orifice, release, take out, unleash, volcano 8 breather, fumarole, spiracle 9 discharge 11 black smoker

venter
3 gut 5 belly 6 paunch 7 abdomen, stomach

ventilate
3 air 5 state, utter 6 aerate, expose 7 discuss, express 9 advertise, broadcast, circulate, verbalize 11 investigate

ventral area
7 abdomen, stomach

ventricle
6 cavity 7 chamber

ventriloquist
9 performer 11 entertainer
companion: 5 dummy
famous: 6 Bergen (Edgar)

venture
3 bet, try 4 dare, face, feat, gest, risk
5 brave, peril, stake, wager 6 chance,
expose, gamble, hazard 7 attempt,
daresay, emprise, exploit 8 endanger,
jeopardy, long shot, make bold
9 challenge, crapshoot, speculate
10 enterprise 11 speculation, undertaking

venturesome
4 bold, rash 5 brave 6 daring 8 reckless
9 audacious, daredevil, foolhardy
11 adventurous, temerarious

venue
4 site 5 arena, forum, place, scene
6 locale, outlet 7 setting 8 locality

Venus
6 planet, Vesper 7 daystar, Lucifer
8 Hesperus
(see also **Aphrodite**)

Venus de _____
4 Milo

_____ vera
4 aloe

veracious
4 just, true 5 exact, frank, right, valid
6 candid, honest 7 correct, factual, sincere
8 accurate, truthful

veracity
4 fact 5 truth 6 candor 7 honesty
8 accuracy, trueness 9 actuality, exactness
11 correctness 12 truthfulness

veranda
5 lanai, porch, stoop 6 piazza 7 gallery,
portico

verb
auxiliary: 3 are, can, did, had, has, may,
was 4 have, must, were, will, word
5 could, might, shall, would 6 should
form: 6 active, gerund 7 passive
10 infinitive, participle
kind: 10 transitive 12 intransitive
linking: 6 copula
mood: 8 optative 10 imperative, indicative
11 subjunctive

tense: 4 past 6 aorist, future 7 perfect,
present 9 predicate 10 pluperfect

verbal
4 oral 5 wordy 6 gerund, spoken 7 literal
9 unwritten 10 infinitive, participle,
rhetorical 11 word-for-word

verbalism
4 term 6 phrase 7 wording 8 phrasing
9 prolixity, windiness, wordiness
11 phraseology

verbalization
4 talk 6 speech 8 speaking 9 discourse,
utterance 12 articulation, vocalization

verbalize
3 air, say 4 talk 5 speak, state, utter,
voice, write 6 broach 7 express
8 bloviate, vocalize 9 ventilate

verbatim
5 exact 6 direct 7 exactly, literal, precise
8 directly 9 literally, literatim, precisely
10 accurately 11 word-for-word

verbiage
4 talk 6 phrase 7 diction, wording
8 parlance, phrasing, pleonasm
9 wordiness 10 redundancy 11 phraseology

verbose
5 gassy, windy, wordy 6 prolix 7 diffuse
9 garrulous, redundant, talkative
10 loquacious, pleonastic 11 tautologous

verbosity
9 prolixity, windiness, wordiness
10 redundancy

verboten
5 taboo 6 banned 7 illegal 8 outlawed
9 forbidden 10 prohibited

verdant
4 lush 5 green, leafy, naive 6 grassy,
unripe

verdict
6 assize, ruling 7 finding, opinion
8 decision, judgment 9 judgement

Verdi opera
4 Aïda 6 Ernani, Oberto, Otello 7 Nabucco
8 Don Carlo, Falstaff, Lombardi (I), Traviata
(La) 9 Don Carlos, Rigoletto, Trovatore (II)
15 Simon Boccanegra

verdure
7 foliage 8 greenery 9 greenness
10 vegetation

verge
3 hem, lip, rim 4 abut, cusp, edge, sink

5 bound, brink, skirt, staff, touch 6 adjoin, border, fringe, margin 7 selvage 8 approach, shoulder 9 threshold 10 borderline

veridical
see **veracious**

verifiable
4 true 6 proven 7 certain 8 provable 9 undoubted

verification
5 proof 10 validation 11 attestation 12 confirmation 13 corroboration

verify
4 aver, test 5 check, prove, vouch 6 attest, settle 7 bear out, confirm 8 document, validate 9 establish, fact-check 11 corroborate, demonstrate 12 authenticate, substantiate

verily
5 truly 6 indeed 7 in truth 9 assuredly, certainly 11 confidently, undoubtedly

veritable
4 real, true 6 actual 7 factual, genuine 8 bona fide 9 authentic, undoubted 10 sure-enough 11 indubitable

verity
5 truth 6 gospel, truism 7 honesty, reality 9 actuality 12 truthfulness

vermiform
8 wormlike

vermilion
3 red

vermin
4 lice, mice, pest, rats, scum 5 fleas, pests, trash 7 bedbugs, varmint

Vermont
capital: 10 Montpelier
city: 7 Rutland 10 Burlington
college, university: 7 Norwich 8 Marlboro 10 Bennington, Middlebury
mountain, range: 5 Green 9 Mansfield
nickname: 13 Green Mountain (State)
river: 11 Connecticut
state bird: 12 hermit thrush
state flower: 9 red clover
state tree: 10 sugar maple

vernacular
4 cant 5 argot, idiom, lingo, slang 6 common, jargon, patois, patter, speech, tongue, vulgar 7 dialect, vulgate 8 language 9 dialectal 10 colloquial 12 mother tongue

vernal
5 fresh, green 6 spring 8 youthful 10 springlike

Verne, Jules
character: 4 Fogg (Phileas), Nemo 12 Passepartout
submarine: 8 Nautilus
work: 16 Mysterious Island (The) 21 From the Earth to the Moon 26 Around the World in Eighty Days

versant
see **conversant**

versatile
5 handy 6 adroit, facile 7 protean 8 variable 9 all-around, competent, many-sided 10 changeable 11 well-rounded 12 ambidextrous

verse
3 lay, ode 4 epic, poem, rune 5 lyric, poesy, rhyme 6 ballad, jingle, poetry, sonnet, stanza 7 passage 8 acquaint 11 composition, familiarize
analysis: 8 scansion
four-line: 8 quatrain
free: 5 blank 8 unrhymed
six-line: 6 sestet
three-line: 6 tercet
two-line: 7 couplet
writer: 4 poet

versed
5 adept 6 au fait 7 abreast, skilled, veteran 8 familiar, informed, seasoned 9 au courant, competent, practiced 10 acquainted 11 experienced 13 knowledgeable

versifier
4 bard, poet 6 rhymer 9 poetaster, rhymester, sonneteer

version
4 copy 5 draft, model 6 flavor, remake 7 account, edition, reading, variant 9 iteration, narrative, redaction, rendition, revision, rewording 10 adaptation, paraphrase 11 arrangement, description, incarnation, restatement, translation

versus
4 anti 6 contra 7 against, vis-à-vis 11 over against

vertebra
7 segment
kind: 6 dorsal, lumbar, sacral 8 cervical, thoracic 9 coccygeal

vertebrae
 4 back 5 spine 6 coccyx, rachis, sacrum
 8 backbone, tailbone 12 spinal column

vertebrate
 6 animal
 characteristic: 5 spine 7 cranium
 12 spinal column
 kind: 4 bird, fish, frog 6 mammal 7 reptile
 9 amphibian

vertex
 3 cap, top 4 acme, apex, peak 5 crest,
 crown 6 apogee, summit, tip-top, zenith

vertical
 5 erect, plumb, sheer, steep 7 upright
 8 straight 10 lengthwise, straight-up
 13 perpendicular

vertiginous
 5 dizzy, giddy, woozy 6 fickle, rotary
 11 light-headed

vertigo
 6 megrim 9 dizziness, giddiness

verve
 3 pep, vim, zip 4 brio, dash, élan, fire, life,
 zest, zing 5 flair, gusto, moxie, oomph,
 style, vigor 6 bounce, energy, spirit, spring
 7 panache 8 vitality, vivacity
 10 enthusiasm, liveliness 13 sprightliness

very
 3 too 4 bare, mere, most, much, pure, real,
 same, true 5 exact, ideal, model, plain,
 quite, sheer, super, truly, utter 6 actual,
 highly, hugely, mighty, really, simple
 7 awfully, genuine, greatly, notably, perfect,
 precise, special 8 absolute, actually, bona
 fide, selfsame, terribly 9 authentic,
 extremely, genuinely, identical, undoubted
 10 absolutely, particular 11 exceedingly
 French: 4 très
 German: 4 sehr
 Italian: 5 molto
 Scottish: 3 gey
 Spanish: 3 muy

vesicle
 3 sac 4 cell, cyst 5 bulla 6 cavity
 7 blister, vacuole

vespers
 8 evensong

_____ Vespucci
 7 Amerigo

vessel
 3 can, cup, jar, pan, pot, tub, urn 4 boat,
 bowl, cask, drum, duct, ewer, pail, ship,
 tank, tube, vase, vein 5 canal, craft, cruse
 6 artery, barrel, bottle, bucket, firkin, flagon,
 kettle, krater, pottle 7 cresset, pitcher
 8 crucible 9 container 10 receptacle,
 watercraft
 combining form: 3 vas 4 angi, vaso
 5 angio
 drinking: 3 cup, mug 4 toby 5 flask,
 glass, gourd, stoup 6 goblet, seidel
 7 tankard, tumbler
 Indian: 4 lota 5 lotah
 Scottish: 6 quaich, quaigh

vest
 6 weskit 9 waistcoat

Vesta
 see **Hestia**

vestal
 4 pure 6 chaste, virgin 8 celibate, virginal,
 virtuous

vestibule
 5 entry, foyer, lobby 6 cavity 7 hallway,
 narthex, passage 8 anteroom, entrance,
 entryway 10 antechapel 11 antechamber

vestige
 4 echo 5 dregs (plural), relic, scrap, stump,
 trace, track 6 shadow 7 memento,
 remains, remnant 8 leftover 9 remainder
 10 hide or hair 11 hide nor hair

vestment
 3 alb 4 cope, garb, gown, robe 5 amice,
 cotta, dress, habit, stole, tunic 6 attire,
 rochet 7 apparel, cassock, garment,
 maniple, pallium, tunicle 8 chasuble,
 cincture, clothing, covering, dalmatic,
 parament, surplice
 ancient Hebrew: 5 ephod 11 breastplate

vestry
 6 closet 8 sacristy 9 sacrarium

vesture
 4 robe 6 clothe 7 apparel, garment
 8 clothing 10 habiliment

Vesuvius
 7 volcano

vet
 5 check 6 go over, review 7 analyze,
 examine, inspect 8 appraise, check out,
 evaluate, look over 10 old soldier

vetch
 4 herb, tare 6 legume
 type: 4 milk (vetch) 5 crown (vetch), hairy
 (vetch)

veteran
4 ex-GI 5 adept 6 expert, master 7 old
hand, skilled 8 old-timer, warhorse
9 practiced, shellback 10 past master
11 experienced

veto
3 nix 4 kill 6 defeat, forbid, refuse, reject
7 decline 8 disallow, negative, prohibit
9 blackball 10 disapprove 11 prohibition
12 interdiction

vex
3 bug, irk 4 fret, gall, itch, roil 5 annoy,
chafe, gripe, rowel, tease 6 badger, baffle,
bother, harass, harrow, harry, nettle, pester,
plague, puzzle, rankle, ruffle, worry
7 chagrin, torment, trouble 8 bullyrag,
distress, irritate

vexation
4 fret, sore 5 chafe, trial 6 bother
7 problem, torment 8 distress, headache
9 annoyance, troubling 10 affliction,
harassment, irritation 11 aggravation,
bedevilment, provocation

vexatious
5 pesky 7 prickly 8 annoying, tiresome
9 troublous 10 bothersome, irritating
11 distressing, troublesome
12 exasperating

vexed
6 sticky, touchy 7 debated, weighty
8 ticklish 9 difficult, discussed, troubling

vexing
5 tough 7 irksome 8 annoying 9 difficult,
harassing, upsetting 10 bothersome,
irritating, troublesome 11 distressing

via
3 per 4 over, with 5 along 7 by way of,
through 9 by means of

viable
6 doable 7 capable 8 feasible, possible,
workable 11 practicable, sustainable

vial
6 ampule 7 ampoule

viands
4 eats, fare, feed, food, grub 7 aliment,
edibles, vittles 8 victuals 9 provender
10 provisions 11 comestibles

vibrant
5 alive, vital, vivid 6 bright, lively, punchy
7 ringing 8 resonant 9 consonant,
pulsating 10 resounding 11 oscillating
12 effervescent

vibrate
3 jar 4 ring 5 quake, shake, swing, throb,
waver 6 quiver, shimmy, thrill, tremor
7 flutter, pulsate 9 undulate 9 fluctuate,
oscillate, vacillate

vibration
4 aura 5 quake, shake, trill 6 motion,
quaver, quiver, shimmy, spirit, tremor
7 flutter, shaking 8 fremitus, wavering
9 emanation, trembling 11 fluctuation,
oscillation, vacillation

vicar
6 pastor, priest 8 minister, reverend
9 clergyman

Vicar of Wakefield, The
author: 9 Goldsmith (Oliver)
character: 8 Primrose

vice
3 sin 4 evil, flaw 5 crime, fault 6 defect
7 devilry, failing, frailty, offense, scandal
8 iniquity 9 deformity, depravity, indecency
10 corruption, debauchery, immorality,
perversion, wickedness 11 shortcoming

vice-president
4 veep 6 deputy 7 officer 9 executive
American: 4 Burr (Aaron), Bush (George),
Ford (Gerald), Gore (Albert), King (William)
5 Adams (John), Agnew (Spiro), Dawes
(Charles), Gerry (Elbridge), Nixon
(Richard), Tyler (John) 6 Arthur (Chester),
Cheney (Richard), Colfax (Schuyler), Curtis
(Charles), Dallas (George), Garner (John
Nance), Hamlin (Hannibal), Hobart
(Garret), Morton (Levi), Quayle (Dan),
Truman (Harry), Wilson (Woodrow)
7 Barkley (Alben), Calhoun (John
Caldwell), Clinton (George), Johnson
(Andrew, Lyndon Baines, Richard Mentor),
Mondale (Walter), Sherman (James
Schoolcraft), Wallace (Henry), Wheeler
(William) 8 Coolidge (Calvin), Fillmore
(Millard), Humphrey (Hubert Horatio),
Marshall (Thomas), Tompkins (Daniel), Van
Buren (Martin) 9 Fairbanks (Charles),
Hendricks (Thomas), Jefferson (Thomas),
Roosevelt (Theodore), Stevenson (Adlai)
11 Rockefeller (Nelson) 12 Breckinridge
(John)

viceroy
5 nabob 6 exarch, satrap 7 khedive
8 alderman, governor 9 butterfly
11 stadtholder

vice versa
10 conversely 12 contrariwise

vicinity
4 area 5 range 6 extent, locale, region, shadow 7 suburbs 8 ballpark, district, environs, locality, nearness, precinct 9 closeness, magnitude, proximity 12 neighborhood

vicious
4 evil, mean, vile 5 cruel 6 fierce, malign, savage, sinful, wicked 7 brutish, corrupt, hateful, immoral, noxious, violent 8 depraved, horrible, perverse, spiteful 9 barbarous, ferocious, malicious, malignant, monstrous, nefarious, reprobate 10 degenerate, flagitious, iniquitous, malevolent, villainous, vindictive

vicissitude
5 rigor, trial 6 chance, change 7 weather 8 hardship, mutation, reversal 9 adversity, mischance 10 affliction, difficulty, misfortune, mutability 11 permutation, progression, tribulation

victim
4 butt, dupe, gull, mark, prey 5 chump, patsy 6 pigeon, martyr, quarry, sucker 7 fall guy 8 casualty, fatality, offering, underdog 9 sacrifice

victimize
4 dupe, fool, gull, hoax 5 cheat, cozen, trick 7 deceive, swindle 8 flimflam, hoodwink 9 bamboozle, sacrifice 11 hornswoggle

victor
5 champ 6 top dog, winner 7 subduer 8 champion 9 conqueror 10 vanquisher

Victorian
4 prim 6 prissy, stuffy 7 prudish 8 priggish 11 puritanical, straitlaced 12 old-fashioned

Victoria, Queen
family: 7 Hanover
father: 6 Edward
husband: 6 Albert
prime minister: 8 Disraeli (Benjamin) 9 Gladstone (William), Melbourne (Lord)
son: 6 Edward

victory
3 win 5 sweep 6 defeat 7 mastery, success, triumph 8 conquest, walkaway, walkover 10 overcoming 11 superiority
costly: 7 Pyrrhic
easy: 8 cakewalk, walkaway
monument: 4 arch 13 Arc de Triomphe
reward: 6 spoils
sign: 3 vee
symbol: 4 flag 6 laurel, wreath

Victory author
6 Conrad (Joseph)

victuals
4 chow, eats, feed, food, grub, prog 6 viands 7 edibles, vittles 9 provender 10 provisions 11 comestibles

_____ Vidal
4 Gore

videlicet
3 viz 5 to wit 6 namely, that is 8 scilicet 11 that is to say

vie
3 pit 5 match 6 oppose, strive 7 compete, contend, contest, counter 8 struggle

Viennese
city hall: 7 Rathaus
family: 8 Habsburg, Hapsburg
palace: 7 Hofburg
park: 6 Prater
river: 6 Danube

Vietnam
capital: 5 Hanoi
city: 3 Hue 6 Da Nang, Saigon 8 Haiphong 13 Ho Chi Minh City
delta: 6 Mekong
gulf: 6 Tonkin 8 Thailand
monetary unit: 4 dong
mountain: 8 Fan-si-pan
neighbor: 4 Laos 5 China 8 Cambodia 9 Kampuchea
river: 3 Red 6 Mekong
sea: 10 South China

Vietnamese New Year
3 Tet

view
3 eye, see 4 espy, look, plan, scan 5 scene, sight, vista, watch 6 behold, belief, look at, notice, notion, regard, review, survey 7 close-up, examine, inspect, lookout, observe, opinion, outlook, picture, scenery, vantage 8 judgment, panorama, perceive, prospect, scrutiny, snapshot 10 conviction, inspection, scrutinize 11 contemplate, examination

viewer
7 witness 8 looker-on, onlooker 9 bystander, spectator 10 eyewitness

viewing instrument
5 glass, scope 6 binocs 7 glasses 8 telescope 10 binoculars, microscope 12 field glasses
combining form: 5 scope

viewpoint
3 eye **5** angle, slant, stand **6** stance
7 outlook **8** attitude, position **9** direction
11 perspective

vigil
4 wake **5** watch **7** lookout, prayers
9 devotions **10** deathwatch **11** wake-
fulness **12** surveillance, watch and ward

vigilance
5 watch **9** alertness **12** surveillance,
watchfulness

vigilant
4 keen, wary **5** alert, awake, aware, chary,
sharp **7** careful, jealous, on guard
8 cautious, open-eyed, watchful
9 attentive, sharp-eyed, wide-awake

vignette
5 scene **6** sketch **7** glimpse, picture
8 ornament

vigor
3 pep, vim, zip **4** brio, push, snap, tuck
5 ardor, drive, force, gusto, moxie, oomph
6 energy, mettle, muscle, spirit, starch
7 potency **8** dynamism, strength, tonicity,
virility, vitality **9** hardihood, lustiness,
puissance **10** get-up-and-go, robustness,
sturdiness

vigorous
5 brisk, hardy, lusty, stout, tough, vital
6 active, hearty, lively, potent, robust,
strong, sturdy, virile **7** dashing, driving,
dynamic, healthy **8** athletic, forceful,
muscular, powerful, spirited, youthful
9 energetic, strenuous **10** mettlesome,
red-blooded

Viking
see **Norse**

vile
4 base, evil, foul, mean, ugly **5** gross,
nasty, slimy **6** filthy, horrid, sordid, vulgar,
wicked **7** low-down, noisome, obscene,
squalid **8** depraved, wretched **9** abhorrent,
loathsome, obnoxious, offensive, perverted,
repugnant, repulsive, revolting
10 despicable, disgusting **12** contemptible

vilify
5 abuse, libel, smear **6** assail, attack,
berate, defame, malign **7** asperse, run
down, slander, spatter, traduce
8 denounce, tear down **9** denigrate,
disparage **10** calumniate

villa
5 dacha, manor **6** estate, quinta
7 château, mansion **9** residence

village
4 burg, town **5** bourg, thorp **6** hamlet
7 townlet
African: 4 dorp **5** kraal
Indian: 6 pueblo
Japanese: 4 mura
Jewish: 6 shtetl
Malay: 7 kampong
Russian: 3 mir

Village Blacksmith author
10 Longfellow (Henry Wadsworth)

villain
4 boor, heel **5** demon, devil, heavy, knave,
rogue **6** rascal, sinner **7** lowlife
8 antihero, criminal, evildoer, offender,
scalawag **9** character, miscreant,
reprobate, scoundrel **10** blackguard,
malefactor
classic: 4 Iago **5** Judas (Iscariot)
6 Brutus (Marcus Junius) **8** Quisling
(Vidkun)

villainous
4 evil **6** rotten, wicked **7** corrupt, debased,
heinous, vicious **8** depraved, wretched
9 atrocious, felonious, miscreant, nefarious
10 detestable, diabolical, flagitious,
iniquitous, perfidious, traitorous
11 treacherous

villainy
4 vice **5** crime **8** evilness **9** depravity,
treachery, turpitude **10** corruption,
wickedness

villein
7 peasant **8** villager

villenage
4 yoke **6** tenure, thrall **7** bondage,
serfdom **9** servitude, thralldom

vim
3 zip **4** brio, dash, élan, gimp, zing
5 gusto, oomph, verve **6** bounce, energy,
esprit, spirit, vigor **7** vinegar **9** animation
10 enthusiasm, razzmatazz

___ vincit omnia
4 Amor

vinculum
3 tie **4** bond, knot, link, yoke **5** nexus
8 ligament, ligature

vindicable
7 tenable **9** excusable **10** condonable,
defendable, defensible, pardonable
11 justifiable, warrantable

vindicate
4 free 5 clear, guard, prove, right 6 acquit, avenge, defend, excuse, refute, shield, uphold, verify 7 absolve, bear out, confirm, deliver, justify, redress, revenge, support, warrant 8 maintain 9 exculpate, exonerate, safeguard 11 corroborate 12 substantiate

vindictive
5 catty, nasty 6 malign 7 hateful, hurtful, vicious 8 punitive, spiteful, vengeful, venomous 9 malicious, malignant, poisonous

vine
3 hop, ivy, pea 5 grape, kudzu, liana, liane, maile, plant 6 maypop 7 chayote, climber, creeper 8 catbrier, clematis 11 bittersweet
Asian: 6 pikake

vinegar
3 vim 6 liquid 8 ill humor, sourness 9 condiment 12 preservative
relating to: 10 acetic acid
steep in: 6 pickle

vinegarish
4 sour 6 bitter, cranky, ornery 7 bearish, waspish 8 snappish 9 crotchety, irascible 12 cantankerous, cross-grained, disagreeable

Vinegar Joe
8 Stilwell (Joseph)

vineyard
French: 3 cru 7 château, domaine

Vinland discoverer
4 Leif (Ericsson, Eriksson) 12 Leif Ericsson, Leif Eriksson

vintage
3 age, old 4 crop, wine 5 yield 7 antique, classic, harvest 8 outdated 9 classical 10 antiquated 12 old-fashioned

Viola
brother: 9 Sebastian
husband: 6 Orsino
play: 12 Twelfth Night

viola da _____
5 gamba

violate
4 rape 5 break, wrong 6 breach, defile, offend, ravish 7 disturb, outrage, profane, traduce 8 fracture, infringe, trespass 9 desecrate, disregard 10 contravene, transgress

violation
4 foul, rape 5 break, crime, wrong 6 breach, injury 7 offense, outrage, perjury, scandal 8 trespass 9 blasphemy, injustice, sacrilege 10 illegality, infraction, ravishment 11 desecration, disturbance, interruption, misdemeanor, profanation 12 encroachment, infringement 13 contravention, transgression

violence
4 fury, riot 5 clash 6 frenzy, mayhem 7 assault, outrage, rampage 8 foul play, savagery, violance 9 onslaught 10 distortion, roughhouse

violent
5 cruel, harsh, rabid 6 fierce, raging, savage, stormy 7 berserk, furious, intense, vicious 8 slam-bang, vehement 9 explosive, ferocious 10 hellacious 11 acrimonious, destructive

violet
5 mauve 6 purple 8 amethyst, lavender 10 heliotrope

violin
6 fiddle 10 instrument
kind: 5 Amati, Strad 8 Guarneri 10 Guarnerius, Stradivari 12 Stradivarius
part: 3 bow, nut, peg 4 neck 6 bridge, scroll, string 8 chin rest 9 tailpiece 10 soundboard 11 fingerboard
precursor: 5 rebec 6 rebeck

violinist
American: 4 Hahn (Hilary) 5 Elman (Mischa), Fodor (Eugene), Ricci (Ruggiero), Stern (Isaac) 6 Midori, Powell (Maud) 7 Heifetz (Jascha), Menuhin (Yehudi), Szigeti (Joseph) 8 Kreisler (Fritz), Milstein (Nathan) 9 Zimbalist (Efrem)
Belgian: 5 Ysaÿe (Eugene) 8 Grumiaux (Arthur)
Czech: 3 Suk (Josef)
English: 7 Menuhin (Yehudi)
French: 12 Francescatti (Zino)
German: 6 Mutter (Anne-Sophie)
Hungarian: 7 Joachim (Joseph)
Israeli: 7 Perlman (Itzhak) 8 Zukerman (Pinchas)
Italian: 6 Viotti (Giovanne Battista) 7 Corelli (Arcangelo), Vivaldi (Antonio) 8 Paganini (Niccolo) 9 Geminiani (Francesco)
Romanian: 6 Enescu (George)
Russian: 8 Oistrakh (David)

violin maker
4 Salò (Gasparo da) 5 Amati (Andrea,

Antonio, Girolamo, Nicolo) **7** Maggini (Giovanni Paolo), Stainer (Jacob) **8** Guarneri (Andrea, del Gesù, Giuseppe, Pietro) **10** Guarnerius (Andrea, Giuseppe, Pietro), Stradivari (Antonio, Francesco, Omobono) **12** Stradivarius (Antonio, Francesco, Omobono)

VIP
4 BMOC, lion **5** mogul, nabob **6** big gun, biggie, bigwig, fat cat, honcho **7** big shot, notable, someone **8** big wheel, luminary, mandarin, somebody **9** big cheese, dignitary **10** panjandrum **13** high-muck-a-muck

viper
3 asp **5** adder, snake **7** serpent **10** bushmaster, copperhead, fer-de-lance **11** rattlesnake **13** water moccasin

virago
5 harpy, scold, shrew, vixen **6** amazon, dragon, gorgon, ogress **8** battle-ax, fishwife, harridan, Xantippe **9** battle-axe, termagant, Xanthippe

Virgil
4 poet **5** guide **6** orator **8** cicerone
epic: 6 Aeneid
poems: 8 Eclogues, Georgics

virgin
3 new **4** pure **5** first, fresh, unwed **6** chaste, intact, maiden, modest, unused, vestal **7** initial **8** celibate, innocent, primeval, pristine, spotless **9** abstinent, undefiled, unmarried, unspoiled, unsullied, untouched **10** immaculate

virginal
4 pure **5** fresh **6** chaste, intact, maiden, spinet **8** pristine, virtuous **9** undefiled, unspoiled, unsullied, untouched

Virgin Goddess
5 Diana **6** Hestia **7** Artemis

Virginia
capital: 8 Richmond
city: 7 Norfolk, Roanoke **10** Alexandria **11** Newport News **13** Virginia Beach
college, university: 3 VMI **7** Hampton **10** Sweet Briar **11** George Mason, Old Dominion **12** James Madison **13** Randolph-Macon **14** William and Mary
historical site: 10 Monticello **11** Mount Vernon **12** Williamsburg
mountain, range: 6 Rogers **9** Blue Ridge
nickname: 11 Old Dominion
river: 5 James **7** Potomac **10** Shenandoah
state bird: 8 cardinal

state flower: 7 dogwood (American)
state tree: 7 dogwood (American)

Virginian, The
author: 6 Wister (Owen)
character: 7 Trampas

Virgin Island
5 Peter **6** Norman, St. John **7** Anegada, St. Croix, Tortola **8** St. Thomas

Virgin Islands (U.S.)
capital: 15 Charlotte Amalie
island: 6 St. John **7** St. Croix **8** St. Thomas
location: 10 West Indies
territory of: 12 United States

Virgin Islands, British
capital: 8 Road Town
island: 5 Peter **6** Norman **7** Anegada, Tortola **11** Jost Van Dyke, Virgin Gorda
location: 10 West Indies

virginity
6 purity **8** celibacy, chastity **10** chasteness, maidenhead, maidenhood

Virgin Queen
9 Elizabeth

Virgo star
5 Spica

virgule
5 comma, slant, slash **7** solidus **8** diagonal

viridity
5 green **7** naïveté **9** freshness, greenness, innocence

virile
4 male **5** macho, manly **6** manful, potent, robust **7** manlike **8** forceful, vigorous **9** energetic, masculine

virtual
5 moral, tacit **7** de facto **8** implicit **9** essential, practical **10** electronic **11** fundamental

virtuality
4 core, pith, soul **5** being, juice, stuff **6** effect, marrow, nature **7** essence, makings **8** quiddity **9** substance **10** capability **12** essentiality, quintessence, potentiality

virtually
4 nigh **6** all but, almost, fairly, nearly, next to **7** morally **8** as good as, in effect, wellnigh **9** basically, in essence, literally **10** implicitly **11** effectively, essentially,

practically **13** approximately, fundamentally, substantially

virtue
5 merit, power, right, trait, valor, value, vigor, worth **7** courage, feature, potency, probity, quality **8** chastity, goodness, morality, strength **9** attribute, character, puissance, rectitude, rightness **10** excellence, excellency, perfection **11** uprightness
cardinal: 4 hope, love **5** faith **7** charity, justice **8** prudence **9** fortitude **10** temperance

virtuosic
5 showy **6** expert, flashy **7** hotshot, skilled **9** brilliant, masterful **10** consummate, prodigious **12** razzle-dazzle

virtuoso
4 whiz **6** expert, master, savant, wizard, wonder **7** artiste, hotshot, maestro, prodigy **10** past master, wunderkind

virtuous
4 good, pure **5** moral, noble, pious, right **6** chaste, decent, modest, proper **7** ethical, sinless **8** innocent, spotless **9** blameless, faultless, guiltless, righteous, unsullied, untainted **10** inculpable, moralistic **11** respectable, right-minded, untarnished

virulent
5 harsh, toxic **6** biting, bitter, malign, poison **7** cutting, hateful, hostile **8** scathing, spiteful, venomous **9** malicious, malignant, pestilent, poisonous, rancorous, vitriolic **10** pathogenic

virus
3 bug **8** pathogen **9** contagion, infection

vis
5 force, might, power

visage
3 mug, pan **4** cast, face, look, mien, phiz, puss **6** aspect, kisser **8** features **9** semblance **10** expression **11** countenance

vis-à-vis
4 date **6** escort, facing, toward **7** against **8** fronting, opposite, together **9** tête-à-tête **10** face-to-face **11** counterpart

visceral
3 gut **4** deep **5** inner **8** internal, intimate **9** intuitive **10** intestinal **11** instinctive, instinctual

viscid
see **viscous**

viscount
4 lord, peer **8** nobleman

viscous
4 limy, ropy **5** gluey, gooey, gummy, limey, slimy, thick **9** glutinous, semifluid **10** gelatinous **12** mucilaginous

vise
5 clamp, screw **7** squeeze

Vishnu
4 Hari
avatar: 4 Rama **5** Kurma **6** Buddha, Matsya, Vamena, Varaha **7** Krishna **9** Narasinha
consort: 3 Sri **4** Shri **7** Lakshmi
home: 4 Meru

visible
6 patent **7** obvious **8** apparent, available, viewable **9** well-known **10** detectable **11** conspicuous, discernible, perceivable, perceptible **12** recognizable

Visigoth
conquest: 4 Rome
king: 6 Alaric

vision
3 eye **5** dream, fancy, image, sense, sight **6** beauty, seeing **7** concept, fantasy, feature, picture, specter **8** daydream, eyesight, phantasm, presence, prophecy **9** foresight, nightmare **10** apparition, perception, phenomenon, revelation **13** manifestation
combining form: 4 opto **5** opsis
deceptive: 6 mirage
relating to: 5 optic **6** visual **7** optical

visionary
4 seer **5** ideal, lofty, noble **6** unreal **7** blue-sky, dreamer, utopian **8** fanciful, idealist, illusory, quixotic, romantic **9** ambitious, ideologue, imaginary **10** abstracted, daydreamer, idealistic, starry-eyed **11** impractical

visionless
5 blind

Vision of Sir Launfal author
6 Lowell (James Russell)

visit
3 gam, see **4** call, chat, stay, talk, tour **5** pop in, run in **6** call on, come by, drop by, drop in, look in, look up, stay at, stop by,

stop in **7** force on, sojourn **8** come over, converse, stay with, stopover **10** social call

visitation
3 woe **4** wake **5** cross, trial **6** misery, ordeal, plague **8** calamity **9** martyrdom **10** affliction **11** tribulation

visitor
5 alien, guest **6** caller, drop-in **7** company, invitee **8** stranger, visitant **9** transient **10** houseguest

visor
4 bill, mask **6** domino **8** eyeshade, disguise, face mask, sunshade

vista
4 view **5** scene, sight **7** lookout, outlook **8** panorama, prospect **9** landscape **11** perspective

visual
5 optic **6** ocular **7** graphic, optical, seeable **8** viewable **9** pictorial **11** discernible, perceivable, perceptible

visualize
3 see **4** view **5** fancy, image **6** call up **7** feature, imagine, picture **8** conceive, envisage, envision **9** conjure up

vital
4 dire **5** alive **6** lively, living, mortal, urgent **7** animate, crucial, pivotal **8** animated, cardinal, critical, decisive, integral, pressing, required, vigorous **9** essential, important, necessary, requisite **10** imperative, red-blooded **11** fundamental **12** invigorating, life-or-death **13** indispensable

vitality
see **vigor**

vitalize
5 liven **6** arouse, excite, infuse, perk up, spirit, vivify **7** animate, enliven, quicken **8** energize **9** encourage, galvanize, stimulate **10** invigorate

vitals
see **viscera**

vitamin
6 biotin, niacin **7** choline, folacin, retinal, retinol **8** thiamine **9** carnitine, cobalamin, folic acid **10** calciferol, pyridoxine, riboflavin, tocopherol **12** ascorbic acid

Vita Nuova author
5 Dante (Alighieri)

vitelline
5 yolky **6** yellow

vitiate
3 mar **4** harm, soil, undo **5** annul, spoil, sully, taint **6** damage, debase, defile, impair, negate **7** blemish, corrupt, debauch, deprave, nullify, pervert, tarnish **8** abrogate **9** undermine **10** bastardize, demoralize, invalidate

vitreous
6 glassy

vitriol
4 bile **5** spite, venom **6** malice, rancor **7** sulfate **8** acrimony **9** virulence **12** sulfuric acid

vitriolic
4 acid **5** acrid **7** acerbic, caustic, cutting, mordant **8** scathing, stinging, virulent **9** rancorous, truculent

vituperate
3 rag **4** lash, rail, rant, rate **5** abuse, baste, curse, scold, score **6** berate, malign, revile, scorch **7** asperse, bawl out, chew out, condemn, cuss out, upbraid **8** lambaste **9** castigate **10** tongue-lash

vituperation
5 abuse **6** rebuke **7** censure, obloquy, reproof **8** scolding **9** contumely, invective **10** scurrility **11** fulmination, mudslinging **12** billingsgate **13** tongue-lashing

vituperative
7 abusive, railing, scurril **8** scathing, scolding, scurrile, venomous, viperish **9** invective **10** censorious, scurrilous **11** opprobrious **12** contumelious

vivace
5 brisk **6** lively **8** animated, spirited

vivacious
3 gay **4** airy, pert **5** perky, spicy, sunny, zesty **6** bouncy, breezy, bubbly, jaunty, lively, sparky **7** buoyant, chipper **8** animated, pixieish, spirited **9** ebullient, sprightly **10** effervescent, high-spirited

vivacity
see **verve**

Vivaldi epithet
9 red priest (the)

_____ vivant
3 bon

vivarium
9 terrarium

viva voce
4 oral **6** orally, spoken **11** word-of-mouth

vivid
5 alive, sharp **6** bright, garish, lively, punchy, visual **7** graphic, intense, vibrant **8** animated, colorful, eloquent, lifelike **9** chromatic, pictorial **10** expressive **11** picturesque

vivify
5 liven, renew **6** excite, infuse, kindle, revive **7** animate, enliven, quicken, refresh, restore **9** stimulate

vixen
3 fox, nag **5** harpy, scold, shrew **6** ogress, virago **8** fishwife, harridan, Xantippe **9** termagant, Xanthippe

viz
5 to wit **6** namely, that is **8** scilicet **9** videlicet **12** in other words

vizard
4 face, mask **5** guise, visor **6** domino **8** disguise

vocabulary
4 cant **5** argot, lingo, slang, words **6** jargon, patois **7** lexicon **8** glossary **9** word-hoard **10** vernacular **11** terminology

vocal
4 oral **5** blunt, frank **6** phonic, spoken, voiced **7** uttered **8** eloquent **9** outspoken **10** articulate, expressive, free-spoken

vocalic
5 vowel

vocalist
4 diva **6** belter, canary, singer **7** crooner, warbler, yodeler **8** minstrel, songbird **9** balladeer, chanteuse, chorister **10** cantatrice, prima donna

vocalization
4 song **5** voice **6** speech **7** diction **8** speaking **9** utterance **11** enunciation **12** articulation **13** pronunciation

vocalize
3 air, hem **4** sing, talk **5** chant, croon, speak, state, utter, voice **6** warble **7** express **9** enunciate, pronounce

vocal organ
6 larynx **8** voice box
bird: **6** syrinx

vocation
3 art, call, job **4** work **5** craft, trade **6** career, métier **7** calling, mission, pursuit **8** business, lifework **10** employment, handicraft, occupation, profession

vociferate
3 bay, cry **4** bark, bray, call, roar, yawp, yell **5** shout **6** bellow, clamor, holler **7** thunder

vociferous
4 loud **5** noisy **6** shrill **7** blatant, clamant, raucous **8** strident **9** clamorous **11** openmouthed **12** obstreperous

vogue
3 cry, fad, ton **4** chic, mode, pose, rage **5** craze, favor, furor, style, trend **6** furore **7** fashion **10** dernier cri, popularity **11** stylishness

voice
3 put, say **4** part, talk, tell, vent **5** say-so, sound, speak, state, utter **6** assert, choice, medium, singer, speech **7** declare, express, opinion, present **8** vocalize **9** condition, enunciate, formulate, pronounce, statement, utterance, verbalize **10** articulate, expression, instrument
female: **4** alto **5** mezzo **7** soprano **9** contralto
high: **5** tenor **7** soprano **8** falsetto
in grammar: **6** active **7** passive
Latin: **3** vox
male: **4** bass **5** tenor **8** baritone
quality: **5** pitch **6** timbre
quiet: **7** whisper
relating to: **5** vocal **8** phonetic
without: **4** dumb, mute

voice box
6 larynx

voiced
4 oral **5** vocal **6** sonant, spoken **7** uttered **8** phonated **9** expressed

voiceless
3 mum **4** dumb, mute, surd **6** silent **8** breathed **12** inarticulate

void
3 gap, nix **4** emit, hole, idle, lack, null, undo **5** abyss, annul, blank, clear, empty, inane, quash **6** bereft, cancel, cavity, hollow, negate, remove, vacant, vacate, vacuum **7** absence, give off, negated, nullify, rescind, reverse, vacuity, vacuous **8** abrogate, deserted, evacuate **9** black hole, discharge, eliminate, emptiness **10** extinguish **11** nothingness

volant
4 fast, spry, yare **5** agile, fleet, quick, zippy **6** flying, lively, nimble **9** dexterous, sprightly

volar
6 palmar

volatile

5 flaky 6 fickle, flying, lively 7 erratic, essence, flighty 8 fleeting, fugitive, skittery, skittish, unstable, variable, volcanic 9 ephemeral, explosive, fugacious, mercurial, momentary, transient 10 capricious, changeable, evanescent, inconstant, short-lived, transitory 11 impermanent 13 temperamental

volatility

10 fickleness 11 flightiness, inconstancy, instability 13 changeability

volcanic

7 violent 8 volatile 9 explosive
explosion: 8 eruption
glass: 8 obsidian
matter: 3 ash 4 lava, tufa, tuff 5 magma 6 scoria
mound: 4 cone
passage: 6 throat 7 conduit
vent: 8 fumarole 9 solfatara

volcano

4 hill, vent 8 mountain
Alaska: 6 Katmai (Mount) 8 Wrangell (Mount) 9 Aniakchak (Crater)
Andes: 5 Omate 12 Huaina Putina
Antarctica: 6 Erebus (Mount)
Azores: 4 Alto (Pico)
California: 6 Lassen (Peak)
Canaries: 5 Teide (Pico de), Teyde (Pico de) 8 Tenerife (Pico de)
Colombia: 5 Huila (Nevado del), Pasto 6 Purace 7 Galeras
Costa Rica: 4 Poás 5 Barba, Irazú
Ecuador: 6 Sangay 8 Antisana, Cotopaxi
extinct: 4 Popa (Mount) 5 Iriga, Kenya (Mount) 8 Mauna Kea 9 Haleakala (Crater)
Guatemala: 4 Agua 5 Fuego 7 Atitlán
Hawaii: 7 Kilauea 8 Mauna Loa
Honshu: 4 Nasu 5 Asama, Azuma 6 Bandai 8 Nasudake 9 Asamayama
Iceland: 5 Askja, Hecla, Hekla
Indonesia: 3 Awu (Gunung) 5 Agung (Gunung) 7 Tambora (Gunung)
island: 5 Thera, Thira 8 Krakatau, Krakatoa, Santorin 9 Santorini
Italy: 8 Vesuvius 9 Stromboli
Iwo Jima: 9 Suribachi (Mount)
Japan: 3 Aso 5 Unzen 6 Asosan
Java: 4 Gede (Gunung) 5 Bromo, Gedeh (Gunung), Kelud (Gunung), Salak (Gunung)
Madeira: 5 Ruivo (Pico)
Martinique: 5 Pelée (Mount)
Mexico: 6 Colima 7 Orizaba 9 Paricutín 12 Popocatepetl

New Zealand: 7 Ruapehu (Mount) 9 Ngauruhoe, Tongariro
Peru: 5 Misti (El)
Philippines: 3 Apo (Mount) 4 Taal 5 Mayon (Mount) 8 Pinatubo (Mount)
Sicily: 4 Etna
Solomons: 5 Balbi
South America: 5 Lanín, Maipo, Maipu
Sumatra: 5 Dempo (Gunumg) 7 Kerinci 8 Kerintji
type: 6 shield 10 cinder cone
Washington: 11 Saint Helens (Mount)
West Indies: 9 Soufrière

___ volente

3 Deo

volition

4 will 6 choice, desire, intent, option 8 decision, election 9 selection 10 preference

volley

4 hail, shot 5 burst, round, salvo, storm 6 return, shower 7 barrage 8 drumfire 9 broadside, cannonade, discharge, fusillade

volplane

5 glide

Volpone

3 Fox (The)
author: 6 Jonson (Ben)
servant: 5 Mosca

Volsung

grandson: 6 Sigurd 9 Siegfried
great-grandfather: 4 Odin
son: 7 Sigmund

voltage

5 power 6 energy 9 intensity

Voltaire

drama: 5 Zaïre 6 Alzire, Brutus, Mèrope, Oedipe 7 Mahomet 8 Tancrède
novel: 5 Zadig 7 Candide
real name: 6 Arouet (François Marie)

volte-face

5 U-turn 8 flip-flop, reversal, turnover 9 about-face, inversion, turnabout 10 switcheroo 13 change of heart

voluble

4 glib 5 gabby, talky, windy 6 chatty, fluent, mouthy, prolix 7 verbose 8 effusive, vocative 9 garrulous, talkative 10 long-winded, loquacious

volume

4 body, book, bulk, mass, size, tome 5 album, flood, folio, space 6 amount,

scroll **7** content **8** capacity, loudness, quantity **9** aggregate **12** displacement

voluminous
4 full **5** bulky **6** legion, prolix **7** copious **8** numerous, prolific **9** capacious **10** convoluted **13** multitudinous

Volumnia's son
10 Coriolanus

voluntary
4 free **7** willful, willing, witting **8** elective, freewill, optional **10** autonomous, deliberate, volitional **11** independent, intentional, spontaneous **13** discretionary

volunteer
5 offer **6** enlist, join up, sign up **7** present, propose, suggest
hospital: 12 candy striper

Volunteer State
9 Tennessee

voluptuous
4 sexy **5** ample, buxom **6** wanton **7** languid, sensual **8** luscious, sensuous **9** bodacious, luxurious **10** curvaceous

volute
5 helix, shell **6** scroll, spiral **7** mollusc, mollusk **8** curlicue

vomit
3 gag **4** barf, cast, gush, hurl, lose, puke, spew, toss **5** expel, retch **6** spit up **7** bring up, throw up, upchuck **8** disgorge **11** regurgitate

vomiting
6 emesis

Vonnegut work
9 Timequake **11** Cat's Cradle, Galapagos, Hocus Pocus **11** Player Piano **13** Sirens of Titan (The) **18** Slaughterhouse Five **20** Breakfast of Champions **22** Happy Birthday Wanda June

voodoo
3 hex **4** jinx, juju **5** charm, magic, mojo, spell **6** amulet, whammy **7** bewitch, enchant, sorcery **8** ensorcel, wizardry **9** ensorcell **10** hocus-pocus, mumbo jumbo, necromancy, witchcraft **11** abracadabra, implausible, unrealistic

voracious
4 avid **5** eager **6** ardent, greedy, hungry **7** piggish, starved **8** edacious, famished, ravenous, starving **9** rapacious **10** gluttonous, insatiable, omnivorous, quenchless

vortex
4 eddy, gyre **5** swirl **7** tornado **9** hurricane, maelstrom, whirlpool, whirlwind **11** tourbillion

votary
3 bug, fan, nut **4** buff **5** lover **6** addict, groupie, zealot **7** admirer, advocate, apostle, devotee, follower, habitué **8** adherent, believer, disciple **9** worshiper **10** aficionado, enthusiast, worshipper

vote
3 opt **4** poll **5** elect, judge, offer **6** ballot, choice, choose, decide, ratify, select, ticket **7** adjudge, declare, endorse, express, opinion, propose, suggest, verdict **8** election, suffrage **9** franchise **10** expression
affirmative: 3 aye, nod, yea, yes **6** placet
kind: 5 proxy, straw, voice **6** secret **7** write-in **8** absentee **10** plebiscite, referendum
negative: 3 nay
right to: 8 suffrage **9** franchise

votive
8 grateful **10** devotional

vouch
5 prove **6** affirm, assert, assure, attest, uphold, verify **7** certify, confirm, support, witness **8** accredit **9** guarantee **11** corroborate **12** substantiate

voucher
3 IOU **4** chit **5** proof **6** coupon, surety **7** receipt **9** affidavit, indenture **10** credential **11** certificate **13** authorization

vouchsafe
4 give **5** award, favor, grant **6** accord, bestow, confer, oblige **7** concede, furnish

vow
4 aver, oath, word **5** swear, troth **6** assert, attest, pledge, plight **7** confirm, declare, promise, warrant **8** covenant **9** assertion, guarantee **10** obligation **11** declaration

vowel
6 letter, symbol **11** speech sound
kind: 4 high, long **5** glide, schwa, short **9** diphthong **11** monophthong
omission: 7 aphesis **11** contraction
variation: 6 ablaut, umlaut

voyage
4 sail, trek, trip **5** jaunt **6** cruise, junket, outing, travel **7** journey, odyssey, set sail

8 traverse **9** excursion **10** expedition, pilgrimage

voyeur
6 peeper **10** peeping Tom

Vronski's lover
12 Anna Karenina

Vulcan
see **Hephaestus**

vulgar
3 low, raw **4** base, lewd, rude, vile **5** crass, crude, gaudy, gross, rough, tacky **6** coarse, earthy, flashy, garish, ribald, sordid, tawdry **7** kitschy, lowbred, lowbrow, obscene, profane, uncouth **8** churlish, improper, indecent, off-color, unseemly **9** barbarous, graceless, low-minded, offensive, tasteless, unrefined **10** indecorous, indelicate, scurrilous, unpolished, vernacular **11** pretentious

vulgate
10 vernacular

Vulgate translator
6 Jerome

vulnerability
8 exposure, soft spot, weakness **10** underbelly **12** Achilles' heel

vulnerable
4 open, weak **6** liable **7** exposed **10** assailable **11** susceptible

vulnerary
4 balm **5** salve, tonic **7** healing, unguent **8** curative, ointment, remedial, salutary, sanative **9** medicinal, wholesome **10** salubrious **11** restorative, therapeutic **12** healthgiving

vulpine
3 sly **4** foxy, wily **5** slick **6** artful, astute, crafty, shrewd, tricky **7** cunning, foxlike **8** guileful

vulture
4 bird **6** condor **11** lammergeier, lammergeyer
food: 7 carrion
relative: 4 hawk **5** eagle **6** falcon **7** buzzard

vulturine
8 ravenous **9** predatory, rapacious, raptorial **10** predacious, predaceous, scavenging

W

wacky
3 fey, mad 4 daft, nuts 5 batty, daffy,
crazy, flaky, kooky, loony, loopy, silly
6 absurd, fruity, insane, screwy 7 bonkers,
cracked, foolish, idiotic, lunatic, offbeat
8 crackers, demented 9 eccentric
10 irrational 11 harebrained
12 preposterous

wad
3 gob 4 lump, mint, pile, plug, quid, roll,
stuff, swab 5 chunk 6 boodle, bundle,
packet, pellet 7 fortune 8 bankroll

waddle
6 toddle

waddy
4 club, cosh 6 cowboy, cudgel 7 rustler
8 bludgeon

wade
4 ford, plod 5 labor 6 drudge, trudge
into: 5 set to 6 attack, plunge, tackle
9 undertake

wadi
3 bed 4 wash 5 gully 6 arroyo, coulee,
course, ravine 9 streambed 10 depression
11 watercourse

wafer
4 chip, disk, host 5 matzo, slice 6 matzoh
7 cracker

waffle
4 yo-yo 5 tripe, waver 6 dither, drivel,
seesaw 7 blather 8 flip-flop 9 fluctuate,
vacillate 10 equivocate

waft
4 flag, gust, puff, wave 5 drift, float, hover
7 pennant

wag
3 bob, nod, wit 4 card, lash, wave
5 clown, cutup, joker, shake, swing, whisk
6 kidder, switch, twitch, waddle 8 brandish,
comedian, funnyman, jokester

wage
3 fee, pay 6 income, reward, salary
7 carry on, payment, stipend 8 earnings,
pittance, receipts 9 emolument
10 recompense 12 compensation,
remuneration

wager
3 bet, lay, pot 4 ante, game, risk 5 stake
6 chance, gamble, hazard 7 venture

waggery
3 gag 4 jest, joke 5 prank, sport 7 devilry,
kidding, roguery 8 deviltry, drollery,
mischief 10 impishness, pleasantry
11 roguishness 12 sportiveness
13 practical joke

waggish
4 arch, pert 5 antic, comic, droll, saucy,
witty 6 impish, jocose 7 comical, jocular,
playful, puckish, roguish 8 humorous,
prankish, sportive 9 facetious
10 frolicsome 11 mischievous

waggle
3 bob 4 reel, sway

Wagner, Richard
birthplace: 7 Leipzig
father-in-law: 5 Liszt (Franz)
festival site: 8 Bayreuth
opera: 4 Ring 6 Rienzi 8 Parsifal
9 Lohengrin, Rheingold (Das), Siegfried
10 Die Walküre, Tannhäuser 12 Das
Rheingold 13 Meistersinger (Die)
14 Flying Dutchman (The)
15 Götterdämmerung 16 Tristan und
Isolde 17 Ring of the Nibelung (The)
recurring theme: 9 leitmotif, leitmotiv
wife: 5 Minna 6 Cosima

wagon
3 van 4 cart, dray, tram, trek, wain
7 caravan, coaster, hayrack

wahoo
3 ono 8 mackerel 9 winged elm

11 burning bush

waif
5 gamin, stray 6 gamine, orphanurchin
8 wanderer 9 foundling 10 ragamuffin
11 guttersnipe

wail
3 bay, cry 4 bawl, blub, fuss, howl, keen,
weep, yowl 5 mourn, whine 6 bemoan,
lament, plaint, repine 7 blubber, ululate
8 complain 9 complaint 11 lamentation

wain
5 wagon 9 Big Dipper

waistband
3 obi 4 belt, sash 6 girdle 8 ceinture,
cincture 10 cummerbund

waistcoat
4 vest 6 jerkin, weskit

wait
4 bide, idle, stay 5 abide, dally, delay,
serve, tarry, watch 6 expect, hold on,
linger, remain 8 hang fire, mark time, sit
tight 10 anticipate 11 stick around

waiter
4 tray 6 garçon, salver, server 7 servant
9 attendant

Waiting for _____
5 Godot, Lefty

wait on
4 tend 5 serve 6 attend, tend to 7 care
for, cater to 9 look after

waive
4 cede, stay 5 allow, defer, delay, forgo,
table, yield 6 give up, hold up, put off,
shelve 7 abandon, concede, dismiss, hold
off, suspend 8 hand over, hold over,
postpone 9 surrender 10 relinquish

wake
4 path, stir, wash 5 alert, arise, get up,
rally, rouse, track, vigil, watch 6 arouse,
bestir, excite, kindle, stir up 7 roll out
8 backwash 9 aftermath, stimulate

wakeful
5 alert 8 restless, vigilant 9 insomniac,
sleepless

waken
see **wake**

Walden author
7 Thoreau (Henry David)

wale
3 rib 4 bend, welt 5 brace, ridge 6 strake

walk
3 pad 4 gait, hike, hoof, pace, path, plod,
roam, slog, step, trip 5 alley, amble, clump,
mince, paseo, stave, strut, stump, trail,
tramp, tread, troop 6 prance, ramble,
sashay, stride, stroll, toddle, trudge,
waddle, wander 7 saunter, shamble,
shuffle, stumble, swagger, traipse
8 ambulate, traverse 9 promenade
11 base on balls, perambulate, peregrinate

walkaway
4 romp, rout

walking shorts
8 Bermudas

walking stick
4 cane 5 staff 6 crutch, insect 7 phasmid,
whangee

walk out
5 leave 6 strike

walk out on
5 leave 6 desert 7 abandon, forsake

Walküre composer
6 Wagner (Richard)

walkway
4 path 7 passage 9 promenade

wall
3 bar, hem 4 side, stop 5 block, close,
fence, hedge 6 immure 7 barrier, close in,
enclose 8 blockade, surround 9 barricade,
enclosure, roadblock, structure
bearing: 7 support
hanging: 8 tapestry
painting: 5 mural
protective: 7 parapet, rampart
top of: 6 coping

wallaby
8 kangaroo

wallet
5 funds 6 folder 8 billfold 9 accessory,
resources 10 pocketbook

Wallis and Futuna Islands
capital: 7 Mata-Utu
island: 4 Uvéa
territory of: 6 France

wallop
3 bop, hit 4 bang, bash, beat, belt, blow,
boil, bust, clip, drub, lick, pelt, slam, slug,
sock, whip, whop, whup 5 baste, paste,
pound, punch, smack, whack 6 buffet,
pummel, thrash, thwack 7 shellac, trounce
8 lambaste

walloping
4 huge **5** giant **7** immense, mammoth, monster **8** colossal, enormous, gigantic, smashing **10** gargantuan, impressive, incredible, prodigious

wallow
4 bask, roll **5** enjoy, revel **6** billow, welter **7** delight, indulge **9** luxuriate

_____ Walpole
4 Hugh **6** Horace

_____ Walton
3 Sam **5** Izaak

waltz
5 dance, valse

Waltz King
7 Strauss (Johann)

Wampanoag chief
9 Massasoit, Metacomet **10** King Philip

wampum
5 beads, money **6** shells

wan
3 dim **4** ashy, gray, pale, waxy, weak, worn **5** ashen, faint, livid, lurid, pasty, waxen **6** anemic, doughy, feeble, infirm, pallid, peaked, sallow, sickly **7** ghastly, languid **8** blanched **9** bloodless, colorless, washed-out **10** cadaverous, white-faced

wand
3 rod **4** pole, tube **5** baton, staff

wander
3 bat, bum, gad **4** mill, roam, rove, swan **5** amble, dally, drift, float, gypsy, mooch, prowl, range, stray, tramp **6** ramble, stroll **7** deviate, digress, diverge, maunder, meander, saunter, traipse **8** divagate, straggle, vagabond **9** expatiate, gallivant **10** kick around

wanderer
4 waif **5** gypsy, nomad, rover, stray **7** pilgrim, vagrant **8** runabout, vagabond

wandering
7 erratic, migrant, nomadic, vagrant **8** vagabond **9** itinerant, migratory, walkabout, wayfaring **10** roundabout **11** peripatetic

wane
3 dim, ebb **4** fail, fall **5** abate, let up **6** lessen, recede, reduce, relent, shrink, weaken **7** decline, dwindle, slacken, subside **8** decrease, diminish, moderate, slack off, taper off

wangle
6 scheme **7** finagle, wheedle **8** inveigle, scrounge **10** manipulate

wannabe
5 clone **7** also-ran, copycat, hopeful, wishful **8** apparent, aspiring, desiring, desirous **9** ambitious, look-alike, potential

want
4 lack, like, need, void, wish **5** covet, crave, fault **6** dearth, desire, penury **7** absence, poverty, require **8** exigency **9** indigence, necessity, neediness, privation **10** deficiency, desiderate, inadequacy, scantiness **11** destitution, requirement **13** insufficiency

wanting
4 away, less, sans **5** minus, scant, short **6** absent, scanty, scarce **7** lacking, missing, without **9** deficient **10** inadequate, incomplete **12** insufficient

wanton
4 doxy, jade, lewd, minx, rank, slut **5** bawdy, cruel, hussy, lavish, loose, tramp, trull, wench **6** coquet, floozy, harlot, immoral, lavish, trifle, unruly **7** baggage, cyprian, jezebel, lustful, obscene, Paphian, sensual, trollop, wayward **8** inhumane, pitiless, ruthless, slattern, spiteful, sportive, strumpet **9** dissolute, luxuriant, malicious, merciless **10** gratuitous, lascivious, malevolent, outrageous, prostitute **11** extravagant, mischievous, uncalled-for

wapiti
3 elk **7** red deer

war
4 feud, odds **5** fight **6** battle, combat, strife **7** contest **8** conflict, struggle, variance **9** hostility **11** antagonism **11** competition
German: 5 Krieg **10** blitzkrieg
god: 3 Tiu, Tyr **4** Ares, Mars, Odin **5** Woden, Wotan
goddess: 4 Enyo **5** Anath **6** Inanna, Ishtar **7** Bellona
Latin: 6 bellum
Muslim: 5 jehad, jihad
relating to: 7 martial

War and Peace
author: 7 Tolstoy (Leo)
composer: 9 Prokofiev (Sergey)

warble
4 sing **5** carol, chirp, trill, tweet **6** gadfly, maggot, quaver **7** descant, melisma, twitter

warbler
4 bird **6** singer **7** kinglet **8** songster

9 blackpoll 11 gnatcatcher
European: 10 chiffchaff

war cry
5 motto 6 slogan
Greek: 5 alala
Japanese: 6 banzai

ward
4 care 5 aegis 6 barrio, charge 7 custody,
defense, keeping 8 district, division,
precinct, security 9 bishopric 10 protection
11 safekeeping 12 guardianship

warden
6 jailer, keeper, regent 7 provost
8 governor, guardian, official 9 castellan,
constable, custodian, protector
10 commandant, supervisor

ward off
5 avert, parry, rebut, repel 6 divert
7 deflect 8 turn away 9 forestall

wardrobe
5 trunk 6 closet 7 apparel, armoire,
clothes 8 clothing 9 garderobe
12 clothespress

warehouse
4 stow 5 depot, lodge, stock, store
7 confine, deposit, shelter, storage,
stowage 8 building 9 stockroom,
storeroom 10 depository, repository
11 accommodate
oriental: 6 godown

wares
4 line 5 goods, stock 9 vendibles
11 commodities, marketables, merchandise

warfare
6 battle, combat, strife 8 conflict, struggle
10 operations 11 hostilities
type: 4 germ 6 trench 10 biological

warhorse
4 hack 7 charger, courser, veteran
8 chestnut, standard

warlike
7 hawkish, martial 8 militant, military
9 bellicose, combative, truculent
10 aggressive, pugnacious 11 belligerent

warlock
3 wiz 4 mage 5 magus 6 wizard
8 conjurer, conjuror, magician, satanist,
sorcerer 9 diabolist, enchanter
11 necromancer

warm
4 bask, heat, kind 5 angry, fresh 6 ardent,
genial, heated, heat up, loving, reheat,
secure, tender 7 affable, cordial, excited,
fervent, sincere 8 friendly, gracious,
spirited 9 heartfelt 10 passionate,
responsive 11 kindhearted, sympathetic
12 affectionate, enthusiastic, wholehearted
13 compassionate
air: 7 thermal

warmed-over
5 banal, stale, tired, trite 6 old-hat
7 clichéd 8 shopworn, timeworn
9 hackneyed

warmhearted
4 kind 6 benign, kindly, loving, tender
7 cordial 8 generous 9 benignant,
unselfish 10 benevolent 11 magnanimous,
sympathetic 12 affectionate
13 compassionate

warmth
4 glow, heat 7 comfort 8 fondness
9 affection 10 cordiality

warn
3 tip 4 clew, clue 5 alert 6 advise, inform,
notify, tip off 7 apprise, caution, counsel
8 admonish

warning
3 tip 4 hint 5 alarm, alert 6 caveat, notice,
signal, tip-off 7 caution, counsel, summons
8 monition, monitory 10 admonition,
cautionary 12 admonishment
legal: 6 caveat

War of the Worlds author
5 Wells (H. G.)

warp
4 base, bend, cast, kink, rope, wind
5 color, curve, twist 6 buckle, debase,
deform, wrench 7 confuse, contort,
corrupt, deflect, distort, pervert, torture,
vitiate 10 bastardize 12 misrepresent

warrant
4 pawn, writ 5 proof, prove, token 6 affirm,
assert, assure, attest, avouch, ensure,
ground, insure, pledge, secure 7 certify,
contend, declare, justify, precept
8 guaranty, maintain, mittimus, sanction,
security 9 assurance, authority, authorize,
guarantee 10 foundation 11 certificate
12 confirmation 13 justification

warranty
4 bail, bond 6 surety 8 covenant, security
9 guarantee

warren
4 maze 7 network, rabbits, tenement

warrior
4 hero 7 battler, fighter, soldier

8 champion **9** combatant **10** serviceman
female: 6 Amazon
Japanese: 7 samurai

Warsaw
castle: 5 Zamek
river: 7 Vistula

wart
4 flaw **6** defect, growth **7** blemish, verruca
11 excrescence

wary
5 alert, cagey, canny, chary, leery
7 careful, dubious, guarded, mindful
8 cautious, skittish, vigilant, watchful
10 suspicious **11** circumspect, distrustful

wash
3 lap, pan, tub **4** hose, lave, suds, wadi
5 bathe, clean, creek, douse, drift, float,
flush, marsh, scrub, slosh, swill **6** drench,
shower, sluice, splash **7** cleanse, coating,
launder, laundry, shampoo, suffuse
8 backwash

washed-out
4 beat **5** all in, faded, spent, tired, weary
6 bushed, effete, sapped, used-up, wasted
7 drained **8** depleted **9** exhausted

washed-up
4 beat, done **5** kaput, spent **6** done in
7 also-ran, defunct, done for, through
8 finished

washing
4 bath **6** lavage **7** laundry **8** ablution,
lavation
ceremonial: 6 lavabo

Washington
capital: 7 Olympia
city: 6 Tacoma **7** Seattle, Spokane
9 Vancouver **10** Walla Walla
college, university: 7 Gonzaga, Whitman
9 Evergreen
dam: 11 Grand Coulee
mountain, range: 7 Cascade, Olympic,
Rainier **8** St. Helens
nickname: 9 Evergreen (State)
river: 6 Yakima **8** Columbia
state bird: 9 goldfinch
state flower: 12 rhododendron
state tree: 7 hemlock

Washington, D.C., designer
7 L'Enfant (Pierre-Charles)

Washington, George
home: 11 Mount Vernon
wife: 6 Martha

Washington Square author
5 James (Henry)

wasp
5 mason **6** digger, hornet, vespid
9 ichneumon, mud dauber **12** yellow jacket

waspish
5 testy **6** snappy, snarky, snippy, touchy
7 peevish, vespine **8** petulant, snappish,
vinegary **9** crotchety, fractious, irritable,
querulous **10** vinegarish **12** cantankerous,
cross-grained

wassail
5 binge, carol, drink, revel, spree, toast
6 bender **7** carouse, revelry, roister
8 carousal, drinking

Wasserstein play
15 Heidi Chronicles (The) **17** Sisters
Rosenzweig (The)

waste
4 arid, fail, kill, loss, ruin, sack, wild
5 empty, offal, scrap, trash **6** barren,
damage, debris, desert, devour, litter,
ravage, refuse, sewage, shrink, weaken
7 badland, consume, despoil, destroy,
fritter, garbage, pillage, plunder, rubbish
8 decrease, desolate, emaciate, enfeeble,
misspend, prodigal, spoilage, squander,
wear away, wildland **9** devastate,
dissipate, excrement, sweepings, throw
away **10** desolation, wilderness
11 prodigality **12** extravagance,
extravagancy
maker: 5 haste
time: 5 dally **6** dawdle, footle, piddle, trifle

waste away
4 fade, fail **6** molder, shrink **7** atrophy,
decline, dwindle, shrivel **10** degenerate

wasted
3 lit **4** high **5** drunk, gaunt **6** peaked,
sickly, stoned **7** elapsed, ravaged
8 skeletal **9** emaciated **10** cadaverous,
skeletonic **11** intoxicated

wasteful
6 lavish **8** prodigal **9** throwaway
10 profligate, thriftless, uneconomic
11 extravagant, improvident, inefficient,
spendthrift

wastefulness
6 excess **10** lavishness **11** prodigality
12 extravagance, immoderation

wasteland
4 wild **5** heath **6** barren **10** desolation,
wilderness

Waste Land author
5 Eliot (T. S.)

wastrel
3 rip 4 rake, roué 7 rounder, spender
8 prodigal 9 fritterer, libertine
10 dissipater, high roller, ne'er-do-well,
profligate, squanderer 11 scattergood,
spendthrift

watch
3 eye, see, spy 4 bide, look, tend, tout,
wait, wake, ward 5 guard, shift, vigil
6 attend, follow, look at, notice, sentry
7 care for, lookout, monitor, surveil
8 bulletin, eagle eye, observe, scrutiny,
sentinel, watchman 9 attention, timepiece,
vigilance 10 duty period, observance
11 chronometer, observation 12 surveillance
chain: 3 fob
maker: 10 horologist

watchdog
5 guard 6 keeper 8 Cerberus, guardian
9 custodian, protector

watcher
6 viewer 7 guarder, lookout 8 beholder,
follower, guardian, observer, onlooker
9 spectator

watchful
4 wary 5 alert, chary 7 on guard, wakeful
8 cautious, vigilant 9 attentive, observant,
sleepless, wide-awake 10 unsleeping
Scottish: 5 tenty 6 tentie

watchman
5 guard, scout 6 patrol, picket, sentry,
warder 7 lookout 8 sentinel

watch out
6 beware 8 take care

watchtower
6 turret 7 lookout 8 barbican, bartizan
10 lighthouse

watchword
3 cry 5 motto 6 mantra, parole, signal,
slogan 8 password 9 principle
10 shibboleth 11 catchphrase, countersign

water
4 soak, thin, tide 5 drink, fluid, spray
6 dilute, liquid, supply 7 moisten 8 irrigate,
moisture, snowmelt, sprinkle 10 excellence
13 amniotic fluid
body: 3 bay, sea 4 gulf, lake, pool
5 ocean 6 lagoon, strait 9 reservoir
combining form: 4 aqui, aquo, hydr
5 hydro

French: 3 eau
goddess: 4 Nina 7 Anahita, Anaitis
Latin: 4 aqua
Spanish: 4 agua

water buffalo
4 arna 5 bovid 7 carabao
female: 5 arnee

water clock
9 clepsydra

water closet
3 loo 4 head, john 5 privy 6 toilet
7 latrine 8 bathroom, lavatory

watercourse
4 dike, duct 5 bayou, canal, ditch 6 arroyo
7 channel, conduit 8 aqueduct, headrace,
tailrace 9 streambed

water cow
6 dugong 7 manatee

watered-down
5 washy 6 dilute 7 diluted

waterfall
5 chute, sault, shoot 7 cascade 8 cataract
Brazil: 6 Iguaçú (Falls), Iguazú (Falls)
California: 8 Yosemite (Falls)
Canada: 5 Grand (Falls) 8 Takkakaw
9 Churchill (Falls)
Canada-U.S.: 7 Niagara (Falls)
Congo: 6 Boyoma (Falls) 7 Stanley
(Falls)
former Nile: 4 Owen (Falls) 5 Ripon
(Falls)
Kentucky: 10 Cumberland (Falls)
New Zealand: 10 Sutherland (Falls)
Niagara: 8 American, Canadian
9 Horseshoe
Norway: 6 Rjukan (Falls)
Oregon: 9 Multnomah (Falls)
South Africa: 6 Tugela (Falls)
Snake River: 4 Twin (Falls) 8 Shoshone
(Falls)
Venezuela: 5 Angel (Falls)
Washington: 10 Snoqualmie (Falls)
world's highest: 5 Angel (Falls)
Wyoming: 11 Yellowstone (Falls)
Zambezi River: 8 Victoria

water finder
6 dowser 11 divining rod

waterfront
8 seacoast 9 lakeshore, riverside

water hole
5 oasis

watering hole
3 bar, pub 4 café 5 oasis 6 lounge, nitery, resort, saloon, tavern 7 barroom, cabaret 9 nightclub, nightspot, roadhouse 10 supper club

waterless
3 dry 4 arid, sere 7 bone-dry 8 droughty 9 anhydrous 10 dehydrated

waterlog
8 saturate

waterloo
4 ruin 6 defeat 7 failure 8 disaster, downfall

water nymph
4 lily 5 naiad 6 mayfly, Nereid 7 Oceanid 9 dragonfly
female: 3 nix 5 nixie

water oscillation
6 seiche

water pipe
4 bong 5 spout 6 hookah 8 narghile, nargileh 12 hubble-bubble

water plant
7 aquatic, seaweed 8 duckweed, wild rice 9 arrowhead, tape grass 10 hydrophyte, manna grass 11 bladderwort

water rat
6 nutria

watershed
6 crisis, divide 12 turning point

water spirit
3 nix 5 nixie, nymph 6 sprite, undine

water tank
7 cistern

watery
4 pale, thin, weak 5 banal, bland, vapid, washy 6 dilute, serous 7 diluted, insipid

wattle
4 gill, grid, jowl 5 frame 8 caruncle 9 framework, interlace 10 interweave

wattle and _____
4 daub

wave
3 wag 4 flag, flap 5 heave, ridge, surge, sweep, swell 6 comber, influx, marcel, motion, period, ripple, signal, waggle 7 breaker, dismiss, flutter, gesture, upsurge 8 activity, brandish, flourish, undulate 9 disregard
large: 7 tsunami

waver
4 reel, sway 5 swing, weave 6 dither, falter, quaver, quiver, teeter, totter, wobble 7 flicker, stagger, whiffle 8 hesitate, undulate 9 oscillate, vacillate 12 shilly-shally

wavering
4 weak 5 shake, shaky 6 unsure, wobbly 7 halting 8 doubtful, insecure, to-and-fro, unstable 9 equivocal, faltering, fluctuant, hesitancy, undecided, vibration, whiffling 10 hesitating, hesitation, indecision 11 fluctuating, irresolute, vacillating, vacillation 12 irresolution, shilly-shally

Waverly author
5 Scott (Walter)

wavy
7 rolling 8 rippling, swelling 9 fluctuant 10 undulating 11 fluctuating

wavy pattern
5 moiré 8 squiggle 10 undulation 11 crenulation

wax
4 come, grow, rise 5 boost, build, mount 6 become, expand, record 7 augment, enlarge 8 heighten, increase, multiply, paraffin, simonize 9 secretion, substance

waxen
3 wan 4 ashy, pale 5 ashen, livid 6 pallid, smooth 7 pliable 8 blanched, moldable 9 colorless

way
3 ilk 4 door, kind, mode, much, path, road, sort, type, very 5 entry, habit, means, order, route, state, style, usage 6 access, artery, action, avenue, course, custom, degree, manner, method, street 7 ability, fashion, feature, ingress, opening, outcome, respect 8 distance, entrance, practice 9 boulevard, condition, direction, procedure, technique 11 opportunity, possibility 12 thoroughfare

wayfarer
5 gypsy, hiker, nomad, tramp 8 traveler 9 itinerant, journeyer

wayfaring
6 roving 7 nomadic, vagrant 8 vagabond 9 itinerant, traveling, wandering 10 travelling 11 peripatetic 13 perambulatory

waylay
5 brace 6 ambush, attack 8 surprise 9 bushwhack, still-hunt

Way of All Flesh author
6 Butler (Samuel)

Way of the World author
8 Congreve (William)

wayward
5 balky 6 fickle, unruly 7 froward, restive, vagrant 8 contrary, perverse, untoward 9 whimsical 10 capricious, headstrong 11 intractable, wrongheaded 12 ungovernable 13 unpredictable

we
French: 4 nous
German: 3 wir
Italian: 3 noi
Spanish: 8 nosotros

weak
3 dim, wan 4 puny, soft, thin 5 faint, frail, shaky, timid 6 dilute, feeble, flimsy, infirm, sickly, unsure, watery, wobbly 7 brittle, diluted, fragile, rickety, spindly, tenuous, unsound 8 decrepit, delicate, helpless, impotent, inferior, insecure, timorous, unstable, wavering 9 deficient, enfeebled, inaudible, powerless, spineless, uncertain 10 improbable, inadequate, unreliable, unstressed 11 debilitated, implausible, ineffective, ineffectual, vacillating, watered-down 12 unconvincing, undependable 13 insubstantial, unsubstantial

weaken
3 lag, sap 4 fail, flag, thin, wane 5 abate 6 damage, dilute, impair, lessen, reduce, soften 7 corrode, decline, disable, dwindle, subvert, unbrace 8 enervate, enfeeble, moderate 9 attenuate, grind down, honeycomb, undermine 10 debilitate, demoralize, invalidate

weak-kneed
5 timid 6 wobbly 7 gutless 8 cowardly, wavering 9 faltering, uncertain, whiffling 10 irresolute, shilly-shally 11 lily-livered, vacillating 12 fainthearted 13 pusillanimous

weakling
4 wimp, wuss 5 mouse, sissy 7 doormat, milksop, sad sack 8 pushover 9 jellyfish 10 namby-pamby 11 milquetoast, mollycoddle 12 invertebrate

weakness
4 flaw, hole, vice 5 crack, fault, taste 6 defect, desire, liking, relish 7 failing, frailty 8 appetite, debility, fondness, soft spot 9 infirmity 10 feebleness 11 decrepitude, shortcoming 12 Achilles'
heel

weal
4 welt 5 ridge 7 welfare 9 well-being

weald
5 woods 6 forest 8 woodland 10 timberland, wilderness

wealth
5 goods, worth 6 assets, estate, plenty, riches 7 capital, fortune 8 holdings, opulence, property 9 abundance, affluence, profusion, resources 11 possessions

Wealth of Nations author
5 Smith (Adam)

wealthy
4 rich 5 flush 6 loaded 7 moneyed, opulent, well-off 8 affluent, well-heeled, well-to-do 9 well-fixed 10 prosperous 12 silk-stocking

wean
4 free, part 5 alien 6 detach 8 accustom, estrange, separate

weapon
3 bow, gun 4 bill, bolo, bomb, club, dart, dirk, mace, nuke, pike 5 A-bomb, arrow, H-bomb, knife, lance, prick, rifle, saber, sabre, sling, spear, steel, sword 6 dagger, Magnum, musket, pistol, poleax, rapier, rocket 7 bazooka, broadax, car bomb, carbine, firearm, gisarme, halberd, javelin, machete, missile, shotgun, sidearm, stun gun, torpedo, war club 8 battle-ax, bludgeon, broadaxe, catapult, crossbow, death ray, nerve gas, nunchaku, partisan, partizan, petronel, revolver, spontoon, tomahawk 9 battle-axe, blackjack, boomerang, derringer, slingshot 10 atomic bomb, machine gun, projectile 11 blunderbuss, depth charge, nuclear bomb 12 quarterstaff 13 brass knuckles

weapons
4 arms 7 arsenal, battery 8 ordnance 9 armaments, artillery, munitions 13 armamentarium

wear
3 rub 4 fray, tire 5 chafe, dress, erode, grind 6 abrade, attire, endure, impair 7 corrode, exhibit, fatigue, fashion 8 abrasion, clothing
and tear: 12 depreciation
thin: 4 fray 5 chafe 6 tatter 7 hackney

wear down
5 drain, erode, grind 6 abrade, weaken

7 corrode, degrade, exhaust, fatigue

weariness
5 ennui 7 boredom, fatigue, languor
8 lethargy 9 lassitude 10 enervation,
exhaustion 12 taedium vitae

wearing
6 taxing, tiring, trying 9 difficult, fatiguing

wearisome
see **tiresome**

wear out
3 fag 4 bust, do in, fray, poop, tire 5 drain
6 efface, tucker 7 consume, deplete,
exhaust, frazzle 8 overstay

weary
4 beat, jade, limp, tire, worn 5 drain, jaded,
spent, tired 6 bushed, done in, pooped,
tucker, wasted 7 drained, fatigue, worn-out
8 dog-tired, fatigued, tiresome 9 apathetic

weasand
6 gullet, throat 7 trachea 8 windpipe
9 esophagus

weasel
5 dodge, evade, hedge, slink, sneak, stoat
6 ermine, escape, ferret, mammal
7 sneaker 8 sidestep 9 pussyfoot
10 equivocate
Scottish: 8 whittret

weather
4 rain 5 storm 6 bear up, endure, expose
7 climate, ride out, undergo 9 withstand
forecasting: 11 meteorology

weathercock
4 vane

weathered
8 hardened, seasoned, tempered

weave
4 cane, lawn, leno, spin, sway 5 braid,
cloth, lurch, twine, waver 6 careen, fabric,
pleach, raddle, wobble, zigzag 7 pattern,
stagger, textile, texture 8 contrive
9 interlace 10 crisscross, intertwine

web
3 net 4 mesh, vane 5 snare, snarl
6 enmesh, fabric, tangle 7 ensnare,
netting, network 8 entangle 10 en-
meshment 12 entanglement

Weber opera
6 Oberon 9 Euryanthe 10 Freischütz (Der)

_____ Webster
4 Noah 6 Daniel

wed
4 join, link, mate, yoke 5 hitch, marry,

merge, unite 6 splice 7 combine, conjoin,
connect, espouse 10 tie the knot

wedded
7 marital, nuptial 8 conjugal, hymeneal
9 connubial 11 matrimonial

wedding
6 bridal 7 spousal 8 espousal, marriage,
nuptials

wedding anniversary
fifteenth: 7 crystal
fifth: 6 wooden
fiftieth: 6 golden
first: 5 paper
seventy-fifth: 7 diamond
tenth: 3 tin
twentieth: 5 china
twenty-fifth: 6 silver

wedge
4 shim 5 chock, stuff 8 golf club, golf shot,
keystone 10 force apart

wedge-shaped
7 cuneate 8 cottered, sphenoid
9 cuneiform

wedlock
4 knot, yoke 8 espousal, marriage
9 matrimony 11 conjugality 12 connubiality

wee
4 tiny 5 bitsy, bitty, early, small, teeny
6 little, minute, teensy 9 itty-bitty, miniature
10 diminutive, teeny-weeny 11 Lilliputian,
little bitty 12 teensy-weensy

weed
4 dock, tare 5 chess, clear, plant 6 cockle,
darnel, dodder, nettle, remove 7 burdock,
burseed, ragweed, ruderal 8 amaranth,
charlock, purslane 9 chickweed, cocklebur,
dandelion, knotgrass, marijuana, poison
ivy, poison oak, stickseed 10 cheatgrass,
lady's thumb, sow thistle
European: 6 spurry 7 spurrey
killer: 8 paraquat 9 herbicide
Western: 4 loco

weedy
4 lean, thin 5 lanky 6 skinny 7 scrawny,
stringy, willowy 8 untended 9 overgrown

week
6 period 8 hebdomad
two weeks: 9 fortnight

weep
3 cry, sob 4 drip, moan, ooze, tear, wail
5 bleed, exude, sweat 6 lament 7 blubber,
dribble, trickle 8 transude

weepy
5 misty, moist, teary **7** tearful **10** lachrymose

weevil
7 billbug **8** curculio

weft
3 web **4** pick, woof, yarn **6** fabric, thread

weigh
3 way **4** heft, rate, tare **5** count, judge, scale, study **6** burden, ponder **7** balance, measure, oppress, perpend **8** appraise, bear down, consider, evaluate, militate **11** contemplate

weigh down
4 load **5** press **6** burden, sadden **7** depress, oppress **8** encumber **10** discourage, overburden

weight
3 tax **4** heft, lade, load, mass, onus, task **5** class, force, power **6** amount, assign, burden, charge, credit, import, moment, saddle **7** oppress, potency, quality **8** encumber, poundage, pressure, prestige, quantity **9** authority, influence, magnitude **10** corpulence, importance **11** consequence **12** significance
allowance: 4 tare
apothecary: 4 dram **5** grain, pound **7** scruple
Asian: 6 cattie
gem: 5 carat
measure of: 3 ton **4** dram, gram **5** grain, ounce, pound **7** long ton, scruple **8** kilogram, short ton **9** metric ton
system: 3 net **4** troy **6** metric **10** apothecary **11** avoirdupois

weightiness
4 pith **6** import, moment **7** dignity, gravity **9** heaviness, magnitude, solemnity **10** importance **11** consequence, massiveness **12** significance **13** momentousness

weight lift
4 pull **5** clean, press, shrug **6** snatch **12** clean and jerk

weighty
3 fat **5** grave, gross, heavy, hefty, obese, sober, staid **6** fleshy, portly, sedate, severe, solemn, somber **7** massive, serious, telling **8** cumbrous, grievous, powerful **9** corpulent, effective, important, momentous, ponderous **10** burdensome, convincing, cumbersome **11** significant, substantial **12** considerable

13 consequential

weir
3 dam **5** stank

weird
3 odd **5** eerie, queer **6** creepy, freaky, spooky **7** bizarre, curious, oddball, strange, uncanny **8** freakish, peculiar, singular, sinister **9** eccentric, fantastic, unearthly **10** mysterious **11** inscrutable **12** supernatural **13** preternatural

weirdo
4 geek, kook **5** freak **7** nutcase, oddball **8** crackpot **9** eccentric, screwball

welcome
4 hail **5** cheer, greet, hello, howdy, invite **6** accept, salute **7** embrace, invited, receive **8** greeting, pleasant, pleasing **9** agreeable, favorable, reception **10** gratifying, hospitable **11** hospitality, pleasurable

weld
4 bond, fuse, join **5** braze, joint, merge, unite **6** solder

welfare
3 aid **4** dole, help, weal **5** pogey **6** health, relief, succor **7** benefit, fortune, success, support **8** interest **9** advantage, happiness, well-being **10** assistance, commonweal, prosperity

welkin
3 sky **5** ether, vault **6** heaven **7** heavens **8** empyrean **9** firmament

well
3 far, fit, pit **4** easy, emit, hale, hole, pool, rise, sane **5** amply, clear, cured, fully, quite, shaft, sound, truly **6** easily, freely, healed, indeed, justly, kindly, likely, nicely, origin, rather, really, source, spring, wholly **7** clearly, healthy, perhaps, readily, rightly **8** entirely, expertly, pleasing, possibly, probably, properly, sensibly, smoothly, suitably **9** advisable, correctly, desirable, elegantly, favorably, fittingly, fortunate, perfectly, wholesome **10** acceptably, adequately, affluently, becomingly, completely, pleasantly, pleasingly, prosperous, reasonably, thoroughly **11** attentively, comfortable, compartment, fortunately, substantial **12** considerably, prosperously, satisfactory, successfully **13** appropriately, significantly

well-being
4 weal **6** health **7** welfare **8** thriving **9** happiness **10** prosperity

well-bred
6 urbane 7 genteel, refined 8 cultured, highborn, polished 9 civilized, patrician 10 cultivated 11 blue-blooded, gentlemanly

well-built
4 buff 5 hunky, solid 8 muscular 9 strapping

well-developed
5 curvy 7 fulsome, rounded, shapely 8 advanced 9 Junoesque 10 curvaceous

well-disposed
7 amiable 8 friendly 9 favorable, receptive 11 sympathetic 13 understanding

Welles movie
5 Trial (The) 7 Macbeth, Othello 8 Jane Eyre, Stranger (The), Third Man (The) 11 Citizen Kane, Touch of Evil 15 Journey into Fear 16 Chimes at Midnight, Lady from Shanghai (The) 20 Magnificent Ambersons (The)

well-favored
4 fair 6 comely, lovely, pretty 8 gorgeous, handsome 9 beauteous, beautiful 10 attractive 11 good-looking

well-fixed
see **well-to-do**

well-founded
5 sound, valid 6 cogent 8 rational 9 justified 10 convincing

well-groomed
4 neat, snug, tidy, trig, trim 5 natty, smart 6 dapper, snappy, spiffy, spruce, sprucy 7 orderly 8 clean-cut 9 shipshape

well-heeled
see **well-to-do**

Wellington
4 duke 7 general 8 Iron Duke
horse: 10 Copenhagen
original name: 9 Wellesley (Arthur)
victory: 7 Vitoria 8 Talavera, Waterloo 9 Salamanca

well-known
5 noted 6 famous 7 big-name, eminent, popular 8 renowned 9 notorious, prominent 10 celebrated 11 illustrious

well-liked
7 beloved, favored, popular 8 favorite 9 cherished, preferred

well-mannered
5 civil, suave 6 poised, polite, proper, urbane 7 genteel, tactful 9 courteous

10 diplomatic

well-nigh
6 all but, almost, fairly, nearly, next to 8 as good as 9 just about, virtually 11 essentially, practically

well-off
see **well-to-do**

well-paying
7 gainful 9 lucrative, rewarding 10 profitable, worthwhile 11 moneymaking 12 advantageous, remunerative

wellspring
4 font, root 5 fount 6 origin, source 7 genesis 8 fountain 10 provenance 11 provenience 12 fountainhead

well-thought-of
6 valued, worthy 7 admired, reputed 8 estimable, reputable 10 creditable 11 respectable

well-timed
6 timely 7 apropos, fitting, timeous 9 favorable, opportune 10 auspicious, felicitous, fortuitous, propitious, seasonable

well-to-do
4 rich 5 flush 6 loaded 7 moneyed, upscale, wealthy 8 affluent 10 prosperous 11 comfortable

well-turned
4 trim 5 plump 7 rounded, shapely 10 curvaceous, felicitous, Rubenesque, statuesque 11 clean-limbed

well-worn
5 banal, musty, stale, stock, tired, trite 6 frayed, old-hat, shabby 7 clichéd 8 bromidic, cobwebby, dog-eared, overused 9 hackneyed 10 threadbare 11 commonplace, stereotyped

Welsh
see **Cymric**

welsh
5 dodge 6 renege, resile 7 back out, default

welt
4 blow, edge, seam, wale, weal 5 ridge, wheal, whelk 6 insert

welter
4 coil, moil, toss 5 chaos, churn, steep, surge 6 flurry, hassle, hubbub, jumble, lather, ruckus, seethe, thrash, wallow, writhe 7 ferment, turmoil 8 disorder 9 confusion

_____ Welty
6 Eudora

wen
4 bleb, cyst 5 blain 6 growth 7 vesicle
11 excrescence

wench
3 gal 4 girl, jade, lass, maid, minx, miss,
puss, slut, tart 5 hussy, nymph, tramp, trull,
whore, woman 6 damsel, gamine, harlot,
hoyden, lassie, maiden, wanton 7 jezebel,
servant, trollop 8 slattern, strumpet

wend
3 hie 4 fare, pass 6 direct, push on, repair,
travel 7 journey, proceed

werewolf
9 loup-garou 11 lycanthrope

Werther's beloved
5 Lotte 9 Charlotte

Wesleyan
9 Methodist

West
8 Occident

western
5 oater 9 Hesperian 10 horse opera,
occidental
hemisphere: 8 Americas, New World

Western novelist
4 Grey (Zane), Ross (Dana Fuller) 5 Brand
(Max), Faust (Frederick), Short (Luke)
6 Judson (E. Z. C.), L'Amour (Louis),
Patten (Lewis), Wister (Owen) 7 Guthrie
(A. B.), Leonard (Elmore) 8 Buntline (Ned),
McMurtry (Larry)

West Indies
country: 4 Cuba 5 Haiti 7 Bahamas,
Grenada, Jamaica 8 Barbados, Dominica
10 Guadeloupe, Martinique, Puerto Rico,
Saint Lucia 17 Dominican Republic
island group: 6 Virgin (Islands)
7 Bahamas, Leeward (Islands) 8 Antilles
(Greater, Lesser), Windward (Islands)

West Point
father of: 6 Thayer (Sylvanus)
freshman: 5 plebe
student: 5 cadet

West Side Story
composer: 9 Bernstein (Leonard)
heroine: 5 Maria
lyricist: 8 Sondheim (Stephen)

West Virginia
capital: 10 Charleston
city: 8 Wheeling 10 Huntington
mountain: 10 Spruce Knob
nickname: 8 Mountain (State)
river: 4 Ohio
state bird: 8 cardinal
state flower: 12 rhododendron
state tree: 10 sugar maple

west wind
see at **wind**

wet
3 sop 4 damp, dank, rain, soak, wash,
weak 5 douse, drown, drunk, humid, moist,
rainy, soggy, soppy, souse, water
6 dampen, drench, soaked, sodden,
soused, sweaty, watery 7 moisten, raining,
soaking, sopping 8 drenched, dripping,
humidify, irrigate, moisture, saturate,
slippery 9 saturated, spineless
combining form: 4 hygr 5 hygro

wet blanket
6 grinch 7 killjoy 8 sourpuss 9 pessimist
10 spoilsport 11 party pooper

wether
4 goat 5 sheep

wetland
3 bog, fen 4 mire, quag 5 marsh, swamp
6 morass, muskeg, slough

whack
3 bat, hit, pop, try 4 bash, belt, biff, blow,
chop, cuff, kill, pelt, shot, sock, stab, wham,
whap, whop 5 crack, punch, smack,
smash 6 strike, wallop 7 bump off
8 knock off, lambaste
up: 4 part 5 divvy, split 6 divide 7 portion
9 apportion

whale
3 hit 4 beat, flog, hide, lash, whip 5 giant
6 defeat, strike, stripe, thrash 7 mammoth
8 cetacean, behemoth 9 leviathan
10 flagellate
arctic: 7 bowhead
group: 3 pod
killer: 4 orca
kind: 3 sei 4 blue 5 right, sperm
6 baleen, beluga, killer 7 narwhal, rorqual
8 cachalot
tale: 8 Moby Dick
toothed: 5 pilot (whale) 9 blackfish
young: 4 calf

whalebone
9 scrimshaw

wham
3 hit 4 bang, beat, blow, boom, clap, slam
5 blast, burst, crack, crash, smash, whack
6 impact, propel, strike 7 explode

whammy
3 hex, zap 4 jinx, juju 5 curse, spell
6 hoodoo, voodoo 7 evil eye

wharf
4 dock, pier, quay 5 jetty, levee

Wharton novel
10 Buccaneers (The), Ethan Frome
12 House of Mirth (The) 14 Age of
Innocence (The) 18 Custom of the Country
(The)

whatnot
7 étagère

wheal
4 lump, welt 5 ridge, whelk

wheat
4 crop 5 emmer, flour, grain, grass, spelt
6 cereal 7 einkorn
beard: 3 awn
beat: 6 thresh
chaff: 4 bran
crushed: 6 bulgur
disease: 4 rust, smut
type: 4 club 5 durum

wheedle
3 con 4 coax 5 cozen 6 cajole, entice,
seduce 7 blarney, flatter 8 blandish,
inveigle, scrounge, soft-soap 9 sweet-talk

wheel
3 VIP 4 auto, gyre, move, reel, spin, turn
5 cycle, drive, motor, pilot, pivot, round,
whirl 6 bigwig, circle, gyrate, league,
rotate, totter travel 7 big shot, circuit,
revolve 8 rotation 9 about-face, volte-face
part: 3 hub, rim 4 tire 5 felly, spoke
spoke: 6 radius
toothed: 3 cog 4 gear

wheeze
3 saw, yuk 4 gasp, hiss, joke, puff, rasp
5 adage, cough 6 saying 7 proverb,
whistle 8 chestnut, rhonchus

whelk
4 wale, weal, welt 5 wheal

whelm
4 bury, sink 5 cover, drown, flood, swamp
6 deluge, engulf 8 bear down, inundate,
overbear, overcome, submerge
9 devastate

whelp
3 cub, kid, pup 4 bear 5 child, puppy
9 youngster

whereas
5 since, while 6 seeing, though 7 howbeit
8 although 11 considering

wherefore
3 why 4 thus 5 proof 6 ground, reason,
whence 8 argument 11 explanation

wherewithal
5 funds, means, money 9 resources

wherry
4 boat 5 barge, scull 7 lighter, rowboat

whet
4 edge, goad, hone 5 drink, rally, rouse,
waken 6 arouse, awaken, excite, kindle
7 sharpen, starter 8 aperitif 9 appetizer,
challenge, stimulate 10 incitement 11 hors
d'oeuvre

whiff
3 fan 4 blow, gust, hint, puff, waft 5 expel,
smoke, tinge, trace 6 breath, exhale, inhale
7 soupçon, whisper 9 strikeout
10 indication, inhalation

whiffet
6 nobody, squirt 9 nonentity

whiffle
4 blow, gust, puff 5 waver 6 dither, falter
9 fluctuate, vacillate 12 shilly-shally

while
4 pass, time, when 5 spell 6 albeit,
moment, though 7 howbeit, stretch,
whereas 8 although, as long as, so long as

whilom
6 bygone, former 7 onetime, quondam
8 formerly, previous, sometime 9 erstwhile

whim
3 bee 4 idea, kink 5 dream, fancy, freak,
humor 6 maggot, megrim, notion, vagary
7 caprice, capstan, conceit, thought
8 crotchet

whimper
3 cry 4 fret, mewl, pule, wail 5 bleat,
whine 6 snivel

whimsical
4 iffy, zany 5 droll, fancy, flaky 6 chancy,
fickle, fitful, quirky, random 7 erratic, flighty,
mutable, puckish, wayward 8 fanciful,
freakish, volatile 9 eccentric, impulsive,
pixilated, screwball, uncertain, vagarious
10 capricious 13 unpredictable

whimsy
3 bee **4** play **5** dream, fancy, freak, humor **6** levity, maggot, megrim, notion, vagary **7** caprice, conceit, fantasy **9** capriccio, frivolity

whim-wham
4 dido **5** curio, fancy, frill **6** bauble, gewgaw, ruffle, trifle **7** bibelot, flounce, trinket **8** furbelow, gimcrack, kickshaw **9** objet d'art **10** knickknack

whine
3 cry **4** cant, fret, fuss, kick, moan, pule, wail **5** bleat, gripe **6** grouse, repine, snivel, whinge, yammer **7** grumble, snuffle, whimper **8** complain **9** bellyache

whinny
5 neigh **6** nicker **7** whicker

whiny
5 fussy **7** fretful, grouchy, peevish **8** petulant **9** irritable, querulous

whip
3 cut, hem, set **4** beat, cane, crop, dash, flog, hide, jerk, lash, lick, pull, rout, wind, wrap **5** abuse, mop up, quirt, spank, sting, whale, whisk **6** defeat, lather, snatch, strike, stroke, subdue, switch, thrash, urge on **7** agitate, dessert, provoke, rawhide, shellac, trounce, utensil **8** coachman, lambaste, overcome, vanquish **9** instigate, overwhelm **10** flagellate **13** cat-o'-nine-tails
braided: 10 blacksnake

whippersnapper
see **whiffet**

whipping boy
4 goat **5** patsy **7** fall guy **9** scapegoat

whippy
6 supple **7** elastic, springy **8** flexible **9** resilient

whir
3 fly, hum **4** burr, buzz, whiz **5** chirr, churr, drone, whizz **7** revolve, vibrate **9** bombinate

whirl
3 ado, gig, pop, try **4** eddy, flit, fuss, gyre, moil, reel, shot, spin, stab, stir, swim, turn, veer **5** hurry, pivot, swirl, whack, wheel **6** bustle, circle, gyrate, hassle, hubbub, pother, rotate **7** circuit, dervish, turmoil **8** ballyhoo, gyration, rotation **9** commotion, pirouette **10** revolution

whirligig
4 gyre, spin **6** beetle, gyrate **8** carousel

9 pirouette **12** merry-go-round

whirlpool
3 ado **4** eddy, fuss **6** bustle, flurry, furore, tumult, vortex **7** turmoil **8** vortices (plural) **9** commotion, maelstrom

whirlwind
4 rush, spout, stir, to-do **5** hasty, swift **6** bustle **7** cyclone, tornado, twister, typhoon **8** headlong **9** commotion, dust devil, dust storm, hurricane **10** waterspout **11** tourbillion

whish
4 fizz, hiss **6** fizzle **8** sibilate

whisk
3 mix, nip, wag, zip **4** beat, flit, fluff, whip **5** broom, brush, hurry, speed **6** switch

whisker
4 hair **7** bristle **8** filament, vibrissa **9** outrigger **11** hairbreadth

whiskered
5 hairy **6** pilose **7** bearded, bristly, hirsute **8** stubbled, unshaven

whiskers
5 beard **6** goatee **7** stubble **8** bristles **9** burnsides, peach fuzz, sideburns, weepers **11** muttonchops

whiskey
3 rye **6** liquor, Scotch **7** alcohol, bourbon
with beer chaser: 11 boilermaker

whisper
4 buzz, hint, hiss, whiz **5** rumor, shade, tinge, touch, trace, whiff **6** breath, gossip, murmur, mutter **8** sibilate, susurrus **9** suspicion, undertone **11** susurration

whist
4 game, hush **5** quiet, still **6** silent **9** noiseless, soundless

whistle
4 pipe, toot **5** flute, whiff **6** signal, tootle, wheeze

whistle-stop
5 stump **8** campaign, politick **9** barnstorm **11** electioneer

whit
3 bit, fig, jot, rap **4** atom, damn, hoot, iota, mite **5** crumb, scrap, shred, speck, whoop **7** dribble, modicum, smidgen **8** molecule, particle

white
4 pure **5** livid, milky, snowy **6** albino, blanch, bleach, pallid **7** silvery **9** colorless

combining form: 4 leuc, leuk 5 leuco, leuko
egg's: 5 glair 6 glaire 7 albumen

White novel
12 Stuart Little 13 Charlotte's Web

white cliffs of _____
5 Dover

White Fang author
6 London (Jack)

White House
designer: 5 Hoban (James)
first occupant: 5 Adams (Abigail, John)

white lightning
5 hooch 7 bootleg, whiskey 9 moonshine
10 bathtub gin 11 mountain dew

whiten
4 fade, pale 5 frost 6 blanch, bleach, blench 8 etiolate 10 decolorize

white plague
8 phthisis 11 consumption 12 tuberculosis

whitewash
6 parget 7 cover up 9 gloss over, gloze over, sugarcoat

whither
5 where 7 whereto 9 whereunto

whiting
3 cod 4 hake 10 silver hake

Whitsunday
9 Pentecost

Whittier poem
9 Snow-Bound 10 Maud Muller
11 Barefoot Boy 16 Barbara Frietchie

whittle
4 form, fret, pare, trim 5 carve, chip, shape, shave, skive 6 reduce, sculpt
8 diminish

whiz
3 fly, hum, zip 4 buzz, flit, hiss, zoom
5 hurry, speed, swish, whirl 6 expert, fizzle, genius, phenom, rotate, whoosh 8 virtuoso
10 wunderkind

whoa
3 hey 4 slow, stop 6 hold up

whole
3 all, fit, sum 4 full, hale, sane 5 sound, total, uncut, unity 6 entire, entity, healed, intact, system, unhurt 7 healthy, perfect, plenary 8 complete, entirely, entirety, flawless, restored, totality, unbroken, unmarred 9 recovered, undamaged, undivided, uninjured, untouched

10 unimpaired, unmodified 11 unblemished 12 concentrated, undistracted
combining form: 3 hol, pan 4 holo

wholehearted
6 ardent 7 devoted, earnest, fervent, sincere 8 bona fide, committed 9 heartfelt, steadfast, unfeigned 10 passionate, unwavering 11 impassioned
12 enthusiastic 13 unquestioning

whole-hog
6 all-out, gung-ho 8 complete, thorough
9 full-scale 11 straight-out
13 thoroughgoing

wholeness
7 oneness 8 entirety, totality 9 integrity, soundness 10 intactness, perfection

whole note
9 semibreve

whole number
5 digit 6 cipher 7 integer, numeral

wholesome
3 fit 4 good, hale, safe, sane, well 5 right, sound 6 benign 7 healthy 8 hygienic, salutary 9 favorable, healthful
10 beneficial, salubrious

wholly
3 all 4 only 6 in toto, singly, solely, purely
7 totally 8 entirely 10 altogether, completely 11 exclusively

whomp
3 hit 4 beat, drub, slap, whip, whup
5 crash, thump 6 crunch, strike, thrash, wallop 7 clobber, shellac, trounce
8 lambaste

whomp up
4 stir 5 rouse, spark 6 arouse, excite, foment

whoopee
3 fun 5 revel, yahoo 6 gaiety, hoopla, yippee 7 jollity, revelry, wassail, whoopla
8 hilarity 9 festivity, high jinks, merriment
10 hurly-burly 11 merrymaking

whoopla
see **hoopla**

whop
3 bat, bop 4 bash, beat, biff, blow, drub, lick, sock 5 baste, pound, smack, thump, whack 6 batter, buffet, defeat, hammer, pummel, strike, thrash, thwack, wallop
7 trounce 8 lambaste

whopping
4 huge, vast 6 mighty 7 amazing,

whorl

immense, massive **8** colossal, enormous, gigantic, whacking **9** bodacious, humongous, monstrous **10** gargantuan, incredible, prodigious **13** extraordinary

whorl

4 coil, eddy, turn **5** swirl **6** spiral

why

5 cause **6** enigma, motive, puzzle, reason, riddle **7** mystery, problem, what for **9** conundrum, rationale, therefore, wherefore **10** puzzlement **11** explanation

wicked

4 evil, mean, very, vile **5** awful, black, wrong **6** fierce, malign, sinful, unholy **7** corrupt, hateful, heinous, immoral, naughty, ungodly, vicious **8** depraved, devilish, fiendish **9** atrocious, barbarous, dangerous, extremely, hazardous, injurious, malicious, malignant, nefarious **10** iniquitous, malevolent, outrageous **11** treacherous

wickedness

3 sin **4** evil, vice **7** devilry **8** enormity, iniquity, satanism **9** depravity **10** corruption, immorality **12** devilishness, fiendishness

wicker

4 twig **5** osier, withe **6** branch

wicket

4 arch, door, gate, hoop **6** window **sticky: 3** fix, jam **4** knot **7** toughie **9** conundrum, tight spot

wide

4 vast **5** broad, fully **8** extended, spacious, straying, sweeping **9** deviating, expansive, extensive, inclusive **10** completely **13** comprehensive

widen

4 ream **6** dilate, expand, extend, open up, spread **7** broaden, distend, enlarge

widespread

4 rife, vast **6** common **7** current, general, popular, rampant, regnant **8** far-flung **9** extensive, pervasive, prevalent **10** far-ranging, ubiquitous

widget

5 gizmo **6** device, dingus, doodad, gadget, hickey, jigger **7** gimmick, whatsit **9** doohickey, thingummy **11** contraption, thingamabob, thingamajig, thingumajig

width

4 gape, kerf, span **5** depth, range **6** spread **7** breadth **9** extension

wield

3 use **5** exert **6** handle **7** control **8** exercise **10** manipulate **the gavel: 7** preside

wiener

3 dog **5** frank **6** hot dog **7** sausage **11** frankfurter **13** Vienna sausage

wife

3 Mrs. **4** mate **5** bride, woman **6** female, matron, missis, missus, spouse **7** consort, partner **8** helpmate, helpmeet **Latin: 4** uxor **of a rajah: 4** rani **5** ranee

wifely

7 uxorial

wig

3 jaw, rap, rug **4** flip, rail, rate **5** chide, freak, scold **6** berate, peruke, rebuke, revile, toupee **7** bawl out, chew out, reproof, upbraid **8** postiche, reproach **9** hairpiece, reprimand **10** tongue-lash

wiggle

4 jerk **5** shake, twist **6** fidget, squirm, writhe **Scottish: 5** hotch

wight

3 man **5** human **6** animal, mortal, person **7** critter **8** creature **10** human being, individual

wild

3 mad **4** fast **5** crazy **6** barren, raging, savage, stormy, unruly **7** erratic, frantic, furious, natural, untamed, vicious **8** barbaric, blustery, desolate, frenetic, frenzied, reckless **9** barbarian, barbarous, delirious, fantastic, turbulent, wasteland **10** incautious, outlandish **11** extravagant, intractable, sensational, tempestuous, uncivilized, uninhabited **12** preposterous, uncontrolled, uncultivated, ungovernable, unmanageable **13** irresponsible, undisciplined

wild ass

5 kiang **6** onager

Wild Duck author

5 Ibsen (Henrik)

wildebeest

3 gnu

wilderness

4 bush **5** heath, waste **6** barren, desert **9** backlands, wasteland **10** hinterland **11** backcountry

Wilder play
7 Our Town 10 Matchmaker (The) 14 Skin of Our Teeth (The)

wild-eyed
6 raving 7 blue-sky, radical 9 visionary

wile
4 ploy, ruse, vamp 5 charm, feint, guile, trick 6 allure, deceit, entice, gambit 7 attract, beguile, bewitch, chicane, cunning, enchant, gimmick 8 artifice, inveigle, maneuver, trickery 9 captivate, chicanery, fascinate, magnetize, stratagem 10 subterfuge

wiliness
5 guile 7 cunning

will
4 like, wish 5 cause, elect, leave order 6 choice, choose, decree, desire, direct, intend, intent, liking, option, ordain, please 7 bequest, consent, control, passion, purpose 8 appetite, bequeath, pleasure, volition 9 intention, testament 10 discipline 11 disposition, inclination, self-control 13 determination, self-restraint
addition: 7 codicil
maker: 8 testator 9 testatrix
without: 9 intestate

willful
5 heady 6 dogged, mulish, unruly 8 perverse, stubborn 9 obstinate, pigheaded, voluntary 10 deliberate, hardheaded, headstrong, purposeful, self-willed 11 intentional, intractable, wrongheaded 12 contumacious, pertinacious, ungovernable

Williams play
10 Camino Real, Rose Tattoo (The) 14 Glass Menagerie (The), Summer and Smoke 16 Cat on a Hot Tin Roof, Night of the Iguana (The), Sweet Bird of Youth 18 Suddenly Last Summer 20 Streetcar Named Desire (A)

William Tell composer
7 Rossini (Gioacchino)

willies
6 creeps, shakes 7 jimjams, jitters, shivers 9 whim-whams 10 goose bumps 13 heebie-jeebies

willing
3 apt 4 fain, game, glad, open 5 prone, ready 6 minded 7 forward, witting 8 amenable, disposed, inclined, obliging, unforced 9 agreeable, compliant, favorable, receptive, voluntary

10 deliberate, volitional 11 intentional, predisposed

williwaw
4 gust, wind 5 blast 8 outburst, paroxysm 9 commotion

will-o'-the-wisp
7 fantasy, figment, phantom 8 daydream, delusion 11 ignis fatuus

willow
5 osier, salix 6 sallow 10 cricket bat
flower cluster: 6 catkin
kind: 5 crack, pussy, white 6 basket 7 weeping

willowy
4 tall 5 lithe 6 pliant, supple, svelte 7 lissome, pliable, slender 8 graceful

Wilson play
6 Fences 11 Piano Lesson (The) 12 Talley's Folly 13 Hot l Baltimore (The) 20 Ma Rainey's Black Bottom

wilt
3 sag 4 swag 5 droop, dry up, wizen 6 wither 7 shrivel 8 languish

wily
3 sly 4 foxy 5 cagey, canny, slick 6 artful, astute, clever, crafty, shrewd, tricky 7 cunning, devious, vulpine 8 guileful, scheming 10 serpentine

wimble
4 bore 5 auger, borer, brace, drill 6 gimlet

Wimbledon's game
6 tennis

wimp
4 nerd, wuss 5 sissy 7 doormat, nebbish 9 jellyfish 11 milquetoast

wimple
4 bend, veil, wrap 5 cover, curve 6 ripple
wearer: 3 nun

wimp out
6 beg off, cave in, give in 8 back down

wimpy
4 lame, puny, weak 5 dinky, inept, timid 6 craven, feeble 7 gutless 8 cowardly, feckless, impotent, pathetic 9 spineless 10 namby-pamby, wishy-washy 11 ineffective, ineffectual

win
3 get 4 beat, earn, gain 5 reach, score 6 attain, defeat, obtain, secure 7 achieve, acquire, conquer, procure, produce, realize, succeed, success, triumph, victory

8 conquest, persuade **9** influence
10 accomplish
over: 6 disarm, induce **8** convince,
persuade, talk into **9** prevail on

wince

5 cower, quail, start **6** blanch, blench,
cringe, flinch, recoil, shrink **7** squinch

wind

3 air, dry, fan, gas **4** bend, blow, clue, coil,
curl, gale, gird, gust, haul, hint, reel, rest,
talk, turn, warp, wrap **5** cover, crank,
curve, force, hoist, raise, sound, spool,
twine, twist **6** breath, breeze, circle,
enlace, girdle, notion, zephyr **7** enclose,
entwine, envelop, inkling, involve,
monsoon, nothing, tighten **8** easterly,
encircle, entangle, surround, tendency,
westerly **9** direction, idle words, influence,
insinuate **10** indication, intimation,
suggestion
California: 8 Santa Ana
cold: 4 bora **7** mistral, pampero
8 williwaw
gentle: 6 breeze, zephyr
god: 6 Boreas (north) **8** Favonius,
Zephyrus (west)
hot: 6 simoom **7** sirocco
instrument: 3 sax **4** horn, oboe, tuba,
vane **5** flute **7** bassoon, trumpet
8 trombone **9** saxophone **10** anemometer
11 weather vane
into: 8 aweather
measure of speed: 4 knot
Mediterranean: 7 sirocco **8** levanter,
libeccio
scale: 8 Beaufort
stormy: 4 gale **7** cyclone, tornado, twister
9 hurricane **11** northeaster
warm: 4 föhn **5** foehn **7** chinook

windbag

6 gabber **7** blabber **8** bigmouth, blowhard,
braggart

windfall

4 boon, gain **5** break **7** jackpot **8** fortuity

winding

4 curl, kink **5** snaky **6** spiral **7** coiling,
curving, devious, sinuous **8** flexuous,
indirect, tortuous, twisting **9** meandrous
10 circuitous, convoluted, meandering,
roundabout, serpentine **11** anfractuous
12 labyrinthine

windmill

4 spin **5** wheel **7** machine
fighter: 10 Don Quixote

window

3 bay, eye **4** pane **5** oriel **6** dormer
7 opening **8** aperture, casement, jalousie
cover: 5 blind **7** curtain, shutter
French: 7 fenêtre
over a door: 7 transom **8** fanlight
part: 4 pane, sash, sill **5** frame
projecting: 3 bay **5** oriel
roof's: 6 dormer **7** lucarne **8** skylight
Scottish: 7 winnock
ship's: 4 port **8** porthole

windpipe

7 trachea
combining form: 6 trache **7** tracheo

windrow

4 bank, heap, hill, mass, pile **5** mound,
ridge, stack

wind up

3 end **4** halt **5** close **6** finish, settle
8 complete, conclude **9** terminate

windup

3 end **5** close **6** ending, finale, finish
9 backswing **10** completion, conclusion
11 termination

windy

4 airy **5** blowy, gassy, gusty, inane, tumid,
wordy **6** breezy, prolix, stormy, turgid
7 diffuse, orotund, pompous, verbose
8 blustery, inflated **9** bombastic, overblown
11 tempestuous **13** grandiloquent

wine

4 vino **5** drink, juice **8** beverage
aromatized: 8 vermouth **9** hippocras
beverage: 5 negus, punch **6** bishop,
cooler **7** sangria **8** sangaree, spritzer
9 hippocras
bottle: 6 fiasco, magnum **8** decanter,
jeroboam **10** methuselah
cabinet: 8 cellaret
cask: 3 tun, vat **4** butt, pipe **8** puncheon
cellar: 6 bodega
discoverer: 4 Noah
distillate: 6 brandy, cognac
dry: 3 sec **4** brut
flavor: 4 mull
fortified: 4 port **6** Malaga, sherry
7 Madeira, marsala, oloroso **8** muscatel
fragrance: 4 nose **7** bouquet
lover: 9 oenophile **11** oenophilist
maker: 7 vintner **8** vigneron **10** wine-
grower **13** viticulturist
merchant: 7 vintner
red: 4 port **5** Gamay, Macon, Medoc,
Rioja **6** Barolo, Beaune, claret, Shiraz

7 Chianti 8 Bordeaux, Burgundy, cabernet
9 Lambrusco, Pinot Noir, St. Emilion,
zinfandel 10 Beaujolais, Sangiovese
11 Petite Sirah 12 Valpolicella
relating to: 6 vinous
residue: 4 marc
rice: 4 sake
richness: 4 body
sediment: 4 lees 5 dregs
shop: 6 bistro, bodega, tavern
sparkling: 8 cold duck, sparkler,
Spumante 9 champagne, Lambrusco
specialist: 9 enologist 10 oenologist
spiced: 6 mulled (wine) 9 hippocras
steward: 9 sommelier
study of: 7 enology 8 oenology
sweet: 4 port 5 Tokay 6 canary, Malaga,
muscat 7 Catawba, Madeira, malmsey,
marsala, oloroso, Vouvray 8 Malvasia,
muscatel, sauterne 9 Sauternes 11 scuppernong
sweeten: 4 mull
vessel: 7 chalice
white: 4 hock 5 Rhine, Soave
7 Catawba, Chablis, Moselle, Orvieto,
Vouvray 8 Bordeaux, Riesling, Semillon,
vermouth 9 champagne, Hermitage,
Meursault 10 chardonnay, Montrachet
11 Chenin Blanc, scuppernong
13 liebfraumilch 14 sauvignon blanc
year: 7 vintage

wing
3 ala, arm, ell, fly 4 sail, unit, vane
5 annex, flank, fleet, pinna, wound 6 flight
7 airfoil, faction, flanker, section
9 appendage, expansion, extension,
improvise 10 projection, protrusion
12 protuberance
relating to: 4 alar 5 alary

wingding
4 bash, fete, gala 5 binge, party
7 blowout, shindig 9 festivity

winged
5 alate, fleet, rapid, swift 7 soaring
8 elevated
deity: 4 Amor, Eros, Nike 5 Cupid
6 Hermes 7 Mercury
horse: 7 Pegasus
monster: 5 harpy

wingless
8 apterous

winglike
4 alar 5 alary
part: 3 ala 4 alae (plural)

wink
3 bat, nap 5 flash, jiffy, shake, trice
6 moment, second, signal 7 connive,
flicker, instant, twinkle 9 nictitate, twinkling
11 split second

winner
3 ace 4 lulu 5 doozy 6 doozie, top dog,
victor 7 success 8 champion 9 conqueror
11 titleholder

Winnie-the-Pooh
author: 5 Milne (A. A.)
character: 3 Roo 5 Kanga 6 Piglet,
Tigger

winning
8 charming, engaging, pleasing
9 agreeable 10 delightful, successful,
triumphant, victorious 11 captivating
13 prepossessing

winnow
3 fan 4 blow, cull, pare, sift, sort 6 delete,
filter, narrow, reduce, remove, screen,
select 8 separate

winsome
5 sweet 6 dulcet, lovely 8 charming,
cheerful, engaging, pleasing 9 easygoing
12 lighthearted

winter
6 season 9 hibernate
French: 5 hiver
Spanish: 8 invierno

Winter's Tale, A
author: 11 Shakespeare (William)
character: 7 Camillo, Leontes, Paulina,
Perdita 8 Florizel, Hermione 9 Antigonus,
Autolycus, Polixenes

wintry
3 icy 4 cold 5 bleak, hoary, nippy, snowy
6 frigid, frosty 8 chilling, freezing, hibernal
12 bone-chilling

wipe
3 dry, rub 4 swab 5 towel, whisk 6 napkin,
smudge, sponge 8 squeegee

wipe out
4 rout 5 crash, erase, smear, sweep 7 blot
out, destroy, expunge 8 decimate
9 eradicate, extirpate 10 annihilate,
obliterate

wipeout
4 fall, rout 5 crash 8 drubbing
11 destruction 12 annihilation

wire
3 rod 4 cord, line, send 5 cable, metal

6 thread 7 message 8 meshwork, telegram 9 cablegram, telegraph 10 finish line

measure: 3 mil 5 gauge

wiry
4 lean, ropy 6 sinewy, supple 7 fibrous, stringy

Wisconsin
capital: 7 Madison
city: 6 Racine 7 Kenosha 8 Green Bay 9 Milwaukee
college, university: 5 Ripon 6 Beloit 9 Marquette
lake: 7 Mendota
motto: 7 Forward
nickname: 6 Badger (State)
peninsula: 4 Door
river: 7 St. Croix 9 Menominee, Wisconsin 11 Mississippi
state bird: 5 robin
state flower: 6 violet
state tree: 10 sugar maple

wisdom
5 sense 7 insight, science 8 judgment, learning, sagacity, sageness, sapience 9 good sense, knowledge 10 horse sense 11 common sense, information

wise
3 hep, hip 4 bold, keen, sage, sane, tell, warn, wily 5 alert, aware, brash, cagey, canny, cocky, fresh, learn, nervy, quick, sassy, sharp, smart 6 artful, astute, bright, cheeky, clever, crafty, fill in, inform, notify, shrewd, sophic, tricky 7 cunning, gnostic, knowing, politic, prudent, sapient 8 discreet, flippant, impudent, insolent, sensible, tactical 9 advisable, bold-faced, expedient, judicious, sagacious, scholarly 10 discerning, insightful, perceptive, reflective, thoughtful 11 foresighted, impertinent, intelligent, quick-witted, sharp-witted, smart-alecky 13 contemplative, knowledgeable, perspicacious
old man: 6 Nestor
person: 4 sage 6 savant 7 scholar

wiseacre
see **wise guy**

wisecrack
3 dig, gag 4 gibe, jape, jest, joke, quip 5 sally 9 witticism

wise guy
6 smarty 7 mobster 8 gangster, smart-ass 9 know-it-all, swellhead 10 smart aleck 11 smarty-pants, wisenheimer

wise man
4 guru, sage 5 magus 6 savant

Wise Men
see **Magi**

wish
3 bid 4 care, goal, like, long, lust, want 5 covet, crave, fancy, foist, order, yearn 6 desire, impose 7 request 10 desiderate

wishbone
7 furcula

wishful
5 eager 7 anxious, hopeful, longing 8 desirous

wishy-washy
4 lame, weak 5 banal, bland, vapid, wimpy 6 jejune, watery 7 insipid, languid 10 namby-pamby 11 ineffective, ineffectual 13 characterless

wisp
3 bit 5 shred, strip, trace 6 sliver, snatch, streak 7 smidgen, snippet 8 fragment 9 scintilla

wispy
4 slim 5 frail 6 flimsy, slight 7 slender, tenuous 8 fleeting, nebulous 10 evanescent

Wister novel
9 Virginian (The)

wistful
3 sad 6 dreamy, triste 7 longing, pensive 8 yearning 9 nostalgic 10 melancholy

wit
3 wag 5 brain, comic, droll, humor, irony, joker 6 banter, esprit, jester, reason, satire, wisdom 7 farceur, punster 8 banterer, comedian, funnyman, judgment, humorist, jokester, quipster, repartee 9 alertness, ingenuity, intellect 10 cleverness, persiflage

witch
3 hag, hex 5 dowse, spell 6 voodoo, Wiccan 7 charmer 8 magician, sorcerer 9 sorceress 11 enchantress
companion: 3 cat
group: 5 coven
male: 6 wizard 7 warlock
meeting: 6 sabbat
town: 5 Endor
vehicle: 5 broom

witchcraft
5 magic, wicca 6 hoodoo, voodoo 7 devilry, hexerei, sorcery 8 wizardry

9 diablerie, sortilege, voodooism 10 black magic, hocus-pocus, mumbo jumbo, necromancy 11 abracadabra, thaumaturgy

witch hazel
5 shrub 6 lotion

witchy
6 Wiccan 7 magical 8 wizardly 9 sorcerous 11 necromantic 12 thaumaturgic

with
3 for, per, pro, via 4 over, upon 5 about 6 having 7 against, by way of, through 8 as well as 9 by means of, in favor of 10 by virtue of
French: 4 avec
German: 3 mit
Italian, Spanish: 3 con
Latin: 3 cum

withal
3 too, yet 4 also 5 still 6 as well, though 7 besides, howbeit, however 8 after all, moreover 11 furthermore, nonetheless 12 additionally, nevertheless

withdraw
4 exit, quit 5 demit, leave, unsay 6 depart, bow out, call in, cash in, desert, detach, recall, recant, recede, recoil, retire, secede, shrink 7 back out, drop out, pull out, retract, retreat, scratch, take off, take out 8 back down, evacuate, fall back, pull away, push back, separate, take back, turn away 9 disengage, stand down 10 disconnect, give ground

withdrawal
4 exit 6 exodus 7 exiting, pullout, removal, retreat 9 departure 10 alienation, detachment, retirement, retraction, revocation

withdrawn
4 cool 5 aloof 6 casual, remote 7 distant, removed 8 detached, isolated, reserved, retiring, solitary 9 incurious, unaffable, uncurious 10 unsociable 11 indifferent, introverted, standoffish, unconcerned, unexpansive 12 uninterested, unresponsive

wither
3 age, dry 4 fade, sear, wilt 5 dry up, parch, quail, wizen 6 scorch 7 mummify, shrivel

withered
4 sere 7 sapless 8 shrunken, wrinkled 9 shriveled

withhold
4 deny 5 check 6 deduct, deprive, detain, refuse, retain 7 abstain, forbear, inhibit, refrain, reserve, subtract 8 restrain 9 constrain

within
4 into 5 among 6 inside 7 indoors, inwards 8 enclosed, interior, inwardly 10 inner place
prefix: 5 infra, intra, intro

with-it
6 modern, modish, trendy 7 à la mode, current, faddish, stylish 8 up-to-date 11 fashionable 12 contemporary

without
4 open, past, sans 5 minus 6 absent 7 lacking, open air, outside, wanting 8 outdoors 10 externally, out-of-doors
Latin: 4 sine

with respect to
4 as to, in re 5 as for 7 apropos 8 touching 9 as regards, regarding 10 concerning

withstand
4 bear, buck, defy 5 fight, repel 6 endure, oppose, resist, suffer 7 hold off, survive, sustain 8 tolerate, traverse

withy
4 twig 5 osier 6 branch, willow 8 flexible 9 resilient

witless
3 mad 4 daft, nuts 5 crazy, daffy, dotty, nutty, silly 6 insane, simple, stupid 7 asinine, cracked, foolish, idiotic 8 demented, deranged, mindless 9 bedlamite, brainless, senseless 10 weak-minded, unbalanced

witlessness
5 folly 6 idiocy, lunacy 7 inanity 8 insanity 9 absurdity, stupidity

witness
3 see 4 note, sign, view 5 proof, vouch 6 attest, depone, depose, notice, viewer 7 bear out, confirm, betoken, certify, testify, watcher 8 attester, beholder, deponent, evidence, looker-on, observer, onlooker 9 bystander, spectator, testament, testifier, testimony 11 affirmation, attestation, corroborate, testimonial 12 confirmation

witticism
3 dig, gag, mot 4 gibe, jape, jest, jibe, joke, quip 5 crack, sally 6 bon mot 8 one-liner,

repartee **9** throwaway, wisecrack

witting
5 aware **7** knowing, willful **8** sensible, sentient **9** cognizant, conscious, voluntary **10** deliberate **11** intentional

witty
5 funny **6** clever, jocose **7** amusing, jocular **8** humorous **9** facetious **13** scintillating

wiz
3 ace **5** adept, fiend **6** artist, expert, phenom **7** artiste **8** virtuoso

wizard
3 ace **4** mage **5** adept, druid, fiend, magus **6** expert, phenom **7** warlock **8** conjurer, magician, sorcerer, virtuoso **9** enchanter **10** past master **11** necromancer, thaumaturge **13** thaumaturgist

wizardly
5 magic **6** mystic, witchy **7** magical **9** sorcerous **10** mysterious **11** necromantic **12** thaumaturgic

Wizard of Menlo Park
6 Edison (Thomas Alva)

Wizard of Oz
author: 4 Baum (L. Frank)
character: 7 Dorothy **9** Scarecrow **10** Tin Woodman **12** Cowardly Lion
dog: 4 Toto

wizardry
5 magic **6** voodoo **7** sorcery **8** witchery **9** diablerie, sortilege **10** black magic, necromancy, witchcraft **11** bewitchment, conjuration, enchantment

wizen
3 dry **4** sere, wilt **5** dry up **6** shrink, wither **7** dried-up, shrivel, wrinkle

wizened
4 aged, sere **5** dried **6** shrunk **7** pinched **8** shrunken, withered, wrinkled

wobble
4 reel, rock, sway **5** quake, shake, waver, weave **6** dither, falter, quaver, teeter, totter **7** stagger, stumble, tremble **8** nutation **9** vacillate

wobbly
4 weak **5** rocky, shaky **6** unsure **7** rackety, rickety **8** insecure, rachitic, unstable, unsteady, wavering **9** faltering, teetering, tottering **10** nutational **11** vacillating

Wodehouse, P. G.
castle: 9 Blandings
character: 6 Bertie (Wooster), Gussie (Fink-Nottle), Jeeves, Psmith **7** Wooster (Bertie) **8** Emsworth (Lord), Mulliner (Mr.) **10** Threepwood (Clarence, Freddie) **12** Lord Emsworth
club: 6 Drones

Woden
see **Odin**

woe
3 rue **4** bale, bane, care **5** grief **6** misery, regret, sorrow **7** anguish, sadness, trouble **8** calamity **9** heartache **10** affliction, heartbreak **11** lamentation, unhappiness **12** wretchedness

woebegone
3 low, sad **4** blue, down, worn **6** shabby **7** doleful, forlorn, ruthful **8** dejected, dolorous, downcast, wretched **9** depressed, miserable, sorrowful **10** despondent, melancholy **11** crestfallen, downhearted, low-spirited **12** disconsolate

woeful
3 sad **5** heavy, sorry **6** dismal, rueful, tragic, triste **7** ruthful **8** dejected, dolorous, downcast, grievous, mournful, stricken, tortured, wretched **9** afflicted, aggrieved, depressed, heartsick, miserable, plaintive, sorrowful **10** deplorable, lamentable, lugubrious, melancholy **11** distressing, downhearted, low-spirited **12** disconsolate **13** heartbreaking

wolf
4 bolt, canid, lobo, rake, roué **6** canine, coyote, devour, gobble, masher **7** Don Juan, poverty **8** Casanova, lothario **10** starvation
genus: 5 Canis
group: 4 pack
young: 5 whelp

Wolfe novel
17 Look Homeward Angel, Of Time and the River **18** You Can't Go Home Again **20** Bonfire of the Vanities (The)

wolfish
4 wild **5** cruel, feral **6** fierce, lupine, savage **7** bestial, brutish, vicious **9** ferocious

wolverine
European: 7 glutton
genus: 4 Gulo

Wolverine State
8 Michigan

woman

4 dame, lady 5 madam 6 female, matron
8 mistress 10 girlfriend
attractive: 5 belle 6 beauty, eyeful, looker
7 stunner 8 knockout
combining form: 4 gyny 5 gynec
6 gynaec, gyneco, gynous 7 gynaeco
courageous: 7 heroine
dignified: 6 matron 7 dowager
10 grande dame
dowdy: 5 frump
English: 6 milady
first, biblical: 3 Eve
first, mythological: 7 Pandora
French: 5 femme
German: 4 Frau 8 Fräulein
Hawaiian: 6 wahine
Indian: 5 squaw
Italian: 5 donna 7 signora .
old: 3 hag 4 dame 5 crone 6 beldam,
carlin, gammer, granny
pregnant: 7 gravida
resembling: 8 gynecoid
royal: 5 queen 8 princess
sailor: 4 Wave
servant: 4 maid
soldier: 3 Wac
Spanish: 4 doña 6 señora
strong: 6 amazon, virago
unmarried: 4 miss 6 maiden 8 spinster
young: 4 girl, lass 6 lassie, maiden

womanize

4 wolf 9 gallivant, philander 10 fool
around, mess around

womanizer

4 stud, wolf 6 masher 7 Don Juan, gallant,
playboy 8 Casanova, lothario 9 ladies'
man 10 lady-killer 11 philanderer

womb

6 uterus
combining form: 6 hyster 7 hystero

women

hatred of: 8 misogyny
organization of: 3 DAR, NOW 8 sorority

Women in Love author

8 Lawrence (D. H.)

wonder

3 awe 4 muse 5 doubt 6 marvel
7 dubiety, miracle, portent, prodigy
8 mistrust, question 9 amazement,
speculate, suspicion 10 admiration,
skepticism 11 incertitude, uncertainty
12 astonishment

wonderful

4 keen 5 grand, great, nifty, super, swell
6 divine, groovy, peachy, spiffy 7 amazing,
strange, too much, topping 8 dynamite,
fabulous, glorious, spiffing, terrific
9 admirable, excellent, marvelous,
wunderbar 10 astounding, delightful,
miraculous, out-of-sight, outstanding,
stupendous 11 astonishing

wondrous

6 mystic 7 amazing, awesome, strange
9 marvelous, remarkable 10 astounding,
formidable, miraculous, portentous,
prodigious, stupendous, surprising
11 astonishing, spectacular
13 extraordinary

wonky

4 awry 5 geeky, nerdy, shaky 7 bookish
8 unsteady

wont

3 apt 4 used 5 habit, usage 6 custom,
manner 8 accustom, habitude, inclined,
practice 10 accustomed, consuetude

wonted

5 usual 7 routine 8 habitual, ordinary
9 customary 10 accustomed

woo

3 sue 5 court 6 pursue 7 address,
entreat, solicit

wood

5 weald 6 forest, lumber, timber 8 golf
club 10 timberland
combining form: 3 xyl 4 lign, xylo 5 ligni,
ligno
decayed: 4 punk
eater: 7 termite
for burning: 5 fagot 6 tinder 8 kindling
golf: 6 driver
hard: 3 elm, oak 4 ebon, rata, teak
5 beech, birch, ebony, maple 6 cherry,
walnut 8 chestnut, mahogany, sycamore
imperfection: 4 knot 5 gnarl
light: 5 balsa
made of: 5 treen
pattern in: 5 grain 6 figure
product: 3 tar 5 paper 10 turpentine
soft: 4 pine

wood alcohol

6 methyl 8 carbinol, methanol

woodchuck

6 marmot 9 groundhog

wood coal

7 lignite

wooded

5 bosky, treed 6 sylvan 8 forested,

timbered

wooden
5 rigid, stiff 6 clumsy 7 awkward, stilted
8 ligneous 10 inflexible

woodland
5 copse, taiga, weald 6 forest, pinery
7 coppice 10 rain forest

wood nymph
5 dryad

woodpecker
4 bird 7 flicker, wryneck 9 sapsucker
genus: 5 Picus
kind: 5 downy, green, hairy 8 imperial,
pileated 9 redheaded 11 ivory-billed

woodsman
6 logger 8 forester 10 bushranger
11 bushwhacker

wood sorrel
3 oca 6 oxalis 8 shamrock 9 carambola

woodsy
6 rustic, sylvan

woodwind
4 oboe, reed 5 flute, shawm 7 bassoon,
piccolo 8 clarinet 9 saxophone
10 instrument 11 English horn
13 contrabassoon

woodworker
9 carpenter 12 cabinetmaker

woody
8 ligneous 12 station wagon

wooer
4 beau 5 lover, spark, swain 6 suitor
7 admirer, gallant, sparker

woof
4 bark, crow, weft, yarn 5 boast, weave
6 fabric, thread 7 texture

wool
3 fur 4 coat, hair 6 fabric, fleece
cut: 5 shear
fabric: 4 felt 5 baize, crepe, serge, tweed
6 covert, kersey, mohair, poplin, shoddy,
velour 7 flannel, worsted 8 cashmere,
chenille 9 gabardine 10 broadcloth
fat: 7 lanolin
kind: 4 hogg 6 angora, hogget, virgin
low-quality: 5 mungo 6 shoddy
musk-ox: 6 qiviut
process: 7 carding
source: 4 goat, lamb 5 camel, llama,
sheep 6 alpaca

woolly
5 fuzzy, hairy, nappy 6 fleecy, shaggy
7 blurred, hirsute 9 roughness
10 indistinct

woozy
4 hazy, sick, weak 5 dazed, dizzy, faint,
fuzzy, muzzy, vague 6 addled, blurry,
groggy, punchy 8 confused, nauseous
9 nauseated, slaphappy 11 light-headed

word
3 vow 4 buzz, news, oath, term 5 logos,
order, rumor 6 advice, gospel, gossip,
phrase, pledge, plight, remark, report,
saying, signal 7 command, message,
promise 8 locution 9 assurance, directive,
discourse, guarantee, statement, utterance
10 commitment, expression
11 declaration, information
12 announcement, conversation,
intelligence
connective: 11 conjunction
group: 6 clause, phrase 8 sentence
misused: 8 malaprop 11 malapropism
naming: 4 noun
new: 7 coinage 9 neologism
of action: 4 verb
of honor: 4 oath 7 promise
origin: 9 etymology
part: 8 syllable
root: 6 etymon
scrambled: 7 anagram
shortened: 11 contraction 12 abbreviation
square: 10 palindrome
with opposite meaning: 7 antonym
with same meaning: 7 synonym
with same pronunciation: 7 homonym
9 homophone
with same spelling: 7 homonym
9 homograph

wordbook
5 vocab 7 lexicon 8 glossary 9 thesaurus
10 dictionary, vocabulary

word-for-word
7 literal 8 ad verbum, verbally, verbatim

wordiness
8 verbiage 9 prolixity, verbosity
10 bloviation, logorrhea

word-of-mouth
4 oral 6 spoken, verbal 8 viva voce
9 unwritten

wordy
5 windy 6 prolix, verbal 7 diffuse, verbose
9 dictional, garrulous, iterative, redundant,
vocabular 10 long-winded, logorrheic,
loquacious, rhetorical

work
3 act, fix, job, run, tug, use 4 duty, line, make, opus, take, task, tend, till, toil 5 chore, craft, drive, forge, grind, guide, labor, shape, solve, sweat, trade 6 create, effect, effort, energy, excite, métier, result, strain, strive, succeed 7 arrange, calling, control, exploit, fashion, operate, perform, product, provoke, pursuit, resolve, travail 8 activity, business, contrive, drudgery, exertion, function, operate, slogging, striving, vocation 9 cultivate, embroider, execution 10 assignment, employment, handicraft, occupation, profession
together: 9 cooperate 11 collaborate
unit: 3 erg 5 joule

workaday
5 plain, usual 7 mundane, prosaic, routine 8 ordinary 9 quotidian 11 commonplace 12 run-of-the-mill

worker
4 doer, hand, serf 6 toiler, wallah 7 artisan, laborer 8 employee, mechanic, operator 9 craftsman, operative 10 roustabout, wage earner
fellow: 7 comrade, partner 9 colleague
group: 4 crew, gang 5 shift, staff, union
hard: 4 slave 6 beaver, drudge
insect: 3 ant, bee 4 wasp 7 termite
itinerant: 6 boomer 7 migrant
slow: 7 plodder
unskilled: 4 peon 7 jackleg, laborer

working
4 busy, live 6 active, useful, viable 7 dynamic, engaged, running 8 employed, occupied 9 operative 11 functioning
not: 5 kaput 6 broken

workman
see **worker**

work out
3 fix 5 solve, train 6 devise, settle 7 arrange, develop, resolve 8 exercise

workout
4 test 5 drill 8 exercise, practice 10 daily dozen

work over
4 beat, redo 5 scrag, study 6 beat up, mess up, redraw, rehash, revamp, revise 7 examine, redraft, restyle, rewrite, rough up 9 manhandle

workroom
3 lab 4 shop 6 studio 7 atelier 10 laboratory

works
4 mill 5 plant 7 factory 8 workshop 11 manufactory

Works and Days author
6 Hesiod

world
5 class, earth, globe, realm 6 career, cosmos, nature, planet, public, society, sphere, system 7 kingdom 8 creation, division, everyone, renowned, universe 9 human race, macrocosm, microcosm 13 distinguished
combining form: 4 cosm 5 cosmo

worldly
5 blasé 6 carnal, earthy, urbane 7 earthly, fleshly, mundane, profane, secular, sensual, terrene 8 material, telluric, temporal 9 sublunary 11 terrestrial 12 cosmopolitan 13 sophisticated

worldly-wise
12 cosmopolitan 13 sophisticated

World War I
battle: 5 Aisne, Marne, Somme, Ypres 6 Isonzo, Verdun 7 Jutland 9 Caporetto 10 Tannenberg 11 Dardanelles
battle line: 9 Siegfried
general: 4 Foch (Ferdinand), Haig (Douglas) 7 Allenby (Edmund) 8 Pershing (John) 10 Hindenburg (Paul von), Ludendorff (Erich)
hero: 4 York (Alvin) 8 Red Baron (The) 10 Richthofen (Manfred von) 12 Rickenbacker (Eddie)
treaty: 10 Versailles

World War II
admiral: 6 Halsey (William "Bull"), Nimitz (Chester)
alliance: 4 Axis 6 Allies
battle: 4 St.-Lô 5 Anzio, Bulge 6 Bataan, Midway, Tarawa, Warsaw 7 Britain, Iwo Jima, Okinawa, Saint-Lô 8 Coral Sea, Normandy 9 El Alamein, Leyte Gulf 10 Stalingrad 11 Guadalcanal
general: 6 Patton (George), Rommel (Erwin), Zhukov (Georgy) 7 Bradley (Omar) 9 MacArthur (Douglas) 10 Eisenhower (Dwight David), Montgomery (Bernard)
hero: 6 Murphy (Audie)
journalist: 4 Pyle (Ernie)
vehicle: 4 jeep
weapon: 5 A-bomb 6 rocket 8 buzz bomb

worldwide
6 cosmic, global 8 catholic 9 planetary, universal 10 ecumenical 12 cosmopolitan

worm
3 cad, cur 4 grub, lout 5 borer, creep, fluke, leech, louse, screw, treat 6 edge in, maggot, no-good, squirm, thread, wiggle, wretch, writhe 7 extract, lowlife, serpent, triclad, wriggle 8 helminth, nematode, squiggle 9 insinuate, planarium, trematode 10 infiltrate
marine: 6 nereid 7 annelid, tubifex
parasitic: 5 fluke, leech 7 ascarid, ascaris, cestode, filaria 8 helminth, trichina 9 strongyle

worn
3 old, wan 4 aged, beat 5 drawn, jaded, tatty, tired, weary 6 eroded, frayed, ragged, shabby 7 haggard 8 fatigued 9 woebegone 10 threadbare

worn-out
4 beat 5 all in, spent, tired, weary 6 bleary, bushed, ragged, used-up 7 drained, run-down 8 decrepit, depleted, fatigued, overused 9 exhausted, worm-eaten 10 broken-down, threadbare, tumbledown 11 debilitated, dilapidated

worried
6 afraid, on edge 7 anxious, nervous 8 bothered, distrait, troubled 9 concerned, tormented 10 distracted, distraught, distressed 12 apprehensive

worry
3 nag, try, vex 4 care, fret, fuss, gnaw, goad, pain, stew, test 5 annoy, beset, shake, tease, trial, upset 6 assail, attack, bother, harass, needle, pester, plague, pull at, unease 7 afflict, anguish, anxiety, concern, disturb, oppress, torment, trouble 8 aggrieve, distress, irritate 9 agitation, annoyance, misgiving 10 irritation, uneasiness

worrywart
7 fusspot 9 Cassandra, doomsayer, pessimist 10 fussbudget

worse
8 inferior

worsen
4 sink 7 decline 10 degenerate 11 deteriorate

worship
4 love 5 adore, honor 6 admire, dote on, homage, revere 7 idolize, lionize, liturgy, respect 8 devotion, idolatry, venerate
9 adoration, affection, reverence 10 admiration, veneration 11 idolization
object of: 3 god 4 icon, idol
place of: 5 altar 6 church, mosque, shrine, temple 9 cathedral, synagogue

worshipper
3 fan 6 votary 7 admirer, devotee 8 adherent, believer, disciple 10 enthusiast

worsted
4 yarn 5 stuff 6 caddis, fabric 7 cheviot, etamine, flannel, lasting 8 shalloon 9 bombazine, sharkskin 10 broadcloth

worth
4 rate 5 merit, price, value 6 regard, riches, wealth 7 caliber, calibre, fortune, quality, stature 9 resources, substance, valuation 10 excellence

worthless
4 vain 6 futile, no-good 7 inutile 8 nugatory 9 no-account

worthwhile
6 paying 7 gainful 9 estimable, honorable, lucrative 10 profitable, well-paying 11 meritorious, moneymaking 12 advantageous, remunerative

worthy
4 good 5 noble 8 laudable, standout 9 admirable, deserving, desirable, estimable, honorable 10 acceptable, creditable 11 commendable, meritorious

Wotan
see **Odin**

Wouk novel
4 Hope (The) 5 Glory (The) 10 Winds of War (The) 11 Caine Mutiny (The) 19 Marjorie Morningstar

would-be
7 hopeful, wishful 8 apparent, aspiring, desiring, desirous 9 ambitious, potential

wound
3 cut 4 blow, harm, hurt, pain, rift 6 damage, injure, injury, insult, lesion, trauma 8 lacerate 10 laceration
discharge: 3 pus
sign: 4 scab, scar 5 blood 7 blister

wow
3 hit 4 boff, grab 5 amaze, boffo, smash 6 dazzle 7 astound, impress, success 8 bedazzle

Wozzeck composer
4 Berg (Alban)

wrack
4 kelp, raze, ruin 5 smash, total 7 destroy,
flotsam, remnant, seaweed 8 decimate,
demolish, shambles, wreckage
11 destruction

wraith
5 ghost, shade, spook 6 double, shadow,
spirit 7 phantom, specter, spectre
8 phantasm 10 apparition

wrangle
3 row 4 spar, spat, tiff 5 argue, brawl,
fight, scrap 6 bicker, fracas, haggle, hassle
7 brabble, dispute, fall out, finagle, quarrel,
quibble 8 squabble 11 altercation

wrangler
6 cowboy 8 buckaroo 9 ranch hand

wrap
3 fur 4 bind, cape, coat, roll 5 cloak,
drape, shawl, stole 6 bundle, clothe,
enfold, invest, jacket, mantle, muffle,
parcel, shroud, swathe 7 bandage,
blanket, conceal, dress up, embrace,
enclose, engross, envelop, involve,
package, swaddle 8 bundle up, enshroud,
surround

wrapped up
4 deep 6 intent 7 engaged 8 absorbed,
consumed, immersed 9 engrossed
11 preoccupied

wrapper
5 cover 6 jacket 10 dust jacket
12 dressing gown

wrap up
6 muffle 8 close out, complete, conclude
9 summarize

wrap-up
4 coda 5 close 6 capper, closer, finale,
report 7 closing 8 epilogue 9 summation
10 denouement

wrath
3 ire 4 fury, rage 5 anger 6 choler
8 ferocity 9 vengeance 10 punishment
11 retribution 12 chastisement

wrathful
3 mad 5 angry, irate 6 heated, raging
7 enraged, furious 8 choleric, incensed,
inflamed 10 infuriated

wreak
5 cause, exact, visit 6 effect, impose

7 inflict 10 bring about

wreath
3 bay, lei 5 crown 6 anadem, laurel
7 chaplet, circlet, coronal, coronet, garland,
laurels

wreathe
4 coil, curl, wind 5 twine, twist 6 spiral
7 entwine 9 corkscrew 10 interweave

wreck
4 do in, heap, hulk, raze, ruin 5 beach,
crack, crash, cream, smash, total 6 beater,
damage, jalopy, junker, pileup, ravage,
strand 7 clunker, crack-up, destroy, scuttle,
smashup, torpedo 8 decimate, demolish
9 vandalize 11 destruction

wreckage
5 wrack 6 debris 7 flotsam 8 detritus,
shambles 11 destruction

wrecker
8 salvager, tow truck

wrench
4 jerk, pull, rack, tool, turn, warp, yank
5 force, twist, wrest, wring 6 change,
injure, injury, snatch, socket, sprain, strain
7 disable, distort, pervert, squeeze
8 distress, twisting
kind: 6 monkey 7 ratchet

wrest
4 rend, rive 5 exact, twist, wring 6 elicit,
extort, snatch, wrench 7 extract, squeeze

wrestle
6 combat, strain, strive, tussle 7 contend,
grapple, scuffle 8 struggle

wrestling
hold: 4 lock 6 nelson 8 headlock,
scissors
kind: 4 sumo
term: 3 pin 4 fall 5 throw 8 takedown

wretch
3 cur, dog 4 scum, toad, worm 5 devil,
knave, louse, rogue, skunk, snake
6 rascal, rotter 7 caitiff, hangdog, lowlife,
outcast, rat fink, stinker, villain 8 scalawag,
stinkard 9 scoundrel 10 blackguard,
sleazeball 11 rapscallion

wretched
3 low, sad 4 base, foul, mean, vile
6 abject, dismal, horrid, scurvy, sordid,
woeful 7 abysmal, doleful, forlorn, ignoble,
inferior, ruthful, servile, squalid, unhappy
8 dejected, dolorous, hopeless 9 afflicted,
execrable, miserable, sorrowful
10 despairing, despicable, deplorable,

despondent, melancholy, villainous

wretchedness
3 woe 6 misery 7 anguish 8 distress

wriggle
4 worm 5 slink 6 squirm, writhe

wring
3 wry 5 choke, exact, screw, twist, wrest
6 extort, squirm, wrench, writhe 7 afflict,
draw out, extract, squeeze, torment
the neck: 5 scrag

wringing-wet
5 soppy 6 soaked, sodden, soused
7 soaking, sopping 8 drenched, dripping
9 saturated

wrinkle
4 fold, ruck, ruga, seam 5 crimp, crisp,
plica, ridge, wizen 6 cockle, crease, fillip,
furrow, pucker, rumple 7 crumple, novelty,
scrunch, shrivel 8 contract 9 corrugate,
crow's-foot, worry line 10 innovation
11 corrugation 12 imperfection, irregularity

wrinkled
5 lined 6 rugose, rumply 7 creased
8 puckered, rugulose

Wrinkle in Time author
6 L'Engle (Madeleine)

wrist
5 joint 6 carpus
bone: 6 carpal, hamate 8 pisiform

writ
5 brief, order 6 assize, capias, decree,
elegit, extent 7 mandate, process,
summons, warrant 8 detainer, document,
mandamus, mittimus, praecipe, replevin,
subpoena 9 execution 10 attachment,
certiorari, court order, injunction 11 fieri
facias, scire facias, supersedeas
12 habeas corpus, venire facias
13 sequestration

write
3 ink, jot, pen 4 note 5 chalk, draft, print,
score, spell 6 answer, author, byline, draw
up, indite, ordain, pencil, record, scrawl,
scribe 7 compose, dissert, engross, fire
off, put down, scratch, set down 8 inscribe,
scribble, spell out 9 autograph, transpose
10 correspond, underwrite

write down
4 note 6 record, reduce 10 transcribe

write off
6 cancel 7 dismiss, expense 8 amortize,
discount 9 eliminate 10 depreciate

write-off
4 debt, loss 7 expense 8 donation
9 allowance, deduction, reduction

writer
4 poet 6 author, penman, scribe
8 composer, novelist 9 scribbler,
wordsmith
bad: 4 hack

write-up
5 blurb, story 7 account, article

writhe
4 curl, worm 5 twist 6 squirm, suffer,
wallow, welter, wiggle, wrench 7 agonize,
contort, distort, wriggle 8 convolve,
squiggle 10 intertwine

writing
4 book, hand, note 5 essay, paper, print,
prose, style, words 6 letter, notice, record,
script 7 epistle 8 document, longhand
9 signature 10 authorship, literature,
manuscript, penmanship 11 calligraphy,
composition, inscription, publication
character: 6 letter 9 cuneiform
10 hieroglyph
combining form: 4 gram 6 grapho,
graphy
for the blind: 7 braille
instrument: 3 pen 5 chalk, quill 6 pencil,
stylus
kind: 5 prose, verse 6 poetry
sacred: 5 Bible, Koran 6 Talmud, Tantra
9 scripture
secret: 4 code
surface: 5 board, paper, slate 6 scroll
9 parchment

wrong
3 bad, ill, off, sin 4 awry, evil, harm, hurt,
tort 5 abuse, amiss, badly, crime, false,
inapt, unfit 6 afield, astray, injure, injury,
malign, offend, sinful, unfair, unjust, untrue
7 defraud, immoral, oppress, outrage,
violate 8 aggrieve, ill-treat, improper,
inequity, iniquity, maltreat, mistaken,
mistreat, opposite 9 discredit, erroneous,
grievance, incorrect, injustice, misguided,
persecute, unethical, unfitting, violation
10 inaccurate, iniquitous, mistakenly,
unfairness, unjustness, unsuitable,
wickedness 11 erroneously, incorrectly,
unfavorably 12 inaccurately, infelicitous
13 inappropriate

wrongdoer
5 felon 6 sinner 8 criminal, offender
9 miscreant, reprobate 10 accomplice,
delinquent, malefactor 12 transgressor

wrongdoing
3 sin **4** evil **5** crime **7** misdeed, offense
8 iniquity **10** misconduct **11** malefaction,
malfeasance, misbehavior

wrongful
6 unjust, unfair **7** illegal, illicit, lawless
8 criminal, improper, unlawful
12 illegitimate

wrongheaded
6 mulish **7** froward **8** contrary, perverse
9 obstinate

wrought
4 made **6** formed, shaped, worked
7 created **8** finished, hammered
9 decorated, fashioned, processed
10 ornamented **11** embellished
12 manufactured
up: 7 excited, stirred

wry
4 bent **5** askew, twist, wrest **6** ironic,
wrench **7** crooked, twisted **8** humorous,
sardonic **11** wrongheaded

wryneck
10 woodpecker **11** torticollis

wurst
7 sausage

Wuthering Heights
author: 6 Brontë (Emily)
character: 5 Cathy **9** Catherine
10 Heathcliff
family: 6 Linton **8** Earnshaw

Wycliffite
7 Lollard

Wyoming
capital: 8 Cheyenne
city: 6 Casper **7** Laramie
mountain, range: 5 Rocky **7** Gannett
(Peak) **9** Wind River **10** Grand Teton
nickname: 8 Equality (State)
river: 5 Green, Snake **6** Powder
7 Bighorn **11** Yellowstone
state bird: 10 meadowlark
state flower: 16 Indian paintbrush
state tree: 10 cottonwood

X

x
    3 chi, ten 4 kiss 5 annul, cross, erase,
    error, times, wrong 6 cancel, delete, efface
    7 mistake, unknown 8 abscissa
    9 signature

Xanthippe
    3 nag 5 scold, shrew 6 nagger
    9 termagant
    husband: 8 Socrates

Xenophon work
    8 Anabasis 9 Cyropedia, Hellenica

xerophyte
    6 cactus

Xerxes
    crossing site: 10 Hellespont
    defeat: 7 Plataea, Salamis
    father: 6 Darius
    kingdom: 6 Persia
    mother: 6 Atossa
    victory: 11 Thermopylae

Xmas
    4 Noel, yule 8 Nativity, yuletide

X-ray
    discoverer: 8 Roentgen (Wilhelm)
    science: 9 radiology

xylophone relative
    7 marimba

Y

yacht
4 race, sail 6 cruise 7 cruiser 8 sailboat
12 cabin cruiser

yahoo
3 hun, yay 4 boor, clod, dolt, hood, lout,
punk, thug 5 brute, chuff, churl, clown,
rough, rowdy, tough 6 hoorah, hooray,
hurrah, savage, terror, vandal, yippie
7 buffoon, bumpkin, hoodlum, ruffian,
toughie 8 bullyboy, hooligan 9 roughneck
10 clodhopper

Yahweh
3 God 6 Adonai, Elohim 7 Jehovah

yak
3 gab, jaw 4 blab, chat 5 clack, prate
6 babble, gabble, jabber, natter, yammer
7 blabber, blather, chatter, palaver, prattle
11 confabulate

Yalta participant
6 Stalin (Joseph) 9 Churchill (Winston),
Roosevelt (Franklin Delano)

yam
7 boniato 11 sweet potato

yammer
3 cry 4 bawl, crab, fuss, moan, wail, yawp,
yell 5 bleat, gripe, whine 6 babble, bellow,
clamor, gabble, grouch, grouse, jabber,
natter, snivel, squawk 7 blather, parttle,
whimper 8 complain 9 bellyache,
caterwaul

yank
3 tug 4 grab, jerk, pull, tear 5 hoick
6 snatch, wrench 7 extract

yap
3 gab 4 bark, hick 5 mouth, prate
6 babble, bowwow, gabble, jabber, natter,
rustic, yammer 7 blather, bumpkin, chatter,
hayseed, prattle 9 hillbilly 10 clodhopper

yard
3 pen 4 herd, quad, spar unit 5 court,
garth, glass 6 length 7 grounds, measure

9 curtilage, enclosure 10 playground,
quadrangle
five and one-half: 3 rod
part of: 4 foot
two hundred and twenty: 7 furlong

yardstick
4 norm, test 5 basis, gauge, model
7 measure, pattern 8 paradigm, standard
9 barometer, benchmark, criterion,
guideline 10 touchstone

yare
4 deft, spry 5 agile, brisk, handy, lithe,
quick, ready, zippy 6 lively, nimble, volant
7 lissome 9 sprightly

yarn
4 tale, talk 5 fiber, story 6 caddis, cotton,
crewel, strand, thread 7 account, caddice
8 anecdote, tall tale 9 adventure, narration,
narrative
ball of: 4 clew
coil: 5 skein 6 skeane
cotton: 10 candlewick
for fastening a sail: 6 roband
woolen: 6 crewel 7 worsted 8 shetland

yaw
4 rock, swag, veer 5 lurch 6 swerve
7 deviate 9 alternate, deviation
10 deflection

yawn
3 gap 4 bore, gape 5 ennui 6 cavity,
tedium 7 boredom, bromide 10 dullsville

yawning
4 deep 5 agape 6 gaping 7 abyssal
9 cavernous

yawp
3 bay, cry, nag 4 bark, bawl, beef, crab,
fuss, gape, wail 5 bleat, gripe 6 clamor,
outcry, squall, squawk, yammer
8 complain 9 bellyache

yaws
9 frambesia

yclept
 5 named **6** called

yea
 3 aye, too **4** also, amen, even, more, okay
 5 truly **6** agreed, assent, as well, indeed,
 really, verily **7** besides, granted **8** likewise,
 moreover, positive **9** certainly **10** definitely
 11 affirmation, affirmative **12** additionally

yeanling
 3 kid **4** lamb

year
 4 time **5** cycle **6** period
 academic division: 4 term **7** quarter,
 session **8** semester **9** trimester
 French: 5 année
 kind: 4 leap **5** solar **6** fiscal **8** academic,
 calendar, sidereal
 Latin: 5 annus
 Scottish: 7 towmond
 Spanish: 3 año

yearbook
 5 annal **6** annual **7** almanac

yearling
 4 colt, foal **5** filly

Yearling, The
 author: 8 Rawlings (Marjorie Kinnan)
 character: 4 Jody
 fawn: 4 Flag

yearly
 6 annual **8** annually

yearn
 4 ache, burn, itch, long, lust, pant, pine,
 sigh, wish **5** dream, spoil **6** hanker,
 hunger, thirst

yearning
 4 wish **5** ardor, drive, eager **6** desire, thirst
 7 craving, wistful **8** appetite **10** aspiration

years
 3 age, era
 five: 7 lustrum **12** quinquennial,
 quinquennium
 four: 11 quadrennial, quadrennium
 one hundred: 7 century **9** centenary
 10 centennial
 one thousand: 10 millennium
 ten: 6 decade **9** decennial, decennium
 three: 9 triennial, triennium
 two: 8 biennial, biennium

yeast
 4 barm, foam, suds **5** froth, spume
 6 lather, leaven **7** ferment

yeasty
 5 dizzy, giddy, light **6** frothy **7** flighty
 8 immature, restless, seething
 9 exuberant, frivolous, unsettled **11** light-
 headed

Yeats, William Butler
 beloved: 9 Maud Gonne
 birthplace: 6 Dublin
 play: 7 Deirdre **9** Herne's Egg (The)
 16 Countess Cathleen (The)
 poetry: 5 Tower (The) **10** Easter 1916
 12 Second Coming (The) **16** Wild Swans
 at Coole (The) **18** Sailing to Byzantium
 theater: 5 Abbey

yegg
 5 thief **6** robber **7** burglar **8** picklock
 11 safecracker

yell
 3 cry **4** call, howl, roar, wail **5** cheer, hallo,
 hollo, shout, whoop **6** bellow, clamor,
 holler, outcry, scream, shriek, squall
 10 vociferate

yellow
 3 age **4** buff, mean, weak, yolk **5** amber,
 blond, color, lemon, straw, tawny, topaz
 6 coward, craven, flaxen, golden, sallow
 7 gutless, ignoble, mustard, saffron
 8 cowardly, discolor **9** dastardly, jaundiced,
 spunkless **11** sensational **12** dishonorable
 13 pusillanimous
 brownish: 3 dun **5** amber, ocher
 dye: 7 annatto
 greenish: 5 olive **6** acacia **10** chartreuse

yellowhammer
 5 finch **7** bunting, flicker

yelp
 3 cry, yap **4** bark **6** outcry, squeal

Yemen
 capital: 4 Sana **5** Sanaa
 city: 4 Aden **5** Ta'izz
 desert: 10 Rub` al-Khali
 gulf: 4 Aden
 island: 7 Socotra
 island group: 7 Kamaran
 language: 6 Arabic
 monetary unit: 4 rial
 neighbor: 4 Oman **11** Saudi Arabia
 peninsula: 7 Arabian
 sea: 3 Red **7** Arabian

yen
 4 ache, itch, long, lust, pine, sigh, urge
 5 taste, yearn **6** desire, hanker, hunger,
 thirst **7** craving, longing, passion
 8 appetite, yearning **9** hankering

yeoman
5 clerk 6 farmer 7 freeman 8 retainer
9 attendant, beefeater, landowner
10 freeholder 11 homesteader

yeomanly
5 loyal 6 sturdy 8 faithful

yes
3 aye, yea, yeh, yep, yup 4 okay, yeah
5 agree 6 agreed, assent, gladly
7 consent, exactly 8 all right 9 assuredly,
certainly, willingly 11 affirmation,
affirmative, undoubtedly
French: 3 oui

yeshiva
6 school 8 seminary

yes-man
5 toady 6 minion, stooge 7 spaniel
8 groveler, truckler 9 flatterer, sycophant
10 bootlicker 13 apple-polisher

yesterday
4 past, yore 8 recently 10 recent time
French: 4 hier
Spanish: 4 ayer

yesteryear
4 past, yore 7 history 8 foretime, lang
syne

yet
3 but, too 4 also, even, more, only, save
5 so far, still 6 as well, though, withal
7 besides, earlier, finally, howbeit, however,
someday, thus far 8 after all, hitherto,
moreover, sometime 10 eventually,
ultimately 11 furthermore, nonetheless, still
and all 12 additionally, nevertheless

Yevtushenko poem
7 Babi Yar, Baby Yar

Ygerne
see **Igraine**

yield
3 bow, net, pay 4 bear, bend, cave, cede,
crop, fold 5 defer, grant, waive 6 accede,
bounty, buckle, comply, impart, output,
profit, relent, render, resign, return, reward,
submit, supply, tender 7 abandon, bring in,
concede, consent, deliver, furnish, harvest,
produce, product, proffer, provide, revenue,
succumb 8 abdicate, collapse, generate,
hand over 9 acquiesce, surrender
10 bring forth, capitulate, production,
relinquish

yielding
4 soft 6 pliant, supple 7 bearing, passive,
pliable 8 flexible 9 adaptable, tractable

10 manageable, productive, submissive
11 acquiescent, unresistant

yin and _____
4 yang

yip
3 cry 4 bark, yelp

yippee
6 hoorah, hooray, hurrah, hurray

yoga posture
5 asana

yoke
3 bar, tie, wed 4 bond, join, link, pair, span,
team 5 clamp, frame, hitch, marry, unite
6 attach, couple, inspan 7 bondage,
connect, control, harness, peonage,
serfdom, slavery 8 marriage 9 servitude
10 crosspiece, oppression
combining form: 3 zyg 4 zygo
part: 5 oxbow

yokel
3 oaf 4 boor, clod, hick, rube 5 churl,
swain 7 bucolic, bumpkin,
hayseed 9 chawbacon, hillbilly
10 clodhopper, countryman

yolk
4 food 6 yellow 10 ovum center

yon
see **yonder**

yonder
5 there 7 farther, further, thither 8 outlying

yore
3 old 7 history 8 foretime, lang syne
9 antiquity, yesterday 10 yesteryear

you
3 one 4 thee, thou
French: 4 vous
German: 3 sie
Spanish: 5 usted 7 ustedes

young
3 fry, new 4 baby, tyro 5 brood, fresh,
green 6 babies, callow, infant, junior, litter,
tender, unripe 7 untried 8 childish,
immature, juvenile, unformed, youthful
9 unfledged 10 unfinished, unseasoned
11 unpracticed 13 inexperienced
animal: 3 cub, fry, kid, kit, pup 4 calf, colt,
fawn, foal, joey 5 puppy 6 kitten, heifer,
piglet
bird: 5 chick 7 gosling
hare: 7 leveret
sheep, goat: 4 lamb 8 yeanling

younger
6 junior

youngster
3 boy, cub, kid, lad, tad, tot 4 girl, lass, tike
5 chick, child 6 moppet, shaver 8 juvenile
9 fledgling

youth
5 prime 6 period, spring 8 juvenile,
preadult, teenager 9 stripling 10 adolescent, springtide, springtime
12 inexperience
ancient Greek: 6 ephebe 7 ephebus
goddess of: 4 Hebe
mythological: 6 Adonis, Apollo, Icarus
8 Ganymede
time of: 9 salad days

youthful
5 fresh, green, young 6 boyish, callow,
maiden, unripe 7 puerile 8 immature,
juvenile, virginal 9 beardless, unfledged

yowl
3 bay, cry 4 bawl, howl, wail 6 scream,
squall, squeal 7 ululate 9 caterwaul

yucca
7 cassava 9 bear grass

Yukon
bay: 9 Mackenzie
capital: 10 Whitehorse
city: 6 Dawson
mountain: 5 Logan
river: 5 Yukon 8 Klondike

yule
4 Noel, Xmas 8 Nativity 9 Christmas
13 Christmastide

Z

Zambia
capital: 6 Lusaka
city: 5 Kitwe, Ndola 11 Livingstone
lake: 5 Mweru 9 Bangweulu 10 Tanganyika
language: 7 English
monetary unit: 6 kwacha
mountain range: 8 Muchinga
neighbor: 5 Congo 6 Angola, Malawi
7 Namibia 8 Tanzania, Zimbabwe
10 Mozambique
river: 5 Kafue 7 Luangwa, Zambezi
waterfall: 13 Victoria Falls

zany
3 nut, wag 4 card, fool, kook 5 antic,
campy, clown, comic, crazy, cutup, dotty,
goofy, idiot, joker, kooky, loony, nutty,
wacky 6 jester, madcap 7 buffoon, farceur,
half-wit 8 clowning, clownish, comedian,
funnyman, jokester 9 harlequin, prankster,
screwball, simpleton, trickster 11 merry-
andrew

zap
3 hit 4 blow, kill, nuke 5 blast, snuff
6 attack 7 destroy, wipe out 8 dissolve
9 eliminate, irradiate, liquidate
10 annihilate

Zauberflöte composer
6 Mozart (Wolfgang Amadeus)

zeal
4 brio, fire, zest 5 ardor, drive, mania
6 desire, energy, esprit, fervor, spirit
7 avidity, passion, urgency 8 devotion,
dynamism, keenness 9 eagerness,
intensity, vehemence 10 enthusiasm,
fanaticism, fierceness

zealot
3 bug, fan, nut 4 buff 5 fiend, freak
6 maniac, votary 7 devotee, fanatic,
sectary 8 partisan 10 aficionado,
enthusiast 12 true believer

zealous
4 avid, keen 5 afire, eager, fiery, fired,
nutty, rabid 6 ardent, fervid, gung-ho
7 devoted, fanatic, fervent 8 frenetic,
obsessed, wild-eyed 9 dedicated,
fanatical, possessed 10 passionate
11 impassioned 12 enthusiastic

zebra
6 equine 7 referee 9 crosswalk
extinct: 6 quagga
type: 6 Grevy's 8 mountain 9 Burchell's

zebu
4 oxen

Zebulun
9 lost tribe
brother: 4 Levi 5 Judah 6 Simeon
father: 5 Jacob
mother: 4 Leah

zecchino
6 sequin

Zechariah
7 prophet

Zedekiah
9 Mattaniah
father: 6 Josiah

zenana
5 harem, serai 8 seraglio

zenith
3 top 4 acme, apex, peak 6 apogee,
height, summit, vertex 8 capstone,
pinnacle 11 culmination 12 highest point
opposite: 5 nadir

Zenobia
husband: 9 Odenathus
kingdom: 7 Palmyra

Zeno follower
5 Stoic

Zephaniah
7 prophet 9 Sophonias

zephyr
6 breeze 8 west wind

Zephyrus
father: 8 Astraeus
mother: 3 Eos 6 Aurora

zeppelin
5 blimp 7 airship 9 dirigible

zero
3 aim, nil, zip 4 love, nada, none, null, void
5 aught, nadir, zilch 6 cipher, naught,
nobody 7 nothing, nullity 8 goose egg
9 nonentity

zest
4 élan, peel, tang, zeal 5 ardor, gusto,
taste 6 fervor, flavor, relish 7 delight,
ecstasy, elation, passion, sparkle
8 appetite, dynamism, piquancy, pleasure
9 eagerness, enjoyment 10 enthusiasm
11 delectation 12 exhilaration, satisfaction

zesty
4 racy, tart 5 sharp, spicy, tangy 6 biting,
lively, savory, snappy 7 peppery, piquant,
pungent 8 exciting, poignant, seasoned,
spirited 9 flavorful

Zetes
brother: 6 Calais
father: 6 Boreas
mother: 8 Orithyia
slayer: 8 Heracles, Hercules

Zethus
brother: 7 Amphion
father: 4 Zeus 7 Jupiter
mother: 7 Antiope

Zeus
7 Jupiter
brother: 5 Hades 8 Poseidon
daughter: 3 Ate 4 Hebe 5 Helen
6 Athena 7 Artemis 9 Aphrodite
10 Persephone, Proserpina
father: 6 Cronus
home: 7 Olympus (Mt.)
lover: 4 Leda, Leto, Maia 5 Danae,
Dione, Metis 6 Aegina, Europa, Latona,
Semele, Themis 7 Alcmene, Antiope,
Demeter 8 Callisto, Eurynome
mother: 4 Rhea
nurse: 9 Almathaea
oracle: 6 Dodona
shield: 5 aegis
sister: 4 Hera, Juno
son: 4 Ares 5 Arcas, Argus, Minos
6 Aeacus, Apollo, Hermes, Zethus
7 Amphion, Perseus 8 Dionysus, Heracles,
Hercules, Sarpedon, Tantalus
tree: 3 oak
wife: 4 Hera, Juno
weapon: 11 thunderbolt

zigzag
4 tack, turn 5 angle, crank, weave
6 jagged 7 chevron 8 flexuous, indirect,
serrated

zilch
3 nil, zip 4 zero 5 aught, squat 6 cipher,
naught, nobody 7 nothing, nullity 8 goose
egg 9 nonentity 11 diddly-squat

Zimbabwe
capital: 6 Harare
city: 5 Gweru 6 Kwekwe, Mutare
8 Bulawayo, Maxvingo 11 Chitungwiza
ethnic group: 5 Shona 7 Ndebele
former name: 8 Rhodesia
lake: 6 Kariba
language: 5 Bantu 7 English
monetary unit: 6 dollar
neighbor: 6 Zambia 8 Botswana
10 Mozambique 11 South Africa
river: 4 Sabi 7 Limpopo, Zambezi
waterfall: 13 Victoria Falls

zinc
7 element
ingot: 7 spelter
ore: 6 blende 10 sphalerite

zing
3 pan, pep, rap, vim, zap, zip 4 brio, dash,
élan, slam, snap, zeal 5 ardor, flair,
oomph, verve, vigor 6 energy, esprit,
fervor, spirit 7 panache, passion, sparkle
8 dynamism, vitality 9 animation,
eagerness 10 ebullience, enthusiasm

Zion
5 bliss 6 heaven, Israel 7 Elysium
8 eternity, paradise 12 New Jerusalem,
promised land

Zionist
American: 5 Szold (Henrietta)
English: 7 Sokolow (Nahum) 8 Zangwill
(Israel)
German: 6 Nordau (Max Simon)
Hungarian: 5 Herzl (Theodor)
Israeli: 5 Buber (Martin) 8 Weizmann
(Chaim)

zip
3 fly, nil, nix, pep, run, vim 4 brio, dash,
hiss, rush, nada, snap, tear, whiz, zero,
zest, zing, zoom 5 drive, gusto, hurry,
oomph, speed, squat, whisk, zilch 6 bustle,

energy, hasten, hustle **7** nothing **8** vitality **10** excitement, liveliness **11** diddly-squat

zippy
4 keen, spry, yare **5** agile, alert, brisk, peppy, quick, ready **6** lively, nimble, snappy, speedy **7** dynamic **8** spirited **9** sprightly

zircon
6 jargon **7** jargoon, mineral
variety: 7 jacinth **8** hyacinth

zit
6 pimple

zither
10 instrument
Chinese: 3 kin **4** ch'in
Japanese: 4 koto
relative: 8 autoharp, dulcimer

zodiac sign
3 Leo (the Lion) **5** Aries (the Ram), Libra (the Balance), Virgo (the Virgin) **6** Cancer (the Crab), Gemini (the Twins), Pisces (the Fishes), Taurus (the Bull) **7** Scorpio (the Scorpion) **8** Aquarius (the Water Bearer) **9** Capricorn (the Goat) **11** Sagittarius (the Archer)

Zola, Emile
work: 4 Nana **7** J'accuse **8** Drunkard (The), Germinal **9** La Débâcle **10** L'Assommoir **13** Thérèse Raquin

zombie
5 robot **8** cocktail **9** automaton

zone
4 area, band, belt **5** layer, tract **6** region, sector **7** portion, quarter, section, segment, stretch **8** district, division, encircle, surround **9** partition, territory

zonked
4 high **5** dazed, doped, drunk, tight **6** ripped, stoned **7** drugged, drunken, smashed **8** hopped-up, tripping, turned on, wiped out **9** spaced-out, strung out, stupefied **10** inebriated, tripped out **11** intoxicated

zoologist
American: 5 Clark (Eugenie), Hyatt (Alpheus) **6** Carson (Rachel), Fossey (Dian), Osborn (Henry Fairfield), Yerkes (Robert) **7** Agassiz (Alexander), Ditmars (Raymond), Merriam (Clinton) **8** Hornaday (William)
Austrian: 6 Frisch (Karl von)
British: 6 Darwin (Charles), Huxley (Julian, Thomas) **7** Goodall (Jane), Medawar (Peter) **9** Lankester (Edwin)
Dutch: 10 Swammerdam (Jan)
French: 6 Buffon (G.-L. Leclerc), Cuvier (Georges)
German: 7 Haeckel (Ernst)
Norwegian: 6 Nansen (Fridtjof)
South African: 5 Broom (Robert)
Swedish: 8 Linnaeus (Carolus)

zoom
3 hum, zip **4** buzz, dash, whiz, zero **5** focus, speed, whizz **6** streak **7** shoot up **9** skyrocket

zoophyte
5 coral **6** sponge **8** bryozoan **9** gorgonian **10** sea anemone

Zoroastrian
demon: 4 deva
god: 10 Ahura Mazda
sacred writings: 6 Avesta

zounds
3 gad **4** egad **8** gadzooks **11** odd's bodkins

zucchetto
7 calotte **8** skullcap

zwieback
5 toast **7** biscuit

zygomatic bone
5 malar **9** cheekbone

zygote
4 cell **6** oocyst